The Bill James Handbook 2009

Baseball Info Solutions

www.baseballinfosolutions.com

Published by ACTA Sports

A Division of ACTA Publications

Cover by Tom A. Wright

Cover Photos by Scott Jordan Levy

First Edition: November 2008

Published by:
ACTA Sports, a division of ACTA Publications
5559 W. Howard Street, Skokie, IL 60077
(800) 397-2282
www.actasports.com www.actapublications.com

ISBN: 978-0-87946-367-0
ISSN: 1940-8668

Printed in the United States of America

Table of Contents

Dedication

This book is dedicated to my mom, Barb, my dad, Mike, and all of my friends for their support and patience these past five baseball seasons.

To my brother Mike, my new sister-in-law Kristin, Bill Sussman, and Al for all of the good times and to my co-workers for all of their hard work throughout the year.

Matt Lorenzo

Acknowledgements

Last year I put a good amount of thought into making the Acknowledgements fun and creative, not exactly an easy thing to do. I inspired my friend Ron Shandler to run an actual contest in the Acknowledgements of his annual publication, so I guess my work here is complete. This year the "Ack" will be dry and boring, like it should be. Don't enjoy!

Thanks to Bill James and John Dewan, the main creative forces of Baseball Info Solutions. They teamed up on the brand new *Bill James Gold Mine* and Bill James Online this year and knocked sabermetrics up another notch.

Thanks to the now expanded Baseball Info Solutions full-time staff for your hard work and dedication to the best baseball data company on the planet. That means you Joe Brekke, Dan Casey, Austin Diamond, Damon Lichtenwalner, Matt Lorenzo, Tony Pellegrino, Pat Quinn, Todd Radcliffe, Jeff Spoljaric, Annemarie Stella, Jim Swavely and Jon Vrecsics. And me.

Thanks to our 2008 Video Scout crew. I personally guarantee no one else has scored or scouted as many games or as random a sample of games from 2008 as these guys: Jake Argue, Steve Gleason, Jeremy Gordon, Brian Johnston, Matt Kelliher-Gibson, Steve Landefeld, Brian Powalish, Kurt Wimpe, Mike Wolverton and J.D. Wyborny. You'll see these guys later on down the line in the baseball world, because they belong here.

Thanks to our two part-time video scouts Dedan Brozino and Joel Kammeyer. Your time and effort is much appreciated.

A special thanks to 2007 Video Scout Joe Werner, who was overlooked in last year's Ack mainly due to my negligence, but also because he had to leave before the season ended for his last year at college. Joe, wherever you are, get in touch and I'll send you a free book.

Thanks to our colleagues at ACTA Sports: Greg Pierce Andrew Yankech, Charles Fiore, Donna Ryding, Mary Eggert and Brendan Gaughan.

Thanks to our remote video crew: Brian Dewberry-Jones, David Dick, Don Masi, John Menna, Gus Papadopoulos, Theo Papadopoulos, Harold Richter, Bob Routier, Wayne Sit and John Wagner.

Thanks to our friends and helpers with a connection to the baseball industry: Greg Ambrosius, Andy Andres, Jeff Barton, Matthew Berry, Jim Callis, Mike Canter, Gary Cohen, David Creamer, Doug Dennis, Jeff Erickson, Steve Goldstein, Jason Grey, Durward Hamil, Gene McCaffrey, Peter Kreutzer, Michael Lehrer, Deric McKamey, Sig Mejdal, Bob Meyerhoff, Mike Murphy, Rob Neyer, Mat Olkin, Scott Pianowski, Mike Phillips, David Pinto, Joe Posnanski, Nate Ravitz, Hal Richman, Mike Salfino, Peter Schoenke, Len Schwartz, Ron Shandler, Joe Sheehan, John Sickels, Dave Studenmund, Tom Tango, Sam Walker, Mark Watson, Rick Wilton, Rick Wolf, Trace Wood and Todd Zola.

Sincerely,

Steve Moyer
President
Baseball Info Solutions

Introduction

It was a season of miracles.

The Tampa Bay Rays, having exorcised the Devil from their surname before the season began, achieved their first winning season in franchise history and won the AL East by two games. To say that no one saw this coming wouldn't be quite true: Bill James himself said in spring training the Rays would win 85 games after losing 96 games and finishing last in 2007. Tampa Bay ascended into first place for good on July 18 and never looked back.

In Chicago, that long-suffering sports town, both the White Sox and the Cubs made the playoffs for the first time in 102 years. The Cubs opened the 2008 season on the 100th Anniversary of their last World Championship—the longest championship drought in professional sports, while the White Sox, having held first place in the AL Central for the majority of the season, faltered in September before beating three teams in three days to claim their spot in the playoffs. Unfortunately for South Side fans, the Pale Hose were quickly dispatched by the miracle Rays in the ALDS.

Across town, the Cubs, riding perhaps unreasonably-high expectations after a 97-win season, stared a century of futility in the face—and ran screaming. Not even a brand new theme song from Eddie Vedder could overcome the curse of appearing on the cover of *Sports Illustrated* shortly before the season ended (see September 29 issue). The Cubbies were swept by the Los Angeles Dodgers in the NLDS...the Dodgers, whose manager Joe Torre walked away from the New York Yankees last offseason only to lead his new franchise on a September bum rush to make the postseason. The Dodgers' swift execution was the first time they'd won a postseason game in twenty years; without Torre at the helm, the Yanks missed the playoffs for the first time since the 1994- 95 strike.

There were miracle performances as well. Indians starter Cliff Lee won 22 games for a Cleveland team that otherwise fell well-short of expectations. Lee spent part of 2007 in the minor leagues, but resurrected himself in 2008 as a near-lock for the AL Cy Young Award. Elsewhere in the American League, Josh Hamilton and Carlos Quentin made unexpected runs at the MVP. Hamilton established himself as a true success story, having overcome personal struggles of biblical proportion too lengthy to chronicle here; while Quentin, acquired by Chicago in the offseason, almost didn't make the White Sox out of spring training. All three players seemed to spring fully-formed from the head of Zeus in 2008.

Francisco Rodriguez saved 62 games and in the process broke Bobby Thigpen's single-season record (57); Omar Vizquel played his 2,654th game at shortstop, cruising past Luis Aparicio's career record (2,583); Ichiro Suzuki tied Wee Willie Keeler for the most consecutive seasons with 200 hits (8); and Albert Pujols became only the third player in MLB history to begin his career with eight straight seasons of 100+ RBI. And as a side note, if this is the year we say goodbye to Frank Thomas, The Big Hurt will retire as only the fourth player to finish his career with a batting average of .300, with 500 home runs, 1,000 runs, and 1,500 walks.

All of which makes this year's *Handbook* maybe the most exciting yet. New for 2009 is Relief Pitching, where basically we're trying to stretch the record book to cover more of the modern bullpen, tabulating 21 categories to rate the best relievers from each team. We've added postseason records to our career registers; baserunning has grown by a column or two. And we still feature the Young Talent Inventory, Manufactured Runs Analysis, and John Dewan's exclusive 2008 Fielding Bible Awards (teaser: *The Fielding Bible—Volume II* will be out in February of 2009!). As always, errata—not that we expect any, but a few always catch us by surprise—will be available beginning February 1 at www.baseballinfosolutions.com.

There was one more miracle too. A certain player who shall remain nameless, but who owns the record for career home runs, didn't make a single plate appearance in 2008. And you know what? He wasn't missed. That is a miracle in and of itself.

LC Fiore
ACTA Sports

2008 Team Statistics

Just before the 2002 Super Bowl, during the pre-game ceremonies, the heavily-favored St. Louis Rams ran out of the clubhouse tunnel as their names were announced. The Rams' roster was packed with stars: Isaac Bruce, Marshall Faulk, Kurt Warner. And the crowd cheered each player as he darted onto the field.

Their opponents that night were the New England Patriots, a collection of guys most casual fans couldn't even name. Troy Brown was their "star" receiver; their offense was led by a quarterback who sounded like a cast-off from *The Brady Bunch*. The Patriots were practically anonymous—which is why, perhaps, when New England was announced, they ran onto the field together, emerging from the tunnel as a unit—as a team.

The Patriots won the Super Bowl that year. They would win two more (at least) before the decade was out.

Move ahead to Major League Baseball's Opening Day 2003. Fenway Park. The Boston Red Sox had a new GM named Theo. During the pregame ceremonies, the New England Patriots made a guest appearance, filtering out from beneath the Green Monster to stand with the home team along the third base line. As a publicity stunt, this was a winner. But it also sent a very clear message to the Red Sox' players and fans: From that day forward, the BoSox would be a team, a franchise worthy of emulation. Boston made the playoffs that year, and won the World Series in 2004 (their first in 86 years) and again in 2007.

This is not to say they won *because* they played as a team. That Brady guy turned out to be pretty good after all, and the 2003 Red Sox could mash (they set a record for team slugging percentage and led the majors in batting average). After all, some would argue that nothing helps team chemistry like winning.

But if a player feels like part of a team, then that player believes each time he takes the field his team is going to win. As a result, personal statistics take a back seat. The player may "selflessly" put the team's performance ahead of individual achievement. He may go 4-for-5 but seem depressed if his team loses anyway. He may move along the runners by hitting into a force out or by laying down a sacrifice bunt.... In short, he'll do whatever it takes to win.

Players like this are considered "team" players—good for the clubhouse—and they sometimes have unreasonably long careers (see Blum, Geoff). Of course, until we invent a stat to quantify "make-up" or "team chemistry," we can only speculate what effect these kind of players actually have, if success breeds chemistry or vice versa. Regardless, for all the attention paid to player statistics in the game of baseball, the context of team is the only place where individual achievements have relevance.

In the next few pages, major league teams are evaluated in aggregate against every other team in baseball. If you want to know how the Kansas City Royals fared in night games, how many double plays the San Francisco Giants turned, or when the Washington Nationals spent their last day in first place, it's all here.

2008 American League Standings

Overall

EAST

Team	W-L	Pct	GB	D1	LD1	LLd
Tampa Bay Rays	97-65	.599	0.0	110	9/30	5.5
Boston Red Sox*	95-67	.586	2.0	68	7/17	3.5
New York Yankees	89-73	.549	8.0	2	4/16	0.0
Toronto Blue Jays	86-76	.531	11.0	1	4/13	0.0
Baltimore Orioles	68-93	.422	28.5	15	4/29	2.5

CENTRAL

Team	W-L	Pct	GB	D1	LD1	LLd
Chicago White Sox	89-74	.546	0.0	148	9/30	6.0
Minnesota Twins	88-75	.540	1.0	47	9/29	2.5
Cleveland Indians	81-81	.500	7.5	7	5/17	1.5
Kansas City Royals	75-87	.463	13.5	12	4/14	1.0
Detroit Tigers	74-88	.457	14.5	0	-	0.0

WEST

Team	W-L	Pct	GB	D1	LD1	LLd
Los Angeles Angels	100-62	.617	0.0	176	9/30	22.0
Texas Rangers	79-83	.488	21.0	1	4/1	0.0
Oakland Athletics	75-86	.466	24.5	31	5/12	2.0
Seattle Mariners	61-101	.377	39.0	3	4/2	0.5

* Clinched Wild Card Birth on 9/23. Division Clinch Dates: Los Angeles 9/10, Tampa Bay 9/26, Chicago 9/30.
D1 = Number of days a team had at least a share of first place of their division; LD1 = Last date the team had at least a share of first place; LLd = The largest number of games that a team led their division

East Division

Tm	AT Home	Road	East	Cent	West	NL	LHS	RHS	Day	Night	Grass	Turf	1-Rn	5+Rn	Xinn	M/A	May	June	July	Aug	Sept	Pre	Post
TB	57-24	40-41	43-29	20-18	22-12	12-6	25-24	72-41	26-21	71-44	38-35	59-30	29-18	27-18	10-6	15-12	19-10	16-10	13-12	21-7	13-14	55-39	42-26
Bos	56-25	39-42	38-34	24-10	22-16	11-7	25-13	70-54	26-20	69-47	88-50	7-17	22-23	33-17	8-3	17-12	17-12	16-11	11-13	18-9	16-10	57-40	38-27
NYY	48-33	41-40	40-32	21-19	18-14	10-8	24-22	65-51	34-22	55-51	82-60	7-13	14-15	14-12	7-3	14-15	14-12	16-12	15-10	13-15	17-9	50-45	39-28
Tor	47-34	39-42	37-35	24-12	17-19	8-10	20-23	66-53	32-18	54-58	34-38	52-38	24-32	24-10	6-9	11-17	20-10	10-16	13-11	16-12	16-10	47-48	39-28
Bal	37-43	31-50	22-50	20-18	15-18	11-7	16-32	52-61	14-30	54-63	62-78	6-15	21-29	20-29	5-6	16-12	11-16	15-12	10-16	11-17	5-20	46-48	22-45

Central Division

Tm	AT Home	Road	East	Cent	West	NL	LHS	RHS	Day	Night	Grass	Turf	1-Rn	5+Rn	Xinn	M/A	May	June	July	Aug	Sept	Pre	Post
CWS	54-28	35-46	15-26	44-29	18-13	12-6	31-20	58-54	33-21	56-53	85-58	4-16	22-17	30-24	8-4	14-13	16-13	17-10	13-12	17-11	12-15	54-41	35-33
Min	53-28	35-47	13-22	43-30	18-19	14-4	29-24	59-51	26-26	62-49	33-42	55-33	26-26	34-18	8-10	13-14	15-13	17-11	15-10	17-12	11-15	53-42	35-33
Cle	45-36	36-45	20-15	36-36	19-18	6-12	21-23	60-58	17-29	64-52	75-72	6-9	14-17	29-20	5-9	13-15	12-15	12-16	10-14	18-10	16-11	41-53	40-28
KC	38-43	37-44	14-26	31-41	17-15	13-5	36-24	39-63	29-24	46-63	70-75	5-12	20-18	16-31	7-6	12-15	10-19	16-11	12-14	7-20	18-8	43-53	32-34
Det	40-41	34-47	15-20	27-45	19-18	13-5	26-22	48-66	25-33	49-55	69-77	5-11	16-25	22-29	3-9	13-15	10-17	19-8	13-13	11-17	8-18	47-47	27-41

West Division

Tm	AT Home	Road	East	Cent	West	NL	LHS	RHS	Day	Night	Grass	Turf	1-Rn	5+Rn	Xinn	M/A	May	June	July	Aug	Sept	Pre	Post
LAA	50-31	50-31	30-16	24-17	36-21	10-8	33-16	67-46	32-11	68-51	94-55	6-7	31-21	20-20	3-5	18-11	15-13	16-10	19-6	15-13	17-9	57-38	43-24
Tex	40-41	39-42	17-26	22-22	30-27	10-8	21-31	58-52	17-24	62-59	73-77	6-6	28-18	24-30	5-6	10-18	19-10	14-13	13-12	11-18	12-12	50-46	29-37
Oak	43-38	32-48	17-23	22-24	26-31	10-8	25-28	50-58	23-29	52-57	69-77	6-9	25-24	21-23	8-7	17-12	12-15	16-10	8-17	10-20	12-12	51-44	24-42
Sea	35-46	26-55	15-29	15-28	22-35	9-9	21-31	40-70	20-33	41-68	56-94	5-7	18-30	13-24	5-7	13-15	8-20	10-16	10-16	12-16	8-18	37-58	24-43

Team vs. Team Breakdown

	EAST TB	Bos	NYY	Tor	Bal	CENTRAL CWS	Min	Cle	KC	Det	WEST LAA	Tex	Oak	Sea
Tampa Bay Rays	-	10	7	11	15	6	3	2	5	4	6	6	6	4
Boston Red Sox	8	-	9	9	12	4	4	5	6	5	1	9	6	6
New York Yankees	11	9	-	9	11	5	6	3	5	2	3	3	5	7
Toronto Blue Jays	7	9	9	-	12	7	6	1	5	5	3	4	6	4
Baltimore Orioles	3	6	7	6	-	4	3	4	5	4	3	4	0	8
Chicago White Sox	4	3	2	1	5	-	9	11	12	12	5	3	5	5
Minnesota Twins	3	3	4	0	3	10	-	10	12	11	3	5	5	5
Cleveland Indians	5	1	4	6	4	7	8	-	10	11	4	6	5	4
Kansas City Royals	3	1	5	2	3	6	6	8	-	11	2	2	6	7
Detroit Tigers	3	2	4	3	3	6	7	7	7	-	3	6	3	7
Los Angeles Angels	3	8	7	6	6	5	5	5	3	6	-	12	10	14
Texas Rangers	3	1	4	4	5	3	5	4	7	3	7	-	12	11
Oakland Athletics	3	4	1	4	5	4	5	4	3	6	9	7	-	10
Seattle Mariners	3	3	2	5	2	1	4	5	2	3	5	8	9	-

2008 National League Standings

Overall

EAST

Team	W-L	Pct	GB	D1	LD1	LLd
Philadelphia Phillies	92-70	.568	0.0	89	9/30	4.0
New York Mets	89-73	.549	3.0	47	9/19	3.5
Florida Marlins	84-77	.522	7.5	49	5/31	3.0
Atlanta Braves	72-90	.444	20.0	1	4/6	0.0
Washington Nationals	59-102	.366	32.5	5	4/3	1.0

CENTRAL

Team	W-L	Pct	GB	D1	LD1	LLd
Chicago Cubs	97-64	.602	0.0	154	9/30	10.5
Milwaukee Brewers*	90-72	.556	7.5	10	7/26	1.0
Houston Astros	86-75	.534	11.0	0	-	0.0
St Louis Cardinals	86-76	.531	11.5	25	5/10	2.5
Cincinnati Reds	74-88	.457	23.5	1	4/3	0.0
Pittsburgh Pirates	67-95	.414	30.5	3	4/3	0.0

WEST

Team	W-L	Pct	GB	D1	LD1	LLd
Los Angeles Dodgers	84-78	.519	0.0	40	9/30	4.5
Arizona Diamondbacks	82-80	.506	2.0	154	9/5	6.5
Colorado Rockies	74-88	.457	10.0	0	-	0.0
San Francisco Giants	72-90	.444	12.0	0	-	0.0
San Diego Padres	63-99	.389	21.0	5	4/5	0.5

* Clinched Wild Card Birth on 9/28. Division Clinch Dates: Chicago 9/20, Los Angeles 9/25, Philadelphia 9/27.
D1 = Number of days a team had at least a share of first place of their division; LD1 = Last date the team had at least a share of first place; LLd = The largest number of games that a team led their division

East Division

Tm	AT Home	AT Road	VERSUS East	Cent	West	AL	LHS	RHS	COND Day	Night	Grass	Turf	GAME 1-Rn	5+Rn	XInn	MONTHLY M/A	May	June	July	Aug	Sept	ALL-STAR Pre	Post
Phi	48-33	44-37	41-31	27-16	20-12	4-11	32-22	60-48	24-24	68-46	92-70	0-0	27-23	21-14	6-7	15-13	17-12	12-14	15-10	16-13	17-8	52-44	40-26
NYM	48-33	41-40	40-32	20-20	20-15	9-6	34-21	55-52	29-25	60-48	89-73	0-0	16-19	29-21	9-9	14-12	13-15	13-15	18-8	18-11	13-12	51-44	38-29
Fla	45-36	39-41	40-31	19-20	20-16	5-10	23-21	61-56	25-18	59-59	83-75	1-2	24-19	21-23	9-5	15-12	16-11	12-16	15-12	11-17	15-9	50-45	34-32
Atl	43-38	29-52	31-41	13-28	20-14	8-7	20-33	52-57	22-30	50-60	71-88	1-2	11-30	28-25	3-10	12-15	17-12	11-16	10-15	9-20	13-12	45-50	27-40
Was	34-46	25-56	27-44	15-25	9-23	8-10	22-36	37-66	19-29	40-73	59-99	0-3	20-29	14-36	7-7	11-17	13-16	9-18	5-19	14-15	7-17	36-60	23-42

Central Division

Tm	AT Home	AT Road	VERSUS East	Cent	West	AL	LHS	RHS	COND Day	Night	Grass	Turf	GAME 1-Rn	5+Rn	XInn	MONTHLY M/A	May	June	July	Aug	Sept	ALL-STAR Pre	Post
ChC	55-26	42-38	20-12	48-33	23-10	6-9	31-16	66-48	48-29	49-35	95-60	2-4	24-22	33-14	10-6	17-10	18-11	15-12	15-11	20-8	12-12	57-38	40-26
Mil	49-32	41-40	16-19	47-32	20-13	7-8	33-20	57-52	36-28	54-44	89-70	1-2	28-17	25-22	12-8	15-12	13-16	16-10	16-11	20-7	10-16	52-43	38-29
Hou	47-33	39-42	17-15	43-35	19-14	7-11	26-20	60-55	23-20	63-55	84-74	2-1	21-21	18-24	5-3	13-16	17-11	10-16	10-14	21-9	15-9	44-51	42-24
StL	46-35	40-41	22-14	36-41	21-13	7-8	27-29	59-47	27-26	59-50	86-76	0-0	24-28	26-19	6-12	18-11	15-13	15-12	13-14	13-12	13-12	46-50	28-38
Cin	43-38	31-50	19-17	31-47	15-18	9-6	30-25	44-63	25-28	49-60	73-86	1-2	28-20	20-30	12-6	11-16	15-13	12-15	12-14	7-21	10-16	44-50	23-45
Pit	39-42	28-53	15-17	32-49	14-20	6-9	14-28	53-67	20-29	47-66	67-95	0-0	22-21	18-32	12-6	11-16	15-13	9-18	5-19	14-15	7-17	44-50	23-45

West Division

Tm	AT Home	AT Road	VERSUS East	Cent	West	AL	LHS	RHS	COND Day	Night	Grass	Turf	GAME 1-Rn	5+Rn	XInn	MONTHLY M/A	May	June	July	Aug	Sept	ALL-STAR Pre	Post
LAD	48-33	36-45	16-18	23-18	40-32	5-10	31-21	53-57	23-24	61-54	84-78	0-0	19-24	29-26	6-12	14-13	13-15	11-16	16-10	13-16	17-8	46-49	38-29
Ari	48-33	34-47	15-21	17-22	44-28	6-9	28-20	54-60	26-28	56-52	82-77	0-3	22-23	26-25	4-6	20-8	11-17	11-16	14-11	13-15	13-13	47-48	35-32
Col	43-38	31-50	15-21	21-18	31-41	7-8	26-21	48-67	17-30	57-58	74-88	0-0	25-20	27-31	10-5	11-17	9-19	15-13	15-10	15-14	13-13	40-55	32-35
SF	37-44	35-46	19-13	11-29	36-36	6-12	16-31	56-59	27-32	45-58	72-90	0-0	16-28	19-27	6-8	11-17	12-17	10-17	9-16	11-16	10-16	37-58	26-41
SD	35-46	28-53	15-16	16-25	29-43	3-15	20-37	43-62	20-24	43-75	63-99	0-0	16-28	19-27	6-8	11-17	12-17	10-17	9-16	11-16	10-16	37-58	26-41

Team vs. Team Breakdown

	EAST Phi	NYM	Fla	Atl	Was	CENTRAL ChC	Mil	Hou	StL	Cin	Pit	WEST LAD	Ari	Col	SF	SD
Philadelphia Phillies	-	7	8	14	12	4	5	4	5	5	4	4	4	5	3	4
New York Mets	11	-	10	7	12	2	4	2	4	4	4	4	3	6	5	2
Florida Marlins	10	8	-	8	14	3	5	4	2	2	3	3	7	3	3	4
Atlanta Braves	4	11	10	-	6	0	3	3	2	3	2	4	5	4	2	5
Washington Nationals	6	6	3	12	-	3	2	2	1	3	4	3	2	3	0	1
Chicago Cubs	3	4	4	6	3	-	9	8	9	8	14	5	4	5	4	5
Milwaukee Brewers	1	2	1	6	6	7	-	8	10	8	14	2	5	3	6	4
Houston Astros	3	5	2	3	4	9	7	-	7	12	8	4	2	3	7	3
St Louis Cardinals	4	3	5	5	5	6	5	8	-	10	7	4	4	4	5	4
Cincinnati Reds	3	3	6	3	4	7	10	3	5	-	6	1	4	1	5	4
Pittsburgh Pirates	2	3	2	5	3	4	1	8	10	9	-	2	3	2	4	3
Los Angeles Dodgers	4	3	4	2	3	2	4	3	2	7	5	-	10	10	9	11
Arizona Diamondbacks	3	3	2	3	4	2	2	4	3	2	4	8	-	15	11	10
Colorado Rockies	0	3	5	3	4	1	4	3	3	5	5	8	3	-	11	9
San Francisco Giants	3	1	3	5	7	3	0	1	4	1	2	9	7	7	-	13
San Diego Padres	2	5	2	1	5	2	3	1	3	4	3	7	8	9	5	-

American League Batting

Tm	G	AB	H	2B	3B	HR	(Hm	Rd)	TB	R	RBI	TBB	IBB	SO	HBP	SH	SF	ShO	SB	CS	SB%	GDP	LOB	Avg	OBP	Slg
Tex	162	5728	1619	376	35	194	(107	87)	2647	901	867	595	43	1207	63	37	54	6	81	25	.76	117	1238	.283	.354	.462
Bos	162	5596	1565	353	33	173	(79	94)	2503	845	807	646	49	1068	70	28	62	7	120	35	.77	148	1262	.280	.358	.447
Min	163	5641	1572	298	49	111	(56	55)	2301	829	791	529	48	979	36	52	72	9	102	42	.71	144	1140	.279	.340	.408
Det	162	5641	1529	293	41	200	(112	88)	2504	821	780	572	23	1076	44	30	44	12	63	31	.67	144	1159	.271	.340	.444
CWS	163	5553	1458	296	13	235	(143	92)	2485	811	785	540	33	1016	63	28	47	11	67	34	.66	158	1067	.263	.332	.448
Cle	162	5543	1455	339	22	171	(89	82)	2351	805	772	560	44	1213	103	43	49	5	77	29	.73	123	1184	.262	.339	.424
NYY	162	5572	1512	289	20	180	(92	88)	2381	789	758	535	36	1015	80	31	39	8	118	39	.75	150	1160	.271	.342	.427
Bal	161	5559	1486	322	30	172	(96	76)	2384	782	750	533	37	990	42	27	48	5	81	37	.69	111	1134	.267	.333	.429
TB	162	5541	1443	284	37	180	(89	91)	2341	774	735	626	33	1224	68	23	52	7	142	50	.74	111	1215	.260	.340	.422
LAA	162	5540	1486	274	25	159	(72	87)	2287	765	721	481	52	987	52	32	50	6	129	48	.73	140	1087	.268	.330	.413
Tor	162	5503	1453	303	32	126	(69	57)	2198	714	681	521	34	938	59	48	56	12	80	27	.75	150	1155	.264	.331	.399
KC	162	5608	1507	303	28	120	(50	70)	2226	699	650	392	31	1005	50	32	36	13	79	38	.68	144	1073	.269	.320	.397
Sea	162	5643	1498	285	20	124	(59	65)	2195	671	631	417	44	890	38	36	42	12	90	32	.74	137	1151	.265	.318	.389
Oak	161	5451	1318	270	23	125	(62	63)	2009	646	610	574	23	1226	48	30	35	10	88	21	.81	126	1166	.242	.318	.369
AL	1134	78119	20901	4285	408	2270	(1175	1095)	32812	10844	10338	7521	530	14834	816	477	686	123	1317	488	.73	1903	16191	.268	.336	.420

American League Pitching

	HOW MUCH THEY PITCHED					WHAT THEY GAVE UP												THE RESULTS									
Tm	G	CG	Rel	IP	BFP	H	R	ER	HR	SH	SF	HB	TBB	IBB	SO	WP	Bk	W	L	Pct.	ShO	Sv-Op	Hld	OAvg	OOBP	OSlg	ERA
Tor	162	15	421	1446.2	6067	1330	610	561	134	31	40	67	467	42	1184	51	4	86	76	.531	13	44-56	72	.244	.309	.380	3.49
TB	162	7	448	1457.2	6145	1349	671	618	166	34	46	46	526	29	1143	52	3	97	65	.599	12	52-68	80	.246	.314	.400	3.82
Oak	161	4	441	1435.0	6112	1364	690	640	135	32	53	54	576	45	1061	30	4	75	86	.466	7	33-52	68	.253	.328	.392	4.01
Bos	162	5	466	1446.1	6180	1369	694	645	147	40	39	68	548	17	1185	43	2	95	67	.586	16	47-69	66	.250	.323	.390	4.01
LAA	162	7	383	1451.1	6161	1455	697	644	160	36	33	63	457	32	1106	50	2	100	62	.617	10	66-89	74	.261	.323	.406	3.99
NYY	162	1	475	1441.2	6175	1478	727	685	143	35	52	51	489	37	1141	55	5	89	73	.549	11	42-51	79	.266	.329	.405	4.28
CWS	163	4	463	1457.2	6218	1471	729	658	156	43	26	48	460	42	1147	54	3	89	74	.546	10	34-52	74	.261	.320	.410	4.06
Min	163	5	485	1459.0	6221	1568	745	675	183	32	37	31	406	38	995	45	4	88	75	.540	10	42-65	75	.274	.324	.431	4.16
Cle	162	10	399	1437.0	6164	1530	761	711	170	28	41	51	444	28	986	44	5	81	81	.500	13	31-51	75	.274	.330	.424	4.45
KC	162	2	439	1445.2	6214	1473	781	720	159	26	59	41	515	15	1085	68	5	75	87	.463	8	44-60	59	.264	.328	.415	4.48
Sea	162	4	469	1435.1	6368	1544	811	754	161	41	61	53	626	37	1016	60	5	61	101	.377	4	36-67	57	.276	.351	.433	4.73
Det	162	1	440	1445.0	6411	1541	857	786	172	33	49	68	644	63	991	65	7	74	88	.457	2	34-62	60	.274	.353	.437	4.90
Bal	161	4	492	1422.0	6414	1538	869	810	184	32	63	80	687	44	922	72	7	68	93	.422	4	35-59	56	.277	.361	.435	5.13
Tex	162	6	458	1442.0	6506	1647	967	860	176	30	55	72	625	44	963	62	9	79	83	.488	8	36-64	73	.288	.362	.455	5.37
AL	1134	75	6279	20222.1	87356	20657	10609	9767	2246	473	653	793	7470	513	14925	751	65	1157	1111	.510	128	576-865	944	.265	.333	.416	4.35

American League Fielding

Team	G	Inn	PO	Ast	OFAst	E	(Throw	Field)	TC	DP	GDP	SB	CS	SB%	CPkof	PPkof	PB	UER	UERA	FPct
Toronto	162	1446.2	4340	1699	31	84	36	48	6123	137	111	86	37	.70	1	5	6	49	0.30	.986
New York	162	1441.2	4325	1586	30	83	41	42	5994	141	111	113	56	.67	1	5	11	42	0.26	.986
Boston	162	1446.1	4339	1597	27	85	41	44	6021	149	119	96	32	.75	0	6	18	49	0.30	.986
Los Angeles	162	1451.1	4354	1646	31	91	47	44	6091	160	141	109	31	.78	3	4	10	53	0.33	.985
Tampa Bay	162	1457.2	4373	1495	33	90	44	46	5958	153	134	76	31	.71	0	4	10	53	0.33	.985
Cleveland	162	1437.0	4311	1689	27	94	34	60	6094	182	161	67	27	.71	0	1	13	50	0.31	.985
Kansas City	162	1445.2	4337	1548	25	96	46	50	5981	160	133	78	26	.75	1	4	8	61	0.38	.984
Seattle	162	1435.1	4306	1654	32	99	43	56	6059	160	139	92	37	.71	1	6	14	57	0.36	.984
Oakland	161	1435.0	4305	1574	35	98	52	46	5977	169	142	70	41	.63	0	16	8	50	0.31	.984
Baltimore	161	1422.0	4266	1661	33	100	52	48	6027	163	142	130	33	.80	1	2	15	59	0.37	.983
Chicago	163	1457.2	4373	1731	17	108	47	61	6212	155	136	139	30	.82	0	5	6	71	0.44	.983
Minnesota	163	1459.0	4377	1682	36	108	61	47	6167	168	143	69	34	.67	1	2	4	70	0.43	.982
Detroit	162	1445.0	4335	1634	28	113	39	74	6082	172	153	69	36	.66	0	5	16	71	0.44	.981
Texas	162	1442.0	4326	1676	30	132	64	68	6134	191	160	114	37	.75	0	5	13	107	0.67	.978
American League	1134	20222.1	60667	22872	415	1381	647	734	84920	2260	1925	1308	488	.73	9	70	152	842	0.37	.984

National League Batting

	BATTING																		BASERUNNING					PERCENTAGES		
Tm	G	AB	H	2B	3B	HR	(Hm	Rd)	TB	R	RBI	TBB	IBB	SO	HBP	SH	SF	ShO	SB	CS	SB%	GDP	LOB	Avg	OBP	Slg
ChC	161	5588	1552	329	21	184	(106	78)	2475	855	811	636	48	1186	50	65	45	8	87	34	.72	134	1237	.278	.354	.443
Phi	162	5509	1407	291	36	214	(109	105)	2412	799	762	586	68	1117	67	71	40	8	136	25	.84	108	1154	.255	.332	.438
NYM	162	5606	1491	274	38	172	(95	77)	2357	799	751	619	71	1024	39	71	49	6	138	36	.79	129	1220	.266	.340	.420
StL	162	5636	1585	283	26	174	(79	95)	2442	779	744	577	63	985	42	71	44	5	73	32	.70	151	1241	.281	.350	.433
Fla	161	5499	1397	302	28	208	(94	114)	2379	770	741	543	50	1371	69	49	46	9	76	28	.73	98	1140	.254	.326	.433
Atl	162	5604	1514	316	33	130	(62	68)	2286	753	721	618	56	1023	42	69	34	14	58	27	.68	143	1274	.270	.345	.408
Mil	162	5535	1398	324	35	198	(100	98)	2386	750	722	550	44	1203	69	54	43	4	108	38	.74	97	1153	.253	.325	.431
Col	162	5557	1462	310	28	160	(92	68)	2308	747	714	570	36	1209	57	90	38	6	141	37	.79	119	1207	.263	.336	.415
Pit	162	5628	1454	314	21	153	(74	79)	2269	735	705	474	40	1039	59	66	51	7	57	19	.75	111	1135	.258	.320	.403
Ari	162	5409	1355	318	47	159	(77	82)	2244	720	683	587	49	1287	49	68	43	6	58	23	.72	105	1142	.251	.327	.415
Hou	161	5451	1432	284	22	167	(92	75)	2261	712	684	449	42	1051	52	57	41	6	114	52	.69	116	1073	.263	.323	.415
Cin	162	5465	1351	269	24	187	(103	84)	2229	704	677	560	50	1125	50	72	41	10	85	47	.64	101	1138	.247	.321	.408
LAD	162	5506	1455	271	29	137	(71	66)	2195	700	659	543	62	1032	43	64	38	12	126	43	.75	153	1161	.264	.333	.399
Was	161	5491	1376	269	26	117	(51	66)	2048	641	608	534	21	1095	67	64	36	21	81	43	.65	153	1178	.251	.323	.373
SF	162	5543	1452	311	37	94	(45	49)	2119	640	606	452	45	1044	48	57	44	13	36	17	.68	128	1181	.262	.321	.382
SD	162	5568	1390	264	27	154	(66	88)	2170	637	615	518	35	1259	53	59	46	13	36	17	.68	129	1181	.250	.317	.390
NL	1294	88595	23071	4729	478	2608	(1316	1292)	36580	11741	11203	8816	780	18050	856	1049	679	148	1482	547	.73	1986	18782	.260	.331	.413

National League Pitching

	HOW MUCH THEY PITCHED					WHAT THEY GAVE UP												THE RESULTS									
Tm	G	CG	Rel	IP	BFP	H	R	ER	HR	SH	SF	HB	TBB	IBB	SO	WP	Bk	W	L	Pct.	ShO	Sv-Op	Hld	OAvg	OOBP	OSlg	ERA
LAD	162	8	461	1447.1	6127	1381	648	591	123	63	43	48	480	58	1205	47	4	84	78	.519	11	35-55	61	.251	.315	.376	3.68
ChC	161	2	478	1450.2	6194	1329	671	624	160	47	38	65	548	45	1264	48	7	97	64	.602	8	44-68	74	.242	.316	.395	3.87
Phi	162	4	468	1449.2	6229	1444	680	625	160	50	24	57	533	64	1081	34	3	92	72	.568	11	47-62	80	.260	.329	.410	3.88
Mil	162	12	445	1455.2	6209	1415	689	623	175	69	40	42	528	32	1110	53	5	90	72	.556	10	45-71	68	.256	.323	.406	3.85
Ari	162	6	444	1434.2	6119	1403	706	635	147	72	47	68	451	41	1229	59	3	82	80	.506	9	39-62	68	.256	.318	.398	3.98
NYM	162	5	557	1464.1	6338	1415	715	662	163	73	40	70	590	53	1181	55	4	89	73	.549	12	43-72	99	.254	.331	.397	4.07
StL	162	2	506	1454.0	6264	1517	725	677	163	52	42	51	496	21	957	50	2	86	76	.531	7	42-73	106	.270	.332	.431	4.19
Hou	161	4	488	1425.1	6125	1453	743	691	197	46	40	49	492	53	1095	22	9	86	75	.534	13	48-65	80	.264	.328	.440	4.36
SF	162	4	478	1442.0	6341	1416	759	701	147	67	57	70	652	59	1240	77	7	72	90	.444	12	41-60	56	.263	.341	.404	4.38
SD	162	3	491	1458.1	6286	1466	764	714	165	64	49	38	561	61	1100	43	4	63	99	.389	6	30-56	55	.263	.332	.409	4.41
Fla	161	2	511	1435.1	6271	1421	767	707	161	77	45	58	586	66	1127	59	4	84	77	.522	8	36-60	87	.258	.333	.407	4.43
Atl	162	2	545	1440.2	6244	1439	778	714	156	86	50	42	586	80	1076	42	5	72	90	.444	7	26-44	76	.263	.336	.423	4.46
Cin	162	2	507	1442.1	6352	1542	800	729	201	77	45	67	557	40	1227	52	7	74	88	.457	6	34-55	58	.275	.345	.450	4.55
Col	162	3	485	1446.0	6338	1547	822	766	148	62	47	53	562	49	1041	61	7	74	88	.457	8	36-59	59	.276	.344	.431	4.77
Was	161	2	517	1434.0	6310	1496	825	742	190	76	49	51	588	44	1063	59	8	59	102	.366	8	28-56	66	.270	.343	.436	4.66
Pit	162	3	497	1455.0	6528	1631	884	822	176	72	56	49	657	31	963	64	9	67	95	.414	7	34-56	65	.263	.333	.417	5.08
NL	1294	61	7878	23135.1	100275	23315	11976	11023	2632	1053	712	879	8867	797	17959	825	88	1271	1317	.491	143	608-974	1158	.263	.333	.417	4.29

National League Fielding

			Fielding																	
Team	G	Inn	PO	Ast	OFAst	E	(Throw	Field)	TC	DP	GDP	SB	CS	SB%	CPkof	PPkof	PB	UER	UERA	FPct
Houston	161	1425.1	4276	1596	35	67	(28	39)	5939	142	120	47	21	.69	1	2	8	52	0.33	.989
St Louis	162	1454.0	4362	1817	31	85	(44	41)	6264	156	134	49	26	.65	7	3	7	48	0.30	.986
New York	162	1464.1	4393	1552	30	83	(35	48)	6086	126	112	66	28	.70	0	6	7	53	0.33	.986
San Diego	162	1458.1	4375	1626	15	85	(48	37)	6137	149	123	168	38	.82	2	3	11	50	0.31	.986
Philadelphia	162	1449.2	4349	1698	36	90	(33	57)	6250	142	127	109	34	.76	2	2	5	55	0.34	.985
Colorado	162	1446.0	4338	1816	27	96	(37	59)	6250	176	142	86	30	.74	1	7	10	56	0.35	.985
Los Angeles	162	1447.1	4342	1795	34	101	(50	51)	6238	138	124	82	26	.76	1	2	9	57	0.35	.984
Milwaukee	162	1455.2	4367	1699	22	101	(48	53)	6167	160	131	71	45	.61	0	4	5	66	0.41	.984
San Francisco	162	1442.0	4326	1393	30	96	(32	64)	5815	129	105	99	41	.71	1	1	8	58	0.36	.983
Chicago	161	1450.2	4352	1446	21	99	(38	61)	5897	118	97	87	36	.71	0	5	8	47	0.29	.983
Pittsburgh	162	1455.0	4365	1830	27	107	(47	60)	6302	180	157	104	46	.69	3	1	13	62	0.38	.983
Atlanta	162	1440.2	4322	1791	29	107	(56	51)	6220	149	129	113	35	.76	2	1	14	64	0.40	.981
Arizona	162	1434.2	4304	1564	22	113	(48	65)	5981	137	114	87	31	.74	0	1	7	71	0.45	.981
Cincinnati	162	1442.1	4327	1568	27	114	(63	51)	6009	156	130	95	40	.70	1	2	17	71	0.44	.980
Florida	161	1435.1	4306	1501	28	117	(59	58)	5924	122	100	110	32	.77	0	2	10	60	0.38	.980
Washington	161	1434.0	4302	1578	26	123	(57	66)	6003	143	119	118	38	.76	1	1	12	83	0.52	.980
National League	1294	23135.1	69406	26270	440	1584	(723	861)	97260	2323	1964	1491	547	.73	22	43	151	953	0.37	.984

Team Efficiency Summary

Bill James

This chart measures three things:

1) How many runs did the team score, compared to the number we would expect them to score based on their hitting stats?

2) How many runs did the team allow, compared to the number we would have expected them to allow?

3) How many games did the team win, based on the number of runs they scored and allowed?

If you have a homer, double, single and a walk in an inning, but you only score one run, that's very inefficient. If you have two walks and a single but you turn it into two runs, that's very efficient.

If you're outscored in a three-game series 7 to 12, but you win two of the three games, that's efficient. If you outscore your opponents 18 to 3 in a double-header, but you split the double-header, that's inefficient.

The most efficient team in the majors in 2008, by far, was the Angels. The least efficient teams were the Braves and the Padres.

2008 American League Team Efficiency Summary

	RC	Runs	Hit Eff	Exp RA	RA	Pit Eff	Exp Wins	Wins	Runs Eff	Eff Wins	Wins	Overall Eff
Los Angeles Angels	741	765	103	698	697	100	89	100	113	86	100	116
Minnesota Twins	783	829	106	755	745	101	90	88	98	84	88	104
Tampa Bay Rays	806	774	96	659	671	98	92	97	105	97	97	100
Kansas City Royals	688	691	100	729	781	93	71	75	105	76	75	98
New York Yankees	802	789	98	710	727	98	88	89	102	91	89	98
Chicago White Sox	792	811	102	704	729	97	90	89	99	91	89	98
Oakland Athletics	644	646	100	664	690	96	75	75	100	78	75	96
Texas Rangers	930	901	97	913	967	94	75	79	105	82	79	96
Baltimore Orioles	786	782	99	880	869	101	72	68	94	71	68	95
Cleveland Indians	790	805	102	741	761	97	86	81	95	86	81	94
Detroit Tigers	834	821	98	844	857	98	78	74	95	80	74	92
Boston Red Sox	894	845	95	672	694	97	97	95	98	104	95	92
Seattle Mariners	686	671	98	821	811	101	66	61	93	67	61	92
Toronto Blue Jays	722	714	99	610	610	100	94	86	92	94	86	91

2008 National League Team Efficiency Summary

	RC	Runs	Hit Eff	Exp RA	RA	Pit Eff	Exp Wins	Wins	Runs Eff	Eff Wins	Wins	Overall Eff
Cincinnati Reds	709	704	99	843	800	105	71	74	105	67	74	110
Houston Astros	713	712	100	731	743	98	77	86	112	79	86	110
Pittsburgh Pirates	721	735	102	893	884	101	66	67	101	64	67	105
Milwaukee Brewers	770	750	97	707	689	103	88	90	102	88	90	102
Florida Marlins	767	770	100	748	767	98	81	84	104	83	84	102
Philadelphia Phillies	805	799	99	714	680	105	94	92	98	91	92	101
San Francisco Giants	666	640	96	750	759	99	67	72	107	71	72	101
New York Mets	811	799	99	724	715	101	90	89	99	90	89	99
Chicago Cubs	871	855	98	669	671	100	100	97	97	101	97	96
Washington Nationals	652	641	98	822	825	100	61	59	97	62	59	95
St Louis Cardinals	844	779	92	743	725	102	87	86	99	91	86	94
Arizona Diamondbacks	729	720	99	676	706	96	83	82	99	87	82	94
Los Angeles Dodgers	722	700	97	632	648	98	87	84	96	92	84	92
Colorado Rockies	779	747	96	774	822	94	73	74	101	82	74	91
San Diego Padres	680	637	94	729	764	95	66	63	95	75	63	84
Atlanta Braves	786	753	96	732	778	94	78	72	92	87	72	83

Albert Pujols   Carl Crawford
Brandon Phillips   Carlos Beltran
Adrian Beltre   Franklin Gutierrez
Jimmy Rollins
                   Yadier Molina
                   Kenny Rogers

THE FIELDING BIBLE AWARDS 2008

The Fielding Bible Awards

John Dewan

Three strikes and you're out. But three wins of a Fielding Bible Award puts you in pretty exclusive company. How does it feel, Albert, to belong to a club that has only you as a member?

This is our third year of The Fielding Bible Awards, and Albert Pujols won his third straight award at first base. There were other repeaters this year as well, but no other player is three for three. Yadier Molina repeated at catcher from last year. Third baseman Adrian Beltre and outfielders Carl Crawford and Carlos Beltran won the award in 2006, took a year off, then won again this year.

Here's a short refresher course on how the awards are determined. We asked our panel of ten experts to rank 10 players at each position from one to ten. We then use the same voting technique as the Major League Baseball MVP voting. A first place vote gets 10 points, second place 9 points, third place 8 points, etc. Total up the points for each player and the player with the most points wins the award. A perfect score is 100.

One important distinction that differentiates our award from most other baseball awards, including the Gold Gloves, is that we only have one winner for all of Major League Baseball, instead of separate winners for each league. Our intention is to stand up and say "This is the best fielder at this position in the major leagues last season."

The Fielding Bible Awards 2008

First Base – Albert Pujols, St. Louis

He was the only repeat winner last year, and now Albert Pujols is the only three-time winner of the Fielding Bible Award. But this time it wasn't so easy. Mark Teixeira gave him a run for his money. Pujols finished with 90 points while Teixeira pulled in 88. One flip-flop would have garnered Teixeira at least a tie for first. Five panelists gave first place to the slugger from St. Louis while the late-season Angels star earned four. Former Angel Casey Kotchman received the final first-place vote.

Second Base – Brandon Phillips, Cincinnati

This one surprised me, but it shouldn't have. Brandon Phillips finished third in our voting last year and now has won his first Fielding Bible Award with 86 points. I voted for Chase Utley, who had the highest Plus/Minus figure at any position this year (+47 – see the Kenny Rogers discussion below for more information about the Plus/Minus System). But the panelists who watched Phillips play more regularly have seen what he can do on the field and rewarded him accordingly.

Third Base – Adrian Beltre, Seattle

It was a runaway victory for Adrian Beltre. Beltre won the award two years ago in the closest vote we've ever had (the tiebreaker was invoked) but this year his 36-point margin of victory, 90 points compared to 64 points for second-place finisher Evan Longoria, was the second largest margin of victory in this year's voting. Longoria showed that the rookie hype for him wasn't just about his prodigious bat. He can flash the leather as well.

Shortstop – Jimmy Rollins, Philadelphia

Jimmy Rollins won his first Gold Glove last year, and this year he wins his first Fielding Bible Award. The year started slow for Rollins. He didn't begin to show up on the Plus/Minus leaderboard at shortstop until well into the season, thanks primarily to his early-season injury. But he got it going and overtook Yunel Escobar in the last week of the season to win the Plus/Minus Crown with +23. Rollins also led all shortstops with the most Good Fielding Plays (65) by a good margin over Orlando Cabrera (55) and Erick Aybar (55). Rollins' 88 points in the voting, compared to 59 points for runner-up J.J. Hardy, represented this year's largest margin of victory. Escobar finished third in our voting, Aybar fourth and Cabrera sixth.

Left Field – Carl Crawford, Tampa Bay

He's baaack! And he didn't even have to play a full season to win it. Carl Crawford missed most of the month of September but still wins the Fielding Bible Award in left field for 2008 with 87 points. It's his second award, having won it in 2006. In 2007, he finished second to Eric Byrnes by a mere three points. Despite the missed time, Crawford held off Willie Harris' late run for the highest Plus/Minus total in left field (+23 to +22).

Center Field – Carlos Beltran, New York Mets

Like Carl Crawford in left, Carlos Beltran won the award for center fielders in 2006, but he finished second to Andruw Jones in a close battle in 2007. Now he wins his second Fielding Bible Award with 82 points. Minnesota's rookie speedster Carlos Gomez (74 points) finished second. Unlike Crawford, Beltran played injury free in 2008, starting 158 games in center field for the Mets, the highest total of his career.

Right Field – Franklin Gutierrez, Cleveland

Franklin Gutierrez led all right fielders in Plus/Minus last year with +20, although he did not win the Fielding Bible Award. To show that 2007 was no fluke, however, Gutierrez led them again this year with +29. Here's the amazing part: he did it while playing only 88 games in right field in 2007 and only 97 games this year. Gutierrez received 85 total points from our panel and is a first-time Fielding Bible Award winner in right field.

Catcher – Yadier Molina, St. Louis

Maybe his brothers are getting jealous; they're creeping up on him. But it's a repeat Fielding Bible Award for Yadier Molina in 2008 (88 points). Jose Molina finished tied for second with Jason Kendall of the Brewers this year at 63 points. With Bengie Molina placing eighth in the voting, it's the first time any set of two brothers, much less three, have cracked the top ten in our Fielding Bible Award voting. That record may stand for quite some time.

Pitcher – Kenny Rogers, Detroit

Greg Maddux of the Dodgers has won the National League Gold Glove Award for pitchers in 17 of the last 18 years. The American League Award has gone to Kenny Rogers of Detroit in five of the last eight years. But are they truly the two best fielding pitchers in baseball? Were they really the best in each and every year that they won? Aren't these two guys getting pretty old? Aren't there some younger studs out there to take their places?

Surely there must be other pitchers who are good fielders and should have won a few of those Gold Glove awards over the years. No other award has a string of repeat winners like this. Think of the MVP Award, the Cy Young Award, the Silver Slugger Award, Relief Man of the Year Award, etc. The key difference between these awards and the Gold Glove awards, however, is that statistics are much more strongly considered in the other awards. Gold Glove voters historically have not relied much on fielding statistics, and with good reason: there haven't been many new reliable statistics in fielding for over 100 years.

Until now (I hope). There are several new systems out there, and the Plus/Minus System from my book, *The Fielding Bible*, seems to be working pretty well. Video Scouts at Baseball Info Solutions chart each and every batted ball, including batted ball speed, type and direction. Using that information, the Plus/Minus System determines how well each fielder handles batted balls within each category compared to other fielders. A plus five (+5) in the system, for example, says this particular fielder successfully handled five more balls than the average fielder at his position.

When we published the first edition of *The Fielding Bible* three years ago, we hadn't yet developed a Plus/Minus System for pitchers. But we have since then. Complete Plus/Minus results for pitchers will be available in *The Fielding Bible – Volume II*, available in February of 2009. So let's see how Maddux and Rogers come out when measured by that system.

Here's what we found: Greg Maddux and Kenny Rogers are far and away the two best fielding pitchers in the Plus/Minus System since we started it in 2003. The Gold Glove voters got this one right by instinct and observation, and now the stats confirm their judgment. Here are the total Plus/Minus numbers for the top three fielding pitchers since 2003:

Greg Maddux	+56
Kenny Rogers	+53
Livan Hernandez	+30

It is incredible that Maddux and Rogers are number one and number two, while the number three guy, Livan Hernandez, is a very distant third. This says two things to me: 1) The Gold Glove voters knew what they're doing when it comes to pitchers. Relying primarily on visual evidence, they've seen the excellent glove work by Maddux and Rogers. 2) The Plus/Minus System works. It comes up with the same answers as the Gold Glove voters.

Of course, there are some huge exceptions to this correlation. For example, Derek Jeter has won three Gold Gloves but has never fared well in the Plus/Minus System, and Adam Everett has worn four "Plus/Minus Crowns" as the highest-rated shortstop in baseball, but he has never won a Gold Glove.

Maddux and Rogers have the highest 6-year Plus/Minus numbers, but that doesn't mean they should win every year, does it? They should have some off years in there somewhere, shouldn't they? Here are their yearly numbers, along with their rank in all of Major League Baseball and their Gold Gloves (GG) and Fielding Bible Awards (FBA):

	Maddux			Rogers		
	+/-	Rank	Award	+/-	Rank	Award
2003	+7	3		+6	6	
2004	+10	2	GG	+10	4	GG
2005	+6	6	GG	+12	1	GG
2006	+10	1	GG, FBA	+8	3	GG
2007	+10	1	GG	+1	---	
2008	+14	2	tba	+16	1	FBA

The real surprise is that either Rogers or Maddux has had the highest Plus/Minus figure among pitchers in each of the last four years, although Johan Santana beat them both out for the Fielding Bible Award for pitchers last year. Mad Dog and The Gambler are not just getting older, they're getting better. Despite his injuries, age, and less-effective pitching, Kenny Rogers had the highest figure again this year, with Maddux right behind him.

Giving the Gold Gloves to Maddux in the National League and Rogers in the American is a no-brainer once again, but this year's Fielding Bible Award goes to Kenny Rogers with the highest point total of the year at any position (95 points). It wasn't simply because his Plus/Minus figure is slightly better. It's because of his control of the running game. Rogers is exceptionally good at it, while Maddux is notoriously bad. Here are the figures: Rogers—only three attempted stolen bases all season, two of them caught, plus three runners picked off; Maddux—29 attempted steals, only five caught, no runners picked off.

Background of the Fielding Bible Awards

While *The Fielding Bible* puts a lot of emphasis on the numbers, especially my Plus-Minus system, I feel that visual observation and subjective judgment are still very important parts of determining the best defensive players. Also, I think people have a right to know who is voting and all the players they are voting for. Therefore, in setting up the Fielding Bible Awards, we took the following steps:

1. *I appointed a panel of experts to vote.* We have a panel of ten experts plus three "tie-breaker" ballots. (See below.)

2. *We rate everybody in one group.* The Gold Glove vote is divided into National League and American League. We make ours different by putting everybody together. Besides, is playing shortstop in the American League one thing and playing shortstop in the National League a different thing, or are they really very much the same thing? We want to say who the best fielder was at each position last year in Major League Baseball, period. So we have a single ballot.

3. *We use a ten-man ballot.* We use a ten-man ballot (I'm referring to the players listed, not the panel of experts). Ten points for first place, nine points for second place, etc, down to one point for tenth place. We feel strongly that a ten-man ballot with weighted positions leads to more accurate outcomes.

4. *We defined the list of candidates.* Only players who actually were regulars at the position are candidates. This eliminates the possibility of a vote going to somebody who wasn't really playing the position.

5. *We are publishing the balloting.* We summarize the voting at each position, clearly identifying whom everybody voted for. Publishing the actual vote totals encourages the voters to take their votes more seriously. Also, we feel the public will have more respect for the voting if they have more insight into the process.

There is something cool about having 10 experts and a 10-man ballot, because that gives each position 100 possible points. If all 10 voters place one player first on their ballot, he scores 100. That hasn't happened yet.

Here are the tie-breaker rules (which came into play in our very first year):
1. Most first-place votes wins.
2. Count the tie-breaker ballots.
3. Award goes to player with the higher plus/minus rating.

Ballots were due on the Tuesday after the end of the regular season. Here is this year's panel:

Since you have this book, you probably know **Bill James**, a baseball writer and analyst published for more than thirty years. Bill is the Senior Baseball Operations Advisor for the Boston Red Sox.

The **BIS Video Scouts** at Baseball Info Solutions (BIS) study every game of the season, sometimes multiple times, with the task of examining a huge list of valuable game details.

The man who created Strat-O-Matic Baseball, **Hal Richman**, continues to lead his company's annual in-depth analysis of each player's season. Hal cautions SOM players that his voting on this ballot may or may not reflect the eventual 2008 fielding ratings for players in his game. Ballots were due prior to the completion of his annual research effort to evaluate player defense.

Named the best sports columnist in America by the Associated Press Sports Editors in 2003 and 2005, **Joe Posnanski** writes for the Kansas City Star.

For over twenty years, BIS owner **John Dewan** has collected, analyzed, and published in-depth baseball statistics. He wrote *The Fielding Bible* in February 2006. An update to this book, *The Fielding Bible – Volume II*, is planned for February 2009.

Mat Olkin has studied, analyzed and written about evaluating player and team performance for fifteen years, the last five as a sabermetrics consultant for major league teams.

On Chicago sports radio for more than fifteen years, **Mike Murphy's** many strengths include keen baseball observations. He currently hosts a daily show on WSCR 670 The Score.

Dan Casey is the Video Scouting Operations Manager at BIS, overseeing Data Collection and managing the Video Scouting staff. Dan began his career in the New York Yankees organization, working in Baseball Operations and Player Development.

Rob Neyer writes baseball for ESPN.com and appears regularly on ESPN radio and ESPNews.

The **Tom Tango Fan Poll** represents the results of a poll taken at the website, Tango on Baseball (www.tangotiger.net). Besides hosting the website, Tom writes research articles devoted to sabermetrics.

Our three tie-breakers are **Steve Moyer**, president of BIS, **Todd Radcliffe**, lead Video Scout at BIS, and **Dave Studenmund**, one of the founders of www.hardballtimes.com and *The Hardball Times Baseball Annual*.

The Fielding Bible Awards

Below we show the final point tally for The Fielding Bible Awards in the 2008 season. We asked a panel of experts to complete a ten-man ballot ranking the defensive ability of players from 1 to 10. We show the ranks in the tables below. We then awarded points in the same way as Major League Baseball's MVP voting: ten points for a first place vote, nine for second, etc., down to one point for tenth place. We cover all nine positions, looking at only their fielding work for the 2008 season. Non-pitchers are only eligible if they played at least 500 innings. Pitchers require a minimum of 100 innings pitched.

First Basemen

First Basemen	Bill James	BIS Video Scouts	Dan Casey	Hal Richman	Joe Posnanski	John Dewan	Mat Olkin	Mike Murphy	Rob Neyer	Tango Fan Poll	Total Points
Albert Pujols	1	2	4	3	1	2	1	4	1	1	90
Mark Teixeira	3	1	1	1	2	1	5	2	2	4	88
Casey Kotchman	7	3	2	4	4	3	3	1	7	10	66
Carlos Pena	4	4	3	8		4	2	3	6		54
Lance Berkman	6	5	5		3	5	6	6	3	7	53
Derrek Lee	5	6	7	2	10	6	4	9	9	2	50
Kevin Youkilis	2	7		6	8	10	8	10	8	6	34
Todd Helton	10	8	8	7	7	8	9	7		5	30
James Loney		9	6	10				5	10	9	17
Joey Votto	8				5	9			5		17
Others receiving points: Adrian Gonzalez 15, Daric Barton 5, Carlos Delgado 2, Justin Morneau 1											

Second Basemen

Second Basemen	Bill James	BIS Video Scouts	Dan Casey	Hal Richman	Joe Posnanski	John Dewan	Mat Olkin	Mike Murphy	Rob Neyer	Tango Fan Poll	Total Points
Brandon Phillips	1	2	1	2	2	3	7	3	2	1	86
Mark Ellis	3	4	5	3	3	2	1		4	2	72
Chase Utley	2	1	7	10	1	1	2	9	1	10	66
Dustin Pedroia	4	3	6	4	4	6	4	10	3	7	59
Orlando Hudson	6	7	2	1	6	7	8	8	7	4	54
Placido Polanco	8	5		7	5	4	5		5	8	41
Asdrubal Cabrera		6		6	10	8	3		6	3	35
Brian Roberts	9		8	5				4		5	24
Alexei Ramirez		8	3			10		6		9	19
Robinson Cano		9	4					2			18
Others receiving points: Adam Kennedy 17, Akinori Iwamura 16, Jose Lopez 10, Freddy Sanchez 7, Ian Kinsler 6, Howie Kendrick 5, Rickie Weeks 4, Jamey Carroll 3, Luis Castillo 3, Mark Grudzielanek 2, Dan Uggla 2, Alexi Casilla 1											

Third Basemen

Third Basemen	Bill James	BIS Video Scouts	Dan Casey	Hal Richman	Joe Posnanski	John Dewan	Mat Olkin	Mike Murphy	Rob Neyer	Tango Fan Poll	Total Points
Adrian Beltre	1	1	1	1	1	1	1	10	1	2	90
Evan Longoria	3	3	5	6	4	9	2	6	5	3	64
Scott Rolen	6	4		2	2	2	7		2	1	62
Jack Hannahan	4	5	2	7	5	5	3		3		54
Joe Crede	5	6	3	10	3	3	6		4		48
David Wright	2	2	4	8	10	6	5	8	8	9	48
Mike Lowell	9	10		3	6	8	4	4	7	6	42
Pedro Feliz				5	7	4	8	5		5	32
Ryan Zimmerman	10	7		4	9	7	10		9	4	28
Alex Rodriguez		8	8					3	6	7	23
Others receiving points: Troy Glaus 20, Kevin Kouzmanoff 9, Chipper Jones 8, Casey Blake 5, Blake DeWitt 4, Edwin Encarnacion 4, Chone Figgins 4, Melvin Mora 2, Aramis Ramirez 2, Bill Hall 1											

Shortstops

Shortstops	Bill James	BIS Video Scouts	Dan Casey	Hal Richman	Joe Posnanski	John Dewan	Mat Olkin	Mike Murphy	Rob Neyer	Tango Fan Poll	Total Points
Jimmy Rollins	2	1	2	1	2	1	1	3	1	8	88
J.J. Hardy	5	3	3		3	3	2	8	2		59
Yunel Escobar	3	4		3	1	7	9	7	3	10	52
Erick Aybar	1	5	1		7	9		10	4	2	49
Jack Wilson		2	5	7		2	6	4		6	45
Orlando Cabrera	6	8	4	6	6	10	8	2	9		40
Cesar Izturis		6		9	4	6	3	5		9	35
Troy Tulowitzki		7		4	8	5	5			3	34
Omar Vizquel		10		2		4			6	1	32
Jose Reyes	4			5			10	9		4	23

Others receiving points: Michael Young 17, Cristian Guzman 15, Miguel Tejada 15, Jason Bartlett 13, Mike Aviles 8, Jhonny Peralta 5, Ryan Theriot 5, Stephen Drew 4, Khalil Greene 4, Yuniesky Betancourt 3, Bobby Crosby 3, Derek Jeter 1

Left Fielders

Left Fielders	Bill James	BIS Video Scouts	Dan Casey	Hal Richman	Joe Posnanski	John Dewan	Mat Olkin	Mike Murphy	Rob Neyer	Tango Fan Poll	Total Points
Carl Crawford	1	1	5	1	1	1	1	9	1	2	87
Willie Harris	4	2		2	3	2	3		2	1	69
Matt Holliday	3	5	8		2	5	2		7	9	47
Fred Lewis	6	4		9	4	8	7		4	5	41
Garret Anderson	10	8	6	6		6	5	4		8	35
Jason Bay		3	1					3		6	31
Johnny Damon	2			5	8				5	7	28
Juan Pierre			3		10		4		6	4	28
Josh Willingham		6	7		9	4		1			28
Luke Scott					6	3			3		21

Others receiving points: Alfonso Soriano 20, Pat Burrell 18, Ben Francisco 17, Conor Jackson 17, Delmon Young 16, Brandon Boggs 14, Ryan Braun 14, Raul Ibanez 11, Adam Lind 4, Chase Headley 2, Carlos Quentin 1, Manny Ramirez 1

Center Fielders

Center Fielders	Bill James	BIS Video Scouts	Dan Casey	Hal Richman	Joe Posnanski	John Dewan	Mat Olkin	Mike Murphy	Rob Neyer	Tango Fan Poll	Total Points
Carlos Beltran	1	1		2	1	2	2	5	2	1	82
Carlos Gomez	2	4	7	6	2	1	1	1	1		74
Grady Sizemore	3	2	3	3	3	6	6	3	7	9	65
Torii Hunter	6	3		1	7		4		4	4	48
Mike Cameron	5	9		5	6	5	3			5	39
Chris Young		6			4	9	5		3	8	31
Adam Jones	9	5					7	10	5	2	28
Corey Patterson			10		5	3			6		20
Shane Victorino	8	7		7	10	7				7	20
Melky Cabrera	4		5					7	9		19
Matt Kemp		6				10	8	6		6	19

Others receiving points: Curtis Granderson 17, Vernon Wells 15, Aaron Rowand 14, Cody Ross 13, B.J. Upton 12, Coco Crisp 10, Nate McLouth 10, Jody Gerut 9, Rick Ankiel 3, Josh Hamilton 1, Willy Taveras 1

Right Fielders

Right Fielders	Bill James	BIS Video Scouts	Dan Casey	Hal Richman	Joe Posnanski	John Dewan	Mat Olkin	Mike Murphy	Rob Neyer	Tango Fan Poll	Total Points
Franklin Gutierrez	2	4	2	2	3	1	2	6	1	2	85
Nick Markakis	6	1	1	3	6	3	3	1	9	5	72
Denard Span	3	5	5	9	4	5	8	2	3	3	63
Ichiro Suzuki	8	2	3	1	2	6	9		6	1	61
Alex Rios	1	3		4		2	1	5	5	8	59
Randy Winn	5	6			1	4	7	7	2	6	50
Brian Giles	4	9	7		5	8	6		4		34
Hunter Pence		7	9	10		10	4	3	8		26
Kosuke Fukudome		8		6		9		10		4	18
J.D. Drew	9			7	10					7	11

Others receiving points: Ryan Church 10, Justin Upton 9, Jermaine Dye 7, Jeff Francoeur 7, Gabe Gross 7, Xavier Nady 7, Jeremy Hermida 6, Austin Kearns 6, Brad Hawpe 3, Geoff Jenkins 3, Andre Ethier 2, Corey Hart 2, Ken Griffey Jr. 1, Ryan Ludwick 1

Catchers

Catchers	Bill James	BIS Video Scouts	Dan Casey	Hal Richman	Joe Posnanski	John Dewan	Mat Olkin	Mike Murphy	Rob Neyer	Tango Fan Poll	Total Points
Yadier Molina	1	1	1	2	4	8	1	2	1	1	88
Jason Kendall	7	5	3	9	5	1	3	1	2		63
Jose Molina		2	2	5		3	2	5	3	3	63
Kurt Suzuki		3	4		1	2	5	7	4	7	55
Joe Mauer	2	4	6	4	3				5	2	51
Rod Barajas		10	5		2	4	7	3			35
Dioner Navarro	3		8		6	5	4	8	9		34
Bengie Molina	4	6		7	8			9	6	10	27
Ivan Rodriguez	10		9		7			6	8	4	22
Russell Martin				1			8		10	6	19
Chris Snyder	5				6		9			5	19

Others receiving points: Jason Varitek 18, Geovany Soto 15, Brian Schneider 13, Kenji Johjima 8, A.J. Pierzynski 8, Gerald Laird 5, Jeff Mathis 4, Brad Ausmus 2, Brian McCann 1

Pitchers

Pitchers	Bill James	BIS Video Scouts	Dan Casey	Hal Richman	Joe Posnanski	John Dewan	Mat Olkin	Mike Murphy	Rob Neyer	Tango Fan Poll	Total Points
Kenny Rogers	1	2	1	3	2	1	1	2	1	1	95
Greg Maddux	4	1	4	1	1	2	5	1	3	2	86
Jesse Litsch	2	5	5	6	6	3		3	4	3	62
Ryan Dempster	6	10			4	7	6	5		4	35
Brandon Webb	10	3		5	3	10		7		5	34
Johan Santana		4	3	2	5						30
Kyle Kendrick	3	7	6					6		8	25
Roy Oswalt		8				4	4		9		19
Jake Peavy	8		2					4			19
Greg Smith							2		2		18

Others receiving points: Aaron Cook 14, Felix Hernandez 13, Jeff Suppan 12, Jon Garland 11, Zack Greinke 9, Javier Vazquez 8, Zach Duke 7, Tim Hudson 7, Mike Mussina 7, Bronson Arroyo 5, Hiroki Kuroda 5, Jason Marquis 5, Dan Haren 4, Dustin McGowan 4, Cole Hamels 3, Rich Harden 3, Mark Buehrle 2, Shaun Marcum 2, Micah Owings 2, Brian Bannister 1, R.A. Dickey 1, Jair Jurrjens 1, Andy Sonnanstine 1

Plus/Minus Leaders

John Dewan

The next two pages summarize the leaders in Plus/Minus by position for the last three years, and for 2008 by itself. Trailers are also included.

The Plus/Minus System is a way to evaluate defensive ability in baseball. A number greater than zero (plus "+") is above average. Below zero (minus "-") is below average. Please see the Glossary (or www.fieldingbible.com) for a more complete description. Also, keep an eye out for my next book on this topic, *The Fielding Bible – Volume II*, scheduled for February 2009.

Some observations on the leader boards:

- The three-year leaders clearly identify the best defensive players in baseball. Take a look at the top five at each position on the 2006-2008 Plus/Minus Leaders page and there's no doubt about it.

- Similarly, the three-year trailers make it pretty clear who baseball's worst defenders are.

- Six winners of a 2008 "Plus/Minus Crown" (the highest Plus/Minus score for the year) at their respective positions also won Fielding Bible Awards in 2008. Of those six, I would expect that at least four of them will also win a Gold Glove. Plus/Minus Crown, Fielding Bible Award and Gold Glove, the triple crown of defense.

- After the release of the Bill James Handbook last year we put "The Manny Adjustment" into the Plus/Minus System. This adjustment came about because of parks with high outfield walls like the Green Monster in Fenway and the Baggie in the Metrodome. This is a specific adjustment to the calculation of Plus/Minus numbers for outfielders. In this adjustment we eliminate from consideration all balls that hit an outfield wall that are too high on the wall and out of reach of the defender in the same way that we remove home runs hit over the wall. The effect was to improve Plus/Minus numbers for Manny Ramirez, and for other outfielders who play in parks with high outfield fences. In 2007, Manny had a -38 before the adjustment and a -24 afterwards. It's still a very poor performance reflecting Manny's ineptitude as a defender, but not incredibly atrocious as represented by -38. As a result, Manny is no longer the 3-year trailer in left field. His three-year Plus/Minus figure of -68 "improves" to second worst as Pat Burrell takes over the dubious distinction of having the worst Plus/Minus figure over the last three years in left field at -73.

2006-2008 Plus/Minus Leaders

First Basemen Leaders			Second Basemen Leaders			Third Basemen Leaders			Shortstops Leaders	
Pujols, Albert	+82		Utley, Chase	+85		Beltre, Adrian	+63		Everett, Adam	+58
Kotchman, Casey	+42		Ellis, Mark	+58		Feliz, Pedro	+55		Rollins, Jimmy	+42
Overbay, Lyle	+32		Hill, Aaron	+45		Crede, Joe	+55		Vizquel, Omar	+36
Mientkiewicz, Doug	+26		Hudson, Orlando	+29		Inge, Brandon	+50		Tulowitzki, Troy	+34
Youkilis, Kevin	+25		Polanco, Placido	+29		Rolen, Scott	+47		Hardy, J.J.	+33
Teixeira, Mark	+22		Valentin, Jose	+27		Zimmerman, Ryan	+33		Bartlett, Jason	+30
Berkman, Lance	+22		Phillips, Brandon	+24		Punto, Nick	+26		Reyes, Jose	+27
Pena, Carlos	+19		Kennedy, Adam	+19		Glaus, Troy	+23		Wilson, Jack	+26
Votto, Joey	+19		Graffanino, Tony	+18		Lowell, Mike	+21		McDonald, John	+26
Shealy, Ryan	+14		Lopez, Jose	+14		Hannahan, Jack	+21		Barmes, Clint	+26

First Basemen Trailers			Second Basemen Trailers			Third Basemen Trailers			Shortstops Trailers	
Jacobs, Mike	-49		Kent, Jeff	-43		Encarnacion, Edwin	-51		Jeter, Derek	-68
Fielder, Prince	-45		Weeks, Rickie	-29		Atkins, Garrett	-42		Ramirez, Hanley	-40
Giambi, Jason	-30		Durham, Ray	-28		Braun, Ryan	-41		Lopez, Felipe	-34
Young, Dmitri	-28		Vidro, Jose	-25		Cabrera, Miguel	-40		Betancourt, Yuniesky	-32
Jackson, Conor	-23		Cantu, Jorge	-22		Bautista, Jose	-38		Young, Michael	-32
Sexson, Richie	-22		Lopez, Felipe	-20		Wigginton, Ty	-26		Harris, Brendan	-28

Left Fielders Leaders			Center Fielders Leaders			Right Fielders Leaders			Pitchers Leaders	
Harris, Willie	+35		Beltran, Carlos	+59		Gutierrez, Franklin	+55		Maddux, Greg	+34
Crawford, Carl	+33		Jones, Andruw	+45		Winn, Randy	+44		Rogers, Kenny	+25
Byrnes, Eric	+23		Patterson, Corey	+37		Rios, Alex	+43		Webb, Brandon	+15
Scott, Luke	+21		Gomez, Carlos	+35		Giles, Brian	+38		Duke, Zach	+13
Cabrera, Melky	+19		Amezaga, Alfredo	+31		Kearns, Austin	+29		Cook, Aaron	+12
Jenkins, Geoff	+18		Young, Chris	+25		Suzuki, Ichiro	+26		Suppan, Jeff	+11
Diaz, Matt	+17		Pierre, Juan	+24		Schierholtz, Nate	+22		Santana, Johan	+11
Hairston, Scott	+16		Granderson, Curtis	+20		Cruz, Nelson	+14		Litsch, Jesse	+11
Podsednik, Scott	+15		Cameron, Mike	+19		Drew, J.D.	+13		Francis, Jeff	+10
Murton, Matt	+15		Logan, Nook	+18		Encarnacion, Juan	+13		Wang, Chien-Ming	+9

Left Fielders Trailers			Center Fielders Trailers			Right Fielders Trailers			Pitchers Trailers	
Burrell, Pat	-73		McLouth, Nate	-49		Dye, Jermaine	-72		Cabrera, Daniel	-15
Ramirez, Manny	-68		Edmonds, Jim	-35		Hawpe, Brad	-66		Kazmir, Scott	-10
Dunn, Adam	-58		Kotsay, Mark	-34		Cuddyer, Michael	-59		Broxton, Jonathan	-9
Ibanez, Raul	-41		Griffey Jr., Ken	-25		Abreu, Bobby	-52		Johnson, Jason	-9
Young, Delmon	-25		Rowand, Aaron	-24		Griffey Jr., Ken	-25		Lee, Cliff	-9
Gonzalez, Luis	-23		Lofton, Kenny	-21		Ordonez, Magglio	-24		Harang, Aaron	-9

2008 Plus/Minus Leaders

First Basemen — Leaders		Second Basemen — Leaders		Third Basemen — Leaders		Shortstops — Leaders	
Teixeira,Mark	+24	Utley,Chase	+47	Beltre,Adrian	+32	Rollins,Jimmy	+23
Pujols,Albert	+20	Ellis,Mark	+26	Hannahan,Jack	+21	Escobar,Yunel	+21
Votto,Joey	+19	Kennedy,Adam	+19	Scutaro,Marco	+15	Hardy,J.J.	+19
Berkman,Lance	+18	Phillips,Brandon	+17	Rolen,Scott	+13	Izturis,Cesar	+19
Pena,Carlos	+14	Pedroia,Dustin	+15	Crede,Joe	+13	Wilson,Jack	+16
Kotchman,Casey	+13	Polanco,Placido	+14	Longoria,Evan	+11	Guzman,Cristian	+15
Overbay,Lyle	+12	Fontenot,Mike	+11	Figgins,Chone	+11	Aviles,Mike	+15
Barton,Daric	+7	Barmes,Clint	+9	DeWitt,Blake	+11	Scutaro,Marco	+12
Youkilis,Kevin	+6	Inglett,Joe	+7	Zimmerman,Ryan	+10	Vizquel,Omar	+9
Helton,Todd	+6	Ojeda,Augie	+6	Jones,Chipper	+9	Lowrie,Jed	+8

First Basemen — Trailers		Second Basemen — Trailers		Third Basemen — Trailers		Shortstops — Trailers	
Jacobs,Mike	-27	Cano,Robinson	-16	Encarnacion,Edwin	-21	Betancourt,Yuniesky	-19
Giambi,Jason	-18	Kinsler,Ian	-15	Reynolds,Mark	-13	Keppinger,Jeff	-14
Delgado,Carlos	-15	Castillo,Luis	-14	Mora,Melvin	-13	Crosby,Bobby	-13
Sexson,Richie	-12	Lopez,Felipe	-14	Ramirez,Aramis	-12	Cintron,Alex	-12
Fielder,Prince	-12	Durham,Ray	-12	Atkins,Garrett	-11	Eckstein,David	-12
Atkins,Garrett	-10	Kent,Jeff	-12	Cantu,Jorge	-11	Jeter,Derek	-12

Left Fielders — Leaders		Center Fielders — Leaders		Right Fielders — Leaders		Pitchers — Leaders	
Crawford,Carl	+23	Gomez,Carlos	+32	Gutierrez,Franklin	+29	Rogers,Kenny	+16
Harris,Willie	+22	Beltran,Carlos	+24	Giles,Brian	+20	Maddux,Greg	+14
Jackson,Conor	+14	Young,Chris	+23	Winn,Randy	+18	Litsch,Jesse	+8
Scott,Luke	+12	Ross,Cody	+15	Rios,Alex	+15	Kendrick,Kyle	+7
Holliday,Matt	+11	Gerut,Jody	+12	Schierholtz,Nate	+14	Dempster,Ryan	+6
Willingham,Josh	+10	Rios,Alex	+11	Markakis,Nick	+12	Webb,Brandon	+5
Boggs,Brandon	+10	Victorino,Shane	+10	Span,Denard	+12	Duke,Zach	+5
Braun,Ryan	+9	Amezaga,Alfredo	+10	Suzuki,Ichiro	+12	Hill,Shawn	+5
Chavez,Endy	+9	Anderson,Josh	+10	Church,Ryan	+11	Acosta,Manny	+5
DeJesus,David	+8	Cameron,Mike	+8	Dukes,Elijah	+11	2 tied with	+4

Left Fielders — Trailers		Center Fielders — Trailers		Right Fielders — Trailers		Pitchers — Trailers	
Young,Delmon	-25	McLouth,Nate	-40	Hawpe,Brad	-37	Johnson,Randy	-7
Burrell,Pat	-20	Edmonds,Jim	-26	Abreu,Bobby	-24	Cabrera,Daniel	-6
Ibanez,Raul	-18	Kotsay,Mark	-16	Griffey Jr.,Ken	-17	Pettitte,Andy	-6
Cust,Jack	-14	Wells,Vernon	-16	Ethier,Andre	-17	Papelbon,Jonathan	-5
Thames,Marcus	-13	Ankiel,Rick	-15	Dye,Jermaine	-17	Green,Sean	-5
Ramirez,Manny	-13	Hamilton,Josh	-13	Francoeur,Jeff	-17	Santana,Ervin	-5

Career Register

The Career Register includes complete career statistics through the 2008 season for every major league player who played in 2008. We added thirty-three bonus players as well, guys who missed the entire 2008 season, for example Kelvim Escobar and Jason Schmidt, or potential foreign imports such as Kenshin Kawakami and Koji Uehara.

New to this year's Career Register are postseason records for every player, where applicable. A player's total career numbers in the postseason appear on one line above his total regular season career numbers. Note that because we work hard to bring you this publication by November 1, career postseason records are only updated through the 2007 World Series.

For players who have appeared in fewer than three major league seasons, we included their full minor league statistics. For those players with three or more years in the big leagues who also spent time in the minor leagues in 2008 (for example, if they had a rehab assignment) we included only their 2008 minor league statistics—indicated by an asterisk. Those players who split time between the majors and the minors last season but have fewer than three years of major league experience will still have their full minor league stats included.

If a player led the league in a particular category, that register total will appear in **boldface**.

The Register also features Runs Created (RC) for hitters and Component ERA (ERC) for pitchers, in addition to the more traditional statistics. Developed by Bill James, Runs Created is a method of measuring every facet of a hitter's strengths and weaknesses and combining those factors into one number, indicative of a player's production. Component ERC estimates what a pitcher's ERA *should* have been based upon his raw pitching statistics and gives us a good indication of whether or not a pitcher actually deserved his ERA. An explanation of Bill's most-current formulas for both RC and ERC can be found in the Baseball Glossary at the end of the *Handbook*.

Some additional definitions:

Age is seasonal as of June 30, 2009.

For pitchers, **BFP** is Batters Facing Pitcher; **TBB** is Total Bases on Balls (or, Total Walks, intentional and unintentional); **Op** is Save Opportunities; **Hld** is Holds.

For varying levels of Class-A ball, we have used "A+" to indicate High A and "A-" to indicate Low A.

The number after the positions listed at the top of each player's chart is games played at that position.

David Aardsma

Pitches: R Bats: R Pos: RP-47 Ht: 6'4" Wt: 205 Born: 12/27/1981 Age: 27

Year	Team	Lg	G	GS	CG	GF	IP	BFP	H	R	ER	HR	SH	SF	HB	TBB	IBB	SO	WP	Bk	W	L	Pct	ShO	Sv-Op	Hld	ERC	ERA
2008	Pwtckt*	AAA	2	0	0	0	2.0	8	0	0	0	0	0	0	0	2	0	2	0	0	0	0	-	0	0- -	-	0.95	0.00
2004	SF	NL	11	0	0	5	10.2	61	20	8	8	1	0	1	2	10	0	5	0	0	1	0	1.000	0	0-1	1	13.38	6.75
2006	ChC	NL	45	0	0	9	53.0	225	41	25	24	4	1	3	1	28	0	49	1	0	3	0	1.000	0	0-0	5	3.88	4.08
2007	CWS	AL	25	0	0	7	32.1	151	39	24	23	4	2	1	1	17	3	36	2	0	1	0	.667	0	0-3	3	5.93	6.40
2008	Bos	AL	47	0	0	7	48.2	228	49	32	30	4	3	2	5	35	2	49	3	0	4	2	.667	0	0-1	4	5.63	5.55
4 ML YEARS			128	0	0	28	144.2	665	149	89	85	18	6	7	9	90	5	139	6	0	10	3	.769	0	0-5	13	5.54	5.29

Reggie Abercrombie

Bats: R Throws: R Pos: PH-13; LF-12; CF-11; PR-6 Ht: 6'3" Wt: 215 Born: 7/15/1981 Age: 27

Year	Team	Lg	G	AB	H	2B	3B	HR	(Hm	Rd)	TB	R	RBI	RC	TBB	IBB	SO	HBP	SH	SF	SB	CS	SB%	GDP	Avg	OBP	Slg
2008	RdRck*	AAA	78	289	79	14	2	12	(-	-)	133	37	36	39	9	0	93	1	0	1	17	9	.65	6	.273	.297	.460
2006	Fla	NL	111	255	54	12	2	5	(1	4)	85	39	24	24	18	2	78	3	4	1	6	5	.55	2	.212	.271	.333
2007	Fla	NL	35	76	15	3	0	2	(0	2)	24	16	5	3	2	0	22	2	0	0	7	1	.88	1	.197	.238	.316
2008	Hou	NL	34	55	17	5	0	2	(1	1)	28	10	5	9	1	0	23	2	1	1	5	2	.71	0	.309	.339	.509
3 ML YEARS			180	386	86	20	2	9	(2	7)	137	65	34	36	21	2	123	7	5	2	18	8	.69	3	.223	.274	.355

Bobby Abreu

Bats: L Throws: R Pos: RF-150; DH-4; PH-4 Ht: 6'0" Wt: 210 Born: 3/11/1974 Age: 35

Year	Team	Lg	G	AB	H	2B	3B	HR	(Hm	Rd)	TB	R	RBI	RC	TBB	IBB	SO	HBP	SH	SF	SB	CS	SB%	GDP	Avg	OBP	Slg
1996	Hou	NL	15	22	5	1	0	0	(0	0)	6	1	1	1	2	0	3	0	0	0	0	0	-	1	.227	.292	.273
1997	Hou	NL	59	188	47	10	2	3	(3	0)	70	22	26	25	21	0	48	1	0	0	7	2	.78	0	.250	.329	.372
1998	Phi	NL	151	497	155	29	6	17	(10	7)	247	68	74	101	84	14	133	0	4	4	19	10	.66	6	.312	.409	.497
1999	Phi	NL	152	546	183	35	11	20	(13	7)	300	118	93	131	109	8	113	3	0	4	27	9	.75	13	.335	.446	.549
2000	Phi	NL	154	576	182	42	10	25	(14	11)	319	103	79	130	100	9	116	1	0	3	28	8	.78	12	.316	.416	.554
2001	Phi	NL	162	588	170	48	4	31	(13	18)	319	118	110	125	106	11	137	1	0	9	36	14	.72	13	.289	.393	.543
2002	Phi	NL	157	572	176	50	6	20	(8	12)	298	102	85	112	104	9	117	3	0	6	31	12	.72	11	.308	.413	.521
2003	Phi	NL	158	577	173	35	1	20	(11	9)	270	99	101	120	109	13	126	2	0	7	22	9	.71	13	.300	.409	.468
2004	Phi	NL	159	574	173	47	1	30	(13	17)	312	118	105	139	127	10	116	5	0	7	40	5	.89	5	.301	.428	.544
2005	Phi	NL	162	588	168	37	1	24	(15	9)	279	104	102	116	117	15	134	6	0	8	31	9	.78	7	.286	.405	.474
2006	2 Tms		156	548	163	41	2	15	(8	7)	253	98	107	123	124	6	138	3	2	9	30	6	.83	13	.297	.424	.462
2007	NYY	AL	158	605	171	40	5	16	(10	6)	269	123	101	101	84	0	115	3	0	7	25	8	.76	11	.283	.369	.445
2008	NYY	AL	156	609	180	39	4	20	(14	6)	287	100	100	108	73	2	109	1	0	1	22	11	.67	14	.296	.371	.471
06	Phi	NL	98	339	94	25	2	8	(5	3)	147	61	65	76	91	5	86	2	0	6	20	4	.83	8	.277	.427	.434
06	NYY	AL	58	209	69	16	0	7	(3	4)	106	37	42	47	33	1	52	1	2	3	10	2	.83	5	.330	.419	.507
	Postseason		11	33	10	2	0	1	(1	0)	15	3	6	6	4	0	7	0	0	0	2	0	1.00	0	.303	.378	.455
13 ML YEARS			1799	6490	1946	454	53	241	(132	109)	3229	1174	1084	1332	1160	97	1405	29	6	65	318	103	.76	119	.300	.405	.498

Tony Abreu

Bats: B Throws: R Pos: 3B Ht: 5'9" Wt: 200 Born: 11/13/1984 Age: 24

Year	Team	Lg	G	AB	H	2B	3B	HR	(Hm	Rd)	TB	R	RBI	RC	TBB	IBB	SO	HBP	SH	SF	SB	CS	SB%	GDP	Avg	OBP	Slg
2003	Ddgrs	R	45	163	48	7	5	0	(-	-)	65	30	20	24	11	1	24	5	0	0	9	3	.75	3	.294	.358	.399
2003	VeroB	A+	3	10	0	0	0	0	(-	-)	0	0	0	0	1	0	2	0	0	0	0	0	-	0	.000	.091	.000
2004	Clmbs	A	104	359	108	21	8	8	(-	-)	169	50	54	54	8	0	59	7	6	3	16	12	.57	5	.301	.326	.471
2004	VeroB	A+	11	43	18	3	1	0	(-	-)	23	8	3	9	1	0	8	1	1	1	4	1	.80	1	.419	.435	.535
2005	VeroB	A+	96	394	129	23	7	4	(-	-)	178	54	43	62	15	1	56	5	3	4	14	10	.58	9	.327	.356	.452
2005	Jaxnvl	AA	24	96	24	3	2	0	(-	-)	31	10	9	8	4	0	21	1	0	1	0	2	.00	2	.250	.284	.323
2006	Jaxnvl	AA	118	457	131	24	3	6	(-	-)	179	66	55	65	33	2	69	9	4	6	9	4	.69	15	.287	.343	.392
2007	LsVgs	AAA	54	234	83	22	5	2	(-	-)	121	48	18	48	14	1	34	4	0	1	5	0	1.00	5	.355	.399	.517
2007	LAD	NL	59	166	45	14	1	2	(0	2)	67	19	17	18	7	1	21	3	0	2	0	0	-	5	.271	.309	.404

Jeremy Accardo

Pitches: R Bats: R Pos: RP-16 Ht: 6'2" Wt: 189 Born: 12/8/1981 Age: 27

Year	Team	Lg	G	GS	CG	GF	IP	BFP	H	R	ER	HR	SH	SF	HB	TBB	IBB	SO	WP	Bk	W	L	Pct	ShO	Sv-Op	Hld	ERC	ERA
2008	Dnedin*	A+	7	1	0	0	7.0	29	8	4	4	2	0	0	0	1	0	3	0	0	0	0	-	0	0- -	-	5.18	5.14
2008	Syrcse*	AAA	5	0	0	1	4.2	22	4	2	1	0	0	0	0	3	0	3	0	0	0	0	-	0	0- -	-	3.21	1.93
2008	B Jays*	R	1	1	0	0	1.0	3	1	0	0	0	0	0	0	0	0	1	0	0	0	0	-	0	0- -	-	2.79	0.00
2005	SF	NL	28	0	0	7	29.2	124	26	13	13	2	1	1	1	9	1	16	1	0	1	5	.167	0	0-1	4	2.87	3.94
2006	2 Tms		65	0	0	27	69.0	297	76	42	41	7	1	4	1	20	5	54	4	1	2	4	.333	0	3-8	10	4.17	5.35
2007	Tor	AL	64	0	0	48	67.1	275	51	19	16	4	0	1	2	24	2	57	0	1	4	4	.500	0	30-35	2	2.44	2.14
2008	Tor	AL	16	0	0	6	12.1	56	15	10	9	1	0	1	1	4	2	5	1	0	0	3	.000	0	4-6	2	4.88	6.57
06	SF	NL	38	0	0	16	40.1	170	38	23	22	2	0	4	1	11	3	40	2	0	1	3	.250	0	3-6	8	2.88	4.91
06	Tor	AL	27	0	0	11	28.2	127	38	19	19	5	1	0	0	9	2	14	2	1	1	1	.500	0	0-2	2	6.25	5.97
4 ML YEARS			173	0	0	88	178.1	752	168	84	79	14	2	7	5	57	10	132	6	2	7	16	.304	0	37-50	18	3.31	3.99

Alfredo Aceves

Pitches: R Bats: R Pos: SP-4; RP-2   Ht: 6'3" Wt: 220 Born: 12/8/1982 Age: 26

			HOW MUCH HE PITCHED						WHAT HE GAVE UP											THE RESULTS							
Year	Team	Lg	G	GS	CG	GF	IP	BFP	H	R	ER	HR	SH	SF	HB	TBB	IBB	SO	WP	Bk	W	L	Pct	ShO	Sv-Op	Hld	ERC	ERA
2008	Tampa	A+	8	8	0	0	47.0	179	32	16	11	1	0	0	1	8	0	37	2	0	4	1	.800	0	0--	-	1.42	2.11
2008	Trntn	AA	7	7	1	0	50.0	184	37	10	10	3	4	0	0	6	0	35	1	0	2	2	.500	1	0--	-	1.64	1.80
2008	S-WB	AAA	10	8	0	1	43.2	186	42	21	20	6	1	3	1	13	0	42	0	0	2	3	.400	0	0--	-	3.75	4.12
2008	NYY	AL	6	4	0	1	30.0	120	25	8	8	4	0	0	0	10	0	16	1	0	1	0	1.000	0	0-0	-	3.23	2.40

Manny Acosta

Pitches: R Bats: B Pos: RP-46   Ht: 6'4" Wt: 170 Born: 5/1/1981 Age: 28

			HOW MUCH HE PITCHED						WHAT HE GAVE UP											THE RESULTS							
Year	Team	Lg	G	GS	CG	GF	IP	BFP	H	R	ER	HR	SH	SF	HB	TBB	IBB	SO	WP	Bk	W	L	Pct	ShO	Sv-Op	Hld	ERC	ERA
2000	Yanks	R	12	10	0	1	62.1	270	64	28	24	3	4	0	0	21	0	46	1	0	4	2	.667	0	0--	-	3.56	3.47
2001	Tampa	A+	2	2	0	0	7.0	31	7	7	6	1	0	0	0	6	0	8	4	0	0	1	.000	0	0--	-	6.78	7.71
2001	Grnsbr	A	10	10	1	0	65.2	267	37	14	11	2	4	1	2	37	0	67	7	2	5	2	.714	1	0--	-	2.09	1.51
2002	Grnsbr	A	13	10	0	0	52.0	257	65	47	37	4	3	3	1	44	0	35	5	0	2	5	.286	0	0--	-	7.41	6.40
2002	StlsInd	A-	3	3	0	0	15.1	70	20	9	7	0	0	1	0	8	0	12	4	0	2	1	.667	0	0--	-	5.74	4.11
2003	Btl Crk	A	15	11	0	3	61.0	290	80	58	45	3	3	7	3	29	0	45	4	0	0	8	.000	0	0--	-	5.97	6.64
2003	MrtlBh	A+	8	0	0	3	12.2	70	19	14	9	1	1	0	0	11	1	10	1	0	2	0	1.000	0	1--	-	8.35	6.39
2004	MrtlBh	A+	11	0	0	4	23.1	102	20	12	11	1	0	0	1	11	0	21	3	0	4	0	1.000	0	0--	-	3.25	4.24
2004	Braves	R	2	0	0	1	2.2	13	5	2	1	0	0	0	0	2	0	2	1	0	0	0	-	0	0--	-	11.62	3.38
2005	Danvle	R+	3	2	0	0	6.0	20	3	2	2	0	1	0	0	1	0	8	2	0	0	0	-	0	0--	-	0.88	3.00
2005	MrtlBh	A+	18	0	0	16	22.1	100	22	12	11	0	2	0	2	9	0	18	3	0	2	2	.500	0	7--	-	3.85	4.43
2006	Missi	AA	13	0	0	9	15.1	68	7	4	4	1	0	0	1	15	3	13	0	0	0	0	-	0	4--	-	2.92	2.35
2006	Rchmd	AAA	38	0	0	33	44.2	204	38	19	18	4	6	2	5	32	3	44	0	0	1	6	.143	0	17--	-	4.72	3.63
2007	Rchmd	AAA	40	0	0	30	59.2	247	46	18	14	0	0	1	1	35	3	56	1	3	9	3	.750	0	12--	-	2.87	2.11
2008	Rchmd	AAA	4	3	0	1	3.2	17	4	0	0	0	0	0	0	2	0	4	0	0	0	0	-	0	0--	-	4.28	0.00
2007	Atl	NL	21	0	0	5	23.2	93	13	6	6	2	0	0	0	14	1	22	1	0	1	1	.500	0	0-0	4	2.39	2.28
2008	Atl	NL	46	0	0	22	53.0	226	48	25	21	7	4	1	1	26	5	31	5	0	3	5	.375	0	3-5	4	4.12	3.57
	2 ML YEARS		67	0	0	27	76.2	319	61	31	27	9	4	1	1	40	6	53	6	0	4	6	.400	0	3-5	8	3.56	3.17

Mike Adams

Pitches: R Bats: R Pos: RP-54   Ht: 6'5" Wt: 190 Born: 7/29/1978 Age: 30

			HOW MUCH HE PITCHED						WHAT HE GAVE UP											THE RESULTS							
Year	Team	Lg	G	GS	CG	GF	IP	BFP	H	R	ER	HR	SH	SF	HB	TBB	IBB	SO	WP	Bk	W	L	Pct	ShO	Sv-Op	Hld	ERC	ERA
2008	Portlnd*	AAA	12	0	0	3	14.2	71	21	12	9	0	0	0	0	9	0	16	3	0	3	1	.750	0	0--	-	6.83	5.52
2004	Mil	NL	46	0	0	13	53.0	225	50	21	20	5	5	2	2	14	2	39	2	0	2	3	.400	0	0-5	12	3.22	3.40
2005	Mil	NL	13	0	0	7	13.1	61	12	4	4	2	0	0	0	10	1	14	1	0	0	1	.000	0	1-2	2	5.12	2.70
2006	Mil	NL	2	0	0	0	2.1	13	4	3	3	1	0	0	0	2	0	1	0	0	0	0	-	0	0-0	0	13.74	11.57
2008	SD	NL	54	0	0	11	65.1	259	49	18	18	7	2	3	0	19	2	74	0	0	2	3	.400	0	0-2	10	2.38	2.48
	4 ML YEARS		115	0	0	31	134.0	558	115	46	45	15	7	5	2	45	5	128	3	0	4	7	.364	0	1-9	24	3.12	3.02

Nick Adenhart

Pitches: R Bats: R Pos: SP-3   Ht: 6'3" Wt: 185 Born: 8/24/1986 Age: 22

			HOW MUCH HE PITCHED						WHAT HE GAVE UP											THE RESULTS							
Year	Team	Lg	G	GS	CG	GF	IP	BFP	H	R	ER	HR	SH	SF	HB	TBB	IBB	SO	WP	Bk	W	L	Pct	ShO	Sv-Op	Hld	ERC	ERA
2005	Angels	R	13	12	1	0	44.0	192	39	26	18	0	3	2	4	24	0	52	3	1	2	3	.400	0	0--	-	3.67	3.68
2005	Orem	R+	1	1	0	0	6.0	21	3	1	0	0	0	0	0	0	0	7	0	0	1	0	1.000	0	0--	-	0.54	0.00
2006	CRpds	A	16	16	1	0	106.0	423	84	33	23	2	1	2	3	26	0	99	17	1	10	2	.833	0	0--	-	2.05	1.95
2006	RCuca	A+	9	9	0	0	52.1	219	51	23	22	1	1	1	3	16	0	46	2	1	5	2	.714	0	0--	-	3.29	3.78
2007	Ark	AA	26	26	0	0	153.0	669	158	72	62	7	6	3	17	65	1	116	13	0	10	8	.556	0	0--	-	4.48	3.65
2008	Salt Lk	AAA	26	26	0	0	145.1	655	173	99	93	15	4	7	3	75	0	110	9	5	9	13	.409	0	0--	-	5.93	5.76
2008	LAA	AL	3	3	0	0	12.0	63	18	12	12	0	0	0	0	13	0	4	2	0	1	0	1.000	0	0-0	-	9.55	9.00

Jon Adkins

Pitches: R Bats: L Pos: RP-4   Ht: 6'0" Wt: 210 Born: 8/30/1977 Age: 31

			HOW MUCH HE PITCHED						WHAT HE GAVE UP											THE RESULTS							
Year	Team	Lg	G	GS	CG	GF	IP	BFP	H	R	ER	HR	SH	SF	HB	TBB	IBB	SO	WP	Bk	W	L	Pct	ShO	Sv-Op	Hld	ERC	ERA
2008	Lsvlle*	AAA	57	0	0	47	62.0	257	62	26	24	5	3	0	3	13	2	39	0	0	1	4	.200	0	30--	-	3.37	3.48
2003	CWS	AL	4	0	0	2	9.1	42	8	5	5	1	1	1	1	7	0	3	0	0	0	0	-	0	0-0	0	5.27	4.82
2004	CWS	AL	50	0	0	19	62.0	271	75	35	32	13	3	1	1	20	3	44	1	0	2	3	.400	0	0-0	5	5.90	4.65
2005	CWS	AL	5	0	0	4	8.1	42	13	8	8	0	0	0	1	4	2	1	0	0	0	0	-	0	0-0	0	6.94	8.64
2006	SD	NL	55	0	0	15	54.1	232	55	26	24	3	5	2	2	20	4	30	0	0	2	1	.667	0	0-0	8	3.77	3.98
2007	NYM	NL	1	0	0	0	1.0	3	0	0	0	0	0	0	0	0	0	0	0	0	0	0	-	0	0-0	0	0.00	0.00
2008	Cin	NL	4	0	0	0	3.2	15	4	1	1	1	0	0	0	3	1	3	0	0	1	0	1.000	0	0-0	0	8.64	2.45
	6 ML YEARS		119	0	0	40	138.2	605	155	75	70	18	9	4	5	54	10	81	1	0	5	5	.500	0	0-0	13	5.05	4.54

Jeremy Affeldt

Pitches: L Bats: L Pos: RP-74   Ht: 6'4" Wt: 225 Born: 6/6/1979 Age: 30

			HOW MUCH HE PITCHED						WHAT HE GAVE UP											THE RESULTS							
Year	Team	Lg	G	GS	CG	GF	IP	BFP	H	R	ER	HR	SH	SF	HB	TBB	IBB	SO	WP	Bk	W	L	Pct	ShO	Sv-Op	Hld	ERC	ERA
2002	KC	AL	34	7	0	4	77.2	353	85	41	40	8	2	1	3	37	4	67	5	2	3	4	.429	0	0-1	1	4.97	4.64
2003	KC	AL	36	18	0	5	126.0	533	126	58	55	12	2	5	5	38	1	98	2	2	7	6	.538	0	4-4	3	3.82	3.93
2004	KC	AL	38	8	0	26	76.1	344	91	49	42	6	4	4	3	32	2	49	4	3	3	4	.429	0	13-17	5	5.26	4.95
2005	KC	AL	49	0	0	13	49.2	232	56	35	29	3	0	1	0	29	2	39	5	0	0	2	.000	0	0-0	12	5.08	5.26

Year	Team	Lg	G	GS	CG	GF	IP	BFP	H	R	ER	HR	SH	SF	HB	TBB	IBB	SO	WP	Bk	W	L	Pct	ShO	Sv-Op	Hld	ERC	ERA
							HOW MUCH HE PITCHED					WHAT HE GAVE UP												THE RESULTS				
2006	2 Tms		54	9	0	12	97.1	448	102	74	67	13	4	4	2	55	3	48	2	0	8	8	.500	0	1-3	5	5.21	6.20
2007	Col	NL	75	0	0	11	59.0	253	47	26	23	3	3	6	3	33	9	46	6	1	4	3	.571	0	0-4	9	3.19	3.51
2008	Cin	NL	74	0	0	20	78.1	335	78	36	29	9	7	0	3	25	0	80	6	0	1	1	.500	0	0-1	5	3.98	3.33
06	KC	AL	27	9	0	3	70.0	320	71	51	46	9	3	3	1	42	0	28	2	0	4	6	.400	0	0-0	2	5.18	5.91
06	Col	NL	27	0	0	9	27.1	128	31	23	21	4	1	1	1	13	3	20	0	0	4	2	.667	0	1-3	3	5.29	6.91
	Postseason		7	0	0	0	5.1	19	3	1	1	1	0	0	0	1	0	4	0	0	0	0	-	0	0-0	2	1.70	1.69
7 ML YEARS			360	42	0	91	564.1	2498	585	319	285	54	22	21	19	249	21	427	30	8	26	28	.481	0	18-30	35	4.47	4.55

Chris Aguila

Bats: R **Throws:** R **Pos:** LF-6; PH-5
Ht: 5'11" **Wt:** 180 **Born:** 2/23/1979 **Age:** 30

Year	Team	Lg	G	AB	H	2B	3B	HR	(Hm	Rd)	TB	R	RBI	RC	TBB	IBB	SO	HBP	SH	SF	SB	CS	SB%	GDP	Avg	OBP	Slg
									BATTING												BASERUNNING				AVERAGES		
2008	NewOr*	AAA	116	420	124	20	2	29	(-	-)	235	74	73	89	53	2	102	4	0	2	13	4	.76	11	.295	.378	.560
2004	Fla	NL	29	45	10	2	1	3	(1	2)	23	10	5	3	2	0	12	0	1	0	0	0	-	0	.222	.255	.511
2005	Fla	NL	65	78	19	3	0	0	(0	0)	22	11	4	4	3	0	19	0	0	0	0	1	.00	0	.244	.272	.282
2006	Fla	NL	47	95	22	8	1	0	(0	0)	32	5	7	7	9	1	26	0	0	0	2	1	.67	2	.232	.298	.337
2008	NYM	NL	8	12	2	0	0	0	(0	0)	2	0	0	0	2	0	4	0	1	0	0	0	-	1	.167	.286	.167
4 ML YEARS			149	230	53	13	2	3	(1	2)	79	26	16	14	16	1	61	0	2	0	2	2	.50	3	.230	.280	.343

Jonathan Albaladejo

Pitches: R **Bats:** R **Pos:** RP-7
Ht: 6'5" **Wt:** 260 **Born:** 10/30/1982 **Age:** 26

Year	Team	Lg	G	GS	CG	GF	IP	BFP	H	R	ER	HR	SH	SF	HB	TBB	IBB	SO	WP	Bk	W	L	Pct	ShO	Sv-Op	Hld	ERC	ERA
							HOW MUCH HE PITCHED					WHAT HE GAVE UP												THE RESULTS				
2001	Pirates	R	10	2	0	5	19.0	85	22	13	10	1	2	3	1	2	0	24	2	0	0	3	.000	0	1--	-	3.44	4.74
2002	Pirates	R	12	10	0	1	60.0	247	71	20	16	2	3	0	3	6	0	37	1	0	3	2	.600	0	0--	-	3.78	2.40
2003	Hkry	A	29	20	5	2	139.0	536	114	53	48	14	2	4	4	19	1	110	5	1	12	5	.706	0	1--	-	2.32	3.11
2004	Lynbrg	A+	24	24	1	0	131.0	561	150	72	63	10	8	7	5	25	0	92	6	0	8	8	.500	1	0--	-	4.04	4.33
2005	Lynbrg	A+	28	6	0	6	78.1	333	74	40	34	9	2	7	2	21	0	76	2	1	4	3	.571	0	2--	-	3.37	3.91
2006	Altna	AA	18	1	0	4	36.0	153	41	18	16	4	3	2	3	5	1	27	1	0	1	2	.333	0	1--	-	4.20	4.00
2006	Pirates	R	3	2	0	0	12.1	48	21	4	4	1	0	0	0	3	0	16	0	0	1	0	1.000	0	0--	-	9.50	2.92
2007	Hrsbrg	AA	21	0	0	13	36.2	156	30	20	17	3	4	0	1	15	3	35	4	0	4	3	.571	0	2--	-	2.92	4.17
2007	Clmbs	AAA	15	0	0	4	24.0	95	14	3	3	2	0	0	3	7	1	21	2	1	3	0	1.000	0	0--	-	1.86	1.13
2008	S-WB	AAA	4	0	0	2	7.0	30	5	2	1	1	0	0	0	4	0	5	0	0	0	0	-	0	0--	-	3.40	1.29
2008	StIsInd	A-	2	2	0	0	4.0	14	3	0	0	0	0	0	0	0	0	4	0	0	0	0	-	0	0--	-	1.21	0.00
2007	Was	NL	14	0	0	1	14.1	51	7	3	3	1	0	1	1	2	0	12	0	0	1	1	.500	0	0-1	2	1.10	1.88
2008	NYY	AL	7	0	0	2	13.2	58	15	6	6	1	1	0	0	6	0	13	0	0	0	1	.000	0	0-0	1	4.82	3.95
2 ML YEARS			21	0	0	3	28.0	109	22	9	9	2	1	1	1	8	0	25	0	0	1	2	.333	0	0-1	3	2.59	2.89

Matt Albers

Pitches: R **Bats:** L **Pos:** RP-25; SP-3
Ht: 6'0" **Wt:** 205 **Born:** 1/20/1983 **Age:** 26

Year	Team	Lg	G	GS	CG	GF	IP	BFP	H	R	ER	HR	SH	SF	HB	TBB	IBB	SO	WP	Bk	W	L	Pct	ShO	Sv-Op	Hld	ERC	ERA
							HOW MUCH HE PITCHED					WHAT HE GAVE UP												THE RESULTS				
2008	Abrdn*	A-	2	0	0	0	2.0	8	1	0	0	0	0	0	0	1	0	4	0	0	0	0	-	0	0--	-	1.41	0.00
2006	Hou	NL	4	2	0	0	15.0	66	17	10	10	1	2	0	0	7	0	11	0	0	0	2	.000	0	0-0	0	4.97	6.00
2007	Hou	NL	31	18	0	2	110.2	508	127	77	72	18	6	8	7	50	6	71	7	0	4	11	.267	0	0-0	0	5.76	5.86
2008	Bal	AL	28	3	0	5	49.0	208	43	21	19	4	1	3	2	22	1	26	1	0	3	3	.500	0	0-2	6	3.62	3.49
3 ML YEARS			63	23	0	7	174.2	782	187	108	101	23	9	11	9	79	7	108	8	0	7	16	.304	0	0-2	6	5.06	5.20

Eliezer Alfonzo

Bats: R **Throws:** R **Pos:** PH-3; C-2
Ht: 5'11" **Wt:** 218 **Born:** 2/7/1979 **Age:** 30

Year	Team	Lg	G	AB	H	2B	3B	HR	(Hm	Rd)	TB	R	RBI	RC	TBB	IBB	SO	HBP	SH	SF	SB	CS	SB%	GDP	Avg	OBP	Slg
									BATTING												BASERUNNING				AVERAGES		
2008	Fresno*	AAA	32	116	36	10	1	5	(-	-)	63	17	24	22	7	1	30	1	0	1	1	0	1.00	2	.310	.352	.543
2008	Augsta*	A	5	16	3	1	0	1	(-	-)	7	1	6	1	1	1	5	0	0	1	0	0	-	1	.188	.222	.438
2008	Conn*	AA	19	80	29	7	0	2	(-	-)	42	8	15	15	2	1	18	2	0	0	0	0	-	4	.363	.393	.525
2006	SF	NL	87	286	76	17	2	12	(3	9)	133	27	39	36	9	7	74	7	4	3	1	0	1.00	10	.266	.302	.465
2007	SF	NL	26	64	16	2	1	1	(1	0)	23	5	6	5	2	2	23	1	0	0	0	2	.00	2	.250	.284	.359
2008	SF	NL	5	11	1	0	0	0	(0	0)	1	0	1	0	0	0	4	0	0	0	0	0	-	2	.091	.091	.091
3 ML YEARS			118	361	93	19	3	13	(4	9)	157	32	46	41	11	9	101	8	4	3	1	2	.33	14	.258	.292	.435

Moises Alou

Bats: R **Throws:** R **Pos:** LF-13; DH-1; PH-1
Ht: 6'3" **Wt:** 229 **Born:** 7/3/1966 **Age:** 42

Year	Team	Lg	G	AB	H	2B	3B	HR	(Hm	Rd)	TB	R	RBI	RC	TBB	IBB	SO	HBP	SH	SF	SB	CS	SB%	GDP	Avg	OBP	Slg
									BATTING												BASERUNNING				AVERAGES		
2008	StLuci*	A+	1	3	3	1	0	0	(-	-)	4	1	0	2	0	0	0	0	0	0	0	0	-	0	1.000	1.000	1.333
2008	Mets*	R	1	3	2	0	0	1	(-	-)	5	1	2	2	0	0	0	0	0	0	0	0	-	0	.667	.667	1.667
2008	Bnghtn*	AA	2	6	1	0	0	0	(-	-)	1	0	0	0	0	0	0	0	0	0	0	0	-	0	.167	.167	.167
1990	2 Tms	NL	16	20	4	0	1	0	(0	0)	6	4	0	1	0	0	3	0	1	0	0	0	-	1	.200	.200	.300
1992	Mon	NL	115	341	96	28	2	9	(3	6)	155	53	56	53	25	0	46	1	5	5	16	2	.89	5	.282	.328	.455
1993	Mon	NL	136	482	138	29	6	18	(10	8)	233	70	85	79	38	9	53	4	3	7	17	6	.74	9	.286	.340	.483
1994	Mon	NL	107	422	143	31	5	22	(9	13)	250	81	78	92	42	10	63	2	0	5	7	6	.54	7	.339	.397	.592
1995	Mon	NL	93	344	94	22	0	14	(4	10)	158	48	58	52	29	6	56	9	0	4	4	3	.57	9	.273	.342	.459
1996	Mon	NL	143	540	152	28	2	21	(14	7)	247	87	96	81	49	7	83	2	0	7	9	4	.69	15	.281	.339	.457
1997	Fla	NL	150	538	157	29	5	23	(12	11)	265	88	115	97	70	9	85	4	0	7	9	5	.64	13	.292	.373	.493
1998	Hou	NL	159	584	182	34	5	38	(19	19)	340	104	124	130	84	11	87	5	0	6	11	3	.79	14	.312	.399	.582

BATTING																				BASERUNNING				AVERAGES		
Year Team	Lg	G	AB	H	2B	3B	HR	(Hm Rd)	TB	R	RBI	RC	TBB	IBB	SO	HBP	SH	SF		SB	CS	SB%	GDP	Avg	OBP	Slg
2000 Hou	NL	126	454	161	28	2	30	(17 13)	283	82	114	104	52	4	45	2	0	9		3	3	.50	21	.355	.416	.623
2001 Hou	NL	136	513	170	31	1	27	(15 12)	284	79	108	104	57	14	57	3	0	8		5	1	.83	18	.331	.396	.554
2002 ChC	NL	132	484	133	23	1	15	(7 8)	203	50	61	59	47	4	61	0	0	3		8	0	1.00	15	.275	.337	.419
2003 ChC	NL	151	565	158	35	1	22	(14 8)	261	83	91	94	63	7	67	7	0	3		3	1	.75	16	.280	.357	.462
2004 ChC	NL	155	601	176	36	3	39	(29 10)	335	106	106	114	68	2	80	0	0	6		3	0	1.00	12	.293	.361	.557
2005 SF	NL	123	427	137	21	3	19	(12 7)	221	67	63	74	56	1	43	3	0	4		5	1	.83	11	.321	.400	.518
2006 SF	NL	98	345	104	25	1	22	(13 9)	197	52	74	65	28	2	31	1	0	4		2	1	.67	15	.301	.352	.571
2007 NYM	NL	87	328	112	19	1	13	(6 7)	172	51	49	52	27	5	30	2	0	3		3	0	1.00	13	.341	.392	.524
2008 NYM	NL	15	49	17	2	0	0	(0 0)	19	4	9	10	2	0	4	2	0	1		1	1	.50	1	.347	.389	.388
90 Pit	NL	2	5	1	0	0	0	(0 0)	1	0	0	0	0	0	0	0	0	0		0	0	-	1	.200	.200	.200
90 Mon	NL	14	15	3	0	1	0	(0 0)	5	4	0	1	0	0	3	0	1	0		0	0	-	0	.200	.200	.333
Postseason		34	134	37	7	0	5	(3 2)	59	14	24	16	7	1	20	0	0	0		2	0	1.00	6	.276	.312	.440
17 ML YEARS		1942	7037	2134	421	39	332	(187 145)	3629	1109	1287	1261	737	91	894	48	9	82		106	37	.74	195	.303	.369	.516

Chip Ambres

Bats: R **Throws:** R **Pos:** PH-14; RF-7; CF-3   **Ht:** 6'1" **Wt:** 232 **Born:** 12/19/1979 **Age:** 29

BATTING																				BASERUNNING				AVERAGES		
Year Team	Lg	G	AB	H	2B	3B	HR	(Hm Rd)	TB	R	RBI	RC	TBB	IBB	SO	HBP	SH	SF		SB	CS	SB%	GDP	Avg	OBP	Slg
2008 Portlnd*	AAA	112	412	115	27	7	22	(- -)	222	82	77	83	56	0	89	4	0	4		8	3	.73	10	.279	.368	.539
2005 KC	AL	53	145	35	8	0	4	(2 2)	55	25	9	13	16	1	32	2	3	1		3	2	.60	5	.241	.323	.379
2007 NYM	NL	3	3	1	0	0	0	(0 0)	1	0	1	1	0	0	1	0	0	0		0	0	-	0	.333	.333	.333
2008 SD	NL	24	41	8	1	0	0	(0 0)	9	3	0	3	7	0	15	0	0	0		1	0	1.00	0	.195	.313	.220
3 ML YEARS		80	189	44	9	0	4	(2 2)	65	28	10	17	23	1	48	2	3	1		4	2	.67	5	.233	.321	.344

Alfredo Amezaga

Bats: B **Throws:** R **Pos:** CF-79; PH-25; SS-19; 3B-15; 2B-10; PR-9   **Ht:** 5'10" **Wt:** 180 **Born:** 1/16/1978 **Age:** 31

BATTING																				BASERUNNING				AVERAGES		
Year Team	Lg	G	AB	H	2B	3B	HR	(Hm Rd)	TB	R	RBI	RC	TBB	IBB	SO	HBP	SH	SF		SB	CS	SB%	GDP	Avg	OBP	Slg
2002 LAA	AL	12	13	7	2	0	0	(0 0)	9	3	2	6	0	0	1	0	0	0		1	0	1.00	1	.538	.538	.692
2003 LAA	AL	37	105	22	3	2	2	(0 2)	35	15	7	7	9	0	23	1	5	0		2	2	.50	2	.210	.278	.333
2004 LAA	AL	73	93	15	2	0	2	(0 2)	23	12	11	5	3	0	24	3	6	0		3	2	.60	2	.161	.212	.247
2005 2 Tms	NL	5	6	1	0	0	0	(0 0)	1	2	0	0	1	0	0	0	0	0		1	0	1.00	0	.167	.286	.167
2006 Fla	NL	132	334	87	9	3	3	(0 3)	111	42	19	32	33	4	46	3	7	1		20	12	.63	5	.260	.332	.332
2007 Fla	NL	133	400	105	14	9	2	(1 1)	143	46	30	38	35	0	52	4	4	5		13	7	.65	4	.263	.324	.358
2008 Fla	NL	125	311	82	13	5	3	(2 1)	114	41	32	37	19	1	47	3	4	0		8	2	.80	6	.264	.312	.367
05 Col	NL	2	3	1	0	0	0	(0 0)	1	1	0	0	0	0	0	0	0	0		0	0	-	0	.333	.333	.333
05 Pit	NL	3	3	0	0	0	0	(0 0)	0	1	0	0	1	0	0	0	0	0		1	0	1.00	0	.000	.250	.000
Postseason		2	2	0	0	0	0	(0 0)	0	0	0	0	0	0	2	0	1	0		0	0	-	0	.000	.000	.000
7 ML YEARS		517	1262	319	43	19	12	(3 9)	436	161	101	125	100	5	193	14	26	6		48	25	.66	20	.253	.313	.345

Brian Anderson

Bats: R **Throws:** R **Pos:** CF-94; PR-20; PH-13; LF-3; RF-2; DH-2   **Ht:** 6'2" **Wt:** 220 **Born:** 3/11/1982 **Age:** 27

BATTING																				BASERUNNING				AVERAGES		
Year Team	Lg	G	AB	H	2B	3B	HR	(Hm Rd)	TB	R	RBI	RC	TBB	IBB	SO	HBP	SH	SF		SB	CS	SB%	GDP	Avg	OBP	Slg
2005 CWS	AL	13	34	6	1	0	2	(0 2)	13	3	3	2	0	0	12	0	1	0		1	0	1.00	1	.176	.176	.382
2006 CWS	AL	134	365	82	23	1	8	(7 1)	131	46	33	32	30	2	90	5	2	3		4	7	.36	3	.225	.290	.359
2007 CWS	AL	13	17	2	1	0	0	(0 0)	3	3	0	0	2	0	7	0	0	0		0	0	-	2	.118	.211	.176
2008 CWS	AL	109	181	42	13	0	8	(5 3)	79	24	26	21	10	0	45	0	2	0		5	1	.83	2	.232	.272	.436
4 ML YEARS		269	597	132	38	1	18	(12 6)	226	76	62	55	42	2	154	5	5	3		10	8	.56	9	.221	.277	.379

Garret Anderson

Bats: L **Throws:** L **Pos:** LF-82; DH-60; PH-5   **Ht:** 6'3" **Wt:** 225 **Born:** 6/30/1972 **Age:** 37

BATTING																				BASERUNNING				AVERAGES		
Year Team	Lg	G	AB	H	2B	3B	HR	(Hm Rd)	TB	R	RBI	RC	TBB	IBB	SO	HBP	SH	SF		SB	CS	SB%	GDP	Avg	OBP	Slg
1994 LAA	AL	5	13	5	0	0	0	(0 0)	5	0	1	2	0	0	2	0	0	0		0	0	-	0	.385	.385	.385
1995 LAA	AL	106	374	120	19	1	16	(7 9)	189	50	69	63	19	4	65	1	2	4		6	2	.75	8	.321	.352	.505
1996 LAA	AL	150	607	173	33	2	12	(7 5)	246	79	72	68	27	5	84	0	5	3		7	9	.44	22	.285	.314	.405
1997 LAA	AL	154	624	189	36	3	8	(5 3)	255	76	92	80	30	6	70	2	1	5		10	4	.71	20	.303	.334	.409
1998 LAA	AL	156	622	183	41	7	15	(4 11)	283	62	79	88	29	8	80	1	3	3		8	3	.73	13	.294	.325	.455
1999 LAA	AL	157	620	188	36	2	21	(10 11)	291	88	80	92	34	8	81	0	0	6		3	4	.43	15	.303	.336	.469
2000 LAA	AL	159	647	185	40	3	35	(20 15)	336	92	117	95	24	5	87	0	1	9		7	6	.54	21	.286	.307	.519
2001 LAA	AL	161	672	194	39	2	28	(13 15)	321	83	123	97	27	4	100	0	0	5		13	6	.68	12	.289	.314	.478
2002 LAA	AL	158	638	195	56	4	29	(13 16)	344	93	123	108	30	11	80	0	0	10		6	4	.60	11	.306	.332	.539
2003 LAA	AL	159	638	201	49	4	29	(12 17)	345	80	116	114	31	10	83	0	0	4		6	3	.67	15	.315	.345	.541
2004 LAA	AL	112	442	133	20	1	14	(4 10)	197	57	75	70	29	6	75	1	0	3		2	1	.67	3	.301	.343	.446
2005 LAA	AL	142	575	163	34	1	17	(5 12)	250	68	96	82	23	8	84	0	0	5		1	1	.50	13	.283	.308	.435
2006 LAA	AL	141	543	152	28	2	17	(8 9)	235	63	85	75	38	11	95	0	0	7		1	0	1.00	8	.280	.323	.433
2007 LAA	AL	108	417	124	31	1	16	(11 5)	205	67	80	65	27	9	54	0	0	6		1	0	1.00	8	.297	.336	.492
2008 LAA	AL	145	557	163	27	3	15	(6 9)	241	66	84	86	29	6	77	1	0	6		7	4	.64	11	.293	.325	.433
Postseason		32	128	33	5	1	5	(2 3)	55	16	22	14	4	0	16	0	0	2		0	1	.00	2	.258	.276	.430
15 ML YEARS		2013	7989	2368	489	35	272	(128 144)	3743	1024	1292	1185	397	101	1117	6	12	76		78	47	.62	180	.296	.327	.469

Josh Anderson

Bats: L **Throws:** R **Pos:** CF-30; LF-6; PH-5; PR-2; RF-1   **Ht:** 6'2" **Wt:** 195 **Born:** 8/10/1982 **Age:** 26

Year	Team	Lg	G	AB	H	2B	3B	HR	(Hm	Rd)	TB	R	RBI	RC	TBB	IBB	SO	HBP	SH	SF	SB	CS	SB%	GDP	Avg	OBP	Slg
2003	TriCity	A-	74	297	85	11	4	3	(-	-)	113	44	30	42	16	2	53	10	2	4	26	9	.74	2	.286	.339	.380
2004	Lxngtn	A	73	299	97	12	3	4	(-	-)	127	69	31	59	33	1	47	7	2	2	47	9	.84	0	.324	.402	.425
2004	Salem	A+	66	280	75	13	6	2	(-	-)	106	45	21	38	13	1	53	6	7	0	31	4	.89	3	.268	.314	.379
2005	CpChr	AA	127	524	148	17	9	1	(-	-)	186	67	25	66	29	2	80	8	10	2	50	18	.74	4	.282	.329	.355
2006	CpChr	AA	131	561	173	26	4	3	(-	-)	216	83	50	81	27	2	73	10	8	4	43	13	.77	9	.308	.349	.385
2007	RdRck	AAA	132	513	140	17	6	2	(-	-)	175	64	43	64	32	2	75	8	10	1	40	8	.83	11	.273	.325	.341
2008	Rchmd	AAA	121	494	155	25	4	4	(-	-)	200	77	44	79	30	3	57	6	8	3	42	7	.86	9	.314	.358	.405
2007	Hou	NL	21	67	24	3	0	0	(0	0)	27	10	11	13	5	0	6	2	0	1	1	1	.50	2	.358	.413	.403
2008	Atl	NL	40	136	40	7	1	3	(0	3)	58	21	12	19	8	2	33	1	1	0	10	1	.91	1	.294	.338	.426
2 ML YEARS			61	203	64	10	1	3	(0	3)	85	31	23	32	13	2	39	3	1	1	11	2	.85	1	.315	.364	.419

Marlon Anderson

Bats: L **Throws:** R **Pos:** PH-60; LF-25; 1B-6; 2B-1; DH-1   **Ht:** 5'11" **Wt:** 200 **Born:** 1/6/1974 **Age:** 35

Year	Team	Lg	G	AB	H	2B	3B	HR	(Hm	Rd)	TB	R	RBI	RC	TBB	IBB	SO	HBP	SH	SF	SB	CS	SB%	GDP	Avg	OBP	Slg
2008	StLuci*	A+	4	13	3	0	0	0	(-	-)	3	0	0	0	1	0	3	0	0	0	0	0	-	0	.231	.286	.231
1998	Phi	NL	17	43	14	3	0	1	(1	0)	20	4	4	7	1	0	6	0	0	1	2	0	1.00	0	.326	.333	.465
1999	Phi	NL	129	452	114	26	4	5	(4	1)	163	48	54	49	24	1	61	2	4	2	13	2	.87	6	.252	.292	.361
2000	Phi	NL	41	162	37	8	1	1	(1	0)	50	10	15	12	12	0	22	0	0	2	2	2	.50	5	.228	.282	.309
2001	Phi	NL	147	522	153	30	2	11	(7	4)	220	69	61	72	35	5	74	2	10	5	8	5	.62	12	.293	.337	.421
2002	Phi	NL	145	539	139	30	6	8	(4	4)	205	64	48	53	42	14	71	5	2	4	5	1	.83	16	.258	.315	.380
2003	TB	AL	145	482	130	27	3	6	(2	4)	181	59	67	70	41	5	60	3	4	5	19	3	.86	6	.270	.328	.376
2004	StL	NL	113	253	60	12	0	8	(2	6)	96	31	28	23	12	1	38	1	0	5	6	2	.75	5	.237	.269	.379
2005	NYM	NL	123	235	62	9	0	7	(3	4)	92	31	19	23	18	0	45	1	4	2	6	1	.86	2	.264	.316	.391
2006	2 Tms	NL	134	279	83	16	4	12	(4	8)	143	43	38	42	25	1	49	1	4	3	4	6	.40	4	.297	.354	.513
2007	2 Tms	NL	66	95	28	7	0	3	(2	1)	44	17	27	17	8	1	17	0	1	2	4	1	.80	2	.295	.343	.463
2008	NYM	NL	87	138	29	6	0	1	(0	1)	38	16	10	4	9	0	27	0	2	2	2	1	.67	2	.210	.255	.275
06	Was	NL	109	215	59	13	2	5	(0	5)	91	31	23	28	18	1	41	1	3	2	2	4	.33	1	.274	.331	.423
06	LAD	NL	25	64	24	3	2	7	(4	3)	52	12	15	14	7	0	8	0	1	1	2	2	.50	3	.375	.431	.813
07	LAD	NL	23	26	6	0	0	0	(0	0)	6	3	2	2	3	0	5	0	0	0	1	0	1.00	0	.231	.310	.231
07	NYM	NL	43	69	22	7	0	3	(2	1)	38	14	25	15	5	1	12	0	1	2	3	1	.75	2	.319	.355	.551
Postseason			15	25	6	3	0	0	(0	0)	9	3	1	2	1	0	3	1	0	0	0	0	-	0	.240	.296	.360
11 ML YEARS			1147	3200	849	174	20	63	(30	33)	1252	392	371	372	227	28	470	15	31	31	71	24	.75	60	.265	.314	.391

Robert Andino

Bats: R **Throws:** R **Pos:** PH-23; 2B-15; SS-4; PR-3; 3B-1; CF-1   **Ht:** 6'0" **Wt:** 170 **Born:** 4/25/1984 **Age:** 25

Year	Team	Lg	G	AB	H	2B	3B	HR	(Hm	Rd)	TB	R	RBI	RC	TBB	IBB	SO	HBP	SH	SF	SB	CS	SB%	GDP	Avg	OBP	Slg
2008	Albq*	AAA	43	181	52	14	3	6	(-	-)	90	28	26	32	18	0	31	2	2	1	9	5	.64	2	.287	.356	.497
2005	Fla	NL	17	44	7	4	0	0	(0	0)	11	4	1	1	5	1	8	0	1	0	1	0	1.00	0	.159	.245	.250
2006	Fla	NL	11	24	4	1	0	0	(0	0)	5	0	2	0	1	0	6	0	1	2	1	0	1.00	0	.167	.185	.208
2007	Fla	NL	7	13	5	1	0	0	(0	0)	6	0	0	1	0	0	2	0	0	0	0	0	-	0	.385	.385	.462
2008	Fla	NL	44	63	13	2	0	2	(1	1)	21	7	9	7	4	0	23	0	1	0	0	0	-	1	.206	.254	.333
4 ML YEARS			79	144	29	8	0	2	(1	1)	43	11	12	9	10	1	39	0	3	2	2	0	1.00	3	.201	.250	.299

Rick Ankiel

Bats: L **Throws:** L **Pos:** CF-89; LF-17; PH-17; RF-1; PR-1   **Ht:** 6'1" **Wt:** 215 **Born:** 7/19/1979 **Age:** 29

Year	Team	Lg	G	AB	H	2B	3B	HR	(Hm	Rd)	TB	R	RBI	RC	TBB	IBB	SO	HBP	SH	SF	SB	CS	SB%	GDP	Avg	OBP	Slg
2005	Sprgfld	AA	34	136	33	7	0	10	(-	-)	70	18	30	21	10	0	29	0	0	0	0	0	-	4	.243	.295	.515
2005	QuadC	A	51	185	50	10	1	11	(-	-)	95	33	45	37	27	1	37	5	0	6	0	0	-	4	.270	.368	.514
2007	Memp	AAA	102	387	104	15	3	32	(-	-)	221	62	89	70	25	5	89	4	0	5	4	3	.57	11	.269	.316	.571
1999	StL	NL	9	10	1	0	0	0	(0	0)	1	0	0	0	0	0	3	0	1	0	0	0	-	0	.100	.100	.100
2000	StL	NL	33	68	17	1	1	2	(2	0)	26	8	9	0	4	0	20	0	1	0	0	0	-	1	.250	.292	.382
2001	StL	NL	6	8	0	0	0	0	(0	0)	0	1	0	0	1	0	5	0	1	0	0	0	-	0	.000	.111	.000
2004	StL	NL	5	1	0	0	0	0	(0	0)	0	0	0	0	1	0	1	0	0	0	0	0	-	0	.000	.500	.000
2007	StL	NL	47	172	49	8	1	11	(9	2)	92	31	39	32	13	0	41	0	1	4	1	0	1.00	4	.285	.328	.535
2008	StL	NL	120	413	109	21	2	25	(11	14)	209	65	71	60	42	3	100	5	0	3	2	1	.67	8	.264	.337	.506
Postseason			3	1	0	0	0	0	(0	0)	0	0	0	0	0	0	0	0	0	0	0	0	-	0	.000	.000	.000
6 ML YEARS			220	672	176	30	4	38	(22	16)	328	105	119	92	61	3	170	5	4	7	3	1	.75	12	.262	.325	.488

Matt Antonelli

Bats: R **Throws:** R **Pos:** 2B-18; PH-3; PR-1   **Ht:** 6'1" **Wt:** 198 **Born:** 4/8/1985 **Age:** 24

Year	Team	Lg	G	AB	H	2B	3B	HR	(Hm	Rd)	TB	R	RBI	RC	TBB	IBB	SO	HBP	SH	SF	SB	CS	SB%	GDP	Avg	OBP	Slg
2006	Eugene	A-	55	189	54	12	1	0	(-	-)	68	38	22	37	46	0	31	4	1	5	9	1	.90	3	.286	.426	.360
2006	FtWyn	A	5	16	2	1	1	0	(-	-)	5	3	0	1	2	0	6	0	0	0	0	0	-	0	.125	.222	.313
2007	Lk Els	A+	82	347	109	14	4	14	(-	-)	173	89	54	73	53	1	58	4	0	2	18	6	.75	4	.314	.409	.499
2007	SnAnt	AA	49	187	55	11	1	7	(-	-)	89	34	24	38	30	0	36	3	0	3	10	3	.77	2	.294	.395	.476
2008	Portlnd	AAA	128	451	97	19	4	7	(-	-)	145	62	39	56	75	0	86	9	0	5	6	4	.60	11	.215	.335	.322
2008	SD	NL	21	57	11	2	0	1	(0	1)	16	6	3	4	5	1	11	3	0	0	0	0	-	1	.193	.292	.281

Greg Aquino

Pitches: R Bats: R Pos: RP-9   Ht: 6'1" Wt: 190 Born: 1/11/1978 Age: 31

Year	Team	Lg	G	GS	CG	GF	IP	BFP	H	R	ER	HR	SH	SF	HB	TBB	IBB	SO	WP	Bk	W	L	Pct	ShO	Sv-Op	Hld	ERC	ERA
2008	Norfolk*	AAA	23	0	0	21	25.1	105	23	10	7	2	3	0	0	6	1	29	2	0	2	2	.500	0	9--	1	2.71	2.49
2008	Frdrck*	A+	1	0	0	0	1.0	4	1	0	0	0	0	0	0	0	0	2	0	0	0	0	-	0	0--	-	1.95	0.00
2008	Abrdn*	A-	1	0	0	0	1.0	3	0	0	0	0	0	0	0	0	0	2	0	0	0	0	-	0	0--	-	0.00	0.00
2008	Dlmrva*	A	1	0	0	1	1.0	3	0	0	0	0	0	0	0	0	0	1	0	0	0	0	-	0	0--	-	0.00	0.00
2008	Bowie*	AA	1	0	0	0	1.0	5	2	0	0	0	0	0	0	0	0	1	0	0	0	0	-	0	0--	-	7.48	0.00
2004	Ari	NL	34	0	0	26	35.1	147	24	15	12	4	2	2	2	17	2	26	4	0	0	2	.000	0	16-19	1	2.87	3.06
2005	Ari	NL	35	0	0	11	31.1	155	42	29	27	7	1	1	4	17	1	34	2	1	0	1	.000	0	1-3	3	8.22	7.76
2006	Ari	NL	42	0	0	12	48.1	220	54	27	24	8	1	0	4	24	2	51	2	0	2	0	1.000	0	0-0	2	5.99	4.47
2007	Mil	NL	15	0	0	8	14.0	59	13	9	7	2	1	0	0	5	1	12	2	0	0	1	.000	0	0-2	2	3.69	4.50
2008	Bal	AL	9	0	0	5	9.1	54	17	13	13	1	1	1	2	9	0	9	0	0	0	0	-	0	0-0	0	13.24	12.54
	5 ML YEARS		135	0	0	62	138.1	635	150	93	83	22	6	4	12	72	6	132	10	1	2	4	.333	0	17-24	8	5.79	5.40

Danny Ardoin

Bats: R Throws: R Pos: C-24; PR-1   Ht: 6'0" Wt: 215 Born: 7/8/1974 Age: 34

										BATTING												BASERUNNING				AVERAGES		
Year	Team	Lg	G	AB	H	2B	3B	HR	(Hm	Rd)	TB	R	RBI	RC	TBB	IBB	SO	HBP	SH	SF	SB	CS	SB%	GDP	Avg	OBP	Slg
2008	LsVgs*	AAA	29	99	30	6	0	4	(-	-)	48	14	16	18	8	0	24	3	3	1	0	0	-	1	.303	.369	.485
2000	Min	AL	15	32	4	1	0	1	(0	1)	8	4	5	2	8	0	10	0	0	0	0	0	-	0	.125	.300	.250
2004	Tex	AL	6	8	1	0	0	0	(0	0)	1	1	1	1	3	0	2	0	0	0	0	0	-	0	.125	.364	.125
2005	Col	NL	80	210	48	10	0	6	(3	3)	76	28	22	21	20	2	69	9	7	2	1	1	.50	8	.229	.320	.362
2006	2 Tms		40	122	22	5	1	0	(0	0)	29	14	3	2	9	2	33	3	1	0	0	0	-	3	.180	.254	.238
2008	LAD	NL	24	51	12	1	0	1	(0	1)	16	3	4	4	2	0	10	1	0	0	1	0	1.00	2	.235	.278	.314
06	Col	NL	35	109	21	5	1	0	(0	0)	28	12	2	2	8	2	27	2	1	0	0	0	-	2	.193	.261	.257
06	Bal	AL	5	13	1	0	0	0	(0	0)	1	2	1	0	1	0	6	1	0	0	0	0	-	1	.077	.200	.077
	5 ML YEARS		165	423	87	17	1	8	(3	5)	130	50	35	30	42	4	124	13	8	2	2	1	.67	13	.206	.296	.307

Alberto Arias

Pitches: R Bats: R Pos: RP-13; SP-2   Ht: 5'11" Wt: 155 Born: 10/14/1983 Age: 25

Year	Team	Lg	G	GS	CG	GF	IP	BFP	H	R	ER	HR	SH	SF	HB	TBB	IBB	SO	WP	Bk	W	L	Pct	ShO	Sv-Op	Hld	ERC	ERA
2003	Casper	R+	13	13	1	0	73.0	313	69	45	29	4	2	2	3	23	0	64	5	1	4	4	.500	0	0--	-	3.23	3.58
2004	Ashvll	A	26	24	4	2	135.0	572	153	86	75	23	5	8	3	36	0	83	6	2	8	9	.471	1	1--	-	5.01	5.00
2005	Mdest	A+	37	7	0	4	90.2	394	99	48	44	4	2	3	6	25	0	53	6	0	4	4	.500	0	2--	-	3.95	4.37
2006	Tulsa	AA	49	9	0	10	111.2	479	102	59	54	15	4	4	10	45	1	83	11	2	8	6	.571	0	0--	-	4.22	4.35
2007	ColSpr	AAA	10	3	0	1	26.1	111	32	12	11	1	1	1	0	8	0	15	1	0	2	2	.500	0	0--	-	4.69	3.76
2008	ColSpr	AAA	30	0	0	8	45.2	200	50	25	24	3	5	1	4	16	1	41	2	0	3	4	.429	0	0--	-	4.53	4.73
2008	RdRck	AAA	8	3	0	2	23.2	95	21	4	4	0	0	0	1	5	0	15	1	0	1	0	1.000	0	1--	-	2.34	1.52
2007	Col	NL	6	0	0	0	7.1	32	8	4	4	1	1	0	0	5	0	3	0	0	1	0	1.000	0	0-1	0	6.51	4.91
2008	2 Tms	NL	15	2	0	4	21.2	95	23	10	10	1	0	0	2	10	0	13	1	0	1	1	.500	0	0-0	0	4.77	4.15
08	Col	NL	12	0	0	4	13.2	56	12	4	4	1	0	0	1	4	0	5	1	0	0	0	-	0	0-0	0	3.17	2.63
08	Hou	NL	3	2	0	0	8.0	39	11	6	6	0	0	0	1	6	0	8	0	0	1	1	.500	0	0-0	0	7.85	6.75
	2 ML YEARS		21	2	0	4	29.0	127	31	14	14	2	1	0	2	15	0	16	1	0	2	1	.667	0	0-1	0	5.19	4.34

Joaquin Arias

Bats: R Throws: R Pos: 2B-30; PH-2; DH-1; PR-1   Ht: 6'1" Wt: 165 Born: 9/21/1984 Age: 24

										BATTING												BASERUNNING				AVERAGES		
Year	Team	Lg	G	AB	H	2B	3B	HR	(Hm	Rd)	TB	R	RBI	RC	TBB	IBB	SO	HBP	SH	SF	SB	CS	SB%	GDP	Avg	OBP	Slg
2002	Yanks	R	57	203	61	7	6	0	(-	-)	80	29	21	26	12	0	16	0	2	1	2	4	.33	4	.300	.338	.394
2003	Btl Crk	A	130	481	128	12	8	3	(-	-)	165	60	48	53	26	0	44	3	7	3	12	5	.71	7	.266	.306	.343
2004	Stcktn	A+	123	500	150	20	8	4	(-	-)	198	77	62	71	31	2	53	5	2	5	30	14	.68	3	.300	.344	.396
2005	Frisco	AA	120	499	157	23	8	5	(-	-)	211	65	56	72	17	1	46	1	3	6	20	10	.67	5	.315	.335	.423
2006	Okla	AAA	124	493	132	14	10	4	(-	-)	178	56	49	55	19	2	64	4	2	7	26	10	.72	6	.268	.296	.361
2007	Rngrs	R	2	7	2	1	0	0	(-	-)	3	1	1	1	0	0	2	0	0	1	0	0	-	0	.286	.250	.429
2007	Okla	AAA	3	11	2	0	0	0	(-	-)	2	3	1	0	0	0	2	0	0	1	1	0	1.00	1	.182	.182	.182
2008	Okla	AAA	104	432	128	15	9	7	(-	-)	182	59	49	63	19	0	53	3	4	2	23	5	.82	10	.296	.329	.421
2006	Tex	AL	6	11	6	1	0	0	(0	0)	7	4	1	3	1	0	0	0	0	0	0	1	.00	0	.545	.583	.636
2008	Tex	AL	32	110	32	7	3	0	(0	0)	45	15	9	15	7	0	12	2	1	0	4	1	.80	4	.291	.345	.409
	2 ML YEARS		38	121	38	8	3	0	(0	0)	52	19	10	18	8	0	12	2	1	0	4	2	.67	4	.314	.366	.430

Tony Armas Jr.

Pitches: R Bats: R Pos: RP-2; SP-1   Ht: 6'3" Wt: 225 Born: 4/29/1978 Age: 31

Year	Team	Lg	G	GS	CG	GF	IP	BFP	H	R	ER	HR	SH	SF	HB	TBB	IBB	SO	WP	Bk	W	L	Pct	ShO	Sv-Op	Hld	ERC	ERA
2008	NewOr*	AAA	17	17	0	0	102.2	400	85	31	29	9	2	2	1	20	1	88	6	0	5	7	.417	0	0--	-	2.42	2.54
1999	Mon	NL	1	1	0	0	6.0	28	8	4	1	0	1	0	0	2	1	2	2	0	1	0	1.000	0	0-0	0	4.53	1.50
2000	Mon	NL	17	17	0	0	95.0	403	74	49	46	10	7	3	3	50	2	59	3	0	7	9	.438	0	0-0	0	3.49	4.36
2001	Mon	NL	34	34	0	0	196.2	851	180	101	88	18	15	6	10	91	6	176	9	1	9	14	.391	0	0-0	0	3.95	4.03
2002	Mon	NL	29	29	0	0	164.1	705	149	87	81	22	6	2	7	78	12	131	14	2	12	12	.500	0	0-0	0	4.19	4.44
2003	Mon	NL	5	5	0	0	31.0	124	25	9	9	4	2	2	1	8	0	23	0	0	2	1	.667	0	0-0	0	2.84	2.61
2004	Mon	NL	16	16	0	0	72.0	320	66	41	39	13	2	2	4	45	6	54	0	0	2	4	.333	0	0-0	0	5.26	4.88
2005	Was	NL	19	19	0	0	101.1	452	100	57	56	16	4	1	5	54	4	59	6	2	7	7	.500	0	0-0	0	5.11	4.97

31

Year Team	Lg	G	GS	CG	GF	IP	BFP	H	R	ER	HR	SH	SF	HB	TBB	IBB	SO	WP	Bk	W	L	Pct	ShO	Sv-Op	Hld	ERC	ERA
		HOW MUCH HE PITCHED						**WHAT HE GAVE UP**												**THE RESULTS**							
2006 Was	NL	30	30	0	0	154.0	693	167	96	86	19	12	6	13	64	7	97	6	1	9	12	.429	0	0-0	0	5.04	5.03
2007 Pit	NL	31	15	0	6	97.0	442	111	68	65	18	2	7	8	38	3	73	2	0	4	5	.444	0	0-0	0	5.77	6.03
2008 NYM	NL	3	1	0	1	8.1	37	11	7	7	2	1	1	0	1	0	6	1	0	1	0	1.000	0	0-0	0	5.65	7.56
10 ML YEARS		185	167	0	7	925.2	4055	891	519	478	122	51	31	51	431	41	680	43	6	53	65	.449	0	0-0	0	4.51	4.65

Jose Arredondo

Pitches: R **Bats:** R **Pos:** RP-52   **Ht:** 6'0" **Wt:** 175 **Born:** 3/30/1984 **Age:** 25

Year Team	Lg	G	GS	CG	GF	IP	BFP	H	R	ER	HR	SH	SF	HB	TBB	IBB	SO	WP	Bk	W	L	Pct	ShO	Sv-Op	Hld	ERC	ERA
		HOW MUCH HE PITCHED						**WHAT HE GAVE UP**												**THE RESULTS**							
2004 Angels	R	8	0	0	4	12.1	56	14	10	4	1	1	0	1	4	0	14	2	0	0	0	-	0	1--	-	4.61	2.92
2005 Ark	AA	5	0	0	3	5.1	22	5	2	2	0	0	0	0	4	0	4	1	0	0	0	-	0	0--	-	4.84	3.38
2005 Orem	R+	15	13	0	0	68.2	295	76	34	32	4	1	1	6	20	0	60	6	0	5	0	1.000	0	0--	-	4.39	4.19
2006 RCuca	A+	15	15	0	0	90.0	360	62	28	23	4	1	5	6	35	0	115	6	0	5	6	.455	0	0--	-	2.36	2.30
2006 Ark	AA	11	11	1	0	60.2	280	80	47	44	8	2	3	1	22	0	48	6	0	2	3	.400	1	0--	-	6.09	6.53
2007 Ark	AA	23	0	0	18	25.0	102	16	10	7	2	1	2	0	12	0	28	1	0	0	1	.000	0	10--	-	2.35	2.52
2007 Salt Lk	AAA	2	0	0	1	3.0	13	2	1	1	0	1	0	0	2	0	1	0	0	0	0	-	0	0--	-	2.54	3.00
2008 Salt Lk	AAA	15	0	0	15	17.0	66	12	4	4	2	1	1	1	4	0	15	1	0	1	1	.500	0	10--	-	2.32	2.12
2008 LAA	AL	52	0	0	10	61.0	244	42	15	11	3	0	0	1	22	0	55	1	0	10	2	.833	0	0-7	16	2.08	1.62

Bronson Arroyo

Pitches: R **Bats:** R **Pos:** SP-34   **Ht:** 6'5" **Wt:** 194 **Born:** 2/24/1977 **Age:** 32

Year Team	Lg	G	GS	CG	GF	IP	BFP	H	R	ER	HR	SH	SF	HB	TBB	IBB	SO	WP	Bk	W	L	Pct	ShO	Sv-Op	Hld	ERC	ERA
		HOW MUCH HE PITCHED						**WHAT HE GAVE UP**												**THE RESULTS**							
2000 Pit	NL	20	12	0	1	71.2	338	88	61	51	10	5	2	4	36	6	50	3	1	2	6	.250	0	0-0	0	6.18	6.40
2001 Pit	NL	24	13	1	1	88.1	390	99	54	50	12	4	6	4	34	6	39	4	1	5	7	.417	0	0-0	2	5.09	5.09
2002 Pit	NL	9	4	0	1	27.0	123	30	14	12	1	1	1	0	15	3	22	0	0	2	1	.667	0	0-0	1	4.64	4.00
2003 Bos	AL	6	0	0	2	17.1	66	10	5	4	0	0	0	1	4	2	14	0	0	0	0	-	0	1-1	0	1.14	2.08
2004 Bos	AL	32	29	0	0	178.2	764	171	99	80	17	5	4	20	47	3	142	5	0	10	9	.526	0	0-0	0	3.65	4.03
2005 Bos	AL	35	32	0	1	205.1	878	213	116	103	22	4	4	14	54	3	100	5	1	14	10	.583	0	0-0	0	4.04	4.51
2006 Cin	NL	35	35	3	0	240.2	992	222	98	88	31	9	2	5	64	7	184	6	0	14	11	.560	1	0-0	0	3.37	3.29
2007 Cin	NL	34	34	1	0	210.2	921	232	109	99	28	10	7	13	63	6	156	4	0	9	15	.375	0	0-0	0	4.68	4.23
2008 Cin	NL	34	34	1	0	200.0	871	219	116	106	29	13	6	6	68	2	163	4	0	15	11	.577	0	0-0	0	4.83	4.77
Postseason		10	2	0	3	17.0	80	19	14	14	5	0	0	2	9	0	20	0	0	0	0	-	0	0-0	2	7.30	7.41
9 ML YEARS		229	193	6	6	1239.2	5343	1284	672	593	150	51	32	67	385	38	870	33	3	71	70	.504	1	1-1	3	4.23	4.31

Jose Ascanio

Pitches: R **Bats:** R **Pos:** RP-6   **Ht:** 6'0" **Wt:** 170 **Born:** 5/2/1985 **Age:** 24

Year Team	Lg	G	GS	CG	GF	IP	BFP	H	R	ER	HR	SH	SF	HB	TBB	IBB	SO	WP	Bk	W	L	Pct	ShO	Sv-Op	Hld	ERC	ERA
		HOW MUCH HE PITCHED						**WHAT HE GAVE UP**												**THE RESULTS**							
2003 Braves	R	8	0	0	0	26.1	104	26	4	4	0	0	1	2	5	0	17	4	0	4	0	1.000	0	0--	-	3.01	1.37
2004 Rome	A	34	0	0	18	65.2	274	58	39	28	6	0	0	4	15	1	64	5	3	3	3	.500	0	9--	-	2.89	3.84
2005 MrtlBh	A+	5	3	0	2	20.2	94	26	17	14	5	1	0	0	9	0	12	2	0	3	1	.750	0	0--	-	6.95	6.10
2006 MrtlBh	A+	8	6	0	0	31.0	148	38	18	17	0	1	2	4	20	0	23	0	0	1	1	.500	0	0--	-	6.24	4.94
2006 Missi	AA	24	0	0	6	38.0	171	37	20	18	2	1	1	6	17	3	37	1	1	4	2	.667	0	0--	-	4.21	4.26
2007 Missi	AA	44	1	0	20	78.0	314	66	26	22	1	4	5	5	18	0	71	8	1	2	2	.500	0	10--	-	2.35	2.54
2008 Iowa	AAA	40	0	0	24	54.2	245	54	35	31	10	3	1	5	23	0	58	2	1	2	1	.667	0	11--	-	4.97	5.10
2007 Atl	NL	13	0	0	6	16.0	74	17	11	9	3	1	0	0	6	2	13	0	0	1	1	.500	0	0-0	0	4.43	5.06
2008 ChC	NL	6	0	0	1	5.2	30	8	5	5	1	1	1	1	4	1	3	0	0	0	0	-	0	0-0	0	8.81	7.94
2 ML YEARS		19	0	0	7	21.2	104	25	16	14	4	2	1	1	10	3	16	0	0	1	1	.500	0	0-0	0	5.50	5.82

Garrett Atkins

Bats: R **Throws:** R **Pos:** 3B-94; 1B-61; PH-2; 2B-1   **Ht:** 6'3" **Wt:** 215 **Born:** 12/12/1979 **Age:** 29

Year Team	Lg	G	AB	H	2B	3B	HR	(Hm	Rd)	TB	R	RBI	RC	TBB	IBB	SO	HBP	SH	SF	SB	CS	SB%	GDP	Avg	OBP	Slg
		BATTING																		**BASERUNNING**				**AVERAGES**		
2003 Col	NL	25	69	11	2	0	0	(0	0)	13	6	4	2	3	0	14	1	0	0	0	0	-	1	.159	.205	.188
2004 Col	NL	15	28	10	2	0	1	(1	0)	15	3	8	8	4	0	3	0	0	1	0	0	-	0	.357	.424	.536
2005 Col	NL	138	519	149	31	1	13	(9	4)	221	62	89	74	45	1	72	5	0	4	0	2	.00	18	.287	.347	.426
2006 Col	NL	157	602	198	48	1	29	(15	14)	335	117	120	129	79	6	76	7	0	7	4	0	1.00	24	.329	.409	.556
2007 Col	NL	157	605	182	35	1	25	(10	15)	294	83	111	106	67	3	96	2	0	10	3	1	.75	16	.301	.367	.486
2008 Col	NL	155	611	175	32	3	21	(9	12)	276	86	99	76	40	0	100	3	0	10	1	1	.50	16	.286	.328	.452
Postseason		11	40	7	3	0	1	(1	0)	13	6	3	4	5	1	5	1	0	0	0	0	-	0	.175	.283	.325
6 ML YEARS		647	2434	725	150	6	89	(44	45)	1154	357	431	395	238	10	361	18	0	32	8	4	.67	79	.298	.360	.474

Michael Aubrey

Bats: L **Throws:** L **Pos:** 1B-12; PH-2; DH-1   **Ht:** 6'0" **Wt:** 195 **Born:** 4/15/1982 **Age:** 27

Year Team	Lg	G	AB	H	2B	3B	HR	(Hm	Rd)	TB	R	RBI	RC	TBB	IBB	SO	HBP	SH	SF	SB	CS	SB%	GDP	Avg	OBP	Slg
		BATTING																		**BASERUNNING**				**AVERAGES**		
2003 Lk Cty	A	38	138	48	13	0	5	(-	-)	76	22	19	30	14	0	22	1	0	1	0	0	-	2	.348	.409	.551
2004 Knstn	A+	60	218	74	14	1	10	(-	-)	120	34	60	52	27	1	26	12	0	1	3	1	.75	4	.339	.438	.550
2004 Akron	AA	38	134	35	7	0	5	(-	-)	57	13	22	21	15	0	18	3	0	4	0	0	-	3	.261	.340	.425
2005 Akron	AA	28	106	30	5	1	4	(-	-)	49	17	20	17	7	2	18	3	0	3	1	0	1.00	3	.283	.336	.462
2006 Knstn	A+	8	28	8	3	0	2	(-	-)	17	8	10	7	5	0	5	2	0	1	0	0	-	0	.286	.417	.607
2006 Akron	AA	6	26	7	2	0	1	(-	-)	12	3	2	4	2	0	4	1	0	0	0	0	-	0	.269	.345	.462
2007 Knstn	A+	13	50	20	5	0	5	(-	-)	40	15	11	17	6	0	7	3	0	0	0	0	-	0	.400	.492	.800

Year	Team	Lg	G	AB	H	2B	3B	HR	(Hm	Rd)	TB	R	RBI	RC	TBB	IBB	SO	HBP	SH	SF	SB	CS	SB%	GDP	Avg	OBP	Slg
2007	Akron	AA	54	207	51	11	0	7	(-	-)	83	22	34	25	11	1	35	3	0	2	0	0	-	5	.246	.291	.401
2008	Akron	AA	25	103	29	10	1	2	(-	-)	47	14	16	16	8	1	12	0	0	1	0	0	-	2	.282	.330	.456
2008	Buffalo	AAA	72	285	80	18	0	7	(-	-)	119	29	37	40	16	5	40	5	1	2	0	0	-	5	.281	.328	.418
2008	Cle	AL	15	45	9	0	0	2	(0	2)	15	2	3	1	5	0	5	0	0	0	0	0	-	2	.200	.280	.333

Rich Aurilia

Bats: R **Throws:** R **Pos:** 1B-82; 3B-63; PH-23; DH-2; 2B-1 **Ht:** 6'1" **Wt:** 199 **Born:** 9/2/1971 **Age:** 37

Year	Team	Lg	G	AB	H	2B	3B	HR	(Hm	Rd)	TB	R	RBI	RC	TBB	IBB	SO	HBP	SH	SF	SB	CS	SB%	GDP	Avg	OBP	Slg
1995	SF	NL	9	19	9	3	0	2	(0	2)	18	4	4	7	1	0	2	0	1	1	1	0	1.00	1	.474	.476	.947
1996	SF	NL	105	318	76	7	1	3	(1	2)	94	27	26	29	25	2	52	1	6	2	4	1	.80	1	.239	.295	.296
1997	SF	NL	46	102	28	8	0	5	(1	4)	51	16	19	16	8	0	15	0	1	2	1	1	.50	3	.275	.321	.500
1998	SF	NL	122	413	110	27	2	9	(5	4)	168	54	49	54	31	3	62	2	5	2	3	3	.50	3	.266	.319	.407
1999	SF	NL	152	558	157	23	1	22	(9	13)	248	68	80	79	43	3	71	5	3	5	2	3	.40	16	.281	.336	.444
2000	SF	NL	141	509	138	24	2	20	(12	8)	226	67	79	74	54	2	90	0	4	4	1	2	.33	15	.271	.339	.444
2001	SF	NL	156	636	206	37	5	37	(15	22)	364	114	97	124	47	2	83	0	3	3	1	3	.25	14	.324	.369	.572
2002	SF	NL	133	538	138	35	2	15	(4	11)	222	76	61	61	37	0	90	4	3	7	1	2	.33	15	.257	.305	.413
2003	SF	NL	129	505	140	26	1	13	(6	7)	207	65	58	56	36	0	82	1	0	3	2	2	.50	18	.277	.325	.410
2004	2 Tms		124	399	98	21	2	6	(3	3)	141	49	44	39	37	1	71	4	7	3	1	0	1.00	12	.246	.314	.353
2005	Cin	NL	114	426	120	23	2	14	(11	3)	189	61	68	70	37	2	67	1	1	3	2	0	1.00	9	.282	.338	.444
2006	Cin	NL	122	440	132	25	1	23	(13	10)	228	61	70	72	34	1	51	1	2	4	3	0	1.00	15	.300	.349	.518
2007	SF	NL	99	329	83	19	2	5	(2	3)	121	40	33	33	22	1	45	4	0	3	0	0	-	8	.252	.304	.368
2008	SF	NL	140	407	115	21	1	10	(5	5)	168	33	52	51	30	4	56	1	0	2	1	1	.50	11	.283	.332	.413
04	Sea	AL	73	261	63	13	0	4	(2	2)	88	27	28	25	22	1	43	2	6	1	1	0	1.00	10	.241	.304	.337
04	SD	NL	51	138	35	8	2	2	(1	1)	53	22	16	14	15	0	28	2	1	2	0	0	-	2	.254	.331	.384
	Postseason		25	98	22	6	0	6	(3	3)	46	17	18	14	7	0	22	1	3	1	0	0	-	1	.224	.280	.469
14 ML YEARS			1592	5599	1550	299	22	184	(87	97)	2445	735	740	765	442	21	837	24	36	44	23	18	.56	135	.277	.330	.437

Brad Ausmus

Bats: R **Throws:** R **Pos:** C-77; PH-4; 1B-2; 2B-1; 3B-1; PR-1 **Ht:** 5'11" **Wt:** 190 **Born:** 4/14/1969 **Age:** 40

Year	Team	Lg	G	AB	H	2B	3B	HR	(Hm	Rd)	TB	R	RBI	RC	TBB	IBB	SO	HBP	SH	SF	SB	CS	SB%	GDP	Avg	OBP	Slg
1993	SD	NL	49	160	41	8	1	5	(4	1)	66	18	12	19	6	0	28	0	0	0	2	0	1.00	2	.256	.283	.413
1994	SD	NL	101	327	82	12	1	7	(6	1)	117	45	24	36	30	12	63	1	6	2	5	1	.83	8	.251	.314	.358
1995	SD	NL	103	328	96	16	4	5	(2	3)	135	44	34	49	31	3	56	2	4	4	16	5	.76	6	.293	.353	.412
1996	2 Tms		125	375	83	16	0	5	(2	3)	114	46	35	32	39	1	72	5	6	2	4	8	.33	8	.221	.302	.304
1997	Hou	NL	130	425	113	25	1	4	(1	3)	152	45	44	51	38	4	78	3	6	6	14	6	.70	8	.266	.326	.358
1998	Hou	NL	128	412	111	10	4	6	(2	4)	147	62	45	55	53	11	60	3	3	1	10	3	.77	18	.269	.356	.357
1999	Det	AL	127	458	126	25	6	9	(5	4)	190	62	54	69	51	0	71	14	3	1	12	9	.57	11	.275	.365	.415
2000	Det	AL	150	523	139	25	3	7	(3	4)	191	75	51	68	69	0	79	6	4	2	11	5	.69	19	.266	.357	.365
2001	Hou	NL	128	422	98	23	4	6	(4	1)	144	45	34	38	30	6	64	1	6	2	4	1	.80	13	.232	.284	.341
2002	Hou	NL	130	447	115	19	3	6	(4	2)	158	57	50	44	38	3	71	6	2	3	2	3	.40	30	.257	.322	.353
2003	Hou	NL	143	450	103	12	2	4	(1	3)	131	43	47	44	46	1	66	4	4	5	5	3	.63	8	.229	.303	.291
2004	Hou	NL	129	403	100	14	1	5	(2	3)	131	38	31	34	33	11	56	2	7	3	2	2	.50	13	.248	.306	.325
2005	Hou	NL	134	387	100	19	0	3	(2	1)	128	35	47	42	51	8	48	5	7	1	5	3	.63	17	.258	.351	.331
2006	Hou	NL	139	439	101	16	1	2	(1	1)	125	37	39	36	45	2	71	6	9	3	1	1	.75	21	.230	.308	.285
2007	Hou	NL	117	349	82	16	3	3	(2	1)	113	38	25	28	37	3	74	6	4	1	6	1	.86	11	.235	.318	.324
2008	Hou	NL	81	216	47	8	0	3	(1	2)	64	15	24	25	25	3	41	2	5	2	0	2	.00	4	.218	.303	.296
96	SD	NL	50	149	27	4	0	1	(0	1)	34	16	13	6	13	0	27	3	1	0	1	4	.20	4	.181	.261	.228
96	Det	AL	75	226	56	12	0	4	(2	2)	80	30	22	26	26	1	45	2	5	2	3	4	.43	4	.248	.328	.354
	Postseason		35	106	26	5	0	3	(2	1)	40	12	7	8	9	3	29	1	2	1	1	0	1.00	5	.245	.308	.377
16 ML YEARS			1914	6121	1537	264	34	79	(42	37)	2106	705	596	666	622	68	998	66	77	37	101	53	.66	197	.251	.325	.344

Mike Aviles

Bats: R **Throws:** R **Pos:** SS-91; 2B-28; 3B-7 **Ht:** 5'9" **Wt:** 195 **Born:** 3/13/1981 **Age:** 28

Year	Team	Lg	G	AB	H	2B	3B	HR	(Hm	Rd)	TB	R	RBI	RC	TBB	IBB	SO	HBP	SH	SF	SB	CS	SB%	GDP	Avg	OBP	Slg
2003	Royals	R	52	212	77	19	5	6	(-	-)	124	51	39	48	13	0	28	5	2	5	11	5	.69	2	.363	.404	.585
2004	Wilmg	A+	126	463	139	40	4	6	(-	-)	205	66	69	73	39	2	57	1	1	6	2	5	.29	8	.300	.352	.443
2005	Wichta	AA	133	521	146	33	6	14	(-	-)	233	79	80	76	30	1	64	1	2	5	12	6	.67	16	.280	.318	.447
2006	Omha	AAA	129	469	125	21	3	8	(-	-)	176	52	47	57	28	1	49	2	0	3	14	5	.74	14	.267	.309	.375
2007	Omha	AAA	133	538	159	27	6	17	(-	-)	249	78	77	83	30	0	59	2	5	6	5	5	.50	24	.296	.332	.463
2008	Omha	AAA	51	214	72	21	6	10	(-	-)	135	42	42	48	11	0	23	1	0	1	3	0	1.00	9	.336	.370	.631
2008	KC	AL	102	419	136	27	4	10	(4	6)	201	68	51	62	18	4	58	2	0	2	8	3	.73	12	.325	.354	.480

Luis Ayala

Pitches: R **Bats:** R **Pos:** RP-81 **Ht:** 6'1" **Wt:** 198 **Born:** 1/12/1978 **Age:** 31

			HOW MUCH HE PITCHED						WHAT HE GAVE UP										THE RESULTS						
Year	Team	Lg	G	GS	CG	GF	IP	BFP	H	R	ER	HR	SH	SF	HB	TBB	IBB	SO	WP	Bk	W	L	Pct	ShO	Sv-Op	Hld	ERC	ERA
2003	Mon	NL	65	0	0	24	71.0	288	65	27	23	8	3	1	5	13	3	46	1	0	10	3	.769	0	5-8	19	3.11	2.92
2004	Mon	NL	81	0	0	28	90.1	367	92	30	27	6	2	2	5	15	2	63	3	1	6	12	.333	0	2-7	21	3.32	2.69
2005	Was	NL	68	0	0	18	71.0	293	75	23	21	7	8	3	6	14	4	40	0	0	8	7	.533	0	1-3	22	3.95	2.66
2007	Was	NL	44	0	0	11	42.1	181	43	16	15	7	3	4	1	12	0	28	1	0	2	2	.500	0	1-2	6	3.88	3.19
2008	2 Tms	NL	81	0	0	25	75.2	335	86	53	48	7	4	3	4	24	4	50	1	0	2	10	.167	0	9-15	19	4.70	5.71
08	Was	NL	62	0	0	12	57.2	257	63	41	37	6	4	2	4	22	4	36	1	0	1	8	.111	0	0-4	19	4.70	5.77
08	NYM	NL	19	0	0	13	18.0	78	23	12	11	3	0	1	0	2	0	14	0	0	1	2	.333	0	9-11	0	4.91	5.50
5 ML YEARS			339	0	0	106	350.1	1464	361	149	134	35	20	13	21	78	13	227	6	1	28	34	.452	0	18-35	87	3.77	3.44

33

Erick Aybar

Bats: B Throws: R Pos: SS-96; PH-4; 2B-2

Ht: 5'10" Wt: 170 Born: 1/14/1984 Age: 25

Year	Team	Lg	G	AB	H	2B	3B	HR	(Hm	Rd)	TB	R	RBI	RC	TBB	IBB	SO	HBP	SH	SF	SB	CS	SB%	GDP	Avg	OBP	Slg
2008	RCuca*	A+	3	10	4	1	0	0	(-	-)	5	2	3	2	0	0	0	0	0	0	2	0	1.00	0	.400	.400	.500
2006	LAA	AL	34	40	10	1	1	0	(0	0)	13	5	2	4	0	0	8	0	0	0	1	0	1.00	1	.250	.250	.325
2007	LAA	AL	79	194	46	5	1	1	(0	1)	56	18	19	16	10	0	32	2	3	2	4	4	.50	8	.237	.279	.289
2008	LAA	AL	98	346	96	18	5	3	(2	1)	133	53	39	49	14	0	45	5	9	1	7	2	.78	2	.277	.314	.384
	Postseason		1	1	0	0	0	0	(0	0)	0	0	0	0	0	0	0	0	0	0	0	0	-	0	.000	.000	.000
	3 ML YEARS		211	580	152	24	7	4	(2	2)	202	76	60	69	24	0	85	7	12	3	12	6	.67	11	.262	.298	.348

Willy Aybar

Bats: B Throws: R Pos: 3B-41; DH-23; 1B-19; PH-14; 2B-10; SS-2

Ht: 5'11" Wt: 200 Born: 3/9/1983 Age: 26

Year	Team	Lg	G	AB	H	2B	3B	HR	(Hm	Rd)	TB	R	RBI	RC	TBB	IBB	SO	HBP	SH	SF	SB	CS	SB%	GDP	Avg	OBP	Slg
2008	VeroB*	A+	3	12	3	0	0	0	(-	-)	3	1	1	0	1	0	2	0	0	0	0	0	-	0	.250	.308	.250
2008	Drham*	AAA	5	20	6	3	0	0	(-	-)	9	3	3	4	4	0	1	0	0	0	0	0	-	0	.300	.417	.450
2005	LAD	NL	26	86	28	8	0	1	(0	1)	39	12	10	21	18	0	11	1	0	0	3	1	.75	0	.326	.448	.453
2006	2 Tms	NL	79	243	68	18	0	4	(3	1)	98	32	30	33	28	0	36	4	3	0	1	2	.33	7	.280	.364	.403
2008	TB	AL	95	324	82	17	2	10	(4	6)	133	33	33	32	32	3	44	4	1	1	2	2	.50	7	.253	.327	.410
	06 LAD	NL	43	128	32	12	0	3	(2	1)	53	15	22	19	18	0	17	3	2	0	1	0	1.00	5	.250	.356	.414
	06 Atl	NL	36	115	36	6	0	1	(1	0)	45	17	8	14	10	0	19	1	1	0	0	2	.00	2	.313	.373	.391
	3 ML YEARS		200	653	178	43	2	15	(7	8)	270	77	73	86	78	3	91	9	4	1	6	5	.55	14	.273	.358	.413

Brandon Backe

Pitches: R Bats: R Pos: SP-31

Ht: 6'0" Wt: 195 Born: 4/5/1978 Age: 31

Year	Team	Lg	G	GS	CG	GF	IP	BFP	H	R	ER	HR	SH	SF	HB	TBB	IBB	SO	WP	Bk	W	L	Pct	ShO	Sv-Op	Hld	ERC	ERA
2002	TB	AL	9	0	0	4	13.0	61	15	10	10	3	0	0	2	7	0	6	0	0	0	0	-	0	0-0	0	7.37	6.92
2003	TB	AL	28	0	0	8	44.2	192	40	28	27	6	2	1	2	25	1	36	3	0	1	1	.500	0	0-0	5	4.64	5.44
2004	Hou	NL	33	9	0	8	67.0	293	75	33	32	10	5	1	1	27	4	54	1	0	5	3	.625	0	0-0	3	5.18	4.30
2005	Hou	NL	26	25	1	0	149.1	653	151	82	79	19	7	1	4	67	1	97	5	2	10	8	.556	1	0-0	0	4.65	4.76
2006	Hou	NL	8	8	0	0	43.0	189	43	18	18	4	1	2	3	18	0	19	2	0	3	2	.600	0	0-0	0	4.37	3.77
2007	Hou	NL	5	5	0	0	28.2	123	27	13	12	4	0	1	2	12	0	11	0	0	3	1	.750	0	0-0	0	4.26	3.77
2008	Hou	NL	31	31	0	0	166.2	756	202	114	112	36	4	2	4	77	2	127	2	0	9	14	.391	0	0-0	0	6.67	6.05
	Postseason		7	6	0	0	36.2	145	24	12	12	3	0	2	3	12	1	32	1	0	1	0	1.000	0	0-0	0	2.21	2.95
	7 ML YEARS		140	78	1	20	512.1	2267	553	298	290	82	19	8	18	232	8	350	13	2	31	29	.517	1	0-0	8	5.37	5.09

Burke Badenhop

Pitches: R Bats: R Pos: SP-8; RP-5

Ht: 6'5" Wt: 220 Born: 2/8/1983 Age: 26

Year	Team	Lg	G	GS	CG	GF	IP	BFP	H	R	ER	HR	SH	SF	HB	TBB	IBB	SO	WP	Bk	W	L	Pct	ShO	Sv-Op	Hld	ERC	ERA
2005	Oneont	A-	14	14	1	0	77.0	321	69	32	25	0	2	0	3	26	0	55	2	0	6	4	.600	1	0--	-	2.77	2.92
2006	WMich	A	27	27	3	0	171.0	702	170	59	54	6	0	2	14	31	0	124	6	0	14	3	.824	1	0--	-	3.14	2.84
2007	Lkland	A+	23	23	1	0	135.1	570	130	61	47	5	4	3	11	34	0	78	2	1	10	6	.625	1	0--	-	3.17	3.13
2007	Erie	AA	3	3	2	0	18.2	68	8	3	3	1	0	1	1	3	0	12	0	0	2	0	1.000	0	0--	-	0.87	1.45
2008	Mrlns	R	1	1	0	0	3.0	10	1	0	0	0	0	0	0	0	0	2	0	0	0	0	-	0	0--	-	0.25	0.00
2008	Carlina	AA	1	1	0	0	6.1	25	6	1	0	0	0	0	0	0	0	3	0	0	1	0	1.000	0	0--	-	1.73	0.00
2008	Fla	NL	13	8	0	2	47.1	218	55	34	32	7	2	2	3	21	1	35	2	0	2	3	.400	0	0-0	0	5.74	6.08

Cha Seung Baek

Pitches: R Bats: R Pos: SP-21; RP-11

Ht: 6'4" Wt: 225 Born: 5/29/1980 Age: 29

Year	Team	Lg	G	GS	CG	GF	IP	BFP	H	R	ER	HR	SH	SF	HB	TBB	IBB	SO	WP	Bk	W	L	Pct	ShO	Sv-Op	Hld	ERC	ERA
2004	Sea	AL	7	5	0	2	31.0	139	35	23	19	5	0	0	2	11	1	20	2	0	2	4	.333	0	0-0	0	5.26	5.52
2006	Sea	AL	6	6	0	0	34.1	140	26	15	14	6	0	0	2	13	0	23	1	0	4	1	.800	0	0-0	0	3.44	3.67
2007	Sea	AL	14	12	1	1	73.1	321	87	45	42	6	1	1	3	14	1	49	1	0	4	3	.571	0	0-0	1	4.24	5.15
2008	2 Tms		32	21	0	2	141.0	602	146	78	75	18	3	8	3	43	3	92	4	0	6	10	.375	0	0-0	1	4.15	4.79
	08 Sea	AL	10	1	0	2	30.0	127	28	18	18	6	0	2	0	13	1	15	1	0	0	1	.000	0	0-0	1	4.54	5.40
	08 SD	NL	22	20	0	0	111.0	475	118	60	57	12	3	6	3	30	2	77	3	0	6	9	.400	0	0-0	0	4.04	4.62
	4 ML YEARS		59	44	1	5	279.2	1202	294	161	150	35	4	9	10	81	5	184	8	0	16	18	.471	0	0-0	1	4.20	4.83

Danys Baez

Pitches: R Bats: R Pos: P

Ht: 6'1" Wt: 230 Born: 9/10/1977 Age: 31

Year	Team	Lg	G	GS	CG	GF	IP	BFP	H	R	ER	HR	SH	SF	HB	TBB	IBB	SO	WP	Bk	W	L	Pct	ShO	Sv-Op	Hld	ERC	ERA
2001	Cle	AL	43	0	0	8	50.1	202	34	22	14	5	0	1	3	20	4	52	3	0	5	3	.625	0	0-1	14	2.51	2.50
2002	Cle	AL	39	26	1	9	165.1	726	160	84	81	14	2	8	9	82	5	130	6	1	10	11	.476	0	6-8	0	4.35	4.41
2003	Cle	AL	73	0	0	46	75.2	318	65	36	32	9	6	1	4	23	0	66	5	0	2	9	.182	0	25-35	5	3.22	3.81
2004	TB	AL	62	0	0	59	68.0	295	60	31	27	6	5	1	7	29	4	52	3	1	4	4	.500	0	30-33	1	3.73	3.57
2005	TB	AL	67	0	0	64	72.1	308	66	27	23	7	4	2	2	30	0	51	0	0	5	4	.556	0	41-49	1	3.74	2.86
2006	2 Tms	NL	57	0	0	28	59.2	257	60	35	30	3	4	5	7	17	3	39	3	0	5	6	.455	0	9-17	12	3.69	4.53
2007	Bal	AL	53	0	0	25	50.1	233	50	36	36	8	3	1	7	29	5	29	0	0	0	6	.000	0	3-5	14	5.56	6.44

		HOW MUCH HE PITCHED						WHAT HE GAVE UP											THE RESULTS						
Year	Team	Lg	G	GS	CG	GF	IP	BFP	H	R	ER	HR	SH	SF	HB	TBB	IBB	SO	WP	Bk	W	L	Pct	ShO	Sv-Op	Hld	ERC	ERA
06	LAD	NL	46	0	0	27	49.2	213	53	29	24	3	4	5	6	11	2	29	3	0	5	5	.500	0	9-16	6	3.90	4.35
06	Atl	NL	11	0	0	1	10.0	44	7	6	6	0	0	0	1	6	1	10	0	0	0	1	.000	0	0-1	6	2.64	5.40
	Postseason		3	0	0	2	3.2	15	4	1	1	0	0	0	0	0	0	6	0	0	0	0	-	0	0-0	0	2.36	2.45
	7 ML YEARS		394	26	1	239	541.2	2339	495	271	243	52	24	19	39	230	21	419	20	2	31	43	.419	0	114-148	46	3.88	4.04

Homer Bailey

Pitches: R Bats: R Pos: SP-8   Ht: 6'4" Wt: 205 Born: 5/3/1986 Age: 23

			HOW MUCH HE PITCHED						WHAT HE GAVE UP											THE RESULTS						
Year	Team	Lg	G	GS	CG	GF	IP	BFP	H	R	ER	HR	SH	SF	HB	TBB	IBB	SO	WP	Bk	W	L	Pct	ShO	Sv-Op	Hld	ERC	ERA
2004	Reds	R	6	3	0	0	12.1	54	14	7	6	0	0	0	0	3	0	9	1	1	0	1	.000	0	0- --		3.42	4.38
2005	Dayton	A	28	21	0	1	103.2	458	89	64	51	5	4	6	3	62	0	125	11	5	8	4	.667	0	0- --		3.76	4.43
2006	Srsota	A+	13	13	0	0	70.2	290	49	35	26	6	2	1	5	22	0	79	2	0	3	5	.375	0	0- --		2.26	3.31
2006	Chatt	AA	13	13	0	0	68.0	276	50	13	12	1	7	0	2	28	0	77	6	0	7	1	.875	0	0- --		2.32	1.59
2007	Lsvlle	AAA	12	12	0	0	67.1	278	49	29	23	4	5	1	0	32	0	59	4	1	6	3	.667	0	0- --		2.65	3.07
2007	Srsota	A+	2	2	0	0	8.0	44	15	9	9	2	0	0	0	5	0	7	0	0	0	1	.000	0	0- --		11.94	10.13
2008	Lsvlle	AAA	19	19	0	0	111.1	480	118	62	59	10	5	6	3	46	0	96	7	2	4	7	.364	0	0- --		4.61	4.77
2007	Cin	NL	9	9	0	0	45.1	205	43	32	29	3	1	6	3	28	1	28	1	1	4	2	.667	0	0-0		4.61	5.76
2008	Cin	NL	8	8	0	0	36.1	180	59	36	32	8	5	2	0	17	1	18	4	1	0	6	.000	0	0-0		9.31	7.93
	2 ML YEARS		17	17	0	0	81.2	385	102	68	61	11	6	8	3	45	2	46	5	2	4	8	.333	0	0-0		6.59	6.72

Jeff Bailey

Bats: R Throws: R Pos: 1B-12; PH-9; LF-5; DH-4; PR-3; RF-1   Ht: 6'2" Wt: 200 Born: 11/26/1978 Age: 30

						BATTING																BASERUNNING				AVERAGES		
Year	Team	Lg	G	AB	H	2B	3B	HR	(Hm	Rd)	TB	R	RBI	RC	TBB	IBB	SO	HBP	SH	SF	SB	CS	SB%	GDP	Avg	OBP	Slg
1997	Mrlns	R	5	7	1	0	0	0	(-	-)	1	0	0	0	1	0	2	0	0	0	0	0	-	1	.143	.250	.143
1998	Mrlns	R	37	127	42	10	0	2	(-	-)	58	21	28	27	19	0	31	7	0	1	3	2	.60	3	.331	.442	.457
1999	Kane	A	76	277	77	19	1	10	(-	-)	128	49	53	48	34	2	77	6	0	5	1	1	.50	8	.278	.363	.462
2000	BrvdCt	A+	125	458	113	19	3	14	(-	-)	180	56	66	62	50	2	116	7	1	4	3	3	.50	9	.247	.328	.393
2001	Portlnd	AA	129	432	104	28	2	13	(-	-)	175	66	66	66	64	1	136	8	0	3	7	2	.78	4	.241	.347	.405
2002	Hrsbrg	AA	99	309	87	17	1	13	(-	-)	145	45	52	64	63	4	78	10	1	3	3	3	.50	3	.282	.416	.469
2003	Hrsbrg	AA	103	362	89	18	3	13	(-	-)	152	54	57	52	35	2	74	8	2	6	2	1	.67	14	.246	.321	.420
2003	Edmtn	AAA	5	17	7	3	0	1	(-	-)	13	5	6	6	3	0	5	1	0	0	0	0	-	1	.412	.524	.765
2004	Portlnd	AA	91	299	88	23	3	13	(-	-)	156	57	58	64	46	0	80	11	0	3	80	0	1.00	7	.294	.404	.522
2004	Pwtckt	AAA	3	10	3	1	0	0	(-	-)	4	2	0	2	3	0	3	0	0	0	0	0	-	0	.300	.462	.400
2005	Pwtckt	AAA	31	95	25	5	0	6	(-	-)	48	15	12	16	8	0	26	1	0	0	1	0	1.00	3	.263	.327	.505
2005	Portlnd	AAA	43	132	33	7	0	7	(-	-)	61	21	26	25	20	0	36	8	1	0	3	1	.75	2	.250	.381	.462
2006	Pwtckt	AAA	134	458	126	22	5	22	(-	-)	224	64	82	89	74	3	116	10	0	6	1	2	.33	11	.275	.383	.489
2007	Pwtckt	AAA	115	404	99	22	1	15	(-	-)	168	64	60	64	59	1	99	13	0	2	9	6	.60	8	.245	.358	.416
2008	Pwtckt	AAA	109	418	126	28	3	25	(-	-)	235	88	75	95	62	1	90	12	0	2	5	2	.71	8	.301	.405	.562
2007	Bos	AL	3	9	1	0	0	1	(0	1)	4	1	1	0	0	0	1	0	0	0	0	0	-	0	.111	.111	.444
2008	Bos	AL	27	50	14	1	1	2	(2	0)	23	10	6	8	9	1	17	0	0	0	0	0	-	2	.280	.390	.460
	2 ML YEARS		30	59	15	1	1	3	(2	1)	27	11	7	8	9	1	18	0	0	0	0	0	-	2	.254	.353	.458

Jeff Baisley

Bats: R Throws: R Pos: 3B-10; 1B-4   Ht: 6'3" Wt: 210 Born: 12/19/1982 Age: 26

						BATTING																BASERUNNING				AVERAGES		
Year	Team	Lg	G	AB	H	2B	3B	HR	(Hm	Rd)	TB	R	RBI	RC	TBB	IBB	SO	HBP	SH	SF	SB	CS	SB%	GDP	Avg	OBP	Slg
2005	Vancvr	A-	61	218	55	15	1	6	(-	-)	90	28	38	34	27	2	27	12	2	3	3	5	.38	9	.252	.362	.413
2006	Kane	A	124	466	139	35	1	22	(-	-)	242	86	110	96	62	4	86	7	0	10	6	1	.86	12	.298	.382	.519
2007	Mdland	AA	101	404	104	22	3	11	(-	-)	165	60	46	53	29	1	84	3	0	6	4	1	.80	5	.257	.308	.408
2008	Scrmto	AAA	81	299	89	25	1	9	(-	-)	143	45	44	54	32	0	43	5	0	1	0	1	1.00	9	.298	.374	.478
2008	As	R	6	22	6	2	0	1	(-	-)	11	4	5	3	0	0	4	2	0	0	0	0	-	0	.273	.333	.500
2008	Oak	AL	14	43	11	1	0	0	(0	0)	12	1	5	4	4	0	7	0	0	0	0	0	-	2	.256	.319	.279

Jeff Baker

Bats: R Throws: R Pos: 2B-49; PH-27; 1B-22; 3B-9; RF-3; DH-3   Ht: 6'2" Wt: 210 Born: 6/21/1981 Age: 28

						BATTING																BASERUNNING				AVERAGES		
Year	Team	Lg	G	AB	H	2B	3B	HR	(Hm	Rd)	TB	R	RBI	RC	TBB	IBB	SO	HBP	SH	SF	SB	CS	SB%	GDP	Avg	OBP	Slg
2005	Col	NL	12	38	8	4	0	1	(1	0)	15	6	4	4	5	0	12	0	0	0	0	0	-	1	.211	.302	.395
2006	Col	NL	18	57	21	7	2	5	(4	1)	47	13	21	17	1	0	14	0	0	0	2	0	1.00	0	.368	.379	.825
2007	Col	NL	85	144	32	2	4	4	(4	0)	50	17	12	8	13	1	40	2	0	0	0	0	-	7	.222	.296	.347
2008	Col	NL	104	299	80	22	1	12	(8	4)	140	55	48	40	26	2	85	1	1	6	4	0	1.00	5	.268	.322	.468
	Postseason		4	4	2	0	0	0	(0	0)	2	0	1	1	0	0	1	0	0	0	0	0	-	0	.500	.500	.500
	4 ML YEARS		219	538	141	35	5	22	(17	5)	252	91	85	69	45	3	151	3	1	6	6	0	1.00	13	.262	.319	.468

John Baker

Bats: L Throws: R Pos: C-59; PH-4   Ht: 6'1" Wt: 210 Born: 1/20/1981 Age: 28

						BATTING																BASERUNNING				AVERAGES		
Year	Team	Lg	G	AB	H	2B	3B	HR	(Hm	Rd)	TB	R	RBI	RC	TBB	IBB	SO	HBP	SH	SF	SB	CS	SB%	GDP	Avg	OBP	Slg
2002	Vancvr	AAA	39	115	27	5	0	1	(-	-)	35	15	13	17	22	0	37	7	0	0	2	0	1.00	3	.235	.389	.304
2003	Kane	A	82	304	94	23	2	6	(-	-)	139	42	49	61	47	2	77	10	0	4	1	0	1.00	4	.309	.414	.457
2003	Mdland	AA	43	150	36	3	0	1	(-	-)	42	16	21	14	14	0	46	4	0	3	0	0	-	0	.240	.316	.280
2004	Mdland	AA	117	439	123	32	5	15	(-	-)	210	67	78	76	37	2	94	17	0	5	1	2	.33	16	.280	.355	.478
2004	Scrmto	AAA	14	49	17	3	0	0	(-	-)	20	11	10	8	6	1	23	1	0	0	0	0	-	0	.347	.429	.408
2005	Scrmto	AAA	103	346	81	24	3	5	(-	-)	126	43	41	40	30	0	90	4	7	0	1	0	1.00	5	.234	.303	.364

Year	Team	Lg	G	AB	H	2B	3B	HR	(Hm	Rd)	TB	R	RBI	RC	TBB	IBB	SO	HBP	SH	SF	SB	CS	SB%	GDP	Avg	OBP	Slg
2006	Scrmto	AAA	83	293	80	19	1	4	(-	-)	113	49	38	45	40	1	77	2	2	3	6	0	1.00	10	.273	.361	.386
2007	Albq	AAA	89	270	77	15	0	8	(-	-)	116	35	41	43	28	1	58	4	0	1	2	0	1.00	7	.285	.360	.430
2008	Albq	AAA	59	193	62	14	1	6	(-	-)	96	35	31	38	24	0	34	2	0	2	1	2	.33	2	.321	.398	.497
2008	Fla	NL	61	197	59	14	0	5	(3	2)	88	32	32	36	30	4	48	2	1	3	0	0	-	6	.299	.392	.447

Scott Baker

Pitches: R **Bats:** R **Pos:** SP-28

Ht: 6'4" **Wt:** 220 **Born:** 9/19/1981 **Age:** 27

			HOW MUCH HE PITCHED					WHAT HE GAVE UP												THE RESULTS							
Year	Team	Lg	G	GS	CG	GF	IP	BFP	H	R	ER	HR	SH	SF	HB	TBB	IBB	SO	WP	Bk	W	L	Pct	ShO	Sv-Op	Hld	ERC	ERA
2008	FtMyrs*	A+	1	1	0	0	5.0	23	7	3	3	0	0	0	0	0	0	4	1	0	1	0	1.000	0	0--	-	3.72	5.40
2005	Min	AL	10	9	0	0	53.2	217	48	21	20	5	2	2	0	14	0	32	0	0	3	3	.500	0	0-0	1	2.97	3.35
2006	Min	AL	16	16	0	0	83.1	377	114	63	59	17	2	4	3	16	1	62	0	0	5	8	.385	0	0-0	0	6.26	6.37
2007	Min	AL	24	23	2	0	143.2	606	162	70	68	15	6	2	5	24	4	102	0	0	9	9	.500	1	0-0	1	4.19	4.26
2008	Min	AL	28	28	0	0	172.1	703	161	66	66	20	2	3	3	42	2	141	6	0	11	4	.733	0	0-0	0	3.31	3.45
	4 ML YEARS		78	76	2	0	453.0	1903	485	220	213	57	12	11	11	101	7	337	6	0	28	24	.538	1	0-0	2	4.05	4.23

Paul Bako

Bats: L **Throws:** R **Pos:** C-96; PH-5; PR-1

Ht: 6'2" **Wt:** 215 **Born:** 6/20/1972 **Age:** 37

									BATTING												BASERUNNING				AVERAGES		
Year	Team	Lg	G	AB	H	2B	3B	HR	(Hm	Rd)	TB	R	RBI	RC	TBB	IBB	SO	HBP	SH	SF	SB	CS	SB%	GDP	Avg	OBP	Slg
1998	Det	AL	96	305	83	12	1	3	(2	1)	106	23	30	34	23	4	82	0	1	4	1	1	.50	3	.272	.319	.348
1999	Hou	NL	73	215	55	14	1	2	(2	0)	77	16	17	26	26	3	57	0	3	3	1	1	.50	4	.256	.332	.358
2000	3 Tms	NL	81	221	50	10	1	2	(2	0)	68	18	20	20	27	10	64	1	1	1	0	0	-	6	.226	.312	.308
2001	Atl	NL	61	137	29	10	1	2	(0	2)	47	19	15	15	20	2	34	0	0	0	1	0	1.00	2	.212	.312	.343
2002	Mil	NL	87	234	55	8	1	4	(2	2)	77	24	20	20	20	3	46	0	3	0	0	2	.00	4	.235	.295	.329
2003	ChC	NL	70	188	43	13	3	0	(0	0)	62	19	17	21	22	3	47	1	1	1	0	1	.00	2	.229	.311	.330
2004	ChC	NL	49	138	28	8	0	1	(1	0)	39	13	10	11	15	3	29	2	1	1	1	0	1.00	2	.203	.288	.283
2005	LAD	NL	13	40	10	2	0	0	(0	0)	12	1	4	6	7	1	12	0	0	0	0	0	-	0	.250	.362	.300
2006	KC	AL	56	153	32	3	0	0	(0	0)	35	7	10	9	11	0	46	0	2	1	0	0	-	3	.209	.261	.229
2007	Bal	AL	60	156	32	3	1	1	(0	1)	39	13	8	6	15	0	50	1	1	0	0	1	.00	0	.205	.277	.256
2008	Cin	NL	99	299	65	11	2	6	(2	4)	98	30	35	28	34	5	90	1	3	1	0	2	.00	9	.217	.299	.328
00	Hou	NL	1	2	0	0	0	0	(0	0)	0	0	0	0	0	0	0	0	0	0	0	0	-	0	.000	.000	.000
00	Fla	NL	56	161	39	6	1	0	(0	0)	47	10	14	16	22	7	48	1	1	0	0	0	-	4	.242	.335	.292
00	Atl	NL	24	58	11	4	0	2	(2	0)	21	8	6	4	5	3	15	0	0	0	0	0	-	2	.190	.254	.362
	Postseason		17	31	6	2	0	1	(1	0)	11	5	5	3	4	0	10	0	1	0	0	0	-	0	.194	.286	.355
	11 ML YEARS		745	2086	482	94	11	21	(11	10)	661	183	186	196	220	34	557	6	16	13	4	8	.33	42	.231	.305	.317

Rocco Baldelli

Bats: R **Throws:** R **Pos:** DH-22; PH-12; RF-6; LF-1

Ht: 6'4" **Wt:** 200 **Born:** 9/25/1981 **Age:** 27

									BATTING												BASERUNNING				AVERAGES		
Year	Team	Lg	G	AB	H	2B	3B	HR	(Hm	Rd)	TB	R	RBI	RC	TBB	IBB	SO	HBP	SH	SF	SB	CS	SB%	GDP	Avg	OBP	Slg
2008	VeroB*	A+	11	37	8	1	0	2	(-	-)	15	3	8	5	4	1	10	1	0	0	2	0	1.00	0	.216	.310	.405
2008	Mont*	AA	13	37	11	1	0	3	(-	-)	21	6	8	8	6	0	7	1	0	0	1	0	1.00	2	.297	.409	.568
2003	TB	AL	156	637	184	32	8	11	(2	9)	265	89	78	77	30	4	128	8	3	6	27	10	.73	10	.289	.326	.416
2004	TB	AL	136	518	145	27	3	16	(6	10)	226	79	74	70	30	2	88	8	3	6	17	4	.81	12	.280	.326	.436
2006	TB	AL	92	364	110	24	6	16	(6	10)	194	59	57	65	14	1	70	7	0	2	10	1	.91	2	.302	.339	.533
2007	TB	AL	35	137	28	6	0	5	(4	1)	49	16	12	14	9	1	35	3	1	0	4	1	.80	1	.204	.268	.358
2008	TB	AL	28	80	21	5	0	4	(0	4)	38	12	13	11	7	0	25	3	0	0	0	0	-	1	.263	.344	.475
	5 ML YEARS		447	1736	488	94	17	52	(18	34)	772	255	234	237	90	8	346	29	7	14	58	16	.78	26	.281	.325	.445

John Bale

Pitches: L **Bats:** L **Pos:** RP-10; SP-3

Ht: 6'4" **Wt:** 220 **Born:** 5/22/1974 **Age:** 35

			HOW MUCH HE PITCHED					WHAT HE GAVE UP												THE RESULTS							
Year	Team	Lg	G	GS	CG	GF	IP	BFP	H	R	ER	HR	SH	SF	HB	TBB	IBB	SO	WP	Bk	W	L	Pct	ShO	Sv-Op	Hld	ERC	ERA
2008	NWArk*	AA	2	1	0	0	1.2	7	3	1	1	0	0	0	0	0	0	3	0	0	0	0	-	0	0--	-	7.19	5.40
2008	Omha*	AAA	10	7	0	0	11.2	57	17	14	14	3	1	1	0	5	0	8	0	0	0	3	.000	0	0--	-	8.11	10.80
1999	Tor	AL	1	0	0	0	2.0	10	2	3	3	1	0	0	0	2	0	4	0	0	0	0	-	0	0-0	0	9.87	13.50
2000	Tor	AL	2	0	0	0	3.2	22	5	7	6	1	0	1	2	3	0	6	0	0	0	0	-	0	0-0	0	11.52	14.73
2001	Bal	AL	14	0	0	3	26.2	113	18	14	9	2	0	2	1	17	0	21	1	0	1	0	1.000	0	0-0	0	3.21	3.04
2003	Cin	NL	10	9	0	0	46.1	195	50	24	23	7	1	2	2	12	2	37	1	0	1	2	.333	0	0-0	0	4.52	4.47
2007	KC	AL	26	0	0	5	40.0	179	45	18	18	1	3	3	1	17	2	42	2	0	1	1	.500	0	0-1	5	4.32	4.05
2008	KC	AL	13	3	0	1	26.2	110	29	13	13	1	3	2	0	6	0	14	1	0	0	3	.000	0	0-0	4	3.54	4.39
	6 ML YEARS		66	12	0	9	145.1	629	149	79	72	13	7	10	6	57	4	124	5	0	3	6	.333	0	0-1	9	4.27	4.46

Wladimir Balentien

Bats: R **Throws:** R **Pos:** RF-35; CF-29; LF-5; PH-4; DH-3; PR-1

Ht: 6'2" **Wt:** 215 **Born:** 7/2/1984 **Age:** 24

									BATTING												BASERUNNING				AVERAGES		
Year	Team	Lg	G	AB	H	2B	3B	HR	(Hm	Rd)	TB	R	RBI	RC	TBB	IBB	SO	HBP	SH	SF	SB	CS	SB%	GDP	Avg	OBP	Slg
2003	Ms	R	50	187	53	12	5	16	(-	-)	123	42	52	44	22	0	55	3	1	3	4	2	.67	4	.283	.363	.658
2004	Wisc	A-	76	260	72	12	3	15	(-	-)	135	39	46	43	12	2	77	3	3	1	10	2	.83	8	.277	.315	.519
2004	InldEm	A+	10	38	11	1	0	2	(-	-)	18	5	5	6	4	0	10	0	0	0	1	0	1.00	0	.289	.357	.474
2005	InldEm	A+	123	492	143	38	8	25	(-	-)	272	76	93	93	33	0	160	6	1	7	9	2	.82	7	.291	.338	.553
2006	SnAnt	AA	121	444	102	23	1	22	(-	-)	193	76	82	69	70	5	140	4	0	4	14	7	.67	10	.230	.337	.435
2007	Tacom	AAA	124	477	139	24	4	24	(-	-)	243	77	84	91	54	3	105	3	2	8	15	4	.79	14	.291	.362	.509

			BATTING																			BASERUNNING				AVERAGES		
Year	Team	Lg	G	AB	H	2B	3B	HR	(Hm	Rd)	TB	R	RBI	RC	TBB	IBB	SO	HBP	SH	SF	SB	CS	SB%	GDP	Avg	OBP	Slg
2008	Tacom	AAA	62	233	62	20	0	18	(-	-)	136	49	55	48	32	0	49	3	1	6	3	4	.43	6	.266	.354	.584
2007	Sea	AL	3	3	2	1	0	1	(1	0)	6	1	4	1	0	0	0	0	0	0	0	0	-	0	.667	.500	2.000
2008	Sea	AL	71	243	49	13	0	7	(3	4)	83	23	24	17	16	1	79	0	0	1	0	1	.00	12	.202	.250	.342
	2 ML YEARS		74	246	51	14	0	8	(4	4)	89	24	28	18	16	1	79	0	0	2	0	1	.00	12	.207	.254	.362

Collin Balester

Pitches: R **Bats:** R **Pos:** SP-15

Ht: 6'5" **Wt:** 194 **Born:** 6/6/1986 **Age:** 23

			HOW MUCH HE PITCHED						WHAT HE GAVE UP											THE RESULTS						
Year	Team	Lg	G	GS	CG	GF	IP	BFP	H	R	ER	HR	SH	SF	HB	TBB	IBB	SO	WP	Bk	W	L	Pct	ShO	Sv-Op	Hld	ERC	ERA
2004	Expos	R	5	4	0	1	24.2	101	20	8	6	0	1	1	1	5	1	21	4	0	1	2	.333	0	0--	-	1.80	2.19
2005	Savann	A	24	23	1	0	125.0	521	105	62	51	11	1	0	6	42	0	95	4	1	8	6	.571	0	0--	-	3.06	3.67
2006	Ptomc	A+	23	22	1	0	117.2	518	126	71	68	12	3	8	4	53	0	87	12	0	4	5	.444	0	0--	-	4.90	5.20
2006	Hrsbrg	AA	3	3	0	0	19.2	77	15	5	4	0	2	2	2	6	1	10	2	0	1	0	1.000	0	0--	-	2.27	1.83
2007	Hrsbrg	AA	17	17	0	0	98.2	423	103	47	41	9	5	2	5	25	0	77	5	0	2	7	.222	0	0--	-	3.85	3.74
2007	Clmbs	AAA	10	10	0	0	51.2	226	49	27	24	3	3	5	3	23	2	40	2	1	2	3	.400	0	0--	-	3.80	4.18
2008	Clmbs	AAA	15	15	0	0	78.2	332	79	37	35	14	2	3	4	23	0	64	4	0	9	3	.750	0	0--	-	4.46	4.00
2008	Was	NL	15	15	0	0	80.0	358	92	53	49	12	2	3	6	28	1	50	4	0	3	7	.300	0	0-0	0	5.40	5.51

Grant Balfour

Pitches: R **Bats:** R **Pos:** RP-51

Ht: 6'2" **Wt:** 192 **Born:** 12/30/1977 **Age:** 31

			HOW MUCH HE PITCHED						WHAT HE GAVE UP											THE RESULTS						
Year	Team	Lg	G	GS	CG	GF	IP	BFP	H	R	ER	HR	SH	SF	HB	TBB	IBB	SO	WP	Bk	W	L	Pct	ShO	Sv-Op	Hld	ERC	ERA
2008	Drham*	AAA	15	0	0	15	23.2	85	5	1	1	1	0	0	0	10	0	39	1	1	1	0	1.000	0	8--	-	0.69	0.38
2001	Min	AL	2	0	0	1	2.2	14	3	4	4	2	1	1	0	3	0	2	0	0	0	0	-	0	0-0	0	13.78	13.50
2003	Min	AL	17	1	0	6	26.0	115	23	12	12	4	2	1	0	14	2	30	0	0	1	0	1.000	0	0-1	4	4.14	4.15
2004	Min	AL	36	0	0	14	39.1	172	35	19	19	4	2	0	2	21	1	42	3	0	4	1	.800	0	0-1	4	4.16	4.35
2007	2 Tms		25	0	0	8	24.2	121	30	21	21	2	2	3	1	20	0	30	0	0	1	2	.333	0	0-0	1	7.15	7.66
2008	TB		51	0	0	12	58.1	224	28	10	10	3	1	3	0	24	1	82	2	0	6	2	.750	0	4-5	14	1.38	1.54
07	Mil	NL	3	0	0	2	2.2	18	4	6	6	1	1	0	1	4	0	3	0	0	0	2	.000	0	0-0	0	15.83	20.25
07	TB	AL	22	0	0	6	22.0	103	26	15	15	1	1	3	0	16	0	27	0	0	1	0	1.000	0	0-0	1	6.19	6.14
	Postseason		2	0	0	0	2.2	7	0	0	0	0	0	0	0	0	0	2	0	0	0	0	-	0	0-0	0	0.00	0.00
	5 ML YEARS		131	1	0	41	151.0	646	119	66	66	15	8	8	3	82	4	186	5	0	12	5	.706	0	4-7	20	3.49	3.93

Josh Banks

Pitches: R **Bats:** R **Pos:** SP-14; RP-3

Ht: 6'3" **Wt:** 210 **Born:** 7/18/1982 **Age:** 26

			HOW MUCH HE PITCHED						WHAT HE GAVE UP											THE RESULTS						
Year	Team	Lg	G	GS	CG	GF	IP	BFP	H	R	ER	HR	SH	SF	HB	TBB	IBB	SO	WP	Bk	W	L	Pct	ShO	Sv-Op	Hld	ERC	ERA
2003	Auburn	A-	15	15	0	0	66.2	264	58	21	18	1	0	4	1	10	0	81	5	0	7	2	.778	0	0--	-	2.03	2.43
2004	Dnedin	A+	11	11	0	0	60.0	230	49	17	12	4	2	1	1	8	0	60	6	0	7	1	.875	0	0--	-	2.07	1.80
2004	NHam	AA	18	17	1	0	91.1	381	89	54	51	15	2	3	0	28	0	76	1	1	6	6	.500	0	0--	-	4.03	5.03
2005	NHam	AA	27	27	0	0	162.1	645	159	76	69	18	4	7	0	11	0	145	3	0	8	11	.421	0	0--	-	2.77	3.83
2006	Syrcse	AAA	29	29	0	0	170.2	727	184	108	98	35	3	3	3	28	0	126	2	0	10	11	.476	0	0--	-	4.25	5.17
2007	Syrcse	AAA	27	27	3	0	169.0	714	192	89	87	22	3	6	4	24	0	101	0	0	12	10	.545	0	0--	-	4.10	4.63
2008	Syrcse	AAA	3	3	0	0	16.2	76	21	15	13	1	1	1	2	5	0	12	0	1	0	2	.000	0	0--	-	5.37	7.02
2008	Portlnd	AAA	9	4	0	2	30.1	137	39	20	20	3	2	0	1	8	0	22	2	0	1	1	.500	0	0--	-	5.25	5.93
2007	Tor	AL	3	1	0	1	7.1	35	11	6	6	1	0	1	0	2	0	2	0	0	0	0	-	0	0-0	0	6.66	7.36
2008	SD	NL	17	14	1	1	85.1	372	94	47	45	12	8	4	3	32	5	43	0	0	3	6	.333	0	0-0	0	4.97	4.75
	2 ML YEARS		20	15	1	2	92.2	407	105	53	51	13	8	5	3	34	5	45	0	0	3	6	.333	0	0-0	0	5.10	4.95

Wes Bankston

Bats: R **Throws:** R **Pos:** 1B-13; DH-4

Ht: 6'4" **Wt:** 215 **Born:** 11/23/1983 **Age:** 25

			BATTING																			BASERUNNING				AVERAGES		
Year	Team	Lg	G	AB	H	2B	3B	HR	(Hm	Rd)	TB	R	RBI	RC	TBB	IBB	SO	HBP	SH	SF	SB	CS	SB%	GDP	Avg	OBP	Slg
2002	Princtn	R+	62	246	74	10	1	18	(-	-)	140	48	57	48	18	1	46	1	0	4	2	1	.67	3	.301	.346	.569
2002	HudVal	A-	8	33	10	1	0	0	(-	-)	11	2	1	3	0	0	6	0	0	0	1	0	1.00	1	.303	.294	.333
2003	CtnSC	A	103	375	96	18	1	12	(-	-)	152	46	60	56	53	3	94	2	0	6	2	3	.40	11	.256	.346	.405
2004	CtnSC	A	127	470	136	30	3	23	(-	-)	241	82	101	98	73	8	104	6	0	2	9	0	1.00	5	.289	.390	.513
2005	Visalia	A+	17	62	24	4	1	3	(-	-)	39	15	23	16	8	1	17	1	0	0	0	2	.00	1	.387	.513	.629
2005	Mont	AA	82	301	88	17	2	12	(-	-)	145	42	47	53	30	3	64	4	0	2	3	3	.50	8	.292	.362	.482
2006	Mont	AA	45	167	44	7	1	4	(-	-)	65	20	19	22	12	0	37	0	0	1	4	1	.80	5	.263	.322	.389
2006	Drham	AAA	52	195	58	13	0	5	(-	-)	86	22	29	28	10	1	40	1	0	1	0	1	.00	2	.297	.333	.441
2007	Drham	AAA	104	390	93	23	1	15	(-	-)	163	46	59	48	25	1	88	2	0	9	2	1	.00	10	.238	.282	.418
2008	Scrmto	AAA	97	375	105	19	1	20	(-	-)	186	56	73	61	21	2	71	7	0	2	0	2	.00	8	.280	.328	.496
2008	Oak	AL	17	59	12	3	0	1	(1	0)	18	4	4	5	2	0	15	1	0	1	0	0	-	0	.203	.238	.305

Brian Bannister

Pitches: R **Bats:** R **Pos:** SP-32

Ht: 6'2" **Wt:** 210 **Born:** 2/28/1981 **Age:** 28

			HOW MUCH HE PITCHED						WHAT HE GAVE UP											THE RESULTS						
Year	Team	Lg	G	GS	CG	GF	IP	BFP	H	R	ER	HR	SH	SF	HB	TBB	IBB	SO	WP	Bk	W	L	Pct	ShO	Sv-Op	Hld	ERC	ERA
2006	NYM	NL	8	6	0	1	38.0	171	34	18	18	4	1	4	2	22	2	19	2	0	2	1	.667	0	0-0	0	4.27	4.26
2007	KC	AL	27	27	1	0	165.0	683	156	76	71	15	2	4	6	44	1	77	4	0	12	9	.571	0	0-0	0	3.36	3.87
2008	KC	AL	32	32	1	0	182.2	811	215	127	117	29	3	10	7	58	1	113	7	1	9	16	.360	0	0-0	0	5.34	5.76
	3 ML YEARS		67	65	2	1	385.2	1665	405	221	206	48	6	18	15	124	4	209	13	1	23	26	.469	0	0-0	0	4.36	4.81

Rod Barajas

Bats: R **Throws:** R **Pos:** C-98; 1B-4; PH-3; DH-2   **Ht:** 6'2" **Wt:** 230 **Born:** 9/5/1975 **Age:** 33

Year Team	Lg	G	AB	H	2B	3B	HR	(Hm	Rd)	TB	R	RBI	RC	TBB	IBB	SO	HBP	SH	SF	SB	CS	SB%	GDP	Avg	OBP	Slg
1999 Ari	NL	5	16	4	1	0	1	(1	0)	8	3	3	2	1	0	1	0	1	0	0	0	-	0	.250	.294	.500
2000 Ari	NL	5	13	3	0	0	1	(1	0)	6	1	3	1	0	0	4	0	0	0	0	0	-	0	.231	.231	.462
2001 Ari	NL	51	106	17	3	0	3	(2	1)	29	9	9	4	4	0	26	0	0	0	0	0	-	0	.160	.191	.274
2002 Ari	NL	70	154	36	10	0	3	(1	2)	55	12	23	15	10	4	25	3	2	3	1	0	1.00	4	.234	.288	.357
2003 Ari	NL	80	220	48	15	0	3	(3	0)	72	19	28	19	14	7	43	1	1	3	0	0	-	6	.218	.265	.327
2004 Tex	AL	108	358	89	26	1	15	(8	7)	162	50	44	43	13	0	63	3	8	7	0	1	.00	3	.249	.276	.453
2005 Tex	AL	120	410	104	24	0	21	(7	14)	191	53	60	56	26	0	70	6	4	3	0	0	-	6	.254	.306	.466
2006 Tex	AL	97	344	88	20	0	11	(6	5)	141	49	41	36	17	0	51	4	5	1	0	0	-	9	.256	.298	.410
2007 Phi	NL	48	122	28	8	0	4	(1	3)	48	16	10	12	21	3	24	2	1	0	0	1	.00	5	.230	.352	.393
2008 Tor	AL	104	349	87	23	0	11	(4	7)	143	44	49	37	17	0	61	7	0	4	0	0	-	9	.249	.294	.410
Postseason		5	9	3	0	0	2	(0	2)	9	2	2	2	0	0	1	0	0	0	0	0	-	0	.333	.333	1.000
10 ML YEARS		688	2092	504	130	1	73	(34	39)	855	256	284	225	123	14	368	26	22	21	1	2	.33	42	.241	.289	.409

Josh Bard

Bats: B **Throws:** R **Pos:** C-49; PH-9   **Ht:** 6'3" **Wt:** 210 **Born:** 3/30/1978 **Age:** 31

Year Team	Lg	G	AB	H	2B	3B	HR	(Hm	Rd)	TB	R	RBI	RC	TBB	IBB	SO	HBP	SH	SF	SB	CS	SB%	GDP	Avg	OBP	Slg
2008 Lk Els*	A+	3	9	1	0	0	0	(-	-)	1	0	0	0	2	0	0	0	0	0	0	0	-	0	.111	.273	.111
2008 Portlnd*	AAA	6	15	2	0	0	0	(-	-)	5	2	1	1	2	0	3	0	0	0	0	0	-	0	.133	.235	.333
2008 Padres*	R	1	3	0	0	0	0	(-	-)	0	0	0	0	0	0	1	0	0	0	0	0	-	0	.000	.000	.000
2002 Cle	AL	24	90	20	5	0	3	(2	1)	34	9	12	7	4	0	13	0	1	0	0	0	-	6	.222	.255	.378
2003 Cle	AL	91	303	74	13	1	8	(5	3)	113	25	36	34	22	1	53	0	1	3	0	2	.00	9	.244	.293	.373
2004 Cle	AL	7	19	8	2	0	1	(1	0)	13	5	4	6	3	0	0	0	0	1	0	0	-	0	.421	.478	.684
2005 Cle	AL	34	83	16	4	0	1	(0	1)	23	6	9	8	9	0	11	0	1	2	0	0	-	2	.193	.266	.277
2006 2 Tms		100	249	83	20	0	9	(5	4)	130	30	40	44	30	1	42	1	2	2	1	0	1.00	9	.333	.404	.522
2007 SD	NL	118	389	111	27	2	5	(4	1)	157	42	51	65	50	7	58	0	1	3	0	1	.00	16	.285	.364	.404
2008 SD	NL	57	178	36	9	0	1	(0	1)	48	11	16	13	18	2	25	1	1	0	0	0	-	5	.202	.279	.270
06 Bos	AL	7	18	5	1	0	0	(0	0)	6	2	0	2	3	0	3	0	0	0	0	0	-	0	.278	.381	.333
06 SD	NL	93	231	78	19	0	9	(5	4)	124	28	40	42	27	1	39	1	2	2	1	0	1.00	9	.338	.406	.537
Postseason		3	7	1	0	0	0	(0	0)	1	0	0	0	1	0	2	1	0	0	0	0	-	0	.143	.333	.143
7 ML YEARS		431	1311	348	80	3	28	(17	11)	518	128	168	177	136	11	202	2	7	11	1	3	.25	47	.265	.333	.395

Brian Barden

Bats: R **Throws:** R **Pos:** PH-5; 3B-4; 1B-1; 2B-1   **Ht:** 5'11" **Wt:** 186 **Born:** 4/2/1981 **Age:** 28

Year Team	Lg	G	AB	H	2B	3B	HR	(Hm	Rd)	TB	R	RBI	RC	TBB	IBB	SO	HBP	SH	SF	SB	CS	SB%	GDP	Avg	OBP	Slg
2002 Yakima	A-	4	15	5	1	0	0	(-	-)	6	5	2	2	1	0	1	1	0	0	0	0	-	1	.333	.412	.400
2002 Lancst	A+	64	269	90	19	1	8	(-	-)	135	58	46	49	16	0	63	1	2	3	3	1	.75	3	.335	.370	.502
2003 ElPaso	AA	109	383	110	24	5	3	(-	-)	153	50	57	56	29	0	78	8	3	3	10	4	.71	8	.287	.348	.399
2004 ElPaso	AA	48	195	59	10	6	3	(-	-)	90	33	28	30	10	1	48	2	1	5	1	2	.33	3	.303	.335	.462
2004 Tucsn	AAA	89	332	94	30	5	8	(-	-)	158	50	50	52	17	0	83	5	2	4	3	1	.75	6	.283	.324	.476
2005 Tucsn	AAA	135	518	159	36	5	15	(-	-)	250	78	85	93	38	3	111	11	3	6	14	5	.74	15	.307	.363	.483
2006 Tucsn	AAA	128	494	147	35	3	16	(-	-)	236	80	96	86	44	2	92	7	2	3	1	3	.25	11	.298	.361	.478
2007 Tucsn	AAA	83	284	77	9	2	2	(-	-)	96	36	25	37	31	1	55	7	5	0	2	3	.40	11	.271	.357	.338
2007 Memp	AAA	20	68	16	3	0	2	(-	-)	25	7	12	7	5	0	13	1	0	3	0	0	-	3	.235	.286	.368
2008 Memp	AAA	103	411	117	21	4	9	(-	-)	173	60	35	62	38	0	72	4	0	3	3	3	.50	13	.285	.349	.421
2007 2 Tms	NL	23	35	6	1	0	0	(0	0)	7	6	0	1	2	0	7	0	0	0	0	0	-	2	.171	.216	.200
2008 StL	NL	9	9	2	0	0	0	(0	0)	2	0	1	0	0	0	4	0	1	0	0	0	-	0	.222	.222	.222
07 Ari	NL	8	12	1	0	0	0	(0	0)	1	0	0	0	0	0	3	0	0	0	0	0	-	0	.083	.083	.083
07 StL	NL	15	23	5	1	0	0	(0	0)	6	6	0	1	2	0	4	0	0	0	0	0	-	2	.217	.280	.261
2 ML YEARS		32	44	8	1	0	0	(0	0)	9	6	1	1	2	0	11	0	1	0	0	0	-	2	.182	.217	.205

Josh Barfield

Bats: R **Throws:** R **Pos:** 2B-9; PR-2; PH-1   **Ht:** 6'0" **Wt:** 190 **Born:** 12/17/1982 **Age:** 26

Year Team	Lg	G	AB	H	2B	3B	HR	(Hm	Rd)	TB	R	RBI	RC	TBB	IBB	SO	HBP	SH	SF	SB	CS	SB%	GDP	Avg	OBP	Slg
2008 Buffalo*	AAA	73	299	75	18	1	5	(-	-)	110	30	23	32	15	0	58	3	1	2	9	5	.64	2	.251	.292	.368
2008 Akron*	AA	2	4	0	0	0	0	(-	-)	0	0	0	0	0	0	2	0	0	0	0	0	-	0	.000	.000	.000
2006 SD	NL	150	539	151	32	3	13	(6	7)	228	72	58	69	30	7	81	2	2	5	21	5	.81	8	.280	.318	.423
2007 Cle	AL	130	420	102	19	3	3	(2	1)	136	53	50	42	14	0	90	3	3	4	14	5	.74	3	.243	.270	.324
2008 Cle	AL	12	33	6	1	0	0	(0	0)	7	3	2	1	0	0	10	0	0	0	0	0	-	0	.182	.182	.212
Postseason		5	8	2	1	0	0	(0	0)	3	0	0	1	1	0	2	0	0	0	1	0	1.00	0	.250	.333	.375
3 ML YEARS		292	992	259	52	6	16	(8	8)	371	128	110	112	44	7	181	5	5	9	35	10	.78	11	.261	.293	.374

Clint Barmes

Bats: R **Throws:** R **Pos:** 2B-61; SS-36; 3B-13; PH-7; PR-3; RF-1   **Ht:** 6'0" **Wt:** 210 **Born:** 3/6/1979 **Age:** 30

Year Team	Lg	G	AB	H	2B	3B	HR	(Hm	Rd)	TB	R	RBI	RC	TBB	IBB	SO	HBP	SH	SF	SB	CS	SB%	GDP	Avg	OBP	Slg
2008 ColSpr*	AAA	5	18	5	0	0	0	(-	-)	5	2	3	1	1	0	1	1	0	0	0	0	-	0	.278	.350	.278
2003 Col	NL	12	25	8	2	0	0	(0	0)	10	2	2	3	0	0	10	2	0	1	0	0	-	0	.320	.357	.400
2004 Col	NL	20	71	20	3	1	2	(0	2)	31	14	10	12	3	0	10	1	2	0	0	1	.00	2	.282	.320	.437
2005 Col	NL	81	350	101	19	1	10	(7	3)	152	55	46	49	16	1	36	6	4	1	6	4	.60	4	.289	.330	.434

BATTING																			BASERUNNING				AVERAGES		
Year	Team	Lg	G	AB	H	2B	3B	HR	(Hm | Rd)	TB	R	RBI	RC	TBB	IBB	SO	HBP	SH	SF	SB	CS	SB%	GDP	Avg	OBP	Slg
2006	Col	NL	131	478	105	26	4	7	(3 | 4)	160	57	56	47	22	6	72	9	19	7	5	4	.56	2	.220	.264	.335
2007	Col	NL	27	37	8	3	0	0	(- | -)	11	5	1	1	1	1	13	0	1	0	0	0	-	1	.216	.237	.297
2008	Col	NL	107	393	114	25	6	11	(8 | 3)	184	47	44	54	17	0	69	2	4	1	13	4	.76	9	.290	.322	.468
6 ML YEARS			378	1354	356	78	12	30	(18 | 12)	548	180	159	166	59	8	210	20	30	10	24	13	.65	18	.263	.301	.405

Michael Barrett

Bats: R **Throws:** R **Pos:** C-30   **Ht:** 6'3" **Wt:** 215 **Born:** 10/22/1976 **Age:** 32

BATTING																			BASERUNNING				AVERAGES		
Year	Team	Lg	G	AB	H	2B	3B	HR	(Hm | Rd)	TB	R	RBI	RC	TBB	IBB	SO	HBP	SH	SF	SB	CS	SB%	GDP	Avg	OBP	Slg
2008	Portlnd*	AAA	3	7	5	2	0	0	(- | -)	7	2	4	3	0	0	0	0	0	0	0	0	-	0	.714	.714	1.000
2008	Lk Els*	A+	1	3	2	0	0	0	(- | -)	2	0	0	1	1	0	1	0	0	0	0	0	-	0	.667	.750	.667
1998	Mon	NL	8	23	7	2	0	1	(0 | 1)	12	3	2	5	3	0	6	1	0	0	0	0	-	0	.304	.407	.522
1999	Mon	NL	126	433	127	32	3	8	(5 | 3)	189	53	52	59	32	4	39	3	0	1	0	2	.00	18	.293	.345	.436
2000	Mon	NL	89	271	58	15	1	1	(0 | 1)	78	28	22	19	23	5	35	1	1	1	0	1	.00	7	.214	.277	.288
2001	Mon	NL	132	472	118	33	2	6	(3 | 3)	173	42	38	46	25	2	54	2	4	3	2	1	.67	14	.250	.289	.367
2002	Mon	NL	117	376	99	20	1	12	(4 | 8)	157	41	49	49	40	7	65	1	6	5	6	3	.67	14	.263	.332	.418
2003	Mon	NL	70	226	47	9	2	10	(5 | 5)	90	33	30	25	21	7	37	2	2	1	0	0	-	6	.208	.280	.398
2004	ChC	NL	134	456	131	32	6	16	(9 | 7)	223	55	65	67	33	4	64	5	4	8	1	4	.20	13	.287	.337	.489
2005	ChC	NL	133	424	117	32	3	16	(9 | 7)	203	48	61	67	40	3	61	7	2	4	0	3	.00	7	.276	.345	.479
2006	ChC	NL	107	375	115	25	3	16	(9 | 7)	194	54	53	58	33	2	41	5	2	3	0	1	.00	12	.307	.368	.517
2007	2 Tms	NL	101	344	84	17	0	9	(6 | 3)	128	29	41	29	19	3	57	0	1	4	2	2	.50	10	.244	.281	.372
2008	SD	NL	30	94	19	3	0	2	(2 | 0)	28	9	9	7	9	0	16	1	1	2	0	0	-	4	.202	.274	.298
07	ChC	NL	57	211	54	9	0	9	(6 | 3)	90	23	29	22	17	3	36	0	0	3	2	2	.50	5	.256	.307	.427
07	SD	NL	44	133	30	8	0	0	(0 | 0)	38	6	12	7	2	0	21	0	1	1	0	0	-	5	.226	.235	.286
11 ML YEARS			1047	3494	922	220	21	97	(52 | 45)	1475	395	422	431	278	37	475	28	22	32	11	17	.39	105	.264	.320	.422

Jimmy Barthmaier

Pitches: R **Bats:** R **Pos:** SP-3   **Ht:** 6'5" **Wt:** 240 **Born:** 1/6/1984 **Age:** 25

HOW MUCH HE PITCHED								WHAT HE GAVE UP											THE RESULTS							
Year	Team	Lg	G	GS	CG	GF	IP	BFP	H	R	ER	HR	SH	SF	HB	TBB	IBB	SO	WP	Bk	W	L	Pct	ShO	Sv-Op	Hld	ERC	ERA
2003	Mrtnsvl	R+	8	3	0	0	21.2	93	19	9	6	0	0	0	2	7	0	18	2	0	1	1	.500	0	0--	-	2.72	2.49
2004	Grnsvle	R+	13	13	0	0	69.0	295	70	32	29	3	3	2	1	22	0	65	3	1	4	3	.571	0	0--	-	3.49	3.78
2005	Lxngtn	A	25	25	0	0	134.2	555	108	41	34	3	2	4	5	55	0	142	7	1	11	6	.647	0	0--	-	2.68	2.27
2005	Salem	A+	1	0	0	0	6.0	28	4	4	1	1	0	0	3	1	0	6	0	0	1	0	1.000	0	0--	-	3.36	1.50
2006	Salem	A+	27	27	0	0	146.2	622	137	64	59	6	2	1	9	67	0	134	3	0	11	8	.579	0	0--	-	3.86	3.62
2007	CpChr	AA	24	16	0	3	90.0	429	116	73	62	11	4	4	5	44	2	73	4	1	2	9	.182	0	0--	-	6.47	6.20
2008	Altna	AA	10	10	0	0	46.1	200	42	27	25	3	3	0	1	21	1	40	2	0	4	3	.333	0	0--	-	3.54	4.86
2008	Indy	AAA	16	16	0	0	79.0	330	69	34	31	5	3	3	4	27	1	71	2	0	3	1	.750	0	0--	-	3.10	3.53
2008	Pit	NL	3	3	0	0	10.1	53	16	12	12	3	1	0	0	8	0	6	0	0	0	2	.000	0	0-0	-	11.15	10.45

Jason Bartlett

Bats: R **Throws:** R **Pos:** SS-125; DH-3; PH-2   **Ht:** 6'0" **Wt:** 185 **Born:** 10/30/1979 **Age:** 29

BATTING																			BASERUNNING				AVERAGES		
Year	Team	Lg	G	AB	H	2B	3B	HR	(Hm | Rd)	TB	R	RBI	RC	TBB	IBB	SO	HBP	SH	SF	SB	CS	SB%	GDP	Avg	OBP	Slg
2004	Min	AL	8	12	1	0	0	0	(0 | 0)	1	2	1	1	1	0	1	0	1	0	2	0	1.00	0	.083	.154	.083
2005	Min	AL	74	224	54	10	1	3	(2 | 1)	75	33	16	22	21	0	37	4	2	1	4	0	1.00	6	.241	.316	.335
2006	Min	AL	99	333	103	18	2	2	(0 | 2)	131	44	32	50	22	1	46	11	1	5	10	5	.67	8	.309	.367	.393
2007	Min	AL	140	510	135	20	7	5	(2 | 3)	184	75	43	65	50	3	73	8	0	2	23	3	.88	8	.265	.339	.361
2008	TB	AL	128	454	130	25	3	1	(1 | 0)	164	48	37	56	22	1	69	9	5	4	20	6	.77	9	.286	.329	.361
Postseason			3	11	3	1	0	0	(0 | 0)	4	0	0	0	0	0	2	0	0	0	0	0	-	0	.273	.273	.364
5 ML YEARS			449	1533	423	73	13	11	(5 | 6)	555	202	129	194	116	5	226	32	9	12	59	14	.81	31	.276	.337	.362

Brian Barton

Bats: R **Throws:** R **Pos:** PH-44; LF-36; RF-10; CF-2; PR-1   **Ht:** 6'3" **Wt:** 187 **Born:** 4/25/1982 **Age:** 27

BATTING																			BASERUNNING				AVERAGES		
Year	Team	Lg	G	AB	H	2B	3B	HR	(Hm | Rd)	TB	R	RBI	RC	TBB	IBB	SO	HBP	SH	SF	SB	CS	SB%	GDP	Avg	OBP	Slg
2005	Lk Cty	A	35	133	55	14	1	4	(- | -)	83	31	32	40	18	1	21	6	0	1	7	2	.78	5	.414	.506	.624
2005	Knstn	A+	64	223	61	15	6	3	(- | -)	97	42	32	42	34	2	57	15	1	0	13	8	.62	6	.274	.404	.435
2006	Knstn	A+	82	295	91	16	3	13	(- | -)	152	56	57	68	39	2	83	16	3	6	26	3	.90	3	.308	.410	.515
2006	Akron	AA	42	151	53	5	0	6	(- | -)	76	32	26	32	13	2	26	5	0	2	15	5	.75	3	.351	.415	.503
2007	Akron	AA	106	389	122	18	2	9	(- | -)	171	56	59	76	41	2	99	28	2	1	21	9	.70	8	.314	.416	.440
2008	Buffalo	AAA	25	87	23	3	0	1	(- | -)	29	7	9	10	7	0	18	2	0	0	1	1	.50	4	.264	.333	.333
2008	Memp	AAA	19	73	19	2	2	3	(- | -)	34	12	11	11	9	0	23	2	0	2	1	4	.20	1	.260	.349	.466
2008	StL	NL	82	153	41	9	2	1	(1 | 1)	60	23	13	19	19	0	39	2	4	1	3	1	.75	5	.268	.354	.392

Daric Barton

Bats: L **Throws:** R **Pos:** 1B-134; PH-8; 3B-1   **Ht:** 6'0" **Wt:** 224 **Born:** 8/16/1985 **Age:** 23

BATTING																			BASERUNNING				AVERAGES		
Year	Team	Lg	G	AB	H	2B	3B	HR	(Hm | Rd)	TB	R	RBI	RC	TBB	IBB	SO	HBP	SH	SF	SB	CS	SB%	GDP	Avg	OBP	Slg
2003	JhsCty	R+	54	170	50	10	0	4	(- | -)	72	29	29	32	37	0	48	2	0	3	0	3	.00	2	.294	.420	.424
2004	Peoria	A	90	313	98	23	0	13	(- | -)	160	63	77	74	69	9	44	8	0	3	4	4	.50	7	.313	.445	.511
2005	Stcktn	A+	79	292	93	16	2	8	(- | -)	137	60	52	64	62	0	49	3	0	4	0	1	.00	6	.318	.438	.469
2005	Mdland	AA	56	212	67	20	1	5	(- | -)	104	38	37	43	35	1	30	0	0	2	1	2	.33	4	.316	.410	.491
2006	Scrmto	AAA	43	147	38	6	4	2	(- | -)	58	25	22	26	32	0	26	0	0	1	1	0	1.00	4	.259	.389	.395
2006	As	R	2	5	1	1	0	0	(- | -)	2	1	0	1	0	0	0	0	0	0	0	0	-	0	.200	.200	.400

Year Team	Lg	G	AB	H	2B	3B	HR	(Hm	Rd)	TB	R	RBI	RC	TBB	IBB	SO	HBP	SH	SF	SB	CS	SB%	GDP	Avg	OBP	Slg
						BATTING															**BASERUNNING**			**AVERAGES**		
2007 Scrmto	AAA	136	516	151	38	5	9	(-	-)	226	84	70	93	78	0	69	6	0	4	3	4	.43	14	.293	.389	.438
2008 Scrmto	AAA	8	31	6	0	0	1	(-	-)	9	4	3	2	2	0	0	0	0	0	0	0	-	0	.194	.242	.290
2007 Oak	AL	18	72	25	9	0	4	(2	2)	46	16	8	14	10	0	11	1	0	1	1	0	1.00	2	.347	.429	.639
2008 Oak	AL	140	446	101	17	5	9	(1	8)	155	59	47	56	65	5	99	3	6	3	2	1	.67	6	.226	.327	.348
2 ML YEARS		158	518	126	26	5	13	(3	10)	201	75	55	70	75	5	110	4	6	4	3	1	.75	8	.243	.341	.388

Brian Bass

Pitches: R **Bats:** R **Pos:** RP-45; SP-4
Ht: 6'2" **Wt:** 213 **Born:** 1/6/1982 **Age:** 27

Year Team	Lg	G	GS	CG	GF	IP	BFP	H	R	ER	HR	SH	SF	HB	TBB	IBB	SO	WP	Bk	W	L	Pct	ShO	Sv-Op	Hld	ERC	ERA
			HOW MUCH HE PITCHED							**WHAT HE GAVE UP**											**THE RESULTS**					
2000 Royals	R	12	9	0	0	44.0	200	36	27	19	0	1	1	9	18	0	44	10	0	3	5	.375	0	0--	-	3.01	3.89
2000 CtnWV	A	1	1	0	0	4.0	18	6	3	3	0	0	0	0	0	0	1	0	0	0	0	-	0	0--	-	4.47	6.75
2001 Burlgtn	A	26	26	1	0	139.1	613	138	82	72	16	3	5	15	53	0	75	14	1	3	10	.231	1	0--	-	4.46	4.65
2002 Burlgtn	A	20	20	1	0	110.1	456	103	57	47	8	1	3	2	31	0	60	9	0	5	7	.417	0	0--	-	3.16	3.83
2003 Wilmg	A+	26	26	2	0	152.1	625	129	59	48	7	5	7	7	43	1	119	7	0	9	8	.529	0	0--	-	2.63	2.84
2004 Wichta	AA	10	10	0	0	36.1	179	53	30	30	4	3	0	3	22	0	20	1	0	0	4	.000	0	0--	-	8.40	7.43
2004 Royals	R	5	5	0	0	17.2	73	17	6	5	0	0	0	1	3	0	23	2	0	1	1	.000	0	0--	-	2.55	2.55
2005 Wichta	AA	27	27	0	0	165.0	713	185	106	96	14	4	8	3	53	0	102	10	0	12	8	.600	0	0--	-	4.46	5.24
2006 Omha	AAA	7	7	0	0	32.0	158	49	35	27	7	0	1	2	14	0	11	4	1	1	5	.167	0	0--	-	8.79	7.59
2006 Wichta	AA	6	5	1	0	27.0	117	29	14	12	2	0	0	3	6	0	18	3	0	4	1	.800	0	0--	-	4.02	4.00
2006 Royals	R	3	3	-	0	12.0	51	15	7	6	0	-	-	1	0	0	9	0	0	1	1	.500	-	0--	-	3.51	4.50
2007 Roch	AAA	37	10	1	12	103.1	424	96	45	40	8	0	4	5	24	2	80	5	0	7	3	.700	0	1--	-	3.08	3.48
2008 Roch	AAA	2	2	0	0	9.0	40	8	5	4	1	0	1	1	4	0	6	0	0	1	0	1.000	0	0--	-	4.05	4.00
2008 2 Tms	AL	49	4	0	14	89.1	388	98	55	48	12	1	1	5	31	4	45	6	0	4	4	.500	0	1-2	3	4.89	4.84
08 Min	AL	44	0	0	14	68.1	303	84	42	37	11	0	1	3	22	3	32	4	0	3	4	.429	0	1-2	3	5.74	4.87
08 Bal	AL	5	4	0	0	21.0	85	14	13	11	1	1	0	2	9	1	13	2	0	1	0	1.000	0	0-0	-	2.42	4.71

Miguel Batista

Pitches: R **Bats:** R **Pos:** RP-24; SP-20
Ht: 6'1" **Wt:** 200 **Born:** 2/19/1971 **Age:** 38

Year Team	Lg	G	GS	CG	GF	IP	BFP	H	R	ER	HR	SH	SF	HB	TBB	IBB	SO	WP	Bk	W	L	Pct	ShO	Sv-Op	Hld	ERC	ERA
			HOW MUCH HE PITCHED							**WHAT HE GAVE UP**											**THE RESULTS**					
1992 Pit	NL	1	0	0	1	2.0	13	4	2	1	0	0	0	0	3	0	1	0	0	0	0	-	0	0-0	0	20.26	9.00
1996 Fla	NL	9	0	0	4	11.1	49	9	8	7	0	3	0	0	7	2	6	1	0	0	0	-	0	0-0	0	2.77	5.56
1997 ChC	NL	11	6	0	2	36.1	168	36	24	23	4	4	4	1	24	2	27	2	0	0	5	.000	0	0-0	0	5.09	5.70
1998 Mon	NL	56	13	0	12	135.0	598	141	66	57	12	7	5	6	65	7	92	6	1	3	5	.375	0	0-3	3	4.70	3.80
1999 Mon	NL	39	17	2	3	134.2	606	146	88	73	10	8	11	7	58	2	95	6	0	8	7	.533	1	1-1	0	4.62	4.88
2000 2 Tms	NL	18	9	0	2	65.1	310	85	68	62	19	1	2	2	37	2	37	4	0	2	7	.222	0	0-2	0	8.37	8.54
2001 Ari	NL	48	18	0	6	139.1	581	113	57	52	13	9	3	10	60	2	90	6	0	11	8	.579	0	0-0	4	3.43	3.36
2002 Ari	NL	36	29	1	2	184.2	790	172	99	88	12	5	8	6	70	3	112	9	2	8	9	.471	0	0-0	2	3.45	4.29
2003 Ari	NL	36	29	2	5	193.1	822	197	85	76	11	3	10	6	83	0	142	7	0	10	9	.526	1	0-0	0	3.77	3.54
2004 Tor	AL	38	31	2	7	198.2	867	206	115	106	22	7	6	3	96	1	104	12	0	10	13	.435	1	5-5	0	4.84	4.80
2005 Tor	AL	71	0	0	62	74.2	331	80	39	34	9	2	2	2	27	5	54	3	0	5	8	.385	0	31-39	0	4.39	4.10
2006 Ari	NL	34	33	3	0	206.1	910	231	116	105	18	12	5	6	84	5	110	14	1	11	8	.579	1	0-0	0	4.82	4.58
2007 Sea	AL	33	32	0	0	193.0	860	209	101	92	18	5	5	8	85	3	133	15	2	16	11	.593	0	0-0	0	4.81	4.29
2008 Sea	AL	44	20	0	9	115.0	556	135	89	80	19	3	11	6	79	6	73	5	0	4	14	.222	0	1-4	4	6.92	6.26
00 Mon	NL	4	0	0	0	8.1	49	19	14	13	2	1	1	2	3	0	7	0	0	0	1	.000	0	0-2	0	14.73	14.04
00 KC	AL	14	9	0	2	57.0	261	66	54	49	17	0	1	0	34	2	30	4	0	2	6	.250	0	0-0	0	7.50	7.74
Postseason		7	4	0	1	25.1	104	18	10	10	3	3	0	1	11	0	14	1	0	1	2	.333	0	0-0	0	2.94	3.55
14 ML YEARS		474	237	10	115	1689.2	7461	1764	957	857	170	76	68	65	755	43	1076	90	6	88	104	.458	4	38-51	13	4.64	4.56

Rick Bauer

Pitches: R **Bats:** R **Pos:** RP-4
Ht: 6'6" **Wt:** 225 **Born:** 1/10/1977 **Age:** 32

Year Team	Lg	G	GS	CG	GF	IP	BFP	H	R	ER	HR	SH	SF	HB	TBB	IBB	SO	WP	Bk	W	L	Pct	ShO	Sv-Op	Hld	ERC	ERA
			HOW MUCH HE PITCHED							**WHAT HE GAVE UP**											**THE RESULTS**					
2008 Buffalo*	AAA	22	0	0	20	23.1	97	17	4	4	0	1	0	1	10	1	30	0	0	0	0	-	0	15--	-	2.18	1.54
2008 Syrcse*	AAA	12	0	0	10	11.1	52	10	7	4	1	0	2	0	7	0	13	1	0	0	0	-	0	3--	-	3.99	3.18
2001 Bal	AL	6	6	0	0	33.0	143	35	22	17	7	0	1	1	9	0	16	0	0	0	5	.000	0	0-0	0	4.74	4.64
2002 Bal	AL	56	1	0	15	83.2	358	84	41	37	12	2	2	4	36	4	45	4	0	6	7	.462	0	1-5	12	4.78	3.98
2003 Bal	AL	35	0	0	10	61.1	259	58	36	31	5	1	3	4	24	3	43	6	0	2	1	.667	0	0-1	3	3.87	4.55
2004 Bal	AL	23	2	0	7	53.2	230	49	31	28	4	0	0	4	20	0	37	1	0	2	1	.667	0	0-1	0	3.59	4.70
2005 Bal	AL	5	0	0	2	8.1	40	13	9	9	2	0	0	4	0	5	0	0	0	0		-	0	0-0	0	9.72	9.72
2006 Tex	AL	58	1	0	19	71.0	302	73	31	28	4	0	5	4	25	0	35	3	0	3	1	.750	0	2-5	7	4.04	3.55
2008 Cle	AL	4	0	0	2	6.0	30	10	9	9	1	0	0	0	3	0	4	0	0	0	0	-	0	0-0	0	9.38	13.50
7 ML YEARS		187	10	0	55	317.0	1362	322	179	159	35	3	11	17	121	7	185	14	0	11	14	.440	0	3-12	22	4.41	4.51

Denny Bautista

Pitches: R **Bats:** R **Pos:** RP-51
Ht: 6'5" **Wt:** 190 **Born:** 8/23/1980 **Age:** 28

Year Team	Lg	G	GS	CG	GF	IP	BFP	H	R	ER	HR	SH	SF	HB	TBB	IBB	SO	WP	Bk	W	L	Pct	ShO	Sv-Op	Hld	ERC	ERA
			HOW MUCH HE PITCHED							**WHAT HE GAVE UP**											**THE RESULTS**					
2008 Toledo*	AAA	5	0	0	0	6.1	26	2	1	0	0	1	0	1	3	0	7	0	0	0	1	.000	0	0--	-	1.10	0.00
2004 2 Tms	AL	7	5	0	0	29.2	142	44	28	28	3	0	1	3	13	1	19	3	2	0	4	.000	0	0-0	0	7.76	8.49
2005 KC	AL	7	7	0	0	35.2	160	36	23	23	2	1	2	1	17	0	23	3	0	2	2	.500	0	0-0	0	4.27	5.80
2006 2 Tms	AL	12	8	0	3	41.2	194	47	34	26	5	1	2	4	21	0	27	5	0	0	3	.000	0	0-0	0	5.75	5.62
2007 Col	NL	9	1	0	2	8.2	48	18	12	12	0	1	0	1	4	0	8	0	0	2	1	.667	0	0-0	2	10.84	12.46
2008 2 Tms	AL	51	0	0	8	60.1	271	61	35	35	6	2	4	2	42	2	44	4	0	4	4	.500	0	0-1	10	5.18	5.22
04 Bal	AL	2	0	0	0	2.0	15	6	8	8	1	0	1	1	2	0	1	1	0	0	0	-	0	0-0	0	28.67	36.00
04 KC	AL	5	5	0	0	27.2	127	38	20	20	2	0	0	2	11	1	18	2	2	0	4	.000	0	0-0	0	6.50	6.51

Year	Team	Lg	G	GS	CG	GF	IP	BFP	H	R	ER	HR	SH	SF	HB	TBB	IBB	SO	WP	Bk	W	L	Pct	ShO	Sv-Op	Hld	ERC	ERA
			HOW MUCH HE PITCHED						WHAT HE GAVE UP												THE RESULTS							
06	KC	AL	8	7	0	0	35.0	161	38	24	22	5	1	2	4	17	0	22	5	0	0	2	.000	0	0-0	0	5.70	5.66
06	Col	NL	4	1	0	3	6.2	33	9	10	4	0	0	0	0	4	0	5	0	0	0	1	.000	0	0-0	0	5.98	5.40
08	Det	AL	16	0	0	3	19.0	83	15	7	7	1	1	1	2	14	0	10	1	0	0	1	.000	0	0-0	0	4.42	3.32
08	Pit	NL	35	0	0	5	41.1	188	46	28	28	5	1	3	0	28	2	34	3	0	4	3	.571	0	0-1	7	6.14	6.10
5 ML YEARS			86	21	0	13	176.0	815	206	132	124	16	5	8	12	97	3	121	15	2	8	14	.364	0	0-1	12	5.93	6.34

Jose Bautista

Bats: R Throws: R Pos: 3B-99; PH-24; DH-7; 1B-5; 2B-2; PR-1

Ht: 6'0" Wt: 195 Born: 10/19/1980 Age: 28

Year	Team	Lg	G	AB	H	2B	3B	HR	(Hm	Rd)	TB	R	RBI	RC	TBB	IBB	SO	HBP	SH	SF	SB	CS	SB%	GDP	Avg	OBP	Slg
			BATTING																		BASERUNNING				AVERAGES		
2008	Indy*	AAA	5	20	6	2	0	2	(-	-)	14	6	8	5	3	0	6	0	0	0	1	0	1.00	0	.300	.391	.700
2004	4 Tms		64	88	18	3	0	0	(0	0)	21	6	2	2	7	0	40	0	1	0	0	1	.00	1	.205	.263	.239
2005	Pit	NL	11	28	4	1	0	0	(0	0)	5	3	1	0	3	0	7	0	0	0	1	0	1.00	2	.143	.226	.179
2006	Pit	NL	117	400	94	20	3	16	(11	5)	168	58	51	55	46	2	110	16	3	4	2	4	.33	12	.235	.335	.420
2007	Pit	NL	142	532	135	36	2	15	(8	7)	220	75	63	71	68	1	101	4	4	6	6	3	.67	16	.254	.339	.414
2008	2 Tms		128	370	88	17	0	15	(5	10)	150	45	54	43	40	5	91	2	8	4	1	1	.50	12	.238	.313	.405
04	Bal	AL	16	11	3	0	0	0	(0	0)	3	3	0	1	1	0	3	0	0	0	0	0	-	0	.273	.333	.273
04	TB	AL	12	12	2	0	0	0	(0	0)	2	1	1	0	3	0	7	0	0	0	0	1	.00	0	.167	.333	.167
04	KC	AL	13	25	5	1	0	0	(0	0)	6	1	1	0	1	0	12	0	0	0	0	0	-	0	.200	.231	.240
04	Pit	NL	23	40	8	2	0	0	(0	0)	10	1	0	1	2	0	18	0	1	0	0	0	-	1	.200	.238	.250
08	Pit	NL	107	314	76	15	0	12	(3	9)	127	38	44	39	38	4	77	2	6	3	1	1	.50	10	.242	.325	.404
08	Tor	AL	21	56	12	2	0	3	(2	1)	23	7	10	4	2	1	14	0	2	1	0	0	-	2	.214	.237	.411
5 ML YEARS			462	1418	339	77	5	46	(24	22)	564	187	171	171	164	8	349	22	16	14	10	9	.53	43	.239	.324	.398

Jason Bay

Bats: R Throws: R Pos: LF-154; PH-1

Ht: 6'2" Wt: 205 Born: 9/20/1978 Age: 30

Year	Team	Lg	G	AB	H	2B	3B	HR	(Hm	Rd)	TB	R	RBI	RC	TBB	IBB	SO	HBP	SH	SF	SB	CS	SB%	GDP	Avg	OBP	Slg
			BATTING																		BASERUNNING				AVERAGES		
2003	2 Tms	NL	30	87	25	7	1	4	(2	2)	46	15	14	19	19	0	29	1	0	0	3	1	.75	0	.287	.421	.529
2004	Pit	NL	120	411	116	24	4	26	(15	11)	226	61	82	75	41	2	129	10	5	5	4	6	.40	9	.282	.358	.550
2005	Pit	NL	162	599	183	44	6	32	(9	23)	335	110	101	128	95	9	142	6	0	7	21	1	.95	12	.306	.402	.559
2006	Pit	NL	159	570	163	29	3	35	(13	22)	303	101	109	103	102	9	156	8	0	9	11	2	.85	15	.286	.396	.532
2007	Pit	NL	145	538	133	25	2	21	(7	14)	225	78	84	74	59	3	141	9	0	8	4	1	.80	8	.247	.327	.418
2008	2 Tms		155	577	165	35	4	31	(18	13)	301	111	101	104	81	4	137	4	0	8	10	0	1.00	7	.286	.373	.522
03	SD	NL	3	8	2	1	0	1	(0	1)	6	2	2	2	1	0	1	1	0	0	0	0	-	0	.250	.400	.750
03	Pit	NL	27	79	23	6	1	3	(2	1)	40	13	12	17	18	0	28	0	0	0	3	1	.75	0	.291	.423	.506
08	Pit	NL	106	393	111	23	2	22	(15	7)	204	72	64	73	59	2	86	2	0	5	7	0	1.00	3	.282	.375	.519
08	Bos	AL	49	184	54	12	2	9	(3	6)	97	39	37	31	22	2	51	2	0	3	3	0	1.00	4	.293	.370	.527
6 ML YEARS			771	2782	785	164	20	149	(64	85)	1436	476	491	503	397	27	734	38	5	37	53	11	.83	51	.282	.375	.516

Yorman Bazardo

Pitches: R Bats: R Pos: RP-3

Ht: 6'2" Wt: 220 Born: 7/11/1984 Age: 24

Year	Team	Lg	G	GS	CG	GF	IP	BFP	H	R	ER	HR	SH	SF	HB	TBB	IBB	SO	WP	Bk	W	L	Pct	ShO	Sv-Op	Hld	ERC	ERA
			HOW MUCH HE PITCHED						WHAT HE GAVE UP												THE RESULTS							
2008	Toledo*	AAA	25	22	0	0	130.0	585	177	100	97	19	7	7	7	44	0	75	9	0	4	13	.235	0	0--	0	6.80	6.72
2005	Fla	NL	1	0	0	0	1.2	12	5	5	4	0	0	0	0	2	0	2	1	0	0	0	-	0	0-0	0	20.56	21.60
2007	Det	AL	11	0	0	6	23.2	96	19	7	6	2	0	1	3	5	0	15	1	0	2	1	.667	0	0-0	1	2.71	2.28
2008	Det	AL	3	0	0	3	3.0	20	7	8	8	0	0	1	0	5	1	5	0	0	0	0	-	0	0-0	1	17.55	24.00
3 ML YEARS			15	2	0	9	28.1	128	31	20	18	2	0	2	3	12	1	20	2	0	2	1	.667	0	0-0	1	4.85	5.72

T.J. Beam

Pitches: R Bats: R Pos: RP-32

Ht: 6'7" Wt: 210 Born: 8/28/1980 Age: 28

Year	Team	Lg	G	GS	CG	GF	IP	BFP	H	R	ER	HR	SH	SF	HB	TBB	IBB	SO	WP	Bk	W	L	Pct	ShO	Sv-Op	Hld	ERC	ERA
			HOW MUCH HE PITCHED						WHAT HE GAVE UP												THE RESULTS							
2003	StlsInd	A-	9	5	0	1	33.1	137	25	14	10	4	1	2	0	9	0	31	1	0	2	1	.667	0	1--	-	2.30	2.70
2003	Btl Crk	A	5	5	0	0	21.2	100	27	16	14	3	0	0	2	8	0	19	0	0	2	1	.667	0	0--	-	6.06	5.82
2004	Btl Crk	A	11	0	0	2	41.1	169	34	20	20	8	5	3	0	17	0	54	1	1	2	5	.286	0	0--	-	3.85	4.35
2004	StlsInd	A-	12	12	1	0	66.2	269	61	28	19	4	0	2	3	14	0	69	1	2	2	4	.333	0	0--	-	2.86	2.57
2005	CtnSC	A	35	2	0	16	59.2	240	45	15	11	2	1	1	1	18	0	78	0	0	3	3	.500	0	2--	-	2.09	1.66
2005	Tampa	A+	12	0	0	5	17.1	72	14	7	6	2	0	0	0	7	1	27	0	0	1	1	.500	0	1--	-	3.06	3.12
2006	Trntn	AA	18	0	0	7	42.0	158	26	5	4	1	1	2	0	12	0	34	0	0	4	0	1.000	0	3--	-	1.48	0.86
2006	Clmbs	AAA	19	0	0	5	31.2	122	16	6	6	1	2	1	0	13	0	37	2	0	2	0	1.000	0	1--	-	1.40	1.71
2007	S-WB	AAA	29	0	0	13	47.1	199	51	20	19	6	3	0	0	10	0	45	0	0	4	3	.571	0	3--	-	3.94	3.61
2007	Yanks	R	4	3	0	0	7.0	29	6	3	2	0	0	0	0	1	0	7	0	0	0	0	-	0	0--	-	1.69	2.57
2008	Indy	AAA	30	0	0	15	43.2	180	36	15	15	2	3	1	0	14	3	41	1	0	2	1	.667	0	5--	-	2.37	3.09
2006	NYY	AL	20	0	0	5	18.0	85	26	17	17	5	0	0	2	6	2	12	1	1	2	0	1.000	0	0-1	2	8.36	8.50
2008	Pit	NL	32	0	0	15	45.2	199	43	21	21	6	4	2	2	20	4	24	0	0	2	2	.500	0	1-1	2	4.12	4.14
2 ML YEARS			52	0	0	13	63.2	284	69	38	38	11	4	2	4	26	6	36	1	1	4	2	.667	0	1-2	4	5.22	5.37

Josh Beckett

Pitches: R **Bats:** R **Pos:** SP-27   **Ht:** 6'5" **Wt:** 222 **Born:** 5/15/1980 **Age:** 29

		HOW MUCH HE PITCHED						WHAT HE GAVE UP												THE RESULTS							
Year	Team	Lg	G	GS	CG	GF	IP	BFP	H	R	ER	HR	SH	SF	HB	TBB	IBB	SO	WP	Bk	W	L	Pct	ShO	Sv-Op	Hld	ERC	ERA
2001	Fla	NL	4	4	0	0	24.0	99	14	9	4	3	0	0	1	11	0	24	1	0	2	2	.500	0	0-0	0	2.36	1.50
2002	Fla	NL	23	21	0	0	107.2	454	93	56	49	13	5	3	1	44	2	113	5	0	6	7	.462	0	0-0	0	3.50	4.10
2003	Fla	NL	24	23	0	1	142.0	601	132	54	48	9	5	1	2	56	4	152	6	1	9	8	.529	0	0-0	0	3.44	3.04
2004	Fla	NL	26	26	1	0	156.2	654	137	72	66	16	9	3	6	54	3	152	5	0	9	9	.500	1	0-0	0	3.32	3.79
2005	Fla	NL	29	29	2	0	178.2	729	153	75	67	14	8	2	7	58	2	166	5	0	15	8	.652	1	0-0	0	3.06	3.38
2006	Bos	AL	33	33	0	0	204.2	869	191	120	114	36	2	3	10	74	1	158	11	1	16	11	.593	0	0-0	0	4.28	5.01
2007	Bos	AL	30	30	1	0	200.2	822	189	76	73	17	3	2	5	40	0	194	3	0	20	7	.741	0	0-0	0	2.99	3.27
2008	Bos	AL	27	27	1	0	174.1	725	173	80	78	18	4	3	9	34	1	172	5	0	12	10	.545	0	0-0	0	3.45	4.03
	Postseason		10	9	3	0	72.2	270	40	14	14	4	2	0	2	14	1	82	3	0	6	2	.750	3	0-0	0	1.21	1.73
	8 ML YEARS		196	193	5	1	1188.2	4953	1082	542	499	126	36	17	41	371	13	1131	41	2	89	62	.589	2	0-0	0	3.41	3.78

Erik Bedard

Pitches: L **Bats:** L **Pos:** SP-15   **Ht:** 6'1" **Wt:** 190 **Born:** 3/6/1979 **Age:** 30

		HOW MUCH HE PITCHED						WHAT HE GAVE UP												THE RESULTS							
Year	Team	Lg	G	GS	CG	GF	IP	BFP	H	R	ER	HR	SH	SF	HB	TBB	IBB	SO	WP	Bk	W	L	Pct	ShO	Sv-Op	Hld	ERC	ERA
2002	Bal	AL	2	0	0	0	0.2	4	2	1	1	0	0	0	0	0	0	0	1	0	0	0	-	0	0-0	0	14.52	13.50
2004	Bal	AL	27	26	0	0	137.1	633	149	83	70	13	0	4	7	71	1	121	7	2	6	10	.375	0	0-0	0	5.11	4.59
2005	Bal	AL	24	24	0	0	141.2	606	139	66	63	10	3	6	5	57	1	125	4	1	6	8	.429	0	0-0	0	3.95	4.00
2006	Bal	AL	33	33	0	0	196.1	844	196	92	82	16	6	4	5	69	0	171	6	0	15	11	.577	0	0-0	0	3.83	3.76
2007	Bal	AL	28	28	1	0	182.0	733	141	66	64	19	2	4	5	57	0	221	3	0	13	5	.722	1	0-0	0	2.71	3.16
2008	Sea	AL	15	15	0	0	81.0	347	70	38	33	9	1	2	4	37	0	72	3	0	6	4	.600	0	0-0	0	3.82	3.67
	6 ML YEARS		129	126	1	0	739.0	3167	697	346	313	67	12	20	26	291	2	711	23	3	46	38	.548	1	0-0	0	3.80	3.81

Joe Beimel

Pitches: L **Bats:** L **Pos:** RP-71   **Ht:** 6'3" **Wt:** 215 **Born:** 4/19/1977 **Age:** 32

		HOW MUCH HE PITCHED						WHAT HE GAVE UP												THE RESULTS							
Year	Team	Lg	G	GS	CG	GF	IP	BFP	H	R	ER	HR	SH	SF	HB	TBB	IBB	SO	WP	Bk	W	L	Pct	ShO	Sv-Op	Hld	ERC	ERA
2001	Pit	NL	42	15	0	9	115.1	511	131	72	67	12	3	1	6	49	4	58	3	0	7	11	.389	0	0-0	0	5.23	5.23
2002	Pit	NL	53	8	0	8	85.1	389	88	49	44	9	7	3	4	45	12	53	2	0	2	5	.286	0	0-1	5	4.68	4.64
2003	Pit	NL	69	0	0	11	62.1	276	69	35	35	7	3	5	4	33	6	42	0	1	1	3	.250	0	0-5	12	5.62	5.05
2004	Min	AL	3	0	0	0	1.2	15	8	8	8	1	0	0	0	2	0	2	0	0	0	0	-	0	0-0	0	44.43	43.20
2005	TB	AL	7	0	0	3	11.0	51	15	4	4	1	0	0	0	4	1	3	1	0	0	0	-	0	0-0	0	5.80	3.27
2006	LAD	NL	62	0	0	10	70.0	295	70	26	23	7	4	3	0	21	3	30	6	1	2	1	.667	0	2-2	10	3.62	2.96
2007	LAD	NL	83	0	0	10	67.1	281	63	30	29	1	5	2	1	24	6	39	3	2	2	1	.667	0	1-1	16	2.93	3.88
2008	LAD	NL	71	0	0	10	49.0	214	50	11	11	0	1	4	3	21	4	32	1	1	5	1	.833	0	0-0	12	3.70	2.02
	8 ML YEARS		390	23	0	61	462.0	2032	494	235	221	38	23	18	18	199	36	259	16	5	21	23	.477	0	3-9	55	4.52	4.31

Matt Belisle

Pitches: R **Bats:** R **Pos:** SP-6   **Ht:** 6'3" **Wt:** 230 **Born:** 6/6/1980 **Age:** 29

		HOW MUCH HE PITCHED						WHAT HE GAVE UP												THE RESULTS							
Year	Team	Lg	G	GS	CG	GF	IP	BFP	H	R	ER	HR	SH	SF	HB	TBB	IBB	SO	WP	Bk	W	L	Pct	ShO	Sv-Op	Hld	ERC	ERA
2008	Srsota*	A+	1	1	0	0	8.2	28	2	0	0	0	0	0	0	0	0	3	0	0	1	0	1.000	0	0--	-	0.12	0.00
2008	Chatt*	AA	1	1	1	1	9.0	35	7	3	2	0	1	0	0	0	0	3	0	0	1	0	1.000	0	0--	-	1.17	2.00
2008	Lsvlle*	AAA	26	1	0	9	38.0	170	43	22	18	1	1	1	4	11	1	27	1	0	5	1	.833	0	4--	-	4.15	4.26
2003	Cin	NL	6	0	0	2	8.2	39	10	5	5	1	2	1	1	2	0	6	0	0	1	1	.500	0	0-1	0	4.73	5.19
2005	Cin	NL	60	5	0	17	85.2	382	101	49	42	11	4	2	6	26	6	59	3	0	4	8	.333	0	1-4	8	5.08	4.41
2006	Cin	NL	30	2	0	5	40.0	180	43	18	16	5	1	2	3	19	1	26	3	0	2	0	1.000	0	0-1	0	5.29	3.60
2007	Cin	NL	30	30	1	0	177.2	771	212	111	105	26	7	9	7	43	4	125	6	1	8	9	.471	0	0-0	0	5.05	5.32
2008	Cin	NL	6	6	0	0	29.2	142	47	27	24	4	1	2	0	6	0	14	2	0	1	4	.200	0	0-0	0	6.87	7.28
	5 ML YEARS		132	43	1	24	341.2	1514	413	210	192	47	15	16	17	96	11	230	14	1	16	22	.421	0	1-6	8	5.24	5.06

Heath Bell

Pitches: R **Bats:** R **Pos:** RP-74   **Ht:** 6'3" **Wt:** 240 **Born:** 9/29/1977 **Age:** 31

		HOW MUCH HE PITCHED						WHAT HE GAVE UP												THE RESULTS							
Year	Team	Lg	G	GS	CG	GF	IP	BFP	H	R	ER	HR	SH	SF	HB	TBB	IBB	SO	WP	Bk	W	L	Pct	ShO	Sv-Op	Hld	ERC	ERA
2004	NYM	NL	17	0	0	2	24.1	94	22	9	9	5	1	0	0	6	0	27	0	0	0	2	.000	0	0-1	1	3.86	3.33
2005	NYM	NL	42	0	0	12	46.2	206	56	30	29	3	4	0	1	13	3	43	0	1	1	3	.250	0	0-0	4	4.42	5.59
2006	NYM	NL	22	0	0	6	37.0	166	51	25	21	6	1	0	0	11	2	35	1	0	0	0	-	0	0-0	0	6.40	5.11
2007	SD	NL	81	0	0	16	93.2	363	60	21	21	3	4	1	2	30	1	102	4	0	6	4	.600	0	2-6	34	1.67	2.02
2008	SD	NL	74	0	0	8	78.0	324	66	31	31	5	4	3	1	28	4	71	2	0	6	6	.500	0	0-7	23	2.93	3.58
	5 ML YEARS		236	0	0	44	279.2	1153	255	116	111	22	13	3	6	88	10	278	7	1	13	15	.464	0	2-14	62	3.20	3.57

Ronnie Belliard

Bats: R **Throws:** R **Pos:** 1B-33; 3B-31; 2B-29; PH-13; SS-5; PR-1   **Ht:** 5'10" **Wt:** 214 **Born:** 4/7/1975 **Age:** 34

		BATTING																				BASERUNNING				AVERAGES		
Year	Team	Lg	G	AB	H	2B	3B	HR	(Hm	Rd)	TB	R	RBI	RC	TBB	IBB	SO	HBP	SH	SF		SB	CS	SB%	GDP		Avg	OBP	Slg
2008	Hrsbrg*	AA	3	12	0	0	0	0	(-	-)	0	0	0	0	0	0	4	0	0	0		0	0	-	1		.000	.000	.000
2008	Ptomc*	A+	1	3	0	0	0	0	(-	-)	0	0	0	0	0	0	0	0	0	0		0	0	-	0		.000	.000	.000
1998	Mil	NL	8	5	1	0	0	0	(0	0)	1	1	0	0	0	0	0	0	0	0		0	0	-	0		.200	.200	.200
1999	Mil	NL	124	457	135	29	4	8	(5	3)	196	60	58	72	64	0	59	0	6	4		4	5	.44	16		.295	.379	.429
2000	Mil	NL	152	571	150	30	9	8	(4	4)	222	83	54	81	82	4	84	3	4	7		7	5	.58	12		.263	.354	.389
2001	Mil	NL	101	364	96	30	3	11	(7	4)	165	69	36	56	35	2	65	5	4	2		5	2	.71	5		.264	.335	.453

Year	Team	Lg	G	AB	H	2B	3B	HR	(Hm	Rd)	TB	R	RBI	RC	TBB	IBB	SO	HBP	SH	SF	SB	CS	SB%	GDP	Avg	OBP	Slg
									BATTING												BASERUNNING				AVERAGES		
2002	Mil	NL	104	289	61	13	0	3	(0	3)	83	30	26	15	18	0	46	1	6	3	2	3	.40	9	.211	.257	.287
2003	Col	NL	116	447	124	31	2	8	(6	2)	183	73	50	71	49	0	71	2	6	1	7	2	.78	7	.277	.351	.409
2004	Cle	AL	152	599	169	48	1	12	(4	8)	255	78	70	87	60	5	98	2	0	2	3	2	.60	18	.282	.348	.426
2005	Cle	AL	145	536	152	36	1	17	(7	10)	241	71	78	71	35	0	72	1	8	7	2	2	.50	17	.284	.325	.450
2006	2 Tms		147	544	148	30	1	13	(5	8)	219	63	67	62	36	2	81	5	3	2	2	3	.40	17	.272	.322	.403
2007	Was	NL	147	511	148	35	1	11	(5	6)	218	57	58	64	34	1	72	1	6	5	3	0	1.00	12	.290	.332	.427
2008	Was	NL	96	296	85	22	0	11	(7	4)	140	37	46	53	37	1	58	3	1	0	2	2	.60	6	.287	.372	.473
06	Cle	AL	93	350	102	21	0	8	(3	5)	147	43	44	47	21	0	45	4	2	2	2	0	1.00	8	.291	.337	.420
06	StL	NL	54	194	46	9	1	5	(2	3)	72	20	23	15	15	2	36	1	1	0	0	3	.00	9	.237	.295	.371
Postseason			14	50	12	1	0	0	(0	0)	13	2	4	5	3	1	6	1	1	0	2	0	1.00	1	.240	.296	.260
11 ML YEARS			1292	4619	1269	304	22	102	(50	52)	1923	622	543	632	450	15	706	23	44	33	38	26	.59	119	.275	.340	.416

Edwin Bellorin

Bats: R Throws: R Pos: C-2; PH-1

Ht: 5'9" Wt: 225 Born: 2/21/1982 Age: 27

Year	Team	Lg	G	AB	H	2B	3B	HR	(Hm	Rd)	TB	R	RBI	RC	TBB	IBB	SO	HBP	SH	SF	SB	CS	SB%	GDP	Avg	OBP	Slg
									BATTING												BASERUNNING				AVERAGES		
2001	Ddgrs	R	28	80	14	1	0	0	(-	-)	15	11	6	5	8	0	6	4	2	0	1	0	1.00	0	.175	.283	.188
2002	SoGA	A	92	318	89	13	1	0	(-	-)	104	28	38	37	19	2	39	6	7	1	4	2	.67	8	.280	.331	.327
2003	VeroB	A+	67	233	57	9	0	3	(-	-)	75	19	28	21	10	0	32	5	2	3	0	2	.00	8	.245	.287	.322
2003	Jaxnvl	AA	17	57	11	2	1	0	(-	-)	15	2	3	2	2	0	13	0	1	0	0	0	-	0	.193	.220	.263
2004	Jaxnvl	AA	86	285	80	15	1	1	(-	-)	100	27	30	35	18	0	51	4	2	1	1	0	1.00	5	.281	.331	.351
2005	VeroB	A+	87	308	84	18	2	3	(-	-)	115	36	33	36	14	2	44	4	1	2	1	1	.50	9	.273	.311	.373
2006	LsVgs	AAA	96	321	75	13	1	7	(-	-)	111	32	49	30	14	1	59	2	8	5	1	2	.33	12	.234	.266	.346
2007	ColSpr	AAA	59	221	72	18	0	9	(-	-)	117	38	45	43	16	1	27	2	0	5	1	0	1.00	6	.326	.369	.529
2008	ColSpr	AAA	87	335	98	27	3	5	(-	-)	146	28	65	48	15	0	43	3	2	1	1	1	.50	11	.293	.328	.436
2007	Col	NL	3	2	0	0	0	0	(0	0)	0	0	0	0	0	0	0	0	0	0	0	0	-	1	.000	.000	.000
2008	Col	NL	3	3	1	0	0	0	(0	0)	1	0	0	0	0	0	0	0	0	0	0	0	-	0	.333	.333	.333
2 ML YEARS			6	5	1	0	0	0	(0	0)	1	0	0	0	0	0	0	0	0	0	0	0	-	1	.200	.200	.200

Carlos Beltran

Bats: B Throws: R Pos: CF-158; PH-2; DH-1

Ht: 6'1" Wt: 205 Born: 4/24/1977 Age: 32

Year	Team	Lg	G	AB	H	2B	3B	HR	(Hm	Rd)	TB	R	RBI	RC	TBB	IBB	SO	HBP	SH	SF	SB	CS	SB%	GDP	Avg	OBP	Slg
									BATTING												BASERUNNING				AVERAGES		
1998	KC	AL	14	58	16	5	3	0	(0	0)	27	12	7	9	3	0	12	1	0	1	3	0	1.00	2	.276	.317	.466
1999	KC	AL	156	663	194	27	7	22	(12	10)	301	112	108	100	46	2	123	4	0	10	27	8	.77	17	.293	.337	.454
2000	KC	AL	98	372	92	15	4	7	(4	3)	136	49	44	43	35	2	69	0	2	4	13	0	1.00	12	.247	.309	.366
2001	KC	AL	155	617	189	32	12	24	(7	17)	317	106	101	118	52	2	120	5	1	5	31	1	.97	12	.306	.362	.514
2002	KC	AL	162	637	174	44	7	29	(19	10)	319	114	105	117	71	1	135	4	3	7	35	7	.83	12	.273	.346	.501
2003	KC	AL	141	521	160	14	10	26	(10	16)	272	102	100	117	72	4	81	2	0	7	41	4	.91	8	.307	.389	.522
2004	2 Tms		159	599	160	36	9	38	(15	23)	328	121	104	124	92	10	101	7	3	7	42	3	.93	6	.267	.367	.548
2005	NYM	NL	151	582	155	34	2	16	(6	10)	241	83	78	88	56	5	96	2	4	6	17	6	.74	9	.266	.330	.414
2006	NYM	NL	140	510	140	38	1	41	(15	26)	303	127	116	121	95	6	99	4	1	7	18	3	.86	6	.275	.388	.594
2007	NYM	NL	144	554	153	33	3	33	(11	22)	291	93	112	97	69	10	111	2	1	10	23	2	.92	3	.276	.353	.525
2008	NYM	NL	161	606	172	40	5	27	(14	13)	303	116	112	116	92	13	96	1	1	6	25	3	.89	11	.284	.376	.500
04	KC	AL	69	266	74	19	2	15	(8	7)	142	51	51	57	37	7	44	2	1	3	14	3	.82	4	.278	.367	.534
04	Hou	NL	90	333	86	17	7	23	(7	16)	186	70	53	67	55	3	57	5	2	4	28	0	1.00	2	.258	.368	.559
Postseason			22	82	30	4	0	11	(4	7)	67	31	19	26	18	1	13	1	0	0	8	0	1.00	1	.366	.485	.817
11 ML YEARS			1481	5719	1605	318	63	263	(113	150)	2838	1035	987	1050	683	55	1043	32	16	70	275	37	.88	100	.281	.357	.496

Francis Beltran

Pitches: R Bats: R Pos: RP-11

Ht: 6'6" Wt: 257 Born: 11/29/1979 Age: 29

Year	Team	Lg	G	GS	CG	GF	IP	BFP	H	R	ER	HR	SH	SF	HB	TBB	IBB	SO	WP	Bk	W	L	Pct	ShO	Sv-Op	Hld	ERC	ERA
					HOW MUCH HE PITCHED							WHAT HE GAVE UP											THE RESULTS					
2008	Toledo*	AAA	37	0	0	24	44.0	184	44	24	23	5	1	0	1	11	2	38	2	0	3	5	.375	0	3- -	-	3.61	4.70
2002	ChC	NL	11	0	0	4	12.0	65	14	11	10	2	3	1	0	16	1	11	2	0	0	0	-	0	0-0	0	9.45	7.50
2004	2 Tms	NL	45	0	0	13	49.1	221	47	31	30	11	4	2	2	27	1	48	2	0	2	2	.500	0	1-1	5	5.40	5.47
2008	Det	NL	11	0	0	4	13.0	56	13	7	3	0	0	0	0	6	1	9	1	0	1	0	1.000	0	0-0	2	5.23	4.85
04	ChC	NL	34	0	0	10	35.0	152	27	19	18	8	3	1	0	22	0	40	1	0	2	2	.500	0	0-0	5	4.58	4.63
04	Mon	NL	11	0	0	3	14.1	69	20	12	12	3	1	1	2	5	1	8	1	0	0	0	-	0	1-1	0	7.56	7.53
3 ML YEARS			67	0	0	21	74.1	342	74	49	47	16	7	3	2	49	3	68	5	0	3	2	.600	0	1-1	7	6.02	5.69

Adrian Beltre

Bats: R Throws: R Pos: 3B-139; DH-5; PH-1

Ht: 5'11" Wt: 225 Born: 4/7/1979 Age: 30

Year	Team	Lg	G	AB	H	2B	3B	HR	(Hm	Rd)	TB	R	RBI	RC	TBB	IBB	SO	HBP	SH	SF	SB	CS	SB%	GDP	Avg	OBP	Slg
									BATTING												BASERUNNING				AVERAGES		
1998	LAD	NL	77	195	42	9	0	7	(5	2)	72	18	22	20	14	0	37	3	2	0	3	1	.75	4	.215	.278	.369
1999	LAD	NL	152	538	148	27	5	15	(6	9)	230	84	67	84	61	12	105	6	4	5	18	7	.72	4	.275	.352	.428
2000	LAD	NL	138	510	148	30	2	20	(7	13)	242	71	85	85	56	2	80	2	3	4	12	5	.71	13	.290	.360	.475
2001	LAD	NL	126	475	126	22	4	13	(4	9)	195	59	60	60	28	1	82	5	2	5	13	4	.76	9	.265	.310	.411
2002	LAD	NL	159	587	151	26	5	21	(7	14)	250	70	75	74	37	4	96	4	1	6	7	5	.58	17	.257	.303	.426
2003	LAD	NL	158	559	134	30	2	23	(13	10)	237	50	80	66	37	4	103	5	1	6	2	2	.50	13	.240	.290	.424
2004	LAD	NL	156	598	200	32	0	48	(23	25)	376	104	121	120	53	9	87	2	0	4	7	2	.78	15	.334	.388	.629
2005	Sea	AL	156	603	154	36	1	19	(7	12)	249	69	87	75	38	6	108	5	0	4	3	1	.75	15	.255	.303	.413
2006	Sea	AL	156	620	166	39	4	25	(16	9)	288	88	89	85	47	4	118	10	1	3	11	5	.69	15	.268	.328	.465

43

BATTING																							BASERUNNING				AVERAGES		
Year Team	Lg	G	AB	H	2B	3B	HR	(Hm	Rd)	TB	R	RBI	RC	TBB	IBB	SO	HBP	SH	SF	SB	CS	SB%	GDP	Avg	OBP	Slg
2007 Sea	AL	149	595	164	41	2	26	(11	15)	287	87	99	79	38	2	104	2	0	4	14	2	.88	18	.276	.319	.482
2008 Sea	AL	143	556	148	29	1	25	(10	15)	254	74	77	71	50	10	90	2	0	4	8	2	.80	11	.266	.327	.457
Postseason		4	15	4	0	0	0	(0	0)	4	1	1	1	0	0	3	0	0	1	0	0	-	0	.267	.250	.267
11 ML YEARS		1570	5836	1581	321	26	242	(109	133)	2680	774	862	819	459	54	1010	46	14	45	98	36	.73	134	.271	.327	.459

Armando Benitez

Pitches: R Bats: R Pos: RP-8

Ht: 6'4" Wt: 260 Born: 11/3/1972 Age: 36

		HOW MUCH HE PITCHED						WHAT HE GAVE UP											THE RESULTS						
Year Team	Lg	G	GS	CG	GF	IP	BFP	H	R	ER	HR	SH	SF	HB	TBB	IBB	SO	WP	Bk	W	L	Pct	ShO	Sv-Op Hld	ERC	ERA
2008 Dnedin*	A+	7	0	0	0	7.0	30	9	3	3	0	0	0	0	0	0	9	1	0	1	0	1.000	0	0- - -	3.32	3.86
2008 Syrcse*	AAA	1	0	0	1	1.0	3	0	0	0	0	0	0	0	0	0	0	0	0	0	0	-	0	0- - -	0.00	0.00
1994 Bal	AL	3	0	0	1	10.0	42	8	1	1	0	0	0	1	4	0	14	0	0	0	0	-	0	0-0 0	2.71	0.90
1995 Bal	AL	44	0	0	18	47.2	221	37	33	30	8	2	3	5	37	2	56	3	1	1	5	.167	0	2-5 6	5.06	5.66
1996 Bal	AL	18	0	0	8	14.1	56	7	6	6	2	0	1	0	6	0	20	1	0	1	0	1.000	0	4-5 1	1.78	3.77
1997 Bal	AL	71	0	0	26	73.1	307	49	22	20	7	2	4	1	43	5	106	1	0	4	5	.444	0	9-10 20	2.92	2.45
1998 Bal	AL	71	0	0	54	68.1	289	48	29	29	10	3	2	4	39	2	87	0	0	5	6	.455	0	22-26 3	3.63	3.82
1999 NYM	NL	77	0	0	42	78.0	312	40	17	16	4	0	0	0	41	4	128	2	0	4	3	.571	0	22-28 17	1.69	1.85
2000 NYM	NL	76	0	0	68	76.0	304	39	24	22	10	2	1	0	38	2	106	2	0	4	4	.500	0	41-46 0	2.08	2.61
2001 NYM	NL	73	0	0	64	76.1	320	59	32	32	12	2	1	1	40	6	93	5	0	6	4	.600	0	43-46 0	3.67	3.77
2002 NYM	NL	62	0	0	52	67.1	275	46	20	17	8	3	2	3	25	0	79	1	0	1	0	1.000	0	33-37 0	2.55	2.27
2003 3 Tms		69	0	0	49	73.0	313	59	27	24	6	0	1	0	41	3	75	3	1	4	4	.500	0	21-29 5	3.45	2.96
2004 Fla	NL	64	0	0	59	69.2	262	36	11	10	6	3	1	0	21	4	62	0	0	2	2	.500	0	47-51 0	1.36	1.29
2005 SF	NL	30	0	0	27	30.0	127	25	17	15	5	0	0	0	16	0	23	0	0	2	3	.400	0	19-23 0	4.24	4.50
2006 SF	NL	41	0	0	33	38.1	171	39	15	15	6	1	3	0	21	2	31	1	0	4	2	.667	0	17-25 1	5.11	3.52
2007 2 Tms		55	0	0	24	50.1	228	49	37	30	8	6	1	1	29	2	57	1	3	2	8	.200	0	9-16 11	5.01	5.36
2008 Tor	AL	8	0	0	2	6.1	26	4	5	4	3	0	0	0	2	0	9	0	0	0	1	.000	0	0-1 2	3.68	5.68
03 NYM		45	0	0	40	49.1	209	41	18	17	5	0	1	0	24	1	50	3	1	3	3	.500	0	21-28 0	3.46	3.10
03 NYY	AL	9	0	0	2	9.1	40	8	4	2	0	0	0	0	6	1	10	0	0	1	1	.500	0	0-0 4	3.43	1.93
03 Sea	AL	15	0	0	7	14.1	64	10	5	5	1	0	0	0	11	1	15	0	0	0	0	-	0	0-1 1	3.40	3.14
07 SF	NL	19	0	0	17	17.1	78	17	9	9	3	2	0	0	9	1	18	0	2	0	3	.000	0	9-11 0	4.77	4.67
07 Fla	NL	36	0	0	7	33.0	150	32	28	21	5	4	1	1	20	1	39	1	1	2	5	.286	0	0-5 11	5.14	5.73
Postseason		28	0	0	13	30.1	135	25	14	12	7	0	2	0	19	3	36	0	0	3	2	.600	0	4-10 5	4.66	3.56
15 ML YEARS		762	0	0	527	779.0	3253	545	296	271	95	24	22	16	403	32	946	18	5	40	47	.460	0	289-348 66	3.06	3.13

Gary Bennett

Bats: R Throws: R Pos: C-10; PH-1

Ht: 6'0" Wt: 210 Born: 4/17/1972 Age: 37

		BATTING																		BASERUNNING				AVERAGES		
Year Team	Lg	G	AB	H	2B	3B	HR	(Hm	Rd)	TB	R	RBI	RC	TBB	IBB	SO	HBP	SH	SF	SB	CS	SB%	GDP	Avg	OBP	Slg
2008 InldEm*	A+	3	7	1	0	0	0	(-	-)	1	1	1	0	1	0	1	0	0	0	0	0	-	0	.143	.250	.143
2008 LsVgs*	AAA	3	5	2	0	0	0	(-	-)	2	1	1	2	4	0	0	0	0	0	0	0	-	1	.400	.667	.400
1995 Phi	NL	1	1	0	0	0	0	(0	0)	0	0	0	0	0	0	1	0	0	0	0	0	-	0	.000	.000	.000
1996 Phi	NL	6	16	4	0	0	0	(0	0)	4	0	1	1	2	1	6	0	0	0	0	0	-	0	.250	.333	.250
1998 Phi	NL	9	31	9	0	0	0	(0	0)	9	4	3	4	5	0	5	0	0	1	0	0	-	0	.290	.378	.290
1999 Phi	NL	36	88	24	4	0	1	(0	1)	31	7	21	7	4	0	11	0	0	2	0	0	-	7	.273	.298	.352
2000 Phi	NL	31	74	18	5	0	2	(0	2)	29	8	5	12	13	0	15	2	0	0	0	0	-	0	.243	.371	.392
2001 3 Tms	NL	46	131	32	6	1	2	(2	0)	46	15	10	15	12	4	24	1	2	2	0	0	-	1	.244	.308	.351
2002 Col	NL	90	291	77	10	2	4	(2	2)	103	26	26	29	15	2	45	6	2	0	1	3	.25	10	.265	.314	.354
2003 SD	NL	96	307	73	15	0	2	(1	1)	94	26	42	33	24	3	48	2	3	2	3	0	1.00	8	.238	.296	.306
2004 Mil	NL	75	219	49	14	0	3	(3	0)	72	18	20	15	22	3	32	2	0	0	1	0	1.00	6	.224	.297	.329
2005 Was	NL	68	199	44	7	0	1	(1	0)	54	11	21	17	21	3	37	2	3	3	0	1	.00	7	.221	.298	.271
2006 StL	NL	60	157	35	5	0	4	(2	2)	52	13	22	13	11	2	30	2	0	0	0	0	-	3	.223	.274	.331
2007 StL	NL	59	155	39	7	0	2	(0	2)	52	12	17	14	8	1	16	1	2	4	1	1	.50	6	.252	.286	.335
2008 LAD	NL	10	21	4	1	0	1	(0	1)	8	1	4	2	2	0	0	0	0	0	0	0	-	1	.190	.261	.381
01 Phi	NL	26	75	16	3	1	1	(1	0)	24	8	6	7	9	1	19	0	1	1	0	0	-	1	.213	.294	.320
01 NYM	NL	1	1	1	0	0	0	(0	0)	1	0	0	1	0	0	0	0	0	0	0	0	-	0	1.000	1.000	1.000
01 Col	NL	19	55	15	3	0	1	(1	0)	21	7	4	7	3	3	5	1	1	1	0	0	-	0	.273	.317	.382
Postseason		3	1	0	0	0	0	(0	0)	0	0	0	0	1	0	0	0	0	0	0	0	-	0	.000	.000	.000
13 ML YEARS		587	1690	408	74	3	22	(11	11)	554	141	192	162	139	19	270	16	14	17	6	5	.55	53	.241	.302	.328

Jeff Bennett

Pitches: R Bats: R Pos: RP-68; SP-4

Ht: 6'3" Wt: 200 Born: 6/10/1980 Age: 29

		HOW MUCH HE PITCHED						WHAT HE GAVE UP											THE RESULTS						
Year Team	Lg	G	GS	CG	GF	IP	BFP	H	R	ER	HR	SH	SF	HB	TBB	IBB	SO	WP	Bk	W	L	Pct	ShO	Sv-Op Hld	ERC	ERA
2008 MrtlBh*	A+	4	4	0	0	4.0	13	3	0	0	0	0	0	0	0	0	3	0	0	0	0	-	0	0- - -	1.30	0.00
2004 Mil	NL	60	0	0	20	71.1	316	78	43	38	12	2	5	2	26	2	45	6	0	1	5	.167	0	0-1 8	4.98	4.79
2007 Atl	NL	3	2	0	0	13.0	57	14	5	5	3	1	1	0	3	1	14	1	0	2	1	.667	0	0-0 0	4.41	3.46
2008 Atl	NL	72	4	0	12	97.1	419	86	44	40	5	6	5	7	47	6	68	5	0	3	7	.300	0	3-4 15	3.62	3.70
3 ML YEARS		135	6	0	32	181.2	792	178	92	83	20	9	11	9	76	9	127	12	0	6	13	.316	0	3-5 23	4.21	4.11

Joaquin Benoit

Pitches: R Bats: R Pos: RP-44

Ht: 6'3" Wt: 220 Born: 7/26/1977 Age: 31

		HOW MUCH HE PITCHED						WHAT HE GAVE UP											THE RESULTS						
Year Team	Lg	G	GS	CG	GF	IP	BFP	H	R	ER	HR	SH	SF	HB	TBB	IBB	SO	WP	Bk	W	L	Pct	ShO	Sv-Op Hld	ERC	ERA
2008 Frisco*	AA	3	1	0	0	1.2	13	4	3	3	0	0	0	1	4	0	2	2	0	0	0	-	0	0- - -	26.61	16.20
2008 Okla*	AAA	2	0	0	0	3.0	9	1	0	0	0	0	0	0	0	0	3	0	0	1	0	1.000	0	0- - -	0.28	0.00
2001 Tex	AL	1	1	0	0	5.0	26	8	6	6	3	0	1	0	3	0	4	0	0	0	0	-	0	0-0 0	13.11	10.80
2002 Tex	AL	17	13	0	2	84.2	405	91	51	50	6	4	3	5	58	2	59	7	0	4	5	.444	0	1-1 0	5.52	5.31

Year	Team	Lg	G	GS	CG	GF	IP	BFP	H	R	ER	HR	SH	SF	HB	TBB	IBB	SO	WP	Bk	W	L	Pct	ShO	Sv-Op	Hld	ERC	ERA
2003	Tex	AL	25	17	0	1	105.0	462	99	67	64	23	1	4	3	51	0	87	3	1	8	5	.615	0	0-0	0	5.03	5.49
2004	Tex	AL	28	15	0	2	103.0	456	113	67	65	19	2	10	8	31	0	95	3	0	5	5	.375	0	0-0	0	5.10	5.68
2005	Tex	AL	32	9	0	6	87.0	369	69	39	36	9	2	1	2	38	0	78	1	0	4	4	.500	0	0-0	5	3.15	3.72
2006	Tex	AL	56	0	0	7	79.2	347	68	49	43	5	0	3	3	38	4	85	3	0	1	1	.500	0	0-2	7	3.30	4.86
2007	Tex	AL	70	0	0	22	82.0	337	68	28	26	6	3	2	2	28	2	87	3	0	7	4	.636	0	6-13	19	2.83	2.85
2008	Tex	AL	44	0	0	8	45.0	209	40	28	25	6	2	0	0	35	2	43	3	0	3	2	.600	0	1-4	13	5.02	5.00
8 ML YEARS			273	55	0	48	591.1	2611	556	335	315	77	14	24	23	282	10	538	23	1	30	26	.536	0	8-20	44	4.33	4.79

Jason Bergmann

Pitches: R Bats: R Pos: SP-22; RP-8

Ht: 6'4" Wt: 216 Born: 9/25/1981 Age: 27

Year	Team	Lg	G	GS	CG	GF	IP	BFP	H	R	ER	HR	SH	SF	HB	TBB	IBB	SO	WP	Bk	W	L	Pct	ShO	Sv-Op	Hld	ERC	ERA
2008	Clmbs*	AAA	5	5	0	0	29.0	123	26	13	12	2	1	2	0	11	0	27	1	0	2	2	.500	0	0--	-	3.18	3.72
2005	Was	NL	15	1	0	4	19.2	85	14	6	6	1	1	1	2	11	1	21	0	0	2	0	1.000	0	0-0	1	3.05	2.75
2006	Was	NL	29	6	0	7	64.2	303	81	49	48	12	6	4	6	27	6	54	3	0	2	0	.000	0	0-0	1	6.50	6.68
2007	Was	NL	21	21	0	0	115.1	480	99	59	57	18	6	1	2	42	1	86	4	0	6	6	.500	0	0-0	3	3.59	4.45
2008	Was	NL	30	22	1	1	139.2	614	153	94	79	25	9	8	1	47	2	96	2	0	2	11	.154	0	0-0	4	4.88	5.09
4 ML YEARS			95	50	1	12	339.1	1482	347	208	190	56	22	14	11	127	10	257	9	0	10	19	.345	0	0-0	2	4.61	5.04

Lance Berkman

Bats: B Throws: L Pos: 1B-152; DH-5; PH-2

Ht: 6'1" Wt: 220 Born: 2/10/1976 Age: 33

Year	Team	Lg	G	AB	H	2B	3B	HR	(Hm	Rd)	TB	R	RBI	RC	TBB	IBB	SO	HBP	SH	SF	SB	CS	SB%	GDP	Avg	OBP	Slg
1999	Hou	NL	34	93	22	2	0	4	(2	2)	36	10	15	12	12	0	21	0	0	1	5	1	.83	2	.237	.321	.387
2000	Hou	NL	114	353	105	28	1	21	(10	11)	198	76	67	76	56	1	73	1	0	7	6	2	.75	6	.297	.388	.561
2001	Hou	NL	156	577	191	55	5	34	(13	21)	358	110	126	144	92	5	121	13	0	6	7	9	.44	8	.331	.430	.620
2002	Hou	NL	158	578	169	35	2	42	(20	22)	334	106	128	130	107	20	118	4	0	3	8	4	.67	10	.292	.405	.578
2003	Hou	NL	153	538	155	35	6	25	(11	14)	277	110	93	115	107	13	108	9	1	3	5	3	.63	10	.288	.412	.515
2004	Hou	NL	160	544	172	40	3	30	(8	22)	308	104	106	126	127	14	101	10	0	6	9	7	.56	10	.316	.450	.566
2005	Hou	NL	132	468	137	34	1	24	(13	11)	245	76	82	88	91	12	72	4	0	2	4	1	.80	18	.293	.411	.524
2006	Hou	NL	152	536	169	29	0	45	(24	21)	333	95	136	138	98	22	106	4	0	8	3	2	.60	11	.315	.420	.621
2007	Hou	NL	153	561	156	24	2	34	(13	21)	286	95	102	105	94	11	125	8	0	5	7	3	.70	11	.278	.386	.510
2008	Hou	NL	159	554	173	46	4	29	(16	13)	314	114	106	129	99	18	108	7	0	5	18	4	.82	13	.312	.420	.567
Postseason			29	106	34	8	0	6	(4	2)	60	18	26	27	20	5	26	1	0	2	2	1	.67	4	.321	.426	.566
10 ML YEARS			1371	4802	1449	328	24	288	(130	158)	2689	896	961	1063	883	116	953	60	1	46	72	36	.67	99	.302	.413	.560

Roger Bernadina

Bats: L Throws: L Pos: CF-14; LF-6; PH-5; PR-1

Ht: 6'1" Wt: 192 Born: 6/12/1984 Age: 25

Year	Team	Lg	G	AB	H	2B	3B	HR	(Hm	Rd)	TB	R	RBI	RC	TBB	IBB	SO	HBP	SH	SF	SB	CS	SB%	GDP	Avg	OBP	Slg
2002	Expos	R	57	196	54	7	0	3	(-	-)	70	22	18	26	19	0	25	4	0	2	1	0	1.00	2	.276	.348	.357
2003	Savann	A	77	278	66	12	3	4	(-	-)	96	36	39	30	19	1	53	4	3	4	11	4	.73	3	.237	.292	.345
2004	Savann	A	129	450	107	24	7	7	(-	-)	166	67	66	66	60	1	113	11	1	6	24	2	.92	7	.238	.338	.369
2005	Savann	A	122	417	97	15	3	12	(-	-)	154	64	54	66	75	0	92	7	2	4	35	8	.81	9	.233	.356	.369
2006	Ptomc	A+	123	434	117	19	3	6	(-	-)	160	60	42	63	56	1	98	4	4	4	28	11	.72	4	.270	.355	.369
2007	Hrsbrg	AA	97	371	100	15	2	6	(-	-)	137	58	36	52	38	0	80	2	3	1	40	13	.75	9	.270	.340	.369
2007	Clmbs	AAA	13	42	7	3	0	0	(-	-)	10	6	1	3	9	0	11	1	1	0	1	0	1.00	0	.167	.327	.238
2008	Hrsbrg	AA	73	266	86	11	7	5	(-	-)	126	47	38	52	31	0	64	2	4	0	26	9	.74	4	.323	.398	.474
2008	Clmbs	AAA	47	191	67	13	3	4	(-	-)	98	33	16	40	16	0	37	1	7	0	15	2	.88	4	.351	.404	.513
2008	Was	NL	26	76	16	1	1	0	(0	0)	19	10	2	4	9	0	21	0	1	0	4	3	.57	3	.211	.294	.250

Doug Bernier

Bats: B Throws: R Pos: 2B-2

Ht: 5'11" Wt: 175 Born: 6/24/1980 Age: 29

Year	Team	Lg	G	AB	H	2B	3B	HR	(Hm	Rd)	TB	R	RBI	RC	TBB	IBB	SO	HBP	SH	SF	SB	CS	SB%	GDP	Avg	OBP	Slg
2002	TriCity	A-	64	208	41	5	0	1	(-	-)	49	26	24	26	58	0	55	4	8	1	3	4	.43	2	.197	.380	.236
2003	Visalia	A+	84	268	54	5	0	0	(-	-)	59	50	21	30	64	1	63	2	6	1	12	2	.86	3	.201	.358	.220
2004	Visalia	A+	102	349	95	13	1	3	(-	-)	119	56	24	46	45	0	94	2	3	0	5	4	.56	8	.272	.359	.341
2005	Tulsa	AA	117	369	75	14	2	3	(-	-)	102	33	39	33	46	1	103	8	11	7	1	4	.20	10	.203	.300	.276
2006	Tulsa	AA	87	246	69	16	3	1	(-	-)	94	44	27	37	30	0	46	2	9	2	4	1	.80	8	.280	.361	.382
2007	ColSpr	AAA	97	216	67	15	0	2	(-	-)	88	27	27	37	31	0	51	1	2	2	4	2	.67	7	.310	.396	.407
2008	ColSpr	AAA	110	337	86	10	4	9	(-	-)	131	58	42	56	64	3	79	8	5	4	1	2	.33	10	.255	.383	.389
2008	Col	NL	2	4	0	0	0	0	(0	0)	0	0	0	0	0	0	1	0	0	0	0	0	-	0	.000	.000	.000

Angel Berroa

Bats: R Throws: R Pos: SS-79; 2B-5; PH-4; PR-3

Ht: 6'0" Wt: 195 Born: 1/27/1978 Age: 31

Year	Team	Lg	G	AB	H	2B	3B	HR	(Hm	Rd)	TB	R	RBI	RC	TBB	IBB	SO	HBP	SH	SF	SB	CS	SB%	GDP	Avg	OBP	Slg
2008	Omha*	AAA	51	189	55	13	0	10	(-	-)	98	34	27	31	8	0	25	2	0	2	4	2	.67	4	.291	.323	.519
2001	KC	AL	15	53	16	2	0	0	(0	0)	18	8	4	6	3	0	10	0	0	0	2	0	1.00	0	.302	.339	.340
2002	KC	AL	20	75	17	7	1	0	(0	0)	26	8	5	8	7	1	10	1	0	0	3	0	1.00	1	.227	.301	.347
2003	KC	AL	158	567	163	28	7	17	(6	11)	256	92	73	82	29	3	100	18	13	8	21	5	.81	13	.287	.338	.451
2004	KC	AL	134	512	134	27	6	8	(3	5)	197	72	43	62	23	0	87	12	5	2	14	8	.64	10	.262	.308	.385
2005	KC	AL	159	608	164	21	5	11	(6	5)	228	68	55	68	18	3	108	14	10	2	7	5	.58	13	.270	.305	.375

Year Team	Lg	G	AB	H	2B	3B	HR	(Hm Rd)	TB	R	RBI	RC	TBB	IBB	SO	HBP	SH	SF	SB	CS	SB%	GDP	Avg	OBP	Slg
2006 KC	AL	132	474	111	18	1	9	(6 3)	158	45	54	32	14	1	88	3	9	3	3	1	.75	21	.234	.259	.333
2007 KC	AL	9	11	1	0	0	0	(0 0)	1	0	1	0	0	0	4	1	1	0	0	1			.091	.167	.091
2008 LAD	NL	84	226	52	13	1	1	(1 0)	70	26	16	14	20	4	41	4	6	0	0	0		13	.230	.304	.310
8 ML YEARS		711	2526	658	116	21	46	(22 24)	954	319	251	272	114	12	448	53	44	15	50	20	.71	74	.260	.305	.378

Rafael Betancourt

Pitches: R **Bats:** R **Pos:** RP-69

Ht: 6'2" **Wt:** 200 **Born:** 4/29/1975 **Age:** 34

Year Team	Lg	G	GS	CG	GF	IP	BFP	H	R	ER	HR	SH	SF	HB	TBB	IBB	SO	WP	Bk	W	L	Pct	ShO	Sv-Op	Hld	ERC	ERA
2003 Cle	AL	33	0	0	13	38.0	154	27	11	9	5	1	1	1	13	2	36	1	0	2	2	.500	0	1-3	4	2.54	2.13
2004 Cle	AL	68	0	0	21	66.2	286	71	32	29	7	1	2	0	18	6	76	5	1	5	6	.455	0	4-11	12	3.77	3.92
2005 Cle	AL	54	0	0	12	67.2	272	57	23	21	5	1	0	0	17	2	73	0	0	4	3	.571	0	1-3	10	2.49	2.79
2006 Cle	AL	50	0	0	17	56.2	231	52	25	24	7	2	2	0	11	5	48	0	0	3	4	.429	0	3-6	7	2.84	3.81
2007 Cle	AL	68	0	0	15	79.1	289	51	13	13	4	0	2	0	9	3	80	0	0	5	1	.833	0	3-6	31	1.24	1.47
2008 Cle	AL	69	0	0	20	71.0	309	76	41	40	11	4	5	0	25	5	64	2	0	3	4	.429	0	4-8	12	4.53	5.07
Postseason		7	0	0	2	10.0	39	7	7	6	1	1	1	0	1	1	9	0	0	0	0	-	0	0-0	2	1.42	5.40
6 ML YEARS		342	0	0	98	379.1	1541	334	145	136	39	9	12	1	93	23	377	8	1	22	20	.524	0	16-37	76	2.79	3.23

Yuniesky Betancourt

Bats: R **Throws:** R **Pos:** SS-153; PH-2; PR-1

Ht: 5'10" **Wt:** 195 **Born:** 1/31/1982 **Age:** 27

Year Team	Lg	G	AB	H	2B	3B	HR	(Hm Rd)	TB	R	RBI	RC	TBB	IBB	SO	HBP	SH	SF	SB	CS	SB%	GDP	Avg	OBP	Slg
2005 Sea	AL	60	211	54	11	5	1	(1 0)	78	24	15	21	11	0	24	2	2	2		3	.25	2	.256	.296	.370
2006 Sea	AL	157	558	161	28	6	8	(2 6)	225	68	47	60	17	0	54	1	7	1	11	8	.58	10	.289	.310	.403
2007 Sea	AL	155	536	155	38	2	9	(6 3)	224	72	67	73	15	3	48	1	3	4	5	4	.56	10	.289	.308	.418
2008 Sea	AL	153	559	156	36	3	7	(3 4)	219	66	51	53	17	0	42	2	6	6	4	4	.50	23	.279	.300	.392
4 ML YEARS		525	1864	526	113	16	25	(12 13)	746	230	180	207	60	3	168	6	18	13	21	19	.53	45	.282	.305	.400

Wilson Betemit

Bats: B **Throws:** R **Pos:** 1B-36; PH-28; 3B-21; SS-14; 2B-3; PR-3; DH-1

Ht: 6'3" **Wt:** 230 **Born:** 11/2/1981 **Age:** 27

Year Team	Lg	G	AB	H	2B	3B	HR	(Hm Rd)	TB	R	RBI	RC	TBB	IBB	SO	HBP	SH	SF	SB	CS	SB%	GDP	Avg	OBP	Slg
2008 S-WB*	AAA	8	27	9	4	0	1	(- -)	16	5	5	7	6	0	7	0	0	0	0	0	-	0	.333	.455	.593
2001 Atl	NL	8	3	0	0	0	0	(0 0)	0	1	0	0	2	0	3	0	0	0	1	0	1.00	0	.000	.400	.000
2004 Atl	NL	22	47	8	0	0	0	(0 0)	8	2	3	0	4	0	16	0	0	1	1	0	1.00	0	.170	.231	.170
2005 Atl	NL	115	246	75	12	4	4	(0 4)	107	36	20	36	22	4	55	0	4	2	1	3	.25	5	.305	.359	.435
2006 2 Tms	NL	143	373	98	23	0	18	(7 11)	175	49	53	52	36	6	102	0	1	2	3	1	.75	11	.263	.326	.469
2007 2 Tms	NL	121	240	55	12	0	14	(8 6)	109	33	50	42	38	0	82	1	2	3	0	0	-	2	.229	.333	.454
2008 NYY	AL	87	189	50	13	0	6	(5 1)	81	24	25	17	6	0	56	1	1	1	0	1	.00	7	.265	.289	.429
06 Atl	NL	88	199	56	16	0	9	(3 6)	99	30	29	35	19	3	57	0	1	0	2	1	.67	4	.281	.344	.497
06 LAD	NL	55	174	42	7	0	9	(4 5)	76	19	24	17	17	3	45	0	0	2	1	0	1.00	1	.241	.306	.437
07 LAD	NL	84	156	36	8	0	10	(6 4)	74	22	26	26	32	0	49	1	0	3	0	0	-	1	.231	.359	.474
07 NYY	AL	37	84	19	4	0	4	(2 2)	35	11	24	16	6	0	33	0	2	0	0	0	-	1	.226	.278	.417
Postseason		6	10	5	1	0	1	(0 1)	9	3	1	2	2	1	2	0	0	0	0	0	-	0	.500	.583	.900
6 ML YEARS		496	1098	286	60	4	42	(20 22)	480	145	151	147	108	10	314	2	8	9	5	6	.45	25	.260	.325	.437

Randor Bierd

Pitches: R **Bats:** R **Pos:** RP-29

Ht: 6'4" **Wt:** 190 **Born:** 3/14/1984 **Age:** 25

Year Team	Lg	G	GS	CG	GF	IP	BFP	H	R	ER	HR	SH	SF	HB	TBB	IBB	SO	WP	Bk	W	L	Pct	ShO	Sv-Op	Hld	ERC	ERA
2004 Tigers	R	11	1	0	3	32.1	127	23	11	10	3	1	0	4	5	0	39	1	2	1	3	.250	0	0- -	-	2.11	2.78
2004 Lkland	A+	4	4	0	0	19.1	85	22	15	14	2	2	1	9	0	18	2	1	0	3	.000	0	0- -	-	5.58	6.52
2005 WMich	A	7	7	0	0	44.1	170	30	14	13	2	1	1	3	10	0	42	3	2	4	1	.800	0	0- -	-	1.79	2.64
2005 Erie	AA	4	4	0	0	21.2	104	28	19	13	2	1	3	8	0	10	1	0	1	3	.250	0	0- -	-	6.03	5.40
2005 Lkland	A+	4	4	0	0	20.2	88	22	14	13	4	0	2	4	0	18	1	0	1	3	.250	0	0- -	-	4.66	5.66
2006 Oneont	A-	20	2	0	7	38.1	182	48	30	28	2	2	1	15	0	41	8	0	5	0	1.000	0	0- -	-	5.28	6.57
2007 WMich	A	15	0	0	10	22.0	88	17	8	5	1	0	0	6	0	29	0	0	1	1	.500	0	0- -	-	2.27	2.05
2007 Erie	AA	27	3	0	8	45.2	180	31	18	17	1	2	0	3	10	0	52	5	0	3	2	.600	0	1- -	-	1.60	3.35
2008 Bowie	AA	5	1	0	0	6.0	28	7	3	3	0	1	0	1	3	0	9	1	0	0	0	-	0	0- -	-	5.37	4.50
2008 Frdrck	A+	3	0	0	1	3.0	11	0	0	0	0	0	0	0	2	0	7	0	0	0	0	-	0	0- -	-	0.46	0.00
2008 Orioles	R	3	0	0	0	4.0	18	3	3	1	0	0	1	0	1	0	5	1	0	0	0	-	0	0- -	-	1.47	2.25
2008 Bal	AL	29	0	0	8	36.2	178	48	21	20	3	1	3	3	19	2	25	4	0	0	2	.000	0	0-0	0	6.40	4.91

Chad Billingsley

Pitches: R **Bats:** R **Pos:** SP-32; RP-3

Ht: 6'1" **Wt:** 245 **Born:** 7/29/1984 **Age:** 24

Year Team	Lg	G	GS	CG	GF	IP	BFP	H	R	ER	HR	SH	SF	HB	TBB	IBB	SO	WP	Bk	W	L	Pct	ShO	Sv-Op	Hld	ERC	ERA
2006 LAD	NL	18	16	0	0	90.0	403	92	43	38	7	4	0	3	58	3	59	5	0	7	4	.636	0	0-0	0	5.22	3.80
2007 LAD	NL	43	20	1	6	147.0	623	131	56	54	15	9	3	3	64	3	141	5	0	12	5	.706	0	0-1	3	3.70	3.31
2008 LAD	NL	35	32	1	1	200.2	859	188	76	70	14	8	5	8	80	6	201	10	0	16	10	.615	1	0-0	1	3.62	3.14
Postseason		2	0	0	0	2.0	6	1	0	0	0	0	0	0	0	0	3	0	0	0	0	-	0	0-0	0	0.63	0.00
3 ML YEARS		96	68	2	7	437.2	1885	411	175	162	36	21	8	14	202	12	401	20	0	35	19	.648	1	0-1	4	3.96	3.33

Kurt Birkins

Pitches: L Bats: L Pos: RP-6   Ht: 6'2" Wt: 192 Born: 8/11/1980 Age: 28

			HOW MUCH HE PITCHED						WHAT HE GAVE UP										THE RESULTS						
Year	Team	Lg	G	GS	CG	GF	IP	BFP	H	R	ER	HR	SH	SF	HB	TBB	IBB	SO	WP	Bk	W	L	Pct	ShO	Sv-Op	Hld	ERC	ERA
2008	Drham*	AAA	36	1	0	6	40.2	207	57	34	34	4	4	1	2	28	0	29	2	0	2	3	.400	0	0- -	-	7.83	7.52
2006	Bal	AL	35	0	0	4	31.0	136	25	19	17	4	2	2	3	16	0	27	3	0	5	2	.714	0	0-1	4	3.98	4.94
2007	Bal	AL	19	2	0	7	34.1	170	52	31	31	3	0	0	3	14	0	30	1	0	1	2	.333	0	0-0	0	7.41	8.13
2008	TB	AL	6	0	0	2	10.0	37	5	1	1	0	0	1	0	5	0	7	0	0	0	0	-	0	0-0	0	1.53	0.90
	3 ML YEARS		60	2	0	13	75.1	343	82	51	49	7	2	3	6	35	0	64	4	0	6	4	.600	0	0-1	4	5.08	5.85

Brian Bixler

Bats: R Throws: R Pos: SS-39; PR-10; PH-5   Ht: 6'1" Wt: 198 Born: 10/22/1982 Age: 26

									BATTING														BASERUNNING				AVERAGES		
Year	Team	Lg	G	AB	H	2B	3B	HR	(Hm	Rd)	TB	R	RBI	RC	TBB	IBB	SO	HBP	SH	SF	SB	CS	SB%	GDP	Avg	OBP	Slg
2004	Wmspt	A-	59	228	63	7	4	0	(-	-)	78	40	21	27	15	0	51	2	1	4	14	5	.74	3	.276	.321	.342
2005	Hkry	A	126	502	141	23	2	9	(-	-)	195	74	50	70	38	0	134	11	3	3	21	10	.68	5	.281	.343	.388
2006	Lynbrg	A+	73	267	81	16	2	5	(-	-)	116	46	33	50	35	1	58	9	6	0	18	7	.72	2	.303	.402	.434
2006	Altna	AA	60	226	68	13	1	3	(-	-)	92	36	19	35	16	0	57	7	2	2	6	2	.75	2	.301	.363	.407
2007	Indy	AAA	129	475	130	23	10	5	(-	-)	188	77	51	78	53	1	131	18	10	0	28	4	.88	6	.274	.346	.396
2008	Indy	AAA	86	321	90	8	5	7	(-	-)	129	44	36	48	27	0	107	7	6	3	23	7	.77	4	.280	.346	.402
2008	Pit	NL	50	108	17	2	1	0	(0	0)	21	16	2	2	6	2	36	4	2	0	1	0	1.00	1	.157	.229	.194

Nick Blackburn

Pitches: R Bats: R Pos: SP-33   Ht: 6'4" Wt: 227 Born: 2/24/1982 Age: 27

				HOW MUCH HE PITCHED					WHAT HE GAVE UP										THE RESULTS						
Year	Team	Lg	G	GS	CG	GF	IP	BFP	H	R	ER	HR	SH	SF	HB	TBB	IBB	SO	WP	Bk	W	L	Pct	ShO	Sv-Op	Hld	ERC	ERA
2002	Elizab	R+	13	13	0	0	66.2	293	70	41	37	6	2	0	2	21	0	62	1	0	3	3	.500	0	0- -	-	3.97	5.00
2003	QuadC	A	16	10	2	4	76.0	320	78	44	41	13	4	3	4	18	0	40	5	0	2	9	.182	1	1- -	-	4.30	4.86
2004	QuadC	A	20	13	1	5	84.1	342	69	37	26	3	3	5	2	23	1	66	2	1	6	4	.600	1	1- -	-	2.31	2.77
2004	FtMyrs	A+	9	7	0	0	37.1	171	51	30	26	7	4	2	2	7	1	21	1	0	3	3	.500	0	0- -	-	6.08	6.27
2005	FtMyrs	A+	15	15	1	0	93.2	381	95	43	35	5	0	2	5	16	0	55	1	0	7	5	.583	0	0- -	-	3.25	3.36
2005	NwBrit	AA	7	7	2	0	49.0	186	35	16	10	1	3	1	2	10	1	27	1	0	2	4	.333	1	0- -	-	1.66	1.84
2005	Roch	AAA	3	3	0	0	14.0	65	20	11	8	2	1	0	0	3	0	7	0	0	0	0	-	0	0- -	-	6.02	5.14
2006	NwBrit	AA	30	19	2	3	132.1	565	141	72	65	11	3	5	8	37	2	81	7	0	7	8	.467	1	0- -	-	4.11	4.42
2007	NwBrit	AA	8	7	0	0	38.0	160	36	21	13	1	1	1	1	7	0	18	1	0	3	1	.750	0	0- -	-	2.51	3.08
2007	Roch	AAA	17	17	3	0	110.2	433	96	32	26	7	3	3	2	12	0	57	0	0	7	3	.700	2	0- -	-	2.17	2.11
2007	Min	AL	6	0	0	3	11.2	54	19	12	10	2	0	0	0	2	0	8	0	0	0	2	.000	0	0-1	1	7.61	7.71
2008	Min	AL	33	33	0	0	193.1	823	224	102	87	23	5	4	7	39	4	96	2	0	11	11	.500	0	0-0	0	4.48	4.05
	2 ML YEARS		39	33	0	3	205.0	877	243	114	97	25	5	4	7	41	4	104	2	0	11	13	.458	0	0-1	1	4.64	4.26

Casey Blake

Bats: R Throws: R Pos: 3B-133; 1B-29; PH-3; 2B-1; SS-1   Ht: 6'2" Wt: 210 Born: 8/23/1973 Age: 35

									BATTING														BASERUNNING				AVERAGES		
Year	Team	Lg	G	AB	H	2B	3B	HR	(Hm	Rd)	TB	R	RBI	RC	TBB	IBB	SO	HBP	SH	SF	SB	CS	SB%	GDP	Avg	OBP	Slg
1999	Tor	AL	14	39	10	2	0	1	(0	1)	15	6	1	4	2	0	7	0	0	0	0	0	-	1	.256	.293	.385
2000	Min	AL	7	16	3	2	0	0	(0	0)	5	1	1	2	3	0	7	1	0	1	0	0	-	1	.188	.333	.313
2001	2 Tms	AL	19	37	9	1	0	1	(0	1)	13	3	4	5	4	1	12	0	0	0	3	0	1.00	0	.243	.317	.351
2002	Min	AL	9	20	4	1	0	0	(0	0)	5	2	1	1	2	0	7	0	0	0	0	0	-	0	.200	.273	.250
2003	Cle	AL	152	557	143	35	4	17	(2	15)	229	80	67	68	38	1	109	10	8	8	7	9	.44	11	.257	.312	.411
2004	Cle	AL	152	587	159	36	3	28	(13	15)	285	93	88	88	68	2	139	9	1	3	5	8	.38	19	.271	.354	.486
2005	Cle	AL	147	523	126	32	1	23	(7	16)	229	72	58	53	43	3	116	10	2	5	4	5	.44	9	.241	.308	.438
2006	Cle	AL	109	401	113	20	1	19	(10	9)	192	63	68	62	45	5	93	4	1	5	6	0	1.00	11	.282	.356	.479
2007	Cle	AL	156	588	159	36	4	18	(11	7)	257	81	78	69	54	2	123	10	5	5	4	5	.44	14	.270	.339	.437
2008	2 Tms	AL	152	536	147	36	1	21	(6	15)	248	71	81	85	49	11	120	11	1	4	3	0	1.00	12	.274	.345	.463
01	Min	AL	13	22	7	1	0	0	(0	0)	8	1	2	4	3	1	8	0	0	0	1	0	1.00	0	.318	.400	.364
01	Bal	AL	6	15	2	0	0	1	(0	1)	5	2	2	1	1	0	4	0	0	0	2	0	1.00	0	.133	.188	.333
08	Cle	AL	94	325	94	24	0	11	(1	10)	151	46	58	64	33	6	68	7	1	2	2	0	1.00	3	.289	.365	.465
08	LAD	NL	58	211	53	12	1	10	(5	5)	97	25	23	21	16	5	52	4	0	2	1	0	1.00	9	.251	.313	.460
	Postseason		11	43	11	3	0	1	(1	0)	17	5	4	4	1	0	12	0	1	0	0	0	-	1	.256	.273	.395
	10 ML YEARS		917	3304	873	201	10	128	(48	80)	1478	472	447	437	308	25	733	55	18	31	32	27	.54	78	.264	.334	.447

Hank Blalock

Bats: L Throws: R Pos: 1B-34; 3B-31   Ht: 6'1" Wt: 200 Born: 11/21/1980 Age: 28

									BATTING														BASERUNNING				AVERAGES		
Year	Team	Lg	G	AB	H	2B	3B	HR	(Hm	Rd)	TB	R	RBI	RC	TBB	IBB	SO	HBP	SH	SF	SB	CS	SB%	GDP	Avg	OBP	Slg
2008	Okla*	AAA	2	5	2	1	0	0	(-	-)	2	1	0	1	1	0	1	0	0	0	0	0	-	0	.400	.500	.400
2008	Frisco*	AA	6	19	8	3	0	0	(-	-)	11	5	4	5	4	1	5	0	0	0	1	0	1.00	1	.421	.522	.579
2002	Tex	AL	49	147	31	8	0	3	(2	1)	48	16	17	15	20	1	43	1	2	2	0	0	-	2	.211	.306	.327
2003	Tex	AL	143	567	170	33	3	29	(18	11)	296	89	90	90	44	1	97	1	0	3	2	3	.40	16	.300	.350	.522
2004	Tex	AL	159	624	172	38	3	32	(16	16)	312	107	110	119	75	7	149	6	0	8	2	2	.50	13	.276	.355	.500
2005	Tex	AL	161	647	170	34	0	25	(20	5)	279	80	92	86	51	1	132	3	0	4	1	0	1.00	16	.263	.318	.431
2006	Tex	AL	152	591	157	26	3	16	(8	8)	237	76	89	87	51	6	98	2	0	2	1	0	1.00	15	.266	.325	.401
2007	Tex	AL	58	208	61	16	3	10	(7	3)	113	32	33	38	21	1	38	1	0	2	4	1	.80	8	.293	.358	.543
2008	Tex	AL	65	258	74	19	1	12	(6	6)	131	37	38	36	19	3	40	2	0	2	1	0	1.00	10	.287	.338	.508
	7 ML YEARS		787	3042	835	174	13	127	(77	50)	1416	437	469	471	281	20	597	16	2	23	11	6	.65	80	.274	.337	.465

Gregor Blanco

Bats: L **Throws:** L **Pos:** LF-77; CF-69; PH-9; PR-6; RF-5   **Ht:** 5'11" **Wt:** 170 **Born:** 12/12/1983 **Age:** 25

									BATTING												BASERUNNING				AVERAGES		
Year	Team	Lg	G	AB	H	2B	3B	HR	(Hm	Rd)	TB	R	RBI	RC	TBB	IBB	SO	HBP	SH	SF	SB	CS	SB%	GDP	Avg	OBP	Slg
2002	Macon	A	132	468	127	14	9	7	(-	-)	180	87	36	81	85	0	120	9	6	2	40	16	.71	2	.271	.392	.385
2003	MrtlBh	A+	126	461	125	19	7	5	(-	-)	173	66	36	67	54	0	114	8	3	1	34	16	.68	4	.271	.357	.375
2004	MrtlBh	A+	119	436	116	17	9	8	(-	-)	175	73	41	64	47	4	114	3	6	3	25	9	.74	5	.266	.339	.401
2005	Missi	AA	123	401	101	11	12	6	(-	-)	154	64	35	64	74	2	124	2	7	3	26	12	.68	7	.252	.369	.384
2006	Missi	AA	66	251	72	16	3	0	(-	-)	94	45	9	42	43	0	57	3	5	0	17	6	.74	3	.287	.397	.375
2006	Rchmd	AAA	73	269	79	12	1	0	(-	-)	93	43	19	43	52	1	53	0	6	0	14	9	.61	5	.294	.408	.346
2007	Rchmd	AAA	124	464	131	18	5	3	(-	-)	168	81	35	66	63	0	85	2	14	2	23	18	.56	5	.282	.369	.362
2008	Atl	NL	144	430	108	14	4	1	(0	1)	133	52	38	60	74	2	99	6	6	3	13	5	.72	3	.251	.366	.309

Henry Blanco

Bats: R **Throws:** R **Pos:** C-45; PH-19; 1B-1   **Ht:** 5'11" **Wt:** 220 **Born:** 8/29/1971 **Age:** 37

									BATTING												BASERUNNING				AVERAGES		
Year	Team	Lg	G	AB	H	2B	3B	HR	(Hm	Rd)	TB	R	RBI	RC	TBB	IBB	SO	HBP	SH	SF	SB	CS	SB%	GDP	Avg	OBP	Slg
1997	LAD	NL	3	5	2	0	0	1	(0	1)	5	1	1	2	0	0	1	0	0	0	0	0	-	0	.400	.400	1.000
1999	Col	NL	88	263	61	12	3	6	(3	3)	97	30	28	32	34	1	38	1	3	2	1	1	.50	4	.232	.320	.369
2000	Mil	NL	93	284	67	24	0	7	(3	4)	112	29	31	33	36	6	60	0	0	4	0	3	.00	9	.236	.318	.394
2001	Mil	NL	104	314	66	18	3	6	(4	2)	108	33	31	30	34	6	72	2	5	2	3	1	.75	10	.210	.290	.344
2002	Atl	NL	81	221	45	9	1	6	(4	2)	74	17	22	15	20	5	51	1	2	5	0	2	.00	5	.204	.267	.335
2003	Atl	NL	55	151	30	8	0	1	(0	1)	41	11	13	13	10	2	21	1	3	1	0	0	-	3	.199	.252	.272
2004	Min	AL	114	315	65	19	1	10	(4	6)	116	36	37	35	21	0	56	3	11	3	0	3	.00	8	.206	.260	.368
2005	ChC	NL	54	161	39	6	0	6	(2	4)	63	16	25	17	11	1	24	0	4	2	0	0	-	6	.242	.287	.391
2006	ChC	NL	74	241	64	15	2	6	(2	4)	101	23	37	26	14	1	38	0	4	2	0	0	-	8	.266	.304	.419
2007	ChC	NL	22	54	9	3	0	0	(0	0)	12	3	4	2	2	0	12	0	1	0	0	0	-	0	.167	.193	.222
2008	ChC	NL	58	120	35	3	0	3	(2	1)	47	15	12	11	6	1	22	0	2	0	0	0	-	4	.292	.325	.392
	Postseason		6	14	3	0	0	1	(1	0)	6	1	2	0	0	0	4	0	0	1	0	0	-	1	.214	.200	.429
	11 ML YEARS		746	2129	483	117	10	52	(24	28)	776	214	241	206	188	23	395	8	35	22	4	10	.29	57	.227	.289	.364

Joe Blanton

Pitches: R **Bats:** R **Pos:** SP-33   **Ht:** 6'3" **Wt:** 255 **Born:** 12/11/1980 **Age:** 28

			HOW MUCH HE PITCHED						WHAT HE GAVE UP											THE RESULTS						
Year	Team	Lg	G	GS	CG	GF	IP	BFP	H	R	ER	HR	SH	SF	HB	TBB	IBB	SO	WP	Bk	W	L	Pct	ShO	Sv-Op	Hld	ERC	ERA
2004	Oak	AL	3	0	0	1	8.0	30	6	5	5	1	0	0	0	2	0	6	0	0	0	0	-	0	0-0	0	2.52	5.63
2005	Oak	AL	33	33	2	0	201.1	835	178	86	79	23	2	7	5	67	3	116	4	2	12	12	.500	0	0-0	0	3.37	3.53
2006	Oak	AL	32	31	1	0	194.1	856	241	111	104	17	3	9	5	58	4	107	3	0	16	12	.571	1	0-0	0	5.09	4.82
2007	Oak	AL	34	34	3	0	230.0	950	240	106	101	16	5	8	4	40	4	140	3	1	14	10	.583	1	0-0	0	3.30	3.95
2008	2 Tms		33	33	0	0	197.2	855	211	110	103	22	2	4	4	66	3	111	2	0	9	12	.429	0	0-0	0	4.33	4.69
08	Oak	AL	20	20	0	0	127.0	550	145	74	70	12	1	2	1	35	3	62	1	0	5	12	.294	0	0-0	0	4.33	4.96
08	Phi	NL	13	13	0	0	70.2	305	66	36	33	10	1	2	3	31	0	49	1	0	4	0	1.000	0	0-0	0	4.33	4.20
	Postseason		1	0	0	1	2.0	8	0	0	0	0	0	0	0	2	0	2	0	0	0	0	-	0	0-0	0	0.95	0.00
	5 ML YEARS		135	131	6	1	831.1	3526	876	418	392	79	12	28	18	233	14	480	12	3	51	46	.526	2	0-0	0	3.95	4.24

Jerry Blevins

Pitches: L **Bats:** L **Pos:** RP-36   **Ht:** 6'6" **Wt:** 175 **Born:** 9/6/1983 **Age:** 25

			HOW MUCH HE PITCHED						WHAT HE GAVE UP											THE RESULTS						
Year	Team	Lg	G	GS	CG	GF	IP	BFP	H	R	ER	HR	SH	SF	HB	TBB	IBB	SO	WP	Bk	W	L	Pct	ShO	Sv-Op	Hld	ERC	ERA
2004	Boise	A-	23	0	0	11	33.1	141	17	7	6	1	0	0	3	21	1	42	2	0	6	1	.857	0	5- -	-	2.13	1.62
2005	Peoria	A	48	2	0	29	76.1	344	75	51	47	6	9	3	5	38	0	96	5	0	3	7	.300	0	14- -	-	4.39	5.54
2006	Dytona	A+	8	0	0	3	11.0	56	18	12	11	0	1	1	1	4	0	9	0	1	0	1	.000	0	1- -	-	7.14	9.00
2006	Boise	A-	16	0	0	6	22.1	109	27	22	15	3	1	3	3	8	0	19	1	0	1	2	.333	0	0- -	-	5.57	6.04
2006	WTenn	AA	5	0	0	2	6.1	25	5	1	1	0	0	0	1	1	0	8	0	0	0	0	-	0	1- -	-	2.11	1.42
2007	Dytona	A+	15	0	0	10	23.2	89	13	1	1	0	1	1	1	5	2	32	0	1	1	0	1.000	0	6- -	-	1.02	0.38
2007	Tenn	AA	23	0	0	11	29.1	120	23	5	5	1	2	2	1	8	1	37	1	0	2	2	.500	0	3- -	-	2.11	1.53
2007	Mdland	AA	17	0	0	11	22.0	86	18	10	8	2	2	2	0	5	1	29	2	0	1	3	.250	0	1- -	-	2.42	3.27
2007	Scrmto	AAA	1	0	0	0	2.2	9	1	0	0	0	0	0	0	0	0	4	0	0	1	0	1.000	0	0- -	-	0.31	0.00
2008	Scrmto	AAA	28	0	0	21	32.1	138	31	16	10	3	1	2	2	6	1	36	2	0	2	2	.500	0	10- -	-	3.05	2.78
2007	Oak	AL	6	0	0	1	4.2	25	8	6	5	1	0	0	0	2	0	3	0	0	0	1	.000	0	0-0	0	9.08	9.64
2008	Oak	AL	36	0	0	8	37.2	156	32	14	13	2	0	1	3	13	2	35	0	0	1	3	.250	0	0-1	5	3.00	3.11
	2 ML YEARS		42	0	0	9	42.1	181	40	20	18	3	0	1	3	15	2	38	0	0	1	4	.200	0	0-1	5	3.59	3.83

Willie Bloomquist

Bats: R **Throws:** R **Pos:** CF-23; PH-18; RF-13; SS-12; PR-10; LF-8; 2B-7; DH-2; 3B-1   **Ht:** 5'11" **Wt:** 195 **Born:** 11/27/1977 **Age:** 31

									BATTING												BASERUNNING				AVERAGES		
Year	Team	Lg	G	AB	H	2B	3B	HR	(Hm	Rd)	TB	R	RBI	RC	TBB	IBB	SO	HBP	SH	SF	SB	CS	SB%	GDP	Avg	OBP	Slg
2002	Sea	AL	12	33	15	4	0	0	(0	0)	19	11	7	10	5	0	2	0	0	0	3	1	.75	0	.455	.526	.576
2003	Sea	AL	89	196	49	7	2	1	(1	0)	63	30	14	18	19	1	39	1	2	2	4	1	.80	6	.250	.317	.321
2004	Sea	AL	93	188	46	10	0	2	(0	2)	62	27	18	18	10	0	48	0	3	0	13	2	.87	2	.245	.283	.330
2005	Sea	AL	82	249	64	15	2	0	(0	0)	83	27	22	26	11	0	38	1	4	2	14	1	.93	5	.257	.289	.333
2006	Sea	AL	102	251	62	6	2	1	(0	1)	75	36	15	27	24	0	40	4	2	2	16	3	.84	3	.247	.320	.299
2007	Sea	AL	91	173	48	3	0	2	(1	1)	57	28	13	16	10	0	35	1	4	0	7	5	.58	7	.277	.321	.329
2008	Sea	AL	71	165	46	1	0	0	(0	0)	47	32	9	24	25	1	29	1	1	0	14	3	.82	1	.279	.377	.285
	7 ML YEARS		540	1255	330	46	6	6	(2	4)	406	191	98	139	104	2	231	8	16	6	71	16	.82	24	.263	.322	.324

Geoff Blum

Bats: B Throws: R Pos: 3B-75; PH-33; 2B-8; 1B-5; SS-4   Ht: 6'3" Wt: 205 Born: 4/26/1973 Age: 36

									BATTING												BASERUNNING				AVERAGES		
Year	Team	Lg	G	AB	H	2B	3B	HR	(Hm	Rd)	TB	R	RBI	RC	TBB	IBB	SO	HBP	SH	SF	SB	CS	SB%	GDP	Avg	OBP	Slg
1999	Mon	NL	45	133	32	7	2	8	(0	8)	67	21	18	22	17	3	25	0	3	0	1	0	1.00	3	.241	.327	.504
2000	Mon	NL	124	343	97	20	2	11	(5	6)	154	40	45	50	26	2	60	3	3	4	1	4	.20	4	.283	.335	.449
2001	Mon	NL	148	453	107	25	0	9	(6	3)	159	57	50	49	43	8	94	10	3	5	9	5	.64	12	.236	.313	.351
2002	Hou	NL	130	368	104	20	4	10	(6	4)	162	45	52	62	49	5	70	1	1	2	2	0	1.00	8	.283	.367	.440
2003	Hou	NL	123	420	110	19	0	10	(6	4)	159	51	52	40	20	1	50	2	2	5	0	0	-	15	.262	.295	.379
2004	TB	AL	112	339	73	21	0	8	(2	6)	118	38	35	29	24	1	58	0	4	2	2	3	.40	4	.215	.266	.348
2005	2 Tms		109	319	73	15	2	6	(1	5)	110	32	25	27	28	0	43	3	0	1	3	3	.50	6	.229	.296	.345
2006	SD	NL	109	276	70	17	1	4	(0	4)	101	27	34	26	17	1	51	0	2	5	0	1	.00	5	.254	.293	.366
2007	SD	NL	122	330	83	21	1	5	(1	4)	121	34	33	38	32	4	52	2	3	3	0	0	-	10	.252	.319	.367
2008	Hou	NL	114	325	78	14	1	14	(6	8)	136	36	53	42	21	2	54	3	0	7	1	2	.33	5	.240	.287	.418
05	SD	NL	78	224	54	13	1	5	(1	4)	84	26	22	23	24	0	28	3	0	1	3	2	.60	5	.241	.321	.375
05	CWS	AL	31	95	19	2	1	1	(0	1)	26	6	3	4	4	0	15	0	0	0	0	1	.00	1	.200	.232	.274
Postseason			6	10	2	1	0	1	(0	1)	6	1	2	1	4	1	1	0	0	1	0	0	-	1	.200	.400	.600
10 ML YEARS			1136	3306	827	179	13	85	(33	52)	1287	381	397	385	277	27	557	24	21	33	19	18	.51	72	.250	.310	.389

Brian Bocock

Bats: R Throws: R Pos: SS-29; PH-3   Ht: 5'11" Wt: 185 Born: 3/9/1985 Age: 24

									BATTING												BASERUNNING				AVERAGES		
Year	Team	Lg	G	AB	H	2B	3B	HR	(Hm	Rd)	TB	R	RBI	RC	TBB	IBB	SO	HBP	SH	SF	SB	CS	SB%	GDP	Avg	OBP	Slg
2006	Salem	A+	39	103	23	6	0	0	(-	-)	29	12	7	10	12	0	29	1	3	2	6	1	.86	3	.223	.305	.282
2006	Augsta	A	2	1	0	0	0	0	(-	-)	0	1	0	0	0	0	0	0	0	1	0	0	-	0	.000	.000	.000
2007	Augsta	A	39	161	47	9	1	1	(-	-)	61	24	20	24	16	0	19	0	0	1	26	8	.76	4	.292	.354	.379
2007	SnJos	A+	87	345	76	19	3	4	(-	-)	113	42	37	35	35	0	105	3	9	6	15	10	.60	7	.220	.293	.328
2008	Fresno	AAA	35	123	20	3	0	0	(-	-)	23	14	3	5	14	0	39	1	3	0	7	3	.70	2	.163	.254	.187
2008	SF	NL	32	77	11	1	0	0	(0	0)	12	4	2	3	12	0	29	0	4	0	4	2	.67	2	.143	.258	.156

Brandon Boggs

Bats: B Throws: R Pos: LF-76; PH-16; DH-15; PR-6; CF-5; RF-3   Ht: 5'11" Wt: 205 Born: 1/9/1983 Age: 26

									BATTING												BASERUNNING				AVERAGES		
Year	Team	Lg	G	AB	H	2B	3B	HR	(Hm	Rd)	TB	R	RBI	RC	TBB	IBB	SO	HBP	SH	SF	SB	CS	SB%	GDP	Avg	OBP	Slg
2004	Spkane	A-	45	149	35	11	0	3	(-	-)	55	27	19	24	29	0	43	5	1	2	6	2	.75	5	.235	.373	.369
2005	Clinton	A	85	309	76	16	2	13	(-	-)	135	54	51	51	50	1	69	2	0	2	14	6	.70	3	.246	.353	.437
2006	Bkrsfld	A+	78	284	74	20	4	8	(-	-)	126	48	37	47	40	1	63	1	0	2	13	4	.76	3	.261	.352	.444
2007	Bkrsfld	A+	26	92	23	9	1	4	(-	-)	46	17	17	17	14	0	28	2	0	0	5	1	.83	0	.250	.361	.500
2007	Frisco	AA	104	354	94	21	4	19	(-	-)	180	69	55	73	70	5	103	1	0	4	11	4	.73	3	.266	.385	.508
2008	Okla	AAA	18	68	21	4	3	0	(-	-)	31	12	6	11	7	0	20	0	0	1	1	1	.50	0	.309	.368	.456
2008	Tex	AL	101	283	64	17	4	8	(6	2)	113	30	41	37	44	1	93	3	1	3	3	2	.60	3	.226	.333	.399

Mitchell Boggs

Pitches: R Bats: R Pos: SP-6; RP-2   Ht: 6'3" Wt: 195 Born: 2/15/1984 Age: 25

			HOW MUCH HE PITCHED						WHAT HE GAVE UP												THE RESULTS					
Year	Team	Lg	G	GS	CG	GF	IP	BFP	H	R	ER	HR	SH	SF	HB	TBB	IBB	SO	WP	Bk	W	L	Pct	ShO	Sv-Op Hld	ERC	ERA
2005	NewJrs	A-	15	14	0	0	71.2	315	77	38	31	5	1	1	5	24	0	61	4	0	4	4	.500	0	0- -	4.28	3.89
2006	PlmBh	A+	27	27	1	0	145.0	634	153	69	55	7	4	6	8	51	0	146	9	0	10	6	.625	1	0- -	4.03	3.41
2007	Sprgfld	AA	26	26	0	0	152.1	688	167	86	65	15	8	8	10	62	2	117	7	0	11	7	.611	0	0- -	4.82	3.84
2008	Memp	AAA	21	21	1	0	125.1	508	107	52	48	11	4	1	2	46	0	81	10	1	9	3	.750	0	0- -	3.24	3.45
2008	StL	NL	8	6	0	1	34.0	164	42	29	28	5	1	1	2	22	0	13	2	0	3	2	.600	0	0-0 0	7.17	7.41

T.J. Bohn

Bats: R Throws: R Pos: LF-12; PR-6; PH-2   Ht: 6'5" Wt: 200 Born: 1/17/1980 Age: 29

									BATTING												BASERUNNING				AVERAGES		
Year	Team	Lg	G	AB	H	2B	3B	HR	(Hm	Rd)	TB	R	RBI	RC	TBB	IBB	SO	HBP	SH	SF	SB	CS	SB%	GDP	Avg	OBP	Slg
2002	Everett	A-	62	212	52	10	0	3	(-	-)	71	28	20	27	29	1	53	3	2	3	7	2	.78	4	.245	.340	.335
2003	Wisc	A	128	471	128	31	2	13	(-	-)	202	75	70	80	70	1	131	8	1	6	16	8	.67	5	.272	.371	.429
2004	InldEm	A+	71	240	68	9	3	7	(-	-)	104	46	37	46	44	2	61	9	2	1	6	4	.60	4	.283	.412	.433
2004	SnAnt	AA	62	220	58	9	4	7	(-	-)	96	24	29	34	22	0	46	3	2	2	6	1	.86	1	.264	.336	.436
2005	SnAnt	AA	113	438	135	30	2	12	(-	-)	205	67	57	77	35	1	96	5	7	1	27	9	.75	8	.308	.365	.468
2005	Tacom	AAA	22	81	26	3	0	1	(-	-)	32	15	7	12	2	0	23	3	0	0	4	0	1.00	5	.321	.360	.395
2006	Tacom	AAA	97	378	107	20	1	9	(-	-)	156	53	43	57	33	2	81	4	2	2	15	3	.83	10	.283	.345	.413
2006	Ms	R	4	16	4	3	1	0	(-	-)	9	4	1	3	1	0	8	0	0	0	3	0	1.00	0	.250	.294	.563
2007	Rchmd	AAA	46	145	35	8	0	1	(-	-)	46	20	14	17	21	0	41	2	1	1	8	4	.67	3	.241	.343	.317
2007	Braves	R	11	31	11	5	0	1	(-	-)	19	8	5	7	5	0	8	0	0	1	1	2	.33	0	.355	.432	.613
2007	Missi	AA	23	85	19	3	0	1	(-	-)	25	15	6	10	14	0	23	1	0	1	3	0	1.00	2	.224	.337	.294
2008	LV	AAA	97	316	68	19	2	4	(-	-)	103	30	27	29	25	1	85	4	2	2	4	2	.67	6	.215	.280	.326
2006	Sea	AL	18	14	2	0	0	1	(0	1)	5	2	2	3	0	0	8	0	0	0	0	0	-	0	.143	.250	.357
2008	Phi	NL	14	5	2	1	0	0	(0	0)	3	1	3	2	0	0	1	0	0	0	0	0	-	0	.400	.400	.600
2 ML YEARS			32	19	4	1	0	1	(0	1)	8	3	5	3	0	0	9	0	0	0	0	0	-	0	.211	.286	.421

Jeremy Bonderman

Pitches: R Bats: R Pos: SP-12 Ht: 6'2" Wt: 220 Born: 10/28/1982 Age: 26

Year	Team	Lg	G	GS	CG	GF	IP	BFP	H	R	ER	HR	SH	SF	HB	TBB	IBB	SO	WP	Bk	W	L	Pct	ShO	Sv-Op	Hld	ERC	ERA
2003	Det	AL	33	28	0	0	162.0	727	193	118	100	23	3	6	4	58	2	108	12	2	6	19	.240	0	0-0	0	5.39	5.56
2004	Det	AL	33	32	2	0	184.0	793	168	101	100	24	10	5	10	73	5	168	7	0	11	13	.458	2	0-0	0	3.93	4.89
2005	Det	AL	29	29	4	0	189.0	801	199	101	96	21	3	3	4	57	0	145	5	1	14	13	.519	0	0-0	0	4.20	4.57
2006	Det	AL	34	34	0	0	214.0	903	214	104	97	18	3	6	3	64	7	202	3	1	14	8	.636	0	0-0	0	3.58	4.08
2007	Det	AL	28	28	0	0	174.1	753	193	105	97	23	2	4	4	48	6	145	12	1	11	9	.550	0	0-0	0	4.44	5.01
2008	Det	AL	12	12	0	0	71.1	319	75	39	34	9	2	3	3	36	2	44	1	0	3	4	.429	0	0-0	0	5.14	4.29
	Postseason		3	3	0	0	20.1	84	17	7	7	1	1	0	0	7	1	11	1	0	1	0	1.000	0	0-0	0	2.58	3.10
6 ML YEARS			169	163	6	0	994.2	4296	1042	568	524	118	23	27	28	336	22	812	40	5	59	66	.472	2	0-0	0	4.31	4.74

Emilio Bonifacio

Bats: B Throws: R Pos: 2B-37; PH-8; RF-2; PR-2; LF-1 Ht: 5'10" Wt: 195 Born: 4/23/1985 Age: 24

Year	Team	Lg	G	AB	H	2B	3B	HR	(Hm	Rd)	TB	R	RBI	RC	TBB	IBB	SO	HBP	SH	SF	SB	CS	SB%	GDP	Avg	OBP	Slg
2003	Msoula	R+	54	146	29	1	1	0	(-	-)	32	20	16	12	18	0	43	3	4	1	15	3	.83	1	.199	.298	.219
2004	Sbend	A	120	411	107	9	6	1	(-	-)	131	59	37	45	25	3	122	3	9	2	40	10	.80	9	.260	.306	.319
2005	Sbend	A	127	522	141	14	7	1	(-	-)	172	81	44	68	56	0	90	2	7	4	55	17	.76	9	.270	.341	.330
2006	Lancst	A+	130	546	175	35	7	7	(-	-)	245	117	50	100	44	0	104	6	8	4	61	14	.81	5	.321	.375	.449
2007	Mobile	AA	132	551	157	21	5	2	(-	-)	194	84	40	70	38	1	105	2	4	1	41	13	.76	6	.285	.333	.352
2008	Tucsn	AAA	85	367	111	18	5	1	(-	-)	142	49	29	51	27	0	64	0	6	2	17	8	.68	3	.302	.348	.387
2008	Clmbs	AAA	8	31	14	2	0	0	(-	-)	16	9	3	7	4	0	4	0	0	1	4	2	.67	0	.452	.500	.516
2007	Ari	NL	11	23	5	1	0	0	(0	0)	6	2	2	4	4	0	3	0	0	0	0	1	.00	0	.217	.333	.261
2008	2 Tms	NL	49	169	41	6	5	0	(0	0)	57	29	14	16	14	0	46	0	0	3	7	4	.64	2	.243	.296	.333
08	Ari	NL	8	12	2	1	0	0	(0	0)	3	3	2	1	0	0	5	0	0	0	1	0	1.00	0	.167	.167	.250
08	Was	NL	41	157	39	5	5	0	(0	0)	54	26	12	15	14	0	41	0	0	3	6	4	.60	2	.248	.305	.344
2 ML YEARS			60	192	46	7	5	0	(0	0)	63	31	16	20	18	0	49	0	0	3	7	5	.58	2	.240	.300	.328

Eddie Bonine

Pitches: R Bats: R Pos: SP-5 Ht: 6'5" Wt: 220 Born: 6/6/1981 Age: 28

Year	Team	Lg	G	GS	CG	GF	IP	BFP	H	R	ER	HR	SH	SF	HB	TBB	IBB	SO	WP	Bk	W	L	Pct	ShO	Sv-Op	Hld	ERC	ERA
2003	Eugene	A-	31	0	0	26	33.1	143	32	15	14	2	1	1	3	10	0	33	1	0	1	2	.333	0	14--	-	3.51	3.78
2004	FtWyn	A	5	5	0	0	27.1	109	25	11	6	2	1	0	0	3	0	31	0	0	2	1	.667	0	0--	-	2.36	1.98
2004	Lk Els	A+	21	21	0	0	112.1	492	121	82	68	12	7	9	8	39	0	96	12	0	5	10	.333	0	0--	-	4.66	5.45
2005	Portlnd	AAA	1	0	0	0	2.0	7	0	0	0	0	0	0	0	0	0	5	0	0	1	0	1.000	0	0--	-	0.00	0.00
2005	Lk Els	A+	36	10	0	7	104.1	494	142	88	75	14	3	5	4	42	0	77	8	0	5	6	.455	0	0--	-	6.62	6.47
2006	Lkland	A+	41	11	0	13	106.1	450	108	62	47	9	2	4	5	27	0	83	8	1	4	4	.500	0	1--	-	3.67	3.98
2006	Erie	AA	1	1	0	0	6.0	26	8	6	6	3	0	0	1	0	0	2	0	0	1	0	1.000	0	0--	-	8.18	9.00
2007	Erie	AA	25	25	2	0	154.2	643	159	77	67	13	5	2	11	24	1	73	11	2	14	5	.737	0	0--	-	3.45	3.90
2007	Toledo	AAA	1	1	0	0	8.0	31	7	2	2	0	0	0	0	1	0	4	1	0	1	0	1.000	0	0--	-	1.87	2.25
2008	Toledo	AAA	17	17	1	0	106.1	440	107	53	49	10	6	3	5	18	0	69	3	0	12	4	.750	0	0--	-	3.36	4.15
2008	Erie	AA	1	1	0	0	3.2	17	4	2	1	0	0	0	1	2	0	1	0	0	0	1	.000	0	0--	-	5.65	2.45
2008	Det	AL	5	5	0	0	26.2	117	36	19	16	3	1	1	2	5	0	9	0	0	2	1	.667	0	0-0	0	5.82	5.40

Boof Bonser

Pitches: R Bats: R Pos: RP-35; SP-12 Ht: 6'4" Wt: 245 Born: 10/14/1981 Age: 27

Year	Team	Lg	G	GS	CG	GF	IP	BFP	H	R	ER	HR	SH	SF	HB	TBB	IBB	SO	WP	Bk	W	L	Pct	ShO	Sv-Op	Hld	ERC	ERA
2006	Min	AL	18	18	0	0	100.1	419	104	50	47	18	2	2	1	24	0	84	2	0	7	6	.538	0	0-0	0	4.25	4.22
2007	Min	AL	31	30	0	0	173.0	772	199	108	98	27	4	3	5	65	4	136	3	1	8	12	.400	0	0-0	0	5.33	5.10
2008	Min	AL	47	12	0	9	118.1	532	139	87	78	16	3	4	1	36	1	97	6	1	3	7	.300	0	0-2	2	4.84	5.93
	Postseason		1	1	0	0	6.0	25	7	2	2	0	0	0	0	1	0	3	0	0	0	0	-	0	0-0	0	3.46	3.00
3 ML YEARS			96	60	0	9	391.2	1723	442	245	223	61	9	9	7	125	5	317	11	2	18	25	.419	0	0-2	2	4.90	5.12

Aaron Boone

Bats: R Throws: R Pos: 1B-54; PH-41; 3B-16; PR-2; 2B-1 Ht: 6'3" Wt: 206 Born: 3/9/1973 Age: 36

Year	Team	Lg	G	AB	H	2B	3B	HR	(Hm	Rd)	TB	R	RBI	RC	TBB	IBB	SO	HBP	SH	SF	SB	CS	SB%	GDP	Avg	OBP	Slg
2008	Nats*	R	1	3	2	1	0	0	(-	-)	3	0	0	1	0	0	0	0	0	0	0	0	-	0	.667	.667	1.000
2008	Clmbs*	AAA	3	8	0	0	0	0	(-	-)	0	0	0	0	0	0	1	1	0	0	0	0	-	1	.000	.111	.000
1997	Cin	NL	16	49	12	1	0	0	(0	0)	13	5	5	3	2	0	5	0	1	0	1	0	1.00	1	.245	.275	.265
1998	Cin	NL	58	181	51	13	2	2	(2	0)	74	24	28	27	15	1	36	5	3	2	6	1	.86	3	.282	.350	.409
1999	Cin	NL	139	472	132	26	5	14	(7	7)	210	56	72	70	30	2	79	8	5	5	17	6	.74	6	.280	.330	.445
2000	Cin	NL	84	291	83	18	0	12	(5	7)	137	44	43	50	24	1	52	10	2	4	6	1	.86	5	.285	.356	.471
2001	Cin	NL	103	381	112	26	2	14	(10	4)	184	54	62	63	29	1	71	8	3	6	6	3	.67	9	.294	.351	.483
2002	Cin	NL	162	606	146	38	2	26	(14	12)	266	83	87	83	56	4	111	10	9	4	32	8	.80	9	.241	.314	.439
2003	2 Tms		160	592	158	32	3	24	(13	11)	268	92	96	89	46	2	104	8	6	2	23	3	.88	13	.267	.327	.453
2005	Cle	AL	143	511	124	19	1	16	(5	11)	193	61	60	52	35	3	92	9	4	6	9	3	.75	14	.243	.299	.378
2006	Cle	AL	104	354	89	19	1	7	(1	6)	131	50	46	46	27	1	62	6	4	1	5	4	.56	4	.251	.314	.370
2007	Fla	NL	69	189	54	11	0	6	(1	4)	80	27	28	32	21	4	41	13	1	4	2	0	1.00	6	.286	.388	.423
2008	Was	NL	104	232	56	13	1	6	(4	2)	89	23	28	22	18	1	52	2	1	2	0	1	.00	8	.241	.299	.384
03	Cin	NL	106	403	110	19	3	18	(10	8)	189	61	65	65	35	2	74	5	3	0	15	3	.83	6	.273	.339	.469
03	NYY	AL	54	189	48	13	0	6	(3	3)	79	31	31	24	11	0	30	3	3	2	8	0	1.00	7	.254	.302	.418
	Postseason		17	53	9	1	0	2	(1	1)	16	4	4	2	1	0	15	1	2	1	2	1	.67	0	.170	.196	.302
11 ML YEARS			1142	3858	1017	216	17	126	(62	64)	1645	519	555	537	303	20	705	79	39	36	107	30	.78	74	.264	.327	.426

Chris Bootcheck

Pitches: R Bats: R Pos: RP-10   Ht: 6'5" Wt: 210 Born: 10/24/1978 Age: 30

			HOW MUCH HE PITCHED						WHAT HE GAVE UP												THE RESULTS							
Year	Team	Lg	G	GS	CG	GF	IP	BFP	H	R	ER	HR	SH	SF	HB	TBB	IBB	SO	WP	Bk	W	L	Pct	ShO	Sv-Op	Hld	ERC	ERA
2008	RCuca*	A+	6	0	0	2	9.2	42	9	7	5	0	0	0	1	6	0	10	3	0	0	1	1.000	0	0--	-	4.40	4.66
2008	Salt Lk*	AAA	19	0	0	8	28.1	136	29	12	9	2	1	1	1	17	0	34	4	0	0	0	-	0	1--	-	4.64	2.86
2003	LAA	AL	4	1	0	2	10.1	53	16	13	11	5	0	0	0	6	0	7	0	0	0	1	.000	0	0-0	0	11.53	9.58
2005	LAA	AL	5	2	0	1	18.2	79	19	7	7	1	0	1	0	4	1	8	1	0	0	1	.000	0	1-1	0	3.00	3.38
2006	LAA	AL	7	0	0	5	10.1	54	16	12	12	3	1	0	0	9	0	7	1	0	0	1	.000	0	0-0	0	11.63	10.45
2007	LAA	AL	51	0	0	17	77.1	331	81	43	41	7	2	4	5	24	3	56	6	1	3	3	.500	0	0-1	4	4.16	4.77
2008	LAA	AL	10	0	0	4	16.0	90	30	18	18	2	0	0	0	12	0	14	2	0	0	1	.000	0	0-0	1	11.28	10.13
5 ML YEARS			77	3	0	29	132.2	607	162	93	89	18	3	5	5	55	4	92	10	1	3	7	.300	0	1-2	5	5.80	6.04

Dave Borkowski

Pitches: R Bats: R Pos: RP-26   Ht: 6'1" Wt: 230 Born: 2/7/1977 Age: 32

			HOW MUCH HE PITCHED						WHAT HE GAVE UP												THE RESULTS							
Year	Team	Lg	G	GS	CG	GF	IP	BFP	H	R	ER	HR	SH	SF	HB	TBB	IBB	SO	WP	Bk	W	L	Pct	ShO	Sv-Op	Hld	ERC	ERA
2008	RdRck*	AAA	27	1	0	12	40.2	165	40	12	11	3	3	2	1	7	2	26	1	0	2	2	.500	0	2--	-	3.00	2.43
1999	Det	AL	17	12	0	2	76.2	351	86	58	52	10	1	2	4	40	0	50	3	0	2	6	.250	0	0-	0	5.75	6.10
2000	Det	AL	2	1	0	0	5.1	34	11	13	13	2	0	1	0	7	1	1	0	0	0	1	.000	0	0-	0	17.78	21.94
2001	Det	AL	15	0	0	7	29.2	135	30	21	21	5	0	2	3	15	3	30	0	0	0	2	.000	0	0-	0	5.28	6.37
2004	Bal	AL	17	8	0	2	56.0	247	65	37	32	6	2	2	3	15	1	45	2	1	3	4	.429	0	0-1	1	4.67	5.14
2006	Hou	NL	40	0	0	12	71.0	299	70	38	37	8	2	2	0	23	7	52	2	0	3	2	.600	0	0-0	1	3.65	4.69
2007	Hou	NL	64	0	0	18	71.2	325	76	46	41	8	3	6	4	34	9	63	3	0	5	3	.625	0	1-4	8	4.76	5.15
2008	Hou	NL	26	0	0	5	36.0	173	54	30	30	9	3	0	1	14	5	24	0	0	0	2	.000	0	0-1	0	8.20	7.50
7 ML YEARS			181	21	0	46	346.1	1564	392	243	226	48	11	15	15	148	26	265	10	1	13	20	.394	0	1-6	10	5.27	5.87

Joe Borowski

Pitches: R Bats: R Pos: RP-18   Ht: 6'2" Wt: 215 Born: 5/4/1971 Age: 38

			HOW MUCH HE PITCHED						WHAT HE GAVE UP												THE RESULTS							
Year	Team	Lg	G	GS	CG	GF	IP	BFP	H	R	ER	HR	SH	SF	HB	TBB	IBB	SO	WP	Bk	W	L	Pct	ShO	Sv-Op	Hld	ERC	ERA
2008	Lk Cty*	A	1	1	0	0	1.0	3	0	0	0	0	0	0	0	0	0	0	0	0	0	0	-	0	0--	-	0.00	0.00
2008	Akron*	AA	1	0	0	0	1.0	4	1	0	0	0	0	0	0	0	0	1	0	0	0	0	-	0	0--	-	1.95	0.00
1995	Bal	AL	6	0	0	3	7.1	30	5	1	1	0	0	0	0	4	0	3	0	0	0	0	-	0	0-0	0	2.32	1.23
1996	Atl	NL	22	0	0	8	26.0	121	33	15	14	4	5	0	1	13	4	15	1	0	2	4	.333	0	0-0	0	6.46	4.85
1997	2 Tms		21	0	0	9	26.0	123	29	13	12	2	1	0	0	20	5	8	0	0	2	3	.400	0	0-0	2	5.74	4.15
1998	NYY	AL	8	0	0	6	9.2	42	11	7	7	0	0	0	0	4	0	7	0	0	1	0	1.000	0	0-0	0	6.47	6.52
2001	ChC	NL	1	1	0	0	1.2	13	6	6	6	1	1	0	0	3	0	1	0	0	0	1	.000	0	0-0	0	39.91	32.40
2002	ChC	NL	73	0	0	25	95.2	391	84	31	29	10	5	3	1	29	6	97	1	0	4	4	.500	0	2-6	12	3.05	2.73
2003	ChC	NL	68	0	0	59	68.1	280	53	23	20	5	4	0	1	19	1	66	0	0	2	2	.500	0	33-37	1	2.26	2.63
2004	ChC	NL	22	0	0	19	21.1	106	27	19	19	3	1	1	0	15	2	17	0	0	2	4	.333	0	9-11	0	6.92	8.02
2005	2 Tms		43	0	0	7	46.1	184	38	23	23	8	1	1	0	12	1	27	1	0	1	5	.167	0	0-4	20	3.04	4.47
2006	Fla	NL	72	0	0	60	69.2	304	63	31	29	7	1	0	2	33	7	64	1	0	3	3	.500	0	36-43	0	3.74	3.75
2007	Cle	AL	69	0	0	58	65.2	292	77	39	37	9	3	4	2	17	4	58	2	0	4	5	.444	0	**45-53**	0	4.68	5.07
2008	Cle	AL	18	0	0	14	16.2	82	24	14	14	4	1	1	0	8	2	9	0	0	1	3	.250	0	6-10	0	7.86	7.56
97	Atl	NL	20	0	0	8	24.0	111	27	11	10	2	1	0	0	16	4	6	0	0	2	2	.500	0	0-0	0	5.51	3.75
97	NYY	AL	1	0	0	1	2.0	12	2	2	2	0	0	0	0	4	1	2	0	0	0	1	.000	0	0-0	0	8.25	9.00
05	ChC	NL	11	0	0	3	11.0	47	12	8	8	5	0	0	0	1	0	11	0	0	0	0	-	0	0-0	1	5.36	6.55
05	TB	AL	32	0	0	4	35.1	137	26	15	15	3	1	1	0	11	1	16	1	0	1	5	.167	0	0-4	19	2.33	3.82
Postseason			11	0	0	9	13.2	62	13	5	4	1	1	1	0	8	1	8	0	0	1	0	1.000	0	3-4	0	4.10	2.63
12 ML YEARS			423	1	0	268	454.1	1968	450	222	211	53	23	9	7	177	32	372	6	0	22	34	.393	0	131-164	36	4.02	4.18

Jason Botts

Bats: B Throws: R Pos: 1B-8; PH-6; LF-4; DH-3   Ht: 6'5" Wt: 250 Born: 7/26/1980 Age: 28

			BATTING																			BASERUNNING				AVERAGES		
Year	Team	Lg	G	AB	H	2B	3B	HR	(Hm	Rd)	TB	R	RBI	RC	TBB	IBB	SO	HBP	SH	SF	SB	CS	SB%	GDP	Avg	OBP	Slg
2008	Okla*	AAA	18	66	16	6	0	4	(-	-)	34	13	11	11	9	2	25	1	0	0	0	0	-	2	.242	.342	.515
2005	Tex	AL	10	27	8	0	0	0	(0	0)	8	4	3	3	3	0	13	0	0	0	0	0	-	1	.296	.367	.296
2006	Tex	AL	20	50	11	4	0	1	(1	0)	18	8	6	6	8	1	18	0	0	2	0	0	-	0	.220	.317	.360
2007	Tex	AL	48	167	40	8	1	2	(1	1)	56	19	14	17	19	0	59	3	0	1	1	0	1.00	8	.240	.326	.335
2008	Tex	AL	15	38	6	3	0	2	(1	1)	15	2	5	5	8	0	18	0	0	0	0	0	-	0	.158	.304	.395
4 ML YEARS			93	282	65	15	1	5	(3	2)	97	33	28	31	38	1	108	3	0	3	1	0	1.00	9	.230	.325	.344

Jason Bourgeois

Bats: R Throws: R Pos: PR-4; DH-2; 2B-1; PH-1   Ht: 5'9" Wt: 190 Born: 1/4/1982 Age: 27

			BATTING																			BASERUNNING				AVERAGES		
Year	Team	Lg	G	AB	H	2B	3B	HR	(Hm	Rd)	TB	R	RBI	RC	TBB	IBB	SO	HBP	SH	SF	SB	CS	SB%	GDP	Avg	OBP	Slg
2000	Rngrs	R	24	88	21	4	0	0	(-	-)	25	18	6	11	14	0	15	2	2	0	9	2	.82	0	.239	.356	.284
2001	Pulaski	R+	62	251	78	12	2	7	(-	-)	115	60	34	47	26	0	47	6	0	1	21	7	.75	3	.311	.387	.458
2002	Savann	A	127	522	133	21	5	8	(-	-)	188	72	49	64	40	1	66	11	8	5	22	11	.67	5	.255	.318	.360
2002	Charltt	A+	9	27	5	1	0	0	(-	-)	6	5	4	1	2	0	4	0	0	1	1	1	.50	0	.185	.233	.222
2003	Stcktn	A+	69	277	91	22	3	4	(-	-)	131	75	34	58	36	0	33	7	3	2	16	3	.84	4	.329	.416	.473
2003	Frisco	AA	55	202	51	5	4	4	(-	-)	76	28	21	25	16	0	45	2	4	4	3	1	.75	4	.252	.308	.376
2004	Frisco	AA	138	530	135	19	7	2	(-	-)	174	73	58	60	44	0	81	3	2	4	30	10	.75	8	.255	.313	.328
2005	Rchmd	AAA	119	388	93	20	2	2	(-	-)	123	33	16	39	31	1	57	4	3	2	5	6	.62	3	.240	.301	.317
2006	SnAnt	AA	107	411	114	22	7	4	(-	-)	162	65	38	59	37	0	66	3	4	5	23	7	.77	6	.277	.338	.394

Year	Team	Lg	G	AB	H	2B	3B	HR	(Hm	Rd)	TB	R	RBI	RC	TBB	IBB	SO	HBP	SH	SF	SB	CS	SB%	GDP	Avg	OBP	Slg
									BATTING												BASERUNNING				AVERAGES		
2007	Brham	AA	43	162	48	10	3	2	(-	-)	70	25	20	28	16	0	20	1	2	3	15	3	.83	0	.296	.357	.432
2007	Charltt	AAA	84	338	105	18	3	7	(-	-)	150	51	34	58	29	1	49	3	3	1	23	6	.79	5	.311	.369	.444
2008	Charltt	AAA	127	510	146	23	5	9	(-	-)	206	83	48	73	33	0	65	5	9	2	30	11	.73	9	.286	.335	.404
2008	CWS	AL	6	3	1	1	0	0	(0	0)	2	0	0	0	0	0	0	0	0	0	0	0	-	0	.333	.333	.667

Michael Bourn

Bats: L **Throws:** R **Pos:** CF-130; PH-11; PR-3   **Ht:** 5'11" **Wt:** 180 **Born:** 12/27/1982 **Age:** 26

Year	Team	Lg	G	AB	H	2B	3B	HR	(Hm	Rd)	TB	R	RBI	RC	TBB	IBB	SO	HBP	SH	SF	SB	CS	SB%	GDP	Avg	OBP	Slg
									BATTING												BASERUNNING				AVERAGES		
2006	Phi	NL	17	8	1	0	0	0	(0	0)	1	2	0	0	1	0	3	0	2	0	1	2	.33	0	.125	.222	.125
2007	Phi	NL	105	119	33	3	3	1	(1	0)	45	29	6	19	13	2	21	0	1	0	18	1	.95	1	.277	.348	.378
2008	Hou	NL	138	467	107	10	4	5	(3	2)	140	57	29	43	37	0	111	2	7	1	41	10	.80	3	.229	.288	.300
	Postseason		2	1	0	0	0	0	(0	0)	0	0	0	0	0	0	0	0	0	0	0	0	-	0	.000	.000	.000
3 ML YEARS			260	594	141	13	7	6	(4	2)	186	88	35	62	51	2	135	2	10	1	60	13	.82	4	.237	.299	.313

Michael Bowden

Pitches: R **Bats:** R **Pos:** SP-1   **Ht:** 6'3" **Wt:** 215 **Born:** 9/9/1986 **Age:** 22

Year	Team	Lg	G	GS	CG	GF	IP	BFP	H	R	ER	HR	SH	SF	HB	TBB	IBB	SO	WP	Bk	W	L	Pct	ShO	Sv-Op	Hld	ERC	ERA
				HOW MUCH HE PITCHED								WHAT HE GAVE UP												THE RESULTS			
2005	RedSx	R	4	2	0	0	6.0	26	4	0	0	0	1	0	0	4	0	10	0	0	1	0	1.000	0	0--	-	2.54	0.00
2006	Grnville	A	24	24	0	0	107.2	443	91	50	42	9	2	1	2	31	0	118	9	0	9	6	.600	0	0--	-	2.77	3.51
2006	Wilmg	A+	1	1	0	0	5.0	25	9	5	5	0	0	1	0	1	0	3	1	0	0	0	-	0	0--	-	7.08	9.00
2007	Lancst	A+	8	8	0	0	46.0	176	35	10	7	1	2	1	0	8	0	46	2	0	2	0	1.000	0	0--	-	1.65	1.37
2007	Portlnd	AA	19	19	1	0	96.2	418	105	51	46	9	1	4	4	33	0	81	3	1	8	6	.571	0	0--	-	4.50	4.28
2008	Portlnd	AA	19	19	0	0	104.1	403	72	31	27	5	3	1	0	24	0	101	3	0	9	4	.692	0	0--	-	1.63	2.33
2008	Pwtckt	AAA	7	6	0	1	40.0	161	40	16	15	5	3	0	0	5	0	29	0	0	3	0	.000	0	0--	-	3.19	3.38
2008	Bos	AL	1	1	0	0	5.0	22	7	2	2	0	0	0	0	1	0	3	0	0	1	0	1.000	0	0-0	0	4.92	3.60

Rob Bowen

Bats: B **Throws:** R **Pos:** C-31; PH-5; 1B-1; DH-1; PR-1   **Ht:** 6'3" **Wt:** 225 **Born:** 2/24/1981 **Age:** 28

Year	Team	Lg	G	AB	H	2B	3B	HR	(Hm	Rd)	TB	R	RBI	RC	TBB	IBB	SO	HBP	SH	SF	SB	CS	SB%	GDP	Avg	OBP	Slg
									BATTING												BASERUNNING				AVERAGES		
2003	Min	AL	7	10	1	0	0	0	(0	0)	1	0	1	0	0	0	4	0	0	1	0	0	-	1	.100	.091	.100
2004	Min	AL	17	27	3	0	0	1	(0	1)	6	1	2	2	4	0	10	0	1	0	0	0	-	1	.111	.226	.222
2006	SD	NL	94	94	23	5	0	3	(2	1)	37	22	13	12	13	0	26	1	1	1	0	1	.00	1	.245	.339	.394
2007	3 Tms		61	156	36	10	0	4	(1	3)	58	21	18	20	27	3	61	1	2	2	1	2	.33	2	.231	.344	.372
2008	Oak	AL	37	91	16	5	1	1	(0	1)	26	6	9	7	4	0	38	1	2	0	0	0	-	2	.176	.219	.286
07	SD	NL	30	82	22	8	0	2	(1	1)	36	12	11	12	13	3	28	1	1	1	1	2	.33	0	.268	.371	.439
07	ChC	NL	10	31	2	1	0	0	(0	0)	3	3	2	0	4	0	13	0	0	1	0	0	-	2	.065	.167	.097
07	Oak	AL	21	43	12	1	0	2	(0	2)	19	6	5	8	10	0	20	0	1	0	0	0	-	0	.279	.415	.442
	Postseason		1	1	1	0	0	0	(0	0)	1	0	0	0	0	0	0	0	0	0	0	0	-	0	1.000	1.000	1.000
5 ML YEARS			216	378	79	20	1	9	(3	6)	128	50	43	41	48	3	139	3	6	4	1	3	.25	7	.209	.300	.339

Cedrick Bowers

Pitches: L **Bats:** B **Pos:** RP-5   **Ht:** 6'2" **Wt:** 220 **Born:** 2/10/1978 **Age:** 31

Year	Team	Lg	G	GS	CG	GF	IP	BFP	H	R	ER	HR	SH	SF	HB	TBB	IBB	SO	WP	Bk	W	L	Pct	ShO	Sv-Op	Hld	ERC	ERA
				HOW MUCH HE PITCHED								WHAT HE GAVE UP												THE RESULTS			
2008	ColSpr	AAA	35	2	0	8	65.0	282	50	28	27	5	2	0	2	43	1	74	4	0	6	1	.857	0	1--	-	3.76	3.74
2008	Col	NL	5	0	0	3	6.2	33	11	10	10	2	0	1	1	5	0	5	1	0	0	0	-	0	0-0	0	13.72	13.50

Micah Bowie

Pitches: L **Bats:** L **Pos:** RP-10   **Ht:** 6'4" **Wt:** 220 **Born:** 11/10/1974 **Age:** 34

Year	Team	Lg	G	GS	CG	GF	IP	BFP	H	R	ER	HR	SH	SF	HB	TBB	IBB	SO	WP	Bk	W	L	Pct	ShO	Sv-Op	Hld	ERC	ERA
				HOW MUCH HE PITCHED								WHAT HE GAVE UP												THE RESULTS			
2008	ColSpr*	AAA	9	0	0	0	7.1	38	12	8	6	1	0	0	0	4	1	8	0	0	0	0	-	0	0--	-	8.50	7.36
2008	RdRck*	AAA	11	0	0	0	14.2	74	22	13	10	2	2	0	1	8	0	15	1	0	1	0	1.000	0	0--	-	8.31	6.14
1999	2 Tms	NL	14	11	0	2	51.0	265	81	60	58	9	3	3	2	34	2	41	4	2	2	7	.222	0	0-0	0	9.69	10.24
2002	Oak	AL	13	0	0	4	12.0	55	12	2	2	1	0	0	1	8	1	8	0	0	2	0	1.000	0	0-0	3	5.26	1.50
2003	Oak	AL	6	0	0	3	8.1	38	13	7	7	1	0	0	1	2	0	4	0	0	0	1	.000	0	0-0	0	7.15	7.56
2006	Was	NL	15	0	0	3	19.2	75	11	3	3	1	1	0	0	7	0	11	0	0	0	0	-	0	0-0	5	1.54	1.37
2007	Was	NL	30	8	0	2	57.1	248	55	30	29	7	4	4	2	27	0	42	0	0	4	3	.571	0	0-1	1	4.48	4.55
2008	Col	NL	10	0	0	1	8.0	38	11	8	8	1	0	1	1	3	0	5	0	0	0	1	.000	0	0-0	0	6.98	9.00
99	Atl	NL	3	0	0	2	4.0	23	8	6	6	1	0	0	0	4	0	2	0	0	0	1	.000	0	0-0	0	15.43	13.50
99	ChC	NL	11	11	0	0	47.0	242	73	54	52	8	3	3	2	30	2	39	4	2	2	6	.250	0	0-0	0	9.23	9.96
	Postseason		1	0	0	1	1.1	4	0	0	0	0	0	0	0	0	0	3	0	0	0	0	-	0	0-0	0	0.00	0.00
6 ML YEARS			88	19	0	15	156.1	719	183	110	107	20	8	8	6	81	3	111	4	2	8	13	.381	0	0-1	9	5.93	6.16

John Bowker

Bats: L **Throws:** L **Pos:** 1B-71; PH-26; RF-14; LF-5; DH-2   **Ht:** 6'2" **Wt:** 200 **Born:** 7/8/1983 **Age:** 25

									BATTING												BASERUNNING				AVERAGES		
Year	Team	Lg	G	AB	H	2B	3B	HR	(Hm	Rd)	TB	R	RBI	RC	TBB	IBB	SO	HBP	SH	SF	SB	CS	SB%	GDP	Avg	OBP	Slg
2004	Giants	R	10	43	22	7	1	2	(-	-)	37	14	11	17	7	0	11	0	0	0	1	0	1.00	1	.512	.580	.860
2004	Salem	A+	31	127	41	9	2	4	(-	-)	66	23	16	25	8	2	25	6	0	0	1	0	1.00	5	.323	.390	.520
2005	SnJos	A+	121	464	124	27	1	13	(-	-)	192	66	67	62	36	0	108	3	2	8	3	7	.30	14	.267	.319	.414
2006	SnJos	A+	112	462	131	32	6	7	(-	-)	196	61	66	68	37	3	100	2	7	3	6	3	.67	12	.284	.337	.424
2006	Fresno	AAA	2	4	2	0	0	0	(-	-)	2	0	0	0	0	0	0	0	0	0	0	0	-	0	.500	.500	.500
2007	Conn	AA	139	522	160	35	6	22	(-	-)	273	79	90	98	41	1	103	12	0	12	3	7	.30	17	.307	.363	.523
2008	Fresno	AAA	23	93	22	3	1	2	(-	-)	33	13	9	10	7	0	23	2	0	0	2	0	1.00	1	.237	.304	.355
2008	SF	NL	111	326	83	14	3	10	(6	4)	133	31	43	41	19	1	74	3	0	2	1	1	.50	7	.255	.300	.408

Blaine Boyer

Pitches: R **Bats:** R **Pos:** RP-76   **Ht:** 6'3" **Wt:** 215 **Born:** 7/11/1981 **Age:** 27

			HOW MUCH HE PITCHED						WHAT HE GAVE UP											THE RESULTS						
Year	Team	Lg	G	GS	CG	GF	IP	BFP	H	R	ER	HR	SH	SF	HB	TBB	IBB	SO	WP	Bk	W	L	Pct	ShO	Sv-Op	Hld	ERC	ERA
2005	Atl	NL	43	0	0	5	37.2	158	32	13	13	1	1	1	2	17	0	33	2	0	4	2	.667	0	0-2	9	3.21	3.11
2006	Atl	NL	2	0	0	0	0.2	7	4	3	3	0	0	0	0	1	0	0	0	0	0	0	-	0	0-0	1	47.92	40.50
2007	Atl	NL	5	0	0	2	5.1	26	10	3	2	0	1	0	0	1	1	3	2	0	0	0	-	0	0-0	1	7.41	3.38
2008	Atl	NL	76	0	0	18	72.0	313	73	51	47	10	3	4	2	25	4	67	2	0	2	6	.250	0	1-5	14	4.19	5.88
4 ML YEARS			126	0	0	25	115.2	504	119	70	65	11	5	5	4	44	5	103	6	0	6	8	.429	0	1-7	25	4.18	5.06

Dallas Braden

Pitches: L **Bats:** L **Pos:** SP-10; RP-9   **Ht:** 6'1" **Wt:** 195 **Born:** 8/13/1983 **Age:** 25

			HOW MUCH HE PITCHED						WHAT HE GAVE UP											THE RESULTS						
Year	Team	Lg	G	GS	CG	GF	IP	BFP	H	R	ER	HR	SH	SF	HB	TBB	IBB	SO	WP	Bk	W	L	Pct	ShO	Sv-Op	Hld	ERC	ERA
2004	Vancvr	A-	7	0	0	4	16.1	63	15	7	5	1	0	0	0	3	0	26	0	0	2	0	1.000	0	2--	-	2.73	2.76
2004	Kane	A	5	5	0	0	23.0	101	22	13	12	2	3	1	0	6	1	33	1	1	2	1	.667	0	0--	-	2.94	4.70
2005	Stckltn	A+	7	7	1	0	43.2	170	31	14	13	4	2	0	3	11	0	64	4	2	6	0	1.000	0	0--	-	2.29	2.68
2005	Mdland	AA	16	16	0	0	97.0	413	104	43	39	5	5	5	1	32	1	71	8	3	9	5	.643	0	0--	-	3.94	3.62
2006	As	R	6	6	0	0	21.0	74	12	2	2	0	2	0	0	3	0	36	1	0	2	0	1.000	0	0--	-	0.98	0.86
2006	Stckltn	A+	3	3	0	0	13.0	57	12	9	9	3	0	0	2	5	0	17	0	0	2	0	1.000	0	0--	-	5.13	6.23
2006	Mdland	AA	1	1	0	0	3.1	19	9	6	6	1	1	0	0	0	0	2	0	0	0	0	-	0	0--	-	15.42	16.20
2007	Mdland	AA	2	2	0	0	12.0	42	5	3	3	2	0	0	0	3	0	13	0	0	1	0	1.000	0	0--	-	1.30	2.25
2007	Scrmto	AAA	11	11	2	0	64.0	263	51	22	21	4	3	0	2	18	1	74	2	2	2	3	.400	0	0--	-	2.38	2.95
2008	Scrmto	AAA	9	9	1	0	53.1	211	49	19	14	7	1	0	0	11	0	54	1	0	3	1	.750	0	0--	-	3.18	2.36
2007	Oak	AL	20	14	0	1	72.1	332	91	59	54	9	4	0	2	26	1	55	6	1	1	8	.111	0	0-0	1	5.63	6.72
2008	Oak	AL	19	10	0	7	71.2	301	77	36	33	8	1	2	2	25	2	41	0	1	5	4	.556	0	0-0	0	4.63	4.14
2 ML YEARS			39	24	0	8	144.0	633	168	95	87	17	5	2	4	51	3	96	6	2	6	12	.333	0	0-0	1	5.13	5.44

Chad Bradford

Pitches: R **Bats:** R **Pos:** RP-68   **Ht:** 6'5" **Wt:** 203 **Born:** 9/14/1974 **Age:** 34

			HOW MUCH HE PITCHED						WHAT HE GAVE UP											THE RESULTS						
Year	Team	Lg	G	GS	CG	GF	IP	BFP	H	R	ER	HR	SH	SF	HB	TBB	IBB	SO	WP	Bk	W	L	Pct	ShO	Sv-Op	Hld	ERC	ERA
1998	CWS	AL	29	0	0	8	30.2	125	27	16	11	0	0	0	0	7	0	11	1	0	2	1	.667	0	1-3	9	2.16	3.23
1999	CWS	AL	3	0	0	0	3.2	24	9	8	8	1	0	0	0	5	0	0	1	0	0	0	-	0	0-0	0	21.34	19.64
2000	CWS	AL	12	0	0	5	13.2	52	13	4	3	0	0	0	0	1	1	9	0	0	1	0	1.000	0	0-0	2	2.01	1.98
2001	Oak	AL	35	0	0	19	36.2	154	41	12	11	6	1	0	1	6	0	34	0	0	2	1	.667	0	1-4	4	4.36	2.70
2002	Oak	AL	75	0	0	14	75.1	311	73	29	26	2	2	2	5	14	5	56	0	1	4	2	.667	0	2-5	24	2.77	3.11
2003	Oak	AL	72	0	0	12	77.0	322	67	28	26	7	1	0	7	30	9	62	0	1	7	4	.636	0	2-5	23	3.50	3.04
2004	Oak	AL	68	0	0	16	59.0	251	51	32	29	5	3	1	5	24	9	34	0	0	5	7	.417	0	1-4	15	3.35	4.42
2005	Bos	AL	31	0	0	2	23.1	104	29	10	10	1	3	1	3	4	1	10	2	0	2	1	.667	0	0-1	8	4.54	3.86
2006	NYM	NL	70	0	0	15	62.0	252	59	22	20	1	4	3	0	13	4	45	0	0	4	2	.667	0	2-3	10	2.48	2.90
2007	Bal	AL	78	0	0	14	64.2	289	77	28	24	1	4	1	6	16	3	29	0	0	4	7	.364	0	2-7	19	4.16	3.34
2008	2 Tms	AL	68	0	0	9	59.1	241	59	20	14	3	3	5	2	15	6	17	0	0	4	3	.571	0	0-2	21	3.24	2.12
08 Bal		AL	47	0	0	5	40.1	160	41	17	11	2	3	2	1	7	3	13	0	0	3	3	.500	0	0-1	16	3.09	2.45
08 TB		AL	21	0	0	4	19.0	81	18	3	3	1	0	3	1	8	3	4	0	0	1	0	1.000	0	0-1	5	3.53	1.42
Postseason			17	0	0	0	15.1	58	12	0	0	0	0	0	2	3	2	10	0	0	0	0	-	0	0-1	1	2.03	0.00
11 ML YEARS			541	0	0	114	505.1	2125	505	209	182	27	21	13	29	135	38	307	4	3	35	28	.556	0	11-34	134	3.37	3.24

Milton Bradley

Bats: B **Throws:** R **Pos:** DH-99; RF-19; PH-9; LF-1   **Ht:** 6'0" **Wt:** 225 **Born:** 4/15/1978 **Age:** 31

									BATTING												BASERUNNING				AVERAGES		
Year	Team	Lg	G	AB	H	2B	3B	HR	(Hm	Rd)	TB	R	RBI	RC	TBB	IBB	SO	HBP	SH	SF	SB	CS	SB%	GDP	Avg	OBP	Slg
2000	Mon	NL	42	154	34	8	1	2	(1	1)	50	20	15	14	14	0	32	1	1	1	2	1	.67	3	.221	.288	.325
2001	2 Tms		77	238	53	17	3	1	(0	1)	79	22	19	21	21	0	65	1	2	0	8	5	.62	7	.223	.288	.332
2002	Cle	AL	98	325	81	18	3	9	(4	5)	132	48	38	40	32	2	58	0	1	0	6	3	.67	12	.249	.317	.406
2003	Cle	AL	101	377	121	34	2	10	(4	6)	189	61	56	77	64	8	73	5	0	5	17	7	.71	10	.321	.421	.501
2004	LAD	NL	141	516	138	24	0	19	(8	11)	219	72	67	70	71	3	123	6	3	1	15	11	.58	12	.267	.362	.424
2005	LAD	NL	75	283	82	14	1	13	(6	7)	137	49	38	40	25	1	47	2	4	1	6	1	.86	6	.290	.350	.484
2006	Oak	AL	96	351	97	14	2	14	(7	7)	157	53	52	60	51	1	65	2	0	1	10	2	.83	13	.276	.370	.447
2007	2 Tms		61	209	64	9	1	13	(7	6)	114	37	37	42	31	3	41	3	0	1	5	2	.71	5	.306	.402	.545
2008	Tex	AL	126	414	133	32	1	22	(16	6)	233	78	77	90	80	13	112	9	0	6	5	3	.63	10	.321	.436	.563
01 Mon		NL	67	220	49	16	3	1	(0	1)	74	19	19	20	19	0	62	1	2	0	7	4	.64	6	.223	.288	.336
01 Cle		AL	10	18	4	1	0	0	(0	0)	5	3	0	1	2	0	3	0	0	0	1	1	.50	1	.222	.300	.278

Year Team	Lg	G	AB	H	2B	3B	HR	(Hm	Rd)	TB	R	RBI	RC	TBB	IBB	SO	HBP	SH	SF	SB	CS	SB%	GDP	Avg	OBP	Slg
07 Oak	AL	19	65	19	4	0	2	(1	1)	29	6	7	10	8	1	14	1	0	1	2	1	.67	2	.292	.373	.446
07 SD	NL	42	144	45	5	1	11	(6	5)	85	31	30	32	23	2	27	2	0	0	3	1	.75	3	.313	.414	.590
Postseason		11	42	13	3	0	4	(3	1)	28	6	8	7	5	0	5	0	0	0	2	0	1.00	3	.310	.383	.667
9 ML YEARS		817	2867	803	170	14	103	(53	50)	1310	440	399	454	389	31	616	29	11	16	74	35	.68	78	.280	.370	.457

Russell Branyan

Bats: L Throws: R Pos: 3B-35; PH-14; 1B-5   **Ht: 6'3" Wt: 195 Born: 12/19/1975 Age: 33**

Year Team	Lg	G	AB	H	2B	3B	HR	(Hm	Rd)	TB	R	RBI	RC	TBB	IBB	SO	HBP	SH	SF	SB	CS	SB%	GDP	Avg	OBP	Slg
2008 Nashv*	AAA	45	153	55	15	0	12	(-	-)	106	24	36	44	25	3	49	1	0	0	4	1	.80	3	.359	.453	.693
1998 Cle	AL	1	4	0	0	0	0	(0	0)	0	0	0	0	0	0	2	0	0	0	0	0	-	0	.000	.000	.000
1999 Cle	AL	11	38	8	2	0	1	(0	1)	13	4	6	4	3	0	19	1	0	0	0	0	-	0	.211	.286	.342
2000 Cle	AL	67	193	46	7	2	16	(13	3)	105	32	38	34	22	1	76	4	0	1	0	0	-	2	.238	.327	.544
2001 Cle	AL	113	315	73	16	2	20	(11	9)	153	48	54	50	38	1	132	3	0	5	1	1	.50	2	.232	.316	.486
2002 2 Tms		134	378	86	13	1	24	(5	19)	173	50	56	49	51	3	151	2	0	5	4	3	.57	5	.228	.320	.458
2003 Cin	NL	74	176	38	12	0	9	(7	2)	77	22	26	23	27	0	69	1	0	1	0	0	-	1	.216	.322	.438
2004 Mil	NL	51	158	37	11	1	11	(8	3)	83	21	27	23	20	0	68	2	0	2	1	0	1.00	1	.234	.324	.525
2005 Mil	NL	85	202	52	11	0	12	(3	9)	99	23	31	38	39	10	80	0	1	0	1	0	1.00	3	.257	.378	.490
2006 2 Tms		91	241	55	11	0	18	(9	9)	120	37	36	34	34	1	89	3	1	3	2	0	1.00	1	.228	.327	.498
2007 3 Tms	NL	89	163	32	5	1	10	(6	4)	69	22	26	27	28	1	69	2	0	1	1	0	1.00	1	.196	.320	.423
2008 Mil	NL	50	132	33	8	0	12	(9	3)	77	24	20	22	19	4	42	0	0	1	1	0	1.00	0	.250	.342	.583
02 Cle	AL	50	161	33	4	0	8	(1	7)	61	16	17	14	17	0	65	0	0	2	1	2	.33	3	.205	.278	.379
02 Cin	NL	84	217	53	9	1	16	(4	12)	112	34	39	35	34	3	86	2	0	2	3	1	.75	2	.244	.349	.516
06 TB	AL	64	169	34	10	0	12	(7	5)	80	23	27	22	19	0	62	2	1	2	2	0	1.00	1	.201	.286	.473
06 SD	NL	27	72	21	1	0	6	(2	4)	40	14	9	12	15	1	27	1	0	1	0	0	-	0	.292	.416	.556
07 SD	NL	61	122	24	5	1	7	(5	2)	52	16	19	18	21	1	48	2	0	1	1	0	1.00	1	.197	.322	.426
07 Phi	NL	7	9	2	0	0	2	(0	2)	8	2	5	2	0	0	6	0	0	0	0	0	-	0	.222	.222	.889
07 StL	NL	21	32	6	0	0	1	(1	0)	9	4	2	3	7	0	15	0	0	0	0	0	-	1	.188	.333	.281
Postseason		6	16	4	1	1	0	(0	0)	7	2	3	1	1	0	6	0	0	0	0	0	-	0	.250	.294	.438
11 ML YEARS		766	2000	460	96	7	133	(71	62)	969	283	320	300	281	21	797	18	2	18	11	4	.73	17	.230	.328	.485

Ryan Braun

Bats: R Throws: R Pos: LF-149; PH-2; DH-1   **Ht: 6'1" Wt: 200 Born: 11/17/1983 Age: 25**

Year Team	Lg	G	AB	H	2B	3B	HR	(Hm	Rd)	TB	R	RBI	RC	TBB	IBB	SO	HBP	SH	SF	SB	CS	SB%	GDP	Avg	OBP	Slg
2005 Helena	R+	10	41	14	2	1	2	(-	-)	24	6	10	9	2	0	6	2	0	2	2	1	.67	0	.341	.383	.585
2005 WV	A	37	152	54	16	2	8	(-	-)	98	21	35	35	9	1	34	2	2	1	2	4	.33	7	.355	.396	.645
2006 BrvdCt	A+	59	226	62	12	2	7	(-	-)	99	34	37	37	23	1	54	4	3	4	14	4	.78	3	.274	.346	.438
2006 Hntsvl	AA	59	231	70	19	1	15	(-	-)	136	42	40	51	21	1	46	3	1	1	12	0	1.00	6	.303	.367	.589
2007 Nashv	AAA	34	117	40	12	0	10	(-	-)	82	28	22	31	15	0	11	1	0	1	4	3	.57	1	.342	.418	.701
2007 Mil	NL	113	451	146	26	6	34	(17	17)	286	91	97	94	29	1	112	7	0	5	15	5	.75	13	.324	.370	**.634**
2008 Mil	NL	151	611	174	39	7	37	(23	14)	338	92	106	100	42	4	129	6	0	4	14	4	.78	13	.285	.335	.553
2 ML YEARS		264	1062	320	65	13	71	(40	31)	624	183	203	194	71	5	241	13	0	9	29	9	.76	26	.301	.350	.588

Bill Bray

Pitches: L Bats: L Pos: RP-63   **Ht: 6'3" Wt: 222 Born: 6/5/1983 Age: 26**

Year Team	Lg	G	GS	CG	GF	IP	BFP	H	R	ER	HR	SH	SF	HB	TBB	IBB	SO	WP	Bk	W	L	Pct	ShO	Sv-Op	Hld	ERC	ERA
2008 Lsvlle*	AAA	9	0	0	1	9.0	38	6	3	3	1	0	0	0	5	0	15	0	0	0	0	-	0	1- -	-	2.90	3.00
2006 2 Tms	NL	48	0	0	10	50.2	223	57	27	23	5	2	1	1	18	3	39	0	0	3	2	.600	0	2-3	3	4.58	4.09
2007 Cin	NL	19	0	0	5	14.1	63	16	10	10	1	0	1	0	5	1	14	0	0	3	3	.500	0	1-1	3	4.16	6.28
2008 Cin	NL	63	0	0	11	47.0	215	50	19	15	4	3	1	1	24	5	54	2	0	2	2	.500	0	0-4	9	4.57	2.87
06 Was	NL	19	0	0	4	23.0	100	24	11	10	2	1	1	1	9	2	16	0	0	1	1	.500	0	0-0	1	4.25	3.91
06 Cin	NL	29	0	0	6	27.2	123	33	16	13	3	1	0	0	9	1	23	0	0	2	1	.667	0	2-3	2	4.85	4.23
3 ML YEARS		130	0	0	26	112.0	501	123	56	48	10	5	3	2	47	9	107	2	0	8	7	.533	0	3-8	15	4.52	3.86

Yhency Brazoban

Pitches: R Bats: R Pos: RP-2   **Ht: 6'1" Wt: 250 Born: 11/6/1980 Age: 28**

Year Team	Lg	G	GS	CG	GF	IP	BFP	H	R	ER	HR	SH	SF	HB	TBB	IBB	SO	WP	Bk	W	L	Pct	ShO	Sv-Op	Hld	ERC	ERA
2008 Jaxnvl*	AA	11	0	0	5	10.2	42	7	3	3	1	0	0	0	2	0	13	0	0	0	1	.000	0	2- -	-	1.54	2.53
2008 LsVgs*	AAA	10	0	0	2	10.0	53	19	12	12	4	0	0	0	5	0	5	0	0	0	0	-	0	1- -	-	13.21	10.80
2008 Ddgrs*	R	2	2	0	0	2.0	10	2	1	1	0	0	0	0	1	0	2	1	0	0	0	-	0	0- -	-	3.21	4.50
2004 LAD	NL	31	0	0	10	32.2	133	25	9	9	2	4	0	0	15	2	27	1	0	6	2	.750	0	0-0	5	2.76	2.48
2005 LAD	NL	74	0	0	44	72.2	317	70	46	43	11	7	2	5	32	4	61	1	0	4	10	.286	0	21-27	8	4.60	5.33
2006 LAD	NL	5	0	0	2	5.0	23	7	3	3	0	0	0	0	2	0	4	1	0	0	0	-	0	0-1	0	5.74	5.40
2007 LAD	NL	4	0	0	1	1.2	12	3	4	3	0	0	0	0	3	1	5	0	0	0	0	-	0	0-0	0	11.51	16.20
2008 LAD	NL	2	0	0	1	3.0	16	4	2	2	0	0	0	0	3	0	3	1	0	0	0	-	0	0-0	0	7.51	6.00
Postseason		2	0	0	1	3.0	13	1	1	1	0	0	0	1	2	0	2	0	0	0	0	-	0	0-0	0	2.02	3.00
5 ML YEARS		116	0	0	58	115.0	501	109	64	60	13	11	3	5	55	7	100	4	0	10	12	.455	0	21-28	13	4.28	4.70

Craig Breslow

Pitches: L Bats: L Pos: RP-49   Ht: 6'0" Wt: 180 Born: 8/8/1980 Age: 28

			HOW MUCH HE PITCHED						WHAT HE GAVE UP									THE RESULTS							
Year	Team	Lg	G	GS	CG	GF	IP	BFP	H	R	ER	HR	SH	SF	HB	TBB	IBB	SO	WP	Bk	W	L	Pct	ShO	Sv-Op Hld	ERC	ERA
2005	SD	NL	14	0	0	3	16.1	78	15	6	4	1	0	1	1	13	0	14	1	0	0	0	-	0	0-0 1	4.98	2.20
2006	Bos	AL	13	0	0	3	12.0	55	12	5	5	0	0	2	1	6	1	12	2	1	0	2	.000	0	0-0 3	3.78	3.75
2008	2 Tms	AL	49	0	0	13	47.0	189	34	12	10	1	2	0	0	19	2	39	4	1	0	2	.000	0	1-2 5	2.12	1.91
08	Cle	AL	7	0	0	3	8.1	40	10	3	3	1	0	0	0	5	0	7	0	0	0	0	-	0	0-0 0	6.09	3.24
08	Min	AL	42	0	0	10	38.2	149	24	9	7	0	2	0	0	14	2	32	4	1	0	2	.000	0	1-2 5	1.49	1.63
3 ML YEARS			76	0	0	19	75.1	322	61	23	19	2	2	3	2	38	3	65	7	2	0	4	.000	0	1-2 9	2.95	2.27

Reid Brignac

Bats: L Throws: R Pos: SS-4; PH-1   Ht: 6'3" Wt: 180 Born: 1/16/1986 Age: 23

							BATTING													BASERUNNING				AVERAGES		
Year	Team	Lg	G	AB	H	2B	3B	HR	(Hm	Rd)	TB	R	RBI	RC	TBB	IBB	SO	HBP	SH	SF	SB	CS	SB%	GDP	Avg	OBP	Slg
2004	Princtn	R+	25	97	35	4	2	1	(-	-)	46	16	25	19	9	0	10	1	0	2	2	1	.67	2	.361	.413	.474
2004	CtnSC	A	3	14	7	1	0	0	(-	-)	8	3	5	3	1	0	2	0	0	0	0	0	-	0	.500	.533	.571
2005	SWMch	A	127	512	135	29	2	15	(-	-)	213	77	61	69	40	0	131	4	4	5	5	5	.50	5	.264	.319	.416
2006	Visalia	A+	100	411	134	26	3	21	(-	-)	229	82	83	85	35	0	82	4	2	3	12	6	.67	6	.326	.382	.557
2006	Mont	AA	28	110	33	6	2	3	(-	-)	52	18	16	19	7	0	31	3	0	1	3	0	1.00	1	.300	.355	.473
2007	Mont	AA	133	527	137	30	5	17	(-	-)	228	91	81	80	55	3	94	3	1	10	15	5	.75	11	.260	.328	.433
2008	Drham	AAA	97	352	88	26	2	9	(-	-)	145	43	43	45	25	2	93	2	1	6	5	2	.71	10	.250	.299	.412
2008	TB	AL	4	10	0	0	0	0	(0	0)	0	1	0	0	1	0	5	0	0	0	0	0	-	0	.000	.091	.000

Chris Britton

Pitches: R Bats: R Pos: RP-15   Ht: 6'3" Wt: 275 Born: 12/16/1982 Age: 26

							HOW MUCH HE PITCHED						WHAT HE GAVE UP								THE RESULTS					
Year	Team	Lg	G	GS	CG	GF	IP	BFP	H	R	ER	HR	SH	SF	HB	TBB	IBB	SO	WP	Bk	W	L	Pct	ShO	Sv-Op Hld	ERC	ERA
2008	S-WB*	AAA	21	0	0	6	27.2	115	28	7	7	2	0	0	0	7	1	26	0	0	3	1	.750	0	0- - 3	3.35	2.28
2008	Yanks*	R	2	2	0	0	3.0	9	0	0	0	0	0	0	0	0	0	3	0	0	0	0	-	0	0- - 0	0.00	0.00
2006	Bal	AL	52	0	0	12	53.2	221	46	22	20	4	1	1	0	17	3	41	0	0	0	2	.000	0	1-3 6	2.74	3.35
2007	NYY	AL	11	0	0	4	12.2	51	9	5	5	2	1	0	0	4	0	5	0	0	1	0	1.000	0	0-0 0	2.55	3.55
2008	NYY	AL	15	0	0	14	23.0	105	28	13	13	4	0	1	0	11	1	12	1	0	0	0	-	0	0-0 0	6.22	5.09
3 ML YEARS			78	0	0	30	89.1	377	83	40	38	10	2	2	0	32	4	58	1	0	0	3	.000	0	1-3 6	3.52	3.83

Lance Broadway

Pitches: R Bats: R Pos: RP-6; SP-1   Ht: 6'3" Wt: 190 Born: 8/20/1983 Age: 25

							HOW MUCH HE PITCHED						WHAT HE GAVE UP								THE RESULTS					
Year	Team	Lg	G	GS	CG	GF	IP	BFP	H	R	ER	HR	SH	SF	HB	TBB	IBB	SO	WP	Bk	W	L	Pct	ShO	Sv-Op Hld	ERC	ERA
2005	WinSa	A+	11	11	0	0	55.0	253	68	31	28	4	4	0	7	20	0	58	2	0	1	3	.250	0	0- - -	5.64	4.58
2006	Brham	AA	25	25	2	0	154.1	659	160	59	47	10	9	5	10	40	0	111	11	0	8	8	.500	1	0- - -	3.74	2.74
2006	Charltt	AAA	2	2	1	0	9.2	40	8	4	4	1	0	0	0	3	0	13	1	0	0	0	-	0	0- - -	2.78	3.72
2007	Charltt	AAA	27	27	2	0	155.0	684	155	86	80	17	7	4	8	78	2	108	12	0	8	9	.471	0	0- - -	4.79	4.65
2008	Charltt	AAA	24	23	1	0	145.0	627	166	87	75	24	8	5	1	44	1	101	13	1	11	7	.611	0	0- - -	5.05	4.66
2007	CWS	AL	4	1	0	1	10.1	41	5	2	1	0	0	0	0	5	0	14	0	0	1	1	.500	0	0-0 0	1.34	0.87
2008	CWS	AL	7	1	0	4	14.0	66	20	11	11	4	0	0	0	5	1	7	0	0	1	0	1.000	0	0-0 0	7.80	7.07
2 ML YEARS			11	2	0	5	24.1	107	25	13	12	4	0	1	0	10	1	21	0	0	2	1	.667	0	0-0 0	4.61	4.44

Doug Brocail

Pitches: R Bats: L Pos: RP-72   Ht: 6'5" Wt: 250 Born: 5/16/1967 Age: 42

							HOW MUCH HE PITCHED						WHAT HE GAVE UP								THE RESULTS					
Year	Team	Lg	G	GS	CG	GF	IP	BFP	H	R	ER	HR	SH	SF	HB	TBB	IBB	SO	WP	Bk	W	L	Pct	ShO	Sv-Op Hld	ERC	ERA
1992	SD	NL	3	3	0	0	14.0	64	17	10	10	2	2	0	0	5	0	15	0	0	0	0	-	0	0-0 0	5.33	6.43
1993	SD	NL	24	24	0	0	128.1	571	143	75	65	16	10	8	4	42	4	70	4	1	4	13	.235	0	0-0 0	4.60	4.56
1994	SD	NL	12	0	0	4	17.0	78	21	13	11	1	1	1	2	5	3	11	1	1	0	0	-	0	0-1 0	4.79	5.82
1995	Hou	NL	36	7	0	12	77.1	339	87	40	36	10	1	4	1	22	2	39	1	1	6	4	.600	0	1-1 0	4.68	4.19
1996	Hou	NL	23	4	0	4	53.0	231	58	31	27	7	3	2	2	23	1	34	0	0	1	5	.167	0	0-0 1	5.26	4.58
1997	Det	AL	61	4	0	20	78.0	332	74	31	28	10	1	3	3	36	4	60	6	0	3	4	.429	0	2-9 16	4.42	3.23
1998	Det	AL	60	0	0	24	62.2	247	47	23	19	2	2	3	1	18	3	55	6	0	5	2	.714	0	0-1 11	1.99	2.73
1999	Det	AL	70	0	0	22	82.0	326	60	23	23	7	4	2	4	25	1	78	4	1	4	4	.500	0	2-4 23	2.43	2.52
2000	Det	AL	49	0	0	10	50.2	221	57	25	23	5	3	3	1	14	2	41	1	1	5	4	.556	0	0-5 19	4.25	4.09
2004	Tex	AL	43	0	0	14	52.1	232	54	29	24	2	4	2	2	20	1	43	2	1	4	1	.800	0	1-1 4	4.05	4.13
2005	Tex	AL	61	0	0	13	73.1	344	90	48	45	2	3	4	4	34	3	61	4	0	5	3	.625	0	1-4 5	5.15	5.52
2006	SD	NL	25	0	0	6	28.1	119	27	16	15	1	3	1	0	8	2	19	1	0	2	2	.500	0	0-0 0	2.80	4.76
2007	SD	NL	67	0	0	16	76.2	319	66	33	26	8	2	1	2	24	3	43	2	0	5	1	.833	0	0-0 10	3.03	3.05
2008	Hou	NL	72	0	0	21	68.2	286	63	30	30	8	1	1	3	21	5	64	1	1	7	5	.583	0	2-5 22	3.45	3.93
14 ML YEARS			606	42	0	166	862.1	3709	864	427	382	81	40	32	35	297	34	633	33	7	51	48	.515	0	9-31 111	3.92	3.99

Ben Broussard

Bats: L Throws: L Pos: 1B-26; PH-1   Ht: 6'2" Wt: 230 Born: 9/24/1976 Age: 32

							BATTING													BASERUNNING				AVERAGES		
Year	Team	Lg	G	AB	H	2B	3B	HR	(Hm	Rd)	TB	R	RBI	RC	TBB	IBB	SO	HBP	SH	SF	SB	CS	SB%	GDP	Avg	OBP	Slg
2008	S-WB*	AAA	64	239	66	18	1	13	(-	-)	125	44	46	44	18	0	45	9	0	1	1	0	1.00	5	.276	.348	.523
2008	Tenn*	AA	2	9	2	0	0	1	(-	-)	5	3	2	1	0	0	1	1	0	0	0	0	-	0	.222	.300	.556
2008	Iowa*	AAA	16	60	16	2	0	3	(-	-)	27	14	13	9	7	1	16	0	0	2	0	0	-	1	.267	.333	.450
2002	Cle	AL	39	112	27	4	0	4	(2	2)	43	10	9	9	7	1	25	1	0	0	0	0	-	3	.241	.292	.384

55

Year	Team	Lg	G	AB	H	2B	3B	HR	(Hm	Rd)	TB	R	RBI	RC	TBB	IBB	SO	HBP	SH	SF	SB	CS	SB%	GDP	Avg	OBP	Slg
2003	Cle	AL	116	386	96	21	3	16	(7	9)	171	53	55	53	32	2	75	5	3	3	5	2	.71	6	.249	.312	.443
2004	Cle	AL	139	418	115	28	5	17	(9	8)	204	57	82	79	52	3	95	12	1	2	4	2	.67	7	.275	.370	.488
2005	Cle	AL	142	466	119	30	5	19	(11	8)	216	59	68	60	32	5	98	4	0	3	2	2	.50	4	.255	.307	.464
2006	2 Tms	AL	144	432	125	21	0	21	(12	9)	209	61	63	64	26	3	103	3	0	4	2	1	.67	8	.289	.331	.484
2007	Sea	AL	99	240	66	10	0	7	(4	3)	97	27	29	30	17	2	50	4	0	3	2	0	1.00	1	.275	.330	.404
2008	Tex	AL	26	82	13	0	0	3	(0	3)	22	8	8	2	5	1	20	2	0	0	0	0	-	2	.159	.225	.268
06	Cle	AL	88	268	86	14	0	13	(11	2)	139	44	46	48	17	1	58	1	0	2	0	1	.00	5	.321	.361	.519
06	Sea	AL	56	164	39	7	0	8	(1	7)	70	17	17	16	9	2	45	2	0	2	2	0	1.00	3	.238	.282	.427
7 ML YEARS			705	2136	561	114	13	87	(45	42)	962	275	314	297	171	17	466	31	4	15	15	7	.68	37	.263	.324	.450

Andrew Brown

Pitches: R Bats: R Pos: RP-31   **Ht: 6'6" Wt: 230 Born: 2/17/1981 Age: 28**

Year	Team	Lg	G	GS	CG	GF	IP	BFP	H	R	ER	HR	SH	SF	HB	TBB	IBB	SO	WP	Bk	W	L	Pct	ShO	Sv-Op	Hld	ERC	ERA
2008	Stcktn*	A+	1	1	0	0	2.0	6	0	0	0	0	0	0	1	0	0	0	0	0	0	0	-	0	0--	-	0.32	0.00
2008	Scrmto*	AAA	1	0	0	0	1.1	5	1	1	1	0	0	0	0	1	0	1	0	0	0	0	-	0	0--	-	3.97	6.75
2006	Cle	AL	9	0	0	4	10.0	44	6	4	4	0	0	0	1	8	1	7	1	0	0	0	-	0	0-0	0	2.87	3.60
2007	Oak	AL	33	0	0	5	41.2	178	38	21	21	1	2	1	3	17	3	43	6	0	3	3	.500	0	0-2	3	3.27	4.54
2008	Oak	AL	31	0	0	13	35.0	147	23	13	12	3	1	1	1	21	1	28	0	0	1	0	1.000	0	0-1	2	2.96	3.09
3 ML YEARS			73	0	0	22	86.2	369	67	38	37	4	3	2	5	46	5	78	7	0	4	3	.571	0	0-3	5	3.11	3.84

Emil Brown

Bats: R Throws: R Pos: LF-65; RF-55; PH-14; DH-7; PR-2; 1B-1; CF-1   **Ht: 6'2" Wt: 210 Born: 12/29/1974 Age: 34**

Year	Team	Lg	G	AB	H	2B	3B	HR	(Hm	Rd)	TB	R	RBI	RC	TBB	IBB	SO	HBP	SH	SF	SB	CS	SB%	GDP	Avg	OBP	Slg
1997	Pit	NL	66	95	17	2	1	2	(1	1)	27	16	6	9	10	1	32	7	0	0	5	1	.83	1	.179	.304	.284
1998	Pit	NL	13	39	10	1	0	0	(0	0)	11	2	3	3	1	0	11	1	0	0	0	0	-	0	.256	.293	.282
1999	Pit	NL	6	14	2	1	0	0	(0	0)	3	0	0	0	0	0	3	0	0	0	0	0	-	0	.143	.143	.214
2000	Pit	NL	50	119	26	5	0	3	(2	1)	40	13	16	11	11	0	34	3	1	1	3	1	.75	3	.218	.299	.336
2001	2 Tms	NL	74	137	26	4	1	3	(2	1)	41	21	13	12	16	1	49	2	0	0	12	4	.75	2	.190	.284	.299
2005	KC	AL	150	545	156	31	5	17	(8	9)	248	75	86	91	48	1	108	8	1	7	10	1	.91	14	.286	.349	.455
2006	KC	AL	147	527	151	41	2	15	(6	9)	241	77	81	79	59	3	95	5	0	10	6	3	.67	15	.287	.358	.457
2007	KC	AL	113	366	94	13	1	6	(1	5)	127	44	62	49	24	2	71	1	0	6	12	2	.86	7	.257	.300	.347
2008	Oak	AL	117	402	98	14	2	13	(6	7)	155	48	59	44	27	2	65	5	0	4	4	2	.67	16	.244	.297	.386
01	Pit	NL	61	123	25	4	1	3	(2	1)	40	18	13	12	15	1	42	2	0	0	10	4	.71	2	.203	.300	.325
01	SD	NL	13	14	1	0	0	0	(0	0)	1	3	0	0	1	0	7	0	0	0	2	0	1.00	0	.071	.133	.071
9 ML YEARS			736	2244	580	112	12	59	(26	33)	893	296	326	298	196	10	468	32	2	28	52	14	.79	58	.258	.323	.398

Matt Brown

Bats: R Throws: R Pos: 3B-10; 2B-1   **Ht: 6'0" Wt: 200 Born: 8/8/1982 Age: 26**

Year	Team	Lg	G	AB	H	2B	3B	HR	(Hm	Rd)	TB	R	RBI	RC	TBB	IBB	SO	HBP	SH	SF	SB	CS	SB%	GDP	Avg	OBP	Slg
2001	Angels	R	46	141	23	7	1	1	(-	-)	35	14	21	9	18	1	30	5	1	3	1	3	.25	1	.163	.275	.248
2002	Angels	R	28	97	35	7	0	2	(-	-)	48	16	22	22	15	0	14	1	0	2	3	1	.75	2	.361	.443	.495
2002	Provo	R+	32	108	32	5	1	0	(-	-)	39	14	11	17	15	0	21	5	0	0	3	3	.50	3	.296	.406	.361
2003	CRpds	A	49	164	34	6	1	3	(-	-)	51	22	15	17	19	0	36	5	0	1	1	0	1.00	4	.207	.307	.311
2003	Provo	R+	65	233	68	19	0	11	(-	-)	120	58	52	51	42	2	56	9	0	5	2	3	.40	1	.292	.412	.515
2004	CRpds	A	122	437	102	20	4	23	(-	-)	199	67	82	62	33	1	126	13	2	5	6	6	.50	4	.233	.303	.455
2005	RCuca	A+	125	488	128	39	4	12	(-	-)	211	68	65	71	40	0	125	11	3	5	4	5	.44	10	.262	.329	.432
2006	Ark	AA	134	515	151	41	3	19	(-	-)	255	77	79	92	47	0	108	10	2	2	7	6	.54	8	.293	.362	.495
2007	Salt Lk	AAA	110	391	108	30	2	19	(-	-)	199	69	60	69	45	0	106	5	1	0	5	9	.36	12	.276	.358	.509
2008	Salt Lk	AAA	97	400	128	33	4	21	(-	-)	232	75	67	84	32	1	80	3	0	2	4	2	.67	7	.320	.373	.580
2007	LAA	AL	4	5	0	0	0	0	(0	0)	0	0	0	0	2	0	1	0	0	0	1	0	1.00	0	.000	.286	.000
2008	LAA	AL	11	19	1	1	0	0	(0	0)	2	0	3	0	1	0	10	0	0	0	0	0	-	0	.053	.100	.105
2 ML YEARS			15	24	1	1	0	0	(0	0)	2	0	3	0	3	0	11	0	0	0	1	0	1.00	0	.042	.148	.083

Jonathan Broxton

Pitches: R Bats: R Pos: RP-70   **Ht: 6'4" Wt: 290 Born: 6/16/1984 Age: 25**

Year	Team	Lg	G	GS	CG	GF	IP	BFP	H	R	ER	HR	SH	SF	HB	TBB	IBB	SO	WP	Bk	W	L	Pct	ShO	Sv-Op	Hld	ERC	ERA
2005	LAD	NL	14	0	0	5	13.2	68	13	11	9	0	0	2	1	12	2	22	2	0	1	0	1.000	0	0-1	1	4.65	5.93
2006	LAD	NL	68	0	0	20	76.1	320	61	25	22	7	3	1	1	33	6	97	7	0	4	1	.800	0	3-7	12	2.97	2.59
2007	LAD	NL	83	0	0	18	82.0	334	69	30	26	6	0	1	1	25	3	99	4	0	4	4	.500	0	2-8	32	2.71	2.85
2008	LAD	NL	70	0	0	32	69.0	285	54	29	24	2	3	3	3	27	5	88	3	0	3	5	.375	0	14-22	13	2.48	3.13
Postseason			2	0	0	1	2.0	14	5	3	3	0	0	0	0	2	0	3	0	0	0	1	.000	0	0-1	0	14.53	13.50
4 ML YEARS			235	0	0	75	241.0	1007	197	95	81	15	6	7	6	97	16	306	16	0	12	10	.545	0	19-38	58	2.84	3.02

Jay Bruce

Bats: L Throws: L Pos: RF-78; CF-35; LF-11; PH-4; PR-1   **Ht: 6'3" Wt: 205 Born: 4/3/1987 Age: 22**

Year	Team	Lg	G	AB	H	2B	3B	HR	(Hm	Rd)	TB	R	RBI	RC	TBB	IBB	SO	HBP	SH	SF	SB	CS	SB%	GDP	Avg	OBP	Slg
2005	Reds	R	37	122	33	9	2	5	(-	-)	61	29	25	19	11	0	31	1	0	2	4	6	.40	2	.270	.331	.500
2005	Billings	R+	17	70	18	2	0	4	(-	-)	32	16	13	11	11	0	22	1	0	0	2	2	.50	2	.257	.358	.457
2006	Dayton	A	117	444	129	42	5	16	(-	-)	229	69	81	82	44	4	106	4	0	6	19	9	.68	7	.291	.355	.516
2007	Srsota	A+	67	268	87	27	5	11	(-	-)	157	49	49	57	24	2	67	2	0	4	4	4	.50	4	.325	.379	.586

Year	Team	Lg	G	AB	H	2B	3B	HR	(Hm Rd)	TB	R	RBI	RC	TBB	IBB	SO	HBP	SH	SF	SB	CS	SB%	GDP	Avg	OBP	Slg
2007	Chatt	AA	16	66	22	7	1	4	(- -)	43	10	15	16	8	0	20	0	0	0	2	1	.67	0	.333	.405	.652
2007	Lsvlle	AAA	50	187	57	12	2	11	(- -)	106	28	25	36	15	1	48	1	0	1	2	2	.50	1	.305	.358	.567
2008	Lsvlle	AAA	49	184	67	9	5	10	(- -)	116	34	37	44	12	4	45	0	0	5	8	1	.89	4	.364	.393	.630
2008	Cin	NL	108	413	105	17	1	21	(13 8)	187	63	52	49	33	1	110	4	0	2	4	6	.40	8	.254	.314	.453

Brian Bruney

Pitches: R **Bats:** R **Pos:** RP-31; SP-1 **Ht:** 6'3" **Wt:** 237 **Born:** 2/17/1982 **Age:** 27

Year	Team	Lg	G	GS	CG	GF	IP	BFP	H	R	ER	HR	SH	SF	HB	TBB	IBB	SO	WP	Bk	W	L	Pct	ShO	Sv-Op	Hld	ERC	ERA
2008	Yanks*	R	3	2	0	0	4.0	17	3	1	1	0	0	0	0	2	0	6	0	0	0	1	.000	0	0--	-	2.40	2.25
2008	Trntn*	AA	2	1	0	0	2.1	10	2	2	1	0	0	0	0	2	0	2	0	0	0	1	.000	0	0--	-	4.61	3.86
2008	S-WB*	AAA	7	1	0	1	7.1	36	7	4	3	0	0	0	1	7	0	7	1	0	0	0	-	0	0--	-	5.73	3.68
2004	Ari	NL	30	0	0	14	31.1	135	20	16	15	2	1	0	1	27	5	34	2	0	3	4	.429	0	0-1	3	3.54	4.31
2005	Ari	NL	47	0	0	21	46.0	230	56	39	38	6	2	1	5	35	2	51	2	0	1	3	.250	0	12-16	4	7.48	7.43
2006	NYY	AL	19	0	0	2	20.2	90	14	2	2	1	0	0	1	15	0	25	2	0	1	1	.500	0	0-0	4	3.37	0.87
2007	NYY	AL	58	0	0	16	50.0	228	44	28	26	5	1	6	3	37	2	39	4	0	3	2	.600	0	0-2	6	4.92	4.68
2008	NYY	AL	32	1	0	5	34.1	137	18	7	7	2	0	2	1	16	0	33	1	0	3	0	1.000	0	1-2	12	1.75	1.83
Postseason			3	0	0	1	2.2	9	1	1	1	1	0	1	0	0	0	4	0	0	0	0	-	0	0-0	0	1.00	3.38
5 ML YEARS			186	1	0	58	182.1	820	152	92	88	16	4	9	11	130	9	182	11	0	11	10	.524	0	13-21	29	4.43	4.34

Eric Bruntlett

Bats: R **Throws:** R **Pos:** SS-35; LF-29; 3B-27; PH-25; PR-18; RF-7; 2B-5; 1B-2 **Ht:** 6'0" **Wt:** 190 **Born:** 3/29/1978 **Age:** 31

Year	Team	Lg	G	AB	H	2B	3B	HR	(Hm Rd)	TB	R	RBI	RC	TBB	IBB	SO	HBP	SH	SF	SB	CS	SB%	GDP	Avg	OBP	Slg
2003	Hou	NL	31	54	14	3	0	1	(1 0)	20	3	4	5	0	0	10	0	1	1	0	0	-	1	.259	.255	.370
2004	Hou	NL	45	52	13	2	0	4	(3 1)	27	14	8	9	7	0	13	0	0	2	4	0	1.00	0	.250	.328	.519
2005	Hou	NL	91	109	24	5	2	4	(2 2)	45	19	14	12	10	0	25	1	1	0	7	2	.78	4	.220	.292	.413
2006	Hou	NL	73	119	33	8	0	0	(0 0)	41	11	10	15	13	1	21	1	2	1	3	1	.75	2	.277	.351	.345
2007	Hou	NL	80	138	34	5	0	0	(0 0)	39	16	14	19	20	1	27	1	6	0	6	3	.67	1	.246	.346	.283
2008	Phi	NL	120	212	46	9	1	2	(1 1)	63	37	15	18	21	3	35	3	2	0	9	2	.82	7	.217	.297	.297
Postseason			16	10	1	0	0	0	(0 0)	1	1	0	0	1	0	5	0	1	0	1	0	1.00	0	.100	.182	.100
6 ML YEARS			440	684	164	32	3	11	(7 4)	235	100	65	78	71	5	131	6	12	4	29	8	.78	15	.240	.315	.344

Clay Buchholz

Pitches: R **Bats:** L **Pos:** SP-15; RP-1 **Ht:** 6'3" **Wt:** 190 **Born:** 8/14/1984 **Age:** 24

Year	Team	Lg	G	GS	CG	GF	IP	BFP	H	R	ER	HR	SH	SF	HB	TBB	IBB	SO	WP	Bk	W	L	Pct	ShO	Sv-Op	Hld	ERC	ERA
2005	Lowell	A-	15	15	0	0	41.1	166	34	15	12	2	0	1	1	9	0	45	0	1	0	1	.000	0	0--	-	2.24	2.61
2006	Grnville	A	21	21	0	0	103.0	411	78	34	30	10	5	3	5	29	0	117	8	1	9	4	.692	0	0--	-	2.55	2.62
2006	Wilmg	A+	3	3	0	0	16.0	61	10	4	2	0	1	1	0	4	0	23	1	0	2	0	1.000	0	0--	-	1.30	1.13
2007	Portlnd	AA	16	15	1	0	86.2	332	55	18	17	4	1	1	2	22	0	116	1	1	7	2	.778	0	0--	-	1.57	1.77
2007	Pwtckt	AAA	8	8	0	0	38.2	164	32	21	17	5	2	3	1	13	0	55	1	3	1	3	.250	0	0--	-	3.08	3.96
2008	Pwtckt	AAA	9	9	0	0	43.2	177	36	13	12	3	2	1	2	17	0	43	3	0	4	2	.667	0	0--	-	3.17	2.47
2008	Portlnd	AA	2	2	0	0	15.0	53	7	4	3	0	1	0	0	1	0	18	0	0	1	0	1.000	0	0--	-	0.57	1.80
2007	Bos	AL	4	3	1	0	22.2	88	14	6	4	0	0	1	1	10	0	22	0	0	3	1	.750	1	0-0	-	1.90	1.59
2008	Bos	AL	16	15	1	0	76.0	357	93	63	57	11	0	3	2	41	1	72	2	1	2	9	.182	0	0-0	-	6.40	6.75
2 ML YEARS			20	18	2	0	98.2	445	107	69	61	11	0	4	3	51	1	94	2	1	5	10	.333	1	0-0	0	5.25	5.56

Taylor Buchholz

Pitches: R **Bats:** R **Pos:** RP-63 **Ht:** 6'4" **Wt:** 220 **Born:** 10/13/1981 **Age:** 27

Year	Team	Lg	G	GS	CG	GF	IP	BFP	H	R	ER	HR	SH	SF	HB	TBB	IBB	SO	WP	Bk	W	L	Pct	ShO	Sv-Op	Hld	ERC	ERA
2006	Hou	NL	22	19	1	1	113.0	479	107	80	74	21	5	6	3	34	4	77	5	0	6	10	.375	1	0-0	0	3.97	5.89
2007	Col	NL	41	8	0	6	93.2	396	105	47	44	8	5	5	2	20	4	61	3	1	6	5	.545	0	0-0	1	3.97	4.23
2008	Col	NL	63	0	0	19	66.1	263	45	23	16	5	2	2	2	18	2	56	5	1	6	6	.500	0	1-3	21	1.87	2.17
3 ML YEARS			126	27	1	26	273.0	1138	257	150	134	34	12	13	7	72	10	194	13	2	18	21	.462	1	1-3	22	3.42	4.42

John Buck

Bats: R **Throws:** R **Pos:** C-107; PH-2; PR-1 **Ht:** 6'3" **Wt:** 220 **Born:** 7/7/1980 **Age:** 28

Year	Team	Lg	G	AB	H	2B	3B	HR	(Hm Rd)	TB	R	RBI	RC	TBB	IBB	SO	HBP	SH	SF	SB	CS	SB%	GDP	Avg	OBP	Slg
2004	KC	AL	71	238	56	9	0	12	(6 6)	101	36	30	26	15	0	79	0	4	1	1	1	.50	6	.235	.280	.424
2005	KC	AL	118	401	97	21	1	12	(6 6)	156	40	47	43	23	2	94	3	1	2	0	2	.50	9	.242	.287	.389
2006	KC	AL	114	371	91	21	1	11	(6 5)	147	37	50	43	26	2	84	7	4	1	0	2	.00	7	.245	.306	.396
2007	KC	AL	113	347	77	18	0	18	(6 12)	149	41	48	37	36	0	92	10	0	6	0	1	.00	11	.222	.308	.429
2008	KC	AL	109	370	83	23	1	9	(4 5)	135	48	48	42	38	2	96	6	0	4	3	3	.00	12	.224	.304	.365
5 ML YEARS			525	1727	404	92	3	62	(25 37)	688	202	223	191	138	6	445	26	9	14	3	9	.25	45	.234	.298	.398

Travis Buck

Bats: L **Throws:** R **Pos:** RF-34; LF-12; PH-1   **Ht:** 6'2" **Wt:** 227 **Born:** 11/18/1983 **Age:** 25

									BATTING												BASERUNNING				AVERAGES		
Year	Team	Lg	G	AB	H	2B	3B	HR	(Hm	Rd)	TB	R	RBI	RC	TBB	IBB	SO	HBP	SH	SF	SB	CS	SB%	GDP	Avg	OBP	Slg
2005	Vancvr	A-	9	36	13	1	0	2	(-	-)	20	7	9	8	5	0	8	0	0	0	1	1	.50	3	.361	.439	.556
2005	Kane	A	32	123	42	13	0	1	(-	-)	58	17	22	25	19	1	19	0	1	1	3	1	.75	4	.341	.427	.472
2006	Stcktn	A+	34	126	44	17	3	3	(-	-)	76	24	26	30	14	0	18	0	0	5	2	1	.67	3	.349	.400	.603
2006	Mdland	AA	50	212	64	22	1	4	(-	-)	100	32	22	39	22	1	39	3	1	0	9	1	.90	5	.302	.376	.472
2007	Scrmto	AAA	2	7	1	0	1	0	(-	-)	3	0	1	1	2	0	2	0	0	0	0	0	-	0	.143	.333	.429
2008	Scrmto	AAA	45	169	50	8	2	2	(-	-)	68	28	17	29	25	0	34	3	0	0	4	1	.80	5	.296	.396	.402
2008	As	R	4	15	10	2	0	1	(-	-)	15	4	6	7	1	0	3	0	0	0	0	0	-	0	.667	.688	1.000
2007	Oak	AL	82	285	82	22	5	7	(3	4)	135	41	34	48	39	2	66	4	2	4	4	1	.80	9	.288	.377	.474
2008	Oak	AL	38	155	35	9	1	7	(3	4)	67	16	25	22	11	0	38	4	0	2	1	0	1.00	2	.226	.291	.432
	2 ML YEARS		120	440	117	31	6	14	(6	8)	202	57	59	70	50	2	104	8	2	6	5	1	.83	11	.266	.347	.459

Billy Buckner

Pitches: R **Bats:** R **Pos:** RP-10   **Ht:** 6'2" **Wt:** 215 **Born:** 8/27/1983 **Age:** 25

			HOW MUCH HE PITCHED						WHAT HE GAVE UP										THE RESULTS						
Year	Team	Lg	G	GS	CG	GF	IP	BFP	H	R	ER	HR	SH	SF	HB	TBB	IBB	SO	WP	Bk	W	L	Pct	ShO	Sv-Op	Hld	ERC	ERA
2004	Idaho	R+	7	5	0	0	30.0	128	36	14	11	4	2	1	1	4	0	37	3	0	2	1	.667	0	0--	-	4.51	3.30
2005	Burlgtn	A	11	11	0	0	60.1	269	66	36	26	9	1	3	2	17	0	60	3	0	3	7	.300	0	0--	-	4.45	3.88
2005	Hi Dsrt	A+	17	17	0	0	94.0	421	105	65	56	10	1	2	4	46	0	92	14	2	5	6	.455	0	0--	-	5.42	5.36
2006	Hi Dsrt	A+	16	16	0	0	90.0	397	92	44	39	6	2	4	4	47	0	85	7	0	7	1	.875	0	0--	-	4.70	3.90
2006	Wichta	AA	13	13	0	0	75.2	344	78	40	39	7	5	1	5	39	0	63	9	0	5	3	.625	0	0--	-	4.88	4.64
2007	Wichta	AA	4	3	0	1	19.1	85	20	10	10	4	0	0	0	6	0	13	1	1	1	3	.250	0	0--	-	4.49	4.66
2007	Omha	AAA	27	15	0	3	104.2	439	108	49	44	11	6	4	5	26	1	83	3	0	9	7	.563	0	0--	-	3.91	3.78
2008	Tucsn	AAA	21	20	0	0	116.1	517	136	74	64	9	7	3	4	43	1	69	7	0	5	10	.333	0	0--	-	4.91	4.95
2007	KC	AL	7	5	0	1	34.0	143	37	20	20	5	0	1	0	16	0	17	0	0	1	2	.333	0	0-0	-	5.57	5.29
2008	Ari	NL	10	0	0	5	14.0	59	16	5	5	3	0	0	1	4	1	11	2	0	1	0	1.000	0	0-0	-	5.72	3.21
	2 ML YEARS		17	5	0	6	48.0	202	53	25	25	8	0	1	1	20	1	28	2	0	2	2	.500	0	0-0	0	5.62	4.69

Ryan Budde

Bats: R **Throws:** R **Pos:** C-7; PR-2; DH-1   **Ht:** 5'11" **Wt:** 205 **Born:** 8/15/1979 **Age:** 29

									BATTING												BASERUNNING				AVERAGES		
Year	Team	Lg	G	AB	H	2B	3B	HR	(Hm	Rd)	TB	R	RBI	RC	TBB	IBB	SO	HBP	SH	SF	SB	CS	SB%	GDP	Avg	OBP	Slg
2002	RCuca	A+	87	307	74	17	1	5	(-	-)	108	40	39	34	27	1	60	2	1	2	2	1	.67	4	.241	.305	.352
2002	Ark	AA	3	9	1	0	0	1	(-	-)	4	1	1	0	1	0	2	0	0	0	0	0	-	0	.111	.200	.444
2003	Ark	AA	96	342	73	9	1	10	(-	-)	114	45	41	34	35	1	76	2	1	2	1	1	.50	5	.213	.289	.333
2003	RCuca	A+	14	50	12	3	1	1	(-	-)	20	6	6	5	2	1	10	0	0	2	0	0	-	1	.240	.259	.400
2004	RCuca	A+	99	359	90	17	0	13	(-	-)	146	54	51	47	27	2	76	8	2	5	3	5	.38	3	.251	.313	.407
2004	Salt Lk	AAA	5	17	4	0	0	0	(-	-)	4	0	1	1	1	0	7	0	0	0	0	0	-	0	.235	.263	.235
2005	Salt Lk	AAA	58	196	45	10	3	6	(-	-)	79	26	25	21	9	0	41	1	2	0	3	1	.75	3	.230	.267	.403
2006	Salt Lk	AAA	72	215	50	15	0	8	(-	-)	89	32	33	30	22	1	55	7	0	0	1	1	.50	8	.233	.324	.414
2007	Clrwtr	A+	3	10	2	1	0	0	(-	-)	3	1	0	0	0	0	3	0	0	0	0	0	-	0	.200	.200	.300
2007	Salt Lk	AAA	47	156	46	12	0	4	(-	-)	70	21	28	26	18	0	27	1	0	2	2	2	.50	10	.295	.367	.449
2008	Salt Lk	AAA	48	173	35	8	2	2	(-	-)	53	16	23	14	10	1	47	3	0	0	3	0	1.00	3	.202	.258	.306
2007	LAA	AL	12	18	3	1	0	0	(0	0)	4	0	1	0	0	0	6	0	0	0	0	0	-	1	.167	.167	.222
2008	LAA	AL	8	2	0	0	0	0	(0	0)	0	0	0	0	0	0	0	0	0	1	0	0	-	1	.000	.000	.000
	2 ML YEARS		20	20	3	1	0	0	(0	0)	4	0	1	0	0	0	6	0	0	1	0	0	-	2	.150	.150	.200

Mark Buehrle

Pitches: L **Bats:** L **Pos:** SP-34   **Ht:** 6'2" **Wt:** 230 **Born:** 3/23/1979 **Age:** 30

			HOW MUCH HE PITCHED						WHAT HE GAVE UP										THE RESULTS						
Year	Team	Lg	G	GS	CG	GF	IP	BFP	H	R	ER	HR	SH	SF	HB	TBB	IBB	SO	WP	Bk	W	L	Pct	ShO	Sv-Op	Hld	ERC	ERA
2000	CWS	AL	28	3	0	6	51.1	225	55	27	24	5	1	0	3	19	1	37	0	0	4	1	.800	0	0-2	5	4.56	4.21
2001	CWS	AL	32	32	4	0	221.1	885	188	89	81	24	9	4	8	48	2	126	1	5	16	8	.667	2	0-0	0	2.79	3.29
2002	CWS	AL	34	34	5	0	239.0	984	236	102	95	25	9	3	3	61	7	134	6	1	19	12	.613	2	0-0	0	3.53	3.58
2003	CWS	AL	35	35	2	0	230.1	978	250	124	106	22	7	7	5	61	2	119	1	0	14	14	.500	0	0-0	0	4.10	4.14
2004	CWS	AL	35	35	4	0	245.1	1016	257	119	106	33	4	6	8	51	2	165	0	0	16	10	.615	1	0-0	0	4.00	3.89
2005	CWS	AL	33	33	3	0	236.2	971	240	99	82	20	7	4	4	40	4	149	2	2	16	8	.667	1	0-0	0	3.21	3.12
2006	CWS	AL	32	32	1	0	204.0	876	247	124	113	36	6	7	6	48	5	98	0	1	12	13	.480	1	0-0	0	5.37	4.99
2007	CWS	AL	30	30	3	0	201.0	835	208	86	81	22	7	5	5	45	5	115	1	0	10	9	.526	1	0-0	0	3.75	3.63
2008	CWS	AL	34	34	1	0	218.2	918	240	106	92	22	2	6	5	52	4	140	4	0	15	12	.556	0	0-0	0	4.12	3.79
	Postseason		5	3	1	2	23.2	94	22	9	9	2	1	1	1	1	1	13	0	0	2	0	1.000	0	1-1	0	2.35	3.42
	9 ML YEARS		293	268	23	6	1847.2	7688	1921	876	780	209	52	42	47	425	32	1083	15	9	122	87	.584	7	0-2	3	3.84	3.80

Francisley Bueno

Pitches: L **Bats:** L **Pos:** RP-1   **Ht:** 5'11" **Wt:** 200 **Born:** 3/5/1981 **Age:** 28

			HOW MUCH HE PITCHED						WHAT HE GAVE UP										THE RESULTS						
Year	Team	Lg	G	GS	CG	GF	IP	BFP	H	R	ER	HR	SH	SF	HB	TBB	IBB	SO	WP	Bk	W	L	Pct	ShO	Sv-Op	Hld	ERC	ERA
2006	Missi	AA	17	14	1	0	80.1	335	77	36	32	10	5	4	2	19	1	84	3	1	1	7	.125	1	0--	-	3.43	3.59
2007	Missi	AA	22	19	0	0	112.2	490	132	55	46	8	8	2	3	26	2	77	5	4	4	6	.400	0	0--	-	4.22	3.67
2007	Rchmd	AAA	3	3	0	0	19.1	81	19	6	6	3	1	0	0	3	0	19	2	1	1	0	1.000	0	0--	-	3.26	2.79
2008	Rchmd	AAA	19	14	0	1	84.1	374	100	51	49	8	4	2	2	29	0	59	6	3	2	6	.250	0	0--	-	4.99	5.23
2008	Atl	NL	1	0	0	0	2.1	13	5	2	2	1	0	0	0	1	0	1	0	0	0	0	-	0	0-0	0	14.73	7.71

Ryan Bukvich

Pitches: R Bats: R Pos: RP-4   Ht: 6'2" Wt: 250 Born: 5/13/1978 Age: 31

		HOW MUCH HE PITCHED						WHAT HE GAVE UP											THE RESULTS						
Year	Team	Lg	G	GS	CG	GF	IP	BFP	H	R	ER	HR	SH	SF	HB	TBB	IBB	SO	WP	Bk	W	L	Pct	ShO	Sv-Op	Hld	ERC	ERA
2008	Norfolk*	AAA	34	9	0	6	85.1	385	82	49	43	4	3	4	3	54	3	60	6	0	8	4	.667	0	1--	-	4.45	4.54
2002	KC	AL	26	0	0	2	25.0	121	26	19	17	2	4	3	1	19	3	20	1	0	1	0	1.000	0	0-1	5	5.39	6.12
2003	KC	AL	9	0	0	6	10.1	52	12	11	11	2	1	1	0	9	0	8	1	0	1	0	1.000	0	0-0	0	7.65	9.58
2004	KC	AL	9	0	0	6	7.1	30	4	3	3	0	1	0	0	7	0	7	0	0	0	0	-	0	1-1	1	3.21	3.68
2005	Tex	AL	4	0	0	0	4.0	19	2	5	5	0	1	0	0	6	0	4	0	0	0	0	-	0	0-0	1	4.74	11.25
2007	CWS	AL	45	0	0	7	35.2	170	36	23	20	5	1	2	3	24	1	18	3	0	1	0	1.000	0	0-1	4	5.70	5.05
2008	Bal	AL	4	0	0	0	5.1	30	9	4	4	2	0	0	0	6	0	5	1	0	0	0	-	0	0-0	0	14.88	6.75
	6 ML YEARS		97	0	0	21	87.2	422	89	65	60	11	8	6	4	71	4	62	6	0	3	0	1.000	0	1-3	11	6.06	6.16

Jason Bulger

Pitches: R Bats: R Pos: RP-14   Ht: 6'4" Wt: 210 Born: 12/6/1978 Age: 30

		HOW MUCH HE PITCHED						WHAT HE GAVE UP											THE RESULTS						
Year	Team	Lg	G	GS	CG	GF	IP	BFP	H	R	ER	HR	SH	SF	HB	TBB	IBB	SO	WP	Bk	W	L	Pct	ShO	Sv-Op	Hld	ERC	ERA
2008	Salt Lk*	AAA	37	0	0	27	43.0	173	25	3	3	0	1	1	1	22	1	75	5	0	4	0	1.000	0	16--	-	1.78	0.63
2005	Ari	NL	9	0	0	5	10.0	48	14	6	6	1	1	0	0	5	1	9	0	0	1	0	1.000	0	0-0	0	6.68	5.40
2006	LAA	AL	2	0	0	1	1.2	9	1	3	3	0	0	0	0	3	0	1	1	0	0	0	-	0	0-0	0	6.15	16.20
2007	LAA	AL	6	0	0	4	6.1	25	5	2	2	0	0	0	0	3	0	8	1	0	0	0	-	0	0-0	0	2.74	2.84
2008	LAA	AL	14	0	0	7	16.0	73	15	13	13	3	0	0	2	9	0	20	0	0	0	0	-	0	0-0	0	5.50	7.31
	4 ML YEARS		31	0	0	17	34.0	155	35	24	24	4	1	0	2	20	1	38	2	0	1	0	1.000	0	0-0	0	5.34	6.35

Bryan Bullington

Pitches: R Bats: R Pos: SP-2; RP-1   Ht: 6'4" Wt: 220 Born: 9/30/1980 Age: 28

		HOW MUCH HE PITCHED						WHAT HE GAVE UP											THE RESULTS						
Year	Team	Lg	G	GS	CG	GF	IP	BFP	H	R	ER	HR	SH	SF	HB	TBB	IBB	SO	WP	Bk	W	L	Pct	ShO	Sv-Op	Hld	ERC	ERA
2008	Indy*	AAA	15	15	0	0	75.0	335	90	54	46	8	3	2	3	25	5	60	1	0	4	6	.400	0	0--	-	5.06	5.52
2008	Buffalo*	AAA	10	8	0	1	53.0	233	65	34	28	7	1	2	2	13	0	47	5	1	1	3	.250	0	1--	-	5.16	4.75
2005	Pit	NL	1	0	0	0	1.1	7	1	2	2	0	0	1	1	1	0	1	0	0	0	0	-	0	0-0	0	5.91	13.50
2007	Pit	NL	5	3	0	0	17.0	76	24	11	10	3	1	0	0	5	0	7	1	0	0	3	.000	0	0-0	0	6.90	5.29
2008	Cle	AL	3	2	0	0	14.2	60	15	9	8	4	0	1	1	2	0	12	1	0	0	2	.000	0	0-0	0	4.63	4.91
	3 ML YEARS		9	5	0	0	33.0	143	40	22	20	7	1	2	2	8	0	20	2	0	0	5	.000	0	0-0	0	5.87	5.45

Ambiorix Burgos

Pitches: R Bats: R Pos: P   Ht: 6'3" Wt: 244 Born: 4/19/1984 Age: 25

		HOW MUCH HE PITCHED						WHAT HE GAVE UP											THE RESULTS						
Year	Team	Lg	G	GS	CG	GF	IP	BFP	H	R	ER	HR	SH	SF	HB	TBB	IBB	SO	WP	Bk	W	L	Pct	ShO	Sv-Op	Hld	ERC	ERA
2008	Kngspt*	R+	2	0	0	0	2.0	9	2	1	1	1	0	0	0	2	0	1	1	0	0	0	-	0	0--	-	11.03	4.50
2008	Mets*	R	3	1	0	0	5.0	21	6	3	3	0	0	0	0	0	0	8	0	0	0	0	-	0	0--	-	2.89	5.40
2008	StLuci*	A+	3	3	0	0	3.0	18	2	2	1	0	0	0	3	3	0	2	0	0	0	1	.000	0	0--	-	6.90	3.00
2005	KC	AL	59	0	0	17	63.1	278	60	29	28	6	2	1	5	31	1	65	8	2	3	5	.375	0	2-6	11	4.41	3.98
2006	KC	AL	68	1	0	41	73.1	336	83	49	45	16	1	4	6	37	4	72	11	3	4	5	.444	0	18-30	5	6.51	5.52
2007	NYM	NL	17	0	0	5	23.2	98	17	10	9	3	1	1	2	9	0	19	2	0	1	0	1.000	0	0-0	1	2.97	3.42
	3 ML YEARS		144	1	0	63	160.1	712	160	88	82	25	4	6	13	77	5	156	21	5	8	10	.444	0	20-36	17	5.10	4.60

Chris Burke

Bats: R Throws: R Pos: PH-30; 2B-18; LF-18; 1B-9; RF-9; PR-7; 3B-4; SS-2; DH-1   Ht: 5'11" Wt: 195 Born: 3/11/1980 Age: 29

			BATTING																			BASERUNNING				AVERAGES		
Year	Team	Lg	G	AB	H	2B	3B	HR	(Hm	Rd)	TB	R	RBI	RC	TBB	IBB	SO	HBP	SH	SF	SB	CS	SB%	GDP	Avg	OBP	Slg
2004	Hou	NL	17	17	1	0	0	0	(0	0)	1	2	0	0	3	0	3	0	0	0	0	0	-	0	.059	.200	.059
2005	Hou	NL	108	318	79	19	2	5	(2	3)	117	49	26	35	23	0	62	6	9	3	11	6	.65	7	.248	.309	.368
2006	Hou	NL	123	366	101	23	1	9	(3	6)	153	58	40	49	27	0	77	14	4	2	11	1	.92	6	.276	.347	.418
2007	Hou	NL	111	319	73	19	2	6	(3	3)	114	39	28	33	27	1	52	8	8	1	9	3	.75	10	.229	.304	.357
2008	Ari	NL	86	165	32	5	1	2	(0	2)	45	20	12	14	27	8	33	2	2	3	5	0	1.00	2	.194	.310	.273
	Postseason		13	28	8	1	1	2	(1	1)	17	7	4	6	4	0	3	0	1	0	2	0	1.00	0	.286	.375	.607
	5 ML YEARS		445	1185	286	66	6	22	(8	14)	430	168	106	131	107	9	227	30	23	9	36	10	.78	25	.241	.318	.363

Jamie Burke

Bats: R Throws: R Pos: C-43; PH-4; 1B-1; 3B-1   Ht: 6'0" Wt: 225 Born: 9/24/1971 Age: 37

			BATTING																			BASERUNNING				AVERAGES		
Year	Team	Lg	G	AB	H	2B	3B	HR	(Hm	Rd)	TB	R	RBI	RC	TBB	IBB	SO	HBP	SH	SF	SB	CS	SB%	GDP	Avg	OBP	Slg
2001	LAA	AL	9	5	1	0	0	0	(0	0)	1	1	0	0	0	0	2	0	0	0	0	0	-	0	.200	.200	.200
2003	CWS	AL	6	8	3	0	0	0	(0	0)	3	0	2	2	0	0	0	0	0	0	0	0	-	0	.375	.375	.375
2004	CWS	AL	57	120	40	9	0	0	(0	0)	49	22	15	21	10	0	13	1	1	1	0	0	-	3	.333	.347	.408
2005	CWS	AL	1	1	0	0	0	0	(0	0)	0	0	0	0	0	0	0	0	0	0	0	0	-	0	.000	.000	.000
2007	Sea	AL	50	113	34	8	0	1	(1	0)	45	19	12	16	7	0	17	4	5	0	0	1	.00	2	.301	.363	.398
2008	Sea	AL	48	92	24	3	0	1	(0	1)	30	10	8	9	5	0	7	1	1	1	0	1	.00	3	.261	.303	.326
	6 ML YEARS		171	339	102	20	0	2	(1	1)	128	52	37	48	22	0	39	6	7	2	0	2	.00	8	.301	.352	.378

A.J. Burnett

Pitches: R Bats: R Pos: SP-34; RP-1

Ht: 6'4" Wt: 230 Born: 1/3/1977 Age: 32

Year	Team	Lg	G	GS	CG	GF	IP	BFP	H	R	ER	HR	SH	SF	HB	TBB	IBB	SO	WP	Bk	W	L	Pct	ShO	Sv-Op	Hld	ERC	ERA
1999	Fla	NL	7	7	0	0	41.1	182	37	23	16	3	1	3	0	25	2	33	0	0	4	2	.667	0	0-0	0	4.00	3.48
2000	Fla	NL	13	13	0	0	82.2	364	80	46	44	8	6	3	2	44	3	57	2	0	3	7	.300	0	0-0	0	4.45	4.79
2001	Fla	NL	27	27	2	0	173.1	733	145	82	78	20	6	8	7	83	3	128	7	1	11	12	.478	1	0-0	0	3.76	4.05
2002	Fla	NL	31	29	7	0	204.1	844	153	84	75	12	9	4	9	90	5	203	14	0	12	9	.571	5	0-1	0	2.77	3.30
2003	Fla	NL	4	4	0	0	23.0	106	18	13	12	2	2	1	2	18	2	21	2	0	0	2	.000	0	0-0	0	4.36	4.70
2004	Fla	NL	20	19	1	0	120.0	490	102	50	49	9	3	3	4	38	0	113	7	0	7	6	.538	0	0-0	0	2.95	3.68
2005	Fla	NL	32	32	4	0	209.0	873	184	97	80	12	7	5	7	79	1	198	12	0	12	12	.500	2	0-0	0	3.20	3.44
2006	Tor	AL	21	21	2	0	135.2	577	138	67	60	14	4	3	8	39	3	118	6	1	10	8	.556	1	0-0	0	3.97	3.98
2007	Tor	AL	25	25	2	0	165.2	691	131	74	69	23	0	2	12	66	2	176	5	0	10	8	.556	0	0-0	0	3.47	3.75
2008	Tor	AL	35	34	1	1	221.1	957	211	109	100	19	8	5	9	86	2	231	11	2	18	10	.643	0	0-0	0	3.78	4.07
10 ML YEARS			215	211	19	1	1376.1	5817	1199	645	583	122	46	37	60	568	23	1278	66	4	87	76	.534	9	0-1	0	3.50	3.81

Sean Burnett

Pitches: L Bats: L Pos: RP-58

Ht: 6'1" Wt: 190 Born: 9/17/1982 Age: 26

Year	Team	Lg	G	GS	CG	GF	IP	BFP	H	R	ER	HR	SH	SF	HB	TBB	IBB	SO	WP	Bk	W	L	Pct	ShO	Sv-Op	Hld	ERC	ERA
2000	Pirates	R	8	6	0	1	31.0	128	31	17	14	0	0	1	0	3	0	24	2	1	2	1	.667	0	0--	-	2.24	4.06
2001	Hkry	A	26	26	1	0	161.0	667	164	63	47	11	6	5	4	33	0	134	7	1	11	8	.579	0	0--	-	3.33	2.63
2002	Lynbrg	A+	26	26	2	0	155.1	605	118	46	31	4	5	5	1	33	0	96	3	1	13	4	.765	0	0--	-	1.78	1.80
2003	Altna	AA	27	27	2	0	159.2	649	158	60	57	2	8	9	7	29	1	86	10	0	14	6	.700	1	0--	-	2.83	3.21
2004	Nashv	AAA	10	10	0	0	47.0	205	58	29	28	5	2	3	2	17	2	25	1	0	1	5	.167	0	0--	-	5.66	5.36
2006	Indy	AAA	25	24	0	0	120.1	530	136	74	69	13	9	6	2	46	1	46	2	0	8	11	.421	0	0--	-	4.89	5.16
2007	Indy	AAA	15	15	0	0	70.1	320	83	39	35	4	5	3	3	39	0	31	4	0	5	4	.444	0	0--	-	5.74	4.48
2008	Indy	AAA	12	0	0	5	17.1	67	9	2	2	1	0	0	0	8	0	15	2	0	1	1	.500	0	3--	-	1.68	1.04
2004	Pit	NL	13	13	1	0	71.2	318	86	41	40	9	2	1	1	28	2	30	2	0	5	5	.500	1	0-0	0	5.49	5.02
2008	Pit	NL	58	0	0	16	56.2	253	57	31	30	7	4	3	2	34	3	42	4	0	1	1	.500	0	0-0	8	5.23	4.76
2 ML YEARS			71	13	1	16	128.1	571	143	72	70	16	6	4	3	62	5	72	6	0	6	6	.500	1	0-0	8	5.38	4.91

Pat Burrell

Bats: R Throws: R Pos: LF-155; PH-3

Ht: 6'4" Wt: 234 Born: 10/10/1976 Age: 32

Year	Team	Lg	G	AB	H	2B	3B	HR	(Hm	Rd)	TB	R	RBI	RC	TBB	IBB	SO	HBP	SH	SF	SB	CS	SB%	GDP	Avg	OBP	Slg
2000	Phi	NL	111	408	106	27	1	18	(7	11)	189	57	79	69	63	2	139	1	0	2	0	0	-	5	.260	.359	.463
2001	Phi	NL	155	539	139	29	2	27	(10	17)	253	70	89	86	70	7	162	5	0	4	2	1	.67	12	.258	.346	.469
2002	Phi	NL	157	586	165	39	2	37	(18	19)	319	96	116	104	89	9	153	3	0	6	1	0	1.00	16	.282	.376	.544
2003	Phi	NL	146	522	109	31	4	21	(9	12)	211	57	64	57	72	2	142	4	0	1	0	0	-	18	.209	.309	.404
2004	Phi	NL	127	448	115	17	0	24	(14	10)	204	66	84	72	78	7	130	4	0	2	0	1.00	16	.257	.365	.455
2005	Phi	NL	154	562	158	27	1	32	(20	12)	283	78	117	109	99	6	160	3	0	5	0	0	-	12	.281	.389	.504
2006	Phi	NL	144	462	119	24	1	29	(12	17)	232	80	95	81	98	5	131	3	0	4	0	0	-	11	.258	.388	.502
2007	Phi	NL	155	472	121	26	0	30	(16	14)	237	77	97	98	114	1	120	4	0	8	0	0	-	10	.256	.400	.502
2008	Phi	NL	157	536	134	33	3	33	(12	21)	272	74	86	93	102	8	136	1	0	6	0	0	-	10	.250	.367	.507
Postseason			3	11	2	0	0	1	(1	0)	5	1	1	1	2	0	3	0	0	0	0	0	-	0	.182	.308	.455
9 ML YEARS			1306	4535	1166	253	14	251	(118	133)	2200	655	827	769	785	47	1273	26	0	42	5	1	.83	104	.257	.367	.485

Brian Burres

Pitches: L Bats: L Pos: SP-22; RP-9

Ht: 6'1" Wt: 181 Born: 4/8/1981 Age: 28

Year	Team	Lg	G	GS	CG	GF	IP	BFP	H	R	ER	HR	SH	SF	HB	TBB	IBB	SO	WP	Bk	W	L	Pct	ShO	Sv-Op	Hld	ERC	ERA
2008	Norfolk*	AAA	4	1	0	0	11.0	44	9	1	1	0	0	0	1	1	0	11	1	0	1	0	1.000	0	0--	-	1.73	0.82
2006	Bal	AL	11	0	0	2	8.0	31	6	2	2	1	0	0	0	1	0	6	0	0	0	0	-	0	0-0	4	1.91	2.25
2007	Bal	AL	37	17	0	9	121.0	559	140	81	80	14	2	2	5	66	1	96	8	0	6	8	.429	0	0-0	0	5.89	5.95
2008	Bal	AL	31	22	0	1	129.2	596	165	90	87	17	1	6	6	50	2	63	3	1	7	10	.412	0	0-1	0	6.03	6.04
3 ML YEARS			79	39	0	12	258.2	1186	311	173	169	32	3	8	11	117	3	165	11	1	13	18	.419	0	0-1	4	5.82	5.88

Emmanuel Burriss

Bats: B Throws: R Pos: SS-47; 2B-41; PR-11; PH-7; RF-1

Ht: 6'0" Wt: 189 Born: 1/17/1985 Age: 24

Year	Team	Lg	G	AB	H	2B	3B	HR	(Hm	Rd)	TB	R	RBI	RC	TBB	IBB	SO	HBP	SH	SF	SB	CS	SB%	GDP	Avg	OBP	Slg
2006	Salem	A+	65	254	78	8	2	1	(-	-)	93	50	27	42	27	1	22	6	4	2	35	11	.76	2	.307	.384	.366
2007	SnJos	A+	36	139	23	2	0	0	(-	-)	25	23	8	7	12	0	20	2	4	3	17	3	.85	2	.165	.237	.180
2007	Augsta	A	89	365	117	14	4	0	(-	-)	139	64	38	59	28	0	49	5	4	3	51	15	.77	3	.321	.374	.381
2008	Fresno	AAA	14	62	16	1	1	0	(-	-)	19	6	6	4	2	0	6	0	0	0	2	2	.50	0	.258	.281	.306
2008	SF	NL	95	240	68	6	1	1	(0	1)	79	37	18	22	23	1	24	5	5	1	13	5	.72	7	.283	.357	.329

Jared Burton

Pitches: R Bats: R Pos: RP-54

Ht: 6'5" Wt: 230 Born: 6/2/1981 Age: 28

Year	Team	Lg	G	GS	CG	GF	IP	BFP	H	R	ER	HR	SH	SF	HB	TBB	IBB	SO	WP	Bk	W	L	Pct	ShO	Sv-Op	Hld	ERC	ERA
2002	Vancvr	A-	13	5	0	2	37.2	164	32	22	15	0	2	1	2	14	0	38	2	1	0	4	.000	0	1--	-	2.57	3.58
2003	Kane	A	15	2	0	3	31.2	120	19	9	8	2	2	0	2	7	0	33	4	0	2	1	.667	0	1--	-	1.55	2.27
2004	As	R	5	5	0	0	21.2	91	21	12	10	2	0	0	2	4	0	15	2	0	1	0	1.000	0	0--	-	3.35	4.15
2004	Mdest	A+	10	3	0	1	32.0	147	34	19	17	6	0	0	1	20	1	25	4	0	3	2	.600	0	0--	-	6.16	4.78

Year	Team	Lg	G	GS	CG	GF	IP	BFP	H	R	ER	HR	SH	SF	HB	TBB	IBB	SO	WP	Bk	W	L	Pct	ShO	Sv-Op	Hld	ERC	ERA
								HOW MUCH HE PITCHED			WHAT HE GAVE UP												THE RESULTS					
2005	Stcktn	A+	52	0	0	35	55.1	234	44	21	16	2	2	0	4	20	0	67	8	1	4	4	.500	0	24--	-	2.63	2.60
2006	Mdland	AA	53	0	0	19	74.0	314	71	36	34	7	4	2	3	27	3	66	9	0	6	5	.545	0	1--	-	3.80	4.14
2007	Lsvlle	AAA	10	0	0	3	14.0	53	11	1	1	0	0	0	0	4	0	13	1	0	1	0	1.000	0	1--	-	2.08	0.64
2007	Chatt	AA	4	0	0	1	5.1	31	10	7	7	0	0	0	1	5	0	3	1	0	0	1	.000	0	0--	-	12.09	11.81
2008	Lsvlle	AAA	2	1	0	0	2.0	8	1	1	1	0	0	0	0	2	0	1	1	0	0	0	-	0	0--	-	3.21	4.50
2007	Cin	NL	47	0	0	12	43.0	176	28	15	12	2	1	1	2	22	4	36	3	1	4	2	.667	0	0-3	11	2.37	2.51
2008	Cin	NL	54	0	0	12	58.2	257	56	24	21	6	2	3	2	25	3	58	2	1	5	1	.833	0	0-2	11	3.93	3.22
2 ML YEARS			101	0	0	24	101.2	433	84	39	33	8	3	4	4	47	7	94	5	2	9	3	.750	0	0-5	22	3.25	2.92

Brian Buscher

Bats: L **Throws:** R **Pos:** 3B-64; 1B-6; PH-6; 2B-1; DH-1; PR-1 **Ht:** 6'0" **Wt:** 222 **Born:** 4/18/1981 **Age:** 28

Year	Team	Lg	G	AB	H	2B	3B	HR	(Hm	Rd)	TB	R	RBI	RC	TBB	IBB	SO	HBP	SH	SF	SB	CS	SB%	GDP	Avg	OBP	Slg
						BATTING															BASERUNNING				AVERAGES		
2003	Hgrstn	A	54	200	55	7	1	0	(-	-)	64	19	26	21	10	0	25	4	0	3	0	0	-	4	.275	.318	.320
2004	SnJos	A+	88	343	100	14	7	4	(-	-)	140	50	56	53	33	0	61	6	0	5	5	4	.56	8	.292	.359	.408
2005	Nrwich	AA	64	215	49	8	1	1	(-	-)	62	19	23	21	20	0	36	6	0	6	3	3	.67	10	.228	.304	.288
2005	SnJos	A+	55	206	58	12	1	5	(-	-)	87	37	29	33	27	0	47	2	0	2	0	2	.00	7	.282	.367	.422
2006	Conn	AA	130	467	121	23	3	7	(-	-)	171	43	49	58	39	3	75	6	7	5	5	4	.56	12	.259	.321	.366
2007	NwBrit	AA	63	247	76	19	1	7	(-	-)	118	37	37	47	31	4	30	4	0	2	2	2	.50	3	.308	.391	.478
2007	Roch	AAA	40	132	41	7	0	7	(-	-)	69	21	22	26	13	1	11	1	0	1	1	0	1.00	1	.311	.374	.523
2008	Roch	AAA	53	185	59	12	0	8	(-	-)	95	27	30	38	20	1	21	7	0	2	1	2	.33	6	.319	.402	.514
2007	Min	AL	33	82	20	1	0	2	(0	2)	27	8	10	8	10	0	16	0	1	1	1	0	1.00	2	.244	.323	.329
2008	Min	AL	70	218	64	9	0	4	(2	2)	85	29	47	36	19	0	42	0	0	7	0	2	.00	6	.294	.340	.390
2 ML YEARS			103	300	84	10	0	6	(2	4)	112	37	57	44	29	0	58	0	1	8	1	2	.33	8	.280	.335	.373

David Bush

Pitches: R **Bats:** R **Pos:** SP-29; RP-2 **Ht:** 6'2" **Wt:** 207 **Born:** 11/9/1979 **Age:** 29

Year	Team	Lg	G	GS	CG	GF	IP	BFP	H	R	ER	HR	SH	SF	HB	TBB	IBB	SO	WP	Bk	W	L	Pct	ShO	Sv-Op	Hld	ERC	ERA
								HOW MUCH HE PITCHED			WHAT HE GAVE UP												THE RESULTS					
2008	Nashv*	AAA	1	1	0	0	6.0	24	3	3	1	1	0	0	0	2	0	7	0	0	0	0	-	0	0--	-	1.62	1.50
2004	Tor	AL	16	16	1	0	97.2	412	95	47	40	11	4	4	6	25	2	64	3	0	5	4	.556	1	0-0	0	3.65	3.69
2005	Tor	AL	25	24	2	1	136.1	575	142	73	68	20	3	2	13	29	3	75	2	0	5	11	.313	0	0-0	0	4.28	4.49
2006	Mil	NL	34	32	3	0	210.0	869	201	111	103	26	9	6	18	38	2	166	6	0	12	11	.522	2	0-0	1	3.47	4.41
2007	Mil	NL	33	31	0	2	186.1	810	217	110	106	27	6	2	11	44	1	134	3	0	12	10	.545	0	0-0	0	4.93	5.12
2008	Mil	NL	31	29	0	0	185.0	763	163	92	86	29	4	3	10	48	3	109	2	1	9	10	.474	0	0-0	0	3.44	4.18
5 ML YEARS			139	132	6	3	815.1	3429	818	433	403	113	26	17	58	184	11	548	16	1	43	46	.483	3	0-0	1	3.94	4.45

Billy Butler

Bats: R **Throws:** R **Pos:** DH-82; 1B-34; PH-9 **Ht:** 6'1" **Wt:** 240 **Born:** 4/18/1986 **Age:** 23

Year	Team	Lg	G	AB	H	2B	3B	HR	(Hm	Rd)	TB	R	RBI	RC	TBB	IBB	SO	HBP	SH	SF	SB	CS	SB%	GDP	Avg	OBP	Slg
						BATTING															BASERUNNING				AVERAGES		
2004	Idaho	R+	74	260	97	22	3	10	(-	-)	155	74	68	75	57	0	63	4	0	3	5	0	1.00	6	.373	.488	.596
2005	Hi Dsrt	A+	92	379	132	30	2	25	(-	-)	241	70	91	95	42	3	80	6	0	3	0	0	-	12	.348	.419	.636
2005	Wichta	AA	29	112	35	9	0	5	(-	-)	59	14	19	20	7	3	18	0	0	0	0	0	-	3	.313	.353	.527
2006	Wichta	AA	119	477	158	33	1	15	(-	-)	238	82	96	93	41	3	67	8	1	8	1	0	1.00	25	.331	.388	.499
2007	Omha	AAA	57	203	59	10	1	13	(-	-)	110	40	46	48	43	2	32	3	1	6	1	0	1.00	4	.291	.412	.542
2008	Omha	AAA	26	101	34	6	1	5	(-	-)	57	18	13	23	14	0	7	0	0	0	0	0	-	4	.337	.417	.564
2007	KC	AL	92	329	96	23	2	8	(5	3)	147	38	52	50	27	5	55	2	0	2	0	0	-	23	.292	.347	.447
2008	KC	AL	124	443	122	22	0	11	(4	7)	177	44	55	57	33	0	57	0	0	2	0	1	.00	23	.275	.324	.400
2 ML YEARS			216	772	218	45	2	19	(9	10)	324	82	107	107	60	5	112	2	0	4	0	1	.00	31	.282	.334	.420

Freddie Bynum

Bats: L **Throws:** R **Pos:** SS-37; PR-5; 2B-1; DH-1; PH-1 **Ht:** 6'1" **Wt:** 190 **Born:** 3/15/1980 **Age:** 29

Year	Team	Lg	G	AB	H	2B	3B	HR	(Hm	Rd)	TB	R	RBI	RC	TBB	IBB	SO	HBP	SH	SF	SB	CS	SB%	GDP	Avg	OBP	Slg
						BATTING															BASERUNNING				AVERAGES		
2008	Bowie*	AA	6	20	7	1	1	1	(-	-)	13	4	3	4	1	0	3	0	1	0	0	1	.00	0	.350	.381	.650
2008	Norfolk*	AAA	37	130	32	4	3	0	(-	-)	42	15	15	17	20	1	39	0	3	2	8	1	.89	1	.246	.342	.323
2005	Oak	AL	7	7	2	1	0	0	(0	0)	3	0	1	1	0	0	3	0	0	0	0	0	-	0	.286	.286	.429
2006	ChC	NL	71	136	35	5	5	4	(3	1)	62	20	12	18	9	0	44	1	2	0	8	4	.67	2	.257	.308	.456
2007	Bal	AL	70	96	25	8	2	2	(0	2)	43	21	11	12	2	0	30	2	1	0	8	1	.89	2	.260	.290	.448
2008	Bal	AL	40	112	20	3	1	0	(0	0)	25	13	8	3	5	0	31	1	3	0	2	3	.40	2	.179	.220	.223
4 ML YEARS			188	351	82	17	8	6	(3	3)	133	54	32	34	16	0	108	4	6	0	18	8	.69	6	.234	.275	.379

Marlon Byrd

Bats: R **Throws:** R **Pos:** CF-57; RF-39; LF-31; PH-7; DH-2 **Ht:** 6'0" **Wt:** 245 **Born:** 8/30/1977 **Age:** 31

Year	Team	Lg	G	AB	H	2B	3B	HR	(Hm	Rd)	TB	R	RBI	RC	TBB	IBB	SO	HBP	SH	SF	SB	CS	SB%	GDP	Avg	OBP	Slg
						BATTING															BASERUNNING				AVERAGES		
2008	Okla*	AAA	4	16	5	2	0	0	(-	-)	7	3	3	2	2	0	6	0	0	0	0	1	.00	0	.313	.389	.438
2002	Phi	NL	10	35	8	2	0	1	(1	0)	13	2	1	0	1	0	8	0	0	0	2	0	1.00	0	.229	.250	.371
2003	Phi	NL	135	495	150	28	4	7	(3	4)	207	86	45	72	44	3	94	7	4	3	11	1	.92	8	.303	.366	.418
2004	Phi	NL	106	346	79	13	2	5	(3	2)	111	48	33	35	22	1	68	7	2	1	2	2	.50	10	.228	.287	.321
2005	2 Tms	NL	79	229	61	15	2	2	(0	2)	86	20	26	30	19	1	50	2	5	4	5	1	.83	5	.266	.323	.376
2006	Was	NL	78	197	44	8	1	5	(1	4)	69	28	18	18	22	1	47	6	1	2	3	3	.50	6	.223	.317	.350
2007	Tex	AL	109	414	127	17	8	10	(4	6)	190	60	70	68	29	3	88	5	0	6	5	3	.63	9	.307	.355	.459

Year	Team	Lg	G	AB	H	2B	3B	HR	(Hm	Rd)	TB	R	RBI	RC	TBB	IBB	SO	HBP	SH	SF	SB	CS	SB%	GDP	Avg	OBP	Slg
																					BASERUNNING				**AVERAGES**		
2008	Tex	AL	122	403	120	28	4	10	(7	3)	186	70	53	63	46	3	62	9	2	2	7	2	.78	10	.298	.380	.462
05	Phi	NL	5	13	4	0	0	0	(0	0)	4	0	0	2	1	0	3	1	0	0	0	0	-	0	.308	.400	.308
05	Was	NL	74	216	57	15	2	2	(0	2)	82	20	26	28	18	1	47	1	5	4	5	1	.83	5	.264	.318	.380
7 ML YEARS			639	2119	589	111	21	40	(19	21)	862	314	246	286	183	12	417	36	14	18	33	14	.70	48	.278	.343	.407

Paul Byrd

Pitches: R Bats: R Pos: SP-30   Ht: 6'1" Wt: 190 Born: 12/3/1970 Age: 38

Year	Team	Lg	G	GS	CG	GF	IP	BFP	H	R	ER	HR	SH	SF	HB	TBB	IBB	SO	WP	Bk	W	L	Pct	ShO	Sv-Op	Hld	ERC	ERA
				HOW MUCH HE PITCHED							**WHAT HE GAVE UP**											**THE RESULTS**					
1995	NYM	NL	17	0	0	6	22.0	91	18	6	5	1	0	2	1	7	1	26	1	2	2	0	1.000	0	0-0	3	2.53	2.05
1996	NYM	NL	38	0	0	14	46.2	204	48	22	22	7	1	1	0	21	4	31	3	0	1	2	.333	0	0-2	3	4.67	4.24
1997	Atl	NL	31	4	0	9	53.0	236	47	34	31	6	2	2	4	28	4	37	3	1	4	4	.500	0	0-0	1	4.15	5.26
1998	2 Tms	NL	9	8	2	0	57.0	233	45	19	17	6	2	1	0	18	1	39	2	0	5	2	.714	1	0-0	1	2.62	2.68
1999	Phi	NL	32	32	1	0	199.2	872	205	119	102	34	5	6	17	31	2	106	11	3	15	11	.577	0	0-0	0	4.87	4.60
2000	Phi	NL	17	15	0	0	83.0	371	89	67	60	17	3	1	3	35	2	53	1	0	2	9	.182	0	0-0	0	5.42	6.51
2001	2 Tms	NL	19	16	1	1	103.1	444	120	54	51	12	4	6	2	26	1	52	2	0	6	7	.462	0	0-0	0	4.62	4.44
2002	KC	AL	33	33	7	0	228.1	935	224	111	99	36	2	13	7	38	1	129	3	1	17	11	.607	2	0-0	0	3.55	3.90
2004	Atl	NL	19	19	0	0	114.1	482	123	57	50	18	3	3	2	19	0	79	1	0	8	7	.533	0	0-0	0	3.98	3.94
2005	LAA	AL	31	31	2	0	204.1	842	216	95	85	22	7	7	7	28	1	102	1	0	12	11	.522	1	0-0	0	3.56	3.74
2006	Cle	AL	31	31	1	0	179.0	805	232	120	97	26	1	6	6	38	3	88	2	0	10	9	.526	0	0-0	0	5.40	4.88
2007	Cle	AL	31	31	2	0	192.1	835	239	107	98	27	4	4	6	28	3	88	5	0	15	8	.652	2	0-0	0	4.80	4.59
2008	2 Tms	AL	30	30	1	0	180.0	761	204	96	92	31	4	4	7	34	0	82	0	0	11	12	.478	0	0-0	0	4.70	4.60
98	Atl	NL	1	0	0	0	2.0	11	4	3	3	0	0	0	0	1	0	0	0	0	0	0	-	0	0-0	0	9.72	13.50
98	Phi	NL	8	8	2	0	55.0	222	41	16	14	6	2	1	0	17	1	38	2	0	5	2	.714	1	0-0	1	2.41	2.29
01	Phi	NL	3	1	0	1	10.0	45	10	9	9	1	2	2	1	4	0	3	1	0	0	1	.000	0	0-0	0	4.36	8.10
01	KC	AL	16	15	1	0	93.1	399	110	45	42	11	2	4	1	22	1	49	1	0	6	6	.500	0	0-0	0	4.65	4.05
08	Cle	AL	22	22	1	0	131.0	553	146	70	66	23	3	4	5	24	0	56	0	0	7	10	.412	0	0-0	0	4.56	4.53
08	Bos	AL	8	8	0	0	49.0	208	58	26	26	8	1	0	2	10	0	26	0	0	4	2	.667	0	0-0	0	5.07	4.78
Postseason			7	5	0	1	30.0	137	39	16	16	6	2	1	2	9	1	13	0	0	3	1	.750	0	0-0	0	6.43	4.80
13 ML YEARS			338	250	17	30	1663.0	7111	1810	907	809	243	38	56	62	390	23	912	35	7	108	93	.537	6	0-2	7	4.36	4.38

Tim Byrdak

Pitches: L Bats: L Pos: RP-59   Ht: 5'11" Wt: 196 Born: 10/31/1973 Age: 35

Year	Team	Lg	G	GS	CG	GF	IP	BFP	H	R	ER	HR	SH	SF	HB	TBB	IBB	SO	WP	Bk	W	L	Pct	ShO	Sv-Op	Hld	ERC	ERA
				HOW MUCH HE PITCHED							**WHAT HE GAVE UP**											**THE RESULTS**					
2008	RdRck*	AAA	7	0	0	2	7.1	30	8	3	3	0	0	0	0	0	0	10	0	0	0	0	-	0	0-0	0	2.36	3.68
1998	KC	AL	3	0	0	0	1.2	9	5	1	1	1	0	0	0	1	0	0	0	0	0	0	-	0	0-0	0	23.52	5.40
1999	KC	AL	33	0	0	5	24.2	128	32	24	21	5	3	0	1	20	2	17	3	1	0	3	.000	0	1-4	10	8.29	7.66
2000	KC	AL	12	0	0	1	6.1	34	11	8	8	3	0	0	1	4	0	8	1	0	0	1	.000	0	0-2	3	13.14	11.37
2005	Bal	AL	41	0	0	3	26.2	131	27	14	12	1	2	1	1	21	1	31	5	0	1	0	1.000	0	1-1	11	5.04	4.05
2006	Bal	AL	16	0	0	2	7.0	42	14	10	10	2	2	0	0	8	1	2	1	0	1	0	1.000	0	0-0	3	15.90	12.86
2007	Det	AL	39	0	0	3	45.0	199	38	23	16	3	2	5	1	26	4	49	3	0	3	0	1.000	0	1-2	8	3.53	3.20
2008	Hou	NL	59	0	0	9	55.1	237	45	24	24	10	2	1	2	29	2	47	0	0	2	1	.667	0	0-0	8	4.18	3.90
7 ML YEARS			203	0	0	23	166.2	780	172	104	92	25	11	7	5	108	10	155	13	1	6	6	.500	0	3-9	43	5.57	4.97

Eric Byrnes

Bats: R Throws: R Pos: LF-51; PH-2; CF-1   Ht: 6'2" Wt: 215 Born: 2/16/1976 Age: 33

Year	Team	Lg	G	AB	H	2B	3B	HR	(Hm	Rd)	TB	R	RBI	RC	TBB	IBB	SO	HBP	SH	SF	SB	CS	SB%	GDP	Avg	OBP	Slg
								BATTING													**BASERUNNING**				**AVERAGES**		
2008	Visalia*	A+	3	12	1	0	0	0	(-	-)	1	1	0	0	1	0	4	1	0	0	0	0	-	0	.083	.214	.083
2000	Oak	AL	10	10	3	0	0	0	(0	0)	3	5	0	1	0	0	1	1	0	0	2	1	.67	0	.300	.364	.300
2001	Oak	AL	19	38	9	1	0	3	(2	1)	19	9	5	7	4	0	6	1	0	0	1	0	1.00	0	.237	.326	.500
2002	Oak	AL	90	94	23	4	2	3	(2	1)	40	24	11	10	4	0	17	3	1	2	3	0	1.00	3	.245	.291	.426
2003	Oak	AL	121	414	109	27	9	12	(7	5)	190	64	51	68	42	4	71	2	0	2	10	2	.83	3	.263	.333	.459
2004	Oak	AL	143	569	161	39	3	20	(10	10)	266	91	73	87	46	0	111	12	0	5	17	1	.94	11	.283	.347	.467
2005	3 Tms		126	412	93	24	3	10	(5	5)	153	49	40	41	32	0	71	4	0	1	7	2	.78	7	.226	.294	.371
2006	Ari	NL	143	562	150	37	3	26	(12	14)	271	82	79	78	34	2	88	5	2	3	25	3	.89	12	.267	.313	.482
2007	Ari	NL	160	626	179	30	8	21	(11	10)	288	103	83	103	57	5	98	10	1	4	50	7	.88	12	.286	.353	.460
2008	Ari	NL	52	206	43	13	1	6	(3	3)	76	28	23	19	16	0	36	2	0	0	4	4	.50	5	.209	.272	.369
05	Oak	AL	59	192	51	15	2	7	(3	4)	91	30	24	29	14	0	27	1	1	1	2	2	.50	1	.266	.336	.474
05	Col	NL	15	53	10	2	0	0	(0	0)	12	2	5	4	7	0	11	0	0	0	2	0	1.00	1	.189	.283	.226
05	Bal	AL	52	167	32	7	1	3	(2	1)	50	17	11	8	11	0	33	1	2	0	3	0	1.00	5	.192	.246	.299
Postseason			16	45	12	2	1	1	(0	1)	19	3	7	3	2	0	14	0	0	0	2	0	1.00	0	.267	.298	.422
9 ML YEARS			864	2931	770	175	29	101	(52	49)	1306	455	365	414	235	11	499	44	7	17	119	20	.86	53	.263	.325	.446

Asdrubal Cabrera

Bats: B Throws: R Pos: 2B-94; SS-20; PR-5; PH-2; DH-1   Ht: 6'0" Wt: 170 Born: 11/13/1985 Age: 23

Year	Team	Lg	G	AB	H	2B	3B	HR	(Hm	Rd)	TB	R	RBI	RC	TBB	IBB	SO	HBP	SH	SF	SB	CS	SB%	GDP	Avg	OBP	Slg
								BATTING													**BASERUNNING**				**AVERAGES**		
2004	Everett	A-	63	239	65	16	3	5	(-	-)	102	44	41	35	21	1	43	2	7	5	7	5	.58	3	.272	.330	.427
2005	Wisc	A	51	192	61	12	3	4	(-	-)	91	26	30	37	30	1	32	1	2	3	2	6	.25	6	.318	.407	.474
2005	InldEm	A+	55	225	64	15	6	1	(-	-)	94	31	26	31	15	0	47	0	1	3	3	1	.75	8	.284	.325	.418
2005	Tacom	AAA	6	23	5	0	1	0	(-	-)	7	4	3	1	1	0	4	0	1	0	0	0	-	1	.217	.250	.304
2006	Tacom	AAA	60	203	48	12	2	3	(-	-)	73	27	22	25	24	1	51	3	1	2	7	5	.58	4	.236	.323	.360
2006	Buffalo	AAA	52	190	50	11	0	1	(-	-)	64	26	14	19	8	0	39	3	4	6	5	4	.56	4	.263	.295	.337
2007	Akron	AA	96	368	114	23	3	8	(-	-)	167	78	54	69	45	0	42	3	2	7	23	7	.77	8	.310	.383	.454
2007	Buffalo	AAA	9	38	12	3	0	0	(-	-)	15	6	3	5	2	0	8	0	0	1	2	0	1.00	1	.316	.350	.395

(continued)

Year Team	Lg	G	AB	H	2B	3B	HR	(Hm Rd)	TB	R	RBI	RC	TBB	IBB	SO	HBP	SH	SF	SB	CS	SB%	GDP	Avg	OBP	Slg
2008 Buffalo	AAA	34	141	46	7	1	4	(- -)	67	25	13	24	7	1	25	4	0	0	2	2	.50	1	.326	.375	.475
2007 Cle	AL	45	159	45	9	2	3	(1 2)	67	30	22	27	17	0	29	2	5	3	0	0	-	7	.283	.354	.421
2008 Cle	AL	114	352	91	20	0	6	(5 1)	129	48	47	48	46	2	77	4	11	5	4	4	.50	8	.259	.346	.366
Postseason		11	46	10	0	0	1	(1 0)	13	5	6	5	2	0	12	0	3	1	0	0	-	2	.217	.245	.283
2 ML YEARS		159	511	136	29	2	9	(6 3)	196	78	69	75	63	2	106	6	16	8	4	4	.50	15	.266	.349	.384

Daniel Cabrera

Pitches: R Bats: R Pos: SP-30 Ht: 6'9" Wt: 269 Born: 5/28/1981 Age: 28

		HOW MUCH HE PITCHED						WHAT HE GAVE UP												THE RESULTS						
Year Team	Lg	G	GS	CG	GF	IP	BFP	H	R	ER	HR	SH	SF	HB	TBB	IBB	SO	WP	Bk	W	L	Pct	ShO	Sv-Op	Hld	ERC	ERA
2004 Bal	AL	28	27	1	1	147.2	662	145	85	82	14	4	7	2	89	2	76	12	0	12	8	.600	1	1-1	0	4.79	5.00
2005 Bal	AL	29	29	0	0	161.1	716	144	92	81	14	2	3	11	87	2	157	9	1	10	13	.435	0	0-0	0	4.13	4.52
2006 Bal	AL	26	26	2	0	148.0	662	130	82	78	11	5	8	5	104	1	157	17	1	9	10	.474	1	0-0	0	4.55	4.74
2007 Bal	AL	34	34	1	0	204.1	922	207	133	126	25	13	5	15	108	6	166	7	2	9	18	.333	0	0-0	0	5.08	5.55
2008 Bal	AL	30	30	2	0	180.0	821	199	109	105	24	5	12	18	90	5	95	15	2	8	10	.444	0	0-0	0	5.77	5.25
5 ML YEARS		147	146	6	1	841.1	3783	825	501	472	88	29	35	51	478	16	651	60	6	48	59	.449	2	1-1	0	4.89	5.05

Fernando Cabrera

Pitches: R Bats: R Pos: RP-22 Ht: 6'4" Wt: 220 Born: 11/16/1981 Age: 27

		HOW MUCH HE PITCHED						WHAT HE GAVE UP												THE RESULTS						
Year Team	Lg	G	GS	CG	GF	IP	BFP	H	R	ER	HR	SH	SF	HB	TBB	IBB	SO	WP	Bk	W	L	Pct	ShO	Sv-Op	Hld	ERC	ERA
2008 Norfolk*	AAA	11	0	0	1	13.0	55	11	1	0	0	0	0	0	7	0	13	0	1	0	0	-	0	0--	0	3.11	0.69
2004 Cle	AL	4	0	0	2	5.1	20	3	3	2	0	0	1	0	1	0	6	0	0	0	0	-	0	0-0	0	0.99	3.38
2005 Cle	AL	15	0	0	6	30.2	124	24	7	5	1	0	0	0	11	1	29	1	1	2	1	.667	0	0-0	1	2.33	1.47
2006 Cle	AL	51	0	0	20	60.2	256	53	36	35	12	1	4	1	32	2	71	5	0	3	3	.500	0	0-4	6	4.72	5.19
2007 2 Tms	AL	33	0	0	13	43.2	207	50	36	35	9	0	2	0	31	3	48	2	0	1	2	.333	0	1-1	1	6.98	7.21
2008 Bal	AL	22	0	0	8	28.1	132	32	18	17	9	0	2	0	17	2	31	3	0	2	1	.667	0	0-1	0	7.24	5.40
07 Cle	AL	24	0	0	9	33.2	157	38	22	21	7	0	2	0	22	3	39	1	0	1	2	.333	0	0-0	1	6.61	5.61
07 Bal	AL	9	0	0	4	10.0	50	12	14	14	2	0	0	0	9	0	9	1	0	0	0	-	0	1-1	0	8.26	12.60
5 ML YEARS		125	0	0	49	168.2	739	162	100	94	31	1	9	1	92	8	185	11	1	8	7	.533	0	1-6	8	5.04	5.02

Jolbert Cabrera

Bats: R Throws: R Pos: LF-17; PH-16; SS-9; 2B-3; 3B-3; RF-3; PR-2 Ht: 6'1" Wt: 214 Born: 12/8/1972 Age: 36

Year Team	Lg	G	AB	H	2B	3B	HR	(Hm Rd)	TB	R	RBI	RC	TBB	IBB	SO	HBP	SH	SF	SB	CS	SB%	GDP	Avg	OBP	Slg
2008 Lsvlle*	AAA	57	215	62	16	5	4	(- -)	100	26	30	35	13	0	39	6	1	4	5	3	.63	6	.288	.340	.465
2008 Dayton*	A	6	22	8	1	1	0	(- -)	11	3	4	4	1	0	4	1	0	0	0	0	-	1	.364	.417	.500
1998 Cle	AL	1	2	0	0	0	0	(0 0)	0	0	0	0	0	0	1	0	0	0	0	0	-	0	.000	.000	.000
1999 Cle	AL	30	37	7	1	0	0	(0 0)	8	6	0	2	1	0	8	1	0	0	3	0	1.00	1	.189	.231	.216
2000 Cle	AL	100	175	44	3	1	2	(2 0)	55	27	15	16	8	0	15	2	1	1	6	4	.60	1	.251	.290	.314
2001 Cle	AL	141	287	75	16	3	1	(1 0)	100	50	38	32	16	0	41	6	1	2	10	4	.71	4	.261	.312	.348
2002 2 Tms		48	84	12	2	0	0	(0 0)	14	8	8	3	7	0	15	1	1	1	1	1	.50	3	.143	.215	.167
2003 LAD	NL	128	347	98	32	2	6	(4 2)	152	43	37	41	17	3	62	10	3	3	6	4	.60	10	.282	.332	.438
2004 Sea	AL	113	359	97	19	2	6	(2 4)	138	38	47	44	16	1	70	8	3	5	10	3	.77	13	.270	.312	.384
2008 Cin	NL	48	115	29	6	1	3	(3 0)	46	17	12	14	8	1	29	2	0	1	2	0	1.00	3	.252	.310	.400
02 Cle	AL	38	72	8	1	0	0	(0 0)	9	5	7	1	5	0	13	1	0	1	1	1	.50	3	.111	.177	.125
02 LAD	NL	10	12	4	1	0	0	(0 0)	5	3	1	2	2	0	2	0	1	0	0	0	-	0	.333	.429	.417
Postseason		2	1	1	0	0	0	(0 0)	1	1	1	1	0	0	0	0	1	0	0	0	-	0	1.000	1.000	1.000
8 ML YEARS		609	1406	362	79	9	18	(12 6)	513	189	157	152	73	5	241	30	9	13	38	16	.70	35	.257	.306	.365

Melky Cabrera

Bats: B Throws: L Pos: CF-117; LF-8; RF-5; PH-4; PR-4 Ht: 5'11" Wt: 200 Born: 8/11/1984 Age: 24

Year Team	Lg	G	AB	H	2B	3B	HR	(Hm Rd)	TB	R	RBI	RC	TBB	IBB	SO	HBP	SH	SF	SB	CS	SB%	GDP	Avg	OBP	Slg
2008 S-WB*	AAA	15	57	19	2	0	0	(- -)	21	8	5	8	8	0	9	0	0	1	1	3	.25	2	.333	.409	.368
2005 NYY	AL	6	19	4	0	0	0	(0 0)	4	1	0	0	0	0	2	0	0	0	0	0	-	0	.211	.211	.211
2006 NYY	AL	130	460	129	26	2	7	(3 4)	180	75	50	68	56	3	59	2	5	1	12	5	.71	9	.280	.360	.391
2007 NYY	AL	150	545	149	24	8	8	(4 4)	213	66	73	70	43	0	68	5	10	9	13	5	.72	14	.273	.327	.391
2008 NYY	AL	129	414	103	12	1	8	(4 4)	141	42	37	37	29	5	58	3	4	3	9	2	.82	11	.249	.301	.341
Postseason		6	19	3	0	0	1	(0 1)	6	2	2	1	0	0	0	0	0	0	0	0	-	0	.158	.158	.316
4 ML YEARS		415	1438	385	62	11	23	(11 12)	538	184	160	175	128	8	187	10	19	13	34	12	.74	34	.268	.329	.374

Miguel Cabrera

Bats: R Throws: R Pos: 1B-143; 3B-14; DH-6; PH-1 Ht: 6'4" Wt: 240 Born: 4/18/1983 Age: 26

Year Team	Lg	G	AB	H	2B	3B	HR	(Hm Rd)	TB	R	RBI	RC	TBB	IBB	SO	HBP	SH	SF	SB	CS	SB%	GDP	Avg	OBP	Slg
2003 Fla	NL	87	314	84	21	3	12	(7 5)	147	39	62	51	25	3	84	2	4	1	0	2	.00	12	.268	.325	.468
2004 Fla	NL	160	603	177	31	1	33	(14 19)	309	101	112	92	68	5	148	6	0	8	5	2	.71	20	.294	.366	.512
2005 Fla	NL	158	613	198	43	2	33	(11 22)	344	106	116	108	64	12	125	2	0	6	1	0	1.00	20	.323	.385	.561
2006 Fla	NL	158	576	195	50	2	26	(15 11)	327	112	114	132	86	27	108	10	0	4	9	6	.60	18	.339	.430	.568
2007 Fla	NL	157	588	188	38	2	34	(19 15)	332	91	119	122	79	23	127	5	1	7	2	1	.67	19	.320	.401	.565
2008 Det	AL	160	616	180	36	2	37	(19 18)	331	85	127	109	56	6	126	3	0	9	1	0	1.00	16	.292	.349	.537
Postseason		17	68	18	2	0	4	(1 3)	32	11	12	9	4	0	19	1	1	0	0	0	-	2	.265	.315	.471
6 ML YEARS		880	3310	1022	219	12	175	(85 90)	1790	534	650	614	378	76	718	28	5	35	18	11	.62	103	.309	.381	.541

Orlando Cabrera

Bats: R **Throws:** R **Pos:** SS-161; PH-1   **Ht:** 5'9" **Wt:** 185 **Born:** 11/2/1974 **Age:** 34

								BATTING												BASERUNNING				AVERAGES		
Year	Team	Lg	G	AB	H	2B	3B	HR	(Hm | Rd)	TB	R	RBI	RC	TBB	IBB	SO	HBP	SH	SF	SB	CS	SB%	GDP	Avg	OBP	Slg
1997	Mon	NL	16	18	4	0	0	0	(0 | 0)	4	4	2	0	1	0	3	0	1	0	1	2	.33	1	.222	.263	.222
1998	Mon	NL	79	261	73	16	5	3	(2 | 1)	108	44	22	34	18	1	27	0	5	1	6	2	.75	6	.280	.325	.414
1999	Mon	NL	104	382	97	23	5	8	(6 | 2)	154	48	39	42	18	4	38	3	4	0	2	2	.50	9	.254	.293	.403
2000	Mon	NL	125	422	100	25	1	13	(7 | 6)	166	47	55	43	25	3	28	1	3	3	4	4	.50	12	.237	.279	.393
2001	Mon	NL	162	626	173	41	6	14	(7 | 7)	268	64	96	85	43	5	54	4	4	7	19	7	.73	15	.276	.324	.428
2002	Mon	NL	153	563	148	43	1	7	(3 | 4)	214	64	56	61	48	4	53	2	9	4	25	7	.78	16	.263	.321	.380
2003	Mon	NL	162	626	186	47	2	17	(8 | 9)	288	95	80	92	52	3	64	1	3	9	24	2	.92	18	.297	.347	.460
2004	2 Tms		161	618	163	38	3	10	(2 | 8)	237	74	62	67	39	0	54	3	3	10	16	4	.80	16	.264	.306	.383
2005	LAA	AL	141	540	139	28	3	8	(2 | 6)	197	70	57	61	38	4	50	3	4	2	21	2	.91	10	.257	.309	.365
2006	LAA	AL	153	607	171	45	1	9	(3 | 6)	245	95	72	77	51	0	58	3	3	11	27	3	.90	12	.282	.335	.404
2007	LAA	AL	155	638	192	35	1	8	(3 | 5)	253	101	86	95	44	0	64	5	3	11	20	4	.83	12	.301	.345	.397
2008	CWS	AL	161	661	186	33	1	8	(5 | 3)	245	93	57	83	56	1	71	1	3	9	19	6	.76	16	.281	.334	.371
04	Mon	NL	103	390	96	19	2	4	(1 | 3)	131	41	31	37	28	0	31	2	2	3	12	3	.80	12	.246	.298	.336
04	Bos	AL	58	228	67	19	1	6	(1 | 5)	106	33	31	30	11	0	23	1	1	7	4	1	.80	4	.294	.320	.465
	Postseason		27	112	29	8	0	1	(1 | 0)	40	13	18	15	9	0	12	1	0	1	1	0	1.00	1	.259	.317	.357
	12 ML YEARS		1572	5962	1632	374	29	105	(48 | 57)	2379	799	684	740	433	25	564	26	45	67	184	45	.80	143	.274	.322	.399

Matt Cain

Pitches: R **Bats:** R **Pos:** SP-34   **Ht:** 6'3" **Wt:** 246 **Born:** 10/1/1984 **Age:** 24

			HOW MUCH HE PITCHED						WHAT HE GAVE UP										THE RESULTS						
Year	Team	Lg	G	GS	CG	GF	IP	BFP	H	R	ER	HR	SH	SF	HB	TBB	IBB	SO	WP	Bk	W	L	Pct	ShO	Sv-Op	Hld	ERC	ERA
2005	SF	NL	7	7	1	0	46.1	181	24	12	12	4	2	1	0	19	1	30	1	0	2	1	.667	0	0-0	0	1.61	2.33
2006	SF	NL	32	31	1	1	190.2	818	157	93	88	18	11	6	6	87	1	179	9	2	13	12	.520	1	0-0	0	3.35	4.15
2007	SF	NL	32	32	1	0	200.0	832	173	84	81	14	8	5	5	79	3	163	12	0	7	16	.304	0	0-0	0	3.23	3.65
2008	SF	NL	34	34	1	0	217.2	933	206	95	91	19	7	7	7	91	9	186	7	2	8	14	.364	1	0-0	0	3.84	3.76
	4 ML YEARS		105	104	4	1	654.2	2764	560	284	272	55	28	19	18	276	14	558	29	4	30	43	.411	2	0-0	0	3.33	3.74

Miguel Cairo

Bats: R **Throws:** R **Pos:** 1B-70; PR-21; 3B-19; PH-16; 2B-5; DH-3; LF-2; SS-1; RF-1   **Ht:** 6'1" **Wt:** 208 **Born:** 5/4/1974 **Age:** 35

								BATTING												BASERUNNING				AVERAGES		
Year	Team	Lg	G	AB	H	2B	3B	HR	(Hm	Rd)	TB	R	RBI	RC	TBB	IBB	SO	HBP	SH	SF	SB	CS	SB%	GDP	Avg	OBP	Slg
1996	Tor	AL	9	27	6	2	0	0	(0	0)	8	5	1	2	2	0	9	1	0	0	0	0	-	1	.222	.300	.296
1997	ChC	NL	16	29	7	1	0	0	(0	0)	8	7	1	3	2	0	3	1	0	0	0	0	-	0	.241	.313	.276
1998	TB	AL	150	515	138	26	5	5	(3	2)	189	49	46	58	24	0	44	6	11	2	19	8	.70	9	.268	.307	.367
1999	TB	AL	120	465	137	15	5	3	(1	2)	171	61	36	57	24	0	46	4	7	5	22	7	.76	13	.295	.335	.368
2000	TB	AL	119	375	98	18	2	1	(0	1)	123	49	34	42	29	0	34	2	6	5	28	7	.80	7	.261	.314	.328
2001	2 Tms	NL	93	156	46	8	1	3	(2	1)	65	25	16	23	18	1	23	0	7	1	2	1	.67	4	.295	.366	.417
2002	StL	NL	108	184	46	9	2	2	(1	1)	65	28	23	19	13	2	36	3	6	2	1	1	.50	5	.250	.307	.353
2003	StL	NL	92	261	64	15	2	5	(2	3)	98	41	32	25	13	1	30	6	3	7	4	1	.80	6	.245	.289	.375
2004	NYY	AL	122	360	105	17	5	6	(4	2)	150	48	42	50	14	12	49	14	12	4	11	3	.79	7	.292	.346	.417
2005	NYM	NL	100	327	82	18	0	2	(1	1)	106	31	19	29	19	2	31	4	12	5	13	3	.81	5	.251	.296	.324
2006	NYY	AL	81	222	53	12	3	0	(0	0)	71	28	30	26	13	0	31	1	5	3	13	1	.93	4	.239	.280	.320
2007	2 Tms		82	174	44	9	2	0	(0	0)	57	20	15	21	11	1	24	2	5	1	10	2	.83	4	.253	.303	.328
2008	Sea	AL	108	221	55	14	2	0	(0	0)	73	34	23	26	18	0	32	4	6	1	5	2	.71	6	.249	.316	.330
01	ChC	NL	66	123	35	3	1	2	(1	1)	46	20	9	17	16	1	21	0	7	1	2	1	.67	3	.285	.364	.374
01	StL	NL	27	33	11	5	0	1	(1	0)	19	5	7	6	2	0	2	0	0	0	0	0	-	1	.333	.371	.576
07	NYY	AL	54	107	27	7	0	0	(0	0)	34	12	10	12	8	1	19	1	4	1	8	1	.89	3	.252	.308	.318
07	StL	NL	28	67	17	2	2	0	(0	0)	23	8	5	9	3	0	5	1	1	0	2	1	.67	0	.254	.296	.343
	Postseason		19	61	20	5	0	1	(1	0)	28	11	6	9	4	0	12	5	2	0	2	1	.67	0	.328	.414	.459
	13 ML YEARS		1200	3316	881	164	29	27	(14	13)	1184	426	318	381	204	8	392	51	80	36	128	36	.78	70	.266	.315	.357

Kiko Calero

Pitches: R **Bats:** R **Pos:** RP-5   **Ht:** 6'1" **Wt:** 210 **Born:** 1/9/1975 **Age:** 34

			HOW MUCH HE PITCHED						WHAT HE GAVE UP										THE RESULTS						
Year	Team	Lg	G	GS	CG	GF	IP	BFP	H	R	ER	HR	SH	SF	HB	TBB	IBB	SO	WP	Bk	W	L	Pct	ShO	Sv-Op	Hld	ERC	ERA
2008	Scrmto*	AAA	8	0	0	4	9.0	44	8	4	4	1	2	0	0	10	1	10	1	0	1	1	.500	0	0--	-	6.16	4.00
2008	Okla*	AAA	18	0	0	9	21.1	98	24	18	18	4	1	3	0	12	1	21	3	0	1	2	.333	0	1--	-	6.06	7.59
2003	StL	NL	26	1	0	7	38.1	162	29	12	12	5	1	3	1	20	2	51	3	1	1	1	.500	0	1-4	1	3.44	2.82
2004	StL	NL	41	0	0	4	45.1	168	27	14	14	5	4	0	1	10	1	47	1	0	3	1	.750	0	2-3	12	1.62	2.78
2005	Oak	AL	58	0	0	15	55.2	229	45	20	20	6	1	1	1	18	2	52	2	0	4	1	.800	0	1-2	12	2.80	3.23
2006	Oak	AL	70	0	0	17	58.0	241	50	22	22	4	0	1	0	24	3	67	1	0	3	2	.600	0	2-5	23	3.13	3.41
2007	Oak	AL	46	0	0	6	40.2	185	46	26	26	3	0	5	2	21	2	31	1	0	1	5	.167	0	1-4	9	5.26	5.75
2008	Oak	AL	5	0	0	3	4.2	20	3	3	2	0	0	0	0	3	0	7	0	0	0	0	-	0	0-0	0	2.35	3.86
	Postseason		12	0	0	1	12.1	55	13	5	5	1	0	0	1	7	0	11	0	0	1	0	1.000	0	0-1	2	5.41	3.65
	6 ML YEARS		246	1	0	52	242.2	1005	200	97	96	23	6	10	5	96	10	255	8	1	12	10	.545	0	7-18	57	3.11	3.56

Alberto Callaspo

Bats: B **Throws:** R **Pos:** 2B-46; SS-18; PH-17; LF-3; 3B-1   **Ht:** 5'9" **Wt:** 180 **Born:** 4/19/1983 **Age:** 26

								BATTING												BASERUNNING				AVERAGES		
Year	Team	Lg	G	AB	H	2B	3B	HR	(Hm	Rd)	TB	R	RBI	RC	TBB	IBB	SO	HBP	SH	SF	SB	CS	SB%	GDP	Avg	OBP	Slg
2008	Omha*	AAA	4	16	3	0	0	0	(-	-)	3	5	0	0	1	0	4	0	0	0	0	0	-	0	.188	.235	.188
2006	Ari	NL	23	42	10	1	1	0	(0	0)	13	2	6	5	4	0	6	0	0	1	0	1	.00	0	.238	.298	.310

			BATTING																		BASERUNNING				AVERAGES		
Year	Team	Lg	G	AB	H	2B	3B	HR	(Hm	Rd)	TB	R	RBI	RC	TBB	IBB	SO	HBP	SH	SF	SB	CS	SB%	GDP	Avg	OBP	Slg
2007	Ari	NL	56	144	31	8	0	0	(0	0)	39	10	7	7	9	0	14	1	1	1	1	1	.50	8	.215	.265	.271
2008	KC	AL	74	213	65	8	3	0	(0	0)	79	21	16	25	19	0	14	0	1	1	2	1	.67	6	.305	.361	.371
	Postseason		2	2	0	0	0	0	(0	0)	0	0	0	0	0	0	0	0	0	0	0	0	-	0	.000	.000	.000
	3 ML YEARS		153	399	106	17	4	0	(0	0)	131	33	29	37	32	0	34	1	2	3	3	3	.50	14	.266	.320	.328

Kevin Cameron

Pitches: R **Bats:** R **Pos:** RP-10

Ht: 6'1" Wt: 191 Born: 12/15/1979 Age: 29

			HOW MUCH HE PITCHED					WHAT HE GAVE UP											THE RESULTS						
Year	Team	Lg	G	GS	CG	GF	IP	BFP	H	R	ER	HR	SH	SF	HB	TBB	IBB	SO	WP	Bk	W	L	Pct	ShO	Sv-Op Hld	ERC	ERA
2001	Elizab	R+	22	0	0	22	23.0	94	16	4	4	0	0	0	3	5	0	30	3	0	1	1	.500	0	13- - -	1.67	1.57
2003	QuadC	A	39	0	0	16	62.0	281	57	30	27	2	5	1	2	33	5	58	13	0	1	5	.167	0	2- - -	3.50	3.92
2004	FtMyrs	A+	22	0	0	10	31.2	131	23	13	11	1	0	0	0	13	1	22	2	0	2	3	.400	0	1- - -	2.16	3.13
2004	NwBrit	AA	26	0	0	10	46.1	209	47	20	12	1	0	0	2	21	2	47	2	0	1	3	.250	0	3- - -	3.78	2.33
2005	NwBrit	AA	42	0	0	16	75.2	331	75	38	24	8	2	2	1	26	1	57	1	1	6	2	.750	0	6- - -	3.76	2.85
2006	Roch	AAA	40	0	0	23	66.1	280	53	25	22	2	3	2	3	26	1	65	3	0	6	4	.600	0	9- - -	2.61	2.98
2008	Portlnd	AAA	15	0	0	2	18.2	73	13	5	4	0	1	0	0	7	0	9	2	0	1	0	1.000	0	1- - -	1.88	1.93
2008	Padres	R	2	1	0	0	2.0	7	0	0	0	0	0	0	0	1	0	1	0	0	0	0	-	0	0- - -	0.00	0.00
2007	SD	NL	48	0	0	20	58.0	263	55	24	18	0	4	2	0	36	5	50	2	0	2	0	1.000	0	0-0 1	3.67	2.79
2008	SD	NL	10	0	0	4	10.0	46	10	9	4	0	1	1	0	6	2	5	0	0	0	0	-	0	0-0 0	3.64	3.60
	2 ML YEARS		58	0	0	24	68.0	309	65	33	22	0	5	3	0	42	7	55	2	0	2	0	1.000	0	0-0 1	3.67	2.91

Mike Cameron

Bats: R **Throws:** R **Pos:** CF-119; PH-1

Ht: 6'2" Wt: 200 Born: 1/8/1973 Age: 36

			BATTING																		BASERUNNING				AVERAGES		
Year	Team	Lg	G	AB	H	2B	3B	HR	(Hm	Rd)	TB	R	RBI	RC	TBB	IBB	SO	HBP	SH	SF	SB	CS	SB%	GDP	Avg	OBP	Slg
2008	Nashv*	AAA	4	15	3	0	0	1	(-	-)	6	4	2	2	3	0	4	0	0	0	0	0	-	0	.200	.333	.400
1995	CWS	AL	28	38	7	2	0	1	(0	1)	12	4	2	3	3	0	15	0	3	0	0	0	-	0	.184	.244	.316
1996	CWS	AL	11	11	1	0	0	0	(0	0)	1	1	0	0	1	0	3	0	0	0	0	1	.00	0	.091	.167	.091
1997	CWS	AL	116	379	98	18	3	14	(10	4)	164	63	55	63	55	1	105	5	2	5	23	2	.92	8	.259	.356	.433
1998	CWS	AL	141	396	83	16	5	8	(5	3)	133	53	43	39	37	0	101	6	1	3	27	11	.71	6	.210	.285	.336
1999	Cin	NL	146	542	139	34	9	21	(12	9)	254	93	66	96	80	2	145	6	5	3	38	12	.76	4	.256	.357	.469
2000	Sea	AL	155	543	145	28	4	19	(5	14)	238	96	78	91	78	0	133	9	7	6	24	7	.77	10	.267	.365	.438
2001	Sea	AL	150	540	144	30	5	25	(7	18)	259	99	110	96	69	3	155	10	1	13	34	5	.87	13	.267	.353	.480
2002	Sea	AL	158	545	130	26	5	25	(7	18)	241	84	80	78	79	3	176	7	4	5	31	8	.79	8	.239	.340	.442
2003	Sea	AL	147	534	135	31	5	18	(11	7)	230	74	76	80	70	1	137	5	1	2	17	7	.71	13	.253	.344	.431
2004	NYM	NL	140	493	114	30	1	30	(11	19)	236	76	76	70	57	2	143	6	1	3	22	6	.79	9	.231	.319	.479
2005	NYM	NL	76	308	84	23	2	12	(5	7)	147	47	39	52	29	0	85	4	1	1	13	1	.93	5	.273	.342	.477
2006	SD	NL	141	552	148	34	9	22	(11	11)	266	88	83	98	71	2	142	6	0	5	25	9	.74	8	.268	.355	.482
2007	SD	NL	151	571	138	33	6	21	(10	11)	246	88	78	83	67	1	160	8	2	4	18	5	.78	9	.242	.328	.431
2008	Mil	NL	120	444	108	25	2	25	(11	11)	212	69	70	70	54	1	142	6	1	3	17	5	.77	5	.243	.331	.477
	Postseason		23	79	14	6	0	1	(1	0)	23	11	7	6	11	0	25	3	2	0	3	1	.75	2	.177	.301	.291
	14 ML YEARS		1680	5896	1474	330	56	241	(103	138)	2639	935	856	919	750	16	1642	80	29	52	289	79	.79	93	.250	.340	.448

Shawn Camp

Pitches: R **Bats:** R **Pos:** RP-40

Ht: 6'1" Wt: 200 Born: 11/18/1975 Age: 33

			HOW MUCH HE PITCHED					WHAT HE GAVE UP											THE RESULTS						
Year	Team	Lg	G	GS	CG	GF	IP	BFP	H	R	ER	HR	SH	SF	HB	TBB	IBB	SO	WP	Bk	W	L	Pct	ShO	Sv-Op Hld	ERC	ERA
2008	Syrcse*	AAA	7	0	0	7	10.0	32	4	0	0	0	0	0	0	0	0	13	0	0	1	0	1.000	0	4- - -	0.38	0.00
2004	KC	AL	42	0	0	12	66.2	286	74	37	29	10	2	3	5	16	1	51	2	1	2	2	.500	0	2-3 5	4.74	3.92
2005	KC	AL	29	0	0	7	49.0	228	69	40	35	4	0	3	4	13	3	28	3	0	1	4	.200	0	0-2 0	6.00	6.43
2006	TB	AL	75	0	0	15	75.0	328	93	43	39	9	2	3	7	19	3	53	4	0	7	4	.636	0	4-6 12	5.48	4.68
2007	TB	AL	50	0	0	8	40.0	198	63	33	32	7	5	1	3	18	6	36	2	0	3	0	.000	0	0-2 11	8.59	7.20
2008	Tor	AL	40	0	0	16	39.1	166	40	18	18	2	0	1	2	11	3	31	0	0	3	1	.750	0	0-0 7	3.47	4.12
	5 ML YEARS		236	0	0	58	270.0	1206	339	171	153	32	9	11	21	77	16	199	11	1	13	14	.481	0	6-13 35	5.51	5.10

Jorge Campillo

Pitches: R **Bats:** R **Pos:** SP-25; RP-14

Ht: 6'1" Wt: 225 Born: 8/10/1978 Age: 30

			HOW MUCH HE PITCHED					WHAT HE GAVE UP											THE RESULTS						
Year	Team	Lg	G	GS	CG	GF	IP	BFP	H	R	ER	HR	SH	SF	HB	TBB	IBB	SO	WP	Bk	W	L	Pct	ShO	Sv-Op Hld	ERC	ERA
2008	Rchmd*	AAA	1	1	0	0	4.1	19	5	0	0	0	0	0	0	0	0	4	0	0	0	0	-	0	0- - -	2.49	0.00
2005	Sea	AL	2	1	0	1	2.0	9	1	0	0	0	0	0	0	1	0	1	0	0	0	0	-	0	0-0 0	1.26	0.00
2006	Sea	AL	1	0	0	0	2.1	11	4	4	4	0	0	0	0	0	0	1	0	0	0	0	-	0	0-0 0	5.71	15.43
2007	Sea	AL	5	0	0	2	13.1	63	18	12	10	2	1	1	1	6	0	6	0	0	0	0	-	0	0-0 0	7.18	6.75
2008	Atl	NL	39	25	1	3	158.2	655	158	74	69	18	9	5	1	38	2	107	2	0	8	7	.533	0	0-0 4	3.55	3.91
	4 ML YEARS		47	26	1	6	176.1	738	181	90	83	20	10	6	2	45	2	118	2	0	8	7	.533	0	0-0 4	3.80	4.24

Robinson Cancel

Bats: R **Throws:** R **Pos:** C-15; PH-13

Ht: 6'0" Wt: 190 Born: 5/4/1976 Age: 33

			BATTING																		BASERUNNING				AVERAGES		
Year	Team	Lg	G	AB	H	2B	3B	HR	(Hm	Rd)	TB	R	RBI	RC	TBB	IBB	SO	HBP	SH	SF	SB	CS	SB%	GDP	Avg	OBP	Slg
1994	Brewrs	R	29	70	12	0	0	0	(-	-)	12	6	8	3	9	1	19	2	0	2	0	2	.00	2	.171	.277	.171
1995	Helena	R+	46	154	37	9	0	0	(-	-)	46	18	24	14	9	0	20	2	1	2	8	3	.73	3	.240	.287	.299
1996	Beloit	A	72	218	48	3	1	1	(-	-)	56	26	29	15	14	0	31	1	5	1	15	5	.72	7	.220	.269	.257
1997	Beloit	A	17	50	15	3	0	0	(-	-)	18	9	4	7	7	0	9	3	0	0	0	2	.00	1	.300	.417	.360
1997	Stcktn	A+	64	211	59	11	0	1	(-	-)	73	25	16	25	13	0	40	2	7	1	9	3	.75	6	.280	.326	.346

Year	Team	Lg	G	AB	H	2B	3B	HR	(Hm	Rd)	TB	R	RBI	RC	TBB	IBB	SO	HBP	SH	SF	SB	CS	SB%	GDP	Avg	OBP	Slg
1998	Stcktn	A+	11	32	6	1	0	0	(-	-)	7	3	2	2	4	0	8	0	0	0	2	1	.67	1	.188	.278	.219
1998	ElPaso	AA	58	158	51	10	0	1	(-	-)	64	17	30	27	22	1	32	0	4	1	2	2	.50	5	.323	.403	.405
1999	Hntsvl	AA	66	223	56	10	1	5	(-	-)	83	35	32	28	23	0	38	3	0	1	8	5	.62	10	.251	.328	.372
1999	Lsvlle	AAA	39	117	43	8	0	5	(-	-)	66	22	28	28	14	0	28	1	1	1	6	2	.75	6	.368	.436	.564
2000	Hntsvl	AA	22	71	19	3	0	1	(-	-)	25	11	12	10	11	0	16	0	0	1	5	1	.83	2	.268	.361	.352
2001	Hntsvl	AA	29	86	15	2	0	0	(-	-)	17	8	5	1	6	0	17	1	2	1	0	5	.00	1	.174	.234	.198
2001	Indy	AAA	51	172	37	5	0	1	(-	-)	45	16	18	11	9	2	38	1	1	3	0	0	-	5	.215	.254	.262
2002	Mdland	AA	108	402	113	21	2	12	(-	-)	174	56	64	59	32	0	70	3	1	1	10	7	.59	12	.281	.338	.433
2003	Smrset	IND	69	236	56	3	0	10	(-	-)	89	27	38	30	20	0	32	3	3	3	11	2	.85	9	.237	.302	.377
2003	Penn	IND	19	67	21	3	0	2	(-	-)	30	7	11	11	7	0	11	0	1	0	3	1	.75	2	.313	.378	.448
2004	Mont	AA	52	159	34	10	1	4	(-	-)	58	15	24	17	15	3	27	2	0	2	0	2	.00	2	.214	.287	.365
2004	Drham	AAA	18	57	15	7	0	1	(-	-)	25	6	4	6	1	0	10	1	0	0	0	1	.00	4	.263	.288	.439
2004	Smrset	IND	6	20	5	1	0	0	(-	-)	6	2	3	2	3	0	2	0	1	0	0	1	.00	1	.250	.348	.300
2005	Sprgfld	AA	65	230	66	13	0	8	(-	-)	103	31	26	40	29	2	36	1	1	4	4	1	.80	4	.287	.364	.448
2005	Memp	AAA	29	95	24	3	1	3	(-	-)	38	12	13	12	8	1	18	1	0	1	0	0	-	0	.253	.314	.400
2006	Ednbg	IND	89	343	102	24	0	10	(-	-)	156	58	52	65	43	2	35	3	2	1	28	4	.88	15	.297	.379	.455
2007	Bnghtn	AA	20	54	14	3	0	2	(-	-)	23	5	6	6	2	0	12	0	1	2	1	2	.33	0	.259	.276	.426
2007	NewOr	AAA	59	182	48	13	1	4	(-	-)	75	18	25	25	13	1	34	1	2	1	3	0	1.00	2	.264	.315	.412
2008	StLuci	A+	4	14	2	0	0	0	(-	-)	2	1	1	0	1	0	1	0	0	0	1	0	1.00	0	.143	.200	.143
2008	NewOr	AAA	15	52	18	4	1	1	(-	-)	27	8	8	10	4	0	5	1	1	1	1	0	1.00	6	.346	.397	.519
1999	Mil	NL	15	44	8	2	0	0	(	)	10	5	5	2	2	0	12	1	1	0	0	0	-	0	.182	.234	.227
2008	NYM	NL	27	49	12	2	0	1	(1	0)	17	5	5	3	3	0	6	0	1	0	1	2	.33	0	.245	.288	.347
2 ML YEARS			42	93	20	4	0	1	(1	0)	27	10	10	5	5	0	18	1	2	0	1	2	.33	0	.215	.263	.290

Andy Cannizaro

Bats: R **Throws:** R **Pos:** SS-1 **Ht:** 5'10" **Wt:** 170 **Born:** 12/19/1978 **Age:** 30

Year	Team	Lg	G	AB	H	2B	3B	HR	(Hm	Rd)	TB	R	RBI	RC	TBB	IBB	SO	HBP	SH	SF	SB	CS	SB%	GDP	Avg	OBP	Slg
2001	StIsInd	A-	67	254	72	9	2	0	(-	-)	85	38	20	33	22	1	21	6	3	3	5	3	.63	15	.283	.351	.335
2002	Tampa	A+	112	366	91	18	1	1	(-	-)	114	52	46	43	38	0	31	14	5	4	3	4	.43	14	.249	.339	.311
2003	Trntn	AA	108	369	102	23	1	1	(-	-)	130	50	39	47	26	1	24	9	8	2	9	4	.69	7	.276	.337	.352
2004	Trntn	AA	85	328	103	18	0	3	(-	-)	130	44	44	52	36	1	31	5	5	5	7	9	.44	7	.314	.385	.396
2005	Trntn	AA	54	202	50	12	0	0	(-	-)	62	28	20	20	11	0	19	4	1	1	5	0	1.00	4	.248	.298	.307
2005	Clmbs	AAA	56	170	43	10	2	1	(-	-)	60	22	18	23	17	0	11	9	6	0	1	1	.50	11	.253	.352	.353
2006	Clmbs	AAA	116	416	115	32	1	3	(-	-)	158	69	32	63	51	0	59	10	7	3	6	5	.55	7	.276	.367	.380
2007	Trntn	AA	8	32	7	1	0	0	(-	-)	8	5	2	2	2	0	3	0	0	0	0	0	-	0	.219	.265	.250
2007	S-WB	AAA	52	166	49	12	0	2	(-	-)	67	27	20	27	21	1	30	3	2	3	0	1	.00	6	.295	.378	.404
2008	Drham	AAA	51	171	41	8	0	1	(-	-)	52	16	14	18	17	0	18	2	5	3	1	0	1.00	1	.240	.311	.304
2008	Buffalo	AAA	25	84	27	4	0	3	(-	-)	40	15	14	15	7	0	7	0	0	0	0	0	-	0	.321	.374	.476
2006	NYY	AL	13	8	2	0	0	1	(0	1)	5	5	1	1	1	0	1	0	0	0	0	0	-	1	.250	.333	.625
2008	TB	AL	1	1	0	0	0	0	(0	0)	0	0	0	0	0	0	0	0	0	0	0	0	-	0	.000	.000	.000
2 ML YEARS			14	9	2	0	0	1	(0	1)	5	5	1	1	1	0	1	0	0	0	0	0	-	1	.222	.300	.556

Robinson Cano

Bats: L **Throws:** R **Pos:** 2B-159; PH-3; PR-1 **Ht:** 6'0" **Wt:** 205 **Born:** 10/22/1982 **Age:** 26

Year	Team	Lg	G	AB	H	2B	3B	HR	(Hm	Rd)	TB	R	RBI	RC	TBB	IBB	SO	HBP	SH	SF	SB	CS	SB%	GDP	Avg	OBP	Slg
2005	NYY	AL	132	522	155	34	4	14	(5	9)	239	78	62	59	16	1	68	3	7	3	1	3	.25	16	.297	.320	.458
2006	NYY	AL	122	482	165	41	1	15	(9	6)	253	62	78	74	18	3	54	2	1	5	5	2	.71	19	.342	.365	.525
2007	NYY	AL	160	617	189	41	7	19	(10	9)	301	93	97	94	39	5	85	8	1	4	4	5	.44	19	.306	.353	.488
2008	NYY	AL	159	597	162	35	3	14	(7	7)	245	70	72	64	26	3	65	5	1	5	2	4	.33	18	.271	.305	.410
Postseason			13	49	12	4	0	2	(1	1)	22	6	8	5	3	0	6	0	0	0	0	2	.00	2	.245	.288	.449
4 ML YEARS			573	2218	671	151	15	62	(31	31)	1038	303	309	291	99	12	272	18	10	17	12	14	.46	72	.303	.335	.468

Jorge Cantu

Bats: R **Throws:** R **Pos:** 3B-129; 1B-66; PH-2 **Ht:** 6'3" **Wt:** 200 **Born:** 1/30/1982 **Age:** 27

Year	Team	Lg	G	AB	H	2B	3B	HR	(Hm	Rd)	TB	R	RBI	RC	TBB	IBB	SO	HBP	SH	SF	SB	CS	SB%	GDP	Avg	OBP	Slg
2004	TB	AL	50	173	52	20	1	2	(0	2)	80	25	17	22	9	0	44	2	0	1	0	0	-	5	.301	.341	.462
2005	TB	AL	150	598	171	40	1	28	(16	12)	297	73	117	88	19	1	83	6	0	7	1	0	1.00	24	.286	.311	.497
2006	TB	AL	107	413	103	18	2	14	(7	7)	167	40	62	42	26	2	91	3	0	6	1	1	.50	16	.249	.295	.404
2007	2 Tms		52	115	29	9	0	1	(0	1)	41	12	13	12	12	0	26	3	0	3	0	0	-	6	.252	.331	.357
2008	Fla	NL	155	628	174	41	0	29	(18	11)	302	92	95	89	40	6	111	10	0	7	6	2	.75	15	.277	.327	.481
07	TB	AL	25	58	12	1	0	0	(0	0)	13	4	4	3	5	0	16	1	0	1	0	0	-	3	.207	.277	.224
07	Cin	NL	27	57	17	8	0	1	(0	1)	28	8	9	9	7	0	10	2	0	2	0	0	-	3	.298	.382	.491
5 ML YEARS			514	1927	529	128	4	74	(41	33)	887	242	304	253	106	9	355	24	0	24	8	3	.73	66	.275	.317	.460

Jose Capellan

Pitches: R **Bats:** R **Pos:** RP-1 **Ht:** 6'4" **Wt:** 235 **Born:** 1/13/1981 **Age:** 28

	HOW MUCH HE PITCHED						WHAT HE GAVE UP												THE RESULTS							
Year	Team	Lg	G	GS	CG	GF	IP	BFP	H	R	ER	HR	SH	SF	HB	TBB	IBB	SO	WP	Bk	W	L	Pct	ShO	Sv-Op	Hld	ERC	ERA
2008	ColSpr*	AAA	3	3	0	0	16.0	65	12	7	7	2	0	0	1	5	0	11	1	1	2	0	1.000	0	0--	-	2.81	3.94
2008	Omha*	AAA	6	5	0	1	37.1	154	35	17	17	3	0	3	0	14	0	20	0	2	2	1	.667	0	0--	-	3.60	4.10
2004	Atl	NL	3	2	0	0	8.0	42	14	10	10	2	1	1	0	5	0	4	0	0	0	1	.000	0	0-0	0	11.31	11.25
2005	Mil	NL	17	0	0	0	15.2	67	17	6	5	1	2	2	0	5	0	14	0	0	1	1	.500	0	0-0	3	4.01	2.87
2006	Mil	NL	61	0	0	12	71.2	310	65	37	35	11	8	2	3	31	7	58	3	0	4	2	.667	0	0-2	16	4.04	4.40
2007	2 Tms		17	0	0	9	26.0	115	28	19	16	7	0	1	1	9	2	20	3	0	0	3	.000	0	0-0	1	5.49	5.54

			HOW MUCH HE PITCHED					WHAT HE GAVE UP											THE RESULTS						
Year	Team	Lg	G	GS	CG	GF	IP	BFP	H	R	ER	HR	SH	SF	HB	TBB	IBB	SO	WP	Bk	W	L	Pct	ShO	Sv-Op	Hld	ERC	ERA
2008	Col	NL	1	0	0	1	2.0	9	3	1	1	0	0	0	0	0	0	2	0	0	0	0	-	0	0-0	0	4.47	4.50
07	Mil	NL	7	0	0	3	12.0	52	10	6	6	2	0	1	0	6	1	8	2	0	0	2	.000	0	0-0	0	3.79	4.50
07	Det	AL	10	0	0	6	14.0	63	18	13	10	5	0	0	1	3	1	12	1	0	0	1	.000	0	0-0	1	7.07	6.43
	5 ML YEARS		99	2	0	29	123.1	543	127	73	67	21	11	6	4	50	9	98	6	0	5	7	.417	0	0-2	20	4.75	4.89

Matt Capps

Pitches: R Bats: R Pos: RP-49

Ht: 6'2" Wt: 255 Born: 9/3/1983 Age: 25

			HOW MUCH HE PITCHED					WHAT HE GAVE UP											THE RESULTS						
Year	Team	Lg	G	GS	CG	GF	IP	BFP	H	R	ER	HR	SH	SF	HB	TBB	IBB	SO	WP	Bk	W	L	Pct	ShO	Sv-Op	Hld	ERC	ERA
2008	Pirates*	R	2	2	0	0	2.0	9	2	1	0	0	0	0	0	0	0	2	0	0	0	0	-	0	0--	1	1.68	0.00
2008	Altna*	AA	3	0	0	0	3.0	10	0	0	0	0	0	0	0	1	0	5	0	0	0	0	-	0	0--	1	0.13	0.00
2008	Indy*	AAA	1	0	0	0	1.2	9	0	0	0	0	0	0	0	3	0	1	0	0	0	0	-	0	0--	1	2.46	0.00
2005	Pit	NL	4	0	0	0	4.0	16	5	2	2	0	0	0	0	1	0	3	0	0	0	0	-	0	0-0	0	4.62	4.50
2006	Pit	NL	85	0	0	15	80.2	329	81	37	34	12	8	2	3	12	5	56	4	0	9	1	.900	0	1-10	13	3.52	3.79
2007	Pit	NL	76	0	0	47	79.0	315	64	22	20	5	3	2	3	16	10	64	1	0	4	7	.364	0	18-21	15	2.10	2.28
2008	Pit	NL	49	0	0	39	53.2	211	47	20	18	5	2	0	2	5	0	39	0	0	2	3	.400	0	21-26	0	2.39	3.02
	4 ML YEARS		214	0	0	101	217.1	871	197	81	74	22	13	4	9	33	15	162	5	0	15	11	.577	0	40-57	28	2.72	3.06

Chris Capuano

Pitches: L Bats: L Pos: P

Ht: 6'2" Wt: 220 Born: 8/19/1978 Age: 30

			HOW MUCH HE PITCHED					WHAT HE GAVE UP											THE RESULTS						
Year	Team	Lg	G	GS	CG	GF	IP	BFP	H	R	ER	HR	SH	SF	HB	TBB	IBB	SO	WP	Bk	W	L	Pct	ShO	Sv-Op	Hld	ERC	ERA
2003	Ari	NL	9	5	0	2	33.0	139	27	19	17	3	4	1	6	11	1	23	3	0	2	4	.333	0	0-0	1	3.45	4.64
2004	Mil	NL	17	17	0	0	88.1	385	91	55	49	18	4	1	5	37	1	80	3	1	6	8	.429	0	0-0	0	5.37	4.99
2005	Mil	NL	35	35	0	0	219.0	949	212	105	97	31	14	5	12	91	6	176	3	4	18	12	.600	0	0-0	0	4.44	3.99
2006	Mil	NL	34	34	3	0	221.1	936	229	108	99	29	9	8	9	47	4	174	7	0	11	12	.478	2	0-0	0	3.84	4.03
2007	Mil	NL	29	25	0	0	150.0	669	170	93	85	20	10	3	8	54	2	132	10	0	5	12	.294	0	0-0	1	5.11	5.10
	5 ML YEARS		124	116	3	2	711.2	3078	729	380	347	101	41	18	40	240	14	585	26	5	42	48	.467	2	0-0	1	4.46	4.39

Luke Carlin

Bats: B Throws: R Pos: C-36; PH-1; PR-1

Ht: 5'10" Wt: 195 Born: 12/20/1980 Age: 28

			BATTING																		BASERUNNING				AVERAGES		
Year	Team	Lg	G	AB	H	2B	3B	HR	(Hm	Rd)	TB	R	RBI	RC	TBB	IBB	SO	HBP	SH	SF	SB	CS	SB%	GDP	Avg	OBP	Slg
2002	Oneont	A-	45	150	34	5	2	0	(-	-)	43	23	10	19	34	0	28	1	1	1	0	2	.00	2	.227	.371	.287
2003	FtWyn	A	17	50	12	0	0	0	(-	-)	12	2	4	3	4	0	11	0	0	0	0	1	.00	2	.240	.296	.240
2003	Eugene	A-	28	100	25	7	0	0	(-	-)	32	14	7	12	14	0	25	2	0	0	1	0	1.00	3	.250	.353	.320
2004	Lk Els	A+	37	107	28	7	0	1	(-	-)	38	12	12	12	10	0	19	0	0	2	1	0	1.00	3	.262	.319	.355
2004	FtWyn	A	27	99	21	6	3	0	(-	-)	33	10	12	10	11	0	23	0	0	1	1	0	1.00	1	.212	.288	.333
2005	Mobile	AA	87	229	60	8	1	2	(-	-)	76	24	25	30	35	3	46	1	1	1	4	3	.57	4	.262	.361	.332
2006	Mobile	AA	2	5	0	0	0	0	(-	-)	0	0	0	0	0	0	1	0	0	0	0	0	-	0	.000	.000	.000
2006	Portlnd	AAA	73	244	65	14	1	4	(-	-)	93	27	29	41	49	0	54	2	1	1	0	0	-	7	.266	.392	.381
2007	Portlnd	AAA	98	300	66	20	2	0	(-	-)	90	35	17	32	47	2	77	0	6	0	0	3	.00	3	.220	.326	.300
2008	Portlnd	AAA	31	88	23	3	0	4	(-	-)	38	12	19	16	19	0	27	2	0	2	0	0	-	1	.261	.396	.432
2008	SD	NL	36	94	14	3	1	1	(0	1)	22	12	6	2	10	0	34	1	0	0	0	0	-	3	.149	.238	.234

Jesse Carlson

Pitches: L Bats: L Pos: RP-69

Ht: 6'1" Wt: 160 Born: 12/31/1980 Age: 28

			HOW MUCH HE PITCHED					WHAT HE GAVE UP											THE RESULTS						
Year	Team	Lg	G	GS	CG	GF	IP	BFP	H	R	ER	HR	SH	SF	HB	TBB	IBB	SO	WP	Bk	W	L	Pct	ShO	Sv-Op	Hld	ERC	ERA
2002	Oneont	A-	19	0	0	4	38.0	143	19	8	7	1	2	0	1	10	0	47	1	1	2	2	.500	0	0--	-	1.11	1.66
2003	Lxngtn	A	53	0	0	27	63.1	241	37	11	11	2	3	0	2	16	3	84	1	0	3	0	1.000	0	13--	-	1.33	1.56
2004	RdRck	AA	41	0	0	19	55.1	248	57	33	31	5	0	4	4	21	3	51	2	0	5	0	1.000	0	1--	-	4.18	5.04
2005	Syrcse	AAA	22	0	0	6	18.2	93	26	10	10	4	1	0	5	7	1	17	0	0	1	1	.500	0	0--	-	8.30	4.82
2005	NHam	AA	39	0	0	14	40.0	150	28	8	8	2	1	1	3	5	0	43	0	1	2	2	.500	0	5--	-	1.65	1.80
2006	Frisco	AA	43	0	0	17	58.0	263	65	39	30	7	3	0	5	18	4	45	0	0	6	5	.545	0	3--	-	4.65	4.66
2006	Okla	AAA	10	0	0	2	11.0	42	6	0	0	0	2	0	0	4	0	5	0	0	0	0	-	0	6--	-	1.31	0.00
2007	NHam	AA	58	0	0	25	70.1	304	77	39	38	4	4	3	4	18	6	81	0	1	8	2	.800	0	6--	-	3.74	4.86
2008	Syrcse	AAA	2	0	0	1	3.2	13	1	0	0	0	1	0	1	0	0	2	1	0	0	0	-	0	0--	-	0.47	0.00
2008	Tor	AL	69	0	0	10	60.0	237	41	16	15	6	1	3	3	21	7	55	2	1	7	2	.778	0	2-2	19	2.32	2.25

Buddy Carlyle

Pitches: R Bats: L Pos: RP-45

Ht: 6'3" Wt: 210 Born: 12/21/1977 Age: 31

			HOW MUCH HE PITCHED					WHAT HE GAVE UP											THE RESULTS						
Year	Team	Lg	G	GS	CG	GF	IP	BFP	H	R	ER	HR	SH	SF	HB	TBB	IBB	SO	WP	Bk	W	L	Pct	ShO	Sv-Op	Hld	ERC	ERA
2008	Rchmd*	AAA	2	2	0	0	7.2	35	11	7	6	0	1	0	0	3	0	7	2	1	0	0	-	0	0--	-	4.95	7.04
1999	SD	NL	7	7	0	0	37.2	162	36	28	25	7	1	2	2	17	0	29	1	0	1	3	.250	0	0-0	0	4.95	5.97
2000	SD	NL	4	0	0	2	3.0	18	6	7	7	0	0	0	0	3	0	2	0	0	0	0	-	0	0-0	0	12.01	21.00
2005	LAD	NL	10	0	0	2	14.0	62	16	13	13	4	2	0	1	4	0	13	0	0	0	1	0	0	0-1	0	6.07	8.36
2007	Atl	NL	22	20	0	0	107.0	462	117	67	62	19	11	5	2	32	8	74	3	0	8	7	.533	0	0-0	0	4.71	5.21
2008	Atl	NL	45	0	0	5	62.2	259	52	26	25	5	4	0	1	26	6	59	4	1	2	0	1.000	0	0-0	0	3.03	3.59
	5 ML YEARS		88	27	0	10	224.1	963	227	141	132	35	18	7	6	82	14	177	8	1	11	10	.524	0	0-1	0	4.43	5.30

Fausto Carmona

Pitches: R Bats: R Pos: SP-22 **Ht: 6'4" Wt: 230 Born: 12/7/1983 Age: 25**

		HOW MUCH HE PITCHED						WHAT HE GAVE UP													THE RESULTS							
Year	Team	Lg	G	GS	CG	GF	IP	BFP	H	R	ER	HR	SH	SF	HB	TBB	IBB	SO	WP	Bk	W	L	Pct	ShO	Sv-Op	Hld	ERC	ERA
2008	Lk Cty*	A	1	1	0	0	4.0	13	1	0	0	0	0	0	0	0	0	3	0	0	0	0	-	0	0--		0.14	0.00
2008	Akron*	AA	1	1	0	0	5.0	21	9	1	1	0	0	0	0	0	0	2	0	0	0	1	1.000	0	0--		7.19	1.80
2006	Cle	AL	38	7	0	12	74.2	340	88	46	45	9	2	4	7	31	3	58	3	1	1	10	.091	0	0-3	10	5.69	5.42
2007	Cle	AL	32	32	2	0	215.0	879	199	78	73	16	2	4	11	61	2	137	5	1	19	8	.704	1	0-0	0	3.32	3.06
2008	Cle	AL	22	22	1	0	120.2	549	126	80	73	7	1	4	9	70	0	58	8	1	8	7	.533	1	0-0	0	5.07	5.44
	Postseason		3	3	0	0	15.0	66	13	12	12	2	0	0	0	11	0	12	0	0	0	1	.000	0	0-0	0	5.02	7.20
	3 ML YEARS		92	61	3	12	410.1	1768	413	204	191	32	5	12	27	162	5	253	16	3	28	25	.528	2	0-3	10	4.24	4.19

Andrew Carpenter

Pitches: R Bats: R Pos: RP-1 **Ht: 6'3" Wt: 225 Born: 5/18/1985 Age: 24**

		HOW MUCH HE PITCHED						WHAT HE GAVE UP													THE RESULTS							
Year	Team	Lg	G	GS	CG	GF	IP	BFP	H	R	ER	HR	SH	SF	HB	TBB	IBB	SO	WP	Bk	W	L	Pct	ShO	Sv-Op	Hld	ERC	ERA
2006	Phillies	R	2	1	0	1	7.0	30	2	0	0	0	0	0	0	0	0	4	0	0	0	0	-	0	0--		1.01	0.00
2006	Batvia	A-	3	3	0	0	11.2	46	10	1	1	0	0	0	1	5	0	12	1	0	0	0	-	0	0--		3.34	0.77
2007	Clrwtr	A+	27	24	3	1	163.0	682	150	65	58	16	2	4	3	53	0	116	1	0	17	6	.739	2	1--		3.41	3.20
2008	Rdng	AA	16	16	0	0	93.2	417	114	68	59	13	8	2	3	30	1	69	3	0	6	8	.429	0	0--		5.44	5.67
2008	Clrwtr	A+	8	8	2	0	52.1	207	44	17	17	2	3	1	1	9	2	32	0	0	3	3	.500	1	0--		2.07	2.92
2008	LV	AAA	1	1	0	0	7.0	29	6	2	2	1	0	0	1	3	0	5	1	0	0	1	.000	0	0--		4.49	2.57
2008	Phi	NL	1	0	0	0	1.0	5	1	0	0	0	1	0	0	1	1	1	0	0	0	0	-	0	0-0		3.46	0.00

Chris Carpenter

Pitches: R Bats: R Pos: SP-3; RP-1 **Ht: 6'6" Wt: 230 Born: 4/27/1975 Age: 34**

		HOW MUCH HE PITCHED						WHAT HE GAVE UP													THE RESULTS							
Year	Team	Lg	G	GS	CG	GF	IP	BFP	H	R	ER	HR	SH	SF	HB	TBB	IBB	SO	WP	Bk	W	L	Pct	ShO	Sv-Op	Hld	ERC	ERA
2008	Sprgfld*	AA	1	1	0	0	4.0	17	1	0	0	0	0	0	0	4	0	4	0	0	0	0	-	0	0--		1.67	0.00
2008	Memp*	AAA	1	1	0	0	5.2	24	4	2	2	0	0	0	2	1	0	5	0	0	0	1	.000	0	0--		2.29	3.18
1997	Tor	AL	14	13	1	1	81.1	374	108	55	46	7	1	2	2	37	0	55	7	1	3	7	.300	1	0-0	0	6.38	5.09
1998	Tor	AL	33	24	1	4	175.0	742	177	97	85	18	4	5	5	61	1	136	5	0	12	7	.632	1	0-0	0	4.12	4.37
1999	Tor	AL	24	24	4	0	150.0	663	177	81	73	16	4	6	3	48	1	106	9	1	9	8	.529	1	0-0	0	4.90	4.38
2000	Tor	AL	34	27	2	1	175.1	795	204	130	122	30	3	1	5	83	1	113	3	0	10	12	.455	0	0-0	0	6.04	6.26
2001	Tor	AL	34	34	3	0	215.2	930	229	112	98	29	3	1	16	75	5	157	5	0	11	11	.500	2	0-0	0	4.82	4.09
2002	Tor	AL	13	13	1	0	73.1	327	89	45	43	11	1	4	4	27	0	45	3	0	4	5	.444	0	0-0	0	5.91	5.28
2004	StL	NL	28	28	1	0	182.0	746	169	75	70	24	6	3	8	38	2	152	4	0	15	5	.750	0	0-0	0	3.32	3.46
2005	StL	NL	33	33	7	0	241.2	953	204	82	76	18	7	7	3	51	0	213	5	0	21	5	.808	4	0-0	0	2.49	2.83
2006	StL	NL	32	32	5	0	221.2	896	194	81	76	21	12	4	10	43	3	184	3	0	15	8	.652	3	0-0	0	2.75	3.09
2007	StL	NL	1	1	0	0	6.0	29	9	5	5	0	1	0	1	1	0	3	0	0	0	1	.000	0	0-0	0	5.80	7.50
2008	StL	NL	4	3	0	0	15.1	63	16	5	3	0	2	1	0	4	0	7	0	0	0	1	.000	0	0-0	0	3.19	1.76
	Postseason		8	8	0	0	53.1	215	45	16	15	5	6	1	2	15	0	35	1	0	5	1	.833	0	0-0	0	2.94	2.53
	11 ML YEARS		250	232	25	6	1537.1	6518	1576	768	697	174	44	34	57	468	13	1171	44	2	100	70	.588	12	0-0	0	4.11	4.08

D.J. Carrasco

Pitches: R Bats: R Pos: RP-31 **Ht: 6'1" Wt: 215 Born: 4/12/1977 Age: 32**

		HOW MUCH HE PITCHED						WHAT HE GAVE UP													THE RESULTS							
Year	Team	Lg	G	GS	CG	GF	IP	BFP	H	R	ER	HR	SH	SF	HB	TBB	IBB	SO	WP	Bk	W	L	Pct	ShO	Sv-Op	Hld	ERC	ERA
2008	Charltt*	AAA	8	1	0	3	25.0	104	24	9	9	0	2	1	2	7	2	24	2	0	2	1	.667	0	1---		2.78	3.24
2003	KC	AL	50	2	0	21	80.1	355	82	44	43	8	1	4	7	40	4	57	6	0	6	5	.545	0	2-5	6	4.94	4.82
2004	KC	AL	30	0	0	11	35.1	163	41	22	19	5	1	1	3	15	3	22	2	0	2	2	.500	0	0-3	4	5.56	4.84
2005	KC	AL	21	20	1	0	114.2	511	129	67	61	11	3	5	6	51	2	69	7	3	6	8	.429	0	0-0	0	5.20	4.79
2008	CWS	AL	31	0	0	6	38.2	158	30	17	17	2	1	5	1	14	1	30	0	0	1	0	1.000	0	0-1	7	2.94	3.96
	4 ML YEARS		132	22	1	38	269.0	1187	282	150	140	26	6	11	21	120	10	158	15	3	15	15	.500	0	2-9	17	4.83	4.68

Brett Carroll

Bats: R Throws: R Pos: PR-13; RF-8; PH-8; LF-7 **Ht: 6'0" Wt: 190 Born: 10/3/1982 Age: 26**

			BATTING																			BASERUNNING				AVERAGES		
Year	Team	Lg	G	AB	H	2B	3B	HR	(Hm	Rd)	TB	R	RBI	RC	TBB	IBB	SO	HBP	SH	SF		SB	CS	SB%	GDP		Avg	OBP	Slg
2004	Jmstwn	A-	60	211	53	16	1	6	(-	-)	89	27	28	29	15	1	57	7	2	1		1	0	1.00	2		.251	.321	.422
2005	Grnsbr	A	118	412	100	28	1	18	(-	-)	184	57	54	54	17	2	108	15	3	2		10	10	.50	4		.243	.296	.447
2006	Jupiter	A+	59	216	52	12	1	8	(-	-)	90	31	30	31	18	1	48	9	0	1		9	3	.75	3		.241	.324	.417
2006	Carlina	AA	74	251	58	15	3	9	(-	-)	106	29	30	33	18	1	62	8	3	0		4	1	.80	8		.231	.303	.422
2007	Carlina	AA	30	100	27	13	0	3	(-	-)	49	9	12	17	12	0	20	3	0	2		2	0	.00	2		.270	.359	.490
2007	Albq	AAA	88	317	100	21	6	19	(-	-)	190	60	70	65	18	0	68	7	0	3		0	4	.00	7		.315	.362	.599
2008	Albq	AAA	18	67	28	5	0	9	(-	-)	60	18	23	23	8	0	18	0	0	0		1	1	.50	2		.418	.480	.896
2008	Mrlns	R	2	8	2	1	0	0	(-	-)	3	1	0	1	1	0	1	0	0	0		0	0	-	2		.250	.333	.375
2008	Jupiter	A+	18	71	12	2	0	2	(-	-)	20	10	9	4	6	0	22	0	0	1		1	0	1.00	2		.169	.231	.282
2007	Fla	NL	23	49	9	1	0	0	(0	0)	10	10	2	0	3	0	15	0	1	0		0	0	-	1		.184	.231	.204
2008	Fla	NL	26	17	1	0	1	0	(0	0)	3	5	1	0	1	0	6	0	0	0		0	0	-	1		.059	.111	.176
	2 ML YEARS		49	66	10	1	1	0	(0	0)	13	15	3	0	4	0	21	0	1	0		0	0	-	1		.152	.200	.197

Jamey Carroll

Bats: R **Throws:** R **Pos:** 2B-74; 3B-43; PR-11; PH-8; LF-1 **Ht:** 5'9" **Wt:** 170 **Born:** 2/18/1974 **Age:** 35

					BATTING															BASERUNNING				AVERAGES		
Year	Team	Lg	G	AB	H	2B	3B	HR	(Hm | Rd)	TB	R	RBI	RC	TBB	IBB	SO	HBP	SH	SF	SB	CS	SB%	GDP	Avg	OBP	Slg
2002	Mon	NL	16	71	22	5	3	1	(1 | 0)	36	16	6	12	4	0	12	0	4	0	1	0	1.00	1	.310	.347	.507
2003	Mon	NL	105	227	59	10	1	1	(1 | 0)	74	31	10	18	19	0	39	3	9	2	5	2	.71	10	.260	.323	.326
2004	Mon	NL	102	218	63	14	2	0	(0 | 0)	81	36	16	28	32	1	21	1	2	3	5	1	.83	3	.289	.378	.372
2005	Was	NL	113	303	76	8	1	0	(0 | 0)	86	44	22	38	34	1	55	5	13	3	3	4	.43	2	.251	.333	.284
2006	Col	NL	136	463	139	23	5	5	(2 | 3)	187	84	36	82	56	1	66	3	9	3	10	12	.45	10	.300	.377	.404
2007	Col	NL	108	227	51	9	1	2	(1 | 1)	68	45	22	24	28	1	34	4	6	3	6	2	.75	2	.225	.317	.300
2008	Cle	AL	113	347	96	13	4	1	(0 | 1)	120	60	36	48	34	0	65	9	10	2	7	3	.70	2	.277	.355	.346
	Postseason		4	2	0	0	0	0	(0 | 0)	0	0	0	0	1	0	0	0	0	0	0	0	-	0	.000	.333	.000
	7 ML YEARS		693	1856	506	82	17	10	(5 | 5)	652	316	148	233	207	4	292	25	53	16	37	24	.61	30	.273	.351	.351

Chris Carter

Bats: L **Throws:** R **Pos:** DH-4; PH-4; LF-3; PR-2 **Ht:** 5'10" **Wt:** 210 **Born:** 9/16/1982 **Age:** 26

					BATTING															BASERUNNING				AVERAGES		
Year	Team	Lg	G	AB	H	2B	3B	HR	(Hm	Rd)	TB	R	RBI	RC	TBB	IBB	SO	HBP	SH	SF	SB	CS	SB%	GDP	Avg	OBP	Slg
2004	Yakima	A-	70	256	86	15	1	15	(-	-)	148	47	63	63	46	1	34	1	0	1	2	3	.40	7	.336	.438	.578
2005	Lancst	A+	103	412	122	26	2	21	(-	-)	215	71	85	81	46	4	66	6	0	6	0	0	-	12	.296	.370	.522
2005	Tenn	AA	36	128	38	4	0	10	(-	-)	72	21	30	27	19	4	11	3	0	1	0	3	.00	1	.297	.397	.563
2006	Tucsn	AAA	136	509	153	36	3	19	(-	-)	246	87	97	100	78	4	69	1	0	0	10	4	.71	14	.301	.395	.483
2007	Tucsn	AAA	126	501	162	39	3	18	(-	-)	261	73	84	100	50	4	68	2	0	6	1	0	1.00	19	.323	.383	.521
2007	Pwtckt	AAA	12	47	11	1	0	1	(-	-)	15	6	4	4	4	0	7	1	0	0	0	0	-	1	.234	.308	.319
2008	Pwtckt	AAA	121	470	141	25	2	24	(-	-)	242	65	81	87	41	6	84	4	0	7	0	0	-	10	.300	.356	.515
2008	Bos	AL	9	18	6	0	0	0	(0	0)	6	5	3	2	2	0	5	0	0	0	0	0	-	0	.333	.400	.333

Raul Casanova

Bats: B **Throws:** R **Pos:** C-13; PH-7 **Ht:** 6'0" **Wt:** 232 **Born:** 8/23/1972 **Age:** 36

					BATTING															BASERUNNING				AVERAGES		
Year	Team	Lg	G	AB	H	2B	3B	HR	(Hm	Rd)	TB	R	RBI	RC	TBB	IBB	SO	HBP	SH	SF	SB	CS	SB%	GDP	Avg	OBP	Slg
2008	NewOr*	AAA	45	157	46	12	0	4	(-	-)	70	18	23	24	11	0	29	1	0	0	0	0	-	4	.293	.343	.446
1996	Det	AL	25	85	16	1	0	4	(1	3)	29	6	9	5	6	0	18	0	0	0	0	0	-	6	.188	.242	.341
1997	Det	AL	101	304	74	10	1	5	(5	0)	101	27	24	29	26	1	48	3	0	1	1	1	.50	10	.243	.308	.332
1998	Det	AL	16	42	6	1	0	1	(1	0)	11	4	3	3	5	0	10	1	0	0	0	0	-	0	.143	.250	.262
2000	Mil	NL	86	231	57	13	3	6	(4	2)	94	20	36	31	26	1	48	4	2	2	1	2	.33	5	.247	.331	.407
2001	Mil	NL	71	192	50	10	0	11	(7	4)	93	21	33	28	12	2	29	1	0	3	0	0	-	3	.260	.303	.484
2002	2 Tms		33	88	16	1	0	1	(0	1)	20	3	8	4	10	4	19	1	0	1	0	0	-	3	.182	.270	.227
2005	CWS	AL	6	5	1	0	0	0	(0	0)	1	0	1	0	0	0	1	0	0	0	0	0	-	0	.200	.200	.200
2007	TB	AL	29	79	20	1	1	6	(0	6)	41	12	11	9	7	1	17	1	0	2	0	0	-	1	.253	.315	.519
2008	NYM	NL	20	55	15	2	0	1	(1	0)	20	5	6	7	6	0	10	0	0	0	0	0	-	4	.273	.344	.364
02	Mil	NL	31	87	16	1	0	1	(0	1)	20	3	8	4	10	4	18	1	0	1	0	0	-	3	.184	.273	.230
02	Bal	AL	2	1	0	0	0	0	(0	0)	0	0	0	0	0	0	1	0	0	0	0	0	-	0	.000	.000	.000
	9 ML YEARS		387	1081	255	40	5	35	(19	16)	410	98	130	117	98	9	200	11	2	9	2	3	.40	31	.236	.304	.379

Sean Casey

Bats: L **Throws:** R **Pos:** 1B-45; PH-19; DH-13 **Ht:** 6'4" **Wt:** 230 **Born:** 7/2/1974 **Age:** 34

					BATTING															BASERUNNING				AVERAGES		
Year	Team	Lg	G	AB	H	2B	3B	HR	(Hm	Rd)	TB	R	RBI	RC	TBB	IBB	SO	HBP	SH	SF	SB	CS	SB%	GDP	Avg	OBP	Slg
2008	Pwtckt*	AAA	2	6	3	1	0	0	(-	-)	4	3	0	2	1	0	1	0	0	0	0	0	-	0	.500	.571	.667
1997	Cle	AL	6	10	2	0	0	0	(0	0)	2	1	1	1	1	0	2	1	0	0	0	0	-	0	.200	.333	.200
1998	Cin	NL	96	302	82	21	1	7	(3	4)	126	44	52	45	43	3	45	3	0	3	1	1	.50	11	.272	.365	.417
1999	Cin	NL	151	594	197	42	3	25	(11	14)	320	103	99	119	61	13	88	9	0	5	0	2	.00	15	.332	.399	.539
2000	Cin	NL	133	480	151	33	2	20	(9	11)	248	69	85	91	52	4	80	7	0	6	1	0	1.00	16	.315	.385	.517
2001	Cin	NL	145	533	165	40	0	13	(5	8)	244	69	89	86	43	8	63	9	0	4	3	1	.75	16	.310	.369	.458
2002	Cin	NL	120	425	111	25	0	6	(3	3)	154	56	42	65	46	4	57	5	0	3	1	2	.67	11	.261	.334	.362
2003	Cin	NL	147	573	167	19	3	14	(8	6)	234	71	80	84	51	4	58	2	0	4	4	0	1.00	19	.291	.350	.408
2004	Cin	NL	146	571	185	44	2	24	(9	15)	305	101	99	104	46	5	36	10	0	6	2	0	1.00	16	.324	.381	.534
2005	Cin	NL	137	529	165	32	0	9	(4	5)	224	75	58	72	48	3	48	5	0	5	2	0	1.00	27	.312	.371	.423
2006	2 Tms		112	397	108	22	0	8	(3	5)	154	47	59	57	33	9	43	7	0	3	2	2	.50	10	.272	.336	.388
2007	Det	AL	143	453	134	30	1	4	(2	2)	178	40	54	57	39	11	42	2	0	4	2	2	.50	9	.296	.353	.393
2008	Bos	AL	69	199	64	14	0	0	(0	0)	78	14	17	27	17	3	25	2	0	0	1	0	1.00	6	.322	.381	.392
06	Pit	NL	59	213	63	15	0	3	(1	2)	87	30	29	33	23	5	22	6	0	2	0	0	-	7	.296	.377	.408
06	Det	AL	53	184	45	7	0	5	(2	3)	67	17	30	24	10	4	21	1	0	1	0	1	.00	3	.245	.286	.364
	Postseason		10	37	16	5	0	2	(0	2)	27	3	9	9	1	0	2	1	0	0	0	0	-	0	.432	.462	.730
	12 ML YEARS		1405	5066	1531	322	12	130	(57	73)	2267	690	735	788	477	69	577	62	0	39	18	8	.69	156	.302	.367	.447

Kevin Cash

Bats: R **Throws:** R **Pos:** C-57; 3B-4; PH-4; DH-2; PR-1 **Ht:** 6'0" **Wt:** 190 **Born:** 12/6/1977 **Age:** 31

					BATTING															BASERUNNING				AVERAGES		
Year	Team	Lg	G	AB	H	2B	3B	HR	(Hm	Rd)	TB	R	RBI	RC	TBB	IBB	SO	HBP	SH	SF	SB	CS	SB%	GDP	Avg	OBP	Slg
2002	Tor	AL	7	14	2	0	0	0	(0	0)	2	1	0	0	1	0	4	0	0	0	0	0	-	1	.143	.200	.143
2003	Tor	AL	34	106	15	3	0	1	(1	0)	21	10	8	0	4	0	22	1	5	1	0	0	-	6	.142	.179	.198
2004	Tor	AL	60	181	35	9	0	4	(2	2)	56	18	21	11	10	0	59	4	0	2	0	0	-	3	.193	.249	.309
2005	TB	AL	13	31	5	1	0	2	(1	1)	12	4	2	0	1	0	13	1	0	0	0	0	-	3	.161	.212	.387
2007	Bos	AL	12	27	3	0	0	0	(0	0)	4	2	4	1	4	0	13	1	0	1	0	0	-	2	.111	.242	.148
2008	Bos	AL	61	142	32	7	0	3	(3	0)	48	11	15	11	18	1	50	0	0	2	0	0	-	6	.225	.309	.338
	6 ML YEARS		187	501	92	21	0	10	(7	3)	143	46	50	23	38	1	161	7	5	6	0	0	-	21	.184	.248	.285

Alexi Casilla

Bats: B **Throws:** R **Pos:** 2B-95; SS-2; PR-2; DH-1
Ht: 5'9" **Wt:** 178 **Born:** 7/20/1984 **Age:** 24

Year	Team	Lg	G	AB	H	2B	3B	HR	(Hm	Rd)	TB	R	RBI	RC	TBB	IBB	SO	HBP	SH	SF	SB	CS	SB%	GDP	Avg	OBP	Slg
2008	Roch*	AAA	32	96	21	3	0	0	(-	-)	24	11	2	10	18	0	18	2	4	1	4	3	.57	2	.219	.350	.250
2008	Beloit*	A	2	7	4	0	0	0	(-	-)	4	2	1	2	2	0	1	0	0	0	0	1	.00	0	.571	.667	.571
2006	Min	AL	9	4	1	0	0	0	(0	0)	1	1	0	1	2	0	1	0	0	0	0	0	-	0	.250	.500	.250
2007	Min	AL	56	189	42	5	1	0	(0	0)	49	15	9	11	9	0	29	0	5	1	11	1	.92	5	.222	.256	.259
2008	Min	AL	98	385	108	15	0	7	(2	5)	144	58	50	50	31	0	45	2	13	6	7	2	.78	5	.281	.333	.374
3 ML YEARS			163	578	151	20	1	7	(2	5)	194	74	59	62	42	0	75	2	18	7	18	3	.86	13	.261	.310	.336

Santiago Casilla

Pitches: R **Bats:** R **Pos:** RP-51
Ht: 6'0" **Wt:** 202 **Born:** 7/25/1980 **Age:** 28

Year	Team	Lg	G	GS	CG	GF	IP	BFP	H	R	ER	HR	SH	SF	HB	TBB	IBB	SO	WP	Bk	W	L	Pct	ShO	Sv-Op	Hld	ERC	ERA
2008	Stcktn*	A+	1	1	0	0	1.0	3	0	0	0	0	0	0	0	0	0	2	0	0	0	0	-	0	0--	-	0.00	0.00
2008	Scrmto*	AAA	2	2	0	0	2.2	12	3	1	1	0	0	1	0	1	0	5	0	0	0	0	-	0	0--	-	3.84	3.38
2004	Oak	AL	4	0	0	2	5.2	32	5	8	8	3	0	0	1	9	0	5	0	0	0	0	-	0	0-0	0	13.22	12.71
2005	Oak	AL	3	0	0	3	3.0	12	2	1	1	0	0	0	0	1	0	1	1	0	0	0	-	0	0-0	0	1.57	3.00
2006	Oak	AL	2	0	0	1	2.1	10	2	3	3	0	0	0	0	2	0	2	0	0	0	0	-	0	0-0	0	4.61	11.57
2007	Oak	AL	46	0	0	10	50.2	219	43	25	25	6	0	3	1	23	6	52	5	0	3	1	.750	0	2-5	12	3.39	4.44
2008	Oak	AL	51	0	0	9	50.1	229	60	22	22	5	3	2	3	20	2	43	6	0	2	1	.667	0	2-3	7	5.34	3.93
5 ML YEARS			106	0	0	25	112.0	502	112	59	59	14	3	5	5	55	8	103	12	0	5	2	.714	0	4-8	19	4.63	4.74

Jack Cassel

Pitches: R **Bats:** R **Pos:** RP-6; SP-3
Ht: 6'2" **Wt:** 190 **Born:** 8/8/1980 **Age:** 28

Year	Team	Lg	G	GS	CG	GF	IP	BFP	H	R	ER	HR	SH	SF	HB	TBB	IBB	SO	WP	Bk	W	L	Pct	ShO	Sv-Op	Hld	ERC	ERA
2000	Idaho	R+	7	0	0	2	12.2	52	10	8	2	1	0	1	0	3	1	13	0	1	0	0	-	0	0--	-	2.06	1.42
2000	FtWyn	A	22	0	0	6	36.1	160	42	24	19	2	0	2	2	12	0	25	4	0	2	2	.500	0	0--	-	4.61	4.71
2001	FtWyn	A	25	23	0	1	128.1	591	163	104	79	7	5	4	12	35	0	89	6	5	4	14	.222	0	0--	-	5.06	5.54
2002	FtWyn	A	27	0	0	9	50.2	222	58	22	17	0	0	2	2	11	3	34	4	1	4	1	.800	0	0--	-	3.44	3.02
2002	Lk Els	A+	23	0	0	4	37.0	154	33	15	10	0	1	0	3	11	0	25	0	1	1	1	.500	0	1--	-	2.76	2.43
2003	Lk Els	A+	64	0	0	22	72.2	300	69	34	29	0	4	0	4	18	1	52	7	0	5	4	.556	0	3--	-	2.78	3.59
2004	Mobile	AA	57	0	0	19	74.2	333	76	35	31	4	1	2	8	27	2	52	6	1	4	2	.667	0	1--	-	3.99	3.74
2005	Mobile	AA	24	3	0	9	43.0	184	45	18	16	1	1	0	2	16	4	29	5	0	3	3	.500	0	0--	-	3.78	3.35
2005	Portlnd	AAA	23	3	0	8	39.0	183	54	25	20	2	2	1	2	17	2	21	2	1	2	2	.600	0	0--	-	6.32	4.62
2006	Portlnd	AAA	18	11	0	0	76.1	346	96	60	55	12	1	1	2	28	2	44	4	0	3	5	.375	0	0--	-	5.98	6.48
2006	Mobile	AA	12	12	1	0	78.2	321	66	30	20	3	0	2	7	18	0	75	4	0	6	3	.667	0	0--	-	2.52	2.29
2007	Portlnd	AAA	27	24	3	0	156.2	705	203	94	68	13	9	3	6	42	6	117	10	1	7	14	.333	0	0--	-	5.21	3.91
2008	RdRck	AAA	19	17	0	0	107.1	453	113	46	44	10	6	3	1	30	1	72	8	0	9	5	.643	0	0--	-	3.90	3.69
2007	SD	NL	6	4	0	0	22.2	98	30	10	10	1	0	0	1	5	0	11	1	0	1	1	.500	0	0-0	0	5.17	3.97
2008	Hou	NL	9	3	0	1	30.1	132	38	21	19	5	1	0	1	8	2	14	2	1	1	1	.500	0	0-0	0	5.63	5.64
2 ML YEARS			15	7	0	1	53.0	230	68	31	29	6	1	0	2	13	2	25	3	1	2	2	.500	0	0-0	0	5.44	4.92

Alberto Castillo

Pitches: L **Bats:** L **Pos:** RP-28
Ht: 6'5" **Wt:** 185 **Born:** 7/5/1975 **Age:** 33

Year	Team	Lg	G	GS	CG	GF	IP	BFP	H	R	ER	HR	SH	SF	HB	TBB	IBB	SO	WP	Bk	W	L	Pct	ShO	Sv-Op	Hld	ERC	ERA
1994	Everett	A-	6	0	0	2	5.1	24	7	4	4	1	0	0	0	1	0	8	0	0	0	0	-	0	0--	-	5.53	6.75
1996	Bllghm	A-	9	7	0	1	24.0	102	20	5	5	2	0	0	3	12	0	18	2	1	3	0	1.000	0	0--	-	4.02	1.88
1997	SnJos	A+	18	1	0	8	33.2	162	41	26	21	2	2	2	4	15	0	30	7	0	2	2	.500	0	0--	-	5.51	5.61
1998	Tampa	A+	12	0	0	3	11.1	75	14	17	17	2	1	2	3	25	1	11	5	2	0	0	-	0	0--	-	15.29	13.50
1998	Grnsbr	A	5	0	0	3	9.2	48	8	6	4	0	0	0	0	14	0	13	2	0	0	0	-	0	0--	-	6.60	3.72
1999	Schbrg	IND	17	16	2	1	97.0	432	97	57	46	9	3	1	8	47	0	70	17	0	7	5	.583	0	0--	-	4.70	4.27
2000	Schbrg	IND	17	17	2	0	102.0	454	107	60	52	10	2	1	5	49	0	77	12	0	7	7	.500	0	0--	-	4.89	4.59
2002	Newark	IND	28	0	0	15	49.2	195	37	19	18	7	1	1	1	15	0	42	3	0	2	2	.500	0	5--	-	2.76	3.26
2003	Newark	IND	28	15	2	7	114.2	507	112	61	56	13	11	5	7	49	7	98	5	1	7	8	.467	0	1--	-	4.23	4.40
2006	RdWar	IND	16	8	0	1	59.1	277	74	42	35	6	0	6	5	28	2	32	8	0	4	3	.571	0	1--	-	6.16	5.31
2007	RdWar	IND	18	0	0	5	33.0	134	28	12	11	1	3	0	2	8	1	38	1	0	3	2	.600	0	0--	-	2.44	3.00
2007	Cam	IND	28	1	0	11	35.0	136	24	10	9	2	1	0	2	7	0	31	2	1	2	0	1.000	0	4--	-	1.73	2.31
2008	Norfolk	AAA	19	0	0	6	26.1	103	16	6	6	2	0	0	4	6	0	26	0	0	3	1	.750	0	0--	-	1.89	2.05
2008	Bal	AL	28	0	0	5	26.0	121	27	11	11	3	0	0	7	10	0	23	1	0	1	0	1.000	0	0-1	0	5.36	3.81

Jose Castillo

Bats: R **Throws:** R **Pos:** 3B-110; PH-15; 2B-12; SS-4
Ht: 6'1" **Wt:** 219 **Born:** 3/19/1981 **Age:** 28

Year	Team	Lg	G	AB	H	2B	3B	HR	(Hm	Rd)	TB	R	RBI	RC	TBB	IBB	SO	HBP	SH	SF	SB	CS	SB%	GDP	Avg	OBP	Slg
2004	Pit	NL	129	383	98	15	2	8	(3	5)	141	44	39	40	23	5	92	1	5	2	3	2	.60	12	.256	.298	.368
2005	Pit	NL	101	370	99	16	3	11	(2	9)	154	49	53	43	23	3	59	0	1	4	2	3	.40	11	.268	.307	.416
2006	Pit	NL	148	518	131	25	0	14	(10	4)	198	54	65	53	32	8	98	5	1	6	6	4	.60	22	.253	.299	.382
2007	Pit	NL	87	221	54	18	1	0	(0	0)	74	18	24	16	6	2	48	2	0	1	0	0	-	11	.244	.270	.335
2008	2 Tms	NL	127	426	105	29	4	6	(1	5)	160	46	37	39	27	1	81	1	0	1	2	2	.50	16	.246	.292	.376
08	SF	NL	112	394	96	28	4	6	(1	5)	150	42	35	36	25	1	71	1	0	0	2	2	.50	16	.244	.290	.381
08	Hou	NL	15	32	9	1	0	0	(0	0)	10	4	2	3	2	0	10	0	0	1	0	0	-	0	.281	.314	.313
5 ML YEARS			592	1918	487	103	10	39	(16	23)	727	211	218	191	111	19	378	9	7	14	13	11	.54	72	.254	.296	.379

Luis Castillo

Bats: B **Throws:** R **Pos:** 2B-81; PH-6   **Ht:** 5'11" **Wt:** 190 **Born:** 9/12/1975 **Age:** 33

Year	Team	Lg	G	AB	H	2B	3B	HR	(Hm	Rd)	TB	R	RBI	RC	TBB	IBB	SO	HBP	SH	SF	SB	CS	SB%	GDP	Avg	OBP	Slg
2008	Mets*	R	3	5	0	0	0	0	(-	-)	0	0	0	0	3	0	0	0	0	0	0	0	-	0	.000	.375	.000
2008	StLuci*	A+	5	15	1	0	0	0	(-	-)	1	1	0	0	4	0	0	0	1	0	0	0	-	0	.067	.263	.067
2008	Bnghtn*	AA	5	16	4	0	0	0	(-	-)	4	1	2	1	2	0	3	0	0	0	0	0	-	0	.250	.333	.250
1996	Fla	NL	41	164	43	2	1	1	(0	1)	50	26	8	19	14	0	46	0	2	0	17	4	.81	0	.262	.320	.305
1997	Fla	NL	75	263	63	8	0	0	(0	0)	71	27	8	21	27	0	53	0	1	0	16	10	.62	6	.240	.310	.270
1998	Fla	NL	44	153	31	3	2	1	(0	1)	41	21	10	14	22	0	33	1	1	0	3	0	1.00	1	.203	.307	.268
1999	Fla	NL	128	487	147	23	4	0	(0	0)	178	76	28	78	67	0	85	0	6	3	50	17	.75	3	.302	.384	.366
2000	Fla	NL	136	539	180	17	3	2	(1	1)	209	101	17	95	78	0	86	0	9	0	62	22	.74	11	.334	.418	.388
2001	Fla	NL	134	537	141	16	10	2	(1	1)	183	76	45	67	67	0	90	1	4	3	33	16	.67	6	.263	.344	.341
2002	Fla	NL	146	606	185	18	5	2	(0	2)	219	86	39	84	55	4	76	2	4	1	48	15	.76	7	.305	.364	.361
2003	Fla	NL	152	595	187	19	6	6	(2	4)	236	99	39	87	63	0	60	2	15	1	21	19	.53	7	.314	.381	.397
2004	Fla	NL	150	564	164	12	7	2	(1	1)	196	91	47	84	75	2	68	1	5	4	21	4	.84	15	.291	.373	.348
2005	Fla	NL	122	439	132	12	4	4	(0	4)	164	72	30	61	65	1	32	1	18	1	10	7	.59	11	.301	.391	.374
2006	Min	AL	142	584	173	22	6	3	(3	0)	216	84	49	80	56	0	58	1	9	2	25	11	.69	14	.296	.358	.370
2007	2 Tms		135	548	165	19	5	1	(0	1)	197	91	38	76	53	0	45	0	12	2	19	6	.76	5	.301	.362	.359
2008	NYM	NL	87	298	73	7	1	3	(2	1)	91	46	28	40	50	2	35	2	7	2	17	2	.89	13	.245	.355	.305
07	Min	AL	85	349	106	11	3	0	(0	0)	123	54	18	45	29	0	28	0	5	1	9	4	.69	3	.304	.356	.352
07	NYM	NL	50	199	59	8	2	1	(0	1)	74	37	20	31	24	0	17	0	7	1	10	2	.83	2	.296	.371	.372
Postseason			20	82	18	4	0	0	(0	0)	22	6	4	6	11	0	15	0	2	0	3	2	.60	0	.220	.312	.268
13 ML YEARS			1492	5777	1684	178	54	27	(10	17)	2051	896	386	806	692	9	767	11	93	19	342	133	.72	99	.292	.367	.355

Wilkin Castillo

Bats: B **Throws:** R **Pos:** PH-8; LF-5; PR-3; 2B-2   **Ht:** 6'0" **Wt:** 200 **Born:** 6/1/1984 **Age:** 25

Year	Team	Lg	G	AB	H	2B	3B	HR	(Hm	Rd)	TB	R	RBI	RC	TBB	IBB	SO	HBP	SH	SF	SB	CS	SB%	GDP	Avg	OBP	Slg
2004	Msoula	R+	63	243	66	13	5	4	(-	-)	101	32	32	32	8	1	40	7	4	5	5	2	.71	1	.272	.308	.416
2004	Tucsn	AAA	6	20	3	1	0	0	(-	-)	4	2	2	1	3	0	3	0	1	0	0	0	-	0	.150	.261	.200
2005	Sbend	A	113	411	124	21	3	6	(-	-)	169	65	53	59	26	0	38	4	16	4	9	9	.50	11	.302	.346	.411
2006	Lancst	A+	56	200	57	10	1	3	(-	-)	78	25	19	27	13	0	24	1	2	2	9	2	.82	6	.285	.329	.390
2006	Tucsn	AAA	6	21	5	1	0	1	(-	-)	9	3	4	2	0	0	8	1	0	0	1	0	1.00	1	.238	.273	.429
2006	Tenn	AA	27	76	19	3	0	0	(-	-)	22	7	5	8	6	1	10	2	2	2	1	0	1.00	1	.250	.314	.289
2007	Mobile	AA	109	410	124	30	3	6	(-	-)	178	50	46	58	17	1	62	3	16	3	18	14	.56	5	.302	.333	.434
2008	Tucsn	AAA	104	386	98	18	2	6	(-	-)	138	40	47	44	24	2	54	6	6	3	4	1	.80	10	.254	.305	.358
2008	Lsvlle	AAA	11	42	8	0	0	0	(-	-)	8	2	0	0	1	0	5	0	0	0	1	2	.33	0	.190	.209	.190
2008	Cin	NL	18	32	9	1	0	0	(0	0)	10	6	1	3	1	0	5	0	1	0	0	0	-	0	.281	.303	.313

Kory Casto

Bats: L **Throws:** R **Pos:** PH-24; 1B-23; 3B-13; LF-8; PR-2; RF-1   **Ht:** 6'0" **Wt:** 207 **Born:** 12/8/1981 **Age:** 27

Year	Team	Lg	G	AB	H	2B	3B	HR	(Hm	Rd)	TB	R	RBI	RC	TBB	IBB	SO	HBP	SH	SF	SB	CS	SB%	GDP	Avg	OBP	Slg
2003	Vrmnt	A-	71	259	62	14	2	4	(-	-)	92	26	28	31	30	1	47	2	0	1	1	1	.50	3	.239	.322	.355
2004	Savann	A	124	483	138	35	4	16	(-	-)	229	67	88	78	31	1	70	8	1	3	1	2	.33	5	.286	.337	.474
2005	Ptomc	A+	135	500	145	36	4	22	(-	-)	255	86	90	104	84	1	98	5	0	5	6	3	.67	5	.290	.394	.510
2006	Hrsbrg	AA	140	489	133	24	6	20	(-	-)	229	84	80	92	81	4	104	8	4	8	6	5	.55	13	.272	.379	.468
2007	Clmbs	AAA	113	408	101	20	2	11	(-	-)	158	56	55	56	54	0	105	2	1	3	4	4	.50	8	.248	.336	.387
2008	Clmbs	AAA	33	130	40	5	0	6	(-	-)	63	19	26	24	19	1	27	0	0	0	1	2	.33	1	.308	.396	.485
2007	Was	NL	16	54	7	2	0	0	(0	0)	9	1	3	0	2	0	17	0	0	1	0	0	-	3	.130	.158	.167
2008	Was	NL	66	163	35	10	0	2	(0	2)	51	15	16	14	19	1	36	0	0	0	1	0	1.00	5	.215	.297	.313
2 ML YEARS			82	217	42	12	0	2			60	16	19	14	21	1	53	0	0	1	1	0	1.00	8	.194	.264	.276

Juan Castro

Bats: R **Throws:** R **Pos:** SS-57; 3B-5; PH-4; 2B-2   **Ht:** 5'11" **Wt:** 190 **Born:** 6/20/1972 **Age:** 37

Year	Team	Lg	G	AB	H	2B	3B	HR	(Hm	Rd)	TB	R	RBI	RC	TBB	IBB	SO	HBP	SH	SF	SB	CS	SB%	GDP	Avg	OBP	Slg
2008	ColSpr*	AAA	18	50	15	2	0	1	(-	-)	20	8	3	7	4	0	7	0	0	0	0	0	-	4	.300	.352	.400
1995	LAD	NL	11	4	1	0	0	0	(0	0)	1	0	0	1	1	0	1	0	0	0	0	0	-	0	.250	.400	.250
1996	LAD	NL	70	132	26	5	3	0	(0	0)	37	16	5	8	10	0	27	0	4	0	1	0	1.00	3	.197	.254	.280
1997	LAD	NL	40	75	11	3	1	0	(0	0)	16	3	4	2	7	1	20	0	2	0	0	0	-	2	.147	.220	.213
1998	LAD	NL	89	220	43	7	0	2	(0	2)	56	25	14	12	15	0	37	0	9	2	0	0	-	5	.195	.245	.255
1999	LAD	NL	2	0	0	0	0	0			0	0	0	0	0	0	1	0	0	0	0	0	-	0	.000	.000	.000
2000	Cin	NL	82	224	54	12	2	4	(1	3)	82	20	23	20	14	1	33	0	4	2	0	0	-	9	.241	.283	.366
2001	Cin	NL	96	242	54	10	0	3	(0	3)	73	27	13	16	13	2	50	0	4	2	0	0	-	9	.223	.261	.302
2002	Cin	NL	54	82	18	3	0	2	(0	2)	27	5	11	11	7	0	18	0	1	1	0	0	-	2	.220	.278	.329
2003	Cin	NL	113	320	81	14	1	9	(4	5)	124	28	33	36	18	1	58	0	7	3	2	3	.40	7	.253	.290	.388
2004	Cin	NL	111	299	73	21	3	5	(3	2)	113	36	26	26	14	1	51	0	2	1	1	0	1.00	11	.244	.277	.378
2005	Min	AL	97	272	70	18	1	5	(2	3)	105	27	33	28	9	1	39	0	9	2	0	1	.00	6	.257	.279	.386
2006	2 Tms		104	251	63	10	3	3	(3	0)	88	18	28	26	11	0	36	0	1	1	1	2	.33	6	.251	.281	.351
2007	Cin	NL	54	89	16	5	0	0	(0	0)	21	5	5	2	4	0	21	0	3	2	0	0	-	5	.180	.211	.236
2008	2 Tms		61	161	31	6	0	2	(0	2)	43	16	16	7	11	0	26	1	2	2	0	0	-	9	.193	.246	.267
06	Min	AL	50	156	36	5	2	1	(1	0)	48	10	14	11	6	0	23	0	1	1	1	1	.50	6	.231	.258	.308
06	Cin	NL	54	95	27	5	1	2	(2	0)	40	8	14	15	5	0	13	0	0	0	0	1	.00	0	.284	.320	.421
08	Cin	NL	7	10	0	0	0	0	(0	0)	0	1	0	0	1	0	0	0	0	0	0	0	-	0	.000	.091	.000
08	Bal	AL	54	151	31	6	0	2	(0	2)	43	15	16	7	10	0	26	1	2	2	0	0	-	9	.205	.256	.285
Postseason			2	5	1	1	0	0	(0	0)	2	0	0	0	1	0	1	0	1	0	0	0	-	0	.200	.333	.400
14 ML YEARS			984	2372	541	114	13	35	(13	22)	786	226	211	195	134	7	418	1	48	18	5	8	.38	71	.228	.268	.331

Ramon Castro

Bats: R **Throws:** R **Pos:** C-47; PH-7 **Ht:** 6'3" **Wt:** 258 **Born:** 3/1/1976 **Age:** 33

Year	Team	Lg	G	AB	H	2B	3B	HR	(Hm	Rd)	TB	R	RBI	RC	TBB	IBB	SO	HBP	SH	SF	SB	CS	SB%	GDP	Avg	OBP	Slg
2008	StLuci*	A+	7	20	7	1	0	2	(-	-)	14	6	5	5	3	0	2	0	0	1	0	0	-	1	.350	.417	.700
1999	Fla	NL	24	67	12	4	0	2	(0	2)	22	4	4	6	10	3	14	0	0	1	0	0	-	1	.179	.282	.328
2000	Fla	NL	50	138	33	4	0	2	(0	2)	43	10	14	14	16	7	36	1	0	2	0	0	-	1	.239	.318	.312
2001	Fla	NL	7	11	2	0	0	0	(0	0)	2	0	1	0	1	0	1	0	0	0	0	0	-	0	.182	.250	.182
2002	Fla	NL	54	101	24	4	0	6	(4	2)	46	11	18	14	14	3	24	0	1	3	0	0	-	4	.238	.322	.455
2003	Fla	NL	40	53	15	2	0	5	(4	1)	32	6	8	8	4	0	11	0	0	0	0	0	-	0	.283	.333	.604
2004	Fla	NL	32	96	13	3	0	3	(0	3)	25	9	8	4	11	2	30	1	0	0	0	0	-	1	.135	.231	.260
2005	NYM	NL	99	209	51	16	0	8	(5	3)	91	26	41	30	25	2	58	0	3	3	1	0	1.00	7	.244	.321	.435
2006	NYM	NL	40	126	30	7	0	4	(1	3)	49	13	12	11	15	2	40	1	1	1	0	0	-	2	.238	.322	.389
2007	NYM	NL	52	144	41	6	0	11	(3	8)	80	24	31	23	10	0	39	1	0	2	0	0	-	1	.285	.331	.556
2008	NYM	NL	52	143	35	7	0	7	(5	2)	63	15	24	23	13	2	34	1	0	0	0	0	-	2	.245	.312	.441
10 ML YEARS			450	1088	256	53	0	48	(22	26)	453	118	161	133	119	21	287	5	5	12	1	0	1.00	19	.235	.310	.416

Frank Catalanotto

Bats: L **Throws:** R **Pos:** 1B-33; LF-26; DH-23; PH-22 **Ht:** 6'0" **Wt:** 205 **Born:** 4/27/1974 **Age:** 35

Year	Team	Lg	G	AB	H	2B	3B	HR	(Hm	Rd)	TB	R	RBI	RC	TBB	IBB	SO	HBP	SH	SF	SB	CS	SB%	GDP	Avg	OBP	Slg
1997	Det	AL	13	26	8	2	0	0	(0	0)	10	2	3	4	3	0	7	0	0	0	0	0	-	0	.308	.379	.385
1998	Det	AL	89	213	60	13	2	6	(3	3)	95	23	25	30	12	1	39	4	0	5	3	2	.60	4	.282	.325	.446
1999	Det	AL	100	286	79	19	0	11	(6	5)	131	41	35	42	15	1	49	9	0	5	3	4	.43	4	.276	.327	.458
2000	Tex	AL	103	282	82	13	2	10	(6	4)	129	55	42	49	33	0	36	6	3	2	6	2	.75	5	.291	.375	.457
2001	Tex	AL	133	463	153	31	5	11	(4	7)	227	77	54	88	39	3	55	8	1	1	15	5	.75	5	.330	.391	.490
2002	Tex	AL	68	212	57	16	6	3	(2	1)	94	42	23	39	25	0	27	8	3	2	9	5	.64	3	.269	.364	.443
2003	Tor	AL	133	489	146	34	6	13	(7	6)	231	83	59	84	35	1	62	6	2	3	2	2	.50	9	.299	.351	.472
2004	Tor	AL	75	249	73	19	1	1	(1	0)	97	27	26	34	17	1	33	4	1	3	1	0	1.00	7	.293	.344	.390
2005	Tor	AL	130	419	126	29	5	8	(3	5)	189	56	59	80	37	0	53	10	4	5	0	2	.00	9	.301	.367	.451
2006	Tor	AL	128	437	131	36	2	7	(2	5)	192	56	56	72	52	0	37	4	2	4	1	3	.25	11	.300	.376	.439
2007	Tex	AL	103	331	86	20	4	11	(9	2)	147	52	44	51	28	0	37	11	6	1	2	1	.67	6	.260	.337	.444
2008	Tex	AL	88	248	68	23	1	2	(0	2)	99	28	21	30	20	0	29	6	3	1	1	1	.50	6	.274	.342	.399
12 ML YEARS			1163	3655	1069	255	34	83	(43	40)	1641	542	447	603	316	7	464	76	25	32	43	27	.61	69	.292	.358	.449

Ronny Cedeno

Bats: R **Throws:** R **Pos:** 2B-43; PH-28; SS-27; 3B-7; PR-7; LF-1; CF-1 **Ht:** 6'0" **Wt:** 180 **Born:** 2/2/1983 **Age:** 26

Year	Team	Lg	G	AB	H	2B	3B	HR	(Hm	Rd)	TB	R	RBI	RC	TBB	IBB	SO	HBP	SH	SF	SB	CS	SB%	GDP	Avg	OBP	Slg
2005	ChC	NL	41	80	24	3	0	1	(0	1)	30	13	6	11	5	1	11	2	2	0	1	0	1.00	4	.300	.356	.375
2006	ChC	NL	151	534	131	18	7	6	(4	2)	181	51	44	41	17	4	109	3	15	3	8	8	.50	10	.245	.271	.339
2007	ChC	NL	38	74	15	2	0	4	(2	2)	29	6	13	8	3	0	18	0	2	1	2	1	.67	0	.203	.231	.392
2008	ChC	NL	99	216	58	12	0	2	(2	0)	76	36	28	23	18	2	41	1	1	0	4	1	.80	6	.269	.328	.352
Postseason			2	0	0	0	0	0	(0	0)	0	0	0	0	0	0	0	0	0	0	0	0	-	0	-	-	-
4 ML YEARS			329	904	228	35	7	13	(8	5)	316	106	88	83	43	7	179	6	20	4	15	10	.60	20	.252	.289	.350

Francisco Cervelli

Bats: B **Throws:** R **Pos:** C-3 **Ht:** 6'1" **Wt:** 210 **Born:** 3/6/1986 **Age:** 23

Year	Team	Lg	G	AB	H	2B	3B	HR	(Hm	Rd)	TB	R	RBI	RC	TBB	IBB	SO	HBP	SH	SF	SB	CS	SB%	GDP	Avg	OBP	Slg
2005	Yanks	R	24	58	11	2	0	1	(-	-)	16	10	9	5	8	0	13	2	0	2	1	0	1.00	0	.190	.300	.276
2006	StIsInd	A-	42	136	42	10	0	2	(-	-)	58	21	16	24	13	1	30	7	1	0	0	0	-	4	.309	.397	.426
2007	Tampa	A+	89	290	81	24	2	2	(-	-)	115	34	32	48	36	0	59	16	4	2	4	3	.57	8	.279	.387	.397
2008	Tampa	A+	3	10	3	0	0	0	(-	-)	3	2	1	1	0	0	3	1	0	0	0	0	-	0	.300	.364	.300
2008	Yanks	R	3	8	2	1	0	0	(-	-)	3	0	0	0	0	0	1	0	0	0	0	0	-	0	.250	.250	.375
2008	Trntn	AA	21	73	23	5	0	0	(-	-)	28	8	8	13	11	0	14	4	0	0	0	0	-	3	.315	.432	.384
2008	NYY	AL	3	5	0	0	0	0	(0	0)	0	0	0	0	0	0	3	0	0	0	0	0	-	1	.000	.000	.000

Mike Cervenak

Bats: R **Throws:** R **Pos:** PH-9; 3B-2 **Ht:** 5'11" **Wt:** 196 **Born:** 8/17/1976 **Age:** 32

Year	Team	Lg	G	AB	H	2B	3B	HR	(Hm	Rd)	TB	R	RBI	RC	TBB	IBB	SO	HBP	SH	SF	SB	CS	SB%	GDP	Avg	OBP	Slg
1999	Chill	IND	68	301	92	17	4	3	(-	-)	126	59	46	44	13	0	21	3	2	2	6	2	.75	4	.306	.339	.419
2000	Chill	IND	40	171	61	9	0	12	(-	-)	106	33	43	41	14	2	13	4	1	1	2	1	.67	5	.357	.415	.620
2000	Grnsbr	A	38	155	51	4	5	3	(-	-)	74	19	20	27	7	0	21	4	3	1	3	3	.50	1	.329	.371	.477
2001	Nrwich	AA	128	463	127	37	1	11	(-	-)	199	63	60	71	44	1	75	9	2	2	2	4	.33	8	.274	.347	.430
2002	Nrwich	AA	134	492	136	34	1	21	(-	-)	235	74	91	79	30	3	78	10	1	2	5	2	.71	12	.276	.330	.478
2003	Nrwich	AA	137	511	138	26	1	20	(-	-)	226	74	91	77	36	3	80	11	0	5	2	1	.67	19	.270	.329	.442
2004	Nrwich	AA	110	410	138	36	1	21	(-	-)	239	77	88	98	52	5	53	6	0	5	6	1	.86	7	.337	.414	.583
2004	Fresno	AAA	10	44	11	1	0	5	(-	-)	27	7	10	7	5	0	7	1	0	0	0	0	-	1	.250	.267	.614
2005	Fresno	AAA	127	494	155	29	3	19	(-	-)	247	67	103	93	38	3	61	10	0	5	4	0	1.00	7	.314	.371	.500
2006	Fresno	AAA	68	269	76	17	1	8	(-	-)	119	36	53	38	13	0	37	1	0	6	0	0	-	12	.283	.311	.442
2007	Norfolk	AAA	140	554	157	25	4	15	(-	-)	235	69	78	76	22	2	80	7	0	6	2	0	1.00	13	.283	.316	.424
2008	LV	AAA	115	456	141	30	2	10	(-	-)	205	64	66	66	13	2	64	7	0	6	5	4	.56	11	.309	.334	.450
2008	Phi	NL	10	13	2	0	0	0	(0	0)	2	0	1	0	0	0	5	0	0	0	0	0	-	1	.154	.154	.154

Shawn Chacon

Pitches: R Bats: R Pos: SP-15

Ht: 6'3" Wt: 220 Born: 12/23/1977 Age: 31

				HOW MUCH HE PITCHED						WHAT HE GAVE UP											THE RESULTS						
Year	Team	Lg	G	GS	CG	GF	IP	BFP	H	R	ER	HR	SH	SF	HB	TBB	IBB	SO	WP	Bk	W	L	Pct	ShO	Sv-Op	Hld	ERC	ERA
2001	Col	NL	27	27	0	0	160.0	711	157	96	90	26	6	3	10	87	10	134	6	0	6	10	.375	0	0-0	0	5.22	5.06
2002	Col	NL	21	21	0	0	119.1	537	122	84	76	25	5	2	7	60	3	67	0	1	5	11	.313	0	0-0	0	5.63	5.73
2003	Col	NL	23	23	0	0	137.0	596	124	73	70	12	10	5	12	58	4	93	8	0	11	8	.579	0	0-0	0	3.82	4.60
2004	Col	NL	66	0	0	60	63.1	316	71	52	50	12	7	0	5	52	7	52	9	0	1	9	.100	0	35-44	0	7.30	7.11
2005	2 Tms		27	24	0	0	151.2	652	135	59	58	14	9	5	14	66	4	79	6	1	8	10	.444	0	0-0	1	3.89	3.44
2006	2 Tms		26	20	0	0	109.0	516	124	86	77	23	7	7	9	63	3	62	4	1	7	6	.538	0	0-0	0	6.76	6.36
2007	Pit	NL	64	4	0	11	96.0	428	95	42	42	9	10	4	7	48	11	79	1	0	5	4	.556	0	1-8	12	4.46	3.94
2008	Hou	NL	15	15	0	0	85.2	374	88	52	48	16	4	1	2	41	5	53	2	0	2	3	.400	0	0-0	0	5.28	5.04
05	Col	NL	13	12	0	0	72.2	322	69	33	33	7	9	4	8	36	4	39	3	0	1	7	.125	0	0-0	0	4.51	4.09
05	NYY	AL	14	12	0	0	79.0	330	66	26	25	7	0	1	6	30	0	40	3	1	7	3	.700	0	0-0	1	3.35	2.85
06	NYY	AL	17	11	0	0	63.0	306	77	54	49	11	3	5	5	36	2	35	3	0	5	3	.625	0	0-0	0	6.86	7.00
06	Pit	NL	9	9	0	0	46.0	210	47	32	28	12	4	2	4	27	1	27	1	1	2	3	.400	0	0-0	0	6.61	5.48
	Postseason		1	1	0	0	6.1	23	4	2	2	0	1	0	0	1	0	5	0	0	0	0	-	0	0-0	0	1.16	2.84
	8 ML YEARS		269	134	0	71	922.0	4130	916	544	511	137	58	27	66	475	47	619	36	3	45	61	.425	0	36-52	13	5.07	4.99

Joba Chamberlain

Pitches: R Bats: R Pos: RP-30; SP-12

Ht: 6'2" Wt: 230 Born: 9/23/1985 Age: 23

				HOW MUCH HE PITCHED						WHAT HE GAVE UP											THE RESULTS						
Year	Team	Lg	G	GS	CG	GF	IP	BFP	H	R	ER	HR	SH	SF	HB	TBB	IBB	SO	WP	Bk	W	L	Pct	ShO	Sv-Op	Hld	ERC	ERA
2007	Tampa	A+	7	7	0	0	40.0	156	25	10	9	0	0	1	1	11	0	51	2	0	4	0	1.000	0	0--	-	1.39	2.03
2007	Trntn	AA	8	7	0	1	40.1	166	32	15	15	4	1	1	2	15	1	66	3	0	4	2	.667	0	0--	-	3.03	3.35
2007	S-WB	AAA	3	1	0	0	8.0	29	5	0	0	0	0	1	0	1	0	18	1	0	1	0	1.000	0	0--	-	1.07	0.00
2007	NYY	AL	19	0	0	3	24.0	91	12	2	1	1	1	0	1	6	0	34	1	0	2	0	1.000	0	1-1	8	1.16	0.38
2008	NYY	AL	42	12	0	5	100.1	417	87	32	29	5	2	1	2	39	3	118	4	2	4	3	.571	0	0-1	19	3.04	2.60
	Postseason		2	0	0	0	3.2	17	3	2	2	0	1	0	1	3	0	4	2	0	0	0	-	0	0-1	0	5.09	4.91
	2 ML YEARS		61	12	0	8	124.1	508	99	34	30	6	3	1	3	45	3	152	5	2	6	3	.667	0	1-2	27	2.59	2.17

Endy Chavez

Bats: L Throws: L Pos: RF-60; LF-54; PH-19; CF-10; PR-4

Ht: 6'0" Wt: 170 Born: 2/7/1978 Age: 31

						BATTING														BASERUNNING				AVERAGES		
Year	Team	Lg	G	AB	H	2B	3B	HR	(Hm	Rd)	TB	R	RBI	RC	TBB	IBB	SO	HBP	SH	SF	SB	CS	SB%	GDP	Avg	OBP	Slg
2001	KC	AL	29	77	16	2	0	0	(0	0)	18	4	5	2	3	0	8	0	0	0	0	2	.00	3	.208	.238	.234
2002	Mon	NL	36	125	37	8	5	1	(0	1)	58	20	9	14	5	0	16	0	7	1	3	5	.38	0	.296	.321	.464
2003	Mon	NL	141	483	121	25	5	5	(4	1)	171	66	47	56	31	3	59	0	9	3	18	7	.72	7	.251	.294	.354
2004	Mon	NL	132	502	139	20	6	5	(4	1)	186	65	34	56	30	0	40	1	12	2	32	7	.82	6	.277	.318	.371
2005	2 Tms		98	116	25	4	3	0	(0	0)	35	19	11	8	7	0	14	0	7	0	2	2	.50	3	.216	.260	.302
2006	NYM	NL	133	353	108	22	5	4	(2	2)	152	48	42	54	24	3	44	0	11	2	12	3	.80	7	.306	.348	.431
2007	NYM	NL	71	150	43	7	2	1	(1	0)	57	20	17	20	9	0	16	0	5	1	5	2	.71	5	.287	.325	.380
2008	NYM	NL	133	270	72	10	2	1	(1	0)	89	30	12	21	17	3	22	0	9	2	6	1	.86	4	.267	.308	.330
05	Was	NL	7	9	2	1	0	0	(0	0)	3	2	1	1	3	0	1	0	0	0	0	1	.00	1	.222	.417	.333
05	Phi	NL	91	107	23	3	3	0	(0	0)	32	17	10	7	4	0	13	0	7	0	2	1	.67	2	.215	.243	.299
	Postseason		10	35	8	2	0	0	(0	0)	10	2	0	0	0	0	1	0	0	0	0	0	-	1	.229	.229	.286
	8 ML YEARS		773	2076	561	98	28	17	(12	5)	766	272	177	231	126	9	219	1	60	11	78	29	.73	37	.270	.311	.369

Eric Chavez

Bats: L Throws: R Pos: 3B-15; DH-8

Ht: 6'1" Wt: 219 Born: 12/7/1977 Age: 31

						BATTING														BASERUNNING				AVERAGES		
Year	Team	Lg	G	AB	H	2B	3B	HR	(Hm	Rd)	TB	R	RBI	RC	TBB	IBB	SO	HBP	SH	SF	SB	CS	SB%	GDP	Avg	OBP	Slg
2008	Scrmto*	AAA	9	30	11	3	0	2	(-	-)	20	7	3	7	3	0	7	0	0	0	0	0	-	1	.367	.424	.667
1998	Oak	AL	16	45	14	4	1	0	(0	0)	20	6	6	7	3	1	5	0	0	0	1	1	.50	1	.311	.354	.444
1999	Oak	AL	115	356	88	21	2	13	(8	5)	152	47	50	50	46	4	56	0	0	0	1	1	.50	7	.247	.333	.427
2000	Oak	AL	153	501	139	23	4	26	(15	11)	248	89	86	86	62	8	94	1	0	5	2	2	.50	9	.277	.355	.495
2001	Oak	AL	151	552	159	43	0	32	(14	18)	298	91	114	99	41	9	99	4	0	7	8	2	.80	7	.288	.338	.540
2002	Oak	AL	153	585	161	31	3	34	(17	17)	300	87	109	103	65	13	119	1	0	2	8	3	.73	8	.275	.348	.513
2003	Oak	AL	156	588	166	39	5	29	(12	17)	302	94	101	97	62	10	89	1	0	3	6	3	.67	14	.282	.350	.514
2004	Oak	AL	125	475	131	20	0	29	(15	14)	238	87	77	84	95	11	99	3	0	4	6	3	.67	21	.276	.397	.501
2005	Oak	AL	160	625	168	40	1	27	(15	12)	291	92	101	95	58	4	129	2	0	9	6	0	1.00	19	.269	.329	.466
2006	Oak	AL	137	485	117	24	2	22	(8	14)	211	74	72	70	84	6	100	1	0	6	3	0	1.00	15	.241	.351	.435
2007	Oak	AL	90	341	82	21	2	15	(10	5)	152	43	46	38	34	2	76	0	0	4	4	2	.67	9	.240	.306	.446
2008	Oak	AL	23	89	22	7	0	2	(1	1)	35	10	14	14	6	0	18	0	0	2	0	0	-	2	.247	.295	.393
	Postseason		27	108	24	7	0	3	(3	0)	40	11	12	12	7	2	22	0	0	0	1	0	1.00	2	.222	.270	.370
	11 ML YEARS		1279	4642	1247	273	20	229	(115	114)	2247	720	776	743	556	67	884	13	0	40	47	17	.73	106	.269	.346	.484

Jesse Chavez

Pitches: R Bats: R Pos: RP-15

Ht: 6'2" Wt: 175 Born: 8/21/1983 Age: 25

						HOW MUCH HE PITCHED						WHAT HE GAVE UP											THE RESULTS				
Year	Team	Lg	G	GS	CG	GF	IP	BFP	H	R	ER	HR	SH	SF	HB	TBB	IBB	SO	WP	Bk	W	L	Pct	ShO	Sv-Op	Hld	ERC	ERA
2003	Spkane	A-	17	8	0	1	55.1	259	63	30	28	5	0	1	7	31	0	48	4	0	2	2	.500	0	0--	-	6.03	4.55
2004	Clinton	A	27	22	0	1	123.0	537	148	75	64	8	7	9	3	35	1	96	4	0	6	10	.375	0	0--	-	4.65	4.68
2005	Bkrsfld	A+	11	0	0	5	24.1	97	16	6	6	2	0	0	0	9	0	31	1	0	0	0	-	0	2--	-	2.09	2.22
2005	Frisco	AA	30	0	0	7	56.0	253	71	43	36	10	1	3	2	25	2	27	8	1	4	3	.571	0	1--	-	6.77	5.79
2006	Frisco	AA	38	0	0	22	59.0	256	54	33	29	5	4	2	2	28	3	70	7	0	2	5	.286	0	4--	-	3.83	4.42
2006	Indy	AAA	12	0	0	1	17.0	77	18	9	8	0	1	0	0	9	1	15	0	0	2	1	.667	0	0--	-	4.00	4.24

			HOW MUCH HE PITCHED						WHAT HE GAVE UP												THE RESULTS							
Year	Team	Lg	G	GS	CG	GF	IP	BFP	H	R	ER	HR	SH	SF	HB	TBB	IBB	SO	WP	Bk	W	L	Pct	ShO	Sv-Op	Hld	ERC	ERA
2006	Okla	AAA	1	0	0	1	2.0	9	3	1	1	0	0	0	0	0	0	3	0	0	0	0	-	0	0--	-	4.47	4.50
2007	Indy	AAA	46	1	0	12	80.1	349	94	41	35	4	1	5	1	18	2	65	3	0	3	3	.500	0	2--	-	3.95	3.92
2008	Indy	AAA	51	0	0	27	68.2	283	58	30	29	8	2	2	0	22	4	70	6	0	2	6	.250	0	14--	-	2.94	3.80
2008	Pit	NL	15	0	0	6	15.0	74	20	11	11	2	3	1	0	9	2	16	2	0	0	1	.000	0	0-2	0	6.76	6.60

Raul Chavez

Bats: R **Throws:** R **Pos:** C-35; PH-7
Ht: 5'11" **Wt:** 210 **Born:** 3/18/1973 **Age:** 36

			BATTING																	BASERUNNING				AVERAGES		
Year	Team	Lg	G	AB	H	2B	3B	HR	(Hm | Rd)	TB	R	RBI	RC	TBB	IBB	SO	HBP	SH	SF	SB	CS	SB%	GDP	Avg	OBP	Slg
2008	Indy*	AAA	26	85	26	5	1	3	(- | -)	42	9	13	14	4	0	11	2	0	0	0	0	-	0	.306	.352	.494
1996	Mon	NL	4	5	1	0	0	0	(0 | 0)	1	1	0	0	1	0	1	0	0	0	1	0	1.00	1	.200	.333	.200
1997	Mon	NL	13	26	7	0	0	0	(0 | 0)	7	0	2	2	1	0	5	0	0	1	1	0	1.00	0	.269	.259	.269
1998	Sea	AL	1	1	0	0	0	0	(0 | 0)	0	0	0	0	0	0	0	0	0	0	0	0	-	0	.000	.000	.000
2000	Hou	NL	14	43	11	2	0	1	(0 | 1)	16	3	5	3	2	2	6	0	0	1	0	0	-	5	.256	.298	.372
2002	Hou	NL	2	4	1	1	0	0	(0 | 0)	2	1	0	1	1	0	1	0	0	0	0	0	-	0	.250	.500	.500
2003	Hou	NL	19	37	10	1	1	1	(0 | 1)	16	5	4	4	1	0	6	0	0	0	0	0	-	3	.270	.289	.432
2004	Hou	NL	64	162	34	8	0	0	(0 | 0)	42	9	23	10	10	3	38	0	4	0	0	1	.00	9	.210	.256	.259
2005	Hou	NL	37	99	17	3	0	2	(1 | 1)	26	6	6	2	4	0	18	1	0	1	1	0	1.00	0	.172	.210	.263
2006	Bal	AL	16	28	5	0	0	0	(0 | 0)	5	1	0	1	0	0	4	0	0	0	0	0	-	0	.179	.179	.179
2008	Pit	NL	42	116	30	4	0	1	(1 | 0)	37	12	10	12	4	1	14	1	0	1	0	0	-	0	.259	.287	.319
	Postseason		5	10	4	0	0	1	(0 | 1)	7	1	2	3	1	0	1	0	1	0	0	0	-	2	.400	.455	.700
	10 ML YEARS		212	521	116	19	1	5	(2 | 3)	152	38	50	34	25	6	92	3	4	4	3	1	.75	25	.223	.260	.292

Rocky Cherry

Pitches: R **Bats:** R **Pos:** RP-18
Ht: 6'5" **Wt:** 225 **Born:** 8/19/1979 **Age:** 29

			HOW MUCH HE PITCHED						WHAT HE GAVE UP												THE RESULTS							
Year	Team	Lg	G	GS	CG	GF	IP	BFP	H	R	ER	HR	SH	SF	HB	TBB	IBB	SO	WP	Bk	W	L	Pct	ShO	Sv-Op	Hld	ERC	ERA
2003	Lansng	A	8	4	0	2	29.1	119	23	16	9	1	2	0	4	7	0	18	3	0	2	0	1.000	0	0--	-	2.45	2.76
2003	Boise	A-	10	10	0	0	54.0	222	36	21	13	1	1	1	2	18	0	55	2	0	5	2	.714	0	0--	-	1.70	2.17
2004	Dytona	A+	27	22	1	0	124.2	557	138	79	72	16	11	8	9	46	1	104	4	0	5	10	.333	1	0--	-	5.03	5.20
2005	WTenn	AA	3	3	0	0	9.1	41	8	5	2	0	1	0	1	4	0	9	0	0	0	0	-	0	0--	-	3.03	1.93
2006	WTenn	AA	31	0	0	16	48.2	200	43	14	12	3	5	3	3	14	3	50	6	0	4	1	.800	0	2--	-	2.95	2.22
2006	Iowa	AAA	2	0	0	0	2.2	12	3	3	3	0	0	0	0	1	0	2	1	0	1	0	1.000	0	0--	-	3.84	10.13
2007	Iowa	AAA	43	1	0	16	51.0	220	50	27	26	5	0	0	1	18	0	56	5	0	2	0	1.000	0	7--	-	3.80	4.59
2007	Cubs	R	2	2	0	0	2.0	7	0	0	0	0	0	0	1	1	0	2	0	0	0	0	-	0	0--	-	1.08	0.00
2008	Bowie	AA	2	0	0	0	2.0	9	1	0	0	0	0	0	0	2	0	3	0	0	0	0	-	0	0--	-	2.80	0.00
2008	Norfolk	AAA	28	0	0	8	37.1	155	35	15	12	3	1	4	2	9	2	37	4	0	0	1	.000	0	0--	-	3.12	2.89
2007	2 Tms		22	0	0	2	31.1	145	30	20	19	4	2	2	3	19	2	23	0	0	1	1	.500	0	0-1	0	5.05	5.46
2008	Bal	AL	18	0	0	4	17.0	85	15	15	12	3	1	2	1	16	3	15	4	0	0	3	.000	0	1-3	2	5.80	6.35
07	ChC	NL	12	0	0	2	15.0	66	13	6	5	1	0	1	1	6	1	13	0	0	1	1	.500	0	0-1	0	3.14	3.00
07	Bal	AL	10	0	0	0	16.1	79	17	14	14	3	2	1	2	13	1	10	0	0	0	0	-	0	0-0	0	7.06	7.71
	2 ML YEARS		40	0	0	6	48.1	230	45	35	31	7	3	4	4	35	5	38	4	0	1	4	.200	0	1-4	2	5.32	5.77

Matt Chico

Pitches: L **Bats:** L **Pos:** SP-8; RP-3
Ht: 5'11" **Wt:** 219 **Born:** 6/10/1983 **Age:** 26

			HOW MUCH HE PITCHED						WHAT HE GAVE UP												THE RESULTS							
Year	Team	Lg	G	GS	CG	GF	IP	BFP	H	R	ER	HR	SH	SF	HB	TBB	IBB	SO	WP	Bk	W	L	Pct	ShO	Sv-Op	Hld	ERC	ERA
2003	Yakima	A-	17	13	0	0	71.1	309	75	28	28	4	3	2	5	25	1	71	9	1	7	4	.636	0	0--	-	4.15	3.53
2004	Sbend	A	14	14	2	0	87.2	344	59	26	25	9	2	1	3	27	0	89	5	0	8	5	.615	1	0--	-	2.22	2.57
2004	ElPaso	AA	14	12	0	0	62.1	300	82	53	40	7	3	5	2	36	1	59	7	1	3	7	.300	0	0--	-	6.91	5.78
2005	Tenn	AA	10	10	0	0	52.2	246	75	44	36	8	5	4	2	15	1	35	2	2	1	7	.125	0	0--	-	6.62	6.15
2005	Lancst	A+	18	18	0	0	110.0	462	101	50	46	13	0	5	3	39	0	102	4	1	7	2	.778	0	0--	-	3.70	3.76
2006	Lancst	A+	10	10	0	0	50.1	215	48	25	21	5	1	1	1	11	0	49	4	0	3	4	.429	0	0--	-	3.06	3.75
2006	Tenn	AA	13	13	0	0	81.0	319	62	22	20	6	1	2	0	21	0	63	8	1	7	2	.778	0	0--	-	2.21	2.22
2006	Hrsbrg	AA	4	4	0	0	22.0	98	28	9	8	3	0	0	2	8	0	13	3	1	2	0	1.000	0	0--	-	6.45	3.27
2007	Clmbs	AAA	2	2	0	0	11.0	44	9	4	4	1	0	0	0	5	0	7	0	0	1	1	.500	0	0--	-	3.42	3.27
2008	Clmbs	AAA	1	1	0	0	4.0	20	7	4	4	1	0	0	0	2	0	1	3	0	0	0	-	0	0--	-	8.49	9.00
2007	Was	NL	31	31	0	0	167.0	747	183	96	86	26	6	10	5	74	3	94	7	0	7	9	.438	0	0-0	0	5.31	4.63
2008	Was	NL	11	8	0	0	48.0	219	63	34	33	10	4	2	1	17	1	31	1	0	0	6	.000	0	0-0	0	6.67	6.19
	2 ML YEARS		42	39	0	0	215.0	966	246	130	119	36	10	12	6	91	4	125	8	0	7	15	.318	0	0-0	0	5.61	4.98

Shin-Soo Choo

Bats: L **Throws:** L **Pos:** RF-51; LF-26; PH-13; DH-11
Ht: 5'11" **Wt:** 200 **Born:** 7/13/1982 **Age:** 26

			BATTING																	BASERUNNING				AVERAGES		
Year	Team	Lg	G	AB	H	2B	3B	HR	(Hm	Rd)	TB	R	RBI	RC	TBB	IBB	SO	HBP	SH	SF	SB	CS	SB%	GDP	Avg	OBP	Slg
2008	Buffalo*	AAA	12	42	11	2	0	1	(-	-)	16	1	3	5	5	0	14	2	0	0	1	3	.25	0	.262	.367	.381
2005	Sea	AL	10	18	1	0	0	0	(0	0)	1	1	1	0	3	0	4	0	0	0	0	0	-	0	.056	.190	.056
2006	2 Tms	AL	49	157	44	12	3	3	(2	1)	71	23	22	24	18	2	50	2	1	1	5	3	.63	3	.280	.360	.452
2007	Cle	AL	6	17	5	0	0	0	(0	0)	5	5	3	2	1		5	0	0	0	0	1	1.00	0	.294	.350	.294
2008	Cle	AL	94	317	98	28	3	14	(10	4)	174	68	66	72	44	4	78	5	0	4	4	3	.57	5	.309	.397	.549
06	Sea	AL	4	11	1	1	0	0	(0	0)	2	0	0	0	0	0	4	1	0	0	0	0	-	1	.091	.167	.182
06	Cle	AL	45	146	43	11	3	3	(2	1)	69	23	22	24	18	2	46	1	1	1	5	3	.63	2	.295	.373	.473
	4 ML YEARS		159	509	148	40	6	17	(12	5)	251	97	94	99	67	7	137	7	1	6	9	7	.56	8	.291	.377	.493

Justin Christian

Bats: R **Throws:** R **Pos:** LF-9; PR-6; RF-5; DH-4; PH-4; CF-3   **Ht:** 6'1" **Wt:** 188 **Born:** 4/30/1980 **Age:** 29

											BATTING										BASERUNNING				AVERAGES		
Year	Team	Lg	G	AB	H	2B	3B	HR	(Hm	Rd)	TB	R	RBI	RC	TBB	IBB	SO	HBP	SH	SF	SB	CS	SB%	GDP	Avg	OBP	Slg
2003	River	IND	38	123	37	5	1	1	(-	-)	47	24	15	22	16	0	18	2	3	0	19	4	.83	2	.301	.390	.382
2004	River	IND	30	120	54	11	2	5	(-	-)	84	31	22	42	17	2	22	0	2	0	26	2	.93	1	.450	.518	.700
2004	Yanks	R	3	7	4	3	0	0	(-	-)	7	1	4	4	4	0	0	0	0	0	0	0	-	0	.571	.727	1.000
2004	StsInd	A-	50	208	57	9	2	7	(-	-)	91	29	33	33	19	0	39	2	0	3	14	2	.88	2	.274	.336	.438
2005	CtnSC	A	29	100	29	5	0	3	(-	-)	43	31	10	20	14	0	12	3	1	0	17	2	.89	2	.290	.393	.430
2005	Tampa	A+	95	372	114	27	6	8	(-	-)	177	52	37	72	33	0	47	6	4	1	38	5	.88	2	.306	.371	.476
2005	Clmbs	AAA	1	0	0	0	0	0	(-	-)	0	0	0	0	0	0	0	0	0	0	0	0	-	0	-	-	-
2006	Trntn	AA	129	467	129	19	9	6	(-	-)	184	76	43	73	43	1	73	3	3	3	68	13	.84	8	.276	.341	.394
2007	Trntn	AA	65	255	60	8	3	3	(-	-)	83	25	32	26	16	2	43	2	2	3	18	4	.82	9	.235	.283	.325
2007	S-WB	AAA	40	169	55	8	4	1	(-	-)	74	32	16	30	10	0	19	2	2	0	17	2	.89	5	.325	.370	.438
2008	S-WB	AAA	74	268	82	17	1	6	(-	-)	119	48	45	46	20	0	34	4	0	5	22	4	.85	10	.306	.357	.444
2008	NYY	AL	24	40	10	3	0	0	(0	0)	13	6	6	7	3	0	4	0	0	0	7	1	.88	1	.250	.302	.325

Vinnie Chulk

Pitches: R **Bats:** R **Pos:** RP-27   **Ht:** 6'2" **Wt:** 195 **Born:** 12/19/1978 **Age:** 30

			HOW MUCH HE PITCHED						WHAT HE GAVE UP											THE RESULTS							
Year	Team	Lg	G	GS	CG	GF	IP	BFP	H	R	ER	HR	SH	SF	HB	TBB	IBB	SO	WP	Bk	W	L	Pct	ShO	Sv-Op	Hld	ERC	ERA
2008	Fresno*	AAA	22	0	0	5	24.2	109	25	10	10	3	0	3	1	13	0	21	4	0	1	0	.000	0	2- -	1	5.07	3.65
2003	Tor	AL	3	0	0	2	5.1	25	6	3	3	0	0	0	0	3	0	2	0	0	0	0	-	0	0-1	0	4.53	5.06
2004	Tor	AL	47	0	0	10	56.0	248	59	30	29	6	1	1	1	27	1	44	2	0	1	3	.250	0	2-5	13	4.83	4.66
2005	Tor	AL	62	0	0	10	72.0	301	68	33	31	9	3	4	1	26	3	39	5	0	1	0	.000	0	0-1	13	3.83	3.88
2006	2 Tms		48	0	0	13	46.1	205	46	29	27	6	0	2	3	20	2	43	1	0	1	3	.250	0	0-2	6	4.53	5.24
2007	SF	NL	57	0	0	15	53.0	222	53	22	21	3	1	4	2	14	2	41	2	0	5	4	.556	0	0-2	9	3.37	3.57
2008	SF	NL	27	0	0	9	31.2	139	33	18	17	6	1	1	2	8	2	16	1	0	0	3	.000	0	0-2	2	4.36	4.83
06	Tor	AL	20	0	0	8	24.0	107	29	16	14	4	0	1	2	5	0	18	1	0	1	0	1.000	0	0-1	1	5.25	5.25
06	SF	NL	28	0	0	5	22.1	98	17	13	13	2	0	1	1	15	2	25	0	0	0	3	.000	0	0-1	5	3.74	5.24
6 ML YEARS			244	0	0	59	264.1	1140	265	135	128	30	6	12	9	98	10	185	14	0	7	14	.333	0	2-'3	43	4.15	4.36

Ryan Church

Bats: L **Throws:** L **Pos:** RF-83; PH-9   **Ht:** 6'1" **Wt:** 190 **Born:** 10/14/1978 **Age:** 30

											BATTING										BASERUNNING				AVERAGES		
Year	Team	Lg	G	AB	H	2B	3B	HR	(Hm	Rd)	TB	R	RBI	RC	TBB	IBB	SO	HBP	SH	SF	SB	CS	SB%	GDP	Avg	OBP	Slg
2008	Bklyn*	A-	2	6	3	1	0	0	(-	-)	4	1	1	1	0	0	2	0	0	0	0	0	-	0	.500	.500	.667
2008	Mets*	R	2	6	1	0	0	0	(-	-)	1	0	1	0	1	1	3	0	0	0	0	0	-	0	.167	.286	.167
2008	NewOr*	AAA	2	5	1	1	0	0	(-	-)	2	0	1	0	1	0	1	0	0	0	0	0	-	0	.200	.333	.400
2008	Bnghtn*	AA	2	8	0	0	0	0	(-	-)	0	0	0	0	0	0	2	0	0	0	0	0	-	0	.000	.000	.000
2004	Mon	NL	30	63	11	1	0	1	(0	1)	15	6	6	2	7	1	16	0	1	0	0	0	-	3	.175	.257	.238
2005	Was	NL	102	268	77	15	3	9	(5	4)	125	41	42	34	24	0	70	5	1	3	3	2	.60	6	.287	.353	.466
2006	Was	NL	71	196	54	17	1	10	(6	4)	103	22	35	36	26	0	60	3	3	2	6	1	.86	4	.276	.366	.526
2007	Was	NL	144	470	128	43	1	15	(5	10)	218	57	70	70	49	4	107	6	4	3	3	2	.60	12	.272	.349	.464
2008	NYM	NL	90	319	88	14	1	12	(6	6)	140	54	49	46	33	3	83	5	1	3	2	3	.40	9	.276	.346	.439
5 ML YEARS			437	1316	358	90	6	47	(22	25)	601	180	202	188	139	8	336	19	6	11	14	8	.64	34	.272	.347	.457

Alex Cintron

Bats: B **Throws:** R **Pos:** SS-45; PH-16; 3B-8; 2B-7; PR-3; 1B-2; DH-2   **Ht:** 6'1" **Wt:** 205 **Born:** 12/17/1978 **Age:** 30

											BATTING										BASERUNNING				AVERAGES		
Year	Team	Lg	G	AB	H	2B	3B	HR	(Hm	Rd)	TB	R	RBI	RC	TBB	IBB	SO	HBP	SH	SF	SB	CS	SB%	GDP	Avg	OBP	Slg
2008	Norfolk*	AAA	16	66	19	1	0	2	(-	-)	26	9	10	8	2	0	11	2	1	0	0	0	-	3	.288	.329	.394
2008	Bowie*	AA	3	9	3	0	0	0	(-	-)	3	0	0	1	1	0	2	0	0	0	0	0	-	0	.333	.400	.333
2008	Frdrck*	A+	2	5	3	0	0	1	(-	-)	6	2	2	2	0	0	1	0	0	0	0	0	-	0	.600	.600	1.200
2001	Ari	NL	8	7	2	0	1	0	(0	0)	4	0	0	1	0	0	0	0	0	0	0	0	-	0	.286	.286	.571
2002	Ari	NL	38	75	16	6	0	0	(0	0)	22	11	4	5	12	2	13	0	3	0	0	0	-	2	.213	.322	.293
2003	Ari	NL	117	448	142	26	6	13	(6	7)	219	70	51	70	29	0	33	2	5	3	2	3	.40	7	.317	.359	.489
2004	Ari	NL	154	564	148	31	7	4	(1	3)	205	56	49	59	31	2	59	2	12	4	3	3	.50	11	.262	.301	.363
2005	Ari	NL	122	330	90	19	2	8	(5	3)	137	36	48	35	12	3	33	1	2	3	1	2	.33	8	.273	.298	.415
2006	CWS	AL	91	288	82	10	3	5	(2	3)	113	35	41	33	10	0	35	2	1	3	10	3	.77	10	.285	.310	.392
2007	CWS	AL	68	185	45	7	1	2	(1	1)	60	23	19	21	9	1	35	1	0	1	2	1	.67	5	.243	.281	.324
2008	Bal	AL	61	133	38	5	1	1	(1	0)	48	12	10	14	7	0	15	0	4	0	0	2	.00	5	.286	.321	.361
	Postseason		2	0	0	0	0	0	(0	0)	0	0	0	0	0	0	0	0	0	0	0	0	-	0	-	-	-
8 ML YEARS			659	2030	563	104	21	33	(17	16)	808	243	222	238	110	8	223	8	27	14	18	14	.56	48	.277	.315	.398

Brady Clark

Bats: R **Throws:** R **Pos:** PH-3; LF-2; RF-2   **Ht:** 6'2" **Wt:** 207 **Born:** 4/18/1973 **Age:** 36

											BATTING										BASERUNNING				AVERAGES		
Year	Team	Lg	G	AB	H	2B	3B	HR	(Hm	Rd)	TB	R	RBI	RC	TBB	IBB	SO	HBP	SH	SF	SB	CS	SB%	GDP	Avg	OBP	Slg
2008	NewOr*	AAA	6	23	7	1	0	0	(-	-)	8	3	1	3	3	0	1	0	0	0	0	0	-	1	.304	.385	.348
2000	Cin	NL	11	11	3	1	0	0	(0	0)	4	1	2	1	0	0	2	0	0	0	0	0	-	0	.273	.273	.364
2001	Cin	NL	89	129	34	3	0	6	(4	2)	55	22	18	21	22	1	16	1	4	1	4	1	.80	6	.264	.373	.426
2002	2 Tms	NL	61	78	15	4	0	0	(0	0)	19	9	10	7	7	2	11	1	1	0	1	2	.33	2	.192	.267	.244
2003	Mil	NL	128	315	86	21	1	6	(5	1)	127	33	40	40	21	0	40	9	2	7	13	2	.87	12	.273	.330	.403
2004	Mil	NL	138	353	99	18	1	7	(1	6)	140	41	46	56	53	2	48	9	1	3	15	8	.65	9	.280	.385	.397
2005	Mil	NL	145	599	183	31	1	13	(8	5)	255	94	53	92	47	1	55	18	8	2	10	13	.43	13	.306	.372	.426
2006	Mil	NL	138	415	109	14	2	4	(3	1)	139	51	29	47	43	4	60	14	5	5	3	9	.25	9	.263	.348	.335
2007	2 Tms	NL	68	107	28	5	2	0	(0	0)	37	13	11	11	14	2	18	1	1	0	1	3	.25	3	.262	.352	.346

Year Team	Lg	G	AB	H	2B	3B	HR	(Hm	Rd)	TB	R	RBI	RC	TBB	IBB	SO	HBP	SH	SF	SB	CS	SB%	GDP	Avg	OBP	Slg
2008 NYM	NL	7	8	2	0	0	0	(0	0)	2	0	1	1	1	0	2	1	1	0	1	0	1.00	1	.250	.400	.250
02 Cin	NL	51	66	10	3	0	0	(0	0)	13	6	9	5	6	2	9	1	1	0	0	1	.33	2	.152	.233	.197
02 NYM	NL	10	12	5	1	0	0	(0	0)	6	3	1	2	1	0	2	0	0	0	0	0	-	0	.417	.462	.500
07 LAD	NL	47	58	13	4	0	0	(0	0)	17	7	5	4	6	0	11	1	1	0	1	2	.33	1	.224	.308	.293
07 SD	NL	21	49	15	1	2	0	(0	0)	20	6	6	7	8	2	7	0	0	0	0	1	.00	1	.306	.404	.408
9 ML YEARS		785	2015	559	97	7	36	(21	15)	778	264	210	276	208	12	252	54	23	18	48	33	.59	55	.277	.358	.386

Howie Clark

Bats: L Throws: R Pos: 1B-2; 2B-1; 3B-1   Ht: 5'10" Wt: 190 Born: 2/13/1974 Age: 35

Year Team	Lg	G	AB	H	2B	3B	HR	(Hm	Rd)	TB	R	RBI	RC	TBB	IBB	SO	HBP	SH	SF	SB	CS	SB%	GDP	Avg	OBP	Slg
2008 Roch*	AAA	93	338	99	17	6	6	(-	-)	146	50	48	51	25	4	30	2	1	5	2	1	.67	12	.293	.341	.432
2002 Bal	AL	14	53	16	5	0	0	(0	0)	21	3	4	3	3	0	6	2	0	0	0	0	-	5	.302	.362	.396
2003 Tor	AL	38	70	25	3	1	0	(0	0)	30	9	7	13	3	0	6	2	2	0	0	1	.00	3	.357	.400	.429
2004 Tor	AL	40	115	25	6	0	3	(3	0)	40	17	12	11	13	0	15	0	3	2	0	0	-	2	.217	.292	.348
2006 Bal	AL	7	7	1	0	0	0	(0	0)	1	1	0	1	2	0	2	0	1	0	0	0	-	0	.143	.333	.143
2007 Tor	AL	31	49	10	2	0	0	(0	0)	12	6	2	3	7	1	5	0	0	1	1	0	1.00	1	.204	.298	.245
2008 Min	AL	4	8	2	2	0	0	(0	0)	4	0	1	1	0	0	2	0	0	0	0	0	-	0	.250	.250	.500
6 ML YEARS		134	302	79	18	1	3	(3	0)	108	36	26	32	28	1	36	4	6	3	1	1	.50	11	.262	.329	.358

Tony Clark

Bats: B Throws: R Pos: PH-76; 1B-26; DH-9; PR-1   Ht: 6'7" Wt: 245 Born: 6/15/1972 Age: 37

Year Team	Lg	G	AB	H	2B	3B	HR	(Hm	Rd)	TB	R	RBI	RC	TBB	IBB	SO	HBP	SH	SF	SB	CS	SB%	GDP	Avg	OBP	Slg
1995 Det	AL	27	101	24	5	1	3	(0	3)	40	10	11	11	8	0	30	0	0	0	0	0	-	2	.238	.294	.396
1996 Det	AL	100	376	94	14	0	27	(17	10)	189	56	72	55	29	1	127	0	0	6	0	1	.00	7	.250	.299	.503
1997 Det	AL	159	580	160	28	3	32	(18	14)	290	105	117	107	93	13	144	3	0	5	1	3	.25	11	.276	.376	.500
1998 Det	AL	157	602	175	37	0	34	(18	16)	314	84	103	107	63	5	128	3	0	5	3	3	.50	16	.291	.358	.522
1999 Det	AL	143	536	150	29	0	31	(12	19)	272	74	99	94	64	7	133	6	0	3	2	1	.67	14	.280	.361	.507
2000 Det	AL	60	208	57	14	0	13	(6	7)	110	32	37	35	24	2	51	0	0	0	0	0	-	10	.274	.349	.529
2001 Det	AL	126	428	123	29	3	16	(7	9)	206	67	75	74	62	10	108	1	0	6	0	1	.00	14	.287	.374	.481
2002 Bos	AL	90	275	57	12	1	3	(1	2)	80	25	29	19	21	0	57	1	0	1	0	0	-	11	.207	.265	.291
2003 NYM	NL	125	254	59	13	0	16	(9	7)	120	29	43	29	24	2	73	1	0	1	0	0	-	8	.232	.300	.472
2004 NYY	AL	106	253	56	12	0	16	(5	11)	116	37	49	37	26	3	92	2	0	2	0	0	-	6	.221	.297	.458
2005 Ari	NL	130	349	106	22	2	30	(19	11)	222	47	87	71	37	6	88	1	0	6	0	0	-	10	.304	.366	.636
2006 Ari	NL	79	132	26	4	0	6	(3	3)	48	13	16	10	13	2	40	2	0	0	0	0	-	5	.197	.279	.364
2007 Ari	NL	113	221	55	5	1	17	(14	3)	113	31	51	28	21	3	59	0	0	3	0	0	-	8	.249	.310	.511
2008 2 Tms	NL	108	151	34	5	0	3	(2	1)	48	12	24	20	31	1	55	0	1	1	0	0	-	8	.225	.359	.318
08 SD	NL	70	88	21	3	0	1	(1	0)	27	5	11	13	19	0	32	0	0	0	0	0	-	2	.239	.374	.307
08 Ari	NL	38	63	13	2	0	2	(1	1)	21	7	13	7	12	1	23	0	1	1	0	0	-	6	.206	.338	.333
Postseason		12	37	5	2	0	0	(0	0)	7	0	1	0	1	1	13	0	0	0	0	0	-	0	.135	.158	.189
14 ML YEARS		1523	4466	1176	229	11	247	(131	116)	2168	622	813	697	516	55	1185	21	0	39	6	9	.40	130	.263	.340	.485

Jeff Clement

Bats: L Throws: R Pos: C-38; DH-21; PH-8   Ht: 6'1" Wt: 215 Born: 8/21/1983 Age: 25

Year Team	Lg	G	AB	H	2B	3B	HR	(Hm	Rd)	TB	R	RBI	RC	TBB	IBB	SO	HBP	SH	SF	SB	CS	SB%	GDP	Avg	OBP	Slg
2005 Wisc	A	30	113	36	5	0	6	(-	-)	59	17	20	22	12	0	25	1	0	1	1	2	.33	0	.319	.386	.522
2006 SnAnt	AA	15	59	17	6	1	2	(-	-)	31	7	10	12	7	0	8	3	0	1	0	0	-	0	.288	.386	.525
2006 Tacom	AAA	67	245	63	10	0	4	(-	-)	85	23	32	28	16	1	53	8	1	2	0	2	.00	8	.257	.321	.347
2007 Tacom	AAA	125	455	125	35	3	20	(-	-)	226	76	80	86	61	4	88	10	0	4	0	0	-	8	.275	.370	.497
2008 Tacom	AAA	48	172	58	17	0	14	(-	-)	117	40	43	50	35	0	29	3	0	0	0	0	-	7	.337	.457	.680
2007 Sea	AL	9	16	6	1	0	2	(2	0)	13	4	3	6	3	0	3	0	0	0	0	0	-	0	.375	.474	.813
2008 Sea	AL	66	203	46	10	1	5	(2	3)	73	17	23	22	15	0	63	5	0	1	0	1	.00	4	.227	.295	.360
2 ML YEARS		75	219	52	11	1	7	(4	3)	86	21	26	28	18	0	66	5	0	1	0	1	.00	4	.237	.309	.393

Brent Clevlen

Bats: R Throws: R Pos: LF-10; CF-3; RF-1; PR-1   Ht: 6'2" Wt: 190 Born: 10/27/1983 Age: 25

Year Team	Lg	G	AB	H	2B	3B	HR	(Hm	Rd)	TB	R	RBI	RC	TBB	IBB	SO	HBP	SH	SF	SB	CS	SB%	GDP	Avg	OBP	Slg
2008 Toledo*	AAA	126	476	133	23	7	22	(-	-)	236	75	82	86	54	5	166	6	1	3	7	2	.78	14	.279	.358	.496
2006 Det	AL	31	39	11	1	2	3	(0	3)	25	9	6	6	2	0	15	0	1	0	0	0	-	0	.282	.317	.641
2007 Det	AL	13	10	1	0	0	0	(0	0)	1	2	0	0	0	0	7	0	0	0	0	0	-	1	.100	.100	.100
2008 Det	AL	11	24	5	0	0	0	(0	0)	5	4	1	2	3	0	8	0	1	0	0	0	-	0	.208	.296	.208
3 ML YEARS		55	73	17	1	2	3	(0	3)	31	15	7	8	5	0	30	0	2	0	0	0	-	1	.233	.282	.425

Tyler Clippard

Pitches: R Bats: R Pos: SP-2   Ht: 6'3" Wt: 199 Born: 2/14/1985 Age: 24

Year Team	Lg	G	GS	CG	GF	IP	BFP	H	R	ER	HR	SH	SF	HB	TBB	IBB	SO	WP	Bk	W	L	Pct	ShO	Sv-Op	Hld	ERC	ERA
2003 Yanks	R	11	5	0	2	43.2	168	33	16	14	3	1	1	5	0	56	4	0	3	3	.500	0	0--	-	2.07	2.89
2004 Btl Crk	A	26	25	1	0	149.0	636	153	71	57	12	7	2	15	32	0	145	4	0	10	10	.500	0	0--	-	3.74	3.44
2005 Tampa	A+	26	25	0	1	147.1	589	118	56	52	12	2	5	9	34	0	169	5	1	10	9	.526	0	0--	-	2.53	3.18
2005 CtnSC	A	1	1	0	0	6.0	29	9	5	5	1	0	0	2	0	0	10	1	0	0	1	.000	0	0--	-	7.19	7.50
2005 Clmbs	AAA	1	0	0	0	1.0	3	0	0	0	0	0	0	0	0	0	2	0	0	0	0	-	0	0--	-	0.00	0.00

Year	Team	Lg	G	GS	CG	GF	IP	BFP	H	R	ER	HR	SH	SF	HB	TBB	IBB	SO	WP	Bk	W	L	Pct	ShO	Sv-Op	Hld	ERC	ERA
2006	Trntn	AA	28	28	1	0	166.1	672	118	72	62	14	6	3	17	55	1	175	3	0	12	10	.545	1	0--	-	2.59	3.35
2007	S-WB	AAA	14	14	0	0	69.1	317	82	40	32	7	2	3	3	35	0	55	3	0	4	4	.500	0	0--	-	5.83	4.15
2007	Trntn	AA	6	6	0	0	26.2	113	22	18	16	5	1	1	2	12	0	28	2	0	2	1	.667	0	0--	-	4.24	5.40
2008	Clmbs	AAA	27	27	0	0	143.0	611	129	80	74	15	7	3	3	66	3	125	2	0	6	13	.316	0	0--	-	3.88	4.66
2007	NYY	AL	6	6	0	0	27.0	124	29	19	19	6	0	0	0	17	1	18	2	1	3	1	.750	0	0-0	0	6.37	6.33
2008	Was	NL	2	2	0	0	10.1	48	12	5	5	2	0	0	0	7	1	8	1	0	1	1	.500	0	0-0	0	6.90	4.35
2 ML YEARS			8	8	0	0	37.1	172	41	24	24	8	0	0	0	24	2	26	3	1	4	2	.667	0	0-0	0	6.51	5.79

Buck Coats

Bats: L **Throws:** R **Pos:** LF-7; PR-3   **Ht:** 6'3" **Wt:** 195 **Born:** 6/9/1982 **Age:** 27

			BATTING																			BASERUNNING				AVERAGES		
Year	Team	Lg	G	AB	H	2B	3B	HR	(Hm	Rd)	TB	R	RBI	RC	TBB	IBB	SO	HBP	SH	SF		SB	CS	SB%	GDP	Avg	OBP	Slg
2008	Syrcse*	AAA	114	447	128	23	5	7	(-	-)	182	67	44	65	36	1	89	4	2	4		14	7	.67	9	.286	.342	.407
2006	ChC	NL	18	18	3	1	0	1	(0	1)	7	2	1	0	0	0	6	0	0	1		0	0	-	1	.167	.167	.389
2007	Cin	NL	20	34	7	4	0	0	(0	0)	11	2	2	2	3	0	15	0	0	1		0	0	-	1	.206	.263	.324
2008	Tor	AL	8	5	1	0	0	0	(0	0)	1	0	0	0	1	0	2	0	0	0		1	0	1.00	0	.200	.333	.200
3 ML YEARS			46	57	11	5	0	1	(0	1)	19	4	3	2	4	0	23	0	0	1		1	0	1.00	2	.193	.242	.333

Todd Coffey

Pitches: R **Bats:** R **Pos:** RP-26   **Ht:** 6'5" **Wt:** 240 **Born:** 9/9/1980 **Age:** 28

Year	Team	Lg	G	GS	CG	GF	IP	BFP	H	R	ER	HR	SH	SF	HB	TBB	IBB	SO	WP	Bk	W	L	Pct	ShO	Sv-Op	Hld	ERC	ERA
2008	Lsvlle*	AAA	34	0	0	13	39.1	181	49	23	19	4	1	1	0	15	0	43	4	1	3	3	.500	0	2--	-	5.34	4.35
2005	Cin	NL	57	0	0	14	58.0	265	84	33	29	5	3	2	5	11	2	26	1	0	4	1	.800	0	1-2	3	6.11	4.50
2006	Cin	NL	81	0	0	28	78.0	340	85	34	31	7	0	1	2	27	5	60	4	0	6	7	.462	0	8-12	15	4.29	3.58
2007	Cin	NL	58	0	0	8	51.0	242	70	36	33	12	1	0	5	19	4	43	4	0	2	1	.667	0	0-3	7	7.58	5.82
2008	2 Tms	NL	26	0	0	9	26.2	116	31	13	13	4	2	1	1	8	0	15	0	0	1	0	1.000	0	0-0	1	5.19	4.39
08	Cin	NL	17	0	0	6	19.1	87	25	13	13	4	1	1	1	6	0	8	0	0	0	0	-	0	0-0	0	6.57	6.05
08	Mil	NL	9	0	0	3	7.1	29	6	0	0	1	0	0	0	2	0	7	0	0	1	0	1.000	0	0-0	1	2.09	0.00
4 ML YEARS			222	0	0	59	213.2	963	270	116	106	28	6	4	13	65	11	144	9	0	13	9	.591	0	9-17	26	5.64	4.46

Phil Coke

Pitches: L **Bats:** L **Pos:** RP-12   **Ht:** 6'1" **Wt:** 210 **Born:** 7/19/1982 **Age:** 26

Year	Team	Lg	G	GS	CG	GF	IP	BFP	H	R	ER	HR	SH	SF	HB	TBB	IBB	SO	WP	Bk	W	L	Pct	ShO	Sv-Op	Hld	ERC	ERA
2003	Yanks	R	10	0	0	3	12.0	53	13	7	5	0	0	1	0	3	0	5	3	0	0	0	-	0	0--	-	3.11	3.75
2004	StIsInd	A-	3	1	0	1	8.0	35	9	6	6	1	0	0	0	3	0	7	2	0	0	0	-	0	0--	-	4.91	6.75
2004	Yanks	R	7	1	0	1	11.1	54	18	7	5	0	1	0	0	3	0	13	1	1	0	1	.000	0	0--	-	6.17	3.97
2005	CtnSC	A	24	18	0	0	103.0	459	122	67	62	11	3	3	2	34	0	68	5	1	8	11	.421	0	0--	-	4.95	5.42
2006	CtnSC	A	5	2	0	2	17.0	64	10	1	1	0	0	0	1	4	0	19	0	0	1	0	1.000	0	1--	-	1.30	0.53
2006	Tampa	A+	22	18	1	1	110.0	470	101	52	44	6	7	3	2	35	0	88	6	0	5	7	.417	0	0--	-	3.00	3.60
2007	Tampa	A+	17	16	1	1	99.0	411	93	36	34	4	0	2	4	37	0	76	3	0	7	3	.700	1	0--	-	3.40	3.09
2008	Trntn	AA	23	20	1	1	118.1	484	105	39	33	7	4	1	0	39	1	115	1	0	9	4	.692	0	0--	-	2.96	2.51
2008	S-WB	AAA	14	1	0	1	17.1	76	19	11	9	0	1	0	0	5	0	22	1	0	2	2	.500	0	0--	-	3.38	4.67
2008	NYY	AL	12	0	0	0	14.2	52	8	1	1	0	0	0	0	2	0	14	1	0	1	0	1.000	0	0-0	5	0.89	0.61

Jesus Colome

Pitches: R **Bats:** R **Pos:** RP-61   **Ht:** 6'2" **Wt:** 238 **Born:** 12/23/1977 **Age:** 31

Year	Team	Lg	G	GS	CG	GF	IP	BFP	H	R	ER	HR	SH	SF	HB	TBB	IBB	SO	WP	Bk	W	L	Pct	ShO	Sv-Op	Hld	ERC	ERA
2001	TB	AL	30	0	0	9	48.2	209	37	22	18	8	2	2	2	25	4	31	2	0	2	3	.400	0	0-0	6	3.62	3.33
2002	TB	AL	32	0	0	15	41.1	204	56	41	38	6	4	1	2	33	5	33	5	0	2	7	.222	0	0-5	3	8.57	8.27
2003	TB	AL	54	0	0	24	74.0	334	69	37	37	9	2	4	3	46	5	69	7	0	3	7	.300	0	2-8	11	4.76	4.50
2004	TB	AL	33	0	0	9	41.1	169	28	16	15	4	5	0	1	18	1	40	1	1	2	2	.500	0	3-4	8	2.54	3.27
2005	TB	AL	36	0	0	18	45.1	212	54	29	23	7	1	0	2	18	3	28	5	0	2	3	.400	0	0-1	2	5.46	4.57
2006	TB	AL	1	0	0	0	0.1	2	0	1	1	0	0	0	0	1	0	0	0	0	0	0	-	0	0-0	0	7.00	27.00
2007	Was	NL	61	0	0	16	66.0	286	64	30	28	6	4	6	1	27	3	43	4	0	5	1	.833	0	1-4	12	3.83	3.82
2008	Was	NL	61	0	0	25	71.0	312	61	38	34	6	7	2	4	39	4	55	7	0	2	2	.500	0	0-2	1	3.86	4.31
8 ML YEARS			308	0	0	116	388.0	1728	369	214	194	46	25	15	15	207	25	299	31	1	18	25	.419	0	6-24	43	4.48	4.50

Bartolo Colon

Pitches: R **Bats:** R **Pos:** SP-7   **Ht:** 5'11" **Wt:** 245 **Born:** 5/24/1973 **Age:** 36

Year	Team	Lg	G	GS	CG	GF	IP	BFP	H	R	ER	HR	SH	SF	HB	TBB	IBB	SO	WP	Bk	W	L	Pct	ShO	Sv-Op	Hld	ERC	ERA
2008	Pwtckt*	AAA	9	9	0	0	31.2	123	23	9	8	2	0	0	0	6	0	21	0	1	3	1	.750	0	0--	-	1.71	2.27
1997	Cle	AL	19	17	1	0	94.0	427	107	66	59	12	4	1	3	45	1	66	5	0	4	7	.364	0	0-0	0	5.53	5.65
1998	Cle	AL	31	31	6	0	204.0	883	205	91	84	15	10	2	3	79	5	158	4	0	14	9	.609	2	0-0	0	3.87	3.71
1999	Cle	AL	32	32	1	0	205.0	858	185	97	90	24	5	4	7	76	5	161	4	0	18	5	.783	1	0-0	0	3.68	3.95
2000	Cle	AL	30	30	2	0	188.0	807	163	86	81	21	2	3	4	98	4	212	4	0	15	8	.652	1	0-0	0	3.97	3.88
2001	Cle	AL	34	34	1	0	222.1	947	220	106	101	26	8	4	2	90	2	201	4	1	14	12	.538	0	0-0	0	4.24	4.09
2002	2 Tms	AL	33	33	8	0	233.1	966	219	85	76	20	19	6	2	70	5	149	2	0	20	8	.714	3	0-0	0	3.29	2.93
2003	CWS	AL	34	34	9	0	242.0	994	223	107	104	30	5	8	5	67	3	173	8	3	15	13	.536	0	0-0	0	3.47	3.87
2004	LAA	AL	34	34	0	0	208.1	897	215	122	116	38	5	8	5	71	1	158	1	0	18	12	.600	0	0-0	0	4.64	5.01
2005	LAA	AL	33	33	2	0	222.2	906	215	93	86	26	9	4	3	43	0	157	2	1	21	8	.724	0	0-0	0	3.28	3.48
2006	LAA	AL	10	10	1	0	56.1	251	71	39	36	11	0	3	0	11	0	31	1	0	1	5	.167	1	0-0	0	5.61	5.11

Year Team Lg	G	GS	CG	GF	IP	BFP	H	R	ER	HR	SH	SF	HB	TBB	IBB	SO	WP	Bk	W	L	Pct	ShO	Sv-Op	Hld	ERC	ERA
2007 LAA AL	19	18	0	0	99.1	453	132	74	70	15	4	3	5	29	1	76	1	0	6	8	.429	0	0-0	1	6.17	6.34
2008 Bos AL	7	7	0	0	39.0	173	44	23	17	5	3	2	2	10	0	27	0	0	4	2	.667	0	0-0	0	4.53	3.92
02 Cle AL	16	16	4	0	116.1	467	104	37	33	11	6	3	2	31	1	75	3	0	10	4	.714	2	0-0	0	3.09	2.55
02 Mon AL	17	17	4	0	117.0	499	115	48	43	9	13	3	0	39	4	74	1	0	10	4	.714	1	0-0	0	3.48	3.31
Postseason	9	9	1	0	52.1	215	49	21	21	5	0	0	1	22	1	41	0	0	2	3	.400	0	0-0	0	4.01	3.61
12 ML YEARS	316	313	31	0	2014.1	8552	1999	989	916	243	78	46	42	689	27	1569	38	5	150	97	.607	8	0-0	1	4.03	4.09

Clay Condrey

Pitches: R Bats: R Pos: RP-56 Ht: 6'3" Wt: 215 Born: 11/19/1975 Age: 33

Year Team Lg	G	GS	CG	GF	IP	BFP	H	R	ER	HR	SH	SF	HB	TBB	IBB	SO	WP	Bk	W	L	Pct	ShO	Sv-Op	Hld	ERC	ERA
2002 SD NL	9	3	0	2	26.2	106	20	7	5	1	2	2	2	8	1	16	1	1	1	2	.333	0	0-0	3	2.29	1.69
2003 SD NL	9	6	0	0	34.0	168	43	32	32	7	3	0	3	21	4	25	0	0	1	2	.333	0	0-0	0	7.50	8.47
2006 Phi NL	21	0	0	10	28.2	122	35	11	10	3	2	1	0	9	2	16	0	0	2	2	.500	0	0-1	1	5.14	3.14
2007 Phi NL	39	0	0	14	50.0	228	61	30	28	4	1	3	5	16	3	27	1	0	5	0	1.000	0	2-2	2	5.14	5.04
2008 Phi NL	56	0	0	30	69.0	303	85	26	25	6	1	0	2	19	8	34	1	0	3	4	.429	0	1-1	1	4.77	3.26
Postseason	1	0	0	0	1.2	8	4	1	1	0	0	0	0	0	0	2	0	0	0	0	-	0	0-0	0	11.50	5.40
5 ML YEARS	134	9	0	56	208.1	927	244	106	100	21	9	6	12	73	18	118	3	1	12	10	.545	0	3-4	7	4.98	4.32

Brooks Conrad

Bats: B Throws: R Pos: 3B-4; 2B-2 Ht: 5'11" Wt: 190 Born: 1/16/1980 Age: 29

Year Team Lg	G	AB	H	2B	3B	HR	(Hm	Rd)	TB	R	RBI	RC	TBB	IBB	SO	HBP	SH	SF	SB	CS	SB%	GDP	Avg	OBP	Slg
2001 Pittsfld A-	65	232	65	16	5	4	(-	-)	103	41	39	44	26	3	52	13	4	6	14	2	.88	1	.280	.375	.444
2002 Mich A	133	499	143	25	14	14	(-	-)	238	94	94	92	62	0	102	7	1	8	18	8	.69	2	.287	.368	.477
2003 Lxngtn A	38	140	26	5	2	3	(-	-)	44	20	11	14	17	0	25	3	1	0	7	1	.88	2	.186	.288	.314
2003 Salem A+	99	345	98	24	3	11	(-	-)	161	50	61	62	42	3	60	6	5	3	4	2	.67	7	.284	.369	.467
2004 RdRck AA	129	480	139	38	6	13	(-	-)	228	84	83	86	63	1	105	1	5	12	8	7	.53	8	.290	.365	.475
2005 RdRck AAA	113	418	110	22	3	21	(-	-)	201	84	58	73	52	3	104	1	4	5	12	3	.80	7	.263	.347	.481
2005 CpChr AA	22	77	18	6	1	2	(-	-)	32	13	11	14	16	1	15	1	0	0	8	0	1.00	1	.234	.372	.416
2006 RdRck AAA	138	533	143	40	16	24	(-	-)	287	101	94	99	54	2	134	4	1	8	15	6	.71	5	.268	.336	.538
2007 RdRck AAA	139	533	116	36	3	22	(-	-)	224	85	70	73	63	5	144	5	1	3	12	3	.80	4	.218	.305	.420
2008 Scrmto AAA	117	465	113	29	5	28	(-	-)	236	86	91	76	46	1	127	2	2	2	4	1	.80	5	.243	.313	.508
2008 Oak AL	6	19	3	1	0	0	(0	0)	4	0	2	1	0	0	9	0	0	0	0	0	-	1	.158	.158	.211

Jose Contreras

Pitches: R Bats: R Pos: SP-20 Ht: 6'4" Wt: 255 Born: 12/6/1971 Age: 37

Year Team Lg	G	GS	CG	GF	IP	BFP	H	R	ER	HR	SH	SF	HB	TBB	IBB	SO	WP	Bk	W	L	Pct	ShO	Sv-Op	Hld	ERC	ERA
2008 Charltt* AAA	1	1	0	0	5.0	19	4	3	3	0	0	0	0	3	0	4	0	0	0	0	-	0	0--	-	3.52	5.40
2003 NYY AL	18	9	0	2	71.0	293	52	27	26	4	0	1	5	30	1	72	2	0	7	2	.778	0	0-1	1	2.71	3.30
2004 2 Tms AL	31	31	0	0	170.1	758	166	114	104	31	3	6	8	84	1	150	17	0	13	9	.591	0	0-0	0	5.05	5.50
2005 CWS AL	32	32	1	0	204.2	857	177	91	82	23	7	2	9	75	2	154	20	2	15	7	.682	0	0-0	0	3.46	3.61
2006 CWS AL	30	30	1	0	196.0	833	194	101	93	20	2	8	10	55	4	134	16	0	13	9	.591	1	0-0	0	3.72	4.27
2007 CWS AL	32	30	2	2	189.0	858	232	134	117	21	8	10	15	62	1	113	3	0	10	17	.370	2	0-0	0	5.49	5.57
2008 CWS AL	20	20	1	0	121.0	522	130	64	61	12	4	2	3	35	0	70	6	0	7	6	.538	0	0-0	0	4.13	4.54
04 NYY AL	18	18	0	0	95.2	425	93	66	60	22	1	4	6	42	1	82	10	0	8	5	.615	0	0-0	0	5.18	5.64
04 CWS AL	13	13	0	0	74.2	333	73	48	44	9	2	2	2	42	0	68	7	0	5	4	.556	0	0-0	0	4.87	5.30
Postseason	12	4	1	3	43.0	176	37	18	18	2	5	1	3	9	0	31	3	0	3	3	.500	0	0-1	2	2.52	3.77
6 ML YEARS	163	152	5	4	952.0	4121	951	531	483	111	24	29	50	341	9	693	64	2	65	50	.565	3	0-1	1	4.20	4.57

Aaron Cook

Pitches: R Bats: R Pos: SP-32 Ht: 6'3" Wt: 215 Born: 2/8/1979 Age: 30

Year Team Lg	G	GS	CG	GF	IP	BFP	H	R	ER	HR	SH	SF	HB	TBB	IBB	SO	WP	Bk	W	L	Pct	ShO	Sv-Op	Hld	ERC	ERA
2002 Col NL	9	5	0	1	35.2	154	41	18	18	4	0	0	2	13	0	14	0	0	2	1	.667	0	0-0	1	5.31	4.54
2003 Col NL	43	16	1	4	124.0	579	160	89	83	8	4	6	8	57	7	43	10	0	4	6	.400	0	0-0	1	5.95	6.02
2004 Col NL	16	16	1	0	96.2	433	112	47	46	7	5	1	7	39	5	40	6	1	6	4	.600	0	0-0	0	5.05	4.28
2005 Col NL	13	13	2	0	83.1	357	101	38	34	8	1	3	2	16	2	24	3	0	7	2	.778	0	0-0	0	4.53	3.67
2006 Col NL	32	32	0	0	212.2	915	242	107	100	17	8	5	7	55	11	92	2	0	9	15	.375	0	0-0	0	4.23	4.23
2007 Col NL	25	25	2	0	166.0	698	178	87	76	15	6	3	6	44	6	61	0	0	8	7	.533	0	0-0	0	4.05	4.12
2008 Col NL	32	32	2	0	211.1	886	236	102	93	13	9	4	4	48	2	96	6	0	16	9	.640	1	0-0	0	3.92	3.96
Postseason	1	1	0	0	6.0	23	6	3	3	1	0	0	0	0	0	2	0	0	0	1	.000	0	0-0	0	3.02	4.50
7 ML YEARS	170	139	8	5	929.2	4022	1070	488	450	72	33	22	36	272	33	370	27	1	52	44	.542	1	0-0	2	4.50	4.36

Alex Cora

Bats: L Throws: R Pos: SS-69; 2B-7; PR-6; PH-1 Ht: 6'0" Wt: 200 Born: 10/18/1975 Age: 33

Year Team Lg	G	AB	H	2B	3B	HR	(Hm	Rd)	TB	R	RBI	RC	TBB	IBB	SO	HBP	SH	SF	SB	CS	SB%	GDP	Avg	OBP	Slg
2008 Pwtckt* AAA	3	11	3	0	0	0	(-	-)	3	2	0	0	0	0	2	0	0	0	0	0	-	1	.273	.273	.273
1998 LAD NL	29	33	4	0	1	0	(0	0)	6	1	0	1	2	0	8	1	2	0	0	0	-	0	.121	.194	.182
1999 LAD NL	11	30	5	1	0	0	(0	0)	6	2	3	0	0	0	4	1	0	0	0	0	-	1	.167	.194	.200
2000 LAD NL	109	353	84	18	6	4	(2	2)	126	39	32	38	26	4	53	7	6	2	4	1	.80	6	.238	.302	.357
2001 LAD NL	134	405	88	18	3	4	(2	2)	124	38	29	30	31	6	58	8	3	2	0	2	.00	16	.217	.285	.306
2002 LAD NL	115	258	75	14	4	5	(4	1)	112	37	28	46	26	4	38	7	2	0	7	2	.78	3	.291	.371	.434

						BATTING																		BASERUNNING					AVERAGES		
Year	Team	Lg	G	AB	H	2B	3B	HR	(Hm	Rd)	TB	R	RBI	RC	TBB	IBB	SO	HBP	SH	SF				SB	CS	SB%	GDP	Avg	OBP	Slg
2003	LAD	NL	148	477	119	24	3	4	(3	1)	161	39	34	46	16	3	59	10	9	2				4	2	.67	5	.249	.287	.338
2004	LAD	NL	138	405	107	9	4	10	(4	6)	154	47	47	63	47	10	41	18	12	2				3	4	.43	9	.264	.364	.380
2005	2 Tms	AL	96	250	58	8	4	3	(1	2)	83	25	24	21	11	0	30	5	4	3				7	2	.78	6	.232	.275	.332
2006	Bos	AL	96	235	56	7	2	1	(1	0)	70	31	18	24	19	1	29	6	4	0				6	2	.75	4	.238	.312	.298
2007	Bos	AL	83	207	51	10	5	3	(0	3)	80	30	18	19	7	2	23	9	7	2				1	1	.50	5	.246	.298	.386
2008	Bos	AL	75	152	41	8	2	0	(0	0)	53	14	9	19	16	1	13	9	1	1				1	1	.50	3	.270	.371	.349
05	Cle	AL	49	146	30	5	2	1	(1	0)	42	11	8	9	5	0	18	4	1	1				6	0	1.00	3	.205	.250	.288
05	Bos	AL	47	104	28	3	2	2	(0	2)	41	14	16	12	6	0	12	1	3	2				1	2	.33	3	.269	.310	.394
	Postseason		9	15	2	0	1	0	(0	0)	4	1	1	0	0	0	3	1	1	0				0	0	-	2	.133	.188	.267
11 ML YEARS			1034	2805	688	117	34	34	(17	17)	975	303	242	307	201	31	356	81	50	14				33	17	.66	58	.245	.313	.348

Roy Corcoran

Pitches: R **Bats:** R **Pos:** RP-50   **Ht:** 5'10" **Wt:** 170 **Born:** 5/11/1980 **Age:** 29

			HOW MUCH HE PITCHED						WHAT HE GAVE UP											THE RESULTS						
Year	Team	Lg	G	GS	CG	GF	IP	BFP	H	R	ER	HR	SH	SF	HB	TBB	IBB	SO	WP	Bk	W	L	Pct	ShO	Sv-Op	Hld	ERC	ERA
2008	Tacom*	AAA	15	0	0	11	14.1	68	14	8	8	1	1	0	2	13	2	11	5	0	0	0	-	0	4- -		6.23	5.02
2003	Mon	NL	5	0	0	2	7.1	31	7	2	1	0	0	0	0	3	0	2	1	0	0	0	-	0	0-0	0	3.20	1.23
2004	Mon	NL	5	0	0	3	5.1	28	7	4	4	0	0	0	0	5	0	4	0	0	0	0	-	0	0-0	0	7.12	6.75
2006	Was	NL	6	0	0	2	5.2	34	12	8	7	1	0	1	0	4	0	6	0	0	0	1	.000	0	0-1	0	12.96	11.12
2008	Sea	AL	50	0	0	13	72.2	316	65	31	26	1	3	3	2	36	4	39	3	0	6	2	.750	0	3-6	8	3.24	3.22
4 ML YEARS			66	0	0	20	91.0	409	91	45	38	2	3	4	2	48	4	51	4	0	6	3	.667	0	3-7	8	3.95	3.76

Chad Cordero

Pitches: R **Bats:** R **Pos:** RP-6   **Ht:** 6'0" **Wt:** 224 **Born:** 3/18/1982 **Age:** 27

			HOW MUCH HE PITCHED						WHAT HE GAVE UP											THE RESULTS						
Year	Team	Lg	G	GS	CG	GF	IP	BFP	H	R	ER	HR	SH	SF	HB	TBB	IBB	SO	WP	Bk	W	L	Pct	ShO	Sv-Op	Hld	ERC	ERA
2008	Ptomc*	A+	2	1	0	1	2.0	7	1	0	0	0	0	0	0	0	0	2	0	0	1	0	1.000	0	0- -	-	0.54	0.00
2003	Mon	NL	12	0	0	4	11.0	40	4	2	2	1	1	0	0	3	1	12	1	0	1	0	1.000	0	1-1	0	0.86	1.64
2004	Mon	NL	69	0	0	40	82.2	357	68	28	27	8	2	4	1	43	4	83	5	0	7	3	.700	0	14-18	8	3.47	2.94
2005	Was	NL	74	0	0	62	74.1	300	55	24	15	9	2	1	2	17	2	61	0	0	2	4	.333	0	47-54	0	2.22	1.82
2006	Was	NL	68	0	0	59	73.1	307	59	27	26	13	6	2	3	22	5	69	0	0	7	4	.636	0	29-33	0	3.10	3.19
2007	Was	NL	76	0	0	59	75.0	321	75	31	28	8	2	1	0	29	3	62	5	1	3	3	.500	0	37-46	1	4.02	3.36
2008	Was	NL	6	0	0	2	4.1	22	6	1	1	0	0	0	0	3	1	5	1	0	0	0	-	0	0-0	1	6.09	2.08
6 ML YEARS			305	0	0	226	320.2	1347	267	113	99	39	13	8	6	117	16	292	12	1	20	14	.588	0	128-152	11	3.12	2.78

Francisco Cordero

Pitches: R **Bats:** R **Pos:** RP-72   **Ht:** 6'3" **Wt:** 238 **Born:** 5/11/1975 **Age:** 34

			HOW MUCH HE PITCHED						WHAT HE GAVE UP											THE RESULTS						
Year	Team	Lg	G	GS	CG	GF	IP	BFP	H	R	ER	HR	SH	SF	HB	TBB	IBB	SO	WP	Bk	W	L	Pct	ShO	Sv-Op	Hld	ERC	ERA
1999	Det	AL	20	0	0	4	19.0	91	19	7	7	2	2	4	0	18	2	19	1	0	2	2	.500	0	0-0	6	6.19	3.32
2000	Tex	AL	56	0	0	13	77.1	365	87	51	46	11	2	6	4	48	3	49	7	0	1	2	.333	0	0-3	4	6.15	5.35
2001	Tex	AL	3	0	0	2	2.1	12	3	1	1	0	0	0	0	2	1	1	1	0	0	1	.000	0	0-0	1	5.73	3.86
2002	Tex	AL	39	0	0	25	45.1	177	33	12	9	2	0	0	2	13	1	41	1	0	2	0	1.000	0	10-12	1	2.11	1.79
2003	Tex	AL	73	0	0	36	82.2	352	70	33	27	4	3	4	2	38	6	90	1	0	5	8	.385	0	15-25	18	3.08	2.94
2004	Tex	AL	67	0	0	63	71.2	304	60	19	17	1	5	1	4	32	2	79	3	2	3	4	.429	0	49-54	0	2.78	2.13
2005	Tex	AL	69	0	0	60	69.0	302	61	28	26	5	4	3	4	30	2	79	0	0	3	1	.750	0	37-45	0	3.47	3.39
2006	2 Tms		77	0	0	47	75.1	322	69	32	31	7	3	5	3	32	2	84	4	0	10	5	.667	0	22-33	16	3.79	3.70
2007	Mil	NL	66	0	0	58	63.1	261	52	23	21	4	2	1	1	18	1	86	2	0	0	4	.000	0	44-51	0	2.45	2.98
2008	Cin	NL	72	0	0	63	70.1	307	61	28	26	6	3	3	3	38	3	78	3	0	5	4	.556	0	34-40	0	3.86	3.33
06	Tex	AL	49	0	0	21	48.2	210	49	27	26	5	1	5	3	16	1	54	3	0	7	4	.636	0	6-15	15	4.05	4.81
06	Mil	NL	28	0	0	26	26.2	112	20	5	5	2	2	0	0	16	1	30	1	0	3	1	.750	0	16-18	1	3.30	1.69
10 ML YEARS			542	0	0	371	576.1	2493	515	234	211	42	24	27	20	269	23	606	23	2	31	31	.500	0	211-263	46	3.60	3.29

Bryan Corey

Pitches: R **Bats:** R **Pos:** RP-46   **Ht:** 6'0" **Wt:** 175 **Born:** 10/21/1973 **Age:** 35

			HOW MUCH HE PITCHED						WHAT HE GAVE UP											THE RESULTS						
Year	Team	Lg	G	GS	CG	GF	IP	BFP	H	R	ER	HR	SH	SF	HB	TBB	IBB	SO	WP	Bk	W	L	Pct	ShO	Sv-Op	Hld	ERC	ERA
2008	Pwtckt*	AAA	5	0	0	4	5.0	20	4	0	0	0	0	0	0	1	0	5	1	0	0	0	-	0	1- -	-	1.70	0.00
2008	Portlnd*	AAA	5	0	0	1	6.2	27	9	1	1	0	0	0	0	1	0	4	1	0	0	0	-	0	0- -	-	4.75	1.35
1998	Ari	NL	3	0	0	2	4.0	20	6	4	4	1	1	0	1	2	0	1	0	0	0	0	-	0	0-0	0	10.40	9.00
2002	LAD	NL	1	0	0	1	1.0	3	0	0	0	0	0	0	0	0	0	0	0	0	0	0	-	0	0-0	0	0.00	0.00
2006	2 Tms	AL	32	0	0	3	39.0	166	35	16	16	1	1	3	2	15	0	28	0	0	2	1	.667	0	0-0	3	3.13	3.69
2007	Bos	AL	9	0	0	2	9.1	32	6	2	2	0	1	1	0	4	0	6	0	0	1	0	1.000	0	0-0	1	2.13	1.93
2008	2 Tms	AL	46	0	0	10	45.0	198	53	34	34	8	3	2	0	12	4	22	2	1	1	3	.250	0	0-2	4	4.90	6.80
06	Tex	AL	16	0	0	3	17.1	75	15	5	5	0	1	1	0	8	0	13	0	0	1	1	.500	0	0-0	0	2.82	2.60
06	Bos	AL	16	0	0	0	21.2	91	20	11	11	1	0	2	2	7	0	15	0	0	1	0	1.000	0	0-0	3	3.39	4.57
08	Bos	AL	7	0	0	2	6.0	31	11	7	7	1	1	0	0	3	1	4	0	0	0	0	-	0	0-0	1	10.18	10.50
08	SD	NL	39	0	0	8	39.0	167	42	27	27	7	2	2	0	9	3	18	2	1	1	3	.250	0	0-2	3	4.19	6.23
5 ML YEARS			91	0	0	18	98.1	419	100	56	56	10	6	6	3	33	4	57	2	1	4	4	.500	0	0-2	8	4.02	5.13

Lance Cormier

Pitches: R **Bats:** R **Pos:** RP-44; SP-1 **Ht:** 6'1" **Wt:** 198 **Born:** 8/19/1980 **Age:** 28

Year	Team	Lg	G	GS	CG	GF	IP	BFP	H	R	ER	HR	SH	SF	HB	TBB	IBB	SO	WP	Bk	W	L	Pct	ShO	Sv-Op	Hld	ERC	ERA
2008	Norfolk*	AAA	9	0	0	2	18.2	72	12	4	2	0	1	0	0	5	2	12	1	0	1	1	.500	0	0--	-	1.29	0.96
2004	Ari	NL	17	5	0	3	45.1	218	62	42	41	13	2	3	2	25	2	24	2	1	1	4	.200	0	0-0	2	8.76	8.14
2005	Ari	NL	67	0	0	13	79.1	356	86	50	45	7	4	1	5	43	5	63	6	0	7	3	.700	0	0-1	13	5.30	5.11
2006	Atl	NL	29	9	0	5	73.2	333	90	44	40	8	1	4	2	39	7	43	2	0	4	5	.444	0	0-0	2	6.13	4.89
2007	Atl	NL	10	9	0	1	45.2	210	56	38	36	16	3	0	0	22	3	27	4	0	2	6	.250	0	0-0	0	7.66	7.09
2008	Bal	AL	45	1	0	10	71.2	319	78	36	32	4	1	3	1	34	3	46	2	1	3	3	.500	0	1-3	0	4.55	4.02
5 ML YEARS			168	24	0	32	315.2	1436	372	210	194	48	11	11	10	163	20	203	16	2	17	21	.447	0	1-4	17	6.13	5.53

Manny Corpas

Pitches: R **Bats:** R **Pos:** RP-76 **Ht:** 6'3" **Wt:** 170 **Born:** 12/3/1982 **Age:** 26

Year	Team	Lg	G	GS	CG	GF	IP	BFP	H	R	ER	HR	SH	SF	HB	TBB	IBB	SO	WP	Bk	W	L	Pct	ShO	Sv-Op	Hld	ERC	ERA
2006	Col	NL	35	0	0	3	32.1	136	36	13	13	3	0	0	2	8	1	27	2	0	1	2	.333	0	0-2	7	4.39	3.62
2007	Col	NL	78	0	0	46	78.0	306	63	20	18	6	2	1	2	20	3	58	0	0	4	2	.667	0	19-22	16	2.51	2.08
2008	Col	NL	76	0	0	20	79.2	346	93	41	40	7	6	1	2	23	4	50	1	0	3	4	.429	0	4-13	19	4.55	4.52
Postseason			9	0	0	8	10.1	37	6	1	1	0	0	0	1	0	0	7	0	0	1	0	1.000	0	5-6	0	0.90	0.87
3 ML YEARS			189	0	0	69	190.0	788	192	74	71	16	8	2	6	51	8	135	3	0	8	8	.500	0	23-37	42	3.65	3.36

Kevin Correia

Pitches: R **Bats:** R **Pos:** SP-19; RP-6 **Ht:** 6'3" **Wt:** 200 **Born:** 8/24/1980 **Age:** 28

Year	Team	Lg	G	GS	CG	GF	IP	BFP	H	R	ER	HR	SH	SF	HB	TBB	IBB	SO	WP	Bk	W	L	Pct	ShO	Sv-Op	Hld	ERC	ERA
2008	SnJos*	A+	1	1	0	0	3.1	12	1	0	0	0	0	0	0	1	0	1	0	0	0	0	-	0	0--	-	0.57	0.00
2008	Fresno*	AAA	2	2	0	0	12.0	43	8	2	2	1	0	0	0	0	0	15	0	0	1	0	1.000	0	0--	-	1.19	1.50
2003	SF	NL	10	7	0	1	39.1	173	41	16	16	6	1	1	4	18	1	28	2	0	3	1	.750	0	0-0	0	5.46	3.66
2004	SF	NL	12	1	0	5	19.0	92	25	20	17	3	3	3	1	10	0	14	0	0	0	1	.000	0	0-0	0	7.12	8.05
2005	SF	NL	16	11	0	1	58.1	264	61	31	30	12	5	1	4	31	2	44	2	0	2	5	.286	0	0-0	0	5.94	4.63
2006	SF	NL	48	0	0	9	69.2	295	64	27	27	5	1	4	3	22	0	57	0	0	2	0	1.000	0	0-1	10	3.25	3.49
2007	SF	NL	59	8	0	9	101.2	437	94	39	39	9	4	3	2	40	7	80	1	1	4	7	.364	0	0-3	12	3.48	3.45
2008	SF	NL	25	19	0	2	110.0	514	141	80	74	15	3	5	4	47	3	66	5	0	3	8	.273	0	0-0	0	6.19	6.05
6 ML YEARS			170	46	0	27	398.0	1775	426	213	203	50	17	17	18	168	13	289	10	1	14	22	.389	0	0-4	22	4.86	4.59

Chris Coste

Bats: R **Throws:** R **Pos:** C-78; PH-23; 1B-1 **Ht:** 6'1" **Wt:** 215 **Born:** 2/4/1973 **Age:** 36

			BATTING																	BASERUNNING				AVERAGES		
Year	Team	Lg	G	AB	H	2B	3B	HR	(Hm Rd)	TB	R	RBI	RC	TBB	IBB	SO	HBP	SH	SF	SB	CS	SB%	GDP	Avg	OBP	Slg
2006	Phi	NL	65	198	65	14	0	7	(4 3)	100	25	32	36	10	1	31	5	0	0	0	0	-	6	.328	.376	.505
2007	Phi	NL	48	129	36	3	0	5	(5 0)	54	15	22	17	4	1	20	2	2	0	0	0	-	1	.279	.311	.419
2008	Phi	NL	98	274	72	17	0	9	(7 2)	116	28	36	37	16	1	51	10	3	2	0	1	.00	7	.263	.325	.423
Postseason			1	1	0	0	0	0	(0 0)	0	0	0	0	0	0	0	0	0	0	0	0	-	0	.000	.000	.000
3 ML YEARS			211	601	173	34	0	21	(16 5)	270	68	90	90	30	3	102	17	5	2	0	1	.00	14	.288	.338	.449

Neal Cotts

Pitches: L **Bats:** L **Pos:** RP-50 **Ht:** 6'1" **Wt:** 200 **Born:** 3/25/1980 **Age:** 29

Year	Team	Lg	G	GS	CG	GF	IP	BFP	H	R	ER	HR	SH	SF	HB	TBB	IBB	SO	WP	Bk	W	L	Pct	ShO	Sv-Op	Hld	ERC	ERA
2008	Iowa*	AAA	19	0	0	5	27.0	110	23	7	6	0	0	1	0	10	2	33	0	0	2	0	1.000	0	3--	-	2.46	2.00
2003	CWS	AL	4	4	0	0	13.1	69	15	12	12	1	1	0	0	17	0	10	0	0	1	1	.500	0	0-0	0	8.43	8.10
2004	CWS	AL	56	1	0	12	65.1	281	61	45	41	13	0	1	3	30	2	58	8	0	4	4	.500	0	0-2	4	4.84	5.65
2005	CWS	AL	69	0	0	10	60.1	248	38	15	13	1	0	3	4	29	5	58	3	0	4	0	1.000	0	0-2	13	2.03	1.94
2006	CWS	AL	70	0	0	14	54.0	251	64	33	31	12	3	1	3	24	6	43	3	0	1	2	.333	0	1-4	14	6.24	5.17
2007	ChC	NL	16	0	0	4	16.2	76	15	9	9	1	1	2	3	9	0	14	0	0	1	0	1.000	0	0-0	2	4.41	4.86
2008	ChC	NL	50	0	0	7	35.2	160	38	18	17	7	3	0	1	13	2	43	3	0	0	2	.000	0	0-2	9	4.87	4.29
Postseason			6	0	0	2	2.1	9	1	0	0	0	0	0	0	1	0	2	0	0	1	0	1.000	0	0-0	2	1.08	0.00
6 ML YEARS			265	5	0	47	245.1	1085	231	132	123	35	8	7	14	122	15	226	17	0	10	10	.500	0	1-10	42	4.54	4.51

Craig Counsell

Bats: L **Throws:** R **Pos:** 3B-38; PH-38; SS-24; 2B-19 **Ht:** 6'0" **Wt:** 179 **Born:** 8/21/1970 **Age:** 38

			BATTING																	BASERUNNING				AVERAGES		
Year	Team	Lg	G	AB	H	2B	3B	HR	(Hm Rd)	TB	R	RBI	RC	TBB	IBB	SO	HBP	SH	SF	SB	CS	SB%	GDP	Avg	OBP	Slg
1995	Col	NL	3	1	0	0	0	0	(0 0)	0	0	0	0	1	0	0	0	0	0	0	0	-	0	.000	.500	.000
1997	2 Tms	NL	52	164	49	9	2	1	(1 0)	65	20	16	24	18	2	17	3	3	1	1	1	.50	5	.299	.376	.396
1998	Fla	NL	107	335	84	19	5	4	(2 2)	125	43	40	48	51	7	47	4	8	1	3	0	1.00	5	.251	.355	.373
1999	2 Tms	NL	87	174	38	7	0	0	(0 0)	45	24	11	12	14	0	24	0	5	2	1	1	1.00	2	.218	.274	.259
2000	Ari	NL	67	152	48	8	1	2	(0 2)	64	23	11	25	20	0	18	2	1	1	3	3	.50	4	.316	.400	.421
2001	Ari	NL	141	458	126	22	3	4	(4 0)	166	76	38	61	61	3	76	2	6	6	8	8	.43	9	.275	.359	.362
2002	Ari	NL	112	436	123	22	1	2	(0 2)	153	63	51	65	45	3	52	1	4	3	7	5	.58	10	.282	.348	.351
2003	Ari	NL	89	303	71	6	3	3	(3 0)	92	40	21	29	41	0	32	2	3	2	11	4	.73	4	.234	.328	.304
2004	Mil	NL	140	473	114	19	5	2	(2 0)	149	59	23	48	59	9	88	5	5	3	17	4	.81	5	.241	.330	.315
2005	Ari	NL	150	578	148	34	4	9	(5 4)	217	85	42	80	78	4	69	8	2	4	26	7	.79	8	.256	.350	.375
2006	Ari	NL	105	372	95	14	4	4	(3 1)	129	56	30	45	31	0	47	9	2	1	15	8	.65	1	.255	.327	.347
2007	Mil	NL	122	282	62	12	2	3	(0 3)	87	31	24	29	41	1	47	3	6	2	4	2	.67	7	.220	.323	.309

Year	Team	Lg	G	AB	H	2B	3B	HR	(Hm	Rd)	TB	R	RBI	RC	TBB	IBB	SO	HBP	SH	SF	SB	CS	SB%	GDP	Avg	OBP	Slg
2008	Ogden	NL	110	248	56	14	1	1	(1	0)	75	31	14	26	46	1	42	5	1	2	3	1	.75	5	.226	.355	.302
97	Col	NL	1	0	0	0	0	0	(0	0)	0	0	0	0	0	0	0	0	0	0	0	0	-	0	-	-	-
97	Fla	NL	51	164	49	9	2	1	(1	0)	65	20	16	24	18	2	17	3	3	1	1	1	.50	5	.299	.376	.396
99	Fla	NL	37	66	10	1	0	0	(0	0)	11	4	2	1	5	0	10	0	2	0	0	0	-	1	.152	.211	.167
99	LAD	NL	50	108	28	6	0	0	(0	0)	34	20	9	11	9	0	14	0	3	2	1	0	1.00	1	.259	.311	.315
	Postseason		31	102	25	5	0	2	(1	1)	36	12	13	11	12	3	20	1	7	1	2	0	1.00	1	.245	.328	.353
13 ML YEARS			1285	3976	1014	186	31	35	(20	15)	1367	551	321	492	506	33	559	44	46	28	97	43	.69	65	.255	.343	.344

Callix Crabbe

Bats: B Throws: R Pos: PH-9; 2B-5; PR-4; SS-3; RF-2; LF-1　　　　**Ht: 5'7" Wt: 184 Born: 2/14/1983 Age: 26**

Year	Team	Lg	G	AB	H	2B	3B	HR	(Hm	Rd)	TB	R	RBI	RC	TBB	IBB	SO	HBP	SH	SF	SB	CS	SB%	GDP	Avg	OBP	Slg
2002	Ogden	R+	67	250	82	16	4	4	(-	-)	118	55	38	50	29	0	34	5	2	1	22	9	.71	2	.328	.407	.472
2003	Beloit	A	129	465	121	25	6	1	(-	-)	161	79	46	66	68	0	52	3	18	3	25	9	.74	12	.260	.356	.346
2004	Hi Dsrt	A+	132	540	157	26	11	7	(-	-)	226	89	61	90	59	0	64	8	4	4	34	11	.76	13	.291	.367	.419
2005	Hntsvl	AA	119	387	94	16	4	1	(-	-)	121	42	33	51	65	4	65	2	20	1	19	6	.76	17	.243	.354	.313
2006	Hntsvl	AA	129	472	126	18	2	5	(-	-)	163	59	46	70	71	2	62	7	16	5	32	13	.71	2	.267	.368	.345
2007	Nashv	AAA	130	457	131	23	9	9	(-	-)	199	84	38	78	67	2	70	3	8	6	17	14	.55	6	.287	.377	.435
2008	Nashv	AAA	69	204	55	9	3	1	(-	-)	73	32	18	33	40	0	41	1	5	4	9	5	.64	3	.270	.386	.358
2008	SD	NL	21	34	6	1	0	0	(0	0)	7	4	2	2	4	0	6	1	0	0	1	0	1.00	0	.176	.282	.206

Jesse Crain

Pitches: R Bats: R Pos: RP-66　　　　**Ht: 6'1" Wt: 215 Born: 7/5/1981 Age: 27**

			HOW MUCH HE PITCHED					WHAT HE GAVE UP										THE RESULTS							
Year	Team	Lg	G	GS	CG	GF	IP	BFP	H	R	ER	HR	SH	SF	HB	TBB	IBB	SO	WP	Bk	W	L	Pct	ShO	Sv-Op	Hld	ERC	ERA
2004	Min	AL	22	0	0	3	27.0	109	17	6	6	2	1	0	1	12	1	14	1	0	3	0	1.000	0	0-1	2	2.25	2.00
2005	Min	AL	75	0	0	17	79.2	326	61	28	24	6	9	3	5	29	7	25	2	0	12	5	.706	0	1-4	11	2.66	2.71
2006	Min	AL	68	0	0	24	76.2	325	79	31	30	6	1	2	2	18	2	60	1	0	4	5	.444	0	1-4	10	3.48	3.52
2007	Min	AL	18	0	0	5	16.1	71	19	16	10	4	0	1	1	4	0	10	0	1	2	.333		0	0-0	6	5.73	5.51
2008	Min	AL	66	0	0	14	62.2	268	62	29	25	6	0	2	1	24	3	50	2	0	5	4	.556	0	0-3	17	3.93	3.59
	Postseason		3	0	0	0	1.1	10	4	3	1	1	0	0	1	0	0	1	0	0	0	0	-	0	0-0	0	24.65	6.75
5 ML YEARS			249	0	0	63	262.1	1099	238	110	95	24	11	8	10	87	13	159	6	1	25	16	.610	0	2-12	46	3.33	3.26

Carl Crawford

Bats: L Throws: L Pos: LF-108; CF-1; DH-1; PH-1; PR-1　　　　**Ht: 6'2" Wt: 215 Born: 8/5/1981 Age: 27**

Year	Team	Lg	G	AB	H	2B	3B	HR	(Hm	Rd)	TB	R	RBI	RC	TBB	IBB	SO	HBP	SH	SF	SB	CS	SB%	GDP	Avg	OBP	Slg
2002	TB	AL	63	259	67	11	6	2	(1	1)	96	23	30	34	9	0	41	3	6	1	9	5	.64	0	.259	.290	.371
2003	TB	AL	151	630	177	18	9	5	(5	0)	228	80	54	80	26	4	102	1	1	3	55	10	.85	5	.281	.309	.362
2004	TB	AL	152	626	185	26	19	11	(6	5)	282	104	55	96	35	2	81	1	4	6	59	15	.80	2	.296	.331	.450
2005	TB	AL	156	644	194	33	15	15	(5	10)	302	101	81	102	27	1	84	5	5	6	46	8	.85	11	.301	.331	.469
2006	TB	AL	151	600	183	20	16	18	(7	11)	289	89	77	113	37	3	85	4	9	2	58	9	.87	8	.305	.348	.482
2007	TB	AL	143	584	184	37	9	11	(6	5)	272	93	80	97	32	5	112	5	1	2	50	10	.83	11	.315	.355	.466
2008	TB	AL	109	443	121	12	10	8	(3	5)	177	69	57	57	30	1	60	2	0	5	25	7	.78	10	.273	.319	.400
7 ML YEARS			925	3786	1111	157	84	70	(33	37)	1646	559	434	579	196	16	565	21	26	25	302	64	.83	47	.293	.330	.435

Joe Crede

Bats: R Throws: R Pos: 3B-97　　　　**Ht: 6'2" Wt: 230 Born: 4/26/1978 Age: 31**

Year	Team	Lg	G	AB	H	2B	3B	HR	(Hm	Rd)	TB	R	RBI	RC	TBB	IBB	SO	HBP	SH	SF	SB	CS	SB%	GDP	Avg	OBP	Slg
2008	Charltt*	AAA	5	16	2	0	0	0	(-	-)	2	0	0	0	0	0	3	0	0	0	0	0	-	1	.125	.125	.125
2000	CWS	AL	7	14	5	1	0	0	(0	0)	6	2	3	2	0	0	3	0	0	0	0	0	-	0	.357	.333	.429
2001	CWS	AL	17	50	11	1	1	0	(0	0)	14	1	7	4	3	0	11	1	0	1	1	0	1.00	1	.220	.273	.280
2002	CWS	AL	53	200	57	10	0	12	(7	5)	103	28	35	31	8	0	40	0	0	1	0	2	.00	1	.285	.311	.515
2003	CWS	AL	151	536	140	31	2	19	(11	8)	232	68	75	69	32	1	75	6	2	4	1	1	.50	11	.261	.308	.433
2004	CWS	AL	144	490	117	25	0	21	(12	9)	205	67	69	58	34	0	81	10	4	5	1	2	.33	14	.239	.299	.418
2005	CWS	AL	132	432	109	21	0	22	(12	10)	196	54	62	62	25	3	66	8	2	4	1	1	.50	7	.252	.303	.454
2006	CWS	AL	150	544	154	31	0	30	(16	14)	275	76	94	84	28	1	58	7	0	7	0	0	-	18	.283	.323	.506
2007	CWS	AL	47	167	36	5	0	4	(0	4)	53	13	22	18	10	0	24	0	0	1	1	0	1.00	1	.216	.258	.317
2008	CWS	AL	97	335	83	18	1	17	(11	6)	154	41	55	45	30	0	45	4	0	4	0	3	.00	10	.248	.314	.460
	Postseason		12	45	13	3	0	4	(2	2)	28	6	11	9	2	0	6	1	1	1	0	1	.00	1	.289	.327	.622
9 ML YEARS			798	2768	712	143	4	125	(69	56)	1238	350	422	373	170	5	403	36	8	28	4	12	.25	63	.257	.306	.447

Coco Crisp

Bats: B Throws: R Pos: CF-114; PR-8; PH-2　　　　**Ht: 6'0" Wt: 180 Born: 11/1/1979 Age: 29**

Year	Team	Lg	G	AB	H	2B	3B	HR	(Hm	Rd)	TB	R	RBI	RC	TBB	IBB	SO	HBP	SH	SF	SB	CS	SB%	GDP	Avg	OBP	Slg
2002	Cle	AL	32	127	33	9	2	1	(1	0)	49	16	9	19	11	0	19	0	3	2	4	1	.80	0	.260	.314	.386
2003	Cle	AL	99	414	110	15	6	3	(3	0)	146	55	27	48	23	1	51	0	7	3	15	9	.63	4	.266	.302	.353
2004	Cle	AL	139	491	146	24	2	15	(8	7)	219	78	71	72	36	4	69	0	9	2	20	13	.61	8	.297	.344	.446
2005	Cle	AL	145	594	178	42	4	16	(4	12)	276	86	69	92	44	1	81	0	13	5	15	6	.71	7	.300	.345	.465
2006	Bos	AL	105	413	109	22	2	8	(4	4)	159	58	36	51	31	1	67	1	7	0	22	4	.85	5	.264	.317	.385

Year Team	Lg	G	AB	H	2B	3B	HR	(Hm	Rd)	TB	R	RBI	RC	TBB	IBB	SO	HBP	SH	SF	SB	CS	SB%	GDP	Avg	OBP	Slg
2007 Bos	AL	145	526	141	28	7	6	(1	5)	201	85	60	68	50	1	84	1	9	5	28	6	.82	12	.268	.330	.382
2008 Bos	AL	118	361	102	18	3	7	(1	6)	147	55	41	49	35	0	59	1	8	4	20	7	.74	6	.283	.344	.407
Postseason		13	33	6	1	0	0	(0	0)	7	3	2	1	1	0	9	0	0	0	2	0	1.00	2	.182	.206	.212
7 ML YEARS		783	2926	819	158	26	56	(22	34)	1197	433	313	399	230	8	430	3	56	21	124	46	.73	42	.280	.331	.409

Bobby Crosby

Bats: R Throws: R Pos: SS-145; PR-1　　　　　　　　**Ht: 6'3" Wt: 206 Born: 1/12/1980 Age: 29**

Year Team	Lg	G	AB	H	2B	3B	HR	(Hm	Rd)	TB	R	RBI	RC	TBB	IBB	SO	HBP	SH	SF	SB	CS	SB%	GDP	Avg	OBP	Slg
2003 Oak	AL	11	12	0	0	0	0	(0	0)	0	1	0	0	1	0	5	1	0	0	0	0	-	0	.000	.143	.000
2004 Oak	AL	151	545	130	34	1	22	(11	11)	232	70	64	60	58	0	141	9	5	6	7	3	.70	20	.239	.319	.426
2005 Oak	AL	84	333	92	25	4	9	(3	6)	152	66	38	47	35	0	54	1	1	0	0	0	-	10	.276	.346	.456
2006 Oak	AL	96	358	82	12	0	9	(3	6)	121	42	40	38	36	1	76	0	2	2	8	1	.89	11	.229	.298	.338
2007 Oak	AL	93	349	79	16	0	8	(7	1)	119	40	31	26	23	1	62	2	0	0	10	2	.83	11	.226	.278	.341
2008 Oak	AL	145	556	132	39	1	7	(2	5)	194	66	61	52	47	0	96	0	0	2	7	3	.70	18	.237	.296	.349
6 ML YEARS		580	2153	515	126	6	55	(26	29)	818	285	234	223	200	2	434	13	8	11	32	9	.78	70	.239	.306	.380

Francisco Cruceta

Pitches: R Bats: R Pos: RP-13　　　　　　　　**Ht: 6'2" Wt: 215 Born: 7/4/1981 Age: 27**

		HOW MUCH HE PITCHED						WHAT HE GAVE UP											THE RESULTS						
Year Team	Lg	G	GS	CG	GF	IP	BFP	H	R	ER	HR	SH	SF	HB	TBB	IBB	SO	WP	Bk	W	L	Pct	ShO	Sv-Op	Hld	ERC	ERA
2008 Toledo*	AAA	32	0	0	11	42.2	188	39	21	20	0	3	1	2	24	2	61	4	0	2	3	.400	0	3- -	-	3.60	4.22
2004 Cle	AL	2	2	0	0	7.2	39	10	9	8	1	0	1	1	4	0	9	1	0	0	1	.000	0	0-0	0	6.85	9.39
2006 Sea	AL	4	1	0	1	6.2	34	10	8	8	2	0	1	0	6	0	2	1	0	0	0	-	0	0-0	0	11.77	10.80
2008 Det	AL	13	0	0	8	11.2	56	13	8	7	2	2	0	0	10	1	11	3	0	0	3	.000	0	0-2	1	7.19	5.40
3 ML YEARS		19	3	0	9	26.0	129	33	25	23	5	2	2	1	20	1	22	5	0	0	4	.000	0	0-2	1	8.17	7.96

Jose Cruz

Bats: B Throws: R Pos: PH-28; LF-10; CF-5; RF-3; PR-1　　　　**Ht: 6'0" Wt: 210 Born: 4/19/1974 Age: 35**

Year Team	Lg	G	AB	H	2B	3B	HR	(Hm	Rd)	TB	R	RBI	RC	TBB	IBB	SO	HBP	SH	SF	SB	CS	SB%	GDP	Avg	OBP	Slg
1997 2 Tms	AL	104	395	98	19	1	26	(11	15)	197	59	68	63	41	2	117	0	1	5	7	2	.78	5	.248	.315	.499
1998 Tor	AL	105	352	89	14	3	11	(4	7)	142	55	42	55	57	3	99	0	0	3	11	4	.73	0	.253	.354	.403
1999 Tor	AL	106	349	84	19	3	14	(8	6)	151	63	45	57	64	5	91	0	1	0	14	4	.78	5	.241	.358	.433
2000 Tor	AL	162	603	146	32	5	31	(15	16)	281	91	76	91	71	3	129	2	2	3	15	5	.75	11	.242	.323	.466
2001 Tor	AL	146	577	158	38	4	34	(15	19)	306	92	88	101	45	4	138	1	2	2	32	5	.86	8	.274	.326	.530
2002 Tor	AL	124	466	114	26	5	18	(11	7)	204	64	70	71	51	1	106	0	1	4	7	1	.88	8	.245	.317	.438
2003 SF	NL	158	539	135	26	1	20	(9	11)	223	90	68	71	102	6	121	0	2	7	5	8	.38	14	.250	.366	.414
2004 TB	AL	153	545	132	25	8	21	(13	8)	236	76	78	79	76	8	117	2	5	8	11	6	.65	6	.242	.333	.433
2005 3 Tms		115	370	93	24	2	18	(11	7)	175	46	50	55	66	3	101	0	0	1	0	2	.00	10	.251	.364	.473
2006 LAD	NL	86	223	52	16	1	5	(2	3)	85	34	17	27	43	2	54	0	4	3	5	1	.83	3	.233	.353	.381
2007 SD	NL	91	256	60	12	3	6	(3	3)	96	37	21	26	31	1	65	0	5	1	6	1	.86	3	.234	.316	.375
2008 Hou	NL	38	49	6	1	0	0	(0	0)	7	6	1	3	11	0	9	0	0	0	0	0	-	0	.122	.283	.143
97 Sea	AL	49	183	49	12	1	12	(7	5)	99	28	34	31	13	0	45	0	1	1	1	0	1.00	3	.268	.315	.541
97 Tor	AL	55	212	49	7	0	14	(4	10)	98	31	34	32	28	2	72	0	0	4	6	2	.75	2	.231	.316	.462
05 Ari	NL	64	202	43	9	0	12	(6	6)	88	23	28	25	42	2	54	0	0	1	0	1	.00	6	.213	.347	.436
05 Bos	AL	4	12	3	1	0	0	(0	0)	4	0	0	1	1	0	4	0	0	0	0	0	-	0	.250	.308	.333
05 LAD	NL	47	156	47	14	2	6	(5	1)	83	23	22	29	23	1	43	0	0	0	0	1	.00	4	.301	.391	.532
Postseason		4	11	0	0	0	0	(0	0)	0	0	1	0	2	1	4	0	1	0	0	0	-	0	.000	.154	.000
12 ML YEARS		1388	4724	1167	252	36	204	(102	102)	2103	713	624	699	658	38	1147	5	23	38	113	39	.74	73	.247	.337	.445

Juan Cruz

Pitches: R Bats: R Pos: RP-57　　　　　　　　**Ht: 6'2" Wt: 145 Born: 10/15/1978 Age: 30**

		HOW MUCH HE PITCHED						WHAT HE GAVE UP											THE RESULTS						
Year Team	Lg	G	GS	CG	GF	IP	BFP	H	R	ER	HR	SH	SF	HB	TBB	IBB	SO	WP	Bk	W	L	Pct	ShO	Sv-Op	Hld	ERC	ERA
2008 Tucsn*	AAA	2	2	0	0	3.0	12	3	1	1	0	0	0	0	0	0	4	0	0	0	0	-	0	0- -	1	1.95	3.00
2001 ChC	NL	8	8	0	0	44.2	185	40	16	16	4	2	0	2	17	1	39	0	0	3	1	.750	0	0-0	0	3.59	3.22
2002 ChC	NL	45	9	0	14	97.1	431	84	56	43	11	7	8	8	59	4	81	1	0	3	11	.214	0	1-4	3	4.49	3.98
2003 ChC	NL	25	6	0	3	61.0	284	66	44	41	7	7	2	7	28	0	65	4	0	2	7	.222	0	0-1	1	5.23	6.05
2004 Atl	NL	50	0	0	22	72.0	300	59	24	22	7	4	1	2	30	1	70	1	0	6	2	.750	0	0-0	2	3.25	2.75
2005 Oak	AL	28	0	0	14	32.2	159	38	33	27	5	0	2	4	22	4	34	3	0	0	3	.000	0	0-0	0	6.87	7.44
2006 Ari	NL	31	15	0	3	94.2	413	80	45	44	7	5	2	11	47	2	88	2	0	5	6	.455	0	0-0	0	3.82	4.18
2007 Ari	NL	53	0	0	15	61.0	262	45	28	21	7	2	2	5	32	3	87	1	2	6	1	.857	0	0-0	4	3.43	3.10
2008 Ari	NL	57	0	0	10	51.2	215	34	17	15	5	2	2	3	31	0	71	1	0	4	0	1.000	0	0-2	8	3.25	2.61
Postseason		8	0	0	2	9.0	44	7	5	4	0	1	0	1	8	0	15	1	0	0	0	-	0	0-0	4	4.12	4.00
8 ML YEARS		297	38	0	83	515.0	2249	446	263	229	53	29	19	42	266	15	535	13	2	29	31	.483	0	1-7	18	4.08	4.00

Luis Cruz

Bats: R Throws: R Pos: SS-20; 2B-2　　　　　　　　**Ht: 6'1" Wt: 200 Born: 2/10/1984 Age: 25**

Year Team	Lg	G	AB	H	2B	3B	HR	(Hm	Rd)	TB	R	RBI	RC	TBB	IBB	SO	HBP	SH	SF	SB	CS	SB%	GDP	Avg	OBP	Slg
2001 RedSx	R	53	197	51	9	0	3	(-	-)	69	18	18	18	7	0	17	1	0	2	1	4	.20	8	.259	.285	.350
2002 Augsta	A	58	202	38	7	1	3	(-	-)	56	15	15	10	9	0	30	0	1	2	0	2	.00	6	.188	.221	.277
2002 RedSx	R	21	72	21	4	0	0	(-	-)	25	10	9	8	3	0	6	1	1	0	2	2	.50	1	.292	.329	.347
2003 FtWyn	A	129	481	111	24	1	8	(-	-)	161	55	53	47	30	1	55	5	5	8	2	2	.50	15	.231	.279	.335

Year	Team	Lg	G	AB	H	2B	3B	HR	(Hm	Rd)	TB	R	RBI	RC	TBB	IBB	SO	HBP	SH	SF	SB	CS	SB%	GDP	Avg	OBP	Slg
2004	Lk Els	A+	124	512	142	35	3	8	(-	-)	207	75	72	64	24	1	56	3	6	6	3	7	.30	9	.277	.310	.404
2005	Mobile	AA	44	151	24	2	1	3	(-	-)	37	14	6	6	9	0	31	2	1	1	0	1	.00	7	.159	.215	.245
2006	Mobile	AA	130	499	130	35	3	12	(-	-)	207	65	65	64	29	1	62	2	5	4	8	4	.67	11	.261	.301	.415
2007	Portlnd	AAA	46	156	26	10	1	5	(-	-)	53	15	17	11	9	1	24	1	0	2	0	0	-	5	.167	.214	.340
2007	SnAnt	AA	69	238	60	10	0	4	(-	-)	82	24	19	25	13	1	20	2	0	3	3	0	1.00	5	.252	.293	.345
2008	Altna	AA	105	375	99	24	1	6	(-	-)	143	41	46	44	19	0	34	4	4	4	3	3	.50	7	.264	.303	.381
2008	Indy	AAA	32	120	39	10	0	3	(-	-)	58	19	15	18	3	1	14	1	3	0	2	4	.33	4	.325	.347	.483
2008	Pit	NL	22	67	15	3	0	0	(0	0)	18	6	3	4	3	0	2	2	2	0	1	1	.50	3	.224	.278	.269

Nelson Cruz

Bats: R Throws: R Pos: RF-31   Ht: 6'3" Wt: 230 Born: 7/1/1980 Age: 28

Year	Team	Lg	G	AB	H	2B	3B	HR	(Hm	Rd)	TB	R	RBI	RC	TBB	IBB	SO	HBP	SH	SF	SB	CS	SB%	GDP	Avg	OBP	Slg
2008	Okla*	AAA	103	383	131	18	3	37	(-	-)	266	93	99	108	56	4	87	5	0	4	24	8	.75	10	.342	.429	.695
2008	Rngrs*	R	1	4	1	1	0	0	(-	-)	2	1	1	1	2	0	1	0	0	0	0	0	-	0	.250	.500	.500
2005	Mil	NL	8	5	1	1	0	0	(0	0)	2	1	0	1	2	0	0	0	0	0	0	0	-	0	.200	.429	.400
2006	Tex	AL	41	130	29	3	0	6	(3	3)	50	15	22	18	7	0	32	0	0	1	1	0	1.00	1	.223	.261	.385
2007	Tex	AL	96	307	72	15	2	9	(4	5)	118	35	34	32	21	1	87	2	1	1	2	4	.33	5	.235	.287	.384
2008	Tex	AL	31	115	38	9	1	7	(4	3)	70	19	26	30	17	2	28	1	0	0	3	1	.75	1	.330	.421	.609
4 ML YEARS			176	557	140	28	3	22	(11	11)	240	70	82	81	47	3	147	3	1	2	6	5	.55	7	.251	.312	.431

Michael Cuddyer

Bats: R Throws: R Pos: RF-58; DH-6; PH-6; 1B-2; CF-1   Ht: 6'2" Wt: 215 Born: 3/27/1979 Age: 30

Year	Team	Lg	G	AB	H	2B	3B	HR	(Hm	Rd)	TB	R	RBI	RC	TBB	IBB	SO	HBP	SH	SF	SB	CS	SB%	GDP	Avg	OBP	Slg
2008	Roch*	AAA	4	10	3	2	0	0	(-	-)	5	3	1	2	3	0	3	0	0	0	0	0	-	1	.300	.462	.500
2001	Min	AL	8	18	4	2	0	0	(0	0)	6	1	1	2	2	0	6	0	0	0	1	0	1.00	0	.222	.300	.333
2002	Min	AL	41	112	29	7	0	4	(2	2)	48	12	13	14	8	0	30	1	1	1	2	0	1.00	3	.259	.311	.429
2003	Min	AL	35	102	25	1	3	4	(1	3)	44	14	8	10	12	0	19	0	0	0	1	1	.50	6	.245	.325	.431
2004	Min	AL	115	339	89	22	1	12	(8	4)	149	49	45	51	37	2	74	3	2	1	5	5	.50	8	.263	.339	.440
2005	Min	AL	126	422	111	25	3	12	(8	4)	178	55	42	43	41	5	93	3	1	3	3	4	.43	19	.263	.330	.422
2006	Min	AL	150	557	158	41	5	24	(15	9)	281	102	109	101	62	5	130	10	0	6	6	0	1.00	11	.284	.362	.504
2007	Min	AL	144	547	151	28	5	16	(8	8)	237	87	81	82	64	1	107	7	0	5	5	0	1.00	19	.276	.356	.433
2008	Min	AL	71	249	62	13	4	3	(1	2)	92	30	36	37	25	4	40	5	0	0	5	1	.83	7	.249	.330	.369
Postseason			16	49	17	1	1	1	(1	0)	23	4	5	2	4	1	12	0	0	0	0	2	.00	1	.347	.396	.469
8 ML YEARS			690	2346	629	139	21	75	(43	32)	1035	350	335	340	251	17	499	29	4	16	28	11	.72	74	.268	.344	.441

Johnny Cueto

Pitches: R Bats: R Pos: SP-31   Ht: 5'10" Wt: 183 Born: 2/15/1986 Age: 23

			HOW MUCH HE PITCHED						WHAT HE GAVE UP												THE RESULTS							
Year	Team	Lg	G	GS	CG	GF	IP	BFP	H	R	ER	HR	SH	SF	HB	TBB	IBB	SO	WP	Bk	W	L	Pct	ShO	Sv-Op	Hld	ERC	ERA
2005	Reds	R	13	6	0	4	43.0	191	49	31	24	2	2	4	5	8	0	38	1	4	2	2	.500	0	1--	-	3.99	5.02
2005	Srsota	A+	2	1	0	0	6.0	25	5	2	2	0	0	0	0	2	0	6	2	0	0	1	.000	0	0--	-	2.26	3.00
2006	Dayton	A	14	14	2	0	76.1	292	52	22	22	5	1	0	4	15	0	82	1	0	8	1	.889	2	0--	-	1.76	2.59
2006	Srsota	A+	12	12	1	0	61.2	255	48	25	24	6	1	1	6	23	0	61	3	3	7	2	.778	1	0--	-	3.16	3.50
2007	Srsota	AA	14	14	1	0	78.1	332	72	34	29	3	2	2	5	21	0	72	0	2	4	5	.444	0	0--	-	2.91	3.33
2007	Lsvlle	AAA	4	4	0	0	22.0	89	22	5	5	2	0	0	2	2	0	21	0	0	2	1	.667	0	0--	-	3.23	2.05
2007	Chatt	AA	10	10	0	0	61.0	252	52	24	21	6	4	4	8	11	0	77	2	1	6	3	.667	0	0--	-	2.91	3.10
2008	Cin	NL	31	31	0	0	174.0	769	178	101	93	29	9	5	14	68	1	158	6	1	9	14	.391	0	0-0	0	4.95	4.81

Aaron Cunningham

Bats: R Throws: R Pos: LF-18; RF-2; PH-2   Ht: 5'11" Wt: 195 Born: 4/24/1986 Age: 23

Year	Team	Lg	G	AB	H	2B	3B	HR	(Hm	Rd)	TB	R	RBI	RC	TBB	IBB	SO	HBP	SH	SF	SB	CS	SB%	GDP	Avg	OBP	Slg
2005	Bristol	R+	56	222	70	10	2	5	(-	-)	99	41	25	40	16	0	45	14	0	3	6	5	.55	3	.315	.392	.446
2005	Knapol	A-	10	26	3	0	0	0	(-	-)	3	7	2	0	3	0	7	0	0	0	1	0	1.00	0	.115	.207	.115
2006	Knapol	A-	95	341	104	26	3	11	(-	-)	169	58	41	66	34	1	72	13	11	3	19	10	.66	4	.305	.386	.496
2007	WinSa	A+	67	252	74	12	5	8	(-	-)	120	51	37	49	34	0	39	4	8	8	22	8	.73	4	.294	.376	.476
2007	Visalia	A+	29	123	44	11	2	3	(-	-)	68	25	20	25	5	0	23	2	3	2	5	3	.63	2	.358	.386	.553
2007	Mobile	AA	31	118	34	8	3	5	(-	-)	63	25	20	21	12	0	27	2	0	0	1	3	.25	1	.288	.364	.534
2008	Mdland	AA	87	347	110	18	6	12	(-	-)	176	65	52	70	38	1	92	5	5	6	12	4	.75	3	.317	.386	.507
2008	Scrmto	AAA	20	76	29	5	0	5	(-	-)	49	21	14	21	11	0	16	1	0	1	3	1	.75	1	.382	.461	.645
2008	Oak	AL	22	80	20	7	1	1	(1	0)	32	7	14	12	6	1	24	1	0	0	2	0	1.00	1	.250	.310	.400

Jack Cust

Bats: L Throws: R Pos: LF-78; DH-61; RF-5; PH-5   Ht: 6'1" Wt: 231 Born: 1/16/1979 Age: 30

Year	Team	Lg	G	AB	H	2B	3B	HR	(Hm	Rd)	TB	R	RBI	RC	TBB	IBB	SO	HBP	SH	SF	SB	CS	SB%	GDP	Avg	OBP	Slg
2001	Ari	NL	3	2	1	0	0	0	(0	0)	1	0	0	1	1	0	0	0	0	0	0	0	-	0	.500	.667	.500
2002	Col	NL	35	65	11	2	0	1	(0	1)	16	8	8	6	12	0	32	0	0	1	0	1	.00	3	.169	.295	.246
2003	Bal	AL	27	73	19	7	0	4	(2	2)	38	7	11	17	10	0	25	1	0	0	0	0	-	0	.260	.357	.521
2004	Bal	AL	1	1	0	0	0	0	(0	0)	0	0	0	0	0	0	1	0	0	0	0	0	-	0	.000	.000	.000

Year Team	Lg	G	AB	H	2B	3B	HR	(Hm	Rd)	TB	R	RBI	RC	TBB	IBB	SO	HBP	SH	SF	SB	CS	SB%	GDP	Avg	OBP	Slg
2006 SD	NL	4	3	1	0	0	0	(0	0)	1	1	0	0	0	0	1	0	0	0	0	0	-	0	.333	.333	.333
2007 Oak	AL	124	395	101	18	1	26	(14	12)	199	61	82	87	105	2	164	1	0	6	0	2	.00	6	.256	.408	.504
2008 Oak	AL	148	481	111	19	0	33	(20	13)	229	77	77	84	111	3	197	2	0	4	0	0	-	7	.231	.375	.476
7 ML YEARS		342	1020	244	46	1	64	(36	28)	484	154	178	195	239	5	420	4	0	11	0	3	.00	16	.239	.382	.475

Johnny Damon

Bats: L **Throws:** L **Pos:** LF-87; CF-34; DH-27; PH-7; PR-2; 1B-1   **Ht:** 6'2" **Wt:** 205 **Born:** 11/5/1973 **Age:** 35

Year Team	Lg	G	AB	H	2B	3B	HR	(Hm	Rd)	TB	R	RBI	RC	TBB	IBB	SO	HBP	SH	SF	SB	CS	SB%	GDP	Avg	OBP	Slg
1995 KC	AL	47	188	53	11	5	3	(1	2)	83	32	23	29	12	0	22	1	2	3	7	0	1.00	2	.282	.324	.441
1996 KC	AL	145	517	140	22	5	6	(3	3)	190	61	50	64	31	3	64	3	10	5	25	5	.83	4	.271	.313	.368
1997 KC	AL	146	472	130	12	8	8	(3	5)	182	70	48	63	42	2	70	3	6	1	16	10	.62	3	.275	.338	.386
1998 KC	AL	161	642	178	30	10	18	(11	7)	282	104	66	98	58	4	84	4	3	3	26	12	.68	4	.277	.339	.439
1999 KC	AL	145	583	179	39	9	14	(5	9)	278	101	77	108	67	5	50	3	3	4	36	6	.86	13	.307	.379	.477
2000 KC	AL	159	655	214	42	10	16	(10	6)	324	136	88	129	65	4	60	1	8	12	46	9	.84	7	.327	.382	.495
2001 Oak	AL	155	644	165	34	4	9	(2	7)	234	108	49	79	61	1	70	5	5	4	27	12	.69	7	.256	.324	.363
2002 Bos	AL	154	623	178	34	11	14	(5	9)	276	118	63	101	65	5	70	6	3	5	31	6	.84	4	.286	.356	.443
2003 Bos	AL	145	608	166	32	6	12	(5	7)	246	103	67	92	68	4	74	2	6	6	30	6	.83	5	.273	.345	.405
2004 Bos	AL	150	621	189	35	6	20	(9	11)	296	123	94	115	76	1	71	2	0	3	19	8	.70	8	.304	.380	.477
2005 Bos	AL	148	624	197	35	6	10	(3	7)	274	117	75	105	53	3	69	2	0	9	18	1	.95	5	.316	.366	.439
2006 NYY	AL	149	593	169	35	5	24	(13	11)	286	115	80	99	67	1	85	4	2	5	25	10	.71	4	.285	.359	.482
2007 NYY	AL	141	533	144	27	2	12	(5	7)	211	93	63	84	66	1	79	2	1	3	27	3	.90	4	.270	.351	.396
2008 NYY	AL	143	555	168	27	5	17	(7	10)	256	95	71	109	64	0	82	1	2	1	29	8	.78	6	.303	.375	.461
Postseason		40	180	50	9	2	7	(3	4)	84	26	21	26	12	0	27	1	0	0	10	1	.91	5	.278	.326	.467
14 ML YEARS		1988	7858	2270	415	92	183	(82	101)	3418	1376	914	1275	795	34	950	39	51	64	362	96	.79	76	.289	.354	.435

John Danks

Pitches: L **Bats:** L **Pos:** SP-33   **Ht:** 6'1" **Wt:** 200 **Born:** 4/15/1985 **Age:** 24

Year Team	Lg	G	GS	CG	GF	IP	BFP	H	R	ER	HR	SH	SF	HB	TBB	IBB	SO	WP	Bk	W	L	Pct	ShO	Sv-Op	Hld	ERC	ERA
2003 Rngrs	R	5	3	0	0	13.0	48	6	3	1	0	0	0	0	4	0	22	1	0	1	0	1.000	0	0--	-	0.97	0.69
2003 Spkane	A-	5	5	0	0	12.2	55	12	12	12	0	1	2	0	7	0	13	0	0	0	2	.000	0	0--	-	3.69	8.53
2004 Clinton	A	14	8	0	2	49.2	200	38	17	12	4	2	2	1	14	0	64	1	0	3	2	.600	0	0--	-	2.35	2.17
2004 Stcktn	A+	13	13	0	0	55.0	247	62	38	32	5	3	6	1	26	0	48	3	1	1	4	.200	0	0--	-	5.13	5.24
2005 Bkrsfld	A+	10	10	0	0	57.2	237	50	18	16	5	0	0	2	16	0	53	1	0	3	3	.500	0	0--	-	2.94	2.50
2005 Frisco	AA	18	17	0	0	98.1	436	117	66	60	12	2	2	5	34	1	85	4	0	4	10	.286	0	0--	-	5.38	5.49
2006 Frisco	AA	13	13	0	0	69.1	300	74	38	32	11	4	1	2	22	0	82	3	0	5	4	.556	0	0--	-	4.65	4.15
2006 Okla	AAA	13	13	0	0	70.2	317	67	43	34	11	4	2	1	34	0	72	2	0	4	5	.444	0	0--	-	4.51	4.33
2007 CWS	AL	26	26	0	0	139.0	622	160	92	85	28	7	4	4	54	4	109	3	0	6	13	.316	0	0-0	0	5.73	5.50
2008 CWS	AL	33	33	0	0	195.0	804	182	74	72	15	2	2	4	57	1	159	7	0	12	9	.571	0	0-0	0	3.26	3.32
2 ML YEARS		59	59	0	0	334.0	1426	342	166	157	43	9	6	8	111	5	268	10	0	18	22	.450	0	0-0	0	4.24	4.23

Jamie D'Antona

Bats: R **Throws:** R **Pos:** PH-17; 1B-2   **Ht:** 6'2" **Wt:** 222 **Born:** 5/12/1982 **Age:** 27

Year Team	Lg	G	AB	H	2B	3B	HR	(Hm	Rd)	TB	R	RBI	RC	TBB	IBB	SO	HBP	SH	SF	SB	CS	SB%	GDP	Avg	OBP	Slg
2003 Yakima	A-	70	271	75	18	1	15	(-	-)	140	46	57	51	35	1	60	1	0	5	0	0	-	5	.277	.356	.517
2004 Lancst	A+	68	273	86	18	1	13	(-	-)	145	45	57	50	16	1	36	2	0	4	2	3	.40	7	.315	.353	.531
2004 ElPaso	AA	19	71	15	3	1	0	(-	-)	20	2	7	4	2	0	16	0	0	1	0	0	-	1	.211	.230	.282
2005 Tenn	AA	125	410	102	25	2	9	(-	-)	158	58	49	52	44	2	67	1	2	1	5	6	.45	10	.249	.322	.385
2006 Tenn	AA	126	461	143	29	0	17	(-	-)	223	72	67	87	54	4	88	2	0	4	2	1	.67	11	.310	.382	.484
2007 Tucsn	AAA	128	483	149	43	5	13	(-	-)	241	79	86	88	40	3	57	4	0	6	3	2	.60	23	.308	.362	.499
2008 Tucsn	AAA	110	419	153	35	1	21	(-	-)	253	69	79	97	30	3	64	1	0	4	1	0	1.00	15	.365	.405	.604
2008 Ari	NL	18	17	3	0	0	0	(0	0)	3	2	1	1	2	0	4	0	0	0	0	0	-	0	.176	.263	.176

Kyle Davies

Pitches: R **Bats:** R **Pos:** SP-21   **Ht:** 6'2" **Wt:** 205 **Born:** 9/9/1983 **Age:** 25

Year Team	Lg	G	GS	CG	GF	IP	BFP	H	R	ER	HR	SH	SF	HB	TBB	IBB	SO	WP	Bk	W	L	Pct	ShO	Sv-Op	Hld	ERC	ERA
2008 Omha*	AAA	11	11	0	0	57.2	233	47	22	13	4	1	1	1	21	0	38	4	0	6	2	.750	0	0--	-	2.89	2.03
2005 Atl	NL	21	14	0	2	87.2	403	98	51	48	8	3	0	1	49	5	62	4	0	7	6	.538	0	0-1	2	5.25	4.93
2006 Atl	NL	14	14	1	0	63.1	312	90	60	59	14	3	2	3	33	0	51	3	0	3	7	.300	0	0-0	0	8.33	8.38
2007 2 Tms		28	28	0	0	136.0	628	155	102	92	22	5	3	5	70	4	99	8	1	7	15	.318	0	0-0	0	5.90	6.09
2008 KC	AL	21	21	0	0	113.0	487	121	57	51	10	1	3	2	43	0	71	8	1	9	7	.563	0	0-0	0	4.46	4.06
07 Atl	NL	17	17	0	0	86.0	389	92	61	55	12	3	2	2	44	3	59	1	1	4	8	.333	0	0-0	0	5.24	5.76
07 KC	AL	11	11	0	0	50.0	239	63	41	37	10	2	1	3	26	1	40	7	0	3	7	.300	0	0-0	0	7.09	6.66
4 ML YEARS		84	77	1	2	400.0	1830	464	270	250	54	12	8	11	195	9	283	23	2	26	35	.426	0	0-1	2	5.70	5.63

Chris Davis

Bats: L Throws: R Pos: 1B-51; 3B-32; PH-1   Ht: 6'4" Wt: 235 Born: 3/17/1986 Age: 23

									BATTING												BASERUNNING				AVERAGES		
Year	Team	Lg	G	AB	H	2B	3B	HR	(Hm	Rd)	TB	R	RBI	RC	TBB	IBB	SO	HBP	SH	SF	SB	CS	SB%	GDP	Avg	OBP	Slg
2006	Spkane	A-	69	253	70	18	1	15	(-	-)	135	38	42	45	23	2	65	3	0	1	2	3	.40	4	.277	.343	.534
2007	Bkrsfld	A+	99	386	115	28	3	24	(-	-)	221	69	93	73	22	2	123	5	0	5	3	3	.50	8	.298	.340	.573
2007	Frisco	AA	30	109	32	7	0	12	(-	-)	75	21	25	26	13	1	27	1	0	1	0	0	-	0	.294	.371	.688
2008	Frisco	AA	46	186	62	14	0	13	(-	-)	115	43	42	42	13	2	44	1	0	2	5	1	.83	3	.333	.376	.618
2008	Okla	AAA	31	111	37	7	1	10	(-	-)	76	25	31	29	13	1	29	1	0	2	2	0	1.00	3	.333	.402	.685
2008	Tex	AL	80	295	84	23	2	17	(8	9)	162	51	55	44	20	1	88	1	0	1	1	2	.33	5	.285	.331	.549

Doug Davis

Pitches: L Bats: R Pos: SP-26   Ht: 6'4" Wt: 213 Born: 9/21/1975 Age: 33

				HOW MUCH HE PITCHED				WHAT HE GAVE UP													THE RESULTS							
Year	Team	Lg	G	GS	CG	GF	IP	BFP	H	R	ER	HR	SH	SF	HB	TBB	IBB	SO	WP	Bk	W	L	Pct	ShO	Sv-Op	Hld	ERC	ERA
2008	Tucsn*	AAA	2	2	0	0	9.2	42	10	4	4	0	0	0	0	3	0	6	2	0	1	1	.500	0	0- -	-	3.14	3.72
1999	Tex	AL	2	0	0	0	2.2	20	12	10	10	3	0	0	0	0	0	3	0	0	0	0	-	0	0-0	0	41.42	33.75
2000	Tex	AL	30	13	1	4	98.2	450	109	61	59	14	6	4	3	58	3	66	5	1	7	6	.538	0	0-3	2	5.93	5.38
2001	Tex	AL	30	30	1	0	186.0	828	220	103	92	14	4	6	3	69	1	115	7	2	11	10	.524	0	0-0	0	4.90	4.45
2002	Tex	AL	10	10	1	0	59.2	262	67	36	33	7	3	3	3	22	0	28	2	2	3	5	.375	1	0-0	0	5.05	4.98
2003	3 Tms		21	20	1	0	109.1	491	123	55	49	16	6	2	1	51	1	62	7	0	7	8	.467	0	0-0	0	5.46	4.03
2004	Mil	NL	34	34	0	0	207.1	880	192	84	78	14	11	5	7	79	3	166	4	1	12	12	.500	0	0-0	0	3.49	3.39
2005	Mil	NL	35	35	2	0	222.2	946	196	103	95	26	12	2	4	93	5	208	3	2	11	11	.500	1	0-0	0	3.62	3.84
2006	Mil	NL	34	34	1	0	203.1	904	206	118	111	19	16	8	5	102	1	159	3	0	11	11	.500	0	0-0	0	4.59	4.91
2007	Ari	NL	33	33	0	0	192.2	862	211	100	91	21	10	2	5	95	7	144	10	1	13	12	.520	0	0-0	0	5.15	4.25
2008	Ari	NL	26	26	0	0	146.0	650	160	76	70	13	10	4	4	64	4	112	7	0	6	8	.429	0	0-0	0	4.77	4.32
03	Tex	AL	1	1	0	0	3.0	17	4	4	4	2	0	0	0	4	0	2	0	0	0	0	-	0	0-0	0	15.81	12.00
03	Tor	AL	12	11	0	0	54.0	250	70	33	30	6	3	0	1	26	1	25	6	0	4	6	.400	0	0-0	0	6.39	5.00
03	Mil	NL	8	8	1	0	52.1	224	49	18	15	8	3	2	0	21	0	35	1	0	3	2	.600	0	0-0	0	4.06	2.58
	Postseason		2	2	0	0	10.2	50	10	6	5	1	1	1	0	8	0	13	0	0	1	0	1.000	0	0-0	0	4.94	4.22
10 ML YEARS			255	235	7	4	1428.1	6293	1496	746	688	147	78	36	35	633	25	1063	48	9	81	83	.494	3	0-3	2	4.62	4.34

Jason Davis

Pitches: R Bats: R Pos: RP-10; SP-4   Ht: 6'6" Wt: 210 Born: 5/8/1980 Age: 29

				HOW MUCH HE PITCHED				WHAT HE GAVE UP													THE RESULTS							
Year	Team	Lg	G	GS	CG	GF	IP	BFP	H	R	ER	HR	SH	SF	HB	TBB	IBB	SO	WP	Bk	W	L	Pct	ShO	Sv-Op	Hld	ERC	ERA
2008	Indy*	AAA	21	20	0	0	116.1	501	113	62	57	4	7	3	11	47	1	68	6	3	6	9	.400	0	0- -	-	3.87	4.41
2002	Cle	AL	3	2	0	0	14.2	60	12	3	3	1	1	0	0	4	0	10	0	1	1	0	1.000	0	0-0	0	2.40	1.84
2003	Cle	AL	27	27	1	0	165.1	696	172	101	86	25	7	3	8	47	4	85	9	2	8	11	.421	0	0-0	0	4.44	4.68
2004	Cle	AL	26	19	0	2	114.1	540	148	81	70	13	7	2	4	51	1	72	7	1	2	7	.222	0	0-1	1	6.17	5.51
2005	Cle	AL	11	4	0	2	40.1	182	44	22	21	4	0	3	3	20	0	32	2	0	4	2	.667	0	0-0	0	5.34	4.69
2006	Cle	AL	39	0	0	10	55.1	246	67	28	23	1	3	4	3	14	2	37	3	0	3	2	.600	0	1-3	6	4.20	3.74
2007	2 Tms	AL	24	0	0	9	37.0	177	42	27	24	4	1	3	2	25	2	19	2	2	2	0	1.000	0	0-0	1	6.14	5.84
2008	Pit	NL	14	4	0	2	34.0	153	38	24	20	2	3	3	3	17	0	13	5	0	2	4	.333	0	0-0	0	5.31	5.29
07	Cle	AL	8	0	0	4	11.1	56	13	6	6	0	0	1	0	9	1	5	0	0	0	0	-	0	0-0	0	5.37	4.76
07	Sea	AL	16	0	0	5	25.2	121	29	21	18	4	1	2	2	16	1	14	2	2	2	0	1.000	0	0-0	1	6.48	6.31
7 ML YEARS			144	56	1	25	461.0	2054	523	286	247	50	22	18	23	178	9	269	28	6	22	26	.458	0	1-3	8	5.04	4.82

Rajai Davis

Bats: R Throws: R Pos: CF-88; PR-28; DH-8; PH-7; LF-3; 2B-1; RF-1   Ht: 5'11" Wt: 195 Born: 10/19/1980 Age: 28

									BATTING												BASERUNNING				AVERAGES		
Year	Team	Lg	G	AB	H	2B	3B	HR	(Hm	Rd)	TB	R	RBI	RC	TBB	IBB	SO	HBP	SH	SF	SB	CS	SB%	GDP	Avg	OBP	Slg
2006	Pit	NL	20	14	2	1	0	0	(0	0)	3	1	0	0	2	0	3	0	1	0	1	3	.25	0	.143	.250	.214
2007	2 Tms	NL	75	190	53	11	2	1	(0	1)	71	32	9	26	21	1	28	4	3	1	22	6	.79	1	.279	.361	.374
2008	2 Tms	NL	113	214	52	5	4	3	(0	3)	74	30	19	24	8	0	40	1	2	1	29	6	.83	1	.243	.272	.346
07	Pit	NL	24	48	13	2	1	0	(0	0)	17	6	2	6	7	0	3	0	1	1	5	2	.71	1	.271	.357	.354
07	SF	NL	51	142	40	9	1	1	(0	1)	54	26	7	20	14	1	25	4	2	0	17	4	.81	0	.282	.363	.380
08	SF	NL	12	18	1	0	0	0	(0	0)	1	2	0	0	1	0	6	0	0	0	4	0	1.00	0	.056	.105	.056
08	Oak	AL	101	196	51	5	4	3	(0	3)	73	28	19	24	7	0	34	1	2	1	25	6	.81	1	.260	.288	.346
3 ML YEARS			208	418	107	17	6	4	(0	4)	148	63	28	50	31	1	71	5	6	2	52	15	.78	2	.256	.314	.354

Alejandro De Aza

Bats: L Throws: L Pos: CF   Ht: 6'0" Wt: 175 Born: 4/11/1984 Age: 25

									BATTING												BASERUNNING				AVERAGES		
Year	Team	Lg	G	AB	H	2B	3B	HR	(Hm	Rd)	TB	R	RBI	RC	TBB	IBB	SO	HBP	SH	SF	SB	CS	SB%	GDP	Avg	OBP	Slg
2002	Ddgrs	R	38	128	29	6	1	1	(-	-)	40	27	14	18	22	0	17	2	2	1	16	2	.89	3	.227	.346	.313
2003	Ogden	R+	55	208	48	11	1	2	(-	-)	67	36	24	26	23	0	34	10	5	0	15	6	.71	2	.231	.336	.322
2004	Clmbs	A	102	341	87	17	2	4	(-	-)	120	63	45	46	38	1	54	10	3	1	24	10	.71	3	.255	.346	.352
2005	Jupiter	A+	123	472	135	24	9	3	(-	-)	186	75	37	75	58	3	87	8	11	5	34	17	.67	8	.286	.370	.394
2006	Carlina	AA	69	230	64	12	2	2	(-	-)	86	40	16	33	21	0	46	4	9	2	28	10	.74	5	.278	.346	.374
2006	Mrlns	R	7	24	11	1	0	0	(-	-)	12	7	4	6	4	0	2	0	0	0	3	2	.60	0	.458	.536	.500
2006	Jupiter	A+	2	7	1	0	1	0	(-	-)	3	1	0	0	0	0	2	0	1	0	0	1	.00	0	.143	.143	.429
2007	Mrlns	R	4	9	6	2	0	0	(-	-)	8	2	1	4	1	0	1	1	0	0	2	2	.50	0	.667	.750	.889
2007	Jupiter	A+	2	8	4	1	1	0	(-	-)	7	1	0	2	1	0	1	0	0	0	0	1	.00	0	.500	.556	.875
2007	Carlina	AA	5	20	7	2	0	2	(-	-)	15	7	3	5	3	0	2	0	0	0	0	0	-	0	.350	.435	.750
2007	Fla	NL	45	144	33	8	2	0	(0	0)	45	14	8	11	6	1	37	1	5	2	2	0	1.00	2	.229	.261	.313

Frankie de la Cruz

Pitches: R Bats: R Pos: RP-5; SP-1   Ht: 5'11" Wt: 175 Born: 3/12/1984 Age: 25

			HOW MUCH HE PITCHED						WHAT HE GAVE UP											THE RESULTS							
Year	Team	Lg	G	GS	CG	GF	IP	BFP	H	R	ER	HR	SH	SF	HB	TBB	IBB	SO	WP	Bk	W	L	Pct	ShO	Sv-Op	Hld	ERC	ERA
2002	Tigers	R	20	0	0	7	37.2	179	40	24	11	0	1	1	2	21	0	46	1	4	1	1	.500	0	1--	-	4.28	2.63
2002	Oneont	A-	2	0	0	1	2.1	20	7	8	6	0	0	1	1	4	0	4	0	0	0	0	-	0	0--	-	24.01	23.14
2003	Tigers	R	22	0	0	18	24.1	105	18	10	7	0	1	0	1	15	0	30	4	0	2	2	.500	0	7--	-	2.92	2.59
2003	Oneont	A-	2	0	0	0	3.1	17	6	4	4	0	0	0	1	1	0	4	1	0	0	0	-	0	0--	-	9.38	10.80
2004	WMich	A	54	0	0	38	54.0	249	51	30	23	2	0	0	3	33	0	44	13	1	2	4	.333	0	17--	-	4.22	3.83
2005	Lkland	A+	40	10	0	11	95.2	395	66	46	36	5	5	3	5	36	0	97	13	0	4	3	.571	0	5--	-	2.22	3.39
2005	Erie	AA	1	0	0	0	1.2	11	2	3	3	0	0	0	0	4	0	0	0	0	1	0	1.000	0	0--	-	12.62	16.20
2006	Erie	AA	38	12	0	9	105.0	454	103	46	40	3	6	1	3	45	4	87	7	2	5	6	.455	0	2--	-	3.63	3.43
2006	Toledo	AAA	1	1	0	0	2.1	14	4	3	3	1	0	0	0	2	0	3	1	0	0	0	-	0	0--	-	12.72	11.57
2007	Erie	AA	11	11	2	0	66.0	262	54	31	25	5	0	2	0	19	0	57	8	1	4	5	.444	1	0--	-	2.60	3.41
2007	Toledo	AAA	22	1	0	5	38.1	167	41	17	15	0	0	4	3	18	1	25	3	0	3	0	1.000	0	0--	-	4.41	3.52
2008	Albq	AAA	25	25	0	0	147.1	629	139	85	71	13	3	7	8	60	0	118	19	0	13	8	.619	0	0--	-	3.97	4.34
2007	Det	AL	6	0	0	4	6.2	32	10	8	5	1	0	0	0	4	1	5	3	0	0	0	-	0	0-0	0	8.47	6.75
2008	Fla	NL	6	1	0	1	9.0	53	15	20	18	2	1	1	0	11	0	4	1	0	0	0	-	0	0-0	0	13.08	18.00
	2 ML YEARS		12	1	0	5	15.2	85	25	28	23	3	1	1	0	15	1	9	4	0	0	0	-	0	0-0	0	11.09	13.21

Jorge de la Rosa

Pitches: L Bats: L Pos: SP-23; RP-5   Ht: 6'1" Wt: 210 Born: 4/5/1981 Age: 28

			HOW MUCH HE PITCHED						WHAT HE GAVE UP											THE RESULTS							
Year	Team	Lg	G	GS	CG	GF	IP	BFP	H	R	ER	HR	SH	SF	HB	TBB	IBB	SO	WP	Bk	W	L	Pct	ShO	Sv-Op	Hld	ERC	ERA
2008	Omha*	AAA	4	4	0	0	22.0	90	18	4	4	0	0	0	0	7	0	23	0	0	3	0	1.000	0	0--	-	2.17	1.64
2004	Mil	NL	5	5	0	0	22.2	113	29	20	16	1	1	3	1	14	0	5	3	0	0	3	.000	0	0-0	0	6.12	6.35
2005	Mil	NL	38	0	0	13	42.1	208	48	23	21	1	2	2	0	38	4	42	6	0	2	2	.500	0	0-2	5	6.04	4.46
2006	2 Tms		28	13	0	4	79.0	367	81	59	57	14	2	4	2	54	1	67	6	1	5	6	.455	0	0-0	1	6.05	6.49
2007	KC	AL	26	23	0	1	130.0	589	160	88	84	20	2	4	3	53	6	82	4	1	8	12	.400	0	0-0	0	5.93	5.82
2008	Col	NL	28	23	0	0	130.0	571	128	77	71	13	6	7	7	62	3	128	14	1	10	8	.556	0	0-0	0	4.50	4.92
06	Mil	NL	18	3	0	4	30.1	146	32	30	29	4	1	3	1	22	1	31	4	0	2	2	.500	0	0-0	1	5.90	8.60
06	KC	AL	10	10	0	0	48.2	221	49	29	28	10	1	1	1	32	0	36	2	1	3	4	.429	0	0-0	0	6.14	5.18
	5 ML YEARS		125	64	0	18	404.0	1848	446	267	249	49	13	20	13	221	14	324	33	3	25	31	.446	0	0-2	6	5.54	5.55

Valerio de los Santos

Pitches: L Bats: L Pos: SP-2   Ht: 6'2" Wt: 210 Born: 10/6/1972 Age: 36

			HOW MUCH HE PITCHED						WHAT HE GAVE UP											THE RESULTS							
Year	Team	Lg	G	GS	CG	GF	IP	BFP	H	R	ER	HR	SH	SF	HB	TBB	IBB	SO	WP	Bk	W	L	Pct	ShO	Sv-Op	Hld	ERC	ERA
2008	ColSpr*	AAA	23	8	0	1	78.1	348	89	55	49	13	4	3	4	28	0	66	1	0	4	5	.444	0	0--	-	5.40	5.63
1998	Mil	NL	13	0	0	3	21.2	75	11	7	7	4	0	0	0	2	0	18	1	0	0	0	-	0	0-0	0	1.25	2.91
1999	Mil	NL	7	0	0	3	8.1	43	12	6	6	1	0	0	1	7	0	5	1	0	0	1	.000	0	0-0	0	9.65	6.48
2000	Mil	NL	66	2	0	15	73.2	320	72	43	42	15	2	1	1	33	7	70	3	1	2	3	.400	0	0-1	9	4.79	5.13
2001	Mil	NL	1	0	0	0	1.0	5	1	1	1	0	0	0	0	1	0	1	0	0	0	0	-	0	0-0	0	5.48	9.00
2002	Mil	NL	51	0	0	12	57.2	237	42	21	20	4	3	7	2	26	3	38	1	0	2	3	.400	0	0-0	7	2.70	3.12
2003	2 Tms	NL	51	0	0	6	52.0	228	45	31	26	8	7	4	5	25	0	39	2	0	4	3	.571	0	1-4	11	4.37	4.50
2004	Tor	AL	17	0	0	1	11.2	56	11	8	8	0	1	1	0	10	2	10	3	0	0	0	-	0	0-1	0	4.29	6.17
2005	Fla	NL	27	0	0	5	22.0	103	25	15	15	4	0	0	2	12	3	16	4	0	1	2	.333	0	0-1	1	6.23	6.14
2008	Col	NL	2	2	0	0	8.0	40	6	5	5	1	0	0	0	11	0	10	0	0	0	1	.000	0	0-0	0	6.76	5.63
03	Mil	NL	45	0	0	5	48.0	205	38	24	22	8	6	4	4	22	0	35	1	0	3	3	.500	0	1-4	11	3.94	4.13
03	Phi	NL	6	0	0	1	4.0	23	7	7	4	0	1	0	1	3	0	4	1	0	1	0	1.000	0	0-0	0	10.26	9.00
	9 ML YEARS		235	4	0	45	256.0	1107	225	137	130	37	13	13	11	127	15	207	15	1	9	13	.409	0	1-7	28	4.17	4.57

David DeJesus

Bats: L Throws: L Pos: LF-71; CF-68; RF-24; DH-1   Ht: 6'0" Wt: 190 Born: 12/20/1979 Age: 29

			BATTING																BASERUNNING				AVERAGES		
Year	Team	Lg	G	AB	H	2B	3B	HR	(Hm	Rd)	TB	R	RBI	RC	TBB	IBB	SO	HBP	SH	SF	SB	CS	SB%	GDP	Avg	OBP	Slg
2003	KC	AL	12	7	2	0	1	0	(0	0)	4	0	0	2	1	0	2	1	1	0	0	0	-	0	.286	.444	.571
2004	KC	AL	96	363	104	15	3	7	(2	5)	146	58	39	53	33	0	53	9	8	6	8	11	.42	6	.287	.360	.402
2005	KC	AL	122	461	135	31	6	9	(6	3)	205	69	56	77	42	1	76	9	5	6	5	5	.50	6	.293	.359	.445
2006	KC	AL	119	491	145	36	7	8	(4	4)	219	83	56	76	43	4	70	12	2	4	6	3	.67	10	.295	.364	.446
2007	KC	AL	157	605	157	29	9	7	(3	4)	225	101	58	87	64	7	83	23	7	4	10	4	.71	10	.260	.351	.372
2008	KC	AL	135	518	159	25	7	12	(6	6)	234	70	73	93	46	3	71	5	4	4	11	8	.58	10	.307	.366	.452
	6 ML YEARS		641	2445	702	136	33	43	(21	22)	1033	381	282	388	229	15	355	59	27	18	40	31	.56	42	.287	.360	.422

Manny Delcarmen

Pitches: R Bats: R Pos: RP-73   Ht: 6'2" Wt: 190 Born: 2/16/1982 Age: 27

			HOW MUCH HE PITCHED						WHAT HE GAVE UP											THE RESULTS							
Year	Team	Lg	G	GS	CG	GF	IP	BFP	H	R	ER	HR	SH	SF	HB	TBB	IBB	SO	WP	Bk	W	L	Pct	ShO	Sv-Op	Hld	ERC	ERA
2005	Bos	AL	10	0	0	2	9.0	41	8	3	3	0	0	0	1	7	0	9	0	0	0	0	-	0	0-0	0	4.68	3.00
2006	Bos	AL	50	0	0	11	53.1	243	68	32	30	2	3	1	2	17	2	45	0	0	2	0	1.000	0	0-4	14	4.90	5.06
2007	Bos	AL	44	0	0	5	44.0	176	28	11	10	4	2	2	2	17	1	41	0	0	0	0	-	0	1-2	11	2.23	2.05
2008	Bos	AL	73	0	0	16	74.1	307	55	28	27	5	4	4	3	28	1	72	0	0	1	2	.333	0	2-5	18	2.51	3.27
	Postseason		6	0	0	1	4.1	24	7	4	4	2	0	0	1	3	0	5	0	0	0	0	-	0	0-0	1	13.67	8.31
	4 ML YEARS		177	0	0	34	180.2	767	159	74	70	11	9	7	8	69	4	167	0	0	3	2	.600	0	3-11	43	3.20	3.49

Carlos Delgado

Bats: L Throws: R Pos: 1B-154; PH-3; DH-2   Ht: 6'3" Wt: 264 Born: 6/25/1972 Age: 37

Year	Team	Lg	G	AB	H	2B	3B	HR	(Hm	Rd)	TB	R	RBI	RC	TBB	IBB	SO	HBP	SH	SF	SB	CS	SB%	GDP	Avg	OBP	Slg
1993	Tor	AL	2	1	0	0	0	0	(0	0)	0	0	0	0	1	0	0	0	0	0	0	0	-	0	.000	.500	.000
1994	Tor	AL	43	130	28	2	0	9	(5	4)	57	17	24	20	25	4	46	3	0	1	1	1	.50	5	.215	.352	.438
1995	Tor	AL	37	91	15	3	0	3	(2	1)	27	7	11	5	6	0	26	0	0	2	0	0	-	1	.165	.212	.297
1996	Tor	AL	138	488	132	28	2	25	(12	13)	239	68	92	83	58	2	139	9	0	8	0	0	-	13	.270	.353	.490
1997	Tor	AL	153	519	136	42	3	30	(17	13)	274	79	91	94	64	9	133	8	0	4	0	3	.00	6	.262	.350	.528
1998	Tor	AL	142	530	155	43	1	38	(20	18)	314	94	115	117	73	13	139	11	0	6	3	0	1.00	8	.292	.385	.592
1999	Tor	AL	152	573	156	39	0	44	(17	27)	327	113	134	121	86	7	141	15	0	7	1	1	.50	11	.272	.377	.571
2000	Tor	AL	162	569	196	57	1	41	(30	11)	378	115	137	164	123	18	104	15	0	4	0	1	.00	12	.344	.470	.664
2001	Tor	AL	162	574	160	31	1	39	(13	26)	310	102	102	126	111	22	136	16	0	3	3	0	1.00	9	.279	.408	.540
2002	Tor	AL	143	505	140	34	2	33	(17	16)	277	103	108	117	102	18	126	13	0	8	1	0	1.00	8	.277	.406	.549
2003	Tor	AL	161	570	172	38	1	42	(24	18)	338	117	145	146	109	23	137	19	0	7	0	0	-	9	.302	.426	.593
2004	Tor	AL	128	458	123	26	0	32	(18	14)	245	74	99	88	69	12	115	13	0	11	0	1	.00	11	.269	.372	.535
2005	Fla	NL	144	521	157	41	3	33	(16	17)	303	81	115	110	72	20	121	17	0	6	0	0	-	16	.301	.399	.582
2006	NYM	NL	144	524	139	30	2	38	(18	20)	287	89	114	101	74	11	120	10	0	10	0	0	-	12	.265	.361	.548
2007	NYM	NL	139	538	139	30	0	24	(9	15)	241	71	87	70	52	8	118	11	0	6	4	0	1.00	12	.258	.333	.448
2008	NYM	NL	159	598	162	32	1	38	(21	17)	310	96	115	104	72	19	124	8	0	8	1	1	.50	16	.271	.353	.518
Postseason			10	37	13	3	0	4	(3	1)	28	8	11	10	6	0	6	0	0	0	0	0	-	0	.351	.442	.757
16 ML YEARS			2009	7189	2010	476	17	469	(239	230)	3927	1226	1489	1466	1097	186	1725	168	0	91	14	8	.64	149	.280	.383	.546

Jesus Delgado

Pitches: R Bats: R Pos: RP-2   Ht: 6'1" Wt: 198 Born: 4/19/1984 Age: 25

Year	Team	Lg	G	GS	CG	GF	IP	BFP	H	R	ER	HR	SH	SF	HB	TBB	IBB	SO	WP	Bk	W	L	Pct	ShO	Sv-Op	Hld	ERC	ERA
2004	Augsta	A	21	16	0	2	58.2	254	61	40	34	10	3	2	1	26	0	34	6	1	1	5	.167	0	0--	-	5.16	5.22
2004	RedSx	R	1	0	0	0	1.2	9	4	2	2	0	0	1	0	0	0	2	0	0	0	0	-	0	0--	-	10.16	10.80
2005	Grnvile	A	33	0	0	7	72.0	310	57	30	28	3	1	3	2	39	0	69	11	0	7	3	.700	0	2--	-	3.15	3.50
2006	Jupiter	A+	28	0	0	6	38.1	168	33	19	11	0	2	1	4	18	0	40	4	0	2	4	.333	0	0--	-	3.22	2.58
2007	Carlina	AA	31	16	0	2	93.2	422	97	59	50	6	6	3	4	45	3	75	6	0	5	7	.417	0	1--	-	4.39	4.80
2008	Carlina	AA	42	0	0	10	57.1	240	46	27	22	2	5	2	1	31	1	52	5	0	5	2	.714	0	1--	-	3.20	3.45
2008	Albq	AAA	6	0	0	1	10.2	51	17	14	14	2	0	0	0	4	0	6	1	0	0	0	-	0	0--	-	8.51	11.81
2008	Fla	NL	2	0	0	1	2.0	10	1	1	1	0	1	0	0	3	0	0	1	0	0	0	-	0	0-0	0	4.47	4.50

David Dellucci

Bats: L Throws: L Pos: LF-56; DH-46; PH-18; PR-2   Ht: 5'11" Wt: 205 Born: 10/31/1973 Age: 35

Year	Team	Lg	G	AB	H	2B	3B	HR	(Hm	Rd)	TB	R	RBI	RC	TBB	IBB	SO	HBP	SH	SF	SB	CS	SB%	GDP	Avg	OBP	Slg
1997	Bal	AL	17	27	6	1	0	1	(0	1)	10	3	3	3	4	1	7	1	0	0	0	0	-	2	.222	.344	.370
1998	Ari	NL	124	416	108	19	12	5	(1	4)	166	43	51	51	33	2	103	3	0	1	3	5	.38	6	.260	.318	.399
1999	Ari	NL	63	109	43	7	1	1	(0	1)	55	27	15	24	11	0	24	3	0	0	2	0	1.00	3	.394	.463	.505
2000	Ari	NL	34	50	15	3	0	0	(0	0)	18	2	2	6	4	0	9	0	0	0	0	2	.00	1	.300	.352	.360
2001	Ari	NL	115	217	60	10	2	10	(5	5)	104	28	40	36	22	4	52	2	0	0	2	1	.67	2	.276	.349	.479
2002	Ari	NL	97	229	56	11	2	7	(2	5)	92	34	29	26	28	5	55	1	0	3	2	4	.33	7	.245	.326	.402
2003	2 Tms		91	216	49	12	3	3	(3	0)	76	26	23	23	23	1	58	5	2	2	12	0	1.00	4	.227	.313	.352
2004	Tex	AL	107	331	80	13	1	17	(9	8)	146	59	61	56	47	3	88	5	1	3	9	4	.69	4	.242	.342	.441
2005	Tex	AL	128	435	109	17	5	29	(14	15)	223	97	65	81	76	0	121	6	0	3	5	3	.63	7	.251	.367	.513
2006	Phi	NL	132	264	77	14	5	13	(6	7)	140	41	39	43	28	0	62	6	0	3	1	3	.25	1	.292	.369	.530
2007	Cle	AL	56	178	41	11	2	4	(0	4)	68	25	20	18	17	2	40	1	0	3	2	1	.67	4	.230	.296	.382
2008	Cle	AL	113	336	80	19	2	11	(4	7)	136	41	47	41	24	1	76	11	0	4	3	2	.60	12	.238	.307	.405
03	Ari	NL	70	165	40	11	3	2	(2	0)	63	18	19	21	19	1	45	3	1	2	9	0	1.00	4	.242	.328	.382
03	NYY	AL	21	51	9	1	0	1	(1	0)	13	8	4	2	4	0	13	2	1	0	3	0	1.00	2	.176	.263	.255
Postseason			17	16	5	0	0	1	(0	1)	8	5	2	2	0	0	2	1	1	0	1	0	1.00	0	.313	.353	.500
12 ML YEARS			1077	2808	724	137	35	101	(44	57)	1234	426	395	408	317	19	695	43	3	21	41	25	.62	55	.258	.340	.439

Ryan Dempster

Pitches: R Bats: R Pos: SP-33   Ht: 6'2" Wt: 215 Born: 5/3/1977 Age: 32

Year	Team	Lg	G	GS	CG	GF	IP	BFP	H	R	ER	HR	SH	SF	HB	TBB	IBB	SO	WP	Bk	W	L	Pct	ShO	Sv-Op	Hld	ERC	ERA
1998	Fla	NL	14	11	0	1	54.2	272	72	47	43	6	5	6	9	38	1	35	5	0	1	5	.167	0	0-1	0	8.14	7.08
1999	Fla	NL	25	25	0	0	147.0	666	146	77	77	21	3	6	6	93	2	126	8	0	7	8	.467	0	0-0	0	5.49	4.71
2000	Fla	NL	33	33	2	0	226.1	974	210	102	92	30	4	5	5	97	7	209	4	0	14	10	.583	1	0-0	0	4.04	3.66
2001	Fla	NL	34	34	2	0	211.1	954	218	123	116	21	15	7	10	112	5	171	5	0	15	12	.556	1	0-0	0	4.91	4.94
2002	2 Tms	NL	33	33	4	0	209.0	915	228	127	125	28	9	6	10	93	2	153	2	0	10	13	.435	0	0-0	0	5.35	5.38
2003	Cin	NL	22	20	0	1	115.2	545	134	89	84	14	9	4	5	70	4	84	3	0	3	7	.300	0	0-0	0	6.11	6.54
2004	ChC	NL	23	0	0	8	20.2	93	16	9	9	1	1	0	2	13	0	18	1	0	1	1	.500	0	2-2	3	3.61	3.92
2005	ChC	NL	63	6	0	53	92.0	401	83	35	32	4	5	0	4	49	7	89	4	0	5	3	.625	0	33-35	0	3.69	3.13
2006	ChC	NL	74	0	0	64	75.0	342	77	47	40	5	5	4	3	36	3	67	6	0	1	9	.100	0	24-33	2	4.26	4.80
2007	ChC	NL	66	0	0	58	66.2	282	59	35	35	8	3	2	1	30	4	55	2	1	2	7	.222	0	28-31	0	3.77	4.73
2008	ChC	NL	33	33	1	0	206.2	856	174	75	68	14	4	3	7	76	1	187	5	0	17	6	.739	0	0-0	0	3.03	2.96
02	Fla	NL	18	18	3	0	120.1	521	126	66	64	12	7	3	7	55	1	87	0	0	5	8	.385	0	0-0	0	4.95	4.79
02	Cin	NL	15	15	1	0	88.2	394	102	61	61	16	2	3	3	38	1	66	2	0	5	5	.500	0	0-0	0	5.90	6.19
Postseason			1	0	0	1	1.0	3	0	0	0	0	0	0	0	0	0	2	0	0	0	0	-	0	0-0	0	0.00	0.00
11 ML YEARS			420	195	9	185	1425.0	6300	1417	767	721	152	63	43	62	707	36	1194	45	1	76	81	.484	2	87-102	5	4.62	4.55

Travis Denker

Bats: R **Throws:** R **Pos:** 2B-13; PH-11; 3B-1   **Ht:** 5'9" **Wt:** 206 **Born:** 8/5/1985 **Age:** 23

									BATTING												BASERUNNING				AVERAGES		
Year	Team	Lg	G	AB	H	2B	3B	HR	(Hm Rd)	TB	R	RBI	RC	TBB	IBB	SO	HBP	SH	SF	SB	CS	SB%	GDP	Avg	OBP	Slg
2003	Ddgrs	R	39	122	33	8	1	3	(- -)	52	17	13	21	20	0	16	2	0	0	2	0	1.00	4	.270	.382	.426
2003	SoGA	A	8	22	5	2	0	0	(- -)	7	2	1	1	2	0	6	0	0	0	0	1	.00	0	.227	.292	.318
2004	Ogden	R+	57	225	70	17	1	12	(- -)	125	44	43	45	24	2	52	0	1	4	2	3	.40	7	.311	.372	.556
2005	Clmbs	A	101	358	111	23	1	21	(- -)	199	65	68	83	67	2	78	3	0	6	2	5	.29	6	.310	.417	.556
2005	VeroB	A+	31	108	20	3	0	2	(- -)	29	14	9	8	15	0	26	2	0	0	1	2	.33	2	.185	.296	.269
2006	VeroB	A+	54	191	42	6	0	5	(- -)	63	24	25	20	24	0	36	2	0	3	0	2	.00	5	.220	.309	.330
2006	Clmbs	A	75	250	67	11	1	11	(- -)	113	47	45	53	65	1	37	2	1	2	2	1	.67	5	.268	.420	.452
2007	InldEm	A+	111	402	118	27	3	10	(- -)	181	65	57	71	48	4	65	4	0	7	8	2	.80	10	.294	.369	.450
2007	SnJos	A+	7	25	10	3	0	1	(- -)	16	7	9	8	7	0	2	0	0	0	1	0	1.00	0	.400	.531	.640
2008	Conn	AA	25	76	14	4	1	0	(- -)	20	4	6	7	14	1	25	0	0	1	1	1	.50	1	.184	.308	.263
2008	Fresno	AAA	62	220	62	20	0	7	(- -)	103	42	30	40	31	0	46	1	1	0	2	0	1.00	9	.282	.373	.468
2008	SnJos	A+	5	18	4	0	0	1	(- -)	7	3	4	2	3	0	2	1	0	0	0	0	-	1	.222	.364	.389
2008	SF	NL	24	37	9	4	1	1	(1 0)	18	6	3	6	5	0	10	0	0	0	0	0	-	0	.243	.333	.486

Chris Denorfia

Bats: R **Throws:** R **Pos:** LF-13; CF-12; DH-5; PR-5; RF-2; PH-2   **Ht:** 6'0" **Wt:** 195 **Born:** 7/15/1980 **Age:** 28

									BATTING												BASERUNNING				AVERAGES		
Year	Team	Lg	G	AB	H	2B	3B	HR	(Hm Rd)	TB	R	RBI	RC	TBB	IBB	SO	HBP	SH	SF	SB	CS	SB%	GDP	Avg	OBP	Slg
2008	Scrmto*	AAA	45	189	57	13	1	2	(- -)	78	34	20	26	12	0	31	0	2	1	5	4	.56	3	.302	.342	.413
2008	Stcktn*	A+	2	9	3	0	0	0	(- -)	3	1	0	0	0	0	1	0	0	0	0	1	.00	0	.333	.333	.333
2005	Cin	NL	18	38	10	3	0	1	(1 0)	16	8	2	3	6	0	9	0	0	0	1	0	1.00	1	.263	.364	.421
2006	Cin	NL	49	106	30	6	0	1	(0 1)	39	14	7	13	11	1	21	1	2	0	1	1	.50	1	.283	.356	.368
2008	Oak	AL	29	62	18	3	0	1	(0 1)	24	10	9	9	6	0	16	1	2	0	2	0	1.00	3	.290	.362	.387
	3 ML YEARS		96	206	58	12	0	3	(1 2)	79	32	18	25	23	1	46	2	4	0	4	1	.80	5	.282	.359	.383

Mark DeRosa

Bats: R **Throws:** R **Pos:** 2B-95; RF-38; LF-27; 3B-22; PH-4; 1B-1; SS-1   **Ht:** 6'1" **Wt:** 205 **Born:** 2/26/1975 **Age:** 34

									BATTING												BASERUNNING				AVERAGES		
Year	Team	Lg	G	AB	H	2B	3B	HR	(Hm Rd)	TB	R	RBI	RC	TBB	IBB	SO	HBP	SH	SF	SB	CS	SB%	GDP	Avg	OBP	Slg
1998	Atl	NL	5	3	1	0	0	0	(0 0)	1	2	0	0	0	0	1	0	0	0	0	0	-	0	.333	.333	.333
1999	Atl	NL	7	8	0	0	0	0	(0 0)	0	0	0	0	0	0	2	0	0	0	0	0	-	0	.000	.000	.000
2000	Atl	NL	22	13	4	1	0	0	(0 0)	5	9	3	2	2	0	1	0	0	0	0	0	-	0	.308	.400	.385
2001	Atl	NL	66	164	47	8	0	3	(3 0)	64	27	20	22	12	6	19	5	1	2	2	1	.67	3	.287	.350	.390
2002	Atl	NL	72	212	63	9	2	5	(3 2)	91	24	23	27	12	3	24	3	2	3	2	3	.40	5	.297	.339	.429
2003	Atl	NL	103	266	70	14	0	6	(3 3)	102	40	22	28	16	0	49	5	0	1	1	0	1.00	6	.263	.316	.383
2004	Atl	NL	118	309	74	16	0	3	(0 3)	99	33	31	24	23	3	53	3	4	6	1	3	.25	6	.239	.293	.320
2005	Tex	AL	66	148	36	5	0	8	(7 1)	65	26	20	20	16	0	35	2	0	0	1	0	1.00	5	.243	.325	.439
2006	Tex	AL	136	520	154	40	2	13	(5 8)	237	78	74	78	44	1	102	6	0	2	4	4	.50	13	.296	.357	.456
2007	ChC	NL	149	502	147	28	3	10	(5 5)	211	64	72	76	58	2	93	7	3	4	1	2	.33	17	.293	.371	.420
2008	ChC	NL	149	505	144	30	3	21	(11 10)	243	103	87	95	69	0	106	9	2	8	6	0	1.00	9	.285	.376	.481
	Postseason		16	28	10	3	1	0	(0 0)	15	5	5	5	4	0	5	1	0	0	0	0	1.00	1	.357	.455	.536
	11 ML YEARS		893	2650	740	151	10	69	(37 32)	1118	406	352	372	252	15	485	40	12	26	18	13	.58	64	.279	.348	.422

Matt DeSalvo

Pitches: R **Bats:** R **Pos:** RP-2   **Ht:** 6'0" **Wt:** 180 **Born:** 9/11/1980 **Age:** 28

			HOW MUCH HE PITCHED						WHAT HE GAVE UP												THE RESULTS					
Year	Team	Lg	G	GS	CG	GF	IP	BFP	H	R	ER	HR	SH	SF	HB	TBB	IBB	SO	WP	Bk	W	L	Pct	ShO	Sv-Op Hld	ERC	ERA
2003	StsInd	A-	10	10	1	0	49.0	205	42	18	10	2	1	0	4	19	1	52	2	2	3	3	.500	0	0- -	3.17	1.84
2003	Btl Crk	A	3	3	0	0	22.0	82	15	5	2	0	0	0	0	5	1	21	0	0	2	0	1.000	0	0- -	1.42	0.82
2004	Tampa	A+	13	13	0	0	75.1	310	48	20	12	1	1	5	3	30	1	80	6	0	6	3	.667	0	0- -	1.75	1.43
2004	Trntn	AA	5	5	0	0	27.1	116	27	20	20	3	1	1	1	10	0	24	5	0	2	2	.500	0	0- -	4.15	6.59
2005	Trntn	AA	25	24	0	1	149.0	609	108	55	49	8	5	4	9	67	1	151	11	0	9	5	.643	0	0- -	2.76	2.96
2006	Clmbs	AAA	11	8	0	1	38.2	193	47	39	33	4	1	0	4	34	0	30	3	1	1	6	.143	0	0- -	8.00	7.68
2006	Trntn	AA	16	16	0	0	78.0	367	80	60	50	7	1	6	3	59	3	52	5	0	5	4	.556	0	0- -	5.67	5.77
2007	S-WB	AAA	20	20	0	0	113.1	483	92	39	34	4	4	2	6	56	2	102	4	0	9	5	.643	0	0- -	3.14	2.70
2008	Rchmd	AAA	34	8	0	5	92.1	419	98	58	50	7	2	5	6	55	2	91	13	2	2	11	.154	0	0- -	5.34	4.87
2007	NYY	AL	7	6	0	0	27.2	135	34	20	19	2	1	0	3	18	0	10	2	0	1	3	.250	0	0-0 -	6.68	6.18
2008	Atl	NL	2	0	0	0	2.0	18	11	7	7	0	0	0	0	2	0	2	0	0	0	0	-	0	0-0 0	43.01	31.50
	2 ML YEARS		9	6	0	0	29.2	153	45	27	26	2	1	0	3	20	0	12	2	0	1	3	.250	0	0-0 0	8.61	7.89

Elmer Dessens

Pitches: R **Bats:** R **Pos:** RP-4   **Ht:** 5'11" **Wt:** 200 **Born:** 1/13/1971 **Age:** 38

			HOW MUCH HE PITCHED						WHAT HE GAVE UP												THE RESULTS					
Year	Team	Lg	G	GS	CG	GF	IP	BFP	H	R	ER	HR	SH	SF	HB	TBB	IBB	SO	WP	Bk	W	L	Pct	ShO	Sv-Op Hld	ERC	ERA
1996	Pit	NL	15	3	0	1	25.0	112	40	23	23	2	3	1	0	4	0	13	0	0	0	2	.000	0	0-0 3	6.77	8.28
1997	Pit	NL	3	0	0	1	3.1	13	2	0	0	0	1	0	1	0	0	2	0	0	0	0	-	0	0-0 0	1.31	0.00
1998	Pit	NL	43	5	0	8	74.2	332	90	50	47	10	4	3	0	25	2	43	1	0	2	6	.250	0	0-1 6	5.19	5.67
2000	Cin	NL	40	16	1	6	147.1	640	170	73	70	10	12	7	3	43	7	85	4	0	11	5	.688	0	1-1 1	4.31	4.28
2001	Cin	NL	34	34	1	0	205.0	862	221	103	102	32	7	7	1	56	1	128	4	1	10	14	.417	1	0-0 0	4.49	4.48
2002	Cin	NL	30	30	0	0	178.0	737	173	70	60	24	7	1	4	49	8	93	3	1	7	8	.467	0	0-0 0	3.82	3.03
2003	Cin	NL	34	30	1	0	175.2	727	212	107	99	22	9	3	4	57	6	113	3	2	8	8	.500	0	0-0 0	5.19	5.07
2004	2 Tms	NL	50	10	0	0	105.0	468	123	61	52	15	4	3	1	31	4	73	2	0	2	6	.250	0	2-5 4	4.83	4.46
2005	LAD	NL	28	7	0	4	65.2	277	63	30	26	6	1	3	1	19	2	37	1	0	1	2	.333	0	0-0 1	3.35	3.56
2006	2 Tms		62	0	0	12	77.0	334	86	43	39	8	5	1	1	22	8	52	3	0	5	5	.385	0	2-7 18	4.17	4.56

(continued)

Year	Team	Lg	G	GS	CG	GF	IP	BFP	H	R	ER	HR	SH	SF	HB	TBB	IBB	SO	WP	Bk	W	L	Pct	ShO	Sv-Op	Hld	ERC	ERA
2007	2 Tms	NL	17	5	0	7	34.0	156	45	32	27	6	2	1	0	12	0	22	0	0	2	2	.500	0	0-0	0	6.37	7.15
2008	Atl	NL	4	0	0	1	4.0	26	10	10	10	1	0	2	0	4	0	2	0	0	0	1	.000	0	0-1	0	18.65	22.50
04	Ari	NL	38	9	0	7	85.1	386	107	54	45	11	4	3	1	23	4	55	2	0	1	6	.143	0	2-4	4	5.08	4.75
04	LAD	NL	12	1	0	2	19.2	82	16	7	7	4	0	0	0	8	0	18	0	0	1	0	1.000	0	0-1	0	3.74	3.20
06	KC	AL	43	0	0	10	54.0	234	63	31	27	4	3	1	1	13	6	36	2	0	5	7	.417	0	2-7	12	4.08	4.50
06	LAD	NL	19	0	0	2	23.0	100	23	12	12	4	2	0	0	9	2	16	1	0	0	1	.000	0	0-0	6	4.37	4.70
07	Mil	NL	12	0	0	7	15.0	69	24	16	11	3	0	1	0	3	0	12	0	0	1	1	.500	0	0-0	0	7.85	6.60
07	Col	NL	5	5	0	0	19.0	87	21	16	16	3	2	0	0	9	0	10	0	0	1	1	.500	0	0-0	0	5.29	7.58
	Postseason		1	0	0	0	1.1	5	1	1	1	1	0	0	0	0	0	1	0	0	0	0	-	0	0-0	0	4.25	6.75
	12 ML YEARS		360	140	2	50	1094.2	4738	1235	602	555	136	54	32	19	322	38	663	21	4	48	62	.436	1	5-15	33	4.59	4.56

Joey Devine

Pitches: R Bats: R Pos: RP-42   Ht: 5'11" Wt: 205 Born: 9/19/1983 Age: 25

Year	Team	Lg	G	GS	CG	GF	IP	BFP	H	R	ER	HR	SH	SF	HB	TBB	IBB	SO	WP	Bk	W	L	Pct	ShO	Sv-Op	Hld	ERC	ERA
2008	Scrmto*	AAA	4	2	0	2	4.0	18	4	4	3	1	0	0	0	1	0	8	0	0	0	1	.000	0	0--	1	4.11	6.75
2005	Atl	NL	5	0	0	1	5.0	26	6	7	7	2	0	0	0	5	1	3	0	0	1	0	1.000	0	0-0	1	9.97	12.60
2006	Atl	NL	10	0	0	1	6.1	36	8	7	7	1	0	0	1	9	1	10	4	1	0	0	-	0	0-1	0	11.11	9.95
2007	Atl	NL	10	0	0	5	8.1	39	7	1	1	0	1	0	0	8	2	7	1	0	1	0	1.000	0	0-0	0	4.08	1.08
2008	Oak	AL	42	0	0	10	45.2	170	23	7	3	0	1	1	0	15	2	49	0	0	6	1	.857	0	1-2	11	1.09	0.59
	Postseason		3	0	0	1	1.2	10	3	2	2	1	0	0	1	1	1	3	0	0	0	1	.000	0	0-0	0	16.60	10.80
	4 ML YEARS		67	0	0	17	65.1	271	44	22	18	3	2	2	1	37	6	69	5	1	7	2	.778	0	1-3	12	2.54	2.48

Blake DeWitt

Bats: L Throws: R Pos: 3B-95; 2B-27; PH-7; PR-3   Ht: 5'11" Wt: 175 Born: 8/20/1985 Age: 23

Year	Team	Lg	G	AB	H	2B	3B	HR	(Hm	Rd)	TB	R	RBI	RC	TBB	IBB	SO	HBP	SH	SF	SB	CS	SB%	GDP	Avg	OBP	Slg
2004	Ogden	R+	70	299	85	19	3	12	(-	-)	146	61	47	51	28	0	78	3	1	1	1	1	.50	6	.284	.350	.488
2005	Clmbs	A	120	481	136	31	3	11	(-	-)	206	61	65	70	34	0	79	4	0	3	0	1	.00	13	.283	.333	.428
2005	VeroB	A+	8	31	13	3	0	1	(-	-)	19	4	7	7	1	0	3	0	0	0	0	0	-		.419	.438	.613
2006	VeroB	A+	106	425	114	18	1	18	(-	-)	188	61	61	66	45	1	79	3	0	5	8	5	.62	8	.268	.339	.442
2006	Jaxnvl	AA	27	104	19	1	0	1	(-	-)	23	6	6	4	8	0	21	0	0	4	0	1	.00	4	.183	.241	.221
2007	InldEm	A+	83	339	101	29	2	8	(-	-)	158	48	46	53	20	0	42	1	0	1	2	3	.40	7	.298	.338	.466
2007	Jaxnvl	AA	45	178	50	13	1	6	(-	-)	83	20	20	25	7	0	26	0	1	1	0	1	.00	1	.281	.306	.466
2008	LsVgs	AAA	27	111	34	4	2	4	(-	-)	54	16	18	20	10	0	14	1	1	1	1	0	1.00	4	.306	.366	.486
2008	LAD	NL	117	368	97	13	2	9	(5	4)	141	45	52	51	45	9	68	3	0	5	3	0	1.00	6	.264	.344	.383

Joselo Diaz

Pitches: R Bats: R Pos: RP-1   Ht: 6'0" Wt: 230 Born: 4/13/1980 Age: 29

Year	Team	Lg	G	GS	CG	GF	IP	BFP	H	R	ER	HR	SH	SF	HB	TBB	IBB	SO	WP	Bk	W	L	Pct	ShO	Sv-Op	Hld	ERC	ERA
2001	Gr Falls	R+	1	0	0	0	1.0	4	0	0	0	0	0	0	1	0	0	2	0	1	0	0	-	0	0--	0	0.95	0.00
2002	SoGA	A	19	0	0	9	25.2	124	14	12	12	1	1	2	8	25	0	33	4	0	3	1	.750	0	1--	4	4.30	4.21
2003	VeroB	A+	15	11	0	1	61.2	277	39	25	24	2	2	0	5	48	1	69	4	4	5	2	.714	0	1--	3	3.20	3.50
2003	Jaxnvl	AA	5	0	0	1	7.2	31	5	1	0	0	0	0	0	3	0	7	1	0	1	0	1.000	0	0--	1	1.65	0.00
2003	StLuci	A+	11	2	0	3	30.1	137	16	12	10	0	5	1	5	25	0	41	5	2	2	2	.500	0	0--	1	2.89	2.97
2004	Bnghtn	AA	21	19	1	0	83.1	391	59	53	48	3	3	1	12	70	0	90	5	2	4	7	.364	0	0--	1	4.08	5.18
2004	Mont	AA	7	6	0	0	30.0	150	26	19	18	4	1	2	7	27	0	37	3	0	1	3	.250	0	0--	0	6.38	5.40
2005	Mont	AA	18	0	0	9	23.2	115	22	24	24	2	1	1	4	20	0	22	4	0	2	2	.500	0	0--	1	5.97	9.13
2005	Akron	AA	8	0	0	2	15.2	52	5	0	0	0	0	0	0	3	0	19	1	0	0	0	-	0	1--	0	0.48	0.00
2005	Buffalo	AAA	20	0	0	7	34.2	156	27	19	15	4	1	3	4	26	3	44	4	0	1	2	.333	0	2--	1	4.66	3.89
2006	Frisco	AA	8	4	0	1	28.0	117	16	5	4	0	1	1	3	20	0	29	3	0	2	0	1.000	0	0--	1	2.73	1.29
2006	Okla	AAA	28	1	0	12	35.2	157	28	14	13	2	0	2	3	22	0	46	3	0	0	0	-	0	4--	1	3.71	3.28
2006	Omha	AAA	13	0	0	8	18.1	85	14	13	11	3	1	3	2	15	2	16	4	0	2	3	.400	0	0--	0	5.06	5.40
2008	NewOr	AAA	12	7	0	2	39.0	184	31	31	29	8	3	2	2	33	0	36	2	1	1	5	.167	0	0--	1	5.55	6.69
2008	Frisco	AA	8	0	0	5	13.2	59	10	6	6	1	0	0	0	11	0	13	1	0	1	0	1.000	0	0--	1	4.07	3.95
2008	Okla	AAA	15	0	0	5	18.0	81	15	12	11	2	1	3	0	14	0	16	3	0	1	1	.500	0	2--	0	4.72	5.50
2006	KC	AL	4	0	0	1	6.2	38	10	8	8	2	0	0	1	8	0	3	2	0	0	0	-	0	0-0	0	13.68	10.80
2008	Tex	AL	1	0	0	1	1.0	6	1	1	0	0	0	1	1	1	0	2	1	0	0	0	-	0	0-0	0	9.51	0.00
	2 ML YEARS		5	0	0	2	7.2	44	11	9	8	2	0	1	2	9	0	5	3	0	0	0	-	0	0-0	0	13.14	9.39

Matt Diaz

Bats: R Throws: R Pos: LF-37; PH-8; PR-1   Ht: 6'1" Wt: 215 Born: 3/3/1978 Age: 31

Year	Team	Lg	G	AB	H	2B	3B	HR	(Hm	Rd)	TB	R	RBI	RC	TBB	IBB	SO	HBP	SH	SF	SB	CS	SB%	GDP	Avg	OBP	Slg
2008	Missi*	AA	7	26	6	0	1	0	(-	-)	9	5	4	2	2	0	5	0	0	0	1	0	1.00	1	.231	.286	.346
2008	Rchmd*	AAA	4	12	2	0	0	0	(-	-)	2	0	1	0	1	0	3	0	0	0	0	0	-	0	.167	.231	.167
2003	TB	AL	4	9	1	0	0	0	(0	0)	1	2	0	0	1	0	3	0	0	0	0	0	-	0	.111	.200	.111
2004	TB	AL	10	21	4	1	1	1	(1	0)	10	3	3	2	1	0	6	2	0	0	0	0	-	0	.190	.292	.476
2005	KC	AL	34	89	25	4	2	1	(0	1)	36	7	9	11	4	0	15	2	1	1	0	1	.00	3	.281	.323	.404
2006	Atl	NL	124	297	97	15	4	7	(3	4)	141	37	32	40	11	3	49	9	1	4	5	5	.50	9	.327	.364	.475
2007	Atl	NL	135	358	121	21	0	12	(5	7)	178	44	45	53	16	3	63	4	1	5	4	0	1.00	6	.338	.368	.497
2008	Atl	NL	43	135	33	2	0	2	(2	0)	41	9	14	14	3	0	32	1	0	1	4	2	.67	4	.244	.264	.304
	6 ML YEARS		350	909	281	43	7	23	(11	12)	407	102	103	116	36	6	168	18	3	11	13	8	.62	24	.309	.344	.448

Robinzon Diaz

Bats: R **Throws:** R **Pos:** C-1; DH-1; PH-1   **Ht:** 5'11" **Wt:** 180 **Born:** 9/19/1983 **Age:** 25

									BATTING												BASERUNNING				AVERAGES		
Year	Team	Lg	G	AB	H	2B	3B	HR	(Hm	Rd)	TB	R	RBI	RC	TBB	IBB	SO	HBP	SH	SF	SB	CS	SB%	GDP	Avg	OBP	Slg
2002	Dnedin	A+	10	25	3	0	0	0	(-	-)	3	3	1	0	1	0	4	0	1	1	0	0	-	0	.120	.148	.120
2002	MdHat	R+	58	192	57	9	0	0	(-	-)	66	29	20	23	13	1	19	1	0	0	7	4	.64	6	.297	.345	.344
2003	Pulaski	R+	48	182	68	20	2	1	(-	-)	95	33	44	36	10	1	14	3	0	4	1	4	.20	5	.374	.407	.522
2004	CtnWV	A	105	407	117	20	2	2	(-	-)	147	62	42	54	27	0	31	8	3	4	10	4	.71	17	.287	.341	.361
2005	Dnedin	A+	100	388	114	17	6	1	(-	-)	146	47	65	49	15	0	28	5	2	4	5	2	.71	11	.294	.325	.376
2006	Dnedin	A+	104	418	128	21	1	3	(-	-)	160	59	44	57	20	2	37	3	4	2	8	1	.89	20	.306	.341	.383
2007	NHam	AA	74	301	95	17	1	3	(-	-)	123	33	29	44	11	2	16	3	2	2	5	0	1.00	11	.316	.344	.409
2007	Syrcse	AAA	19	65	22	3	0	1	(-	-)	28	10	10	11	1	0	6	1	2	0	0	0	-	2	.338	.358	.431
2008	Syrcse	AAA	36	131	32	7	1	1	(-	-)	44	7	13	11	5	2	10	0	2	3	0	1	.00	5	.244	.266	.336
2008	B Jays	R	15	44	17	3	0	2	(-	-)	26	9	10	10	2	0	4	2	0	0	0	0	-	0	.386	.420	.591
2008	Dnedin	A+	6	25	8	1	0	1	(-	-)	12	3	3	3	0	0	0	0	0	0	0	0	-	1	.320	.320	.480
2008	Indy	AAA	5	14	5	0	1	0	(-	-)	7	0	3	1	0	0	0	0	0	0	1	2	.33	0	.357	.357	.500
2008	2 Tms		3	10	3	0	0	0	(0	0)	3	0	1	2	0	0	2	0	0	0	1	0	1.00	0	.300	.300	.300
08	Tor	AL	1	4	0	0	0	0	(0	0)	0	0	0	0	0	0	1	0	0	0	0	0	-	0	.000	.000	.000
08	Pit	NL	2	6	3	0	0	0	(0	0)	3	0	1	2	0	0	1	0	0	0	1	0	1.00	0	.500	.500	.500

Chris Dickerson

Bats: L **Throws:** L **Pos:** LF-28; CF-7; PH-5   **Ht:** 6'3" **Wt:** 226 **Born:** 4/10/1982 **Age:** 27

									BATTING												BASERUNNING				AVERAGES		
Year	Team	Lg	G	AB	H	2B	3B	HR	(Hm	Rd)	TB	R	RBI	RC	TBB	IBB	SO	HBP	SH	SF	SB	CS	SB%	GDP	Avg	OBP	Slg
2003	Billings	R+	58	201	49	6	4	6	(-	-)	81	36	38	34	39	0	66	4	5	1	9	4	.69	0	.244	.376	.403
2004	Dayton	A	84	314	95	15	3	4	(-	-)	128	50	34	57	51	1	92	8	2	3	27	14	.66	1	.303	.410	.408
2004	Ptomc	A+	15	45	9	2	0	0	(-	-)	11	5	5	4	7	0	14	1	3	0	3	1	.75	1	.200	.321	.244
2005	Srsota	A+	119	436	103	17	7	11	(-	-)	167	68	43	61	53	2	124	6	7	3	19	3	.86	2	.236	.325	.383
2006	Chatt	AA	116	389	94	21	7	12	(-	-)	165	65	48	65	65	4	129	5	3	3	21	6	.78	2	.242	.355	.424
2007	Chatt	AA	30	114	31	4	1	1	(-	-)	40	11	11	14	7	1	31	2	0	0	7	2	.78	2	.272	.325	.351
2007	Lsvlle	AAA	104	354	92	11	6	13	(-	-)	154	58	44	61	52	4	131	5	3	2	23	5	.82	2	.260	.361	.435
2008	Lsvlle	AAA	97	349	100	16	9	11	(-	-)	167	65	53	69	54	2	102	3	5	3	26	7	.79	2	.287	.384	.479
2008	Cin	NL	31	102	31	9	2	6	(4	2)	62	20	15	22	17	0	35	2	1	0	5	3	.63	0	.304	.413	.608

R.A. Dickey

Pitches: R **Bats:** R **Pos:** RP-18; SP-14   **Ht:** 6'3" **Wt:** 220 **Born:** 10/29/1974 **Age:** 34

			HOW MUCH HE PITCHED							WHAT HE GAVE UP												THE RESULTS					
Year	Team	Lg	G	GS	CG	GF	IP	BFP	H	R	ER	HR	SH	SF	HB	TBB	IBB	SO	WP	Bk	W	L	Pct	ShO	Sv-Op	Hld	ERC	ERA
2008	Tacom*	AAA	7	7	0	0	49.2	211	58	25	19	2	2	3	3	8	0	30	2	0	2	5	.286	0	0- -	-	3.93	3.44
2001	Tex	AL	4	0	0	1	12.0	53	13	9	9	3	0	0	0	7	1	4	1	0	0	1	.000	0	0-0	-	6.57	6.75
2003	Tex	AL	38	13	1	6	116.2	513	135	68	66	16	4	3	5	38	5	94	5	2	9	8	.529	1	1-1	3	5.09	5.09
2004	Tex	AL	25	15	0	2	104.1	480	136	77	65	17	3	3	4	33	1	57	5	1	6	7	.462	0	1-1	0	6.08	5.61
2005	Tex	AL	9	4	0	2	29.2	134	29	23	22	4	0	1	2	17	0	15	2	0	1	2	.333	0	0-0	0	5.18	6.67
2006	Tex	AL	1	1	0	0	3.1	18	8	7	7	6	0	0	0	1	0	1	1	0	0	1	.000	0	0-0	0	32.05	18.90
2008	Sea	AL	32	14	0	9	112.1	500	124	65	65	15	4	6	2	51	4	58	11	1	5	8	.385	0	0-0	0	5.19	5.21
	6 ML YEARS		109	47	1	20	378.1	1698	445	249	234	61	11	13	13	147	11	229	24	4	21	27	.438	1	2-2	3	5.62	5.57

Mark DiFelice

Pitches: R **Bats:** R **Pos:** RP-15   **Ht:** 6'2" **Wt:** 190 **Born:** 8/23/1976 **Age:** 32

			HOW MUCH HE PITCHED							WHAT HE GAVE UP												THE RESULTS					
Year	Team	Lg	G	GS	CG	GF	IP	BFP	H	R	ER	HR	SH	SF	HB	TBB	IBB	SO	WP	Bk	W	L	Pct	ShO	Sv-Op	Hld	ERC	ERA
1998	Portlnd	AA	15	13	0	2	81.2	343	83	45	30	6	1	2	3	11	0	62	3	1	4	6	.400	0	0- -	-	3.03	3.31
1999	Salem	A+	27	23	3	1	156.1	642	142	71	67	20	4	6	4	36	0	142	3	1	8	12	.400	0	0- -	-	3.19	3.86
2000	Carlina	AA	23	22	2	0	133.0	556	152	58	53	15	2	3	0	19	0	98	2	0	7	5	.583	0	0- -	-	3.96	3.59
2001	Carlina	AA	19	18	2	0	123.0	498	108	47	43	13	3	5	3	23	0	98	1	0	6	4	.600	1	0- -	-	2.73	3.15
2001	ColSpr	AAA	8	8	0	0	46.0	207	56	29	27	11	2	1	8	8	3	43	1	0	3	2	.600	0	0- -	-	6.02	5.28
2002	TriCity	A-	6	1	0	0	17.0	77	18	12	10	2	1	1	2	0	0	13	1	0	0	0	-	0	0- -	-	3.03	5.29
2002	Salem	A+	6	6	0	0	35.1	146	40	12	11	3	1	0	2	5	0	21	0	0	3	0	1.000	0	0- -	-	4.03	2.80
2003	Tulsa	AA	21	21	0	0	113.2	479	121	61	47	16	4	2	4	24	2	75	7	0	7	6	.538	0	0- -	-	4.09	3.72
2004	Ottawa	AAA	36	4	0	3	89.0	365	73	42	34	10	1	1	2	27	1	70	3	1	9	4	.692	0	1- -	-	2.88	3.44
2005	NewOr	AAA	14	2	0	4	31.0	148	39	35	28	10	3	3	1	13	1	21	1	0	1	2	.333	0	0- -	-	7.27	8.13
2005	Smrset	IND	14	11	1	1	75.2	297	72	26	26	11	1	1	1	8	0	53	1	1	7	4	.636	0	0- -	-	3.08	3.09
2006	Cam	IND	25	25	7	0	158.0	656	163	66	56	12	6	7	4	24	2	132	0	0	12	9	.571	2	0- -	-	3.19	3.19
2007	Hntsvl	AA	26	3	0	5	66.2	250	50	12	12	3	1	1	1	6	1	60	3	0	6	1	.857	0	0- -	-	1.54	1.62
2007	Nashv	AAA	10	10	0	0	58.0	229	45	21	20	6	2	3	3	9	0	63	1	0	4	2	.667	0	0- -	-	2.21	3.10
2008	Nashv	AAA	13	12	0	0	64.1	252	50	25	23	5	2	2	4	8	0	65	3	0	5	1	.833	0	0- -	-	2.01	3.22
2008	Mil	NL	15	0	0	5	19.0	78	17	7	6	4	0	0	0	4	0	20	1	0	1	0	1.000	0	0-0	1	3.39	2.84

Mike DiFelice

Bats: R **Throws:** R **Pos:** C-7   **Ht:** 6'2" **Wt:** 223 **Born:** 5/28/1969 **Age:** 40

									BATTING												BASERUNNING				AVERAGES		
Year	Team	Lg	G	AB	H	2B	3B	HR	(Hm	Rd)	TB	R	RBI	RC	TBB	IBB	SO	HBP	SH	SF	SB	CS	SB%	GDP	Avg	OBP	Slg
2008	Drham*	AAA	69	217	47	13	0	3	(-	-)	69	19	24	19	15	0	53	2	0	2	0	0	-	5	.217	.271	.318
1996	StL	NL	4	7	2	1	0	0	(0	0)	3	0	2	1	0	0	1	0	0	0	0	0	-	0	.286	.286	.429
1997	StL	NL	93	260	62	10	1	4	(1	3)	86	16	30	23	19	0	61	3	6	1	1	1	.50	11	.238	.297	.331
1998	TB	AL	84	248	57	12	3	3	(1	2)	84	17	23	19	15	0	56	1	3	2	0	0	-	12	.230	.274	.339
1999	TB	AL	51	179	55	11	0	6	(5	1)	84	21	27	29	8	0	23	3	0	1	0	0	-	1	.307	.346	.469
2000	TB	AL	60	204	49	13	1	6	(4	2)	82	23	19	21	12	0	40	0	5	0	0	0	-	8	.240	.280	.402

									BATTING												BASERUNNING				AVERAGES		
Year	Team	Lg	G	AB	H	2B	3B	HR	(Hm	Rd)	TB	R	RBI	RC	TBB	IBB	SO	HBP	SH	SF	SB	CS	SB%	GDP	Avg	OBP	Slg
2001	2 Tms		60	170	32	5	1	2	(0	2)	45	14	10	10	8	0	49	4	3	2	1	1	.50	3	.188	.239	.265
2002	StL	NL	70	174	40	11	0	4	(3	1)	63	17	19	17	17	3	42	1	1	3	0	0	-	4	.230	.297	.362
2003	KC	AL	62	189	48	16	1	3	(1	2)	75	29	25	26	9	0	30	4	1	2	1	0	1.00	6	.254	.299	.397
2004	2 Tms		17	25	3	0	1	0	(0	0)	5	3	2	1	3	0	4	0	0	0	0	0	-	3	.120	.214	.200
2005	NYM	NL	11	17	2	0	0	0	(0	0)	2	0	0	0	2	0	5	0	0	0	0	0	-	1	.118	.211	.118
2006	NYM	NL	15	25	2	1	0	0	(0	0)	3	3	1	1	5	0	10	0	0	0	0	0	-	0	.080	.233	.120
2007	NYM	NL	16	40	10	2	1	0	(0	0)	14	1	5	6	2	0	12	2	2	1	0	0	-	2	.250	.311	.350
2008	TB	AL	7	20	6	1	0	0	(0	0)	7	1	4	4	1	0	1	1	0	0	0	0	-	0	.300	.364	.350
01	TB	AL	48	149	31	5	1	2	(0	2)	44	13	9	10	8	0	39	3	2	2	1	1	.50	3	.208	.259	.295
01	Ari	NL	12	21	1	0	0	0	(0	0)	1	1	1	0	0	0	10	1	1	0	0	0	-	0	.048	.091	.048
04	Det	AL	13	22	3	0	1	0	(0	0)	5	3	2	1	3	0	3	0	0	0	0	0	-	3	.136	.240	.227
04	ChC	NL	4	3	0	0	0	0	(0	0)	0	0	0	0	0	0	1	0	0	0	0	0	-	0	.000	.000	.000
Postseason			1	1	0	0	0	0	(0	0)	0	0	0	0	0	0	0	0	0	0	0	0	-	0	.000	.000	.000
13 ML YEARS			550	1558	368	83	9	28	(15	13)	553	145	167	158	101	3	334	19	22	14	3	2	.60	51	.236	.288	.355

Tim Dillard

Pitches: R **Bats:** B **Pos:** RP-13   **Ht:** 6'4" **Wt:** 215 **Born:** 7/19/1983 **Age:** 25

			HOW MUCH HE PITCHED						WHAT HE GAVE UP										THE RESULTS						
Year	Team	Lg	G	GS	CG	GF	IP	BFP	H	R	ER	HR	SH	SF	HB	TBB	IBB	SO	WP	Bk	W	L	Pct	ShO	Sv-Op Hld	ERC	ERA
2003	Brewrs	R	11	4	0	3	35.2	154	36	19	15	1	1	1	9	5	0	32	1	0	1	2	.333	0	0- - -	3.58	3.79
2003	Helena	R+	3	0	0	1	5.0	22	5	0	0	0	0	0	0	2	0	6	2	0	0	0	-	0	0- - -	3.28	0.00
2004	Beloit	A	43	1	0	28	77.2	349	89	46	34	4	0	1	8	22	2	61	6	0	2	5	.286	0	10- - -	4.37	3.94
2005	BrvdCt	A+	28	28	5	0	185.1	740	150	64	51	9	5	7	13	31	0	128	13	0	12	10	.545	2	0- - -	2.17	2.48
2006	Hntsvl	AA	29	25	1	2	163.0	698	166	76	57	10	9	6	6	36	0	108	12	0	10	7	.588	1	0- - -	3.28	3.15
2007	Nashv	AAA	34	16	1	4	133.0	584	167	72	71	13	6	5	7	37	2	62	3	0	8	4	.667	0	0- - -	5.35	4.80
2008	Nashv	AAA	37	0	0	15	63.1	272	57	21	14	5	6	1	2	28	2	55	1	0	6	1	.857	0	2- - -	3.60	1.99
2008	Mil	NL	13	0	0	5	14.1	65	17	12	7	2	0	1	0	6	2	5	1	0	0	0	-	0	0-0 1	5.24	4.40

Joe Dillon

Bats: R **Throws:** R **Pos:** PH-45; 2B-6; 1B-4; LF-2; 3B-1   **Ht:** 6'2" **Wt:** 214 **Born:** 8/2/1975 **Age:** 33

									BATTING												BASERUNNING				AVERAGES		
Year	Team	Lg	G	AB	H	2B	3B	HR	(Hm	Rd)	TB	R	RBI	RC	TBB	IBB	SO	HBP	SH	SF	SB	CS	SB%	GDP	Avg	OBP	Slg
2008	Nashv*	AAA	46	171	45	8	1	5	(-	-)	70	35	23	28	29	1	30	3	0	3	1	2	.33	5	.263	.374	.409
2005	Fla	NL	27	36	6	1	0	1	(1	0)	10	6	1	0	1	0	8	1	1	0	0	0	-	3	.167	.211	.278
2007	Mil	NL	39	76	26	8	2	0	(0	0)	38	12	10	13	5	0	14	1	0	0	0	0	-	2	.342	.390	.500
2008	Mil	NL	56	75	16	3	0	1	(0	1)	22	13	6	9	13	0	21	1	1	0	1	0	1.00	1	.213	.337	.293
3 ML YEARS			122	187	48	12	2	2	(1	1)	70	31	17	22	19	0	43	3	2	0	1	0	1.00	6	.257	.335	.374

Lenny DiNardo

Pitches: L **Bats:** L **Pos:** RP-9; SP-2   **Ht:** 6'2" **Wt:** 208 **Born:** 9/19/1979 **Age:** 29

			HOW MUCH HE PITCHED						WHAT HE GAVE UP										THE RESULTS						
Year	Team	Lg	G	GS	CG	GF	IP	BFP	H	R	ER	HR	SH	SF	HB	TBB	IBB	SO	WP	Bk	W	L	Pct	ShO	Sv-Op Hld	ERC	ERA
2008	Scrmto*	AAA	15	13	0	0	71.1	328	107	56	53	7	2	1	5	16	1	49	2	0	6	5	.545	0	0- - -	6.72	6.69
2004	Bos	AL	22	0	0	6	27.2	130	34	17	13	1	1	1	2	12	1	21	1	0	0	0	-	0	0-0 0	5.17	4.23
2005	Bos	AL	8	1	0	3	14.2	62	13	6	3	1	1	1	0	5	1	15	1	0	0	1	.000	0	0-0 0	2.86	1.84
2006	Bos	AL	13	6	0	0	39.0	190	61	35	34	6	0	1	1	20	1	17	1	0	1	2	.333	0	0-0 1	8.80	7.85
2007	Oak	AL	35	20	0	9	131.1	555	136	74	60	13	7	6	3	50	2	59	2	0	8	10	.444	0	0-0 0	4.39	4.11
2008	Oak	AL	11	2	0	8	23.0	114	31	20	19	3	1	0	2	13	2	12	1	0	1	2	.333	0	0-0 0	7.21	7.43
5 ML YEARS			89	29	0	26	235.2	1051	275	152	129	24	10	9	8	100	7	124	6	0	10	15	.400	0	0-0 1	5.32	4.93

Greg Dobbs

Bats: L **Throws:** R **Pos:** PH-72; 3B-52; RF-4; LF-3; 1B-2; DH-2   **Ht:** 6'1" **Wt:** 205 **Born:** 7/2/1978 **Age:** 30

									BATTING												BASERUNNING				AVERAGES		
Year	Team	Lg	G	AB	H	2B	3B	HR	(Hm	Rd)	TB	R	RBI	RC	TBB	IBB	SO	HBP	SH	SF	SB	CS	SB%	GDP	Avg	OBP	Slg
2004	Sea	AL	18	53	12	1	0	1	(1	0)	16	4	9	5	1	0	14	1	0	1	0	0	-	0	.226	.250	.302
2005	Sea	AL	59	142	35	7	1	1	(0	1)	47	8	20	16	9	3	25	0	1	2	1	0	1.00	4	.246	.288	.331
2006	Sea	AL	23	27	10	3	1	0	(0	0)	15	4	3	5	0	0	4	1	0	0	1	1	.00	0	.370	.393	.556
2007	Phi	NL	142	324	88	20	4	10	(5	5)	146	45	55	42	29	4	67	1	0	4	3	0	1.00	4	.272	.330	.451
2008	Phi	NL	128	226	68	14	1	9	(3	6)	111	30	40	38	11	1	40	1	0	2	3	1	.75	4	.301	.333	.491
Postseason			3	3	0	0	0	0	(0	0)	0	0	0	0	1	0	1	0	0	0	0	0	-	0	.000	.250	.000
5 ML YEARS			370	772	213	45	7	21	(9	12)	335	91	127	106	50	8	150	4	1	9	7	2	.78	15	.276	.320	.434

Scott Dohmann

Pitches: R **Bats:** R **Pos:** RP-12   **Ht:** 6'1" **Wt:** 200 **Born:** 2/13/1978 **Age:** 31

			HOW MUCH HE PITCHED						WHAT HE GAVE UP										THE RESULTS						
Year	Team	Lg	G	GS	CG	GF	IP	BFP	H	R	ER	HR	SH	SF	HB	TBB	IBB	SO	WP	Bk	W	L	Pct	ShO	Sv-Op Hld	ERC	ERA
2008	Drham*	AAA	33	0	0	29	41.2	170	35	16	16	2	1	2	1	12	0	49	2	0	0	2	.000	0	20- - -	2.57	3.46
2004	Col	NL	41	0	0	13	46.0	198	41	22	21	8	2	3	0	19	0	49	3	0	0	3	.000	0	0-4 4	3.94	4.11
2005	Col	NL	32	0	0	10	31.0	143	33	21	21	6	0	0	0	19	1	35	0	0	2	1	.667	0	0-3 7	5.94	6.10
2006	2 Tms		48	0	0	18	48.1	231	59	39	38	9	4	0	4	33	7	44	5	0	2	4	.333	0	1-3 6	7.54	7.08
2007	TB	AL	31	0	0	8	32.2	136	29	13	12	3	1	1	0	18	1	26	0	0	3	0	1.000	0	0-0 4	4.13	3.31
2008	TB	AL	12	0	0	6	14.2	66	18	10	10	2	0	1	0	7	1	12	0	0	2	0	1.000	0	0-0 0	6.03	6.14
06	Col	NL	27	0	0	9	24.2	114	26	18	17	4	2	0	2	15	2	22	2	0	1	1	.500	0	1-2 3	5.94	6.20
06	KC	AL	21	0	0	9	23.2	117	33	21	21	5	2	0	2	18	5	22	3	0	1	3	.250	0	0-1 3	9.34	7.99
5 ML YEARS			164	0	0	55	172.2	774	180	105	102	28	8	7	4	96	10	166	8	0	9	8	.529	0	1-10 21	5.47	5.32

Freddy Dolsi

Pitches: R Bats: R Pos: RP-42   Ht: 6'0" Wt: 160 Born: 1/9/1983 Age: 26

			HOW MUCH HE PITCHED						WHAT HE GAVE UP													THE RESULTS							
Year	Team	Lg	G	GS	CG	GF	IP	BFP	H	R	ER	HR	SH	SF	HB	TBB	IBB	SO	WP	Bk	W	L	Pct	ShO	Sv-Op	Hld	ERC	ERA
2003	Tigers	R	8	2	0	0	23.0	114	27	20	12	1	1	1	2	12	0	19	3	1	1	1	.500	0	0--	-	5.13	4.70
2005	WMich	A	23	0	0	6	37.0	163	36	16	10	5	0	2	1	14	0	27	7	0	1	0	1.000	0	0--	-	4.07	2.43
2006	Lkland	A+	30	0	0	11	42.2	190	47	25	19	5	1	2	1	17	0	29	7	1	4	4	.500	0	1--	-	4.84	4.01
2007	Lkland	A+	48	0	0	42	51.2	222	52	24	20	3	3	4	3	17	3	44	3	1	5	3	.625	0	23--	-	3.67	3.48
2007	Erie	AA	1	0	0	1	1.0	5	1	0	0	0	0	0	0	1	0	0	0	0	0	0	-	0	0--	-	5.48	0.00
2008	Lkland	A+	9	0	0	8	7.1	34	7	5	5	1	0	0	2	3	0	11	0	1	0	1	.000	0	5--	-	5.10	6.14
2008	Erie	AA	3	0	0	3	3.0	10	1	0	0	0	0	0	0	1	0	1	0	0	0	0	-	0	2--	-	0.75	0.00
2008	Toledo	AAA	4	0	0	1	9.0	33	5	1	1	0	0	0	0	3	0	7	1	0	0	0	-	0	1--	-	1.32	1.00
2008	Det	AL	42	0	0	13	47.2	218	50	21	21	3	0	0	3	28	5	29	4	1	1	5	.167	0	2-3	7	4.89	3.97

Brendan Donnelly

Pitches: R Bats: R Pos: RP-15   Ht: 6'3" Wt: 250 Born: 7/4/1971 Age: 37

			HOW MUCH HE PITCHED						WHAT HE GAVE UP													THE RESULTS							
Year	Team	Lg	G	GS	CG	GF	IP	BFP	H	R	ER	HR	SH	SF	HB	TBB	IBB	SO	WP	Bk	W	L	Pct	ShO	Sv-Op	Hld	ERC	ERA
2008	Indns*	R	3	2	0	0	2.2	15	7	4	4	0	0	1	0	0	0	1	0	0	0	1	.000	0	0--	-	11.75	13.50
2008	Knstn*	A+	2	0	0	0	2.0	7	1	0	0	0	0	0	0	0	0	2	0	0	0	0	-	0	0--	-	0.54	0.00
2008	Buffalo*	AAA	6	0	0	0	6.0	24	5	1	1	1	0	0	0	1	0	5	1	0	0	1	1.000	0	0--	-	2.66	1.50
2002	LAA	AL	46	0	0	11	49.2	199	32	13	12	2	3	1	2	19	3	54	1	0	1	1	.500	0	1-3	13	1.89	2.17
2003	LAA	AL	63	0	0	15	74.0	307	55	14	13	2	3	1	4	24	1	79	1	0	2	2	.500	0	3-5	29	2.12	1.58
2004	LAA	AL	40	0	0	10	42.0	172	34	14	14	5	2	2	1	15	0	56	0	0	5	2	.714	0	0-0	5	3.12	3.00
2005	LAA	AL	66	0	0	14	65.1	271	60	30	27	9	3	1	2	19	3	53	3	0	9	3	.750	0	0-5	16	3.52	3.72
2006	LAA	AL	62	0	0	17	64.0	278	58	32	28	8	2	2	4	28	3	53	6	0	6	0	1.000	0	0-11	11	4.02	3.94
2007	Bos	AL	27	0	0	4	20.2	90	19	8	7	0	0	0	4	5	0	15	2	0	2	1	.667	0	0-0	8	3.00	3.05
2008	Cle	AL	15	0	0	3	13.2	69	20	13	13	2	0	2	0	10	0	8	0	0	1	0	1.000	0	0-0	4	8.84	8.56
Postseason			17	0	0	3	20.0	83	14	12	11	2	0	0	1	9	2	23	2	0	1	0	1.000	0	0-0	4	2.69	4.95
7 ML YEARS			319	0	0	74	329.1	1386	278	124	114	28	13	9	17	120	10	318	13	0	26	9	.743	0	4-14	86	3.12	3.12

Octavio Dotel

Pitches: R Bats: R Pos: RP-72   Ht: 6'0" Wt: 215 Born: 11/25/1973 Age: 35

			HOW MUCH HE PITCHED						WHAT HE GAVE UP													THE RESULTS							
Year	Team	Lg	G	GS	CG	GF	IP	BFP	H	R	ER	HR	SH	SF	HB	TBB	IBB	SO	WP	Bk	W	L	Pct	ShO	Sv-Op	Hld	ERC	ERA
1999	NYM	NL	19	14	0	1	85.1	368	69	52	51	12	3	5	6	49	1	85	3	2	8	3	.727	0	0-0	0	4.30	5.38
2000	Hou	NL	50	16	0	25	125.0	563	127	80	75	26	7	8	7	61	3	142	6	0	3	7	.300	0	16-23	0	5.47	5.40
2001	Hou	NL	61	4	0	20	105.0	438	79	35	31	5	2	2	2	47	2	145	4	0	7	5	.583	0	2-4	14	2.62	2.66
2002	Hou	NL	83	0	0	22	97.1	376	58	21	20	7	3	7	4	27	2	118	2	0	6	4	.600	0	6-10	31	1.61	1.85
2003	Hou	NL	76	0	0	13	87.0	346	53	25	24	9	2	1	3	31	2	97	2	0	6	4	.600	0	4-6	33	2.02	2.48
2004	2 Tms		77	0	0	70	85.1	356	68	38	35	13	4	2	4	33	7	122	4	1	6	6	.500	0	36-45	0	3.31	3.69
2005	Oak	AL	15	0	0	13	15.1	65	10	6	6	2	0	0	0	11	2	16	1	0	1	2	.333	0	7-11	0	3.44	3.52
2006	NYY	AL	14	0	0	7	10.0	59	18	13	12	2	0	1	0	11	1	7	3	0	0	0	-	0	0-0	1	12.97	10.80
2007	2 Tms		33	0	0	25	30.2	138	29	16	14	4	1	0	4	12	4	41	2	0	2	1	.667	0	11-15	1	4.12	4.11
2008	CWS	AL	72	0	0	10	67.0	288	52	34	28	12	4	0	5	29	3	92	4	0	4	4	.500	0	1-5	21	3.64	3.76
04	Hou	NL	32	0	0	29	34.2	146	27	15	12	4	2	1	1	15	4	50	3	1	4	0	1.000	0	14-17	0	3.01	3.12
04	Oak	AL	45	0	0	41	50.2	210	41	23	23	9	2	1	3	18	3	72	1	0	2	6	.250	0	22-28	0	3.52	4.09
07	KC	AL	24	0	0	22	23.0	108	24	11	10	3	1	0	4	11	4	29	2	0	2	1	.667	0	11-14	0	5.13	3.91
07	Atl	NL	9	0	0	3	7.2	30	5	5	4	1	0	0	0	1	0	12	0	0	0	0	-	0	0-1	1	1.51	4.70
Postseason			4	0	0	1	6.2	34	10	5	5	1	0	0	1	4	1	10	0	0	1	0	1.000	0	0-0	0	8.88	6.75
10 ML YEARS			500	34	0	206	708.0	2997	563	320	296	92	26	26	35	311	27	865	31	3	43	36	.544	0	83-119	101	3.42	3.76

Ryan Doumit

Bats: B Throws: R Pos: C-106; PH-12; 1B-1; DH-1   Ht: 6'1" Wt: 210 Born: 4/3/1981 Age: 28

			BATTING													BASERUNNING				AVERAGES						
Year	Team	Lg	G	AB	H	2B	3B	HR	(Hm	Rd)	TB	R	RBI	RC	TBB	IBB	SO	HBP	SH	SF	SB	CS	SB%	GDP	Avg	OBP	Slg
2008	Altna*	AA	3	7	3	0	0	0	(-	-)	3	0	0	1	0	0	2	0	0	0	0	0	-	0	.429	.429	.429
2005	Pit	NL	75	231	59	13	1	6	(4	2)	92	25	35	32	11	1	48	13	1	1	2	1	.67	5	.255	.324	.398
2006	Pit	NL	61	149	31	9	0	6	(3	3)	58	15	17	17	15	1	42	11	1	2	0	0	-	3	.208	.322	.389
2007	Pit	NL	83	252	69	19	2	9	(7	2)	119	33	32	34	22	2	59	4	0	1	1	2	.33	5	.274	.341	.472
2008	Pit	NL	116	431	137	34	0	15	(8	7)	216	71	69	79	23	4	55	6	0	5	2	2	.50	10	.318	.357	.501
4 ML YEARS			335	1063	296	75	3	36	(22	14)	485	144	153	162	71	8	204	34	2	9	5	5	.50	23	.278	.341	.456

Scott Downs

Pitches: L Bats: L Pos: RP-66   Ht: 6'2" Wt: 190 Born: 3/17/1976 Age: 33

			HOW MUCH HE PITCHED						WHAT HE GAVE UP													THE RESULTS							
Year	Team	Lg	G	GS	CG	GF	IP	BFP	H	R	ER	HR	SH	SF	HB	TBB	IBB	SO	WP	Bk	W	L	Pct	ShO	Sv-Op	Hld	ERC	ERA
2000	2 Tms	NL	19	19	0	0	97.0	442	122	62	57	13	2	4	5	40	1	63	1	0	4	3	.571	0	0-0	0	6.19	5.29
2003	Mon	NL	1	1	0	0	3.0	17	5	5	5	2	0	0	0	3	2	4	0	1	0	1	.000	0	0-0	0	15.01	15.00
2004	Mon	NL	12	12	1	0	63.0	284	79	47	36	9	2	1	3	23	2	38	2	0	3	6	.333	1	0-0	0	5.97	5.14
2005	Tor	AL	26	13	0	0	94.0	407	93	49	45	12	0	1	5	34	0	75	3	0	4	3	.571	0	0-0	0	4.25	4.31
2006	Tor	AL	59	5	0	13	79.0	327	73	38	35	9	1	1	2	30	6	61	7	0	6	2	.750	0	1-4	6	3.87	4.09
2007	Tor	AL	81	0	0	13	58.0	239	47	15	14	3	1	2	1	24	3	57	2	1	4	2	.667	0	1-4	24	2.81	2.17
2008	Tor	AL	66	0	0	14	70.2	290	54	15	14	3	5	0	4	27	7	57	3	0	0	3	.000	0	5-9	24	2.47	1.78
00	ChC	NL	18	18	0	0	94.0	426	117	59	54	13	2	4	5	37	1	63	1	0	4	3	.571	0	0-0	0	5.17	5.17
00	Mon	NL	1	1	0	0	3.0	16	5	3	3	0	0	0	0	3	0	0	0	0	0	0	-	0	0-0	0	10.34	9.00
7 ML YEARS			264	50	1	40	462.0	2006	473	231	206	51	11	9	20	181	21	355	18	2	21	20	.512	1	7-17	54	4.37	4.01

J.D. Drew

Bats: L **Throws:** R **Pos:** RF-106; DH-2; CF-1; PH-1   **Ht:** 6'1" **Wt:** 200 **Born:** 11/20/1975 **Age:** 33

Year	Team	Lg	G	AB	H	2B	3B	HR	(Hm	Rd)	TB	R	RBI	RC	TBB	IBB	SO	HBP	SH	SF	SB	CS	SB%	GDP	Avg	OBP	Slg
1998	StL	NL	14	36	15	3	1	5	(4	1)	35	9	13	12	4	0	10	0	0	1	0	0	-	4	.417	.463	.972
1999	StL	NL	104	368	89	16	6	13	(5	8)	156	72	39	58	50	4	77	6	3	3	19	3	.86	3	.242	.340	.424
2000	StL	NL	135	407	120	17	2	18	(11	7)	195	73	57	80	67	4	99	6	5	1	17	9	.65	3	.295	.401	.479
2001	StL	NL	109	375	121	18	5	27	(15	12)	230	80	73	92	57	4	75	4	3	4	13	3	.81	6	.323	.414	.613
2002	StL	NL	135	424	107	19	1	18	(9	9)	182	61	56	65	57	4	104	8	3	4	8	2	.80	4	.252	.349	.429
2003	StL	NL	100	287	83	13	3	15	(7	8)	147	60	42	58	36	0	48	3	2	0	2	2	.50	6	.289	.374	.512
2004	Atl	NL	145	518	158	28	8	31	(14	17)	295	118	93	121	118	2	116	5	1	3	12	3	.80	7	.305	.436	.569
2005	LAD	NL	72	252	72	12	1	15	(10	5)	131	48	36	49	51	3	50	5	0	3	1	1	.50	3	.286	.412	.520
2006	LAD	NL	146	494	140	34	6	20	(12	8)	246	84	100	92	89	8	106	4	1	6	2	3	.40	4	.283	.393	.498
2007	Bos	AL	140	466	126	30	4	11	(4	7)	197	84	64	68	79	10	100	1	0	6	4	2	.67	12	.270	.373	.423
2008	Bos	AL	109	368	103	23	4	19	(10	9)	191	79	64	72	79	5	80	4	0	5	4	1	.80	11	.280	.408	.519
	Postseason		41	137	36	4	0	4	(2	2)	52	15	17	13	13	0	25	1	2	0	3	1	.75	3	.263	.331	.380
11 ML YEARS			1209	3995	1134	213	41	192	(101	91)	2005	768	637	767	687	40	865	46	18	36	82	29	.74	64	.284	.392	.502

Stephen Drew

Bats: L **Throws:** R **Pos:** SS-151; PH-2   **Ht:** 6'0" **Wt:** 185 **Born:** 3/16/1983 **Age:** 26

Year	Team	Lg	G	AB	H	2B	3B	HR	(Hm	Rd)	TB	R	RBI	RC	TBB	IBB	SO	HBP	SH	SF	SB	CS	SB%	GDP	Avg	OBP	Slg
2006	Ari	NL	59	209	66	13	7	5	(3	2)	108	27	23	31	14	4	50	0	2	1	2	0	1.00	1	.316	.357	.517
2007	Ari	NL	150	543	129	28	4	12	(6	6)	201	60	60	71	60	5	100	3	5	8	9	0	1.00	4	.238	.313	.370
2008	Ari	NL	152	611	178	44	11	21	(9	12)	307	91	67	97	41	6	109	1	3	7	3	3	.50	5	.291	.333	.502
	Postseason		7	31	12	1	1	2	(1	1)	21	6	4	5	1	0	7	0	0	0	1	0	1.00	1	.387	.406	.677
3 ML YEARS			361	1363	373	85	22	38	(18	20)	616	178	150	199	115	15	259	4	10	16	14	3	.82	10	.274	.328	.452

Justin Duchscherer

Pitches: R **Bats:** R **Pos:** SP-22   **Ht:** 6'2" **Wt:** 201 **Born:** 11/19/1977 **Age:** 31

Year	Team	Lg	G	GS	CG	GF	IP	BFP	H	R	ER	HR	SH	SF	HB	TBB	IBB	SO	WP	Bk	W	L	Pct	ShO	Sv-Op	Hld	ERC	ERA
2008 Scrmto*		AAA	1	1	0	0	2.2	13	5	2	2	0	0	0	1	0	0	1	0	0	0	1	.000	0	0- --		9.01	6.75
2001	Tex	AL	5	2	0	1	14.2	76	24	20	20	5	0	0	4	4	0	11	1	0	1	1	.500	0	0-0	0	10.68	12.27
2003	Oak	AL	4	3	0	0	16.1	71	17	7	6	1	1	0	2	3	0	15	0	0	1	1	.500	0	0-0	0	3.58	3.31
2004	Oak	AL	53	0	0	18	96.1	398	85	37	35	13	7	1	5	32	6	59	1	1	7	6	.538	0	0-2	6	3.57	3.27
2005	Oak	AL	65	0	0	24	85.2	338	67	25	21	7	4	2	2	19	3	85	2	0	7	4	.636	0	5-7	10	2.23	2.21
2006	Oak	AL	53	0	0	17	55.2	224	52	18	18	4	1	0	1	9	0	51	3	0	2	1	.667	0	9-11	17	2.73	2.91
2007	Oak	AL	17	0	0	2	16.1	75	18	9	9	3	1	2	0	8	3	13	0	0	3	3	.500	0	0-2	5	5.22	4.96
2008	Oak	AL	22	22	1	0	141.2	557	107	45	40	11	1	4	8	34	2	95	1	0	10	8	.556	1	0-0	0	2.31	2.54
	Postseason		2	0	0	0	4.0	13	1	1	1	0	0	0	0	0	0	4	0	0	0	0	-	0	0-0	2	0.46	2.25
7 ML YEARS			219	27	1	62	426.2	1739	370	161	149	44	15	9	22	109	14	329	8	1	31	24	.564	1	14-22	38	3.00	3.14

Brandon Duckworth

Pitches: R **Bats:** R **Pos:** SP-7   **Ht:** 6'1" **Wt:** 215 **Born:** 1/23/1976 **Age:** 33

Year	Team	Lg	G	GS	CG	GF	IP	BFP	H	R	ER	HR	SH	SF	HB	TBB	IBB	SO	WP	Bk	W	L	Pct	ShO	Sv-Op	Hld	ERC	ERA
2008 Omha*		AAA	27	17	1	3	134.2	574	132	78	71	23	4	4	2	49	1	103	8	0	5	11	.313	0	1- --		4.38	4.75
2001	Phi	NL	11	11	0	0	69.0	289	57	29	27	2	7	3	6	29	5	40	2	0	3	2	.600	0	0-0	0	2.98	3.52
2002	Phi	NL	30	29	0	0	163.0	725	167	103	98	26	7	3	7	69	5	167	10	0	8	9	.471	0	0-0	0	4.80	5.41
2003	Phi	NL	24	18	0	2	93.0	424	98	58	51	12	9	1	10	44	3	68	5	0	4	7	.364	0	0-0	0	5.25	4.94
2004	Hou	NL	19	6	0	6	39.1	180	55	30	30	11	3	1	0	13	3	23	3	0	1	2	.333	0	0-0	0	7.56	6.86
2005	Hou	NL	7	2	0	1	16.1	82	24	20	20	4	0	1	5	7	1	10	0	0	0	1	.000	0	0-0	0	9.78	11.02
2006	KC	AL	10	8	0	0	45.2	216	62	36	31	3	1	2	2	24	4	27	4	0	1	5	.167	0	0-0	0	6.58	6.11
2007	KC	AL	26	3	0	6	46.2	211	51	30	24	3	1	1	3	23	2	21	7	0	3	5	.375	0	1-1	5	4.69	4.63
2008	KC	AL	7	7	0	0	38.0	167	38	20	19	2	0	2	3	19	0	20	0	0	3	3	.500	0	0-0	0	4.52	4.50
8 ML YEARS			134	84	0	15	511.0	2294	552	326	300	63	28	14	34	228	23	376	31	0	23	34	.404	0	1-1	5	5.09	5.28

Zach Duke

Pitches: L **Bats:** L **Pos:** SP-31   **Ht:** 6'2" **Wt:** 220 **Born:** 4/19/1983 **Age:** 26

Year	Team	Lg	G	GS	CG	GF	IP	BFP	H	R	ER	HR	SH	SF	HB	TBB	IBB	SO	WP	Bk	W	L	Pct	ShO	Sv-Op	Hld	ERC	ERA
2005	Pit	NL	14	14	0	0	84.2	341	79	20	17	3	3	1	2	23	2	58	1	0	8	2	.800	0	0-0	0	2.96	1.81
2006	Pit	NL	34	34	2	0	215.1	935	255	116	107	17	13	4	7	68	6	117	8	1	10	15	.400	1	0-0	0	4.82	4.47
2007	Pit	NL	20	19	0	0	107.1	482	161	74	66	14	2	4	3	25	2	41	0	1	3	8	.273	0	0-0	0	6.96	5.53
2008	Pit	NL	31	31	1	0	185.0	829	230	111	99	19	14	4	7	47	1	87	2	2	5	14	.263	1	0-0	0	4.99	4.82
4 ML YEARS			99	98	3	0	592.1	2587	725	321	289	53	32	13	19	163	11	303	11	4	26	39	.400	2	0-0	0	4.95	4.39

Elijah Dukes

Bats: R **Throws:** R **Pos:** RF-69; LF-10; PH-4; CF-1   **Ht:** 6'1" **Wt:** 241 **Born:** 6/26/1984 **Age:** 25

Year	Team	Lg	G	AB	H	2B	3B	HR	(Hm	Rd)	TB	R	RBI	RC	TBB	IBB	SO	HBP	SH	SF	SB	CS	SB%	GDP	Avg	OBP	Slg
2003	CtnSC	A	117	383	94	17	4	7	(-	-)	140	51	53	53	45	1	130	10	4	3	33	11	.75	5	.245	.338	.366
2004	CtnSC	A	43	163	47	12	2	2	(-	-)	69	26	15	28	18	3	47	3	0	1	14	1	.93	1	.288	.368	.423
2004	Bkrsfld	A+	58	211	70	16	2	8	(-	-)	114	44	34	47	26	1	50	5	1	1	16	7	.70	1	.332	.416	.540
2005	Mont	AA	120	446	128	21	5	18	(-	-)	213	73	75	78	45	2	83	4	0	3	21	8	.72	11	.287	.355	.478

Year	Team	Lg	G	AB	H	2B	3B	HR	(Hm	Rd)	TB	R	RBI	RC	TBB	IBB	SO	HBP	SH	SF	SB	CS	SB%	GDP	Avg	OBP	Slg
2006	Drham	AAA	80	283	83	15	5	10	(-	-)	138	58	50	57	44	3	47	7	0	0	9	4	.69	5	.293	.401	.488
2008	Ptomc	A+	6	17	3	1	0	0	(-	-)	4	1	1	1	4	0	5	1	0	0	0	1	.00	0	.176	.364	.235
2008	Clmbs	AAA	17	47	11	3	1	1	(-	-)	19	8	6	7	8	0	17	2	0	0	2	2	.50	1	.234	.368	.404
2008	Nats	R	2	5	0	0	0	0	(-	-)	0	0	0	0	0	0	0	0	0	0	0	0	-	0	.000	.000	.000
2007	TB	AL	52	184	35	3	2	10	(4	6)	72	27	21	20	33	0	44	2	0	1	2	4	.33	6	.190	.318	.391
2008	Was	NL	81	276	73	16	2	13	(7	6)	132	48	44	46	50	1	79	6	0	2	13	4	.76	10	.264	.386	.478
2 ML YEARS			133	460	108	19	4	23	(11	12)	204	75	65	66	83	1	123	8	0	3	15	8	.65	16	.235	.359	.443

Phil Dumatrait

Pitches: L Bats: R Pos: SP-11; RP-10

Ht: 6'2" Wt: 195 Born: 7/12/1981 Age: 27

			HOW MUCH HE PITCHED						WHAT HE GAVE UP											THE RESULTS								
Year	Team	Lg	G	GS	CG	GF	IP	BFP	H	R	ER	HR	SH	SF	HB	TBB	IBB	SO	WP	Bk	W	L	Pct	ShO	Sv-Op	Hld	ERC	ERA
2000	RedSx	R	6	6	0	0	16.1	73	10	6	3	0	1	0	2	12	0	12	0	0	0	1	.000	0	0--	-	2.88	1.65
2001	RedSx	R	8	8	0	0	32.2	128	27	10	10	0	1	0	0	9	0	33	1	0	3	0	1.000	0	0--	-	2.17	2.76
2001	Lowell	A-	2	2	0	0	10.1	44	9	4	4	0	0	0	0	4	0	15	1	0	1	1	.500	0	0--	-	2.60	3.48
2002	Augsta	A	22	22	1	0	120.1	492	109	44	37	5	1	1	5	47	0	108	7	0	8	5	.615	1	0--	-	3.43	2.77
2002	Srsota	A+	4	4	0	0	14.0	68	10	9	6	0	0	1	0	15	0	16	2	0	0	2	.000	0	0--	-	4.07	3.86
2003	Srsota	A+	21	20	0	1	104.1	429	74	41	35	4	2	2	4	59	0	74	4	0	7	5	.583	0	1--	-	2.96	3.02
2003	Ptomc	A+	7	7	1	0	37.2	162	36	17	14	2	2	0	1	14	0	32	3	0	4	1	.800	0	0--	-	3.46	3.35
2005	Srsota	A+	3	2	0	0	10.0	41	8	4	3	0	0	0	0	3	0	13	0	0	0	0	-	0	0--	-	2.00	2.70
2005	Chatt	AA	24	24	0	0	127.2	551	115	58	45	4	6	4	2	70	4	101	13	0	4	12	.250	0	0--	-	3.66	3.17
2006	Chatt	AA	10	10	0	0	49.2	206	39	24	20	4	1	3	1	22	2	45	3	1	3	4	.429	0	0--	-	2.99	3.62
2006	Lsvlle	AAA	16	15	1	0	87.2	392	104	49	46	10	7	2	1	36	1	58	1	0	5	7	.417	0	0--	-	5.38	4.72
2007	Lsvlle	AAA	22	22	0	0	125.0	537	114	57	49	10	9	1	6	49	0	76	1	0	10	6	.625	0	0--	-	3.58	3.53
2007	Cin	NL	6	6	0	0	18.0	104	39	30	30	6	2	2	1	12	0	9	0	0	0	4	.000	0	0-0	0	15.81	15.00
2008	Pit	NL	21	11	0	4	78.2	351	82	48	46	7	1	3	2	42	2	52	1	0	3	4	.429	0	0-0	0	4.87	5.26
2 ML YEARS			27	17	0	4	96.2	455	121	78	76	13	3	5	3	54	2	61	1	0	3	8	.273	0	0-0	0	6.64	7.08

Chris Duncan

Bats: L Throws: R Pos: LF-43; 1B-21; PH-17; RF-2; DH-1

Ht: 6'5" Wt: 230 Born: 5/5/1981 Age: 28

									BATTING											BASERUNNING				AVERAGES		
Year	Team	Lg	G	AB	H	2B	3B	HR	(Hm	Rd)	TB	R	RBI	RC	TBB	IBB	SO	HBP	SH	SF	SB	CS	SB%	GDP	Avg	OBP	Slg
2008	Memp*	AAA	7	25	4	2	0	0	(-	-)	6	5	3	2	4	0	5	1	0	0	0	0	-	1	.160	.300	.240
2005	StL	NL	9	10	2	1	0	1	(1	0)	6	2	3	1	0	0	5	0	0	0	0	0	-	1	.200	.200	.600
2006	StL	NL	90	280	82	11	3	22	(9	13)	165	60	43	47	30	0	69	2	0	2	0	0	-	4	.293	.363	.589
2007	StL	NL	127	375	97	20	0	21	(8	13)	180	51	70	69	55	3	123	1	0	1	2	1	.67	4	.259	.354	.480
2008	StL	NL	76	222	55	8	0	6	(4	2)	81	26	27	27	34	3	52	0	0	1	2	1	.67	9	.248	.346	.365
Postseason			10	22	3	1	0	1	(1	0)	7	3	2	2	4	0	7	0	0	0	0	0	-	0	.136	.269	.318
4 ML YEARS			302	887	236	40	3	50	(22	28)	432	139	143	144	119	6	249	3	0	4	4	2	.67	18	.266	.353	.487

Shelley Duncan

Bats: R Throws: R Pos: 1B-16; RF-4; PH-4; DH-1; PR-1

Ht: 6'5" Wt: 225 Born: 9/29/1979 Age: 29

									BATTING											BASERUNNING				AVERAGES		
Year	Team	Lg	G	AB	H	2B	3B	HR	(Hm	Rd)	TB	R	RBI	RC	TBB	IBB	SO	HBP	SH	SF	SB	CS	SB%	GDP	Avg	OBP	Slg
2001	StlsInd	A-	70	273	67	17	2	8	(-	-)	112	43	39	36	21	1	62	6	0	2	5	3	.63	5	.245	.311	.410
2002	Grnsbr	A	101	356	95	23	2	14	(-	-)	164	58	56	66	59	1	88	3	0	1	15	3	.83	4	.267	.375	.461
2003	Tampa	A+	91	330	87	19	2	8	(-	-)	134	42	47	48	35	0	83	4	0	6	5	1	.83	8	.264	.336	.406
2004	Tampa	A+	123	424	105	27	1	19	(-	-)	191	65	78	68	54	5	119	7	0	9	6	3	.67	7	.248	.336	.450
2005	Trntn	AA	142	537	130	28	2	34	(-	-)	264	86	92	88	56	3	140	11	0	2	3	2	.60	14	.242	.325	.492
2006	Trntn	AA	92	351	90	24	0	19	(-	-)	171	47	61	58	34	3	77	5	0	4	3	1	.75	9	.256	.327	.487
2006	Clmbs	AAA	12	43	8	1	0	1	(-	-)	12	1	4	3	5	1	10	0	0	0	0	0	-	1	.186	.271	.279
2007	S-WB	AAA	91	336	99	18	1	25	(-	-)	194	58	79	73	45	3	82	3	0	3	2	2	.50	4	.295	.380	.577
2008	S-WB	AAA	58	205	49	14	0	12	(-	-)	99	38	44	39	41	3	55	2	0	4	6	1	.86	5	.239	.365	.483
2008	Yanks	R	2	7	0	0	0	0	(-	-)	0	0	0	0	1	0	3	0	0	0	0	0	-	0	.000	.125	.000
2007	NYY	AL	34	74	19	1	0	7	(6	1)	41	16	17	14	8	0	20	0	0	1	0	0	-	2	.257	.329	.554
2008	NYY	AL	23	57	10	3	0	1	(1	0)	16	7	6	4	7	0	13	0	0	1	0	0	-	1	.175	.262	.281
Postseason			3	4	2	0	0	0	(0	0)	2	1	0	1	0	0	1	0	0	0	0	0	-	0	.500	.500	.500
2 ML YEARS			57	131	29	4	0	8	(7	1)	57	23	23	18	15	0	33	0	0	1	0	0	-	3	.221	.299	.435

Adam Dunn

Bats: L Throws: R Pos: LF-119; RF-23; 1B-19; DH-2; PH-2

Ht: 6'6" Wt: 275 Born: 11/9/1979 Age: 29

									BATTING											BASERUNNING				AVERAGES		
Year	Team	Lg	G	AB	H	2B	3B	HR	(Hm	Rd)	TB	R	RBI	RC	TBB	IBB	SO	HBP	SH	SF	SB	CS	SB%	GDP	Avg	OBP	Slg
2001	Cin	NL	66	244	64	18	1	19	(8	11)	141	54	43	51	38	2	74	4	0	0	4	2	.67	4	.262	.371	.578
2002	Cin	NL	158	535	133	28	2	26	(13	13)	243	84	71	96	128	13	170	9	1	3	19	9	.68	8	.249	.400	.454
2003	Cin	NL	116	381	82	12	1	27	(16	11)	177	70	57	61	74	8	126	10	0	4	8	2	.80	4	.215	.354	.465
2004	Cin	NL	161	568	151	34	0	46	(25	21)	323	105	102	108	108	11	195	5	0	0	6	1	.86	8	.266	.388	.569
2005	Cin	NL	160	543	134	35	2	40	(26	14)	293	107	101	112	114	14	168	12	0	2	4	2	.67	6	.247	.387	.540
2006	Cin	NL	160	561	131	24	0	40	(22	18)	275	99	92	96	112	12	194	6	1	3	7	0	1.00	8	.234	.365	.490
2007	Cin	NL	152	522	138	27	2	40	(19	21)	289	101	106	103	101	8	165	5	0	4	9	2	.82	12	.264	.386	.554
2008	2 Tms	NL	158	517	122	23	0	40	(21	19)	265	79	100	101	122	13	164	7	0	5	2	1	.67	7	.236	.386	.513
08	Cin	NL	114	373	87	14	0	32	(16	16)	197	58	74	74	80	6	120	6	0	5	1	1	.50	4	.233	.373	.528
08	Ari	NL	44	144	35	9	0	8	(5	3)	68	21	26	27	42	7	44	1	0	0	1	0	1.00	3	.243	.417	.472
8 ML YEARS			1131	3871	955	201	8	278	(150	128)	2006	699	672	728	797	81	1256	58	2	21	59	19	.76	57	.247	.381	.518

94

German Duran

Bats: R Throws: R Pos: 3B-30; 2B-17; PH-8; LF-6; SS-2; RF-2; PR-2   Ht: 5'10" Wt: 185 Born: 8/3/1984 Age: 24

									BATTING													BASERUNNING				AVERAGES		
Year	Team	Lg	G	AB	H	2B	3B	HR	(Hm	Rd)	TB	R	RBI	RC	TBB	IBB	SO	HBP	SH	SF	SB	CS	SB%	GDP	Avg	OBP	Slg
2005	Spkane	A-	62	252	66	17	2	4	(-	-)	99	36	33	31	18	0	56	1	2	1	6	4	.60	6	.262	.313	.393
2006	Bkrsfld	A+	114	457	130	31	2	13	(-	-)	204	81	72	69	35	0	89	1	2	8	15	9	.63	11	.284	.331	.446
2007	Frisco	AA	130	480	144	32	5	22	(-	-)	252	81	84	90	34	0	77	7	4	4	11	2	.85	13	.300	.352	.525
2008	Okla	AAA	21	77	20	3	2	1	(-	-)	30	12	6	9	7	0	12	0	1	1	0	1	.00	2	.260	.318	.390
2008	Tex	AL	60	143	33	6	1	3	(1	2)	50	22	16	12	7	0	32	2	5	1	1	1	.50	4	.231	.275	.350

Chad Durbin

Pitches: R Bats: B Pos: RP-71   Ht: 6'2" Wt: 200 Born: 12/3/1977 Age: 31

			HOW MUCH HE PITCHED						WHAT HE GAVE UP											THE RESULTS							
Year	Team	Lg	G	GS	CG	GF	IP	BFP	H	R	ER	HR	SH	SF	HB	TBB	IBB	SO	WP	Bk	W	L	Pct	ShO	Sv-Op	Hld	ERC	ERA
1999	KC	AL	1	0	0	0	2.1	9	1	0	0	0	0	0	0	1	0	3	1	0	0	0	-	0	0-0	0	1.08	0.00
2000	KC	AL	16	16	0	0	72.1	349	91	71	66	14	1	3	0	43	1	37	7	0	2	5	.286	0	0-0	0	7.05	8.21
2001	KC	AL	29	29	2	0	179.0	777	201	109	98	26	2	7	11	58	0	95	6	0	9	16	.360	0	0-0	0	5.15	4.93
2002	KC	AL	2	2	0	0	8.1	43	13	11	11	3	0	0	1	4	0	5	0	0	0	1	.000	0	0-0	0	10.58	11.88
2003	Cle	AL	3	1	0	0	8.2	45	18	12	7	2	0	0	1	3	0	8	2	0	1	0	.000	0	0-0	0	12.37	7.27
2004	2 Tms		24	8	1	5	60.2	291	72	50	47	11	2	2	5	35	3	48	5	0	6	7	.462	0	0-0	1	6.75	6.97
2006	Det	AL	3	0	0	1	6.0	24	6	1	1	1	0	0	0	3	0	3	0	0	0	0	-	0	0-0	0	2.87	1.50
2007	Det	AL	36	19	0	7	127.2	561	133	71	67	21	1	7	8	49	4	66	2	0	8	7	.533	0	1-2	3	4.92	4.72
2008	Phi	NL	71	0	0	12	87.2	365	81	33	28	5	4	2	4	35	7	63	3	0	5	4	.556	0	1-7	17	3.51	2.87
04	Cle	AL	17	8	1	5	51.1	239	63	40	38	10	0	2	4	24	3	38	3	0	5	6	.455	0	0-0	0	6.70	6.66
04	Ari	NL	7	0	0	0	9.1	52	9	10	9	1	2	0	1	11	0	10	2	0	1	1	.500	0	0-0	1	6.92	8.68
9 ML YEARS			185	75	3	25	552.2	2464	616	358	325	83	10	21	29	228	15	328	26	0	30	41	.423	0	2-9	21	5.36	5.29

Ray Durham

Bats: B Throws: R Pos: 2B-95; PH-37; DH-1   Ht: 5'8" Wt: 204 Born: 11/30/1971 Age: 37

									BATTING													BASERUNNING				AVERAGES		
Year	Team	Lg	G	AB	H	2B	3B	HR	(Hm	Rd)	TB	R	RBI	RC	TBB	IBB	SO	HBP	SH	SF	SB	CS	SB%	GDP	Avg	OBP	Slg
1995	CWS	AL	125	471	121	27	6	7	(1	6)	181	68	51	57	31	2	83	6	5	4	18	5	.78	8	.257	.309	.384
1996	CWS	AL	156	557	153	33	5	10	(3	7)	226	79	65	87	58	4	95	10	7	7	30	4	.88	6	.275	.350	.406
1997	CWS	AL	155	634	172	27	5	11	(3	8)	242	106	53	83	61	0	96	6	2	8	33	16	.67	14	.271	.337	.382
1998	CWS	AL	158	635	181	35	8	19	(10	9)	289	126	67	110	73	3	105	6	6	3	36	9	.80	5	.285	.363	.455
1999	CWS	AL	153	612	181	30	8	13	(7	6)	266	109	60	103	73	1	105	4	3	2	34	11	.76	9	.296	.373	.435
2000	CWS	AL	151	614	172	35	9	17	(5	12)	276	121	75	100	75	0	105	7	5	8	25	13	.66	13	.280	.361	.450
2001	CWS	AL	152	611	163	42	10	20	(9	11)	285	104	65	97	64	3	110	4	6	8	23	10	.70	10	.267	.337	.466
2002	2 Tms	AL	150	564	163	34	6	15	(11	4)	254	114	70	96	73	1	93	7	10	5	26	7	.79	15	.289	.374	.450
2003	SF	NL	110	410	117	30	5	8	(3	5)	181	61	33	56	50	2	82	3	4	2	7	7	.50	4	.285	.366	.441
2004	SF	NL	120	471	133	28	8	17	(8	9)	228	95	65	83	57	3	60	6	4	4	10	4	.71	6	.282	.364	.484
2005	SF	NL	142	497	144	33	0	12	(6	6)	213	67	62	67	48	2	59	7	1	7	6	3	.67	19	.290	.356	.429
2006	SF	NL	137	498	146	30	7	26	(10	16)	268	79	93	93	51	6	61	2	2	2	7	2	.78	17	.293	.360	.538
2007	SF	NL	138	464	101	21	2	11	(2	9)	159	56	71	47	53	6	75	2	0	9	10	2	.83	18	.218	.295	.343
2008	2 Tms		128	370	107	35	0	6	(3	3)	160	64	45	59	53	1	72	2	0	1	8	4	.67	7	.289	.380	.432
02	CWS	AL	96	345	103	20	2	9	(6	3)	154	71	48	61	49	0	59	5	8	4	20	5	.80	13	.299	.390	.446
02	Oak	AL	54	219	60	14	4	6	(5	1)	100	43	22	35	24	1	34	2	2	1	6	2	.75	2	.274	.350	.457
08	SF	NL	87	263	77	23	0	3	(1	2)	109	43	32	39	38	0	49	2	0	0	6	2	.75	6	.293	.385	.414
08	Mil	NL	41	107	30	12	0	3	(2	1)	51	21	13	20	15	1	23	0	0	0	2	2	.50	1	.280	.369	.477
Postseason			12	48	13	4	0	3	(2	1)	26	11	3	7	6	0	12	2	1	0	1	0	1.00	2	.271	.375	.542
14 ML YEARS			1975	7408	2054	440	79	192	(81	111)	3228	1249	875	1138	820	34	1201	72	55	68	273	97	.74	151	.277	.352	.436

Jermaine Dye

Bats: R Throws: R Pos: RF-151; DH-2; PH-1   Ht: 6'5" Wt: 245 Born: 1/28/1974 Age: 35

									BATTING													BASERUNNING				AVERAGES		
Year	Team	Lg	G	AB	H	2B	3B	HR	(Hm	Rd)	TB	R	RBI	RC	TBB	IBB	SO	HBP	SH	SF	SB	CS	SB%	GDP	Avg	OBP	Slg
1996	Atl	NL	98	292	82	16	0	12	(4	8)	134	32	37	36	8	0	67	3	0	3	1	4	.20	11	.281	.304	.459
1997	KC	AL	75	263	62	14	0	7	(3	4)	97	26	22	26	17	0	51	1	1	1	2	1	.67	6	.236	.284	.369
1998	KC	AL	60	214	50	5	1	5	(3	2)	72	24	23	17	11	2	46	1	0	4	2	2	.50	8	.234	.270	.336
1999	KC	AL	158	608	179	44	8	27	(15	12)	320	96	119	106	58	4	119	1	0	6	2	3	.40	17	.294	.354	.526
2000	KC	AL	157	601	193	41	2	33	(15	18)	337	107	118	125	69	6	99	3	0	6	0	1	.00	12	.321	.390	.561
2001	2 Tms	AL	158	599	169	31	1	26	(16	10)	280	91	106	99	57	6	112	7	1	11	9	1	.90	8	.282	.346	.467
2002	Oak	AL	131	488	123	27	1	24	(13	11)	224	74	86	70	52	2	108	10	0	5	2	0	1.00	15	.252	.333	.459
2003	Oak	AL	65	221	38	6	0	4	(3	1)	56	28	20	10	25	2	42	3	0	4	1	0	1.00	11	.172	.261	.253
2004	Oak	AL	137	532	141	29	4	23	(12	11)	247	87	80	69	49	4	128	4	0	5	4	2	.67	16	.265	.329	.464
2005	CWS	AL	145	529	145	29	2	31	(15	16)	271	74	86	80	39	3	99	9	0	2	11	4	.73	15	.274	.333	.512
2006	CWS	AL	146	539	170	27	3	44	(21	23)	335	103	120	116	59	4	118	6	0	7	7	3	.70	15	.315	.385	.622
2007	CWS	AL	138	508	129	34	0	28	(14	14)	247	68	78	67	45	2	107	4	0	4	2	1	.67	17	.254	.317	.486
2008	CWS	AL	154	590	172	41	2	34	(18	16)	319	96	96	91	44	3	104	6	0	5	3	2	.60	18	.292	.344	.541
01	KC	AL	97	367	100	14	0	13	(8	5)	153	50	47	54	30	3	68	6	1	6	7	1	.88	2	.272	.333	.417
01	Oak	AL	61	232	69	17	1	13	(8	5)	127	41	59	45	27	3	44	1	0	5	2	0	1.00	6	.297	.366	.547
Postseason			40	147	38	8	0	4	(1	3)	58	15	16	15	11	0	30	3	1	2	2	1	.67	1	.259	.319	.395
13 ML YEARS			1622	5984	1653	344	24	298	(152	146)	2939	906	991	912	533	38	1200	58	2	63	46	24	.66	169	.276	.338	.491

Damion Easley

Bats: R Throws: R Pos: 2B-64; PH-35; SS-8; LF-7; 1B-4; 3B-1; DH-1; PR-1   Ht: 5'11" Wt: 195 Born: 11/11/1969 Age: 39

Year Team	Lg	G	AB	H	2B	3B	HR	(Hm	Rd)	TB	R	RBI	RC	TBB	IBB	SO	HBP	SH	SF	SB	CS	SB%	GDP	Avg	OBP	Slg
1992 LAA	AL	47	151	39	5	0	1	(1	0)	47	14	12	14	8	0	26	3	2	1	9	5	.64	2	.258	.307	.311
1993 LAA	AL	73	230	72	13	2	2	(0	2)	95	33	22	37	28	2	35	3	1	2	6	6	.50	5	.313	.392	.413
1994 LAA	AL	88	316	68	16	1	6	(4	2)	104	41	30	28	29	0	48	4	4	2	4	5	.44	8	.215	.288	.329
1995 LAA	AL	114	357	77	14	2	4	(1	3)	107	35	35	30	32	1	47	6	6	4	5	2	.71	11	.216	.288	.300
1996 2 Tms	AL	49	112	30	2	0	4	(1	3)	44	14	17	16	10	0	25	1	5	1	3	1	.75	0	.268	.331	.393
1997 Det	AL	151	527	139	37	3	22	(12	10)	248	97	72	88	68	3	102	16	4	5	28	13	.68	18	.264	.362	.471
1998 Det	AL	153	594	161	38	2	27	(19	8)	284	84	100	94	39	2	112	16	0	2	15	5	.75	8	.271	.332	.478
1999 Det	AL	151	549	146	30	1	20	(12	8)	238	83	65	65	51	2	124	19	2	6	11	3	.79	15	.266	.346	.434
2000 Det	AL	126	464	120	27	2	14	(5	9)	193	76	58	69	55	1	79	11	4	1	13	4	.76	11	.259	.350	.416
2001 Det	AL	154	585	146	27	7	11	(4	7)	220	77	65	72	52	3	90	13	4	4	10	5	.67	10	.250	.323	.376
2002 Det	AL	85	304	68	14	1	8	(4	4)	108	24	30	29	27	3	43	11	1	3	1	3	.25	4	.224	.307	.355
2003 TB	AL	36	107	20	3	1	1	(0	1)	28	8	7	3	2	0	18	0	1	0	0	0	-	3	.187	.202	.262
2004 Fla	NL	98	223	53	20	1	9	(5	4)	102	26	43	34	24	1	36	8	0	2	4	1	.80	6	.238	.331	.457
2005 Fla	NL	102	267	64	19	1	9	(5	4)	112	37	30	33	26	3	47	4	3	4	4	1	.80	4	.240	.312	.419
2006 Ari	NL	90	189	44	6	1	9	(3	6)	79	24	28	29	21	0	30	5	3	2	1	1	.50	4	.233	.323	.418
2007 NYM	NL	76	193	54	6	0	10	(6	4)	90	24	26	34	19	1	35	5	0	1	0	1	.00	1	.280	.358	.466
2008 NYM	NL	113	316	85	10	2	6	(2	4)	117	33	44	37	19	0	38	7	2	3	0	0	-	15	.269	.322	.370
96 LAA	AL	28	45	7	1	0	2	(1	1)	14	4	7	4	6	0	12	0	3	0	0	0	-	0	.156	.255	.311
96 Det	AL	21	67	23	1	0	2	(0	2)	30	10	10	12	4	0	13	1	2	1	3	1	.75	0	.343	.384	.448
17 ML YEARS		1706	5484	1386	287	27	163	(84	79)	2216	735	684	729	510	22	935	132	42	43	114	56	.67	128	.253	.329	.404

Adam Eaton

Pitches: R Bats: R Pos: SP-19; RP-2   Ht: 6'2" Wt: 200 Born: 11/23/1977 Age: 31

Year Team	Lg	G	GS	CG	GF	IP	BFP	H	R	ER	HR	SH	SF	HB	TBB	IBB	SO	WP	Bk	W	L	Pct	ShO	Sv-Op	Hld	ERC	ERA
2008 Lakwd*	A	1	1	0	0	3.2	16	5	4	4	1	0	0	0	1	0	2	0	0	0	1	.000	0	0--	-	7.34	9.82
2008 Rdng*	AA	5	5	0	0	26.2	125	34	24	21	8	1	0	4	4	0	23	0	0	0	3	.000	0	0--	-	6.47	7.09
2008 LV*	AAA	1	1	0	0	3.0	14	5	3	1	0	1	0	0	1	0	2	0	0	1	0	1.000	0	0--	-	7.34	3.00
2000 SD	NL	22	22	0	0	135.0	583	134	63	62	14	1	3	2	61	3	90	3	0	7	4	.636	0	0-0	0	4.34	4.13
2001 SD	NL	17	17	2	0	116.2	499	108	61	56	20	3	2	5	40	3	109	3	0	8	5	.615	0	0-0	0	4.01	4.32
2002 SD	NL	6	6	0	0	33.1	142	28	20	20	5	2	2	2	17	0	25	2	0	1	1	.500	0	0-0	0	4.28	5.40
2003 SD	NL	31	31	1	0	183.0	789	173	91	83	20	5	5	7	68	6	146	7	1	9	12	.429	0	0-0	0	3.78	4.08
2004 SD	NL	33	33	0	0	199.1	848	204	113	102	28	12	7	10	52	3	153	5	0	11	14	.440	0	0-0	0	4.10	4.61
2005 SD	NL	24	22	0	0	128.2	568	140	70	64	14	4	6	5	44	6	100	5	0	11	5	.688	0	0-0	0	4.44	4.27
2006 Tex	AL	13	13	0	0	65.0	291	78	38	37	11	1	1	4	24	0	43	0	0	7	4	.636	0	0-0	0	5.98	5.12
2007 Phi	NL	30	30	0	0	161.2	734	192	117	113	30	10	5	11	71	4	97	6	0	10	10	.500	0	0-0	0	6.33	6.29
2008 Phi	NL	21	19	0	0	107.0	478	131	71	69	15	3	2	6	44	5	57	2	0	4	8	.333	0	0-0	0	6.07	5.80
9 ML YEARS		197	193	3	2	1129.2	4932	1188	644	603	157	41	33	52	421	30	820	33	1	68	63	.519	0	0-0	0	4.70	4.80

David Eckstein

Bats: R Throws: R Pos: SS-57; 2B-24; DH-9; PR-4; PH-2   Ht: 5'7" Wt: 177 Born: 1/20/1975 Age: 34

Year Team	Lg	G	AB	H	2B	3B	HR	(Hm	Rd)	TB	R	RBI	RC	TBB	IBB	SO	HBP	SH	SF	SB	CS	SB%	GDP	Avg	OBP	Slg
2008 Dnedin*	A+	5	14	2	1	0	0	(-	-)	3	4	0	1	2	0	1	1	0	0	0	0	-	0	.143	.294	.214
2001 LAA	AL	153	582	166	26	2	4	(3	1)	208	82	41	80	43	0	60	21	16	2	29	4	.88	11	.285	.355	.357
2002 LAA	AL	152	608	178	22	6	8	(3	5)	236	107	63	93	45	0	44	27	14	8	21	13	.62	7	.293	.363	.388
2003 LAA	AL	120	452	114	22	1	3	(1	2)	147	59	31	53	36	0	45	15	10	4	16	5	.76	9	.252	.325	.325
2004 LAA	AL	142	566	156	24	1	2	(2	0)	188	92	35	60	42	1	49	13	14	2	16	5	.76	11	.276	.339	.332
2005 StL	NL	158	630	185	26	7	8	(3	5)	249	90	61	103	58	0	44	13	8	4	11	8	.58	13	.294	.363	.395
2006 StL	NL	123	500	146	18	1	2	(0	2)	172	68	23	60	31	0	41	15	3	3	7	6	.54	7	.292	.350	.344
2007 StL	NL	117	434	134	23	0	3	(1	2)	166	58	31	55	24	0	22	12	7	7	10	1	.91	9	.309	.356	.382
2008 2 Tms	NL	94	324	86	21	0	2	(2	0)	113	32	27	42	31	1	32	9	9	3	2	1	.67	7	.265	.343	.349
08 Tor	AL	76	260	72	18	0	1	(1	0)	93	27	23	37	24	1	27	8	9	2	2	1	.67	6	.277	.354	.358
08 Ari	NL	18	64	14	3	0	1	(1	0)	20	5	4	5	7	0	5	1	0	1	0	0	-	1	.219	.301	.313
Postseason		44	176	49	4	0	2	(1	1)	59	26	18	25	12	0	9	7	3	2	7	1	.88	2	.278	.345	.335
8 ML YEARS		1059	4096	1165	182	18	32	(15	17)	1479	588	312	546	310	2	337	125	81	33	112	43	.72	74	.284	.351	.361

Jim Edmonds

Bats: L Throws: L Pos: CF-103; PH-10   Ht: 6'1" Wt: 212 Born: 6/27/1970 Age: 39

Year Team	Lg	G	AB	H	2B	3B	HR	(Hm	Rd)	TB	R	RBI	RC	TBB	IBB	SO	HBP	SH	SF	SB	CS	SB%	GDP	Avg	OBP	Slg
2008 Lk Els*	A+	2	6	2	0	0	0	(-	-)	2	0	0	0	0	0	1	0	0	0	0	0	-	0	.333	.333	.333
1993 LAA	AL	18	61	15	4	1	0	(0	0)	21	5	4	4	2	1	16	0	0	0	0	2	.00	1	.246	.270	.344
1994 LAA	AL	94	289	79	13	1	5	(3	2)	109	35	37	38	30	3	72	1	1	1	4	2	.67	3	.273	.343	.377
1995 LAA	AL	141	558	162	30	4	33	(16	17)	299	120	107	100	51	4	130	5	1	5	1	4	.20	10	.290	.352	.536
1996 LAA	AL	114	431	131	28	3	27	(17	10)	246	73	66	88	46	2	101	4	0	2	4	0	1.00	6	.304	.375	.571
1997 LAA	AL	133	502	146	27	0	26	(14	12)	276	79	80	80	60	5	80	4	0	5	5	7	.42	8	.291	.368	.550
1998 LAA	AL	154	599	184	42	1	25	(9	16)	303	115	91	104	57	7	114	1	1	1	7	5	.58	16	.307	.368	.506
1999 LAA	AL	55	204	51	17	2	5	(3	2)	87	34	23	30	28	0	45	0	0	1	5	4	.56	3	.250	.339	.426
2000 StL	NL	152	525	155	25	0	42	(22	20)	306	129	108	126	103	3	167	6	1	8	10	3	.77	5	.295	.411	.583
2001 StL	NL	150	500	152	38	1	30	(16	14)	282	95	110	113	93	12	136	4	1	10	5	5	.50	8	.304	.410	.564
2002 StL	NL	144	476	148	31	2	28	(17	11)	267	96	83	101	86	14	134	8	0	6	4	3	.57	9	.311	.420	.561
2003 StL	NL	137	447	123	32	2	39	(17	22)	276	89	89	87	77	6	127	4	1	2	1	3	.25	11	.275	.385	.617
2004 StL	NL	153	498	150	38	3	42	(24	18)	320	102	111	115	101	12	150	5	0	8	8	3	.73	4	.301	.418	.643
2005 StL	NL	142	467	123	37	1	29	(15	14)	249	88	89	95	91	10	139	4	1	4	5	5	.50	6	.263	.385	.533
2006 StL	NL	110	350	90	18	0	19	(11	8)	165	52	70	64	53	7	101	0	0	5	4	0	1.00	11	.257	.350	.471

			BATTING																			BASERUNNING				AVERAGES		
Year	Team	Lg	G	AB	H	2B	3B	HR	(Hm	Rd)	TB	R	RBI	RC	TBB	IBB	SO	HBP	SH	SF		SB	CS	SB%	GDP		Avg	OBP	Slg
2007	StL	NL	117	365	92	15	2	12	(5	7)	147	39	53	43	41	2	75	0	2	3		0	2	.00	9		.252	.325	.403
2008	2 Tms	NL	111	340	80	19	2	20	(11	9)	163	53	55	48	55	3	82	2	1	3		2	2	.50	8		.235	.343	.479
08	SD	NL	26	90	16	2	0	1	(0	1)	21	6	6	5	10	1	24	1	1	1		2	1	.67	1		.178	.265	.233
08	ChC	NL	85	250	64	17	2	19	(11	8)	142	47	49	43	45	2	58	1	0	2		0	1	.00	7		.256	.369	.568
Postseason			61	220	61	15	0	13	(7	6)	115	32	41	37	30	3	70	2	0	1		2	2	.50	1		.277	.368	.523
16 ML YEARS			1925	6612	1881	414	25	382	(200	182)	3491	1207	1176	1233	974	91	1669	48	10	64		65	50	.57	120		.284	.377	.528

Mike Ekstrom

Pitches: R Bats: R Pos: RP-8   Ht: 5'11" Wt: 190 Born: 8/30/1983 Age: 25

			HOW MUCH HE PITCHED						WHAT HE GAVE UP											THE RESULTS						
Year	Team	Lg	G	GS	CG	GF	IP	BFP	H	R	ER	HR	SH	SF	HB	TBB	IBB	SO	WP	Bk	W	L	Pct	ShO	Sv-Op Hld		ERC	ERA
2004	Eugene	A-	12	7	0	1	39.0	171	38	18	16	1	1	4	4	10	0	42	2	0	3	1	.750	0	0-- -		3.14	3.69
2004	FtWyn	A	3	3	0	0	14.1	62	21	15	13	1	1	1	4	3	0	10	3	0	0	2	.000	0	0-- -		6.14	8.16
2005	FtWyn	A	28	28	1	0	167.2	703	167	76	69	11	6	6	5	36	0	112	4	0	13	6	.684	1	0-- -		3.19	3.70
2006	Lk Els	A+	14	14	1	0	82.1	335	76	32	21	2	3	1	7	21	0	68	3	0	7	4	.636	1	0-- -		3.02	2.30
2006	Mobile	AA	14	14	3	0	84.1	360	87	46	36	2	4	2	2	19	3	49	5	0	3	7	.300	1	0-- -		5.12	4.76
2007	SnAnt	AA	27	27	0	0	143.2	643	183	85	76	6	9	1	5	47	0	98	8	0	7	10	.412	0	1-- -		5.74	4.58
2008	SnAnt	AA	41	15	0	10	108.0	496	137	66	55	14	3	2	8	34	2	101	4	0	11	8	.579	0	1-- -		5.74	4.58
2008	SD	NL	8	0	0	1	9.2	47	14	8	8	2	0	0	0	7	1	6	0	0	0	2	.000	0	0-0 0		9.38	7.45

Scott Elarton

Pitches: R Bats: R Pos: RP-8   Ht: 6'8" Wt: 240 Born: 2/23/1976 Age: 33

			HOW MUCH HE PITCHED						WHAT HE GAVE UP											THE RESULTS						
Year	Team	Lg	G	GS	CG	GF	IP	BFP	H	R	ER	HR	SH	SF	HB	TBB	IBB	SO	WP	Bk	W	L	Pct	ShO	Sv-Op Hld		ERC	ERA
2008	Buffalo*	AAA	15	0	0	1	25.2	102	21	9	7	2	1	0	0	7	2	18	0	0	1	2	.333	0	0-- -		2.44	2.45
1998	Hou	NL	28	2	0	7	57.0	227	40	21	21	5	1	1	1	20	0	56	1	0	2	1	.667	0	2-3 2		2.35	3.32
1999	Hou	NL	42	15	0	3	124.0	524	111	55	48	8	7	4	4	43	0	121	3	0	9	5	.643	0	1-4 5		3.16	3.48
2000	Hou	NL	30	30	2	0	192.2	855	198	117	103	29	5	7	6	84	1	131	8	0	17	7	.708	0	0-0 0		4.82	4.81
2001	2 Tms	NL	24	24	0	0	132.2	595	146	105	104	34	7	2	6	59	2	87	5	0	4	10	.286	0	0-0 0		6.21	7.06
2003	Col	NL	11	10	0	0	51.2	253	73	46	36	13	3	4	4	20	3	20	3	0	4	4	.500	0	0-0 0		7.79	6.27
2004	2 Tms		29	29	1	0	158.2	697	164	107	104	33	5	7	4	62	3	103	8	0	11	9	.550	0	0-0 0		5.04	5.90
2005	Cle	AL	31	31	1	0	181.2	774	189	100	93	32	3	10	6	48	1	103	4	1	11	9	.550	0	0-0 0		4.40	4.61
2006	KC	AL	20	20	0	0	114.2	501	117	73	68	26	2	4	6	52	1	49	3	0	4	9	.308	0	0-0 0		5.64	5.34
2007	KC	AL	9	9	0	0	37.0	185	53	44	43	12	0	3	3	21	0	13	2	0	2	4	.333	0	0-0 0		9.76	10.46
2008	Cle	AL	8	0	0	4	15.1	70	16	7	6	0	0	0	0	9	2	15	2	0	0	1	.000	0	0-0 0		4.01	3.52
01	Hou	NL	20	20	0	0	109.2	499	126	88	87	26	7	2	6	49	1	76	5	0	4	8	.333	0	0-0 0		6.42	7.14
01	Col	NL	4	4	0	0	23.0	96	20	17	17	8	0	0	0	10	1	11	0	0	0	2	.000	0	0-0 0		5.18	6.65
04	Col	NL	8	8	0	0	41.1	199	57	45	45	8	2	3	0	20	1	23	5	0	0	6	.000	0	0-0 0		7.35	9.80
04	Cle	AL	21	21	1	0	117.1	498	107	62	59	25	3	4	4	42	2	80	3	0	5	3	.375	1	0-0 0		4.28	4.53
Postseason			3	0	0	1	4.1	20	5	2	2	1	1	0	1	2	0	6	2	0	0	1	.000	0	0-0 0		7.50	4.15
10 ML YEARS			232	170	4	19	1065.1	4681	1107	675	626	192	33	40	40	418	13	698	39	1	56	61	.479	1	3-7 7		4.96	5.29

Scott Elbert

Pitches: L Bats: L Pos: RP-10   Ht: 6'2" Wt: 210 Born: 8/13/1985 Age: 23

			HOW MUCH HE PITCHED						WHAT HE GAVE UP											THE RESULTS						
Year	Team	Lg	G	GS	CG	GF	IP	BFP	H	R	ER	HR	SH	SF	HB	TBB	IBB	SO	WP	Bk	W	L	Pct	ShO	Sv-Op Hld		ERC	ERA
2004	Ogden	R+	12	12	0	0	49.2	217	47	33	29	5	6	2	5	30	0	45	5	0	2	3	.400	0	0-- -		5.21	5.26
2005	Clmbs	A	25	24	1	0	115.0	482	83	37	34	8	0	5	4	57	0	128	5	0	8	5	.615	1	0-- -		2.86	2.66
2006	VeroB	A+	17	15	0	0	83.2	346	57	27	22	4	4	0	5	41	0	97	6	0	5	5	.500	0	0-- -		2.62	2.37
2006	Jaxnvl	AA	11	11	0	0	62.1	267	40	26	25	11	6	2	1	44	0	76	1	0	6	4	.600	0	0-- -		3.89	3.61
2007	Jaxnvl	AA	3	3	0	0	14.0	57	6	6	6	0	0	0	0	10	0	24	0	0	1	0	1.000	0	0-- -		1.66	3.86
2008	Jaxnvl	AA	25	1	0	7	41.1	162	22	14	11	2	1	1	1	19	1	46	1	0	4	1	.800	0	0-- -		1.70	2.40
2008	LAD	NL	10	0	0	1	6.0	31	9	8	8	2	0	0	1	4	0	8	0	0	0	1	.000	0	0-0 2		11.46	12.00

A.J. Ellis

Bats: R Throws: R Pos: C-3; PR-1   Ht: 6'3" Wt: 230 Born: 4/9/1981 Age: 28

			BATTING																			BASERUNNING				AVERAGES		
Year	Team	Lg	G	AB	H	2B	3B	HR	(Hm	Rd)	TB	R	RBI	RC	TBB	IBB	SO	HBP	SH	SF		SB	CS	SB%	GDP		Avg	OBP	Slg
2003	SoGA	A	3	6	0	0	0	0	(-	-)	0	0	0	0	0	0	0	1	0	0		0	1	.00	0		.000	.143	.000
2004	VeroB	A+	40	114	25	4	0	2	(-	-)	35	15	22	15	24	0	20	1	1	1		1	0	1.00	3		.219	.357	.307
2005	VeroB	A+	57	176	45	8	0	3	(-	-)	62	27	22	23	22	0	26	6	1	1		1	3	.25	3		.256	.356	.352
2006	Jaxnvl	AA	82	252	63	9	1	0	(-	-)	74	34	21	36	53	2	53	3	3	3		2	0	1.00	3		.250	.383	.294
2007	Jaxnvl	AA	110	357	96	22	2	8	(-	-)	146	59	57	60	60	1	61	8	1	4		1	4	.20	12		.269	.382	.409
2008	LsVgs	AAA	84	274	88	17	4	4	(-	-)	125	44	59	58	50	0	44	8	2	3		0	2	.00	8		.321	.436	.456
2008	LAD	NL	4	3	0	0	0	0	(0	0)	0	1	0	0	0	0	2	0	0	0		0	0	-	0		.000	.000	.000

Mark Ellis

Bats: R Throws: R Pos: 2B-115; PH-2; DH-1; PR-1   Ht: 5'11" Wt: 190 Born: 6/6/1977 Age: 32

			BATTING																			BASERUNNING				AVERAGES		
Year	Team	Lg	G	AB	H	2B	3B	HR	(Hm	Rd)	TB	R	RBI	RC	TBB	IBB	SO	HBP	SH	SF		SB	CS	SB%	GDP		Avg	OBP	Slg
2002	Oak	AL	98	345	94	16	4	6	(6	0)	136	58	35	55	44	1	54	4	8	3		4	2	.67	3		.272	.359	.394
2003	Oak	AL	154	553	137	31	5	9	(7	2)	205	78	52	69	48	4	94	7	9	5		6	2	.75	7		.248	.313	.371
2005	Oak	AL	122	434	137	21	5	13	(5	8)	207	76	52	78	44	1	51	4	4	0		1	3	.25	10		.316	.384	.477
2006	Oak	AL	124	441	110	25	1	11	(7	4)	170	64	52	53	40	1	76	8	4	7		4	0	1.00	13		.249	.319	.385

97

Year	Team	Lg	G	AB	H	2B	3B	HR	(Hm	Rd)	TB	R	RBI	RC	TBB	IBB	SO	HBP	SH	SF	SB	CS	SB%	GDP	Avg	OBP	Slg
																					BASERUNNING				AVERAGES		
2007	Oak	AL	150	583	161	33	3	19	(10	9)	257	84	76	76	44	1	94	10	2	3	9	4	.69	10	.276	.336	.441
2008	Oak	AL	117	442	103	20	3	12	(7	5)	165	55	41	54	53	2	65	5	5	2	14	2	.88	11	.233	.321	.373
	Postseason		12	43	11	2	0	1	(1	0)	16	3	4	6	5	0	11	1	0	0	0	0	-	0	.256	.347	.372
	6 ML YEARS		765	2798	742	146	21	70	(42	28)	1140	415	308	385	273	10	434	38	32	20	38	13	.75	54	.265	.337	.407

Jason Ellison

Bats: R **Throws:** R **Pos:** RF-3; LF-2; CF-2; DH-2; PH-2; PR-2   **Ht:** 5'10" **Wt:** 180 **Born:** 4/4/1978 **Age:** 31

Year	Team	Lg	G	AB	H	2B	3B	HR	(Hm	Rd)	TB	R	RBI	RC	TBB	IBB	SO	HBP	SH	SF	SB	CS	SB%	GDP	Avg	OBP	Slg
									BATTING												BASERUNNING				AVERAGES		
2008	Okla*	AAA	120	477	114	21	4	2	(-	-)	149	65	45	55	63	1	77	8	4	4	14	10	.58	14	.239	.335	.312
2003	SF	NL	7	10	1	0	0	0	(0	0)	1	1	0	0	0	0	1	0	0	0	0	0	-	0	.100	.100	.100
2004	SF	NL	13	4	2	0	0	0	(0	1)	5	4	3	3	0	0	1	0	0	0	2	0	1.00	0	.500	.500	1.250
2005	SF	NL	131	352	93	18	2	4	(2	2)	127	49	24	34	24	1	44	3	6	1	14	6	.70	7	.264	.316	.361
2006	SF	NL	84	81	18	5	1	2	(0	2)	31	14	4	4	5	0	14	1	3	1	2	2	.50	3	.222	.273	.383
2007	2 Tms		100	94	22	1	0	1	(0	1)	26	16	2	5	6	0	27	1	3	0	4	3	.57	1	.234	.287	.277
2008	Tex	AL	9	13	3	0	0	0	(0	0)	3	5	2	1	1	0	1	0	0	0	0	0	-	0	.231	.286	.231
07	Sea	AL	63	46	13	0	0	0	(0	0)	13	9	0	2	1	0	12	0	1	0	3	3	.50	1	.283	.298	.283
07	Cin	NL	37	48	9	1	0	1	(0	1)	13	7	2	3	5	0	15	1	2	0	1	0	1.00	0	.188	.278	.271
	6 ML YEARS		344	554	139	24	3	8	(2	6)	193	89	35	47	36	1	88	5	12	2	22	11	.67	11	.251	.302	.348

Jacoby Ellsbury

Bats: L **Throws:** L **Pos:** CF-66; LF-58; RF-36; PR-5; DH-2; PH-1   **Ht:** 6'1" **Wt:** 185 **Born:** 9/11/1983 **Age:** 25

Year	Team	Lg	G	AB	H	2B	3B	HR	(Hm	Rd)	TB	R	RBI	RC	TBB	IBB	SO	HBP	SH	SF	SB	CS	SB%	GDP	Avg	OBP	Slg
									BATTING												BASERUNNING				AVERAGES		
2005	Lowell	A-	35	139	44	3	5	1	(-	-)	60	28	19	30	24	0	20	1	0	1	23	3	.88	4	.317	.418	.432
2006	Wilmg	A+	61	244	73	7	5	4	(-	-)	102	35	32	42	25	3	28	7	4	1	25	9	.74	5	.299	.379	.418
2006	Portlnd	AA	50	198	61	10	3	3	(-	-)	86	29	19	34	24	2	25	2	0	1	16	8	.67	1	.308	.387	.434
2007	Portlnd	AA	17	73	33	10	2	0	(-	-)	47	16	13	23	6	0	7	4	0	0	8	1	.89	0	.452	.518	.644
2007	Pwtckt	AAA	87	363	108	14	5	2	(-	-)	138	66	28	56	32	2	47	4	1	1	33	6	.85	5	.298	.360	.380
2007	Bos	AL	33	116	41	7	1	3	(3	0)	59	20	18	26	8	0	15	1	0	2	9	0	1.00	2	.353	.394	.509
2008	Bos	AL	145	554	155	22	7	9	(4	5)	218	98	47	71	41	2	80	7	4	3	50	11	.82	10	.280	.336	.394
	Postseason		11	25	9	4	0	0	(0	0)	13	8	4	7	3	1	3	0	0	0	2	0	1.00	1	.360	.429	.520
	2 ML YEARS		178	670	196	29	8	12	(7	5)	277	118	65	97	49	2	95	8	4	5	59	11	.84	12	.293	.346	.413

Alan Embree

Pitches: L **Bats:** L **Pos:** RP-70   **Ht:** 6'2" **Wt:** 200 **Born:** 1/23/1970 **Age:** 39

Year	Team	Lg	G	GS	CG	GF	IP	BFP	H	R	ER	HR	SH	SF	HB	TBB	IBB	SO	WP	Bk	W	L	Pct	ShO	Sv-Op	Hld	ERC	ERA
			HOW MUCH HE PITCHED						WHAT HE GAVE UP												THE RESULTS							
1992	Cle	AL	4	4	0	0	18.0	81	19	14	14	3	0	2	1	8	0	12	1	1	0	2	.000	0	0-0	0	5.25	7.00
1995	Cle	AL	23	0	0	8	24.2	111	23	16	14	2	2	2	0	16	0	23	1	0	3	2	.600	0	1-1	6	4.51	5.11
1996	Cle	AL	24	0	0	2	31.0	141	30	26	22	10	1	3	0	21	3	33	3	0	1	1	.500	0	0-0	1	6.58	6.39
1997	Atl	NL	66	0	0	15	46.0	190	36	13	13	1	4	1	2	20	2	45	3	1	3	1	.750	0	0-0	16	2.66	2.54
1998	2 Tms	NL	55	0	0	16	53.2	237	56	32	25	7	4	1	1	23	0	43	3	0	4	2	.667	0	1-3	12	4.71	4.19
1999	SF	NL	68	0	0	13	58.2	244	42	22	22	6	3	2	3	26	2	53	3	0	3	2	.600	0	0-3	22	2.86	3.38
2000	SF	NL	63	0	0	21	60.0	263	62	34	33	4	4	5	3	25	2	49	1	0	3	5	.375	0	2-5	9	4.24	4.95
2001	2 Tms		61	0	0	17	54.0	245	65	47	44	14	0	6	3	17	2	59	3	0	1	4	.200	0	0-3	9	6.20	7.33
2002	2 Tms		68	0	0	20	62.0	251	47	19	15	6	1	2	1	20	3	81	1	0	4	6	.400	0	2-7	18	2.48	2.18
2003	Bos	AL	65	0	0	15	55.0	221	49	26	26	5	0	2	0	16	3	45	0	0	4	1	.800	0	1-2	14	3.01	4.25
2004	Bos	AL	71	0	0	11	52.1	217	49	28	24	7	2	2	1	11	1	37	0	0	2	2	.500	0	0-1	20	3.21	4.13
2005	2 Tms	NL	67	0	0	15	52.0	231	62	47	44	10	3	3	2	14	3	38	1	1	2	5	.286	0	1-3	10	5.34	7.62
2006	SD	NL	73	0	0	11	52.1	221	50	21	19	4	2	3	0	15	2	53	0	0	4	3	.571	0	0-0	16	3.13	3.27
2007	Oak	AL	68	0	0	36	68.0	284	67	30	30	5	1	4	0	19	5	51	0	0	1	2	.333	0	17-21	16	3.24	3.97
2008	Oak	AL	70	0	0	11	61.2	270	59	36	34	8	2	3	2	30	5	57	2	0	2	5	.286	0	0-5	18	4.39	4.96
98	Atl	NL	20	0	0	5	18.2	87	23	14	9	2	1	1	0	10	0	19	0	0	1	0	1.000	0	0-1	6	6.06	4.34
98	Ari	NL	35	0	0	11	35.0	150	33	18	16	5	3	0	1	13	0	24	3	0	3	2	.600	0	1-2	6	4.03	4.11
01	SF	NL	22	0	0	7	20.0	106	34	26	25	7	0	3	2	10	2	25	1	0	0	2	.000	0	0-1	0	11.29	11.25
01	CWS	AL	39	0	0	10	34.0	139	31	21	19	7	0	3	1	7	0	34	2	0	1	2	.333	0	0-2	9	3.61	5.03
02	SD	NL	36	0	0	13	28.2	118	23	7	4	2	0	0	0	9	2	38	1	0	3	4	.429	0	0-2	10	2.38	1.26
02	Bos	AL	32	0	0	7	33.1	133	24	12	11	4	1	2	1	11	1	43	0	0	1	2	.333	0	2-5	8	2.56	2.97
05	Bos	AL	43	0	0	11	37.2	163	42	33	32	8	1	2	1	11	2	30	1	0	1	4	.200	0	1-3	4	5.14	7.65
05	NYY	AL	24	0	0	4	14.1	68	20	14	12	2	2	1	1	3	1	8	0	1	1	1	.200	0	0-0	6	5.85	7.53
	Postseason		31	0	0	6	21.2	84	16	5	4	0	2	2	1	5	2	13	0	0	1	0	1.000	0	0-1	5	1.64	1.66
	15 ML YEARS		846	4	0	211	749.1	3207	716	411	379	92	29	41	19	281	33	679	22	3	37	43	.463	0	25-54	187	3.91	4.55

Edwin Encarnacion

Bats: R **Throws:** R **Pos:** 3B-143; PH-2; PR-1   **Ht:** 6'1" **Wt:** 216 **Born:** 1/7/1983 **Age:** 26

Year	Team	Lg	G	AB	H	2B	3B	HR	(Hm	Rd)	TB	R	RBI	RC	TBB	IBB	SO	HBP	SH	SF	SB	CS	SB%	GDP	Avg	OBP	Slg
									BATTING												BASERUNNING				AVERAGES		
2005	Cin	NL	69	211	49	16	0	9	(3	6)	92	25	31	24	20	2	60	3	0	0	3	0	1.00	8	.232	.308	.436
2006	Cin	NL	117	406	112	33	1	15	(7	8)	192	60	72	66	41	3	78	13	0	3	6	3	.67	9	.276	.359	.473
2007	Cin	NL	139	502	145	25	1	16	(10	6)	220	66	76	86	39	4	86	14	0	1	8	1	.89	5	.289	.356	.438
2008	Cin	NL	146	506	127	29	1	26	(15	11)	236	75	68	72	61	1	102	10	0	5	1	0	1.00	13	.251	.340	.466
	4 ML YEARS		471	1625	433	103	3	66	(35	31)	740	226	247	248	161	10	326	40	0	9	18	4	.82	35	.266	.346	.455

Morgan Ensberg

Bats: R **Throws:** R **Pos:** 3B-21; 1B-7; PH-3; PR-2; DH-1   **Ht:** 6'2" **Wt:** 210 **Born:** 8/26/1975 **Age:** 33

								BATTING												BASERUNNING				AVERAGES		
Year	Team	Lg	G	AB	H	2B	3B	HR	(Hm | Rd)	TB	R	RBI	RC	TBB	IBB	SO	HBP	SH	SF	SB	CS	SB%	GDP	Avg	OBP	Slg
2008	Buffalo*	AAA	52	159	30	9	0	5	(- | -)	54	24	23	19	31	2	43	1	4	1	1	1	.50	5	.189	.323	.340
2000	Hou	NL	4	7	2	0	0	0	(0 | 0)	2	0	0	1	0	0	1	0	0	0	0	0	-	0	.286	.286	.286
2002	Hou	NL	49	132	32	7	2	3	(2 | 1)	52	14	19	13	18	0	25	3	0	0	2	0	1.00	8	.242	.346	.394
2003	Hou	NL	127	385	112	15	1	25	(16 | 9)	204	69	60	71	48	1	60	6	1	1	7	2	.78	10	.291	.377	.530
2004	Hou	NL	131	411	113	20	3	10	(9 | 1)	169	51	66	57	36	1	46	0	5	4	6	4	.60	17	.275	.330	.411
2005	Hou	NL	150	526	149	30	3	36	(20 | 16)	293	86	101	107	85	9	119	8	0	5	6	7	.46	12	.283	.388	.557
2006	Hou	NL	127	387	91	17	1	23	(16 | 7)	179	67	58	73	101	7	96	4	0	3	1	4	.20	3	.235	.396	.463
2007	2 Tms	NL	115	282	65	13	0	12	(5 | 7)	114	47	39	34	38	0	67	0	2	2	0	1	.00	7	.230	.320	.404
2008	NYY	AL	28	74	15	0	0	1	(0 | 1)	18	6	4	3	6	0	22	0	0	0	0	0	-	1	.203	.263	.243
07	Hou		85	224	52	10	0	8	(2 | 6)	86	36	31	27	31	0	48	0	2	2	0	1	.00	6	.232	.323	.384
07	SD	NL	30	58	13	3	0	4	(3 | 1)	28	11	8	7	7	0	19	0	0	0	0	0	-	1	.224	.308	.483
	Postseason		26	98	22	5	0	2	(0 | 2)	33	8	18	9	9	1	16	2	0	1	0	2	.00	5	.224	.300	.337
	8 ML YEARS		731	2204	579	102	10	110	(68 | 42)	1031	340	347	359	332	18	436	21	8	15	22	19	.54	58	.263	.362	.468

Darin Erstad

Bats: L **Throws:** L **Pos:** LF-56; PH-51; CF-40; 1B-12; RF-6; PR-2   **Ht:** 6'2" **Wt:** 220 **Born:** 6/4/1974 **Age:** 35

								BATTING												BASERUNNING				AVERAGES		
Year	Team	Lg	G	AB	H	2B	3B	HR	(Hm | Rd)	TB	R	RBI	RC	TBB	IBB	SO	HBP	SH	SF	SB	CS	SB%	GDP	Avg	OBP	Slg
1996	LAA	AL	57	208	59	5	1	4	(1 | 3)	78	34	20	26	17	1	29	0	1	3	3	3	.50	3	.284	.333	.375
1997	LAA	AL	139	539	161	34	4	16	(8 | 8)	251	99	77	92	51	4	86	4	5	6	23	8	.74	5	.299	.360	.466
1998	LAA	AL	133	537	159	39	3	19	(9 | 10)	261	84	82	94	43	7	77	6	1	3	20	6	.77	2	.296	.353	.486
1999	LAA	AL	142	585	148	22	5	13	(7 | 6)	219	84	53	64	47	3	101	1	2	4	13	7	.65	16	.253	.308	.374
2000	LAA	AL	157	676	240	39	6	25	(11 | 14)	366	121	100	145	64	9	82	1	2	4	28	8	.78	8	.355	.409	.541
2001	LAA	AL	157	631	163	35	1	9	(3 | 6)	227	89	63	79	62	7	113	10	1	7	24	10	.71	8	.258	.331	.360
2002	LAA	AL	150	625	177	28	4	10	(2 | 8)	243	99	73	74	27	4	67	2	5	4	23	3	.88	9	.283	.313	.389
2003	LAA	AL	67	258	65	7	1	4	(1 | 3)	86	35	17	22	18	1	40	4	2	2	9	1	.90	8	.252	.309	.333
2004	LAA	AL	125	495	146	29	1	7	(3 | 4)	198	79	69	76	37	1	74	4	3	4	16	1	.94	9	.295	.346	.400
2005	LAA	AL	153	609	166	33	3	7	(4 | 3)	226	86	66	79	47	3	109	1	4	2	10	3	.77	8	.273	.325	.371
2006	LAA	AL	40	95	21	8	1	0	(0 | 0)	31	8	5	6	6	0	18	2	1	1	1	1	.50	2	.221	.279	.326
2007	CWS	AL	87	310	77	13	1	4	(2 | 2)	104	33	32	36	28	0	44	0	6	1	7	2	.78	4	.248	.310	.335
2008	Hou	NL	140	322	89	16	0	4	(2 | 2)	117	49	31	39	14	3	68	2	2	2	2	3	.40	7	.276	.309	.363
	Postseason		29	118	40	9	0	3	(2 | 1)	58	18	12	17	5	0	17	1	2	1	4	0	1.00	3	.339	.368	.492
	13 ML YEARS		1547	5890	1671	308	31	122	(53 | 69)	2407	900	688	832	461	43	908	37	35	42	179	56	.76	85	.284	.337	.409

Alcides Escobar

Bats: R **Throws:** R **Pos:** PR-4; PH-3; SS-2   **Ht:** 6'1" **Wt:** 175 **Born:** 12/16/1986 **Age:** 22

								BATTING												BASERUNNING				AVERAGES		
Year	Team	Lg	G	AB	H	2B	3B	HR	(Hm | Rd)	TB	R	RBI	RC	TBB	IBB	SO	HBP	SH	SF	SB	CS	SB%	GDP	Avg	OBP	Slg
2004	Helena	R+	68	231	65	8	0	2	(- | -)	79	38	24	30	20	0	44	4	6	1	20	9	.69	6	.281	.348	.342
2005	WV	A-	127	520	141	25	8	2	(- | -)	188	80	36	60	20	0	90	7	11	4	30	13	.70	4	.271	.305	.362
2006	BrvdCt	A+	87	350	90	9	1	2	(- | -)	107	47	33	36	19	1	56	3	7	7	28	8	.78	4	.257	.296	.306
2007	BrvdCt	A+	63	268	87	8	3	0	(- | -)	101	37	25	35	7	0	35	0	2	2	18	10	.64	4	.325	.345	.377
2007	Hntsvl	AA	62	226	64	5	4	1	(- | -)	80	27	26	25	11	4	36	0	6	2	4	3	.57	6	.283	.314	.354
2008	Hntsvl	AA	131	547	180	25	5	8	(- | -)	239	95	76	92	31	0	82	3	9	7	35	8	.81	10	.329	.364	.437
2008	Mil	NL	9	4	2	0	0	0	(0 | 0)	2	0	0	0	0	0	1	0	0	0	0	0	-	0	.500	.500	.500

Kelvim Escobar

Pitches: R **Bats:** R **Pos:** P   **Ht:** 6'1" **Wt:** 230 **Born:** 4/11/1976 **Age:** 33

			HOW MUCH HE PITCHED					WHAT HE GAVE UP											THE RESULTS						
Year	Team	Lg	G	GS	CG	GF	IP	BFP	H	R	ER	HR	SH	SF	HB	TBB	IBB	SO	WP	Bk	W	L	Pct	ShO	Sv-Op Hld	ERC	ERA
2008	Angels*	R	1	1	0	0	2.0	8	2	1	1	0	0	1	0	0	0	2	0	0	0	0	-	0	0- -	1.95	4.50
2008	RCuca*	A+	1	1	0	0	3.0	10	1	0	0	0	0	0	0	0	0	4	0	0	0	0	-	0	0- -	0.25	0.00
1997	Tor	AL	27	0	0	23	31.0	139	28	12	10	1	2	0	0	19	2	36	0	0	3	2	.600	0	14-17 1	3.68	2.90
1998	Tor	AL	22	10	0	2	79.2	342	72	37	33	5	0	3	0	35	0	72	0	0	7	3	.700	0	0-1 5	3.41	3.73
1999	Tor	AL	33	30	1	2	174.0	795	203	118	110	19	2	8	10	81	2	129	6	1	14	11	.560	0	0-0 0	5.62	5.69
2000	Tor	AL	43	24	3	8	180.0	794	186	118	107	26	5	4	3	85	3	142	4	0	10	15	.400	1	2-3 3	4.94	5.35
2001	Tor	AL	59	11	1	15	126.0	517	93	51	49	8	2	5	3	52	5	121	2	0	6	8	.429	1	0-0 13	2.54	3.50
2002	Tor	AL	76	0	0	68	78.0	355	75	39	37	10	1	0	5	44	6	85	4	0	5	7	.417	0	38-46 0	4.77	4.27
2003	Tor	AL	41	26	1	12	180.1	797	189	94	86	15	5	5	9	78	3	159	9	0	13	9	.591	1	4-5 0	4.53	4.29
2004	LAA	AL	33	33	0	0	208.1	878	192	91	91	21	3	6	7	76	2	191	9	0	11	12	.478	0	0-0 0	3.65	3.93
2005	LAA	AL	16	7	0	2	59.2	242	45	21	20	4	2	0	2	21	1	63	4	0	3	2	.600	0	1-1 2	2.51	3.02
2006	LAA	AL	30	30	1	0	189.1	789	192	93	76	17	6	3	4	50	2	147	7	0	11	14	.440	0	0-0 0	3.67	3.61
2007	LAA	AL	30	30	3	0	195.2	812	182	79	74	11	5	4	3	66	2	160	9	0	18	7	.720	0	0-0 0	3.25	3.40
	Postseason		8	2	0	2	19.2	92	15	12	8	2	0	2	0	17	2	24	2	0	1	2	.333	0	0-1 2	4.22	3.66
	11 ML YEARS		410	201	10	132	1502.0	6460	1457	753	693	137	33	38	46	607	28	1305	54	1	101	90	.529	4	59-73 24	3.97	4.15

Yunel Escobar

Bats: R **Throws:** R **Pos:** SS-127; PH-8; PR-1   **Ht:** 6'2" **Wt:** 200 **Born:** 11/2/1982 **Age:** 26

								BATTING												BASERUNNING				AVERAGES		
Year	Team	Lg	G	AB	H	2B	3B	HR	(Hm | Rd)	TB	R	RBI	RC	TBB	IBB	SO	HBP	SH	SF	SB	CS	SB%	GDP	Avg	OBP	Slg
2005	Danvle	R	8	30	12	2	1	2	(- | -)	22	9	9	9	5	0	4	0	0	1	0	0	-	1	.400	.472	.733
2005	Rome	A	48	198	62	13	3	4	(- | -)	93	30	19	32	14	0	30	1	0	2	0	2	.00	6	.313	.358	.470
2006	Missi	AA	121	428	112	21	4	2	(- | -)	147	55	45	57	58	1	76	9	2	4	7	9	.44	20	.262	.359	.343

			BATTING																		BASERUNNING				AVERAGES		
Year Team	Lg	G	AB	H	2B	3B	HR	(Hm Rd)	TB	R	RBI	RC	TBB	IBB	SO	HBP	SH	SF	SB	CS	SB%	GDP	Avg	OBP	Slg
2007 Rchmd	AAA	46	180	60	10	3	2	(- -)	82	20	29	31	14	1	27	0	0	1	7	3	.70	10	.333	.379	.456
2007 Atl	NL	94	319	104	25	0	5	(3 2)	144	54	28	52	27	1	44	5	2	2	5	3	.63	6	.326	.385	.451
2008 Atl	NL	136	514	148	24	2	10	(5 5)	206	71	60	70	59	4	62	5	7	2	2	5	.29	24	.288	.366	.401
2 ML YEARS		230	833	252	49	2	15	(8 7)	350	125	88	122	86	5	106	10	9	4	7	8	.47	30	.303	.373	.420

Geno Espineli

Pitches: L Bats: L Pos: RP-15

Ht: 6'4" Wt: 195 Born: 9/8/1982 Age: 26

		HOW MUCH HE PITCHED						WHAT HE GAVE UP											THE RESULTS						
Year Team	Lg	G	GS	CG	GF	IP	BFP	H	R	ER	HR	SH	SF	HB	TBB	IBB	SO	WP	Bk	W	L	Pct	ShO	Sv-Op Hld	ERC	ERA
2004 Salem	A+	22	0	0	11	30.0	128	29	18	17	0	1	2	1	8	0	37	1	0	1	3	.250	0	3- -	2.77	5.10
2004 SnJos	A+	1	0	0	1	1.0	3	0	0	0	0	0	0	0	0	0	1	0	0	0	0	-	0	1- -	0.00	0.00
2005 SnJos	A+	40	0	0	7	64.1	271	57	22	19	2	5	4	2	24	0	55	0	1	4	0	1.000	0	1- -	3.00	2.66
2005 Fresno	AAA	12	0	0	2	18.1	83	22	13	13	3	2	0	1	8	0	12	0	1	1	1	.500	0	0- -	6.21	6.38
2006 Conn	AA	35	13	1	8	107.1	459	117	53	49	6	8	5	3	29	3	65	2	0	8	7	.533	1	2- -	3.84	4.11
2007 Conn	AA	29	24	0	4	140.2	586	142	63	54	8	5	4	3	37	0	105	1	1	8	10	.444	0	0- -	3.43	3.45
2008 Fresno	AAA	38	0	0	8	61.0	247	56	22	18	2	2	4	2	11	1	48	4	0	1	1	.500	0	1- -	2.50	2.66
2008 SF	NL	15	0	0	5	16.0	69	17	10	9	5	0	0	0	8	2	8	2	0	2	0	1.000	0	0-0 0	6.48	5.06

Shawn Estes

Pitches: L Bats: R Pos: SP-8; RP-1

Ht: 6'2" Wt: 200 Born: 2/18/1973 Age: 36

		HOW MUCH HE PITCHED						WHAT HE GAVE UP											THE RESULTS						
Year Team	Lg	G	GS	CG	GF	IP	BFP	H	R	ER	HR	SH	SF	HB	TBB	IBB	SO	WP	Bk	W	L	Pct	ShO	Sv-Op Hld	ERC	ERA
2008 Portlnd*	AAA	8	8	0	0	44.2	188	45	20	18	3	0	1	4	10	0	29	1	1	5	2	.714	0	0- -	3.58	3.63
2008 Lk Els*	A+	2	2	0	0	5.2	25	6	3	3	1	0	0	0	3	0	5	0	0	1	0	1.000	0	0- -	5.63	4.76
1995 SF	NL	3	3	0	0	17.1	76	16	14	13	2	0	0	1	5	0	14	4	0	0	3	.000	0	0-0 0	3.37	6.75
1996 SF	NL	11	11	0	0	70.0	305	63	30	28	3	5	0	2	39	3	60	4	0	3	5	.375	0	0-0 0	3.78	3.60
1997 SF	NL	32	32	3	0	201.0	849	162	80	71	12	13	2	8	100	2	181	10	2	19	5	.792	2	0-0 0	3.28	3.18
1998 SF	NL	25	25	1	0	149.1	661	150	89	84	14	15	4	5	80	6	136	6	1	7	12	.368	1	0-0 0	4.71	5.06
1999 SF	NL	32	32	1	0	203.0	914	209	121	111	21	14	3	5	112	2	159	15	1	11	11	.500	1	0-0 0	4.96	4.92
2000 SF	NL	30	30	4	0	190.1	829	194	99	90	11	7	6	3	108	1	136	11	0	15	6	.714	2	0-0 0	4.75	4.26
2001 SF	NL	27	27	0	0	159.0	693	151	78	71	11	5	9	5	77	7	109	10	2	9	8	.529	0	0-0 0	3.96	4.02
2002 2 Tms	NL	29	29	1	0	160.2	713	171	94	91	13	7	6	9	83	9	109	3	1	5	12	.294	1	0-0 0	5.00	5.10
2003 ChC	NL	29	28	1	0	152.1	699	182	113	97	20	11	7	1	83	1	103	6	0	8	11	.421	1	0-0 0	6.15	5.73
2004 Col	NL	34	34	1	0	202.0	904	223	133	131	36	13	8	11	105	5	117	4	2	15	8	.652	0	0-0 0	5.86	5.84
2005 Ari	NL	21	21	2	0	123.2	535	132	70	66	15	10	4	4	45	0	63	4	0	7	8	.467	0	0-0 0	4.65	4.80
2006 SD	NL	1	1	0	0	6.0	27	5	3	3	0	0	0	0	3	0	4	0	0	1	0	1.000	0	0-0 0	3.35	4.50
2008 SD	NL	9	8	0	0	43.2	198	50	26	23	6	2	2	1	18	0	19	2	0	2	3	.400	0	0-0 0	5.39	4.74
02 NYM	NL	23	23	1	0	132.2	580	133	70	67	12	7	4	5	66	9	92	2	1	4	9	.308	1	0-0 0	4.51	4.55
02 Cin	NL	6	6	0	0	28.0	133	38	24	24	1	0	2	4	17	0	17	1	0	1	3	.250	0	0-0 0	7.52	7.71
Postseason		2	2	0	0	6.0	34	8	7	7	1	0	0	1	7	0	6	0	0	0	0	-	0	0-0 0	10.63	10.50
13 ML YEARS		283	281	14	0	1678.1	7403	1708	950	879	158	102	49	57	858	36	1210	79	9	101	93	.521	8	0-0 0	4.73	4.71

Johnny Estrada

Bats: B Throws: R Pos: C-14; PH-11

Ht: 5'11" Wt: 254 Born: 6/27/1976 Age: 33

			BATTING																		BASERUNNING				AVERAGES		
Year Team	Lg	G	AB	H	2B	3B	HR	(Hm Rd)	TB	R	RBI	RC	TBB	IBB	SO	HBP	SH	SF	SB	CS	SB%	GDP	Avg	OBP	Slg
2008 Clmbs*	AAA	4	16	4	0	0	0	(- -)	4	1	1	1	1	0	1	0	0	0	0	0	-	0	.250	.294	.250
2008 Nats*	R	3	7	2	0	0	0	(- -)	2	1	3	0	0	0	1	0	0	0	0	0	-	0	.286	.286	.286
2008 Ptomc*	A+	4	14	5	1	0	0	(- -)	6	1	3	2	1	1	1	0	0	0	0	0	-	1	.357	.400	.429
2008 Hrsbrg*	AA	5	20	5	0	0	1	(- -)	8	2	3	2	0	0	2	0	0	0	0	0	-	1	.250	.250	.400
2001 Phi	NL	89	298	68	15	0	8	(7 1)	107	26	37	25	16	6	32	4	2	4	0	0	-	15	.228	.273	.359
2002 Phi	NL	10	17	2	1	0	0	(0 0)	3	0	2	0	2	1	2	0	0	0	0	0	-	0	.118	.211	.176
2003 Atl	NL	16	36	11	0	0	0	(0 0)	11	2	2	2	0	0	3	3	0	0	0	0	-	1	.306	.359	.306
2004 Atl	NL	134	462	145	36	0	9	(4 5)	208	56	76	78	39	7	66	11	1	4	0	0	-	18	.314	.378	.450
2005 Atl	NL	105	357	93	26	0	4	(2 2)	131	31	39	36	20	6	38	3	0	3	0	0	-	13	.261	.303	.367
2006 Ari	NL	115	414	125	26	0	11	(7 4)	184	43	71	59	13	7	40	7	1	8	0	0	-	17	.302	.328	.444
2007 Mil	NL	120	442	123	25	0	10	(3 7)	178	40	54	41	12	3	43	2	1	7	0	0	-	16	.278	.296	.403
2008 Was	NL	23	53	9	0	0	0	(0 0)	9	0	4	4	1	0	4	1	0	0	0	0	-	0	.170	.200	.170
Postseason		6	21	7	0	0	2	(1 1)	13	3	5	4	3	0	5	0	0	1	0	0	-	0	.333	.400	.619
8 ML YEARS		612	2079	576	129	0	42	(23 19)	831	198	285	245	103	30	228	31	5	26	0	0	-	80	.277	.317	.400

Marco Estrada

Pitches: R Bats: R Pos: RP-11

Ht: 6'0" Wt: 180 Born: 7/5/1983 Age: 25

		HOW MUCH HE PITCHED						WHAT HE GAVE UP											THE RESULTS						
Year Team	Lg	G	GS	CG	GF	IP	BFP	H	R	ER	HR	SH	SF	HB	TBB	IBB	SO	WP	Bk	W	L	Pct	ShO	Sv-Op Hld	ERC	ERA
2006 Nats	R	5	4	0	0	23.2	91	14	4	4	1	0	0	0	6	0	27	0	0	2	0	1.000	0	0- -	1.34	1.52
2006 Savann	A	8	8	0	0	37.0	166	44	23	23	6	1	1	4	14	0	29	2	0	1	4	.200	0	0- -	6.15	5.59
2007 Hgrstn	A	8	8	0	0	36.0	163	39	24	21	4	3	2	1	17	0	35	0	1	1	5	.167	0	0- -	4.98	5.25
2007 Ptomc	A+	11	11	0	0	58.1	249	67	32	32	7	1	1	0	17	0	54	0	1	5	3	.625	0	0- -	4.72	4.94
2007 Nats	R	4	4	0	0	11.1	57	19	6	4	1	0	1	1	3	0	13	0	0	0	0	-	0	0- -	7.74	3.18
2008 Hrsbrg	AA	13	13	1	0	74.1	314	62	27	22	5	1	1	2	32	1	67	0	0	6	3	.667	1	0- -	3.14	2.66
2008 Clmbs	AAA	12	12	0	0	65.1	281	73	28	26	3	0	2	4	21	1	52	0	1	3	3	.500	0	0- -	4.36	3.58
2008 Was	NL	11	0	0	3	12.2	63	17	13	11	4	0	0	2	5	1	10	0	0	0	0	-	0	0-1 3	8.13	7.82

100

Andre Ethier

Bats: L **Throws:** L **Pos:** RF-109; LF-41; PH-8   **Ht:** 6'2" **Wt:** 212 **Born:** 4/10/1982 **Age:** 27

Year	Team	Lg	G	AB	H	2B	3B	HR	(Hm	Rd)	TB	R	RBI	RC	TBB	IBB	SO	HBP	SH	SF	SB	CS	SB%	GDP	Avg	OBP	Slg
2006	LAD	NL	126	396	122	20	7	11	(9	2)	189	50	55	62	34	2	77	5	0	6	5	5	.50	11	.308	.365	.477
2007	LAD	NL	153	447	127	32	2	13	(8	5)	202	50	64	65	46	12	68	4	0	8	0	4	.00	10	.284	.350	.452
2008	LAD	NL	141	525	160	38	5	20	(10	10)	268	90	77	99	59	0	88	4	1	7	6	3	.67	6	.305	.375	.510
Postseason			2	1	0	0	0	0	(-	-)	0	0	0	0	0	0	0	0	0	0	0	0	-	0	.000	.000	.000
3 ML YEARS			420	1368	409	90	14	44	(27	17)	659	190	196	226	139	14	233	13	1	21	11	12	.48	27	.299	.364	.482

Nick Evans

Bats: R **Throws:** R **Pos:** LF-28; PH-20; 1B-3; PR-2   **Ht:** 6'3" **Wt:** 210 **Born:** 1/30/1986 **Age:** 23

Year	Team	Lg	G	AB	H	2B	3B	HR	(Hm	Rd)	TB	R	RBI	RC	TBB	IBB	SO	HBP	SH	SF	SB	CS	SB%	GDP	Avg	OBP	Slg
2004	Mets	R	50	182	47	10	3	7	(-	-)	84	36	27	26	14	0	51	0	0	0	3	2	.60	3	.258	.311	.462
2005	Kngspt	R+	15	64	22	7	0	6	(-	-)	47	11	22	16	4	1	17	0	0	0	1	0	1.00	1	.344	.382	.734
2005	Bklyn	A-	57	226	57	11	3	6	(-	-)	92	30	33	28	17	1	34	0	0	2	1	1	.00	3	.252	.302	.407
2006	Hgrstn	A	137	511	130	33	3	15	(-	-)	214	55	67	72	45	3	99	6	0	3	2	0	1.00	17	.254	.320	.419
2007	StLuci	A+	103	378	108	25	1	15	(-	-)	180	65	54	71	53	4	64	3	2	4	3	0	1.00	10	.286	.374	.476
2008	Bnghtn	AA	75	296	92	18	7	14	(-	-)	166	52	53	59	26	1	64	1	0	3	2	1	.67	7	.311	.365	.561
2008	NYM	NL	50	109	28	10	0	2	(0	2)	44	18	9	10	7	2	24	1	0	2	0	0	-	1	.257	.303	.404

Dana Eveland

Pitches: L **Bats:** L **Pos:** SP-29   **Ht:** 6'0" **Wt:** 170 **Born:** 10/29/1983 **Age:** 25

Year	Team	Lg	G	GS	CG	GF	IP	BFP	H	R	ER	HR	SH	SF	HB	TBB	IBB	SO	WP	Bk	W	L	Pct	ShO	Sv-Op	Hld	ERC	ERA
2008	Scrmto*	AAA	3	3	0	0	21.0	91	23	9	6	2	1	0	0	4	0	21	1	0	3	0	1.000	0	0--	-	3.61	2.57
2005	Mil	NL	27	0	0	3	31.2	146	40	21	21	2	0	1	1	18	3	23	1	0	1	1	.500	0	1-2	7	6.16	5.97
2006	Mil	NL	9	5	0	1	27.2	141	39	25	25	4	1	1	5	16	2	32	2	0	0	3	.000	0	0-1	0	8.30	8.13
2007	Ari	NL	5	1	0	0	5.0	28	8	8	8	0	0	1	0	5	0	3	1	0	1	0	1.000	0	0-0	0	9.25	14.40
2008	Oak	AL	29	29	1	0	168.0	737	172	82	81	10	2	5	12	77	2	118	6	1	9	9	.500	0	0-0	0	4.47	4.34
4 ML YEARS			70	35	1	4	232.1	1052	259	136	135	16	3	8	18	116	7	176	10	1	11	13	.458	0	1-3	7	5.22	5.23

Adam Everett

Bats: R **Throws:** R **Pos:** SS-44; PH-3; PR-3; DH-2; 2B-1   **Ht:** 6'0" **Wt:** 178 **Born:** 2/5/1977 **Age:** 32

Year	Team	Lg	G	AB	H	2B	3B	HR	(Hm	Rd)	TB	R	RBI	RC	TBB	IBB	SO	HBP	SH	SF	SB	CS	SB%	GDP	Avg	OBP	Slg
2008	Twins*	R	4	12	6	1	0	0	(-	-)	7	1	1	3	0	0	1	0	0	1	1	0	1.00	0	.500	.462	.583
2008	FtMyrs*	A+	2	8	0	0	0	0	(-	-)	0	0	0	0	0	0	2	0	0	0	0	0	-	0	.000	.000	.000
2008	Roch*	AAA	5	19	6	0	0	0	(-	-)	6	5	3	2	2	0	4	0	0	0	0	0	-	1	.316	.381	.316
2001	Hou	NL	9	3	0	0	0	0	(0	0)	0	1	0	0	0	0	1	0	0	0	1	0	1.00	0	.000	.000	.000
2002	Hou	NL	40	88	17	3	0	0	(0	0)	20	11	4	6	12	1	19	1	2	0	3	0	1.00	1	.193	.297	.227
2003	Hou	NL	128	387	99	18	3	8	(5	3)	147	51	51	50	28	6	66	9	11	1	8	1	.89	7	.256	.320	.380
2004	Hou	NL	104	384	105	15	2	8	(5	3)	148	66	31	51	17	0	56	9	22	3	13	2	.87	4	.273	.317	.385
2005	Hou	NL	152	549	136	27	2	11	(7	4)	200	58	54	61	26	1	103	8	8	4	21	7	.75	5	.248	.290	.364
2006	Hou	NL	150	514	123	28	6	6	(2	4)	181	52	59	50	34	5	71	4	10	4	9	6	.60	5	.239	.290	.352
2007	Hou	NL	66	220	51	11	1	2	(1	1)	70	18	15	21	14	0	31	1	1	0	4	2	.67	3	.232	.281	.318
2008	Min	AL	48	127	27	6	1	2	(2	0)	41	19	20	15	12	1	15	1	6	4	0	0	-	0	.213	.278	.323
Postseason			19	53	11	1	1	0	(0	0)	14	5	3	1	2	0	9	0	2	1	0	1	.00	2	.208	.232	.264
8 ML YEARS			697	2272	558	108	15	37	(22	15)	807	276	234	254	143	14	362	33	60	16	59	18	.77	25	.246	.298	.355

Scott Eyre

Pitches: L **Bats:** L **Pos:** RP-38   **Ht:** 6'1" **Wt:** 220 **Born:** 5/30/1972 **Age:** 37

Year	Team	Lg	G	GS	CG	GF	IP	BFP	H	R	ER	HR	SH	SF	HB	TBB	IBB	SO	WP	Bk	W	L	Pct	ShO	Sv-Op	Hld	ERC	ERA
2008	Dytona*	A+	3	1	0	1	2.2	14	5	4	4	0	1	0	0	1	0	2	0	0	0	0	-	0	1--	-	8.33	13.50
2008	Tenn*	AA	3	0	0	1	3.0	11	1	0	0	0	0	0	0	1	0	3	0	0	0	0	-	0	0--	-	0.69	0.00
2008	Iowa*	AAA	1	0	0	0	1.0	5	2	1	1	0	0	0	0	0	0	2	0	0	0	0	-	0	0--	-	16.28	9.00
2008	Peoria*	A	2	1	0	0	2.1	13	6	3	3	0	0	1	0	0	0	3	0	0	0	0	-	0	0--	-	11.37	11.57
2008	Cubs*	R	1	0	0	0	1.0	3	0	0	0	0	0	0	0	1	0	0	0	0	0	0	-	0	0--	-	1.26	0.00
1997	CWS	AL	11	11	0	0	60.2	267	62	36	34	11	1	2	1	31	1	36	2	0	4	4	.500	0	0-0	0	5.37	5.04
1998	CWS	AL	33	17	0	10	107.0	491	114	78	64	24	2	3	2	64	0	73	7	0	3	8	.273	0	0-0	0	6.31	5.38
1999	CWS	AL	21	0	0	8	25.0	129	38	22	21	6	0	1	1	15	2	17	1	0	1	1	.500	0	0-0	1	9.23	7.56
2000	CWS	AL	13	1	0	3	19.0	93	29	15	14	3	0	2	1	12	0	16	0	0	1	1	.500	0	0-0	0	9.49	6.63
2001	Tor	AL	17	0	0	5	15.2	66	15	6	6	1	0	1	1	7	2	16	2	0	1	2	.333	0	2-3	3	3.96	3.45
2002	2 Tms		70	3	0	6	74.2	333	80	41	37	4	2	4	0	36	8	58	5	0	2	4	.333	0	0-1	18	4.26	4.46
2003	SF	NL	74	0	0	10	57.0	256	60	23	21	4	2	3	1	26	0	35	6	0	4	2	.667	0	1-3	20	4.37	3.32
2004	SF	NL	83	0	0	12	52.2	229	43	26	24	8	3	3	0	27	3	49	3	0	2	2	.500	0	1-5	23	3.67	4.10
2005	SF	NL	86	0	0	15	68.1	277	48	21	20	3	4	3	4	26	0	65	3	0	2	2	.500	0	0-2	32	2.32	2.63
2006	ChC	NL	74	0	0	15	61.1	266	61	25	23	7	1	2	4	30	4	73	6	0	1	3	.250	0	0-3	18	4.94	3.38
2007	ChC	NL	55	0	0	17	52.1	240	59	26	24	3	2	1	1	35	5	45	3	0	2	1	.667	0	0-4	5	5.61	4.13
2008	2 Tms		38	0	0	3	25.2	106	23	12	12	2	0	2	2	7	2	32	1	0	5	0	1.000	0	0-2	5	3.09	4.21
02	Tor	AL	49	3	0	3	63.1	283	69	37	35	4	2	4	0	29	7	51	4	0	2	4	.333	0	0-1	12	4.32	4.97
02	SF	NL	21	0	0	3	11.1	50	11	4	2	0	0	0	0	7	1	7	1	0	0	0	-	0	0-0	6	3.91	1.59
08	ChC	NL	19	0	0	1	11.1	53	15	9	9	1	0	0	2	4	1	14	1	0	2	0	1.000	0	0-1	4	5.86	7.15
08	Phi	NL	19	0	0	2	14.1	53	8	3	3	1	0	1	0	3	1	18	0	0	3	0	1.000	0	0-1	1	1.39	1.88
Postseason			12	0	0	2	6.1	28	9	1	0	0	0	0	0	1	1	2	0	0	0	0	-	0	0-0	1	4.54	0.00
12 ML YEARS			575	32	0	104	619.1	2753	632	331	300	80	18	29	14	316	27	515	39	0	26	29	.473	0	4-23	128	4.88	4.36

Brandon Fahey

Bats: L **Throws:** R **Pos:** SS-46; 2B-10; PR-8; PH-3; DH-1   **Ht:** 6'2" **Wt:** 160 **Born:** 1/18/1981 **Age:** 28

Year	Team	Lg	G	AB	H	2B	3B	HR	(Hm	Rd)	TB	R	RBI	RC	TBB	IBB	SO	HBP	SH	SF	SB	CS	SB%	GDP	Avg	OBP	Slg
									BATTING												BASERUNNING				AVERAGES		
2008	Norfolk*	AAA	64	222	56	8	0	1	(-	-)	67	26	24	21	21	1	47	1	2	2	1	4	.20	0	.252	.317	.302
2006	Bal	AL	91	251	59	8	2	2	(2	0)	77	36	23	27	23	0	48	3	9	0	3	3	.50	2	.235	.307	.307
2007	Bal	AL	40	54	9	1	1	0	(0	0)	12	10	1	2	2	0	9	0	0	0	2	1	.67	1	.167	.196	.222
2008	Bal	AL	58	106	24	9	2	0	(0	0)	37	8	12	10	3	0	25	1	2	1	0	0	-	3	.226	.252	.349
	3 ML YEARS		189	411	92	18	5	2	(2	0)	126	54	36	39	28	0	82	4	11	1	5	4	.56	6	.224	.279	.307

Brian Falkenborg

Pitches: R **Bats:** R **Pos:** RP-25   **Ht:** 6'7" **Wt:** 235 **Born:** 1/18/1978 **Age:** 31

Year	Team	Lg	G	GS	CG	GF	IP	BFP	H	R	ER	HR	SH	SF	HB	TBB	IBB	SO	WP	Bk	W	L	Pct	ShO	Sv-Op	Hld	ERC	ERA
			HOW MUCH HE PITCHED						WHAT HE GAVE UP												THE RESULTS							
2008	LsVgs*	AAA	32	0	0	27	35.0	145	33	14	14	3	0	1	1	8	1	41	5	0	1	1	.500	0	13- -	-	3.06	3.60
1999	Bal	AL	2	0	0	0	3.0	12	2	0	0	0	0	0	0	2	0	1	0	0	0	0	-	0	0-0	0	2.79	0.00
2004	LAD	NL	6	0	0	1	14.1	73	19	14	12	2	2	0	3	9	0	11	1	0	0	1	.000	0	0-0	0	8.19	7.53
2005	SD	NL	10	0	0	3	11.0	54	17	11	10	2	0	0	0	5	1	10	2	0	0	0	-	0	0-0	0	8.14	8.18
2006	StL	NL	5	0	0	3	6.1	25	5	2	2	0	1	0	1	0	0	5	0	0	0	1	.000	0	0-0	0	1.57	2.84
2007	StL	NL	16	0	0	2	18.2	84	22	10	10	2	0	0	1	8	0	16	1	0	0	1	.000	0	0-0	1	5.58	4.82
2008	2 Tms	NL	25	0	0	8	22.1	102	26	13	13	4	2	0	0	12	2	19	0	0	2	3	.400	0	0-1	1	6.11	5.24
08	LAD	NL	16	0	0	2	11.2	49	11	8	8	2	1	0	0	4	1	9	0	0	2	2	.500	0	0-1	1	3.89	6.17
08	SD	NL	9	0	0	6	10.2	53	15	5	5	2	1	0	0	8	1	10	0	0	0	1	.000	0	0-0	0	8.80	4.22
	6 ML YEARS		64	0	0	17	75.2	350	91	50	47	10	5	0	5	36	3	62	4	0	3	5	.375	0	0-1	2	6.05	5.59

Kyle Farnsworth

Pitches: R **Bats:** R **Pos:** RP-61   **Ht:** 6'4" **Wt:** 235 **Born:** 4/14/1976 **Age:** 33

Year	Team	Lg	G	GS	CG	GF	IP	BFP	H	R	ER	HR	SH	SF	HB	TBB	IBB	SO	WP	Bk	W	L	Pct	ShO	Sv-Op	Hld	ERC	ERA
			HOW MUCH HE PITCHED						WHAT HE GAVE UP												THE RESULTS							
1999	ChC	NL	27	21	1	1	130.0	579	140	80	73	28	6	2	3	52	1	70	7	1	5	9	.357	1	0-0	0	5.39	5.05
2000	ChC	NL	46	5	0	8	77.0	371	90	58	55	14	4	4	4	50	8	74	3	0	2	9	.182	0	1-6	6	6.72	6.43
2001	ChC	NL	76	0	0	24	82.0	339	65	26	25	8	2	2	1	29	2	107	2	2	4	6	.400	0	2-3	24	2.76	2.74
2002	ChC	NL	45	0	0	17	46.2	213	53	47	38	9	2	5	1	24	7	46	1	0	4	6	.400	0	1-7	6	5.89	7.33
2003	ChC	NL	77	0	0	13	76.1	312	53	31	28	6	4	1	0	36	1	92	6	0	3	2	.600	0	0-3	19	2.58	3.30
2004	ChC	NL	72	0	0	25	66.2	298	67	39	35	10	5	0	2	33	1	78	1	0	4	5	.444	0	0-4	18	4.91	4.73
2005	2 Tms		72	0	0	34	70.0	277	44	18	17	5	2	1	3	27	0	87	3	1	1	1	.500	0	16-18	19	2.12	2.19
2006	NYY	AL	72	0	0	24	66.0	289	62	34	32	8	3	2	1	28	3	75	5	1	3	6	.333	0	6-10	19	3.88	4.36
2007	NYY	AL	64	0	0	11	60.0	266	60	35	32	9	1	2	2	27	2	48	4	2	2	1	.667	0	0-3	15	4.67	4.80
2008	2 Tms		61	0	0	11	60.1	261	70	32	30	15	3	1	1	24	4	61	1	1	2	3	.400	0	1-4	14	6.11	4.48
05	Det	AL	46	0	0	16	42.2	174	29	12	11	1	1	1	1	20	0	55	2	0	1	1	.500	0	6-8	15	2.26	2.32
05	Atl	NL	26	0	0	18	27.1	103	15	6	6	4	1	0	2	7	0	32	1	1	0	0	-	0	10-10	4	1.86	1.98
08	NYY	AL	45	0	0	6	44.1	185	43	18	18	11	3	1	1	17	3	43	1	1	1	2	.333	0	1-1	11	5.02	3.65
08	Det	AL	16	0	0	5	16.0	76	27	14	12	4	0	0	0	7	1	18	0	0	1	1	.500	0	0-3	3	9.43	6.75
	Postseason		13	0	0	3	14.0	58	11	9	9	2	1	1	0	5	2	16	0	0	0	0	-	0	0-0	2	2.78	5.79
	10 ML YEARS		612	26	1	168	735.0	3205	704	400	365	112	32	20	18	328	29	738	33	8	30	48	.385	1	27-58	140	4.40	4.47

Sal Fasano

Bats: R **Throws:** R **Pos:** C-15; 1B-1   **Ht:** 6'2" **Wt:** 225 **Born:** 8/10/1971 **Age:** 37

Year	Team	Lg	G	AB	H	2B	3B	HR	(Hm	Rd)	TB	R	RBI	RC	TBB	IBB	SO	HBP	SH	SF	SB	CS	SB%	GDP	Avg	OBP	Slg
									BATTING												BASERUNNING				AVERAGES		
2008	Rchmd*	AAA	26	83	16	3	1	2	(-	-)	27	6	9	7	5	1	22	4	0	0	0	0	-	2	.193	.272	.325
1996	KC	AL	51	143	29	2	0	6	(1	5)	49	20	19	13	14	0	25	2	1	0	1	1	.50	3	.203	.283	.343
1997	KC	AL	13	38	8	2	0	1	(0	1)	13	4	1	2	1	0	12	0	0	0	0	0	-	1	.211	.231	.342
1998	KC	AL	74	216	49	10	0	8	(4	4)	83	21	31	26	10	1	56	16	3	2	1	0	1.00	4	.227	.307	.384
1999	Oak	AL	23	60	14	2	0	5	(2	3)	31	11	16	12	7	0	17	7	0	1	0	1	.00	4	.233	.373	.517
2000	Oak	AL	52	126	27	6	0	7	(4	3)	54	21	19	16	14	0	47	3	0	1	0	0	-	3	.214	.306	.429
2001	3 Tms		39	85	17	5	0	3	(3	0)	31	12	9	10	5	0	31	4	2	0	0	0	-	3	.200	.277	.365
2002	LAA	AL	2	1	0	0	0	0	(0	0)	0	0	0	0	0	0	0	0	0	0	0	0	-	0	.000	.000	.000
2005	Bal	AL	64	160	40	3	0	11	(1	10)	76	25	20	17	9	0	41	5	0	0	0	0	-	5	.250	.310	.475
2006	2 Tms		78	189	41	12	0	5	(2	3)	68	12	15	12	7	0	61	6	4	0	0	1	.00	5	.217	.267	.360
2007	Tor	AL	16	45	8	3	0	1	(0	1)	14	5	4	2	2	0	19	1	1	0	0	0	-	0	.178	.229	.311
2008	Cle	AL	15	46	12	4	0	0	(0	0)	16	5	6	6	3	0	17	3	1	1	0	0	-	1	.261	.340	.348
01	Oak	AL	11	21	1	0	0	0	(0	0)	1	2	0	0	1	0	12	1	0	0	0	0	-	1	.048	.130	.048
01	KC	AL	3	1	0	0	0	0	(0	0)	0	0	0	0	0	0	0	0	0	0	0	0	-	0	.000	.000	.000
01	Col	NL	25	63	16	5	0	3	(3	0)	30	10	9	10	4	0	19	3	2	0	0	0	-	1	.254	.329	.476
06	Phi	NL	50	140	34	8	0	4	(2	2)	54	9	10	9	5	0	47	3	1	0	0	1	.00	4	.243	.284	.386
06	NYY	AL	28	49	7	4	0	1	(0	1)	14	3	5	3	2	0	14	3	3	0	0	0	-	1	.143	.222	.286
	Postseason		1	0	0	0	0	0	(0	0)	0	0	0	0	0	0	0	0	0	0	0	0	-	0	-	-	-
	11 ML YEARS		427	1109	245	49	0	47	(17	30)	435	136	140	116	72	1	327	47	12	5	2	3	.40	26	.221	.295	.392

Ryan Feierabend

Pitches: L **Bats:** L **Pos:** SP-8   **Ht:** 6'3" **Wt:** 228 **Born:** 8/22/1985 **Age:** 23

Year	Team	Lg	G	GS	CG	GF	IP	BFP	H	R	ER	HR	SH	SF	HB	TBB	IBB	SO	WP	Bk	W	L	Pct	ShO	Sv-Op	Hld	ERC	ERA
			HOW MUCH HE PITCHED						WHAT HE GAVE UP												THE RESULTS							
2008	Tacom*	AAA	13	13	0	0	75.0	295	64	21	17	5	2	2	0	15	0	48	4	0	7	1	.875	0	0- -	-	2.40	2.04
2008	Ms*	R	2	2	0	0	4.2	19	4	4	2	0	0	0	0	3	0	1	0	0	1	0	1.000	0	0- -	-	3.81	3.86
2008	Everett*	A-	2	2	0	0	10.2	44	12	6	6	1	0	0	1	0	0	10	2	1	0	0	-	0	0- -	-	3.53	5.06

	HOW MUCH HE PITCHED						WHAT HE GAVE UP												THE RESULTS						
Year Team	Lg	G	GS	CG	GF	IP	BFP	H	R	ER	HR	SH	SF	HB	TBB	IBB	SO	WP	Bk	W	L	Pct	ShO	Sv-Op	Hld	ERC	ERA
2006 Sea	AL	4	2	0	2	17.0	73	15	7	7	3	1	0	0	7	0	11	1	2	0	1	.000	0	0-0	0	3.91	3.71
2007 Sea	AL	13	9	0	0	49.1	236	73	44	44	10	0	2	4	23	2	27	3	0	1	6	.143	0	0-0	0	8.71	8.03
2008 Sea	AL	8	8	0	0	39.2	183	59	34	34	7	1	1	1	14	0	26	1	0	1	4	.200	0	0-0	0	7.83	7.71
3 ML YEARS		25	19	0	2	106.0	492	147	85	85	20	2	3	5	44	2	64	5	2	2	11	.154	0	0-0	0	7.54	7.22

Scott Feldman

Pitches: R **Bats:** L **Pos:** SP-25; RP-3   **Ht:** 6'5" **Wt:** 210 **Born:** 2/7/1983 **Age:** 26

	HOW MUCH HE PITCHED						WHAT HE GAVE UP												THE RESULTS						
Year Team	Lg	G	GS	CG	GF	IP	BFP	H	R	ER	HR	SH	SF	HB	TBB	IBB	SO	WP	Bk	W	L	Pct	ShO	Sv-Op	Hld	ERC	ERA
2008 Frisco*	AA	2	2	0	0	12.2	53	11	6	6	0	0	1	2	2	0	4	0	0	2	0	1.000	0	0--	-	2.36	4.26
2005 Tex	AL	8	0	0	3	9.1	37	9	1	1	0	0	0	0	2	1	4	0	0	0	1	.000	0	0-0	1	2.48	0.96
2006 Tex	AL	36	0	0	5	41.1	175	42	19	18	4	2	1	4	10	0	30	0	0	0	2	.000	0	0-1	7	3.94	3.92
2007 Tex	AL	29	0	0	10	39.0	192	44	26	25	3	0	2	3	32	5	19	2	2	1	2	.333	0	0-0	6	6.40	5.77
2008 Tex	AL	28	25	0	2	151.1	651	161	103	89	22	1	9	10	56	2	74	4	2	6	8	.429	0	0-0	0	5.03	5.29
4 ML YEARS		101	25	0	20	241.0	1055	256	149	133	29	3	12	17	100	8	127	6	4	7	13	.350	0	0-1	8	4.96	4.97

Pedro Feliciano

Pitches: L **Bats:** L **Pos:** RP-86   **Ht:** 5'10" **Wt:** 192 **Born:** 8/25/1976 **Age:** 32

	HOW MUCH HE PITCHED						WHAT HE GAVE UP												THE RESULTS						
Year Team	Lg	G	GS	CG	GF	IP	BFP	H	R	ER	HR	SH	SF	HB	TBB	IBB	SO	WP	Bk	W	L	Pct	ShO	Sv-Op	Hld	ERC	ERA
2002 NYM	NL	6	0	0	3	6.0	26	9	5	5	0	0	0	0	1	0	4	0	0	0	0	-	0	0-0	0	5.56	7.50
2003 NYM	NL	23	0	0	8	48.1	218	52	21	18	5	0	1	3	21	3	43	3	1	0	0	-	0	0-0	0	4.77	3.35
2004 NYM	NL	22	0	0	3	18.1	82	14	12	11	2	1	1	1	12	0	14	1	0	1	1	.500	0	0-0	2	3.93	5.40
2006 NYM	NL	64	0	0	10	60.1	256	56	15	14	4	4	3	3	20	1	54	1	0	7	2	.778	0	0-3	10	3.34	2.09
2007 NYM	NL	78	0	0	12	64.0	275	47	26	22	3	2	2	5	31	4	61	1	1	2	2	.500	0	2-3	18	5.11	3.09
2008 NYM	NL	86	0	0	14	53.1	237	57	24	24	7	2	3	3	26	8	50	2	0	3	4	.429	0	2-4	21	5.11	4.05
Postseason		6	0	0	0	4.2	18	2	1	1	1	0	0	0	2	0	3	1	0	1	0	1.000	0	0-0	1	1.92	1.93
6 ML YEARS		279	0	0	50	250.1	1094	235	103	94	21	9	10	15	111	16	226	8	2	13	9	.591	0	4-10	51	3.89	3.38

Pedro Feliz

Bats: R **Throws:** R **Pos:** 3B-129; PH-17; SS-1   **Ht:** 6'1" **Wt:** 208 **Born:** 4/27/1975 **Age:** 34

		BATTING																			BASERUNNING				AVERAGES		
Year Team	Lg	G	AB	H	2B	3B	HR	(Hm	Rd)	TB	R	RBI	RC	TBB	IBB	SO	HBP	SH	SF	SB	CS	SB%	GDP	Avg	OBP	Slg
2008 Clrwtr*	A+	1	3	0	0	0	0	(-	-)	0	0	0	0	1	0	1	0	0	0	0	0	-	0	.000	.250	.000
2008 Rdng*	AA	2	8	4	0	0	2	(-	-)	10	2	2	3	0	0	2	0	0	0	0	0	-	0	.500	.500	1.250
2000 SF	NL	8	7	2	0	0	0	(0	0)	2	1	0	1	0	0	1	0	0	0	0	0	-	0	.286	.286	.286
2001 SF	NL	94	220	50	9	1	7	(3	4)	82	23	22	20	10	2	50	2	3	3	2	1	.67	5	.227	.264	.373
2002 SF	NL	67	146	37	4	1	2	(1	1)	49	14	13	12	6	1	27	0	0	1	0	0	-	2	.253	.281	.336
2003 SF	NL	95	235	58	9	3	16	(6	10)	121	31	48	34	10	0	53	1	1	2	2	2	.50	7	.247	.278	.515
2004 SF	NL	144	503	139	33	3	22	(11	11)	244	72	84	56	23	1	85	0	0	5	5	2	.71	18	.276	.305	.485
2005 SF	NL	156	569	142	30	4	20	(10	10)	240	69	81	58	38	1	102	1	1	6	2	0	.00	20	.250	.295	.422
2006 SF	NL	160	603	147	35	5	22	(6	16)	258	75	98	71	33	4	112	1	1	6	1	1	.50	18	.244	.281	.428
2007 SF	NL	150	557	141	28	2	20	(8	12)	233	61	72	67	29	2	70	1	0	3	2	2	.50	15	.253	.290	.418
2008 Phi	NL	133	425	106	19	2	14	(8	6)	171	43	58	47	33	3	54	1	0	3	0	0	-	14	.249	.302	.402
Postseason		8	10	2	0	1	0	(0	0)	4	1	1	2	0	0	4	0	0	0	0	0	-	0	.200	.200	.400
9 ML YEARS		1007	3265	822	167	21	123	(53	70)	1400	389	476	366	182	14	554	6	9	28	12	10	.55	99	.252	.290	.429

Prince Fielder

Bats: L **Throws:** R **Pos:** 1B-155; DH-4   **Ht:** 5'11" **Wt:** 270 **Born:** 5/9/1984 **Age:** 25

		BATTING																			BASERUNNING				AVERAGES		
Year Team	Lg	G	AB	H	2B	3B	HR	(Hm	Rd)	TB	R	RBI	RC	TBB	IBB	SO	HBP	SH	SF	SB	CS	SB%	GDP	Avg	OBP	Slg
2005 Mil	NL	39	59	17	4	0	2	(2	0)	27	2	10	10	2	0	17	0	0	1	0	0	-	0	.288	.306	.458
2006 Mil	NL	157	569	154	35	1	28	(11	17)	275	82	81	84	59	5	125	12	0	8	7	2	.78	17	.271	.347	.483
2007 Mil	NL	158	573	165	35	2	50	(27	23)	354	109	119	125	90	21	121	14	0	4	2	2	.50	9	.288	.395	.618
2008 Mil	NL	159	588	162	30	2	34	(18	16)	298	86	102	105	84	19	134	12	0	10	3	2	.60	12	.276	.372	.507
4 ML YEARS		513	1789	498	104	5	114	(58	56)	954	279	312	324	235	45	397	38	0	23	12	6	.67	38	.278	.370	.533

Josh Fields

Bats: R **Throws:** R **Pos:** 3B-12; DH-2; PH-2   **Ht:** 6'1" **Wt:** 220 **Born:** 12/14/1982 **Age:** 26

		BATTING																			BASERUNNING				AVERAGES		
Year Team	Lg	G	AB	H	2B	3B	HR	(Hm	Rd)	TB	R	RBI	RC	TBB	IBB	SO	HBP	SH	SF	SB	CS	SB%	GDP	Avg	OBP	Slg
2008 Charltt*	AAA	75	276	68	15	3	10	(-	-)	119	41	35	43	37	1	98	3	1	1	8	2	.80	6	.246	.341	.431
2008 WinSa*	A+	4	9	3	1	0	0	(-	-)	4	1	1	2	5	0	2	0	0	0	0	1	.00	0	.333	.571	.444
2006 CWS	AL	11	20	3	2	0	1	(1	0)	8	4	2	1	5	0	8	0	0	0	0	0	-	0	.150	.320	.400
2007 CWS	AL	100	373	91	17	1	23	(15	8)	179	54	67	56	35	0	125	1	6	3	1	1	.50	11	.244	.308	.480
2008 CWS	AL	14	32	5	1	0	0	(0	0)	6	3	2	1	3	0	17	0	0	0	0	0	-	0	.156	.229	.188
3 ML YEARS		125	425	99	20	1	24	(16	8)	193	61	71	58	43	0	150	1	6	3	1	1	.50	11	.233	.303	.454

Chone Figgins

Bats: B **Throws:** R **Pos:** 3B-105; 2B-9; DH-2; PH-1; PR-1   **Ht:** 5'8" **Wt:** 180 **Born:** 1/22/1978 **Age:** 31

Year Team	Lg	G	AB	H	2B	3B	HR	(Hm	Rd)	TB	R	RBI	RC	TBB	IBB	SO	HBP	SH	SF	SB	CS	SB%	GDP	Avg	OBP	Slg
2008 Salt Lk*	AAA	3	10	2	0	0	0	(-	-)	2	2	0	0	2	0	3	0	0	0	0	0	-	0	.200	.333	.200
2002 LAA	AL	15	12	2	1	0	0	(0	0)	3	6	1	7	0	0	5	0	0	0	2	1	.67	1	.167	.167	.250
2003 LAA	AL	71	240	71	9	4	0	(0	0)	88	34	27	39	20	0	38	0	6	4	13	7	.65	1	.296	.345	.367
2004 LAA	AL	148	577	171	22	17	5	(3	2)	242	83	60	93	49	0	94	0	10	2	34	13	.72	6	.296	.350	.419
2005 LAA	AL	158	642	186	25	10	8	(2	6)	255	113	57	94	64	1	101	0	9	5	62	17	.78	9	.290	.352	.397
2006 LAA	AL	155	604	161	23	8	9	(2	7)	227	93	62	84	65	1	100	2	5	7	52	16	.76	6	.267	.336	.376
2007 LAA	AL	115	442	146	26	6	3	(1	2)	191	81	58	88	51	0	81	0	2	8	41	12	.77	7	.330	.393	.432
2008 LAA	AL	116	453	125	14	1	1	(0	1)	144	72	22	59	62	3	80	3	2	0	34	13	.72	7	.276	.367	.318
Postseason		22	66	11	4	1	0	(0	0)	17	8	4	3	2	0	20	1	2	0	3	1	.75	1	.167	.203	.258
7 ML YEARS		778	2970	862	118	46	26	(8	18)	1150	482	287	457	311	5	499	5	34	26	238	79	.75	37	.290	.356	.387

Nelson Figueroa

Pitches: R **Bats:** R **Pos:** RP-10; SP-6   **Ht:** 6'1" **Wt:** 205 **Born:** 5/18/1974 **Age:** 35

Year Team	Lg	G	GS	CG	GF	IP	BFP	H	R	ER	HR	SH	SF	HB	TBB	IBB	SO	WP	Bk	W	L	Pct	ShO	Sv-Op	Hld	ERC	ERA
2008 NewOr*	AAA	20	16	0	0	113.2	483	120	62	56	15	4	6	4	33	0	97	1	0	4	7	.364	0	0- -	-	4.37	4.43
2000 Ari	NL	3	3	0	0	15.2	68	17	13	13	4	1	2	0	5	0	7	2	0	0	1	.000	0	0-0	0	5.31	7.47
2001 Phi	NL	19	13	0	1	89.0	393	95	40	39	8	4	0	7	37	3	61	2	0	4	5	.444	0	0-0	0	4.76	3.94
2002 Mil	NL	30	11	0	4	93.0	412	96	59	52	18	11	5	4	37	6	51	5	0	1	7	.125	0	0-0	1	4.94	5.03
2003 Pit	NL	12	3	0	1	35.1	146	28	13	13	8	2	2	2	13	2	23	2	0	2	1	.667	0	0-0	0	3.80	3.31
2004 Pit	NL	10	3	0	0	28.1	121	32	18	18	4	4	0	0	11	1	10	3	0	0	3	.000	0	0-0	0	5.21	5.72
2008 NYM	NL	16	6	0	2	45.1	211	48	26	23	3	2	1	2	26	1	36	0	0	3	3	.500	0	0-1	0	4.88	4.57
6 ML YEARS		90	39	0	8	306.2	1351	316	169	158	45	24	10	15	129	13	188	14	0	10	20	.333	0	0-1	1	4.80	4.64

Jeff Fiorentino

Bats: L **Throws:** R **Pos:** CF-2; PR-2   **Ht:** 6'1" **Wt:** 186 **Born:** 4/14/1983 **Age:** 26

Year Team	Lg	G	AB	H	2B	3B	HR	(Hm	Rd)	TB	R	RBI	RC	TBB	IBB	SO	HBP	SH	SF	SB	CS	SB%	GDP	Avg	OBP	Slg
2008 Scrmto*	AAA	8	22	6	0	0	0	(-	-)	6	3	3	4	4	0	5	0	0	2	1	0	1.00	0	.273	.357	.273
2008 Norfolk*	AAA	68	228	61	12	1	2	(-	-)	81	25	25	33	34	2	52	1	1	3	7	3	.70	2	.268	.361	.355
2005 Bal	AL	13	44	11	2	0	1	(1	0)	16	7	5	2	2	0	10	0	0	1	1	0	1.00	0	.250	.277	.364
2006 Bal	AL	19	39	10	2	0	0	(0	0)	12	8	7	6	7	0	3	1	2	1	1	0	1.00	1	.256	.375	.308
2008 Oak	AL	2	1	1	0	0	0	(0	0)	1	0	1	1	0	0	0	0	0	0	0	0	-	0	1.000	1.000	1.000
3 ML YEARS		34	84	22	4	0	1	(1	0)	29	15	13	9	9	0	13	1	2	2	2	0	1.00	1	.262	.333	.345

Jesus Flores

Bats: R **Throws:** R **Pos:** C-82; PH-10   **Ht:** 6'0" **Wt:** 230 **Born:** 10/26/1984 **Age:** 24

Year Team	Lg	G	AB	H	2B	3B	HR	(Hm	Rd)	TB	R	RBI	RC	TBB	IBB	SO	HBP	SH	SF	SB	CS	SB%	GDP	Avg	OBP	Slg
2004 Mets	R	45	141	45	12	3	4	(-	-)	75	16	25	27	8	0	26	4	1	2	1	1	.50	2	.319	.368	.532
2004 Bklyn	A-	3	6	2	0	0	1	(-	-)	5	1	3	1	0	0	1	0	0	0	0	0	-	1	.333	.333	.833
2005 Hgrstn	A	82	319	69	18	0	7	(-	-)	108	34	42	26	12	0	90	3	1	2	2	2	.50	6	.216	.250	.339
2006 StLuci	A+	120	429	114	32	0	21	(-	-)	209	66	70	72	28	1	127	18	2	3	2	0	1.00	6	.266	.335	.487
2008 Clmbs	AAA	17	59	9	3	0	1	(-	-)	15	8	7	4	8	1	20	2	0	0	0	0	-	2	.153	.275	.254
2007 Was	NL	79	180	44	9	0	4	(1	3)	65	21	25	19	14	0	48	3	0	0	0	1	.00	5	.244	.310	.361
2008 Was	NL	90	301	77	18	1	8	(2	6)	121	23	59	45	15	1	78	4	0	4	0	1	.00	7	.256	.296	.402
2 ML YEARS		169	481	121	27	1	12	(3	9)	186	44	84	64	29	1	126	7	0	4	0	2	.00	12	.252	.301	.387

Randy Flores

Pitches: L **Bats:** L **Pos:** RP-43   **Ht:** 6'0" **Wt:** 180 **Born:** 7/31/1975 **Age:** 33

Year Team	Lg	G	GS	CG	GF	IP	BFP	H	R	ER	HR	SH	SF	HB	TBB	IBB	SO	WP	Bk	W	L	Pct	ShO	Sv-Op	Hld	ERC	ERA
2008 Memp*	AAA	15	0	0	3	18.1	80	20	6	5	2	1	1	0	6	0	14	2	0	0	1	.000	0	1- -	-	4.32	2.45
2002 2 Tms		28	2	0	9	29.0	140	40	26	24	7	2	2	3	16	3	14	4	0	0	2	.000	0	1-2	2	8.69	7.45
2004 StL	NL	9	1	0	3	14.0	57	13	3	3	0	1	1	3	3	1	7	0	0	1	0	1.000	0	0-0	3	1.53	1.93
2005 StL	NL	50	0	0	6	41.2	174	37	22	16	5	1	3	3	13	0	43	2	0	3	1	.750	0	1-3	11	3.55	3.46
2006 StL	NL	65	0	0	10	41.2	196	49	29	26	5	3	1	1	22	3	40	1	0	1	1	.500	0	0-1	18	5.64	5.62
2007 StL	NL	70	0	0	11	55.0	253	71	31	26	2	4	2	3	15	0	47	3	0	1	1	.500	0	1-2	14	4.87	4.25
2008 StL	NL	43	0	0	3	25.2	131	34	16	15	2	0	2	1	20	3	17	1	0	1	0	1.000	0	1-3	14	7.23	5.26
02 Tex	AL	20	0	0	5	12.0	52	11	7	6	2	1	2	0	8	2	7	3	0	0	0		0	1-2	2	5.07	4.50
02 Col	NL	8	2	0	4	17.0	88	29	19	18	5	1	0	3	8	1	7	1	0	0	2	.000	0	0-0	0	11.52	9.53
Postseason		12	0	0	0	9.0	34	7	1	1	1	0	0	0	2	0	7	0	0	1	0	1.000	0	0-0	3	2.45	1.00
6 ML YEARS		265	3	0	42	207.0	951	244	127	110	21	11	11	14	89	10	168	11	0	9	4	.692	0	4-11	59	5.40	4.78

Cliff Floyd

Bats: L **Throws:** R **Pos:** DH-76; PH-8   **Ht:** 6'4" **Wt:** 230 **Born:** 12/5/1972 **Age:** 36

Year Team	Lg	G	AB	H	2B	3B	HR	(Hm	Rd)	TB	R	RBI	RC	TBB	IBB	SO	HBP	SH	SF	SB	CS	SB%	GDP	Avg	OBP	Slg
1993 Mon	NL	10	31	7	0	0	1	(0	1)	10	3	2	2	0	0	9	0	0	0	0	0	-	0	.226	.226	.323
1994 Mon	NL	100	334	94	19	4	4	(2	2)	133	43	41	46	24	0	63	3	2	3	10	3	.77	3	.281	.332	.398
1995 Mon	NL	29	69	9	1	0	1	(1	0)	13	6	8	2	7	0	22	1	0	0	3	0	1.00	1	.130	.221	.188
1996 Mon	NL	117	227	55	15	4	6	(3	3)	96	29	26	35	30	1	52	5	1	3	7	1	.88	3	.242	.340	.423

Year	Team	Lg	G	AB	H	2B	3B	HR	(Hm	Rd)	TB	R	RBI	RC	TBB	IBB	SO	HBP	SH	SF	SB	CS	SB%	GDP	Avg	OBP	Slg
1997	Fla	NL	61	137	32	9	1	6	(2	4)	61	23	19	23	24	0	33	2	1	1	6	2	.75	3	.234	.354	.445
1998	Fla	NL	153	588	166	45	3	22	(10	12)	283	85	90	92	47	7	112	3	0	3	27	14	.66	10	.282	.337	.481
1999	Fla	NL	69	251	76	19	1	11	(4	7)	130	37	49	45	30	5	47	2	0	2	5	6	.45	8	.303	.379	.518
2000	Fla	NL	121	420	126	30	0	22	(13	9)	222	75	91	88	50	5	82	8	0	9	24	3	.89	4	.300	.378	.529
2001	Fla	NL	149	555	176	44	4	31	(16	15)	321	123	103	121	59	19	101	10	0	5	18	3	.86	9	.317	.390	.578
2002	3 Tms		146	520	150	43	0	28	(13	15)	277	86	79	92	76	19	106	10	0	3	15	5	.75	6	.288	.388	.533
2003	NYM	NL	108	365	106	25	2	18	(10	8)	189	57	68	69	51	2	66	3	0	6	3	0	1.00	10	.290	.376	.518
2004	NYM	NL	113	396	103	26	0	18	(7	11)	183	55	63	64	47	6	103	11	0	3	11	4	.73	8	.260	.352	.462
2005	NYM	NL	150	550	150	22	2	34	(21	13)	278	85	98	99	63	13	98	11	0	2	12	2	.86	5	.273	.358	.505
2006	NYM	NL	97	332	81	19	1	11	(5	6)	135	45	44	45	29	3	58	12	0	3	6	0	1.00	5	.244	.324	.407
2007	ChC	NL	108	282	80	10	1	9	(3	6)	119	40	45	43	35	5	47	5	0	0	0	0	-	6	.284	.373	.422
2008	TB	AL	80	246	66	13	0	11	(9	2)	112	32	39	36	28	2	58	5	0	5	1	0	1.00	4	.268	.349	.455
02	Fla	NL	84	296	85	20	0	18	(7	11)	159	49	57	64	58	18	68	7	0	1	10	5	.67	5	.287	.414	.537
02	Mon	NL	15	53	11	2	0	3	(3	0)	22	7	4	2	3	1	10	1	0	0	1	0	1.00	1	.208	.263	.415
02	Bos	AL	47	171	54	21	4	7	(3	4)	96	30	18	26	15	0	28	2	0	2	4	0	1.00	6	.316	.374	.561
	Postseason		12	19	4	0	0	1	(1	0)	7	4	2	3	4	2	6	1	0	0	0	0	-	0	.211	.375	.368
	16 ML YEARS		1611	5303	1477	340	23	233	(119	114)	2562	824	865	902	600	87	1057	91	4	48	148	43	.77	85	.279	.359	.483

Gavin Floyd

Pitches: R Bats: R Pos: SP-33   Ht: 6'5" Wt: 230 Born: 1/27/1983 Age: 26

			HOW MUCH HE PITCHED						WHAT HE GAVE UP										THE RESULTS					
Year	Team	Lg	G	GS	CG	GF	IP	BFP	H	R	ER	HR	SH	SF	HB	TBB	IBB	SO	WP	Bk	W	L	Pct	ShO	Sv-Op Hld	ERC	ERA
2004	Phi	NL	6	4	0	0	28.1	126	25	11	11	1	1	0	5	16	0	24	1	1	2	0	1.000	0	0-0 0	4.33	3.49
2005	Phi	NL	7	4	0	0	26.0	127	30	31	29	5	1	1	3	16	2	17	2	0	1	2	.333	0	0-0 0	6.82	10.04
2006	Phi	NL	11	11	1	0	54.1	264	70	48	44	14	2	5	3	32	3	34	2	0	4	3	.571	1	0-0 0	8.02	7.29
2007	CWS	AL	16	10	0	4	70.0	314	85	45	41	17	3	2	6	19	0	49	1	0	1	5	.167	0	0-0 0	6.22	5.27
2008	CWS	AL	33	33	1	0	206.1	878	190	107	88	30	7	5	9	70	6	145	9	0	17	8	.680	0	0-0 0	3.80	3.84
	5 ML YEARS		73	62	2	4	385.0	1709	400	242	213	67	14	13	26	153	11	269	15	1	25	18	.581	1	0-0 0	5.02	4.98

Josh Fogg

Pitches: R Bats: R Pos: SP-14; RP-8   Ht: 6'0" Wt: 205 Born: 12/13/1976 Age: 32

			HOW MUCH HE PITCHED						WHAT HE GAVE UP										THE RESULTS					
Year	Team	Lg	G	GS	CG	GF	IP	BFP	H	R	ER	HR	SH	SF	HB	TBB	IBB	SO	WP	Bk	W	L	Pct	ShO	Sv-Op Hld	ERC	ERA
2008	Srsota*	A+	3	3	0	0	19.0	81	24	7	7	1	0	0	1	3	0	14	0	0	1	0	1.000	0	0- - 1	4.60	3.32
2008	Lsvlle*	AAA	2	2	1	0	17.0	65	14	4	3	0	1	1	0	3	0	12	0	0	1	1	.500	0	0- - 1	1.84	1.59
2001	CWS	AL	11	0	0	4	13.1	53	10	3	3	0	0	1	1	3	1	17	0	0	0	0	-	0	0-0 2	1.73	2.03
2002	Pit	NL	33	33	0	0	194.1	832	199	102	94	28	6	3	8	69	12	113	2	0	12	12	.500	0	0-0 0	4.46	4.35
2003	Pit	NL	26	26	1	0	142.0	625	166	90	83	22	6	4	9	40	0	71	2	0	10	9	.526	0	0-0 0	5.25	5.26
2004	Pit	NL	32	32	0	0	178.1	770	193	98	92	17	9	6	4	66	8	82	4	1	11	10	.524	0	0-0 0	4.59	4.64
2005	Pit	NL	34	28	0	1	169.1	742	196	106	95	27	4	6	6	53	11	85	2	1	6	11	.353	0	0-0 0	5.13	5.05
2006	Col	NL	31	31	0	0	172.0	765	206	115	105	24	6	5	6	60	13	93	3	0	11	9	.550	1	0-0 0	5.36	5.49
2007	Col	NL	30	29	0	0	165.2	745	194	99	91	23	5	5	13	59	7	94	3	0	10	9	.526	0	0-0 0	5.44	4.94
2008	Cin	NL	22	14	0	3	78.1	362	97	69	66	17	6	2	6	27	1	45	1	0	2	7	.222	0	0-0 0	6.36	7.58
	Postseason		3	2	0	0	10.2	49	18	7	7	1	0	0	0	3	1	6	0	0	2	1	.667	0	0-0 0	8.00	5.91
	8 ML YEARS		219	193	2	8	1113.1	4894	1261	682	629	158	42	32	57	377	53	600	17	2	62	67	.481	1	0-0 3	5.06	5.08

Mike Fontenot

Bats: L Throws: R Pos: 2B-82; PH-42; PR-3; SS-1   Ht: 5'8" Wt: 170 Born: 6/9/1980 Age: 29

			BATTING																	BASERUNNING				AVERAGES		
Year	Team	Lg	G	AB	H	2B	3B	HR	(Hm	Rd)	TB	R	RBI	RC	TBB	IBB	SO	HBP	SH	SF	SB	CS	SB%	GDP	Avg	OBP	Slg
2005	ChC	NL	7	2	0	0	0	0	(0	0)	0	4	0	1	2	0	0	1	0	0	0	0	-	0	.000	.600	.000
2007	ChC	NL	86	234	65	12	4	3			94	32	29	26	22	0	43	0	1	3	5	4	.56	5	.278	.336	.402
2008	ChC	NL	119	243	74	22	1	9	(4	5)	125	42	40	49	34	2	51	3	3	1	2	0	1.00	1	.305	.395	.514
	Postseason		2	2	0	0	0	0	(0	0)	0	0	0	0	0	0	1	0	0	0	0	0	-	0	.000	.000	.000
	3 ML YEARS		212	479	139	34	5	12	(6	6)	219	78	69	76	58	2	94	4	4	4	7	4	.64	6	.290	.369	.457

Casey Fossum

Pitches: L Bats: L Pos: RP-31   Ht: 6'1" Wt: 170 Born: 1/6/1978 Age: 31

			HOW MUCH HE PITCHED						WHAT HE GAVE UP										THE RESULTS					
Year	Team	Lg	G	GS	CG	GF	IP	BFP	H	R	ER	HR	SH	SF	HB	TBB	IBB	SO	WP	Bk	W	L	Pct	ShO	Sv-Op Hld	ERC	ERA
2008	Toledo*	AAA	11	4	0	2	46.0	176	21	11	10	4	0	0	5	19	1	48	1	2	3	0	1.000	0	0- - 1	1.75	1.96
2001	Bos	AL	13	7	0	3	44.1	197	44	26	24	7	1	6	1	20	1	26	1	1	3	2	.600	0	0-0 0	4.70	4.87
2002	Bos	AL	43	12	0	13	106.2	461	113	56	41	12	2	4	4	30	0	101	0	3	5	4	.556	0	1-1 3	4.14	3.46
2003	Bos	AL	19	14	0	2	79.0	346	82	55	48	9	1	3	4	34	0	63	4	0	6	5	.545	0	1-1 0	4.77	5.47
2004	Ari	NL	27	27	0	0	142.0	652	171	111	105	31	8	4	10	63	5	117	4	2	4	15	.211	0	0-0 0	6.67	6.65
2005	TB	AL	36	25	0	1	162.2	725	170	100	89	21	3	5	18	60	3	128	8	1	8	12	.400	0	0-1 0	4.80	4.92
2006	TB	AL	25	25	0	0	130.0	594	136	89	77	18	2	3	12	63	3	88	4	1	6	6	.500	0	0-0 0	5.25	5.33
2007	TB	AL	40	10	0	7	76.0	364	109	71	65	15	2	7	6	27	1	53	3	0	5	8	.385	0	0-4 2	7.59	7.70
2008	Det	AL	31	0	0	9	41.1	179	44	26	26	4	0	0	3	18	1	28	1	0	3	1	.750	0	0-0 0	4.98	5.66
	8 ML YEARS		234	120	0	35	782.0	3518	869	534	475	114	18	27	63	315	14	604	28	5	40	53	.430	0	2-8 11	5.37	5.47

Keith Foulke

Pitches: R Bats: R Pos: RP-31

Ht: 6'0" Wt: 210 Born: 10/19/1972 Age: 36

			HOW MUCH HE PITCHED						WHAT HE GAVE UP												THE RESULTS							
Year	Team	Lg	G	GS	CG	GF	IP	BFP	H	R	ER	HR	SH	SF	HB	TBB	IBB	SO	WP	Bk	W	L	Pct	ShO	Sv-Op	Hld	ERC	ERA
2008	Scrmto*	AAA	4	1	0	0	6.1	30	12	9	9	3	0	0	0	0	0	7	0	1	0	0	-	0	0--	-	11.22	12.79
2008	Stcktn*	A+	2	1	0	0	2.0	8	2	1	1	1	0	0	0	0	0	1	0	1	0	0	-	0	0--	-	4.70	4.50
2008	As*	R	1	1	0	0	1.0	4	1	0	0	0	0	0	0	1	0	1	0	0	0	0	-	0	0--	-	6.99	0.00
1997	2 Tms		27	8	0	5	73.1	326	88	52	52	13	3	1	4	23	2	54	1	0	4	5	.444	0	3-6	5	5.68	6.38
1998	CWS	AL	54	0	0	18	65.1	267	51	31	30	9	2	2	4	20	3	57	3	1	3	2	.600	0	1-2	13	2.95	4.13
1999	CWS	AL	67	0	0	31	105.1	411	72	28	26	11	3	0	3	21	4	123	1	0	3	3	.500	0	9-13	22	1.80	2.22
2000	CWS	AL	72	0	0	58	88.0	350	66	31	29	9	5	2	2	22	2	91	1	0	3	1	.750	0	34-39	3	2.28	2.97
2001	CWS	AL	72	0	0	69	81.0	322	57	21	21	3	4	1	8	22	1	75	1	0	4	9	.308	0	42-45	0	2.06	2.33
2002	CWS	AL	65	0	0	35	77.2	306	65	26	25	7	2	4	1	13	2	58	1	0	2	4	.333	0	11-14	8	2.38	2.90
2003	Oak	AL	72	0	0	67	86.2	338	57	21	20	10	1	1	7	20	2	88	0	1	9	1	.900	0	43-48	0	2.07	2.08
2004	Bos	AL	72	0	0	61	83.0	333	63	22	20	8	2	4	6	15	5	79	3	0	5	3	.625	0	32-39	0	2.14	2.17
2005	Bos	AL	43	0	0	37	45.2	210	53	30	30	8	2	1	5	18	1	34	0	0	5	5	.500	0	15-19	1	5.93	5.91
2006	Bos	AL	44	0	0	16	49.2	205	52	24	24	9	0	4	2	7	0	36	2	0	3	1	.750	0	0-0	14	4.03	4.35
2008	Oak	AL	31	0	0	9	31.0	133	28	14	14	7	1	2	1	13	2	23	1	0	0	3	.000	0	1-2	8	4.49	4.06
97	SF	NL	11	8	0	0	44.2	209	60	41	41	9	2	0	4	18	1	33	1	0	1	5	.167	0	0-1	0	7.41	8.26
97	CWS	AL	16	0	0	5	28.2	117	28	11	11	4	1	1	0	5	1	21	0	0	3	0	1.000	0	3-5	5	3.27	3.45
	Postseason		16	0	0	12	21.1	93	15	6	6	3	1	0	1	12	3	24	0	0	1	2	.333	0	3-5	0	3.21	2.53
11 ML YEARS			619	8	0	406	786.2	3201	652	300	291	94	25	18	44	194	24	718	14	2	41	37	.526	0	191-227	74	2.87	3.33

Dexter Fowler

Bats: B Throws: R Pos: CF-9; PH-3; PR-3; RF-1

Ht: 6'4" Wt: 175 Born: 3/22/1986 Age: 23

			BATTING																		BASERUNNING				AVERAGES		
Year	Team	Lg	G	AB	H	2B	3B	HR	(Hm	Rd)	TB	R	RBI	RC	TBB	IBB	SO	HBP	SH	SF		SB	CS	SB%	GDP	Avg	OBP	Slg
2005	Casper	R+	62	220	60	10	4	4	(-	-)	90	43	23	35	27	1	73	2	3	0		18	6	.75	2	.273	.357	.409
2006	Ashvll	A	99	405	120	31	6	8	(-	-)	187	92	46	71	43	0	79	7	2	1		43	23	.65	8	.296	.373	.462
2007	Mdest	A+	65	245	67	7	5	2	(-	-)	90	43	23	40	44	0	64	7	2	1		20	11	.65	4	.273	.397	.367
2008	Tulsa	AA	108	421	141	31	9	9	(-	-)	217	92	64	96	65	4	89	8	8	3		20	8	.71	6	.335	.431	.515
2008	Col	NL	13	26	4	0	0	0	(0	0)	4	0	0	5	0	0	5	1	0	0		0	1	.00	0	.154	.185	.154

Chad Fox

Pitches: R Bats: R Pos: RP-3

Ht: 6'3" Wt: 215 Born: 9/3/1970 Age: 38

			HOW MUCH HE PITCHED						WHAT HE GAVE UP												THE RESULTS							
Year	Team	Lg	G	GS	CG	GF	IP	BFP	H	R	ER	HR	SH	SF	HB	TBB	IBB	SO	WP	Bk	W	L	Pct	ShO	Sv-Op	Hld	ERC	ERA
2008	Dytona*	A+	3	3	0	0	4.0	15	1	0	0	0	0	0	1	1	0	4	0	0	0	0	-	0	0--	-	0.75	0.00
2008	Tenn*	AA	1	0	0	0	0.2	6	3	4	4	1	0	0	0	0	0	2	1	0	0	1	.000	0	0--	-	38.55	54.00
1997	Atl	NL	30	0	0	8	27.1	120	24	12	10	4	0	0	0	16	0	28	4	0	0	1	.000	0	0-1	7	4.44	3.29
1998	Mil	NL	49	0	0	12	57.0	242	56	27	25	4	6	0	1	20	0	64	5	0	1	4	.200	0	0-2	20	3.66	3.95
1999	Mil	NL	6	0	0	2	6.2	36	11	8	8	1	0	0	0	4	0	12	1	1	0	0	-	0	0-0	1	9.96	10.80
2001	Mil	NL	65	0	0	9	66.2	287	44	16	14	6	2	1	5	36	7	80	5	1	5	2	.714	0	2-4	20	2.75	1.89
2002	Mil	NL	3	0	0	0	4.2	25	6	3	3	0	1	0	0	5	1	3	0	0	1	0	1.000	0	0-0	0	7.03	5.79
2003	2 Tms		38	0	0	13	43.1	198	35	16	15	3	5	5	1	31	4	46	6	0	3	3	.500	0	3-5	7	3.80	3.12
2004	Fla	NL	12	0	0	1	10.2	49	9	8	8	1	0	0	1	8	0	17	1	0	0	1	.000	0	0-2	5	4.88	6.75
2005	ChC	NL	11	0	0	4	8.0	38	8	6	6	2	0	1	0	8	0	11	0	0	0	0	-	0	1-1	3	8.11	6.75
2008	ChC	NL	3	0	0	0	3.1	14	2	2	2	1	1	0	0	3	0	1	1	0	0	1	.000	0	0-0	0	5.57	5.40
03	Bos	AL	17	0	0	10	18.0	93	19	10	9	2	2	1	1	17	2	19	1	0	1	2	.333	0	3-5	0	6.42	4.50
03	Fla	NL	21	0	0	3	25.1	105	16	6	6	1	3	4	0	14	2	27	5	0	2	1	.667	0	0-0	7	2.18	2.13
	Postseason		9	0	0	1	11.1	53	12	5	5	2	2	0	0	9	3	9	0	0	1	0	1.000	0	0-0	1	6.25	3.97
9 ML YEARS			217	0	0	50	227.2	1009	195	98	91	22	15	7	9	131	12	262	23	2	10	12	.455	0	6-15	63	3.94	3.60

Jeff Francis

Pitches: L Bats: L Pos: SP-24

Ht: 6'5" Wt: 205 Born: 1/8/1981 Age: 28

			HOW MUCH HE PITCHED						WHAT HE GAVE UP												THE RESULTS							
Year	Team	Lg	G	GS	CG	GF	IP	BFP	H	R	ER	HR	SH	SF	HB	TBB	IBB	SO	WP	Bk	W	L	Pct	ShO	Sv-Op	Hld	ERC	ERA
2008	Tulsa*	AA	3	3	0	0	14.1	55	12	1	1	0	0	1	0	2	0	19	2	0	1	0	1.000	0	0- -	-	1.76	0.63
2004	Col	NL	7	7	0	0	36.2	164	42	22	21	8	2	1	1	13	1	32	2	0	3	2	.600	0	0-0	0	5.62	5.15
2005	Col	NL	33	33	0	0	183.2	828	228	119	116	26	6	10	8	70	5	128	2	0	14	12	.538	0	0-0	0	5.94	5.68
2006	Col	NL	32	32	1	0	199.0	843	187	100	92	18	7	7	13	69	15	117	0	0	13	11	.542	1	0-0	0	3.63	4.16
2007	Col	NL	34	34	1	0	215.1	922	234	103	101	25	7	4	7	63	7	165	1	1	17	9	.654	1	0-0	0	4.37	4.22
2008	Col	NL	24	24	0	0	143.2	636	164	84	80	21	6	4	3	49	4	94	0	0	4	10	.286	0	0-0	0	5.00	5.01
	Postseason		3	3	0	0	16.2	75	21	9	9	3	0	0	2	6	2	15	0	0	2	1	.667	0	0-0	0	6.57	4.86
5 ML YEARS			130	130	2	0	778.1	3393	855	429	410	98	28	26	32	264	32	536	5	1	51	44	.537	2	0-0	0	4.71	4.74

Ben Francisco

Bats: R Throws: R Pos: LF-83; RF-32; DH-15; PH-12; CF-2

Ht: 6'1" Wt: 190 Born: 10/23/1981 Age: 27

			BATTING																		BASERUNNING				AVERAGES		
Year	Team	Lg	G	AB	H	2B	3B	HR	(Hm	Rd)	TB	R	RBI	RC	TBB	IBB	SO	HBP	SH	SF		SB	CS	SB%	GDP	Avg	OBP	Slg
2002	MhVlly	A-	58	235	82	23	2	3	(-	-)	118	55	23	51	22	1	28	7	2	3		22	6	.79	5	.349	.416	.502
2003	Lk Cty	A	80	289	83	21	1	11	(-	-)	139	57	48	52	31	1	50	4	1	5		15	6	.71	7	.287	.359	.481
2004	Akron	AA	133	497	126	29	3	15	(-	-)	206	72	71	73	50	2	86	6	4	6		21	5	.81	10	.254	.326	.414
2005	Akron	AA	83	323	99	19	7	7	(-	-)	153	45	46	56	24	1	60	2	2	1		15	4	.79	4	.307	.357	.474
2005	Buffalo	AAA	4	16	8	1	0	0	(-	-)	9	4	3	4	1	0	3	0	0	0		1	0	1.00	1	.500	.500	.563
2006	Buffalo	AAA	134	515	143	32	4	17	(-	-)	234	80	59	86	45	0	72	10	5	4		25	5	.83	9	.278	.345	.454
2007	Buffalo	AAA	95	377	120	27	2	12	(-	-)	187	60	51	73	36	3	66	4	6	2		22	8	.73	11	.318	.382	.496

		BATTING																	BASERUNNING				AVERAGES		
Year Team	Lg	G	AB	H	2B	3B	HR	(Hm Rd)	TB	R	RBI	RC	TBB	IBB	SO	HBP	SH	SF	SB	CS	SB%	GDP	Avg	OBP	Slg
2008 Buffalo	AAA	24	92	21	3	1	1	(- -)	29	9	6	10	11	0	25	0	0	1	3	0	1.00	4	.228	.308	.315
2007 Cle	AL	25	62	17	5	0	3	(2 1)	31	10	12	6	3	0	19	0	0	1	0	2	.00	2	.274	.303	.500
2008 Cle	AL	121	447	119	32	0	15	(7 8)	196	65	54	57	40	0	86	6	2	4	4	3	.57	10	.266	.332	.438
2 ML YEARS		146	509	136	37	0	18	(9 9)	227	75	66	63	43	0	105	6	2	5	4	5	.44	12	.267	.329	.446

Frank Francisco

Pitches: R Bats: R Pos: RP-58   Ht: 6'3" Wt: 230 Born: 9/11/1979 Age: 29

		HOW MUCH HE PITCHED						WHAT HE GAVE UP										THE RESULTS						
Year Team	Lg	G	GS	CG	GF	IP	BFP	H	R	ER	HR	SH	SF	HB	TBB	IBB	SO	WP	Bk	W	L	Pct	ShO	Sv-Op Hld	ERC	ERA
2008 Okla*	AAA	8	0	0	7	9.0	33	3	0	0	0	0	0	0	3	0	16	0	0	0	0	-	0	5--	0.69	0.00
2004 Tex	AL	45	0	0	7	51.1	216	36	19	19	4	2	1	3	28	2	60	4	1	5	1	.833	0	0-3 10	3.04	3.33
2006 Tex	AL	8	0	0	2	7.1	32	8	4	4	2	0	0	0	2	0	6	1	0	0	1	.000	0	0-0 2	5.17	4.91
2007 Tex	AL	59	0	0	16	59.1	268	57	33	30	3	6	1	2	38	4	49	8	0	1	1	.500	0	0-0 21	4.44	4.55
2008 Tex	AL	58	0	0	18	63.1	264	47	24	22	7	0	3	0	26	2	83	5	0	3	5	.375	0	5-11 12	2.70	3.13
4 ML YEARS		170	0	0	43	181.1	780	148	80	75	16	8	5	5	94	8	198	18	1	9	8	.529	0	5-14 45	3.45	3.72

Jeff Francoeur

Bats: R Throws: R Pos: RF-152; PH-4   Ht: 6'4" Wt: 220 Born: 1/8/1984 Age: 25

		BATTING																	BASERUNNING				AVERAGES		
Year Team	Lg	G	AB	H	2B	3B	HR	(Hm Rd)	TB	R	RBI	RC	TBB	IBB	SO	HBP	SH	SF	SB	CS	SB%	GDP	Avg	OBP	Slg
2008 Missi*	AA	3	13	7	0	1	0	(- -)	9	3	2	4	1	0	2	0	0	0	0	0	-	0	.538	.571	.692
2005 Atl	NL	70	257	77	20	1	14	(11 3)	141	41	45	50	11	3	58	4	0	2	3	2	.60	4	.300	.336	.549
2006 Atl	NL	162	651	169	24	6	29	(19 10)	292	83	103	91	23	6	132	9	0	3	1	6	.14	15	.260	.293	.449
2007 Atl	NL	162	642	188	40	4	19	(7 12)	285	84	105	97	42	5	129	5	0	7	5	2	.71	14	.293	.338	.444
2008 Atl	NL	155	599	143	33	3	11	(5 6)	215	70	71	49	39	5	111	10	0	4	0	1	.00	18	.239	.294	.359
Postseason		4	17	4	1	1	0	(0 0)	7	2	1	2	2	1	4	1	1	0	0	0	-	1	.235	.350	.412
4 ML YEARS		549	2149	577	117	10	73	(42 31)	933	278	324	287	115	19	430	28	0	16	9	11	.45	51	.268	.312	.434

Kevin Frandsen

Bats: R Throws: R Pos: PH-1   Ht: 6'0" Wt: 184 Born: 5/24/1982 Age: 27

		BATTING																	BASERUNNING				AVERAGES		
Year Team	Lg	G	AB	H	2B	3B	HR	(Hm Rd)	TB	R	RBI	RC	TBB	IBB	SO	HBP	SH	SF	SB	CS	SB%	GDP	Avg	OBP	Slg
2006 SF	NL	41	93	20	4	0	2	(0 2)	30	12	7	7	3	0	14	6	0	0	0	1	.00	3	.215	.284	.323
2007 SF	NL	109	264	71	12	1	5	(1 4)	100	26	31	29	21	3	24	5	3	3	4	3	.57	17	.269	.331	.379
2008 SF	NL	1	1	0	0	0	0	(0 0)	0	0	0	0	0	0	0	0	0	0	0	0	-	0	.000	.000	.000
3 ML YEARS		151	358	91	16	1	7	(1 6)	130	38	38	36	24	3	38	11	3	3	4	4	.50	20	.254	.318	.363

Ryan Franklin

Pitches: R Bats: R Pos: RP-74   Ht: 6'3" Wt: 190 Born: 3/5/1973 Age: 36

		HOW MUCH HE PITCHED						WHAT HE GAVE UP										THE RESULTS						
Year Team	Lg	G	GS	CG	GF	IP	BFP	H	R	ER	HR	SH	SF	HB	TBB	IBB	SO	WP	Bk	W	L	Pct	ShO	Sv-Op Hld	ERC	ERA
1999 Sea	AL	6	0	0	2	11.1	51	10	6	6	2	0	0	1	8	1	6	0	0	0	0	-	0	0-0 1	5.52	4.76
2001 Sea	AL	38	0	0	14	78.1	335	76	32	31	13	1	2	4	24	4	60	2	0	5	1	.833	0	0-1 5	4.08	3.56
2002 Sea	AL	41	12	0	10	118.2	495	117	62	53	14	5	5	5	22	1	65	0	0	7	5	.583	0	0-1 3	3.40	4.02
2003 Sea	AL	32	32	2	0	212.0	877	199	93	84	34	8	5	9	61	3	99	1	2	11	13	.458	1	0-0 0	3.90	3.57
2004 Sea	AL	32	32	2	0	200.1	870	224	116	109	33	2	11	10	61	1	104	0	0	4	16	.200	1	0-0 0	5.08	4.90
2005 Sea	AL	32	30	2	0	190.2	832	212	110	108	28	3	3	7	62	4	93	3	1	8	15	.348	1	0-0 0	4.89	5.10
2006 2 Tms	NL	66	0	0	19	77.1	343	86	42	39	13	2	2	4	33	10	43	2	0	6	7	.462	0	0-3 8	4.54	4.54
2007 StL	NL	69	0	0	8	80.0	317	70	28	27	8	2	2	3	11	0	44	2	0	4	4	.500	0	1-6 25	2.59	3.04
2008 StL	NL	74	0	0	39	78.2	346	86	34	31	10	2	2	3	30	4	51	3	0	6	6	.500	0	17-25 13	4.82	3.55
06 Phi	NL	46	0	0	13	53.0	233	59	28	27	10	0	1	4	17	4	25	1	0	1	5	.167	0	0-1 8	5.26	4.58
06 Cin	NL	20	0	0	6	24.1	110	27	14	12	3	2	1	0	16	6	18	1	0	5	2	.714	0	0-2 0	5.67	4.44
9 ML YEARS		390	106	6	92	1047.1	4466	1080	523	488	155	25	32	46	312	28	565	13	6	51	67	.432	3	18-36 55	4.34	4.19

Jason Frasor

Pitches: R Bats: R Pos: RP-49   Ht: 5'10" Wt: 170 Born: 8/9/1977 Age: 31

		HOW MUCH HE PITCHED						WHAT HE GAVE UP										THE RESULTS						
Year Team	Lg	G	GS	CG	GF	IP	BFP	H	R	ER	HR	SH	SF	HB	TBB	IBB	SO	WP	Bk	W	L	Pct	ShO	Sv-Op Hld	ERC	ERA
2004 Tor	AL	63	0	0	37	68.1	299	64	31	31	4	3	3	2	36	3	54	4	2	4	6	.400	0	17-19 8	3.97	4.08
2005 Tor	AL	67	0	0	12	74.2	305	67	31	27	8	2	1	3	28	2	62	1	0	3	5	.375	0	1-3 15	3.72	3.25
2006 Tor	AL	51	0	0	12	50.0	215	47	24	24	8	0	3	2	17	1	51	3	0	3	2	.600	0	0-1 12	3.98	4.32
2007 Tor	AL	51	0	0	18	57.0	242	47	29	29	3	1	2	2	23	1	59	2	1	1	5	.167	0	3-6 4	2.88	4.58
2008 Tor	AL	49	0	0	21	47.1	208	36	23	22	4	0	2	1	32	4	42	6	0	1	2	.333	0	0-1 4	3.62	4.18
5 ML YEARS		281	0	0	100	297.1	1269	261	138	133	27	6	11	10	136	11	268	16	3	12	20	.375	0	21-30 43	3.64	4.03

Ryan Freel

Bats: R Throws: R Pos: CF-23; LF-13; PH-12; RF-5; PR-5; 3B-4; 2B-3   Ht: 5'10" Wt: 184 Born: 3/8/1976 Age: 33

		BATTING																	BASERUNNING				AVERAGES		
Year Team	Lg	G	AB	H	2B	3B	HR	(Hm Rd)	TB	R	RBI	RC	TBB	IBB	SO	HBP	SH	SF	SB	CS	SB%	GDP	Avg	OBP	Slg
2001 Tor	AL	9	22	6	1	0	0	(0 0)	7	1	3	3	1	0	4	1	0	0	2	1	.67	0	.273	.333	.318
2003 Cin	NL	43	137	39	6	1	4	(0 4)	59	23	12	17	9	1	13	4	2	1	4	2	.69	2	.285	.344	.431
2004 Cin	NL	143	505	140	21	8	3	(1 2)	186	74	28	73	67	0	88	12	8	7	37	10	.79	7	.277	.375	.368
2005 Cin	NL	103	369	100	19	3	4	(2 2)	137	69	21	55	51	0	59	8	3	0	36	10	.78	9	.271	.371	.371

107

Year	Team	Lg	G	AB	H	2B	3B	HR	(Hm	Rd)	TB	R	RBI	RC	TBB	IBB	SO	HBP	SH	SF	SB	CS	SB%	GDP	Avg	OBP	Slg
									BATTING													**BASERUNNING**				**AVERAGES**	
2006	Cin	NL	132	454	123	30	2	8	(6	2)	181	67	27	59	57	0	98	9	3	0	37	11	.77	5	.271	.363	.399
2007	Cin	NL	75	277	68	13	3	3	(2	1)	96	44	16	31	18	0	47	7	2	0	15	8	.65	4	.245	.308	.347
2008	Cin	NL	48	131	39	8	0	0	(0	0)	47	17	10	19	8	0	18	1	2	1	6	4	.60	3	.298	.340	.359
7 ML YEARS			553	1895	515	98	17	22	(11	11)	713	295	117	257	211	1	327	42	20	2	142	48	.75	30	.272	.357	.376

Brian Fuentes

Pitches: L Bats: L Pos: RP-67

Ht: 6'4" Wt: 230 Born: 8/9/1975 Age: 33

Year	Team	Lg	G	GS	CG	GF	IP	BFP	H	R	ER	HR	SH	SF	HB	TBB	IBB	SO	WP	Bk	W	L	Pct	ShO	Sv-Op	Hld	ERC	ERA
				HOW MUCH HE PITCHED								**WHAT HE GAVE UP**											**THE RESULTS**					
2001	Sea	AL	10	0	0	3	11.2	47	6	6	6	2	0	1	3	8	0	10	1	0	1	1	.500	0	0-1	1	4.39	4.63
2002	Col	NL	31	0	0	9	26.2	118	25	14	14	4	0	2	3	13	0	38	1	0	2	0	1.000	0	0-0	0	4.91	4.73
2003	Col	NL	75	0	0	23	75.1	320	64	24	23	7	0	3	6	34	2	82	2	1	3	3	.500	0	4-6	19	3.71	2.75
2004	Col	NL	47	0	0	12	44.2	201	46	30	28	5	7	0	4	19	6	48	3	0	2	4	.333	0	0-1	13	4.50	5.64
2005	Col	NL	78	0	0	55	74.1	321	59	25	24	6	5	1	10	34	4	91	8	0	2	5	.286	0	31-34	6	3.44	2.91
2006	Col	NL	66	0	0	58	65.1	274	50	25	25	8	2	1	6	26	4	73	6	0	3	4	.429	0	30-36	3	3.19	3.44
2007	Col	NL	64	0	0	38	61.1	255	46	26	21	6	1	1	7	23	0	56	2	0	3	5	.375	0	20-27	8	3.06	3.08
2008	Col	NL	67	0	0	48	62.2	256	47	22	19	3	3	1	1	22	1	82	1	0	1	5	.167	0	30-34	6	2.27	2.73
Postseason			10	0	0	0	9.2	47	14	7	7	2	0	0	0	5	0	11	1	0	1	0	1.000	0	0-0	3	8.22	6.52
8 ML YEARS			438	0	0	246	422.0	1792	343	172	160	41	18	10	40	179	17	480	24	1	17	27	.386	0	115-139	53	3.43	3.41

Kosuke Fukudome

Bats: L Throws: R Pos: RF-137; PH-15; CF-12; DH-1; PR-1

Ht: 6'0" Wt: 187 Born: 4/26/1977 Age: 32

Year	Team	Lg	G	AB	H	2B	3B	HR	(Hm	Rd)	TB	R	RBI	RC	TBB	IBB	SO	HBP	SH	SF	SB	CS	SB%	GDP	Avg	OBP	Slg
									BATTING													**BASERUNNING**				**AVERAGES**	
1999	Chnchi	Jap	132	461	131	25	2	16	(-	-)	208	76	52	68	50	-	121	5	8	2	4	7	.36	3	.284	.359	.451
2000	Chnchi	Jap	97	316	80	18	2	13	(-	-)	141	50	42	51	45	-	79	3	2	2	8	5	.62	5	.253	.350	.446
2001	Chnchi	Jap	120	375	94	22	2	15	(-	-)	165	51	56	62	56	-	90	4	4	3	8	4	.67	4	.251	.352	.440
2002	Chnchi	Jap	140	542	186	42	3	19	(-	-)	291	85	65	116	56	2	96	5	0	5	4	2	.67	4	.343	.406	.537
2003	Chnchi	Jap	140	528	165	30	11	34	(-	-)	319	107	96	125	78	1	118	4	1	6	10	5	.67	5	.313	.401	.604
2004	Chnchi	Jap	92	350	97	19	7	23	(-	-)	199	61	81	73	48	0	93	3	1	2	8	3	.73	3	.277	.367	.569
2005	Chnchi	Jap	142	515	169	39	6	28	(-	-)	304	102	103	128	93	3	128	1	0	3	13	5	.72	8	.328	.430	.590
2006	Chnchi	Jap	130	496	174	47	5	31	(-	-)	324	117	104	135	76	4	94	3	0	3	11	2	.85	4	.351	.438	.653
2007	Chnchi	Jap	81	269	79	22	0	13	(-	-)	140	64	48	67	69	2	66	6	0	4	5	2	.71	5	.294	.443	.520
2008	ChC	NL	150	501	129	25	3	10	(6	4)	190	79	58	77	81	9	104	1	2	5	12	4	.75	7	.257	.359	.379

Kazuo Fukumori

Pitches: R Bats: R Pos: RP-4

Ht: 6'0" Wt: 175 Born: 8/4/1976 Age: 32

Year	Team	Lg	G	GS	CG	GF	IP	BFP	H	R	ER	HR	SH	SF	HB	TBB	IBB	SO	WP	Bk	W	L	Pct	ShO	Sv-Op	Hld	ERC	ERA
				HOW MUCH HE PITCHED								**WHAT HE GAVE UP**											**THE RESULTS**					
1995	Yokha	Jap	2	1	0	0	5.0	23	5	0	0	0	-	-	0	3	-	4	0	0	0	0	-	0	0- -	-	3.99	0.00
1996	Yokha	Jap	1	0	0	1	1.0	4	2	0	0	0	-	-	0	0	-	1	0	0	0	0	-	0	0- -	-	9.49	0.00
1997	Yokha	Jap	25	10	0	8	71.1	296	58	26	23	7	-	-	4	28	-	42	2	1	4	4	.500	0	0- -	-	3.27	2.90
1998	Yokha	Jap	3	3	0	0	18.2	82	20	8	6	1	-	-	1	6	-	13	3	0	1	2	.333	0	0- -	-	4.00	2.89
1999	Yokha	Jap	30	19	1	4	132.2	576	151	65	63	15	-	-	3	45	-	96	8	0	9	9	.500	0	0- -	-	4.88	4.27
2000	Yokha	Jap	40	8	0	16	88.0	380	92	40	35	7	-	-	2	27	-	49	9	1	6	6	.500	0	10- -	-	3.87	3.58
2001	Yokha	Jap	5	5	0	0	31.0	120	20	12	12	5	-	-	0	10	-	23	0	0	1	2	.333	0	0- -	-	2.35	3.48
2002	Yokha	Jap	33	2	0	12	48.2	211	45	21	16	2	-	-	3	15	-	47	1	0	2	3	.400	0	2- -	-	3.04	2.96
2003	Yokha	Jap	62	0	0	20	60.0	255	55	32	30	6	-	-	4	17	2	34	3	0	1	3	.250	0	1- -	-	3.32	4.50
2004	Kintets	Jap	43	0	0	33	48.2	218	53	29	28	5	5	1	3	24	4	27	0	0	2	5	.286	0	10- -	-	5.16	5.18
2005	Tohoku	Jap	49	0	0	32	63.0	286	75	26	25	5	7	7	2	24	7	36	4	0	4	3	.571	0	11- -	-	4.82	3.57
2006	Tohoku	Jap	50	0	0	34	58.0	253	50	18	14	2	7	0	3	27	4	55	7	0	0	3	.000	0	21- -	-	3.13	2.17
2007	Tohoku	Jap	34	0	0	23	36.0	167	44	20	19	1	3	1	2	17	2	33	1	0	4	2	.667	0	17- -	-	5.20	4.75
2008	Okla	AAA	38	4	0	15	64.0	284	79	41	39	7	1	1	1	18	0	40	4	0	1	6	.143	0	2- -	-	5.07	5.48
2008	Tex	AL	4	0	0	0	4.0	26	11	9	9	2	0	0	0	4	1	1	2	0	0	0	-	0	0-0	0	23.91	20.25

Jeff Fulchino

Pitches: R Bats: R Pos: RP-12

Ht: 6'5" Wt: 252 Born: 11/26/1979 Age: 29

Year	Team	Lg	G	GS	CG	GF	IP	BFP	H	R	ER	HR	SH	SF	HB	TBB	IBB	SO	WP	Bk	W	L	Pct	ShO	Sv-Op	Hld	ERC	ERA
				HOW MUCH HE PITCHED								**WHAT HE GAVE UP**											**THE RESULTS**					
2001	Utica	A-	14	13	0	1	60.2	267	48	34	24	2	1	0	8	31	0	33	3	3	3	8	.273	0	0- -	-	3.32	3.56
2002	Kane	A	24	22	0	0	132.2	114	114	67	57	7	5	5	10	51	0	94	9	1	5	5	.500	0	0- -	-	18.04	3.87
2003	Grnsbr	A	5	4	0	0	25.1	113	28	14	11	1	1	1	3	7	0	16	0	2	1	2	.333	0	0- -	-	4.14	3.91
2003	Jupiter	A+	17	16	1	0	78.0	341	76	41	35	1	1	3	10	32	0	47	5	0	2	4	.333	0	0- -	-	3.87	4.04
2004	Jupiter	A+	8	8	0	0	43.0	173	39	17	13	1	3	4	1	16	0	28	3	0	2	2	.500	0	0- -	-	3.20	2.72
2004	Carlina	AA	17	17	0	0	90.2	391	93	45	45	5	5	3	3	37	3	84	3	0	6	5	.545	0	0- -	-	4.06	4.47
2005	Albq	AAA	29	29	0	0	153.0	698	179	102	86	21	13	3	11	67	3	101	9	0	11	7	.611	0	0- -	-	5.79	5.06
2006	Albq	AAA	25	24	0	1	140.0	613	144	82	70	12	7	3	15	56	0	109	9	1	6	10	.375	0	0- -	-	4.62	4.50
2007	Albq	AAA	16	16	0	0	88.0	410	108	63	57	13	1	3	4	39	3	55	3	0	6	2	.750	0	0- -	-	6.02	5.83
2008	NWArk	AA	2	0	0	1	3.1	15	3	3	2	0	0	0	1	1	0	6	0	0	0	0	-	0	1- -	-	2.26	5.40
2008	Omha	AAA	25	5	0	11	61.1	273	71	38	33	2	1	2	0	27	1	53	4	1	3	4	.429	0	5- -	-	4.64	4.84
2006	Fla	NL	1	0	0	0	0.1	2	0	0	0	0	0	0	0	1	0	0	0	0	0	0	-	0	0-0	0	7.00	0.00
2008	KC	AL	12	0	0	7	14.0	72	21	15	14	2	0	1	1	8	0	12	1	0	0	1	.000	0	0-0	0	8.38	9.00
2 ML YEARS			13	0	0	7	14.1	74	21	15	14	2	0	1	1	9	0	12	1	0	0	1	.000	0	0-0	0	8.37	8.79

Rafael Furcal

Bats: B **Throws:** R **Pos:** SS-36; PH-1 **Ht:** 5'9" **Wt:** 195 **Born:** 10/24/1977 **Age:** 31

								BATTING												BASERUNNING				AVERAGES		
Year Team	Lg	G	AB	H	2B	3B	HR	(Hm Rd)	TB	R	RBI	RC	TBB	IBB	SO	HBP	SH	SF	SB	CS	SB%	GDP	Avg	OBP	Slg
2008 LsVgs*	AAA	1	3	1	1	0	0	(- -)	2	0	1	0	0	0	0	0	0	0	0	0	-	0	.333	.333	.667
2000 Atl	NL	131	455	134	20	4	4	(1 3)	174	87	37	78	73	0	80	3	9	2	40	14	.74	2	.295	.394	.382
2001 Atl	NL	79	324	89	19	0	4	(3 1)	120	39	30	41	24	1	56	1	4	6	22	6	.79	5	.275	.321	.370
2002 Atl	NL	154	636	175	31	8	8	(4 4)	246	95	47	80	43	0	114	3	9	2	27	15	.64	8	.275	.323	.387
2003 Atl	NL	156	664	194	35	10	15	(4 11)	294	130	61	107	60	2	76	3	3	4	25	2	.93	1	.292	.352	.443
2004 Atl	NL	143	563	157	24	5	14	(5 9)	233	103	59	82	58	4	71	1	5	5	29	6	.83	9	.279	.344	.414
2005 Atl	NL	154	616	175	31	11	12	(9 3)	264	100	58	98	62	3	78	1	5	5	46	10	.82	11	.284	.348	.429
2006 LAD	NL	159	654	196	32	9	15	(12 3)	291	113	63	110	73	3	98	1	5	3	37	13	.74	7	.300	.369	.445
2007 LAD	NL	138	581	157	23	4	6	(4 2)	206	87	47	65	55	3	68	1	2	3	25	6	.81	11	.270	.333	.355
2008 LAD	NL	36	143	51	12	2	5	(3 2)	82	34	16	33	20	0	17	1	0	0	8	3	.73	3	.357	.439	.573
Postseason		25	106	24	1	2	2	(2 0)	35	14	7	12	15	1	17	1	3	0	11	2	.85	1	.226	.328	.330
9 ML YEARS		1150	4636	1328	227	53	83	(45 38)	1910	788	418	694	468	16	658	15	42	30	259	75	.78	57	.286	.352	.412

Kason Gabbard

Pitches: L **Bats:** L **Pos:** SP-12 **Ht:** 6'3" **Wt:** 200 **Born:** 4/8/1982 **Age:** 27

			HOW MUCH HE PITCHED					WHAT HE GAVE UP												THE RESULTS						
Year Team	Lg	G	GS	CG	GF	IP	BFP	H	R	ER	HR	SH	SF	HB	TBB	IBB	SO	WP	Bk	W	L	Pct	ShO	Sv-Op	Hld	ERC	ERA
2008 Frisco*	AA	1	1	0	0	4.0	16	1	1	1	0	0	0	0	3	0	6	0	0	0	0	-	0	0--	-	1.18	2.25
2008 Okla*	AAA	2	2	0	0	12.2	58	17	8	7	2	2	0	0	4	0	12	0	0	0	1	.000	0	0--	-	6.16	4.97
2006 Bos	AL	7	4	0	1	25.2	111	24	11	10	0	1	0	0	16	0	15	1	1	1	3	.250	0	0-0	0	3.96	3.51
2007 2 Tms	AL	15	15	1	0	81.1	344	68	42	42	8	1	1	7	41	1	55	5	0	6	1	.857	1	0-0	0	3.99	4.65
2008 Tex	AL	12	12	0	0	56.0	263	64	36	30	5	2	2	1	39	4	33	4	0	2	3	.400	0	0-0	0	6.04	4.82
07 Bos	AL	7	7	1	0	41.0	165	28	17	17	3	0	0	4	18	0	29	0	0	4	0	1.000	1	0-0	0	2.83	3.73
07 Tex	AL	8	8	0	0	40.1	179	40	25	25	5	1	1	3	23	1	26	5	0	2	1	.667	0	0-0	0	5.27	5.58
3 ML YEARS		34	31	1	1	163.0	718	156	89	82	13	4	3	8	96	5	103	10	1	9	7	.563	1	0-0	0	4.67	4.53

Eric Gagne

Pitches: R **Bats:** R **Pos:** RP-50 **Ht:** 6'0" **Wt:** 240 **Born:** 1/7/1976 **Age:** 33

			HOW MUCH HE PITCHED					WHAT HE GAVE UP												THE RESULTS						
Year Team	Lg	G	GS	CG	GF	IP	BFP	H	R	ER	HR	SH	SF	HB	TBB	IBB	SO	WP	Bk	W	L	Pct	ShO	Sv-Op	Hld	ERC	ERA
2008 Nashv*	AAA	2	2	0	0	1.2	9	2	2	2	0	0	0	0	1	0	3	1	0	0	0	-	0	0--	-	7.49	10.80
1999 LAD	NL	5	5	0	0	30.0	119	18	8	7	3	1	0	0	15	0	30	1	0	1	1	.500	0	0-0	0	2.42	2.10
2000 LAD	NL	20	19	0	0	101.1	464	106	62	58	20	5	3	6	60	1	79	4	0	4	6	.400	0	0-0	0	5.97	5.15
2001 LAD	NL	33	24	0	3	151.2	649	144	90	80	24	6	8	16	46	1	130	3	1	6	7	.462	0	0-0	0	4.22	4.75
2002 LAD	NL	77	0	0	68	82.1	314	55	18	18	6	3	2	2	16	4	114	1	0	4	1	.800	0	52-56	1	1.60	1.97
2003 LAD	NL	77	0	0	67	82.1	306	37	12	11	2	4	0	3	20	2	137	2	0	2	3	.400	0	55-55	0	0.93	1.20
2004 LAD	NL	70	0	0	59	82.1	326	53	24	20	5	4	2	5	22	3	114	2	0	7	3	.700	0	45-47	0	1.72	2.19
2005 LAD	NL	14	0	0	13	13.1	53	10	4	4	2	0	0	0	3	0	22	3	0	1	0	1.000	0	8-8	0	2.38	2.70
2006 LAD	NL	2	0	0	2	2.0	8	0	0	0	0	0	0	1	1	0	3	0	0	0	0	-	0	1-1	0	0.95	0.00
2007 2 Tms	AL	54	0	0	41	52.0	222	49	22	22	3	0	0	1	21	0	51	1	0	4	2	.667	0	16-20	4	3.56	3.81
2008 Mil	NL	50	0	0	16	46.1	203	46	28	28	11	1	0	2	22	2	38	1	0	4	3	.571	0	10-17	7	5.51	5.44
07 Tex	AL	34	0	0	30	33.1	133	23	8	8	2	0	0	1	12	0	29	1	0	2	0	1.000	0	16-17	1	2.21	2.16
07 Bos	AL	20	0	0	11	18.2	89	26	14	14	1	0	0	0	9	0	22	0	0	2	2	.500	0	0-3	3	6.37	6.75
Postseason		7	0	0	6	7.1	29	5	3	3	0	0	1	0	3	0	9	1	0	0	1	.000	0	0-0	0	1.90	3.68
10 ML YEARS		402	48	0	269	643.2	2664	518	268	248	76	24	15	33	226	13	718	18	1	33	26	.559	0	187-204	12	3.12	3.47

Armando Galarraga

Pitches: R **Bats:** R **Pos:** SP-28; RP-2 **Ht:** 6'4" **Wt:** 180 **Born:** 1/15/1982 **Age:** 27

			HOW MUCH HE PITCHED					WHAT HE GAVE UP												THE RESULTS						
Year Team	Lg	G	GS	CG	GF	IP	BFP	H	R	ER	HR	SH	SF	HB	TBB	IBB	SO	WP	Bk	W	L	Pct	ShO	Sv-Op	Hld	ERC	ERA
2001 Expos	R	14	1	0	5	34.2	157	37	21	12	2	2	2	3	15	1	24	3	1	1	3	.250	0	2--	-	4.51	3.12
2002 Expos	R	2	2	0	0	3.2	12	1	1	1	0	0	0	0	0	0	1	0	0	0	0	-	0	0--	-	0.55	2.45
2003 Expos	R	5	5	0	0	15.0	60	13	5	3	0	0	0	1	5	0	7	1	0	1	1	.500	0	0--	-	2.84	1.80
2004 Savann	A	23	19	2	1	110.1	470	104	64	57	14	6	6	8	31	0	94	3	1	5	5	.500	0	0--	-	3.71	4.65
2005 Ptomc	A+	14	14	0	0	80.0	337	69	30	22	7	1	1	10	23	0	79	4	2	3	4	.429	0	0--	-	3.28	2.48
2005 Hrsbrg	AA	14	13	1	0	77.1	328	80	46	43	10	5	3	4	22	0	59	2	1	3	4	.429	1	0--	-	4.27	5.00
2006 Frisco	AA	9	9	0	0	41.0	192	56	34	25	5	1	1	6	13	0	38	1	1	1	6	.143	0	0--	-	6.76	5.49
2006 Rngrs	R	6	6	0	0	16.1	69	18	8	6	0	0	0	1	6	0	16	4	0	0	2	.000	0	0--	-	4.24	3.31
2006 Spkane	A-	1	1	0	0	4.0	16	4	2	2	1	0	0	0	0	0	3	0	0	0	1	.000	0	0--	-	3.33	4.50
2006 Bkrsfld	A+	2	2	0	0	8.2	41	6	9	6	2	0	0	0	7	0	7	1	0	0	1	.000	0	0--	-	4.55	6.23
2007 Frisco	AA	23	22	2	0	127.2	542	122	58	57	14	4	0	12	47	0	114	4	0	9	6	.600	2	0--	-	4.23	4.02
2007 Okla	AAA	4	4	1	0	24.2	109	23	13	13	1	0	0	1	11	0	21	2	1	2	2	.500	1	0--	-	3.52	4.74
2008 Toledo	AAA	2	2	0	0	12.0	44	7	3	3	1	0	0	1	1	0	11	0	0	2	0	1.000	0	0--	-	1.11	2.25
2007 Tex	AL	3	1	0	2	8.2	40	8	6	6	2	0	1	0	7	0	6	0	0	0	0	-	0	0-0	0	6.35	6.23
2008 Det	AL	30	28	0	0	178.2	746	152	83	74	28	2	4	6	61	2	126	6	0	13	7	.650	0	0-1	0	3.50	3.73
2 ML YEARS		33	29	0	2	187.1	786	160	89	80	30	2	5	6	68	2	132	6	0	13	7	.650	0	0-1	0	3.62	3.84

Sean Gallagher

Pitches: R Bats: R Pos: SP-21; RP-2

Ht: 6'2" Wt: 235 Born: 12/30/1985 Age: 23

			HOW MUCH HE PITCHED						WHAT HE GAVE UP											THE RESULTS							
Year	Team	Lg	G	GS	CG	GF	IP	BFP	H	R	ER	HR	SH	SF	HB	TBB	IBB	SO	WP	Bk	W	L	Pct	ShO	Sv-Op	Hld	ERC	ERA
2004	Cubs	R	10	9	0	0	34.2	152	38	19	12	0	0	0	3	11	0	44	1	0	1	2	.333	0	0--	-	3.91	3.12
2005	Peoria	A	26	26	0	0	146.0	600	107	53	44	10	6	5	15	55	0	139	5	0	14	5	.737	0	0--	-	2.77	2.71
2005	Dytona	A+	1	1	0	0	5.0	21	6	1	1	1	0	0	0	0	0	7	0	0	0	0	-	0	0--	-	4.14	1.80
2006	Dytona	A+	13	13	0	0	78.1	322	75	24	20	5	6	2	5	21	0	80	3	0	4	0	1.000	0	0--	-	3.42	2.30
2006	WTenn	AA	15	15	0	0	86.1	374	74	30	26	4	5	3	1	55	2	91	9	0	7	5	.583	0	0--	-	3.88	2.71
2007	Tenn	AA	11	11	0	0	61.0	260	54	25	23	3	0	1	3	24	0	54	3	0	7	2	.778	0	0--	-	3.24	3.39
2007	Iowa	AAA	8	8	0	0	40.2	163	33	12	12	1	3	2	3	13	0	37	3	0	3	1	.750	0	0--	-	2.65	2.66
2008	Iowa	AAA	5	5	0	0	29.0	117	21	11	10	2	1	0	0	9	1	30	3	0	2	2	.500	0	0--	-	2.05	3.10
2007	ChC	NL	8	0	0	3	14.2	74	19	15	14	3	0	1	1	12	0	5	0	0	0	0	-	0	1-1	0	8.95	8.59
2008	2 Tms		23	21	0	1	115.1	522	118	73	66	13	3	6	6	58	2	103	2	0	5	7	.417	0	0-0	0	4.83	5.15
08	ChC	NL	12	10	0	0	58.2	256	58	31	29	6	2	1	4	22	1	49	2	0	3	4	.429	0	0-0	0	4.14	4.45
08	Oak	AL	11	11	0	0	56.2	266	60	42	37	7	1	5	2	36	1	54	0	0	2	3	.400	0	0-0	0	5.57	5.88
	2 ML YEARS		31	21	0	4	130.0	596	137	88	80	16	3	7	7	70	2	108	2	0	5	7	.417	0	1-1	0	5.26	5.54

Yovani Gallardo

Pitches: R Bats: R Pos: SP-4

Ht: 6'2" Wt: 220 Born: 2/27/1986 Age: 23

			HOW MUCH HE PITCHED						WHAT HE GAVE UP											THE RESULTS							
Year	Team	Lg	G	GS	CG	GF	IP	BFP	H	R	ER	HR	SH	SF	HB	TBB	IBB	SO	WP	Bk	W	L	Pct	ShO	Sv-Op	Hld	ERC	ERA
2004	Brewrs	R	6	6	0	0	19.1	74	14	3	1	0	0	0	1	4	0	23	2	0	0	0	-	0	0--	-	1.65	0.47
2004	Beloit	A	2	2	0	0	7.1	34	12	10	10	2	0	0	0	4	0	8	3	0	0	1	.000	0	0--	-	11.30	12.27
2005	WV	A	26	18	0	5	121.1	503	100	46	37	5	7	1	8	51	0	110	8	0	8	3	.727	0	1--	-	3.12	2.74
2006	BrvdCt	A+	13	13	0	0	77.2	307	54	24	19	4	4	1	4	23	0	103	5	0	6	3	.667	0	0--	-	2.05	2.20
2006	Hntsvl	AA	13	13	0	0	77.1	303	50	18	14	2	6	1	1	28	0	85	3	0	5	2	.714	0	0--	-	1.78	1.63
2007	Nashv	AAA	13	13	0	0	77.2	315	53	26	25	4	3	1	2	28	0	110	4	0	8	3	.727	0	0--	-	2.06	2.90
2008	Nashv	AAA	3	3	1	0	15.2	68	20	9	9	2	0	0	0	5	0	18	0	0	1	0	1.000	0	0--	-	5.78	5.17
2007	Mil	NL	20	17	0	1	110.1	466	103	48	45	8	4	3	2	37	2	101	3	0	9	5	.643	0	0-0	0	3.30	3.67
2008	Mil	NL	4	4	0	0	24.0	97	22	5	5	3	2	1	0	8	0	20	0	0	0	0	-	0	0-0	0	3.66	1.88
	2 ML YEARS		24	21	0	1	134.1	563	125	53	50	11	6	4	2	45	2	121	3	0	9	5	.643	0	0-0	0	3.36	3.35

Mat Gamel

Bats: L Throws: R Pos: PH-2; 3B-1

Ht: 6'0" Wt: 194 Born: 7/26/1985 Age: 23

			BATTING																		BASERUNNING				AVERAGES		
Year	Team	Lg	G	AB	H	2B	3B	HR	(Hm	Rd)	TB	R	RBI	RC	TBB	IBB	SO	HBP	SH	SF	SB	CS	SB%	GDP	Avg	OBP	Slg
2005	Helena	R+	50	199	65	15	2	5	(-	-)	99	34	37	36	12	1	49	4	0	1	7	4	.64	6	.327	.375	.497
2005	WV	A-	8	23	4	0	0	1	(-	-)	7	2	1	2	5	1	9	0	0	0	0	0	-	0	.174	.321	.304
2006	WV	A-	129	493	142	28	5	17	(-	-)	231	65	88	86	52	8	81	5	0	5	9	2	.82	7	.288	.359	.469
2007	BrvdCt	A+	128	466	140	37	8	9	(-	-)	220	78	60	86	58	9	98	3	2	5	14	7	.67	5	.300	.378	.472
2008	Hntsvl	AA	127	508	167	35	7	19	(-	-)	273	96	97	105	55	5	111	4	0	5	7	7	.50	8	.329	.395	.537
2008	Nashv	AAA	5	21	5	0	0	1	(-	-)	8	3	3	2	2	0	10	0	0	0	0	0	-	0	.238	.304	.381
2008	Mil	NL	2	2	1	0	0	0	(0	0)	2	0	0	1	0	0	1	0	0	0	0	0	-	0	.500	.500	1.000

Freddy Garcia

Pitches: R Bats: R Pos: SP-3

Ht: 6'4" Wt: 260 Born: 6/10/1976 Age: 33

			HOW MUCH HE PITCHED						WHAT HE GAVE UP											THE RESULTS							
Year	Team	Lg	G	GS	CG	GF	IP	BFP	H	R	ER	HR	SH	SF	HB	TBB	IBB	SO	WP	Bk	W	L	Pct	ShO	Sv-Op	Hld	ERC	ERA
2008	Lkland*	A+	1	1	0	0	2.0	9	3	0	0	0	0	0	0	0	0	1	0	0	0	0	-	0	0--	-	7.26	0.00
2008	Toledo*	AAA	1	1	0	0	3.0	10	2	0	0	0	0	0	0	0	0	4	0	0	0	0	-	0	0--	-	1.01	0.00
1999	Sea	AL	33	33	2	0	201.1	888	205	96	91	18	3	6	10	90	4	170	12	3	17	8	.680	1	0-0	0	4.46	4.07
2000	Sea	AL	21	20	0	0	124.1	538	112	62	54	16	6	1	2	64	4	79	4	2	9	5	.643	0	0-0	0	4.20	3.91
2001	Sea	AL	34	34	4	0	238.2	971	199	88	81	16	8	5	5	69	6	163	3	1	18	6	.750	3	0-0	0	2.61	3.05
2002	Sea	AL	34	34	1	0	223.2	955	227	110	109	30	4	8	6	63	3	181	7	1	16	10	.615	0	0-0	0	3.98	4.39
2003	Sea	AL	33	33	1	0	201.1	862	196	109	101	31	2	8	11	71	2	144	11	0	12	14	.462	0	0-0	0	4.33	4.51
2004	2 Tms		31	31	1	0	210.0	878	192	92	89	22	8	3	7	64	3	184	6	0	13	11	.542	0	0-0	0	3.37	3.81
2005	CWS	AL	33	33	2	0	228.0	943	225	102	98	26	5	5	3	60	2	146	20	1	14	8	.636	0	0-0	0	3.65	3.87
2006	CWS	AL	33	33	1	0	216.1	917	228	116	109	32	1	6	7	48	3	135	4	0	17	9	.654	0	0-0	0	4.09	4.53
2007	Phi	NL	11	11	0	0	58.0	264	74	39	38	12	4	3	5	19	3	50	5	0	1	5	.167	0	0-0	0	6.57	5.90
2008	Det	AL	3	3	0	0	15.0	61	11	8	7	3	0	0	1	6	0	12	0	0	1	1	.500	0	0-0	0	3.61	4.20
04	Sea	AL	15	15	1	0	107.0	446	96	39	38	8	4	1	2	32	1	82	5	0	4	7	.364	0	0-0	0	3.00	3.20
04	CWS	AL	16	16	0	0	103.0	432	96	53	51	14	4	2	5	32	2	102	1	0	9	4	.692	0	0-0	0	3.77	4.46
	Postseason		9	9	1	0	55.0	230	51	20	19	5	2	0	2	22	1	45	1	0	6	2	.750	0	0-0	0	3.82	3.11
	10 ML YEARS		266	265	12	0	1716.2	7277	1669	822	777	206	41	45	57	554	30	1264	74	8	118	77	.605	4	0-0	0	3.86	4.07

Jaime Garcia

Pitches: L Bats: L Pos: RP-9; SP-1

Ht: 6'2" Wt: 200 Born: 7/8/1986 Age: 22

			HOW MUCH HE PITCHED						WHAT HE GAVE UP											THE RESULTS							
Year	Team	Lg	G	GS	CG	GF	IP	BFP	H	R	ER	HR	SH	SF	HB	TBB	IBB	SO	WP	Bk	W	L	Pct	ShO	Sv-Op	Hld	ERC	ERA
2006	QuadC	A	13	13	1	0	77.2	317	67	28	25	1	5	0	2	18	0	80	7	4	5	4	.556	0	0--	-	2.25	2.90
2006	PlmBh	A+	12	12	0	0	77.1	319	84	33	33	2	1	1	1	16	0	51	5	5	5	4	.556	0	0--	-	3.52	3.84
2007	Sprgfld	AA	18	18	0	0	103.1	440	93	47	43	14	10	3	3	45	1	97	13	1	5	9	.357	0	0--	-	4.03	3.75
2008	Sprgfld	AA	6	6	1	0	35.0	145	26	10	8	0	1	0	2	16	0	41	1	0	3	2	.600	0	0--	-	2.49	2.06
2008	Memp	AAA	13	12	0	0	71.0	310	74	41	35	6	4	3	3	26	0	59	9	3	4	4	.500	0	0--	-	4.22	4.44
2008	StL	NL	10	1	0	4	16.0	69	14	10	10	4	0	0	1	8	0	8	3	0	1	1	.500	0	0-0	3	5.15	5.63

Nomar Garciaparra

Bats: R **Throws:** R **Pos:** SS-31; 3B-11; 1B-8; PH-8   **Ht:** 6'0" **Wt:** 190 **Born:** 7/23/1973 **Age:** 35

Year	Team	Lg	G	AB	H	2B	3B	HR	(Hm	Rd)	TB	R	RBI	RC	TBB	IBB	SO	HBP	SH	SF	SB	CS	SB%	GDP	Avg	OBP	Slg
2008	LsVgs*	AAA	7	20	9	1	0	1	(-	-)	13	4	4	6	3	0	2	0	0	0	0	0	-	1	.450	.522	.650
1996	Bos	AL	24	87	21	2	3	4	(3	1)	41	11	16	13	4	0	14	0	1	1	5	0	1.00	0	.241	.272	.471
1997	Bos	AL	153	684	209	44	11	30	(11	19)	365	122	98	122	35	2	92	6	2	7	22	9	.71	9	.306	.342	.534
1998	Bos	AL	143	604	195	37	8	35	(17	18)	353	111	122	117	33	1	62	8	0	7	12	6	.67	20	.323	.362	.584
1999	Bos	AL	135	532	190	42	4	27	(14	13)	321	103	104	125	51	7	39	8	0	4	14	3	.82	11	.357	.418	.603
2000	Bos	AL	140	529	197	51	3	21	(7	14)	317	104	96	127	61	20	50	2	0	7	5	2	.71	8	.372	.434	.599
2001	Bos	AL	21	83	24	3	0	4	(3	1)	39	13	8	13	7	0	9	1	0	0	0	1	.00	1	.289	.352	.470
2002	Bos	AL	156	635	197	56	5	24	(10	14)	335	101	120	113	41	4	63	6	0	11	5	2	.71	17	.310	.352	.528
2003	Bos	AL	156	658	198	37	13	28	(18	10)	345	120	105	114	39	1	61	11	1	10	19	5	.79	10	.301	.345	.524
2004	2 Tms		81	321	99	21	3	9	(6	3)	153	52	41	53	24	2	30	6	1	2	4	1	.80	10	.308	.365	.477
2005	ChC	NL	62	230	65	12	0	9	(5	4)	104	28	30	28	12	0	24	2	0	3	0	0	-	6	.283	.320	.452
2006	LAD	NL	122	469	142	31	2	20	(9	11)	237	82	93	87	42	9	30	8	0	4	3	0	1.00	15	.303	.367	.505
2007	LAD	NL	121	431	122	17	0	7	(6	1)	160	39	59	60	31	5	41	0	0	4	3	1	.75	6	.283	.328	.371
2008	LAD	NL	55	163	43	9	0	8	(5	3)	76	24	28	20	15	2	11	1	0	2	1	1	.50	12	.264	.326	.466
04	Bos	AL	38	156	50	7	3	5	(3	2)	78	24	21	26	8	2	16	4	0	1	2	0	1.00	4	.321	.367	.500
04	ChC	AL	43	165	49	14	0	4	(3	1)	75	28	20	27	16	0	14	2	1	1	2	1	.67	6	.297	.364	.455
Postseason			28	105	33	7	1	7	(3	4)	63	16	23	19	11	4	16	1	0	2	2	0	1.00	3	.314	.378	.600
13 ML YEARS			1369	5426	1702	362	52	226	(114	112)	2846	910	920	992	395	53	526	59	5	62	93	31	.75	125	.314	.363	.525

Brett Gardner

Bats: L **Throws:** L **Pos:** CF-22; LF-17; PR-5; PH-1   **Ht:** 5'10" **Wt:** 180 **Born:** 8/24/1983 **Age:** 25

Year	Team	Lg	G	AB	H	2B	3B	HR	(Hm	Rd)	TB	R	RBI	RC	TBB	IBB	SO	HBP	SH	SF	SB	CS	SB%	GDP	Avg	OBP	Slg
2005	StIsInd	A-	73	282	80	9	1	5	(-	-)	106	62	32	47	39	1	49	6	3	5	19	3	.86	4	.284	.377	.376
2006	Tampa	A+	63	232	75	12	5	0	(-	-)	97	46	22	48	43	0	51	2	1	0	30	7	.81	1	.323	.433	.418
2006	Trntn	AA	55	217	59	4	3	0	(-	-)	69	41	13	31	27	1	39	2	1	4	28	5	.85	1	.272	.352	.318
2007	Trntn	AA	54	203	61	14	5	0	(-	-)	85	43	17	38	33	0	32	0	1	4	18	4	.82	5	.300	.392	.419
2007	S-WB	AAA	45	181	47	4	3	1	(-	-)	60	37	9	25	21	0	43	2	3	0	21	3	.88	0	.260	.343	.331
2008	S-WB	AAA	94	341	101	12	11	3	(-	-)	144	68	32	70	70	2	76	1	11	3	37	9	.80	2	.296	.414	.422
2008	NYY	AL	42	127	29	5	2	0	(0	0)	38	18	16	17	8	0	30	2	3	1	13	1	.93	0	.228	.283	.299

Lee Gardner

Pitches: R **Bats:** R **Pos:** RP-7   **Ht:** 6'0" **Wt:** 220 **Born:** 1/16/1975 **Age:** 34

	HOW MUCH HE PITCHED						WHAT HE GAVE UP											THE RESULTS							
Year	Team	Lg	G	GS	CG	GF	IP	BFP	H	R	ER	HR	SH	SF	HB	TBB	IBB	SO	WP	Bk	W	L	Pct	ShO	Sv-Op	Hld	ERC	ERA
2002	TB	AL	12	0	0	3	13.1	65	12	11	6	3	1	2	3	8	0	8	0	0	1	1	.500	0	0-2	1	5.86	4.05
2005	TB	AL	5	0	0	2	7.1	37	12	9	4	2	0	1	0	2	0	4	0	0	0	0	-	0	0-0	0	8.45	4.91
2007	Fla	NL	62	0	0	20	74.1	311	72	19	16	2	3	3	3	18	4	52	1	0	3	4	.429	0	2-2	9	2.87	1.94
2008	Fla	NL	7	0	0	0	6.2	38	14	8	8	2	1	0	0	4	0	4	0	0	0	0	-	0	0-0	0	14.00	10.80
4 ML YEARS			86	0	0	25	101.2	451	110	47	34	9	5	6	6	32	4	68	1	0	4	5	.444	0	2-4	10	4.20	3.01

Ryan Garko

Bats: R **Throws:** R **Pos:** 1B-121; DH-14; PH-7   **Ht:** 6'2" **Wt:** 225 **Born:** 1/2/1981 **Age:** 28

Year	Team	Lg	G	AB	H	2B	3B	HR	(Hm	Rd)	TB	R	RBI	RC	TBB	IBB	SO	HBP	SH	SF	SB	CS	SB%	GDP	Avg	OBP	Slg
2005	Cle	AL	1	1	0	0	0	0	(0	0)	0	0	0	0	0	0	1	0	0	0	0	0	-	0	.000	.000	.000
2006	Cle	AL	50	185	54	12	0	7	(4	3)	87	28	45	32	14	0	37	7	0	3	0	0	-	5	.292	.359	.470
2007	Cle	AL	138	484	140	29	1	21	(12	9)	234	62	61	71	34	1	94	20	0	3	0	1	.00	12	.289	.359	.483
2008	Cle	AL	141	495	135	21	1	14	(8	6)	200	61	90	81	45	1	86	15	0	8	0	0	-	10	.273	.346	.404
Postseason			9	35	11	2	1	1	(1	0)	18	7	5	6	1	0	6	3	0	0	0	0	-	1	.314	.385	.514
4 ML YEARS			330	1165	329	62	2	42	(24	18)	521	151	196	184	93	2	218	42	0	14	0	1	.00	27	.282	.353	.447

Jon Garland

Pitches: R **Bats:** R **Pos:** SP-32   **Ht:** 6'6" **Wt:** 210 **Born:** 9/27/1979 **Age:** 29

	HOW MUCH HE PITCHED						WHAT HE GAVE UP											THE RESULTS							
Year	Team	Lg	G	GS	CG	GF	IP	BFP	H	R	ER	HR	SH	SF	HB	TBB	IBB	SO	WP	Bk	W	L	Pct	ShO	Sv-Op	Hld	ERC	ERA
2000	CWS	AL	15	13	0	1	69.2	324	82	55	50	10	2	2	1	40	0	42	4	0	4	8	.333	0	0-0	1	6.26	6.46
2001	CWS	AL	35	16	0	8	117.0	510	123	59	48	16	2	5	4	55	2	61	3	0	6	7	.462	0	1-1	2	5.16	3.69
2002	CWS	AL	33	33	1	0	192.2	827	188	109	98	23	3	4	9	83	1	112	5	0	12	12	.500	1	0-0	0	4.46	4.58
2003	CWS	AL	32	32	1	0	191.2	813	188	103	96	28	4	8	4	74	1	108	8	0	12	13	.480	0	0-0	0	4.38	4.51
2004	CWS	AL	34	33	1	0	217.0	923	223	125	118	34	9	5	4	76	2	113	3	0	12	11	.522	0	0-0	0	4.56	4.89
2005	CWS	AL	32	32	3	0	221.0	901	212	93	86	26	9	8	7	47	3	115	2	0	18	10	.643	3	0-0	0	3.39	3.50
2006	CWS	AL	33	32	1	0	211.1	900	247	112	106	26	7	6	4	44	1	112	4	0	18	7	.720	1	0-0	0	4.50	4.51
2007	CWS	AL	32	32	2	0	208.1	883	219	114	98	19	3	7	4	57	3	98	1	0	10	13	.435	1	0-0	0	3.87	4.23
2008	LAA	AL	32	32	1	0	196.2	864	237	116	107	23	8	8	8	59	4	90	4	0	14	8	.636	0	0-0	0	5.18	4.90
Postseason			2	2	1	0	16.0	58	11	6	4	2	2	0	0	3	0	11	0	0	1	0	1.000	0	0-0	0	2.00	2.25
9 ML YEARS			278	255	9	9	1625.1	6945	1719	886	807	205	43	55	47	532	20	851	34	0	106	89	.544	6	1-1	3	4.45	4.47

Matt Garza

Pitches: R Bats: R Pos: SP-30   Ht: 6'4" Wt: 205 Born: 11/26/1983 Age: 25

Year	Team	Lg	G	GS	CG	GF	IP	BFP	H	R	ER	HR	SH	SF	HB	TBB	IBB	SO	WP	Bk	W	L	Pct	ShO	Sv-Op	Hld	ERC	ERA
2008	VeroB*	A+	1	1	0	0	3.2	20	8	4	4	0	0	0	0	3	0	4	0	0	0	0	-	0	0- -	-	13.77	9.82
2006	Min	AL	10	9	0	0	50.0	232	62	33	32	6	0	3	0	23	0	38	1	0	3	6	.333	0	0-0	0	5.82	5.76
2007	Min	AL	16	15	0	1	83.0	367	96	44	34	8	1	4	4	32	4	67	4	0	5	7	.417	0	0-0	0	5.08	3.69
2008	TB	AL	30	30	3	0	184.2	772	170	83	76	19	3	9	6	59	2	128	3	2	11	9	.550	2	0-0	0	3.47	3.70
3 ML YEARS			56	54	3	1	317.2	1371	328	160	142	33	4	16	10	114	6	233	8	2	19	22	.463	2	0-0	0	4.23	4.02

Joey Gathright

Bats: L Throws: R Pos: CF-100; PR-8; PH-4; LF-3   Ht: 5'10" Wt: 170 Born: 4/27/1981 Age: 28

Year	Team	Lg	G	AB	H	2B	3B	HR	(Hm	Rd)	TB	R	RBI	RC	TBB	IBB	SO	HBP	SH	SF	SB	CS	SB%	GDP	Avg	OBP	Slg
2008	Omha*	AAA	9	33	5	0	0	0	(-	-)	5	3	0	1	0	1	2	0	0	1	0	1.00	0	.152	.222	.152
2004	TB	AL	19	52	13	0	0	0	(0	0)	13	11	1	4	2	0	14	3	0	0	6	1	.86	2	.250	.316	.250
2005	TB	AL	76	203	56	7	3	0	(0	0)	69	29	13	22	10	0	39	2	3	0	20	5	.80	5	.276	.316	.340
2006	2 Tms	AL	134	383	91	12	3	1	(1	0)	112	59	41	46	42	0	75	7	9	4	22	9	.71	3	.238	.321	.292
2007	KC	AL	74	228	70	8	0	0	(0	0)	78	28	19	31	20	0	36	3	10	0	9	8	.53	2	.307	.371	.342
2008	KC	AL	105	279	71	3	1	0	(0	0)	76	41	22	31	20	0	40	4	10	2	21	4	.84	3	.254	.311	.272
06	TB	AL	55	154	31	6	0	0	(0	0)	37	25	13	15	20	0	30	3	5	0	12	3	.80	1	.201	.305	.240
06	KC	AL	79	229	60	6	3	1	(1	0)	75	34	28	31	22	0	45	4	4	4	10	6	.63	2	.262	.332	.328
5 ML YEARS			408	1145	301	30	7	1	(1	0)	348	168	96	134	94	0	204	19	32	6	78	27	.74	15	.263	.328	.304

Chad Gaudin

Pitches: R Bats: R Pos: RP-44; SP-6   Ht: 5'10" Wt: 188 Born: 3/24/1983 Age: 26

Year	Team	Lg	G	GS	CG	GF	IP	BFP	H	R	ER	HR	SH	SF	HB	TBB	IBB	SO	WP	Bk	W	L	Pct	ShO	Sv-Op	Hld	ERC	ERA
2003	TB	AL	15	3	0	5	40.0	173	37	18	16	4	0	2	1	16	0	23	1	0	2	0	1.000	0	0-0	0	3.70	3.60
2004	TB	AL	26	4	0	5	42.2	201	59	27	23	4	2	4	4	16	4	30	0	0	1	2	.333	0	0-1	5	6.46	4.85
2005	Tor	AL	5	3	0	0	13.0	74	31	19	19	6	0	1	1	6	0	12	0	0	1	3	.250	0	0-0	0	18.35	13.15
2006	Oak	AL	55	0	0	13	64.0	276	51	24	22	3	0	3	1	42	2	36	2	2	4	2	.667	0	2-3	11	3.62	3.09
2007	Oak	AL	34	34	1	0	199.1	886	205	108	98	21	3	6	8	100	8	154	3	1	11	13	.458	0	0-0	4	4.80	4.42
2008	2 Tms		50	6	0	14	90.0	382	92	50	44	11	2	2	3	27	3	71	2	2	9	5	.643	0	0-1	4	4.06	4.40
08	Oak	AL	26	6	0	9	62.2	263	63	29	25	6	2	1	3	17	1	44	2	1	5	3	.625	0	0-0	2	3.78	3.59
08	ChC	NL	24	0	0	5	27.1	119	29	21	19	5	0	1	0	10	2	27	0	1	4	2	.667	0	0-1	2	4.74	6.26
Postseason			3	0	0	0	3.1	15	2	0	0	0	1	0	0	3	1	1	0	0	0	0	-	0	0-0	0	2.46	0.00
6 ML YEARS			185	50	1	37	449.0	1992	475	246	222	49	7	18	18	207	17	326	8	5	28	25	.528	0	2-5	20	4.84	4.45

Geoff Geary

Pitches: R Bats: R Pos: RP-55   Ht: 6'0" Wt: 180 Born: 8/26/1976 Age: 32

Year	Team	Lg	G	GS	CG	GF	IP	BFP	H	R	ER	HR	SH	SF	HB	TBB	IBB	SO	WP	Bk	W	L	Pct	ShO	Sv-Op	Hld	ERC	ERA
2003	Phi	NL	5	0	0	2	6.0	28	8	3	3	0	1	0	0	3	0	3	0	0	0	0	-	0	0-0	0	5.70	4.50
2004	Phi	NL	33	0	0	16	44.2	200	52	29	27	8	1	2	3	16	3	30	2	1	1	0	1.000	0	0-0	0	5.63	5.44
2005	Phi	NL	40	0	0	12	58.0	247	54	29	24	5	2	4	1	21	4	42	3	0	2	1	.667	0	0-1	3	3.38	3.72
2006	Phi	NL	81	0	0	17	91.1	390	103	34	30	6	3	1	6	20	4	60	2	0	7	1	.875	0	1-4	15	4.07	2.96
2007	Phi	NL	57	0	0	10	67.1	296	72	44	33	8	5	3	9	25	6	38	3	0	3	2	.600	0	0-3	9	4.98	4.41
2008	Hou	NL	55	0	0	8	64.0	262	45	18	18	3	3	1	2	28	5	45	0	1	2	3	.400	0	0-2	12	2.32	2.53
6 ML YEARS			271	0	0	65	331.1	1423	334	157	135	30	15	11	21	113	22	218	10	2	15	7	.682	0	1-10	39	3.99	3.67

Josh Geer

Pitches: R Bats: R Pos: SP-5   Ht: 6'3" Wt: 190 Born: 6/2/1983 Age: 26

Year	Team	Lg	G	GS	CG	GF	IP	BFP	H	R	ER	HR	SH	SF	HB	TBB	IBB	SO	WP	Bk	W	L	Pct	ShO	Sv-Op	Hld	ERC	ERA
2005	Eugene	A-	7	6	0	0	31.2	131	35	13	13	5	2	1	1	4	0	13	1	0	3	1	.750	0	0- -	-	4.14	3.69
2005	FtWyn	A	5	5	0	0	29.2	125	29	16	14	3	2	1	1	9	0	23	0	0	1	1	.500	0	0- -	-	3.73	4.25
2006	FtWyn	A	12	11	1	0	72.2	295	72	27	25	3	0	3	5	13	0	46	2	0	6	2	.750	1	0- -	-	3.14	3.10
2006	Lk Els	A+	15	15	0	0	89.0	392	116	60	49	7	4	2	3	16	0	56	3	2	7	4	.636	0	0- -	-	4.92	4.96
2007	SnAnt	AA	26	26	2	0	171.1	699	163	67	61	9	12	2	11	27	1	102	7	0	16	6	.727	0	0- -	-	2.84	3.20
2007	Portlnd	AAA	1	1	0	0	6.0	23	6	2	2	0	0	1	0	1	0	6	1	0	1	0	1.000	0	0- -	-	2.76	3.00
2008	Portlnd	AAA	28	27	0	0	166.2	718	187	95	84	22	6	6	4	45	1	107	6	1	8	9	.471	0	0- -	-	4.58	4.54
2008	SD	NL	5	5	0	0	27.0	117	29	8	8	2	0	0	0	9	2	16	0	0	2	1	.667	0	0-0	0	3.90	2.67

Esteban German

Bats: R Throws: R Pos: LF-39; 2B-35; PH-11; PR-10; 3B-6; DH-4; SS-3   Ht: 5'9" Wt: 165 Born: 1/26/1978 Age: 31

Year	Team	Lg	G	AB	H	2B	3B	HR	(Hm	Rd)	TB	R	RBI	RC	TBB	IBB	SO	HBP	SH	SF	SB	CS	SB%	GDP	Avg	OBP	Slg
2002	Oak	AL	9	35	7	0	0	0	(0	0)	7	4	0	2	4	0	11	1	0	1	1	0	1.00	0	.200	.300	.200
2003	Oak	AL	5	4	1	0	0	0	(0	0)	1	0	1	1	0	0	1	0	0	0	0	0	-	1	.250	.250	.250
2004	Oak	AL	31	60	15	1	1	0	(0	0)	18	9	7	8	4	0	13	0	1	0	1	.00	1	.250	.297	.300
2005	Tex	AL	5	4	3	1	0	0	(0	0)	4	3	1	2	0	0	1	0	0	0	2	0	1.00	0	.750	.750	1.000
2006	KC	AL	106	279	91	18	5	3	(2	1)	128	44	34	55	40	0	49	6	6	0	7	3	.70	8	.326	.422	.459
2007	KC	AL	121	348	92	15	6	4	(3	1)	131	49	37	48	43	0	60	5	6	3	11	7	.61	11	.264	.351	.376
2008	KC	AL	89	216	53	14	3	0	(0	0)	73	30	22	26	18	1	42	1	4	3	7	3	.70	5	.245	.303	.338
7 ML YEARS			366	946	262	49	15	7	(5	2)	362	139	102	142	109	1	177	13	17	6	28	14	.67	26	.277	.358	.383

Franklyn German

Pitches: R **Bats:** R **Pos:** RP-17 **Ht:** 6'7" **Wt:** 260 **Born:** 1/20/1980 **Age:** 29

Year	Team	Lg	G	GS	CG	GF	IP	BFP	H	R	ER	HR	SH	SF	HB	TBB	IBB	SO	WP	Bk	W	L	Pct	ShO	Sv-Op	Hld	ERC	ERA
2008	Indy*	AAA	24	0	0	8	27.2	126	24	12	11	3	3	1	1	17	2	22	1	0	1	1	.500	0	0- -	-	4.11	3.58
2008	Charltt*	AAA	5	0	0	2	6.1	32	6	7	3	1	0	0	0	6	1	9	0	0	1	1	.500	0	0- -	-	5.81	4.26
2002	Det	AL	7	0	0	1	6.2	25	3	0	0	0	2	0	1	2	1	6	0	0	1	0	1.000	0	1-1	1	1.09	0.00
2003	Det	AL	45	0	0	15	44.2	222	47	32	30	5	2	1	2	45	3	41	8	1	2	4	.333	0	5-7	4	7.06	6.04
2004	Det	AL	16	0	0	5	14.2	73	17	15	12	4	1	0	0	11	1	8	2	0	1	0	1.000	0	0-1	1	7.53	7.36
2005	Det	AL	58	0	0	19	59.0	270	63	26	24	7	2	5	7	34	4	38	4	1	4	0	1.000	0	1-3	4	5.80	3.66
2006	Fla	NL	12	0	0	3	12.0	57	7	4	4	1	1	0	1	14	2	6	0	0	0	0	-	0	0-1	1	4.52	3.00
2008	Tex	AL	17	0	0	9	21.2	93	18	5	5	0	3	3	0	13	1	15	1	0	1	3	.250	0	0-1	0	3.15	2.08
6 ML YEARS			155	0	0	52	158.2	740	155	82	75	17	11	9	11	119	12	114	15	2	9	7	.563	0	7-14	11	5.57	4.25

Justin Germano

Pitches: R **Bats:** R **Pos:** SP-6; RP-6 **Ht:** 6'3" **Wt:** 205 **Born:** 8/6/1982 **Age:** 26

Year	Team	Lg	G	GS	CG	GF	IP	BFP	H	R	ER	HR	SH	SF	HB	TBB	IBB	SO	WP	Bk	W	L	Pct	ShO	Sv-Op	Hld	ERC	ERA
2008	Portlnd*	AAA	17	16	1	0	98.0	437	119	67	60	12	7	6	2	25	1	67	3	0	2	9	.182	0	0- -	-	4.86	5.51
2004	SD	NL	7	5	0	0	21.1	109	31	24	21	2	3	1	0	14	0	16	0	0	1	2	.333	0	0-0	0	7.69	8.86
2006	Cin	NL	2	1	0	0	6.2	31	8	4	4	1	0	0	1	3	1	8	0	0	0	1	.000	0	0-0	0	6.26	5.40
2007	SD	NL	26	23	0	3	133.1	566	133	72	66	14	4	0	8	40	3	78	1	0	7	10	.412	0	0-0	0	3.93	4.46
2008	SD	NL	12	6	0	4	43.2	194	54	31	29	8	2	1	1	13	2	17	4	0	0	3	.000	0	0-0	0	5.69	5.98
4 ML YEARS			47	35	0	7	205.0	900	226	131	120	25	9	2	10	70	6	119	5	0	8	16	.333	0	0-0	0	4.74	5.27

Jody Gerut

Bats: L **Throws:** L **Pos:** CF-80; PH-21; RF-9; PR-2 **Ht:** 6'0" **Wt:** 210 **Born:** 9/18/1977 **Age:** 31

Year	Team	Lg	G	AB	H	2B	3B	HR	(Hm	Rd)	TB	R	RBI	RC	TBB	IBB	SO	HBP	SH	SF	SB	CS	SB%	GDP	Avg	OBP	Slg
2008	Portlnd*	AAA	27	107	33	9	2	5	(-	-)	61	22	18	23	13	0	11	1	0	2	4	1	.80	1	.308	.382	.570
2003	Cle	AL	127	480	134	33	2	22	(13	9)	237	66	75	73	35	4	70	7	1	2	4	5	.44	13	.279	.336	.494
2004	Cle	AL	134	481	121	31	5	11	(3	8)	195	72	51	60	54	4	59	7	3	3	13	6	.68	9	.252	.334	.405
2005	3 Tms		59	170	43	11	1	1	(1	0)	59	15	14	18	20	1	20	0	0	1	1	1	.50	4	.253	.330	.347
2008	SD	NL	100	328	97	15	4	14	(4	10)	162	46	43	55	28	0	52	0	0	6	6	4	.60	1	.296	.351	.494
05	Cle	AL	44	138	38	9	1	1	(1	0)	52	12	12	17	18	1	14	0	0	1	1	1	.50	3	.275	.357	.377
05	ChC	NL	11	14	1	1	0	0	(0	0)	2	1	0	0	2	0	3	0	0	0	0	0	-	0	.071	.188	.143
05	Pit	NL	4	18	4	1	0	0	(0	0)	5	2	2	1	0	0	3	0	0	0	0	0	-	1	.222	.222	.278
4 ML YEARS			420	1459	395	90	12	48	(21	27)	653	199	183	206	137	9	201	14	4	6	24	16	.60	27	.271	.338	.448

Chris Getz

Bats: L **Throws:** R **Pos:** 2B-7; PR-5; DH-2; PH-1 **Ht:** 6'0" **Wt:** 185 **Born:** 8/30/1983 **Age:** 25

Year	Team	Lg	G	AB	H	2B	3B	HR	(Hm	Rd)	TB	R	RBI	RC	TBB	IBB	SO	HBP	SH	SF	SB	CS	SB%	GDP	Avg	OBP	Slg
2005	Gr Falls	R+	6	24	8	1	0	0	(-	-)	9	3	4	3	1	0	2	0	1	1	2	1	.67	0	.333	.346	.375
2005	Knapol	A-	55	214	65	13	2	1	(-	-)	85	38	28	39	35	1	10	3	0	1	11	4	.73	5	.304	.407	.397
2006	Brham	AA	130	508	130	15	6	2	(-	-)	163	67	36	59	52	3	47	2	9	2	19	6	.76	10	.256	.326	.321
2007	Brham	AA	72	278	83	10	2	3	(-	-)	106	40	29	44	36	2	30	2	2	1	13	7	.65	4	.299	.382	.381
2008	Charltt	AAA	112	404	122	24	1	11	(-	-)	181	61	52	70	41	2	53	3	4	5	12	4	.75	5	.302	.366	.448
2008	CWS	AL	10	7	2	0	0	0	(0	0)	2	2	1	1	0	0	1	0	0	0	1	1	.50	0	.286	.286	.286

Jason Giambi

Bats: L **Throws:** R **Pos:** 1B-113; DH-26; PH-7 **Ht:** 6'3" **Wt:** 235 **Born:** 1/8/1971 **Age:** 38

Year	Team	Lg	G	AB	H	2B	3B	HR	(Hm	Rd)	TB	R	RBI	RC	TBB	IBB	SO	HBP	SH	SF	SB	CS	SB%	GDP	Avg	OBP	Slg
1995	Oak	AL	54	176	45	7	0	6	(3	3)	70	27	25	27	28	0	31	3	1	2	2	1	.67	4	.256	.364	.398
1996	Oak	AL	140	536	156	40	1	20	(6	14)	258	84	79	88	51	3	95	5	1	5	0	1	.00	15	.291	.355	.481
1997	Oak	AL	142	519	152	41	2	20	(14	6)	257	66	81	91	55	3	89	6	0	8	0	1	.00	11	.293	.362	.495
1998	Oak	AL	153	562	166	28	0	27	(12	15)	275	92	110	103	81	7	102	5	0	9	2	2	.50	16	.295	.384	.489
1999	Oak	AL	158	575	181	36	1	33	(17	16)	318	115	123	132	105	6	106	7	0	8	1	1	.50	11	.315	.422	.553
2000	Oak	AL	152	510	170	29	1	43	(23	20)	330	108	137	152	137	6	96	9	0	8	2	0	1.00	9	.333	.476	.647
2001	Oak	AL	154	520	178	47	2	38	(27	11)	343	109	120	153	129	24	83	13	0	9	2	0	1.00	5	.342	.477	.660
2002	NYY	AL	155	560	176	34	1	41	(19	22)	335	120	122	139	109	4	112	15	0	5	2	2	.50	18	.314	.435	.598
2003	NYY	AL	156	535	134	25	0	41	(12	29)	282	97	107	120	129	9	140	21	0	5	2	1	.67	9	.250	.412	.527
2004	NYY	AL	80	264	55	9	0	12	(5	7)	100	33	40	42	47	1	62	8	0	3	0	1	.00	5	.208	.342	.379
2005	NYY	AL	139	417	113	14	0	32	(16	16)	223	74	87	102	108	5	109	19	0	1	0	0	-	7	.271	.440	.535
2006	NYY	AL	139	446	113	25	0	37	(20	17)	249	92	113	106	110	12	106	16	0	7	2	0	1.00	10	.253	.413	.558
2007	NYY	AL	83	254	60	8	0	14	(6	8)	110	31	39	41	40	2	66	8	0	1	1	0	1.00	6	.236	.356	.433
2008	NYY	AL	145	458	113	19	1	32	(16	16)	230	68	96	79	76	5	111	22	0	9	2	1	.67	6	.247	.373	.502
Postseason			42	135	39	6	0	7	(5	2)	66	18	18	25	30	2	29	4	0	2	2	0	1.00	3	.289	.427	.489
14 ML YEARS			1850	6332	1812	362	9	396	(196	200)	3380	1116	1279	1375	1205	87	1308	157	2	80	18	11	.62	139	.286	.408	.534

Dan Giese

Pitches: R Bats: R Pos: RP-17; SP-3   Ht: 6'3" Wt: 195 Born: 5/19/1977 Age: 32

			HOW MUCH HE PITCHED						WHAT HE GAVE UP													THE RESULTS						
Year	Team	Lg	G	GS	CG	GF	IP	BFP	H	R	ER	HR	SH	SF	HB	TBB	IBB	SO	WP	Bk	W	L	Pct	ShO	Sv-Op	Hld	ERC	ERA
1999	Lowell	A-	18	0	0	8	34.1	131	17	8	7	2	1	1	2	10	1	27	2	0	3	0	1.000	0	2--	-	1.31	1.83
1999	Augsta	A	9	0	0	1	17.1	71	15	4	4	1	1	0	3	5	0	11	1	0	1	0	1.000	0	0--	-	3.42	2.08
2000	Lowell	A-	15	0	0	13	19.2	75	12	3	2	1	1	0	0	1	0	20	1	0	0	0	-	0	9--	-	0.98	0.92
2000	Srsota	A+	8	0	0	2	14.1	64	19	8	5	2	0	1	0	2	0	13	0	0	1	0	1.000	0	0--	-	5.05	3.14
2001	Augsta	A	46	0	0	39	74.0	297	65	27	18	2	0	0	1	8	3	95	2	0	6	4	.600	0	9--	-	1.89	2.19
2002	Trntn	AA	23	0	0	9	49.1	204	53	24	21	6	3	3	1	9	3	39	1	0	1	2	.333	0	3--	-	3.82	3.83
2002	Mobile	AA	32	0	0	8	52.2	222	56	24	17	3	2	3	0	13	6	51	1	0	4	5	.444	0	0--	-	3.36	2.91
2003	Mobile	AA	2	0	0	0	4.0	15	1	1	1	1	0	0	2	0	0	4	0	0	1	0	1.000	0	0--	-	1.58	2.25
2003	Portlnd	AAA	3	0	0	1	6.0	32	12	9	9	0	0	0	0	3	0	6	0	0	1	0	1.000	0	0--	-	13.48	13.50
2003	Rdng	AA	9	0	0	4	12.1	46	8	2	2	1	1	0	1	1	0	16	0	0	2	1	.667	0	1--	-	1.49	1.46
2003	S-WB	AAA	34	0	0	11	48.1	189	37	19	17	8	0	2	1	10	0	49	0	0	2	0	1.000	0	0--	-	2.61	3.17
2004	S-WB	AAA	54	0	0	23	83.1	332	63	27	26	8	0	0	1	18	3	54	1	0	12	5	.706	0	3--	-	2.08	2.81
2005	S-WB	AAA	26	0	0	5	38.0	166	51	28	24	9	2	1	1	1	0	28	1	1	3	4	.429	0	2--	-	5.49	5.68
2006	Rdng	AA	23	0	0	10	36.1	144	27	11	10	5	1	2	0	14	1	27	0	0	1	2	.333	0	1--	-	2.94	2.48
2006	S-WB	AAA	25	0	0	8	35.2	154	46	17	12	3	3	2	0	4	1	33	0	1	2	2	.500	0	0--	-	4.39	3.03
2007	Fresno	AAA	47	0	0	14	73.1	291	65	26	23	2	2	2	1	10	1	76	3	1	3	1	.750	0	2--	-	2.10	2.82
2008	S-WB	AAA	13	10	1	0	59.0	231	43	16	13	2	0	0	3	14	0	51	2	0	4	2	.667	1	0--	-	1.91	1.98
2007	SF	NL	8	0	0	3	9.1	37	8	5	5	4	1	0	0	2	0	7	0	0	0	2	.000	0	0-0	0	4.61	4.82
2008	NYY	AL	20	3	0	6	43.1	186	39	22	17	3	0	3	1	14	1	29	1	0	1	3	.250	0	0-0	0	2.98	3.53
	2 ML YEARS		28	3	0	9	52.2	223	47	27	22	7	1	3	1	16	1	36	1	0	1	5	.167	0	0-0	0	3.29	3.76

Brian Giles

Bats: L Throws: L Pos: RF-144; PH-5; CF-2   Ht: 5'10" Wt: 205 Born: 1/20/1971 Age: 38

						BATTING														BASERUNNING				AVERAGES		
Year	Team	Lg	G	AB	H	2B	3B	HR	(Hm	Rd)	TB	R	RBI	RC	TBB	IBB	SO	HBP	SH	SF	SB	CS	SB%	GDP	Avg	OBP	Slg
1995	Cle	AL	6	9	5	0	0	1	(0	1)	8	6	3	3	0	0	1	0	0	0	0	0	-	0	.556	.556	.889
1996	Cle	AL	51	121	43	14	1	5	(2	3)	74	26	27	29	19	4	13	0	0	3	3	0	1.00	6	.355	.434	.612
1997	Cle	AL	130	377	101	15	3	17	(7	10)	173	62	61	66	63	2	50	1	3	7	13	3	.81	10	.268	.368	.459
1998	Cle	AL	112	350	94	19	0	16	(10	6)	161	56	66	66	73	8	75	3	1	3	10	5	.67	7	.269	.396	.460
1999	Pit	NL	141	521	164	33	3	39	(24	15)	320	109	115	127	95	7	80	3	0	8	6	2	.75	14	.315	.418	.614
2000	Pit	NL	156	559	176	37	7	35	(19	16)	332	111	123	139	114	13	69	7	0	8	6	0	1.00	15	.315	.432	.594
2001	Pit	NL	160	576	178	37	7	37	(18	19)	340	116	95	131	90	14	67	4	0	4	13	6	.68	10	.309	.404	.590
2002	Pit	NL	153	497	148	37	5	38	(15	23)	309	95	103	128	135	24	74	7	0	5	15	6	.71	10	.298	.450	.622
2003	2 Tms	NL	134	492	147	34	6	20	(12	8)	253	93	88	102	105	12	58	8	0	4	4	3	.57	12	.299	.427	.514
2004	SD	NL	159	609	173	33	7	23	(10	13)	289	97	94	102	89	6	80	4	0	9	10	3	.77	12	.284	.374	.475
2005	SD	NL	158	545	164	38	8	15	(6	9)	263	92	83	112	119	9	64	2	0	8	13	5	.72	14	.301	.423	.483
2006	SD	NL	158	604	159	37	1	14	(8	6)	240	87	83	95	104	6	60	5	0	4	9	4	.69	18	.263	.374	.397
2007	SD	NL	121	483	131	27	2	13	(1	12)	201	72	51	74	64	5	61	4	0	6	4	6	.40	8	.271	.361	.416
2008	SD	NL	147	559	171	40	4	12	(6	6)	255	81	63	92	87	2	52	2	0	5	2	2	.50	18	.306	.398	.456
03	Pit	NL	105	388	116	30	4	16	(10	6)	202	70	70	79	85	11	48	6	0	2	0	3	.00	8	.299	.430	.521
03	SD	NL	29	104	31	4	2	4	(2	2)	51	23	18	23	20	1	10	2	0	2	4	0	1.00	4	.298	.414	.490
	Postseason		29	77	16	6	0	0	(0	0)	22	4	4	6	11	0	21	1	0	1	1	1	.50	2	.208	.311	.286
	14 ML YEARS		1786	6302	1854	401	54	285	(131	154)	3218	1103	1055	1266	1157	112	804	50	4	69	108	45	.71	154	.294	.404	.511

Conor Gillaspie

Bats: L Throws: R Pos: PH-6; 3B-2; PR-1   Ht: 6'1" Wt: 200 Born: 7/18/1987 Age: 21

						BATTING														BASERUNNING				AVERAGES		
Year	Team	Lg	G	AB	H	2B	3B	HR	(Hm	Rd)	TB	R	RBI	RC	TBB	IBB	SO	HBP	SH	SF	SB	CS	SB%	GDP	Avg	OBP	Slg
2008	Giants	R	6	22	6	3	0	0	(-	-)	9	2	7	3	3	0	1	0	0	0	1	0	1.00	2	.273	.360	.409
2008	Salem	A+	18	71	19	4	0	0	(-	-)	23	4	8	9	9	0	13	0	0	0	2	0	1.00	2	.268	.350	.324
2008	SF	NL	8	5	1	0	0	0	(0	0)	1	1	0	1	2	0	0	0	0	0	0	0	-	0	.200	.429	.200

Matt Ginter

Pitches: R Bats: R Pos: SP-4   Ht: 6'1" Wt: 220 Born: 12/24/1977 Age: 31

			HOW MUCH HE PITCHED						WHAT HE GAVE UP													THE RESULTS						
Year	Team	Lg	G	GS	CG	GF	IP	BFP	H	R	ER	HR	SH	SF	HB	TBB	IBB	SO	WP	Bk	W	L	Pct	ShO	Sv-Op	Hld	ERC	ERA
2008	Buffalo*	AAA	18	17	0	1	100.0	439	110	57	50	10	3	3	5	32	0	65	2	0	6	6	.500	0	0--	-	4.50	4.50
2000	CWS	AL	7	0	0	3	9.1	52	18	14	14	5	0	1	0	7	0	6	1	0	1	0	1.000	0	0-1	0	16.24	13.50
2001	CWS	AL	20	0	0	7	39.2	167	34	23	23	2	0	3	7	14	2	24	2	0	1	0	1.000	0	0-0	0	3.44	5.22
2002	CWS	AL	33	0	0	15	54.1	236	59	34	27	6	0	2	1	21	0	37	2	0	1	0	1.000	0	1-1	0	4.72	4.47
2003	CWS	AL	3	0	0	0	3.1	15	2	5	5	1	1	0	2	1	0	0	0	0	0	0	-	0	0-0	0	5.16	13.50
2004	NYM	NL	15	14	0	0	69.1	313	82	41	35	8	3	1	5	20	5	38	1	0	1	3	.250	0	0-0	0	4.87	4.54
2005	Det	AL	14	1	0	2	35.0	157	49	25	24	6	1	1	2	9	1	15	0	0	0	1	.000	0	0-0	0	6.81	6.17
2008	Cle	AL	4	4	0	0	21.0	87	25	12	12	3	1	0	0	3	1	12	2	0	1	3	.250	0	0-0	0	4.46	5.14
	7 ML YEARS		96	19	0	27	232.0	1027	269	154	140	31	6	8	17	75	9	132	8	0	5	7	.417	0	1-2	0	5.20	5.43

Troy Glaus

Bats: R Throws: R Pos: 3B-146; 1B-4; PH-3   Ht: 6'5" Wt: 240 Born: 8/3/1976 Age: 32

						BATTING														BASERUNNING				AVERAGES		
Year	Team	Lg	G	AB	H	2B	3B	HR	(Hm	Rd)	TB	R	RBI	RC	TBB	IBB	SO	HBP	SH	SF	SB	CS	SB%	GDP	Avg	OBP	Slg
1998	LAA	AL	48	165	36	9	0	1	(0	1)	48	19	23	13	15	0	51	0	0	2	1	0	1.00	3	.218	.280	.291
1999	LAA	AL	154	551	132	29	0	29	(12	17)	248	85	79	84	71	1	143	6	0	3	5	1	.83	9	.240	.331	.450
2000	LAA	AL	159	563	160	37	1	47	(24	23)	340	120	102	129	112	6	163	2	0	1	14	11	.56	14	.284	.404	.604
2001	LAA	AL	161	588	147	38	2	41	(22	19)	312	100	108	114	107	7	158	6	0	7	10	3	.77	16	.250	.367	.531

114

Year	Team	Lg	G	AB	H	2B	3B	HR	Hm	Rd	TB	R	RBI	RC	TBB	IBB	SO	HBP	SH	SF	SB	CS	SB%	GDP	Avg	OBP	Slg
2002	LAA	AL	156	569	142	24	1	30	(13	17)	258	99	111	100	88	4	144	6	0	8	10	3	.77	12	.250	.352	.453
2003	LAA	AL	91	319	79	17	2	16	(9	7)	148	53	50	48	46	4	73	1	0	1	7	2	.78	8	.248	.343	.464
2004	LAA	AL	58	207	52	11	1	18	(9	9)	119	47	42	41	31	3	52	3	0	1	2	3	.40	6	.251	.355	.575
2005	Ari	NL	149	538	139	29	1	37	(20	17)	281	78	97	87	84	2	145	7	0	5	4	2	.67	7	.258	.363	.522
2006	Tor	AL	153	540	136	27	0	38	(25	13)	277	105	104	84	86	6	134	3	0	5	3	2	.60	25	.252	.355	.513
2007	Tor	AL	115	385	101	19	1	20	(7	13)	182	60	62	65	61	2	102	5	0	5	0	1	.00	7	.262	.366	.473
2008	StL	NL	151	544	147	33	1	27	(13	14)	263	69	99	88	87	3	104	3	0	3	0	1	.00	14	.270	.372	.483
Postseason			19	72	25	5	1	9	(4	5)	59	18	16	15	9	2	18	1	0	0	0	0	-	1	.347	.427	.819
11 ML YEARS			1395	4969	1271	273	10	304	(154	150)	2476	835	877	853	788	38	1269	42	0	41	56	29	.66	121	.256	.360	.498

Tom Glavine

Pitches: L Bats: L Pos: SP-13   Ht: 6'0" Wt: 204 Born: 3/25/1966 Age: 43

Year	Team	Lg	G	GS	CG	GF	IP	BFP	H	R	ER	HR	SH	SF	HB	TBB	IBB	SO	WP	Bk	W	L	Pct	ShO	Sv-Op	Hld	ERC	ERA
2008	MrtlBh*	A+	1	1	0	0	4.0	16	3	1	1	0	0	0	1	1	0	4	0	0	0	0	-	0	0- -	-	2.58	2.25
2008	Missi*	AA	1	1	0	0	5.0	20	4	3	2	0	0	1	0	1	0	1	0	0	0	1	.000	0	0- -	-	1.70	3.60
1987	Atl	NL	9	9	0	0	50.1	238	55	34	31	5	2	3	3	33	4	20	1	1	2	4	.333	0	0-0	0	5.70	5.54
1988	Atl	NL	34	34	1	0	195.1	844	201	111	99	12	17	11	8	63	7	84	2	2	7	17	.292	0	0-0	0	3.74	4.56
1989	Atl	NL	29	29	6	0	186.0	766	172	88	76	20	11	4	2	40	3	90	2	0	14	8	.636	4	0-0	0	2.99	3.68
1990	Atl	NL	33	33	1	0	214.1	929	232	111	102	18	21	2	1	78	10	129	8	1	10	12	.455	0	0-0	0	4.24	4.28
1991	Atl	NL	34	34	9	0	246.2	989	201	83	70	17	7	6	2	69	6	192	10	2	20	11	.645	1	0-0	0	2.47	2.55
1992	Atl	NL	33	33	7	0	225.0	919	197	81	69	6	2	6	2	70	7	129	5	0	20	8	.714	5	0-0	0	2.61	2.76
1993	Atl	NL	36	36	4	0	239.1	1014	236	91	85	16	10	2	2	90	7	120	4	0	22	6	.786	2	0-0	0	3.70	3.20
1994	Atl	NL	25	25	2	0	165.1	731	173	76	73	10	9	6	1	70	10	140	8	1	13	9	.591	0	0-0	0	4.02	3.97
1995	Atl	NL	29	29	3	0	198.2	822	182	76	68	9	7	5	5	66	0	127	3	0	16	7	.696	1	0-0	0	3.14	3.08
1996	Atl	NL	36	36	1	0	235.1	994	222	91	78	14	15	2	0	85	7	181	4	0	15	10	.600	0	0-0	0	3.29	2.98
1997	Atl	NL	33	33	5	0	240.0	970	197	86	79	20	11	6	4	79	9	152	3	0	14	7	.667	2	0-0	0	2.80	2.96
1998	Atl	NL	33	33	4	0	229.1	934	202	67	63	13	6	2	2	74	2	157	3	0	20	6	.769	3	0-0	0	2.93	2.47
1999	Atl	NL	35	35	2	0	234.0	1023	259	115	107	18	22	10	4	83	14	138	2	0	14	11	.560	0	0-0	0	4.31	4.12
2000	Atl	NL	35	35	4	0	241.0	992	222	101	91	24	9	5	4	65	6	152	0	0	21	9	.700	2	0-0	0	3.19	3.40
2001	Atl	NL	35	35	1	0	219.1	929	213	92	87	24	5	8	2	97	10	116	2	0	16	7	.696	1	0-0	0	4.21	3.57
2002	Atl	NL	36	36	2	0	224.2	936	210	85	74	21	12	6	8	78	8	127	2	0	18	11	.621	1	0-0	0	3.61	2.96
2003	NYM	NL	32	32	0	0	183.1	791	205	94	92	21	7	4	2	66	7	82	2	0	9	14	.391	0	0-0	0	4.77	4.52
2004	NYM	NL	33	33	1	0	212.1	904	204	94	85	20	13	10	0	70	10	109	0	0	11	14	.440	1	0-0	0	3.43	3.60
2005	NYM	NL	33	33	2	0	211.1	901	227	88	83	12	19	3	3	61	5	105	1	0	13	13	.500	1	0-0	0	3.79	3.53
2006	NYM	NL	32	32	0	0	198.0	842	202	94	84	22	11	7	6	62	7	131	1	0	15	7	.682	0	0-0	0	4.01	3.82
2007	NYM	NL	34	34	1	0	200.1	855	219	102	99	23	5	2	4	64	2	89	2	0	13	8	.619	1	0-0	0	4.53	4.45
2008	Atl	NL	13	13	0	0	63.1	281	67	40	39	11	7	3	1	37	4	37	0	0	2	4	.333	0	0-0	0	5.85	5.54
Postseason			35	35	3	0	218.1	912	191	91	80	21	10	2	7	87	11	143	3	1	14	16	.467	0	0-0	0	3.45	3.30
22 ML YEARS			682	682	56	0	4413.1	18604	4298	1900	1734	356	228	113	66	1500	145	2607	65	7	305	203	.600	25	0-0	0	3.60	3.54

Ross Gload

Bats: L Throws: L Pos: 1B-111; LF-8; PR-5; PH-4; RF-3   Ht: 6'1" Wt: 190 Born: 4/5/1976 Age: 33

Year	Team	Lg	G	AB	H	2B	3B	HR	Hm	Rd	TB	R	RBI	RC	TBB	IBB	SO	HBP	SH	SF	SB	CS	SB%	GDP	Avg	OBP	Slg
2000	ChC	NL	18	31	6	0	1	1	(0	1)	11	4	3	3	3	0	10	0	0	1	0	0	-	1	.194	.257	.355
2002	Col	NL	26	31	8	1	0	1	(1	0)	12	4	4	3	3	0	7	0	0	0	0	0	-	0	.258	.324	.387
2004	CWS	AL	110	234	75	16	0	7	(3	4)	112	28	44	41	20	1	37	2	1	3	0	3	.00	11	.321	.375	.479
2005	CWS	AL	28	42	7	2	0	0	(0	0)	9	2	5	2	2	0	9	0	0	0	0	1	-	1	.167	.205	.214
2006	CWS	AL	77	156	51	8	2	3	(1	2)	72	22	18	24	6	0	15	1	3	1	6	0	1.00	3	.327	.354	.462
2007	KC	AL	102	320	92	22	3	7	(2	5)	141	37	51	45	16	2	39	2	0	8	2	2	.50	13	.288	.318	.441
2008	KC	AL	122	388	106	18	1	3	(2	1)	135	46	37	41	23	4	39	3	1	3	4	.43	12	.273	.317	.348
7 ML YEARS			483	1202	345	67	7	22	(9	13)	492	143	162	159	73	7	156	8	5	16	11	9	.55	41	.287	.328	.409

Gary Glover

Pitches: R Bats: R Pos: RP-47   Ht: 6'5" Wt: 225 Born: 12/3/1976 Age: 32

Year	Team	Lg	G	GS	CG	GF	IP	BFP	H	R	ER	HR	SH	SF	HB	TBB	IBB	SO	WP	Bk	W	L	Pct	ShO	Sv-Op	Hld	ERC	ERA
2008	Toledo*	AAA	3	0	0	1	4.0	14	3	0	0	0	0	0	0	0	0	4	0	0	0	0	-	0	1- -	-	1.21	0.00
1999	Tor	AL	1	0	0	1	1.0	3	0	0	0	0	0	0	0	1	0	0	0	0	0	0	-	0	0-0	0	1.26	0.00
2001	CWS	AL	46	11	0	10	100.1	429	98	61	55	16	2	2	4	32	3	63	4	0	5	5	.500	0	0-1	7	4.12	4.93
2002	CWS	AL	41	22	0	10	138.1	604	136	86	80	21	6	2	7	52	1	70	6	0	7	8	.467	0	1-1	2	4.39	5.20
2003	2 Tms	AL	42	0	0	15	62.2	279	77	33	33	6	0	5	3	22	3	37	2	0	2	0	1.000	0	0-0	1	5.37	4.74
2004	Mil	NL	4	3	0	0	18.0	82	18	9	7	2	2	2	2	8	1	8	1	0	2	1	.667	0	0-0	0	4.57	3.50
2005	Mil	NL	15	11	0	1	64.2	284	74	41	40	10	3	2	2	20	0	58	3	0	5	4	.556	0	0-0	0	5.06	5.57
2007	TB	AL	67	0	0	18	77.1	334	87	44	42	12	1	3	1	27	3	51	2	0	6	5	.545	0	2-4	11	5.07	4.89
2008	2 Tms	AL	47	0	0	15	54.1	246	64	33	32	7	1	0	2	22	6	37	4	0	2	3	.400	0	0-1	5	5.29	5.30
03	CWS	AL	24	0	0	8	35.2	160	43	18	18	3	0	3	2	14	2	23	1	0	1	0	1.000	0	0-0	1	5.32	4.54
03	LAA	AL	18	0	0	7	27.0	119	34	15	15	3	0	2	1	8	1	14	1	0	1	0	1.000	0	0-0	0	5.44	5.00
08	TB	AL	29	0	0	10	34.0	160	42	22	22	3	1	0	1	18	5	22	4	0	1	2	.333	0	0-0	2	5.71	5.82
08	Det	AL	18	0	0	5	20.1	86	22	11	10	4	0	0	1	4	1	15	0	0	1	1	.500	0	0-1	3	4.52	4.43
8 ML YEARS			263	47	0	70	516.2	2261	554	307	289	74	15	16	21	184	17	324	22	0	29	26	.527	0	3-7	26	4.73	5.03

Jimmy Gobble

Pitches: L Bats: L Pos: RP-39   Ht: 6'3" Wt: 205 Born: 7/19/1981 Age: 27

			HOW MUCH HE PITCHED						WHAT HE GAVE UP											THE RESULTS							
Year Team	Lg	G	GS	CG	GF	IP	BFP	H	R	ER	HR	SH	SF	HB	TBB	IBB	SO	WP	Bk	W	L	Pct	ShO	Sv-Op	Hld	ERC	ERA
2008 Omha*	AAA	8	4	0	0	14.1	67	16	9	9	1	0	0	1	9	0	16	0	0	1	1	.500	0	0- -	-	5.75	5.65
2003 KC	AL	9	9	0	0	52.2	230	56	32	27	8	1	3	4	15	0	31	1	0	4	5	.444	0	0-0	0	4.61	4.61
2004 KC	AL	25	24	1	0	148.0	638	157	94	88	24	4	7	3	43	0	49	4	0	9	8	.529	0	0-0	0	4.47	5.35
2005 KC	AL	28	4	0	11	53.2	249	64	34	34	9	3	1	1	30	4	38	2	0	1	1	.500	0	0-0	4	6.39	5.70
2006 KC	AL	60	6	0	17	84.0	370	95	51	48	12	3	0	1	29	1	80	4	0	4	6	.400	0	2-4	11	4.93	5.14
2007 KC	AL	74	0	0	12	53.2	233	56	23	18	6	1	5	2	23	6	50	6	1	4	1	.800	0	1-3	16	4.56	3.02
2008 KC	AL	39	0	0	10	31.2	159	39	31	31	5	0	1	2	23	1	27	6	0	0	2	.000	0	1-2	4	7.36	8.81
6 ML YEARS		235	43	1	50	423.2	1879	467	265	246	64	12	17	13	163	12	275	23	1	22	23	.489	0	4-9	35	5.04	5.23

Greg Golson

Bats: R Throws: R Pos: PR-4; CF-2; RF-1; PH-1   Ht: 6'0" Wt: 190 Born: 9/17/1985 Age: 23

								BATTING											BASERUNNING				AVERAGES		
Year Team	Lg	G	AB	H	2B	3B	HR	(Hm	Rd)	TB	R	RBI	RC	TBB	IBB	SO	HBP	SH	SF	SB	CS	SB%	GDP	Avg	OBP	Slg
2004 Phillies	R	47	183	54	8	5	1	(-	-)	75	34	22	28	10	0	54	5	1	2	12	2	.86	2	.295	.345	.410
2005 Lakwd	A	89	375	99	19	8	4	(-	-)	146	51	27	49	26	0	106	6	2	0	25	9	.74	4	.264	.322	.389
2006 Lakwd	A	93	387	85	15	4	7	(-	-)	129	56	31	35	19	1	107	2	8	3	23	7	.77	2	.220	.258	.333
2006 Clrwtr	A+	40	159	42	11	2	6	(-	-)	75	31	17	24	11	1	53	3	1	0	7	3	.70	3	.264	.324	.472
2007 Clrwtr	A+	99	418	119	27	3	12	(-	-)	188	66	52	63	21	2	124	4	2	4	25	8	.76	3	.285	.322	.450
2007 Rdng	AA	37	153	37	5	2	3	(-	-)	55	20	16	14	2	0	49	1	1	1	5	0	1.00	0	.242	.255	.359
2008 Rdng	AA	106	426	120	18	4	13	(-	-)	185	64	60	65	34	0	130	1	4	5	22	5	.81	3	.282	.333	.434
2008 Phi	NL	6	6	0	0	0	0	(0	0)	0	2	0	0	0	0	4	0	0	0	1	0	1.00	0	.000	.000	.000

Jonny Gomes

Bats: R Throws: R Pos: DH-36; PH-22; RF-21; LF-9; PR-7   Ht: 6'1" Wt: 225 Born: 11/22/1980 Age: 28

								BATTING											BASERUNNING				AVERAGES		
Year Team	Lg	G	AB	H	2B	3B	HR	(Hm	Rd)	TB	R	RBI	RC	TBB	IBB	SO	HBP	SH	SF	SB	CS	SB%	GDP	Avg	OBP	Slg
2008 Drhm*	AAA	26	107	27	11	0	2	(-	-)	44	19	14	15	12	0	32	3	0	1	0	1	.00	1	.252	.341	.411
2003 TB	AL	8	15	2	1	0	0	(0	0)	3	1	0	0	0	0	6	1	0	0	0	0	-	0	.133	.188	.200
2004 TB	AL	5	14	1	0	0	0	(0	0)	1	0	1	0	1	0	6	0	0	0	0	0	-	0	.071	.133	.071
2005 TB	AL	101	348	98	13	6	21	(11	10)	186	61	54	62	39	1	113	14	1	5	9	5	.64	6	.282	.372	.534
2006 TB	AL	117	385	83	21	1	20	(7	13)	166	53	59	53	61	2	116	6	0	9	1	5	.17	10	.216	.325	.431
2007 TB	AL	107	348	85	20	2	17	(10	7)	160	48	49	47	35	1	126	7	0	4	12	4	.75	1	.244	.322	.460
2008 TB	AL	77	154	28	5	1	8	(2	6)	59	23	21	18	15	1	46	7	0	1	8	1	.89	1	.182	.282	.383
6 ML YEARS		415	1264	297	60	10	66	(30	36)	575	186	184	180	151	5	413	35	1	19	30	15	.67	18	.235	.329	.455

Carlos Gomez

Bats: R Throws: R Pos: CF-151; PR-5   Ht: 6'4" Wt: 195 Born: 12/4/1985 Age: 23

								BATTING											BASERUNNING				AVERAGES		
Year Team	Lg	G	AB	H	2B	3B	HR	(Hm	Rd)	TB	R	RBI	RC	TBB	IBB	SO	HBP	SH	SF	SB	CS	SB%	GDP	Avg	OBP	Slg
2004 Kngspt	R+	38	150	43	10	4	1	(-	-)	64	24	20	23	5	1	29	6	1	1	8	1	.89	2	.287	.333	.427
2004 Mets	R	19	71	19	7	0	0	(-	-)	26	10	11	9	2	0	9	2	0	1	9	1	.90	1	.268	.303	.366
2005 Hgrstn	A	120	487	134	13	6	8	(-	-)	183	75	48	66	32	0	88	9	10	1	64	24	.73	6	.275	.331	.376
2006 Bnghtn	AA	120	430	121	24	8	7	(-	-)	182	53	48	71	27	0	97	20	6	3	41	9	.82	6	.281	.350	.423
2007 StLuci	A+	5	13	2	0	0	0	(-	-)	2	1	0	0	1	0	4	1	0	0	2	0	1.00	0	.154	.267	.154
2007 NewOr	AAA	36	140	40	8	2	2	(-	-)	58	24	13	23	15	0	23	2	0	0	17	4	.81	2	.286	.363	.414
2007 NYM	NL	58	125	29	3	0	2	(1	1)	38	14	12	11	8	2	27	3	0	3	12	3	.80	0	.232	.288	.304
2008 Min	AL	153	577	149	24	7	7	(3	4)	208	79	59	66	25	0	142	7	3	2	33	11	.75	7	.258	.296	.360
2 ML YEARS		211	702	178	27	7	9	(4	5)	246	93	71	77	33	2	169	10	3	5	45	14	.76	7	.254	.295	.350

Chris Gomez

Bats: R Throws: R Pos: PH-43; 3B-20; 2B-18; SS-13; 1B-5   Ht: 6'1" Wt: 190 Born: 6/16/1971 Age: 38

								BATTING											BASERUNNING				AVERAGES		
Year Team	Lg	G	AB	H	2B	3B	HR	(Hm	Rd)	TB	R	RBI	RC	TBB	IBB	SO	HBP	SH	SF	SB	CS	SB%	GDP	Avg	OBP	Slg
1993 Det	AL	46	128	32	7	1	0	(0	0)	41	11	11	12	9	0	17	1	3	0	2	2	.50	2	.250	.304	.320
1994 Det	AL	84	296	76	19	0	8	(5	3)	119	32	53	39	33	0	64	3	3	1	5	3	.63	8	.257	.336	.402
1995 Det	AL	123	431	96	20	2	11	(5	6)	153	49	50	43	41	0	96	3	3	4	4	1	.80	13	.223	.292	.355
1996 2 Tms		137	456	117	21	1	4	(2	2)	152	53	45	52	57	1	84	7	6	2	3	5	.50	16	.257	.347	.333
1997 SD	NL	150	522	132	19	2	5	(2	3)	170	62	54	57	53	1	114	5	3	5	5	8	.38	16	.253	.326	.326
1998 SD	NL	145	449	120	32	3	4	(3	1)	170	55	39	58	51	7	87	5	7	3	1	3	.25	11	.267	.346	.379
1999 SD	NL	76	234	59	8	1	1	(1	0)	72	20	15	23	27	3	49	1	2	1	1	2	.33	6	.252	.331	.308
2000 SD	NL	33	54	12	0	0	0	(0	0)	12	4	3	4	7	0	5	0	1	1	0	0	-	1	.222	.306	.222
2001 2 Tms		98	301	78	19	0	8	(5	3)	121	37	43	36	17	0	38	2	6	5	4	0	1.00	9	.259	.298	.402
2002 TB	AL	130	461	122	31	3	10	(2	8)	189	51	46	51	21	0	58	7	6	3	1	3	.25	8	.265	.305	.410
2003 Min	AL	58	175	44	9	3	1	(0	1)	62	14	15	15	7	1	13	0	2	1	2	1	.67	10	.251	.279	.354
2004 Tor	AL	109	341	96	11	1	3	(1	2)	118	41	37	48	28	0	41	2	3	2	3	2	.60	4	.282	.337	.346
2005 Bal	AL	89	219	61	11	0	1	(0	1)	75	27	18	24	27	1	17	1	6	1	2	1	.67	14	.279	.359	.342
2006 Bal	AL	55	132	45	7	0	2	(1	1)	58	14	17	22	7	1	11	3	0	0	1	2	.33	5	.341	.387	.439
2007 2 Tms	AL	92	222	66	12	1	1	(1	0)	83	21	21	23	10	1	26	0	6	2	1	2	.33	6	.297	.325	.374
2008 Pit	NL	90	183	50	8	0	1	(0	1)	61	26	20	22	13	1	30	1	1	2	0	0	-	3	.273	.322	.333
96 Det	AL	48	128	31	5	0	1	(1	0)	39	21	16	13	18	0	20	1	3	0	1	1	.50	5	.242	.340	.305
96 SD	NL	89	328	86	16	1	3	(1	2)	113	32	29	39	39	1	64	6	3	2	2	5	.50	11	.262	.349	.345
01 SD	NL	40	112	21	3	0	0	(0	0)	24	6	7	4	9	0	14	0	2	2	1	0	1.00	5	.188	.244	.214
01 TB	AL	58	189	57	16	0	8	(5	3)	97	31	36	32	8	0	24	2	4	3	3	0	1.00	4	.302	.332	.513

116

Year	Team	Lg	G	AB	H	2B	3B	HR	(Hm	Rd)	TB	R	RBI	RC	TBB	IBB	SO	HBP	SH	SF	SB	CS	SB%	GDP	Avg	OBP	Slg
07	Bal	AL	73	169	51	10	1	1	(1	0)	66	17	16	20	10	1	20	0	5	1	1	2	.33	5	.302	.339	.391
07	Cle	AL	19	53	15	2	0	0	(0	0)	17	4	5	3	0	0	6	0	1	1	0	0	-	1	.283	.278	.321
	Postseason		19	55	12	1	1	0	(0	0)	15	5	1	4	7	0	12	0	0	0	0	0	-	3	.218	.306	.273
	16 ML YEARS		1515	4604	1206	234	18	60	(27	33)	1656	517	487	524	408	17	750	41	58	32	35	33	.51	134	.262	.325	.360

Adrian Gonzalez

Bats: L **Throws:** L **Pos:** 1B-161; PH-2   **Ht:** 6'2" **Wt:** 225 **Born:** 5/8/1982 **Age:** 27

Year	Team	Lg	G	AB	H	2B	3B	HR	(Hm	Rd)	TB	R	RBI	RC	TBB	IBB	SO	HBP	SH	SF	SB	CS	SB%	GDP	Avg	OBP	Slg
2004	Tex	AL	16	42	10	3	0	1	(1	0)	16	7	7	7	2	0	6	0	0	0	0	0	-	0	.238	.273	.381
2005	Tex	AL	43	150	34	7	1	6	(3	3)	61	17	17	13	10	2	37	0	0	2	0	0	-	3	.227	.272	.407
2006	SD	NL	156	570	173	38	1	24	(10	14)	285	83	82	82	52	9	113	3	1	5	0	1	.00	24	.304	.362	.500
2007	SD	NL	161	646	182	46	3	30	(10	20)	324	101	100	108	65	9	140	3	0	6	0	0	-	6	.282	.347	.502
2008	SD	NL	162	616	172	32	1	36	(14	22)	314	103	119	107	74	10	142	7	0	3	0	0	-	24	.279	.361	.510
	Postseason		4	14	5	0	0	0	(0	0)	5	2	0	1	3	0	3	0	0	0	0	0	-	0	.357	.471	.357
	5 ML YEARS		538	2024	571	126	6	97	(38	59)	1000	311	325	317	203	38	438	13	1	16	0	1	.00	57	.282	.349	.494

Alberto Gonzalez

Bats: R **Throws:** R **Pos:** SS-26; 3B-14; PH-7; 2B-4; PR-3   **Ht:** 5'11" **Wt:** 160 **Born:** 4/18/1983 **Age:** 26

Year	Team	Lg	G	AB	H	2B	3B	HR	(Hm	Rd)	TB	R	RBI	RC	TBB	IBB	SO	HBP	SH	SF	SB	CS	SB%	GDP	Avg	OBP	Slg
2004	Sbend	A	100	319	76	15	6	2	(-	-)	109	39	25	33	16	0	44	11	5	2	9	7	.56	10	.238	.296	.342
2005	Sbend	A	95	352	112	21	7	1	(-	-)	150	60	42	56	20	1	42	5	5	5	12	5	.71	7	.318	.359	.426
2006	Tenn	AA	129	434	126	20	3	6	(-	-)	170	67	50	65	37	6	42	8	13	2	5	1	.83	11	.290	.356	.392
2006	Tucsn	AAA	4	15	3	0	0	0	(-	-)	3	2	1	0	1	0	1	1	0	0	0	0	-	0	.200	.294	.200
2007	S-WB	AAA	106	384	95	21	10	1	(-	-)	139	44	35	44	24	2	49	6	9	3	12	5	.71	12	.247	.300	.362
2007	Trntn	AA	28	109	36	10	1	0	(-	-)	48	18	16	19	10	0	14	1	3	2	1	1	.50	3	.330	.385	.440
2008	S-WB	AAA	47	188	47	8	0	4	(-	-)	67	23	23	22	16	1	30	3	2	4	4	2	.67	7	.250	.313	.356
2008	Clmbs	AAA	8	33	10	3	0	1	(-	-)	16	2	6	5	0	0	5	1	0	0	0	0	-	1	.303	.324	.485
2007	NYY	AL	12	14	1	0	0	0	(0	0)	1	3	1	0	1	0	1	0	0	0	0	1	.00	1	.071	.133	.071
2008	2 Tms		45	101	26	8	0	1	(0	1)	37	13	10	11	8	0	14	1	2	0	0	1	.00	6	.257	.318	.366
08	NYY	AL	28	52	9	2	0	0	(0	0)	11	4	1	0	4	0	8	0	2	0	0	0	-	4	.173	.232	.212
08	Was	NL	17	49	17	6	0	1	(0	1)	26	9	9	11	4	0	6	1	0	0	0	1	.00	2	.347	.407	.531
	2 ML YEARS		57	115	27	8	0	1	(0	1)	38	16	11	11	9	0	15	1	2	0	0	2	.00	7	.235	.296	.330

Alex Gonzalez

Bats: R **Throws:** R **Pos:** SS   **Ht:** 6'0" **Wt:** 200 **Born:** 2/15/1977 **Age:** 32

Year	Team	Lg	G	AB	H	2B	3B	HR	(Hm	Rd)	TB	R	RBI	RC	TBB	IBB	SO	HBP	SH	SF	SB	CS	SB%	GDP	Avg	OBP	Slg
1998	Fla	NL	25	86	13	2	0	3	(1	2)	24	11	7	5	9	0	30	1	2	0	0	0	-	2	.151	.240	.279
1999	Fla	NL	136	560	155	28	8	14	(7	7)	241	81	59	69	15	0	113	12	1	3	3	5	.38	13	.277	.308	.430
2000	Fla	NL	109	385	77	17	4	7	(5	2)	123	35	42	26	13	0	77	2	5	2	7	1	.88	7	.200	.229	.319
2001	Fla	NL	145	515	129	36	1	9	(5	4)	194	57	48	56	30	6	107	10	3	3	2	2	.50	13	.250	.303	.377
2002	4 Tms	NL	42	151	34	7	1	2	(1	1)	49	15	18	14	12	1	32	4	3	2	3	1	.75	2	.225	.296	.325
2003	Fla	NL	150	528	135	33	6	18	(7	11)	234	52	77	67	33	13	106	13	3	5	0	4	.00	8	.256	.313	.443
2004	Fla	NL	159	561	130	30	3	23	(13	10)	235	67	79	58	27	9	126	9	3	4	3	1	.75	17	.232	.270	.419
2005	Fla	NL	130	435	115	30	0	5	(2	3)	160	45	45	47	31	10	81	5	4	3	5	3	.63	11	.264	.319	.368
2006	Bos	AL	111	388	99	24	2	9	(4	5)	154	48	50	40	22	1	67	5	7	7	1	0	1.00	6	.255	.299	.397
2007	Cin	NL	110	393	107	27	1	16	(8	8)	184	55	55	51	24	1	75	8	2	3	0	1	.00	13	.272	.325	.468
02	Fla	NL	42	151	34	7	1	2	(1	1)	49	15	18	14	12	1	32	4	3	2	3	1	.75	2	.225	.296	.325
02	Fla	NL	42	151	34	7	1	2	(1	1)	49	15	18	14	12	1	32	4	3	2	3	1	.75	2	.225	.296	.325
	Postseason		17	62	10	4	0	1	(1	0)	17	6	6	2	1	0	16	0	1	0	0	1	.00	2	.161	.175	.274
	10 ML YEARS		1117	4002	994	234	26	106	(53	53)	1598	466	480	433	216	41	814	64	33	32	24	18	.57	92	.248	.295	.399

Andy Gonzalez

Bats: R **Throws:** R **Pos:** 1B-7; PR-3; 3B-2; DH-1; PH-1   **Ht:** 6'3" **Wt:** 205 **Born:** 12/15/1981 **Age:** 27

Year	Team	Lg	G	AB	H	2B	3B	HR	(Hm	Rd)	TB	R	RBI	RC	TBB	IBB	SO	HBP	SH	SF	SB	CS	SB%	GDP	Avg	OBP	Slg
2001	WhSox	R	48	189	61	18	1	5	(-	-)	96	33	30	38	15	0	36	3	0	0	13	2	.87	5	.323	.382	.508
2002	Bristol	R+	66	254	71	17	0	1	(-	-)	91	48	45	36	32	1	43	3	0	7	5	4	.56	3	.280	.358	.358
2003	Knapol	A-	123	429	99	17	1	1	(-	-)	121	58	39	50	69	1	82	7	4	0	22	10	.69	8	.231	.347	.282
2004	Knapol	A-	14	48	13	1	0	1	(-	-)	17	6	3	5	4	0	6	1	0	1	1	2	.33	0	.271	.333	.354
2004	WinSa	A+	80	309	78	18	0	8	(-	-)	120	59	28	48	49	0	53	7	1	2	2	3	.40	4	.252	.365	.388
2004	Brham	AA	36	112	19	3	0	3	(-	-)	31	19	8	8	10	0	17	4	1	0	1	0	1.00	4	.170	.262	.277
2005	Brham	AA	122	433	120	19	2	4	(-	-)	155	51	63	63	60	1	91	5	5	8	5	5	.50	9	.277	.366	.358
2006	Charltt	AAA	117	403	110	27	0	6	(-	-)	155	48	51	59	46	2	77	7	5	2	16	8	.67	9	.273	.356	.385
2007	Charltt	AAA	35	124	30	7	1	3	(-	-)	48	15	17	19	22	1	39	1	0	1	6	1	.86	2	.242	.358	.387
2008	Buffalo	AAA	83	289	70	13	0	7	(-	-)	104	37	35	39	39	2	71	6	2	4	2	2	.50	10	.242	.340	.360
2007	CWS	AL	67	189	35	6	0	2	(1	1)	47	17	11	12	25	1	61	0	1	0	1	5	.17	4	.185	.280	.249
2008	Cle	AL	10	24	5	0	0	1	(1	0)	8	3	2	3	6	0	5	0	0	0	0	1	.00	1	.208	.367	.333
	2 ML YEARS		77	213	40	6	0	3	(2	1)	55	20	13	15	31	1	66	0	1	0	1	6	.14	5	.188	.291	.258

Carlos Gonzalez

Bats: L **Throws:** L **Pos:** CF-69; RF-36; PH-6   **Ht:** 6'1" **Wt:** 200 **Born:** 10/17/1985 **Age:** 23

Year	Team	Lg	G	AB	H	2B	3B	HR	(Hm	Rd)	TB	R	RBI	RC	TBB	IBB	SO	HBP	SH	SF	SB	CS	SB%	GDP	Avg	OBP	Slg
2003	Msoula	R+	72	275	71	14	4	6	(-	-)	111	45	25	35	16	1	61	5	0	3	12	7	.63	3	.258	.308	.404
2004	Sbend	A	14	51	14	4	0	1	(-	-)	21	5	8	5	1	0	13	0	0	0	0	2	.00	0	.275	.288	.412
2004	Yakima	A-	73	300	82	15	2	9	(-	-)	128	44	44	43	22	0	70	3	2	2	2	0	1.00	4	.273	.327	.427
2005	Sbend	A	129	515	158	28	6	18	(-	-)	252	91	92	94	48	8	86	5	0	1	7	3	.70	12	.307	.371	.489
2006	Lancst	A+	104	403	121	35	4	21	(-	-)	227	82	94	81	30	7	104	10	0	9	15	8	.65	6	.300	.356	.563
2006	Tenn	AA	18	61	13	6	0	2	(-	-)	25	11	5	7	7	1	12	0	1	0	1	0	1.00	3	.213	.294	.410
2007	Mobile	AA	120	458	131	33	3	16	(-	-)	218	63	74	73	32	2	103	1	2	6	9	5	.64	7	.286	.330	.476
2007	Tucsn	AAA	10	42	13	5	0	1	(-	-)	21	9	11	8	6	1	6	0	0	0	1	0	1.00	1	.310	.396	.500
2008	Scrmto	AAA	46	173	49	9	1	4	(-	-)	72	23	28	25	16	3	35	0	0	0	1	1	.50	5	.283	.344	.416
2008	Oak	AL	85	302	73	22	1	4	(3	1)	109	31	26	30	13	1	81	0	1	0	4	1	.80	7	.242	.273	.361

Edgar G. Gonzalez

Pitches: R **Bats:** R **Pos:** RP-11; SP-6   **Ht:** 6'2" **Wt:** 210 **Born:** 2/23/1983 **Age:** 26

Year	Team	Lg	G	GS	CG	GF	IP	BFP	H	R	ER	HR	SH	SF	HB	TBB	IBB	SO	WP	Bk	W	L	Pct	ShO	Sv-Op	Hld	ERC	ERA
2003	Ari	NL	9	2	0	1	18.1	85	28	10	10	3	1	1	0	7	2	14	2	0	2	1	.667	0	0-1	0	7.81	4.91
2004	Ari	NL	10	10	0	0	46.1	228	72	49	48	15	5	1	5	18	4	31	3	1	0	9	.000	0	0-0	0	9.78	9.32
2005	Ari	NL	1	0	0	0	0.1	5	2	4	4	1	0	0	0	2	0	1	1	0	0	0	-	0	0-0	0	124.7	108.0
2006	Ari	NL	11	5	0	1	42.2	182	45	20	20	7	4	1	3	9	0	28	2	0	3	4	.429	0	0-0	1	4.33	4.22
2007	Ari	NL	32	12	0	5	102.0	437	110	61	57	18	2	3	4	28	4	62	5	1	8	4	.667	0	0-0	0	4.67	5.03
2008	Ari	NL	17	6	0	3	48.0	221	58	34	32	8	4	1	3	21	2	32	4	0	1	3	.250	0	0-0	0	6.16	6.00
6 ML YEARS			80	35	0	10	257.2	1158	315	178	171	52	16	7	15	85	12	168	17	2	14	21	.400	0	0-1	1	6.05	5.97

Edgar Gonzalez

Bats: R **Throws:** R **Pos:** 2B-72; PH-34; 3B-4; SS-3; RF-3; LF-2   **Ht:** 6'0" **Wt:** 180 **Born:** 6/14/1978 **Age:** 31

Year	Team	Lg	G	AB	H	2B	3B	HR	(Hm	Rd)	TB	R	RBI	RC	TBB	IBB	SO	HBP	SH	SF	SB	CS	SB%	GDP	Avg	OBP	Slg
2000	HudVal	A-	41	145	32	4	4	0	(-	-)	44	17	8	13	12	0	32	1	0	0	5	1	.83	3	.221	.280	.303
2000	Princtn	R+	20	63	17	3	3	0	(-	-)	26	6	8	12	13	0	14	1	1	0	4	1	.80	2	.270	.403	.413
2001	HudVal	A-	73	277	92	19	4	9	(-	-)	146	49	34	60	37	6	56	3	2	4	6	3	.67	5	.332	.411	.527
2002	CtnSC	A	134	447	123	28	1	8	(-	-)	177	68	62	73	74	3	75	4	1	7	21	14	.60	14	.275	.378	.396
2003	Bkrsfld	A+	100	349	104	34	3	6	(-	-)	162	51	62	63	45	0	82	5	1	5	8	7	.53	7	.298	.381	.464
2004	Frisco	AA	106	394	114	25	4	8	(-	-)	171	58	55	63	36	0	83	6	1	3	6	2	.75	12	.289	.355	.434
2005	Hrsbrg	AA	99	333	93	24	3	8	(-	-)	147	41	49	54	42	1	74	4	2	6	5	7	.42	6	.279	.361	.441
2005	NewOr	AAA	23	48	17	4	0	0	(-	-)	21	12	4	7	1	0	10	0	1	0	0	0	-	2	.354	.367	.438
2006	Jupiter	A+	21	75	22	8	0	2	(-	-)	36	10	10	11	6	0	18	0	1	1	1	3	.25	1	.293	.341	.480
2006	Carlina	AA	64	210	62	10	3	6	(-	-)	96	19	25	36	24	0	37	3	0	3	9	6	.60	7	.295	.371	.457
2006	Albq	AAA	46	143	56	10	1	5	(-	-)	83	29	36	37	20	1	32	4	1	2	1	1	.50	4	.392	.473	.580
2007	Memp	AAA	126	459	142	34	3	8	(-	-)	206	64	53	81	50	1	69	2	4	2	15	4	.79	13	.309	.378	.449
2008	Portlnd	AAA	27	82	24	1	0	4	(-	-)	37	10	12	14	12	0	12	2	0	1	0	4	.00	3	.293	.392	.451
2008	SD	NL	111	325	89	15	0	7	(2	5)	125	38	33	34	25	1	76	2	0	1	1	3	.25	11	.274	.329	.385

Enrique Gonzalez

Pitches: R **Bats:** R **Pos:** RP-4   **Ht:** 5'10" **Wt:** 210 **Born:** 7/14/1982 **Age:** 26

Year	Team	Lg	G	GS	CG	GF	IP	BFP	H	R	ER	HR	SH	SF	HB	TBB	IBB	SO	WP	Bk	W	L	Pct	ShO	Sv-Op	Hld	ERC	ERA
2008	Portlnd*	AAA	35	13	0	6	99.1	448	106	58	49	10	5	3	1	50	1	82	4	0	7	5	.583	0	0- -	-	4.86	4.44
2006	Ari	NL	22	18	0	1	106.1	462	114	71	67	14	7	3	4	34	0	66	1	0	3	7	.300	0	0-0	0	4.53	5.67
2007	Ari	NL	1	0	0	1	2.0	11	4	4	3	0	0	0	0	1	0	0	0	0	0	0	-	0	0-0	0	9.72	13.50
2008	SD	NL	4	0	0	3	3.1	15	4	4	4	0	0	0	0	2	0	1	0	0	1	0	1.000	0	0-1	0	5.47	10.80
3 ML YEARS			27	18	0	5	111.2	488	122	79	74	14	7	3	4	37	0	67	1	0	4	7	.364	0	0-1	0	4.65	5.96

Gio Gonzalez

Pitches: L **Bats:** R **Pos:** SP-7; RP-3   **Ht:** 5'11" **Wt:** 185 **Born:** 9/19/1985 **Age:** 23

Year	Team	Lg	G	GS	CG	GF	IP	BFP	H	R	ER	HR	SH	SF	HB	TBB	IBB	SO	WP	Bk	W	L	Pct	ShO	Sv-Op	Hld	ERC	ERA
2004	Bristol	R+	7	6	0	0	24.0	94	17	8	6	0	1	3	0	8	0	36	4	1	1	2	.333	0	0- -	-	1.78	2.25
2004	Knapol	A-	6	6	0	0	32.2	147	30	13	11	1	2	1	0	13	0	27	1	1	1	1	.500	0	0- -	-	2.92	3.03
2005	Knapol	A-	11	10	0	0	57.2	231	36	16	12	3	0	1	2	22	0	84	2	3	5	3	.625	0	0- -	-	1.91	1.87
2005	WinSa	A+	13	13	0	0	73.1	297	61	33	29	5	2	1	1	25	0	79	2	3	8	3	.727	0	0- -	-	2.85	3.56
2006	Rdng	AA	27	27	1	0	154.2	684	140	88	80	24	4	5	8	81	2	166	9	2	7	12	.368	0	0- -	-	4.58	4.66
2007	Brham	AA	27	27	0	0	150.0	611	116	57	53	10	9	5	2	57	1	185	5	2	9	7	.563	0	0- -	-	2.64	3.18
2008	Scrmto	AAA	23	22	1	0	123.0	524	106	65	58	12	3	3	2	61	1	128	5	0	8	7	.533	0	0- -	-	3.75	4.24
2008	Oak	AL	10	7	0	3	34.0	163	32	34	29	9	2	1	3	25	1	34	1	0	1	4	.200	0	0-0	0	6.54	7.68

Luis Gonzalez

Bats: L **Throws:** R **Pos:** LF-64; PH-52; RF-22; DH-2   **Ht:** 6'2" **Wt:** 210 **Born:** 9/3/1967 **Age:** 41

Year Team	Lg	G	AB	H	2B	3B	HR	(Hm	Rd)	TB	R	RBI	RC	TBB	IBB	SO	HBP	SH	SF	SB	CS	SB%	GDP	Avg	OBP	Slg
1990 Hou	NL	12	21	4	2	0	0	(0	0)	6	1	0	2	2	1	5	0	0	0	0	0	-	0	.190	.261	.286
1991 Hou	NL	137	473	120	28	9	13	(4	9)	205	51	69	64	40	4	101	8	1	4	10	7	.59	9	.254	.320	.433
1992 Hou	NL	122	387	94	19	3	10	(4	6)	149	40	55	41	24	3	52	2	1	2	7	7	.50	6	.243	.289	.385
1993 Hou	NL	154	540	162	34	3	15	(8	7)	247	82	72	90	47	7	83	10	3	10	20	9	.69	9	.300	.361	.457
1994 Hou	NL	112	392	107	29	4	8	(3	5)	168	57	67	57	49	6	57	3	0	6	15	13	.54	10	.273	.353	.429
1995 2 Tms	NL	133	471	130	29	8	13	(6	7)	214	69	69	72	57	8	63	6	1	6	6	8	.43	16	.276	.357	.454
1996 ChC	NL	146	483	131	30	4	15	(6	9)	214	70	79	75	61	8	49	4	1	6	9	6	.60	13	.271	.354	.443
1997 Hou	NL	152	550	142	31	2	10	(4	6)	207	78	68	73	71	7	67	5	0	5	10	7	.59	12	.258	.345	.376
1998 Det	AL	154	547	146	35	5	23	(15	8)	260	84	71	89	57	7	62	8	0	8	12	7	.63	9	.267	.340	.475
1999 Ari	NL	153	614	**206**	45	4	26	(10	16)	337	112	111	129	66	6	63	7	1	5	9	5	.64	13	.336	.403	.549
2000 Ari	NL	**162**	618	192	47	2	31	(14	17)	336	106	114	128	78	6	85	12	2	12	2	4	.33	13	.311	.392	.544
2001 Ari	NL	**162**	609	198	36	7	57	(26	31)	419	128	142	164	100	24	83	14	0	5	1	1	.50	14	.325	.429	.688
2002 Ari	NL	148	524	151	19	3	28	(11	17)	260	90	103	114	97	8	76	5	0	7	9	2	.82	12	.288	.400	.496
2003 Ari	NL	156	579	176	46	4	26	(6	20)	308	92	104	113	94	17	67	3	0	3	5	3	.63	19	.304	.402	.532
2004 Ari	NL	105	379	98	28	5	17	(10	7)	187	69	48	62	68	11	58	2	0	2	2	2	.50	9	.259	.373	.493
2005 Ari	NL	155	579	157	37	4	24	(10	14)	266	90	79	87	78	12	90	11	0	4	4	1	.80	14	.271	.366	.459
2006 Ari	NL	153	586	159	52	2	15	(8	7)	260	93	73	81	69	10	58	7	0	6	0	1	.00	14	.271	.352	.444
2007 LAD	NL	139	464	129	23	2	15	(5	10)	201	70	68	65	56	4	56	4	0	2	6	2	.75	11	.278	.359	.433
2008 Fla	NL	136	341	89	26	1	8	(5	3)	141	30	47	48	41	1	43	0	0	5	1	2	.33	10	.261	.336	.413
95 Hou	NL	56	209	54	10	4	6	(1	5)	90	35	35	26	18	3	30	3	1	3	1	3	.25	8	.258	.322	.431
95 ChC	NL	77	262	76	19	4	7	(5	2)	124	34	34	46	39	5	33	3	0	3	5	5	.50	8	.290	.384	.473
Postseason		24	87	22	3	0	4	(2	2)	37	12	12	12	11	3	20	4	0	0	0	0	-	1	.253	.363	.425
19 ML YEARS		2591	9157	2591	596	68	354	(155	199)	4385	1412	1439	1554	1155	150	1218	111	10	98	128	87	.60	213	.283	.367	.479

Mike Gonzalez

Pitches: L **Bats:** R **Pos:** RP-36   **Ht:** 6'2" **Wt:** 213 **Born:** 5/23/1978 **Age:** 31

Year Team	Lg	G	GS	CG	GF	IP	BFP	H	R	ER	HR	SH	SF	HB	TBB	IBB	SO	WP	Bk	W	L	Pct	ShO	Sv-Op	Hld	ERC	ERA
2008 Missi*	AA	4	0	0	0	5.0	20	7	0	0	0	0	0	0	0	0	4	0	0	-	0		0	0--	-	4.37	0.00
2008 Rchmd*	AAA	5	0	0	1	6.0	23	5	1	1	0	0	0	0	1	0	8	0	0	1	0	1.000	0	1--	-	1.84	1.50
2003 Pit	NL	16	0	0	2	8.1	38	7	7	7	4	1	1	0	6	0	6	1	0	0	1	.000	0	0-0	3	7.18	7.56
2004 Pit	NL	47	0	0	12	43.1	169	32	7	6	2	3	0	1	6	0	55	4	0	3	1	.750	0	1-4	13	1.60	1.25
2005 Pit	NL	51	0	0	15	50.0	212	35	15	15	2	0	2	1	31	2	58	3	0	1	3	.250	0	3-3	15	2.90	2.70
2006 Pit	NL	54	0	0	47	54.0	234	42	13	13	1	3	1	2	31	2	64	0	0	3	4	.429	0	24-24	3	3.00	2.17
2007 Atl	NL	18	0	0	5	17.0	70	15	3	3	0	0	1	0	8	0	13	0	0	2	0	1.000	0	2-2	5	3.13	1.59
2008 Atl	NL	36	0	0	29	33.2	142	26	21	16	6	1	2	1	14	3	44	0	0	0	3	.000	0	14-16	0	3.33	4.28
6 ML YEARS		222	0	0	110	206.1	865	157	66	60	15	8	7	5	96	7	240	8	0	9	12	.429	0	44-49	39	2.88	2.62

Alex Gordon

Bats: L **Throws:** R **Pos:** 3B-133; DH-1   **Ht:** 6'1" **Wt:** 220 **Born:** 2/10/1984 **Age:** 25

Year Team	Lg	G	AB	H	2B	3B	HR	(Hm	Rd)	TB	R	RBI	RC	TBB	IBB	SO	HBP	SH	SF	SB	CS	SB%	GDP	Avg	OBP	Slg
2006 Wichta	AA	130	485	158	39	1	29	(-	-)	286	111	100	123	73	0	112	16	0	2	23	3	.88	4	.326	.429	.590
2007 KC	AL	151	543	134	36	4	15	(8	7)	223	60	60	69	41	4	137	13	1	2	14	4	.78	12	.247	.314	.411
2008 KC	AL	134	493	128	35	1	16	(9	7)	213	72	59	71	66	5	120	6	1	5	9	2	.82	8	.260	.351	.432
2 ML YEARS		285	1036	262	71	5	31	(17	14)	436	132	119	140	107	9	257	19	2	7	23	6	.79	20	.253	.332	.421

Brian Gordon

Pitches: R **Bats:** L **Pos:** RP-3   **Ht:** 6'0" **Wt:** 180 **Born:** 8/16/1978 **Age:** 30

Year Team	Lg	G	GS	CG	GF	IP	BFP	H	R	ER	HR	SH	SF	HB	TBB	IBB	SO	WP	Bk	W	L	Pct	ShO	Sv-Op	Hld	ERC	ERA
2007 CpChr	AA	30	0	0	13	50.1	215	44	17	16	3	1	1	2	19	6	43	0	1	5	1	.833	0	1--	-	2.95	2.86
2007 RdRck	AAA	9	0	0	5	11.0	45	14	7	6	1	0	3	0	1	0	8	0	0	1	1	.500	0	0--	-	4.52	4.91
2008 CpChr	AA	1	0	0	0	2.0	8	2	1	1	1	0	0	0	1	0	1	0	0	0	0	-	0	0--	-	8.28	4.50
2008 Frisco	AA	15	0	0	9	22.0	79	9	1	0	0	1	0	0	4	0	18	2	1	2	0	1.000	0	3--	-	0.62	0.00
2008 Okla	AAA	18	11	0	1	71.0	304	85	43	36	14	1	2	2	15	0	51	2	1	4	5	.444	0	0--	-	5.34	4.56
2008 Tex	AL	3	0	0	0	4.0	16	4	1	1	0	0	0	0	0	0	1	0	0	0	0	-	0	0-0	0	1.95	2.25

Tom Gordon

Pitches: R **Bats:** R **Pos:** RP-34   **Ht:** 5'10" **Wt:** 200 **Born:** 11/18/1967 **Age:** 41

Year Team	Lg	G	GS	CG	GF	IP	BFP	H	R	ER	HR	SH	SF	HB	TBB	IBB	SO	WP	Bk	W	L	Pct	ShO	Sv-Op	Hld	ERC	ERA
2008 Clrwtr*	A+	2	2	0	0	1.0	6	1	2	2	1	0	0	0	2	0	1	0	0	0	1	.000	0	0--	-	20.50	18.00
1988 KC	AL	5	2	0	0	15.2	67	16	9	9	1	0	0	0	7	0	18	0	0	0	2	.000	0	0-0	2	4.22	5.17
1989 KC	AL	49	16	1	16	163.0	677	122	67	66	10	4	4	1	86	4	153	12	0	17	9	.654	1	1-7	9	2.97	3.64
1990 KC	AL	32	32	6	0	195.1	858	192	99	81	17	8	2	3	99	1	175	11	0	12	11	.522	1	0-0	0	4.37	3.73
1991 KC	AL	45	14	1	11	158.0	684	129	76	68	16	5	3	4	87	6	167	5	0	9	14	.391	0	1-4	4	3.67	3.87
1992 KC	AL	40	11	0	13	117.2	516	116	67	60	9	2	4	4	55	4	98	5	2	6	10	.375	0	0-2	0	4.17	4.59
1993 KC	AL	48	14	2	18	155.2	651	125	65	62	11	6	6	1	77	5	143	17	0	12	6	.667	0	1-6	2	3.18	3.58
1994 KC	AL	24	24	0	0	155.1	675	136	79	75	15	3	8	3	87	3	126	12	1	11	7	.611	0	0-0	0	4.04	4.35
1995 KC	AL	31	31	2	0	189.0	843	204	110	93	12	7	11	4	89	4	119	9	0	12	12	.500	0	0-0	0	4.59	4.43
1996 Bos	AL	34	34	4	0	215.2	998	249	143	**134**	28	2	11	6	105	5	171	6	1	12	9	.571	1	0-0	0	5.50	5.59
1997 Bos	AL	42	25	2	16	182.2	774	155	85	76	10	3	4	3	78	1	159	5	0	6	10	.375	1	11-13	1	3.08	3.74
1998 Bos	AL	73	0	0	**69**	79.1	317	55	24	24	2	2	2	0	25	1	78	9	0	7	4	.636	0	**46-47**	1	1.72	2.72

Year	Team	Lg	G	GS	CG	GF	IP	BFP	H	R	ER	HR	SH	SF	HB	TBB	IBB	SO	WP	Bk	W	L	Pct	ShO	Sv-Op	Hld	ERC	ERA
1999	Bos	AL	21	0	0	15	17.2	82	17	11	11	2	0	0	1	12	2	24	0	0	0	2	.000	0	11-13	1	5.04	5.60
2001	ChC	NL	47	0	0	40	45.1	187	32	18	17	4	0	0	1	16	1	67	2	0	1	2	.333	0	27-31	0	2.27	3.38
2002	2 Tms	NL	34	0	0	10	42.2	181	42	19	16	3	3	0	1	16	3	48	0	0	1	3	.250	0	0-0	6	3.71	3.38
2003	CWS	AL	66	0	0	35	74.0	310	57	29	26	4	4	3	4	31	3	91	5	0	7	6	.538	0	12-17	7	2.74	3.16
2004	NYY	AL	80	0	0	15	89.2	342	56	23	22	5	5	2	1	23	5	96	3	0	9	4	.692	0	4-10	36	1.50	2.21
2005	NYY	AL	79	0	0	17	80.2	324	59	25	23	8	1	3	0	29	4	69	1	1	5	4	.556	0	2-9	33	2.45	2.57
2006	Phi	NL	59	0	0	53	59.1	253	53	23	22	9	2	1	1	22	4	68	3	0	3	4	.429	0	34-39	0	3.62	3.34
2007	Phi	NL	44	0	0	11	40.0	170	40	21	21	7	1	2	2	13	0	32	1	0	3	2	.600	0	6-11	14	4.55	4.73
2008	Phi	NL	34	0	0	7	29.2	139	31	19	17	3	0	1	0	17	1	26	4	0	5	4	.556	0	2-3	14	4.77	5.16
02	ChC	NL	19	0	0	7	23.2	104	27	12	9	1	1	0	1	10	1	31	0	0	1	1	.500	0	0-0	2	4.75	3.42
02	Hou	NL	15	0	0	3	19.0	77	15	7	7	2	2	0	0	6	2	17	0	0	0	2	.000	0	0-0	4	2.53	3.32
Postseason			21	0	0	6	21.2	100	24	18	17	6	0	1	2	9	1	19	3	0	0	1	.000	0	0-1	5	6.28	7.06
20 ML YEARS			887	203	18	346	2106.1	9048	1886	1012	923	176	58	69	38	974	57	1928	110	5	138	125	.525	4	158-212	122	3.64	3.94

Tom Gorzelanny

Pitches: L Bats: L Pos: SP-21   Ht: 6'2" Wt: 220 Born: 7/12/1982 Age: 26

			HOW MUCH HE PITCHED						WHAT HE GAVE UP												THE RESULTS						
Year	Team	Lg	G	GS	CG	GF	IP	BFP	H	R	ER	HR	SH	SF	HB	TBB	IBB	SO	WP	Bk	W	L	Pct	ShO	Sv-Op	Hld	ERC	ERA
2008	Indy*	AAA	7	7	0	0	35.0	135	28	11	8	1	0	0	1	4	0	33	1	0	3	1	.750	0	0--	-	1.74	2.06
2005	Pit	NL	3	1	0	0	6.0	32	10	8	8	1	1	0	0	3	0	3	0	0	0	1	.000	0	0-0	0	8.76	12.00
2006	Pit	NL	11	11	0	0	61.2	267	50	29	26	3	7	4	4	31	2	40	3	0	2	5	.286	0	0-0	0	3.23	3.79
2007	Pit	NL	32	32	1	0	201.2	874	214	90	87	18	3	9	11	68	3	135	5	1	14	10	.583	1	0-0	0	4.31	3.88
2008	Pit	NL	21	21	0	0	105.1	490	120	79	78	20	3	6	1	70	0	67	5	1	6	9	.400	0	0-0	0	6.86	6.66
4 ML YEARS			67	65	1	0	374.2	1663	394	206	199	42	14	19	16	172	5	245	13	2	22	25	.468	1	0-0	0	4.86	4.78

Ruben Gotay

Bats: B Throws: R Pos: PH-76; 3B-10; 2B-3; PR-2   Ht: 5'11" Wt: 190 Born: 12/25/1982 Age: 26

			BATTING																	BASERUNNING				AVERAGES		
Year	Team	Lg	G	AB	H	2B	3B	HR	(Hm	Rd)	TB	R	RBI	RC	TBB	IBB	SO	HBP	SH	SF	SB	CS	SB%	GDP	Avg	OBP	Slg
2008	Rchmd*	AAA	3	12	3	0	0	0	(-	-)	3	1	1	1	1	0	2	1	0	0	0	0	-	0	.250	.357	.250
2004	KC	AL	44	152	41	7	3	1	(1	0)	57	17	16	17	9	0	36	2	1	2	0	1	.00	4	.270	.315	.375
2005	KC	AL	86	282	64	14	2	5	(2	3)	97	32	29	31	22	0	51	4	4	5	2	2	.50	3	.227	.288	.344
2007	NYM	NL	98	190	56	12	0	4	(2	2)	80	25	24	28	16	1	42	1	3	1	3	3	.50	2	.295	.351	.421
2008	Atl	NL	88	102	24	5	0	2	(2	0)	35	10	8	9	13	0	32	0	2	0	1	1	.50	4	.235	.322	.343
4 ML YEARS			316	726	185	38	5	12	(7	5)	269	84	77	85	60	1	161	7	10	8	6	7	.46	13	.255	.315	.371

John Grabow

Pitches: L Bats: L Pos: RP-74   Ht: 6'2" Wt: 205 Born: 11/4/1978 Age: 30

			HOW MUCH HE PITCHED						WHAT HE GAVE UP												THE RESULTS						
Year	Team	Lg	G	GS	CG	GF	IP	BFP	H	R	ER	HR	SH	SF	HB	TBB	IBB	SO	WP	Bk	W	L	Pct	ShO	Sv-Op	Hld	ERC	ERA
2003	Pit	NL	5	0	0	1	5.0	22	6	3	2	0	0	0	0	0	0	9	0	0	0	0	-	0	0-0	0	2.73	3.60
2004	Pit	NL	68	0	0	10	61.2	286	81	39	35	8	6	1	0	28	7	64	5	0	2	5	.286	0	1-7	11	6.21	5.11
2005	Pit	NL	63	0	0	8	52.0	222	46	31	28	6	2	0	2	25	2	42	1	0	2	3	.400	0	0-1	14	4.00	4.85
2006	Pit	NL	72	0	0	17	69.2	303	68	34	32	7	5	3	3	30	3	66	0	0	4	2	.667	0	0-2	11	4.17	4.13
2007	Pit	NL	63	0	0	14	51.2	228	56	27	26	6	4	2	1	19	2	42	3	0	3	2	.600	0	1-2	8	4.51	4.53
2008	Pit	NL	74	0	0	18	76.0	322	60	25	24	9	3	2	1	37	2	62	4	2	6	3	.667	0	4-8	16	3.37	2.84
6 ML YEARS			345	0	0	68	316.0	1383	317	159	147	36	20	8	7	139	16	285	13	2	17	15	.531	0	6-20	60	4.35	4.19

Curtis Granderson

Bats: L Throws: R Pos: CF-140; PH-3   Ht: 6'1" Wt: 185 Born: 3/16/1981 Age: 28

			BATTING																	BASERUNNING				AVERAGES		
Year	Team	Lg	G	AB	H	2B	3B	HR	(Hm	Rd)	TB	R	RBI	RC	TBB	IBB	SO	HBP	SH	SF	SB	CS	SB%	GDP	Avg	OBP	Slg
2008	WMich*	A	3	11	4	0	2	0	(-	-)	8	1	1	3	1	0	2	0	0	0	0	0	-	0	.364	.417	.727
2008	Toledo*	AAA	2	9	3	1	0	0	(-	-)	4	1	0	1	0	0	1	0	0	0	0	0	-	0	.333	.333	.444
2004	Det	AL	9	25	6	1	1	0	(0	0)	9	2	0	2	3	0	8	0	0	0	0	0	-	1	.240	.321	.360
2005	Det	AL	47	162	44	6	3	8	(5	3)	80	18	20	26	10	0	43	0	2	0	1	1	.50	2	.272	.314	.494
2006	Det	AL	159	596	155	31	9	19	(7	12)	261	90	68	89	66	0	174	4	7	6	8	5	.62	4	.260	.335	.438
2007	Det	AL	158	612	185	38	23	23	(10	13)	338	122	74	106	52	3	141	5	1	3	26	1	.96	3	.302	.361	.552
2008	Det	AL	141	553	155	26	13	22	(11	11)	273	112	66	100	71	1	111	3	1	1	12	4	.75	7	.280	.365	.494
Postseason			13	53	12	3	1	3	(1	2)	26	8	7	8	5	0	10	0	0	1	2	0	1.00	1	.226	.288	.491
5 ML YEARS			514	1948	545	102	49	72	(33	39)	961	344	228	323	202	4	477	12	15	9	47	11	.81	17	.280	.350	.493

Jeff Gray

Pitches: R Bats: R Pos: RP-5   Ht: 6'2" Wt: 208 Born: 11/19/1981 Age: 27

			HOW MUCH HE PITCHED						WHAT HE GAVE UP												THE RESULTS						
Year	Team	Lg	G	GS	CG	GF	IP	BFP	H	R	ER	HR	SH	SF	HB	TBB	IBB	SO	WP	Bk	W	L	Pct	ShO	Sv-Op	Hld	ERC	ERA
2004	As	R	14	2	0	2	38.0	152	30	14	8	0	1	1	5	3	0	32	4	1	3	0	1.000	0	0--	-	1.69	1.89
2005	Vancvr	A-	12	11	0	0	46.2	183	33	16	13	0	4	0	1	5	0	24	4	1	4	2	.667	0	0--	-	1.24	2.51
2006	Kane	A	22	11	0	2	78.1	322	77	47	41	2	2	1	7	19	0	62	7	0	5	5	.500	0	0--	-	3.32	4.71
2006	Stcktn	A+	19	0	0	6	31.2	129	32	15	12	0	2	2	0	6	0	26	0	0	1	1	.500	0	1--	-	2.71	3.41
2007	Mdland	AA	8	0	0	8	12.1	44	7	1	0	0	1	0	1	2	0	12	0	0	2	0	1.000	0	3--	-	1.18	0.00
2007	Scrmto	AAA	46	0	0	31	50.0	239	58	27	25	2	1	1	3	22	4	45	2	2	2	4	.333	0	12--	-	4.07	4.09
2008	Scrmto	AAA	54	0	0	23	67.2	306	86	33	33	9	3	1	4	23	4	50	6	0	2	7	.222	0	4--	-	5.87	4.39
2008	Oak	AL	5	0	0	2	4.2	24	8	4	4	1	0	0	1	1	0	4	0	0	0	0	-	0	0-0	0	9.48	7.71

Sean Green

Pitches: R Bats: R Pos: RP-72   Ht: 6'6" Wt: 235 Born: 4/20/1979 Age: 30

Year	Team	Lg	G	GS	CG	GF	IP	BFP	H	R	ER	HR	SH	SF	HB	TBB	IBB	SO	WP	Bk	W	L	Pct	ShO	Sv-Op	Hld	ERC	ERA
2006	Sea	AL	24	0	0	11	32.0	139	34	16	16	2	1	1	2	13	1	15	2	0	0	0	-	0	0-1	3	4.47	4.50
2007	Sea	AL	64	0	0	10	68.0	304	77	31	29	2	4	5	3	34	6	53	2	0	5	2	.714	0	0-3	13	4.81	3.84
2008	Sea	AL	72	0	0	13	79.0	358	80	47	41	3	3	7	6	36	1	62	5	1	4	5	.444	0	1-4	17	4.09	4.67
3 ML YEARS			160	0	0	34	179.0	801	191	94	86	7	8	13	11	83	8	130	9	1	9	7	.563	0	1-8	33	4.42	4.32

Khalil Greene

Bats: R Throws: R Pos: SS-105   Ht: 5'11" Wt: 186 Born: 10/21/1979 Age: 29

Year	Team	Lg	G	AB	H	2B	3B	HR	(Hm	Rd)	TB	R	RBI	RC	TBB	IBB	SO	HBP	SH	SF	SB	CS	SB%	GDP	Avg	OBP	Slg
2003	SD	NL	20	65	14	4	1	2	(0	2)	26	8	6	4	4	0	19	1	0	0	0	1	.00	3	.215	.271	.400
2004	SD	NL	139	484	132	31	4	15	(3	12)	216	67	65	73	53	10	94	8	1	8	4	2	.67	9	.273	.349	.446
2005	SD	NL	121	436	109	30	2	15	(6	9)	188	51	70	58	25	3	93	6	3	6	5	0	1.00	8	.250	.296	.431
2006	SD	NL	122	412	101	26	2	15	(6	9)	176	56	55	48	39	0	87	7	0	2	5	1	.83	15	.245	.320	.427
2007	SD	NL	153	611	155	44	3	27	(12	15)	286	89	97	77	32	3	128	5	0	11	4	0	1.00	12	.254	.291	.468
2008	SD	NL	105	389	83	15	2	10	(7	3)	132	30	35	26	22	1	100	5	0	7	5	1	.83	7	.213	.260	.339
Postseason			6	14	4	2	0	0	(0	0)	6	2	1	1	1	0	4	0	0	1	0	0	-	0	.286	.313	.429
6 ML YEARS			660	2397	594	150	14	84	(34	50)	1024	301	328	286	175	17	521	32	4	34	23	5	.82	54	.248	.304	.427

Kevin Gregg

Pitches: R Bats: R Pos: RP-72   Ht: 6'6" Wt: 238 Born: 6/20/1978 Age: 31

Year	Team	Lg	G	GS	CG	GF	IP	BFP	H	R	ER	HR	SH	SF	HB	TBB	IBB	SO	WP	Bk	W	L	Pct	ShO	Sv-Op	Hld	ERC	ERA
2003	LAA	AL	5	3	0	0	24.2	97	18	9	9	3	0	0	1	8	0	14	0	0	2	0	1.000	0	0-0	0	2.74	3.28
2004	LAA	AL	55	0	0	23	87.2	377	86	43	41	6	4	5	3	28	3	84	13	1	5	2	.714	0	1-2	3	3.47	4.21
2005	LAA	AL	33	2	0	9	64.1	290	70	37	36	8	1	1	3	29	2	52	5	0	1	2	.333	0	0-1	1	5.08	5.04
2006	LAA	AL	32	3	0	12	78.1	341	88	41	36	10	0	3	2	21	0	71	6	0	3	4	.429	0	0-0	0	4.51	4.14
2007	Fla	NL	74	0	0	55	84.0	355	63	34	33	7	3	0	6	40	1	87	6	0	0	5	.000	0	32-36	6	3.15	3.54
2008	Fla	NL	72	0	0	59	68.2	296	51	30	26	3	3	1	4	37	4	58	7	0	7	8	.467	0	29-38	4	2.90	3.41
Postseason			2	0	0	0	4.0	18	4	0	0	0	0	0	0	2	0	3	1	0	0	0	-	0	0-0	0	3.63	0.00
6 ML YEARS			271	8	0	158	407.2	1756	376	194	181	37	11	10	19	163	10	366	37	1	18	21	.462	0	62-77	14	3.70	4.00

Zack Greinke

Pitches: R Bats: R Pos: SP-32   Ht: 6'2" Wt: 185 Born: 10/21/1983 Age: 25

Year	Team	Lg	G	GS	CG	GF	IP	BFP	H	R	ER	HR	SH	SF	HB	TBB	IBB	SO	WP	Bk	W	L	Pct	ShO	Sv-Op	Hld	ERC	ERA
2004	KC	AL	24	24	0	0	145.0	599	143	64	64	26	3	2	8	26	3	100	1	1	8	11	.421	0	0-0	0	3.85	3.97
2005	KC	AL	33	33	2	0	183.0	829	233	125	118	23	4	4	13	53	0	114	4	2	5	17	.227	0	0-0	0	5.71	5.80
2006	KC	AL	3	0	0	1	6.1	28	7	3	3	1	0	0	0	3	2	5	0	0	1	0	1.000	0	0-0	0	4.93	4.26
2007	KC	AL	52	14	0	7	122.0	507	122	52	50	12	3	4	3	36	5	106	3	1	7	7	.500	0	1-1	12	3.77	3.69
2008	KC	AL	32	32	1	0	202.1	851	202	87	78	21	2	4	4	56	1	183	8	1	13	10	.565	0	0-0	0	3.68	3.47
5 ML YEARS			144	103	3	8	658.2	2814	707	331	313	83	12	14	28	174	11	508	16	5	34	45	.430	0	1-1	12	4.29	4.28

Ken Griffey Jr.

Bats: L Throws: L Pos: RF-91; CF-32; DH-13; PH-7   Ht: 6'3" Wt: 228 Born: 11/21/1969 Age: 39

Year	Team	Lg	G	AB	H	2B	3B	HR	(Hm	Rd)	TB	R	RBI	RC	TBB	IBB	SO	HBP	SH	SF	SB	CS	SB%	GDP	Avg	OBP	Slg
1989	Sea	AL	127	455	120	23	0	16	(10	6)	191	61	61	64	44	8	83	2	1	4	16	7	.70	4	.264	.329	.420
1990	Sea	AL	155	597	179	28	7	22	(8	14)	287	91	80	80	63	12	81	2	0	4	16	11	.59	12	.300	.366	.481
1991	Sea	AL	154	548	179	42	1	22	(16	6)	289	76	100	112	71	21	82	1	4	9	18	6	.75	10	.327	.399	.527
1992	Sea	AL	142	565	174	39	4	27	(16	11)	302	83	103	102	44	15	67	5	0	3	10	5	.67	15	.308	.361	.535
1993	Sea	AL	156	582	180	38	3	45	(21	24)	359	113	109	137	96	25	91	6	0	7	17	9	.65	14	.309	.408	.617
1994	Sea	AL	111	433	140	24	4	40	(18	22)	292	94	90	107	56	19	73	2	0	2	11	3	.79	9	.323	.402	.674
1995	Sea	AL	72	260	67	7	0	17	(13	4)	125	52	42	49	52	6	53	0	0	2	4	2	.67	4	.258	.379	.481
1996	Sea	AL	140	545	165	26	2	49	(26	23)	342	125	140	131	78	13	104	7	1	7	16	1	.94	7	.303	.392	.628
1997	Sea	AL	157	608	185	34	3	56	(27	29)	393	125	147	142	76	23	121	8	0	12	15	4	.79	12	.304	.382	.646
1998	Sea	AL	161	633	180	33	3	56	(30	26)	387	120	146	136	76	11	121	7	0	4	20	5	.80	14	.284	.365	.611
1999	Sea	AL	160	606	173	26	3	48	(27	21)	349	123	134	132	91	17	108	7	0	2	24	7	.77	8	.285	.384	.576
2000	Cin	NL	145	520	141	22	3	40	(22	18)	289	100	118	111	94	17	117	9	0	8	6	4	.60	7	.271	.387	.556
2001	Cin	NL	111	364	104	20	2	22	(12	10)	194	57	65	69	44	6	72	4	1	4	2	0	1.00	8	.286	.365	.533
2002	Cin	NL	70	197	52	8	0	8	(4	4)	84	17	23	27	28	6	39	3	0	4	1	2	.33	6	.264	.358	.426
2003	Cin	NL	53	166	41	12	1	13	(5	8)	94	34	26	26	27	5	44	6	1	1	1	0	1.00	3	.247	.370	.566
2004	Cin	NL	83	300	76	18	0	20	(11	9)	154	49	60	60	44	3	67	2	0	2	1	0	1.00	6	.253	.351	.513
2005	Cin	NL	128	491	148	30	0	35	(15	20)	283	85	92	89	54	3	93	3	0	7	0	1	.00	9	.301	.369	.576
2006	Cin	NL	109	428	108	19	0	27	(13	14)	208	62	72	55	39	6	78	2	0	3	0	0	-	13	.252	.316	.486
2007	Cin	NL	144	528	146	24	1	30	(17	13)	262	78	93	87	85	14	99	1	0	9	6	1	.86	14	.277	.372	.496
2008	2 Tms		143	490	122	30	1	18	(8	10)	208	67	71	79	78	14	89	3	0	4	0	1	.00	13	.249	.353	.424
08	Cin	NL	102	359	88	20	1	15	(7	8)	155	51	53	59	61	13	64	2	0	3	0	1	.00	7	.245	.355	.432
08	CWS	AL	41	131	34	10	0	3	(1	2)	53	16	18	20	17	1	25	1	0	1	0	0	-	6	.260	.347	.405
Postseason			15	59	18	2	0	6	(3	3)	38	11	11	14	7	1	11	1	0	1	5	1	.83	0	.305	.382	.644
20 ML YEARS			2521	9316	2680	503	38	611	(319	292)	5092	1612	1772	1812	1240	244	1682	80	8	98	184	69	.73	190	.288	.373	.547

121

Jason Grilli

Pitches: R **Bats:** R **Pos:** RP-60   **Ht:** 6'5" **Wt:** 225 **Born:** 11/11/1976 **Age:** 32

Year	Team	Lg	G	GS	CG	GF	IP	BFP	H	R	ER	HR	SH	SF	HB	TBB	IBB	SO	WP	Bk	W	L	Pct	ShO	Sv-Op	Hld	ERC	ERA
2000	Fla	NL	1	1	0	0	6.2	35	11	4	4	0	2	0	2	2	0	3	0	0	1	0	1.000	0	0-0	0	7.84	5.40
2001	Fla	NL	6	5	0	1	26.2	115	30	18	18	6	1	0	2	11	0	17	0	0	2	2	.500	0	0-0	0	6.44	6.08
2004	CWS	AL	8	8	1	0	45.0	203	52	38	37	11	2	1	3	20	0	26	2	0	2	3	.400	0	0-0	0	6.67	7.40
2005	Det	AL	3	2	0	0	16.0	63	14	6	6	1	1	1	0	6	0	5	0	0	1	1	.500	0	0-0	0	3.27	3.38
2006	Det	AL	51	0	0	18	62.0	270	61	31	29	6	2	4	5	25	3	31	5	0	2	3	.400	0	0-0	9	4.23	4.21
2007	Det	AL	57	0	0	13	79.2	352	81	46	42	5	1	5	5	32	1	62	5	0	5	3	.625	0	0-2	11	4.09	4.74
2008	2 Tms		60	0	0	16	75.0	323	67	27	25	2	1	3	2	38	7	69	4	0	3	3	.500	0	1-2	4	3.34	3.00
08	Det	AL	9	0	0	4	13.2	59	12	5	5	1	0	0	1	7	1	10	1	0	0	1	.000	0	0-1	0	3.85	3.29
08	Col	NL	51	0	0	12	61.1	264	55	22	20	1	1	3	1	31	6	59	3	0	3	2	.600	0	1-1	4	3.23	2.93
	Postseason		5	0	0	0	3.0	14	1	0	0	0	0	0	0	4	1	1	0	0	0	0	-	0	0-0	1	2.44	0.00
	7 ML YEARS		186	16	1	48	311.0	1361	316	170	161	31	10	14	19	134	11	213	16	0	16	15	.516	0	1-4	24	4.51	4.66

Gabe Gross

Bats: L **Throws:** R **Pos:** RF-121; CF-18; PH-14; LF-2   **Ht:** 6'3" **Wt:** 222 **Born:** 10/21/1979 **Age:** 29

Year	Team	Lg	G	AB	H	2B	3B	HR	(Hm	Rd)	TB	R	RBI	RC	TBB	IBB	SO	HBP	SH	SF	SB	CS	SB%	GDP	Avg	OBP	Slg
2004	Tor	AL	44	129	27	4	0	3	(2	1)	40	18	16	15	19	0	31	0	0	0	2	2	.50	1	.209	.311	.310
2005	Tor	AL	40	92	23	4	1	1	(1	0)	32	11	7	11	10	0	21	0	0	0	1	1	.50	0	.250	.324	.348
2006	Mil	NL	117	208	57	15	0	9	(5	4)	99	42	38	42	36	3	60	2	3	3	1	0	1.00	3	.274	.382	.476
2007	Mil	NL	93	183	43	12	2	7	(4	3)	80	28	24	23	25	2	37	1	0	1	3	1	.75	1	.235	.329	.437
2008	2 Tms		143	345	82	16	3	13	(7	6)	143	46	40	46	50	0	82	2	0	2	4	2	.67	6	.238	.336	.414
08	Mil	NL	16	43	9	3	0	0	(0	0)	12	6	2	6	10	0	7	0	0	1	2	0	1.00	0	.209	.352	.279
08	TB	AL	127	302	73	13	3	13	(7	6)	131	40	38	40	40	0	75	2	0	1	2	2	.50	6	.242	.333	.434
	5 ML YEARS		437	957	232	51	6	33	(19	14)	394	145	125	137	140	5	231	5	3	6	11	6	.65	11	.242	.340	.412

Mark Grudzielanek

Bats: R **Throws:** R **Pos:** 2B-85; PH-1   **Ht:** 6'1" **Wt:** 190 **Born:** 6/30/1970 **Age:** 39

Year	Team	Lg	G	AB	H	2B	3B	HR	(Hm	Rd)	TB	R	RBI	RC	TBB	IBB	SO	HBP	SH	SF	SB	CS	SB%	GDP	Avg	OBP	Slg
1995	Mon	NL	78	269	66	12	2	1	(1	0)	85	27	20	24	14	4	47	7	3	0	8	3	.73	7	.245	.300	.316
1996	Mon	NL	153	657	201	34	4	6	(5	1)	261	99	49	90	26	3	83	9	1	3	33	7	.83	10	.306	.340	.397
1997	Mon	NL	156	649	177	54	3	4	(1	3)	249	76	51	75	23	0	76	10	3	3	25	9	.74	13	.273	.307	.384
1998	2 Tms	NL	156	589	160	21	1	10	(5	5)	213	62	62	64	26	2	73	11	8	7	18	5	.78	18	.272	.311	.362
1999	LAD	NL	123	488	159	23	5	7	(4	3)	213	72	46	76	31	1	65	10	2	3	6	6	.50	13	.326	.376	.436
2000	LAD	NL	148	617	172	35	6	7	(4	3)	240	101	49	80	45	0	81	9	2	3	12	3	.80	16	.279	.335	.389
2001	LAD	NL	133	539	146	21	3	13	(8	5)	212	83	55	66	28	0	83	11	3	5	4	4	.50	9	.271	.317	.393
2002	LAD	NL	150	536	145	23	0	9	(5	4)	195	56	50	53	22	4	89	3	1	4	4	1	.80	17	.271	.301	.364
2003	ChC	NL	121	481	151	38	1	3	(2	1)	200	73	38	71	30	0	64	11	7	2	6	2	.75	12	.314	.366	.416
2004	ChC	NL	81	257	79	12	1	6	(3	3)	111	32	23	35	15	0	32	1	4	1	1	1	.50	7	.307	.347	.432
2005	StL	NL	137	528	155	30	3	8	(3	5)	215	64	59	68	26	3	81	7	0	2	8	6	.57	14	.294	.334	.407
2006	KC	AL	134	548	163	32	4	7	(5	2)	224	85	52	69	28	4	69	2	3	5	3	2	.60	12	.297	.331	.409
2007	KC	AL	116	453	137	32	3	6	(4	2)	193	70	51	64	23	2	60	8	0	2	1	2	.33	14	.302	.346	.426
2008	KC	AL	86	331	99	24	0	3	(2	1)	132	36	24	41	19	1	41	5	3	2	2	1	.67	8	.299	.345	.399
98	Mon	NL	105	396	109	15	1	8	(3	5)	150	51	41	47	21	1	50	9	5	4	11	5	.69	11	.275	.323	.379
98	LAD	NL	51	193	51	6	0	2	(2	0)	63	11	21	17	5	1	23	2	3	3	7	0	1.00	7	.264	.286	.326
	Postseason		21	85	16	1	1	0	(0	0)	19	8	5	4	3	0	13	1	2	0	0	0	-	2	.188	.225	.224
	14 ML YEARS		1772	6942	2010	391	36	90	(52	38)	2743	936	629	876	356	24	944	104	40	42	131	52	.72	170	.290	.332	.395

Eddie Guardado

Pitches: L **Bats:** R **Pos:** RP-64   **Ht:** 6'0" **Wt:** 225 **Born:** 10/2/1970 **Age:** 38

Year	Team	Lg	G	GS	CG	GF	IP	BFP	H	R	ER	HR	SH	SF	HB	TBB	IBB	SO	WP	Bk	W	L	Pct	ShO	Sv-Op	Hld	ERC	ERA
1993	Min	AL	19	16	0	2	94.2	426	123	68	65	13	1	3	1	36	2	46	0	0	3	8	.273	0	0-0	0	6.18	6.18
1994	Min	AL	4	4	0	0	17.0	81	26	16	16	3	1	2	0	4	0	8	0	0	0	2	.000	0	0-0	0	7.01	8.47
1995	Min	AL	51	5	0	10	91.1	410	99	54	52	13	6	5	0	45	2	71	5	1	4	9	.308	0	2-5	5	5.20	5.12
1996	Min	AL	83	0	0	17	73.2	313	61	45	43	12	6	4	3	33	4	74	3	0	6	5	.545	0	4-7	18	3.81	5.25
1997	Min	AL	69	0	0	20	46.0	201	45	23	20	7	2	1	2	17	2	54	2	0	0	4	.000	0	1-1	13	4.23	3.91
1998	Min	AL	79	0	0	12	65.2	286	66	34	33	10	3	6	0	28	6	53	2	0	3	1	.750	0	0-4	16	4.42	4.52
1999	Min	AL	63	0	0	13	48.0	197	37	24	24	6	2	1	2	25	4	50	0	0	2	5	.286	0	2-4	15	3.63	4.50
2000	Min	AL	70	0	0	36	61.2	262	55	27	27	14	3	2	1	25	3	52	1	1	7	4	.636	0	9-11	8	4.34	3.94
2001	Min	AL	67	0	0	26	66.2	270	47	27	26	5	5	3	1	23	4	67	4	0	7	1	.875	0	12-14	14	2.13	3.51
2002	Min	AL	68	0	0	62	67.2	270	53	22	22	9	2	2	1	18	2	70	0	0	1	3	.250	0	45-51	0	2.66	2.93
2003	Min	AL	66	0	0	60	65.1	260	50	22	21	7	3	2	0	14	2	60	5	0	3	5	.375	0	41-45	0	2.14	2.89
2004	Sea	AL	41	0	0	35	45.1	176	31	14	14	8	0	1	1	14	0	45	0	0	2	2	.500	0	18-25	0	2.69	2.78
2005	Sea	AL	58	0	0	55	56.1	238	52	23	17	7	3	2	0	15	3	48	1	0	2	3	.400	0	36-41	0	3.12	2.72
2006	2 Tms		43	0	0	26	37.0	166	44	19	16	10	3	1	1	13	2	39	0	0	1	3	.250	0	13-18	2	6.26	3.89
2007	Cin	NL	15	0	0	2	13.2	62	16	11	11	2	0	1	1	4	0	8	0	0	0	0	-	0	0-2	1	5.14	7.24
2008	2 Tms		64	0	0	14	56.1	227	50	26	26	4	2	2	0	19	2	33	1	0	4	4	.500	0	4-5	25	3.09	4.15
06	Sea	AL	28	0	0	15	23.0	108	29	14	14	8	3	0	0	11	1	22	0	0	1	3	.250	0	5-8	2	7.78	5.48
06	Cin	NL	15	0	0	11	14.0	58	15	5	2	2	0	1	1	2	1	17	0	0	0	0	-	0	8-10	0	3.98	1.29
08	Tex	AL	55	0	0	14	49.1	194	38	20	20	3	2	2	0	17	2	28	1	0	3	3	.500	0	4-4	23	2.45	3.65
08	Min	AL	9	0	0	0	7.0	33	12	6	6	1	0	0	0	2	0	5	0	0	1	1	.500	0	0-1	2	8.69	7.71
	Postseason		5	0	0	5	5.0	27	10	5	5	2	0	0	0	2	0	5	0	0	0	0	-	0	3-3	0	13.18	9.00
	16 ML YEARS		860	25	0	390	906.1	3845	855	455	433	130	42	38	14	333	38	778	24	2	45	59	.433	0	187-233	117	3.93	4.30

Vladimir Guerrero

Bats: R **Throws:** R **Pos:** RF-99; DH-44　　　　**Ht:** 6'3" **Wt:** 235 **Born:** 2/9/1976 **Age:** 33

							BATTING														BASERUNNING				AVERAGES		
Year	Team	Lg	G	AB	H	2B	3B	HR	(Hm	Rd)	TB	R	RBI	RC	TBB	IBB	SO	HBP	SH	SF	SB	CS	SB%	GDP	Avg	OBP	Slg
1996	Mon	NL	9	27	5	0	0	1	(0	1)	8	2	1	1	0	0	3	0	0	0	0	0	-	1	.185	.185	.296
1997	Mon	NL	90	325	98	22	2	11	(5	6)	157	44	40	51	19	2	39	7	0	3	3	4	.43	11	.302	.350	.483
1998	Mon	NL	159	623	202	37	7	38	(19	19)	367	108	109	124	42	13	95	7	0	5	11	9	.55	15	.324	.371	.589
1999	Mon	NL	160	610	193	37	5	42	(23	19)	366	102	131	127	55	14	62	7	0	2	14	7	.67	18	.316	.378	.600
2000	Mon	NL	154	571	197	28	11	44	(25	19)	379	101	123	137	58	23	74	8	0	4	9	10	.47	15	.345	.410	.664
2001	Mon	NL	159	599	184	45	4	34	(21	13)	339	107	108	116	40	24	88	9	0	3	37	16	.70	24	.307	.377	.566
2002	Mon	NL	161	614	206	37	2	39	(20	19)	364	106	111	123	84	32	70	6	0	5	40	20	.67	20	.336	.417	.593
2003	Mon	NL	112	394	130	20	3	25	(15	10)	231	71	79	83	63	22	53	6	0	4	9	5	.64	18	.330	.426	.586
2004	LAA	AL	156	612	206	39	2	39	(19	20)	366	124	126	122	52	14	74	8	0	8	15	3	.83	19	.337	.391	.598
2005	LAA	AL	141	520	165	29	2	32	(19	13)	294	95	108	108	61	26	48	8	0	5	13	1	.93	16	.317	.394	.565
2006	LAA	AL	156	607	200	34	1	33	(14	19)	335	92	116	109	50	25	68	4	0	4	15	5	.75	16	.329	.382	.552
2007	LAA	AL	150	574	186	45	1	27	(13	14)	314	89	125	127	71	28	62	9	0	6	2	3	.40	19	.324	.403	.547
2008	LAA	AL	143	541	164	31	3	27	(13	14)	282	85	91	96	51	16	77	4	0	4	5	3	.63	27	.303	.365	.521
Postseason			16	60	11	0	0	1	(0	1)	14	6	7	5	5	2	7	2	0	0	1	1	.50	2	.183	.269	.233
13 ML YEARS			1750	6617	2136	404	43	392	(206	186)	3802	1126	1268	1324	666	239	813	83	0	53	173	86	.67	219	.323	.389	.575

Matt Guerrier

Pitches: R **Bats:** R **Pos:** RP-76　　　　**Ht:** 6'3" **Wt:** 195 **Born:** 8/2/1978 **Age:** 30

			HOW MUCH HE PITCHED						WHAT HE GAVE UP										THE RESULTS						
Year	Team	Lg	G	GS	CG	GF	IP	BFP	H	R	ER	HR	SH	SF	HB	TBB	IBB	SO	WP	Bk	W	L	Pct	ShO	Sv-Op Hld	ERC	ERA
2004	Min	AL	9	2	0	5	19.0	84	22	13	12	5	2	0	1	6	0	11	0	0	0	1	.000	0	0-0 0	6.10	5.68
2005	Min	AL	43	0	0	14	71.2	306	71	29	27	6	4	1	3	24	5	46	3	0	0	3	.000	0	0-0 1	3.71	3.39
2006	Min	AL	39	1	0	13	69.2	300	78	29	26	9	3	4	0	21	0	37	6	0	1	0	1.000	0	1-1 2	4.59	3.36
2007	Min	AL	73	0	0	16	88.0	351	71	23	23	9	0	3	5	21	1	68	6	0	2	4	.333	0	1-4 14	2.70	2.35
2008	Min	AL	76	0	0	15	76.1	344	84	47	44	12	1	1	0	37	9	59	2	0	6	9	.400	0	1-5 20	5.20	5.19
Postseason			1	0	0	1	1.0	3	0	0	0	0	0	0	0	0	0	0	0	0	0	0	-	0	0-0 0	0.00	0.00
5 ML YEARS			240	3	0	63	324.2	1385	326	141	132	41	10	9	9	109	15	221	17	0	9	17	.346	0	3-10 37	4.08	3.66

Carlos Guevara

Pitches: R **Bats:** R **Pos:** RP-10　　　　**Ht:** 5'11" **Wt:** 190 **Born:** 3/18/1982 **Age:** 27

			HOW MUCH HE PITCHED						WHAT HE GAVE UP										THE RESULTS						
Year	Team	Lg	G	GS	CG	GF	IP	BFP	H	R	ER	HR	SH	SF	HB	TBB	IBB	SO	WP	Bk	W	L	Pct	ShO	Sv-Op Hld	ERC	ERA
2003	Billings	R+	2	2	0	0	11.0	40	4	1	1	0	0	0	0	3	0	14	2	0	1	0	1.000	0	0-- -	0.66	0.82
2003	Dayton	A	12	3	0	3	39.1	171	37	17	15	4	4	0	3	14	1	39	6	0	0	1	.000	0	0-- -	3.78	3.43
2004	Dayton	A	44	0	0	28	56.2	240	47	22	18	6	0	0	3	24	0	90	7	0	3	4	.429	0	9-- -	3.47	2.86
2005	Srsota	A+	44	0	0	29	51.1	211	39	17	14	2	3	0	2	14	0	65	6	0	4	3	.571	0	14-- -	2.06	2.45
2006	Chatt	AA	49	0	0	37	77.1	332	74	35	32	6	2	1	2	27	0	89	7	0	2	3	.400	0	1-- -	3.54	3.72
2007	Chatt	AAA	51	0	0	37	62.0	258	51	17	16	4	3	3	3	23	0	87	4	1	1	2	.333	0	16-- -	2.96	2.32
2008	Portlnd	AAA	16	0	0	8	18.0	80	16	13	13	1	0	1	1	9	0	20	2	0	0	2	.000	0	2-- -	3.65	6.50
2008	SD	NL	10	0	0	6	12.1	60	13	9	8	2	1	0	2	9	2	11	3	0	1	0	1.000	0	0-0 0	5.68	5.84

Carlos Guillen

Bats: B **Throws:** R **Pos:** 3B-89; 1B-24; DH-4; LF-2; PH-2　　　　**Ht:** 6'1" **Wt:** 213 **Born:** 9/30/1975 **Age:** 33

							BATTING														BASERUNNING				AVERAGES		
Year	Team	Lg	G	AB	H	2B	3B	HR	(Hm	Rd)	TB	R	RBI	RC	TBB	IBB	SO	HBP	SH	SF	SB	CS	SB%	GDP	Avg	OBP	Slg
1998	Sea	AL	10	39	13	1	1	0	(0	0)	16	9	5	7	3	0	9	0	0	0	2	0	1.00	0	.333	.381	.410
1999	Sea	AL	5	19	3	0	0	1	(1	0)	6	2	3	1	1	0	6	0	1	0	0	0	-	1	.158	.200	.316
2000	Sea	AL	90	288	74	15	2	7	(3	4)	114	45	42	36	28	0	53	2	7	3	1	3	.25	6	.257	.324	.396
2001	Sea	AL	140	456	118	21	4	5	(2	3)	162	72	53	56	53	0	89	1	7	6	4	1	.80	9	.259	.333	.355
2002	Sea	AL	134	475	124	24	6	9	(4	5)	187	73	56	58	46	4	91	1	3	3	4	5	.44	8	.261	.326	.394
2003	Sea	AL	109	388	107	19	3	7	(4	3)	153	63	52	52	52	2	64	1	5	5	4	4	.50	12	.276	.359	.394
2004	Det	AL	136	522	166	37	10	20	(7	13)	283	97	97	97	52	3	87	2	4	4	12	5	.71	12	.318	.379	.542
2005	Det	AL	87	334	107	15	4	5	(3	2)	145	48	23	39	24	3	45	2	0	1	2	3	.40	9	.320	.368	.434
2006	Det	AL	153	543	174	41	5	19	(10	9)	282	100	85	106	71	10	87	4	0	4	20	9	.69	16	.320	.400	.519
2007	Det	AL	151	564	167	35	9	21	(12	9)	283	86	102	94	55	10	93	3	0	8	13	8	.62	14	.296	.357	.502
2008	Det	AL	113	420	120	29	2	10	(8	2)	183	68	54	65	60	3	67	3	2	4	9	3	.75	11	.286	.376	.436
Postseason			19	61	21	5	1	2	(0	2)	34	8	7	10	8	0	12	0	0	0	1	1	.50	2	.344	.420	.557
11 ML YEARS			1128	4048	1173	237	46	104	(54	50)	1814	663	572	613	445	35	691	19	28	38	71	41	.63	98	.290	.360	.448

Jose Guillen

Bats: R **Throws:** R **Pos:** RF-67; LF-45; DH-43; PH-2　　　　**Ht:** 5'11" **Wt:** 195 **Born:** 5/17/1976 **Age:** 33

							BATTING														BASERUNNING				AVERAGES		
Year	Team	Lg	G	AB	H	2B	3B	HR	(Hm	Rd)	TB	R	RBI	RC	TBB	IBB	SO	HBP	SH	SF	SB	CS	SB%	GDP	Avg	OBP	Slg
1997	Pit	NL	143	498	133	20	5	14	(5	9)	205	58	70	56	17	0	88	8	0	3	1	2	.33	16	.267	.300	.412
1998	Pit	NL	153	573	153	38	2	14	(10	4)	237	60	84	68	21	0	100	6	1	4	3	5	.38	7	.267	.298	.414
1999	2 Tms		87	288	73	16	0	3	(1	2)	98	42	31	28	20	2	57	7	1	2	1	0	1.00	6	.253	.315	.340
2000	TB	AL	105	316	80	16	5	10	(5	5)	136	40	41	43	18	1	65	13	2	0	3	1	.75	6	.253	.320	.430
2001	TB	AL	41	135	37	5	0	3	(0	3)	51	14	11	15	6	2	26	3	0	1	2	3	.40	2	.274	.317	.378
2002	2 Tms	NL	85	240	57	7	0	8	(5	3)	88	25	31	16	14	1	43	3	1	1	4	5	.44	13	.238	.287	.367
2003	2 Tms		136	485	151	28	2	31	(14	17)	276	77	86	86	24	2	95	14	0	3	1	3	.25	16	.311	.359	.569
2004	LAA	AL	148	565	166	28	3	27	(13	14)	281	88	104	98	37	5	92	15	0	3	5	4	.56	14	.294	.352	.497
2005	Was	NL	148	551	156	32	2	24	(3	21)	264	81	76	72	31	6	102	19	1	9	1	1	.50	14	.283	.338	.479
2006	Was	NL	69	241	52	15	1	9	(4	5)	96	28	40	28	15	4	48	7	0	5	1	0	1.00	8	.216	.276	.398
2007	Sea	AL	153	593	172	28	2	23	(12	11)	273	84	99	90	41	2	118	19	0	5	5	1	.83	17	.290	.353	.460

Year	Team	Lg	G	AB	H	2B	3B	HR	(Hm	Rd)	TB	R	RBI	RC	TBB	IBB	SO	HBP	SH	SF	SB	CS	SB%	GDP	Avg	OBP	Slg
																			BATTING				BASERUNNING				AVERAGES	
2008	KC	AL	153	598	158	42	1	20	(8	12)	262	66	97	68	23	3	106	9	0	3	2	1	.67	23	.264	.300	.438
99	Pit	NL	40	120	32	6	0	1	(0	1)	41	18	18	12	10	1	21	0	1	1	1	0	1.00	7	.267	.321	.342
99	TB	AL	47	168	41	10	0	2	(1	1)	57	24	13	16	10	1	36	7	0	1	0	0	-	9	.244	.312	.339
02	Ari	NL	54	131	30	4	0	4	(3	1)	46	13	15	7	7	1	25	2	0	1	3	4	.43	7	.229	.277	.351
02	Cin	NL	31	109	27	3	0	4	(2	2)	42	12	16	9	7	0	18	1	1	0	1	1	.50	6	.248	.299	.385
03	Cin	NL	91	315	106	21	1	23	(10	13)	198	52	63	64	17	1	63	9	6	2	1	3	.25	8	.337	.385	.629
03	Oak	AL	45	170	45	7	1	8	(4	4)	78	25	23	22	7	1	32	5	2	1	0	0	-	8	.265	.311	.459
	Postseason		4	11	5	1	0	0	(0	0)	6	1	1	3	3	0	2	0	0	0	0	0	-	0	.455	.571	.545
	12 ML YEARS		1421	5083	1388	275	23	186	(80	106)	2267	663	770	663	267	28	940	123	14	39	29	26	.53	152	.273	.323	.446

Jeremy Guthrie

Pitches: R **Bats:** R **Pos:** SP-30 **Ht:** 6'1" **Wt:** 196 **Born:** 4/8/1979 **Age:** 30

			HOW MUCH HE PITCHED					WHAT HE GAVE UP											THE RESULTS							
Year	Team	Lg	G	GS	CG	GF	IP	BFP	H	R	ER	HR	SH	SF	HB	TBB	IBB	SO	WP	Bk	W	L	Pct	ShO	Sv-Op	Hld	ERC	ERA
2004	Cle	AL	6	0	0	2	11.2	49	9	6	6	1	0	0	1	6	0	7	1	0	0	0	-	0	0-0	0	3.58	4.63
2005	Cle	AL	1	0	0	1	6.0	29	4	2	1	1	1	0	0	2	0	3	0	0	0	0	-	0	0-0	0	8.58	6.00
2006	Cle	AL	9	1	0	1	19.1	93	24	15	15	2	0	0	2	15	1	14	3	0	0	0	-	0	0-0	0	7.78	6.98
2007	Bal	AL	32	26	0	3	175.1	723	165	78	72	23	4	6	4	47	2	123	8	1	7	5	.583	0	0-1	0	3.55	3.70
2008	Bal	AL	30	30	1	0	190.2	796	176	82	77	24	2	2	7	58	2	120	3	0	10	12	.455	0	0-0	0	3.59	3.63
	5 ML YEARS		78	57	1	7	403.0	1690	383	185	174	52	7	9	14	128	5	267	15	1	17	17	.500	0	0-1	0	3.82	3.89

Franklin Gutierrez

Bats: R **Throws:** R **Pos:** RF-97; PH-17; CF-12; LF-11; DH-6; PR-4 **Ht:** 6'2" **Wt:** 190 **Born:** 2/21/1983 **Age:** 26

									BATTING											BASERUNNING				AVERAGES		
Year	Team	Lg	G	AB	H	2B	3B	HR	(Hm	Rd)	TB	R	RBI	RC	TBB	IBB	SO	HBP	SH	SF	SB	CS	SB%	GDP	Avg	OBP	Slg
2005	Cle	AL	7	1	0	0	0	0	(0	0)	0	2	0	0	1	0	0	0	0	0	0	0	-	0	.000	.500	.000
2006	Cle	AL	43	136	37	9	0	1	(1	0)	49	21	8	12	3	0	28	0	2	0	0	0	-	4	.272	.288	.360
2007	Cle	AL	100	271	72	13	2	13	(10	3)	128	41	36	36	21	1	77	1	5	3	8	3	.73	7	.266	.318	.472
2008	Cle	AL	134	399	99	26	2	8	(6	4)	153	54	41	37	27	1	87	8	4	2	9	3	.75	10	.248	.307	.383
	Postseason		10	29	6	0	0	1	(0	1)	9	5	4	3	5	0	11	0	0	0	0	0	-	1	.207	.324	.310
	4 ML YEARS		284	807	208	48	4	22	(17	5)	330	118	85	85	52	2	192	9	11	5	17	6	.74	21	.258	.308	.409

Angel Guzman

Pitches: R **Bats:** R **Pos:** RP-5; SP-1 **Ht:** 6'3" **Wt:** 200 **Born:** 12/14/1981 **Age:** 27

			HOW MUCH HE PITCHED					WHAT HE GAVE UP											THE RESULTS							
Year	Team	Lg	G	GS	CG	GF	IP	BFP	H	R	ER	HR	SH	SF	HB	TBB	IBB	SO	WP	Bk	W	L	Pct	ShO	Sv-Op	Hld	ERC	ERA
2008	Dytona*	A+	2	2	0	0	5.0	20	4	4	2	0	0	0	1	1	0	6	0	0	0	0	-	0	0--	0	2.46	3.60
2008	Tenn*	AA	1	1	0	0	3.0	11	3	0	0	0	0	0	0	0	0	2	0	0	0	0	-	0	0--	0	2.18	0.00
2008	Iowa*	AAA	4	4	0	1	9.0	35	7	1	1	0	1	1	0	3	0	12	0	0	1	0	1.000	0	0--	0	2.15	1.00
2006	ChC	NL	15	10	0	1	56.0	272	68	48	46	9	5	3	6	37	1	60	8	1	0	6	.000	0	0-0	0	7.41	7.39
2007	ChC	NL	12	3	0	3	30.1	128	32	12	12	2	1	1	2	9	0	26	3	0	0	1	.000	0	0-1	0	4.10	3.56
2008	ChC	NL	6	1	0	1	9.2	44	10	6	6	1	0	0	1	4	0	10	1	0	0	0	-	0	0-0	0	4.65	5.59
	3 ML YEARS		33	14	0	5	96.0	444	110	66	64	12	6	4	9	50	1	96	12	1	0	7	.000	0	0-1	0	6.03	6.00

Cristian Guzman

Bats: B **Throws:** R **Pos:** SS-136; PH-4; PR-1 **Ht:** 6'0" **Wt:** 213 **Born:** 3/21/1978 **Age:** 31

									BATTING											BASERUNNING				AVERAGES		
Year	Team	Lg	G	AB	H	2B	3B	HR	(Hm	Rd)	TB	R	RBI	RC	TBB	IBB	SO	HBP	SH	SF	SB	CS	SB%	GDP	Avg	OBP	Slg
1999	Min	AL	131	420	95	12	3	1	(1	0)	116	47	26	29	22	0	90	3	7	4	9	7	.56	6	.226	.267	.276
2000	Min	AL	156	631	156	25	20	8	(3	5)	245	89	54	76	46	1	101	2	7	4	28	10	.74	5	.247	.299	.388
2001	Min	AL	118	493	149	28	14	10	(7	3)	235	80	51	79	21	0	78	5	8	0	25	8	.76	6	.302	.337	.477
2002	Min	AL	148	623	170	31	6	9	(6	3)	240	80	59	63	17	2	79	2	4	8	12	13	.48	12	.273	.292	.385
2003	Min	AL	143	534	143	15	14	3	(1	2)	195	78	53	62	30	0	79	5	12	4	18	9	.67	4	.268	.311	.365
2004	Min	AL	145	576	158	31	4	8	(5	3)	221	84	46	66	30	4	64	1	13	4	10	5	.67	15	.274	.309	.384
2005	Was	NL	142	456	100	19	6	4	(0	4)	143	39	31	26	25	6	76	1	8	2	7	4	.64	12	.219	.260	.314
2007	Was	NL	46	174	57	6	6	2	(1	1)	81	31	14	30	15	1	21	1	0	2	2	0	1.00	1	.328	.380	.466
2008	Was	NL	138	579	183	35	5	9	(4	5)	255	77	55	84	23	1	57	5	1	4	6	5	.55	10	.316	.345	.440
	Postseason		18	67	16	3	0	1	(0	1)	22	9	2	5	5	0	12	1	2	0	3	0	1.00	0	.239	.301	.328
	9 ML YEARS		1167	4486	1211	202	78	54	(28	26)	1731	605	389	515	229	15	645	25	64	30	117	61	.66	71	.270	.307	.386

Tony Gwynn

Bats: L **Throws:** R **Pos:** PH-16; CF-7; PR-3; RF-2; LF-1; DH-1 **Ht:** 5'11" **Wt:** 191 **Born:** 10/4/1982 **Age:** 26

									BATTING											BASERUNNING				AVERAGES		
Year	Team	Lg	G	AB	H	2B	3B	HR	(Hm	Rd)	TB	R	RBI	RC	TBB	IBB	SO	HBP	SH	SF	SB	CS	SB%	GDP	Avg	OBP	Slg
2008	Nashv*	AAA	93	375	103	9	3	2	(-	-)	124	47	26	45	29	1	54	2	4	2	20	6	.77	9	.275	.328	.331
2006	Mil	NL	32	77	20	2	1	0	(0	0)	24	5	4	5	2	0	15	0	0	1	3	1	.75	2	.260	.275	.312
2007	Mil	NL	69	123	32	3	2	0	(0	0)	39	13	10	16	12	1	24	0	0	0	8	1	.89	6	.260	.326	.317
2008	Mil	NL	29	42	8	1	0	0	(0	0)	9	5	1	2	4	0	7	1	1	1	3	1	.75	1	.190	.271	.214
	3 ML YEARS		130	242	60	6	3	0	(0	0)	72	23	15	23	18	1	46	1	1	2	14	3	.82	3	.248	.300	.298

Charlie Haeger

Pitches: R Bats: R Pos: RP-4   Ht: 6'1" Wt: 220 Born: 9/19/1983 Age: 25

			HOW MUCH HE PITCHED						WHAT HE GAVE UP											THE RESULTS					
Year Team	Lg	G	GS	CG	GF	IP	BFP	H	R	ER	HR	SH	SF	HB	TBB	IBB	SO	WP	Bk	W	L	Pct	ShO	Sv-Op Hld	ERC	ERA
2008 Charltt*	AAA	28	25	3	1	178.0	772	167	96	88	13	2	12	15	77	0	117	9	2	10	13	.435	0	0--	-	4.02	4.45
2006 CWS	AL	7	1	0	4	18.1	79	12	10	7	0	0	0	0	13	0	19	0	0	1	1	.500	0	1-1	0	2.65	3.44
2007 CWS	AL	8	0	0	5	11.1	59	17	11	9	3	1	1	1	8	2	1	0	0	0	1	.000	0	0-0	1	10.02	7.15
2008 SD	NL	4	0	0	1	4.1	28	8	10	8	2	0	0	2	5	0	4	0	0	0	0	-	0	0-0	0	19.18	16.62
3 ML YEARS		19	1	0	10	34.0	166	37	31	24	5	1	1	3	26	2	24	0	0	1	2	.333	0	1-1	1	6.67	6.35

Travis Hafner

Bats: L Throws: R Pos: DH-54; PH-3   Ht: 6'3" Wt: 240 Born: 6/3/1977 Age: 32

								BATTING													BASERUNNING				AVERAGES		
Year Team	Lg	G	AB	H	2B	3B	HR	(Hm	Rd)	TB	R	RBI	RC	TBB	IBB	SO	HBP	SH	SF		SB	CS	SB%	GDP	Avg	OBP	Slg
2008 Buffalo*	AAA	7	22	7	3	0	0	(-	-)	10	4	4	4	3	0	4	0	0	0		0	0	-	1	.318	.400	.455
2002 Tex	AL	23	62	15	4	1	1	(0	1)	24	6	6	7	8	1	15	0	0	0		0	1	.00	0	.242	.329	.387
2003 Cle	AL	91	291	74	19	3	14	(7	7)	141	35	40	42	22	2	81	10	0	1		2	1	.67	7	.254	.327	.485
2004 Cle	AL	140	482	150	41	3	28	(7	21)	281	96	109	103	68	7	111	17	0	6		3	2	.60	11	.311	.410	.583
2005 Cle	AL	137	486	148	42	0	33	(14	19)	289	94	108	115	79	7	123	9	0	4		0	0	-	9	.305	.408	.595
2006 Cle	AL	129	454	140	31	1	42	(21	21)	299	100	117	118	100	16	111	7	0	2		0	0	-	10	.308	.439	.659
2007 Cle	AL	152	545	145	25	2	24	(12	12)	246	80	100	94	102	17	115	7	0	5		1	1	.50	15	.266	.385	.451
2008 Cle	AL	57	198	39	10	0	5	(2	3)	64	21	24	21	27	6	55	5	0	3		1	1	.50	4	.197	.305	.323
Postseason		11	43	8	1	0	2	(1	1)	15	6	4	3	7	1	15	0	0	0		0	0	-	1	.186	.300	.349
7 ML YEARS		729	2518	711	172	10	147	(63	84)	1344	432	504	500	406	56	611	55	0	21		7	6	.54	56	.282	.391	.534

Jerry Hairston

Bats: R Throws: R Pos: SS-36; LF-24; CF-17; RF-12; PH-10; 2B-7; 3B-1   Ht: 5'10" Wt: 185 Born: 5/29/1976 Age: 33

								BATTING													BASERUNNING				AVERAGES		
Year Team	Lg	G	AB	H	2B	3B	HR	(Hm	Rd)	TB	R	RBI	RC	TBB	IBB	SO	HBP	SH	SF		SB	CS	SB%	GDP	Avg	OBP	Slg
2008 Lsvlle*	AAA	20	79	30	8	2	4	(-	-)	54	11	19	19	3	0	9	1	1	1		1	1	.50	1	.380	.405	.684
1998 Bal	AL	6	7	0	0	0	0	(0	0)	0	2	0	0	0	0	1	0	0	0		0	0	-	0	.000	.000	.000
1999 Bal	AL	50	175	47	12	1	4	(1	3)	73	26	17	24	11	0	24	3	4	0		9	4	.69	2	.269	.323	.417
2000 Bal	AL	49	180	46	5	0	5	(2	3)	66	27	19	22	21	0	22	6	5	0		8	5	.62	8	.256	.353	.367
2001 Bal	AL	159	532	124	25	5	8	(5	3)	183	63	47	57	44	0	73	13	9	4		29	11	.73	12	.233	.305	.344
2002 Bal	AL	122	426	114	25	3	5	(2	3)	160	55	32	55	34	0	55	7	8	4		21	6	.78	5	.268	.329	.376
2003 Bal	AL	58	218	59	12	2	2	(1	1)	81	25	21	32	23	0	25	6	10	2		14	5	.74	8	.271	.353	.372
2004 Bal	AL	86	287	87	19	1	2	(0	2)	114	43	24	45	29	1	29	8	6	4		13	8	.62	3	.303	.378	.397
2005 ChC	NL	114	380	99	25	2	4	(3	1)	140	51	30	46	31	0	46	12	7	0		8	9	.47	5	.261	.336	.368
2006 2 Tms	NL	101	170	35	6	1	0	(0	0)	43	25	10	9	13	2	34	2	7	0		5	2	.71	5	.206	.270	.253
2007 Tex	AL	73	159	30	7	0	3	(1	2)	46	22	16	12	11	0	24	3	4	1		5	1	.83	5	.189	.249	.289
2008 Cin	NL	80	261	85	20	2	6	(3	3)	127	47	36	52	23	0	36	3	8	2		15	3	.83	0	.326	.384	.487
06 ChC	NL	38	82	17	3	0	0	(0	0)	20	8	4	5	4	2	14	1	5	0		3	0	1.00	1	.207	.253	.244
06 Tex	NL	63	88	18	3	1	0	(0	0)	23	17	6	4	9	0	20	1	2	0		2	2	.50	4	.205	.286	.261
11 ML YEARS		898	2795	726	156	17	39	(18	21)	1033	386	252	354	240	3	369	63	71	20		127	54	.70	53	.260	.330	.370

Scott Hairston

Bats: R Throws: R Pos: CF-51; LF-49; PH-30; 2B-1; PR-1   Ht: 6'0" Wt: 185 Born: 5/25/1980 Age: 29

								BATTING													BASERUNNING				AVERAGES		
Year Team	Lg	G	AB	H	2B	3B	HR	(Hm	Rd)	TB	R	RBI	RC	TBB	IBB	SO	HBP	SH	SF		SB	CS	SB%	GDP	Avg	OBP	Slg
2004 Ari	NL	101	339	84	15	6	13	(6	7)	150	39	29	32	21	0	88	1	2	1		3	3	.50	4	.248	.293	.442
2005 Ari	NL	15	20	2	1	0	0	(0	0)	3	0	0	0	0	0	6	0	0	0		0	0	-	1	.100	.100	.150
2006 Ari	NL	9	15	6	2	0	0	(0	0)	8	2	2	2	1	0	5	0	0	0		0	0	-	0	.400	.438	.533
2007 2 Tms	NL	107	263	64	18	2	11	(6	5)	119	37	36	36	26	0	55	1	3	1		2	0	1.00	4	.243	.313	.452
2008 SD	NL	112	326	81	18	9	7	(9	8)	156	42	31	43	28	2	84	3	3	2		3	1	.75	2	.248	.312	.479
07 Ari	NL	76	176	39	13	1	3	(1	2)	63	21	16	19	19	0	37	1	3	0		2	0	1.00	4	.222	.301	.358
07 SD	NL	31	87	25	5	1	8	(5	3)	56	16	20	17	7	0	18	0	0	1		0	0	-	0	.287	.337	.644
5 ML YEARS		344	963	237	54	11	41	(21	20)	436	120	98	113	76	2	238	5	8	4		8	4	.67	12	.246	.303	.453

Bill Hall

Bats: R Throws: R Pos: 3B-113; PH-18; 2B-6   Ht: 6'0" Wt: 209 Born: 12/28/1979 Age: 29

								BATTING													BASERUNNING				AVERAGES		
Year Team	Lg	G	AB	H	2B	3B	HR	(Hm	Rd)	TB	R	RBI	RC	TBB	IBB	SO	HBP	SH	SF		SB	CS	SB%	GDP	Avg	OBP	Slg
2002 Mil	NL	19	36	7	1	1	1	(0	1)	13	3	5	3	3	0	13	0	0	0		0	1	.00	1	.194	.256	.361
2003 Mil	NL	52	142	37	9	2	5	(2	3)	65	23	20	18	7	0	28	1	4	1		1	2	.33	5	.261	.298	.458
2004 Mil	NL	126	390	93	20	3	9	(5	4)	146	43	53	41	20	1	119	1	2	2		12	6	.67	4	.238	.276	.374
2005 Mil	NL	146	501	146	39	6	17	(12	5)	248	69	62	73	39	2	103	1	3	3		18	6	.75	11	.291	.342	.495
2006 Mil	NL	148	537	145	39	4	35	(18	17)	297	101	85	87	63	6	162	1	3	4		8	9	.47	12	.270	.345	.553
2007 Mil	NL	136	452	115	35	0	14	(10	4)	192	59	63	59	40	1	128	3	1	7		4	5	.44	9	.254	.315	.425
2008 Mil	NL	128	404	91	22	1	15	(10	5)	160	50	55	43	37	2	124	3	1	3		5	6	.45	4	.225	.293	.396
7 ML YEARS		755	2462	634	165	17	96	(57	39)	1121	348	343	324	209	12	677	10	13	20		48	35	.58	46	.258	.316	.455

Toby Hall

Bats: R **Throws:** R **Pos:** C-37; PH-4; DH-3; PR-1   **Ht:** 6'2" **Wt:** 255 **Born:** 10/21/1975 **Age:** 33

Year	Team	Lg	G	AB	H	2B	3B	HR	(Hm	Rd)	TB	R	RBI	RC	TBB	IBB	SO	HBP	SH	SF	SB	CS	SB%	GDP	Avg	OBP	Slg
2000	TB	AL	4	12	2	0	0	1	(0	1)	5	1	1	1	1	0	0	0	0	0	0	0	-	0	.167	.231	.417
2001	TB	AL	49	188	56	16	0	4	(1	3)	84	28	30	25	4	0	16	3	0	1	2	2	.50	5	.298	.321	.447
2002	TB	AL	85	330	85	19	1	6	(2	4)	124	37	42	39	17	3	27	1	2	3	0	1	.00	14	.258	.293	.376
2003	TB	AL	130	463	117	23	0	12	(4	8)	176	50	47	45	23	4	40	7	0	5	0	1	.00	14	.253	.295	.380
2004	TB	AL	119	404	103	21	0	8	(6	2)	148	35	60	42	24	1	41	5	1	7	0	2	.00	20	.255	.300	.366
2005	TB	AL	135	432	124	20	0	5	(1	4)	159	28	48	46	16	1	39	5	3	7	0	0	-	15	.287	.315	.368
2006	2 Tms		85	278	72	17	0	8	(6	2)	113	17	31	25	10	4	22	2	0	4	0	2	.00	10	.259	.286	.406
2007	CWS	AL	38	116	24	4	0	0	(0	0)	28	8	3	3	3	0	12	0	0	1	0	0	-	0	.207	.225	.241
2008	CWS	AL	41	127	33	3	0	2	(2	0)	42	7	7	14	6	1	19	2	1	0	0	0	-	0	.260	.304	.331
06	TB	AL	64	221	51	13	0	8	(6	2)	88	15	23	18	8	2	17	2	0	3	0	2	.00	8	.231	.261	.398
06	LAD	NL	21	57	21	4	0	0	(0	0)	25	2	8	7	2	2	5	0	0	1	0	0	-	2	.368	.383	.439
9 ML YEARS			686	2350	616	123	1	46	(22	24)	879	211	269	240	104	14	216	25	7	28	2	8	.20	80	.262	.297	.374

Roy Halladay

Pitches: R **Bats:** R **Pos:** SP-33; RP-1   **Ht:** 6'6" **Wt:** 225 **Born:** 5/14/1977 **Age:** 32

Year	Team	Lg	G	GS	CG	GF	IP	BFP	H	R	ER	HR	SH	SF	HB	TBB	IBB	SO	WP	Bk	W	L	Pct	ShO	Sv-Op	Hld	ERC	ERA
1998	Tor	AL	2	2	1	0	14.0	53	9	4	3	2	0	0	0	2	0	13	0	0	1	0	1.000	0	0-0	0	1.61	1.93
1999	Tor	AL	36	18	1	2	149.1	668	156	76	65	19	3	4	4	79	1	82	6	0	8	7	.533	1	1-1	2	5.19	3.92
2000	Tor	AL	19	13	0	4	67.2	349	107	87	80	14	2	3	2	42	0	44	6	1	4	7	.364	0	0-0	0	9.70	10.64
2001	Tor	AL	17	16	1	0	105.1	432	97	41	37	3	3	1	1	25	0	96	4	1	5	3	.625	1	0-0	0	2.61	3.16
2002	Tor	AL	34	34	2	0	239.1	993	223	93	78	10	9	2	7	62	6	168	4	1	19	7	.731	1	0-0	0	2.85	2.93
2003	Tor	AL	36	36	9	0	266.0	1071	253	111	96	26	3	2	9	32	1	204	6	1	22	7	.759	2	0-0	0	2.86	3.25
2004	Tor	AL	21	21	1	0	133.0	561	140	66	62	13	4	3	1	39	1	95	2	2	8	8	.500	1	0-0	0	4.00	4.20
2005	Tor	AL	19	19	5	0	141.2	553	118	39	38	11	2	1	7	18	2	108	2	1	12	4	.750	2	0-0	0	2.26	2.41
2006	Tor	AL	32	32	4	0	220.0	876	208	82	78	19	3	5	5	34	5	132	3	0	16	5	.762	0	0-0	0	2.87	3.19
2007	Tor	AL	31	31	7	0	225.1	927	232	101	93	15	2	7	3	48	3	139	4	0	16	7	.696	1	0-0	0	3.37	3.71
2008	Tor	AL	34	33	9	0	246.0	987	220	88	76	18	5	4	12	39	3	206	4	0	20	11	.645	2	0-0	1	2.62	2.78
11 ML YEARS			281	255	40	6	1807.2	7470	1763	788	706	150	36	32	51	420	22	1287	41	7	131	66	.665	11	1-1	3	3.29	3.52

Cole Hamels

Pitches: L **Bats:** L **Pos:** SP-33   **Ht:** 6'3" **Wt:** 190 **Born:** 12/27/1983 **Age:** 25

Year	Team	Lg	G	GS	CG	GF	IP	BFP	H	R	ER	HR	SH	SF	HB	TBB	IBB	SO	WP	Bk	W	L	Pct	ShO	Sv-Op	Hld	ERC	ERA
2006	Phi	NL	23	23	0	0	132.1	558	117	66	60	19	6	8	3	48	4	145	5	0	9	8	.529	0	0-0	0	3.61	4.08
2007	Phi	NL	28	28	2	0	183.1	743	163	72	69	25	5	5	3	43	4	177	5	0	15	5	.750	0	0-0	0	3.12	3.39
2008	Phi	NL	33	33	2	0	227.1	914	193	89	78	28	6	2	1	53	7	196	0	0	14	10	.583	2	0-0	0	2.76	3.09
Postseason			1	1	0	0	6.2	27	3	3	3	0	1	0	0	4	0	7	0	0	0	1	.000	0	0-0	0	1.47	4.05
3 ML YEARS			84	84	4	0	543.0	2215	473	227	207	72	17	15	7	144	15	518	10	0	38	23	.623	2	0-0	0	3.08	3.43

Josh Hamilton

Bats: L **Throws:** L **Pos:** CF-111; RF-34; DH-15; PH-1   **Ht:** 6'4" **Wt:** 235 **Born:** 5/21/1981 **Age:** 28

Year	Team	Lg	G	AB	H	2B	3B	HR	(Hm	Rd)	TB	R	RBI	RC	TBB	IBB	SO	HBP	SH	SF	SB	CS	SB%	GDP	Avg	OBP	Slg
1999	Princtn	R+	56	236	82	20	4	10	(-	-)	140	49	48	52	13	0	43	0	1	2	17	3	.85	0	.347	.378	.593
1999	HudVal	A-	16	72	14	3	0	0	(-	-)	17	7	7	2	1	0	14	1	0	1	1	1	.50	2	.194	.213	.236
2000	CtnSC	A	96	391	118	23	3	13	(-	-)	186	62	61	65	27	3	71	2	0	3	14	6	.70	5	.302	.348	.476
2001	Orlndo	AA	23	89	16	5	0	0	(-	-)	21	5	4	4	5	2	22	0	0	1	2	0	1.00	1	.180	.221	.236
2001	CtnSC	A	4	11	4	1	0	1	(-	-)	8	3	2	3	2	0	3	0	0	0	0	0	-	0	.364	.462	.727
2002	Bkrsfld	A+	56	211	64	14	1	9	(-	-)	107	32	44	40	20	3	46	0	1	3	10	1	.91	4	.303	.359	.507
2006	HudVal	A-	15	50	13	3	1	0	(-	-)	18	7	5	5	5	0	11	0	0	0	0	1	.00	2	.260	.327	.360
2007	Lsvlle	AAA	11	40	14	1	0	4	(-	-)	27	9	8	11	5	0	9	0	0	0	3	0	1.00	0	.350	.422	.675
2007	Cin	NL	90	298	87	17	2	19	(11	8)	165	52	47	58	33	4	65	4	0	2	3	3	.50	6	.292	.368	.554
2008	Tex	AL	156	624	190	35	5	32	(19	13)	331	98	130	119	64	9	126	7	0	9	9	1	.90	8	.304	.371	.530
2 ML YEARS			246	922	277	52	7	51	(30	21)	496	150	177	177	97	13	191	11	0	11	12	4	.75	14	.300	.370	.538

Jason Hammel

Pitches: R **Bats:** R **Pos:** RP-35; SP-5   **Ht:** 6'6" **Wt:** 220 **Born:** 9/2/1982 **Age:** 26

Year	Team	Lg	G	GS	CG	GF	IP	BFP	H	R	ER	HR	SH	SF	HB	TBB	IBB	SO	WP	Bk	W	L	Pct	ShO	Sv-Op	Hld	ERC	ERA
2006	TB	AL	9	9	0	0	44.0	208	61	38	38	7	0	3	1	21	0	32	3	2	0	6	.000	0	0-0	0	7.40	7.77
2007	TB	AL	24	14	0	2	85.0	384	100	58	58	12	2	0	2	40	1	64	3	0	3	5	.375	0	0-0	0	5.86	6.14
2008	TB	AL	40	5	0	21	78.1	346	83	45	40	11	2	2	2	35	4	44	7	0	4	4	.500	0	2-2	1	4.94	4.60
3 ML YEARS			73	28	0	23	207.1	938	244	141	136	30	4	5	5	96	5	140	13	2	7	15	.318	0	2-2	1	5.82	5.90

Robby Hammock

Bats: R Throws: R Pos: C-15; PH-3; PR-2   Ht: 5'10" Wt: 187 Born: 5/13/1977 Age: 32

Year	Team	Lg	G	AB	H	2B	3B	HR	(Hm	Rd)	TB	R	RBI	RC	TBB	IBB	SO	HBP	SH	SF	SB	CS	SB%	GDP	Avg	OBP	Slg
2008	Tucsn*	AAA	62	217	52	6	2	5	(-	-)	77	29	27	24	18	1	47	1	3	3	1	0	1.00	10	.240	.297	.355
2003	Ari	NL	65	195	55	10	2	8	(5	3)	93	30	28	28	17	3	44	2	0	2	3	2	.60	5	.282	.343	.477
2004	Ari	NL	62	195	47	16	2	4	(1	3)	79	22	18	14	13	6	39	0	1	1	3	3	.50	9	.241	.287	.405
2006	Ari	NL	1	2	1	1	0	0	(0	0)	2	1	0	0	0	0	0	0	0	0	0	0	-	0	.500	.500	1.000
2007	Ari	NL	34	45	11	2	0	0	(0	0)	13	5	0	4	3	0	7	1	0	0	0	0	-	3	.244	.306	.289
2008	Ari	NL	18	42	8	1	0	0	(0	0)	9	4	2	3	5	1	9	1	0	0	0	0	-	0	.190	.292	.214
5 ML YEARS			180	479	122	30	4	12	(6	6)	196	62	48	49	38	10	99	4	1	3	6	5	.55	17	.255	.313	.409

Justin Hampson

Pitches: L Bats: L Pos: RP-35   Ht: 6'1" Wt: 206 Born: 5/24/1980 Age: 29

Year	Team	Lg	G	GS	CG	GF	IP	BFP	H	R	ER	HR	SH	SF	HB	TBB	IBB	SO	WP	Bk	W	L	Pct	ShO	Sv-Op	Hld	ERC	ERA
2008	Lk Els*	A+	5	0	0	0	6.0	19	1	0	0	0	0	0	0	1	0	4	0	0	0	0	-	0	0--	-	0.20	0.00
2008	Portlnd*	AAA	10	0	0	2	10.1	46	11	5	4	1	0	0	0	3	0	16	0	0	1	2	.333	0	0--	-	3.79	3.48
2006	Col	NL	5	1	0	0	12.0	60	19	10	10	3	0	1	0	5	0	9	1	0	1	0	1.000	0	0-1	0	9.41	7.50
2007	SD	NL	39	0	0	12	53.1	219	48	17	16	1	1	1	3	16	4	34	0	0	2	3	.400	0	0-0	4	2.77	2.70
2008	SD	NL	35	0	0	8	30.2	126	31	11	10	1	1	4	0	10	2	19	0	0	2	1	.667	0	0-0	0	3.41	2.93
3 ML YEARS			79	1	0	20	96.0	405	98	38	36	5	2	5	4	31	6	62	1	0	5	4	.556	0	0-1	4	3.69	3.38

Mike Hampton

Pitches: L Bats: R Pos: SP-13   Ht: 5'10" Wt: 195 Born: 9/9/1972 Age: 36

Year	Team	Lg	G	GS	CG	GF	IP	BFP	H	R	ER	HR	SH	SF	HB	TBB	IBB	SO	WP	Bk	W	L	Pct	ShO	Sv-Op	Hld	ERC	ERA
2008	Rchmd*	AAA	2	2	0	0	6.1	27	6	1	1	0	0	0	0	3	0	6	0	0	0	1	.000	0	0--	-	3.41	1.42
2008	Braves*	R	2	2	0	0	5.2	22	4	0	0	0	0	0	0	0	0	4	0	0	0	0	-	0	0--	-	0.97	0.00
2008	Rome*	A	1	1	0	0	3.0	18	8	4	3	0	0	0	0	0	0	5	1	0	0	0	-	0	0--	-	11.35	9.00
2008	MrtlBh*	A+	1	1	0	0	5.0	19	5	0	0	0	1	0	0	0	0	6	0	0	0	0	-	0	0--	-	2.09	0.00
2008	Missi*	AA	2	2	0	0	7.0	28	7	3	3	1	1	0	0	1	0	6	0	0	0	0	-	0	0--	-	3.42	3.86
1993	Sea	AL	13	3	0	2	17.0	95	28	20	18	3	1	1	0	17	3	8	1	1	1	3	.250	0	1-1	2	11.09	9.53
1994	Hou	NL	44	0	0	7	41.1	181	46	19	17	4	0	2	2	16	1	24	5	1	2	1	.667	0	0-1	10	4.88	3.70
1995	Hou	NL	24	24	0	0	150.2	641	141	73	56	13	11	5	4	49	3	115	3	1	9	8	.529	0	0-0	0	3.37	3.35
1996	Hou	NL	27	27	2	0	160.1	691	175	79	64	12	10	3	3	49	1	101	7	2	10	10	.500	1	0-0	0	4.11	3.59
1997	Hou	NL	34	34	7	0	223.0	941	217	105	95	16	11	7	2	77	2	139	6	1	15	10	.600	2	0-0	0	3.56	3.83
1998	Hou	NL	32	32	1	0	211.2	917	227	92	79	18	7	7	5	81	1	137	4	2	11	7	.611	1	0-0	0	4.45	3.36
1999	Hou	NL	34	34	3	0	239.0	979	206	86	77	12	10	9	5	101	2	177	9	0	22	4	.846	3	0-0	0	3.25	2.90
2000	NYM	NL	33	33	3	0	217.2	929	194	89	76	10	11	5	8	99	5	151	10	0	15	10	.600	1	0-0	0	3.44	3.14
2001	Col	NL	32	32	2	0	203.0	904	236	138	122	31	8	6	8	85	7	122	6	0	14	13	.519	1	0-0	0	5.69	5.41
2002	Col	NL	30	30	0	0	178.2	838	228	135	122	24	2	9	7	91	4	74	9	2	7	15	.318	0	0-0	0	6.61	6.15
2003	Atl	NL	31	31	1	0	190.0	823	186	91	81	14	10	5	1	78	4	110	10	1	14	8	.636	0	0-0	0	3.77	3.84
2004	Atl	NL	29	29	1	0	172.1	760	198	86	82	15	8	3	1	65	3	87	3	2	13	9	.591	0	0-0	0	4.76	4.28
2005	Atl	NL	12	12	1	0	69.1	284	74	28	27	5	2	1	0	18	0	27	1	0	5	3	.625	1	0-0	0	3.85	3.50
2008	Atl	NL	13	13	0	0	78.0	331	83	45	42	10	5	2	1	28	6	38	0	0	3	4	.429	0	0-0	0	4.52	4.85
Postseason			11	10	1	0	65.0	271	48	27	27	8	2	0	1	32	2	53	4	0	2	4	.333	1	0-0	0	3.19	3.74
14 ML YEARS			388	334	21	9	2152.0	9314	2239	1086	958	187	96	63	47	854	42	1310	74	13	141	105	.573	9	1-2	12	4.29	4.01

Ryan Hanigan

Bats: R Throws: R Pos: C-30; PH-3   Ht: 6'0" Wt: 195 Born: 8/16/1980 Age: 28

Year	Team	Lg	G	AB	H	2B	3B	HR	(Hm	Rd)	TB	R	RBI	RC	TBB	IBB	SO	HBP	SH	SF	SB	CS	SB%	GDP	Avg	OBP	Slg
2002	Dayton	A	6	11	3	1	0	0	(-	-)	4	1	0	1	1	0	2	0	0	0	0	0	-	0	.273	.333	.364
2003	Dayton	A	92	311	86	12	0	1	(-	-)	101	43	31	40	40	1	44	4	1	3	3	4	.43	3	.277	.363	.325
2003	Lsvlle	AAA	1	3	1	0	0	0	(-	-)	1	1	0	0	0	0	1	1	0	0	0	0	-	0	.333	.500	.333
2004	Ptomc	A+	119	429	127	21	0	5	(-	-)	163	58	56	65	49	1	51	6	5	9	6	5	.55	12	.296	.369	.380
2005	Chatt	AA	100	333	107	14	1	4	(-	-)	135	45	29	61	50	1	41	5	2	0	4	1	.80	8	.321	.418	.405
2006	Chatt	AA	56	126	31	2	0	0	(-	-)	33	17	14	14	19	0	23	2	0	3	0	0	-	1	.246	.347	.262
2006	Lsvlle	AAA	8	13	2	0	0	0	(-	-)	2	2	1	1	6	0	2	0	0	0	0	0	-	0	.154	.421	.154
2007	Chatt	AA	60	197	59	14	1	3	(-	-)	84	30	27	39	41	2	30	3	2	4	0	2	.00	4	.299	.420	.426
2007	Lsvlle	AAA	41	127	32	5	0	1	(-	-)	40	16	9	15	14	2	15	2	6	1	0	0	-	3	.252	.333	.315
2008	Lsvlle	AAA	75	272	88	14	0	4	(-	-)	114	37	35	47	25	0	39	8	2	4	1	0	1.00	9	.324	.392	.419
2007	Cin	NL	5	10	3	1	0	0	(0	0)	4	3	2	2	1	1	2	0	0	0	0	0	-	0	.300	.364	.400
2008	Cin	NL	31	85	23	2	0	2	(1	1)	31	9	9	12	10	1	9	3	0	0	0	0	-	2	.271	.367	.365
2 ML YEARS			36	95	26	3	0	2	(1	1)	35	12	11	14	11	2	11	3	0	0	0	0	-	2	.274	.367	.368

Jack Hannahan

Bats: L Throws: R Pos: 3B-126; 1B-10; PH-9; DH-5; PR-3   Ht: 6'2" Wt: 205 Born: 3/4/1980 Age: 29

Year	Team	Lg	G	AB	H	2B	3B	HR	(Hm	Rd)	TB	R	RBI	RC	TBB	IBB	SO	HBP	SH	SF	SB	CS	SB%	GDP	Avg	OBP	Slg
2006	Det	AL	3	9	0	0	0	0	(0	0)	0	0	0	0	1	0	1	0	0	0	0	0	-	0	.000	.100	.000
2007	Oak	AL	41	144	40	12	0	3	(1	2)	61	16	24	23	21	0	39	1	1	2	1	0	1.00	6	.278	.369	.424
2008	Oak	AL	143	436	95	27	0	9	(4	5)	149	48	47	38	55	4	131	2	3	5	2	0	1.00	5	.218	.305	.342
3 ML YEARS			187	589	135	39	0	12	(5	7)	210	64	71	61	77	4	171	3	4	7	3	0	1.00	11	.229	.318	.357

Joel Hanrahan

Pitches: R Bats: R Pos: RP-69   **Ht: 6'4" Wt: 248 Born: 10/6/1981 Age: 27**

Year	Team	Lg	G	GS	CG	GF	IP	BFP	H	R	ER	HR	SH	SF	HB	TBB	IBB	SO	WP	Bk	W	L	Pct	ShO	Sv-Op	Hld	ERC	ERA
2000	Gr Falls	R+	12	11	0	0	55.0	240	49	32	29	4	0	0	5	23	0	40	4	0	3	1	.750	0	0--	-	3.65	4.75
2001	Wilmg	A+	27	26	0	1	144.0	615	136	71	54	13	5	1	11	55	0	116	8	1	9	11	.450	0	0--	-	3.97	3.38
2002	VeroB	A+	25	25	2	0	143.1	608	129	74	67	11	4	7	11	51	1	139	7	1	10	6	.625	1	0--	-	3.49	4.21
2002	Jaxnvl	AA	3	3	0	0	11.0	55	15	14	13	2	0	2	0	7	0	10	0	0	1	1	.500	0	0--	-	7.81	10.64
2003	Jaxnvl	AA	23	23	1	0	133.1	556	117	44	36	5	4	2	7	53	2	130	4	0	10	4	.714	0	0--	-	3.21	2.43
2003	LsVgs	AAA	5	5	0	0	25.0	130	36	28	28	2	1	2	2	20	1	13	2	0	1	2	.333	0	0--	-	8.57	10.08
2004	LsVgs	AAA	25	22	0	1	119.1	548	128	78	67	22	9	7	7	75	0	97	9	0	7	7	.500	0	0--	-	6.45	5.05
2005	VeroB	A+	5	5	0	0	21.1	97	25	15	14	5	0	0	0	11	0	25	2	0	1	0	1.000	0	0--	-	6.69	5.91
2005	Jaxnvl	AA	23	21	0	0	111.2	499	118	71	61	17	6	4	1	55	1	102	9	0	9	8	.529	0	0--	-	5.18	4.92
2006	Jaxnvl	AA	12	12	0	0	66.1	273	49	19	19	4	4	1	3	38	1	67	7	0	7	2	.778	0	0--	-	3.33	2.58
2006	LsVgs	AAA	14	14	0	0	74.1	331	70	47	37	7	5	3	3	39	1	46	3	0	4	3	.571	0	0--	-	4.28	4.48
2007	LsVgs	AAA	15	15	0	0	75.1	330	65	36	31	10	1	1	4	36	0	71	2	0	5	4	.556	0	0--	-	3.98	3.70
2007	Was	NL	12	11	0	0	51.0	247	59	35	34	9	2	1	0	38	0	43	3	0	5	3	.625	0	0-0	0	7.01	6.00
2008	Was	NL	69	0	0	34	84.1	364	73	40	37	9	2	6	1	42	7	93	6	0	6	3	.667	0	9-13	3	3.65	3.95
	2 ML YEARS		81	11	0	34	135.1	611	132	75	71	18	4	7	1	80	7	136	9	0	11	6	.647	0	9-13	3	4.84	4.72

Devern Hansack

Pitches: R Bats: R Pos: RP-4   **Ht: 6'2" Wt: 180 Born: 2/5/1978 Age: 31**

Year	Team	Lg	G	GS	CG	GF	IP	BFP	H	R	ER	HR	SH	SF	HB	TBB	IBB	SO	WP	Bk	W	L	Pct	ShO	Sv-Op	Hld	ERC	ERA
2008	Pwtckt*	AAA	25	25	2	0	139.0	570	123	68	63	16	2	4	3	41	0	128	4	1	6	10	.375	0	0--	-	3.26	4.08
2006	Bos	AL	2	2	1	0	10.0	36	6	3	3	2	0	0	0	1	0	8	0	0	1	1	.500	1	0-0	0	1.59	2.70
2007	Bos	AL	3	1	0	0	7.2	38	9	5	4	2	0	0	0	5	0	5	0	0	0	1	.000	0	0-0	0	7.11	4.70
2008	Bos	AL	4	0	0	3	6.2	26	6	5	3	0	0	1	0	1	0	5	0	0	1	0	1.000	0	0-0	0	2.08	4.05
	3 ML YEARS		9	3	1	3	24.1	100	21	13	10	4	0	1	0	7	0	18	0	0	2	2	.500	1	0-0	0	3.29	3.70

Craig Hansen

Pitches: R Bats: R Pos: RP-48   **Ht: 6'6" Wt: 230 Born: 11/15/1983 Age: 25**

Year	Team	Lg	G	GS	CG	GF	IP	BFP	H	R	ER	HR	SH	SF	HB	TBB	IBB	SO	WP	Bk	W	L	Pct	ShO	Sv-Op	Hld	ERC	ERA
2008	Pwtckt*	AAA	11	0	0	2	16.2	65	6	4	3	0	0	1	3	5	0	17	0	1	1	0	1.000	0	0--	-	0.98	1.62
2008	Indy*	AAA	2	0	0	1	2.0	10	4	2	2	0	1	0	0	1	0	2	1	0	0	0	-	0	0--	-	10.75	9.00
2005	Bos	AL	4	0	0	1	3.0	16	6	2	2	1	0	1	0	1	0	3	0	0	0	0	-	0	0-1	0	12.18	6.00
2006	Bos	AL	38	0	0	11	38.0	176	46	32	28	5	3	3	4	15	0	30	1	0	2	2	.500	0	0-2	8	5.93	6.63
2008	2 Tms		48	0	0	15	46.1	224	40	37	32	3	2	1	2	43	2	32	6	0	2	7	.222	0	3-7	7	5.05	6.22
08	Bos	AL	32	0	0	6	30.2	146	29	23	19	2	0	1	1	23	1	25	3	0	1	3	.250	0	2-4	7	4.78	5.58
08	Pit	NL	16	0	0	9	15.2	78	11	14	13	1	2	0	1	20	1	7	3	0	1	4	.200	0	1-3	0	5.55	7.47
	3 ML YEARS		90	0	0	27	87.1	416	92	71	62	9	5	5	6	59	2	65	7	0	4	9	.308	0	3-10	15	5.66	6.39

J.A. Happ

Pitches: L Bats: L Pos: SP-4; RP-4   **Ht: 6'6" Wt: 200 Born: 10/19/1982 Age: 26**

Year	Team	Lg	G	GS	CG	GF	IP	BFP	H	R	ER	HR	SH	SF	HB	TBB	IBB	SO	WP	Bk	W	L	Pct	ShO	Sv-Op	Hld	ERC	ERA
2004	Batvia	A-	11	11	0	0	35.2	143	22	8	8	1	1	2	3	18	0	37	0	0	1	2	.333	0	0--	-	2.38	2.02
2005	Lakwd	A	14	12	0	0	72.1	300	57	26	19	3	1	0	5	26	0	70	4	1	4	4	.500	0	0--	-	2.66	2.36
2005	Rdng	AA	1	1	0	0	6.0	23	3	1	1	0	0	1	0	2	0	8	0	0	1	0	1.000	0	0--	-	1.09	1.50
2006	Clrwtr	A+	13	13	0	0	80.0	319	63	35	25	9	4	3	2	19	0	77	1	2	3	7	.300	0	0--	-	2.52	2.81
2006	Rdng	AA	12	12	0	0	74.2	307	58	27	22	2	2	2	3	29	0	81	0	0	2	6	.250	0	0--	-	2.54	2.65
2006	S-WB	AAA	1	1	0	0	6.0	24	3	1	1	1	0	0	1	1	0	4	0	0	1	0	1.000	0	0--	-	1.62	1.50
2007	Ottawa	AAA	24	24	0	0	118.1	515	118	74	66	12	4	4	0	62	1	117	2	1	4	6	.400	0	0--	-	4.63	5.02
2008	LV	AAA	24	23	0	1	135.0	552	116	58	54	14	5	2	1	48	0	151	4	0	8	7	.533	0	0--	-	3.25	3.60
2007	Phi	NL	1	1	0	0	4.0	21	7	5	5	3	0	0	0	2	0	5	0	0	0	1	.000	0	0-0	0	15.13	11.25
2008	Phi	NL	8	4	0	1	31.2	138	28	13	13	3	2	1	1	14	1	26	1	0	1	0	1.000	0	0-0	1	3.55	3.69
	2 ML YEARS		9	5	0	1	35.2	159	35	18	18	6	2	1	1	16	1	31	1	0	1	1	.500	0	0-0	1	4.62	4.54

Aaron Harang

Pitches: R Bats: R Pos: SP-29; RP-1   **Ht: 6'7" Wt: 275 Born: 5/9/1978 Age: 31**

Year	Team	Lg	G	GS	CG	GF	IP	BFP	H	R	ER	HR	SH	SF	HB	TBB	IBB	SO	WP	Bk	W	L	Pct	ShO	Sv-Op	Hld	ERC	ERA
2008	Lsvlle*	AAA	1	1	0	0	6.0	21	5	0	0	0	0	0	0	0	0	6	0	0	1	0	1.000	0	0--	-	1.50	0.00
2002	Oak	AL	16	15	0	0	78.1	354	78	44	42	7	3	4	3	45	2	64	1	0	5	4	.556	0	0-0	0	4.76	4.83
2003	2 Tms		16	15	0	1	76.1	327	89	47	45	11	5	1	1	19	0	42	3	1	5	6	.455	0	0-0	0	4.84	5.31
2004	Cin	NL	28	28	1	0	161.0	711	177	90	87	26	13	6	5	53	5	125	7	0	10	9	.526	1	0-0	0	4.81	4.86
2005	Cin	NL	32	32	1	0	211.2	887	217	93	90	22	11	5	8	51	3	163	6	0	11	13	.458	0	0-0	0	3.77	3.83
2006	Cin	NL	36	35	6	0	234.1	993	242	109	98	28	21	8	8	56	8	216	6	1	16	11	.593	2	0-0	0	3.82	3.76
2007	Cin	NL	34	34	2	0	231.2	948	213	100	96	28	4	5	8	52	3	218	12	1	16	6	.727	1	0-0	0	3.22	3.73
2008	Cin	NL	30	29	1	0	184.1	793	205	104	98	35	11	7	2	50	5	153	2	0	6	17	.261	1	0-0	0	4.83	4.78
03	Oak	AL	7	6	0	0	30.1	136	41	19	18	5	2	1	0	9	0	16	0	1	1	3	.250	0	0-0	0	6.32	5.34
03	Cin	NL	9	9	0	0	46.0	191	48	28	27	6	3	0	1	10	0	26	3	0	4	3	.571	0	0-0	0	3.94	5.28
	7 ML YEARS		192	188	11	1	1177.2	5013	1221	587	556	157	68	36	35	326	26	981	37	3	69	66	.511	5	0-0	0	4.11	4.25

Rich Harden

Pitches: R Bats: L Pos: SP-25   Ht: 6'1" Wt: 195 Born: 11/30/1981 Age: 27

			HOW MUCH HE PITCHED						WHAT HE GAVE UP														THE RESULTS						
Year	Team	Lg	G	GS	CG	GF	IP	BFP	H	R	ER	HR	SH	SF	HB	TBB	IBB	SO	WP	Bk	W	L	Pct	ShO	Sv-Op	Hld	ERC	ERA
2008	Scrmto*	AAA	1	1	0	0	3.2	14	3	1	1	0	0	0	0	0	0	4	0	0	0	0	-	0	0--	-	1.32	2.45
2008	Stcktn*	A+	1	1	0	0	6.0	22	3	0	0	0	0	0	3	0	0	9	0	0	0	1	1.000	0	0--	-	1.54	0.00
2003	Oak	AL	15	13	0	0	74.2	324	72	38	37	5	2	3	1	40	1	67	6	0	5	4	.556	0	0-0	0	4.28	4.46
2004	Oak	AL	31	31	0	0	189.2	803	171	90	84	16	5	6	3	81	6	167	4	1	11	7	.611	0	0-0	0	3.57	3.99
2005	Oak	AL	22	19	2	0	128.0	514	93	42	36	7	4	2	2	43	0	121	6	0	10	5	.667	1	0-0	1	2.20	2.53
2006	Oak	AL	9	9	0	0	46.2	191	31	22	22	5	0	2	1	26	0	49	0	0	4	0	1.000	0	0-0	0	3.07	4.24
2007	Oak	AL	7	4	0	2	25.2	100	18	7	7	3	0	0	0	11	1	27	0	0	1	2	.333	0	0-0	0	2.80	2.45
2008	2 Tms		25	25	0	0	148.0	595	96	38	34	11	2	3	3	61	2	181	3	0	10	2	.833	0	0-0	0	2.20	2.07
08	Oak	AL	13	13	0	0	77.0	311	57	21	20	5	0	2	1	31	0	92	1	0	5	1	.833	0	0-0	0	2.56	2.34
08	ChC	NL	12	12	0	0	71.0	284	39	17	14	6	2	1	2	30	1	89	2	0	5	1	.833	0	0-0	0	1.84	1.77
	Postseason		3	1	0	2	7.0	34	7	5	5	2	0	0	0	7	1	5	1	0	1	2	.333	0	0-0	0	7.94	6.43
	6 ML YEARS		109	101	2	2	612.2	2527	481	237	220	47	13	16	10	262	10	612	19	1	41	20	.672	1	0-0	1	2.94	3.23

J.J. Hardy

Bats: R Throws: R Pos: SS-145; PH-1   Ht: 6'2" Wt: 191 Born: 8/19/1982 Age: 26

						BATTING															BASERUNNING				AVERAGES		
Year	Team	Lg	G	AB	H	2B	3B	HR	(Hm	Rd)	TB	R	RBI	RC	TBB	IBB	SO	HBP	SH	SF	SB	CS	SB%	GDP	Avg	OBP	Slg
2005	Mil	NL	124	372	92	22	1	9	(6	3)	143	46	50	49	44	7	48	1	8	2	0	0	-	10	.247	.327	.384
2006	Mil	NL	35	128	31	5	0	5	(4	1)	51	13	14	13	10	0	23	0	0	1	1	1	.50	4	.242	.295	.398
2007	Mil	NL	151	592	164	30	1	26	(15	11)	274	89	80	84	40	1	73	1	4	1	2	3	.40	13	.277	.323	.463
2008	Mil	NL	146	569	161	31	4	24	(14	10)	272	78	74	78	52	3	98	1	5	2	2	1	.67	18	.283	.343	.478
	4 ML YEARS		456	1661	448	88	6	64	(39	25)	740	226	218	224	146	11	242	3	17	6	5	5	.50	45	.270	.329	.446

Dan Haren

Pitches: R Bats: R Pos: SP-33   Ht: 6'5" Wt: 215 Born: 9/17/1980 Age: 28

				HOW MUCH HE PITCHED						WHAT HE GAVE UP										THE RESULTS						
Year	Team	Lg	G	GS	CG	GF	IP	BFP	H	R	ER	HR	SH	SF	HB	TBB	IBB	SO	WP	Bk	W	L	Pct	ShO	Sv-Op	Hld	ERC	ERA
2003	StL	NL	14	14	0	0	72.2	320	84	44	41	9	4	2	5	22	0	43	3	0	3	7	.300	0	0-0	0	5.07	5.08
2004	StL	NL	14	5	0	2	46.0	195	45	23	23	4	4	2	2	17	2	32	1	0	3	3	.500	0	0-0	0	3.91	4.50
2005	Oak	AL	34	34	3	0	217.0	897	212	101	90	26	3	5	6	53	5	163	6	0	14	12	.538	0	0-0	0	3.58	3.73
2006	Oak	AL	34	34	2	0	223.0	930	224	109	102	31	3	3	10	45	6	176	10	0	14	13	.519	0	0-0	0	3.72	4.12
2007	Oak	AL	34	34	0	0	222.2	935	214	91	76	24	2	8	3	55	1	192	10	0	15	9	.625	0	0-0	0	3.32	3.07
2008	Ari	NL	33	33	1	0	216.0	881	204	86	80	19	7	3	6	40	4	206	11	0	16	8	.667	1	0-0	0	2.96	3.33
	Postseason		7	2	0	0	19.1	86	24	7	7	3	1	0	0	7	0	16	2	0	2	0	1.000	0	0-0	0	5.83	3.26
	6 ML YEARS		163	154	6	2	997.1	4158	983	454	412	113	23	23	32	232	18	812	41	0	65	52	.556	1	0-0	0	3.53	3.72

Brad Harman

Bats: R Throws: R Pos: PH-4; 2B-3; 3B-1   Ht: 6'1" Wt: 195 Born: 11/19/1985 Age: 23

						BATTING															BASERUNNING				AVERAGES		
Year	Team	Lg	G	AB	H	2B	3B	HR	(Hm	Rd)	TB	R	RBI	RC	TBB	IBB	SO	HBP	SH	SF	SB	CS	SB%	GDP	Avg	OBP	Slg
2004	Clrwtr	A+	1	0	0	0	0	0	(-	-)	0	1	0	0	1	0	0	0	0	0	0	0	-	0	-	1.000	-
2004	Phillies	R	51	183	42	10	0	2	(-	-)	58	23	19	17	11	0	41	3	1	2	2	1	.67	2	.230	.281	.317
2005	Lakwd	A	105	419	127	23	1	11	(-	-)	185	63	58	69	45	1	89	7	1	0	5	11	.31	8	.303	.380	.442
2006	Clrwtr	A+	119	423	102	19	1	2	(-	-)	129	59	25	46	48	2	102	3	7	1	6	2	.75	7	.241	.322	.305
2007	Clrwtr	A+	122	448	126	26	5	13	(-	-)	201	63	62	70	40	0	105	3	4	4	1	1	.50	4	.281	.341	.449
2008	Rdng	AA	117	443	93	17	1	17	(-	-)	163	49	56	48	43	1	138	2	2	4	3	1	.75	7	.210	.280	.368
2008	Phi	NL	6	10	1	1	0	0	(0	0)	2	1	1	0	1	0	1	0	0	0	0	0	-	1	.100	.182	.200

Brendan Harris

Bats: R Throws: R Pos: SS-55; 2B-39; 3B-34; PH-11; 1B-2; DH-2   Ht: 6'1" Wt: 210 Born: 8/26/1980 Age: 28

						BATTING															BASERUNNING				AVERAGES		
Year	Team	Lg	G	AB	H	2B	3B	HR	(Hm	Rd)	TB	R	RBI	RC	TBB	IBB	SO	HBP	SH	SF	SB	CS	SB%	GDP	Avg	OBP	Slg
2004	2 Tms	NL	23	59	10	3	0	1	(0	1)	16	4	3	2	3	0	12	1	0	0	0	0	-	0	.169	.222	.271
2005	Was	NL	4	9	3	1	0	1	(0	1)	7	1	3	3	0	0	0	1	0	0	0	0	-	2	.333	.400	.778
2006	2 Tms	NL	25	42	10	2	0	1	(1	0)	15	5	3	4	4	0	7	1	0	0	0	0	-	2	.238	.319	.357
2007	TB	AL	137	521	149	35	3	12	(5	7)	226	72	59	70	42	1	96	4	8	1	4	1	.80	19	.286	.343	.434
2008	Min	NL	130	434	115	29	3	7	(3	4)	171	57	49	52	39	0	98	4	7	6	1	1	.50	13	.265	.327	.394
04	ChC	NL	3	9	2	1	0	0	(0	0)	3	0	1	1	1	0	1	0	0	0	0	0	-	0	.222	.300	.333
04	Mon	NL	20	50	8	2	0	1	(0	1)	13	4	2	1	2	0	11	1	0	0	0	0	-	0	.160	.208	.260
06	Was	NL	17	32	8	2	0	0	(0	0)	10	3	2	3	3	0	3	1	0	0	0	0	-	1	.250	.333	.313
06	Cin	NL	8	10	2	0	0	1	(1	0)	5	2	1	1	1	0	4	0	0	0	0	0	-	1	.200	.273	.500
	5 ML YEARS		319	1065	287	70	6	22	(9	13)	435	139	117	131	88	1	213	11	15	7	5	2	.71	36	.269	.330	.408

Willie Harris

Bats: L Throws: R Pos: LF-86; PH-22; CF-17; 2B-14; 3B-14; PR-9; SS-3   Ht: 5'9" Wt: 186 Born: 6/22/1978 Age: 31

						BATTING															BASERUNNING				AVERAGES		
Year	Team	Lg	G	AB	H	2B	3B	HR	(Hm	Rd)	TB	R	RBI	RC	TBB	IBB	SO	HBP	SH	SF	SB	CS	SB%	GDP	Avg	OBP	Slg
2001	Bal	AL	9	24	3	1	0	0	(0	0)	4	3	0	0	0	0	7	0	1	0	0	0	-	0	.125	.125	.167
2002	CWS	AL	49	163	38	4	0	2	(2	0)	48	14	12	15	9	0	21	0	3	2	8	0	1.00	3	.233	.270	.294
2003	CWS	AL	79	137	28	3	1	0	(0	0)	33	19	5	11	10	0	28	0	3	0	12	2	.86	1	.204	.259	.241
2004	CWS	AL	129	409	107	15	2	2	(2	0)	132	68	27	53	51	0	79	1	7	3	19	7	.73	4	.262	.343	.323
2005	CWS	AL	56	121	31	2	1	1	(1	0)	38	17	8	15	13	0	25	1	4	0	10	3	.77	1	.256	.333	.314

Year	Team	Lg	G	AB	H	2B	3B	HR	(Hm	Rd)	TB	R	RBI	RC	TBB	IBB	SO	HBP	SH	SF	SB	CS	SB%	GDP	Avg	OBP	Slg
2006	Bos	AL	47	45	7	2	0	0	(0	0)	9	17	1	1	4	0	11	2	0	1	6	3	.67	0	.156	.250	.200
2007	Atl	NL	117	344	93	20	8	2	(1	1)	135	56	32	47	40	0	71	3	1	3	17	11	.61	3	.270	.349	.392
2008	Was	NL	140	367	92	14	4	13	(4	9)	153	58	43	50	50	2	66	3	3	1	13	3	.81	8	.251	.344	.417
Postseason			3	2	2	0	0	0	(0	0)	2	1	1	2	0	0	0	0	0	0	1	0	1.00	0	1.000	1.000	1.000
8 ML YEARS			626	1610	399	61	16	20	(10	10)	552	252	128	192	177	2	308	10	22	10	85	29	.75	20	.248	.324	.343

Matt Harrison

Pitches: L **Bats:** L **Pos:** SP-15

Ht: 6'4" Wt: 225 Born: 8/16/1985 Age: 23

Year	Team	Lg	G	GS	CG	GF	IP	BFP	H	R	ER	HR	SH	SF	HB	TBB	IBB	SO	WP	Bk	W	L	Pct	ShO	Sv-Op	Hld	ERC	ERA
2003	Braves	R	11	6	0	1	39.0	161	40	18	16	2	0	0	0	9	0	33	3	0	3	1	.750	0	1--	-	3.28	3.69
2004	Danvle	R+	13	12	1	0	66.0	278	72	36	30	3	4	4	1	10	1	49	3	1	4	4	.500	0	0--	-	3.24	4.09
2005	Rome	A	27	27	2	0	167.0	672	151	65	60	17	1	3	6	30	0	118	3	2	12	7	.632	1	0--	-	2.89	3.23
2006	MrtlBh	A+	13	13	2	0	81.1	327	77	30	28	6	1	1	4	16	0	60	0	1	8	4	.667	1	0--	-	3.11	3.10
2006	Missi	AA	13	12	1	0	77.1	330	83	36	31	6	4	1	3	17	0	54	5	5	3	4	.429	0	0--	-	3.62	3.61
2007	Missi	AA	20	20	0	0	116.2	487	118	51	44	6	2	3	1	34	0	78	2	3	5	7	.417	0	0--	-	3.46	3.39
2008	Frisco	AA	9	9	1	0	46.0	200	49	23	17	3	0	0	0	14	0	35	0	1	3	2	.600	1	0--	-	3.75	3.33
2008	Okla	AAA	6	6	0	0	38.0	159	40	15	15	3	1	2	0	14	0	20	1	0	3	1	.750	0	0--	-	4.25	3.55
2008	Tex	AL	15	15	1	0	83.2	372	100	57	51	12	1	5	2	31	2	42	2	2	9	3	.750	1	0-0	0	5.53	5.49

Corey Hart

Bats: R **Throws:** R **Pos:** RF-156; PH-1

Ht: 6'6" Wt: 218 Born: 3/24/1982 Age: 27

Year	Team	Lg	G	AB	H	2B	3B	HR	(Hm	Rd)	TB	R	RBI	RC	TBB	IBB	SO	HBP	SH	SF	SB	CS	SB%	GDP	Avg	OBP	Slg
2004	Mil	NL	1	1	0	0	0	0	(0	0)	0	0	0	0	0	0	1	0	0	0	0	0	-	0	.000	.000	.000
2005	Mil	NL	21	57	11	2	1	1	(2	0)	21	9	7	4	6	0	11	0	0	0	2	0	1.00	6	.193	.270	.368
2006	Mil	NL	87	237	67	13	2	9	(6	3)	111	32	33	30	17	1	58	0	0	2	5	8	.38	7	.283	.328	.468
2007	Mil	NL	140	505	149	33	9	24	(15	9)	272	86	81	94	36	3	99	13	5	7	23	7	.77	6	.295	.353	.539
2008	Mil	NL	157	612	164	45	6	20	(7	13)	281	76	91	81	27	2	109	5	4	9	23	7	.77	17	.268	.300	.459
5 ML YEARS			406	1412	391	93	18	55	(30	25)	685	203	212	209	86	6	278	18	9	18	53	22	.71	36	.277	.323	.485

Kevin Hart

Pitches: R **Bats:** R **Pos:** RP-21

Ht: 6'4" Wt: 220 Born: 11/29/1982 Age: 26

Year	Team	Lg	G	GS	CG	GF	IP	BFP	H	R	ER	HR	SH	SF	HB	TBB	IBB	SO	WP	Bk	W	L	Pct	ShO	Sv-Op	Hld	ERC	ERA
2004	Abrdn	A-	9	0	0	2	14.1	61	10	7	6	0	0	0	0	7	2	16	2	1	3	0	1.000	0	1--	-	2.13	3.77
2004	Dlmrva	A	4	2	0	0	14.1	63	13	6	6	0	0	1	1	5	0	16	1	0	2	0	1.000	0	0--	-	2.83	3.77
2005	Dlmrva	A	28	28	0	0	152.1	687	170	101	77	9	2	8	12	54	0	164	14	3	9	8	.529	0	0--	-	4.49	4.55
2006	Frdrck	A+	28	27	0	0	148.1	661	149	97	76	18	4	5	10	65	0	122	11	0	6	11	.353	0	0--	-	4.63	4.61
2007	Tenn	AA	18	17	0	0	102.0	431	100	59	48	13	2	4	5	27	2	92	11	1	8	5	.615	0	0--	-	3.77	4.24
2007	Iowa	AAA	9	8	1	0	56.0	240	56	23	22	6	6	3	1	23	0	39	6	0	4	1	.800	0	0--	-	4.30	3.54
2008	Iowa	AAA	26	10	0	14	57.2	228	38	19	18	3	1	0	4	20	1	63	3	2	2	2	.667	0	5--	-	2.10	2.81
2008	Tenn	AA	1	1	0	0	3.0	12	2	1	1	0	0	0	0	2	0	3	0	0	0	0	-	0	0--	-	2.79	3.00
2007	ChC	NL	8	0	0	2	11.0	42	7	1	1	0	1	0	0	4	0	13	0	0	0	0	-	0	0-0	0	1.62	0.82
2008	ChC	NL	21	0	0	4	27.2	142	39	24	20	2	1	0	3	18	3	23	1	0	2	2	.500	0	0-0	1	7.48	6.51
Postseason			1	0	0	0	1.0	5	0	2	2	0	0	0	0	2	0	2	1	0	0	0	-	0	0-0	0	3.47	18.00
2 ML YEARS			29	0	0	6	38.2	184	46	25	21	2	2	0	3	22	3	36	1	0	2	2	.500	0	0-0	1	5.60	4.89

Scott Hatteberg

Bats: L **Throws:** R **Pos:** PH-19; 1B-16

Ht: 6'1" Wt: 212 Born: 12/14/1969 Age: 39

Year	Team	Lg	G	AB	H	2B	3B	HR	(Hm	Rd)	TB	R	RBI	RC	TBB	IBB	SO	HBP	SH	SF	SB	CS	SB%	GDP	Avg	OBP	Slg
1995	Bos	AL	2	2	1	0	0	0	(0	0)	1	1	0	0	0	0	0	0	0	0	0	0	-	0	.500	.500	.500
1996	Bos	AL	10	11	2	1	0	0	(0	0)	3	3	0	1	3	0	2	0	0	0	0	0	-	2	.182	.357	.273
1997	Bos	AL	114	350	97	23	1	10	(5	5)	152	46	44	52	40	2	70	2	2	1	0	1	.00	11	.277	.354	.434
1998	Bos	AL	112	359	99	23	1	12	(4	8)	160	46	43	56	43	3	58	5	0	3	0	0	-	11	.276	.359	.446
1999	Bos	AL	30	80	22	5	0	1	(1	0)	30	12	11	14	18	0	14	1	0	1	0	0	-	2	.275	.410	.375
2000	Bos	AL	92	230	61	15	0	8	(2	6)	100	21	36	36	38	3	39	0	1	2	0	1	.00	8	.265	.367	.435
2001	Bos	AL	94	278	68	19	0	3	(2	1)	96	34	25	32	33	0	26	4	0	1	1	1	.50	7	.245	.332	.345
2002	Oak	AL	136	492	138	22	4	15	(8	7)	213	58	61	77	68	1	56	6	1	1	0	0	-	8	.280	.374	.433
2003	Oak	AL	147	541	137	34	0	12	(6	6)	207	63	61	80	66	0	53	9	3	3	0	1	.00	14	.253	.342	.383
2004	Oak	AL	152	550	156	30	0	15	(8	7)	231	87	82	90	72	5	48	5	3	8	0	0	-	10	.284	.367	.420
2005	Oak	AL	134	464	119	19	0	7	(4	3)	159	52	59	64	51	4	54	4	2	2	0	1	.00	22	.256	.334	.343
2006	Cin	NL	141	456	132	28	0	13	(10	3)	199	62	51	76	74	3	41	2	2	2	2	2	.50	13	.289	.389	.436
2007	Cin	NL	116	361	112	27	1	10	(6	4)	171	50	47	61	49	6	35	3	1	3	0	0	-	8	.310	.394	.474
2008	Cin	NL	34	52	9	3	0	0	(0	0)	12	3	7	4	7	0	7	0	0	2	0	1	.00	0	.173	.262	.231
Postseason			17	42	12	2	0	1	(0	1)	17	9	4	6	11	0	5	0	0	0	0	0	-	0	.286	.434	.405
14 ML YEARS			1314	4226	1153	249	7	106	(56	50)	1734	538	527	639	562	27	503	42	15	31	3	8	.27	117	.273	.361	.410

LaTroy Hawkins

Pitches: R **Bats:** R **Pos:** RP-57 **Ht:** 6'5" **Wt:** 215 **Born:** 12/21/1972 **Age:** 36

				HOW MUCH HE PITCHED						WHAT HE GAVE UP										THE RESULTS							
Year	Team	Lg	G	GS	CG	GF	IP	BFP	H	R	ER	HR	SH	SF	HB	TBB	IBB	SO	WP	Bk	W	L	Pct	ShO	Sv-Op	Hld	ERC	ERA
1995	Min	AL	6	6	1	0	27.0	131	39	29	26	3	0	3	1	12	0	9	1	1	2	3	.400	0	0-0	0	7.14	8.67
1996	Min	AL	7	6	0	1	26.1	124	42	24	24	8	1	1	0	9	0	24	1	1	1	1	.500	0	0-0	0	9.49	8.20
1997	Min	AL	20	20	0	0	103.1	478	134	71	67	19	2	2	4	47	0	58	6	3	6	12	.333	0	0-0	0	7.01	5.84
1998	Min	AL	33	33	0	0	190.1	840	227	126	111	27	4	10	5	61	1	105	10	2	7	14	.333	0	0-0	0	5.31	5.25
1999	Min	AL	33	33	1	0	174.1	803	238	136	129	29	1	5	1	60	2	103	9	0	10	14	.417	0	0-0	0	6.55	6.66
2000	Min	AL	66	0	0	38	87.2	370	85	34	33	7	4	1	1	32	1	59	6	0	2	5	.286	0	14-14	7	3.70	3.39
2001	Min	AL	62	0	0	51	51.1	248	59	34	34	3	1	4	1	39	3	36	7	0	1	5	.167	0	28-37	1	6.02	5.96
2002	Min	AL	65	0	0	15	80.1	310	63	23	19	5	2	3	0	15	1	63	5	0	6	0	1.000	0	0-3	13	1.99	2.13
2003	Min	AL	74	0	0	12	77.1	310	69	20	16	4	4	1	1	15	1	75	5	0	9	3	.750	0	2-8	28	2.48	1.86
2004	ChC	NL	77	0	0	50	82.0	333	72	27	24	10	6	2	2	14	5	69	2	0	5	4	.556	0	25-34	4	2.66	2.63
2005	2 Tms	NL	66	0	0	21	56.1	247	58	27	24	7	3	1	0	24	3	43	1	0	2	8	.200	0	6-15	15	4.41	3.83
2006	Bal	NL	60	0	0	12	60.1	261	73	30	30	4	1	2	0	15	3	27	2	0	3	2	.600	0	0-4	16	4.37	4.48
2007	Col	NL	62	0	0	10	55.1	225	52	21	21	6	2	1	0	16	1	29	2	0	2	5	.286	0	0-5	18	3.43	3.42
2008	2 Tms		57	0	0	15	62.0	252	53	29	27	3	1	3	0	22	4	48	3	0	3	1	.750	0	1-2	13	2.75	3.92
05	ChC	NL	21	0	0	12	19.0	80	18	9	7	4	1	0	0	7	0	13	0	0	1	4	.200	0	4-8	0	4.44	3.32
05	SF	NL	45	0	0	9	37.1	167	40	18	17	3	2	1	0	17	3	30	1	0	1	4	.200	0	2-7	15	4.36	4.10
08	NYY	AL	33	0	0	11	41.0	173	42	26	26	3	1	2	0	17	3	23	2	0	1	1	.500	0	0-1	1	4.09	5.71
08	Hou	NL	24	0	0	4	21.0	79	11	3	1	0	0	1	0	5	1	25	1	0	2	0	1.000	0	1-1	12	0.95	0.43
	Postseason		15	0	0	4	11.2	48	11	7	6	0	2	1	0	2	0	14	0	0	1	0	1.000	0	0-0	4	2.24	4.63
14 ML YEARS			688	98	2	225	1134.0	4932	1264	631	585	135	32	39	16	381	25	748	60	7	59	77	.434	0	76-122	115	4.65	4.64

Brad Hawpe

Bats: L **Throws:** L **Pos:** RF-133; PH-6 **Ht:** 6'3" **Wt:** 205 **Born:** 6/22/1979 **Age:** 30

						BATTING														BASERUNNING				AVERAGES		
Year	Team	Lg	G	AB	H	2B	3B	HR	(Hm	Rd)	TB	R	RBI	RC	TBB	IBB	SO	HBP	SH	SF	SB	CS	SB%	GDP	Avg	OBP	Slg
2008	ColSpr*	AAA	3	11	1	0	0	0	(-	-)	1	0	0	1	0	4	0	0	0		0	0	-	0	.091	.167	.091
2004	Col	NL	42	105	26	3	2	3	(1	2)	42	12	9	11	11	3	34	1	0	1	1	1	.50	4	.248	.322	.400
2005	Col	NL	101	305	80	10	3	9	(5	4)	123	38	47	44	43	3	70	0	0	3	2	2	.50	5	.262	.350	.403
2006	Col	NL	150	499	146	33	6	22	(6	16)	257	67	84	85	74	11	123	0	0	2	5	5	.50	8	.293	.383	.515
2007	Col	NL	152	516	150	33	4	29	(19	10)	278	80	116	103	81	11	137	3	1	5	0	2	.00	13	.291	.387	.539
2008	Col	NL	138	488	138	24	4	25	(14	11)	243	69	85	86	76	6	134	3	0	2	2	2	.50	7	.283	.381	.498
	Postseason		11	39	11	0	1	1	(1	0)	16	4	4	6	8	0	16	0	0	0	0	0	-	0	.282	.404	.410
5 ML YEARS			583	1913	540	103	18	88	(45	43)	943	266	341	329	285	34	498	7	1	13	10	12	.45	37	.282	.375	.493

Dirk Hayhurst

Pitches: R **Bats:** L **Pos:** RP-7; SP-3 **Ht:** 6'2" **Wt:** 215 **Born:** 3/24/1981 **Age:** 28

						HOW MUCH HE PITCHED						WHAT HE GAVE UP								THE RESULTS					
Year	Team	Lg	G	GS	CG	GF	IP	BFP	H	R	ER	HR	SH	SF	HB	TBB	IBB	SO	WP	Bk	W	L	Pct	ShO	Sv-Op	Hld	ERC	ERA
2003	Eugene	A-	25	1	0	5	37.2	168	38	23	16	3	1	0	4	12	0	49	0	0	4	3	.571	0	0- -	-	3.95	3.82
2004	FtWyn	A	26	17	0	1	118.1	475	114	41	35	6	5	5	4	19	0	106	4	1	9	4	.692	0	0- -	-	2.84	2.66
2004	Lk Els	A+	5	5	0	0	22.2	109	25	18	14	2	0	1	1	16	0	18	1	1	1	2	.333	0	0- -	-	5.92	5.56
2005	Lk Els	A+	38	7	0	7	93.2	414	106	66	56	9	1	7	4	27	0	69	3	1	5	5	.500	0	1- -	-	4.46	5.38
2005	Mobile	AA	1	1	1	0	7.0	26	5	2	2	1	0	0	0	4	0	4	1	0	1	0	1.000	0	0- -	-	4.01	2.57
2006	Lk Els	A+	12	11	0	0	59.0	259	61	34	26	3	2	2	5	20	0	51	4	0	2	7	.222	0	0- -	-	3.97	3.97
2006	Portlnd	AAA	4	4	0	0	20.0	95	29	15	15	4	0	2	0	9	0	12	0	0	1	2	.333	0	0- -	-	7.94	6.75
2006	Mobile	AA	12	10	0	1	52.1	230	58	35	28	6	1	1	3	18	3	49	1	0	3	5	.375	0	0- -	-	4.73	4.82
2007	Lk Els	A+	13	0	0	4	20.0	87	23	11	4	0	0	0	1	6	2	16	1	0	0	1	.000	0	0- -	-	3.86	1.80
2007	SnAnt	AA	32	1	0	8	59.1	242	54	24	21	6	2	0	2	9	1	55	4	0	4	1	.800	0	2- -	-	2.72	3.19
2007	Portlnd	AAA	2	0	0	0	2.2	17	9	7	7	2	1	0	0	1	0	1	1	0	0	0	-	0	0- -	-	30.21	23.63
2008	Portlnd	AAA	46	2	0	7	84.0	362	84	36	35	7	4	3	3	28	4	98	3	1	2	3	.400	0	2- -	-	3.73	3.75
2008	SD	NL	10	3	0	3	16.2	84	27	18	18	2	0	0	0	10	1	14	4	0	0	2	.000	0	0-0	0	8.97	9.72

Nathan Haynes

Bats: L **Throws:** L **Pos:** RF-15; PR-3; LF-2; CF-2; PH-2; DH-1 **Ht:** 5'9" **Wt:** 170 **Born:** 9/7/1979 **Age:** 29

						BATTING														BASERUNNING				AVERAGES		
Year	Team	Lg	G	AB	H	2B	3B	HR	(Hm	Rd)	TB	R	RBI	RC	TBB	IBB	SO	HBP	SH	SF	SB	CS	SB%	GDP	Avg	OBP	Slg
1997	As	R	17	54	15	1	0	0	(-	-)	16	8	6	7	7	0	9	2	1	0	5	1	.83	3	.278	.381	.296
1997	SoOre	A-	24	82	23	1	1	0	(-	-)	26	18	9	18	26	0	21	2	0	1	19	3	.86	1	.280	.459	.317
1998	Mdest	A+	125	507	128	13	7	1	(-	-)	158	89	41	57	54	2	139	4	6	2	42	18	.70	10	.252	.328	.312
1999	Visalia	A+	35	145	45	7	1	1	(-	-)	57	28	14	22	17	0	27	3	2	1	12	10	.55	1	.310	.392	.393
1999	Lk Els	A+	26	110	36	5	5	1	(-	-)	54	19	15	21	12	0	19	1	0	1	10	5	.67	2	.327	.395	.491
1999	Erie	AA	5	19	3	1	0	0	(-	-)	4	3	0	2	5	0	5	1	0	0	0	0	-	0	.158	.360	.211
2000	Erie	AA	118	457	116	16	4	6	(-	-)	158	56	43	52	33	0	107	9	8	2	37	20	.65	3	.254	.315	.346
2001	Ark	AA	79	316	98	11	5	5	(-	-)	134	49	23	53	32	2	65	3	2	0	33	15	.69	4	.310	.379	.424
2002	RCuca	A+	11	50	14	0	0	0	(-	-)	14	6	2	6	4	0	8	1	0	0	6	2	.75	0	.280	.345	.280
2002	Salt Lk	AAA	67	283	80	14	6	2	(-	-)	112	37	12	33	12	0	53	1	1	1	10	10	.50	3	.283	.313	.396
2003	Ark	AA	91	372	110	16	10	5	(-	-)	161	59	42	58	34	3	74	2	4	2	27	9	.75	6	.296	.356	.433
2003	Salt Lk	AAA	28	120	26	3	3	1	(-	-)	38	16	7	11	9	1	20	2	0	1	6	0	1.00	2	.217	.280	.317
2004	Fresno	AAA	1	4	1	0	1	0	(-	-)	3	1	0	0	0	0	1	0	0	0	0	0	1.00	0	.250	.250	.750
2005	Giants	R	7	16	4	1	2	0	(-	-)	9	4	1	3	3	0	0	0	0	0	3	0	1.00	0	.250	.368	.563
2006	Gary	IND	31	114	30	4	1	5	(-	-)	51	24	17	18	9	0	22	1	0	0	8	1	.89	2	.263	.323	.447
2006	Ark	AA	52	207	58	14	3	2	(-	-)	84	38	19	30	22	1	49	1	3	1	19	10	.66	5	.280	.351	.406
2006	Salt Lk	AAA	16	50	13	1	2	1	(-	-)	21	7	11	6	4	0	15	1	2	1	3	2	.60	0	.228	.286	.368
2007	Salt Lk	AAA	44	171	66	9	6	4	(-	-)	99	33	32	43	22	2	36	2	3	0	14	7	.67	5	.386	.462	.579
2008	Drham	AAA	77	277	70	8	2	2	(-	-)	88	28	24	27	11	1	59	3	4	2	13	3	.81	7	.253	.287	.318

131

				BATTING																BASERUNNING				AVERAGES		
Year Team	Lg	G	AB	H	2B	3B	HR	(Hm Rd)	TB	R	RBI	RC	TBB	IBB	SO	HBP	SH	SF	SB	CS	SB%	GDP	Avg	OBP	Slg
2007 LAA	AL	40	45	12	0	1	0	(0 0)	14	10	1	5	3	0	11	0	0	0	1	2	.33	0	.267	.313	.311
2008 TB	AL	20	44	10	0	0	0	(0 0)	10	3	3	3	3	0	12	0	0	0	4	1	.80	1	.227	.277	.227
Postseason		1	1	0	0	0	0	(0 0)	0	0	0	0	0	0	1	0	0	0	0	0	-	0	.000	.000	.000
2 ML YEARS		60	89	22	0	1	0	(0 0)	24	13	4	8	6	0	23	0	0	0	5	3	.63	1	.247	.295	.270

Chase Headley

Bats: B **Throws:** R **Pos:** LF-82; 3B-7; PH-3   **Ht:** 6'2" **Wt:** 195 **Born:** 5/9/1984 **Age:** 25

				BATTING																BASERUNNING				AVERAGES		
Year Team	Lg	G	AB	H	2B	3B	HR	(Hm Rd)	TB	R	RBI	RC	TBB	IBB	SO	HBP	SH	SF	SB	CS	SB%	GDP	Avg	OBP	Slg
2005 Eugene	A-	57	220	59	14	3	6	(- -)	97	29	33	38	34	1	48	4	0	1	1	1	.50	6	.268	.375	.441
2005 FtWyn	A	4	15	3	0	0	0	(- -)	3	2	1	0	1	0	4	0	0	0	0	0	-	1	.200	.250	.200
2006 Lk Els	A+	129	484	141	33	0	12	(- -)	210	79	73	86	74	3	96	5	5	3	4	5	.44	10	.291	.389	.434
2007 SnAnt	AA	121	433	143	38	5	20	(- -)	251	82	78	109	74	7	114	11	0	4	1	0	1.00	7	.330	.437	.580
2008 Portlnd	AAA	65	259	79	24	1	13	(- -)	144	49	40	54	31	0	65	3	0	2	0	0	-	10	.305	.383	.556
2007 SD	NL	8	18	4	1	0	0	(0 0)	5	1	0	1	2	0	4	1	0	0	0	0	-	2	.222	.333	.278
2008 SD	NL	91	331	89	19	2	9	(4 5)	139	34	38	42	30	1	104	5	0	2	4	1	.80	5	.269	.337	.420
2 ML YEARS		99	349	93	20	2	9	(4 5)	144	35	38	43	32	1	108	6	0	2	4	1	.80	7	.266	.337	.413

Aaron Heilman

Pitches: R **Bats:** R **Pos:** RP-78   **Ht:** 6'5" **Wt:** 227 **Born:** 11/12/1978 **Age:** 30

		HOW MUCH HE PITCHED						WHAT HE GAVE UP											THE RESULTS							
Year Team	Lg	G	GS	CG	GF	IP	BFP	H	R	ER	HR	SH	SF	HB	TBB	IBB	SO	WP	Bk	W	L	Pct	ShO	Sv-Op	Hld	ERC	ERA
2003 NYM	NL	14	13	0	0	65.1	315	79	53	49	13	5	3	3	41	2	51	5	0	2	7	.222	0	0-0	0	7.16	6.75
2004 NYM	NL	5	5	0	0	28.0	119	27	17	17	4	1	0	0	13	0	22	0	0	1	3	.250	0	0-0	0	4.54	5.46
2005 NYM	NL	53	7	1	20	108.0	439	87	40	38	6	4	1	6	37	4	106	1	1	5	3	.625	1	5-6	5	2.74	3.17
2006 NYM	NL	74	0	0	14	87.0	356	73	37	35	5	7	2	3	28	2	73	5	0	4	5	.444	0	0-5	27	2.76	3.62
2007 NYM	NL	81	0	0	28	86.0	352	72	36	29	8	4	2	5	20	1	63	2	0	7	7	.500	0	1-6	22	2.71	3.03
2008 NYM	NL	78	0	0	23	76.0	356	75	48	44	10	8	2	9	46	8	80	2	0	3	8	.273	0	3-8	15	5.26	5.21
Postseason		6	0	0	1	7.1	30	7	3	3	2	0	0	0	1	1	6	1	0	1	0	1.000	0	0-0	1	3.60	3.68
6 ML YEARS		305	25	1	85	450.1	1937	413	231	212	46	29	10	26	185	17	395	15	1	22	33	.400	1	9-25	69	3.83	4.24

Wes Helms

Bats: R **Throws:** R **Pos:** 3B-60; PH-46; 1B-42; PR-7; LF-1   **Ht:** 6'4" **Wt:** 220 **Born:** 5/12/1976 **Age:** 33

				BATTING																BASERUNNING				AVERAGES		
Year Team	Lg	G	AB	H	2B	3B	HR	(Hm Rd)	TB	R	RBI	RC	TBB	IBB	SO	HBP	SH	SF	SB	CS	SB%	GDP	Avg	OBP	Slg
1998 Atl	NL	7	13	4	1	0	1	(0 1)	8	2	2	2	0	0	4	0	0	0	0	0	-	0	.308	.308	.615
2000 Atl	NL	6	5	1	0	0	0	(0 0)	1	0	0	0	0	0	2	0	0	0	0	0	-	0	.200	.200	.200
2001 Atl	NL	100	216	48	10	3	10	(6 4)	94	28	36	27	21	2	56	1	0	1	1	1	.50	3	.222	.293	.435
2002 Atl	NL	85	210	51	16	0	6	(4 2)	85	20	22	15	11	2	57	3	1	6	1	1	.50	5	.243	.283	.405
2003 Mil	NL	134	476	124	21	0	23	(16 7)	214	56	67	66	43	3	131	10	0	7	0	1	.00	10	.261	.330	.450
2004 Mil	NL	92	274	72	13	1	4	(3 1)	99	24	28	28	24	1	60	5	1	2	0	1	.00	6	.263	.331	.361
2005 Mil	NL	95	168	50	13	1	4	(2 2)	77	18	24	26	14	0	30	3	0	3	0	1	.00	7	.298	.356	.458
2006 Fla	NL	140	240	79	19	5	10	(4 6)	138	30	47	45	21	1	55	6	6	5	0	4	.00	7	.329	.390	.575
2007 Phi	NL	112	280	69	19	0	5	(3 2)	103	21	39	24	19	2	62	3	2	4	0	0	-	10	.246	.297	.368
2008 Fla	NL	132	251	61	11	0	5	(1 4)	87	28	31	29	17	0	65	5	0	5	0	0	-	6	.243	.299	.347
Postseason		3	2	0	0	0	0	(0 0)	0	1	0	0	1	0	0	0	0	0	0	0	-	0	.000	.333	.000
10 ML YEARS		903	2133	559	123	10	68	(39 29)	906	227	296	262	170	11	522	36	10	33	2	9	.18	58	.262	.323	.425

Todd Helton

Bats: L **Throws:** L **Pos:** 1B-81; PH-2   **Ht:** 6'2" **Wt:** 210 **Born:** 8/20/1973 **Age:** 35

				BATTING																BASERUNNING				AVERAGES		
Year Team	Lg	G	AB	H	2B	3B	HR	(Hm Rd)	TB	R	RBI	RC	TBB	IBB	SO	HBP	SH	SF	SB	CS	SB%	GDP	Avg	OBP	Slg
1997 Col	NL	35	93	26	2	1	5	(3 2)	45	13	11	15	8	0	11	0	0	0	0	1	.00	1	.280	.337	.484
1998 Col	NL	152	530	167	37	1	25	(13 12)	281	78	97	101	53	5	54	6	1	5	3	3	.50	15	.315	.380	.530
1999 Col	NL	159	578	185	39	5	35	(23 12)	339	114	113	124	68	6	77	6	0	4	7	6	.54	14	.320	.395	.587
2000 Col	NL	160	580	216	59	2	42	(27 15)	405	138	147	169	103	22	61	4	0	10	5	3	.63	12	.372	.463	.698
2001 Col	NL	159	587	197	54	2	49	(27 22)	402	132	146	157	98	15	104	5	1	5	7	5	.58	14	.336	.432	.685
2002 Col	NL	156	553	182	39	4	30	(18 12)	319	107	109	127	99	21	91	5	0	10	5	1	.83	10	.329	.429	.577
2003 Col	NL	160	583	209	49	5	33	(23 10)	367	135	117	160	111	21	72	2	0	7	0	4	.00	19	.358	.458	.630
2004 Col	NL	154	547	190	49	2	32	(21 11)	339	115	96	143	127	19	72	3	0	6	3	0	1.00	12	.347	.469	.620
2005 Col	NL	144	509	163	45	2	20	(13 7)	272	92	79	114	106	22	80	9	1	1	3	0	1.00	14	.320	.445	.534
2006 Col	NL	145	546	165	40	5	15	(8 7)	260	94	81	118	91	15	64	6	0	6	3	2	.60	10	.302	.404	.476
2007 Col	NL	154	557	178	42	2	17	(9 8)	275	86	91	115	116	16	74	2	0	7	0	1	.00	15	.320	.434	.494
2008 Col	NL	83	299	79	16	0	7	(5 2)	116	39	29	45	61	8	50	1	0	0	0	0	-	9	.264	.391	.388
Postseason		11	41	9	2	1	0	(0 0)	13	6	2	2	5	0	9	0	0	1	0	0	-	0	.220	.298	.317
12 ML YEARS		1661	5962	1957	471	31	310	(190 120)	3420	1143	1116	1388	1041	170	810	49	3	61	36	26	.58	145	.328	.428	.574

Mark Hendrickson

Pitches: L **Bats:** L **Pos:** SP-19; RP-17   **Ht:** 6'9" **Wt:** 230 **Born:** 6/23/1974 **Age:** 35

		HOW MUCH HE PITCHED						WHAT HE GAVE UP											THE RESULTS							
Year Team	Lg	G	GS	CG	GF	IP	BFP	H	R	ER	HR	SH	SF	HB	TBB	IBB	SO	WP	Bk	W	L	Pct	ShO	Sv-Op	Hld	ERC	ERA
2002 Tor	AL	16	4	0	0	36.2	142	25	11	10	1	2	2	2	12	3	21	0	0	3	0	1.000	0	0-1	1	1.90	2.45
2003 Tor	AL	30	30	1	0	158.1	703	207	111	97	24	1	8	0	40	3	76	4	0	9	9	.500	1	0-0	0	5.64	5.51
2004 TB	AL	32	30	2	1	183.1	803	211	113	98	21	4	5	7	46	5	87	5	2	10	15	.400	0	0-0	0	4.51	4.81
2005 TB	AL	31	31	1	0	178.1	796	227	126	117	24	8	7	2	49	1	89	4	1	11	8	.579	0	0-0	0	5.44	5.90

			HOW MUCH HE PITCHED						WHAT HE GAVE UP											THE RESULTS							
Year	Team	Lg	G	GS	CG	GF	IP	BFP	H	R	ER	HR	SH	SF	HB	TBB	IBB	SO	WP	Bk	W	L	Pct	ShO	Sv-Op	Hld	ERC	ERA
2006	2 Tms		31	25	1	0	164.2	719	173	87	77	17	5	4	4	62	0	99	6	1	6	15	.286	1	0-0	1	4.38	4.21
2007	LAD	NL	39	15	0	4	122.2	532	142	75	71	15	12	4	1	29	4	92	4	0	4	8	.333	0	0-1	2	4.42	5.21
2008	Fla	NL	36	19	0	4	133.2	590	148	87	81	17	9	5	5	48	7	81	4	0	7	8	.467	0	0-0	3	4.78	5.45
06	TB	AL	13	13	1	0	89.2	377	81	42	38	10	2	3	2	34	0	51	4	0	4	8	.333	1	0-0	0	3.65	3.81
06	LAD	NL	18	12	0	0	75.0	342	92	45	39	7	3	1	2	28	0	48	2	1	2	7	.222	0	0-0	1	5.29	4.68
	Postseason		3	0	0	0	2.2	10	1	0	0	0	0	0	1	1	0	1	0	0	0	0	-	0	0-0	0	1.70	0.00
	7 ML YEARS		215	154	5	9	977.2	4285	1133	610	551	119	41	35	21	286	23	545	27	4	50	63	.442	2	0-2	7	4.75	5.07

Sean Henn

Pitches: L Bats: R Pos: RP-4   Ht: 6'4" Wt: 225 Born: 4/23/1981 Age: 28

			HOW MUCH HE PITCHED						WHAT HE GAVE UP											THE RESULTS							
Year	Team	Lg	G	GS	CG	GF	IP	BFP	H	R	ER	HR	SH	SF	HB	TBB	IBB	SO	WP	Bk	W	L	Pct	ShO	Sv-Op	Hld	ERC	ERA
2008	Tampa*	A+	3	0	0	0	4.0	16	5	0	0	0	0	0	0	0	0	5	0	0	0	0	-	0	0--	-	3.37	0.00
2008	S-WB*	AAA	5	0	0	0	6.2	27	5	2	1	0	1	1	0	1	0	7	0	0	1	0	1.000	0	0--	-	1.38	1.35
2008	Portlnd*	AAA	9	0	0	3	6.1	38	10	10	10	1	1	1	0	10	0	3	1	0	0	0	-	0	0--	-	13.81	14.21
2005	NYY	AL	3	3	0	0	11.1	61	18	16	14	3	0	0	0	11	0	3	0	0	0	3	.000	0	0-0	0	12.12	11.12
2006	NYY	AL	4	1	0	0	9.1	44	11	5	5	2	0	1	1	5	0	7	0	0	0	1	.000	0	0-0	0	7.09	4.82
2007	NYY	AL	29	1	0	8	36.2	181	44	32	29	6	1	0	3	27	1	28	1	0	2	2	.500	0	0-0	2	7.47	7.12
2008	SD	NL	4	0	0	2	9.1	47	11	8	8	1	1	0	0	9	1	9	1	0	0	0	-	0	0-0	1	7.32	7.71
	4 ML YEARS		40	5	0	10	66.2	333	84	61	56	12	2	1	4	52	2	47	2	0	2	6	.250	0	0-0	2	8.15	7.56

Brad Hennessey

Pitches: R Bats: R Pos: RP-13; SP-4   Ht: 6'2" Wt: 193 Born: 2/7/1980 Age: 29

			HOW MUCH HE PITCHED						WHAT HE GAVE UP											THE RESULTS							
Year	Team	Lg	G	GS	CG	GF	IP	BFP	H	R	ER	HR	SH	SF	HB	TBB	IBB	SO	WP	Bk	W	L	Pct	ShO	Sv-Op	Hld	ERC	ERA
2008	Fresno*	AAA	21	21	3	0	132.1	568	157	78	71	22	6	5	1	37	0	69	2	0	7	10	.412	0	0--	-	5.29	4.83
2004	SF	NL	7	7	0	0	34.1	163	42	24	19	2	4	1	0	15	1	25	1	0	2	2	.500	0	0-0	0	4.91	4.98
2005	SF	NL	21	21	0	0	118.1	521	127	63	61	15	2	3	4	52	3	64	3	1	5	8	.385	0	0-0	0	5.00	4.64
2006	SF	NL	34	12	0	0	99.1	428	92	53	47	12	6	2	10	42	1	42	3	0	5	6	.455	0	1-1	2	4.34	4.26
2007	SF	NL	69	0	0	34	68.1	287	66	26	26	7	4	0	3	23	1	40	2	0	4	5	.444	0	19-24	13	3.87	3.42
2008	SF	NL	17	4	1	4	40.1	196	63	35	35	8	3	1	1	15	1	21	1	0	1	2	.333	0	0-1	0	8.28	7.81
	5 ML YEARS		148	44	1	47	360.2	1595	390	201	188	44	19	7	18	147	7	192	10	1	17	23	.425	0	20-26	15	4.92	4.69

Clay Hensley

Pitches: R Bats: R Pos: RP-31; SP-1   Ht: 5'11" Wt: 185 Born: 8/31/1979 Age: 29

			HOW MUCH HE PITCHED						WHAT HE GAVE UP											THE RESULTS							
Year	Team	Lg	G	GS	CG	GF	IP	BFP	H	R	ER	HR	SH	SF	HB	TBB	IBB	SO	WP	Bk	W	L	Pct	ShO	Sv-Op	Hld	ERC	ERA
2008	Lk Els*	A+	1	0	0	0	1.0	4	1	0	0	0	0	0	0	0	0	1	0	0	1	0	1.000	0	0--	-	1.95	0.00
2008	Portlnd*	AAA	16	10	0	0	48.0	204	46	23	21	7	0	0	3	16	0	34	3	0	1	1	.500	0	0--	-	4.17	3.94
2005	SD	NL	24	1	0	5	47.2	189	33	12	9	0	1	2	0	17	2	28	2	0	1	1	.500	0	0-0	2	1.70	1.70
2006	SD	NL	37	29	1	2	187.0	787	174	82	77	15	10	3	3	76	7	122	3	0	11	12	.478	1	0-1	1	3.64	3.71
2007	SD	NL	13	9	0	1	50.0	238	62	40	38	5	2	1	1	32	2	30	4	1	2	3	.400	0	0-0	0	6.54	6.84
2008	SD	NL	32	1	0	8	39.0	173	36	27	23	2	1	3	1	25	3	26	1	0	1	2	.333	0	0-1	3	4.23	5.31
	Postseason		5	0	0	1	7.1	32	6	2	2	0	1	0	0	4	0	1	0	0	0	0	-	0	0-0	0	2.87	2.45
	4 ML YEARS		106	40	1	16	323.2	1387	305	161	147	22	14	9	5	150	14	206	10	1	15	18	.455	1	0-2	6	3.81	4.09

Matt Herges

Pitches: R Bats: L Pos: RP-58   Ht: 6'0" Wt: 210 Born: 4/1/1970 Age: 39

			HOW MUCH HE PITCHED						WHAT HE GAVE UP											THE RESULTS							
Year	Team	Lg	G	GS	CG	GF	IP	BFP	H	R	ER	HR	SH	SF	HB	TBB	IBB	SO	WP	Bk	W	L	Pct	ShO	Sv-Op	Hld	ERC	ERA
2008	ColSpr*	AAA	2	0	0	0	2.0	11	2	1	1	1	0	0	0	0	0	1	0	0	0	0	-	0	0--	-	4.70	4.50
1999	LAD	NL	17	0	0	9	24.1	104	24	13	11	5	1	0	1	8	0	18	0	0	0	2	.000	0	0-2	1	4.61	4.07
2000	LAD	NL	59	4	0	17	110.2	461	100	43	39	7	9	4	6	40	5	75	4	0	11	3	.786	0	1-3	4	3.35	3.17
2001	LAD	NL	75	0	0	22	99.1	435	97	39	38	8	4	3	8	46	12	76	2	0	9	8	.529	0	1-8	15	4.20	3.44
2002	Mon	NL	62	0	0	25	64.2	298	80	33	29	10	6	2	2	26	8	50	3	0	2	5	.286	0	6-14	9	5.74	4.04
2003	2 Tms	NL	67	0	0	24	79.0	332	68	27	24	3	2	6	3	29	2	68	1	1	3	2	.600	0	3-6	9	2.87	2.62
2004	SF	NL	70	0	0	43	65.1	301	90	44	38	8	7	4	3	21	4	39	2	0	4	5	.444	0	23-31	5	6.29	5.23
2005	2 Tms	NL	28	0	0	7	29.0	132	35	23	23	6	2	2	1	12	1	9	0	0	1	1	.500	0	0-0	3	6.26	7.14
2006	Fla	NL	66	0	0	21	71.0	328	94	42	34	5	3	1	3	28	5	36	1	0	2	3	.400	0	0-4	9	5.81	4.31
2007	Col	NL	35	0	0	9	48.2	191	34	17	16	4	3	1	0	15	2	30	0	0	5	1	.833	0	0-2	3	2.05	2.96
2008	Col	NL	58	0	0	10	64.1	294	79	40	36	5	1	4	5	24	5	46	3	1	3	4	.429	0	0-5	4	5.29	5.04
03	SD	NL	40	0	0	21	44.0	192	40	16	14	2	1	5	2	20	2	40	1	0	2	2	.500	0	3-5	4	3.45	2.86
03	SF	NL	27	0	0	3	35.0	140	28	11	9	1	1	1	1	9	0	28	0	1	1	0	1.000	0	0-1	5	2.18	2.31
05	SF	NL	21	0	0	5	21.0	90	23	11	11	2	2	1	0	7	1	6	0	0	1	1	.500	0	0-0	3	4.29	4.71
05	Ari	NL	7	0	0	2	8.0	42	12	12	12	4	0	1	1	5	0	3	0	0	0	0	-	0	0-0	0	12.23	13.50
	Postseason		10	0	0	0	11.1	41	3	0	0	1	0	1	0	5	0	11	0	0	1	0	1.000	0	0-0	1	0.88	0.00
	10 ML YEARS		537	4	0	187	656.1	2876	701	321	287	61	38	27	32	249	44	447	16	2	40	34	.541	0	34-75	62	4.43	3.94

Jeremy Hermida

Bats: L **Throws:** R **Pos:** RF-132; PH-14; PR-2   **Ht:** 6'3" **Wt:** 210 **Born:** 1/30/1984 **Age:** 25

								BATTING												BASERUNNING				AVERAGES		
Year Team	Lg	G	AB	H	2B	3B	HR	(Hm	Rd)	TB	R	RBI	RC	TBB	IBB	SO	HBP	SH	SF	SB	CS	SB%	GDP	Avg	OBP	Slg
2008 Jupiter*	A+	5	15	5	1	0	1	(-	-)	9	6	1	4	4	1	3	0	0	0	0	0	-	1	.333	.474	.600
2005 Fla	NL	23	41	12	2	0	4	(4	0)	26	9	11	10	6	1	12	0	0	0	2	0	1.00	1	.293	.383	.634
2006 Fla	NL	99	307	77	19	1	5	(3	2)	113	37	28	38	33	3	70	5	2	1	4	1	.80	6	.251	.332	.368
2007 Fla	NL	123	429	127	32	1	18	(8	10)	215	54	63	69	47	2	105	4	1	3	3	4	.43	10	.296	.369	.501
2008 Fla	NL	142	502	125	22	3	17	(4	13)	204	74	61	65	48	5	138	7	1	1	6	1	.86	12	.249	.323	.406
4 ML YEARS		387	1279	341	75	5	44	(19	25)	558	174	163	182	134	11	325	16	4	5	15	6	.71	29	.267	.342	.436

Anderson Hernandez

Bats: B **Throws:** R **Pos:** 2B-16; PH-9; SS-3   **Ht:** 5'9" **Wt:** 170 **Born:** 10/30/1982 **Age:** 26

								BATTING												BASERUNNING				AVERAGES		
Year Team	Lg	G	AB	H	2B	3B	HR	(Hm	Rd)	TB	R	RBI	RC	TBB	IBB	SO	HBP	SH	SF	SB	CS	SB%	GDP	Avg	OBP	Slg
2008 NewOr*	AAA	125	479	97	21	7	5	(-	-)	147	57	36	38	38	1	95	1	3	2	11	8	.58	12	.203	.262	.307
2005 NYM	NL	6	18	1	0	0	0	(0	0)	1	1	0	0	1	0	4	0	0	0	0	1	.00	0	.056	.105	.056
2006 NYM	NL	25	66	10	1	1	1	(1	0)	16	4	3	0	1	0	12	0	0	0	0	0	-	3	.152	.164	.242
2007 NYM	NL	4	3	1	0	0	0	(0	0)	1	1	0	0	0	0	1	0	0	0	0	0	-	0	.333	.333	.333
2008 Was	NL	28	81	27	4	0	0	(0	0)	31	11	17	18	10	0	8	0	0	0	0	0	-	1	.333	.407	.383
Postseason		2	1	0	0	0	0	(0	0)	0	0	0	0	0	0	1	0	0	0	0	0	-	0	.000	.000	.000
4 ML YEARS		63	168	39	5	1	1	(1	0)	49	17	20	18	12	0	25	0	0	0	0	1	.00	4	.232	.283	.292

Felix Hernandez

Pitches: R **Bats:** R **Pos:** SP-31   **Ht:** 6'3" **Wt:** 230 **Born:** 4/8/1986 **Age:** 23

		HOW MUCH HE PITCHED						WHAT HE GAVE UP											THE RESULTS						
Year Team	Lg	G	GS	CG	GF	IP	BFP	H	R	ER	HR	SH	SF	HB	TBB	IBB	SO	WP	Bk	W	L	Pct	ShO	Sv-Op Hld	ERC	ERA
2005 Sea	AL	12	12	0	0	84.1	328	61	26	25	5	1	2	2	23	0	77	3	0	4	4	.500	0	0-0 0	2.08	2.67
2006 Sea	AL	31	31	2	0	191.0	816	195	105	96	23	2	3	6	60	2	176	11	0	12	14	.462	1	0-0 0	4.11	4.52
2007 Sea	AL	30	30	1	0	190.1	808	209	88	83	20	6	1	3	53	4	165	7	1	14	7	.667	1	0-0 0	4.27	3.92
2008 Sea	AL	31	31	2	0	200.2	857	198	85	77	17	4	6	8	80	7	175	8	1	9	11	.450	0	0-0 0	4.05	3.45
4 ML YEARS		104	104	5	0	666.1	2809	663	304	281	65	13	12	19	216	13	593	29	2	39	36	.520	2	0-0 0	3.86	3.80

Fernando Hernandez

Pitches: R **Bats:** R **Pos:** RP-3   **Ht:** 5'11" **Wt:** 190 **Born:** 7/31/1984 **Age:** 24

		HOW MUCH HE PITCHED						WHAT HE GAVE UP											THE RESULTS						
Year Team	Lg	G	GS	CG	GF	IP	BFP	H	R	ER	HR	SH	SF	HB	TBB	IBB	SO	WP	Bk	W	L	Pct	ShO	Sv-Op Hld	ERC	ERA
2003 Gr Falls	R+	24	0	0	23	23.1	101	23	10	7	0	1	1	1	10	0	14	7	0	1	3	.250	0	7-- -	3.58	2.70
2004 Knapol	A-	28	0	0	11	45.1	198	43	20	15	2	0	0	3	16	1	59	3	0	3	3	.500	0	4-- -	3.36	2.98
2004 WinSa	A+	2	0	0	2	2.0	8	1	0	0	0	0	0	0	1	0	1	0	0	0	0	-	0	0-- -	1.41	0.00
2005 WinSa	A+	45	0	0	16	70.0	317	83	44	40	6	5	4	4	30	0	59	3	0	4	1	.800	0	1-- -	5.44	5.14
2006 WinSa	A+	57	0	0	34	65.1	281	50	24	14	4	2	1	4	32	0	81	4	0	7	5	.583	0	13-- -	3.06	1.93
2007 Brham	AA	60	0	0	27	85.1	349	73	30	29	4	5	2	2	23	0	84	4	0	1	3	.250	0	9-- -	2.56	3.06
2008 Brham	AA	41	0	0	12	58.0	260	60	32	30	2	5	3	4	29	1	47	1	0	6	5	.545	0	0-- -	4.43	4.66
2008 Oak	AL	3	0	0	1	3.0	19	4	6	6	0	0	0	1	5	0	2	0	0	1	0	1.000	0	0-0 0	11.80	18.00

Livan Hernandez

Pitches: R **Bats:** R **Pos:** SP-31   **Ht:** 6'2" **Wt:** 245 **Born:** 2/20/1975 **Age:** 34

		HOW MUCH HE PITCHED						WHAT HE GAVE UP											THE RESULTS						
Year Team	Lg	G	GS	CG	GF	IP	BFP	H	R	ER	HR	SH	SF	HB	TBB	IBB	SO	WP	Bk	W	L	Pct	ShO	Sv-Op Hld	ERC	ERA
1996 Fla	NL	1	0	0	0	3.0	13	3	0	0	0	0	0	0	2	0	2	0	0	0	0	-	0	0-0 0	4.60	0.00
1997 Fla	NL	17	17	0	0	96.1	405	81	39	34	5	4	7	3	38	1	72	0	0	9	3	.750	0	0-0 0	2.96	3.18
1998 Fla	NL	33	33	9	0	234.1	1040	265	133	123	37	8	5	6	104	8	162	4	3	10	12	.455	0	0-0 0	5.58	4.72
1999 2 Tms	NL	30	30	2	0	199.2	886	227	110	103	23	7	6	2	76	5	144	2	2	8	12	.400	0	0-0 0	4.88	4.64
2000 SF	NL	33	33	5	0	240.0	1030	254	114	100	22	12	9	4	73	3	165	3	0	17	11	.607	2	0-0 0	4.01	3.75
2001 SF	NL	34	34	2	0	226.2	1008	266	143	132	24	12	12	4	85	7	138	7	0	13	15	.464	0	0-0 0	5.03	5.24
2002 SF	NL	33	33	5	0	216.0	921	233	113	105	19	14	8	4	71	5	134	1	1	12	16	.429	3	0-0 0	4.26	4.38
2003 Mon	NL	33	33	8	0	233.1	967	225	92	83	27	6	4	10	57	3	178	6	1	15	10	.600	0	0-0 0	3.55	3.20
2004 Mon	NL	35	35	9	0	255.0	1053	234	105	102	26	11	4	10	83	9	186	1	0	11	15	.423	1	0-0 0	3.52	3.60
2005 Was	NL	35	35	2	0	246.1	1065	268	116	109	25	15	9	13	84	14	147	3	2	15	10	.600	0	0-0 0	4.54	3.98
2006 2 Tms	NL	34	34	0	0	216.0	959	246	125	116	29	16	8	4	78	6	128	1	0	13	13	.500	0	0-0 0	4.97	4.83
2007 Ari	NL	33	33	1	0	204.1	913	247	116	112	34	17	8	6	79	1	90	3	2	11	11	.500	0	0-0 0	5.94	4.93
2008 2 Tms	NL	31	31	2	0	180.0	811	257	129	121	25	5	9	2	43	4	67	3	1	13	11	.542	0	0-0 0	6.35	6.05
99 Fla	NL	20	20	2	0	136.0	612	161	78	72	17	3	4	2	55	3	97	2	1	5	9	.357	0	0-0 0	5.37	4.76
99 SF	NL	10	10	0	0	63.2	274	66	32	31	6	4	2	0	21	2	47	0	1	3	3	.500	0	0-0 0	3.88	4.38
06 Was	NL	24	24	0	0	146.2	661	176	94	87	22	10	7	2	52	4	89	0	0	9	8	.529	0	0-0 0	5.38	5.34
06 Ari	NL	10	10	0	0	69.1	298	70	31	29	7	6	1	2	26	2	39	1	0	4	5	.444	0	0-0 0	4.13	3.76
08 Min	AL	23	23	2	0	139.2	627	199	93	85	18	4	9	1	29	3	54	2	1	10	8	.556	0	0-0 0	6.06	5.48
08 Col	NL	8	8	0	0	40.1	184	58	36	36	7	1	0	1	14	1	13	1	0	3	3	.500	0	0-0 0	7.38	8.03
Postseason		12	10	1	0	68.0	305	67	32	30	6	5	2	4	36	3	47	1	0	7	3	.700	0	0-0 0	4.56	3.97
13 ML YEARS		382	381	45	0	2551.0	11071	2806	1335	1240	296	127	89	67	873	66	1613	34	12	147	139	.514	7	0-0 0	4.63	4.37

Luis Hernandez

Bats: B **Throws:** R **Pos:** SS-30; 2B-5; PR-2; PH-1 **Ht:** 5'10" **Wt:** 182 **Born:** 6/26/1984 **Age:** 25

Year	Team	Lg	G	AB	H	2B	3B	HR	(Hm	Rd)	TB	R	RBI	RC	TBB	IBB	SO	HBP	SH	SF	SB	CS	SB%	GDP	Avg	OBP	Slg
2002	Braves	R	53	201	51	8	4	0	(-	-)	67	34	20	23	19	0	29	4	1	0	11	6	.65	1	.254	.330	.333
2003	Rome	A	111	337	78	4	1	2	(-	-)	90	27	25	27	24	2	42	2	18	0	7	3	.70	7	.231	.287	.267
2004	MrtlBh	A+	117	402	109	23	4	6	(-	-)	158	49	45	49	16	0	70	5	10	2	8	6	.57	12	.271	.306	.393
2005	Missi	AA	122	415	101	12	5	2	(-	-)	129	47	32	43	41	2	56	4	6	3	5	5	.50	11	.243	.315	.311
2005	Braves	R	1	4	1	0	0	0	(-	-)	4	1	1	1	0	0	2	0	0	0	0	0	-	0	.250	.250	1.000
2006	Missi	AA	104	380	102	12	4	1	(-	-)	125	39	29	39	20	1	46	3	7	3	4	4	.50	8	.268	.308	.329
2006	Rchmd	AAA	19	73	14	4	0	1	(-	-)	21	3	5	3	0	0	8	0	1	0	0	1	.00	0	.192	.192	.288
2007	Bowie	AA	92	364	88	15	6	0	(-	-)	115	42	37	32	18	0	50	1	6	4	6	5	.55	6	.242	.276	.316
2007	Norfolk	AAA	9	33	9	0	0	0	(-	-)	9	4	3	2	0	0	5	0	1	0	0	0	-	1	.273	.273	.273
2008	Norfolk	AAA	57	205	38	7	0	0	(-	-)	45	18	11	7	8	0	27	0	3	0	2	2	.50	8	.185	.216	.220
2007	Bal	AL	30	69	20	2	0	1	(1	0)	25	5	7	6	1	0	10	0	1	0	2	2	.50	1	.290	.300	.362
2008	Bal	AL	36	79	19	1	0	0	(0	0)	20	9	3	6	7	0	11	0	3	2	2	0	1.00	2	.241	.295	.253
	2 ML YEARS		66	148	39	3	0	1	(1	0)	45	14	10	12	8	0	21	0	4	2	4	2	.67	3	.264	.297	.304

Michel Hernandez

Bats: R **Throws:** R **Pos:** C-4; DH-1; PH-1 **Ht:** 6'0" **Wt:** 211 **Born:** 8/12/1978 **Age:** 30

Year	Team	Lg	G	AB	H	2B	3B	HR	(Hm	Rd)	TB	R	RBI	RC	TBB	IBB	SO	HBP	SH	SF	SB	CS	SB%	GDP	Avg	OBP	Slg
1998	Oneont	A-	61	205	52	8	2	0	(-	-)	64	29	24	18	20	0	19	0	1	1	4	4	.50	10	.254	.319	.312
1999	Tampa	A+	82	281	69	10	1	2	(-	-)	87	26	23	24	18	0	49	3	3	2	2	2	.50	8	.246	.296	.310
2000	Nrwich	AA	21	66	14	2	0	0	(-	-)	16	7	4	4	4	0	13	0	2	1	1	0	1.00	1	.212	.254	.242
2000	Tampa	A+	75	231	51	12	0	1	(-	-)	66	17	28	21	29	0	23	3	4	3	3	4	.43	4	.221	.312	.286
2001	Nrwich	AA	51	128	29	6	0	2	(-	-)	41	10	10	11	10	0	20	2	2	1	1	0	1.00	5	.227	.291	.320
2001	Yanks	R	2	5	0	0	0	0	(-	-)	0	0	0	0	0	0	1	1	0	0	0	0	-	1	.000	.167	.000
2002	Nrwich	AA	20	61	19	6	0	1	(-	-)	28	11	12	9	5	0	6	0	0	1	0	1	.00	2	.311	.358	.459
2002	Clmbs	AAA	41	121	34	5	1	1	(-	-)	44	11	12	13	8	0	13	2	1	0	1	3	.25	5	.281	.336	.364
2003	Clmbs	AAA	89	282	79	14	0	4	(-	-)	105	39	30	39	37	1	35	3	1	2	0	2	.00	9	.280	.367	.372
2004	S-WB	AAA	77	232	59	9	0	6	(-	-)	86	34	31	28	25	0	24	2	2	3	0	1	.00	8	.254	.328	.371
2005	Portlnd	AAA	82	264	76	9	1	3	(-	-)	96	19	31	39	37	3	35	0	2	6	0	1	.00	13	.288	.368	.364
2006	Memp	AAA	90	285	78	10	1	2	(-	-)	96	24	28	35	27	0	29	2	3	4	3	1	.75	13	.274	.336	.337
2007	Smrset	IND	25	76	26	6	0	3	(-	-)	41	11	16	20	19	2	3	3	0	0	1	1	.50	2	.342	.490	.539
2007	Drham	AAA	51	170	47	4	0	4	(-	-)	63	22	19	22	16	0	13	1	2	0	1	0	1.00	3	.276	.342	.371
2008	Indy	AAA	76	252	67	14	2	3	(-	-)	94	29	17	30	17	0	35	2	0	0	0	2	.00	10	.266	.317	.373
2003	NYY	AL	5	4	1	0	0	0	(0	0)	1	0	0	1	1	0	1	0	0	0	0	0	-	0	.250	.400	.250
2008	TB	AL	5	15	3	0	0	0	(0	0)	3	2	0	0	0	0	3	0	0	0	0	0	-	0	.200	.200	.200
	2 ML YEARS		10	19	4	0	0	0	(0	0)	4	2	0	1	1	0	4	0	0	0	0	0	-	0	.211	.250	.211

Orlando Hernandez

Pitches: R **Bats:** R **Pos:** P **Ht:** 6'2" **Wt:** 220 **Born:** 10/11/1969 **Age:** 39

Year	Team	Lg	G	GS	CG	GF	IP	BFP	H	R	ER	HR	SH	SF	HB	TBB	IBB	SO	WP	Bk	W	L	Pct	ShO	Sv-Op	Hld	ERC	ERA
2008	Bnghtn*	AA	1	1	0	0	1.0	7	2	2	2	0	0	0	0	2	0	1	0	0	0	1	.000	0	0--	-	16.69	18.00
2008	StLuci*	A+	2	2	0	0	10.2	41	6	4	4	1	0	0	3	2	0	11	1	0	0	0	-	0	0--	-	2.14	3.38
2008	Mets*	R	1	1	0	0	4.0	19	4	2	1	0	0	0	0	1	0	6	0	0	0	0	-	0	0--	-	2.42	2.25
1998	NYY	AL	21	21	3	0	141.0	574	113	53	49	11	3	5	6	52	1	131	5	2	12	4	.750	1	0-0	0	2.96	3.13
1999	NYY	AL	33	33	2	0	214.1	910	187	108	98	24	3	11	8	87	2	157	4	0	17	9	.654	1	0-0	0	3.60	4.12
2000	NYY	AL	29	29	3	0	195.2	820	186	104	98	34	4	5	6	51	2	141	1	0	12	13	.480	0	0-0	0	3.82	4.51
2001	NYY	AL	17	16	0	0	94.2	414	90	51	51	19	2	2	5	42	1	77	0	0	4	7	.364	0	0-0	0	4.87	4.85
2002	NYY	AL	24	22	0	1	146.0	606	131	63	59	17	1	5	8	36	2	113	8	0	8	5	.615	0	1-1	1	3.20	3.64
2004	NYY	AL	15	15	0	0	84.2	359	73	31	31	9	0	1	5	36	0	84	3	0	8	2	.800	0	0-0	0	3.71	3.30
2005	CWS	AL	24	22	0	1	128.1	568	137	77	73	18	3	5	12	50	1	91	3	2	9	9	.500	0	1-1	1	5.12	5.12
2006	2 Tms	NL	29	29	1	0	162.1	699	155	90	84	22	7	5	12	61	5	164	1	3	11	11	.500	0	0-0	0	4.23	4.66
2007	NYM	AL	27	24	0	0	147.2	608	109	64	61	23	8	3	5	64	4	128	2	0	9	5	.643	0	0-0	0	3.26	3.72
06	Ari	NL	9	9	0	0	45.2	204	52	32	31	8	2	0	4	20	3	52	0	0	2	4	.333	0	0-0	0	6.00	6.11
06	NYM	NL	20	20	1	0	116.2	495	103	58	53	14	5	5	8	41	2	112	1	3	9	7	.563	0	0-0	0	3.60	4.09
	Postseason		19	14	0	0	106.0	443	77	32	30	9	4	4	4	55	3	107	1	0	9	3	.750	0	0-0	0	3.07	2.55
	9 ML YEARS		219	211	9	2	1314.2	5558	1181	641	604	177	31	42	67	479	18	1086	27	7	90	65	.581	2	2-2	2	3.79	4.13

Ramon Hernandez

Bats: R **Throws:** R **Pos:** C-127; PH-10; 1B-2; DH-1 **Ht:** 6'0" **Wt:** 235 **Born:** 5/20/1976 **Age:** 33

Year	Team	Lg	G	AB	H	2B	3B	HR	(Hm	Rd)	TB	R	RBI	RC	TBB	IBB	SO	HBP	SH	SF	SB	CS	SB%	GDP	Avg	OBP	Slg
1999	Oak	AL	40	136	38	7	0	3	(1	2)	54	13	21	20	18	0	11	1	1	2	1	0	1.00	5	.279	.363	.397
2000	Oak	AL	143	419	101	19	0	14	(7	7)	162	52	62	49	38	1	64	7	10	5	1	0	1.00	14	.241	.311	.387
2001	Oak	AL	136	453	115	25	0	15	(5	10)	185	55	60	58	37	3	68	6	9	4	1	1	.50	10	.254	.316	.408
2002	Oak	AL	136	403	94	20	0	7	(3	4)	135	51	42	41	43	1	64	5	3	3	0	0	-	11	.233	.313	.335
2003	Oak	AL	140	483	132	24	1	21	(9	12)	221	70	78	69	33	2	79	12	2	6	0	0	-	14	.273	.331	.458
2004	SD	NL	111	384	106	23	0	18	(10	8)	183	45	63	50	35	0	45	5	4	4	1	0	1.00	16	.276	.341	.477
2005	SD	NL	99	369	107	19	2	12	(5	7)	166	36	58	44	18	0	40	1	1	3	1	0	1.00	14	.290	.322	.450
2006	Bal	AL	144	501	138	29	2	23	(17	6)	240	66	91	82	43	2	79	11	0	5	1	0	1.00	13	.275	.343	.479
2007	Bal	AL	106	364	94	19	0	9	(4	5)	139	40	62	56	36	1	59	6	0	3	1	3	.25	9	.258	.333	.382
2008	Bal	AL	133	463	119	22	1	15	(10	5)	188	49	65	59	32	3	62	5	1	6	0	0	-	9	.257	.308	.406
	Postseason		22	69	15	2	0	1	(1	0)	20	6	6	7	5	0	13	3	2	0	0	0	-	2	.217	.299	.290
	10 ML YEARS		1188	3975	1044	206	6	137	(71	66)	1673	477	602	528	333	13	571	59	31	41	7	4	.64	115	.263	.326	.421

135

Runelvys Hernandez

Pitches: R Bats: R Pos: SP-4
Ht: 6'1" Wt: 250 Born: 4/27/1978 Age: 31

		HOW MUCH HE PITCHED						WHAT HE GAVE UP												THE RESULTS							
Year	Team	Lg	G	GS	CG	GF	IP	BFP	H	R	ER	HR	SH	SF	HB	TBB	IBB	SO	WP	Bk	W	L	Pct	ShO	Sv-Op	Hld	ERC	ERA
2008	RdRck*	AAA	24	23	1	0	124.2	528	120	72	68	18	5	6	4	43	0	95	3	0	8	8	.500	0	0--	-	4.11	4.91
2002	KC	AL	12	12	0	0	74.1	316	79	36	36	8	1	3	1	22	0	45	2	0	4	4	.500	0	0-0	0	4.16	4.36
2003	KC	AL	16	16	0	0	91.2	397	87	51	47	9	1	4	6	37	0	48	2	1	7	5	.583	0	0-0	0	4.05	4.61
2005	KC	AL	29	29	0	0	159.2	706	172	101	98	18	1	6	7	70	0	88	4	0	8	14	.364	0	0-0	0	4.99	5.52
2006	KC	AL	21	21	1	0	109.2	508	145	87	79	22	3	8	6	48	0	50	3	2	6	10	.375	1	0-0	0	7.35	6.48
2008	Hou	NL	4	4	0	0	19.1	98	32	19	18	4	1	0	0	11	1	15	0	0	0	3	.000	0	0-0	0	9.88	8.38
	5 ML YEARS		82	82	1	0	454.2	2025	515	294	278	61	7	21	20	188	1	246	11	3	25	36	.410	1	0-0	0	5.38	5.50

Daniel Ray Herrera

Pitches: L Bats: L Pos: RP-7
Ht: 5'7" Wt: 145 Born: 10/21/1984 Age: 24

		HOW MUCH HE PITCHED						WHAT HE GAVE UP												THE RESULTS							
Year	Team	Lg	G	GS	CG	GF	IP	BFP	H	R	ER	HR	SH	SF	HB	TBB	IBB	SO	WP	Bk	W	L	Pct	ShO	Sv-Op	Hld	ERC	ERA
2006	Rngrs	R+	3	0	0	3	8.2	29	5	2	2	0	0	0	0	0	0	11	1	0	0	1	.000	0	2--	-	0.75	2.08
2006	Bkrsfld	A+	14	5	0	3	53.1	211	39	16	8	0	0	0	5	12	0	61	3	0	4	2	.667	0	1--	-	1.82	1.35
2007	Bkrsfld	A+	7	1	0	4	11.0	52	14	4	4	1	0	0	0	5	1	11	0	0	2	0	1.000	0	1--	-	5.51	3.27
2007	Frisco	AA	34	0	0	10	52.1	212	43	24	22	3	2	2	3	20	1	64	2	0	5	2	.714	0	0--	-	3.06	3.78
2008	Chatt	AA	10	0	0	1	17.2	69	12	6	5	0	1	3	1	7	0	10	0	0	3	0	1.000	0	0--	-	2.08	2.55
2008	Lsvlle	AAA	48	0	0	12	55.0	221	47	20	17	4	3	1	0	10	2	50	0	1	4	4	.500	0	6--	-	2.26	2.78
2008	Cin	NL	7	0	0	0	7.1	37	10	7	6	1	2	0	2	3	2	8	0	0	0	0	-	0	0-0	0	7.05	7.36

Jonathan Herrera

Bats: B Throws: R Pos: 2B-21; PH-8; SS-2; PR-1
Ht: 5'9" Wt: 150 Born: 11/3/1984 Age: 24

		BATTING																		BASERUNNING				AVERAGES		
Year	Team	Lg	G	AB	H	2B	3B	HR	(Hm	Rd)	TB	R	RBI	RC	TBB	IBB	SO	HBP	SH	SF	SB	CS	SB%	GDP	Avg	OBP	Slg
2003	Casper	R+	39	159	49	7	1	1	(-	-)	61	27	25	23	10	0	25	2	4	1	12	3	.80	2	.308	.355	.384
2004	Ashvll	A	95	380	106	20	2	6	(-	-)	148	71	35	51	26	0	80	7	3	2	21	12	.64	5	.279	.335	.389
2005	Ashvll	A	19	87	27	2	0	0	(-	-)	29	17	5	11	8	0	11	3	0	1	6	6	.50	1	.310	.384	.333
2006	Mdest	A+	73	310	80	9	4	2	(-	-)	103	48	30	34	23	0	52	3	8	1	9	4	.69	9	.258	.315	.332
2006	Mdest	A+	127	487	151	20	8	7	(-	-)	208	87	77	85	58	0	67	3	13	7	34	15	.69	5	.310	.382	.427
2007	Tulsa	AA	131	509	131	24	4	3	(-	-)	172	65	40	57	36	0	69	8	17	3	18	12	.60	5	.257	.315	.338
2008	ColSpr	AAA	66	226	70	7	0	3	(-	-)	86	40	31	35	19	0	30	2	2	1	15	2	.88	6	.310	.367	.381
2008	Col	NL	28	61	14	1	1	0	(0	0)	17	5	3	6	4	0	10	0	1	0	1	1	.50	0	.230	.277	.279

Yoslan Herrera

Pitches: R Bats: R Pos: SP-5
Ht: 6'2" Wt: 200 Born: 4/28/1981 Age: 28

		HOW MUCH HE PITCHED						WHAT HE GAVE UP												THE RESULTS							
Year	Team	Lg	G	GS	CG	GF	IP	BFP	H	R	ER	HR	SH	SF	HB	TBB	IBB	SO	WP	Bk	W	L	Pct	ShO	Sv-Op	Hld	ERC	ERA
2007	Altna	AA	25	25	1	0	128.2	569	151	72	67	11	6	9	6	38	2	70	10	4	6	9	.400	0	0--	-	4.69	4.69
2008	Altna	AA	21	21	0	0	114.1	481	114	51	44	9	4	8	1	36	1	69	7	1	6	9	.400	0	0--	-	3.63	3.46
2008	Indy	AAA	1	1	0	0	7.0	27	7	2	2	1	0	0	0	1	0	6	0	0	1	0	1.000	0	0--	-	3.56	2.57
2008	Pit	NL	5	5	0	0	18.1	100	35	20	20	1	3	2	1	12	0	10	1	0	1	1	.500	0	0-0	0	10.94	9.82

Mike Hessman

Bats: R Throws: R Pos: 3B-12; PH-1
Ht: 6'5" Wt: 215 Born: 3/5/1978 Age: 31

		BATTING																		BASERUNNING				AVERAGES		
Year	Team	Lg	G	AB	H	2B	3B	HR	(Hm	Rd)	TB	R	RBI	RC	TBB	IBB	SO	HBP	SH	SF	SB	CS	SB%	GDP	Avg	OBP	Slg
2008	Toledo*	AAA	108	399	108	20	5	34	(-	-)	240	83	72	89	59	3	140	10	0	5	3	3	.50	2	.271	.374	.602
2003	Atl	NL	19	21	6	2	0	2	(1	1)	14	2	3	5	5	1	6	0	0	0	0	0	-	2	.286	.423	.667
2004	Atl	NL	29	69	9	3	0	2	(2	0)	18	8	5	1	1	0	24	1	0	0	0	0	-	0	.130	.155	.261
2007	Det	AL	17	51	12	0	0	4	(3	1)	24	7	12	7	5	0	17	0	0	1	0	0	-	0	.235	.298	.471
2008	Det	AL	12	27	8	1	0	5	(4	1)	24	6	7	7	2	0	9	2	0	0	0	0	-	0	.296	.387	.889
	4 ML YEARS		77	168	35	6	0	13	(10	3)	80	23	27	20	13	1	56	3	0	1	0	0	-	2	.208	.276	.476

Aaron Hill

Bats: R Throws: R Pos: 2B-55
Ht: 5'11" Wt: 195 Born: 3/21/1982 Age: 27

		BATTING																		BASERUNNING				AVERAGES		
Year	Team	Lg	G	AB	H	2B	3B	HR	(Hm	Rd)	TB	R	RBI	RC	TBB	IBB	SO	HBP	SH	SF	SB	CS	SB%	GDP	Avg	OBP	Slg
2005	Tor	AL	105	361	99	25	3	3	(3	0)	139	49	40	50	34	0	41	5	3	4	2	1	.67	5	.274	.342	.385
2006	Tor	AL	155	546	159	28	3	6	(4	2)	211	70	50	68	42	5	66	9	4	5	5	2	.71	15	.291	.349	.386
2007	Tor	AL	160	608	177	47	2	17	(8	9)	279	87	78	88	41	1	102	0	3	5	4	3	.57	21	.291	.333	.459
2008	Tor	AL	55	205	54	14	0	2	(1	1)	74	19	20	24	16	0	31	3	4	1	4	2	.67	4	.263	.324	.361
	4 ML YEARS		475	1720	489	114	8	28	(16	12)	703	225	188	230	133	6	240	17	14	15	15	8	.65	45	.284	.339	.409

Koyie Hill

Bats: B Throws: R Pos: C-9; PH-4
Ht: 6'0" Wt: 190 Born: 3/9/1979 Age: 30

		BATTING																		BASERUNNING				AVERAGES		
Year	Team	Lg	G	AB	H	2B	3B	HR	(Hm	Rd)	TB	R	RBI	RC	TBB	IBB	SO	HBP	SH	SF	SB	CS	SB%	GDP	Avg	OBP	Slg
2008	Iowa*	AAA	113	364	100	24	2	17	(-	-)	179	56	64	64	40	1	77	3	3	2	3	2	.60	6	.275	.350	.492
2003	LAD	NL	3	3	1	1	0	0	(0	0)	2	0	0	0	0	0	2	0	0	0	0	0	-	0	.333	.333	.667
2004	Ari	NL	13	36	9	1	0	1	(1	0)	13	3	6	5	2	1	6	0	0	0	1	0	1.00	1	.250	.289	.361

Year Team	Lg	G	AB	H	2B	3B	HR	(Hm	Rd)	TB	R	RBI	RC	TBB	IBB	SO	HBP	SH	SF	SB	CS	SB%	GDP	Avg	OBP	Slg
2005 Ari	NL	34	78	17	5	0	0	(0	0)	22	6	6	6	11	0	27	0	0	2	0	1	.00	0	.218	.308	.282
2007 ChC	NL	36	93	15	4	0	2	(1	1)	25	7	12	3	8	0	18	1	1	2	0	0	-	4	.161	.231	.269
2008 ChC	NL	10	21	2	1	0	0	(0	0)	3	0	1	0	0	0	12	0	1	0	0	0	-	0	.095	.095	.143
5 ML YEARS		96	231	44	12	0	3	(2	1)	65	16	25	14	21	1	65	1	2	4	1	1	.50	5	.190	.257	.281

Rich Hill

Pitches: L Bats: L Pos: SP-5   Ht: 6'5" Wt: 205 Born: 3/11/1980 Age: 29

Year Team	Lg	G	GS	CG	GF	IP	BFP	H	R	ER	HR	SH	SF	HB	TBB	IBB	SO	WP	Bk	W	L	Pct	ShO	Sv-Op	Hld	ERC	ERA
2008 Iowa*	AAA	7	7	0	0	26.0	127	22	19	17	4	2	1	2	28	0	32	3	0	2	4	.333	0	0- -		6.69	5.88
2008 Cubs*	R	3	3	0	0	9.1	38	5	5	3	0	0	1	1	5	0	11	1	0	1	1	.500	0	0- -		1.94	2.89
2008 Dytona*	A+	3	3	0	0	12.1	61	12	12	11	0	0	1	3	11	0	14	1	0	1	2	.333	0	0- -		6.05	8.03
2005 ChC	NL	10	4	0	1	23.2	115	25	24	24	3	1	0	1	17	1	21	0	0	0	2	.000	0	0-0	0	5.81	9.13
2006 ChC	NL	17	16	2	1	99.1	417	83	51	46	16	8	3	2	39	1	90	3	0	6	7	.462	1	0-0	0	3.59	4.17
2007 ChC	NL	32	32	0	0	195.0	812	170	89	85	27	9	4	12	63	3	183	1	1	11	8	.579	0	0-0	0	3.56	3.92
2008 ChC	NL	5	5	0	0	19.2	89	13	9	9	2	0	2	1	18	0	15	1	0	1	0	1.000	0	0-0	0	4.38	4.12
Postseason		1	1	0	0	3.0	18	6	3	3	1	0	0	1	2	0	3	0	0	0	1	.000	0	0-0	0	15.68	9.00
4 ML YEARS		64	57	2	2	337.2	1433	291	173	164	48	18	9	16	137	5	309	5	1	18	17	.514	1	0-0	0	3.78	4.37

Shawn Hill

Pitches: R Bats: R Pos: SP-12   Ht: 6'2" Wt: 226 Born: 4/28/1981 Age: 28

Year Team	Lg	G	GS	CG	GF	IP	BFP	H	R	ER	HR	SH	SF	HB	TBB	IBB	SO	WP	Bk	W	L	Pct	ShO	Sv-Op	Hld	ERC	ERA
2008 Ptomc*	A+	1	1	0	0	5.0	19	4	0	0	0	0	0	0	1	0	4	0	0	1	0	1.000	0	0- -		1.82	0.00
2008 Clmbs*	AAA	1	1	0	0	6.0	27	9	6	5	1	0	1	0	0	0	2	0	0	1	0	1.000	0	0- -		5.69	7.50
2004 Mon	NL	3	3	0	0	9.0	51	17	16	16	1	0	2	1	7	0	10	0	0	1	2	.333	0	0-0	0	12.14	16.00
2006 Was	NL	6	6	0	0	36.2	163	43	20	19	2	2	1	3	12	2	16	1	0	1	3	.250	0	0-0	0	4.70	4.66
2007 Was	NL	16	16	0	0	97.1	399	86	42	37	9	2	1	5	25	2	65	2	0	4	5	.444	0	0-0	0	3.03	3.42
2008 Was	NL	12	12	0	0	63.1	296	88	47	41	5	3	3	1	23	2	39	2	1	1	5	.167	0	0-0	0	6.04	5.83
4 ML YEARS		37	37	0	0	206.1	909	234	125	113	17	7	7	10	67	6	130	5	1	7	15	.318	0	0-0	0	4.55	4.93

Mike Hinckley

Pitches: L Bats: R Pos: RP-14   Ht: 6'2" Wt: 199 Born: 10/5/1982 Age: 26

Year Team	Lg	G	GS	CG	GF	IP	BFP	H	R	ER	HR	SH	SF	HB	TBB	IBB	SO	WP	Bk	W	L	Pct	ShO	Sv-Op	Hld	ERC	ERA
2001 Expos	R	8	5	0	0	34.1	158	46	23	20	1	1	2	3	12	0	28	6	1	2	2	.500	0	0- -		5.74	5.24
2002 Vrmnt	A-	16	16	0	0	91.2	357	60	19	14	4	3	1	4	30	0	66	6	3	6	2	.750	0	0- -		1.92	1.37
2003 Savann	A	23	23	2	0	121.0	515	124	54	49	4	2	6	9	41	1	111	8	2	9	5	.643	1	0- -		3.86	3.64
2003 BrvdCt	A+	4	4	1	0	25.0	89	14	2	2	1	0	0	0	1	0	23	2	0	4	0	1.000	0	0- -		0.85	0.72
2004 BrvdCt	A+	10	10	0	0	62.0	250	47	23	18	6	2	1	6	18	0	51	1	0	6	2	.750	0	0- -		2.76	2.61
2004 Hrsbrg	AA	16	16	0	0	94.0	376	83	34	30	5	8	5	7	23	0	80	1	0	5	2	.714	0	0- -		2.94	2.87
2005 Ptomc	A+	22	21	1	-	127.2	585	151	90	70	10	-	-	9	51	0	80	6	2	3	9	.250	0	0- -		5.20	4.93
2006 Ptomc	A+	28	28	-	0	148.1	686	178	102	91	18	-	-	9	63	-	79	10	5	6	8	.429	-	0- -		5.70	5.52
2007 Hrsbrg	AA	25	23	0	0	117.1	553	145	85	76	15	6	1	10	59	2	70	9	1	9	10	.474	0	0- -		6.45	5.83
2008 Hrsbrg	AA	23	6	0	6	65.0	305	79	40	37	6	3	2	3	40	3	53	4	1	5	3	.625	0	0- -		6.38	5.12
2008 Clmbs	AAA	20	1	0	4	25.2	114	27	11	9	0	1	1	6	15	0	20	1	0	2	2	.000	0	1- -		4.42	3.16
2008 Was	NL	14	0	0	2	13.2	49	8	1	0	0	0	0	1	3	0	9	0	1	0	0	-	0	0-0	4	1.35	0.00

Alex Hinshaw

Pitches: L Bats: L Pos: RP-48   Ht: 6'4" Wt: 190 Born: 10/31/1982 Age: 26

Year Team	Lg	G	GS	CG	GF	IP	BFP	H	R	ER	HR	SH	SF	HB	TBB	IBB	SO	WP	Bk	W	L	Pct	ShO	Sv-Op	Hld	ERC	ERA
2005 Salem	A+	25	0	0	2	22.0	102	17	9	9	1	3	3	3	18	0	33	2	0	0	1	.000	0	0- -		4.50	3.68
2006 SnJos	A+	30	10	0	8	69.2	330	58	48	33	6	1	4	10	60	0	78	6	0	6	3	.667	0	0- -		5.38	4.26
2007 Conn	AA	17	5	0	0	41.1	165	22	13	9	2	1	1	2	19	0	50	2	0	3	1	.750	0	0- -		1.78	1.96
2008 Fresno	AAA	13	0	0	9	15.2	55	5	1	1	0	0	0	0	4	0	21	0	0	0	0	-	0	7- -		0.55	0.57
2008 SF	NL	48	0	0	12	39.2	179	31	16	15	5	4	2	3	29	4	47	5	0	2	1	.667	0	0-0	4	4.43	3.40

Eric Hinske

Bats: L Throws: R Pos: RF-49; LF-40; DH-20; PH-16; 1B-11; 3B-8   Ht: 6'2" Wt: 235 Born: 8/5/1977 Age: 31

Year Team	Lg	G	AB	H	2B	3B	HR	(Hm	Rd)	TB	R	RBI	RC	TBB	IBB	SO	HBP	SH	SF	SB	CS	SB%	GDP	Avg	OBP	Slg
2002 Tor	AL	151	566	158	38	2	24	(15	9)	272	99	84	103	77	5	138	2	0	5	13	1	.93	12	.279	.365	.481
2003 Tor	AL	124	449	109	45	3	12	(4	8)	196	74	63	66	59	1	104	1	0	5	12	2	.86	11	.243	.329	.437
2004 Tor	AL	155	570	140	23	3	15	(6	9)	214	66	69	60	54	2	109	4	0	6	12	8	.60	14	.246	.312	.375
2005 Tor	AL	147	477	125	31	2	15	(7	8)	205	79	68	71	46	4	121	8	0	6	8	4	.67	8	.262	.333	.430
2006 2 Tms	AL	109	277	75	17	2	13	(7	6)	135	43	34	39	35	2	79	0	0	0	2	2	.50	8	.271	.353	.487
2007 Bos	AL	84	186	38	12	3	6	(4	2)	74	25	21	22	28	2	54	3	0	1	3	0	1.00	7	.204	.317	.398
2008 TB	AL	133	381	94	21	1	20	(8	12)	177	59	60	53	47	4	88	3	0	1	10	3	.77	13	.247	.333	.465
06 Tor	AL	78	197	52	9	2	12	(6	6)	101	35	29	29	27	2	49	0	0	0	1	1	.50	6	.264	.353	.513
06 Bos	AL	31	80	23	8	0	1	(1	0)	34	8	5	10	8	0	30	0	0	0	1	1	.50	2	.288	.352	.425
Postseason		3	2	0	0	0	0	(0	0)	0	1	0	0	0	0	2	0	0	0	0	0	-	0	.000	.000	.000
7 ML YEARS		903	2906	739	187	16	105	(51	54)	1273	445	399	414	346	20	693	21	0	24	60	20	.75	73	.254	.335	.438

Jason Hirsh

Pitches: R **Bats:** R **Pos:** RP-3; SP-1   **Ht:** 6'8" **Wt:** 250 **Born:** 2/20/1982 **Age:** 27

			HOW MUCH HE PITCHED						WHAT HE GAVE UP										THE RESULTS							
Year	Team	Lg	G	GS	CG	GF	IP	BFP	H	R	ER	HR	SH	SF	HB	TBB	IBB	SO	WP	Bk	W	L	Pct	ShO	Sv-Op Hld	ERC	ERA
2008	ColSpr*	AAA	18	17	0	1	99.1	455	115	66	64	16	4	3	3	52	3	51	5	0	4	4	.500	0	0-- -	6.10	5.80
2006	Hou	NL	9	9	0	0	44.2	206	48	32	30	11	0	1	3	22	2	29	4	0	3	4	.429	0	0-0 0	6.11	6.04
2007	Col	NL	19	19	1	0	112.1	483	103	63	60	18	6	4	2	48	5	75	5	1	5	7	.417	0	0-0 0	4.12	4.81
2008	Col	NL	4	1	0	1	8.2	46	15	10	8	3	0	0	0	4	0	6	0	0	0	0	-	0	0-0 0	10.73	8.31
3 ML YEARS			32	29	1	1	165.2	735	166	105	98	32	6	5	5	74	7	110	9	1	8	11	.421	0	0-0 0	4.94	5.32

Luke Hochevar

Pitches: R **Bats:** R **Pos:** SP-22   **Ht:** 6'5" **Wt:** 205 **Born:** 9/15/1983 **Age:** 25

			HOW MUCH HE PITCHED						WHAT HE GAVE UP										THE RESULTS							
Year	Team	Lg	G	GS	CG	GF	IP	BFP	H	R	ER	HR	SH	SF	HB	TBB	IBB	SO	WP	Bk	W	L	Pct	ShO	Sv-Op Hld	ERC	ERA
2006	FtWth	IND	4	4	0	0	22.2	96	20	7	6	1	0	1	2	11	0	34	1	0	1	1	.500	0	0-- -	3.82	2.38
2006	Burlgtn	A	4	4	0	0	15.1	57	8	3	2	0	0	0	1	2	0	16	1	0	0	1	.000	0	0-- -	1.32	1.17
2007	Wichta	AAA	17	16	0	0	94.0	418	110	62	49	13	1	1	6	26	0	94	6	0	3	6	.333	0	0-- -	5.05	4.69
2007	Omha	AAA	10	10	0	0	58.0	245	53	34	33	11	2	2	3	21	0	44	2	0	1	3	.250	0	0-- -	4.29	5.12
2008	Omha	AAA	3	3	0	0	17.1	68	11	7	5	2	1	0	0	6	0	12	3	1	1	1	.500	0	0-- -	2.11	2.60
2007	KC	AL	4	1	0	1	12.2	54	11	4	3	1	1	0	3	4	0	5	1	0	0	1	.000	0	0-0 0	3.86	2.13
2008	KC	AL	22	22	0	0	129.0	566	143	84	79	12	1	2	5	47	1	72	7	0	6	12	.333	0	0-0 0	4.67	5.51
2 ML YEARS			26	23	0	1	141.2	620	154	88	82	13	2	2	8	51	1	77	8	0	6	13	.316	0	0-0 0	4.60	5.21

Jim Hoey

Pitches: R **Bats:** R **Pos:** P   **Ht:** 6'6" **Wt:** 210 **Born:** 12/30/1982 **Age:** 26

			HOW MUCH HE PITCHED						WHAT HE GAVE UP										THE RESULTS							
Year	Team	Lg	G	GS	CG	GF	IP	BFP	H	R	ER	HR	SH	SF	HB	TBB	IBB	SO	WP	Bk	W	L	Pct	ShO	Sv-Op Hld	ERC	ERA
2003	Bluefld	R+	11	8	0	0	42.0	177	33	19	13	3	0	0	6	19	0	20	2	0	2	3	.400	0	0-- -	3.53	2.79
2004	Abrdn	A-	2	2	0	0	6.2	34	12	8	7	1	0	1	0	1	0	6	0	0	0	1	.000	0	0-- -	7.91	9.45
2005	Abrdn	A-	9	0	0	2	15.0	67	11	10	8	1	2	1	3	10	0	15	1	0	1	1	.500	0	0-- -	4.17	4.80
2006	Dlmrva	A	27	0	0	23	28.1	113	17	8	8	2	5	1	0	10	0	46	1	0	2	1	.667	0	18-- -	1.68	2.54
2006	Frdrck	A+	14	0	0	14	14.0	63	13	3	1	0	0	0	1	5	0	16	1	0	0	0	-	0	11-- -	2.91	0.64
2006	Bowie	AA	8	0	0	6	9.0	41	9	5	4	1	0	1	0	3	0	11	0	0	0	0	-	0	4-- -	3.59	4.00
2007	Bowie	AA	20	0	0	20	18.2	72	13	0	0	0	2	0	1	4	0	28	0	0	1	0	1.000	0	14-- -	1.57	0.00
2007	Norfolk	AAA	20	0	0	6	27.0	106	15	4	4	1	1	1	1	10	0	41	1	0	2	0	1.000	0	2-- -	1.55	1.33
2006	Bal	AL	12	0	0	2	9.2	49	14	11	11	1	1	2	2	5	0	6	0	1	0	1	.000	0	0-1 4	8.22	10.24
2007	Bal	AL	23	0	0	1	24.2	115	25	21	20	2	0	4	1	18	1	18	1	0	3	4	.429	0	0-3 4	5.43	7.30
2 ML YEARS			35	0	0	3	34.1	164	39	32	31	3	1	6	3	23	1	24	1	1	3	5	.375	0	0-4 8	6.18	8.13

Trevor Hoffman

Pitches: R **Bats:** R **Pos:** RP-48   **Ht:** 6'0" **Wt:** 221 **Born:** 10/13/1967 **Age:** 41

			HOW MUCH HE PITCHED						WHAT HE GAVE UP										THE RESULTS							
Year	Team	Lg	G	GS	CG	GF	IP	BFP	H	R	ER	HR	SH	SF	HB	TBB	IBB	SO	WP	Bk	W	L	Pct	ShO	Sv-Op Hld	ERC	ERA
1993	2 Tms	NL	67	0	0	26	90.0	391	80	43	39	10	4	5	1	39	13	79	5	0	4	6	.400	0	5-8 15	3.40	3.90
1994	SD	NL	47	0	0	41	56.0	225	39	16	16	4	1	2	0	20	6	68	3	0	4	4	.500	0	20-23 1	2.02	2.57
1995	SD	NL	55	0	0	51	53.1	218	48	25	23	10	0	0	0	14	3	52	1	0	7	4	.636	0	31-38 0	3.48	3.88
1996	SD	NL	70	0	0	62	88.0	348	50	23	22	6	2	2	2	31	5	111	2	0	9	5	.643	0	42-49 0	1.58	2.25
1997	SD	NL	70	0	0	59	81.1	322	59	25	24	9	2	1	0	24	4	111	7	0	6	4	.600	0	37-44 0	2.27	2.66
1998	SD	NL	66	0	0	61	73.0	274	41	12	12	2	3	0	1	21	2	86	8	0	4	2	.667	0	53-54 0	1.32	1.48
1999	SD	NL	64	0	0	54	67.1	263	48	23	16	5	1	3	0	15	2	73	4	0	2	3	.400	0	40-43 0	1.78	2.14
2000	SD	NL	70	0	0	59	72.1	291	61	29	24	7	3	5	0	11	4	85	4	0	4	7	.364	0	43-50 0	2.18	2.99
2001	SD	NL	62	0	0	55	60.1	248	48	25	23	10	2	2	1	21	2	63	3	0	3	4	.429	0	43-46 0	3.20	3.43
2002	SD	NL	61	0	0	52	59.1	245	52	20	18	2	2	2	1	18	2	69	3	0	2	5	.286	0	38-41 0	2.63	2.73
2003	SD	NL	9	0	0	7	9.0	36	7	2	2	1	0	0	1	3	0	11	0	0	0	0	-	0	0-0 0	2.76	2.00
2004	SD	NL	55	0	0	51	54.2	209	42	14	14	5	2	0	0	8	1	53	2	0	3	3	.500	0	41-45 0	1.92	2.30
2005	SD	NL	60	0	0	54	57.2	240	52	23	19	3	2	3	1	12	1	54	1	0	1	6	.143	0	43-46 0	2.49	2.97
2006	SD	NL	65	0	0	50	63.0	248	48	16	15	8	1	0	0	13	1	50	2	0	0	2	.000	0	46-51 0	2.14	2.14
2007	SD	NL	61	0	0	50	57.1	235	49	21	19	2	3	2	0	15	5	44	0	0	4	5	.444	0	42-49 0	2.23	2.98
2008	SD	NL	48	0	0	42	45.1	180	38	19	19	8	1	0	0	9	2	46	0	0	3	6	.333	0	30-34 0	2.86	3.77
93	Fla	NL	28	0	0	13	35.2	152	24	13	13	5	2	1	0	19	7	26	3	0	2	2	.500	0	2-3 8	2.71	3.28
93	SD	NL	39	0	0	13	54.1	239	56	30	26	5	2	4	1	20	6	53	2	0	2	4	.333	0	3-5 7	3.88	4.31
Postseason			12	0	0	11	13.0	55	11	6	5	2	0	1	0	5	1	14	0	0	1	2	.333	0	4-6 0	3.35	3.46
16 ML YEARS			930	0	0	774	988.0	3973	762	336	305	90	28	27	8	274	53	1055	45	0	56	66	.459	0	554-621 16	2.31	2.78

Micah Hoffpauir

Bats: L **Throws:** L **Pos:** PH-16; LF-7; 1B-6; RF-5; DH-1   **Ht:** 6'3" **Wt:** 215 **Born:** 3/1/1980 **Age:** 29

			BATTING																		BASERUNNING				AVERAGES		
Year	Team	Lg	G	AB	H	2B	3B	HR	(Hm	Rd)	TB	R	RBI	RC	TBB	IBB	SO	HBP	SH	SF		SB	CS	SB%	GDP	Avg	OBP	Slg
2002	Boise	A-	60	216	65	10	3	10	(-	-)	111	35	41	34	7	1	35	3	1	1		2	6	.25	1	.301	.330	.514
2003	Dytona	A+	124	477	121	33	2	8	(-	-)	182	59	58	62	44	7	96	7	0	5		2	1	.67	11	.254	.323	.382
2004	WTenn	AA	94	340	104	20	6	11	(-	-)	169	58	75	59	27	6	61	1	1	12		1	4	.20	4	.306	.347	.497
2004	Iowa	AAA	1	3	1	1	0	0	(-	-)	2	0	1	0	1	0	0	0	0	0		0	0	-	0	.333	.500	.667
2005	Iowa	AAA	119	392	105	14	3	3	(-	-)	134	48	47	49	38	4	59	3	1	4		3	0	1.00	11	.268	.334	.342
2005	WTenn	AA	7	25	4	0	0	1	(-	-)	7	1	2	0	0	0	6	0	0	0		0	0	-	0	.160	.160	.280
2006	WTenn	AA	40	138	37	11	2	10	(-	-)	82	28	31	30	20	2	29	2	0	3		0	0	-	2	.268	.362	.594

Year	Team	Lg	G	AB	H	2B	3B	HR	(Hm	Rd)	TB	R	RBI	RC	TBB	IBB	SO	HBP	SH	SF	SB	CS	SB%	GDP	Avg	OBP	Slg
2006	Iowa	AAA	77	255	68	9	1	12	(-	-)	115	34	49	41	33	4	59	1	1	7	1	2	.33	6	.267	.345	.451
2007	Iowa	AAA	82	310	99	24	0	16	(-	-)	171	56	73	62	24	3	34	2	0	6	2	1	.67	3	.319	.365	.552
2008	Iowa	AAA	71	290	105	34	2	25	(-	-)	218	63	100	79	17	1	46	1	0	5	2	0	1.00	4	.362	.393	.752
2008	ChC	NL	33	73	25	8	0	2	(0	2)	39	14	8	14	6	0	24	1	0	0	1	0	1.00	0	.342	.400	.534

Matt Holliday

Bats: R **Throws:** R **Pos:** LF-139   **Ht:** 6'4" **Wt:** 235 **Born:** 1/15/1980 **Age:** 29

Year	Team	Lg	G	AB	H	2B	3B	HR	(Hm	Rd)	TB	R	RBI	RC	TBB	IBB	SO	HBP	SH	SF	SB	CS	SB%	GDP	Avg	OBP	Slg
2008	ColSpr*	AAA	3	10	6	1	0	1	(-	-)	10	4	3	4	1	0	3	0	0	0	0	0	-	0	.600	.636	1.000
2004	Col	NL	121	400	116	31	3	14	(10	4)	195	65	57	61	31	0	86	6	1	1	3	3	.50	9	.290	.349	.488
2005	Col	NL	125	479	147	24	7	19	(12	7)	242	68	87	88	36	1	79	7	0	4	14	3	.82	11	.307	.361	.505
2006	Col	NL	155	602	196	45	5	34	(22	12)	353	119	114	112	47	3	110	15	0	3	10	5	.67	22	.326	.387	.586
2007	Col	NL	158	636	216	50	6	36	(25	11)	386	120	137	134	63	7	126	10	0	4	11	4	.73	23	.340	.405	.607
2008	Col	NL	139	539	173	38	2	25	(15	10)	290	107	88	104	74	6	104	8	0	2	28	2	.93	9	.321	.409	.538
	Postseason		11	45	13	0	0	5	(3	2)	28	6	10	7	1	0	12	1	0	0	0	0	-	1	.289	.319	.622
	5 ML YEARS		698	2656	848	188	23	128	(84	44)	1466	479	483	499	251	17	505	46	1	14	66	17	.80	74	.319	.386	.552

Michael Hollimon

Bats: B **Throws:** R **Pos:** SS-6; PR-3; 2B-2; 3B-2; PH-1   **Ht:** 6'1" **Wt:** 185 **Born:** 6/14/1982 **Age:** 27

Year	Team	Lg	G	AB	H	2B	3B	HR	(Hm	Rd)	TB	R	RBI	RC	TBB	IBB	SO	HBP	SH	SF	SB	CS	SB%	GDP	Avg	OBP	Slg
2005	Oneont	A-	72	255	70	13	10	13	(-	-)	142	66	53	57	50	1	76	2	1	5	8	3	.73	5	.275	.391	.557
2006	WMich	A	128	449	125	29	13	15	(-	-)	225	69	54	92	77	6	124	4	3	4	19	5	.79	1	.278	.386	.501
2007	Erie	AA	127	471	133	34	8	14	(-	-)	225	91	76	87	64	2	121	5	7	5	16	6	.73	7	.282	.371	.478
2007	Toledo	AAA	5	19	4	1	1	0	(-	-)	7	2	2	1	1	0	4	0	0	0	0	0	-	0	.211	.250	.368
2008	Toledo	AAA	91	331	70	16	4	15	(-	-)	139	56	33	45	45	0	109	2	3	4	7	3	.70	4	.211	.306	.420
2008	Det	AL	11	23	6	2	1	1	(0	1)	13	4	2	1	1	0	6	0	0	0	0	0	-	0	.261	.280	.565

Steve Holm

Bats: R **Throws:** R **Pos:** C-42; PH-9; PR-3   **Ht:** 6'0" **Wt:** 210 **Born:** 10/21/1979 **Age:** 29

Year	Team	Lg	G	AB	H	2B	3B	HR	(Hm	Rd)	TB	R	RBI	RC	TBB	IBB	SO	HBP	SH	SF	SB	CS	SB%	GDP	Avg	OBP	Slg
2001	Salem	A+	33	72	15	3	1	0	(-	-)	20	8	2	7	10	0	16	1	1	1	1	0	1.00	4	.208	.310	.278
2002	Salem	A+	50	128	22	4	0	0	(-	-)	26	15	11	6	15	0	16	1	0	4	0	0	-	4	.172	.255	.203
2003	Hgrstn	A	55	173	38	10	1	1	(-	-)	53	12	17	14	8	0	32	3	2	1	3	1	.75	5	.220	.265	.306
2004	SnJos	A+	61	201	52	12	0	9	(-	-)	91	27	29	35	33	0	52	4	4	0	1	2	.33	5	.259	.374	.453
2005	Augsta	A	56	176	41	7	0	5	(-	-)	63	16	31	20	17	0	36	3	2	3	1	1	.50	2	.233	.307	.358
2005	Nrwich	AA	11	23	5	1	0	0	(-	-)	6	4	2	3	4	0	7	2	2	0	1	0	1.00	1	.217	.379	.261
2006	SnJos	A+	69	229	59	13	0	15	(-	-)	117	44	30	40	24	0	59	5	5	0	0	0	-	0	.258	.341	.511
2007	Conn	AA	84	254	69	14	0	9	(-	-)	110	35	28	46	42	2	39	6	3	0	3	1	.75	7	.272	.387	.433
2008	Fresno	AAA	22	66	18	4	0	0	(-	-)	22	7	11	9	10	1	12	1	0	2	0	0	-	0	.273	.367	.333
2008	SF	NL	49	84	22	9	0	1	(1	0)	34	10	6	8	10	1	16	3	0	1	0	1	.00	3	.262	.357	.405

Paul Hoover

Bats: R **Throws:** R **Pos:** C-13   **Ht:** 6'1" **Wt:** 210 **Born:** 4/14/1976 **Age:** 33

Year	Team	Lg	G	AB	H	2B	3B	HR	(Hm	Rd)	TB	R	RBI	RC	TBB	IBB	SO	HBP	SH	SF	SB	CS	SB%	GDP	Avg	OBP	Slg
2008	Albq*	AAA	50	175	44	8	0	6	(-	-)	70	27	19	22	14	0	44	3	0	1	1	1	.50	8	.251	.316	.400
2001	TB	AL	3	4	1	0	0	0	(0	0)	1	1	0	0	0	0	1	0	0	0	0	0	-	0	.250	.250	.250
2002	TB	AL	5	17	3	0	0	0	(0	0)	3	1	2	1	0	0	5	0	0	0	0	0	-	0	.176	.176	.176
2006	Fla	NL	4	5	2	0	0	0	(0	0)	2	0	1	1	0	0	0	0	0	0	0	0	-	0	.400	.400	.400
2007	Fla	NL	3	8	3	0	0	0	(0	0)	3	1	0	0	0	0	2	0	0	0	0	0	-	0	.375	.375	.375
2008	Fla	NL	13	40	8	1	0	0	(0	0)	9	1	2	0	2	1	17	0	0	0	0	0	-	2	.200	.238	.225
	5 ML YEARS		28	74	17	1	0	0	(0	0)	18	4	5	2	2	1	25	0	0	0	0	0	-	2	.230	.250	.243

Norris Hopper

Bats: R **Throws:** R **Pos:** PH-12; LF-8; CF-7; RF-4   **Ht:** 5'10" **Wt:** 209 **Born:** 3/24/1979 **Age:** 30

Year	Team	Lg	G	AB	H	2B	3B	HR	(Hm	Rd)	TB	R	RBI	RC	TBB	IBB	SO	HBP	SH	SF	SB	CS	SB%	GDP	Avg	OBP	Slg
2008	Srsota*	A+	2	7	2	0	0	0	(-	-)	2	3	0	1	2	0	0	0	0	0	0	0	-	0	.286	.444	.286
2008	Lsvlle*	AAA	4	17	5	1	0	0	(-	-)	6	3	0	1	0	0	4	0	1	0	0	0	-	0	.294	.294	.353
2006	Cin	NL	21	39	14	1	0	1	(1	0)	18	6	5	8	6	0	4	0	1	1	2	2	.50	1	.359	.435	.462
2007	Cin	NL	121	307	101	14	2	0	(0	0)	119	51	14	43	20	1	33	1	6	1	14	6	.70	8	.329	.371	.388
2008	Cin	NL	26	50	10	0	0	0	(0	0)	10	3	1	4	5	0	6	1	2	0	1	0	1.00	0	.200	.286	.200
	3 ML YEARS		168	396	125	15	2	1	(1	0)	147	60	20	55	31	1	43	2	9	2	17	8	.68	9	.316	.367	.371

Brian Horwitz

Bats: R **Throws:** R **Pos:** PH-12; LF-9; RF-2 **Ht:** 6'1" **Wt:** 187 **Born:** 11/7/1982 **Age:** 26

Year	Team	Lg	G	AB	H	2B	3B	HR	(Hm	Rd)	TB	R	RBI	RC	TBB	IBB	SO	HBP	SH	SF	SB	CS	SB%	GDP	Avg	OBP	Slg
2004	Salem	A+	71	268	93	24	1	2	(-	-)	125	41	44	51	21	0	34	8	0	3	3	3	.50	7	.347	.407	.466
2005	Augsta	A	123	470	164	38	4	2	(-	-)	216	77	88	92	50	2	39	8	0	7	6	6	.50	12	.349	.415	.460
2006	SnJos	A+	56	207	67	11	2	2	(-	-)	88	26	31	38	30	2	23	4	0	3	0	2	.00	8	.324	.414	.425
2006	Fresno	AAA	5	16	2	1	0	0	(-	-)	3	1	1	0	2	0	2	0	0	0	0	0	-	2	.125	.222	.188
2006	Conn	AA	78	269	77	9	1	2	(-	-)	94	23	29	37	31	0	35	4	0	3	4	3	.57	10	.286	.365	.349
2007	Conn	AA	35	136	42	5	0	2	(-	-)	53	17	10	20	13	0	10	1	0	1	2	1	.67	0	.309	.371	.390
2007	Fresno	AAA	84	264	86	21	2	1	(-	-)	114	32	21	45	21	1	22	4	0	1	2	0	1.00	11	.326	.383	.432
2008	Fresno	AAA	86	264	73	11	1	7	(-	-)	107	40	29	40	31	1	42	2	2	3	1	1	.50	9	.277	.353	.405
2008	SF	NL	21	36	8	0	0	2	(1	1)	14	5	4	5	5	0	10	0	0	1	0	0	-	0	.222	.310	.389

J.R. House

Bats: R **Throws:** R **Pos:** PH-3 **Ht:** 6'0" **Wt:** 210 **Born:** 11/11/1979 **Age:** 29

Year	Team	Lg	G	AB	H	2B	3B	HR	(Hm	Rd)	TB	R	RBI	RC	TBB	IBB	SO	HBP	SH	SF	SB	CS	SB%	GDP	Avg	OBP	Slg
2008	RdRck*	AAA	127	454	139	25	0	18	(-	-)	218	63	60	84	53	0	52	2	0	4	1	2	.33	11	.306	.378	.480
2003	Pit	NL	1	1	1	0	0	0	(0	0)	1	0	0	1	0	0	0	0	0	0	0	0	-	0	1.000	1.000	1.000
2004	Pit	NL	5	9	1	1	0	0	(0	0)	2	1	0	0	0	0	2	0	0	0	0	0	-	0	.111	.111	.222
2006	Hou	NL	4	9	0	0	0	0	(0	0)	0	0	0	0	0	0	2	0	0	0	0	0	-	1	.000	.000	.000
2007	Bal	AL	19	38	8	2	0	3	(2	1)	19	5	3	1	1	0	11	2	0	0	0	0	-	0	.211	.268	.500
2008	Hou	NL	3	3	0	0	0	0	(0	0)	0	0	1	0	0	0	1	0	0	0	0	0	-	0	.000	.000	.000
	5 ML YEARS		32	60	10	3	0	3	(2	1)	22	6	4	2	1	0	16	2	0	0	0	0	-	2	.167	.206	.367

Ryan Howard

Bats: L **Throws:** L **Pos:** 1B-159; PH-4; DH-2 **Ht:** 6'4" **Wt:** 256 **Born:** 11/19/1979 **Age:** 29

Year	Team	Lg	G	AB	H	2B	3B	HR	(Hm	Rd)	TB	R	RBI	RC	TBB	IBB	SO	HBP	SH	SF	SB	CS	SB%	GDP	Avg	OBP	Slg
2004	Phi	NL	19	39	11	0	1	2	(1	1)	22	5	5	7	2	0	13	1	0	0	0	0	-	2	.282	.333	.564
2005	Phi	NL	88	312	90	17	2	22	(11	11)	177	52	63	50	33	8	100	1	0	2	0	1	.00	6	.288	.356	.567
2006	Phi	NL	159	581	182	25	1	58	(29	29)	383	104	149	138	108	37	181	9	0	6	0	0	-	7	.313	.425	.659
2007	Phi	NL	144	529	142	26	0	47	(23	24)	309	94	136	119	107	35	199	5	0	7	1	0	1.00	13	.268	.392	.584
2008	Phi	NL	162	610	153	26	4	48	(26	22)	331	105	146	117	81	17	199	3	0	6	1	1	.50	11	.251	.339	.543
	Postseason		3	12	3	0	0	1	(1	0)	6	1	1	1	0	0	7	1	0	0	0	0	-	0	.250	.308	.500
	5 ML YEARS		572	2071	578	99	7	177	(90	87)	1222	360	499	431	331	97	692	19	0	21	2	2	.50	39	.279	.380	.590

J.P. Howell

Pitches: L **Bats:** L **Pos:** RP-64 **Ht:** 6'0" **Wt:** 175 **Born:** 4/25/1983 **Age:** 26

			HOW MUCH HE PITCHED						WHAT HE GAVE UP											THE RESULTS						
Year	Team	Lg	G	GS	CG	GF	IP	BFP	H	R	ER	HR	SH	SF	HB	TBB	IBB	SO	WP	Bk	W	L	Pct	ShO	Sv-Op	Hld	ERC	ERA
2005	KC	AL	15	15	0	0	72.2	328	73	55	50	9	3	3	6	39	0	54	7	0	3	5	.375	0	0-0	0	5.18	6.19
2006	TB	AL	8	8	0	0	42.1	187	52	25	24	4	0	2	3	14	0	33	1	0	1	3	.250	0	0-0	0	5.51	5.10
2007	TB	AL	10	10	0	0	51.0	244	69	45	43	8	2	1	3	21	0	49	3	0	1	6	.143	0	0-0	0	6.84	7.59
2008	TB	AL	64	0	0	9	89.1	370	62	29	22	6	6	1	4	39	1	92	5	0	6	1	.857	0	3-5	14	2.51	2.22
	4 ML YEARS		97	33	0	9	255.1	1129	256	154	139	27	11	7	16	113	1	228	16	0	11	15	.423	0	3-5	14	4.53	4.90

Bob Howry

Pitches: R **Bats:** L **Pos:** RP-72 **Ht:** 6'5" **Wt:** 220 **Born:** 8/4/1973 **Age:** 35

			HOW MUCH HE PITCHED						WHAT HE GAVE UP											THE RESULTS						
Year	Team	Lg	G	GS	CG	GF	IP	BFP	H	R	ER	HR	SH	SF	HB	TBB	IBB	SO	WP	Bk	W	L	Pct	ShO	Sv-Op	Hld	ERC	ERA
1998	CWS	AL	44	0	0	15	54.1	217	37	20	19	7	2	3	2	19	2	51	2	0	0	3	.000	0	9-11	19	2.50	3.15
1999	CWS	AL	69	0	0	54	67.2	298	58	34	27	8	3	1	3	38	3	80	3	1	5	3	.625	0	28-34	1	4.11	3.59
2000	CWS	AL	65	0	0	29	71.0	289	54	26	25	6	2	4	4	29	2	60	2	0	2	4	.333	0	7-12	14	2.96	3.17
2001	CWS	AL	69	0	0	23	78.2	346	85	41	41	11	4	3	4	30	9	64	6	0	4	5	.444	0	5-11	21	4.78	4.69
2002	2 Tms	AL	67	0	0	26	68.2	292	67	37	32	9	4	6	5	21	4	45	2	0	3	5	.375	0	0-1	15	4.00	4.19
2003	Bos	AL	4	0	0	3	4.1	27	11	6	6	1	0	1	0	3	1	4	0	0	0	0	-	0	0-1	0	16.51	12.46
2004	Cle	AL	37	0	0	6	42.2	178	37	14	13	5	1	1	2	12	0	39	0	0	4	2	.667	0	0-2	8	3.15	2.74
2005	Cle	AL	79	0	0	24	73.0	277	49	23	20	4	3	2	0	16	1	48	0	0	7	4	.636	0	3-5	29	1.58	2.47
2006	ChC	NL	84	0	0	26	76.2	314	70	28	27	8	5	3	3	17	4	71	1	0	4	4	.500	0	5-9	21	3.03	3.17
2007	ChC	NL	78	0	0	32	81.1	336	76	31	30	8	4	1	2	19	3	72	1	0	6	7	.462	0	8-12	22	3.10	3.32
2008	ChC	NL	72	0	0	27	70.2	311	90	44	42	13	1	4	2	13	5	59	0	0	7	5	.583	0	1-5	15	5.37	5.35
02	CWS	AL	47	0	0	17	50.2	209	45	22	22	7	1	4	3	17	2	31	1	0	2	2	.500	0	0-0	10	3.72	3.91
02	Bos	AL	20	0	0	9	18.0	83	22	15	10	2	3	2	2	4	2	14	1	0	1	3	.250	0	0-1	5	4.79	5.00
	Postseason		4	0	0	1	5.2	21	3	1	1	0	1	0	0	2	0	10	0	0	0	0	-	0	0-0	1	1.27	1.59
	11 ML YEARS		668	0	0	265	689.0	2885	634	304	282	80	29	29	27	217	34	593	17	1	42	43	.494	0	66-103	165	3.50	3.68

Chin-lung Hu

Bats: R **Throws:** R **Pos:** SS-35; 2B-30; PR-9; PH-1 **Ht:** 5'11" **Wt:** 191 **Born:** 2/2/1984 **Age:** 25

Year	Team	Lg	G	AB	H	2B	3B	HR	(Hm	Rd)	TB	R	RBI	RC	TBB	IBB	SO	HBP	SH	SF	SB	CS	SB%	GDP	Avg	OBP	Slg
2003	Ogden	R+	53	220	67	9	5	3	(-	-)	95	34	23	32	14	0	33	0	4	2	5	4	.56	2	.305	.343	.432
2004	Clmbs	A	84	332	99	15	4	6	(-	-)	140	58	25	50	20	0	50	3	11	2	17	7	.71	7	.298	.342	.422
2004	VeroB	A+	20	75	23	4	1	0	(-	-)	29	12	10	10	5	0	6	0	3	0	3	1	.75	1	.307	.350	.387
2005	VeroB	A+	116	470	147	29	1	8	(-	-)	202	80	56	73	19	1	40	7	7	2	23	6	.79	6	.313	.347	.430

Year	Team	Lg		BATTING																				BASERUNNING				AVERAGES		
			G	AB	H	2B	3B	HR	(Hm	Rd)	TB	R	RBI	RC	TBB	IBB	SO	HBP	SH	SF		SB	CS	SB%	GDP		Avg	OBP	Slg
2006	Jaxnvl	AA	125	488	124	20	2	5	(-	-)	163	71	34	58	49	1	63	4	13	2		11	5	.69	10		.254	.326	.334
2007	Jaxnvl	AA	82	325	107	30	5	6	(-	-)	165	56	34	63	26	1	33	1	3	1		12	4	.75	5		.329	.380	.508
2007	LsVgs	AAA	45	192	61	10	1	8	(-	-)	97	33	28	31	6	0	18	0	1	1		3	4	.43	5		.318	.337	.505
2008	LsVgs	AAA	41	156	46	5	3	1	(-	-)	60	21	15	20	7	1	19	0	4	1		2	0	1.00	10		.295	.323	.385
2007	LAD	NL	12	29	7	0	1	2	(2	0)	15	5	5	5	0	0	8	0	2	0		0	0	-	5		.241	.241	.517
2008	LAD	NL	65	116	21	2	2	0	(0	0)	27	16	9	5	11	4	23	0	2	0		2	0	1.00	5		.181	.252	.233
2 ML YEARS			77	145	28	2	3	2	(2	0)	42	21	14	10	11	4	31	0	4	0		2	0	1.00	5		.193	.250	.290

Justin Huber

Bats: R **Throws:** R **Pos:** LF-22; PH-10; DH-1; PR-1   **Ht:** 6'2" **Wt:** 205 **Born:** 7/1/1982 **Age:** 26

Year	Team	Lg		BATTING																				BASERUNNING				AVERAGES		
			G	AB	H	2B	3B	HR	(Hm	Rd)	TB	R	RBI	RC	TBB	IBB	SO	HBP	SH	SF		SB	CS	SB%	GDP		Avg	OBP	Slg
2008	Portlnd	AAA	61	199	49	12	0	3	(-	-)	70	17	27	23	18	1	51	4	0	2		0	1	.00	9		.246	.318	.352
2005	KC	AL	25	78	17	3	0	0	(0	0)	20	6	6	4	5	0	20	1	0	1		0	0	-	1		.218	.271	.256
2006	KC	AL	5	10	2	1	0	0	(0	0)	3	1	1	1	1	0	4	0	0	0		1	0	1.00	0		.200	.273	.300
2007	KC	AL	8	10	1	0	0	0	(0	0)	1	2	0	0	0	0	2	0	0	0		0	0	-	0		.100	.100	.100
2008	SD	NL	33	61	15	3	0	2	(0	2)	24	5	8	9	3	0	19	2	1	0		0	0	-	0		.246	.303	.393
4 ML YEARS			71	159	35	7	0	2	(0	2)	48	14	15	14	9	0	45	3	1	1		1	0	1.00	1		.220	.273	.302

Luke Hudson

Pitches: R **Bats:** R **Pos:** P   **Ht:** 6'3" **Wt:** 205 **Born:** 5/2/1977 **Age:** 32

Year	Team	Lg		HOW MUCH HE PITCHED					WHAT HE GAVE UP											THE RESULTS							
			G	GS	CG	GF	IP	BFP	H	R	ER	HR	SH	SF	HB	TBB	IBB	SO	WP	Bk	W	L	Pct	ShO	Sv-Op	Hld	ERC	ERA
2002	Cin	NL	3	0	0	0	6.0	28	5	5	3	1	0	0	0	6	0	7	2	0	0	0	-	0	0-0	1	6.15	4.50
2004	Cin	NL	9	9	0	0	48.1	204	36	16	13	3	2	2	2	25	1	38	5	0	4	2	.667	0	0-0	0	3.01	2.42
2005	Cin	NL	19	16	0	1	84.2	380	83	62	60	14	5	4	11	50	2	53	5	0	6	9	.400	0	0-0	0	5.88	6.38
2006	KC	AL	26	15	0	1	102.0	440	109	62	58	7	0	3	4	38	1	64	6	0	7	6	.538	0	0-1	1	4.34	5.12
2007	KC	AL	1	1	0	0	2.0	13	2	5	4	1	0	0	0	4	0	0	0	0	0	1	.000	0	0-0	0	13.81	18.00
5 ML YEARS			58	41	0	2	243.0	1065	235	150	138	26	7	9	17	123	4	162	18	0	17	18	.486	0	0-1	2	4.68	5.11

Orlando Hudson

Bats: B **Throws:** R **Pos:** 2B-105; DH-1; PH-1   **Ht:** 6'0" **Wt:** 190 **Born:** 12/12/1977 **Age:** 31

Year	Team	Lg		BATTING																				BASERUNNING				AVERAGES		
			G	AB	H	2B	3B	HR	(Hm	Rd)	TB	R	RBI	RC	TBB	IBB	SO	HBP	SH	SF		SB	CS	SB%	GDP		Avg	OBP	Slg
2002	Tor	AL	54	192	53	10	5	4	(2	2)	85	20	23	30	11	0	27	2	0	2		0	1	.00	6		.276	.319	.443
2003	Tor	AL	142	474	127	21	6	9	(5	4)	187	54	57	64	39	1	87	5	0	3		5	4	.56	13		.268	.328	.395
2004	Tor	AL	135	489	132	32	7	12	(5	7)	214	73	58	71	51	0	98	4	3	4		7	3	.70	12		.270	.341	.438
2005	Tor	AL	131	461	125	25	5	10	(4	6)	190	62	63	59	30	1	65	3	0	7		7	1	.88	10		.271	.315	.412
2006	Ari	NL	157	579	166	34	9	15	(7	8)	263	87	67	89	61	5	78	2	4	4		9	6	.60	17		.287	.354	.454
2007	Ari	NL	139	517	152	28	9	10	(7	3)	228	69	63	82	70	1	87	2	5	7		10	2	.83	21		.294	.376	.441
2008	Ari	NL	107	407	124	29	3	8	(6	2)	183	54	41	66	40	2	62	2	3	3		4	1	.80	18		.305	.367	.450
7 ML YEARS			865	3119	879	179	44	68	(36	32)	1350	419	372	461	302	10	504	20	15	30		42	18	.70	97		.282	.346	.433

Tim Hudson

Pitches: R **Bats:** R **Pos:** SP-22; RP-1   **Ht:** 6'1" **Wt:** 170 **Born:** 7/14/1975 **Age:** 33

Year	Team	Lg		HOW MUCH HE PITCHED					WHAT HE GAVE UP											THE RESULTS							
			G	GS	CG	GF	IP	BFP	H	R	ER	HR	SH	SF	HB	TBB	IBB	SO	WP	Bk	W	L	Pct	ShO	Sv-Op	Hld	ERC	ERA
1999	Oak	AL	21	21	1	0	136.1	580	121	56	49	8	1	2	4	62	2	132	6	0	11	2	.846	0	0-0	0	3.50	3.23
2000	Oak	AL	32	32	2	0	202.1	847	169	100	93	24	5	7	7	82	5	169	7	0	20	6	.769	2	0-0	0	3.43	4.14
2001	Oak	AL	35	35	3	0	235.0	980	216	100	88	20	12	8	6	71	5	181	9	1	18	9	.667	0	0-0	0	3.22	3.37
2002	Oak	AL	34	34	4	0	238.1	983	237	87	79	16	9	6	8	62	9	152	7	1	15	9	.625	2	0-0	0	3.51	2.98
2003	Oak	AL	34	34	3	0	240.0	967	197	84	72	15	11	2	10	61	9	162	6	0	16	7	.696	2	0-0	0	2.47	2.70
2004	Oak	AL	27	27	3	0	188.2	793	194	82	74	8	7	4	12	44	3	103	4	1	12	6	.667	2	0-0	0	3.44	3.53
2005	Atl	NL	29	29	2	0	192.0	817	194	79	75	20	9	1	9	65	5	115	4	0	14	9	.609	0	0-0	0	4.12	3.52
2006	Atl	NL	35	35	2	0	218.1	959	235	129	118	25	8	3	9	79	10	141	7	0	13	12	.520	1	0-0	0	4.54	4.86
2007	Atl	NL	34	34	1	0	224.1	925	221	87	83	10	11	6	8	53	8	132	5	2	16	10	.615	1	0-0	0	3.12	3.33
2008	Atl	NL	23	22	1	0	142.0	573	125	53	50	11	5	6	3	40	5	85	3	1	11	7	.611	1	0-0	0	2.90	3.17
Postseason			9	8	1	0	47.2	207	50	27	21	5	4	2	2	16	1	32	1	0	1	3	.250	0	0-0	0	4.25	3.97
10 ML YEARS			304	303	22	0	2017.1	8424	1909	857	781	160	75	42	75	619	61	1372	58	6	146	77	.655	11	0-0	0	3.41	3.48

Aubrey Huff

Bats: L **Throws:** R **Pos:** DH-98; 3B-33; 1B-24; PH-2   **Ht:** 6'4" **Wt:** 234 **Born:** 12/20/1976 **Age:** 32

Year	Team	Lg		BATTING																				BASERUNNING				AVERAGES		
			G	AB	H	2B	3B	HR	(Hm	Rd)	TB	R	RBI	RC	TBB	IBB	SO	HBP	SH	SF		SB	CS	SB%	GDP		Avg	OBP	Slg
2000	TB	AL	39	122	35	7	0	4	(3	1)	54	12	14	15	5	1	18	1	0	1		0	0	-	6		.287	.318	.443
2001	TB	AL	111	411	102	25	1	8	(5	3)	153	42	45	37	23	2	72	0	0	0		1	3	.25	18		.248	.288	.372
2002	TB	AL	113	454	142	25	0	23	(17	6)	236	67	59	66	37	7	55	1	0	2		4	1	.80	17		.313	.364	.520
2003	TB	AL	162	636	198	47	3	34	(15	19)	353	91	107	112	53	17	80	8	0	9		2	3	.40	19		.311	.367	.555
2004	TB	AL	157	600	178	27	2	29	(16	13)	296	92	104	96	56	6	74	6	0	5		5	1	.83	9		.297	.360	.493
2005	TB	AL	154	575	150	26	2	22	(9	13)	246	70	92	77	49	13	88	5	0	7		8	7	.53	12		.261	.321	.428
2006	2 Tms		131	454	121	25	2	21	(9	12)	213	57	66	55	50	6	64	7	0	6		0	0	-	11		.267	.344	.469
2007	Bal	AL	151	550	154	34	5	15	(8	7)	243	68	72	79	48	2	87	1	0	4		1	1	.50	13		.280	.337	.442

Year	Team	Lg	G	AB	H	2B	3B	HR	(Hm	Rd)	TB	R	RBI	RC	TBB	IBB	SO	HBP	SH	SF	SB	CS	SB%	GDP	Avg	OBP	Slg
									BATTING												**BASERUNNING**				**AVERAGES**		
2008	Bal	AL	154	598	182	48	2	32	(18	14)	330	96	108	111	53	7	89	3	0	7	4	0	1.00	9	.304	.360	.552
06	TB	AL	63	230	65	15	1	8	(4	4)	106	26	28	28	24	3	25	0	0	2	0	0	-	4	.283	.348	.461
06	Hou	NL	68	224	56	10	1	13	(5	8)	107	31	38	27	26	3	39	7	0	4	0	0	-	7	.250	.341	.478
9 ML YEARS			1172	4400	1262	264	17	188	(100	88)	2124	595	667	648	374	61	627	32	0	41	25	16	.61	114	.287	.344	.483

Phil Hughes

Pitches: R Bats: R Pos: SP-8   Ht: 6'5" Wt: 230 Born: 6/24/1986 Age: 23

Year	Team	Lg	G	GS	CG	GF	IP	BFP	H	R	ER	HR	SH	SF	HB	TBB	IBB	SO	WP	Bk	W	L	Pct	ShO	Sv-Op	Hld	ERC	ERA
			HOW MUCH HE PITCHED						**WHAT HE GAVE UP**												**THE RESULTS**							
2004	Yanks	R	3	3	0	0	5.0	18	4	0	0	0	0	0	0	0	0	8	0	0	0	0	-	0	0--	-	1.34	0.00
2005	CtnSC	A	12	12	1	0	68.2	265	46	19	15	1	2	4	3	16	0	72	3	0	7	1	.875	0	0--	-	1.55	1.97
2005	Tampa	A+	5	4	0	0	17.2	65	8	6	6	0	1	0	3	4	0	21	0	0	2	0	1.000	0	0--	-	1.13	3.06
2006	Tampa	A+	5	5	0	0	30.0	110	19	7	6	0	0	0	1	2	0	30	0	0	2	3	.400	0	0--	-	1.03	1.80
2006	Trntn	AA	21	21	0	0	116.0	448	73	30	29	5	4	2	2	32	0	138	5	0	10	3	.769	0	0--	-	1.57	2.25
2007	S-WB	AAA	5	5	0	0	28.2	106	16	7	7	0	1	0	1	8	0	28	2	0	4	1	.800	0	0--	-	1.27	2.20
2007	Tampa	A+	1	1	0	0	2.0	8	0	1	0	0	0	0	0	2	0	3	0	0	0	0	-	0	0--	-	0.95	0.00
2007	Trntn	AA	2	2	0	0	7.0	27	5	1	1	0	0	0	0	2	0	11	0	0	0	0	-	0	0--	-	1.68	1.29
2008	CtnSC	A	2	0	0	0	6.2	24	3	0	0	0	0	0	0	2	0	6	2	0	2	0	1.000	0	0--	-	0.94	0.00
2008	S-WB	AAA	6	6	0	0	29.0	132	34	19	19	2	0	0	2	9	0	31	0	0	1	0	1.000	0	0--	-	4.63	5.90
2007	NYY	AL	13	13	0	0	72.2	306	64	39	36	8	2	1	2	29	0	58	4	0	5	3	.625	0	0-0	0	3.61	4.46
2008	NYY	AL	8	8	0	0	34.0	157	43	26	25	3	1	3	1	15	0	23	2	0	0	4	.000	0	0-0	0	5.84	6.62
Postseason			2	0	0	1	5.2	21	3	1	1	1	0	0	0	0	0	6	1	0	1	0	1.000	0	0-0	0	0.99	1.59
2 ML YEARS			21	21	0	0	106.2	463	107	65	61	11	3	4	3	44	0	81	6	0	5	7	.417	0	0-0	0	4.29	5.15

Tug Hulett

Bats: L Throws: R Pos: DH-13; PH-13; 2B-4; SS-4; PR-4; 3B-1   Ht: 5'10" Wt: 185 Born: 2/28/1983 Age: 26

Year	Team	Lg	G	AB	H	2B	3B	HR	(Hm	Rd)	TB	R	RBI	RC	TBB	IBB	SO	HBP	SH	SF	SB	CS	SB%	GDP	Avg	OBP	Slg
									BATTING												**BASERUNNING**				**AVERAGES**		
2004	Spkane	A-	70	247	69	17	0	0	(-	-)	86	54	23	48	68	0	67	5	1	0	19	7	.73	1	.279	.444	.348
2005	Clinton	A	106	385	102	22	3	1	(-	-)	133	70	45	66	90	0	87	2	9	5	20	6	.77	7	.265	.402	.345
2006	Bkrsfld	A+	77	289	84	19	7	2	(-	-)	123	46	37	58	61	0	61	3	4	4	15	5	.75	2	.291	.415	.426
2006	Frisco	AA	48	185	57	8	4	0	(-	-)	73	36	15	34	31	0	36	1	3	3	9	2	.82	5	.308	.405	.395
2007	Okla	AAA	132	517	141	30	2	11	(-	-)	208	95	67	82	64	0	114	7	1	6	20	5	.80	11	.273	.357	.402
2008	Tacom	AAA	91	336	100	22	5	14	(-	-)	174	71	47	68	49	3	73	0	8	7	10	5	.67	4	.298	.380	.518
2008	Sea	AL	30	49	11	1	0	1	(0	1)	15	2	2	2	5	0	17	1	1	0	0	0	-	3	.224	.309	.306

Philip Humber

Pitches: R Bats: R Pos: RP-5   Ht: 6'4" Wt: 224 Born: 12/21/1982 Age: 26

Year	Team	Lg	G	GS	CG	GF	IP	BFP	H	R	ER	HR	SH	SF	HB	TBB	IBB	SO	WP	Bk	W	L	Pct	ShO	Sv-Op	Hld	ERC	ERA
			HOW MUCH HE PITCHED						**WHAT HE GAVE UP**												**THE RESULTS**							
2008	Roch*	AAA	31	23	2	3	136.1	593	145	76	69	21	0	6	6	49	1	106	6	0	10	8	.556	0	0--	-	4.86	4.56
2006	NYM	NL	2	0	0	1	2.0	7	0	0	0	0	0	0	0	1	0	2	0	0	0	0	-	0	0-0	0	0.27	0.00
2007	NYM	NL	3	1	0	2	7.0	32	9	6	6	1	0	0	0	2	0	2	0	0	0	0	-	0	0-0	0	5.46	7.71
2008	Min	AL	5	0	0	2	11.2	50	11	6	6	4	0	0	1	5	0	6	0	0	0	0	-	0	0-0	0	6.11	4.63
3 ML YEARS			10	1	0	5	20.2	89	20	12	12	5	0	0	1	8	0	10	0	0	0	0	-	0	0-0	0	5.06	5.23

Nick Hundley

Bats: R Throws: R Pos: C-59; PH-1   Ht: 6'1" Wt: 210 Born: 9/8/1983 Age: 25

Year	Team	Lg	G	AB	H	2B	3B	HR	(Hm	Rd)	TB	R	RBI	RC	TBB	IBB	SO	HBP	SH	SF	SB	CS	SB%	GDP	Avg	OBP	Slg
									BATTING												**BASERUNNING**				**AVERAGES**		
2005	Eugene	A-	43	148	37	7	1	7	(-	-)	67	30	22	29	33	1	35	2	0	1	1	0	1.00	2	.250	.391	.453
2005	FtWyn	A	10	36	8	2	0	0	(-	-)	10	2	5	3	4	0	9	1	0	1	0	0	-	0	.222	.310	.278
2006	FtWyn	A	57	215	59	19	0	8	(-	-)	102	29	44	37	25	0	45	4	0	4	1	1	.50	3	.274	.355	.474
2006	Lk Els	A+	47	176	49	13	0	3	(-	-)	71	18	23	26	20	1	44	2	1	1	1	1	.50	2	.278	.357	.403
2007	SnAnt	AA	101	373	92	22	1	20	(-	-)	176	55	71	58	42	0	75	2	2	3	0	2	.00	7	.247	.324	.472
2008	Portlnd	AAA	58	224	52	13	0	12	(-	-)	101	33	39	29	17	0	44	0	1	1	0	0	-	8	.232	.285	.451
2008	SD	NL	60	198	47	7	1	5	(4	1)	71	21	24	17	11	0	52	2	0	5	0	0	-	1	.237	.278	.359

Tommy Hunter

Pitches: R Bats: R Pos: SP-3   Ht: 6'3" Wt: 255 Born: 7/3/1986 Age: 22

Year	Team	Lg	G	GS	CG	GF	IP	BFP	H	R	ER	HR	SH	SF	HB	TBB	IBB	SO	WP	Bk	W	L	Pct	ShO	Sv-Op	Hld	ERC	ERA
			HOW MUCH HE PITCHED						**WHAT HE GAVE UP**												**THE RESULTS**							
2007	Spkane	A-	10	0	0	5	17.2	69	15	7	5	0	0	0	0	1	0	13	0	0	2	3	.400	0	1--	-	1.53	2.55
2008	Bkrsfld	A+	9	9	0	0	58.1	241	63	26	23	6	4	1	2	8	0	50	4	0	5	4	.556	0	0--	-	3.68	3.55
2008	Frisco	AA	8	8	0	0	52.1	218	52	24	22	5	2	1	3	17	1	28	2	0	4	2	.667	0	0--	-	4.04	3.78
2008	Okla	AAA	8	8	0	0	53.0	219	55	18	17	6	0	2	0	9	0	28	1	0	4	2	.667	0	0--	-	3.47	2.89
2008	Tex	AL	3	3	0	0	11.0	63	23	20	20	4	0	0	1	3	0	9	0	0	0	2	.000	0	0-0	0	12.66	16.36

Torii Hunter

Bats: R Throws: R Pos: CF-137; DH-9   Ht: 6'2" Wt: 225 Born: 7/18/1975 Age: 33

Year	Team	Lg	G	AB	H	2B	3B	HR	(Hm	Rd)	TB	R	RBI	RC	TBB	IBB	SO	HBP	SH	SF	SB	CS	SB%	GDP	Avg	OBP	Slg
1997	Min	AL	1	0	0	0	0	0	(0	0)	0	0	0	0	0	0	0	0	0	0	0	0	-	-	-	-	-
1998	Min	AL	6	17	4	1	0	0	(0	0)	5	0	2	1	2	0	6	0	0	0	0	1	.00	1	.235	.316	.294
1999	Min	AL	135	384	98	17	2	9	(2	7)	146	52	35	44	26	1	72	6	1	5	10	6	.63	9	.255	.309	.380
2000	Min	AL	99	336	94	14	7	5	(4	1)	137	44	44	39	18	2	68	2	0	2	4	3	.57	13	.280	.318	.408
2001	Min	AL	148	564	147	32	5	27	(13	14)	270	82	92	79	29	0	125	8	1	1	9	6	.60	12	.261	.306	.479
2002	Min	AL	148	561	162	37	4	29	(13	16)	294	89	94	85	35	3	118	5	0	3	23	8	.74	17	.289	.334	.524
2003	Min	AL	154	581	145	31	4	26	(12	14)	262	83	102	76	50	7	106	5	0	6	6	7	.46	15	.250	.312	.451
2004	Min	AL	138	520	141	37	0	23	(9	14)	247	79	81	69	40	4	101	7	0	2	21	7	.75	23	.271	.330	.475
2005	Min	AL	98	372	100	24	1	14	(6	8)	168	63	56	53	34	3	65	6	0	4	23	7	.77	8	.269	.337	.452
2006	Min	AL	147	557	155	21	2	31	(15	16)	273	86	98	81	45	2	108	5	0	4	12	6	.67	19	.278	.336	.490
2007	Min	AL	160	600	172	45	1	28	(11	17)	303	94	107	99	40	10	101	5	0	5	18	9	.67	17	.287	.334	.505
2008	LAA	AL	146	551	153	37	2	21	(10	11)	257	85	78	80	50	6	108	6	0	1	19	5	.79	15	.278	.344	.466
Postseason			21	80	24	8	1	3	(0	3)	43	15	8	9	5	1	11	0	2	1	2	0	1.00	2	.300	.337	.538
12 ML YEARS			1380	5043	1371	296	28	213	(95	118)	2362	757	789	706	369	38	978	55	2	33	145	65	.69	149	.272	.326	.468

Eric Hurley

Pitches: R Bats: R Pos: SP-5   Ht: 6'4" Wt: 195 Born: 9/17/1985 Age: 23

Year	Team	Lg	G	GS	CG	GF	IP	BFP	H	R	ER	HR	SH	SF	HB	TBB	IBB	SO	WP	Bk	W	L	Pct	ShO	Sv-Op	Hld	ERC	ERA
2004	Rngrs	R	6	2	0	1	15.1	69	20	8	4	1	0	1	1	4	0	15	1	0	0	1	.000	0	0- -	-	5.31	2.35
2004	Spkane	A-	8	6	0	0	28.1	115	31	18	17	6	1	2	1	6	1	21	0	0	0	2	.000	0	0- -	-	4.97	5.40
2005	Clinton	A	28	28	0	0	155.1	653	135	72	65	11	2	7	8	59	0	152	11	0	12	6	.667	0	0- -	-	3.30	3.77
2006	Bkrsfld	A+	18	18	1	0	100.2	425	92	60	46	12	1	3	4	32	0	106	4	0	5	6	.455	0	0- -	-	3.54	4.11
2006	Frisco	AA	6	6	0	0	37.0	140	21	9	8	4	1	0	3	11	0	31	0	0	3	1	.750	0	0- -	-	1.94	1.95
2007	Frisco	AA	15	14	1	0	88.2	357	71	39	32	13	1	0	4	27	0	76	2	1	7	2	.778	1	0- -	-	3.16	3.25
2007	Okla	AAA	13	13	0	0	73.1	313	65	45	40	13	4	2	3	28	0	59	4	0	4	7	.364	0	0- -	-	4.02	4.91
2008	Okla	AAA	13	13	0	0	74.2	338	86	51	44	15	1	2	4	29	0	72	1	1	2	5	.286	0	0- -	-	5.86	5.30
2008	Frisco	AA	1	1	0	0	7.1	24	4	0	0	0	0	0	0	1	0	2	0	0	1	0	1.000	0	0- -	-	0.96	0.00
2008	Tex	AL	5	5	0	0	24.2	107	26	15	15	5	0	0	1	9	0	13	1	0	1	2	.333	0	0-0	0	5.19	5.47

Chris Iannetta

Bats: R Throws: R Pos: C-100; PH-5; 3B-1   Ht: 6'0" Wt: 225 Born: 4/8/1983 Age: 26

Year	Team	Lg	G	AB	H	2B	3B	HR	(Hm	Rd)	TB	R	RBI	RC	TBB	IBB	SO	HBP	SH	SF	SB	CS	SB%	GDP	Avg	OBP	Slg
2006	Col	NL	21	77	20	4	0	2	(0	2)	30	12	10	9	13	2	17	1	1	1	0	1	.00	1	.260	.370	.390
2007	Col	NL	67	197	43	8	3	4	(1	3)	69	22	27	27	29	3	58	5	1	2	0	0	-	3	.218	.330	.350
2008	Col	NL	104	333	88	22	2	18	(11	7)	168	50	65	65	56	0	92	14	2	2	0	0	-	6	.264	.390	.505
3 ML YEARS			192	607	151	34	5	24	(12	12)	267	84	102	101	98	5	167	20	4	5	0	1	.00	10	.249	.368	.440

Raul Ibanez

Bats: L Throws: R Pos: LF-153; DH-9   Ht: 6'2" Wt: 225 Born: 6/2/1972 Age: 37

Year	Team	Lg	G	AB	H	2B	3B	HR	(Hm	Rd)	TB	R	RBI	RC	TBB	IBB	SO	HBP	SH	SF	SB	CS	SB%	GDP	Avg	OBP	Slg
1996	Sea	AL	4	5	0	0	0	0	(0	0)	0	0	0	0	0	0	1	1	0	0	0	0	-	0	.000	.167	.000
1997	Sea	AL	11	26	4	0	1	1	(1	0)	9	3	4	1	0	0	6	0	0	0	0	0	-	0	.154	.154	.346
1998	Sea	AL	37	98	25	7	1	2	(1	1)	40	12	12	10	5	0	22	0	0	0	0	0	-	4	.255	.291	.408
1999	Sea	AL	87	209	54	7	0	9	(3	6)	88	23	27	28	17	1	32	0	0	1	5	1	.83	4	.258	.313	.421
2000	Sea	AL	92	140	32	8	0	2	(2	0)	46	21	15	15	14	1	25	1	0	1	2	0	1.00	1	.229	.301	.329
2001	KC	AL	104	279	78	11	5	13	(5	8)	138	44	54	46	32	2	51	0	0	1	0	2	.00	6	.280	.353	.495
2002	KC	AL	137	497	146	37	6	24	(14	10)	267	70	103	89	40	5	76	2	1	4	5	3	.63	11	.294	.346	.537
2003	KC	AL	157	608	179	33	5	18	(8	10)	276	95	90	91	49	5	81	3	1	10	8	4	.67	10	.294	.345	.454
2004	Sea	AL	123	481	146	31	1	16	(9	7)	227	67	62	67	36	5	72	3	0	4	1	2	.33	10	.304	.353	.472
2005	Sea	AL	162	614	172	32	2	20	(9	11)	268	92	89	99	71	6	99	2	0	3	9	4	.69	12	.280	.355	.436
2006	Sea	AL	159	626	181	33	5	33	(17	16)	323	103	123	114	65	15	115	1	0	7	2	4	.33	13	.289	.353	.516
2007	Sea	AL	149	573	167	35	5	21	(7	14)	275	80	105	101	53	4	97	3	0	4	0	0	-	14	.291	.351	.480
2008	Sea	AL	162	635	186	43	3	23	(14	9)	304	85	110	107	64	11	110	3	0	5	2	4	.33	13	.293	.358	.479
Postseason			9	17	3	0	0	0	(0	0)	3	2	0	1	0	0	2	0	0	0	0	0	-	0	.176	.176	.176
13 ML YEARS			1384	4791	1370	277	34	182	(90	92)	2261	695	794	768	446	55	787	19	2	43	34	24	.59	98	.286	.346	.472

Kei Igawa

Pitches: L Bats: L Pos: SP-1; RP-1   Ht: 6'1" Wt: 212 Born: 7/13/1979 Age: 29

Year	Team	Lg	G	GS	CG	GF	IP	BFP	H	R	ER	HR	SH	SF	HB	TBB	IBB	SO	WP	Bk	W	L	Pct	ShO	Sv-Op	Hld	ERC	ERA
1999	Hnshn	Jap	7	3	0	1	15.1	80	23	11	11	1	-	-	1	13	-	14	0	0	1	1	.500	0	0- -	-	9.21	6.46
2000	Hnshn	Jap	9	5	0	1	39.1	172	36	19	19	5	-	-	0	19	-	37	7	0	1	3	.250	0	0- -	-	4.05	4.35
2001	Hnshn	Jap	29	28	3	0	192.0	829	174	76	57	11	-	-	3	89	-	171	6	0	9	13	.409	2	0- -	-	3.54	2.67
2002	Hnshn	Jap	31	29	8	2	209.2	830	163	63	58	15	-	-	7	53	-	206	8	0	14	9	.609	4	0- -	-	2.35	2.49
2003	Hnshn	Jap	29	29	8	0	206.0	839	184	72	64	15	0	0	3	58	3	179	5	0	20	5	.800	2	0- -	-	2.94	2.80
2004	Hnshn	Jap	29	29	6	0	200.1	840	190	95	83	29	11	2	6	54	0	228	5	0	14	11	.560	3	0- -	-	3.67	3.73
2005	Hnshn	Jap	27	27	2	0	172.1	778	199	91	74	23	-	-	1	60	-	145	4	0	13	9	.591	1	0- -	-	4.90	3.86
2006	Hnshn	Jap	28	28	7	0	200.0	820	174	77	69	17	-	-	6	46	-	184	4	0	13	9	.591	2	0- -	-	2.73	3.11
2007	Tampa	A+	2	2	0	0	9.0	37	7	4	2	0	0	0	0	3	0	6	0	0	1	1	.500	0	0- -	-	2.01	2.00
2007	S-WB	AAA	11	11	0	0	68.1	282	68	30	28	10	2	1	2	15	0	71	0	1	5	4	.556	0	0- -	-	3.80	3.69

	HOW MUCH HE PITCHED						WHAT HE GAVE UP													THE RESULTS							
Year Team	Lg	G	GS	CG	GF	IP	BFP	H	R	ER	HR	SH	SF	HB	TBB	IBB	SO	WP	Bk	W	L	Pct	ShO	Sv-Op	Hld	ERC	ERA
2008 S-WB	AAA	26	24	2	1	156.1	644	141	65	60	15	7	3	4	45	0	117	5	0	14	6	.700	0	0--	-	3.20	3.45
2007 NYY	AL	14	12	0	0	67.2	313	76	48	47	15	0	0	4	37	1	53	5	1	2	3	.400	0	0-0	0	6.60	6.25
2008 NYY	AL	2	1	0	1	4.0	24	13	6	6	0	0	0	0	0	0	0	0	0	0	1	.000	0	0-0	0	17.14	13.50
2 ML YEARS		16	13	0	1	71.2	337	89	54	53	15	0	1	4	37	1	53	5	1	2	4	.333	0	0-0	0	7.12	6.66

Tadahito Iguchi

Bats: R **Throws:** R **Pos:** 2B-78; PH-8; PR-1 **Ht:** 5'10" **Wt:** 185 **Born:** 12/4/1974 **Age:** 34

	BATTING																		BASERUNNING				AVERAGES		
Year Team	Lg	G	AB	H	2B	3B	HR	(Hm	Rd)	TB	R	RBI	RC	TBB	IBB	SO	HBP	SH	SF	SB	CS	SB%	GDP	Avg	OBP	Slg
2008 Lk Els*	A+	3	10	4	0	0	2	(-	-)	10	4	3	3	1	0	2	0	0	0	0	0	-	0	.400	.455	1.000
2005 CWS	AL	135	511	142	25	6	15	(7	8)	224	74	71	74	47	0	114	6	11	6	15	5	.75	16	.278	.342	.438
2006 CWS	AL	138	555	156	24	0	18	(12	6)	234	97	67	87	59	0	110	3	8	2	11	5	.69	7	.281	.352	.422
2007 2 Tms	AL	135	465	124	27	4	9	(6	3)	186	67	43	68	57	1	88	3	2	6	14	2	.88	6	.267	.347	.400
2008 2 Tms	NL	85	310	72	15	1	2	(1	1)	95	29	24	25	26	0	75	0	1	0	8	1	.89	11	.232	.292	.306
07 CWS	AL	90	327	82	17	4	6	(4	2)	125	45	31	46	44	1	65	2	1	3	8	1	.89	5	.251	.340	.382
07 Phi	NL	45	138	42	10	0	3	(2	1)	61	22	12	22	13	0	23	1	1	3	6	1	.86	1	.304	.361	.442
08 SD	NL	81	303	70	14	1	2	(1	1)	92	29	24	25	26	0	75	0	1	0	8	1	.89	11	.231	.292	.304
08 Phi	NL	4	7	2	1	0	0	(0	0)	3	0	0	0	0	0	0	0	0	0	0	0	-	0	.286	.286	.429
Postseason		15	48	9	1	0	1	(1	0)	13	7	5	6	4	0	12	3	3	0	0	1	.00	1	.188	.291	.271
4 ML YEARS		493	1841	494	91	11	44	(26	18)	739	267	205	254	189	1	387	12	22	14	48	13	.79	40	.268	.338	.401

Omar Infante

Bats: R **Throws:** R **Pos:** LF-34; 3B-32; SS-20; PH-15; 2B-10; CF-3 **Ht:** 6'0" **Wt:** 180 **Born:** 12/26/1981 **Age:** 27

	BATTING																		BASERUNNING				AVERAGES		
Year Team	Lg	G	AB	H	2B	3B	HR	(Hm	Rd)	TB	R	RBI	RC	TBB	IBB	SO	HBP	SH	SF	SB	CS	SB%	GDP	Avg	OBP	Slg
2008 Rchmd*	AAA	3	11	4	1	0	0	(-	-)	5	3	3	2	1	0	1	0	0	0	0	0	-	0	.364	.417	.455
2002 Det	AL	18	72	24	3	0	1	(0	1)	30	4	6	12	3	0	10	0	0	0	0	1	.00	0	.333	.360	.417
2003 Det	AL	69	221	49	6	1	0	(0	0)	57	24	8	16	18	0	37	0	3	2	6	3	.67	1	.222	.278	.258
2004 Det	AL	142	503	133	27	9	16	(7	9)	226	69	55	69	40	3	112	1	7	5	13	7	.65	4	.264	.317	.449
2005 Det	AL	121	406	90	28	2	9	(3	6)	149	36	43	38	16	0	73	2	8	2	8	0	1.00	5	.222	.254	.367
2006 Det	AL	78	224	62	11	4	4	(0	4)	93	35	25	26	14	0	45	3	2	2	3	2	.60	5	.277	.325	.415
2007 Det	AL	66	166	45	6	1	2	(0	2)	59	24	17	23	9	0	29	0	2	1	4	1	.80	4	.271	.307	.355
2008 Atl	NL	96	317	93	24	3	3	(1	2)	132	45	40	45	22	2	44	2	2	5	0	1	.00	4	.293	.338	.416
Postseason		2	3	1	0	0	0	(0	0)	1	0	0	1	1	0	1	0	0	0	1	0	1.00	0	.333	.500	.333
7 ML YEARS		590	1909	496	105	20	35	(11	24)	746	237	194	229	122	5	350	8	24	17	34	15	.69	23	.260	.304	.391

Brandon Inge

Bats: R **Throws:** R **Pos:** C-60; 3B-51; CF-13; LF-2; PH-2; PR-2 **Ht:** 5'11" **Wt:** 188 **Born:** 5/19/1977 **Age:** 32

	BATTING																		BASERUNNING				AVERAGES		
Year Team	Lg	G	AB	H	2B	3B	HR	(Hm	Rd)	TB	R	RBI	RC	TBB	IBB	SO	HBP	SH	SF	SB	CS	SB%	GDP	Avg	OBP	Slg
2008 Toledo*	AAA	3	10	3	0	0	1	(-	-)	6	2	4	2	2	0	2	0	0	0	0	0	-	0	.300	.417	.600
2001 Det	AL	79	189	34	11	0	0	(0	0)	45	13	15	6	9	0	41	0	2	2	1	4	.20	2	.180	.215	.238
2002 Det	AL	95	321	65	15	3	7	(3	4)	107	27	24	24	24	0	101	4	1	1	1	3	.25	7	.202	.266	.333
2003 Det	AL	104	330	67	15	3	8	(4	4)	112	32	30	23	24	0	79	5	4	3	4	4	.50	8	.203	.265	.339
2004 Det	AL	131	408	117	15	7	13	(9	4)	185	43	64	63	32	0	72	4	8	6	5	4	.56	4	.287	.340	.453
2005 Det	AL	160	616	161	31	9	16	(10	6)	258	75	72	82	63	1	140	3	6	6	7	6	.54	14	.261	.330	.419
2006 Det	AL	159	542	137	29	2	27	(12	15)	251	83	83	79	43	2	128	7	4	5	7	4	.64	12	.253	.313	.463
2007 Det	AL	151	508	120	25	2	14	(5	9)	191	64	71	65	47	5	150	11	7	4	9	2	.82	8	.236	.312	.376
2008 Det	AL	113	347	71	16	4	11	(8	3)	128	41	51	44	43	2	94	8	5	4	4	3	.57	4	.205	.303	.369
Postseason		13	44	12	3	0	1	(0	1)	18	4	4	5	4	2	15	0	1	1	0	0	-	1	.273	.327	.409
8 ML YEARS		992	3261	772	157	30	96	(55	41)	1277	378	410	386	285	10	805	42	37	31	38	30	.56	59	.237	.304	.392

Joe Inglett

Bats: L **Throws:** R **Pos:** 2B-66; LF-22; PH-13; RF-12; 3B-6; SS-2; DH-2; CF-1; PR-1 **Ht:** 5'10" **Wt:** 180 **Born:** 6/29/1978 **Age:** 31

	BATTING																		BASERUNNING				AVERAGES		
Year Team	Lg	G	AB	H	2B	3B	HR	(Hm	Rd)	TB	R	RBI	RC	TBB	IBB	SO	HBP	SH	SF	SB	CS	SB%	GDP	Avg	OBP	Slg
2008 Syrcse*	AAA	15	54	22	2	2	1	(-	-)	31	12	6	13	7	0	7	1	0	0	1	2	.33	0	.407	.484	.574
2006 Cle	AL	64	201	57	8	3	2	(1	1)	77	26	21	28	14	0	39	1	5	1	5	1	.83	1	.284	.332	.383
2007 Tor	AL	2	5	3	0	1	0	(0	0)	5	0	2	3	0	0	0	0	0	0	1	0	1.00	0	.600	.600	1.000
2008 Tor	AL	109	344	102	15	7	3	(2	1)	140	45	39	52	28	0	43	4	8	1	9	2	.82	5	.297	.355	.407
3 ML YEARS		175	550	162	23	11	5	(3	2)	222	71	62	83	42	0	82	5	13	2	15	3	.83	6	.295	.349	.404

Hernan Iribarren

Bats: L **Throws:** R **Pos:** PH-10; 2B-2; CF-1 **Ht:** 6'1" **Wt:** 180 **Born:** 6/29/1984 **Age:** 25

	BATTING																		BASERUNNING				AVERAGES		
Year Team	Lg	G	AB	H	2B	3B	HR	(Hm	Rd)	TB	R	RBI	RC	TBB	IBB	SO	HBP	SH	SF	SB	CS	SB%	GDP	Avg	OBP	Slg
2004 Brewrs	R	46	189	83	6	9	4	(-	-)	119	40	36	52	19	2	23	0	3	0	15	7	.68	2	.439	.490	.630
2004 Beloit	A	15	67	25	6	5	1	(-	-)	44	12	10	17	5	0	16	0	0	1	1	0	1.00	1	.373	.411	.657
2005 WV	A-	126	486	141	15	8	4	(-	-)	184	72	48	73	51	2	99	5	13	5	38	15	.72	9	.290	.360	.379
2006 BrvdCt	A+	108	398	127	12	4	2	(-	-)	153	50	50	60	39	0	57	1	11	6	19	15	.56	8	.319	.376	.384
2007 Hntsvl	AA	124	479	147	23	12	4	(-	-)	206	72	52	75	44	2	109	1	13	5	18	16	.53	5	.307	.363	.430
2008 Nashv	AAA	99	361	100	17	3	0	(-	-)	123	47	30	43	28	0	61	1	5	2	19	8	.70	6	.277	.329	.341
2008 Mil	NL	12	14	2	1	0	0	(0	0)	3	1	1	1	1	0	3	0	0	0	0	0	-	0	.143	.200	.214

Travis Ishikawa

Bats: L **Throws:** L **Pos:** 1B-29; PH-6   **Ht:** 6'3" **Wt:** 225 **Born:** 9/24/1983 **Age:** 25

Year	Team	Lg	G	AB	H	2B	3B	HR	(Hm	Rd)	TB	R	RBI	RC	TBB	IBB	SO	HBP	SH	SF	SB	CS	SB%	GDP	Avg	OBP	Slg
2002	Giants	R	19	68	19	4	2	1	(-	-)	30	10	10	12	7	1	20	2	0	0	7	0	1.00	1	.279	.364	.441
2002	SlmKzr	A-	23	88	27	2	1	1	(-	-)	34	14	17	12	5	0	22	1	1	1	1	1	.50	2	.307	.347	.386
2003	Hgrstn	A	57	194	40	5	0	3	(-	-)	54	20	22	19	33	5	69	3	1	1	3	4	.43	7	.206	.329	.278
2003	SlmKzr	A-	66	248	63	17	4	3	(-	-)	97	53	31	40	44	0	77	5	0	1	0	0	-	2	.254	.376	.391
2004	Hgrstn	A	97	355	91	19	2	15	(-	-)	159	59	54	59	45	0	110	11	1	1	10	5	.67	8	.256	.357	.448
2004	SnJos	A+	16	56	13	7	0	1	(-	-)	23	10	10	9	10	2	16	1	0	1	0	0	-	1	.232	.353	.411
2005	SnJos	A+	127	432	122	28	7	22	(-	-)	230	87	79	90	70	3	129	7	2	5	1	4	.20	1	.282	.387	.532
2006	Conn	AA	86	298	69	13	4	10	(-	-)	120	33	42	40	35	3	88	3	1	3	0	0	-	4	.232	.316	.403
2007	Conn	AA	48	173	37	3	1	3	(-	-)	51	17	17	15	17	1	48	2	0	0	1	0	1.00	4	.214	.292	.295
2007	SnJos	A+	56	198	53	15	1	13	(-	-)	109	35	34	37	19	0	78	4	0	1	0	0	-	1	.268	.342	.551
2008	Conn	AA	64	234	68	16	0	8	(-	-)	108	34	48	44	35	3	45	2	2	4	10	4	.71	3	.291	.382	.462
2008	Fresno	AAA	48	171	53	19	3	16	(-	-)	126	35	46	44	14	0	36	4	0	3	0	1	.00	2	.310	.370	.737
2006	SF	NL	12	24	7	3	1	0	(0	0)	12	1	4	4	1	0	6	0	0	0	0	0	-	1	.292	.320	.500
2008	SF	NL	33	95	26	6	0	3	(1	2)	41	12	15	17	9	1	27	0	0	0	1	0	1.00	1	.274	.337	.432
	2 ML YEARS		45	119	33	9	1	3	(1	2)	53	13	19	21	10	1	33	0	0	0	1	0	1.00	2	.277	.333	.445

Jason Isringhausen

Pitches: R **Bats:** R **Pos:** RP-42   **Ht:** 6'3" **Wt:** 230 **Born:** 9/7/1972 **Age:** 36

Year	Team	Lg	G	GS	CG	GF	IP	BFP	H	R	ER	HR	SH	SF	HB	TBB	IBB	SO	WP	Bk	W	L	Pct	ShO	Sv-Op	Hld	ERC	ERA
2008	PlmBh*	A+	1	1	0	0	2.0	7	1	0	0	0	0	0	0	0	0	1	0	0	0	0	-	0	0--	-	0.54	0.00
2008	Sprgfld*	AA	1	1	0	0	1.2	6	1	0	0	0	0	0	0	0	0	2	0	0	0	0	-	0	0--	-	0.75	0.00
1995	NYM	NL	14	14	1	0	93.0	385	88	29	29	6	3	3	2	31	2	55	4	1	9	2	.818	0	0-0	0	3.40	2.81
1996	NYM	NL	27	27	2	0	171.2	766	190	103	91	13	7	9	8	73	5	114	14	0	6	14	.300	1	0-0	0	4.75	4.77
1997	NYM	NL	6	6	0	0	29.2	145	40	27	25	3	1	2	1	22	0	25	3	0	2	2	.500	0	0-0	0	7.99	7.58
1999	2 Tms		33	5	0	20	64.2	286	64	35	34	9	0	1	3	34	4	51	4	0	1	4	.200	0	9-9	0	4.94	4.73
2000	Oak	AL	66	0	0	57	69.0	304	67	34	29	6	2	1	3	32	5	57	5	1	6	4	.600	0	33-40	0	4.09	3.78
2001	Oak	AL	65	0	0	54	71.1	293	54	24	21	5	3	1	0	23	5	74	2	0	4	3	.571	0	34-43	0	2.18	2.65
2002	StL	NL	60	0	0	51	65.1	257	46	22	18	0	4	3	1	18	1	68	0	0	3	2	.600	0	32-37	0	1.61	2.48
2003	StL	NL	40	0	0	31	42.0	174	31	14	11	2	1	0	0	18	1	41	6	0	0	1	.000	0	22-25	1	2.40	2.36
2004	StL	NL	74	0	0	66	75.1	308	55	27	24	5	6	1	2	23	4	71	1	0	4	2	.667	0	47-54	0	2.09	2.87
2005	StL	NL	63	0	0	52	59.0	245	43	14	14	4	3	1	1	27	5	51	2	0	1	2	.333	0	39-43	1	2.56	2.14
2006	StL	NL	59	0	0	51	58.1	257	47	25	23	10	1	3	3	38	3	52	3	0	4	8	.333	0	33-43	0	4.63	3.55
2007	StL	NL	63	0	0	54	65.1	267	42	21	18	4	1	1	2	28	3	54	3	0	4	0	1.000	0	32-34	0	2.11	2.48
2008	StL	NL	42	0	0	27	42.2	200	48	28	27	5	0	1	5	22	0	36	1	0	1	5	.167	0	12-19	2	5.84	5.70
99	NYM	NL	13	5	0	2	39.1	179	43	29	28	7	0	1	2	22	2	31	2	0	1	3	.250	0	1-1	0	6.07	6.41
99	Oak	AL	20	0	0	18	25.1	107	21	6	6	2	0	0	1	12	2	20	2	0	0	1	.000	0	8-8	0	3.33	2.13
	Postseason		23	0	0	22	26.2	110	17	8	7	2	2	1	1	12	4	23	0	0	1	1	.500	0	11-12	0	2.10	2.36
	13 ML YEARS		612	52	3	463	907.1	3887	815	403	364	72	32	27	31	389	38	749	48	2	45	49	.479	1	293-347	4	3.54	3.61

Akinori Iwamura

Bats: L **Throws:** R **Pos:** 2B-152   **Ht:** 5'9" **Wt:** 176 **Born:** 2/9/1979 **Age:** 30

Year	Team	Lg	G	AB	H	2B	3B	HR	(Hm	Rd)	TB	R	RBI	RC	TBB	IBB	SO	HBP	SH	SF	SB	CS	SB%	GDP	Avg	OBP	Slg
1998	Yakult	Jap	1	3	0	0	0	0	(-	-)	0	0	0	0	0	-	2	0	0	0	0	0	-	0	.000	.000	.000
1999	Yakult	Jap	83	252	74	11	4	11	(-	-)	126	28	35	44	18	-	46	1	0	2	7	1	.88	3	.294	.341	.500
2000	Yakult	Jap	130	436	121	13	9	18	(-	-)	206	67	66	74	39	-	103	4	9	1	13	1	.93	7	.278	.342	.472
2001	Yakult	Jap	136	520	149	24	4	19	(-	-)	238	79	81	80	32	-	111	3	5	4	15	6	.71	6	.287	.329	.458
2002	Yakult	Jap	140	510	163	35	2	23	(-	-)	271	67	75	104	58	6	114	3	2	4	5	4	.56	10	.320	.390	.531
2003	Yakult	Jap	60	232	61	6	2	12	(-	-)	107	43	31	36	22	3	55	1	2	1	5	1	.83	3	.263	.328	.461
2004	Yakult	Jap	138	533	160	19	0	44	(-	-)	311	99	103	117	70	3	173	4	0	4	8	3	.73	5	.300	.383	.583
2005	Yakult	Jap	144	548	175	31	4	30	(-	-)	304	83	102	114	63	2	146	2	0	5	6	3	.67	4	.319	.388	.555
2006	Yakult	Jap	145	546	170	27	2	32	(-	-)	297	84	77	113	67	5	128	1	1	3	8	1	.89	5	.311	.386	.544
2007	TB	AL	123	491	140	21	10	7	(4	3)	202	82	34	68	58	0	114	1	4	5	12	8	.60	2	.285	.359	.411
2008	TB	AL	152	627	172	30	9	6	(3	3)	238	91	48	85	70	3	131	4	3	3	8	6	.57	2	.274	.349	.380
	2 ML YEARS		275	1118	312	51	19	13	(7	6)	440	173	82	153	128	3	245	5	7	8	20	14	.59	4	.279	.353	.394

Hitoki Iwase

Pitches: L **Bats:** L **Pos:** P   **Ht:** 5'11" **Wt:** 178 **Born:** 11/10/1974 **Age:** 34

Year	Team	Lg	G	GS	CG	GF	IP	BFP	H	R	ER	HR	SH	SF	HB	TBB	IBB	SO	WP	Bk	W	L	Pct	ShO	Sv-Op	Hld	ERC	ERA
1999	Chnchi	Jap	65	0	0	13	74.1	307	67	16	13	3	-	-	2	22	-	73	4	0	10	2	.833	0	1--	-	2.87	1.57
2000	Chnchi	Jap	58	1	0	12	80.1	323	66	20	17	3	-	-	1	28	-	65	1	0	10	5	.667	0	1--	-	2.65	1.90
2001	Chnchi	Jap	61	0	0	9	62.2	252	51	23	23	3	-	-	3	16	-	62	0	0	8	3	.727	0	0--	-	2.43	3.30
2002	Chnchi	Jap	52	0	0	7	59.2	231	38	8	7	2	-	-	3	15	-	66	1	0	4	2	.667	0	0--	-	1.57	1.06
2003	Chnchi	Jap	58	0	0	9	63.2	244	47	10	10	3	-	-	1	12	6	69	1	1	5	2	.714	0	4--	-	1.66	1.41
2004	Chnchi	Jap	60	0	0	38	64.1	259	53	20	20	4	5	1	3	14	2	53	1	0	2	3	.400	0	22--	-	2.37	2.80
2005	Chnchi	Jap	60	0	0	55	57.1	229	51	12	12	0	3	0	2	8	2	52	1	0	1	2	.333	0	46--	-	2.01	1.88
2006	Chnchi	Jap	56	0	0	46	55.1	214	40	8	8	3	1	1	0	8	2	44	0	0	2	2	.500	0	40--	-	1.51	1.30
2007	Chnchi	Jap	61	0	0	-	59.0	233	53	18	16	3	-	-	0	9	3	50	0	0	2	4	.333	0	43--	-	2.28	2.44
2008	Chnchi	Jap	51	0	0	46	49.0	212	55	16	16	2	-	-	0	10	-	41	0	0	3	3	.500	0	36--	-	3.49	2.94

Cesar Izturis

Bats: B Throws: R Pos: SS-130; 3B-8; PH-7; PR-1   Ht: 5'9" Wt: 190 Born: 2/10/1980 Age: 29

Year	Team	Lg	G	AB	H	2B	3B	HR	(Hm	Rd)	TB	R	RBI	RC	TBB	IBB	SO	HBP	SH	SF	SB	CS	SB%	GDP	Avg	OBP	Slg
2001	Tor	AL	46	134	36	6	2	2	(1	1)	52	19	9	16	2	0	15	0	4	0	8	1	.89	0	.269	.279	.388
2002	LAD	NL	135	439	102	24	2	1	(0	1)	133	43	31	26	14	1	39	0	10	5	7	7	.50	12	.232	.253	.303
2003	LAD	NL	158	558	140	21	6	1	(0	1)	176	47	40	42	25	8	70	0	7	3	10	5	.67	8	.251	.282	.315
2004	LAD	NL	159	670	193	32	9	4	(1	3)	255	90	62	95	43	2	70	0	12	3	25	9	.74	6	.288	.330	.381
2005	LAD	NL	106	444	114	19	2	2	(1	1)	143	48	31	37	25	1	51	4	4	1	8	8	.50	11	.257	.302	.322
2006	2 Tms	NL	54	192	47	9	1	1	(1	0)	61	14	18	14	12	3	14	2	1	1	1	4	.20	4	.245	.295	.318
2007	2 Tms	NL	110	314	81	14	2	0	(0	0)	99	31	16	27	19	2	19	1	3	0	3	3	.50	7	.258	.302	.315
2008	StL	NL	135	414	109	10	3	1	(0	1)	128	50	24	39	29	1	26	6	3	2	24	6	.80	6	.263	.319	.309
06	LAD	NL	32	119	30	7	1	1	(1	0)	42	10	12	10	7	3	6	2	0	1	1	3	.25	1	.252	.302	.353
06	ChC	NL	22	73	17	2	0	0	(0	0)	19	4	6	4	5	0	8	0	1	0	0	1	.00	3	.233	.282	.260
07	ChC	NL	65	191	47	11	0	0	(0	0)	58	15	8	13	13	2	16	1	2	0	3	0	1.00	6	.246	.298	.304
07	Pit	NL	45	123	34	3	2	0	(0	0)	41	16	8	14	6	0	3	0	1	0	0	3	.00	1	.276	.310	.333
	Postseason		4	17	3	1	0	0	(0	0)	4	1	0	0	1	0	2	0	0	0	0	0	-	0	.176	.222	.235
	8 ML YEARS		903	3165	822	135	27	12	(4	8)	1047	342	231	296	169	18	304	13	44	15	86	43	.67	54	.260	.299	.331

Maicer Izturis

Bats: B Throws: R Pos: SS-52; 2B-23; 3B-5; PR-2; PH-1   Ht: 5'8" Wt: 170 Born: 9/12/1980 Age: 28

Year	Team	Lg	G	AB	H	2B	3B	HR	(Hm	Rd)	TB	R	RBI	RC	TBB	IBB	SO	HBP	SH	SF	SB	CS	SB%	GDP	Avg	OBP	Slg
2008	RCuca*	A+	1	2	1	0	0	0	(-	-)	1	0	0	0	0	0	1	0	0	0	0	0	-	0	.500	.500	.500
2004	Mon	NL	32	107	22	5	2	1	(1	0)	34	10	4	8	10	1	20	2	2	0	4	0	1.00	1	.206	.286	.318
2005	LAA	AL	77	191	47	8	4	1	(0	1)	66	18	15	25	17	2	21	0	1	1	9	3	.75	5	.246	.306	.346
2006	LAA	AL	104	352	103	21	3	5	(1	4)	145	64	44	56	38	1	35	3	5	1	14	6	.70	7	.293	.365	.412
2007	LAA	AL	102	336	97	17	2	6	(4	2)	136	47	51	65	33	2	39	0	1	4	7	1	.88	4	.289	.349	.405
2008	LAA	AL	79	290	78	14	2	3	(1	2)	105	44	37	39	26	0	27	1	2	2	11	2	.85	9	.269	.329	.362
	Postseason		4	12	4	2	0	0	(0	0)	6	1	0	1	0	0	2	0	0	0	2	0	1.00	0	.333	.333	.500
	5 ML YEARS		394	1276	347	65	13	16	(7	9)	486	183	151	193	124	6	142	6	11	8	45	12	.79	26	.272	.337	.381

Conor Jackson

Bats: R Throws: R Pos: LF-77; 1B-68; PH-2   Ht: 6'2" Wt: 215 Born: 5/7/1982 Age: 27

Year	Team	Lg	G	AB	H	2B	3B	HR	(Hm	Rd)	TB	R	RBI	RC	TBB	IBB	SO	HBP	SH	SF	SB	CS	SB%	GDP	Avg	OBP	Slg
2005	Ari	NL	40	85	17	3	0	2	(2	0)	26	8	8	6	12	0	11	1	0	1	0	0	-	6	.200	.303	.306
2006	Ari	NL	140	485	141	26	1	15	(8	7)	214	75	79	77	54	2	73	9	1	7	1	0	1.00	18	.291	.368	.441
2007	Ari	NL	130	415	118	29	1	15	(8	7)	194	56	60	67	53	2	50	4	2	3	2	2	.50	8	.284	.368	.467
2008	Ari	NL	144	540	162	31	6	12	(6	6)	241	87	75	88	59	3	61	9	1	3	10	2	.83	14	.300	.376	.446
	Postseason		6	17	4	1	0	0	(0	0)	5	1	2	1	0	0	3	0	0	0	1	0	-	0	.235	.222	.294
	4 ML YEARS		454	1525	438	89	8	44	(24	20)	675	226	222	238	178	7	195	23	4	14	13	4	.76	46	.287	.367	.443

Edwin Jackson

Pitches: R Bats: R Pos: SP-31; RP-1   Ht: 6'3" Wt: 210 Born: 9/9/1983 Age: 25

Year	Team	Lg	G	GS	CG	GF	IP	BFP	H	R	ER	HR	SH	SF	HB	TBB	IBB	SO	WP	Bk	W	L	Pct	ShO	Sv-Op	Hld	ERC	ERA
2003	LAD	NL	4	3	0	0	22.0	91	17	6	6	2	1	1	1	11	1	19	3	0	2	1	.667	0	0-0	0	3.36	2.45
2004	LAD	NL	8	5	0	1	24.2	113	31	20	20	7	1	0	0	11	1	16	0	0	2	1	.667	0	0-0	0	7.21	7.30
2005	LAD	NL	7	6	0	0	28.2	134	31	22	20	2	0	2	1	17	0	13	2	1	2	2	.500	0	0-0	0	5.13	6.28
2006	TB	AL	23	1	0	7	36.1	174	42	27	22	2	2	2	1	25	0	27	3	1	0	0	-	0	0-0	0	5.86	5.45
2007	TB	AL	32	31	1	0	161.0	755	195	116	103	19	5	6	4	88	3	128	7	1	5	15	.250	1	0-0	0	6.11	5.76
2008	TB	AL	32	31	0	0	183.1	792	199	91	90	23	3	3	2	77	1	108	7	1	14	11	.560	0	0-1	0	4.99	4.42
	6 ML YEARS		106	77	1	8	456.0	2059	515	282	261	55	12	14	9	229	6	311	22	4	25	30	.455	1	0-1	0	5.50	5.15

Zach Jackson

Pitches: L Bats: L Pos: SP-9; RP-2   Ht: 6'5" Wt: 220 Born: 5/13/1983 Age: 26

Year	Team	Lg	G	GS	CG	GF	IP	BFP	H	R	ER	HR	SH	SF	HB	TBB	IBB	SO	WP	Bk	W	L	Pct	ShO	Sv-Op	Hld	ERC	ERA
2004	Auburn	A-	4	4	0	0	15.0	69	20	9	9	1	0	1	0	6	0	11	1	0	0	0	-	0	0--	-	5.80	5.40
2005	Dnedin	A+	10	10	0	0	59.1	240	56	25	19	3	2	3	0	6	0	48	0	0	8	1	.889	0	0--	-	2.31	2.88
2005	NHam	AA	9	9	0	0	54.0	227	57	27	24	3	3	3	3	12	0	43	0	0	4	3	.571	0	0--	-	3.64	4.00
2005	Syrcse	AAA	8	8	0	0	47.1	216	61	33	27	3	3	1	2	21	1	33	1	0	4	4	.500	0	0--	-	5.93	5.13
2006	Nashv	AAA	18	18	1	0	107.0	458	106	55	49	11	2	1	7	44	0	58	4	0	4	6	.400	0	0--	-	4.45	4.12
2007	Nashv	AAA	29	28	1	1	169.2	741	184	95	84	13	9	7	11	64	0	123	8	2	11	10	.524	0	0--	-	4.62	4.46
2008	Nashv	AAA	22	6	0	6	57.1	276	81	54	50	10	3	4	4	18	0	34	5	0	1	5	.167	0	0--	-	6.89	7.85
2008	Buffalo	AAA	8	4	0	0	26.2	112	25	13	12	3	1	1	2	5	1	20	1	0	3	1	.750	0	0--	-	3.16	4.05
2006	Mil	NL	8	7	0	1	38.1	178	48	26	23	6	1	1	4	14	0	22	1	0	2	2	.500	0	0-0	0	6.26	5.40
2008	2 Tms	NL	11	9	0	2	58.1	256	69	38	36	7	1	1	3	16	0	31	2	0	2	3	.400	0	0-0	0	5.00	5.55
08	Mil	NL	2	0	0	2	3.2	18	5	2	2	0	0	0	0	2	0	1	1	0	0	0	-	0	0-0	0	5.84	4.91
08	Cle	AL	9	9	0	0	54.2	238	64	36	34	7	1	1	3	14	0	30	1	0	2	3	.400	0	0-0	0	4.94	5.60
	2 ML YEARS		19	16	0	3	96.2	434	117	64	59	13	2	2	7	30	0	53	3	0	4	5	.444	0	0-0	0	5.49	5.49

Mike Jacobs

Bats: L Throws: R Pos: 1B-119; PH-16; DH-6   Ht: 6'3" Wt: 215 Born: 10/30/1980 Age: 28

								BATTING													BASERUNNING				AVERAGES		
Year	Team	Lg	G	AB	H	2B	3B	HR	(Hm	Rd)	TB	R	RBI	RC	TBB	IBB	SO	HBP	SH	SF	SB	CS	SB%	GDP	Avg	OBP	Slg
2005	NYM	NL	30	100	31	7	0	11	(6	5)	71	19	23	21	10	0	22	1	0	1	0	0	-	5	.310	.375	.710
2006	Fla	NL	136	469	123	37	1	20	(12	8)	222	54	77	66	45	2	105	1	0	5	3	0	1.00	16	.262	.325	.473
2007	Fla	NL	114	426	113	27	2	17	(10	7)	195	57	54	51	31	3	101	2	0	1	1	2	.33	12	.265	.317	.458
2008	Fla	NL	141	477	118	27	2	32	(14	18)	245	67	93	69	36	10	119	1	0	5	1	0	1.00	7	.247	.299	.514
	4 ML YEARS		421	1472	385	98	5	80	(42	38)	733	197	247	207	122	15	347	5	0	12	5	2	.71	40	.262	.318	.498

Chuck James

Pitches: L Bats: L Pos: SP-7   Ht: 6'0" Wt: 190 Born: 11/9/1981 Age: 27

			HOW MUCH HE PITCHED						WHAT HE GAVE UP										THE RESULTS						
Year	Team	Lg	G	GS	CG	GF	IP	BFP	H	R	ER	HR	SH	SF	HB	TBB	IBB	SO	WP	Bk	W	L	Pct	ShO	Sv-Op Hld	ERC	ERA
2008	Rchmd*	AAA	16	15	0	1	86.1	373	76	34	28	5	5	5	3	39	0	74	3	0	5	5	.500	0	0-- -	3.42	2.92
2005	Atl	NL	2	0	0	0	5.2	23	4	1	1	0	0	0	0	3	0	5	1	0	0	0	-	0	0-0 0	2.41	1.59
2006	Atl	NL	25	18	0	0	119.0	504	101	54	50	20	8	7	6	47	2	91	2	0	11	4	.733	0	0-0 0	3.84	3.78
2007	Atl	NL	30	30	0	0	161.1	691	164	77	76	32	9	4	1	58	5	116	1	1	11	10	.524	0	0-0 0	4.69	4.24
2008	Atl	NL	7	7	0	0	29.2	146	36	30	30	10	4	3	3	20	2	22	1	1	2	5	.286	0	0-0 0	8.81	9.10
	4 ML YEARS		64	55	0	0	315.2	1364	305	162	157	62	21	14	10	128	9	234	5	2	24	19	.558	0	0-0 0	4.67	4.48

Paul Janish

Bats: R Throws: R Pos: SS-36; PR-3; PH-2   Ht: 6'2" Wt: 190 Born: 10/12/1982 Age: 26

								BATTING													BASERUNNING				AVERAGES		
Year	Team	Lg	G	AB	H	2B	3B	HR	(Hm	Rd)	TB	R	RBI	RC	TBB	IBB	SO	HBP	SH	SF	SB	CS	SB%	GDP	Avg	OBP	Slg
2004	Billings	R+	66	205	54	11	0	2	(-	-)	71	39	22	35	45	0	45	5	7	1	7	3	.70	2	.263	.406	.346
2005	Dayton	A	55	208	51	10	2	5	(-	-)	80	30	29	31	29	2	38	5	8	4	5	2	.71	1	.245	.346	.385
2006	Dayton	A	26	98	39	6	0	5	(-	-)	60	19	18	24	7	0	10	1	0	2	0	0	-	0	.398	.435	.612
2006	Srsota	A+	91	335	93	17	2	9	(-	-)	141	53	55	55	38	0	39	6	7	7	8	2	.80	8	.278	.355	.421
2006	Chatt	AA	4	15	4	1	0	0	(-	-)	5	1	2	1	1	0	5	0	0	0	0	0	-	1	.267	.313	.333
2007	Chatt	AA	88	324	79	21	2	1	(-	-)	107	46	20	45	50	1	54	9	5	3	10	3	.77	5	.244	.358	.330
2007	Lsvlle	AAA	55	199	44	8	1	3	(-	-)	63	20	19	18	14	1	31	2	11	1	2	0	1.00	7	.221	.278	.317
2008	Lsvlle	AAA	92	318	80	20	1	7	(-	-)	123	45	42	43	26	3	71	9	10	2	2	0	1.00	8	.252	.324	.387
2008	Cin	NL	38	80	15	2	0	1	(1	0)	20	5	6	5	7	0	18	2	0	0	0	0	-	2	.188	.270	.250

Casey Janssen

Pitches: R Bats: R Pos: P   Ht: 6'4" Wt: 205 Born: 9/17/1981 Age: 27

			HOW MUCH HE PITCHED						WHAT HE GAVE UP										THE RESULTS						
Year	Team	Lg	G	GS	CG	GF	IP	BFP	H	R	ER	HR	SH	SF	HB	TBB	IBB	SO	WP	Bk	W	L	Pct	ShO	Sv-Op Hld	ERC	ERA
2004	Auburn	A-	10	10	0	0	51.2	208	47	21	20	2	0	0	2	10	0	45	2	0	3	1	.750	0	0-- -	2.61	3.48
2005	Lansng	A	7	7	0	0	46.0	163	27	8	7	0	0	3	1	4	0	38	1	0	4	0	1.000	0	0-- -	0.95	1.37
2005	Dnedin	A+	10	10	0	0	59.2	228	46	16	15	2	1	1	2	12	0	51	1	0	6	1	.857	0	0-- -	1.98	2.26
2005	NHam	AA	9	9	0	0	43.0	177	49	20	14	3	1	0	2	4	0	47	2	0	3	3	.500	0	0-- -	3.69	2.93
2006	Syrcse	AAA	9	9	0	0	42.2	178	47	23	23	3	1	1	2	8	0	32	2	0	1	5	.167	0	0-- -	3.86	4.85
2006	Tor	AL	19	17	0	1	94.0	407	103	58	53	12	2	2	7	21	3	44	3	2	6	10	.375	0	0-0 0	4.32	5.07
2007	Tor	AL	70	0	0	21	72.2	297	67	22	19	4	0	3	3	20	2	39	4	0	2	3	.400	0	6-11 24	3.06	2.35
	2 ML YEARS		89	17	0	22	166.2	704	170	80	72	16	2	5	10	41	5	83	7	2	8	13	.381	0	6-11 24	3.76	3.89

John Jaso

Bats: L Throws: R Pos: C-3; PH-3   Ht: 6'2" Wt: 205 Born: 9/19/1983 Age: 25

								BATTING													BASERUNNING				AVERAGES		
Year	Team	Lg	G	AB	H	2B	3B	HR	(Hm	Rd)	TB	R	RBI	RC	TBB	IBB	SO	HBP	SH	SF	SB	CS	SB%	GDP	Avg	OBP	Slg
2003	HudVal	A-	47	154	35	7	0	2	(-	-)	48	20	20	20	25	3	26	4	2	3	2	0	1.00	2	.227	.344	.312
2004	HudVal	A-	57	199	60	17	2	2	(-	-)	87	34	35	34	22	2	32	3	0	1	1	0	1.00	10	.302	.378	.437
2005	SWMch	A	92	332	102	25	1	14	(-	-)	171	61	50	67	42	2	53	4	0	8	3	1	.75	10	.307	.383	.515
2006	Visalia	A+	95	366	113	22	0	10	(-	-)	165	58	55	61	31	1	48	3	0	6	1	2	.33	8	.309	.362	.451
2007	Mont	AA	109	380	120	24	2	12	(-	-)	184	62	71	78	59	1	49	4	2	5	2	2	.50	8	.316	.408	.484
2008	Mont	AA	85	284	77	13	2	7	(-	-)	115	51	43	54	62	1	33	6	1	3	1	0	1.00	12	.271	.408	.405
2008	Drham	AAA	31	108	30	7	0	5	(-	-)	52	14	24	17	10	0	14	0	0	0	1	1	.50	2	.278	.339	.481
2008	TB	AL	5	10	2	0	0	0	(0	0)	2	2	0	0	0	0	2	0	0	0	0	0	-	1	.200	.200	.200

Geoff Jenkins

Bats: L Throws: R Pos: RF-90; PH-26; DH-2; PR-2   Ht: 6'1" Wt: 215 Born: 7/21/1974 Age: 34

								BATTING													BASERUNNING				AVERAGES		
Year	Team	Lg	G	AB	H	2B	3B	HR	(Hm	Rd)	TB	R	RBI	RC	TBB	IBB	SO	HBP	SH	SF	SB	CS	SB%	GDP	Avg	OBP	Slg
1998	Mil	NL	84	262	60	12	1	9	(4	5)	101	33	28	26	20	4	61	2	0	1	1	3	.25	7	.229	.288	.385
1999	Mil	NL	135	447	140	43	3	21	(10	11)	252	70	82	88	35	7	87	7	3	1	5	1	.83	10	.313	.371	.564
2000	Mil	NL	135	512	155	36	4	34	(15	19)	301	100	94	104	33	6	135	15	0	4	11	1	.92	9	.303	.360	.588
2001	Mil	NL	105	397	105	21	1	20	(11	9)	188	60	63	60	36	7	120	8	0	5	4	2	.67	11	.264	.334	.474
2002	Mil	NL	67	243	59	17	1	10	(4	6)	108	35	29	28	22	1	60	6	0	1	2	.33	8	.243	.320	.444
2003	Mil	NL	124	487	144	30	2	28	(16	12)	262	81	95	90	58	10	120	6	0	3	0	0	-	12	.296	.375	.538
2004	Mil	NL	157	617	163	36	6	27	(13	14)	292	88	93	76	46	10	152	12	0	6	3	1	.75	19	.264	.325	.473
2005	Mil	NL	148	538	157	42	1	25	(10	15)	276	87	86	87	56	9	138	19	1	5	0	0	-	13	.292	.375	.513

147

Year Team	Lg	G	AB	H	2B	3B	HR	(Hm Rd)	TB	R	RBI	RC	TBB	IBB	SO	HBP	SH	SF	SB	CS	SB%	GDP	Avg	OBP	Slg
							BATTING												**BASERUNNING**				**AVERAGES**		
2006 Mil	NL	147	484	131	26	1	17	(8 9)	210	62	70	76	56	8	129	11	0	4	4	1	.80	9	.271	.357	.434
2007 Mil	NL	132	420	107	24	2	21	(11 10)	198	45	64	60	32	10	116	9	0	3	2	2	.50	9	.255	.319	.471
2008 Phi	NL	115	293	72	16	0	9	(5 4)	115	27	29	30	24	5	68	1	0	4	1	1	.50	6	.246	.301	.392
11 ML YEARS		1349	4700	1293	303	22	221	(107 114)	2303	688	733	725	418	77	1186	96	3	37	32	14	.70	113	.275	.344	.490

Bobby Jenks

Pitches: R **Bats:** R **Pos:** RP-57   **Ht:** 6'3" **Wt:** 275 **Born:** 3/14/1981 **Age:** 28

Year Team	Lg	G	GS	CG	GF	IP	BFP	H	R	ER	HR	SH	SF	HB	TBB	IBB	SO	WP	Bk	W	L	Pct	ShO	Sv-Op	Hld	ERC	ERA
				HOW MUCH HE PITCHED						**WHAT HE GAVE UP**												**THE RESULTS**					
2008 WinSa*	A+	1	1	0	0	1.0	6	3	1	1	0	0	1	0	0	0	0	0	0	0	0	-	0	0--	-	14.52	9.00
2008 Brham*	AA	1	1	0	0	1.0	3	0	0	0	0	0	0	0	0	0	3	0	0	0	0	-	0	0--	-	0.00	0.00
2005 CWS	AL	32	0	0	18	39.1	168	34	15	12	3	1	0	1	15	3	50	4	0	1	1	.500	0	6-8	3	3.02	2.75
2006 CWS	AL	67	0	0	58	69.2	300	66	32	31	5	4	2	2	31	10	80	3	0	3	4	.429	0	41-45	0	3.65	4.00
2007 CWS	AL	66	0	0	62	65.0	249	45	20	20	2	5	3	1	13	4	56	4	0	3	5	.375	0	40-46	0	1.49	2.77
2008 CWS	AL	57	0	0	52	61.2	243	51	18	18	3	2	1	1	17	4	38	3	0	3	1	.750	0	30-34	0	2.43	2.63
Postseason		6	0	0	4	8.0	32	4	2	2	0	1	0	1	3	0	8	0	0	0	0	-	0	4-5	0	1.41	2.25
4 ML YEARS		222	0	0	190	235.2	960	196	85	81	13	12	6	5	76	21	224	14	0	10	11	.476	0	117-133	3	2.57	3.09

Jason Jennings

Pitches: R **Bats:** L **Pos:** SP-6   **Ht:** 6'2" **Wt:** 235 **Born:** 7/17/1978 **Age:** 30

Year Team	Lg	G	GS	CG	GF	IP	BFP	H	R	ER	HR	SH	SF	HB	TBB	IBB	SO	WP	Bk	W	L	Pct	ShO	Sv-Op	Hld	ERC	ERA
				HOW MUCH HE PITCHED						**WHAT HE GAVE UP**												**THE RESULTS**					
2001 Col	NL	7	7	1	0	39.1	174	42	21	20	2	1	1	1	19	0	26	1	0	4	1	.800	1	0-0	0	4.58	4.58
2002 Col	NL	32	32	0	0	185.1	808	201	102	93	26	9	3	8	70	2	127	10	0	16	8	.667	0	0-0	0	4.98	4.52
2003 Col	NL	32	32	1	0	181.1	820	212	115	103	20	11	6	5	88	7	119	7	0	12	13	.480	0	0-0	0	5.60	5.11
2004 Col	NL	33	33	0	0	201.0	925	241	125	123	27	9	3	7	101	14	133	6	1	11	12	.478	0	0-0	0	5.99	5.51
2005 Col	NL	20	20	1	0	122.0	551	130	73	68	11	6	3	5	64	4	75	8	0	6	9	.400	0	0-0	0	4.91	5.02
2006 Col	NL	32	32	3	0	212.0	902	206	94	89	17	8	6	3	85	7	142	10	0	9	13	.409	2	0-0	0	3.83	3.78
2007 Hou	NL	19	18	0	0	99.0	445	119	73	71	19	6	7	2	34	2	71	5	0	2	9	.182	0	0-0	0	5.72	6.45
2008 Tex	AL	6	6	0	0	27.1	135	35	27	26	8	2	0	1	18	2	12	1	0	0	5	.000	0	0-0	0	8.42	8.56
8 ML YEARS		181	180	6	0	1067.1	4760	1186	630	593	130	52	29	32	477	38	705	48	1	60	70	.462	3	0-0	0	5.16	5.00

Kevin Jepsen

Pitches: R **Bats:** R **Pos:** RP-9   **Ht:** 6'3" **Wt:** 215 **Born:** 7/26/1984 **Age:** 24

Year Team	Lg	G	GS	CG	GF	IP	BFP	H	R	ER	HR	SH	SF	HB	TBB	IBB	SO	WP	Bk	W	L	Pct	ShO	Sv-Op	Hld	ERC	ERA
				HOW MUCH HE PITCHED						**WHAT HE GAVE UP**												**THE RESULTS**					
2002 Angels	R	8	5	0	1	26.1	125	29	22	20	3	0	2	5	12	0	19	1	0	1	3	.250	0	0--	-	5.63	6.84
2003 CRpds	A	10	10	0	0	51.0	211	32	24	15	2	1	2	2	28	0	42	0	0	6	3	.667	0	0--	-	2.42	2.65
2004 CRpds	A	27	27	1	0	144.1	628	122	68	55	6	10	2	12	77	1	136	14	2	8	10	.444	1	0--	-	3.63	3.43
2005 Angels	R	7	7	0	0	14.2	67	8	10	9	1	0	0	3	11	0	17	4	1	0	1	.000	0	0--	-	3.31	5.52
2005 RCuca	A+	4	4	0	0	12.2	68	19	18	15	2	0	0	1	10	0	11	0	0	0	1	.000	0	0--	-	9.56	10.66
2006 RCuca	A+	47	0	0	41	50.1	237	51	26	20	2	7	3	4	34	0	46	6	0	4	4	.500	0	16--	-	5.02	3.58
2007 RCuca	A+	44	0	0	16	53.2	252	61	29	25	2	1	1	3	38	2	50	4	0	1	5	.167	0	3--	-	5.88	4.19
2008 Ark	AA	25	0	0	21	31.2	131	22	5	5	0	2	0	0	18	1	35	3	0	1	1	.667	0	11--	-	2.40	1.42
2008 Salt Lk	AAA	15	0	0	9	23.0	95	17	9	6	3	3	0	0	12	1	21	2	0	1	3	.250	0	2--	-	3.32	2.35
2008 LAA	AL	9	0	0	0	8.1	36	8	5	4	0	0	0	0	4	0	7	1	0	0	1	.000	0	0-0	3	3.46	4.32

Derek Jeter

Bats: R **Throws:** R **Pos:** SS-148; DH-2   **Ht:** 6'3" **Wt:** 195 **Born:** 6/26/1974 **Age:** 35

Year Team	Lg	G	AB	H	2B	3B	HR	(Hm Rd)	TB	R	RBI	RC	TBB	IBB	SO	HBP	SH	SF	SB	CS	SB%	GDP	Avg	OBP	Slg
								BATTING											**BASERUNNING**				**AVERAGES**		
1995 NYY	AL	15	48	12	4	1	0	(0 0)	18	5	7	5	3	0	11	0	0	0	0	0	-	0	.250	.294	.375
1996 NYY	AL	157	582	183	25	6	10	(3 7)	250	104	78	92	48	1	102	9	6	9	14	7	.67	13	.314	.370	.430
1997 NYY	AL	159	654	190	31	7	10	(5 5)	265	116	70	99	74	0	125	10	8	2	23	12	.66	14	.291	.370	.405
1998 NYY	AL	149	626	203	25	8	19	(9 10)	301	127	84	115	57	1	119	5	3	3	30	6	.83	13	.324	.384	.481
1999 NYY	AL	158	627	219	37	9	24	(15 9)	346	134	102	146	91	5	116	12	3	6	19	8	.70	12	.349	.438	.552
2000 NYY	AL	148	593	201	31	4	15	(8 7)	285	119	73	118	68	4	99	12	3	3	22	4	.85	14	.339	.416	.481
2001 NYY	AL	150	614	191	35	3	21	(13 8)	295	110	74	112	56	3	99	10	5	1	27	3	.90	13	.311	.377	.480
2002 NYY	AL	157	644	191	26	0	18	(8 10)	271	124	75	108	73	2	114	7	3	3	32	3	.91	14	.297	.373	.421
2003 NYY	AL	119	482	156	25	3	10	(7 3)	217	87	52	86	43	2	88	13	3	1	11	5	.69	10	.324	.393	.450
2004 NYY	AL	154	643	188	44	1	23	(11 12)	303	111	78	100	46	1	99	14	16	2	23	4	.85	19	.292	.352	.471
2005 NYY	AL	159	654	202	25	5	19	(12 7)	294	122	70	105	77	3	117	11	7	3	14	5	.74	15	.309	.389	.450
2006 NYY	AL	154	623	214	39	3	14	(8 6)	301	118	97	132	69	4	102	12	7	4	34	5	.87	13	.343	.417	.483
2007 NYY	AL	156	639	206	39	4	12	(4 8)	289	102	73	112	56	3	100	14	3	2	15	8	.65	21	.322	.388	.452
2008 NYY	AL	150	596	179	25	3	11	(3 8)	243	88	69	88	52	0	85	9	7	4	11	5	.69	24	.300	.363	.408
Postseason		123	495	153	22	3	17	(10 7)	232	85	49	77	51	1	96	5	8	4	16	4	.80	10	.309	.377	.469
14 ML YEARS		1985	8025	2535	411	57	206	(106 100)	3678	1467	1002	1418	813	29	1376	138	74	43	275	75	.79	195	.316	.387	.458

Cesar Jimenez

Pitches: L Bats: L Pos: RP-29; SP-2   Ht: 5'11" Wt: 215 Born: 11/12/1984 Age: 24

			HOW MUCH HE PITCHED						WHAT HE GAVE UP												THE RESULTS							
Year	Team	Lg	G	GS	CG	GF	IP	BFP	H	R	ER	HR	SH	SF	HB	TBB	IBB	SO	WP	Bk	W	L	Pct	ShO	Sv-Op	Hld	ERC	ERA
2002	Ms	R	1	0	0	0	2.2	11	3	2	1	0	1	0	0	0	0	3	0	0	0	0	-	0	0--	-	2.52	3.38
2002	Everett	A	8	0	0	2	20.0	81	12	7	6	2	3	1	3	5	0	25	1	0	2	1	.667	0	0--	-	1.97	2.70
2003	Wisc	A	28	20	0	3	126.1	552	134	61	41	7	8	6	2	46	2	76	10	0	8	11	.421	0	0--	-	3.96	2.92
2004	InldEm	A+	43	2	0	26	86.1	360	80	28	22	3	1		5	19	0	81	6	3	6	7	.462	0	6--	-	2.76	2.29
2005	SnAnt	AA	45	1	0	19	68.2	288	64	21	20	3	4	2	2	24	0	54	4	0	3	5	.375	0	4--	-	3.26	2.62
2005	Tacom	AAA	4	0	0	2	7.2	33	9	8	8	5	0	1	0	1	0	9	0	0	0	0	-	0	0--	-	7.56	9.39
2006	SnAnt	AA	3	3	0	0	16.1	62	10	5	5	0	0	0	1	5	0	10	1	0	0	2	.000	0	0--	-	1.55	2.76
2006	Tacom	AAA	24	19	1	3	107.1	468	107	54	52	8	4	3	4	55	1	66	5	1	5	10	.333	1	3--	-	4.54	4.36
2007	Ms	R	3	2	0	0	6.0	22	4	0	0	0	0	0	1	0	0	6	0	0	0	0	-	0	0--	-	1.29	0.00
2007	Tacom	AAA	16	0	0	7	25.1	117	28	15	10	2	0	1	0	12	1	23	1	1	2	1	.667	0	2--	-	4.58	3.55
2008	Tacom	AAA	29	0	0	7	38.0	165	37	19	15	3	0	0	2	8	1	47	3	0	1	3	.250	0	3--	-	3.06	3.55
2006	Sea	AL	4	1	0	1	7.1	38	13	12	12	4	0	0	0	4	0	3	2	0	0	0	-	0	0-0	0	14.01	14.73
2008	Sea	AL	31	2	0	8	34.1	141	32	13	13	2	2	1	1	13	0	26	2	0	0	2	.000	0	0-4	4	3.59	3.41
2 ML YEARS			35	3	0	9	41.2	179	45	25	25	6	2	1	1	17	0	29	4	0	0	2	.000	0	0-4	4	5.14	5.40

Kelvin Jimenez

Pitches: R Bats: R Pos: RP-15   Ht: 6'2" Wt: 195 Born: 10/27/1980 Age: 28

			HOW MUCH HE PITCHED						WHAT HE GAVE UP												THE RESULTS							
Year	Team	Lg	G	GS	CG	GF	IP	BFP	H	R	ER	HR	SH	SF	HB	TBB	IBB	SO	WP	Bk	W	L	Pct	ShO	Sv-Op	Hld	ERC	ERA
2001	Pulaski	R+	4	4	0	0	14.1	73	24	14	10	2	0	0	1	4	0	10	1	0	0	3	.000	0	0--	-	8.04	6.28
2001	Rngrs	R	9	6	1	1	45.2	183	36	19	13	2	1	3	2	9	0	51	2	0	3	3	.500	1	1--	-	2.03	2.56
2002	Savann	A	29	16	0	4	121.0	524	122	63	43	9	7	1	7	37	2	116	4	0	5	10	.333	0	0--	-	3.72	3.20
2003	Stcktn	A+	34	18	0	4	131.1	565	135	81	69	14	2	3	9	43	1	101	11	2	6	5	.545	0	2--	-	4.28	4.73
2004	Frisco	AA	26	21	0	0	129.0	584	135	76	65	13	6	6	7	67	1	101	12	1	3	5	.375	0	0--	-	5.02	4.53
2005	Frisco	AA	6	0	0	3	13.0	60	12	5	5	0	1	1	2	6	0	12	2	0	0	0	-	0	2--	-	3.57	3.46
2005	Okla	AAA	37	5	0	11	79.1	345	79	40	32	6	3	3	4	33	3	64	4	1	4	6	.400	0	3--	-	4.09	3.63
2006	Okla	AAA	26	0	0	4	38.0	179	40	22	22	4	1	2	1	24	1	40	6	0	4	2	.667	0	1--	-	5.28	5.21
2007	Memp	AAA	30	0	0	8	39.2	174	46	16	12	2	1	2	1	11	4	34	2	1	2	3	.400	0	1--	-	4.03	2.72
2008	Memp	AAA	46	0	0	23	52.1	220	55	22	17	3	3	4	3	12	1	28	1	0	1	6	.143	0	12--	-	3.63	2.92
2007	StL	NL	34	0	0	15	42.0	198	56	36	35	2	1	1	4	17	1	24	0	0	3	0	1.000	0	0-0	1	5.99	7.50
2008	StL	NL	15	0	0	5	24.0	114	28	15	15	5	1	1	1	15	0	11	3	0	0	0	-	0	0-0	0	7.03	5.63
2 ML YEARS			49	0	0	20	66.0	312	84	51	50	7	2	2	5	32	1	35	3	0	3	0	1.000	0	0-0	1	6.37	6.82

Ubaldo Jimenez

Pitches: R Bats: R Pos: SP-34   Ht: 6'4" Wt: 200 Born: 1/22/1984 Age: 25

			HOW MUCH HE PITCHED						WHAT HE GAVE UP												THE RESULTS							
Year	Team	Lg	G	GS	CG	GF	IP	BFP	H	R	ER	HR	SH	SF	HB	TBB	IBB	SO	WP	Bk	W	L	Pct	ShO	Sv-Op	Hld	ERC	ERA
2006	Col	NL	2	1	0	0	7.2	30	5	4	3	1	0	0	0	3	0	3	0	0	0	0	-	0	0-0	0	2.48	3.52
2007	Col	NL	15	15	0	0	82.0	354	70	46	39	10	3	1	6	37	4	68	3	0	4	4	.500	0	0-0	0	3.80	4.28
2008	Col	NL	34	34	1	0	198.2	868	182	97	88	11	7	4	10	103	4	172	16	0	12	12	.500	0	0-0	0	3.92	3.99
Postseason			3	3	0	0	16.0	71	11	4	4	1	0	1	1	13	1	13	1	0	0	1	.000	0	0-0	0	3.80	2.25
3 ML YEARS			51	50	1	0	288.1	1252	257	147	130	22	10	5	16	143	8	243	19	0	16	16	.500	0	0-0	0	3.85	4.06

Charlton Jimerson

Bats: R Throws: R Pos: LF-1; PR-1   Ht: 6'3" Wt: 215 Born: 9/22/1979 Age: 29

			BATTING																				BASERUNNING				AVERAGES		
Year	Team	Lg	G	AB	H	2B	3B	HR	(Hm	Rd)	TB	R	RBI	RC	TBB	IBB	SO	HBP	SH	SF	SB	CS	SB%	GDP	Avg	OBP	Slg
2008	Tacom*	AAA	55	210	49	8	1	11	(-	-)	92	23	31	23	3	0	80	2	3	1	14	7	.67	6	.233	.250	.438
2005	Hou	NL	1	0	0	0	0	0	(0	0)	0	0	0	0	0	0	0	0	0	0	0	0	-	0	-	-	-
2006	Hou	NL	17	6	2	0	0	1	(0	1)	5	2	1	1	0	0	3	0	0	0	2	0	1.00	0	.333	.333	.833
2007	Sea	AL	11	2	2	0	0	1	(1	0)	5	5	1	2	0	0	0	0	0	0	2	0	1.00	0	1.000	1.000	2.500
2008	Sea	AL	2	1	0	0	0	0	(0	0)	0	0	1	0	0	0	0	0	0	0	0	0	-	0	.000	.000	.000
4 ML YEARS			31	9	4	0	0	2	(1	1)	10	8	2	3	0	0	3	0	0	0	4	0	1.00	1	.444	.444	1.111

Kenji Johjima

Bats: R Throws: R Pos: C-100; DH-10; PH-3   Ht: 6'0" Wt: 205 Born: 6/8/1976 Age: 33

			BATTING																				BASERUNNING				AVERAGES		
Year	Team	Lg	G	AB	H	2B	3B	HR	(Hm	Rd)	TB	R	RBI	RC	TBB	IBB	SO	HBP	SH	SF	SB	CS	SB%	GDP	Avg	OBP	Slg
2006	Sea	AL	144	506	147	25	1	18	(6	12)	228	61	76	79	20	1	46	13	0	3	3	1	.75	15	.291	.332	.451
2007	Sea	AL	135	485	139	29	1	14	(8	6)	210	52	61	55	15	0	41	11	0	2	0	2	.00	22	.287	.322	.433
2008	Sea	AL	112	379	86	19	0	7	(3	4)	126	29	39	37	19	1	33	8	1	2	2	0	1.00	12	.227	.277	.332
3 ML YEARS			391	1370	372	73	1	39	(17	22)	564	142	176	171	54	2	120	32	1	7	5	3	.63	49	.272	.313	.412

Dan Johnson

Bats: L Throws: R Pos: 1B-8; PH-3; LF-1; DH-1; PR-1   Ht: 6'2" Wt: 216 Born: 8/10/1979 Age: 29

			BATTING																				BASERUNNING				AVERAGES		
Year	Team	Lg	G	AB	H	2B	3B	HR	(Hm	Rd)	TB	R	RBI	RC	TBB	IBB	SO	HBP	SH	SF	SB	CS	SB%	GDP	Avg	OBP	Slg
2008	Drham*	AAA	113	394	120	23	0	25	(-	-)	218	85	83	94	84	1	75	1	0	7	0	1	.00	6	.305	.422	.553
2005	Oak	AL	109	375	103	21	0	15	(2	13)	169	54	58	56	50	1	52	1	0	8	0	0	-	6	.275	.355	.451
2006	Oak	AL	91	286	67	13	1	9	(4	5)	109	30	37	33	40	2	45	0	0	5	0	0	-	6	.234	.323	.381
2007	Oak	AL	117	416	98	20	1	18	(9	9)	174	53	62	58	72	4	77	3	0	4	0	0	-	12	.236	.349	.418

Year Team	Lg	G	AB	H	2B	3B	HR	(Hm	Rd)	TB	R	RBI	RC	TBB	IBB	SO	HBP	SH	SF	SB	CS	SB%	GDP	Avg	OBP	Slg
								BATTING												BASERUNNING				AVERAGES		
2008 2 Tms	AL	11	26	5	0	0	2	(1	1)	11	3	4	3	3	0	7	0	0	0	0	0	-	0	.192	.276	.423
08 Oak	AL	1	1	0	0	0	0	(0	0)	0	0	0	0	0	0	0	0	0	0	0	0	-	0	.000	.000	.000
08 TB	AL	10	25	5	0	0	2	(1	1)	11	3	4	3	3	0	7	0	0	0	0	0	-	0	.200	.286	.440
4 ML YEARS		328	1103	273	54	2	44	(16	28)	463	140	161	150	165	7	181	4	0	17	0	1	.00	29	.248	.343	.420

Elliot Johnson

Bats: B Throws: R Pos: SS-2; DH-2; 2B-1; CF-1; RF-1; PH-1   Ht: 6'0" Wt: 185 Born: 3/9/1984 Age: 25

Year Team	Lg	G	AB	H	2B	3B	HR	(Hm	Rd)	TB	R	RBI	RC	TBB	IBB	SO	HBP	SH	SF	SB	CS	SB%	GDP	Avg	OBP	Slg
								BATTING												BASERUNNING				AVERAGES		
2002 Princtn	R+	42	152	40	10	1	1	(-	-)	55	21	13	22	18	0	48	1	1	0	14	2	.88	2	.263	.345	.362
2003 CtnSC	A	54	151	32	4	0	0	(-	-)	36	22	15	17	38	0	32	0	0	0	8	5	.62	2	.212	.370	.238
2004 CtnSC	A	126	503	132	22	7	6	(-	-)	186	92	41	70	54	1	91	5	10	2	43	15	.74	2	.262	.339	.370
2005 Visalia	A+	56	227	62	10	3	8	(-	-)	102	42	33	40	24	1	49	3	2	0	28	5	.85	2	.273	.350	.449
2005 Mont	AA	63	264	69	9	6	3	(-	-)	99	31	22	32	13	0	68	4	1	1	14	4	.78	3	.261	.305	.375
2006 Mont	AA	122	494	139	21	10	15	(-	-)	225	69	50	74	39	1	121	2	4	3	21	18	.54	6	.281	.335	.455
2007 Drham	AAA	129	463	96	17	6	11	(-	-)	158	56	45	48	43	2	139	8	9	1	16	6	.73	1	.207	.285	.341
2008 Drham	AAA	107	387	101	26	5	9	(-	-)	164	49	50	56	33	1	104	2	5	0	15	3	.83	6	.261	.322	.424
2008 TB	AL	7	19	3	0	0	0	(0	0)	3	0	0	0	0	0	7	0	0	0	0	1	.00	0	.158	.158	.158

Jason Johnson

Pitches: R Bats: R Pos: RP-14; SP-2   Ht: 6'6" Wt: 225 Born: 10/27/1973 Age: 35

Year Team	Lg	G	GS	CG	GF	IP	BFP	H	R	ER	HR	SH	SF	HB	TBB	IBB	SO	WP	Bk	W	L	Pct	ShO	Sv-Op	Hld	ERC	ERA
		HOW MUCH HE PITCHED						WHAT HE GAVE UP												THE RESULTS							
2008 LsVgs*	AAA	20	16	0	3	113.0	492	127	55	48	15	5	5	5	30	0	95	3	0	11	5	.688	0	0- -	-	4.64	3.82
1997 Pit	NL	3	0	0	0	6.0	27	10	4	4	2	0	1	0	1	0	3	0	0	0	0	-	0	0-0	0	9.59	6.00
1998 TB	AL	13	13	0	0	60.0	274	74	38	38	9	1	1	3	27	0	36	2	0	2	5	.286	0	0-0	0	6.35	5.70
1999 Bal	AL	22	21	0	0	115.1	515	120	74	70	16	2	4	3	55	0	71	5	1	8	7	.533	0	0-0	0	4.99	5.46
2000 Bal	AL	25	13	0	3	107.2	501	119	95	84	21	3	5	4	61	2	79	3	0	1	10	.091	0	0-0	2	6.18	7.02
2001 Bal	AL	32	32	2	0	196.0	856	194	109	89	28	6	6	13	77	3	114	9	0	10	12	.455	0	0-0	0	4.53	4.09
2002 Bal	AL	22	22	1	0	131.1	561	141	68	67	19	0	3	6	41	2	97	4	0	5	14	.263	0	0-0	0	4.70	4.59
2003 Bal	AL	32	32	0	0	189.2	858	216	100	88	22	3	1	10	80	8	118	7	0	10	10	.500	0	0-0	0	5.21	4.18
2004 Det	AL	33	33	2	0	196.2	859	222	121	112	22	1	10	5	60	3	125	7	1	8	15	.348	1	0-0	0	4.58	5.13
2005 Det	AL	33	33	1	0	210.0	888	233	117	106	23	9	7	6	49	4	93	17	0	8	13	.381	0	0-0	0	4.24	4.54
2006 3 Tms		24	20	0	0	115.0	527	160	86	78	14	1	8	5	35	0	54	8	0	3	12	.200	0	0-0	0	6.43	6.10
2008 LAD	NL	16	2	0	5	29.1	130	32	19	17	5	1	0	2	12	3	20	3	0	1	2	.333	0	0-0	1	5.32	5.22
06 Cle	AL	14	14	0	0	77.0	348	108	55	51	10	1	6	2	22	0	32	6	0	3	8	.273	0	0-0	0	6.47	5.96
06 Bos	AL	6	6	0	0	29.1	141	41	26	24	3	0	2	2	13	0	18	2	0	0	4	.000	0	0-0	0	6.94	7.36
06 Cin	NL	4	0	0	0	8.2	38	11	5	3	1	0	0	1	0	0	4	0	0	0	0	-	0	0-0	0	4.45	3.12
11 ML YEARS		255	221	6	8	1357.0	5996	1521	831	753	181	27	46	57	498	25	810	65	2	56	100	.359	1	0-0	3	5.04	4.99

Jim Johnson

Pitches: R Bats: R Pos: RP-54   Ht: 6'5" Wt: 224 Born: 6/27/1983 Age: 26

Year Team	Lg	G	GS	CG	GF	IP	BFP	H	R	ER	HR	SH	SF	HB	TBB	IBB	SO	WP	Bk	W	L	Pct	ShO	Sv-Op	Hld	ERC	ERA
		HOW MUCH HE PITCHED						WHAT HE GAVE UP												THE RESULTS							
2008 Norfolk*	AAA	1	1	0	0	4.0	16	2	1	1	0	0	0	1	1	0	2	0	0	0	1	.000	0	0- -	-	1.41	2.25
2006 Bal	AL	1	1	0	0	3.0	21	9	8	8	1	0	1	0	3	0	0	0	0	0	1	.000	0	0-0	0	26.81	24.00
2007 Bal	AL	1	0	0	1	2.0	11	3	2	2	0	0	1	0	2	0	1	0	0	0	0	-	0	0-0	0	8.58	9.00
2008 Bal	AL	54	0	0	18	68.2	281	54	18	17	0	2	1	3	28	3	38	1	1	2	4	.333	0	1-1	19	2.45	2.23
3 ML YEARS		56	1	0	19	73.2	313	66	28	27	1	2	3	4	33	3	39	1	1	2	5	.286	0	1-1	19	3.27	3.30

Josh Johnson

Pitches: R Bats: L Pos: SP-14   Ht: 6'7" Wt: 230 Born: 1/31/1984 Age: 25

Year Team	Lg	G	GS	CG	GF	IP	BFP	H	R	ER	HR	SH	SF	HB	TBB	IBB	SO	WP	Bk	W	L	Pct	ShO	Sv-Op	Hld	ERC	ERA
		HOW MUCH HE PITCHED						WHAT HE GAVE UP												THE RESULTS							
2008 Grnsbr*	A	1	1	0	0	5.0	23	8	2	2	0	1	0	0	0	0	7	0	0	0	1	.000	0	0- -	-	5.03	3.60
2008 Jupiter*	A+	1	1	0	0	5.1	24	6	3	3	1	0	0	0	2	0	2	0	0	0	0	-	0	0- -	-	5.21	5.06
2008 Carlina*	AA	3	3	0	0	19.0	82	22	9	7	0	2	1	0	3	1	14	0	0	1	1	.500	0	0- -	-	3.15	3.32
2005 Fla	NL	4	4	0	0	12.1	55	11	5	5	0	1	0	1	10	0	10	0	0	0	0	-	0	0-0	0	4.82	3.65
2006 Fla	NL	31	24	0	1	157.0	659	136	63	54	14	11	0	4	68	6	133	3	1	12	7	.632	0	0-1	0	3.48	3.10
2007 Fla	NL	4	4	0	0	15.2	82	26	17	13	1	2	1	0	12	3	14	1	0	0	3	.000	0	0-0	0	9.16	7.47
2008 Fla	NL	14	14	1	0	87.1	365	91	36	35	7	5	1	1	27	1	77	4	0	7	1	.875	0	0-0	0	3.94	3.61
4 ML YEARS		53	43	1	1	272.1	1161	264	121	107	22	19	2	6	117	10	234	8	1	19	11	.633	0	0-1	0	3.98	3.54

Kelly Johnson

Bats: L Throws: R Pos: 2B-144; PH-12   Ht: 6'1" Wt: 205 Born: 2/22/1982 Age: 27

Year Team	Lg	G	AB	H	2B	3B	HR	(Hm	Rd)	TB	R	RBI	RC	TBB	IBB	SO	HBP	SH	SF	SB	CS	SB%	GDP	Avg	OBP	Slg
								BATTING												BASERUNNING				AVERAGES		
2005 Atl	NL	87	290	70	12	3	9	(2	7)	115	46	40	41	40	1	75	1	2	1	2	1	.67	11	.241	.334	.397
2007 Atl	NL	147	521	144	26	10	16	(5	11)	238	91	68	87	79	3	117	4	2	2	9	5	.64	8	.276	.375	.457
2008 Atl	NL	150	547	157	39	6	12	(5	7)	244	86	69	87	52	2	113	2	9	4	11	6	.65	3	.287	.349	.446
Postseason		4	2	0	0	0	0	(0	0)	0	0	0	0	1	0	0	0	0	0	0	0	-	0	.000	.333	.000
3 ML YEARS		384	1358	371	77	19	37	(12	25)	597	223	177	215	171	6	305	7	13	7	22	12	.65	22	.273	.356	.440

Mark Johnson

Bats: L **Throws:** R **Pos:** C-10; PH-1   **Ht:** 6'0" **Wt:** 200 **Born:** 9/12/1975 **Age:** 33

Year	Team	Lg	G	AB	H	2B	3B	HR	(Hm	Rd)	TB	R	RBI	RC	TBB	IBB	SO	HBP	SH	SF	SB	CS	SB%	GDP	Avg	OBP	Slg
2008	Memp*	AAA	66	201	53	9	0	1	(-	-)	65	17	31	28	33	1	28	2	2	1	1	1	.50	9	.264	.371	.323
1998	CWS	AL	7	23	2	0	2	0	(0	0)	6	2	1	0	1	0	8	0	0	0	0	0	-	0	.087	.125	.261
1999	CWS	AL	73	207	47	11	0	4	(2	2)	70	27	16	27	36	0	58	2	1	2	3	1	.75	2	.227	.344	.338
2000	CWS	AL	75	213	48	11	0	3	(2	1)	68	29	23	23	27	0	40	1	10	0	3	2	.60	3	.225	.315	.319
2001	CWS	AL	61	173	43	6	1	5	(2	3)	66	21	18	23	23	1	31	2	10	3	2	1	.67	5	.249	.338	.382
2002	CWS	AL	86	263	55	8	1	4	(1	3)	77	31	18	24	30	1	52	3	6	0	0	0	-	4	.209	.297	.293
2003	Oak	AL	13	27	3	1	0	0	(0	0)	4	3	3	0	3	0	4	1	1	1	0	0	-	0	.111	.219	.148
2004	Mil	NL	7	11	1	0	0	0	(0	0)	1	1	2	1	3	1	2	0	0	1	0	0	-	0	.091	.267	.091
2008	StL	NL	10	17	5	0	0	0	(0	0)	5	1	2	2	1	0	2	0	0	0	0	0	-	0	.294	.333	.294
8 ML YEARS			332	934	204	37	4	16	(7	9)	297	115	83	100	124	3	197	9	28	7	8	4	.67	14	.218	.314	.318

Nick Johnson

Bats: L **Throws:** L **Pos:** 1B-35; PH-4   **Ht:** 6'3" **Wt:** 237 **Born:** 9/19/1978 **Age:** 30

Year	Team	Lg	G	AB	H	2B	3B	HR	(Hm	Rd)	TB	R	RBI	RC	TBB	IBB	SO	HBP	SH	SF	SB	CS	SB%	GDP	Avg	OBP	Slg
2001	NYY	AL	23	67	13	2	0	2	(1	1)	21	6	8	6	7	0	15	4	0	0	0	0	-	3	.194	.308	.313
2002	NYY	AL	129	378	92	15	0	15	(7	8)	152	56	58	59	48	5	98	12	3	0	1	3	.25	11	.243	.347	.402
2003	NYY	AL	96	324	92	19	0	14	(8	6)	153	60	47	65	70	4	57	8	3	1	5	2	.71	9	.284	.422	.472
2004	Mon	NL	73	251	63	16	0	7	(4	3)	100	35	33	36	40	2	58	3	0	1	6	3	.67	5	.251	.359	.398
2005	Was	NL	131	453	131	35	3	15	(7	8)	217	66	74	83	80	8	87	12	0	2	3	8	.27	15	.289	.408	.479
2006	Was	NL	147	500	145	46	0	23	(10	13)	260	100	77	104	110	15	99	13	2	3	10	3	.77	12	.290	.428	.520
2008	Was	NL	38	109	24	8	0	5	(2	3)	47	15	20	21	33	4	25	4	0	1	0	0	-	2	.220	.415	.431
Postseason			20	67	14	3	0	1	(1	0)	20	10	6	6	8	1	14	1	0	0	0	0	-	2	.209	.303	.299
7 ML YEARS			637	2082	560	141	3	81	(39	42)	950	338	317	374	388	38	439	56	8	8	25	19	.57	57	.269	.396	.456

Randy Johnson

Pitches: L **Bats:** R **Pos:** SP-30   **Ht:** 6'10" **Wt:** 225 **Born:** 9/10/1963 **Age:** 45

			HOW MUCH HE PITCHED						WHAT HE GAVE UP												THE RESULTS							
Year	Team	Lg	G	GS	CG	GF	IP	BFP	H	R	ER	HR	SH	SF	HB	TBB	IBB	SO	WP	Bk	W	L	Pct	ShO	Sv-Op	Hld	ERC	ERA
2008	Tucsn*	AAA	2	2	0	0	10.0	43	11	8	8	1	1	0	0	3	0	8	2	0	0	0	-	0	0--	-	4.25	7.20
1988	Mon	NL	4	4	1	0	26.0	109	23	8	7	3	0	0	0	7	0	25	3	0	3	0	1.000	0	0-0	0	2.96	2.42
1989	2 Tms		29	28	2	1	160.2	715	147	100	86	13	10	13	3	96	2	130	7	7	7	13	.350	0	0-0	0	4.26	4.82
1990	Sea	AL	33	33	5	0	219.2	944	174	103	89	26	7	6	5	120	2	194	4	2	14	11	.560	2	0-0	0	3.68	3.65
1991	Sea	AL	33	33	2	0	201.1	889	151	96	89	15	9	8	12	152	0	228	12	2	13	10	.565	1	0-0	0	4.15	3.98
1992	Sea	AL	31	31	6	0	210.1	922	154	104	88	13	3	8	18	144	1	241	13	1	12	14	.462	2	0-0	0	3.75	3.77
1993	Sea	AL	35	34	10	1	255.1	1043	185	97	92	22	8	7	16	99	1	308	8	2	19	8	.704	3	1-1	0	2.73	3.24
1994	Sea	AL	23	23	9	0	172.0	694	132	65	61	14	3	1	6	72	2	204	5	0	13	6	.684	4	0-0	0	2.99	3.19
1995	Sea	AL	30	30	6	0	214.1	866	159	65	59	12	2	1	6	65	1	294	5	2	18	2	.900	3	0-0	0	2.18	2.48
1996	Sea	AL	14	8	0	2	61.1	256	48	27	25	8	1	0	2	25	0	85	3	1	5	0	1.000	0	1-2	0	3.24	3.67
1997	Sea	AL	30	29	5	0	213.0	850	147	60	54	20	4	1	10	77	2	291	4	0	20	4	.833	2	0-0	0	2.47	2.28
1998	2 Tms		34	34	10	0	244.1	1014	203	102	89	23	5	2	14	86	1	329	7	2	19	11	.633	6	0-0	0	3.16	3.28
1999	Ari	NL	35	35	12	0	271.2	1079	207	86	75	30	4	3	9	70	3	364	4	2	17	9	.654	2	0-0	0	2.49	2.48
2000	Ari	NL	35	35	8	0	248.2	1001	202	89	73	23	14	5	6	76	2	347	5	2	19	7	.731	3	0-0	0	2.80	2.64
2001	Ari	NL	35	34	3	1	249.2	994	181	74	69	19	10	5	18	71	2	372	8	1	21	6	.778	2	0-0	0	2.35	2.49
2002	Ari	NL	35	35	8	0	260.0	1035	197	78	67	26	4	2	13	71	1	334	3	2	24	5	.828	4	0-0	0	2.54	2.32
2003	Ari	NL	18	18	1	0	114.0	489	125	61	54	16	4	3	8	27	3	125	1	1	6	8	.429	1	0-0	0	4.52	4.26
2004	Ari	NL	35	35	4	0	245.2	964	177	88	71	18	7	5	10	44	1	290	3	1	16	14	.533	2	0-0	0	1.82	2.60
2005	NYY	AL	34	34	4	0	225.2	920	207	102	95	32	5	5	12	47	2	211	3	1	17	8	.680	0	0-0	0	3.38	3.79
2006	NYY	AL	33	33	2	0	205.0	860	194	125	114	28	6	7	10	60	1	172	3	2	17	11	.607	0	0-0	0	3.80	5.00
2007	Ari	NL	10	10	0	0	56.2	233	52	26	24	7	4	0	4	13	3	72	1	0	4	3	.571	0	0-0	0	3.34	3.81
2008	Ari	NL	30	30	2	0	184.0	778	184	92	80	24	13	6	6	44	6	173	2	1	11	10	.524	0	0-0	0	3.69	3.91
89	Mon	NL	7	6	0	1	29.2	143	29	25	22	2	3	4	0	26	1	26	2	2	0	4	.000	0	0-0	0	5.42	6.67
89	Sea	AL	22	22	2	0	131.0	572	118	75	64	11	7	9	3	70	1	104	5	5	7	9	.438	0	0-0	0	4.01	4.40
98	Sea	AL	23	23	6	0	160.0	685	146	90	77	19	5	1	11	60	0	213	7	2	9	10	.474	2	0-0	0	3.88	4.33
98	Hou	NL	11	11	4	0	84.1	329	57	12	12	4	0	1	3	26	1	116	0	0	10	1	.909	4	0-0	0	1.93	1.28
Postseason			19	16	3	2	121.0	493	106	51	47	15	5	5	0	32	2	132	0	0	7	9	.438	2	0-0	0	3.02	3.50
21 ML YEARS			596	586	100	5	4039.1	16655	3249	1648	1461	392	123	88	188	1466	35	4789	104	32	295	160	.648	37	2-3	0	3.04	3.26

Reed Johnson

Bats: R **Throws:** R **Pos:** CF-78; LF-26; PH-24; RF-6   **Ht:** 5'10" **Wt:** 180 **Born:** 12/8/1976 **Age:** 32

Year	Team	Lg	G	AB	H	2B	3B	HR	(Hm	Rd)	TB	R	RBI	RC	TBB	IBB	SO	HBP	SH	SF	SB	CS	SB%	GDP	Avg	OBP	Slg
2003	Tor	AL	114	412	121	21	2	10	(6	4)	176	79	52	64	20	1	67	20	1	4	5	3	.63	10	.294	.353	.427
2004	Tor	AL	141	537	145	25	2	10	(8	2)	204	68	61	65	28	2	98	12	3	2	6	3	.67	17	.270	.320	.380
2005	Tor	AL	142	398	107	21	6	8	(4	4)	164	55	58	57	22	1	82	16	2	1	5	6	.45	8	.269	.332	.412
2006	Tor	AL	134	461	147	34	2	12	(4	8)	221	86	49	76	33	4	81	21	1	1	8	2	.80	9	.319	.390	.479
2007	Tor	AL	79	275	65	13	2	2	(1	1)	88	31	14	24	16	0	56	11	5	0	4	2	.67	7	.236	.305	.320
2008	ChC	NL	109	333	101	21	0	6	(3	3)	140	52	50	57	19	1	68	12	5	5	5	6	.45	3	.303	.358	.420
6 ML YEARS			719	2416	686	135	14	48	(26	22)	993	371	284	343	138	9	452	92	17	13	33	22	.60	54	.284	.344	.411

Rob Johnson

Bats: R **Throws:** R **Pos:** C-10; DH-3; PR-2   **Ht:** 6'1" **Wt:** 208 **Born:** 7/22/1983 **Age:** 25

Year	Team	Lg	G	AB	H	2B	3B	HR	(Hm	Rd)	TB	R	RBI	RC	TBB	IBB	SO	HBP	SH	SF	SB	CS	SB%	GDP	Avg	OBP	Slg
2004	Everett	A-	20	77	18	3	1	1	(-	-)	26	17	7	8	4	0	10	2	0	1	6	2	.75	1	.234	.286	.338
2004	Ms	R	8	27	6	1	0	0	(-	-)	7	4	1	2	3	0	7	1	0	0	1	1	.50	1	.222	.323	.259
2005	Wisc	A	77	305	83	19	1	9	(-	-)	131	41	51	44	20	0	31	3	3	4	10	3	.77	8	.272	.319	.430
2005	InldEm	A+	19	70	22	3	0	2	(-	-)	31	15	12	13	10	0	14	0	2	4	2	0	1.00	1	.314	.381	.443
2006	Tacom	AAA	97	337	78	9	4	4	(-	-)	107	28	33	27	13	1	74	1	6	2	14	7	.67	9	.231	.261	.318
2007	Tacom	AAA	112	422	113	26	0	6	(-	-)	157	57	40	53	39	2	62	1	3	0	7	7	.50	11	.268	.331	.372
2008	Tacom	AAA	112	417	127	36	0	9	(-	-)	184	55	49	68	37	1	61	3	3	3	7	6	.54	13	.305	.363	.441
2007	Sea	AL	6	3	1	0	0	0	(0	0)	1	1	0	0	0	0	0	0	0	0	1	0	1.00	0	.333	.333	.333
2008	Sea	AL	14	31	4	0	0	1	(1	0)	7	2	2	0	0	0	6	0	1	0	0	0	-	1	.129	.129	.226
	2 ML YEARS		20	34	5	0	0	1	(1	0)	8	3	2	0	0	0	6	0	1	0	1	0	1.00	1	.147	.147	.235

Tyler Johnson

Pitches: L **Bats:** B **Pos:** P   **Ht:** 6'2" **Wt:** 205 **Born:** 6/7/1981 **Age:** 28

			HOW MUCH HE PITCHED						WHAT HE GAVE UP												THE RESULTS					
Year	Team	Lg	G	GS	CG	GF	IP	BFP	H	R	ER	HR	SH	SF	HB	TBB	IBB	SO	WP	Bk	W	L	Pct	ShO	Sv-Op Hld	ERC	ERA
2005	StL	NL	5	0	0	1	2.2	13	3	0	0	0	0	0	0	3	0	4	0	0	0	0	-	0	0-1 1	7.28	0.00
2006	StL	NL	56	0	0	12	36.1	164	33	21	20	5	1	1	4	23	2	37	2	0	2	4	.333	0	0-2 11	5.16	4.95
2007	StL	NL	55	0	0	6	38.0	164	31	18	17	4	1	1	3	16	2	24	2	0	1	1	.500	0	0-1 5	3.33	4.03
	Postseason		10	0	0	1	7.1	31	4	1	1	0	0	0	2	2	0	12	0	0	0	0	-	0	0-0 4	1.59	1.23
	3 ML YEARS		116	0	0	19	77.0	341	67	39	37	9	2	2	7	42	4	65	4	0	3	5	.375	0	0-4 17	4.29	4.32

Adam Jones

Bats: R **Throws:** R **Pos:** CF-129; PH-2; PR-2   **Ht:** 6'2" **Wt:** 210 **Born:** 8/1/1985 **Age:** 23

Year	Team	Lg	G	AB	H	2B	3B	HR	(Hm	Rd)	TB	R	RBI	RC	TBB	IBB	SO	HBP	SH	SF	SB	CS	SB%	GDP	Avg	OBP	Slg
2006	Sea	AL	32	74	16	4	0	1	(0	1)	23	6	8	4	2	0	22	0	0	0	3	1	.75	3	.216	.237	.311
2007	Sea	AL	41	65	16	2	1	2	(1	1)	26	16	4	5	4	0	21	1	0	0	2	1	.67	0	.246	.300	.400
2008	Bal	AL	132	477	129	21	7	9	(4	5)	191	61	57	56	23	0	108	7	2	5	10	3	.77	12	.270	.311	.400
	3 ML YEARS		205	616	161	27	8	12	(5	7)	240	83	69	65	29	0	151	8	3	5	15	5	.75	15	.261	.301	.390

Andruw Jones

Bats: R **Throws:** R **Pos:** CF-66; PH-9; DH-1; PR-1   **Ht:** 6'1" **Wt:** 240 **Born:** 4/23/1977 **Age:** 32

Year	Team	Lg	G	AB	H	2B	3B	HR	(Hm	Rd)	TB	R	RBI	RC	TBB	IBB	SO	HBP	SH	SF	SB	CS	SB%	GDP	Avg	OBP	Slg
2008	LsVgs*	AAA	11	31	10	0	0	4	(-	-)	22	7	11	8	3	0	5	0	0	2	2	0	1.00	2	.323	.361	.710
1996	Atl	NL	31	106	23	7	1	5	(3	2)	47	11	13	13	7	0	29	0	0	0	3	0	1.00	1	.217	.265	.443
1997	Atl	NL	153	399	92	18	1	18	(5	13)	166	60	70	54	56	2	107	4	5	3	20	11	.65	11	.231	.329	.416
1998	Atl	NL	159	582	158	33	8	31	(16	15)	300	89	90	97	40	8	129	4	1	4	27	4	.87	10	.271	.321	.515
1999	Atl	NL	162	592	163	35	5	26	(10	16)	286	97	84	103	76	11	103	9	0	2	24	12	.67	12	.275	.365	.483
2000	Atl	NL	161	656	199	36	6	36	(15	21)	355	122	104	127	59	0	100	9	0	5	21	6	.78	12	.303	.366	.541
2001	Atl	NL	161	625	157	25	2	34	(16	18)	288	104	104	90	56	3	142	3	0	9	11	4	.73	10	.251	.312	.461
2002	Atl	NL	154	560	148	34	0	35	(18	17)	287	91	94	94	83	4	135	10	0	6	8	3	.73	14	.264	.366	.513
2003	Atl	NL	156	595	165	28	2	36	(16	20)	305	101	116	92	53	2	125	5	0	6	4	3	.57	18	.277	.338	.513
2004	Atl	NL	154	570	149	34	4	29	(13	16)	278	85	91	75	71	9	147	3	0	2	6	6	.50	24	.261	.345	.488
2005	Atl	NL	160	586	154	24	3	51	(21	30)	337	95	128	91	64	13	112	15	0	7	5	3	.63	19	.263	.347	.575
2006	Atl	NL	156	565	148	29	0	41	(19	22)	300	107	129	108	82	9	127	13	0	9	4	1	.80	13	.262	.363	.531
2007	Atl	NL	154	572	127	27	2	26	(16	10)	236	83	94	71	70	4	138	8	0	9	5	2	.71	16	.222	.311	.413
2008	LAD		75	209	33	8	1	3	(0	3)	52	21	14	6	27	0	76	1	0	1	0	1	.00	5	.158	.256	.249
	Postseason		75	238	65	8	0	10	(5	5)	103	43	33	34	34	2	50	2	1	3	5	5	.50	7	.273	.365	.433
	13 ML YEARS		1836	6617	1716	338	35	371	(168	203)	3237	1066	1131	1021	744	65	1470	84	6	63	138	56	.71	165	.259	.339	.489

Brandon Jones

Bats: L **Throws:** R **Pos:** LF-29; PH-9; RF-7; PR-1   **Ht:** 6'1" **Wt:** 210 **Born:** 12/10/1983 **Age:** 25

Year	Team	Lg	G	AB	H	2B	3B	HR	(Hm	Rd)	TB	R	RBI	RC	TBB	IBB	SO	HBP	SH	SF	SB	CS	SB%	GDP	Avg	OBP	Slg
2004	Danvle	R	57	209	62	6	5	3	(-	-)	87	35	33	33	23	0	33	1	0	2	4	2	.67	5	.297	.366	.416
2005	Braves	R	2	8	1	0	0	0	(-	-)	1	0	2	0	0	0	2	0	0	0	0	1	.00	0	.125	.125	.125
2005	Danvle	R	2	7	2	0	0	0	(-	-)	2	0	1	0	1	0	0	0	0	0	0	0	-	0	.286	.375	.286
2005	Rome	A	43	156	48	12	3	8	(-	-)	90	37	27	38	29	0	29	3	0	1	4	1	.80	3	.308	.423	.577
2005	MrtlBh	A+	17	60	21	4	0	0	(-	-)	25	7	5	11	9	0	9	1	0	1	0	1	1.00	1	.350	.437	.417
2006	MrtlBh	A+	59	226	58	10	3	7	(-	-)	95	27	35	32	25	6	49	1	0	3	11	6	.65	6	.257	.329	.420
2006	Missi	AA	48	176	48	9	3	7	(-	-)	84	18	25	28	15	1	38	0	1	2	4	2	.67	3	.273	.326	.477
2007	Missi	AA	94	365	107	21	6	15	(-	-)	185	58	74	69	44	2	84	3	0	6	12	7	.63	6	.293	.368	.507
2007	Rchmd	AAA	44	170	51	12	1	4	(-	-)	77	26	26	29	17	2	36	1	1	2	5	0	1.00	4	.300	.363	.453
2008	Rchmd	AAA	95	346	90	24	1	8	(-	-)	140	44	52	51	46	4	76	0	0	4	9	6	.60	9	.260	.343	.405
2007	Atl	NL	5	19	3	1	0	0	(0	0)	4	0	4	1	0	0	8	1	0	1	0	0	-	0	.158	.190	.211
2008	Atl	NL	41	116	31	10	1	1	(0	1)	46	16	17	15	7	2	28	1	3	1	1	0	1.00	3	.267	.312	.397
	2 ML YEARS		46	135	34	11	1	1	(0	1)	50	16	21	16	7	2	36	2	3	2	1	0	1.00	3	.252	.295	.370

Chipper Jones

Bats: B Throws: R Pos: 3B-115; PH-10; DH-3 Ht: 6'4" Wt: 210 Born: 4/24/1972 Age: 37

Year	Team	Lg	G	AB	H	2B	3B	HR	(Hm	Rd)	TB	R	RBI	RC	TBB	IBB	SO	HBP	SH	SF	SB	CS	SB%	GDP	Avg	OBP	Slg
1993	Atl	NL	8	3	2	1	0	0	(0	0)	3	2	0	2	1	0	1	0	0	0	0	0	-	0	.667	.750	1.000
1995	Atl	NL	140	524	139	22	3	23	(15	8)	236	87	86	84	73	1	99	0	1	4	8	4	.67	10	.265	.353	.450
1996	Atl	NL	157	598	185	32	5	30	(18	12)	317	114	110	123	87	0	88	0	1	7	14	1	.93	14	.309	.393	.530
1997	Atl	NL	157	597	176	41	3	21	(7	14)	286	100	111	104	76	8	88	0	0	6	20	5	.80	19	.295	.371	.479
1998	Atl	NL	160	601	188	29	5	34	(17	17)	329	123	107	129	96	1	93	1	1	8	16	6	.73	17	.313	.404	.547
1999	Atl	NL	157	567	181	41	1	45	(25	20)	359	116	110	150	126	18	94	2	0	6	25	3	.89	20	.319	.441	.633
2000	Atl	NL	156	579	180	38	1	36	(18	18)	328	118	111	128	95	10	64	2	0	10	14	7	.67	14	.311	.404	.566
2001	Atl	NL	159	572	189	33	5	38	(19	19)	346	113	102	136	98	20	82	2	0	5	9	10	.47	13	.330	.427	.605
2002	Atl	NL	158	548	179	35	1	26	(17	9)	294	90	100	119	107	23	89	2	0	5	8	2	.80	18	.327	.435	.536
2003	Atl	NL	153	555	169	33	2	27	(16	11)	287	103	106	110	94	13	83	1	0	6	2	2	.50	10	.305	.402	.517
2004	Atl	NL	137	472	117	20	1	30	(19	11)	229	69	96	82	84	8	96	4	0	7	2	0	1.00	14	.248	.362	.485
2005	Atl	NL	109	358	106	30	0	21	(9	12)	199	66	72	78	72	5	56	0	0	2	5	1	.83	9	.296	.412	.556
2006	Atl	NL	110	411	133	28	3	26	(12	14)	245	87	86	94	61	4	73	1	0	4	6	1	.86	12	.324	.409	.596
2007	Atl	NL	134	513	173	42	4	29	(14	15)	310	108	102	110	82	10	75	0	0	5	5	1	.83	21	.337	.425	.604
2008	Atl	NL	128	439	160	24	1	22	(10	12)	252	82	75	98	90	16	61	1	0	4	4	0	1.00	13	.364	.470	.574
Postseason			92	333	96	18	0	13	(7	6)	153	58	47	60	72	11	60	1	1	5	8	3	.73	10	.288	.411	.459
15 ML YEARS			2023	7337	2277	449	35	408	(218	190)	4020	1378	1374	1547	1242	137	1142	16	3	79	138	43	.76	204	.310	.408	.548

Jacque Jones

Bats: L Throws: L Pos: LF-27; PH-9; CF-5; RF-3; DH-1 Ht: 5'10" Wt: 200 Born: 4/25/1975 Age: 34

Year	Team	Lg	G	AB	H	2B	3B	HR	(Hm	Rd)	TB	R	RBI	RC	TBB	IBB	SO	HBP	SH	SF	SB	CS	SB%	GDP	Avg	OBP	Slg
1999	Min	AL	95	322	93	24	2	9	(5	4)	148	54	44	46	17	1	63	4	1	3	3	4	.43	7	.289	.329	.460
2000	Min	AL	154	523	149	26	5	19	(11	8)	242	66	76	70	26	4	111	0	1	7	7	5	.58	17	.285	.319	.463
2001	Min	AL	149	475	131	25	0	14	(5	9)	198	57	49	63	39	2	92	3	2	0	12	9	.57	10	.276	.335	.417
2002	Min	AL	149	577	173	37	2	27	(6	21)	295	96	85	100	37	2	129	2	4	6	6	7	.46	8	.300	.341	.511
2003	Min	AL	136	517	157	33	1	16	(7	9)	240	76	69	73	21	2	105	4	1	5	13	1	.93	10	.304	.333	.464
2004	Min	AL	151	555	141	22	1	24	(9	15)	237	69	80	73	40	2	117	10	2	1	13	10	.57	12	.254	.315	.427
2005	Min	AL	142	523	130	22	4	23	(9	14)	229	74	73	72	51	12	120	5	2	4	13	4	.76	17	.249	.319	.438
2006	ChC	NL	149	533	152	31	1	27	(12	15)	266	73	81	82	35	6	116	5	2	2	9	1	.90	17	.285	.334	.499
2007	ChC	NL	135	453	129	33	2	5	(3	2)	181	52	66	62	34	5	70	2	3	3	6	3	.67	15	.285	.335	.400
2008	2 Tms		42	116	17	2	1	1	(1	0)	24	15	7	3	14	1	26	1	0	3	0	1	.00	3	.147	.239	.207
08	Det	AL	24	79	13	2	1	1	(1	0)	20	10	5	2	8	0	18	1	0	2	0	1	.00	2	.165	.244	.253
08	Fla	NL	18	37	4	0	0	0	(0	0)	4	5	2	1	6	1	8	0	0	1	0	0	-	1	.108	.227	.108
Postseason			21	85	17	6	0	2	(1	1)	29	7	5	4	4	0	24	1	0	1	0	1	.00	3	.200	.242	.341
10 ML YEARS			1302	4594	1272	255	19	165	(68	97)	2060	632	630	644	314	37	949	36	18	27	82	45	.65	116	.277	.326	.448

Todd Jones

Pitches: R Bats: L Pos: RP-45 Ht: 6'3" Wt: 230 Born: 4/24/1968 Age: 41

Year	Team	Lg	G	GS	CG	GF	IP	BFP	H	R	ER	HR	SH	SF	HB	TBB	IBB	SO	WP	Bk	W	L	Pct	ShO	Sv-Op	Hld	ERC	ERA
1993	Hou	NL	27	0	0	8	37.1	150	28	14	13	4	2	1	1	15	2	25	1	1	1	2	.333	0	2-3	6	2.90	3.13
1994	Hou	NL	48	0	0	20	72.2	288	52	23	22	3	1	1	1	26	4	63	1	0	5	2	.714	0	5-9	8	2.10	2.72
1995	Hou	NL	68	0	0	40	99.2	442	89	38	34	8	5	4	6	52	17	96	5	0	6	5	.545	0	15-20	8	3.73	3.07
1996	Hou	NL	51	0	0	37	57.1	263	61	30	28	5	2	1	5	32	6	44	3	0	6	3	.667	0	17-23	1	5.16	4.40
1997	Det	AL	68	0	0	51	70.0	301	60	29	24	3	1	4	1	35	2	70	7	0	5	4	.556	0	31-36	5	3.27	3.09
1998	Det	AL	65	0	0	53	63.1	279	58	38	35	7	2	6	2	36	4	57	5	0	1	4	.200	0	28-32	0	4.37	4.97
1999	Det	AL	65	0	0	62	66.1	287	64	30	28	7	3	1	1	35	1	64	2	0	4	4	.500	0	30-35	0	4.55	3.80
2000	Det	AL	67	0	0	60	64.0	271	67	28	25	6	1	1	1	25	1	67	2	0	2	4	.333	0	**42**-46	0	4.43	3.52
2001	2 Tms		69	0	0	36	68.0	314	87	39	32	9	3	3	0	29	1	54	3	0	5	5	.500	0	13-21	10	6.03	4.24
2002	Col	NL	79	0	0	20	82.1	352	84	43	43	10	6	3	3	28	3	73	1	0	1	4	.200	0	1-3	30	4.72	4.70
2003	2 Tms		59	1	0	14	68.2	326	93	58	54	10	3	3	1	31	2	59	0	0	3	5	.375	0	0-5	4	6.73	7.08
2004	2 Tms		78	0	0	16	82.1	358	84	39	38	7	5	6	6	33	5	59	2	0	11	5	.688	0	2-8	27	4.32	4.15
2005	Fla	NL	68	0	0	55	73.0	289	61	19	17	2	6	1	3	14	2	62	2	0	1	5	.167	0	40-45	1	2.15	2.10
2006	Det	AL	62	0	0	56	64.0	272	70	31	28	6	3	2	0	11	3	28	2	0	1	4	.200	0	37-43	0	3.53	3.94
2007	Det	AL	63	0	0	54	61.1	265	64	29	29	2	3	2	0	23	6	33	3	0	1	4	.200	0	38-44	0	3.70	4.26
2008	Det	AL	45	0	0	37	41.2	193	50	30	23	5	1	2	4	18	3	14	4	0	4	1	.800	0	18-21	0	5.78	4.97
01	Det	AL	45	0	0	28	48.2	225	60	31	25	6	2	3	0	22	1	39	3	0	4	5	.444	0	11-17	3	5.74	4.62
01	Min	AL	24	0	0	8	19.1	89	27	8	7	3	1	0	0	7	0	15	0	0	1	0	1.000	0	2-4	7	6.80	3.26
03	Col	NL	33	1	0	7	39.1	193	61	39	36	8	3	2	1	18	0	28	0	0	1	4	.200	0	0-5	3	8.77	8.24
03	Bos	AL	26	0	0	7	29.1	133	32	19	18	2	0	1	0	13	2	31	0	0	2	1	.667	0	0-0	1	4.30	5.52
04	Cin	NL	51	0	0	10	57.0	235	49	25	24	4	2	5	1	25	2	37	2	0	8	2	.800	0	1-6	22	3.37	3.79
04	Phi	NL	27	0	0	6	25.1	123	35	14	14	3	3	1	5	8	3	22	0	0	3	3	.500	0	1-2	5	6.65	4.97
Postseason			8	0	0	6	7.0	33	8	1	0	0	0	0	1	2	0	5	0	0	0	0	-	0	4-4	0	3.99	0.00
16 ML YEARS			982	1	0	619	1072.0	4650	1072	518	473	93	48	38	38	443	62	868	43	1	58	63	.479	0	319-394	100	4.09	3.97

Ryan Jorgensen

Bats: R Throws: R Pos: C-2 Ht: 6'2" Wt: 220 Born: 5/4/1979 Age: 30

Year	Team	Lg	G	AB	H	2B	3B	HR	(Hm	Rd)	TB	R	RBI	RC	TBB	IBB	SO	HBP	SH	SF	SB	CS	SB%	GDP	Avg	OBP	Slg
2008	Roch*	AAA	65	198	49	12	0	8	(-	-)	85	27	25	28	18	0	54	2	5	2	0	0	-	3	.247	.314	.429
2005	Fla	NL	4	4	0	0	0	0	(0	0)	0	0	0	0	0	0	3	0	0	0	0	0	-	0	.000	.000	.000
2007	Cin	NL	4	15	3	0	0	2	(1	1)	9	3	6	4	0	0	5	0	0	0	0	0	-	0	.200	.200	.600
2008	Min	AL	2	1	0	0	0	0	(0	0)	0	0	0	0	0	0	0	0	0	0	0	0	-	0	.000	.000	.000
3 ML YEARS			10	20	3	0	0	2	(1	1)	9	3	6	4	0	0	8	0	0	0	0	0	-	0	.150	.150	.450

Matt Joyce

Bats: L **Throws:** R **Pos:** LF-60; RF-25; PH-10; DH-2; PR-2   **Ht:** 6'2" **Wt:** 185 **Born:** 8/3/1984 **Age:** 24

Year	Team	Lg	G	AB	H	2B	3B	HR	(Hm	Rd)	TB	R	RBI	RC	TBB	IBB	SO	HBP	SH	SF	SB	CS	SB%	GDP	Avg	OBP	Slg
2005	Oneont	A-	65	247	82	10	4	4	(-	-)	112	51	46	46	28	0	29	1	1	6	9	5	.64	4	.332	.394	.453
2006	WMich	A	122	465	120	30	5	11	(-	-)	193	75	86	69	56	2	70	3	1	5	5	4	.56	7	.258	.338	.415
2007	Erie	AA	130	456	117	33	3	17	(-	-)	207	61	70	70	51	1	127	3	1	3	4	6	.40	7	.257	.333	.454
2008	Toledo	AAA	56	200	54	13	2	13	(-	-)	110	36	41	38	24	1	62	2	0	1	2	3	.40	1	.270	.352	.550
2008	Det	AL	92	242	61	16	3	12	(6	6)	119	40	33	36	31	0	65	2	0	2	0	2	.00	3	.252	.339	.492

Jorge Julio

Pitches: R **Bats:** R **Pos:** RP-27   **Ht:** 6'1" **Wt:** 223 **Born:** 3/3/1979 **Age:** 30

Year	Team	Lg	G	GS	CG	GF	IP	BFP	H	R	ER	HR	SH	SF	HB	TBB	IBB	SO	WP	Bk	W	L	Pct	ShO	Sv-Op	Hld	ERC	ERA
2008	Rchmd*	AAA	38	0	0	29	39.2	169	33	15	9	1	0	0	3	23	0	45	7	1	1	2	.333	0	13-	-	3.71	2.04
2001	Bal	AL	18	0	0	8	21.1	99	25	13	9	2	2	0	1	9	0	22	1	0	1	1	.500	0	0-1	3	5.17	3.80
2002	Bal	AL	67	0	0	61	68.0	289	55	22	15	5	1	1	2	27	3	55	8	0	5	6	.455	0	25-31	1	2.83	1.99
2003	Bal	AL	64	0	0	51	61.2	273	60	36	30	10	2	1	2	34	4	52	0	0	0	7	.000	0	36-44	2	5.05	4.38
2004	Bal	AL	65	0	0	50	69.0	306	59	35	35	11	2	3	3	39	4	70	7	0	2	5	.286	0	22-26	2	4.35	4.57
2005	Bal	AL	67	0	0	19	71.2	313	76	50	47	14	1	3	2	24	4	58	10	0	3	5	.375	0	0-2	12	4.82	5.90
2006	2 Tms	NL	62	0	0	44	66.0	285	52	35	31	10	1	0	1	35	2	88	9	0	2	4	.333	0	16-20	1	3.72	4.23
2007	2 Tms	NL	68	0	0	14	62.0	280	68	39	36	8	2	4	3	31	2	56	6	1	0	5	.000	0	0-7	17	5.44	5.23
2008	2 Tms		27	0	0	11	30.0	132	27	12	12	3	0	2	1	19	2	34	6	0	3	0	1.000	0	0-1	0	4.52	3.60
06	NYM	NL	18	0	0	12	21.1	96	21	15	12	4	0	0	1	10	1	33	2	0	1	2	.333	0	1-1	0	4.90	5.06
06	Ari	NL	44	0	0	32	44.2	189	31	20	19	6	1	0	0	25	1	55	7	0	1	2	.333	0	15-19	1	3.18	3.83
07	Fla	NL	10	0	0	5	9.1	59	18	14	13	2	1	0	2	11	1	6	1	1	0	2	.000	0	0-2	1	15.51	12.54
07	Col	NL	58	0	0	9	52.2	221	50	25	23	6	1	4	1	20	1	50	5	0	0	3	.000	0	0-5	16	3.93	3.93
08	Cle	AL	15	0	0	6	17.2	78	18	11	11	3	0	2	0	11	1	15	3	0	0	0	-	0	0-0	0	5.70	5.60
08	Atl	NL	12	0	0	5	12.1	54	9	1	1	0	0	0	1	8	1	19	3	0	3	0	1.000	0	0-1	0	2.97	0.73
8 ML YEARS			438	0	0	258	449.2	1977	422	242	215	63	11	14	15	218	21	435	47	1	16	33	.327	0	99-132	38	4.37	4.30

Jair Jurrjens

Pitches: R **Bats:** R **Pos:** SP-31   **Ht:** 6'1" **Wt:** 200 **Born:** 1/29/1986 **Age:** 23

Year	Team	Lg	G	GS	CG	GF	IP	BFP	H	R	ER	HR	SH	SF	HB	TBB	IBB	SO	WP	Bk	W	L	Pct	ShO	Sv-Op	Hld	ERC	ERA
2003	Tigers	R	7	2	0	3	28.0	121	33	16	10	3	1	0	4	3	0	20	0	0	2	1	.667	0	0-	-	4.55	3.21
2004	Tigers	R	6	6	2	1	39.2	158	25	16	10	2	1	0	1	10	1	39	4	0	4	2	.667	1	0-	-	1.49	2.27
2004	Oneont	A-	7	7	0	0	39.0	178	50	25	23	0	0	2	3	10	1	31	5	1	1	5	.167	0	0-	-	4.55	5.31
2005	WMich	A	26	26	0	0	142.2	586	132	62	54	5	3	4	6	36	0	108	12	3	12	6	.667	0	0-	-	2.87	3.41
2006	Lkland	A+	12	12	0	0	73.2	281	53	23	17	4	1	0	2	10	0	59	3	0	5	0	1.000	0	0-	-	1.60	2.08
2006	Erie	AA	12	12	0	0	67.0	283	71	30	25	7	2	0	4	21	2	53	4	0	4	3	.571	0	0-	-	4.42	3.36
2007	Erie	AA	19	19	1	0	112.2	470	112	43	40	7	1	1	1	31	3	94	9	1	7	5	.583	1	0-	-	3.32	3.20
2007	Det	AL	7	7	0	0	30.2	122	24	16	16	4	0	1	1	11	0	13	2	0	3	1	.750	0	0-0	0	3.19	4.70
2008	Atl	NL	31	31	0	0	188.1	813	188	87	77	11	12	5	4	70	9	139	3	0	13	10	.565	0	0-0	0	3.65	3.68
2 ML YEARS			38	38	0	0	219.0	935	212	103	93	15	12	6	5	81	9	152	5	0	16	11	.593	0	0-0	0	3.59	3.82

Kila Ka'aihue

Bats: L **Throws:** R **Pos:** DH-5; PH-5; 1B-4; PR-1   **Ht:** 6'3" **Wt:** 230 **Born:** 3/29/1984 **Age:** 25

Year	Team	Lg	G	AB	H	2B	3B	HR	(Hm	Rd)	TB	R	RBI	RC	TBB	IBB	SO	HBP	SH	SF	SB	CS	SB%	GDP	Avg	OBP	Slg
2002	Royals	R	43	139	36	8	0	3	(-	-)	53	15	21	22	26	0	35	2	0	1	0	0	-	4	.259	.381	.381
2003	Burlgtn	A	114	395	94	21	1	11	(-	-)	150	53	63	59	67	1	87	8	6	6	1	3	.25	13	.238	.355	.380
2004	Burlgtn	A	125	390	96	23	2	15	(-	-)	168	57	62	66	64	4	98	9	3	5	1	0	1.00	6	.246	.361	.431
2005	Hi Dsrt	A+	132	493	150	31	2	20	(-	-)	245	84	90	110	97	2	97	12	0	3	2	1	.67	12	.304	.428	.497
2006	Wichta	AA	103	327	65	15	0	6	(-	-)	98	40	45	34	49	0	73	4	5	10	0	1	.00	5	.199	.303	.300
2007	Wilmg	A+	60	207	52	8	0	9	(-	-)	87	28	42	35	35	0	38	4	0	7	1	0	1.00	5	.251	.360	.420
2007	Wichta	AA	70	244	60	13	0	12	(-	-)	109	37	40	41	41	3	40	2	1	0	0	0	-	4	.246	.359	.447
2008	NWArk	AA	91	287	90	11	0	26	(-	-)	179	64	79	83	80	7	41	4	0	5	3	2	.60	3	.314	.463	.624
2008	Omha	AAA	33	114	36	4	0	11	(-	-)	73	27	21	31	24	0	26	1	0	0	0	0	-	1	.316	.439	.640
2008	KC	AL	12	21	6	0	0	1	(1	0)	9	4	1	3	3	0	2	0	0	0	0	0	-	0	.286	.375	.429

Gabe Kapler

Bats: R **Throws:** R **Pos:** CF-36; PH-33; LF-17; RF-14   **Ht:** 6'2" **Wt:** 188 **Born:** 7/31/1975 **Age:** 33

Year	Team	Lg	G	AB	H	2B	3B	HR	(Hm	Rd)	TB	R	RBI	RC	TBB	IBB	SO	HBP	SH	SF	SB	CS	SB%	GDP	Avg	OBP	Slg
1998	Det	AL	7	25	5	0	1	0	(0	0)	7	3	0	2	1	0	4	0	0	0	2	0	1.00	0	.200	.231	.280
1999	Det	AL	130	416	102	22	4	18	(12	6)	186	60	49	59	42	0	74	2	4	4	11	5	.69	7	.245	.315	.447
2000	Tex	AL	116	444	134	32	1	14	(11	3)	210	59	66	72	42	2	57	0	2	3	8	4	.67	12	.302	.360	.473
2001	Tex	AL	134	483	129	29	1	17	(11	6)	211	77	72	77	61	2	70	3	2	7	23	6	.79	10	.267	.348	.437
2002	2 Tms		112	315	88	16	4	2	(1	1)	118	37	34	44	16	0	53	1	7	3	11	4	.73	5	.279	.313	.375
2003	2 Tms		107	225	61	13	1	4	(2	2)	88	39	27	28	22	1	41	0	0	0	6	2	.75	8	.271	.336	.391
2004	Bos	AL	136	290	79	14	1	6	(3	3)	113	51	33	32	15	0	49	2	1	2	5	4	.56	5	.272	.311	.390
2005	Bos	AL	36	97	24	7	0	1	(0	1)	34	15	9	7	3	0	15	2	1	1	1	0	1.00	1	.247	.282	.351
2006	Bos	AL	72	130	33	7	0	2	(1	1)	46	21	12	14	14	0	15	3	0	0	1	1	.50	5	.254	.340	.354
2008	Mil	NL	96	229	69	17	2	8	(4	4)	114	36	38	35	13	0	39	1	1	1	3	1	.75	3	.301	.340	.498
02	Tex	AL	72	196	51	12	1	0	(0	0)	65	25	17	20	8	0	30	0	7	3	5	2	.71	3	.260	.285	.332
02	Col	NL	40	119	37	4	3	2	(1	1)	53	12	17	24	8	0	23	1	0	0	6	2	.75	2	.311	.359	.445

			BATTING																			BASERUNNING				AVERAGES		
Year	Team	Lg	G	AB	H	2B	3B	HR	(Hm	Rd)	TB	R	RBI	RC	TBB	IBB	SO	HBP	SH	SF	SB	CS	SB%	GDP	Avg	OBP	Slg
03	Col	NL	39	67	15	2	0	0	(0	0)	17	10	4	5	8	1	18	0	0	0	2	0	1.00	3	.224	.307	.254
03	Bos	AL	68	158	46	11	1	4	(2	2)	71	29	23	23	14	0	23	0	0	0	4	2	.67	5	.291	.349	.449
	Postseason		15	27	3	0	0	0	(0	0)	3	2	0	1	0	0	7	0	0	0	0	1	.00	2	.111	.111	.111
10 ML YEARS			946	2654	724	157	15	72	(45	27)	1127	398	340	370	229	5	417	14	18	21	71	27	.72	56	.273	.331	.425

Jeff Karstens

Pitches: R Bats: R Pos: SP-9   Ht: 6'3" Wt: 185 Born: 9/24/1982 Age: 26

			HOW MUCH HE PITCHED						WHAT HE GAVE UP												THE RESULTS							
Year	Team	Lg	G	GS	CG	GF	IP	BFP	H	R	ER	HR	SH	SF	HB	TBB	IBB	SO	WP	Bk	W	L	Pct	ShO	Sv-Op	Hld	ERC	ERA
2008	S-WB*	AAA	12	12	0	0	68.2	278	66	31	29	8	2	3	0	15	1	55	2	0	6	4	.600	0	0- -	-	3.30	3.80
2006	NYY	AL	8	6	0	2	42.2	179	40	20	18	6	0	2	1	11	2	16	3	1	2	1	.667	0	0-0	0	3.42	3.80
2007	NYY	AL	7	3	0	2	14.2	80	27	21	18	4	2	1	0	9	0	5	2	0	1	4	.200	0	0-0	0	11.86	11.05
2008	Pit	NL	9	9	1	0	51.1	220	56	32	23	7	2	4	0	13	0	23	1	0	2	6	.250	1	0-0	0	4.22	4.03
3 ML YEARS			24	18	1	4	108.2	479	123	73	59	17	4	7	1	33	2	44	6	1	5	11	.313	1	0-0	0	4.78	4.89

Kenshin Kawakami

Pitches: R Bats: R Pos: P   Ht: 5'10" Wt: 198 Born: 6/22/1975 Age: 34

			HOW MUCH HE PITCHED						WHAT HE GAVE UP												THE RESULTS							
Year	Team	Lg	G	GS	CG	GF	IP	BFP	H	R	ER	HR	SH	SF	HB	TBB	IBB	SO	WP	Bk	W	L	Pct	ShO	Sv-Op	Hld	ERC	ERA
1998	Chnchi	Jap	26	25	4	1	161.1	649	123	48	46	14	-	-	2	51	-	124	4	0	14	6	.700	3	0- -	-	2.48	2.57
1999	Chnchi	Jap	29	25	3	1	162.0	695	173	84	80	20	-	-	2	43	-	102	3	0	8	9	.471	1	1- -	-	4.10	4.44
2000	Chnchi	Jap	14	10	0	2	60.1	260	65	32	32	10	-	-	1	20	-	24	1	0	2	3	.400	0	0- -	-	4.81	4.77
2001	Chnchi	Jap	26	25	3	1	145.0	608	153	61	60	12	-	-	4	36	-	127	4	0	6	10	.375	1	0- -	-	3.83	3.72
2002	Chnchi	Jap	27	27	3	0	187.2	760	170	54	49	13	-	-	8	34	-	149	0	0	12	6	.667	3	0- -	-	2.72	2.35
2003	Chnchi	Jap	8	8	1	0	53.2	234	60	22	18	2	-	-	1	14	-	37	3	0	4	3	.571	0	0- -	-	3.76	3.02
2004	Chnchi	Jap	27	27	5	0	193.1	774	173	72	71	27	11	1	4	38	2	176	2	0	17	7	.708	2	0- -	-	3.08	3.31
2005	Chnchi	Jap	25	25	3	0	180.1	738	186	75	75	20	9	3	4	28	4	138	1	0	11	8	.579	2	0- -	-	3.45	3.74
2006	Chnchi	Jap	29	28	6	0	215.0	841	166	74	60	22	11	2	5	39	1	194	3	0	17	7	.708	3	0- -	-	2.19	2.51
2007	Chnchi	Jap	26	26	0	0	167.1	696	175	72	66	18	-	-	6	23	2	145	1	0	12	8	.600	0	0- -	-	3.45	3.55
2008	Chnchi	Jap	19	16	1	1	115.1	466	95	33	30	11	-	-	5	24	-	110	1	0	9	5	.643	0	0- -	-	2.54	2.34

Sean Kazmar

Bats: R Throws: R Pos: SS-15; 2B-2; PH-1; PR-1   Ht: 5'9" Wt: 170 Born: 8/5/1984 Age: 24

			BATTING																			BASERUNNING				AVERAGES		
Year	Team	Lg	G	AB	H	2B	3B	HR	(Hm	Rd)	TB	R	RBI	RC	TBB	IBB	SO	HBP	SH	SF	SB	CS	SB%	GDP	Avg	OBP	Slg
2004	Eugene	A-	65	274	69	13	3	6	(-	-)	106	29	27	30	9	1	55	1	1	0	6	0	1.00	5	.252	.278	.387
2004	FtWyn	A	5	23	5	3	0	0	(-	-)	8	5	2	2	1	0	6	2	0	0	0	0	-	1	.217	.308	.348
2005	FtWyn	A	125	469	125	26	4	10	(-	-)	181	47	48	62	44	2	69	1	2	3	7	4	.64	8	.267	.329	.386
2006	Lk Els	A+	133	540	135	19	5	13	(-	-)	203	86	72	73	63	0	80	2	5	6	10	1	.91	11	.250	.327	.376
2007	SnAnt	AA	78	269	56	10	2	6	(-	-)	88	30	33	26	24	1	46	3	0	3	6	1	.86	8	.208	.278	.327
2007	Lk Els	A+	47	201	57	20	0	3	(-	-)	86	27	24	31	16	0	27	3	2	0	4	1	.80	3	.284	.345	.428
2008	SnAnt	AA	111	382	101	21	3	3	(-	-)	137	53	39	49	38	0	66	3	6	4	7	4	.64	14	.264	.333	.359
2008	SD	NL	19	39	8	1	0	0	(0	0)	9	2	2	3	5	0	14	0	1	1	0	0	-	0	.205	.289	.231

Scott Kazmir

Pitches: L Bats: L Pos: SP-27   Ht: 6'0" Wt: 190 Born: 1/24/1984 Age: 25

			HOW MUCH HE PITCHED						WHAT HE GAVE UP												THE RESULTS							
Year	Team	Lg	G	GS	CG	GF	IP	BFP	H	R	ER	HR	SH	SF	HB	TBB	IBB	SO	WP	Bk	W	L	Pct	ShO	Sv-Op	Hld	ERC	ERA
2008	VeroB*	A+	2	2	0	0	7.2	32	8	5	4	2	0	0	0	0	0	7	0	0	0	1	.000	0	0- -	-	3.50	4.70
2008	Drham*	AAA	1	1	0	0	5.0	19	3	1	1	1	0	0	0	1	0	3	0	0	0	0	-	0	0- -	-	1.85	1.80
2004	TB	AL	8	7	0	0	33.1	152	33	22	21	4	0	2	0	21	0	41	3	0	2	3	.400	0	0-0	0	5.36	5.67
2005	TB	AL	32	32	0	0	186.0	818	172	90	78	12	6	9	10	100	3	174	7	1	10	9	.526	0	0-0	0	4.13	3.77
2006	TB	AL	24	24	1	0	144.2	610	132	59	52	15	0	5	2	52	3	163	6	0	10	8	.556	1	0-0	0	3.47	3.24
2007	TB	AL	34	34	0	0	206.2	887	196	91	80	18	6	3	7	89	1	239	10	0	13	9	.591	0	0-0	0	3.97	3.48
2008	TB	AL	27	27	0	0	152.1	641	123	61	59	23	4	5	4	70	2	166	5	0	12	8	.600	0	0-0	0	3.69	3.49
5 ML YEARS			125	124	1	0	723.0	3108	656	323	290	72	16	22	25	332	9	783	31	1	47	37	.560	1	0-0	0	3.92	3.61

Austin Kearns

Bats: R Throws: R Pos: RF-85; PH-2   Ht: 6'3" Wt: 238 Born: 5/20/1980 Age: 29

			BATTING																			BASERUNNING				AVERAGES		
Year	Team	Lg	G	AB	H	2B	3B	HR	(Hm	Rd)	TB	R	RBI	RC	TBB	IBB	SO	HBP	SH	SF	SB	CS	SB%	GDP	Avg	OBP	Slg
2008	Hgrstn*	A	2	3	1	0	0	0	(-	-)	1	2	1	1	3	0	1	0	0	0	0	0	-	0	.333	.667	.333
2008	Clmbs*	AAA	5	14	6	1	1	1	(-	-)	12	2	6	5	3	0	2	1	0	1	0	0	-	0	.429	.526	.857
2002	Cin	NL	107	372	117	24	3	13	(7	6)	186	66	56	70	54	3	81	6	0	3	6	3	.67	11	.315	.407	.500
2003	Cin	NL	82	292	77	11	0	15	(8	7)	133	39	58	52	41	1	68	5	0	0	5	2	.71	7	.264	.364	.455
2004	Cin	NL	64	217	50	10	2	9	(3	6)	91	28	32	26	28	0	71	1	0	0	2	1	.67	8	.230	.321	.419
2005	Cin	NL	112	387	93	26	1	18	(9	9)	175	62	67	55	48	2	107	8	0	5	0	0	-	4	.240	.333	.452
2006	2 Tms	NL	150	537	142	33	2	24	(12	12)	251	86	86	81	76	4	135	10	1	5	9	4	.69	18	.264	.363	.467
2007	Was	NL	161	587	156	35	1	16	(8	8)	241	84	74	87	71	5	106	12	0	4	2	2	.50	20	.266	.355	.411
2008	Was	NL	86	313	68	10	0	7	(1	6)	99	40	32	28	35	0	63	8	0	1	2	2	.50	11	.217	.311	.316
06	Cin	NL	87	325	89	21	1	16	(8	8)	160	53	50	46	35	2	85	5	0	3	7	1	.88	14	.274	.351	.492
06	Was	NL	63	212	53	12	1	8	(4	4)	91	33	36	35	41	2	50	5	1	2	2	3	.40	4	.250	.381	.429
7 ML YEARS			762	2705	703	149	9	102	(48	54)	1176	405	405	399	353	15	631	50	1	18	26	14	.65	76	.260	.354	.435

Matt Kemp

Bats: R Throws: R Pos: CF-101; RF-63; PH-7; PR-2   Ht: 6'2" Wt: 230 Born: 9/23/1984 Age: 24

Year Team	Lg	G	AB	H	2B	3B	HR	(Hm Rd)	TB	R	RBI	RC	TBB	IBB	SO	HBP	SH	SF	SB	CS	SB%	GDP	Avg	OBP	Slg
2006 LAD	NL	52	154	39	7	1	7	(4 3)	69	30	23	20	9	1	53	0	0	3	6	0	1.00	1	.253	.289	.448
2007 LAD	NL	98	292	100	12	5	10	(9 1)	152	47	42	49	16	0	66	0	0	3	10	5	.67	6	.342	.373	.521
2008 LAD	NL	155	606	176	38	5	18	(14 4)	278	93	76	86	46	6	153	1	1	3	35	11	.76	11	.290	.340	.459
3 ML YEARS		305	1052	315	57	11	35	(27 8)	499	170	141	155	71	7	272	1	1	9	51	16	.76	18	.299	.342	.474

Jason Kendall

Bats: R Throws: R Pos: C-149; PH-2   Ht: 6'0" Wt: 204 Born: 6/26/1974 Age: 35

Year Team	Lg	G	AB	H	2B	3B	HR	(Hm Rd)	TB	R	RBI	RC	TBB	IBB	SO	HBP	SH	SF	SB	CS	SB%	GDP	Avg	OBP	Slg
1996 Pit	NL	130	414	124	23	5	3	(2 1)	166	54	42	63	35	11	30	15	3	4	5	2	.71	7	.300	.372	.401
1997 Pit	NL	144	486	143	36	4	8	(5 3)	211	71	49	86	49	2	53	31	1	5	18	6	.75	11	.294	.391	.434
1998 Pit	NL	149	535	175	36	3	12	(6 6)	253	95	75	110	51	3	51	31	2	8	26	5	.84	6	.327	.411	.473
1999 Pit	NL	78	280	93	20	3	8	(5 3)	143	61	41	63	38	3	32	12	0	4	22	3	.88	8	.332	.428	.511
2000 Pit	NL	152	579	185	33	6	14	(7 7)	272	112	58	112	79	3	79	15	1	4	22	12	.65	13	.320	.412	.470
2001 Pit	NL	157	606	161	22	2	10	(3 7)	217	84	53	68	44	4	48	20	0	2	13	14	.48	18	.266	.335	.358
2002 Pit	NL	145	545	154	25	3	3	(1 2)	194	59	44	66	49	1	29	9	0	2	15	8	.65	11	.283	.350	.356
2003 Pit	NL	150	587	191	29	3	6	(3 3)	244	84	58	97	49	3	40	25	1	3	8	7	.53	9	.325	.399	.416
2004 Pit	NL	147	574	183	32	0	3	(2 1)	224	86	51	95	60	2	41	19	1	4	11	8	.58	12	.319	.399	.390
2005 Oak	AL	150	601	163	28	1	0	(0 0)	193	70	53	79	50	0	39	20	0	5	8	3	.73	27	.271	.345	.321
2006 Oak	AL	143	552	163	23	0	1	(1 0)	189	76	50	80	53	2	54	12	4	5	11	5	.69	19	.295	.367	.342
2007 2 Tms		137	466	113	20	1	3	(1 2)	144	45	41	43	31	2	42	9	5	3	3	4	.43	8	.242	.301	.309
2008 Mil	NL	151	516	127	30	2	2	(1 1)	167	46	49	59	50	7	45	13	6	2	8	3	.73	5	.246	.327	.324
07 Oak	AL	80	292	66	10	0	2	(0 2)	82	24	22	18	12	0	27	3	2	3	3	1	.75	7	.226	.261	.281
07 ChC		57	174	47	10	1	1	(1 0)	62	21	19	25	19	2	15	6	3	0	0	3	.00	1	.270	.362	.356
Postseason		8	35	9	1	0	0	(0 0)	10	1	2	3	2	0	7	0	0	0	0	0	-	0	.257	.297	.286
13 ML YEARS		1833	6741	1975	357	33	73	(37 36)	2617	943	664	1021	638	43	583	231	24	51	170	80	.68	154	.293	.371	.388

Howie Kendrick

Bats: R Throws: R Pos: 2B-92   Ht: 5'10" Wt: 195 Born: 7/12/1983 Age: 25

Year Team	Lg	G	AB	H	2B	3B	HR	(Hm Rd)	TB	R	RBI	RC	TBB	IBB	SO	HBP	SH	SF	SB	CS	SB%	GDP	Avg	OBP	Slg
2008 RCuca*	A+	2	6	5	0	0	2	(- -)	11	3	2	5	0	0	0	0	0	0	1	0	1.00	0	.833	.833	1.833
2008 Salt Lk*	AAA	2	5	1	0	0	0	(- -)	1	0	1	0	0	0	1	0	0	0	0	0	-	0	.200	.200	.200
2006 LAA	AL	72	267	76	21	1	4	(2 2)	111	25	30	32	9	2	44	4	0	3	6	0	1.00	5	.285	.314	.416
2007 LAA	AL	88	338	109	24	2	5	(3 2)	152	55	39	41	9	2	61	4	1	1	5	4	.56	15	.322	.347	.450
2008 LAA	AL	92	340	104	26	2	3	(1 2)	143	43	37	50	12	3	58	4	1	4	11	4	.73	8	.306	.333	.421
Postseason		3	10	2	0	0	0	(0 0)	2	0	1	0	0	0	1	0	0	1	2	0	1.00	1	.200	.182	.200
3 ML YEARS		252	945	289	71	5	12	(6 6)	406	123	106	123	30	7	163	12	2	8	22	8	.73	28	.306	.333	.430

Kyle Kendrick

Pitches: R Bats: R Pos: SP-30; RP-1   Ht: 6'3" Wt: 190 Born: 8/26/1984 Age: 24

Year Team	Lg	G	GS	CG	GF	IP	BFP	H	R	ER	HR	SH	SF	HB	TBB	IBB	SO	WP	Bk	W	L	Pct	ShO	Sv-Op Hld	ERC	ERA
2003 Phillies	R	9	5	0	0	31.1	145	40	24	19	3	1	1	0	12	0	26	2	0	0	4	.000	0	0- - -	5.49	5.46
2004 Lakwd	A	15	15	0	0	66.2	318	85	56	45	9	6	4	8	33	0	36	4	0	3	8	.273	0	0- - -	6.92	6.08
2004 Batvia	A-	13	12	0	0	70.2	317	94	52	43	6	3	6	5	18	1	53	1	1	2	8	.200	0	0- - -	5.64	5.48
2005 Lakwd	A	5	5	0	0	22.2	117	38	24	23	2	0	2	2	10	0	11	1	0	0	3	.000	0	0- - -	8.61	9.13
2005 Clrwtr	A+	1	1	0	0	4.0	18	5	1	0	0	0	0	1	2	0	1	0	0	0	1	.000	0	0- - -	6.70	0.00
2005 Batvia	A-	14	14	1	0	91.1	391	94	49	38	7	5	1	4	22	0	70	2	1	5	4	.556	0	0- - -	3.57	3.74
2006 Lakwd	A	7	7	0	0	46.0	188	34	14	11	0	0	1	1	15	0	54	0	0	3	2	.600	0	0- - -	1.88	2.15
2006 Clrwtr	A+	21	20	2	0	130.0	533	117	59	51	15	4	2	3	37	0	79	1	0	9	7	.563	1	0- - -	3.31	3.53
2007 Rdng	AA	12	12	1	0	81.1	337	82	38	29	3	4	3	2	18	0	50	2	0	4	7	.364	0	0- - -	3.13	3.21
2007 Phi	NL	20	20	0	0	121.0	499	129	53	52	16	4	2	7	25	3	49	0	0	10	4	.714	0	0-0 0	4.23	3.87
2008 Phi	NL	31	30	0	0	155.2	722	194	103	95	23	8	4	14	57	2	68	4	1	11	9	.550	0	0-0 0	6.05	5.49
Postseason		1	1	0	0	3.2	18	5	5	5	2	0	0	0	2	1	2	0	0	0	1	.000	0	0-0 0	9.97	12.27
2 ML YEARS		51	50	0	1	276.2	1221	323	156	147	39	12	6	21	82	5	117	4	1	21	13	.618	0	0-0 0	5.24	4.78

Adam Kennedy

Bats: L Throws: R Pos: 2B-84; PH-25; RF-9; 1B-3; LF-1; DH-1   Ht: 6'1" Wt: 196 Born: 1/10/1976 Age: 33

Year Team	Lg	G	AB	H	2B	3B	HR	(Hm Rd)	TB	R	RBI	RC	TBB	IBB	SO	HBP	SH	SF	SB	CS	SB%	GDP	Avg	OBP	Slg
1999 StL	NL	33	102	26	10	1	1	(1 0)	41	12	16	12	3	0	8	2	1	2	0	1	.00	1	.255	.284	.402
2000 LAA	AL	156	598	159	33	11	9	(7 2)	241	82	72	72	28	5	73	3	8	4	22	8	.73	10	.266	.300	.403
2001 LAA	AL	137	478	129	25	3	6	(4 2)	178	48	40	57	27	3	71	11	7	9	12	7	.63	7	.270	.318	.372
2002 LAA	AL	144	474	148	32	6	7	(6 1)	213	65	52	70	19	1	80	7	5	4	17	4	.81	5	.312	.345	.449
2003 LAA	AL	143	449	121	17	1	13	(8 5)	179	71	49	61	45	4	73	9	2	2	22	9	.71	7	.269	.344	.399
2004 LAA	AL	144	468	130	20	5	10	(5 5)	190	70	48	66	41	7	92	13	9	2	15	5	.75	10	.278	.351	.406
2005 LAA	AL	129	416	125	23	0	2	(1 1)	154	49	37	62	29	1	64	7	5	3	19	4	.83	5	.300	.354	.370
2006 LAA	AL	139	451	123	26	6	4	(3 1)	173	50	55	62	39	5	72	5	3	5	16	10	.62	15	.273	.334	.384
2007 StL	NL	87	279	61	9	1	3	(0 3)	81	27	18	19	22	6	33	3	1	1	6	2	.75	9	.219	.282	.290
2008 StL	NL	115	339	95	17	4	2	(1 1)	126	42	36	39	21	4	43	1	0	2	21	1	.88	13	.280	.321	.372
Postseason		25	78	24	3	1	4	(4 0)	41	13	13	11	1	0	15	1	3	2	1	2	.33	1	.308	.317	.526
10 ML YEARS		1227	4054	1117	212	38	57	(36 21)	1576	516	423	514	274	36	609	61	41	39	136	51	.73	82	.276	.328	.389

Ian Kennedy

Pitches: R **Bats:** R **Pos:** SP-9; RP-1   **Ht:** 6'0" **Wt:** 195 **Born:** 12/19/1984 **Age:** 24

Year	Team	Lg	G	GS	CG	GF	IP	BFP	H	R	ER	HR	SH	SF	HB	TBB	IBB	SO	WP	Bk	W	L	Pct	ShO	Sv-Op Hld	ERC	ERA
2006	StIsInd	A-	1	1	0	0	2.2	12	2	0	0	0	0	0	0	2	0	2	0	0	0	0	-	0	0- -	-	3.21	0.00
2007	Tampa	A+	11	10	1	0	63.0	250	39	9	9	2	1	1	1	22	0	72	1	0	6	1	.857	0	0- -	-	1.63	1.29
2007	Trntn	AA	9	9	0	0	48.2	186	27	14	14	2	1	0	2	17	0	57	2	0	5	1	.833	0	0- -	-	1.57	2.59
2007	S-WB	AAA	6	6	0	0	34.2	137	25	8	8	2	1	0	3	11	1	34	0	0	1	1	.500	0	0- -	-	2.40	2.08
2008	S-WB	AAA	13	12	0	0	69.0	280	52	19	18	4	3	1	5	17	0	72	2	1	5	3	.625	0	0- -	-	2.20	2.35
2008	Yanks	R	1	0	0	0	3.0	13	3	1	1	0	0	0	1	0	0	7	1	0	1	0	1.000	0	0- -	-	3.05	3.00
2008	Tampa	A+	1	1	0	0	5.0	18	2	0	0	0	0	0	0	1	0	4	0	0	0	0	-	0	0- -	-	0.63	0.00
2007	NYY	AL	3	3	0	0	19.0	77	13	6	4	1	0	0	0	9	0	15	0	0	1	0	1.000	0	0-0 0	2.42	1.89
2008	NYY	AL	10	9	0	1	39.2	194	50	37	36	5	1	4	1	26	0	27	3	0	0	4	.000	0	0-0 0	6.93	8.17
	2 ML YEARS		13	12	0	1	58.2	271	63	43	40	6	1	4	1	35	0	42	3	0	1	4	.200	0	0-0 0	5.33	6.14

Logan Kensing

Pitches: R **Bats:** R **Pos:** RP-48   **Ht:** 6'1" **Wt:** 185 **Born:** 7/3/1982 **Age:** 26

Year	Team	Lg	G	GS	CG	GF	IP	BFP	H	R	ER	HR	SH	SF	HB	TBB	IBB	SO	WP	Bk	W	L	Pct	ShO	Sv-Op Hld	ERC	ERA
2008	Albq*	AAA	13	0	0	8	12.2	61	8	10	9	3	1	0	2	12	1	17	3	0	1	0	1.000	0	3- - -	5.47	6.39
2004	Fla	NL	5	3	0	0	13.2	66	19	15	15	5	0	1	1	9	0	7	2	0	0	3	.000	0	0-0 0	10.74	9.88
2005	Fla	NL	3	0	0	0	5.2	31	11	7	7	2	0	1	0	3	0	4	0	0	0	0	-	0	0-0 1	12.96	11.12
2006	Fla	NL	37	0	0	10	37.2	161	30	19	19	6	3	0	3	19	2	45	0	0	1	3	.250	0	1-7 14	4.02	4.54
2007	Fla	NL	9	0	0	0	13.1	59	11	2	2	0	1	0	2	7	2	13	0	0	3	0	1.000	0	0-0 0	3.15	1.35
2008	Fla	NL	48	0	0	7	55.1	254	50	26	26	7	1	2	4	33	5	55	7	0	3	1	.750	0	0-3 5	4.50	4.23
	5 ML YEARS		102	3	0	19	125.2	571	121	69	69	20	5	4	10	71	9	124	9	0	7	7	.500	0	1-10 20	5.12	4.94

Jeff Kent

Bats: R **Throws:** R **Pos:** 2B-116; PH-6; 1B-1   **Ht:** 6'2" **Wt:** 210 **Born:** 3/7/1968 **Age:** 41

Year	Team	Lg	G	AB	H	2B	3B	HR	(Hm	Rd)	TB	R	RBI	RC	TBB	IBB	SO	HBP	SH	SF	SB	CS	SB%	GDP	Avg	OBP	Slg
1992	2 Tms		102	305	73	21	2	11	(4	7)	131	52	50	40	27	0	76	7	0	4	2	3	.40	5	.239	.312	.430
1993	NYM	NL	140	496	134	24	0	21	(9	12)	221	65	80	68	30	2	88	8	6	4	4	4	.50	11	.270	.320	.446
1994	NYM	NL	107	415	121	24	5	14	(10	4)	197	53	68	64	23	3	84	10	1	3	1	4	.20	7	.292	.341	.475
1995	NYM	NL	125	472	131	22	3	20	(11	9)	219	65	65	69	29	3	89	8	1	4	3	3	.50	9	.278	.327	.464
1996	2 Tms		128	437	124	27	1	12	(4	8)	189	61	55	55	31	1	78	2	1	6	6	4	.60	8	.284	.330	.432
1997	SF	NL	155	580	145	38	2	29	(13	16)	274	90	121	86	48	6	133	13	0	10	11	3	.79	14	.250	.316	.472
1998	SF	NL	137	526	156	37	3	31	(17	14)	292	94	128	100	48	4	110	9	1	10	9	4	.69	16	.297	.359	.555
1999	SF	NL	138	511	148	40	2	23	(11	12)	261	86	101	93	61	3	112	5	0	8	13	6	.68	12	.290	.366	.511
2000	SF	NL	159	587	196	41	7	33	(14	19)	350	114	125	138	90	6	107	9	0	9	12	9	.57	17	.334	.424	.596
2001	SF	NL	159	607	181	49	6	22	(8	14)	308	84	106	112	65	4	96	11	0	13	7	6	.54	11	.298	.369	.507
2002	SF	NL	152	623	195	42	2	37	(11	26)	352	102	108	105	52	3	101	4	0	3	5	1	.83	20	.313	.368	.565
2003	Hou	NL	130	505	150	39	1	22	(9	13)	257	77	93	92	39	2	85	5	0	3	6	2	.75	13	.297	.351	.509
2004	Hou	NL	145	540	156	34	8	27	(14	13)	287	96	107	94	47	3	96	6	0	11	3	3	.70	23	.289	.348	.531
2005	LAD	NL	149	553	160	36	0	29	(15	14)	283	100	105	105	72	8	85	8	0	4	6	2	.75	19	.289	.377	.512
2006	LAD	NL	115	407	119	27	3	14	(10	4)	194	61	68	71	55	8	69	8	0	3	1	2	.33	9	.292	.385	.477
2007	LAD	NL	136	494	149	36	1	20	(9	11)	247	78	79	75	57	4	61	5	0	6	1	3	.25	17	.302	.375	.500
2008	LAD	NL	121	440	123	23	1	12	(5	7)	184	42	59	49	25	1	52	7	0	2	0	1	.00	13	.280	.327	.418
92	Tor	AL	65	192	46	13	1	8	(2	6)	85	36	35	28	20	0	47	6	0	4	2	1	.67	3	.240	.324	.443
92	NYM	NL	37	113	27	8	1	3	(2	1)	46	16	15	12	7	0	29	1	0	0	0	2	.00	2	.239	.289	.407
96	NYM	NL	89	335	97	20	1	9	(2	7)	146	45	39	46	21	1	56	1	1	3	4	3	.57	7	.290	.331	.436
96	Cle	AL	39	102	27	7	0	3	(2	1)	43	16	16	15	10	0	22	1	0	3	2	1	.67	1	.265	.328	.422
	Postseason		43	161	47	11	0	9	(7	2)	85	25	23	27	13	0	33	4	1	1	1	0	1.00	3	.292	.358	.528
	17 ML YEARS		2298	8498	2461	560	47	377	(174	203)	4246	1320	1518	1415	801	61	1522	125	10	103	94	60	.61	224	.290	.356	.500

Jeff Keppinger

Bats: R **Throws:** R **Pos:** SS-108; 3B-10; PH-5; 1B-3; 2B-3   **Ht:** 6'0" **Wt:** 180 **Born:** 4/21/1980 **Age:** 29

Year	Team	Lg	G	AB	H	2B	3B	HR	(Hm	Rd)	TB	R	RBI	RC	TBB	IBB	SO	HBP	SH	SF	SB	CS	SB%	GDP	Avg	OBP	Slg
2008	Srsota*	R	2	7	2	0	0	0	(-	-)	2	1	1	0	0	0	0	0	0	0	0	0	-	0	.286	.286	.286
2008	Lsvlle*	AAA	6	22	11	2	0	1	(-	-)	16	3	2	7	2	0	1	0	1	0	0	0	-	1	.500	.542	.727
2004	NYM	NL	33	116	33	2	0	3	(3	0)	44	9	9	12	6	0	7	0	0	1	2	1	.67	6	.284	.317	.379
2006	KC	AL	22	60	16	2	0	2	(0	2)	24	11	8	8	5	1	6	0	2	0	0	0	-	2	.267	.323	.400
2007	Cin	NL	67	241	80	16	2	5	(2	3)	115	39	32	42	24	0	12	4	6	1	2	1	.67	11	.332	.400	.477
2008	Cin	NL	121	459	122	24	2	3	(3	0)	159	45	43	52	30	3	24	2	6	5	3	1	.75	14	.266	.310	.346
	4 ML YEARS		243	876	251	44	4	13	(8	5)	342	104	92	114	65	4	49	6	14	7	7	3	.70	33	.287	.338	.390

Clayton Kershaw

Pitches: L **Bats:** L **Pos:** SP-21; RP-1   **Ht:** 6'3" **Wt:** 220 **Born:** 3/19/1988 **Age:** 21

Year	Team	Lg	G	GS	CG	GF	IP	BFP	H	R	ER	HR	SH	SF	HB	TBB	IBB	SO	WP	Bk	W	L	Pct	ShO	Sv-Op Hld	ERC	ERA
2006	Ddgrs	R	10	8	0	1	37.0	144	28	16	9	0	0	0	0	5	0	54	8	0	2	0	1.000	0	1- - -	1.42	1.95
2007	Gt Lks	A	20	20	0	0	97.1	413	72	39	30	5	5	1	2	50	0	134	8	0	7	5	.583	0	0- - -	2.82	2.77
2007	Jaxnvl	AA	5	5	0	0	24.2	107	17	13	10	4	2	0	0	17	0	29	1	1	1	2	.333	0	0- - -	3.88	3.65
2008	Jaxnvl	AA	13	11	0	0	61.1	241	39	19	13	0	2	2	0	19	0	59	7	2	2	3	.400	0	0- - -	1.44	1.91
2008	LAD	NL	22	21	0	0	107.2	470	109	51	51	11	3	3	1	52	3	100	7	0	5	5	.500	0	0-0 1	4.53	4.26

Ray King

Pitches: L **Bats:** L **Pos:** RP-12　　　　**Ht:** 6'0" **Wt:** 239 **Born:** 1/15/1974 **Age:** 35

Year	Team	Lg	G	GS	CG	GF	IP	BFP	H	R	ER	HR	SH	SF	HB	TBB	IBB	SO	WP	Bk	W	L	Pct	ShO	Sv-Op	Hld	ERC	ERA
2008	Charltt*	AAA	4	0	0	2	4.2	20	6	2	2	1	0	0	0	1	1	5	0	0	0	0	-	0	0- -	-	5.61	3.86
2008	RdRck*	AAA	32	0	0	10	32.0	132	23	10	8	1	0	0	1	14	1	23	0	0	2	1	.667	0	5- -	-	2.35	2.25
1999	ChC	NL	10	0	0	0	10.2	50	11	8	7	2	1	0	1	10	0	5	1	0	0	0	-	0	0-0	2	8.10	5.91
2000	Mil	NL	36	0	0	8	28.2	111	18	7	4	1	0	1	0	10	1	19	1	0	3	2	.600	0	0-1	5	1.64	1.26
2001	Mil	NL	82	0	0	19	55.0	234	49	22	22	5	3	2	1	25	7	49	2	0	0	4	.000	0	1-4	18	3.51	3.60
2002	Mil	NL	76	0	0	15	65.0	273	61	24	22	5	5	2	3	24	6	50	0	1	3	2	.600	0	0-1	15	3.55	3.05
2003	Atl	NL	80	0	0	9	59.0	247	46	30	23	3	1	2	1	27	2	43	4	0	3	4	.429	0	0-1	18	2.79	3.51
2004	StL	NL	86	0	0	9	62.0	248	43	19	18	1	2	1	3	24	0	40	2	0	5	2	.714	0	0-1	31	2.13	2.61
2005	StL	NL	77	0	0	18	44.0	177	46	17	15	4	0	1	3	16	0	23	1	0	4	4	.500	0	0-6	16	5.37	3.38
2006	Col	NL	67	0	0	7	44.2	199	56	26	22	6	3	3	2	20	0	23	3	0	1	4	.200	0	1-2	15	6.51	4.43
2007	2 Tms	NL	67	0	0	10	39.2	175	37	21	21	6	1	2	2	21	1	25	2	0	1	1	.500	0	0-0	11	4.75	4.76
2008	Was	NL	12	0	0	2	6.1	33	9	4	4	1	1	0	1	4	0	1	0	0	0	0	-	0	0-0	4	8.66	5.68
07	Was	NL	55	0	0	7	33.2	149	31	17	17	5	1	2	2	18	1	18	2	0	1	1	.500	0	0-0	10	4.70	4.54
07	Mil	NL	12	0	0	3	6.0	26	6	4	4	1	0	0	0	3	0	7	0	0	0	0	-	0	0-0	1	5.06	6.00
	Postseason		14	0	0	1	7.2	27	6	2	2	2	0	0	0	2	0	3	0	0	0	0	-	0	0-0	3	3.86	2.35
10 ML YEARS			593	0	0	97	411.0	1747	376	178	158	34	17	14	17	181	17	278	16	1	20	23	.465	0	2-17	135	3.79	3.46

Josh Kinney

Pitches: R **Bats:** R **Pos:** RP-7　　　　**Ht:** 6'1" **Wt:** 195 **Born:** 3/31/1979 **Age:** 30

Year	Team	Lg	G	GS	CG	GF	IP	BFP	H	R	ER	HR	SH	SF	HB	TBB	IBB	SO	WP	Bk	W	L	Pct	ShO	Sv-Op	Hld	ERC	ERA
2001	River	IND	3	3	0	0	21.0	86	18	7	4	1	1	0	2	7	0	18	0	0	1	0	1.000	0	0- -	-	3.15	1.71
2001	NewJrs	A-	3	0	0	0	5.2	18	2	0	0	0	0	0	0	0	0	5	0	0	2	0	1.000	0	0- -	-	0.30	0.00
2001	Peoria	A	27	0	0	5	41.0	192	47	24	20	1	4	2	7	15	0	35	4	1	1	4	.200	0	0- -	-	4.75	4.39
2002	Ptomc	A+	44	0	0	28	55.0	239	52	21	14	2	2	1	3	23	1	42	6	0	1	3	.250	0	7- -	-	3.55	2.29
2003	PlmBh	A+	31	0	0	10	41.1	167	38	7	7	0	2	0	0	10	4	35	5	0	3	0	1.000	0	3- -	-	2.31	1.52
2003	Tenn	AA	29	0	0	12	39.2	147	19	4	3	2	1	0	0	12	0	48	1	0	2	1	.667	0	2- -	-	1.18	0.68
2004	Tenn	AA	50	0	0	25	55.2	270	67	40	34	6	0	0	3	34	0	48	6	0	3	8	.273	0	4- -	-	6.30	5.50
2004	PlmBh	A+	7	0	0	7	8.1	39	8	6	4	1	0	0	1	6	2	12	0	0	0	1	.000	0	0- -	-	5.33	4.32
2005	Sprgfld	AA	32	0	0	22	42.0	165	28	9	6	2	0	2	0	12	0	42	1	0	5	2	.714	0	11- -	-	1.67	1.29
2005	Memp	AAA	26	0	0	8	25.2	135	40	21	21	4	0	1	2	19	1	25	4	0	1	2	.333	0	0- -	-	9.84	7.36
2006	Memp	AAA	51	0	0	17	71.0	286	46	16	12	4	2	1	5	29	4	76	12	0	2	2	.500	0	3- -	-	2.03	1.52
2008	Sprgfld	AA	4	0	0	0	3.2	15	4	3	3	0	0	0	1	0	0	5	0	0	0	1	.000	0	0- -	-	3.55	7.36
2006	StL	NL	21	0	0	4	25.0	99	17	9	9	3	0	0	1	8	0	22	0	0	0	0	-	0	0-0	2	2.40	3.24
2008	StL	NL	7	0	0	1	7.0	25	3	0	0	0	0	0	0	1	0	8	0	0	0	0	-	0	0-0	0	0.60	0.00
	Postseason		7	0	0	1	6.1	25	3	0	0	0	0	0	1	4	0	6	0	0	1	0	1.000	0	0-0	3	2.24	0.00
2 ML YEARS			28	0	0	5	32.0	124	20	9	9	3	0	0	1	9	0	30	0	0	0	0	-	0	0-0	2	1.84	2.53

Ian Kinsler

Bats: R **Throws:** R **Pos:** 2B-121; PH-1　　　　**Ht:** 6'0" **Wt:** 200 **Born:** 6/22/1982 **Age:** 27

Year	Team	Lg	G	AB	H	2B	3B	HR	(Hm	Rd)	TB	R	RBI	RC	TBB	IBB	SO	HBP	SH	SF	SB	CS	SB%	GDP	Avg	OBP	Slg
2006	Tex	AL	120	423	121	27	1	14	(10	4)	192	65	55	65	40	1	64	3	1	7	11	4	.73	12	.286	.347	.454
2007	Tex	AL	130	483	127	22	2	20	(12	8)	213	96	61	79	62	2	83	9	8	4	23	2	.92	14	.263	.355	.441
2008	Tex	AL	121	518	165	41	4	18	(4	14)	268	102	71	106	45	1	67	6	7	7	26	2	.93	12	.319	.375	.517
3 ML YEARS			371	1424	413	90	7	52	(26	26)	673	263	187	250	147	4	214	18	16	18	60	8	.88	38	.290	.360	.473

Brandon Knight

Pitches: R **Bats:** L **Pos:** SP-2; RP-2　　　　**Ht:** 6'0" **Wt:** 195 **Born:** 10/1/1975 **Age:** 33

Year	Team	Lg	G	GS	CG	GF	IP	BFP	H	R	ER	HR	SH	SF	HB	TBB	IBB	SO	WP	Bk	W	L	Pct	ShO	Sv-Op	Hld	ERC	ERA
2008	NewOr*	AAA	12	5	0	2	43.1	164	28	12	11	5	1	0	0	12	0	55	3	0	5	1	.833	0	1- -	-	1.98	2.28
2001	NYY	AL	4	0	0	2	10.2	52	18	12	12	5	0	0	0	3	0	7	0	0	0	0	-	0	0-0	0	11.03	10.13
2002	NYY	AL	7	0	0	5	8.2	41	11	12	11	2	0	0	0	5	0	7	1	0	0	0	-	0	0-0	0	7.53	11.42
2008	NYM	NL	4	2	0	0	12.0	57	14	7	7	0	0	1	2	7	0	10	0	0	1	0	1.000	0	0-0	0	5.70	5.25
3 ML YEARS			15	2	0	7	31.1	150	43	31	30	7	0	1	2	15	0	24	1	0	1	0	1.000	0	0-0	0	8.02	8.62

Masa Kobayashi

Pitches: R **Bats:** R **Pos:** RP-57　　　　**Ht:** 6'0" **Wt:** 195 **Born:** 5/24/1974 **Age:** 35

Year	Team	Lg	G	GS	CG	GF	IP	BFP	H	R	ER	HR	SH	SF	HB	TBB	IBB	SO	WP	Bk	W	L	Pct	ShO	Sv-Op	Hld	ERC	ERA
1999	Chiba	Jap	46	10	3	9	124.1	507	93	42	37	8	-	-	4	55	-	107	6	4	5	5	.500	0	0- -	-	2.84	2.68
2000	Chiba	Jap	65	3	0	33	109.2	441	87	34	26	4	-	-	1	37	-	72	6	0	11	6	.647	0	14- -	-	2.42	2.13
2001	Chiba	Jap	48	0	0	41	52.0	218	54	25	25	7	-	-	1	13	-	47	1	0	0	4	.000	0	33- -	-	4.04	4.33
2002	Chiba	Jap	43	0	0	43	43.1	158	26	4	4	1	-	-	0	6	-	41	1	0	2	1	.667	0	37- -	-	1.10	0.83
2003	Chiba	Jap	44	0	0	40	47.0	192	45	18	15	2	-	-	1	11	-	30	1	0	2	0	.000	0	33- -	-	2.96	2.87
2004	Chiba	Jap	51	0	0	46	57.2	235	51	25	25	4	2	2	2	19	6	50	3	0	8	5	.615	0	20- -	-	3.03	3.90
2005	Chiba	Jap	46	0	0	43	45.1	186	49	14	13	6	2	0	1	9	1	33	0	0	2	2	.500	0	29- -	-	4.13	2.58
2006	Chiba	Jap	53	0	0	48	53.2	214	49	16	16	4	4	1	2	8	0	48	0	0	6	2	.750	0	34- -	-	2.68	2.68
2007	Chiba	Jap	49	0	0	-	47.1	207	53	24	19	4	-	-	2	12	4	35	0	0	2	7	.222	0	27- -	-	4.03	3.61
2008	Cle	AL	57	0	0	31	55.2	244	65	30	28	8	1	1	1	14	2	35	4	0	4	5	.444	0	6-9	2	4.71	4.53

Paul Konerko

Bats: R Throws: R Pos: 1B-116; DH-5; PH-1   Ht: 6'2" Wt: 220 Born: 3/5/1976 Age: 33

										BATTING													BASERUNNING				AVERAGES		
Year	Team	Lg	G	AB	H	2B	3B	HR	(Hm	Rd)	TB	R	RBI	RC	TBB	IBB	SO	HBP	SH	SF	SB	CS	SB%	GDP	Avg	OBP	Slg
2008	Charltt*	AAA	4	11	6	2	0	0	(-	-)	8	3	3	5	6	1	1	0	0	1	0	0	-	0	.545	.667	.727
1997	LAD	NL	6	7	1	0	0	0	(-	-)	1	0	0	0	1	0	2	0	0	0	0	0	-	1	.143	.250	.143
1998	2 Tms	NL	75	217	47	4	0	7	(2	5)	72	21	29	17	16	0	40	3	0	3	0	1	.00	10	.217	.276	.332
1999	CWS	AL	142	513	151	31	4	24	(16	8)	262	71	81	86	45	0	68	2	1	3	1	0	1.00	19	.294	.352	.511
2000	CWS	AL	143	524	156	31	1	21	(10	11)	252	84	97	86	47	0	72	10	0	5	1	0	1.00	22	.298	.363	.481
2001	CWS	AL	156	582	164	35	0	32	(19	13)	295	92	99	99	54	6	89	9	0	5	1	0	1.00	17	.282	.349	.507
2002	CWS	AL	151	570	173	30	0	27	(13	14)	284	81	104	96	44	2	72	9	0	7	0	0	-	17	.304	.359	.498
2003	CWS	AL	137	444	104	19	0	18	(9	9)	177	49	65	42	43	7	50	4	0	4	0	0	-	28	.234	.305	.399
2004	CWS	AL	155	563	156	22	0	41	(29	12)	301	84	117	106	69	5	107	6	0	5	1	0	1.00	23	.277	.359	.535
2005	CWS	AL	158	575	163	24	0	40	(23	17)	307	98	100	106	81	10	109	5	0	3	0	0	-	9	.283	.375	.534
2006	CWS	AL	152	566	177	30	0	35	(21	14)	312	97	113	110	66	3	104	8	0	6	1	0	1.00	25	.313	.381	.551
2007	CWS	AL	151	549	142	34	0	31	(17	14)	269	71	90	88	78	9	102	3	0	6	0	1	.00	11	.259	.351	.490
2008	CWS	AL	122	438	105	19	1	22	(15	7)	192	59	62	60	65	4	80	7	0	4	2	0	1.00	17	.240	.344	.438
98	LAD	NL	49	144	31	1	0	4	(2	2)	44	14	16	10	10	0	30	2	0	2	0	1	.00	5	.215	.272	.306
98	Cin	NL	26	73	16	3	0	3	(0	3)	28	7	13	7	6	0	10	1	0	1	0	0	-	5	.219	.284	.384
	Postseason		15	58	13	2	0	5	(2	3)	30	7	15	11	4	2	9	1	0	0	0	0	-	2	.224	.286	.517
	12 ML YEARS		1548	5548	1539	279	6	298	(174	124)	2724	807	957	896	603	46	895	66	1	54	7	2	.78	209	.277	.352	.491

Bobby Korecky

Pitches: R Bats: R Pos: RP-16   Ht: 5'11" Wt: 185 Born: 9/16/1979 Age: 29

			HOW MUCH HE PITCHED						WHAT HE GAVE UP										THE RESULTS							
Year	Team	Lg	G	GS	CG	GF	IP	BFP	H	R	ER	HR	SH	SF	HB	TBB	IBB	SO	WP	Bk	W	L	Pct	ShO	Sv-Op	Hld	ERC	ERA
2002	Batvia	A-	7	5	0	0	35.0	132	30	12	9	2	1	1	0	6	0	25	2	0	2	2	.500	0	0- -	-	2.37	2.31
2002	Lakwd	A	8	4	2	3	27.0	106	25	10	9	0	1	0	0	3	0	15	1	0	2	2	.500	0	1- -	-	2.05	3.00
2003	Clrwtr	A+	49	0	0	44	59.2	234	52	19	15	3	3	0	2	9	1	46	2	0	5	4	.556	0	25- -	-	2.32	2.26
2004	NwBrit	AA	55	0	0	48	67.0	275	52	29	25	5	1	0	3	20	2	58	3	0	3	4	.429	0	31- -	-	2.45	3.36
2005	NwBrit	AA	2	0	0	1	1.1	7	2	1	1	0	0	0	0	1	0	1	0	0	0	0	-	0	0- -	-	7.52	6.75
2006	NwBrit	AA	16	0	0	13	25.0	118	30	15	9	1	1	2	1	13	5	14	1	0	1	2	.333	0	5- -	-	4.94	3.24
2006	Roch	AAA	34	0	0	22	51.1	219	52	25	19	4	1	2	0	16	7	28	5	0	5	3	.625	0	8- -	-	3.41	3.33
2007	Roch	AAA	66	0	0	59	85.0	358	80	42	35	5	3	4	0	34	9	71	3	0	5	6	.455	0	35- -	-	3.34	3.71
2008	Roch	AAA	53	0	0	44	74.1	308	66	26	24	3	4	3	1	22	3	71	3	0	6	5	.545	0	26- -	-	2.67	2.91
2008	Min	AL	16	0	0	9	17.2	74	19	9	9	2	0	0	0	8	0	6	0	0	2	0	1.000	0	0-0	0	5.13	4.58

Joe Koshansky

Bats: L Throws: L Pos: 1B-11; PH-8   Ht: 6'4" Wt: 225 Born: 5/26/1982 Age: 27

										BATTING													BASERUNNING				AVERAGES		
Year	Team	Lg	G	AB	H	2B	3B	HR	(Hm	Rd)	TB	R	RBI	RC	TBB	IBB	SO	HBP	SH	SF	SB	CS	SB%	GDP	Avg	OBP	Slg
2004	TriCity	A-	66	239	56	18	0	12	(-	-)	110	41	43	38	31	1	84	4	2	2	1	0	1.00	4	.234	.330	.460
2005	Ashvll	A	120	453	132	31	4	36	(-	-)	273	92	103	100	53	7	122	11	0	8	6	6	.50	14	.291	.373	.603
2005	Tulsa	AA	12	45	12	3	0	2	(-	-)	21	5	12	6	2	0	15	0	0	1	0	0	-	0	.267	.292	.467
2006	Tulsa	AA	130	500	142	28	0	31	(-	-)	263	84	109	98	64	5	134	6	1	2	3	2	.60	12	.284	.371	.526
2007	ColSpr	AAA	136	498	147	30	2	21	(-	-)	244	79	99	94	67	4	128	2	0	2	4	3	.57	14	.295	.380	.490
2008	ColSpr	AAA	122	457	137	36	4	31	(-	-)	274	90	121	103	60	7	158	3	0	6	1	0	1.00	5	.300	.380	.600
2007	Col	NL	17	12	1	1	0	0	(0	0)	2	0	2	1	2	0	5	0	0	1	0	0	-	0	.083	.200	.167
2008	Col	NL	18	38	8	3	0	3	(2	1)	20	5	8	5	1	0	17	1	0	0	0	0	-	2	.211	.250	.526
	2 ML YEARS		35	50	9	4	0	3	(2	1)	22	5	10	6	3	0	22	1	0	1	0	0	-	2	.180	.236	.440

Casey Kotchman

Bats: L Throws: L Pos: 1B-141; PH-6   Ht: 6'3" Wt: 215 Born: 2/22/1983 Age: 26

										BATTING													BASERUNNING				AVERAGES		
Year	Team	Lg	G	AB	H	2B	3B	HR	(Hm	Rd)	TB	R	RBI	RC	TBB	IBB	SO	HBP	SH	SF	SB	CS	SB%	GDP	Avg	OBP	Slg
2004	LAA	AL	38	116	26	6	0	0	(0	0)	32	7	15	14	7	3	11	4	0	1	3	0	1.00	3	.224	.289	.276
2005	LAA	AL	47	126	35	5	0	7	(5	2)	61	16	22	21	15	0	18	0	1	1	1	1	.50	3	.278	.352	.484
2006	LAA	AL	29	79	12	2	0	1	(0	1)	17	6	6	1	7	0	13	0	2	0	0	1	.00	2	.152	.221	.215
2007	LAA	AL	137	443	131	37	3	11	(5	6)	207	64	68	74	53	1	43	4	3	5	2	4	.33	17	.296	.372	.467
2008	2 Tms		143	525	143	28	1	14	(3	11)	215	65	74	70	36	5	39	9	0	3	2	1	.67	18	.272	.328	.410
08	LAA	AL	100	373	107	24	0	12	(2	10)	167	47	54	53	18	3	23	5	0	2	2	1	.67	14	.287	.327	.448
08	Atl	NL	43	152	36	4	1	2	(1	1)	48	18	20	17	18	2	16	4	0	1	0	0	-	4	.237	.331	.316
	Postseason		8	15	2	1	0	0	(0	0)	3	1	1	1	3	0	2	0	0	0	0	0	-	0	.133	.278	.200
	5 ML YEARS		394	1289	347	78	4	33	(13	20)	532	158	185	180	118	9	124	17	6	10	8	7	.53	43	.269	.336	.413

Mark Kotsay

Bats: L Throws: L Pos: CF-84; RF-19; 1B-6; PH-6   Ht: 6'0" Wt: 204 Born: 12/2/1975 Age: 33

										BATTING													BASERUNNING				AVERAGES		
Year	Team	Lg	G	AB	H	2B	3B	HR	(Hm	Rd)	TB	R	RBI	RC	TBB	IBB	SO	HBP	SH	SF	SB	CS	SB%	GDP	Avg	OBP	Slg
2008	Missi*	AA	5	18	6	1	0	0	(-	-)	7	4	1	2	1	0	4	0	0	0	0	0	-	0	.333	.368	.389
1997	Fla	NL	14	52	10	1	1	0	(0	0)	13	5	4	3	4	0	7	1	0	0	3	0	1.00	1	.192	.250	.250
1998	Fla	NL	154	578	161	25	7	11	(5	6)	233	72	68	70	34	2	61	1	7	3	10	5	.67	17	.279	.318	.403
1999	Fla	NL	148	495	134	23	9	8	(5	3)	199	57	50	58	29	5	50	0	2	9	7	6	.54	11	.271	.306	.402
2000	Fla	NL	152	530	158	31	5	12	(5	7)	235	87	57	78	42	2	46	0	2	4	19	9	.68	17	.298	.347	.443
2001	SD	NL	119	406	118	29	1	10	(3	7)	179	67	58	65	48	1	58	2	1	3	13	5	.72	11	.291	.366	.441
2002	SD	NL	153	578	169	27	7	17	(11	6)	261	82	61	92	59	0	89	3	2	4	11	9	.55	10	.292	.359	.452
2003	SD	NL	128	482	128	28	4	7	(1	6)	185	64	38	59	56	3	82	1	1	1	6	3	.67	8	.266	.343	.384
2004	Oak	AL	148	606	190	37	3	15	(9	6)	278	78	63	94	55	5	70	2	5	5	8	5	.62	6	.314	.370	.459

Year	Team	Lg	G	AB	H	2B	3B	HR	(Hm	Rd)	TB	R	RBI	RC	TBB	IBB	SO	HBP	SH	SF	SB	CS	SB%	GDP	Avg	OBP	Slg
									BATTING												**BASERUNNING**				**AVERAGES**		
2005	Oak	AL	139	582	163	35	1	15	(4	11)	245	75	82	86	40	3	51	1	2	4	5	5	.50	13	.280	.325	.421
2006	Oak	AL	129	502	138	29	3	7	(1	6)	194	57	59	63	44	1	55	2	4	6	6	3	.67	18	.275	.332	.386
2007	Oak	AL	56	206	44	14	0	1	(0	1)	61	20	20	19	19	3	20	0	0	1	1	1	.50	4	.214	.279	.296
2008	2 Tms		110	402	111	25	4	6	(4	2)	162	45	49	49	32	3	45	0	1	1	2	4	.33	14	.276	.329	.403
08	Atl	NL	88	318	92	17	3	6	(4	2)	133	39	37	37	25	2	34	0	1	1	2	3	.40	13	.289	.340	.418
08	Bos	AL	22	84	19	8	1	0	(0	0)	29	6	12	12	7	1	11	0	0	0	0	1	.00	1	.226	.286	.345
	Postseason		7	30	6	2	0	1	(0	1)	11	5	2	2	2	0	5	0	0	0	0	0	-	3	.200	.250	.367
	12 ML YEARS		1450	5419	1524	304	45	109	(48	61)	2245	709	609	736	462	28	634	12	28	41	91	55	.62	130	.281	.337	.414

George Kottaras

Bats: L **Throws:** R **Pos:** C-2; PR-1   **Ht:** 6'0" **Wt:** 185 **Born:** 5/16/1983 **Age:** 26

Year	Team	Lg	G	AB	H	2B	3B	HR	(Hm	Rd)	TB	R	RBI	RC	TBB	IBB	SO	HBP	SH	SF	SB	CS	SB%	GDP	Avg	OBP	Slg
									BATTING												**BASERUNNING**				**AVERAGES**		
2003	Idaho	R+	42	143	37	8	1	7	(-	-)	68	27	24	24	19	1	36	1	0	1	1	1	.50	2	.259	.348	.476
2004	FtWyn	A	78	271	84	18	1	7	(-	-)	125	40	46	55	51	2	41	0	1	3	0	0	-	7	.310	.415	.461
2005	Lk Els	A+	91	337	102	29	0	9	(-	-)	158	54	50	64	50	2	60	1	2	4	2	1	.67	6	.303	.390	.469
2005	Mobile	AA	29	101	29	7	0	2	(-	-)	42	16	15	18	19	1	23	0	0	1	0	0	-	1	.287	.397	.416
2006	Mobile	AA	78	257	71	19	1	8	(-	-)	116	40	34	46	50	4	68	1	0	2	0	1	.00	9	.276	.394	.451
2006	Portlnd	AAA	33	119	25	10	1	2	(-	-)	43	14	17	13	12	0	30	1	0	0	0	0	-	6	.210	.286	.361
2007	Pwtckt	AAA	87	294	71	22	0	9	(-	-)	120	32	39	40	32	1	71	2	2	4	1	1	.50	12	.241	.316	.408
2008	Pwtckt	AAA	107	395	96	18	0	22	(-	-)	180	63	65	66	64	3	110	1	0	2	0	0	-	6	.243	.348	.456
2008	Bos	AL	3	5	1	1	0	0	(0	0)	2	1	0	0	0	0	2	0	0	0	0	0	-	0	.200	.200	.400

Kevin Kouzmanoff

Bats: R **Throws:** R **Pos:** 3B-154   **Ht:** 6'1" **Wt:** 210 **Born:** 7/25/1981 **Age:** 27

Year	Team	Lg	G	AB	H	2B	3B	HR	(Hm	Rd)	TB	R	RBI	RC	TBB	IBB	SO	HBP	SH	SF	SB	CS	SB%	GDP	Avg	OBP	Slg
									BATTING												**BASERUNNING**				**AVERAGES**		
2006	Cle	AL	16	56	12	2	0	3	(0	3)	23	4	11	7	5	0	12	0	0	0	0	0	-	3	.214	.279	.411
2007	SD	NL	145	484	133	30	2	18	(5	13)	221	57	74	69	32	2	94	10	2	6	1	0	1.00	9	.275	.329	.457
2008	SD	NL	154	624	162	31	4	23	(11	12)	270	71	84	70	23	3	139	15	0	6	0	0	-	14	.260	.299	.433
	3 ML YEARS		315	1164	307	63	6	44	(16	28)	514	132	169	146	60	5	245	25	2	12	1	0	1.00	26	.264	.311	.442

Jason Kubel

Bats: L **Throws:** R **Pos:** DH-83; RF-32; PH-19; LF-18; PR-1   **Ht:** 6'0" **Wt:** 210 **Born:** 5/25/1982 **Age:** 27

Year	Team	Lg	G	AB	H	2B	3B	HR	(Hm	Rd)	TB	R	RBI	RC	TBB	IBB	SO	HBP	SH	SF	SB	CS	SB%	GDP	Avg	OBP	Slg
									BATTING												**BASERUNNING**				**AVERAGES**		
2004	Min	AL	23	60	18	2	0	2	(0	2)	26	10	7	13	6	0	9	0	0	1	1	1	.50	0	.300	.358	.433
2006	Min	AL	73	220	53	8	0	8	(3	5)	85	23	26	20	12	0	45	0	2	1	2	0	1.00	9	.241	.279	.386
2007	Min	AL	128	418	114	31	2	13	(6	7)	188	49	65	64	41	2	79	1	1	5	5	0	1.00	19	.273	.335	.450
2008	Min	AL	141	463	126	22	5	20	(9	11)	218	74	78	66	47	2	91	0	0	7	0	1	.00	12	.272	.335	.471
	Postseason		2	7	1	1	0	0	(0	0)	2	0	0	0	0	0	2	0	0	0	0	0	-	0	.143	.143	.286
	4 ML YEARS		365	1161	311	63	7	43	(18	25)	517	156	176	163	106	4	224	1	3	14	8	2	.80	34	.268	.326	.445

Eddie Kunz

Pitches: R **Bats:** R **Pos:** RP-4   **Ht:** 6'6" **Wt:** 265 **Born:** 4/8/1986 **Age:** 23

Year	Team	Lg	G	GS	CG	GF	IP	BFP	H	R	ER	HR	SH	SF	HB	TBB	IBB	SO	WP	Bk	W	L	Pct	ShO	Sv-Op	Hld	ERC	ERA
			HOW MUCH HE PITCHED						**WHAT HE GAVE UP**												**THE RESULTS**							
2007	Bklyn	A-	12	0	0	9	12.0	52	8	9	9	0	1	0	1	8	1	9	1	0	0	1	.000	0	5- -		2.73	6.75
2008	Bnghtn	AA	44	0	0	39	48.1	207	39	19	15	0	4	1	1	25	3	43	4	0	1	4	.200	0	27- -		2.74	2.79
2008	NewOr	AAA	6	0	0	5	5.2	28	9	5	5	1	0	0	0	2	0	4	0	0	1	0	1.000	0	0- -		7.94	7.94
2008	NYM	NL	4	0	0	0	2.2	14	5	4	4	1	1	0	1	1	0	1	2	0	0	0	-	0	0-0	0	14.88	13.50

Hong-Chih Kuo

Pitches: L **Bats:** L **Pos:** RP-39; SP-3   **Ht:** 6'1" **Wt:** 235 **Born:** 7/23/1981 **Age:** 27

Year	Team	Lg	G	GS	CG	GF	IP	BFP	H	R	ER	HR	SH	SF	HB	TBB	IBB	SO	WP	Bk	W	L	Pct	ShO	Sv-Op	Hld	ERC	ERA
			HOW MUCH HE PITCHED						**WHAT HE GAVE UP**												**THE RESULTS**							
2005	LAD	NL	9	0	0	0	5.1	26	5	4	4	1	0	0	0	5	1	10	0	1	0	1	.000	0	0-1	3	6.10	6.75
2006	LAD	NL	28	5	0	6	59.2	258	54	30	28	3	2	1	1	33	5	71	2	0	1	5	.167	0	0-0	2	3.76	4.22
2007	LAD	NL	8	6	0	1	30.1	140	35	26	25	3	1	1	1	14	0	27	1	0	1	4	.200	0	0-0	0	5.25	7.42
2008	LAD	NL	42	3	0	10	80.0	323	60	21	19	4	4	1	3	21	2	96	1	1	5	3	.625	0	1-3	12	2.05	2.14
	Postseason		1	1	0	0	4.1	19	4	2	2	0	1	0	0	2	1	4	1	0	1	0	1.000	0	0-0	0	2.74	4.15
	4 ML YEARS		87	14	0	17	175.1	747	154	81	76	11	7	3	5	73	8	204	4	2	7	13	.350	0	1-4	17	3.24	3.90

Hiroki Kuroda

Pitches: R **Bats:** R **Pos:** SP-31   **Ht:** 6'1" **Wt:** 210 **Born:** 2/10/1975 **Age:** 34

Year	Team	Lg	G	GS	CG	GF	IP	BFP	H	R	ER	HR	SH	SF	HB	TBB	IBB	SO	WP	Bk	W	L	Pct	ShO	Sv-Op	Hld	ERC	ERA
			HOW MUCH HE PITCHED						**WHAT HE GAVE UP**												**THE RESULTS**							
1997	Hrshm	Jap	23	23	4	0	135.0	601	147	72	66	17	-	-	4	63	-	64	8	1	6	9	.400	1	0- -		5.21	4.40
1998	Hrshm	Jap	18	6	0	3	45.0	199	53	34	33	5	-	-	1	24	-	25	1	0	1	4	.200	0	0- -		6.14	6.60
1999	Hrshm	Jap	21	16	2	1	87.2	406	106	70	66	20	-	-	3	39	-	55	4	0	5	8	.385	1	0- -		6.58	6.78
2000	Hrshm	Jap	29	21	7	3	144.0	623	147	73	69	21	-	-	1	61	-	116	3	0	9	6	.600	1	0- -		4.69	4.31
2001	Hrshm	Jap	27	27	13	0	190.0	786	175	72	64	19	-	-	1	45	-	146	7	0	12	8	.600	3	0- -		3.17	3.03
2002	Hrshm	Jap	23	23	8	0	164.1	671	166	69	67	16	-	-	1	34	-	144	1	0	10	10	.500	2	0- -		3.44	3.67

Year	Team	Lg	G	GS	CG	GF	IP	BFP	H	R	ER	HR	SH	SF	HB	TBB	IBB	SO	WP	Bk	W	L	Pct	ShO	Sv-Op	Hld	ERC	ERA
			HOW MUCH HE PITCHED						**WHAT HE GAVE UP**												**THE RESULTS**							
2003	Hrshm	Jap	28	28	8	0	205.2	827	197	77	71	18	-	-	3	45	2	137	5	1	13	9	.591	1	0--	-	3.20	3.11
2004	Hrshm	Jap	21	21	7	0	147.0	639	187	81	76	17	6	6	2	29	1	138	1	0	7	9	.438	1	0--	-	5.02	4.65
2005	Hrshm	Jap	29	29	11	0	212.2	863	183	76	75	17	-	-	7	42	-	165	7	0	15	12	.556	1	0--	-	2.55	3.17
2006	Hrshm	Jap	25	25	7	0	189.0	757	169	49	39	12	-	-	7	21	-	143	5	0	13	6	.684	2	0--	-	2.34	1.86
2007	Hrshm	Jap	26	26	7	0	179.2	738	176	78	71	20	-	-	5	42	3	123	1	0	12	8	.600	1	0--	-	3.53	3.56
2008	LAD	NL	31	31	2	0	183.1	776	181	85	76	13	7	5	7	42	8	116	5	0	9	10	.474	2	0-0	0	3.18	3.73

John Lackey

Pitches: R Bats: R Pos: SP-24   Ht: 6'6" Wt: 235 Born: 10/23/1978 Age: 30

Year	Team	Lg	G	GS	CG	GF	IP	BFP	H	R	ER	HR	SH	SF	HB	TBB	IBB	SO	WP	Bk	W	L	Pct	ShO	Sv-Op	Hld	ERC	ERA
			HOW MUCH HE PITCHED						**WHAT HE GAVE UP**												**THE RESULTS**							
2008	RCuca*	A+	3	3	0	0	9.0	40	8	4	4	1	0	1	2	2	0	11	1	0	0	0	-	0	0--	-	3.53	4.00
2002	LAA	AL	18	18	1	0	108.1	465	113	52	44	10	0	4	4	33	0	69	7	2	9	4	.692	0	0-0	0	4.03	3.66
2003	LAA	AL	33	33	2	0	204.0	885	223	117	105	31	2	4	4	66	4	151	11	1	10	16	.385	2	0-0	0	4.88	4.63
2004	LAA	AL	33	32	1	0	198.1	855	215	108	103	22	9	4	8	60	4	144	11	1	14	13	.519	1	0-0	0	4.39	4.67
2005	LAA	AL	33	33	1	0	209.0	892	208	85	80	13	1	2	11	71	3	199	18	0	14	5	.737	0	0-0	0	3.76	3.44
2006	LAA	AL	33	33	3	0	217.2	922	203	98	86	14	8	6	9	72	4	190	16	0	13	11	.542	2	0-0	0	3.31	3.56
2007	LAA	AL	33	33	2	0	224.0	929	219	87	75	18	1	1	12	52	2	179	9	1	19	9	.679	2	0-0	0	3.40	**3.01**
2008	LAA	AL	24	24	3	0	163.1	675	161	71	68	26	5	1	10	40	1	130	5	0	12	5	.706	0	0-0	0	4.10	3.75
Postseason			9	7	0	0	44.2	187	45	18	18	3	2	2	0	18	4	33	3	0	2	2	.500	0	0-0	0	3.88	3.63
7 ML YEARS			207	206	13	0	1324.2	5623	1342	618	561	134	26	24	64	394	18	1062	77	5	91	63	.591	7	0-0	0	3.95	3.81

Aaron Laffey

Pitches: L Bats: L Pos: SP-16   Ht: 6'0" Wt: 180 Born: 4/15/1985 Age: 24

Year	Team	Lg	G	GS	CG	GF	IP	BFP	H	R	ER	HR	SH	SF	HB	TBB	IBB	SO	WP	Bk	W	L	Pct	ShO	Sv-Op	Hld	ERC	ERA
			HOW MUCH HE PITCHED						**WHAT HE GAVE UP**												**THE RESULTS**							
2003	Burlgtn	A	9	4	0	1	34.0	143	22	13	11	0	0	1	7	15	0	46	4	1	3	1	.750	0	0--	-	2.44	2.91
2004	Lk Cty	A	19	15	0	2	73.0	346	79	58	53	6	3	3	8	44	0	67	3	1	3	7	.300	0	1--	-	5.60	6.53
2004	MhVlly	A-	8	8	0	0	43.2	180	38	15	6	1	1	1	2	10	0	30	2	0	3	1	.750	0	0--	-	2.39	1.24
2005	Lk Cty	A	25	23	1	2	142.1	581	123	62	51	5	9	1	4	52	0	69	2	2	7	7	.500	0	1--	-	2.97	3.22
2005	Akron	AA	1	1	0	0	5.0	24	8	2	2	0	0	0	0	2	0	6	1	0	1	0	1.000	0	0--	-	6.98	3.60
2006	Knstn	A+	10	4	1	2	41.1	170	38	16	10	0	3	0	3	6	0	24	2	0	4	1	.800	1	1--	-	2.30	2.18
2006	Akron	AA	19	19	0	0	112.1	476	121	50	44	9	8	3	8	33	0	61	4	0	8	3	.727	0	0--	-	4.35	3.53
2007	Akron	AA	6	6	0	0	35.0	141	29	13	9	2	1	1	3	7	0	24	0	0	4	1	.800	0	0--	-	2.49	2.31
2007	Buffalo	AAA	16	15	2	0	96.1	395	89	36	33	5	2	0	3	23	0	75	0	1	9	3	.750	1	0--	-	2.87	3.08
2008	Buffalo	AAA	11	11	0	0	61.2	271	72	33	30	2	1	2	2	18	0	47	2	2	6	2	.750	0	0--	-	4.22	4.38
2007	Cle	AL	9	9	0	0	49.1	207	54	26	25	2	1	2	4	12	0	25	2	1	4	2	.667	0	0-0	0	4.02	4.56
2008	Cle	AL	16	16	0	0	93.2	409	103	52	44	10	2	0	9	31	1	43	5	1	5	7	.417	0	0-0	0	4.86	4.23
Postseason			1	0	0	0	4.2	16	1	0	0	0	0	0	0	1	0	3	0	0	0	0	-	0	0-0	0	0.30	0.00
2 ML YEARS			25	25	0	0	143.0	616	157	78	69	12	3	2	13	43	1	68	7	2	9	9	.500	0	0-0	0	4.56	4.34

Bryan LaHair

Bats: L Throws: R Pos: 1B-36; DH-6; PH-4   Ht: 6'5" Wt: 220 Born: 11/5/1982 Age: 26

Year	Team	Lg	G	AB	H	2B	3B	HR	(Hm	Rd)	TB	R	RBI	RC	TBB	IBB	SO	HBP	SH	SF	SB	CS	SB%	GDP	Avg	OBP	Slg
			BATTING																		**BASERUNNING**				**AVERAGES**		
2003	Everett	A-	57	201	49	14	0	2	(-	-)	69	26	20	19	11	1	40	1	0	0	4	3	.57	3	.244	.286	.343
2004	Everett	A-	7	25	11	6	0	1	(-	-)	20	5	7	8	1	0	3	1	0	1	0	0	-	1	.440	.464	.800
2004	Wisc	A	67	262	73	24	0	5	(-	-)	112	30	28	34	16	1	66	1	1	0	0	6	.00	5	.279	.323	.427
2005	InldEm	A+	126	509	158	28	2	22	(-	-)	256	81	113	96	51	4	125	3	0	6	0	1	.00	19	.310	.373	.503
2006	SnAnt	AA	60	222	65	12	0	6	(-	-)	95	22	30	36	24	3	52	4	1	1	0	0	-	3	.293	.371	.428
2006	Tacom	AAA	54	202	66	10	0	10	(-	-)	106	36	44	42	23	0	49	1	1	3	3	0	1.00	4	.327	.393	.525
2007	Tacom	AAA	138	552	152	46	2	12	(-	-)	238	79	81	81	49	1	126	0	1	4	0	1	.00	10	.275	.332	.431
2008	Tacom	AAA	86	316	83	26	1	12	(-	-)	147	39	53	54	45	4	87	1	0	0	1	1	.50	5	.263	.356	.465
2008	Sea	AL	45	136	34	4	0	3	(0	3)	47	15	10	14	13	1	40	0	1	0	0	1	.00	4	.250	.315	.346

Gerald Laird

Bats: R Throws: R Pos: C-88; DH-5; PH-3; 3B-2; PR-1   Ht: 6'1" Wt: 225 Born: 11/13/1979 Age: 29

Year	Team	Lg	G	AB	H	2B	3B	HR	(Hm	Rd)	TB	R	RBI	RC	TBB	IBB	SO	HBP	SH	SF	SB	CS	SB%	GDP	Avg	OBP	Slg
			BATTING																		**BASERUNNING**				**AVERAGES**		
2008	Okla*	AAA	4	12	0	0	0	0	(-	-)	0	1	2	0	1	0	3	2	0	2	0	0	-	0	.000	.176	.000
2003	Tex	AL	19	44	12	2	1	1	(0	1)	19	9	4	5	5	0	11	1	0	0	0	0	-	2	.273	.360	.432
2004	Tex	AL	49	147	33	6	0	1	(1	0)	42	20	16	11	12	0	35	2	4	3	0	1	.00	5	.224	.287	.286
2005	Tex	AL	13	40	9	2	0	1	(0	1)	14	7	4	4	2	0	7	0	0	0	0	0	-	1	.225	.262	.350
2006	Tex	AL	78	243	72	20	1	7	(3	4)	115	46	22	24	12	0	54	2	1	2	3	1	.75	7	.296	.332	.473
2007	Tex	AL	120	407	91	18	3	9	(6	3)	142	48	47	45	30	1	103	2	5	4	6	2	.75	3	.224	.278	.349
2008	Tex	AL	95	344	95	24	0	6	(3	3)	137	54	41	46	23	2	63	6	4	4	2	4	.33	5	.276	.329	.398
6 ML YEARS			374	1225	312	72	5	25	(13	12)	469	184	134	135	84	3	273	13	14	13	11	8	.58	23	.255	.306	.383

Mike Lamb

Bats: L **Throws:** R **Pos:** 3B-56; PH-28; 1B-9; DH-8   **Ht:** 6'1" **Wt:** 207 **Born:** 8/9/1975 **Age:** 33

Year Team	Lg	G	AB	H	2B	3B	HR	(Hm	Rd)	TB	R	RBI	RC	TBB	IBB	SO	HBP	SH	SF	SB	CS	SB%	GDP	Avg	OBP	Slg
2000 Tex	AL	138	493	137	25	2	6	(4	2)	184	65	47	59	34	6	60	4	5	2	0	2	.00	10	.278	.328	.373
2001 Tex	AL	76	284	87	18	0	4	(1	3)	117	42	35	40	14	1	27	5	1	2	2	1	.67	6	.306	.348	.412
2002 Tex	AL	115	314	89	13	0	9	(7	2)	129	54	33	46	33	5	48	3	2	3	0	0	-	7	.283	.354	.411
2003 Tex	AL	28	38	5	0	0	0	(0	0)	5	3	2	0	2	0	7	1	0	1	1	0	1.00	1	.132	.190	.132
2004 Hou	NL	112	278	80	14	3	14	(8	6)	142	38	58	51	31	3	63	0	0	3	1	1	.50	4	.288	.356	.511
2005 Hou	NL	125	322	76	13	5	12	(4	8)	135	41	53	38	22	1	65	1	0	4	1	1	.50	2	.236	.284	.419
2006 Hou	NL	126	381	117	22	3	12	(5	7)	181	70	45	52	35	6	55	0	0	5	2	4	.33	10	.307	.361	.475
2007 Hou	NL	124	311	90	14	2	11	(5	6)	141	45	40	48	36	5	45	3	1	2	0	0	-	5	.289	.366	.453
2008 2 Tms		92	247	58	12	3	1	(0	1)	79	22	32	29	17	4	33	0	0	8	0	1	.00	3	.235	.276	.320
08 Min	AL	81	236	55	12	3	1	(0	1)	76	20	32	28	17	4	32	0	0	8	0	1	.00	3	.233	.276	.322
08 Mil	NL	11	11	3	0	0	0	(0	0)	3	2	0	1	0	0	1	0	0	0	0	0	-	0	.273	.273	.273
Postseason		16	40	10	2	0	5	(2	3)	27	7	7	5	5	3	7	0	0	1	0	0	-	1	.250	.326	.675
9 ML YEARS		936	2668	739	131	18	69	(34	35)	1113	380	345	363	224	31	403	17	9	30	7	10	.41	56	.277	.333	.417

Chris Lambert

Pitches: R **Bats:** R **Pos:** RP-5; SP-3   **Ht:** 6'1" **Wt:** 205 **Born:** 3/8/1983 **Age:** 26

Year Team	Lg	G	GS	CG	GF	IP	BFP	H	R	ER	HR	SH	SF	HB	TBB	IBB	SO	WP	Bk	W	L	Pct	ShO	Sv-Op	Hld	ERC	ERA
2004 Peoria	A	9	9	0	0	38.1	169	31	15	11	2	0	2	1	24	1	46	2	0	1	1	.500	0	0-	-	3.56	2.58
2005 PlmBh	A+	10	10	0	0	54.2	231	53	20	16	4	2	1	5	15	0	46	6	1	7	1	.875	0	0-	-	3.61	2.63
2005 Sprgfld	AA	18	18	0	0	85.0	403	97	69	60	10	2	10	10	48	0	69	8	3	3	7	.300	0	0-	-	6.17	6.35
2006 Sprgfld	AA	23	23	0	0	120.2	548	126	84	71	20	3	6	5	63	1	113	13	1	10	9	.526	0	0-	-	5.44	5.30
2006 Memp	AAA	1	1	0	0	4.0	17	5	3	3	0	1	1	0	0	0	2	1	0	1	0	1.000	0	0-	-	4.32	6.75
2007 Sprgfld	AA	5	5	0	0	26.1	108	24	11	10	5	0	0	2	8	0	17	2	0	0	2	.000	0	0-	-	4.24	3.42
2007 Memp	AAA	28	4	0	6	57.2	271	74	49	48	10	5	2	3	29	1	50	4	0	1	4	.200	0	0-	-	7.04	7.49
2007 Toledo	AAA	1	1	0	0	6.0	22	1	0	0	0	0	0	0	2	0	10	0	0	0	0	-	0	0-	-	0.57	0.00
2008 Toledo	AAA	26	26	3	0	149.1	631	143	69	58	7	6	9	2	48	0	124	3	1	12	8	.600	1	0-	-	3.22	3.50
2008 Det	AL	8	3	0	1	20.2	102	31	18	13	3	0	1	2	7	1	15	0	0	1	2	.333	0	0-0	0	7.37	5.66

Ryan Langerhans

Bats: L **Throws:** L **Pos:** PH-37; LF-24; RF-12; 1B-2; PR-2; DH-1   **Ht:** 6'3" **Wt:** 229 **Born:** 2/20/1980 **Age:** 29

Year Team	Lg	G	AB	H	2B	3B	HR	(Hm	Rd)	TB	R	RBI	RC	TBB	IBB	SO	HBP	SH	SF	SB	CS	SB%	GDP	Avg	OBP	Slg
2008 Clmbs*	AAA	62	213	66	16	2	3	(-	-)	95	40	31	43	40	4	57	1	1	2	12	3	.80	1	.310	.418	.446
2002 Atl	NL	1	1	0	0	0	0	(0	0)	0	0	0	0	0	0	0	0	0	0	0	0	-	0	.000	.000	.000
2003 Atl	NL	16	15	4	0	0	0	(0	0)	4	2	0	1	0	0	6	0	0	0	0	0	-	1	.267	.267	.267
2005 Atl	NL	128	326	87	22	3	8	(3	5)	139	48	42	53	37	3	75	5	2	3	0	2	.00	2	.267	.348	.426
2006 Atl	NL	131	315	76	16	3	7	(3	4)	119	46	28	45	50	8	91	3	0	1	1	2	.33	9	.241	.350	.378
2007 3 Tms		125	210	35	7	2	6	(1	5)	64	27	23	22	29	2	81	2	1	2	3	1	.75	4	.167	.272	.305
2008 Was	NL	73	111	26	5	2	3	(1	2)	44	17	12	18	25	1	31	1	2	0	2	0	1.00	2	.234	.380	.396
07 Atl	NL	20	44	3	1	0	0	(0	0)	4	3	1	0	6	1	16	1	0	1	1	0	.00	3	.068	.192	.091
07 Oak	NL	2	4	0	0	0	0	(0	0)	0	0	0	0	1	0	2	0	0	0	0	0	-	0	.000	.200	.000
07 Was	NL	103	162	32	6	2	6	(1	5)	60	24	22	22	22	1	63	1	1	1	3	0	1.00	1	.198	.296	.370
Postseason		4	12	4	1	0	0	(0	0)	5	1	0	2	3	1	3	1	0	1	1	0	1.00	0	.333	.500	.417
6 ML YEARS		474	978	228	50	10	24	(8	16)	370	140	105	139	141	14	284	11	5	6	6	5	.55	17	.233	.335	.378

John Lannan

Pitches: L **Bats:** L **Pos:** SP-31   **Ht:** 6'4" **Wt:** 225 **Born:** 9/27/1984 **Age:** 24

Year Team	Lg	G	GS	CG	GF	IP	BFP	H	R	ER	HR	SH	SF	HB	TBB	IBB	SO	WP	Bk	W	L	Pct	ShO	Sv-Op	Hld	ERC	ERA
2005 Vrmnt	A-	14	11	0	1	63.1	296	74	46	37	5	0	3	4	31	0	41	5	3	3	5	.375	0	0-	-	5.43	5.26
2006 Savann	A	27	25	1	1	138.0	613	149	83	73	11	4	8	6	54	0	114	4	0	6	8	.429	1	0-	-	4.49	4.76
2007 Ptomc	A+	8	8	0	0	50.2	198	31	13	12	3	1	0	0	15	0	35	1	0	6	0	1.000	0	0-	-	1.56	2.13
2007 Hrsbrg	AA	6	5	0	0	36.0	149	31	14	13	2	0	0	1	15	1	20	0	0	3	2	.600	0	0-	-	3.22	3.25
2007 Clmbs	AAA	7	6	0	1	38.0	155	30	8	7	1	0	0	2	12	0	19	1	0	3	1	.750	0	0-	-	2.38	1.66
2007 Was	NL	6	6	0	0	34.2	153	36	17	16	3	2	0	2	17	1	10	1	0	2	2	.500	0	0-0	0	4.82	4.15
2008 Was	NL	31	31	0	0	182.0	779	172	89	79	23	13	5	7	72	1	117	6	2	9	15	.375	0	0-0	0	4.09	3.91
2 ML YEARS		37	37	0	0	216.2	932	208	106	95	26	15	5	9	89	2	127	7	2	11	17	.393	0	0-0	0	4.21	3.95

Jeff Larish

Bats: L **Throws:** R **Pos:** 3B-12; DH-12; PH-12; 1B-8; PR-1   **Ht:** 6'2" **Wt:** 200 **Born:** 10/11/1982 **Age:** 26

Year Team	Lg	G	AB	H	2B	3B	HR	(Hm	Rd)	TB	R	RBI	RC	TBB	IBB	SO	HBP	SH	SF	SB	CS	SB%	GDP	Avg	OBP	Slg
2005 Tigers	R	6	18	4	1	0	0	(-	-)	5	1	4	2	4	0	5	1	0	1	0	1	.00	0	.222	.375	.278
2005 Oneont	A-	18	64	19	3	0	6	(-	-)	40	16	13	17	13	0	6	2	0	0	0	0	-	0	.297	.430	.625
2006 Lkland	A+	135	457	118	34	2	18	(-	-)	210	76	65	84	81	8	101	10	0	4	9	7	.56	10	.258	.379	.460
2007 Erie	AA	132	454	121	25	2	28	(-	-)	234	71	101	96	87	9	108	9	0	6	5	2	.71	2	.267	.390	.515
2008 Toledo	AAA	103	384	96	20	2	21	(-	-)	183	49	64	64	50	4	109	4	0	2	1	1	.00	13	.250	.341	.477
2008 Det	AL	42	104	27	6	0	2	(1	1)	39	12	16	14	7	0	34	0	0	0	2	2	.50	2	.260	.306	.375

Adam LaRoche

Bats: L Throws: L Pos: 1B-129; PH-6; DH-2   Ht: 6'3" Wt: 200 Born: 11/6/1979 Age: 29

Year Team	Lg	G	AB	H	2B	3B	HR	(Hm	Rd)	TB	R	RBI	RC	TBB	IBB	SO	HBP	SH	SF	SB	CS	SB%	GDP	Avg	OBP	Slg
2008 Hkry*	A	3	10	6	1	0	1	(-	-)	10	2	4	5	2	0	1	0	0	0	0	0	-	0	.600	.667	1.000
2004 Atl	NL	110	324	90	27	1	13	(7	6)	158	45	45	43	27	1	78	1	2	2	0	0	-	10	.278	.333	.488
2005 Atl	NL	141	451	117	28	0	20	(11	9)	205	53	78	63	39	7	87	4	2	6	0	2	.00	15	.259	.320	.455
2006 Atl	NL	149	492	140	38	1	32	(11	21)	276	89	90	83	55	5	128	2	1	7	0	2	.00	9	.285	.354	.561
2007 Pit	NL	152	563	153	42	0	21	(10	11)	258	71	88	84	62	5	131	3	0	4	1	1	.50	18	.272	.345	.458
2008 Pit	NL	136	492	133	32	3	25	(14	11)	246	66	85	76	54	7	122	2	0	6	1	1	.50	9	.270	.341	.500
Postseason		8	25	8	2	0	2	(0	2)	16	3	10	6	5	1	6	0	1	0	0	0	-	1	.320	.433	.640
5 ML YEARS		688	2322	633	167	5	111	(53	58)	1143	324	386	349	237	25	546	12	5	25	2	6	.25	61	.273	.340	.492

Andy LaRoche

Bats: R Throws: R Pos: 3B-59; PH-16; 2B-3; 1B-1   Ht: 6'1" Wt: 223 Born: 9/13/1983 Age: 25

Year Team	Lg	G	AB	H	2B	3B	HR	(Hm	Rd)	TB	R	RBI	RC	TBB	IBB	SO	HBP	SH	SF	SB	CS	SB%	GDP	Avg	OBP	Slg
2003 Ogden	R+	6	19	4	1	0	0	(-	-)	5	1	5	1	1	0	4	0	0	1	0	0	-	0	.211	.238	.263
2004 Clmbs	A	65	244	69	20	0	13	(-	-)	128	52	42	49	29	1	30	8	2	2	12	5	.71	6	.283	.375	.525
2004 VeroB	A+	62	219	52	13	0	10	(-	-)	95	26	34	28	17	0	42	2	2	3	2	3	.40	1	.237	.295	.434
2005 VeroB	A+	63	249	83	14	1	21	(-	-)	162	54	51	59	19	3	38	1	0	2	6	1	.86	6	.333	.380	.651
2005 Jaxnvl	AA	64	227	62	12	0	9	(-	-)	101	41	43	39	32	2	54	3	0	2	2	1	.67	9	.273	.367	.445
2006 Jaxnvl	AA	62	230	71	13	0	9	(-	-)	111	42	46	49	41	1	32	4	0	2	6	3	.67	2	.309	.419	.483
2006 LsVgs	AAA	55	202	65	14	1	10	(-	-)	111	35	35	43	25	0	32	2	0	1	3	2	.60	7	.322	.400	.550
2007 LsVgs	AAA	73	265	82	18	1	18	(-	-)	156	55	48	61	39	0	42	3	0	4	2	2	.50	8	.309	.399	.589
2008 Jaxnvl	AA	6	22	7	1	0	0	(-	-)	8	5	1	3	3	0	6	0	0	0	1	0	1.00	1	.318	.400	.364
2008 LsVgs	AAA	40	123	36	3	0	5	(-	-)	54	35	28	28	37	1	14	2	0	4	2	1	.67	7	.293	.452	.439
2007 LAD	NL	35	93	21	5	0	1	(0	1)	29	16	10	12	20	5	24	1	0	1	2	1	.67	1	.226	.365	.312
2008 2 Tms	NL	76	223	37	5	0	5	(1	4)	57	17	18	10	24	1	37	2	2	1	2	0	1.00	6	.166	.252	.256
08 LAD	NL	27	59	12	1	0	2	(0	2)	19	6	6	3	10	0	7	0	0	0	0	0	-	5	.203	.319	.322
08 Pit	NL	49	164	25	4	0	3	(1	2)	38	11	12	7	14	1	30	2	2	1	2	0	1.00	3	.152	.227	.232
2 ML YEARS		111	316	58	10	0	6	(1	5)	86	33	28	22	44	6	61	3	2	2	4	1	.80	9	.184	.288	.272

Jason LaRue

Bats: R Throws: R Pos: C-57; 1B-3; PH-3; PR-2   Ht: 5'11" Wt: 205 Born: 3/19/1974 Age: 35

Year Team	Lg	G	AB	H	2B	3B	HR	(Hm	Rd)	TB	R	RBI	RC	TBB	IBB	SO	HBP	SH	SF	SB	CS	SB%	GDP	Avg	OBP	Slg
1999 Cin	NL	36	90	19	7	0	3	(1	2)	35	12	10	10	11	1	32	2	0	0	4	1	.80	4	.211	.311	.389
2000 Cin	NL	31	98	23	3	0	5	(1	4)	41	12	12	12	5	2	19	4	0	0	0	0	-	1	.235	.299	.418
2001 Cin	NL	121	364	86	21	2	12	(3	9)	147	39	43	42	27	4	106	9	1	2	3	3	.50	11	.236	.303	.404
2002 Cin	NL	113	353	88	17	1	12	(5	7)	143	42	52	44	27	6	117	13	2	2	1	2	.33	13	.249	.324	.405
2003 Cin	NL	118	379	87	23	1	16	(12	4)	160	52	50	47	33	4	111	20	1	4	3	3	.50	9	.230	.321	.422
2004 Cin	NL	114	390	98	24	2	14	(3	11)	168	46	55	53	26	5	108	24	2	3	0	2	.00	7	.251	.334	.431
2005 Cin	NL	110	361	94	27	0	14	(6	8)	163	38	60	63	41	7	101	13	5	2	0	0	-	8	.260	.355	.452
2006 Cin	NL	72	191	37	5	0	8	(5	3)	66	22	21	17	27	9	51	8	3	1	1	0	1.00	3	.194	.317	.346
2007 KC	AL	66	169	25	9	0	4	(2	2)	46	14	13	7	17	0	66	4	3	2	1	0	1.00	6	.148	.240	.272
2008 StL	NL	61	164	35	8	1	4	(1	3)	57	17	21	16	15	1	20	5	3	2	0	0	-	6	.213	.296	.348
10 ML YEARS		842	2559	592	144	7	92	(39	53)	1026	294	337	311	229	39	731	102	20	18	13	11	.54	68	.231	.317	.401

Brandon League

Pitches: R Bats: R Pos: RP-31   Ht: 6'3" Wt: 192 Born: 3/16/1983 Age: 26

Year Team	Lg	G	GS	CG	GF	IP	BFP	H	R	ER	HR	SH	SF	HB	TBB	IBB	SO	WP	Bk	W	L	Pct	ShO	Sv-Op	Hld	ERC	ERA
2008 Syrcse*	AAA	20	0	0	8	34.1	152	36	19	15	2	1	1	2	10	0	32	7	0	2	3	.400	0	2- -		3.73	3.93
2004 Tor	AL	3	0	0	0	4.2	18	3	0	0	0	0	0	0	1	0	2	0	0	1	0	1.000	0	0-0	1	1.26	0.00
2005 Tor	AL	20	0	0	4	35.2	162	42	27	26	8	0	1	2	20	1	17	5	0	1	0	1.000	0	0-0	1	7.24	6.56
2006 Tor	AL	33	0	0	8	42.2	173	34	17	12	3	2	0	3	9	2	29	0	0	1	2	.333	0	1-4	12	2.30	2.53
2007 Tor	AL	14	0	0	2	11.2	58	19	8	1	0	1	0	7	0	7	3	0	0	0	0	-	0	0-1	0	8.98	6.17
2008 Tor	AL	31	0	0	8	33.0	141	28	9	8	2	1	0	3	15	2	23	2	0	1	2	.333	0	1-1	5	3.45	2.18
5 ML YEARS		101	0	0	22	127.2	552	126	61	54	14	3	2	8	52	5	78	10	0	4	4	.500	0	2-6	19	4.33	3.81

Wade LeBlanc

Pitches: L Bats: L Pos: SP-4; RP-1   Ht: 6'3" Wt: 202 Born: 8/7/1984 Age: 24

Year Team	Lg	G	GS	CG	GF	IP	BFP	H	R	ER	HR	SH	SF	HB	TBB	IBB	SO	WP	Bk	W	L	Pct	ShO	Sv-Op	Hld	ERC	ERA
2006 Eugene	A-	7	3	0	0	21.0	85	19	10	10	2	1	0	1	6	0	20	1	0	1	0	1.000	0	0- -		2.54	4.29
2006 FtWyn	A	7	7	0	0	32.2	136	31	8	8	1	1	0	1	10	0	27	0	0	4	1	.800	0	0- -		3.12	2.20
2007 Lk Els	A+	16	16	0	0	92.0	363	72	32	27	5	2	4	1	17	0	90	7	0	6	5	.545	0	0- -		1.93	2.64
2007 SnAnt	AA	12	11	0	0	57.1	233	48	22	22	8	1	0	0	19	0	55	1	0	7	3	.700	0	0- -		3.22	3.45
2008 Portlnd	AAA	26	25	0	0	138.2	587	136	85	82	21	8	5	7	42	0	139	2	0	11	9	.550	0	0- -		4.16	5.32
2008 SD	NL	5	4	0	0	21.1	104	29	19	19	7	1	0	0	15	2	14	0	0	1	3	.250	0	0-0	0	9.57	8.02

Wil Ledezma

Pitches: L Bats: L Pos: RP-22; SP-6   Ht: 6'4" Wt: 212 Born: 1/21/1981 Age: 28

Year	Team	Lg	G	GS	CG	GF	IP	BFP	H	R	ER	HR	SH	SF	HB	TBB	IBB	SO	WP	Bk	W	L	Pct	ShO	Sv-Op	Hld	ERC	ERA
2008	Portlnd*	AAA	11	0	0	2	16.1	66	14	8	8	1	1	0	1	4	0	20	1	0	1	0	1.000	0	1--	-	2.75	4.41
2003	Det	AL	34	8	0	13	84.0	376	99	55	54	12	1	4	3	35	3	49	2	0	3	7	.300	0	0-1	1	5.67	5.79
2004	Det	AL	15	8	0	1	53.1	225	55	28	26	3	0	3	2	18	0	29	3	1	4	3	.571	0	0-1	0	3.94	4.39
2005	Det	AL	10	10	0	0	49.2	234	61	46	39	10	4	4	2	24	0	30	2	2	2	4	.333	0	0-0	0	6.66	7.07
2006	Det	AL	24	7	0	2	60.1	264	60	28	24	5	2	1	2	23	0	39	2	0	3	3	.500	0	0-1	2	3.92	3.58
2007	3 Tms		44	1	0	13	59.1	280	70	42	37	7	2	3	0	38	4	47	3	2	3	3	.500	0	0-2	4	6.13	5.61
2008	2 Tms	NL	28	6	0	8	58.1	266	51	29	27	4	4	4	3	41	2	53	4	0	2	0	.000	0	0-0	0	4.41	4.17
07	Det	AL	23	0	0	5	35.2	166	38	21	19	4	2	1	0	26	2	24	3	2	3	1	.750	0	0-2	2	5.83	4.79
07	Atl	NL	12	0	0	4	9.1	45	12	10	8	1	0	1	0	4	0	7	0	0	0	2	.000	0	0-0	2	5.64	7.71
07	SD	NL	9	1	0	4	14.1	69	20	11	10	2	0	1	0	8	2	16	0	0	0	0	-	0	0-0	0	7.23	6.28
08	SD	NL	25	6	0	6	54.1	249	49	29	27	4	4	4	3	38	2	49	4	0	0	0	.000	0	0-0	0	4.61	4.47
08	Ari	NL	3	0	0	2	4.0	17	2	0	0	0	0	0	0	3	0	4	0	0	0	0	-	0	0-0	0	2.03	0.00
	Postseason		4	0	0	1	4.0	17	4	1	1	1	0	0	0	1	0	2	0	0	1	0	1.000	0	0-0	1	4.38	2.25
6 ML YEARS			155	40	0	37	365.0	1645	396	228	207	41	12	19	12	179	9	247	16	5	15	22	.405	0	0-5	7	5.11	5.10

Carlos Lee

Bats: R Throws: R Pos: LF-110; DH-4; PH-1   Ht: 6'2" Wt: 240 Born: 6/20/1976 Age: 33

							BATTING												BASERUNNING				AVERAGES		
Year	Team	Lg	G	AB	H	2B	3B	HR	(Hm | Rd)	TB	R	RBI	RC	TBB	IBB	SO	HBP	SH	SF	SB	CS	SB%	GDP	Avg	OBP	Slg
1999	CWS	AL	127	492	144	32	2	16	(10 | 6)	228	66	84	68	13	0	72	4	1	7	4	2	.67	11	.293	.312	.463
2000	CWS	AL	152	572	172	29	2	24	(12 | 12)	277	107	92	91	38	1	94	3	1	5	13	4	.76	17	.301	.345	.484
2001	CWS	AL	150	558	150	33	3	24	(12 | 12)	261	75	84	81	38	2	85	6	1	2	17	7	.71	15	.269	.321	.468
2002	CWS	AL	140	492	130	26	2	26	(14 | 12)	238	82	80	86	75	4	73	2	0	7	1	4	.20	5	.264	.359	.484
2003	CWS	AL	158	623	181	35	1	31	(18 | 13)	311	100	113	105	37	2	91	4	0	7	18	4	.82	20	.291	.331	.499
2004	CWS	AL	153	591	180	37	3	31	(17 | 14)	310	103	99	112	54	3	86	7	0	6	11	5	.69	10	.305	.366	.525
2005	Mil	NL	162	618	164	41	0	32	(15 | 17)	301	85	114	98	57	7	87	2	0	11	13	4	.76	8	.265	.324	.487
2006	2 Tms		161	624	187	37	1	37	(15 | 22)	337	102	116	113	58	6	65	2	0	11	19	2	.90	22	.300	.355	.540
2007	Hou	NL	162	627	190	43	1	32	(15 | 17)	331	93	119	104	53	10	63	4	0	13	10	5	.67	27	.303	.354	.528
2008	Hou	NL	115	436	137	27	0	28	(11 | 17)	248	61	100	85	37	7	49	3	0	5	4	1	.80	8	.314	.368	.569
06	Mil	NL	102	388	111	18	0	28	(10 | 18)	213	60	81	75	38	4	39	2	0	7	12	2	.86	13	.286	.347	.549
06	Tex	AL	59	236	76	19	1	9	(5 | 4)	124	42	35	38	20	2	26	0	0	4	7	0	1.00	9	.322	.369	.525
	Postseason		3	11	1	1	0	0	(0 | 0)	2	0	1	0	0	0	2	0	0	1	0	0	-	0	.091	.083	.182
10 ML YEARS			1480	5633	1635	340	12	281	(141 | 140)	2842	874	1001	943	460	42	765	37	3	74	110	38	.74	143	.290	.344	.505

Cliff Lee

Pitches: L Bats: L Pos: SP-31   Ht: 6'3" Wt: 190 Born: 8/30/1978 Age: 30

Year	Team	Lg	G	GS	CG	GF	IP	BFP	H	R	ER	HR	SH	SF	HB	TBB	IBB	SO	WP	Bk	W	L	Pct	ShO	Sv-Op	Hld	ERC	ERA
2002	Cle	AL	2	2	0	0	10.1	44	6	2	2	0	1	0	0	8	1	6	0	1	0	0	.000	0	0-0	0	2.38	1.74
2003	Cle	AL	9	9	0	0	52.1	210	41	28	21	7	1	1	2	20	1	44	3	0	3	3	.500	0	0-0	0	3.29	3.61
2004	Cle	AL	33	33	0	0	179.0	802	188	113	108	30	2	6	11	81	1	161	6	0	14	8	.636	0	0-0	0	5.31	5.43
2005	Cle	AL	32	32	1	0	202.0	838	194	91	85	22	5	7	0	52	1	143	4	0	18	5	.783	0	0-0	0	3.35	3.79
2006	Cle	AL	33	33	1	0	200.2	882	224	114	99	29	3	6	8	58	3	129	3	0	14	11	.560	0	0-0	0	4.69	4.40
2007	Cle	AL	20	16	1	1	97.1	443	112	73	68	17	3	2	7	36	1	66	5	0	5	8	.385	0	0-0	0	5.59	6.29
2008	Cle	AL	31	31	4	0	223.1	891	214	68	63	12	2	3	5	34	1	170	4	0	22	3	.880	2	0-0	0	2.75	2.54
7 ML YEARS			160	156	7	1	965.0	4110	979	489	445	117	17	25	33	289	9	719	25	1	76	39	.661	2	0-0	0	4.03	4.15

Derrek Lee

Bats: R Throws: R Pos: 1B-153; DH-2; PH-1   Ht: 6'5" Wt: 245 Born: 9/6/1975 Age: 33

							BATTING												BASERUNNING				AVERAGES		
Year	Team	Lg	G	AB	H	2B	3B	HR	(Hm | Rd)	TB	R	RBI	RC	TBB	IBB	SO	HBP	SH	SF	SB	CS	SB%	GDP	Avg	OBP	Slg
1997	SD	NL	22	54	14	3	0	1	(0 | 1)	20	9	4	8	9	0	24	0	0	0	0	0	-	1	.259	.365	.370
1998	Fla	NL	141	454	106	29	1	17	(4 | 13)	188	62	74	59	47	1	120	10	0	2	5	2	.71	12	.233	.318	.414
1999	Fla	NL	70	218	45	9	1	5	(0 | 5)	71	21	20	18	17	1	70	0	0	1	2	1	.67	3	.206	.263	.326
2000	Fla	NL	158	477	134	18	3	28	(9 | 19)	242	70	70	84	63	6	123	4	0	2	0	3	.00	14	.281	.368	.507
2001	Fla	NL	158	561	158	37	4	21	(8 | 13)	266	83	75	88	50	1	126	8	0	6	4	2	.67	18	.282	.346	.474
2002	Fla	NL	162	581	157	35	2	27	(9 | 18)	287	95	86	96	98	8	164	5	0	4	19	9	.68	14	.270	.378	.494
2003	Fla	NL	155	539	146	31	2	31	(11 | 20)	274	91	92	99	88	7	131	10	0	6	21	8	.72	9	.271	.379	.508
2004	ChC	NL	161	605	168	39	1	32	(18 | 14)	305	90	98	101	68	4	128	8	2	5	12	5	.71	14	.278	.356	.504
2005	ChC	NL	158	594	199	50	3	46	(24 | 22)	393	120	107	135	85	23	109	5	0	7	15	3	.83	12	.335	.418	.662
2006	ChC	NL	50	175	50	9	0	8	(5 | 3)	83	30	30	27	25	1	41	0	0	4	8	4	.67	11	.286	.368	.474
2007	ChC	NL	150	567	180	43	1	22	(16 | 6)	291	91	82	108	71	8	114	9	0	3	6	5	.55	15	.317	.400	.513
2008	ChC	NL	155	623	181	41	3	20	(15 | 5)	288	93	90	93	71	3	119	0	0	4	8	2	.80	27	.291	.361	.462
	Postseason		20	84	19	3	0	1	(0 | 1)	25	7	8	4	4	0	21	3	0	0	2	0	1.00	4	.226	.286	.298
12 ML YEARS			1540	5448	1538	344	26	258	(119 | 139)	2708	855	828	916	692	63	1269	59	2	44	100	44	.69	150	.282	.367	.497

Anthony Lerew

Pitches: R Bats: L Pos: P   Ht: 6'3" Wt: 220 Born: 10/28/1982 Age: 26

Year	Team	Lg	G	GS	CG	GF	IP	BFP	H	R	ER	HR	SH	SF	HB	TBB	IBB	SO	WP	Bk	W	L	Pct	ShO	Sv-Op	Hld	ERC	ERA
2008	Rchmd*	AAA	9	8	0	0	37.0	170	43	24	17	5	1	1	2	20	2	22	3	0	1	4	.200	0	0--	-	6.08	4.14
2008	Braves*	R	5	5	0	0	11.2	54	11	9	7	0	0	0	1	6	0	8	0	0	0	1	.000	0	0--	-	3.61	5.40

Year Team	Lg	HOW MUCH HE PITCHED						WHAT HE GAVE UP												THE RESULTS							
		G	GS	CG	GF	IP	BFP	H	R	ER	HR	SH	SF	HB	TBB	IBB	SO	WP	Bk	W	L	Pct	ShO	Sv-Op	Hld	ERC	ERA
2005 Atl	NL	7	0	0	4	8.0	37	9	5	5	1	1	0	0	5	2	5	0	0	0	0	-	0	0-1	0	5.47	5.63
2006 Atl	NL	1	0	0	0	2.0	15	5	5	5	0	0	0	1	3	0	1	0	0	0	0	-	0	0-0	0	20.57	22.50
2007 Atl	NL	3	3	0	0	11.2	57	14	10	10	4	3	0	0	7	1	9	1	0	0	2	.000	0	0-0	0	7.62	7.71
3 ML YEARS		11	3	0	4	21.2	109	28	20	20	5	4	0	1	15	3	15	1	0	0	2	.000	0	0-1	0	7.95	8.31

Jon Lester

Pitches: L Bats: L Pos: SP-33   Ht: 6'2" Wt: 190 Born: 1/7/1984 Age: 25

Year Team	Lg	HOW MUCH HE PITCHED						WHAT HE GAVE UP												THE RESULTS							
		G	GS	CG	GF	IP	BFP	H	R	ER	HR	SH	SF	HB	TBB	IBB	SO	WP	Bk	W	L	Pct	ShO	Sv-Op	Hld	ERC	ERA
2006 Bos	AL	15	15	0	0	81.1	367	91	43	43	7	2	8	5	43	1	60	5	0	7	2	.778	0	0-0	0	5.52	4.76
2007 Bos	AL	12	11	0	0	63.0	275	61	33	32	10	1	5	1	31	0	50	1	0	4	0	1.000	0	0-0	0	4.78	4.57
2008 Bos	AL	33	33	2	0	210.1	874	202	78	75	14	6	3	10	66	1	152	3	1	16	6	.727	2	0-0	0	3.55	3.21
Postseason		3	1	0	2	9.1	38	6	2	2	1	0	0	0	4	0	8	0	0	1	0	1.000	0	0-0	0	2.33	1.93
3 ML YEARS		60	59	2	0	354.2	1516	354	154	150	31	9	16	16	140	2	262	9	1	27	8	.771	2	0-0	0	4.20	3.81

Colby Lewis

Pitches: R Bats: R Pos: P   Ht: 6'4" Wt: 230 Born: 8/2/1979 Age: 29

Year Team	Lg	HOW MUCH HE PITCHED						WHAT HE GAVE UP												THE RESULTS							
		G	GS	CG	GF	IP	BFP	H	R	ER	HR	SH	SF	HB	TBB	IBB	SO	WP	Bk	W	L	Pct	ShO	Sv-Op	Hld	ERC	ERA
2008 Hrshm*	Jap	25	25	3	0	174.0	680	142	48	45	10	-	-	6	26	-	177	1	3	15	7	.682	2	0--	-	2.10	2.33
2002 Tex	AL	15	4	0	4	34.1	168	42	26	24	4	2	0	2	26	2	28	3	1	1	3	.250	0	0-2	1	7.22	6.29
2003 Tex	AL	26	26	0	0	127.0	594	163	104	103	23	2	2	5	70	1	88	5	0	10	9	.526	0	0-0	0	7.38	7.30
2004 Tex	AL	3	3	0	0	15.1	71	13	7	7	1	0	0	1	13	0	11	0	0	1	1	.500	0	0-0	0	4.98	4.11
2006 Det	AL	2	0	0	1	3.0	18	8	1	1	1	0	0	0	1	0	5	0	0	0	0	-	0	0-0	0	17.35	3.00
2007 Oak	AL	26	1	0	8	37.2	170	44	28	27	7	1	2	3	14	3	23	1	1	0	2	.000	0	0-1	3	5.79	6.45
5 ML YEARS		72	34	0	13	217.1	1021	270	166	162	36	5	4	11	124	6	155	9	2	12	15	.444	0	0-3	4	7.03	6.71

Fred Lewis

Bats: L Throws: R Pos: LF-112; PH-20; CF-14; RF-2   Ht: 6'2" Wt: 198 Born: 12/9/1980 Age: 28

Year Team	Lg	BATTING																		BASERUNNING				AVERAGES		
		G	AB	H	2B	3B	HR	(Hm	Rd)	TB	R	RBI	RC	TBB	IBB	SO	HBP	SH	SF	SB	CS	SB%	GDP	Avg	OBP	Slg
2006 SF	NL	13	11	5	1	0	0	(0	0)	6	5	2	4	0	0	3	0	0	0	0	0	-	0	.455	.455	.545
2007 SF	NL	58	157	45	6	2	3	(0	3)	64	34	19	27	19	0	32	3	1	0	5	1	.83	4	.287	.374	.408
2008 SF	NL	133	468	132	25	11	9	(4	5)	206	81	40	67	51	3	124	0	0	2	21	7	.75	5	.282	.351	.440
3 ML YEARS		204	636	182	32	13	12	(4	8)	276	120	61	98	70	3	159	3	1	2	26	8	.76	9	.286	.359	.434

Jensen Lewis

Pitches: R Bats: R Pos: RP-51   Ht: 6'3" Wt: 210 Born: 5/16/1984 Age: 25

Year Team	Lg	HOW MUCH HE PITCHED						WHAT HE GAVE UP												THE RESULTS							
		G	GS	CG	GF	IP	BFP	H	R	ER	HR	SH	SF	HB	TBB	IBB	SO	WP	Bk	W	L	Pct	ShO	Sv-Op	Hld	ERC	ERA
2005 MhVlly	A-	13	11	0	0	59.0	249	58	24	21	6	2	1	6	11	0	59	2	0	4	2	.667	0	0--	-	3.53	3.20
2006 Knstn	A+	21	20	0	0	108.1	460	110	59	48	11	0	1	9	29	0	94	5	0	7	6	.538	0	0--	-	4.01	3.99
2006 Akron	AA	7	7	0	0	39.1	170	41	21	17	4	1	1	4	12	0	44	0	0	1	2	.333	0	0--	-	4.39	3.89
2007 Akron	AA	24	0	0	12	39.0	154	27	12	8	2	0	2	1	13	1	49	1	0	2	0	1.000	0	1--	-	2.04	1.85
2007 Buffalo	AAA	10	0	0	2	13.0	48	5	2	2	1	0	1	0	4	0	12	0	0	1	0	1.000	0	1--	-	1.00	1.38
2008 Buffalo	AAA	11	0	0	5	20.0	87	16	11	8	2	3	2	1	8	1	18	1	0	1	2	.333	0	1--	-	2.96	3.60
2007 Cle	AL	26	0	0	5	29.1	125	26	8	7	1	2	1	1	10	1	34	1	0	1	1	.500	0	0-0	5	2.81	2.15
2008 Cle	AL	51	0	0	28	66.0	292	68	29	28	8	2	2	5	27	3	52	0	0	0	4	.000	0	13-14	4	4.66	3.82
Postseason		7	0	0	1	7.2	27	6	4	4	2	0	0	0	0	0	7	0	0	0	0	-	0	0-0	1	2.46	4.70
2 ML YEARS		77	0	0	33	95.1	417	94	37	35	9	4	3	6	37	4	86	1	0	1	5	.167	0	13-14	9	4.06	3.30

Scott Lewis

Pitches: L Bats: B Pos: SP-4   Ht: 6'0" Wt: 185 Born: 9/26/1983 Age: 25

Year Team	Lg	HOW MUCH HE PITCHED						WHAT HE GAVE UP												THE RESULTS							
		G	GS	CG	GF	IP	BFP	H	R	ER	HR	SH	SF	HB	TBB	IBB	SO	WP	Bk	W	L	Pct	ShO	Sv-Op	Hld	ERC	ERA
2004 MhVlly	A-	3	3	0	0	5.1	21	5	3	3	0	0	0	0	1	0	13	2	0	0	2	.000	0	0--	-	2.40	5.06
2005 MhVlly	A-	7	6	0	0	15.2	66	13	8	8	2	0	0	2	6	0	24	3	0	1	0	1.000	0	0--	-	3.81	4.60
2006 Knstn	A+	27	26	0	0	115.2	445	84	24	19	3	3	0	0	28	0	123	4	0	3	3	.500	0	0--	-	1.73	1.48
2007 Akron	AA	27	25	0	0	134.2	556	135	58	55	13	2	2	3	34	0	121	4	0	7	9	.438	0	0--	-	3.64	3.68
2008 Akron	AA	13	13	0	0	73.1	288	62	22	19	2	1	0	1	9	0	61	2	0	6	2	.750	0	0--	-	1.89	2.33
2008 Buffalo	AAA	4	4	1	0	24.0	93	19	8	7	2	0	4	0	4	0	21	0	0	2	2	.500	0	0--	-	2.07	2.63
2008 Cle	AL	4	4	0	0	24.0	97	20	9	7	4	1	0	0	6	0	15	1	0	4	0	1.000	0	0-0	0	3.01	2.63

Brad Lidge

Pitches: R Bats: R Pos: RP-72   Ht: 6'5" Wt: 210 Born: 12/23/1976 Age: 32

Year Team	Lg	HOW MUCH HE PITCHED						WHAT HE GAVE UP												THE RESULTS							
		G	GS	CG	GF	IP	BFP	H	R	ER	HR	SH	SF	HB	TBB	IBB	SO	WP	Bk	W	L	Pct	ShO	Sv-Op	Hld	ERC	ERA
2008 Clrwtr*	A+	1	1	0	0	1.0	6	2	1	1	1	0	0	0	1	0	2	0	0	0	0	-	0	0--	-	23.01	9.00
2002 Hou	NL	6	1	0	2	8.2	48	12	6	6	0	1	0	2	9	1	12	0	0	1	0	1.000	0	0-0	0	8.90	6.23
2003 Hou	NL	78	1	0	9	85.0	349	60	36	34	6	2	3	5	42	7	97	4	1	6	3	.667	0	1-6	28	2.82	3.60
2004 Hou	NL	80	0	0	44	94.2	369	57	21	20	8	3	2	6	30	5	157	3	1	6	5	.545	0	29-33	17	1.85	1.90
2005 Hou	NL	70	0	0	65	70.2	291	58	21	18	5	4	1	3	23	1	103	8	0	4	4	.500	0	42-46	0	2.79	2.29
2006 Hou	NL	78	0	0	52	75.0	340	69	47	44	10	6	2	6	36	4	104	11	0	1	5	.167	0	32-38	6	4.25	5.28

			HOW MUCH HE PITCHED						WHAT HE GAVE UP											THE RESULTS						
Year	Team	Lg	G	GS	CG	GF	IP	BFP	H	R	ER	HR	SH	SF	HB	TBB	IBB	SO	WP	Bk	W	L	Pct	ShO	Sv-Op Hld	ERC	ERA
2007	Hou	NL	66	0	0	34	67.0	287	54	29	25	9	5	1	4	30	4	88	6	0	5	3	.625	0	19-27 7	3.52	3.36
2008	Phi	NL	72	0	0	61	69.1	292	50	17	15	2	2	1	4	35	4	92	5	0	2	0	1.000	0	41-41 0	2.45	1.95
	Postseason		17	0	0	12	25.0	99	17	7	7	2	2	0	1	9	0	38	0	0	1	3	.250	0	6-8 0	2.33	2.52
	7 ML YEARS		450	1	0	267	470.1	1976	360	177	162	40	23	10	27	205	26	653	37	2	25	20	.556	0	164-191 58	2.97	3.10

Jon Lieber

Pitches: R **Bats:** L **Pos:** RP-25; SP-1

Ht: 6'2" **Wt:** 240 **Born:** 4/2/1970 **Age:** 39

			HOW MUCH HE PITCHED						WHAT HE GAVE UP											THE RESULTS						
Year	Team	Lg	G	GS	CG	GF	IP	BFP	H	R	ER	HR	SH	SF	HB	TBB	IBB	SO	WP	Bk	W	L	Pct	ShO	Sv-Op Hld	ERC	ERA
2008	Cubs*	R	1	1	0	0	3.0	11	4	0	0	0	0	0	0	0	0	1	0	0	0	0	-	0	0- -	4.31	0.00
2008	Peoria*	A	3	1	0	0	7.0	29	8	4	3	1	0	0	1	0	0	6	0	0	1	0	1.000	0	0- -	4.20	3.86
1994	Pit	NL	17	17	1	0	108.2	460	116	62	45	12	3	3	1	25	3	71	2	3	6	7	.462	0	0-0 0	3.83	3.73
1995	Pit	NL	21	12	0	3	72.2	327	103	56	51	7	5	6	4	14	0	45	3	0	4	7	.364	0	0-1 3	5.96	6.32
1996	Pit	NL	51	15	0	6	142.0	600	156	70	63	19	7	2	3	28	2	94	0	0	9	5	.643	0	1-4 9	4.12	3.99
1997	Pit	NL	33	32	1	0	188.1	799	193	102	94	23	6	7	1	51	8	160	3	1	11	14	.440	0	0-0 0	3.78	4.49
1998	Pit	NL	29	28	2	1	171.0	731	182	93	78	23	7	4	3	40	4	138	0	3	8	14	.364	0	1-1 0	4.00	4.11
1999	ChC	NL	31	31	3	0	203.1	875	226	107	92	28	7	11	1	46	6	186	2	2	10	11	.476	1	0-0 0	4.19	4.07
2000	ChC	NL	35	35	6	0	251.0	1047	248	130	123	36	9	7	10	54	3	192	2	2	12	11	.522	1	0-0 0	3.70	4.41
2001	ChC	NL	34	34	5	0	232.1	958	226	104	98	25	13	9	7	41	4	148	4	1	20	6	.769	1	0-0 0	3.19	3.80
2002	ChC	NL	21	21	3	0	141.0	582	153	64	58	15	10	6	1	12	2	87	0	0	8	8	.429	0	0-0 0	3.33	3.70
2004	NYY	AL	27	27	0	0	176.2	749	216	95	85	20	3	7	2	18	2	102	7	0	14	8	.636	0	0-0 0	4.26	4.33
2005	Phi	NL	35	35	1	0	218.1	912	223	107	102	33	13	5	5	41	6	149	3	0	17	13	.567	0	0-0 0	3.72	4.20
2006	Phi	NL	27	27	2	0	168.0	714	196	100	92	27	6	4	6	24	3	100	3	0	9	11	.450	1	0-0 0	4.53	4.93
2007	Phi	NL	14	12	1	1	78.0	342	91	44	41	7	2	4	3	22	5	54	1	1	3	6	.333	1	0-0 0	4.53	4.73
2008	ChC	NL	26	1	0	7	46.2	204	59	24	21	10	2	1	2	6	4	27	0	0	2	3	.400	0	0-1 3	5.30	4.05
	Postseason		3	3	0	0	21.0	80	19	8	8	1	0	1	1	2	0	9	1	0	1	1	.500	0	0-0 0	2.43	3.43
	14 ML YEARS		401	327	25	18	2198.0	9300	2388	1158	1043	285	93	76	49	422	52	1553	30	13	131	124	.514	5	2-7 15	3.97	4.27

Brent Lillibridge

Bats: R **Throws:** R **Pos:** SS-23; PR-8; 3B-1; PH-1

Ht: 5'11" **Wt:** 192 **Born:** 9/18/1983 **Age:** 25

			BATTING																				BASERUNNING				AVERAGES		
Year	Team	Lg	G	AB	H	2B	3B	HR	(Hm	Rd)	TB	R	RBI	RC	TBB	IBB	SO	HBP	SH	SF	SB	CS	SB%	GDP	Avg	OBP	Slg
2005	Wmspt	A-	42	169	41	12	4	4	(-	-)	73	19	18	24	14	0	35	2	4	2	10	3	.77	0	.243	.305	.432
2006	Hkry	A	74	274	82	18	5	11	(-	-)	143	59	43	63	51	0	61	4	2	2	29	8	.78	4	.299	.414	.522
2006	Lynbrg	A+	54	201	63	10	3	2	(-	-)	85	47	28	42	36	0	43	5	8	2	24	5	.83	4	.313	.426	.423
2007	Missi	AA	52	204	56	8	3	3	(-	-)	79	31	17	30	20	0	60	6	6	1	14	7	.67	1	.275	.355	.387
2007	Rchmd	AAA	87	321	92	14	2	10	(-	-)	140	47	41	51	20	0	59	3	8	5	28	5	.85	2	.287	.331	.436
2008	Rchmd	AAA	90	355	78	18	7	4	(-	-)	122	46	39	40	33	0	90	6	5	4	24	7	.77	6	.220	.294	.344
2008	Atl	NL	29	80	16	6	1	1	(0	1)	27	9	8	6	3	0	23	1	1	0	2	0	1.00	0	.200	.238	.338

Ted Lilly

Pitches: L **Bats:** L **Pos:** SP-34

Ht: 6'1" **Wt:** 190 **Born:** 1/4/1976 **Age:** 33

			HOW MUCH HE PITCHED						WHAT HE GAVE UP											THE RESULTS						
Year	Team	Lg	G	GS	CG	GF	IP	BFP	H	R	ER	HR	SH	SF	HB	TBB	IBB	SO	WP	Bk	W	L	Pct	ShO	Sv-Op Hld	ERC	ERA
1999	Mon	NL	9	3	0	1	23.2	110	30	20	20	7	0	1	3	9	0	28	1	0	0	1	.000	0	0-0 0	7.76	7.61
2000	NYY	AL	7	0	0	1	8.0	39	8	6	5	1	0	0	0	5	0	11	1	0	0	0	-	0	0-0 0	4.76	5.63
2001	NYY	AL	26	21	0	2	120.2	537	126	81	72	20	2	5	7	51	1	112	9	2	5	6	.455	0	0-0 0	5.10	5.37
2002	2 Tms	AL	22	16	2	1	100.0	413	80	43	41	15	0	3	6	31	3	77	6	1	5	7	.417	1	0-0 0	3.14	3.69
2003	Oak	AL	32	31	0	0	178.1	773	179	92	86	24	3	4	5	58	3	147	5	4	12	10	.545	1	0-0 0	4.06	4.34
2004	Tor	AL	32	32	2	0	197.1	845	171	92	89	26	3	3	6	89	2	168	6	4	12	10	.545	1	0-0 0	3.84	4.06
2005	Tor	AL	25	25	0	0	126.1	566	135	79	78	23	3	5	3	58	1	96	2	2	10	11	.476	0	0-0 0	5.38	5.56
2006	Tor	AL	32	32	0	0	181.2	797	179	98	87	28	4	2	4	81	6	160	7	4	15	13	.536	0	0-0 0	4.57	4.31
2007	ChC	NL	34	34	0	0	207.0	847	181	91	88	28	11	9	3	55	2	174	7	0	15	8	.652	0	0-0 0	3.14	3.83
2008	ChC	NL	34	34	0	0	204.2	861	187	96	93	32	5	3	7	64	2	184	4	4	17	9	.654	0	0-0 0	3.73	4.09
02	NYY	AL	16	11	2	1	76.2	314	57	31	29	10	0	3	6	24	3	59	6	0	3	6	.333	1	0-0 0	2.74	3.40
02	Oak	AL	6	5	0	0	23.1	99	23	12	12	5	0	0	1	7	0	18	0	1	2	1	.667	0	0-0 0	4.56	4.63
	Postseason		5	2	0	0	16.1	76	19	13	12	2	1	0	1	7	0	14	1	0	0	2	.000	0	0-1 0	5.43	6.61
	10 ML YEARS		253	228	4	5	1347.2	5788	1276	698	659	204	31	35	44	501	20	1157	48	22	91	75	.548	2	0-0 0	4.10	4.40

Tim Lincecum

Pitches: R **Bats:** L **Pos:** SP-33; RP-1

Ht: 5'11" **Wt:** 170 **Born:** 6/15/1984 **Age:** 25

			HOW MUCH HE PITCHED						WHAT HE GAVE UP											THE RESULTS						
Year	Team	Lg	G	GS	CG	GF	IP	BFP	H	R	ER	HR	SH	SF	HB	TBB	IBB	SO	WP	Bk	W	L	Pct	ShO	Sv-Op Hld	ERC	ERA
2006	SlmKzr	A-	2	2	0	0	4.0	14	1	0	0	0	0	0	0	0	0	10	1	0	0	0	-	0	0- -	0.13	0.00
2006	SnJos	A+	6	6	0	0	27.2	108	13	7	6	3	0	0	0	12	0	48	2	0	2	0	1.000	0	0- -	1.61	1.95
2007	Fresno	AAA	5	5	0	0	31.0	114	12	1	1	0	0	1	1	11	0	46	1	0	4	0	1.000	0	0- -	0.92	0.29
2007	SF	NL	24	24	0	0	146.1	618	122	70	65	12	5	7	2	65	5	150	10	0	7	5	.583	0	0-0 0	3.21	4.00
2008	SF	NL	34	33	2	0	227.0	928	182	72	66	11	11	3	6	84	1	265	17	2	18	5	.783	1	0-0 0	2.69	2.62
	2 ML YEARS		58	57	2	0	373.1	1546	304	142	131	23	16	10	8	149	6	415	27	2	25	10	.714	1	0-0 0	2.89	3.16

Mike Lincoln

Pitches: R **Bats:** R **Pos:** RP-64   **Ht:** 6'2" **Wt:** 213 **Born:** 4/10/1975 **Age:** 34

Year	Team	Lg	G	GS	CG	GF	IP	BFP	H	R	ER	HR	SH	SF	HB	TBB	IBB	SO	WP	Bk	W	L	Pct	ShO	Sv-Op	Hld	ERC	ERA
1999	Min	AL	18	15	0	0	76.1	353	102	59	58	11	2	6	1	26	0	27	4	0	3	10	.231	0	0-0	1	6.16	6.84
2000	Min	AL	8	4	0	1	20.2	109	36	25	25	10	0	0	2	13	0	15	1	0	0	3	.000	0	0-0	0	14.32	10.89
2001	Pit	NL	31	0	0	5	40.1	168	34	16	12	3	1	1	4	11	0	24	2	0	2	1	.667	0	0-2	7	2.94	2.68
2002	Pit	NL	55	0	0	9	72.1	309	80	28	25	7	2	4	0	27	8	50	2	0	4	4	.333	0	0-3	11	4.49	3.11
2003	Pit	NL	36	0	0	14	36.1	153	38	22	21	5	1	1	1	13	0	28	1	0	3	4	.429	0	5-8	5	4.70	5.20
2004	StL	NL	13	0	0	1	17.1	71	10	12	10	1	1	2	1	6	0	14	0	0	3	2	.600	0	0-2	1	1.63	5.19
2008	Cin	NL	64	0	0	12	70.1	297	66	37	35	10	3	3	3	24	1	57	3	0	2	5	.286	0	0-1	10	3.96	4.48
7 ML YEARS			225	19	0	42	333.2	1460	366	199	186	47	10	17	12	120	9	215	13	0	15	29	.341	0	5-16	35	4.89	5.02

Adam Lind

Bats: L **Throws:** L **Pos:** LF-71; DH-16; PH-1   **Ht:** 6'2" **Wt:** 195 **Born:** 7/17/1983 **Age:** 25

			BATTING																		BASERUNNING				AVERAGES		
Year	Team	Lg	G	AB	H	2B	3B	HR	(Hm	Rd)	TB	R	RBI	RC	TBB	IBB	SO	HBP	SH	SF	SB	CS	SB%	GDP	Avg	OBP	Slg
2008	Syrcse*	AAA	51	189	62	17	2	6	(-	-)	101	24	50	39	19	2	36	3	0	2	1	1	.50	4	.328	.394	.534
2006	Tor	AL	18	60	22	8	0	2	(0	2)	36	8	8	13	5	0	12	0	0	0	0	0	-	0	.367	.415	.600
2007	Tor	AL	89	290	69	14	0	11	(10	1)	116	34	46	38	16	0	65	1	2	2	1	2	.33	7	.238	.278	.400
2008	Tor	AL	88	326	92	16	4	9	(2	7)	143	48	40	39	16	3	59	2	1	4	2	0	1.00	8	.282	.316	.439
3 ML YEARS			195	676	183	38	4	22	(12	10)	295	90	94	90	37	3	136	3	3	6	3	2	.60	15	.271	.309	.436

Matt Lindstrom

Pitches: R **Bats:** R **Pos:** RP-66   **Ht:** 6'4" **Wt:** 210 **Born:** 2/11/1980 **Age:** 29

Year	Team	Lg	G	GS	CG	GF	IP	BFP	H	R	ER	HR	SH	SF	HB	TBB	IBB	SO	WP	Bk	W	L	Pct	ShO	Sv-Op	Hld	ERC	ERA
2002	Kngspt	R+	12	11	0	1	48.1	228	56	45	26	6	1	4	2	21	0	39	4	1	0	6	.000	0	0--	-	5.25	4.84
2003	CptCty	A	12	11	0	0	56.2	237	46	21	18	2	0	1	1	33	0	50	6	3	2	3	.400	0	0--	-	3.48	2.86
2003	Bklyn	A-	14	14	0	0	65.1	280	61	28	25	2	0	2	7	27	0	52	6	0	7	3	.700	0	0--	-	3.74	3.44
2004	CptCty	A	13	12	0	0	56.0	222	47	26	20	3	1	3	4	10	0	64	7	0	3	2	.600	0	0--	-	2.43	3.21
2004	StLuci	A+	14	14	1	0	79.2	329	83	44	33	5	6	6	3	20	0	50	4	0	5	5	.500	0	0--	-	3.73	3.73
2005	Bnghtn	AA	35	10	0	11	73.1	366	90	61	44	11	3	4	5	55	2	58	11	1	2	5	.286	0	0--	-	7.48	5.40
2006	StLuci	A+	11	0	0	5	18.0	75	14	7	5	2	1	0	0	7	0	16	1	0	1	0	1.000	0	2--	-	2.86	2.50
2006	Bnghtn	AA	35	0	0	22	40.2	179	42	19	17	2	0	2	5	14	1	54	3	2	4	4	.333	0	11--	-	4.11	3.76
2008	Albq	AAA	3	0	0	2	4.0	18	5	4	4	1	0	0	0	1	0	4	0	0	0	0	-	0	0--	-	5.88	9.00
2007	Fla	NL	71	0	0	11	67.0	284	66	27	23	2	3	1	3	21	4	62	5	0	3	4	.429	0	0-2	19	3.26	3.09
2008	Fla	NL	66	0	0	27	57.1	245	57	21	20	1	6	1	1	26	4	43	4	0	3	3	.500	0	5-6	14	3.69	3.14
2 ML YEARS			137	0	0	38	124.1	529	123	48	43	3	9	2	4	47	8	105	9	0	6	7	.462	0	5-8	33	3.46	3.11

Scott Linebrink

Pitches: R **Bats:** R **Pos:** RP-50   **Ht:** 6'2" **Wt:** 215 **Born:** 8/4/1976 **Age:** 32

Year	Team	Lg	G	GS	CG	GF	IP	BFP	H	R	ER	HR	SH	SF	HB	TBB	IBB	SO	WP	Bk	W	L	Pct	ShO	Sv-Op	Hld	ERC	ERA
2000	2 Tms	NL	11	0	0	4	12.0	63	18	8	8	4	0	0	3	8	0	6	0	0	0	0	-	0	0-0	0	11.88	6.00
2001	Hou	NL	9	0	0	2	10.1	44	6	4	3	0	1	1	2	6	0	9	1	0	0	0	-	0	0-0	0	2.54	2.61
2002	Hou	NL	22	0	0	4	24.1	120	31	21	19	2	0	2	1	13	4	24	0	0	0	0	-	0	0-0	1	5.70	7.03
2003	2 Tms	NL	52	6	0	8	92.1	397	93	37	34	9	4	6	6	36	4	68	11	0	3	2	.600	0	0-0	6	4.32	3.31
2004	SD	NL	73	0	0	7	84.0	326	61	22	20	8	2	3	3	26	2	83	3	0	7	3	.700	0	0-5	28	2.48	2.14
2005	SD	NL	73	0	0	19	73.2	288	55	17	15	4	2	0	0	23	4	70	3	0	8	1	.889	0	1-6	26	2.15	1.83
2006	SD	NL	73	0	0	11	75.2	314	70	31	30	9	1	2	1	22	3	68	2	0	7	4	.636	0	2-11	36	3.36	3.57
2007	2 Tms	NL	71	0	0	11	70.1	295	68	33	29	12	0	0	1	25	3	50	6	0	5	6	.455	0	1-8	21	4.26	3.71
2008	CWS	AL	50	0	0	13	46.1	186	41	20	19	8	2	0	0	9	1	40	3	0	2	2	.500	0	1-4	19	3.09	3.69
00	SF	NL	3	0	0	1	2.1	16	7	3	3	1	0	0	2	0	0	0	0	0	0	0	-	0	0-0	0	24.13	11.57
00	Hou	NL	8	0	0	3	9.2	47	11	5	5	3	0	0	1	6	0	6	0	0	0	0	-	0	0-0	0	9.21	4.66
03	Hou	NL	9	6	0	0	31.2	140	38	15	15	4	2	1	3	14	1	17	5	0	1	1	.500	0	0-0	0	6.27	4.26
03	SD	NL	43	0	0	6	60.2	257	55	22	19	5	2	5	3	22	3	51	6	0	2	1	.667	0	0-0	6	3.41	2.82
07	SD	NL	44	0	0	7	45.0	186	41	19	19	9	0	0	1	14	1	25	4	0	3	3	.500	0	1-7	15	3.99	3.80
07	Mil	NL	27	0	0	4	25.1	109	27	14	10	3	0	0	0	11	2	25	2	0	2	3	.400	0	0-1	6	4.71	3.55
Postseason			3	0	0	2	2.1	10	3	1	1	0	0	0	0	1	0	1	0	0	0	0	-	0	0-0	1	9.24	3.86
9 ML YEARS			434	6	0	77	489.0	2033	443	193	177	56	12	14	17	168	21	418	29	0	32	18	.640	0	5-34	137	3.55	3.26

Francisco Liriano

Pitches: L **Bats:** L **Pos:** SP-14   **Ht:** 6'2" **Wt:** 225 **Born:** 10/26/1983 **Age:** 25

Year	Team	Lg	G	GS	CG	GF	IP	BFP	H	R	ER	HR	SH	SF	HB	TBB	IBB	SO	WP	Bk	W	L	Pct	ShO	Sv-Op	Hld	ERC	ERA
2008	FtMyrs*	A+	1	1	0	0	5.1	24	6	4	4	0	1	1	0	2	0	8	0	0	0	1	.000	0	0--	-	3.84	6.75
2008	Roch*	AAA	19	19	0	0	118.0	480	102	44	43	8	3	2	3	31	1	113	4	0	10	2	.833	0	0--	-	2.72	3.28
2005	Min	AL	6	4	0	2	23.2	93	19	15	15	4	0	0	0	7	0	33	0	0	1	2	.333	0	0-0	0	3.15	5.70
2006	Min	AL	28	16	0	2	121.0	473	89	31	29	9	4	2	1	32	0	144	9	1	12	3	.800	0	1-1	1	2.12	2.16
2008	Min	AL	14	14	0	0	76.0	329	74	40	33	7	2	3	1	32	1	67	3	0	6	4	.600	0	0-0	0	3.97	3.91
3 ML YEARS			48	34	0	4	220.2	895	182	86	77	20	6	5	2	71	1	244	12	1	19	9	.679	0	1-1	1	2.84	3.14

Jesse Litsch

Pitches: R Bats: R Pos: SP-28; RP-1
Ht: 6'1" Wt: 175 Born: 3/9/1985 Age: 24

Year	Team	Lg	G	GS	CG	GF	IP	BFP	H	R	ER	HR	SH	SF	HB	TBB	IBB	SO	WP	Bk	W	L	Pct	ShO	Sv-Op	Hld	ERC	ERA
2005	Pulaski	R+	11	11	0	0	65.2	255	51	22	20	6	0	0	4	10	0	67	2	1	5	1	.833	0	0--	-	2.22	2.74
2005	Auburn	A-	4	3	0	0	10.0	50	11	9	4	0	1	2	0	6	0	7	1	0	1	0	1.000	0	0--	-	4.23	3.60
2006	Dnedin	A+	16	15	2	0	89.1	367	94	39	35	5	1	1	5	8	0	81	5	0	6	6	.500	1	0--	-	3.10	3.53
2006	NHam	AA	12	12	1	0	69.1	298	85	44	39	6	1	3	6	13	0	54	3	0	3	4	.429	0	0--	-	4.89	5.06
2007	NHam	AA	10	10	1	0	61.1	252	51	24	16	5	1	0	4	14	0	46	2	0	7	2	.778	0	0--	-	2.62	2.35
2007	Syrcse	AAA	2	2	0	0	15.0	58	12	3	3	0	1	1	0	3	0	10	0	0	1	0	1.000	0	0--	-	1.78	1.80
2008	Syrcse	AAA	3	3	0	0	20.0	81	18	10	8	1	0	1		4	0	18	1	0	1	1	.500	0	0--	-	2.68	3.60
2007	Tor	AL	20	20	0	0	111.0	478	116	56	47	14	3	3	7	36	2	50	2	0	7	9	.438	0	0-0	0	4.48	3.81
2008	Tor	AL	29	28	2	0	176.0	735	178	79	70	20	1	4	8	39	2	99	4	0	13	9	.591	2	0-0	0	3.71	3.58
	2 ML YEARS		49	48	2	0	287.0	1213	294	135	117	34	4	7	15	75	4	149	6	0	20	18	.526	2	0-0	0	4.00	3.67

Wes Littleton

Pitches: R Bats: R Pos: RP-12
Ht: 6'3" Wt: 200 Born: 9/2/1982 Age: 26

Year	Team	Lg	G	GS	CG	GF	IP	BFP	H	R	ER	HR	SH	SF	HB	TBB	IBB	SO	WP	Bk	W	L	Pct	ShO	Sv-Op	Hld	ERC	ERA
2008	Okla*	AAA	44	0	0	19	58.1	252	55	27	26	3	0	3	2	25	1	58	5	0	7	1	.875	0	6--	-	3.62	4.01
2006	Tex	AL	33	0	0	6	36.1	138	23	7	7	2	0	1	2	13	0	17	0	0	2	1	.667	0	1-1	7	2.10	1.73
2007	Tex	AL	35	0	0	11	48.0	205	48	23	23	6	0	3	3	16	1	24	1	0	3	2	.600	0	2-3	2	4.24	4.31
2008	Tex	AL	12	0	0	4	18.0	80	18	12	12	1	0	1	3	8	0	14	0	0	0	0	-	0	0-1	0	4.64	6.00
	3 ML YEARS		80	0	0	21	102.1	423	89	42	42	9	0	5	8	37	1	55	1	0	5	3	.625	0	3-5	9	3.51	3.69

Radhames Liz

Pitches: R Bats: R Pos: SP-17
Ht: 6'2" Wt: 186 Born: 6/10/1983 Age: 26

Year	Team	Lg	G	GS	CG	GF	IP	BFP	H	R	ER	HR	SH	SF	HB	TBB	IBB	SO	WP	Bk	W	L	Pct	ShO	Sv-Op	Hld	ERC	ERA
2005	Dlmrva	A	10	10	0	0	38.1	170	33	23	19	2	2	1	1	23	0	55	5	0	2	3	.400	0	0--	-	3.78	4.46
2005	Abrdn	A-	11	11	0	0	56.0	214	36	14	11	1	2	0	2	19	0	82	4	3	5	4	.556	0	0--	-	1.77	1.77
2006	Frdrck	A+	16	16	0	0	83.0	341	57	32	26	8	0	1	5	44	0	95	2	0	6	5	.545	0	0--	-	3.17	2.82
2006	Bowie	AA	10	10	0	0	50.1	230	55	31	30	9	1	0	2	31	1	54	4	0	3	1	.750	0	0--	-	6.37	5.36
2007	Bowie	AA	25	25	2	0	137.0	584	101	60	49	13	3	3	12	70	0	161	11	0	11	4	.733	1	0--	-	3.36	3.22
2008	Norfolk	AAA	15	15	1	0	87.0	364	77	42	35	6	4	3	4	32	1	85	3	0	3	7	.300	0	0--	-	3.30	3.62
2007	Bal	AL	9	4	0	5	24.2	122	25	21	19	3	1	1	1	23	1	24	3	0	2	0	.000	0	0-0	0	6.49	6.93
2008	Bal	AL	17	17	0	0	84.1	393	99	67	63	16	1	3	3	51	3	57	6	0	6	6	.500	0	0-0	0	6.84	6.72
	2 ML YEARS		26	21	0	5	109.0	515	124	88	82	19	2	4	4	74	4	81	9	0	6	8	.429	0	0-0	0	6.77	6.77

Paul Lo Duca

Bats: R Throws: R Pos: C-26; PH-21; 1B-17; LF-5; DH-1
Ht: 5'9" Wt: 213 Born: 4/12/1972 Age: 37

Year	Team	Lg	G	AB	H	2B	3B	HR	(Hm	Rd)	TB	R	RBI	RC	TBB	IBB	SO	HBP	SH	SF	SB	CS	SB%	GDP	Avg	OBP	Slg
2008	Ptomc*	A+	5	14	2	1	0	0	(-	-)	3	0	1	1	3	0	2	0	0	0	0	0	-	2	.143	.294	.214
2008	Clmbs*	AAA	4	13	2	0	0	0	(-	-)	2	0	2	0	2	0	3	0	0	0	0	0	-	0	.154	.267	.154
2008	Albq*	AAA	7	26	11	1	0	0	(-	-)	12	5	7	6	5	0	4	0	0	0	0	0	-	0	.423	.516	.462
1998	LAD	NL	6	14	4	1	0	0	(0	0)	5	2	1	1	0	0	1	0	0	0	0	0	-	0	.286	.286	.357
1999	LAD	NL	36	95	22	1	0	3	(1	2)	32	11	11	9	10	4	9	2	1	2	1	2	.33	3	.232	.312	.337
2000	LAD	NL	34	65	16	2	0	2	(0	2)	24	6	8	6	6	0	8	0	2	2	0	2	.00	2	.246	.301	.369
2001	LAD	NL	125	460	147	28	0	25	(11	14)	250	71	90	89	39	2	30	6	5	9	2	4	.33	11	.320	.374	.543
2002	LAD	NL	149	580	163	38	1	10	(5	5)	233	74	64	73	34	2	31	10	4	4	3	1	.75	20	.281	.330	.402
2003	LAD	NL	147	568	155	34	2	7	(4	3)	214	64	52	67	44	6	54	10	7	1	0	2	.00	21	.273	.335	.377
2004	2 Tms	NL	143	535	153	29	2	13	(8	5)	225	68	80	78	36	0	49	9	8	6	4	5	.44	22	.286	.338	.421
2005	Fla	NL	132	445	126	23	1	6	(2	4)	169	45	57	50	34	5	31	4	5	8	4	3	.57	16	.283	.334	.380
2006	NYM	NL	124	512	163	39	1	5	(2	3)	219	80	49	71	24	0	38	6	7	2	3	0	1.00	15	.318	.355	.428
2007	NYM	NL	119	445	121	18	1	9	(3	6)	168	46	54	48	24	4	33	6	3	10	2	0	1.00	18	.272	.311	.378
2008	2 Tms	NL	67	173	42	9	0	0	(0	0)	51	16	15	18	15	0	11	5	0	0	1	0	1.00	10	.243	.321	.295
04	LAD	NL	91	349	105	18	1	10	(6	4)	155	41	49	51	22	0	27	6	2	2	2	4	.33	15	.301	.351	.444
04	Fla	NL	52	186	48	11	1	3	(2	1)	70	27	31	27	14	0	22	3	6	4	2	1	.67	7	.258	.314	.376
08	Was	NL	46	139	32	7	0	0	(0	0)	39	13	12	13	9	0	9	5	0	0	1	0	1.00	9	.230	.301	.281
08	Fla	NL	21	34	10	2	0	0	(0	0)	12	3	3	5	6	0	2	0	0	0	0	0	-	1	.294	.400	.353
	Postseason		10	40	11	2	0	0	(0	0)	13	5	6	6	3	0	3	1	1	1	0	0	-	0	.275	.333	.325
	11 ML YEARS		1082	3892	1112	222	8	80	(36	44)	1590	483	481	510	266	23	295	58	42	44	20	19	.51	138	.286	.337	.409

Esteban Loaiza

Pitches: R Bats: R Pos: RP-7; SP-3
Ht: 6'2" Wt: 228 Born: 12/31/1971 Age: 37

Year	Team	Lg	G	GS	CG	GF	IP	BFP	H	R	ER	HR	SH	SF	HB	TBB	IBB	SO	WP	Bk	W	L	Pct	ShO	Sv-Op	Hld	ERC	ERA
2008	InldEm*	A+	1	1	0	0	3.0	11	3	1	1	0	0	0	0	0	0	2	0	0	0	1	.000	0	0--	-	2.18	3.00
2008	Charltt*	AAA	5	5	0	0	11.0	51	18	9	8	2	0	3	0	0	0	5	2	0	0	2	.000	0	0--	-	6.66	6.55
2008	Brham*	AA	3	1	0	0	6.0	21	3	0	0	0	0	0	0	1	0	3	0	0	0	0	-	0	0--	-	0.84	0.00
1995	Pit	NL	32	31	1	0	172.2	762	205	115	99	21	10	9	5	55	3	85	6	1	8	9	.471	0	0-0	0	5.10	5.16
1996	Pit	NL	10	10	1	0	52.2	236	65	32	29	11	3	1	2	19	2	32	0	0	2	3	.400	1	0-0	0	6.30	4.96
1997	Pit	NL	33	32	1	0	196.1	851	214	99	90	17	10	7	12	56	9	122	2	3	11	11	.500	1	0-0	0	4.20	4.13
1998	2 Tms		35	28	1	3	171.0	751	199	107	98	28	7	12	5	52	4	108	4	2	9	11	.450	0	0-1	0	5.19	5.16
1999	Tex	AL	30	15	0	4	120.1	517	128	65	61	10	7	4	0	40	2	77	2	0	9	5	.643	0	0-0	0	4.03	4.56
2000	2 Tms	AL	34	31	1	2	199.1	871	228	112	101	29	4	5	13	57	1	137	1	0	10	13	.435	1	1-1	0	5.07	4.56
2001	Tor	AL	36	30	1	1	190.0	837	239	113	106	27	6	4	9	40	1	110	1	1	11	11	.500	1	0-0	0	5.30	5.02

Year	Team	Lg	G	GS	CG	GF	IP	BFP	H	R	ER	HR	SH	SF	HB	TBB	IBB	SO	WP	Bk	W	L	Pct	ShO	Sv-Op	Hld	ERC	ERA
2002	Tor	AL	25	25	3	0	151.1	670	192	102	96	18	1	6	4	38	3	87	1	0	9	10	.474	1	0-0	0	5.26	5.71
2003	CWS	AL	34	34	1	0	226.1	922	196	75	73	17	7	6	10	56	2	207	3	1	21	9	.700	1	0-0	0	2.79	2.90
2004	2 Tms	AL	31	27	2	1	183.0	818	217	124	116	32	1	10	3	71	5	117	4	0	10	7	.588	1	0-0	0	5.72	5.70
2005	Was	NL	34	34	0	0	217.0	912	227	93	91	18	4	3	5	55	3	173	6	0	12	10	.545	0	0-0	0	3.74	3.77
2006	Oak	AL	26	26	2	0	154.2	679	179	92	84	17	5	8	5	40	3	97	2	0	11	9	.550	1	0-0	0	4.53	4.89
2007	2 Tms		7	7	0	0	37.1	164	36	24	24	10	3	1	1	20	1	20	0	1	2	4	.333	0	0-0	0	5.79	5.79
2008	2 Tms		10	3	0	5	27.0	116	27	17	16	4	0	3	1	5	1	10	0	0	1	2	.333	0	0-0	0	3.49	5.33
98	Pit	NL	21	14	0	3	91.2	394	96	50	46	13	5	7	3	30	1	53	1	2	6	5	.545	0	0-1	0	4.48	4.52
98	Tex	AL	14	14	1	0	79.1	357	103	57	52	15	2	5	2	22	3	55	3	0	3	6	.333	0	0-0	0	6.04	5.90
00	Tex	AL	20	17	0	2	107.1	480	133	67	64	21	2	4	3	31	1	75	1	0	5	6	.455	0	1-1	0	5.81	5.37
00	Tor	AL	14	14	1	0	92.0	391	95	45	37	8	2	1	10	26	0	62	0	0	5	7	.417	1	0-0	0	4.22	3.62
04	CWS	AL	21	21	2	0	140.2	604	156	81	76	23	1	5	1	45	3	83	2	0	9	5	.643	1	0-0	0	4.89	4.86
04	NYY	AL	10	6	0	1	42.1	214	61	43	40	9	0	5	2	26	2	34	2	0	1	2	.333	0	0-0	0	8.70	8.50
07	Oak	AL	2	2	0	0	14.2	56	10	3	3	1	0	0	0	4	0	5	0	0	1	0	1.000	0	0-0	0	1.87	1.84
07	LAD	NL	5	5	0	0	22.2	108	26	21	21	9	3	1	1	16	1	15	0	1	1	4	.200	0	0-0	0	8.92	8.34
08	LAD	NL	7	3	0	2	24.0	103	24	15	15	3	0	3	1	5	1	9	0	0	1	2	.333	0	0-0	0	3.47	5.63
08	CWS	AL	3	0	0	3	3.0	13	3	2	1	1	0	0	0	0	0	1	0	0	0	0	-	0	0-0	0	3.45	3.00
Postseason			6	3	0	1	26.1	111	31	13	13	4	0	2	0	5	0	16	0	0	0	3	.000	0	0-0	0	4.67	4.44
14 ML YEARS			377	333	14	16	2099.0	9106	2352	1170	1084	259	73	79	75	604	40	1382	32	9	126	114	.525	6	1-2	0	4.60	4.65

Kameron Loe

Pitches: R Bats: R Pos: RP-14   Ht: 6'8" Wt: 240 Born: 9/10/1981 Age: 27

Year	Team	Lg	G	GS	CG	GF	IP	BFP	H	R	ER	HR	SH	SF	HB	TBB	IBB	SO	WP	Bk	W	L	Pct	ShO	Sv-Op	Hld	ERC	ERA
2008	Okla*	AAA	26	4	0	8	58.0	259	70	41	36	7	2	1	2	20	0	31	4	0	3	5	.375	0	1--	-	5.37	5.59
2004	Tex	AL	2	1	0	0	6.2	29	6	5	4	0	0	0	1	6	0	3	0	0	0	0	-	0	0-0	0	5.87	5.40
2005	Tex	AL	48	8	0	13	92.0	392	89	43	35	7	5	1	2	31	6	45	2	0	9	6	.600	0	1-4	4	3.45	3.42
2006	Tex	AL	15	15	1	0	78.1	358	105	54	51	10	1	3	1	22	0	34	3	0	3	6	.333	1	0-0	0	5.79	5.86
2007	Tex	AL	28	23	0	0	136.0	615	162	96	81	13	1	5	4	56	6	78	6	0	6	11	.353	0	0-0	0	5.24	5.36
2008	Tex	AL	14	0	0	4	30.2	134	36	18	11	3	0	1	0	8	1	20	0	0	1	0	1.000	0	0-1	2	4.40	3.23
5 ML YEARS			107	47	1	17	343.2	1528	398	216	182	33	7	10	8	123	13	180	11	0	19	23	.452	1	1-5	6	4.80	4.77

Adam Loewen

Pitches: L Bats: L Pos: SP-4; RP-3   Ht: 6'5" Wt: 235 Born: 4/9/1984 Age: 25

Year	Team	Lg	G	GS	CG	GF	IP	BFP	H	R	ER	HR	SH	SF	HB	TBB	IBB	SO	WP	Bk	W	L	Pct	ShO	Sv-Op	Hld	ERC	ERA
2008	Frdrck*	A+	3	1	0	0	3.0	10	1	0	0	0	0	0	0	0	0	5	0	0	0	0	-	0	0--	-	0.25	0.00
2008	Bowie*	AA	6	0	0	1	6.2	30	7	3	1	1	0	1	2	2	0	6	0	0	1	0	1.000	0	0--	-	5.63	1.35
2006	Bal	AL	22	19	0	1	112.1	504	111	72	67	8	1	4	8	62	0	98	3	1	6	6	.500	0	0-0	1	4.70	5.37
2007	Bal	AL	6	6	0	0	30.1	143	27	14	12	1	1	0	3	26	0	22	1	1	2	0	1.000	0	0-0	0	5.11	3.56
2008	Bal	AL	7	4	0	0	21.1	102	25	19	19	5	0	2	0	18	0	14	2	0	0	2	.000	0	0-0	1	8.37	8.02
3 ML YEARS			35	29	0	1	164.0	749	163	105	98	14	2	6	11	106	0	134	6	2	8	8	.500	0	0-0	2	5.22	5.38

Boone Logan

Pitches: L Bats: R Pos: RP-55   Ht: 6'5" Wt: 210 Born: 8/13/1984 Age: 24

Year	Team	Lg	G	GS	CG	GF	IP	BFP	H	R	ER	HR	SH	SF	HB	TBB	IBB	SO	WP	Bk	W	L	Pct	ShO	Sv-Op	Hld	ERC	ERA
2008	Charltt*	AAA	5	0	0	1	9.0	46	10	8	6	2	1	2	3	6	0	7	1	0	0	1	.000	0	0--	-	8.15	6.00
2006	CWS	AL	21	0	0	4	17.1	93	21	18	16	2	1	1	3	15	2	15	1	0	0	0	-	0	1-2	2	7.56	8.31
2007	CWS	AL	68	0	0	13	50.2	226	59	30	28	7	2	6	0	20	3	35	2	0	2	1	.667	0	0-2	11	5.18	4.97
2008	CWS	AL	55	0	0	12	42.1	197	57	31	28	7	2	0	1	14	3	42	1	0	2	3	.400	0	0-1	3	6.24	5.95
3 ML YEARS			144	0	0	29	110.1	516	137	79	72	16	5	7	4	49	8	92	4	0	4	4	.500	0	1-5	16	5.97	5.87

Kyle Lohse

Pitches: R Bats: R Pos: SP-33   Ht: 6'2" Wt: 209 Born: 10/4/1978 Age: 30

Year	Team	Lg	G	GS	CG	GF	IP	BFP	H	R	ER	HR	SH	SF	HB	TBB	IBB	SO	WP	Bk	W	L	Pct	ShO	Sv-Op	Hld	ERC	ERA
2001	Min	AL	19	16	0	2	90.1	402	102	60	57	16	1	5	8	29	0	64	5	0	4	7	.364	0	0-0	0	5.43	5.68
2002	Min	AL	32	31	1	0	180.2	783	181	92	85	26	3	3	9	70	2	124	8	0	13	8	.619	1	0-1	0	4.55	4.23
2003	Min	AL	33	33	2	0	201.0	850	211	107	103	28	8	3	5	45	1	130	10	1	14	11	.560	1	0-0	0	4.00	4.61
2004	Min	AL	35	34	1	1	194.0	883	240	128	115	28	5	7	7	76	5	111	6	0	9	13	.409	1	0-0	0	5.89	5.34
2005	Min	AL	31	30	0	1	178.2	769	211	85	83	22	3	7	9	44	5	86	4	1	9	13	.409	0	0-0	0	4.91	4.18
2006	2 Tms		34	19	0	6	126.2	567	150	83	82	15	8	5	6	44	4	97	3	1	5	10	.333	0	0-0	0	5.20	5.83
2007	2 Tms	NL	34	32	2	0	192.2	829	207	109	99	22	14	4	12	57	3	122	3	0	9	12	.429	1	0-0	0	4.45	4.62
2008	StL	NL	33	33	0	0	200.0	839	211	88	84	18	6	4	3	49	3	119	5	0	15	6	.714	0	0-0	0	3.77	3.78
06	Min	AL	22	8	0	5	63.2	295	80	50	50	8	1	3	6	25	2	46	1	1	2	5	.286	0	0-0	0	6.10	7.07
06	Cin	NL	12	11	0	1	63.0	272	70	33	32	7	7	2	0	19	2	51	2	0	3	5	.375	0	0-0	0	4.34	4.57
07	Cin	NL	21	21	2	0	131.2	561	143	76	67	14	8	4	6	33	1	80	3	0	6	12	.333	1	0-0	0	4.32	4.58
07	Phi	NL	13	11	0	0	61.0	268	64	33	32	6	6	0	6	24	2	42	0	0	3	0	1.000	0	0-0	0	4.71	4.72
Postseason			6	1	0	3	13.1	52	10	5	5	2	0	0	0	2	0	15	1	0	0	2	.000	0	0-0	0	2.12	3.38
8 ML YEARS			251	228	6	10	1364.0	5922	1513	752	708	175	48	40	59	414	23	853	44	3	78	80	.494	4	0-1	0	4.68	4.67

James Loney

Bats: L Throws: L Pos: 1B-158; PH-5; PR-1   Ht: 6'3" Wt: 220 Born: 5/7/1984 Age: 25

Year	Team	Lg	G	AB	H	2B	3B	HR	(Hm	Rd)	TB	R	RBI	RC	TBB	IBB	SO	HBP	SH	SF	SB	CS	SB%	GDP	Avg	OBP	Slg
2006	LAD	NL	48	102	29	6	5	4	(1	3)	57	20	18	17	8	1	10	1	0	0	1	0	1.00	8	.284	.342	.559
2007	LAD	NL	96	344	114	18	4	15	(5	10)	185	41	67	71	28	5	48	1	0	2	0	1	.00	6	.331	.381	.538
2008	LAD	NL	161	595	172	35	6	13	(5	8)	258	66	90	79	45	6	85	3	1	7	7	4	.64	25	.289	.338	.434
	Postseason		1	4	3	0	0	0	(0	0)	3	0	3	1	1	0	0	0	0	0	0	0	-	1	.750	.800	.750
	3 ML YEARS		305	1041	315	59	15	32	(11	21)	500	127	175	167	81	12	143	5	1	9	8	5	.62	39	.303	.353	.480

Evan Longoria

Bats: R Throws: R Pos: 3B-119; SS-1; DH-1; PH-1   Ht: 6'2" Wt: 210 Born: 10/7/1985 Age: 23

Year	Team	Lg	G	AB	H	2B	3B	HR	(Hm	Rd)	TB	R	RBI	RC	TBB	IBB	SO	HBP	SH	SF	SB	CS	SB%	GDP	Avg	OBP	Slg
2006	HudVal	A-	8	33	14	1	1	4	(-	-)	29	5	11	12	5	0	5	0	0	1	1	0	1.00	0	.424	.487	.879
2006	Visalia	A+	28	110	36	8	0	8	(-	-)	68	22	28	26	13	4	19	2	1	2	1	1	.50	2	.327	.402	.618
2006	Mont	AA	26	105	28	5	0	6	(-	-)	51	14	19	14	14	0	20	0	0	3	2	1	.67	1	.267	.266	.486
2007	Mont	AA	105	381	117	21	0	21	(-	-)	201	78	76	83	51	5	81	12	0	3	4	0	1.00	1	.307	.403	.528
2007	Drham	AAA	31	104	28	8	0	5	(-	-)	51	19	19	21	22	0	29	1	0	1	0	0	-	1	.269	.398	.490
2008	Drham	AAA	7	25	5	0	0	0	(-	-)	5	2	1	2	4	1	5	1	0	0	0	0	-	1	.200	.333	.200
2008	TB	AL	122	448	122	31	2	27	(18	9)	238	67	85	72	46	4	122	6	0	8	7	0	1.00	8	.272	.343	.531

Braden Looper

Pitches: R Bats: R Pos: SP-33   Ht: 6'3" Wt: 220 Born: 10/28/1974 Age: 34

Year	Team	Lg	G	GS	CG	GF	IP	BFP	H	R	ER	HR	SH	SF	HB	TBB	IBB	SO	WP	Bk	W	L	Pct	ShO	Sv-Op	Hld	ERC	ERA
1998	StL	NL	4	0	0	3	3.1	16	5	4	2	1	0	1	0	1	0	4	1	0	0	1	.000	0	0-2	0	8.14	5.40
1999	Fla	NL	72	0	0	22	83.0	370	96	43	35	7	5	5	1	31	6	50	2	2	3	3	.500	0	0-4	8	4.65	3.80
2000	Fla	NL	73	0	0	23	67.1	311	71	41	33	3	3	2	5	36	6	29	5	0	5	1	.833	0	2-5	18	4.55	4.41
2001	Fla	NL	71	0	0	21	71.0	295	63	28	28	8	0	3	2	30	3	52	0	0	3	3	.500	0	3-6	16	3.77	3.55
2002	Fla	NL	78	0	0	40	86.0	349	73	31	30	8	3	0	1	28	3	55	1	0	2	5	.286	0	13-16	16	2.98	3.14
2003	Fla	NL	74	0	0	64	80.2	347	82	34	33	4	3	1	1	29	1	56	2	0	6	4	.600	0	28-34	0	3.67	3.68
2004	NYM	NL	71	0	0	60	83.1	346	86	28	25	5	2	2	3	16	3	60	1	0	2	5	.286	0	29-34	0	3.28	2.70
2005	NYM	NL	60	0	0	54	59.1	271	65	31	26	7	4	0	5	22	3	27	1	0	4	7	.364	0	28-36	0	4.75	3.94
2006	StL	NL	69	0	0	28	73.1	308	76	30	29	3	7	5	2	20	5	41	0	0	9	3	.750	0	0-2	15	3.41	3.56
2007	StL	NL	31	30	0	0	175.0	746	183	100	96	22	4	6	4	51	2	87	0	3	12	12	.500	0	0-0	0	4.16	4.94
2008	StL	NL	33	33	1	0	199.0	842	216	101	92	25	7	5	11	45	1	108	3	1	12	14	.462	1	0-0	0	4.31	4.16
	Postseason		15	0	0	10	15.2	69	17	9	8	3	2	0	1	3	2	7	0	0	2	0	1.000	0	1-1	2	4.24	4.60
	11 ML YEARS		636	63	1	315	981.1	4201	1016	471	429	93	38	32	35	309	33	569	16	6	58	58	.500	1	103-139	73	4.00	3.93

Aquilino Lopez

Pitches: R Bats: R Pos: RP-48   Ht: 6'3" Wt: 187 Born: 4/21/1975 Age: 34

Year	Team	Lg	G	GS	CG	GF	IP	BFP	H	R	ER	HR	SH	SF	HB	TBB	IBB	SO	WP	Bk	W	L	Pct	ShO	Sv-Op	Hld	ERC	ERA
2008	Toledo*	AAA	3	2	0	0	11.0	39	5	3	3	1	0	0	1	0	0	14	0	0	0	0	-	0	0--	0	0.81	2.45
2003	Tor	AL	72	0	0	34	73.2	316	58	31	28	5	2	2	5	34	5	64	2	1	1	3	.250	0	14-16	16	3.04	3.42
2004	Tor	AL	18	0	0	6	21.0	95	21	15	14	5	0	1	2	13	3	13	0	0	1	1	.500	0	0-0	3	6.32	6.00
2005	2 Tms	NL	11	0	0	5	16.2	72	16	5	4	2	1	0	0	7	1	22	1	0	1	0	1.000	0	0-0	0	3.95	2.16
2007	Det	AL	10	0	0	6	17.1	76	18	10	10	2	0	2	2	6	0	7	0	0	0	0	-	0	1-1	4	4.68	5.19
2008	Det	AL	48	0	0	18	78.2	344	86	33	31	9	0	10	2	22	4	61	6	1	4	1	.800	0	0-1	4	4.17	3.55
05	Col	NL	1	0	0	0	4.0	15	3	1	1	0	0	0	0	0	0	6	0	0	0	0	-	0	0-0	0	1.13	2.25
05	Phi	NL	10	0	0	5	12.2	57	13	4	3	2	1	0	0	7	1	16	1	0	1	0	.000	0	0-0	0	5.12	2.13
	5 ML YEARS		159	0	0	69	207.1	903	199	94	87	23	3	15	11	82	13	167	9	2	6	6	.500	0	15-18	24	3.98	3.78

Felipe Lopez

Bats: B Throws: R Pos: 2B-101; LF-16; 3B-13; SS-13; PH-12; PR-3; 1B-1; RF-1   Ht: 6'0" Wt: 203 Born: 5/12/1980 Age: 29

Year	Team	Lg	G	AB	H	2B	3B	HR	(Hm	Rd)	TB	R	RBI	RC	TBB	IBB	SO	HBP	SH	SF	SB	CS	SB%	GDP	Avg	OBP	Slg
2001	Tor	AL	49	177	46	5	4	5	(3	2)	74	21	23	22	12	1	39	0	1	2	4	3	.57	2	.260	.304	.418
2002	Tor	AL	85	282	64	15	3	8	(5	3)	109	35	34	32	23	1	90	1	2	1	5	4	.56	4	.227	.287	.387
2003	Cin	NL	59	197	42	7	2	2	(0	2)	59	28	13	21	28	1	59	1	2	1	8	5	.62	2	.213	.313	.299
2004	Cin	NL	79	264	64	18	2	7	(3	4)	107	35	31	34	25	0	81	3	2	1	1	1	.50	1	.242	.314	.405
2005	Cin	NL	148	580	169	34	5	23	(16	7)	282	97	85	95	57	2	111	1	3	7	15	7	.68	8	.291	.352	.486
2006	2 Tms	NL	156	617	169	27	3	11	(5	6)	235	98	52	84	81	1	126	2	11	3	44	12	.79	9	.274	.358	.381
2007	Was	NL	154	603	148	25	6	9	(2	7)	212	70	50	63	53	1	109	4	5	6	24	9	.73	11	.245	.308	.352
2008	2 Tms	NL	143	481	136	28	2	6	(2	4)	186	64	46	56	43	2	82	3	2	3	8	1	.50	13	.283	.343	.387
06	Cin	NL	85	343	92	14	1	9	(5	4)	135	55	30	48	47	1	66	0	3	1	23	6	.79	6	.268	.355	.394
06	Was	NL	71	274	77	13	2	2	(0	2)	100	43	22	36	34	0	60	2	8	2	21	6	.78	3	.281	.362	.365
08	Was	NL	100	325	76	20	0	2	(1	1)	102	34	25	25	32	1	54	2	2	2	4	5	.44	13	.234	.305	.314
08	StL	NL	43	156	60	8	2	4	(1	3)	84	30	21	31	11	1	28	1	0	1	4	3	.57	0	.385	.426	.538
	8 ML YEARS		873	3201	838	159	27	71	(36	35)	1264	448	334	407	322	9	697	15	28	24	109	49	.69	50	.262	.330	.395

Javier Lopez

Pitches: L **Bats:** L **Pos:** RP-70 **Ht:** 6'4" **Wt:** 220 **Born:** 7/11/1977 **Age:** 31

			HOW MUCH HE PITCHED							WHAT HE GAVE UP											THE RESULTS							
Year	Team	Lg	G	GS	CG	GF	IP	BFP	H	R	ER	HR	SH	SF	HB	TBB	IBB	SO	WP	Bk	W	L	Pct	ShO	Sv-Op	Hld	ERC	ERA
2003	Col	NL	75	0	0	11	58.1	242	58	25	24	5	1	0	4	12	2	40	1	3	4	1	.800	0	1-2	15	3.44	3.70
2004	Col	NL	64	0	0	10	40.2	187	45	34	34	1	1	0	3	26	4	20	3	0	1	2	.333	0	0-1	12	5.28	7.52
2005	2 Tms	NL	32	0	0	6	16.1	87	26	20	20	2	1	0	1	11	3	11	0	0	1	1	.500	0	2-4	6	8.82	11.02
2006	Bos	AL	27	0	0	8	16.2	69	13	10	5	1	0	1	1	10	1	11	0	0	1	0	1.000	0	1-1	6	3.96	2.70
2007	Bos	AL	61	0	0	11	40.2	174	36	16	14	2	1	1	4	18	2	26	1	0	2	1	.667	0	0-2	13	3.59	3.10
2008	Bos	AL	70	0	0	10	59.1	247	53	18	16	4	1	1	2	27	0	38	1	0	2	0	1.000	0	0-1	10	3.73	2.43
05	Col	NL	3	0	0	1	2.0	13	7	5	5	0	0	0	0	0	0	0	1	0	0	0	-	0	0-1	0	18.39	22.50
05	Ari	NL	29	0	0	5	14.1	74	19	15	15	2	1	0	1	11	3	11	0	0	1	1	.500	0	2-3	6	7.63	9.42
	Postseason		5	0	0	0	2.1	14	5	4	4	0	0	1	0	2	1	0	1	0	0	0	-	0	0-0	0	11.29	15.43
	6 ML YEARS		329	0	0	56	232.0	1006	231	123	113	15	5	3	16	104	12	147	6	3	11	5	.688	0	4-11	62	4.25	4.38

Jose Lopez

Bats: R **Throws:** R **Pos:** 2B-139; 1B-13; DH-7; PH-1 **Ht:** 6'0" **Wt:** 205 **Born:** 11/24/1983 **Age:** 25

						BATTING															BASERUNNING			AVERAGES		
Year	Team	Lg	G	AB	H	2B	3B	HR	(Hm	Rd)	TB	R	RBI	RC	TBB	IBB	SO	HBP	SH	SF	SB	CS	SB%	GDP	Avg	OBP	Slg
2004	Sea	AL	57	207	48	13	0	5	(4	1)	76	28	22	20	8	0	31	1	1	1	0	1	.00	1	.232	.263	.367
2005	Sea	AL	54	190	47	19	0	2	(1	1)	72	18	25	24	6	0	25	4	1	2	4	2	.67	5	.247	.282	.379
2006	Sea	AL	151	603	170	28	8	10	(4	6)	244	78	79	84	26	1	80	9	12	5	5	2	.71	17	.282	.319	.405
2007	Sea	AL	149	524	132	17	2	11	(5	6)	186	58	62	52	20	0	64	5	9	3	2	3	.40	16	.252	.284	.355
2008	Sea	AL	159	644	191	41	1	17	(13	4)	285	80	89	83	27	5	67	1	6	9	6	3	.67	14	.297	.322	.443
	5 ML YEARS		570	2168	588	118	11	45	(27	18)	863	262	277	263	87	6	267	20	29	20	17	11	.61	53	.271	.303	.398

Rodrigo Lopez

Pitches: R **Bats:** R **Pos:** P **Ht:** 6'1" **Wt:** 185 **Born:** 12/14/1975 **Age:** 33

						HOW MUCH HE PITCHED					WHAT HE GAVE UP											THE RESULTS						
Year	Team	Lg	G	GS	CG	GF	IP	BFP	H	R	ER	HR	SH	SF	HB	TBB	IBB	SO	WP	Bk	W	L	Pct	ShO	Sv-Op	Hld	ERC	ERA
2008	Braves*	R	2	2	0	0	3.0	11	2	0	0	0	0	0	0	0	0	4	0	0	0	0	-	0	0- -	-	0.91	0.00
2008	Rome*	A	1	1	0	0	2.0	16	8	9	9	2	0	1	0	2	0	1	0	0	0	1	.000	0	0- -	-	41.46	40.50
2000	SD	NL	6	6	0	0	24.2	120	40	24	24	5	0	1	0	13	0	17	0	0	3	3	.000	0	0-0	0	9.78	8.76
2002	Bal	AL	33	28	1	0	196.2	809	172	83	78	23	2	4	5	62	4	136	2	1	15	9	.625	0	0-0	0	3.27	3.57
2003	Bal	AL	26	26	3	0	147.0	663	188	101	95	24	3	7	10	43	6	103	2	1	7	10	.412	1	0-0	0	6.00	5.82
2004	Bal	AL	37	23	1	3	170.2	714	164	71	68	21	5	2	2	54	2	121	4	1	14	9	.609	1	0-1	4	3.74	3.59
2005	Bal	AL	35	35	0	0	209.1	918	232	126	114	28	3	5	7	63	1	118	5	1	15	12	.556	0	0-0	0	4.62	4.90
2006	Bal	AL	36	29	0	2	189.0	847	234	129	124	32	5	5	4	59	2	136	6	1	9	18	.333	0	0-0	0	5.68	5.90
2007	Col	NL	14	14	0	0	79.1	333	83	43	39	11	3	5	0	21	6	43	0	0	5	4	.556	0	0-0	0	3.97	4.42
	7 ML YEARS		187	161	5	5	1016.2	4404	1113	577	542	144	21	29	28	315	21	674	19	5	65	65	.500	2	0-1	4	4.64	4.80

Mark Loretta

Bats: R **Throws:** R **Pos:** 2B-46; PH-35; 3B-17; SS-5; 1B-2 **Ht:** 6'0" **Wt:** 185 **Born:** 8/14/1971 **Age:** 37

						BATTING															BASERUNNING			AVERAGES		
Year	Team	Lg	G	AB	H	2B	3B	HR	(Hm	Rd)	TB	R	RBI	RC	TBB	IBB	SO	HBP	SH	SF	SB	CS	SB%	GDP	Avg	OBP	Slg
1995	Mil	AL	19	50	13	3	0	1	(0	1)	19	13	3	6	4	0	7	1	1	0	1	1	.50	1	.260	.327	.380
1996	Mil	AL	73	154	43	3	0	1	(0	1)	49	20	13	16	14	0	15	0	2	0	2	1	.67	7	.279	.339	.318
1997	Mil	AL	132	418	120	17	5	5	(2	3)	162	56	47	56	47	2	60	2	5	10	5	5	.50	15	.287	.354	.388
1998	Mil	NL	140	434	137	29	0	6	(3	3)	184	55	54	68	42	1	47	7	4	4	9	6	.60	14	.316	.382	.424
1999	Mil	NL	153	587	170	34	5	5	(2	3)	229	93	67	82	52	1	59	10	9	6	4	1	.80	14	.290	.354	.390
2000	Mil	NL	91	352	99	21	1	7	(3	4)	143	49	40	48	37	2	38	1	8	1	3	0	.00	9	.281	.350	.406
2001	Mil	NL	102	384	111	14	2	2	(0	2)	135	40	29	48	28	0	46	7	7	3	1	2	.33	6	.289	.346	.352
2002	2 Tms	NL	107	283	86	18	0	4	(2	2)	116	33	27	50	32	1	37	5	6	3	1	1	.50	7	.304	.381	.410
2003	SD	NL	154	589	185	28	4	13	(10	3)	260	74	72	93	54	2	62	3	3	4	5	4	.56	17	.314	.372	.441
2004	SD	NL	154	620	208	47	2	16	(11	5)	307	108	76	112	58	3	45	9	4	16	5	3	.63	10	.335	.391	.495
2005	SD	NL	105	404	113	16	1	3	(1	2)	140	54	38	53	45	4	34	8	2	4	8	4	.67	11	.280	.360	.347
2006	Bos	AL	155	635	181	33	0	5	(4	1)	229	75	59	80	49	1	63	12	2	5	4	1	.80	16	.285	.345	.361
2007	Hou	NL	133	460	132	23	2	4	(4	0)	171	52	41	60	44	0	41	3	3	1	1	2	.33	15	.287	.352	.372
2008	Hou	NL	101	261	73	15	0	4	(3	1)	100	27	38	37	29	1	30	2	0	5	0	0	-	9	.280	.350	.383
02	Mil	NL	86	217	58	14	0	2	(1	1)	78	23	19	33	23	1	32	5	6	1	0	0	-	6	.267	.350	.359
02	Hou	NL	21	66	28	4	0	2	(1	1)	38	10	8	17	9	0	5	0	0	2	1	1	.50	1	.424	.481	.576
	Postseason		3	15	4	0	0	0	(0	0)	4	0	2	1	0	0	0	0	0	0	0	0	-	1	.267	.267	.267
	14 ML YEARS		1619	5631	1671	301	22	76	(45	31)	2244	749	604	809	535	18	584	70	56	62	46	34	.58	151	.297	.361	.399

Shane Loux

Pitches: R **Bats:** R **Pos:** RP-7 **Ht:** 6'2" **Wt:** 210 **Born:** 8/31/1979 **Age:** 29

						HOW MUCH HE PITCHED					WHAT HE GAVE UP											THE RESULTS						
Year	Team	Lg	G	GS	CG	GF	IP	BFP	H	R	ER	HR	SH	SF	HB	TBB	IBB	SO	WP	Bk	W	L	Pct	ShO	Sv-Op	Hld	ERC	ERA
2008	Salt Lk*	AAA	22	22	1	0	138.0	595	154	69	61	14	1	3	6	40	0	77	3	0	12	6	.667	0	0- -	-	4.53	3.98
2002	Det	AL	3	3	0	0	14.0	64	19	16	14	4	0	1	0	3	0	7	1	0	0	3	.000	0	0-0	0	7.12	9.00
2003	Det	AL	11	4	0	1	30.1	140	37	24	24	4	1	1	4	12	1	8	1	0	1	1	.500	0	0-0	0	6.12	7.12
2008	LAA	AL	7	0	0	5	16.0	66	16	6	5	1	1	0	2	2	0	4	0	0	0	0	-	0	0-0	0	3.28	2.81
	3 ML YEARS		21	7	0	6	60.1	270	72	46	43	9	2	1	7	17	1	19	2	0	1	4	.200	0	0-0	0	5.55	6.41

Derek Lowe

Pitches: R **Bats:** R **Pos:** SP-34

Ht: 6'6" **Wt:** 230 **Born:** 6/1/1973 **Age:** 36

Year	Team	Lg	G	GS	CG	GF	IP	BFP	H	R	ER	HR	SH	SF	HB	TBB	IBB	SO	WP	Bk	W	L	Pct	ShO	Sv-Op	Hld	ERC	ERA
1997	2 Tms	AL	20	9	0	1	69.0	298	74	49	47	11	4	2	4	23	3	52	2	0	2	6	.250	0	0-2	1	4.88	6.13
1998	Bos	AL	63	10	0	8	123.0	527	126	65	55	5	4	5	4	42	5	77	8	0	3	9	.250	0	4-9	12	3.64	4.02
1999	Bos	AL	74	0	0	32	109.1	436	84	35	32	7	1	2	4	25	1	80	1	0	6	3	.667	0	15-20	22	2.14	2.63
2000	Bos	AL	74	0	0	64	91.1	379	90	27	26	6	4	1	2	22	5	79	2	1	4	4	.500	0	42-47	0	3.17	2.56
2001	Bos	AL	67	3	0	50	91.2	404	103	39	36	7	5	1	5	29	9	82	4	0	5	10	.333	0	24-30	4	4.31	3.53
2002	Bos	AL	32	32	1	0	219.2	854	166	65	63	12	5	2	12	48	0	127	5	0	21	8	.724	1	0-0	0	2.13	2.58
2003	Bos	AL	33	33	1	0	203.1	886	216	113	101	17	3	5	11	72	4	110	3	0	17	7	.708	0	0-0	0	4.32	4.47
2004	Bos	AL	33	33	0	0	182.2	839	224	138	110	15	8	4	8	71	2	105	3	0	14	12	.538	0	0-0	0	5.31	5.42
2005	LAD	NL	35	35	2	0	222.0	934	223	113	89	28	12	5	5	55	1	146	3	2	12	15	.444	2	0-0	0	3.75	3.61
2006	LAD	NL	35	34	1	1	218.0	913	221	97	88	14	7	2	5	55	2	123	3	2	16	8	.667	0	0-0	0	3.42	3.63
2007	LAD	NL	33	32	3	0	199.1	831	194	100	86	20	6	2	1	59	2	147	3	1	12	14	.462	0	0-0	0	3.55	3.88
2008	LAD	NL	34	34	1	0	211.0	851	194	84	76	14	8	7	1	45	7	147	2	0	14	11	.560	0	0-0	0	2.72	3.24
97	Sea	AL	12	9	0	1	53.0	234	59	43	41	11	2	1	2	20	2	39	2	0	2	4	.333	0	0-0	0	5.55	6.96
97	Bos	AL	8	0	0	0	16.0	64	15	6	6	0	2	1	2	3	1	13	0	0	0	2	.000	0	0-2	1	2.78	3.38
	Postseason		18	7	0	3	67.1	283	53	31	25	6	5	0	4	23	5	43	1	0	4	4	.500	0	1-2	1	2.70	3.34
	12 ML YEARS		533	255	9	156	1940.1	8152	1915	925	809	156	67	38	62	546	41	1275	39	6	126	107	.541	3	85-108	40	3.51	3.75

Mark Lowe

Pitches: R **Bats:** R **Pos:** RP-57

Ht: 6'3" **Wt:** 198 **Born:** 6/7/1983 **Age:** 26

Year	Team	Lg	G	GS	CG	GF	IP	BFP	H	R	ER	HR	SH	SF	HB	TBB	IBB	SO	WP	Bk	W	L	Pct	ShO	Sv-Op	Hld	ERC	ERA
2006	Sea	AL	15	0	0	3	18.2	75	12	4	4	1	1	0	2	9	1	20	1	0	1	0	1.000	0	0-0	6	2.61	1.93
2007	Sea	AL	4	0	0	1	2.2	13	2	2	2	1	0	0	0	3	0	3	0	0	0	0	-	0	0-0	2	7.69	6.75
2008	Sea	AL	57	0	0	19	63.2	303	78	44	38	6	3	3	4	34	0	55	2	0	1	5	.167	0	1-5	1	6.10	5.37
	3 ML YEARS		76	0	0	23	85.0	391	92	50	44	8	4	3	6	46	1	78	3	0	2	5	.286	0	1-5	9	5.32	4.66

Mike Lowell

Bats: R **Throws:** R **Pos:** 3B-110; DH-2; PH-1

Ht: 6'3" **Wt:** 210 **Born:** 2/24/1974 **Age:** 35

Year	Team	Lg	G	AB	H	2B	3B	HR	(Hm	Rd)	TB	R	RBI	RC	TBB	IBB	SO	HBP	SH	SF	SB	CS	SB%	GDP	Avg	OBP	Slg
2008	Pwtckt*	AAA	3	13	3	0	0	0	(-	-)	3	0	3	0	0	0	1	0	0	1	0	0	-	0	.231	.214	.231
1998	NYY	AL	8	15	4	0	0	0	(0	0)	4	1	0	1	0	0	1	0	0	0	0	0	-	0	.267	.267	.267
1999	Fla	NL	97	308	78	15	0	12	(5	7)	129	32	47	40	26	1	69	5	0	5	0	0	-	8	.253	.317	.419
2000	Fla	NL	140	508	137	38	0	22	(11	11)	241	73	91	86	54	4	75	9	0	11	4	0	1.00	4	.270	.344	.474
2001	Fla	NL	146	551	156	37	0	18	(12	6)	247	65	100	84	43	3	79	10	0	10	1	2	.33	9	.283	.340	.448
2002	Fla	NL	160	597	165	44	0	24	(13	11)	281	88	92	84	65	5	92	4	0	11	4	3	.57	16	.276	.346	.471
2003	Fla	NL	130	492	136	27	1	32	(14	18)	261	76	105	88	56	6	78	3	0	6	3	1	.75	14	.276	.350	.530
2004	Fla	NL	158	598	175	44	1	27	(14	13)	302	87	85	96	64	8	77	6	0	3	5	1	.83	17	.293	.365	.505
2005	Fla	NL	150	500	118	36	1	8	(5	3)	180	56	58	46	46	1	58	2	1	9	4	0	1.00	14	.236	.298	.360
2006	Bos	AL	153	573	163	47	1	20	(9	11)	272	79	80	77	47	5	61	4	0	7	2	2	.50	22	.284	.339	.475
2007	Bos	AL	154	589	191	37	2	21	(14	7)	295	79	120	106	53	4	71	3	0	9	3	2	.60	19	.324	.378	.501
2008	Bos	AL	113	419	115	27	0	17	(6	11)	193	58	73	59	38	2	61	5	0	6	2	2	.50	14	.274	.338	.461
	Postseason		29	97	27	8	0	4	(2	2)	47	16	20	16	11	2	12	1	0	3	1	0	1.00	2	.278	.348	.485
	11 ML YEARS		1409	5150	1438	352	6	201	(105	96)	2405	694	851	767	492	39	722	51	1	76	28	13	.68	137	.279	.343	.467

Devon Lowery

Pitches: R **Bats:** L **Pos:** RP-5

Ht: 6'1" **Wt:** 195 **Born:** 3/24/1983 **Age:** 26

Year	Team	Lg	G	GS	CG	GF	IP	BFP	H	R	ER	HR	SH	SF	HB	TBB	IBB	SO	WP	Bk	W	L	Pct	ShO	Sv-Op	Hld	ERC	ERA
2001	Royals	R	11	6	0	4	41.0	178	38	25	19	2	0	3	2	12	0	19	3	0	2	3	.400	0	1--	-	2.98	4.17
2002	Royals	R	15	0	0	12	25.2	114	25	13	11	1	3	1	1	11	1	26	2	2	3	0	.000	0	4--	-	3.60	3.86
2003	Burlgtn	A	26	10	0	11	96.1	394	78	39	36	9	4	2	3	34	0	74	4	0	6	4	.600	0	5--	-	2.98	3.36
2004	Wilmg	A+	28	28	1	0	145.0	607	139	74	59	16	8	5	6	52	0	115	2	0	9	9	.500	1	0--	-	4.01	3.66
2005	Wichta	AA	4	4	0	0	8.1	57	21	24	23	1	0	3	0	14	0	5	2	2	0	4	.000	0	0--	-	21.81	24.84
2005	Hi Dsrt	A+	14	11	0	-	70.1	306	70	34	30	8	-	0	0	25	0	50	1	0	6	3	.667	0	0--	-	3.88	3.84
2006	Wichta	AA	24	0	0	13	33.1	151	29	22	21	5	0	2	3	19	2	31	0	1	5	1	.833	0	4--	-	4.53	5.67
2007	Wichta	AA	6	0	0	4	7.1	43	12	11	9	2	1	0	1	10	1	7	2	1	0	1	.000	0	0--	-	15.12	11.05
2007	Royals	R	2	2	0	0	4.0	16	4	1	1	0	0	0	0	0	0	9	0	0	0	0	-	0	0--	-	1.95	2.25
2008	NWArk	AA	9	0	0	5	13.0	54	8	2	1	0	0	0	1	5	0	17	0	0	1	0	1.000	0	2--	-	1.66	0.69
2008	Omha	AAA	31	0	0	18	59.1	250	48	19	14	4	2	1	2	30	2	43	1	0	1	1	.500	0	5--	-	3.33	2.12
2008	KC	AL	5	0	0	2	4.1	21	6	5	5	2	0	0	0	2	0	6	0	0	0	0	-	0	0-0	0	9.49	10.38

Jed Lowrie

Bats: B **Throws:** R **Pos:** SS-49; 3B-45; 2B-3; PR-3; PH-2

Ht: 6'0" **Wt:** 180 **Born:** 4/17/1984 **Age:** 25

Year	Team	Lg	G	AB	H	2B	3B	HR	(Hm	Rd)	TB	R	RBI	RC	TBB	IBB	SO	HBP	SH	SF	SB	CS	SB%	GDP	Avg	OBP	Slg
2005	Lowell	A-	53	201	66	12	0	4	(-	-)	90	36	32	40	34	0	30	2	2	1	7	5	.58	3	.328	.429	.448
2006	Wilmg	A+	97	374	98	21	6	3	(-	-)	140	43	50	54	54	1	65	2	0	8	2	2	.50	11	.262	.352	.374
2007	Portlnd	AA	93	337	100	31	7	8	(-	-)	169	61	49	72	65	2	58	1	3	2	5	3	.63	11	.297	.410	.501
2007	Pwtckt	AAA	40	160	48	16	1	5	(-	-)	81	21	21	28	12	0	33	3	0	2	0	1	.00	0	.300	.356	.506
2008	Pwtckt	AAA	53	198	53	14	2	5	(-	-)	86	35	32	33	31	2	43	0	0	5	1	0	1.00	5	.268	.359	.434
2008	Bos	AL	81	260	67	25	3	2	(0	2)	104	34	46	35	35	0	68	1	2	8	1	0	1.00	8	.258	.339	.400

Noah Lowry

Pitches: L Bats: R Pos: P

Ht: 6'2" Wt: 205 Born: 10/10/1980 Age: 28

			HOW MUCH HE PITCHED						WHAT HE GAVE UP											THE RESULTS						
Year	Team	Lg	G	GS	CG	GF	IP	BFP	H	R	ER	HR	SH	SF	HB	TBB	IBB	SO	WP	Bk	W	L	Pct	ShO	Sv-Op	Hld	ERC	ERA
2003	SF	NL	4	0	0	3	6.1	24	1	0	0	0	0	0	1	2	0	5	0	0	0	0	-	0	0-0	0	0.50	0.00
2004	SF	NL	16	14	2	0	92.0	383	91	41	39	10	2	1	0	28	1	72	2	0	6	0	1.000	1	0-0	0	3.73	3.82
2005	SF	NL	33	33	0	0	204.2	875	193	92	86	21	13	3	7	76	1	172	2	0	13	13	.500	0	0-0	0	3.78	3.78
2006	SF	NL	27	27	1	0	159.1	689	166	89	84	21	11	7	6	56	2	84	2	1	7	10	.412	1	0-0	0	4.49	4.74
2007	SF	NL	26	26	1	0	156.0	694	155	76	68	12	14	4	5	87	2	87	5	0	14	8	.636	0	0-0	0	4.63	3.92
5 ML YEARS			106	100	4	3	618.1	2665	606	298	277	64	40	15	19	249	6	420	11	1	40	31	.563	2	0-0	0	4.12	4.03

Ryan Ludwick

Bats: R Throws: L Pos: RF-124; LF-29; CF-14; PH-13; PR-1

Ht: 6'3" Wt: 218 Born: 7/13/1978 Age: 30

									BATTING												BASERUNNING				AVERAGES		
Year	Team	Lg	G	AB	H	2B	3B	HR	(Hm	Rd)	TB	R	RBI	RC	TBB	IBB	SO	HBP	SH	SF	SB	CS	SB%	GDP	Avg	OBP	Slg
2002	Tex	AL	23	81	19	6	0	1	(1	0)	28	10	9	6	7	0	24	0	0	0	2	1	.67	4	.235	.295	.346
2003	2 Tms	AL	47	162	40	8	1	7	(2	5)	71	17	26	28	12	1	48	0	1	0	2	0	1.00	1	.247	.299	.438
2004	Cle	AL	15	50	11	2	0	2	(0	2)	19	3	4	4	2	0	14	2	0	0	0	0	-	0	.220	.278	.380
2005	Cle	AL	19	41	9	0	0	4	(3	1)	21	8	5	3	7	0	13	0	0	1	0	1	.00	1	.220	.333	.512
2007	StL	NL	120	303	81	22	0	14	(7	7)	145	42	52	45	26	1	72	7	3	0	4	4	.50	1	.267	.339	.479
2008	StL	NL	152	538	161	40	3	37	(18	19)	318	104	113	100	62	3	146	8	1	8	4	4	.50	9	.299	.375	.591
03	Tex	AL	8	26	4	1	0	0	(0	0)	5	3	0	1	4	0	9	0	0	0	0	0	-	0	.154	.267	.192
03	Cle	AL	39	136	36	7	1	7	(2	5)	66	14	26	27	8	1	39	0	1	0	2	0	1.00	1	.265	.306	.485
6 ML YEARS			376	1175	321	78	4	65	(31	34)	602	184	209	186	116	5	317	17	5	8	12	10	.55	16	.273	.345	.512

Julio Lugo

Bats: R Throws: R Pos: SS-81; LF-1; PH-1

Ht: 6'1" Wt: 175 Born: 11/16/1975 Age: 33

									BATTING												BASERUNNING				AVERAGES		
Year	Team	Lg	G	AB	H	2B	3B	HR	(Hm	Rd)	TB	R	RBI	RC	TBB	IBB	SO	HBP	SH	SF	SB	CS	SB%	GDP	Avg	OBP	Slg
2000	Hou	NL	116	420	119	22	5	10	(6	4)	181	78	40	62	37	0	93	4	3	1	22	9	.71	9	.283	.346	.431
2001	Hou	NL	140	513	135	20	3	10	(6	4)	191	93	37	63	46	0	116	5	15	7	12	11	.52	7	.263	.326	.372
2002	Hou	NL	88	322	84	15	1	8	(6	2)	125	45	35	43	28	3	74	2	4	2	9	3	.75	6	.261	.322	.388
2003	2 Tms		139	498	135	16	4	15	(5	10)	204	64	55	68	44	1	100	4	7	3	12	4	.75	7	.271	.333	.410
2004	TB	AL	157	581	160	41	4	7	(3	4)	230	83	75	86	54	0	106	5	7	8	21	5	.81	8	.275	.338	.396
2005	TB	AL	158	616	182	36	6	6	(0	6)	248	89	57	94	61	0	72	6	3	4	39	11	.78	5	.295	.362	.403
2006	2 Tms		122	435	121	22	2	12	(7	5)	183	69	37	65	39	0	76	4	5	3	24	9	.73	9	.278	.341	.421
2007	Bos	AL	147	570	135	36	2	8	(2	6)	199	71	73	65	48	0	82	0	8	4	33	6	.85	9	.237	.294	.349
2008	Bos	AL	82	261	70	13	0	1	(1	0)	86	27	22	20	34	0	51	4	3	5	12	4	.75	13	.268	.355	.330
03	Hou	NL	22	65	16	3	0	0	(0	0)	19	6	2	7	9	1	12	0	0	0	2	1	.67	2	.246	.338	.292
03	TB	AL	117	433	119	13	4	15	(5	10)	185	58	53	61	35	0	88	4	7	3	10	3	.77	5	.275	.333	.427
06	TB	AL	73	289	89	17	1	12	(7	5)	144	53	27	52	27	0	47	3	3	0	18	4	.82	7	.308	.373	.498
06	LAD	NL	49	146	32	5	1	0	(0	0)	39	16	10	9	12	0	29	1	2	3	6	5	.55	2	.219	.278	.267
Postseason			19	60	14	4	0	0	(0	0)	18	8	3	3	6	0	12	0	0	2	1	1	.50	6	.233	.303	.300
9 ML YEARS			1149	4216	1141	221	27	77	(36	41)	1647	619	431	562	391	4	770	34	55	37	184	62	.75	73	.271	.335	.391

Hector Luna

Bats: R Throws: R Pos: PH-1; PR-1

Ht: 6'1" Wt: 190 Born: 2/1/1980 Age: 29

									BATTING												BASERUNNING				AVERAGES		
Year	Team	Lg	G	AB	H	2B	3B	HR	(Hm	Rd)	TB	R	RBI	RC	TBB	IBB	SO	HBP	SH	SF	SB	CS	SB%	GDP	Avg	OBP	Slg
2008	Syrcse*	AAA	116	429	120	24	1	11	(-	-)	179	67	43	61	30	1	73	5	0	2	6	2	.75	4	.280	.333	.417
2004	StL	NL	83	173	43	7	2	3	(1	2)	63	25	22	20	13	0	37	2	1	3	6	3	.67	2	.249	.304	.364
2005	StL	NL	64	137	39	10	2	1	(0	1)	56	26	18	19	9	0	25	4	2	1	10	2	.83	4	.285	.344	.409
2006	2 Tms		113	350	100	21	2	6	(1	5)	143	41	38	46	27	1	60	1	0	1	5	4	.56	7	.286	.338	.409
2007	Tor	AL	22	42	7	0	0	1	(1	0)	10	5	4	1	2	0	10	1	0	1	2	0	1.00	0	.167	.217	.238
2008	Tor	AL	2	1	1	0	0	0	(0	0)	1	0	0	0	0	0	0	0	0	0	0	0	-	0	1.000	1.000	1.000
06	StL	NL	76	223	65	14	1	4	(1	3)	93	27	21	32	21	1	34	1	0	0	5	3	.63	3	.291	.355	.417
06	Cle	AL	37	127	35	7	1	2	(0	2)	50	14	17	14	6	0	26	0	0	1	0	1	.00	4	.276	.306	.394
Postseason			5	9	0	0	0	0	(0	0)	0	0	0	0	0	0	5	0	0	0	0	0	-	0	.000	.000	.000
5 ML YEARS			284	703	190	38	6	11	(3	8)	273	97	82	86	51	1	132	8	3	6	23	10	.70	13	.270	.324	.388

Brandon Lyon

Pitches: R Bats: R Pos: RP-61

Ht: 6'1" Wt: 195 Born: 8/10/1979 Age: 29

			HOW MUCH HE PITCHED						WHAT HE GAVE UP											THE RESULTS						
Year	Team	Lg	G	GS	CG	GF	IP	BFP	H	R	ER	HR	SH	SF	HB	TBB	IBB	SO	WP	Bk	W	L	Pct	ShO	Sv-Op	Hld	ERC	ERA
2001	Tor	AL	11	11	0	0	63.0	261	63	31	30	6	2	6	1	15	0	35	0	1	5	4	.556	0	0-0	0	3.50	4.29
2002	Tor	AL	15	10	0	0	62.0	279	78	47	45	14	3	2	2	19	2	30	2	0	1	4	.200	0	0-1	0	6.24	6.53
2003	Bos	AL	49	0	0	31	59.0	273	73	33	27	6	1	4	2	19	5	50	0	0	4	6	.400	0	9-12	2	4.96	4.12
2005	Ari	NL	32	0	0	22	29.1	144	44	25	21	6	2	1	2	10	2	17	1	1	0	2	.000	0	14-15	1	7.72	6.44
2006	Ari	NL	68	0	0	22	69.1	293	68	32	30	7	3	4	0	22	7	46	1	0	2	4	.333	0	0-7	23	3.49	3.89
2007	Ari	NL	73	0	0	20	74.0	307	70	25	22	2	3	2	1	22	2	40	3	1	3	2	.600	0	2-5	35	2.93	2.68
2008	Ari	NL	61	0	0	50	59.1	265	75	34	31	7	2	1	0	13	1	44	1	0	3	5	.375	0	26-31	3	4.86	4.70
Postseason			5	0	0	1	6.0	20	1	0	0	0	0	0	0	1	0	5	0	0	0	0	-	0	0-0	2	0.19	0.00
7 ML YEARS			309	21	0	145	416.0	1822	471	227	206	48	16	20	8	120	19	262	8	3	21	29	.420	0	51-71	64	4.45	4.46

Mike MacDougal

Pitches: R Bats: R Pos: RP-16   Ht: 6'4" Wt: 175 Born: 3/5/1977 Age: 32

Year	Team	Lg	G	GS	CG	GF	IP	BFP	H	R	ER	HR	SH	SF	HB	TBB	IBB	SO	WP	Bk	W	L	Pct	ShO	Sv-Op	Hld	ERC	ERA
2008	Charltt*	AAA	38	2	0	21	49.1	227	47	22	21	2	1	2	2	30	3	65	14	0	0	4	.000	0	4- -	-	4.11	3.83
2001	KC	AL	3	3	0	0	15.1	67	18	10	8	2	0	0	1	4	0	7	3	0	1	1	.500	0	0-0	0	5.04	4.70
2002	KC	AL	6	0	0	1	9.0	38	5	5	5	0	0	0	0	7	1	10	1	0	0	1	.000	0	0-0	0	2.26	5.00
2003	KC	AL	68	0	0	61	64.0	285	64	36	29	4	3	2	8	32	0	57	6	0	3	5	.375	0	27-35	1	4.76	4.08
2004	KC	AL	13	0	0	8	11.1	61	16	8	7	2	0	0	1	9	0	14	2	0	1	1	.500	0	1-3	0	9.04	5.56
2005	KC	AL	68	0	0	53	70.1	298	69	32	26	6	1	1	3	24	2	72	6	1	5	6	.455	0	21-25	0	3.80	3.33
2006	2 Tms		29	0	0	7	29.0	110	21	5	5	1	1	0	1	6	0	21	1	0	1	1	.500	0	1-2	11	1.80	1.55
2007	CWS	AL	54	0	0	8	42.1	208	50	37	32	3	0	1	2	33	3	39	8	0	2	5	.286	0	0-3	19	6.49	6.80
2008	CWS	AL	16	0	0	8	17.0	78	16	4	4	0	0	0	2	12	2	12	4	1	0	0	-	0	0-0	0	4.45	2.12
06	KC	AL	4	0	0	3	4.0	13	2	0	0	0	0	0	0	0	0	2	0	0	0	0	-	0	1-1	0	0.58	0.00
06	CWS	AL	25	0	0	4	25.0	97	19	5	5	1	1	0	1	6	0	19	1	0	1	1	.500	0	0-1	11	2.10	1.80
8 ML YEARS			257	3	0	146	258.1	1145	259	137	116	18	5	4	18	127	8	232	31	2	13	20	.394	0	50-68	31	4.48	4.04

Drew Macias

Bats: L Throws: L Pos: PH-12; LF-4; RF-3   Ht: 6'3" Wt: 175 Born: 3/7/1983 Age: 26

Year	Team	Lg	G	AB	H	2B	3B	HR	(Hm	Rd)	TB	R	RBI	RC	TBB	IBB	SO	HBP	SH	SF	SB	CS	SB%	GDP	Avg	OBP	Slg
2003	Idaho	R+	61	239	60	10	4	2	(-	-)	84	41	13	30	19	1	32	5	6	1	15	4	.79	8	.251	.318	.351
2003	FtWyn	A	1	2	0	0	0	0	(-	-)	0	0	0	0	0	0	1	0	1	0	0	0	-	1	.000	.000	.000
2004	FtWyn	A	129	478	127	18	5	8	(-	-)	179	60	55	64	49	1	68	8	4	6	16	14	.53	7	.266	.340	.374
2005	Lk Els	A+	128	492	142	23	6	6	(-	-)	195	79	66	70	46	3	78	6	5	2	15	15	.50	7	.289	.355	.396
2006	Mobile	AA	134	430	110	20	3	7	(-	-)	157	43	46	52	44	3	94	8	1	3	4	12	.25	5	.256	.334	.365
2007	SnAnt	AA	100	331	83	15	5	8	(-	-)	132	43	50	49	51	3	53	5	0	4	5	8	.38	6	.251	.355	.399
2007	Portlnd	AAA	31	110	31	6	1	2	(-	-)	45	14	11	19	21	0	25	0	0	1	3	1	.75	1	.282	.397	.409
2008	SnAnt	AA	136	504	145	27	4	11	(-	-)	213	92	66	92	83	1	81	8	3	5	18	6	.75	14	.288	.393	.423
2007	SD	NL	1	0	0	0	0	0	(0	0)	0	0	0	0	0	0	0	0	0	0	0	0	-	0	-	-	-
2008	SD	NL	17	20	4	0	0	2	(1	1)	10	2	5	1	2	0	6	0	1	2	0	0	-	1	.200	.250	.500
2 ML YEARS			18	20	4	0	0	2	(1	1)	10	3	5	1	2	0	6	0	1	2	0	0	-	1	.200	.250	.500

Rob Mackowiak

Bats: L Throws: R Pos: PH-24; LF-12; RF-2   Ht: 5'11" Wt: 181 Born: 6/20/1976 Age: 33

Year	Team	Lg	G	AB	H	2B	3B	HR	(Hm	Rd)	TB	R	RBI	RC	TBB	IBB	SO	HBP	SH	SF	SB	CS	SB%	GDP	Avg	OBP	Slg
2008	Lsvlle*	AAA	49	141	36	2	1	5	(-	-)	55	31	15	28	37	2	42	5	1	0	4	1	.80	2	.255	.426	.390
2001	Pit	NL	83	214	57	15	2	4	(3	1)	88	30	21	28	15	5	52	3	2	3	4	3	.57	3	.266	.319	.411
2002	Pit	NL	136	385	94	22	0	16	(9	7)	164	57	48	57	42	5	120	7	3	2	9	3	.75	0	.244	.328	.426
2003	Pit	NL	77	174	47	4	4	6	(1	5)	77	20	19	27	15	2	53	4	0	0	6	0	1.00	1	.270	.342	.443
2004	Pit	NL	155	491	121	22	6	17	(11	6)	206	65	75	73	50	2	114	6	1	7	13	4	.76	3	.246	.319	.420
2005	Pit	NL	142	463	126	21	3	9	(7	2)	180	57	58	59	43	4	100	3	2	1	8	4	.67	7	.272	.337	.389
2006	CWS	AL	112	255	74	12	1	5	(2	3)	103	31	23	35	28	3	59	3	2	2	5	2	.71	1	.290	.365	.404
2007	2 Tms		113	293	77	14	2	6	(4	2)	113	40	38	37	26	1	71	8	0	2	4	1	.80	7	.263	.337	.386
2008	Was	NL	38	53	7	1	0	1	(0	1)	11	7	4	4	8	0	17	1	0	1	0	0	-	1	.132	.254	.208
07	CWS	AL	85	237	66	11	2	6	(4	2)	99	34	36	37	23	1	53	6	0	2	3	1	.75	5	.278	.341	.418
07	SD	NL	28	56	11	3	0	0	(0	0)	14	6	2	0	3	0	18	2	0	0	1	0	1.00	2	.196	.262	.250
8 ML YEARS			856	2328	603	111	18	64	(37	27)	942	307	286	320	227	22	586	35	10	18	49	17	.74	23	.259	.332	.405

Matt Macri

Bats: R Throws: R Pos: 3B-11; PH-4; 1B-2; 2B-2   Ht: 6'2" Wt: 215 Born: 5/29/1982 Age: 27

Year	Team	Lg	G	AB	H	2B	3B	HR	(Hm	Rd)	TB	R	RBI	RC	TBB	IBB	SO	HBP	SH	SF	SB	CS	SB%	GDP	Avg	OBP	Slg
2004	TriCity	A-	52	195	65	17	4	7	(-	-)	111	33	43	44	23	1	52	5	0	4	5	4	.44	8	.333	.410	.569
2005	Mdest	A+	64	244	69	16	1	7	(-	-)	108	40	34	44	33	0	67	7	6	2	6	1	.86	3	.283	.381	.443
2005	Tulsa	AA	1	3	0	0	0	0	(-	-)	0	1	0	0	1	0	0	0	0	0	0	0	-	0	.000	.250	.000
2006	Tulsa	AA	83	288	67	12	2	8	(-	-)	107	35	35	32	22	1	66	5	6	5	2	4	.33	4	.233	.294	.372
2007	Tulsa	AA	79	275	82	23	0	11	(-	-)	138	46	33	47	20	0	58	2	0	1	4	4	.50	4	.298	.349	.502
2007	ColSpr	AAA	3	9	6	2	0	1	(-	-)	11	1	4	5	0	0	0	0	0	0	1	0	1.00	0	.667	.667	1.222
2007	Roch	AAA	14	47	10	1	0	3	(-	-)	20	5	6	5	3	0	13	0	0	0	1	0	1.00	0	.213	.260	.426
2008	Roch	AAA	89	313	81	24	4	11	(-	-)	146	35	48	48	26	0	84	5	3	3	2	2	.50	4	.259	.323	.466
2008	Min	AL	18	34	11	1	0	1	(0	1)	15	3	4	5	2	0	10	0	0	0	1	1	.50	0	.324	.361	.441

Greg Maddux

Pitches: R Bats: R Pos: SP-33   Ht: 6'0" Wt: 197 Born: 4/14/1966 Age: 43

Year	Team	Lg	G	GS	CG	GF	IP	BFP	H	R	ER	HR	SH	SF	HB	TBB	IBB	SO	WP	Bk	W	L	Pct	ShO	Sv-Op	Hld	ERC	ERA
1986	ChC	NL	6	5	1	1	31.0	144	44	20	19	3	1	0	1	11	2	20	2	0	2	4	.333	0	0-0	0	6.45	5.52
1987	ChC	NL	30	27	1	2	155.2	701	181	111	97	17	7	1	4	74	13	101	4	7	6	14	.300	1	0-0	0	5.42	5.61
1988	ChC	NL	34	34	9	0	249.0	1047	230	97	88	13	11	2	9	81	16	140	3	6	18	8	.692	3	0-0	0	3.09	3.18
1989	ChC	NL	35	35	7	0	238.1	1002	222	90	78	13	18	6	6	82	13	135	5	3	19	12	.613	1	0-0	0	3.20	2.95
1990	ChC	NL	35	35	8	0	237.0	1011	242	116	91	11	18	5	4	71	10	144	3	0	15	15	.500	2	0-0	0	3.41	3.46
1991	ChC	NL	37	37	7	0	263.0	1070	232	113	98	18	16	3	6	66	9	198	6	3	15	11	.577	2	0-0	0	2.73	3.35
1992	ChC	NL	35	35	9	0	268.0	1061	201	68	65	7	15	3	14	70	7	199	5	0	20	11	.645	4	0-0	0	2.01	2.18
1993	Atl	NL	36	36	8	0	267.0	1064	228	85	70	14	15	7	6	52	7	197	5	1	20	10	.667	1	0-0	0	2.32	2.36
1994	Atl	NL	25	25	10	0	202.0	774	150	44	35	4	6	5	6	31	3	156	3	1	16	6	.727	3	0-0	0	1.59	1.56
1995	Atl	NL	28	28	10	0	209.2	785	147	39	38	8	9	1	4	23	3	181	1	0	19	2	.905	3	0-0	0	1.41	1.63

(continued)

Year	Team	Lg	G	GS	CG	GF	IP	BFP	H	R	ER	HR	SH	SF	HB	TBB	IBB	SO	WP	Bk	W	L	Pct	ShO	Sv-Op	Hld	ERC	ERA
1996	Atl	NL	35	35	5	0	245.0	978	225	85	74	11	8	5	3	28	11	172	4	0	15	11	.577	1	0-0	0	2.22	2.72
1997	Atl	NL	33	33	5	0	232.2	893	200	58	57	9	11	7	6	20	6	177	0	0	19	4	.826	2	0-0	0	1.95	2.20
1998	Atl	NL	34	34	9	0	251.0	987	201	75	62	13	15	5	7	45	10	204	4	0	18	9	.667	5	0-0	0	2.01	2.22
1999	Atl	NL	33	33	4	0	219.1	940	258	103	87	16	15	5	4	37	8	136	1	0	19	9	.679	0	0-0	0	3.95	3.57
2000	Atl	NL	35	35	0	0	249.1	1012	225	91	83	19	8	5	10	42	12	190	1	2	19	9	.679	3	0-0	0	2.60	3.00
2001	Atl	NL	34	34	3	0	233.0	927	220	86	79	20	12	11	7	27	10	173	2	0	17	11	.607	3	0-0	0	2.70	3.05
2002	Atl	NL	34	34	0	0	199.1	820	194	67	58	14	13	4	4	45	7	118	1	0	16	6	.727	0	0-0	0	3.11	2.62
2003	Atl	NL	36	36	1	0	218.1	901	225	112	96	24	10	9	8	33	7	124	3	0	16	11	.593	0	0-0	0	3.44	3.96
2004	ChC	NL	33	33	2	0	212.2	872	218	103	95	35	12	8	9	33	4	151	2	0	16	11	.593	1	0-0	0	3.86	4.02
2005	ChC	NL	35	35	3	0	225.0	936	239	112	106	29	19	6	7	36	4	136	8	0	13	15	.464	0	0-0	0	3.77	4.24
2006	2 Tms	NL	34	34	0	0	210.0	862	219	109	98	20	11	5	0	37	7	117	0	0	15	14	.517	0	0-0	0	3.39	4.20
2007	SD	NL	34	34	1	0	198.0	830	221	92	91	14	15	8	6	25	3	104	5	0	14	11	.560	0	0-0	0	3.54	4.14
2008	2 Tms	NL	33	33	0	0	194.0	804	204	105	91	21	9	8	6	30	5	98	2	2	8	13	.381	0	0-0	0	3.55	4.22
06	ChC	NL	22	22	0	0	136.1	572	153	78	71	14	7	3	0	23	3	81	0	0	9	11	.450	0	0-0	0	3.83	4.69
06	LAD	NL	12	12	0	0	73.2	290	66	31	27	6	4	2	0	14	4	36	0	0	6	3	.667	0	0-0	0	2.61	3.30
08	SD	NL	26	26	0	0	153.1	638	161	80	68	16	6	6	5	26	4	80	2	2	6	9	.400	0	0-0	0	3.57	3.99
08	LAD	NL	7	7	0	0	40.2	166	43	25	23	5	3	2	1	4	1	18	0	0	2	4	.333	0	0-0	0	3.44	5.09
Postseason			32	30	2	1	194.0	818	191	95	72	14	10	2	9	50	15	122	4	0	11	14	.440	0	1-1	0	3.30	3.34
23 ML YEARS			744	740	109	3	5008.1	20421	4726	1981	1756	353	274	119	137	999	177	3371	70	28	355	227	.610	35	0-0	0	2.88	3.16

Warner Madrigal

Pitches: R Bats: R Pos: RP-30; SP-1   Ht: 6'0" Wt: 200 Born: 3/21/1984 Age: 25

Year	Team	Lg	G	GS	CG	GF	IP	BFP	H	R	ER	HR	SH	SF	HB	TBB	IBB	SO	WP	Bk	W	L	Pct	ShO	Sv-Op	Hld	ERC	ERA
2006	Angels	R	12	0	0	11	12.0	50	11	5	5	0	2	0	1	3	0	13	0	1	2	1	.667	0	5--	-	2.71	3.75
2007	CRpds	A	54	0	0	40	61.0	247	44	18	14	3	4	1	1	23	1	75	3	1	5	4	.556	0	20--	-	2.26	2.07
2008	Frisco	AA	14	0	0	13	15.2	64	11	4	3	1	0	1	0	8	1	18	1	0	1	0	1.000	0	10--	-	2.62	1.72
2008	Okla	AAA	17	0	0	11	20.1	91	20	10	9	2	0	2	0	8	2	25	3	0	0	0	-	0	4--	-	3.61	3.98
2008	Tex	AL	31	1	0	10	36.0	154	36	22	19	4	1	2	0	14	0	22	2	0	0	2	.000	0	1-3	3	4.13	4.75

Ryan Madson

Pitches: R Bats: L Pos: RP-76   Ht: 6'6" Wt: 200 Born: 8/28/1980 Age: 28

Year	Team	Lg	G	GS	CG	GF	IP	BFP	H	R	ER	HR	SH	SF	HB	TBB	IBB	SO	WP	Bk	W	L	Pct	ShO	Sv-Op	Hld	ERC	ERA
2003	Phi	NL	1	0	0	0	2.0	6	0	0	0	0	0	0	0	0	0	0	0	0	0	0	-	0	0-0	0	0.00	0.00
2004	Phi	NL	52	1	0	14	77.0	312	68	23	20	6	1	1	5	19	4	55	7	0	9	3	.750	0	1-2	7	2.95	2.34
2005	Phi	NL	78	0	0	10	87.0	365	84	44	40	11	5	5	6	25	6	79	6	1	6	5	.545	0	0-7	32	3.83	4.14
2006	Phi	NL	50	17	0	0	134.1	620	176	92	85	20	9	3	10	50	4	99	12	0	11	9	.550	0	2-4	6	6.50	5.69
2007	Phi	NL	38	0	0	9	56.0	237	48	19	19	5	2	2	2	23	4	43	2	2	2	2	.500	0	1-2	7	3.28	3.05
2008	Phi	NL	76	0	0	14	82.2	340	79	29	28	6	3	2	1	23	4	67	2	1	4	2	.667	0	1-3	17	3.20	3.05
6 ML YEARS			295	18	0	55	439.0	1880	455	207	192	48	20	13	24	140	22	343	29	4	32	21	.604	0	5-18	69	4.20	3.94

Ron Mahay

Pitches: L Bats: L Pos: RP-57   Ht: 6'2" Wt: 190 Born: 6/28/1971 Age: 38

Year	Team	Lg	G	GS	CG	GF	IP	BFP	H	R	ER	HR	SH	SF	HB	TBB	IBB	SO	WP	Bk	W	L	Pct	ShO	Sv-Op	Hld	ERC	ERA
1997	Bos	AL	28	0	0	7	25.0	105	19	7	7	3	1	0	0	11	0	22	3	0	3	0	1.000	0	0-1	5	3.01	2.52
1998	Bos	AL	29	0	0	6	26.0	120	26	16	10	2	0	4	2	15	1	14	3	0	1	1	.500	0	1-2	7	4.76	3.46
1999	Oak	AL	6	1	0	2	19.1	68	8	4	4	2	0	0	0	3	0	15	0	0	2	0	1.000	0	1-1	0	0.88	1.86
2000	2 Tms		23	2	0	7	41.1	199	57	35	33	10	1	2	0	25	1	32	4	0	1	1	.500	0	0-0	2	8.55	7.19
2001	ChC	NL	17	0	0	4	20.2	86	14	6	6	4	0	0	0	15	1	24	1	0	0	0	-	0	0-0	2	4.32	2.61
2002	ChC	NL	11	0	0	1	14.2	65	13	14	14	6	0	0	0	8	0	14	0	0	2	0	1.000	0	0-0	0	6.11	8.59
2003	Tex	AL	35	0	0	5	45.1	189	33	19	16	3	0	0	0	20	7	38	4	0	3	3	.500	0	0-3	9	2.31	3.18
2004	Tex	AL	60	0	0	12	67.0	290	60	23	19	5	4	0	2	29	5	54	2	0	3	0	1.000	0	0-2	14	3.39	2.55
2005	Tex	AL	30	0	0	9	35.2	167	47	28	27	8	0	1	0	16	1	30	2	0	2	0	.000	0	1-1	6	7.10	6.81
2006	Tex	AL	62	0	0	14	57.0	246	54	30	25	7	1	1	0	28	2	56	1	0	1	3	.250	0	0-1	9	4.28	3.95
2007	2 Tms		58	0	0	8	67.0	281	52	20	19	4	3	2	1	37	2	55	1	1	3	0	1.000	0	1-2	7	3.23	2.55
2008	KC	AL	57	0	0	3	64.2	278	61	27	25	6	0	6	1	29	0	49	1	0	5	0	1.000	0	0-1	21	3.98	3.48
00	Oak	AL	5	2	0	1	16.0	82	26	18	16	4	1	1	0	9	0	5	2	0	0	1	.000	0	0-0	0	9.97	9.00
00	Fla	NL	18	0	0	6	25.1	117	31	17	17	6	0	1	0	16	1	27	2	0	1	0	1.000	0	0-0	2	7.67	6.04
07	Tex	AL	28	0	0	8	39.0	164	33	12	12	3	1	1	1	21	0	32	0	1	1	0	1.000	0	1-1	1	3.81	2.77
07	Atl	NL	30	0	0	0	28.0	117	19	8	7	1	2	1	0	16	2	23	1	0	1	0	1.000	0	0-1	6	2.47	2.25
12 ML YEARS			416	3	0	78	483.2	2094	444	229	205	60	10	16	6	236	20	403	22	1	24	10	.706	0	4-14	82	4.11	3.81

Paul Maholm

Pitches: L Bats: L Pos: SP-31   Ht: 6'2" Wt: 220 Born: 6/25/1982 Age: 27

Year	Team	Lg	G	GS	CG	GF	IP	BFP	H	R	ER	HR	SH	SF	HB	TBB	IBB	SO	WP	Bk	W	L	Pct	ShO	Sv-Op	Hld	ERC	ERA
2005	Pit	NL	6	6	0	0	41.1	168	31	16	10	2	0	3	0	17	0	26	0	0	3	1	.750	0	0-0	0	2.79	2.18
2006	Pit	NL	30	30	0	0	176.0	788	202	98	93	19	7	4	12	81	6	117	3	1	8	10	.444	0	0-0	0	5.58	4.76
2007	Pit	NL	29	29	2	0	177.2	765	204	110	99	22	13	6	6	49	3	105	5	0	10	15	.400	1	0-0	0	4.77	5.02
2008	Pit	NL	31	31	1	0	206.1	853	201	89	85	21	8	8	9	63	2	139	2	1	9	9	.500	0	0-0	0	3.84	3.71
4 ML YEARS			96	96	3	0	601.1	2574	638	307	287	64	28	18	30	210	11	387	10	2	30	35	.462	1	0-0	0	4.53	4.30

Mitch Maier

Bats: L **Throws:** R **Pos:** CF-34; RF-4; PR-2; PH-1 **Ht:** 6'2" **Wt:** 210 **Born:** 6/30/1982 **Age:** 27

Year	Team	Lg	G	AB	H	2B	3B	HR	(Hm	Rd)	TB	R	RBI	RC	TBB	IBB	SO	HBP	SH	SF	SB	CS	SB%	GDP	Avg	OBP	Slg
2003	Royals	R	51	203	71	14	6	2	(-	-)	103	41	45	41	18	0	25	2	0	3	7	3	.70	4	.350	.403	.507
2004	Burlgtn	A	82	317	95	24	3	4	(-	-)	137	41	36	52	27	4	51	0	0	1	34	10	.77	3	.300	.354	.432
2004	Wilmg	A+	51	174	46	9	2	3	(-	-)	68	25	17	24	15	0	29	2	1	2	9	2	.82	3	.264	.326	.391
2005	Hi Dsrt	A+	50	211	71	26	1	8	(-	-)	123	42	32	44	12	1	43	1	0	3	6	1	.86	5	.336	.370	.583
2005	Wichta	AA	80	322	82	21	5	7	(-	-)	134	55	49	40	15	1	47	2	0	3	10	3	.77	4	.255	.289	.416
2006	Wichta	AA	138	543	166	35	7	14	(-	-)	257	95	92	92	41	1	96	7	3	9	13	12	.52	8	.306	.357	.473
2007	Omha	AAA	140	544	152	29	5	14	(-	-)	233	75	62	78	33	0	89	4	6	9	7	2	.78	8	.279	.320	.428
2008	Omha	AAA	85	345	109	24	1	9	(-	-)	162	57	41	61	29	0	42	1	3	5	12	3	.80	3	.316	.366	.470
2006	KC	AL	5	13	2	0	0	0	(0	0)	2	3	0	0	2	0	4	0	0	0	0	0	-	1	.154	.267	.154
2008	KC	AL	34	91	26	1	1	0	(0	0)	29	9	9	7	2	0	18	2	2	0	0	2	.00	3	.286	.316	.319
2 ML YEARS			39	104	28	1	1	0	(0	0)	31	12	9	7	4	0	22	2	2	0	0	2	.00	4	.269	.309	.298

John Maine

Pitches: R **Bats:** R **Pos:** SP-25 **Ht:** 6'4" **Wt:** 200 **Born:** 5/8/1981 **Age:** 28

Year	Team	Lg	G	GS	CG	GF	IP	BFP	H	R	ER	HR	SH	SF	HB	TBB	IBB	SO	WP	Bk	W	L	Pct	ShO	Sv-Op	Hld	ERC	ERA
2004	Bal	AL	1	1	0	0	3.2	19	7	4	4	1	0	0	0	3	0	1	1	0	0	1	.000	0	0-0	0	14.87	9.82
2005	Bal	AL	10	8	0	1	40.0	184	39	30	28	8	0	2	1	24	0	24	0	1	2	3	.400	0	0-0	0	5.47	6.30
2006	NYM	NL	16	15	1	1	90.0	365	69	40	36	15	3	1	2	33	1	71	3	0	6	5	.545	1	0-0	0	3.22	3.60
2007	NYM	NL	32	32	1	0	191.0	810	168	90	83	23	11	4	5	75	3	180	2	0	15	10	.600	1	0-0	0	3.58	3.91
2008	NYM	NL	25	25	0	0	140.0	608	122	70	65	16	10	5	4	67	2	122	10	0	10	8	.556	0	0-0	0	3.81	4.18
Postseason			3	3	0	0	13.2	62	10	5	4	1	1	0	1	11	2	13	0	0	1	0	1.000	0	0-0	0	3.93	2.63
5 ML YEARS			84	81	2	2	464.2	1986	405	234	216	63	24	12	12	202	6	398	16	1	33	27	.550	2	0-0	0	3.80	4.18

Gary Majewski

Pitches: R **Bats:** R **Pos:** RP-37 **Ht:** 6'1" **Wt:** 219 **Born:** 2/26/1980 **Age:** 29

Year	Team	Lg	G	GS	CG	GF	IP	BFP	H	R	ER	HR	SH	SF	HB	TBB	IBB	SO	WP	Bk	W	L	Pct	ShO	Sv-Op	Hld	ERC	ERA
2008	Lsvlle*	AAA	22	0	0	8	26.1	107	27	11	11	2	0	0	0	7	0	22	3	0	2	1	.667	0	3- -		3.67	3.76
2004	Mon	NL	16	0	0	7	21.0	95	28	15	9	2	1	1	2	5	1	12	0	0	0	1	.000	0	1-2	0	5.68	3.86
2005	Was	NL	79	0	0	24	86.0	376	80	32	28	2	5	4	7	37	6	50	1	0	4	4	.500	0	1-5	24	3.43	2.93
2006	2 Tms	NL	65	0	0	21	70.1	316	79	38	36	5	1	3	4	29	3	43	6	0	4	4	.500	0	0-7	6	4.76	4.61
2007	Cin	NL	32	0	0	3	23.0	113	43	22	21	3	0	0	2	3	1	10	0	0	0	4	.000	0	0-3	6	9.01	8.22
2008	Cin	NL	37	0	0	8	40.0	192	61	31	29	6	2	4	3	15	0	27	1	0	1	0	1.000	0	0-1	2	8.04	6.53
06	Was	NL	46	0	0	14	55.1	237	49	24	22	4	1	0	1	25	1	34	6	0	3	2	.600	0	0-5	6	3.48	3.58
06	Cin	NL	19	0	0	7	15.0	79	30	14	14	1	0	3	3	4	2	9	0	0	1	2	.333	0	0-2	2	10.33	8.40
5 ML YEARS			229	0	0	63	240.1	1092	291	138	123	18	9	12	18	89	11	142	8	0	9	13	.409	0	2-18	40	5.21	4.61

Charlie Manning

Pitches: L **Bats:** L **Pos:** RP-57 **Ht:** 6'2" **Wt:** 185 **Born:** 3/31/1979 **Age:** 30

Year	Team	Lg	G	GS	CG	GF	IP	BFP	H	R	ER	HR	SH	SF	HB	TBB	IBB	SO	WP	Bk	W	L	Pct	ShO	Sv-Op	Hld	ERC	ERA
2001	StIslnd	A-	14	14	0	0	80.0	326	73	33	31	4	0	2	5	21	0	87	5	0	8	4	.667	0	0- -		3.06	3.49
2002	Tampa	A+	17	16	0	0	100.0	419	82	48	36	4	3	4	10	31	0	85	5	3	6	4	.600	0	0- -		2.72	3.24
2002	Nrwich	AA	11	11	1	0	63.0	263	55	27	25	1	0	1	2	26	0	61	3	0	4	2	.667	1	0- -		3.03	3.57
2003	Trntn	AA	23	6	0	5	46.0	216	53	34	32	1	2	3	1	35	2	34	5	0	2	2	.000	0	0- -		5.94	6.26
2003	Tampa	A+	6	6	0	0	31.1	134	27	14	12	2	1	1	1	15	1	25	2	0	2	4	.333	0	0- -		3.44	3.45
2003	Ptomc	A+	6	6	0	0	37.2	145	24	7	5	1	0	1	1	11	0	31	1	0	5	0	1.000	0	0- -		1.60	1.19
2004	Chatt	AA	13	13	1	0	70.1	303	79	42	40	5	3	6	2	21	0	71	1	0	4	4	.500	0	0- -		4.32	5.12
2004	Trntn	AA	15	1	0	3	24.1	109	31	11	11	1	0	1	3	6	0	19	0	1	2	1	.667	0	0- -		5.16	4.07
2004	Clmbs	AAA	11	0	0	4	12.1	54	10	6	5	0	0	0	1	6	0	11	0	0	1	1	.500	0	0- -		2.91	3.65
2005	Trntn	AA	45	0	0	16	73.0	321	66	33	27	6	1	3	6	37	2	68	3	0	4	3	.571	0	2- -		4.10	3.33
2005	Clmbs	AAA	7	0	0	0	9.2	46	8	6	6	0	0	0	0	9	1	6	0	0	1	1	.500	0	0- -		4.06	5.59
2006	Trntn	AA	48	1	0	14	83.0	340	60	30	25	5	2	3	3	28	2	81	2	0	8	3	.727	0	1- -		2.21	2.71
2006	Clmbs	AAA	1	0	0	0	1.0	7	3	3	0	0	0	0	0	0	0	1	0	0	0	0	-	0	-		12.36	0.00
2007	S-WB	AAA	34	1	0	18	51.2	225	41	27	25	2	2	1	3	24	1	59	2	0	3	2	.600	0	2- -		2.87	4.35
2007	Trntn	AA	7	0	0	2	9.2	36	4	0	0	0	0	0	0	2	0	9	0	0	1	0	1.000	0	1- -		0.65	0.00
2008	Clmbs	AAA	19	0	0	7	27.2	114	20	8	6	1	1	2	1	13	1	34	2	0	0	0	-	0	6- -		2.55	1.95
2008	Was	NL	57	0	0	7	42.0	189	35	25	24	8	2	0	0	31	2	37	2	0	1	3	.250	0	0-2	7	5.04	5.14

Shaun Marcum

Pitches: R **Bats:** R **Pos:** SP-25 **Ht:** 6'0" **Wt:** 180 **Born:** 12/14/1981 **Age:** 27

Year	Team	Lg	G	GS	CG	GF	IP	BFP	H	R	ER	HR	SH	SF	HB	TBB	IBB	SO	WP	Bk	W	L	Pct	ShO	Sv-Op	Hld	ERC	ERA
2008	Dnedin*	A+	1	1	0	0	4.0	14	0	0	0	0	0	0	0	0	0	6	1	0	0	0	-	0	0- -		0.00	0.00
2008	Syrcse*	AAA	2	2	0	0	13.0	53	10	5	4	0	0	1	0	3	0	15	0	0	0	1	.000	0	0- -		1.64	2.77
2005	Tor	AL	5	0	0	3	8.0	32	6	0	0	0	0	0	0	4	0	4	0	0	0	0	-	0	0-0	0	2.58	0.00
2006	Tor	AL	21	14	0	3	78.1	357	87	44	44	14	1	2	4	38	3	65	1	0	3	4	.429	0	0-0	0	5.80	5.06
2007	Tor	AL	38	25	0	6	159.0	660	149	76	73	27	3	3	5	49	1	122	1	0	12	6	.667	0	1-2	1	4.00	4.13
2008	Tor	AL	25	25	0	0	151.1	630	126	60	57	21	1	3	8	50	2	123	3	0	9	7	.563	0	0-0	0	3.32	3.39
4 ML YEARS			89	64	0	12	396.2	1679	368	180	174	62	5	8	17	141	6	314	5	0	24	17	.585	0	1-2	1	4.04	3.95

Nick Markakis

Bats: L Throws: L Pos: RF-156; PH-2   Ht: 6'2" Wt: 195 Born: 11/17/1983 Age: 25

																			BASERUNNING				AVERAGES		
Year	Team	Lg	G	AB	H	2B	3B	HR	(Hm | Rd)	TB	R	RBI	RC	TBB	IBB	SO	HBP	SH	SF	SB	CS	SB%	GDP	Avg	OBP	Slg
2006	Bal	AL	147	491	143	25	2	16	(9 | 7)	220	72	62	67	43	3	72	3	3	2	2	0	1.00	15	.291	.351	.448
2007	Bal	AL	161	637	191	43	3	23	(15 | 8)	309	97	112	103	61	5	112	5	1	6	18	6	.75	22	.300	.362	.485
2008	Bal	AL	157	595	182	48	1	20	(11 | 9)	292	106	87	113	99	7	113	2	0	1	10	7	.59	10	.306	.406	.491
3 ML YEARS			465	1723	516	116	6	59	(35 | 24)	821	275	261	283	203	15	297	10	4	9	30	13	.70	47	.299	.375	.476

Carlos Marmol

Pitches: R Bats: R Pos: RP-82   Ht: 6'2" Wt: 180 Born: 10/14/1982 Age: 26

			HOW MUCH HE PITCHED						WHAT HE GAVE UP										THE RESULTS						
Year	Team	Lg	G	GS	CG	GF	IP	BFP	H	R	ER	HR	SH	SF	HB	TBB	IBB	SO	WP	Bk	W	L	Pct	ShO	Sv-Op	Hld	ERC	ERA
2006	ChC	NL	19	13	0	1	77.0	356	71	54	52	14	6	2	5	59	2	59	3	1	5	7	.417	0	0-0	0	6.01	6.08
2007	ChC	NL	59	0	0	6	69.1	285	41	11	11	3	1	2	4	35	3	96	5	1	5	1	.833	0	1-2	16	2.11	1.43
2008	ChC	NL	82	0	0	22	87.1	348	40	30	26	10	2	3	6	41	3	114	6	1	2	4	.333	0	7-9	30	1.86	2.68
Postseason			2	0	0	0	3.0	15	3	3	3	2	0	1	0	3	0	6	0	0	0	1	.000	0	0-0	0	11.34	9.00
3 ML YEARS			160	13	0	29	233.2	989	152	95	89	27	9	7	15	135	8	269	14	3	12	12	.500	0	8-11	46	3.15	3.43

Jason Marquis

Pitches: R Bats: L Pos: SP-28; RP-1   Ht: 6'1" Wt: 210 Born: 8/21/1978 Age: 30

			HOW MUCH HE PITCHED						WHAT HE GAVE UP										THE RESULTS						
Year	Team	Lg	G	GS	CG	GF	IP	BFP	H	R	ER	HR	SH	SF	HB	TBB	IBB	SO	WP	Bk	W	L	Pct	ShO	Sv-Op	Hld	ERC	ERA
2000	Atl	NL	15	0	0	7	23.1	103	23	16	13	4	1	1	1	12	1	17	1	0	1	0	1.000	0	0-1	1	5.13	5.01
2001	Atl	NL	38	16	0	9	129.1	556	113	62	50	14	6	5	4	59	4	98	1	2	5	6	.455	0	0-2	2	3.70	3.48
2002	Atl	NL	22	22	0	0	114.1	507	127	66	64	19	4	3	3	49	3	84	4	0	8	9	.471	0	0-0	0	5.43	5.04
2003	Atl	NL	21	2	0	10	40.2	182	43	27	25	3	0	3	2	18	2	19	2	0	0	0	-	0	1-1	0	4.45	5.53
2004	StL	NL	32	32	0	0	201.1	874	215	90	83	26	5	6	10	70	1	138	6	0	15	7	.682	0	0-0	0	4.69	3.71
2005	StL	NL	33	33	3	0	207.0	868	206	110	95	29	4	3	5	69	2	100	10	3	13	14	.481	1	0-0	0	4.23	4.13
2006	StL	NL	33	33	0	0	194.1	870	221	136	130	35	12	3	16	75	2	96	2	1	14	16	.467	0	0-0	0	5.79	6.02
2007	ChC	NL	34	33	1	0	191.2	846	190	111	98	22	13	1	13	76	6	109	3	0	12	9	.571	1	0-0	0	4.28	4.60
2008	ChC	NL	29	28	0	0	167.0	738	172	87	84	15	10	7	8	70	6	91	8	1	11	9	.550	0	0-0	1	4.35	4.53
Postseason			9	3	0	4	21.2	107	23	16	11	5	4	1	0	18	1	13	0	0	0	2	.000	0	0-0	0	6.99	4.57
9 ML YEARS			257	198	4	26	1269.0	5544	1310	705	642	167	55	32	62	498	27	752	37	7	79	70	.530	2	1-4	4	4.63	4.55

Sean Marshall

Pitches: L Bats: L Pos: RP-27; SP-7   Ht: 6'7" Wt: 220 Born: 8/30/1982 Age: 26

			HOW MUCH HE PITCHED						WHAT HE GAVE UP										THE RESULTS						
Year	Team	Lg	G	GS	CG	GF	IP	BFP	H	R	ER	HR	SH	SF	HB	TBB	IBB	SO	WP	Bk	W	L	Pct	ShO	Sv-Op	Hld	ERC	ERA
2008	Iowa*	AAA	7	7	0	0	31.2	126	26	13	12	2	0	1	1	6	1	25	0	0	1	1	.500	0	0-	-	2.22	3.41
2006	ChC	NL	24	24	0	0	125.2	563	132	85	78	20	7	1	7	59	3	77	6	0	6	9	.400	0	0-0	0	5.27	5.59
2007	ChC	NL	21	19	0	0	103.1	446	107	52	45	13	7	2	1	35	3	67	4	0	7	8	.467	0	0-0	0	4.18	3.92
2008	ChC	NL	34	7	0	6	65.1	279	60	28	28	9	4	3	4	23	4	58	3	0	3	5	.375	0	1-2	3	3.82	3.86
3 ML YEARS			79	50	0	6	294.1	1288	299	165	151	42	18	6	12	117	10	202	13	0	16	22	.421	0	1-2	3	4.55	4.62

Lou Marson

Bats: R Throws: R Pos: C-1   Ht: 6'1" Wt: 202 Born: 6/26/1986 Age: 23

																			BASERUNNING				AVERAGES		
Year	Team	Lg	G	AB	H	2B	3B	HR	(Hm | Rd)	TB	R	RBI	RC	TBB	IBB	SO	HBP	SH	SF	SB	CS	SB%	GDP	Avg	OBP	Slg
2004	Phillies	R	38	113	29	3	0	4	(- | -)	44	18	8	16	13	0	18	0	0	0	4	0	1.00	4	.257	.333	.389
2005	Batvia	A-	60	220	54	11	3	5	(- | -)	86	25	25	29	27	0	52	1	3	1	0	1	.00	12	.245	.329	.391
2006	Lakwd	A	104	350	85	16	5	4	(- | -)	123	44	39	47	49	1	82	5	1	5	4	0	1.00	13	.243	.343	.351
2007	Clrwtr	A+	111	393	113	24	1	7	(- | -)	160	68	63	64	52	2	80	5	1	6	3	1	.75	10	.288	.373	.407
2008	Rdng	AA	94	322	101	18	0	5	(- | -)	134	55	46	64	68	2	70	2	0	3	3	3	.50	10	.314	.433	.416
2008	Phi	NL	1	4	2	0	0	1	(1 | 0)	5	2	2	2	0	0	2	0	0	0	0	0	-	0	.500	.500	1.250

Andy Marte

Bats: R Throws: R Pos: 3B-76; PH-7; 1B-1; DH-1   Ht: 6'1" Wt: 205 Born: 10/21/1983 Age: 25

																			BASERUNNING				AVERAGES		
Year	Team	Lg	G	AB	H	2B	3B	HR	(Hm | Rd)	TB	R	RBI	RC	TBB	IBB	SO	HBP	SH	SF	SB	CS	SB%	GDP	Avg	OBP	Slg
2005	Atl	NL	24	57	8	2	1	0	(0 | 0)	12	3	4	1	7	0	13	0	0	2	0	1	.00	2	.140	.227	.211
2006	Cle	AL	50	164	37	15	1	5	(3 | 2)	69	20	23	21	13	0	38	1	0	0	0	0	-	3	.226	.287	.421
2007	Cle	AL	20	57	11	4	0	1	(0 | 1)	18	3	8	4	2	0	9	1	0	0	0	0	-	0	.193	.233	.316
2008	Cle	AL	80	235	52	11	1	3	(2 | 1)	74	21	17	17	14	0	52	1	7	0	1	2	.33	5	.221	.268	.315
4 ML YEARS			174	513	108	32	3	9	(5 | 4)	173	47	52	43	36	0	112	3	7	2	1	3	.25	10	.211	.265	.337

Damaso Marte

Pitches: L Bats: L Pos: RP-72   Ht: 6'2" Wt: 213 Born: 2/14/1975 Age: 34

			HOW MUCH HE PITCHED						WHAT HE GAVE UP										THE RESULTS						
Year	Team	Lg	G	GS	CG	GF	IP	BFP	H	R	ER	HR	SH	SF	HB	TBB	IBB	SO	WP	Bk	W	L	Pct	ShO	Sv-Op	Hld	ERC	ERA
1999	Sea	AL	5	0	0	2	8.2	47	16	9	9	3	0	0	0	6	0	3	0	0	0	1	.000	0	0-0	0	13.32	9.35
2001	Pit	NL	23	0	0	4	36.1	154	34	21	19	5	1	2	3	12	3	39	1	0	0	1	.000	0	0-0	0	3.93	4.71
2002	CWS	AL	68	0	0	22	60.1	240	44	19	19	5	1	1	4	18	2	72	3	1	1	1	.500	0	10-12	14	2.42	2.83
2003	CWS	AL	71	0	0	25	79.2	314	50	16	14	3	3	3	3	34	6	87	1	0	4	2	.667	0	11-18	14	1.96	1.58
2004	CWS	AL	74	0	0	24	73.2	303	56	28	28	10	2	6	3	34	4	68	3	0	6	5	.545	0	6-12	21	3.39	3.42

Year Team	Lg	G	GS	CG	GF	IP	BFP	H	R	ER	HR	SH	SF	HB	TBB	IBB	SO	WP	Bk	W	L	Pct	ShO	Sv-Op	Hld	ERC	ERA
2005 CWS	AL	66	0	0	15	45.1	213	45	21	19	5	1	0	3	33	4	54	1	1	3	4	.429	0	4-8	22	5.51	3.77
2006 Pit	NL	75	0	0	15	58.1	255	51	30	24	5	8	3	4	31	6	63	3	1	1	7	.125	0	0-4	13	3.88	3.70
2007 Pit	NL	65	0	0	11	45.1	182	32	14	12	2	0	2	2	18	1	51	0	1	2	0	1.000	0	0-0	15	2.35	2.38
2008 2 Tms		72	0	0	10	65.0	272	52	29	29	5	1	0	2	26	2	71	1	0	5	3	.625	0	5-7	25	2.90	4.02
08 Pit	NL	47	0	0	8	46.2	192	38	18	18	4	0	0	1	16	1	47	1	0	4	0	1.000	0	5-7	15	2.82	3.47
08 NYY	AL	25	0	0	8	18.1	80	14	11	11	1	1	0	1	10	1	24	0	0	1	3	.250	0	0-0	10	3.07	5.40
Postseason		2	0	0	0	1.2	11	1	0	0	0	0	0	0	4	0	3	0	0	1	0	1.000	0	0-0	0	7.68	0.00
9 ML YEARS		519	0	0	128	472.2	1980	380	187	173	43	17	17	24	212	28	508	13	4	22	24	.478	0	36-61	124	3.27	3.29

Russell Martin

Bats: R **Throws:** R **Pos:** C-149; 3B-11; PH-7; DH-1 **Ht:** 5'10" **Wt:** 210 **Born:** 2/15/1983 **Age:** 26

Year Team	Lg	G	AB	H	2B	3B	HR	(Hm	Rd)	TB	R	RBI	RC	TBB	IBB	SO	HBP	SH	SF	SB	CS	SB%	GDP	Avg	OBP	Slg
2006 LAD	NL	121	415	117	26	4	10	(8	2)	181	65	65	58	45	8	57	4	1	3	10	5	.67	17	.282	.355	.436
2007 LAD	NL	151	540	158	32	3	19	(8	11)	253	87	87	84	67	1	89	7	0	6	21	9	.70	16	.293	.374	.469
2008 LAD	NL	155	553	155	25	0	13	(6	7)	219	87	69	89	90	8	83	5	0	2	18	6	.75	16	.280	.385	.396
Postseason		3	12	4		0	0	(0	0)	4	2	0	1	1	0	2	0	0	0	0	0	-	0	.333	.385	.333
3 ML YEARS		427	1508	430	83	7	42	(22	20)	653	239	221	231	202	17	229	16	1	11	49	20	.71	49	.285	.373	.433

Pedro Martinez

Pitches: R **Bats:** R **Pos:** SP-20 **Ht:** 5'11" **Wt:** 193 **Born:** 10/25/1971 **Age:** 37

Year Team	Lg	G	GS	CG	GF	IP	BFP	H	R	ER	HR	SH	SF	HB	TBB	IBB	SO	WP	Bk	W	L	Pct	ShO	Sv-Op	Hld	ERC	ERA
2008 StLuci*	A+	1	1	0	0	6.0	23	4	2	2	0	0	0	0	0	0	6	0	0	0	1	.000	0	0--	-	0.87	3.00
1992 LAD	NL	2	1	0	1	8.0	31	6	2	2	0	0	0	0	1	0	8	0	0	0	1	.000	0	0-0	0	1.38	2.25
1993 LAD	NL	65	2	0	20	107.0	444	76	34	31	5	0	5	4	57	4	119	3	1	10	5	.667	0	2-3	14	2.79	2.61
1994 Mon	NL	24	23	1	1	144.2	584	115	58	55	11	2	3	11	45	3	142	6	0	11	5	.688	1	1-1	0	2.81	3.42
1995 Mon	NL	30	30	2	0	194.2	784	158	79	76	21	7	3	11	66	1	174	5	2	14	10	.583	2	0-0	0	3.19	3.51
1996 Mon	NL	33	33	4	0	216.2	901	189	100	89	19	9	6	3	70	3	222	6	0	13	10	.565	1	0-0	0	3.02	3.70
1997 Mon	NL	31	31	13	0	241.1	947	158	65	51	16	9	1	9	67	5	305	3	1	17	8	.680	4	0-0	0	1.79	1.90
1998 Bos	AL	33	33	3	0	233.2	951	188	82	75	26	4	7	8	67	3	251	9	0	19	7	.731	2	0-0	0	2.78	2.89
1999 Bos	AL	31	29	5	1	213.1	835	160	56	49	9	3	6	9	37	1	313	6	0	23	4	.852	1	0-0	0	1.79	2.07
2000 Bos	AL	29	29	7	0	217.0	817	128	44	42	17	2	1	14	32	0	284	1	0	18	6	.750	4	0-0	0	1.39	1.74
2001 Bos	AL	18	18	1	0	116.2	456	84	33	31	5	2	0	6	25	0	163	4	0	7	3	.700	0	0-0	0	1.84	2.39
2002 Bos	AL	30	30	2	0	199.1	787	144	62	50	13	2	4	15	40	1	239	3	0	20	4	.833	1	0-0	0	1.98	2.26
2003 Bos	AL	29	29	3	0	186.2	749	147	52	46	7	4	4	9	47	0	206	5	0	14	4	.778	0	0-0	0	2.22	2.22
2004 Bos	AL	33	33	1	0	217.0	903	193	99	94	26	5	9	16	61	0	227	2	0	16	9	.640	1	0-0	0	3.44	3.90
2005 NYM	NL	31	31	4	0	217.0	843	159	69	68	19	9	2	4	47	3	208	4	0	15	8	.652	1	0-0	0	2.03	2.82
2006 NYM	NL	23	23	0	0	132.2	550	108	72	66	19	6	5	10	39	2	137	2	1	9	8	.529	0	0-0	0	3.18	4.48
2007 NYM	NL	5	5	0	0	28.0	128	33	11	8	0	1	2	2	7	1	32	1	0	3	1	.750	0	0-0	0	3.80	2.57
2008 NYM	NL	20	20	0	0	109.0	493	127	70	68	19	7	4	6	44	3	87	2	1	5	6	.455	0	0-0	0	5.80	5.61
Postseason		13	11	0	1	79.1	324	63	30	30	7	0	0	6	26	0	80	1	0	6	2	.750	0	0-0	0	2.95	3.40
17 ML YEARS		467	400	46	23	2782.2	11203	2173	988	901	232	72	62	137	752	30	3117	62	6	214	99	.684	17	3-4	14	2.51	2.91

Ramon Martinez

Bats: R **Throws:** R **Pos:** 2B-5; PH-1; PR-1 **Ht:** 6'0" **Wt:** 190 **Born:** 10/10/1972 **Age:** 36

Year Team	Lg	G	AB	H	2B	3B	HR	(Hm	Rd)	TB	R	RBI	RC	TBB	IBB	SO	HBP	SH	SF	SB	CS	SB%	GDP	Avg	OBP	Slg
2008 LsVgs*	AAA	28	101	29	7	0	2	(-	-)	42	15	13	15	9	0	6	2	1	2	0	0	-	5	.287	.351	.416
2008 Ddgrs*	R	2	6	1	0	0	0	(-	-)	1	1	0	0	1	0	2	0	0	0	0	0	-	0	.167	.286	.167
2008 NewOr*	AAA	25	86	25	1	0	0	(-	-)	26	8	5	11	12	1	11	1	1	2	1	1	.50	3	.291	.376	.302
1998 SF	NL	19	19	6	1	0	0	(0	0)	7	4	0	4	4	0	2	0	1	0	0	0	-	0	.316	.435	.368
1999 SF	NL	61	144	38	6	0	5	(3	2)	59	21	19	19	14	0	17	0	6	1	1	2	.33	2	.264	.327	.410
2000 SF	NL	88	189	57	13	2	6	(4	2)	92	30	25	31	15	1	22	1	4	1	3	2	.60	6	.302	.354	.487
2001 SF	NL	128	391	99	18	3	5	(1	4)	138	48	37	44	38	6	52	5	6	6	1	2	.33	11	.253	.323	.353
2002 SF	NL	72	181	49	10	2	4	(4	0)	75	26	25	33	14	2	26	4	0	1	2	0	1.00	5	.271	.335	.414
2003 ChC	NL	108	293	83	16	1	3	(3	0)	110	30	34	34	24	1	50	2	6	8	0	1	.00	8	.283	.333	.375
2004 ChC	NL	102	260	64	15	1	3	(1	2)	90	22	30	28	26	3	40	1	7	4	1	0	1.00	5	.246	.313	.346
2005 2 Tms		52	112	31	3	0	1	(1	0)	37	11	14	14	6	0	11	1	4	4	0	0	-	2	.277	.309	.330
2006 LAD	NL	82	176	49	7	1	2	(1	1)	64	20	24	22	15	1	20	1	2	0	0	0	-	9	.278	.339	.364
2007 LAD	NL	67	129	25	4	0	0	(0	0)	29	10	27	11	11	0	15	0	2	5	1	0	1.00	5	.194	.248	.225
2008 NYM	NL	7	16	4	3	0	0	(0	0)	7	0	3	2	2	0	3	0	0	0	0	0	-	1	.250	.333	.438
05 Det	AL	19	56	15	1	0	0	(0	0)	16	4	5	7	3	0	4	0	2	1	0	0	-	1	.268	.300	.286
05 Phi	NL	33	56	16	2	0	1	(1	0)	21	7	9	7	3	0	7	1	2	3	0	0	-	1	.286	.317	.375
Postseason		16	20	3	1	0	0	(0	0)	4	0	2	1	1	0	8	0	1	0	0	0	-	0	.150	.190	.200
11 ML YEARS		786	1910	505	96	10	29	(18	11)	708	222	238	242	169	14	258	15	38	30	9	7	.56	45	.264	.324	.371

Victor Martinez

Bats: B **Throws:** R **Pos:** C-55; 1B-10; DH-5; PH-5 **Ht:** 6'2" **Wt:** 210 **Born:** 12/23/1978 **Age:** 30

Year Team	Lg	G	AB	H	2B	3B	HR	(Hm	Rd)	TB	R	RBI	RC	TBB	IBB	SO	HBP	SH	SF	SB	CS	SB%	GDP	Avg	OBP	Slg
2008 Akron*	AA	2	6	2	0	0	1	(-	-)	5	1	1	1	1	0	2	0	0	0	0	0	-	0	.333	.429	.833
2008 Buffalo*	AAA	6	20	6	2	0	0	(-	-)	8	2	2	3	4	0	4	0	0	1	0	0	-	0	.300	.400	.400
2002 Cle	AL	12	32	9	1	0	1	(1	0)	13	2	5	5	3	0	2	0	0	1	0	0	-	1	.281	.333	.406
2003 Cle	AL	49	159	46	4	0	1	(1	0)	53	15	16	17	13	0	21	1	0	1	1	1	.50	8	.289	.345	.333
2004 Cle	AL	141	520	147	38	1	23	(8	15)	256	77	108	90	60	11	69	5	0	6	0	0	.00	16	.283	.359	.492
2005 Cle	AL	147	547	167	33	0	20	(10	10)	260	73	80	90	63	9	78	5	0	7	0	1	.00	16	.305	.378	.475

Year	Team	Lg	G	AB	H	2B	3B	HR	(Hm	Rd)	TB	R	RBI	RC	TBB	IBB	SO	HBP	SH	SF	SB	CS	SB%	GDP	Avg	OBP	Slg
2006	Cle	AL	153	572	181	37	0	16	(4	12)	266	82	93	96	71	8	78	3	0	6	0	0	-	27	.316	.391	.465
2007	Cle	AL	147	562	169	40	0	25	(12	13)	284	78	114	108	62	12	76	10	0	11	0	0	-	19	.301	.374	.505
2008	Cle	AL	73	266	74	17	0	2	(2	0)	97	30	35	36	24	4	32	1	0	3	0	0	-	12	.278	.337	.365
Postseason			11	44	14	2	0	2	(1	1)	22	6	7	8	4	3	8	1	0	0	0	0	-	0	.318	.388	.500
7 ML YEARS			722	2658	793	170	1	88	(37	51)	1229	357	451	442	296	44	356	25	0	35	1	3	.25	99	.298	.370	.462

Shairon Martis

Pitches: R **Bats:** R **Pos:** SP-4; RP-1   **Ht:** 6'1" **Wt:** 175 **Born:** 3/30/1987 **Age:** 22

Year	Team	Lg	G	GS	CG	GF	IP	BFP	H	R	ER	HR	SH	SF	HB	TBB	IBB	SO	WP	Bk	W	L	Pct	ShO	Sv-Op	Hld	ERC	ERA
2005	Giants	R	11	5	0	4	34.0	137	28	10	7	1	3	0	1	9	0	50	3	0	2	1	.667	0	1--	-	2.33	1.85
2006	Augsta	A	15	15	0	0	76.2	325	76	39	31	3	2	2	4	21	0	66	3	0	6	4	.600	0	0--	-	3.31	3.64
2006	Savann	A	4	4	0	0	21.1	86	23	9	9	2	0	1	0	4	0	14	0	1	1	1	.500	0	0--	-	3.79	3.80
2006	Ptomc	A+	2	2	0	0	12.0	47	9	5	4	0	0	0	1	3	0	7	1	0	2	0	.000	0	0--	-	1.99	3.00
2006	Hrsbrg	AA	1	1	0	0	5.0	26	8	7	7	4	0	0	0	3	0	1	0	0	0	1	.000	0	0--	-	14.97	12.60
2007	Ptomc	A+	27	26	1	0	151.0	645	150	83	71	9	3	4	5	52	0	108	11	2	14	8	.636	0	0--	-	3.68	4.23
2007	Hrsbrg	AA	14	14	0	0	74.2	317	73	35	33	5	4	2	0	28	1	57	3	0	4	4	.500	0	0--	-	3.62	3.98
2008	Clmbs	AAA	7	7	0	0	41.2	182	42	17	14	2	0	3	1	17	0	42	3	1	1	2	.333	0	0--	-	3.85	3.02
2008	Was	NL	5	4	0	0	20.2	92	18	14	13	5	0	1	0	12	0	23	1	0	1	3	.250	0	0-0	0	4.98	5.66

Nick Masset

Pitches: R **Bats:** R **Pos:** RP-41; SP-1   **Ht:** 6'4" **Wt:** 235 **Born:** 5/17/1982 **Age:** 27

Year	Team	Lg	G	GS	CG	GF	IP	BFP	H	R	ER	HR	SH	SF	HB	TBB	IBB	SO	WP	Bk	W	L	Pct	ShO	Sv-Op	Hld	ERC	ERA
2006	Tex	AL	8	0	0	7	8.0	36	9	4	4	0	0	2	2	2	0	4	0	0	0	0	-	0	0-0	0	4.05	4.15
2007	CWS	AL	27	1	0	4	39.1	193	52	33	31	2	1	3	2	26	5	21	4	0	2	3	.400	0	0-1	2	6.63	7.09
2008	2 Tms		42	1	0	12	62.0	271	71	32	27	7	3	1	2	26	4	43	3	1	2	0	1.000	0	1-3	2	5.27	3.92
08	CWS	AL	32	1	0	11	44.2	203	55	26	23	4	3	1	2	21	4	32	2	1	1	0	1.000	0	1-1	1	5.78	4.63
08	Cin	NL	10	0	0	1	17.1	68	16	6	4	3	0	0	0	5	0	11	1	0	1	0	1.000	0	0-2	1	3.93	2.08
3 ML YEARS			77	2	0	23	110.0	500	132	69	62	9	4	6	6	54	9	68	7	1	4	3	.571	0	1-4	4	5.66	5.07

Justin Masterson

Pitches: R **Bats:** R **Pos:** RP-27; SP-9   **Ht:** 6'6" **Wt:** 250 **Born:** 3/22/1985 **Age:** 24

Year	Team	Lg	G	GS	CG	GF	IP	BFP	H	R	ER	HR	SH	SF	HB	TBB	IBB	SO	WP	Bk	W	L	Pct	ShO	Sv-Op	Hld	ERC	ERA
2006	Lowell	A-	14	0	0	1	31.2	120	20	4	3	0	0	0	3	2	0	33	1	0	3	1	.750	0	0--	-	1.12	0.85
2007	Lancst	A+	17	17	0	0	95.2	410	103	56	46	4	2	5	6	22	0	56	1	0	8	5	.615	0	0--	-	3.66	4.33
2007	Portlnd	AA	10	10	0	0	58.0	239	49	29	28	4	1	0	2	18	0	59	3	0	4	3	.571	0	0--	-	2.83	4.34
2008	Portlnd	AA	8	8	0	0	38.1	169	37	22	18	0	0	1	3	16	0	37	2	0	1	3	.250	0	0--	-	3.48	4.23
2008	Pwtckt	AAA	4	1	0	0	9.1	35	6	4	3	1	2	0	1	1	0	8	1	0	1	0	1.000	0	0--	-	1.70	2.89
2008	Bos	AL	36	9	0	6	88.1	365	68	31	31	10	1	1	8	40	3	68	1	0	6	5	.545	0	0-1	3	3.51	3.16

Tom Mastny

Pitches: R **Bats:** R **Pos:** RP-13; SP-1   **Ht:** 6'6" **Wt:** 225 **Born:** 2/4/1981 **Age:** 28

Year	Team	Lg	G	GS	CG	GF	IP	BFP	H	R	ER	HR	SH	SF	HB	TBB	IBB	SO	WP	Bk	W	L	Pct	ShO	Sv-Op	Hld	ERC	ERA
2008	Buffalo*	AAA	28	0	0	7	35.1	141	26	10	7	1	0	0	3	12	2	43	4	0	2	2	.500	0	0--	-	2.31	1.78
2006	Cle	AL	15	0	0	12	16.1	73	17	10	10	1	1	2	1	8	1	14	0	0	0	1	.000	0	5-7	0	4.53	5.51
2007	Cle	AL	51	0	0	18	57.2	262	63	30	30	6	3	2	2	32	9	52	5	0	7	2	.778	0	0-0	7	5.16	4.68
2008	Cle	AL	14	1	0	4	20.0	100	28	24	24	6	0	1	0	11	2	19	0	0	2	2	.500	0	0-1	0	8.39	10.80
Postseason			3	0	0	1	4.2	18	2	0	0	0	2	0	0	2	0	3	0	0	1	0	1.000	0	0-0	0	1.08	0.00
3 ML YEARS			80	1	0	34	94.0	435	108	64	64	13	4	5	3	51	12	85	5	0	9	5	.643	0	5-8	7	5.71	6.13

Joe Mather

Bats: R **Throws:** R **Pos:** LF-25; PH-19; CF-15; RF-15; 1B-4; PR-4; 3B-1   **Ht:** 6'4" **Wt:** 195 **Born:** 7/23/1982 **Age:** 26

Year	Team	Lg	G	AB	H	2B	3B	HR	(Hm	Rd)	TB	R	RBI	RC	TBB	IBB	SO	HBP	SH	SF	SB	CS	SB%	GDP	Avg	OBP	Slg
2001	JhsCty	R+	45	165	41	3	0	5	(-	-)	59	25	21	17	7	0	60	3	1	2	2	2	.50	5	.248	.288	.358
2002	JhsCty	R+	62	224	52	15	2	8	(-	-)	95	29	39	33	27	0	57	3	0	2	9	1	.90	5	.232	.320	.424
2003	NewJrs	A-	65	196	45	12	1	2	(-	-)	65	23	22	21	18	0	38	6	3	0	4	4	.50	4	.230	.314	.332
2004	NewJrs	A-	3	8	1	0	0	0	(-	-)	1	0	0	0	0	0	2	0	0	0	2	0	1.00	0	.125	.125	.125
2004	Peoria	A	65	241	61	18	2	7	(-	-)	104	34	31	35	24	0	70	5	0	5	3	3	.50	7	.253	.333	.432
2005	QuadC	A	54	209	46	15	2	9	(-	-)	92	30	33	28	20	3	49	3	0	2	0	0	-	8	.220	.295	.440
2005	PlmBh	A+	57	200	55	12	2	8	(-	-)	95	37	27	34	12	1	39	9	3	1	4	0	1.00	5	.275	.342	.475
2006	PlmBh	A+	124	443	119	33	1	16	(-	-)	202	64	74	71	36	3	91	8	3	4	9	0	1.00	8	.269	.332	.456
2007	Sprgfld	AA	64	234	71	17	0	18	(-	-)	142	48	46	55	29	6	32	5	1	3	4	0	1.00	2	.303	.387	.607
2007	Memp	AAA	70	253	61	10	1	13	(-	-)	112	32	31	39	23	0	51	10	2	0	6	0	1.00	12	.241	.329	.443
2008	Memp	AAA	59	211	64	14	2	17	(-	-)	133	45	41	54	32	0	36	8	1	2	7	2	.78	6	.303	.411	.630
2008	StL	NL	54	133	32	7	0	8	(2	6)	63	20	18	18	12	1	32	1	0	1	1	0	1.00	2	.241	.306	.474

Doug Mathis

Pitches: R Bats: R Pos: SP-4; RP-4   Ht: 6'3" Wt: 222 Born: 6/7/1983 Age: 26

Year	Team	Lg	G	GS	CG	GF	IP	BFP	H	R	ER	HR	SH	SF	HB	TBB	IBB	SO	WP	Bk	W	L	Pct	ShO	Sv-Op	Hld	ERC	ERA
2005	Spkane	A-	17	16	0	0	84.0	346	78	33	25	2	2	0	6	17	0	78	7	0	4	7	.364	0	0- -	-	2.72	2.68
2006	Bkrsfld	A+	26	25	2	1	150.2	641	160	76	70	14	2	2	8	47	0	109	8	1	10	7	.588	1	0- -	-	4.32	4.18
2006	Frisco	AA	2	2	0	0	10.0	49	14	5	4	0	0	0	1	5	1	10	0	0	0	0	-	0	0- -	-	6.21	3.60
2007	Okla	AAA	3	2	0	0	12.2	63	21	16	15	2	0	1	0	6	0	8	1	0	0	3	.000	0	0- -	-	9.09	10.66
2007	Frisco	AA	22	22	1	0	131.2	559	140	59	55	7	3	4	5	40	0	92	3	0	11	7	.611	1	0- -	-	3.93	3.76
2007	Rngrs	R	1	1	0	0	2.2	15	7	5	5	0	0	0	0	1	0	2	0	0	0	0	-	0	0- -	-	14.52	16.88
2008	Okla	AAA	10	10	0	0	53.2	222	51	28	20	7	2	4	1	14	0	36	0	0	5	1	.833	0	0- -	-	3.55	3.35
2008	Rngrs	R	1	1	0	0	2.0	7	1	1	1	1	0	0	0	0	0	3	0	0	0	0	-	0	0- -	-	1.73	4.50
2008	Tex	AL	8	4	0	3	22.1	112	37	20	17	3	1	0	0	14	2	9	1	0	2	1	.667	0	0-0	0	9.60	6.85

Jeff Mathis

Bats: R Throws: R Pos: C-94   Ht: 6'0" Wt: 200 Born: 3/31/1983 Age: 26

Year	Team	Lg	G	AB	H	2B	3B	HR	(Hm	Rd)	TB	R	RBI	RC	TBB	IBB	SO	HBP	SH	SF	SB	CS	SB%	GDP	Avg	OBP	Slg
2005	LAA	AL	5	3	1	0	0	0	(0	0)	1	1	0	0	0	0	1	0	0	0	0	0	-	0	.333	.333	.333
2006	LAA	AL	23	55	8	2	0	2	(1	1)	16	9	6	4	7	1	14	0	0	1	0	0	-	0	.145	.238	.291
2007	LAA	AL	59	171	36	12	0	4	(3	1)	60	24	23	13	15	0	49	2	3	4	0	1	.00	3	.211	.276	.351
2008	LAA	AL	94	283	55	8	0	9	(4	5)	90	35	42	33	30	4	90	3	8	4	2	2	.50	1	.194	.275	.318
	Postseason		2	3	0	0	0	0	(0	0)	0	0	1	0	0	0	0	0	0	0	0	0	-	0	.000	.000	.000
	4 ML YEARS		181	512	100	22	0	15	(8	7)	167	69	71	50	52	5	154	5	11	9	2	3	.40	4	.195	.272	.326

Osiris Matos

Pitches: R Bats: R Pos: RP-20   Ht: 6'1" Wt: 202 Born: 8/6/1984 Age: 24

Year	Team	Lg	G	GS	CG	GF	IP	BFP	H	R	ER	HR	SH	SF	HB	TBB	IBB	SO	WP	Bk	W	L	Pct	ShO	Sv-Op	Hld	ERC	ERA
2002	Giants	R	13	13	0	0	62.0	268	63	35	32	3	1	5	3	22	0	51	1	1	4	2	.667	0	0- -	-	3.81	4.65
2003	Giants	R	9	6	0	0	34.2	151	35	21	18	1	1	4	2	0	0	28	3	0	2	2	.500	0	0- -	-	2.15	4.67
2004	Giants	R	11	8	0	2	48.0	212	43	23	13	1	1	1	3	20	0	47	2	1	2	0	1.000	0	1- -	-	3.14	2.44
2005	Augsta	A	29	22	0	3	135.1	594	162	83	75	12	4	6	8	31	0	79	1	1	8	8	.500	0	0- -	-	4.66	4.99
2006	Augsta	A	44	0	0	30	61.1	237	42	13	12	3	3	4	0	12	0	81	3	0	7	3	.700	0	13- -	-	1.53	1.76
2006	Conn	AA	6	0	0	3	9.2	41	11	4	4	0	0	0	0	2	1	5	0	0	0	0	-	0	2- -	-	3.23	3.72
2007	Conn	AA	35	0	0	12	56.0	239	50	20	18	3	5	2	1	21	2	43	1	0	5	0	1.000	0	4- -	-	3.04	2.89
2007	Augsta	A	7	0	0	6	9.0	29	1	0	0	0	0	0	0	1	0	9	0	0	5	0	1.000	0	4- -	-	0.09	0.00
2008	Conn	AA	27	0	0	14	36.2	144	25	5	5	0	1	0	1	11	0	37	1	0	0	0	-	0	8- -	-	1.64	1.23
2008	Fresno	AAA	5	0	0	1	9.2	36	5	0	0	0	0	0	0	2	0	13	0	0	1	0	1.000	0	1- -	-	0.91	0.00
2008	SF	NL	20	0	0	5	20.2	98	26	17	11	3	1	3	1	9	1	16	0	0	1	2	.333	0	0-1	0	6.06	4.79

Hideki Matsui

Bats: L Throws: R Pos: DH-66; LF-21; PH-5; RF-3   Ht: 6'2" Wt: 210 Born: 6/12/1974 Age: 35

Year	Team	Lg	G	AB	H	2B	3B	HR	(Hm	Rd)	TB	R	RBI	RC	TBB	IBB	SO	HBP	SH	SF	SB	CS	SB%	GDP	Avg	OBP	Slg
2008	Tampa*	A+	3	8	2	0	0	1	(-	-)	5	1	1	2	2	0	0	0	0	0	0	0	-	0	.250	.400	.625
2003	NYY	AL	163	623	179	42	1	16	(9	7)	271	82	106	96	63	5	86	3	0	6	2	2	.50	25	.287	.353	.435
2004	NYY	AL	162	584	174	34	2	31	(18	13)	305	109	108	117	88	2	103	3	0	5	3	0	1.00	11	.298	.390	.522
2005	NYY	AL	162	629	192	45	3	23	(15	8)	312	108	116	109	63	7	78	3	0	8	2	2	.50	16	.305	.367	.496
2006	NYY	AL	51	172	52	9	0	8	(1	7)	85	32	29	30	27	2	23	0	0	2	1	0	1.00	6	.302	.393	.494
2007	NYY	AL	143	547	156	28	4	25	(16	9)	267	100	103	91	73	2	73	3	0	10	4	2	.67	9	.285	.367	.488
2008	NYY	AL	93	337	99	17	0	9	(3	6)	143	43	45	56	38	6	47	3	0	0	0	0	-	10	.294	.370	.424
	Postseason		41	162	49	13	1	6	(2	4)	82	27	26	25	18	2	23	1	0	2	0	0	-	4	.302	.372	.506
	6 ML YEARS		774	2892	852	175	10	112	(62	50)	1383	474	507	499	352	24	410	15	0	31	12	6	.67	77	.295	.371	.478

Kaz Matsui

Bats: B Throws: R Pos: 2B-94; PH-2   Ht: 5'10" Wt: 185 Born: 10/23/1975 Age: 33

Year	Team	Lg	G	AB	H	2B	3B	HR	(Hm	Rd)	TB	R	RBI	RC	TBB	IBB	SO	HBP	SH	SF	SB	CS	SB%	GDP	Avg	OBP	Slg
2008	CpChr*	AA	2	7	3	3	0	0	(-	-)	6	1	0	2	0	0	1	0	1	0	0	0	-	1	.429	.429	.857
2008	RdRck*	AAA	3	11	2	1	0	1	(-	-)	6	1	1	1	1	0	2	0	0	0	0	0	-	0	.182	.250	.545
2004	NYM	NL	114	460	125	32	2	7	(4	3)	182	65	44	63	40	4	97	2	5	2	14	3	.82	3	.272	.331	.396
2005	NYM	NL	87	267	68	9	4	3	(1	2)	94	31	24	27	14	1	43	5	5	4	6	1	.86	2	.255	.300	.352
2006	2 Tms	NL	70	243	65	12	3	3	(0	3)	92	32	26	28	16	1	46	0	4	2	10	1	.91	1	.267	.310	.379
2007	Col	NL	104	410	118	24	6	4	(4	0)	166	84	37	61	34	1	69	0	8	1	32	4	.89	1	.288	.342	.405
2008	Hou	NL	96	375	110	26	3	6	(4	2)	160	58	33	53	37	0	53	0	7	3	20	5	.80	3	.293	.354	.427
06	NYM	NL	38	130	26	6	1	0	(0	1)	35	10	7	5	6	1	19	0	3	0	2	0	1.00	1	.200	.235	.269
06	Col	NL	32	113	39	6	3	2	(0	2)	57	22	19	23	10	0	27	0	1	2	8	1	.89	0	.345	.392	.504
	Postseason		11	46	14	2	2	1	(0	1)	23	5	8	9	3	1	12	0	1	0	2	0	1.00	0	.304	.347	.500
	5 ML YEARS		471	1755	486	103	18	23	(13	10)	694	270	164	232	141	7	308	7	29	12	82	14	.85	10	.277	.331	.395

Daisuke Matsuzaka

Pitches: R Bats: R Pos: SP-29 　　　　Ht: 6'0" Wt: 200 Born: 9/13/1980 Age: 28

			HOW MUCH HE PITCHED						WHAT HE GAVE UP										THE RESULTS							
Year	Team	Lg	G	GS	CG	GF	IP	BFP	H	R	ER	HR	SH	SF	HB	TBB	IBB	SO	WP	Bk	W	L	Pct	ShO	Sv-Op	Hld	ERC	ERA
1999	Seibu	Jap	25	24	6	1	180.0	743	124	55	52	14	-	-	8	87	-	151	5	2	16	5	.762	2	0--	-	2.77	2.60
2000	Seibu	Jap	27	24	6	2	167.2	727	132	85	74	12	-	-	4	95	-	144	2	0	14	7	.667	2	1--	-	3.40	3.97
2001	Seibu	Jap	33	32	12	1	240.1	1004	184	104	96	27	-	-	8	117	-	214	9	1	15	15	.500	2	0--	-	3.38	3.60
2002	Seibu	Jap	14	11	2	0	73.1	302	60	30	30	13	-	-	7	15	-	78	2	1	6	2	.750	0	0--	-	3.14	3.68
2003	Seibu	Jap	29	27	8	1	194.0	801	165	71	61	13	-	-	9	63	3	215	4	0	16	7	.696	2	0--	-	2.94	2.83
2004	Seibu	Jap	23	19	10	0	146.0	601	127	50	47	7	8	6	6	42	0	127	5	0	10	6	.625	5	0--	-	2.78	2.90
2005	Seibu	Jap	28	28	15	0	215.0	868	172	63	55	13	11	1	10	49	0	226	9	0	14	13	.519	3	0--	-	2.30	2.30
2006	Seibu	Jap	25	25	13	0	186.1	722	138	50	44	13	10	6	3	34	0	200	5	0	17	5	.773	2	0--	-	1.86	2.13
2008	Pwtckt	AAA	1	1	0	0	5.0	19	4	2	2	0	0	0	1	0	5	1	0	1	0	1.000	0	0--	-	1.82	3.60
2007	Bos	AL	32	32	1	0	204.2	874	191	100	100	25	3	2	13	80	1	201	5	0	15	12	.556	0	0-0	0	4.10	4.40
2008	Bos	AL	29	29	0	0	167.2	716	128	58	54	12	3	4	7	94	1	154	5	0	18	3	.857	0	0-0	0	3.36	2.90
	Postseason		4	4	0	0	19.2	89	22	11	11	1	0	1	1	8	0	17	3	0	2	1	.667	0	0-0	0	4.55	5.03
	2 ML YEARS		61	61	1	0	372.1	1590	319	158	154	37	6	6	20	174	2	355	10	0	33	15	.688	0	0-0	0	3.76	3.72

Gary Matthews Jr.

Bats: B Throws: R Pos: RF-43; LF-37; CF-31; DH-13; PH-8; PR-4 　　　　Ht: 6'3" Wt: 225 Born: 8/25/1974 Age: 34

			BATTING																BASERUNNING				AVERAGES		
Year	Team	Lg	G	AB	H	2B	3B	HR	(Hm | Rd)	TB	R	RBI	RC	TBB	IBB	SO	HBP	SH	SF	SB	CS	SB%	GDP	Avg	OBP	Slg
1999	SD	NL	23	36	8	0	0	0	(0 | 0)	8	4	7	4	9	0	9	0	0	0	2	0	1.00	1	.222	.378	.222
2000	ChC	NL	80	158	30	1	2	4	(2 | 2)	47	24	14	13	15	1	28	1	1	0	3	0	1.00	2	.190	.264	.297
2001	2 Tms	NL	152	405	92	15	2	14	(4 | 10)	153	63	44	51	60	2	100	1	5	1	8	5	.62	8	.227	.328	.378
2002	2 Tms		111	345	95	25	3	7	(6 | 1)	147	54	38	55	43	1	69	1	5	4	15	5	.75	4	.275	.354	.426
2003	2 Tms		144	468	116	31	2	6	(3 | 3)	169	71	42	51	43	0	95	2	0	0	12	8	.60	8	.248	.314	.361
2004	Tex	AL	87	280	77	17	1	11	(7 | 4)	129	37	36	48	33	5	64	1	0	3	5	1	.83	1	.275	.350	.461
2005	Tex	AL	131	475	121	25	5	17	(8 | 9)	207	72	55	63	47	1	90	0	1	3	9	2	.82	11	.255	.320	.436
2006	Tex	AL	147	620	194	44	6	19	(11 | 8)	307	102	79	109	58	5	99	4	0	8	10	7	.59	8	.313	.371	.495
2007	LAA	AL	140	516	130	26	3	18	(7 | 11)	216	79	72	66	55	6	102	2	0	6	18	4	.82	12	.252	.323	.419
2008	LAA	AL	127	426	103	19	3	8	(2 | 6)	152	53	46	47	45	2	95	4	0	2	8	3	.73	12	.242	.319	.357
01	ChC	NL	106	258	56	9	1	9	(2 | 7)	94	41	30	31	38	2	55	1	5	0	5	3	.63	4	.217	.320	.364
01	Pit	NL	46	147	36	6	1	5	(2 | 3)	59	22	14	20	22	0	45	0	0	1	3	2	.60	4	.245	.341	.401
02	NYM	NL	2	1	0	0	0	0	(0 | 0)	0	0	0	0	0	0	0	0	0	0	0	0	-	0	.000	.000	.000
02	Bal	AL	109	344	95	25	3	7	(6 | 1)	147	54	38	55	43	1	69	1	5	4	15	5	.75	4	.276	.355	.427
03	Bal	AL	41	162	33	12	1	2	(2 | 0)	53	21	20	15	9	0	29	1	0	0	0	3	.00	4	.204	.250	.327
03	SD	NL	103	306	83	19	1	4	(1 | 3)	116	50	22	36	34	0	66	1	0	0	12	5	.71	4	.271	.346	.379
	10 ML YEARS		1142	3729	966	203	27	104	(50 | 54)	1535	559	433	507	408	23	751	16	12	27	90	35	.72	67	.259	.333	.412

Joe Mauer

Bats: L Throws: R Pos: C-139; PH-7; DH-5 　　　　Ht: 6'5" Wt: 230 Born: 4/19/1983 Age: 26

			BATTING																BASERUNNING				AVERAGES		
Year	Team	Lg	G	AB	H	2B	3B	HR	(Hm | Rd)	TB	R	RBI	RC	TBB	IBB	SO	HBP	SH	SF	SB	CS	SB%	GDP	Avg	OBP	Slg
2004	Min	AL	35	107	33	8	1	6	(4 | 2)	61	18	17	21	11	0	14	1	0	3	1	0	1.00	1	.308	.369	.570
2005	Min	AL	131	489	144	26	2	9	(4 | 5)	201	61	55	78	61	12	64	1	0	9	13	1	.93	9	.294	.372	.411
2006	Min	AL	140	521	181	36	4	13	(3 | 10)	264	86	84	103	79	21	54	1	0	7	8	3	.73	24	.347	.429	.507
2007	Min	AL	109	406	119	27	3	7	(2 | 5)	173	62	60	69	57	10	51	3	2	3	7	1	.88	11	.293	.382	.426
2008	Min	AL	146	536	176	31	4	9	(7 | 2)	242	98	85	103	84	8	50	1	1	11	1	1	.50	21	.328	.413	.451
	Postseason		3	11	2	0	0	0	(0 | 0)	2	0	0	0	1	0	0	0	0	0	0	0	-	0	.182	.250	.182
	5 ML YEARS		561	2059	653	128	14	44	(20 | 24)	941	325	301	374	292	51	233	7	3	27	30	6	.83	66	.317	.399	.457

Cameron Maybin

Bats: R Throws: R Pos: CF-8 　　　　Ht: 6'4" Wt: 205 Born: 4/4/1987 Age: 22

			BATTING																BASERUNNING				AVERAGES		
Year	Team	Lg	G	AB	H	2B	3B	HR	(Hm | Rd)	TB	R	RBI	RC	TBB	IBB	SO	HBP	SH	SF	SB	CS	SB%	GDP	Avg	OBP	Slg
2006	WMich	A	101	385	117	20	6	9	(- | -)	176	59	69	73	50	3	116	5	0	5	27	7	.79	9	.304	.387	.457
2007	Lkland	A+	83	296	90	14	5	10	(- | -)	144	58	44	61	43	0	83	4	1	6	25	6	.81	5	.304	.393	.486
2007	Tigers	R	2	7	4	0	0	0	(- | -)	4	1	1	2	2	0	2	0	0	0	0	0	-	0	.571	.667	.571
2007	Erie	AA	6	20	8	1	0	4	(- | -)	21	9	8	9	6	0	6	0	0	0	0	0	-	1	.400	.538	1.050
2008	Carlina	AA	108	390	108	15	8	13	(- | -)	178	73	49	71	60	1	124	3	3	3	22	7	.76	4	.277	.375	.456
2007	Det	AL	24	49	7	3	0	1	(0 | 1)	13	8	2	2	3	0	21	1	0	0	5	0	1.00	0	.143	.208	.265
2008	Fla	NL	8	32	16	2	0	0	(0 | 0)	18	9	2	8	3	0	8	0	1	0	4	0	1.00	0	.500	.543	.563
	2 ML YEARS		32	81	23	5	0	1	(0 | 1)	31	17	4	10	6	0	29	1	1	0	9	0	1.00	0	.284	.341	.383

Edwin Maysonet

Bats: R Throws: R Pos: SS-4; 2B-3; PH-2; PR-2 　　　　Ht: 6'1" Wt: 180 Born: 10/17/1981 Age: 27

			BATTING																BASERUNNING				AVERAGES		
Year	Team	Lg	G	AB	H	2B	3B	HR	(Hm | Rd)	TB	R	RBI	RC	TBB	IBB	SO	HBP	SH	SF	SB	CS	SB%	GDP	Avg	OBP	Slg
2003	TriCity	A-	45	138	38	7	1	1	(- | -)	50	30	13	26	29	0	28	5	3	3	9	1	.90	0	.275	.411	.362
2004	Lxngtn	A	109	391	102	22	10	11	(- | -)	177	79	63	72	64	1	91	9	14	7	18	7	.72	4	.261	.372	.453
2005	Salem	A+	66	236	46	9	2	1	(- | -)	62	29	16	19	26	0	69	3	12	4	4	2	.67	4	.195	.279	.263
2005	Lxngtn	A	45	173	45	11	1	4	(- | -)	70	29	17	27	15	0	29	10	2	1	11	4	.73	0	.260	.352	.405
2006	Salem	A+	113	378	96	32	0	8	(- | -)	152	58	38	51	20	1	58	8	11	4	21	3	.88	3	.254	.302	.402
2007	CpChr	AA	107	341	92	14	2	5	(- | -)	125	35	39	40	17	0	65	2	10	2	5	2	.71	9	.270	.307	.367
2008	RdRck	AAA	117	406	110	24	1	6	(- | -)	154	59	34	57	44	0	70	4	6	6	4	3	.57	5	.271	.343	.379
2008	Hou	NL	7	7	1	0	0	0	(0 | 0)	1	0	0	0	0	0	2	0	0	0	0	0	-	0	.143	.143	.143

Luis Maza

Bats: R Throws: R Pos: 2B-35; SS-16; PH-3; PR-3   Ht: 5'9" Wt: 180 Born: 6/22/1980 Age: 29

								BATTING													BASERUNNING				AVERAGES		
Year	Team	Lg	G	AB	H	2B	3B	HR	(Hm	Rd)	TB	R	RBI	RC	TBB	IBB	SO	HBP	SH	SF	SB	CS	SB%	GDP	Avg	OBP	Slg
1999	Twins	R	25	61	16	4	0	0	(-	-)	20	11	10	9	10	0	15	3	1	0	1	1	.50	1	.262	.392	.328
2000	Elizab	R+	56	210	62	16	3	8	(-	-)	108	40	35	43	19	1	41	12	7	1	12	4	.75	1	.295	.384	.514
2001	QuadC	A	116	429	120	24	1	9	(-	-)	173	74	46	66	30	0	66	23	2	2	12	4	.75	9	.280	.357	.403
2002	FtMyrs	A+	105	344	83	15	3	4	(-	-)	116	44	38	36	19	0	53	13	10	5	4	6	.40	6	.241	.302	.337
2003	FtMyrs	A+	111	410	119	18	6	5	(-	-)	164	70	61	65	34	0	79	19	9	5	1	1	.50	6	.290	.368	.400
2004	NwBrit	AA	126	492	153	26	8	12	(-	-)	231	84	66	84	28	0	70	15	4	2	5	6	.45	12	.311	.365	.470
2004	Roch	AAA	9	35	8	2	1	0	(-	-)	12	6	1	3	1	0	3	2	1	0	1	0	1.00	2	.229	.289	.343
2005	NwBrit	AA	49	197	49	9	0	6	(-	-)	76	28	23	23	12	1	34	3	1	2	0	1	.00	4	.249	.299	.386
2005	Roch	AAA	76	275	80	14	2	11	(-	-)	131	43	43	42	11	1	34	2	1	4	2	1	.67	11	.291	.318	.476
2006	Roch	AAA	95	305	63	10	6	3	(-	-)	94	29	35	24	15	1	57	6	10	3	2	2	.50	5	.207	.255	.308
2007	Jaxnvl	AA	26	97	23	3	1	3	(-	-)	37	14	8	13	14	0	17	1	1	1	1	2	.33	2	.237	.336	.381
2007	LsVgs	AAA	68	227	75	21	0	3	(-	-)	105	31	34	41	17	1	36	4	4	4	2	0	1.00	11	.330	.381	.463
2008	LsVgs	AAA	63	238	90	11	5	2	(-	-)	117	51	29	52	31	1	30	1	2	1	1	2	.33	7	.378	.450	.492
2008	LAD	NL	45	79	18	1	0	1	(1	0)	22	7	4	6	5	0	11	1	3	0	0	0	-	5	.228	.282	.278

Paul McAnulty

Bats: L Throws: R Pos: LF-35; PH-23; RF-15; PR-1   Ht: 5'10" Wt: 220 Born: 2/24/1981 Age: 28

								BATTING													BASERUNNING				AVERAGES		
Year	Team	Lg	G	AB	H	2B	3B	HR	(Hm	Rd)	TB	R	RBI	RC	TBB	IBB	SO	HBP	SH	SF	SB	CS	SB%	GDP	Avg	OBP	Slg
2008	Portlnd*	AAA	53	181	62	14	1	13	(-	-)	117	34	50	50	35	1	38	2	0	7	0	0	-	2	.343	.440	.646
2005	SD	NL	22	24	5	0	0	0	(0	0)	5	4	0	1	3	1	7	1	1	0	1	0	1.00	0	.208	.321	.208
2006	SD	NL	16	13	3	1	0	1	(1	0)	7	3	3	3	2	0	4	0	0	0	0	0	-	0	.231	.333	.538
2007	SD	NL	20	40	8	1	0	1	(0	1)	12	5	5	3	3	1	10	0	0	0	0	0	-	0	.200	.256	.300
2008	SD	NL	66	135	28	7	1	3	(1	2)	46	9	13	19	26	2	41	2	0	1	0	0	-	0	.207	.341	.341
	4 ML YEARS		124	212	44	9	1	5	(2	3)	70	21	21	26	34	4	62	3	1	1	1	0	1.00	0	.208	.324	.330

Macay McBride

Pitches: L Bats: L Pos: P   Ht: 5'11" Wt: 210 Born: 10/24/1982 Age: 26

			HOW MUCH HE PITCHED						WHAT HE GAVE UP											THE RESULTS						
Year	Team	Lg	G	GS	CG	GF	IP	BFP	H	R	ER	HR	SH	SF	HB	TBB	IBB	SO	WP	Bk	W	L	Pct	ShO	Sv-Op	Hld	ERC	ERA
2008	Toledo*	AAA	1	1	0	0	1.0	4	1	0	0	0	0	0	0	0	0	0	0	0	0	0	-	0	0- -	-	1.95	0.00
2005	Atl	NL	23	0	0	4	14.0	68	18	11	9	0	1	1	0	7	0	22	2	0	1	0	1.000	0	1-1	6	5.12	5.79
2006	Atl	NL	71	0	0	13	56.2	249	53	28	23	2	2	0	1	32	4	46	3	0	4	1	.800	0	1-2	10	3.85	3.65
2007	2 Tms		38	0	0	5	32.2	156	33	21	18	4	1	0	2	25	0	30	2	0	1	1	.500	0	0-0	4	5.98	4.96
07	Atl	NL	18	0	0	4	15.0	75	14	9	6	1	0	0	1	15	0	17	1	0	1	0	1.000	0	0-0	0	5.93	3.60
07	Det	AL	20	0	0	1	17.2	81	19	12	12	3	1	0	1	10	0	13	1	0	0	1	.000	0	0-0	4	5.99	6.11
	Postseason		1	0	0	1	1.0	3	0	0	0	0	0	0	0	0	0	0	0	0	0	0	-	0	0-0	0	0.00	0.00
	3 ML YEARS		132	0	0	22	103.1	473	104	60	50	6	4	1	3	64	4	98	7	0	6	2	.750	0	2-3	20	4.67	4.35

Brian McCann

Bats: L Throws: R Pos: C-138; PH-13   Ht: 6'3" Wt: 230 Born: 2/20/1984 Age: 25

								BATTING													BASERUNNING				AVERAGES		
Year	Team	Lg	G	AB	H	2B	3B	HR	(Hm	Rd)	TB	R	RBI	RC	TBB	IBB	SO	HBP	SH	SF	SB	CS	SB%	GDP	Avg	OBP	Slg
2005	Atl	NL	59	180	50	7	0	5	(2	3)	72	20	23	25	18	5	26	1	4	1	1	1	.50	5	.278	.345	.400
2006	Atl	NL	130	442	147	34	0	24	(10	14)	253	61	93	94	41	8	54	3	0	6	2	0	1.00	12	.333	.388	.572
2007	Atl	NL	139	504	136	38	0	18	(6	12)	228	51	92	68	35	7	74	5	2	6	0	1	.00	19	.270	.320	.452
2008	Atl	NL	145	509	153	42	1	23	(10	13)	266	68	87	84	57	4	64	4	0	3	5	0	1.00	17	.301	.373	.523
	Postseason		3	16	3	0	0	2	(1	1)	9	2	5	2	0	0	6	0	0	0	0	0	-	0	.188	.188	.563
	4 ML YEARS		473	1635	486	121	1	70	(28	42)	819	200	295	271	151	24	218	13	6	16	8	2	.80	53	.297	.358	.501

Brandon McCarthy

Pitches: R Bats: R Pos: SP-5   Ht: 6'7" Wt: 200 Born: 7/7/1983 Age: 25

			HOW MUCH HE PITCHED						WHAT HE GAVE UP											THE RESULTS						
Year	Team	Lg	G	GS	CG	GF	IP	BFP	H	R	ER	HR	SH	SF	HB	TBB	IBB	SO	WP	Bk	W	L	Pct	ShO	Sv-Op	Hld	ERC	ERA
2008	Rngrs*	R	2	2	0	0	5.0	21	7	2	2	0	0	0	0	1	0	5	1	0	0	0	-	0	0- -	-	5.19	3.60
2008	Okla*	AAA	5	5	0	0	26.2	108	21	10	10	2	1	0	0	8	0	23	1	0	1	1	.500	0	0- -	-	2.41	3.38
2005	CWS	AL	12	10	0	0	67.0	277	62	30	30	13	1	1	2	17	0	48	1	1	3	2	.600	0	0-0	0	3.83	4.03
2006	CWS	AL	53	2	0	13	84.2	354	77	44	44	17	3	1	0	33	9	69	5	0	4	7	.364	0	0-1	11	4.10	4.68
2007	Tex	AL	23	22	0	0	101.2	459	111	62	55	9	3	5	3	48	0	59	4	1	5	10	.333	0	0-0	0	4.89	4.87
2008	Tex	AL	5	5	0	0	22.0	93	20	11	10	3	0	2	1	8	0	10	0	0	1	1	.500	0	0-0	0	3.87	4.09
	4 ML YEARS		93	39	0	13	275.1	1183	270	147	139	42	7	9	6	106	9	186	10	2	13	20	.394	0	0-1	11	4.32	4.54

Scott McClain

Bats: R Throws: R Pos: PH-6; 1B-4; 3B-4   Ht: 6'4" Wt: 231 Born: 5/19/1972 Age: 37

								BATTING													BASERUNNING				AVERAGES		
Year	Team	Lg	G	AB	H	2B	3B	HR	(Hm	Rd)	TB	R	RBI	RC	TBB	IBB	SO	HBP	SH	SF	SB	CS	SB%	GDP	Avg	OBP	Slg
2008	Fresno*	AAA	134	477	143	32	1	29	(-	-)	264	87	108	103	72	6	98	1	0	6	5	2	.71	6	.300	.388	.553
1998	TB	AL	9	20	2	0	0	0	(	)	2	2	0	0	2	0	6	1	0	0	0	0	-	0	.100	.217	.100
2005	ChC	NL	13	14	2	1	0	0	(0	0)	3	1	1	0	2	0	2	0	0	0	0	0	-	1	.143	.250	.214
2007	SF	NL	8	11	2	0	0	0	(0	0)	2	1	0	0	0	0	2	0	0	0	0	0	-	0	.182	.182	.182
2008	SF	NL	14	33	9	1	0	2	(1	1)	16	7	7	5	5	0	8	0	0	1	0	1	.00	0	.273	.368	.485
	4 ML YEARS		44	78	15	2	0	2	(1	1)	23	11	8	5	9	0	18	1	0	1	0	1	.00	1	.192	.284	.295

Kyle McClellan

Pitches: R Bats: R Pos: RP-68   Ht: 6'2" Wt: 205 Born: 6/12/1984 Age: 25

		HOW MUCH HE PITCHED						WHAT HE GAVE UP									THE RESULTS					
Year	Team	Lg	G	GS	CG	GF	IP	BFP	H	R	ER	HR	SH	SF	HB	TBB	IBB	SO	WP	Bk	W	L	Pct	ShO	Sv-Op Hld	ERC	ERA
2002	JhsCty	R+	7	3	0	1	12.0	60	17	17	15	3	0	0	1	7	0	8	3	0	0	2	.000	0	0- - -	9.06	11.25
2003	JhsCty	R+	12	12	0	0	67.2	298	74	34	30	4	1	1	5	16	1	44	5	0	3	6	.333	0	0- - -	3.83	3.99
2004	Peoria	A	24	24	1	0	128.0	562	143	85	76	12	4	5	14	34	1	84	18	0	4	12	.250	0	0- - -	4.59	5.34
2005	QuadC	A	17	8	0	4	54.0	243	59	33	29	4	1	4	6	26	0	36	7	0	1	4	.200	0	1- - -	5.28	4.83
2006	JhsCty	R+	3	3	0	0	6.2	32	7	7	7	0	1	0	1	3	0	4	0	0	0	1	.000	0	0- - -	4.11	9.45
2007	PlmBh	A+	16	1	0	4	29.0	112	22	4	4	0	1	0	2	4	0	24	2	0	4	1	.800	0	0- - -	1.63	1.24
2007	Sprgfld	AA	24	0	0	8	30.2	118	24	9	8	2	0	0	0	6	1	30	2	0	2	0	1.000	0	0- - -	2.01	2.35
2008	StL	NL	68	0	0	7	75.2	327	79	37	34	7	2	1	4	26	2	59	6	0	2	7	.222	0	1-6 30	4.24	4.04

Seth McClung

Pitches: R Bats: R Pos: RP-25; SP-12   Ht: 6'6" Wt: 252 Born: 2/7/1981 Age: 28

		HOW MUCH HE PITCHED						WHAT HE GAVE UP									THE RESULTS					
Year	Team	Lg	G	GS	CG	GF	IP	BFP	H	R	ER	HR	SH	SF	HB	TBB	IBB	SO	WP	Bk	W	L	Pct	ShO	Sv-Op Hld	ERC	ERA
2003	TB	AL	12	5	0	2	38.2	167	33	23	23	6	1	1	3	25	1	25	2	0	4	1	.800	0	0-0 1	5.11	5.35
2005	TB	AL	34	17	0	3	109.1	500	106	85	80	20	0	5	7	62	1	92	6	0	7	11	.389	0	0-1 2	5.36	6.59
2006	TB	AL	39	15	0	20	103.0	489	120	77	72	14	1	9	3	68	5	59	7	0	6	12	.333	0	6-7 0	6.44	6.29
2007	Mil	NL	14	0	0	1	12.0	51	11	9	5	0	0	1	1	5	0	11	0	0	1	0	1.000	0	0-0 0	3.35	3.75
2008	Mil	NL	37	12	0	10	105.1	456	93	47	47	10	5	6	7	55	3	87	5	0	6	6	.500	0	0-0 1	4.13	4.02
	5 ML YEARS		136	49	0	36	368.1	1663	363	241	227	50	7	22	21	215	10	274	20	0	23	31	.426	0	6-8 4	5.20	5.55

Bob McCrory

Pitches: R Bats: R Pos: RP-8   Ht: 6'1" Wt: 205 Born: 5/3/1982 Age: 27

		HOW MUCH HE PITCHED						WHAT HE GAVE UP									THE RESULTS					
Year	Team	Lg	G	GS	CG	GF	IP	BFP	H	R	ER	HR	SH	SF	HB	TBB	IBB	SO	WP	Bk	W	L	Pct	ShO	Sv-Op Hld	ERC	ERA
2004	Dlmrva	A	8	0	0	1	10.2	59	13	16	9	3	0	0	0	15	0	11	5	0	0	1	.000	0	0- - -	11.55	7.59
2004	Bluefld	R+	11	11	0	0	51.2	222	42	21	11	3	1	2	1	32	0	51	8	1	4	3	.571	0	0- - -	3.72	1.92
2004	Abrdn	A-	1	1	0	0	1.0	8	3	3	3	1	0	0	0	2	0	0	0	0	0	1	.000	0	0- - -	38.33	27.00
2005	Abrdn	A-	5	5	0	0	24.2	101	21	9	9	2	0	0	3	8	0	21	3	0	2	1	.667	0	0- - -	3.43	3.28
2006	Abrdn	A-	20	1	0	4	38.2	161	32	12	10	2	3	1	2	16	0	57	3	0	2	2	.500	0	2- - -	3.11	2.33
2007	Frdrck	A+	22	0	0	18	22.0	93	16	4	3	1	0	1	2	12	1	22	5	0	0	0	-	0	14- - -	3.08	1.23
2007	Bowie	AA	22	0	0	19	23.0	113	23	17	10	1	0	0	3	16	0	22	3	0	1	2	.333	0	13- - -	4.72	3.91
2008	Norfolk	AAA	35	1	0	18	45.0	199	41	22	19	1	4	5	2	24	1	35	2	0	2	3	.400	0	5- - -	3.63	3.80
2008	Abrdn	A-	1	0	0	0	1.0	6	1	2	2	0	0	0	0	2	0	2	0	0	0	0	-	0	0- - -	9.51	18.00
2008	Bal	AL	8	0	0	2	6.1	37	10	12	11	0	1	1	0	8	0	5	1	0	0	0	-	0	0-0 0	10.26	15.63

James McDonald

Pitches: R Bats: L Pos: RP-4   Ht: 6'5" Wt: 195 Born: 10/19/1984 Age: 24

		HOW MUCH HE PITCHED						WHAT HE GAVE UP									THE RESULTS					
Year	Team	Lg	G	GS	CG	GF	IP	BFP	H	R	ER	HR	SH	SF	HB	TBB	IBB	SO	WP	Bk	W	L	Pct	ShO	Sv-Op Hld	ERC	ERA
2003	Ddgrs	R	12	9	0	0	48.2	199	39	20	18	3	1	0	6	15	0	47	3	0	2	4	.333	0	0- - -	2.93	3.33
2005	Ogden	R+	4	0	0	0	6.0	26	4	3	1	0	0	0	1	2	0	9	0	0	0	0	-	0	0- - -	1.92	1.50
2006	Clmbs	A	30	22	2	4	142.1	600	119	72	63	15	2	2	11	65	0	146	12	0	5	10	.333	1	0- - -	3.80	3.98
2007	InldEm	A+	16	15	0	0	82.0	341	79	37	36	8	0	3	5	21	0	104	3	0	6	7	.462	0	0- - -	3.57	3.95
2007	Jaxnvl	AA	10	10	0	0	52.2	215	41	14	9	5	3	1	2	16	0	64	1	1	7	2	.778	0	0- - -	2.63	1.54
2008	Jaxnvl	AA	22	22	0	0	118.2	491	98	47	42	12	6	2	6	46	2	113	4	2	5	3	.625	0	0- - -	3.30	3.19
2008	LsVgs	AAA	5	4	0	0	22.1	95	17	9	9	3	0	0	3	7	0	28	0	0	2	1	.667	0	0- - -	3.10	3.63
2008	LAD	NL	4	0	0	1	6.0	24	5	0	0	1	0	0	0	2	0	2	0	0	0	0	-	0	0-0 0	1.74	0.00

John McDonald

Bats: R Throws: R Pos: SS-67; PR-12; DH-5; 3B-4; PH-2; 2B-1   Ht: 5'11" Wt: 185 Born: 9/24/1974 Age: 34

			BATTING																			BASERUNNING				AVERAGES		
Year	Team	Lg	G	AB	H	2B	3B	HR	(Hm	Rd)	TB	R	RBI	RC	TBB	IBB	SO	HBP	SH	SF	SB	CS	SB%	GDP	Avg	OBP	Slg
2008	Dnedin*	A+	3	11	4	0	0	0	(-	-)	4	2	1	1	1	0	1	0	0	0	0	0	-	0	.364	.417	.364
1999	Cle	AL	18	21	7	0	0	0	(0	0)	7	2	0	1	0	0	3	0	0	0	0	1	.00	2	.333	.333	.333
2000	Cle	AL	9	9	4	0	0	0	(0	0)	4	0	0	2	0	0	1	0	0	0	0	0	-	0	.444	.444	.444
2001	Cle	AL	17	22	2	1	0	0	(0	0)	3	1	0	0	1	0	7	1	1	0	0	0	-	0	.091	.167	.136
2002	Cle	AL	93	264	66	11	3	1	(0	1)	86	35	12	24	10	0	50	5	7	2	3	0	1.00	4	.250	.288	.326
2003	Cle	AL	82	214	46	9	1	1	(0	1)	60	21	14	18	11	0	31	2	4	2	3	3	.50	4	.215	.258	.280
2004	Cle	AL	66	93	19	5	1	2	(0	2)	32	17	7	6	4	0	11	0	3	0	0	0	-	2	.204	.237	.344
2005	2 Tms	AL	68	166	46	6	1	0	(0	0)	54	18	16	19	11	0	24	2	3	2	6	1	.86	6	.277	.326	.325
2006	Tor	AL	104	260	58	7	3	3	(1	2)	80	35	23	20	16	0	41	2	6	2	7	2	.78	8	.223	.271	.308
2007	Tor	AL	123	327	82	20	2	1	(1	0)	109	32	31	35	11	0	48	2	12	1	7	2	.78	5	.251	.279	.333
2008	Tor	AL	84	186	39	8	0	1	(1	0)	50	21	18	11	10	0	25	2	7	2	3	1	.75	3	.210	.255	.269
05	Ogden	AL	37	93	27	3	0	0	(0	0)	30	8	12	13	6	0	12	2	3	2	5	0	1.00	3	.290	.340	.323
05	Det	AL	31	73	19	3	1	0	(0	0)	24	10	4	6	5	0	12	0	0	0	1	1	.50	3	.260	.308	.329
	10 ML YEARS		664	1562	369	67	11	9	(3	6)	485	182	121	136	74	0	241	16	43	11	29	10	.74	33	.236	.276	.310

Casey McGehee

Bats: R Throws: R Pos: 3B-6; PH-3

Ht: 6'1" Wt: 195 Born: 10/12/1982 Age: 26

Year	Team	Lg	G	AB	H	2B	3B	HR	(Hm	Rd)	TB	R	RBI	RC	TBB	IBB	SO	HBP	SH	SF	SB	CS	SB%	GDP	Avg	OBP	Slg
2003	Lansng	A	64	243	66	18	1	3	(-	-)	95	24	23	28	10	0	46	2	0	3	2	3	.40	8	.272	.302	.391
2004	Dytona	A+	119	449	117	30	0	10	(-	-)	177	56	66	57	33	3	69	1	4	4	2	1	.67	9	.261	.310	.394
2005	WTenn	AA	124	455	135	31	1	8	(-	-)	192	67	72	71	43	5	64	1	0	6	2	2	.50	21	.297	.354	.422
2006	Iowa	AAA	135	497	139	28	1	11	(-	-)	202	56	68	69	41	0	70	3	1	4	0	3	.00	17	.280	.336	.406
2007	Iowa	AAA	18	52	9	2	0	1	(-	-)	14	3	5	2	3	0	10	1	0	1	0	1	.00	2	.173	.228	.269
2007	Tenn	AA	105	384	105	26	2	9	(-	-)	162	53	54	57	40	5	73	0	0	5	1	2	.33	15	.273	.338	.422
2008	Iowa	AAA	133	497	147	30	0	12	(-	-)	213	68	92	76	40	0	89	3	0	10	0	3	.00	14	.296	.345	.429
2008	ChC	NL	9	24	4	1	0	0	(0	0)	5	1	5	0	0	0	8	0	0	1	0	0	-	1	.167	.160	.208

Dustin McGowan

Pitches: R Bats: R Pos: SP-19

Ht: 6'3" Wt: 220 Born: 3/24/1982 Age: 27

Year	Team	Lg	G	GS	CG	GF	IP	BFP	H	R	ER	HR	SH	SF	HB	TBB	IBB	SO	WP	Bk	W	L	Pct	ShO	Sv-Op	Hld	ERC	ERA
2005	Tor	AL	13	7	0	2	45.1	205	49	34	32	7	0	4	7	17	0	34	7	0	1	3	.250	0	0-0	1	5.47	6.35
2006	Tor	AL	16	3	0	3	27.1	143	35	27	22	2	0	1	2	25	2	22	3	1	1	2	.333	0	0-1	1	7.72	7.24
2007	Tor	AL	27	27	2	0	169.2	705	146	80	77	14	0	6	2	61	3	144	13	0	12	10	.545	1	0-0	0	3.07	4.08
2008	Tor	AL	19	19	1	0	111.1	474	115	60	54	9	2	8	5	38	1	85	5	0	6	7	.462	0	0-0	0	4.13	4.37
4 ML YEARS			75	56	3	5	353.2	1527	345	201	185	32	2	19	16	141	6	285	28	1	20	22	.476	1	0-1	2	4.03	4.71

Nate McLouth

Bats: L Throws: R Pos: CF-149; LF-4; RF-2; PH-1

Ht: 5'11" Wt: 180 Born: 10/28/1981 Age: 27

Year	Team	Lg	G	AB	H	2B	3B	HR	(Hm	Rd)	TB	R	RBI	RC	TBB	IBB	SO	HBP	SH	SF	SB	CS	SB%	GDP	Avg	OBP	Slg
2005	Pit	NL	41	109	28	6	0	5	(2	3)	49	20	12	9	3	0	20	5	2	1	2	0	1.00	3	.257	.305	.450
2006	Pit	NL	106	270	63	16	2	7	(3	4)	104	50	16	25	18	0	59	5	3	1	10	1	.91	7	.233	.293	.385
2007	Pit	NL	137	329	85	21	3	13	(5	8)	151	62	38	52	39	2	77	9	3	2	22	1	.96	2	.258	.351	.459
2008	Pit	NL	152	597	165	46	4	26	(15	11)	297	113	94	105	65	11	93	12	5	6	23	3	.88	5	.276	.356	.497
4 ML YEARS			436	1305	341	89	9	51	(25	26)	601	245	160	191	125	13	249	31	13	10	57	5	.92	17	.261	.338	.461

Dallas McPherson

Bats: L Throws: R Pos: PH-9; 3B-2

Ht: 6'4" Wt: 230 Born: 7/23/1980 Age: 28

Year	Team	Lg	G	AB	H	2B	3B	HR	(Hm	Rd)	TB	R	RBI	RC	TBB	IBB	SO	HBP	SH	SF	SB	CS	SB%	GDP	Avg	OBP	Slg
2008	Albq*	AAA	127	448	123	22	3	42	(-	-)	277	94	98	104	76	3	168	2	0	4	14	6	.70	6	.275	.379	.618
2004	LAA	AL	16	40	9	1	0	3	(2	1)	19	5	6	5	3	0	17	0	0	0	1	0	1.00	6	.225	.279	.475
2005	LAA	AL	61	205	50	14	2	8	(6	2)	92	29	26	28	14	0	64	1	0	0	3	3	.50	5	.244	.295	.449
2006	LAA	AL	40	115	30	4	0	7	(3	4)	55	16	13	16	6	0	40	0	0	0	1	0	1.00	3	.261	.298	.478
2008	Fla	NL	11	11	2	2	0	0	(0	0)	4	3	0	1	4	1	5	0	0	0	0	0	-	0	.182	.400	.364
Postseason			3	9	1	0	0	0	(0	0)	1	0	1	0	0	0	4	0	0	0	0	0	-	0	.111	.111	.111
4 ML YEARS			128	371	91	21	2	18	(11	7)	170	53	45	50	27	1	126	1	0	0	5	3	.63	8	.245	.298	.458

Gil Meche

Pitches: R Bats: R Pos: SP-34

Ht: 6'3" Wt: 220 Born: 9/8/1978 Age: 30

Year	Team	Lg	G	GS	CG	GF	IP	BFP	H	R	ER	HR	SH	SF	HB	TBB	IBB	SO	WP	Bk	W	L	Pct	ShO	Sv-Op	Hld	ERC	ERA
1999	Sea	AL	16	15	0	0	85.2	375	73	48	45	9	5	3	2	57	1	47	1	0	8	4	.667	0	0-0	0	4.47	4.73
2000	Sea	AL	15	15	1	0	85.2	363	75	37	36	7	5	4	1	40	0	60	2	0	4	4	.500	1	0-0	0	3.60	3.78
2003	Sea	AL	32	32	1	0	186.1	785	187	97	95	30	3	5	3	63	2	130	7	0	15	13	.536	0	0-0	0	4.39	4.59
2004	Sea	AL	23	23	1	0	127.2	565	139	73	71	21	1	3	5	47	0	99	4	0	7	7	.500	1	0-0	0	5.06	5.01
2005	Sea	AL	29	26	0	2	143.1	638	153	92	81	18	1	5	2	72	1	83	4	0	10	8	.556	0	0-0	0	5.15	5.09
2006	Sea	AL	32	32	1	0	186.2	811	183	106	93	24	3	2	8	84	2	156	4	2	11	8	.579	0	0-0	0	4.56	4.48
2007	KC	AL	34	34	1	0	216.0	906	218	98	88	22	5	7	3	62	2	156	3	0	9	13	.409	0	0-0	0	3.77	3.67
2008	KC	AL	34	34	0	0	210.1	886	204	98	93	19	4	10	0	73	2	183	5	0	14	11	.560	0	0-0	0	3.64	3.98
8 ML YEARS			215	211	5	2	1241.2	5329	1232	649	602	150	27	39	24	498	10	914	30	2	78	68	.534	2	0-0	0	4.28	4.36

Brandon Medders

Pitches: R Bats: R Pos: RP-18

Ht: 6'1" Wt: 200 Born: 1/26/1980 Age: 29

Year	Team	Lg	G	GS	CG	GF	IP	BFP	H	R	ER	HR	SH	SF	HB	TBB	IBB	SO	WP	Bk	W	L	Pct	ShO	Sv-Op	Hld	ERC	ERA
2008	Tucsn*	AAA	26	0	0	8	38.2	187	45	35	32	4	1	1	4	24	1	33	2	0	1	2	.333	0	0- -	-	6.27	7.45
2005	Ari	NL	27	0	0	10	30.1	122	21	6	6	2	0	2	1	11	0	31	1	0	4	1	.800	0	0-0	2	2.25	1.78
2006	Ari	NL	60	0	0	13	71.2	316	76	37	29	5	3	2	2	28	3	47	2	0	5	3	.625	0	0-1	10	4.17	3.64
2007	Ari	NL	30	0	0	7	29.1	128	30	16	14	9	1	0	1	16	0	23	1	0	1	2	.333	0	0-1	1	6.76	4.30
2008	Ari	NL	18	0	0	3	19.2	88	17	11	10	2	1	2	2	11	2	8	1	0	1	0	1.000	0	0-1	0	4.13	4.58
4 ML YEARS			135	0	0	33	151.0	654	144	70	59	18	5	6	6	66	5	109	5	0	11	6	.647	0	0-3	13	4.21	3.52

Evan Meek

Pitches: R Bats: R Pos: RP-9   Ht: 6'0" Wt: 220 Born: 5/12/1983 Age: 26

			HOW MUCH HE PITCHED						WHAT HE GAVE UP													THE RESULTS							
Year	Team	Lg	G	GS	CG	GF	IP	BFP	H	R	ER	HR	SH	SF	HB	TBB	IBB	SO	WP	Bk	W	L	Pct	ShO	Sv-Op	Hld	ERC	ERA
2003	Elizab	R+	14	8	0	3	51.0	209	33	15	14	2	0	0	0	24	0	47	6	0	7	1	.875	0	1--	-	2.10	2.47
2004	QuadC	A	3	3	0	0	5.2	39	7	7	7	0	1	0	2	15	0	3	4	0	0	0	-	0	0--	-	16.39	11.12
2004	Elizab	R+	12	3	0	3	22.1	117	18	26	20	1	2	3	8	25	0	23	11	0	1	2	.333	0	0--	-	6.65	8.06
2005	Beloit	A	13	0	0	2	18.0	107	15	26	20	0	1	3	2	36	0	11	8	1	0	1	.000	0	0--	-	8.86	10.00
2006	Lk Els	A+	26	25	0	0	119.1	546	136	80	66	5	1	3	8	62	0	113	9	1	6	6	.500	0	0--	-	5.23	4.98
2006	Visalia	A+	2	0	0	0	5.0	26	6	5	5	0	0	0	2	4	0	7	1	0	0	1	.000	0	0--	-	7.80	9.00
2007	Mont	AA	44	0	0	9	67.0	297	74	36	32	2	2	2	1	34	5	69	11	0	1	1	.667	0	1--	-	4.58	4.30
2008	Altna	AA	9	0	0	7	16.0	65	14	5	5	0	2	0	1	3	0	17	3	1	1	1	.500	0	2--	-	2.22	2.81
2008	Indy	AAA	23	0	0	9	41.1	167	30	12	11	2	0	0	0	14	4	34	4	0	0	0	-	0	2--	-	1.96	2.40
2008	Pit	NL	9	0	0	7	13.0	61	11	11	10	3	1	1	2	12	2	7	3	0	0	1	.000	0	0-0	-	6.46	6.92

Adam Melhuse

Bats: B Throws: R Pos: C-10; PH-3; 3B-2; PR-1   Ht: 6'2" Wt: 210 Born: 3/27/1972 Age: 37

			BATTING																			BASERUNNING				AVERAGES		
Year	Team	Lg	G	AB	H	2B	3B	HR	(Hm	Rd)	TB	R	RBI	RC	TBB	IBB	SO	HBP	SH	SF		SB	CS	SB%	GDP		Avg	OBP	Slg
2008	TriCity*	A-	5	12	1	1	0	0	(-	-)	2	1	1	0	2	0	5	1	0	0		0	0	-	0		.083	.267	.167
2008	ColSpr*	AAA	32	90	28	7	0	3	(-	-)	44	14	16	18	15	1	22	1	0	1		0	0	-	5		.311	.411	.489
2000	2 Tms	NL	24	24	4	0	1	0	(0	0)	6	3	4	2	3	0	6	0	0	0		0	0	-	1		.167	.259	.250
2001	Col	NL	40	71	13	2	0	1	(0	1)	18	5	8	4	6	0	18	0	0	2		1	0	1.00	1		.183	.241	.254
2003	Oak	AL	40	77	23	7	0	5	(2	3)	45	13	14	15	9	0	19	0	0	0		0	0	-	2		.299	.372	.584
2004	Oak	AL	69	214	55	11	0	11	(3	8)	99	23	31	21	16	1	47	0	1	0		0	1	.00	4		.257	.309	.463
2005	Oak	AL	39	97	24	7	0	2	(1	1)	37	11	12	12	5	0	28	0	0	0		0	0	-	3		.247	.284	.381
2006	Oak	AL	49	128	28	8	0	4	(2	2)	48	10	18	10	9	1	34	1	0	1		0	1	.00	6		.219	.273	.375
2007	2 Tms	AL	35	94	20	4	0	1	(1	0)	27	8	9	9	7	0	26	1	1	0		0	0	-	3		.213	.275	.287
2008	2 Tms		15	30	5	1	0	0	(0	0)	6	3	2	1	2	0	15	0	0	0		0	0	-	0		.167	.219	.200
00	LAD	NL	1	1	0	0	0	0	(0	0)	0	0	0	0	0	0	1	0	0	0		0	0	-	0		.000	.000	.000
00	Col	NL	23	23	4	0	1	0	(0	0)	6	3	4	2	3	0	5	0	0	0		0	0	-	1		.174	.269	.261
07	Oak	AL	12	26	6	1	0	0	(0	0)	7	2	2	3	4	0	8	0	0	0		0	0	-	0		.231	.333	.269
07	Tex	AL	23	68	14	3	0	1	(1	0)	20	6	7	6	3	0	18	1	1	0		0	0	-	3		.206	.250	.294
08	Tex	AL	8	20	4	0	0	0	(0	0)	4	1	1	0	2	0	11	0	0	0		0	0	-	0		.200	.273	.200
08	Col	NL	7	10	1	1	0	0	(0	0)	2	2	1	1	0	0	4	0	0	0		0	0	-	0		.100	.100	.200
Postseason			3	6	3	0	1	0	(0	0)	5	1	1	2	0	0	2	0	0	0		0	0	-	0		.500	.500	.833
8 ML YEARS			311	735	172	40	1	24	(9	15)	286	76	98	74	57	2	193	2	2	3		1	2	.33	19		.234	.290	.389

John Meloan

Pitches: R Bats: R Pos: RP-2   Ht: 6'3" Wt: 230 Born: 7/11/1984 Age: 24

			HOW MUCH HE PITCHED						WHAT HE GAVE UP													THE RESULTS							
Year	Team	Lg	G	GS	CG	GF	IP	BFP	H	R	ER	HR	SH	SF	HB	TBB	IBB	SO	WP	Bk	W	L	Pct	ShO	Sv-Op	Hld	ERC	ERA
2005	Ogden	R+	16	6	0	5	39.0	166	30	16	16	4	1	2	2	18	0	54	6	1	0	2	.000	0	1--	-	3.23	3.69
2006	Clmbs	A	12	0	0	7	23.1	84	9	5	4	2	0	1	0	7	0	41	0	0	1	1	.500	0	1--	-	1.04	1.54
2006	VeroB	A+	4	3	0	0	18.0	73	15	6	5	2	0	0	1	4	0	27	2	0	1	0	1.000	0	0--	-	2.79	2.50
2006	Jaxnvl	AA	5	0	0	0	10.2	40	3	2	2	1	0	0	0	5	0	23	0	0	1	0	1.000	0	0--	-	1.09	1.69
2007	Jaxnvl	AA	35	0	0	33	45.1	176	24	13	11	3	0	1	2	18	0	70	3	0	5	2	.714	0	19--	-	1.69	2.18
2007	LsVgs	AAA	14	0	0	4	21.1	87	12	5	4	2	0	1	1	9	0	21	1	0	2	0	1.000	0	1--	-	1.99	1.69
2008	LsVgs	AAA	21	20	0	0	105.0	488	119	72	58	7	2	5	9	60	1	99	2	2	5	10	.333	0	5--	-	5.65	4.97
2008	Buffalo	AAA	12	0	0	2	14.2	64	12	8	7	1	2	1	1	9	0	12	0	0	0	1	.000	0	0--	-	3.96	4.30
2007	LAD	NL	5	0	0	3	7.1	38	8	9	9	1	1	0	1	8	0	7	0	0	0	0	-	0	0-0	0	8.45	11.05
2008	Cle	AL	2	0	0	1	2.0	6	0	0	0	0	0	0	0	1	0	2	0	0	0	0	-	0	0-0	0	0.32	0.00
2 ML YEARS			7	0	0	4	9.1	44	8	9	9	1	1	0	1	9	0	9	0	0	0	0	-	0	0-0	0	6.14	8.68

Kevin Mench

Bats: R Throws: R Pos: LF-21; RF-15; DH-15; PH-12; PR-2   Ht: 6'0" Wt: 215 Born: 1/7/1978 Age: 31

			BATTING																			BASERUNNING				AVERAGES		
Year	Team	Lg	G	AB	H	2B	3B	HR	(Hm	Rd)	TB	R	RBI	RC	TBB	IBB	SO	HBP	SH	SF		SB	CS	SB%	GDP		Avg	OBP	Slg
2008	Okla*	AAA	29	110	31	7	2	3	(-	-)	51	18	18	18	11	0	11	0	0	1		0	0	-	7		.282	.344	.464
2008	Syrcse*	AAA	22	74	21	5	0	1	(-	-)	29	7	12	9	3	1	14	0	0	0		0	0	-	4		.284	.312	.392
2002	Tex	AL	110	366	95	20	2	15	(8	7)	164	52	60	59	31	0	83	8	2	5		1	1	.50	4		.260	.327	.448
2003	Tex	AL	38	125	40	12	0	2	(1	1)	58	15	11	23	10	0	17	3	0	1		1	1	.50	2		.320	.381	.464
2004	Tex	AL	125	438	122	30	3	26	(14	12)	236	69	71	72	33	2	63	6	0	4		0	0	-	6		.279	.335	.539
2005	Tex	AL	150	557	147	33	4	25	(13	12)	261	71	73	75	50	4	68	5	0	3		4	3	.57	6		.264	.328	.469
2006	2 Tms	NL	127	446	120	24	2	13	(9	4)	187	45	68	57	27	5	59	4	0	5		1	0	1.00	8		.269	.313	.419
2007	Mil	NL	101	288	77	20	3	8	(3	5)	127	39	37	42	16	2	21	1	0	3		3	1	.75	3		.267	.305	.441
2008	Tor	AL	51	115	28	11	1	0	(0	0)	41	18	10	13	14	2	18	0	0	2		2	0	1.00	3		.243	.321	.357
06	Tex	AL	87	320	91	18	1	12	(8	4)	147	36	50	48	23	5	42	4	0	2		1	0	1.00	4		.284	.338	.459
06	Mil	NL	40	126	29	6	1	1	(1	0)	40	9	18	9	4	0	17	0	0	3		0	0	-	4		.230	.248	.317
7 ML YEARS			702	2335	629	150	14	89	(48	41)	1074	309	330	341	181	15	329	27	2	23		12	6	.67	32		.269	.326	.460

Luis Mendoza

Pitches: R Bats: R Pos: RP-14; SP-11　　　　Ht: 6'3" Wt: 210 Born: 10/31/1983 Age: 25

Year	Team	Lg	G	GS	CG	GF	IP	BFP	H	R	ER	HR	SH	SF	HB	TBB	IBB	SO	WP	Bk	W	L	Pct	ShO	Sv-Op	Hld	ERC	ERA
2002	RedSx	R	13	10	0	2	57.2	245	76	36	27	3	2	1	3	8	0	21	4	0	3	4	.429	0	1--	-	4.89	4.21
2003	Augsta	A-	13	11	0	0	59.2	241	46	19	15	1	2	1	5	14	0	29	2	0	3	3	.500	0	0--	-	2.06	2.26
2003	RedSx	R	2	2	0	0	5.0	19	4	0	0	0	0	0	0	1	0	3	0	0	0	0	-	0	0--	-	1.82	0.00
2004	Srsota	A+	25	25	1	0	137.0	596	133	76	57	12	6	8	6	54	5	51	10	0	8	7	.533	0	0--	-	3.88	3.74
2005	Wilmg	A+	23	22	1	1	119.1	539	145	91	84	17	5	8	7	36	0	60	8	0	4	9	.308	0	0--	-	5.43	6.34
2005	Lk Els	A+	2	2	0	0	10.2	51	18	14	11	1	1	0	0	4	0	3	1	0	0	1	.000	0	0--	-	8.46	9.28
2006	Wilmg	A+	13	13	0	0	63.0	270	67	26	22	4	0	2	3	14	-	46	6	0	5	4	.556	0	0--	-	3.62	3.14
2006	Portlnd	AA	9	9	0	0	48.0	226	73	35	34	4	4	0	3	14	1	29	3	1	1	5	.167	0	0--	-	6.93	6.38
2006	Frisco	AA	7	7	0	0	38.1	181	55	33	33	2	0	3	2	11	0	21	7	0	2	4	.333	0	0--	-	5.93	7.75
2007	Frisco	AA	26	25	3	1	148.2	633	145	75	65	11	4	3	10	48	0	93	10	1	15	4	.789	1	0--	-	3.74	3.93
2008	Okla	AAA	8	8	0	0	35.0	153	43	21	20	1	1	1	0	8	0	19	1	1	2	3	.400	0	0--	-	4.15	5.14
2008	Frisco	AA	1	1	0	0	1.1	8	1	2	1	0	0	0	0	2	0	1	1	0	0	0	-	0	0--	-	5.10	6.75
2007	Tex	AL	6	3	0	2	16.0	64	13	4	4	1	0	2	2	4	0	7	0	0	1	0	1.000	0	0-0	0	2.83	2.25
2008	Tex	AL	25	11	0	6	63.1	316	97	74	61	7	0	2	6	25	4	35	5	0	3	8	.273	0	1-2	0	7.53	8.67
2 ML YEARS			31	14	0	8	79.2	380	110	78	65	8	0	4	8	29	4	42	5	0	4	8	.333	0	1-2	0	6.50	7.37

Kent Mercker

Pitches: L Bats: L Pos: RP-15　　　　Ht: 6'2" Wt: 205 Born: 2/1/1968 Age: 41

Year	Team	Lg	G	GS	CG	GF	IP	BFP	H	R	ER	HR	SH	SF	HB	TBB	IBB	SO	WP	Bk	W	L	Pct	ShO	Sv-Op	Hld	ERC	ERA
2008	Dayton*	A	1	0	0	0	1.0	3	0	0	0	0	0	0	0	0	0	1	0	0	0	0	-	0	0--	-	0.00	0.00
2008	Lsvlle*	AAA	2	1	0	0	1.2	8	2	1	1	0	0	0	0	1	0	0	0	0	0	1	.000	0	0--	-	5.10	5.40
1989	Atl	NL	2	1	0	1	4.1	26	8	6	6	0	0	0	0	6	0	4	0	0	0	0	-	0	0-0	0	13.19	12.46
1990	Atl	NL	36	0	0	28	48.1	211	43	22	17	6	1	2	2	24	3	39	2	0	4	7	.364	0	7-10	0	4.04	3.17
1991	Atl	NL	50	4	0	28	73.1	306	56	23	21	5	2	2	1	35	3	62	4	1	5	3	.625	0	6-8	3	2.88	2.58
1992	Atl	NL	53	0	0	18	68.1	289	51	27	26	4	4	1	3	35	1	49	6	0	3	2	.600	0	6-9	6	2.99	3.42
1993	Atl	NL	43	6	0	9	66.0	283	52	24	21	2	0	0	2	36	3	59	5	1	3	1	.750	0	0-3	4	3.02	2.86
1994	Atl	NL	20	17	2	0	112.1	461	90	46	43	16	4	3	0	45	3	111	4	1	9	4	.692	1	0-0	0	3.27	3.45
1995	Atl	NL	29	26	0	1	143.0	612	140	73	66	16	8	7	3	61	2	102	6	2	7	8	.467	0	0-0	0	4.19	4.15
1996	2 Tms	AL	24	12	0	2	69.2	329	83	60	54	13	3	6	3	38	2	29	3	1	4	6	.400	0	0-0	2	6.56	6.98
1997	Cin	NL	28	25	0	0	144.2	616	135	65	63	16	8	4	2	62	6	75	2	1	8	11	.421	0	0-0	0	3.91	3.92
1998	StL	NL	30	29	0	1	161.2	716	199	99	91	11	10	9	3	53	4	72	6	4	11	11	.500	0	0-0	0	4.96	5.07
1999	2 Tms	NL	30	23	0	2	129.1	589	148	85	69	16	8	4	3	64	3	81	3	1	8	5	.615	0	0-0	0	5.54	4.80
2000	LAA	AL	21	7	0	2	48.1	225	57	35	35	12	3	1	2	29	3	30	2	0	1	3	.250	0	0-0	1	7.35	6.52
2002	Col	NL	58	0	0	8	44.0	208	55	33	30	12	0	0	2	22	2	37	1	0	3	1	.750	0	0-3	9	7.45	6.14
2003	2 Tms	NL	67	0	0	15	55.1	242	46	16	12	6	6	1	0	32	4	48	4	1	2	0	.000	0	1-5	11	3.72	1.95
2004	ChC	NL	71	0	0	7	53.0	223	39	15	15	4	0	3	3	27	2	51	4	1	3	1	.750	0	0-3	16	3.07	2.55
2005	Cin	NL	78	0	0	23	61.2	265	64	27	25	8	4	2	3	19	4	45	1	0	3	1	.750	0	4-7	20	4.23	3.65
2006	Cin	NL	37	0	0	7	28.1	123	28	15	13	6	3	1	0	11	1	17	1	1	1	1	.500	0	1-3	6	4.63	4.13
2008	Cin	NL	15	0	0	5	13.2	58	13	5	5	1	1	0	0	8	1	6	1	0	1	0	1.000	0	0-0	0	4.42	3.29
96	Bal	AL	14	12	0	2	58.0	283	73	56	50	12	3	4	3	35	1	22	3	1	3	6	.333	0	0-0	0	7.45	7.76
96	Cle	AL	10	0	0	2	11.2	46	10	4	4	1	0	2	0	3	1	7	0	0	1	0	1.000	0	0-0	2	2.65	3.09
99	StL	NL	25	18	0	2	103.2	476	125	73	59	16	8	3	2	51	3	64	3	1	6	5	.545	0	0-0	0	6.15	5.12
99	Bos	AL	5	5	0	0	25.2	113	23	12	10	0	0	1	1	13	0	17	0	0	2	0	1.000	0	0-0	0	3.29	3.51
03	Cin	NL	49	0	0	8	38.1	169	31	13	10	5	6	0	0	25	2	41	2	1	0	2	.000	0	0-3	10	4.09	2.35
03	Atl	NL	18	0	0	7	17.0	73	15	3	2	1	0	1	0	7	2	7	2	0	0	0	-	0	1-2	1	2.95	1.06
Postseason			16	3	0	2	22.1	100	20	9	9	2	1	1	1	15	0	15	0	0	0	2	.000	0	0-0	1	4.69	3.63
18 ML YEARS			692	150	2	157	1325.1	5792	1307	676	612	154	65	46	32	607	47	917	55	15	74	67	.525	1	25-51	78	4.39	4.16

Cla Meredith

Pitches: R Bats: R Pos: RP-73　　　　Ht: 6'0" Wt: 189 Born: 6/4/1983 Age: 26

Year	Team	Lg	G	GS	CG	GF	IP	BFP	H	R	ER	HR	SH	SF	HB	TBB	IBB	SO	WP	Bk	W	L	Pct	ShO	Sv-Op	Hld	ERC	ERA
2008	Portlnd*	AAA	6	0	0	3	6.2	29	6	2	2	0	0	0	0	3	0	4	0	1	0	0	-	0	0--	-	2.95	2.70
2005	Bos	AL	3	0	0	0	2.1	18	6	7	7	1	0	0	1	4	0	0	1	0	0	0	-	0	0-0	0	27.60	27.00
2006	SD	NL	45	0	0	11	50.2	185	30	6	6	3	1	0	2	6	3	37	0	2	5	1	.833	0	0-2	16	1.19	1.07
2007	SD	NL	80	0	0	18	79.2	342	94	38	31	6	1	3	3	17	4	59	3	1	5	6	.455	0	0-5	10	4.28	3.50
2008	SD	NL	73	0	0	19	70.1	302	79	34	32	6	2	3	1	24	3	49	2	0	0	3	.000	0	0-6	11	4.52	4.09
Postseason			2	0	0	0	3.2	15	3	2	0	0	1	0	1	0	0	3	0	0	0	0	-	0	0-0	0	2.00	0.00
4 ML YEARS			201	0	0	48	203.0	847	209	85	76	16	4	6	7	51	10	145	6	3	10	10	.500	0	0-13	37	3.62	3.37

Randy Messenger

Pitches: R Bats: R Pos: RP-13　　　　Ht: 6'6" Wt: 270 Born: 8/13/1981 Age: 27

Year	Team	Lg	G	GS	CG	GF	IP	BFP	H	R	ER	HR	SH	SF	HB	TBB	IBB	SO	WP	Bk	W	L	Pct	ShO	Sv-Op	Hld	ERC	ERA
2008	Fresno*	AAA	29	0	0	15	41.0	173	47	24	22	4	3	0	0	12	0	30	3	0	3	4	.429	0	3--	-	4.60	4.83
2008	Tacom*	AAA	12	0	0	5	22.2	95	19	7	6	2	2	0	0	11	4	16	0	0	6	0	1.000	0	1--	-	3.21	2.38
2005	Fla	NL	29	0	0	8	37.0	178	39	22	22	5	2	3	0	30	7	29	1	0	0	0	-	0	0-0	5	5.91	5.35
2006	Fla	NL	59	0	0	10	60.1	275	72	42	38	8	5	2	1	24	2	45	3	0	2	7	.222	0	0-1	9	5.38	5.67
2007	2 Tms	NL	60	0	0	21	64.1	291	85	30	30	4	6	5	1	21	5	34	1	0	2	4	.333	0	1-5	11	5.32	4.20
2008	Sea	AL	13	0	0	3	12.2	57	16	5	5	1	0	0	1	5	1	7	0	0	0	0	-	0	1-1	2	5.78	3.55
07	Fla	NL	23	0	0	8	23.2	103	27	7	7	0	4	1	0	9	2	12	0	0	1	1	.500	0	0-0	6	3.97	2.66
07	SF	NL	37	0	0	13	40.2	188	58	23	23	4	2	4	1	12	3	22	1	0	1	3	.250	0	1-5	5	6.14	5.09
4 ML YEARS			161	0	0	42	174.1	801	212	99	95	18	13	10	2	80	15	115	5	0	4	11	.267	0	2-7	24	5.50	4.90

Travis Metcalf

Bats: R **Throws:** R **Pos:** 3B-19; PH-2; SS-1; DH-1; PR-1   **Ht:** 6'3" **Wt:** 215 **Born:** 8/17/1982 **Age:** 26

									BATTING													BASERUNNING				AVERAGES		
Year	Team	Lg	G	AB	H	2B	3B	HR	(Hm	Rd)	TB	R	RBI	RC	TBB	IBB	SO	HBP	SH	SF	SB	CS	SB%	GDP	Avg	OBP	Slg
2004	Spkane	A-	72	290	78	21	1	15	(-	-)	146	48	62	52	37	1	74	3	1	6	1	2	.33	6	.269	.351	.503
2005	Bkrsfld	A+	132	505	147	32	7	22	(-	-)	259	80	94	94	49	0	129	6	1	5	8	2	.80	14	.291	.358	.513
2006	Frisco	AA	121	425	94	16	2	8	(-	-)	138	51	37	43	45	2	112	3	0	4	9	7	.56	9	.221	.298	.325
2007	Frisco	AA	55	200	56	18	0	7	(-	-)	95	38	34	34	21	2	44	1	0	4	2	1	.67	3	.280	.345	.475
2007	Okla	AAA	18	61	9	3	0	0	(-	-)	12	2	6	2	7	0	17	0	1	1	0	0	-	3	.148	.232	.197
2008	Okla	AAA	71	265	67	14	1	5	(-	-)	98	36	37	30	18	0	59	1	1	3	0	1	.00	6	.253	.300	.370
2007	Tex	AL	57	161	41	12	1	5	(1	4)	70	25	21	20	13	0	41	0	5	2	0	1	.00	6	.255	.307	.435
2008	Tex	AL	23	56	13	2	0	6	(5	1)	33	11	14	7	3	0	12	1	0	1	0	0	-	2	.232	.279	.589
	2 ML YEARS		80	217	54	14	1	11	(6	5)	103	36	35	27	16	0	53	1	5	3	0	1	.00	8	.249	.300	.475

Dan Meyer

Pitches: L **Bats:** R **Pos:** RP-7; SP-4   **Ht:** 6'3" **Wt:** 222 **Born:** 7/3/1981 **Age:** 27

			HOW MUCH HE PITCHED					WHAT HE GAVE UP										THE RESULTS						
Year	Team	Lg	G	GS	CG	GF	IP	BFP	H	R	ER	HR	SH	SF	HB	TBB	IBB	SO	WP	Bk	W	L	Pct	ShO	Sv-Op	Hld	ERC	ERA
2008	Scrmto*	AAA	22	20	0	0	122.2	523	113	65	61	10	6	2	1	52	1	109	10	0	10	5	.667	0	0--	-	3.21	4.48
2004	Atl	NL	2	0	0	1	2.0	8	2	0	0	0	0	0	0	1	1	1	0	0	0	0	-	0	0-0	-	3.21	0.00
2007	Oak	AL	6	3	0	2	16.1	79	20	19	16	2	1	1	0	9	0	11	3	0	0	2	.000	0	0-0	0	5.97	8.82
2008	Oak	AL	11	4	0	5	27.2	132	35	28	23	6	0	2	1	14	0	20	0	0	0	4	.000	0	0-0	0	7.10	7.48
	3 ML YEARS		19	7	0	8	46.0	219	57	47	39	8	1	3	1	24	1	32	3	0	0	6	.000	0	0-0	0	6.52	7.63

Jason Michaels

Bats: R **Throws:** R **Pos:** PH-50; RF-43; LF-34; CF-8; PR-3   **Ht:** 6'0" **Wt:** 206 **Born:** 5/4/1976 **Age:** 33

									BATTING													BASERUNNING				AVERAGES		
Year	Team	Lg	G	AB	H	2B	3B	HR	(Hm	Rd)	TB	R	RBI	RC	TBB	IBB	SO	HBP	SH	SF	SB	CS	SB%	GDP	Avg	OBP	Slg
2001	Phi	NL	6	6	1	0	0	0	(0	0)	1	0	1	0	0	0	2	0	0	0	0	0	-	0	.167	.167	.167
2002	Phi	NL	81	105	28	10	3	2	(0	2)	50	16	11	14	13	1	33	1	0	2	1	1	.50	1	.267	.347	.476
2003	Phi	NL	76	109	36	11	0	5	(1	4)	62	20	17	19	15	1	22	1	0	0	0	0	-	3	.330	.416	.569
2004	Phi	NL	115	299	82	12	0	10	(5	5)	124	44	40	47	42	1	80	2	0	3	2	2	.50	3	.274	.364	.415
2005	Phi	NL	105	289	88	16	2	4	(1	3)	120	54	31	47	44	1	45	4	2	4	3	3	.50	3	.304	.399	.415
2006	Cle	AL	123	494	132	32	1	9	(4	5)	193	77	55	62	43	0	101	3	2	6	9	5	.64	6	.267	.326	.391
2007	Cle	AL	105	267	72	11	1	7	(5	2)	106	43	39	37	20	1	50	3	2	3	3	4	.43	3	.270	.324	.397
2008	2 Tms		123	286	64	13	1	8	(4	4)	103	28	53	37	27	0	65	2	2	4	2	1	.67	9	.224	.292	.360
08	Cle	AL	21	58	12	4	0	0	(0	0)	16	3	9	5	4	0	13	1	1	3	1	1	.50	0	.207	.258	.276
08	Pit	NL	102	228	52	9	1	8	(4	4)	87	25	44	32	23	0	52	1	1	1	1	0	1.00	9	.228	.300	.382
	Postseason		2	1	1	1	0	0	(0	0)	2	1	0	1	0	0	0	0	1	0	0	0	-	0	1.000	1.000	2.000
	8 ML YEARS		734	1855	503	105	8	45	(20	25)	759	282	247	263	204	5	398	16	8	22	20	16	.56	28	.271	.345	.409

Kam Mickolio

Pitches: R **Bats:** R **Pos:** RP-9   **Ht:** 6'9" **Wt:** 256 **Born:** 5/10/1984 **Age:** 25

			HOW MUCH HE PITCHED					WHAT HE GAVE UP										THE RESULTS						
Year	Team	Lg	G	GS	CG	GF	IP	BFP	H	R	ER	HR	SH	SF	HB	TBB	IBB	SO	WP	Bk	W	L	Pct	ShO	Sv-Op	Hld	ERC	ERA
2006	Everett	A-	21	0	0	11	32.1	140	34	14	10	1	1	0	3	7	0	26	3	1	1	0	1.000	0	4--	-	3.47	2.78
2007	WTenn	AA	18	0	0	8	29.2	123	24	9	6	0	1	1	2	12	1	27	2	0	3	1	.750	0	2--	-	2.63	1.82
2007	Tacom	AAA	14	0	0	7	24.0	102	19	12	10	3	1	0	2	10	0	28	3	1	3	3	.500	0	1--	-	3.46	3.75
2008	Bowie	AA	28	0	0	6	38.1	178	39	21	20	2	2	2	3	22	0	40	3	0	2	1	.667	0	1--	-	4.71	4.70
2008	Norfolk	AAA	17	0	0	3	20.0	87	13	7	4	0	1	0	2	9	0	23	0	0	1	0	1.000	0	2--	-	2.01	1.80
2008	Bal	AL	9	0	0	5	7.2	36	8	5	5	0	1	1	0	4	0	8	2	0	0	1	.000	0	0-1	0	3.81	5.87

Doug Mientkiewicz

Bats: L **Throws:** R **Pos:** PH-53; 1B-37; 3B-33; RF-10; PR-1   **Ht:** 6'2" **Wt:** 210 **Born:** 6/19/1974 **Age:** 35

									BATTING													BASERUNNING				AVERAGES		
Year	Team	Lg	G	AB	H	2B	3B	HR	(Hm	Rd)	TB	R	RBI	RC	TBB	IBB	SO	HBP	SH	SF	SB	CS	SB%	GDP	Avg	OBP	Slg
1998	Min	AL	8	25	5	1	0	0	(0	0)	6	1	2	2	4	0	3	0	0	0	1	1	.50	0	.200	.310	.240
1999	Min	AL	118	327	75	21	3	2	(0	2)	108	34	32	34	43	3	51	4	3	2	1	1	.50	13	.229	.324	.330
2000	Min	AL	3	14	6	0	0	0	(0	0)	6	0	4	2	0	0	0	0	0	1	0	0	-	1	.429	.400	.429
2001	Min	AL	151	543	166	39	1	15	(11	4)	252	77	74	96	67	6	92	9	0	7	2	6	.25	10	.306	.387	.464
2002	Min	AL	143	467	122	29	1	10	(6	4)	183	60	64	76	74	8	69	6	0	7	1	2	.33	7	.261	.365	.392
2003	Min	AL	142	487	146	38	1	11	(6	5)	219	67	65	89	74	4	55	5	2	6	4	1	.80	9	.300	.393	.450
2004	2 Tms		127	391	93	24	1	6	(1	5)	137	47	35	46	48	2	56	4	2	2	2	3	.40	12	.238	.326	.350
2005	NYM	NL	87	275	66	13	0	11	(3	8)	112	36	29	28	32	7	39	2	2	2	0	1	.00	11	.240	.322	.407
2006	KC	AL	91	314	89	24	2	4	(1	3)	129	37	43	48	35	1	50	5	1	5	3	0	1.00	6	.283	.359	.411
2007	NYY	AL	72	166	46	12	0	5	(4	1)	73	26	24	25	16	0	23	3	6	1	0	0	-	3	.277	.349	.440
2008	Pit	NL	125	285	79	19	2	2	(0	2)	108	37	30	47	44	3	28	2	0	3	0	0	-	6	.277	.374	.379
04	Min	AL	78	284	70	18	0	5	(1	4)	103	34	25	34	38	2	38	3	2	1	2	2	.50	9	.246	.340	.363
04	Bos	AL	49	107	23	6	1	1	(0	1)	34	13	10	12	10	0	18	1	0	1	0	1	.00	3	.215	.286	.318
	Postseason		29	68	16	2	0	2	(1	1)	24	4	7	8	4	0	6	0	2	0	0	0	-	0	.235	.278	.353
	11 ML YEARS		1067	3294	893	220	11	66	(32	34)	1333	422	402	493	437	34	466	40	16	36	14	15	.48	78	.271	.360	.405

Jose Mijares

Pitches: L Bats: L Pos: RP-10

Ht: 6'0" Wt: 231 Born: 10/29/1984 Age: 24

				HOW MUCH HE PITCHED						WHAT HE GAVE UP										THE RESULTS							
Year	Team	Lg	G	GS	CG	GF	IP	BFP	H	R	ER	HR	SH	SF	HB	TBB	IBB	SO	WP	Bk	W	L	Pct	ShO	Sv-Op Hld	ERC	ERA
2004	Twins	R	19	0	0	13	29.2	126	22	9	8	1	2	1	2	15	0	25	3	1	4	0	1.000	0	5-- -	2.87	2.43
2005	Beloit	A	20	6	0	5	54.1	240	43	28	26	6	1	1	2	40	0	78	3	1	6	3	.667	0	2-- -	4.50	4.31
2005	FtMyrs	A+	5	1	0	1	12.0	49	5	4	2	1	0	0	0	5	0	17	0	0	0	0	.-	0	0-- -	1.24	1.50
2006	FtMyrs	A+	27	5	0	6	63.0	267	52	30	25	10	4	2	4	27	0	77	5	0	3	5	.375	0	0-- -	3.88	3.57
2007	NwBrit	AA	46	0	0	31	61.0	275	40	26	24	7	5	2	2	48	1	75	3	0	5	3	.625	0	9-- -	3.75	3.54
2007	Roch	AAA	5	0	0	0	8.2	41	9	7	6	3	0	1	1	5	1	6	0	0	0	1	.000	0	0-- -	7.11	6.23
2008	Twins	R	7	0	0	1	11.0	44	10	3	1	0	0	0	0	1	0	16	0	0	2	1	.667	0	0-- -	1.84	0.82
2008	FtMyrs	A+	5	0	0	1	10.1	40	7	3	3	0	0	1	0	3	0	8	2	0	0	0	.-	0	0-- -	1.55	2.61
2008	NwBrit	AA	11	0	0	3	15.1	69	16	5	5	2	0	0	0	7	0	17	0	0	1	1	.500	0	2-- -	4.66	2.93
2008	Min	AL	10	0	0	3	10.1	34	3	1	1	0	0	0	0	0	0	5	1	0	0	1	.000	0	0-0 2	0.19	0.87

Aaron Miles

Bats: B Throws: R Pos: 2B-85; PH-34; SS-27; 3B-11; LF-4; CF-1; RF-1

Ht: 5'8" Wt: 185 Born: 12/15/1976 Age: 32

						BATTING															BASERUNNING				AVERAGES		
Year	Team	Lg	G	AB	H	2B	3B	HR	(Hm	Rd)	TB	R	RBI	RC	TBB	IBB	SO	HBP	SH	SF	SB	CS	SB%	GDP	Avg	OBP	Slg
2003	CWS	AL	8	12	4	3	0	0	(0	0)	7	3	2	3	0	0	0	0	0	0	0	0	.-	0	.333	.333	.583
2004	Col	NL	134	522	153	15	3	6	(4	2)	192	75	47	70	29	0	53	2	7	6	12	7	.63	12	.293	.329	.368
2005	Col	NL	99	324	91	12	3	2	(0	2)	115	37	28	42	8	1	38	4	10	1	4	2	.67	6	.281	.306	.355
2006	StL	NL	135	426	112	20	5	2	(1	1)	148	48	30	49	38	9	42	2	4	3	2	1	.67	8	.263	.324	.347
2007	StL	NL	133	414	120	16	1	2	(0	2)	144	55	32	49	25	1	40	1	4	5	2	1	.67	11	.290	.328	.348
2008	StL	NL	134	379	120	15	2	4	(1	3)	151	49	31	44	23	2	37	0	5	1	3	3	.50	13	.317	.355	.398
	Postseason		7	11	4	0	1	0	(0	0)	6	2	0	2	1	1	2	0	0	0	1	0	1.00	0	.364	.417	.545
	6 ML YEARS		643	2077	600	81	14	16	(6	10)	757	267	170	257	123	13	210	9	28	16	23	14	.62	50	.289	.329	.364

Kevin Millar

Bats: R Throws: R Pos: 1B-130; DH-14; PH-2

Ht: 6'0" Wt: 217 Born: 9/24/1971 Age: 37

						BATTING															BASERUNNING				AVERAGES		
Year	Team	Lg	G	AB	H	2B	3B	HR	(Hm	Rd)	TB	R	RBI	RC	TBB	IBB	SO	HBP	SH	SF	SB	CS	SB%	GDP	Avg	OBP	Slg
1998	Fla	NL	2	2	1	0	0	0	(0	0)	1	1	0	1	1	0	0	0	0	0	0	0	.-	0	.500	.667	.500
1999	Fla	NL	105	351	100	17	4	9	(3	6)	152	48	67	57	40	2	64	7	1	8	1	0	1.00	7	.285	.362	.433
2000	Fla	NL	123	259	67	14	3	14	(6	8)	129	36	42	47	36	0	47	8	0	2	0	0	.-	5	.259	.364	.498
2001	Fla	NL	144	449	141	39	5	20	(13	7)	250	62	85	89	39	2	70	5	0	2	0	0	.-	8	.314	.374	.557
2002	Fla	NL	126	438	134	41	0	16	(11	5)	223	58	57	63	40	0	74	5	0	6	2	0	.00	15	.306	.366	.509
2003	Bos	AL	148	544	150	30	1	25	(10	15)	257	83	96	87	60	5	108	5	0	9	3	2	.60	14	.276	.348	.472
2004	Bos	AL	150	508	151	36	0	18	(12	6)	241	74	74	90	57	0	91	17	0	6	1	1	.50	16	.297	.383	.474
2005	Bos	AL	134	449	122	28	1	9	(8	1)	179	57	50	58	54	0	74	8	0	8	0	1	.00	12	.272	.355	.399
2006	Bal	AL	132	430	117	26	0	15	(7	8)	188	64	64	67	59	3	74	12	0	2	1	1	.50	14	.272	.374	.437
2007	Bal	AL	140	476	121	26	1	17	(12	5)	200	63	63	71	76	2	94	8	0	2	1	1	.50	8	.254	.365	.420
2008	Bal	AL	145	531	124	25	0	20	(11	9)	209	73	72	67	71	3	93	2	0	6	0	1	.00	8	.234	.323	.394
	Postseason		28	95	23	5	0	2	(0	2)	34	11	10	9	11	0	21	1	0	0	0	0	.-	2	.242	.327	.358
	11 ML YEARS		1349	4437	1228	282	15	163	(93	70)	2029	619	670	697	533	17	789	77	1	51	7	9	.44	107	.277	.361	.457

Lastings Milledge

Bats: R Throws: R Pos: CF-134; PH-4

Ht: 6'0" Wt: 207 Born: 4/5/1985 Age: 24

						BATTING															BASERUNNING				AVERAGES		
Year	Team	Lg	G	AB	H	2B	3B	HR	(Hm	Rd)	TB	R	RBI	RC	TBB	IBB	SO	HBP	SH	SF	SB	CS	SB%	GDP	Avg	OBP	Slg
2008	Nats*	R	2	4	1	0	0	1	(-	-)	4	1	1	0	0	0	0	0	0	0	0	0	.-	0	.250	.250	1.000
2008	Clmbs*	AAA	3	13	1	0	0	0	(-	-)	1	0	2	0	0	0	4	0	0	0	0	0	.-	1	.077	.077	.077
2006	NYM	NL	56	166	40	7	2	4	(2	2)	63	14	22	21	12	4	39	5	1	1	1	2	.33	4	.241	.310	.380
2007	NYM	NL	59	184	50	9	1	7	(6	1)	82	27	29	27	13	2	42	7	1	1	3	2	.60	5	.272	.341	.446
2008	Was	NL	138	523	140	24	2	14	(7	7)	210	65	61	60	38	1	96	14	5	7	24	9	.73	19	.268	.330	.402
	3 ML YEARS		253	873	230	40	5	25	(15	10)	355	106	112	108	63	7	177	26	7	9	28	13	.68	28	.263	.329	.407

Andrew Miller

Pitches: L Bats: L Pos: SP-20; RP-9

Ht: 6'6" Wt: 210 Born: 5/21/1985 Age: 24

				HOW MUCH HE PITCHED						WHAT HE GAVE UP										THE RESULTS							
Year	Team	Lg	G	GS	CG	GF	IP	BFP	H	R	ER	HR	SH	SF	HB	TBB	IBB	SO	WP	Bk	W	L	Pct	ShO	Sv-Op Hld	ERC	ERA
2008	Mrlns*	R	1	1	0	0	1.0	6	2	2	2	0	0	0	0	1	0	0	0	0	0	1	.000	0	0-- -	12.01	18.00
2008	Jupiter*	A+	4	2	0	0	12.2	48	10	1	1	1	1	0	0	1	0	11	2	0	1	0	1.000	0	0-- -	1.75	0.71
2008	Carlina*	AA	1	1	0	0	5.2	23	2	2	2	0	1	0	1	4	0	6	0	0	0	0	.-	0	0-- -	1.87	3.18
2006	Det	AL	8	0	0	3	10.1	51	8	9	7	0	0	0	2	10	0	6	1	0	0	1	.000	0	0-0 1	4.79	6.10
2007	Det	AL	13	13	0	0	64.0	309	73	43	40	8	3	1	7	39	0	56	4	1	5	5	.500	0	0-0 0	6.31	5.63
2008	Fla	NL	29	20	0	1	107.1	492	120	78	70	7	10	7	4	56	4	89	4	0	6	10	.375	0	0-0 2	5.04	5.87
	3 ML YEARS		50	33	0	4	181.2	852	201	130	117	15	13	8	13	105	4	151	9	1	11	16	.407	0	0-0 3	5.47	5.80

Corky Miller

Bats: R **Throws:** R **Pos:** C-29; PH-4   **Ht:** 6'1" **Wt:** 246 **Born:** 3/18/1976 **Age:** 33

Year	Team	Lg	G	AB	H	2B	3B	HR	(Hm	Rd)	TB	R	RBI	RC	TBB	IBB	SO	HBP	SH	SF	SB	CS	SB%	GDP	Avg	OBP	Slg
2008	Rchmd*	AAA	16	56	19	3	0	5	(-	-)	37	9	12	15	9	1	11	2	0	0	0	1	.00	4	.339	.448	.661
2001	Cin	NL	17	49	9	2	0	3	(1	2)	20	5	7	6	4	0	16	2	0	2	1	0	1.00	1	.184	.263	.408
2002	Cin	NL	39	114	29	10	0	3	(2	1)	48	9	15	15	9	2	20	4	1	1	0	0	-	7	.254	.328	.421
2003	Cin	NL	14	30	8	0	0	0	(0	0)	8	4	1	5	5	0	7	2	0	1	0	0	-	1	.267	.395	.267
2004	Cin	NL	13	39	1	0	0	0	(0	0)	1	2	3	0	6	0	12	3	0	1	0	0	-	3	.026	.204	.026
2005	Min	AL	5	12	0	0	0	0	(0	0)	0	0	0	0	0	0	2	0	0	0	0	0	-	0	.000	.000	.000
2006	Bos	AL	1	4	0	0	0	0	(0	0)	0	0	0	0	0	0	1	0	0	0	0	0	-	0	.000	.000	.000
2007	Atl	NL	12	27	7	2	0	1	(0	1)	12	3	4	4	1	0	5	1	0	0	0	0	-	1	.259	.310	.444
2008	Atl	NL	31	60	5	0	0	1	(0	1)	8	4	5	0	5	0	15	0	1	1	0	0	-	2	.083	.152	.133
	8 ML YEARS		132	335	59	14	0	8	(3	5)	97	27	35	30	30	2	78	12	2	6	1	0	1.00	15	.176	.264	.290

Jai Miller

Bats: R **Throws:** R **Pos:** CF-1   **Ht:** 6'4" **Wt:** 195 **Born:** 1/17/1985 **Age:** 24

Year	Team	Lg	G	AB	H	2B	3B	HR	(Hm	Rd)	TB	R	RBI	RC	TBB	IBB	SO	HBP	SH	SF	SB	CS	SB%	GDP	Avg	OBP	Slg
2003	Mrlns	R	46	146	29	4	1	1	(-	-)	38	17	15	11	15	0	45	2	1	2	9	3	.75	4	.199	.279	.260
2003	Jmstwn	A-	11	43	10	3	0	0	(-	-)	13	5	6	3	3	0	15	1	0	1	1	1	.50	0	.233	.292	.302
2004	Grnsbr	A	113	390	80	15	3	12	(-	-)	137	51	49	38	32	0	163	5	5	1	11	4	.73	10	.205	.273	.351
2005	Grnsbr	A	115	415	86	14	2	13	(-	-)	143	69	34	46	57	1	139	3	1	3	16	11	.59	5	.207	.305	.345
2006	Jupiter	A+	111	344	72	16	2	0	(-	-)	92	40	24	32	45	1	115	5	5	2	24	10	.71	5	.209	.308	.267
2007	Carlina	AA	129	406	106	26	2	14	(-	-)	178	54	58	67	55	5	127	5	4	3	12	5	.71	10	.261	.354	.438
2008	Albq	AAA	117	434	116	22	5	19	(-	-)	205	67	56	75	52	3	133	5	2	5	19	6	.76	5	.267	.349	.472
2008	Fla	NL	1	1	0	0	0	0	(0	0)	0	0	0	0	0	0	1	0	0	0	0	0	-	0	.000	.000	.000

Jim Miller

Pitches: R **Bats:** R **Pos:** RP-8   **Ht:** 6'1" **Wt:** 200 **Born:** 4/28/1982 **Age:** 27

Year	Team	Lg	G	GS	CG	GF	IP	BFP	H	R	ER	HR	SH	SF	HB	TBB	IBB	SO	WP	Bk	W	L	Pct	ShO	Sv-Op	Hld	ERC	ERA
2004	TriCity	A-	34	0	0	32	37.0	145	21	6	4	1	0	0	2	11	0	65	1	0	1	1	.500	0	17- -	-	1.42	0.97
2005	Mdest	A+	48	0	0	44	47.2	201	39	22	20	3	0	0	1	17	0	68	3	0	1	3	.250	0	25- -	-	2.70	3.78
2005	Tulsa	AA	16	0	0	13	15.0	61	6	5	1	2	0	0	2	8	0	19	2	0	1	1	.500	0	9- -	-	2.14	0.60
2006	Tulsa	AA	45	0	0	27	44.1	205	50	23	19	10	1	3	5	14	2	41	1	1	0	3	.000	0	12- -	-	5.58	3.86
2007	Bowie	AA	30	0	0	13	38.2	167	26	13	12	0	0	1	3	25	0	49	3	0	2	3	.400	0	4- -	-	2.81	2.79
2007	Norfolk	AAA	22	0	0	13	27.2	126	25	13	13	3	2	0	1	16	0	30	2	0	1	2	.333	0	3- -	-	4.29	4.23
2008	Bowie	AA	7	0	0	2	13.0	57	11	5	5	1	0	1	3	5	0	17	0	0	1	0	1.000	0	0- -	-	3.87	3.46
2008	Norfolk	AAA	49	0	0	29	67.0	271	50	26	23	4	4	1	0	22	1	79	1	1	3	5	.375	0	10- -	-	2.20	3.09
2008	Bal	AL	8	0	0	5	7.2	39	9	3	1	0	1	1	1	5	2	8	1	0	0	2	.000	0	1-2	0	4.99	1.17

Justin Miller

Pitches: R **Bats:** R **Pos:** RP-46   **Ht:** 6'2" **Wt:** 200 **Born:** 8/27/1977 **Age:** 31

Year	Team	Lg	G	GS	CG	GF	IP	BFP	H	R	ER	HR	SH	SF	HB	TBB	IBB	SO	WP	Bk	W	L	Pct	ShO	Sv-Op	Hld	ERC	ERA
2008	Mrlns*	R	1	0	0	0	1.0	6	2	1	1	0	0	0	0	0	0	2	1	0	0	0	-	0	0- -	-	6.14	9.00
2008	Jupiter*	A+	3	0	0	0	3.0	12	2	0	0	0	0	0	0	1	0	3	0	0	1	0	1.000	0	0- -	-	1.57	0.00
2008	Albq*	AAA	1	0	0	0	0.2	6	4	3	3	1	0	0	0	0	0	1	0	0	0	0	-	0	0- -	-	61.64	40.50
2002	Tor	AL	25	18	0	2	102.1	469	103	70	63	12	1	6	11	66	2	68	6	0	9	5	.643	0	0-0	1	5.73	5.54
2004	Tor	AL	19	15	0	0	81.2	375	101	58	55	14	2	6	5	42	3	47	3	1	3	4	.429	0	0-0	0	6.16	6.06
2005	Tor	AL	1	0	0	0	2.1	12	5	4	4	3	0	0	0	0	0	2	0	0	0	0	-	0	0-0	0	20.19	15.43
2007	Fla	NL	62	0	0	10	61.2	259	53	27	25	5	3	0	0	24	6	74	4	1	5	0	1.000	0	0-3	17	2.98	3.65
2008	Fla	NL	46	0	0	8	46.2	202	46	26	22	4	0	1	3	20	3	43	1	1	4	2	.667	0	0-1	7	4.21	4.24
	5 ML YEARS		153	33	0	20	294.2	1317	308	185	169	38	6	13	19	152	14	234	14	3	21	11	.656	0	0-4	25	5.27	5.16

Trever Miller

Pitches: L **Bats:** R **Pos:** RP-68   **Ht:** 6'3" **Wt:** 200 **Born:** 5/29/1973 **Age:** 36

Year	Team	Lg	G	GS	CG	GF	IP	BFP	H	R	ER	HR	SH	SF	HB	TBB	IBB	SO	WP	Bk	W	L	Pct	ShO	Sv-Op	Hld	ERC	ERA
1996	Det	AL	5	4	0	0	16.2	88	28	17	17	3	2	2	2	9	0	8	0	0	0	4	.000	0	0-0	0	10.15	9.18
1998	Hou	NL	37	1	0	15	53.1	235	57	21	18	4	0	0	1	20	1	30	1	0	2	0	1.000	0	1-2	1	4.18	3.04
1999	Hou	NL	47	0	0	11	49.2	232	58	29	28	6	2	2	5	29	1	37	4	0	3	2	.600	0	1-1	4	6.48	5.07
2000	2 Tms		16	0	0	2	16.1	90	27	22	19	3	1	1	2	12	1	11	1	0	0	0	-	0	0-0	0	10.68	10.47
2003	Tor	AL	79	0	0	18	52.2	233	46	30	27	7	1	0	5	28	3	44	2	0	2	2	.500	0	3-4	16	4.38	4.61
2004	TB	AL	60	0	0	15	49.0	208	48	21	17	3	3	0	3	15	4	43	2	0	1	1	.500	0	1-3	9	3.45	3.12
2005	TB	AL	61	0	0	13	44.1	206	45	23	20	4	3	5	7	29	6	35	2	0	2	2	.500	0	0-3	11	5.57	4.06
2006	Hou	NL	70	0	0	14	50.2	207	42	17	17	7	1	2	4	13	2	56	1	0	2	3	.400	0	1-3	12	3.11	3.02
2007	Hou	NL	76	0	0	12	46.1	211	45	26	25	6	3	0	4	23	6	46	1	0	0	0	-	0	1-3	12	4.52	4.86
2008	TB	AL	68	0	0	16	43.1	187	39	21	20	2	1	1	4	20	1	44	1	0	2	0	1.000	0	2-3	11	3.73	4.15
00	Phi	NL	14	0	0	2	14.0	72	19	16	13	3	1	1	1	9	1	10	1	0	0	0	-	0	0-0	0	8.14	8.36
00	LAD	NL	2	0	0	0	2.1	18	8	6	6	0	0	0	1	3	0	1	0	0	0	0	-	0	0-0	0	28.18	23.14
	Postseason		3	0	0	0	1.1	6	1	0	0	0	0	0	0	1	0	2	1	0	0	0	-	0	0-0	1	3.21	0.00
	10 ML YEARS		519	5	0	116	422.1	1897	435	227	208	45	17	13	37	198	25	354	15	0	14	14	.500	0	10-22	76	4.81	4.43

Kevin Millwood

Pitches: R **Bats:** R **Pos:** SP-29   **Ht:** 6'4" **Wt:** 230 **Born:** 12/24/1974 **Age:** 34

			HOW MUCH HE PITCHED						WHAT HE GAVE UP										THE RESULTS							
Year	Team	Lg	G	GS	CG	GF	IP	BFP	H	R	ER	HR	SH	SF	HB	TBB	IBB	SO	WP	Bk	W	L	Pct	ShO	Sv-Op	Hld	ERC	ERA
2008	Frisco*	AA	1	1	0	0	4.0	18	5	2	1	0	0	0	0	2	0	6	0	0	0	1	.000	0	0--	-	5.31	2.25
1997	Atl	NL	12	8	0	2	51.1	227	55	26	23	1	3	5	2	21	1	42	1	0	5	3	.625	0	0-0	0	4.03	4.03
1998	Atl	NL	31	29	3	1	174.1	748	175	86	79	18	8	3	3	56	3	163	6	1	17	8	.680	1	0-0	1	3.81	4.08
1999	Atl	NL	33	33	2	0	228.0	906	168	80	68	24	9	3	4	59	2	205	5	0	18	7	.720	0	0-0	0	2.26	2.68
2000	Atl	NL	36	35	0	0	212.2	903	213	115	110	26	8	5	3	62	2	168	4	0	10	13	.435	0	0-0	0	3.83	4.66
2001	Atl	NL	21	21	0	0	121.0	515	121	66	58	20	7	2	1	40	6	84	5	1	7	7	.500	0	0-0	0	4.20	4.31
2002	Atl	NL	35	34	1	0	217.0	895	186	83	78	16	9	4	8	65	7	178	4	0	18	8	.692	1	0-0	0	2.85	3.24
2003	Phi	NL	35	35	5	0	222.0	930	210	103	99	19	12	5	4	68	6	169	2	0	14	12	.538	3	0-0	0	3.35	4.01
2004	Phi	NL	25	25	0	0	141.0	628	155	81	76	14	11	2	7	51	5	125	4	0	9	6	.600	0	0-0	0	4.57	4.85
2005	Cle	AL	30	30	1	0	192.0	799	182	72	61	20	6	4	4	52	0	146	2	0	9	11	.450	0	0-0	0	3.40	2.86
2006	Tex	AL	34	34	2	0	215.0	907	228	114	108	23	8	3	4	53	4	157	6	0	16	12	.571	0	0-0	0	3.92	4.52
2007	Tex	AL	31	31	0	0	172.2	788	213	111	99	19	1	4	8	67	2	123	4	0	10	14	.417	0	0-0	0	5.64	5.16
2008	Tex	AL	29	29	3	0	168.2	767	220	104	95	18	5	2	6	49	3	125	2	1	9	10	.474	0	0-0	0	5.54	5.07
	Postseason		9	7	1	1	41.1	164	33	20	18	7	1	1	0	6	0	38	1	1	3	3	.500	0	1-1	0	2.41	3.92
	12 ML YEARS		352	344	17	3	2115.2	9013	2126	1041	954	218	87	42	54	643	41	1685	45	3	142	111	.561	5	0-0	1	3.80	4.06

Eric Milton

Pitches: L **Bats:** L **Pos:** P   **Ht:** 6'3" **Wt:** 218 **Born:** 8/4/1975 **Age:** 33

			HOW MUCH HE PITCHED						WHAT HE GAVE UP										THE RESULTS							
Year	Team	Lg	G	GS	CG	GF	IP	BFP	H	R	ER	HR	SH	SF	HB	TBB	IBB	SO	WP	Bk	W	L	Pct	ShO	Sv-Op	Hld	ERC	ERA
1998	Min	AL	32	32	1	0	172.1	772	195	113	108	25	2	6	2	70	0	107	1	0	8	14	.364	0	0-0	0	5.21	5.64
1999	Min	AL	34	34	4	0	206.1	858	190	111	103	28	3	6	3	63	2	163	2	0	7	11	.389	2	0-0	0	3.56	4.49
2000	Min	AL	33	33	0	0	200.0	849	205	123	108	35	4	6	7	44	0	160	5	0	13	10	.565	0	0-0	0	4.09	4.86
2001	Min	AL	35	34	2	0	220.2	944	222	109	106	35	8	6	5	61	0	157	2	0	15	7	.682	1	0-0	0	4.05	4.32
2002	Min	AL	29	29	2	0	171.0	707	173	96	92	24	0	4	3	30	0	121	4	0	13	9	.591	1	0-0	0	3.59	4.84
2003	Min	AL	3	3	0	0	17.0	66	15	5	5	2	0	1	0	1	0	7	0	0	1	0	1.000	0	0-0	0	2.29	2.65
2004	Phi	NL	34	34	0	0	201.0	862	196	110	106	43	11	6	1	75	6	161	3	0	14	6	.700	0	0-0	0	4.57	4.75
2005	Cin	NL	34	34	0	0	186.1	855	237	141	134	40	6	6	7	52	2	123	8	0	8	15	.348	0	0-0	0	6.03	6.47
2006	Cin	NL	26	26	0	0	152.2	662	163	94	88	29	6	3	5	42	4	90	2	0	8	8	.500	0	0-0	0	4.62	5.19
2007	Cin	NL	6	6	0	0	31.1	143	39	21	18	4	3	0	0	9	0	18	2	0	0	4	.000	0	0-0	0	5.07	5.17
	Postseason		3	2	0	0	16.1	65	13	3	3	2	0	0	0	3	0	9	0	0	1	0	1.000	0	0-0	0	2.30	1.65
	10 ML YEARS		266	265	9	0	1558.2	6718	1635	923	868	265	43	44	33	447	14	1107	29	0	87	84	.509	4	0-0	0	4.41	5.01

Zach Miner

Pitches: R **Bats:** R **Pos:** RP-32; SP-13   **Ht:** 6'3" **Wt:** 200 **Born:** 3/12/1982 **Age:** 27

			HOW MUCH HE PITCHED						WHAT HE GAVE UP										THE RESULTS							
Year	Team	Lg	G	GS	CG	GF	IP	BFP	H	R	ER	HR	SH	SF	HB	TBB	IBB	SO	WP	Bk	W	L	Pct	ShO	Sv-Op	Hld	ERC	ERA
2008	Toledo*	AAA	4	2	0	1	10.2	45	11	4	4	0	0	1	0	3	0	15	0	0	0	1	.000	0	0--	-	3.11	3.38
2006	Det	AL	27	16	1	4	93.0	398	100	53	50	11	2	2	0	32	1	59	1	0	7	6	.538	0	0-0	1	4.44	4.84
2007	Det	AL	34	1	0	8	53.2	232	56	22	18	3	4	1	0	22	4	34	1	0	3	4	.429	0	0-2	9	3.95	3.02
2008	Det	AL	45	13	0	3	118.0	509	118	60	56	10	4	3	6	46	3	62	4	0	8	5	.615	0	0-3	6	4.12	4.27
	Postseason		1	0	0	1	0.2	2	0	0	0	0	0	0	0	1	0	0	0	1	0	0	-	0	0-0	0	3.22	0.00
	3 ML YEARS		106	30	1	15	264.2	1139	274	135	124	24	10	6	6	100	8	155	6	0	18	15	.545	0	0-5	16	4.20	4.22

Juan Miranda

Bats: L **Throws:** L **Pos:** 1B-5   **Ht:** 6'0" **Wt:** 220 **Born:** 4/25/1983 **Age:** 26

			BATTING																	BASERUNNING				AVERAGES		
Year	Team	Lg	G	AB	H	2B	3B	HR	(Hm	Rd)	TB	R	RBI	RC	TBB	IBB	SO	HBP	SH	SF	SB	CS	SB%	GDP	Avg	OBP	Slg
2007	Tampa	A+	67	250	66	17	3	9	(-	-)	116	35	50	43	29	3	60	7	0	7	1	0	1.00	1	.264	.348	.464
2007	Trntn	AA	55	196	52	17	2	7	(-	-)	94	29	46	34	23	2	46	5	0	3	0	1	.00	4	.265	.352	.480
2008	S-WB	AAA	99	356	102	22	0	12	(-	-)	160	40	52	65	55	3	79	3	0	3	2	1	.67	6	.287	.384	.449
2008	NYY	AL	5	10	4	1	0	0	(0	0)	5	2	1	3	2	0	4	1	0	1	0	0	-	0	.400	.500	.500

Pat Misch

Pitches: L **Bats:** R **Pos:** RP-8; SP-7   **Ht:** 6'2" **Wt:** 196 **Born:** 8/18/1981 **Age:** 27

			HOW MUCH HE PITCHED						WHAT HE GAVE UP										THE RESULTS							
Year	Team	Lg	G	GS	CG	GF	IP	BFP	H	R	ER	HR	SH	SF	HB	TBB	IBB	SO	WP	Bk	W	L	Pct	ShO	Sv-Op	Hld	ERC	ERA
2008	Fresno*	AAA	20	13	0	3	87.0	386	101	58	52	15	11	1	6	27	1	56	0	1	6	5	.545	0	0--	-	5.45	5.38
2006	SF	NL	1	0	0	0	1.0	5	2	0	0	0	0	0	0	0	0	1	0	0	0	0	-	0	0-0	0	7.48	0.00
2007	SF	NL	18	4	0	2	40.1	176	47	21	19	3	1	2	2	12	2	26	0	0	0	4	.000	0	0-0	2	4.59	4.24
2008	SF	NL	15	7	0	6	52.1	230	56	34	33	11	3	4	3	15	2	38	1	1	0	3	.000	0	0-0	0	4.88	5.68
	3 ML YEARS		34	11	0	8	93.2	411	105	55	52	14	4	6	5	27	4	65	1	1	0	7	.000	0	0-0	2	4.79	5.00

Sergio Mitre

Pitches: R **Bats:** R **Pos:** P   **Ht:** 6'3" **Wt:** 225 **Born:** 2/16/1981 **Age:** 28

			HOW MUCH HE PITCHED						WHAT HE GAVE UP										THE RESULTS							
Year	Team	Lg	G	GS	CG	GF	IP	BFP	H	R	ER	HR	SH	SF	HB	TBB	IBB	SO	WP	Bk	W	L	Pct	ShO	Sv-Op	Hld	ERC	ERA
2003	ChC	NL	3	2	0	1	8.2	43	15	8	8	1	0	1	0	4	1	3	0	0	0	1	.000	0	0-0	0	9.02	8.31
2004	ChC	NL	12	9	0	2	51.2	244	71	38	38	6	3	0	4	20	1	37	5	1	2	4	.333	0	0-0	0	6.69	6.62

Year Team	Lg	G	GS	CG	GF	IP	BFP	H	R	ER	HR	SH	SF	HB	TBB	IBB	SO	WP	Bk	W	L	Pct	ShO	Sv-Op	Hld	ERC	ERA
												HOW MUCH HE PITCHED			WHAT HE GAVE UP								THE RESULTS				
2005 ChC	NL	21	7	1	7	60.1	268	62	37	36	11	1	3	3	23	2	37	5	0	2	5	.286	1	0-0	0	4.81	5.37
2006 Fla	NL	15	7	0	3	41.0	189	44	28	26	7	2	1	6	20	3	31	1	0	1	5	.167	0	0-1	2	5.87	5.71
2007 Fla	NL	27	27	0	0	149.0	662	180	88	77	9	6	10	10	41	3	80	6	0	5	8	.385	0	0-0	0	4.71	4.65
5 ML YEARS		78	52	1	13	310.2	1406	372	199	185	34	12	15	23	108	10	188	17	1	10	23	.303	1	0-1	2	5.31	5.36

Garrett Mock

Pitches: R Bats: R Pos: RP-23; SP-3   Ht: 6'3" Wt: 238 Born: 4/25/1983 Age: 26

Year Team	Lg	G	GS	CG	GF	IP	BFP	H	R	ER	HR	SH	SF	HB	TBB	IBB	SO	WP	Bk	W	L	Pct	ShO	Sv-Op	Hld	ERC	ERA
2004 Yakima	A-	5	5	0	0	23.1	86	18	8	4	1	1	2	0	4	0	14	0	0	2	0	1.000	0	0- --	-	1.89	1.54
2004 Sbend	A	8	8	1	0	54.0	215	49	21	18	2	5	1	2	12	0	37	2	2	3	2	.600	0	0- --	-	2.73	3.00
2005 Lancst	A+	28	28	0	0	174.1	757	202	95	81	19	2	2	9	33	0	160	7	0	14	7	.667	0	0- --	-	4.36	4.18
2006 Tenn	AA	23	23	0	0	131.0	583	144	81	72	14	7	4	7	50	0	117	5	0	4	8	.333	0	0- --	-	4.82	4.95
2006 Hrsbrg	AA	4	4	0	0	16.2	84	29	21	19	2	0	2	2	5	0	9	2	0	0	4	.000	0	0- --	-	8.97	10.26
2007 Ptomc	A+	1	1	0	0	6.0	23	3	0	0	0	0	0	1	1	0	5	0	0	1	0	1.000	0	0- --	-	1.09	0.00
2007 Nats	R	3	2	0	0	7.2	34	11	7	4	3	0	0	0	1	0	8	0	0	0	2	.000	0	0- --	-	7.80	4.70
2007 Hrsbrg	AA	11	11	0	0	51.1	254	66	41	33	5	6	5	3	28	0	41	8	0	1	5	.167	0	0- --	-	6.36	5.79
2008 Clmbs	AAA	19	17	0	0	104.2	436	98	41	35	9	7	5	6	25	0	96	5	1	6	3	.667	0	0- --	-	3.23	3.01
2008 Was	NL	26	3	0	5	41.0	180	37	20	19	4	1	1	0	23	3	46	3	1	1	3	.250	0	0-0	0	4.00	4.17

Brian Moehler

Pitches: R Bats: R Pos: SP-26; RP-5   Ht: 6'3" Wt: 235 Born: 12/31/1971 Age: 37

Year Team	Lg	G	GS	CG	GF	IP	BFP	H	R	ER	HR	SH	SF	HB	TBB	IBB	SO	WP	Bk	W	L	Pct	ShO	Sv-Op	Hld	ERC	ERA
1996 Det	AL	2	2	0	0	10.1	51	11	10	5	1	1	0	0	8	1	2	1	0	0	1	.000	0	0-0	0	5.49	4.35
1997 Det	AL	31	31	2	0	175.1	770	198	97	91	22	1	8	5	61	1	97	3	0	11	12	.478	1	0-0	0	4.92	4.67
1998 Det	AL	33	33	4	0	221.1	912	220	103	96	30	3	3	2	56	1	123	4	0	14	13	.519	3	0-0	0	3.79	3.90
1999 Det	AL	32	32	2	0	196.1	859	229	116	110	22	8	5	7	59	5	106	4	0	10	16	.385	2	0-0	0	4.85	5.04
2000 Det	AL	29	29	2	0	178.0	776	222	99	89	20	3	4	2	40	0	103	2	1	12	9	.571	0	0-0	0	4.95	4.50
2001 Det	AL	1	1	0	0	8.0	30	6	3	3	0	0	0	0	1	0	2	0	0	0	0	-	0	0-0	0	1.43	3.38
2002 2 Tms		13	12	0	0	63.0	278	78	39	34	11	4	2	1	13	0	31	0	0	3	5	.375	0	0-0	0	5.20	4.86
2003 Hou	NL	3	3	0	0	13.2	66	22	12	12	4	1	1	0	6	0	5	0	0	0	0	-	0	0-0	0	9.97	7.90
2005 Fla	NL	37	25	0	4	158.1	696	198	82	80	16	13	4	5	42	9	95	1	0	6	12	.333	0	0-0	1	5.07	4.55
2006 Fla	NL	29	21	0	2	122.0	556	164	95	89	19	7	2	5	38	3	58	2	1	7	11	.389	0	0-1	0	6.36	6.57
2007 Hou	NL	42	0	0	29	59.2	257	67	29	27	8	1	1	0	17	3	36	1	0	4	.200	0	1-1	1	4.48	4.07
2008 Hou	NL	31	26	0	0	150.0	650	166	79	76	20	7	8	4	36	1	82	3	0	11	8	.579	0	0-0	0	4.31	4.56
02 Det	AL	3	3	0	0	19.2	77	17	5	5	3	1	1	0	2	0	13	0	0	1	1	.500	0	0-0	0	2.54	2.29
02 Cin	NL	10	9	0	0	43.1	201	61	34	29	8	3	1	1	11	0	18	0	0	2	4	.333	0	0-0	0	6.56	6.02
12 ML YEARS		283	215	10	35	1356.0	5901	1581	764	712	173	49	38	31	377	24	740	21	2	75	91	.452	6	1-2	2	4.82	4.73

Chad Moeller

Bats: R Throws: R Pos: C-33; PH-6; 3B-3; 1B-2; DH-2; PR-1   Ht: 6'4" Wt: 215 Born: 2/18/1975 Age: 34

Year Team	Lg	G	AB	H	2B	3B	HR	(Hm	Rd)	TB	R	RBI	RC	TBB	IBB	SO	HBP	SH	SF	SB	CS	SB%	GDP	Avg	OBP	Slg
2008 S-WB*	AAA	23	81	19	4	0	1	(-	-)	26	6	7	7	5	0	22	0	0	3	0	0	-	2	.235	.270	.321
2000 Min	AL	48	128	27	3	1	1	(1	0)	35	13	9	8	9	0	33	0	1	1	1	0	1.00	3	.211	.261	.273
2001 Ari	NL	25	56	13	0	1	1	(1	0)	18	8	2	5	6	1	12	0	1	0	0	0	-	2	.232	.306	.321
2002 Ari	NL	37	105	30	11	1	2	(2	0)	49	10	16	17	17	3	23	0	1	0	0	1	.00	6	.286	.385	.467
2003 Ari	NL	78	239	64	17	1	7	(2	5)	104	29	29	28	23	11	59	2	3	2	1	2	.33	7	.268	.335	.435
2004 Mil	NL	101	317	66	13	1	5	(3	2)	96	25	27	14	21	1	74	4	6	1	0	1	.00	12	.208	.265	.303
2005 Mil	NL	66	199	41	9	1	7	(5	2)	73	23	23	14	13	1	48	1	2	1	0	0	-	9	.206	.257	.367
2006 Mil	NL	29	98	18	3	0	2	(2	0)	27	9	5	3	4	0	26	2	0	0	0	0	-	3	.184	.231	.276
2007 2 Tms	NL	37	56	9	1	0	1	(1	0)	13	8	2	0	0	0	18	1	1	0	0	0	-	3	.161	.175	.232
2008 NYY	AL	41	91	21	6	0	1	(0	1)	30	13	9	9	7	1	18	4	0	1	0	0	-	2	.231	.311	.330
07 Cin	NL	30	48	8	1	0	1	(1	0)	12	6	2	0	0	0	17	0	1	0	0	0	-	2	.167	.167	.250
07 LAD	NL	7	8	1	0	0	0	(0	0)	1	2	0	0	0	0	1	1	0	0	0	0	-	1	.125	.222	.125
Postseason		3	5	2	0	0	0	(0	0)	2	0	0	1	0	0	1	0	0	0	0	0	-	0	.400	.400	.400
9 ML YEARS		462	1289	289	63	6	27	(17	10)	445	138	122	98	100	18	311	14	15	6	2	4	.33	47	.224	.286	.345

Bengie Molina

Bats: R Throws: R Pos: C-136; PH-11; DH-1   Ht: 5'11" Wt: 225 Born: 7/20/1974 Age: 34

Year Team	Lg	G	AB	H	2B	3B	HR	(Hm	Rd)	TB	R	RBI	RC	TBB	IBB	SO	HBP	SH	SF	SB	CS	SB%	GDP	Avg	OBP	Slg
1998 LAA	AL	2	1	0	0	0	0	(0	0)	0	0	0	0	0	0	0	0	0	0	0	0	-	0	.000	.000	.000
1999 LAA	AL	31	101	26	5	0	1	(0	1)	34	8	10	9	6	0	6	2	0	0	0	1	.00	5	.257	.312	.337
2000 LAA	AL	130	473	133	20	2	14	(11	3)	199	59	71	60	23	0	33	6	4	7	1	0	1.00	17	.281	.318	.421
2001 LAA	AL	96	325	85	11	0	6	(6	0)	114	31	40	34	16	3	51	8	2	4	0	1	.00	8	.262	.309	.351
2002 LAA	AL	122	428	105	18	0	5	(2	3)	138	34	47	33	15	3	34	4	6	6	0	0	-	15	.245	.274	.322
2003 LAA	AL	119	409	115	24	0	14	(7	7)	181	37	71	57	13	2	31	2	2	4	1	1	.50	17	.281	.304	.443
2004 LAA	AL	97	337	93	13	0	10	(5	5)	136	36	54	44	18	1	35	2	2	4	0	0	-	18	.276	.313	.404
2005 LAA	AL	119	410	121	17	0	15	(8	7)	183	45	69	53	27	2	41	1	5	6	0	2	.00	14	.295	.336	.446
2006 Tor	AL	143	433	123	20	1	19	(12	7)	202	44	57	58	19	1	47	4	0	2	1	1	.50	15	.284	.319	.467
2007 SF	NL	134	497	137	19	1	19	(9	10)	215	38	81	64	15	2	53	2	1	2	0	0	-	13	.276	.298	.433
2008 SF	NL	145	530	155	33	0	16	(9	7)	236	46	95	70	19	5	38	9	0	11	0	0	-	23	.292	.322	.445
Postseason		29	91	24	4	1	3	(2	1)	39	7	12	14	4	2	8	3	2	0	0	0	-	3	.264	.316	.429
11 ML YEARS		1112	3944	1093	180	4	119	(69	50)	1638	378	595	482	171	19	369	40	22	46	3	7	.30	145	.277	.310	.415

191

Gustavo Molina

Bats: R **Throws:** R **Pos:** C-2 **Ht:** 6'0" **Wt:** 220 **Born:** 2/24/1982 **Age:** 27

Year	Team	Lg	G	AB	H	2B	3B	HR	(Hm	Rd)	TB	R	RBI	RC	TBB	IBB	SO	HBP	SH	SF	SB	CS	SB%	GDP	Avg	OBP	Slg
2000	WhSox	R	31	115	28	10	0	1	(-	-)	41	15	22	15	13	0	13	2	1	3	3	1	.75	0	.243	.323	.357
2001	Bristol	R+	46	166	47	9	0	2	(-	-)	62	18	24	22	9	1	26	5	1	3	3	1	.75	2	.283	.333	.373
2002	Knapol	A	94	310	70	13	1	2	(-	-)	91	37	34	31	27	1	61	9	7	6	7	2	.78	6	.226	.301	.294
2003	Knapol	A	96	315	72	15	1	5	(-	-)	104	30	41	31	17	0	56	9	8	1	5	3	.63	4	.229	.287	.330
2004	Knapol	A	37	105	17	3	0	4	(-	-)	32	16	17	9	12	0	24	4	3	0	2	1	.67	6	.162	.273	.305
2004	WinSa	A+	25	77	22	6	0	3	(-	-)	37	10	14	12	5	0	16	1	1	1	0	0	-	0	.286	.333	.481
2005	WinSa	A+	109	345	90	20	1	11	(-	-)	145	38	41	49	30	0	47	6	8	3	1	2	.33	16	.261	.328	.420
2006	Brham	AA	103	344	78	14	0	7	(-	-)	113	26	34	32	25	0	65	4	8	1	5	6	.45	8	.227	.286	.328
2006	Charltt	AAA	10	30	5	0	0	0	(-	-)	5	0	0	0	1	0	5	0	0	0	0	0	-	3	.167	.194	.167
2007	Charltt	AAA	43	139	29	4	0	2	(-	-)	39	13	9	9	9	0	27	2	5	1	0	2	.00	7	.209	.265	.281
2007	Bowie	AA	22	77	28	4	0	0	(-	-)	32	5	6	12	3	0	9	0	0	0	0	0	-	3	.364	.388	.416
2008	NewOr	AAA	74	228	47	7	0	7	(-	-)	75	22	27	21	16	0	56	5	0	1	0	0	-	10	.206	.272	.329
2007	2 Tms	AL	17	27	3	1	0	0	(0	0)	4	1	1	1	1	0	7	0	1	1	0	0	-	0	.111	.138	.148
2008	NYM	NL	2	7	1	0	0	0	(0	0)	1	0	0	0	1	0	1	0	0	0	0	0	-	0	.143	.250	.143
07	CWS	AL	10	18	1	0	0	0	(0	0)	1	0	1	0	1	0	4	0	1	0	0	0	-	0	.056	.100	.056
07	Bal	AL	7	9	2	1	0	0	(0	0)	3	1	0	1	0	0	3	0	0	0	0	0	-	0	.222	.222	.333
2 ML YEARS			19	34	4	1	0	0	(0	0)	5	1	1	1	2	0	8	0	1	1	0	0	-	0	.118	.162	.147

Jose Molina

Bats: R **Throws:** R **Pos:** C-97; PH-4; 1B-1 **Ht:** 6'2" **Wt:** 235 **Born:** 6/3/1975 **Age:** 34

Year	Team	Lg	G	AB	H	2B	3B	HR	(Hm	Rd)	TB	R	RBI	RC	TBB	IBB	SO	HBP	SH	SF	SB	CS	SB%	GDP	Avg	OBP	Slg
1999	ChC	NL	10	19	5	1	0	0	(0	0)	6	3	1	2	2	1	4	0	0	0	0	0	-	0	.263	.333	.316
2001	LAA	AL	15	37	10	3	0	2	(0	2)	19	8	4	6	3	0	8	0	2	0	0	0	-	2	.270	.325	.514
2002	LAA	AL	29	70	19	3	0	0	(0	0)	22	5	5	4	5	0	15	0	4	2	0	2	.00	2	.271	.312	.314
2003	LAA	AL	53	114	21	4	0	0	(0	0)	25	12	6	5	1	0	26	3	4	1	0	0	-	1	.184	.210	.219
2004	LAA	AL	73	203	53	10	2	3	(1	2)	76	26	25	19	10	0	52	0	5	0	4	1	.80	6	.261	.296	.374
2005	LAA	AL	75	184	42	4	0	6	(2	4)	64	14	25	19	13	0	41	2	4	0	2	0	1.00	5	.228	.286	.348
2006	LAA	AL	78	225	54	17	0	4	(0	4)	83	18	22	21	9	0	49	2	7	2	1	0	1.00	6	.240	.273	.369
2007	2 Tms	AL	69	191	49	13	0	1	(1	0)	65	18	19	20	5	0	43	0	5	1	2	1	.67	4	.257	.274	.340
2008	NYY	AL	100	268	58	17	0	3	(2	1)	84	32	18	15	12	0	52	6	8	3	0	0	-	9	.216	.263	.313
07	LAA	AL	40	125	28	8	0	0	(0	0)	36	9	10	9	3	0	30	0	3	0	2	1	.67	3	.224	.242	.288
07	NYY	AL	29	66	21	5	0	1	(1	0)	29	9	9	11	2	0	13	0	2	1	0	0	-	1	.318	.333	.439
Postseason			10	8	3	0	0	0	(0	0)	3	3	1	2	2	0	0	0	1	0	0	0	-	0	.375	.500	.375
9 ML YEARS			502	1311	311	72	2	19	(6	13)	444	136	125	111	60	1	290	13	39	9	9	4	.69	35	.237	.276	.339

Yadier Molina

Bats: R **Throws:** R **Pos:** C-119; PH-5; 1B-2; DH-1 **Ht:** 5'11" **Wt:** 215 **Born:** 7/13/1982 **Age:** 26

Year	Team	Lg	G	AB	H	2B	3B	HR	(Hm	Rd)	TB	R	RBI	RC	TBB	IBB	SO	HBP	SH	SF	SB	CS	SB%	GDP	Avg	OBP	Slg
2004	StL	NL	51	135	36	6	0	2	(1	1)	48	12	15	15	13	3	20	0	2	1	0	1	.00	4	.267	.329	.356
2005	StL	NL	114	385	97	15	1	8	(6	2)	138	36	49	46	23	3	30	2	8	3	2	3	.40	10	.252	.295	.358
2006	StL	NL	129	417	90	26	0	6	(2	4)	134	29	49	35	26	2	41	8	8	2	1	2	.33	15	.216	.274	.321
2007	StL	NL	111	353	97	15	0	6	(4	2)	130	30	40	38	34	5	43	3	2	4	1	1	.50	18	.275	.340	.368
2008	StL	NL	124	444	135	18	0	7	(2	5)	174	37	56	57	32	4	29	1	3	5	0	2	.00	21	.304	.349	.392
Postseason			29	95	30	7	0	2	(1	1)	43	7	11	12	6	1	9	0	0	0	0	1	.00	3	.316	.356	.453
5 ML YEARS			529	1734	455	80	1	29	(15	14)	624	144	209	191	128	17	163	14	23	15	4	9	.31	68	.262	.316	.360

Craig Monroe

Bats: R **Throws:** R **Pos:** DH-36; PH-13; CF-7; RF-3; LF-1 **Ht:** 6'1" **Wt:** 215 **Born:** 2/27/1977 **Age:** 32

Year	Team	Lg	G	AB	H	2B	3B	HR	(Hm	Rd)	TB	R	RBI	RC	TBB	IBB	SO	HBP	SH	SF	SB	CS	SB%	GDP	Avg	OBP	Slg
2001	Tex	AL	27	52	11	1	0	2	(1	1)	18	8	5	6	6	0	18	0	0	0	2	0	1.00	1	.212	.293	.346
2002	Det	AL	13	25	3	1	0	1	(0	1)	7	3	1	0	0	0	5	1	0	0	0	2	.00	1	.120	.154	.280
2003	Det	AL	128	425	102	18	1	23	(10	13)	191	51	70	61	27	2	89	2	1	3	4	2	.67	10	.240	.287	.449
2004	Det	AL	128	447	131	27	3	18	(9	9)	218	65	72	66	29	1	79	2	0	3	3	4	.43	8	.293	.337	.488
2005	Det	AL	157	567	157	30	3	20	(9	11)	253	69	89	77	40	4	95	3	1	12	8	3	.73	16	.277	.322	.446
2006	Det	AL	147	541	138	35	2	28	(12	16)	261	89	92	76	37	3	126	1	0	6	2	2	.50	14	.255	.301	.482
2007	2 Tms		122	392	86	23	0	12	(5	7)	145	53	59	36	26	0	107	2	1	6	0	4	.00	13	.219	.268	.370
2008	Min	AL	58	163	33	9	0	8	(5	3)	66	22	29	22	16	1	48	0	0	0	0	1	.00	3	.202	.274	.405
07	Det	AL	99	343	76	19	0	11	(5	6)	128	47	55	32	20	0	94	2	1	6	0	3	.00	10	.222	.264	.373
07	ChC	NL	23	49	10	4	0	1	(0	1)	17	6	4	4	6	0	13	0	0	0	0	1	.00	3	.204	.291	.347
Postseason			13	50	12	4	0	5	(4	1)	31	11	9	6	4	0	12	0	0	1	0	0	-	0	.240	.291	.620
8 ML YEARS			780	2612	661	144	9	112	(51	61)	1159	360	417	344	181	11	567	11	3	30	19	18	.51	66	.253	.301	.444

Lou Montanez

Bats: R **Throws:** R **Pos:** LF-26; CF-5; RF-5; PH-5; DH-3; PR-2 **Ht:** 6'2" **Wt:** 180 **Born:** 12/15/1981 **Age:** 27

Year	Team	Lg	G	AB	H	2B	3B	HR	(Hm	Rd)	TB	R	RBI	RC	TBB	IBB	SO	HBP	SH	SF	SB	CS	SB%	GDP	Avg	OBP	Slg
2000	Cubs	R	50	192	66	16	7	2	(-	-)	102	50	37	44	25	1	42	8	3	1	11	6	.65	9	.344	.438	.531
2000	Lansng	A	8	29	4	1	0	0	(-	-)	5	2	0	0	3	0	6	0	0	0	0	1	.00	0	.138	.219	.172
2001	Lansng	A	124	499	127	33	6	5	(-	-)	187	70	54	63	34	0	121	12	3	3	20	7	.74	12	.255	.316	.375
2002	Dytona	A+	124	487	129	21	5	4	(-	-)	172	69	59	61	44	0	89	9	0	7	14	8	.64	16	.265	.333	.353
2003	Dytona	A+	126	486	123	18	3	5	(-	-)	162	51	38	53	33	0	89	6	6	6	11	4	.73	11	.253	.305	.333

192

Year	Team	Lg	G	AB	H	2B	3B	HR	(Hm	Rd)	TB	R	RBI	RC	TBB	IBB	SO	HBP	SH	SF	SB	CS	SB%	GDP	Avg	OBP	Slg
2004	Dytona	A+	21	79	17	4	2	1	(-	-)	28	8	7	8	7	0	16	2	1	1	2	3	.40	0	.215	.292	.354
2004	Boise	A-	72	266	79	15	7	8	(-	-)	132	47	48	50	35	2	53	3	2	3	5	5	.50	5	.297	.381	.496
2005	Peoria	A	82	315	96	28	2	12	(-	-)	164	54	48	64	32	1	46	10	2	2	10	4	.71	6	.305	.384	.521
2005	WTenn	AA	45	153	41	9	1	2	(-	-)	58	20	14	19	12	1	21	2	2	2	0	2	.00	1	.268	.325	.379
2006	WTenn	AA	38	141	52	11	0	2	(-	-)	69	24	25	30	15	1	26	3	2	1	5	3	.63	2	.369	.438	.489
2006	Iowa	AAA	82	245	55	12	0	8	(-	-)	91	23	31	26	17	0	44	3	2	2	0	1	.00	8	.224	.281	.371
2007	Norfolk	AAA	69	212	55	11	0	7	(-	-)	87	27	26	29	22	0	35	2	3	2	1	3	.25	9	.259	.332	.410
2007	Bowie	AA	31	121	41	2	0	3	(-	-)	52	24	11	21	10	0	16	2	2	0	3	2	.60	1	.339	.398	.430
2008	Bowie	AA	116	451	151	32	5	26	(-	-)	271	90	97	101	36	2	63	6	0	8	4	4	.50	9	.335	.385	.601
2008	Bal	AL	38	112	33	6	1	3	(2	1)	50	18	14	17	4	0	20	0	0	1	0	0	-	0	.295	.316	.446

Miguel Montero

Bats: L Throws: R Pos: C-53; PH-24

Ht: 5'11" Wt: 190 Born: 7/9/1983 Age: 25

Year	Team	Lg	G	AB	H	2B	3B	HR	(Hm	Rd)	TB	R	RBI	RC	TBB	IBB	SO	HBP	SH	SF	SB	CS	SB%	GDP	Avg	OBP	Slg
2008	Tucsn*	AAA	11	32	9	2	0	1	(-	-)	14	3	5	5	5	1	3	1	0	0	0	0	-	1	.281	.395	.438
2006	Ari	NL	6	16	4	1	0	0	(0	0)	5	0	3	2	1	0	3	0	0	0	0	0	-	0	.250	.294	.313
2007	Ari	NL	84	214	48	7	0	10	(7	3)	85	30	37	19	20	2	35	3	1	6	0	0	-	7	.224	.292	.397
2008	Ari	NL	70	184	47	16	1	5	(1	4)	80	24	18	21	19	3	49	2	1	1	0	0	-	0	.255	.330	.435
	Postseason		4	7	2	0	0	0	(0	0)	2	1	0	0	1	0	0	0	0	0	0	0	-	0	.286	.375	.286
	3 ML YEARS		160	414	99	24	1	15	(8	7)	170	54	58	42	40	5	87	5	2	7	0	0	-	8	.239	.309	.411

Luke Montz

Bats: R Throws: R Pos: C-8; PH-2

Ht: 6'2" Wt: 205 Born: 7/7/1983 Age: 25

Year	Team	Lg	G	AB	H	2B	3B	HR	(Hm	Rd)	TB	R	RBI	RC	TBB	IBB	SO	HBP	SH	SF	SB	CS	SB%	GDP	Avg	OBP	Slg
2003	Expos	R	32	103	23	0	0	2	(-	-)	29	8	9	8	9	0	21	0	1	0	1	1	.50	2	.223	.286	.282
2004	BrvdCt	A+	1	2	1	0	0	0	(-	-)	2	0	0	1	2	0	1	0	0	0	0	0	-	0	.500	.750	1.000
2004	Vrmnt	A-	62	204	51	11	0	10	(-	-)	92	31	34	35	33	0	42	3	1	1	2	1	.67	5	.250	.361	.451
2005	Savann	A	100	343	77	24	1	19	(-	-)	160	66	68	55	50	0	95	3	2	5	1	1	.50	6	.224	.324	.466
2006	Ptomc	A+	131	449	103	27	3	16	(-	-)	184	59	76	62	51	1	91	8	2	4	3	3	.50	7	.229	.313	.410
2007	Ptomc	A+	60	201	54	15	1	7	(-	-)	92	43	39	40	45	0	54	3	2	2	3	2	.60	4	.269	.406	.458
2007	Hrsbrg	AA	40	146	34	5	1	5	(-	-)	56	22	19	15	8	0	50	1	1	2	0	0	-	2	.233	.274	.384
2008	Hrsbrg	AA	63	220	62	14	0	14	(-	-)	118	30	53	43	31	1	46	0	1	2	0	1	.00	1	.282	.368	.536
2008	Clmbs	AAA	48	168	43	8	1	2	(-	-)	59	18	18	18	13	0	37	0	0	0	1	1	.50	6	.256	.309	.351
2008	Was	NL	10	21	3	0	0	1	(0	1)	6	2	3	3	5	0	9	0	0	0	0	0	-	0	.143	.308	.286

Scott Moore

Bats: L Throws: R Pos: PH-2; 2B-1; 3B-1

Ht: 6'2" Wt: 195 Born: 11/17/1983 Age: 25

Year	Team	Lg	G	AB	H	2B	3B	HR	(Hm	Rd)	TB	R	RBI	RC	TBB	IBB	SO	HBP	SH	SF	SB	CS	SB%	GDP	Avg	OBP	Slg
2008	Norfolk*	AAA	78	287	71	21	2	7	(-	-)	117	41	44	39	23	0	67	8	0	0	3	0	1.00	7	.247	.321	.408
2006	ChC	NL	16	38	10	2	0	2	(1	1)	18	6	5	5	2	0	10	1	1	0	0	0	-	1	.263	.317	.474
2007	2 Tms		19	52	12	2	0	1	(1	0)	17	2	11	6	1	0	17	0	0	0	0	1	.00	1	.231	.236	.327
2008	Bal	AL	4	8	1	0	0	1	(0	1)	4	1	1	1	1	0	3	0	0	0	0	0	-	0	.125	.222	.500
07	ChC	NL	2	5	0	0	0	0	(0	0)	0	0	0	0	0	0	2	0	0	0	0	0	-	0	.000	.000	.000
07	Bal	AL	17	47	12	2	0	1	(1	0)	17	2	11	6	1	0	15	0	0	2	0	1	.00	1	.255	.260	.362
	3 ML YEARS		39	98	23	4	0	4	(2	2)	39	9	17	12	4	0	30	1	1	2	0	1	.00	2	.235	.267	.398

Melvin Mora

Bats: R Throws: R Pos: 3B-124; DH-6; PH-5; SS-1

Ht: 5'11" Wt: 200 Born: 2/2/1972 Age: 37

Year	Team	Lg	G	AB	H	2B	3B	HR	(Hm	Rd)	TB	R	RBI	RC	TBB	IBB	SO	HBP	SH	SF	SB	CS	SB%	GDP	Avg	OBP	Slg
1999	NYM	NL	66	31	5	0	0	0	(0	0)	5	6	1	2	4	0	7	1	3	0	2	1	.67	0	.161	.278	.161
2000	2 Tms		132	414	114	22	5	8	(5	3)	170	60	47	56	35	3	80	6	4	5	12	11	.52	5	.275	.337	.411
2001	Bal	AL	128	436	109	28	0	7	(6	1)	158	49	48	55	41	2	91	14	5	7	11	4	.73	6	.250	.329	.362
2002	Bal	AL	149	557	130	30	4	19	(8	11)	225	86	64	78	70	2	108	20	1	4	6	3	.67	3	.233	.338	.404
2003	Bal	AL	96	344	109	17	1	15	(8	7)	173	68	48	67	49	0	71	12	6	2	6	3	.67	3	.317	.418	.503
2004	Bal	AL	140	550	187	41	0	27	(15	12)	309	111	104	115	66	0	95	11	6	3	11	6	.65	10	.340	.419	.562
2005	Bal	AL	149	593	168	30	1	27	(13	14)	281	86	88	88	50	0	112	11	6	3	7	4	.64	9	.283	.348	.474
2006	Bal	AL	155	624	171	25	0	16	(8	8)	244	96	83	93	54	1	99	14	6	7	11	1	.92	9	.274	.342	.391
2007	Bal	AL	126	467	128	23	1	14	(7	7)	195	67	58	61	47	3	83	3	5	5	9	3	.75	22	.274	.341	.418
2008	Bal	AL	135	513	146	29	2	23	(15	8)	248	77	104	88	37	3	70	11	3	6	3	7	.30	14	.285	.342	.483
00	NYM	NL	79	215	56	13	2	6	(4	2)	91	35	30	29	18	3	48	2	2	5	7	3	.70	3	.260	.317	.423
00	Bal	AL	53	199	58	9	3	2	(1	1)	79	25	17	27	17	0	32	4	2	0	5	8	.38	2	.291	.359	.397
	Postseason		9	15	6	0	0	1	(0	1)	9	4	2	4	3	0	2	0	1	0	2	0	1.00	0	.400	.500	.600
	10 ML YEARS		1276	4529	1267	245	14	156	(85	71)	2008	706	645	703	453	14	816	102	47	42	88	50	.64	85	.280	.355	.443

Franklin Morales

Pitches: L Bats: L Pos: SP-5   Ht: 6'0" Wt: 170 Born: 1/24/1986 Age: 23

Year	Team	Lg	G	GS	CG	GF	IP	BFP	H	R	ER	HR	SH	SF	HB	TBB	IBB	SO	WP	Bk	W	L	Pct	ShO	Sv-Op	Hld	ERC	ERA
2004	Casper	R+	15	15	1	0	65.0	320	92	61	55	8	2	2	5	39	0	82	7	4	6	4	.600	1	0- -	-	8.09	7.62
2005	Ashvll	A	21	15	0	3	96.1	399	73	40	33	6	1	1	8	48	0	108	7	7	8	4	.667	0	1- -	-	3.29	3.08
2006	Mdest	A+	27	26	0	0	154.0	671	126	77	63	9	3	2	11	89	0	179	24	10	10	9	.526	0	0- -	-	3.75	3.68
2007	Tulsa	AA	17	17	1	0	95.2	401	77	41	37	8	4	3	8	45	0	77	6	2	3	4	.429	0	0- -	-	3.56	3.48
2007	ColSpr	AAA	3	3	0	0	17.0	75	20	8	7	1	0	0	0	13	1	16	3	0	2	0	1.000	0	0- -	-	6.78	3.71
2008	ColSpr	AAA	21	21	0	0	110.1	500	108	72	67	14	5	4	6	82	1	83	3	5	10	5	.667	0	0- -	-	5.95	5.47
2007	Col	NL	8	8	0	0	39.1	163	34	15	15	2	4	2	2	14	1	26	0	0	3	2	.600	0	0-0	0	3.04	3.43
2008	Col	NL	5	5	0	0	25.1	120	28	18	18	2	2	2	1	17	2	9	1	3	1	2	.333	0	0-0	0	5.58	6.39
	Postseason		4	2	0	0	10.0	49	15	11	11	1	0	0	2	4	0	6	0	1	0	0	-	0	0-0	0	8.14	9.90
	2 ML YEARS		13	13	0	0	64.2	283	62	33	33	4	6	4	3	31	3	35	1	3	4	4	.500	0	0-0	0	3.99	4.59

Kendry Morales

Bats: B Throws: R Pos: RF-12; PH-8; 1B-6; DH-3; PR-1   Ht: 6'1" Wt: 225 Born: 6/20/1983 Age: 26

Year	Team	Lg	G	AB	H	2B	3B	HR	(Hm	Rd)	TB	R	RBI	RC	TBB	IBB	SO	HBP	SH	SF	SB	CS	SB%	GDP	Avg	OBP	Slg
2008	Salt Lk*	AAA	78	317	108	19	0	15	(-	-)	172	46	64	62	19	3	43	1	0	3	1	3	.25	9	.341	.376	.543
2008	Angels*	R	5	21	11	3	0	1	(-	-)	17	4	10	7	1	0	1	0	0	0	0	0	-	1	.524	.545	.810
2006	LAA	AL	57	197	46	10	1	5	(1	4)	73	21	22	19	17	1	28	0	0	1	1	1	.50	11	.234	.293	.371
2007	LAA	AL	43	119	35	10	0	4	(2	2)	57	12	15	15	6	2	21	1	0	0	0	1	.00	5	.294	.333	.479
2008	LAA	AL	27	61	13	2	0	3	(0	3)	24	7	8	3	4	0	7	1	0	0	0	1	.00	5	.213	.273	.393
	Postseason		3	9	1	0	0	0	(0	0)	1	1	0	0	0	0	2	0	0	0	0	0	-	0	.111	.111	.111
	3 ML YEARS		127	377	94	22	1	12	(3	9)	154	40	45	37	27	3	56	2	0	1	1	3	.25	19	.249	.302	.408

Nyjer Morgan

Bats: L Throws: L Pos: LF-23; CF-17; PH-17; RF-6; PR-1   Ht: 6'0" Wt: 175 Born: 7/2/1980 Age: 28

Year	Team	Lg	G	AB	H	2B	3B	HR	(Hm	Rd)	TB	R	RBI	RC	TBB	IBB	SO	HBP	SH	SF	SB	CS	SB%	GDP	Avg	OBP	Slg
2003	Wmspt	A-	72	268	92	7	4	0	(-	-)	107	49	23	50	33	1	44	13	10	0	26	17	.60	2	.343	.439	.399
2004	Hkry	A	134	514	131	16	7	4	(-	-)	173	83	41	75	53	2	120	33	10	6	55	16	.77	1	.255	.358	.337
2005	Lynbrg	A+	60	252	72	12	3	0	(-	-)	90	36	24	32	11	0	40	7	3	4	24	10	.71	0	.286	.328	.357
2006	Lynbrg	A+	61	228	69	7	3	0	(-	-)	82	43	22	39	20	1	40	15	7	4	38	11	.78	1	.303	.390	.360
2006	Altna	AA	56	219	67	6	5	1	(-	-)	86	39	10	32	15	0	28	3	7	0	21	11	.66	2	.306	.359	.393
2007	Indy	AAA	44	164	50	4	2	0	(-	-)	58	30	10	25	15	1	28	3	2	0	26	7	.79	1	.305	.374	.354
2007	Pirates	R	4	13	4	0	0	1	(-	-)	7	3	1	3	2	0	3	1	0	0	0	0	-	0	.308	.438	.538
2008	Indy	AAA	82	322	96	13	4	1	(-	-)	120	54	33	49	18	1	47	7	5	0	44	8	.85	4	.298	.349	.373
2007	Pit	NL	28	107	32	3	4	1	(1	0)	46	15	7	18	9	0	19	1	1	0	7	3	.70	0	.299	.359	.430
2008	Pit	NL	58	160	47	13	0	0	(0	0)	60	26	7	18	10	0	32	3	1	1	9	5	.64	0	.294	.345	.375
	2 ML YEARS		86	267	79	16	4	1	(1	0)	106	41	14	36	19	0	51	4	2	1	16	8	.67	0	.296	.351	.397

Juan Morillo

Pitches: R Bats: R Pos: RP-1   Ht: 6'3" Wt: 190 Born: 11/5/1983 Age: 25

Year	Team	Lg	G	GS	CG	GF	IP	BFP	H	R	ER	HR	SH	SF	HB	TBB	IBB	SO	WP	Bk	W	L	Pct	ShO	Sv-Op	Hld	ERC	ERA
2008	ColSpr*	AAA	52	0	0	20	59.2	283	53	38	35	3	3	5	2	56	0	55	5	0	1	0	1.000	0	0- -	-	5.30	5.28
2006	Col	NL	1	1	0	0	4.0	24	8	7	7	3	1	0	1	3	0	4	0	0	0	0	-	0	0-0	0	20.26	15.75
2007	Col	NL	4	0	0	1	3.2	16	3	4	4	1	0	0	1	1	0	3	0	0	0	0	-	0	0-0	0	4.74	9.82
2008	Col	NL	1	0	0	1	1.0	4	1	0	0	0	0	0	0	0	0	0	0	0	0	0	-	0	0-0	0	1.95	0.00
	3 ML YEARS		6	1	0	2	8.2	44	12	11	11	4	1	0	2	4	0	7	0	0	0	0	-	0	0-0	0	10.71	11.42

Justin Morneau

Bats: L Throws: R Pos: 1B-155; DH-8   Ht: 6'4" Wt: 230 Born: 5/15/1981 Age: 28

Year	Team	Lg	G	AB	H	2B	3B	HR	(Hm	Rd)	TB	R	RBI	RC	TBB	IBB	SO	HBP	SH	SF	SB	CS	SB%	GDP	Avg	OBP	Slg
2003	Min	AL	40	106	24	4	0	4	(1	3)	40	14	16	11	9	1	30	0	0	0	0	0	-	4	.226	.287	.377
2004	Min	AL	74	280	76	17	0	19	(9	10)	150	39	58	48	28	8	54	2	0	2	0	0	-	4	.271	.340	.536
2005	Min	AL	141	490	117	23	4	22	(9	13)	214	62	79	58	44	8	94	4	0	5	0	2	.00	12	.239	.304	.437
2006	Min	AL	157	592	190	37	4	34	(17	17)	331	97	130	118	53	9	93	5	0	11	3	3	.50	10	.321	.375	.559
2007	Min	AL	157	590	160	31	3	31	(15	16)	290	84	111	95	64	11	91	5	0	9	1	1	.50	17	.271	.343	.492
2008	Min	AL	163	623	187	47	4	23	(12	11)	311	97	129	122	76	16	85	3	0	10	0	1	.00	20	.300	.374	.499
	Postseason		7	29	9	3	0	2	(1	1)	18	4	4	3	0	0	3	0	0	0	0	0	-	0	.310	.310	.621
	6 ML YEARS		732	2681	754	159	12	133	(63	70)	1336	393	523	452	274	53	447	19	0	37	4	7	.36	67	.281	.348	.498

Matt Morris

Pitches: R Bats: R Pos: SP-5   Ht: 6'5" Wt: 225 Born: 8/9/1974 Age: 34

Year	Team	Lg	G	GS	CG	GF	IP	BFP	H	R	ER	HR	SH	SF	HB	TBB	IBB	SO	WP	Bk	W	L	Pct	ShO	Sv-Op	Hld	ERC	ERA
1997	StL	NL	33	33	3	0	217.0	900	208	88	77	12	11	7	7	69	2	149	5	3	12	9	.571	0	0-0	0	3.41	3.19
1998	StL	NL	17	17	2	0	113.2	468	101	37	32	8	6	1	3	42	6	79	3	0	7	5	.583	1	0-0	0	3.25	2.53
2000	StL	NL	31	0	0	12	53.0	226	53	22	21	3	3	1	2	17	1	34	0	0	3	3	.500	0	4-7	7	3.58	3.57
2001	StL	NL	34	34	2	0	216.1	909	218	86	76	13	14	5	13	54	3	185	5	1	22	8	.733	1	0-0	0	3.50	3.16
2002	StL	NL	32	32	1	0	210.1	890	210	86	80	16	7	8	6	64	3	171	3	0	17	9	.654	1	0-0	0	3.63	3.42
2003	StL	NL	27	27	5	0	172.1	703	164	76	72	20	5	3	4	39	1	120	3	0	11	8	.579	3	0-0	0	3.37	3.76

Year	Team	Lg	G	GS	CG	GF	IP	BFP	H	R	ER	HR	SH	SF	HB	TBB	IBB	SO	WP	Bk	W	L	Pct	ShO	Sv-Op	Hld	ERC	ERA
			HOW MUCH HE PITCHED						WHAT HE GAVE UP												THE RESULTS							
2004	StL	NL	32	32	3	0	202.0	850	205	116	106	35	13	5	6	56	3	131	3	1	15	10	.600	2	0-0	0	4.30	4.72
2005	StL	NL	31	31	2	0	192.2	818	209	101	88	22	10	5	8	37	3	117	1	1	14	10	.583	0	0-0	0	3.95	4.11
2006	SF	NL	33	33	2	0	207.2	903	218	123	115	22	9	5	14	63	9	117	1	3	10	15	.400	0	0-0	0	4.19	4.98
2007	2 Tms	NL	32	32	3	0	198.2	884	240	123	108	18	10	8	9	61	4	102	4	0	10	11	.476	0	0-0	0	4.98	4.89
2008	Pit	NL	5	5	0	0	22.1	118	41	31	24	6	2	2	2	7	1	9	2	0	0	4	.000	0	0-0	0	10.53	9.67
07	SF	NL	21	21	3	0	136.2	603	162	79	66	12	5	6	5	39	3	73	1	0	7	7	.500	0	0-0	0	4.69	4.35
07	Pit	NL	11	11	0	0	62.0	281	78	44	42	6	5	2	4	22	1	29	3	0	3	4	.429	0	0-0	0	5.66	6.10
	Postseason		15	11	0	1	73.1	326	73	35	33	9	5	3	6	34	4	44	2	1	2	6	.250	0	0-0	0	4.70	4.05
11 ML YEARS			307	276	23	12	1806.0	7669	1867	889	799	175	90	50	74	509	36	1214	30	9	121	92	.568	8	4-7	7	3.93	3.98

Brandon Morrow

Pitches: R Bats: R Pos: RP-40; SP-5   Ht: 6'3" Wt: 184 Born: 7/26/1984 Age: 24

Year	Team	Lg	G	GS	CG	GF	IP	BFP	H	R	ER	HR	SH	SF	HB	TBB	IBB	SO	WP	Bk	W	L	Pct	ShO	Sv-Op	Hld	ERC	ERA
			HOW MUCH HE PITCHED						WHAT HE GAVE UP												THE RESULTS							
2006	Ms	R	7	4	0	0	13.0	53	10	4	4	0	0	0	0	9	0	13	3	0	0	2	.000	0	0--	-	3.46	2.77
2006	InldEm	A+	1	1	0	0	3.0	9	0	0	0	0	0	0	0	0	0	4	0	0	0	0	-	0	0--	-	0.00	0.00
2008	WTenn	AA	6	0	0	1	7.1	30	3	1	0	0	0	0	0	6	0	8	2	0	0	0	-	0	0--	-	1.91	0.00
2008	Tacom	AAA	6	5	0	0	23.1	98	17	13	13	2	1	1	0	11	0	26	3	0	1	2	.333	0	0--	-	2.75	5.01
2007	Sea	AL	60	0	0	18	63.1	289	56	29	29	3	4	4	1	50	5	66	4	0	3	4	.429	0	0-2	18	4.47	4.12
2008	Sea	AL	45	5	0	24	64.2	265	40	26	24	10	1	0	0	34	1	75	5	0	3	4	.429	0	10-12	3	2.84	3.34
2 ML YEARS			105	5	0	42	128.0	554	96	55	53	13	5	4	1	84	6	141	9	0	6	8	.429	0	10-14	21	3.65	3.73

Mike Morse

Bats: R Throws: R Pos: RF-5; PH-1   Ht: 6'4" Wt: 230 Born: 3/22/1982 Age: 27

Year	Team	Lg	G	AB	H	2B	3B	HR	(Hm	Rd)	TB	R	RBI	RC	TBB	IBB	SO	HBP	SH	SF	SB	CS	SB%	GDP	Avg	OBP	Slg
			BATTING																		BASERUNNING				AVERAGES		
2005	Sea	AL	72	230	64	10	1	3	(3	0)	85	27	23	28	18	0	50	8	0	2	3	1	.75	9	.278	.349	.370
2006	Sea	AL	21	43	16	5	0	0	(0	0)	21	5	11	9	3	0	7	0	0	2	1	0	1.00	2	.372	.396	.488
2007	Sea	AL	9	18	8	2	0	0	(0	0)	10	1	3	6	1	0	4	1	0	0	0	0	-	0	.444	.500	.556
2008	Sea	AL	5	9	2	1	0	0	(0	0)	3	0	0	1	1	0	4	1	0	0	0	0	-	0	.222	.364	.333
4 ML YEARS			107	300	90	18	1	3	(3	0)	119	33	37	44	23	0	65	10	0	4	4	1	.80	11	.300	.365	.397

Charlie Morton

Pitches: R Bats: R Pos: SP-15; RP-1   Ht: 6'4" Wt: 190 Born: 10/12/1983 Age: 25

Year	Team	Lg	G	GS	CG	GF	IP	BFP	H	R	ER	HR	SH	SF	HB	TBB	IBB	SO	WP	Bk	W	L	Pct	ShO	Sv-Op	Hld	ERC	ERA
			HOW MUCH HE PITCHED						WHAT HE GAVE UP												THE RESULTS							
2002	Braves	R	11	5	0	1	39.2	186	37	34	20	1	1	1	2	30	0	32	5	0	1	7	.125	0	0--	-	4.63	4.54
2003	Danvle	R+	14	13	0	0	54.0	246	65	32	8	3	2	3	1	25	0	46	9	5	2	5	.286	0	0--	-	5.27	1.33
2004	Rome	A	27	18	0	3	117.2	558	140	76	63	7	4	8	7	68	2	102	10	0	7	9	.438	0	2--	-	5.76	4.82
2005	Rome	A	26	22	0	4	124.2	561	124	84	72	7	2	7	14	62	0	86	12	2	5	9	.357	0	1--	-	4.54	5.20
2006	MrtlBh	A+	30	14	0	6	100.0	466	116	70	60	14	7	3	4	54	0	75	9	0	6	7	.462	0	0--	-	6.03	5.40
2007	Missi	AA	41	6	0	9	79.2	350	80	41	38	3	6	4	6	37	2	67	11	0	4	6	.400	0	0--	-	4.19	4.29
2008	Rchmd	AAA	13	12	0	1	79.0	312	51	20	18	0	2	0	2	27	0	72	2	0	5	2	.714	0	0--	-	1.60	2.05
2008	Atl	NL	16	15	0	0	74.2	345	80	56	51	9	5	4	2	41	2	48	2	0	4	8	.333	0	0-0	0	5.21	6.15

Colt Morton

Bats: R Throws: R Pos: C-7; PH-2; PR-2   Ht: 6'5" Wt: 230 Born: 4/10/1982 Age: 27

Year	Team	Lg	G	AB	H	2B	3B	HR	(Hm	Rd)	TB	R	RBI	RC	TBB	IBB	SO	HBP	SH	SF	SB	CS	SB%	GDP	Avg	OBP	Slg
			BATTING																		BASERUNNING				AVERAGES		
2003	Eugene	A-	25	97	27	6	0	7	(-	-)	54	14	20	18	10	0	29	0	0	0	0	0	-	1	.278	.346	.557
2003	FtWyn	A	22	76	13	4	0	2	(-	-)	23	5	7	4	5	1	28	0	0	0	0	0	-	2	.171	.222	.303
2004	FtWyn	A	36	127	19	5	1	4	(-	-)	38	10	11	10	16	0	45	3	0	0	0	0	-	0	.150	.260	.299
2004	Eugene	A-	66	243	58	13	0	17	(-	-)	122	43	45	43	33	1	75	6	0	3	2	0	1.00	3	.239	.340	.502
2004	Mobile	AA	1	3	1	0	0	1	(-	-)	4	1	1	1	1	0	0	0	0	0	0	0	-	0	.333	.500	1.333
2005	FtWyn	A	63	222	58	15	0	10	(-	-)	103	27	46	40	35	1	57	3	0	5	0	0	-	4	.261	.362	.464
2005	Lk Els	A+	26	96	31	4	0	9	(-	-)	62	19	19	24	14	0	30	1	0	2	0	1	.00	1	.323	.407	.646
2006	Lk Els	A+	53	176	40	15	0	5	(-	-)	70	30	22	29	36	0	44	7	0	3	0	1	.00	7	.227	.374	.398
2006	Mobile	AA	41	139	37	10	0	6	(-	-)	65	15	21	21	11	0	44	2	0	0	0	0	-	4	.266	.329	.468
2007	Padres	R	11	31	9	4	0	0	(-	-)	13	9	8	5	5	0	11	1	0	4	0	0	-	1	.290	.366	.419
2007	Lk Els	A+	6	24	12	7	0	3	(-	-)	28	5	8	12	4	0	3	2	0	0	0	0	-	0	.500	.600	1.167
2007	SnAnt	AA	29	94	25	3	0	6	(-	-)	46	17	19	18	15	1	34	4	1	2	0	0	-	0	.266	.383	.489
2008	SnAnt	AA	49	165	31	8	0	3	(-	-)	48	18	18	11	11	0	55	1	0	0	1	0	1.00	4	.188	.243	.291
2008	PortInd	AAA	17	53	9	1	1	2	(-	-)	18	6	6	4	6	0	15	0	0	0	0	0	-	2	.170	.254	.340
2007	SD	NL	1	1	0	0	0	0	(0	0)	0	0	0	0	0	0	0	0	0	0	0	0	-	0	.000	.000	.000
2008	SD	NL	9	15	1	0	0	0	(0	0)	1	2	1	0	2	0	5	0	0	1	0	0	-	0	.067	.167	.067
2 ML YEARS			10	16	1	0	0	0	(0	0)	1	2	1	0	2	0	5	0	0	1	0	0	-	0	.063	.158	.063

Dustin Moseley

Pitches: R Bats: R Pos: SP-10; RP-2   Ht: 6'4" Wt: 215 Born: 12/26/1981 Age: 27

Year	Team	Lg	G	GS	CG	GF	IP	BFP	H	R	ER	HR	SH	SF	HB	TBB	IBB	SO	WP	Bk	W	L	Pct	ShO	Sv-Op	Hld	ERC	ERA
			HOW MUCH HE PITCHED						WHAT HE GAVE UP												THE RESULTS							
2008	RCuca*	A+	1	1	0	0	3.2	16	3	0	0	0	0	0	0	2	0	6	0	0	0	0	-	0	0--	-	2.87	0.00
2008	Salt Lk*	AAA	20	20	0	0	116.2	520	150	93	90	23	1	3	5	34	0	83	5	2	7	10	.412	0	0--	-	6.33	6.94
2006	LAA	AL	3	2	0	1	11.0	54	22	11	11	3	0	1	0	2	0	3	0	0	1	0	1.000	0	0-0	0	11.45	9.00

Year	Team	Lg	G	GS	CG	GF	IP	BFP	H	R	ER	HR	SH	SF	HB	TBB	IBB	SO	WP	Bk	W	L	Pct	ShO	Sv-Op	Hld	ERC	ERA
2007	LAA	AL	46	8	0	13	92.0	383	97	45	45	7	1	2	3	27	3	50	6	1	4	3	.571	0	0-0	4	4.00	4.40
2008	LAA	AL	12	10	0	1	50.1	237	70	38	38	6	1	3	2	20	0	37	3	1	2	4	.333	0	0-0	0	6.74	6.79
	Postseason		1	0	0	1	1.0	3	1	0	0	0	0	0	0	0	0	1	0	0	0	0	-	0	0-0	0	2.79	0.00
	3 ML YEARS		61	20	0	15	153.1	674	189	94	94	16	2	6	5	49	3	90	9	2	7	7	.500	0	0-0	4	5.34	5.52

Brandon Moss

Bats: L **Throws:** R **Pos:** LF-36; RF-32; PH-9; PR-4; DH-3; 1B-2 **Ht:** 6'0" **Wt:** 205 **Born:** 9/16/1983 **Age:** 25

							BATTING													BASERUNNING				AVERAGES		
Year	Team	Lg	G	AB	H	2B	3B	HR	(Hm | Rd)	TB	R	RBI	RC	TBB	IBB	SO	HBP	SH	SF	SB	CS	SB%	GDP	Avg	OBP	Slg
2002	RedSx	R	42	113	23	6	2	0	(- | -)	33	10	6	10	13	0	40	2	1	1	1	2	.33	2	.204	.295	.292
2003	Lowell	A-	65	228	54	15	4	7	(- | -)	98	29	34	29	15	0	53	4	0	5	7	5	.58	1	.237	.290	.430
2004	Augsta	A	109	433	147	25	6	13	(- | -)	223	66	101	90	46	4	75	4	0	7	19	8	.70	8	.339	.402	.515
2004	Srsota	A+	23	83	35	2	1	2	(- | -)	45	16	10	20	7	2	15	0	0	1	2	0	1.00	2	.422	.462	.542
2005	Portlnd	AA	135	503	136	31	4	16	(- | -)	223	87	61	79	53	6	129	3	1	8	6	3	.67	6	.270	.339	.443
2006	Portlnd	AA	133	508	145	36	3	12	(- | -)	223	76	83	82	56	5	108	3	2	4	8	5	.62	13	.285	.357	.439
2007	Pwtckt	AAA	133	493	139	41	2	16	(- | -)	232	66	78	85	61	3	148	3	0	2	3	5	.38	7	.282	.363	.471
2008	Pwtckt	AAA	43	163	46	8	4	8	(- | -)	86	29	30	30	16	0	47	1	0	2	2	0	1.00	1	.282	.346	.528
2007	Bos	AL	15	25	7	2	1	0	(0 | 0)	11	6	1	3	4	0	6	0	0	0	0	0	-	1	.280	.379	.440
2008	2 Tms		79	236	58	15	3	8	(4 | 4)	103	19	34	30	21	1	70	1	0	5	1	2	.33	2	.246	.304	.436
08	Bos	AL	34	78	23	5	1	2	(1 | 1)	36	7	11	11	6	0	25	0	0	2	1	1	.50	0	.295	.337	.462
08	Pit	NL	45	158	35	10	2	6	(3 | 3)	67	12	23	19	15	1	45	1	0	3	0	1	.00	2	.222	.288	.424
	2 ML YEARS		94	261	65	17	4	8	(4 | 4)	114	25	35	33	25	1	76	1	0	5	1	2	.33	3	.249	.312	.437

Guillermo Mota

Pitches: R **Bats:** R **Pos:** RP-58 **Ht:** 6'6" **Wt:** 210 **Born:** 7/25/1973 **Age:** 35

Year	Team	Lg	G	GS	CG	GF	IP	BFP	H	R	ER	HR	SH	SF	HB	TBB	IBB	SO	WP	Bk	W	L	Pct	ShO	Sv-Op	Hld	ERC	ERA
1999	Mon	NL	51	0	0	18	55.1	243	54	24	18	5	3	3	2	25	3	27	1	1	2	4	.333	0	0-1	3	4.10	2.93
2000	Mon	NL	29	0	0	7	30.0	126	27	21	20	3	1	1	2	12	0	24	1	1	1	0	.500	0	0-0	5	3.86	6.00
2001	Mon	NL	53	0	0	12	49.2	212	51	30	29	9	3	2	1	18	1	31	1	0	1	3	.250	0	0-3	12	4.77	5.26
2002	LAD	NL	43	0	0	11	60.2	256	45	30	28	4	3	1	2	27	6	49	3	0	1	3	.250	0	0-1	4	2.57	4.15
2003	LAD	NL	76	0	0	18	105.0	410	78	23	23	7	3	1	1	26	4	99	0	0	6	3	.667	0	1-3	13	2.01	1.97
2004	2 Tms		78	0	0	18	96.2	393	75	33	33	8	5	3	4	37	6	85	5	0	9	8	.529	0	4-8	30	2.82	3.07
2005	Fla	NL	56	0	0	24	67.0	293	65	38	35	5	1	3	1	32	7	60	4	0	2	2	.500	0	2-4	14	3.90	4.70
2006	2 Tms		52	0	0	17	55.2	241	55	29	28	11	0	3	0	24	4	46	2	0	4	3	.571	0	0-0	9	4.71	4.53
2007	NYM	NL	52	0	0	18	59.1	261	63	39	38	8	2	0	2	18	2	47	2	0	2	2	.500	0	0-3	6	4.26	5.76
2008	Mil	NL	58	0	0	18	57.0	244	52	28	26	7	1	3	0	28	0	50	4	1	5	6	.455	0	1-4	11	4.14	4.11
04	LAD	NL	52	0	0	11	63.0	259	51	15	15	4	4	2	2	27	5	52	5	0	8	4	.667	0	1-1	17	2.98	2.14
04	Fla	NL	26	0	0	7	33.2	134	24	18	18	4	1	1	2	10	1	33	0	0	1	4	.200	0	3-7	13	2.51	4.81
06	Cle	AL	34	0	0	13	37.2	173	45	27	26	9	0	3	0	19	3	27	2	0	1	3	.250	0	0-0	5	6.62	6.21
06	NYM	NL	18	0	0	4	18.0	68	10	2	2	2	0	0	0	5	1	19	0	0	3	0	1.000	0	0-0	4	1.51	1.00
	Postseason		7	0	0	2	8.1	36	10	5	5	0	0	0	0	2	0	7	0	0	1	0	1.000	0	0-2	3	3.86	5.40
	10 ML YEARS		548	0	0	153	636.1	2679	565	295	278	67	22	20	15	247	33	518	23	3	33	35	.485	0	8-27	107	3.47	3.93

Jason Motte

Pitches: R **Bats:** R **Pos:** RP-12 **Ht:** 6'0" **Wt:** 200 **Born:** 6/22/1982 **Age:** 27

Year	Team	Lg	G	GS	CG	GF	IP	BFP	H	R	ER	HR	SH	SF	HB	TBB	IBB	SO	WP	Bk	W	L	Pct	ShO	Sv-Op	Hld	ERC	ERA
2006	StCol	A-	21	0	0	16	26.1	114	30	12	9	1	1	2	0	4	0	25	0	0	1	2	.333	0	8--	-	3.33	3.08
2006	QuadC	A	8	0	0	0	12.2	58	16	8	7	1	0	0	1	3	0	13	0	0	1	1	.500	0	0--	-	4.97	4.97
2007	PlmBh	A+	9	0	0	8	10.0	40	7	2	1	0	0	1	0	1	0	6	0	0	1	0	1.000	0	3--	-	1.13	0.90
2007	Sprgfld	AA	45	0	0	23	49.0	200	36	13	11	3	1	1	3	22	2	63	2	0	3	3	.500	0	8--	-	2.82	2.02
2008	Memp	AAA	63	0	0	28	66.2	290	64	25	24	6	2	0	1	26	3	110	7	0	4	3	.571	0	9--	-	3.66	3.24
2008	StL	NL	12	0	0	4	11.0	40	5	2	1	0	1	0	0	3	0	16	0	0	0	0	-	0	1-1	4	0.89	0.82

Jamie Moyer

Pitches: L **Bats:** L **Pos:** SP-33 **Ht:** 6'0" **Wt:** 185 **Born:** 11/18/1962 **Age:** 46

Year	Team	Lg	G	GS	CG	GF	IP	BFP	H	R	ER	HR	SH	SF	HB	TBB	IBB	SO	WP	Bk	W	L	Pct	ShO	Sv-Op	Hld	ERC	ERA
1986	ChC	NL	16	16	1	0	87.1	395	107	52	49	10	3	3	3	42	1	45	3	3	7	4	.636	1	0-0	0	6.13	5.05
1987	ChC	NL	35	33	1	1	201.0	899	210	127	114	28	14	7	5	97	9	147	11	2	12	15	.444	0	0-0	0	4.96	5.10
1988	ChC	NL	34	30	3	1	202.0	855	212	84	78	20	14	4	4	55	7	121	4	0	9	15	.375	1	0-2	0	3.89	3.48
1989	Tex	AL	15	15	1	0	76.0	337	84	51	41	10	1	4	2	33	0	44	1	0	4	9	.308	0	0-0	0	5.20	4.86
1990	Tex	AL	33	10	1	6	102.1	447	115	59	53	6	1	7	4	39	4	58	1	0	2	6	.250	0	0-0	1	4.57	4.66
1991	StL	NL	8	7	0	1	31.1	142	38	21	20	5	4	2	1	16	0	20	2	1	0	5	.000	0	0-0	0	6.58	5.74
1993	Bal	AL	25	25	3	0	152.0	630	154	63	58	15	3	1	6	38	2	90	1	1	12	9	.571	1	0-0	0	3.58	3.43
1994	Bal	AL	23	23	0	0	149.0	631	158	81	79	23	5	2	2	38	3	87	1	0	5	7	.417	0	0-0	0	4.24	4.77
1995	Bal	AL	27	18	0	3	115.2	483	117	70	67	18	5	3	3	30	0	65	0	0	8	6	.571	0	0-0	0	4.11	5.21
1996	2 Tms		34	21	0	1	160.2	703	177	86	71	23	7	6	2	46	5	79	3	1	13	3	.813	0	0-0	0	4.42	3.98
1997	Sea	AL	30	30	2	0	188.2	787	187	82	81	21	6	1	7	43	2	113	3	1	17	5	.773	0	0-0	0	3.56	3.86
1998	Sea	AL	34	34	4	0	234.1	974	234	99	92	23	4	3	10	42	2	158	3	1	15	9	.625	3	0-0	0	3.34	3.53
1999	Sea	AL	32	32	4	0	228.0	945	235	108	98	23	6	2	9	48	1	137	3	0	14	8	.636	0	0-0	0	3.71	3.87
2000	Sea	AL	26	26	0	0	154.0	678	173	103	94	27	3	3	3	53	2	98	4	1	13	10	.565	0	0-0	0	4.91	5.49
2001	Sea	AL	33	33	1	0	209.2	851	187	84	80	24	5	11	10	44	4	119	1	0	20	6	.769	0	0-0	0	3.03	3.43
2002	Sea	AL	34	34	4	0	230.2	931	198	89	85	28	5	7	9	50	4	147	3	0	13	8	.619	2	0-0	0	2.89	3.32
2003	Sea	AL	33	33	1	0	215.0	897	199	83	78	19	7	6	8	66	3	129	0	0	21	7	.750	0	0-0	0	3.37	3.27
2004	Sea	AL	34	33	1	0	202.0	888	217	127	117	44	9	6	11	63	3	125	1	0	7	13	.350	0	0-0	0	5.13	5.21

Year	Team	Lg	G	GS	CG	GF	IP	BFP	H	R	ER	HR	SH	SF	HB	TBB	IBB	SO	WP	Bk	W	L	Pct	ShO	Sv-Op	Hld	ERC	ERA
2005	Sea	AL	32	32	1	0	200.0	868	225	99	95	23	6	6	8	52	2	102	3	0	13	7	.650	0	0-0	0	4.46	4.28
2006	2 Tms		33	33	2	0	211.1	894	228	110	101	33	5	9	5	51	5	108	3	1	11	14	.440	1	0-0	0	4.36	4.30
2007	Phi	NL	33	33	1	0	199.1	867	222	118	111	30	11	5	5	66	3	133	2	0	14	12	.538	0	0-0	0	4.92	5.01
2008	Phi	NL	33	33	0	0	196.1	841	199	85	81	20	7	2	11	62	4	123	3	0	16	7	.696	0	0-0	0	4.03	3.71
96	Bos	AL	23	10	0	1	90.0	405	111	50	45	14	4	3	1	27	2	50	2	1	7	1	.875	0	0-0	1	5.37	4.50
96	Sea	AL	11	11	0	0	70.2	298	66	36	26	9	3	3	1	19	3	29	1	0	6	2	.750	0	0-0	0	3.31	3.31
06	Sea	AL	25	25	2	0	160.0	685	179	85	78	25	3	7	3	44	3	82	3	1	6	12	.333	1	0-0	0	4.74	4.39
06	Phi	NL	8	8	0	0	51.1	209	49	25	23	8	2	2	2	7	2	26	0	0	5	2	.714	0	0-0	0	3.24	4.03
Postseason			5	5	0	0	29.2	114	22	8	8	2	1	0	1	6	0	19	0	0	3	1	.750	0	0-0	0	2.02	2.43
22 ML YEARS			637	584	31	14	3746.2	15943	3876	1881	1743	464	131	100	128	1074	66	2248	56	11	246	185	.571	9	0-2	2	4.11	4.19

Peter Moylan

Pitches: R **Bats:** R **Pos:** RP-7   **Ht:** 6'2" **Wt:** 200 **Born:** 12/2/1978 **Age:** 30

Year	Team	Lg	G	GS	CG	GF	IP	BFP	H	R	ER	HR	SH	SF	HB	TBB	IBB	SO	WP	Bk	W	L	Pct	ShO	Sv-Op	Hld	ERC	ERA
2006	Atl	NL	15	0	0	5	15.0	68	18	8	8	1	1	0	0	5	1	14	0	0	0	0	-	0	0-0	0	4.47	4.80
2007	Atl	NL	80	0	0	16	90.0	359	65	27	18	6	4	4	7	31	12	63	2	0	5	3	.625	0	1-2	8	2.36	1.80
2008	Atl	NL	7	0	0	2	5.2	25	5	1	1	0	0	1	1	1	0	5	0	0	0	1	.000	0	1-2	4	3.51	1.59
3 ML YEARS			102	0	0	23	110.2	452	88	36	27	8	5	4	8	37	13	82	2	0	5	4	.556	0	2-4	12	2.69	2.20

Edward Mujica

Pitches: R **Bats:** R **Pos:** RP-33   **Ht:** 6'2" **Wt:** 215 **Born:** 5/10/1984 **Age:** 25

Year	Team	Lg	G	GS	CG	GF	IP	BFP	H	R	ER	HR	SH	SF	HB	TBB	IBB	SO	WP	Bk	W	L	Pct	ShO	Sv-Op	Hld	ERC	ERA
2008	Buffalo*	AAA	18	0	0	8	26.0	118	29	14	12	2	1	4	1	10	0	27	0	0	0	2	.000	0	4--	-	4.54	4.15
2006	Cle	AL	10	0	0	2	18.1	78	25	6	6	1	0	2	1	0	0	12	0	0	0	1	.000	0	0-0	0	4.50	2.95
2007	Cle	AL	10	0	0	5	13.0	60	19	12	12	3	0	1	0	2	0	7	0	0	0	0	-	0	0-0	0	6.63	8.31
2008	Cle	AL	33	0	0	13	38.2	168	46	29	29	5	0	4	1	10	3	27	1	0	3	2	.600	0	0-2	1	4.82	6.75
3 ML YEARS			53	0	0	20	70.0	306	90	47	47	9	0	7	2	12	3	46	1	0	3	3	.500	0	0-2	1	5.06	6.04

Mark Mulder

Pitches: L **Bats:** L **Pos:** RP-2; SP-1   **Ht:** 6'6" **Wt:** 215 **Born:** 8/5/1977 **Age:** 31

Year	Team	Lg	G	GS	CG	GF	IP	BFP	H	R	ER	HR	SH	SF	HB	TBB	IBB	SO	WP	Bk	W	L	Pct	ShO	Sv-Op	Hld	ERC	ERA
2008	PlmBh*	A+	1	1	0	0	5.0	20	6	2	1	1	0	0	0	0	0	1	0	0	0	0	-	0	0--	-	4.38	1.80
2008	Sprgfld*	AA	3	3	0	0	16.0	65	14	4	4	1	0	0	0	7	0	9	2	0	3	0	1.000	0	0--	-	3.44	2.25
2008	Memp*	AAA	3	3	0	0	13.1	75	28	22	20	3	1	2	3	5	0	8	0	0	0	3	.000	0	0--	-	13.40	13.50
2000	Oak	AL	27	27	0	0	154.0	705	191	106	93	22	3	8	4	69	3	88	6	0	9	10	.474	0	0-0	0	6.14	5.44
2001	Oak	AL	34	34	6	0	229.1	927	214	92	88	16	8	3	5	51	4	153	4	0	21	8	.724	4	0-0	0	2.95	3.45
2002	Oak	AL	30	30	2	0	207.1	862	182	88	80	21	6	4	11	55	3	159	7	1	19	7	.731	1	0-0	0	3.06	3.47
2003	Oak	AL	26	26	9	0	186.2	747	180	66	65	15	7	2	2	40	2	128	7	0	15	9	.625	2	0-0	0	3.17	3.13
2004	Oak	AL	33	33	5	0	225.2	952	223	119	111	25	7	6	12	83	1	140	10	0	17	8	.680	1	0-0	0	4.27	4.43
2005	StL	NL	32	32	3	0	205.0	868	212	90	83	19	9	4	9	70	1	111	9	0	16	8	.667	2	0-0	0	4.25	3.64
2006	StL	NL	17	17	0	0	93.1	430	124	77	74	19	10	1	5	35	1	50	3	0	6	7	.462	0	0-0	0	7.04	7.14
2007	StL	NL	3	3	0	0	11.0	59	22	17	15	4	1	0	1	7	0	3	0	0	0	3	.000	0	0-0	0	15.59	12.27
2008	StL	NL	3	1	0	1	1.2	12	4	2	2	0	0	1	1	2	0	2	1	0	0	0	-	0	0-1	0	18.81	10.80
Postseason			7	7	0	0	42.1	181	50	14	11	2	4	1	4	9	2	29	3	0	3	4	.429	0	0-0	0	4.39	2.34
9 ML YEARS			205	203	25	1	1314.0	5562	1352	657	611	141	51	29	50	412	15	834	47	1	103	60	.632	10	0-1	0	4.14	4.18

Carlos Muniz

Pitches: R **Bats:** R **Pos:** RP-18   **Ht:** 6'1" **Wt:** 190 **Born:** 3/12/1981 **Age:** 28

Year	Team	Lg	G	GS	CG	GF	IP	BFP	H	R	ER	HR	SH	SF	HB	TBB	IBB	SO	WP	Bk	W	L	Pct	ShO	Sv-Op	Hld	ERC	ERA
2003	Bklyn	A-	19	0	0	15	20.0	73	12	1	1	1	1	0	0	5	2	23	3	0	0	0	-	0	13--	-	1.38	0.45
2004	CptCty	A	16	0	0	14	21.0	84	11	10	10	1	0	0	3	8	0	19	0	0	4	0	1.000	0	7--	-	1.78	4.29
2004	Bklyn	A-	12	0	0	11	14.2	62	14	8	5	1	0	0	1	3	2	20	2	0	3	2	.600	0	3--	-	2.86	3.07
2005	Hgrstn	A	30	0	0	26	37.2	169	37	22	20	6	3	1	2	19	0	43	1	2	3	4	.429	0	14--	-	5.00	4.78
2005	Mets	R	2	0	0	1	1.2	11	6	4	3	0	0	0	0	0	0	0	0	0	0	1	.000	0	0--	-	19.18	16.20
2005	StLuci	A+	14	0	0	3	17.0	73	13	11	11	3	1	1	0	9	0	19	1	0	3	0	1.000	0	0--	-	3.73	5.82
2006	StLuci	A+	48	0	0	44	49.2	208	39	21	17	5	2	3	2	18	0	45	1	0	4	3	.571	0	31--	-	2.88	3.08
2007	Bnghtn	AA	44	0	0	36	58.2	241	43	20	16	2	3	1	2	17	5	62	2	0	2	4	.333	0	23--	-	1.84	2.45
2007	NewOr	AAA	3	0	0	0	5.2	22	4	0	0	0	0	0	0	1	0	4	0	0	0	0	-	0	0--	-	1.36	0.00
2008	NewOr	AAA	33	0	0	27	36.2	150	30	16	16	5	3	0	0	14	1	31	2	0	4	4	.333	0	9--	-	3.26	3.93
2007	NYM	NL	2	0	0	1	2.1	10	1	2	2	0	0	0	0	2	0	2	0	0	0	0	-	0	0-0	0	2.03	7.71
2008	NYM	NL	18	0	0	8	23.1	100	24	14	14	4	0	1	2	7	0	16	2	0	1	1	.500	0	0-1	1	4.74	5.40
2 ML YEARS			20	0	0	9	25.2	110	25	16	16	4	0	1	2	9	0	18	2	0	1	1	.500	0	0-1	1	4.47	5.61

Daniel Murphy

Bats: L **Throws:** R **Pos:** LF-32; PH-19   **Ht:** 6'2" **Wt:** 214 **Born:** 4/1/1985 **Age:** 24

			BATTING															BASERUNNING				AVERAGES		
Year	Team	Lg	G	AB	H	2B	3B	HR	(Hm Rd)	TB	R	RBI	RC	TBB	IBB	SO	HBP	SH	SF	SB	CS	SB%	GDP	Avg	OBP	Slg
2006	Mets	R	8	18	1	0	0	0	(- -)	1	2	0	0	4	0	3	0	0	0	0	0	-	0	.056	.227	.056
2006	Kngspt	R+	9	33	9	0	0	2	(- -)	15	2	7	5	4	0	1	0	0	0	0	0	-	4	.273	.351	.455
2006	Bklyn	A-	8	29	7	1	0	0	(- -)	8	2	3	3	4	1	3	0	0	0	0	0	-	0	.241	.324	.276
2007	StLuci	A+	135	502	143	34	3	11	(- -)	216	68	78	77	42	5	61	4	0	11	6	3	.67	8	.285	.338	.430

Year	Team	Lg	G	AB	H	2B	3B	HR	(Hm	Rd)	TB	R	RBI	RC	TBB	IBB	SO	HBP	SH	SF	SB	CS	SB%	GDP	Avg	OBP	Slg
2008	Bnghtn	AA	95	357	110	26	1	13	(-	-)	177	56	67	69	39	7	46	3	1	7	14	5	.74	10	.308	.374	.496
2008	Bklyn	A-	3	14	7	0	0	0	(-	-)	7	1	2	3	0	0	2	0	0	0	0	0	-	0	.500	.500	.500
2008	NewOr	AAA	1	4	1	0	0	0	(-	-)	1	2	0	0	1	0	0	0	0	0	0	0	-	0	.250	.400	.250
2008	NYM	NL	49	131	41	9	3	2	(1	1)	62	24	17	26	18	1	28	1	0	1	0	2	.00	4	.313	.397	.473

David Murphy

Bats: L **Throws:** L **Pos:** RF-56; LF-54; CF-13; PH-3; DH-2; PR-1 **Ht:** 6'4" **Wt:** 205 **Born:** 10/18/1981 **Age:** 27

Year	Team	Lg	G	AB	H	2B	3B	HR	(Hm	Rd)	TB	R	RBI	RC	TBB	IBB	SO	HBP	SH	SF	SB	CS	SB%	GDP	Avg	OBP	Slg
2006	Bos	AL	20	22	5	1	0	1	(0	1)	9	4	2	2	4	0	4	0	0	0	0	0	-	1	.227	.346	.409
2007	2 Tms	AL	46	105	36	12	2	2	(1	1)	58	17	14	23	7	0	20	0	0	0	0	0	-	1	.343	.384	.552
2008	Tex	AL	108	415	114	28	3	15	(8	7)	193	64	74	62	31	3	70	0	2	6	7	2	.78	7	.275	.321	.465
07	Bos	AL	3	2	1	0	1	0	(0	0)	3	1	0	1	0	0	1	0	0	0	0	0	-	0	.500	.500	1.500
07	Tex	AL	43	103	35	12	1	2	(1	1)	55	16	14	22	7	0	19	0	0	0	0	0	-	1	.340	.382	.534
3 ML YEARS			174	542	155	41	5	18	(9	9)	260	85	90	87	42	3	94	0	2	6	7	2	.78	9	.286	.334	.480

Donnie Murphy

Bats: R **Throws:** R **Pos:** 3B-24; SS-13; 2B-10; PR-4; LF-1; PH-1 **Ht:** 5'10" **Wt:** 185 **Born:** 3/10/1983 **Age:** 26

Year	Team	Lg	G	AB	H	2B	3B	HR	(Hm	Rd)	TB	R	RBI	RC	TBB	IBB	SO	HBP	SH	SF	SB	CS	SB%	GDP	Avg	OBP	Slg
2008	Stcktn*	A+	1	3	1	1	0	0	(-	-)	2	1	0	0	0	0	2	0	0	0	0	0	-	0	.333	.333	.667
2008	Scrmto*	AAA	36	141	38	10	2	11	(-	-)	85	25	27	27	8	0	46	2	2	1	1	0	1.00	1	.270	.316	.603
2004	KC	AL	7	27	5	3	0	0	(0	0)	8	1	3	2	0	0	7	0	0	0	1	0	1.00	1	.185	.185	.296
2005	KC	AL	32	77	12	5	0	1	(0	1)	20	4	8	1	9	0	23	0	1	1	0	1	.00	1	.156	.241	.260
2007	Oak	AL	42	118	26	8	0	6	(2	4)	52	21	21	16	10	0	35	2	1	1	0	1	1.00	3	.220	.290	.441
2008	Oak	AL	46	103	19	3	0	3	(2	1)	31	10	13	6	11	0	38	2	0	1	2	1	.67	1	.184	.274	.301
4 ML YEARS			127	325	62	19	0	10	(4	6)	111	36	45	25	30	0	103	4	2	3	2	3	.67	8	.191	.265	.342

A.J. Murray

Pitches: L **Bats:** B **Pos:** SP-2 **Ht:** 6'3" **Wt:** 200 **Born:** 3/17/1982 **Age:** 27

			HOW MUCH HE PITCHED						WHAT HE GAVE UP											THE RESULTS							
Year	Team	Lg	G	GS	CG	GF	IP	BFP	H	R	ER	HR	SH	SF	HB	TBB	IBB	SO	WP	Bk	W	L	Pct	ShO	Sv-Op	Hld	ERC	ERA
2001	Rngrs	R	12	8	0	2	53.1	207	48	15	11	1	1	1	1	10	2	45	4	1	3	3	.500	0	0--	-	2.38	1.86
2002	Savann	A	14	8	0	2	62.2	255	63	22	20	0	2	6	0	14	0	51	5	0	5	3	.625	0	0--	-	2.83	2.87
2002	Charltt	A+	19	14	0	3	83.1	339	77	31	28	4	1	0	0	20	0	68	3	1	3	3	.500	0	2--	-	2.75	3.02
2003	Frisco	AA	27	25	0	1	144.0	611	134	68	58	13	5	12	4	63	2	90	9	0	10	4	.714	0	0--	-	3.92	3.63
2005	Bkrsfld	A+	14	11	0	0	60.0	266	75	36	35	6	0	2	2	13	0	64	2	0	2	5	.286	0	0--	-	4.86	5.25
2005	Frisco	AA	11	10	0	0	58.0	239	62	27	21	3	1	4	1	15	0	49	1	0	4	4	.500	0	0--	-	3.77	3.26
2005	Okla	AAA	2	2	0	0	10.0	42	11	7	7	4	0	0	0	2	0	11	0	0	1	0	1.000	0	0--	-	5.90	6.30
2007	Okla	AAA	41	1	0	21	52.2	221	42	19	18	2	3	1	2	25	0	51	1	0	3	3	.500	0	5--	-	3.01	3.08
2008	Okla	AAA	9	9	2	0	45.0	199	51	23	20	3	0	1	1	15	1	36	1	0	2	2	.500	0	0--	-	4.33	4.00
2007	Tex	AL	14	2	0	6	28.0	123	25	15	14	6	1	1	0	15	1	18	0	0	1	2	.333	0	0-0	0	4.71	4.50
2008	Tex	AL	2	2	0	0	7.2	38	12	4	3	0	0	0	0	3	0	5	0	0	1	0	1.000	0	0-0	0	6.43	3.52
2 ML YEARS			16	4	0	6	35.2	161	37	19	17	6	1	1	0	18	1	23	0	0	2	2	.500	0	0-0	0	5.09	4.29

Matt Murton

Bats: R **Throws:** R **Pos:** LF-17; PH-14; RF-2 **Ht:** 6'1" **Wt:** 220 **Born:** 10/3/1981 **Age:** 27

Year	Team	Lg	G	AB	H	2B	3B	HR	(Hm	Rd)	TB	R	RBI	RC	TBB	IBB	SO	HBP	SH	SF	SB	CS	SB%	GDP	Avg	OBP	Slg
2008	Iowa*	AAA	54	191	57	11	1	1	(-	-)	73	26	15	32	29	0	20	3	1	1	4	2	.67	7	.298	.397	.382
2008	Scrmto*	AAA	32	130	36	12	2	1	(-	-)	55	19	13	20	13	0	20	1	0	1	3	1	.75	8	.277	.345	.423
2005	ChC	NL	51	140	45	3	2	7	(2	5)	73	19	14	19	16	4	22	0	2	2	2	1	.67	4	.321	.386	.521
2006	ChC	NL	144	455	135	22	3	13	(7	6)	202	70	62	68	45	1	62	5	1	2	5	2	.71	16	.297	.365	.444
2007	ChC	NL	94	235	66	13	0	8	(2	6)	103	35	22	28	26	0	39	0	0	0	1	0	1.00	4	.281	.352	.438
2008	2 Tms		28	70	13	3	0	0	(0	0)	16	3	8	2	2	0	12	1	0	0	0	0	-	3	.186	.219	.229
08	ChC	NL	19	40	10	2	0	0	(0	0)	12	2	6	2	1	0	5	1	0	0	0	0	-	2	.250	.286	.300
08	Oak	AL	9	30	3	1	0	0	(0	0)	4	1	2	0	1	0	7	0	0	0	0	0	-	1	.100	.129	.133
Postseason			1	4	1	0	0	0	(0	0)	1	1	0	0	0	0	0	0	0	0	0	0	-	0	.250	.250	.250
4 ML YEARS			317	900	259	41	5	28	(11	17)	394	127	106	117	89	5	135	6	3	4	8	3	.73	27	.288	.354	.438

Neal Musser

Pitches: L **Bats:** L **Pos:** RP-1 **Ht:** 6'1" **Wt:** 235 **Born:** 8/25/1980 **Age:** 28

			HOW MUCH HE PITCHED						WHAT HE GAVE UP											THE RESULTS							
Year	Team	Lg	G	GS	CG	GF	IP	BFP	H	R	ER	HR	SH	SF	HB	TBB	IBB	SO	WP	Bk	W	L	Pct	ShO	Sv-Op	Hld	ERC	ERA
1999	Mets	R	8	7	0	0	31.1	134	26	13	7	1	0	0	0	18	0	22	4	0	2	1	.667	0	0--	-	3.36	2.01
2000	Kngspt	R+	7	7	0	0	34.1	138	33	10	8	1	0	0	1	6	0	21	3	0	3	2	.600	0	0--	-	2.72	2.10
2001	Clmbia	A	17	17	1	0	95.0	387	86	38	30	3	4	3	3	18	0	98	8	1	7	4	.636	0	0--	-	2.46	2.84
2001	StLuci	A+	9	9	0	0	45.2	201	45	24	18	2	0	2	5	19	0	40	2	0	3	4	.429	0	0--	-	4.08	3.55
2002	StLuci	A+	4	4	0	0	19.0	80	20	4	3	1	0	1	1	5	0	12	1	0	2	0	1.000	0	0--	-	3.77	1.42
2002	Bklyn	A-	4	4	0	0	13.0	49	7	2	1	0	0	0	1	5	0	12	0	0	0	0	-	0	0--	-	1.54	0.69
2003	StLuci	A+	7	6	0	0	34.2	155	41	20	18	5	1	1	3	9	0	16	1	1	3	0	1.000	0	0--	-	5.19	4.67
2003	Bnghtn	AA	20	20	0	0	100.1	436	108	57	51	9	4	4	4	39	0	76	5	1	9	5	.357	0	0--	-	4.72	4.57
2004	Bnghtn	AA	19	19	0	0	108.1	458	103	52	41	7	8	5	4	40	0	70	3	1	9	6	.600	0	0--	-	3.62	3.41
2004	Norfolk	AAA	7	7	0	0	36.0	161	39	30	25	4	5	5	0	17	2	24	3	0	2	4	.333	0	0--	-	4.81	6.25
2005	Norfolk	AAA	24	24	0	0	123.2	561	141	75	69	12	6	6	5	52	0	89	7	1	6	11	.353	0	0--	-	5.23	5.02

Year	Team	Lg	G	GS	CG	GF	IP	BFP	H	R	ER	HR	SH	SF	HB	TBB	IBB	SO	WP	Bk	W	L	Pct	ShO	Sv-Op	Hld	ERC	ERA
			HOW MUCH HE PITCHED						WHAT HE GAVE UP												THE RESULTS							
2006	Tucsn	AAA	8	7	0	0	36.1	174	44	26	22	4	1	0	5	24	0	18	6	0	1	3	.250	0	0--	-	7.25	5.45
2006	Omha	AAA	2	2	0	0	9.2	38	7	2	2	2	0	0	0	3	0	6	0	0	1	0	1.000	0	0--	-	2.96	1.86
2006	Wichta	AA	18	11	0	3	83.2	372	80	53	46	12	2	3	5	48	3	67	6	1	6	3	.667	0	2--	-	5.08	4.95
2007	Omha	AAA	32	0	0	20	55.1	204	32	5	3	1	2	3	3	11	0	47	4	0	4	1	.800	0	8--	-	1.27	0.49
2008	Omha	AAA	37	3	0	21	56.0	254	47	32	27	9	1	0	3	37	0	64	5	1	3	5	.375	0	6--	-	4.77	4.34
2008	Royals	R	3	3	0	0	2.2	11	3	1	1	0	0	0	0	0	0	6	0	0	0	1	.000	0	0--	-	2.52	3.38
2007	KC	AL	17	0	0	3	24.2	116	32	13	12	5	0	0	0	14	3	19	2	0	0	1	.000	0	0-0	1	7.27	4.38
2008	KC	AL	1	0	0	1	1.0	3	0	0	0	0	0	0	0	1	0	0	0	0	0	0	-	0	0-0	0	1.26	0.00
2 ML YEARS			18	0	0	4	25.2	119	32	13	12	5	0	0	0	15	3	19	2	0	0	1	.000	0	0-0	1	7.01	4.21

Mike Mussina

Pitches: R Bats: L Pos: SP-34   Ht: 6'2" Wt: 190 Born: 12/8/1968 Age: 40

Year	Team	Lg	G	GS	CG	GF	IP	BFP	H	R	ER	HR	SH	SF	HB	TBB	IBB	SO	WP	Bk	W	L	Pct	ShO	Sv-Op	Hld	ERC	ERA
			HOW MUCH HE PITCHED						WHAT HE GAVE UP												THE RESULTS							
1991	Bal	AL	12	12	2	0	87.2	349	77	31	28	7	3	2	1	21	0	52	3	1	4	5	.444	0	0-0	0	2.80	2.87
1992	Bal	AL	32	32	8	0	241.0	957	212	70	68	16	13	6	2	48	2	130	6	0	18	5	.783	4	0-0	0	2.54	2.54
1993	Bal	AL	25	25	3	0	167.2	693	163	84	83	20	6	4	3	44	2	117	5	0	14	6	.700	2	0-0	0	3.61	4.46
1994	Bal	AL	24	24	3	0	176.1	712	163	63	60	19	3	9	1	42	1	99	0	0	16	5	.762	0	0-0	0	3.16	3.06
1995	Bal	AL	32	32	7	0	221.2	882	187	86	81	24	2	2	1	50	4	158	2	0	19	9	.679	4	0-0	0	2.66	3.29
1996	Bal	AL	36	36	4	0	243.1	1039	264	137	130	31	4	4	3	69	0	204	3	0	19	11	.633	1	0-0	0	4.36	4.81
1997	Bal	AL	33	33	4	0	224.2	905	197	87	80	27	3	2	3	54	3	218	5	0	15	8	.652	1	0-0	0	3.00	3.20
1998	Bal	AL	29	29	4	0	206.1	835	189	85	80	22	6	3	4	41	3	175	10	0	13	10	.565	2	0-0	0	2.96	3.49
1999	Bal	AL	31	31	4	0	203.1	842	207	88	79	16	9	7	1	52	0	172	2	0	18	7	.720	2	0-0	0	3.54	3.50
2000	Bal	AL	34	34	6	0	237.2	987	236	105	100	28	8	6	3	46	0	210	3	0	11	15	.423	1	0-0	0	3.37	3.79
2001	NYY	AL	34	34	4	0	228.2	909	202	87	80	20	5	6	4	42	2	214	6	0	17	11	.607	3	0-0	0	2.65	3.15
2002	NYY	AL	33	33	2	0	215.2	886	208	103	97	27	5	5	5	48	1	182	7	0	18	10	.643	2	0-0	0	2.75	3.40
2003	NYY	AL	31	31	2	0	214.2	855	192	86	81	21	1	4	3	40	4	195	4	0	17	8	.680	1	0-0	0	4.19	4.59
2004	NYY	AL	27	27	1	0	164.2	697	178	91	84	22	5	4	2	40	1	132	5	0	12	9	.571	0	0-0	0	4.55	4.41
2005	NYY	AL	30	30	2	0	179.2	766	199	93	88	23	6	4	7	47	0	142	2	0	13	8	.619	2	0-0	0	3.01	3.51
2006	NYY	AL	32	32	1	0	197.1	804	184	88	77	22	1	1	5	35	1	172	3	0	15	7	.682	0	0-0	0	4.87	5.15
2007	NYY	AL	28	27	0	0	152.0	656	188	90	87	14	6	6	4	35	2	91	1	0	11	10	.524	0	0-0	0	3.61	3.37
2008	NYY	AL	34	34	0	0	200.1	819	214	85	75	17	4	7	8	31	3	150	4	0	20	9	.690	0	0-0	0	3.61	3.37
Postseason			23	21	0	0	139.2	571	121	56	53	19	6	4	3	33	7	145	2	0	7	8	.467	0	0-0	0	2.94	3.42
18 ML YEARS			537	536	57	0	3562.2	14593	3460	1559	1458	376	90	82	60	785	29	2813	71	1	270	153	.638	23	0-0	0	3.35	3.68

Brett Myers

Pitches: R Bats: R Pos: SP-30   Ht: 6'4" Wt: 238 Born: 8/17/1980 Age: 28

Year	Team	Lg	G	GS	CG	GF	IP	BFP	H	R	ER	HR	SH	SF	HB	TBB	IBB	SO	WP	Bk	W	L	Pct	ShO	Sv-Op	Hld	ERC	ERA
			HOW MUCH HE PITCHED						WHAT HE GAVE UP												THE RESULTS							
2008	LV*	AAA	2	2	0	0	12.1	53	12	6	5	0	0	1	1	4	0	12	1	0	1	1	.500	0	0--	-	3.23	3.65
2008	Rdng*	AA	1	1	0	0	8.0	33	5	3	2	1	0	0	0	2	0	10	0	0	0	1	.000	0	0--	-	1.64	2.25
2008	Clrwtr*	A+	1	1	1	0	6.2	27	7	3	2	0	1	0	1	1	1	6	0	0	0	1	.000	0	0--	-	2.57	2.70
2002	Phi	NL	12	12	1	0	72.0	307	73	38	34	11	6	2	6	29	1	34	2	1	4	5	.444	0	0-0	0	5.04	4.25
2003	Phi	NL	32	32	1	0	193.0	848	205	99	95	20	6	3	9	76	8	143	9	0	14	9	.609	1	0-0	0	4.56	4.43
2004	Phi	NL	32	31	1	1	176.0	778	196	113	108	31	9	3	6	62	4	116	5	0	11	11	.500	1	0-0	0	5.17	5.52
2005	Phi	NL	34	34	2	0	215.1	905	193	94	89	31	9	3	11	68	2	208	4	4	13	8	.619	0	0-0	0	3.64	3.72
2006	Phi	NL	31	31	3	0	198.0	833	194	93	86	29	7	4	3	63	3	189	3	0	12	7	.632	0	0-0	0	4.02	3.91
2007	Phi	NL	51	3	0	37	68.2	293	61	33	33	9	3	1	1	27	1	83	5	0	5	7	.417	0	21-24	3	3.63	4.33
2008	Phi	NL	30	30	2	0	190.0	817	197	103	96	29	4	3	6	65	6	163	2	0	10	13	.435	1	0-0	0	4.53	4.55
Postseason			2	0	0	2	1.1	6	2	0	0	0	0	0	0	0	0	3	0	0	0	0	-	0	0-0	0	4.47	0.00
7 ML YEARS			222	173	8	38	1113.0	4781	1119	573	541	160	44	19	42	390	25	936	30	5	69	60	.535	3	21-24	3	4.34	4.37

Brian Myrow

Bats: L Throws: R Pos: PH-20; 1B-2   Ht: 5'11" Wt: 210 Born: 9/4/1976 Age: 32

Year	Team	Lg	G	AB	H	2B	3B	HR	(Hm	Rd)	TB	R	RBI	RC	TBB	IBB	SO	HBP	SH	SF	SB	CS	SB%	GDP	Avg	OBP	Slg
			BATTING																		BASERUNNING				AVERAGES		
2008	PortInd*	AAA	97	328	103	23	1	12	(-	-)	164	60	59	78	81	1	72	4	0	4	0	1	.00	4	.314	.451	.500
2005	LAD	NL	19	20	4	1	0	0	(0	0)	5	2	0	3	5	0	8	0	0	0	0	0	-	0	.200	.360	.250
2007	SD	NL	12	10	1	1	0	0	(0	0)	2	0	1	1	1	0	4	1	0	0	0	0	-	1	.100	.250	.200
2008	SD	NL	21	21	3	0	0	1	(1	0)	6	1	3	0	2	0	5	0	0	1	0	0	-	1	.143	.208	.286
3 ML YEARS			52	51	8	2	0	1	(1	0)	13	3	4	4	8	0	17	1	0	1	0	0	-	2	.157	.279	.255

Xavier Nady

Bats: R Throws: R Pos: RF-89; LF-46; DH-8; PH-7; 1B-3   Ht: 6'2" Wt: 215 Born: 11/14/1978 Age: 30

Year	Team	Lg	G	AB	H	2B	3B	HR	(Hm	Rd)	TB	R	RBI	RC	TBB	IBB	SO	HBP	SH	SF	SB	CS	SB%	GDP	Avg	OBP	Slg
			BATTING																		BASERUNNING				AVERAGES		
2000	SD	NL	1	1	1	0	0	0	(0	0)	1	1	0	1	0	0	0	0	0	0	0	0	-	0	1.000	1.000	1.000
2003	SD	NL	110	371	99	17	1	9	(5	4)	145	50	39	39	24	0	74	6	2	1	6	2	.75	14	.267	.321	.391
2004	SD	NL	34	77	19	4	0	3	(1	2)	32	7	9	8	5	0	13	1	1	0	0	0	-	4	.247	.301	.416
2005	SD	NL	124	326	85	15	2	13	(5	8)	143	40	43	37	22	0	77	7	1	0	2	1	.67	5	.261	.321	.439
2006	2 Tms	NL	130	468	131	28	1	17	(10	7)	212	57	63	62	30	7	85	11	2	1	3	3	.50	12	.280	.337	.453
2007	Pit	NL	125	431	120	23	1	20	(7	13)	205	55	72	60	23	2	101	12	0	4	3	1	.75	16	.278	.330	.476
2008	2 Tms	NL	148	555	169	37	1	25	(11	14)	283	76	97	93	39	2	103	9	0	4	2	1	.67	14	.305	.357	.510
06	NYM	NL	75	265	70	15	1	14	(10	4)	129	37	40	35	19	4	51	6	1	1	2	1	.67	7	.264	.326	.487
06	Pit	NL	55	203	61	13	0	3	(0	3)	83	20	23	27	11	3	34	5	1	0	1	2	.33	5	.300	.352	.409

Year Team	Lg	G	AB	H	2B	3B	HR	(Hm Rd)	TB	R	RBI	RC	TBB	IBB	SO	HBP	SH	SF	SB	CS	SB%	GDP	Avg	OBP	Slg
08 Pit	NL	89	327	108	26	1	13	(6 7)	175	50	57	59	25	1	55	5	0	3	1	0	1.00	9	.330	.383	.535
08 NYY	AL	59	228	61	11	0	12	(5 7)	108	26	40	34	14	1	48	4	0	1	1	1	.50	5	.268	.320	.474
Postseason		2	3	1	0	0	0	(0 0)	1	0	2	1	0	0	1	2	0	0	0	0	-	5	.333	.600	.333
7 ML YEARS		672	2229	624	124	6	87	(39 48)	1021	286	323	300	143	12	443	46	6	10	16	8	.67	65	.280	.335	.458

Mike Napoli

Bats: R Throws: R Pos: C-75; PH-5

Ht: 6'0" Wt: 215 Born: 10/31/1981 Age: 27

Year Team	Lg	G	AB	H	2B	3B	HR	(Hm Rd)	TB	R	RBI	RC	TBB	IBB	SO	HBP	SH	SF	SB	CS	SB%	GDP	Avg	OBP	Slg
2008 RCuca*	A+	5	14	8	3	0	1	(- -)	14	3	4	6	2	0	2	0	0	1	0	0	-	0	.571	.588	1.000
2006 LAA	AL	99	268	61	13	0	16	(10 6)	122	47	42	40	51	0	90	5	0	1	2	3	.40	2	.228	.360	.455
2007 LAA	AL	75	219	54	11	1	10	(5 5)	97	40	34	35	33	2	63	5	1	5	5	2	.71	5	.247	.351	.443
2008 LAA	AL	78	227	62	9	1	20	(10 10)	133	39	49	46	35	5	70	5	1	6	7	3	.70	3	.273	.374	.586
Postseason		3	6	1	0	0	0	(0 0)	1	0	0	0	0	0	3	0	0	0	0	0	-	0	.167	.167	.167
3 ML YEARS		252	714	177	33	2	46	(25 21)	352	126	125	121	119	7	223	15	2	12	14	8	.64	10	.248	.362	.493

Joe Nathan

Pitches: R Bats: R Pos: RP-68

Ht: 6'4" Wt: 225 Born: 11/22/1974 Age: 34

Year Team	Lg	G	GS	CG	GF	IP	BFP	H	R	ER	HR	SH	SF	HB	TBB	IBB	SO	WP	Bk	W	L	Pct	ShO	Sv-Op	Hld	ERC	ERA
1999 SF	NL	19	14	0	2	90.1	395	84	45	42	17	2	0	1	46	0	54	2	0	7	4	.636	0	1-1	0	4.78	4.18
2000 SF	NL	20	15	0	0	93.1	426	89	63	54	12	5	5	4	63	4	61	5	0	5	2	.714	0	0-1	0	5.23	5.21
2002 SF	NL	4	0	0	3	3.2	12	1	0	0	0	0	0	0	2	0	2	0	0	0	0	-	0	0-0	0	0.17	0.00
2003 SF	NL	78	0	0	9	79.0	316	51	26	26	7	2	4	3	33	3	83	4	1	12	4	.750	0	0-3	20	2.34	2.96
2004 Min	AL	73	0	0	63	72.1	284	48	14	13	3	2	0	2	23	3	89	5	0	1	2	.333	0	44-47	0	1.78	1.62
2005 Min	AL	69	0	0	58	70.0	276	46	22	21	5	1	2	0	22	1	94	2	0	7	4	.636	0	43-48	0	1.83	2.70
2006 Min	AL	64	0	0	61	68.1	262	38	12	12	3	3	2	1	16	4	95	3	0	7	0	1.000	0	36-38	0	1.18	1.58
2007 Min	AL	68	0	0	60	71.2	282	54	15	15	4	2	2	1	19	2	77	3	0	4	2	.667	0	37-41	0	2.08	1.88
2008 Min	AL	68	0	0	57	67.2	261	43	13	10	5	1	0	2	18	4	74	2	0	1	2	.333	0	39-45	0	1.67	1.33
Postseason		6	0	0	2	6.0	31	7	5	5	1	0	0	0	6	2	8	1	0	0	2	.000	0	1-2	0	7.30	7.50
9 ML YEARS		463	29	0	313	616.1	2514	454	210	193	56	18	15	14	240	21	629	26	1	44	20	.688	0	200-224	20	2.62	2.82

Dioner Navarro

Bats: B Throws: R Pos: C-117; PH-6

Ht: 5'9" Wt: 205 Born: 2/9/1984 Age: 25

Year Team	Lg	G	AB	H	2B	3B	HR	(Hm Rd)	TB	R	RBI	RC	TBB	IBB	SO	HBP	SH	SF	SB	CS	SB%	GDP	Avg	OBP	Slg
2008 VeroB*	A+	4	10	4	1	0	1	(- -)	8	4	4	5	6	0	1	2	0	0	1	0	1.00	0	.400	.667	.800
2004 NYY	AL	5	7	3	0	0	0	(0 0)	3	2	1	1	0	0	0	0	0	0	0	0	-	1	.429	.429	.429
2005 LAD	NL	50	176	48	9	0	3	(3 0)	66	21	14	18	20	1	21	2	1	0	0	0	-	3	.273	.354	.375
2006 2 Tms		81	268	68	9	0	6	(4 2)	95	28	28	27	31	6	51	1	1	1	2	1	.67	7	.254	.332	.354
2007 TB	AL	119	388	88	19	2	9	(5 4)	138	46	44	35	33	3	67	1	7	5	3	1	.75	11	.227	.286	.356
2008 TB	AL	120	427	126	27	0	7	(4 3)	174	43	54	59	34	1	49	3	3	3	0	4	.00	16	.295	.349	.407
06 LAD	NL	25	75	21	2	0	2	(1 1)	29	5	8	8	11	4	18	0	0	0	1	0	1.00	1	.280	.372	.387
06 TB	AL	56	193	47	7	0	4	(3 1)	66	23	20	19	20	2	33	1	1	1	1	1	.50	6	.244	.316	.342
5 ML YEARS		375	1266	333	64	2	25	(16 9)	476	140	141	140	118	11	188	7	12	9	5	6	.45	38	.263	.327	.376

Brad Nelson

Bats: L Throws: R Pos: PH-7; 1B-2

Ht: 6'2" Wt: 253 Born: 12/23/1982 Age: 26

Year Team	Lg	G	AB	H	2B	3B	HR	(Hm Rd)	TB	R	RBI	RC	TBB	IBB	SO	HBP	SH	SF	SB	CS	SB%	GDP	Avg	OBP	Slg
2001 Brewrs	R	17	63	19	6	1	0	(- -)	27	10	13	11	8	0	18	2	1	1	0	0	-	1	.302	.392	.429
2001 Ogden	R+	13	42	11	4	0	0	(- -)	15	5	10	4	3	0	9	0	0	2	0	0	-	4	.262	.298	.357
2002 Beloit	A	106	417	124	38	2	17	(- -)	217	70	99	77	34	4	86	4	0	4	4	1	.80	9	.297	.353	.520
2002 Hi Dsrt	A+	26	102	26	11	0	3	(- -)	46	24	17	15	12	1	28	0	0	0	0	0	-	4	.255	.333	.451
2003 Hi Dsrt	A+	41	167	52	9	1	1	(- -)	66	23	18	24	12	0	22	2	0	1	2	2	.50	3	.311	.363	.395
2003 Hntsvl	AA	39	143	30	12	0	1	(- -)	45	15	14	12	11	2	34	2	0	1	2	2	.50	4	.210	.274	.315
2004 Hntsvl	AA	137	500	127	31	1	19	(- -)	217	61	77	71	47	3	146	6	1	6	11	10	.52	9	.254	.321	.434
2005 Nashv	AAA	81	281	71	16	2	7	(- -)	112	50	39	42	45	4	74	2	2	1	4	5	.44	5	.253	.359	.399
2005 Hntsvl	AA	55	208	61	8	1	6	(- -)	89	27	38	34	26	5	42	1	0	3	1	2	.33	5	.293	.370	.428
2006 Nashv	AAA	40	130	28	10	0	3	(- -)	47	22	17	16	18	0	36	2	0	2	4	3	.57	5	.215	.316	.362
2006 Hntsvl	AA	80	265	70	14	1	6	(- -)	104	47	39	48	63	4	62	0	0	4	6	3	.67	6	.264	.401	.392
2007 Nashv	AAA	116	411	108	23	1	20	(- -)	193	54	65	61	31	1	98	2	0	1	9	6	.60	5	.263	.317	.470
2008 Nashv	AAA	132	475	136	36	1	18	(- -)	228	78	78	89	73	3	77	1	0	4	13	8	.62	13	.286	.380	.480
2008 Mil	NL	9	7	2	2	0	0	(0 0)	4	0	0	1	1	0	0	0	0	0	0	0	-	0	.286	.375	.571

Joe Nelson

Pitches: R Bats: R Pos: RP-59

Ht: 6'1" Wt: 200 Born: 10/25/1974 Age: 34

Year Team	Lg	G	GS	CG	GF	IP	BFP	H	R	ER	HR	SH	SF	HB	TBB	IBB	SO	WP	Bk	W	L	Pct	ShO	Sv-Op	Hld	ERC	ERA
2008 Albq*	AAA	19	0	0	19	25.2	98	17	6	6	1	0	0	1	6	0	36	1	0	1	1	.500	0	11--	-	1.63	2.10
2001 Atl	NL	2	0	0	0	2.0	16	7	9	8	1	0	1	1	2	0	0	0	0	0	0	-	0	0-0	0	33.03	36.00
2004 Bos	AL	3	0	0	1	2.2	17	4	5	5	0	1	0	2	3	0	5	0	0	0	0	-	0	0-0	0	12.43	16.88
2006 KC	AL	43	0	0	20	44.2	193	37	22	22	5	3	1	1	24	4	44	1	0	1	1	.500	0	9-10	5	3.67	4.43
2008 Fla	NL	59	0	0	20	54.0	230	42	16	12	5	2	0	2	22	4	60	3	0	3	1	.750	0	1-5	11	2.80	2.00
4 ML YEARS		107	0	0	41	103.1	456	90	52	47	11	6	2	6	51	8	109	4	0	4	2	.667	0	10-15	16	3.79	4.09

Pat Neshek

Pitches: R Bats: B Pos: RP-15
Ht: 6'3" Wt: 210 Born: 9/4/1980 Age: 28

Year Team	Lg	G	GS	CG	GF	IP	BFP	H	R	ER	HR	SH	SF	HB	TBB	IBB	SO	WP	Bk	W	L	Pct	ShO	Sv-Op	Hld	ERC	ERA
2006 Min	AL	32	0	0	3	37.0	138	23	9	9	6	0	1	0	6	0	53	0	0	4	2	.667	0	0-2	10	1.68	2.19
2007 Min	AL	74	0	0	20	70.1	278	44	25	23	7	4	5	2	27	5	74	2	0	7	2	.778	0	0-3	15	2.12	2.94
2008 Min	AL	15	0	0	3	13.1	56	12	7	7	2	1	1	0	4	1	15	0	0	0	1	.000	0	0-2	6	3.29	4.73
Postseason		2	0	0	1	1.0	4	1	1	1	0	0	0	0	0	0	1	0	0	0	1	.000	0	0-0		1.95	9.00
3 ML YEARS		121	0	0	26	120.2	472	79	41	39	15	5	7	2	37	6	142	2	0	11	5	.688	0	0-7	31	2.11	2.91

David Newhan

Bats: L Throws: R Pos: PH-38; 2B-28; LF-2; PR-1
Ht: 5'10" Wt: 185 Born: 9/7/1973 Age: 35

Year Team	Lg	G	AB	H	2B	3B	HR	(Hm	Rd)	TB	R	RBI	RC	TBB	IBB	SO	HBP	SH	SF	SB	CS	SB%	GDP	Avg	OBP	Slg
2008 RdRck*	AAA	60	198	61	14	2	9	(-	-)	106	39	36	38	14	0	33	1	2	1	8	2	.80	2	.308	.355	.535
1999 SD	NL	32	43	6	1	0	2	(1	1)	13	7	6	1	1	0	11	0	0	0	2	1	.67	0	.140	.159	.302
2000 2 Tms	NL	24	37	6	1	0	1	(1	0)	10	8	2	2	8	1	13	0	0	0	0	0	-	2	.162	.311	.270
2001 Phi	NL	7	6	2	1	0	0	(0	0)	3	2	1	1	1	0	0	0	0	1	0	0	-	0	.333	.375	.500
2004 Bal	AL	95	373	116	15	7	8	(3	5)	169	66	54	70	27	0	72	4	5	3	11	1	.92	4	.311	.361	.453
2005 Bal	AL	96	218	44	9	0	5	(1	4)	68	31	21	19	22	1	45	2	5	2	9	2	.82	2	.202	.279	.312
2006 Bal	AL	39	131	33	4	0	4	(3	1)	49	14	18	10	7	1	22	2	0	3	4	2	.67	4	.252	.294	.374
2007 NYM	NL	56	74	15	1	1	1	(1	0)	21	9	6	8	8	0	19	1	0	0	2	0	1.00	1	.203	.289	.284
2008 Hou	NL	64	104	27	5	2	2	(1	1)	42	11	12	10	6	0	28	0	0	1	1	0	1.00	3	.260	.297	.404
00 SD	NL	14	20	3	1	0	1	(1	0)	7	5	2	2	6	1	7	0	0	0	0	0	-	0	.150	.346	.350
00 Phi	NL	10	17	3	0	0	0	(0	0)	3	3	0	0	2	0	6	0	0	0	0	0	-	0	.176	.263	.176
8 ML YEARS		413	986	249	37	10	23	(11	12)	375	148	120	121	80	3	210	9	10	10	29	6	.83	16	.253	.312	.380

Josh Newman

Pitches: L Bats: L Pos: RP-12
Ht: 6'1" Wt: 200 Born: 6/11/1982 Age: 27

Year Team	Lg	G	GS	CG	GF	IP	BFP	H	R	ER	HR	SH	SF	HB	TBB	IBB	SO	WP	Bk	W	L	Pct	ShO	Sv-Op	Hld	ERC	ERA
2004 Casper	R+	27	0	0	8	33.2	139	30	17	13	2	0	0	0	8	0	46	1	0	1	2	.333	0	1- -	-	2.57	3.48
2005 Mdest	A+	41	0	0	16	63.1	268	45	22	22	5	1	0	0	40	0	59	2	0	5	2	.714	0	0- -	-	3.27	3.13
2006 Tulsa	AA	62	0	0	22	77.0	303	56	27	27	8	1	1	3	24	1	77	2	0	9	5	.643	0	2- -	-	2.53	3.16
2007 ColSpr	AAA	55	0	0	14	62.0	288	73	34	28	3	2	2	4	30	1	49	4	0	3	2	.600	0	0- -	-	5.23	4.06
2008 ColSpr	AAA	20	0	0	6	22.0	91	16	9	6	0	0	1	1	9	0	18	1	0	1	1	.500	0	1- -	-	2.18	2.45
2008 Omha	AAA	7	2	0	1	22.0	99	23	13	12	1	0	1	0	13	0	22	2	0	0	1	.000	0	0- -	-	4.71	4.91
2007 Col	NL	2	0	0	2	2.0	8	2	1	1	0	0	0	0	0	0	3	1	0	0	0	-	0	0-0	0	1.95	4.50
2008 2 Tms		12	0	0	6	15.2	84	25	18	15	4	0	1	2	12	1	8	0	1	0	0	-	0	0-0	0	11.44	8.62
08 Col	NL	8	0	0	3	8.2	49	15	9	9	3	0	0	2	6	1	6	0	1	0	0	-	0	0-0	0	13.09	9.35
08 KC	AL	4	0	0	3	7.0	35	10	9	6	1	0	1	0	6	0	2	0	0	0	0	-	0	0-0	0	9.42	7.71
2 ML YEARS		14	0	0	8	17.2	92	27	19	16	4	0	1	2	12	1	11	1	1	0	0	-	0	0-0	0	10.16	8.15

Jeff Niemann

Pitches: R Bats: R Pos: RP-3; SP-2
Ht: 6'9" Wt: 280 Born: 2/28/1983 Age: 26

Year Team	Lg	G	GS	CG	GF	IP	BFP	H	R	ER	HR	SH	SF	HB	TBB	IBB	SO	WP	Bk	W	L	Pct	ShO	Sv-Op	Hld	ERC	ERA
2005 Visalia	A+	5	5	0	0	20.1	83	12	10	9	3	-	-	2	10	0	28	1	0	0	1	.000	0	0- -	-	2.95	3.98
2005 Mont	AA	6	3	0	1	10.1	43	7	7	5	0	0	0	0	5	0	14	0	0	0	1	.000	0	0- -	-	2.02	4.35
2006 Mont	AA	14	14	0	0	77.1	320	56	24	23	6	4	3	7	29	0	84	3	0	5	5	.500	0	0- -	-	2.70	2.68
2007 Drhm	AAA	25	25	0	0	131.0	580	144	69	58	13	3	3	9	46	1	123	8	0	12	6	.667	0	0- -	-	4.69	3.98
2008 Drhm	AAA	24	24	3	0	133.0	547	101	60	53	15	2	1	5	50	0	128	2	0	9	5	.643	1	0- -	-	2.92	3.59
2008 TB	AL	5	2	0	2	16.0	76	18	12	9	3	2	0	1	8	0	14	0	0	2	2	.500	0	0-0	0	5.93	5.06

Jonathon Niese

Pitches: L Bats: L Pos: SP-3
Ht: 6'4" Wt: 215 Born: 10/27/1986 Age: 22

Year Team	Lg	G	GS	CG	GF	IP	BFP	H	R	ER	HR	SH	SF	HB	TBB	IBB	SO	WP	Bk	W	L	Pct	ShO	Sv-Op	Hld	ERC	ERA
2005 Mets	R	7	5	0	0	24.2	105	23	10	10	1	0	0	1	10	0	24	2	0	1	0	1.000	0	0- -	-	3.49	3.65
2006 Hgrstn	A	25	25	1	0	123.2	549	121	67	54	7	3	3	9	62	0	132	15	1	11	9	.550	1	0- -	-	4.33	3.93
2006 StLuci	A+	2	2	0	0	10.0	45	8	8	5	0	2	1	0	5	0	10	1	0	0	2	.000	0	0- -	-	2.49	4.50
2007 StLuci	A+	27	27	2	0	134.1	575	151	78	64	9	4	4	7	31	0	110	7	0	11	7	.611	1	0- -	-	4.11	4.29
2008 Bnghtn	AA	22	22	2	0	124.1	521	118	53	42	5	5	3	2	44	0	112	7	0	6	7	.462	1	0- -	-	3.31	3.04
2008 NewOr	AAA	7	7	0	0	39.2	167	34	15	15	4	2	2	2	14	0	32	1	0	5	1	.833	0	0- -	-	3.29	3.40
2008 NYM	NL	3	3	0	0	14.0	69	20	11	11	2	1	0	0	8	0	11	0	0	1	1	.500	0	0-0	0	7.71	7.07

Fernando Nieve

Pitches: R Bats: R Pos: RP-11
Ht: 6'0" Wt: 195 Born: 7/15/1982 Age: 26

Year Team	Lg	G	GS	CG	GF	IP	BFP	H	R	ER	HR	SH	SF	HB	TBB	IBB	SO	WP	Bk	W	L	Pct	ShO	Sv-Op	Hld	ERC	ERA
2001 Mrtnsvl	R+	12	8	1	0	38.0	161	27	20	16	2	0	0	3	21	0	49	3	1	4	2	.667	0	0- -	-	3.08	3.79
2002 Mrtnsvl	R+	13	13	0	0	67.2	280	46	23	18	5	1	2	2	27	0	60	1	0	4	1	.800	0	0- -	-	2.28	2.39
2002 Lxngtn	A	1	1	0	0	3.0	18	6	5	2	0	0	0	1	0	0	2	0	0	0	1	.000	0	0- -	-	7.91	6.00
2003 Lxngtn	A	28	28	1	0	150.1	638	133	69	61	10	4	8	0	65	0	144	7	1	14	9	.609	0	0- -	-	3.33	3.65
2004 Salem	A+	24	24	2	0	149.0	599	136	52	49	9	10	6	1	40	0	117	5	0	10	6	.625	2	0- -	-	2.95	2.96
2004 RdRck	AA	3	3	0	0	17.1	69	12	4	3	0	1	0	1	8	0	17	0	0	2	0	1.000	0	0- -	-	2.35	1.56

Year	Team	Lg	G	GS	CG	GF	IP	BFP	H	R	ER	HR	SH	SF	HB	TBB	IBB	SO	WP	Bk	W	L	Pct	ShO	Sv-Op	Hld	ERC	ERA
			HOW MUCH HE PITCHED						**WHAT HE GAVE UP**												**THE RESULTS**							
2005	CpChr	AA	14	14	0	0	85.0	341	62	27	25	7	2	3	3	29	0	96	4	0	4	3	.571	0	0--	-	2.48	2.65
2005	RdRck	AAA	13	13	2	0	82.0	372	92	45	44	10	2	5	5	33	2	75	3	0	4	4	.500	2	0--	-	5.09	4.83
2006	RdRck	AAA	4	0	0	2	5.1	19	2	0	0	0	0	0	0	0	0	7	0	0	0	0	-	0	2--	-	0.30	0.00
2007	RdRck	AAA	5	5	0	0	21.2	105	30	19	15	1	0	2	1	15	1	13	2	0	1	3	.250	0	0--	-	7.51	6.23
2008	RdRck	AAA	36	7	0	15	72.1	329	87	50	46	13	2	4	3	27	0	63	4	0	2	5	.286	0	6--	-	5.89	5.72
2006	Hou	NL	40	11	0	11	96.1	411	87	46	45	18	5	3	2	41	5	70	1	0	3	3	.500	0	0-0	0	4.24	4.20
2008	Hou	NL	11	0	0	1	10.2	49	17	10	10	2	0	0	0	2	0	12	0	0	0	1	.000	0	0-1	0	7.62	8.44
	2 ML YEARS		51	11	0	12	107.0	460	104	56	55	20	5	3	2	43	5	82	1	0	3	4	.429	0	0-1	0	4.55	4.63

Wil Nieves

Bats: R Throws: R Pos: C-61; PH-8; PR-2　　　　　**Ht: 5'11" Wt: 187 Born: 9/25/1977 Age: 31**

Year	Team	Lg	G	AB	H	2B	3B	HR	(Hm	Rd)	TB	R	RBI	RC	TBB	IBB	SO	HBP	SH	SF	SB	CS	SB%	GDP	Avg	OBP	Slg
								BATTING													**BASERUNNING**				**AVERAGES**		
2008	Clmbs*	AAA	9	25	6	1	0	0	(-	-)	7	3	2	2	3	0	6	0	1	0	1	0	1.00	0	.240	.321	.280
2002	SD	NL	28	72	13	3	1	0	(0	0)	18	2	3	4	4	4	15	0	0	0	1	0	1.00	1	.181	.224	.250
2005	NYY	AL	3	4	0	0	0	0	(0	0)	0	0	0	0	0	0	1	0	0	0	0	0	-	0	.000	.000	.000
2006	NYY	AL	6	6	0	0	0	0	(0	0)	0	0	0	0	0	0	0	0	0	0	0	0	-	0	.000	.000	.000
2007	NYY	AL	26	61	10	4	0	0	(0	0)	14	6	8	4	2	0	9	0	3	0	0	0	-	3	.164	.190	.230
2008	Was	NL	68	176	46	9	1	1	(1	0)	60	15	20	20	13	1	29	0	5	2	0	1	.00	7	.261	.309	.341
	5 ML YEARS		131	319	69	16	2	1	(1	0)	92	23	31	28	19	5	55	0	8	2	1	1	.50	11	.216	.259	.288

Dustin Nippert

Pitches: R Bats: R Pos: RP-14; SP-6　　　　　**Ht: 6'8" Wt: 225 Born: 5/6/1981 Age: 28**

Year	Team	Lg	G	GS	CG	GF	IP	BFP	H	R	ER	HR	SH	SF	HB	TBB	IBB	SO	WP	Bk	W	L	Pct	ShO	Sv-Op	Hld	ERC	ERA
			HOW MUCH HE PITCHED						**WHAT HE GAVE UP**												**THE RESULTS**							
2008	Okla*	AAA	12	10	1	0	63.1	262	65	28	28	8	0	4	2	16	0	43	4	0	6	2	.750	0	0--	-	4.04	3.98
2005	Ari	NL	3	3	0	0	14.2	68	10	9	9	1	0	0	1	13	0	11	1	0	1	0	1.000	0	0-0	0	4.09	5.52
2006	Ari	NL	2	2	0	0	10.0	51	15	13	13	5	1	0	0	7	0	9	0	0	0	2	.000	0	0-0	0	12.21	11.70
2007	Ari	NL	36	0	0	8	45.1	196	48	30	28	5	0	0	1	16	1	38	4	0	1	1	.500	0	0-0	2	4.25	5.56
2008	Tex	AL	20	6	0	6	71.2	341	92	52	51	10	3	1	1	37	3	55	1	1	3	5	.375	0	0-0	0	6.47	6.40
	Postseason		2	0	0	1	2.1	8	1	0	0	0	0	0	0	0	0	2	0	0	0	0	-	0	0-0	0	0.40	0.00
	4 ML YEARS		61	11	0	14	141.2	656	165	104	101	21	4	1	2	73	4	113	6	1	5	8	.385	0	0-0	2	5.84	6.42

Jayson Nix

Bats: R Throws: R Pos: 2B-20; PH-2　　　　　**Ht: 5'11" Wt: 185 Born: 8/26/1982 Age: 26**

Year	Team	Lg	G	AB	H	2B	3B	HR	(Hm	Rd)	TB	R	RBI	RC	TBB	IBB	SO	HBP	SH	SF	SB	CS	SB%	GDP	Avg	OBP	Slg
								BATTING													**BASERUNNING**				**AVERAGES**		
2001	Casper	R+	42	153	45	10	1	5	(-	-)	72	28	24	27	21	1	43	3	0	2	1	5	.17	1	.294	.385	.471
2002	Ashvll	A	132	487	120	29	2	14	(-	-)	195	73	79	72	62	2	105	9	3	4	14	5	.74	10	.246	.340	.400
2003	Visalia	A+	137	562	158	46	0	21	(-	-)	267	107	86	98	54	2	131	10	3	6	24	8	.75	3	.281	.351	.475
2004	Tulsa	AA	123	456	97	17	1	14	(-	-)	158	58	58	50	40	1	101	12	1	6	14	3	.82	9	.213	.292	.346
2005	Tulsa	AA	131	501	118	27	0	11	(-	-)	178	68	47	53	29	1	92	11	4	6	10	6	.63	6	.236	.289	.355
2006	ColSpr	AAA	103	358	90	14	1	2	(-	-)	112	39	26	40	32	0	61	3	3	1	15	3	.83	4	.251	.317	.313
2007	ColSpr	AAA	124	439	128	33	2	11	(-	-)	198	80	58	70	31	1	79	4	7	2	24	8	.75	9	.292	.342	.451
2008	ColSpr	AAA	67	264	80	21	2	17	(-	-)	156	63	51	58	27	1	64	5	3	4	11	5	.69	6	.303	.373	.591
2008	Col	NL	22	56	7	2	0	0	(0	0)	9	2	2	0	7	2	17	1	1	0	1	0	1.00	1	.125	.234	.161

Laynce Nix

Bats: L Throws: L Pos: PH-8; LF-2　　　　　**Ht: 6'1" Wt: 220 Born: 10/30/1980 Age: 28**

Year	Team	Lg	G	AB	H	2B	3B	HR	(Hm	Rd)	TB	R	RBI	RC	TBB	IBB	SO	HBP	SH	SF	SB	CS	SB%	GDP	Avg	OBP	Slg
								BATTING													**BASERUNNING**				**AVERAGES**		
2008	Nashv*	AAA	103	380	108	22	3	23	(-	-)	205	63	60	71	36	3	88	2	0	2	5	3	.63	9	.284	.348	.539
2003	Tex	AL	53	184	47	10	0	8	(7	1)	81	25	30	25	9	0	53	0	1	1	3	0	1.00	1	.255	.289	.440
2004	Tex	AL	115	371	92	20	4	14	(9	5)	162	58	46	44	23	4	113	2	1	3	1	1	.50	6	.248	.293	.437
2005	Tex	AL	63	229	55	12	3	6	(3	3)	91	28	32	26	9	3	45	0	0	2	2	0	1.00	3	.240	.267	.397
2006	2 Tms		19	67	11	2	0	1	(1	0)	16	3	10	3	0	0	28	2	0	1	0	0	-	1	.164	.186	.239
2007	Mil	NL	10	12	0	0	0	0	(0	0)	0	0	0	0	0	0	4	0	0	0	0	0	-	0	.000	.000	.000
2008	Mil	NL	10	12	1	0	0	0	(0	0)	1	1	0	0	1	0	3	0	0	0	0	0	-	0	.083	.154	.083
	06 Tex	AL	9	32	3	1	0	0	(0	0)	4	1	4	0	0	0	17	1	0	1	0	0	-	0	.094	.118	.125
	06 Mil	NL	10	35	8	1	0	1	(1	0)	12	2	6	3	0	0	11	1	0	0	0	0	-	1	.229	.250	.343
	6 ML YEARS		270	875	206	44	7	29	(20	9)	351	115	118	98	42	7	246	4	2	7	6	1	.86	11	.235	.272	.401

Trot Nixon

Bats: L Throws: L Pos: LF-6; RF-5; PH-1　　　　　**Ht: 6'0" Wt: 210 Born: 4/11/1974 Age: 35**

Year	Team	Lg	G	AB	H	2B	3B	HR	(Hm	Rd)	TB	R	RBI	RC	TBB	IBB	SO	HBP	SH	SF	SB	CS	SB%	GDP	Avg	OBP	Slg
								BATTING													**BASERUNNING**				**AVERAGES**		
2008	Tucsn*	AAA	58	181	56	15	0	10	(-	-)	101	39	31	45	40	4	25	1	0	0	1	0	1.00	5	.309	.437	.558
2008	Mets*	R	3	10	6	2	0	0	(-	-)	8	1	1	4	1	0	0	0	0	0	0	0	-	0	.600	.636	.800
2008	NewOr*	AAA	10	41	12	1	0	4	(-	-)	25	9	13	10	8	0	9	0	0	0	1	0	1.00	1	.293	.408	.610
1996	Bos	AL	2	4	2	1	0	0	(0	0)	3	2	0	1	0	0	1	0	0	0	1	0	1.00	0	.500	.500	.750
1998	Bos	AL	13	27	7	1	0	0	(0	0)	8	3	0	2	1	0	3	0	0	0	0	0	-	0	.259	.286	.296
1999	Bos	AL	124	381	103	22	5	15	(3	12)	180	67	52	66	53	1	75	3	2	8	3	1	.75	7	.270	.357	.472
2000	Bos	AL	123	427	118	27	8	12	(4	8)	197	66	60	74	63	2	85	2	5	5	8	1	.89	11	.276	.368	.461
2001	Bos	AL	148	535	150	31	4	27	(14	13)	270	100	88	102	79	1	113	7	6	6	7	4	.64	8	.280	.376	.505
2002	Bos	AL	152	532	136	36	3	24	(8	16)	250	81	94	85	65	2	109	5	3	7	4	2	.67	7	.256	.338	.470

Year	Team	Lg	G	AB	H	2B	3B	HR	(Hm	Rd)	TB	R	RBI	RC	TBB	IBB	SO	HBP	SH	SF	SB	CS	SB%	GDP	Avg	OBP	Slg
																									BATTING	BASERUNNING	AVERAGES
2003	Bos	AL	134	441	135	24	6	28	(10	18)	255	81	87	90	65	4	96	3	1	3	4	2	.67	3	.306	.396	.578
2004	Bos	AL	48	149	47	9	1	6	(3	3)	76	24	23	24	15	1	24	1	0	2	0	0	-	3	.315	.377	.510
2005	Bos	AL	124	408	112	29	1	13	(5	8)	182	64	67	70	53	3	59	3	0	6	2	1	.67	7	.275	.357	.446
2006	Bos	AL	114	381	104	24	0	8	(1	7)	150	59	52	55	60	1	56	7	0	5	0	2	.00	10	.268	.373	.394
2007	Cle	AL	99	307	77	17	0	3	(2	1)	103	30	31	34	44	7	59	0	0	3	0	0	-	9	.251	.342	.336
2008	NYM	NL	11	35	6	1	0	1	(0	1)	10	2	1	2	6	1	9	0	0	0	1	0	1.00	0	.171	.293	.286
Postseason			42	138	39	11	0	6	(3	3)	68	18	25	25	14	1	30	1	0	2	1	2	.33	2	.283	.348	.493
12 ML YEARS			1092	3627	995	222	28	137	(50	87)	1684	579	555	605	504	23	689	31	17	45	30	13	.70	65	.274	.364	.464

Ricky Nolasco

Pitches: R Bats: R Pos: SP-32; RP-2   Ht: 6'2" Wt: 220 Born: 12/13/1982 Age: 26

Year	Team	Lg	G	GS	CG	GF	IP	BFP	H	R	ER	HR	SH	SF	HB	TBB	IBB	SO	WP	Bk	W	L	Pct	ShO	Sv-Op	Hld	ERC	ERA
			HOW MUCH HE PITCHED						WHAT HE GAVE UP												THE RESULTS						
2006	Fla	NL	35	22	0	0	140.0	613	157	86	75	20	8	6	10	41	5	99	7	0	11	11	.500	0	0-0	2	4.89	4.82
2007	Fla	NL	5	4	0	0	21.1	99	26	16	13	3	3	5	1	9	2	11	1	0	1	2	.333	0	0-0	0	5.71	5.48
2008	Fla	NL	34	32	1	0	212.1	868	192	88	83	28	6	9	6	42	6	186	1	3	15	8	.652	1	0-0	0	3.03	3.52
3 ML YEARS			74	58	1	0	373.2	1580	375	190	171	51	17	20	17	92	13	296	9	3	27	21	.563	1	0-0	2	3.85	4.12

Hideo Nomo

Pitches: R Bats: R Pos: RP-3   Ht: 6'2" Wt: 220 Born: 8/31/1968 Age: 40

Year	Team	Lg	G	GS	CG	GF	IP	BFP	H	R	ER	HR	SH	SF	HB	TBB	IBB	SO	WP	Bk	W	L	Pct	ShO	Sv-Op	Hld	ERC	ERA
			HOW MUCH HE PITCHED						WHAT HE GAVE UP												THE RESULTS						
1995	LAD	NL	28	28	4	0	191.1	780	124	63	54	14	11	4	5	78	2	236	19	5	13	6	.684	3	0-0	0	2.16	2.54
1996	LAD	NL	33	33	3	0	228.1	932	180	93	81	23	12	6	2	85	6	234	11	3	16	11	.593	2	0-0	0	2.86	3.19
1997	LAD	NL	33	33	1	0	207.1	904	193	104	98	23	7	1	9	92	2	233	10	4	14	12	.538	0	0-0	0	4.06	4.25
1998	2 Tms	NL	29	28	3	0	157.1	687	130	88	86	19	8	5	4	94	2	167	13	4	6	12	.333	0	0-0	0	4.10	4.92
1999	Mil	NL	28	28	0	0	176.1	767	173	96	89	27	5	5	3	78	2	161	10	1	12	8	.600	0	0-0	0	4.57	4.54
2000	Det	AL	32	31	1	0	190.0	828	191	102	100	31	6	3	3	89	1	181	16	0	8	12	.400	0	0-0	0	4.95	4.74
2001	Bos	AL	33	33	2	0	198.0	849	171	105	99	26	4	7	3	96	2	220	6	0	13	10	.565	2	0-0	0	3.90	4.50
2002	LAD	NL	34	34	0	0	220.1	926	189	92	83	26	17	4	2	101	5	193	6	0	16	6	.727	0	0-0	0	3.68	3.39
2003	LAD	NL	33	33	2	0	218.1	897	175	82	75	24	11	3	1	98	6	177	11	0	16	13	.552	2	0-0	0	3.30	3.09
2004	LAD	NL	18	18	0	0	84.0	393	105	77	77	19	7	3	4	42	1	54	3	0	4	11	.267	0	0-0	0	7.22	8.25
2005	TB	AL	19	19	0	0	100.2	472	127	82	81	16	6	8	2	51	2	59	3	0	5	8	.385	0	0-0	0	6.58	7.24
2008	KC	AL	3	0	0	2	4.1	27	10	9	9	3	0	1	0	4	0	3	1	0	0	0		0	0-0	0	21.77	18.69
98	LAD	NL	12	12	2	0	67.2	295	57	39	38	8	2	2	3	38	0	73	4	1	2	7	.222	0	0-0	0	4.13	5.05
98	NYM	NL	17	16	1	0	89.2	392	73	49	48	11	6	3	1	56	2	94	9	3	4	5	.444	0	0-0	0	4.07	4.82
Postseason			2	2	0	0	8.2	45	12	10	10	3	1	0	0	7	1	9	1	0	0	2	.000	0	0-0	0	10.00	10.38
12 ML YEARS			323	318	16	2	1976.1	8462	1768	993	932	251	94	50	38	908	31	1918	109	17	123	109	.530	9	0-0	0	3.97	4.24

Greg Norton

Bats: B Throws: R Pos: PH-75; LF-25; 1B-11; DH-8; RF-2   Ht: 6'1" Wt: 205 Born: 7/6/1972 Age: 36

Year	Team	Lg	G	AB	H	2B	3B	HR	(Hm	Rd)	TB	R	RBI	RC	TBB	IBB	SO	HBP	SH	SF	SB	CS	SB%	GDP	Avg	OBP	Slg
																					BATTING				BASERUNNING	AVERAGES	
2008	Tacom*	AAA	8	22	9	2	0	0	(-	-)	11	3	3	5	2	0	3	0	0	1	1	0	1.00	0	.409	.440	.500
1996	CWS	AL	11	23	5	0	0	2	(0	2)	11	4	3	3	4	0	6	0	0	0	0	1	.00	0	.217	.333	.478
1997	CWS	AL	18	34	9	2	2	0	(0	0)	15	5	1	5	2	0	8	0	1	0	0	0	-	0	.265	.306	.441
1998	CWS	AL	105	299	71	17	2	9	(6	3)	119	38	36	33	26	1	77	2	1	2	3	3	.50	11	.237	.301	.398
1999	CWS	AL	132	436	111	26	0	16	(5	11)	185	62	50	66	69	3	93	2	1	2	4	4	.50	11	.255	.358	.424
2000	CWS	AL	71	201	49	6	1	6	(4	2)	75	25	28	27	26	0	47	2	0	2	1	0	1.00	2	.244	.333	.373
2001	Col	NL	117	225	60	13	2	13	(7	6)	116	30	40	36	19	2	65	0	0	1	1	0	1.00	6	.267	.321	.516
2002	Col	NL	113	168	37	8	1	7	(3	4)	68	19	37	22	24	0	52	0	1	2	2	3	.40	4	.220	.314	.405
2003	Col	NL	114	179	47	15	0	6	(2	4)	80	19	31	26	16	0	47	1	0	1	2	1	.67	8	.263	.325	.447
2004	Det	AL	41	86	15	1	0	2	(1	1)	22	9	2	1	12	1	21	0	1	0	0	0	-	3	.174	.296	.256
2006	TB	AL	98	294	87	15	0	17	(9	8)	153	47	45	53	35	2	69	3	1	2	1	1	.50	9	.296	.374	.520
2007	TB	AL	75	202	49	9	0	4	(2	2)	70	25	23	28	37	3	55	0	0	1	1	1	.50	1	.243	.358	.347
2008	2 Tms	AL	117	187	49	12	0	7	(2	5)	82	29	35	32	33	4	44	0	0	0	0	0	-	7	.262	.373	.439
08	Sea	AL	6	16	7	2	0	0	(0	0)	9	2	4	6	2	0	4	0	0	0	0	0	-	0	.438	.500	.563
08	Atl	NL	111	171	42	10	0	7	(2	5)	73	27	31	26	31	4	40	0	0	0	0	0	-	7	.246	.361	.427
12 ML YEARS			1012	2334	589	124	8	89	(41	48)	996	312	331	332	303	16	584	10	6	14	15	18	.45	51	.252	.339	.427

Abraham Nunez

Bats: B Throws: R Pos: PH-2   Ht: 5'11" Wt: 201 Born: 3/16/1976 Age: 33

Year	Team	Lg	G	AB	H	2B	3B	HR	(Hm	Rd)	TB	R	RBI	RC	TBB	IBB	SO	HBP	SH	SF	SB	CS	SB%	GDP	Avg	OBP	Slg
																					BATTING				BASERUNNING	AVERAGES	
2008	Nashv*	AAA	33	105	22	2	0	0	(-	-)	24	14	8	9	14	0	18	1	2	1	5	0	1.00	2	.210	.306	.229
2008	NewOr*	AAA	72	218	46	4	0	4	(-	-)	62	26	20	26	42	4	38	2	3	0	4	1	.80	8	.211	.344	.284
1997	Pit	NL	19	40	9	2	2	0	(0	0)	15	3	6	4	3	0	10	1	0	1	1	0	1.00	1	.225	.289	.375
1998	Pit	NL	24	52	10	2	0	1	(0	1)	15	6	2	6	12	0	14	0	3	0	4	2	.67	1	.192	.344	.288
1999	Pit	NL	90	259	57	8	0	0	(0	0)	65	25	17	22	28	0	54	1	13	0	9	1	.90	2	.220	.299	.251
2000	Pit	NL	40	91	20	1	0	1	(0	1)	24	10	8	6	8	1	14	0	0	0	0	0	-	3	.220	.283	.264
2001	Pit	NL	115	301	79	11	4	1	(0	1)	101	30	21	36	28	1	53	1	4	1	8	2	.80	0	.262	.326	.336
2002	Pit	NL	112	253	59	14	1	2	(2	0)	81	28	15	25	27	1	44	2	3	1	3	4	.43	2	.233	.311	.320
2003	Pit	NL	118	311	77	8	7	4	(2	2)	111	37	35	28	26	1	53	3	9	2	9	3	.75	8	.248	.310	.357
2004	Pit	NL	112	182	43	9	0	2	(1	1)	58	17	13	12	10	0	36	0	2	1	3	1	.25	8	.236	.275	.319
2005	StL	NL	139	421	120	13	2	5	(3	2)	152	64	44	54	37	4	63	0	9	0	1	1	1.00	6	.285	.343	.361
2006	Phi	NL	123	322	68	10	2	2	(2	0)	88	42	32	27	41	8	58	2	3	1	1	0	1.00	7	.211	.303	.273

							BATTING															BASERUNNING				AVERAGES		
Year	Team	Lg	G	AB	H	2B	3B	HR	(Hm	Rd)	TB	R	RBI	RC	TBB	IBB	SO	HBP	SH	SF	SB	CS	SB%	GDP	Avg	OBP	Slg
2007	Phi	NL	136	252	59	10	1	0	(0	0)	71	24	16	21	30	5	48	1	4	0	2	0	1.00	10	.234	.318	.282
2008	NYM	NL	2	2	0	0	0	0	(0	0)	0	0	0	0	0	0	0	0	0	0	0	0	-	0	.000	.000	.000
	Postseason		10	26	9	1	0	0	(0	0)	10	4	0	4	2	0	4	0	0	0	1	0	1.00	1	.346	.393	.385
	12 ML YEARS		1030	2486	601	88	19	18	(10	8)	781	286	209	241	250	21	447	11	50	7	38	16	.70	48	.242	.313	.314

Leo Nunez

Pitches: R **Bats:** R **Pos:** RP-45

Ht: 6'1" **Wt:** 165 **Born:** 8/14/1983 **Age:** 25

			HOW MUCH HE PITCHED						WHAT HE GAVE UP											THE RESULTS							
Year	Team	Lg	G	GS	CG	GF	IP	BFP	H	R	ER	HR	SH	SF	HB	TBB	IBB	SO	WP	Bk	W	L	Pct	ShO	Sv-Op	Hld	ERC	ERA
2008	Omha*	AAA	4	0	0	2	4.0	20	7	3	3	1	0	0	0	1	0	3	0	0	0	0	-	0	0--	-	9.18	6.75
2008	NWArk*	AA	1	1	0	0	2.0	6	0	0	0	0	0	0	0	0	0	2	0	0	0	0	-	0	0--	-	0.00	0.00
2005	KC	AL	41	0	0	10	53.2	246	73	45	45	9	1	2	3	18	2	32	1	0	3	2	.600	0	0-1	2	6.76	7.55
2006	KC	AL	7	0	0	5	13.1	58	15	7	7	2	0	1	2	5	0	7	0	0	0	0	-	0	0-0	0	5.98	4.73
2007	KC	AL	13	6	0	3	43.2	182	44	21	19	8	0	2	0	10	0	37	1	0	2	4	.333	0	0-0	1	3.98	3.92
2008	KC	AL	45	0	0	12	48.1	205	45	19	16	2	3	2	4	15	2	26	3	0	4	1	.800	0	0-3	7	3.20	2.98
	4 ML YEARS		106	6	0	29	159.0	691	177	92	87	21	4	7	9	48	4	102	5	0	9	7	.563	0	0-4	10	4.78	4.92

Vladimir Nunez

Pitches: R **Bats:** R **Pos:** RP-23

Ht: 6'4" **Wt:** 240 **Born:** 3/15/1975 **Age:** 34

			HOW MUCH HE PITCHED						WHAT HE GAVE UP											THE RESULTS							
Year	Team	Lg	G	GS	CG	GF	IP	BFP	H	R	ER	HR	SH	SF	HB	TBB	IBB	SO	WP	Bk	W	L	Pct	ShO	Sv-Op	Hld	ERC	ERA
2008	Rchmd*	AAA	37	0	0	13	57.1	251	54	23	22	1	2	4	2	28	1	61	0	0	3	1	.750	0	3--	-	3.59	3.45
1998	Ari	NL	4	0	0	2	5.1	25	7	6	6	0	0	1	0	2	0	2	0	1	0	0	-	0	0-0	0	4.87	10.13
1999	2 Tms	NL	44	12	0	12	108.2	463	95	63	49	11	7	6	4	54	6	86	8	1	7	10	.412	0	1-3	4	3.88	4.06
2000	Fla	NL	17	12	0	3	68.1	322	88	63	60	12	5	5	2	34	2	45	5	0	6	0	.000	0	0-0	1	6.88	7.90
2001	Fla	NL	52	3	0	13	92.0	380	79	33	28	9	2	5	5	30	5	64	1	1	4	5	.444	0	0-1	4	3.17	2.74
2002	Fla	NL	77	0	0	43	97.2	404	80	38	37	8	6	4	0	37	1	73	2	0	6	5	.545	0	20-28	11	2.88	3.41
2003	Fla	NL	14	0	0	4	10.2	63	21	21	19	7	1	2	0	7	0	10	0	0	0	3	.000	0	0-3	2	16.12	16.03
2004	Col	NL	22	0	0	6	25.2	114	26	22	20	6	1	5	1	14	0	22	4	0	3	3	.500	0	0-3	3	6.01	7.01
2008	Atl	NL	23	0	0	7	32.2	146	32	14	14	0	0	3	1	19	5	24	2	0	1	2	.333	0	0-0	-	3.77	3.86
99	Ari	NL	27	0	0	11	34.0	146	29	15	11	2	2	3	1	20	5	28	3	0	3	2	.600	0	1-2	3	3.63	2.91
99	Fla	NL	17	12	0	1	74.2	317	66	48	38	9	5	3	3	34	1	58	5	1	4	8	.333	0	0-1	1	3.98	4.58
	8 ML YEARS		253	27	0	90	441.0	1917	428	260	233	53	22	31	13	197	19	326	22	3	21	34	.382	0	21-38	25	4.29	4.76

Ivan Ochoa

Bats: R **Throws:** R **Pos:** SS-35; 2B-8; PH-4; PR-1

Ht: 5'9" **Wt:** 177 **Born:** 12/16/1982 **Age:** 26

							BATTING															BASERUNNING				AVERAGES		
Year	Team	Lg	G	AB	H	2B	3B	HR	(Hm	Rd)	TB	R	RBI	RC	TBB	IBB	SO	HBP	SH	SF	SB	CS	SB%	GDP	Avg	OBP	Slg
2001	Burlgtn	R+	51	176	38	2	0	0	(-	-)	40	30	14	18	24	0	57	11	5	0	14	5	.74	1	.216	.346	.227
2002	Clmbs	AAA	125	391	85	9	3	0	(-	-)	100	54	28	43	54	0	87	9	9	3	47	10	.82	4	.217	.324	.256
2003	Knstn	A+	82	296	75	12	3	0	(-	-)	93	42	23	36	31	1	67	6	7	0	28	10	.74	2	.253	.336	.314
2004	Knstn	A+	66	257	61	9	3	1	(-	-)	79	41	26	27	21	1	56	6	6	2	11	4	.73	1	.237	.308	.307
2005	Akron	AA	126	422	114	13	6	2	(-	-)	145	46	30	50	30	0	80	12	8	3	14	12	.54	7	.270	.334	.344
2006	Akron	AA	104	335	84	10	2	1	(-	-)	101	53	28	41	37	0	63	8	6	3	20	4	.83	6	.251	.337	.301
2006	Buffalo	AAA	16	39	8	2	1	0	(-	-)	12	4	2	5	4	0	5	3	1	0	4	0	1.00	0	.205	.326	.308
2007	Fresno	AAA	47	179	53	11	2	3	(-	-)	77	22	20	27	10	1	30	2	3	2	8	2	.80	4	.296	.337	.430
2008	Fresno	AAA	84	292	93	11	4	6	(-	-)	130	54	32	54	34	0	62	7	2	3	20	11	.65	9	.318	.399	.445
2008	SF	NL	47	120	24	8	0	0	(0	0)	32	7	3	4	4	1	28	3	7	0	0	1	.00	3	.200	.244	.267

Mike O'Connor

Pitches: L **Bats:** L **Pos:** RP-4; SP-1

Ht: 6'3" **Wt:** 186 **Born:** 8/17/1980 **Age:** 28

			HOW MUCH HE PITCHED						WHAT HE GAVE UP											THE RESULTS							
Year	Team	Lg	G	GS	CG	GF	IP	BFP	H	R	ER	HR	SH	SF	HB	TBB	IBB	SO	WP	Bk	W	L	Pct	ShO	Sv-Op	Hld	ERC	ERA
2002	Vrmnt	A-	21	0	0	11	43.0	177	25	17	15	2	1	3	1	27	2	66	4	0	2	3	.400	0	4--	-	2.41	3.14
2003	Savann	A	42	0	0	24	70.0	301	56	36	30	6	2	1	3	35	1	83	6	1	8	3	.727	0	1--	-	3.37	3.86
2004	BrvdCt	A+	26	14	0	0	103.0	438	98	51	47	5	4	6	4	42	0	104	6	2	8	8	.500	0	0--	-	3.68	4.11
2005	Ptomc	A+	26	26	2	0	167.2	695	144	73	66	14	6	4	3	48	0	158	11	1	10	11	.476	1	0--	-	2.81	3.54
2006	NewOr	AAA	6	6	0	0	26.1	109	21	10	8	2	0	1	2	11	1	28	0	0	1	0	1.000	0	0--	-	3.18	2.73
2007	Hrsbrg	AA	15	15	1	0	71.1	321	86	59	56	21	2	1	2	19	2	46	5	0	3	7	.300	0	0--	-	6.08	7.07
2008	Clmbs	AA	16	11	0	0	99.2	385	82	29	24	10	0	2	0	17	0	70	2	0	5	3	.625	0	0--	-	2.36	2.17
2008	Nats	R	1	1	0	0	5.1	24	4	5	1	0	0	0	0	1	0	6	0	0	0	0	-	0	0--	-	1.33	1.69
2006	Was	NL	21	20	0	0	105.0	455	96	61	56	15	6	4	7	45	5	59	8	0	3	8	.273	0	0-0	0	4.19	4.80
2008	Was	NL	5	1	0	0	9.0	48	11	13	13	3	2	1	0	11	0	4	2	0	1	1	.500	0	0-1	0	11.25	13.00
	2 ML YEARS		26	21	0	0	114.0	503	107	74	69	18	8	5	7	56	5	63	10	0	4	9	.308	0	0-1	0	4.67	5.45

Darren O'Day

Pitches: R **Bats:** R **Pos:** RP-30

Ht: 6'4" **Wt:** 225 **Born:** 10/22/1982 **Age:** 26

			HOW MUCH HE PITCHED						WHAT HE GAVE UP											THE RESULTS							
Year	Team	Lg	G	GS	CG	GF	IP	BFP	H	R	ER	HR	SH	SF	HB	TBB	IBB	SO	WP	Bk	W	L	Pct	ShO	Sv-Op	Hld	ERC	ERA
2006	Orem	R+	14	0	0	13	14.1	60	11	5	4	1	0	1	1	5	0	15	3	0	0	1	.000	0	7--	-	2.66	2.51
2006	CRpds	A	17	0	0	6	23.1	90	20	8	7	1	1	1	1	2	0	14	2	0	3	1	.750	0	1--	-	2.05	2.70
2007	RCuca	A+	24	0	0	22	24.0	90	10	3	2	1	0	1	6	2	0	26	1	1	4	0	1.000	0	11--	-	0.87	0.75
2007	Ark	AA	29	0	0	26	29.1	126	27	13	13	3	2	1	2	14	0	22	1	0	3	4	.429	0	10--	-	4.30	3.99
2008	Salt Lk	AAA	21	0	0	16	33.0	130	29	13	12	3	1	2	1	7	0	30	0	0	2	2	.500	0	7--	-	2.87	3.27
2008	LAA	AL	30	0	0	17	43.1	194	49	24	22	2	1	4	4	14	6	29	1	0	0	1	.000	0	0-0	1	4.20	4.57

Eric O'Flaherty

Pitches: L Bats: L Pos: RP-7 **Ht:** 6'2" **Wt:** 220 **Born:** 2/5/1985 **Age:** 24

Year	Team	Lg	G	GS	CG	GF	IP	BFP	H	R	ER	HR	SH	SF	HB	TBB	IBB	SO	WP	Bk	W	L	Pct	ShO	Sv-Op	Hld	ERC	ERA
2008	WTenn*	AA	1	0	0	1	2.0	7	1	0	0	0	0	0	0	0	0	2	0	0	0	0	-	0	0--	-	0.54	0.00
2008	Tacom*	AAA	14	0	0	7	16.1	79	23	9	9	1	1	0	0	9	0	19	2	0	1	0	1.000	0	2--	-	6.84	4.96
2006	Sea	AL	15	0	0	5	11.0	57	18	9	5	2	1	0	0	6	3	6	2	0	0	0	-	0	0-0	1	8.63	4.09
2007	Sea	AL	56	0	0	9	52.1	221	45	26	26	1	0	2	5	20	1	36	4	1	7	1	.875	0	0-1	4	3.04	4.47
2008	Sea	AL	7	0	0	1	6.2	42	16	15	15	2	0	1	2	4	2	4	0	0	0	1	.000	0	0-0	2	17.12	20.25
3 ML YEARS			78	0	0	15	70.0	320	79	50	46	5	1	3	7	30	6	46	6	1	7	2	.778	0	0-1	7	4.93	5.91

Ross Ohlendorf

Pitches: R Bats: R Pos: RP-25; SP-5 **Ht:** 6'4" **Wt:** 235 **Born:** 8/8/1982 **Age:** 26

Year	Team	Lg	G	GS	CG	GF	IP	BFP	H	R	ER	HR	SH	SF	HB	TBB	IBB	SO	WP	Bk	W	L	Pct	ShO	Sv-Op	Hld	ERC	ERA
2004	Yakima	A-	7	7	0	0	29.0	128	22	14	9	1	0	0	4	19	0	28	9	0	2	3	.400	0	0--	-	3.79	2.79
2005	Sbend	A	27	26	1	1	157.0	699	181	89	79	10	4	4	10	48	0	144	9	0	11	10	.524	1	0--	-	4.52	4.53
2006	Tenn	AA	27	27	4	0	177.2	713	180	70	65	13	8	2	8	29	2	125	16	1	10	8	.556	2	0--	-	3.33	3.29
2006	Tucsn	AAA	1	1	0	0	5.0	21	6	1	1	0	0	0	1	0	0	4	0	0	0	0	-	0	0--	-	3.80	1.80
2007	S-WB	AAA	22	9	0	1	68.1	308	89	41	39	7	2	3	2	24	2	49	4	1	3	4	.429	0	0--	-	5.83	5.14
2007	Yanks	R	4	4	0	0	16.0	62	13	8	7	2	0	0	3	1	0	17	1	0	1	1	.500	0	0--	-	2.78	3.94
2008	S-WB	AAA	5	5	0	0	22.1	101	28	11	10	0	1	0	2	5	0	25	2	0	1	1	.500	0	0--	-	4.35	4.03
2008	Indy	AAA	7	7	0	0	46.2	189	46	18	18	7	2	1	2	8	0	39	1	0	4	3	.571	0	0--	-	3.67	3.47
2007	NYY	AL	6	0	0	3	6.1	26	5	2	2	1	0	0	0	2	0	9	0	0	0	0	-	0	0-0	1	2.94	2.84
2008	2 Tms		30	5	0	3	62.2	300	86	49	45	10	1	1	1	31	3	49	10	1	1	4	.200	0	0-0	4	7.16	6.46
08	NYY	AL	25	0	0	0	40.0	187	50	31	29	7	0	0	1	19	3	36	6	0	1	1	.500	0	0-0	4	6.39	6.53
08	Pit	NL	5	5	0	0	22.2	113	36	18	16	3	1	1	0	12	0	13	4	1	0	3	.000	0	0-0	8	7.63	6.35
Postseason			1	0	0	0	1.0	9	4	3	3	1	0	0	1	0	0	0	0	0	0	0	-	0	0-0	0	47.63	27.00
2 ML YEARS			36	5	0	6	69.0	326	91	51	47	11	1	1	1	33	3	58	10	1	1	4	.200	0	0-0	5	6.74	6.13

Will Ohman

Pitches: L Bats: L Pos: RP-83 **Ht:** 6'2" **Wt:** 210 **Born:** 8/13/1977 **Age:** 31

Year	Team	Lg	G	GS	CG	GF	IP	BFP	H	R	ER	HR	SH	SF	HB	TBB	IBB	SO	WP	Bk	W	L	Pct	ShO	Sv-Op	Hld	ERC	ERA
2000	ChC	NL	6	0	0	2	3.1	17	4	3	3	0	0	0	0	4	1	2	1	0	1	0	1.000	0	0-0	1	7.25	8.10
2001	ChC	NL	11	0	0	0	11.2	54	14	10	10	2	0	0	0	6	0	12	2	0	0	1	.000	0	0-0	1	6.26	7.71
2005	ChC	NL	69	0	0	13	43.1	187	32	14	14	6	1	0	3	24	3	45	6	1	2	2	.500	0	0-3	13	3.62	2.91
2006	ChC	NL	78	0	0	14	65.1	286	51	30	30	6	0	2	5	34	2	74	4	0	1	1	.500	0	0-0	9	3.44	4.13
2007	ChC	NL	56	0	0	11	36.1	168	42	20	20	3	2	0	1	16	4	33	2	0	2	4	.333	0	1-1	12	4.79	4.95
2008	Atl	NL	83	0	0	16	58.2	248	51	27	24	3	3	0	1	22	4	53	2	0	4	1	.800	0	1-4	23	2.87	3.68
6 ML YEARS			303	0	0	56	218.2	960	194	104	101	20	6	2	10	106	14	219	17	1	10	9	.526	0	2-8	59	3.73	4.16

Augie Ojeda

Bats: B Throws: R Pos: 2B-44; 3B-28; PH-26; SS-22; PR-5 **Ht:** 5'9" **Wt:** 174 **Born:** 12/20/1974 **Age:** 34

Year	Team	Lg	G	AB	H	2B	3B	HR	(Hm	Rd)	TB	R	RBI	RC	TBB	IBB	SO	HBP	SH	SF	SB	CS	SB%	GDP	Avg	OBP	Slg
2000	ChC	NL	28	77	17	3	1	2	(1	1)	28	10	8	9	10	1	9	0	1	1	0	1	.00	1	.221	.307	.364
2001	ChC	NL	78	144	29	5	1	1	(1	0)	39	16	12	10	12	1	20	2	2	2	1	0	1.00	2	.201	.269	.271
2002	ChC	NL	30	70	13	4	0	0	(0	0)	17	4	4	4	5	0	5	1	4	1	1	0	1.00	2	.186	.247	.243
2003	ChC	NL	12	25	3	0	0	0	(0	0)	3	2	0	2	1	1	5	1	0	0	0	0	-	1	.120	.185	.120
2004	Min	AL	30	59	20	1	0	2	(0	2)	27	16	7	11	10	0	3	0	2	1	1	1	.50	0	.339	.429	.458
2007	Ari	NL	57	113	31	2	2	1	(0	1)	40	16	12	16	15	3	13	0	2	2	1	0	1.00	1	.274	.354	.354
2008	Ari	NL	105	231	56	9	2	0	(0	0)	69	27	17	27	26	2	24	10	4	1	0	0	-	6	.242	.343	.299
Postseason			7	21	6	1	0	0	(0	0)	7	1	1	2	1	0	3	1	0	0	0	0	-	3	.286	.348	.333
7 ML YEARS			340	719	169	24	6	6	(2	4)	223	91	60	77	79	8	79	14	15	8	4	2	.67	13	.235	.320	.310

Hideki Okajima

Pitches: L Bats: L Pos: RP-64 **Ht:** 6'1" **Wt:** 194 **Born:** 12/25/1975 **Age:** 33

Year	Team	Lg	G	GS	CG	GF	IP	BFP	H	R	ER	HR	SH	SF	HB	TBB	IBB	SO	WP	Bk	W	L	Pct	ShO	Sv-Op	Hld	ERC	ERA
1995	Yomiuri	Jap	1	1	0	0	5.0	20	5	1	1	0	-	-	0	2	0	9	0	0	0	0	-	0	0--	-	3.66	1.80
1996	Yomiuri	Jap	5	1	0	2	12.2	60	13	2	1	0	-	-	1	9	0	8	1	0	1	0	1.000	0	0--	-	4.92	0.71
1997	Yomiuri	Jap	25	21	2	2	109.1	477	92	47	42	7	-	-	4	59	0	102	3	0	4	9	.308	1	0--	-	3.59	3.46
1998	Yomiuri	Jap	14	12	0	2	62.1	273	61	31	30	7	-	-	2	32	0	54	3	1	3	6	.333	0	0--	-	4.68	4.33
1999	Yomiuri	Jap	37	3	0	9	69.2	275	42	25	23	6	-	-	3	28	0	77	3	0	4	1	.800	0	0--	-	2.15	2.97
2000	Yomiuri	Jap	56	0	0	26	72.1	300	53	26	25	4	-	-	2	31	0	102	5	0	5	4	.556	0	7--	-	2.56	3.11
2001	Yomiuri	Jap	58	0	0	43	62.0	281	62	21	19	5	9	2	2	39	6	70	2	0	2	1	.667	0	25--	-	4.82	2.76
2002	Yomiuri	Jap	52	0	0	13	55.2	231	42	21	21	8	-	-	3	22	0	58	4	0	6	3	.667	0	0--	-	3.21	3.40
2003	Yomiuri	Jap	41	0	0	7	38.2	175	45	22	21	6	-	-	1	20	3	29	1	0	2	3	.400	0	0--	-	5.95	4.89
2004	Yomiuri	Jap	53	0	0	21	46.2	192	33	16	16	5	0	0	1	20	1	53	2	0	4	3	.571	0	5--	-	2.71	3.09
2005	Yomiuri	Jap	42	0	0	18	53.0	231	55	31	28	10	2	3	4	19	0	56	1	0	1	0	1.000	0	0--	-	5.10	4.75
2006	HNHF	Jap	55	0	0	13	54.2	220	46	14	13	5	3	2	1	14	2	63	6	0	2	2	.500	0	4--	-	2.68	2.14
2007	Bos	AL	66	0	0	13	69.0	272	50	17	17	6	5	1	1	17	2	63	0	0	3	2	.600	0	5-7	27	2.03	2.22
2008	Bos	AL	64	0	0	11	62.0	258	49	18	18	6	0	3	1	23	1	60	2	0	3	2	.600	0	1-9	23	2.82	2.61
Postseason			8	0	0	0	11.0	45	9	3	3	2	0	0	0	3	1	11	0	0	0	0	-	0	0-0	4	2.94	2.45
2 ML YEARS			130	0	0	24	131.0	530	99	35	35	12	5	4	2	40	3	123	2	0	6	4	.600	0	6-16	50	2.40	2.40

Darren Oliver

Pitches: L Bats: R Pos: RP-54   Ht: 6'2" Wt: 200 Born: 10/6/1970 Age: 38

Year	Team	Lg	G	GS	CG	GF	IP	BFP	H	R	ER	HR	SH	SF	HB	TBB	IBB	SO	WP	Bk	W	L	Pct	ShO	Sv-Op	Hld	ERC	ERA
1993	Tex	AL	2	0	0	0	3.1	14	2	1	1	1	0	0	0	1	1	4	0	0	0	0	-	0	0-0	0	2.15	2.70
1994	Tex	AL	43	0	0	10	50.0	226	40	24	19	4	6	0	6	35	4	50	2	2	4	0	1.000	0	2-3	9	4.29	3.42
1995	Tex	AL	17	7	0	2	49.0	222	47	25	23	3	5	1	1	32	1	39	4	0	4	2	.667	0	0-0	0	4.59	4.22
1996	Tex	AL	30	30	1	0	173.2	777	190	97	90	20	2	7	10	76	3	112	5	1	14	6	.700	1	0-0	0	5.10	4.66
1997	Tex	AL	32	32	3	0	201.1	887	213	111	94	29	2	5	11	82	3	104	7	0	13	12	.520	1	0-0	0	4.98	4.20
1998	2 Tms		29	29	2	0	160.1	749	204	115	102	18	8	8	10	66	2	87	7	4	10	11	.476	0	0-0	0	6.01	5.73
1999	StL	NL	30	30	2	0	196.1	842	197	96	93	16	11	4	11	74	4	119	6	2	9	9	.500	1	0-0	0	4.11	4.26
2000	Tex	AL	21	21	0	0	108.0	501	151	95	89	16	5	4	4	42	3	49	4	1	2	9	.182	0	0-0	0	7.04	7.42
2001	Tex	AL	28	28	1	0	154.0	696	189	109	103	23	1	5	6	65	0	104	8	2	11	11	.500	0	0-0	0	6.14	6.02
2002	Bos	AL	14	9	1	0	58.0	258	70	30	30	7	1	3	6	27	0	32	1	0	4	5	.444	1	0-0	0	6.49	4.66
2003	Col	NL	33	32	1	0	180.1	786	201	108	101	21	4	5	8	61	3	88	0	0	13	11	.542	0	0-0	0	4.80	5.04
2004	2 Tms		27	10	0	5	72.2	314	87	50	48	14	4	3	1	21	1	46	1	0	3	3	.500	0	0-0	0	5.59	5.94
2006	NYM	NL	45	0	0	10	81.0	333	70	33	31	13	2	4	3	21	2	60	1	0	4	1	.800	0	0-0	0	3.27	3.44
2007	LAA	AL	61	0	0	20	64.1	273	58	31	27	5	2	4	1	23	2	51	1	1	3	1	.750	0	0-0	8	3.19	3.78
2008	LAA	AL	54	0	0	9	72.0	291	67	24	23	5	4	3	4	16	2	48	3	0	7	1	.875	0	0-2	12	3.07	2.88
98	Tex	AL	19	19	2	0	103.1	493	140	84	75	11	3	6	10	43	1	58	6	1	6	7	.462	0	0-0	0	6.68	6.53
98	StL	NL	10	10	0	0	57.0	256	64	31	27	7	5	2	0	23	1	29	1	3	4	4	.500	0	0-0	0	4.85	4.26
04	Fla	NL	18	8	0	3	58.2	260	75	44	42	13	4	3	1	17	1	33	1	0	2	3	.400	0	0-0	0	6.30	6.44
04	Hou	NL	9	2	0	2	14.0	54	12	6	6	1	0	0	0	4	0	13	0	0	1	0	1.000	0	0-0	0	2.89	3.86
	Postseason		4	1	0	0	16.0	62	14	8	8	2	2	0	1	3	0	6	1	0	1	0	1.000	0	0-0	0	3.16	4.50
15 ML YEARS			466	228	11	56	1624.1	7169	1786	949	874	195	57	56	82	642	31	993	50	13	101	82	.552	4	2-5	32	4.99	4.84

Miguel Olivo

Bats: R Throws: R Pos: C-58; DH-21; PH-6   Ht: 6'0" Wt: 220 Born: 7/15/1978 Age: 30

Year	Team	Lg	G	AB	H	2B	3B	HR	(Hm	Rd)	TB	R	RBI	RC	TBB	IBB	SO	HBP	SH	SF	SB	CS	SB%	GDP	Avg	OBP	Slg
2002	CWS	AL	6	19	4	1	0	1	(0	1)	8	2	5	4	2	0	5	0	0	0	0	0	-	1	.211	.286	.421
2003	CWS	AL	114	317	75	19	1	6	(4	2)	114	37	27	32	19	0	80	4	4	2	6	4	.60	3	.237	.287	.360
2004	2 Tms	AL	96	301	70	15	4	13	(8	5)	132	46	40	33	20	2	84	3	4	1	7	6	.54	4	.233	.286	.439
2005	2 Tms		91	267	58	11	1	9	(5	4)	98	30	34	23	8	2	80	3	1	2	7	2	.78	7	.217	.246	.367
2006	Fla	NL	127	430	113	22	3	16	(7	9)	189	52	58	49	9	4	103	7	3	3	2	3	.40	9	.263	.287	.440
2007	Fla	NL	122	452	107	20	4	16	(11	5)	183	43	60	43	14	2	123	2	0	1	3	2	.60	13	.237	.262	.405
2008	KC	AL	84	306	78	22	0	12	(3	9)	136	29	41	35	7	2	82	3	0	1	7	0	1.00	6	.255	.278	.444
04	CWS	AL	46	141	38	7	2	7	(4	3)	70	21	26	21	10	1	29	0	4	1	4	4	.56	2	.270	.316	.496
04	Sea	AL	50	160	32	8	2	6	(4	2)	62	25	14	12	10	1	55	3	0	0	2	2	.50	2	.200	.260	.388
05	Sea	AL	54	152	23	4	0	5	(4	1)	42	14	18	6	4	0	49	0	0	1	1	1	.50	3	.151	.172	.276
05	SD	NL	37	115	35	7	1	4	(1	3)	56	16	16	17	4	2	31	3	1	1	6	1	.86	4	.304	.341	.487
	Postseason		1	1	0	0	0	0	(0	0)	0	0	0	0	0	0	0	0	0	0	0	0	-	1	.000	.000	.000
7 ML YEARS			640	2092	505	110	13	73	(38	35)	860	239	265	219	79	12	557	22	12	10	32	17	.65	43	.241	.275	.411

Scott Olsen

Pitches: L Bats: L Pos: SP-33   Ht: 6'5" Wt: 215 Born: 1/12/1984 Age: 25

Year	Team	Lg	G	GS	CG	GF	IP	BFP	H	R	ER	HR	SH	SF	HB	TBB	IBB	SO	WP	Bk	W	L	Pct	ShO	Sv-Op	Hld	ERC	ERA
2005	Fla	NL	5	4	0	0	20.1	91	21	13	9	5	0	0	0	10	0	21	1	0	1	1	.500	0	0-0	0	5.66	3.98
2006	Fla	NL	31	31	0	0	180.2	761	160	94	81	23	7	2	7	75	1	166	8	0	12	10	.545	0	0-0	0	3.88	4.04
2007	Fla	NL	33	33	0	0	176.2	826	226	134	114	29	14	8	1	85	4	133	8	0	10	15	.400	0	0-0	0	6.54	5.81
2008	Fla	NL	33	33	0	0	201.2	855	195	106	94	30	7	4	3	69	13	113	5	0	8	11	.421	0	0-0	0	3.96	4.20
4 ML YEARS			102	101	0	0	579.1	2533	602	347	298	87	28	14	11	239	18	433	22	0	31	37	.456	0	0-0	0	4.74	4.63

Garrett Olson

Pitches: L Bats: L Pos: SP-26   Ht: 6'1" Wt: 197 Born: 10/18/1983 Age: 25

Year	Team	Lg	G	GS	CG	GF	IP	BFP	H	R	ER	HR	SH	SF	HB	TBB	IBB	SO	WP	Bk	W	L	Pct	ShO	Sv-Op	Hld	ERC	ERA
2005	Abrdn	A-	11	6	0	2	40.0	153	22	7	7	1	4	0	2	13	0	40	1	0	2	1	.667	0	1--	-	1.45	1.58
2005	Frdrck	A+	3	3	0	0	14.1	61	10	5	5	0	0	0	2	7	0	19	1	0	0	0	-	0	0--	-	2.61	3.14
2006	Frdrck	A+	14	14	0	0	81.1	342	81	32	25	7	3	5	10	19	0	77	2	0	4	4	.500	0	0--	-	3.85	2.77
2006	Bowie	AA	14	14	0	0	84.1	357	78	33	32	5	4	3	6	31	0	86	4	1	6	5	.545	0	0--	-	3.57	3.42
2007	Norfolk	AAA	22	22	1	0	128.0	510	95	49	45	13	4	5	5	39	0	120	1	0	9	7	.563	0	0--	-	2.55	3.16
2008	Norfolk	AAA	7	7	0	0	36.1	159	35	14	12	1	5	3	1	16	0	39	1	2	2	2	.333	0	0--	-	3.58	2.97
2007	Bal	AL	7	7	0	0	32.1	162	42	28	28	4	0	3	2	28	1	28	1	1	1	3	.250	0	0-0	0	8.46	7.79
2008	Bal	AL	26	26	0	0	132.2	621	168	100	98	17	4	4	8	62	1	83	6	0	9	10	.474	0	0-0	0	6.40	6.65
2 ML YEARS			33	33	0	0	165.0	783	210	128	126	21	4	7	10	90	2	111	7	1	10	13	.435	0	0-0	0	6.80	6.87

Magglio Ordonez

Bats: R Throws: R Pos: RF-135; DH-10; PH-2   Ht: 6'0" Wt: 215 Born: 1/28/1974 Age: 35

Year	Team	Lg	G	AB	H	2B	3B	HR	(Hm	Rd)	TB	R	RBI	RC	TBB	IBB	SO	HBP	SH	SF	SB	CS	SB%	GDP	Avg	OBP	Slg
2008	WMich*	A	1	4	1	0	0	0	(-	-)	1	1	0	0	0	0	0	0	0	0	0	0	-	0	.250	.250	.250
1997	CWS	AL	21	69	22	6	0	4	(2	2)	40	12	11	12	2	0	8	0	1	0	1	2	.33	1	.319	.338	.580
1998	CWS	AL	145	535	151	25	2	20	(8	6)	222	70	65	67	28	1	53	9	2	4	9	7	.56	19	.282	.326	.415
1999	CWS	AL	157	624	188	34	3	30	(16	14)	318	100	117	102	47	4	64	1	0	5	13	6	.68	24	.301	.349	.510
2000	CWS	AL	153	588	185	34	3	32	(21	11)	321	102	126	112	60	3	64	2	0	15	18	4	.82	28	.315	.371	.546
2001	CWS	AL	160	593	181	40	1	31	(17	14)	316	97	113	117	70	7	70	5	0	3	25	7	.78	14	.305	.382	.533

Year	Team	Lg	G	AB	H	2B	3B	HR	(Hm	Rd)	TB	R	RBI	RC	TBB	IBB	SO	HBP	SH	SF	SB	CS	SB%	GDP	Avg	OBP	Slg
2002	CWS	AL	153	590	189	47	1	38	(24	14)	352	116	135	119	53	2	77	7	0	3	7	5	.58	21	.320	.381	.597
2003	CWS	AL	160	606	192	46	3	29	(17	12)	331	95	99	109	57	1	73	7	0	4	9	5	.64	20	.317	.380	.546
2004	CWS	AL	52	202	59	8	2	9	(4	5)	98	32	37	39	16	2	22	3	0	1	0	2	.00	4	.292	.351	.485
2005	Det	AL	82	305	92	17	0	8	(2	6)	133	38	46	51	30	1	35	1	0	7	0	0	-	8	.302	.359	.436
2006	Det	AL	155	593	177	32	1	24	(8	16)	283	82	104	97	45	3	87	4	0	4	1	4	.20	13	.298	.350	.477
2007	Det	AL	157	595	216	54	0	28	(17	11)	354	117	139	146	76	8	79	2	0	5	4	1	.80	20	**.363**	.434	.595
2008	Was	AL	146	561	178	32	2	21	(13	8)	277	72	103	92	53	2	76	3	0	6	1	5	.17	27	.317	.376	.494
Postseason			16	62	12	1	1	3	(3	0)	24	8	9	4	6	0	10	0	0	0	1	1	.50	3	.194	.265	.387
12 ML YEARS			1541	5861	1830	375	18	268	(149	119)	3045	933	1095	1063	537	34	708	44	3	57	88	48	.65	199	.312	.371	.520

Pete Orr

Bats: L Throws: R Pos: PH-25; 3B-8; SS-8; 2B-7; PR-7; LF-2   Ht: 5'11" Wt: 195 Born: 6/8/1979 Age: 30

Year	Team	Lg	G	AB	H	2B	3B	HR	(Hm	Rd)	TB	R	RBI	RC	TBB	IBB	SO	HBP	SH	SF	SB	CS	SB%	GDP	Avg	OBP	Slg
2008	Clmbs*	AAA	73	284	78	16	11	2	(-	-)	122	46	33	44	21	1	56	4	5	2	19	4	.83	5	.275	.331	.430
2005	Atl	NL	112	150	45	8	1	1	(0	1)	58	32	8	18	6	0	23	1	5	0	7	1	.88	2	.300	.331	.387
2006	Atl	NL	102	154	39	3	4	1	(1	0)	53	22	8	16	5	1	30	0	5	0	2	4	.33	1	.253	.277	.344
2007	Atl	NL	57	65	13	1	0	0	(0	0)	14	11	2	3	3	0	14	0	1	0	1	0	1.00	1	.200	.235	.215
2008	Was	NL	49	75	19	2	1	0	(0	0)	23	10	7	6	2	0	16	1	1	0	1	0	1.00	0	.253	.282	.307
Postseason			3	2	0	0	0	0	(0	0)	0	0	0	0	0	0	0	0	0	0	0	0	-	0	.000	.000	.000
4 ML YEARS			320	444	116	14	6	2	(1	1)	148	75	25	43	16	1	83	2	12	0	11	5	.69	4	.261	.290	.333

David Ortiz

Bats: L Throws: L Pos: DH-109; PH-1   Ht: 6'4" Wt: 230 Born: 11/18/1975 Age: 33

Year	Team	Lg	G	AB	H	2B	3B	HR	(Hm	Rd)	TB	R	RBI	RC	TBB	IBB	SO	HBP	SH	SF	SB	CS	SB%	GDP	Avg	OBP	Slg
2008	Pwtckt*	AAA	3	9	3	0	0	3	(-	-)	12	4	5	4	3	0	2	0	0	0	0	0	-	0	.333	.500	1.333
2008	PortInd*	AA	3	8	2	0	0	0	(-	-)	2	2	1	1	2	0	1	0	0	0	0	0	-	1	.250	.400	.250
1997	Min	AL	15	49	16	3	0	1	(0	1)	22	10	6	7	2	0	19	0	0	0	0	0	-	1	.327	.353	.449
1998	Min	AL	86	278	77	20	0	9	(2	7)	124	47	46	46	39	3	72	5	0	4	1	0	1.00	8	.277	.371	.446
1999	Min	AL	10	20	0	0	0	0	(0	0)	0	1	0	0	5	0	12	0	0	0	0	0	-	2	.000	.200	.000
2000	Min	AL	130	415	117	36	1	10	(7	3)	185	59	63	66	57	2	81	0	0	6	1	0	1.00	13	.282	.364	.446
2001	Min	AL	89	303	71	17	1	18	(6	12)	144	46	48	46	40	8	68	1	1	2	1	0	1.00	6	.234	.324	.475
2002	Min	AL	125	412	112	32	1	20	(5	15)	206	52	75	62	43	0	87	3	0	8	1	2	.33	5	.272	.339	.500
2003	Bos	AL	128	448	129	39	2	31	(17	14)	265	79	101	80	58	8	83	1	0	2	0	0	-	9	.288	.369	.592
2004	Bos	AL	150	582	175	47	3	41	(17	24)	351	94	139	127	75	8	133	4	0	8	0	0	-	12	.301	.380	.603
2005	Bos	AL	159	601	180	40	1	47	(20	27)	363	119	148	137	102	9	124	1	0	4	1	0	1.00	13	.300	.397	.604
2006	Bos	AL	151	558	160	29	2	54	(22	32)	355	115	137	129	119	23	117	4	0	5	1	0	1.00	12	.287	.413	.636
2007	Bos	AL	149	549	182	52	1	35	(16	19)	341	116	117	138	111	12	103	4	0	3	3	1	.75	16	.332	**.445**	.621
2008	Bos	AL	109	416	110	30	1	23	(12	11)	211	74	89	82	70	12	74	1	1	3	1	0	1.00	11	.264	.369	.507
Postseason			52	189	60	16	1	11	(6	5)	111	35	42	46	32	6	47	2	0	2	0	1	.00	3	.317	.418	.587
12 ML YEARS			1301	4631	1329	345	13	289	(124	165)	2567	812	969	920	721	85	973	24	2	50	10	3	.77	108	.287	.382	.554

Russ Ortiz

Pitches: R Bats: R Pos: P   Ht: 6'1" Wt: 220 Born: 6/5/1974 Age: 35

Year	Team	Lg	G	GS	CG	GF	IP	BFP	H	R	ER	HR	SH	SF	HB	TBB	IBB	SO	WP	Bk	W	L	Pct	ShO	Sv-Op	Hld	ERC	ERA
1998	SF	NL	22	13	0	3	88.1	394	90	51	49	11	5	4	4	46	1	75	3	0	4	4	.500	0	0-0	1	5.05	4.99
1999	SF	NL	33	33	3	0	207.2	922	189	109	88	24	11	6	6	125	5	164	13	0	18	9	.667	0	0-0	0	4.56	3.81
2000	SF	NL	33	32	0	0	195.2	871	192	117	109	28	10	6	7	112	1	167	8	0	14	12	.538	0	0-0	0	5.17	5.01
2001	SF	NL	33	33	1	0	218.2	911	187	90	80	13	10	4	0	91	3	169	8	1	17	9	.654	1	0-0	0	3.08	3.29
2002	SF	NL	33	33	2	0	214.1	911	191	89	86	15	15	6	4	94	5	137	5	0	14	10	.583	0	0-0	0	3.46	3.61
2003	Atl	NL	34	34	1	0	212.1	912	177	101	90	17	6	7	4	102	7	149	5	0	21	7	.750	1	0-0	0	3.32	3.81
2004	Atl	NL	34	34	2	0	204.2	896	197	98	94	23	10	7	3	112	7	143	4	1	15	9	.625	1	0-0	0	4.60	4.13
2005	Ari	NL	22	22	0	0	115.0	551	147	92	88	18	5	8	4	65	3	46	5	0	5	11	.313	0	0-0	0	6.96	6.89
2006	2 Tms		26	11	0	5	63.0	303	86	60	57	18	1	1	3	40	1	44	2	0	0	8	.000	0	0-0	0	9.39	8.14
2007	SF	NL	12	8	0	1	49.0	223	57	32	30	4	3	1	6	20	1	27	0	0	2	3	.400	0	0-0	0	5.42	5.51
06	Ari	NL	6	6	0	0	22.2	113	27	21	19	3	1	0	1	22	1	21	0	0	0	5	.000	0	0-0	0	8.19	7.54
06	Bal	AL	20	5	0	5	40.1	190	59	39	38	15	0	1	2	18	0	23	2	0	0	3	.000	0	0-0	0	9.99	8.48
Postseason			9	9	0	0	44.0	204	51	28	28	5	0	2	0	25	3	27	3	0	3	1	.750	0	0-0	0	5.65	5.73
10 ML YEARS			282	253	9	9	1568.2	6894	1513	839	771	171	76	50	41	807	34	1121	53	2	110	82	.573	3	0-0	1	4.48	4.42

Dan Ortmeier

Bats: R Throws: R Pos: 1B-13; LF-13; PH-11; PR-3; RF-2   Ht: 6'4" Wt: 230 Born: 5/11/1981 Age: 28

Year	Team	Lg	G	AB	H	2B	3B	HR	(Hm	Rd)	TB	R	RBI	RC	TBB	IBB	SO	HBP	SH	SF	SB	CS	SB%	GDP	Avg	OBP	Slg
2008	SnJos*	A+	8	29	4	0	0	1	(-	-)	7	1	1	2	5	0	15	1	0	0	1	0	1.00	0	.138	.286	.241
2008	Fresno*	AAA	28	97	20	4	0	1	(-	-)	27	12	9	6	5	0	21	0	1	0	4	1	.80	1	.206	.245	.278
2005	SF	NL	15	22	3	0	0	0	(0	0)	3	1	1	1	3	0	5	1	0	0	1	0	1.00	2	.136	.269	.136
2006	SF	NL	9	12	3	1	0	0	(0	0)	4	0	2	2	0	0	4	0	0	0	0	0	-	0	.250	.250	.333
2007	SF	NL	62	157	45	7	4	6	(1	5)	78	20	16	20	7	1	41	1	0	2	2	1	.67	2	.287	.317	.497
2008	SF	NL	38	64	14	6	0	0	(0	0)	20	4	5	3	7	1	18	2	0	0	2	2	.50	1	.219	.315	.313
4 ML YEARS			124	255	65	14	4	6	(1	5)	105	25	24	26	17	2	68	4	0	2	5	3	.63	5	.255	.309	.412

Franquelis Osoria

Pitches: R Bats: R Pos: RP-43 Ht: 6'0" Wt: 201 Born: 9/12/1981 Age: 27

Year	Team	Lg	G	GS	CG	GF	IP	BFP	H	R	ER	HR	SH	SF	HB	TBB	IBB	SO	WP	Bk	W	L	Pct	ShO	Sv-Op	Hld	ERC	ERA
2008	Indy*	AAA	10	0	0	5	12.2	53	13	5	5	1	0	1	0	3	1	14	1	0	2	1	.667	0	1--	-	3.32	3.55
2005	LAD	NL	24	0	0	6	29.2	122	28	14	13	3	3	0	3	8	0	15	0	0	0	2	.000	0	0-2	3	3.78	3.94
2006	LAD	NL	12	0	0	1	17.2	86	27	14	14	4	1	0	1	9	1	13	0	0	0	2	.000	0	0-0	0	9.30	7.13
2007	Pit	NL	25	0	0	3	28.1	126	33	16	15	3	0	0	4	8	2	13	2	0	0	2	.000	0	0-0	4	5.09	4.76
2008	Pit	NL	43	0	0	10	60.2	276	87	43	41	10	1	0	4	12	0	31	0	0	4	3	.571	0	0-2	3	6.67	6.08
4 ML YEARS			104	0	0	20	136.1	610	175	87	83	20	5	0	12	37	3	72	2	0	4	9	.308	0	0-4	10	5.99	5.48

Roy Oswalt

Pitches: R Bats: R Pos: SP-32 Ht: 6'0" Wt: 185 Born: 8/29/1977 Age: 31

Year	Team	Lg	G	GS	CG	GF	IP	BFP	H	R	ER	HR	SH	SF	HB	TBB	IBB	SO	WP	Bk	W	L	Pct	ShO	Sv-Op	Hld	ERC	ERA
2001	Hou	NL	28	20	3	4	141.2	575	126	48	43	13	4	4	6	24	2	144	0	0	14	3	.824	1	0-0	0	2.68	2.73
2002	Hou	NL	35	34	0	0	233.0	956	215	86	78	17	12	7	5	62	4	208	3	0	19	9	.679	0	0-0	0	3.05	3.01
2003	Hou	NL	21	21	0	0	127.1	514	116	48	42	15	7	1	5	29	0	108	1	0	10	5	.667	0	0-0	0	3.26	2.97
2004	Hou	NL	36	35	2	0	237.0	983	233	100	92	17	11	4	11	62	5	206	5	1	20	10	.667	2	0-0	0	3.46	3.49
2005	Hou	NL	35	35	4	0	241.2	1002	243	85	79	18	12	7	8	48	3	184	5	1	20	12	.625	1	0-0	0	3.27	2.94
2006	Hou	NL	33	32	2	1	220.2	896	220	76	73	18	12	4	6	38	4	166	1	1	15	8	.652	0	0-0	0	3.19	2.98
2007	Hou	NL	33	32	1	0	212.0	910	221	80	75	14	6	4	7	60	6	154	1	1	14	7	.667	0	0-0	1	3.68	3.18
2008	Hou	NL	32	32	3	0	208.2	862	199	89	82	23	8	9	10	47	2	165	1	0	17	10	.630	2	0-0	0	3.40	3.54
Postseason			8	7	0	1	46.2	206	48	19	19	5	2	2	4	19	0	32	0	0	4	0	1.000	0	0-0	0	4.67	3.66
8 ML YEARS			253	241	15	5	1622.0	6698	1573	612	564	135	72	40	58	370	26	1335	17	4	129	64	.668	6	0-0	1	3.27	3.13

Josh Outman

Pitches: L Bats: L Pos: SP-4; RP-2 Ht: 6'1" Wt: 186 Born: 9/14/1984 Age: 24

Year	Team	Lg	G	GS	CG	GF	IP	BFP	H	R	ER	HR	SH	SF	HB	TBB	IBB	SO	WP	Bk	W	L	Pct	ShO	Sv-Op	Hld	ERC	ERA
2005	Batvia	A-	11	4	0	0	29.1	128	23	14	9	1	1	0	2	14	0	31	3	0	2	1	.667	0	0--	-	2.91	2.76
2006	Lakwd	A	27	27	1	0	155.1	652	119	61	51	5	5	5	8	75	0	161	12	1	14	6	.700	1	0--	-	2.88	2.95
2007	Clrwtr	A+	20	18	0	0	117.1	504	104	35	32	7	2	2	5	54	0	117	4	0	10	4	.714	0	0--	-	3.57	2.45
2007	Rdng	AA	7	7	1	0	42.0	184	38	25	21	5	1	2	1	23	1	34	2	0	2	3	.400	1	0--	-	4.32	4.50
2008	Rdng	AA	33	5	0	7	70.1	310	68	27	25	3	3	3	2	37	0	66	3	0	5	4	.556	0	1--	-	4.08	3.20
2008	Mdland	AA	4	4	0	0	12.2	54	13	7	6	1	1	0	0	3	0	5	1	0	1	0	1.000	0	0--	-	3.36	4.26
2008	Scrmto	AAA	5	2	0	1	15.1	59	9	3	3	1	0	0	0	5	1	15	2	0	1	0	1.000	0	0--	-	1.54	1.76
2008	Oak	AL	6	4	0	0	25.2	116	34	14	13	1	0	2	2	8	1	19	1	0	1	2	.333	0	0-0	0	5.49	4.56

Lyle Overbay

Bats: L Throws: L Pos: 1B-156; PH-3 Ht: 6'2" Wt: 236 Born: 1/28/1977 Age: 32

Year	Team	Lg	G	AB	H	2B	3B	HR	(Hm	Rd)	TB	R	RBI	RC	TBB	IBB	SO	HBP	SH	SF	SB	CS	SB%	GDP	Avg	OBP	Slg
2001	Ari	NL	2	2	1	0	0	0	(0	0)	1	0	0	0	0	0	1	0	0	0	0	0	-	0	.500	.500	.500
2002	Ari	NL	10	10	1	0	0	0	(0	0)	1	0	1	0	0	0	5	0	0	0	0	0	-	0	.100	.100	.100
2003	Ari	NL	86	254	70	20	0	4	(2	2)	102	23	28	34	35	7	67	2	0	2	1	0	1.00	6	.276	.365	.402
2004	Mil	NL	159	579	174	53	1	16	(6	10)	277	83	87	94	81	9	128	2	0	6	2	1	.67	11	.301	.385	.478
2005	Mil	NL	158	537	148	34	1	19	(10	9)	241	80	72	84	78	8	98	2	1	4	1	0	1.00	17	.276	.367	.449
2006	Tor	AL	157	581	181	46	1	22	(17	5)	295	82	92	89	55	7	96	2	0	2	5	3	.63	19	.312	.372	.508
2007	Tor	AL	122	425	102	30	2	10	(6	4)	166	49	44	45	47	4	78	1	0	3	2	0	1.00	12	.240	.315	.391
2008	Tor	AL	158	544	147	32	2	15	(7	8)	228	74	69	73	74	3	116	3	1	5	1	2	.33	24	.270	.358	.419
8 ML YEARS			852	2932	824	215	7	86	(48	38)	1311	391	393	419	370	38	589	12	2	22	12	6	.67	91	.281	.362	.447

Henry Owens

Pitches: R Bats: R Pos: P Ht: 6'3" Wt: 230 Born: 4/23/1979 Age: 30

Year	Team	Lg	G	GS	CG	GF	IP	BFP	H	R	ER	HR	SH	SF	HB	TBB	IBB	SO	WP	Bk	W	L	Pct	ShO	Sv-Op	Hld	ERC	ERA
2001	Pirates	R	6	0	0	5	7.0	28	5	1	1	0	0	0	0	2	0	8	0	0	1	0	1.000	0	1--	-	1.62	1.29
2002	Wmspt	A-	23	0	0	15	44.2	177	23	18	13	4	0	1	3	16	0	63	8	0	0	3	.000	0	7--	-	1.65	2.62
2003	Hkry	A	22	0	0	17	34.0	143	21	14	11	1	1	0	6	17	0	52	7	0	2	1	.667	0	9--	-	2.60	2.91
2003	Lynbrg	A+	13	0	0	11	14.2	65	9	6	4	0	2	0	1	11	0	21	0	0	1	2	.333	0	5--	-	2.77	2.45
2004	Lynbrg	A+	39	0	0	27	54.2	240	46	26	26	4	0	0	4	26	1	49	10	0	3	4	.429	0	4--	-	3.47	4.28
2005	StLuci	A+	38	1	0	16	54.1	240	49	29	19	2	0	1	5	24	2	74	7	0	2	5	.286	0	4--	-	3.46	3.15
2006	Bnghtn	AA	37	0	0	36	40.0	154	19	9	7	1	1	0	3	10	1	74	5	0	2	2	.500	0	20--	-	1.07	1.58
2007	Jupiter	A+	3	0	0	0	3.0	10	1	0	0	0	0	0	0	0	0	5	1	0	1	0	1.000	0	0--	-	0.25	0.00
2006	NYM	NL	3	0	0	1	4.0	19	4	4	4	0	0	1	0	4	0	2	0	0	0	0	-	0	0-0	0	5.79	9.00
2007	Fla	NL	22	0	0	10	23.0	98	19	7	5	3	0	0	0	10	1	16	2	0	2	0	1.000	0	4-5	5	3.33	1.96
2 ML YEARS			25	0	0	11	27.0	117	23	11	9	3	0	1	0	14	1	18	2	0	2	0	1.000	0	4-5	5	3.69	3.00

Jerry Owens

Bats: L Throws: L Pos: LF-7; PR-5; CF-4; PH-1   Ht: 6'3" Wt: 195 Born: 2/16/1981 Age: 28

Year	Team	Lg	G	AB	H	2B	3B	HR	(Hm	Rd)	TB	R	RBI	RC	TBB	IBB	SO	HBP	SH	SF	SB	CS	SB%	GDP	Avg	OBP	Slg
2008	Charltt*	AAA	89	351	97	11	0	1	(-	-)	111	39	21	44	38	4	56	2	2	5	30	13	.70	4	.276	.346	.316
2006	CWS	AL	12	9	3	1	0	0	(0	0)	4	4	0	1	0	0	2	0	0	0	1	0	1.00	0	.333	.333	.444
2007	CWS	AL	93	356	95	9	2	1	(1	0)	111	44	17	41	27	0	63	3	3	0	32	8	.80	5	.267	.324	.312
2008	CWS	AL	12	16	4	0	0	0	(0	0)	4	1	1	0	0	0	4	0	1	0	2	1	.67	0	.250	.250	.250
3 ML YEARS			117	381	102	10	2	1	(1	0)	119	49	18	42	27	0	69	3	4	0	35	9	.80	5	.268	.321	.312

Micah Owings

Pitches: R Bats: R Pos: SP-18; RP-4   Ht: 6'5" Wt: 220 Born: 9/28/1982 Age: 26

Year	Team	Lg	G	GS	CG	GF	IP	BFP	H	R	ER	HR	SH	SF	HB	TBB	IBB	SO	WP	Bk	W	L	Pct	ShO	Sv-Op	Hld	ERC	ERA
2005	Lancst	A+	16	0	0	1	22.0	83	17	6	6	0	1	1	0	4	0	30	0	0	1	1	.500	0	0- -	-	1.65	2.45
2006	Tenn	AA	12	12	0	0	74.1	297	66	24	24	4	4	2	6	17	2	69	2	0	6	2	.750	0	0- -	-	2.90	2.91
2006	Tucsn	AAA	15	15	1	0	87.2	381	96	40	36	4	6	5	5	34	0	61	5	0	10	0	1.000	0	0- -	-	4.49	3.70
2007	Tucsn	AAA	1	1	0	0	5.0	18	4	0	0	0	1	0	0	1	0	7	0	0	0	0	-	0	0- -	-	1.95	0.00
2008	Tucsn	AAA	2	2	0	0	11.0	49	8	5	5	3	0	0	4	6	0	9	1	0	0	0	-	0	0- -	-	6.01	4.09
2007	Ari	NL	29	27	2	0	152.2	651	146	81	73	22	7	3	14	50	2	106	5	0	8	8	.500	1	0-0	0	4.13	4.30
2008	2 Tms	NL	22	18	0	2	104.2	466	104	73	69	14	2	4	12	41	0	87	4	0	6	9	.400	0	0-0	1	4.66	5.93
Postseason			1	1	0	0	3.2	21	6	6	2	1	0	0	1	2	0	2	0	0	0	1	.000	0	0-0	0	10.83	4.91
2 ML YEARS			51	45	2	2	257.1	1117	250	154	142	34	9	7	26	91	2	193	9	0	14	17	.452	1	0-0	1	4.34	4.97

Pablo Ozuna

Bats: R Throws: R Pos: 2B-37; 3B-17; PR-17; PH-5; SS-4; LF-2; DH-2   Ht: 5'11" Wt: 200 Born: 8/25/1974 Age: 34

Year	Team	Lg	G	AB	H	2B	3B	HR	(Hm	Rd)	TB	R	RBI	RC	TBB	IBB	SO	HBP	SH	SF	SB	CS	SB%	GDP	Avg	OBP	Slg
2000	Fla	NL	14	24	8	1	0	0	(0	0)	9	2	0	3	0	0	2	0	2	0	1	0	1.00	0	.333	.333	.375
2002	Fla	NL	34	47	13	2	2	0	(0	0)	19	4	3	4	1	0	3	1	0	1	1	1	.50	2	.277	.300	.404
2003	Col	NL	17	40	8	1	0	0	(0	0)	9	5	2	4	2	0	6	2	1	0	3	0	1.00	1	.200	.273	.225
2005	CWS	AL	70	203	56	7	2	0	(0	0)	67	27	11	20	7	0	26	4	3	0	14	7	.67	5	.276	.313	.330
2006	CWS	AL	79	189	62	12	2	2	(2	0)	84	25	17	30	7	0	16	4	3	0	6	6	.50	3	.328	.365	.444
2007	CWS	AL	27	78	19	3	0	0	(0	0)	22	9	3	5	3	0	9	1	3	0	3	0	1.00	1	.244	.280	.282
2008	2 Tms	NL	68	96	25	3	1	1	(1	0)	33	11	9	8	3	0	8	1	2	0	1	3	.25	3	.260	.290	.344
08	CWS	AL	32	64	18	3	0	0	(0	0)	21	5	6	6	2	0	3	1	2	0	0	2	.00	2	.281	.313	.328
08	LAD	NL	36	32	7	0	1	1	(1	0)	12	6	3	2	1	0	5	0	0	0	1	1	.50	1	.219	.242	.375
Postseason			2	0	0	0	0	0	(0	0)	0	1	0	0	0	0	0	0	0	0	1	0	1.00	0	-	-	-
7 ML YEARS			309	677	191	29	7	3	(3	0)	243	83	45	74	23	0	70	13	14	1	29	17	.63	15	.282	.318	.359

Vicente Padilla

Pitches: R Bats: R Pos: SP-29   Ht: 6'2" Wt: 220 Born: 9/27/1977 Age: 31

Year	Team	Lg	G	GS	CG	GF	IP	BFP	H	R	ER	HR	SH	SF	HB	TBB	IBB	SO	WP	Bk	W	L	Pct	ShO	Sv-Op	Hld	ERC	ERA
1999	Ari	NL	5	0	0	2	2.2	19	7	5	5	1	1	0	0	3	0	0	0	0	0	1	.000	0	0-1	1	20.65	16.88
2000	2 Tms	NL	55	0	0	16	65.1	291	72	33	27	3	5	3	1	28	7	51	1	0	4	7	.364	0	2-7	15	4.22	3.72
2001	Phi	NL	23	0	0	5	34.0	144	36	18	16	1	0	0	0	12	0	29	1	0	3	1	.750	0	0-3	1	3.80	4.24
2002	Phi	NL	32	32	1	0	206.0	862	198	83	75	16	10	3	15	53	5	128	6	2	14	11	.560	1	0-0	0	3.42	3.28
2003	Phi	NL	32	32	1	0	208.2	876	196	94	84	22	11	7	16	62	4	133	3	2	14	12	.538	1	0-0	0	3.68	3.62
2004	Phi	NL	20	20	0	0	115.1	503	119	63	58	16	7	5	10	36	6	82	2	0	7	7	.500	0	0-0	0	4.42	4.53
2005	Phi	NL	27	27	0	0	147.0	654	146	79	77	22	7	3	8	74	9	103	1	0	9	12	.429	0	0-0	0	4.94	4.71
2006	Tex	AL	33	33	0	0	200.0	872	206	108	100	21	6	6	17	70	2	156	4	2	15	10	.600	0	0-0	0	4.41	4.50
2007	Tex	AL	23	23	0	0	120.1	553	146	88	77	16	3	2	9	50	1	71	2	0	6	10	.375	0	0-0	0	5.95	5.76
2008	Tex	AL	29	29	1	0	171.0	757	185	100	90	26	1	3	15	65	4	127	12	3	14	8	.636	1	0-0	0	5.20	4.74
00	Ari	NL	27	0	0	12	35.0	143	32	10	9	0	0	1	0	10	2	30	0	0	2	1	.667	0	0-1	7	2.48	2.31
00	Phi	NL	28	0	0	4	30.1	148	40	23	18	3	5	2	1	18	5	21	1	0	2	6	.250	0	2-6	8	6.52	5.34
10 ML YEARS			279	196	3	23	1270.1	5531	1311	671	609	144	51	32	91	453	38	880	32	9	86	79	.521	3	2-11	17	4.43	4.31

Angel Pagan

Bats: B Throws: R Pos: LF-21; PH-8; CF-2; RF-1   Ht: 6'2" Wt: 195 Born: 7/2/1981 Age: 27

Year	Team	Lg	G	AB	H	2B	3B	HR	(Hm	Rd)	TB	R	RBI	RC	TBB	IBB	SO	HBP	SH	SF	SB	CS	SB%	GDP	Avg	OBP	Slg
2008	Mets*	R	2	5	3	1	0	0	(-	-)	4	1	0	2	0	0	0	0	1	0	2	0	1.00	0	.600	.600	.800
2008	StLuci*	A+	1	4	0	0	0	0	(-	-)	0	1	0	0	1	0	0	0	0	0	0	0	-	0	.000	.200	.000
2008	Bklyn*	A-	4	13	4	0	0	0	(-	-)	4	0	1	2	1	0	0	0	0	0	3	0	1.00	0	.308	.357	.308
2006	ChC	NL	77	170	42	6	2	5	(4	1)	67	28	18	21	15	0	28	0	1	1	4	2	.67	3	.247	.306	.394
2007	ChC	NL	71	148	39	10	2	4	(3	1)	65	21	21	23	10	0	32	0	1	2	4	1	.80	0	.264	.306	.439
2008	NYM	NL	31	91	25	7	1	0	(0	0)	34	12	13	15	11	0	18	0	1	2	4	0	1.00	0	.275	.346	.374
3 ML YEARS			179	409	106	23	5	9	(7	2)	166	61	52	59	36	0	78	0	3	5	12	3	.80	3	.259	.316	.406

Matt Palmer

Pitches: R **Bats:** R **Pos:** SP-3   **Ht:** 6'2" **Wt:** 228 **Born:** 3/21/1979 **Age:** 30

Year	Team	Lg	G	GS	CG	GF	IP	BFP	H	R	ER	HR	SH	SF	HB	TBB	IBB	SO	WP	Bk	W	L	Pct	ShO	Sv-Op	Hld	ERC	ERA
2002	Salem	A+	16	9	0	3	53.2	217	44	15	11	0	0	1	3	23	0	49	5	0	3	2	.600	0	0--	-	2.89	1.84
2003	Hgrstn	A	44	0	0	41	52.1	195	21	7	7	3	2	0	4	15	0	56	3	1	5	0	1.000	0	25--	-	1.10	1.20
2003	Nrwich	AA	5	0	0	1	6.2	41	12	11	10	0	0	1	2	5	0	5	3	0	0	0	-	0	0--	-	10.28	13.50
2004	Nrwich	AA	42	5	0	17	79.1	358	66	35	27	4	4	4	7	51	4	81	7	0	4	7	.364	0	8--	-	3.91	3.06
2005	Nrwich	AA	11	2	0	4	26.0	115	22	14	8	2	0	2	3	9	1	20	2	0	1	0	1.000	0	1--	-	3.09	2.77
2006	Conn	AA	15	9	0	2	62.1	253	50	20	9	1	4	0	7	10	0	51	1	0	5	3	.625	0	0--	-	2.03	1.30
2006	Fresno	AAA	15	15	0	0	91.0	387	91	45	41	10	5	0	9	30	0	64	3	1	6	4	.600	0	0--	-	4.35	4.05
2007	Fresno	AAA	29	25	1	1	150.0	644	155	80	72	17	7	1	12	51	0	98	6	0	11	8	.579	0	0--	-	4.52	4.32
2007	Conn	AA	1	1	0	0	5.0	26	8	6	6	2	2	0	1	2	0	3	1	0	0	0	-	0	0--	-	11.25	10.80
2008	Fresno	AAA	26	25	1	0	142.0	629	138	71	66	11	7	6	10	72	0	143	11	0	6	10	.375	0	0--	-	4.47	4.18
2008	SF	NL	3	3	0	0	12.2	67	17	13	12	1	1	0	2	13	1	3	0	0	0	2	.000	0	0-0	0	9.37	8.53

Jonathan Papelbon

Pitches: R **Bats:** R **Pos:** RP-67   **Ht:** 6'4" **Wt:** 225 **Born:** 11/23/1980 **Age:** 28

Year	Team	Lg	G	GS	CG	GF	IP	BFP	H	R	ER	HR	SH	SF	HB	TBB	IBB	SO	WP	Bk	W	L	Pct	ShO	Sv-Op	Hld	ERC	ERA
2005	Bos	AL	17	3	0	4	34.0	148	33	11	10	4	1	0	3	17	2	34	1	0	3	1	.750	0	0-1	4	4.82	2.65
2006	Bos	AL	59	0	0	49	68.1	257	40	8	7	3	1	2	1	13	2	75	2	0	4	2	.667	0	35-41	1	1.22	0.92
2007	Bos	AL	59	0	0	53	58.1	224	30	12	12	5	0	0	4	15	0	84	0	0	1	3	.250	0	37-40	2	1.43	1.85
2008	Bos	AL	67	0	0	62	69.1	273	58	24	18	4	4	1	0	8	0	77	2	0	5	4	.556	0	41-46	0	1.92	2.34
	Postseason		9	0	0	7	14.2	55	7	0	0	0	0	0	0	4	1	9	0	0	1	0	1.000	0	4-4	0	0.87	0.00
	4 ML YEARS		202	3	0	168	230.0	902	161	55	47	16	6	3	8	53	4	270	5	0	13	10	.565	0	113-128	7	1.86	1.84

Mike Parisi

Pitches: R **Bats:** R **Pos:** RP-10; SP-2   **Ht:** 6'3" **Wt:** 215 **Born:** 4/18/1983 **Age:** 26

Year	Team	Lg	G	GS	CG	GF	IP	BFP	H	R	ER	HR	SH	SF	HB	TBB	IBB	SO	WP	Bk	W	L	Pct	ShO	Sv-Op	Hld	ERC	ERA
2004	NewJrs	A-	7	7	0	0	36.1	147	40	18	18	3	0	2	1	6	0	26	1	0	4	2	.667	0	0--	-	3.87	4.46
2004	Peoria	A	6	6	0	0	35.2	151	30	16	13	1	2	4	4	15	1	36	2	0	1	1	.500	0	0--	-	3.21	3.28
2005	QuadC	A	14	14	0	0	86.0	379	98	42	39	5	3	4	4	25	0	66	2	2	5	5	.500	0	0--	-	4.28	4.08
2005	PlmBh	A+	13	13	1	0	78.0	329	79	31	28	6	3	1	4	22	0	63	3	0	5	6	.455	0	0--	-	3.77	3.23
2006	Sprgfld	AA	27	27	0	0	150.2	672	168	92	77	13	4	2	5	63	1	107	7	0	9	8	.529	0	0--	-	4.83	4.60
2007	Memp	AAA	28	28	0	0	165.0	733	192	100	90	21	10	4	10	65	0	111	5	1	8	13	.381	0	0--	-	5.55	4.91
2008	Memp	AAA	15	15	1	0	84.0	355	80	38	36	7	2	0	3	33	0	58	0	0	8	2	.800	0	0--	-	3.87	3.86
2008	StL	NL	12	2	0	6	23.0	121	37	24	21	2	1	0	0	15	2	13	3	0	0	4	.000	0	0-0	0	8.44	8.22

Chan Ho Park

Pitches: R **Bats:** R **Pos:** RP-49; SP-5   **Ht:** 6'2" **Wt:** 212 **Born:** 6/30/1973 **Age:** 36

Year	Team	Lg	G	GS	CG	GF	IP	BFP	H	R	ER	HR	SH	SF	HB	TBB	IBB	SO	WP	Bk	W	L	Pct	ShO	Sv-Op	Hld	ERC	ERA
1994	LAD	NL	2	0	0	1	4.0	23	5	5	5	1	0	0	1	5	0	6	0	0	0	0	-	0	0-0	0	11.69	11.25
1995	LAD	NL	2	1	0	0	4.0	16	2	2	2	1	0	0	0	2	0	7	0	1	0	0	-	0	0-0	0	2.70	4.50
1996	LAD	NL	48	10	0	7	108.2	477	82	48	44	7	8	1	4	71	3	119	4	3	5	5	.500	0	0-0	4	3.50	3.64
1997	LAD	NL	32	29	2	1	192.0	792	149	80	72	24	9	5	8	70	1	166	4	1	14	8	.636	0	0-0	0	3.04	3.38
1998	LAD	NL	34	34	2	0	220.2	946	199	101	91	16	11	10	11	97	1	191	6	2	15	9	.625	0	0-0	0	3.69	3.71
1999	LAD	NL	33	33	0	0	194.1	883	208	120	113	31	10	5	14	100	4	174	11	1	13	11	.542	0	0-0	0	5.68	5.23
2000	LAD	NL	34	34	3	0	226.0	963	173	92	82	21	12	5	12	124	4	217	13	0	18	10	.643	1	0-0	0	3.51	3.27
2001	LAD	NL	36	35	2	0	234.0	981	183	98	91	23	16	7	20	91	1	218	3	3	15	11	.577	1	0-0	0	3.15	3.50
2002	Tex	AL	25	25	0	0	145.2	666	154	95	93	20	4	3	17	78	2	121	9	0	9	8	.529	0	0-0	0	5.75	5.75
2003	Tex	AL	7	7	0	0	29.2	146	34	26	25	5	1	3	6	25	0	16	1	1	1	3	.250	0	0-0	0	8.56	7.58
2004	Tex	AL	16	16	0	0	95.2	428	105	63	58	22	4	4	13	33	0	63	1	1	4	7	.364	0	0-0	0	5.97	5.46
2005	2 Tms		30	29	0	0	155.1	715	180	103	99	11	7	3	10	80	1	113	6	0	12	8	.600	0	0-0	0	5.52	5.74
2006	SD	NL	24	21	1	0	136.2	606	146	81	73	20	10	4	10	44	7	96	5	0	7	7	.500	1	0-0	0	4.62	4.81
2007	NYM	NL	1	1	0	0	4.0	20	6	7	7	2	0	0	0	2	0	4	1	0	0	1	.000	0	0-0	0	10.88	15.75
2008	LAD	NL	54	5	0	11	95.1	412	97	43	36	12	4	0	4	36	7	79	2	1	4	4	.500	0	2-5	5	4.34	3.40
05	Tex	AL	20	20	0	0	109.2	502	130	70	69	8	5	2	6	54	1	80	3	0	8	5	.615	0	0-0	0	5.58	5.66
05	SD	NL	10	9	0	0	45.2	213	50	33	30	3	2	1	4	26	0	33	3	0	4	3	.571	0	0-0	0	5.36	5.91
	Postseason		1	0	0	0	2.0	6	1	0	0	0	0	0	1	0	0	0	0	0	0	0	-	0	0-0	0	1.96	0.00
	15 ML YEARS		378	280	10	20	1846.0	8074	1723	964	891	216	96	50	130	858	31	1590	66	14	117	92	.560	3	2-5	9	4.33	4.34

Bobby Parnell

Pitches: R **Bats:** R **Pos:** RP-6   **Ht:** 6'4" **Wt:** 200 **Born:** 9/8/1984 **Age:** 24

Year	Team	Lg	G	GS	CG	GF	IP	BFP	H	R	ER	HR	SH	SF	HB	TBB	IBB	SO	WP	Bk	W	L	Pct	ShO	Sv-Op	Hld	ERC	ERA
2005	Bklyn	A-	15	14	0	1	73.0	294	48	20	14	1	0	2	4	29	0	67	3	0	2	3	.400	0	0--	-	1.97	1.73
2006	Hgrstn	A	18	18	1	0	93.2	401	84	56	42	7	1	2	6	40	0	84	12	0	5	10	.333	0	0--	-	3.70	4.04
2006	StLuci	A+	3	3	0	0	11.2	58	16	13	12	3	0	1	0	9	0	13	2	0	1	0	1.000	0	0--	-	9.50	9.26
2007	StLuci	A+	12	12	0	0	55.1	242	56	22	20	0	0	0	4	22	0	62	3	1	3	3	.500	0	0--	-	3.69	3.25
2007	Bnghtn	AA	17	17	0	0	88.2	401	98	54	47	9	1	2	4	38	1	74	3	0	5	5	.500	0	0--	-	4.91	4.77
2008	Bnghtn	AA	24	24	0	0	127.2	556	126	66	61	14	2	3	6	57	1	91	9	0	10	6	.625	0	0--	-	4.46	4.30
2008	NewOr	AAA	5	4	0	0	20.1	94	25	16	15	0	1	0	0	9	0	23	1	0	2	2	.500	0	0--	-	4.72	6.64
2008	NYM	NL	6	0	0	3	5.0	19	3	3	0	0	0	0	0	2	0	3	1	0	0	0	-	0	0-0	0	1.59	5.40

Chad Paronto

Pitches: R Bats: R Pos: RP-6   Ht: 6'5" Wt: 250 Born: 7/28/1975 Age: 33

Year	Team	Lg	G	GS	CG	GF	IP	BFP	H	R	ER	HR	SH	SF	HB	TBB	IBB	SO	WP	Bk	W	L	Pct	ShO	Sv-Op	Hld	ERC	ERA
2008	RdRck*	AAA	35	0	0	13	52.2	231	61	19	18	2	3	1	3	14	3	57	1	0	2	.000	0	3- -		4.11	3.08
2001	Bal	AL	24	0	0	9	27.0	128	33	24	15	5	1	1	1	11	0	16	1	0	1	3	.250	0	0-1	5	5.98	5.00
2002	Cle	AL	29	0	0	11	35.2	154	34	19	16	3	0	4	2	11	1	23	2	0	0	2	.000	0	0-0	0	3.45	4.04
2003	Cle	AL	6	0	0	5	6.2	29	7	8	7	1	1	1	0	3	0	6	0	0	0	2	.000	0	0-0	0	5.00	9.45
2006	Atl	NL	65	0	0	11	56.2	237	53	23	20	5	4	1	3	19	3	41	3	0	2	3	.400	0	0-2	8	3.56	3.18
2007	Atl	NL	41	0	0	12	40.1	180	47	20	16	1	2	3	3	19	5	14	2	0	3	1	.750	0	1-2	2	4.95	3.57
2008	Hou	NL	6	0	0	3	10.1	41	11	5	5	2	1	0	0	2	0	4	0	0	1		.000	0	0-0	0	4.49	4.35
	6 ML YEARS		171	0	0	51	176.2	769	185	99	79	17	9	10	9	65	9	104	8	0	6	12	.333	0	1-5	15	4.32	4.02

James Parr

Pitches: R Bats: R Pos: SP-5   Ht: 6'1" Wt: 185 Born: 2/27/1986 Age: 23

Year	Team	Lg	G	GS	CG	GF	IP	BFP	H	R	ER	HR	SH	SF	HB	TBB	IBB	SO	WP	Bk	W	L	Pct	ShO	Sv-Op	Hld	ERC	ERA
2004	Braves	R	10	10	0	0	40.1	167	39	19	19	2	0	0	0	12	0	40	2	1	3	2	.600	0	0- -	-	3.20	4.24
2005	Rome	A	26	18	0	7	126.2	537	134	54	48	13	3	7	4	24	0	98	1	0	13	4	.765	0	3- -	-	3.67	3.41
2006	MrtlBh	A+	24	22	2	1	134.2	566	138	76	72	14	6	9	1	37	0	90	2	1	7	8	.467	0	1- -	-	3.80	4.81
2007	MrtlBh	A+	8	8	1	0	39.2	153	36	14	14	1	1	2	1	6	0	37	1	2	3	4	.429	1	0- -	-	2.41	3.18
2007	Missi	AA	18	16	0	0	98.0	416	111	51	50	8	10	3	2	25	0	75	0	1	4	5	.444	0	0- -	-	4.27	4.59
2008	Missi	AA	18	17	0	0	95.0	397	87	40	39	9	2	3	2	37	0	81	3	1	8	4	.667	0	0- -	-	3.68	3.69
2008	Rchmd	AAA	10	9	0	0	55.2	226	49	20	20	4	0	1	1	14	0	44	0	1	5	3	.625	0	0- -	-	2.78	3.23
2008	Atl	NL	5	5	0	0	22.1	102	29	13	12	4	1	0	0	9	0	14	1	0	1	0	1.000	0	0-0	0	6.53	4.84

Manny Parra

Pitches: L Bats: L Pos: SP-29; RP-3   Ht: 6'3" Wt: 208 Born: 10/30/1982 Age: 26

Year	Team	Lg	G	GS	CG	GF	IP	BFP	H	R	ER	HR	SH	SF	HB	TBB	IBB	SO	WP	Bk	W	L	Pct	ShO	Sv-Op	Hld	ERC	ERA
2002	Brewrs	R	1	1	0	0	2.0	7	1	1	1	0	0	0	0	0	0	4	0	0	0		0- -	-	1.73	4.50
2002	Ogden	R+	11	10	0	0	47.2	213	59	30	17	3	0	1	4	10	0	51	5	0	3	1	.750	0	0- -	-	4.69	3.21
2003	Beloit	A	23	23	1	0	138.2	551	127	50	42	9	5	0	0	24	0	117	5	3	11	2	.846	0	0- -	-	2.59	2.73
2004	Hi Dsrt	A+	13	12	1	0	67.1	295	76	41	26	3	6	6	2	19	0	64	3	1	5	2	.714	1	0- -	-	4.01	3.48
2004	Hntsvl	AA	3	3	0	0	6.0	23	5	3	2	0	0	0	0	0	0	10	1	0	0	1	.000	0	0- -	-	1.37	3.00
2005	Hntsvl	AA	16	16	0	0	91.0	404	111	47	40	4	5	1	2	21	0	85	7	3	5	6	.455	0	0- -	-	4.25	3.96
2006	BrvdCt	A+	15	14	0	0	54.2	239	47	29	18	4	3	1	3	32	0	61	1	0	1	3	.250	0	0- -	-	4.06	2.96
2006	Hntsvl	AA	6	6	0	0	31.1	125	26	13	10	0	1	2	2	8	0	29	1	0	3	0	1.000	0	0- -	-	2.31	2.87
2007	Hntsvl	AA	13	13	0	0	80.2	334	70	28	24	2	3	3	3	26	1	81	2	2	7	3	.700	0	0- -	-	2.71	2.68
2007	Nashv	AAA	4	4	1	0	26.0	101	15	6	5	1	5	0	2	7	0	25	1	0	3	1	.750	1	0- -	-	1.50	1.73
2007	Mil	NL	9	2	0	3	26.1	116	25	13	11	1	1	3	2	12	0	26	1	0	1	0	1.000	0	0-0	1	3.83	3.76
2008	Mil	NL	32	29	0	0	166.0	741	181	91	81	18	10	2	2	75	1	147	17	2	10	8	.556	0	0-0	0	4.89	4.39
	2 ML YEARS		41	31	0	3	192.1	857	206	104	92	19	11	5	4	87	1	173	18	2	10	9	.526	0	0-0	1	4.74	4.31

John Parrish

Pitches: L Bats: L Pos: RP-7; SP-6   Ht: 5'11" Wt: 210 Born: 11/26/1977 Age: 31

Year	Team	Lg	G	GS	CG	GF	IP	BFP	H	R	ER	HR	SH	SF	HB	TBB	IBB	SO	WP	Bk	W	L	Pct	ShO	Sv-Op	Hld	ERC	ERA
2008	Syrcse*	AAA	17	13	0	0	91.0	389	80	42	29	5	1	5	3	39	1	100	4	0	10	1	.909	0	0- -	0	3.30	2.87
2000	Bal	AL	8	8	0	0	36.1	180	40	32	29	6	0	0	1	35	0	28	1	0	2	4	.333	0	0-0	0	7.75	7.18
2001	Bal	AL	16	1	0	7	22.0	107	22	17	15	5	0	0	3	17	1	20	1	0	1	2	.333	0	0-0	0	7.06	6.14
2003	Bal	AL	14	0	0	2	23.2	93	17	7	5	2	0	1	1	8	2	15	2	0	0	1	.000	0	0-2	1	2.39	1.90
2004	Bal	AL	56	1	0	17	78.0	353	68	39	30	4	3	6	3	55	6	71	6	0	6	3	.667	0	1-1	2	4.17	3.46
2005	Bal	AL	14	0	0	2	17.1	86	19	6	6	1	1	0	0	17	1	25	6	0	1	0	1.000	0	0-0	1	6.53	3.12
2007	2 Tms	AL	53	0	0	14	52.0	254	63	34	33	2	1	1	2	37	4	41	3	0	2	2	.500	0	0-2	10	6.03	5.71
2008	Tor	AL	13	6	0	1	42.1	179	47	19	19	5	0	1	0	15	0	21	4	0	1	1	.500	0	0-0	0	4.82	4.04
07	Bal	AL	45	0	0	9	41.2	199	41	26	25	2	0	1	2	33	4	36	2	0	2	2	.500	0	0-2	9	5.05	5.40
07	Sea	AL	8	0	0	5	10.1	55	22	8	8	0	1	0	0	4	0	5	1	0	0		-	0	0-0	1	10.48	6.97
	7 ML YEARS		174	16	0	43	271.2	1252	276	154	137	25	5	9	10	184	14	221	23	0	13	13	.500	0	1-5	14	5.29	4.54

Corey Patterson

Bats: L Throws: R Pos: CF-124; PH-22; PR-5   Ht: 5'9" Wt: 175 Born: 8/13/1979 Age: 29

Year	Team	Lg	G	AB	H	2B	3B	HR	(Hm	Rd)	TB	R	RBI	RC	TBB	IBB	SO	HBP	SH	SF	SB	CS	SB%	GDP	Avg	OBP	Slg
2008	Lsvlle*	AAA	5	22	9	2	0	0	(-	-)	11	3	0	4	1	0	5	0	0	0	1	1	.50	1	.409	.435	.500
2000	ChC	NL	11	42	7	1	0	2	(1	1)	14	9	2	3	3	0	14	1	1	0	1	1	.50	0	.167	.239	.333
2001	ChC	NL	59	131	29	3	0	4	(1	3)	44	26	14	13	6	0	33	3	2	3	4	0	1.00	1	.221	.266	.336
2002	ChC	NL	153	592	150	30	5	14	(7	7)	232	71	54	61	19	1	142	8	4	5	18	3	.86	8	.253	.284	.392
2003	ChC	NL	83	329	98	17	7	13	(7	6)	168	49	55	55	15	2	77	1	0	2	16	5	.76	5	.298	.329	.511
2004	ChC	NL	157	631	168	33	6	24	(14	10)	285	91	72	87	45	7	168	5	5	1	32	9	.78	7	.266	.320	.452
2005	ChC	NL	126	451	97	15	3	13	(9	4)	157	47	34	32	23	3	118	1	5	1	15	5	.75	5	.215	.254	.348
2006	Bal	AL	135	463	128	19	5	16	(9	7)	205	75	53	66	21	5	94	5	8	1	45	9	.83	0	.276	.314	.443
2007	Bal	AL	132	461	124	26	2	8	(5	3)	178	65	45	51	21	1	65	4	13	4	37	9	.80	3	.269	.304	.386
2008	Cin	NL	135	366	75	17	2	10	(2	8)	126	46	34	23	16	0	57	1	5	4	14	9	.61	3	.205	.238	.344
	9 ML YEARS		991	3466	876	161	30	104	(55	49)	1409	479	363	391	169	19	768	29	43	21	182	50	.78	32	.253	.291	.407

Eric Patterson

Bats: L Throws: R Pos: 2B-22; LF-17; PH-4; PR-3; CF-1; DH-1   Ht: 5'11" Wt: 170 Born: 4/8/1983 Age: 26

								BATTING														BASERUNNING				AVERAGES		
Year	Team	Lg	G	AB	H	2B	3B	HR	(Hm	Rd)	TB	R	RBI	RC	TBB	IBB	SO	HBP	SH	SF	SB	CS	SB%	GDP	Avg	OBP	Slg
2005	Peoria	A	110	432	144	26	11	13	(-	-)	231	90	71	97	53	3	94	4	4	7	40	11	.78	7	.333	.405	.535
2005	WTenn	AA	9	30	6	2	0	0	(-	-)	8	5	2	3	6	0	7	0	0	1	3	2	.60	0	.200	.324	.267
2006	WTenn	AA	121	441	116	22	9	8	(-	-)	180	66	48	65	46	2	89	1	7	6	38	12	.76	2	.263	.330	.408
2006	Iowa	AAA	17	67	24	1	1	2	(-	-)	33	14	12	15	6	0	9	0	0	3	8	0	1.00	2	.358	.395	.493
2007	Iowa	AAA	128	516	153	28	6	14	(-	-)	235	94	65	89	54	2	85	2	4	6	24	9	.73	4	.297	.362	.455
2008	Iowa	AAA	52	203	65	16	3	6	(-	-)	105	33	28	39	12	0	45	1	2	2	11	0	1.00	1	.320	.358	.517
2008	Scrmto	AAA	25	109	36	8	2	4	(-	-)	60	18	19	23	9	0	28	1	3	2	8	2	.80	1	.330	.380	.550
2007	ChC	NL	7	8	2	1	0	0	(0	0)	3	0	0	0	0	0	3	0	1	0	0	0	-	0	.250	.250	.375
2008	2 Tms		43	130	25	4	0	1	(1	0)	32	16	15	11	17	0	36	0	0	1	10	1	.91	1	.192	.284	.246
08	ChC	NL	13	38	9	1	0	1	(1	0)	13	5	7	5	5	0	12	0	0	1	2	1	.67	1	.237	.318	.342
08	Oak	AL	30	92	16	3	0	0	(0	0)	19	11	8	6	12	0	24	0	0	0	8	0	1.00	0	.174	.269	.207
	2 ML YEARS		50	138	27	5	0	1	(1	0)	35	16	15	11	17	0	39	0	1	1	10	1	.91	1	.196	.282	.254

Scott Patterson

Pitches: R Bats: R Pos: RP-4   Ht: 6'6" Wt: 230 Born: 6/20/1979 Age: 30

			HOW MUCH HE PITCHED						WHAT HE GAVE UP											THE RESULTS						
Year	Team	Lg	G	GS	CG	GF	IP	BFP	H	R	ER	HR	SH	SF	HB	TBB	IBB	SO	WP	Bk	W	L	Pct	ShO	Sv-Op	Hld	ERC	ERA
2002	Gtwy	IND	13	2	1	6	42.1	173	33	18	16	4	0	0	1	13	0	51	1	0	2	2	.500	1	1--	-	2.59	3.40
2003	Gtwy	IND	20	11	3	6	129.2	527	119	45	42	6	3	2	7	24	2	120	2	0	8	3	.727	2	0--	-	2.68	2.92
2004	Gtwy	IND	20	20	1	0	129.2	536	127	67	62	18	3	11	4	31	0	120	4	0	11	2	.846	0	0--	-	3.64	4.30
2005	Lancst	A+	28	9	0	12	73.2	321	85	40	39	16	3	1	2	20	0	62	0	1	4	2	.667	0	6--	-	5.40	4.76
2005	Gtwy	IND	19	0	0	17	27.1	109	21	5	5	4	0	0	1	8	0	41	0	0	1	1	.500	0	9--	-	2.91	1.65
2006	Lancst	A+	20	0	0	17	23.0	87	13	2	2	1	1	0	1	5	1	31	1	0	2	0	1.000	0	14--	-	1.27	0.78
2006	Trntn	AA	26	0	0	16	38.2	152	26	11	10	6	2	0	1	8	0	43	0	0	0	1	.000	0	1--	-	2.05	2.33
2007	Trntn	AA	43	3	0	16	74.1	284	45	13	9	1	1	1	2	15	2	91	2	0	4	2	.667	0	2--	-	1.21	1.09
2007	S-WB	AAA	1	0	0	0	3.0	9	0	0	0	0	0	0	0	0	0	1	0	0	0	0	-	0	0--	-	0.00	0.00
2008	S-WB	AAA	42	0	0	21	47.1	200	47	22	20	7	1	3	1	13	2	54	2	0	2	1	.667	0	5--	-	3.87	3.80
2008	2 Tms		4	0	0	2	4.2	22	2	1	1	0	0	0	0	6	1	7	1	0	0	0	-	0	0-0	0	2.97	1.93
08	NYY	AL	1	0	0	0	1.1	7	1	1	1	0	0	0	0	2	0	2	0	0	0	0	-	0	0-0	0	5.91	6.75
08	SD	NL	3	0	0	2	3.1	15	1	0	0	0	0	0	0	4	1	5	1	0	0	0	-	0	0-0	0	1.96	0.00

Troy Patton

Pitches: L Bats: B Pos: P   Ht: 6'1" Wt: 185 Born: 9/3/1985 Age: 23

			HOW MUCH HE PITCHED						WHAT HE GAVE UP											THE RESULTS						
Year	Team	Lg	G	GS	CG	GF	IP	BFP	H	R	ER	HR	SH	SF	HB	TBB	IBB	SO	WP	Bk	W	L	Pct	ShO	Sv-Op	Hld	ERC	ERA
2004	Grnsvle	R	6	6	0	0	28.0	111	23	8	6	1	0	3	1	5	0	32	0	0	2	2	.500	0	0--	-	2.08	1.93
2005	Lxngtn	A	15	15	0	0	78.2	310	59	24	17	3	4	0	5	20	0	94	0	0	5	2	.714	0	0--	-	2.14	1.94
2005	Salem	A+	10	9	0	0	41.0	162	34	12	12	2	0	2	2	8	0	38	1	0	1	4	.200	0	0--	-	2.33	2.63
2006	Salem	A+	19	19	1	0	101.1	435	92	49	33	4	6	4	5	37	0	102	3	0	7	7	.500	0	0--	-	3.16	2.93
2006	CpChr	AA	8	8	0	0	45.1	195	48	26	22	6	2	1	2	13	0	37	3	0	2	5	.286	0	0--	-	4.36	4.37
2007	CpChr	AA	16	16	0	0	102.1	437	96	38	34	10	5	1	9	33	1	69	2	0	6	6	.500	0	0--	-	3.73	2.99
2007	RdRck	AAA	8	8	0	0	49.0	200	44	26	25	5	4	3	3	11	0	25	0	0	4	2	.667	0	0--	-	3.13	4.59
2007	Hou	NL	3	2	0	1	12.2	54	10	6	5	3	1	0	2	4	0	8	0	0	0	2	.000	0	0-0	0	4.04	3.55

David Pauley

Pitches: R Bats: R Pos: RP-4; SP-2   Ht: 6'2" Wt: 210 Born: 6/17/1983 Age: 26

			HOW MUCH HE PITCHED						WHAT HE GAVE UP											THE RESULTS						
Year	Team	Lg	G	GS	CG	GF	IP	BFP	H	R	ER	HR	SH	SF	HB	TBB	IBB	SO	WP	Bk	W	L	Pct	ShO	Sv-Op	Hld	ERC	ERA
2001	Idaho	R+	15	15	0	0	68.2	315	88	57	46	8	1	3	1	24	0	53	6	0	4	9	.308	0	0--	-	5.64	6.03
2002	Eugene	A	15	15	0	0	80.0	335	81	32	25	6	3	4	6	18	1	62	7	0	6	1	.857	0	0--	-	3.60	2.81
2003	FtWyn	A	22	21	0	1	117.2	495	109	51	43	9	2	2	8	38	0	117	5	0	7	7	.500	0	1--	-	3.50	3.29
2004	Lk Els	A+	27	26	0	0	153.1	665	155	89	71	8	8	9	8	60	0	128	6	0	7	12	.368	0	0--	-	3.98	4.17
2005	Portlnd	AA	27	27	1	0	156.0	666	169	86	66	18	5	5	5	34	0	104	6	0	9	7	.563	0	0--	-	4.00	3.81
2006	Portlnd	AAA	10	10	0	0	60.1	245	54	20	16	6	5	3	2	17	1	47	0	0	2	3	.400	0	0--	-	3.22	2.39
2006	Pwtckt	AAA	9	9	0	0	50.1	227	60	40	31	10	3	3	5	18	0	25	1	0	1	3	.250	0	0--	-	6.26	5.54
2007	Pwtckt	AAA	27	26	0	0	153.2	672	164	90	74	18	3	3	7	49	1	110	8	1	6	6	.500	0	0--	-	4.39	4.33
2008	Pwtckt	AAA	25	25	0	0	147.0	617	147	68	58	10	3	5	10	41	0	103	3	0	14	4	.778	0	0--	-	3.73	3.55
2006	Bos	AL	3	3	0	0	16.0	82	31	14	14	1	0	0	2	6	1	10	0	0	0	2	.000	0	0-0	0	10.41	7.88
2008	Bos	AL	6	2	0	3	12.1	67	23	17	16	2	0	1	1	5	0	11	0	0	0	1	.000	0	0-0	0	10.16	11.68
	2 ML YEARS		9	5	0	3	28.1	149	54	31	30	3	0	1	3	11	1	21	0	0	0	3	.000	0	0-0	0	10.30	9.53

Felipe Paulino

Pitches: R Bats: R Pos: P   Ht: 6'2" Wt: 180 Born: 10/5/1983 Age: 25

			HOW MUCH HE PITCHED						WHAT HE GAVE UP											THE RESULTS						
Year	Team	Lg	G	GS	CG	GF	IP	BFP	H	R	ER	HR	SH	SF	HB	TBB	IBB	SO	WP	Bk	W	L	Pct	ShO	Sv-Op	Hld	ERC	ERA
2003	Mrtnsvl	R+	16	0	0	6	25.2	126	23	20	16	0	0	1	8	19	0	27	8	0	2	2	.500	0	1--	-	5.12	5.61
2004	Grnsvle	R	10	10	0	0	32.0	149	30	30	27	4	0	1	4	22	0	37	6	0	1	3	.250	0	0--	-	5.55	7.59
2005	TriCity	A-	13	2	0	10	30.2	126	21	15	13	2	1	0	3	11	0	34	8	0	2	2	.500	0	1--	-	2.39	3.82
2005	Lxngtn	A	7	5	0	0	24.1	100	21	8	5	2	3	1	0	6	0	30	2	0	1	1	.500	0	0--	-	2.61	1.85
2006	Salem	A+	27	26	0	0	126.1	546	119	67	61	13	2	2	7	59	0	91	9	0	9	7	.563	0	0--	-	4.31	4.35
2007	CpChr	AA	22	21	0	0	112.0	480	103	55	45	6	0	4	3	49	0	110	7	1	4	5	.444	0	0--	-	3.49	3.62
2008	RdRck	AAA	1	0	0	0	0.2	4	1	0	0	0	0	0	0	1	0	1	0	0	0	0	-	0	0--	-	10.76	0.00
2007	Hou	NL	5	3	0	0	19.0	85	22	15	15	5	2	0	0	7	1	11	1	0	2	1	.667	0	0-0	1	5.93	7.11

Ronny Paulino

Bats: R Throws: R Pos: C-32; PH-9   Ht: 6'2" Wt: 240 Born: 4/21/1981 Age: 28

			BATTING																		BASERUNNING				AVERAGES		
Year Team	Lg	G	AB	H	2B	3B	HR	(Hm	Rd)	TB	R	RBI	RC	TBB	IBB	SO	HBP	SH	SF	SB	CS	SB%	GDP	Avg	OBP	Slg
2008 Indy*	AAA	30	111	34	13	1	4	(-	-)	61	16	18	22	13	1	31	0	0	2	0	2	.00	3	.306	.373	.550
2008 Pirates*	R	8	28	8	1	0	1	(-	-)	12	3	6	4	2	0	3	0	0	0	0	0	-	3	.286	.333	.429
2005 Pit	NL	2	4	2	0	0	0	(0	0)	2	1	0	1	1	0	0	0	0	0	0	0	-	0	.500	.600	.500
2006 Pit	NL	129	442	137	19	0	6	(2	4)	174	37	55	60	34	5	79	2	1	2	0	0	-	17	.310	.360	.394
2007 Pit	NL	133	457	120	25	0	11	(7	4)	178	56	55	49	33	0	79	2	0	2	2	2	.50	14	.263	.314	.389
2008 Pit	NL	40	118	25	5	0	2	(0	2)	36	8	18	14	11	1	24	0	0	1	0	0	-	4	.212	.277	.305
4 ML YEARS		304	1021	284	49	0	19	(9	10)	390	102	128	124	79	6	182	4	1	5	2	2	.50	35	.278	.331	.382

Carl Pavano

Pitches: R Bats: R Pos: SP-7   Ht: 6'5" Wt: 241 Born: 1/8/1976 Age: 33

		HOW MUCH HE PITCHED						WHAT HE GAVE UP											THE RESULTS						
Year Team	Lg	G	GS	CG	GF	IP	BFP	H	R	ER	HR	SH	SF	HB	TBB	IBB	SO	WP	Bk	W	L	Pct	ShO	Sv-Op	Hld	ERC	ERA
2008 CtnSC*	A	2	2	0	0	5.0	21	6	1	1	0	0	0	0	1	0	6	0	0	0	0	-	0	0--	-	3.80	1.80
2008 Trntn*	AA	3	3	0	0	14.0	59	14	6	6	3	0	0	2	3	0	13	2	0	1	1	.500	0	0--	-	4.77	3.86
1998 Mon	NL	24	23	0	0	134.2	580	130	70	63	18	5	6	8	43	1	83	1	0	6	9	.400	0	0-0	0	3.97	4.21
1999 Mon	NL	19	18	1	0	104.0	457	117	66	65	8	5	2	4	35	1	70	1	3	6	8	.429	1	0-0	0	4.51	5.63
2000 Mon	NL	15	15	0	0	97.0	408	89	40	33	8	4	3	8	34	1	64	1	1	8	4	.667	0	0-0	0	3.67	3.06
2001 Mon	NL	8	8	0	0	42.2	199	59	33	30	7	2	1	2	16	1	36	0	1	1	6	.143	0	0-0	0	6.99	6.33
2002 2 Tms	NL	37	22	0	2	136.0	619	174	88	78	19	4	4	10	45	8	92	3	2	6	10	.375	0	0-0	0	5.98	5.16
2003 Fla	NL	33	32	2	1	201.0	846	204	99	96	19	9	10	7	49	10	133	3	2	12	13	.480	0	0-0	0	3.57	4.30
2004 Fla	NL	31	31	2	0	222.1	909	212	80	74	16	7	4	11	49	13	139	2	3	18	8	.692	2	0-0	0	3.10	3.00
2005 NYY	AL	17	17	1	0	100.0	442	129	66	53	17	4	3	8	18	1	56	2	1	4	6	.400	1	0-0	0	5.74	4.77
2007 NYY	AL	2	2	0	0	11.1	46	12	7	6	1	0	0	0	2	0	4	0	0	1	0	1.000	0	0-0	0	3.54	4.76
2008 NYY	AL	7	7	0	0	34.1	154	41	23	22	5	3	3	4	10	0	15	0	1	4	2	.667	0	0-0	0	5.60	5.77
02 Mon	NL	15	14	0	0	74.1	350	98	55	52	14	2	2	7	31	5	51	2	1	3	8	.273	0	0-0	0	7.07	6.30
02 Fla	NL	22	8	0	2	61.2	269	76	33	26	5	2	2	3	14	3	41	1	1	3	2	.600	0	0-0	3	4.74	3.79
Postseason		8	2	0	1	19.1	75	17	3	3	0	1	1	1	3	1	15	0	0	2	0	1.000	0	0-0	0	2.13	1.40
10 ML YEARS		193	175	6	3	1083.1	4660	1167	572	520	118	43	36	62	301	36	692	13	14	66	66	.500	4	0-0	3	4.28	4.32

Jay Payton

Bats: R Throws: R Pos: LF-71; CF-38; PH-21; PR-9; RF-4   Ht: 5'10" Wt: 207 Born: 11/22/1972 Age: 36

			BATTING																		BASERUNNING				AVERAGES		
Year Team	Lg	G	AB	H	2B	3B	HR	(Hm	Rd)	TB	R	RBI	RC	TBB	IBB	SO	HBP	SH	SF	SB	CS	SB%	GDP	Avg	OBP	Slg
1998 NYM	NL	15	22	7	1	0	0	(0	0)	8	2	0	3	1	0	4	0	0	0	0	0	-	0	.318	.348	.364
1999 NYM	NL	13	8	2	1	0	0	(0	0)	3	1	1	0	0	0	2	1	0	0	1	2	.33	0	.250	.333	.375
2000 NYM	NL	149	488	142	23	1	17	(9	8)	218	63	62	68	30	0	60	3	0	8	5	11	.31	9	.291	.331	.447
2001 NYM	NL	104	361	92	16	1	8	(6	2)	134	44	34	37	18	1	52	5	0	2	4	3	.57	11	.255	.298	.371
2002 2 Tms	NL	134	445	135	20	7	16	(9	7)	217	69	59	71	29	0	54	4	2	1	7	4	.64	11	.303	.351	.488
2003 Col	NL	157	600	181	32	5	28	(13	15)	307	93	89	95	43	3	77	7	5	3	6	4	.60	27	.302	.354	.512
2004 SD	NL	143	458	119	17	4	8	(0	8)	168	57	55	61	43	2	56	4	2	4	2	0	1.00	12	.260	.326	.367
2005 2 Tms	NL	124	408	109	16	1	18	(11	7)	181	62	63	56	24	2	47	0	0	3	0	1	.00	8	.267	.306	.444
2006 Oak	AL	142	557	165	32	3	10	(5	5)	233	78	59	76	22	1	52	4	0	5	8	4	.67	12	.296	.325	.418
2007 Bal	AL	131	434	111	21	5	7	(6	1)	163	48	58	49	22	0	42	3	5	6	5	2	.71	9	.256	.292	.376
2008 Bal	AL	127	338	82	10	2	7	(2	5)	117	41	41	37	22	1	53	1	2	0	8	1	.89	7	.243	.291	.346
02 NYM	NL	87	275	78	6	3	8	(4	4)	114	33	31	38	21	0	34	1	2	1	4	1	.80	8	.284	.336	.415
02 Col	NL	47	170	57	14	4	8	(5	3)	103	36	28	33	8	0	20	3	0	0	3	3	.50	3	.335	.376	.606
05 Bos	AL	55	133	35	7	0	5	(2	3)	57	24	21	16	10	0	14	0	0	1	0	0	-	4	.263	.313	.429
05 Oak	AL	69	275	74	9	1	13	(9	4)	124	38	42	40	14	2	33	0	0	2	0	1	.00	4	.269	.302	.451
Postseason		21	83	21	2	0	3	(0	3)	32	9	10	5	3	0	17	1	0	1	1	1	.50	2	.253	.284	.386
11 ML YEARS		1239	4119	1145	189	29	119	(61	58)	1749	558	521	553	254	10	499	32	16	32	46	32	.59	106	.278	.323	.425

Steve Pearce

Bats: R Throws: R Pos: RF-29; PH-9; LF-1   Ht: 5'11" Wt: 205 Born: 4/13/1983 Age: 26

			BATTING																		BASERUNNING				AVERAGES		
Year Team	Lg	G	AB	H	2B	3B	HR	(Hm	Rd)	TB	R	RBI	RC	TBB	IBB	SO	HBP	SH	SF	SB	CS	SB%	GDP	Avg	OBP	Slg
2005 Wmspt	A-	72	272	82	26	0	7	(-	-)	129	48	52	49	35	0	43	2	0	3	2	4	.33	9	.301	.381	.474
2006 Hkry	A	41	160	46	13	1	12	(-	-)	97	35	38	33	15	1	32	4	0	0	1	3	.25	3	.288	.363	.606
2006 Lynbrg	A+	90	328	87	27	1	14	(-	-)	158	48	60	56	34	0	65	10	1	4	7	5	.58	9	.265	.348	.482
2007 Lynbrg	A+	19	75	26	4	1	11	(-	-)	65	19	24	24	8	0	13	1	0	1	2	0	1.00	1	.347	.412	.867
2007 Altna	AA	81	290	97	27	2	14	(-	-)	170	57	72	68	33	0	45	4	0	8	7	2	.78	10	.334	.400	.586
2007 Indy	AAA	34	122	39	9	1	6	(-	-)	68	18	17	25	6	0	12	3	0	0	5	0	1.00	2	.320	.366	.557
2008 Indy	AAA	103	386	97	26	1	12	(-	-)	161	47	60	53	32	2	75	5	4	6	11	4	.73	8	.251	.312	.417
2007 Pit	NL	23	68	20	5	1	0	(0	0)	27	13	6	9	5	0	12	0	0	0	2	1	.67	2	.294	.342	.397
2008 Pit	NL	37	109	27	7	0	4	(0	4)	46	6	15	13	5	0	22	3	0	2	2	0	1.00	1	.248	.294	.422
2 ML YEARS		60	177	47	12	1	4	(0	4)	73	19	21	22	10	0	34	3	0	2	4	1	.80	3	.266	.313	.412

Jake Peavy

Pitches: R Bats: R Pos: SP-27   Ht: 6'1" Wt: 193 Born: 5/31/1981 Age: 28

		HOW MUCH HE PITCHED						WHAT HE GAVE UP											THE RESULTS						
Year Team	Lg	G	GS	CG	GF	IP	BFP	H	R	ER	HR	SH	SF	HB	TBB	IBB	SO	WP	Bk	W	L	Pct	ShO	Sv-Op	Hld	ERC	ERA
2002 SD	NL	17	17	0	0	97.2	430	106	54	49	11	5	2	3	33	4	90	1	2	6	7	.462	0	0-0	0	4.41	4.52
2003 SD	NL	32	32	0	0	194.2	827	173	94	89	33	7	5	6	82	3	156	2	0	12	11	.522	0	0-0	0	4.13	4.11
2004 SD	NL	27	27	0	0	166.1	694	146	49	42	13	5	6	11	53	4	173	1	1	15	6	.714	0	0-0	0	3.18	2.27
2005 SD	NL	30	30	3	0	203.0	812	162	70	65	18	4	5	7	50	3	216	3	1	13	7	.650	3	0-0	0	2.49	2.88

213

			HOW MUCH HE PITCHED						WHAT HE GAVE UP													THE RESULTS							
Year	Team	Lg	G	GS	CG	GF	IP	BFP	H	R	ER	HR	SH	SF	HB	TBB	IBB	SO	WP	Bk	W	L	Pct	ShO	Sv-Op	Hld	ERC	ERA
2006	SD	NL	32	32	2	0	202.1	846	187	93	92	23	5	1	6	62	11	215	4	0	11	14	.440	0	0-0	0	3.42	4.09
2007	SD	NL	34	34	0	0	223.1	898	169	67	63	13	5	7	6	68	5	240	4	0	19	6	.760	0	0-0	0	2.27	2.54
2008	SD	NL	27	27	1	0	173.2	709	146	57	55	17	7	1	5	59	1	166	6	0	10	11	.476	0	0-0	0	3.12	2.85
Postseason			2	2	0	0	9.2	49	19	13	13	3	1	1	0	4	3	5	1	0	0	2	.000	0	0-0	0	12.16	12.10
7 ML YEARS			199	199	6	0	1261.0	5216	1089	484	455	128	38	27	44	407	31	1256	24	3	86	62	.581	3	0-0	0	3.16	3.25

Dustin Pedroia

Bats: R **Throws:** R **Pos:** 2B-157; PH-2   **Ht:** 5'9" **Wt:** 180 **Born:** 8/17/1983 **Age:** 25

			BATTING																		BASERUNNING				AVERAGES		
Year	Team	Lg	G	AB	H	2B	3B	HR	(Hm	Rd)	TB	R	RBI	RC	TBB	IBB	SO	HBP	SH	SF	SB	CS	SB%	GDP	Avg	OBP	Slg
2006	Bos	AL	31	89	17	4	0	2	(1	1)	27	5	7	3	7	0	7	1	1	0	0	1	.00	1	.191	.258	.303
2007	Bos	AL	139	520	165	39	1	8	(5	3)	230	86	50	79	47	1	42	7	5	2	7	1	.88	8	.317	.380	.442
2008	Bos	AL	157	653	213	54	2	17	(7	10)	322	118	83	107	50	1	52	7	7	9	20	1	.95	17	.326	.376	.493
Postseason			14	60	17	6	0	2	(2	0)	29	12	10	11	6	0	7	0	1	0	0	0	-	2	.283	.348	.483
3 ML YEARS			327	1262	395	97	3	27	(13	14)	579	209	140	189	104	2	101	15	13	11	27	3	.90	26	.313	.369	.459

Jailen Peguero

Pitches: R **Bats:** R **Pos:** RP-7   **Ht:** 6'0" **Wt:** 185 **Born:** 1/4/1981 **Age:** 28

			HOW MUCH HE PITCHED						WHAT HE GAVE UP													THE RESULTS							
Year	Team	Lg	G	GS	CG	GF	IP	BFP	H	R	ER	HR	SH	SF	HB	TBB	IBB	SO	WP	Bk	W	L	Pct	ShO	Sv-Op	Hld	ERC	ERA
2002	TriCity	A-	25	3	0	14	49.2	208	49	20	19	3	1	2	0	17	1	42	6	0	1	1	.500	0	6- -	-	3.52	3.44
2003	Lxngtn	A	31	21	0	5	146.0	609	110	74	59	11	2	6	8	69	1	111	10	0	5	13	.278	0	1- -	-	3.08	3.64
2004	Salem	A+	51	1	0	31	86.0	384	93	51	37	7	0	0	4	32	3	79	5	1	5	6	.455	0	8- -	-	4.34	3.87
2005	CpChr	AA	50	0	0	36	64.1	280	62	25	21	3	4	3	4	25	5	63	2	0	2	2	.500	0	12- -	-	3.53	2.94
2006	CpChr	AA	27	0	0	26	38.2	149	18	4	3	0	1	1	6	16	0	48	2	0	2	0	1.000	0	14- -	-	1.52	0.70
2006	RdRck	AAA	21	0	0	6	36.1	162	34	18	14	3	2	2	1	18	2	30	4	1	1	2	.333	0	1- -	-	3.88	3.47
2007	Tucsn	AAA	53	0	0	22	66.2	268	47	19	14	5	4	2	2	26	1	68	3	0	6	2	.750	0	4- -	-	2.46	1.89
2008	Tucsn	AAA	51	0	0	37	70.1	321	71	41	33	5	1	4	4	40	2	68	10	0	6	4	.600	0	5- -	-	4.71	4.22
2007	Ari	NL	18	0	0	6	14.2	71	17	15	15	2	1	1	1	13	1	9	1	0	0	1	1.000	0	0-0	3	7.79	9.20
2008	Ari	NL	7	0	0	0	9.1	38	9	6	5	0	1	0	1	4	0	5	0	0	0	0	-	0	0-0	0	4.01	4.82
2 ML YEARS			25	0	0	6	24.0	109	26	21	20	2	2	1	2	17	1	14	1	0	1	0	1.000	0	0-0	3	6.25	7.50

Mike Pelfrey

Pitches: R **Bats:** R **Pos:** SP-32   **Ht:** 6'7" **Wt:** 230 **Born:** 1/14/1984 **Age:** 25

			HOW MUCH HE PITCHED						WHAT HE GAVE UP													THE RESULTS							
Year	Team	Lg	G	GS	CG	GF	IP	BFP	H	R	ER	HR	SH	SF	HB	TBB	IBB	SO	WP	Bk	W	L	Pct	ShO	Sv-Op	Hld	ERC	ERA
2006	NYM	NL	4	4	0	0	21.1	99	25	14	13	1	1	1	3	12	0	13	2	0	2	1	.667	0	0-0	0	6.05	5.48
2007	NYM	NL	15	13	0	0	72.2	342	85	47	45	6	6	3	9	39	1	45	3	0	3	8	.273	0	0-0	0	5.99	5.57
2008	NYM	NL	32	32	2	0	200.2	851	209	86	83	12	11	5	13	64	1	110	2	0	13	11	.542	0	0-0	0	4.04	3.72
3 ML YEARS			51	49	2	0	294.2	1292	319	147	141	19	18	9	25	115	2	168	7	0	18	20	.474	0	0-0	0	4.65	4.31

Brayan Pena

Bats: B **Throws:** R **Pos:** PH-14   **Ht:** 5'11" **Wt:** 210 **Born:** 1/7/1982 **Age:** 27

			BATTING																		BASERUNNING				AVERAGES		
Year	Team	Lg	G	AB	H	2B	3B	HR	(Hm	Rd)	TB	R	RBI	RC	TBB	IBB	SO	HBP	SH	SF	SB	CS	SB%	GDP	Avg	OBP	Slg
2008	Omha*	AAA	60	234	71	17	1	6	(-	-)	108	33	31	42	26	1	17	2	3	1	7	3	.70	8	.303	.376	.462
2005	Atl	NL	18	39	7	2	0	0	(0	0)	9	2	4	0	1	1	7	0	0	0	0	0	-	0	.179	.200	.231
2006	Atl	NL	23	41	11	2	0	1	(0	1)	16	9	5	4	2	0	5	0	0	0	0	0	-	2	.268	.302	.390
2007	Atl	NL	16	33	7	0	0	1	(1	0)	10	2	3	0	0	0	3	0	0	0	0	1	.00	2	.212	.212	.303
2008	Atl	NL	14	14	4	1	0	0	(0	0)	5	3	0	0	1	0	2	0	0	0	0	0	-	0	.286	.333	.357
4 ML YEARS			71	127	29	5	0	2	(1	1)	40	16	12	4	4	1	17	0	0	0	0	1	.00	5	.228	.252	.315

Carlos Pena

Bats: L **Throws:** L **Pos:** 1B-132; DH-5; PH-2   **Ht:** 6'2" **Wt:** 215 **Born:** 5/17/1978 **Age:** 31

			BATTING																		BASERUNNING				AVERAGES		
Year	Team	Lg	G	AB	H	2B	3B	HR	(Hm	Rd)	TB	R	RBI	RC	TBB	IBB	SO	HBP	SH	SF	SB	CS	SB%	GDP	Avg	OBP	Slg
2008	VeroB*	A+	1	4	0	0	0	0	(-	-)	0	0	1	0	1	0	0	0	0	0	0	0	-	0	.000	.200	.000
2001	Tex	AL	22	62	16	4	1	3	(2	1)	31	6	12	11	10	0	17	0	0	0	0	0	-	1	.258	.361	.500
2002	2 Tms	AL	115	397	96	17	4	19	(10	9)	178	43	52	56	41	0	111	3	0	2	2	2	.50	7	.242	.316	.448
2003	Det	AL	131	452	112	21	6	18	(8	10)	199	51	50	61	53	1	123	6	1	4	4	5	.44	6	.248	.332	.440
2004	Det	AL	142	481	116	22	4	27	(10	17)	227	89	82	73	70	2	146	3	2	5	7	1	.88	11	.241	.338	.472
2005	Det	AL	79	260	61	9	0	18	(14	4)	124	37	44	40	31	2	95	4	0	0	0	1	.00	3	.235	.325	.477
2006	Bos	AL	18	33	9	2	0	1	(1	0)	14	3	3	3	4	0	10	0	0	0	0	0	-	1	.273	.351	.424
2007	TB	AL	148	490	138	29	1	46	(23	23)	307	99	121	114	103	10	142	10	1	8	1	0	1.00	7	.282	.411	.627
2008	TB	AL	139	490	121	24	2	31	(14	17)	242	76	102	92	96	7	166	12	0	9	1	1	.50	6	.247	.377	.494
02	Oak	AL	40	124	27	4	0	7	(5	2)	52	12	16	17	15	0	38	1	0	1	0	0	-	2	.218	.305	.419
02	Det	AL	75	273	69	13	4	12	(5	7)	126	31	36	39	26	0	73	2	0	1	2	2	.50	5	.253	.321	.462
8 ML YEARS			794	2665	669	128	18	163	(82	81)	1322	404	466	450	408	22	810	38	4	28	15	10	.60	42	.251	.355	.496

Tony Pena

Pitches: R Bats: R Pos: RP-72   Ht: 6'2" Wt: 219 Born: 1/9/1982 Age: 27

Year	Team	Lg	G	GS	CG	GF	IP	BFP	H	R	ER	HR	SH	SF	HB	TBB	IBB	SO	WP	Bk	W	L	Pct	ShO	Sv-Op	Hld	ERC	ERA
2006	Ari	NL	25	0	0	6	30.2	135	36	21	19	6	2	1	0	8	0	21	1	0	3	4	.429	0	1-1	2	5.12	5.58
2007	Ari	NL	75	0	0	13	85.1	344	63	36	31	8	1	3	5	31	4	63	3	1	5	4	.556	0	2-5	30	2.71	3.27
2008	Ari	NL	72	0	0	20	72.2	313	80	38	35	5	4	4	3	17	5	52	4	0	3	2	.600	0	3-8	23	3.79	4.33
	Postseason		5	0	0	1	5.1	17	3	0	0	0	0	0	0	0	0	7	0	0	0	0	-	0	0-0	1	0.75	0.00
	3 ML YEARS		172	0	0	39	188.2	792	179	95	85	19	7	8	8	56	9	136	8	1	11	10	.524	0	6-14	55	3.50	4.05

Tony F Pena

Bats: R Throws: R Pos: SS-94; PR-5; PH-3; DH-1   Ht: 6'2" Wt: 180 Born: 3/23/1981 Age: 28

									BATTING												BASERUNNING				AVERAGES		
Year	Team	Lg	G	AB	H	2B	3B	HR	(Hm	Rd)	TB	R	RBI	RC	TBB	IBB	SO	HBP	SH	SF	SB	CS	SB%	GDP	Avg	OBP	Slg
2006	Atl	NL	40	44	10	2	0	1	(1	0)	15	12	3	3	2	1	10	0	0	0	0	0	-	1	.227	.261	.341
2007	KC	AL	152	509	136	25	7	2	(1	1)	181	58	47	48	10	0	78	4	8	5	5	6	.45	13	.267	.284	.356
2008	KC	AL	95	225	38	4	1	1	(0	1)	47	22	14	7	6	2	49	0	2	2	3	1	.75	4	.169	.189	.209
	3 ML YEARS		287	778	184	31	8	4	(2	2)	243	92	64	58	18	3	137	4	10	7	8	7	.53	18	.237	.255	.312

Wily Mo Pena

Bats: R Throws: R Pos: LF-54; PH-9; DH-2   Ht: 6'3" Wt: 268 Born: 1/23/1982 Age: 27

									BATTING												BASERUNNING				AVERAGES		
Year	Team	Lg	G	AB	H	2B	3B	HR	(Hm	Rd)	TB	R	RBI	RC	TBB	IBB	SO	HBP	SH	SF	SB	CS	SB%	GDP	Avg	OBP	Slg
2008	Clmbs*	AAA	1	2	0	0	0	0	(-	-)	0	0	0	0	0	0	2	0	0	0	0	0	-	0	.000	.000	.000
2002	Cin	NL	13	18	4	0	0	1	(1	0)	7	1	1	1	0	0	11	0	0	0	0	0	-	0	.222	.222	.389
2003	Cin	NL	80	165	36	6	1	5	(1	4)	59	20	16	14	12	2	53	3	1	0	3	2	.60	2	.218	.283	.358
2004	Cin	NL	110	336	87	10	1	26	(13	13)	177	45	66	54	22	1	108	6	0	0	5	2	.71	7	.259	.316	.527
2005	Cin	NL	99	311	79	17	0	19	(11	8)	153	42	51	40	20	0	116	3	0	1	2	1	.67	7	.254	.304	.492
2006	Bos	AL	84	276	83	15	2	11	(5	6)	135	36	42	39	20	0	90	3	0	5	0	1	.00	7	.301	.349	.489
2007	2 Tms		110	289	73	13	1	13	(3	10)	127	42	39	31	22	2	94	6	0	0	2	1	.67	7	.253	.319	.439
2008	Was	NL	64	195	40	6	0	2	(2	0)	52	10	10	9	10	0	48	0	0	1	0	1	.00	5	.205	.243	.267
07	Bos	AL	73	156	34	9	1	5	(1	4)	60	18	17	11	14	0	58	2	0	0	0	1	.00	5	.218	.291	.385
07	Was	NL	37	133	39	4	0	8	(2	6)	67	24	22	20	8	2	36	4	0	0	2	0	1.00	2	.293	.352	.504
	7 ML YEARS		560	1590	402	67	5	77	(36	41)	710	196	225	188	106	5	520	21	1	7	12	8	.60	35	.253	.307	.447

Hunter Pence

Bats: R Throws: R Pos: RF-156; PH-2   Ht: 6'4" Wt: 210 Born: 4/13/1983 Age: 26

									BATTING												BASERUNNING				AVERAGES		
Year	Team	Lg	G	AB	H	2B	3B	HR	(Hm	Rd)	TB	R	RBI	RC	TBB	IBB	SO	HBP	SH	SF	SB	CS	SB%	GDP	Avg	OBP	Slg
2004	TriCity	A-	51	199	59	18	1	8	(-	-)	103	36	37	37	23	1	30	1	0	2	3	5	.38	4	.296	.369	.518
2005	Lxngtn	A	80	302	102	14	3	25	(-	-)	197	59	60	77	38	2	53	1	0	0	8	3	.73	2	.338	.413	.652
2005	Salem	A+	41	151	46	8	1	6	(-	-)	74	24	30	27	18	0	37	0	0	2	1	2	.33	6	.305	.374	.490
2006	CpChr	AA	136	523	148	31	8	28	(-	-)	279	97	95	102	60	6	109	3	1	5	17	4	.81	11	.283	.357	.533
2007	RdRck	AAA	25	95	31	11	1	3	(-	-)	53	17	21	20	10	0	15	0	0	1	2	0	1.00	4	.326	.387	.558
2007	Hou	NL	108	456	147	30	9	17	(7	10)	246	57	69	77	26	0	95	1	0	1	11	5	.69	10	.322	.360	.539
2008	Hou	NL	157	595	160	34	4	25	(14	11)	277	78	83	82	40	2	124	4	0	3	11	10	.52	14	.269	.318	.466
	2 ML YEARS		265	1051	307	64	13	42	(21	21)	523	135	152	159	66	2	219	5	0	4	22	15	.59	24	.292	.336	.498

Cliff Pennington

Bats: B Throws: R Pos: 2B-16; SS-10; 3B-9; PR-3   Ht: 5'11" Wt: 188 Born: 6/15/1984 Age: 25

									BATTING												BASERUNNING				AVERAGES		
Year	Team	Lg	G	AB	H	2B	3B	HR	(Hm	Rd)	TB	R	RBI	RC	TBB	IBB	SO	HBP	SH	SF	SB	CS	SB%	GDP	Avg	OBP	Slg
2005	Kane	A	69	290	80	15	0	3	(-	-)	104	49	29	44	39	0	47	2	2	1	25	6	.81	4	.276	.364	.359
2006	Stcktn	A+	46	177	36	7	0	2	(-	-)	49	36	21	17	24	0	35	1	0	0	7	1	.88	5	.203	.302	.277
2006	As	R	9	28	13	3	1	0	(-	-)	18	3	6	8	4	0	2	0	0	0	0	0	-	0	.464	.531	.643
2007	Stcktn	A+	68	286	73	17	3	6	(-	-)	114	50	36	44	43	2	54	0	0	4	9	2	.82	2	.255	.348	.399
2007	Mdland	AA	70	271	68	13	2	2	(-	-)	91	41	21	35	38	0	35	1	2	2	8	2	.80	5	.251	.343	.336
2008	Mdland	AA	50	204	53	7	2	0	(-	-)	64	42	18	32	39	0	36	0	1	0	20	1	.95	7	.260	.379	.314
2008	Scrmto	AAA	65	236	70	9	3	2	(-	-)	91	47	16	45	54	2	34	0	3	1	11	5	.69	2	.297	.426	.386
2008	Oak	AL	36	99	24	5	0	0	(0	0)	29	14	9	12	13	0	18	2	2	1	4	1	.80	1	.242	.339	.293

Brad Penny

Pitches: R Bats: R Pos: SP-17; RP-2   Ht: 6'4" Wt: 260 Born: 5/24/1978 Age: 31

Year	Team	Lg	G	GS	CG	GF	IP	BFP	H	R	ER	HR	SH	SF	HB	TBB	IBB	SO	WP	Bk	W	L	Pct	ShO	Sv-Op	Hld	ERC	ERA
2008	LsVgs*	AAA	1	1	0	0	4.0	19	6	2	2	0	1	0	0	1	0	4	0	0	0	0	0--	0	5.46	4.50
2000	Fla	NL	23	22	0	0	119.2	529	120	70	64	13	6	2	5	60	4	80	4	1	8	7	.533	0	0-0	0	4.70	4.81
2001	Fla	NL	31	31	1	0	205.0	833	183	92	84	15	8	2	7	54	3	154	2	0	10	10	.500	1	0-0	0	2.96	3.69
2002	Fla	NL	24	24	1	0	129.1	574	148	76	67	18	6	4	1	50	7	93	4	0	8	7	.533	1	0-0	0	5.08	4.66
2003	Fla	NL	32	32	0	0	196.1	811	195	96	90	21	7	5	3	56	6	138	3	4	14	10	.583	0	0-0	0	3.73	4.13
2004	2 Tms	NL	24	24	0	0	143.0	590	130	55	50	12	3	3	3	45	6	111	5	0	9	10	.474	0	0-0	0	3.20	3.15
2005	LAD	NL	29	29	1	0	175.1	738	185	78	76	17	7	1	3	41	2	122	3	0	7	9	.438	0	0-0	0	3.77	3.90
2006	LAD	NL	34	33	0	0	189.0	813	206	94	91	19	8	3	9	54	4	148	6	0	16	9	.640	0	0-0	1	4.32	4.33
2007	LAD	NL	33	33	0	0	208.0	865	199	75	70	9	13	9	5	73	2	135	6	0	16	4	.800	0	0-0	0	3.41	3.03
2008	LAD	NL	19	17	0	1	94.2	426	112	68	66	13	10	2	3	42	0	51	1	1	6	9	.400	0	0-0	0	5.82	6.27

Year	Team	Lg	G	GS	CG	GF	IP	BFP	H	R	ER	HR	SH	SF	HB	TBB	IBB	SO	WP	Bk	W	L	Pct	ShO	Sv-Op Hld	ERC	ERA
04	Fla	NL	21	21	0	0	131.1	545	124	50	46	10	3	3	3	39	6	105	5	0	8	8	.500	0	0-0 0	3.26	3.15
04	LAD	NL	3	3	0	0	11.2	45	6	5	4	2	0	0	0	6	0	6	0	0	1	2	.333	0	0-0 0	2.51	3.09
	Postseason		8	4	0	0	23.0	106	31	17	16	3	2	1	0	11	1	14	0	0	3	2	.600	0	0-1 0	6.81	6.26
	9 ML YEARS		249	245	3	1	1460.1	6179	1478	704	658	137	68	31	39	475	34	1032	34	6	94	75	.556	2	0-0 1	3.92	4.06

Jhonny Peralta

Bats: R **Throws:** R **Pos:** SS-146; DH-6; PH-3; 3B-1   **Ht:** 6'1" **Wt:** 210 **Born:** 5/28/1982 **Age:** 27

						BATTING															BASERUNNING				AVERAGES		
Year	Team	Lg	G	AB	H	2B	3B	HR	(Hm	Rd)	TB	R	RBI	RC	TBB	IBB	SO	HBP	SH	SF	SB	CS	SB%	GDP	Avg	OBP	Slg
2003	Cle	AL	77	242	55	10	1	4	(3	1)	79	24	21	24	20	0	65	4	2	2	1	3	.25	5	.227	.295	.326
2004	Cle	AL	8	25	6	1	0	0	(0	0)	7	2	2	2	3	0	6	0	0	0	0	1	.00	0	.240	.321	.280
2005	Cle	AL	141	504	147	35	4	24	(14	10)	262	82	78	87	58	3	128	3	1	4	0	2	.00	12	.292	.366	.520
2006	Cle	AL	149	569	146	28	3	13	(7	6)	219	84	68	66	56	0	152	1	3	3	0	1	.00	19	.257	.323	.385
2007	Cle	AL	152	574	155	27	1	21	(16	5)	247	87	72	85	61	2	146	4	1	7	4	4	.50	12	.270	.341	.430
2008	Cle	AL	154	605	167	42	4	23	(11	12)	286	104	89	84	48	2	126	4	2	5	3	1	.75	26	.276	.331	.473
	Postseason		11	42	14	5	0	2	(1	1)	25	6	10	9	5	0	11	0	0	1	1	0	1.00	2	.333	.396	.595
	6 ML YEARS		681	2519	676	143	13	85	(51	34)	1100	383	330	348	246	7	623	16	9	21	8	12	.40	74	.268	.335	.437

Joel Peralta

Pitches: R **Bats:** R **Pos:** RP-40   **Ht:** 5'11" **Wt:** 180 **Born:** 3/23/1976 **Age:** 33

					HOW MUCH HE PITCHED						WHAT HE GAVE UP									THE RESULTS						
Year	Team	Lg	G	GS	CG	GF	IP	BFP	H	R	ER	HR	SH	SF	HB	TBB	IBB	SO	WP	Bk	W	L	Pct	ShO	Sv-Op Hld	ERC	ERA
2008	Omha*	AAA	10	0	0	5	18.2		9	0	0	0	0	0	0	6	0	19	0	0	1	0	1.000	0	2-- -	1.07	0.00
2005	LAA	AL	28	0	0	10	34.2	145	28	15	15	6	2	1	0	14	2	30	2	0	1	0	1.000	0	0-0 0	3.40	3.89
2006	KC	AL	64	0	0	21	73.2	304	74	37	36	10	1	3	2	17	2	57	5	0	1	3	.250	0	1-3 17	3.80	4.40
2007	KC	AL	62	0	0	18	87.2	366	93	39	37	9	2	4	2	19	5	66	2	0	1	3	.250	0	1-5 7	3.75	3.80
2008	KC	AL	40	0	0	12	52.2	224	56	37	35	15	1	3	2	14	0	38	1	0	1	2	.333	0	0-1 1	5.38	5.98
	4 ML YEARS		194	0	0	61	248.2	1039	251	128	123	40	6	11	6	64	9	191	10	0	4	8	.333	0	2-9 25	4.05	4.45

Troy Percival

Pitches: R **Bats:** R **Pos:** RP-50   **Ht:** 6'3" **Wt:** 240 **Born:** 8/9/1969 **Age:** 39

					HOW MUCH HE PITCHED						WHAT HE GAVE UP									THE RESULTS						
Year	Team	Lg	G	GS	CG	GF	IP	BFP	H	R	ER	HR	SH	SF	HB	TBB	IBB	SO	WP	Bk	W	L	Pct	ShO	Sv-Op Hld	ERC	ERA
1995	LAA	AL	62	0	0	16	74.0	284	37	19	16	6	4	1	1	26	2	94	2	2	3	2	.600	0	3-6 29	1.44	1.95
1996	LAA	AL	62	0	0	52	74.0	291	38	20	19	8	2	1	2	31	4	100	2	0	0	2	.000	0	36-39 2	1.76	2.31
1997	LAA	AL	55	0	0	46	52.0	224	40	20	20	6	1	2	4	22	2	72	5	0	5	5	.500	0	27-31 0	3.15	3.46
1998	LAA	AL	67	0	0	60	66.2	287	45	31	27	5	3	2	3	37	4	87	3	0	2	7	.222	0	42-48 0	2.74	3.65
1999	LAA	AL	60	0	0	50	57.0	230	38	24	24	9	0	1	3	22	0	58	3	0	4	6	.400	0	31-39 0	2.83	3.79
2000	LAA	AL	54	0	0	45	50.0	221	42	27	25	7	3	2	2	30	4	49	1	0	5	5	.500	0	32-42 0	4.24	4.50
2001	LAA	AL	57	0	0	50	57.2	230	39	19	17	3	1	0	2	18	1	71	2	0	4	2	.667	0	39-42 0	1.90	2.65
2002	LAA	AL	58	0	0	50	56.1	228	38	12	12	5	0	1	0	25	1	68	5	0	4	1	.800	0	40-44 0	2.45	1.92
2003	LAA	AL	52	0	0	49	49.1	206	33	22	19	7	0	1	3	23	1	48	1	0	0	5	.000	0	33-37 0	2.99	3.47
2004	LAA	AL	52	0	0	48	49.2	211	43	19	16	7	0	2	3	19	3	33	2	0	2	3	.400	0	33-38 0	3.67	2.90
2005	Det	AL	26	0	0	23	25.0	107	19	16	16	7	1	1	2	11	3	20	0	0	1	3	.250	0	8-11 0	4.17	5.76
2007	StL	NL	34	1	0	9	40.0	150	24	8	8	3	0	0	0	10	0	36	2	0	3	0	1.000	0	0-0 3	1.52	1.80
2008	TB	AL	50	0	0	38	45.2	194	29	26	23	9	1	2	1	27	0	38	2	0	2	1	.667	0	28-32 4	3.50	4.53
	Postseason		9	0	0	9	9.2	39	8	3	3	1	0	0	1	1	0	10	0	0	0	0	-	0	7-7 0	2.42	2.79
	13 ML YEARS		689	1	0	536	697.1	2863	465	263	242	82	16	16	26	301	25	774	30	2	35	42	.455	0	352-409 38	2.61	3.12

Chris Perez

Pitches: R **Bats:** R **Pos:** RP-41   **Ht:** 6'4" **Wt:** 225 **Born:** 7/1/1985 **Age:** 23

					HOW MUCH HE PITCHED						WHAT HE GAVE UP									THE RESULTS						
Year	Team	Lg	G	GS	CG	GF	IP	BFP	H	R	ER	HR	SH	SF	HB	TBB	IBB	SO	WP	Bk	W	L	Pct	ShO	Sv-Op Hld	ERC	ERA
2006	QuadC	A	25	0	0	21	29.1	126	20	9	6	0	1	1	4	19	0	32	9	0	2	0	1.000	0	12-- -	3.13	1.84
2007	Sprgfld	AA	39	0	0	37	40.2	172	17	11	11	3	1	0	8	28	0	62	2	0	2	0	1.000	0	27-- -	2.61	2.43
2007	Memp	AAA	15	0	0	15	14.0	58	6	7	7	2	2	0	1	13	0	15	2	0	0	1	.000	0	9-- -	3.75	4.50
2008	Memp	AAA	26	0	0	21	25.1	105	18	9	9	3	1	0	1	12	0	38	4	0	1	1	.500	0	11-- -	3.08	3.20
2008	StL	NL	41	0	0	23	41.2	177	34	18	16	5	1	3	1	22	0	42	2	0	3	3	.500	0	7-11 6	3.83	3.46

Fernando Perez

Bats: B **Throws:** R **Pos:** CF-15; LF-8; PH-3; PR-3; RF-2   **Ht:** 6'1" **Wt:** 195 **Born:** 4/28/1983 **Age:** 26

						BATTING															BASERUNNING				AVERAGES		
Year	Team	Lg	G	AB	H	2B	3B	HR	(Hm	Rd)	TB	R	RBI	RC	TBB	IBB	SO	HBP	SH	SF	SB	CS	SB%	GDP	Avg	OBP	Slg
2004	HudVal	A-	69	267	62	8	5	2	(-	-)	86	46	20	32	30	0	70	3	1	3	24	4	.86	0	.232	.314	.322
2005	SWMch	A	134	522	151	17	13	6	(-	-)	212	93	48	85	58	0	80	3	6	5	57	17	.77	14	.289	.361	.406
2006	Visalia	A+	133	547	168	19	9	4	(-	-)	217	123	56	94	78	0	134	6	8	2	33	16	.67	5	.307	.398	.397
2007	Mont	AA	102	393	121	24	10	8	(-	-)	189	84	33	82	76	0	104	2	5	0	32	18	.64	2	.308	.423	.481
2008	Drham	AAA	129	511	147	17	11	5	(-	-)	201	86	36	80	58	2	156	2	5	3	43	12	.78	3	.288	.361	.393
2008	TB	AL	23	60	15	2	0	3	(2	1)	26	18	8	10	8	1	16	1	3	0	5	0	1.00	3	.250	.348	.433

Odalis Perez

Pitches: L **Bats:** L **Pos:** SP-30   **Ht:** 6'0" **Wt:** 212 **Born:** 6/11/1977 **Age:** 32

		HOW MUCH HE PITCHED						WHAT HE GAVE UP												THE RESULTS							
Year Team	Lg	G	GS	CG	GF	IP	BFP	H	R	ER	HR	SH	SF	HB	TBB	IBB	SO	WP	Bk	W	L	Pct	ShO	Sv-Op	Hld	ERC	ERA
2008 Ptomc*	A+	1	1	0	0	4.0	15	3	1	1	0	0	0	0	0	0	5	0	0	0	0	-	0	0--	-	1.13	2.25
1998 Atl	NL	10	0	0	0	10.2	45	10	5	5	1	0	0	0	4	0	5	0	0	0	1	.000	0	0-1	5	3.60	4.22
1999 Atl	NL	18	17	0	0	93.0	424	100	65	62	12	3	4	1	53	2	82	5	3	4	6	.400	0	0-0	0	5.42	6.00
2001 Atl	NL	24	16	0	1	95.1	418	108	55	52	7	3	3	1	39	0	71	2	3	7	8	.467	0	0-0	0	4.79	4.91
2002 LAD	NL	32	32	4	0	222.1	869	182	76	74	21	13	7	4	38	5	155	2	3	15	10	.600	2	0-0	0	2.31	3.00
2003 LAD	NL	30	30	0	0	185.1	772	191	98	93	28	5	3	3	46	4	141	2	1	12	12	.500	0	0-0	0	4.07	4.52
2004 LAD	NL	31	31	0	0	196.1	787	180	76	71	26	16	3	3	44	4	128	2	2	7	6	.538	0	0-0	0	3.26	3.25
2005 LAD	NL	19	19	0	0	108.2	453	109	59	55	13	8	1	0	28	2	74	3	0	7	8	.467	0	0-0	0	3.65	4.56
2006 2 Tms	NL	32	20	0	6	126.1	573	169	93	87	18	4	7	3	31	2	81	6	2	6	8	.429	0	0-1	0	5.77	6.20
2007 KC	AL	26	26	0	0	137.1	626	178	90	85	14	6	7	4	50	5	64	3	0	8	11	.421	0	0-0	0	5.77	5.57
2008 Was	NL	30	30	0	0	159.2	711	182	87	77	22	12	1	8	55	4	119	5	2	7	12	.368	0	0-0	0	5.07	4.34
06 LAD	NL	20	8	0	6	59.1	275	89	49	45	9	1	2	2	13	1	33	4	1	4	4	.500	0	0-1	0	6.85	6.83
06 KC	AL	12	12	0	0	67.0	298	80	44	42	9	3	5	1	18	1	48	2	1	2	4	.333	0	0-0	0	4.86	5.64
Postseason		5	2	0	1	6.0	38	13	10	10	4	1	0	0	9	1	4	0	0	1	1	.500	0	0-0	0	24.43	15.00
10 ML YEARS		252	221	4	7	1335.0	5678	1409	704	661	162	70	36	27	388	28	920	30	16	73	82	.471	2	0-2	5	4.17	4.46

Oliver Perez

Pitches: L **Bats:** L **Pos:** SP-34   **Ht:** 6'3" **Wt:** 217 **Born:** 8/15/1981 **Age:** 27

		HOW MUCH HE PITCHED						WHAT HE GAVE UP												THE RESULTS							
Year Team	Lg	G	GS	CG	GF	IP	BFP	H	R	ER	HR	SH	SF	HB	TBB	IBB	SO	WP	Bk	W	L	Pct	ShO	Sv-Op	Hld	ERC	ERA
2002 SD	NL	16	15	0	0	90.0	387	71	37	35	13	5	3	5	48	1	94	3	0	4	5	.444	0	0-0	0	3.93	3.50
2003 2 Tms	NL	24	24	0	0	126.2	579	129	80	77	22	5	2	4	77	3	141	7	1	4	10	.286	0	0-0	0	5.66	5.47
2004 Pit	NL	30	30	2	0	196.0	805	145	71	65	22	9	5	9	81	2	239	2	1	12	10	.545	1	0-0	0	2.99	2.98
2005 Pit	NL	20	20	0	0	103.0	471	102	68	67	23	5	4	6	70	1	97	3	0	7	5	.583	0	0-0	0	6.44	5.85
2006 2 Tms	NL	22	22	1	0	112.2	529	129	90	82	20	5	10	6	68	0	102	5	1	3	13	.188	1	0-0	0	6.62	6.55
2007 NYM	NL	29	29	0	0	177.0	765	153	90	70	22	4	7	7	79	1	174	6	0	15	10	.600	0	0-0	0	3.76	3.56
2008 NYM	NL	34	34	0	0	194.0	847	167	100	91	24	9	7	11	105	4	180	9	1	10	7	.588	0	0-0	0	4.21	4.22
03 SD	NL	19	19	0	0	103.2	473	103	65	62	20	4	2	3	65	2	117	6	1	4	7	.364	0	0-0	0	5.74	5.38
03 Pit	NL	5	5	0	0	23.0	106	26	15	15	2	1	0	1	12	1	24	1	0	0	3	.000	0	0-0	0	5.29	5.87
06 Pit	NL	15	15	0	0	76.0	364	88	64	56	13	5	8	3	51	0	61	4	1	2	10	.167	0	0-0	0	6.85	6.63
06 NYM	NL	7	7	1	0	36.2	165	41	26	26	7	0	2	3	17	0	41	1	0	1	3	.250	1	0-0	0	6.16	6.38
Postseason		2	2	0	0	11.2	50	13	6	6	3	2	0	1	3	1	7	0	0	1	0	1.000	0	0-0	0	5.61	4.63
7 ML YEARS		175	174	3	0	999.1	4383	896	536	487	146	42	38	48	528	12	1027	35	4	55	60	.478	2	0-0	0	4.50	4.39

Rafael Perez

Pitches: L **Bats:** L **Pos:** RP-73   **Ht:** 6'3" **Wt:** 195 **Born:** 5/15/1982 **Age:** 27

		HOW MUCH HE PITCHED						WHAT HE GAVE UP												THE RESULTS							
Year Team	Lg	G	GS	CG	GF	IP	BFP	H	R	ER	HR	SH	SF	HB	TBB	IBB	SO	WP	Bk	W	L	Pct	ShO	Sv-Op	Hld	ERC	ERA
2006 Cle	AL	18	0	0	5	12.1	56	10	6	6	2	1	0	0	6	1	15	4	1	0	0	-	0	0-1	1	3.37	4.38
2007 Cle	AL	44	0	0	11	60.2	236	41	15	12	5	1	1	0	15	2	62	4	0	1	2	.333	0	1-2	12	1.74	1.78
2008 Cle	AL	73	0	0	14	76.1	313	67	32	30	8	2	0	2	23	3	86	3	0	4	4	.500	0	2-7	25	3.14	3.54
Postseason		6	0	0	2	7.0	34	10	9	6	3	0	0	0	3	0	6	0	0	1	0	1.000	0	0-0	0	9.36	7.71
3 ML YEARS		135	0	0	30	149.1	605	118	53	48	15	4	1	2	44	6	163	11	1	5	6	.455	0	3-10	38	2.56	2.89

Tomas Perez

Bats: B **Throws:** R **Pos:** 2B-5; PH-3; 3B-1   **Ht:** 5'11" **Wt:** 180 **Born:** 12/29/1973 **Age:** 35

		BATTING																			BASERUNNING				AVERAGES		
Year Team	Lg	G	AB	H	2B	3B	HR	(Hm	Rd)	TB	R	RBI	RC	TBB	IBB	SO	HBP	SH	SF	SB	CS	SB%	GDP	Avg	OBP	Slg
2008 RdRck*	AAA	79	306	84	15	5	1	(-	-)	112	32	25	36	22	1	44	1	4	6	1	6	.14	2	.275	.319	.366
1995 Tor	AL	41	98	24	3	1	1	(1	0)	32	12	8	7	7	0	18	0	0	1	0	1	.00	6	.245	.292	.327
1996 Tor	AL	91	295	74	13	4	1	(1	0)	98	24	19	28	25	0	29	1	6	1	1	2	.33	10	.251	.311	.332
1997 Tor	AL	40	123	24	3	2	0	(0	0)	31	9	9	8	11	0	28	1	3	0	1	1	.50	2	.195	.267	.252
1998 Tor	AL	6	9	1	0	0	0	(0	0)	1	1	0	0	1	0	3	0	1	0	0	0	-	1	.111	.200	.111
2000 Phi	NL	45	140	31	7	1	1	(0	1)	43	12	13	11	11	2	30	0	1	0	1	1	.50	3	.221	.278	.307
2001 Phi	NL	62	135	41	7	1	3	(2	1)	59	11	19	20	7	1	22	2	1	0	0	1	.00	3	.304	.347	.437
2002 Phi	NL	92	212	53	13	1	5	(2	3)	83	22	20	20	21	6	40	1	2	1	1	0	1.00	5	.250	.319	.392
2003 Phi	NL	125	298	79	18	1	5	(2	3)	114	39	33	29	23	11	54	0	4	2	0	1	.00	7	.265	.316	.383
2004 Phi	NL	86	176	38	13	2	6	(4	2)	73	22	21	20	9	2	44	1	3	1	0	0	-	3	.216	.257	.415
2005 Phi	NL	94	159	37	7	0	0	(0	0)	44	17	22	14	11	2	27	2	3	1	1	0	1.00	6	.233	.289	.277
2006 TB	AL	99	241	51	12	0	2	(2	0)	69	31	16	11	5	0	44	0	4	4	1	0	1.00	3	.212	.224	.286
2008 Hou	NL	8	10	2	0	0	0	(0	0)	2	1	0	0	0	0	2	0	0	0	0	0	-	0	.200	.200	.200
12 ML YEARS		789	1896	455	96	13	24	(14	10)	649	205	180	168	131	24	341	8	28	11	6	7	.46	47	.240	.290	.342

Glen Perkins

Pitches: L **Bats:** L **Pos:** SP-26   **Ht:** 6'0" **Wt:** 200 **Born:** 3/2/1983 **Age:** 26

		HOW MUCH HE PITCHED						WHAT HE GAVE UP												THE RESULTS							
Year Team	Lg	G	GS	CG	GF	IP	BFP	H	R	ER	HR	SH	SF	HB	TBB	IBB	SO	WP	Bk	W	L	Pct	ShO	Sv-Op	Hld	ERC	ERA
2008 Roch*	AAA	7	6	1	0	33.1	149	28	15	11	2	1	1	1	19	0	27	1	1	2	1	.667	1	0--	-	3.56	2.97
2006 Min	AL	4	0	0	1	5.2	20	3	1	1	0	0	0	0	0	0	6	0	0	0	0	-	0	0-0	1	0.60	1.59
2007 Min	AL	19	0	0	3	28.2	115	23	10	10	2	1	1	2	12	0	20	2	0	0	0	-	0	0-0	3	3.32	3.14
2008 Min	AL	26	26	0	0	151.0	661	183	81	74	25	7	4	3	39	0	74	2	1	12	4	.750	0	0-0	0	5.30	4.41
Postseason		1	0	0	0	0.1	3	2	0	0	0	0	0	0	0	0	0	0	0	0	0	-	0	0-0	0	39.65	0.00
3 ML YEARS		49	26	0	4	185.1	796	209	92	85	27	8	5	5	51	0	100	4	1	12	4	.750	0	0-0	4	4.79	4.13

Jason Perry

Bats: L **Throws:** R **Pos:** RF-4; PR-1   **Ht:** 6'0" **Wt:** 216 **Born:** 8/18/1980 **Age:** 28

								BATTING													BASERUNNING				AVERAGES		
Year	Team	Lg	G	AB	H	2B	3B	HR	(Hm	Rd)	TB	R	RBI	RC	TBB	IBB	SO	HBP	SH	SF	SB	CS	SB%	GDP	Avg	OBP	Slg
2002	MdHat	R+	30	106	45	6	2	10	(-	-)	85	25	36	36	12	2	19	6	0	0	0	2	.00	3	.425	.508	.802
2002	Dnedin	A+	13	45	13	3	0	1	(-	-)	19	7	5	8	5	0	11	3	0	1	0	0	-	0	.289	.389	.422
2003	Dnedin	A+	39	135	41	11	1	1	(-	-)	57	17	17	21	10	0	32	2	2	2	1	0	1.00	5	.304	.356	.422
2003	Mdest	A+	50	190	58	9	1	4	(-	-)	81	28	26	33	21	0	46	7	0	1	0	1	.00	5	.305	.393	.426
2004	Mdland	AA	28	81	16	5	1	1	(-	-)	26	11	11	7	4	0	23	5	1	1	3	1	.75	3	.198	.275	.321
2004	Mdland	A+	83	325	110	39	1	24	(-	-)	223	81	80	89	34	2	87	21	1	3	4	4	.50	5	.338	.431	.686
2005	Mdland	AA	124	435	112	21	4	22	(-	-)	207	68	77	72	45	0	126	13	0	4	1	4	.20	9	.257	.342	.476
2006	Mdland	AA	28	107	43	8	2	4	(-	-)	67	28	17	29	12	2	23	4	0	1	2	1	.67	2	.402	.476	.626
2006	Scrmto	AAA	90	318	80	15	2	8	(-	-)	123	36	47	39	23	0	84	4	2	3	3	2	.60	8	.252	.307	.387
2007	Mdland	AA	21	78	20	7	0	5	(-	-)	42	15	17	16	11	0	20	6	0	0	0	0	-	2	.256	.389	.538
2007	Scrmto	AAA	78	284	76	16	1	18	(-	-)	148	59	58	56	41	1	89	5	1	2	4	0	1.00	13	.268	.367	.521
2007	Toledo	AAA	16	49	9	3	0	2	(-	-)	18	10	3	6	8	0	16	1	0	0	0	0	-	0	.184	.310	.367
2008	Missi	AA	38	137	42	11	1	13	(-	-)	94	34	41	38	23	2	44	5	0	3	1	0	1.00	1	.307	.417	.686
2008	Rchmd	AAA	66	228	56	10	1	10	(-	-)	98	38	25	37	25	0	65	11	0	1	5	0	1.00	3	.246	.347	.430
2008	Atl	NL	4	17	2	0	1	0	(0	0)	4	0	1	0	0	0	4	0	0	0	0	0	-	1	.118	.118	.235

Gregorio Petit

Bats: R **Throws:** R **Pos:** SS-8; 2B-4; DH-2; PR-2   **Ht:** 5'10" **Wt:** 191 **Born:** 12/10/1984 **Age:** 24

								BATTING													BASERUNNING				AVERAGES		
Year	Team	Lg	G	AB	H	2B	3B	HR	(Hm	Rd)	TB	R	RBI	RC	TBB	IBB	SO	HBP	SH	SF	SB	CS	SB%	GDP	Avg	OBP	Slg
2003	As	R	32	117	31	6	0	0	(-	-)	37	13	12	11	10	0	22	0	2	0	3	5	.38	5	.265	.323	.316
2004	Vancvr	AAA	68	254	65	9	2	4	(-	-)	90	34	35	29	20	0	67	3	4	2	3	3	.50	9	.256	.315	.354
2005	Kane	A	87	287	83	10	4	9	(-	-)	128	55	33	46	26	0	44	1	3	1	8	2	.80	9	.289	.349	.446
2006	Stcktn	A+	137	519	133	25	7	8	(-	-)	196	71	63	63	38	0	96	5	9	5	22	13	.63	15	.256	.310	.378
2007	Mdland	AA	66	268	82	14	0	4	(-	-)	108	33	31	42	25	0	44	1	4	1	9	3	.75	5	.306	.366	.403
2007	Scrmto	AAA	67	235	65	12	0	2	(-	-)	83	20	28	28	16	0	48	3	3	3	1	2	.33	15	.277	.327	.353
2008	Scrmto	AAA	79	308	83	14	3	1	(-	-)	106	39	35	34	23	0	60	1	7	0	3	5	.38	11	.269	.322	.344
2008	Oak	AL	14	23	8	2	0	0	(0	0)	10	4	0	2	2	0	9	0	0	0	0	0	-	0	.348	.400	.435

Yusmeiro Petit

Pitches: R **Bats:** R **Pos:** RP-11; SP-8   **Ht:** 6'0" **Wt:** 253 **Born:** 11/22/1984 **Age:** 24

			HOW MUCH HE PITCHED						WHAT HE GAVE UP											THE RESULTS						
Year	Team	Lg	G	GS	CG	GF	IP	BFP	H	R	ER	HR	SH	SF	HB	TBB	IBB	SO	WP	Bk	W	L	Pct	ShO	Sv-Op Hld	ERC	ERA
2008	Tucsn*	AAA	11	11	0	0	60.0	249	64	34	32	7	3	1	0	8	0	67	2	0	3	3	.500	0	0- -	3.48	4.80
2006	Fla	NL	15	1	0	5	26.1	129	46	28	28	7	1	1	0	9	1	20	0	0	1	1	.500	0	0-0 0	10.07	9.57
2007	Ari	NL	14	10	0	2	57.0	243	58	30	29	12	1	1	0	18	1	40	0	1	3	4	.429	0	0-0 0	4.56	4.58
2008	Ari	NL	19	8	0	6	56.1	229	45	29	27	12	4	2	1	14	2	42	3	1	3	5	.375	0	0-0 0	3.08	4.31
	3 ML YEARS		48	19	0	13	139.2	601	149	87	84	31	6	4	1	41	4	102	3	2	7	10	.412	0	0-0 0	4.83	5.41

Andy Pettitte

Pitches: L **Bats:** L **Pos:** SP-33   **Ht:** 6'5" **Wt:** 225 **Born:** 6/15/1972 **Age:** 37

			HOW MUCH HE PITCHED						WHAT HE GAVE UP											THE RESULTS						
Year	Team	Lg	G	GS	CG	GF	IP	BFP	H	R	ER	HR	SH	SF	HB	TBB	IBB	SO	WP	Bk	W	L	Pct	ShO	Sv-Op Hld	ERC	ERA
1995	NYY	AL	31	26	3	1	175.0	745	183	86	81	15	4	5	1	63	3	114	8	1	12	9	.571	0	0-0 0	4.13	4.17
1996	NYY	AL	35	34	2	1	221.0	929	229	105	95	23	7	3	3	72	2	162	6	1	21	8	.724	0	0-0 0	4.14	3.87
1997	NYY	AL	35	35	4	0	240.1	986	233	86	77	7	6	2	3	65	0	166	7	0	18	7	.720	1	0-0 0	3.05	2.88
1998	NYY	AL	33	32	5	0	216.1	932	226	110	102	20	6	7	6	87	1	146	5	0	16	11	.593	0	0-0 0	4.46	4.24
1999	NYY	AL	31	31	0	0	191.2	851	216	105	100	20	6	6	3	89	3	121	3	1	14	11	.560	0	0-0 0	5.22	4.70
2000	NYY	AL	32	32	3	0	204.2	903	219	111	99	17	7	4	4	80	4	125	2	3	19	9	.679	1	0-0 0	4.32	4.35
2001	NYY	AL	31	31	2	0	200.2	858	224	103	89	14	8	7	6	41	3	164	2	2	15	10	.600	0	0-0 0	3.82	3.99
2002	NYY	AL	22	22	3	0	134.2	570	144	58	49	6	3	2	4	32	2	97	2	1	13	5	.722	1	0-0 0	3.55	3.27
2003	NYY	AL	33	33	1	0	208.1	896	227	109	93	21	5	5	1	50	3	180	5	0	21	8	.724	0	0-0 0	3.89	4.02
2004	Hou	NL	15	15	0	0	83.0	346	71	37	36	8	1	0	0	31	2	79	4	0	6	4	.600	0	0-0 0	3.12	3.90
2005	Hou	NL	33	33	0	0	222.1	875	188	66	59	17	10	4	3	41	0	171	2	0	17	9	.654	0	0-0 0	2.40	2.39
2006	Hou	NL	36	35	2	1	214.1	929	238	114	100	27	14	5	2	70	9	178	2	1	14	13	.519	1	0-0 0	4.58	4.20
2007	NYY	AL	36	34	0	0	215.1	916	238	106	97	16	5	9	1	69	1	141	3	0	15	9	.625	0	0-0 1	4.27	4.05
2008	NYY	AL	33	33	0	0	204.0	881	233	112	103	19	8	7	7	55	4	158	6	1	14	14	.500	0	0-0 0	4.45	4.54
	Postseason		35	35	0	0	218.1	923	235	100	96	24	11	6	3	60	3	139	3	1	14	9	.609	0	0-0 0	4.16	3.96
	14 ML YEARS		436	426	25	3	2731.2	11617	2869	1308	1180	230	90	66	44	845	37	2002	57	11	215	127	.629	4	0-0 1	3.96	3.89

Adam Pettyjohn

Pitches: L **Bats:** R **Pos:** RP-2; SP-1   **Ht:** 6'3" **Wt:** 200 **Born:** 6/11/1977 **Age:** 32

			HOW MUCH HE PITCHED						WHAT HE GAVE UP											THE RESULTS						
Year	Team	Lg	G	GS	CG	GF	IP	BFP	H	R	ER	HR	SH	SF	HB	TBB	IBB	SO	WP	Bk	W	L	Pct	ShO	Sv-Op Hld	ERC	ERA
1998	Jmstwn	A-	4	4	0	0	22.0	93	21	10	7	0	1	2	2	4	0	24	1	1	2	2	.500	0	0- -	2.62	2.86
1998	WMich	A	8	8	1	0	50.1	210	46	15	11	3	3	0	4	9	0	64	1	0	4	2	.667	1	0- -	2.76	1.97
1999	Lkland	A+	9	9	2	0	59.2	255	62	35	25	2	2	0	1	11	0	51	2	0	3	4	.429	0	0- -	2.98	3.77
1999	Jaxnvl	AA	20	20	0	0	126.2	548	134	75	66	13	3	5	8	35	0	92	4	0	9	5	.643	0	0- -	4.16	4.69
2000	Jaxnvl	AA	8	8	0	0	50.1	203	43	20	19	4	1	0	4	12	0	45	2	0	2	2	.500	0	0- -	2.91	3.40
2000	Toledo	AAA	7	7	0	0	39.0	182	45	34	29	5	2	3	2	22	0	23	1	0	0	4	.000	0	0- -	6.08	6.69
2001	Toledo	AAA	17	17	0	0	107.1	449	107	51	41	9	3	6	4	26	0	78	5	1	5	8	.385	0	0- -	3.49	3.44
2003	Erie	AA	19	10	1	5	81.0	340	87	39	36	9	-	-	3	18	0	49	0	-	1	4	.200	0	0- -	4.06	4.00
2004	Fresno	AAA	21	14	0	2	79.2	352	103	58	48	7	-	-	3	25	1	43	2	-	3	6	.333	0	0- -	5.63	5.42
2004	Scrmto	AAA	10	9	1	0	52.2	222	55	38	37	10	-	-	3	14	0	44	3	-	3	1	.750	0	0- -	4.73	6.32

218

			HOW MUCH HE PITCHED					WHAT HE GAVE UP											THE RESULTS							
Year	Team	Lg	G	GS	CG	GF	IP	BFP	H	R	ER	HR	SH	SF	HB	TBB	IBB	SO	WP	Bk	W	L	Pct	ShO	Sv-Op	Hld	ERC	ERA
2005	Long Beach	IND	16	16	3	0	110.1	457	109	53	48	11	9	1	9	23	3	73	3	1	10	2	.833	1	0- -	-	3.59	3.92
2006	SnAnt	AA	17	3	0	8	52.2	207	46	18	17	5	2	2	1	14	1	45	1	2	2	4	.333	0	1- -	-	3.04	2.91
2006	Long Beach	IND	2	2	0	0	11.0	46	10	4	2	0	1	0	0	3	0	11	0	0	1	1	.500	0	0- -	-	2.41	1.64
2006	Scrmto	AAA	11	9	0	1	63.0	281	74	34	32	6	3	3	1	21	1	43	0	0	3	2	.600	0	1- -	-	4.76	4.57
2007	Hntsvl	AA	11	11	0	0	56.2	244	61	31	28	5	3	0	1	15	0	54	2	0	4	2	.667	0	0- -	-	3.92	4.45
2007	Nashv	AAA	17	17	1	0	104.2	431	99	50	45	19	2	3	0	19	1	83	3	1	12	4	.750	1	0- -	-	3.37	3.87
2008	Lsville	AAA	28	28	0	0	174.1	740	188	97	89	20	9	6	7	43	0	95	3	0	15	6	.714	0	0- -	-	4.20	4.59
2001	Det	AL	16	9	0	1	65.0	293	81	48	42	10	3	3	4	21	2	40	2	0	1	6	.143	0	0-0	1	5.84	5.82
2008	Cin	NL	3	1	0	1	4.0	26	11	9	9	2	0	0	1	2	1	1	0	0	0	1	.000	0	0-0	0	21.60	20.25
2 ML YEARS			19	10	0	2	69.0	319	92	57	51	12	3	3	5	23	3	41	2	0	1	7	.125	0	0-0	1	6.61	6.65

Josh Phelps

Bats: R Throws: R Pos: PH-11; 1B-4; LF-3; RF-2; PR-1   Ht: 6'3" Wt: 225 Born: 5/12/1978 Age: 31

			BATTING																BASERUNNING				AVERAGES		
Year	Team	Lg	G	AB	H	2B	3B	HR	(Hm | Rd)	TB	R	RBI	RC	TBB	IBB	SO	HBP	SH	SF	SB	CS	SB%	GDP	Avg	OBP	Slg
2008	Memp*	AAA	126	461	134	31	2	31	(- | -)	262	90	97	97	56	4	109	7	0	4	2	2	.50	14	.291	.373	.568
2000	Tor	AL	1	1	0	0	0	0	(0 | 0)	0	0	0	0	0	0	1	0	0	0	0	0	-	0	.000	.000	.000
2001	Tor	AL	8	12	0	0	0	0	(0 | 0)	0	3	1	0	2	0	5	0	0	0	1	0	1.00	1	.000	.143	.000
2002	Tor	AL	74	265	82	20	1	15	(6 | 9)	149	41	58	52	19	0	82	3	0	0	0	0	-	7	.309	.362	.562
2003	Tor	AL	119	396	106	18	1	20	(11 | 9)	186	57	66	65	39	3	115	17	0	1	1	2	.33	12	.268	.358	.470
2004	2 Tms	AL	103	371	93	19	2	17	(9 | 8)	167	51	61	50	22	2	93	7	0	1	0	0	-	13	.251	.304	.450
2005	TB	AL	47	158	42	10	0	5	(4 | 1)	67	21	26	23	12	1	48	4	0	3	0	0	-	3	.266	.328	.424
2007	2 Tms		94	157	48	6	2	7	(2 | 5)	79	21	31	26	20	0	42	5	0	1	0	0	-	6	.306	.399	.503
2008	StL	NL	19	34	9	1	0	0	(0 | 0)	10	4	1	2	2	0	11	0	0	0	0	0	-	0	.265	.306	.294
04	Tor	AL	79	295	70	13	2	12	(7 | 5)	123	38	51	40	18	2	73	7	0	1	0	0	-	9	.237	.296	.417
04	Cle	AL	24	76	23	6	0	5	(2 | 3)	44	13	10	10	4	0	20	0	0	0	0	0	-	4	.303	.338	.579
07	NYY	AL	36	80	21	2	0	2	(1 | 1)	29	8	12	8	6	0	19	2	0	0	0	0	-	5	.263	.330	.363
07	Pit	NL	58	77	27	4	2	5	(1 | 4)	50	13	19	18	14	0	23	3	0	1	0	0	-	1	.351	.463	.649
8 ML YEARS			465	1394	380	74	6	64	(32 | 32)	658	198	244	218	116	6	397	36	0	6	2	2	.50	42	.273	.343	.472

Andy Phillips

Bats: R Throws: R Pos: PH-39; 3B-8; 2B-6; 1B-5; LF-2   Ht: 6'0" Wt: 210 Born: 4/6/1977 Age: 32

			BATTING																BASERUNNING				AVERAGES		
Year	Team	Lg	G	AB	H	2B	3B	HR	(Hm | Rd)	TB	R	RBI	RC	TBB	IBB	SO	HBP	SH	SF	SB	CS	SB%	GDP	Avg	OBP	Slg
2008	Lsville*	AAA	40	146	46	9	1	5	(- | -)	72	27	22	29	20	2	19	1	0	3	2	0	1.00	2	.315	.394	.493
2004	NYY	AL	5	8	2	0	0	1	(0 | 1)	5	1	2	1	0	0	1	0	0	0	0	0	-	2	.250	.250	.625
2005	NYY	AL	27	40	6	4	0	1	(1 | 0)	13	7	4	2	1	0	13	0	0	0	0	0	-	1	.150	.171	.325
2006	NYY	AL	110	246	59	11	3	7	(5 | 2)	97	30	29	22	15	0	56	0	0	2	3	2	.60	9	.240	.281	.394
2007	NYY	AL	61	185	54	7	1	2	(1 | 1)	69	27	25	23	12	0	26	2	6	2	0	3	.00	5	.292	.338	.373
2008	2 Tms		56	78	18	3	0	3	(3 | 0)	30	12	10	5	6	0	14	1	0	0	0	0	-	4	.231	.294	.385
08	Cin	NL	52	73	17	3	0	3	(3 | 0)	29	11	10	5	6	0	14	1	0	0	0	0	-	3	.233	.300	.397
08	NYM	NL	4	5	1	0	0	0	(0 | 0)	1	1	0	0	0	0	0	0	0	0	0	0	-	1	.200	.200	.200
Postseason			1	1	0	0	0	0	(0 | 0)	0	0	0	0	0	0	0	0	0	0	0	0	-	0	.000	.000	.000
5 ML YEARS			259	557	139	25	4	14	(10 | 4)	214	77	70	53	34	0	110	3	6	4	3	5	.38	20	.250	.294	.384

Brandon Phillips

Bats: R Throws: R Pos: 2B-140; PH-1   Ht: 6'0" Wt: 196 Born: 6/28/1981 Age: 28

			BATTING																BASERUNNING				AVERAGES		
Year	Team	Lg	G	AB	H	2B	3B	HR	(Hm | Rd)	TB	R	RBI	RC	TBB	IBB	SO	HBP	SH	SF	SB	CS	SB%	GDP	Avg	OBP	Slg
2002	Cle	AL	11	31	8	3	1	0	(0 | 0)	13	5	4	5	3	0	6	1	1	0	0	0	-	0	.258	.343	.419
2003	Cle	AL	112	370	77	18	1	6	(3 | 3)	115	36	33	22	14	0	77	3	5	1	4	5	.44	12	.208	.242	.311
2004	Cle	AL	6	22	4	2	0	0	(0 | 0)	6	1	1	0	2	0	5	0	0	0	0	2	.00	1	.182	.250	.273
2005	Cle	AL	6	9	0	0	0	0	(0 | 0)	0	1	0	0	0	0	4	0	0	0	0	0	-	0	.000	.000	.000
2006	Cin	NL	149	536	148	28	1	17	(9 | 8)	229	65	75	74	35	3	88	6	4	6	25	2	.93	19	.276	.324	.427
2007	Cin	NL	158	650	187	26	6	30	(17 | 13)	315	107	94	88	33	4	109	12	2	5	32	8	.80	26	.288	.331	.485
2008	Cin	NL	141	559	146	24	7	21	(13 | 8)	247	80	78	74	39	6	93	5	0	6	23	10	.70	13	.261	.312	.442
7 ML YEARS			583	2177	570	101	16	74	(42 | 32)	925	295	285	263	126	13	382	27	12	18	84	27	.76	71	.262	.308	.425

Paul Phillips

Bats: R Throws: R Pos: C-4; PH-1   Ht: 5'11" Wt: 205 Born: 4/15/1977 Age: 32

			BATTING																BASERUNNING				AVERAGES		
Year	Team	Lg	G	AB	H	2B	3B	HR	(Hm | Rd)	TB	R	RBI	RC	TBB	IBB	SO	HBP	SH	SF	SB	CS	SB%	GDP	Avg	OBP	Slg
2008	Charltt*	AAA	73	253	68	15	0	2	(- | -)	89	22	17	29	17	1	32	1	3	0	0	0	-	5	.269	.317	.352
2004	KC	AL	4	5	1	0	0	0	(0 | 0)	1	2	0	0	0	0	1	0	0	0	0	0	-	0	.200	.333	.200
2005	KC	AL	23	67	18	4	1	1	(0 | 1)	27	6	9	8	0	0	5	0	0	0	0	0	-	4	.269	.269	.403
2006	KC	AL	23	65	18	3	0	1	(0 | 1)	24	8	5	8	1	0	8	0	2	1	0	0	-	0	.277	.284	.369
2007	KC	AL	8	14	2	1	0	0	(0 | 0)	3	2	2	1	1	0	1	0	0	0	0	0	-	1	.143	.200	.214
2008	CWS	AL	4	2	0	0	0	0	(0 | 0)	0	0	0	0	0	0	1	0	0	0	0	0	-	0	.000	.000	.000
5 ML YEARS			62	153	39	8	1	2	(0 | 2)	55	18	16	17	2	0	16	1	2	1	0	0	-	5	.255	.268	.359

Felix Pie

Bats: L Throws: L Pos: CF-39; PH-7; PR-3; LF-1 **Ht: 6'2" Wt: 170 Born: 2/8/1985 Age: 24**

								BATTING													BASERUNNING				AVERAGES		
Year	Team	Lg	G	AB	H	2B	3B	HR	(Hm	Rd)	TB	R	RBI	RC	TBB	IBB	SO	HBP	SH	SF	SB	CS	SB%	GDP	Avg	OBP	Slg
2002	Cubs	R	55	218	70	16	13	4	(-	-)	124	42	37	47	21	1	47	4	1	4	17	8	.68	1	.321	.385	.569
2002	Boise	A-	2	8	1	1	0	0	(-	-)	2	1	1	0	1	0	1	0	0	0	0	0	-	0	.125	.222	.250
2003	Lansng	A	124	505	144	22	9	4	(-	-)	196	72	47	69	41	2	98	6	3	0	19	13	.59	3	.285	.346	.388
2004	Dytona	A+	106	415	125	17	10	8	(-	-)	186	79	47	70	39	2	113	5	7	5	32	16	.67	5	.301	.364	.448
2005	WTenn	AA	59	240	73	17	5	11	(-	-)	133	40	25	45	16	1	53	2	1	3	13	8	.62	0	.304	.349	.554
2006	Iowa	AAA	141	559	158	33	8	15	(-	-)	252	78	57	87	46	3	126	5	10	3	17	11	.61	11	.283	.341	.451
2007	Iowa	AAA	55	229	83	9	5	9	(-	-)	129	51	43	49	19	1	40	0	1	1	9	6	.60	3	.362	.410	.563
2008	Iowa	AAA	85	335	96	20	5	10	(-	-)	156	57	55	53	23	0	54	3	5	2	11	7	.61	3	.287	.336	.466
2008	Cubs	R	1	3	2	0	0	1	(-	-)	5	3	5	2	1	0	0	0	0	0	0	0	-	0	.667	.750	1.667
2007	ChC	NL	87	177	38	9	3	2	(0	2)	59	26	20	21	14	0	43	0	2	1	8	1	.89	0	.215	.271	.333
2008	ChC	NL	43	83	20	2	1	1	(1	0)	27	9	10	9	7	0	29	2	0	1	3	0	1.00	3	.241	.312	.325
	Postseason		1	1	0	0	0	0	(0	0)	0	0	0	0	0	0	1	0	0	0	0	0	-	0	.000	.000	.000
	2 ML YEARS		130	260	58	11	4	3	(1	2)	86	35	30	30	21	0	72	2	2	2	11	1	.92	3	.223	.284	.331

Juan Pierre

Bats: L Throws: L Pos: LF-84; PH-31; CF-18; DH-1; PR-1 **Ht: 5'11" Wt: 180 Born: 8/14/1977 Age: 31**

								BATTING													BASERUNNING				AVERAGES		
Year	Team	Lg	G	AB	H	2B	3B	HR	(Hm	Rd)	TB	R	RBI	RC	TBB	IBB	SO	HBP	SH	SF	SB	CS	SB%	GDP	Avg	OBP	Slg
2008	LsVgs*	AAA	2	6	3	1	0	0	(-	-)	4	2	0	2	2	0	1	0	0	0	0	0	-	1	.500	.625	.667
2000	Col	NL	51	200	62	2	0	0	(0	0)	64	26	20	23	13	0	15	1	4	1	7	6	.54	2	.310	.353	.320
2001	Col	NL	156	617	202	26	11	2	(0	2)	256	108	55	101	41	1	29	10	14	1	46	17	.73	6	.327	.378	.415
2002	Col	NL	152	592	170	20	5	1	(0	1)	203	90	35	79	31	0	52	9	8	0	47	12	.80	7	.287	.332	.343
2003	Fla	NL	162	668	204	28	7	1	(1	0)	249	100	41	92	55	1	35	5	15	3	65	20	.76	9	.305	.361	.373
2004	Fla	NL	162	678	221	22	12	3	(1	2)	276	100	49	101	45	1	35	8	15	2	45	24	.65	9	.326	.374	.407
2005	Fla	NL	162	656	181	19	13	2	(1	1)	232	96	47	76	41	1	45	9	10	2	57	17	.77	10	.276	.326	.354
2006	ChC	NL	162	699	204	32	13	3	(1	2)	271	87	40	84	32	0	38	8	10	5	58	20	.74	6	.292	.330	.388
2007	LAD	NL	162	668	196	24	8	0	(0	0)	236	96	41	75	33	0	37	6	20	2	64	15	.81	10	.293	.331	.353
2008	LAD	NL	119	375	106	10	2	1	(0	1)	123	44	28	48	22	1	24	3	5	1	40	12	.77	3	.283	.327	.328
	Postseason		17	73	22	4	2	0	(0	0)	30	12	7	13	8	2	4	1	1	0	3	4	.43	0	.301	.378	.411
	9 ML YEARS		1288	5153	1546	183	71	13	(4	9)	1910	747	356	679	313	5	310	59	101	13	429	143	.75	62	.300	.346	.371

A.J. Pierzynski

Bats: L Throws: R Pos: C-131; PH-7 **Ht: 6'4" Wt: 240 Born: 12/30/1976 Age: 32**

								BATTING													BASERUNNING				AVERAGES		
Year	Team	Lg	G	AB	H	2B	3B	HR	(Hm	Rd)	TB	R	RBI	RC	TBB	IBB	SO	HBP	SH	SF	SB	CS	SB%	GDP	Avg	OBP	Slg
1998	Min	AL	7	10	3	0	0	0	(0	0)	3	1	1	2	1	0	2	1	0	1	0	0	-	0	.300	.385	.300
1999	Min	AL	9	22	6	2	0	0	(0	0)	8	3	3	3	1	0	4	1	0	0	0	0	-	0	.273	.333	.364
2000	Min	AL	33	88	27	5	1	2	(1	1)	40	12	11	14	5	0	14	2	0	1	1	0	1.00	1	.307	.354	.455
2001	Min	AL	114	381	110	17	1	7	(3	4)	168	51	55	50	16	4	57	4	1	3	1	7	.13	7	.289	.322	.441
2002	Min	AL	130	440	132	31	6	6	(2	4)	193	54	49	60	13	1	61	11	2	3	1	2	.33	14	.300	.334	.439
2003	Min	AL	137	487	152	35	3	11	(6	5)	226	63	74	80	24	12	55	15	2	5	3	1	.75	13	.312	.360	.464
2004	SF	NL	131	471	128	28	2	11	(3	8)	193	45	77	58	19	4	27	15	2	3	0	1	.00	27	.272	.319	.410
2005	CWS	AL	128	460	118	21	0	18	(12	6)	193	61	56	55	23	5	68	12	1	1	0	2	.00	13	.257	.308	.420
2006	CWS	AL	140	509	150	24	0	16	(9	7)	222	65	64	68	22	6	72	8	3	1	1	0	1.00	10	.295	.333	.436
2007	CWS	AL	136	472	124	24	0	14	(8	6)	190	54	50	49	25	5	66	8	1	1	1	1	.50	21	.263	.309	.403
2008	CWS	AL	134	534	150	31	1	13	(7	6)	222	66	60	64	19	5	71	8	3	6	1	0	1.00	14	.281	.312	.416
	Postseason		26	87	25	4	1	5	(3	2)	46	15	16	16	8	1	12	1	1	1	2	2	.50	2	.287	.351	.529
	11 ML YEARS		1099	3874	1100	234	15	98	(51	47)	1658	475	500	503	168	42	497	85	15	27	9	14	.39	120	.284	.326	.428

Carmen Pignatiello

Pitches: L Bats: R Pos: RP-2 **Ht: 6'0" Wt: 205 Born: 9/12/1982 Age: 26**

			HOW MUCH HE PITCHED					WHAT HE GAVE UP											THE RESULTS					
Year	Team	Lg	G	GS	CG	GF	IP	BFP	H	R	ER	HR	SH	SF	HB	TBB	IBB	SO	WP	Bk	W	L	Pct	ShO	Sv-Op Hld	ERC	ERA
2000	Cubs	R	9	3	0	1	36.1	169	48	26	18	1	1	1	5	13	0	32	1	2	4	1	.800	0	0- -	5.25	4.46
2001	Boise	A-	16	12	0	3	78.0	337	70	37	26	2	4	1	6	22	0	83	6	0	7	3	.700	0	1- -	2.75	3.00
2002	Lansng	A	27	27	1	0	167.1	702	152	76	59	10	7	5	6	51	0	139	4	1	9	11	.450	0	0- -	3.06	3.17
2003	Dytona	A+	26	26	1	0	156.1	674	144	87	76	13	5	3	13	55	0	140	7	2	8	11	.421	0	0- -	3.62	4.38
2003	WTenn	AA	1	1	0	0	6.0	22	3	1	1	1	0	0	0	2	0	11	0	0	1	0	1.000	0	0- -	1.80	1.50
2004	WTenn	AA	27	27	1	0	148.0	637	167	89	75	16	16	7	9	39	1	137	5	0	9	7	.563	0	0- -	4.61	4.56
2005	WTenn	AA	16	10	0	1	80.2	329	68	26	24	3	5	1	2	28	1	77	3	0	5	4	.556	0	0- -	2.75	2.68
2005	Iowa	AAA	22	5	0	6	47.1	213	52	34	29	6	1	0	2	20	2	43	2	0	1	5	.167	0	0- -	4.98	5.51
2006	WTenn	AA	38	1	0	8	60.1	254	52	19	18	3	2	1	5	19	1	74	6	0	3	1	.750	0	0- -	2.93	2.69
2006	Iowa	AAA	8	0	0	1	6.2	28	7	4	2	0	0	0	0	2	0	4	1	0	0	0	-	0	0- -	3.32	2.70
2007	Tenn	AA	5	0	0	2	6.2	27	2	2	0	0	0	0	0	2	0	6	0	0	1	0	1.000	0	2- -	0.50	0.00
2007	Iowa	AAA	45	0	0	11	69.0	205	40	20	15	5	3	0	1	16	0	44	2	0	1	0	1.000	0	2- -	2.83	2.76
2008	Iowa	AAA	45	0	0	12	39.2	187	52	35	35	6	2	0	1	19	1	35	0	0	1	1	.000	0	3- -	6.72	7.94
2007	ChC	NL	4	0	0	0	2.0	8	3	1	1	1	0	0	0	0	0	3	0	0	0	0	-	0	0-0 1	9.22	4.50
2008	ChC	NL	2	0	0	0	0.2	7	2	1	1	0	0	0	1	2	0	0	1	0	0	0	-	0	0-0 0	37.18	13.50
	2 ML YEARS		6	0	0	0	2.2	15	5	2	2	1	0	0	1	2	0	3	1	0	0	0	-	0	0-0 1	16.91	6.75

Joel Pineiro

Pitches: R Bats: R Pos: SP-25; RP-1   Ht: 6'1" Wt: 200 Born: 9/25/1978 Age: 30

			HOW MUCH HE PITCHED						WHAT HE GAVE UP										THE RESULTS						
Year	Team	Lg	G	GS	CG	GF	IP	BFP	H	R	ER	HR	SH	SF	HB	TBB	IBB	SO	WP	Bk	W	L	Pct	ShO	Sv-Op Hld	ERC	ERA
2008	Memp*	AAA	1	1	0	0	6.0	24	6	2	2	0	0	0	0	1	0	5	0	0	0	0	-	0	0- - -	2.62	3.00
2000	Sea	AL	8	1	0	5	19.1	94	25	13	12	3	0	2	0	13	0	10	0	0	1	0	1.000	0	0-0	0	7.44	5.59
2001	Sea	AL	17	11	0	1	75.1	289	50	24	17	2	1	2	3	21	0	56	2	0	6	2	.750	0	0-0	2	1.71	2.03
2002	Sea	AL	37	28	2	4	194.1	812	189	75	70	24	5	7	7	54	1	136	8	0	14	7	.667	1	0-0	3	3.77	3.24
2003	Sea	AL	32	32	3	0	211.2	890	192	94	89	19	3	9	6	76	3	151	5	0	16	11	.593	2	0-0	0	3.43	3.78
2004	Sea	AL	21	21	1	0	140.2	596	144	77	73	21	1	5	4	43	1	111	4	0	6	11	.353	0	0-0	0	4.32	4.67
2005	Sea	AL	30	30	2	0	189.0	822	224	118	118	23	5	7	6	56	4	107	7	1	7	11	.389	0	0-0	0	5.05	5.62
2006	Sea	AL	40	25	1	6	165.2	753	209	123	117	23	1	6	10	64	13	87	4	1	8	13	.381	0	1-2	4	6.05	6.36
2007	2 Tms		42	11	0	15	97.2	419	110	49	47	14	3	1	2	26	0	60	3	0	7	5	.583	0	0-0	1	4.68	4.33
2008	StL	NL	26	25	0	1	148.2	645	180	89	85	22	7	3	2	35	0	81	1	0	7	7	.500	0	1-1	0	5.05	5.15
07	Bos	AL	31	0	0	15	34.0	157	41	20	19	3	1	1	1	14	0	20	3	0	1	1	.500	0	0-0	1	5.25	5.03
07	StL	NL	11	11	0	0	63.2	262	69	29	28	11	2	0	1	12	0	40	0	0	6	4	.600	0	0-0	0	4.36	3.96
	Postseason		1	0	0	0	2.0	12	4	1	1	0	0	0	0	2	0	5	1	0	0	0	-	0	0-0	0	12.01	4.50
	9 ML YEARS		253	184	9	32	1242.1	5320	1323	662	628	151	26	42	40	388	22	799	34	2	72	67	.518	3	2-3	10	4.39	4.55

Renyel Pinto

Pitches: L Bats: L Pos: RP-67   Ht: 6'4" Wt: 215 Born: 7/8/1982 Age: 26

			HOW MUCH HE PITCHED						WHAT HE GAVE UP										THE RESULTS						
Year	Team	Lg	G	GS	CG	GF	IP	BFP	H	R	ER	HR	SH	SF	HB	TBB	IBB	SO	WP	Bk	W	L	Pct	ShO	Sv-Op Hld	ERC	ERA
2006	Fla	NL	27	0	0	7	29.2	135	20	12	10	3	0	1	1	27	0	36	4	0	0	0	-	0	1-1	3	4.33	3.03
2007	Fla	NL	57	0	0	4	58.2	242	45	25	24	7	1	3	3	32	2	56	2	0	2	4	.333	0	1-6	16	3.79	3.68
2008	Fla	NL	67	0	0	11	64.2	284	52	33	32	9	6	5	4	39	2	56	8	0	2	5	.286	0	0-2	17	4.24	4.45
	3 ML YEARS		151	0	0	22	153.0	661	117	70	66	19	7	9	8	98	4	148	14	0	4	9	.308	0	2-9	36	4.09	3.88

Scott Podsednik

Bats: L Throws: L Pos: PH-57; CF-36; LF-10; PR-5; DH-2; RF-1   Ht: 6'2" Wt: 190 Born: 3/18/1976 Age: 33

			BATTING																		BASERUNNING				AVERAGES		
Year	Team	Lg	G	AB	H	2B	3B	HR	(Hm	Rd)	TB	R	RBI	RC	TBB	IBB	SO	HBP	SH	SF	SB	CS	SB%	GDP	Avg	OBP	Slg
2008	ColSpr*	AAA	4	16	7	0	0	0	(-	-)	7	2	3	4	3	0	0	0	0	0	3	0	1.00	1	.438	.526	.438
2001	Sea	AL	5	6	1	0	1	0	(0	0)	3	1	3	0	0	0	1	0	0	0	0	0	-	1	.167	.167	.500
2002	Sea	AL	14	20	4	0	0	1	(0	1)	7	2	5	3	4	0	6	0	0	1	0	0	-	1	.200	.320	.350
2003	Mil	NL	154	558	175	29	8	9	(7	2)	247	100	58	101	56	2	91	4	8	2	43	10	.81	11	.314	.379	.443
2004	Mil	NL	154	640	156	27	7	12	(3	9)	233	85	39	76	58	2	105	7	6	1	70	13	.84	7	.244	.313	.364
2005	CWS	AL	129	507	147	28	1	0	(0	0)	177	80	25	64	47	0	75	3	6	5	59	23	.72	7	.290	.351	.349
2006	CWS	AL	139	524	137	27	6	3	(2	1)	185	86	45	65	54	1	96	2	8	4	40	19	.68	7	.261	.330	.353
2007	CWS	AL	62	214	52	13	4	2	(1	1)	79	30	11	17	13	0	36	4	4	0	12	5	.71	9	.243	.299	.369
2008	Col	NL	93	162	41	8	1	1	(0	1)	54	22	15	19	16	0	28	1	1	1	12	4	.75	3	.253	.322	.333
	Postseason		12	49	14	1	3	2	(2	0)	27	9	6	10	7	0	10	2	1	0	6	3	.67	1	.286	.397	.551
	8 ML YEARS		750	2631	713	132	28	28	(13	15)	985	406	201	345	248	5	438	21	33	14	236	74	.76	46	.271	.337	.374

Placido Polanco

Bats: R Throws: R Pos: 2B-141; PH-2   Ht: 5'10" Wt: 194 Born: 10/10/1975 Age: 33

			BATTING																		BASERUNNING				AVERAGES		
Year	Team	Lg	G	AB	H	2B	3B	HR	(Hm	Rd)	TB	R	RBI	RC	TBB	IBB	SO	HBP	SH	SF	SB	CS	SB%	GDP	Avg	OBP	Slg
1998	StL	NL	45	114	29	3	2	1	(1	0)	39	10	11	12	5	0	9	1	2	0	2	0	1.00	1	.254	.292	.342
1999	StL	NL	88	220	61	9	3	1	(0	1)	79	24	19	23	15	1	24	0	3	2	1	3	.25	7	.277	.321	.359
2000	StL	NL	118	323	102	12	3	5	(2	3)	135	50	39	44	16	0	26	1	7	3	4	4	.50	8	.316	.347	.418
2001	StL	NL	144	564	173	26	4	3	(1	2)	216	87	38	70	25	0	43	6	14	1	12	3	.80	22	.307	.342	.383
2002	2 Tms	NL	147	548	158	32	2	9	(8	1)	221	75	49	64	26	1	41	8	13	0	5	3	.63	15	.288	.330	.403
2003	Phi	NL	122	492	142	30	3	14	(7	7)	220	87	63	74	42	1	38	8	8	4	14	2	.88	16	.289	.352	.447
2004	Phi	NL	126	503	150	21	0	17	(10	7)	222	74	55	71	27	0	39	12	7	6	7	4	.64	13	.298	.345	.441
2005	2 Tms	NL	129	501	166	27	2	9	(6	3)	224	84	56	86	33	0	25	11	2	4	4	3	.57	12	.331	.383	.447
2006	Det	AL	110	461	136	18	1	4	(2	2)	168	58	52	65	17	0	27	7	8	2	1	2	.33	18	.295	.329	.364
2007	Det	AL	142	587	200	36	3	9	(7	2)	269	105	67	100	37	3	30	11	2	4	7	3	.70	9	.341	.388	.458
2008	Det	AL	141	580	178	34	3	8	(2	6)	242	90	58	81	35	2	43	6	4	4	7	1	.88	14	.307	.350	.417
02	StL	NL	94	342	97	19	1	5	(5	0)	133	47	27	38	12	1	27	4	9	0	3	1	.75	12	.284	.316	.389
02	Phi	NL	53	206	61	13	1	4	(3	1)	88	28	22	26	14	0	14	4	4	0	2	2	.50	3	.296	.353	.427
05	Phi	NL	43	158	50	7	0	3	(2	1)	66	26	20	26	12	0	9	3	0	0	0	0	-	3	.316	.376	.418
05	Det	AL	86	343	116	20	2	6	(4	2)	158	58	36	60	21	0	16	8	2	4	4	3	.57	9	.338	.386	.461
	Postseason		25	81	24	2	0	0	(0	0)	26	7	8	8	8	2	5	1	3	1	2	1	.67	1	.296	.363	.321
	11 ML YEARS		1312	4893	1495	248	26	80	(46	34)	2035	744	507	690	278	8	345	71	70	30	64	28	.70	135	.306	.350	.416

Sidney Ponson

Pitches: R Bats: R Pos: SP-24; RP-1   Ht: 6'1" Wt: 258 Born: 11/2/1976 Age: 32

			HOW MUCH HE PITCHED						WHAT HE GAVE UP										THE RESULTS						
Year	Team	Lg	G	GS	CG	GF	IP	BFP	H	R	ER	HR	SH	SF	HB	TBB	IBB	SO	WP	Bk	W	L	Pct	ShO	Sv-Op Hld	ERC	ERA
2008	Okla*	AAA	5	4	0	0	23.1	100	25	9	9	3	1	2	0	9	0	12	2	0	1	2	.333	0	0- - -	4.72	3.47
2008	S-WB*	AAA	1	1	0	0	4.0	17	3	2	1	0	0	0	0	3	0	2	0	0	0	0	-	0	0- - -	3.44	2.25
1998	Bal	AL	31	20	0	5	135.0	588	157	82	79	19	3	4	3	42	2	85	4	1	8	9	.471	0	1-2	5	5.07	5.27
1999	Bal	AL	32	32	6	0	210.0	897	227	118	110	35	4	7	1	80	2	112	4	0	12	12	.500	0	0-0	0	5.08	4.71
2000	Bal	AL	32	32	6	0	222.0	953	223	125	119	30	3	3	3	83	0	152	5	0	9	13	.409	1	0-0	0	4.26	4.82
2001	Bal	AL	23	23	3	0	138.1	605	161	83	76	21	3	2	6	37	0	84	2	0	5	10	.333	1	0-0	0	5.04	4.94
2002	Bal	AL	28	28	3	0	176.0	736	172	84	80	26	2	3	2	63	1	120	3	0	7	9	.438	0	0-0	0	4.24	4.09
2003	2 Tms		31	31	4	0	216.0	898	211	94	90	16	6	5	5	61	5	134	9	0	17	12	.586	0	0-0	0	3.41	3.75

Year	Team	Lg	G	GS	CG	GF	IP	BFP	H	R	ER	HR	SH	SF	HB	TBB	IBB	SO	WP	Bk	W	L	Pct	ShO	Sv-Op	Hld	ERC	ERA
2004	Bal	AL	33	33	5	0	215.2	954	265	136	127	23	6	3	8	69	3	115	8	2	11	15	.423	2	0-0	0	5.33	5.30
2005	Bal	AL	23	23	1	0	130.1	595	177	97	90	16	2	8	3	48	1	68	10	0	7	11	.389	0	0-0	0	6.45	6.21
2006	2 Tms	AL	19	16	0	1	85.0	384	108	62	59	10	4	0	4	36	1	48	2	0	4	5	.444	0	0-0	0	6.25	6.25
2007	Min	AL	7	7	0	0	37.2	181	54	31	29	7	0	0	3	17	1	23	0	0	2	5	.286	0	0-0	0	8.04	6.93
2008	2 Tms	AL	25	24	1	1	135.2	612	170	89	76	14	2	8	7	48	2	58	4	0	8	5	.615	0	0-0	0	5.63	5.04
03	Bal	AL	21	21	4	0	148.0	622	147	65	62	10	2	3	4	43	2	100	6	0	14	6	.700	0	0-0	0	3.50	3.77
03	SF	NL	10	10	0	0	68.0	276	64	29	28	6	4	2	1	18	3	34	3	0	3	6	.333	0	0-0	0	3.23	3.71
06	StL	NL	14	13	0	0	68.2	303	82	42	40	7	4	0	4	29	1	33	2	0	4	4	.500	0	0-0	0	5.74	5.24
06	NYY	AL	5	3	0	1	16.1	81	26	20	19	3	0	0	0	7	0	15	0	0	0	1	.000	0	0-0	0	8.48	10.47
08	Tex	AL	9	9	1	0	55.2	252	71	36	24	3	0	3	2	16	0	25	2	0	4	1	.800	0	0-0	0	4.96	3.88
08	NYY	AL	16	15	0	1	80.0	360	99	53	52	11	2	5	5	32	2	33	2	0	4	4	.500	0	0-0	0	6.11	5.85
Postseason			1	1	0	0	5.0	22	7	4	4	0	0	0	0	0	0	3	1	0	0	0	-	0	0-0	0	3.92	7.20
11 ML YEARS			284	269	29	7	1701.2	7403	1925	1001	935	217	35	43	43	584	18	999	51	3	90	106	.459	4	1-2	0	4.95	4.95

Jorge Posada

Bats: B Throws: R Pos: C-30; DH-15; 1B-7; PH-5   Ht: 6'2" Wt: 215 Born: 8/17/1971 Age: 37

Year	Team	Lg	G	AB	H	2B	3B	HR	(Hm	Rd)	TB	R	RBI	RC	TBB	IBB	SO	HBP	SH	SF	SB	CS	SB%	GDP	Avg	OBP	Slg
1995	NYY	AL	1	0	0	0	0	0	(0	0)	0	0	0	0	0	0	0	0	0	0	0	0	-	0	-	-	-
1996	NYY	AL	8	14	1	0	0	0	(0	0)	1	1	0	0	1	0	6	0	0	0	0	0	-	1	.071	.133	.071
1997	NYY	AL	60	188	47	12	0	6	(2	4)	77	29	25	29	30	2	33	3	1	2	1	2	.33	2	.250	.359	.410
1998	NYY	AL	111	358	96	23	0	17	(6	11)	170	56	63	56	47	7	92	0	0	4	0	1	.00	14	.268	.350	.475
1999	NYY	AL	112	379	93	19	2	12	(4	8)	152	50	57	52	53	2	91	3	0	2	1	0	1.00	9	.245	.341	.401
2000	NYY	AL	151	505	145	35	1	28	(18	10)	266	92	86	110	107	10	151	8	0	4	2	2	.50	11	.287	.417	.527
2001	NYY	AL	138	484	134	28	1	22	(14	8)	230	59	95	80	62	10	132	6	0	5	2	6	.25	10	.277	.363	.475
2002	NYY	AL	143	511	137	40	1	20	(12	8)	239	79	99	92	81	9	143	3	0	3	1	0	1.00	23	.268	.370	.468
2003	NYY	AL	142	481	135	24	0	30	(15	15)	249	83	101	98	93	6	110	10	0	4	2	4	.33	13	.281	.405	.518
2004	NYY	AL	137	449	122	31	0	21	(11	10)	216	72	81	78	88	5	92	9	0	1	1	3	.25	24	.272	.400	.481
2005	NYY	AL	142	474	124	23	0	19	(11	8)	204	67	71	71	66	5	94	2	0	4	1	0	1.00	8	.262	.352	.430
2006	NYY	AL	143	465	129	27	2	23	(11	12)	229	65	93	89	64	1	97	11	0	5	3	0	1.00	10	.277	.374	.492
2007	NYY	AL	144	506	171	42	1	20	(11	9)	275	91	90	99	74	7	98	6	0	3	2	0	1.00	18	.338	.426	.543
2008	NYY	AL	51	168	45	13	1	3	(1	2)	69	18	22	23	24	3	38	2	0	1	0	0	-	7	.268	.364	.411
Postseason			96	322	76	19	0	9	(4	5)	122	41	31	36	57	8	77	2	0	2	2	3	.40	13	.236	.352	.379
14 ML YEARS			1483	4982	1379	317	9	221	(116	105)	2377	762	883	877	790	67	1177	63	1	38	16	18	.47	150	.277	.380	.477

Martin Prado

Bats: R Throws: R Pos: 3B-24; PH-18; 1B-17; 2B-17; LF-3; PR-3; SS-2   Ht: 6'1" Wt: 190 Born: 10/27/1983 Age: 25

Year	Team	Lg	G	AB	H	2B	3B	HR	(Hm	Rd)	TB	R	RBI	RC	TBB	IBB	SO	HBP	SH	SF	SB	CS	SB%	GDP	Avg	OBP	Slg
2008	Missi*	AA	5	19	5	2	0	0	(-	-)	7	2	3	2	3	0	2	0	0	0	0	0	-	0	.263	.364	.368
2006	Atl	NL	24	42	11	1	1	1	(1	0)	17	3	9	9	5	0	7	0	2	0	0	0	-	0	.262	.340	.405
2007	Atl	NL	28	59	17	3	0	0	(0	0)	20	5	2	6	3	0	6	0	0	0	0	0	-	0	.288	.323	.339
2008	Atl	NL	78	228	73	18	4	2	(1	1)	105	36	33	39	21	0	29	1	2	2	3	1	.75	3	.320	.377	.461
3 ML YEARS			130	329	101	22	5	3	(2	1)	142	44	44	54	29	0	42	1	4	2	3	1	.75	5	.307	.363	.432

David Price

Pitches: L Bats: L Pos: RP-4; SP-1   Ht: 6'6" Wt: 225 Born: 8/26/1985 Age: 23

Year	Team	Lg	G	GS	CG	GF	IP	BFP	H	R	ER	HR	SH	SF	HB	TBB	IBB	SO	WP	Bk	W	L	Pct	ShO	Sv-Op	Hld	ERC	ERA
2008	VeroB	A+	6	6	0	0	34.2	134	28	7	7	0	0	0	0	7	0	37	1	0	4	0	1.000	0	0--	-	1.83	1.82
2008	Mont	AA	9	9	1	0	57.0	224	42	13	12	7	0	0	4	16	1	55	1	0	7	0	1.000	0	0--	-	2.70	1.89
2008	Drham	AAA	4	4	0	0	18.0	82	22	10	9	0	0	0	0	9	0	17	1	0	1	1	.500	0	0--	-	5.04	4.50
2008	TB	AL	5	1	0	0	14.0	57	9	4	3	1	0	1	1	4	0	12	0	0	0	0	-	0	0-0	1	1.86	1.93

Jason Pridie

Bats: L Throws: R Pos: PR-5; LF-3; RF-3; PH-3; DH-2   Ht: 6'1" Wt: 200 Born: 10/9/1983 Age: 25

Year	Team	Lg	G	AB	H	2B	3B	HR	(Hm	Rd)	TB	R	RBI	RC	TBB	IBB	SO	HBP	SH	SF	SB	CS	SB%	GDP	Avg	OBP	Slg
2002	Princtn	R+	67	285	105	12	9	7	(-	-)	156	60	33	60	19	1	35	2	1	1	13	9	.59	2	.368	.410	.547
2002	HudVal	A-	8	32	11	1	1	1	(-	-)	17	4	1	6	3	1	6	0	0	0	0	0	-	0	.344	.400	.531
2003	CtnSC	A	128	530	138	28	10	7	(-	-)	207	75	48	63	30	1	113	4	3	5	26	17	.60	2	.260	.302	.391
2004	CtnSC	A	128	515	142	27	11	17	(-	-)	242	103	86	82	37	3	114	6	9	8	17	6	.74	1	.276	.327	.470
2005	Visalia	A+	1	2	1	0	0	0	(-	-)	1	0	0	0	0	0	0	0	0	0	0	0	-	0	.500	.500	.500
2005	Mont	AA	28	95	20	4	2	3	(-	-)	37	14	8	10	8	0	30	0	2	0	5	1	.83	3	.211	.272	.389
2006	Mont	AA	132	461	106	11	4	5	(-	-)	140	39	34	41	31	5	93	3	4	5	16	5	.76	6	.230	.280	.304
2007	Mont	AA	71	280	81	16	7	4	(-	-)	123	42	27	41	14	1	45	4	1	2	14	7	.67	8	.289	.330	.439
2007	Drham	AAA	63	245	78	16	4	10	(-	-)	132	47	39	50	22	2	47	2	2	3	12	3	.80	1	.318	.375	.520
2008	Roch	AAA	138	559	151	21	16	13	(-	-)	243	84	61	77	30	2	152	1	7	6	25	9	.74	8	.270	.305	.435
2008	Min	AL	10	4	0	0	0	0	(0	0)	0	3	0	0	1	0	1	0	1	0	0	0	-	0	.000	.200	.000

Scott Proctor

Pitches: R **Bats:** R **Pos:** RP-41   **Ht:** 6'1" **Wt:** 195 **Born:** 1/2/1977 **Age:** 32

Year	Team	Lg	G	GS	CG	GF	IP	BFP	H	R	ER	HR	SH	SF	HB	TBB	IBB	SO	WP	Bk	W	L	Pct	ShO	Sv-Op	Hld	ERC	ERA
2008	InldEm*	A+	1	0	0	0	0.2	6	3	3	1	0	0	0	0	0	0	1	0	0	0	0	-	0	0--	-	22.06	13.50
2008	LsVgs*	AAA	2	0	0	0	3.0	11	2	0	0	0	0	0	0	0	0	5	0	0	1	0	1.000	0	0--	-	0.91	0.00
2004	NYY	AL	26	0	0	12	25.0	118	29	15	15	5	0	2	0	14	0	21	1	0	2	1	.667	0	0-0	2	6.32	5.40
2005	NYY	AL	29	1	0	11	44.2	199	46	32	30	10	0	1	2	17	4	36	4	1	1	0	1.000	0	0-0	4	4.98	6.04
2006	NYY	AL	83	0	0	12	102.1	426	89	41	40	12	2	6	2	33	6	89	2	0	6	4	.600	0	1-8	26	3.15	3.52
2007	2 Tms		83	0	0	14	86.1	382	78	41	35	12	3	7	6	44	4	64	5	1	5	5	.500	0	0-6	18	4.41	3.65
2008	LAD	NL	41	0	0	11	38.2	184	41	30	26	7	1	2	0	24	1	46	6	0	2	0	1.000	0	0-1	2	5.67	6.05
07	NYY	AL	52	0	0	10	54.1	245	53	27	23	8	1	6	3	29	3	37	3	0	2	5	.286	0	0-4	11	4.90	3.81
07	LAD	NL	31	0	0	4	32.0	137	25	14	12	4	2	1	3	15	1	27	2	1	3	0	1.000	0	0-2	7	3.61	3.38
	Postseason		5	0	0	2	6.0	26	8	1	1	0	0	0	0	1	0	2	1	0	0	0	-	0	0-0	1	4.37	1.50
	5 ML YEARS		262	1	0	60	297.0	1309	283	162	146	46	6	18	10	132	15	256	18	3	16	10	.615	0	1-15	48	4.36	4.42

Albert Pujols

Bats: R **Throws:** R **Pos:** 1B-144; PH-4; DH-3; 2B-1   **Ht:** 6'3" **Wt:** 230 **Born:** 1/16/1980 **Age:** 29

										BATTING													BASERUNNING				AVERAGES		
Year	Team	Lg	G	AB	H	2B	3B	HR	(Hm	Rd)	TB	R	RBI	RC	TBB	IBB	SO	HBP	SH	SF	SB	CS	SB%	GDP	Avg	OBP	Slg
2001	StL	NL	161	590	194	47	4	37	(18	19)	360	112	130	132	69	6	93	9	1	7	1	3	.25	21	.329	.403	.610
2002	StL	NL	157	590	185	40	2	34	(14	20)	331	118	127	121	72	13	69	9	0	4	2	4	.33	20	.314	.394	.561
2003	StL	NL	157	591	212	51	1	43	(21	22)	394	137	124	160	79	12	65	10	0	5	5	1	.83	13	.359	.439	.667
2004	StL	NL	154	592	196	51	2	46	(18	28)	389	133	123	143	84	12	52	7	0	9	5	5	.50	21	.331	.415	.657
2005	StL	NL	161	591	195	38	2	41	(23	18)	360	129	117	139	97	27	65	9	0	3	16	2	.89	19	.330	.430	.609
2006	StL	NL	143	535	177	33	1	49	(24	25)	359	119	137	146	92	28	50	4	0	3	7	2	.78	20	.331	.431	.671
2007	StL	NL	158	565	185	38	1	32	(12	20)	321	99	103	118	99	22	58	7	0	8	2	6	.25	27	.327	.429	.568
2008	StL	NL	148	524	187	44	0	37	(19	18)	342	100	116	130	104	34	54	5	0	8	7	3	.70	16	.357	.462	.653
	Postseason		53	189	61	10	1	13	(7	6)	112	39	35	43	33	9	27	3	0	1	0	1	.00	5	.323	.429	.593
	8 ML YEARS		1239	4578	1531	342	13	319	(149	170)	2856	947	977	1089	696	154	506	60	1	47	45	26	.63	157	.334	.425	.624

Nick Punto

Bats: B **Throws:** R **Pos:** SS-61; 2B-26; 3B-12; CF-3; PH-2; PR-2; DH-1   **Ht:** 5'9" **Wt:** 195 **Born:** 11/8/1977 **Age:** 31

										BATTING													BASERUNNING				AVERAGES		
Year	Team	Lg	G	AB	H	2B	3B	HR	(Hm	Rd)	TB	R	RBI	RC	TBB	IBB	SO	HBP	SH	SF	SB	CS	SB%	GDP	Avg	OBP	Slg
2008	FtMyrs*	A+	3	12	3	0	0	0	(-	-)	3	0	1	1	1	0	1	0	0	0	1	0	1.00	0	.250	.308	.250
2001	Phi	NL	4	5	2	0	0	0	(0	0)	2	0	0	0	0	0	0	0	0	0	0	0	-	0	.400	.400	.400
2002	Phi	NL	9	6	1	0	0	0	(0	0)	1	0	0	0	0	0	3	0	1	0	0	0	-	0	.167	.167	.167
2003	Phi	NL	64	92	20	2	0	1	(0	1)	25	14	4	7	7	1	22	0	0	0	2	1	.67	0	.217	.273	.272
2004	Min	AL	38	91	23	0	0	2	(2	0)	29	17	12	15	12	0	19	0	0	0	6	0	1.00	2	.253	.340	.319
2005	Min	AL	112	394	94	18	4	4	(3	1)	132	45	26	35	36	0	86	0	7	2	13	8	.62	9	.239	.301	.335
2006	Min	AL	135	459	133	21	7	1	(0	1)	171	73	45	59	47	0	68	1	10	7	17	5	.77	8	.290	.352	.373
2007	Min	AL	150	472	99	18	4	1	(0	1)	128	53	25	37	55	1	90	0	6	3	16	6	.73	7	.210	.291	.271
2008	Min	AL	99	338	96	19	4	2	(1	1)	129	43	28	42	32	1	57	0	5	2	15	6	.71	10	.284	.344	.382
	Postseason		3	12	2	0	0	0	(0	0)	2	0	0	0	0	0	1	0	1	0	0	0	-	0	.167	.167	.167
	8 ML YEARS		611	1857	468	78	19	11	(6	5)	617	245	140	196	189	3	345	1	29	14	69	26	.73	36	.252	.319	.332

David Purcey

Pitches: L **Bats:** L **Pos:** SP-12   **Ht:** 6'5" **Wt:** 240 **Born:** 4/22/1982 **Age:** 27

Year	Team	Lg	G	GS	CG	GF	IP	BFP	H	R	ER	HR	SH	SF	HB	TBB	IBB	SO	WP	Bk	W	L	Pct	ShO	Sv-Op	Hld	ERC	ERA
2004	Auburn	A-	3	2	0	0	12.0	43	6	2	2	0	1	2	1	1	0	13	0	0	1	0	1.000	0	0--	-	0.82	1.50
2005	Dnedin	A+	21	21	0	0	94.1	422	80	51	38	8	2	4	10	56	0	116	8	0	5	4	.556	0	0--	-	4.25	3.63
2005	NHam	AA	8	8	1	0	43.0	184	32	17	14	2	0	2	1	25	0	45	4	0	4	3	.571	0	0--	-	3.08	2.93
2006	Syrcse	AAA	12	12	1	0	51.2	242	49	41	31	7	1	4	2	38	0	45	2	0	2	7	.222	0	0--	-	5.48	5.40
2006	NHam	AA	16	16	0	0	88.1	414	101	59	55	9	4	1	12	44	0	81	6	0	4	5	.444	0	0--	-	5.86	5.60
2007	NHam	AA	11	11	1	0	62.0	266	67	41	37	4	1	3	4	16	0	55	4	1	3	5	.375	1	0--	-	3.99	5.37
2008	Syrcse	AAA	19	19	0	0	117.0	471	97	41	35	8	4	3	4	34	0	120	11	1	8	6	.571	0	0--	-	2.73	2.69
2008	Tor	AL	12	12	1	0	65.0	289	67	41	40	9	2	3	4	29	0	58	3	0	3	6	.333	0	0-0	0	4.96	5.54

J.J. Putz

Pitches: R **Bats:** R **Pos:** RP-47   **Ht:** 6'5" **Wt:** 250 **Born:** 2/22/1977 **Age:** 32

Year	Team	Lg	G	GS	CG	GF	IP	BFP	H	R	ER	HR	SH	SF	HB	TBB	IBB	SO	WP	Bk	W	L	Pct	ShO	Sv-Op	Hld	ERC	ERA
2008	Ms*	R	2	2	0	0	3.0	10	2	0	0	0	0	0	0	0	0	4	0	0	0	0	-	0	0--	-	1.01	0.00
2008	Tacom*	AAA	1	1	0	0	1.2	5	0	0	0	0	0	0	0	0	0	1	0	0	0	0	-	0	0--	-	0.00	0.00
2003	Sea	AL	3	0	0	3	3.2	18	4	2	2	0	0	0	0	3	0	3	0	0	0	0	-	0	0-0	0	5.31	4.91
2004	Sea	AL	54	0	0	30	63.0	275	66	35	33	10	3	2	5	24	4	47	1	0	0	3	.000	0	9-13	9	4.71	4.71
2005	Sea	AL	64	0	0	24	60.0	259	58	27	24	8	3	3	2	23	2	45	2	0	6	5	.545	0	1-4	21	4.11	3.60
2006	Sea	AL	72	0	0	57	78.1	303	59	20	20	4	1	2	2	13	1	104	1	0	4	1	.800	0	36-43	5	1.78	2.30
2007	Sea	AL	68	0	0	65	71.2	260	37	11	11	6	2	1	2	13	0	82	3	0	6	1	.857	0	40-42	0	1.21	1.38
2008	Sea	AL	47	0	0	35	46.1	211	46	20	20	4	0	1	2	28	2	56	2	0	6	5	.545	0	15-23	0	4.82	3.88
	6 ML YEARS		308	0	0	207	323.0	1326	270	115	110	32	9	9	13	104	9	337	9	0	22	15	.595	0	101-125	29	3.02	3.07

Chad Qualls

Pitches: R Bats: R Pos: RP-77   Ht: 6'5" Wt: 220 Born: 8/17/1978 Age: 30

		HOW MUCH HE PITCHED						WHAT HE GAVE UP												THE RESULTS							
Year	Team	Lg	G	GS	CG	GF	IP	BFP	H	R	ER	HR	SH	SF	HB	TBB	IBB	SO	WP	Bk	W	L	Pct	ShO	Sv-Op	Hld	ERC	ERA
2004	Hou	NL	25	0	0	4	33.0	141	34	13	13	3	0	1	4	8	1	24	0	0	4	0	1.000	0	1-2	9	4.02	3.55
2005	Hou	NL	77	0	0	19	79.2	329	73	33	29	7	4	3	6	23	2	60	1	0	6	4	.600	0	0-0	22	3.42	3.28
2006	Hou	NL	81	0	0	13	88.2	356	76	38	37	10	4	4	6	28	6	56	0	0	7	3	.700	0	0-6	23	3.36	3.76
2007	Hou	NL	79	0	0	16	82.2	345	84	29	28	10	6	2	3	25	5	78	2	0	6	5	.545	0	5-10	21	4.07	3.05
2008	Ari	NL	77	0	0	21	73.2	300	61	29	23	4	4	3	3	18	2	71	6	0	4	8	.333	0	9-17	22	2.40	2.81
	Postseason		15	0	0	0	21.0	85	20	11	11	2	1	0	0	7	3	17	0	0	1	1	.500	0	0-2	2	3.45	4.71
	5 ML YEARS		339	0	0	73	357.2	1471	328	142	130	34	18	13	22	102	16	289	9	0	27	20	.574	0	15-35	97	3.38	3.27

Carlos Quentin

Bats: R Throws: R Pos: LF-130   Ht: 6'2" Wt: 220 Born: 8/28/1982 Age: 26

							BATTING													BASERUNNING				AVERAGES		
Year	Team	Lg	G	AB	H	2B	3B	HR	(Hm	Rd)	TB	R	RBI	RC	TBB	IBB	SO	HBP	SH	SF	SB	CS	SB%	GDP	Avg	OBP	Slg
2006	Ari	NL	57	166	42	13	3	9	(3	6)	88	23	32	29	15	2	34	8	1	1	0	1	1.00	6	.253	.342	.530
2007	Ari	NL	81	229	49	16	0	5	(5	0)	80	29	31	27	18	1	54	11	1	4	2	2	.50	5	.214	.298	.349
2008	CWS	AL	130	480	138	26	1	36	(21	15)	274	96	100	104	66	0	80	20	0	3	7	3	.70	16	.288	.394	.571
	3 ML YEARS		268	875	229	55	4	50	(29	21)	442	148	163	160	99	3	168	39	2	8	10	5	.67	27	.262	.359	.505

Robb Quinlan

Bats: R Throws: R Pos: 3B-39; 1B-22; DH-4; PH-4; LF-3; RF-3; PR-2   Ht: 6'1" Wt: 200 Born: 3/17/1977 Age: 32

							BATTING													BASERUNNING				AVERAGES		
Year	Team	Lg	G	AB	H	2B	3B	HR	(Hm	Rd)	TB	R	RBI	RC	TBB	IBB	SO	HBP	SH	SF	SB	CS	SB%	GDP	Avg	OBP	Slg
2003	LAA	AL	38	94	27	4	2	0	(0	0)	35	13	4	8	6	0	16	0	1	0	1	2	.33	3	.287	.330	.372
2004	LAA	AL	56	160	55	14	0	5	(3	2)	84	23	23	33	14	0	26	2	0	1	3	1	.75	1	.344	.401	.525
2005	LAA	AL	54	134	31	8	0	5	(3	2)	54	17	14	11	7	0	26	1	0	1	0	1	.00	4	.231	.273	.403
2006	LAA	AL	86	234	75	11	1	9	(3	6)	115	28	32	36	7	1	28	2	0	1	2	1	.67	6	.321	.344	.491
2007	LAA	AL	79	178	44	9	0	3	(1	2)	62	21	21	15	14	1	27	1	0	1	3	2	.60	6	.247	.304	.348
2008	LAA	AL	68	164	43	1	2	1	(1	0)	51	15	11	17	14	0	28	2	0	1	4	2	.67	5	.262	.326	.311
	Postseason		4	6	2	0	0	1	(0	1)	5	1	1	2	0	0	2	0	0	0	0	0	-	0	.333	.333	.833
	6 ML YEARS		381	964	275	47	5	23	(11	12)	401	117	105	120	62	2	151	8	1	5	13	9	.59	25	.285	.332	.416

Omar Quintanilla

Bats: L Throws: R Pos: 2B-40; SS-39; PH-5   Ht: 5'9" Wt: 190 Born: 10/24/1981 Age: 27

							BATTING													BASERUNNING				AVERAGES		
Year	Team	Lg	G	AB	H	2B	3B	HR	(Hm	Rd)	TB	R	RBI	RC	TBB	IBB	SO	HBP	SH	SF	SB	CS	SB%	GDP	Avg	OBP	Slg
2008	ColSpr*	AAA	20	73	24	4	0	1	(-	-)	31	18	8	16	16	1	11	1	0	1	3	0	1.00	1	.329	.451	.425
2005	Col	NL	39	128	28	1	1	0	(0	0)	31	16	7	9	9	0	15	0	6	0	2	1	.67	3	.219	.270	.242
2006	Col	NL	11	34	6	1	1	0	(0	0)	9	3	3	2	3	1	9	0	1	0	1	1	.50	1	.176	.243	.265
2007	Col	NL	27	70	16	4	0	0	(0	0)	20	6	5	6	5	0	15	0	0	0	0	0	-	3	.229	.280	.286
2008	Col	NL	81	210	50	17	0	2	(1	1)	73	28	15	18	15	3	46	0	8	1	0	0	-	3	.238	.288	.348
	4 ML YEARS		158	442	100	23	2	2	(1	1)	133	53	30	35	32	4	85	0	15	1	3	2	.60	10	.226	.278	.301

Humberto Quintero

Bats: R Throws: R Pos: C-59; PH-1   Ht: 5'9" Wt: 215 Born: 8/2/1979 Age: 29

							BATTING													BASERUNNING				AVERAGES		
Year	Team	Lg	G	AB	H	2B	3B	HR	(Hm	Rd)	TB	R	RBI	RC	TBB	IBB	SO	HBP	SH	SF	SB	CS	SB%	GDP	Avg	OBP	Slg
2008	RdRck*	AAA	32	118	28	2	2	3	(-	-)	43	13	18	11	5	0	15	1	0	0	0	2	.00	2	.237	.274	.364
2008	CpChr*	AA	3	12	3	2	0	0	(-	-)	5	0	1	1	0	0	1	0	0	0	0	0	-	1	.250	.250	.417
2003	SD	NL	12	23	5	0	0	0	(0	0)	5	1	2	2	1	1	6	0	0	0	0	0	-	0	.217	.250	.217
2004	SD	NL	23	72	18	3	0	2	(1	1)	27	7	10	6	5	0	16	0	0	1	0	2	.00	0	.250	.295	.375
2005	Hou	NL	18	54	10	1	0	1	(1	0)	14	6	8	2	1	1	10	0	2	0	0	0	-	3	.185	.200	.259
2006	Hou	NL	11	21	7	2	0	0	(0	0)	9	2	2	1	1	0	3	0	0	0	0	0	-	2	.333	.364	.429
2007	Hou	NL	29	53	12	2	0	0	(0	0)	14	2	1	3	2	1	13	2	0	0	0	0	-	2	.226	.281	.264
2008	Hou	NL	59	168	38	6	0	2	(1	1)	50	16	12	10	6	0	34	4	5	0	0	0	-	5	.226	.270	.298
	6 ML YEARS		152	391	90	14	0	5	(3	2)	119	34	35	24	16	3	82	6	7	1	0	2	.00	17	.230	.271	.304

Guillermo Quiroz

Bats: R Throws: R Pos: C-54; PH-4   Ht: 6'1" Wt: 200 Born: 11/29/1981 Age: 27

							BATTING													BASERUNNING				AVERAGES		
Year	Team	Lg	G	AB	H	2B	3B	HR	(Hm	Rd)	TB	R	RBI	RC	TBB	IBB	SO	HBP	SH	SF	SB	CS	SB%	GDP	Avg	OBP	Slg
2004	Tor	AL	17	52	11	2	0	0	(0	0)	13	2	6	4	2	0	8	2	0	1	1	0	1.00	1	.212	.263	.250
2005	Tor	AL	12	36	7	2	0	0	(0	0)	9	3	4	3	2	0	13	1	0	0	0	0	-	0	.194	.256	.250
2006	Sea	AL	1	2	0	0	0	0	(0	0)	0	0	0	0	0	0	2	0	0	0	0	0	-	0	.000	.000	.000
2007	Tex	AL	9	10	4	1	0	0	(0	0)	5	1	2	3	1	0	2	0	0	0	0	0	-	0	.400	.455	.500
2008	Bal	AL	56	134	25	5	0	2	(1	1)	36	12	14	10	12	0	34	1	1	0	0	0	-	3	.187	.259	.269
	5 ML YEARS		95	234	47	10	0	2	(1	1)	63	18	26	20	17	0	59	4	1	1	1	0	1.00	4	.201	.266	.269

Mike Rabelo

Bats: B Throws: R Pos: C-32; PH-2   Ht: 6'1" Wt: 210 Born: 1/17/1980 Age: 29

Year	Team	Lg	G	AB	H	2B	3B	HR	(Hm	Rd)	TB	R	RBI	RC	TBB	IBB	SO	HBP	SH	SF	SB	CS	SB%	GDP	Avg	OBP	Slg
2008	Jupiter*	A+	8	30	6	2	0	0	(-	-)	8	2	1	1	2	0	8	0	0	0	0	0	-	1	.200	.250	.267
2008	Albq*	AAA	9	29	7	1	0	1	(-	-)	11	2	2	2	1	1	8	0	0	0	0	0	-	1	.241	.267	.379
2006	Det	AL	1	1	0	0	0	0	(0	0)	0	0	0	0	0	0	1	0	0	0	0	0	-	0	.000	.000	.000
2007	Det	AL	51	168	43	10	2	1	(0	1)	60	14	18	16	6	0	41	5	5	0	0	0	-	4	.256	.300	.357
2008	Fla	NL	34	109	22	1	0	3	(0	3)	32	9	10	8	8	0	25	1	1	3	0	1	.00	1	.202	.256	.294
	3 ML YEARS		86	278	65	11	2	4	(0	4)	92	23	28	24	14	0	67	6	6	4	0	1	.00	5	.234	.281	.331

Ryan Raburn

Bats: R Throws: R Pos: LF-30; RF-22; 3B-18; 2B-16; PH-9; PR-8; CF-6; DH-3   Ht: 6'0" Wt: 185 Born: 4/17/1981 Age: 28

Year	Team	Lg	G	AB	H	2B	3B	HR	(Hm	Rd)	TB	R	RBI	RC	TBB	IBB	SO	HBP	SH	SF	SB	CS	SB%	GDP	Avg	OBP	Slg
2008	Toledo*	AAA	5	19	6	2	0	2	(-	-)	14	6	6	5	4	0	5	0	0	0	0	0	-	1	.316	.435	.737
2004	Det	AL	12	29	4	1	0	0	(0	0)	5	4	1	1	2	0	15	0	0	0	1	0	1.00	0	.138	.194	.172
2007	Det	AL	49	138	42	12	2	4	(2	2)	70	28	27	21	8	1	33	0	1	1	3	0	1.00	7	.304	.340	.507
2008	Det	AL	92	182	43	10	1	4	(2	2)	67	26	20	20	16	1	49	0	1	0	3	1	.75	2	.236	.298	.368
	3 ML YEARS		153	349	89	23	3	8	(4	4)	142	58	48	42	26	2	97	0	2	1	7	1	.88	9	.255	.306	.407

Alexei Ramirez

Bats: R Throws: R Pos: 2B-121; SS-16; CF-11; PH-2; PR-2; 3B-1; DH-1   Ht: 6'3" Wt: 185 Born: 9/22/1981 Age: 27

Year	Team	Lg	G	AB	H	2B	3B	HR	(Hm	Rd)	TB	R	RBI	RC	TBB	IBB	SO	HBP	SH	SF	SB	CS	SB%	GDP	Avg	OBP	Slg
2008	CWS	AL	136	480	139	22	2	21	(13	8)	228	65	77	78	18	3	61	3	4	4	13	9	.59	14	.290	.317	.475

Aramis Ramirez

Bats: R Throws: R Pos: 3B-147; DH-1; PH-1   Ht: 6'1" Wt: 215 Born: 6/25/1978 Age: 31

Year	Team	Lg	G	AB	H	2B	3B	HR	(Hm	Rd)	TB	R	RBI	RC	TBB	IBB	SO	HBP	SH	SF	SB	CS	SB%	GDP	Avg	OBP	Slg
1998	Pit	NL	72	251	59	9	1	6	(3	3)	88	23	24	26	18	0	72	4	1	1	0	1	.00	3	.235	.296	.351
1999	Pit	NL	18	56	10	2	1	0	(0	0)	14	2	7	4	6	0	9	0	1	1	0	0	-	0	.179	.254	.250
2000	Pit	NL	73	254	65	15	2	6	(4	2)	102	19	35	28	10	0	36	5	1	4	0	0	-	9	.256	.293	.402
2001	Pit	NL	158	603	181	40	0	34	(16	18)	323	83	112	108	40	4	100	8	0	4	5	4	.56	9	.300	.350	.536
2002	Pit	NL	142	522	122	26	0	18	(7	11)	202	51	71	49	29	3	95	8	0	11	2	0	1.00	17	.234	.279	.387
2003	2 Tms	NL	159	607	165	32	2	27	(10	17)	282	75	106	88	42	3	99	10	0	11	2	2	.50	21	.272	.324	.465
2004	ChC	NL	145	547	174	32	1	36	(22	14)	316	99	103	100	49	6	62	3	0	7	0	2	.00	15	.318	.373	.578
2005	ChC	NL	123	463	140	30	4	31	(11	20)	263	72	92	79	35	4	60	6	0	2	0	1	.00	15	.302	.358	.568
2006	ChC	NL	157	594	173	38	4	38	(14	24)	333	93	119	109	50	4	63	9	0	7	2	1	.67	15	.291	.352	.561
2007	ChC	NL	132	506	157	35	4	26	(17	9)	278	72	101	95	43	8	66	4	0	5	0	0	-	13	.310	.366	.549
2008	ChC	NL	149	554	160	44	1	27	(17	10)	287	97	111	108	74	7	94	11	0	6	2	2	.50	13	.289	.380	.518
03	Pit	NL	96	375	105	25	1	12	(6	6)	168	44	67	49	25	3	68	7	0	8	1	1	.50	17	.280	.330	.448
03	ChC	NL	63	232	60	7	1	15	(4	11)	114	31	39	39	17	0	31	3	0	3	1	1	.50	4	.259	.314	.491
	Postseason		15	56	11	1	1	4	(1	3)	26	6	10	8	8	0	13	1	0	0	0	0	-	4	.196	.308	.464
	11 ML YEARS		1328	4957	1406	303	16	249	(121	128)	2488	686	881	794	396	39	756	68	3	59	13	13	.50	140	.284	.341	.502

Edwar Ramirez

Pitches: R Bats: R Pos: RP-55   Ht: 6'3" Wt: 164 Born: 3/28/1981 Age: 28

			HOW MUCH HE PITCHED					WHAT HE GAVE UP										THE RESULTS						
Year	Team	Lg	G	GS	CG	GF	IP	BFP	H	R	ER	HR	SH	SF	HB	TBB	IBB	SO	WP	Bk	W	L	Pct	ShO	Sv-Op Hld	ERC	ERA
2002	Angels	R	13	7	0	1	46.1	197	47	22	19	1	0	1	4	13	0	45	1	0	2	5	.286	0	0-- -	3.51	3.69
2002	Provo	R+	2	1	0	0	9.2	47	14	10	10	0	0	2	3	4	0	4	2	0	0	1	1.000	0	0-- -	7.58	9.31
2003	RCuca	A+	4	4	0	0	16.2	83	29	16	15	5	1	0	0	7	0	9	1	0	0	2	.000	0	0-- -	10.81	8.10
2003	CRpds	A	6	1	0	0	19.0	83	17	7	7	2	0	1	1	8	0	15	1	0	1	1	.500	0	0-- -	3.73	3.32
2005	Pnscla	IND	43	0	0	29	62.0	243	37	12	10	4	1	1	8	15	2	93	4	1	2	2	.500	0	11-- -	1.69	1.45
2005	Salt Lk	AAA	1	0	0	0	2.0	6	0	0	0	0	0	0	0	0	0	2	0	0	0	0	-	0	0-- -	0.00	0.00
2006	Ednbg	IND	25	0	0	24	25.1	101	14	6	3	2	3	1	1	10	0	46	4	0	1	1	.500	0	16-- -	1.79	1.07
2006	Tampa	A+	19	0	0	12	30.2	112	14	4	4	0	0	0	1	6	0	47	2	0	4	1	.800	0	3-- -	0.81	1.17
2007	Trntn	AA	9	0	0	3	16.2	67	6	1	1	1	0	0	1	8	1	33	1	0	3	0	1.000	0	1-- -	1.24	0.54
2007	S-WB	AAA	25	0	0	10	40.0	153	20	4	4	0	2	0	3	14	0	69	3	1	1	0	1.000	0	6-- -	1.30	0.90
2008	S-WB	AAA	8	0	0	5	9.0	31	2	0	0	0	0	1	0	1	0	13	1	0	1	0	1.000	0	0-- -	0.32	0.00
2007	NYY	AL	21	0	0	5	21.0	103	24	19	19	6	1	1	3	14	2	31	4	0	1	1	.500	0	1-3 3	7.95	8.14
2008	NYY	AL	55	0	0	16	55.1	233	44	25	24	7	1	2	3	24	2	63	3	0	5	1	.833	0	1-4 5	3.42	3.90
	2 ML YEARS		76	0	0	21	76.1	336	68	44	43	13	2	6	38	4	94	7	0	6	2	.750	0	2-7 8	4.55	5.07

Elizardo Ramirez

Pitches: R Bats: B Pos: RP-1   Ht: 6'0" Wt: 190 Born: 1/28/1983 Age: 26

			HOW MUCH HE PITCHED					WHAT HE GAVE UP										THE RESULTS						
Year	Team	Lg	G	GS	CG	GF	IP	BFP	H	R	ER	HR	SH	SF	HB	TBB	IBB	SO	WP	Bk	W	L	Pct	ShO	Sv-Op Hld	ERC	ERA
2008	Okla*	AAA	27	23	0	1	160.0	701	193	97	80	24	3	2	7	33	0	85	2	1	10	7	.588	0	0-- -	4.99	4.50
2004	Phi	NL	7	0	0	5	15.0	67	17	8	8	3	0	1	1	5	1	9	1	0	0	0	-	0	0-0 0	5.44	4.80
2005	Cin	NL	6	4	0	1	22.1	110	33	22	21	5	2	0	2	10	1	9	2	0	0	3	.000	0	0-0 0	8.45	8.46

Year	Team	Lg	G	GS	CG	GF	IP	BFP	H	R	ER	HR	SH	SF	HB	TBB	IBB	SO	WP	Bk	W	L	Pct	ShO	Sv-Op	Hld	ERC	ERA
			HOW MUCH HE PITCHED						**WHAT HE GAVE UP**												**THE RESULTS**							
2006	Cin	NL	21	19	0	1	104.0	465	123	70	62	14	5	3	8	29	2	69	0	3	4	9	.308	0	0-0	0	5.13	5.37
2007	Cin	NL	4	3	0	0	16.1	73	20	14	14	5	1	0	0	8	0	8	0	0	0	2	.000	0	0-0	0	7.69	7.71
2008	Tex	AL	1	0	0	0	2.2	19	8	9	9	1	0	0	1	2	0	1	1	0	0	1	.000	0	0-0	0	24.96	30.38
5 ML YEARS			39	26	0	7	160.1	734	201	123	114	28	8	4	12	54	5	96	4	3	4	15	.211	0	0-0	0	6.12	6.40

Hanley Ramirez

Bats: R **Throws:** R **Pos:** SS-150; DH-1; PH-1; PR-1 **Ht:** 6'3" **Wt:** 200 **Born:** 12/23/1983 **Age:** 25

Year	Team	Lg	G	AB	H	2B	3B	HR	(Hm	Rd)	TB	R	RBI	RC	TBB	IBB	SO	HBP	SH	SF	SB	CS	SB%	GDP	Avg	OBP	Slg
			BATTING																		**BASERUNNING**				**AVERAGES**		
2005	Bos	AL	2	2	0	0	0	0	(0	0)	0	0	0	0	0	0	2	0	0	0	0	0	-	0	.000	.000	.000
2006	Fla	NL	158	633	185	46	11	17	(9	8)	304	119	59	101	56	0	128	4	5	2	51	15	.77	7	.292	.353	.480
2007	Fla	NL	154	639	212	48	6	29	(15	14)	359	125	81	115	52	3	95	7	4	4	51	14	.78	10	.332	.386	.562
2008	Fla	NL	153	589	177	34	4	33	(17	16)	318	**125**	67	116	92	9	122	8	0	4	35	12	.74	5	.301	.400	.540
4 ML YEARS			467	1863	574	128	21	79	(41	38)	981	369	207	332	200	12	347	19	9	10	137	41	.77	22	.308	.379	.527

Horacio Ramirez

Pitches: L **Bats:** L **Pos:** RP-32 **Ht:** 6'1" **Wt:** 220 **Born:** 11/24/1979 **Age:** 29

Year	Team	Lg	G	GS	CG	GF	IP	BFP	H	R	ER	HR	SH	SF	HB	TBB	IBB	SO	WP	Bk	W	L	Pct	ShO	Sv-Op	Hld	ERC	ERA
			HOW MUCH HE PITCHED						**WHAT HE GAVE UP**												**THE RESULTS**							
2008	Omha*	AAA	3	3	0	0	19.0	71	13	5	3	2	0	1	0	3	0	8	0	0	1	1	.500	0	0- -	-	1.69	1.42
2003	Atl	NL	29	29	1	0	182.1	781	181	91	81	21	12	3	6	72	10	100	5	1	12	4	.750	0	0-0	0	4.21	4.00
2004	Atl	NL	10	9	1	0	60.1	259	51	24	16	7	2	1	0	30	5	31	0	2	2	4	.333	0	0-0	0	3.55	2.39
2005	Atl	NL	33	32	1	0	202.1	847	214	108	104	31	13	5	2	67	4	80	4	1	11	9	.550	1	0-0	0	4.66	4.63
2006	Atl	NL	14	14	0	0	76.1	337	85	42	38	6	3	3	4	31	2	37	0	1	5	5	.500	0	0-0	0	4.82	4.48
2007	Sea	AL	20	20	0	0	98.0	459	139	86	78	13	1	1	2	42	1	40	1	0	8	7	.533	0	0-0	0	7.17	7.16
2008	2 Tms		32	0	0	7	37.1	168	45	20	18	1	3	1	2	9	1	13	2	0	1	4	.200	0	0-0	2	4.13	4.34
08	CWS	AL	17	0	0	3	13.0	72	24	11	11	0	3	0	0	8	1	2	1	0	0	3	.000	0	0-0	1	8.89	7.62
08	KC	AL	15	0	0	4	24.1	96	21	9	7	1	0	1	2	1	0	11	1	0	1	1	.500	0	0-0	1	1.99	2.59
6 ML YEARS			138	104	3	7	656.2	2851	715	371	335	79	34	14	16	251	23	301	12	5	39	33	.542	1	0-0	2	4.77	4.59

Manny Ramirez

Bats: R **Throws:** R **Pos:** LF-119; DH-31; PH-3 **Ht:** 6'0" **Wt:** 200 **Born:** 5/30/1972 **Age:** 37

Year	Team	Lg	G	AB	H	2B	3B	HR	(Hm	Rd)	TB	R	RBI	RC	TBB	IBB	SO	HBP	SH	SF	SB	CS	SB%	GDP	Avg	OBP	Slg
			BATTING																		**BASERUNNING**				**AVERAGES**		
1993	Cle	AL	22	53	9	1	0	2	(0	2)	16	5	5	2	2	0	8	0	0	0	0	0	-	3	.170	.200	.302
1994	Cle	AL	91	290	78	22	0	17	(9	8)	151	51	60	53	42	4	72	0	0	4	4	2	.67	6	.269	.357	.521
1995	Cle	AL	137	484	149	26	1	31	(12	19)	270	85	107	103	75	6	112	5	2	5	6	6	.50	13	.308	.402	.558
1996	Cle	AL	152	550	170	45	3	33	(19	14)	320	94	112	120	85	8	104	3	0	9	8	5	.62	18	.309	.399	.582
1997	Cle	AL	150	561	184	40	0	26	(14	12)	302	99	88	117	79	5	115	7	0	4	2	3	.40	19	.328	.415	.538
1998	Cle	AL	150	571	168	35	2	45	(25	20)	342	108	145	121	76	6	121	6	0	10	5	3	.63	18	.294	.377	.599
1999	Cle	AL	147	522	174	34	3	44	(21	23)	346	131	**165**	**141**	96	9	131	13	0	9	2	4	.33	12	.333	.442	**.663**
2000	Cle	AL	118	439	154	34	2	38	(22	16)	306	92	122	127	86	9	117	3	0	4	1	1	.50	9	.351	.457	**.697**
2001	Bos	AL	142	529	162	33	2	41	(21	20)	322	93	125	122	81	**25**	147	8	0	2	0	1	.00	9	.306	.405	.609
2002	Bos	AL	120	436	152	31	0	33	(18	15)	282	84	107	125	73	14	85	8	0	1	0	0	-	13	**.349**	**.450**	.647
2003	Bos	AL	154	569	185	36	1	37	(18	19)	334	117	104	128	97	**28**	94	8	0	5	3	1	.75	22	.325	**.427**	.587
2004	Bos	AL	152	568	175	44	0	**43**	(23	20)	348	108	130	124	82	15	124	6	0	7	2	4	.33	17	.308	.397	**.613**
2005	Bos	AL	152	554	162	30	1	45	(22	23)	329	112	144	134	80	9	119	10	0	6	1	0	1.00	6	.292	.388	.594
2006	Bos	AL	130	449	144	27	1	35	(16	19)	278	79	102	114	100	16	102	1	0	0	0	1	.00	13	.321	**.439**	.619
2007	Bos	AL	133	483	143	33	1	20	(10	10)	238	84	88	78	71	13	92	7	0	8	0	0	-	21	.296	.388	.493
2008	2 Tms		153	552	183	36	1	37	(17	20)	332	102	121	133	87	24	124	11	0	4	3	0	1.00	17	.332	.430	.601
08	Bos	AL	100	365	109	22	1	20	(8	12)	193	66	68	69	52	8	86	8	0	0	1	0	1.00	12	.299	.398	.529
08	LAD	NL	53	187	74	14	0	17	(9	8)	139	36	53	64	35	16	38	3	0	4	2	0	1.00	5	.396	.489	.743
Postseason			95	353	95	14	0	24	(10	14)	181	55	64	66	59	8	81	5	0	6	1	1	.50	11	.269	.376	.513
16 ML YEARS			2103	7610	2392	507	18	527	(267	260)	4516	1444	1725	1742	1212	191	1667	96	2	86	37	31	.54	230	.314	.411	.593

Max Ramirez

Bats: R **Throws:** R **Pos:** C-12; 1B-3; DH-2; PH-2 **Ht:** 5'11" **Wt:** 175 **Born:** 10/11/1984 **Age:** 24

Year	Team	Lg	G	AB	H	2B	3B	HR	(Hm	Rd)	TB	R	RBI	RC	TBB	IBB	SO	HBP	SH	SF	SB	CS	SB%	GDP	Avg	OBP	Slg
			BATTING																		**BASERUNNING**				**AVERAGES**		
2004	Braves	R	57	204	56	16	1	8	(-	-)	98	20	35	34	19	0	50	3	0	4	1	0	1.00	4	.275	.339	.480
2005	Danvle	R+	63	239	83	19	0	8	(-	-)	126	45	47	53	31	2	41	4	0	4	1	2	.33	5	.347	.424	.527
2006	Rome	A	80	267	76	17	0	9	(-	-)	120	50	37	53	54	0	72	3	0	2	2	0	1.00	6	.285	.408	.449
2006	Lk Cty	A	37	127	39	6	1	4	(-	-)	59	19	26	28	30	0	27	1	0	3	0	0	-	3	.307	.435	.465
2007	Knstn	A+	77	277	84	20	0	12	(-	-)	140	46	62	62	53	2	63	6	0	6	1	0	1.00	9	.303	.418	.505
2007	Bkrsfld	A+	32	114	35	10	0	4	(-	-)	57	16	20	25	21	1	39	2	0	1	1	0	1.00	1	.307	.420	.500
2008	Frisco	AA	69	243	86	16	2	17	(-	-)	157	49	50	66	37	0	56	7	0	2	2	2	.50	4	.354	.450	.646
2008	Okla	AAA	10	37	9	1	0	2	(-	-)	16	5	6	4	3	0	13	0	0	1	0	0	-	2	.243	.293	.432
2008	Rngrs	R	2	5	4	2	0	0	(-	-)	6	4	1	3	2	0	0	0	0	0	0	0	-	0	.800	.857	1.200
2008	Tex	AL	17	46	10	1	0	2	(1	1)	17	8	9	8	6	0	15	3	0	0	0	0	-	0	.217	.345	.370

Ramon Ramirez

Pitches: R Bats: R Pos: RP-71   Ht: 5'11" Wt: 190 Born: 8/31/1981 Age: 27

			HOW MUCH HE PITCHED						WHAT HE GAVE UP											THE RESULTS							
Year	Team	Lg	G	GS	CG	GF	IP	BFP	H	R	ER	HR	SH	SF	HB	TBB	IBB	SO	WP	Bk	W	L	Pct	ShO	Sv-Op	Hld	ERC	ERA
2006	Col	NL	61	0	0	14	67.2	285	58	28	26	5	2	3	1	27	3	61	2	0	4	3	.571	0	0-2	10	3.09	3.46
2007	Col	NL	22	0	0	5	17.1	78	21	16	16	2	2	2	1	6	2	15	2	0	2	2	.500	0	0-0	3	5.24	8.31
2008	KC	AL	71	0	0	15	71.2	295	57	23	21	2	4	3	0	31	6	70	6	1	3	2	.600	0	1-5	21	2.53	2.64
3 ML YEARS			154	0	0	34	156.2	658	136	67	63	9	8	8	2	64	11	146	10	1	9	7	.563	0	1-7	34	3.05	3.62

Ramon A Ramirez

Pitches: R Bats: R Pos: SP-4; RP-1   Ht: 5'10" Wt: 172 Born: 9/16/1982 Age: 26

			HOW MUCH HE PITCHED						WHAT HE GAVE UP											THE RESULTS							
Year	Team	Lg	G	GS	CG	GF	IP	BFP	H	R	ER	HR	SH	SF	HB	TBB	IBB	SO	WP	Bk	W	L	Pct	ShO	Sv-Op	Hld	ERC	ERA
2004	Billings	R+	17	12	0	2	74.1	310	63	36	28	7	10	3	9	36	0	60	5	2	3	6	.333	0	1--	-	4.19	3.39
2005	Dayton	A	30	19	0	2	114.0	502	114	69	57	8	0	7	15	50	0	90	9	1	5	7	.417	0	0--	-	4.60	4.50
2006	Srsota	A+	15	11	1	2	65.0	279	66	33	31	11	1	1	3	21	0	53	5	2	4	5	.444	0	0--	-	4.53	4.29
2007	Srsota	A+	15	12	0	1	73.1	303	64	37	33	5	1	0	1	25	0	86	4	0	5	2	.714	0	1--	-	3.02	4.05
2007	Chatt	AA	16	0	0	3	31.1	132	30	16	16	3	2	0	0	12	1	34	3	1	5	1	.833	0	1--	-	3.74	4.60
2007	Lsvlle	AAA	5	2	0	1	14.2	54	7	0	0	1	0	0	0	6	0	16	1	0	1	0	1.000	0	0--	-	1.24	0.00
2008	Chatt	AA	11	9	0	2	46.0	193	41	29	24	6	1	2	2	15	0	52	4	0	2	3	.400	0	1--	-	3.55	4.70
2008	Lsvlle	AAA	19	15	0	2	99.1	400	76	37	34	8	3	0	1	42	1	93	4	1	4	5	.444	0	1--	-	2.89	3.08
2008	Cin	NL	5	4	0	0	27.0	105	17	8	8	3	0	0	1	11	0	21	0	1	1	1	.500	0	0-0	0	2.48	2.67

Cody Ransom

Bats: R Throws: R Pos: 1B-19; SS-9; PR-5; 3B-4; 2B-2; PH-1   Ht: 6'2" Wt: 190 Born: 2/17/1976 Age: 33

			BATTING																			BASERUNNING				AVERAGES		
Year	Team	Lg	G	AB	H	2B	3B	HR	(Hm	Rd)	TB	R	RBI	RC	TBB	IBB	SO	HBP	SH	SF	SB	CS	SB%	GDP	Avg	OBP	Slg
2008	S-WB*	AAA	116	423	108	24	3	22	(-	-)	204	69	71	71	50	0	115	4	2	2	9	5	.64	9	.255	.338	.482
2001	SF	NL	9	7	0	0	0	0	(0	0)	0	1	0	0	0	0	5	0	0	0	0	0	-	0	.000	.000	.000
2002	SF	NL	7	3	2	0	0	0	(0	0)	2	2	1	1	1	1	1	0	0	0	0	0	-	0	.667	.750	.667
2003	SF	NL	20	27	6	1	0	1	(1	0)	10	7	1	1	1	0	11	0	0	0	0	0	-	0	.222	.250	.370
2004	SF	NL	78	68	17	6	0	1	(0	1)	26	13	11	9	6	0	20	1	3	0	2	2	.50	2	.250	.320	.382
2007	Hou	NL	19	35	8	2	0	1	(1	0)	13	9	3	6	9	1	9	2	0	0	0	0	-	1	.229	.413	.371
2008	NYY	AL	33	43	13	3	0	4	(1	3)	28	9	8	10	6	0	12	1	1	0	0	0	-	0	.302	.400	.651
6 ML YEARS			166	183	46	12	0	7	(3	4)	79	41	24	27	23	2	58	4	4	0	2	2	.50	3	.251	.348	.432

Clay Rapada

Pitches: L Bats: R Pos: RP-25   Ht: 6'5" Wt: 200 Born: 3/9/1981 Age: 28

			HOW MUCH HE PITCHED						WHAT HE GAVE UP											THE RESULTS							
Year	Team	Lg	G	GS	CG	GF	IP	BFP	H	R	ER	HR	SH	SF	HB	TBB	IBB	SO	WP	Bk	W	L	Pct	ShO	Sv-Op	Hld	ERC	ERA
2002	Boise	A-	12	0	0	0	18.0	85	18	7	3	0	0	2	3	8	0	12	0	0	0	0	-	0	1--	-	3.92	1.50
2003	Boise	A-	1	0	0	0	3.0	12	2	0	0	0	1	0	0	1	0	3	0	0	0	0	-	0	0--	-	1.57	0.00
2003	Lansng	A	21	4	0	2	42.1	193	46	29	25	3	0	3	3	19	0	24	1	0	1	2	.333	0	0--	-	4.76	5.31
2004	Lansng	A	57	0	0	18	85.0	353	65	30	22	2	0	0	4	30	4	91	4	0	6	6	.500	0	3--	-	2.24	2.33
2005	Dytona	A+	27	0	0	12	42.1	186	40	21	18	2	4	0	3	16	0	61	2	2	1	3	.250	0	5--	-	3.50	3.83
2006	WTenn	AA	33	0	0	28	43.2	169	30	7	4	1	0	4	2	10	2	45	0	0	3	2	.600	0	21--	-	1.60	0.82
2006	Iowa	AAA	28	0	0	5	23.2	109	27	8	8	0	3	2	2	15	1	21	3	1	3	2	.600	0	0--	-	5.44	3.04
2007	Iowa	AAA	55	0	0	39	55.1	234	55	24	22	4	0	4	3	25	3	50	2	0	7	2	.778	0	17--	-	4.36	3.58
2007	Toledo	AAA	2	0	0	0	2.1	13	5	3	3	0	0	0	0	1	0	3	2	0	0	0	-	0	0--	-	10.38	11.57
2008	Toledo	AAA	28	0	0	9	35.0	151	32	10	9	2	2	2	2	14	3	45	0	0	0	1	.000	0	2--	-	3.36	2.31
2007	2 Tms		5	0	0	2	2.2	13	3	3	3	2	0	0	0	2	0	4	2	0	0	0	-	0	0-0	0	11.59	10.13
2008	Det	AL	25	0	0	3	21.1	94	19	11	10	0	1	0	1	14	1	15	1	0	3	0	1.000	0	0-0	2	3.87	4.22
07	ChC	NL	1	0	0	0	0.1	3	1	0	0	0	0	0	0	0	0	0	0	0	0	0	-	0	0-0	0	0.00	0.00
07	Det	AL	4	0	0	2	2.1	12	3	3	3	2	0	0	0	2	0	4	2	0	0	0	-	0	0-0	0	14.48	11.57
2 ML YEARS			30	0	0	5	24.0	107	22	14	13	2	1	0	1	16	1	19	3	0	3	0	1.000	0	0-0	2	4.69	4.88

Darrell Rasner

Pitches: R Bats: R Pos: SP-20; RP-4   Ht: 6'3" Wt: 210 Born: 1/13/1981 Age: 28

			HOW MUCH HE PITCHED						WHAT HE GAVE UP											THE RESULTS							
Year	Team	Lg	G	GS	CG	GF	IP	BFP	H	R	ER	HR	SH	SF	HB	TBB	IBB	SO	WP	Bk	W	L	Pct	ShO	Sv-Op	Hld	ERC	ERA
2008	S-WB*	AAA	5	5	0	0	31.0	114	18	4	3	0	1	1	0	6	0	27	0	0	4	0	1.000	0	0--	-	1.08	0.87
2005	Was	NL	5	1	0	1	7.1	31	5	3	3	0	1	0	2	2	1	4	0	0	0	1	.000	0	0-0	0	2.03	3.68
2006	NYY	AL	6	3	0	1	20.1	83	18	10	10	2	1	0	1	5	0	11	1	0	3	1	.750	0	0-0	0	3.07	4.43
2007	NYY	AL	6	6	0	0	24.2	111	29	14	11	4	0	1	2	8	0	11	0	0	1	3	.250	0	0-0	0	5.56	4.01
2008	NYY	AL	24	20	0	1	113.1	513	135	74	68	14	5	3	5	39	1	67	4	0	5	10	.333	0	0-0	0	5.23	5.40
4 ML YEARS			41	30	0	3	165.2	738	187	101	92	20	7	4	10	54	2	93	5	0	9	15	.375	0	0-0	0	4.84	5.00

Jon Rauch

Pitches: R Bats: R Pos: RP-74   Ht: 6'11" Wt: 291 Born: 9/27/1978 Age: 30

			HOW MUCH HE PITCHED						WHAT HE GAVE UP											THE RESULTS							
Year	Team	Lg	G	GS	CG	GF	IP	BFP	H	R	ER	HR	SH	SF	HB	TBB	IBB	SO	WP	Bk	W	L	Pct	ShO	Sv-Op	Hld	ERC	ERA
2002	CWS	AL	8	6	0	1	28.2	130	28	26	21	7	0	1	2	14	2	19	1	1	2	1	.667	0	0-0	0	5.41	6.59
2004	2 Tms		11	4	0	1	32.0	131	30	10	10	1	2	1	0	11	2	22	2	0	4	1	.800	0	0-0	0	3.05	2.81
2005	Was	NL	15	1	0	4	30.0	124	24	12	12	3	1	1	1	11	2	23	2	0	2	4	.333	0	0-0	0	2.90	3.60
2006	Was	NL	85	0	0	19	91.1	383	78	37	34	13	1	6	2	36	6	86	4	1	4	5	.444	0	2-5	18	3.52	3.35
2007	Was	NL	88	0	0	26	87.1	354	75	37	35	7	2	5	0	21	4	71	2	0	8	4	.667	0	4-10	33	2.53	3.61

Year	Team	Lg	G	GS	CG	GF	IP	BFP	H	R	ER	HR	SH	SF	HB	TBB	IBB	SO	WP	Bk	W	L	Pct	ShO	Sv-Op	Hld	ERC	ERA
2008	2 Tms	NL	74	0	0	51	71.2	295	69	36	33	11	6	3	0	16	2	66	1	0	4	8	.333	0	18-24	6	3.48	4.14
04	CWS	AL	2	2	0	0	8.2	43	16	6	6	0	1	1	0	4	0	4	1	0	1	1	.500	0	0-0	0	9.15	6.23
04	Mon	NL	9	2	0	1	23.1	88	14	4	4	1	1	0	0	7	2	18	1	0	3	0	1.000	0	0-0	0	1.44	1.54
08	Was	NL	48	0	0	41	48.1	192	42	18	16	5	3	1	0	7	1	44	0	0	4	2	.667	0	17-22	0	2.41	2.98
08	Ari	NL	26	0	0	10	23.1	103	27	18	17	6	3	2	0	9	1	22	1	0	0	6	.000	0	1-2	6	6.09	6.56
6 ML YEARS			281	11	0	102	341.0	1417	304	158	145	42	12	17	5	109	18	287	12	2	24	23	.511	0	24-39	57	3.30	3.83

Chris Ray

Pitches: R Bats: R Pos: P Ht: 6'3" Wt: 214 Born: 1/12/1982 Age: 27

Year	Team	Lg	G	GS	CG	GF	IP	BFP	H	R	ER	HR	SH	SF	HB	TBB	IBB	SO	WP	Bk	W	L	Pct	ShO	Sv-Op	Hld	ERC	ERA
2008	Orioles*	R	3	3	0	0	3.0	12	3	0	0	0	0	0	0	0	0	3	0	0	0	0	-	0	0--	-	1.95	0.00
2008	Frdrck*	A+	1	0	0	0	1.0	6	3	2	2	1	0	0	0	0	0	1	1	0	0	0	-	0	0--	-	25.51	18.00
2008	Abrdn*	A-	3	0	0	0	3.0	13	4	0	0	0	0	0	0	0	0	5	0	0	0	0	-	0	0--	-	3.56	0.00
2008	Dlmrva*	A	1	0	0	0	1.0	3	1	0	0	0	0	0	0	0	0	2	0	0	0	0	-	0	0--	-	2.79	0.00
2008	Bowie*	AA	1	0	0	0	1.0	3	0	0	0	0	0	0	0	0	0	2	0	0	0	0	-	0	0--	-	0.00	0.00
2005	Bal	AL	41	0	0	8	40.2	174	34	15	12	5	1	1	1	18	3	43	0	1	1	3	.250	0	0-4	8	3.43	2.66
2006	Bal	AL	61	0	0	56	66.0	267	45	22	20	10	2	4	1	27	2	51	2	0	4	4	.500	0	33-38	0	2.77	2.73
2007	Bal	AL	43	0	0	37	42.2	179	35	22	21	5	0	1	2	18	2	44	1	0	5	6	.455	0	16-20	0	3.42	4.43
3 ML YEARS			145	0	0	101	149.1	620	114	59	53	20	3	6	4	63	7	138	3	1	10	13	.435	0	49-62	8	3.13	3.19

Tim Redding

Pitches: R Bats: R Pos: SP-33 Ht: 5'11" Wt: 225 Born: 2/12/1978 Age: 31

Year	Team	Lg	G	GS	CG	GF	IP	BFP	H	R	ER	HR	SH	SF	HB	TBB	IBB	SO	WP	Bk	W	L	Pct	ShO	Sv-Op	Hld	ERC	ERA
2001	Hou	NL	13	9	0	1	55.2	249	62	38	34	11	2	3	3	24	0	55	2	0	3	1	.750	0	0-0	0	5.87	5.50
2002	Hou	NL	18	14	0	1	73.1	325	78	49	44	10	4	3	0	35	3	63	5	1	3	6	.333	0	0-0	0	4.96	5.40
2003	Hou	NL	33	32	0	0	176.0	769	179	85	72	16	7	3	7	65	4	116	3	0	10	14	.417	0	0-0	0	4.07	3.68
2004	Hou	NL	27	17	0	2	100.2	465	125	73	64	15	10	3	5	43	3	56	2	0	5	7	.417	0	0-0	0	6.14	5.72
2005	2 Tms		10	7	0	0	30.2	154	44	41	36	7	3	3	2	17	1	19	1	0	0	6	.000	0	0-0	0	8.60	10.57
2007	Was	NL	15	15	0	0	84.0	366	84	35	34	10	6	1	4	38	4	47	1	1	3	6	.333	0	0-0	0	4.59	3.64
2008	Was	NL	33	33	1	0	182.0	791	195	110	100	27	5	5	7	65	5	120	10	0	10	11	.476	0	0-0	0	4.80	4.95
05	SD	NL	9	6	0	0	29.2	143	40	35	30	7	3	3	2	13	1	17	1	0	0	5	.000	0	0-0	0	7.56	9.10
05	NYY	AL	1	1	0	0	1.0	11	4	6	6	0	0	0	0	4	0	2	0	0	0	1	.000	0	0-0	0	43.35	54.00
7 ML YEARS			149	127	1	4	702.1	3119	767	431	384	96	37	21	28	287	20	476	24	2	34	51	.400	0	0-0	0	5.03	4.92

Mark Redman

Pitches: L Bats: L Pos: SP-9; RP-1 Ht: 6'5" Wt: 245 Born: 1/5/1974 Age: 35

Year	Team	Lg	G	GS	CG	GF	IP	BFP	H	R	ER	HR	SH	SF	HB	TBB	IBB	SO	WP	Bk	W	L	Pct	ShO	Sv-Op	Hld	ERC	ERA
2008	ColSpr*	AAA	18	12	0	1	85.0	363	96	53	50	5	5	3	2	22	0	51	6	0	8	4	.667	0	0--	0	4.09	5.29
1999	Min	AL	5	1	0	0	12.2	65	17	13	12	3	0	0	1	7	0	11	0	0	1	0	1.000	0	0-0	0	7.86	8.53
2000	Min	AL	32	24	0	3	151.1	651	168	81	80	22	3	2	3	45	0	117	6	0	12	9	.571	0	0-0	0	4.73	4.76
2001	2 Tms	AL	11	11	0	0	58.0	261	68	32	29	7	2	0	1	23	0	33	6	0	2	6	.250	0	0-0	0	5.26	4.50
2002	Det	AL	30	30	3	0	203.0	858	211	107	95	15	5	8	6	51	2	109	11	1	8	15	.348	0	0-0	0	3.64	4.21
2003	Fla	NL	29	29	3	0	190.2	802	172	82	76	16	10	5	5	61	3	151	8	2	14	9	.609	0	0-0	0	3.17	3.59
2004	Oak	AL	32	32	2	0	191.0	832	218	110	100	28	5	7	6	68	6	102	6	1	11	12	.478	0	0-0	0	5.23	4.71
2005	Pit	NL	30	30	2	0	178.1	751	188	110	97	18	11	5	2	56	3	101	7	3	5	15	.250	1	0-0	0	4.15	4.90
2006	KC	AL	29	29	2	0	167.0	740	202	110	106	19	6	4	8	63	1	76	12	2	11	10	.524	1	0-0	0	5.63	5.71
2007	2 Tms	NL	11	8	0	0	41.1	200	59	37	35	6	0	2	2	17	2	27	1	1	2	4	.333	0	0-0	0	7.09	7.62
2008	Col	NL	10	9	0	1	45.1	211	61	40	38	7	5	1	1	16	2	20	1	0	2	5	.286	0	0-0	0	6.31	7.54
01	Min	AL	9	9	0	0	49.0	219	57	26	24	6	1	0	0	19	0	29	6	0	2	4	.333	0	0-0	0	5.11	4.22
01	Det	AL	2	2	0	0	9.0	42	11	6	6	1	1	0	1	4	0	4	0	0	0	2	.000	0	0-0	0	6.12	6.00
07	Atl	NL	6	5	0	0	21.2	116	38	29	28	4	0	2	2	11	2	13	1	0	0	4	.000	0	0-0	0	10.10	11.63
07	Col	NL	5	3	0	0	19.2	84	21	8	7	2	0	0	0	6	0	14	0	1	2	0	1.000	0	0-0	0	4.10	3.20
Postseason			4	4	0	0	18.0	87	25	13	13	3	2	1	2	9	1	10	1	0	0	1	.000	0	0-0	0	7.89	6.50
10 ML YEARS			219	203	12	4	1238.2	5371	1364	712	668	141	47	34	35	407	19	747	58	10	68	85	.444	2	0-0	0	4.58	4.85

Mike Redmond

Bats: R Throws: R Pos: C-30; DH-4; PH-4 Ht: 5'11" Wt: 200 Born: 5/5/1971 Age: 38

Year	Team	Lg	G	AB	H	2B	3B	HR	(Hm	Rd)	TB	R	RBI	RC	TBB	IBB	SO	HBP	SH	SF	SB	CS	SB%	GDP	Avg	OBP	Slg
1998	Fla	NL	37	118	39	9	0	2	(1	1)	54	10	12	18	5	2	16	2	4	0	0	0	-	6	.331	.368	.458
1999	Fla	NL	84	242	73	9	0	1	(0	1)	85	22	27	33	26	2	34	5	5	0	0	0	-	6	.302	.381	.351
2000	Fla	NL	87	210	53	8	1	0	(0	0)	63	17	15	20	13	3	19	8	1	3	0	0	-	5	.252	.316	.300
2001	Fla	NL	48	141	44	4	0	4	(3	1)	60	19	14	21	13	4	13	2	1	1	0	0	-	6	.312	.376	.426
2002	Fla	NL	89	256	78	15	0	2	(1	1)	99	19	28	37	21	8	34	8	2	3	0	2	.00	2	.305	.372	.387
2003	Fla	NL	59	125	30	7	1	0	(0	0)	39	12	11	10	7	0	16	5	2	2	0	0	-	2	.240	.302	.312
2004	Fla	NL	81	246	63	15	0	2	(0	2)	84	19	25	27	14	0	28	8	3	2	1	0	1.00	10	.256	.315	.341
2005	Min	AL	45	148	46	9	0	1	(1	0)	58	17	26	23	6	0	14	3	2	0	0	0	-	9	.311	.350	.392
2006	Min	AL	47	179	61	13	0	0	(0	0)	74	20	23	22	4	0	18	4	1	2	0	0	-	9	.341	.365	.413
2007	Min	AL	82	272	80	13	0	1	(1	0)	96	23	38	38	18	3	23	5	0	3	0	0	-	9	.294	.346	.353
2008	Min	AL	38	129	37	6	0	0	(0	0)	43	14	12	12	5	0	11	2	0	1	0	0	-	6	.287	.321	.333
Postseason			2	1	0	0	0	0	(0	0)	0	1	0	0	1	0	0	0	0	0	0	0	-	0	.000	.500	.000
11 ML YEARS			697	2066	604	108	2	13	(6	7)	755	192	231	261	132	22	226	52	21	17	1	2	.33	74	.292	.348	.365

Jeremy Reed

Bats: L **Throws:** L **Pos:** CF-58; PH-17; RF-14; LF-6; DH-5; PR-2; 1B-1   **Ht:** 6'0" **Wt:** 200 **Born:** 6/15/1981 **Age:** 28

									BATTING											BASERUNNING				AVERAGES		
Year	Team	Lg	G	AB	H	2B	3B	HR	(Hm	Rd)	TB	R	RBI	RC	TBB	IBB	SO	HBP	SH	SF	SB	CS	SB%	GDP	Avg	OBP	Slg
2008	Tacom*	AAA	38	149	52	11	1	6	(-	-)	83	26	21	34	16	0	14	1	1	1	6	1	.86	3	.349	.413	.557
2004	Sea	AL	18	58	23	4	0	0	(0	0)	27	11	5	11	7	1	4	1	0	0	3	1	.75	2	.397	.470	.466
2005	Sea	AL	141	488	124	33	3	3	(0	3)	172	61	45	49	48	1	74	2	4	2	12	11	.52	10	.254	.322	.352
2006	Sea	AL	67	212	46	6	5	6	(1	5)	80	27	17	13	11	1	31	2	2	2	2	3	.40	5	.217	.260	.377
2007	Sea	AL	13	17	3	0	1	0	(0	0)	5	2	0	0	0	0	3	0	0	0	0	0	-	0	.176	.176	.294
2008	Sea	AL	97	286	77	18	1	2	(1	1)	103	30	31	31	18	0	38	2	3	3	2	3	.40	5	.269	.314	.360
	5 ML YEARS		336	1061	273	61	10	11	(2	9)	387	131	98	104	84	3	150	7	9	7	19	18	.51	22	.257	.314	.365

Steven Register

Pitches: R **Bats:** R **Pos:** RP-10   **Ht:** 6'1" **Wt:** 180 **Born:** 5/16/1983 **Age:** 26

			HOW MUCH HE PITCHED						WHAT HE GAVE UP											THE RESULTS						
Year	Team	Lg	G	GS	CG	GF	IP	BFP	H	R	ER	HR	SH	SF	HB	TBB	IBB	SO	WP	Bk	W	L	Pct	ShO	Sv-Op Hld	ERC	ERA
2004	TriCity	A-	15	15	0	0	79.1	326	68	41	32	5	6	2	7	20	0	63	2	0	6	7	.462	0	0- - -	2.85	3.63
2005	Mdest	A+	27	27	1	0	156.0	676	184	98	77	16	3	4	1	35	0	108	6	0	9	11	.450	0	0- - -	4.41	4.44
2006	Tulsa	AA	27	27	2	0	155.0	694	189	114	96	25	10	7	10	53	1	77	5	1	4	10	.286	0	0- - -	5.91	5.57
2007	Tulsa	AA	61	0	0	55	58.0	250	63	27	26	3	3	4	1	16	1	48	3	0	1	3	.250	0	37- - -	3.74	4.03
2008	ColSpr	AAA	56	0	0	45	59.0	251	57	25	22	4	3	1	3	19	0	52	3	0	5	3	.625	0	16- - -	3.56	3.36
2008	Col	NL	10	0	0	5	10.0	49	13	10	10	4	0	1	0	6	1	8	0	0	0	0	-	0	0-0 0	8.89	9.00

Chad Reineke

Pitches: R **Bats:** R **Pos:** SP-3; RP-1   **Ht:** 6'6" **Wt:** 210 **Born:** 4/9/1982 **Age:** 27

			HOW MUCH HE PITCHED						WHAT HE GAVE UP											THE RESULTS						
Year	Team	Lg	G	GS	CG	GF	IP	BFP	H	R	ER	HR	SH	SF	HB	TBB	IBB	SO	WP	Bk	W	L	Pct	ShO	Sv-Op Hld	ERC	ERA
2004	TriCity	A-	23	0	0	16	36.2	160	27	13	10	0	0	0	0	23	0	52	3	0	1	2	.333	0	3- - -	2.74	2.45
2005	Lxngtn	A	42	11	0	16	102.1	425	84	46	40	5	5	1	4	49	0	108	6	0	10	8	.556	0	4- - -	3.29	3.52
2006	Salem	A+	17	17	1	0	99.2	414	82	42	33	5	4	4	5	29	0	87	7	0	6	5	.545	0	0- - -	2.55	2.98
2006	CpChr	AA	15	4	0	2	44.1	187	33	17	15	3	2	0	1	26	1	45	1	0	1	3	.250	0	0- - -	3.27	3.05
2007	RdRck	AAA	32	16	0	4	100.0	439	99	61	52	7	4	4	0	52	7	95	7	0	5	5	.500	0	0- - -	4.17	4.68
2008	RdRck	AAA	20	19	1	0	112.1	480	112	62	55	15	3	1	1	35	0	100	2	0	5	9	.357	0	0- - -	3.93	4.41
2008	Portlnd	AAA	3	3	0	0	17.1	72	17	8	8	0	0	0	0	6	0	13	0	0	1	0	1.000	0	0- - -	5.17	4.15
2008	SD	NL	4	3	0	1	18.0	78	14	10	10	1	1	1	0	12	1	13	0	0	2	1	.667	0	0-0 0	3.48	5.00

Edgar Renteria

Bats: R **Throws:** R **Pos:** SS-138; PH-1   **Ht:** 6'1" **Wt:** 200 **Born:** 8/7/1975 **Age:** 33

									BATTING											BASERUNNING				AVERAGES		
Year	Team	Lg	G	AB	H	2B	3B	HR	(Hm	Rd)	TB	R	RBI	RC	TBB	IBB	SO	HBP	SH	SF	SB	CS	SB%	GDP	Avg	OBP	Slg
1996	Fla	NL	106	431	133	18	3	5	(2	3)	172	68	31	62	33	0	68	2	2	3	16	2	.89	12	.309	.358	.399
1997	Fla	NL	154	617	171	21	3	4	(3	1)	210	90	52	68	45	1	108	4	19	6	32	15	.68	17	.277	.327	.340
1998	Fla	NL	133	517	146	18	2	3	(1	2)	177	79	31	61	48	1	78	4	9	2	41	22	.65	13	.282	.347	.342
1999	StL	NL	154	585	161	36	2	11	(6	5)	234	92	63	81	53	0	82	2	6	7	37	8	.82	16	.275	.334	.400
2000	StL	NL	150	562	156	32	1	16	(4	12)	238	94	76	80	63	3	77	1	8	9	21	13	.62	19	.278	.346	.423
2001	StL	NL	141	493	128	19	3	10	(3	7)	183	54	57	57	39	4	73	3	8	6	17	4	.81	15	.260	.314	.371
2002	StL	NL	152	544	166	36	2	11	(4	7)	239	77	83	94	49	7	57	4	7	5	22	7	.76	17	.305	.364	.439
2003	StL	NL	157	587	194	47	1	13	(4	9)	282	96	100	103	65	12	54	1	7	3	34	7	.83	21	.330	.394	.480
2004	StL	NL	149	586	168	37	0	10	(7	3)	235	84	72	74	39	5	78	1	6	10	17	11	.61	14	.287	.327	.401
2005	Bos	AL	153	623	172	36	4	8	(3	5)	240	100	70	82	55	0	100	3	6	5	9	4	.69	15	.276	.335	.385
2006	Atl	NL	149	598	175	40	2	14	(4	10)	261	100	70	89	62	0	89	3	8	2	17	6	.74	17	.293	.361	.436
2007	Atl	NL	124	494	164	30	1	12	(5	7)	232	87	57	82	46	0	77	1	2	0	11	2	.85	14	.332	.390	.470
2008	Det	AL	138	503	136	22	2	10	(5	5)	192	69	55	61	37	1	64	0	2	5	6	3	.67	19	.270	.317	.382
	Postseason		55	207	51	12	0	1	(1	0)	66	30	17	23	23	1	34	3	6	2	9	1	.90	6	.246	.328	.319
	13 ML YEARS		1860	7140	2070	392	26	127	(52	75)	2895	1090	817	994	634	34	1005	29	86	67	280	104	.73	209	.290	.347	.405

Jason Repko

Bats: R **Throws:** R **Pos:** LF-12; RF-7; PH-5; PR-3; CF-2   **Ht:** 5'11" **Wt:** 190 **Born:** 12/27/1980 **Age:** 28

									BATTING											BASERUNNING				AVERAGES		
Year	Team	Lg	G	AB	H	2B	3B	HR	(Hm	Rd)	TB	R	RBI	RC	TBB	IBB	SO	HBP	SH	SF	SB	CS	SB%	GDP	Avg	OBP	Slg
2008	LsVgs*	AAA	121	459	130	26	7	12	(-	-)	206	89	50	82	50	2	108	18	4	4	20	6	.77	6	.283	.373	.449
2005	LAD	NL	129	276	61	15	3	8	(4	4)	106	43	30	28	16	1	80	7	2	0	5	0	1.00	7	.221	.281	.384
2006	LAD	NL	69	130	33	5	1	3	(1	2)	49	21	16	21	15	1	24	3	2	0	10	4	.71	2	.254	.345	.377
2008	LAD	NL	22	18	3	1	0	0	(0	0)	4	0	0	0	2	0	9	0	0	0	1	0	1.00	0	.167	.250	.222
	Postseason		1	0	0	0	0	0	(0	0)	0	0	0	0	0	0	0	0	0	0	0	0	-	0	-	-	-
	3 ML YEARS		220	424	97	21	4	11	(5	6)	159	64	46	49	33	2	113	10	4	0	16	4	.80	9	.229	.300	.375

Chris Resop

Pitches: R **Bats:** R **Pos:** RP-16   **Ht:** 6'3" **Wt:** 215 **Born:** 11/4/1982 **Age:** 26

			HOW MUCH HE PITCHED						WHAT HE GAVE UP											THE RESULTS						
Year	Team	Lg	G	GS	CG	GF	IP	BFP	H	R	ER	HR	SH	SF	HB	TBB	IBB	SO	WP	Bk	W	L	Pct	ShO	Sv-Op Hld	ERC	ERA
2008	Rchmd*	AAA	9	2	0	2	18.0	78	14	4	3	0	0	0	0	12	0	22	0	0	2	0	1.000	0	0- - -	3.17	1.50
2005	Fla	NL	15	0	0	6	17.0	80	22	16	16	1	0	2	1	9	0	15	3	0	2	0	1.000	0	0-0 0	6.35	8.47

Year	Team	Lg	G	GS	CG	GF	IP	BFP	H	R	ER	HR	SH	SF	HB	TBB	IBB	SO	WP	Bk	W	L	Pct	ShO	Sv-Op	Hld	ERC	ERA
2006	Fla	NL	22	0	0	10	21.1	101	26	9	8	1	0	0	1	16	5	10	0	0	1	2	.333	0	0-1	2	6.30	3.38
2007	LAA	AL	4	0	0	3	4.1	17	4	2	2	1	2	1	0	1	0	2	0	0	0	0	-	0	0-0	0	4.00	4.15
2008	Atl	NL	16	0	0	9	18.1	82	16	12	12	2	2	1	2	10	2	13	0	0	0	1	.000	0	0-0	2	4.19	5.89
	4 ML YEARS		57	0	0	28	61.0	280	68	39	38	5	4	4	4	36	7	40	3	0	3	3	.500	0	0-1	4	5.51	5.61

Al Reyes

Pitches: R Bats: R Pos: RP-26   Ht: 6'1" Wt: 230 Born: 4/10/1970 Age: 39

Year	Team	Lg	G	GS	CG	GF	IP	BFP	H	R	ER	HR	SH	SF	HB	TBB	IBB	SO	WP	Bk	W	L	Pct	ShO	Sv-Op	Hld	ERC	ERA
2008	VeroB*	A+	6	6	0	0	6.0	23	4	2	2	1	0	0	0	0	0	6	0	0	0	1	.000	0	0- -	-	1.35	3.00
2008	Bnghtn*	AA	5	0	0	2	5.0	20	4	0	0	0	0	0	1	2	0	3	0	0	0	0	-	0	1- -	-	3.31	0.00
1995	Mil	AL	27	0	0	13	33.1	138	19	9	9	3	1	2	3	18	2	29	0	0	1	1	.500	0	1-1	4	2.51	2.43
1996	Mil	AL	5	0	0	2	5.2	27	8	5	5	1	0	0	0	2	0	2	2	0	1	0	1.000	0	0-0	0	6.79	7.94
1997	Mil	AL	19	0	0	7	29.2	131	32	19	18	4	2	0	3	9	0	28	1	0	1	2	.333	0	1-1	1	4.76	5.46
1998	Mil	NL	50	0	0	13	57.0	253	55	26	25	9	2	1	2	31	1	58	0	0	5	1	.833	0	0-1	10	5.01	3.95
1999	2 Tms		53	0	0	12	65.2	287	50	33	33	9	4	3	6	41	3	67	3	0	4	3	.571	0	0-4	6	4.19	4.52
2000	2 Tms		19	0	0	6	19.2	86	15	10	10	2	1	2	0	12	1	18	0	0	1	0	1.000	0	0-1	3	3.43	4.58
2001	LAD	NL	19	0	0	9	25.2	120	28	13	11	3	0	2	1	13	1	23	0	1	2	1	.667	0	1-2	0	5.07	3.86
2002	Pit	NL	15	0	0	6	17.0	67	9	5	5	1	1	1	2	7	0	21	1	0	0	0	-	0	0-1	3	1.93	2.65
2003	NYY	AL	13	0	0	2	17.0	73	13	7	6	1	0	0	0	9	1	9	1	0	0	0	-	0	0-1	0	2.86	3.18
2004	StL	NL	12	2	0	4	12.0	41	3	1	1	0	2	0	0	2	0	11	0	0	0	0	-	0	0-0	0	0.31	0.75
2005	StL	NL	65	0	0	18	62.2	244	38	15	15	5	3	1	5	20	2	67	1	0	4	2	.667	0	3-3	16	1.94	2.15
2007	TB	AL	61	0	0	52	60.2	254	49	35	33	13	1	2	2	21	1	70	0	1	2	4	.333	0	26-30	0	3.60	4.90
2008	TB	AL	26	0	0	6	22.2	96	21	12	11	2	0	2	1	10	2	19	1	0	2	2	.500	0	0-1	2	3.86	4.37
99	Mil	NL	26	0	0	6	36.0	161	27	17	17	5	1	1	3	25	1	39	2	0	2	0	1.000	0	0-1	2	4.35	4.25
99	Bal	AL	27	0	0	6	29.2	126	23	16	16	4	3	2	3	16	2	28	1	0	2	3	.400	0	0-3	4	3.99	4.85
00	Bal	AL	13	0	0	2	13.0	62	13	10	10	2	1	2	0	11	1	10	0	0	1	0	1.000	0	0-1	2	6.14	6.92
00	LAD	NL	6	0	0	4	6.2	24	2	0	0	0	0	0	0	1	0	8	0	0	0	0	-	0	0-0	1	0.35	0.00
	Postseason		2	0	0	1	1.1	4	0	0	0	0	0	0	0	0	0	0	0	0	0	0	-	0	0-0	0	0.00	0.00
	13 ML YEARS		384	2	0	150	428.2	1817	340	190	182	53	17	16	25	195	14	422	13	1	23	16	.590	0	32-46	45	3.48	3.82

Anthony Reyes

Pitches: R Bats: R Pos: RP-10; SP-6   Ht: 6'2" Wt: 230 Born: 10/16/1981 Age: 27

Year	Team	Lg	G	GS	CG	GF	IP	BFP	H	R	ER	HR	SH	SF	HB	TBB	IBB	SO	WP	Bk	W	L	Pct	ShO	Sv-Op	Hld	ERC	ERA
2008	Memp*	AAA	11	11	0	0	52.2	223	51	21	19	4	2	1	3	21	0	47	3	1	2	3	.400	0	0- -	-	4.05	3.25
2008	Buffalo*	AAA	2	2	0	0	13.0	52	10	4	4	3	0	0	0	4	0	8	0	0	2	0	1.000	0	0- -	-	3.31	2.77
2005	StL	NL	4	1	0	0	13.1	51	6	4	4	2	1	1	0	4	1	12	2	0	1	1	.500	0	0-0	0	1.32	2.70
2006	StL	NL	17	17	1	0	85.1	370	84	48	48	17	5	3	7	34	0	72	2	0	5	8	.385	0	0-0	0	5.08	5.06
2007	StL	NL	22	20	1	1	107.1	474	108	77	72	16	1	7	9	43	0	74	1	2	2	14	.125	0	0-0	0	4.78	6.04
2008	2 Tms		16	6	0	6	49.0	203	47	15	15	4	1	0	1	15	0	25	0	0	4	2	.667	0	1-1	2	3.50	2.76
08	StL	NL	10	0	0	6	14.2	61	16	8	8	2	0	0	0	3	0	10	0	0	2	1	.667	0	1-1	2	4.11	4.91
08	Cle	AL	6	6	0	0	34.1	142	31	7	7	2	1	0	1	12	0	15	0	0	2	1	.667	0	0-0	0	3.24	1.83
	Postseason		2	2	0	0	12.0	48	7	4	4	3	0	0	0	5	0	8	0	0	1	0	1.000	0	0-0	0	2.81	3.00
	4 ML YEARS		59	44	2	7	255.0	1098	245	144	139	39	8	11	17	96	1	183	5	2	12	25	.324	0	1-1	2	4.41	4.91

Argenis Reyes

Bats: B Throws: R Pos: 2B-27; PH-25   Ht: 5'10" Wt: 165 Born: 9/25/1982 Age: 26

Year	Team	Lg	G	AB	H	2B	3B	HR	(Hm	Rd)	TB	R	RBI	RC	TBB	IBB	SO	HBP	SH	SF	SB	CS	SB%	GDP	Avg	OBP	Slg
2003	Burlgtn	R+	39	151	42	2	0	0	(-	-)	44	26	9	17	7	1	23	3	1	1	14	1	.93	3	.278	.321	.291
2004	MhVlly	A-	73	324	101	11	0	0	(-	-)	112	53	20	43	15	2	36	5	0	3	27	9	.75	4	.312	.349	.346
2005	Lk Cty	A	71	317	102	14	5	2	(-	-)	132	51	36	48	16	1	36	1	3	2	16	6	.73	4	.322	.354	.416
2005	Knstn	A+	52	202	52	4	1	1	(-	-)	61	23	13	18	8	0	38	1	5	1	8	3	.73	7	.257	.288	.302
2006	Knstn	A+	130	516	137	16	6	2	(-	-)	171	71	58	64	48	2	73	4	10	8	24	6	.80	14	.266	.328	.331
2007	Akron	AA	126	467	130	21	4	3	(-	-)	168	66	32	56	23	0	56	1	11	1	27	8	.77	14	.278	.313	.360
2008	NewOr	AAA	81	311	88	11	1	0	(-	-)	101	41	22	39	31	1	47	1	7	3	13	6	.68	2	.283	.347	.325
2008	NYM	NL	49	110	24	0	0	1	(1	0)	27	13	3	4	4	0	20	2	5	0	2	0	1.00	2	.218	.259	.245

Dennys Reyes

Pitches: L Bats: R Pos: RP-75   Ht: 6'3" Wt: 250 Born: 4/19/1977 Age: 32

Year	Team	Lg	G	GS	CG	GF	IP	BFP	H	R	ER	HR	SH	SF	HB	TBB	IBB	SO	WP	Bk	W	L	Pct	ShO	Sv-Op	Hld	ERC	ERA
1997	LAD	NL	14	0	0	4	47.0	207	51	21	20	4	5	1	4	18	3	36	2	1	2	3	.400	0	0-0	0	4.34	3.83
1998	2 Tms	NL	19	10	0	4	67.1	300	62	36	34	3	7	2	1	47	5	77	6	1	3	5	.375	0	0-0	0	4.37	4.54
1999	Cin	NL	65	1	0	12	61.2	277	53	30	26	5	4	3	3	39	1	72	5	1	2	2	.500	0	2-3	14	4.16	3.79
2000	Cin	NL	62	0	0	15	43.2	200	43	31	22	5	3	3	1	29	0	36	5	0	2	1	.667	0	0-1	10	5.24	4.53
2001	Cin	NL	35	6	0	2	53.0	246	51	35	29	5	2	2	1	35	1	52	5	0	2	6	.250	0	0-0	6	4.77	4.92
2002	2 Tms	NL	58	5	0	15	82.2	378	98	52	49	10	3	2	0	45	4	59	10	1	4	4	.500	0	0-0	4	5.90	5.33
2003	2 Tms	NL	15	0	0	4	12.2	63	15	16	15	2	1	2	0	10	1	16	5	0	0	0	-	0	0-0	2	6.96	10.66
2004	KC	AL	40	12	0	5	108.0	483	114	64	57	12	7	5	4	50	3	91	6	2	4	8	.333	0	0-1	5	4.81	4.75
2005	SD	NL	36	1	0	9	43.2	215	57	30	25	3	1	0	1	32	2	35	3	1	3	2	.600	0	0-1	4	7.06	5.15
2006	Min	AL	66	0	0	8	50.2	194	35	8	5	3	1	0	0	15	2	49	4	0	5	0	1.000	0	0-1	16	1.90	0.89
2007	Min	AL	50	0	0	7	29.1	139	34	14	13	1	3	3	2	21	1	21	4	0	2	1	.667	0	0-0	8	6.08	3.99
2008	Min	AL	75	0	0	16	46.1	188	40	12	12	4	4	0	2	15	2	39	5	0	1	0	1.000	0	0-3	17	3.14	2.33
98	LAD	NL	11	3	0	4	28.2	130	27	17	15	1	3	1	0	20	4	33	1	1	0	4	.000	0	0-0	0	4.16	4.71
98	Cin	NL	8	7	0	0	38.2	170	35	19	19	2	4	1	1	27	1	44	5	0	3	1	.750	0	0-0	0	4.54	4.42

Year	Team	Lg	G	GS	CG	GF	IP	BFP	H	R	ER	HR	SH	SF	HB	TBB	IBB	SO	WP	Bk	W	L	Pct	ShO	Sv-Op	Hld	ERC	ERA
																											HOW MUCH HE PITCHED / WHAT HE GAVE UP / THE RESULTS	
02	Col	NL	43	0	0	13	40.1	182	43	19	19	1	2	2	0	24	3	30	4	0	0	1	.000	0	0-0	4	4.55	4.24
02	Tex	AL	15	5	0	2	42.1	196	55	33	30	9	1	0	0	21	1	29	6	1	4	3	.571	0	0-0	0	7.24	6.38
03	Pit	NL	12	0	0	4	10.1	50	10	13	12	1	1	2	0	9	1	11	5	0	0	0	-	0	0-0	2	5.43	10.45
03	Ari	NL	3	0	0	0	2.1	13	5	3	3	1	0	0	0	1	0	5	0	0	0	0	-	0	0-0	0	14.73	11.57
Postseason			2	0	0	0	1.0	6	1	3	1	1	0	0	0	2	1	0	0	0	0	0	-	0	0-0	0	17.98	9.00
12 ML YEARS			535	40	0	97	646.0	2890	653	349	307	57	38	23	16	356	25	583	60	7	32	32	.500	0	2-10	82	4.69	4.28

Jo-Jo Reyes

Pitches: L Bats: L Pos: SP-22; RP-1   Ht: 6'2" Wt: 230 Born: 11/20/1984 Age: 24

Year	Team	Lg	G	GS	CG	GF	IP	BFP	H	R	ER	HR	SH	SF	HB	TBB	IBB	SO	WP	Bk	W	L	Pct	ShO	Sv-Op	Hld	ERC	ERA
2003	Braves	R	11	10	0	0	45.2	181	34	16	13	1	0	0	1	14	0	55	3	0	5	3	.625	0	0--	-	2.04	2.56
2004	Rome	A	15	14	1	1	74.1	328	84	49	44	10	7	4	2	25	2	71	3	3	2	4	.333	0	0--	-	4.86	5.33
2005	Braves	R	3	2	0	0	5.1	23	6	2	1	0	0	0	0	1	0	6	0	0	0	1	.000	0	0--	-	3.17	1.69
2005	Danvle	R	9	8	0	0	43.1	170	37	18	17	3	1	1	0	6	0	27	2	1	3	0	1.000	0	0--	-	2.17	3.53
2006	Rome	A	13	13	1	0	75.1	311	62	26	25	5	1	2	7	25	0	84	5	0	8	1	.889	1	0--	-	3.03	2.99
2006	MrtlBh	A+	14	14	0	0	65.2	281	52	36	30	0	3	3	3	36	0	58	1	0	4	4	.500	0	0--	-	2.99	4.11
2007	Missi	AA	13	13	0	0	73.1	308	63	31	29	5	2	5	3	35	0	71	0	0	8	1	.889	0	0--	-	3.62	3.56
2007	Rchmd	AAA	6	6	0	0	36.0	143	25	7	4	2	1	0	0	12	0	39	0	0	4	0	1.000	0	0--	-	2.00	1.00
2008	Rchmd	AAA	8	8	0	0	39.0	163	31	11	10	2	3	0	2	16	0	38	2	1	1	1	.500	0	0--	-	2.88	2.31
2007	Atl	NL	11	10	0	0	50.2	230	55	39	35	9	5	2	1	30	2	27	1	0	2	2	.500	0	0-0	0	6.06	6.22
2008	Atl	NL	23	22	0	0	113.0	512	134	77	73	18	9	3	3	52	4	78	2	0	3	11	.214	0	0-0	0	5.97	5.81
2 ML YEARS			34	32	0	0	163.2	742	189	116	108	27	14	5	4	82	6	105	3	0	5	13	.278	0	0-0	0	6.00	5.94

Jose Reyes

Bats: B Throws: R Pos: SS-159   Ht: 6'1" Wt: 200 Born: 6/11/1983 Age: 26

Year	Team	Lg	G	AB	H	2B	3B	HR	(Hm	Rd)	TB	R	RBI	RC	TBB	IBB	SO	HBP	SH	SF	SB	CS	SB%	GDP	Avg	OBP	Slg
2003	NYM	NL	69	274	84	12	4	5	(1	4)	119	47	32	46	13	0	36	0	2	3	13	3	.81	1	.307	.334	.434
2004	NYM	NL	53	220	56	16	2	2	(1	1)	82	33	14	25	5	0	31	0	4	0	19	2	.90	1	.255	.271	.373
2005	NYM	NL	161	696	190	24	17	7	(2	5)	269	99	58	84	27	0	78	2	4	4	60	15	.80	7	.273	.300	.386
2006	NYM	NL	153	647	194	30	17	19	(9	10)	315	122	81	121	53	6	81	1	2	0	64	17	.79	6	.300	.354	.487
2007	NYM	NL	160	681	191	36	12	12	(7	5)	287	119	57	99	77	13	78	1	5	1	78	21	.79	6	.280	.354	.421
2008	NYM	NL	159	688	204	37	19	16	(9	7)	327	113	68	117	66	8	82	1	5	3	56	15	.79	9	.297	.358	.475
Postseason			10	44	11	1	1	1	(1	0)	17	7	5	6	3	1	5	0	0	0	3	1	.75	0	.250	.298	.386
6 ML YEARS			755	3206	919	155	71	61	(29	32)	1399	533	310	492	241	27	386	5	22	11	290	73	.80	30	.287	.336	.436

Greg Reynolds

Pitches: R Bats: R Pos: SP-13; RP-1   Ht: 6'7" Wt: 225 Born: 7/3/1985 Age: 23

Year	Team	Lg	G	GS	CG	GF	IP	BFP	H	R	ER	HR	SH	SF	HB	TBB	IBB	SO	WP	Bk	W	L	Pct	ShO	Sv-Op	Hld	ERC	ERA
2006	Mdest	A+	11	11	0	0	48.2	205	51	22	18	1	0	0	3	14	0	29	3	0	2	1	.667	0	0--	-	3.67	3.33
2007	Tulsa	AA	8	8	0	0	50.2	196	32	10	8	2	1	0	2	9	0	35	0	0	4	1	.800	0	0--	-	1.41	1.42
2008	ColSpr	AAA	13	13	0	0	63.1	286	84	38	30	4	2	3	3	22	0	37	0	0	1	3	.250	0	0--	-	5.81	4.26
2008	Col	NL	14	13	0	0	62.0	294	83	58	56	14	4	2	4	26	3	22	2	0	2	8	.200	0	0-0	0	7.36	8.13

Mark Reynolds

Bats: R Throws: R Pos: 3B-150; PH-2; 1B-1   Ht: 6'2" Wt: 220 Born: 8/3/1983 Age: 25

Year	Team	Lg	G	AB	H	2B	3B	HR	(Hm	Rd)	TB	R	RBI	RC	TBB	IBB	SO	HBP	SH	SF	SB	CS	SB%	GDP	Avg	OBP	Slg
2004	Yakima	A-	64	234	64	19	1	12	(-	-)	121	58	41	46	25	3	65	13	3	2	4	1	.80	3	.274	.372	.517
2004	Sbend	A	4	15	1	1	0	0	(-	-)	2	0	0	0	1	0	5	0	0	0	0	0	-	0	.067	.125	.133
2004	Lancst	A+	4	12	1	0	0	0	(-	-)	1	1	1	0	0	0	4	0	0	0	0	0	-	0	.083	.083	.083
2005	Sbend	A	118	434	110	26	2	19	(-	-)	197	65	76	65	37	2	107	6	5	2	4	1	.80	7	.253	.319	.454
2006	Lancst	A+	76	273	92	18	2	23	(-	-)	183	64	77	73	41	1	72	3	0	5	1	1	.50	3	.337	.422	.670
2006	Tenn	AA	30	114	31	7	0	8	(-	-)	62	23	21	21	11	0	37	2	0	0	0	1	.00	1	.272	.346	.544
2007	Mobile	AA	37	134	41	9	2	6	(-	-)	72	28	21	28	20	2	32	0	0	1	3	1	.75	6	.306	.394	.537
2007	Ari	NL	111	366	102	20	4	17	(7	10)	181	62	62	62	37	4	129	5	1	0	0	0	.00	5	.279	.349	.495
2008	Ari	NL	152	539	129	28	3	28	(13	15)	247	87	97	82	64	0	204	3	1	6	11	2	.85	10	.239	.320	.458
Postseason			7	26	4	0	0	2	(1	1)	10	3	2	1	2	0	9	1	0	0	0	0	-	0	.154	.241	.385
2 ML YEARS			263	905	231	48	7	45	(20	25)	428	149	159	144	101	4	333	8	2	11	11	3	.79	15	.255	.332	.473

Arthur Rhodes

Pitches: L Bats: L Pos: RP-61   Ht: 6'2" Wt: 212 Born: 10/24/1969 Age: 39

Year	Team	Lg	G	GS	CG	GF	IP	BFP	H	R	ER	HR	SH	SF	HB	TBB	IBB	SO	WP	Bk	W	L	Pct	ShO	Sv-Op	Hld	ERC	ERA
2008	WTenn*	AA	1	1	0	0	0.1	4	2	3	1	0	0	0	0	1	0	1	0	0	0	0	1.000	0	0--	-	56.02	27.00
1991	Bal	AL	8	8	0	0	36.0	174	47	35	32	4	1	3	0	23	0	23	2	0	0	3	.000	0	0-0	0	7.00	8.00
1992	Bal	AL	15	15	2	0	94.1	394	87	39	38	6	5	1	1	38	2	77	2	1	7	5	.583	1	0-0	0	3.48	3.63
1993	Bal	AL	17	17	0	0	85.2	387	91	62	62	16	2	3	1	49	1	49	2	0	5	6	.455	0	0-0	0	5.88	6.51
1994	Bal	AL	10	10	3	0	52.2	238	51	34	34	8	2	3	2	30	1	47	3	0	3	5	.375	2	0-0	0	5.03	5.81
1995	Bal	AL	19	9	0	3	75.1	336	68	53	52	13	4	0	0	48	1	77	3	1	2	5	.286	0	0-1	0	4.97	6.21
1996	Bal	AL	28	2	0	5	53.0	224	48	28	24	6	1	1	0	23	3	62	0	0	9	1	.900	0	1-1	2	3.72	4.08
1997	Bal	AL	53	0	0	6	95.1	378	75	32	32	9	0	4	4	26	5	102	2	0	10	3	.769	0	1-2	9	2.58	3.02
1998	Bal	AL	45	0	0	10	77.0	321	65	30	30	8	2	5	1	34	2	83	1	1	4	4	.500	0	4-8	10	3.47	3.51

			HOW MUCH HE PITCHED						WHAT HE GAVE UP												THE RESULTS							
Year	Team	Lg	G	GS	CG	GF	IP	BFP	H	R	ER	HR	SH	SF	HB	TBB	IBB	SO	WP	Bk	W	L	Pct	ShO	Sv-Op	Hld	ERC	ERA
1999	Bal	AL	43	0	0	11	53.0	244	43	37	32	9	2	2	0	45	6	59	4	0	3	4	.429	0	3-5	5	5.07	5.43
2000	Sea	AL	72	0	0	9	69.1	281	51	34	33	6	1	2	0	29	3	77	4	0	5	8	.385	0	0-7	24	2.62	4.28
2001	Sea	AL	71	0	0	16	68.0	258	46	14	13	5	1	0	1	12	0	83	3	0	8	0	1.000	0	3-7	32	1.61	1.72
2002	Sea	AL	66	0	0	9	69.2	257	45	18	18	4	2	1	0	13	1	81	2	0	10	4	.714	0	2-7	27	1.46	2.33
2003	Sea	AL	67	0	0	14	54.0	228	53	25	25	4	2	0	1	18	2	48	2	0	3	3	.500	0	3-6	18	3.57	4.17
2004	Oak	AL	37	0	0	25	38.2	182	46	23	22	9	3	1	0	21	4	34	2	0	3	3	.500	0	9-14	3	6.54	5.12
2005	Cle	AL	47	0	0	8	43.1	175	33	13	10	2	0	2	1	12	2	43	0	0	3	1	.750	0	0-3	16	2.06	2.08
2006	Phi	NL	55	0	0	10	45.2	214	47	27	27	2	1	0	2	30	7	48	7	0	0	5	.000	0	4-7	23	4.63	5.32
2008	2 Tms		61	0	0	6	35.1	146	28	9	8	0	4	1	0	16	4	40	1	0	4	1	.800	0	2-3	24	2.36	2.04
08	Sea	AL	36	0	0	4	22.0	92	17	8	7	0	3	1	0	13	2	26	1	0	2	1	.667	0	1-2	13	2.79	2.86
08	Fla	NL	25	0	0	2	13.1	54	11	1	1	0	1	0	0	3	2	14	0	0	2	0	1.000	0	1-1	11	1.69	0.68
Postseason			20	0	0	0	17.0	75	16	9	9	2	2	1	0	10	2	19	4	0	0	1	.000	0	0-3	4	4.44	4.76
17 ML YEARS			714	61	5	132	1046.1	4437	924	513	492	111	33	29	14	467	44	1033	40	3	79	61	.564	3	32-71	193	3.66	4.23

Danny Richar

Bats: L Throws: R Pos: 2B-10; PH-9; SS-1   Ht: 6'1" Wt: 195 Born: 6/9/1983 Age: 26

			BATTING																		BASERUNNING				AVERAGES		
Year	Team	Lg	G	AB	H	2B	3B	HR	(Hm	Rd)	TB	R	RBI	RC	TBB	IBB	SO	HBP	SH	SF	SB	CS	SB%	GDP	Avg	OBP	Slg
2002	Lancst	A+	85	251	58	7	1	1	(-	-)	70	27	17	18	12	0	49	3	10	0	4	5	.44	2	.231	.274	.279
2002	Yakima	A-	25	88	20	5	1	0	(-	-)	27	7	9	6	6	0	21	0	1	1	0	3	.00	2	.227	.274	.307
2003	Lancst	A+	123	405	123	19	9	1	(-	-)	163	51	42	54	14	0	70	3	10	1	6	3	.67	10	.304	.331	.402
2004	ElPaso	AA	26	82	17	3	0	0	(-	-)	20	6	5	6	7	0	17	2	0	0	2	0	1.00	0	.207	.286	.244
2004	Lancst	A+	96	383	108	13	4	6	(-	-)	147	51	44	48	16	0	78	2	13	3	22	8	.73	2	.282	.312	.384
2005	Lancst	A+	121	454	136	32	8	20	(-	-)	244	78	79	85	32	0	64	3	10	4	9	3	.75	10	.300	.347	.537
2006	Tenn	AA	129	480	140	25	5	8	(-	-)	199	79	42	77	52	2	77	3	6	7	15	5	.75	2	.292	.360	.415
2007	Tucsn	AAA	66	265	75	19	4	8	(-	-)	126	39	46	43	27	2	47	0	3	2	3	5	.38	2	.283	.347	.475
2007	Charltt	AAA	32	133	46	5	4	5	(-	-)	74	21	15	29	10	2	24	2	0	0	4	0	1.00	4	.346	.400	.556
2008	Charltt	AAA	62	248	65	12	1	9	(-	-)	106	35	39	36	20	0	45	2	0	1	11	2	.85	2	.262	.321	.427
2008	Lsvlle	AAA	29	114	29	9	2	2	(-	-)	48	16	16	15	11	1	26	1	1	2	3	3	.50	2	.254	.320	.421
2007	CWS	AL	56	187	43	9	3	6	(3	3)	76	30	15	21	16	0	33	0	2	1	1	3	.25	5	.230	.289	.406
2008	Cin	NL	16	36	8	2	0	0	(0	0)	10	4	3	1	0	0	9	0	1	0	1	0	1.00	1	.222	.222	.278
2 ML YEARS			72	223	51	11	3	6	(3	3)	86	34	18	22	16	0	42	0	3	1	2	3	.40	6	.229	.279	.386

Clayton Richard

Pitches: L Bats: L Pos: SP-8; RP-5   Ht: 6'5" Wt: 240 Born: 9/12/1983 Age: 25

			HOW MUCH HE PITCHED						WHAT HE GAVE UP												THE RESULTS							
Year	Team	Lg	G	GS	CG	GF	IP	BFP	H	R	ER	HR	SH	SF	HB	TBB	IBB	SO	WP	Bk	W	L	Pct	ShO	Sv-Op	Hld	ERC	ERA
2005	Gr Falls	R+	10	9	0	0	41.0	168	37	19	13	2	0	1	1	12	0	39	0	1	2	1	.667	0	0--	-	2.93	2.85
2005	Knapol	A-	3	2	0	1	10.1	44	14	7	6	1	0	0	0	1	0	8	1	2	0	1	.000	0	0--	-	4.97	5.23
2006	Knapol	A-	18	17	0	0	95.2	423	117	49	39	0	4	6	7	28	0	54	8	0	6	6	.500	0	0--	-	4.52	3.67
2006	WinSa	A+	4	4	1	0	23.2	104	29	18	12	2	2	3	1	6	0	12	1	0	1	3	.250	0	0--	-	4.86	4.56
2007	WinSa	A+	28	27	1	1	161.1	684	159	86	65	11	5	8	5	59	0	99	4	2	8	12	.400	0	0--	-	3.81	3.63
2008	Brham	AA	13	13	1	0	83.2	327	66	29	23	2	2	1	4	16	0	53	3	0	6	6	.500	1	0--	-	1.98	2.47
2008	Charltt	AAA	7	7	1	0	44.0	167	33	12	12	3	0	0	1	4	0	33	0	2	6	0	1.000	0	0--	-	1.64	2.45
2008	CWS	AL	13	8	0	3	47.2	215	61	37	32	5	0	1	0	13	2	29	1	1	2	5	.286	0	0-0	0	5.06	6.04

Scott Richmond

Pitches: R Bats: R Pos: SP-5   Ht: 6'5" Wt: 225 Born: 8/30/1979 Age: 29

			HOW MUCH HE PITCHED						WHAT HE GAVE UP												THE RESULTS							
Year	Team	Lg	G	GS	CG	GF	IP	BFP	H	R	ER	HR	SH	SF	HB	TBB	IBB	SO	WP	Bk	W	L	Pct	ShO	Sv-Op	Hld	ERC	ERA
2008	NHam	AA	16	16	0	0	89.2	390	89	55	49	14	1	1	3	30	0	84	4	3	5	8	.385	0	0--	-	4.22	4.92
2008	Syrcse	AAA	8	8	1	0	48.0	197	44	20	19	6	2	1	1	13	0	40	2	0	1	3	.250	0	0--	-	3.39	3.56
2008	Tor	AL	5	5	1	0	27.0	113	32	12	12	2	0	1	2	2	0	20	0	0	1	3	.250	1	0-0	0	3.99	4.00

Jeff Ridgway

Pitches: L Bats: R Pos: RP-10   Ht: 6'3" Wt: 210 Born: 8/17/1980 Age: 28

			HOW MUCH HE PITCHED						WHAT HE GAVE UP												THE RESULTS							
Year	Team	Lg	G	GS	CG	GF	IP	BFP	H	R	ER	HR	SH	SF	HB	TBB	IBB	SO	WP	Bk	W	L	Pct	ShO	Sv-Op	Hld	ERC	ERA
2000	Princtn	R+	12	12	0	0	54.2	237	47	24	15	2	0	2	1	30	0	60	6	0	3	4	.429	0	0--	-	3.49	2.47
2001	CtnSC	A	22	22	0	0	104.0	458	110	55	47	4	2	2	9	42	0	71	11	0	7	8	.467	0	0--	-	4.34	4.07
2003	CtnSC	A	24	19	0	1	99.1	444	102	63	46	2	7	4	12	41	0	74	5	1	5	8	.385	0	0--	-	4.14	4.17
2004	Bkrsfld	A+	15	1	0	1	35.0	155	32	17	9	0	1	0	2	19	1	27	3	0	2	3	.400	0	1--	-	3.57	2.31
2005	Visalia	A+	24	0	0	9	45.0	218	43	31	26	2	7	5	3	36	0	56	7	0	3	4	.429	0	0--	-	5.06	5.20
2006	Mont	AA	16	0	0	4	19.1	79	10	5	5	1	4	0	2	7	0	29	1	0	1	0	1.000	0	2--	-	1.57	2.33
2006	Drham	AAA	34	0	0	9	38.2	166	35	15	13	3	2	2	2	13	0	38	2	0	1	4	.200	0	0--	-	3.28	3.03
2007	Drham	AAA	54	0	0	15	64.2	275	54	25	22	8	4	2	2	30	1	67	4	0	2	3	.400	0	4--	-	3.67	3.06
2008	Rchmd	AAA	44	0	0	12	52.2	246	67	38	33	3	2	2	3	26	1	57	4	0	4	0	1.000	0	4--	-	5.97	5.47
2007	TB	AL	3	0	0	0	0.1	10	7	7	7	1	0	0	1	0	0	0	0	0	0	0	-	0	0-0	0	276.0	189.0
2008	Atl	NL	10	0	0	2	9.2	38	7	4	4	3	0	0	1	1	0	8	0	0	1	0	1.000	0	0-1	0	3.03	3.72
2 ML YEARS			13	0	0	2	10.0	48	14	11	11	4	0	0	2	2	0	8	0	0	1	0	1.000	0	0-1	0	8.77	9.90

Shawn Riggans

Bats: R Throws: R Pos: C-41; PH-5; LF-1   Ht: 6'2" Wt: 210 Born: 7/25/1980 Age: 28

Year	Team	Lg	G	AB	H	2B	3B	HR	(Hm	Rd)	TB	R	RBI	RC	TBB	IBB	SO	HBP	SH	SF	SB	CS	SB%	GDP	Avg	OBP	Slg
2006	TB	AL	10	29	5	1	0	0	(0	0)	6	3	1	0	4	0	7	0	0	0	0	0	-	1	.172	.273	.207
2007	TB	AL	3	10	1	0	0	0	(0	0)	1	1	2	0	0	0	1	0	0	0	0	0	-	1	.100	.100	.100
2008	TB	AL	44	135	30	7	0	6	(3	3)	55	21	24	17	12	0	30	1	2	2	0	0	-	4	.222	.287	.407
3 ML YEARS			57	174	36	8	0	6	(3	3)	62	25	27	17	16	0	38	1	2	2	0	0	-	6	.207	.275	.356

Juan Rincon

Pitches: R Bats: R Pos: RP-47   Ht: 5'11" Wt: 210 Born: 1/23/1979 Age: 30

Year	Team	Lg	G	GS	CG	GF	IP	BFP	H	R	ER	HR	SH	SF	HB	TBB	IBB	SO	WP	Bk	W	L	Pct	ShO	Sv-Op	Hld	ERC	ERA
2008	Buffalo*	AAA	4	0	0	0	5.1	32	11	7	4	1	0	0	0	3	1	4	0	0	0	1	.000	0	0- -	-	11.14	6.75
2001	Min	AL	4	0	0	0	5.2	28	7	5	4	1	1	0	0	5	0	4	0	0	0	0	-	0	0-0	0	8.33	6.35
2002	Min	AL	10	3	0	0	28.2	135	44	23	20	5	0	1	0	9	0	21	2	0	0	2	.000	0	0-1	0	7.62	6.28
2003	Min	AL	58	0	0	20	85.2	370	74	38	35	5	2	5	4	38	7	63	7	0	6	5	.455	0	0-1	5	3.21	3.68
2004	Min	AL	77	0	0	18	82.0	327	52	27	24	5	3	3	2	32	1	106	2	0	11	6	.647	0	2-6	16	2.00	2.63
2005	Min	AL	75	0	0	18	77.0	319	63	26	21	2	4	1	3	30	3	84	5	1	6	6	.500	0	0-5	25	2.68	2.45
2006	Min	AL	75	0	0	22	74.1	315	76	30	24	2	5	1	3	24	3	65	2	0	3	1	.750	0	1-3	26	3.53	2.91
2007	Min	AL	63	0	0	16	59.2	272	65	38	34	9	2	1	3	28	3	49	4	0	3	3	.500	0	0-2	14	5.31	5.13
2008	2 Tms	AL	47	0	0	15	55.1	254	67	39	36	8	2	0	3	24	2	39	5	0	3	3	.500	0	0-0	3	5.96	5.86
08	Min	AL	24	0	0	6	28.0	133	33	21	19	5	2	0	2	16	2	20	3	0	2	2	.500	0	0-0	1	6.59	6.11
08	Cle	AL	23	0	0	9	27.1	121	34	18	17	3	0	0	1	8	0	19	2	0	1	1	.500	0	0-0	2	5.33	5.60
Postseason			8	0	0	2	8.2	36	6	5	5	1	0	0	0	6	0	9	1	0	0	0	-	0	0-0	1	3.77	5.19
8 ML YEARS			409	3	0	110	468.1	2020	448	226	198	37	19	12	18	190	19	431	27	1	31	27	.534	0	3-18	89	3.79	3.80

Ricardo Rincon

Pitches: L Bats: L Pos: RP-8   Ht: 5'9" Wt: 190 Born: 4/13/1970 Age: 39

Year	Team	Lg	G	GS	CG	GF	IP	BFP	H	R	ER	HR	SH	SF	HB	TBB	IBB	SO	WP	Bk	W	L	Pct	ShO	Sv-Op	Hld	ERC	ERA
2008	NewOr*	AAA	1	0	0	0	1.0	3	0	0	0	0	0	0	0	0	0	1	0	0	0	0	-	0	0- -	-	0.00	0.00
1997	Pit	NL	62	0	0	23	60.0	254	51	26	23	5	5	1	2	24	6	71	2	3	4	8	.333	0	4-6	18	3.10	3.45
1998	Pit	NL	60	0	0	27	65.0	272	50	31	21	6	1	2	0	29	2	64	2	0	0	2	.000	0	14-17	11	2.88	2.91
1999	Cle	AL	59	0	0	14	44.2	193	41	22	22	6	2	1	1	24	5	30	2	1	2	3	.400	0	0-2	11	4.38	4.43
2000	Cle	AL	35	0	0	4	20.0	90	17	7	6	1	0	1	0	13	1	20	1	0	2	0	1.000	0	0-0	10	3.89	2.70
2001	Cle	AL	67	0	0	19	54.0	223	44	18	17	3	2	3	0	21	5	50	1	0	2	1	.667	0	2-4	12	2.62	2.83
2002	2 Tms	AL	71	0	0	9	56.0	222	47	28	26	4	2	4	1	11	1	49	0	0	1	4	.200	0	1-5	27	2.36	4.18
2003	Oak	AL	64	0	0	16	55.1	241	45	21	20	4	8	2	3	32	4	40	0	0	8	4	.667	0	0-3	13	3.62	3.25
2004	Oak	AL	67	0	0	10	44.0	201	45	22	18	3	1	1	1	22	4	40	4	0	1	1	.500	0	0-4	18	4.16	3.68
2005	Oak	AL	67	0	0	4	37.1	162	34	19	18	7	2	1	1	20	4	27	1	0	1	1	.500	0	0-2	16	4.73	4.34
2006	StL	NL	5	0	0	1	3.1	21	6	4	4	1	0	0	1	4	0	6	0	0	0	0	-	0	0-0	2	16.33	10.80
2008	NYM	NL	8	0	0	1	4.0	16	4	2	2	1	0	0	0	1	0	3	1	0	0	0	-	0	0-0	1	4.69	4.50
02	Cle	AL	46	0	0	6	35.2	150	36	21	19	3	2	2	1	8	1	30	0	0	1	4	.200	0	0-3	11	3.38	4.79
02	Oak	AL	25	0	0	3	20.1	72	11	7	7	1	0	2	0	3	0	19	0	0	0	0	-	0	1-2	16	1.06	3.10
Postseason			10	0	0	1	9.2	40	10	7	7	3	0	0	0	2	0	9	1	0	0	0	-	0	0-1	2	4.92	6.52
11 ML YEARS			565	0	0	128	443.2	1895	384	200	177	41	23	15	11	201	32	400	14	4	21	24	.467	0	21-43	139	3.46	3.59

Royce Ring

Pitches: L Bats: L Pos: RP-42   Ht: 6'0" Wt: 220 Born: 12/21/1980 Age: 28

Year	Team	Lg	G	GS	CG	GF	IP	BFP	H	R	ER	HR	SH	SF	HB	TBB	IBB	SO	WP	Bk	W	L	Pct	ShO	Sv-Op	Hld	ERC	ERA
2008	Rchmd*	AAA	11	0	0	1	9.0	38	5	3	3	0	1	0	0	7	0	7	2	0	0	1	.000	0	0- -	-	2.44	3.00
2005	NYM	NL	15	0	0	2	10.2	51	10	6	6	0	1	0	0	10	1	8	0	0	0	2	.000	0	0-0	3	4.80	5.06
2006	NYM	NL	11	0	0	2	12.2	48	7	3	3	2	0	0	0	3	0	8	0	0	0	0	-	0	0-0	2	1.60	2.13
2007	2 Tms	NL	26	0	0	7	20.0	88	13	8	6	1	0	1	0	17	2	21	2	0	1	0	1.000	0	0-0	0	3.33	2.70
2008	Atl	NL	42	0	0	8	22.1	113	32	25	21	2	3	2	2	10	3	16	0	1	2	1	.667	0	0-0	4	6.61	8.46
07	SD	NL	15	0	0	4	15.0	69	11	8	6	1	0	0	0	14	2	17	2	0	1	0	1.000	0	0-0	0	4.10	3.60
07	Atl	NL	11	0	0	3	5.0	19	2	0	0	0	0	1	0	3	0	4	0	0	0	0	-	0	0-0	0	1.39	0.00
4 ML YEARS			94	0	0	19	65.2	300	62	42	36	5	4	3	2	40	6	53	2	1	3	3	.500	0	0-0	9	4.27	4.93

Alex Rios

Bats: R Throws: R Pos: RF-93; CF-62; DH-2; PH-2   Ht: 6'5" Wt: 194 Born: 2/18/1981 Age: 28

Year	Team	Lg	G	AB	H	2B	3B	HR	(Hm	Rd)	TB	R	RBI	RC	TBB	IBB	SO	HBP	SH	SF	SB	CS	SB%	GDP	Avg	OBP	Slg
2004	Tor	AL	111	426	122	24	7	1	(0	1)	163	55	28	49	31	0	84	2	1	0	15	3	.83	14	.286	.338	.383
2005	Tor	AL	146	481	126	23	6	10	(5	5)	191	71	59	56	28	1	101	5	0	5	14	9	.61	14	.262	.306	.397
2006	Tor	AL	128	450	136	33	6	17	(12	5)	232	68	82	83	35	1	89	3	0	10	15	6	.71	10	.302	.349	.516
2007	Tor	AL	161	643	191	43	7	24	(13	11)	320	114	85	105	55	3	103	6	0	7	17	4	.81	9	.297	.354	.498
2008	Tor	AL	155	635	185	47	8	15	(9	6)	293	91	79	92	44	2	112	2	0	5	32	8	.80	20	.291	.337	.461
5 ML YEARS			701	2635	760	170	34	67	(39	28)	1199	399	333	385	193	7	489	18	1	27	93	30	.76	67	.288	.338	.455

David Riske

Pitches: R Bats: R Pos: RP-45

Ht: 6'2" Wt: 180 Born: 10/23/1976 Age: 32

			HOW MUCH HE PITCHED						WHAT HE GAVE UP											THE RESULTS							
Year	Team	Lg	G	GS	CG	GF	IP	BFP	H	R	ER	HR	SH	SF	HB	TBB	IBB	SO	WP	Bk	W	L	Pct	ShO	Sv-Op	Hld	ERC	ERA
2008	Nashv*	AAA	1	1	0	0	1.0	3	0	0	0	0	0	0	0	0	0	3	0	0	0	0	-	0	0- -	-	0.00	0.00
1999	Cle	AL	12	0	0	3	14.0	68	20	15	13	2	1	1	0	6	0	16	0	0	1	1	.500	0	0-1	0	6.96	8.36
2001	Cle	AL	26	0	0	6	27.1	118	20	7	6	3	0	1	2	18	3	29	1	0	2	0	1.000	0	1-1	3	3.81	1.98
2002	Cle	AL	51	0	0	17	51.1	237	49	32	30	8	4	3	4	35	4	65	1	0	2	2	.500	0	1-1	5	5.55	5.26
2003	Cle	AL	68	0	0	24	74.2	293	52	21	19	9	4	1	3	20	3	82	1	0	2	2	.500	0	8-13	17	2.26	2.29
2004	Cle	AL	72	0	0	27	77.1	336	69	32	32	11	3	2	2	41	4	78	3	0	7	3	.700	0	5-12	9	4.32	3.72
2005	Cle	AL	58	0	0	33	72.2	288	55	28	25	11	3	1	4	15	0	48	0	0	3	4	.429	0	1-1	0	2.59	3.10
2006	2 Tms	AL	41	0	0	12	44.0	189	40	20	19	6	1	2	3	17	1	28	0	0	1	2	.333	0	0-1	2	3.98	3.89
2007	KC	AL	65	0	0	27	69.2	289	61	19	19	8	4	3	1	27	4	52	0	0	1	4	.200	0	4-8	16	3.46	2.45
2008	Mil	NL	45	0	0	6	42.1	193	47	25	25	6	4	0	0	25	0	27	1	0	1	2	.333	0	2-7	11	5.88	5.31
06	Bos	AL	8	0	0	2	9.2	42	8	4	4	2	1	0	2	3	0	5	0	0	0	1	.000	0	0-0	0	4.23	3.72
06	CWS	AL	33	0	0	10	34.1	147	32	16	15	4	0	2	1	14	1	23	0	0	1	1	.500	0	0-1	2	3.91	3.93
	Postseason		3	0	0	0	3.2	14	2	0	0	0	0	0	0	1	0	5	0	0	0	0	-	0	0-0	0	1.10	0.00
	9 ML YEARS		438	0	0	155	473.1	2011	413	199	188	64	20	18	19	204	19	425	7	0	20	20	.500	0	22-45	63	3.84	3.57

Luis Rivas

Bats: R Throws: R Pos: SS-31; 2B-29; PH-25; PR-3; 3B-1

Ht: 5'11" Wt: 190 Born: 8/30/1979 Age: 29

			BATTING																		BASERUNNING				AVERAGES		
Year	Team	Lg	G	AB	H	2B	3B	HR	(Hm	Rd)	TB	R	RBI	RC	TBB	IBB	SO	HBP	SH	SF	SB	CS	SB%	GDP	Avg	OBP	Slg
2000	Min	AL	16	58	18	4	1	0	(0	0)	24	8	6	8	2	0	4	0	2	2	2	0	1.00	2	.310	.323	.414
2001	Min	AL	153	563	150	21	6	7	(3	4)	204	70	47	65	40	0	99	6	5	5	31	11	.74	15	.266	.319	.362
2002	Min	AL	93	316	81	23	4	4	(2	2)	124	46	35	35	19	2	51	3	8	0	9	4	.69	12	.256	.305	.392
2003	Min	AL	135	475	123	16	9	8	(4	4)	181	69	43	46	30	0	65	5	8	3	17	7	.71	20	.259	.308	.381
2004	Min	AL	109	336	86	19	5	10	(4	6)	145	44	34	34	13	0	53	1	5	3	15	1	.94	8	.256	.283	.432
2005	Min	AL	59	136	35	3	1	1	(0	1)	43	21	12	16	9	0	17	2	0	1	4	0	1.00	3	.257	.311	.316
2007	Cle	AL	4	11	3	0	1	1	(0	1)	8	3	4	2	0	0	0	0	0	0	0	0	-	0	.273	.273	.727
2008	Pit	NL	79	206	45	6	2	3	(2	1)	64	25	20	14	13	0	27	1	2	1	3	2	.60	7	.218	.267	.311
	Postseason		16	38	6	1	0	0	(0	0)	7	3	1	0	2	0	9	0	2	1	0	0	-	5	.158	.195	.184
	8 ML YEARS		648	2101	541	92	29	34	(15	19)	793	286	201	220	126	2	316	18	30	15	81	25	.76	66	.257	.303	.377

Juan Rivera

Bats: R Throws: R Pos: LF-41; RF-19; DH-17; PH-14; 1B-1; 2B-1; CF-1

Ht: 6'2" Wt: 205 Born: 7/3/1978 Age: 30

			BATTING																		BASERUNNING				AVERAGES		
Year	Team	Lg	G	AB	H	2B	3B	HR	(Hm	Rd)	TB	R	RBI	RC	TBB	IBB	SO	HBP	SH	SF	SB	CS	SB%	GDP	Avg	OBP	Slg
2001	NYY	AL	3	4	0	0	0	0	(0	0)	0	0	0	0	0	0	0	0	0	0	0	0	-	0	.000	.000	.000
2002	NYY	AL	28	83	22	5	0	1	(0	1)	30	9	6	8	6	0	10	0	1	1	1	1	.50	4	.265	.311	.361
2003	NYY	AL	57	173	46	14	0	7	(4	3)	81	22	26	23	10	1	27	0	1	1	0	0	-	8	.266	.304	.468
2004	Mon	NL	134	391	120	24	1	12	(6	6)	182	48	49	60	34	7	45	1	0	0	6	2	.75	11	.307	.364	.465
2005	LAA	AL	106	350	95	17	1	15	(8	7)	159	46	59	49	23	0	44	0	2	1	1	9	.10	15	.271	.316	.454
2006	LAA	AL	124	448	139	27	0	23	(12	11)	235	65	85	80	33	0	59	7	0	6	0	4	.00	14	.310	.362	.525
2007	LAA	AL	14	43	12	1	0	2	(1	1)	19	3	8	5	1	0	4	0	0	0	0	0	-	5	.279	.295	.442
2008	LAA	AL	89	256	63	13	0	12	(5	7)	112	31	45	28	16	0	33	0	0	8	1	1	.50	10	.246	.282	.438
	Postseason		24	61	16	3	0	1	(1	0)	22	8	5	5	5	2	9	0	1	0	0	0	-	1	.262	.318	.361
	8 ML YEARS		555	1748	497	101	2	72	(36	36)	818	224	278	253	123	8	222	8	4	17	9	17	.35	67	.284	.331	.468

Mariano Rivera

Pitches: R Bats: R Pos: RP-64

Ht: 6'2" Wt: 185 Born: 11/29/1969 Age: 39

			HOW MUCH HE PITCHED						WHAT HE GAVE UP											THE RESULTS							
Year	Team	Lg	G	GS	CG	GF	IP	BFP	H	R	ER	HR	SH	SF	HB	TBB	IBB	SO	WP	Bk	W	L	Pct	ShO	Sv-Op	Hld	ERC	ERA
1995	NYY	AL	19	10	0	2	67.0	301	71	43	41	11	0	2	2	30	0	51	0	1	5	3	.625	0	0-1	0	5.14	5.51
1996	NYY	AL	61	0	0	14	107.2	425	73	25	25	1	2	1	2	34	3	130	1	0	8	3	.727	0	5-8	27	1.65	2.09
1997	NYY	AL	66	0	0	56	71.2	301	65	17	15	5	3	4	0	20	6	68	2	0	6	4	.600	0	43-52	0	2.73	1.88
1998	NYY	AL	54	0	0	49	61.1	246	48	13	13	3	2	3	1	17	1	36	0	0	3	0	1.000	0	36-41	0	2.21	1.91
1999	NYY	AL	66	0	0	63	69.0	268	43	15	14	2	0	2	3	18	3	52	2	1	4	3	.571	0	45-49	0	1.47	1.83
2000	NYY	AL	66	0	0	61	75.2	311	58	26	24	4	5	2	0	25	3	58	2	0	7	4	.636	0	36-41	0	2.20	2.85
2001	NYY	AL	71	0	0	66	80.2	310	61	24	21	5	4	1	1	12	2	83	1	0	4	6	.400	0	50-57	0	1.74	2.34
2002	NYY	AL	45	0	0	36	46.0	187	35	16	14	3	2	0	2	11	2	41	1	1	1	4	.200	0	28-32	2	2.08	2.74
2003	NYY	AL	64	0	0	57	70.2	277	61	15	13	3	1	2	4	10	1	63	0	0	5	2	.714	0	40-46	0	2.29	1.66
2004	NYY	AL	74	0	0	69	78.2	316	65	17	17	3	2	0	5	20	3	66	0	0	4	2	.667	0	53-57	0	2.45	1.94
2005	NYY	AL	71	0	0	67	78.1	306	50	18	12	2	0	1	4	18	0	80	0	0	7	4	.636	0	43-47	0	1.48	1.38
2006	NYY	AL	63	0	0	59	75.0	293	61	16	15	3	1	2	5	11	4	55	0	0	5	5	.500	0	34-37	0	2.03	1.80
2007	NYY	AL	67	0	0	59	71.1	295	68	25	25	4	1	1	6	12	2	74	1	0	3	4	.429	0	30-34	0	2.92	3.15
2008	NYY	AL	64	0	0	60	70.2	259	41	11	11	4	1	1	2	6	0	77	1	0	6	5	.545	0	39-40	0	1.09	1.40
	Postseason		76	0	0	61	117.1	438	72	12	10	2	5	3	3	16	3	93	3	0	8	1	.889	0	34-39	4	1.13	0.77
	14 ML YEARS		851	10	0	718	1023.2	4095	800	281	260	53	24	22	37	244	30	934	11	3	68	49	.581	0	482-542	29	2.14	2.29

Mike Rivera

Bats: R Throws: R Pos: C-17; 1B-3; PH-2

Ht: 6'1" Wt: 229 Born: 9/8/1976 Age: 32

			BATTING																		BASERUNNING				AVERAGES		
Year	Team	Lg	G	AB	H	2B	3B	HR	(Hm	Rd)	TB	R	RBI	RC	TBB	IBB	SO	HBP	SH	SF	SB	CS	SB%	GDP	Avg	OBP	Slg
2001	Det	AL	4	12	4	2	0	0	(0	0)	6	2	1	2	0	0	2	0	0	0	0	0	-	0	.333	.333	.500
2002	Det	AL	39	132	30	8	1	1	(0	1)	43	11	11	8	4	0	35	1	0	1	0	0	-	5	.227	.254	.326
2003	SD	NL	19	53	9	1	0	1	(0	1)	13	2	2	0	5	0	11	0	0	0	0	0	-	4	.170	.241	.245

234

Year	Team	Lg	G	AB	H	2B	3B	HR	(Hm	Rd)	TB	R	RBI	RC	TBB	IBB	SO	HBP	SH	SF	SB	CS	SB%	GDP	Avg	OBP	Slg
2006	Mil	NL	46	142	38	9	0	6	(3	3)	65	16	24	19	10	5	21	3	1	2	0	0	-	3	.268	.325	.458
2007	Mil	NL	11	13	3	0	0	2	(1	1)	9	2	3	2	1	0	3	0	1	0	0	0	-	0	.231	.286	.692
2008	Mil	NL	21	62	19	5	0	1	(0	1)	27	8	14	13	6	0	10	1	0	0	2	0	1.00	2	.306	.377	.435
6 ML YEARS			140	414	103	25	1	11	(4	7)	163	41	55	44	26	5	82	5	2	3	2	0	1.00	14	.249	.299	.394

Saul Rivera

Pitches: R Bats: B Pos: RP-76   Ht: 5'10" Wt: 184 Born: 12/7/1977 Age: 31

	HOW MUCH HE PITCHED						WHAT HE GAVE UP											THE RESULTS						
Year	Team	Lg	G	GS	CG	GF	IP	BFP	H	R	ER	HR	SH	SF	HB	TBB	IBB	SO	WP	Bk	W	L	Pct	ShO	Sv-Op Hld	ERC	ERA
2006	Was	NL	54	0	0	16	60.1	277	59	28	23	4	4	1	4	32	6	41	3	0	3	0	1.000	0	1-3 9	4.17	3.43
2007	Was	NL	85	0	0	17	93.0	398	88	39	38	1	5	4	2	42	4	64	4	0	4	6	.400	0	3-5 19	3.39	3.68
2008	Was	NL	76	0	0	14	84.0	371	90	41	37	3	3	6	2	35	2	65	4	1	5	6	.455	0	0-6 17	4.11	3.96
3 ML YEARS			215	0	0	47	237.1	1046	237	108	98	8	12	11	8	109	12	170	11	1	12	12	.500	0	4-14 45	3.84	3.72

Brian Roberts

Bats: B Throws: R Pos: 2B-155; PH-3   Ht: 5'9" Wt: 175 Born: 10/9/1977 Age: 31

									BATTING												BASERUNNING				AVERAGES		
Year	Team	Lg	G	AB	H	2B	3B	HR	(Hm	Rd)	TB	R	RBI	RC	TBB	IBB	SO	HBP	SH	SF	SB	CS	SB%	GDP	Avg	OBP	Slg
2001	Bal	AL	75	273	69	12	3	2	(0	2)	93	42	17	27	13	0	36	0	3	3	12	3	.80	3	.253	.284	.341
2002	Bal	AL	38	128	29	6	0	1	(1	0)	38	18	11	12	15	0	21	1	3	2	9	2	.82	3	.227	.308	.297
2003	Bal	AL	112	460	124	22	4	5	(3	2)	169	65	41	62	46	1	58	1	4	1	23	6	.79	9	.270	.337	.367
2004	Bal	AL	159	641	175	50	2	4	(0	4)	241	107	53	91	71	1	95	1	15	6	29	12	.71	3	.273	.344	.376
2005	Bal	AL	143	561	176	45	7	18	(9	9)	289	92	73	106	67	5	83	3	5	4	27	10	.73	6	.314	.387	.515
2006	Bal	AL	138	563	161	34	3	10	(6	4)	231	85	55	74	55	4	66	0	6	5	36	7	.84	16	.286	.347	.410
2007	Bal	AL	156	621	180	42	5	12	(6	6)	268	103	57	105	89	6	99	0	2	4	50	7	.88	8	.290	.377	.432
2008	Bal	AL	155	611	181	51	8	9	(6	3)	275	107	57	101	82	3	104	2	3	6	40	10	.80	8	.296	.378	.450
8 ML YEARS			976	3858	1095	262	32	61	(31	30)	1604	619	364	578	438	20	562	8	41	31	226	57	.80	56	.284	.355	.416

Dave Roberts

Bats: L Throws: L Pos: LF-32; PH-24; PR-1   Ht: 5'10" Wt: 180 Born: 5/31/1972 Age: 37

									BATTING												BASERUNNING				AVERAGES		
Year	Team	Lg	G	AB	H	2B	3B	HR	(Hm	Rd)	TB	R	RBI	RC	TBB	IBB	SO	HBP	SH	SF	SB	CS	SB%	GDP	Avg	OBP	Slg
2008	Fresno*	AAA	11	31	12	4	1	2	(-	-)	24	4	5	9	6	0	6	0	0	0	2	0	.00	1	.387	.486	.774
1999	Cle	AL	41	143	34	4	0	2	(1	1)	44	26	12	14	9	0	16	0	3	1	11	3	.79	0	.238	.281	.308
2000	Cle	AL	19	10	2	0	0	0	(0	0)	2	1	0	1	2	0	2	0	1	0	1	1	.50	0	.200	.333	.200
2001	Cle	AL	15	12	4	1	0	0	(0	0)	5	3	2	2	1	0	2	0	0	0	0	1	.00	0	.333	.385	.417
2002	LAD	NL	127	422	117	14	7	3	(0	3)	154	63	34	67	48	0	51	2	6	1	45	10	.82	1	.277	.353	.365
2003	LAD	NL	107	388	97	6	5	2	(1	1)	119	56	16	43	43	1	39	4	5	0	40	14	.74	0	.250	.331	.307
2004	2 Tms		113	319	81	14	7	4	(2	2)	121	64	35	52	38	0	48	5	3	6	38	3	.93	4	.254	.337	.379
2005	SD	NL	115	411	113	19	10	8	(5	3)	176	65	38	69	53	3	59	1	11	4	23	12	.66	9	.275	.356	.428
2006	SD	NL	129	499	146	18	13	2	(1	1)	196	80	44	81	51	2	61	4	7	5	49	6	.89	5	.293	.360	.393
2007	SF	NL	114	396	103	17	9	2	(1	1)	144	61	23	51	42	1	66	0	4	0	31	5	.86	4	.260	.331	.364
2008	SF	NL	52	107	24	2	2	0	(0	0)	30	18	9	11	20	1	18	0	1	2	5	3	.63	2	.224	.341	.280
04	LAD	NL	68	233	59	4	7	4	(1	1)	83	45	21	41	28	0	31	4	2	3	33	1	.97	2	.253	.340	.356
04	Bos	AL	45	86	22	10	0	2	(1	1)	38	19	14	11	10	0	17	1	1	3	5	2	.71	2	.256	.330	.442
Postseason			12	28	9	0	1	1	(1	0)	14	4	1	2	1	0	7	0	1	0	2	1	.67	0	.321	.345	.500
10 ML YEARS			832	2707	721	95	53	23	(11	12)	991	437	213	381	307	8	362	16	41	19	243	58	.81	23	.266	.342	.366

Ryan Roberts

Bats: R Throws: R Pos: DH-1; PH-1   Ht: 5'11" Wt: 190 Born: 9/19/1980 Age: 28

									BATTING												BASERUNNING				AVERAGES		
Year	Team	Lg	G	AB	H	2B	3B	HR	(Hm	Rd)	TB	R	RBI	RC	TBB	IBB	SO	HBP	SH	SF	SB	CS	SB%	GDP	Avg	OBP	Slg
2008	Okla*	AAA	130	453	136	28	8	10	(-	-)	210	71	66	87	67	0	78	2	1	6	15	3	.83	19	.300	.388	.464
2006	Tor	AL	9	13	1	0	0	1	(0	1)	4	1	1	0	1	0	4	0	0	0	0	0	-	1	.077	.143	.308
2007	Tor	AL	8	13	1	0	0	0	(0	0)	1	2	0	0	2	0	7	1	0	0	0	0	-	0	.077	.250	.077
2008	Tex	AL	1	1	0	0	0	0	(0	0)	0	0	0	0	0	0	1	0	0	0	0	0	-	0	.000	.000	.000
3 ML YEARS			18	27	2	0	0	1	(0	1)	5	3	1	0	3	0	12	1	0	0	0	0	-	1	.074	.194	.185

Connor Robertson

Pitches: R Bats: R Pos: RP-6   Ht: 6'2" Wt: 220 Born: 9/10/1981 Age: 27

	HOW MUCH HE PITCHED						WHAT HE GAVE UP											THE RESULTS						
Year	Team	Lg	G	GS	CG	GF	IP	BFP	H	R	ER	HR	SH	SF	HB	TBB	IBB	SO	WP	Bk	W	L	Pct	ShO	Sv-Op Hld	ERC	ERA
2004	As	R	25	0	0	22	29.1	120	17	8	3	2	0	2	2	8	0	46	0	0	2	2	.500	0	13-- -	1.53	0.92
2004	Vancvr	A	3	0	0	2	5.0	21	4	2	2	1	0	0	0	2	0	5	0	0	0	0	-	0	0-- -	3.57	3.60
2005	Kane	A	20	0	0	6	27.2	118	23	10	9	0	2	0	3	14	0	47	3	1	2	2	.500	0	1-- -	3.32	2.93
2005	Stcktn	A+	32	0	0	7	42.1	189	37	17	13	1	1	1	2	23	0	68	4	0	5	2	.714	0	1-- -	3.47	2.76
2005	Scrmto	AAA	3	0	0	1	5.0	22	2	1	1	0	1	0	1	3	1	5	0	0	0	0	-	0	0-- -	1.44	1.80
2006	Mdland	AA	55	0	0	19	83.2	325	73	28	26	1	2	1	2	22	2	97	2	0	7	2	.778	0	6-- -	2.53	2.80
2007	Scrmto	AAA	31	0	0	10	39.1	175	43	25	19	3	0	1	1	21	0	40	6	0	4	1	.800	0	2-- -	5.19	4.35
2007	As	R	1	0	0	0	1.0	5	0	0	0	0	0	0	0	0	0	2	0	0	1	0	1.000	0	0-- -	0.00	0.00
2008	Tucsn	AAA	47	0	0	14	71.2	307	69	45	40	7	2	5	4	30	0	72	10	0	7	4	.636	0	1-- -	4.21	5.02
2007	Oak	AL	3	0	0	2	2.0	15	6	4	4	0	0	1	1	2	1	2	0	0	0	0	-	0	0-0 0	20.56	18.00
2008	Ari	NL	6	0	0	3	7.0	32	8	4	4	1	1	0	1	2	1	2	0	0	0	1	.000	0	0-0 0	4.96	5.14
2 ML YEARS			9	0	0	3	9.0	47	14	8	8	1	1	1	2	4	2	4	0	0	0	1	.000	0	0-0 0	8.09	8.00

David Robertson

Pitches: R Bats: R Pos: RP-25

Ht: 5'11" Wt: 180 Born: 4/9/1985 Age: 24

Year	Team	Lg	G	GS	CG	GF	IP	BFP	H	R	ER	HR	SH	SF	HB	TBB	IBB	SO	WP	Bk	W	L	Pct	ShO	Sv-Op	Hld	ERC	ERA
2007	CtnSC	A	24	0	0	4	47.0	183	25	5	4	0	1	1	0	15	0	67	5	0	5	2	.714	0	3--	-	1.14	0.77
2007	Tampa	A+	18	0	0	7	33.1	129	18	6	4	0	1	0	0	15	0	37	2	0	3	1	.750	0	1--	-	1.48	1.08
2007	Trntn	AA	2	0	0	0	4.0	16	2	1	1	0	0	0	0	2	0	9	1	0	0	0	-	0	0--	-	1.41	2.25
2008	Trntn	AA	9	0	0	5	18.2	68	8	2	2	0	1	0	1	6	0	26	1	0	0	0	-	0	2--	-	1.03	0.96
2008	S-WB	AAA	21	0	0	4	35.0	146	20	11	8	1	0	2	1	17	1	51	1	0	4	0	1.000	0	1--	-	1.74	2.06
2008	NYY	AL	25	0	0	8	30.1	131	29	18	18	3	0	3	0	15	2	36	6	0	4	0	1.000	0	0-0	0	4.12	5.34

Nate Robertson

Pitches: L Bats: R Pos: SP-28; RP-4

Ht: 6'2" Wt: 225 Born: 9/3/1977 Age: 31

Year	Team	Lg	G	GS	CG	GF	IP	BFP	H	R	ER	HR	SH	SF	HB	TBB	IBB	SO	WP	Bk	W	L	Pct	ShO	Sv-Op	Hld	ERC	ERA
2002	Fla	NL	6	1	0	1	8.1	46	15	11	11	3	0	0	2	4	1	3	0	0	0	1	.000	0	0-0	0	12.69	11.88
2003	Det	AL	8	8	0	0	44.2	203	55	27	27	6	0	0	0	23	2	33	3	0	1	2	.333	0	0-0	0	6.24	5.44
2004	Det	AL	34	32	1	1	196.2	852	210	116	107	30	12	4	4	66	1	155	5	1	12	10	.545	0	1-1	0	4.65	4.90
2005	Det	AL	32	32	2	0	196.2	846	202	113	98	28	3	11	7	65	2	122	6	1	7	16	.304	0	0-0	0	4.38	4.48
2006	Det	AL	32	32	1	0	208.2	881	206	98	89	29	4	7	8	67	2	137	6	0	13	13	.500	0	0-0	0	4.14	3.84
2007	Det	AL	30	30	0	0	177.2	781	199	98	94	22	5	6	3	63	2	119	5	1	9	13	.409	0	0-0	0	4.80	4.76
2008	Det	AL	32	28	0	1	168.2	761	218	124	119	26	4	0	2	62	7	108	5	0	7	11	.389	0	0-0	0	6.14	6.35
Postseason			3	3	0	0	15.2	74	23	9	9	1	0	0	2	6	1	8	0	0	1	2	.333	0	0-0	0	7.15	5.17
7 ML YEARS			174	163	4	3	1001.1	4370	1105	587	545	144	28	28	26	350	17	677	30	3	49	66	.426	0	1-1	0	4.88	4.90

Fernando Rodney

Pitches: R Bats: R Pos: RP-38

Ht: 5'11" Wt: 218 Born: 3/18/1977 Age: 32

Year	Team	Lg	G	GS	CG	GF	IP	BFP	H	R	ER	HR	SH	SF	HB	TBB	IBB	SO	WP	Bk	W	L	Pct	ShO	Sv-Op	Hld	ERC	ERA
2008	Toledo*	AAA	4	0	0	1	5.1	25	3	4	4	1	0	0	1	5	0	8	1	0	1	0	1.000	0	0--	-	5.00	6.75
2002	Det	AL	20	0	0	10	18.0	89	25	15	12	2	2	1	0	10	2	10	0	1	1	3	.250	0	0-4	0	6.77	6.00
2003	Det	AL	27	0	0	11	29.2	143	35	20	20	2	3	3	1	17	1	33	0	0	1	3	.250	0	3-6	3	5.46	6.07
2005	Det	AL	39	0	0	26	44.0	185	39	14	14	5	2	0	2	17	3	42	2	0	2	3	.400	0	9-15	3	3.59	2.86
2006	Det	AL	63	0	0	30	71.2	304	51	36	28	6	2	0	8	34	4	65	3	0	7	4	.636	0	7-11	18	3.01	3.52
2007	Det	AL	48	0	0	12	50.2	223	46	27	24	5	4	2	3	21	0	54	4	0	2	6	.250	0	1-3	12	3.74	4.26
2008	Det	AL	38	0	0	25	40.1	188	34	22	22	3	1	2	3	30	5	49	3	0	0	6	.000	0	13-19	5	4.29	4.91
Postseason			7	0	0	0	7.2	33	6	4	2	0	2	0	0	5	1	9	0	0	0	0	-	0	0-1	2	2.94	2.35
6 ML YEARS			235	0	0	114	254.1	1132	230	134	120	23	14	8	17	129	15	253	12	1	13	25	.342	0	33-58	41	3.98	4.25

Alex Rodriguez

Bats: R Throws: R Pos: 3B-131; DH-7

Ht: 6'3" Wt: 225 Born: 7/27/1975 Age: 33

Year	Team	Lg	G	AB	H	2B	3B	HR	(Hm	Rd)	TB	R	RBI	RC	TBB	IBB	SO	HBP	SH	SF	SB	CS	SB%	GDP	Avg	OBP	Slg
1994	Sea	AL	17	54	11	0	0	0	(0	0)	11	4	2	3	3	0	20	0	1	1	3	0	1.00	0	.204	.241	.204
1995	Sea	AL	48	142	33	6	2	5	(1	4)	58	15	19	15	6	0	42	0	1	0	4	2	.67	0	.232	.264	.408
1996	Sea	AL	146	601	215	54	1	36	(18	18)	379	141	123	144	59	1	104	4	6	7	15	4	.79	15	.358	.414	.631
1997	Sea	AL	141	587	176	40	3	23	(16	7)	291	100	84	100	41	1	99	5	4	1	29	6	.83	14	.300	.350	.496
1998	Sea	AL	161	686	213	35	5	42	(18	24)	384	123	124	135	45	0	121	10	3	4	46	13	.78	12	.310	.360	.560
1999	Sea	AL	129	502	143	25	0	42	(20	22)	294	110	111	102	56	2	109	5	1	8	21	7	.75	12	.285	.357	.586
2000	Sea	AL	148	554	175	34	2	41	(13	28)	336	134	132	138	100	5	121	7	0	11	15	4	.79	10	.316	.420	.606
2001	Tex	AL	162	632	201	34	1	52	(26	26)	393	133	135	148	75	6	131	16	0	9	18	3	.86	17	.318	.399	.622
2002	Tex	AL	162	624	187	27	2	57	(34	23)	389	125	142	152	87	12	122	10	0	4	9	4	.69	14	.300	.392	.623
2003	Tex	AL	161	607	181	30	6	47	(26	21)	364	124	118	131	87	10	126	15	0	6	17	3	.85	16	.298	.396	.600
2004	NYY	AL	155	601	172	24	2	36	(17	19)	308	112	106	112	80	6	131	10	0	7	28	4	.88	18	.286	.375	.512
2005	NYY	AL	162	605	194	29	1	48	(26	22)	369	124	130	137	91	8	139	16	0	3	21	6	.78	8	.321	.421	.610
2006	NYY	AL	154	572	166	26	1	35	(20	15)	299	113	121	112	90	8	139	8	0	4	15	4	.79	22	.290	.392	.523
2007	NYY	AL	158	583	183	31	0	54	(26	28)	376	143	156	159	95	11	120	21	0	9	24	4	.86	15	.314	.422	.645
2008	NYY	AL	138	510	154	33	0	35	(21	14)	292	104	103	97	65	9	117	14	0	5	18	3	.86	16	.302	.392	.573
Postseason			39	147	41	9	0	7	(3	4)	71	21	17	21	17	1	38	5	1	0	4	3	.57	4	.279	.373	.483
15 ML YEARS			2042	7860	2404	428	26	553	(282	271)	4543	1605	1606	1685	980	79	1641	141	16	79	283	67	.81	189	.306	.389	.578

Francisco Rodriguez

Pitches: R Bats: R Pos: RP-76

Ht: 6'0" Wt: 190 Born: 1/7/1982 Age: 27

Year	Team	Lg	G	GS	CG	GF	IP	BFP	H	R	ER	HR	SH	SF	HB	TBB	IBB	SO	WP	Bk	W	L	Pct	ShO	Sv-Op	Hld	ERC	ERA
2002	LAA	AL	5	0	0	4	5.2	21	3	0	0	0	0	0	0	2	1	13	0	0	0	0	-	0	0-0	0	1.52	0.00
2003	LAA	AL	59	0	0	23	86.0	334	50	30	29	12	2	4	2	35	5	95	7	0	8	3	.727	0	2-6	7	2.25	3.03
2004	LAA	AL	69	0	0	29	84.0	335	51	21	17	2	2	1	1	33	1	123	5	0	4	1	.800	0	12-19	27	1.64	1.82
2005	LAA	AL	66	0	0	58	67.1	279	45	20	20	7	1	1	0	32	3	91	8	0	2	5	.286	0	45-50	0	2.52	2.67
2006	LAA	AL	69	0	0	58	73.0	296	52	16	14	6	3	0	1	28	5	98	10	0	2	3	.400	0	47-51	0	2.35	1.73
2007	LAA	AL	64	0	0	56	67.1	285	50	22	21	3	1	4	1	34	0	90	7	1	5	2	.714	0	40-46	0	2.74	2.81
2008	LAA	AL	76	0	0	69	68.1	288	54	21	17	4	1	1	2	34	4	77	6	0	2	3	.400	0	62-69	0	3.06	2.24
Postseason			19	0	0	7	29.1	121	22	12	9	4	0	3	1	12	2	39	5	0	5	3	.625	0	3-5	3	3.03	2.76
7 ML YEARS			408	0	0	297	451.2	1838	305	130	118	34	10	11	8	198	19	587	43	1	23	17	.575	0	208-241	34	2.37	2.35

Ivan Rodriguez

Bats: R Throws: R Pos: C-112; PH-4; DH-2; PR-2   Ht: 5'9" Wt: 190 Born: 11/30/1971 Age: 37

Year	Team	Lg	G	AB	H	2B	3B	HR	(Hm	Rd)	TB	R	RBI	RC	TBB	IBB	SO	HBP	SH	SF	SB	CS	SB%	GDP	Avg	OBP	Slg
1991	Tex	AL	88	280	74	16	0	3	(3	0)	99	24	27	23	5	0	42	0	2	1	0	1	.00	10	.264	.276	.354
1992	Tex	AL	123	420	109	16	1	8	(4	4)	151	39	37	41	24	2	73	1	7	2	0	0	-	15	.260	.300	.360
1993	Tex	AL	137	473	129	28	4	10	(7	3)	195	56	66	57	29	3	70	4	5	8	8	7	.53	16	.273	.315	.412
1994	Tex	AL	99	363	108	19	1	16	(7	9)	177	56	57	61	31	5	42	7	0	4	6	3	.67	10	.298	.360	.488
1995	Tex	AL	130	492	149	32	2	12	(5	7)	221	56	67	68	16	2	48	4	0	5	0	2	.00	11	.303	.327	.449
1996	Tex	AL	153	639	192	47	3	19	(10	9)	302	116	86	99	38	7	55	4	0	4	5	0	1.00	15	.300	.342	.473
1997	Tex	AL	150	597	187	34	4	20	(12	8)	289	98	77	98	38	7	89	8	1	4	7	3	.70	18	.313	.360	.484
1998	Tex	AL	145	579	186	40	4	21	(12	9)	297	88	91	100	32	4	88	3	0	3	9	0	1.00	18	.321	.358	.513
1999	Tex	AL	144	600	199	29	1	35	(12	23)	335	116	113	104	24	2	64	1	0	5	25	12	.68	31	.332	.356	.558
2000	Tex	AL	91	363	126	27	4	27	(16	11)	242	66	83	78	19	5	48	1	0	6	5	5	.50	17	.347	.375	.667
2001	Tex	AL	111	442	136	24	2	25	(16	9)	239	70	65	77	23	3	73	4	0	1	10	3	.77	13	.308	.347	.541
2002	Tex	AL	108	408	128	32	2	19	(15	4)	221	67	60	63	25	2	71	2	1	4	5	4	.56	13	.314	.353	.542
2003	Fla	NL	144	511	152	36	3	16	(8	8)	242	90	85	91	55	6	92	6	1	5	10	6	.63	18	.297	.369	.474
2004	Det	AL	135	527	176	32	2	19	(7	12)	269	72	86	98	41	6	91	3	0	4	7	4	.64	15	.334	.383	.510
2005	Det	AL	129	504	139	33	5	14	(8	6)	224	71	50	44	11	2	93	2	1	7	7	3	.70	19	.276	.290	.444
2006	Det	AL	136	547	164	28	4	13	(5	8)	239	74	69	82	26	4	86	1	4	2	8	3	.73	16	.300	.332	.437
2007	Det	AL	129	502	141	31	3	11	(4	7)	211	50	63	55	9	1	96	1	1	2	2	2	.50	16	.281	.294	.420
2008	2 Tms		115	398	110	20	3	7	(5	2)	157	44	35	40	23	2	67	3	3	2	10	1	.91	15	.276	.319	.394
08	Det	AL	82	302	89	16	3	5	(3	2)	126	33	32	36	19	1	52	2	3	2	6	1	.86	9	.295	.338	.417
08	NYY	AL	33	96	21	4	0	2	(2	0)	31	11	3	4	4	1	15	1	0	0	4	0	1.00	6	.219	.257	.323
	Postseason		40	153	39	9	0	4	(2	2)	60	17	25	22	14	3	32	1	0	2	1	0	1.00	3	.255	.314	.392
18 ML YEARS			2267	8645	2605	524	48	295	(156	139)	4110	1253	1217	1279	469	63	1288	55	26	69	124	59	.68	286	.301	.339	.475

Luis Rodriguez

Bats: B Throws: R Pos: SS-52; PH-8; 2B-7; 1B-2; 3B-1   Ht: 5'9" Wt: 188 Born: 6/27/1980 Age: 29

Year	Team	Lg	G	AB	H	2B	3B	HR	(Hm	Rd)	TB	R	RBI	RC	TBB	IBB	SO	HBP	SH	SF	SB	CS	SB%	GDP	Avg	OBP	Slg
2008	Portlnd*	AAA	31	96	29	5	1	1	(-	-)	39	10	8	15	10	0	3	0	1	0	0	0	-	4	.302	.368	.406
2005	Min	AL	79	175	47	10	2	2	(1	1)	67	21	20	27	18	0	23	1	6	3	2	2	.50	4	.269	.335	.383
2006	Min	AL	59	115	27	4	0	2	(1	1)	37	11	6	8	14	1	16	0	2	1	0	0	-	3	.235	.315	.322
2007	Min	AL	68	155	34	5	1	2	(1	1)	47	18	12	11	12	0	14	2	2	2	1	0	1.00	8	.219	.281	.303
2008	SD	NL	64	202	58	11	1	0	(0	0)	71	22	12	19	13	0	13	0	7	3	1	1	.50	9	.287	.326	.351
4 ML YEARS			270	647	166	30	4	6	(3	3)	222	72	50	65	57	1	66	3	17	9	4	3	.57	24	.257	.316	.343

Sean Rodriguez

Bats: R Throws: R Pos: 2B-51; SS-4; PR-3; DH-2; PH-2; 3B-1   Ht: 6'1" Wt: 215 Born: 4/26/1985 Age: 24

Year	Team	Lg	G	AB	H	2B	3B	HR	(Hm	Rd)	TB	R	RBI	RC	TBB	IBB	SO	HBP	SH	SF	SB	CS	SB%	GDP	Avg	OBP	Slg
2003	Angels	R	54	216	58	8	5	2	(-	-)	82	30	25	29	14	0	37	7	1	1	11	4	.73	6	.269	.332	.380
2004	CRpds	A	57	196	49	8	4	4	(-	-)	77	35	17	28	18	0	54	7	2	1	14	4	.78	2	.250	.333	.393
2004	Provo	R+	64	225	76	14	4	10	(-	-)	128	64	55	64	51	0	62	15	0	1	9	3	.75	2	.338	.486	.569
2005	CRpds	A	124	448	112	29	3	14	(-	-)	189	86	45	78	78	0	85	9	9	2	27	11	.71	8	.250	.371	.422
2006	RCuca	A+	116	455	137	29	5	24	(-	-)	248	78	77	95	47	0	124	12	3	6	15	3	.83	9	.301	.377	.545
2006	Ark	AA	18	65	23	5	0	5	(-	-)	43	16	9	17	11	0	18	2	1	0	0	3	.00	1	.354	.462	.662
2006	Salt Lk	AAA	1	2	0	0	0	0	(-	-)	0	0	0	0	0	0	2	0	0	0	0	0	-	0	.000	.000	.000
2007	Ark	AA	136	508	129	31	2	17	(-	-)	215	84	73	79	54	0	132	19	2	4	15	8	.65	5	.254	.345	.423
2008	Salt Lk	AAA	66	248	76	19	1	21	(-	-)	160	68	52	62	29	0	45	9	2	1	4	1	.80	5	.306	.397	.645
2008	LAA	AL	59	167	34	8	1	3	(2	1)	53	18	10	12	14	0	55	3	2	1	3	1	.75	3	.204	.276	.317

Wandy Rodriguez

Pitches: L Bats: B Pos: SP-25   Ht: 5'11" Wt: 180 Born: 1/18/1979 Age: 30

Year	Team	Lg	G	GS	CG	GF	IP	BFP	H	R	ER	HR	SH	SF	HB	TBB	IBB	SO	WP	Bk	W	L	Pct	ShO	Sv-Op	Hld	ERC	ERA
2008	CpChr*	AA	1	1	0	0	6.0	22	4	1	1	1	0	0	0	1	0	0	0	0	0	0	-	0	0--	-	1.99	1.50
2005	Hou	NL	25	22	0	0	128.2	560	135	82	79	19	3	3	8	53	2	80	3	3	10	10	.500	0	0-0	0	5.08	5.53
2006	Hou	NL	30	24	0	1	135.2	611	154	96	85	17	7	4	6	63	7	98	6	0	9	10	.474	0	0-0	0	5.45	5.64
2007	Hou	NL	31	31	1	0	182.2	782	179	102	93	22	6	4	5	62	2	158	3	0	9	13	.409	1	0-0	0	3.94	4.58
2008	Hou	NL	25	25	0	0	137.1	587	136	65	54	14	2	5	5	44	3	131	2	3	9	7	.563	0	0-0	0	3.82	3.54
	Postseason		3	0	0	1	4.2	22	5	2	2	2	1	0	0	5	1	4	0	0	0	1	1.000	0	0-0	0	10.58	3.86
4 ML YEARS			111	102	1	1	584.1	2540	604	345	311	72	18	16	24	222	14	467	14	6	37	40	.481	1	0-0	0	4.49	4.79

Josh Roenicke

Pitches: R Bats: R Pos: RP-5   Ht: 6'3" Wt: 200 Born: 8/4/1982 Age: 26

Year	Team	Lg	G	GS	CG	GF	IP	BFP	H	R	ER	HR	SH	SF	HB	TBB	IBB	SO	WP	Bk	W	L	Pct	ShO	Sv-Op	Hld	ERC	ERA
2006	Reds	R	7	0	0	4	7.2	36	8	2	1	0	1	0	1	3	0	9	1	0	1	0	1.000	0	0--	-	3.81	1.17
2006	Billings	R+	14	0	0	12	15.2	68	10	11	11	1	0	0	0	12	0	24	1	0	1	0	1.000	0	6--	-	3.22	6.32
2007	Srsota	A+	27	0	0	25	27.2	119	23	10	10	1	1	0	1	15	2	41	1	0	2	1	.667	0	16--	-	3.28	3.25
2007	Chatt	AA	19	0	0	14	19.0	72	12	3	2	0	1	0	0	6	0	15	0	0	1	1	.500	0	8--	-	1.49	0.95
2008	Chatt	AA	22	0	0	19	22.0	100	21	10	8	2	2	3	0	12	1	28	1	0	4	2	.667	0	10--	-	4.10	3.27
2008	Lsvlle	AAA	35	0	0	12	39.0	161	34	11	11	2	1	1	0	14	3	43	8	0	2	0	1.000	0	3--	-	2.81	2.54
2008	Cin	NL	5	0	0	0	3.0	18	6	3	3	0	0	0	1	2	0	6	0	0	0	0	-	0	0-0	0	12.01	9.00

Kenny Rogers

Pitches: L **Bats:** L **Pos:** SP-30   **Ht:** 6'1" **Wt:** 190 **Born:** 11/10/1964 **Age:** 44

			HOW MUCH HE PITCHED						WHAT HE GAVE UP										THE RESULTS								
Year	Team	Lg	G	GS	CG	GF	IP	BFP	H	R	ER	HR	SH	SF	HB	TBB	IBB	SO	WP	Bk	W	L	Pct	ShO	Sv-Op	Hld	ERC	ERA
1989	Tex	AL	73	0	0	24	73.2	314	60	28	24	2	6	3	4	42	9	63	6	0	3	4	.429	0	2-5	15	3.26	2.93
1990	Tex	AL	69	3	0	46	97.2	428	93	40	34	6	7	4	1	42	5	74	5	0	10	6	.625	0	15-23	6	3.53	3.13
1991	Tex	AL	63	9	0	20	109.2	511	121	80	66	14	9	5	6	61	7	73	3	1	10	10	.500	0	5-6	11	5.57	5.42
1992	Tex	AL	81	0	0	38	78.2	337	80	32	27	7	4	1	0	26	8	70	4	1	3	6	.333	0	6-10	16	3.63	3.09
1993	Tex	AL	35	33	5	0	208.1	885	210	108	95	18	7	5	4	71	2	140	6	5	16	10	.615	0	0-0	1	3.88	4.10
1994	Tex	AL	24	24	6	0	167.1	714	169	93	83	24	3	6	3	52	1	120	3	1	11	8	.579	2	0-0	0	4.12	4.46
1995	Tex	AL	31	31	3	0	208.0	877	192	87	78	26	3	5	2	76	1	140	8	1	17	7	.708	1	0-0	0	3.72	3.38
1996	NYY	AL	30	30	2	0	179.0	786	179	97	93	16	6	3	8	83	2	92	5	0	12	8	.600	1	0-0	0	4.43	4.68
1997	NYY	AL	31	22	1	4	145.0	651	161	100	91	18	2	4	7	62	1	78	2	2	6	7	.462	0	0-0	1	5.18	5.65
1998	Oak	AL	34	34	7	0	238.2	970	215	96	84	19	4	5	7	67	0	138	5	2	16	8	.667	1	0-0	0	3.13	3.17
1999	2 Tms		31	31	5	0	195.1	845	206	101	91	16	7	7	13	69	1	126	4	1	10	4	.714	1	0-0	0	4.38	4.19
2000	Tex	AL	34	34	2	0	227.1	998	257	126	115	20	3	4	11	78	2	127	1	1	13	13	.500	0	0-0	0	4.72	4.55
2001	Tex	AL	20	20	0	0	120.2	552	150	88	83	18	1	6	8	49	2	74	4	1	5	7	.417	0	0-0	0	6.22	6.19
2002	Tex	AL	33	33	2	0	210.2	892	212	101	90	21	3	1	6	70	1	107	5	1	13	8	.619	1	0-0	0	3.99	3.84
2003	Min	AL	33	31	0	0	195.0	851	227	108	99	22	9	3	11	50	5	116	6	4	13	8	.619	0	0-0	0	4.73	4.57
2004	Tex	AL	35	35	2	0	211.2	935	248	117	112	24	7	4	9	66	0	126	2	1	18	9	.667	1	0-0	0	4.99	4.76
2005	Tex	AL	30	30	1	0	195.1	828	205	86	75	15	5	6	8	53	1	87	0	0	14	8	.636	1	0-0	0	3.87	3.46
2006	Det	AL	34	33	0	1	204.0	849	195	97	87	23	1	7	9	62	2	99	5	0	17	8	.680	0	0-0	0	3.76	3.84
2007	Det	AL	11	11	0	0	63.0	275	65	36	31	8	0	3	1	25	0	36	1	0	3	4	.429	0	0-0	0	4.48	4.43
2008	Det	AL	30	30	0	0	173.2	782	212	118	110	22	7	10	9	71	3	82	4	1	9	13	.409	0	0-0	0	5.90	5.70
99	Oak	AL	19	19	3	0	119.1	528	135	66	57	8	4	6	9	41	0	68	3	1	5	3	.625	0	0-0	0	4.68	4.30
99	NYM	NL	12	12	2	0	76.0	317	71	35	34	8	3	1	4	28	1	58	1	0	5	1	.833	1	0-0	0	3.91	4.03
	Postseason		12	8	0	1	43.1	189	41	20	20	4	2	1	3	23	3	34	1	0	3	3	.500	0	0-0	0	4.48	4.15
20 ML YEARS			762	474	36	133	3302.2	14280	3457	1739	1568	339	94	92	127	1175	53	1968	79	23	219	156	.584	9	28-44	50	4.33	4.27

Ryan Rohlinger

Bats: R **Throws:** R **Pos:** 3B-14; PR-6; PH-3; 2B-1   **Ht:** 6'1" **Wt:** 195 **Born:** 10/7/1983 **Age:** 25

									BATTING												BASERUNNING				AVERAGES		
Year	Team	Lg	G	AB	H	2B	3B	HR	(Hm	Rd)	TB	R	RBI	RC	TBB	IBB	SO	HBP	SH	SF	SB	CS	SB%	GDP	Avg	OBP	Slg
2006	Salem	A+	65	234	59	13	1	3	(-	-)	83	34	28	30	27	1	27	5	2	5	0	2	.00	13	.252	.336	.355
2007	Augsta	A	135	506	119	31	3	18	(-	-)	210	86	78	74	62	3	83	13	1	4	3	3	.50	7	.235	.332	.415
2008	SnJos	A+	73	277	79	16	0	7	(-	-)	116	45	46	46	34	0	50	5	1	5	5	1	.83	6	.285	.368	.419
2008	Conn	AA	44	159	47	12	1	6	(-	-)	79	27	19	28	13	0	20	3	3	1	1	1	.50	8	.296	.358	.497
2008	SF	NL	21	32	3	1	1	0	(0	0)	6	2	2	0	1	0	8	0	0	0	0	1	.00	2	.094	.121	.188

Scott Rolen

Bats: R **Throws:** R **Pos:** 3B-115   **Ht:** 6'4" **Wt:** 240 **Born:** 4/4/1975 **Age:** 34

									BATTING												BASERUNNING				AVERAGES		
Year	Team	Lg	G	AB	H	2B	3B	HR	(Hm	Rd)	TB	R	RBI	RC	TBB	IBB	SO	HBP	SH	SF	SB	CS	SB%	GDP	Avg	OBP	Slg
2008	Dnedin*	A+	3	9	0	0	0	0	(-	-)	0	0	0	0	0	0	1	0	0	0	0	0	-	0	.000	.000	.000
1996	Phi	NL	37	130	33	7	0	4	(2	2)	52	10	18	16	13	0	27	1	0	2	0	2	.00	4	.254	.322	.400
1997	Phi	NL	156	561	159	35	3	21	(11	10)	263	93	92	103	76	4	138	13	0	7	16	6	.73	6	.283	.377	.469
1998	Phi	NL	160	601	174	45	4	31	(19	12)	320	120	110	124	93	6	141	11	0	6	14	7	.67	10	.290	.391	.532
1999	Phi	NL	112	421	113	28	1	26	(9	17)	221	74	77	83	67	2	114	3	0	6	12	2	.86	8	.268	.368	.525
2000	Phi	NL	128	483	144	32	6	26	(12	14)	266	88	89	97	51	9	99	5	0	2	8	1	.89	4	.298	.370	.551
2001	Phi	NL	151	554	160	39	1	25	(12	13)	276	96	107	108	74	6	127	13	0	12	16	5	.76	6	.289	.378	.498
2002	2 Tms	NL	155	580	154	29	8	31	(14	17)	292	89	110	98	72	4	102	12	0	3	8	4	.67	22	.266	.357	.503
2003	StL	NL	154	559	160	49	1	28	(12	16)	295	98	104	104	82	5	104	9	0	7	13	3	.81	19	.286	.382	.528
2004	StL	NL	142	500	157	32	4	34	(10	24)	299	109	124	124	72	5	92	13	1	7	4	3	.57	6	.314	.409	.598
2005	StL	NL	56	196	46	12	1	5	(2	3)	75	28	28	22	25	1	28	1	0	1	1	2	.33	3	.235	.323	.383
2006	StL	NL	142	521	154	48	1	22	(12	10)	270	94	95	89	56	7	69	9	0	8	7	4	.64	10	.296	.369	.518
2007	StL	NL	112	392	104	24	2	8	(4	4)	156	55	58	47	37	2	56	5	0	7	5	3	.63	13	.265	.331	.398
2008	Tor	AL	115	408	107	30	3	11	(6	5)	176	58	50	57	46	2	71	10	0	3	5	0	1.00	12	.262	.349	.431
02	Phi	NL	100	375	97	21	4	17	(8	9)	177	52	66	60	52	2	68	8	0	3	5	2	.71	12	.259	.358	.472
02	StL	NL	55	205	57	8	4	14	(6	8)	115	37	44	38	20	2	34	4	0	0	3	2	.60	10	.278	.354	.561
	Postseason		32	114	26	7	0	5	(3	2)	48	17	11	14	14	0	22	2	0	1	0	1	.00	5	.228	.321	.421
13 ML YEARS			1620	5906	1665	410	35	272	(125	147)	2961	1012	1062	1072	764	53	1168	105	1	71	109	42	.72	125	.282	.370	.501

Jimmy Rollins

Bats: B **Throws:** R **Pos:** SS-132; PH-5   **Ht:** 5'8" **Wt:** 174 **Born:** 11/27/1978 **Age:** 30

									BATTING												BASERUNNING				AVERAGES		
Year	Team	Lg	G	AB	H	2B	3B	HR	(Hm	Rd)	TB	R	RBI	RC	TBB	IBB	SO	HBP	SH	SF	SB	CS	SB%	GDP	Avg	OBP	Slg
2008	Clrwtr*	A+	1	3	0	0	0	0	(-	-)	0	2	0	0	1	0	0	0	0	0	0	0	-	0	.000	.250	.000
2000	Phi	NL	14	53	17	1	1	0	(0	0)	20	5	5	8	2	0	7	0	0	0	3	0	1.00	0	.321	.345	.377
2001	Phi	NL	158	656	180	29	12	14	(8	6)	275	97	54	96	48	2	108	2	9	5	46	8	.85	5	.274	.323	.419
2002	Phi	NL	154	637	156	33	10	11	(3	8)	242	82	60	72	54	3	103	4	6	4	31	13	.70	14	.245	.306	.380
2003	Phi	NL	156	628	165	42	6	8	(5	3)	243	85	62	76	54	4	113	0	5	2	20	12	.63	9	.263	.320	.387
2004	Phi	NL	154	657	190	43	12	14	(8	6)	299	119	73	108	57	3	73	3	6	2	30	9	.77	4	.289	.348	.455
2005	Phi	NL	158	677	196	38	11	12	(5	7)	292	115	54	100	47	8	71	4	2	2	41	6	.87	6	.290	.338	.431
2006	Phi	NL	158	689	191	45	9	25	(15	10)	329	127	83	114	57	2	80	5	0	7	36	4	.90	12	.277	.334	.478
2007	Phi	NL	162	716	212	38	20	30	(10	20)	380	139	94	127	49	5	85	7	0	6	41	6	.87	11	.296	.344	.531
2008	Phi	NL	137	556	154	38	9	11	(5	6)	243	76	59	95	58	7	55	5	3	3	47	3	.94	11	.277	.349	.437
	Postseason		3	11	2	0	1	1	(1	0)	7	1	4	2	2	0	3	0	0	0	1	0	1.00	1	.182	.308	.636
9 ML YEARS			1251	5269	1461	307	90	125	(67	58)	2323	845	544	793	426	34	695	30	31	31	295	61	.83	75	.277	.333	.441

Alex Romero

Bats: L **Throws:** R **Pos:** RF-38; PH-33; LF-13; PR-6; CF-2   **Ht:** 6'0" **Wt:** 198 **Born:** 9/9/1983 **Age:** 25

								BATTING														BASERUNNING				AVERAGES		
Year	Team	Lg	G	AB	H	2B	3B	HR	(Hm	Rd)	TB	R	RBI	RC	TBB	IBB	SO	HBP	SH	SF	SB	CS	SB%	GDP	Avg	OBP	Slg
2002	Twins	R	56	186	62	13	2	2	(-	-)	85	31	42	40	29	3	14	5	3	7	16	6	.73	5	.333	.423	.457
2003	QuadC	A	120	423	125	16	3	4	(-	-)	159	50	40	60	43	3	43	1	5	4	11	8	.58	10	.296	.359	.376
2004	FtMyrs	A+	105	380	111	21	2	6	(-	-)	154	59	42	64	54	3	47	6	5	2	6	4	.60	4	.292	.387	.405
2005	NwBrit	AA	139	510	153	31	2	15	(-	-)	233	65	77	83	36	5	69	8	4	2	14	10	.58	11	.300	.354	.457
2006	Roch	AAA	71	236	59	8	2	0	(-	-)	71	20	26	23	15	2	22	3	5	3	6	2	.75	11	.250	.300	.301
2006	NwBrit	AA	48	167	47	11	2	5	(-	-)	77	29	16	31	26	2	19	3	2	2	15	7	.68	2	.281	.384	.461
2007	Tucsn	AAA	131	533	166	32	6	5	(-	-)	225	82	66	81	37	2	52	1	8	3	13	10	.57	20	.311	.355	.422
2008	Tucsn	AAA	41	173	56	9	2	3	(-	-)	78	28	19	28	11	0	19	1	1	0	4	3	.57	4	.324	.368	.451
2008	Ari	NL	78	135	31	8	2	1	(1	0)	46	13	12	11	3	0	20	1	2	1	4	0	1.00	3	.230	.250	.341

J.C. Romero

Pitches: L **Bats:** B **Pos:** RP-81   **Ht:** 5'11" **Wt:** 203 **Born:** 6/4/1976 **Age:** 33

			HOW MUCH HE PITCHED						WHAT HE GAVE UP											THE RESULTS							
Year	Team	Lg	G	GS	CG	GF	IP	BFP	H	R	ER	HR	SH	SF	HB	TBB	IBB	SO	WP	Bk	W	L	Pct	ShO	Sv-Op	Hld	ERC	ERA
1999	Min	AL	5	0	0	3	9.2	39	13	4	4	0	0	0	0	0	0	4	0	0	0	0	-	0	0-0	0	3.95	3.72
2000	Min	AL	12	11	0	0	57.2	268	72	51	45	8	4	2	1	30	0	50	2	1	2	7	.222	0	0-0	0	6.48	7.02
2001	Min	AL	14	11	0	1	65.0	286	71	48	45	10	3	2	1	24	1	39	1	0	1	4	.200	0	0-0	0	4.89	6.23
2002	Min	AL	81	0	0	15	81.0	332	62	17	17	3	1	0	4	36	4	76	9	0	9	2	.818	0	1-5	33	2.74	1.89
2003	Min	AL	73	0	0	17	63.0	295	66	37	35	7	4	0	6	42	7	50	9	2	2	0	1.000	0	0-4	22	5.72	5.00
2004	Min	AL	74	0	0	12	74.1	319	61	32	29	4	3	1	5	38	6	69	5	0	7	4	.636	0	1-8	16	3.33	3.51
2005	Min	AL	68	0	0	11	57.0	264	50	26	22	6	5	1	6	39	8	48	1	1	4	3	.571	0	0-1	11	4.62	3.47
2006	LAA	AL	65	0	0	16	48.1	226	57	40	36	3	1	5	1	28	2	31	1	0	1	2	.333	0	0-1	7	5.54	6.70
2007	2 Tms		74	0	0	10	56.1	237	39	12	12	3	1	1	2	40	5	42	4	0	2	2	.500	0	1-2	24	3.35	1.92
2008	Phi	NL	81	0	0	14	59.0	255	41	18	18	5	4	0	5	38	5	52	2	1	4	4	.500	0	1-5	24	3.42	2.75
	07 Bos		23	0	0	5	20.0	94	24	7	7	2	0	1	0	15	3	11	0	0	1	0	1.000	0	1-1	2	6.61	3.15
	07 Phi		51	0	0	5	36.1	143	15	5	5	1	1	0	2	25	2	31	4	0	1	2	.333	0	0-1	22	1.86	1.24
	Postseason		15	0	0	3	11.2	54	13	7	7	1	2	1	0	6	1	8	1	0	0	2	.000	0	0-0	2	4.80	5.40
	10 ML YEARS		547	22	0	99	571.1	2521	532	285	263	49	26	12	31	315	38	461	34	5	32	28	.533	0	4-26	137	4.30	4.14

Sergio Romo

Pitches: R **Bats:** R **Pos:** RP-29   **Ht:** 5'11" **Wt:** 191 **Born:** 3/4/1983 **Age:** 26

			HOW MUCH HE PITCHED						WHAT HE GAVE UP											THE RESULTS							
Year	Team	Lg	G	GS	CG	GF	IP	BFP	H	R	ER	HR	SH	SF	HB	TBB	IBB	SO	WP	Bk	W	L	Pct	ShO	Sv-Op	Hld	ERC	ERA
2005	Salem	A+	15	14	0	0	68.2	283	70	24	21	7	3	0	3	9	0	65	1	1	7	1	.875	0	0--	-	3.31	2.75
2006	Augsta	A	31	10	0	10	103.1	405	78	33	29	9	0	6	5	19	0	95	2	0	10	2	.833	0	4--	-	2.13	2.53
2007	SnJos	A+	41	0	0	27	66.1	247	35	12	10	4	2	3	1	15	1	106	2	0	6	2	.750	0	9--	-	1.20	1.36
2008	Conn	AA	24	0	0	21	27.0	108	22	15	12	1	2	1	2	7	2	30	0	0	1	3	.250	0	11--	-	2.40	4.00
2008	Fresno	AAA	3	0	0	2	6.0	22	3	0	0	0	0	0	0	2	1	7	0	0	0	0	-	0	0--	-	1.00	0.00
2008	SF	NL	29	0	0	8	34.0	130	16	13	8	3	2	1	3	8	1	33	0	0	3	1	.750	0	0-0	5	1.27	2.12

Carlos Rosa

Pitches: R **Bats:** R **Pos:** RP-2   **Ht:** 6'1" **Wt:** 185 **Born:** 9/21/1984 **Age:** 24

			HOW MUCH HE PITCHED						WHAT HE GAVE UP											THE RESULTS							
Year	Team	Lg	G	GS	CG	GF	IP	BFP	H	R	ER	HR	SH	SF	HB	TBB	IBB	SO	WP	Bk	W	L	Pct	ShO	Sv-Op	Hld	ERC	ERA
2002	Royals	R	10	9	0	0	32.0	161	52	32	22	3	1	2	2	12	0	11	3	1	0	4	.000	0	0--	-	7.89	6.19
2003	Royals	R	15	11	0	0	69.1	297	79	36	28	4	1	0	4	18	1	54	9	1	5	3	.625	0	0--	-	4.29	3.63
2004	Burlgtn	A	8	8	0	0	34.2	159	41	24	18	1	2	0	2	17	0	23	0	0	0	5	.000	0	0--	-	5.21	4.67
2004	Burlgtn	A	4	4	0	0	11.0	53	14	6	6	1	0	0	1	9	0	8	2	2	0	0	-	0	0--	-	8.21	4.91
2006	Burlgtn	A	24	24	1	0	138.2	575	121	50	39	6	5	2	7	54	0	102	4	3	8	6	.571	1	0--	-	3.22	2.53
2006	Hi Dsrt	A+	3	3	0	0	11.1	59	20	12	9	1	1	2	1	4	0	13	0	0	0	1	.000	0	0--	-	8.72	7.15
2007	Wilmg	A+	4	4	0	0	23.0	89	18	2	1	0	0	0	0	3	0	15	0	0	2	1	.667	0	0--	-	1.51	0.39
2007	Wichta	AA	21	17	0	0	97.0	419	101	53	47	8	3	1	1	43	1	70	4	0	6	6	.500	0	1--	-	4.46	4.36
2008	NWArk	AA	8	8	0	0	45.0	166	30	8	6	2	0	0	0	7	0	42	3	0	4	2	.667	0	0--	-	1.41	1.20
2008	Omha	AAA	11	11	0	0	50.2	204	51	24	23	3	0	1	0	12	0	44	3	1	4	3	.571	0	0--	-	3.34	4.09
2008	KC	AL	2	0	0	1	3.1	12	3	1	1	0	0	0	0	0	0	3	0	0	0	0	-	0	0-0	0	1.70	2.70

Adam Rosales

Bats: R **Throws:** R **Pos:** PH-13; 3B-4; 2B-2   **Ht:** 6'1" **Wt:** 195 **Born:** 5/20/1983 **Age:** 26

								BATTING														BASERUNNING				AVERAGES		
Year	Team	Lg	G	AB	H	2B	3B	HR	(Hm	Rd)	TB	R	RBI	RC	TBB	IBB	SO	HBP	SH	SF	SB	CS	SB%	GDP	Avg	OBP	Slg
2005	Billings	R+	34	140	45	14	0	5	(-	-)	74	29	25	28	13	0	37	5	0	1	2	2	.50	0	.321	.396	.529
2005	Dayton	A	32	134	44	8	0	9	(-	-)	79	24	21	29	10	0	24	2	0	2	3	1	.75	3	.328	.378	.590
2006	Srsota	A+	34	122	26	8	2	2	(-	-)	44	15	14	15	20	0	27	2	1	2	3	3	.50	1	.213	.329	.361
2006	Dayton	A	55	222	60	9	3	6	(-	-)	93	36	29	32	15	1	40	5	0	2	5	1	.83	1	.270	.328	.419
2007	Srsota	A+	69	248	73	23	5	5	(-	-)	121	47	48	51	31	1	46	13	2	6	9	2	.82	8	.294	.393	.488
2007	Chatt	AA	67	255	71	18	6	13	(-	-)	140	51	31	53	37	3	66	5	2	3	4	4	.50	1	.278	.377	.549
2008	Lsvlle	AAA	117	432	124	29	7	11	(-	-)	200	70	58	70	22	0	82	14	1	4	7	1	.88	6	.287	.339	.463
2008	Cin	NL	18	29	6	1	0	0	(0	0)	7	0	2	2	1	0	4	0	0	0	1	0	1.00	0	.207	.233	.241

Leo Rosales

Pitches: R Bats: R Pos: RP-27 Ht: 6'0" Wt: 205 Born: 5/28/1981 Age: 28

			HOW MUCH HE PITCHED					WHAT HE GAVE UP												THE RESULTS							
Year	Team	Lg	G	GS	CG	GF	IP	BFP	H	R	ER	HR	SH	SF	HB	TBB	IBB	SO	WP	Bk	W	L	Pct	ShO	Sv-Op	Hld	ERC	ERA
2003	Eugene	A-	36	0	0	11	43.0	178	32	13	10	4	0	2	1	16	0	58	1	0	3	1	.750	0	3--	-	2.61	2.09
2004	FtWyn	A	53	1	0	40	57.2	230	38	11	9	4	0	0	0	15	1	66	1	0	6	1	.857	0	26--	-	1.62	1.40
2005	Lk Els	A+	61	0	0	56	65.0	275	53	26	23	5	5	3	1	24	0	77	1	0	8	7	.533	0	27--	-	2.79	3.18
2006	Mobile	AA	53	0	0	21	61.2	264	53	35	22	6	2	4	2	18	6	54	5	0	5	6	.455	0	0--	-	2.74	3.21
2006	Lk Els	A+	5	0	0	0	6.1	23	1	0	0	0	1	0	0	2	0	7	0	0	1	0	1.000	0	0--	-	0.31	0.00
2007	Portlnd	AAA	24	0	0	22	24.2	104	23	9	9	3	0	0	0	10	1	27	0	0	1	1	.500	0	14--	-	3.85	3.28
2008	Tucsn	AAA	29	0	0	25	36.1	159	39	22	18	5	1	2	0	14	1	28	4	0	2	2	.500	0	9--	-	4.65	4.46
2008	Ari	NL	27	0	0	6	30.0	136	32	15	14	2	1	1	1	15	3	18	2	0	1	1	.500	0	0-1	1	4.51	4.20

Francisco Rosario

Pitches: R Bats: R Pos: P Ht: 6'0" Wt: 197 Born: 9/28/1980 Age: 28

			HOW MUCH HE PITCHED					WHAT HE GAVE UP												THE RESULTS							
Year	Team	Lg	G	GS	CG	GF	IP	BFP	H	R	ER	HR	SH	SF	HB	TBB	IBB	SO	WP	Bk	W	L	Pct	ShO	Sv-Op	Hld	ERC	ERA
2001	MdHat	R+	16	15	0	0	75.2	344	79	61	47	8	1	4	9	38	0	55	6	6	3	7	.300	0	0--	-	5.28	5.59
2002	CtnWV	A	13	13	1	0	66.2	265	50	22	19	5	2	2	4	14	0	78	2	0	6	1	.857	0	0--	-	2.15	2.57
2002	Dnedin	A+	13	12	0	0	63.0	248	33	10	9	3	1	1	3	25	0	65	1	2	3	3	.500	0	0--	-	1.58	1.29
2004	Dnedin	A+	6	6	0	0	17.1	80	16	12	9	2	0	2	0	11	0	16	1	0	1	1	.500	0	0--	-	4.51	4.67
2004	NHam	AA	12	12	0	0	48.0	199	48	25	23	6	1	3	2	16	0	45	1	0	2	4	.333	0	0--	-	4.31	4.31
2005	Syrcse	AAA	30	18	0	4	116.1	489	111	59	51	16	5	1	10	42	1	80	5	1	2	7	.222	0	2--	-	4.38	3.95
2006	Syrcse	AAA	14	8	0	2	42.0	168	29	14	13	2	1	1	5	13	0	50	2	0	0	3	.000	0	1--	-	2.28	2.79
2007	Clrwtr	A+	6	5	0	0	13.1	56	9	6	6	1	0	1	2	5	16	0	0	0	0	0	-	0	0--	-	1.08	4.05
2008	Clrwtr	A+	3	3	0	0	2.2	10	0	2	2	0	0	0	0	2	0	1	0	0	0	0	-	0	0--	-	0.57	6.75
2006	Tor	AL	17	1	0	4	23.0	108	24	17	17	4	0	0	1	16	2	21	3	0	1	2	.333	0	0-0	1	6.12	6.65
2007	Phi	NL	23	0	0	10	26.1	127	34	16	16	3	2	2	4	13	1	25	1	0	0	3	.000	0	1-1	1	6.89	5.47
	2 ML YEARS		40	1	0	14	49.1	235	58	33	33	7	2	2	5	29	3	46	4	0	1	5	.167	0	1-1	2	6.53	6.02

Cody Ross

Bats: R Throws: L Pos: CF-109; RF-35; LF-17; PH-17; PR-2; DH-1 Ht: 5'9" Wt: 203 Born: 12/23/1980 Age: 28

			BATTING																		BASERUNNING				AVERAGES		
Year	Team	Lg	G	AB	H	2B	3B	HR	(Hm	Rd)	TB	R	RBI	RC	TBB	IBB	SO	HBP	SH	SF	SB	CS	SB%	GDP	Avg	OBP	Slg
2003	Det	AL	6	19	4	1	0	1	(1	0)	8	1	5	4	1	0	3	1	1	0	0	0	-	0	.211	.286	.421
2005	LAD	NL	14	25	4	1	0	0	(0	0)	5	1	1	0	1	0	10	0	0	0	0	0	-	1	.160	.192	.200
2006	3 Tms	NL	101	269	61	12	2	13	(6	7)	116	34	46	36	22	0	65	4	1	2	1	1	.50	8	.227	.293	.431
2007	Fla	NL	66	173	58	19	0	12	(8	4)	113	35	39	42	20	3	38	3	0	1	2	0	1.00	2	.335	.411	.653
2008	Fla	NL	145	461	120	29	5	22	(7	15)	225	59	73	68	33	2	116	7	0	5	6	1	.86	5	.260	.316	.488
06	LAD	NL	8	14	7	1	1	2	(0	2)	16	4	9	6	0	0	2	0	0	0	1	0	1.00	0	.500	.500	1.143
06	Cin	NL	2	5	1	0	0	0	(0	0)	1	0	0	1	0	0	2	0	0	0	0	0	-	0	.200	.200	.200
06	Fla	NL	91	250	53	11	1	11	(6	5)	99	30	37	29	22	0	61	4	1	2	0	1	.00	8	.212	.284	.396
	5 ML YEARS		332	947	247	62	7	48	(22	26)	467	130	164	150	77	5	232	15	2	8	9	2	.82	16	.261	.324	.493

David Ross

Bats: R Throws: R Pos: C-54; PH-7; PR-1 Ht: 6'2" Wt: 238 Born: 3/19/1977 Age: 32

			BATTING																		BASERUNNING				AVERAGES		
Year	Team	Lg	G	AB	H	2B	3B	HR	(Hm	Rd)	TB	R	RBI	RC	TBB	IBB	SO	HBP	SH	SF	SB	CS	SB%	GDP	Avg	OBP	Slg
2008	Srsota*	A+	4	11	2	0	0	0	(-	-)	2	2	1	1	3	0	4	0	0	1	0	0	-	0	.182	.333	.182
2008	Lsvlle*	AAA	9	30	5	1	1	1	(-	-)	11	4	2	2	3	0	12	0	0	1	0	0	-	0	.167	.235	.367
2008	Pwtckt*	AAA	6	28	7	1	0	1	(-	-)	11	4	3	3	1	0	7	0	0	0	0	0	-	1	.250	.276	.393
2002	LAD	NL	8	10	2	1	0	1	(0	1)	6	2	2	2	2	0	4	1	0	0	0	0	-	0	.200	.385	.600
2003	LAD	NL	40	124	32	7	0	10	(5	5)	69	19	18	18	13	0	42	2	0	1	0	0	-	4	.258	.336	.556
2004	LAD	NL	70	165	28	3	1	5	(2	3)	48	13	15	11	15	1	62	5	0	5	0	0	-	3	.170	.253	.291
2005	2 Tms	NL	51	125	30	8	1	3	(2	1)	49	11	15	13	6	0	28	2	2	3	0	0	-	3	.240	.279	.392
2006	Cin	NL	90	247	63	15	1	21	(13	8)	143	37	52	43	37	7	75	3	4	5	0	0	-	9	.255	.353	.579
2007	Cin	NL	112	311	63	10	0	17	(12	5)	124	32	39	27	30	4	92	0	5	2	0	0	-	9	.203	.271	.399
2008	2 Tms	NL	60	142	32	9	0	3	(1	2)	50	18	13	19	32	4	39	1	6	1	0	1	.00	3	.225	.369	.352
05	Pit	NL	40	108	24	8	0	3	(2	1)	41	9	15	9	6	0	24	1	1	3	0	0	-	3	.222	.263	.380
05	SD	NL	11	17	6	0	1	0	(0	0)	8	2	0	4	0	0	4	1	1	0	0	0	-	0	.353	.389	.471
08	Cin	NL	52	134	31	9	0	3	(1	2)	49	17	13	19	32	4	36	1	5	1	0	1	.00	3	.231	.381	.366
08	Bos	AL	8	8	1	0	0	0	(0	0)	1	1	0	0	0	0	3	0	1	0	0	0	-	0	.125	.125	.125
	Postseason		2	3	0	0	0	0	(0	0)	0	0	0	0	1	0	1	0	0	0	0	0	-	0	.000	.250	.000
	7 ML YEARS		431	1124	250	53	3	60	(35	25)	489	132	154	133	135	16	342	14	17	17	0	1	.00	26	.222	.309	.435

Vinny Rottino

Bats: R Throws: R Pos: PH-1 Ht: 6'1" Wt: 206 Born: 4/7/1980 Age: 29

			BATTING																		BASERUNNING				AVERAGES		
Year	Team	Lg	G	AB	H	2B	3B	HR	(Hm	Rd)	TB	R	RBI	RC	TBB	IBB	SO	HBP	SH	SF	SB	CS	SB%	GDP	Avg	OBP	Slg
2008	Nashv*	AAA	118	431	112	30	3	7	(-	-)	169	59	55	56	31	0	72	6	1	8	9	4	.69	16	.260	.313	.392
2006	Mil	NL	9	14	3	1	0	0	(0	0)	4	1	1	1	1	0	2	0	0	0	1	0	1.00	0	.214	.267	.286
2007	Mil	NL	8	9	2	1	0	0	(0	0)	3	0	3	2	0	0	1	0	0	0	0	0	-	0	.222	.222	.333
2008	Mil	NL	1	1	0	0	0	0	(0	0)	0	0	0	0	0	0	0	0	0	0	0	0	-	0	.000	.000	.000
	3 ML YEARS		18	24	5	2	0	0	(0	0)	7	1	4	3	1	0	3	0	0	0	1	0	1.00	0	.208	.240	.292

Aaron Rowand

Bats: R **Throws:** R **Pos:** CF-149; PH-3; DH-1   **Ht:** 6'0" **Wt:** 219 **Born:** 8/29/1977 **Age:** 31

Year	Team	Lg	G	AB	H	2B	3B	HR	(Hm	Rd)	TB	R	RBI	RC	TBB	IBB	SO	HBP	SH	SF	SB	CS	SB%	GDP	Avg	OBP	Slg
2001	CWS	AL	63	123	36	5	0	4	(3	1)	53	21	20	22	15	0	28	4	5	1	5	1	.83	2	.293	.385	.431
2002	CWS	AL	126	302	78	16	2	7	(5	2)	119	41	29	37	12	1	54	6	9	2	0	1	.00	8	.258	.298	.394
2003	CWS	AL	93	157	45	8	0	6	(5	1)	71	22	24	28	7	0	21	3	2	1	0	0	-	1	.287	.327	.452
2004	CWS	AL	140	487	151	38	2	24	(12	12)	265	94	69	92	30	1	91	10	5	2	17	5	.77	5	.310	.361	.544
2005	CWS	AL	157	578	156	30	5	13	(8	5)	235	77	69	78	32	3	116	21	5	4	16	5	.76	17	.270	.329	.407
2006	Phi	NL	109	405	106	24	3	12	(6	6)	172	59	47	47	18	2	76	18	2	2	10	4	.71	13	.262	.321	.425
2007	Phi	NL	161	612	189	45	0	27	(17	10)	315	105	89	100	47	3	119	19	2	4	6	3	.67	18	.309	.374	.515
2008	SF	NL	152	549	149	37	0	13	(6	7)	225	57	70	67	44	7	126	14	0	4	2	4	.33	21	.271	.339	.410
	Postseason		15	57	13	6	0	1	(1	0)	22	9	4	3	4	1	13	1	0	1	1	0	1.00	3	.228	.286	.386
	8 ML YEARS		1001	3213	910	203	12	106	(62	44)	1455	476	417	471	205	17	631	95	30	20	56	23	.71	85	.283	.342	.453

Ryan Rowland-Smith

Pitches: L **Bats:** L **Pos:** RP-35; SP-12   **Ht:** 6'3" **Wt:** 240 **Born:** 1/26/1983 **Age:** 26

	HOW MUCH HE PITCHED							WHAT HE GAVE UP											THE RESULTS							
Year	Team	Lg	G	GS	CG	GF	IP	BFP	H	R	ER	HR	SH	SF	HB	TBB	IBB	SO	WP	Bk	W	L	Pct	ShO	Sv-Op	Hld	ERC	ERA
2001	Ms	R	17	0	0	10	33.1	128	25	11	11	1	1	0	2	9	1	39	0	0	1	1	.500	0	5- -	-	2.17	2.97
2002	Wisc	A	12	8	0	2	41.1	198	50	39	31	7	2	1	3	19	0	38	1	4	1	2	.333	0	0- -	-	6.19	6.75
2002	Everett	A-	18	6	0	5	61.2	267	58	22	19	2	3	2	4	22	0	58	4	3	4	1	.800	0	2- -	-	3.31	2.77
2003	Wisc	A	13	0	0	5	32.1	141	22	13	4	0	2	1	3	14	0	37	0	0	3	0	1.000	0	1- -	-	2.06	1.11
2003	InldEm	A+	15	0	0	3	19.2	80	12	9	7	0	0	3	3	8	0	15	0	1	0	1	.000	0	0- -	-	2.01	3.20
2004	InldEm	A+	29	12	0	4	99.2	425	107	50	42	10	4	3	3	30	0	119	5	1	5	3	.625	0	3- -	-	4.27	3.79
2005	SnAnt	AA	33	17	0	4	122.0	537	134	72	59	7	5	6	5	51	0	102	15	2	6	7	.462	0	0- -	-	4.61	4.35
2006	InldEm	A+	7	0	0	1	6.1	31	8	7	4	1	2	1	0	2	0	9	1	0	0	1	.000	0	0- -	-	5.17	5.68
2006	SnAnt	AA	23	1	0	9	41.1	182	38	18	13	2	4	1	1	18	1	48	2	0	1	3	.250	0	4- -	-	3.36	2.83
2007	Tacom	AAA	25	0	0	7	41.2	183	35	20	17	2	2	1	3	22	1	50	1	0	3	4	.429	0	1- -	-	3.51	3.67
2008	Tacom	AAA	3	3	0	0	18.2	74	12	6	6	1	1	1	0	7	0	12	1	0	2	0	1.000	0	0- -	-	1.89	2.89
2007	Sea	AL	26	0	0	6	38.2	168	39	19	17	4	1	4	2	15	1	42	0	0	1	0	1.000	0	0-0	3	4.27	3.96
2008	Sea	AL	47	12	0	10	118.1	506	114	49	45	13	2	3	2	48	0	77	2	1	5	3	.625	0	2-3	1	4.05	3.42
	2 ML YEARS		73	12	0	15	157.0	674	153	68	62	17	3	7	4	63	1	119	2	1	6	3	.667	0	2-3	4	4.11	3.55

Justin Ruggiano

Bats: R **Throws:** R **Pos:** LF-26; RF-15; PH-7; CF-5; DH-1; PR-1   **Ht:** 6'2" **Wt:** 205 **Born:** 4/12/1982 **Age:** 27

Year	Team	Lg	G	AB	H	2B	3B	HR	(Hm	Rd)	TB	R	RBI	RC	TBB	IBB	SO	HBP	SH	SF	SB	CS	SB%	GDP	Avg	OBP	Slg
2004	Ogden	R+	46	155	51	12	0	7	(-	-)	84	26	36	37	23	0	38	6	0	3	6	1	.86	7	.329	.428	.542
2005	VeroB	A	71	242	75	15	4	9	(-	-)	125	47	37	51	28	2	65	9	0	1	16	5	.76	6	.310	.400	.517
2005	Jaxnvl	AA	53	161	55	10	1	6	(-	-)	85	23	29	35	17	0	56	6	0	1	8	3	.73	1	.342	.422	.528
2006	Jaxnvl	AA	89	292	76	19	3	9	(-	-)	128	51	45	50	46	3	74	5	0	3	10	5	.67	6	.260	.367	.438
2006	Mont	AA	31	108	36	14	3	4	(-	-)	68	25	27	28	19	0	29	2	1	0	4	4	.50	3	.333	.442	.630
2007	Drham	AAA	127	482	149	29	2	20	(-	-)	242	78	73	94	53	2	151	8	2	1	26	11	.70	5	.309	.386	.502
2008	Drham	AAA	66	257	81	18	3	11	(-	-)	138	49	51	54	22	1	77	5	0	5	20	3	.87	6	.315	.374	.537
2007	TB	AL	7	14	3	0	0	0	(0	0)	3	2	3	1	1	0	5	0	0	0	0	0	-	0	.214	.267	.214
2008	TB	AL	45	76	15	4	0	2	(2	0)	25	9	7	4	4	0	27	1	0	0	2	0	1.00	2	.197	.247	.329
	2 ML YEARS		52	90	18	4	0	2	(2	0)	28	11	10	5	5	0	32	1	0	0	2	0	1.00	2	.200	.250	.311

Carlos Ruiz

Bats: R **Throws:** R **Pos:** C-110; PH-9; PR-4; 3B-1   **Ht:** 5'10" **Wt:** 202 **Born:** 1/22/1979 **Age:** 30

Year	Team	Lg	G	AB	H	2B	3B	HR	(Hm	Rd)	TB	R	RBI	RC	TBB	IBB	SO	HBP	SH	SF	SB	CS	SB%	GDP	Avg	OBP	Slg
2006	Phi	NL	27	69	18	1	1	3	(2	1)	30	5	10	10	5	2	8	1	2	1	0	0	-	3	.261	.316	.435
2007	Phi	NL	115	374	97	29	2	6	(4	2)	148	42	54	49	42	10	49	5	5	3	6	1	.86	17	.259	.340	.396
2008	Phi	NL	117	320	70	14	0	4	(2	2)	96	47	31	28	44	6	38	4	4	1	1	2	.33	14	.219	.320	.300
	Postseason		3	9	3	1	0	0	(0	0)	4	1	0	1	1	0	1	0	0	0	1	0	1.00	1	.333	.400	.444
	3 ML YEARS		259	763	185	44	3	13	(8	5)	274	94	95	87	91	18	95	10	11	5	7	3	.70	34	.242	.329	.359

Randy Ruiz

Bats: R **Throws:** R **Pos:** DH-17; PH-7   **Ht:** 6'3" **Wt:** 235 **Born:** 10/19/1977 **Age:** 31

Year	Team	Lg	G	AB	H	2B	3B	HR	(Hm	Rd)	TB	R	RBI	RC	TBB	IBB	SO	HBP	SH	SF	SB	CS	SB%	GDP	Avg	OBP	Slg
1999	Reds	R	33	102	29	8	0	3	(-	-)	46	12	9	18	12	0	33	4	0	1	5	2	.71	5	.284	.378	.451
1999	Clinton	A	2	8	5	2	0	0	(-	-)	7	3	2	3	1	0	0	0	0	1	0	0	-	1	.625	.600	.875
2000	Billings	R+	61	231	88	15	1	10	(-	-)	135	55	55	60	29	0	56	10	1	2	1	2	.33	6	.381	.467	.584
2001	Dayton	A	123	466	125	34	3	20	(-	-)	225	82	92	82	48	4	116	14	0	3	21	9	.70	10	.268	.352	.483
2002	Stcktn	A+	28	100	26	9	0	3	(-	-)	44	16	17	15	13	0	29	2	0	0	0	3	.00	4	.260	.357	.440
2002	Dayton	A	78	285	86	17	4	8	(-	-)	135	49	44	55	36	1	88	8	0	4	9	3	.75	8	.302	.390	.474
2003	Frdrck	A+	17	68	17	4	1	1	(-	-)	26	7	8	7	4	0	24	1	0	0	0	0	-	1	.250	.301	.382
2003	Dlmrva	A	67	239	74	18	2	11	(-	-)	129	33	51	50	29	1	70	5	0	3	3	3	.50	6	.310	.391	.540
2004	Lakwd	A	110	417	120	31	2	17	(-	-)	206	85	91	77	42	0	140	13	0	5	1	1	.50	10	.288	.367	.494
2005	Rdng	AA	89	345	122	29	0	27	(-	-)	232	59	89	88	30	11	85	6	0	5	0	2	.00	6	.354	.409	.672
2006	Wichta	AA	6	23	5	1	0	2	(-	-)	12	3	3	4	6	0	8	0	0	0	0	0	-	0	.217	.379	.522
2006	Trntn	AA	119	468	134	35	1	26	(-	-)	249	72	87	90	41	6	132	15	0	2	2	0	1.00	12	.286	.361	.532
2007	Altna	AA	47	162	47	9	1	7	(-	-)	79	20	30	29	18	1	32	2	0	3	1	0	1.00	2	.290	.362	.488
2007	Rdng	AA	22	82	31	10	0	3	(-	-)	50	16	12	19	6	0	21	1	0	0	1	0	1.00	1	.378	.427	.610

			BATTING																			BASERUNNING					AVERAGES		
Year	Team	Lg	G	AB	H	2B	3B	HR	(Hm	Rd)	TB	R	RBI	RC	TBB	IBB	SO	HBP	SH	SF	SB	CS	SB%	GDP	Avg	OBP	Slg
2007	Ottawa	AAA	22	79	17	4	0	4	(-	-)	33	11	11	10	9	0	23	0	0	0	0	0	-	3	.215	.295	.418
2007	Conn	AA	39	151	44	6	3	8	(-	-)	80	25	27	27	11	1	40	3	0	0	0	0	-	2	.291	.352	.530
2008	Roch	AAA	111	416	133	33	3	17	(-	-)	223	58	68	80	23	1	115	11	0	6	1	2	.33	10	.320	.366	.536
2008	Min	AL	22	62	17	2	0	1	(0	1)	22	13	7	11	6	1	21	0	0	0	0	0	-	1	.274	.338	.355

Rich Rundles

Pitches: L **Bats:** L **Pos:** RP-8

Ht: 6'5" **Wt:** 210 **Born:** 6/3/1981 **Age:** 28

			HOW MUCH HE PITCHED					WHAT HE GAVE UP											THE RESULTS						
Year	Team	Lg	G	GS	CG	GF	IP	BFP	H	R	ER	HR	SH	SF	HB	TBB	IBB	SO	WP	Bk	W	L	Pct	ShO	Sv-Op Hld	ERC	ERA
1999	RedSx	R	5	1	0	0	12.2	53	13	3	3	1	0	1	0	1	0	11	2	0	1	0	1.000	0	0- - -	2.73	2.13
2000	RedSx	R	9	6	0	0	40.1	158	31	15	11	3	2	0	4	10	0	32	0	1	3	1	.750	0	0- - -	2.60	2.45
2001	Augsta	A	19	19	0	0	115.0	468	109	46	31	5	5	5	7	10	0	94	4	0	7	6	.538	0	0- - -	2.46	2.43
2001	Clinton	A	4	4	0	0	27.0	112	26	10	7	0	0	1	3	3	1	20	1	0	1	1	.500	0	0- - -	2.47	2.33
2002	BrvdCt	A+	12	11	0	0	57.1	243	66	34	26	5	1	1	2	16	1	31	2	0	2	7	.222	0	0- - -	4.62	4.08
2003	BrvdCt	A+	19	19	2	0	106.2	446	111	44	35	2	4	2	2	24	0	76	4	1	5	6	.455	1	0- - -	3.16	2.95
2004	Hrsbrg	AA	20	20	0	0	102.2	441	107	50	39	7	3	5	8	35	2	65	8	0	3	6	.333	0	0- - -	4.20	3.42
2004	BrvdCt	A+	1	1	0	0	3.0	13	4	2	2	0	0	0	0	2	0	0	0	0	0	1	.000	0	0- - -	7.18	6.00
2005	Hrsbrg	AA	27	26	2	0	159.1	695	177	95	73	14	6	2	6	49	1	91	5	0	6	13	.316	0	0- - -	4.38	4.12
2006	Sprgfld	AA	15	14	1	0	86.0	379	100	52	44	9	1	4	4	28	0	47	3	0	5	6	.455	0	0- - -	4.97	4.60
2006	Bnghtn	AA	12	7	0	2	43.1	206	53	32	22	4	4	1	4	23	1	23	1	0	1	3	.250	0	0- - -	6.18	4.57
2006	StLuci	A+	3	3	0	0	19.2	89	27	8	4	2	0	0	1	6	0	9	0	0	1	2	.333	0	0- - -	6.25	1.83
2007	Akron	AA	23	2	0	6	34.1	140	27	10	7	0	1	0	4	10	0	29	0	0	3	0	1.000	0	2- - -	2.36	1.83
2007	Buffalo	AAA	17	0	0	8	26.2	131	28	15	8	1	1	1	5	16	3	19	2	0	2	4	.333	0	0- - -	4.97	2.70
2008	Buffalo	AAA	55	0	0	22	52.2	221	40	18	17	3	1	0	1	24	1	60	1	0	5	4	.556	0	4- - -	2.73	2.91
2008	Cle	AL	8	0	0	0	5.0	22	5	1	1	0	0	0	0	3	0	6	0	0	0	0	-	0	0-0 1	4.20	1.80

Josh Rupe

Pitches: R **Bats:** R **Pos:** RP-46

Ht: 6'2" **Wt:** 210 **Born:** 8/18/1982 **Age:** 26

			HOW MUCH HE PITCHED					WHAT HE GAVE UP											THE RESULTS						
Year	Team	Lg	G	GS	CG	GF	IP	BFP	H	R	ER	HR	SH	SF	HB	TBB	IBB	SO	WP	Bk	W	L	Pct	ShO	Sv-Op Hld	ERC	ERA
2005	Tex	AL	4	1	0	1	9.2	39	7	4	3	0	1	0	2	4	0	6	1	0	1	0	1.000	0	0-0 0	2.91	2.79
2006	Tex	AL	16	0	0	3	29.0	126	33	11	11	2	1	0	1	9	0	14	2	0	0	1	.000	0	0-1 1	4.45	3.41
2008	Tex	AL	46	0	0	10	89.1	392	93	52	51	8	2	7	10	46	3	53	3	0	3	1	.750	0	0-2 2	5.30	5.14
	3 ML YEARS		66	1	0	14	128.0	557	133	67	65	10	4	7	13	59	3	73	6	0	4	2	.667	0	0-3 3	4.92	4.57

Glendon Rusch

Pitches: L **Bats:** L **Pos:** RP-26; SP-9

Ht: 6'1" **Wt:** 225 **Born:** 11/7/1974 **Age:** 34

			HOW MUCH HE PITCHED					WHAT HE GAVE UP											THE RESULTS						
Year	Team	Lg	G	GS	CG	GF	IP	BFP	H	R	ER	HR	SH	SF	HB	TBB	IBB	SO	WP	Bk	W	L	Pct	ShO	Sv-Op Hld	ERC	ERA
2008	ColSpr*	AAA	7	7	0	0	41.0	176	48	21	21	4	2	2	1	13	1	24	0	0	1	2	.333	0	0- - -	4.90	4.61
1997	KC	AL	30	27	1	0	170.1	758	206	111	104	28	8	7	7	52	0	116	0	1	6	9	.400	0	0-0 0	5.56	5.50
1998	KC	AL	29	24	1	2	154.2	686	191	104	101	22	1	2	4	50	0	94	1	0	6	15	.286	1	1-1 0	5.62	5.88
1999	2 Tms		4	0	0	2	5.0	26	8	7	7	1	0	0	1	3	0	4	0	0	0	0	1.000	0	0-0 0	10.75	12.60
2000	NYM	NL	31	30	2	0	190.2	802	196	91	85	18	10	7	6	44	2	157	2	0	11	11	.500	0	0-0 0	3.64	4.01
2001	NYM	NL	33	33	1	0	179.0	785	216	110	92	23	11	5	7	43	2	156	3	2	8	12	.400	0	0-0 0	4.97	4.63
2002	Mil	NL	34	34	4	0	210.2	913	227	118	110	30	14	5	5	76	1	140	6	0	10	16	.385	1	0-0 0	4.80	4.70
2003	Mil	NL	32	19	1	1	123.1	573	171	93	88	11	5	2	4	45	3	93	3	0	1	12	.077	0	1-1 7	6.27	6.42
2004	ChC	NL	32	16	0	5	129.2	545	127	54	50	10	8	2	4	33	1	90	1	1	6	2	.750	0	2-2 3	3.33	3.47
2005	ChC	NL	46	19	1	6	145.1	655	175	79	73	14	13	9	1	53	8	111	1	1	9	8	.529	1	0-1 3	4.97	4.52
2006	ChC	NL	25	9	0	5	66.1	311	86	57	55	21	7	1	1	33	2	59	0	0	3	8	.273	0	0-0 0	8.09	7.46
2008	2 Tms	NL	35	9	0	9	83.2	367	94	50	48	10	5	5	0	25	7	55	2	0	5	5	.500	0	0-1 1	4.31	5.16
99	KC	AL	3	0	0	1	4.0	23	7	7	7	1	0	0	1	3	0	4	0	0	0	1	.000	0	0-0 0	12.89	15.75
99	NYM	NL	1	0	0	1	1.0	3	1	0	0	0	0	0	0	0	0	0	0	0	0	0	-	0	0-0 0	2.79	0.00
08	SD	NL	12	0	0	6	19.2	92	22	15	14	2	1	1	0	11	4	12	1	0	1	2	.333	0	0-0 0	4.92	6.41
08	Col	NL	23	9	0	3	64.0	275	72	35	34	8	4	4	0	14	3	43	1	0	4	3	.571	0	0-1 1	4.11	4.78
	Postseason		6	0	0	1	8.1	35	9	1	1	0	0	1	1	2	1	7	2	0	1	0	1.000	0	0-0 0	3.58	1.08
	11 ML YEARS		331	220	11	30	1458.2	6421	1697	865	813	188	82	45	40	457	26	1075	19	5	65	99	.396	3	4-6 14	4.96	5.02

Adam Russell

Pitches: R **Bats:** R **Pos:** RP-22

Ht: 6'8" **Wt:** 250 **Born:** 4/14/1983 **Age:** 26

			HOW MUCH HE PITCHED					WHAT HE GAVE UP											THE RESULTS						
Year	Team	Lg	G	GS	CG	GF	IP	BFP	H	R	ER	HR	SH	SF	HB	TBB	IBB	SO	WP	Bk	W	L	Pct	ShO	Sv-Op Hld	ERC	ERA
2004	Gr Falls	R+	15	4	0	2	38.0	158	31	11	10	2	3	1	0	18	0	33	0	0	4	0	1.000	0	0- - -	3.08	2.37
2004	Knapol	A-	2	2	0	0	10.0	52	18	11	10	3	0	0	1	7	0	3	1	0	0	2	.000	0	0- - -	13.80	9.00
2005	Knapol	A-	24	24	0	0	126.1	542	116	61	53	10	4	5	6	55	0	82	5	0	9	7	.563	0	0- - -	3.82	3.78
2006	WinSa	A+	17	17	0	0	94.2	393	80	35	28	5	4	2	7	39	0	61	4	0	7	3	.700	0	0- - -	3.32	2.66
2006	Brham	AA	10	10	0	0	55.0	242	59	33	29	5	0	1	3	19	0	47	3	1	3	3	.500	0	0- - -	4.39	4.75
2007	Brham	AA	38	20	0	1	138.2	622	158	81	73	8	7	2	6	58	0	95	4	0	9	11	.450	0	1- - -	4.81	4.74
2008	Charltt	AAA	25	0	0	7	37.1	160	28	13	12	3	1	1	1	19	0	28	2	0	3	2	.600	0	0- - -	3.04	2.89
2008	CWS	AL	22	0	0	16	26.0	118	30	15	15	1	2	1	2	10	1	22	3	0	4	0	1.000	0	0-0 0	4.63	5.19

B.J. Ryan

Pitches: L Bats: L Pos: RP-60   Ht: 6'6" Wt: 260 Born: 12/28/1975 Age: 33

Year	Team	Lg	G	GS	CG	GF	IP	BFP	H	R	ER	HR	SH	SF	HB	TBB	IBB	SO	WP	Bk	W	L	Pct	ShO	Sv-Op	Hld	ERC	ERA
2008	Dnedin*	A+	4	1	0	0	4.0	13	2	1	1	0	0	0	0	1	0	5	1	1	0	1	.000	0	0--	-	1.09	2.25
1999	2 Tms		14	0	0	3	20.1	82	13	7	7	0	0	1	0	13	1	29	1	0	1	0	1.000	0	0-0	0	2.42	3.10
2000	Bal	AL	42	0	0	9	42.2	193	36	29	28	7	1	1	0	31	1	41	2	1	2	3	.400	0	0-3	7	4.87	5.91
2001	Bal	AL	61	0	0	9	53.0	237	47	31	25	6	1	2	2	30	4	54	0	0	2	4	.333	0	2-4	14	4.13	4.25
2002	Bal	AL	67	0	0	13	57.2	252	51	31	30	7	3	0	4	33	4	56	4	0	2	1	.667	0	1-2	12	4.48	4.68
2003	Bal	AL	76	0	0	17	50.1	219	42	19	19	1	1	3	3	27	0	63	2	0	4	1	.800	0	0-2	19	3.33	3.40
2004	Bal	AL	76	0	0	19	87.0	361	64	24	22	4	3	2	1	35	9	122	0	0	4	6	.400	0	3-7	21	2.20	2.28
2005	Bal	AL	69	0	0	61	70.1	290	54	20	19	4	1	1	2	26	2	100	5	0	1	4	.200	0	36-41	0	2.50	2.43
2006	Tor	AL	65	0	0	57	72.1	270	42	12	11	3	1	1	0	20	1	86	4	0	2	2	.500	0	38-42	1	1.39	1.37
2007	Tor	AL	5	0	0	4	4.1	25	7	7	6	1	0	0	0	4	0	3	0	0	0	2	.000	0	3-5	0	10.86	12.46
2008	Tor	AL	60	0	0	48	58.0	249	46	21	19	4	2	1	4	28	3	58	2	1	2	4	.333	0	32-36	1	3.20	2.95
99	Cin	NL	1	0	0	0	2.0	9	4	1	1	0	0	0	0	1	0	1	0	0	0	0	-	0	0-0	0	12.01	4.50
99	Bal		13	0	0	3	18.1	73	9	6	6	0	0	1	0	12	1	28	1	0	1	0	1.000	0	0-0	0	1.73	2.95
10 ML YEARS			535	0	0	240	516.0	2178	402	201	186	37	13	12	16	247	25	612	20	2	20	27	.426	0	115-142	75	3.02	3.24

Brendan Ryan

Bats: R Throws: R Pos: SS-40; 2B-23; PH-16; PR-7; 3B-5; RF-3; LF-1   Ht: 6'2" Wt: 195 Born: 3/26/1982 Age: 27

Year	Team	Lg	G	AB	H	2B	3B	HR	(Hm	Rd)	TB	R	RBI	RC	TBB	IBB	SO	HBP	SH	SF	SB	CS	SB%	GDP	Avg	OBP	Slg
2003	NewJrs	A-	53	193	60	14	4	0	(-	-)	82	20	13	31	14	1	25	3	1	2	11	3	.79	4	.311	.363	.425
2004	Peoria	A	105	426	137	21	4	2	(-	-)	172	72	59	67	24	2	42	4	9	9	30	7	.81	13	.322	.356	.404
2005	PlmBh	A+	49	188	57	17	0	1	(-	-)	77	29	16	29	15	0	20	0	4	0	8	1	.89	4	.303	.355	.410
2005	Sprgfld	AA	43	154	42	8	1	2	(-	-)	58	28	9	22	15	0	19	2	2	1	7	0	1.00	3	.273	.343	.377
2006	StCol	AA	8	34	8	0	0	0	(-	-)	8	5	3	2	3	0	4	0	1	2	1	0	1.00	0	.235	.282	.235
2006	PlmBh	A+	3	14	6	1	0	0	(-	-)	7	2	1	2	0	0	0	0	0	0	1	0	1.00	0	.429	.429	.500
2006	Sprgfld	AA	10	43	13	1	0	0	(-	-)	14	6	3	5	3	0	6	0	1	0	1	1	.50	0	.302	.348	.326
2006	Memp	AAA	7	26	4	0	0	1	(-	-)	7	4	6	1	1	0	3	0	0	0	1	0	1.00	1	.154	.185	.269
2007	Memp	AAA	81	321	87	8	5	1	(-	-)	108	55	15	38	25	0	39	2	2	1	17	6	.74	6	.271	.327	.336
2008	PlmBh	A+	3	12	3	1	0	0	(-	-)	4	1	0	1	1	0	1	0	0	0	1	1	.50	0	.250	.308	.333
2008	Sprgfld	AA	4	19	7	3	0	1	(-	-)	13	5	3	5	1	0	6	1	0	0	1	0	1.00	1	.368	.429	.684
2008	Memp	AAA	21	80	19	5	0	3	(-	-)	33	13	10	9	4	0	17	1	2	1	1	0	1.00	5	.238	.279	.413
2007	StL	NL	67	180	52	9	0	4	(2	2)	73	30	12	21	15	0	19	1	3	0	7	0	1.00	3	.289	.347	.406
2008	StL	NL	80	197	48	9	0	0	(0	0)	57	30	10	12	16	0	31	2	3	0	7	2	.78	4	.244	.307	.289
2 ML YEARS			147	377	100	18	0	4	(2	2)	130	60	22	33	31	0	50	3	6	0	14	2	.88	7	.265	.326	.345

Dusty Ryan

Bats: R Throws: R Pos: C-15   Ht: 6'4" Wt: 220 Born: 9/2/1984 Age: 24

Year	Team	Lg	G	AB	H	2B	3B	HR	(Hm	Rd)	TB	R	RBI	RC	TBB	IBB	SO	HBP	SH	SF	SB	CS	SB%	GDP	Avg	OBP	Slg
2004	Oneont	A-	54	157	43	11	1	4	(-	-)	68	20	26	26	24	0	52	2	2	4	6	4	.60	1	.274	.369	.433
2005	WMich	A	75	241	44	11	0	4	(-	-)	67	21	16	16	22	0	70	2	4	2	3	3	.50	6	.183	.255	.278
2006	WMich	A	98	322	79	13	2	6	(-	-)	114	49	35	42	44	2	102	5	3	1	3	4	.43	6	.245	.344	.354
2007	Lkland	A+	46	145	31	0	0	7	(-	-)	52	17	22	17	18	0	52	3	0	2	0	1	.00	5	.214	.310	.359
2007	Tigers	R	6	16	1	0	0	0	(-	-)	1	1	1	0	4	0	5	0	0	0	0	0	-	2	.063	.250	.063
2008	Erie	AA	82	296	75	17	2	15	(-	-)	141	46	50	49	38	1	95	2	0	2	2	1	.67	6	.253	.340	.476
2008	Toledo	AAA	20	73	23	7	2	2	(-	-)	40	12	13	14	6	0	27	1	0	1	0	0	-	2	.315	.370	.548
2008	Det	AL	15	44	14	2	0	2	(1	1)	22	6	7	9	5	0	13	0	0	1	0	0	-	0	.318	.380	.500

Jae Kuk Ryu

Pitches: R Bats: R Pos: RP-1   Ht: 6'3" Wt: 225 Born: 5/30/1983 Age: 26

Year	Team	Lg	G	GS	CG	GF	IP	BFP	H	R	ER	HR	SH	SF	HB	TBB	IBB	SO	WP	Bk	W	L	Pct	ShO	Sv-Op	Hld	ERC	ERA
2008	Drham*	AAA	5	5	0	0	24.2	107	26	12	12	1	3	2	0	9	0	19	2	0	1	2	.333	0	0--	-	3.80	4.38
2006	ChC	NL	10	1	0	4	15.0	77	23	14	14	7	3	0	2	6	1	17	1	0	0	1	.000	0	0-0	0	10.72	8.40
2007	TB	AL	17	0	0	7	23.1	110	31	19	19	2	0	0	4	11	0	14	2	0	1	2	.333	0	0-1	1	7.17	7.33
2008	TB	AL	1	0	0	1	1.1	5	0	0	0	0	0	0	0	1	0	1	0	0	0	0	-	0	0-0	0	0.57	0.00
3 ML YEARS			28	1	0	12	39.2	192	54	33	33	9	3	0	6	18	1	32	3	0	1	3	.250	0	0-1	1	8.21	7.49

Kirk Saarloos

Pitches: R Bats: R Pos: RP-7; SP-1   Ht: 6'0" Wt: 180 Born: 5/23/1979 Age: 30

Year	Team	Lg	G	GS	CG	GF	IP	BFP	H	R	ER	HR	SH	SF	HB	TBB	IBB	SO	WP	Bk	W	L	Pct	ShO	Sv-Op	Hld	ERC	ERA
2008	Scrmto*	AAA	22	22	1	0	140.2	602	150	73	66	18	2	4	7	36	2	79	4	0	9	4	.692	0	0--	-	4.25	4.22
2002	Hou	NL	17	17	1	0	85.1	372	100	59	57	12	5	2	6	27	5	54	1	0	6	7	.462	1	0-0	0	5.35	6.01
2003	Hou	NL	36	6	0	11	49.1	218	55	31	27	4	1	1	3	17	3	43	0	0	2	1	.667	0	0-0	4	4.51	4.93
2004	Oak	AL	6	5	0	0	24.1	112	27	13	12	4	2	1	2	12	0	10	0	0	2	1	.667	0	0-0	0	5.91	4.44
2005	Oak	AL	29	27	2	0	159.2	682	170	75	74	11	3	3	11	54	8	53	1	0	10	9	.526	1	0-0	0	4.27	4.17
2006	Oak	AL	35	16	0	7	121.1	548	149	70	64	19	2	6	3	53	3	52	3	0	7	7	.500	0	2-3	6	6.17	4.75
2007	Cin	NL	34	3	0	7	42.2	201	54	36	34	8	2	0	3	19	1	27	1	0	1	5	.167	0	0-1	4	6.75	7.17
2008	Oak	AL	8	1	0	1	26.1	118	37	17	16	2	1	1	0	4	1	12	0	0	1	0	1.000	0	0-0	0	5.13	5.47
7 ML YEARS			165	73	3	27	509.0	2251	592	301	284	60	16	14	28	186	21	251	6	0	29	30	.492	2	2-4	8	5.24	5.02

CC Sabathia

Pitches: L Bats: L Pos: SP-35   Ht: 6'7" Wt: 290 Born: 7/21/1980 Age: 28

			HOW MUCH HE PITCHED						WHAT HE GAVE UP													THE RESULTS						
Year	Team	Lg	G	GS	CG	GF	IP	BFP	H	R	ER	HR	SH	SF	HB	TBB	IBB	SO	WP	Bk	W	L	Pct	ShO	Sv-Op	Hld	ERC	ERA
2001	Cle	AL	33	33	0	0	180.1	763	149	93	88	19	3	5	7	95	1	171	7	3	17	5	.773	0	0-0	0	3.86	4.39
2002	Cle	AL	33	33	2	0	210.0	891	198	109	102	17	5	10	1	88	2	149	6	3	13	11	.542	0	0-0	0	3.74	4.37
2003	Cle	AL	30	30	2	0	197.2	832	190	85	79	19	10	4	6	66	3	141	4	2	13	9	.591	1	0-0	0	3.70	3.60
2004	Cle	AL	30	30	1	0	188.0	787	176	90	86	20	3	6	7	72	3	139	1	1	11	10	.524	1	0-0	0	3.91	4.12
2005	Cle	AL	31	31	1	0	196.2	823	185	92	88	19	6	3	7	62	1	161	7	0	15	10	.600	0	0-0	0	3.55	4.03
2006	Cle	AL	28	28	6	0	192.2	802	182	83	69	17	8	5	7	44	3	172	3	0	12	11	.522	2	0-0	0	3.13	3.22
2007	Cle	AL	34	34	4	0	241.0	975	238	94	86	20	6	6	8	37	1	209	1	0	19	7	.731	1	0-0	0	3.12	3.21
2008	2 Tms		35	35	10	0	253.0	1023	223	85	76	19	9	6	7	59	1	251	2	2	17	10	.630	5	0-0	0	2.78	2.70
08	Cle	AL	18	18	3	0	122.1	507	117	54	52	13	3	3	3	34	1	123	1	2	6	8	.429	2	0-0	0	3.52	3.83
08	Mil	NL	17	17	7	0	130.2	516	106	31	24	6	6	3	4	25	0	128	1	0	11	2	.846	3	0-0	0	2.13	1.65
	Postseason		4	4	0	0	21.1	105	27	17	17	3	1	0	3	18	3	19	1	0	2	2	.500	0	0-0	0	8.61	7.17
	8 ML YEARS		254	254	26	0	1659.1	6896	1541	731	674	150	50	45	50	523	15	1393	31	11	117	73	.616	10	0-0	0	3.43	3.66

Mark Saccomanno

Bats: R Throws: R Pos: PH-9; 1B-2   Ht: 6'4" Wt: 200 Born: 4/30/1980 Age: 29

							BATTING														BASERUNNING				AVERAGES		
Year	Team	Lg	G	AB	H	2B	3B	HR	(Hm	Rd)	TB	R	RBI	RC	TBB	IBB	SO	HBP	SH	SF	SB	CS	SB%	GDP	Avg	OBP	Slg
2003	Mrtnsvl	R+	34	136	44	5	1	3	(-	-)	60	25	21	22	9	0	18	1	1	1	1	1	.50	3	.324	.367	.441
2004	Salem	A+	136	513	134	25	2	22	(-	-)	229	71	80	78	48	2	134	6	0	3	2	1	.67	13	.261	.330	.446
2005	CpChr	AA	134	514	143	37	1	12	(-	-)	218	66	51	70	27	1	108	4	0	1	5	2	.71	11	.278	.319	.424
2006	CpChr	AA	83	298	73	15	3	20	(-	-)	154	42	63	47	23	1	84	2	2	2	2	1	.67	7	.245	.302	.517
2007	RdRck	AAA	131	470	130	23	5	22	(-	-)	229	64	85	75	33	1	114	2	0	6	1	2	.33	7	.277	.323	.487
2008	RdRck	AAA	137	528	157	33	2	27	(-	-)	275	83	84	93	35	2	94	1	1	6	4	3	.57	16	.297	.339	.521
2008	Hou	NL	10	10	2	1	0	1	(1	0)	6	1	2	1	0	0	3	0	0	0	0	0	-	0	.200	.200	.600

Billy Sadler

Pitches: R Bats: R Pos: RP-33   Ht: 6'0" Wt: 194 Born: 9/21/1981 Age: 27

						HOW MUCH HE PITCHED						WHAT HE GAVE UP												THE RESULTS						
Year	Team	Lg	G	GS	CG	GF	IP	BFP	H	R	ER	HR	SH	SF	HB	TBB	IBB	SO	WP	Bk	W	L	Pct	ShO	Sv-Op	Hld	ERC	ERA
2003	Hgrstn	A	12	0	0	6	15.0	72	15	8	8	4	0	0	2	13	0	10	0	0	0	0		0	1--	-	8.17	4.80
2004	SnJos	A+	30	3	0	3	56.0	241	29	17	15	1	1	1	4	40	0	16	3	2	2	2	.500	0	0--	-	2.34	2.41
2004	Nrwich	AA	17	0	0	6	30.1	134	22	16	13	3	0	0	3	18	0	24	8	0	0	3	.000	0	0--	-	3.60	3.86
2005	Nrwich	AA	47	0	0	22	84.1	350	64	34	31	4	4	2	12	33	0	81	9	0	6	5	.545	0	5--	-	2.98	3.31
2006	Conn	AA	44	0	0	34	45.2	190	23	14	13	1	2	0	2	29	2	67	2	0	4	3	.571	0	20--	-	1.93	2.56
2006	Fresno	AAA	7	0	0	5	10.0	34	5	2	2	1	0	0	0	2	0	12	1	0	2	0	1.000	0	1--	-	1.27	1.80
2007	Fresno	AAA	40	0	0	24	42.1	195	36	31	28	5	1	1	1	35	0	59	8	0	3	2	.600	0	6--	-	5.14	5.95
2007	Conn	AA	9	0	0	3	12.1	44	3	1	1	1	1	1	0	6	0	18	1	0	0	0		0	1--	-	1.02	0.73
2008	Fresno	AAA	22	0	0	7	33.0	136	19	7	4	0	2	1	0	21	0	41	3	0	1	0	1.000	0	1--	-	2.09	1.09
2006	SF	NL	5	0	0	2	4.0	20	5	3	3	2	0	1	0	2	0	6	0	0	0	0		0	0-0	0	10.38	6.75
2008	SF	NL	33	0	0	8	44.1	197	34	21	20	6	2	2	8	27	4	42	8	0	0	1	.000	0	0-0	1	4.42	4.06
	2 ML YEARS		38	0	0	10	48.1	217	39	24	23	8	2	2	9	29	4	48	8	0	0	1	.000	0	0-0	1	4.87	4.28

Takashi Saito

Pitches: R Bats: R Pos: RP-45   Ht: 6'2" Wt: 214 Born: 2/14/1970 Age: 39

						HOW MUCH HE PITCHED						WHAT HE GAVE UP												THE RESULTS						
Year	Team	Lg	G	GS	CG	GF	IP	BFP	H	R	ER	HR	SH	SF	HB	TBB	IBB	SO	WP	Bk	W	L	Pct	ShO	Sv-Op	Hld	ERC	ERA
2006	LAD	NL	72	0	0	48	78.1	303	48	19	18	3	3	4	2	23	3	107	2	0	6	2	.750	0	24-26	7	1.52	2.07
2007	LAD	NL	63	0	0	55	64.1	234	33	10	10	5	0	0	3	13	0	78	0	0	2	1	.667	0	39-43	1	1.28	1.40
2008	LAD	NL	45	0	0	35	47.0	197	40	14	13	1	0	2	2	16	3	60	1	0	4	4	.500	0	18-22	0	2.57	2.49
	Postseason		2	0	0	2	2.2	9	0	0	0	0	0	0	0	0	0	4	0	0	0	0	-	0	0-0	0	0.00	0.00
	3 ML YEARS		180	0	0	138	189.2	734	121	43	41	9	3	6	7	52	6	245	3	0	12	7	.632	0	81-91	8	1.63	1.95

Juan Salas

Pitches: R Bats: R Pos: RP-5   Ht: 6'2" Wt: 230 Born: 11/7/1978 Age: 30

						HOW MUCH HE PITCHED						WHAT HE GAVE UP												THE RESULTS						
Year	Team	Lg	G	GS	CG	GF	IP	BFP	H	R	ER	HR	SH	SF	HB	TBB	IBB	SO	WP	Bk	W	L	Pct	ShO	Sv-Op	Hld	ERC	ERA
2008	Drham*	AAA	28	0	0	7	44.2	174	32	13	13	2	0	2	2	11	0	53	3	1	4	5	.444	0	1--	-	1.94	2.62
2006	TB	AL	8	0	0	4	10.0	48	13	7	6	1	0	1	0	3	0	8	0	0	0	0		0	0-1	1	5.03	5.40
2007	TB	AL	34	0	0	10	36.1	168	36	19	15	7	1	0	5	17	0	26	3	0	1	1	.500	0	0-1	2	5.39	3.72
2008	TB	AL	5	0	0	2	6.1	27	5	5	5	0	0	0	0	4	0	8	1	0	0	0		0	0-0	0	3.15	7.11
	3 ML YEARS		47	0	0	14	52.2	243	54	31	26	8	1	1	5	24	0	42	7	0	1	1	.500	0	0-2	3	5.05	4.44

Marino Salas

Pitches: R Bats: R Pos: RP-13   Ht: 6'0" Wt: 195 Born: 10/2/1981 Age: 27

						HOW MUCH HE PITCHED						WHAT HE GAVE UP												THE RESULTS						
Year	Team	Lg	G	GS	CG	GF	IP	BFP	H	R	ER	HR	SH	SF	HB	TBB	IBB	SO	WP	Bk	W	L	Pct	ShO	Sv-Op	Hld	ERC	ERA
2001	Orioles	R	15	0	0	13	18.2	89	21	12	10	1	1	1	1	13	4	10	0	1	1	5	.167	0	6--	-	4.95	4.82
2002	Bluefld	R+	27	0	0	7	36.2	177	44	31	22	6	1	1	3	21	1	34	7	3	3	0	1.000	0	0--	-	6.67	5.40
2003	Bluefld	R+	23	0	0	5	35.0	150	36	22	19	1	3	1	4	9	0	27	4	2	1	2	.333	0	0--	-	3.63	4.89
2004	Dlmrva	A	40	0	0	34	50.1	220	51	15	12	5	0	0	1	17	3	46	2	0	2	4	.333	0	13--	-	3.79	2.15
2005	Frdrck	A+	50	0	0	38	62.0	266	54	32	25	7	2	2	2	28	0	63	9	0	4	2	.667	0	16--	-	3.76	3.63
2006	Bowie	AA	44	0	0	37	49.1	204	38	16	16	3	3	3	1	17	1	46	4	0	2	6	.250	0	19--	-	2.41	2.92

244

			HOW MUCH HE PITCHED						WHAT HE GAVE UP													THE RESULTS							
Year	Team	Lg	G	GS	CG	GF	IP	BFP	H	R	ER	HR	SH	SF	HB	TBB	IBB	SO	WP	Bk	W	L	Pct	ShO	Sv-Op	Hld	ERC	ERA
2007	Hntsvl	AA	37	0	0	31	38.0	149	25	7	6	2	0	1	2	14	1	29	1	0	0	0	-	0	17--	-	2.13	1.42
2007	Nashv	AAA	14	0	0	7	23.2	107	27	13	13	7	0	0	2	8	1	25	3	0	0	1	.000	0	0--	-	6.32	4.94
2008	Indy	AAA	40	0	0	16	57.0	238	40	23	22	6	2	1	0	30	3	54	4	1	4	4	.500	0	4--	-	2.90	3.47
2008	Pit	NL	13	0	0	4	17.0	88	25	16	16	4	1	1	2	14	3	9	4	0	1	0	1.000	0	0-0	0	10.53	8.47

Jeff Salazar

Bats: L **Throws:** L **Pos:** PH-48; LF-27; RF-18; CF-4; PR-3   **Ht:** 6'0" **Wt:** 194 **Born:** 11/24/1980 **Age:** 28

							BATTING														BASERUNNING				AVERAGES		
Year	Team	Lg	G	AB	H	2B	3B	HR	(Hm	Rd)	TB	R	RBI	RC	TBB	IBB	SO	HBP	SH	SF	SB	CS	SB%	GDP	Avg	OBP	Slg
2008	Tucsn*	AAA	24	99	36	6	3	4	(-	-)	60	29	18	25	14	0	14	0	1	1	3	0	1.00	1	.364	.439	.606
2006	Col	NL	19	53	15	4	0	1	(1	0)	22	13	8	11	11	2	16	1	1	1	2	0	1.00	0	.283	.409	.415
2007	Ari	NL	38	94	26	6	1	1	(0	1)	37	13	10	16	9	0	19	0	0	0	2	0	1.00	1	.277	.340	.394
2008	Ari	NL	90	128	27	5	3	2	(0	2)	44	17	12	17	21	1	41	2	1	0	0	2	.00	2	.211	.331	.344
Postseason			6	10	1	0	0	0	(0	0)	1	0	0	0	1	0	3	0	0	0	0	0	-	0	.100	.182	.100
3 ML YEARS			147	275	68	15	4	4	(1	3)	103	43	30	44	41	3	76	3	2	1	4	2	.67	3	.247	.350	.375

Oscar Salazar

Bats: R **Throws:** R **Pos:** PH-13; 1B-10; 3B-7; DH-6; SS-1; PR-1   **Ht:** 6'0" **Wt:** 190 **Born:** 6/27/1978 **Age:** 31

							BATTING														BASERUNNING				AVERAGES		
Year	Team	Lg	G	AB	H	2B	3B	HR	(Hm	Rd)	TB	R	RBI	RC	TBB	IBB	SO	HBP	SH	SF	SB	CS	SB%	GDP	Avg	OBP	Slg
1998	As	R	26	102	33	7	5	2	(-	-)	56	29	18	21	12	0	15	1	0	0	4	1	.80	1	.324	.400	.549
1998	SoOre	A-	28	101	32	4	1	5	(-	-)	53	19	28	22	16	0	22	0	1	3	5	2	.71	0	.317	.400	.525
1999	Mdest	A+	130	525	155	26	18	18	(-	-)	271	100	105	89	39	1	106	1	0	9	14	6	.70	10	.295	.340	.516
2000	Mdland	AA	111	427	128	27	1	13	(-	-)	196	70	57	67	39	0	71	2	2	3	4	4	.50	9	.300	.359	.459
2000	Scrmto	AAA	4	13	2	1	0	0	(-	-)	3	0	1	0	1	0	1	0	0	0	1	0	1.00	2	.154	.214	.231
2001	Mdland	AA	130	521	139	31	4	18	(-	-)	232	75	95	74	49	2	100	2	1	6	10	3	.77	11	.267	.329	.445
2001	Scrmto	AAA	5	16	1	0	0	0	(-	-)	1	0	1	0	1	0	5	0	0	0	0	0	-	1	.063	.118	.063
2002	Toledo	AAA	8	19	6	0	0	0	(-	-)	6	0	1	2	3	0	1	0	0	0	0	1	.00	0	.316	.409	.316
2002	Erie	AA	53	191	41	18	1	6	(-	-)	79	16	26	19	14	0	36	3	0	0	2	1	.67	6	.215	.279	.414
2002	Bnghtn	AA	28	75	13	2	0	1	(-	-)	18	6	5	2	5	0	19	1	0	1	0	1	.00	2	.173	.232	.240
2003	Ark	AA	39	143	47	6	2	4	(-	-)	69	22	21	29	19	1	20	2	1	2	2	1	.67	1	.329	.410	.483
2003	Salt Lk	AAA	7	26	8	2	1	1	(-	-)	15	5	4	5	3	0	4	0	0	1	0	0	-	1	.308	.367	.577
2003	Wichta	AA	78	287	80	15	2	7	(-	-)	120	34	43	37	24	4	48	0	0	3	4	4	.50	7	.279	.331	.418
2004	Akron	AA	44	163	36	6	2	4	(-	-)	60	18	21	14	11	0	30	0	0	1	2	1	.67	4	.221	.269	.368
2007	Bowie	AA	136	532	154	39	2	22	(-	-)	263	73	96	85	26	4	77	3	1	4	3	3	.50	12	.289	.324	.494
2008	Norfolk	AAA	112	443	140	42	3	13	(-	-)	227	73	85	85	42	1	56	0	0	6	8	2	.80	12	.316	.371	.512
2002	Det	AL	8	21	4	1	0	1	(0	1)	8	2	3	3	1	0	2	0	1	0	0	0	-	0	.190	.227	.381
2008	Bal	AL	34	81	23	3	0	5	(4	1)	41	13	15	14	12	0	13	0	0	1	0	1	.00	1	.284	.372	.506
2 ML YEARS			42	102	27	4	0	6	(4	2)	49	15	18	17	13	0	15	0	1	1	0	1	.00	1	.265	.345	.480

Angel Salome

Bats: R **Throws:** R **Pos:** PH-3   **Ht:** 5'7" **Wt:** 198 **Born:** 6/8/1986 **Age:** 23

							BATTING														BASERUNNING				AVERAGES		
Year	Team	Lg	G	AB	H	2B	3B	HR	(Hm	Rd)	TB	R	RBI	RC	TBB	IBB	SO	HBP	SH	SF	SB	CS	SB%	GDP	Avg	OBP	Slg
2004	Brewrs	R	20	81	19	7	0	0	(-	-)	26	7	8	7	4	1	14	0	0	0	2	0	1.00	6	.235	.271	.321
2005	Helena	R+	37	159	66	11	0	8	(-	-)	107	34	50	45	15	3	16	1	0	0	6	2	.75	6	.415	.469	.673
2005	WV	A-	29	118	30	7	1	4	(-	-)	51	15	21	15	8	0	17	0	0	0	1	0	1.00	0	.254	.302	.432
2006	WV	A-	105	418	122	31	2	10	(-	-)	187	63	85	68	39	3	63	2	0	8	7	3	.70	18	.292	.349	.447
2007	BrvdCt	A+	68	258	82	20	0	6	(-	-)	120	33	53	41	12	0	32	0	0	6	1	0	1.00	4	.318	.341	.465
2008	Hntsvl	AA	98	367	132	30	2	13	(-	-)	205	67	83	82	33	3	57	5	1	5	3	2	.60	13	.360	.415	.559
2008	Mil	NL	3	3	0	0	0	0	(0	0)	0	0	0	0	0	0	1	0	0	0	0	0	-	0	.000	.000	.000

Jarrod Saltalamacchia

Bats: B **Throws:** R **Pos:** C-54; DH-5; PH-4; PR-1   **Ht:** 6'4" **Wt:** 235 **Born:** 5/2/1985 **Age:** 24

							BATTING														BASERUNNING				AVERAGES		
Year	Team	Lg	G	AB	H	2B	3B	HR	(Hm	Rd)	TB	R	RBI	RC	TBB	IBB	SO	HBP	SH	SF	SB	CS	SB%	GDP	Avg	OBP	Slg
2003	Braves	R	46	134	32	11	2	2	(-	-)	53	23	14	22	28	0	33	3	0	0	0	0	-	0	.239	.382	.396
2004	Rome	A	91	323	88	19	2	10	(-	-)	141	42	51	51	34	2	83	5	1	3	1	0	1.00	6	.272	.348	.437
2005	MrtlBh	A+	129	459	144	35	1	19	(-	-)	238	70	81	95	57	11	99	7	1	5	2	2	.67	14	.314	.394	.519
2006	Missi	AA	92	313	72	18	1	9	(-	-)	119	30	39	46	55	5	71	6	0	3	0	1	.00	8	.230	.353	.380
2007	Missi	AA	22	81	25	7	0	6	(-	-)	50	18	13	20	13	1	17	0	0	0	2	0	1.00	1	.309	.404	.617
2008	Okla	AAA	15	55	16	3	1	2	(-	-)	27	10	13	10	7	1	15	2	0	0	0	0	-	1	.291	.391	.491
2007	2 Tms		93	308	82	13	1	11	(6	5)	130	39	33	32	19	1	75	1	0	1	0	0	-	8	.266	.310	.422
2008	Tex	AL	61	198	50	13	0	3	(2	1)	72	27	26	29	31	1	74	0	0	1	0	2	.00	1	.253	.352	.364
07	Atl	NL	47	141	40	6	0	4	(4	0)	58	11	12	13	10	1	28	1	0	1	0	0	-	4	.284	.333	.411
07	Tex	AL	46	167	42	7	1	7	(2	5)	72	28	21	19	9	0	47	0	0	0	0	0	-	4	.251	.290	.431
2 ML YEARS			154	506	132	26	1	14	(8	6)	202	66	59	61	50	2	149	1	0	2	0	2	.00	9	.261	.327	.399

Jeff Samardzija

Pitches: R Bats: R Pos: RP-26 Ht: 6'5" Wt: 218 Born: 1/23/1985 Age: 24

Year	Team	Lg	G	GS	CG	GF	IP	BFP	H	R	ER	HR	SH	SF	HB	TBB	IBB	SO	WP	Bk	W	L	Pct	ShO	Sv-Op	Hld	ERC	ERA
2006	Boise	A-	5	5	0	0	19.0	84	18	5	5	1	0	0	5	6	0	13	2	0	1	1	.500	0	0--	-	4.13	2.37
2006	Peoria	A	2	2	0	0	11.0	43	6	5	4	1	0	1	0	6	0	4	0	0	1	1	.000	0	0--	-	2.30	3.27
2007	Dytona	A+	24	20	1	0	107.1	479	142	69	59	8	2	2	1	35	1	45	3	0	3	8	.273	0	0--	-	5.60	4.95
2007	Tenn	AA	6	6	0	0	34.1	145	33	15	13	8	2	1	1	9	0	20	0	0	3	3	.500	0	0--	-	4.26	3.41
2008	Tenn	AA	16	15	0	0	76.0	332	71	43	41	6	4	2	2	42	0	44	4	0	3	5	.375	0	0--	-	4.30	4.86
2008	Iowa	AAA	6	6	1	0	37.1	152	32	13	13	5	1	1	1	16	0	40	3	0	4	1	.800	0	0--	-	3.91	3.13
2008	ChC	NL	26	0	0	6	27.2	124	24	12	7	0	1	1	1	15	2	25	2	0	1	0	1.000	0	1-4	3	3.08	2.28

Clint Sammons

Bats: R Throws: R Pos: C-22; PH-2 Ht: 6'0" Wt: 200 Born: 5/15/1983 Age: 26

Year	Team	Lg	G	AB	H	2B	3B	HR	(Hm	Rd)	TB	R	RBI	RC	TBB	IBB	SO	HBP	SH	SF	SB	CS	SB%	GDP	Avg	OBP	Slg
2004	Danvle	R	40	132	38	7	2	0	(-	-)	49	19	17	20	18	1	26	0	1	2	5	1	.83	3	.288	.368	.371
2005	Rome	A	121	427	122	29	4	0	(-	-)	163	60	62	66	55	0	66	5	0	7	4	1	.80	15	.286	.368	.382
2006	MrtlBh	A+	103	360	93	21	0	8	(-	-)	138	36	56	47	32	1	65	5	4	6	4	4	.50	7	.258	.323	.383
2007	MrtlBh	A+	23	78	21	6	0	4	(-	-)	39	13	13	14	10	0	14	2	0	1	1	1	.50	0	.269	.363	.500
2007	Missi	AA	83	296	72	10	0	5	(-	-)	97	27	36	31	26	0	72	1	2	3	1	1	.50	5	.243	.304	.328
2008	Rchmd	AAA	81	278	66	18	0	1	(-	-)	87	23	22	27	21	1	60	2	3	1	7	2	.78	2	.237	.295	.313
2007	Atl	NL	2	3	2	1	0	0	(0	0)	3	0	0	1	0	0	0	0	0	0	0	0	-	0	.667	.667	1.000
2008	Atl	NL	23	54	8	0	0	1	(1	0)	11	2	4	2	5	0	12	0	0	0	0	0	-	2	.148	.220	.204
2 ML YEARS			25	57	10	1	0	1	(1	0)	14	2	4	3	5	0	12	0	0	0	0	0	-	3	.175	.242	.246

Chris Sampson

Pitches: R Bats: R Pos: RP-43; SP-11 Ht: 6'1" Wt: 190 Born: 5/23/1978 Age: 31

Year	Team	Lg	G	GS	CG	GF	IP	BFP	H	R	ER	HR	SH	SF	HB	TBB	IBB	SO	WP	Bk	W	L	Pct	ShO	Sv-Op	Hld	ERC	ERA
2006	Hou	NL	12	3	0	0	34.0	130	25	10	8	3	1	1	1	5	1	15	0	0	2	1	.667	0	0-0	0	1.84	2.12
2007	Hou	NL	24	19	0	2	121.2	522	138	64	62	20	6	6	7	30	2	51	3	0	7	8	.467	0	0-0	0	4.96	4.59
2008	Hou	NL	54	11	0	6	117.1	478	118	60	55	8	3	5	3	23	5	61	0	0	6	4	.600	0	0-2	11	3.21	4.22
3 ML YEARS			90	33	0	8	273.0	1130	281	134	125	31	10	12	11	58	8	127	3	0	15	13	.536	0	0-2	11	3.77	4.12

Brian Sanches

Pitches: R Bats: R Pos: RP-12 Ht: 6'0" Wt: 197 Born: 8/8/1978 Age: 30

Year	Team	Lg	G	GS	CG	GF	IP	BFP	H	R	ER	HR	SH	SF	HB	TBB	IBB	SO	WP	Bk	W	L	Pct	ShO	Sv-Op	Hld	ERC	ERA
2008	Clmbs*	AAA	32	0	0	26	33.2	133	24	9	9	2	1	0	1	9	2	45	3	0	2	1	.667	0	13--	-	1.91	2.41
2006	Phi	NL	18	0	0	5	21.1	98	23	14	14	5	0	0	0	13	3	22	0	1	0	0	-	0	0-0	0	6.18	5.91
2007	Phi	NL	12	0	0	4	14.2	68	13	11	9	6	1	0	1	12	2	9	1	0	1	1	.500	0	0-0	1	7.73	5.52
2008	Was	NL	12	0	0	2	11.0	54	16	10	9	2	0	1	1	5	0	10	0	0	2	0	1.000	0	0-1	0	8.15	7.36
3 ML YEARS			42	0	0	11	47.0	220	52	35	32	13	1	1	2	30	5	41	1	1	3	1	.750	0	0-1	1	7.11	6.13

Anibal Sanchez

Pitches: R Bats: R Pos: SP-10 Ht: 6'0" Wt: 180 Born: 2/27/1984 Age: 25

Year	Team	Lg	G	GS	CG	GF	IP	BFP	H	R	ER	HR	SH	SF	HB	TBB	IBB	SO	WP	Bk	W	L	Pct	ShO	Sv-Op	Hld	ERC	ERA
2008	Mrlns*	R	1	1	0	0	5.0	18	4	2	2	0	1	0	0	1	0	4	0	0	1	0	1.000	0	0--	-	1.95	3.60
2008	Jupiter*	A+	2	2	0	0	10.0	40	7	2	2	0	0	0	0	4	0	9	0	0	0	0	-	0	0--	-	1.93	1.80
2008	Carlina*	AA	2	2	0	0	13.0	52	12	5	5	0	1	0	0	5	0	12	1	0	1	0	1.000	0	0--	-	3.11	3.46
2006	Fla	NL	18	17	2	0	114.1	469	90	39	36	9	3	1	4	46	1	72	4	1	10	3	.769	1	0-0	0	2.96	2.83
2007	Fla	NL	6	6	0	0	30.0	151	43	17	16	3	2	2	2	19	1	14	3	0	2	1	.667	0	0-0	0	7.90	4.80
2008	Fla	NL	10	10	0	0	51.2	241	54	35	32	7	4	2	6	27	2	50	1	0	2	5	.286	0	0-0	0	5.40	5.57
3 ML YEARS			34	33	2	0	196.0	861	187	91	84	19	9	5	12	92	4	136	8	1	14	9	.609	1	0-0	0	4.27	3.86

Duaner Sanchez

Pitches: R Bats: R Pos: RP-66 Ht: 6'2" Wt: 210 Born: 10/14/1979 Age: 29

Year	Team	Lg	G	GS	CG	GF	IP	BFP	H	R	ER	HR	SH	SF	HB	TBB	IBB	SO	WP	Bk	W	L	Pct	ShO	Sv-Op	Hld	ERC	ERA
2008	StLuci*	A+	3	0	0	0	4.0	18	6	2	2	2	0	0	1	0	0	6	0	0	0	0	-	0	0--	-	10.07	4.50
2008	NewOr*	AAA	2	0	0	0	2.0	6	0	0	0	0	0	0	0	1	0	1	0	0	0	0	-	0	0--	-	0.32	0.00
2002	2 Tms	NL	9	0	0	5	6.0	31	6	6	6	2	0	0	0	7	0	6	0	0	0	0	-	0	0-1	1	9.19	9.00
2003	Pit	NL	6	0	0	2	6.0	34	15	11	11	2	0	1	2	1	0	3	0	0	1	0	1.000	0	0-0	0	17.96	16.50
2004	LAD	NL	67	0	0	27	80.0	342	81	34	30	9	2	3	6	27	2	44	6	0	3	1	.750	0	0-1	4	4.31	3.38
2005	LAD	NL	79	0	0	31	82.0	353	75	36	34	8	10	1	3	36	6	71	7	1	7	4	.364	0	8-12	13	3.76	3.73
2006	NYM	NL	49	0	0	15	55.1	229	43	19	16	3	4	4	4	24	6	44	1	0	5	1	.833	0	0-1	14	2.85	2.60
2008	NYM	NL	66	0	0	14	58.1	254	54	28	28	6	0	1	3	23	3	44	2	0	5	1	.833	0	0-1	21	3.71	4.32
02	Ari	NL	6	0	0	3	3.2	19	3	2	2	1	0	0	0	5	0	4	0	0	0	0	-	0	0-1	1	8.32	4.91
02	Pit	NL	3	0	0	2	2.1	12	3	4	4	1	0	0	0	2	0	2	0	0	0	0	-	0	0-0	0	10.55	15.43
Postseason			2	0	0	2	2.0	8	1	0	0	0	0	0	0	1	0	3	0	0	0	0	-	0	0-0	0	1.41	0.00
6 ML YEARS			276	0	0	94	287.2	1243	274	134	125	30	16	10	18	118	17	212	16	1	18	10	.643	0	8-16	53	4.04	3.91

Freddy Sanchez

Bats: R **Throws:** R **Pos:** 2B-131; PH-13; DH-1   **Ht:** 5'10" **Wt:** 188 **Born:** 12/21/1977 **Age:** 31

							BATTING													BASERUNNING				AVERAGES		
Year	Team	Lg	G	AB	H	2B	3B	HR	(Hm | Rd)	TB	R	RBI	RC	TBB	IBB	SO	HBP	SH	SF	SB	CS	SB%	GDP	Avg	OBP	Slg
2002	Bos	AL	12	16	3	0	0	0	(0 | 0)	3	3	2	1	2	0	3	0	0	0	0	0	-	0	.188	.278	.188
2003	Bos	AL	20	34	8	2	0	0	(0 | 0)	10	6	2	1	0	0	8	0	0	0	0	0	-	0	.235	.235	.294
2004	Pit	NL	9	19	3	0	0	0	(0 | 0)	3	2	2	2	0	0	3	0	1	0	0	0	-	0	.158	.158	.158
2005	Pit	NL	132	453	132	26	4	5	(3 | 2)	181	54	35	57	27	1	36	5	4	3	2	2	.50	6	.291	.336	.400
2006	Pit	NL	157	582	200	**53**	2	6	(2 | 4)	275	85	85	101	31	6	52	7	3	9	3	2	.60	12	**.344**	.378	.473
2007	Pit	NL	147	602	183	42	4	11	(5 | 6)	266	77	81	94	32	2	76	8	2	9	0	1	.00	13	.304	.343	.442
2008	Pit	NL	145	569	154	26	2	9	(1 | 8)	211	75	52	61	21	1	63	4	8	6	0	1	.00	13	.271	.298	.371
	7 ML YEARS		622	2275	683	149	12	31	(11 | 20)	949	302	259	317	113	10	241	24	18	27	5	6	.45	44	.300	.336	.417

Gaby Sanchez

Bats: R **Throws:** R **Pos:** 1B-3; PH-3   **Ht:** 6'2" **Wt:** 225 **Born:** 9/2/1983 **Age:** 25

							BATTING													BASERUNNING				AVERAGES		
Year	Team	Lg	G	AB	H	2B	3B	HR	(Hm | Rd)	TB	R	RBI	RC	TBB	IBB	SO	HBP	SH	SF	SB	CS	SB%	GDP	Avg	OBP	Slg
2005	Jmstwn	A-	62	234	83	16	0	5	(- | -)	114	34	42	46	16	0	24	4	0	3	11	5	.69	6	.355	.401	.487
2006	Grnsbr	A	55	189	60	12	0	14	(- | -)	114	43	40	51	39	2	20	7	0	2	6	2	.75	4	.317	.444	.603
2006	Mrlns	R	3	6	2	1	0	0	(- | -)	3	1	3	2	5	0	0	0	0	0	0	0	-	0	.333	.636	.500
2006	Jupiter	A+	16	55	10	3	1	1	(- | -)	18	13	7	7	12	0	12	0	0	1	1	0	1.00	0	.182	.324	.327
2007	Jupiter	A+	133	473	132	40	3	9	(- | -)	205	89	70	79	64	0	74	6	0	4	6	6	.50	15	.279	.369	.433
2008	Carlina	AA	133	478	150	42	1	17	(- | -)	245	70	92	101	69	4	70	6	0	4	17	8	.68	13	.314	.404	.513
2008	Fla	NL	5	8	3	2	0	0	(0 | 0)	5	0	1	2	0	0	2	0	0	0	0	0	-	0	.375	.375	.625

Humberto Sanchez

Pitches: R **Bats:** R **Pos:** RP-2   **Ht:** 6'6" **Wt:** 270 **Born:** 5/28/1983 **Age:** 26

			HOW MUCH HE PITCHED						WHAT HE GAVE UP											THE RESULTS					
Year	Team	Lg	G	GS	CG	GF	IP	BFP	H	R	ER	HR	SH	SF	HB	TBB	IBB	SO	WP	Bk	W	L	Pct	ShO	Sv-Op	Hld	ERC	ERA
2002	Oneont	A-	9	9	0	0	32.1	141	29	18	13	1	0	0	1	21	0	26	2	0	2	2	.500	0	0- -		4.19	3.62
2003	WMich	A	23	23	0	0	116.0	525	107	71	57	3	6	1	11	78	2	96	9	3	7	7	.500	0	0- -		4.53	4.42
2004	Lkland	A+	19	19	3	0	105.1	452	103	67	61	9	2	6	2	51	0	115	12	1	7	11	.389	0	0- -		4.36	5.21
2004	Erie	AA	2	2	0	0	12.2	56	10	5	3	1	0	1	2	6	0	15	1	0	1	0	1.000	0	0- -		3.57	2.13
2005	Erie	AA	15	11	0	0	64.2	287	72	42	39	10	1	3	2	27	1	65	5	1	3	5	.375	0	0- -		5.34	5.43
2006	Erie	AA	11	11	0	0	71.2	282	47	17	14	2	2	2	3	27	0	86	4	0	5	3	.625	0	0- -		1.98	1.76
2006	Toledo	AAA	9	9	0	0	51.1	217	50	23	22	2	1	1	3	20	0	43	1	0	5	3	.625	0	0- -		3.78	3.86
2008	Yanks	R	12	9	0	0	11.2	48	9	4	3	0	0	0	1	4	0	15	0	0	1	0	1.000	0	0- -		2.33	2.31
2008	Tampa	A+	2	2	0	0	3.0	13	3	2	2	0	0	0	1	1	0	4	0	0	0	1	.000	0	0- -		3.05	6.00
2008	Trntn	AA	1	1	0	0	1.0	5	2	1	1	0	1	0	0	1	0	2	0	0	0	0	-	0	0- -		7.48	9.00
2008	NYY	AL	2	0	0	0	2.0	8	1	1	1	0	0	0	0	2	0	1	0	0	0	0	-	0	0-0	0	3.21	4.50

Jonathan Sanchez

Pitches: L **Bats:** L **Pos:** SP-29   **Ht:** 6'2" **Wt:** 189 **Born:** 11/19/1982 **Age:** 26

			HOW MUCH HE PITCHED						WHAT HE GAVE UP											THE RESULTS					
Year	Team	Lg	G	GS	CG	GF	IP	BFP	H	R	ER	HR	SH	SF	HB	TBB	IBB	SO	WP	Bk	W	L	Pct	ShO	Sv-Op	Hld	ERC	ERA
2006	SF	NL	27	4	0	4	40.0	185	39	26	22	2	0	2	4	23	0	33	2	0	3	1	.750	0	0-0	5	4.54	4.95
2007	SF	NL	33	4	0	8	52.0	238	57	34	34	8	2	2	5	28	1	62	4	0	1	5	.167	0	0-0	2	6.06	5.88
2008	SF	NL	29	29	0	0	158.0	695	154	90	88	14	9	5	7	75	1	157	7	0	9	12	.429	0	0-0	0	4.31	5.01
	3 ML YEARS		89	37	0	12	250.0	1118	250	150	144	24	11	9	16	126	2	252	13	0	13	18	.419	0	0-0	7	4.69	5.18

Romulo Sanchez

Pitches: R **Bats:** R **Pos:** RP-10   **Ht:** 6'5" **Wt:** 258 **Born:** 4/28/1984 **Age:** 25

			HOW MUCH HE PITCHED						WHAT HE GAVE UP											THE RESULTS					
Year	Team	Lg	G	GS	CG	GF	IP	BFP	H	R	ER	HR	SH	SF	HB	TBB	IBB	SO	WP	Bk	W	L	Pct	ShO	Sv-Op	Hld	ERC	ERA
2005	Pirates	R	2	1	0	0	10.0	38	7	2	2	1	0	0	0	4	0	7	0	0	1	0	1.000	0			2.70	1.80
2005	Altna	AA	2	2	0	0	10.0	44	11	4	4	0	2	1	0	4	0	5	1	0	1	0	1.000	0	0- -		5.40	3.60
2005	Hkry	A	10	10	0	0	53.2	235	59	34	28	5	3	1	10	19	0	24	4	1	3	3	.500	0	0- -		5.37	4.70
2006	Hkry	A	21	3	0	12	40.2	198	51	36	32	4	1	3	6	18	0	28	6	1	0	3	.000	0	4- -		6.16	7.08
2006	Lynbrg	A+	8	0	0	7	8.2	38	7	1	1	0	0	0	1	4	0	6	0	0	0	0	-	0	1- -		2.92	1.04
2006	Altna	AA	8	0	0	4	9.0	41	8	5	5	1	0	0	0	8	0	5	0	0	0	0	-	0	0- -		5.63	5.00
2007	Altna	AA	40	0	0	16	57.2	236	43	24	18	8	2	3	3	17	2	52	5	1	6	3	.667	0	1- -		2.68	2.81
2008	Indy	AAA	33	0	0	8	54.2	227	50	27	21	5	2	1	3	19	2	32	2	0	5	1	.833	0	4- -		3.58	3.46
2007	Pit	NL	16	0	0	7	18.0	73	16	10	10	2	0	1	1	8	0	11	1	0	1	0	1.000	0	0-0	2	4.20	5.00
2008	Pit	NL	10	0	0	5	13.1	57	14	6	6	0	0	2	1	6	0	3	4	0	0	0	-	0	1-1	0	4.30	4.05
	2 ML YEARS		26	0	0	12	31.1	130	30	16	16	2	0	3	2	14	0	14	5	0	1	0	1.000	0	1-1	2	4.25	4.60

Freddy Sandoval

Bats: B **Throws:** R **Pos:** DH-4; PR-3; 1B-1; 3B-1; PH-1   **Ht:** 6'1" **Wt:** 200 **Born:** 8/16/1982 **Age:** 26

							BATTING													BASERUNNING				AVERAGES		
Year	Team	Lg	G	AB	H	2B	3B	HR	(Hm	Rd)	TB	R	RBI	RC	TBB	IBB	SO	HBP	SH	SF	SB	CS	SB%	GDP	Avg	OBP	Slg
2005	CRpds	A	117	427	120	34	4	4	(-	-)	174	54	63	66	53	3	58	4	6	7	17	12	.59	11	.281	.360	.407
2006	RCuca	A+	113	434	112	28	2	5	(-	-)	159	60	54	63	59	0	98	1	7	8	30	8	.79	14	.258	.343	.366
2007	Ark	AA	127	472	144	32	6	11	(-	-)	221	84	72	91	67	3	78	5	12	7	21	11	.66	12	.305	.392	.468
2008	Salt Lk	AAA	131	525	176	45	2	15	(-	-)	270	92	88	105	47	4	74	4	4	7	6	3	.67	20	.335	.389	.514
2008	LAA	AL	6	6	1	0	0	0	(0	0)	1	0	0	0	1	0	0	0	0	0	0	0	-	0	.167	.286	.167

Pablo Sandoval

Bats: B **Throws:** R **Pos:** 1B-17; 3B-12; C-11; PH-7   **Ht:** 5'11" **Wt:** 246 **Born:** 8/11/1986 **Age:** 22

								BATTING												BASERUNNING				AVERAGES		
Year	Team	Lg	G	AB	H	2B	3B	HR	(Hm | Rd)	TB	R	RBI	RC	TBB	IBB	SO	HBP	SH	SF	SB	CS	SB%	GDP	Avg	OBP	Slg
2004	Giants	R	46	177	47	9	5	0	(- | -)	66	21	26	20	5	1	17	2	3	4	4	1	.80	2	.266	.287	.373
2005	Salem	A+	75	294	97	15	2	3	(- | -)	125	46	50	49	21	3	33	6	3	3	2	3	.40	9	.330	.383	.425
2006	Augsta	A	117	438	116	20	1	1	(- | -)	141	43	49	45	22	4	74	8	1	4	3	4	.43	18	.265	.309	.322
2007	SnJos	A+	102	401	115	33	5	11	(- | -)	191	56	52	60	16	6	52	0	3	3	3	1	.75	10	.287	.312	.476
2008	SnJos	A+	68	273	98	25	2	12	(- | -)	163	61	59	64	23	2	39	3	0	2	2	1	.67	1	.359	.412	.597
2008	Conn	AA	44	175	59	13	0	8	(- | -)	96	29	37	33	8	2	20	0	0	1	0	1	.00	4	.337	.364	.549
2008	SF	NL	41	145	50	10	1	3	(1 | 2)	71	24	24	24	4	1	14	1	0	4	0	0	-	6	.345	.357	.490

Ervin Santana

Pitches: R **Bats:** R **Pos:** SP-32   **Ht:** 6'2" **Wt:** 185 **Born:** 12/12/1982 **Age:** 26

			HOW MUCH HE PITCHED					WHAT HE GAVE UP											THE RESULTS						
Year	Team	Lg	G	GS	CG	GF	IP	BFP	H	R	ER	HR	SH	SF	HB	TBB	IBB	SO	WP	Bk	W	L	Pct	ShO	Sv-Op Hld	ERC	ERA
2005	LAA	AL	23	23	1	0	133.2	583	139	73	69	17	1	4	8	47	2	99	4	0	12	8	.600	1	0-0 0	4.51	4.65
2006	LAA	AL	33	33	0	0	204.0	846	181	106	97	21	4	10	11	70	2	141	10	2	16	8	.667	0	0-0 0	3.51	4.28
2007	LAA	AL	28	26	0	1	150.0	675	174	103	96	26	3	2	8	58	3	126	7	0	7	14	.333	0	0-0 0	5.69	5.76
2008	LAA	AL	32	32	2	0	219.0	897	198	89	85	23	3	5	8	47	2	214	5	1	16	7	.696	1	0-0 0	3.00	3.49
	Postseason		3	1	0	1	11.2	49	8	9	8	3	0	1	2	5	0	6	0	0	1	1	.500	0	0-0 0	4.21	6.17
	4 ML YEARS		116	114	3	1	706.2	3001	692	371	347	87	11	21	35	222	9	580	26	3	51	37	.580	2	0-0 0	3.97	4.42

Johan Santana

Pitches: L **Bats:** L **Pos:** SP-34   **Ht:** 6'0" **Wt:** 208 **Born:** 3/13/1979 **Age:** 30

			HOW MUCH HE PITCHED					WHAT HE GAVE UP											THE RESULTS						
Year	Team	Lg	G	GS	CG	GF	IP	BFP	H	R	ER	HR	SH	SF	HB	TBB	IBB	SO	WP	Bk	W	L	Pct	ShO	Sv-Op Hld	ERC	ERA
2000	Min	AL	30	5	0	9	86.0	398	102	64	62	11	1	3	2	54	0	64	5	2	2	3	.400	0	0-0 0	6.59	6.49
2001	Min	AL	15	4	0	5	43.2	195	50	25	23	6	2	3	3	16	0	28	3	0	1	0	1.000	0	0-0 0	5.36	4.74
2002	Min	AL	27	14	0	2	108.1	452	84	41	36	7	3	3	1	49	0	137	15	2	8	6	.571	0	1-1 3	2.86	2.99
2003	Min	AL	45	18	0	7	158.1	644	127	56	54	17	2	4	3	47	1	169	6	2	12	3	.800	0	0-0 5	2.73	3.07
2004	Min	AL	34	34	1	0	228.0	881	156	70	66	24	3	3	9	54	0	265	7	0	20	6	.769	1	0-0 0	2.07	2.61
2005	Min	AL	33	33	3	0	231.2	910	180	77	74	22	6	2	1	45	1	238	8	0	16	7	.696	2	0-0 0	2.14	2.87
2006	Min	AL	34	34	1	0	233.2	923	186	79	72	24	6	4	4	47	0	245	4	1	19	6	.760	0	0-0 0	2.36	2.77
2007	Min	AL	33	33	1	0	219.0	878	183	88	81	33	4	4	4	52	0	235	7	1	15	13	.536	1	0-0 0	2.98	3.33
2008	NYM	NL	34	34	3	0	234.1	964	206	74	66	23	9	1	4	63	5	206	9	2	16	7	.696	2	0-0 0	2.93	2.53
	Postseason		11	5	0	0	34.0	143	35	15	15	2	0	0	1	10	1	32	2	0	1	3	.250	0	0-0 1	3.66	3.97
	9 ML YEARS		285	209	9	23	1543.0	6245	1274	574	534	167	36	27	31	427	7	1587	64	10	109	51	.681	6	1-1 8	2.81	3.11

Ramon Santiago

Bats: B **Throws:** R **Pos:** SS-33; 2B-21; 3B-6; PR-6; PH-3   **Ht:** 5'11" **Wt:** 175 **Born:** 8/31/1979 **Age:** 29

								BATTING												BASERUNNING				AVERAGES		
Year	Team	Lg	G	AB	H	2B	3B	HR	(Hm	Rd)	TB	R	RBI	RC	TBB	IBB	SO	HBP	SH	SF	SB	CS	SB%	GDP	Avg	OBP	Slg
2008	Toledo*	AAA	8	28	6	2	0	0	(-	-)	8	3	3	2	2	0	7	2	1	0	0	0	-	0	.214	.313	.286
2002	Det	AL	65	222	54	5	5	4	(3	1)	81	33	20	23	13	0	48	8	4	2	8	5	.62	2	.243	.306	.365
2003	Det	AL	141	444	100	18	1	2	(1	1)	126	41	29	38	33	0	66	10	18	2	10	4	.71	9	.225	.292	.284
2004	Sea	AL	19	39	7	1	0	0	(0	0)	8	8	2	1	3	0	3	1	2	0	0	0	-	1	.179	.256	.205
2005	Sea	AL	8	8	1	0	0	0	(0	0)	1	2	0	1	1	0	2	3	1	0	0	0	-	0	.125	.417	.125
2006	Det	AL	43	80	18	1	1	0	(0	0)	21	9	3	3	1	0	14	1	4	0	2	0	1.00	1	.225	.244	.263
2007	Det	AL	32	67	19	5	1	0	(0	0)	26	10	7	11	1	0	10	3	3	0	3	0	1.00	1	.284	.324	.388
2008	Det	AL	58	124	35	6	2	4	(4	0)	57	30	18	26	22	0	17	5	5	0	1	0	1.00	1	.282	.411	.460
	Postseason		6	12	1	0	0	0	(0	0)	1	0	0	0	1	0	2	0	1	0	0	0	-	0	.083	.154	.083
	7 ML YEARS		366	984	234	36	10	10	(8	2)	320	133	79	103	74	0	160	31	37	4	24	9	.73	14	.238	.310	.325

Omir Santos

Bats: R **Throws:** R **Pos:** C-9; DH-1; PH-1; PR-1   **Ht:** 6'0" **Wt:** 200 **Born:** 4/29/1981 **Age:** 28

								BATTING												BASERUNNING				AVERAGES		
Year	Team	Lg	G	AB	H	2B	3B	HR	(Hm	Rd)	TB	R	RBI	RC	TBB	IBB	SO	HBP	SH	SF	SB	CS	SB%	GDP	Avg	OBP	Slg
2001	StsInd	A-	44	117	32	5	1	0	(-	-)	39	11	8	12	6	0	25	1	1	2	0	1	.00	2	.274	.310	.333
2002	Grnsbr	A	23	73	17	2	1	1	(-	-)	24	7	8	6	2	0	15	3	0	2	0	0	-	2	.233	.275	.329
2002	StsInd	A-	61	232	67	10	0	7	(-	-)	98	22	44	33	12	0	32	4	0	3	2	1	.67	6	.289	.331	.422
2003	Btl Crk	A	82	277	65	11	0	2	(-	-)	82	35	30	27	25	0	36	3	6	8	0	0	-	8	.235	.297	.296
2003	Yanks	R	1	0	0	0	0	0	(-	-)	0	0	0	0	0	0	0	0	0	0	0	0	-	0	-	-	-
2004	Btl Crk	A	56	171	41	7	0	2	(-	-)	54	21	16	16	7	0	27	3	0	3	4	0	1.00	2	.240	.277	.316
2004	Tampa	A+	37	119	34	6	1	2	(-	-)	48	18	13	17	6	0	17	4	1	0	1	0	1.00	5	.286	.341	.403
2005	Trntn	AA	111	401	102	17	0	10	(-	-)	149	44	48	43	11	1	75	9	1	3	0	1	.00	12	.254	.288	.372
2006	Trntn	AA	101	324	87	18	0	4	(-	-)	117	31	38	39	19	0	65	6	3	4	1	0	1.00	10	.269	.317	.361
2007	Trntn	AA	10	38	8	2	0	0	(-	-)	10	4	0	2	1	0	8	0	0	0	0	0	-	0	.211	.231	.263
2007	S-WB	AAA	51	167	39	8	0	3	(-	-)	56	13	19	15	10	1	35	1	2	2	1	1	.50	7	.234	.278	.335
2008	Norfolk	AAA	84	297	80	13	0	1	(-	-)	96	31	36	33	20	0	57	8	3	4	1	2	.33	5	.269	.328	.323
2008	Bal	AL	11	10	1	0	0	0	(0	0)	1	0	0	0	0	0	2	0	0	0	0	0	-	0	.100	.100	.100

248

Dane Sardinha

Bats: R Throws: R Pos: C-17   Ht: 6'0" Wt: 215 Born: 4/8/1979 Age: 30

Year	Team	Lg	G	AB	H	2B	3B	HR	(Hm	Rd)	TB	R	RBI	RC	TBB	IBB	SO	HBP	SH	SF	SB	CS	SB%	GDP	Avg	OBP	Slg
									BATTING												BASERUNNING				AVERAGES		
2008	Toledo*	AAA	54	183	37	9	0	6	(-	-)	64	19	18	15	8	1	59	1	4	1	1	0	1.00	6	.202	.238	.350
2003	Cin	NL	1	2	0	0	0	0	(0	0)	0	0	0	0	0	0	1	0	0	0	0	0	-	0	.000	.000	.000
2005	Cin	NL	1	3	0	0	0	0	(0	0)	0	0	0	0	0	0	1	0	0	0	0	0	-	0	.000	.000	.000
2008	Det	AL	17	44	7	0	1	0	(0	0)	9	2	3	3	4	0	11	0	1	0	0	0	-	1	.159	.229	.205
3 ML YEARS			19	49	7	0	1	0	(0	0)	9	2	3	3	4	0	13	0	1	0	0	0	-	1	.143	.208	.184

Dennis Sarfate

Pitches: R Bats: R Pos: RP-53; SP-4   Ht: 6'4" Wt: 225 Born: 4/9/1981 Age: 28

Year	Team	Lg	G	GS	CG	GF	IP	BFP	H	R	ER	HR	SH	SF	HB	TBB	IBB	SO	WP	Bk	W	L	Pct	ShO	Sv-Op	Hld	ERC	ERA
				HOW MUCH HE PITCHED							WHAT HE GAVE UP											THE RESULTS					
2006	Mil	NL	8	0	0	5	8.1	38	9	4	4	0	0	0	4	1	11	2	0	0	0	-	0	0-0	3	3.77	4.32
2007	Hou	NL	7	0	0	1	8.1	31	5	1	1	0	0	1	0	1	0	14	0	0	1	0	1.000	0	0-0	3	0.96	1.08
2008	Bal	AL	57	4	0	15	79.2	359	62	47	42	8	2	3	7	62	2	86	6	1	4	3	.571	0	0-2	6	4.65	4.74
3 ML YEARS			72	4	0	21	96.1	428	76	52	47	8	2	4	7	67	3	111	8	1	5	3	.625	0	0-2	6	4.16	4.39

Joe Saunders

Pitches: L Bats: L Pos: SP-31   Ht: 6'3" Wt: 210 Born: 6/16/1981 Age: 28

Year	Team	Lg	G	GS	CG	GF	IP	BFP	H	R	ER	HR	SH	SF	HB	TBB	IBB	SO	WP	Bk	W	L	Pct	ShO	Sv-Op	Hld	ERC	ERA
				HOW MUCH HE PITCHED							WHAT HE GAVE UP											THE RESULTS					
2005	LAA	AL	2	2	0	0	9.1	41	10	8	8	3	0	0	0	4	0	4	1	0	0	0	-	0	0-0	0	6.27	7.71
2006	LAA	AL	13	13	0	0	70.2	302	71	42	37	6	1	2	1	29	1	51	2	1	7	3	.700	0	0-0	0	4.13	4.71
2007	LAA	AL	18	18	0	0	107.1	473	129	56	53	11	0	5	1	34	1	69	3	0	8	5	.615	0	0-0	0	4.96	4.44
2008	LAA	AL	31	31	1	0	198.0	807	187	82	75	21	5	2	6	53	2	103	3	0	17	7	.708	0	0-0	0	3.49	3.41
4 ML YEARS			64	64	1	0	385.1	1623	397	188	173	41	6	9	8	120	4	227	9	1	32	15	.681	0	0-0	0	4.07	4.04

Max Scherzer

Pitches: R Bats: R Pos: RP-9; SP-7   Ht: 6'3" Wt: 213 Born: 7/27/1984 Age: 24

Year	Team	Lg	G	GS	CG	GF	IP	BFP	H	R	ER	HR	SH	SF	HB	TBB	IBB	SO	WP	Bk	W	L	Pct	ShO	Sv-Op	Hld	ERC	ERA
				HOW MUCH HE PITCHED							WHAT HE GAVE UP											THE RESULTS					
2007	FtWth	IND	3	3	0	0	16.0	60	9	2	1	0	0	0	1	4	0	25	2	1	1	0	1.000	0	0- -	-	1.27	0.56
2007	Visalia	A+	3	3	0	0	17.0	59	5	1	1	0	0	0	1	2	0	30	0	0	2	0	1.000	0	0- -	-	0.39	0.53
2007	Mobile	AA	14	14	0	0	73.2	320	64	38	32	3	3	1	4	40	0	76	3	0	4	4	.500	0	0- -	-	3.71	3.91
2008	Tucsn	AAA	13	10	0	0	53.0	219	35	19	16	2	1	2	2	22	0	79	1	0	1	1	.500	0	0- -	-	2.07	2.72
2008	Ari	NL	16	7	0	2	56.0	237	48	24	19	5	4	2	5	21	1	66	2	0	0	4	.000	0	0-0	0	3.45	3.05

Nate Schierholtz

Bats: L Throws: R Pos: RF-19; PH-1   Ht: 6'2" Wt: 217 Born: 2/15/1984 Age: 25

Year	Team	Lg	G	AB	H	2B	3B	HR	(Hm	Rd)	TB	R	RBI	RC	TBB	IBB	SO	HBP	SH	SF	SB	CS	SB%	GDP	Avg	OBP	Slg
									BATTING												BASERUNNING				AVERAGES		
2003	Giants	R	11	45	18	0	2	0	(-	-)	22	5	5	10	3	0	8	1	0	0	4	0	1.00	6	.400	.449	.489
2003	SlmKzr	A-	35	124	38	6	2	3	(-	-)	57	23	29	22	12	1	15	5	0	3	0	1	.00	1	.306	.382	.460
2004	Hgrstn	A	58	233	69	22	0	15	(-	-)	136	41	53	47	18	3	52	4	0	3	1	0	1.00	4	.296	.353	.584
2004	SnJos	A+	62	258	76	18	9	3	(-	-)	121	39	31	41	15	1	41	3	3	2	3	1	.75	6	.295	.338	.469
2005	SnJos	A+	128	502	160	37	8	15	(-	-)	258	83	86	91	32	0	132	6	3	5	5	7	.42	10	.319	.363	.514
2006	Conn	AA	125	470	127	25	7	14	(-	-)	208	55	54	69	27	8	81	12	0	1	8	3	.73	11	.270	.325	.443
2007	Fresno	AAA	110	411	137	31	7	16	(-	-)	230	67	68	82	17	3	58	7	1	4	10	4	.71	8	.333	.367	.560
2008	Fresno	AAA	93	350	112	22	10	18	(-	-)	208	62	73	74	21	1	51	4	0	2	9	3	.75	7	.320	.363	.594
2007	SF	NL	39	112	34	5	3	0	(0	0)	45	9	10	14	2	0	19	1	0	2	3	1	.75	0	.304	.316	.402
2008	SF	NL	19	75	24	8	1	1	(1	0)	37	12	5	12	3	0	8	3	0	0	0	1	.00	1	.320	.370	.493
2 ML YEARS			58	187	58	13	4	1	(1	0)	82	21	15	26	5	0	27	4	0	2	3	2	.60	1	.310	.338	.439

Curt Schilling

Pitches: R Bats: R Pos: P   Ht: 6'5" Wt: 235 Born: 11/14/1966 Age: 42

Year	Team	Lg	G	GS	CG	GF	IP	BFP	H	R	ER	HR	SH	SF	HB	TBB	IBB	SO	WP	Bk	W	L	Pct	ShO	Sv-Op	Hld	ERC	ERA
				HOW MUCH HE PITCHED							WHAT HE GAVE UP											THE RESULTS					
1988	Bal	AL	4	4	0	0	14.2	76	22	19	16	3	0	3	1	10	1	4	2	0	0	3	.000	0	0-0	0	9.43	9.82
1989	Bal	AL	5	1	0	0	8.2	38	10	6	6	2	0	0	0	3	0	6	1	0	0	1	.000	0	0-0	0	5.74	6.23
1990	Bal	AL	35	0	0	16	46.0	191	38	13	13	1	2	4	0	19	0	32	0	0	1	2	.333	0	3-9	5	2.68	2.54
1991	Hou	NL	56	0	0	34	75.2	336	79	35	32	2	5	1	0	39	7	71	4	1	3	5	.375	0	8-11	5	4.08	3.81
1992	Phi	NL	42	26	10	10	226.1	895	165	67	59	11	7	8	1	59	4	147	4	0	14	11	.560	4	2-3	0	1.86	2.35
1993	Phi	NL	34	34	7	0	235.1	982	234	114	105	23	9	7	4	57	6	186	9	3	16	7	.696	2	0-0	0	3.44	4.02
1994	Phi	NL	13	13	1	0	82.1	360	87	42	41	10	4	1	3	28	3	58	3	1	2	8	.200	0	0-0	0	4.36	4.48
1995	Phi	NL	17	17	1	0	116.0	473	96	52	46	12	5	2	3	26	2	114	0	1	7	5	.583	0	0-0	0	2.55	3.57
1996	Phi	NL	26	26	8	0	183.1	732	149	69	65	16	6	4	3	50	5	182	5	0	9	10	.474	2	0-0	0	2.59	3.19
1997	Phi	NL	35	35	7	0	254.1	1009	208	96	84	25	8	8	5	58	3	319	5	1	17	11	.607	2	0-0	0	2.55	2.97
1998	Phi	NL	35	35	15	0	268.2	1089	236	101	97	23	14	7	6	61	3	300	12	0	15	14	.517	2	0-0	0	2.75	3.25
1999	Phi	NL	24	24	8	0	180.1	735	159	74	71	25	11	3	6	44	0	152	4	0	15	6	.714	1	0-0	0	3.20	3.54
2000	2 Tms	NL	29	29	8	0	210.1	862	204	90	89	27	11	4	1	45	4	168	4	0	11	12	.478	2	0-0	0	3.38	3.81
2001	Ari	NL	35	35	6	0	256.2	1021	237	86	85	37	8	5	1	39	0	293	4	0	22	6	.786	1	0-0	0	3.03	2.98
2002	Ari	NL	36	35	5	0	259.1	1017	218	95	93	29	4	3	3	33	1	316	6	0	23	7	.767	1	0-0	0	2.33	3.23
2003	Ari	NL	24	24	3	0	168.0	673	144	58	55	17	11	1	3	32	2	194	4	0	8	9	.471	0	0-0	0	2.59	2.95
2004	Bos	AL	32	32	3	0	226.2	910	206	84	82	23	3	6	5	35	0	203	3	0	21	6	.778	0	0-0	0	2.75	3.26

Year	Team	Lg	HOW MUCH HE PITCHED						WHAT HE GAVE UP										THE RESULTS						
			G	GS	CG	GF	IP	BFP	H	R	ER	HR	SH	SF	HB	TBB	IBB	SO	WP	Bk	W	L	Pct	ShO	Sv-Op	Hld	ERC	ERA
2005	Bos	AL	32	11	0	21	93.1	418	121	59	59	12	3	5	3	22	0	87	1	1	8	8	.500	0	9-11	0	5.45	5.69
2006	Bos	AL	31	31	0	0	204.0	834	220	90	90	28	5	2	3	28	1	183	1	0	15	7	.682	0	0-0	0	3.83	3.97
2007	Bos	AL	24	24	1	0	151.0	633	165	68	65	21	4	3	2	23	1	101	0	0	9	8	.529	1	0-0	0	3.90	3.87
00	Phi	NL	16	16	4	0	112.2	474	110	49	49	17	5	1	1	32	4	96	4	0	6	6	.500	1	0-0	0	3.79	3.91
00	Ari	NL	13	13	4	0	97.2	388	94	41	40	10	6	3	0	19	0	72	0	0	5	6	.455	1	0-0	0	2.91	3.69
	Postseason		19	19	4	0	133.1	525	115	41	36	12	3	4	3	30	0	139	0	0	11	2	.846	2	0-0	0	2.79	2.43
	20 ML YEARS		569	436	83	81	3261.0	13284	2998	1318	1253	347	122	77	52	711	43	3116	72	8	216	146	.597	20	22-34	10	3.03	3.46

Jason Schmidt

Pitches: R Bats: R Pos: P **Ht: 6'5" Wt: 210 Born: 1/29/1973 Age: 36**

Year	Team	Lg	HOW MUCH HE PITCHED						WHAT HE GAVE UP										THE RESULTS						
			G	GS	CG	GF	IP	BFP	H	R	ER	HR	SH	SF	HB	TBB	IBB	SO	WP	Bk	W	L	Pct	ShO	Sv-Op	Hld	ERC	ERA
2008	LsVgs*	AAA	5	5	0	0	12.1	64	19	13	10	3	0	1	1	8	0	5	1	0	0	1	.000	0	0- --	-	10.16	7.30
2008	InldEm*	A+	4	4	0	0	10.1	44	8	5	4	0	0	1	0	4	0	9	2	0	0	0	-	0	0- --	-	2.09	3.48
1995	Atl	NL	9	2	0	1	25.0	119	27	17	16	2	2	4	1	18	3	19	1	0	2	2	.500	0	0-1	0	5.56	5.76
1996	2 Tms	NL	19	17	1	0	96.1	445	108	67	61	10	4	9	2	53	0	74	8	1	5	6	.455	0	0-0	0	5.46	5.70
1997	Pit	NL	32	32	2	0	187.2	825	193	106	96	16	10	3	9	76	2	136	8	0	10	9	.526	0	0-0	0	4.31	4.60
1998	Pit	NL	33	33	0	0	214.1	916	228	106	97	24	10	3	4	71	3	158	15	1	11	14	.440	0	0-0	0	4.35	4.07
1999	Pit	NL	33	33	2	0	212.2	937	219	110	99	24	7	7	3	85	4	148	6	4	13	11	.542	0	0-0	0	4.30	4.19
2000	Pit	NL	11	11	0	0	63.1	295	71	43	38	6	1	2	1	41	2	51	1	0	2	5	.286	0	0-0	0	5.77	5.40
2001	2 Tms	NL	25	25	1	0	150.1	641	138	75	68	13	5	3	7	61	3	142	8	1	13	7	.650	0	0-0	0	3.72	4.07
2002	SF	NL	29	29	2	0	185.1	769	148	78	71	15	11	5	2	73	1	196	12	0	13	8	.619	2	0-0	0	2.87	3.45
2003	SF	NL	29	29	5	0	207.2	819	152	56	54	14	6	3	5	46	1	208	7	1	17	5	.773	3	0-0	0	1.93	2.34
2004	SF	NL	32	32	4	0	225.0	907	165	84	80	18	7	3	3	77	3	251	7	1	18	7	.720	3	0-0	0	2.37	3.20
2005	SF	NL	29	29	0	0	172.0	757	160	90	84	16	8	8	5	85	4	165	7	1	12	7	.632	0	0-0	0	4.04	4.40
2006	SF	NL	32	32	3	0	213.1	894	189	94	85	21	7	7	6	80	6	180	11	1	11	9	.550	1	0-0	0	3.43	3.59
2007	LAD	NL	6	6	0	0	25.2	125	32	20	18	4	2	0	1	14	2	22	2	0	1	4	.200	0	0-0	0	6.40	6.31
96	Atl	NL	13	11	0	0	58.2	274	69	48	44	8	3	6	0	32	0	48	5	1	3	4	.429	0	0-0	0	5.92	6.75
96	Pit	NL	6	6	1	0	37.2	171	39	19	17	2	1	3	2	21	0	26	3	0	2	2	.500	0	0-0	0	4.75	4.06
01	Pit	NL	14	14	1	0	84.0	357	81	46	43	11	3	2	7	28	2	77	3	1	6	6	.500	0	0-0	0	4.17	4.61
01	SF	NL	11	11	0	0	66.1	284	57	29	25	2	2	1	0	33	1	65	5	0	7	1	.875	0	0-0	0	3.16	3.39
	Postseason		5	5	1	0	32.1	132	26	11	11	3	2	1	0	9	1	32	1	0	3	1	.750	1	0-0	0	2.45	3.06
	13 ML YEARS		319	310	20	1	1978.2	8449	1830	946	867	183	80	57	49	780	34	1750	93	11	128	94	.577	9	0-1	0	3.64	3.94

Brian Schneider

Bats: L Throws: R Pos: C-109; PH-3; PR-1 **Ht: 6'1" Wt: 196 Born: 11/26/1976 Age: 32**

Year	Team	Lg	BATTING														BASERUNNING				AVERAGES		
			G	AB	H	2B	3B	HR	(Hm | Rd)	TB	R	RBI	RC	TBB	IBB	SO	HBP	SH	SF	SB	CS	SB%	GDP	Avg	OBP	Slg
2000	Mon	NL	45	115	27	6	0	0	(0 | 0)	33	6	11	8	7	2	24	0	0	1	0	1	.00	1	.235	.276	.287
2001	Mon	NL	27	41	13	3	0	1	(1 | 0)	19	4	6	8	6	1	3	0	0	1	0	0	-	0	.317	.396	.463
2002	Mon	NL	73	207	57	19	2	5	(3 | 2)	95	21	29	29	21	8	41	0	2	2	1	2	.33	7	.275	.339	.459
2003	Mon	NL	108	335	77	26	1	9	(9 | 0)	132	34	46	36	37	8	75	2	1	2	0	2	.00	12	.230	.309	.394
2004	Mon	NL	135	436	112	20	3	12	(5 | 7)	174	40	49	52	42	10	63	3	5	2	0	1	.00	8	.257	.325	.399
2005	Was	NL	116	369	99	20	1	10	(5 | 5)	151	38	44	48	29	7	48	6	2	2	1	0	1.00	10	.268	.330	.409
2006	Was	NL	124	410	105	18	0	4	(3 | 1)	135	30	55	45	38	10	67	2	2	3	2	2	.50	14	.256	.320	.329
2007	Was	NL	129	408	96	21	1	6	(2 | 4)	137	33	54	41	56	7	56	2	4	7	0	0	-	15	.235	.326	.336
2008	NYM	NL	110	335	86	10	0	9	(4 | 5)	123	30	38	36	42	9	53	1	4	2	0	0	-	11	.257	.339	.367
	9 ML YEARS		867	2656	672	143	8	56	(32 | 24)	999	236	332	303	278	62	430	16	20	22	4	8	.33	78	.253	.325	.376

Scott Schoeneweis

Pitches: L Bats: L Pos: RP-73 **Ht: 6'0" Wt: 190 Born: 10/2/1973 Age: 35**

Year	Team	Lg	HOW MUCH HE PITCHED						WHAT HE GAVE UP										THE RESULTS						
			G	GS	CG	GF	IP	BFP	H	R	ER	HR	SH	SF	HB	TBB	IBB	SO	WP	Bk	W	L	Pct	ShO	Sv-Op	Hld	ERC	ERA
1999	LAA	AL	31	0	0	6	39.1	175	47	27	24	4	0	1	0	14	1	22	1	0	1	1	.500	0	0-0	3	4.99	5.49
2000	LAA	AL	27	27	1	0	170.0	742	183	112	103	21	2	5	6	67	2	78	4	3	7	10	.412	1	0-0	0	4.84	5.45
2001	LAA	AL	32	32	1	0	205.1	910	227	122	116	21	3	8	14	77	2	104	4	1	10	11	.476	0	0-0	0	4.87	5.08
2002	LAA	AL	54	15	0	4	118.0	510	119	68	64	17	1	5	5	49	4	65	1	1	9	8	.529	0	1-4	11	4.68	4.88
2003	2 Tms	AL	59	0	0	19	64.2	276	63	35	30	3	2	1	4	19	5	56	3	0	3	2	.600	0	0-2	4	3.25	4.18
2004	CWS	AL	20	19	0	0	112.2	500	129	74	70	17	3	2	3	49	0	69	3	0	6	9	.400	0	0-0	0	5.65	5.59
2005	Tor	AL	80	0	0	15	57.0	250	54	23	21	2	1	0	4	25	5	43	2	0	3	4	.429	0	1-4	21	3.56	3.32
2006	2 Tms	AL	71	0	0	16	51.2	221	48	28	28	4	1	0	2	24	6	29	3	0	4	2	.667	0	4-6	19	3.79	4.88
2007	NYM	NL	70	0	0	17	59.0	265	62	36	33	8	4	1	3	28	5	41	3	1	0	2	.000	0	2-3	11	4.97	5.03
2008	NYM	NL	73	0	0	12	56.2	243	55	23	21	7	2	2	4	23	6	34	3	0	2	6	.250	0	1-5	15	4.28	3.34
03	LAA	AL	39	0	0	12	38.2	163	37	19	17	2	1	1	3	10	3	29	1	0	1	1	.500	0	0-1	4	3.14	3.96
03	CWS	AL	20	0	0	7	26.0	113	26	16	13	1	1	0	1	9	2	27	2	0	2	1	.667	0	0-1	0	3.41	4.50
06	Tor	AL	55	0	0	8	37.1	161	39	27	27	3	1	0	1	16	5	18	2	0	2	2	.500	0	1-3	18	4.27	6.51
06	Cin	NL	16	0	0	8	14.1	60	9	1	1	1	0	0	1	8	1	11	1	0	2	0	1.000	0	3-3	1	2.64	0.63
	Postseason		6	0	0	1	3.0	12	3	1	1	0	0	0	0	1	0	2	0	0	0	0	-	0	0-1	0	3.35	3.00
	10 ML YEARS		517	93	2	89	934.1	4092	987	548	510	104	19	25	45	375	36	541	27	6	45	55	.450	1	9-24	84	4.65	4.91

Chris Schroder

Pitches: R Bats: R Pos: RP-4   Ht: 6'1" Wt: 210 Born: 8/20/1978 Age: 30

			HOW MUCH HE PITCHED						WHAT HE GAVE UP										THE RESULTS						
Year	Team	Lg	G	GS	CG	GF	IP	BFP	H	R	ER	HR	SH	SF	HB	TBB	IBB	SO	WP	Bk	W	L	Pct	ShO	Sv-Op	Hld	ERC	ERA
2008	Clmbs*	AAA	43	0	0	20	45.1	203	48	21	20	3	4	1	5	20	2	55	2	0	5	4	.556	0	8- -	-	4.27	3.97
2006	Was	NL	21	0	0	3	28.1	127	23	21	20	7	1	3	5	15	3	39	0	0	0	2	.000	0	0-1	1	5.07	6.35
2007	Was	NL	37	0	0	8	45.1	192	36	19	16	2	2	0	2	15	1	43	0	0	2	3	.400	0	0-0	1	2.40	3.18
2008	Was	NL	4	0	0	0	5.0	27	6	3	3	2	1	0	0	6	0	3	0	0	0	0	-	0	0-0	0	11.40	5.40
3 ML YEARS			62	0	0	11	78.2	346	65	43	39	11	4	3	7	36	4	85	0	0	2	5	.286	0	0-1	2	3.77	4.46

Skip Schumaker

Bats: L Throws: R Pos: CF-79; LF-56; RF-33; PH-12; PR-1   Ht: 5'10" Wt: 195 Born: 2/3/1980 Age: 29

			BATTING																	BASERUNNING				AVERAGES		
Year	Team	Lg	G	AB	H	2B	3B	HR	(Hm	Rd)	TB	R	RBI	RC	TBB	IBB	SO	HBP	SH	SF	SB	CS	SB%	GDP	Avg	OBP	Slg
2005	StL	NL	27	24	6	1	0	0	(0	0)	7	9	1	2	2	0	2	0	0	0	1	0	1.00	0	.250	.308	.292
2006	StL	NL	28	54	10	1	0	1	(0	1)	14	3	2	2	5	1	6	0	1	0	2	1	.67	1	.185	.254	.259
2007	StL	NL	88	177	59	12	2	2	(1	1)	81	19	19	30	8	0	20	0	1	1	1	1	.50	5	.333	.358	.458
2008	StL	NL	153	540	163	22	5	8	(4	4)	219	87	46	74	47	2	60	2	4	1	8	2	.80	19	.302	.359	.406
4 ML YEARS			296	795	238	36	7	11	(5	6)	321	118	68	108	62	3	88	2	6	3	12	4	.75	25	.299	.350	.404

Luke Scott

Bats: L Throws: R Pos: LF-106; DH-26; PH-21   Ht: 6'0" Wt: 210 Born: 6/25/1978 Age: 31

			BATTING																	BASERUNNING				AVERAGES		
Year	Team	Lg	G	AB	H	2B	3B	HR	(Hm	Rd)	TB	R	RBI	RC	TBB	IBB	SO	HBP	SH	SF	SB	CS	SB%	GDP	Avg	OBP	Slg
2005	Hou	NL	34	80	15	4	2	0	(0	0)	23	6	4	6	9	1	23	0	0	0	1	1	.50	0	.188	.270	.288
2006	Hou	NL	65	214	72	19	6	10	(8	2)	133	31	37	48	30	4	43	4	0	1	2	1	.67	2	.336	.426	.621
2007	Hou	NL	132	369	94	28	5	18	(8	10)	186	49	64	55	53	4	95	2	0	1	3	1	.75	8	.255	.351	.504
2008	Bal	AL	148	475	122	29	2	23	(11	12)	224	67	65	68	53	10	102	5	0	3	2	2	.50	7	.257	.336	.472
Postseason			2	2	0	0	0	0	(0	0)	0	1	0	0	1	0	1	0	0	0	0	0	-	0	.000	.333	.000
4 ML YEARS			379	1138	303	80	15	51	(27	24)	566	153	170	177	145	19	263	11	0	5	8	5	.62	17	.266	.353	.497

Marco Scutaro

Bats: R Throws: R Pos: SS-56; 2B-50; 3B-41; PH-4; 1B-3; LF-3; DH-2; PR-2   Ht: 5'10" Wt: 186 Born: 10/30/1975 Age: 33

			BATTING																	BASERUNNING				AVERAGES		
Year	Team	Lg	G	AB	H	2B	3B	HR	(Hm	Rd)	TB	R	RBI	RC	TBB	IBB	SO	HBP	SH	SF	SB	CS	SB%	GDP	Avg	OBP	Slg
2002	NYM	NL	27	36	8	0	1	1	(1	0)	13	2	6	2	0	0	11	0	1	1	0	1	.00	1	.222	.216	.361
2003	NYM	NL	48	75	16	4	0	2	(0	2)	26	10	6	10	13	2	14	1	1	1	2	0	1.00	1	.213	.333	.347
2004	Oak	AL	137	455	124	32	1	7	(6	1)	179	50	43	48	16	1	58	0	5	1	0	0	-	9	.273	.297	.393
2005	Oak	AL	118	381	94	22	3	9	(5	4)	149	48	37	45	36	1	48	0	4	2	5	2	.71	6	.247	.310	.391
2006	Oak	AL	117	365	97	21	6	5	(1	4)	145	52	41	47	50	0	66	0	3	5	5	1	.83	16	.266	.350	.397
2007	Oak	AL	104	338	88	13	0	7	(2	5)	122	49	41	42	35	1	40	2	2	2	2	1	.67	13	.260	.332	.361
2008	Tor	AL	145	517	138	23	1	7	(5	2)	184	76	60	72	57	0	65	5	6	7	7	2	.78	8	.267	.341	.356
Postseason			7	27	5	4	0	0	(0	0)	9	1	6	3	0	0	4	0	0	0	0	0	-	1	.185	.185	.333
7 ML YEARS			696	2167	565	115	12	38	(20	18)	818	287	234	266	207	5	302	8	22	19	21	7	.75	54	.261	.325	.377

Rudy Seanez

Pitches: R Bats: R Pos: RP-42   Ht: 6'1" Wt: 225 Born: 10/20/1968 Age: 40

			HOW MUCH HE PITCHED						WHAT HE GAVE UP										THE RESULTS						
Year	Team	Lg	G	GS	CG	GF	IP	BFP	H	R	ER	HR	SH	SF	HB	TBB	IBB	SO	WP	Bk	W	L	Pct	ShO	Sv-Op	Hld	ERC	ERA
2008	LV*	AAA	1	0	0	0	1.0	3	0	0	0	0	0	0	0	0	0	1	0	0	1	0	1.000	0	0- -	-	0.00	0.00
2008	Lakwd*	A	1	0	0	0	1.0	6	2	2	0	0	0	0	0	0	0	1	0	0	1	0	1.000	0	0- -	-	6.14	0.00
1989	Cle	AL	5	0	0	2	5.0	20	1	2	2	0	0	2	0	4	1	7	1	1	0	0	-	0	0-0	0	0.94	3.60
1990	Cle	AL	24	0	0	12	27.1	127	22	17	17	2	0	1	1	25	1	24	5	0	2	1	.667	0	0-0	3	4.85	5.60
1991	Cle	AL	5	0	0	0	5.0	33	10	12	9	2	0	0	0	7	0	7	2	0	0	0	-	0	0-1	0	17.96	16.20
1993	SD	NL	3	0	0	3	3.1	20	8	6	5	1	1	0	0	2	0	1	0	0	0	0	-	0	0-0	0	16.31	13.50
1994	LAD	NL	17	0	0	6	23.2	104	24	7	7	2	4	2	1	9	1	18	3	0	1	1	.500	0	0-1	1	4.01	2.66
1995	LAD	NL	37	0	0	12	34.2	159	39	27	26	5	3	0	1	18	3	29	0	0	1	3	.250	0	3-4	6	5.57	6.75
1998	Atl	NL	34	0	0	8	36.0	148	25	13	11	2	1	2	1	16	0	50	2	0	4	1	.800	0	2-4	8	2.44	2.75
1999	Atl	NL	56	0	0	13	53.2	225	47	21	20	3	0	2	1	21	1	41	3	0	6	1	.857	0	3-8	18	3.12	3.35
2000	Atl	NL	23	0	0	8	21.0	89	15	11	10	3	1	0	1	9	1	20	0	0	2	4	.333	0	2-3	6	2.95	4.29
2001	2 Tms	NL	38	0	0	8	36.0	150	23	12	11	4	0	1	1	19	0	41	4	0	2	0	1.000	0	1-3	9	2.78	2.75
2002	Tex	AL	33	0	0	4	33.0	150	28	25	21	5	3	1	0	24	1	40	6	0	1	3	.250	0	0-4	10	4.77	5.73
2003	Bos	AL	9	0	0	4	8.2	44	11	7	6	2	0	1	0	6	1	9	3	0	1	0	1.000	0	0-1	0	7.45	6.23
2004	2 Tms	NL	39	0	0	15	46.0	193	39	17	17	3	0	3	0	19	3	46	4	0	3	2	.600	0	0-2	4	2.96	3.33
2005	SD	NL	57	0	0	9	60.1	248	49	19	18	4	2	1	2	22	4	84	4	0	7	1	.875	0	0-2	11	2.76	2.69
2006	2 Tms	NL	49	0	0	22	53.0	249	58	32	29	8	0	1	1	32	4	54	7	0	3	3	.500	0	0-2	3	5.68	4.92
2007	LAD	NL	73	0	0	19	76.0	329	78	33	32	10	2	3	4	27	3	73	2	0	6	3	.667	0	1-3	4	4.43	3.79
2008	Phi	NL	42	0	0	14	43.1	189	38	24	17	2	2	1	2	25	4	30	2	0	5	4	.556	0	0-1	2	3.64	3.53
01	SD	NL	26	0	0	8	24.0	102	15	8	7	3	0	1	1	15	0	24	1	0	2	0	.000	0	1-3	5	3.21	2.63
01	Atl	NL	12	0	0	0	12.0	48	8	4	4	1	0	0	0	4	0	17	3	0	0	0	-	0	0-0	4	1.99	3.00
04	KC	AL	16	0	0	7	23.0	100	21	10	10	0	0	3	0	11	2	21	3	0	1	0	1.000	0	0-1	1	3.01	3.91
04	Fla	NL	23	0	0	8	23.0	93	18	7	7	3	0	0	0	8	1	25	1	0	2	2	.500	0	0-1	3	2.87	2.74
06	Bos	AL	41	0	0	16	46.2	216	51	28	25	6	0	1	1	26	1	48	7	0	2	1	.667	0	0-1	3	5.44	4.82
06	SD	NL	8	0	0	6	6.1	33	7	4	4	2	0	0	0	6	3	6	0	0	1	2	.333	0	0-1	0	7.49	5.68
Postseason			11	0	0	1	11.2	46	6	4	4	0	0	0	0	6	2	13	0	0	1	0	1.000	0	0-0	1	1.35	3.09
17 ML YEARS			544	0	0	159	566.0	2477	515	285	258	58	19	22	15	285	28	574	48	1	41	30	.577	0	12-39	85	3.99	4.10

251

Bobby Seay

Pitches: L Bats: L Pos: RP-60   Ht: 6'2" Wt: 235 Born: 6/20/1978 Age: 31

			HOW MUCH HE PITCHED						WHAT HE GAVE UP										THE RESULTS						
Year	Team	Lg	G	GS	CG	GF	IP	BFP	H	R	ER	HR	SH	SF	HB	TBB	IBB	SO	WP	Bk	W	L	Pct	ShO	Sv-Op	Hld	ERC	ERA
2001	TB	AL	12	0	0	4	13.0	58	13	11	9	3	2	0	1	5	1	12	1	0	1	1	.500	0	0-0	0	5.03	6.23
2003	TB	AL	12	0	0	2	9.0	39	7	3	3	0	0	2	0	6	0	5	0	0	0	0	-	0	0-1	0	3.17	3.00
2004	TB	AL	21	0	0	6	22.2	95	21	6	6	2	0	0	2	5	1	17	1	0	0	0	-	0	0-0	0	3.15	2.38
2005	Col	NL	17	0	0	5	11.2	58	18	11	11	3	1	0	0	8	1	11	0	1	0	0	-	0	0-1	1	10.28	8.49
2006	Det	AL	14	0	0	6	15.1	71	14	11	11	1	1	1	3	9	1	12	0	0	0	0	-	0	0-0	0	4.65	6.46
2007	Det	AL	58	0	0	19	46.1	189	38	12	12	1	2	2	2	15	4	38	1	1	3	0	1.000	0	1-2	10	2.39	2.33
2008	Det	AL	60	0	0	14	56.1	246	59	28	28	4	3	4	2	25	7	58	3	0	1	2	.333	0	0-1	13	4.29	4.47
	7 ML YEARS		194	0	0	56	174.1	756	170	82	80	14	9	9	10	73	15	153	6	2	5	3	.625	0	1-5	24	3.97	4.13

Alex Serrano

Pitches: R Bats: R Pos: RP-1   Ht: 6'1" Wt: 200 Born: 2/18/1981 Age: 28

			HOW MUCH HE PITCHED						WHAT HE GAVE UP										THE RESULTS						
Year	Team	Lg	G	GS	CG	GF	IP	BFP	H	R	ER	HR	SH	SF	HB	TBB	IBB	SO	WP	Bk	W	L	Pct	ShO	Sv-Op	Hld	ERC	ERA
1999	Rckies	R	18	0	0	13	30.0	126	21	10	4	1	3	0	1	14	0	23	5	0	3	2	.600	0	5--	-	2.38	1.20
2000	Rckies	R	6	0	0	4	6.1	23	2	0	0	0	0	0	0	1	0	5	0	0	0	0	-	0	1--	-	0.39	0.00
2001	Casper	R+	12	0	0	10	18.0	66	10	0	0	0	2	0	1	1	0	23	1	0	2	0	1.000	0	6--	-	0.84	0.00
2001	Ashvll	A	14	0	0	9	13.2	61	13	4	1	0	0	0	2	5	1	13	0	1	0	0	-	0	0--	-	3.30	0.66
2002	Ashvll	A	48	0	0	28	61.2	277	81	37	34	7	5	1	8	14	3	61	3	0	5	5	.500	0	8--	-	5.86	4.96
2003	Visalia	A+	49	0	0	20	75.2	314	74	34	26	4	0	3	6	13	3	71	1	0	4	5	.444	0	4--	-	3.01	3.09
2004	Tulsa	AA	14	0	0	3	24.0	99	22	9	9	2	2	1	0	4	1	27	0	0	3	4	.429	0	0--	-	2.51	3.38
2005	Tulsa	AA	11	0	0	8	14.1	50	10	1	1	1	1	0	0	1	0	5	0	0	1	0	1.000	0	4--	-	1.47	0.63
2005	ColSpr	AAA	21	0	0	6	32.1	143	33	25	21	6	2	0	1	11	1	24	1	0	4	3	.571	0	0--	-	4.49	5.85
2005	Ark	AA	24	0	0	22	26.0	106	24	9	5	1	1	0	1	6	0	18	0	1	1	3	.250	0	11--	-	2.80	1.73
2007	Salt Lk	AAA	47	0	0	19	69.2	310	93	44	39	8	0	1	4	10	0	46	0	1	3	5	.375	0	4--	-	5.29	5.04
2008	Salt Lk	AAA	14	0	0	5	18.0	81	26	13	13	7	0	0	0	5	0	12	0	1	2	0	1.000	0	0--	-	8.81	6.50
2008	Angels	R	10	2	0	2	12.2	49	11	6	4	0	0	0	0	0	0	7	0	1	1	1	.500	0	1--	-	1.47	2.84
2008	LAA	AL	1	0	0	1	1.0	4	1	0	0	0	0	0	0	0	0	1	0	0	0	0	-	0	0-0	0	1.95	0.00

Richie Sexson

Bats: R Throws: R Pos: 1B-92; PH-5; DH-2; PR-2   Ht: 6'8" Wt: 240 Born: 12/29/1974 Age: 34

			BATTING																	BASERUNNING				AVERAGES		
Year	Team	Lg	G	AB	H	2B	3B	HR	(Hm	Rd)	TB	R	RBI	RC	TBB	IBB	SO	HBP	SH	SF	SB	CS	SB%	GDP	Avg	OBP	Slg
1997	Cle	AL	5	11	3	0	0	0	(0	0)	3	1	0	0	0	0	2	0	0	0	0	0	-	2	.273	.273	.273
1998	Cle	AL	49	174	54	14	1	11	(9	2)	103	28	35	33	6	0	42	3	0	0	1	1	.50	3	.310	.344	.592
1999	Cle	AL	134	479	122	17	7	31	(18	13)	246	72	116	70	34	0	117	4	0	8	3	3	.50	19	.255	.305	.514
2000	2 Tms		148	537	146	30	1	30	(15	15)	268	89	91	91	59	2	159	7	0	4	2	0	1.00	11	.272	.349	.499
2001	Mil	NL	158	598	162	24	3	45	(28	17)	327	94	125	103	60	5	178	6	0	4	2	4	.33	20	.271	.342	.547
2002	Mil	NL	157	570	159	37	2	29	(13	16)	287	86	102	98	70	7	136	8	0	4	0	0	-	17	.279	.363	.504
2003	Mil	NL	162	606	165	28	2	45	(23	22)	332	97	124	116	98	7	151	9	0	5	2	3	.40	18	.272	.379	.548
2004	Ari	NL	23	90	21	4	0	9	(6	3)	52	20	23	18	14	0	21	0	0	0	0	0	-	2	.233	.337	.578
2005	Sea	AL	156	558	147	36	1	39	(21	18)	302	99	121	117	89	4	167	6	0	3	1	1	.50	14	.263	.369	.541
2006	Sea	AL	158	591	156	40	0	34	(17	17)	298	75	107	92	64	5	154	4	0	4	1	1	.50	17	.264	.338	.504
2007	Sea	AL	121	434	89	21	0	21	(12	9)	173	58	63	46	51	1	100	5	0	1	1	0	1.00	12	.205	.295	.399
2008	2 Tms	AL	96	280	62	9	0	12	(3	9)	107	29	36	30	43	0	86	0	0	4	1	0	1.00	9	.221	.321	.382
00	Cle	AL	91	324	83	16	1	16	(8	8)	149	45	44	45	25	0	96	4	0	3	1	0	1.00	8	.256	.315	.460
00	Mil	NL	57	213	63	14	0	14	(7	7)	119	44	47	46	34	2	63	3	0	1	1	0	1.00	3	.296	.398	.559
08	Sea	AL	74	252	55	8	0	11	(3	8)	96	27	30	25	37	0	76	0	0	3	1	0	1.00	8	.218	.315	.381
08	NYY	AL	22	28	7	1	0	1	(0	1)	11	2	6	5	6	0	10	0	0	1	0	0	-	1	.250	.371	.393
	Postseason		9	14	1	0	0	0	(0	0)	1	1	1	0	3	0	7	0	0	0	0	0	-	1	.071	.235	.071
	12 ML YEARS		1367	4928	1286	260	17	306	(165	141)	2498	748	943	814	588	31	1313	52	0	36	14	13	.52	144	.261	.344	.507

Ryan Shealy

Bats: R Throws: R Pos: 1B-20   Ht: 6'5" Wt: 240 Born: 8/29/1979 Age: 29

			BATTING																	BASERUNNING				AVERAGES		
Year	Team	Lg	G	AB	H	2B	3B	HR	(Hm	Rd)	TB	R	RBI	RC	TBB	IBB	SO	HBP	SH	SF	SB	CS	SB%	GDP	Avg	OBP	Slg
2008	Omha*	AAA	111	400	113	22	0	22	(-	-)	201	53	65	78	55	0	93	8	0	5	0	1	.00	22	.283	.376	.503
2005	Col	NL	36	91	30	7	0	2	(0	2)	43	14	16	14	13	0	22	0	0	0	1	0	1.00	6	.330	.413	.473
2006	2 Tms		56	202	56	12	1	7	(5	2)	91	31	37	32	15	1	54	2	0	0	1	1	.50	5	.277	.333	.450
2007	KC	AL	52	172	38	6	0	3	(0	3)	53	18	21	15	13	0	53	3	0	1	0	0	-	4	.221	.286	.308
2008	KC	AL	20	73	22	1	0	7	(3	4)	44	12	20	15	5	0	19	1	0	0	0	0	-	2	.301	.354	.603
06	Col	NL	5	9	2	2	0	0	(0	0)	4	2	1	0	0	0	4	0	0	0	0	0	-	0	.222	.222	.444
06	KC	AL	51	193	54	10	1	7	(5	2)	87	29	36	32	15	1	50	2	0	0	1	1	.50	5	.280	.338	.451
	4 ML YEARS		164	538	146	26	1	19	(8	11)	231	75	94	76	46	1	148	6	0	1	2	1	.67	17	.271	.335	.429

Ben Sheets

Pitches: R Bats: R Pos: SP-31   Ht: 6'1" Wt: 226 Born: 7/18/1978 Age: 30

			HOW MUCH HE PITCHED						WHAT HE GAVE UP										THE RESULTS						
Year	Team	Lg	G	GS	CG	GF	IP	BFP	H	R	ER	HR	SH	SF	HB	TBB	IBB	SO	WP	Bk	W	L	Pct	ShO	Sv-Op	Hld	ERC	ERA
2001	Mil	NL	25	25	1	0	151.1	653	166	89	80	23	8	5	5	48	6	94	3	0	11	10	.524	1	0-0	0	4.78	4.76
2002	Mil	NL	34	34	1	0	216.2	934	237	105	100	21	10	0	10	70	10	170	9	0	11	16	.407	0	0-0	0	4.45	4.15
2003	Mil	NL	34	34	1	0	220.2	932	232	122	109	29	11	6	6	43	2	157	7	0	11	13	.458	0	0-0	0	3.83	4.45
2004	Mil	NL	34	34	5	0	237.0	937	201	85	71	25	6	4	4	32	1	264	8	1	12	14	.462	0	0-0	0	2.37	2.70
2005	Mil	NL	22	22	3	0	156.2	633	142	66	58	19	6	2	2	25	1	141	7	0	10	9	.526	0	0-0	0	2.81	3.33

252

			HOW MUCH HE PITCHED					WHAT HE GAVE UP												THE RESULTS							
Year	Team	Lg	G	GS	CG	GF	IP	BFP	H	R	ER	HR	SH	SF	HB	TBB	IBB	SO	WP	Bk	W	L	Pct	ShO	Sv-Op	Hld	ERC	ERA
2006	Mil	NL	17	17	0	0	106.0	430	105	47	45	9	6	5	2	11	1	116	3	0	6	7	.462	0	0-0	0	2.84	3.82
2007	Mil	NL	24	24	2	0	141.1	592	138	62	60	17	4	5	1	37	2	106	4	0	12	5	.706	0	0-0	0	3.53	3.82
2008	Mil	NL	31	31	5	0	198.1	812	181	74	68	17	6	7	1	47	2	158	8	0	13	9	.591	3	0-0	0	2.89	3.09
8 ML YEARS			221	221	18	0	1428.0	5922	1402	650	591	160	57	34	31	313	25	1206	49	1	86	83	.509	4	0-0	0	3.41	3.72

Gary Sheffield

Bats: R **Throws:** R **Pos:** DH-106; LF-6; PH-2   **Ht:** 6'0" **Wt:** 215 **Born:** 11/18/1968 **Age:** 40

							BATTING														BASERUNNING				AVERAGES		
Year	Team	Lg	G	AB	H	2B	3B	HR	(Hm	Rd)	TB	R	RBI	RC	TBB	IBB	SO	HBP	SH	SF	SB	CS	SB%	GDP	Avg	OBP	Slg
2008 Lkland*	A+	5	13	2	0	0	2	(-	-)	8	7	2	3	6	1	1	0	0	0	0	0	-	0	.154	.421	.615
1988	Mil	AL	24	80	19	1	0	4	(1	3)	32	12	12	8	7	0	7	0	1	1	3	1	.75	5	.238	.295	.400
1989	Mil	AL	95	368	91	18	0	5	(2	3)	124	34	32	38	27	0	33	4	3	3	10	6	.63	4	.247	.303	.337
1990	Mil	AL	125	487	143	30	1	10	(3	7)	205	67	67	73	44	1	41	3	4	9	25	10	.71	11	.294	.350	.421
1991	Mil	AL	50	175	34	12	2	2	(2	0)	56	25	22	15	19	1	15	3	1	5	5	5	.50	3	.194	.277	.320
1992	SD	NL	146	557	184	34	3	33	(23	10)	323	87	100	113	48	5	40	6	0	7	5	6	.45	19	.330	.385	.580
1993	2 Tms	NL	140	494	145	20	5	20	(10	10)	235	67	73	84	47	6	64	9	0	7	17	5	.77	11	.294	.361	.476
1994	Fla	NL	87	322	89	16	1	27	(15	12)	188	61	78	68	51	11	50	6	0	5	12	6	.67	10	.276	.380	.584
1995	Fla	NL	63	213	69	8	0	16	(4	12)	125	46	46	60	55	8	45	4	0	2	19	4	.83	3	.324	.467	.587
1996	Fla	NL	161	519	163	33	1	42	(19	23)	324	118	120	144	142	19	66	10	0	6	16	9	.64	16	.314	.465	.624
1997	Fla	NL	135	444	111	22	1	21	(13	8)	198	86	71	92	121	11	79	15	0	2	11	7	.61	7	.250	.424	.446
1998	2 Tms	NL	130	437	132	27	2	22	(11	11)	229	73	85	102	95	12	46	8	0	9	22	7	.76	7	.302	.428	.524
1999	LAD	NL	152	549	165	20	0	34	(15	19)	287	103	101	118	101	4	64	4	0	9	11	5	.69	10	.301	.407	.523
2000	LAD	NL	141	501	163	24	3	43	(23	20)	322	105	109	131	101	7	71	4	0	6	4	6	.40	13	.325	.438	.643
2001	LAD	NL	143	515	160	28	2	36	(16	20)	300	98	100	120	94	13	67	4	0	5	10	4	.71	12	.311	.417	.583
2002	Atl	NL	135	492	151	26	0	25	(10	15)	252	82	84	102	72	2	53	11	0	4	12	2	.86	16	.307	.404	.512
2003	Atl	NL	155	576	190	37	2	39	(20	19)	348	126	132	134	86	6	55	8	0	8	18	4	.82	16	.330	.419	.604
2004	NYY	AL	154	573	166	30	1	36	(19	17)	306	117	121	123	92	7	83	11	0	6	5	6	.45	16	.290	.393	.534
2005	NYY	AL	154	584	170	27	0	34	(19	15)	299	104	123	130	78	7	76	8	0	5	10	2	.83	11	.291	.379	.512
2006	NYY	AL	39	151	45	5	0	6	(5	1)	68	22	25	21	13	2	16	1	0	1	5	1	.83	6	.298	.355	.450
2007	Det	AL	133	494	131	20	1	25	(14	11)	228	107	75	90	84	2	71	9	0	4	22	5	.81	10	.265	.378	.462
2008	Det	AL	114	418	94	16	0	19	(13	6)	167	52	57	51	58	3	83	5	0	1	9	2	.82	19	.225	.326	.400
93	SD	NL	68	258	76	12	2	10	(6	4)	122	34	36	40	18	0	30	3	0	3	5	1	.83	9	.295	.344	.473
93	Fla	NL	72	236	69	8	3	10	(4	6)	113	33	37	44	29	6	34	6	0	4	12	4	.75	2	.292	.378	.479
98	Fla	NL	40	136	37	11	1	6	(6	0)	68	21	28	27	26	1	16	2	0	2	4	2	.67	3	.272	.392	.500
98	LAD	NL	90	301	95	16	1	16	(5	11)	161	52	57	75	69	11	30	6	0	7	18	5	.78	4	.316	.444	.535
Postseason		44	161	40	6	0	6	(4	2)	64	27	19	27	39	2	26	2	0	0	1	1	.50	6	.248	.401	.398
21 ML YEARS		2476	8949	2615	454	25	499	(257	242)	4616	1592	1633	1817	1435	127	1125	133	9	109	251	103	.71	225	.292	.394	.516

Steven Shell

Pitches: R **Bats:** R **Pos:** RP-39   **Ht:** 6'4" **Wt:** 217 **Born:** 3/10/1983 **Age:** 26

			HOW MUCH HE PITCHED						WHAT HE GAVE UP											THE RESULTS							
Year	Team	Lg	G	GS	CG	GF	IP	BFP	H	R	ER	HR	SH	SF	HB	TBB	IBB	SO	WP	Bk	W	L	Pct	ShO	Sv-Op	Hld	ERC	ERA
2001	Angels	R	3	0	0	1	4.0	15	1	0	0	0	0	0	0	2	0	3	0	0	1	0	1.000	0	0--	-	0.75	0.00
2001	Provo	R+	14	4	0	3	37.2	182	52	31	30	3	0	1	9	15	0	33	3	0	1	3	.000	0	1--	-	7.31	7.17
2002	CRpds	A	22	21	1	0	121.0	506	119	59	50	12	1	3	9	26	0	86	3	2	11	4	.733	0	0--	-	3.56	3.72
2003	RCuca	A+	22	21	1	0	127.1	540	123	66	60	13	4	3	12	26	0	100	3	1	6	8	.429	1	0--	-	3.45	4.24
2004	RCuca	A+	28	28	2	0	165.1	672	151	76	66	19	6	2	16	40	0	190	4	1	12	7	.632	1	0--	-	3.57	3.59
2005	Ark	AA	27	27	1	0	159.2	712	175	90	81	18	-	-	9	58	0	126	10	0	10	8	.556	1	0--	-	4.75	4.57
2006	Ark	AA	3	3	0	0	18.0	75	20	12	8	1	0	0	1	4	0	10	0	0	1	2	.333	0	0--	-	4.04	4.00
2006	Salt Lk	AAA	24	22	0	1	122.2	542	156	91	84	16	3	5	12	32	0	82	2	1	5	9	.357	0	0--	-	5.88	6.16
2007	Ark	AA	5	0	0	0	13.1	54	10	1	1	1	0	0	3	1	0	19	0	0	0	0	-	0	0--	-	2.21	0.68
2007	Salt Lk	AAA	31	7	0	10	70.1	297	83	43	37	15	1	4	2	19	0	52	1	0	7	3	.700	0	0--	-	5.76	4.73
2008	Clmbs	AAA	22	4	0	3	58.1	232	49	19	17	5	2	1	3	14	1	54	2	1	3	2	.600	0	1--	-	2.77	2.62
2008	Was	NL	39	0	0	7	50.0	199	34	14	12	5	1	1	2	20	1	41	1	0	2	2	.500	0	2-3	7	2.58	2.16

Chris Shelton

Bats: R **Throws:** R **Pos:** 1B-39; PH-9; 3B-1; PR-1   **Ht:** 6'0" **Wt:** 215 **Born:** 6/26/1980 **Age:** 29

							BATTING														BASERUNNING				AVERAGES		
Year	Team	Lg	G	AB	H	2B	3B	HR	(Hm	Rd)	TB	R	RBI	RC	TBB	IBB	SO	HBP	SH	SF	SB	CS	SB%	GDP	Avg	OBP	Slg
2008 Okla*	AAA	67	256	87	22	2	11	(-	-)	146	38	51	58	31	0	54	1	0	3	0	0	-	7	.340	.409	.570
2004	Det	AL	27	46	9	1	0	1	(1	0)	13	6	3	4	9	0	14	0	0	1	0	0	-	2	.196	.321	.283
2005	Det	AL	107	388	116	22	3	18	(10	8)	198	61	59	65	34	0	87	5	0	4	0	0	-	11	.299	.360	.510
2006	Det	AL	115	373	102	16	4	16	(5	11)	174	50	47	50	34	1	107	4	0	1	1	2	.33	10	.273	.340	.466
2008	Tex	AL	41	97	21	5	0	2	(1	1)	32	14	11	11	17	0	33	0	3	0	1	0	1.00	3	.216	.333	.330
4 ML YEARS		290	904	248	44	7	37	(17	20)	417	131	120	130	94	1	241	9	3	6	2	2	.50	26	.274	.346	.461

George Sherrill

Pitches: L **Bats:** L **Pos:** RP-57   **Ht:** 6'0" **Wt:** 230 **Born:** 4/19/1977 **Age:** 32

			HOW MUCH HE PITCHED						WHAT HE GAVE UP											THE RESULTS							
Year	Team	Lg	G	GS	CG	GF	IP	BFP	H	R	ER	HR	SH	SF	HB	TBB	IBB	SO	WP	Bk	W	L	Pct	ShO	Sv-Op	Hld	ERC	ERA
2004	Sea	AL	21	0	0	4	23.2	104	24	12	10	3	0	1	1	9	1	16	4	1	2	1	.667	0	0-0	3	4.31	3.80
2005	Sea	AL	29	0	0	2	19.0	77	13	12	11	3	1	1	1	7	2	24	0	0	4	3	.571	0	0-0	9	2.70	5.21
2006	Sea	AL	72	0	0	6	40.0	174	30	19	19	0	4	2	0	27	4	42	0	0	2	4	.333	0	1-1	17	2.86	4.28
2007	Sea	AL	73	0	0	16	45.2	182	28	12	12	4	4	4	1	17	1	56	1	1	2	0	1.000	0	3-7	22	1.96	2.36
2008	Bal	AL	57	0	0	49	53.1	239	47	28	28	6	1	3	1	33	6	58	1	0	3	5	.375	0	31-37	0	4.18	4.73
5 ML YEARS		252	0	0	77	181.2	776	142	83	80	16	10	11	4	93	14	196	6	2	13	13	.500	0	35-45	51	3.17	3.96

James Shields

Pitches: R **Bats:** R **Pos:** SP-33 **Ht:** 6'4" **Wt:** 214 **Born:** 12/20/1981 **Age:** 27

Year	Team	Lg	G	GS	CG	GF	IP	BFP	H	R	ER	HR	SH	SF	HB	TBB	IBB	SO	WP	Bk	W	L	Pct	ShO	Sv-Op	Hld	ERC	ERA
2006	TB	AL	21	21	1	0	124.2	540	141	69	67	18	4	3	5	38	5	104	9	0	6	8	.429	0	0-0	0	4.92	4.84
2007	TB	AL	31	31	1	0	215.0	874	202	99	92	28	4	5	10	36	0	184	9	0	12	8	.600	0	0-0	0	3.24	3.85
2008	TB	AL	33	33	3	0	215.0	877	208	94	85	24	6	0	12	40	0	160	6	0	14	8	.636	2	0-0	0	3.41	3.56
3 ML YEARS			85	85	5	0	554.2	2291	551	261	244	70	14	8	27	114	5	448	24	0	32	24	.571	2	0-0	0	3.67	3.96

Scot Shields

Pitches: R **Bats:** R **Pos:** RP-64 **Ht:** 6'1" **Wt:** 180 **Born:** 7/22/1975 **Age:** 33

Year	Team	Lg	G	GS	CG	GF	IP	BFP	H	R	ER	HR	SH	SF	HB	TBB	IBB	SO	WP	Bk	W	L	Pct	ShO	Sv-Op	Hld	ERC	ERA
2008 Salt Lk*	AAA		1	0	0	0	1.0	5	2	0	0	0	0	0	0	0	0	3	0	0	0	0	-	0	0- -	-	7.48	0.00
2001	LAA	AL	8	0	0	6	11.0	48	8	1	0	0	0	0	1	7	0	7	2	0	0	0	-	0	0-0	0	3.10	0.00
2002	LAA	AL	29	1	0	13	49.0	188	31	13	12	4	1	0	1	21	1	30	3	0	5	3	.625	0	0-0	3	2.35	2.20
2003	LAA	AL	44	13	0	5	148.1	609	138	56	47	12	3	4	5	38	6	111	4	0	5	6	.455	0	1-1	3	3.12	2.85
2004	LAA	AL	60	0	0	12	105.1	454	97	42	39	6	2	2	3	40	5	109	4	0	8	2	.800	0	4-7	17	3.24	3.33
2005	LAA	AL	78	0	0	21	91.2	375	66	33	28	5	4	3	2	37	2	98	12	0	10	11	.476	0	7-13	33	2.37	2.75
2006	LAA	AL	74	0	0	13	87.2	351	70	30	28	8	3	1	1	24	4	84	8	0	7	7	.500	0	2-8	31	2.48	2.87
2007	LAA	AL	71	0	0	13	77.0	320	62	36	33	7	0	1	4	33	0	77	6	0	4	5	.444	0	2-8	31	3.31	3.86
2008	LAA	AL	64	0	0	12	63.1	270	56	29	19	6	1	1	2	29	2	64	2	0	6	4	.600	0	4-9	31	3.72	2.70
Postseason			13	0	0	2	19.2	85	18	10	6	3	0	1	0	10	2	18	0	0	1	1	.500	0	0-1	1	4.25	2.75
8 ML YEARS			428	14	0	95	633.1	2615	528	240	206	48	14	12	19	229	20	580	41	0	45	38	.542	0	20-46	149	2.96	2.93

Kelly Shoppach

Bats: R **Throws:** R **Pos:** C-110; PH-4; DH-1 **Ht:** 6'0" **Wt:** 220 **Born:** 4/29/1980 **Age:** 29

Year	Team	Lg	G	AB	H	2B	3B	HR	(Hm	Rd)	TB	R	RBI	RC	TBB	IBB	SO	HBP	SH	SF	SB	CS	SB%	GDP	Avg	OBP	Slg
2005	Bos	AL	9	15	0	0	0	0	(0	0)	0	1	0	0	0	0	7	1	0	0	0	0	-	0	.000	.063	.000
2006	Cle	AL	41	110	27	6	0	3	(2	1)	42	7	16	13	8	0	45	0	2	0	0	0	-	2	.245	.297	.382
2007	Cle	AL	59	161	42	13	0	7	(4	3)	76	26	30	24	11	0	76	1	3	1	0	0	-	2	.261	.310	.472
2008	Cle	AL	112	352	92	27	0	21	(9	12)	182	67	55	58	36	3	133	11	3	1	0	0	-	7	.261	.348	.517
Postseason			2	6	3	2	0	0	(0	0)	5	1	0	2	0	0	2	2	0	0	0	0	-	0	.500	.625	.833
4 ML YEARS			221	638	161	46	0	31	(15	16)	300	101	101	95	55	3	241	13	8	2	0	0	-	11	.252	.323	.470

Brian Shouse

Pitches: L **Bats:** L **Pos:** RP-69 **Ht:** 5'10" **Wt:** 196 **Born:** 9/26/1968 **Age:** 40

Year	Team	Lg	G	GS	CG	GF	IP	BFP	H	R	ER	HR	SH	SF	HB	TBB	IBB	SO	WP	Bk	W	L	Pct	ShO	Sv-Op	Hld	ERC	ERA
1993	Pit	NL	6	0	0	1	4.0	22	7	4	4	1	0	1	0	2	0	3	1	0	0	0	-	0	0-0	0	9.92	9.00
1998	Bos	AL	7	0	0	4	8.0	36	9	5	5	2	0	0	0	4	0	5	0	0	0	1	.000	0	0-0	1	6.42	5.63
2002	KC	AL	23	0	0	7	14.2	71	15	10	10	3	1	1	2	9	1	11	2	0	0	0	-	0	0-0	2	6.11	6.14
2003	Tex	AL	62	0	0	14	61.0	253	62	24	21	1	3	0	4	14	6	40	0	0	0	1	.000	0	1-1	10	3.10	3.10
2004	Tex	AL	53	0	0	14	44.1	184	36	12	11	3	2	2	1	18	3	34	0	0	2	0	1.000	0	0-0	12	2.87	2.23
2005	Tex	AL	64	0	0	12	53.1	233	55	37	31	7	2	3	8	18	4	35	2	0	3	2	.600	0	0-2	11	4.29	5.23
2006	2 Tms		65	0	0	10	38.1	174	40	18	17	4	1	1	6	18	5	23	0	1	1	3	.250	0	2-5	15	5.06	3.99
2007	Mil	NL	73	0	0	13	47.2	201	46	19	16	0	4	2	2	14	5	32	0	1	1	1	.500	0	1-4	21	2.79	3.02
2008	Mil	NL	69	0	0	17	51.1	212	46	19	16	5	4	1	0	14	4	33	1	0	5	1	.833	0	2-5	15	2.87	2.81
06	Tex	AL	6	0	0	2	4.1	20	6	2	2	1	0	0	0	1	1	3	0	0	0	0	-	0	0-1	1	6.09	4.15
06	Mil	NL	59	0	0	8	34.0	154	34	16	15	3	1	1	6	17	4	20	0	1	1	3	.250	0	2-4	14	4.92	3.97
9 ML YEARS			422	0	0	92	322.2	1386	316	148	131	26	17	11	18	111	28	216	6	1	12	9	.571	0	6-17	87	3.68	3.65

Carlos Silva

Pitches: R **Bats:** R **Pos:** SP-28 **Ht:** 6'4" **Wt:** 246 **Born:** 4/23/1979 **Age:** 30

Year	Team	Lg	G	GS	CG	GF	IP	BFP	H	R	ER	HR	SH	SF	HB	TBB	IBB	SO	WP	Bk	W	L	Pct	ShO	Sv-Op	Hld	ERC	ERA
2002	Phi	NL	68	0	0	21	84.0	350	88	34	30	4	9	3	4	22	6	41	3	0	5	0	1.000	0	1-5	8	3.60	3.21
2003	Phi	NL	62	1	0	15	87.1	381	92	43	43	7	6	1	8	37	5	48	12	1	3	1	.750	0	1-3	4	4.71	4.43
2004	Min	AL	33	33	1	0	203.0	869	255	100	95	23	6	0	5	35	2	76	5	1	14	8	.636	1	0-0	0	4.89	4.21
2005	Min	AL	27	27	2	0	188.1	749	212	83	72	25	2	5	3	9	2	71	0	0	9	8	.529	0	0-0	0	3.78	3.44
2006	Min	AL	36	31	0	3	180.1	811	246	130	119	38	6	7	7	32	4	70	1	0	11	15	.423	0	0-0	2	6.23	5.94
2007	Min	AL	33	33	2	0	202.0	848	229	99	94	20	6	5	4	36	2	89	4	1	13	14	.481	1	0-0	0	4.05	4.19
2008	Sea	AL	28	28	1	0	153.1	689	213	114	110	20	3	7	4	32	2	69	1	0	4	15	.211	0	0-0	0	5.93	6.46
Postseason			1	1	0	0	5.0	24	10	6	6	1	0	0	0	0	0	1	0	0	1	0	1.000	0	0-0	0	9.65	10.80
7 ML YEARS			287	153	6	38	1098.1	4697	1335	603	563	137	38	28	35	203	23	464	26	3	59	61	.492	2	2-8	14	4.78	4.61

Alfredo Simon

Pitches: R **Bats:** R **Pos:** RP-3; SP-1 **Ht:** 6'4" **Wt:** 230 **Born:** 5/8/1981 **Age:** 28

Year	Team	Lg	G	GS	CG	GF	IP	BFP	H	R	ER	HR	SH	SF	HB	TBB	IBB	SO	WP	Bk	W	L	Pct	ShO	Sv-Op	Hld	ERC	ERA
2001	Phillies	R	10	8	0	0	43.1	194	35	23	14	2	2	3	7	23	0	40	6	3	2	2	.500	0	0- -	-	3.67	2.91
2002	Batvia	A-	15	14	0	1	90.1	388	79	44	36	5	2	2	5	46	0	77	3	1	9	2	.818	0	0- -	-	3.75	3.59
2003	Lakwd	A	14	7	0	0	71.1	298	59	32	30	4	4	3	3	25	0	66	5	1	5	0	1.000	0	2- -	-	2.80	3.79
2004	Clrwtr	A+	22	21	4	0	134.2	552	121	58	49	13	8	2	5	38	2	107	10	4	7	9	.438	3	0- -	-	3.21	3.27
2004	SnJos	A+	6	6	0	0	31.2	142	44	24	20	7	3	2	0	12	0	21	5	0	1	2	.333	0	0- -	-	7.62	5.68

Year	Team	Lg	G	GS	CG	GF	IP	BFP	H	R	ER	HR	SH	SF	HB	TBB	IBB	SO	WP	Bk	W	L	Pct	ShO	Sv-Op	Hld	ERC	ERA
2005	Nrwich	AA	43	9	0	28	91.1	395	104	54	51	6	7	5	3	24	2	60	5	0	3	8	.273	0	19--	-	4.17	5.03
2006	Fresno	AAA	10	10	0	0	52.0	245	76	41	39	8	3	2	3	19	0	35	7	0	0	6	.000	-	0--	-	7.52	6.75
2006	SnJos	A+	18	7	-	-	36.1	166	43	28	26	7	-	-	1	14	-	35	1	1	2	4	.333	-	0--	-	5.80	6.44
2007	Okla	AAA	22	22	1	0	119.0	539	152	92	85	19	3	1	6	46	0	73	4	0	5	10	.333	0	0--	-	6.46	6.43
2008	Norfolk	AAA	1	1	0	0	4.2	25	9	7	4	1	0	1	1	2	0	5	0	0	0	1	.000	0	0--	-	12.56	7.71
2008	Bal	AL	4	1	0	0	13.0	59	16	10	9	4	0	1	2	2	0	8	2	0	0	0	-	0	0-0	0	6.45	6.23

Andy Sisco

Pitches: L Bats: L Pos: P   Ht: 6'10" Wt: 270 Born: 1/13/1983 Age: 26

			HOW MUCH HE PITCHED						WHAT HE GAVE UP												THE RESULTS						
Year	Team	Lg	G	GS	CG	GF	IP	BFP	H	R	ER	HR	SH	SF	HB	TBB	IBB	SO	WP	Bk	W	L	Pct	ShO	Sv-Op	Hld	ERC	ERA
2005	KC	AL	67	0	0	13	75.1	329	68	27	26	6	2	3	2	42	4	76	2	0	2	5	.286	0	0-5	14	4.04	3.11
2006	KC	AL	65	0	0	16	58.1	278	66	47	46	8	4	5	1	40	6	52	4	0	1	3	.250	0	1-5	5	6.14	7.10
2007	CWS	AL	19	0	0	6	14.0	74	19	13	13	2	0	0	1	11	0	13	3	0	0	1	.000	0	0-0	4	8.28	8.36
3 ML YEARS			151	0	0	35	147.2	681	153	87	85	16	6	8	4	93	10	141	9	0	3	9	.250	0	1-10	23	5.23	5.18

Grady Sizemore

Bats: L Throws: L Pos: CF-151; DH-6   Ht: 6'2" Wt: 200 Born: 8/2/1982 Age: 26

			BATTING																			BASERUNNING				AVERAGES		
Year	Team	Lg	G	AB	H	2B	3B	HR	(Hm	Rd)	TB	R	RBI	RC	TBB	IBB	SO	HBP	SH	SF		SB	CS	SB%	GDP		Avg	OBP	Slg
2004	Cle	AL	43	138	34	6	2	4	(2	2)	56	15	24	21	14	0	34	5	0	2		0	0	1.00	0		.246	.333	.406
2005	Cle	AL	158	640	185	37	11	22	(10	12)	310	111	81	101	52	1	132	7	5	2		22	10	.69	17		.289	.348	.484
2006	Cle	AL	162	655	190	53	11	28	(14	14)	349	134	76	121	78	8	153	13	1	4		22	6	.79	2		.290	.375	.533
2007	Cle	AL	162	628	174	34	5	24	(11	13)	290	118	78	123	101	9	155	17	0	2		33	10	.77	3		.277	.390	.462
2008	Cle	AL	157	634	170	39	5	33	(21	12)	318	101	90	121	98	14	130	11	0	2		38	5	.88	5		.268	.374	.502
Postseason			11	43	12	2	1	2	(0	2)	22	9	3	5	8	3	9	1	0	1		2	1	.67	2		.279	.396	.512
5 ML YEARS			682	2695	753	169	34	111	(58	53)	1323	479	349	487	343	32	604	53	6	12		117	31	.79	27		.279	.370	.491

Doug Slaten

Pitches: L Bats: L Pos: RP-45   Ht: 6'5" Wt: 215 Born: 2/4/1980 Age: 29

			HOW MUCH HE PITCHED						WHAT HE GAVE UP												THE RESULTS						
Year	Team	Lg	G	GS	CG	GF	IP	BFP	H	R	ER	HR	SH	SF	HB	TBB	IBB	SO	WP	Bk	W	L	Pct	ShO	Sv-Op	Hld	ERC	ERA
2008	Tucsn*	AAA	6	0	0	0	6.2	30	6	3	3	1	0	2	0	4	0	9	0	0	0	0	-	0	0--	-	4.56	4.05
2006	Ari	NL	9	0	0	0	5.2	21	3	0	0	0	1	0	0	2	1	3	0	0	0	0	-	0	0-0	2	1.11	0.00
2007	Ari	NL	61	0	0	13	36.1	163	41	15	11	4	0	0	4	14	0	28	3	0	3	2	.600	0	0-1	7	4.74	2.72
2008	Ari	NL	45	0	0	13	32.1	147	33	20	17	4	1	1	4	14	1	20	0	0	0	3	.000	0	0-0	4	4.86	4.73
Postseason			3	0	0	1	1.1	7	1	0	0	0	0	0	0	2	1	1	1	0	0	0	-	0	0-0	4	4.29	0.00
3 ML YEARS			115	0	0	26	74.1	331	77	35	28	8	2	1	4	30	2	51	3	0	3	5	.375	0	0-1	13	4.45	3.39

Brian Slocum

Pitches: R Bats: R Pos: RP-2   Ht: 6'3" Wt: 210 Born: 3/27/1981 Age: 28

			HOW MUCH HE PITCHED						WHAT HE GAVE UP												THE RESULTS						
Year	Team	Lg	G	GS	CG	GF	IP	BFP	H	R	ER	HR	SH	SF	HB	TBB	IBB	SO	WP	Bk	W	L	Pct	ShO	Sv-Op	Hld	ERC	ERA
2002	MhVlly	A	11	11	0	0	55.1	223	47	19	16	1	2	1	2	14	0	48	3	0	5	2	.714	0	0--	-	2.38	2.60
2003	Knstn	A	22	21	0	1	107.0	469	112	61	53	7	0	2	5	41	0	66	1	0	6	7	.462	0	1--	-	4.20	4.46
2004	Knstn	A	25	25	2	0	135.0	568	136	66	65	13	5	7	6	41	0	102	11	0	15	6	.714	2	0--	-	3.95	4.33
2005	Akron	AA	21	18	1	2	102.1	436	98	52	50	9	7	3	6	36	0	95	2	0	7	5	.583	0	0--	-	3.82	4.40
2006	Buffalo	AAA	27	15	0	4	94.0	394	78	42	35	5	2	2	9	37	2	91	6	0	6	3	.667	0	1--	-	3.18	3.35
2007	Buffalo	AAA	5	5	0	0	26.0	118	21	13	12	3	0	0	1	16	1	28	0	0	2	2	.500	0	0--	-	3.87	4.15
2008	Buffalo	AAA	30	11	0	6	85.1	381	82	50	45	12	3	2	6	42	1	81	3	0	3	7	.300	0	1--	-	4.74	4.75
2006	Cle	AL	8	2	0	1	17.2	85	27	11	11	3	0	0	1	9	0	11	2	0	0	0	-	0	0-0	0	8.99	5.60
2008	Cle	AL	2	0	0	0	2.0	15	8	6	6	2	0	1	1	0	0	1	0	0	0	0	-	0	0-0	0	38.27	27.00
2 ML YEARS			10	2	0	1	19.2	100	35	17	17	5	0	1	2	9	0	12	2	0	0	0	-	0	0-0	0	11.54	7.78

Kevin Slowey

Pitches: R Bats: R Pos: SP-27   Ht: 6'3" Wt: 205 Born: 5/4/1984 Age: 25

			HOW MUCH HE PITCHED						WHAT HE GAVE UP												THE RESULTS						
Year	Team	Lg	G	GS	CG	GF	IP	BFP	H	R	ER	HR	SH	SF	HB	TBB	IBB	SO	WP	Bk	W	L	Pct	ShO	Sv-Op	Hld	ERC	ERA
2005	Elizab	R+	4	0	0	2	7.2	25	2	1	1	1	0	0	0	0	0	15	0	0	0	0	-	0	1--	-	0.33	1.17
2005	Beloit	A	13	9	1	2	64.1	243	42	18	16	4	1	2	2	8	0	69	0	0	3	2	.600	1	0--	-	1.40	2.24
2006	FtMyrs	A+	14	14	0	0	89.2	333	52	19	10	2	1	1	4	9	0	99	0	0	4	2	.667	0	0--	-	1.03	1.00
2006	NwBrit	AA	9	9	1	0	59.1	242	50	23	21	6	1	2	2	13	0	52	0	0	4	3	.571	0	0--	-	2.65	3.19
2007	Roch	AAA	20	20	5	0	133.2	523	110	31	28	4	8	1	3	18	0	107	1	1	10	5	.667	1	0--	-	1.88	1.89
2008	FtMyrs	A+	2	2	0	0	8.0	27	1	1	1	1	0	0	0	2	0	10	0	0	0	0	-	0	0--	-	0.44	1.13
2008	Roch	AAA	1	1	0	0	5.0	20	3	2	2	2	0	0	0	2	0	9	0	0	0	1	.000	0	0--	-	3.65	3.60
2007	Min	AL	13	11	0	0	66.2	297	82	39	35	16	0	1	0	11	0	47	3	0	4	1	.800	0	0-0	0	5.22	4.73
2008	Min	AL	27	27	3	0	160.1	653	161	74	71	22	1	5	4	24	1	123	1	0	12	11	.522	2	0-0	0	3.48	3.99
2 ML YEARS			40	38	3	0	227.0	950	243	113	106	38	1	6	4	35	1	170	4	0	16	12	.571	2	0-0	0	3.98	4.20

Chris Smith

Pitches: R Bats: R Pos: RP-12   Ht: 6'2" Wt: 200 Born: 4/9/1981 Age: 28

Year	Team	Lg	G	GS	CG	GF	IP	BFP	H	R	ER	HR	SH	SF	HB	TBB	IBB	SO	WP	Bk	W	L	Pct	ShO	Sv-Op	Hld	ERC	ERA
2002	Lowell	A-	14	14	0	0	56.2	237	54	29	26	3	1	0	2	14	0	50	5	0	3	3	.500	0	0--	-	3.03	4.13
2003	RedSx	R	3	2	0	0	8.1	39	11	8	6	0	0	0	0	4	0	3	1	0	0	2	.000	0	0--	-	5.47	6.48
2003	Augsta	A	8	8	0	0	46.1	188	48	22	22	4	1	3	3	5	0	25	3	1	3	3	.500	0	0--	-	3.37	4.27
2003	Srsota	A+	2	2	0	0	12.0	47	8	2	0	0	0	0	1	2	0	9	0	0	2	0	1.000	0	0--	-	1.40	0.00
2004	Portlnd	AA	14	14	0	0	74.1	317	77	34	31	10	4	1	2	21	0	85	1	3	5	2	.714	0	0--	-	4.15	3.75
2005	Portlnd	AA	15	15	0	0	75.2	331	95	46	44	13	6	4	4	15	1	49	3	0	4	4	.500	0	0--	-	5.50	5.23
2005	RedSx	R	1	1	0	0	3.0	19	0	0	0	0	0	-	0	0	0	4	0	0	0	0	-	0	0--	-	0.00	0.00
2006	Portlnd	AA	20	20	1	0	115.2	492	114	57	52	9	6	4	10	29	3	78	4	3	9	6	.600	1	0--	-	3.54	4.05
2006	Pwtckt	AAA	7	6	0	0	33.2	144	33	16	12	2	2	0	1	9	0	23	1	0	1	1	.500	0	0--	-	3.22	3.21
2007	Pwtckt	AAA	30	14	0	4	104.0	466	126	57	51	10	5	3	8	42	2	80	7	1	6	9	.400	0	1--	-	5.72	4.41
2007	Pwtckt	AAA	2	0	0	0	5.0	29	12	5	1	1	0	1	1	0	0	2	0	0	0	0	-	0	0--	-	12.68	1.80
2008	Pwtckt	AAA	37	4	0	27	59.1	239	54	23	21	6	1	2	2	11	2	52	2	0	1	5	.167	0	15--	-	2.89	3.19
2008	Bos	AL	12	0	0	3	18.1	78	18	16	16	6	1	1	0	7	0	13	0	0	1	0	1.000	0	0-0	0	5.53	7.85

Greg Smith

Pitches: L Bats: L Pos: SP-32   Ht: 6'2" Wt: 190 Born: 12/22/1983 Age: 25

Year	Team	Lg	G	GS	CG	GF	IP	BFP	H	R	ER	HR	SH	SF	HB	TBB	IBB	SO	WP	Bk	W	L	Pct	ShO	Sv-Op	Hld	ERC	ERA
2005	Msoula	R+	16	14	0	0	82.1	326	69	40	38	8	2	2	5	18	0	100	6	0	8	5	.615	0	0--	-	2.82	4.15
2006	Lancst	A+	13	13	2	0	88.1	339	57	21	16	3	3	1	4	31	0	71	2	1	9	0	1.000	2	0--	-	1.95	1.63
2006	Tenn	AA	11	11	0	0	60.0	261	65	32	26	4	3	2	4	23	0	38	2	4	5	4	.556	0	0--	-	4.59	3.90
2007	Mobile	AA	12	12	2	0	69.2	278	64	30	26	7	5	2	2	14	0	62	2	1	5	3	.625	0	0--	-	3.07	3.36
2007	Tucsn	AAA	10	10	1	0	52.1	224	61	27	22	4	0	0	0	18	0	34	3	1	4	2	.667	0	0--	-	4.78	3.78
2008	Scrmto	AAA	1	1	0	0	6.0	25	6	2	2	0	0	1	0	1	0	4	0	0	0	1	.000	0	0--	-	2.49	3.00
2008	Oak	AL	32	32	2	0	190.1	800	169	92	88	21	5	10	3	87	5	111	5	1	7	16	.304	0	0-0	0	3.84	4.16

Jason Smith

Bats: L Throws: R Pos: PR-11; 2B-9; 3B-5; PH-5; DH-4; 1B-1; LF-1   Ht: 6'3" Wt: 200 Born: 7/24/1977 Age: 31

Year	Team	Lg	G	AB	H	2B	3B	HR	(Hm	Rd)	TB	R	RBI	RC	TBB	IBB	SO	HBP	SH	SF	SB	CS	SB%	GDP	Avg	OBP	Slg
2008	Omha*	AAA	110	423	107	20	7	20	(-	-)	201	52	62	60	23	0	128	1	6	6	3	1	.75	4	.253	.289	.475
2001	ChC	NL	2	1	0	0	0	0	(0	0)	0	0	0	0	0	0	1	0	0	0	0	0	-	0	.000	.000	.000
2002	TB	AL	26	65	13	1	2	1	(0	1)	21	9	6	5	2	0	24	0	2	0	3	0	1.00	0	.200	.224	.323
2003	TB	AL	1	4	1	0	0	0	(0	0)	1	0	0	0	0	0	0	0	0	0	0	0	-	0	.250	.250	.250
2004	Det	AL	61	155	37	7	4	5	(0	5)	67	20	19	13	8	0	37	1	5	0	1	2	.33	0	.239	.280	.432
2005	Det	AL	27	58	11	1	2	0	(0	0)	16	4	2	4	0	0	16	1	4	0	2	1	.67	0	.190	.203	.276
2006	Col	NL	49	99	26	1	0	5	(1	4)	42	9	13	15	7	1	29	2	0	0	3	0	1.00	0	.263	.324	.424
2007	3 Tms		69	141	28	3	2	6	(0	6)	53	16	18	11	6	0	53	1	0	1	0	0	-	2	.199	.235	.376
2008	KC	AL	22	28	6	2	0	0	(0	0)	8	6	1	1	0	0	12	0	0	0	0	1	.00	0	.214	.214	.286
07	Tor	AL	27	52	11	1	1	0	(0	0)	14	7	4	3	3	0	22	1	0	0	0	0	-	0	.212	.268	.269
07	Ari	NL	2	4	1	0	0	0	(0	0)	1	0	0	0	0	0	2	0	0	0	0	0	-	0	.250	.250	.250
07	KC	AL	40	85	16	2	1	6	(0	6)	38	9	14	8	3	0	29	0	0	1	0	0	-	2	.188	.213	.447
8 ML YEARS			257	551	122	15	10	17	(1	16)	208	64	59	49	23	1	172	5	11	1	9	4	.69	3	.221	.259	.377

Joe Smith

Pitches: R Bats: R Pos: RP-82   Ht: 6'2" Wt: 210 Born: 3/22/1984 Age: 25

Year	Team	Lg	G	GS	CG	GF	IP	BFP	H	R	ER	HR	SH	SF	HB	TBB	IBB	SO	WP	Bk	W	L	Pct	ShO	Sv-Op	Hld	ERC	ERA
2006	Bklyn	A-	17	0	0	15	20.0	78	10	3	1	0	0	0	4	3	0	28	2	0	0	1	.000	0	9--	-	1.11	0.45
2006	Bnghtn	AA	10	0	0	5	12.2	59	12	8	8	1	2	0	1	11	1	12	1	0	0	2	.000	0	0--	-	5.80	5.68
2007	NewOr	AAA	8	0	0	4	9.0	35	7	3	2	0	0	1	0	4	0	5	0	0	0	0	-	0	2--	-	2.60	2.00
2007	NYM	NL	54	0	0	14	44.1	205	48	18	17	3	2	0	7	21	4	45	2	0	3	2	.600	0	0-0	10	5.04	3.45
2008	NYM	NL	82	0	0	12	63.1	271	51	28	25	4	4	0	4	31	4	52	1	0	6	3	.667	0	0-3	18	3.23	3.55
2 ML YEARS			136	0	0	26	107.2	476	99	46	42	7	6	0	11	52	8	97	3	0	9	5	.643	0	0-3	28	3.95	3.51

Seth Smith

Bats: L Throws: L Pos: PH-43; RF-14; CF-9; LF-8   Ht: 6'3" Wt: 215 Born: 9/30/1982 Age: 26

Year	Team	Lg	G	AB	H	2B	3B	HR	(Hm	Rd)	TB	R	RBI	RC	TBB	IBB	SO	HBP	SH	SF	SB	CS	SB%	GDP	Avg	OBP	Slg
2004	Casper	R+	56	233	86	21	3	9	(-	-)	140	46	61	58	25	0	47	0	0	2	9	1	.90	7	.369	.427	.601
2004	TriCity	A-	9	27	7	1	1	2	(-	-)	16	6	5	4	1	1	3	0	0	1	0	0	-	1	.259	.276	.593
2005	Mdest	A+	129	533	160	45	6	9	(-	-)	244	87	72	87	44	1	115	1	4	3	5	3	.63	16	.300	.353	.458
2006	Tulsa	AA	130	524	154	46	4	15	(-	-)	253	79	71	92	51	1	74	4	3	0	4	4	.50	7	.294	.361	.483
2007	ColSpr	AAA	129	451	143	32	6	17	(-	-)	238	68	82	90	39	0	73	10	1	4	7	3	.70	10	.317	.381	.528
2008	ColSpr	AAA	68	248	80	16	2	10	(-	-)	130	55	53	59	46	0	46	3	0	6	11	0	1.00	8	.323	.426	.524
2007	Col	NL	7	8	5	0	1	0	(0	0)	7	4	0	3	0	0	1	0	0	0	0	0	-	0	.625	.625	.875
2008	Col	NL	67	108	28	7	0	4	(2	2)	47	13	15	18	15	0	23	0	0	0	1	0	1.00	0	.259	.350	.435
	Postseason		6	6	3	1	0	0	(0	0)	4	2	2	2	0	0	1	0	0	0	0	0	-	0	.500	.500	.667
2 ML YEARS			74	116	33	7	1	4	(2	2)	54	17	15	21	15	0	24	0	0	0	1	0	1.00	0	.284	.366	.466

John Smoltz

Pitches: R Bats: R Pos: SP-5; RP-1   Ht: 6'3" Wt: 220 Born: 5/15/1967 Age: 42

Year Team	Lg	G	GS	CG	GF	IP	BFP	H	R	ER	HR	SH	SF	HB	TBB	IBB	SO	WP	Bk	W	L	Pct	ShO	Sv-Op	Hld	ERC	ERA
2008 Missi*	AA	1	0	0	1	1.0	4	1	0	0	0	0	0	0	0	0	0	0	0	0	0	-	0	0--	-	1.95	0.00
2008 Rome*	A	2	1	0	0	3.0	11	1	0	0	0	0	0	0	0	0	4	0	0	0	0	-	0	0--	-	0.23	0.00
1988 Atl	NL	12	12	0	0	64.0	297	74	40	39	10	2	0	2	33	4	37	2	1	2	7	.222	0	0-0	0	5.86	5.48
1989 Atl	NL	29	29	5	0	208.0	847	160	79	68	15	10	7	2	72	2	168	8	3	12	11	.522	0	0-0	0	2.50	2.94
1990 Atl	NL	34	34	6	0	231.1	966	206	109	99	20	9	8	1	90	3	170	14	3	14	11	.560	2	0-0	0	3.37	3.85
1991 Atl	NL	36	36	5	0	229.2	947	206	101	97	16	9	9	3	77	1	148	20	2	14	13	.519	0	0-0	0	3.15	3.80
1992 Atl	NL	35	35	9	0	246.2	1021	206	90	78	17	7	8	5	80	5	215	17	1	15	12	.556	3	0-0	0	2.73	2.85
1993 Atl	NL	35	35	3	0	243.2	1028	208	104	98	23	13	4	6	100	12	208	13	1	15	11	.577	1	0-0	0	3.29	3.62
1994 Atl	NL	21	21	1	0	134.2	568	120	69	62	15	7	6	4	48	4	113	7	0	6	10	.375	0	0-0	0	3.44	4.14
1995 Atl	NL	29	29	2	0	192.2	808	166	76	68	15	13	5	4	72	8	193	13	0	12	7	.632	1	0-0	0	3.08	3.18
1996 Atl	NL	35	35	6	0	253.2	995	199	93	83	19	12	4	2	55	3	276	10	1	24	8	.750	2	0-0	0	2.17	2.94
1997 Atl	NL	35	35	7	0	256.0	1043	234	97	86	21	10	3	1	63	9	241	10	1	15	12	.556	2	0-0	0	2.89	3.02
1998 Atl	NL	26	26	2	0	167.2	681	145	58	54	10	4	2	4	44	2	173	3	1	17	3	.850	2	0-0	0	2.67	2.90
1999 Atl	NL	29	29	1	0	186.1	746	168	70	66	14	10	5	4	40	2	156	2	0	11	8	.579	1	0-0	0	2.81	3.19
2001 Atl	NL	36	5	0	20	59.0	238	53	24	22	7	1	2	2	10	2	57	0	0	3	3	.500	0	10-11	5	2.85	3.36
2002 Atl	NL	75	0	0	68	80.1	314	59	30	29	4	2	1	0	24	1	85	1	1	3	2	.600	0	55-59	0	2.06	3.25
2003 Atl	NL	62	0	0	55	64.1	244	48	9	8	2	0	1	0	8	1	73	2	0	0	2	.000	0	45-49	0	1.50	1.12
2004 Atl	NL	73	0	0	61	81.2	323	75	25	25	8	4	0	1	13	2	85	6	0	0	1	.000	0	44-49	0	2.73	2.76
2005 Atl	NL	33	33	3	0	229.2	931	210	83	78	18	10	3	1	53	7	169	2	1	14	7	.667	1	0-0	0	2.83	3.06
2006 Atl	NL	35	35	3	0	232.0	960	221	93	90	23	4	10	9	55	4	211	5	0	16	9	.640	1	0-0	0	3.32	3.49
2007 Atl	NL	32	32	0	0	205.2	853	196	78	71	18	10	5	4	47	9	197	8	0	14	8	.636	0	0-0	0	3.07	3.11
2008 Atl	NL	6	5	0	0	28.0	117	25	8	8	2	0	0	0	8	1	36	2	0	3	2	.600	0	0-1	0	2.77	2.57
Postseason		40	27	2	11	207.0	846	168	66	61	17	4	3	3	67	6	194	6	0	15	4	.789	1	4-5	0	2.68	2.65
20 ML YEARS		708	466	53	204	3395.0	13927	2979	1336	1229	277	137	83	54	992	82	3011	145	16	210	147	.588	16	154-169	5	2.92	3.26

Ian Snell

Pitches: R Bats: R Pos: SP-31   Ht: 5'11" Wt: 198 Born: 10/30/1981 Age: 27

Year Team	Lg	G	GS	CG	GF	IP	BFP	H	R	ER	HR	SH	SF	HB	TBB	IBB	SO	WP	Bk	W	L	Pct	ShO	Sv-Op	Hld	ERC	ERA
2004 Pit	NL	3	1	0	1	12.0	56	14	10	10	2	0	0	0	9	0	9	0	0	1	0	1.000	0	0-0	0	7.31	7.50
2005 Pit	NL	15	5	0	1	42.0	189	43	25	24	5	2	1	1	24	3	34	4	0	1	2	.333	0	0-0	1	5.03	5.14
2006 Pit	NL	32	32	0	0	186.0	813	198	104	98	29	16	6	2	74	4	169	8	0	14	11	.560	0	0-0	0	4.86	4.74
2007 Pit	NL	32	32	1	0	208.0	882	209	94	87	22	6	7	8	68	4	177	12	0	9	12	.429	0	0-0	0	4.02	3.76
2008 Pit	NL	31	31	0	0	164.1	766	201	107	99	18	7	6	2	89	0	135	8	1	7	12	.368	0	0-0	0	6.11	5.42
5 ML YEARS		113	101	1	3	612.1	2706	665	340	318	76	31	20	13	264	11	524	32	1	31	38	.449	0	0-0	1	4.95	4.67

Chris Snelling

Bats: L Throws: L Pos: PH-4   Ht: 5'10" Wt: 205 Born: 12/3/1981 Age: 27

Year Team	Lg	G	AB	H	2B	3B	HR	(Hm	Rd)	TB	R	RBI	RC	TBB	IBB	SO	HBP	SH	SF	SB	CS	SB%	GDP	Avg	OBP	Slg
2008 LV*	AAA	35	96	22	1	0	1	(-	-)	26	14	8	12	19	0	23	3	0	2	1	0	1.00	3	.229	.367	.271
2008 Clrwtr*	A+	4	14	2	0	0	0	(-	-)	2	4	1	1	3	0	2	1	0	0	0	0	-	0	.143	.333	.143
2002 Sea	AL	8	27	4	0	0	1	(0	1)	7	2	3	3	2	0	4	0	0	0	0	0	-	2	.148	.207	.259
2005 Sea	AL	15	29	8	2	0	1	(1	0)	13	4	1	3	5	0	2	0	1	0	0	2	.00	0	.276	.382	.448
2006 Sea	AL	36	96	24	6	1	3	(2	1)	41	14	8	11	13	0	38	4	5	1	2	1	.67	0	.250	.360	.427
2007 2 Tms		30	69	17	1	1	1	(0	1)	23	10	7	10	14	1	15	3	0	0	0	1	.00	1	.246	.395	.333
2008 Phi	NL	4	4	2	1	0	1	(1	0)	6	1	1	2	0	0	0	0	0	0	0	0	-	0	.500	.500	1.500
07 Was	NL	24	49	10	1	1	1	(0	1)	16	6	7	6	9	1	11	3	0	0	0	1	.00	1	.204	.361	.327
07 Oak	AL	6	20	7	0	0	0	(0	0)	7	4	0	4	5	0	4	0	0	0	0	0	-	0	.350	.480	.350
5 ML YEARS		93	225	55	10	2	7	(4	3)	90	31	20	29	34	1	59	7	6	1	2	4	.33	3	.244	.360	.400

Travis Snider

Bats: L Throws: L Pos: LF-13; RF-7; DH-4; PH-1   Ht: 5'11" Wt: 245 Born: 2/2/1988 Age: 21

Year Team	Lg	G	AB	H	2B	3B	HR	(Hm	Rd)	TB	R	RBI	RC	TBB	IBB	SO	HBP	SH	SF	SB	CS	SB%	GDP	Avg	OBP	Slg
2006 Pulaski	R+	54	194	63	12	1	11	(-	-)	110	36	41	44	30	4	47	0	0	2	6	3	.67	2	.325	.412	.567
2007 Lansng	A	118	457	143	35	7	16	(-	-)	240	72	93	87	49	5	129	3	0	8	3	10	.23	8	.313	.377	.525
2008 Dnedin	A+	17	61	17	5	0	4	(-	-)	34	15	7	11	5	0	22	0	0	0	1	0	1.00	1	.279	.333	.557
2008 NHam	AA	98	362	95	21	0	17	(-	-)	167	65	67	62	52	0	116	4	0	5	1	1	.50	10	.262	.357	.461
2008 Syrcse	AAA	18	64	22	5	0	2	(-	-)	33	9	17	12	4	0	16	1	0	1	1	0	1.00	1	.344	.386	.516
2008 Tor	AL	24	73	22	6	0	2	(1	1)	34	9	13	13	5	0	23	0	0	2	0	0	-	0	.301	.338	.466

J.T. Snow

Bats: L Throws: L Pos: 1B-1   Ht: 6'2" Wt: 210 Born: 2/26/1968 Age: 41

Year Team	Lg	G	AB	H	2B	3B	HR	(Hm	Rd)	TB	R	RBI	RC	TBB	IBB	SO	HBP	SH	SF	SB	CS	SB%	GDP	Avg	OBP	Slg
1992 NYY	AL	7	14	2	1	0	0	(0	0)	3	1	2	2	5	1	5	0	0	0	0	0	-	0	.143	.368	.214
1993 LAA	AL	129	419	101	18	2	16	(10	6)	171	60	57	57	55	4	88	2	7	6	3	0	1.00	10	.241	.328	.408
1994 LAA	AL	61	223	49	4	0	8	(7	1)	77	22	30	22	19	1	48	3	2	1	0	1	.00	2	.220	.289	.345
1995 LAA	AL	143	544	157	22	1	24	(14	10)	253	80	102	85	52	4	91	3	5	2	2	1	.67	16	.289	.353	.465
1996 LAA	AL	155	575	148	20	1	17	(8	9)	221	69	67	67	56	6	96	5	2	3	1	6	.14	19	.257	.327	.384
1997 SF	NL	157	531	149	36	1	28	(14	14)	271	81	104	105	96	13	124	1	2	7	6	4	.60	8	.281	.387	.510
1998 SF	NL	138	435	108	29	1	15	(9	6)	184	65	79	60	58	3	84	0	0	7	1	2	.33	12	.248	.332	.423
1999 SF	NL	161	570	156	25	2	24	(7	17)	257	90	98	93	86	7	121	5	1	6	0	4	.00	16	.274	.370	.451

Year	Team	Lg	G	AB	H	2B	3B	HR	(Hm	Rd)	TB	R	RBI	RC	TBB	IBB	SO	HBP	SH	SF	SB	CS	SB%	GDP	Avg	OBP	Slg
									BATTING												BASERUNNING				AVERAGES		
2000	SF	NL	155	536	152	33	2	19	(10	9)	246	82	96	87	66	6	129	11	0	14	1	3	.25	20	.284	.365	.459
2001	SF	NL	101	285	70	12	1	8	(3	5)	108	43	34	44	55	10	81	4	0	4	0	0	-	2	.246	.371	.379
2002	SF	NL	143	422	104	26	2	6	(1	5)	152	47	53	54	59	5	90	7	0	6	0	0	-	11	.246	.344	.360
2003	SF	NL	103	330	90	18	3	8	(2	6)	138	48	51	59	55	0	55	8	1	2	1	2	.33	7	.273	.387	.418
2004	SF	NL	107	346	113	32	1	12	(5	7)	183	62	60	79	58	0	61	7	2	4	4	0	1.00	5	.327	.429	.529
2005	SF	NL	117	367	101	17	2	4	(1	3)	134	40	40	48	32	1	61	7	2	2	1	0	1.00	6	.275	.343	.365
2006	Bos	AL	38	44	9	0	0	0	(0	0)	9	5	4	5	8	0	8	1	0	0	0	0	-	1	.205	.340	.205
2008	SF	NL	1	0	0	0	0	0	(0	0)	0	0	0	0	0	0	0	0	0	0	0	0	-	0	-	-	-
	Postseason		28	98	32	4	1	3	(1	2)	47	11	15	16	9	3	15	0	0	0	0	0	-	1	.327	.383	.480
	16 ML YEARS		1716	5641	1509	293	19	189	(91	98)	2407	798	877	867	760	61	1142	64	24	64	20	23	.47	135	.268	.357	.427

Chris Snyder

Bats: R **Throws:** R **Pos:** C-112; PH-5   **Ht:** 6'4" **Wt:** 245 **Born:** 2/12/1981 **Age:** 28

Year	Team	Lg	G	AB	H	2B	3B	HR	(Hm	Rd)	TB	R	RBI	RC	TBB	IBB	SO	HBP	SH	SF	SB	CS	SB%	GDP	Avg	OBP	Slg
									BATTING												BASERUNNING				AVERAGES		
2008	Visalia*	A+	1	5	2	0	0	1	(-	-)	5	1	4	1	0	0	2	0	0	0	0	0	-	0	.400	.400	1.000
2004	Ari	NL	29	96	23	6	0	5	(1	4)	44	10	15	11	13	1	25	0	0	1	0	0	-	0	.240	.327	.458
2005	Ari	NL	115	326	66	14	0	6	(2	4)	98	24	28	25	40	5	87	4	3	0	0	1	.00	6	.202	.297	.301
2006	Ari	NL	61	184	51	9	0	6	(4	2)	78	19	32	27	22	4	39	1	1	5	0	0	-	5	.277	.349	.424
2007	Ari	NL	110	326	82	20	0	13	(4	9)	141	37	47	48	40	3	67	7	3	4	0	1	.00	9	.252	.342	.433
2008	Ari	NL	115	334	79	22	1	16	(6	10)	151	47	64	53	56	5	101	4	5	5	0	0	-	7	.237	.348	.452
	Postseason		6	19	5	2	0	1	(0	1)	10	3	3	2	2	0	6	0	0	0	0	0	-	3	.263	.333	.526
	5 ML YEARS		430	1266	301	71	1	46	(17	29)	512	137	186	164	171	18	319	16	12	15	0	2	.00	27	.238	.332	.404

Kyle Snyder

Pitches: R **Bats:** B **Pos:** RP-2   **Ht:** 6'8" **Wt:** 230 **Born:** 9/9/1977 **Age:** 31

Year	Team	Lg	G	GS	CG	GF	IP	BFP	H	R	ER	HR	SH	SF	HB	TBB	IBB	SO	WP	Bk	W	L	Pct	ShO	Sv-Op	Hld	ERC	ERA
			HOW MUCH HE PITCHED						WHAT HE GAVE UP												THE RESULTS							
2008	Pwtckt*	AAA	14	7	0	4	37.2	165	34	23	22	5	0	2	6	12	0	30	3	1	1	4	.200	0	1--	-	3.98	5.26
2008	RedSx*	R	6	3	0	0	10.2	40	8	4	4	1	0	0	0	1	0	12	2	0	0	0	-	0	0--	-	1.71	3.38
2008	Lowell*	A-	1	1	0	0	2.1	9	1	2	0	0	0	0	0	0	0	1	0	0	0	0	-	0	0--	-	0.36	0.00
2003	KC	AL	15	15	0	0	85.1	364	94	52	49	11	0	9	2	21	3	39	4	0	1	6	.143	0	0-0	0	4.29	5.17
2005	KC	AL	13	3	0	4	36.0	169	55	29	27	3	0	2	1	10	1	19	1	0	1	3	.250	0	0-0	0	6.70	6.75
2006	2 Tms	AL	17	11	0	3	60.1	287	87	51	44	12	0	2	2	20	3	57	3	0	4	5	.444	0	0-0	1	7.21	6.56
2007	Bos	AL	46	0	0	17	54.1	242	45	29	23	7	1	1	6	32	2	41	4	0	2	3	.400	0	0-0	1	4.41	3.81
2008	Bos	AL	2	0	0	0	1.2	9	2	4	4	1	1	0	0	2	0	1	1	0	0	0	-	0	0-1	0	13.35	21.60
06	KC	AL	1	1	0	0	2.0	19	10	9	5	1	0	0	0	1	0	2	0	0	0	0	-	0	0-0	0	36.36	22.50
06	Bos	AL	16	10	0	3	58.1	268	77	42	39	11	0	2	2	19	3	55	3	0	4	5	.444	0	0-0	1	6.38	6.02
	5 ML YEARS		93	29	0	24	237.2	1071	283	165	147	34	2	14	11	85	9	157	13	0	8	17	.320	0	0-1	2	5.44	5.57

Andy Sonnanstine

Pitches: R **Bats:** L **Pos:** SP-32   **Ht:** 6'3" **Wt:** 185 **Born:** 3/18/1983 **Age:** 26

Year	Team	Lg	G	GS	CG	GF	IP	BFP	H	R	ER	HR	SH	SF	HB	TBB	IBB	SO	WP	Bk	W	L	Pct	ShO	Sv-Op	Hld	ERC	ERA
			HOW MUCH HE PITCHED						WHAT HE GAVE UP												THE RESULTS							
2004	HudVal	A-	9	2	0	1	27.0	105	18	4	3	0	0	0	0	3	0	24	0	0	3	1	.750	0	1--	-	1.09	1.00
2004	CtnSC	A	8	5	0	1	30.2	116	18	5	2	0	1	0	0	7	0	42	0	0	2	0	1.000	0	0--	-	1.14	0.59
2005	SWMch	A	18	18	1	0	116.2	461	103	42	33	10	2	2	2	11	0	103	5	0	10	4	.714	0	0--	-	2.29	2.55
2005	Visalia	A+	10	10	0	0	64.0	266	71	29	27	5	0	2	1	7	0	75	2	0	4	1	.800	0	0--	-	3.45	3.80
2006	Mont	AA	28	28	4	0	185.2	721	151	63	55	15	3	4	5	34	1	152	3	0	15	8	.652	4	0--	-	2.33	2.67
2007	Drham	AAA	11	11	0	0	71.0	283	60	24	21	8	3	1	2	13	0	66	2	0	6	4	.600	0	0--	-	2.63	2.66
2007	TB	AL	22	22	0	0	130.2	554	151	87	85	18	3	5	5	26	2	97	2	0	6	10	.375	0	0-0	0	4.62	5.85
2008	TB	AL	32	32	1	0	193.1	819	212	105	94	21	4	9	5	37	2	124	6	0	13	9	.591	1	0-0	0	3.92	4.38
	2 ML YEARS		54	54	1	0	324.0	1373	363	192	179	39	7	14	10	63	4	221	8	0	19	19	.500	1	0-0	0	4.20	4.97

Joakim Soria

Pitches: R **Bats:** R **Pos:** RP-63   **Ht:** 6'3" **Wt:** 185 **Born:** 5/18/1984 **Age:** 25

Year	Team	Lg	G	GS	CG	GF	IP	BFP	H	R	ER	HR	SH	SF	HB	TBB	IBB	SO	WP	Bk	W	L	Pct	ShO	Sv-Op	Hld	ERC	ERA
			HOW MUCH HE PITCHED						WHAT HE GAVE UP												THE RESULTS							
2002	Ddgrs	R	4	0	0	2	5.0	21	6	2	2	0	0	0	0	0	0	6	0	0	0	0	-	0	0--	-	2.89	3.60
2006	FtWyn	A	7	0	0	2	11.2	40	5	3	3	1	0	0	0	2	0	11	0	0	1	0	1.000	0	0--	-	0.93	2.31
2007	KC	AL	62	0	0	38	69.0	270	46	20	19	3	1	3	1	19	3	75	2	0	2	3	.400	0	17-21	9	1.63	2.48
2008	KC	AL	63	0	0	57	67.1	260	39	13	12	5	2	2	6	19	1	66	1	1	2	3	.400	0	42-45	0	1.72	1.60
	2 ML YEARS		125	0	0	95	136.1	530	85	33	31	8	3	5	7	38	4	141	3	1	4	6	.400	0	59-66	9	1.67	2.05

Alfonso Soriano

Bats: R **Throws:** R **Pos:** LF-108; PH-2; 2B-1   **Ht:** 6'1" **Wt:** 180 **Born:** 1/7/1976 **Age:** 33

Year	Team	Lg	G	AB	H	2B	3B	HR	(Hm	Rd)	TB	R	RBI	RC	TBB	IBB	SO	HBP	SH	SF	SB	CS	SB%	GDP	Avg	OBP	Slg
									BATTING												BASERUNNING				AVERAGES		
2008	Cubs*	R	1	2	0	0	0	0	(Hm	Rd)	0	1	0	2	1	0	1	0	0	0	0	0	-	0	.000	.333	.000
2008	Iowa*	AAA	1	3	1	0	0	0	(-	-)	1	0	0	0	0	0	1	0	0	0	0	0	-	0	.333	.333	.333
1999	NYY	AL	9	8	1	0	0	1	(1	0)	4	2	1	0	0	0	3	0	0	0	0	1	.00	0	.125	.125	.500
2000	NYY	AL	22	50	9	3	0	2	(0	2)	18	5	3	4	1	0	15	0	2	0	2	0	1.00	0	.180	.196	.360
2001	NYY	AL	158	574	154	34	3	18	(8	10)	248	77	73	77	29	0	125	3	3	5	43	14	.75	7	.268	.304	.432
2002	NYY	AL	156	696	209	51	2	39	(17	22)	381	128	102	121	23	1	157	14	1	7	41	13	.76	8	.300	.332	.547
2003	NYY	AL	156	682	198	36	5	38	(15	23)	358	114	91	110	38	7	130	12	0	2	35	8	.81	8	.290	.338	.525

Year	Team	Lg	G	AB	H	2B	3B	HR	(Hm	Rd)	TB	R	RBI	RC	TBB	IBB	SO	HBP	SH	SF	SB	CS	SB%	GDP	Avg	OBP	Slg
2004	Tex	AL	145	608	170	32	4	28	(12	16)	294	77	91	90	33	4	121	10	0	7	18	5	.78	7	.280	.324	.484
2005	Tex	AL	156	637	171	43	2	36	(25	11)	326	102	104	93	33	3	125	7	0	5	30	2	**.94**	6	.268	.309	.512
2006	Was	NL	159	647	179	41	2	46	(24	22)	362	119	95	114	67	16	160	9	2	3	41	17	.71	3	.277	.351	.560
2007	ChC	NL	135	579	173	42	5	33	(13	20)	324	97	70	91	31	4	130	4	0	3	19	6	.76	9	.299	.337	.560
2008	ChC	NL	109	453	127	27	0	29	(17	12)	241	76	75	77	43	11	103	3	0	4	19	3	.86	9	.280	.344	.532
Postseason			41	160	36	3	0	4	(3	1)	51	14	18	14	9	0	49	3	0	0	10	3	.77	3	.225	.279	.319
10 ML YEARS			1205	4934	1391	309	23	270	(132	138)	2556	797	705	777	298	46	1069	62	8	36	248	69	.78	57	.282	.329	.518

Rafael Soriano

Pitches: R Bats: R Pos: RP-14

Ht: 6'1" Wt: 220 Born: 12/19/1979 Age: 29

	HOW MUCH HE PITCHED						WHAT HE GAVE UP											THE RESULTS						
Year	Team	Lg	G	GS	CG	GF	IP	BFP	H	R	ER	HR	SH	SF	HB	TBB	IBB	SO	WP	Bk	W	L	Pct	ShO	Sv-Op	Hld	ERC	ERA
2008	Missi*	AA	2	1	0	0	2.0	7	1	0	0	0	0	0	0	1	0	2	0	0	0	0	-	0	0- -	-	1.62	0.00
2002	Sea	AL	10	8	0	1	47.1	202	45	25	24	8	1	0	0	16	1	32	2	0	0	3	.000	0	1-1	0	3.93	4.56
2003	Sea	AL	40	0	0	12	53.0	201	30	9	9	2	0	1	3	12	1	68	0	0	3	0	1.000	0	1-2	5	1.32	1.53
2004	Sea	AL	6	0	0	0	3.1	23	9	6	5	0	0	0	0	3	0	3	0	0	0	3	.000	0	0-1	0	15.97	13.50
2005	Sea	AL	7	0	0	4	7.1	30	6	2	2	0	0	1	1	1	0	9	0	0	0	0	-	0	0-0	1	2.00	2.45
2006	Sea	AL	53	0	0	14	60.0	241	44	15	15	6	1	1	2	21	0	65	2	0	1	2	.333	0	2-6	18	2.64	2.25
2007	Atl	NL	71	0	0	28	72.0	276	47	26	24	12	0	0	2	21	5	70	0	0	3	3	.500	0	9-12	19	2.05	3.00
2008	Atl	NL	14	0	0	5	14.0	57	7	5	4	1	0	0	1	2	0	16	1	0	0	1	.000	0	3-4	0	2.27	2.57
7 ML YEARS			201	8	0	64	257.0	1030	188	88	83	29	2	3	9	77	6	263	5	0	7	12	.368	0	16-26	43	2.47	2.91

Jorge Sosa

Pitches: R Bats: R Pos: RP-20

Ht: 6'2" Wt: 218 Born: 4/28/1977 Age: 32

	HOW MUCH HE PITCHED						WHAT HE GAVE UP											THE RESULTS						
Year	Team	Lg	G	GS	CG	GF	IP	BFP	H	R	ER	HR	SH	SF	HB	TBB	IBB	SO	WP	Bk	W	L	Pct	ShO	Sv-Op	Hld	ERC	ERA
2008	RdRck*	AAA	17	0	0	11	21.2	93	20	11	10	5	0	1	0	8	0	24	1	0	1	2	.333	0	2- -	-	4.32	4.15
2008	Tacom*	AAA	10	0	0	5	14.2	70	14	6	6	0	1	1	1	13	1	12	0	0	1	0	1.000	0	2- -	-	5.07	3.68
2002	TB	AL	31	14	0	10	99.1	434	88	63	61	16	0	5	2	54	0	48	5	0	2	7	.222	0	0-0	1	4.51	5.53
2003	TB	AL	29	19	1	4	128.2	566	137	71	66	14	4	5	4	60	4	72	8	1	5	12	.294	1	0-0	0	4.93	4.62
2004	TB	AL	43	8	0	6	99.1	447	100	67	61	17	2	4	1	54	3	94	2	0	4	7	.364	0	1-1	6	5.17	5.53
2005	Atl	NL	44	20	0	5	134.0	577	122	42	38	12	5	2	0	64	4	85	3	0	13	3	**.813**	0	0-0	4	3.70	2.55
2006	2 Tms	NL	45	13	0	12	118.0	524	138	79	71	30	7	4	1	40	6	75	2	0	3	11	.214	0	4-7	0	5.88	5.42
2007	NYM	NL	42	14	0	2	112.2	481	109	58	56	10	10	3	0	41	2	69	0	0	9	8	.529	0	0-2	5	3.63	4.47
2008	NYM	NL	20	0	0	8	21.2	107	30	23	17	4	3	0	0	11	4	12	2	0	4	1	.800	0	0-0	1	6.95	7.06
06	Atl	NL	26	13	0	8	87.1	394	105	61	53	20	5	4	1	32	5	58	2	0	3	10	.231	0	3-6	0	6.00	5.46
06	StL	NL	19	0	0	4	30.2	130	33	18	18	10	2	0	0	8	1	17	0	0	0	1	.000	0	1-1	0	5.48	5.28
Postseason			1	1	0	0	6.0	27	7	3	3	1	0	1	1	2	2	3	0	0	0	1	.000	0	0-0	0	5.45	4.50
7 ML YEARS			254	88	1	47	713.2	3136	724	403	370	103	31	23	8	324	27	455	22	1	40	49	.449	1	5-10	21	4.67	4.67

Geovany Soto

Bats: R Throws: R Pos: C-136; PH-6; DH-3

Ht: 6'1" Wt: 225 Born: 1/20/1983 Age: 26

			BATTING																		BASERUNNING				AVERAGES		
Year	Team	Lg	G	AB	H	2B	3B	HR	(Hm	Rd)	TB	R	RBI	RC	TBB	IBB	SO	HBP	SH	SF	SB	CS	SB%	GDP	Avg	OBP	Slg
2005	ChC	NL	1	1	0	0	0	0	(0	0)	0	0	0	0	0	0	0	0	0	0	0	0	-	0	.000	.000	.000
2006	ChC	NL	11	25	5	1	0	0	(0	0)	6	1	2	0	0	0	5	1	0	0	0	0	-	0	.200	.231	.240
2007	ChC	NL	18	54	21	6	0	3	(2	1)	36	12	8	13	5	0	14	0	0	1	0	0	-	1	.389	.433	.667
2008	ChC	NL	141	494	141	35	2	23	(11	12)	249	66	86	81	62	6	121	2	0	5	0	1	.00	11	.285	.364	.504
Postseason			2	6	1	0	0	1	(0	1)	4	1	2	1	2	0	1	0	0	0	0	0	-	0	.167	.375	.667
4 ML YEARS			171	574	167	42	2	26	(13	13)	291	79	96	94	67	6	140	3	0	6	0	1	.00	12	.291	.365	.507

Jeremy Sowers

Pitches: L Bats: L Pos: SP-22

Ht: 6'1" Wt: 180 Born: 5/17/1983 Age: 26

	HOW MUCH HE PITCHED						WHAT HE GAVE UP											THE RESULTS						
Year	Team	Lg	G	GS	CG	GF	IP	BFP	H	R	ER	HR	SH	SF	HB	TBB	IBB	SO	WP	Bk	W	L	Pct	ShO	Sv-Op	Hld	ERC	ERA
2008	Buffalo*	AAA	10	10	1	0	60.2	245	56	16	14	4	4	1	0	17	0	43	0	0	4	3	.571	0	0- -	-	3.06	2.08
2006	Cle	AL	14	14	2	0	88.1	360	85	36	35	10	1	0	2	20	1	35	1	0	7	4	.636	2	0-0	0	3.41	3.57
2007	Cle	AL	13	13	0	0	67.1	303	84	49	48	10	0	5	4	21	2	24	3	0	1	6	.143	0	0-0	0	5.75	6.42
2008	Cle	AL	22	22	0	0	121.0	533	141	84	75	18	3	4	3	39	1	64	3	1	4	9	.308	0	0-0	0	5.17	5.58
3 ML YEARS			49	49	2	0	276.2	1196	310	169	158	38	4	9	9	80	4	123	7	1	12	19	.387	2	0-0	0	4.72	5.14

Denard Span

Bats: L Throws: L Pos: RF-85; CF-19; PR-2

Ht: 6'0" Wt: 205 Born: 2/27/1984 Age: 25

			BATTING																		BASERUNNING				AVERAGES		
Year	Team	Lg	G	AB	H	2B	3B	HR	(Hm	Rd)	TB	R	RBI	RC	TBB	IBB	SO	HBP	SH	SF	SB	CS	SB%	GDP	Avg	OBP	Slg
2003	Elizab	R+	50	207	56	5	1	1	(-	-)	66	34	18	26	23	0	34	4	0	0	14	5	.74	2	.271	.355	.319
2004	QuadC	A	64	240	64	4	3	0	(-	-)	74	29	14	31	34	0	49	3	4	1	15	8	.65	2	.267	.363	.308
2005	FtMyrs	A+	49	186	63	3	3	1	(-	-)	75	38	19	33	22	0	25	1	2	1	13	4	.76	3	.339	.410	.403
2005	NwBrit	AA	68	267	76	6	5	0	(-	-)	92	47	26	34	22	1	41	8	5	2	10	8	.56	2	.285	.355	.345
2006	NwBrit	AA	134	536	153	16	6	2	(-	-)	187	80	45	68	40	0	78	5	15	1	25	11	.69	11	.285	.340	.349
2007	Roch	AAA	139	487	130	20	7	3	(-	-)	173	59	55	58	40	1	90	0	21	0	25	14	.64	10	.267	.323	.355
2008	Roch	AAA	40	156	53	11	1	3	(-	-)	75	32	14	33	26	1	36	0	2	0	15	8	.65	1	.340	.434	.481
2008	Min	AL	93	347	102	16	7	6	(2	4)	150	70	47	68	50	3	60	4	8	2	18	7	.72	3	.294	.387	.432

Justin Speier

Pitches: R Bats: R Pos: RP-62   Ht: 6'4" Wt: 205 Born: 11/6/1973 Age: 35

Year	Team	Lg	HOW MUCH HE PITCHED						WHAT HE GAVE UP												THE RESULTS							
			G	GS	CG	GF	IP	BFP	H	R	ER	HR	SH	SF	HB	TBB	IBB	SO	WP	Bk	W	L	Pct	ShO	Sv-Op	Hld	ERC	ERA
1998	2 Tms	NL	19	0	0	10	20.2	99	27	20	20	7	2	1	0	13	1	17	3	0	0	3	.000	0	0-1	1	8.94	8.71
1999	Atl	NL	19	0	0	8	28.2	127	28	18	18	8	0	1	0	13	1	22	0	0	0	0	-	0	0-0	0	5.27	5.65
2000	Cle	AL	47	0	0	12	68.1	290	57	27	25	9	2	4	4	28	3	69	7	1	5	2	.714	0	0-1	6	3.56	3.29
2001	2 Tms	AL	54	0	0	10	76.2	324	71	40	39	13	2	7	8	20	3	62	6	1	6	3	.667	0	0-1	4	3.93	4.58
2002	Col	NL	63	0	0	7	62.1	259	51	31	30	9	0	1	3	19	4	47	1	2	5	1	.833	0	1-4	18	3.06	4.33
2003	Col	NL	72	0	0	31	73.1	319	73	37	33	11	1	4	7	23	6	66	0	0	3	1	.750	0	9-12	12	4.27	4.05
2004	Tor	AL	62	0	0	32	69.0	294	61	32	30	8	6	3	5	25	6	52	4	0	3	8	.273	0	7-11	7	3.52	3.91
2005	Tor	AL	65	0	0	36	66.2	264	48	20	19	10	4	0	3	15	2	56	1	1	3	2	.600	0	0-4	11	2.38	2.57
2006	Tor	AL	58	0	0	8	51.1	222	47	18	17	5	0	0	1	21	3	55	4	0	2	0	1.000	0	0-3	25	3.55	2.98
2007	LAA	AL	51	0	0	9	50.0	198	36	17	16	6	2	2	4	12	1	47	2	0	2	3	.400	0	0-1	24	2.43	2.88
2008	LAA	AL	62	0	0	19	68.0	305	69	41	38	15	4	4	6	27	5	56	8	0	2	8	.200	0	0-2	10	5.17	5.03
98	ChC	NL	1	0	0	0	1.1	7	2	2	2	0	0	0	0	1	0	2	1	0	0	0	-	0	0-0	0	7.52	13.50
98	Fla	NL	18	0	0	10	19.1	92	25	18	18	7	2	1	0	12	1	15	2	0	0	3	.000	0	0-1	1	9.02	8.38
01	Cle	AL	12	0	0	2	20.2	96	24	16	16	5	0	3	3	8	0	15	2	0	2	0	1.000	0	0-0	0	6.61	6.97
01	Col	NL	42	0	0	8	56.0	228	47	24	23	8	2	4	5	12	3	47	4	1	4	3	.571	0	0-1	4	3.04	3.70
Postseason			2	0	0	0	1.2	10	4	5	5	0	0	1	0	1	0	0	0	0	0	1	.000	0	0-0	0	13.02	27.00
11 ML YEARS			572	0	0	182	635.0	2701	568	301	285	101	23	27	41	216	35	549	36	5	31	31	.500	0	17-40	118	3.79	4.04

Ryan Speier

Pitches: R Bats: R Pos: RP-43   Ht: 6'7" Wt: 210 Born: 7/24/1979 Age: 29

Year	Team	Lg	HOW MUCH HE PITCHED						WHAT HE GAVE UP												THE RESULTS							
			G	GS	CG	GF	IP	BFP	H	R	ER	HR	SH	SF	HB	TBB	IBB	SO	WP	Bk	W	L	Pct	ShO	Sv-Op	Hld	ERC	ERA
2008	ColSpr*	AAA	11	0	0	10	13.1	53	10	3	3	1	1	0	0	4	0	9	1	1	1	0	1.000	0	5--	-	2.27	2.03
2008	Ashvll*	A	2	0	0	0	1.2	9	1	2	2	0	1	0	1	2	0	3	1	0	0	0	-	0	0--	-	3.47	10.80
2005	Col	NL	22	0	0	10	24.2	111	26	12	10	0	2	1	1	13	0	10	2	0	2	1	.667	0	0-1	2	4.29	3.65
2007	Col	NL	20	0	0	5	18.0	77	20	8	8	1	1	0	1	8	1	13	2	1	3	1	.750	0	0-1	2	4.95	4.00
2008	Col	NL	43	0	0	8	51.0	217	52	23	23	3	1	3	4	18	2	33	2	0	2	1	.667	0	0-1	3	4.05	4.06
Postseason			3	0	0	1	2.1	11	1	1	0	0	0	0	0	3	0	1	0	0	0	0	-	0	1-1	0	3.36	0.00
3 ML YEARS			85	0	0	23	93.2	405	98	43	41	4	4	4	6	39	3	56	6	1	7	3	.700	0	0-3	7	4.28	3.94

Levale Speigner

Pitches: R Bats: R Pos: RP-7   Ht: 5'11" Wt: 175 Born: 9/24/1980 Age: 28

Year	Team	Lg	HOW MUCH HE PITCHED						WHAT HE GAVE UP												THE RESULTS							
			G	GS	CG	GF	IP	BFP	H	R	ER	HR	SH	SF	HB	TBB	IBB	SO	WP	Bk	W	L	Pct	ShO	Sv-Op	Hld	ERC	ERA
2003	Elizab	R+	22	0	0	19	29.2	122	31	13	13	1	0	0	1	4	0	35	2	0	5	2	.714	0	4--	-	3.01	3.94
2004	QuadC	A	22	0	0	15	31.2	144	27	14	10	1	1	1	2	15	4	29	3	0	2	2	.500	0	9--	-	2.90	2.84
2004	FtMyrs	A+	22	1	0	7	73.1	201	46	15	9	3	1	0	2	14	1	49	3	0	4	3	.571	0	2--	-	1.98	1.10
2005	NwBrit	AA	23	23	2	0	143.2	605	149	75	66	14	5	2	12	28	1	94	1	1	6	10	.375	1	0--	-	3.79	4.13
2005	Roch	AAA	2	1	0	0	7.1	38	14	7	6	0	0	2	0	1	0	5	0	0	1	0	1.000	0	0--	-	7.29	7.36
2006	NwBrit	AA	40	0	0	31	58.0	252	61	27	21	5	4	2	3	14	1	37	0	0	3	2	.600	0	13--	-	3.73	3.26
2006	Roch	AAA	9	0	0	4	12.2	60	16	7	7	1	1	0	0	5	1	8	0	0	1	1	.500	0	1--	-	5.05	4.97
2007	Clmbs	AAA	17	6	0	1	49.0	230	63	30	27	1	2	4	1	20	1	33	1	0	3	4	.429	0	0--	-	5.08	4.96
2008	Hrsbrg	AA	10	0	0	2	14.2	56	8	1	1	0	1	0	0	5	0	4	2	0	1	0	1.000	0	0--	-	1.25	0.61
2008	Clmbs	AAA	25	1	0	7	44.2	172	36	13	11	3	2	0	0	8	2	36	0	0	3	0	1.000	0	0--	-	2.06	2.22
2007	Was	NL	19	6	0	3	40.0	198	58	39	39	4	2	3	0	23	2	19	1	0	2	3	.400	0	0-0	0	7.38	8.78
2008	Was	NL	7	0	0	2	8.0	42	13	10	10	1	1	0	2	6	1	1	0	0	0	1	.000	0	0-0	0	11.19	11.25
2 ML YEARS			26	6	0	5	48.0	240	71	49	49	5	3	3	2	29	3	20	1	0	2	4	.333	0	0-0	0	7.98	9.19

Ryan Spilborghs

Bats: R Throws: R Pos: PH-31; LF-22; RF-22; CF-17; DH-4   Ht: 6'1" Wt: 190 Born: 9/5/1979 Age: 29

Year	Team	Lg	BATTING																		BASERUNNING				AVERAGES		
			G	AB	H	2B	3B	HR	(Hm	Rd)	TB	R	RBI	RC	TBB	IBB	SO	HBP	SH	SF	SB	CS	SB%	GDP	Avg	OBP	Slg
2008	ColSpr*	AAA	11	30	9	1	0	1	(-	-)	13	9	4	5	5	0	6	0	0	1	0	1	.00	2	.300	.389	.433
2005	Col	NL	1	4	2	0	0	0	(0	0)	2	0	1	1	0	0	1	0	0	0	0	0	-	0	.500	.500	.500
2006	Col	NL	67	167	48	6	3	4	(3	1)	72	26	21	22	14	0	30	0	2	3	5	2	.71	7	.287	.337	.431
2007	Col	NL	97	264	79	14	1	11	(5	6)	128	40	51	48	28	1	45	2	0	6	4	1	.80	5	.299	.363	.485
2008	Col	NL	89	233	73	14	2	6	(3	3)	109	38	36	42	38	0	41	1	0	3	7	4	.64	8	.313	.407	.468
Postseason			9	20	3	0	0	0	(0	0)	3	3	0	1	5	0	7	0	0	0	0	0	-	0	.150	.320	.150
4 ML YEARS			254	668	202	34	6	21	(11	10)	311	104	109	113	80	1	117	3	2	12	16	7	.70	20	.302	.374	.466

Russ Springer

Pitches: R Bats: R Pos: RP-70   Ht: 6'4" Wt: 225 Born: 11/7/1968 Age: 40

Year	Team	Lg	HOW MUCH HE PITCHED						WHAT HE GAVE UP												THE RESULTS							
			G	GS	CG	GF	IP	BFP	H	R	ER	HR	SH	SF	HB	TBB	IBB	SO	WP	Bk	W	L	Pct	ShO	Sv-Op	Hld	ERC	ERA
1992	NYY	AL	14	0	0	5	16.0	75	18	11	11	0	0	0	0	10	0	12	0	0	0	0	-	0	0-0	2	5.15	6.19
1993	LAA	AL	14	9	1	3	60.0	278	73	48	48	11	1	1	3	32	1	31	6	0	1	6	.143	0	0-0	0	6.87	7.20
1994	LAA	AL	18	5	0	6	45.2	198	53	28	28	9	1	1	0	14	0	28	2	0	2	2	.500	0	2-3	1	5.38	5.52
1995	2 Tms	AL	33	6	0	6	78.1	350	82	48	46	16	2	2	7	35	4	70	2	0	2	2	.333	0	1-2	0	5.63	5.29
1996	Phi	NL	51	7	0	12	96.2	437	106	60	50	12	5	3	1	38	6	94	5	0	3	10	.231	0	0-3	6	4.57	4.66
1997	Hou	NL	54	0	0	13	55.1	241	48	28	26	4	1	2	4	27	2	74	4	0	3	3	.500	0	3-7	9	3.69	4.23
1998	2 Tms	NL	48	0	0	14	52.2	232	51	26	24	4	2	1	4	30	4	56	5	0	5	4	.556	0	0-4	4	4.38	4.10
1999	Atl	NL	49	0	0	8	47.1	194	31	20	18	5	0	2	2	22	2	49	0	0	2	1	.667	0	1-1	8	2.63	3.42
2000	Ari	NL	52	0	0	10	62.0	282	63	36	35	11	2	3	2	34	6	59	3	0	2	4	.333	0	0-2	3	5.25	5.08
2001	Ari	NL	18	0	0	9	17.2	79	20	16	14	5	1	1	0	4	0	12	2	0	0	0	-	0	1-1	2	5.13	7.13

	HOW MUCH HE PITCHED						WHAT HE GAVE UP												THE RESULTS						
Year	Team	Lg	G	GS	CG	GF	IP	BFP	H	R	ER	HR	SH	SF	HB	TBB	IBB	SO	WP	Bk	W	L	Pct	ShO	Sv-Op	Hld	ERC	ERA
2003	StL	NL	17	0	0	4	17.1	77	19	16	16	8	0	0	1	6	0	11	1	0	1	1	.500	0	0-1	5	7.27	8.31
2004	Hou	NL	16	0	0	3	13.2	62	15	4	4	1	0	0	1	6	0	9	2	0	0	1	.000	0	0-0	5	4.84	2.63
2005	Hou	NL	62	0	0	11	59.0	246	49	34	31	9	1	0	3	21	3	54	2	0	4	4	.500	0	0-3	10	3.45	4.73
2006	Hou	NL	72	0	0	17	59.2	240	46	23	23	10	2	0	4	16	1	46	2	0	1	1	.500	0	0-0	9	3.03	3.47
2007	StL	NL	76	0	0	18	66.0	257	41	18	16	3	3	6	3	19	1	66	1	0	8	1	.889	0	0-2	11	1.63	2.18
2008	StL	NL	70	0	0	9	50.1	205	39	14	13	4	2	0	1	18	0	45	2	0	2	1	.667	0	0-2	15	2.68	2.32
95	LAA	AL	19	6	0	3	51.2	238	60	37	35	11	1	0	5	25	1	38	1	0	1	2	.333	0	1-2	0	6.69	6.10
95	Phi	AL	14	0	0	3	26.2	112	22	11	11	5	1	2	2	10	3	32	1	0	0	0	-	0	0-0	0	3.73	3.71
98	Ari	NL	26	0	0	13	32.2	140	29	16	15	4	0	0	1	14	1	37	3	0	4	3	.571	0	0-3	1	3.77	4.13
98	Atl	NL	22	0	0	1	20.0	92	22	10	9	0	2	1	0	16	3	19	2	0	1	1	.500	0	0-1	6	5.36	4.05
	Postseason		14	0	0	4	14.1	63	15	7	7	1	0	1	0	6	0	14	0	0	1	1	.500	0	0-0	0	4.51	4.40
16 ML YEARS			664	27	1	148	797.2	3453	754	430	403	112	23	23	34	332	30	716	39	0	35	41	.461	0	8-31	93	4.21	4.55

Matt Stairs

Bats: L **Throws:** R **Pos:** DH-81; PH-28; RF-10; LF-9   **Ht:** 5'9" **Wt:** 215 **Born:** 2/27/1968 **Age:** 41

							BATTING															BASERUNNING				AVERAGES		
Year	Team	Lg	G	AB	H	2B	3B	HR	(Hm	Rd)	TB	R	RBI	RC	TBB	IBB	SO	HBP	SH	SF	SB	CS	SB%	GDP	Avg	OBP	Slg
1992	Mon	NL	13	30	5	2	0	0	(0	0)	7	2	5	3	7	0	7	0	0	1	0	0	-	0	.167	.316	.233
1993	Mon	NL	6	8	3	1	0	0	(0	0)	4	1	2	1	0	0	1	0	0	0	0	0	-	1	.375	.375	.500
1995	Bos	AL	39	88	23	7	1	1	(0	1)	35	8	17	9	4	0	14	1	1	1	0	1	.00	4	.261	.298	.398
1996	Oak	AL	61	137	38	5	1	10	(5	5)	75	21	23	27	19	2	23	1	0	1	1	1	.50	2	.277	.367	.547
1997	Oak	AL	133	352	105	19	0	27	(20	7)	205	62	73	77	50	1	60	3	1	4	3	2	.60	6	.298	.386	.582
1998	Oak	AL	149	523	154	33	1	26	(16	10)	267	88	106	96	59	4	93	6	1	4	8	3	.73	13	.294	.370	.511
1999	Oak	AL	146	531	137	26	3	38	(15	23)	283	94	102	101	89	6	124	2	0	1	2	7	.22	8	.258	.366	.533
2000	Oak	AL	143	476	108	26	0	21	(9	12)	197	74	81	69	78	4	122	1	1	6	5	2	.71	7	.227	.333	.414
2001	ChC	NL	128	340	85	21	0	17	(5	12)	157	48	61	57	52	7	76	7	1	3	2	3	.40	4	.250	.358	.462
2002	Mil	NL	107	270	66	15	0	16	(6	10)	129	41	41	38	36	4	50	8	0	1	2	0	1.00	7	.244	.349	.478
2003	Pit	NL	121	305	89	20	1	20	(13	7)	171	49	57	58	45	3	64	5	0	2	0	1	.00	7	.292	.389	.561
2004	KC	AL	126	439	117	21	3	18	(6	12)	198	48	66	65	49	2	92	5	0	3	1	0	1.00	15	.267	.345	.451
2005	KC	AL	127	396	109	26	1	13	(5	8)	176	55	66	70	60	4	69	5	0	5	1	2	.33	9	.275	.373	.444
2006	3 Tms	AL	117	348	86	21	0	13	(6	7)	146	42	51	51	40	3	86	3	0	2	0	0	-	5	.247	.328	.420
2007	Tor	AL	125	357	103	28	1	21	(7	14)	196	58	64	65	44	5	66	2	0	2	2	1	.67	7	.289	.368	.549
2008	2 Tms	NL	121	337	85	12	1	13	(7	6)	138	46	49	44	42	9	90	5	0	3	1	1	.50	10	.252	.341	.409
06	KC	AL	77	226	59	14	0	8	(3	5)	97	31	32	35	31	2	52	2	0	2	0	0	-	5	.261	.352	.429
06	Tex	AL	26	81	17	4	0	3	(2	1)	30	6	11	10	6	1	22	1	0	0	0	0	-	1	.210	.273	.370
06	Det	AL	14	41	10	3	0	2	(1	1)	19	5	8	6	3	0	12	0	0	0	0	0	-	1	.244	.295	.463
08	Tor	AL	105	320	80	11	1	11	(6	5)	126	42	44	41	41	9	87	5	0	2	1	1	.50	10	.250	.342	.394
08	Phi	NL	16	17	5	1	0	2	(1	1)	12	4	5	3	1	0	3	0	0	1	0	0	-	0	.294	.316	.706
	Postseason		4	10	1	1	0	0	(0	0)	2	0	0	0	0	0	2	0	0	0	0	0	-	0	.100	.100	.200
16 ML YEARS			1662	4937	1313	283	13	254	(120	134)	2384	737	864	831	674	54	1037	54	5	39	28	24	.54	107	.266	.358	.483

Craig Stansberry

Bats: R **Throws:** R **Pos:** PH-7; 2B-4; DH-1; PR-1   **Ht:** 6'0" **Wt:** 185 **Born:** 3/8/1982 **Age:** 27

							BATTING															BASERUNNING				AVERAGES		
Year	Team	Lg	G	AB	H	2B	3B	HR	(Hm	Rd)	TB	R	RBI	RC	TBB	IBB	SO	HBP	SH	SF	SB	CS	SB%	GDP	Avg	OBP	Slg
2003	Wmspt	A-	45	166	51	9	3	2	(-	-)	72	19	21	27	13	1	25	4	3	1	5	3	.63	2	.307	.370	.434
2004	Hkry	A	106	391	112	14	5	9	(-	-)	163	57	67	66	52	0	88	5	2	2	20	8	.71	6	.286	.376	.417
2005	Lynbrg	A+	24	94	33	7	2	3	(-	-)	53	17	19	23	11	1	13	2	0	0	7	1	.88	1	.351	.430	.564
2005	Altna	AA	116	421	100	22	11	18	(-	-)	198	62	67	66	44	0	116	6	5	7	15	5	.75	8	.238	.314	.470
2006	Altna	AA	72	260	67	18	3	10	(-	-)	121	46	30	43	31	0	62	4	1	1	8	3	.73	6	.258	.345	.465
2006	Indy	AAA	61	201	44	10	3	2	(-	-)	67	30	25	27	35	0	36	2	3	1	11	3	.79	5	.219	.339	.333
2007	Portlnd	AAA	124	466	127	33	3	14	(-	-)	208	83	75	80	70	3	95	6	0	6	10	10	.50	6	.273	.370	.446
2008	Portlnd	AAA	75	273	68	13	3	7	(-	-)	108	44	27	40	45	1	55	1	1	1	5	6	.45	5	.249	.356	.396
2007	SD	NL	11	7	2	0	0	0	(0	0)	2	1	1	1	0	0	3	1	2	0	0	0	-	0	.286	.375	.286
2008	SD	NL	12	16	6	1	0	0	(0	0)	7	4	2	4	2	0	3	0	0	0	0	0	-	0	.375	.444	.438
2 ML YEARS			23	23	8	1	0	0	(0	0)	9	5	3	5	2	0	6	1	2	0	0	0	-	0	.348	.423	.391

Tim Stauffer

Pitches: R **Bats:** R **Pos:** P   **Ht:** 6'1" **Wt:** 205 **Born:** 6/2/1982 **Age:** 27

							HOW MUCH HE PITCHED			WHAT HE GAVE UP													THE RESULTS					
Year	Team	Lg	G	GS	CG	GF	IP	BFP	H	R	ER	HR	SH	SF	HB	TBB	IBB	SO	WP	Bk	W	L	Pct	ShO	Sv-Op	Hld	ERC	ERA
2005	SD	NL	15	14	0	0	81.0	355	92	50	48	10	2	0	2	29	0	49	0	0	3	6	.333	0	0-0	0	5.00	5.33
2006	SD	NL	1	1	0	0	6.0	21	3	2	1	0	0	0	0	1	0	2	0	0	0	0	1.000	0	0-0	0	0.84	1.50
2007	SD	NL	2	2	0	0	7.2	45	15	18	18	5	0	0	1	6	0	6	0	0	0	1	.000	0	0-0	0	18.32	21.13
3 ML YEARS			18	17	0	0	94.2	421	110	70	67	15	2	0	3	36	0	57	0	0	4	7	.364	0	0-0	0	5.54	6.37

Nick Stavinoha

Bats: R **Throws:** R **Pos:** PH-14; LF-13; RF-5; DH-4; PR-1   **Ht:** 6'2" **Wt:** 225 **Born:** 5/3/1982 **Age:** 27

							BATTING															BASERUNNING				AVERAGES		
Year	Team	Lg	G	AB	H	2B	3B	HR	(Hm	Rd)	TB	R	RBI	RC	TBB	IBB	SO	HBP	SH	SF	SB	CS	SB%	GDP	Avg	OBP	Slg
2005	QuadC	A	65	250	86	9	2	14	(-	-)	141	54	53	55	23	1	25	2	0	4	4	0	1.00	7	.344	.398	.564
2006	Sprgfld	AA	111	417	124	26	3	12	(-	-)	192	55	73	66	28	0	81	2	0	6	2	1	.67	10	.297	.340	.460
2007	Memp	AAA	139	499	130	17	0	13	(-	-)	186	50	49	60	31	0	81	4	1	2	7	1	.88	7	.261	.308	.373
2008	Memp	AAA	112	427	144	23	3	16	(-	-)	221	67	74	79	20	0	50	2	0	4	2	1	.67	12	.337	.366	.518
2008	StL	NL	29	57	11	1	0	0	(0	0)	12	4	4	0	2	1	11	0	1	1	0	0	-	2	.193	.217	.211

Mitch Stetter

Pitches: L Bats: L Pos: RP-30 Ht: 6'4" Wt: 199 Born: 1/16/1981 Age: 28

			HOW MUCH HE PITCHED						WHAT HE GAVE UP													THE RESULTS							
Year	Team	Lg	G	GS	CG	GF	IP	BFP	H	R	ER	HR	SH	SF	HB	TBB	IBB	SO	WP	Bk	W	L	Pct	ShO	Sv-Op	Hld	ERC	ERA
2003	Helena	R+	15	8	0	0	54.2	239	55	34	24	3	1	2	6	12	0	63	7	0	6	2	.750	0	0--	-	3.40	3.95
2004	Beloit	A	24	3	0	14	53.0	198	31	12	10	4	2	0	0	12	0	57	1	0	4	0	1.000	0	6--	-	1.41	1.70
2004	Hi Dsrt	A+	8	7	0	0	38.2	185	54	39	35	6	2	3	2	14	0	29	4	0	1	4	.200	0	0--	-	6.83	8.15
2005	Hntsvl	AA	32	0	0	22	51.2	205	45	15	14	3	1	0	2	11	1	47	0	0	2	3	.400	0	8--	-	2.61	2.44
2005	Nashv	AAA	27	0	0	4	25.1	111	23	17	13	5	2	1	0	11	1	23	2	0	1	1	.500	0	0--	-	4.17	4.62
2006	Nashv	AAA	51	0	0	6	38.1	169	38	20	19	3	6	3	3	16	3	36	3	0	2	5	.286	0	0--	-	4.09	4.46
2007	Nashv	AAA	24	0	0	0	14.2	55	8	7	7	1	0	2	0	5	0	19	1	0	1	0	1.000	0	1--	-	1.54	4.30
2007	Brewrs	R	7	5	0	0	6.0	22	4	1	1	0	0	0	1	0	0	9	0	0	0	0	-	0	0--	-	1.29	1.50
2007	Hntsvl	AA	2	0	0	0	1.0	3	0	0	0	0	0	0	0	0	0	2	0	0	0	0	-	0	0--	-	0.00	0.00
2008	Nashv	AAA	29	0	0	13	29.0	112	21	10	8	2	0	0	0	7	0	30	0	0	3	3	.500	0	0--	-	1.94	2.48
2007	Mil	NL	6	0	0	2	5.0	20	2	2	2	0	0	1	2	2	0	4	3	0	1	0	1.000	0	0-0	0	1.86	3.60
2008	Mil	NL	30	0	0	7	25.1	109	14	9	9	2	1	0	4	19	1	31	1	0	3	1	.750	0	0-1	4	3.40	3.20
	2 ML YEARS		36	0	0	9	30.1	129	16	11	11	2	1	1	6	21	1	35	4	0	4	1	.800	0	0-1	4	3.13	3.26

Chris Stewart

Bats: R Throws: R Pos: C-1 Ht: 6'4" Wt: 210 Born: 2/19/1982 Age: 27

						BATTING																BASERUNNING				AVERAGES		
Year	Team	Lg	G	AB	H	2B	3B	HR	(Hm	Rd)	TB	R	RBI	RC	TBB	IBB	SO	HBP	SH	SF		SB	CS	SB%	GDP	Avg	OBP	Slg
2008	S-WB*	AAA	86	272	76	19	0	2	(-	-)	101	32	24	38	28	2	38	3	5	1		2	1	.67	12	.279	.352	.371
2006	CWS	AL	6	8	0	0	0	0	(0	0)	0	0	0	0	0	0	2	0	0	0		0	0	-	0	.000	.000	.000
2007	Tex	AL	17	37	9	2	0	0	(0	0)	11	4	3	3	3	0	6	0	3	0		0	0	-	2	.243	.300	.297
2008	NYY	AL	1	3	0	0	0	0	(0	0)	0	0	0	0	0	0	1	0	0	0		0	0	-	0	.000	.000	.000
	3 ML YEARS		24	48	9	2	0	0	(0	0)	11	4	3	3	3	0	9	0	3	0		0	0	-	2	.188	.235	.229

Ian Stewart

Bats: L Throws: R Pos: 3B-65; 2B-12; PH-8 Ht: 6'3" Wt: 205 Born: 4/5/1985 Age: 24

						BATTING																BASERUNNING				AVERAGES		
Year	Team	Lg	G	AB	H	2B	3B	HR	(Hm	Rd)	TB	R	RBI	RC	TBB	IBB	SO	HBP	SH	SF		SB	CS	SB%	GDP	Avg	OBP	Slg
2003	Casper	R+	57	224	71	14	5	10	(-	-)	125	40	43	49	29	3	54	3	0	1		4	1	.80	5	.317	.401	.558
2004	Ashvll	A	131	505	161	31	9	30	(-	-)	300	92	101	117	66	6	112	4	1	5		19	9	.68	7	.319	.398	.594
2005	Mdest	A+	112	435	119	32	7	17	(-	-)	216	83	86	78	52	0	113	5	0	7		2	2	.50	13	.274	.353	.497
2006	Tulsa	AA	120	462	124	41	7	10	(-	-)	209	75	71	74	50	2	103	11	1	4		3	8	.27	13	.268	.351	.452
2007	ColSpr	AAA	112	414	126	23	2	15	(-	-)	198	72	65	78	49	6	92	3	4	4		11	2	.85	10	.304	.379	.478
2008	ColSpr	AAA	69	257	72	15	6	19	(-	-)	156	65	57	58	34	3	66	5	0	2		7	2	.78	10	.280	.372	.607
2007	Col	NL	35	43	9	4	0	1	(1	0)	16	3	9	5	1	0	17	2	0	0		0	0	-	0	.209	.261	.372
2008	Col	NL	81	266	69	18	2	10	(5	5)	121	33	41	44	30	4	94	7	0	1		1	1	.50	3	.259	.349	.455
	2 ML YEARS		116	309	78	22	2	11	(6	5)	137	36	50	49	31	4	111	9	0	1		1	1	.50	3	.252	.337	.443

Shannon Stewart

Bats: R Throws: R Pos: LF-40; DH-9; PH-7 Ht: 5'11" Wt: 210 Born: 2/25/1974 Age: 35

						BATTING																BASERUNNING				AVERAGES		
Year	Team	Lg	G	AB	H	2B	3B	HR	(Hm	Rd)	TB	R	RBI	RC	TBB	IBB	SO	HBP	SH	SF		SB	CS	SB%	GDP	Avg	OBP	Slg
2008	B Jays*	R	2	6	4	1	0	0	(-	-)	5	1	1	2	1	0	1	0	0	0		0	0	-	0	.667	.714	.833
2008	Dnedin*	A+	6	16	2	0	0	0	(-	-)	2	0	3	1	6	0	4	0	0	1		0	0	-	1	.125	.348	.125
2008	Syrcse*	AAA	1	4	0	0	0	0	(-	-)	0	0	0	0	0	0	0	0	0	0		0	0	-	0	.000	.000	.000
1995	Tor	AL	12	38	8	0	0	0	(0	0)	8	2	1	3	5	0	5	1	0	0		2	0	1.00	0	.211	.318	.211
1996	Tor	AL	7	17	3	1	0	0	(0	0)	4	2	2	1	1	0	4	0	0	0		1	0	1.00	1	.176	.222	.235
1997	Tor	AL	44	168	48	13	7	0	(0	0)	75	25	22	29	19	1	24	4	0	2		10	3	.77	3	.286	.368	.446
1998	Tor	AL	144	516	144	29	3	12	(6	6)	215	90	55	88	67	1	77	15	6	1		51	18	.74	5	.279	.377	.417
1999	Tor	AL	145	608	185	28	2	11	(4	7)	250	102	67	95	59	0	83	8	3	4		37	14	.73	12	.304	.371	.411
2000	Tor	AL	136	583	186	43	5	21	(12	9)	302	107	69	106	37	1	79	6	1	4		20	5	.80	12	.319	.363	.518
2001	Tor	AL	155	640	202	44	7	12	(6	6)	296	103	60	109	46	1	72	11	0	1		27	10	.73	9	.316	.371	.463
2002	Tor	AL	141	577	175	38	6	10	(4	6)	255	103	45	92	54	2	60	9	0	1		14	2	.88	17	.303	.371	.442
2003	2 Tms	AL	136	573	176	44	2	13	(7	6)	263	90	73	93	52	3	66	6	2	11		4	6	.40	10	.307	.364	.459
2004	Min	AL	92	378	115	17	2	11	(5	6)	169	46	47	68	47	4	44	1	1	3		6	3	.67	5	.304	.380	.447
2005	Min	AL	132	551	151	27	3	10	(4	6)	214	69	56	68	34	2	73	8	1	5		7	5	.58	11	.274	.323	.388
2006	Min	AL	44	174	51	5	1	2	(0	2)	64	21	21	26	14	0	19	1	0	1		3	1	.75	7	.293	.347	.368
2007	Oak	AL	146	576	167	22	1	12	(2	10)	227	79	48	75	47	0	60	3	1	3		11	3	.79	15	.290	.345	.394
2008	Min	AL	52	175	42	4	2	1	(0	1)	53	14	14	17	22	1	18	1	0	2		3	1	.75	8	.240	.325	.303
03	Tor	AL	71	303	89	22	2	7	(3	4)	136	47	35	51	27	2	30	2	0	8		1	2	.33	6	.294	.347	.449
03	Min	AL	65	270	87	22	0	6	(4	2)	127	43	38	42	25	1	36	4	2	3		3	4	.43	4	.322	.384	.470
	Postseason		8	35	10	2	0	0	(0	0)	12	1	2	3	2	0	6	0	0	0		1	0	1.00	0	.286	.316	.343
	14 ML YEARS		1386	5574	1653	315	41	115	(50	65)	2395	853	580	870	504	16	684	74	15	38		196	71	.73	115	.297	.360	.430

Phil Stockman

Pitches: R Bats: R Pos: RP-6 Ht: 6'8" Wt: 251 Born: 1/25/1980 Age: 29

						HOW MUCH HE PITCHED						WHAT HE GAVE UP											THE RESULTS							
Year	Team	Lg	G	GS	CG	GF	IP	BFP	H	R	ER	HR	SH	SF	HB	TBB	IBB	SO	WP	Bk	W	L	Pct	ShO	Sv-Op	Hld	ERC	ERA
1998	DBcks	R	1	0	0	0	0.1	3	2	0	0	0	0	0	0	2	0	1	0	0	0	0	-	0	0--	-	120.2	0.00
2000	DBcks	R	14	2	0	5	41.2	194	40	22	12	2	0	0	2	23	0	40	3	1	3	2	.600	0	1--	-	4.04	2.59
2000	Msoula	R+	2	2	0	0	11.0	46	10	3	3	0	0	0	0	3	0	4	0	0	2	0	1.000	0	0--	-	2.41	2.45
2001	Lancst	A+	8	0	0	1	17.2	70	11	11	10	2	1	4	1	9	0	18	1	0	0	0	-	0	0--	-	2.92	5.09
2001	Yakima	A-	15	14	0	0	76.0	329	81	39	36	5	3	1	5	22	0	48	5	0	3	4	.429	0	0--	-	4.02	4.26
2002	Lancst	A+	20	20	0	0	108.1	463	91	58	53	10	4	1	7	58	0	108	7	0	7	5	.583	0	0--	-	3.99	4.40

Year	Team	Lg	G	GS	CG	GF	IP	BFP	H	R	ER	HR	SH	SF	HB	TBB	IBB	SO	WP	Bk	W	L	Pct	ShO	Sv-Op	Hld	ERC	ERA
2003	ElPaso	AA	26	26	0	0	147.2	648	137	75	65	9	8	6	9	64	0	146	2	0	11	7	.611	0	0--	-	3.70	3.96
2003	Tucsn	AAA	2	1	0	0	9.0	37	8	1	1	0	1	0	1	4	0	5	0	1	1	1	.500	0	0--	-	3.56	1.00
2004	Tucsn	AAA	12	12	0	0	56.1	263	60	39	36	2	7	8	0	36	0	35	1	1	3	2	.600	0	0--	-	4.81	5.75
2004	ElPaso	AA	6	6	1	0	27.0	120	17	13	8	1	2	2	4	20	0	21	2	0	1	3	.250	0	0--	-	3.41	2.67
2005	Tucsn	AAA	17	4	0	1	31.2	158	35	29	22	4	3	3	1	27	0	16	1	0	1	1	.500	0	0--	-	6.75	6.25
2005	Tenn	AA	47	1	0	7	36.0	165	31	16	13	2	4	3	4	24	2	30	2	0	1	3	.250	0	1--	-	4.27	3.25
2006	Missi	AA	3	0	0	0	7.1	25	1	0	0	0	0	0	0	2	0	12	0	0	0	0	-	0	0--	-	0.25	0.00
2006	Rchmd	AAA	18	0	0	10	33.1	122	13	3	3	0	0	1	0	10	1	41	1	0	0	0	-	0	2--	-	0.75	0.81
2006	Rome	A	3	3	0	0	3.0	15	5	3	0	0	0	0	0	3	0	6	0	0	0	1	.000	0	0--	-	11.06	0.00
2007	Rchmd	AAA	9	0	0	1	15.2	59	7	3	3	1	0	0	0	6	0	15	0	0	1	0	1.000	0	0--	-	1.29	1.72
2007	Braves	R	3	0	0	0	5.0	22	5	4	4	0	0	0	1	1	0	9	1	0	0	0	-	0	0--	-	3.28	7.20
2007	Missi	AA	12	0	0	6	15.1	61	8	2	1	0	0	0	0	7	1	17	0	0	1	0	1.000	0	3--	-	1.33	0.59
2008	Rchmd	AAA	19	0	0	6	30.0	120	15	7	7	3	0	0	0	18	0	26	0	0	1	1	.500	0	2--	-	2.26	2.10
2006	Atl	NL	4	0	0	0	4.0	19	3	1	1	0	2	0	0	4	2	4	0	0	0	0	-	0	0-0	0	3.15	2.25
2008	Atl	NL	6	0	0	4	7.1	28	2	0	0	0	0	0	1	4	0	9	1	0	0	0	-	0	0-0	0	1.16	0.00
2 ML YEARS			10	0	0	5	11.1	47	5	1	1	0	2	0	1	8	2	13	1	0	0	0	-	0	0-0	0	1.69	0.79

Brian Stokes

Pitches: R Bats: R Pos: RP-23; SP-1   Ht: 6'1" Wt: 210 Born: 9/7/1979 Age: 29

Year	Team	Lg	G	GS	CG	GF	IP	BFP	H	R	ER	HR	SH	SF	HB	TBB	IBB	SO	WP	Bk	W	L	Pct	ShO	Sv-Op	Hld	ERC	ERA
2008	NewOr*	AAA	23	22	1	0	130.2	556	124	74	64	7	9	4	1	48	1	97	5	1	10	8	.556	1	0--	-	3.35	4.41
2006	TB	AL	5	4	0	0	24.0	110	31	13	13	2	0	3	1	9	0	15	0	0	1	0	1.000	0	0-0	0	5.75	4.88
2007	TB	AL	59	0	0	22	62.1	294	90	49	49	11	1	3	3	25	1	35	1	0	2	7	.222	0	0-2	8	7.70	7.07
2008	NYM	NL	24	1	0	5	33.1	138	35	13	13	5	2	3	0	8	3	26	1	0	1	0	1.000	0	1-3	4	3.99	3.51
3 ML YEARS			88	5	0	27	119.2	542	156	75	75	18	3	9	4	42	4	76	2	0	4	7	.364	0	1-5	12	6.22	5.64

Huston Street

Pitches: R Bats: R Pos: RP-63   Ht: 6'0" Wt: 200 Born: 8/2/1983 Age: 25

Year	Team	Lg	G	GS	CG	GF	IP	BFP	H	R	ER	HR	SH	SF	HB	TBB	IBB	SO	WP	Bk	W	L	Pct	ShO	Sv-Op	Hld	ERC	ERA
2005	Oak	AL	67	0	0	47	78.1	306	53	17	15	3	3	2	2	26	4	72	1	0	5	1	.833	0	23-27	0	1.87	1.72
2006	Oak	AL	69	0	0	55	70.2	290	64	28	26	4	3	3	2	13	3	67	4	0	4	5	.500	0	37-48	1	2.49	3.31
2007	Oak	AL	48	0	0	35	50.0	199	35	20	16	5	2	1	0	12	3	63	0	0	5	2	.714	0	16-21	5	1.84	2.88
2008	Oak	AL	63	0	0	37	70.0	287	58	29	29	6	3	3	1	27	6	69	2	0	7	5	.583	0	18-25	6	2.98	3.73
Postseason			5	0	0	5	6.1	26	8	5	5	2	0	0	0	1	0	4	0	0	0	1	.000	0	2-2	0	6.51	7.11
4 ML YEARS			247	0	0	174	269.0	1082	210	94	86	18	11	9	5	78	16	271	7	0	21	12	.636	0	94-121	12	2.30	2.88

Eric Stults

Pitches: L Bats: L Pos: SP-7   Ht: 6'0" Wt: 227 Born: 12/9/1979 Age: 29

Year	Team	Lg	G	GS	CG	GF	IP	BFP	H	R	ER	HR	SH	SF	HB	TBB	IBB	SO	WP	Bk	W	L	Pct	ShO	Sv-Op	Hld	ERC	ERA
2008	LsVgs*	AAA	20	20	0	0	117.2	497	118	53	50	14	1	3	1	35	1	102	6	0	7	7	.500	0	0--	-	3.84	3.82
2006	LAD	NL	6	2	0	2	17.2	73	17	12	11	4	2	0	0	7	0	5	0	0	1	0	1.000	0	0-0	0	4.91	5.60
2007	LAD	NL	12	5	0	0	38.2	179	50	26	25	5	1	1	1	17	2	30	2	0	1	4	.200	0	0-0	1	6.25	5.82
2008	LAD	NL	7	7	1	0	38.2	167	38	18	15	6	2	0	1	13	2	30	0	0	2	3	.400	1	0-0	0	4.07	3.49
3 ML YEARS			25	14	1	2	95.0	419	105	56	51	15	5	1	2	37	4	65	2	0	4	7	.364	1	0-0	1	5.09	4.83

Tanyon Sturtze

Pitches: R Bats: R Pos: RP-3   Ht: 6'5" Wt: 230 Born: 10/12/1970 Age: 38

Year	Team	Lg	G	GS	CG	GF	IP	BFP	H	R	ER	HR	SH	SF	HB	TBB	IBB	SO	WP	Bk	W	L	Pct	ShO	Sv-Op	Hld	ERC	ERA
2008	Jaxnvl*	AA	18	1	0	1	23.0	109	31	16	12	2	1	2	0	6	0	16	3	0	1	1	.500	0	0--	-	5.13	4.70
2008	LsVgs*	AAA	21	0	0	12	28.1	122	25	15	13	4	4	1	0	12	0	23	1	0	1	1	.500	0	5--	-	3.72	4.13
1995	ChC	NL	2	0	0	0	2.0	9	2	2	2	1	0	0	0	1	0	0	0	0	0	0	-	0	0-0	0	7.30	9.00
1996	ChC	NL	6	0	0	3	11.0	51	16	11	11	3	0	0	0	5	0	7	0	0	1	0	1.000	0	0-0	0	8.87	9.00
1997	Tex	AL	9	5	0	1	32.2	155	45	30	30	6	0	4	0	18	0	18	1	1	1	1	.500	0	0-0	0	7.84	8.27
1999	CWS	AL	1	1	0	0	6.0	22	4	0	0	0	0	0	0	2	0	2	0	0	0	0	-	0	0-0	0	1.73	0.00
2000	2 Tms	AL	29	6	0	9	68.1	300	72	39	36	8	1	2	3	29	1	44	2	0	5	2	.714	0	0-0	0	4.80	4.74
2001	TB	AL	39	27	0	6	195.1	837	200	98	96	23	2	10	9	79	0	110	11	0	11	12	.478	0	1-3	3	4.65	4.42
2002	TB	AL	33	33	4	0	224.0	1008	271	141	129	33	7	6	9	89	2	137	7	2	4	18	.182	0	0-0	0	5.87	5.18
2003	Tor	AL	40	8	0	7	89.1	415	107	67	59	14	2	2	7	43	3	54	6	0	7	6	.538	0	0-0	1	6.30	5.94
2004	NYY	AL	28	3	0	7	77.1	337	75	49	47	9	2	4	6	33	2	56	2	1	6	2	.750	0	1-1	1	4.42	5.47
2005	NYY	AL	64	1	0	12	78.0	332	76	43	41	10	1	2	6	27	1	45	3	0	5	3	.625	0	1-6	16	4.26	4.73
2006	NYY	AL	18	0	0	2	10.2	56	17	10	9	3	0	1	1	6	0	6	0	0	0	0	-	0	0-0	3	10.37	7.59
2008	LAD	NL	3	0	0	1	2.1	9	1	0	0	0	0	0	0	1	0	1	0	0	0	0	-	0	0-0	0	1.08	0.00
00 CWS		AL	10	1	0	2	15.2	85	25	23	21	4	0	2	2	15	0	6	1	0	1	2	.333	0	0-0	0	12.84	12.06
00 TB		AL	19	5	0	7	52.2	215	47	16	15	4	1	0	1	14	1	38	1	0	4	0	1.000	0	0-0	0	2.89	2.56
Postseason			8	0	0	1	6.2	31	7	4	4	3	0	0	0	5	0	6	0	0	0	0	-	0	0-0	2	8.82	5.40
12 ML YEARS			272	84	4	48	797.0	3531	886	490	460	110	15	28	41	333	9	480	32	4	40	44	.476	0	3-10	24	5.33	5.19

Cory Sullivan

Bats: L Throws: L Pos: PH-7; CF-5; RF-5; LF-2; PR-2   Ht: 6'0" Wt: 180 Born: 8/20/1979 Age: 29

Year	Team	Lg	G	AB	H	2B	3B	HR	(Hm	Rd)	TB	R	RBI	RC	TBB	IBB	SO	HBP	SH	SF	SB	CS	SB%	GDP	Avg	OBP	Slg
2008	ColSpr*	AAA	94	381	122	32	3	7	(-	-)	181	70	47	68	31	1	63	3	1	3	13	7	.65	5	.320	.373	.475
2005	Col	NL	139	378	111	15	4	4	(1	3)	146	64	30	54	28	0	83	3	10	5	12	3	.80	6	.294	.343	.386
2006	Col	NL	126	386	103	26	10	2	(0	2)	155	47	30	47	32	3	100	1	19	5	10	6	.63	5	.267	.321	.402
2007	Col	NL	72	140	40	6	1	2	(0	2)	54	19	14	20	9	1	25	2	1	1	2	0	1.00	5	.286	.336	.386
2008	Col	NL	18	23	5	0	1	0	(0	0)	7	3	4	3	0	0	5	1	0	0	1	0	1.00	0	.217	.250	.304
	Postseason		6	6	2	0	0	0	(0	0)	2	0	0	0	0	0	1	0	0	0	0	0	-	0	.333	.333	.333
	4 ML YEARS		355	927	259	47	16	8	(1	7)	362	133	78	124	69	4	213	7	30	11	25	9	.74	16	.279	.330	.391

Jeff Suppan

Pitches: R Bats: R Pos: SP-31   Ht: 6'2" Wt: 237 Born: 1/2/1975 Age: 34

Year	Team	Lg	G	GS	CG	GF	IP	BFP	H	R	ER	HR	SH	SF	HB	TBB	IBB	SO	WP	Bk	W	L	Pct	ShO	Sv-Op	Hld	ERC	ERA
1995	Bos	AL	8	3	1	0	22.2	100	29	15	15	4	1	0	0	5	1	19	0	0	1	2	.333	0	0-0	1	5.43	5.96
1996	Bos	AL	8	4	0	2	22.2	107	29	19	19	3	1	4	1	13	0	13	3	0	1	1	.500	0	0-0	0	7.03	7.54
1997	Bos	AL	23	22	0	1	112.1	503	140	75	71	12	0	4	4	36	1	67	5	0	7	3	.700	0	0-0	0	5.39	5.69
1998	2 Tms		17	14	1	2	78.2	345	91	56	50	13	3	2	1	22	1	51	2	0	1	7	.125	0	0-0	0	4.95	5.72
1999	KC	AL	32	32	4	0	208.2	887	222	113	105	28	7	5	3	62	4	103	5	1	10	12	.455	1	0-0	0	4.33	4.53
2000	KC	AL	35	33	3	0	217.0	948	240	121	119	36	5	6	7	84	3	128	7	1	10	9	.526	1	0-0	0	5.31	4.94
2001	KC	AL	34	34	1	0	218.1	946	227	120	106	26	5	6	12	74	3	120	6	0	10	14	.417	0	0-0	0	4.40	4.37
2002	KC	AL	33	33	3	0	208.0	912	229	134	123	32	4	11	7	68	3	109	10	1	9	16	.360	1	0-0	0	4.84	5.32
2003	2 Tms		32	31	3	0	204.0	873	217	98	95	23	11	6	8	51	5	110	7	0	13	11	.542	2	0-0	0	4.03	4.19
2004	StL	NL	31	31	0	0	188.0	811	192	98	87	25	8	5	8	65	1	110	4	1	16	9	.640	0	0-0	0	4.38	4.16
2005	StL	NL	32	32	0	0	194.1	834	206	93	77	24	11	5	7	63	1	114	6	1	16	10	.615	0	0-0	0	4.46	3.57
2006	StL	NL	32	32	0	0	190.0	837	207	100	87	21	9	3	8	69	6	104	8	0	12	7	.632	0	0-0	0	4.62	4.12
2007	Mil	NL	34	34	1	0	206.2	919	243	113	106	18	14	11	11	68	10	114	7	0	12	12	.500	0	0-0	0	4.84	4.62
2008	Mil	NL	31	31	0	0	177.2	780	207	110	98	30	10	4	4	67	7	90	3	1	10	10	.500	0	0-0	0	5.58	4.96
98	Ari	NL	13	13	1	0	66.0	299	82	55	49	12	3	2	1	21	1	39	2	0	1	7	.125	0	0-0	0	5.73	6.68
98	KC	AL	4	1	0	2	12.2	46	9	1	1	1	0	0	0	1	0	12	0	0	0	0	-	0	0-0	0	1.51	0.71
03	Pit	NL	21	21	3	0	141.0	597	147	57	56	11	10	2	6	31	5	78	3	0	10	7	.588	2	0-0	0	3.55	3.57
03	Bos	AL	11	10	0	0	63.0	276	70	41	39	12	1	4	2	20	0	32	4	0	3	4	.429	0	0-0	0	5.15	5.57
	Postseason		9	9	0	0	54.0	225	40	19	18	6	1	2	3	22	3	33	0	0	3	3	.500	0	0-0	0	2.89	3.00
	14 ML YEARS		382	366	16	6	2249.0	9802	2479	1265	1158	295	89	73	81	747	46	1252	73	6	128	123	.510	5	0-0	1	4.74	4.63

Ichiro Suzuki

Bats: L Throws: R Pos: RF-91; CF-69; DH-2; PH-1   Ht: 5'11" Wt: 172 Born: 10/22/1973 Age: 35

Year	Team	Lg	G	AB	H	2B	3B	HR	(Hm	Rd)	TB	R	RBI	RC	TBB	IBB	SO	HBP	SH	SF	SB	CS	SB%	GDP	Avg	OBP	Slg
2001	Sea	AL	157	692	242	34	8	8	(5	3)	316	127	69	124	30	10	53	8	4	4	56	14	.80	3	.350	.381	.457
2002	Sea	AL	157	647	208	27	8	8	(4	4)	275	111	51	110	68	27	62	5	3	5	31	15	.67	8	.321	.388	.425
2003	Sea	AL	159	679	212	29	8	13	(8	5)	296	111	62	107	36	7	69	6	3	1	34	8	.81	3	.312	.352	.436
2004	Sea	AL	161	704	262	24	5	8	(4	4)	320	101	60	125	49	19	63	4	2	3	36	11	.77	6	.372	.414	.455
2005	Sea	AL	162	679	206	21	12	15	(8	7)	296	111	68	109	48	23	66	4	2	6	33	8	.80	5	.303	.350	.436
2006	Sea	AL	161	695	224	20	9	9	(6	3)	289	110	49	107	49	16	71	5	1	2	45	2	.96	2	.322	.370	.416
2007	Sea	AL	161	678	238	22	7	6	(3	3)	292	111	68	128	49	13	77	3	4	2	37	8	.82	7	.351	.396	.431
2008	Sea	AL	162	686	213	20	7	6	(3	3)	265	103	42	100	51	12	65	5	3	4	43	4	.91	8	.310	.361	.386
	Postseason		10	38	16	2	0	0	(0	0)	18	7	3	8	5	2	4	0	0	0	3	2	.60	0	.421	.488	.474
	8 ML YEARS		1280	5460	1805	197	64	73	(41	32)	2349	885	469	910	380	127	526	40	22	27	315	70	.82	42	.331	.377	.430

Kurt Suzuki

Bats: R Throws: R Pos: C-141; PH-8; DH-1   Ht: 6'0" Wt: 197 Born: 10/4/1983 Age: 25

Year	Team	Lg	G	AB	H	2B	3B	HR	(Hm	Rd)	TB	R	RBI	RC	TBB	IBB	SO	HBP	SH	SF	SB	CS	SB%	GDP	Avg	OBP	Slg
2004	Vancvr	A	46	175	52	10	3	3	(-	-)	77	27	31	32	18	0	26	12	3	3	0	1	.00	5	.297	.394	.440
2005	Stcktn	A+	114	441	122	26	5	12	(-	-)	194	85	65	79	63	0	61	12	2	5	5	3	.63	16	.277	.378	.440
2006	Mdland	AA	99	376	107	26	1	7	(-	-)	156	64	55	66	58	1	50	9	0	1	5	3	.63	15	.285	.392	.415
2007	Scrmto	AAA	55	211	59	9	0	3	(-	-)	77	32	27	29	21	1	41	4	1	3	0	0	-	10	.280	.351	.365
2007	Oak	AL	68	213	53	13	0	7	(4	3)	87	27	39	33	24	0	39	3	3	5	0	0	-	4	.249	.327	.408
2008	Oak	AL	148	530	148	25	1	7	(5	2)	196	54	42	66	44	2	69	11	2	1	2	3	.40	20	.279	.346	.370
	2 ML YEARS		216	743	201	38	1	14	(9	5)	283	81	81	99	68	2	108	14	5	6	2	3	.40	24	.271	.341	.381

Mark Sweeney

Bats: L Throws: L Pos: PH-94; 1B-2; DH-2; LF-1   Ht: 6'1" Wt: 195 Born: 10/26/1969 Age: 39

Year	Team	Lg	G	AB	H	2B	3B	HR	(Hm	Rd)	TB	R	RBI	RC	TBB	IBB	SO	HBP	SH	SF	SB	CS	SB%	GDP	Avg	OBP	Slg
2008	LsVgs*	AAA	4	16	4	0	0	0	(-	-)	4	2	0	1	1	0	2	0	0	0	0	0	-	0	.250	.294	.250
1995	StL	NL	37	77	21	2	0	2	(0	2)	29	5	13	10	10	0	15	0	1	2	1	1	.50	3	.273	.348	.377
1996	StL	NL	98	170	45	9	0	3	(0	3)	63	32	22	27	33	2	29	1	5	0	3	0	1.00	4	.265	.387	.371
1997	2 Tms	NL	115	164	46	7	0	2	(2	0)	59	16	23	22	20	1	32	1	1	2	2	3	.40	3	.280	.358	.360
1998	SD	NL	122	192	45	8	3	2	(1	1)	65	17	15	21	26	0	37	1	0	3	1	2	.33	5	.234	.324	.339
1999	Cin	NL	37	31	11	3	0	2	(1	1)	20	6	7	7	4	1	9	0	0	0	0	0	-	2	.355	.429	.645
2000	Mil	NL	71	73	16	6	0	1	(0	1)	25	9	6	9	12	1	18	1	1	0	0	0	-	1	.219	.337	.342
2001	Mil	NL	48	89	23	3	1	3	(1	2)	37	9	11	14	12	0	23	0	2	0	2	1	.67	0	.258	.347	.416
2002	SD	NL	48	65	11	3	0	1	(0	1)	17	3	4	1	4	0	19	0	0	0	0	0	-	1	.169	.217	.262
2003	Col	NL	67	97	25	9	0	2	(1	1)	40	13	14	15	9	1	27	0	0	0	0	1	.00	2	.258	.321	.412

Year	Team	Lg	G	AB	H	2B	3B	HR	(Hm	Rd)	TB	R	RBI	RC	TBB	IBB	SO	HBP	SH	SF	SB	CS	SB%	GDP	Avg	OBP	Slg
2004	Col	NL	122	177	47	12	2	9	(6	3)	90	25	40	36	32	2	51	2	0	4	1	0	1.00	2	.266	.377	.508
2005	SD	NL	135	221	65	12	1	8	(3	5)	103	31	40	37	40	3	58	0	1	5	4	0	1.00	6	.294	.395	.466
2006	SF	NL	114	259	65	15	2	5	(0	5)	99	32	37	34	28	3	50	3	0	1	0	1	.00	6	.251	.330	.382
2007	2 Tms	NL	106	123	32	9	0	2	(0	2)	47	20	13	15	14	0	29	3	1	0	2	0	1.00	0	.260	.350	.382
2008	LAD	NL	98	92	12	3	0	0	(0	0)	15	2	5	3	15	0	28	0	0	1	0	0	-	0	.130	.250	.163
97	StL	NL	44	61	13	3	0	0	(0	0)	16	5	4	5	9	1	14	1	1	1	0	1	.00	2	.213	.319	.262
97	SD	NL	71	103	33	4	0	2	(2	0)	43	11	19	17	11	0	18	0	0	1	2	2	.50	1	.320	.383	.417
07	SF	NL	76	90	23	8	0	2	(0	2)	37	18	10	13	13	0	18	3	1	0	2	0	1.00	0	.256	.368	.411
07	LAD	NL	30	33	9	1	0	0	(0	0)	10	2	3	2	1	0	11	0	0	0	0	0	-	0	.273	.294	.303
	Postseason		17	14	5	1	0	0	(0	0)	6	3	1	2	4	0	4	0	1	0	0	1	.00	0	.357	.500	.429
	14 ML YEARS		1218	1830	464	101	9	42	(15	27)	709	220	250	251	259	14	425	12	12	18	16	9	.64	35	.254	.347	.387

Mike Sweeney

Bats: R Throws: R Pos: DH-19; PH-14; 1B-13   Ht: 6'3" Wt: 220 Born: 7/22/1973 Age: 35

Year	Team	Lg	G	AB	H	2B	3B	HR	(Hm	Rd)	TB	R	RBI	RC	TBB	IBB	SO	HBP	SH	SF	SB	CS	SB%	GDP	Avg	OBP	Slg
2008	Scrmto*	AAA	9	27	6	1	0	1	(-	-)	10	4	6	2	2	0	4	0	0	0	0	0	-	1	.222	.276	.370
1995	KC	AL	4	4	1	0	0	0	(0	0)	1	1	0	0	0	0	0	0	0	0	0	0	-	0	.250	.250	.250
1996	KC	AL	50	165	46	10	0	4	(1	3)	68	23	24	23	18	0	21	4	0	3	1	2	.33	7	.279	.358	.412
1997	KC	AL	84	240	58	8	0	7	(5	2)	87	30	31	25	17	0	33	6	1	2	3	2	.60	8	.242	.306	.363
1998	KC	AL	92	282	73	18	0	8	(6	2)	115	32	35	35	24	1	38	2	2	1	2	3	.40	7	.259	.320	.408
1999	KC	AL	150	575	185	44	2	22	(10	12)	299	101	102	109	54	0	48	10	0	4	6	1	.86	21	.322	.387	.520
2000	KC	AL	159	618	206	30	0	29	(17	12)	323	105	144	128	71	5	67	15	0	13	8	3	.73	15	.333	.407	.523
2001	KC	AL	147	559	170	46	1	29	(14	15)	303	97	99	109	64	13	64	2	1	6	10	3	.77	13	.304	.374	.542
2002	KC	AL	126	471	160	31	1	24	(14	10)	265	81	86	112	61	10	46	6	0	7	9	7	.56	9	.340	.417	.563
2003	KC	AL	108	392	115	18	1	16	(7	9)	183	62	83	83	64	5	56	2	0	5	3	2	.60	13	.293	.391	.467
2004	KC	AL	106	411	118	23	0	22	(8	14)	207	56	79	75	33	9	44	6	0	2	3	2	.60	7	.287	.347	.504
2005	KC	AL	122	470	141	39	0	21	(7	14)	243	63	83	80	33	7	61	4	1	6	3	0	1.00	16	.300	.347	.517
2006	KC	AL	60	217	56	15	0	8	(4	4)	95	23	33	33	28	5	48	4	0	3	2	0	1.00	5	.258	.349	.438
2007	KC	AL	74	265	69	15	1	7	(6	1)	107	26	38	39	17	4	29	5	0	2	0	0	-	9	.260	.315	.404
2008	Oak	AL	42	126	36	8	0	2	(1	1)	50	13	12	16	7	0	6	2	0	1	0	0	-	3	.286	.331	.397
	14 ML YEARS		1324	4795	1434	305	5	199	(100	99)	2346	713	849	867	491	59	561	68	5	55	50	25	.67	133	.299	.368	.489

Ryan Sweeney

Bats: L Throws: L Pos: RF-75; CF-51; LF-13; PH-6; PR-3   Ht: 6'4" Wt: 215 Born: 2/20/1985 Age: 24

Year	Team	Lg	G	AB	H	2B	3B	HR	(Hm	Rd)	TB	R	RBI	RC	TBB	IBB	SO	HBP	SH	SF	SB	CS	SB%	GDP	Avg	OBP	Slg
2008	Scrmto*	AAA	8	34	14	4	0	1	(-	-)	21	5	5	8	3	0	4	0	0	0	0	0	-	0	.412	.459	.618
2008	As*	R	1	3	0	0	0	0	(-	-)	0	0	0	0	2	0	0	0	0	0	0	0	-	1	.000	.400	.000
2006	CWS	AL	18	35	8	0	0	0	(0	0)	8	1	5	1	0	0	7	0	0	0	0	0	-	1	.229	.229	.229
2007	CWS	AL	15	45	9	3	0	1	(1	0)	15	5	5	2	4	0	5	0	0	0	0	1	.00	2	.200	.265	.333
2008	CWS	AL	115	384	110	18	2	5	(1	4)	147	53	45	56	38	3	67	3	2	6	9	1	.90	9	.286	.350	.383
	3 ML YEARS		148	464	127	21	2	6	(2	4)	170	59	55	59	42	3	79	3	2	6	9	2	.82	12	.274	.334	.366

R.J. Swindle

Pitches: L Bats: L Pos: RP-3   Ht: 6'3" Wt: 190 Born: 7/7/1983 Age: 25

			HOW MUCH HE PITCHED						WHAT HE GAVE UP												THE RESULTS							
Year	Team	Lg	G	GS	CG	GF	IP	BFP	H	R	ER	HR	SH	SF	HB	TBB	IBB	SO	WP	Bk	W	L	Pct	ShO	Sv-Op	Hld	ERC	ERA
2004	Lowell	A-	12	1	0	0	51.0	199	42	18	11	0	3	3	2	4	0	56	1	0	5	1	.833	0	0--	-	1.60	1.94
2005	Schbrg	IND	18	16	2	0	118.1	491	117	46	43	5	8	4	3	27	0	102	1	0	6	4	.600	0	0--	-	3.08	3.27
2006	Schbrg	IND	5	5	0	0	31.2	131	32	15	12	1	1	0	1	8	0	22	0	0	2	2	.500	0	0--	-	3.28	3.41
2006	CtnSC	A	21	0	0	6	44.1	174	35	5	3	0	1	0	1	5	0	46	1	0	4	2	.667	0	2--	-	1.52	0.61
2006	Clmbs	AAA	1	0	0	1	2.0	7	1	0	0	0	0	0	0	0	0	0	0	0	0	0	-	0	1--	-	1.62	0.00
2007	Newark	IND	9	0	0	1	9.1	40	8	3	2	0	0	0	1	3	0	9	0	0	1	0	1.000	0	0--	-	2.67	1.93
2007	Lakwd	A	20	0	0	16	29.0	107	16	3	3	0	2	4	1	5	2	37	1	0	1	1	.667	0	10--	-	0.96	0.93
2007	Clrwtr	A+	12	0	0	8	15.0	62	15	8	8	3	0	0	0	3	0	20	0	0	1	1	.000	0	3--	-	3.93	4.80
2008	Rdng	AA	11	0	0	4	16.2	60	8	1	1	0	2	0	1	1	1	16	0	1	1	0	1.000	0	0--	-	0.64	0.54
2008	LV	AAA	27	0	0	11	36.1	147	33	9	8	1	1	1	1	7	1	51	0	0	2	1	.667	0	1--	-	2.43	1.98
2008	Phi	NL	3	0	0	0	4.2	24	9	4	4	2	0	0	0	2	0	4	0	0	0	0	-	0	0-0	0	13.63	7.71

Nick Swisher

Bats: B Throws: L Pos: 1B-71; CF-70; LF-18; RF-18; PH-5; DH-1   Ht: 6'0" Wt: 215 Born: 11/25/1980 Age: 28

Year	Team	Lg	G	AB	H	2B	3B	HR	(Hm	Rd)	TB	R	RBI	RC	TBB	IBB	SO	HBP	SH	SF	SB	CS	SB%	GDP	Avg	OBP	Slg
2004	Oak	AL	20	60	15	4	0	2	(1	1)	25	11	8	8	8	0	11	2	0	1	0	0	-	2	.250	.352	.417
2005	Oak	AL	131	462	109	32	1	21	(11	10)	206	66	74	62	55	3	110	4	0	1	0	1	.00	9	.236	.322	.446
2006	Oak	AL	157	556	141	24	2	35	(17	18)	274	106	95	95	97	7	152	11	2	6	1	2	.33	13	.254	.372	.493
2007	Oak	AL	150	539	141	36	1	22	(8	14)	245	84	78	89	100	12	131	10	1	9	2	3	.60	14	.262	.381	.455
2008	CWS	AL	153	497	109	21	1	24	(19	5)	204	86	69	69	82	6	135	4	1	4	3	3	.50	14	.219	.332	.410
	Postseason		7	20	4	2	0	0	(0	0)	6	3	1	3	7	0	7	0	0	0	0	0	-	0	.200	.407	.300
	5 ML YEARS		611	2114	515	117	5	104	(56	48)	954	353	324	323	342	28	539	31	4	21	7	8	.47	51	.244	.354	.451

So Taguchi

Bats: R **Throws:** R **Pos:** LF-38; PH-38; PR-22; RF-11; CF-1   **Ht:** 5'10" **Wt:** 169 **Born:** 7/2/1969 **Age:** 39

Year	Team	Lg	G	AB	H	2B	3B	HR	(Hm	Rd)	TB	R	RBI	RC	TBB	IBB	SO	HBP	SH	SF	SB	CS	SB%	GDP	Avg	OBP	Slg
2002	StL	NL	19	15	6	0	0	0	(0	0)	6	4	2	4	2	0	1	0	2	0	1	0	1.00	0	.400	.471	.400
2003	StL	NL	43	54	14	3	1	3	(1	2)	28	9	13	11	4	1	11	0	1	0	0	0	-	2	.259	.310	.519
2004	StL	NL	109	179	52	10	2	3	(1	2)	75	26	25	27	12	1	23	2	10	3	6	3	.67	6	.291	.337	.419
2005	StL	NL	143	396	114	21	2	8	(5	3)	163	45	53	59	20	2	62	2	2	4	11	2	.85	11	.288	.322	.412
2006	StL	NL	134	316	84	19	1	2	(0	2)	111	46	31	35	32	1	48	2	9	2	11	3	.79	9	.266	.335	.351
2007	StL	NL	130	307	89	15	0	3	(0	3)	113	48	30	41	23	0	32	6	3	1	7	4	.64	10	.290	.350	.368
2008	Phi	NL	88	91	20	5	1	0	(0	0)	27	18	9	8	8	0	14	0	4	0	3	0	1.00	2	.220	.283	.297
	Postseason		26	28	7	1	0	2	(1	1)	14	6	5	4	1	0	8	0	3	0	0	0	-	0	.250	.276	.500
	7 ML YEARS		666	1358	379	73	7	19	(7	12)	523	196	163	185	101	5	191	12	31	10	39	12	.76	40	.279	.332	.385

Mitch Talbot

Pitches: R **Bats:** R **Pos:** RP-2; SP-1   **Ht:** 6'2" **Wt:** 200 **Born:** 10/17/1983 **Age:** 25

Year	Team	Lg	G	GS	CG	GF	IP	BFP	H	R	ER	HR	SH	SF	HB	TBB	IBB	SO	WP	Bk	W	L	Pct	ShO	Sv-Op	Hld	ERC	ERA
2003	Mrtnsvl	R+	12	12	0	0	54.0	223	45	26	17	1	4	1	6	11	0	46	1	0	4	4	.500	0	0- -		2.32	2.83
2004	Lxngtn	A	27	27	1	0	152.2	647	145	78	65	16	7	3	11	49	1	115	6	1	10	10	.500	0	0- -		3.81	3.83
2005	Salem	A+	27	27	1	0	151.1	667	169	90	73	15	8	2	8	46	0	100	9	1	8	11	.421	1	0- -		4.52	4.34
2006	CpChr	AA	18	17	0	1	90.1	390	94	49	34	4	3	2	6	29	0	96	2	2	6	4	.600	0	1- -		3.87	3.39
2006	Mont	AA	10	10	0	0	66.1	264	51	16	14	2	2	1	4	18	0	59	5	0	4	3	.571	0	0- -		2.22	1.90
2007	Drhm	AAA	29	29	1	0	161.0	695	169	89	81	13	5	5	10	59	0	124	4	3	13	9	.591	1	0- -		4.40	4.53
2008	Drhm	AAA	28	28	1	0	161.0	683	165	79	69	9	3	6	11	35	0	141	7	0	13	9	.591	0	0- -		3.45	3.86
2008	TB	AL	3	1	0	0	9.2	54	16	12	12	3	0	0	1	11	0	5	1	0	0	0	-	0	0-0	0	14.85	11.17

Brian Tallet

Pitches: L **Bats:** L **Pos:** RP-51   **Ht:** 6'7" **Wt:** 220 **Born:** 9/21/1977 **Age:** 31

Year	Team	Lg	G	GS	CG	GF	IP	BFP	H	R	ER	HR	SH	SF	HB	TBB	IBB	SO	WP	Bk	W	L	Pct	ShO	Sv-Op	Hld	ERC	ERA
2008	Syrcse*	AAA	2	0	0	0	2.0	9	2	1	1	0	0	1	0	1	0	1	1	0	0	0	-	0	0- -		3.63	4.50
2002	Cle	AL	2	2	0	0	12.0	47	9	3	2	0	0	0	1	4	0	5	0	0	1	0	1.000	0	0-0		2.31	1.50
2003	Cle	AL	5	3	0	1	19.0	87	23	14	10	2	2	0	1	8	0	9	0	0	0	2	.000	0	0-0		5.65	4.74
2005	Cle	AL	2	0	0	0	4.2	24	6	4	4	2	0	0	1	3	0	2	0	0	0	0	-	0	0-0		10.55	7.71
2006	Tor	AL	44	1	0	8	54.1	229	45	24	23	5	1	5	3	31	4	37	2	1	3	0	1.000	0	0-0	5	3.97	3.81
2007	Tor	AL	48	0	0	11	62.1	267	49	26	24	1	2	3	6	28	7	54	1	0	2	4	.333	0	0-3	1	2.68	3.47
2008	Tor	AL	51	0	0	15	56.1	240	52	19	18	4	1	2	1	22	3	47	0	0	1	2	.333	0	0-0	3	3.39	2.88
	6 ML YEARS		152	6	0	35	208.2	894	184	90	81	14	6	10	13	96	14	154	3	1	7	8	.467	0	0-3	10	3.58	3.49

Taylor Tankersley

Pitches: L **Bats:** L **Pos:** RP-25   **Ht:** 6'1" **Wt:** 220 **Born:** 3/7/1983 **Age:** 26

Year	Team	Lg	G	GS	CG	GF	IP	BFP	H	R	ER	HR	SH	SF	HB	TBB	IBB	SO	WP	Bk	W	L	Pct	ShO	Sv-Op	Hld	ERC	ERA
2008	Albq*	AAA	29	0	0	4	31.2	143	32	8	6	2	3	2	3	17	1	28	2	0	2	1	.667	0	0- -		4.74	1.71
2006	Fla	NL	49	0	0	10	41.0	178	33	14	13	4	3	3	1	26	5	46	3	0	2	1	.667	0	3-7	22	3.92	2.85
2007	Fla	NL	67	0	0	12	47.1	205	42	22	21	4	2	3	3	29	3	49	2	0	6	1	.857	0	1-3	16	4.45	3.99
2008	Fla	NL	25	0	0	3	17.2	84	22	16	16	6	1	0	1	8	0	13	3	0	0	1	.000	0	0-2	4	7.76	8.15
	3 ML YEARS		141	0	0	25	106.0	467	97	52	50	14	4	5	5	63	8	108	8	0	8	3	.727	0	4-12	42	4.72	4.25

Jack Taschner

Pitches: L **Bats:** L **Pos:** RP-67   **Ht:** 6'3" **Wt:** 207 **Born:** 4/21/1978 **Age:** 31

Year	Team	Lg	G	GS	CG	GF	IP	BFP	H	R	ER	HR	SH	SF	HB	TBB	IBB	SO	WP	Bk	W	L	Pct	ShO	Sv-Op	Hld	ERC	ERA
2005	SF	NL	24	0	0	7	22.2	95	15	5	4	0	0	1	0	13	0	19	0	0	2	0	1.000	0	0-1	3	2.25	1.59
2006	SF	NL	24	0	0	6	19.1	101	31	23	18	4	0	2	2	7	0	15	3	0	0	1	.000	0	0-1	3	8.55	8.38
2007	SF	NL	63	0	0	16	50.0	222	44	31	30	4	2	3	1	29	2	51	2	0	3	1	.750	0	0-2	13	3.92	5.40
2008	SF	NL	67	0	0	7	48.0	227	57	27	26	5	3	3	2	24	2	39	5	0	3	2	.600	0	0-4	14	5.56	4.88
	4 ML YEARS		178	0	0	36	140.0	645	147	86	78	13	5	9	5	73	4	124	10	0	8	4	.667	0	0-8	33	4.76	5.01

Fernando Tatis

Bats: R **Throws:** R **Pos:** LF-51; RF-39; PH-20; 1B-6; 3B-4   **Ht:** 5'11" **Wt:** 195 **Born:** 1/1/1975 **Age:** 34

Year	Team	Lg	G	AB	H	2B	3B	HR	(Hm	Rd)	TB	R	RBI	RC	TBB	IBB	SO	HBP	SH	SF	SB	CS	SB%	GDP	Avg	OBP	Slg
2008	NewOr*	AAA	37	120	29	6	0	12	(-	-)	71	18	31	24	17	0	23	2	0	0	0	0	-	3	.242	.345	.592
1997	Tex	AL	60	223	57	9	0	8	(6	2)	90	29	29	26	14	0	42	0	2	2	3	0	1.00	6	.256	.297	.404
1998	2 Tms		150	532	147	33	4	11	(6	5)	221	69	58	69	36	3	123	6	4	1	13	5	.72	16	.276	.329	.415
1999	StL	NL	149	537	160	31	2	34	(16	18)	297	104	107	117	82	4	128	16	0	4	21	9	.70	11	.298	.404	.553
2000	StL	NL	96	324	82	21	1	18	(11	7)	159	59	64	58	57	1	94	10	1	2	2	3	.40	13	.253	.399	.491
2001	Mon	NL	41	145	37	9	0	2	(2	0)	52	20	11	18	16	0	43	4	0	3	0	0	-	5	.255	.339	.359
2002	Mon	NL	114	381	87	18	1	15	(5	10)	152	43	55	39	35	1	90	8	1	5	2	2	.50	15	.228	.303	.399
2003	Mon	NL	53	175	34	6	0	2	(1	1)	46	15	15	15	18	0	40	3	0	0	2	1	.67	7	.194	.281	.263
2006	Bal	AL	28	56	14	6	1	2	(1	1)	28	7	8	9	6	1	17	0	0	2	0	0	-	2	.250	.313	.500
2008	NYM	NL	92	273	81	16	1	11	(6	5)	132	33	47	55	29	3	59	3	0	1	3	0	1.00	7	.297	.369	.484

Year	Team	Lg	G	AB	H	2B	3B	HR	(Hm	Rd)	TB	R	RBI	RC	TBB	IBB	SO	HBP	SH	SF	SB	CS	SB%	GDP	Avg	OBP	Slg
									BATTING												BASERUNNING				AVERAGES		
98	Tex	AL	95	330	89	17	2	3	(1	2)	119	41	32	33	12	2	66	4	4	0	6	2	.75	10	.270	.303	.361
98	StL	NL	55	202	58	16	2	8	(5	3)	102	28	26	36	24	1	57	2	0	1	7	3	.70	6	.287	.367	.505
Postseason			5	13	3	2	0	0	(0	0)	5	1	2	1	1	0	5	0	0	1	0	0	-	0	.231	.267	.385
9 ML YEARS			783	2646	699	149	10	103	(52	51)	1177	379	394	406	293	13	636	50	8	20	46	20	.70	82	.264	.346	.445

Ty Taubenheim

Pitches: R Bats: R Pos: SP-1   Ht: 6'5" Wt: 255 Born: 11/17/1982 Age: 26

Year	Team	Lg	G	GS	CG	GF	IP	BFP	H	R	ER	HR	SH	SF	HB	TBB	IBB	SO	WP	Bk	W	L	Pct	ShO	Sv-Op	Hld	ERC	ERA
			HOW MUCH HE PITCHED						WHAT HE GAVE UP												THE RESULTS						
2008	Indy*	AAA	19	19	0	0	98.0	431	102	66	61	12	10	7	6	39	3	66	2	0	4	9	.308	0	0--	-	4.66	5.60
2006	Tor	AL	12	7	0	1	35.0	167	40	22	19	5	1	2	4	18	0	26	1	0	1	5	.167	0	0-0	0	6.05	4.89
2007	Tor	AL	1	1	0	0	5.0	24	5	5	5	1	0	1	1	4	0	4	1	0	0	0	-	0	0-0	0	7.56	9.00
2008	Pit	NL	1	1	0	0	6.0	27	7	2	2	0	0	1	0	3	0	4	0	0	0	0	-	0	0-0	0	4.72	3.00
3 ML YEARS			14	9	0	1	46.0	218	52	29	26	6	1	4	5	25	0	34	2	0	1	5	.167	0	0-0	0	6.03	5.09

Julian Tavarez

Pitches: R Bats: L Pos: RP-52   Ht: 6'2" Wt: 195 Born: 5/22/1973 Age: 36

Year	Team	Lg	G	GS	CG	GF	IP	BFP	H	R	ER	HR	SH	SF	HB	TBB	IBB	SO	WP	Bk	W	L	Pct	ShO	Sv-Op	Hld	ERC	ERA
			HOW MUCH HE PITCHED						WHAT HE GAVE UP												THE RESULTS						
1993	Cle	AL	8	7	0	0	37.0	172	53	29	27	7	0	1	2	13	2	19	3	1	2	2	.500	0	0-0	0	7.48	6.57
1994	Cle	AL	1	1	0	0	1.2	14	6	8	4	1	0	1	0	1	1	0	0	0	0	1	.000	0	0-0	0	24.13	21.60
1995	Cle	AL	57	0	0	15	85.0	350	76	36	23	7	0	2	3	21	0	68	3	2	10	2	.833	0	0-4	19	2.93	2.44
1996	Cle	AL	51	4	0	13	80.2	353	101	49	48	9	5	4	1	22	5	46	1	0	4	7	.364	0	0-0	13	5.12	5.36
1997	SF	NL	89	0	0	13	88.1	378	91	43	38	6	3	8	4	34	5	38	4	0	6	4	.600	0	0-3	26	4.13	3.87
1998	SF	NL	60	0	0	12	85.1	374	96	41	36	5	5	3	8	36	11	52	1	1	5	3	.625	0	1-6	10	4.89	3.80
1999	SF	NL	47	0	0	12	54.2	258	65	38	36	7	3	2	8	25	3	33	4	1	2	0	1.000	0	0-2	5	6.10	5.93
2000	Col	NL	51	12	1	8	120.0	530	124	68	59	11	3	4	7	53	9	62	2	1	11	5	.688	0	1-1	6	4.49	4.43
2001	ChC	NL	34	28	0	1	161.1	712	172	98	81	8	4	11	69	4	107	2	1	10	9	.526	0	0--	2	4.70	4.52
2002	Fla	NL	29	27	0	1	153.2	714	188	100	92	9	13	2	15	74	7	67	7	2	10	12	.455	0	0-0	0	5.75	5.39
2003	Pit	NL	64	0	0	29	83.2	350	75	37	34	1	9	1	5	27	8	39	3	0	3	3	.500	0	11-14	9	2.72	3.66
2004	StL	NL	77	0	0	27	64.1	268	57	21	17	1	3	1	6	19	0	48	2	1	7	4	.636	0	4-6	19	2.87	2.38
2005	StL	NL	74	0	0	16	65.2	278	68	28	25	6	3	3	8	19	4	47	1	0	2	3	.400	0	4-6	32	4.29	3.43
2006	Bos	AL	58	6	1	11	98.2	431	110	54	49	10	3	3	6	44	3	56	2	0	4	4	.556	0	1-3	5	5.32	4.47
2007	Bos	AL	34	23	0	2	134.2	604	151	89	77	14	3	5	7	51	4	77	4	0	7	11	.389	0	0-0	1	4.83	5.15
2008	3 Tms		52	0	0	15	54.2	267	73	42	31	5	5	2	3	28	4	51	2	1	1	5	.167	0	0-0	6	6.42	5.10
08	Bos	AL	9	0	0	2	12.2	64	18	12	9	0	1	1	1	9	0	6	1	0	0	1	.000	0	0-0	0	7.43	6.39
08	Mil	NL	7	0	0	1	7.1	41	13	10	7	0	1	0	0	5	0	10	0	0	0	1	.000	0	0-0	0	8.77	8.59
08	Atl	NL	36	0	0	12	34.2	162	42	20	15	5	3	1	2	14	4	35	1	1	1	3	.250	0	0-0	6	5.56	3.89
Postseason			31	13	0	7	30.2	135	31	13	12	6	2	0	4	10	3	16	3	0	2	4	.333	0	0-1	4	4.86	3.52
16 ML YEARS			786	108	2	175	1369.1	6053	1506	781	677	112	66	46	94	536	70	810	41	11	85	75	.531	0	22-46	150	4.70	4.45

Willy Taveras

Bats: R Throws: R Pos: CF-124; PH-17; PR-4   Ht: 6'0" Wt: 160 Born: 12/25/1981 Age: 27

Year	Team	Lg	G	AB	H	2B	3B	HR	(Hm	Rd)	TB	R	RBI	RC	TBB	IBB	SO	HBP	SH	SF	SB	CS	SB%	GDP	Avg	OBP	Slg
									BATTING												BASERUNNING				AVERAGES		
2004	Hou	NL	10	1	0	0	0	0	(0	0)	0	2	0	0	0	0	1	0	1	0	1	0	1.00	0	.000	.000	.000
2005	Hou	NL	152	592	172	13	4	3	(2	1)	202	82	29	61	25	1	103	7	7	4	34	11	.76	4	.291	.325	.341
2006	Hou	NL	149	529	147	19	5	1	(0	1)	179	83	30	64	34	0	88	11	11	2	33	9	.79	6	.278	.333	.338
2007	Col	NL	97	372	119	13	2	2	(2	0)	142	64	24	56	21	0	55	7	7	1	33	9	.79	1	.320	.367	.382
2008	Col	NL	133	479	120	15	2	1	(0	1)	142	64	26	49	36	0	79	5	15	3	68	7	.91	4	.251	.308	.296
Postseason			21	69	18	4	1	0	(0	0)	24	9	1	8	4	0	13	3	4	0	2	1	.67	0	.261	.329	.348
5 ML YEARS			541	1973	558	60	13	7	(4	3)	665	295	109	230	116	1	326	30	41	10	169	36	.82	15	.283	.331	.337

Taylor Teagarden

Bats: R Throws: R Pos: C-12; DH-4; PH-2   Ht: 6'1" Wt: 200 Born: 12/21/1983 Age: 25

Year	Team	Lg	G	AB	H	2B	3B	HR	(Hm	Rd)	TB	R	RBI	RC	TBB	IBB	SO	HBP	SH	SF	SB	CS	SB%	GDP	Avg	OBP	Slg
									BATTING												BASERUNNING				AVERAGES		
2005	Spkane	A-	31	96	27	5	4	7	(-	-)	61	23	16	25	23	0	32	2	0	1	1	1	.50	1	.281	.426	.635
2006	Rngrs	R	20	1	0	0	0	0	(-	-)	1	4	1	1	9	0	7	0	0	1	1	0	1.00	0	.050	.345	.050
2007	Bkrsfld	A+	81	292	92	25	0	20	(-	-)	177	75	67	78	65	0	89	6	0	1	2	1	.67	4	.315	.448	.606
2007	Frisco	AA	29	102	30	3	0	7	(-	-)	54	19	16	19	10	0	39	1	0	2	0	0	-	1	.294	.357	.529
2008	Frisco	AA	16	59	10	2	0	2	(-	-)	18	6	6	5	8	0	23	1	0	1	1	0	1.00	6	.169	.279	.305
2008	Okla	AAA	57	187	42	5	3	7	(-	-)	74	26	16	26	28	0	59	2	1	0	0	0	-	6	.225	.332	.396
2008	Tex	AL	16	47	15	5	0	6	(3	3)	38	10	17	15	5	0	19	1	0	0	0	0	-	0	.319	.396	.809

Mark Teahen

Bats: L Throws: R Pos: RF-92; LF-31; 3B-19; 1B-14; CF-1; DH-1; PR-1   Ht: 6'3" Wt: 210 Born: 9/6/1981 Age: 27

Year	Team	Lg	G	AB	H	2B	3B	HR	(Hm	Rd)	TB	R	RBI	RC	TBB	IBB	SO	HBP	SH	SF	SB	CS	SB%	GDP	Avg	OBP	Slg
									BATTING												BASERUNNING				AVERAGES		
2005	KC	AL	130	447	110	29	4	7	(3	4)	168	60	55	52	40	2	107	1	2	1	7	2	.78	13	.246	.309	.376
2006	KC	AL	109	393	114	21	7	18	(9	9)	203	70	69	79	40	2	85	2	2	2	10	0	1.00	5	.290	.357	.517
2007	KC	AL	144	544	155	31	8	7	(6	1)	223	78	60	82	55	8	127	3	4	2	13	5	.72	23	.285	.353	.410
2008	KC	AL	149	572	146	31	4	15	(4	11)	230	66	59	66	46	4	131	3	0	2	4	3	.57	6	.255	.313	.402
4 ML YEARS			532	1956	525	112	23	47	(22	25)	824	274	243	279	181	16	450	9	8	7	34	10	.77	47	.268	.332	.421

Mark Teixeira

Bats: B **Throws:** R **Pos:** 1B-153; DH-4 **Ht:** 6'3" **Wt:** 220 **Born:** 4/11/1980 **Age:** 29

								BATTING											BASERUNNING				AVERAGES		
Year	Team	Lg	G	AB	H	2B	3B	HR	(Hm | Rd)	TB	R	RBI	RC	TBB	IBB	SO	HBP	SH	SF	SB	CS	SB%	GDP	Avg	OBP	Slg
2003	Tex	AL	146	529	137	29	5	26	(19 | 7)	254	66	84	78	44	5	120	14	0	2	1	2	.33	14	.259	.331	.480
2004	Tex	AL	145	545	153	34	2	38	(18 | 20)	305	101	112	120	68	12	117	10	0	2	4	1	.80	6	.281	.370	.560
2005	Tex	AL	162	644	194	41	3	43	(30 | 13)	370	112	144	148	72	5	124	11	0	3	4	0	1.00	18	.301	.379	.575
2006	Tex	AL	162	628	177	45	1	33	(12 | 21)	323	99	110	114	89	12	128	4	0	6	2	0	1.00	17	.282	.371	.514
2007	2 Tms		132	494	151	33	2	30	(14 | 16)	278	86	105	116	72	13	112	7	0	2	0	0	-	7	.306	.400	.563
2008	2 Tms		157	574	177	41	0	33	(19 | 14)	317	102	121	119	97	13	93	7	0	7	2	0	1.00	17	.308	.410	.552
07	Tex	AL	78	286	85	24	1	13	(5 | 8)	150	48	49	58	45	10	66	3	0	1	0	0	-	5	.297	.397	.524
07	Atl	NL	54	208	66	9	1	17	(9 | 8)	128	38	56	58	27	3	46	4	0	1	0	0	-	2	.317	.404	.615
08	Atl	NL	103	381	108	27	0	20	(11 | 9)	195	63	78	69	65	9	70	3	0	2	0	0	-	13	.283	.390	.512
08	LAA	AL	54	193	69	14	0	13	(8 | 5)	122	39	43	50	32	4	23	4	0	5	2	0	1.00	4	.358	.449	.632
	6 ML YEARS		904	3414	989	223	13	203	(112 | 91)	1847	566	676	695	442	60	694	53	0	22	13	3	.81	79	.290	.378	.541

Miguel Tejada

Bats: R **Throws:** R **Pos:** SS-157; PH-2 **Ht:** 5'9" **Wt:** 213 **Born:** 5/25/1974 **Age:** 35

								BATTING											BASERUNNING				AVERAGES		
Year	Team	Lg	G	AB	H	2B	3B	HR	(Hm | Rd)	TB	R	RBI	RC	TBB	IBB	SO	HBP	SH	SF	SB	CS	SB%	GDP	Avg	OBP	Slg
1997	Oak	AL	26	99	20	3	2	2	(1 | 1)	33	10	10	7	2	0	22	3	0	0	2	0	1.00	3	.202	.240	.333
1998	Oak	AL	105	365	85	20	1	11	(5 | 6)	140	53	45	40	28	0	86	7	4	3	5	6	.45	8	.233	.298	.384
1999	Oak	AL	159	593	149	33	4	21	(12 | 9)	253	93	84	82	57	3	94	10	9	5	8	7	.53	11	.251	.325	.427
2000	Oak	AL	160	607	167	32	1	30	(16 | 14)	291	105	115	99	66	6	102	4	2	2	6	0	1.00	15	.275	.349	.479
2001	Oak	AL	162	622	166	31	3	31	(17 | 14)	296	107	113	94	43	5	89	13	1	4	11	5	.69	14	.267	.326	.476
2002	Oak	AL	162	662	204	30	0	34	(17 | 17)	336	108	131	123	38	3	84	11	0	4	7	2	.78	21	.308	.354	.508
2003	Oak	AL	162	636	177	42	0	27	(15 | 12)	300	98	106	103	53	7	65	6	0	8	10	0	1.00	12	.278	.336	.472
2004	Bal	AL	162	653	203	40	2	34	(17 | 17)	349	107	150	124	48	6	73	10	0	14	4	1	.80	24	.311	.360	.534
2005	Bal	AL	162	654	199	50	5	26	(16 | 10)	337	89	98	102	40	9	83	7	0	3	5	1	.83	26	.304	.349	.515
2006	Bal	AL	162	648	214	37	0	24	(17 | 7)	323	99	100	99	46	10	79	9	0	6	6	2	.75	28	.330	.379	.498
2007	Bal	AL	133	514	152	19	1	18	(12 | 6)	227	72	81	76	41	9	55	10	0	3	2	1	.67	22	.296	.357	.442
2008	Hou	NL	158	632	179	38	3	13	(8 | 5)	262	92	66	61	24	4	72	6	1	3	7	7	.50	32	.283	.314	.415
	Postseason		20	85	18	7	0	1	(0 | 1)	28	9	8	6	3	0	16	1	0	2	1	0	1.00	0	.212	.242	.329
	12 ML YEARS		1713	6685	1915	375	22	271	(153 | 118)	3147	1033	1099	1010	486	62	904	96	17	55	73	32	.70	216	.286	.341	.471

Robinson Tejeda

Pitches: R **Bats:** R **Pos:** RP-28; SP-1 **Ht:** 6'3" **Wt:** 230 **Born:** 3/24/1982 **Age:** 27

			HOW MUCH HE PITCHED					WHAT HE GAVE UP											THE RESULTS					
Year	Team	Lg	G	GS	CG	GF	IP	BFP	H	R	ER	HR	SH	SF	HB	TBB	IBB	SO	WP	Bk	W	L	Pct	ShO	Sv-Op Hld	ERC	ERA
2008	Okla*	AAA	10	4	0	3	33.0	128	20	8	8	2	0	1	1	10	0	39	0	0	1	1	.500	0	1- -	1.65	2.18
2005	Phi	NL	26	13	0	5	85.2	371	67	36	34	5	3	2	8	51	4	72	3	1	4	3	.571	0	0-0 1	3.64	3.57
2006	Tex	AL	14	14	0	0	73.2	329	83	40	35	10	1	5	3	32	1	40	1	1	5	5	.500	0	0-0 0	5.41	4.28
2007	Tex	AL	19	19	0	0	95.1	454	110	78	70	17	3	6	6	60	2	69	10	0	5	9	.357	0	0-0 0	6.77	6.61
2008	2 Tms	AL	29	1	0	15	45.1	186	27	23	20	4	0	3	1	24	0	45	5	0	2	2	.500	0	0-1 1	2.43	3.97
08	Tex	AL	4	0	0	1	6.0	29	5	6	6	1	0	1	0	5	0	4	0	0	0	0	-	0	0-1 0	5.04	9.00
08	KC	AL	25	1	0	14	39.1	157	22	17	14	3	0	2	1	19	0	41	5	0	2	2	.500	0	0-0 1	2.08	3.20
	4 ML YEARS		88	47	0	20	300.0	1340	287	177	159	36	7	16	18	167	7	226	19	2	16	19	.457	0	0-1 2	4.81	4.77

Marcus Thames

Bats: R **Throws:** R **Pos:** LF-73; DH-14; PH-10; 1B-9; RF-7 **Ht:** 6'2" **Wt:** 220 **Born:** 3/6/1977 **Age:** 32

								BATTING											BASERUNNING				AVERAGES		
Year	Team	Lg	G	AB	H	2B	3B	HR	(Hm | Rd)	TB	R	RBI	RC	TBB	IBB	SO	HBP	SH	SF	SB	CS	SB%	GDP	Avg	OBP	Slg
2002	NYY	AL	7	13	3	1	0	1	(1 | 0)	7	2	2	2	0	0	4	0	0	0	0	0	-	0	.231	.231	.538
2003	Tex	AL	30	73	15	2	0	1	(0 | 1)	20	12	4	5	8	0	18	2	0	1	0	1	.00	2	.205	.298	.274
2004	Det	AL	61	165	42	12	0	10	(5 | 5)	84	24	33	30	16	0	42	2	0	1	0	1	.00	3	.255	.326	.509
2005	Det	AL	38	107	21	2	0	7	(3 | 4)	44	11	16	10	9	1	38	1	0	1	0	0	-	1	.196	.263	.411
2006	Det	AL	110	348	89	20	2	26	(11 | 15)	191	61	60	60	37	0	92	4	0	1	1	1	.50	0	.256	.333	.549
2007	Det	AL	86	269	65	15	0	18	(14 | 4)	134	37	54	39	13	1	72	1	0	1	2	1	.67	6	.242	.278	.498
2008	Det	AL	103	316	76	12	0	25	(10 | 15)	163	50	56	44	24	0	95	0	0	2	0	3	.00	6	.241	.292	.516
	Postseason		8	21	5	2	0	0	(0 | 0)	7	3	1	3	1	0	6	0	0	0	0	0	-	0	.238	.273	.333
	7 ML YEARS		435	1291	311	64	2	88	(44 | 44)	643	197	225	190	107	2	361	10	0	7	3	7	.30	18	.241	.302	.498

Joe Thatcher

Pitches: L **Bats:** L **Pos:** RP-25 **Ht:** 6'2" **Wt:** 223 **Born:** 10/4/1981 **Age:** 27

			HOW MUCH HE PITCHED					WHAT HE GAVE UP											THE RESULTS					
Year	Team	Lg	G	GS	CG	GF	IP	BFP	H	R	ER	HR	SH	SF	HB	TBB	IBB	SO	WP	Bk	W	L	Pct	ShO	Sv-Op Hld	ERC	ERA
2004	River	IND	29	0	0	14	42.1	179	38	15	14	3	2	1	2	15	4	55	2	0	2	3	.400	0	5- -	3.17	2.98
2005	River	IND	18	0	0	17	21.1	87	18	5	3	0	2	1	1	4	0	27	2	0	4	2	.667	0	5- -	1.99	1.27
2005	Helena	R+	6	0	0	6	7.2	33	8	3	3	1	0	0	1	1	0	10	0	0	2	0	1.000	0	2- -	3.89	3.52
2005	BrvdCt	A+	7	0	0	4	9.0	32	6	0	0	0	0	0	0	0	0	14	3	0	0	0	-	0	2- -	0.94	0.00
2006	WV	A	26	0	0	25	29.2	126	28	13	8	2	0	1	4	6	0	42	1	0	1	3	.250	0	10- -	3.26	2.43
2006	BrvdCt	A+	16	0	0	12	30.2	114	12	6	1	1	2	0	2	9	0	32	0	0	3	1	.750	0	2- -	0.98	0.29
2006	Hntsvl	AA	4	0	0	1	5.1	21	2	2	1	0	0	1	0	2	0	6	0	0	1	0	1.000	0	0- -	1.18	1.69
2007	Hntsvl	AA	14	0	0	3	16.1	61	11	1	1	0	1	0	1	2	0	20	0	0	1	0	1.000	0	0- -	1.32	0.55
2007	Nashv	AAA	24	0	0	5	21.2	94	19	5	5	0	2	0	1	7	1	33	4	1	2	1	.667	0	1- -	2.44	2.08
2007	Portlnd	AAA	8	0	0	1	8.2	38	10	4	1	0	0	0	1	1	0	11	1	0	1	0	1.000	0	0- -	3.47	1.04

			HOW MUCH HE PITCHED						WHAT HE GAVE UP													THE RESULTS							
Year	Team	Lg	G	GS	CG	GF	IP	BFP	H	R	ER	HR	SH	SF	HB	TBB	IBB	SO	WP	Bk	W	L	Pct	ShO	Sv-Op	Hld	ERC	ERA
2008	Portlnd	AAA	37	0	0	10	39.0	168	38	17	12	2	1	1	2	11	1	44	4	0	5	2	.714	0	3- -	-	3.23	2.77
2007	SD	NL	22	0	0	5	21.0	85	13	6	3	1	0	0	1	6	2	16	0	0	2	2	.500	0	0-0	2	1.49	1.29
2008	SD	NL	25	0	0	7	25.2	128	42	25	24	4	2	3	0	13	2	17	0	0	0	4	.000	0	0-3	5	8.91	8.42
2 ML YEARS			47	0	0	12	46.2	213	55	31	27	5	2	3	1	19	4	33	0	0	2	6	.250	0	0-3	7	5.05	5.21

Ryan Theriot

Bats: R **Throws:** R **Pos:** SS-149; PH-6   **Ht:** 5'11" **Wt:** 175 **Born:** 12/7/1979 **Age:** 29

			BATTING																	BASERUNNING				AVERAGES		
Year	Team	Lg	G	AB	H	2B	3B	HR	(Hm	Rd)	TB	R	RBI	RC	TBB	IBB	SO	HBP	SH	SF	SB	CS	SB%	GDP	Avg	OBP	Slg
2005	ChC	NL	9	13	2	1	0	0	(0	0)	3	3	0	0	1	0	2	0	0	0	0	0	-	0	.154	.214	.231
2006	ChC	NL	53	134	44	11	3	3	(3	0)	70	34	16	31	17	0	18	2	6	0	13	2	.87	5	.328	.412	.522
2007	ChC	NL	148	537	143	30	2	3	(3	0)	186	80	45	64	49	1	50	0	8	3	28	4	.88	12	.266	.326	.346
2008	ChC	NL	149	580	178	19	4	1	(1	0)	208	85	38	78	73	1	58	3	4	1	22	13	.63	19	.307	.387	.359
Postseason			3	12	3	0	0	0	(0	0)	3	0	1	1	1	0	1	0	0	0	1	0	1.00	1	.250	.308	.250
4 ML YEARS			359	1264	367	61	9	7	(7	0)	467	202	99	173	140	2	128	5	18	4	63	19	.77	36	.290	.362	.369

Curtis Thigpen

Bats: R **Throws:** R **Pos:** C-9; 1B-1; PH-1; PR-1   **Ht:** 5'11" **Wt:** 190 **Born:** 4/19/1983 **Age:** 26

			BATTING																	BASERUNNING				AVERAGES		
Year	Team	Lg	G	AB	H	2B	3B	HR	(Hm	Rd)	TB	R	RBI	RC	TBB	IBB	SO	HBP	SH	SF	SB	CS	SB%	GDP	Avg	OBP	Slg
2004	Auburn	A-	45	166	50	11	2	7	(-	-)	86	34	29	34	23	0	32	3	1	3	1	1	.50	2	.301	.390	.518
2005	Lansng	A	79	293	84	18	2	5	(-	-)	121	41	35	54	54	0	34	1	2	2	5	0	1.00	10	.287	.397	.413
2005	NHam	AA	39	141	40	8	0	4	(-	-)	60	18	15	21	9	0	19	3	4	0	0	0	-	1	.284	.340	.426
2006	NHam	AA	87	309	80	25	5	5	(-	-)	130	49	36	53	52	0	61	4	5	3	5	1	.83	7	.259	.370	.421
2006	Syrcse	AAA	13	53	14	3	0	1	(-	-)	20	2	9	5	2	0	9	1	0	0	0	1	.00	0	.264	.304	.377
2007	Syrcse	AAA	50	179	51	10	0	3	(-	-)	70	20	20	26	17	2	23	2	1	3	1	0	1.00	5	.285	.348	.391
2008	Syrcse	AAA	96	361	80	23	0	3	(-	-)	112	28	41	30	21	0	58	3	5	5	2	1	.67	15	.222	.267	.310
2007	Tor	AL	47	101	24	5	0	0	(0	0)	29	13	11	13	8	0	17	0	1	0	2	0	1.00	4	.238	.294	.287
2008	Tor	AL	10	17	3	0	0	1	(0	1)	6	2	1	1	1	0	8	1	2	0	0	0	-	0	.176	.263	.353
2 ML YEARS			57	118	27	5	0	1	(0	1)	35	15	12	14	9	0	25	1	3	0	2	0	1.00	4	.229	.289	.297

Clete Thomas

Bats: L **Throws:** R **Pos:** LF-25; CF-16; RF-3; PH-3; PR-2   **Ht:** 5'11" **Wt:** 195 **Born:** 11/14/1983 **Age:** 25

			BATTING																	BASERUNNING				AVERAGES		
Year	Team	Lg	G	AB	H	2B	3B	HR	(Hm	Rd)	TB	R	RBI	RC	TBB	IBB	SO	HBP	SH	SF	SB	CS	SB%	GDP	Avg	OBP	Slg
2005	Oneont	A-	18	70	27	5	1	1	(-	-)	37	19	14	19	12	1	11	2	0	0	9	0	1.00	0	.386	.488	.529
2005	WMich	A	51	194	55	8	5	0	(-	-)	73	39	11	29	21	3	37	2	2	2	11	3	.79	3	.284	.356	.376
2006	Lkland	A+	132	529	136	30	5	6	(-	-)	194	67	40	70	56	3	127	6	1	3	34	13	.72	8	.257	.333	.367
2007	Erie	AA	137	528	148	30	6	8	(-	-)	214	97	53	80	59	0	110	7	3	3	18	11	.62	3	.280	.359	.405
2008	Toledo	AAA	76	291	72	18	2	9	(-	-)	121	44	45	43	37	2	88	1	3	1	29	11	.73	9	.247	.333	.416
2008	Det	AL	40	116	33	9	1	1	(1	0)	47	7	9	17	14	1	26	1	2	0	2	0	1.00	1	.284	.366	.405

Frank Thomas

Bats: R **Throws:** R **Pos:** DH-69; PH-2   **Ht:** 6'5" **Wt:** 275 **Born:** 5/27/1968 **Age:** 41

			BATTING																	BASERUNNING				AVERAGES		
Year	Team	Lg	G	AB	H	2B	3B	HR	(Hm	Rd)	TB	R	RBI	RC	TBB	IBB	SO	HBP	SH	SF	SB	CS	SB%	GDP	Avg	OBP	Slg
1990	CWS	AL	60	191	63	11	3	7	(2	5)	101	39	31	46	44	0	54	2	0	3	0	1	.00	5	.330	.454	.529
1991	CWS	AL	158	559	178	31	2	32	(24	8)	309	104	109	134	138	13	112	1	0	2	1	2	.33	20	.318	.453	.553
1992	CWS	AL	160	573	185	46	2	24	(10	14)	307	108	115	132	122	6	88	5	0	11	6	3	.67	19	.323	.439	.536
1993	CWS	AL	153	549	174	36	0	41	(26	15)	333	106	128	137	112	23	54	2	0	13	4	2	.67	10	.317	.426	.607
1994	CWS	AL	113	399	141	34	1	38	(22	16)	291	106	101	127	109	12	61	2	0	7	2	3	.40	15	.353	.487	.729
1995	CWS	AL	145	493	152	27	0	40	(15	25)	299	102	111	132	136	29	74	6	0	12	3	2	.60	14	.308	.454	.606
1996	CWS	AL	141	527	184	26	0	40	(16	24)	330	110	134	137	109	26	70	5	0	8	1	1	.50	25	.349	.459	.626
1997	CWS	AL	146	530	184	35	0	35	(16	19)	324	110	125	139	109	9	69	3	0	7	1	1	.50	15	.347	.456	.611
1998	CWS	AL	160	585	155	35	2	29	(15	14)	281	109	109	111	110	2	93	6	0	11	7	0	1.00	14	.265	.381	.480
1999	CWS	AL	135	486	148	36	0	15	(9	6)	229	74	77	95	87	13	66	9	0	8	3	3	.50	15	.305	.414	.471
2000	CWS	AL	159	582	191	44	0	43	(30	13)	364	115	143	148	112	18	94	5	0	8	1	3	.25	13	.328	.436	.625
2001	CWS	AL	20	68	15	3	0	4	(2	2)	30	8	10	10	10	2	12	0	0	1	0	0	-	0	.221	.316	.441
2002	CWS	AL	148	523	132	29	1	28	(24	4)	247	77	92	96	88	2	115	7	0	10	3	0	1.00	10	.252	.361	.472
2003	CWS	AL	153	546	146	35	0	42	(29	13)	307	87	105	115	100	4	115	12	0	4	0	0	-	11	.267	.390	.562
2004	CWS	AL	74	240	65	16	0	18	(14	4)	135	53	49	59	64	3	57	6	0	1	0	2	.00	2	.271	.434	.563
2005	CWS	AL	34	105	23	3	0	12	(9	3)	62	19	26	18	16	0	31	0	0	3	0	0	-	2	.219	.315	.590
2006	Oak	AL	137	466	126	11	0	39	(23	16)	254	77	114	99	81	3	81	6	0	6	0	0	-	13	.270	.381	.545
2007	Tor	AL	155	531	147	30	0	26	(19	7)	255	63	95	97	81	3	94	7	0	5	0	0	-	14	.277	.377	.480
2008	2 Tms	AL	71	246	59	7	1	8	(7	1)	92	27	30	34	39	0	57	3	0	3	0	0	-	9	.240	.349	.374
08	Tor	AL	16	60	10	1	0	3	(3	0)	20	7	11	8	11	0	13	1	0	0	0	0	-	3	.167	.306	.333
08	Oak	AL	55	186	49	6	1	5	(4	1)	72	20	19	26	28	0	44	2	0	1	0	0	-	6	.263	.364	.387
Postseason			16	49	11	1	0	3	(0	3)	21	5	5	12	18	4	10	1	0	0	0	0	-	1	.224	.441	.429
19 ML YEARS			2322	8199	2468	495	12	521	(312	209)	4550	1494	1704	1866	1667	168	1397	87	0	121	32	23	.58	226	.301	.419	.555

Justin Thomas

Pitches: L Bats: L Pos: RP-8   Ht: 6'3" Wt: 226 Born: 1/18/1984 Age: 25

Year	Team	Lg	G	GS	CG	GF	IP	BFP	H	R	ER	HR	SH	SF	HB	TBB	IBB	SO	WP	Bk	W	L	Pct	ShO	Sv-Op	Hld	ERC	ERA
2005	Everett	A-	18	6	0	2	59.0	256	63	31	25	2	0	0	4	20	0	48	5	0	3	3	.500	0	0--	-	4.04	3.81
2006	Wisc	A	11	11	0	0	61.0	268	69	29	21	4	5	2	3	17	0	51	2	0	5	5	.500	0	0--	-	4.24	3.10
2006	InldEm	A+	17	17	1	0	105.1	454	108	58	48	10	2	3	3	45	0	111	6	0	9	4	.692	1	0--	-	4.49	4.10
2007	WTenn	AA	24	24	0	0	119.1	559	147	82	73	11	10	6	5	61	0	100	12	0	4	9	.308	0	0--	-	5.99	5.51
2008	WTenn	AA	25	17	1	1	118.2	525	116	66	57	11	6	1	10	57	1	106	6	3	7	7	.500	1	0--	-	4.55	4.32
2008	Tacom	AAA	7	1	0	4	17.0	71	15	7	7	2	0	0	0	9	0	21	2	0	2	1	.667	0	1--	-	4.21	3.71
2008	Sea	AL	8	0	0	2	4.0	22	9	3	3	0	1	0	0	2	0	2	1	0	0	1	.000	0	0-1	1	12.01	6.75

Jim Thome

Bats: L Throws: R Pos: DH-139; PH-10   Ht: 6'3" Wt: 255 Born: 8/27/1970 Age: 38

Year	Team	Lg	G	AB	H	2B	3B	HR	(Hm	Rd)	TB	R	RBI	RC	TBB	IBB	SO	HBP	SH	SF	SB	CS	SB%	GDP	Avg	OBP	Slg
1991	Cle	AL	27	98	25	4	2	1	(0	1)	36	7	9	9	5	1	16	1	0	0	1	1	.50	4	.255	.298	.367
1992	Cle	AL	40	117	24	3	1	2	(1	1)	35	8	12	9	10	2	34	2	0	2	2	0	1.00	3	.205	.275	.299
1993	Cle	AL	47	154	41	11	0	7	(5	2)	73	28	22	30	29	1	36	4	0	5	2	1	.67	3	.266	.385	.474
1994	Cle	AL	98	321	86	20	1	20	(10	10)	168	58	52	56	46	5	84	0	1	1	3	3	.50	11	.268	.359	.523
1995	Cle	AL	137	452	142	29	3	25	(13	12)	252	92	73	109	97	3	113	5	0	3	4	3	.57	3	.314	.438	.558
1996	Cle	AL	151	505	157	28	5	38	(18	20)	309	122	116	132	123	8	141	6	0	2	2	2	.50	13	.311	.450	.612
1997	Cle	AL	147	496	142	25	0	40	(17	23)	287	104	102	120	120	9	146	3	0	8	1	1	.50	9	.286	.423	.579
1998	Cle	AL	123	440	129	34	2	30	(18	12)	257	89	85	104	89	8	141	4	0	4	1	0	1.00	7	.293	.413	.584
1999	Cle	AL	146	494	137	27	2	33	(19	14)	267	101	108	116	127	13	171	4	0	4	0	0	-	6	.277	.426	.540
2000	Cle	AL	158	557	150	33	1	37	(21	16)	296	106	106	119	118	4	171	4	0	5	1	0	1.00	9	.269	.398	.531
2001	Cle	AL	156	526	153	26	1	49	(30	19)	328	101	124	130	111	14	185	4	0	3	0	1	.00	9	.291	.416	.624
2002	Cle	AL	147	480	146	19	2	52	(30	22)	325	101	118	139	122	18	139	5	0	6	1	2	.33	5	.304	.445	.677
2003	Phi	NL	159	578	154	30	3	47	(28	19)	331	111	131	125	111	11	182	4	0	5	0	3	.00	5	.266	.385	.573
2004	Phi	NL	143	508	139	28	1	42	(19	23)	295	97	105	97	104	26	144	2	0	4	0	2	.00	10	.274	.396	.581
2005	Phi	NL	59	193	40	7	0	7	(6	1)	68	26	30	25	45	4	59	2	0	2	0	0	-	5	.207	.360	.352
2006	CWS	AL	143	490	141	26	0	42	(25	17)	293	108	109	120	107	12	147	6	0	7	0	0	-	4	.288	.416	.598
2007	CWS	AL	130	432	119	19	0	35	(21	14)	243	79	96	104	95	11	134	6	0	3	0	1	.00	10	.275	.410	.563
2008	CWS	AL	149	503	123	28	0	34	(19	15)	253	93	90	96	91	9	147	4	0	4	1	0	1.00	18	.245	.362	.503
Postseason			55	188	43	1	1	17	(13	4)	97	32	36	29	25	1	61	2	1	0	0	0	-	3	.229	.326	.516
18 ML YEARS			2160	7344	2048	397	24	541	(300	241)	4116	1431	1488	1640	1550	159	2190	66	1	68	19	20	.49	138	.279	.406	.560

Brad Thompson

Pitches: R Bats: R Pos: RP-20; SP-6   Ht: 6'1" Wt: 190 Born: 1/31/1982 Age: 27

Year	Team	Lg	G	GS	CG	GF	IP	BFP	H	R	ER	HR	SH	SF	HB	TBB	IBB	SO	WP	Bk	W	L	Pct	ShO	Sv-Op	Hld	ERC	ERA
2008	Memp*	AAA	3	3	0	0	12.2	62	22	13	11	4	0	0	0	2	0	4	0	0	1	1	.500	0	0--	-	9.19	7.82
2005	StL	NL	40	0	0	8	55.0	225	46	22	18	5	3	0	4	15	2	29	0	0	4	0	1.000	0	1-1	7	2.90	2.95
2006	StL	NL	43	1	0	16	56.2	245	58	23	21	4	3	0	5	20	3	32	1	0	1	2	.333	0	0-0	3	4.11	3.34
2007	StL	NL	44	17	0	10	129.1	580	157	76	68	23	4	2	13	40	2	53	4	0	8	6	.571	0	0-0	0	5.99	4.73
2008	StL	NL	26	6	0	10	64.2	273	72	38	37	5	2	3	3	19	1	32	2	0	6	3	.667	0	0-1	1	4.44	5.15
Postseason			8	0	0	1	4.1	23	8	5	4	2	0	1	0	1	0	4	0	0	0	1	.000	0	0-0	0	11.13	8.31
4 ML YEARS			153	24	0	44	305.2	1323	333	159	144	37	12	5	25	94	8	146	7	0	19	11	.633	0	1-2	11	4.72	4.24

Daryl Thompson

Pitches: R Bats: R Pos: SP-3   Ht: 6'0" Wt: 180 Born: 11/2/1985 Age: 23

Year	Team	Lg	G	GS	CG	GF	IP	BFP	H	R	ER	HR	SH	SF	HB	TBB	IBB	SO	WP	Bk	W	L	Pct	ShO	Sv-Op	Hld	ERC	ERA
2003	Expos	R	12	10	0	1	46.0	185	49	16	11	1	2	0	2	11	0	18	2	0	1	2	.333	0	0--	-	3.67	2.15
2004	Savann	A	25	21	0	1	102.2	442	117	66	58	13	4	4	9	30	0	79	4	2	4	9	.308	0	0--	-	5.14	5.08
2005	Savann	A	11	11	0	0	53.2	225	46	23	20	3	0	2	1	24	0	48	3	1	2	3	.400	0	0--	-	3.29	3.35
2006	Vrmnt	A-	4	4	0	0	6.2	31	5	5	5	0	0	0	1	5	0	8	1	0	0	1	.000	0	0--	-	3.72	6.75
2006	Reds	R	5	4	0	0	14.0	52	10	4	4	1	0	1	2	4	0	16	0	0	0	0	-	0	0--	-	2.80	2.57
2007	Dayton	A	5	5	0	0	28.0	99	16	3	3	1	0	0	0	2	0	24	0	0	5	0	1.000	0	0--	-	0.94	0.96
2007	Srsota	A+	22	22	0	0	105.0	446	106	51	44	19	3	2	5	31	0	97	1	3	9	5	.643	0	0--	-	4.49	3.77
2008	Chatt	AA	10	10	0	0	61.1	233	43	19	12	2	4	3	0	14	0	56	5	0	2	2	.600	0	0--	-	1.64	1.76
2008	Lsvlle	AAA	7	7	0	0	45.2	181	39	15	14	4	2	0	2	9	0	33	1	0	5	0	1.000	0	0--	-	2.68	2.76
2008	Reds	R	1	0	0	0	4.0	15	2	1	0	0	0	0	0	0	0	3	0	0	0	0	-	0	0--	-	0.50	0.00
2008	Srsota	A+	3	3	0	0	15.2	70	20	12	12	2	3	1	0	7	0	7	0	0	0	2	.000	0	0--	-	6.34	6.89
2008	Cin	NL	3	3	0	0	14.1	69	20	11	11	3	0	0	1	7	0	6	1	1	0	2	.000	0	0-0	0	8.14	6.91

Rich Thompson

Pitches: R Bats: R Pos: RP-2   Ht: 6'1" Wt: 180 Born: 7/1/1984 Age: 24

Year	Team	Lg	G	GS	CG	GF	IP	BFP	H	R	ER	HR	SH	SF	HB	TBB	IBB	SO	WP	Bk	W	L	Pct	ShO	Sv-Op	Hld	ERC	ERA
2002	Angels	R	15	0	0	2	23.1	96	14	12	7	0	1	1	3	9	0	29	1	1	2	0	1.000	0	1--	-	1.54	2.70
2003	CRpds	A	31	0	0	23	37.2	145	18	5	1	1	2	1	0	13	0	54	6	0	1	2	.333	0	9--	-	1.14	0.24
2003	RCuca	A+	24	0	0	18	29.1	135	28	19	16	4	0	1	2	18	1	33	5	0	2	2	.500	0	8--	-	5.08	4.91
2004	RCuca	A+	41	5	0	17	77.2	339	76	36	34	9	1	0	3	33	2	71	4	1	3	2	.600	0	4--	-	4.26	3.94
2005	RCuca	A+	42	15	0	14	121.1	539	132	76	71	20	2	5	2	53	0	92	12	2	6	8	.429	0	3--	-	5.28	5.27
2006	Ark	AA	42	0	0	30	66.2	276	52	39	38	13	2	4	4	27	0	60	6	1	3	4	.429	0	10--	-	3.79	5.13
2006	Salt Lk	AAA	4	0	0	2	4.1	25	9	6	6	1	0	3	0	4	0	3	0	0	0	1	.000	0	1--	-	15.35	12.46
2007	RCuca	A+	1	0	0	0	2.0	7	1	0	0	1	0	0	0	0	0	3	1	0	0	0	-	0	0--	-	0.54	0.00

Year	Team	Lg	HOW MUCH HE PITCHED						WHAT HE GAVE UP												THE RESULTS							
			G	GS	CG	GF	IP	BFP	H	R	ER	HR	SH	SF	HB	TBB	IBB	SO	WP	Bk	W	L	Pct	ShO	Sv-Op	Hld	ERC	ERA
2007	Ark	AA	21	3	0	7	49.1	196	34	15	11	5	2	1	3	14	1	50	3	1	2	3	.400	0	0- -	-	2.25	2.01
2007	Salt Lk	AAA	16	0	0	10	24.2	100	17	7	6	2	2	1	3	6	0	32	3	0	3	0	1.000	0	1- -	-	2.18	2.19
2008	Salt Lk	AAA	10	0	0	5	13.1	61	12	6	6	1	0	1	1	9	0	11	1	0	1	0	1.000	0	0- -	-	4.66	4.05
2008	Angels	R	7	0	0	2	9.0	33	6	3	3	0	0	0	0	2	0	13	2	0	0	0	-	0	2- -	-	1.42	3.00
2007	LAA	AL	7	0	0	2	6.2	32	10	8	8	4	0	0	0	3	0	9	2	0	0	0	-	0	0-0	0	11.85	10.80
2008	LAA	AL	2	0	0	1	2.0	12	4	5	5	0	0	0	0	2	0	1	1	0	0	0	-	0	0-0	0	12.01	22.50
2 ML YEARS			9	0	0	3	8.2	44	14	13	13	4	0	0	0	5	0	10	3	0	0	0	-	0	0-0	0	12.09	13.50

Matt Thornton

Pitches: L Bats: L Pos: RP-74   Ht: 6'5" Wt: 245 Born: 9/15/1976 Age: 32

Year	Team	Lg	HOW MUCH HE PITCHED						WHAT HE GAVE UP												THE RESULTS							
			G	GS	CG	GF	IP	BFP	H	R	ER	HR	SH	SF	HB	TBB	IBB	SO	WP	Bk	W	L	Pct	ShO	Sv-Op	Hld	ERC	ERA
2004	Sea	AL	19	1	0	8	32.2	148	30	15	15	2	2	1	0	25	1	30	2	0	1	2	.333	0	0-0	0	4.75	4.13
2005	Sea	AL	55	0	0	15	57.0	262	54	33	33	13	1	1	0	42	2	57	7	0	0	4	.000	0	0-1	5	6.06	5.21
2006	CWS	AL	63	0	0	20	54.0	227	46	20	20	5	1	3	1	21	4	49	1	0	5	3	.625	0	2-5	18	3.12	3.33
2007	CWS	AL	68	0	0	13	56.1	249	59	31	30	4	0	2	2	26	6	55	3	0	4	4	.500	0	2-7	17	4.35	4.79
2008	CWS	AL	74	0	0	12	67.1	268	48	20	20	5	1	1	2	19	2	77	3	0	5	3	.625	0	1-6	20	2.07	2.67
5 ML YEARS			279	1	0	68	267.1	1154	237	119	118	29	5	8	5	133	15	268	16	0	15	16	.484	0	5-19	60	3.86	3.97

Erick Threets

Pitches: L Bats: L Pos: RP-7   Ht: 6'5" Wt: 240 Born: 11/4/1981 Age: 27

Year	Team	Lg	HOW MUCH HE PITCHED						WHAT HE GAVE UP												THE RESULTS							
			G	GS	CG	GF	IP	BFP	H	R	ER	HR	SH	SF	HB	TBB	IBB	SO	WP	Bk	W	L	Pct	ShO	Sv-Op	Hld	ERC	ERA
2001	SnJos	A+	14	14	0	0	59.1	270	49	34	28	2	1	3	7	40	0	60	14	3	0	10	.000	0	0- -	-	4.07	4.25
2001	Hgrstn	A-	12	0	0	3	24.0	94	13	3	2	1	0	0	1	9	0	32	2	1	2	0	1.000	0	1- -	-	1.55	0.75
2002	SnJos	A+	26	0	0	4	28.1	136	23	24	21	2	2	1	3	28	1	43	6	1	0	1	.000	0	0- -	-	5.42	6.67
2003	Nrwich	AA	11	0	0	4	11.1	72	15	20	20	1	0	0	2	21	0	16	6	0	0	0	-	0	0- -	-	12.88	15.88
2003	Hgrstn	A-	22	0	0	0	49.2	215	26	20	18	2	0	2	7	42	0	47	9	1	2	3	.400	0	0- -	-	3.32	3.26
2005	Nrwich	AA	30	0	0	7	42.2	201	43	28	24	2	1	0	2	31	0	35	6	0	1	2	.333	0	2- -	-	5.13	5.06
2006	Fresno	AAA	49	0	0	11	62.2	284	51	26	20	4	4	2	5	44	0	51	7	0	2	1	.667	0	0- -	-	4.20	2.87
2007	Fresno	AAA	40	3	0	12	54.2	238	46	26	21	4	3	2	2	35	0	40	2	1	3	1	.750	0	1- -	-	4.14	3.46
2008	Fresno	AAA	37	4	0	4	66.1	288	53	30	25	5	4	2	1	36	0	46	5	0	4	5	.444	0	0- -	-	3.35	3.39
2007	SF	NL	3	0	0	1	2.1	15	5	5	5	0	0	0	0	3	0	1	1	0	0	0	-	0	0-0	0	14.38	19.29
2008	SF	NL	7	0	0	6	10.0	50	11	4	4	1	1	0	3	9	2	6	1	0	0	1	.000	0	0-0	0	7.86	3.60
2 ML YEARS			10	0	0	7	12.1	65	16	9	9	1	1	0	3	12	2	7	2	0	0	1	.000	0	0-0	0	9.04	6.57

Joe Thurston

Bats: L Throws: R Pos: LF-4   Ht: 5'11" Wt: 190 Born: 9/29/1979 Age: 29

Year	Team	Lg	BATTING																	BASERUNNING				AVERAGES		
			G	AB	H	2B	3B	HR	(Hm	Rd)	TB	R	RBI	RC	TBB	IBB	SO	HBP	SH	SF	SB	CS	SB%	GDP	Avg	OBP	Slg
2008	Pwtckt*	AAA	126	507	160	28	5	11	(-	-)	231	84	64	87	35	1	75	11	14	8	19	11	.63	8	.316	.367	.456
2002	LAD	NL	8	13	6	1	0	0	(0	0)	7	1	1	3	0	0	1	0	1	1	0	0	-	0	.462	.429	.538
2003	LAD	NL	12	10	2	0	0	0	(0	0)	2	2	0	0	1	0	1	0	0	0	0	0	-	0	.200	.273	.200
2004	LAD	NL	17	17	3	1	1	0	(0	0)	6	1	1	1	0	0	5	0	0	1	0	0	-	0	.176	.167	.353
2006	Phi	NL	18	18	4	1	0	0	(0	0)	5	3	0	1	1	0	2	1	0	0	0	0	-	0	.222	.300	.278
2008	Bos	AL	4	8	0	0	0	0	(0	0)	0	0	0	0	0	0	1	1	0	0	0	0	-	0	.000	.111	.000
5 ML YEARS			59	66	15	3	1	0	(0	0)	20	7	2	5	2	0	10	2	1	2	0	0	-	0	.227	.264	.303

Terry Tiffee

Bats: B Throws: R Pos: PH-5; LF-1   Ht: 6'3" Wt: 213 Born: 4/21/1979 Age: 30

Year	Team	Lg	BATTING																	BASERUNNING				AVERAGES		
			G	AB	H	2B	3B	HR	(Hm	Rd)	TB	R	RBI	RC	TBB	IBB	SO	HBP	SH	SF	SB	CS	SB%	GDP	Avg	OBP	Slg
2008	LsVgs*	AAA	93	392	148	39	3	9	(-	-)	220	73	69	87	27	5	43	2	0	4	1	2	.33	17	.378	.416	.561
2004	Min	AL	17	44	12	4	0	2	(1	1)	22	7	8	5	3	0	3	1	0	0	0	0	-	2	.273	.333	.500
2005	Min	AL	54	150	31	8	1	1	(1	0)	44	9	15	8	8	1	15	0	0	1	1	0	1.00	10	.207	.245	.293
2006	Min	AL	20	45	11	1	0	2	(1	1)	18	4	6	5	4	1	8	0	0	0	0	1	.00	2	.244	.306	.400
2008	LAD	NL	6	4	1	0	0	0	(0	0)	1	0	0	1	0	0	0	1	0	0	0	0	-	0	.250	.400	.250
4 ML YEARS			97	243	55	13	1	5	(3	2)	85	20	29	19	15	2	26	2	0	1	1	1	.50	14	.226	.276	.350

Mike Timlin

Pitches: R Bats: R Pos: RP-47   Ht: 6'4" Wt: 210 Born: 3/10/1966 Age: 43

Year	Team	Lg	HOW MUCH HE PITCHED						WHAT HE GAVE UP												THE RESULTS							
			G	GS	CG	GF	IP	BFP	H	R	ER	HR	SH	SF	HB	TBB	IBB	SO	WP	Bk	W	L	Pct	ShO	Sv-Op	Hld	ERC	ERA
2008	Pwtckt*	AAA	5	1	0	0	5.0	17	2	0	0	0	0	0	0	0	0	4	0	0	0	0	-	0	0- -	-	0.35	0.00
1991	Tor	AL	63	3	0	17	108.1	463	94	43	38	6	6	2	1	50	11	85	5	0	11	6	.647	0	3-8	9	3.14	3.16
1992	Tor	AL	26	0	0	14	43.2	190	45	23	20	0	2	1	1	20	5	35	0	0	0	2	.000	0	1-1	1	3.68	4.12
1993	Tor	AL	54	0	0	27	55.2	254	63	32	29	7	1	3	1	27	3	49	1	0	4	2	.667	0	1-4	9	5.32	4.69
1994	Tor	AL	34	0	0	16	40.0	179	41	25	23	5	0	0	2	20	0	38	3	0	0	1	.000	0	2-4	5	5.01	5.18
1995	Tor	AL	31	0	0	19	42.0	179	38	13	10	1	3	0	2	17	5	36	3	1	4	3	.571	0	5-9	4	3.04	2.14
1996	Tor	AL	59	0	0	56	56.2	230	47	25	23	4	2	3	2	18	4	52	3	0	1	6	.143	0	31-38	2	2.74	3.65
1997	2 Tms		64	0	0	31	72.2	297	69	30	26	8	6	1	1	20	5	45	1	1	6	4	.600	0	10-18	9	3.40	3.22
1998	Sea	AL	70	0	0	40	79.1	321	78	26	26	5	4	2	3	16	2	60	0	0	3	3	.500	0	19-24	6	3.17	2.95
1999	Bal	AL	62	0	0	52	63.0	261	51	30	25	9	1	1	5	23	3	50	1	0	3	9	.250	0	27-36	0	3.46	3.57
2000	2 Tms		62	0	0	40	64.2	295	67	33	30	8	7	2	4	35	6	52	0	0	5	4	.556	0	12-18	6	5.08	4.18
2001	StL	NL	67	0	0	19	72.2	307	78	35	33	7	4	2	4	19	4	47	3	1	4	5	.444	0	3-7	12	3.95	4.09

Year	Team	Lg	G	GS	CG	GF	IP	BFP	H	R	ER	HR	SH	SF	HB	TBB	IBB	SO	WP	Bk	W	L	Pct	ShO	Sv-Op	Hld	ERC	ERA
2002	2 Tms	NL	72	1	0	17	96.2	376	75	35	32	15	2	1	5	14	2	50	3	0	4	6	.400	0	0-4	20	2.46	2.98
2003	Bos	AL	72	0	0	13	83.2	340	77	37	33	11	4	1	4	9	3	65	0	0	6	4	.600	0	2-6	17	2.81	3.55
2004	Bos	AL	76	0	0	12	76.1	320	75	35	35	8	3	1	5	19	3	56	1	0	5	4	.556	0	1-4	20	3.64	4.13
2005	Bos	AL	81	0	0	27	80.1	342	86	23	20	2	3	6	2	20	5	59	3	0	7	3	.700	0	13-20	24	3.35	2.24
2006	Bos	AL	68	0	0	22	64.0	279	78	33	31	7	4	1	2	16	4	30	3	0	6	6	.500	0	9-17	21	4.86	4.36
2007	Bos	AL	50	0	0	19	55.1	222	46	23	21	7	5	2	3	14	3	31	0	0	2	1	.667	0	1-1	8	2.96	3.42
2008	Bos	AL	47	0	0	26	49.1	227	60	32	31	9	4	3	1	20	4	32	1	0	4	4	.500	0	1-1	0	5.85	5.66
97	Tor	AL	38	0	0	26	47.0	190	41	17	15	6	4	1	1	15	4	36	1	1	3	2	.600	0	9-13	2	3.30	2.87
97	Sea	AL	26	0	0	5	25.2	107	28	13	11	2	2	0	0	5	1	9	0	0	3	2	.600	0	1-5	7	3.59	3.86
00	Bal	AL	37	0	0	31	35.0	157	37	22	19	6	5	1	2	15	3	26	0	0	2	3	.400	0	11-15	1	5.08	4.89
00	StL	NL	25	0	0	9	29.2	138	30	11	11	2	2	1	2	20	3	26	0	0	1	1	.750	0	1-3	5	5.05	3.34
02	StL	NL	42	1	0	10	61.0	236	48	19	17	9	2	0	4	7	2	35	1	0	1	3	.250	0	0-2	12	2.41	2.51
02	Phi	NL	30	0	0	7	35.2	140	27	16	15	6	0	1	1	7	0	15	2	0	3	3	.500	0	0-2	8	2.55	3.79
Postseason			44	0	0	8	48.0	209	44	26	21	4	5	3	1	15	3	41	1	0	0	2	.000	0	1-3	11	3.00	3.94
18 ML YEARS			1058	4	0	467	1204.1	5082	1168	533	486	118	58	32	47	377	72	872	31	3	75	73	.507	0	141-220	173	3.63	3.63

Clay Timpner

Bats: L **Throws:** L **Pos:** LF-1; PH-1 **Ht:** 6'2" **Wt:** 197 **Born:** 5/13/1983 **Age:** 26

								BATTING												BASERUNNING				AVERAGES		
Year	Team	Lg	G	AB	H	2B	3B	HR	(Hm Rd)	TB	R	RBI	RC	TBB	IBB	SO	HBP	SH	SF	SB	CS	SB%	GDP	Avg	OBP	Slg
2004	Salem	A+	68	294	86	7	2	5	(- -)	112	37	28	40	20	0	35	1	4	1	16	5	.76	3	.293	.339	.381
2004	SnJos	A+	6	25	7	2	0	0	(- -)	9	4	2	3	1	0	2	0	0	1	1	0	1.00	0	.280	.296	.360
2005	SnJos	A+	126	549	160	22	12	4	(- -)	218	85	39	76	34	1	93	3	2	3	34	13	.72	7	.291	.334	.397
2006	Conn	AA	66	261	58	11	2	3	(- -)	82	26	13	21	13	1	31	1	5	2	11	6	.65	6	.222	.260	.314
2006	Fresno	AAA	62	238	68	8	3	3	(- -)	91	33	19	27	10	0	31	0	3	0	5	7	.42	5	.286	.315	.382
2007	Fresno	AAA	109	392	118	11	4	6	(- -)	155	51	39	56	37	0	68	2	5	1	9	11	.45	7	.301	.363	.395
2008	Fresno	AAA	119	436	107	19	3	3	(- -)	141	64	46	45	33	1	61	3	5	3	13	6	.68	8	.245	.301	.323
2008	SF	NL	2	2	0	0	0	0	(0 0)	0	0	0	0	0	0	2	0	0	0	0	0	-	0	.000	.000	.000

Matt Tolbert

Bats: B **Throws:** R **Pos:** 3B-17; SS-14; 2B-11; PH-6; DH-3; PR-3 **Ht:** 6'0" **Wt:** 185 **Born:** 5/4/1982 **Age:** 27

								BATTING												BASERUNNING				AVERAGES		
Year	Team	Lg	G	AB	H	2B	3B	HR	(Hm Rd)	TB	R	RBI	RC	TBB	IBB	SO	HBP	SH	SF	SB	CS	SB%	GDP	Avg	OBP	Slg
2004	Elizab	R+	33	104	32	7	2	3	(- -)	52	23	18	19	12	0	13	0	1	1	3	2	.60	4	.308	.376	.500
2005	FtMyrs	A+	111	417	111	20	6	3	(- -)	152	55	46	53	35	1	80	3	15	2	11	4	.73	3	.266	.326	.365
2006	NwBrit	AA	72	248	64	15	1	3	(- -)	90	33	35	34	30	1	43	4	5	5	5	1	.83	3	.258	.341	.363
2006	FtMyrs	A+	40	155	47	6	3	4	(- -)	71	20	24	27	14	1	17	1	1	2	7	2	.78	4	.303	.360	.458
2007	Roch	AAA	121	417	122	24	7	6	(- -)	178	65	53	67	37	0	56	5	12	6	11	3	.79	4	.293	.353	.427
2008	NwBrit	AA	14	56	14	3	0	0	(- -)	17	6	6	3	1	0	6	0	0	0	4	3	.57	0	.250	.263	.304
2008	Min	AL	41	113	32	6	3	0	(0 0)	44	18	6	13	7	0	19	0	2	1	7	1	.88	5	.283	.322	.389

Brett Tomko

Pitches: R **Bats:** R **Pos:** RP-12; SP-10 **Ht:** 6'4" **Wt:** 220 **Born:** 4/7/1973 **Age:** 36

Year	Team	Lg	G	GS	CG	GF	IP	BFP	H	R	ER	HR	SH	SF	HB	TBB	IBB	SO	WP	Bk	W	L	Pct	ShO	Sv-Op	Hld	ERC	ERA
2008	Lk Els*	A+	1	0	0	0	1.0	3	0	0	0	0	0	0	0	0	0	1	0	0	0	0	-	0	0--	-	0.00	0.00
2008	Portlnd*	AAA	5	2	0	0	5.0	22	4	5	5	1	0	0	0	3	0	6	0	0	0	0	-	0	0--	-	4.36	9.00
1997	Cin	NL	22	19	0	1	126.0	519	106	50	48	14	5	9	4	47	4	95	5	0	11	7	.611	0	0-0	0	3.31	3.43
1998	Cin	NL	34	34	1	0	210.2	887	198	111	104	22	12	2	7	64	3	162	9	1	13	12	.520	0	0-0	0	3.50	4.44
1999	Cin	NL	33	26	1	1	172.0	744	175	103	99	31	9	5	4	60	10	132	8	0	5	7	.417	0	0-0	1	4.51	4.92
2000	Sea	AL	32	8	0	10	92.1	401	92	53	48	12	5	3	5	40	4	59	1	1	7	5	.583	0	1-2	3	4.49	4.68
2001	Sea	AL	11	4	0	1	34.2	164	42	24	20	9	1	2	0	15	2	22	1	0	3	1	.750	0	0-1	0	6.31	5.19
2002	SD	NL	32	32	3	0	204.1	871	212	107	102	31	6	8	2	60	9	126	3	0	10	10	.500	0	0-0	0	4.18	4.49
2003	StL	NL	33	32	2	0	202.2	903	252	126	119	35	12	3	5	57	2	114	6	0	13	9	.591	0	0-0	0	5.63	5.28
2004	SF	NL	32	31	2	1	194.0	825	196	98	87	19	7	1	6	64	3	108	10	0	11	7	.611	1	0-0	0	3.82	4.04
2005	SF	NL	33	30	3	1	190.2	823	205	99	95	20	6	5	7	57	11	114	5	0	8	15	.348	0	1-1	1	4.18	4.48
2006	LAD	NL	44	15	0	2	112.1	491	123	67	59	17	7	7	2	29	0	76	3	1	8	7	.533	0	0-3	5	4.37	4.73
2007	2 Tms	NL	40	19	0	3	131.1	588	149	89	81	18	8	6	2	48	1	105	5	0	4	12	.250	0	0-0	0	4.96	5.55
2008	2 Tms		22	10	0	3	70.0	307	83	51	49	11	1	2	0	18	2	49	4	0	2	7	.222	0	0-2	0	4.88	6.30
07	LAD	NL	33	15	0	8	104.0	475	124	75	67	13	6	6	2	42	1	79	3	0	2	11	.154	0	0-0	0	5.39	5.80
07	SD	NL	7	4	0	0	27.1	113	25	14	14	5	3	0	0	6	0	26	2	0	2	1	.667	0	0-0	0	3.37	4.61
08	KC	AL	16	10	0	1	60.2	271	80	49	47	11	1	2	0	13	0	40	4	0	2	7	.222	0	0-2	0	5.73	6.97
08	SD	NL	6	0	0	2	9.1	36	3	2	2	0	0	0	0	5	2	9	0	0	0	0	-	0	0-0	0	0.81	1.93
Postseason			5	0	0	0	8.2	40	8	8	5	0	1	1	0	7	1	4	2	1	0	0	-	0	0-0	0	4.23	5.19
12 ML YEARS			368	260	12	29	1741.0	7523	1833	978	906	239	79	55	36	559	51	1162	60	3	95	99	.490	1	2-9	10	4.34	4.68

Yorvit Torrealba

Bats: R **Throws:** R **Pos:** C-67; PH-4 **Ht:** 5'11" **Wt:** 200 **Born:** 7/19/1978 **Age:** 30

								BATTING												BASERUNNING				AVERAGES		
Year	Team	Lg	G	AB	H	2B	3B	HR	(Hm Rd)	TB	R	RBI	RC	TBB	IBB	SO	HBP	SH	SF	SB	CS	SB%	GDP	Avg	OBP	Slg
2001	SF	NL	3	4	2	0	1	0	(0 0)	4	0	2	2	0	0	0	0	0	0	0	0	-	0	.500	.500	1.000
2002	SF	NL	53	136	38	10	0	2	(0 2)	54	17	14	16	14	2	20	2	3	0	0	0	-	11	.279	.355	.397
2003	SF	NL	66	200	52	10	2	4	(2 2)	78	22	29	25	14	1	39	2	3	2	1	0	1.00	7	.260	.312	.390
2004	SF	NL	64	172	39	7	3	6	(3 3)	70	19	24	17	13	3	31	2	4	1	2	0	1.00	7	.227	.302	.407
2005	2 Tms	NL	76	201	47	12	0	3	(2 1)	68	32	15	14	16	1	50	2	5	0	1	0	1.00	8	.234	.297	.338
2006	Col	NL	65	223	55	16	3	7	(3 4)	98	23	43	30	11	1	49	4	2	1	4	3	.57	7	.247	.293	.439
2007	Col	NL	113	396	101	22	1	8	(6 2)	149	47	47	34	34	1	73	6	6	1	2	1	.67	19	.255	.323	.376

			BATTING																		BASERUNNING				AVERAGES		
Year	Team	Lg	G	AB	H	2B	3B	HR	(Hm	Rd)	TB	R	RBI	RC	TBB	IBB	SO	HBP	SH	SF	SB	CS	SB%	GDP	Avg	OBP	Slg
2008	Col	NL	70	236	58	17	0	6	(5	1)	93	19	31	23	12	0	44	5	5	3	0	4	.00	10	.246	.293	.394
05	SF	NL	34	93	21	6	0	1	(1	0)	32	18	7	7	9	1	25	1	2	0	1	0	1.00	3	.226	.301	.344
05	Sea	AL	42	108	26	4	0	2	(1	1)	36	14	8	7	7	0	25	1	3	0	0	0	-	5	.241	.293	.333
	Postseason		13	42	10	2	0	1	(1	0)	15	5	9	6	4	1	6	0	2	1	0	0	-	2	.238	.298	.357
	8 ML YEARS		510	1568	392	94	10	36	(22	14)	614	179	204	162	118	9	306	23	28	8	10	8	.56	65	.250	.310	.392

Eider Torres

Bats: B **Throws:** R **Pos:** SS-5; DH-2; PR-2; 2B-1   **Ht:** 5'9" **Wt:** 175 **Born:** 1/16/1983 **Age:** 26

			BATTING																		BASERUNNING				AVERAGES		
Year	Team	Lg	G	AB	H	2B	3B	HR	(Hm	Rd)	TB	R	RBI	RC	TBB	IBB	SO	HBP	SH	SF	SB	CS	SB%	GDP	Avg	OBP	Slg
2002	Burlgtn	A	45	194	62	6	1	0	(-	-)	70	26	13	32	15	0	22	1	8	0	28	3	.90	4	.320	.371	.361
2002	MhVlly	A-	19	75	23	5	0	0	(-	-)	28	9	8	9	3	1	9	1	0	0	9	5	.64	2	.307	.342	.373
2003	Knstn	A+	124	447	111	13	0	1	(-	-)	127	63	39	46	39	1	73	4	16	1	43	14	.75	4	.248	.314	.284
2004	Knstn	A+	113	440	133	24	3	3	(-	-)	172	68	46	67	22	5	46	3	8	4	48	6	.89	6	.302	.337	.391
2005	Akron	AA	108	453	129	27	5	6	(-	-)	184	73	56	64	16	0	66	11	18	5	34	9	.79	5	.285	.322	.406
2006	Akron	AA	104	428	117	12	2	2	(-	-)	139	49	42	51	32	0	54	2	11	2	41	12	.77	12	.273	.325	.325
2006	Buffalo	AAA	11	44	9	0	0	0	(-	-)	9	5	2	2	2	0	4	0	2	0	3	1	.75	1	.205	.239	.205
2007	Norfolk	AAA	108	393	105	16	0	4	(-	-)	133	38	41	43	24	0	55	1	12	5	22	11	.67	7	.267	.307	.338
2008	Norfolk	AAA	115	473	145	20	6	1	(-	-)	180	69	46	69	38	1	60	1	10	3	28	11	.72	9	.307	.357	.381
2008	Bal	AL	8	9	2	0	0	0	(0	0)	2	2	0	0	0	0	2	0	0	0	0	0	-	1	.222	.222	.222

Salomon Torres

Pitches: R **Bats:** R **Pos:** RP-71   **Ht:** 5'11" **Wt:** 220 **Born:** 3/11/1972 **Age:** 37

			HOW MUCH HE PITCHED						WHAT HE GAVE UP										THE RESULTS							
Year	Team	Lg	G	GS	CG	GF	IP	BFP	H	R	ER	HR	SH	SF	HB	TBB	IBB	SO	WP	Bk	W	L	Pct	ShO	Sv-Op	Hld	ERC	ERA
1993	SF	NL	8	8	0	0	44.2	196	37	21	20	5	7	1	1	27	3	23	3	1	3	5	.375	0	0-0	0	3.95	4.03
1994	SF	NL	16	14	1	2	84.1	378	95	55	51	10	4	8	7	34	2	42	4	1	2	8	.200	0	0-0	0	5.29	5.44
1995	2 Tms		20	14	1	4	80.0	384	100	61	56	16	1	0	2	49	3	47	1	2	3	9	.250	0	0-0	0	7.30	6.30
1996	Sea	AL	10	7	1	1	49.0	212	44	27	25	5	3	1	3	15	0	36	1	0	3	3	.500	1	0-0	0	3.98	4.59
1997	2 Tms		14	0	0	4	25.2	127	32	29	28	2	3	1	3	15	0	11	3	0	0	0	-	0	0-0	0	6.44	9.82
2002	Pit	NL	5	5	0	0	30.0	127	28	10	9	2	2	0	3	13	1	12	0	0	2	1	.667	0	0-0	0	4.07	2.70
2003	Pit	NL	41	16	0	7	121.0	518	128	65	64	19	4	1	7	42	5	84	3	0	7	5	.583	0	2-3	6	4.88	4.76
2004	Pit	NL	84	0	0	20	92.0	380	87	33	27	6	9	3	6	22	6	62	5	0	7	7	.500	0	0-4	30	3.12	2.64
2005	Pit	NL	78	0	0	32	94.2	388	76	34	29	7	3	2	5	36	7	55	5	0	5	5	.500	0	3-3	8	2.91	2.76
2006	Pit	NL	94	0	0	24	93.1	411	98	42	34	6	7	2	6	38	9	72	3	0	3	6	.333	0	12-15	20	4.23	3.28
2007	Pit	NL	56	0	0	28	52.2	231	57	34	32	7	1	3	4	17	0	45	3	0	2	4	.333	0	12-18	5	4.78	5.47
2008	Mil	NL	71	0	0	46	80.0	344	75	35	31	6	7	4	4	33	5	51	2	0	7	5	.583	0	28-35	5	3.70	3.49
95	SF	NL	4	1	0	2	8.0	40	13	8	8	4	0	0	0	7	0	2	0	0	0	1	.000	0	0-0	0	15.31	9.00
95	Sea	AL	16	13	1	2	72.0	344	87	53	48	12	1	0	2	42	3	45	1	2	3	8	.273	0	0-0	0	6.55	6.00
97	Sea	AL	2	0	0	1	3.1	21	7	10	10	0	0	0	1	3	0	0	0	0	0	0	-	0	0-0	0	13.67	27.00
97	Mon	NL	12	0	0	3	22.1	106	25	19	18	2	3	1	2	12	0	11	3	0	0	0	-	0	0-0	0	5.47	7.25
	12 ML YEARS		497	64	3	168	847.1	3696	857	446	406	91	51	26	51	349	43	540	33	4	44	58	.431	1	57-78	74	4.42	4.31

J.R. Towles

Bats: R **Throws:** R **Pos:** C-53; PH-2   **Ht:** 6'2" **Wt:** 190 **Born:** 2/11/1984 **Age:** 25

			BATTING																		BASERUNNING				AVERAGES		
Year	Team	Lg	G	AB	H	2B	3B	HR	(Hm	Rd)	TB	R	RBI	RC	TBB	IBB	SO	HBP	SH	SF	SB	CS	SB%	GDP	Avg	OBP	Slg
2004	Grnsvle	R	39	111	27	6	0	0	(-	-)	33	17	8	14	12	0	23	11	1	1	4	3	.57	1	.243	.370	.297
2005	Lxngtn	A	45	162	56	14	2	5	(-	-)	89	35	23	37	16	0	29	10	5	0	11	7	.61	3	.346	.436	.549
2006	Lxngtn	A	81	284	90	19	2	12	(-	-)	149	39	55	57	21	0	46	10	4	2	13	5	.72	5	.317	.382	.525
2007	Salem	A+	26	90	18	3	2	0	(-	-)	25	14	11	9	12	0	15	9	0	4	3	5	.38	2	.200	.339	.278
2007	CpChr	AA	61	216	70	12	2	11	(-	-)	119	47	49	50	23	1	35	15	3	0	9	4	.69	2	.324	.425	.551
2007	RdRck	AAA	13	43	12	0	0	0	(-	-)	12	5	2	3	4	0	7	1	2	0	2	4	.33	0	.279	.354	.279
2008	RdRck	AAA	48	168	51	8	2	7	(-	-)	84	28	28	31	13	1	31	6	3	2	4	3	.57	6	.304	.370	.500
2007	Hou	NL	14	40	15	5	0	1	(0	1)	23	9	12	11	3	1	1	0	0	0	0	1	.00	1	.375	.432	.575
2008	Hou	NL	54	146	20	5	0	4	(3	1)	37	10	16	10	16	1	40	6	3	0	0	0	-	3	.137	.250	.253
	2 ML YEARS		68	186	35	10	0	5	(3	2)	60	19	28	21	19	2	41	7	3	0	0	1	.00	4	.188	.288	.323

Billy Traber

Pitches: L **Bats:** L **Pos:** RP-19   **Ht:** 6'5" **Wt:** 205 **Born:** 9/18/1979 **Age:** 29

			HOW MUCH HE PITCHED						WHAT HE GAVE UP										THE RESULTS							
Year	Team	Lg	G	GS	CG	GF	IP	BFP	H	R	ER	HR	SH	SF	HB	TBB	IBB	SO	WP	Bk	W	L	Pct	ShO	Sv-Op	Hld	ERC	ERA
2008	S-WB*	AAA	40	2	0	9	47.2	202	46	19	18	3	1	0	4	13	2	41	4	0	2	1	.667	0	4--	-	3.39	3.40
2003	Cle	AL	33	18	1	0	111.2	503	132	67	65	15	4	3	5	40	4	88	6	0	6	9	.400	1	0-0	1	5.31	5.24
2006	Was	NL	15	8	0	0	43.1	202	53	33	31	5	3	1	8	14	2	25	0	0	4	3	.571	0	0-0	2	5.81	6.44
2007	Was	NL	28	2	0	5	39.2	182	50	22	21	4	3	5	2	13	3	27	0	0	2	2	.500	0	0-1	2	5.34	4.76
2008	NYY	AL	19	0	0	3	16.2	80	23	13	13	3	0	0	2	7	1	11	2	0	0	0	-	0	0-0	1	7.54	7.02
	4 ML YEARS		95	28	1	8	211.1	967	258	135	130	27	10	9	17	74	10	151	8	0	12	14	.462	1	0-1	6	5.58	5.54

Steve Trachsel

Pitches: R Bats: R Pos: SP-8; RP-2

Ht: 6'4" Wt: 205 Born: 10/31/1970 Age: 38

			HOW MUCH HE PITCHED					WHAT HE GAVE UP											THE RESULTS							
Year	Team	Lg	G	GS	CG	GF	IP	BFP	H	R	ER	HR	SH	SF	HB	TBB	IBB	SO	WP	Bk	W	L	Pct	ShO	Sv-Op	Hld	ERC	ERA
1993	ChC	NL	3	3	0	0	19.2	78	16	10	10	4	1	1	0	3	0	14	1	0	0	2	.000	0	0-0	0	2.71	4.58
1994	ChC	NL	22	22	1	0	146.0	612	133	57	52	19	3	3	3	54	4	108	6	0	9	7	.563	0	0-0	0	3.74	3.21
1995	ChC	NL	30	29	2	0	160.2	722	174	104	92	25	12	5	0	76	8	117	2	1	7	13	.350	0	0-0	0	5.13	5.15
1996	ChC	NL	31	31	3	0	205.0	845	181	82	69	30	3	3	8	62	3	132	5	2	13	9	.591	2	0-0	0	3.52	3.03
1997	ChC	NL	34	34	0	0	201.1	878	225	110	101	32	8	11	5	69	6	160	4	1	8	12	.400	0	0-0	0	5.04	4.51
1998	ChC	NL	33	33	1	0	208.0	894	204	107	103	27	9	7	8	84	5	149	3	2	15	8	.652	0	0-0	0	4.35	4.46
1999	ChC	NL	34	34	4	0	205.2	894	226	133	127	32	6	14	3	64	4	149	8	3	8	18	.308	0	0-0	0	4.69	5.56
2000	2 Tms	AL	34	34	3	0	200.2	882	232	116	107	26	6	6	6	74	2	110	4	0	8	15	.348	1	0-0	0	5.25	4.80
2001	NYM	NL	28	28	1	0	173.2	726	168	90	86	28	8	7	3	47	7	144	4	0	11	13	.458	1	0-0	0	3.80	4.46
2002	NYM	NL	30	30	1	0	173.2	741	170	80	65	16	9	3	0	69	4	105	4	0	11	11	.500	1	0-0	0	3.88	3.37
2003	NYM	NL	33	33	2	0	204.2	857	204	90	86	26	8	8	3	65	9	111	5	2	16	10	.615	2	0-0	0	3.97	3.78
2004	NYM	NL	33	33	0	0	202.2	881	203	104	90	25	11	8	5	83	9	117	4	2	12	13	.480	0	0-0	0	4.31	4.00
2005	NYM	NL	6	6	0	0	37.0	157	37	20	17	6	2	2	1	12	0	24	1	0	1	4	.200	0	0-0	0	4.34	4.14
2006	NYM	NL	30	30	1	0	164.2	736	185	94	91	23	4	7	4	78	1	79	4	0	15	8	.652	0	0-0	0	5.55	4.97
2007	2 Tms		29	29	1	0	158.0	702	176	89	86	19	5	9	2	76	1	56	7	3	7	11	.389	0	0-0	0	5.34	4.90
2008	Bal	AL	10	8	0	1	39.2	194	53	41	37	10	1	0	1	27	0	16	2	0	2	5	.286	0	0-0	0	8.85	8.39
00	TB	AL	23	23	3	0	137.2	606	160	76	70	16	2	5	6	49	1	78	3	0	6	10	.375	1	0-0	0	5.19	4.58
00	Tor	AL	11	11	0	0	63.0	276	72	40	37	10	4	1	0	25	1	32	1	0	2	5	.286	0	0-0	0	5.38	5.29
07	Bal	AL	25	25	1	0	140.2	623	151	73	70	16	3	7	2	69	0	45	6	3	6	8	.429	0	0-0	0	5.08	4.48
07	ChC	NL	4	4	0	0	17.1	79	25	16	16	3	2	2	0	7	1	11	1	0	1	3	.250	0	0-0	0	7.56	8.31
	Postseason		2	2	0	0	4.1	29	11	7	7	1	0	0	0	6	0	3	0	0	0	1	.000	0	0-0	0	21.46	14.54
16 ML YEARS			420	417	20	1	2501.0	10799	2587	1327	1219	348	96	94	52	943	63	1591	64	16	143	159	.474	7	0-0	0	4.53	4.39

Andy Tracy

Bats: L Throws: R Pos: PH-4

Ht: 6'3" Wt: 220 Born: 12/11/1973 Age: 35

						BATTING															BASERUNNING				AVERAGES		
Year	Team	Lg	G	AB	H	2B	3B	HR	(Hm	Rd)	TB	R	RBI	RC	TBB	IBB	SO	HBP	SH	SF	SB	CS	SB%	GDP	Avg	OBP	Slg
2008	LV*	AAA	124	430	124	34	0	22	(-	-)	224	71	85	89	65	8	96	4	2	6	5	0	1.00	16	.288	.382	.521
2000	Mon	NL	83	192	50	8	1	11	(	)	93	29	32	31	22	1	61	2	0	2	1	0	1.00	3	.260	.339	.484
2001	Mon	NL	38	55	6	1	0	2	(	)	13	4	8	1	6	0	26	0	0	2	0	0	-	1	.109	.190	.236
2004	Col	NL	15	16	3	1	0	0	(0	0)	4	1	1	1	1	0	8	0	0	0	0	0	-	0	.188	.235	.250
2008	Phi	NL	4	2	0	0	0	0	(0	0)	0	0	1	0	1	0	1	0	0	1	0	0	-	0	.000	.250	.000
4 ML YEARS			140	265	59	10	1	13	(0	0)	110	34	42	33	30	1	96	2	0	5	1	0	1.00	4	.223	.301	.415

Chad Tracy

Bats: L Throws: R Pos: 1B-65; PH-17; DH-5; 3B-2

Ht: 6'2" Wt: 215 Born: 5/22/1980 Age: 29

						BATTING															BASERUNNING				AVERAGES		
Year	Team	Lg	G	AB	H	2B	3B	HR	(Hm	Rd)	TB	R	RBI	RC	TBB	IBB	SO	HBP	SH	SF	SB	CS	SB%	GDP	Avg	OBP	Slg
2008	Tucsn*	AAA	12	49	15	2	0	0	(-	-)	17	5	6	5	1	0	4	0	0	0	0	0	-	2	.306	.320	.347
2004	Ari	NL	143	481	137	29	3	8	(6	2)	196	45	53	63	45	3	60	0	1	5	2	3	.40	11	.285	.343	.407
2005	Ari	NL	145	503	155	34	4	27	(9	18)	278	73	72	82	35	4	78	8	1	6	3	1	.75	10	.308	.359	.553
2006	Ari	NL	154	597	168	41	0	20	(14	6)	269	91	80	85	54	5	129	5	1	5	5	1	.83	11	.281	.343	.451
2007	Ari	NL	76	227	60	18	2	7	(3	4)	103	30	35	33	29	4	43	1	0	3	0	0	-	8	.264	.346	.454
2008	Ari	NL	88	273	73	16	0	8	(3	5)	113	25	39	32	16	2	49	1	0	2	0	0	-	5	.267	.308	.414
5 ML YEARS			606	2081	593	138	9	70	(35	35)	959	264	279	295	179	18	359	15	3	21	10	5	.67	45	.285	.343	.461

Matt Treanor

Bats: R Throws: R Pos: C-65

Ht: 6'0" Wt: 210 Born: 3/3/1976 Age: 33

						BATTING															BASERUNNING				AVERAGES		
Year	Team	Lg	G	AB	H	2B	3B	HR	(Hm	Rd)	TB	R	RBI	RC	TBB	IBB	SO	HBP	SH	SF	SB	CS	SB%	GDP	Avg	OBP	Slg
2008	Jupiter*	A+	5	16	5	1	0	1	(-	-)	9	7	5	4	6	0	3	0	0	1	0	0	-	1	.313	.478	.563
2004	Fla	NL	29	55	13	2	0	0	(0	0)	15	7	1	4	4	0	13	2	0	0	0	0	-	3	.236	.311	.273
2005	Fla	NL	58	134	27	8	0	0	(0	0)	35	10	13	13	16	1	28	3	1	0	0	0	-	5	.201	.301	.261
2006	Fla	NL	67	157	36	6	1	2	(0	2)	50	12	14	16	19	4	34	5	2	2	0	1	.00	4	.229	.328	.318
2007	Fla	NL	55	171	46	7	1	4	(2	2)	67	16	19	26	19	1	29	5	2	1	0	0	-	2	.269	.357	.392
2008	Fla	NL	65	206	49	7	0	2	(1	1)	62	18	23	25	18	1	53	3	5	2	1	0	1.00	2	.238	.306	.301
5 ML YEARS			274	723	171	30	2	8	(3	5)	229	63	70	84	76	7	157	18	10	5	1	1	.50	16	.237	.322	.317

Ramon Troncoso

Pitches: R Bats: R Pos: RP-32

Ht: 6'2" Wt: 200 Born: 2/16/1983 Age: 26

					HOW MUCH HE PITCHED					WHAT HE GAVE UP											THE RESULTS							
Year	Team	Lg	G	GS	CG	GF	IP	BFP	H	R	ER	HR	SH	SF	HB	TBB	IBB	SO	WP	Bk	W	L	Pct	ShO	Sv-Op	Hld	ERC	ERA
2005	Clmbs	A	13	6	0	3	37.2	183	58	33	28	2	0	5	4	13	0	27	2	0	3	3	.400	0	1--	-	7.19	6.69
2005	Ogden	R+	29	0	0	27	36.2	167	40	19	15	0	1	2	8	12	0	30	4	0	6	2	.750	0	13--	-	4.37	3.68
2006	VeroB	A+	18	0	0	9	29.1	146	43	27	22	1	4	1	3	14	3	31	1	0	1	3	.250	0	0--	-	6.79	6.75
2006	Clmbs	A	23	0	0	23	33.2	129	28	11	9	1	1	1	4	7	0	22	1	0	4	0	1.000	0	15--	-	2.66	2.41
2007	InldEm	A+	16	0	0	12	26.0	100	18	6	3	0	2	1	1	3	0	30	2	0	3	1	.750	0	7--	-	1.28	1.04
2007	Jaxnvl	AA	35	0	0	22	52.0	219	52	19	18	3	1	1	1	18	1	39	1	0	7	3	.700	0	7--	-	3.68	3.12
2008	LsVgs	AAA	22	0	0	6	30.2	149	43	24	17	1	2	0	3	16	0	18	1	0	4	0	1.000	0	0--	-	6.90	4.99
2008	LAD	NL	32	0	0	12	38.0	160	37	19	18	2	4	3	3	12	1	38	2	0	1	1	.500	0	0-0	2	3.60	4.26

Ryan Tucker

Pitches: R Bats: R Pos: RP-7; SP-6   Ht: 6'2" Wt: 190 Born: 12/6/1986 Age: 22

			HOW MUCH HE PITCHED						WHAT HE GAVE UP											THE RESULTS							
Year	Team	Lg	G	GS	CG	GF	IP	BFP	H	R	ER	HR	SH	SF	HB	TBB	IBB	SO	WP	Bk	W	L	Pct	ShO	Sv-Op	Hld	ERC	ERA
2005	Mrlns	R	8	7	0	0	31.2	137	35	13	13	0	6	2	2	16	0	23	3	0	3	3	.500	0	0- -	-	4.85	3.69
2005	Jmstwn	A-	4	4	0	0	14.0	76	21	14	13	3	0	1	2	8	0	18	3	0	1	1	.500	0	0- -	-	8.98	8.36
2006	Grnsbr	A	25	25	2	0	131.1	580	123	86	73	14	4	1	7	67	0	133	11	2	7	13	.350	0	0- -	-	4.40	5.00
2007	Jupiter	A+	24	24	1	0	138.1	601	142	64	57	6	4	3	11	46	1	104	9	1	5	8	.385	1	0- -	-	3.85	3.71
2008	Carlina	AA	25	12	0	0	91.0	375	64	17	16	2	2	2	6	36	0	74	6	0	5	3	.625	0	0- -	-	2.23	1.58
2008	Fla	NL	13	6	0	3	37.0	178	46	34	34	8	1	1	2	23	1	28	1	0	2	3	.400	0	0-1	0	7.63	8.27

Matt Tuiasosopo

Bats: R Throws: R Pos: 3B-13; DH-1   Ht: 6'2" Wt: 223 Born: 5/10/1986 Age: 23

					BATTING														BASERUNNING				AVERAGES		
Year	Team	Lg	G	AB	H	2B	3B	HR	(Hm | Rd)	TB	R	RBI	RC	TBB	IBB	SO	HBP	SH	SF	SB	CS	SB%	GDP	Avg	OBP	Slg
2004	Ms	R	20	68	28	5	2	4	(- | -)	49	18	12	23	13	1	14	6	0	2	1	2	.33	2	.412	.528	.721
2004	Everett	A-	29	101	25	6	1	2	(- | -)	39	18	14	13	10	0	36	4	0	1	4	3	.57	3	.248	.336	.386
2005	Wisc	A	107	409	113	21	3	6	(- | -)	158	72	45	60	44	2	96	9	1	1	8	5	.62	7	.276	.359	.386
2006	InldEm	A+	59	232	71	14	0	1	(- | -)	88	31	34	31	14	1	58	5	2	0	5	6	.45	8	.306	.359	.379
2006	SnAnt	AA	62	216	40	4	0	1	(- | -)	47	16	10	11	20	0	64	2	2	1	2	1	.67	4	.185	.259	.218
2007	WTenn	AA	129	446	116	27	5	9	(- | -)	180	74	57	73	76	2	113	11	1	14	4	8	.33	14	.260	.371	.404
2008	Tacom	AAA	111	437	123	32	2	13	(- | -)	198	87	73	76	47	0	104	12	0	4	4	0	1.00	9	.281	.364	.453
2008	Sea	AL	14	44	7	2	1	0	(0 | 0)	11	1	2	1	2	0	16	1	0	0	0	0	-	0	.159	.213	.250

Troy Tulowitzki

Bats: R Throws: R Pos: SS-101; PH-1   Ht: 6'3" Wt: 205 Born: 10/10/1984 Age: 24

					BATTING														BASERUNNING				AVERAGES		
Year	Team	Lg	G	AB	H	2B	3B	HR	(Hm | Rd)	TB	R	RBI	RC	TBB	IBB	SO	HBP	SH	SF	SB	CS	SB%	GDP	Avg	OBP	Slg
2008	Mdest*	A+	5	12	4	3	0	0	(- | -)	7	3	1	3	5	0	2	0	0	1	0	0	-	0	.333	.500	.583
2008	Tulsa*	AA	5	21	7	0	0	2	(- | -)	13	5	3	5	3	0	1	0	0	0	0	0	-	1	.333	.417	.619
2008	ColSpr*	AAA	2	7	3	1	0	0	(- | -)	4	2	1	2	1	0	1	0	0	0	1	0	1.00	1	.429	.500	.571
2006	Col	NL	25	96	23	2	0	1	(0 | 1)	28	15	6	10	10	3	25	1	1	0	3	0	1.00	1	.240	.318	.292
2007	Col	NL	155	609	177	33	5	24	(15 | 9)	292	104	99	95	57	3	130	9	5	2	7	6	.54	14	.291	.359	.479
2008	Col	NL	101	377	99	24	2	8	(4 | 4)	151	48	46	42	38	5	56	2	2	2	1	6	.14	16	.263	.332	.401
	Postseason		11	41	8	3	0	1	(0 | 1)	14	3	3	2	4	0	15	0	0	0	0	1	.00	1	.195	.267	.341
	3 ML YEARS		281	1082	299	59	7	33	(19 | 14)	471	167	151	147	105	11	211	12	8	4	11	12	.48	31	.276	.346	.435

Matt Tupman

Bats: L Throws: R Pos: C-1; PH-1   Ht: 5'11" Wt: 180 Born: 11/25/1979 Age: 29

					BATTING														BASERUNNING				AVERAGES		
Year	Team	Lg	G	AB	H	2B	3B	HR	(Hm | Rd)	TB	R	RBI	RC	TBB	IBB	SO	HBP	SH	SF	SB	CS	SB%	GDP	Avg	OBP	Slg
2002	Spkane	A-	51	170	46	7	0	2	(- | -)	59	26	23	25	22	0	22	4	3	2	3	0	1.00	4	.271	.364	.347
2003	Burlgtn	A	81	296	66	12	3	2	(- | -)	90	32	38	27	27	1	41	3	0	7	1	2	.33	4	.223	.288	.304
2004	Wilmg	A+	108	330	99	24	0	3	(- | -)	132	38	35	50	33	0	59	2	4	6	0	1	.00	6	.300	.361	.400
2005	Wichta	AA	109	366	96	15	2	2	(- | -)	121	57	32	48	46	2	62	8	2	3	1	2	.33	13	.262	.355	.331
2006	Wichta	AA	73	220	67	8	1	1	(- | -)	80	35	31	40	48	0	27	1	7	4	1	1	.50	3	.305	.425	.364
2006	Omha	AAA	20	70	16	0	0	0	(- | -)	16	9	4	5	8	0	5	0	0	0	0	0	-	3	.229	.308	.229
2007	Omha	AAA	86	299	84	16	0	1	(- | -)	103	21	32	40	36	1	34	2	6	1	2	2	.50	8	.281	.361	.344
2008	Omha	AAA	81	288	66	10	1	4	(- | -)	90	36	34	26	22	0	44	2	4	4	0	1	.00	9	.229	.285	.313
2008	KC	AL	1	1	1	0	0	0	(0 | 0)	1	0	0	1	0	0	0	0	0	0	0	0	-	0	1.000	1.000	1.000

Derrick Turnbow

Pitches: R Bats: R Pos: RP-8   Ht: 6'3" Wt: 222 Born: 1/25/1978 Age: 31

			HOW MUCH HE PITCHED						WHAT HE GAVE UP											THE RESULTS							
Year	Team	Lg	G	GS	CG	GF	IP	BFP	H	R	ER	HR	SH	SF	HB	TBB	IBB	SO	WP	Bk	W	L	Pct	ShO	Sv-Op	Hld	ERC	ERA
2008	Nashv*	AAA	18	0	0	0	18.0	113	17	21	21	0	1	1	1	41	0	28	10	0	2	2	.500	0	0- -	-	10.54	10.50
2000	LAA	AL	24	1	0	16	38.0	181	36	21	20	7	0	0	2	36	0	25	3	1	0	0	-	0	0-0	1	7.05	4.74
2003	LAA	AL	11	0	0	7	15.1	53	7	1	1	0	0	0	0	3	0	15	0	0	2	0	1.000	0	0-0	0	0.79	0.59
2004	LAA	AL	4	0	0	4	6.1	26	2	0	0	0	0	0	0	7	0	3	0	0	0	0	-	0	0-0	0	2.47	0.00
2005	Mil	NL	69	0	0	62	67.1	271	49	15	13	5	0	0	1	24	2	64	9	0	7	1	.875	ShO	39-43	2	2.35	1.74
2006	Mil	NL	64	0	0	49	56.1	266	56	51	43	8	2	1	4	39	2	69	6	1	4	9	.308	0	24-32	4	5.69	6.87
2007	Mil	NL	77	0	0	13	68.0	292	44	36	35	4	1	2	2	46	0	84	7	0	4	5	.444	0	1-4	33	3.02	4.63
2008	Mil	NL	8	0	0	5	6.1	44	12	11	11	1	1	0	1	13	1	5	0	0	0	1	.000	0	1-1	0	18.86	15.63
	7 ML YEARS		257	1	0	156	257.2	1133	206	135	123	25	4	3	10	168	5	265	25	2	17	16	.515	0	65-80	40	4.03	4.30

Jason Tyner

Bats: L Throws: L Pos: LF-1   Ht: 6'1" Wt: 175 Born: 4/23/1977 Age: 32

					BATTING														BASERUNNING				AVERAGES		
Year	Team	Lg	G	AB	H	2B	3B	HR	(Hm | Rd)	TB	R	RBI	RC	TBB	IBB	SO	HBP	SH	SF	SB	CS	SB%	GDP	Avg	OBP	Slg
2008	Buffalo*	AAA	76	238	56	9	0	1	(- | -)	68	31	14	26	28	1	20	3	9	1	8	0	1.00	6	.235	.322	.286
2008	Charltt*	AAA	21	69	20	3	0	0	(- | -)	23	8	4	9	8	0	6	1	1	0	3	1	.75	1	.290	.372	.333
2000	2 Tms		50	124	28	4	0	0	(0 | 0)	32	9	13	9	5	0	16	2	8	3	7	2	.78	2	.226	.261	.258
2001	TB	AL	105	396	111	8	5	0	(0 | 0)	129	51	21	43	15	0	42	3	5	1	31	6	.84	6	.280	.311	.326
2002	TB	AL	44	168	36	2	1	0	(0 | 0)	40	17	9	8	7	0	19	1	3	1	7	1	.88	1	.214	.249	.238
2003	TB	AL	46	90	25	7	0	0	(0 | 0)	32	12	6	12	10	0	12	0	2	0	2	1	.67	1	.278	.350	.356
2005	Min	AL	18	56	18	1	1	0	(0 | 0)	21	8	5	8	4	0	4	0	0	0	2	0	1.00	2	.321	.367	.375

Year	Team	Lg	G	AB	H	2B	3B	HR	(Hm	Rd)	TB	R	RBI	RC	TBB	IBB	SO	HBP	SH	SF	SB	CS	SB%	GDP	Avg	OBP	Slg
2006	Min	AL	62	218	68	5	2	0	(0	0)	77	29	18	30	11	2	18	1	0	2	4	2	.67	5	.312	.345	.353
2007	Min	AL	114	304	87	14	2	1	(0	1)	108	42	22	31	16	0	26	5	2	1	8	3	.73	12	.286	.331	.355
2008	Cle	AL	1	2	0	0	0	0	(0	0)	0	0	0	0	0	0	0	1	0	0	0	0		0	.000	.000	.000
00	NYM	NL	13	41	8	2	0	0	(0	0)	10	3	5	2	1	0	4	1	3	2	1	1	.50	1	.195	.222	.244
00	TB		37	83	20	2	0	0	(0	0)	22	6	8	7	4	0	12	1	5	1	6	1	.86	1	.241	.281	.265
Postseason			2	6	0	0	0	0	(0	0)	0	0	0	0	2	0	2	0	0	0	1	0	1.00	1	.000	.250	.000
8 ML YEARS			440	1358	373	41	11	1	(0	1)	439	168	94	141	68	2	137	13	20	8	61	15	.80	29	.275	.314	.323

Koji Uehara

Pitches: R **Bats:** R **Pos:** P **Ht:** 6'1" **Wt:** 187 **Born:** 4/3/1975 **Age:** 34

Year	Team	Lg	G	GS	CG	GF	IP	BFP	H	R	ER	HR	SH	SF	HB	TBB	IBB	SO	WP	Bk	W	L	Pct	ShO	Sv-Op	Hld	ERC	ERA
1999	Yomiuri	Jap	25	25	12	0	197.2	769	153	49	46	12	-	-	4	24	-	179	3	0	20	4	.833	1	0-	-	1.75	2.09
2000	Yomiuri	Jap	20	20	6	0	131.0	519	112	53	52	20	-	-	1	22	-	126	1	0	9	7	.563	1	0-	-	2.78	3.57
2001	Yomiuri	Jap	24	22	4	0	138.2	573	133	66	62	18	15	3	5	28	3	108	2	0	10	7	.588	1	0-	-	3.38	4.02
2002	Yomiuri	Jap	26	26	8	0	204.0	808	173	65	59	18	-	-	6	23	-	182	2	0	17	5	.773	3	0-	-	2.24	2.60
2003	Yomiuri	Jap	27	27	11	0	207.1	821	190	76	73	28	-	-	5	23	3	194	0	0	16	5	.762	1	0-	-	2.84	3.17
2004	Yomiuri	Jap	22	22	2	0	163.0	637	135	54	47	24	6	3	5	23	0	153	1	0	13	5	.722	0	0-	-	2.62	2.60
2005	Yomiuri	Jap	27	27	6	0	187.1	747	164	73	69	24	19	3	0	22	0	145	0	1	9	12	.429	2	0-	-	2.48	3.31
2006	Yomiuri	Jap	24	24	5	0	168.1	673	157	67	60	24	15	5	1	21	3	151	0	1	8	9	.471	0	0-	-	2.92	3.21
2007	Yomiuri	Jap	55	0	0		62.0	237	47	12	12	4	-	-	1	4	1	66	1	0	4	3	.571	0	32-	-	1.54	1.74
2008	Yomiuri	Jap	26	12	2	3	89.2	345	90	43	38	11	-	-	0	16	-	72	0	0	6	5	.545	0	1-	-	3.65	3.81

Dan Uggla

Bats: R **Throws:** R **Pos:** 2B-144; PH-2 **Ht:** 5'11" **Wt:** 200 **Born:** 3/11/1980 **Age:** 29

Year	Team	Lg	G	AB	H	2B	3B	HR	(Hm	Rd)	TB	R	RBI	RC	TBB	IBB	SO	HBP	SH	SF	SB	CS	SB%	GDP	Avg	OBP	Slg
2006	Fla	NL	154	611	172	26	7	27	(10	17)	293	105	90	97	48	1	123	9	7	8	6	6	.50	5	.282	.339	.480
2007	Fla	NL	159	632	155	49	3	31	(18	13)	303	113	88	81	68	0	167	13	4	11	2	1	.67	10	.245	.326	.479
2008	Fla	NL	146	531	138	37	1	32	(15	17)	273	97	92	93	77	6	171	8	0	3	5	5	.50	10	.260	.360	.514
3 ML YEARS			459	1774	465	112	11	90	(43	47)	869	315	270	271	193	7	461	30	11	22	13	12	.52	25	.262	.341	.490

B.J. Upton

Bats: R **Throws:** R **Pos:** CF-143; PH-2; DH-1 **Ht:** 6'3" **Wt:** 185 **Born:** 8/21/1984 **Age:** 24

Year	Team	Lg	G	AB	H	2B	3B	HR	(Hm	Rd)	TB	R	RBI	RC	TBB	IBB	SO	HBP	SH	SF	SB	CS	SB%	GDP	Avg	OBP	Slg
2004	TB	AL	45	159	41	8	2	4	(2	2)	65	19	12	22	15	0	46	1	1	1	4	1	.80	1	.258	.324	.409
2006	TB	AL	50	175	43	5	0	1	(1	0)	51	20	10	17	13	0	40	1	0	2	11	3	.79	1	.246	.302	.291
2007	TB	AL	129	474	142	25	1	24	(13	11)	241	86	82	93	65	4	154	4	1	4	22	8	.73	14	.300	.386	.508
2008	TB	AL	145	531	145	37	2	9	(4	5)	213	85	67	87	97	4	134	2	3	7	44	**16**	.73	13	.273	.383	.401
4 ML YEARS			369	1339	371	75	5	38	(20	18)	570	210	171	219	190	8	374	8	5	12	81	28	.74	29	.277	.367	.426

Justin Upton

Bats: R **Throws:** R **Pos:** RF-101; PH-8 **Ht:** 6'2" **Wt:** 205 **Born:** 8/25/1987 **Age:** 21

Year	Team	Lg	G	AB	H	2B	3B	HR	(Hm	Rd)	TB	R	RBI	RC	TBB	IBB	SO	HBP	SH	SF	SB	CS	SB%	GDP	Avg	OBP	Slg
2006	Sbend	A	113	438	115	28	1	12	(-	-)	181	71	66	66	52	3	96	5	0	6	15	7	.68	6	.263	.343	.413
2007	Visalia	A+	32	126	43	6	2	5	(-	-)	68	27	17	29	19	1	28	3	0	2	9	4	.69	2	.341	.433	.540
2007	Mobile	AA	71	259	80	17	4	13	(-	-)	144	48	53	57	37	4	51	5	0	5	10	7	.59	6	.309	.399	.556
2008	Tucsn	AAA	15	61	17	3	1	3	(-	-)	31	13	10	11	7	0	26	0	0	0	2	0	1.00	0	.279	.353	.508
2007	Ari	NL	43	140	31	8	3	2	(2	0)	51	17	11	13	11	4	37	1	0	0	2	0	1.00	3	.221	.283	.364
2008	Ari	NL	108	356	89	19	6	15	(12	3)	165	52	42	47	54	6	121	4	0	3	1	4	.20	3	.250	.353	.463
Postseason			6	14	5	1	0	0	(0	0)	8	2	1	4	3	0	3	0	0	0	1	0	1.00	0	.357	.526	.571
2 ML YEARS			151	496	120	27	9	17	(14	3)	216	69	53	60	65	10	158	5	0	3	3	4	.43	6	.242	.334	.435

Juan Uribe

Bats: R **Throws:** R **Pos:** 3B-57; 2B-52; PH-7; SS-4; DH-1 **Ht:** 6'0" **Wt:** 225 **Born:** 3/22/1979 **Age:** 30

Year	Team	Lg	G	AB	H	2B	3B	HR	(Hm	Rd)	TB	R	RBI	RC	TBB	IBB	SO	HBP	SH	SF	SB	CS	SB%	GDP	Avg	OBP	Slg
2008	Charltt*	AAA	3	11	2	0	0	0	(-	-)	2	0	2	0	0	0	3	0	0	0	0	0	-	0	.182	.182	.182
2001	Col	NL	72	273	82	15	11	8	(3	5)	143	32	53	44	8	1	55	2	0	6	3	0	1.00	6	.300	.325	.524
2002	Col	NL	155	566	136	25	7	6	(4	2)	193	69	49	53	34	1	120	5	7	6	9	2	.82	17	.240	.286	.341
2003	Col	NL	87	316	80	19	3	10	(6	4)	135	45	33	45	17	0	60	3	6	1	7	2	.78	3	.253	.297	.427
2004	CWS	AL	134	502	142	31	6	23	(16	7)	234	82	74	81	32	1	96	3	1	6	9	11	.45	10	.283	.327	.506
2005	CWS	AL	146	481	121	23	4	16	(10	6)	198	58	71	59	34	0	77	4	11	10	4	6	.40	7	.252	.301	.412
2006	CWS	AL	132	463	109	28	2	21	(13	8)	204	53	71	52	13	1	82	3	9	7	1	1	.50	10	.235	.257	.441
2007	CWS	AL	150	513	120	18	2	20	(15	5)	200	55	68	52	34	2	112	4	7	5	1	9	.10	6	.234	.284	.394
2008	CWS	AL	110	324	80	22	1	7	(5	2)	125	38	40	43	22	0	64	1	5	1	1	3	.25	5	.247	.296	.386
Postseason			12	42	12	5	0	1	(1	0)	20	7	6	7	5	0	8	0	1	0	1	0	1.00	1	.286	.362	.476
8 ML YEARS			986	3438	870	181	35	111	(72	39)	1454	432	459	429	194	6	666	25	56	35	35	34	.51	64	.253	.295	.423

Chase Utley

Bats: L Throws: R Pos: 2B-159; 1B-2   Ht: 6'1" Wt: 200 Born: 12/17/1978 Age: 30

						BATTING														BASERUNNING				AVERAGES		
Year	Team	Lg	G	AB	H	2B	3B	HR	(Hm	Rd)	TB	R	RBI	RC	TBB	IBB	SO	HBP	SH	SF	SB	CS	SB%	GDP	Avg	OBP	Slg
2003	Phi	NL	43	134	32	10	1	2	(1	1)	50	13	21	19	11	0	22	6	0	1	2	0	1.00	3	.239	.322	.373
2004	Phi	NL	94	267	71	11	2	13	(8	5)	125	36	57	37	15	1	40	2	1	2	4	1	.80	6	.266	.308	.468
2005	Phi	NL	147	543	158	39	6	28	(12	16)	293	93	105	102	69	5	109	9	0	7	16	3	.84	10	.291	.376	.540
2006	Phi	NL	160	658	203	40	4	32	(16	16)	347	131	102	122	63	1	132	14	0	4	15	4	.79	9	.309	.379	.527
2007	Phi	NL	132	530	176	48	5	22	(14	8)	300	104	103	111	50	1	89	25	1	7	9	1	.90	7	.332	.410	.566
2008	Phi	NL	159	607	177	41	4	33	(20	13)	325	113	104	113	64	14	104	27	1	8	14	2	.88	9	.292	.380	.535
	Postseason		3	11	2	0	0	0	(0	0)	2	0	0		2	0	5	0	0	0	0	0	-	0	.182	.308	.182
	6 ML YEARS		735	2739	817	189	22	130	(71	59)	1440	490	492	504	272	22	496	83	3	29	60	11	.85	44	.298	.375	.526

Luis Valbuena

Bats: L Throws: R Pos: 2B-16; PR-2; SS-1; PH-1   Ht: 5'10" Wt: 199 Born: 11/30/1985 Age: 23

						BATTING														BASERUNNING				AVERAGES		
Year	Team	Lg	G	AB	H	2B	3B	HR	(Hm	Rd)	TB	R	RBI	RC	TBB	IBB	SO	HBP	SH	SF	SB	CS	SB%	GDP	Avg	OBP	Slg
2005	Tacom	AAA	3	4	0	0	0	0	(-	-)	0	0	0	0	1	0	2	0	0	0	0	0	-	0	.000	.200	.000
2005	Everett	A-	74	287	75	10	3	12	(-	-)	127	47	51	45	31	0	37	2	1	4	14	6	.70	3	.261	.333	.443
2006	Wisc	A	89	325	93	16	6	3	(-	-)	130	45	38	53	44	0	44	1	1	2	21	7	.75	8	.286	.371	.400
2006	InldEm	A+	43	163	41	10	1	2	(-	-)	59	18	10	18	14	2	26	1	3	0	1	3	.25	5	.252	.315	.362
2007	WTenn	AA	122	444	106	23	3	11	(-	-)	168	55	44	55	48	2	83	1	6	6	10	6	.63	9	.239	.311	.378
2008	WTenn	AA	70	240	73	12	2	9	(-	-)	116	43	40	45	31	0	37	0	4	2	8	4	.67	4	.304	.381	.483
2008	Tacom	AAA	58	212	64	9	0	2	(-	-)	79	41	20	33	28	0	32	0	6	0	10	4	.71	1	.302	.383	.373
2008	Sea	AL	18	49	12	5	0	0	(0	0)	17	6	1	5	4	0	11	1	0	0	0	0	-	0	.245	.315	.347

Merkin Valdez

Pitches: R Bats: R Pos: RP-16; SP-1   Ht: 6'5" Wt: 232 Born: 11/10/1981 Age: 27

			HOW MUCH HE PITCHED					WHAT HE GAVE UP											THE RESULTS							
Year	Team	Lg	G	GS	CG	GF	IP	BFP	H	R	ER	HR	SH	SF	HB	TBB	IBB	SO	WP	Bk	W	L	Pct	ShO	Sv-Op	Hld	ERC	ERA
2002	Braves	R	12	8	1	3	68.1	266	47	18	15	0	2	1	2	12	0	76	2	0	7	3	.700	1	0- -	-	1.37	1.98
2003	Hgrstn	A	26	26	2	0	156.0	617	119	42	39	11	2	1	5	49	0	166	4	0	9	5	.643	1	0- -	-	2.51	2.25
2004	SnJos	A+	7	7	0	0	35.2	146	30	12	10	4	0	0	4	5	0	44	1	0	3	1	.750	0	0- -	-	2.70	2.52
2004	Fresno	AAA	1	1	0	0	5.0	25	6	4	4	0	1	1	0	4	0	5	0	0	0	0	-	0	0- -	-	5.88	7.20
2004	Nrwich	AA	10	7	0	1	41.2	172	35	21	21	3	1	3	0	15	0	31	1	0	1	4	.200	0	1- -	-	2.88	4.32
2005	Nrwich	AA	24	19	1	1	107.0	465	99	48	42	7	4	5	8	45	0	96	6	0	5	6	.455	0	0- -	-	3.77	3.53
2006	Fresno	AAA	46	3	0	20	49.2	240	52	42	32	6	4	3	5	39	0	48	8	2	0	4	.000	0	5- -	-	6.50	5.80
2008	SnJos	A+	1	0	0	0	1.0	5	1	0	0	0	1	0	0	0	0	3	0	0	0	0	-	0	0- -	-	1.51	0.00
2004	SF	NL	2	0	0	0	1.2	12	4	5	5	1	0	0	0	3	0	2	0	0	0	0	-	0	0-0	0	26.50	27.00
2008	SF	NL	17	1	0	3	16.0	69	14	5	3	1	1	0	2	7	2	13	2	1	1	0	1.000	0	0-0	2	3.57	1.69
	2 ML YEARS		19	1	0	3	17.2	81	18	10	8	2	1	0	2	10	2	15	2	1	1	0	1.000	0	0-0	2	5.21	4.08

Javier Valentin

Bats: B Throws: R Pos: PH-70; C-17; 1B-11; 3B-4   Ht: 5'10" Wt: 215 Born: 9/19/1975 Age: 33

						BATTING														BASERUNNING				AVERAGES		
Year	Team	Lg	G	AB	H	2B	3B	HR	(Hm	Rd)	TB	R	RBI	RC	TBB	IBB	SO	HBP	SH	SF	SB	CS	SB%	GDP	Avg	OBP	Slg
1997	Min	AL	4	7	2	0	0	0	(0	0)	2	1	0	1	0	0	3	0	0	0	0	0	-	0	.286	.286	.286
1998	Min	AL	55	162	32	7	1	3	(1	2)	50	11	18	10	11	1	30	0	3	1	0	0	-	7	.198	.247	.309
1999	Min	AL	78	218	54	12	1	5	(2	3)	83	22	28	27	22	0	39	1	1	5	0	0	-	2	.248	.313	.381
2002	Min	AL	4	4	2	0	0	0	(0	0)	2	0	0	0	0	0	0	0	0	0	0	0	-	0	.500	.500	.500
2003	TB	AL	49	135	30	7	1	3	(2	1)	48	13	15	11	5	0	31	1	0	1	0	0	-	7	.222	.254	.356
2004	Cin	NL	82	202	47	10	1	6	(2	4)	77	18	20	20	17	3	36	1	0	2	0	0	-	4	.233	.293	.381
2005	Cin	NL	76	221	62	11	0	14	(7	7)	115	36	50	41	30	3	37	0	0	3	0	0	-	5	.281	.362	.520
2006	Cin	NL	92	186	50	6	1	8	(6	2)	82	24	27	17	13	3	29	0	0	2	0	0	-	5	.269	.313	.441
2007	Cin	NL	97	243	67	21	0	2	(2	0)	94	19	34	31	19	2	25	1	0	2	0	0	-	7	.276	.328	.387
2008	Cin	NL	94	129	33	8	0	4	(1	3)	53	10	18	15	14	0	27	0	0	1	0	0	-	2	.256	.326	.411
	10 ML YEARS		631	1507	379	82	5	45	(23	22)	606	154	210	173	131	12	257	4	4	17	0	0	-	39	.251	.310	.402

Jose Valverde

Pitches: R Bats: R Pos: RP-74   Ht: 6'4" Wt: 254 Born: 3/24/1979 Age: 30

			HOW MUCH HE PITCHED					WHAT HE GAVE UP											THE RESULTS							
Year	Team	Lg	G	GS	CG	GF	IP	BFP	H	R	ER	HR	SH	SF	HB	TBB	IBB	SO	WP	Bk	W	L	Pct	ShO	Sv-Op	Hld	ERC	ERA
2003	Ari	NL	54	0	0	33	50.1	204	24	16	12	4	0	1	2	26	2	71	2	0	2	1	.667	0	10-11	8	1.77	2.15
2004	Ari	NL	29	0	0	20	29.2	131	23	17	14	7	3	2	1	17	4	38	4	0	1	2	.333	0	8-10	5	4.25	4.25
2005	Ari	NL	61	0	0	34	66.1	268	51	19	18	5	3	1	2	20	1	75	3	0	3	4	.429	0	15-17	7	2.43	2.44
2006	Ari	NL	44	0	0	35	49.1	223	50	32	32	6	1	3	2	22	3	69	2	0	2	3	.400	0	18-22	1	4.42	5.84
2007	Ari	NL	65	0	0	59	64.1	265	46	21	19	7	0	1	3	26	1	78	1	0	1	4	.200	0	47-54	0	2.77	2.66
2008	Hou	NL	74	0	0	71	72.0	303	62	28	27	10	0	2	2	23	6	83	3	2	6	3	.667	0	44-51	0	3.18	3.38
	Postseason		4	0	0	3	4.2	21	2	1	1	0	0	0	0	4	0	8	0	0	0	1	.000	0	1-1	0	1.91	1.93
	6 ML YEARS		327	0	0	252	332.0	1394	256	133	122	39	7	10	12	134	17	414	15	2	15	17	.469	0	142-165	21	2.98	3.31

John Van Benschoten

Pitches: R **Bats:** R **Pos:** SP-5; RP-4   **Ht:** 6'4" **Wt:** 230 **Born:** 4/14/1980 **Age:** 29

		HOW MUCH HE PITCHED						WHAT HE GAVE UP										THE RESULTS						
Year	Team	Lg	G	GS	CG	GF	IP	BFP	H	R	ER	HR	SH	SF	HB	TBB	IBB	SO	WP	Bk	W	L	Pct	ShO	Sv-Op Hld	ERC	ERA
2008	Indy*	AAA	22	13	0	2	80.1	332	70	36	35	3	6	1	4	32	1	62	1	0	7	4	.636	0	0- - -	3.20	3.92
2004	Pit	NL	6	5	0	0	28.2	135	33	27	22	3	2	2	2	19	0	18	1	0	1	3	.250	0	0-0 0	6.47	6.91
2007	Pit	NL	11	9	0	1	39.0	203	55	45	44	4	3	2	5	29	1	26	1	0	0	7	.000	0	0-0 0	8.51	10.15
2008	Pit	NL	9	5	0	2	22.1	125	37	28	26	7	1	0	3	20	1	21	0	1	1	3	.250	0	0-0 0	13.13	10.48
3 ML YEARS			26	19	0	3	90.0	463	125	100	92	14	6	4	10	68	2	65	2	1	2	13	.133	0	0-0 0	8.93	9.20

Jonathan Van Every

Bats: L **Throws:** L **Pos:** RF-8; PR-4; LF-1; CF-1; PH-1   **Ht:** 6'1" **Wt:** 190 **Born:** 11/27/1979 **Age:** 29

			BATTING															BASERUNNING				AVERAGES		
Year	Team	Lg	G	AB	H	2B	3B	HR	(Hm | Rd)	TB	R	RBI	RC	TBB	IBB	SO	HBP	SH	SF	SB	CS	SB%	GDP	Avg	OBP	Slg
2001	MhVlly	A-	41	135	34	4	2	6	(- | -)	60	30	17	26	28	1	50	7	0	0	1	2	.33	1	.252	.406	.444
2002	MhVlly	A-	42	140	36	7	6	6	(- | -)	73	31	26	27	20	0	45	1	1	2	6	0	1.00	3	.257	.350	.521
2002	Clmbs	A	15	43	6	0	1	3	(- | -)	17	10	4	7	13	1	25	2	0	0	1	0	1.00	0	.140	.362	.395
2003	Lk Cty	A	59	197	38	9	2	5	(- | -)	66	22	24	18	12	0	89	7	3	2	15	5	.75	0	.193	.261	.335
2003	MhVlly	A-	22	65	17	6	1	1	(- | -)	28	13	9	11	9	0	23	3	0	2	7	4	.64	1	.262	.367	.431
2004	Knstn	A+	113	392	108	22	2	21	(- | -)	197	67	71	76	53	0	129	8	0	6	11	3	.79	3	.276	.368	.503
2005	Akron	AA	118	389	96	14	2	27	(- | -)	195	71	64	75	65	5	155	8	3	1	16	5	.76	3	.247	.365	.501
2006	Akron	AA	66	236	61	16	5	10	(- | -)	117	35	40	41	26	4	80	5	0	5	5	1	.83	1	.258	.338	.496
2006	Buffalo	AAA	47	151	39	9	2	5	(- | -)	67	23	16	23	16	0	51	3	0	1	5	2	.71	2	.258	.339	.444
2007	Akron	AA	44	151	52	14	5	4	(- | -)	88	27	34	34	19	2	48	1	3	2	4	5	.44	1	.344	.416	.583
2007	Buffalo	AAA	51	158	43	5	1	8	(- | -)	74	17	23	27	23	1	57	2	2	1	2	3	.40	1	.272	.370	.468
2008	Pwtckt	AAA	119	380	100	15	3	26	(- | -)	199	84	70	73	54	1	157	4	3	1	6	1	.86	4	.263	.360	.524
2008	Bos	AL	11	17	4	0	1	0	(0 | 0)	6	0	5	3	1	0	6	0	0	0	0	0	-	0	.235	.278	.353

Rick VandenHurk

Pitches: R **Bats:** R **Pos:** SP-4   **Ht:** 6'5" **Wt:** 195 **Born:** 5/22/1985 **Age:** 24

			HOW MUCH HE PITCHED						WHAT HE GAVE UP										THE RESULTS						
Year	Team	Lg	G	GS	CG	GF	IP	BFP	H	R	ER	HR	SH	SF	HB	TBB	IBB	SO	WP	Bk	W	L	Pct	ShO	Sv-Op Hld	ERC	ERA
2003	Mrlns	R	11	10	0	0	38.2	190	49	30	23	2	3	1	7	20	0	30	4	3	2	6	.250	0	0- - -	6.40	5.35
2004	Jupiter	A+	14	14	0	0	58.0	252	54	22	21	2	2	7	4	31	0	43	6	0	2	3	.400	0	0- - -	4.09	3.26
2005	Grnsbr	A	4	4	1	0	22.0	91	17	7	6	1	0	0	1	11	0	26	1	0	1	2	.333	0	0- - -	3.11	2.45
2005	Jupiter	A+	2	2	0	0	6.2	28	7	4	3	0	0	0	1	0	0	6	0	0	0	1	.000	0	0- - -	2.67	4.05
2006	Mrlns	R	5	5	0	0	15.0	56	4	2	2	0	1	0	0	8	0	26	1	0	0	0	-	0	0- - -	0.86	1.20
2006	Jupiter	A+	3	3	0	0	10.0	40	5	4	3	1	0	0	0	6	0	15	0	0	0	0	-	0	0- - -	2.26	2.70
2007	Carlina	AA	9	9	0	0	53.2	220	42	23	21	5	5	1	2	20	0	61	4	1	2	2	.500	0	0- - -	2.93	3.52
2007	Albq	AAA	2	2	0	0	12.0	44	6	3	3	3	0	0	0	4	0	14	1	0	2	0	1.000	0	0- - -	2.21	2.25
2008	Carlina	AA	10	10	0	0	55.1	231	49	32	26	8	5	1	2	19	0	55	2	0	3	3	.500	0	0- - -	3.68	4.23
2008	Albq	AAA	4	4	0	0	17.2	77	13	11	8	3	0	0	0	11	0	21	1	0	2	1	.667	0	0- - -	3.89	4.08
2007	Fla	NL	18	17	0	0	81.2	379	94	63	62	15	5	3	3	48	5	82	4	4	4	6	.400	0	0-0 0	6.50	6.83
2008	Fla	NL	4	4	0	0	14.0	74	20	12	12	1	2	0	2	10	0	20	0	0	1	1	.500	0	0-0 0	8.20	7.71
2 ML YEARS			22	21	0	0	95.2	453	114	75	74	16	7	3	5	58	5	102	4	4	5	7	.417	0	0-0 0	6.75	6.96

Claudio Vargas

Pitches: R **Bats:** R **Pos:** RP-7; SP-4   **Ht:** 6'4" **Wt:** 238 **Born:** 6/19/1978 **Age:** 31

			HOW MUCH HE PITCHED						WHAT HE GAVE UP										THE RESULTS						
Year	Team	Lg	G	GS	CG	GF	IP	BFP	H	R	ER	HR	SH	SF	HB	TBB	IBB	SO	WP	Bk	W	L	Pct	ShO	Sv-Op Hld	ERC	ERA
2008	StLuci*	A+	1	1	0	0	5.0	17	3	2	1	0	0	1	0	0	0	6	0	0	0	0	-	0	0- - -	0.80	1.80
2008	NewOr*	AAA	8	8	0	0	43.1	187	47	24	21	5	4	2	0	13	1	43	1	0	5	2	.714	0	0- - -	4.20	4.36
2003	Mon	NL	23	20	0	0	114.0	492	111	59	55	16	5	4	7	41	5	62	2	0	6	8	.429	0	0-0 0	4.21	4.34
2004	Mon	NL	45	14	0	6	118.1	530	120	75	69	26	4	4	7	64	7	89	8	0	5	5	.500	0	0-0 3	5.84	5.25
2005	2 Tms	NL	25	23	0	0	132.1	586	146	81	77	25	6	1	7	47	5	95	6	0	9	9	.500	0	0-0 0	5.28	5.24
2006	Ari	NL	31	30	0	1	167.2	747	185	101	90	27	8	3	8	52	2	123	9	1	12	10	.545	0	0-0 0	4.81	4.83
2007	Mil	NL	29	23	0	1	134.1	605	153	80	76	23	5	7	2	54	3	107	4	0	11	6	.647	0	1-2 0	5.38	5.09
2008	NYM	NL	11	4	0	2	37.0	150	33	20	19	4	1	1	2	11	0	20	1	0	3	2	.600	0	0-1 1	3.46	4.62
05	Was	NL	4	4	0	0	12.2	66	22	15	13	4	0	0	0	7	2	5	0	0	0	3	.000	0	0-0 0	11.04	9.24
05	Ari	NL	21	19	0	0	119.2	520	124	66	64	21	6	1	7	40	3	90	6	0	9	6	.600	0	0-0 0	4.74	4.81
6 ML YEARS			164	114	0	10	703.2	3110	748	416	386	121	29	20	33	269	22	496	30	1	46	40	.535	0	1-3 4	5.00	4.94

Jason Varitek

Bats: B **Throws:** R **Pos:** C-131; PH-4   **Ht:** 6'2" **Wt:** 230 **Born:** 4/11/1972 **Age:** 37

			BATTING															BASERUNNING				AVERAGES		
Year	Team	Lg	G	AB	H	2B	3B	HR	(Hm | Rd)	TB	R	RBI	RC	TBB	IBB	SO	HBP	SH	SF	SB	CS	SB%	GDP	Avg	OBP	Slg
1997	Bos	AL	1	1	1	0	0	0	(0 | 0)	1	0	0	1	0	0	0	0	0	0	0	0	-	0	1.000	1.000	1.000
1998	Bos	AL	86	221	56	13	0	7	(1 | 6)	90	31	33	26	17	1	45	2	4	3	2	2	.50	8	.253	.309	.407
1999	Bos	AL	144	483	130	39	2	20	(12 | 8)	233	70	76	75	46	2	85	2	5	8	1	2	.33	13	.269	.330	.482
2000	Bos	AL	139	448	111	31	1	10	(2 | 8)	174	55	65	59	60	3	84	6	1	4	1	1	.50	16	.248	.342	.388
2001	Bos	AL	51	174	51	11	1	7	(2 | 5)	85	19	25	30	21	3	35	1	1	1	0	0	-	6	.293	.371	.489
2002	Bos	AL	132	467	124	27	1	10	(6 | 4)	183	58	61	52	41	3	95	7	1	3	4	3	.57	13	.266	.332	.392
2003	Bos	AL	142	451	123	31	1	25	(13 | 12)	231	63	85	79	51	8	106	7	5	7	3	2	.60	10	.273	.351	.512
2004	Bos	AL	137	463	137	30	1	18	(8 | 10)	223	67	73	79	62	9	126	10	0	1	10	3	.77	11	.296	.390	.482
2005	Bos	AL	133	470	132	30	1	22	(7 | 15)	230	70	70	78	62	3	117	3	1	3	2	0	1.00	10	.281	.366	.489
2006	Bos	AL	103	365	87	19	2	12	(2 | 10)	146	46	55	45	46	7	87	2	1	2	1	2	.33	10	.238	.325	.400

278

							BATTING														BASERUNNING				AVERAGES		
Year	Team	Lg	G	AB	H	2B	3B	HR	(Hm	Rd)	TB	R	RBI	RC	TBB	IBB	SO	HBP	SH	SF	SB	CS	SB%	GDP	Avg	OBP	Slg
2007	Bos	AL	131	435	111	15	3	17	(9	8)	183	57	68	61	71	9	122	8	0	4	1	2	.33	9	.255	.367	.421
2008	Bos	AL	131	423	93	20	0	13	(4	9)	152	34	43	36	52	3	122	6	0	2	0	1	.00	13	.220	.313	.359
	Postseason		53	194	50	12	2	10	(3	7)	96	33	32	27	12	4	47	4	1	3	0	0	-	4	.258	.310	.495
	12 ML YEARS		1330	4401	1156	266	13	161	(66	95)	1931	573	654	621	529	51	1024	54	19	38	25	18	.58	119	.263	.346	.439

Javier Vazquez

Pitches: R **Bats:** R **Pos:** SP-33

Ht: 6'2" **Wt:** 210 **Born:** 7/25/1976 **Age:** 32

			HOW MUCH HE PITCHED					WHAT HE GAVE UP												THE RESULTS						
Year	Team	Lg	G	GS	CG	GF	IP	BFP	H	R	ER	HR	SH	SF	HB	TBB	IBB	SO	WP	Bk	W	L	Pct	ShO	Sv-Op	Hld	ERC	ERA
1998	Mon	NL	33	32	0	1	172.1	764	196	121	116	31	9	4	11	68	2	139	2	0	5	15	.250	0	0-0	0	5.79	6.06
1999	Mon	NL	26	26	3	0	154.2	667	154	98	86	20	3	3	4	52	4	113	2	0	9	8	.529	1	0-0	0	4.02	5.00
2000	Mon	NL	33	33	2	0	217.2	945	247	104	98	24	11	3	5	61	10	196	3	0	11	9	.550	1	0-0	0	4.45	4.05
2001	Mon	NL	32	32	5	0	223.2	898	197	92	85	24	9	2	3	44	4	208	3	1	16	11	.593	3	0-0	0	2.75	3.42
2002	Mon	NL	34	34	2	0	230.1	971	243	111	100	28	15	7	4	49	6	179	3	0	10	13	.435	0	0-0	0	3.80	3.91
2003	Mon	NL	34	34	4	0	230.2	938	198	93	83	28	6	6	4	57	5	241	11	1	13	12	.520	1	0-0	0	2.90	3.24
2004	NYY	AL	32	32	0	0	198.0	849	195	114	108	33	4	8	11	60	3	150	12	2	14	10	.583	0	0-0	0	4.23	4.91
2005	Ari	NL	33	33	3	0	215.2	904	223	112	106	35	13	5	3	46	4	192	7	0	11	15	.423	1	0-0	0	4.00	4.42
2006	CWS	AL	33	32	1	0	202.2	872	206	116	109	23	2	4	15	56	2	184	7	0	11	12	.478	0	0-0	0	4.02	4.84
2007	CWS	AL	32	32	2	0	216.2	882	197	95	90	25	5	7	7	50	2	213	5	0	15	8	.652	0	0-0	0	3.29	3.74
2008	CWS	AL	33	33	1	0	208.1	890	214	113	108	25	4	4	6	61	2	200	2	0	12	16	.429	0	0-0	0	4.03	4.67
	Postseason		3	1	0	0	11.1	58	16	12	12	4	0	2	2	9	0	12	0	0	1	0	1.000	0	0-0	0	11.94	9.53
	11 ML YEARS		355	353	23	1	2270.2	9580	2270	1169	1089	300	81	51	75	604	44	2015	57	4	127	129	.496	7	0-0	0	3.86	4.32

Ramon Vazquez

Bats: L **Throws:** R **Pos:** 3B-70; SS-26; PH-15; 2B-11; 1B-1

Ht: 5'11" **Wt:** 195 **Born:** 8/21/1976 **Age:** 32

							BATTING														BASERUNNING				AVERAGES		
Year	Team	Lg	G	AB	H	2B	3B	HR	(Hm	Rd)	TB	R	RBI	RC	TBB	IBB	SO	HBP	SH	SF	SB	CS	SB%	GDP	Avg	OBP	Slg
2001	Sea	AL	17	35	8	0	0	0	(0	0)	8	5	4	2	0	0	3	0	1	1	0	0	-	0	.229	.222	.229
2002	SD	NL	128	423	116	21	5	2	(0	2)	153	50	32	55	45	3	79	1	3	2	7	2	.78	6	.274	.344	.362
2003	SD	NL	116	422	110	17	4	3	(1	2)	144	56	30	49	52	2	88	2	5	3	10	3	.77	4	.261	.342	.341
2004	SD	NL	52	115	27	3	2	1	(1	0)	37	12	13	9	11	2	24	0	4	2	1	1	.50	2	.235	.297	.322
2005	2 Tms	AL	39	85	18	5	0	0	(0	0)	23	7	5	5	5	0	17	0	2	0	0	0	-	0	.212	.256	.271
2006	Cle	AL	34	67	14	2	0	1	(1	0)	19	11	8	7	6	0	18	0	2	0	0	0	-	3	.209	.267	.284
2007	Tex	AL	104	300	69	13	3	8	(2	6)	112	42	28	36	29	0	72	2	12	2	1	0	1.00	4	.230	.300	.373
2008	Tex	AL	105	300	87	18	3	6	(1	2)	129	44	40	46	38	3	66	0	5	4	0	1	.00	4	.290	.365	.430
05	Bos	AL	27	61	12	2	0	0	(0	0)	14	6	4	3	3	0	14	0	2	0	0	0	-	0	.197	.234	.230
05	Cle	AL	12	24	6	3	0	0	(0	0)	9	1	1	2	2	0	3	0	0	0	0	0	-	0	.250	.308	.375
	Postseason		1	0	0	0	0	0	(0	0)	0	0	0	0	0	0	0	0	0	0	0	0	-	0			
	8 ML YEARS		595	1747	449	79	17	21	(9	12)	625	227	160	209	186	10	367	5	34	16	19	7	.73	23	.257	.328	.358

Jorge Velandia

Bats: R **Throws:** R **Pos:** SS-4; PH-3; 2B-2; DH-2; PR-2

Ht: 5'9" **Wt:** 190 **Born:** 1/12/1975 **Age:** 34

							BATTING														BASERUNNING				AVERAGES		
Year	Team	Lg	G	AB	H	2B	3B	HR	(Hm	Rd)	TB	R	RBI	RC	TBB	IBB	SO	HBP	SH	SF	SB	CS	SB%	GDP	Avg	OBP	Slg
2008	Syrcse*	AAA	28	94	27	2	1	3	(-	-)	40	16	12	16	14	0	18	1	1	0	0	0	-	1	.287	.385	.426
2008	Buffalo*	AAA	52	206	43	3	0	0	(-	-)	46	18	8	14	20	0	49	4	4	0	2	0	1.00	5	.209	.291	.223
1997	SD	NL	14	29	3	2	0	0	(0	0)	5	0	0	1	1	0	7	0	0	0	0	0	-	0	.103	.133	.172
1998	Oak	AL	8	4	1	0	0	0	(0	0)	1	0	0	0	0	0	1	0	0	0	0	0	-	0	.250	.250	.250
1999	Oak	AL	63	48	9	1	0	0	(0	0)	10	4	2	3	2	0	13	1	0	0	2	0	1.00	0	.188	.235	.208
2000	2 Tms		33	31	3	1	0	0	(0	0)	4	2	2	1	2	0	8	1	0	0	0	0	-	0	.097	.176	.129
2001	NYM	NL	9	9	0	0	0	0	(0	0)	0	0	0	0	2	0	1	0	0	0	0	0	-	0	.000	.182	.000
2003	NYM	NL	23	58	11	3	1	0	(0	0)	16	6	8	6	10	1	15	0	3	1	0	0	-	1	.190	.304	.276
2007	TB	AL	14	50	16	4	0	2	(1	1)	26	7	11	12	8	0	17	1	1	0	0	0	-	1	.320	.424	.520
2008	2 Tms	AL	10	15	3	1	0	0	(0	0)	4	1	0	1	1	0	4	0	0	0	0	0	-	0	.200	.250	.267
00	Oak	AL	18	24	3	1	0	0	(0	0)	4	1	2	1	0	0	6	1	0	0	0	0	-	0	.125	.160	.167
00	NYM	NL	15	7	0	0	0	0	(0	0)	0	1	0	0	2	0	2	0	0	0	0	0	-	0	.000	.222	.000
08	Tor	AL	3	7	0	0	0	0	(0	0)	0	0	0	0	0	0	2	0	0	0	0	0	-	0	.000	.000	.000
08	Cle	AL	7	8	3	1	0	0	(0	0)	4	1	0	1	1	0	2	0	0	0	0	0	-	0	.375	.444	.500
	8 ML YEARS		174	244	46	12	1	2	(1	1)	66	21	23	24	26	1	66	3	4	1	2	0	1.00	1	.189	.274	.270

Gil Velazquez

Bats: R **Throws:** R **Pos:** 2B-2; SS-1; PR-1

Ht: 6'3" **Wt:** 190 **Born:** 10/17/1979 **Age:** 29

							BATTING														BASERUNNING				AVERAGES		
Year	Team	Lg	G	AB	H	2B	3B	HR	(Hm	Rd)	TB	R	RBI	RC	TBB	IBB	SO	HBP	SH	SF	SB	CS	SB%	GDP	Avg	OBP	Slg
1998	Kngspt	R+	12	29	3	1	0	0	(-	-)	4	2	4	0	2	0	7	0	3	1	2	0	1.00	0	.103	.156	.138
1998	Mets	R	33	97	18	3	0	0	(-	-)	21	7	7	5	8	0	10	2	3	1	2	1	.67	1	.186	.259	.216
1999	Clmbia	A	21	75	17	4	1	0	(-	-)	23	9	6	5	3	0	14	1	2	3	0	1	.00	2	.227	.256	.307
1999	Kngspt	R+	62	225	59	8	0	1	(-	-)	70	24	19	25	19	0	43	3	2	4	4	1	.80	5	.262	.323	.311
2000	StLuci	A+	125	440	101	16	1	1	(-	-)	122	37	43	33	25	0	69	9	4	3	3	9	.25	15	.230	.283	.277
2001	Bnghtn	AA	106	358	74	11	2	3	(-	-)	98	33	19	25	26	1	84	3	4	0	1	1	.50	12	.207	.266	.274
2002	Bnghtn	AA	27	72	14	2	0	0	(-	-)	16	6	5	3	7	0	15	1	1	0	0	3	.00	3	.194	.275	.222
2002	StLuci	A+	33	118	25	6	0	0	(-	-)	31	13	16	7	6	0	30	0	1	0	2	0	1.00	1	.212	.250	.263
2002	Norfolk	AAA	12	33	7	1	0	0	(-	-)	8	2	1	2	4	0	9	0	0	0	0	0	-	0	.212	.297	.242
2003	Bnghtn	AA	59	141	32	6	0	3	(-	-)	47	17	19	14	15	0	30	0	5	1	1	3	.25	4	.227	.299	.333
2003	Norfolk	AAA	5	16	4	0	0	0	(-	-)	4	0	1	0	0	0	5	0	0	0	0	1	.00	0	.250	.250	.250
2003	StLuci	A+	19	57	12	3	0	1	(-	-)	18	6	6	5	6	0	5	0	1	0	0	0	-	2	.211	.286	.316
2004	Norfolk	AAA	17	33	3	1	0	0	(-	-)	4	4	0	0	5	0	12	0	2	0	1	0	1.00	1	.091	.211	.121

Year	Team	Lg	G	AB	H	2B	3B	HR	(Hm	Rd)	TB	R	RBI	RC	TBB	IBB	SO	HBP	SH	SF	SB	CS	SB%	GDP	Avg	OBP	Slg
2004	Bnghtn	AA	105	359	86	16	3	5	(-	-)	123	42	37	39	32	1	94	2	6	2	4	3	.57	3	.240	.304	.343
2005	NwBrit	AA	81	286	66	13	0	1	(-	-)	82	36	28	26	22	0	52	6	6	3	3	2	.60	2	.231	.287	.287
2005	Roch	AAA	17	34	9	1	1	0	(-	-)	12	3	3	3	0	0	8	0	0	0	0	0	-	1	.265	.265	.353
2006	NwBrit	AA	6	16	6	2	0	0	(-	-)	8	1	3	3	3	0	2	0	2	0	0	0	-	0	.375	.474	.500
2006	Roch	AAA	56	164	41	4	1	1	(-	-)	50	26	17	15	11	0	33	2	3	2	2	2	.50	5	.250	.302	.305
2007	NwBrit	AA	17	45	12	2	3	1	(-	-)	23	6	13	10	10	0	13	0	3	3	1	0	1.00	6	.267	.379	.511
2007	Roch	AAA	69	183	44	9	1	1	(-	-)	58	26	16	19	13	0	35	3	5	2	3	0	1.00	6	.240	.299	.317
2008	Pwtckt	AAA	101	350	90	17	4	10	(-	-)	145	54	46	46	22	0	73	5	5	4	3	3	.50	13	.257	.307	.414
2008	Bos	AL	3	8	1	0	0	0	(0	0)	1	0	1	1	0	0	0	0	0	0	0	0	-	0	.125	.125	.125

Eugenio Velez

Bats: B Throws: R Pos: 2B-69; PH-26; LF-8; RF-7; PR-3; CF-2   Ht: 6'1" Wt: 162 Born: 5/16/1982 Age: 27

Year	Team	Lg	G	AB	H	2B	3B	HR	(Hm	Rd)	TB	R	RBI	RC	TBB	IBB	SO	HBP	SH	SF	SB	CS	SB%	GDP	Avg	OBP	Slg
2003	Pulaski	R+	50	186	48	7	2	2	(-	-)	65	20	24	18	8	0	49	1	0	1	3	4	.43	7	.258	.291	.349
2003	Auburn	A-	7	26	5	2	0	1	(-	-)	10	2	7	2	1	0	10	0	0	0	0	0	-	0	.192	.222	.385
2004	Pulaski	R+	44	168	49	14	4	1	(-	-)	74	27	27	24	12	1	32	1	1	2	1	4	.20	4	.292	.339	.440
2004	Auburn	A-	10	19	5	0	0	0	(-	-)	5	5	2	2	3	0	5	1	1	0	0	0	-	2	.263	.391	.263
2005	Lansng	A	67	239	68	11	3	4	(-	-)	97	25	34	30	9	0	40	2	0	4	7	5	.58	2	.285	.311	.406
2006	Augsta	A	126	460	145	29	20	14	(-	-)	256	90	90	99	34	2	81	8	1	5	64	15	.81	9	.315	.369	.557
2007	Conn	AA	96	376	112	17	9	1	(-	-)	150	55	25	56	26	0	66	2	4	3	49	17	.74	6	.298	.344	.399
2007	Fresno	AAA	4	18	5	0	0	0	(-	-)	5	5	0	3	2	0	3	1	0	0	5	0	1.00	0	.278	.381	.278
2008	Fresno	AAA	42	171	53	11	4	5	(-	-)	87	25	15	31	17	0	32	0	0	0	13	9	.59	5	.310	.372	.509
2007	SF	NL	14	11	3	0	2	0	(0	0)	7	5	2	4	2	0	3	0	0	0	4	0	1.00	0	.273	.385	.636
2008	SF	NL	98	275	72	16	7	1	(0	1)	105	32	30	29	14	2	40	1	1	1	15	6	.71	11	.262	.299	.382
2 ML YEARS			112	286	75	16	9	1	(0	1)	112	37	32	33	16	2	43	1	1	1	19	6	.76	11	.262	.303	.392

Will Venable

Bats: L Throws: L Pos: CF-27; PH-1   Ht: 6'2" Wt: 205 Born: 10/29/1982 Age: 26

Year	Team	Lg	G	AB	H	2B	3B	HR	(Hm	Rd)	TB	R	RBI	RC	TBB	IBB	SO	HBP	SH	SF	SB	CS	SB%	GDP	Avg	OBP	Slg
2005	Padres	R	15	59	19	4	2	1	(-	-)	30	13	12	12	2	0	9	4	0	0	4	0	1.00	1	.322	.385	.508
2005	Eugene	A-	42	139	30	5	2	2	(-	-)	45	17	14	14	14	0	38	2	0	1	2	1	.67	1	.216	.295	.324
2006	FtWyn	A	124	472	148	34	5	11	(-	-)	225	86	91	92	55	4	81	7	1	6	18	5	.78	8	.314	.389	.477
2007	SnAnt	AA	134	515	143	19	3	8	(-	-)	192	66	68	72	38	3	84	10	5	4	21	2	.91	8	.278	.337	.373
2008	Portlnd	AAA	120	442	129	26	4	14	(-	-)	205	70	58	76	44	0	104	5	3	2	7	3	.70	7	.292	.361	.464
2008	SD	NL	28	110	29	4	2	2	(0	2)	43	16	10	15	13	1	21	0	0	1	1	1	.50	1	.264	.339	.391

Jose Veras

Pitches: R Bats: R Pos: RP-60   Ht: 6'5" Wt: 236 Born: 10/20/1980 Age: 28

Year	Team	Lg	G	GS	CG	GF	IP	BFP	H	R	ER	HR	SH	SF	HB	TBB	IBB	SO	WP	Bk	W	L	Pct	ShO	Sv-Op	Hld	ERC	ERA
2008 S-WB*	AAA	13	0	0	13	13.0	53	8	3	2	1	0	0	2	4	0	21	0	0	0	0	-	0	9--	-	2.14	1.38
2006 NYY	AL	12	0	0	4	11.0	43	8	5	5	2	0	0	0	5	0	6	1	1	0	0	-	0	1-1		3.55	4.09
2007 NYY	AL	9	0	0	3	9.1	41	6	6	6	0	0	0	0	7	1	7	1	0	0	0	-	0	2-2	1	2.52	5.79
2008 NYY	AL	60	0	0	15	57.2	253	52	23	23	7	2	1	3	29	6	63	4	0	5	3	.625	0	0-2	10	4.09	3.59
Postseason		2	0	0	0	0.2	4	1	0	0	0	0	0	0	1	1	1	0	0	0	0	-	0	0-0	0	6.98	0.00
3 ML YEARS		81	0	0	22	78.0	337	66	34	34	9	2	1	3	41	7	76	6	1	5	3	.625	0	3-5	12	3.82	3.92

Justin Verlander

Pitches: R Bats: R Pos: SP-33   Ht: 6'5" Wt: 200 Born: 2/20/1983 Age: 26

Year	Team	Lg	G	GS	CG	GF	IP	BFP	H	R	ER	HR	SH	SF	HB	TBB	IBB	SO	WP	Bk	W	L	Pct	ShO	Sv-Op	Hld	ERC	ERA
2005 Det	AL	2	2	0	0	11.1	54	15	9	9	1	0	0	1	5	0	7	1	0	0	2	.000	0	0-0	0	6.41	7.15
2006 Det	AL	30	30	1	0	186.0	776	187	78	75	21	2	4	6	60	1	124	5	1	17	9	.654	1	0-0	0	4.12	3.63
2007 Det	AL	32	32	1	0	201.2	866	181	88	82	20	3	1	19	67	3	183	17	2	18	6	.750	1	0-0	0	3.53	3.66
2008 Det	AL	33	33	1	0	201.0	880	195	119	108	18	4	6	14	87	8	163	6	3	11	17	.393	0	0-0	0	4.17	4.84
Postseason		4	4	0	0	21.2	100	26	17	14	5	1	0	0	10	0	23	3	1	1	2	.333	0	0-0	0	6.45	5.82
4 ML YEARS		97	97	3	0	600.0	2576	578	294	274	60	9	11	40	219	12	477	29	6	46	34	.575	2	0-0	0	3.98	4.11

Shane Victorino

Bats: B Throws: R Pos: CF-139; PH-8; RF-5   Ht: 5'9" Wt: 180 Born: 11/30/1980 Age: 28

Year	Team	Lg	G	AB	H	2B	3B	HR	(Hm	Rd)	TB	R	RBI	RC	TBB	IBB	SO	HBP	SH	SF	SB	CS	SB%	GDP	Avg	OBP	Slg
2008 Clrwtr*	A+	2	5	2	0	0	0	(-	-)	2	1	1	1	2	0	1	0	0	0	0	1	.00	0	.400	.571	.400
2008 Rdng*	AA	1	3	1	0	0	0	(-	-)	1	0	0	0	0	0	0	0	0	0	0	0	-	0	.333	.333	.333
2008 LV*	AAA	2	8	3	0	0	0	(-	-)	3	0	0	1	0	0	0	0	0	0	0	0	-	0	.375	.375	.375
2003 SD	NL	36	73	11	2	0	0	(0	0)	13	8	4	1	7	0	17	1	1	1	7	2	.78	5	.151	.232	.178
2005 Phi	NL	21	17	5	0	0	2	(1	1)	11	5	8	4	0	0	3	0	0	2	0	0	-	0	.294	.263	.647
2006 Phi	NL	153	415	119	19	8	6	(3	3)	172	70	46	58	24	0	54	14	8	1	4	3	.57	5	.287	.346	.414
2007 Phi	NL	131	456	128	23	3	12	(6	6)	193	78	46	65	37	1	62	10	5	2	37	4	.90	10	.281	.347	.423
2008 Phi	NL	146	570	167	30	8	14	(6	8)	255	102	58	86	45	2	69	7	5	0	36	11	.77	8	.293	.352	.447
Postseason		3	9	2	0	0	1	(0	1)	5	2	1	1	0	0	1	0	0	0	1	0	1.00	0	.222	.222	.556
5 ML YEARS		487	1531	430	74	19	34	(16	18)	644	263	162	214	113	3	205	32	19	6	84	20	.81	28	.281	.342	.421

280

Jose Vidro

Bats: B Throws: R Pos: DH-70; 1B-9; PH-8   Ht: 6'0" Wt: 200 Born: 8/27/1974 Age: 34

										BATTING													BASERUNNING				AVERAGES		
Year	Team	Lg	G	AB	H	2B	3B	HR	(Hm	Rd)	TB	R	RBI	RC	TBB	IBB	SO	HBP	SH	SF	SB	CS	SB%	GDP	Avg	OBP	Slg
1997	Mon	NL	67	169	42	12	1	2	(0	2)	62	19	17	19	11	0	20	2	0	3	1	0	1.00	1	.249	.297	.367
1998	Mon	NL	83	205	45	12	0	0	(0	0)	57	24	18	19	27	0	33	4	6	3	2	2	.50	5	.220	.318	.278
1999	Mon	NL	140	494	150	45	2	12	(5	7)	235	67	59	76	29	2	51	4	2	2	0	4	.00	12	.304	.346	.476
2000	Mon	NL	153	606	200	51	2	24	(11	13)	327	101	97	115	49	4	69	2	0	6	5	4	.56	17	.330	.379	.540
2001	Mon	NL	124	486	155	34	1	15	(6	9)	236	82	59	81	31	2	49	10	2	2	4	1	.80	18	.319	.371	.486
2002	Mon	NL	152	604	190	43	3	19	(11	8)	296	103	96	112	60	1	70	3	11	3	2	1	.67	12	.315	.378	.490
2003	Mon	NL	144	509	158	36	0	15	(7	8)	239	77	65	89	69	6	50	7	2	5	3	2	.60	16	.310	.397	.470
2004	Mon	NL	110	412	121	24	0	14	(6	8)	187	51	60	59	49	7	43	0	4	2	3	1	.75	14	.294	.367	.454
2005	Was	NL	87	309	85	21	2	7	(2	5)	131	38	32	41	31	3	30	1	2	4	0	0	-	8	.275	.339	.424
2006	Was	NL	126	463	134	26	1	7	(3	4)	183	52	47	60	41	3	48	3	0	4	1	0	1.00	16	.289	.348	.395
2007	Sea	AL	147	548	172	26	0	6	(2	4)	216	78	59	82	63	5	57	1	5	8	0	0	-	21	.314	.381	.394
2008	Sea	AL	85	308	72	11	0	7	(3	4)	104	28	45	28	18	2	36	0	2	2	2	1	.67	5	.234	.274	.338
12 ML YEARS			1418	5113	1524	341	12	128	(56	72)	2273	720	654	781	478	35	556	37	36	44	23	16	.59	145	.298	.359	.445

Carlos Villanueva

Pitches: R Bats: B Pos: RP-38; SP-9   Ht: 6'2" Wt: 213 Born: 11/28/1983 Age: 25

			HOW MUCH HE PITCHED						WHAT HE GAVE UP												THE RESULTS						
Year	Team	Lg	G	GS	CG	GF	IP	BFP	H	R	ER	HR	SH	SF	HB	TBB	IBB	SO	WP	Bk	W	L	Pct	ShO	Sv-Op	Hld	ERC	ERA
2006	Mil	NL	10	6	0	2	53.2	215	43	22	22	8	1	0	4	11	1	39	0	0	2	2	.500	0	0-0	1	2.85	3.69
2007	Mil	NL	59	6	0	8	114.1	489	101	52	50	16	4	1	3	53	3	99	3	0	8	5	.615	0	1-3	16	4.03	3.94
2008	Mil	NL	47	9	0	9	108.1	464	112	53	49	18	9	1	3	30	1	93	4	0	4	7	.364	0	1-1	11	4.29	4.07
3 ML YEARS			116	21	0	19	276.1	1168	256	127	121	42	14	2	10	94	5	231	7	0	14	14	.500	0	2-4	27	3.90	3.94

Oscar Villarreal

Pitches: R Bats: L Pos: RP-35   Ht: 6'0" Wt: 217 Born: 11/22/1981 Age: 27

			HOW MUCH HE PITCHED						WHAT HE GAVE UP												THE RESULTS						
Year	Team	Lg	G	GS	CG	GF	IP	BFP	H	R	ER	HR	SH	SF	HB	TBB	IBB	SO	WP	Bk	W	L	Pct	ShO	Sv-Op	Hld	ERC	ERA
2008	Tacom*	AAA	5	0	0	1	9.2	41	7	7	5	2	0	0	0	4	0	11	2	0	1	0	1.000	0	1--	-	3.17	4.66
2008	ColSpr*	AAA	3	3	0	0	13.0	61	17	11	9	1	2	1	0	7	0	7	1	0	0	1	.000	0	0--	-	6.35	6.23
2003	Ari	NL	86	1	0	14	98.0	422	80	40	28	6	9	3	3	46	10	80	3	2	10	7	.588	0	0-4	10	2.97	2.57
2004	Ari	NL	17	0	0	4	18.0	84	25	14	14	3	3	0	1	7	1	17	5	0	0	2	.000	0	0-0	7	7.13	7.00
2005	Ari	NL	11	0	0	0	13.2	57	11	8	8	2	2	1	1	6	2	5	0	0	2	0	1.000	0	0-2	2	3.59	5.27
2006	Atl	NL	58	4	0	11	92.1	397	93	41	37	13	5	4	5	27	3	55	4	0	9	1	.900	0	0-4	2	4.10	3.61
2007	Atl	NL	51	0	0	11	76.1	336	75	40	36	6	3	9	4	32	8	58	6	0	2	2	.500	0	1-2	2	3.88	4.24
2008	Hou	NL	35	0	0	13	37.2	168	42	25	21	12	1	1	2	17	0	21	2	0	1	3	.250	0	0-1	2	6.98	5.02
6 ML YEARS			258	5	0	53	336.0	1464	326	168	144	42	23	18	16	135	24	236	20	2	24	15	.615	0	1-13	20	4.13	3.86

Ron Villone

Pitches: L Bats: L Pos: RP-74   Ht: 6'3" Wt: 240 Born: 1/16/1970 Age: 39

			HOW MUCH HE PITCHED						WHAT HE GAVE UP												THE RESULTS						
Year	Team	Lg	G	GS	CG	GF	IP	BFP	H	R	ER	HR	SH	SF	HB	TBB	IBB	SO	WP	Bk	W	L	Pct	ShO	Sv-Op	Hld	ERC	ERA
1995	2 Tms		38	0	0	15	45.0	212	44	31	29	11	3	1	1	34	0	63	3	0	2	3	.400	0	1-5	6	6.57	5.80
1996	2 Tms		44	0	0	19	43.0	182	31	15	15	6	0	2	5	25	0	38	2	0	1	1	.500	0	2-3	9	4.08	3.14
1997	Mil	AL	50	0	0	15	52.2	238	54	23	20	4	2	0	1	36	2	40	3	0	1	0	1.000	0	0-2	8	5.30	3.42
1998	Cle	AL	25	0	0	6	27.0	129	30	18	18	3	2	2	2	22	0	15	0	0	0	0	-	0	0-0	1	7.01	6.00
1999	Cin	NL	29	22	0	2	142.2	610	114	70	67	8	9	3	5	73	2	97	6	0	9	7	.563	0	2-2	0	3.20	4.23
2000	Cin	NL	35	23	2	5	141.0	643	154	95	85	22	10	8	9	78	3	77	7	0	10	10	.500	0		1	5.97	5.43
2001	2 Tms	NL	53	12	0	12	114.2	523	133	81	75	18	1	1	5	53	5	113	4	1	6	10	.375	0	0-0	6	5.81	5.89
2002	Pit	NL	45	7	0	6	93.0	399	95	63	60	8	5	3	5	34	3	55	1	0	4	6	.400	0	0-1	1	4.18	5.81
2003	Hou	NL	19	19	0	0	106.2	449	91	51	49	16	3	3	5	48	1	91	1	0	6	6	.500	0	0-0	0	4.04	4.13
2004	Sea	AL	56	10	0	14	117.0	523	102	64	53	12	4	4	12	64	3	86	6	0	8	6	.571	0	0-1	7	4.26	4.08
2005	2 Tms	NL	79	0	0	24	64.0	287	57	34	29	4	3	5	7	35	2	70	3	1	5	5	.500	0	1-9	21	4.09	4.08
2006	NYY	AL	70	0	0	19	80.1	365	75	48	45	9	6	4	4	51	9	72	5	0	3	3	.500	0	0-1	6	4.69	5.04
2007	NYY	AL	37	0	0	13	42.1	176	36	20	20	5	0	1	3	18	3	25	4	0	0	0	-	0	0-1	4	3.74	4.25
2008	StL	NL	74	0	0	11	50.0	229	45	27	26	4	2	3	2	37	2	50	2	0	1	2	.333	0	1-2	16	4.77	4.68
95	Sea	AL	19	0	0	7	19.1	101	20	19	17	6	3	0	1	23	0	26	1	0	0	2	.000	0	0-3	3	9.67	7.91
95	SD	NL	19	0	0	8	25.2	111	24	12	12	5	0	1	0	11	0	37	2	0	2	1	.667	0	1-2	3	4.44	4.21
96	SD	NL	21	0	0	9	18.1	78	17	6	6	2	0	0	1	7	0	19	0	0	1	1	.500	0	0-1	4	3.90	2.95
96	Mil	NL	23	0	0	10	24.2	104	14	9	9	4	0	2	4	18	0	19	2	0	0	0	-	0	2-2	5	4.21	3.28
01	Col	NL	22	6	0	6	46.2	222	56	35	33	6	1	1	1	29	4	48	2	0	1	3	.250	0	0-0	2	6.30	6.36
01	Hou	NL	31	6	0	6	68.0	301	77	46	42	12	0	0	4	24	1	65	2	1	5	7	.417	0	0-0	4	5.46	5.56
05	Sea	AL	52	0	0	14	40.1	178	33	14	11	2	1	3	5	23	1	41	2	1	2	3	.400	0	1-6	17	3.79	2.45
05	Fla	NL	27	0	0	10	23.2	109	24	20	18	2	2	2	2	12	1	29	1	0	3	2	.600	0	0-3	4	4.61	6.85
Postseason			3	0	0	2	2.0	8	1	0	0	0	0	0	0	1	0	1	0	0	0	0	-	0	0-0	0	1.41	0.00
14 ML YEARS			654	93	2	161	1119.1	4965	1061	640	591	130	50	40	66	608	35	892	47	2	56	59	.487	0	7-27	85	4.67	4.75

Luis Vizcaino

Pitches: R Bats: R Pos: RP-43   Ht: 5'11" Wt: 210 Born: 8/6/1974 Age: 34

			HOW MUCH HE PITCHED						WHAT HE GAVE UP												THE RESULTS						
Year	Team	Lg	G	GS	CG	GF	IP	BFP	H	R	ER	HR	SH	SF	HB	TBB	IBB	SO	WP	Bk	W	L	Pct	ShO	Sv-Op	Hld	ERC	ERA
2008	ColSpr*	AAA	4	0	0	0	4.0	13	1	0	0	0	0	0	0	0	0	4	0	0	0	0	-	0	0--	-	0.14	0.00
1999	Oak	AL	1	0	0	1	3.1	16	3	2	2	1	0	0	0	3	0	2	1	0	0	0	-	0	0-0	1	7.01	5.40
2000	Oak	AL	12	0	0	1	19.1	96	25	17	16	2	0	1	2	11	0	18	1	0	0	1	.000	0	0-0	0	6.83	7.45
2001	Oak	AL	36	0	0	15	36.2	156	38	19	19	8	0	1	0	12	1	31	3	0	2	1	.667	0	1-1	3	4.80	4.66

Year	Team	Lg	G	GS	CG	GF	IP	BFP	H	R	ER	HR	SH	SF	HB	TBB	IBB	SO	WP	Bk	W	L	Pct	ShO	Sv-Op	Hld	ERC	ERA
2002	Mil	NL	76	0	0	30	81.1	326	55	27	27	6	3	3	3	30	4	79	3	2	5	3	.625	0	5-6	19	2.20	2.99
2003	Mil	NL	75	0	0	21	62.0	272	64	45	44	16	2	1	1	25	3	61	3	0	4	3	.571	0	0-6	9	5.37	6.39
2004	Mil	NL	73	0	0	21	72.0	298	61	35	30	12	1	5	1	24	3	63	9	0	4	4	.500	0	1-5	21	3.40	3.75
2005	CWS	AL	65	0	0	20	70.0	305	74	30	29	8	4	1	2	29	6	43	3	0	6	5	.545	0	0-3	9	4.58	3.73
2006	Ari	NL	70	0	0	15	65.1	272	51	26	26	8	2	0	4	29	6	72	1	0	6	4	.600	0	0-2	25	3.34	3.58
2007	NYY	AL	77	0	0	13	75.1	334	66	37	36	6	2	6	2	43	11	62	1	0	8	2	.800	0	0-3	14	3.70	4.30
2008	Col	NL	43	0	0	13	46.0	203	48	28	27	10	1	2	1	19	1	49	0	0	1	2	.333	0	0-1	1	5.25	5.28
Postseason			2	0	0	1	1.2	10	2	1	1	0	1	0	0	3	1	0	0	0	0	1	.000	0	0-0	0	8.50	5.40
10 ML YEARS			528	0	0	150	531.1	2278	485	266	256	77	15	20	16	225	35	480	25	2	34	27	.557	0	7-27	101	4.00	4.34

Omar Vizquel

Bats: B **Throws:** R **Pos:** SS-84; PH-12   **Ht:** 5'9" **Wt:** 175 **Born:** 4/24/1967 **Age:** 42

Year	Team	Lg	G	AB	H	2B	3B	HR	(Hm	Rd)	TB	R	RBI	RC	TBB	IBB	SO	HBP	SH	SF	SB	CS	SB%	GDP	Avg	OBP	Slg
2008	Fresno*	AAA	2	5	1	0	0	0	(-	-)	1	0	0	0	0	0	0	0	0	0	0	0	-	0	.200	.200	.200
2008	SnJos*	A+	3	8	3	0	0	0	(-	-)	3	3	1	1	2	0	0	0	0	0	0	0	-	0	.375	.500	.375
1989	Sea	AL	143	387	85	7	3	1	(1	0)	101	45	20	25	28	0	40	1	13	2	1	4	.20	6	.220	.273	.261
1990	Sea	AL	81	255	63	3	2	2	(0	2)	76	19	18	22	18	0	22	0	10	2	4	1	.80	7	.247	.295	.298
1991	Sea	AL	142	426	98	16	4	1	(1	0)	125	42	41	39	45	0	37	0	8	3	7	2	.78	8	.230	.302	.293
1992	Sea	AL	136	483	142	20	4	0	(0	0)	170	49	21	54	32	0	38	2	9	1	15	13	.54	14	.294	.340	.352
1993	Sea	AL	158	560	143	14	2	2	(1	1)	167	68	31	53	50	2	71	4	13	3	12	14	.46	7	.255	.319	.298
1994	Cle	AL	69	286	78	10	1	1	(0	1)	93	39	33	32	23	0	23	0	11	2	13	4	.76	4	.273	.325	.325
1995	Cle	AL	136	542	144	28	0	6	(3	3)	190	87	56	70	59	0	59	1	10	10	29	11	.73	4	.266	.333	.351
1996	Cle	AL	151	542	161	36	1	9	(2	7)	226	98	64	87	56	0	42	4	12	9	35	9	.80	10	.297	.362	.417
1997	Cle	AL	153	565	158	23	6	5	(3	2)	208	89	49	75	57	1	58	2	16	2	43	12	.78	16	.280	.347	.368
1998	Cle	AL	151	576	166	30	6	2	(0	2)	214	86	50	82	62	1	64	4	12	6	37	12	.76	10	.288	.358	.372
1999	Cle	AL	144	574	191	36	4	5	(3	2)	250	112	66	106	65	0	50	1	17	7	42	9	.82	8	.333	.397	.436
2000	Cle	AL	156	613	176	27	3	7	(1	6)	230	101	66	92	87	0	72	5	7	5	22	10	.69	13	.287	.377	.375
2001	Cle	AL	155	611	156	26	8	2	(2	0)	204	84	50	66	61	0	72	2	15	4	13	9	.59	14	.255	.323	.334
2002	Cle	AL	151	582	160	31	5	14	(9	5)	243	85	72	91	56	3	64	8	7	10	18	10	.64	7	.275	.341	.418
2003	Cle	AL	64	250	61	13	2	2	(2	0)	84	43	19	25	29	0	20	0	5	1	8	3	.73	11	.244	.321	.336
2004	Cle	AL	148	567	165	28	3	7	(2	5)	220	82	59	86	57	0	62	1	20	6	19	6	.76	12	.291	.353	.388
2005	SF	NL	152	568	154	28	4	3	(0	3)	199	66	45	76	56	0	58	5	20	2	24	10	.71	10	.271	.341	.350
2006	SF	NL	153	579	171	22	10	4	(2	2)	225	88	58	90	56	3	51	6	13	5	24	7	.77	13	.295	.361	.389
2007	SF	NL	145	513	126	18	3	4	(2	2)	162	54	51	53	44	6	48	1	14	3	14	6	.70	14	.246	.305	.316
2008	SF	NL	92	266	59	10	1	0	(0	0)	71	24	23	24	24	9	29	0	7	3	5	4	.56	4	.222	.283	.267
Postseason			57	228	57	7	4	0	(0	0)	72	28	20	27	25	0	36	2	7	2	23	3	.88	0	.250	.327	.316
20 ML YEARS			2680	9745	2657	426	72	77	(34	43)	3458	1361	892	1248	965	25	980	47	239	86	385	156	.71	192	.273	.338	.355

Edinson Volquez

Pitches: R **Bats:** R **Pos:** SP-32; RP-1   **Ht:** 6'0" **Wt:** 200 **Born:** 7/3/1983 **Age:** 25

Year	Team	Lg	G	GS	CG	GF	IP	BFP	H	R	ER	HR	SH	SF	HB	TBB	IBB	SO	WP	Bk	W	L	Pct	ShO	Sv-Op	Hld	ERC	ERA
2005	Tex	AL	6	3	0	0	12.2	75	25	22	20	3	0	1	2	10	0	11	0	0	0	4	.000	0	0-0	0	14.15	14.21
2006	Tex	AL	8	8	0	0	33.1	164	52	28	27	7	0	1	1	17	0	15	0	0	1	6	.143	0	0-0	0	9.27	7.29
2007	Tex	AL	6	6	0	0	34.0	149	34	18	17	4	0	2	2	15	0	29	0	0	2	1	.667	0	0-0	0	4.63	4.50
2008	Cin	NL	33	32	0	1	196.0	838	167	82	70	14	6	5	14	93	5	206	10	1	17	6	.739	0	0-0	0	3.61	3.21
4 ML YEARS			53	49	0	1	276.0	1226	278	150	134	28	6	9	19	135	5	261	10	1	20	17	.541	0	0-0	0	4.75	4.37

Chris Volstad

Pitches: R **Bats:** R **Pos:** SP-14; RP-1   **Ht:** 6'7" **Wt:** 190 **Born:** 9/23/1986 **Age:** 22

Year	Team	Lg	G	GS	CG	GF	IP	BFP	H	R	ER	HR	SH	SF	HB	TBB	IBB	SO	WP	Bk	W	L	Pct	ShO	Sv-Op	Hld	ERC	ERA
2005	Fla	R	6	6	0	0	27.0	111	25	14	7	1	1	1	2	4	0	26	1	0	1	1	.500	0	0--	-	2.58	2.33
2005	Jmstwn	A-	7	7	0	0	38.0	170	43	19	9	0	1	1	3	11	0	29	2	1	3	2	.600	0	0--	-	3.88	2.13
2006	Grnsbr	A	26	26	0	0	152.0	636	161	73	52	12	6	2	6	36	0	99	6	0	11	8	.579	0	0--	-	3.84	3.08
2007	Jupiter	A+	21	20	2	0	126.0	567	152	76	63	8	2	4	6	37	1	93	9	0	8	9	.471	1	0--	-	4.67	4.50
2007	Carlina	AA	7	7	0	0	42.2	177	41	19	15	4	3	0	1	10	0	25	3	0	4	2	.667	0	0--	-	3.27	3.16
2008	Carlina	AA	15	15	1	0	91.0	383	86	37	34	0	7	2	2	30	3	55	3	0	4	4	.500	0	0--	-	2.86	3.36
2008	Fla	NL	15	14	0	0	84.1	365	76	30	27	3	6	1	5	36	4	52	0	0	6	4	.600	0	0-0	0	3.30	2.88

Joey Votto

Bats: L **Throws:** R **Pos:** 1B-144; PH-9   **Ht:** 6'3" **Wt:** 220 **Born:** 9/10/1983 **Age:** 25

Year	Team	Lg	G	AB	H	2B	3B	HR	(Hm	Rd)	TB	R	RBI	RC	TBB	IBB	SO	HBP	SH	SF	SB	CS	SB%	GDP	Avg	OBP	Slg
2002	Reds	R	50	175	47	13	3	9	(-	-)	93	29	33	33	21	1	45	1	0	5	7	2	.78	3	.269	.342	.531
2003	Dayton	A	60	195	45	8	0	1	(-	-)	56	19	20	21	34	0	64	2	0	2	2	5	.29	3	.231	.348	.287
2003	Billings	R+	70	240	76	17	3	6	(-	-)	117	47	38	57	56	3	80	4	0	1	4	0	1.00	4	.317	.452	.488
2004	Dayton	A	111	391	118	26	2	14	(-	-)	190	60	72	84	79	1	110	1	0	2	9	2	.82	6	.302	.419	.486
2004	Ptomc	A+	24	84	25	7	0	5	(-	-)	47	11	20	17	11	1	21	1	0	0	1	1	.50	1	.298	.385	.560
2005	Srsota	A+	124	464	119	23	2	17	(-	-)	197	64	83	68	52	2	122	3	1	9	4	5	.44	9	.256	.330	.425
2006	Chatt	AA	136	508	162	46	2	22	(-	-)	278	85	77	115	78	5	109	1	0	3	24	7	.77	13	.319	.408	.547
2007	Lsvlle	AAA	133	496	146	21	2	22	(-	-)	237	74	92	94	70	5	110	5	0	9	17	10	.63	7	.294	.381	.478
2007	Cin	NL	24	84	27	7	0	4	(4	0)	46	11	17	17	5	1	15	0	0	0	1	0	1.00	0	.321	.360	.548
2008	Cin	NL	151	526	156	32	3	24	(14	10)	266	69	84	91	59	9	102	2	0	2	7	5	.58	7	.297	.368	.506
2 ML YEARS			175	610	183	39	3	28	(18	10)	312	80	101	108	64	10	117	2	0	2	8	5	.62	7	.300	.367	.511

Cory Wade

Pitches: R Bats: R Pos: RP-55 — Ht: 6'2" Wt: 185 Born: 5/28/1983 Age: 26

Year	Team	Lg	G	GS	CG	GF	IP	BFP	H	R	ER	HR	SH	SF	HB	TBB	IBB	SO	WP	Bk	W	L	Pct	ShO	Sv-Op	Hld	ERC	ERA
2004	Ddgrs	R	11	2	0	6	32.2	129	28	12	11	2	1	0	4	1	0	26	0	0	2	1	.667	0	1--	-	2.19	3.03
2004	Ogden	R+	8	0	0	2	14.0	70	24	9	8	0	0	0	0	4	1	19	1	0	1	2	.333	0	0--	-	6.77	5.14
2005	Clmbs	A	12	0	0	8	20.0	102	29	19	9	2	3	3	1	10	0	14	1	0	0	2	.000	0	2--	-	7.11	4.05
2005	Ogden	R+	16	11	1	0	72.1	306	81	42	35	12	3	1	5	19	0	60	3	0	2	3	.400	0	0--	-	5.13	4.35
2006	Clmbs	A	23	14	1	5	94.1	401	101	56	52	9	1	3	10	11	0	94	5	0	6	5	.545	1	2--	-	3.69	4.96
2006	VeroB	A+	7	7	0	0	39.1	184	52	40	36	9	1	2	4	13	0	32	0	0	2	4	.333	0	0--	-	7.13	8.24
2007	InldEm	A+	25	2	0	7	66.0	265	50	19	18	6	0	1	6	17	1	67	4	0	7	0	1.000	0	6--	-	2.55	2.45
2007	Jaxnvl	AA	14	0	0	3	33.0	136	22	5	5	2	3	1	0	11	2	33	0	0	1	0	1.000	0	0--	-	1.72	1.36
2008	Jaxnvl	AA	5	0	0	2	14.2	58	14	7	7	3	0	0	2	1	0	13	1	0	0	0	-	0	1--	-	3.87	4.30
2008	Gt Lks	A	1	1	0	0	1.0	4	1	0	0	0	0	0	0	0	0	0	0	0	0	0	-	0	0--	-	1.95	0.00
2008	LAD	NL	55	0	0	21	71.1	275	51	22	18	7	2	1	4	15	3	51	2	0	2	1	.667	0	0-1	9	2.11	2.27

Doug Waechter

Pitches: R Bats: R Pos: RP-48 — Ht: 6'4" Wt: 209 Born: 1/28/1981 Age: 28

Year	Team	Lg	G	GS	CG	GF	IP	BFP	H	R	ER	HR	SH	SF	HB	TBB	IBB	SO	WP	Bk	W	L	Pct	ShO	Sv-Op	Hld	ERC	ERA
2008	Albq*	AAA	2	2	0	0	10.2	49	17	5	5	3	0	0	0	2	1	4	0	0	1	0	1.000	0	0--	-	8.23	4.22
2008	Mrlns*	R	1	1	0	0	1.0	4	1	0	0	0	0	0	0	0	0	2	0	0	0	0	-	0	0--	-	1.95	0.00
2008	Jupiter*	A+	2	0	0	0	1.2	9	3	3	1	0	0	0	0	0	0	2	1	0	0	0	-	0	0--	-	5.47	5.40
2003	TB	AL	6	5	1	0	35.1	145	29	13	13	4	0	0	1	15	0	29	0	0	3	2	.600	1	0-0	0	3.48	3.31
2004	TB	AL	14	14	0	0	70.1	309	68	54	47	20	0	2	4	33	1	36	1	1	5	7	.417	0	0-0	0	5.74	6.01
2005	TB	AL	29	25	0	3	157.0	692	191	109	98	29	4	4	3	38	5	87	4	2	5	12	.294	0	0-0	0	5.29	5.62
2006	TB	AL	11	10	0	0	53.0	249	67	40	39	6	3	6	5	19	1	25	0	0	1	4	.200	0	0-0	0	5.79	6.62
2008	Fla	NL	48	0	0	10	63.1	275	63	29	26	7	2	2	2	21	3	46	2	0	4	2	.667	0	0-1	9	3.82	3.69
	5 ML YEARS		108	54	1	13	379.0	1670	418	245	223	66	9	14	15	126	10	223	7	3	18	27	.400	1	0-1	9	5.02	5.30

Billy Wagner

Pitches: L Bats: L Pos: RP-45 — Ht: 5'11" Wt: 203 Born: 7/25/1971 Age: 37

Year	Team	Lg	G	GS	CG	GF	IP	BFP	H	R	ER	HR	SH	SF	HB	TBB	IBB	SO	WP	Bk	W	L	Pct	ShO	Sv-Op	Hld	ERC	ERA
2008	Bnghtn*	AA	1	0	0	0	1.0	3	0	0	0	0	0	0	0	0	0	2	0	0	0	0	-	0	0--	-	0.00	0.00
1995	Hou	NL	1	0	0	0	0.1	1	0	0	0	0	0	0	0	0	0	0	0	0	0	0	-	0	0-0	0	0.00	0.00
1996	Hou	NL	37	0	0	20	51.2	212	28	16	14	6	7	2	3	30	2	67	1	0	2	2	.500	0	9-13	1	2.61	2.44
1997	Hou	NL	62	0	0	49	66.1	277	49	23	21	5	3	1	3	30	1	106	3	0	7	8	.467	0	23-29	1	2.85	2.85
1998	Hou	NL	58	0	0	50	60.0	247	46	19	18	6	4	0	0	25	1	97	2	0	4	3	.571	0	30-35	1	2.87	2.70
1999	Hou	NL	66	0	0	55	74.2	286	35	14	13	5	2	1	1	23	1	124	2	0	4	1	.800	0	39-42	1	1.20	1.57
2000	Hou	NL	28	0	0	19	27.2	129	28	19	19	6	0	0	1	18	0	28	7	0	2	4	.333	0	6-15	0	6.15	6.18
2001	Hou	NL	64	0	0	58	62.2	251	44	19	19	5	3	1	5	20	0	79	3	0	2	5	.286	0	39-41	0	2.42	2.73
2002	Hou	NL	70	0	0	61	75.0	289	51	21	21	7	3	3	2	22	5	88	6	0	4	2	.667	0	35-41	0	2.08	2.52
2003	Hou	NL	78	0	0	67	86.0	335	52	18	17	8	1	0	3	23	5	105	4	0	1	4	.200	0	44-47	0	1.63	1.78
2004	Phi	NL	45	0	0	38	48.1	182	31	16	13	5	3	0	2	6	1	59	1	0	4	0	1.000	0	21-25	1	1.52	2.42
2005	Phi	NL	75	0	0	70	77.2	297	45	17	13	6	0	2	3	20	2	87	3	1	4	3	.571	0	38-41	0	1.53	1.51
2006	NYM	NL	70	0	0	59	72.1	297	59	22	18	7	2	0	4	21	1	94	2	0	3	2	.600	0	40-45	0	2.83	2.24
2007	NYM	NL	66	0	0	57	68.1	282	55	22	20	6	1	2	2	22	4	80	4	0	2	2	.500	0	34-39	0	2.66	2.63
2008	NYM	NL	45	0	0	34	47.0	184	32	17	12	4	0	1	0	10	0	52	2	0	0	1	.000	0	27-34	0	1.68	2.30
	Postseason		11	0	0	9	10.1	51	18	11	11	3	0	0	1	1	0	11	1	0	1	1	.500	0	3-4	0	9.19	9.58
	14 ML YEARS		765	0	0	637	818.0	3269	555	243	218	76	28	13	29	270	23	1066	40	1	39	37	.513	0	385-447	7	2.20	2.40

Ryan Wagner

Pitches: R Bats: R Pos: P — Ht: 6'4" Wt: 210 Born: 7/15/1982 Age: 26

Year	Team	Lg	G	GS	CG	GF	IP	BFP	H	R	ER	HR	SH	SF	HB	TBB	IBB	SO	WP	Bk	W	L	Pct	ShO	Sv-Op	Hld	ERC	ERA
2008	Clmbs*	AAA	16	0	0	4	19.0	93	26	14	12	3	1	1	0	12	1	14	2	0	0	3	.000	0	1--	-	7.67	5.68
2008	Ptomc*	A+	7	1	0	0	7.1	32	5	1	1	0	0	0	0	5	0	6	1	0	0	0	-	0	1--	-	2.66	1.23
2003	Cin	NL	17	0	0	3	21.2	88	13	4	4	2	0	1	0	12	1	25	4	0	2	0	1.000	0	0-1	6	2.46	1.66
2004	Cin	NL	49	0	0	5	51.2	242	59	31	27	7	2	3	2	27	2	37	6	0	3	2	.600	0	0-3	8	5.66	4.70
2005	Cin	NL	42	0	0	8	45.2	210	56	33	31	4	1	3	4	17	1	39	2	0	3	2	.600	0	0-1	12	5.48	6.11
2006	Was	NL	26	0	0	5	30.2	141	36	21	16	3	1	0	2	15	3	20	3	1	3	3	.500	0	0-2	3	5.55	4.70
2007	Was	NL	14	0	0	2	15.2	73	20	11	10	2	1	0	0	8	2	9	1	0	0	2	.000	0	0-0	1	6.18	5.74
	5 ML YEARS		148	0	0	23	165.1	754	184	100	88	18	5	7	8	79	9	130	16	1	11	9	.550	0	0-7	30	5.18	4.79

Adam Wainwright

Pitches: R Bats: R Pos: SP-20 — Ht: 6'7" Wt: 229 Born: 8/30/1981 Age: 27

Year	Team	Lg	G	GS	CG	GF	IP	BFP	H	R	ER	HR	SH	SF	HB	TBB	IBB	SO	WP	Bk	W	L	Pct	ShO	Sv-Op	Hld	ERC	ERA
2008	Memp*	AAA	2	2	0	0	3.2	20	8	5	5	1	0	0	0	2	0	3	0	0	0	1	.000	0	0--	-	14.78	12.27
2008	Sprgfld*	AA	1	1	0	0	4.2	18	4	0	0	0	0	0	0	0	0	7	0	0	0	0	-	0	0--	-	1.44	0.00
2005	StL	NL	2	0	0	1	2.0	9	2	3	3	1	0	0	0	1	0	0	0	0	0	0	-	0	0-0	0	7.30	13.50
2006	StL	NL	61	0	0	10	75.0	309	64	26	26	6	4	1	4	22	2	72	3	0	2	1	.667	0	3-5	17	2.92	3.12
2007	StL	NL	32	32	1	0	202.0	882	212	93	83	13	9	5	9	70	4	136	6	0	14	12	.538	0	0-0	0	4.01	3.70
2008	StL	NL	20	20	1	0	132.0	544	122	51	47	12	6	4	3	34	1	91	3	0	11	3	.786	0	0-0	0	3.14	3.20
	Postseason		9	0	0	9	9.2	38	7	0	0	0	0	0	0	2	0	15	1	0	1	0	1.000	0	4-5	0	1.48	0.00
	4 ML YEARS		115	52	2	11	411.0	1744	400	173	159	32	19	10	16	127	7	299	12	0	27	16	.628	0	3-5	17	3.54	3.48

Tim Wakefield

Pitches: R Bats: R Pos: SP-30   Ht: 6'2" Wt: 210 Born: 8/2/1966 Age: 42

Year	Team	Lg	G	GS	CG	GF	IP	BFP	H	R	ER	HR	SH	SF	HB	TBB	IBB	SO	WP	Bk	W	L	Pct	ShO	Sv-Op	Hld	ERC	ERA
1992	Pit	NL	13	13	4	0	92.0	373	76	26	22	3	6	4	1	35	1	51	3	1	8	1	.889	1	0-0	0	2.72	2.15
1993	Pit	NL	24	20	3	1	128.1	595	145	83	80	14	7	5	9	75	2	59	6	0	6	11	.353	2	0-0	0	5.97	5.61
1995	Bos	AL	27	27	6	0	195.1	804	163	76	64	22	3	7	9	68	0	119	11	0	16	8	.667	1	0-0	0	3.28	2.95
1996	Bos	AL	32	32	6	0	211.2	963	238	151	121	38	1	9	12	90	0	140	4	1	14	13	.519	0	0-0	0	5.68	5.14
1997	Bos	AL	35	29	4	2	201.1	866	193	109	95	24	3	7	16	87	5	151	6	0	12	15	.444	2	0-0	1	4.47	4.25
1998	Bos	AL	36	33	2	1	216.0	939	211	123	110	30	1	8	14	79	1	146	6	1	17	8	.680	0	0-0	0	4.30	4.58
1999	Bos	AL	49	17	0	28	140.0	635	146	93	79	19	1	8	5	72	2	104	1	0	6	11	.353	0	15-18	0	5.12	5.08
2000	Bos	AL	51	17	0	13	159.1	706	170	107	97	31	4	8	4	65	3	102	4	0	6	10	.375	0	0-1	3	5.23	5.48
2001	Bos	AL	45	17	0	5	168.2	732	156	84	73	13	3	9	18	73	5	148	5	1	9	12	.429	0	3-5	3	4.02	3.90
2002	Bos	AL	45	15	0	10	163.1	657	121	57	51	15	1	4	9	51	2	134	5	2	11	5	.688	0	3-5	5	2.54	2.81
2003	Bos	AL	35	33	0	2	202.1	872	193	106	92	23	2	4	12	71	0	169	8	0	11	7	.611	0	1-1	0	3.92	4.09
2004	Bos	AL	32	30	0	0	188.1	831	197	121	102	29	2	4	16	63	3	116	9	0	12	10	.545	0	0-0	1	4.73	4.87
2005	Bos	AL	33	33	3	0	225.1	943	210	113	104	35	1	6	11	68	4	151	8	0	16	12	.571	0	0-0	0	3.87	4.15
2006	Bos	AL	23	23	1	0	140.0	610	135	80	72	19	1	3	10	51	0	90	6	0	7	11	.389	0	0-0	0	4.22	4.63
2007	Bos	AL	31	31	0	0	189.0	800	191	104	100	22	2	6	4	64	1	110	10	0	17	12	.586	0	0-0	0	4.14	4.76
2008	Bos	AL	30	30	1	0	181.0	754	154	89	83	25	2	4	13	60	0	117	12	0	10	11	.476	0	0-0	0	3.54	4.13
	Postseason		17	10	2	2	69.1	313	62	51	49	10	1	3	9	36	2	52	1	0	5	6	.455	0	0-0	0	4.67	6.36
16 ML YEARS			541	400	30	62	2802.0	12080	2699	1522	1345	362	40	96	163	1072	29	1907	104	6	178	157	.531	6	22-30	13	4.22	4.32

Jamie Walker

Pitches: L Bats: L Pos: RP-59   Ht: 6'2" Wt: 194 Born: 7/1/1971 Age: 37

Year	Team	Lg	G	GS	CG	GF	IP	BFP	H	R	ER	HR	SH	SF	HB	TBB	IBB	SO	WP	Bk	W	L	Pct	ShO	Sv-Op	Hld	ERC	ERA
2008	Bowie*	AA	1	0	0	0	1.0	7	5	3	3	1	1	0	0	0	0	0	0	0	0	0	-	0	0- -	-	51.05	27.00
2008	Frdrck*	A+	1	0	0	0	1.0	4	1	0	0	0	0	0	0	0	0	0	0	0	0	0	-	0	0- -	-	1.95	0.00
1997	KC	AL	50	0	0	15	43.0	197	46	28	26	6	2	2	3	20	3	24	2	0	3	3	.500	0	0-1	3	5.10	5.44
1998	KC	AL	6	2	0	2	17.1	86	30	20	19	5	1	1	2	3	0	15	0	0	0	1	.000	0	0-0	1	9.69	9.87
2002	Det	AL	57	0	0	16	43.2	175	32	19	18	9	0	1	4	9	1	40	1	1	1	1	.500	0	1-4	5	2.86	3.71
2003	Det	AL	78	0	0	19	65.0	273	61	30	24	9	5	2	2	17	1	45	1	0	4	3	.571	0	3-7	12	3.51	3.32
2004	Det	AL	70	0	0	18	64.2	277	69	28	23	8	1	1	1	12	3	53	4	0	3	4	.429	0	1-7	18	3.65	3.20
2005	Det	AL	66	0	0	11	48.2	208	49	22	20	5	1	1	2	13	3	30	0	0	3	4	.571	0	0-2	14	3.63	3.70
2006	Det	AL	56	0	0	14	48.0	196	47	15	15	8	1	0	0	8	3	37	1	0	0	1	.000	0	0-0	11	3.38	2.81
2007	Bal	AL	81	0	0	19	61.1	258	57	25	22	6	0	5	2	17	4	41	3	0	3	2	.600	0	7-13	21	3.19	3.23
2008	Bal	AL	59	0	0	11	38.0	178	53	31	29	12	1	2	1	11	3	24	2	0	1	3	.250	0	0-4	9	7.53	6.87
	Postseason		5	0	0	3	4.1	16	3	2	2	2	0	0	0	1	0	3	1	0	1	0	1.000	0	0-0	0	4.01	4.15
9 ML YEARS			523	2	0	125	429.2	1848	444	218	196	68	12	15	17	110	21	309	14	1	19	21	.475	0	12-38	94	4.11	4.11

Tyler Walker

Pitches: R Bats: R Pos: RP-65   Ht: 6'3" Wt: 275 Born: 5/15/1976 Age: 33

Year	Team	Lg	G	GS	CG	GF	IP	BFP	H	R	ER	HR	SH	SF	HB	TBB	IBB	SO	WP	Bk	W	L	Pct	ShO	Sv-Op	Hld	ERC	ERA
2002	NYM	NL	5	1	0	3	10.2	49	11	7	7	3	0	0	0	5	1	7	0	0	1	0	1.000	0	0-0	0	5.46	5.91
2004	SF	NL	52	0	0	13	63.2	275	69	31	30	8	3	7	1	24	1	48	1	0	5	1	.833	0	1-1	5	4.76	4.24
2005	SF	NL	67	0	0	39	61.2	279	68	31	29	9	5	1	3	27	6	54	4	0	6	4	.600	0	23-28	2	5.15	4.23
2006	2 Tms		26	0	0	17	25.1	111	27	20	20	1	1	0	0	12	0	19	1	0	1	4	.200	0	10-14	1	4.35	7.11
2007	SF	NL	15	0	0	1	14.1	53	12	2	2	0	0	1	0	4	1	9	0	0	2	0	1.000	0	0-1	7	2.30	1.26
2008	SF	NL	65	0	0	19	53.1	226	47	29	27	7	2	1	1	21	3	49	5	0	5	8	.385	0	0-4	19	3.57	4.56
06	SF	NL	6	0	0	1	5.1	28	9	9	9	1	0	0	0	5	0	3	1	0	0	1	.000	0	0-2	1	12.35	15.19
06	TB	AL	20	0	0	16	20.0	83	18	11	11	0	1	0	0	7	0	16	0	0	1	3	.250	0	10-12	0	2.70	4.95
6 ML YEARS			230	1	0	92	229.0	993	234	120	115	28	11	10	5	93	12	186	11	0	20	17	.541	0	34-48	34	4.41	4.52

Les Walrond

Pitches: L Bats: L Pos: RP-6   Ht: 6'3" Wt: 205 Born: 11/7/1976 Age: 32

Year	Team	Lg	G	GS	CG	GF	IP	BFP	H	R	ER	HR	SH	SF	HB	TBB	IBB	SO	WP	Bk	W	L	Pct	ShO	Sv-Op	Hld	ERC	ERA
2008	Iowa*	AAA	7	0	0	1	11.0	60	20	11	8	1	2	0	0	5	2	14	3	0	1	1	.500	0	0- -	-	8.46	6.55
2008	LV*	AAA	21	17	2	0	111.0	471	106	47	41	4	4	7	5	42	2	105	5	1	5	8	.385	2	0- -	-	3.48	3.32
2003	KC	AL	7	0	0	2	8.0	41	11	9	9	2	0	0	0	7	1	6	1	0	0	2	.000	0	0-0	1	9.58	10.13
2006	ChC	NL	10	2	0	0	17.1	84	19	13	12	2	1	1	0	12	1	21	0	0	0	1	.000	0	0-0	0	5.62	6.23
2008	Phi	NL	6	0	0	1	10.1	49	13	7	7	0	2	0	0	9	4	12	2	0	1	1	.500	0	0-0	0	6.21	6.10
3 ML YEARS			23	2	0	3	35.2	174	43	29	28	4	3	1	0	28	6	39	3	0	1	4	.200	0	0-0	1	6.66	7.07

Chien-Ming Wang

Pitches: R Bats: R Pos: SP-15   Ht: 6'3" Wt: 225 Born: 3/31/1980 Age: 29

Year	Team	Lg	G	GS	CG	GF	IP	BFP	H	R	ER	HR	SH	SF	HB	TBB	IBB	SO	WP	Bk	W	L	Pct	ShO	Sv-Op	Hld	ERC	ERA
2005	NYY	AL	18	17	0	0	116.1	486	113	58	52	9	3	4	6	32	3	47	3	0	8	5	.615	0	0-0	0	3.47	4.02
2006	NYY	AL	34	33	2	1	218.0	902	233	92	88	12	3	2	2	52	4	76	6	1	19	6	.760	1	1-1	0	3.62	3.63
2007	NYY	AL	30	30	1	0	199.1	823	199	84	82	9	2	3	8	59	1	104	9	1	19	7	.731	0	0-0	0	3.54	3.70
2008	NYY	AL	15	15	1	0	95.0	402	90	44	43	4	0	3	3	35	1	54	0	0	8	2	.800	0	0-0	0	3.39	4.07
	Postseason		4	4	0	0	19.0	90	28	19	16	5	2	0	3	5	0	7	0	0	1	3	.250	0	0-0	0	8.53	7.58
4 ML YEARS			97	95	4	1	628.2	2611	635	278	265	34	8	12	19	178	9	281	18	2	54	20	.730	1	1-1	0	3.53	3.79

Daryle Ward

Bats: L **Throws:** L **Pos:** PH-73; 1B-13; LF-6; RF-3; DH-1   **Ht:** 6'2" **Wt:** 240 **Born:** 6/27/1975 **Age:** 34

								BATTING													BASERUNNING				AVERAGES		
Year	Team	Lg	G	AB	H	2B	3B	HR	(Hm	Rd)	TB	R	RBI	RC	TBB	IBB	SO	HBP	SH	SF	SB	CS	SB%	GDP	Avg	OBP	Slg
2008 Iowa*	AAA	3	10	5	0	0	0	(-	-)	5	3	0	2	1	0	1	0	0	0	0	0	-	0	.500	.545	.500
1998 Hou	NL	4	3	1	0	0	0	(0	0)	1	1	0	1	1	0	2	0	0	0	0	0	-	0	.333	.500	.333
1999 Hou	NL	64	150	41	6	0	8	(2	6)	71	11	30	21	9	0	31	0	0	2	0	0	-	4	.273	.311	.473
2000 Hou	NL	119	264	68	10	2	20	(13	7)	142	36	47	40	15	2	61	0	0	2	0	0	-	6	.258	.295	.538
2001 Hou	NL	95	213	56	15	0	9	(5	4)	98	21	39	31	19	4	48	1	0	2	0	0	-	3	.263	.323	.460
2002 Hou	NL	136	453	125	31	0	12	(9	3)	192	41	72	61	33	5	82	1	0	4	1	3	.25	9	.276	.324	.424
2003 LAD	NL	52	109	20	1	0	0	(0	0)	21	6	9	1	3	0	19	1	0	1	0	0	-	0	.183	.211	.193
2004 Pit	NL	79	293	73	17	2	15	(8	7)	139	39	57	40	22	3	45	3	0	3	0	0	-	8	.249	.305	.474
2005 Pit	NL	133	407	106	21	1	12	(7	5)	165	46	63	49	37	10	60	1	0	8	0	2	.00	18	.260	.318	.405
2006 2 Tms	NL	98	130	40	10	0	7	(3	4)	71	17	26	26	15	1	27	2	0	3	0	1	.00	5	.308	.380	.546
2007 ChC	NL	79	110	36	13	0	3	(2	1)	58	16	19	19	22	8	23	0	0	1	0	0	-	6	.327	.436	.527
2008 ChC	NL	89	102	22	7	0	4	(1	3)	41	8	17	10	16	3	24	0	0	1	0	0	-	4	.216	.319	.402
06 Was	NL	78	104	32	9	0	6	(3	3)	59	15	19	19	14	1	21	2	0	3	0	1	.00	5	.308	.390	.567
06 Atl	NL	20	26	8	1	0	1	(0	1)	12	2	7	7	1	0	6	0	0	0	0	0	-	0	.308	.333	.462
Postseason		8	11	3	1	0	2	(0	2)	10	2	5	2	1	0	3	0	0	0	0	0	-	0	.273	.333	.909
11 ML YEARS		948	2234	588	131	5	90	(50	40)	999	242	379	299	192	36	422	9	0	27	1	6	.14	67	.263	.320	.447

Jarrod Washburn

Pitches: L **Bats:** L **Pos:** SP-26; RP-2   **Ht:** 6'1" **Wt:** 195 **Born:** 8/13/1974 **Age:** 34

			HOW MUCH HE PITCHED						WHAT HE GAVE UP											THE RESULTS						
Year	Team	Lg	G	GS	CG	GF	IP	BFP	H	R	ER	HR	SH	SF	HB	TBB	IBB	SO	WP	Bk	W	L	Pct	ShO	Sv-Op	Hld	ERC	ERA
1998 LAA	AL	15	11	0	0	74.0	317	70	40	38	11	2	3	3	27	1	48	0	0	6	3	.667	0	0-0	1	4.09	4.62
1999 LAA	AL	16	10	0	3	61.2	264	61	36	36	6	1	2	1	26	0	39	2	0	4	5	.444	0	0-0	1	4.20	5.25
2000 LAA	AL	14	14	0	0	84.1	340	64	38	35	16	1	3	1	37	0	49	1	0	7	2	.778	0	0-0	0	3.66	3.74
2001 LAA	AL	30	30	1	0	193.1	813	196	89	81	25	4	4	7	54	4	126	3	0	11	10	.524	0	0-0	0	4.03	3.77
2002 LAA	AL	32	32	1	0	206.0	852	183	75	72	19	4	7	3	59	1	139	5	1	18	6	.750	0	0-0	0	3.02	3.15
2003 LAA	AL	32	32	2	0	207.1	876	205	106	102	34	5	6	11	54	4	118	4	1	10	15	.400	0	0-0	0	4.07	4.43
2004 LAA	AL	25	25	1	0	149.1	640	159	81	77	20	2	4	4	40	1	86	5	0	11	8	.579	1	0-0	0	4.23	4.64
2005 LAA	AL	29	29	1	0	177.1	740	184	66	63	19	4	6	8	51	0	94	2	0	8	8	.500	1	0-0	0	4.19	3.20
2006 Sea	AL	31	31	0	0	187.0	809	198	103	97	25	3	6	7	55	2	103	3	0	8	14	.364	0	0-0	0	4.33	4.67
2007 Sea	AL	32	32	1	0	193.2	839	201	102	93	23	9	6	8	67	5	114	2	1	10	15	.400	1	0-0	0	4.33	4.32
2008 Sea	AL	28	26	1	1	153.2	675	174	87	80	19	6	5	7	50	2	87	2	0	5	14	.263	0	1-1	0	4.88	4.69
Postseason		8	7	0	1	36.2	164	40	26	20	8	3	3	2	14	2	21	0	0	1	3	.250	0	0-0	0	5.48	4.91
11 ML YEARS		284	272	8	4	1687.2	7165	1695	823	774	217	41	52	60	520	20	1003	29	3	98	100	.495	3	1-1	2	4.07	4.13

Rico Washington

Bats: L **Throws:** R **Pos:** PH-9; 3B-4; 2B-1; LF-1; RF-1   **Ht:** 5'9" **Wt:** 195 **Born:** 5/30/1978 **Age:** 31

								BATTING													BASERUNNING				AVERAGES		
Year	Team	Lg	G	AB	H	2B	3B	HR	(Hm	Rd)	TB	R	RBI	RC	TBB	IBB	SO	HBP	SH	SF	SB	CS	SB%	GDP	Avg	OBP	Slg
1997 Pirates	R	28	98	24	6	0	1	(-	-)	33	12	11	10	4	1	13	4	0	1	1	0	1.00	2	.245	.299	.337
1998 Erie	A-	51	197	65	14	2	6	(-	-)	101	31	31	39	17	2	33	7	0	0	1	2	.33	4	.330	.403	.513
1998 Augsta	A	12	50	15	2	1	2	(-	-)	25	12	12	10	7	0	9	2	0	1	2	0	1.00	0	.300	.400	.500
1999 Hkry	A	76	287	102	15	1	13	(-	-)	158	70	50	73	48	7	45	8	0	6	5	1	.83	4	.355	.453	.551
1999 Lynbrg	A+	57	205	58	7	0	7	(-	-)	86	31	32	35	30	0	45	4	1	2	4	1	.80	8	.283	.382	.420
2000 Altna	AA	135	503	130	22	7	8	(-	-)	190	74	59	66	55	1	74	5	9	4	4	9	.31	11	.258	.335	.378
2001 Altna	AA	75	291	88	17	0	4	(-	-)	117	31	29	42	21	3	49	5	1	0	5	5	.50	5	.302	.360	.402
2002 Altna	AA	112	359	80	11	3	8	(-	-)	121	53	34	46	60	3	66	12	3	1	3	4	.43	7	.223	.352	.337
2003 Mobile	AA	111	402	98	19	2	14	(-	-)	163	60	60	57	44	4	73	9	0	4	2	2	.50	7	.244	.329	.405
2003 Portlnd	AAA	17	58	13	2	1	3	(-	-)	26	11	10	9	10	0	14	1	0	1	0	0	.00	1	.224	.343	.448
2004 Portlnd	AAA	47	104	20	6	0	1	(-	-)	29	10	13	9	13	2	15	2	0	1	0	0	-	3	.192	.292	.279
2004 Mobile	AA	68	244	71	12	1	9	(-	-)	112	36	45	43	33	0	42	2	1	3	0	2	.00	6	.291	.376	.459
2005 Mont	AA	126	454	136	31	2	19	(-	-)	228	83	77	91	63	1	62	7	0	8	6	5	.55	6	.300	.387	.502
2006 Sprgfld	AA	66	232	75	23	3	13	(-	-)	143	49	56	63	49	3	48	3	0	2	4	1	.80	3	.323	.444	.616
2006 Memp	AAA	68	219	53	10	1	5	(-	-)	80	28	20	28	28	2	38	2	2	0	4	2	.67	5	.242	.333	.365
2007 Sprgfld	AA	25	95	25	4	0	4	(-	-)	41	13	20	13	7	0	10	2	0	1	0	0	-	2	.263	.324	.432
2007 Memp	AAA	53	167	52	12	2	7	(-	-)	89	24	23	33	17	0	24	1	0	4	2	0	1.00	4	.311	.370	.533
2007 Cards	R	6	14	6	0	1	1	(-	-)	11	6	5	5	5	0	1	0	0	0	0	0	-	0	.429	.579	.786
2008 Memp	AAA	92	252	64	15	0	13	(-	-)	118	54	40	49	52	1	49	7	0	3	0	2	.00	6	.254	.392	.468
2008 StL	NL	14	19	3	2	0	0	(0	0)	5	2	3	1	3	0	6	0	0	0	0	0	-	1	.158	.273	.263

Ehren Wassermann

Pitches: R **Bats:** B **Pos:** RP-24   **Ht:** 6'0" **Wt:** 185 **Born:** 12/6/1980 **Age:** 28

			HOW MUCH HE PITCHED						WHAT HE GAVE UP											THE RESULTS						
Year	Team	Lg	G	GS	CG	GF	IP	BFP	H	R	ER	HR	SH	SF	HB	TBB	IBB	SO	WP	Bk	W	L	Pct	ShO	Sv-Op	Hld	ERC	ERA
2003 Bristol	R+	4	0	0	2	3.2	22	9	6	6	0	0	0	0	3	1	4	3	0	0	1	.000	0	0--	-	14.40	14.73
2003 Knapol	A-	6	0	0	5	9.0	36	8	1	1	0	2	0	1	3	1	10	1	0	1	1	.500	0	0--	-	2.98	1.00
2004 Knapol	A-	50	0	0	47	55.2	230	44	20	17	1	1	0	4	16	3	42	4	0	2	3	.400	0	30--	-	2.19	2.75
2004 WinSa	A+	10	0	0	4	10.0	47	11	4	3	1	0	0	1	5	3	5	1	0	1	0	1.000	0	1--	-	4.78	2.70
2005 WinSa	A+	42	0	0	38	46.0	183	41	10	7	0	3	3	2	9	0	37	3	0	4	2	.667	0	20--	-	2.33	1.37
2005 Brham	AA	15	0	0	5	22.0	95	24	6	5	0	0	1	2	8	1	21	2	0	2	1	.000	0	0--	-	4.10	2.05
2006 Brham	AA	61	0	0	54	63.1	274	60	26	18	3	5	1	6	25	2	47	7	1	4	8	.333	0	22--	-	3.72	2.56
2007 Charltt	AAA	38	0	0	14	42.2	178	34	13	10	0	4	1	5	18	2	33	1	0	2	4	.333	0	5--	-	2.80	2.11
2008 Charltt	AAA	32	0	0	17	39.0	156	29	8	5	1	4	1	1	13	2	42	6	0	3	0	1.000	0	7--	-	2.08	1.15
2007 CWS	AL	33	0	0	6	23.0	94	20	9	7	0	4	2	2	7	4	14	1	0	1	1	.500	0	0-1	9	2.47	2.74
2008 CWS	AL	24	0	0	6	19.2	101	27	19	17	0	4	1	4	14	4	9	1	0	1	2	.333	0	0-0	2	6.35	7.78
2 ML YEARS		57	0	0	12	42.2	195	47	28	24	0	4	3	6	21	8	23	2	0	2	3	.400	0	0-1	11	4.16	5.06

Chris Waters

Pitches: L **Bats:** L **Pos:** SP-11   **Ht:** 6'1" **Wt:** 185 **Born:** 8/17/1980 **Age:** 28

					HOW MUCH HE PITCHED			WHAT HE GAVE UP											THE RESULTS						
Year	Team	Lg	G	GS	CG	GF	IP	BFP	H	R	ER	HR	SH	SF	HB	TBB	IBB	SO	WP	Bk	W	L	Pct	ShO	Sv-Op Hld	ERC	ERA
2000	Danvle	R+	13	13	1	0	69.0	286	64	33	30	4	2	2	2	29	0	73	6	0	5	3	.625	0	0- - -	3.71	3.91
2001	Macon	A	25	24	3	0	147.2	616	131	71	55	14	4	4	7	52	0	78	8	2	8	6	.571	1	0- - -	3.45	3.35
2002	MrtlBh	A+	28	28	2	0	182.2	752	154	63	56	12	7	7	24	43	0	103	12	0	13	7	.650	1	0- - -	2.90	2.76
2003	MrtlBh	A+	2	2	0	0	9.1	43	7	7	3	0	1	3	1	6	0	6	3	0	1	1	.500	0	0- - -	3.13	2.89
2003	Grnville	A	17	17	0	0	85.2	381	104	53	42	11	7	6	1	26	1	54	2	1	3	8	.273	0	0- - -	5.13	4.41
2004	MrtlBh	A+	4	1	0	0	7.1	39	14	10	10	0	0	0	0	4	0	5	1	0	0	1	.000	0	0- - -	9.57	12.27
2005	MrtlBh	A+	17	17	1	0	103.1	434	106	54	49	10	1	5	4	31	0	67	0	0	4	5	.444	0	0- - -	4.04	4.27
2006	Missi	AA	27	27	0	0	155.0	673	152	90	83	24	9	6	2	79	1	117	5	2	8	14	.364	0	0- - -	4.93	4.82
2007	Bowie	AA	27	27	0	0	152.1	673	144	83	76	17	4	2	6	86	3	117	12	2	8	9	.471	0	0- - -	4.67	4.49
2007	Norfolk	AAA	1	1	0	0	6.0	28	9	2	2	0	0	0	0	3	0	3	0	0	0	-	-	0	0- - -	6.98	3.00
2008	Bowie	AA	6	6	0	0	32.0	120	20	6	6	2	0	0	0	8	0	22	2	0	5	0	1.000	0	0- - -	1.56	1.69
2008	Norfolk	AAA	18	16	1	1	90.0	406	97	62	57	10	4	4	7	43	1	72	4	1	3	6	.333	0	0- - -	5.24	5.70
2008	Bal	AL	11	11	1	0	64.2	291	70	38	36	9	0	3	3	29	0	33	1	1	3	5	.375	1	0-0 0	5.20	5.01

David Weathers

Pitches: R **Bats:** R **Pos:** RP-72   **Ht:** 6'3" **Wt:** 237 **Born:** 9/25/1969 **Age:** 39

					HOW MUCH HE PITCHED			WHAT HE GAVE UP											THE RESULTS						
Year	Team	Lg	G	GS	CG	GF	IP	BFP	H	R	ER	HR	SH	SF	HB	TBB	IBB	SO	WP	Bk	W	L	Pct	ShO	Sv-Op Hld	ERC	ERA
2008	Lsvlle*	AAA	1	0	0	1	1.0	3	0	0	0	0	0	0	0	0	0	1	0	0	0	0	-	0	0- - -	0.00	0.00
2008	Dayton*	A	2	1	0	0	2.0	6	0	0	0	0	0	0	0	0	0	3	0	0	0	0	-	0	0- - -	0.00	0.00
1991	Tor	AL	15	0	0	4	14.2	79	15	9	8	1	2	1	2	17	3	13	0	0	1	0	1.000	0	0-0 1	6.88	4.91
1992	Tor	AL	2	0	0	0	3.1	15	5	3	3	1	0	0	0	2	0	3	0	0	0	0	-	0	0-0 0	10.97	8.10
1993	Fla	NL	14	6	0	2	45.2	202	57	26	26	3	2	0	1	13	1	34	6	0	2	3	.400	0	0-0 0	4.86	5.12
1994	Fla	NL	24	24	0	0	135.0	621	166	87	79	13	12	4	4	59	9	72	7	1	8	12	.400	0	0-0 0	5.52	5.27
1995	Fla	NL	28	15	0	0	90.1	419	104	68	60	8	7	3	5	52	3	60	3	0	4	5	.444	0	0-0 1	5.79	5.98
1996	2 Tms		42	12	0	9	88.2	409	108	60	54	8	5	2	6	42	5	53	3	0	2	4	.333	0	0-0 3	5.80	5.48
1997	2 Tms	AL	19	1	0	5	25.2	126	38	24	24	3	2	1	1	15	0	18	3	0	1	3	.250	0	0-1 0	8.27	8.42
1998	2 Tms	NL	44	9	0	9	110.0	492	130	69	60	6	6	2	3	41	3	94	7	2	6	5	.545	0	0-1 3	4.73	4.91
1999	Mil	NL	63	0	0	14	93.0	414	102	49	48	14	4	4	2	38	3	74	1	1	7	4	.636	0	2-6 9	5.04	4.65
2000	Mil	NL	69	0	0	23	76.1	320	73	29	26	7	4	1	2	32	8	50	0	0	3	5	.375	0	1-7 14	3.90	3.07
2001	2 Tms	NL	80	0	0	25	86.0	351	65	24	23	6	10	3	3	34	8	66	0	0	4	5	.444	0	4-10 16	2.59	2.41
2002	NYM	NL	71	0	0	12	77.1	331	69	30	25	6	6	4	3	36	7	61	2	0	6	3	.667	0	0-5 18	3.60	2.91
2003	NYM	NL	77	0	0	20	87.2	384	87	33	30	6	8	0	6	40	6	75	1	0	1	6	.143	0	7-9 26	4.21	3.08
2004	3 Tms	NL	66	2	0	20	82.1	357	85	44	38	12	5	2	5	35	2	61	1	1	7	7	.500	0	0-4 12	5.01	4.15
2005	Cin	NL	73	0	0	41	77.2	331	71	36	34	7	4	2	2	29	2	61	4	0	7	4	.636	0	15-19 8	3.46	3.94
2006	Cin	NL	67	0	0	32	73.2	314	61	31	29	12	5	3	2	34	4	50	0	0	4	4	.500	0	12-19 9	3.79	3.54
2007	Cin	NL	70	0	0	20	77.2	328	67	33	31	4	5	4	5	27	4	48	1	0	2	6	.250	0	33-39 0	2.95	3.59
2008	Cin	NL	72	0	0	17	69.1	311	76	27	25	6	2	1	3	30	8	46	1	1	4	6	.400	0	0-4 19	4.61	3.25
96	Fla	NL	31	8	0	8	71.1	319	85	41	36	7	5	1	4	28	4	40	2	0	2	2	.500	0	0-0 3	5.35	4.54
96	NYY	AL	11	4	0	1	17.1	90	23	19	18	1	0	1	2	14	1	13	1	0	0	2	.000	0	0-0 0	7.66	9.35
97	NYY	AL	10	0	0	3	9.0	47	15	10	10	1	0	0	0	7	0	4	2	0	0	1	.000	0	0-1 0	10.26	10.00
97	Cle	AL	9	1	0	2	16.2	79	23	14	14	2	2	1	1	8	0	14	1	0	1	2	.333	0	0-0 0	7.23	7.56
98	Cin	NL	16	9	0	0	62.1	294	86	47	43	3	4	1	1	27	2	51	5	1	2	4	.333	0	0-0 0	6.04	6.21
98	Mil	NL	28	0	0	9	47.2	198	44	22	17	3	2	1	2	14	1	43	2	1	4	1	.800	0	0-1 3	3.15	3.21
01	Mil	NL	52	0	0	21	57.2	233	37	14	13	3	8	1	2	25	7	46	0	0	3	4	.429	0	4-7 10	2.01	2.03
01	ChC	NL	28	0	0	4	28.1	118	28	10	10	3	2	2	1	9	1	20	0	0	1	1	.500	0	0-3 6	3.90	3.18
04	NYM	NL	32	0	0	10	33.2	156	41	19	16	5	2	2	2	15	0	25	1	1	5	3	.625	0	0-1 6	6.15	4.28
04	Hou	NL	26	0	0	9	32.0	137	31	20	17	5	2	0	3	13	1	26	0	0	1	4	.200	0	0-3 5	4.77	4.78
04	Fla	NL	8	2	0	1	16.2	64	13	5	5	2	1	0	0	7	1	10	0	0	1	0	1.000	0	0-0 1	3.28	2.70
	Postseason		7	0	0	2	11.0	41	6	1	1	0	1	1	0	3	1	8	0	1	2	0	1.000	0	0-0 1	1.05	0.82
18 ML YEARS			896	69	0	293	1314.1	5804	1379	682	623	123	89	37	55	576	76	939	40	6	69	82	.457	0	74-124 139	4.54	4.27

Jered Weaver

Pitches: R **Bats:** R **Pos:** SP-30   **Ht:** 6'7" **Wt:** 205 **Born:** 10/4/1982 **Age:** 26

					HOW MUCH HE PITCHED			WHAT HE GAVE UP											THE RESULTS						
Year	Team	Lg	G	GS	CG	GF	IP	BFP	H	R	ER	HR	SH	SF	HB	TBB	IBB	SO	WP	Bk	W	L	Pct	ShO	Sv-Op Hld	ERC	ERA
2006	LAA	AL	19	19	0	0	123.0	490	94	36	35	15	2	2	3	33	1	105	2	0	11	2	.846	0	0-0 0	2.57	2.56
2007	LAA	AL	28	28	0	0	161.0	695	178	77	70	17	5	5	2	45	3	115	4	0	13	7	.650	0	0-0 0	4.24	3.91
2008	LAA	AL	30	30	0	0	176.2	745	173	88	85	20	1	4	6	54	4	152	3	0	11	10	.524	0	0-0 0	3.80	4.33
	Postseason		1	1	0	0	5.0	21	4	2	2	2	0	0	0	3	0	5	0	0	1	0	1.000	0	0-0 0	6.06	3.60
3 ML YEARS			77	77	0	0	460.2	1930	445	201	190	52	8	11	11	132	8	372	9	0	35	19	.648	0	0-0 0	3.60	3.71

Brandon Webb

Pitches: R **Bats:** R **Pos:** SP-34   **Ht:** 6'2" **Wt:** 228 **Born:** 5/9/1979 **Age:** 30

					HOW MUCH HE PITCHED			WHAT HE GAVE UP											THE RESULTS						
Year	Team	Lg	G	GS	CG	GF	IP	BFP	H	R	ER	HR	SH	SF	HB	TBB	IBB	SO	WP	Bk	W	L	Pct	ShO	Sv-Op Hld	ERC	ERA
2003	Ari	NL	29	28	1	1	180.2	750	140	65	57	12	9	1	13	68	4	172	9	1	10	9	.526	1	0-0 0	2.80	2.84
2004	Ari	NL	35	35	1	0	208.0	933	194	111	83	17	14	6	11	119	11	164	17	1	7	16	.304	0	0-0 0	4.32	3.59
2005	Ari	NL	33	33	1	0	229.0	943	229	98	90	21	10	7	2	59	4	172	14	1	14	12	.538	0	0-0 0	3.54	3.54
2006	Ari	NL	33	33	5	0	235.0	950	216	91	81	15	10	6	6	50	4	178	5	2	16	8	.667	3	0-0 0	2.81	3.10
2007	Ari	NL	34	34	4	0	236.1	975	209	91	79	12	9	6	5	72	6	194	3	0	18	10	.643	3	0-0 0	2.82	3.01
2008	Ari	NL	34	34	3	0	226.2	944	206	95	83	13	8	9	12	65	5	183	8	1	22	7	.759	1	0-0 0	3.04	3.30
	Postseason		2	2	0	0	13.0	55	11	5	5	0	0	0	1	5	0	13	2	0	1	1	.500	0	0-0 0	2.79	3.46
6 ML YEARS			198	197	15	1	1315.2	5495	1194	551	473	90	60	35	49	433	34	1063	56	6	87	62	.584	8	0-0 0	3.20	3.24

Rickie Weeks

Bats: R Throws: R Pos: 2B-120; PH-9   Ht: 5'10" Wt: 213 Born: 9/13/1982 Age: 26

										BATTING													BASERUNNING				AVERAGES		
Year	Team	Lg	G	AB	H	2B	3B	HR	(Hm	Rd)	TB	R	RBI	RC	TBB	IBB	SO	HBP	SH	SF	SB	CS	SB%	GDP	Avg	OBP	Slg
2003	Mil	NL	7	12	2	1	0	0	(0	0)	3	1	0	0	1	0	6	1	0	0	0	0	-	0	.167	.286	.250
2005	Mil	NL	96	360	86	13	2	13	(8	5)	142	56	42	49	40	2	96	11	2	1	15	2	.88	11	.239	.333	.394
2006	Mil	NL	95	359	100	15	3	8	(6	2)	145	73	34	53	30	1	92	19	2	3	19	5	.79	6	.279	.363	.404
2007	Mil	NL	118	409	96	21	6	16	(5	11)	177	87	36	65	78	5	116	14	3	2	25	2	.93	3	.235	.374	.433
2008	Mil	NL	129	475	111	22	7	14	(3	11)	189	89	46	67	66	0	115	14	1	4	19	5	.79	5	.234	.342	.398
5 ML YEARS			445	1615	395	72	18	51	(22	29)	656	306	158	234	215	8	425	59	8	10	78	14	.85	25	.245	.352	.406

Todd Wellemeyer

Pitches: R Bats: R Pos: SP-32   Ht: 6'3" Wt: 225 Born: 8/30/1978 Age: 30

				HOW MUCH HE PITCHED						WHAT HE GAVE UP												THE RESULTS						
Year	Team	Lg	G	GS	CG	GF	IP	BFP	H	R	ER	HR	SH	SF	HB	TBB	IBB	SO	WP	Bk	W	L	Pct	ShO	Sv-Op	Hld	ERC	ERA
2003	ChC	NL	15	0	0	8	27.2	122	25	22	20	5	1	0	0	19	1	30	0	0	1	1	.500	0	1-1	1	5.33	6.51
2004	ChC	NL	20	0	0	7	24.1	119	27	16	16	1	3	2	0	20	2	30	0	1	2	1	.667	0	0-0	0	5.67	5.92
2005	ChC	NL	22	0	0	6	32.1	146	32	23	22	7	2	1	0	22	1	32	3	0	2	1	.667	0	1-1	3	6.09	6.12
2006	2 Tms		46	0	0	10	78.1	345	68	38	36	6	3	6	4	50	3	54	9	0	1	4	.200	0	1-1	3	4.28	4.14
2007	2 Tms		32	11	0	7	79.1	353	77	50	40	11	3	4	3	40	2	60	4	0	3	3	.500	0	0-0	2	4.68	4.54
2008	StL	NL	32	32	0	0	191.2	807	178	84	79	25	6	6	7	62	1	134	7	1	13	9	.591	0	0-0	0	3.72	3.71
06 Fla		NL	18	0	0	6	21.1	97	20	13	13	1	1	3	2	13	1	17	2	0	0	2	.000	0	0-0	1	4.41	5.48
06 KC		AL	28	0	0	4	57.0	248	48	25	23	5	2	3	2	37	2	37	7	0	1	2	.333	0	1-1	3	4.23	3.63
07 KC		AL	12	0	0	5	15.2	84	25	19	18	4	1	0	1	11	2	9	2	0	0	1	.000	0	0-0	1	10.40	10.34
07 StL		NL	20	11	0	2	63.2	269	52	31	22	7	2	4	2	29	0	51	2	0	3	2	.600	0	0-0	1	3.48	3.11
6 ML YEARS			167	43	0	38	433.2	1892	407	233	213	55	18	19	14	213	10	340	23	2	22	19	.537	0	3-3	9	4.38	4.42

Jared Wells

Pitches: R Bats: R Pos: RP-8   Ht: 6'4" Wt: 200 Born: 10/31/1981 Age: 27

				HOW MUCH HE PITCHED						WHAT HE GAVE UP												THE RESULTS						
Year	Team	Lg	G	GS	CG	GF	IP	BFP	H	R	ER	HR	SH	SF	HB	TBB	IBB	SO	WP	Bk	W	L	Pct	ShO	Sv-Op	Hld	ERC	ERA
2003	Eugene	A-	14	14	0	0	78.2	341	77	34	24	6	3	2	3	32	1	53	2	0	4	6	.400	0	0- -		3.94	2.75
2004	FtWyn	A	14	14	1	0	81.1	349	91	42	37	6	1	5	2	19	0	72	4	1	4	6	.400	0	0- -		3.99	4.09
2004	Lk Els	A+	13	12	0	0	71.2	317	81	44	36	5	5	2	1	30	0	38	3	2	4	6	.400	0	0- -		4.77	4.52
2005	Lk Els	A+	19	19	2	0	120.1	492	116	51	46	6	1	6	7	26	0	80	5	1	11	3	.786	1	0- -		3.13	3.44
2005	Mobile	AA	7	7	0	0	43.0	187	51	25	20	3	3	2	0	16	1	22	3	0	2	5	.286	0	0- -		4.89	4.19
2006	Mobile	AA	12	12	1	0	61.1	261	53	20	18	4	3	1	4	27	2	49	1	0	4	3	.571	0	0- -		3.46	2.64
2006	Portlnd	AAA	15	15	0	0	73.0	351	87	66	59	8	3	1	7	46	0	55	5	0	2	9	.182	0	0- -		6.64	7.27
2007	Portlnd	AAA	47	10	0	21	92.2	433	107	59	54	9	9	5	5	48	3	87	10	0	4	7	.364	0	5- -		5.52	5.24
2008	Portlnd	AAA	19	0	0	18	20.0	90	19	13	13	1	0	2	1	12	1	14	2	0	1	1	.500	0	4- -		5.85	5.85
2008	Tacom	AAA	33	0	0	26	40.2	185	44	30	29	6	2	2	1	23	2	42	2	0	0	4	.000	0	11- -		5.63	6.42
2008	2 Tms		8	0	0	2	8.1	44	11	8	8	2	2	0	0	7	0	5	2	0	0	0	-	0	0-0	0	8.76	8.64
08 SD		NL	2	0	0	0	3.0	14	4	2	2	0	1	0	0	1	0	2	0	0	0	0	-	0	0-0	0	4.83	6.00
08 Sea		AL	6	0	0	2	5.1	30	7	6	6	2	1	0	0	6	0	3	2	0	0	0	-	0	0-0	0	11.19	10.13

Kip Wells

Pitches: R Bats: R Pos: RP-23; SP-2   Ht: 6'3" Wt: 205 Born: 4/21/1977 Age: 32

				HOW MUCH HE PITCHED						WHAT HE GAVE UP												THE RESULTS						
Year	Team	Lg	G	GS	CG	GF	IP	BFP	H	R	ER	HR	SH	SF	HB	TBB	IBB	SO	WP	Bk	W	L	Pct	ShO	Sv-Op	Hld	ERC	ERA
2008	ColSpr*	AAA	4	4	0	0	18.1	92	32	25	18	4	2	1	0	6	0	15	3	0	0	3	.000	0	0- -	-	9.35	8.84
2008	Tulsa*	AA	1	1	0	0	6.2	27	6	2	2	0	1	0	1	0	8	0	0	0	0	0	-	0	0- -	-	1.98	2.70
1999	CWS	AL	7	7	0	0	35.2	153	33	17	16	2	0	2	3	15	0	29	1	2	4	1	.800	0	0-0	0	3.80	4.04
2000	CWS	AL	20	20	0	0	98.2	468	126	76	66	15	1	3	2	58	4	71	7	0	6	9	.400	0	0-0	0	7.01	6.02
2001	CWS	AL	40	20	0	3	133.1	603	145	80	71	14	8	6	12	61	5	99	14	0	10	11	.476	0	0-2	6	5.16	4.79
2002	Pit	NL	33	33	1	0	198.1	845	197	92	79	21	7	5	7	71	11	134	7	0	12	14	.462	1	0-0	0	4.00	3.58
2003	Pit	NL	31	31	1	0	197.1	835	171	77	72	24	15	2	7	76	7	147	7	0	10	9	.526	1	0-0	0	3.49	3.28
2004	Pit	NL	24	24	0	0	138.1	621	145	70	70	14	5	6	6	66	4	116	3	0	5	7	.417	0	0-0	0	4.77	4.55
2005	Pit	NL	33	33	1	0	182.0	828	186	116	103	23	9	10	12	99	8	132	8	0	8	18	.308	1	0-0	0	5.14	5.09
2006	2 Tms		9	9	0	0	44.1	208	61	33	32	3	1	1	4	21	1	20	5	0	2	5	.286	0	0-0	0	6.90	6.50
2007	StL	NL	34	26	0	4	162.2	750	186	116	103	19	8	7	9	78	9	122	8	1	7	17	.292	0	0-0	0	5.44	5.70
2008	2 Tms		25	2	0	8	37.2	176	39	29	26	4	3	0	2	30	2	31	3	0	1	3	.250	0	0-0	0	6.20	6.21
06 Pit		NL	7	7	0	0	36.1	168	46	27	27	3	1	1	4	18	1	16	5	0	1	5	.167	0	0-0	0	6.51	6.69
06 Tex		AL	2	2	0	0	8.0	40	15	6	5	0	0	0	0	3	0	4	0	0	1	0	1.000	0	0-0	0	8.77	5.63
08 Col		NL	15	0	0	6	27.1	126	29	19	16	3	3	0	1	19	2	22	2	0	1	2	.333	0	0-0	0	5.82	5.27
08 KC		AL	10	0	0	2	10.1	50	10	10	10	1	0	0	1	11	0	9	1	0	0	1	.000	0	0-0	0	7.23	8.71
10 ML YEARS			256	205	3	15	1228.1	5487	1289	707	638	139	57	42	64	575	51	901	63	3	65	94	.409	2	0-2	7	4.87	4.67

Randy Wells

Pitches: R Bats: R Pos: RP-4   Ht: 6'3" Wt: 230 Born: 8/28/1982 Age: 26

				HOW MUCH HE PITCHED						WHAT HE GAVE UP												THE RESULTS						
Year	Team	Lg	G	GS	CG	GF	IP	BFP	H	R	ER	HR	SH	SF	HB	TBB	IBB	SO	WP	Bk	W	L	Pct	ShO	Sv-Op	Hld	ERC	ERA
2003	Lansng	A	1	0	0	1	1.0	3	1	0	0	0	0	0	0	0	0	0	0	0	0	0	-	0	0- -	-	2.79	0.00
2003	Cubs	R	3	0	0	0	5.0	25	5	2	2	0	1	0	0	4	0	4	0	0	0	0	-	0	0- -	-	4.51	3.60
2004	Lansng	A	36	15	0	4	107.2	466	112	64	53	9	0	4	5	40	1	121	4	1	6	6	.500	0	1- -	-	4.28	4.43
2005	Dytona	A+	41	10	0	12	98.2	407	93	33	30	5	3	0	3	22	0	106	5	0	10	2	.833	0	2- -	-	2.88	2.74
2005	WTenn	AA	6	0	0	0	8.1	41	12	4	4	0	2	1	0	6	1	4	0	0	1	0	1.000	0	1- -	-	7.12	4.32
2006	WTenn	AA	12	12	0	0	62.1	247	45	13	11	2	3	4	2	13	1	54	1	0	4	2	.667	0	0- -	-	1.71	1.59
2006	Iowa	AAA	13	12	0	0	69.0	314	87	42	38	7	5	3	1	23	1	59	2	0	5	5	.500	0	0- -	-	5.30	4.96

Year	Team	Lg	G	GS	CG	GF	IP	BFP	H	R	ER	HR	SH	SF	HB	TBB	IBB	SO	WP	Bk	W	L	Pct	ShO	Sv-Op	Hld	ERC	ERA
2007	Iowa	AAA	40	9	0	6	95.2	425	100	54	48	11	4	2	5	41	0	101	2	1	5	6	.455	0	2- -	-	4.75	4.52
2008	Iowa	AAA	27	19	0	1	118.2	513	127	64	53	15	2	3	1	34	1	102	3	0	10	4	.714	0	0- -	-	4.17	4.02
2008	2 Tms		4	0	0	2	5.1	18	0	0	0	0	0	0	0	3	0	1	0	0	0	0	-	0	0-0	0	0.35	0.00
08	Tor	AL	1	0	0	1	1.0	4	0	0	0	0	0	0	0	1	0	0	0	0	0	0	-	0	0-0	0	0.95	0.00
08	ChC	NL	3	0	0	1	4.1	14	0	0	0	0	0	0	0	2	0	1	0	0	0	0	-	0	0-0	0	0.25	0.00

Vernon Wells

Bats: R Throws: R Pos: CF-100; DH-8　　　　　　　　**Ht: 6'1" Wt: 225 Born: 12/8/1978 Age: 30**

						BATTING															BASERUNNING				AVERAGES		
Year	Team	Lg	G	AB	H	2B	3B	HR	(Hm	Rd)	TB	R	RBI	RC	TBB	IBB	SO	HBP	SH	SF	SB	CS	SB%	GDP	Avg	OBP	Slg
2008	Dnedin*	A+	2	8	4	0	0	0	(-	-)	4	3	4	1	0	0	3	0	0	0	0	0	-	0	.500	.500	.500
2008	Syrcse*	AAA	2	6	0	0	0	0	(-	-)	0	0	0	0	1	0	0	0	0	0	0	0	-	1	.000	.143	.000
1999	Tor	AL	24	88	23	5	0	1	(1	0)	31	8	8	7	4	0	18	0	0	0	1	1	.50	6	.261	.293	.352
2000	Tor	AL	3	2	0	0	0	0	(0	0)	0	0	0	0	0	0	0	0	0	0	0	0	-	0	.000	.000	.000
2001	Tor	AL	30	96	30	8	0	1	(1	0)	41	14	6	16	5	0	15	1	0	1	5	0	1.00	6	.313	.350	.427
2002	Tor	AL	159	608	167	34	4	23	(10	13)	278	87	100	88	27	0	85	3	2	8	9	4	.69	15	.275	.305	.457
2003	Tor	AL	161	678	215	49	5	33	(13	20)	373	118	117	124	42	2	80	7	0	8	4	1	.80	21	.317	.359	.550
2004	Tor	AL	134	536	146	34	2	23	(14	9)	253	82	67	72	51	2	83	2	0	1	9	2	.82	17	.272	.337	.472
2005	Tor	AL	156	620	167	30	3	28	(14	14)	287	78	97	96	47	3	86	3	0	8	8	3	.73	13	.269	.320	.463
2006	Tor	AL	154	611	185	40	5	32	(24	8)	331	91	106	107	54	9	90	3	0	9	17	4	.81	13	.303	.357	.542
2007	Tor	AL	149	584	143	36	4	16	(8	8)	235	85	80	74	49	4	89	3	0	6	10	4	.71	9	.245	.304	.402
2008	Tor	AL	108	427	128	22	1	20	(11	9)	212	63	78	68	29	5	46	3	0	7	4	2	.67	16	.300	.343	.496
	10 ML YEARS		1078	4250	1204	258	24	177	(96	81)	2041	626	659	652	308	16	592	25	2	48	67	21	.76	110	.283	.332	.480

Jayson Werth

Bats: R Throws: R Pos: RF-88; CF-31; LF-28; PH-18; PR-2　　　　　**Ht: 6'5" Wt: 225 Born: 5/20/1979 Age: 30**

						BATTING															BASERUNNING				AVERAGES		
Year	Team	Lg	G	AB	H	2B	3B	HR	(Hm	Rd)	TB	R	RBI	RC	TBB	IBB	SO	HBP	SH	SF	SB	CS	SB%	GDP	Avg	OBP	Slg
2008	Clrwtr*	A+	2	6	1	0	0	0	(-	-)	1	0	0	0	1	0	3	1	0	0	0	0	-	0	.167	.375	.167
2002	Tor	AL	15	46	12	2	1	0	(0	0)	16	4	6	5	6	0	11	0	0	1	1	0	1.00	4	.261	.340	.348
2003	Tor	AL	26	48	10	4	0	2	(0	2)	20	7	10	6	3	0	22	0	0	0	1	0	1.00	0	.208	.255	.417
2004	LAD	NL	89	290	76	11	3	16	(11	5)	141	56	47	47	30	0	85	4	1	1	4	1	.80	1	.262	.338	.486
2005	LAD	NL	102	337	79	22	2	7	(1	6)	126	46	43	44	48	2	114	6	1	3	11	2	.85	10	.234	.338	.374
2007	Phi	NL	94	255	76	11	3	8	(1	7)	117	43	49	57	44	1	73	2	2	1	7	1	.88	5	.298	.404	.459
2008	Phi	NL	134	418	114	16	3	24	(11	13)	208	73	67	74	57	1	119	4	0	3	20	1	**.95**	2	.273	.363	.498
	Postseason		6	17	4	1	0	2	(1	1)	11	3	3	3	4	0	5	0	0	0	0	0	-	0	.235	.381	.647
	6 ML YEARS		460	1394	367	66	12	57	(24	33)	628	229	222	233	188	4	424	16	4	9	44	5	.90	17	.263	.355	.451

Jake Westbrook

Pitches: R Bats: R Pos: SP-5　　　　　　　　　　　**Ht: 6'3" Wt: 215 Born: 9/29/1977 Age: 31**

				HOW MUCH HE PITCHED					WHAT HE GAVE UP											THE RESULTS						
Year	Team	Lg	G	GS	CG	GF	IP	BFP	H	R	ER	HR	SH	SF	HB	TBB	IBB	SO	WP	Bk	W	L	Pct	ShO	Sv-Op	Hld	ERC	ERA
2008	Lk Cty*	A	1	1	0	0	3.2	14	3	1	1	0	0	0	0	1	0	4	0	0	0	0	-	0	0- -	-	2.18	2.45
2008	Akron*	AA	1	1	0	0	6.0	22	3	0	0	0	0	0	0	4	0	2	0	0	0	0	-	0	0- -	-	2.11	0.00
2000	NYY	AL	3	2	0	1	6.2	38	15	10	10	1	0	2	0	4	1	1	0	0	0	2	.000	0	0-0	0	13.53	13.50
2001	Cle	AL	23	6	0	3	64.2	290	79	43	42	6	1	5	4	22	4	48	4	0	4	4	.500	0	0-0	5	5.25	5.85
2002	Cle	AL	11	4	0	1	41.2	185	50	30	27	6	2	1	1	12	1	20	1	0	1	3	.250	0	0-2	1	5.12	5.83
2003	Cle	AL	34	22	1	4	133.0	580	142	70	64	9	4	3	12	56	1	58	3	0	7	10	.412	0	0-0	0	4.78	4.33
2004	Cle	AL	33	30	5	2	215.2	895	208	95	81	19	6	6	5	61	3	116	4	1	14	9	.609	1	0-0	0	3.45	3.38
2005	Cle	AL	34	34	2	0	210.2	895	218	121	105	19	5	4	7	56	3	119	3	0	15	15	.500	0	0-0	0	3.78	4.49
2006	Cle	AL	32	32	3	0	211.1	904	**247**	106	98	15	5	4	4	55	4	109	5	0	15	10	.600	**2**	0-0	0	4.39	4.17
2007	Cle	AL	25	25	0	0	152.0	648	159	78	73	13	6	4	6	55	5	93	3	0	6	9	.400	0	0-0	0	4.28	4.32
2008	Cle	AL	5	5	1	0	34.2	139	33	13	12	5	0	2	1	7	0	19	1	0	1	2	.333	0	0-0	0	3.54	3.12
	Postseason		3	3	0	0	17.2	74	25	11	11	2	0	1	0	4	1	8	0	0	1	2	.333	0	0-0	0	6.33	5.60
	9 ML YEARS		200	160	12	11	1070.1	4574	1151	566	512	93	29	31	40	328	22	583	24	1	63	64	.496	3	0-2	7	4.21	4.31

Dan Wheeler

Pitches: R Bats: R Pos: RP-70　　　　　　　　　　**Ht: 6'3" Wt: 222 Born: 12/10/1977 Age: 31**

				HOW MUCH HE PITCHED					WHAT HE GAVE UP											THE RESULTS						
Year	Team	Lg	G	GS	CG	GF	IP	BFP	H	R	ER	HR	SH	SF	HB	TBB	IBB	SO	WP	Bk	W	L	Pct	ShO	Sv-Op	Hld	ERC	ERA
1999	TB	AL	6	6	0	0	30.2	136	35	20	20	7	1	0	0	13	1	32	1	0	1	4	.000	0	0-0	0	5.96	5.87
2000	TB	AL	11	2	0	6	23.0	111	29	14	14	2	1	1	2	11	2	17	2	0	1	1	.500	0	0-1	1	5.87	5.48
2001	TB	AL	13	0	0	3	17.2	87	30	17	17	3	0	2	0	5	0	12	1	1	1	0	1.000	0	0-0	0	8.38	8.66
2003	NYM	NL	35	0	0	10	51.0	215	49	23	21	6	0	3	1	17	4	35	1	0	1	3	.250	0	2-3	0	3.69	3.71
2004	2 Tms	NL	46	1	0	11	65.0	287	76	33	31	10	2	1	1	20	2	55	4	1	3	1	.750	0	0-0	5	5.05	4.29
2005	Hou	NL	71	0	0	20	73.1	288	53	18	18	7	5	1	3	19	3	69	0	0	2	3	.400	0	3-5	17	2.22	2.21
2006	Hou	NL	75	0	0	25	71.1	295	58	22	20	5	3	3	2	24	8	68	0	0	3	5	.375	0	9-12	24	2.57	2.52
2007	2 Tms	NL	70	0	0	29	74.2	321	74	48	44	11	3	3	3	23	3	82	2	0	1	9	.100	0	11-18	18	4.04	5.30
2008	TB	AL	70	0	0	26	66.1	264	44	25	23	10	0	0	2	22	4	53	1	0	5	6	.455	0	13-18	26	2.28	3.12
04	NYM	NL	32	1	0	7	50.2	232	65	29	27	9	2	1	0	17	2	46	4	1	3	1	.750	0	0-0	3	5.91	4.80
04	Hou	NL	14	0	0	4	14.1	55	11	4	4	1	0	0	1	3	0	9	0	0	0	0	-	0	0-0	2	2.35	2.51
07	Hou	NL	45	0	0	25	49.2	205	46	28	28	8	1	1	2	13	1	56	1	0	1	4	.200	0	11-15	6	3.69	5.07
07	TB	AL	25	0	0	4	25.0	116	28	20	16	3	2	2	1	10	2	26	1	0	0	5	.000	0	0-3	12	4.72	5.76
	Postseason		13	0	0	3	17.0	72	12	4	4	0	1	0	3	4	1	17	0	0	1	0	1.000	0	0-0	3	1.78	2.12
	9 ML YEARS		397	9	0	130	473.0	2004	448	220	208	61	15	16	12	154	27	423	12	2	17	32	.347	0	38-57	91	3.68	3.96

Bill White

Pitches: L Bats: L Pos: RP-8 Ht: 6'3" Wt: 215 Born: 11/20/1978 Age: 30

			HOW MUCH HE PITCHED						WHAT HE GAVE UP										THE RESULTS							
Year	Team	Lg	G	GS	CG	GF	IP	BFP	H	R	ER	HR	SH	SF	HB	TBB	IBB	SO	WP	Bk	W	L	Pct	ShO	Sv-Op	Hld	ERC	ERA
2000	DBcks	R	4	1	0	0	6.0	25	3	4	4	0	0	0	1	5	0	9	3	0	0	1	.000	0	0- -	-	2.39	6.00
2000	Sbend	A	1	1	0	0	2.2	14	3	1	1	0	0	0	0	3	0	5	1	0	0	0	-	0	0- -	-	6.72	3.38
2001	Sbend	A	19	19	0	0	111.1	465	90	53	47	9	4	2	4	53	0	103	5	1	9	3	.750	0	0- -	-	3.39	3.80
2001	ElPaso	AA	7	7	0	0	37.2	165	38	23	19	2	2	2	3	20	0	26	6	1	0	4	.000	0	0- -	-	4.76	4.54
2002	Yakima	A-	3	3	0	0	8.2	46	10	9	9	2	0	0	0	10	0	11	1	1	0	1	.000	0	0- -	-	9.22	9.35
2002	Lancst	A+	6	6	0	0	19.1	102	31	23	22	4	0	2	0	16	0	15	2	0	0	3	.000	0	0- -	-	10.89	10.24
2003	ElPaso	AA	15	6	0	2	39.0	179	42	27	27	4	1	2	8	22	0	25	5	1	1	3	.250	0	0- -	-	6.26	6.23
2004	Lancst	A+	14	0	0	6	18.1	81	16	8	4	2	0	0	3	7	0	23	2	0	1	1	.500	0	1- -	-	3.91	1.96
2004	ElPaso	AA	31	0	0	10	35.1	198	42	37	29	2	0	1	1	34	3	40	8	0	2	3	.400	0	0- -	-	6.35	7.39
2005	Tenn	AA	60	0	0	7	42.1	192	40	28	20	1	3	1	4	26	0	33	4	0	0	2	.000	0	0- -	-	4.39	4.25
2006	Tenn	AA	54	0	0	20	63.2	280	59	27	25	6	2	5	5	33	2	76	3	1	0	1	.000	0	12- -	-	4.37	3.53
2007	Okla	AAA	1	0	0	0	1.2	10	2	0	0	0	0	0	0	2	0	2	0	0	0	0	-	0	0- -	-	6.68	0.00
2007	Frisco	AA	43	0	0	7	48.2	227	48	26	24	4	3	1	7	26	0	64	7	1	2	0	1.000	0	2- -	-	4.84	4.44
2008	Okla	AAA	50	0	0	19	53.1	233	45	24	21	4	5	2	3	30	3	62	4	0	4	1	.800	0	6- -	-	3.78	3.54
2008	Bkrsfld	A+	1	0	0	0	1.0	4	0	0	0	0	1	0	0	0	0	2	0	0	0	0	-	0	0- -	-	0.95	0.00
2007	Tex	AL	9	0	0	1	9.1	42	8	5	5	1	0	0	2	7	1	9	0	0	2	0	1.000	0	0-0	3	5.63	4.82
2008	Tex	AL	8	0	0	2	4.0	30	7	9	9	1	0	0	0	11	1	1	0	0	0	0	-	0	0-0	0	20.85	20.25
	2 ML YEARS		17	0	0	3	13.1	72	15	14	14	2	0	0	2	18	2	10	0	0	2	0	1.000	0	0-0	3	9.85	9.45

Josh Whitesell

Bats: L Throws: L Pos: PH-6; 1B-1 Ht: 6'1" Wt: 225 Born: 4/14/1982 Age: 27

						BATTING														BASERUNNING				AVERAGES		
Year	Team	Lg	G	AB	H	2B	3B	HR	(Hm	Rd)	TB	R	RBI	RC	TBB	IBB	SO	HBP	SH	SF	SB	CS	SB%	GDP	Avg	OBP	Slg
2003	Vrmnt	A-	49	167	41	10	1	5	(-	-)	68	13	19	27	28	2	53	4	0	1	0	0	-	2	.246	.365	.407
2004	Savann	A	113	380	95	29	0	16	(-	-)	172	56	54	63	58	2	91	2	1	2	0	1	.00	5	.250	.351	.453
2005	Ptomc	A+	113	389	114	32	2	18	(-	-)	204	59	66	87	74	3	125	9	1	1	1	1	.50	3	.293	.416	.524
2006	Hrsbrg	AA	127	402	106	11	0	19	(-	-)	174	47	56	63	53	3	125	4	6	2	2	6	.25	17	.264	.354	.433
2007	Hrsbrg	AA	119	387	110	23	1	21	(-	-)	198	78	74	87	87	5	107	10	0	3	6	2	.75	6	.284	.425	.512
2008	Tucsn	AAA	127	475	156	36	0	26	(-	-)	270	86	110	112	74	4	136	8	0	3	1	2	.33	9	.328	.425	.568
2008	Ari	NL	7	7	2	0	0	1	(0	1)	5	1	1	2	1	0	2	1	0	0	0	0	-	0	.286	.444	.714

Ty Wigginton

Bats: R Throws: R Pos: 3B-82; LF-31; PH-3 Ht: 6'0" Wt: 225 Born: 10/11/1977 Age: 31

						BATTING														BASERUNNING				AVERAGES		
Year	Team	Lg	G	AB	H	2B	3B	HR	(Hm	Rd)	TB	R	RBI	RC	TBB	IBB	SO	HBP	SH	SF	SB	CS	SB%	GDP	Avg	OBP	Slg
2008	RdRck*	AAA	3	9	1	0	1	0	(-	-)	3	1	1	1	2	1	3	2	0	0	0	1	.00	0	.111	.385	.333
2002	NYM	NL	46	116	35	8	0	6	(4	2)	61	18	18	15	8	0	19	2	0	1	2	1	.67	4	.302	.354	.526
2003	NYM	NL	156	573	146	36	6	11	(4	7)	227	73	71	76	46	2	124	9	1	4	12	2	.86	15	.255	.318	.396
2004	2 Tms	NL	144	494	129	30	2	17	(6	11)	214	63	66	59	45	6	82	2	1	3	7	1	.88	15	.261	.324	.433
2005	Pit	NL	57	155	40	9	1	7	(1	6)	72	20	25	24	14	0	30	1	1	0	1	0	1.00	3	.258	.324	.465
2006	TB	AL	122	444	122	25	1	24	(18	6)	221	55	79	69	32	3	97	6	1	3	4	3	.57	11	.275	.330	.498
2007	2 Tms	NL	148	547	152	33	0	22	(15	7)	251	71	67	64	41	0	113	8	0	4	6	4	.40	16	.278	.333	.459
2008	Hou	NL	111	386	110	22	1	23	(15	8)	203	50	58	57	32	1	69	8	0	3	4	6	.40	9	.285	.350	.526
04	NYM	NL	86	312	89	23	2	12	(5	7)	152	46	42	38	23	4	48	1	1	2	6	1	.86	11	.285	.334	.487
04	Pit	NL	58	182	40	7	0	5	(1	4)	62	17	24	21	22	2	34	1	0	1	1	0	1.00	4	.220	.306	.341
07	TB	AL	98	378	104	21	0	16	(9	7)	173	47	49	42	28	0	73	5	0	6	4	2	.67	8	.275	.329	.458
07	Hou	NL	50	169	48	12	0	6	(6	0)	78	24	18	22	13	0	40	3	0	2	2	0	1.00	8	.284	.342	.462
	7 ML YEARS		784	2715	734	163	11	110	(63	47)	1249	350	384	362	218	12	534	36	4	22	32	18	.64	73	.270	.330	.460

Brad Wilkerson

Bats: L Throws: L Pos: RF-64; LF-29; PH-10; PR-6; CF-5; 1B-4; DH-1 Ht: 6'0" Wt: 205 Born: 6/1/1977 Age: 32

						BATTING														BASERUNNING				AVERAGES		
Year	Team	Lg	G	AB	H	2B	3B	HR	(Hm	Rd)	TB	R	RBI	RC	TBB	IBB	SO	HBP	SH	SF	SB	CS	SB%	GDP	Avg	OBP	Slg
2008	Dnedin*	A+	3	11	5	3	0	1	(-	-)	11	4	1	4	1	0	2	0	0	0	0	0	-	0	.455	.500	1.000
2001	Mon	NL	47	117	24	7	2	1	(1	0)	38	11	5	12	17	1	41	0	1	1	2	1	.67	2	.205	.304	.325
2002	Mon	NL	153	507	135	27	8	20	(12	8)	238	92	59	83	81	7	161	5	6	4	7	8	.47	5	.266	.370	.469
2003	Mon	NL	146	504	135	34	4	19	(9	10)	234	78	77	90	89	0	155	4	2	3	13	10	.57	5	.268	.380	.464
2004	Mon	NL	160	572	146	39	2	32	(15	17)	285	112	67	95	106	8	152	4	3	3	13	6	.68	6	.255	.374	.498
2005	Was	NL	148	565	140	42	7	11	(6	5)	229	76	57	83	84	9	147	7	3	2	8	10	.44	6	.248	.351	.405
2006	Tex	AL	95	320	71	15	2	15	(5	10)	135	56	44	39	37	1	116	3	2	1	3	2	.60	6	.222	.306	.422
2007	Tex	AL	119	338	79	17	1	20	(12	8)	158	54	62	58	43	0	107	1	3	4	4	1	.80	2	.234	.319	.467
2008	2 Tms	AL	104	264	58	12	2	4	(3	1)	86	21	28	25	35	4	68	1	4	5	3	5	.38	4	.220	.308	.326
08	Sea	AL	19	56	13	4	0	0	(0	0)	17	1	5	5	10	0	15	0	2	0	1	2	.33	1	.232	.348	.304
08	Tor	AL	85	208	45	8	2	4	(3	1)	69	20	23	20	25	4	53	1	2	5	2	3	.40	3	.216	.297	.332
	8 ML YEARS		972	3187	788	193	28	122	(63	59)	1403	500	399	485	492	30	947	25	24	25	53	43	.55	36	.247	.350	.440

Josh Willingham

Bats: R Throws: R Pos: LF-98; PH-4 Ht: 6'2" Wt: 215 Born: 2/17/1979 Age: 30

						BATTING														BASERUNNING				AVERAGES		
Year	Team	Lg	G	AB	H	2B	3B	HR	(Hm	Rd)	TB	R	RBI	RC	TBB	IBB	SO	HBP	SH	SF	SB	CS	SB%	GDP	Avg	OBP	Slg
2008	Carlina*	AA	8	26	6	2	0	0	(-	-)	8	6	5	3	2	0	5	2	0	0	0	0	-	0	.231	.333	.308
2004	Fla	NL	12	25	5	0	0	1	(0	1)	8	2	1	1	4	0	8	0	0	0	0	0	-	1	.200	.310	.320
2005	Fla	NL	16	23	7	1	0	0	(0	0)	8	3	4	3	2	0	5	2	1	0	0	0	-	1	.304	.407	.348

Year	Team	Lg	G	AB	H	2B	3B	HR	(Hm	Rd)	TB	R	RBI	RC	TBB	IBB	SO	HBP	SH	SF	SB	CS	SB%	GDP	Avg	OBP	Slg
2006	Fla	NL	142	502	139	28	2	26	(11	15)	249	62	74	74	54	2	109	11	0	6	2	0	1.00	13	.277	.356	.496
2007	Fla	NL	144	521	138	32	4	21	(10	11)	241	75	89	94	66	1	122	16	0	1	8	1	.89	11	.265	.364	.463
2008	Fla	NL	102	351	89	21	5	15	(6	9)	165	54	51	56	48	2	82	14	1	2	3	2	.60	7	.254	.364	.470
5 ML YEARS			416	1422	378	82	11	63	(27	36)	671	196	219	228	174	5	326	43	2	9	13	3	.81	33	.266	.361	.472

Dontrelle Willis

Pitches: L Bats: L Pos: SP-7; RP-1   Ht: 6'4" Wt: 225 Born: 1/12/1982 Age: 27

Year	Team	Lg	G	GS	CG	GF	IP	BFP	H	R	ER	HR	SH	SF	HB	TBB	IBB	SO	WP	Bk	W	L	Pct	ShO	Sv-Op	Hld	ERC	ERA
2008	Toledo*	AAA	6	6	0	0	28.1	128	34	16	14	2	0	0	0	14	1	20	1	0	3	1	.750	0	0--	-	5.41	4.45
2008	Lkland*	A+	6	5	0	0	28.0	121	30	15	14	2	0	0	0	11	0	18	2	0	3	0	.000	0	0--	-	4.29	4.50
2003	Fla	NL	27	27	2	0	160.2	668	148	61	59	13	3	1	3	58	0	142	7	1	14	6	.700	2	0-0	0	3.49	3.30
2004	Fla	NL	32	32	2	0	197.0	848	210	99	88	20	8	2	8	61	8	139	2	0	10	11	.476	0	0-0	0	4.21	4.02
2005	Fla	NL	34	34	7	0	236.1	960	213	79	69	11	14	5	8	55	3	170	2	1	22	10	.688	5	0-0	0	2.71	2.63
2006	Fla	NL	34	34	4	0	223.1	975	234	106	96	21	11	6	19	83	6	160	6	1	12	12	.500	1	0-0	0	4.53	3.87
2007	Fla	NL	35	35	0	0	205.1	942	241	131	118	29	15	7	14	87	4	146	9	1	10	15	.400	0	0-0	0	5.72	5.17
2008	Det	AL	8	7	0	0	24.0	122	18	25	25	4	0	0	1	35	1	18	5	1	0	2	.000	0	0-0	0	7.65	9.38
Postseason			7	2	0	0	12.2	63	15	12	12	1	1	2	0	10	0	10	1	0	0	1	.000	0	0-0	1	6.43	8.53
6 ML YEARS			170	169	15	0	1046.2	4515	1064	501	455	98	51	21	53	379	22	775	31	5	68	56	.548	8	0-0	0	4.16	3.91

Reggie Willits

Bats: B Throws: R Pos: LF-30; RF-22; PH-18; PR-11; CF-9; DH-5   Ht: 5'11" Wt: 185 Born: 5/30/1981 Age: 28

Year	Team	Lg	G	AB	H	2B	3B	HR	(Hm	Rd)	TB	R	RBI	RC	TBB	IBB	SO	HBP	SH	SF	SB	CS	SB%	GDP	Avg	OBP	Slg
2008	Salt Lk*	AAA	10	37	14	2	1	0	(-	-)	18	7	4	8	5	0	6	0	1	0	1	1	.50	0	.378	.452	.486
2008	RCuca*	A+	4	14	5	0	0	0	(-	-)	5	4	0	2	2	0	1	0	0	0	2	0	1.00	0	.357	.438	.357
2006	LAA	AL	28	45	12	1	0	0	(0	0)	13	12	2	6	11	0	10	0	2	0	4	3	.57	0	.267	.411	.289
2007	LAA	AL	136	430	126	20	1	0	(0	0)	148	74	34	68	69	2	83	3	11	5	27	8	.77	7	.293	.391	.344
2008	LAA	AL	82	108	21	4	0	0	(0	0)	25	21	7	10	21	0	26	0	5	2	2	1	.67	1	.194	.321	.231
Postseason			3	4	0	0	0	0	(0	0)	0	0	0	0	1	0	2	0	0	0	1	0	1.00	0	.000	.200	.000
3 ML YEARS			246	583	159	25	1	0	(0	0)	186	107	43	84	101	2	119	3	18	7	33	12	.73	8	.273	.379	.319

Bobby Wilson

Bats: R Throws: R Pos: C-7   Ht: 6'0" Wt: 220 Born: 4/8/1983 Age: 26

Year	Team	Lg	G	AB	H	2B	3B	HR	(Hm	Rd)	TB	R	RBI	RC	TBB	IBB	SO	HBP	SH	SF	SB	CS	SB%	GDP	Avg	OBP	Slg
2003	Provo	R+	57	236	67	12	0	6	(-	-)	97	36	62	33	18	0	31	0	0	4	0	0	-	11	.284	.329	.411
2004	CRpds	A	105	396	106	23	0	8	(-	-)	153	45	64	52	30	3	55	5	1	9	5	2	.71	3	.268	.320	.386
2005	RCuca	A+	115	466	135	32	1	14	(-	-)	211	66	77	71	30	0	61	2	0	3	2	1	.67	5	.290	.333	.453
2006	Ark	AA	103	374	107	26	0	9	(-	-)	160	46	53	56	33	2	47	5	4	2	1	6	.14	7	.286	.350	.428
2007	Ark	AA	50	181	49	9	0	6	(-	-)	76	24	27	27	22	1	26	0	0	1	5	3	.63	5	.271	.348	.420
2008	Salt Lk	AAA	40	132	39	13	1	3	(-	-)	63	15	22	21	8	1	18	0	1	0	1	0	1.00	6	.295	.336	.477
2008	Salt Lk	AAA	72	260	81	20	0	4	(-	-)	113	33	45	45	29	1	45	4	3	2	0	0	-	5	.312	.386	.435
2008	LAA	AL	7	6	1	0	0	0	(0	0)	1	0	1	0	1	0	3	0	0	0	0	0	-	0	.167	.286	.167

Brian Wilson

Pitches: R Bats: R Pos: RP-63   Ht: 6'1" Wt: 196 Born: 3/16/1982 Age: 27

Year	Team	Lg	G	GS	CG	GF	IP	BFP	H	R	ER	HR	SH	SF	HB	TBB	IBB	SO	WP	Bk	W	L	Pct	ShO	Sv-Op	Hld	ERC	ERA
2006	SF	NL	31	0	0	9	30.0	141	32	19	18	1	1	4	1	21	2	23	0	0	2	3	.400	0	1-2	4	5.11	5.40
2007	SF	NL	24	0	0	9	23.2	93	16	6	6	1	0	0	1	7	0	18	0	0	1	2	.333	0	6-7	9	1.87	2.28
2008	SF	NL	63	0	0	54	62.1	274	62	32	32	7	2	5	3	28	4	67	2	0	3	2	.600	0	41-47	0	4.41	4.62
3 ML YEARS			118	0	0	72	116.0	508	110	57	56	9	3	9	5	56	6	108	2	0	6	7	.462	0	48-56	13	4.03	4.34

C.J. Wilson

Pitches: L Bats: L Pos: RP-50   Ht: 6'1" Wt: 210 Born: 11/18/1980 Age: 28

Year	Team	Lg	G	GS	CG	GF	IP	BFP	H	R	ER	HR	SH	SF	HB	TBB	IBB	SO	WP	Bk	W	L	Pct	ShO	Sv-Op	Hld	ERC	ERA
2005	Tex	AL	24	6	0	5	48.0	220	63	39	37	5	1	2	2	18	1	30	4	1	1	7	.125	0	1-1	4	6.03	6.94
2006	Tex	AL	44	0	0	12	44.1	191	39	23	20	7	1	0	5	18	1	43	0	0	2	4	.333	0	1-2	7	4.25	4.06
2007	Tex	AL	66	0	0	22	68.1	285	50	25	23	4	2	4	6	33	1	63	5	0	2	1	.667	0	12-14	15	3.01	3.03
2008	Tex	AL	50	0	0	41	46.1	214	49	35	31	8	1	1	2	27	2	41	3	0	2	2	.500	0	24-28	5	5.77	6.02
4 ML YEARS			184	6	0	80	207.0	910	201	122	111	24	5	7	15	96	5	177	12	1	7	14	.333	0	38-45	27	4.55	4.83

Jack Wilson

Bats: R Throws: R Pos: SS-80; PH-7   Ht: 6'0" Wt: 198 Born: 12/29/1977 Age: 31

Year	Team	Lg	G	AB	H	2B	3B	HR	(Hm	Rd)	TB	R	RBI	RC	TBB	IBB	SO	HBP	SH	SF	SB	CS	SB%	GDP	Avg	OBP	Slg
2008	Indy*	AAA	4	12	4	1	0	0	(-	-)	5	2	2	1	0	0	1	0	0	0	0	0	-	0	.333	.333	.417
2008	Altna*	AA	7	19	6	0	0	0	(-	-)	6	1	0	3	4	0	2	1	1	0	2	0	1.00	0	.316	.458	.316
2001	Pit	NL	108	390	87	17	1	3	(0	3)	115	44	25	27	16	2	70	1	17	1	1	3	.25	4	.223	.255	.295
2002	Pit	NL	147	527	133	22	4	4	(2	2)	175	77	47	60	37	2	74	4	17	1	5	2	.71	7	.252	.306	.332
2003	Pit	NL	150	558	143	21	3	9	(2	7)	197	58	62	62	36	3	74	4	11	6	5	5	.50	11	.256	.303	.353

Year	Team	Lg	G	AB	H	2B	3B	HR	(Hm	Rd)	TB	R	RBI	RC	TBB	IBB	SO	HBP	SH	SF	SB	CS	SB%	GDP	Avg	OBP	Slg
2004	Pit	NL	157	652	201	41	12	11	(7	4)	299	82	59	84	26	0	71	3	7	5	8	4	.67	15	.308	.335	.459
2005	Pit	NL	158	587	151	24	7	8	(3	5)	213	60	52	60	31	6	58	6	11	4	7	3	.70	11	.257	.299	.363
2006	Pit	NL	142	543	148	27	1	8	(5	3)	201	70	35	58	33	0	65	4	9	5	4	3	.57	15	.273	.316	.370
2007	Pit	NL	135	477	141	29	2	12	(3	9)	210	67	56	70	38	9	46	6	7	7	2	5	.29	8	.296	.350	.440
2008	Pit	NL	87	305	83	18	1	1	(1	0)	106	24	22	32	13	0	27	5	6	1	2	2	.50	6	.272	.312	.348
8 ML YEARS			1084	4039	1087	199	31	56	(23	33)	1516	482	358	453	230	22	485	33	85	30	34	27	.56	77	.269	.312	.375

Randy Winn

Bats: B **Throws:** R **Pos:** RF-133; LF-15; CF-10; PH-5; DH-2　　　　**Ht:** 6'2" **Wt:** 193 **Born:** 6/9/1974 **Age:** 35

Year	Team	Lg	G	AB	H	2B	3B	HR	(Hm	Rd)	TB	R	RBI	RC	TBB	IBB	SO	HBP	SH	SF	SB	CS	SB%	GDP	Avg	OBP	Slg
1998	TB	AL	109	338	94	9	9	1	(0	1)	124	51	17	44	29	0	69	1	11	0	26	12	.68	2	.278	.337	.367
1999	TB	AL	79	303	81	16	4	2	(2	0)	111	44	24	32	17	0	63	1	1	2	9	9	.50	3	.267	.307	.366
2000	TB	AL	51	159	40	5	0	1	(1	0)	48	28	16	18	26	0	25	2	2	1	6	7	.46	2	.252	.362	.302
2001	TB	AL	128	429	117	25	6	6	(3	3)	172	54	50	56	38	0	81	6	5	2	12	10	.55	10	.273	.339	.401
2002	TB	AL	152	607	181	39	9	14	(9	5)	280	87	75	104	55	3	109	6	1	5	27	8	.77	9	.298	.360	.461
2003	Sea	AL	157	600	177	37	4	11	(6	5)	255	103	75	96	41	0	108	8	6	5	23	5	.82	9	.295	.346	.425
2004	Sea	AL	157	626	179	34	6	14	(6	8)	267	84	81	91	53	1	98	8	9	7	21	7	.75	16	.286	.346	.427
2005	2 Tms		160	617	189	47	6	20	(9	11)	308	85	63	95	48	4	91	5	10	3	19	11	.63	11	.306	.360	.499
2006	SF	NL	149	573	150	34	5	11	(5	6)	227	82	56	69	48	3	63	7	3	4	10	8	.56	7	.262	.324	.396
2007	SF	NL	155	593	178	42	1	14	(4	10)	264	73	65	86	44	3	85	7	4	5	15	3	.83	12	.300	.353	.445
2008	SF	NL	155	598	183	38	2	10	(6	4)	255	84	64	90	59	6	88	0	1	9	25	2	.93	6	.306	.363	.426
05	Sea	AL	102	386	106	25	1	6	(2	4)	151	46	37	52	37	3	53	4	6	3	12	6	.67	7	.275	.342	.391
05	SF	NL	58	231	83	22	5	14	(7	7)	157	39	26	43	11	1	38	1	4	0	7	5	.58	4	.359	.391	.680
11 ML YEARS			1452	5443	1569	326	52	104	(49	55)	2311	775	586	781	458	20	880	51	53	43	193	82	.70	87	.288	.347	.425

Dewayne Wise

Bats: L **Throws:** L **Pos:** LF-24; CF-23; PH-13; PR-7; RF-6; DH-4　　　　**Ht:** 6'1" **Wt:** 194 **Born:** 2/24/1978 **Age:** 31

Year	Team	Lg	G	AB	H	2B	3B	HR	(Hm	Rd)	TB	R	RBI	RC	TBB	IBB	SO	HBP	SH	SF	SB	CS	SB%	GDP	Avg	OBP	Slg
2008	Charltt*	AAA	55	191	61	14	3	9	(-	-)	108	39	23	43	22	0	32	5	3	1	15	7	.68	5	.319	.402	.565
2000	Tor	AL	28	22	3	0	0	0	(0	0)	3	3	0	0	1	0	5	1	0	0	1	0	1.00	0	.136	.208	.136
2002	Tor	AL	42	112	20	4	1	3	(2	1)	35	14	13	8	4	0	15	0	0	0	5	0	1.00	0	.179	.207	.313
2004	Atl	NL	77	162	37	9	4	6	(3	3)	72	24	17	20	9	1	28	1	2	1	6	1	.86	1	.228	.272	.444
2006	Cin	NL	31	38	7	2	0	0	(0	0)	9	3	1	0	0	0	6	0	2	0	0	0	-	2	.184	.184	.237
2007	Cin	NL	5	5	1	0	1	0	(0	0)	3	1	1	1	1	1	1	0	0	0	0	0	-	0	.200	.333	.600
2008	CWS	AL	57	129	32	4	2	6	(2	4)	58	20	18	14	8	0	32	1	3	2	9	0	1.00	1	.248	.293	.450
	Postseason		5	5	1	1	0	0	(0	0)	2	1	0	0	0	0	2	0	0	0	0	0	-	0	.200	.200	.400
6 ML YEARS			240	468	100	19	8	15	(7	8)	180	65	50	43	23	2	87	3	7	3	21	1	.95	8	.214	.254	.385

Matt Wise

Pitches: R **Bats:** R **Pos:** RP-8　　　　**Ht:** 6'4" **Wt:** 200 **Born:** 11/18/1975 **Age:** 33

Year	Team	Lg	G	GS	CG	GF	IP	BFP	H	R	ER	HR	SH	SF	HB	TBB	IBB	SO	WP	Bk	W	L	Pct	ShO	Sv-Op	Hld	ERC	ERA
2008	StLuci*	A+	3	0	0	0	4.0	12	0	0	0	0	0	0	0	0	0	6	0	0	0	0	-	0	0- -	-	0.00	0.00
2000	LAA	AL	8	6	0	0	37.1	163	40	23	23	7	0	2	1	13	1	20	1	0	3	3	.500	0	0-0	0	4.96	5.54
2001	LAA	AL	11	9	0	2	49.1	211	47	27	24	11	2	1	2	18	1	50	0	0	1	4	.200	0	0-0	0	4.65	4.38
2002	LAA	AL	7	0	0	6	8.1	33	7	3	3	0	1	0	1	1	0	6	0	0	0	0	-	0	0-0	0	2.07	3.24
2004	Mil	NL	30	3	0	5	52.2	222	51	27	26	3	1	2	2	15	1	30	2	0	1	2	.333	0	0-0	3	3.27	4.44
2005	Mil	NL	49	0	0	11	64.1	262	37	25	24	6	1	2	3	25	5	62	1	1	4	4	.500	0	1-3	10	1.83	3.36
2006	Mil	NL	40	0	0	9	44.1	188	45	24	19	6	3	1	2	14	2	27	0	1	5	6	.455	0	0-4	14	4.23	3.86
2007	Mil	NL	56	0	0	9	53.2	236	61	30	25	5	1	3	1	17	1	43	0	1	3	2	.600	0	1-2	13	4.49	4.19
2008	NYM	NL	8	0	0	5	7.0	34	10	5	5	2	0	0	0	3	1	6	0	0	0	1	.000	0	0-0	1	7.88	6.43
8 ML YEARS			209	18	0	47	317.0	1349	298	164	149	40	9	11	12	106	12	244	4	3	17	22	.436	0	2-9	41	3.73	4.23

Randy Wolf

Pitches: L **Bats:** L **Pos:** SP-33　　　　**Ht:** 5'10" **Wt:** 198 **Born:** 8/22/1976 **Age:** 32

Year	Team	Lg	G	GS	CG	GF	IP	BFP	H	R	ER	HR	SH	SF	HB	TBB	IBB	SO	WP	Bk	W	L	Pct	ShO	Sv-Op	Hld	ERC	ERA
1999	Phi	NL	22	21	0	0	121.2	552	126	78	75	20	5	1	5	67	0	116	4	0	6	9	.400	0	0-0	0	5.54	5.55
2000	Phi	NL	32	32	1	0	206.1	889	210	107	100	25	10	8	8	83	2	160	1	0	11	9	.550	0	0-0	0	4.54	4.36
2001	Phi	NL	28	25	4	1	163.0	684	150	74	67	15	11	7	10	51	4	152	1	0	10	11	.476	2	0-0	0	3.46	3.70
2002	Phi	NL	31	31	3	0	210.2	855	172	77	75	23	7	6	7	63	5	172	4	0	11	9	.550	2	0-0	0	2.88	3.20
2003	Phi	NL	33	33	2	0	200.0	850	176	101	94	27	8	4	6	78	4	177	6	0	16	10	.615	2	0-0	0	3.67	4.23
2004	Phi	NL	23	23	1	0	136.2	585	145	73	65	20	6	3	5	36	4	89	2	0	5	8	.385	1	0-0	0	4.29	4.28
2005	Phi	NL	13	13	0	0	80.0	346	87	40	39	14	4	1	6	26	2	61	1	0	4	6	.400	0	0-0	0	5.17	4.39
2006	Phi	NL	12	12	0	0	56.2	261	63	37	35	13	2	3	2	33	2	44	2	0	4	0	1.000	0	0-0	0	6.63	5.56
2007	LAD	NL	18	18	0	0	102.2	458	110	55	54	10	5	5	6	39	2	94	4	0	9	6	.600	0	0-0	0	4.52	4.73
2008	2 Tms	NL	33	33	1	0	190.1	823	191	100	91	21	10	4	12	71	4	162	3	0	12	12	.500	1	0-0	0	4.30	4.30
08	SD	NL	21	21	0	0	119.2	522	123	69	63	14	6	2	8	47	2	105	2	0	6	10	.375	0	0-0	0	4.63	4.74
08	Hou	NL	12	12	1	0	70.2	301	68	31	28	7	4	2	4	24	2	57	1	0	6	2	.750	1	0-0	0	3.77	3.57
10 ML YEARS			245	241	12	1	1468.0	6303	1430	742	695	188	68	42	67	547	29	1227	28	0	90	78	.536	8	0-0	0	4.18	4.26

Brian Wolfe

Pitches: R Bats: R Pos: RP-20   Ht: 6'2" Wt: 200 Born: 11/29/1980 Age: 28

			HOW MUCH HE PITCHED						WHAT HE GAVE UP												THE RESULTS						
Year	Team	Lg	G	GS	CG	GF	IP	BFP	H	R	ER	HR	SH	SF	HB	TBB	IBB	SO	WP	Bk	W	L	Pct	ShO	Sv-Op	Hld	ERC	ERA
1999	Twins	R	9	5	2	0	38.0	153	33	14	12	2	1	1	1	9	0	40	2	0	4	0	1.000	0	0--	-	2.59	2.84
2000	QuadC	A	31	18	0	2	123.1	541	148	73	65	13	2	6	4	34	1	91	7	1	5	9	.357	0	0--	-	4.90	4.74
2001	QuadC	A	28	23	2	2	160.0	641	128	64	50	11	2	4	5	32	2	128	8	0	13	8	.619	2	0--	-	2.18	2.81
2002	FtMyrs	A+	25	23	0	0	132.0	584	160	84	68	17	5	4	7	34	0	85	5	3	6	9	.400	0	0--	-	5.15	4.64
2003	FtMyrs	A+	7	7	0	0	46.1	185	41	15	13	3	0	1	1	6	0	22	2	0	2	1	.667	0	0--	-	2.31	2.53
2003	NwBrit	AA	30	10	1	11	82.2	375	111	65	59	10	2	5	3	24	2	42	0	1	5	7	.417	0	3--	-	5.95	6.42
2004	NwBrit	AA	7	0	0	1	11.0	50	16	10	10	3	1	0	0	3	0	6	0	0	1	1	.500	0	0--	-	7.80	8.18
2005	Roch	AAA	3	0	0	0	6.1	31	10	8	6	1	0	0	0	2	0	5	0	0	0	2	.000	0	0--	-	7.54	8.53
2005	NwBrit	AA	5	0	0	2	7.2	37	10	6	6	0	0	0	0	7	1	4	0	0	1	0	1.000	0	0--	-	7.28	7.04
2005	BrvdCt	A+	18	0	0	13	22.2	91	19	3	2	0	0	0	0	8	0	22	1	0	1	1	.500	0	8--	-	2.47	0.79
2005	Hntsvl	AA	16	0	0	7	24.0	115	32	12	9	1	2	1	1	8	2	19	3	0	3	2	.600	0	0--	-	5.07	3.38
2006	Dnedin	A+	5	5	0	0	24.0	110	33	20	16	3	0	1	2	3	0	17	1	0	1	4	.200	0	0--	-	5.53	6.00
2006	NHam	AA	24	2	0	6	42.1	198	54	30	27	5	2	1	1	15	1	34	2	1	1	3	.250	0	0--	-	5.52	5.74
2007	Syrcse	AAA	17	0	0	6	26.0	100	18	4	3	1	0	0	0	6	1	23	1	0	2	0	1.000	0	0--	-	1.58	1.04
2008	Dnedin	A+	1	0	0	0	1.0	4	0	0	0	0	0	0	0	1	1	0	0	0	0	0	-	0	0--	-	0.95	0.00
2008	Syrcse	AAA	17	6	0	8	36.2	154	39	17	14	2	1	2	0	10	1	29	0	0	2	3	.400	0	1--	-	3.62	3.44
2007	Tor	AL	38	0	0	12	45.1	174	36	17	15	5	0	2	2	9	2	22	0	0	3	1	.750	0	0-2	6	2.52	2.98
2008	Tor	AL	20	0	0	4	22.0	86	18	6	6	2	2	1	0	6	1	14	1	0	0	2	.000	0	0-0	3	2.61	2.45
	2 ML YEARS		58	0	0	16	67.1	260	54	23	21	7	2	3	2	15	3	36	1	0	3	3	.500	0	0-2	9	2.55	2.81

Brandon Wood

Bats: R Throws: R Pos: 3B-32; SS-28; PR-1   Ht: 6'3" Wt: 190 Born: 3/2/1985 Age: 24

			BATTING																	BASERUNNING				AVERAGES		
Year	Team	Lg	G	AB	H	2B	3B	HR	(Hm	Rd)	TB	R	RBI	RC	TBB	IBB	SO	HBP	SH	SF	SB	CS	SB%	GDP	Avg	OBP	Slg
2003	Angels	R	19	78	24	8	2	0	(-	-)	36	14	13	13	4	0	15	2	0	2	3	0	1.00	1	.308	.349	.462
2003	Provo	R+	42	162	45	13	2	5	(-	-)	77	25	31	27	16	0	48	2	0	1	1	1	.50	2	.278	.348	.475
2004	CRpds	A	125	478	120	30	5	11	(-	-)	193	65	64	67	46	3	117	5	4	2	21	5	.81	8	.251	.322	.404
2005	RCuca	A+	130	536	172	51	4	43	(-	-)	360	109	115	131	48	5	128	7	2	2	7	3	.70	12	.321	.383	.672
2005	Salt Lk	AAA	4	19	6	2	1	0	(-	-)	10	1	1	3	0	0	6	0	0	0	0	0	-	0	.316	.316	.526
2006	Ark	AA	118	453	125	42	4	25	(-	-)	250	74	83	92	54	1	149	6	2	7	19	3	.86	10	.276	.356	.552
2007	Salt Lk	AAA	111	437	119	27	1	23	(-	-)	217	73	77	76	45	0	120	1	0	5	10	1	.91	10	.272	.338	.497
2008	Salt Lk	AAA	103	395	117	21	2	31	(-	-)	235	82	84	85	45	1	104	6	0	2	6	5	.55	9	.296	.375	.595
2007	LAA	AL	13	33	5	1	0	1	(0	1)	9	2	3	1	0	0	12	0	0	0	0	0	-	0	.152	.152	.273
2008	LAA	AL	55	150	30	4	0	5	(2	3)	49	12	13	7	4	0	43	1	1	1	4	0	1.00	3	.200	.224	.327
	2 ML YEARS		68	183	35	5	0	6	(2	4)	58	14	16	8	4	0	55	1	1	1	4	0	1.00	3	.191	.212	.317

Jason Wood

Bats: R Throws: R Pos: PH-3   Ht: 6'1" Wt: 170 Born: 12/16/1969 Age: 39

			BATTING																	BASERUNNING				AVERAGES		
Year	Team	Lg	G	AB	H	2B	3B	HR	(Hm	Rd)	TB	R	RBI	RC	TBB	IBB	SO	HBP	SH	SF	SB	CS	SB%	GDP	Avg	OBP	Slg
2008	Albq*	AAA	105	346	93	14	0	4	(-	-)	119	53	42	42	27	1	59	6	2	3	3	0	1.00	9	.269	.330	.344
1998	2 Tms	AL	13	24	8	2	0	1	(0	1)	13	6	1	4	3	0	5	0	0	0	0	1	.00	0	.333	.407	.542
1999	Det	AL	27	44	7	1	0	1	(1	0)	11	5	8	7	2	0	13	0	1	0	0	0	-	0	.159	.196	.250
2006	Fla	NL	12	13	6	2	0	0	(0	0)	8	3	1	4	1	0	2	0	0	0	1	0	1.00	0	.462	.500	.615
2007	Fla	NL	98	117	28	6	0	3	(2	1)	43	11	26	16	8	0	38	0	1	1	0	0	-	1	.239	.286	.368
2008	Fla	NL	3	2	0	0	0	0	(0	0)	0	0	0	0	1	0	1	0	0	0	0	0	-	0	.000	.333	.000
98	Oak	AL	3	1	0	0	0	0	(0	0)	0	1	0	0	0	0	1	0	0	0	0	0	-	0	.000	.000	.000
98	Det	AL	10	23	8	2	0	1	(0	1)	13	5	1	4	3	0	4	0	0	0	0	1	.00	0	.348	.423	.565
	5 ML YEARS		153	200	49	11	0	5	(3	2)	75	25	36	25	15	0	59	0	2	1	1	1	.50	1	.245	.296	.375

Kerry Wood

Pitches: R Bats: R Pos: RP-65   Ht: 6'5" Wt: 211 Born: 6/16/1977 Age: 32

			HOW MUCH HE PITCHED						WHAT HE GAVE UP												THE RESULTS						
Year	Team	Lg	G	GS	CG	GF	IP	BFP	H	R	ER	HR	SH	SF	HB	TBB	IBB	SO	WP	Bk	W	L	Pct	ShO	Sv-Op	Hld	ERC	ERA
1998	ChC	NL	26	26	1	0	166.2	699	117	69	63	14	2	4	11	85	1	233	6	3	13	6	.684	1	0-0	0	3.03	3.40
2000	ChC	NL	23	23	1	0	137.0	603	112	77	73	17	7	5	9	87	0	132	5	1	8	7	.533	0	0-0	0	4.43	4.80
2001	ChC	NL	28	28	1	0	174.1	740	127	70	65	16	4	5	10	92	3	217	9	0	12	6	.667	1	0-0	0	3.22	3.36
2002	ChC	NL	33	33	4	0	213.2	895	169	92	87	22	13	5	16	97	5	217	8	1	12	11	.522	1	0-0	0	3.46	3.66
2003	ChC	NL	32	32	4	0	211.0	887	152	77	75	24	11	6	21	100	2	266	10	0	14	11	.560	2	0-0	0	3.31	3.20
2004	ChC	NL	22	22	0	0	140.1	595	127	62	58	16	6	6	11	51	0	144	7	0	8	9	.471	0	0-0	0	3.83	3.72
2005	ChC	NL	21	10	0	4	66.0	273	52	32	31	14	2	1	2	26	0	77	0	0	3	4	.429	0	0-0	4	3.75	4.23
2006	ChC	NL	4	4	0	0	19.2	86	19	13	9	5	0	2	1	8	0	13	1	0	1	2	.333	0	0-0	0	5.17	4.12
2007	ChC	NL	22	0	0	2	24.1	101	18	9	9	0	1	0	0	13	1	24	1	0	1	1	.500	0	0-0	0	2.49	3.33
2008	ChC	NL	65	0	0	56	66.1	276	54	24	24	3	2	2	7	18	4	84	1	0	5	4	.556	0	34-40	0	2.52	3.26
	Postseason		7	5	0	1	35.2	151	27	15	15	3	1	0	0	18	1	38	1	0	2	2	.500	0	0-0	0	2.97	3.79
	10 ML YEARS		276	178	11	62	1219.1	5155	947	525	494	131	48	36	88	577	16	1407	48	5	77	61	.558	5	34-40	4	3.46	3.65

Jake Woods

Pitches: L Bats: L Pos: RP-15   Ht: 6'1" Wt: 200 Born: 9/3/1981 Age: 27

Year	Team	Lg	G	GS	CG	GF	IP	BFP	H	R	ER	HR	SH	SF	HB	TBB	IBB	SO	WP	Bk	W	L	Pct	ShO	Sv-Op	Hld	ERC	ERA
2008	Tacom*	AAA	32	2	0	3	64.0	274	64	29	29	7	2	0	2	27	1	54	2	0	6	1	.857	0	1--	-	4.42	4.08
2005	LAA	AL	28	0	0	10	27.2	122	30	18	14	7	1	0	2	8	0	20	2	0	1	1	.500	0	0-0	2	5.44	4.55
2006	Sea	AL	37	8	0	10	105.0	473	115	51	49	12	2	2	2	53	5	66	4	0	7	4	.636	0	1-1	2	5.16	4.20
2007	Sea	AL	4	0	0	2	10.2	49	9	8	7	1	0	0	1	7	0	4	0	0	0	0	-	0	0-0	0	4.41	5.91
2008	Sea	AL	15	0	0	3	19.0	87	22	13	13	5	0	0	1	11	2	9	2	1	0	0	-	0	0-1	1	7.29	6.16
4 ML YEARS			84	8	0	25	162.1	731	176	90	83	25	3	2	6	79	7	99	8	1	8	5	.615	0	1-2	5	5.41	4.60

Mark Worrell

Pitches: R Bats: R Pos: RP-4   Ht: 6'1" Wt: 215 Born: 3/8/1983 Age: 26

Year	Team	Lg	G	GS	CG	GF	IP	BFP	H	R	ER	HR	SH	SF	HB	TBB	IBB	SO	WP	Bk	W	L	Pct	ShO	Sv-Op	Hld	ERC	ERA
2004	JhsCty	R+	17	0	0	17	22.1	86	12	3	3	1	0	0	0	7	0	35	0	0	1	0	1.000	0	6--	-	1.32	1.21
2004	Peoria	A	12	0	0	11	14.2	60	9	10	7	2	0	0	1	6	0	20	0	0		2	.000	0	6--	-	2.53	4.30
2005	PlmBh	A+	53	0	0	52	56.0	225	38	20	14	6	2	1	4	19	0	53	6	0	2	3	.400	0	35--	-	2.49	2.25
2006	Sprgfld	AA	57	0	0	51	61.2	257	52	34	31	10	3	3	1	20	2	75	2	0	3	7	.300	0	27--	-	3.30	4.52
2007	Memp	AAA	49	0	0	17	67.0	289	58	25	23	6	5	6	7	25	5	66	4	0	3	2	.600	0	4--	-	3.40	3.09
2008	Memp	AAA	53	0	0	18	58.2	249	45	21	14	2	2	1	1	31	2	80	3	0	3	3	.500	0	5--	-	2.85	2.15
2008	StL	NL	4	0	0	1	5.2	27	8	5	5	1	1	0	0	4	1	4	0	0	0	1	.000	0	0-0	0	8.66	7.94

David Wright

Bats: R Throws: R Pos: 3B-159; DH-1   Ht: 6'0" Wt: 217 Born: 12/20/1982 Age: 26

Year	Team	Lg	G	AB	H	2B	3B	HR	(Hm	Rd)	TB	R	RBI	RC	TBB	IBB	SO	HBP	SH	SF	SB	CS	SB%	GDP	Avg	OBP	Slg
2004	NYM	NL	69	263	77	17	1	14	(8	6)	138	41	40	42	14	0	40	3	0	3	6	0	1.00	7	.293	.332	.525
2005	NYM	NL	160	575	176	42	1	27	(12	15)	301	99	102	105	72	2	113	7	0	3	17	7	.71	16	.306	.388	.523
2006	NYM	NL	154	582	181	40	5	26	(13	13)	309	96	116	119	66	13	113	5	0	8	20	5	.80	15	.311	.381	.531
2007	NYM	NL	160	604	196	42	1	30	(16	14)	330	113	107	127	94	6	115	6	0	7	34	5	.87	14	.325	.416	.546
2008	NYM	NL	160	626	189	42	2	33	(21	12)	334	115	124	116	94	5	118	4	0	11	15	5	.75	15	.302	.390	.534
Postseason			10	37	8	3	0	1	(0	1)	14	3	6	5	5	1	8	0	0	0	0	0	-	0	.216	.310	.378
5 ML YEARS			703	2650	819	183	10	130	(70	60)	1412	464	489	509	340	26	499	25	0	32	92	22	.81	67	.309	.389	.533

Jamey Wright

Pitches: R Bats: R Pos: RP-75   Ht: 6'5" Wt: 230 Born: 12/24/1974 Age: 34

Year	Team	Lg	G	GS	CG	GF	IP	BFP	H	R	ER	HR	SH	SF	HB	TBB	IBB	SO	WP	Bk	W	L	Pct	ShO	Sv-Op	Hld	ERC	ERA
1996	Col	NL	16	15	0	0	91.1	406	105	60	50	8	4	2	7	41	1	45	1	2	4	4	.500	0	0-0	1	5.50	4.93
1997	Col	NL	26	26	1	0	149.2	698	198	113	104	19	8	3	11	71	3	59	6	2	8	12	.400	0	0-0	0	6.96	6.25
1998	Col	NL	34	34	1	0	206.1	919	235	143	130	24	8	6	11	95	3	86	6	3	9	14	.391	0	0-0	0	5.57	5.67
1999	Col	NL	16	16	0	0	94.1	423	110	52	51	10	3	4	4	54	3	49	3	0	4	3	.571	0	0-0	0	6.19	4.87
2000	Mil	NL	26	25	0	1	164.2	718	157	81	75	12	4	6	18	88	5	96	9	2	7	9	.438	0	0-0	0	4.67	4.10
2001	Mil	NL	33	33	1	0	194.2	868	201	115	106	26	7	5	20	98	10	129	6	1	11	12	.478	1	0-0	0	5.36	4.90
2002	2 Tms	NL	33	22	1	0	129.1	585	130	80	76	17	9	6	11	75	9	77	9	0	7	13	.350	1	0-0	0	5.35	5.29
2003	KC	AL	4	4	2	0	25.1	106	23	14	12	1	0	0	1	11	0	19	0	0	1	2	.333	1	0-0	0	3.53	4.26
2004	Col	NL	14	14	0	0	78.2	361	82	39	36	8	1	1	6	45	3	41	3	0	2	3	.400	0	0-0	0	5.26	4.12
2005	Col	NL	34	27	0	1	171.1	782	201	119	104	22	4	3	15	81	4	101	2	2	8	16	.333	0	0-0	1	6.02	5.46
2006	SF	NL	34	21	0	2	156.0	676	167	95	90	16	5	4	10	64	4	79	6	0	6	10	.375	0	0-0	1	4.89	5.19
2007	Tex	AL	20	9	0	3	77.0	330	72	35	31	6	3	2	5	41	2	39	4	0	5	4	.444	0	0-0	1	4.44	3.62
2008	Tex	AL	75	0	0	17	84.1	379	93	57	48	5	3	4	8	35	3	60	5	0	8	7	.533	0	0-6	17	4.74	5.12
02	Mil	NL	19	19	1	0	114.1	515	115	72	68	15	9	6	11	63	8	69	8	0	5	13	.278	1	0-0	0	5.28	5.35
02	StL	NL	4	3	0	0	15.0	70	15	8	8	2	0	0	0	12	1	8	1	0	2	0	1.000	0	0-0	0	5.87	4.80
13 ML YEARS			355	246	6	24	1623.0	7251	1774	1003	913	174	59	46	127	799	50	880	60	12	79	110	.418	3	0-6	20	5.42	5.06

Wesley Wright

Pitches: L Bats: R Pos: RP-71   Ht: 5'11" Wt: 160 Born: 1/28/1985 Age: 24

Year	Team	Lg	G	GS	CG	GF	IP	BFP	H	R	ER	HR	SH	SF	HB	TBB	IBB	SO	WP	Bk	W	L	Pct	ShO	Sv-Op	Hld	ERC	ERA
2003	Ddgrs	R	14	5	0	1	37.2	157	37	15	15	1	0	0	1	19	0	26	4	0	3	1	.750	0	0--	-	4.21	3.58
2005	Clmbs	A	30	0	0	9	60.2	254	38	21	13	2	0	1	7	33	0	68	5	0	1	5	.167	0	1--	-	2.62	1.93
2005	VeroB	A+	6	0	0	1	6.2	37	8	7	7	0	0	0	0	10	0	8	0	0	0	0	-	0	0--	-	8.99	9.45
2006	VeroB	A+	26	0	0	15	42.1	174	29	11	7	0	3	0	1	23	1	51	6	0	3	3	.500	0	0--	-	2.37	1.49
2006	Jaxnvl	AA	15	0	0	11	21.1	90	14	13	11	2	1	2	2	11	0	28	4	1	1	1	.500	0	1--	-	2.96	4.64
2007	Jaxnvl	AA	30	1	0	9	61.1	258	45	19	17	4	2	4	0	31	0	67	6	1	6	2	.750	0	2--	-	2.79	2.49
2007	LsVgs	AAA	14	1	0	6	16.2	92	28	23	17	4	2	2	1	18	1	18	2	0	1	2	.333	0	0--	-	13.54	9.18
2008	Hou	NL	71	0	0	15	55.2	250	45	34	31	8	1	1	4	34	4	57	2	1	4	3	.571	0	1-1	13	4.21	5.01

Mike Wuertz

Pitches: R **Bats:** R **Pos:** RP-45   **Ht:** 6'3" **Wt:** 205 **Born:** 12/15/1978 **Age:** 30

Year	Team	Lg	HOW MUCH HE PITCHED						WHAT HE GAVE UP											THE RESULTS						
			G	GS	CG	GF	IP	BFP	H	R	ER	HR	SH	SF	HB	TBB	IBB	SO	WP	Bk	W	L	Pct	ShO	Sv-Op Hld	ERC	ERA
2008	Iowa*	AAA	17	0	0	14	20.0	86	13	8	8	2	1	1	0	14	2	29	4	0	0	1	.000	0	4- - -	3.13	3.60
2004	ChC	NL	31	0	0	11	29.0	124	22	14	14	4	4	2	0	17	1	30	2	1	1	0	1.000	0	1-1 1	3.67	4.34
2005	ChC	NL	75	0	0	12	75.2	319	60	36	32	6	3	2	0	40	7	89	7	0	6	2	.750	0	0-3 18	3.17	3.81
2006	ChC	NL	41	0	0	4	40.2	175	35	14	12	5	3	0	1	16	2	42	1	0	3	1	.750	0	0-1 6	3.37	2.66
2007	ChC	NL	73	0	0	19	72.1	312	64	30	28	8	3	1	0	35	6	79	6	0	2	3	.400	0	0-0 8	3.68	3.48
2008	ChC	NL	45	0	0	13	44.2	189	44	23	18	4	1	3	0	20	2	30	2	0	1	1	.500	0	0-3 3	4.15	3.63
	Postseason		2	0	0	0	1.2	7	0	0	0	0	0	0	0	1	0	2	1	0	0	0	-	0	0-0 0	0.32	0.00
	5 ML YEARS		265	0	0	59	262.1	1119	225	117	104	27	14	8	1	128	18	270	18	1	13	7	.650	0	1-8 36	3.56	3.57

Keiichi Yabu

Pitches: R **Bats:** R **Pos:** RP-60   **Ht:** 6'1" **Wt:** 232 **Born:** 9/28/1968 **Age:** 40

Year	Team	Lg	HOW MUCH HE PITCHED						WHAT HE GAVE UP											THE RESULTS						
			G	GS	CG	GF	IP	BFP	H	R	ER	HR	SH	SF	HB	TBB	IBB	SO	WP	Bk	W	L	Pct	ShO	Sv-Op Hld	ERC	ERA
1994	Hnshn	Jap	26	25	8	-	181.1	762	174	67	64	12	-	-	2	42	-	110	2	1	9	9	.500	1	0- - -	2.97	3.18
1995	Hnshn	Jap	27	27	7	0	196.0	833	185	73	65	19	-	-	10	50	-	118	4	1	7	13	.350	2	0- - -	3.31	2.98
1996	Hnshn	Jap	30	30	6	0	195.1	852	204	97	87	14	-	-	11	51	-	145	1	1	11	14	.440	1	0- - -	3.71	4.01
1997	Hnshn	Jap	29	22	4	-	183.0	794	172	79	73	23	-	-	11	62	-	111	9	0	10	12	.455	1	0- - -	3.83	3.59
1998	Hnshn	Jap	24	24	3	0	164.0	710	159	74	64	11	-	-	8	51	-	90	4	2	11	10	.524	2	0- - -	3.44	3.51
1999	Hnshn	Jap	28	27	4	-	173.1	763	175	80	76	16	-	-	11	57	-	95	4	0	6	16	.273	2	0- - -	3.95	3.95
2000	Hnshn	Jap	25	24	1	-	151.0	649	162	76	70	19	-	-	4	30	-	95	7	0	6	10	.375	1	0- - -	3.88	4.17
2001	Hnshn	Jap	17	8	0	-	55.0	258	55	32	25	2	-	-	5	33	-	26	5	0	4	4	.000	0	0- - -	4.61	4.09
2002	Hnshn	Jap	20	15	5	-	131.2	549	118	48	46	14	-	-	6	30	-	97	3	0	10	6	.625	2	0- - -	3.01	3.14
2003	Hnshn	Jap	23	15	0	-	97.2	419	97	50	43	13	-	-	2	27	-	67	4	0	8	3	.727	0	0- - -	3.77	3.96
2004	Hnshn	Jap	19	19	1	0	116.1	499	108	44	33	8	-	-	6	36	-	75	5	0	6	9	.400	1	0- - -	3.25	2.55
2008	Fresno	AAA	3	0	0	1	5.0	25	4	1	1	0	1	0	0	6	0	7	2	1	0	0	-	0	0- - -	5.08	1.80
2005	Oak	AL	40	0	0	15	58.0	262	64	34	29	6	2	3	8	26	3	44	2	0	4	0	1.000	0	1-2 1	5.45	4.50
2008	SF	NL	60	0	0	10	68.0	302	63	33	27	3	3	0	8	32	4	48	5	1	3	6	.333	0	0-1 9	3.86	3.57
	2 ML YEARS		100	0	0	25	126.0	564	127	67	56	9	5	3	16	58	7	92	7	1	7	6	.538	0	1-3 10	4.57	4.00

Yasuhiko Yabuta

Pitches: R **Bats:** R **Pos:** RP-31   **Ht:** 6'2" **Wt:** 185 **Born:** 6/19/1973 **Age:** 36

Year	Team	Lg	HOW MUCH HE PITCHED						WHAT HE GAVE UP											THE RESULTS						
			G	GS	CG	GF	IP	BFP	H	R	ER	HR	SH	SF	HB	TBB	IBB	SO	WP	Bk	W	L	Pct	ShO	Sv-Op Hld	ERC	ERA
1996	Chiba	Jap	18	11	1	3	92.0	376	79	39	37	8	-	-	3	29	-	58	5	0	4	6	.400	0	0- - -	3.07	3.62
1997	Chiba	Jap	25	24	4	0	146.1	621	144	69	64	16	-	-	3	48	-	74	7	2	5	9	.357	0	0- - -	3.85	3.94
1998	Chiba	Jap	17	16	2	0	100.1	448	123	61	54	15	-	-	1	40	-	45	8	6	2	9	.182	0	0- - -	5.91	4.84
1999	Chiba	Jap	12	10	0	1	57.0	260	68	33	31	9	-	-	2	30	-	33	3	1	5	4	.556	0	0- - -	6.48	4.89
2000	Chiba	Jap	2	2	0	0	6.2	31	9	10	10	3	-	-	0	2	-	3	0	0	0	1	.000	0	0- - -	8.30	13.50
2001	Chiba	Jap	27	13	0	8	97.1	414	94	46	42	15	-	-	3	40	-	70	4	0	4	6	.400	0	0- - -	4.51	3.88
2002	Chiba	Jap	3	3	0	0	11.1	52	16	11	11	4	-	-	0	4	-	8	0	0	1	2	.333	0	0- - -	8.57	8.74
2003	Chiba	Jap	17	13	0	1	68.2	304	74	45	45	12	-	-	2	27	-	44	3	0	5	6	.455	0	0- - -	5.13	5.90
2004	Chiba	Jap	66	1	0	24	77.1	328	62	26	24	4	5	2	3	34	4	71	2	1	3	4	.429	0	2- - -	2.86	2.79
2005	Chiba	Jap	51	0	0	15	55.2	220	42	20	19	7	4	0	2	13	1	54	1	0	7	4	.636	0	2- - -	2.45	3.07
2006	Chiba	Jap	47	0	0	16	55.0	232	43	19	16	3	6	3	0	26	4	48	0	0	4	2	.667	0	1- - -	2.73	2.62
2007	Chiba	Jap	58	0	0	-	62.2	264	64	21	19	5	-	-	2	10	2	45	1	0	4	6	.400	0	4- - -	3.13	2.73
2008	Omha	AAA	20	0	0	15	40.1	178	46	24	24	3	3	1	0	16	0	33	1	0	4	3	.571	0	3- - -	4.70	5.36
2008	KC	AL	31	0	0	12	37.2	168	41	21	20	6	1	1	0	17	0	25	1	0	1	3	.250	0	0-1 0	5.21	4.78

Tyler Yates

Pitches: R **Bats:** R **Pos:** RP-72   **Ht:** 6'4" **Wt:** 240 **Born:** 8/7/1977 **Age:** 31

Year	Team	Lg	HOW MUCH HE PITCHED						WHAT HE GAVE UP											THE RESULTS						
			G	GS	CG	GF	IP	BFP	H	R	ER	HR	SH	SF	HB	TBB	IBB	SO	WP	Bk	W	L	Pct	ShO	Sv-Op Hld	ERC	ERA
2004	NYM	NL	21	7	0	2	46.2	228	61	36	33	6	2	2	3	25	3	35	1	1	2	4	.333	0	0-0 2	6.73	6.36
2006	Atl	NL	56	0	0	11	50.0	217	42	23	22	6	2	0	0	31	8	46	1	0	2	5	.286	0	1-6 12	3.95	3.96
2007	Atl	NL	75	0	0	14	66.0	294	64	44	38	6	4	1	3	31	8	69	2	0	2	3	.400	0	2-3 13	4.02	5.18
2008	Pit	NL	72	0	0	16	73.1	331	72	39	38	6	4	1	2	41	4	63	5	0	6	3	.667	0	1-5 14	4.43	4.66
	4 ML YEARS		224	7	0	43	236.0	1070	239	142	131	24	12	4	8	128	23	213	9	1	12	15	.444	0	4-14 41	4.64	5.00

Kevin Youkilis

Bats: R **Throws:** R **Pos:** 1B-126; 3B-36; RF-2; PR-1   **Ht:** 6'1" **Wt:** 220 **Born:** 3/15/1979 **Age:** 30

Year	Team	Lg	BATTING																		BASERUNNING				AVERAGES		
			G	AB	H	2B	3B	HR	(Hm	Rd)	TB	R	RBI	RC	TBB	IBB	SO	HBP	SH	SF	SB	CS	SB%	GDP	Avg	OBP	Slg
2004	Bos	AL	72	208	54	11	0	7	(2	5)	86	38	35	36	33	0	45	4	0	3	0	1	.00	1	.260	.367	.413
2005	Bos	AL	44	79	22	7	0	1	(0	1)	32	11	9	13	14	0	19	2	0	0	0	1	.00	0	.278	.400	.405
2006	Bos	AL	147	569	159	42	2	13	(6	7)	244	100	72	104	91	0	120	9	0	11	5	2	.71	12	.279	.381	.429
2007	Bos	AL	145	528	152	35	2	16	(8	8)	239	85	83	101	77	0	105	15	0	5	4	2	.67	9	.288	.390	.453
2008	Bos	AL	145	538	168	43	4	29	(17	12)	306	91	115	120	62	7	108	12	0	9	3	5	.38	11	.312	.390	.569
	Postseason		15	51	19	4	1	4	(2	2)	37	16	10	15	9	0	9	0	0	0	0	0	-	2	.373	.459	.725
	5 ML YEARS		553	1922	555	138	8	66	(33	33)	907	325	314	374	277	7	397	42	0	28	12	11	.52	33	.289	.385	.472

Chris Young

Pitches: R Bats: R Pos: SP-18   Ht: 6'10" Wt: 278 Born: 5/25/1979 Age: 30

Year Team	Lg	G	GS	CG	GF	IP	BFP	H	R	ER	HR	SH	SF	HB	TBB	IBB	SO	WP	Bk	W	L	Pct	ShO	Sv-Op	Hld	ERC	ERA
		HOW MUCH HE PITCHED						WHAT HE GAVE UP												THE RESULTS							
2008 Lk Els*	A+	2	2	0	0	8.2	32	5	3	3	3	0	0	0	1	0	7	0	0	0	1	.000	0	0--	-	2.06	3.12
2004 Tex	AL	7	7	0	0	36.1	158	36	21	19	7	1	0	2	10	0	27	1	0	3	2	.600	0	0-0	0	4.26	4.71
2005 Tex	AL	31	31	0	0	164.2	700	162	84	78	19	2	4	7	45	2	137	3	0	12	7	.632	0	0-0	0	3.71	4.26
2006 SD	NL	31	31	0	0	179.1	735	134	72	69	28	8	3	6	69	4	164	6	1	11	5	.688	0	0-0	0	3.12	3.46
2007 SD	NL	30	30	0	0	173.0	705	118	66	60	10	3	6	7	72	0	167	7	4	9	8	.529	0	0-0	0	2.35	3.12
2008 SD	NL	18	18	1	0	102.1	434	84	46	45	13	4	1	1	48	4	93	3	1	7	6	.538	0	0-0	0	3.50	3.96
Postseason		1	1	0	0	6.2	25	4	0	0	0	0	0	0	2	1	9	0	0	1	0	1.000	0			1.22	0.00
5 ML YEARS		117	117	1	0	655.2	2732	534	289	271	77	18	14	23	244	10	588	20	6	42	28	.600	0	0-0	0	3.18	3.72

Chris Young

Bats: R Throws: R Pos: CF-159; PH-2   Ht: 6'2" Wt: 200 Born: 9/5/1983 Age: 25

Year Team	Lg	G	AB	H	2B	3B	HR	(Hm	Rd)	TB	R	RBI	RC	TBB	IBB	SO	HBP	SH	SF	SB	CS	SB%	GDP	Avg	OBP	Slg
		BATTING																		BASERUNNING				AVERAGES		
2006 Ari	NL	30	70	17	4	0	2	(1	1)	27	10	10	11	6	0	12	1	0	1	2	1	.67	0	.243	.308	.386
2007 Ari	NL	148	569	135	29	3	32	(14	18)	266	85	68	68	43	1	141	6	1	5	27	6	.82	5	.237	.295	.467
2008 Ari	NL	160	625	155	42	7	22	(9	13)	277	85	85	84	62	2	165	1	6	5	14	5	.74	10	.248	.315	.443
Postseason		7	25	7	1	0	2	(1	1)	14	4	5	7	7	0	13	1	0	0	1	2	.33	0	.280	.455	.560
3 ML YEARS		338	1264	307	75	10	56	(24	32)	570	180	163	163	111	3	318	8	7	11	43	12	.78	15	.243	.306	.451

Delmon Young

Bats: R Throws: R Pos: LF-151; PH-1; PR-1   Ht: 6'3" Wt: 200 Born: 9/14/1985 Age: 23

Year Team	Lg	G	AB	H	2B	3B	HR	(Hm	Rd)	TB	R	RBI	RC	TBB	IBB	SO	HBP	SH	SF	SB	CS	SB%	GDP	Avg	OBP	Slg
		BATTING																		BASERUNNING				AVERAGES		
2006 TB	AL	30	126	40	9	1	3	(1	2)	60	16	10	15	1	0	24	3	0	1	2	2	.50	0	.317	.336	.476
2007 TB	AL	162	645	186	38	4	13	(9	4)	263	65	93	90	26	2	127	3	0	7	10	3	.77	23	.288	.316	.408
2008 Min	AL	152	575	167	28	4	10	(7	3)	233	80	69	74	35	7	105	7	1	5	14	5	.74	19	.290	.336	.405
3 ML YEARS		344	1346	393	75	5	26	(17	9)	556	161	172	179	62	9	256	13	1	13	26	10	.72	42	.292	.326	.413

Delwyn Young

Bats: B Throws: R Pos: PH-58; LF-15; RF-11; 2B-5; PR-2; DH-1   Ht: 5'10" Wt: 209 Born: 6/30/1982 Age: 27

Year Team	Lg	G	AB	H	2B	3B	HR	(Hm	Rd)	TB	R	RBI	RC	TBB	IBB	SO	HBP	SH	SF	SB	CS	SB%	GDP	Avg	OBP	Slg
		BATTING																		BASERUNNING				AVERAGES		
2008 LsVgs*	AAA	13	49	17	5	1	3	(-	-)	33	14	10	13	7	0	8	0	0	0	0	0	-	5	.347	.429	.673
2006 LAD	NL	8	5	0	0	0	0	(0	0)	0	0	0	0	0	0	1	0	0	0	0	0	-	0	.000	.000	.000
2007 LAD	NL	19	34	13	1	1	2	(2	0)	22	4	3	8	2	0	5	0	0	0	1	0	1.00	0	.382	.417	.647
2008 LAD	NL	83	126	31	9	0	1	(1	0)	43	10	7	11	14	0	34	0	3	0	0	0	-	2	.246	.321	.341
3 ML YEARS		110	165	44	10	1	3	(3	0)	65	14	10	19	16	0	40	0	3	0	1	0	1.00	2	.267	.331	.394

Dmitri Young

Bats: B Throws: R Pos: 1B-38; PH-7; DH-6   Ht: 6'2" Wt: 298 Born: 10/11/1973 Age: 35

Year Team	Lg	G	AB	H	2B	3B	HR	(Hm	Rd)	TB	R	RBI	RC	TBB	IBB	SO	HBP	SH	SF	SB	CS	SB%	GDP	Avg	OBP	Slg
		BATTING																		BASERUNNING				AVERAGES		
2008 Hrsbrg*	AA	3	8	3	1	0	0	(-	-)	4	0	0	2	3	0	1	0	0	0	0	0	-	0	.375	.545	.500
2008 Vrmnt*	A-	5	12	4	2	0	0	(-	-)	6	0	2	1	0	0	0	0	0	0	0	0	-	0	.333	.333	.500
1996 StL	NL	16	29	7	0	0	0	(0	0)	7	3	2	2	4	0	5	1	0	0	0	1	.00	1	.241	.353	.241
1997 StL	NL	110	333	86	14	3	5	(2	3)	121	38	34	40	38	3	63	2	1	3	6	5	.55	8	.258	.335	.363
1998 Cin	NL	144	536	166	48	1	14	(3	11)	258	81	83	88	47	4	94	2	0	5	2	4	.33	16	.310	.364	.481
1999 Cin	NL	127	373	112	30	2	14	(9	5)	188	63	56	63	30	1	71	2	0	4	3	1	.75	11	.300	.352	.504
2000 Cin	NL	152	548	166	37	6	18	(6	12)	269	68	88	86	36	6	80	3	1	5	0	3	.00	16	.303	.346	.491
2001 Cin	NL	142	540	163	28	3	21	(8	13)	260	68	69	83	37	10	77	5	1	3	8	5	.62	22	.302	.350	.481
2002 Det	AL	54	201	57	14	0	7	(5	2)	92	25	27	27	12	5	39	2	0	1	2	0	1.00	16	.284	.329	.458
2003 Det	AL	155	562	167	34	7	29	(10	19)	302	78	85	101	58	16	130	11	0	4	2	1	.67	16	.297	.372	.537
2004 Det	AL	104	389	106	23	2	18	(8	10)	187	72	60	57	33	4	71	6	0	4	0	1	.00	8	.272	.336	.481
2005 Det	AL	126	469	127	25	3	21	(10	11)	221	61	72	60	29	7	100	9	0	1	1	0	1.00	16	.271	.325	.471
2006 Det	AL	48	172	43	4	1	7	(2	5)	70	19	23	20	11	0	39	0	0	1	1	1	.50	3	.250	.293	.407
2007 Was	NL	136	460	147	38	1	13	(7	6)	226	57	74	74	44	6	74	1	0	3	0	0	-	13	.320	.378	.491
2008 Was	NL	50	150	42	6	0	4	(1	3)	60	15	10	16	28	4	28	1	0	1	0	0	-	8	.280	.394	.400
Postseason		4	7	2	0	1	0	(0	0)	4	1	2	1	0	0	2	0	0	0	0	0	-	0	.286	.286	.571
13 ML YEARS		1364	4762	1389	301	29	171	(71	100)	2261	648	683	717	407	66	871	45	3	35	25	22	.53	150	.292	.351	.475

Michael Young

Bats: R Throws: R Pos: SS-152; DH-3; PH-1   Ht: 6'1" Wt: 200 Born: 10/19/1976 Age: 32

Year Team	Lg	G	AB	H	2B	3B	HR	(Hm	Rd)	TB	R	RBI	RC	TBB	IBB	SO	HBP	SH	SF	SB	CS	SB%	GDP	Avg	OBP	Slg
		BATTING																		BASERUNNING				AVERAGES		
2000 Tex	AL	2	2	0	0	0	0	(0	0)	0	0	0	0	0	0	1	0	0	0	0	0	-	0	.000	.000	.000
2001 Tex	AL	106	386	96	18	4	11	(7	4)	155	57	49	45	26	0	91	3	9	5	3	1	.75	9	.249	.298	.402
2002 Tex	AL	156	573	150	26	8	9	(3	6)	219	77	62	64	41	1	112	0	13	6	6	7	.46	14	.262	.308	.382
2003 Tex	AL	160	666	204	33	9	14	(9	5)	297	106	72	106	36	1	103	1	3	7	13	2	.87	14	.306	.339	.446
2004 Tex	AL	160	690	216	33	9	22	(9	13)	333	114	99	124	44	1	89	1	0	4	12	3	.80	11	.313	.353	.483
2005 Tex	AL	159	668	221	40	5	24	(12	12)	343	114	91	131	58	0	91	3	0	3	5	2	.71	20	.331	.385	.513

Year	Team	Lg	G	AB	H	2B	3B	HR	(Hm	Rd)	TB	R	RBI	RC	TBB	IBB	SO	HBP	SH	SF	SB	CS	SB%	GDP	Avg	OBP	Slg
									BATTING												BASERUNNING				AVERAGES		
2006	Tex	AL	162	691	217	52	3	14	(8	6)	317	93	103	120	48	0	96	1	0	8	7	3	.70	27	.314	.356	.459
2007	Tex	AL	156	639	201	37	1	9	(8	1)	267	80	94	107	47	5	107	5	0	1	13	3	.81	21	.315	.366	.418
2008	Tex	AL	155	645	183	36	2	12	(8	4)	259	102	82	86	55	0	109	2	0	6	10	0	1.00	19	.284	.339	.402
9 ML YEARS			1216	4960	1488	275	41	115	(64	51)	2190	743	652	783	355	8	799	16	25	40	69	21	.77	135	.300	.346	.442

Carlos Zambrano

Pitches: R Bats: B Pos: SP-30

Ht: 6'5" Wt: 255 Born: 6/1/1981 Age: 28

Year	Team	Lg	G	GS	CG	GF	IP	BFP	H	R	ER	HR	SH	SF	HB	TBB	IBB	SO	WP	Bk	W	L	Pct	ShO	Sv-Op	Hld	ERC	ERA
			HOW MUCH HE PITCHED						WHAT HE GAVE UP												THE RESULTS							
2001	ChC	NL	6	1	0	1	7.2	42	11	13	13	2	1	1	1	8	0	4	1	0	1	2	.333	0	0-1	0	11.86	15.26
2002	ChC	NL	32	16	0	3	108.1	477	94	53	44	9	9	1	4	63	2	93	6	0	4	8	.333	0	0-0	0	4.02	3.66
2003	ChC	NL	32	32	3	0	214.0	907	188	88	74	9	11	6	10	94	12	168	6	0	13	11	.542	1	0-0	0	3.28	3.11
2004	ChC	NL	31	31	1	0	209.2	887	174	73	64	14	10	3	20	81	4	188	6	2	16	8	.667	1	0-0	0	3.20	2.75
2005	ChC	NL	33	33	2	0	223.1	909	170	88	81	21	9	5	8	86	3	202	7	0	14	6	.700	0	0-0	0	2.86	3.26
2006	ChC	NL	33	33	0	0	214.0	917	162	91	81	20	11	4	9	115	4	210	9	1	16	7	.696	0	0-0	0	3.34	3.41
2007	ChC	NL	34	34	1	0	216.1	925	187	100	95	23	6	3	14	101	4	177	3	0	18	13	.581	0	0-0	0	3.88	3.95
2008	ChC	NL	30	30	1	0	188.2	796	172	85	82	18	5	0	6	72	1	130	4	0	14	6	.700	1	0-0	0	3.62	3.91
Postseason			4	4	0	0	22.2	102	29	12	11	5	1	1	1	6	0	20	1	0	0	1	.000	0	0-0	0	6.24	4.37
8 ML YEARS			231	210	8	4	1382.0	5860	1158	591	534	116	62	23	72	620	30	1172	42	4	96	61	.611	3	0-1	0	3.44	3.48

Gregg Zaun

Bats: B Throws: R Pos: C-79; PH-8; DH-3

Ht: 5'10" Wt: 190 Born: 4/14/1971 Age: 38

Year	Team	Lg	G	AB	H	2B	3B	HR	(Hm	Rd)	TB	R	RBI	RC	TBB	IBB	SO	HBP	SH	SF	SB	CS	SB%	GDP	Avg	OBP	Slg
									BATTING												BASERUNNING				AVERAGES		
2008	Syrcse*	AAA	2	8	2	0	0	1	(-	-)	5	1	1	1	0	0	2	0	0	0	0	0	-	1	.250	.250	.625
1995	Bal	AL	40	104	27	5	0	3	(1	2)	41	18	14	15	16	0	14	0	2	0	1	1	.50	2	.260	.358	.394
1996	2 Tms		60	139	34	9	1	2	(1	1)	51	20	15	16	14	3	20	2	1	2	1	0	1.00	5	.245	.318	.367
1997	Fla	NL	58	143	43	10	2	2	(0	2)	63	21	20	27	26	4	18	2	1	0	1	0	1.00	3	.301	.415	.441
1998	Fla	NL	106	298	56	12	2	5	(2	3)	87	19	29	23	35	2	52	1	2	2	5	2	.71	7	.188	.274	.292
1999	Tex	AL	43	93	23	2	1	1	(0	1)	30	12	12	10	10	0	7	0	1	2	1	0	1.00	4	.247	.314	.323
2000	KC	AL	83	234	64	11	0	7	(2	5)	96	36	33	40	43	3	34	3	0	2	7	3	.70	4	.274	.390	.410
2001	KC	AL	39	125	40	9	0	6	(1	5)	67	15	18	24	12	0	16	0	0	1	1	2	.33	2	.320	.377	.536
2002	Hou	NL	76	185	41	7	1	3	(3	0)	59	18	24	17	12	1	36	2	2	1	1	0	1.00	4	.222	.275	.319
2003	2 Tms	NL	74	166	38	8	0	4	(1	3)	58	15	21	20	19	0	21	1	1	2	1	1	.50	5	.229	.309	.349
2004	Tor	AL	107	338	91	24	0	6	(2	4)	133	46	36	50	47	3	61	6	0	1	0	2	-	4	.269	.367	.393
2005	Tor	AL	133	434	109	18	1	11	(7	4)	162	61	61	65	73	2	70	0	0	5	2	3	.40	11	.251	.355	.373
2006	Tor	AL	99	290	79	19	0	12	(7	5)	134	39	40	41	43	2	42	3	0	5	0	2	.00	10	.272	.363	.462
2007	Tor	AL	110	331	80	24	1	10	(6	4)	136	43	52	48	51	8	55	2	1	6	0	0	-	9	.242	.341	.411
2008	Tor	AL	86	245	58	12	0	6	(5	1)	88	29	30	32	38	1	38	1	3	1	2	1	.67	6	.237	.340	.359
96	Bal	AL	50	108	25	8	1	1	(1	0)	38	16	13	12	11	2	15	2	0	2	0	0	-	3	.231	.309	.352
96	Fla	NL	10	31	9	1	0	1	(0	1)	13	4	2	4	3	1	5	0	1	0	1	0	1.00	2	.290	.353	.419
03	Hou	NL	59	120	26	7	0	1	(1	0)	36	9	13	12	14	0	14	1	1	2	1	0	1.00	5	.217	.299	.300
03	Col	NL	15	46	12	1	0	3	(0	3)	22	6	8	8	5	0	7	0	0	0	0	1	.00	0	.261	.333	.478
Postseason			3	2	0	0	0	0	(0	0)	0	0	0	0	0	0	0	0	0	0	0	0	-	0	.000	.000	.000
14 ML YEARS			1114	3125	783	170	9	78	(38	40)	1205	392	405	428	437	30	484	23	14	30	23	17	.58	77	.251	.344	.386

Brad Ziegler

Pitches: R Bats: R Pos: RP-47

Ht: 6'4" Wt: 200 Born: 10/10/1979 Age: 29

Year	Team	Lg	G	GS	CG	GF	IP	BFP	H	R	ER	HR	SH	SF	HB	TBB	IBB	SO	WP	Bk	W	L	Pct	ShO	Sv-Op	Hld	ERC	ERA
			HOW MUCH HE PITCHED						WHAT HE GAVE UP												THE RESULTS							
2003	Batvia	A-	3	0	0	1	6.0	23	5	1	1	0	0	0	0	1	0	6	0	0	1	0	1.000	0	0- -	-	1.84	1.50
2004	Schbrg	IND	4	4	1	0	24.0	84	12	5	4	0	1	0	2	1	0	26	0	0	3	0	1.000	0	0- -	-	0.76	1.50
2004	Mdest	A+	16	15	0	1	92.1	389	94	51	40	11	4	2	2	22	0	77	0	1	9	2	.818	0	0- -	-	3.74	3.90
2005	Mdland	AA	4	4	0	0	21.0	96	27	16	16	1	1	1	3	4	0	20	1	0	2	1	.667	0	0- -	-	4.98	6.86
2005	Stcktn	A+	24	24	0	0	141.0	605	166	84	73	13	1	2	6	20	0	144	4	0	9	7	.563	0	0- -	-	4.13	4.66
2006	Mdland	AA	23	22	1	0	141.2	596	151	60	53	17	5	5	7	37	0	88	3	1	9	6	.600	0	0- -	-	4.32	3.37
2006	Scrmto	AAA	4	4	0	0	21.0	97	32	17	14	3	1	1	1	5	0	11	1	0	0	1	.000	0	0- -	-	7.24	6.00
2007	Mdland	AA	15	0	0	4	23.2	94	19	6	3	0	1	2	0	4	0	18	0	0	4	0	1.000	0	1- -	-	1.64	1.14
2007	Scrmto	AAA	35	0	0	5	54.2	218	46	20	18	0	2	1	2	14	0	44	0	1	8	3	.727	0	1- -	-	2.27	2.96
2008	Scrmto	AAA	19	0	0	14	24.1	91	15	2	1	0	1	0	0	4	1	20	0	0	2	0	1.000	0	8- -	-	1.07	0.37
2008	Oak	AL	47	0	0	21	59.2	229	47	8	7	2	4	3	1	22	3	30	0	0	3	0	1.000	0	11-13	9	2.60	1.06

Ryan Zimmerman

Bats: R Throws: R Pos: 3B-104; PH-2

Ht: 6'3" Wt: 228 Born: 9/28/1984 Age: 24

Year	Team	Lg	G	AB	H	2B	3B	HR	(Hm	Rd)	TB	R	RBI	RC	TBB	IBB	SO	HBP	SH	SF	SB	CS	SB%	GDP	Avg	OBP	Slg
									BATTING												BASERUNNING				AVERAGES		
2008	Ptomc*	A+	2	10	3	2	0	0	(-	-)	5	1	0	1	0	0	1	0	0	0	0	0	-	0	.300	.300	.500
2008	Clmbs*	AAA	4	15	4	1	0	1	(-	-)	8	4	3	2	2	1	3	0	0	0	0	0	-	0	.267	.353	.533
2005	Was	NL	20	58	23	10	0	0	(0	0)	33	6	6	9	3	0	12	0	0	1	0	0	-	1	.397	.419	.569
2006	Was	NL	157	614	176	47	3	20	(10	10)	289	84	110	101	61	7	120	2	1	4	11	8	.58	15	.287	.351	.471
2007	Was	NL	162	653	174	43	5	24	(11	13)	299	99	91	83	61	3	125	3	0	5	4	1	.80	26	.266	.330	.458
2008	Was	NL	106	428	121	24	1	14	(7	7)	189	51	51	48	31	1	71	3	0	4	1	1	.50	12	.283	.333	.442
4 ML YEARS			445	1753	494	124	9	58	(28	30)	810	240	258	241	156	11	328	8	1	14	16	10	.62	54	.282	.341	.462

Charlie Zink

Pitches: R Bats: R Pos: SP-1   Ht: 6'1" Wt: 190 Born: 8/26/1979 Age: 29

		HOW MUCH HE PITCHED						WHAT HE GAVE UP											THE RESULTS						
Year	Team	Lg	G	GS	CG	GF	IP	BFP	H	R	ER	HR	SH	SF	HB	TBB	IBB	SO	WP	Bk	W	L	Pct	ShO	Sv-Op	Hld	ERC	ERA
2001	Yuma	IND	4	0	0	2	5.0	23	4	3	3	1	1	1	0	4	0	6	1	0	0	0	-	0	0--	-	5.17	5.40
2002	Augsta	A	26	0	0	10	48.1	200	42	17	9	1	2	3	4	16	0	48	2	0	1	2	.333	0	0--	-	2.94	1.68
2002	Srsota	A+	4	0	0	2	9.0	33	2	1	0	0	1	1	0	3	1	11	0	0	0	0	-	0	0--	-	0.38	0.00
2003	Srsota	A+	24	19	2	0	136.0	576	123	69	59	10	0	6	4	64	0	94	3	1	7	9	.438	0	0--	-	3.83	3.90
2003	Portlnd	AA	6	6	0	0	39.1	159	21	16	15	1	1	1	7	14	0	18	2	0	3	2	.600	0	0--	-	1.72	3.43
2004	Portlnd	AA	18	18	0	0	93.1	442	101	70	60	3	4	4	7	72	0	50	4	1	1	8	.111	0	0--	-	5.90	5.79
2004	Srsota	A+	3	3	0	0	14.1	66	22	13	9	0	1	2	0	9	0	3	2	0	0	2	.000	0	0--	-	8.17	5.65
2005	Portlnd	AA	29	15	1	7	105.1	464	102	65	57	12	4	7	9	53	1	70	0	0	8	5	.615	1	0--	-	4.80	4.87
2005	Pwtckt	AAA	4	1	0	0	10.1	53	17	12	12	1	0	0	1	8	0	5	1	0	2	1	.667	0	0--	-	10.75	10.45
2006	Pwtckt	AAA	2	1	0	0	7.1	33	6	3	1	1	0	0	0	5	0	7	0	0	1	0	1.000	0	0--	-	4.33	1.23
2006	Pwtckt	AAA	23	15	0	2	109.1	475	100	54	49	7	2	2	6	60	0	58	5	2	9	4	.692	0	0--	-	4.21	4.03
2007	Pwtckt	AAA	16	16	1	0	92.2	407	92	50	41	6	2	4	10	44	0	55	3	0	9	3	.750	0	0--	-	4.58	3.98
2007	Pwtckt	AAA	8	8	0	0	47.1	224	51	37	31	8	0	1	5	27	0	23	2	0	2	3	.400	0	0--	-	6.09	5.89
2008	Pwtckt	AAA	28	28	2	0	174.1	716	144	73	56	13	5	6	11	49	0	106	8	0	14	6	.700	1	0--	-	2.77	2.89
2008	Bos	AL	1	1	0	0	4.1	25	11	8	8	0	0	0	0	1	0	1	1	0	0	0	-	0	0-0	0	12.25	16.62

Barry Zito

Pitches: L Bats: L Pos: SP-32   Ht: 6'4" Wt: 206 Born: 5/13/1978 Age: 31

		HOW MUCH HE PITCHED						WHAT HE GAVE UP											THE RESULTS						
Year	Team	Lg	G	GS	CG	GF	IP	BFP	H	R	ER	HR	SH	SF	HB	TBB	IBB	SO	WP	Bk	W	L	Pct	ShO	Sv-Op	Hld	ERC	ERA
2000	Oak	AL	14	14	1	0	92.2	376	64	30	28	6	1	0	2	45	2	78	2	0	7	4	.636	1	0-0	0	2.63	2.72
2001	Oak	AL	35	35	3	0	214.1	902	184	92	83	18	5	4	13	80	0	205	6	1	17	8	.680	2	0-0	0	3.33	3.49
2002	Oak	AL	35	35	1	0	229.1	939	182	79	70	24	9	7	9	78	2	182	2	1	23	5	.821	0	0-0	0	2.92	2.75
2003	Oak	AL	35	35	4	0	231.2	957	186	98	85	19	7	7	6	88	3	146	4	0	14	12	.538	1	0-0	0	2.91	3.30
2004	Oak	AL	34	34	0	0	213.0	926	216	116	106	28	7	9	9	81	2	163	4	1	11	11	.500	0	0-0	0	4.45	4.48
2005	Oak	AL	35	35	0	0	228.1	953	185	106	98	26	8	7	13	89	0	171	4	0	14	13	.519	0	0-0	0	3.32	3.86
2006	Oak	AL	34	34	0	0	221.0	945	211	99	94	27	7	6	13	99	5	151	4	2	16	10	.615	0	0-0	0	4.47	3.83
2007	SF	NL	34	33	0	0	196.2	850	182	105	99	24	12	4	4	83	4	131	5	0	11	13	.458	0	0-0	0	3.91	4.53
2008	SF	NL	32	32	0	0	180.0	818	186	115	103	16	8	14	4	102	10	120	3	0	10	17	.370	0	0-0	0	4.81	5.15
	Postseason		7	7	0	0	44.1	184	34	16	16	6	1	0	3	17	0	33	1	0	4	3	.571	0	0-0	0	3.24	3.25
	9 ML YEARS		288	287	9	0	1807.0	7666	1596	840	766	188	64	58	73	745	28	1347	34	5	123	93	.569	4	0-0	0	3.65	3.82

Ben Zobrist

Bats: B Throws: R Pos: SS-35; LF-14; PH-10; 2B-8; CF-5; RF-2; DH-2; 3B-1   Ht: 6'3" Wt: 200 Born: 5/26/1981 Age: 28

			BATTING																			BASERUNNING				AVERAGES		
Year	Team	Lg	G	AB	H	2B	3B	HR	(Hm	Rd)	TB	R	RBI	RC	TBB	IBB	SO	HBP	SH	SF	SB	CS	SB%	GDP	Avg	OBP	Slg
2008	VeroB*	A+	4	14	4	1	0	0	(-	-)	5	1	2	1	0	0	2	0	0	1	0	0	-	-	.286	.267	.357
2008	Drhm*	AAA	20	71	26	2	0	0	(-	-)	40	15	13	19	15	0	16	0	1	1	4	1	.80	0	.366	.471	.563
2006	TB	AL	52	183	41	6	2	2	(2	0)	57	10	18	13	10	1	26	0	2	3	2	3	.40	2	.224	.260	.311
2007	TB	AL	31	97	15	2	0	1	(0	1)	20	8	9	0	3	0	21	1	2	2	2	0	1.00	1	.155	.184	.206
2008	TB	AL	62	198	50	10	2	12	(4	8)	100	32	30	31	25	1	37	2	0	2	3	0	1.00	4	.253	.339	.505
	3 ML YEARS		145	478	106	18	4	15	(6	9)	177	50	57	44	38	2	84	3	4	7	7	3	.70	7	.222	.279	.370

Joel Zumaya

Pitches: R Bats: R Pos: RP-21   Ht: 6'3" Wt: 210 Born: 11/9/1984 Age: 24

			HOW MUCH HE PITCHED						WHAT HE GAVE UP											THE RESULTS						
Year	Team	Lg	G	GS	CG	GF	IP	BFP	H	R	ER	HR	SH	SF	HB	TBB	IBB	SO	WP	Bk	W	L	Pct	ShO	Sv-Op	Hld	ERC	ERA
2008	Lkland*	A+	2	0	0	1	3.0	11	1	0	0	0	0	0	0	1	0	2	0	0	0	0	-	0	0--	-	0.69	0.00
2008	Toledo*	AAA	4	0	0	0	4.0	20	5	3	1	0	0	0	0	2	0	4	0	0	0	0	-	0	0--	-	4.72	2.25
2006	Det	AL	62	0	0	12	83.1	350	56	20	18	6	2	4	2	42	2	97	4	0	6	3	.667	0	1-6	30	2.55	1.94
2007	Det	AL	28	0	0	7	33.2	142	23	16	16	3	1	1	1	17	2	27	3	0	2	3	.400	0	1-5	8	2.68	4.28
2008	Det	AL	21	0	0	5	23.1	114	24	13	9	3	0	1	0	22	4	22	6	0	0	2	.000	0	1-5	5	6.32	3.47
	Postseason		6	0	0	2	6.0	24	2	4	2	0	0	0	0	3	0	6	1	0	0	1	.000	0	0-0	1	0.92	3.00
	3 ML YEARS		111	0	0	24	140.1	606	103	49	43	12	3	6	3	81	8	146	13	0	8	8	.500	0	3-16	43	3.14	2.76

2008 Fielding Statistics

The following pages offer all of the traditional fielding statistics for the 2008 season. But keep in mind, these fielding stats are not official; there will most likely be a few discrepancies when the official, Major League Baseball-sanctioned results arrive later this year. But we had a choice: publish the book in November or wait for the official totals. Well, we hope you'll agree it's worth putting the book out early. Our totals may not be official, but they're no less accurate.

Each position is broken down into "The Regulars" and "The Rest." This way, we get a clearer sense of how the starters at each position compare to one another, and we don't have to sift through the handful of games played by players away from their regular positions. September call-ups and players playing out of position have their own lists, so if you want to know how the LaRoche brothers compared at the infield corners, or how Felipe Lopez performed at six different positions in 2008, we have that too.

The last column for the non-catchers is Range Factor, labeled "Rng." Range Factor is the number of successful chances (putouts plus assists) times nine, divided by the number of defensive innings played.

Don't miss our "Catchers Special" section where we offer catcher statistics like catcher ERA and caught stealing percentages. There are three Molina brothers playing in the big leagues right now—so which one is Mama Molina most proud of?

A few clarifications before you start reading: One, **PCS** is the number of Total Caught Stealing attributed to the pitcher, not to the catcher in question. So **CS%** is the percentage of runners caught stealing not including **PCS**. Two, if you are looking for a pitcher's fielding statistics, you will find them in the "Pitchers Hitting, Fielding & Holding Runners" section. And third, if you are interested in seeing fielding leader boards you can find them for position players in the Leader Board section and in The 2008 Fielding Bible Awards section.

First Basemen - Regulars

Player	Tm	G	GS	Inn	PO	A	E	DP	Pct.	Rng
Kotchman,Casey	TOT	141	135	1210.1	1205	96	2	125	.998	-
Pena,Carlos	TB	132	131	1168.2	991	106	2	117	.998	-
Morneau,Justin	Min	155	155	1363.2	1316	89	4	149	.997	-
Sexson,Richie	TOT	92	78	684.0	646	56	2	58	.997	-
Teixeira,Mark	TOT	153	153	1335.0	1394	99	5	131	.997	-
Helton,Todd	Col	81	81	715.1	830	57	3	79	.997	-
Overbay,Lyle	Tor	156	151	1354.2	1316	155	5	112	.997	-
Garko,Ryan	Cle	121	121	1058.2	1039	80	4	123	.996	-
Berkman,Lance	Hou	152	151	1307.1	1240	132	5	122	.996	-
Youkilis,Kevin	Bos	126	110	984.2	923	87	4	92	.996	-
Gonzalez,Adrian	SD	161	159	1417.1	1306	130	6	129	.996	-
Pujols,Albert	StL	144	140	1215.0	1297	135	6	119	.996	-
Gload,Ross	KC	111	95	878.1	837	43	4	87	.995	-
Millar,Kevin	Bal	130	128	1131.1	1099	110	6	128	.995	-
Delgado,Carlos	NYM	154	154	1376.1	1237	105	8	106	.994	-
Konerko,Paul	CWS	116	116	995.2	1010	75	7	94	.994	-
LaRoche,Adam	Pit	129	128	1135.2	1130	81	8	122	.993	-
Lee,Derrek	ChC	153	152	1339.1	1193	110	9	98	.993	-
Cabrera,Miguel	Det	143	139	1204.0	1117	73	9	116	.992	-
Loney,James	LAD	158	150	1362.2	1364	121	13	123	.991	-
Votto,Joey	Cin	144	138	1223.2	1050	136	11	119	.991	-
Giambi,Jason	NYY	113	112	898.0	870	36	9	77	.990	-
Fielder,Prince	Mil	155	155	1383.2	1369	89	17	132	.988	-
Barton,Daric	Oak	134	124	1121.2	1021	73	13	128	.988	-
Jacobs,Mike	Fla	119	119	927.1	825	62	11	67	.988	-
Howard,Ryan	Phi	159	156	1402.2	1408	101	19	128	.988	-

First Basemen - The Rest

Player	Tm	G	GS	Inn	PO	A	E	DP	Pct.	Rng
Anderson,Marlon	NYM	6	3	26.0	22	4	0	4	1.000	-
Atkins,Garrett	Col	61	60	527.2	551	23	6	55	.990	-
Aubrey,Michael	Cle	12	11	94.1	99	6	0	14	1.000	-
Aurilia,Rich	SF	82	49	477.0	384	26	4	52	.990	-
Ausmus,Brad	Hou	2	0	4.0	5	0	0	0	1.000	-
Aybar,Willy	TB	19	18	155.0	144	11	0	10	1.000	-
Bailey,Jeff	Bos	12	7	67.0	77	3	0	10	1.000	-
Baisley,Jeff	Oak	4	4	33.0	37	1	1	3	.974	-
Baker,Jeff	Col	22	13	128.2	143	5	0	14	1.000	-
Bankston,Wes	Oak	13	12	108.0	104	6	1	10	.991	-
Barajas,Rod	Tor	4	3	27.0	27	5	0	4	1.000	-
Barden,Brian	StL	1	0	1.0	0	0	0	0	-	-
Bautista,Jose	Tor	5	4	27.0	29	0	0	1	1.000	-
Belliard,Ronnie	Was	33	21	201.0	185	14	2	14	.990	-
Betemit,Wilson	NYY	36	21	207.0	191	13	1	23	.995	-
Blake,Casey	Cle	27	17	160.0	171	10	1	20	.995	-
Blake,Casey	LAD	2	2	17.0	27	0	1	2	.964	-
Blalock,Hank	Tex	34	34	296.0	262	13	1	24	.996	-
Blanco,Henry	ChC	1	0	1.2	3	0	0	0	1.000	-
Blum,Geoff	Hou	5	2	24.2	17	1	0	1	1.000	-
Boone,Aaron	Was	54	35	342.0	313	17	1	32	.997	-
Botts,Jason	Tex	8	5	41.0	51	2	2	7	.964	-
Bowen,Rob	Oak	1	0	2.0	2	0	0	2	1.000	-
Bowker,John	SF	71	67	550.1	448	39	6	43	.988	-
Branyan,Russell	Mil	5	2	24.0	26	1	0	3	1.000	-
Broussard,Ben	Tex	26	23	204.0	202	22	3	32	.987	-
Brown,Emil	Oak	1	0	0.1	1	0	0	0	1.000	-
Bruntlett,Eric	Phi	2	2	16.0	18	1	0	2	1.000	-
Burke,Chris	Ari	9	6	63.0	67	4	0	6	1.000	-
Burke,Jamie	Sea	1	0	2.0	4	0	0	1	1.000	-
Buscher,Brian	Min	6	1	14.0	13	0	0	1	1.000	-
Butler,Billy	KC	34	33	260.0	233	9	2	27	.992	-
Cairo,Miguel	Sea	70	37	394.0	414	23	1	43	.998	-
Cantu,Jorge	Fla	66	23	286.2	260	14	2	23	.993	-
Casey,Sean	Bos	45	40	342.2	331	13	3	25	.991	-
Casto,Kory	Was	23	20	175.2	149	13	2	13	.988	-
Catalanotto,Frank	Tex	33	25	224.2	215	15	0	31	1.000	-
Cintron,Alex	Bal	2	0	3.0	3	1	0	1	1.000	-
Clark,Howie	Min	2	0	5.0	3	1	0	0	1.000	-
Clark,Tony	SD	1	1	22.0	17	1	0	4	1.000	-
Clark,Tony	Ari	25	12	133.0	148	14	2	15	.988	-
Coste,Chris	Phi	1	1	9.0	7	1	0	0	1.000	-

Player	Tm	G	GS	Inn	PO	A	E	DP	Pct.	Rng
Cuddyer,Michael	Min	2	2	18.0	22	1	1	5	.958	-
Damon,Johnny	NYY	1	0	1.0	1	0	0	0	1.000	-
D'Antona,Jamie	Ari	2	1	7.0	7	2	0	2	1.000	-
Davis,Chris	Tex	51	46	404.0	358	34	1	52	.997	-
DeRosa,Mark	ChC	1	0	2.0	2	0	0	0	1.000	-
Dillon,Joe	Mil	4	3	25.0	25	3	0	4	1.000	-
Dobbs,Greg	Phi	2	1	8.0	6	2	0	1	1.000	-
Doumit,Ryan	Pit	1	0	1.0	1	0	0	0	1.000	-
Duncan,Chris	StL	21	15	142.0	143	13	0	13	1.000	-
Duncan,Shelley	NYY	16	12	107.0	98	5	3	8	.972	-
Dunn,Adam	Ari	19	14	128.0	123	7	3	14	.977	-
Easley,Damion	NYM	4	3	31.0	25	1	0	1	1.000	-
Ensberg,Morgan	NYY	7	3	35.0	38	0	0	1	1.000	-
Erstad,Darin	Hou	12	6	66.1	71	2	0	4	1.000	-
Evans,Nick	NYM	3	1	12.0	7	0	0	3	1.000	-
Fasano,Sal	Cle	1	0	3.0	0	0	0	0	-	-
Garciaparra,Nomar	LAD	8	6	38.2	49	4	0	2	1.000	-
Glaus,Troy	StL	4	3	28.2	29	2	0	5	1.000	-
Gomez,Chris	Pit	5	4	35.0	39	4	0	6	1.000	-
Gonzalez,Andy	Cle	7	4	38.0	39	0	2	4	.951	-
Guillen,Carlos	Det	24	18	162.0	142	11	2	22	.987	-
Hannahan,Jack	Oak	10	10	80.0	82	5	2	7	.978	-
Harris,Brendan	Min	2	0	3.0	1	1	0	0	1.000	-
Hatteberg,Scott	Cin	16	8	87.2	69	6	1	3	.987	-
Helms,Wes	Fla	42	18	209.1	185	13	2	19	.990	-
Hernandez,Ramon	Bal	2	1	10.0	11	0	0	1	1.000	-
Hinske,Eric	TB	11	9	87.0	78	8	1	11	.989	-
Hoffpauir,Micah	ChC	6	5	47.2	37	1	1	3	.974	-
Huff,Aubrey	Bal	24	23	194.1	177	16	0	16	1.000	-
Ishikawa,Travis	SF	29	26	213.1	161	20	3	14	.984	-
Jackson,Conor	Ari	68	66	571.2	533	30	4	34	.993	-
Johnson,Dan	TB	8	4	47.0	39	5	0	4	1.000	-
Johnson,Nick	Was	35	34	300.1	302	14	0	21	1.000	-
Ka'aihue,Kila	KC	4	1	15.0	12	1	0	2	1.000	-
Kennedy,Adam	StL	3	2	18.0	23	3	1	4	.963	-
Kent,Jeff	LAD	1	1	4.0	7	1	0	1	1.000	-
Keppinger,Jeff	Cin	3	2	18.2	15	1	0	0	1.000	-
Koshansky,Joe	Col	11	8	74.1	71	6	1	8	.987	-
Kotchman,Casey	LAA	100	95	857.0	838	73	2	86	.998	-
Kotchman,Casey	Atl	41	40	353.1	367	23	0	39	1.000	-
Kotsay,Mark	Bos	6	4	39.0	35	3	1	7	.974	-
LaHair,Bryan	Sea	36	33	273.0	277	18	2	37	.993	-
Lamb,Mike	Min	9	5	52.1	46	8	0	4	1.000	-
Langerhans,Ryan	Was	2	0	7.0	8	0	0	1	1.000	-
Larish,Jeff	Det	8	2	38.0	41	3	0	9	1.000	-
LaRoche,Andy	LAD	1	1	8.0	11	1	0	1	1.000	-
LaRue,Jason	StL	3	0	7.1	7	1	0	1	1.000	-
Lo Duca,Paul	Was	16	14	118.0	113	8	3	16	.976	-
Lo Duca,Paul	Fla	1	0	1.0	1	0	0	0	1.000	-
Lopez,Felipe	StL	1	0	1.0	2	0	0	0	1.000	-
Lopez,Jose	Sea	13	12	100.0	100	11	1	5	.991	-
Loretta,Mark	Hou	2	2	17.0	14	0	0	1	1.000	-
Macri,Matt	Min	2	0	3.0	3	0	0	1	1.000	-
Marte,Andy	Cle	1	0	1.0	2	1	0	1	1.000	-
Martinez,Victor	Cle	10	9	82.0	82	4	1	9	.989	-
Mather,Joe	StL	4	0	13.0	9	1	0	1	1.000	-
McClain,Scott	SF	4	3	28.1	26	2	0	1	1.000	-
Mientkiewicz,Doug	Pit	37	30	283.1	290	19	0	34	1.000	-
Miranda,Juan	NYY	5	3	32.2	30	2	0	1	1.000	-
Moeller,Chad	NYY	2	0	3.0	4	0	0	1	1.000	-
Molina,Jose	NYY	1	0	1.0	0	0	0	0	-	-
Molina,Yadier	StL	2	1	11.0	13	3	0	1	1.000	-
Morales,Kendry	LAA	6	4	41.0	30	3	0	7	1.000	-
Moss,Brandon	Bos	2	1	13.0	10	0	0	1	1.000	-
Myrow,Brian	SD	2	1	9.0	9	0	0	1	1.000	-
Nady,Xavier	NYY	3	0	4.0	3	1	0	0	1.000	-
Nelson,Brad	Mil	2	0	2.0	1	0	0	0	1.000	-
Norton,Greg	Sea	1	1	6.0	7	1	1	2	.889	-
Norton,Greg	Atl	10	6	64.1	73	2	2	6	.974	-
Ortmeier,Dan	SF	13	4	52.0	41	6	0	3	1.000	-
Phelps,Josh	StL	4	1	17.0	18	0	0	1	1.000	-
Phillips,Andy	Cin	4	4	30.2	35	0	1	3	.972	-
Phillips,Andy	NYM	1	0	1.0	0	0	0	0	-	-
Posada,Jorge	NYY	7	3	31.0	25	0	0	2	1.000	-

Player	Tm	G	GS	Inn	PO	A	E	DP	Pct.	Rng
Prado,Martin	Atl	17	14	124.1	123	11	1	10	.993	-
Quinlan,Robb	LAA	22	12	114.0	105	11	0	11	1.000	-
Ramirez,Max	Tex	3	3	23.0	20	4	0	5	1.000	-
Ransom,Cody	NYY	19	2	42.0	47	1	0	2	1.000	-
Reed,Jeremy	Sea	1	0	1.0	2	0	1	0	.667	-
Reynolds,Mark	Ari	1	0	2.0	1	0	1	0	.500	-
Rivera,Juan	LAA	1	0	2.0	5	0	0	1	1.000	-
Rivera,Mike	Mil	3	2	21.0	20	3	0	3	1.000	-
Rodriguez,Luis	SD	2	1	10.0	3	2	0	0	1.000	-
Saccomanno,Mark	Hou	2	0	6.0	6	0	0	0	1.000	-
Salazar,Oscar	Bal	10	9	83.1	79	5	0	5	1.000	-
Sanchez,Gaby	Fla	3	1	11.0	13	1	0	1	1.000	-
Sandoval,Freddy	LAA	1	0	1.0	0	0	0	0	-	-
Sandoval,Pablo	SF	17	13	121.0	100	12	1	7	.991	-
Scutaro,Marco	Tor	3	2	15.0	15	1	0	2	1.000	-
Sexson,Richie	Sea	73	72	604.0	568	48	2	52	.997	-
Sexson,Richie	NYY	19	6	80.0	78	8	0	6	1.000	-
Shealy,Ryan	KC	20	20	169.0	155	12	2	18	.988	-
Shelton,Chris	Tex	39	26	247.1	241	20	3	21	.989	-
Smith,Jason	KC	1	0	2.0	2	0	0	0	1.000	-
Snow,J.T.	SF	0	0	0.0	0	0	0	0	-	-
Sweeney,Mark	LAD	2	2	17.0	18	1	0	1	1.000	-
Sweeney,Mike	Oak	13	11	90.0	89	11	0	9	1.000	-
Swisher,Nick	CWS	71	47	462.0	447	32	2	52	.996	-
Tatis,Fernando	NYM	6	1	18.0	16	1	2	0	.895	-
Teahen,Mark	KC	14	13	121.1	130	10	1	13	.993	-
Teixeira,Mark	Atl	102	102	898.2	963	65	2	85	.998	-
Teixeira,Mark	LAA	51	51	436.1	431	34	3	46	.994	-
Thames,Marcus	Det	9	3	41.0	34	1	0	10	1.000	-
Thigpen,Curtis	Tor	1	0	3.0	1	0	0	0	1.000	-
Tracy,Chad	Ari	65	62	523.0	528	26	4	49	.993	-
Utley,Chase	Phi	2	2	14.0	16	2	0	1	1.000	-
Valentin,Javier	Cin	11	10	81.2	75	4	0	10	1.000	-
Vazquez,Ramon	Tex	1	0	2.0	2	0	0	1	1.000	-
Vidro,Jose	Sea	9	7	55.1	54	5	1	6	.983	-
Ward,Daryle	ChC	13	4	60.0	54	4	0	4	1.000	-
Whitesell,Josh	Ari	1	1	7.0	7	0	0	0	1.000	-
Wilkerson,Brad	Tor	4	2	20.0	22	0	0	0	1.000	-
Young,Dmitri	Was	38	37	290.0	275	15	7	32	.976	-

Second Basemen - Regulars

Player	Tm	G	GS	Inn	PO	A	E	DP	Pct.	Rng
Kinsler,Ian	Tex	121	120	1064.0	292	390	18	123	.974	5.77
Cabrera,Asdrubal	Cle	94	87	776.2	202	281	3	83	.994	5.60
Lopez,Jose	Sea	139	139	1226.1	259	468	11	99	.985	5.32
Polanco,Placido	Det	141	136	1201.1	323	374	8	100	.989	5.22
Kennedy,Adam	StL	84	74	635.2	144	224	7	56	.981	5.21
Utley,Chase	Phi	159	157	1395.2	340	463	13	102	.984	5.18
Johnson,Kelly	Atl	144	135	1198.2	262	425	14	89	.980	5.16
Cano,Robinson	NYY	159	154	1376.2	305	482	13	103	.984	5.15
Kendrick,Howie	LAA	92	90	776.0	155	287	4	67	.991	5.13
Sanchez,Freddy	Pit	131	131	1135.2	291	355	7	104	.989	5.12
Phillips,Brandon	Cin	140	140	1237.2	298	401	7	85	.990	5.08
Weeks,Rickie	Mil	120	118	1056.0	256	333	15	84	.975	5.02
Ellis,Mark	Oak	115	114	1011.2	228	336	4	88	.993	5.02
Ramirez,Alexei	CWS	121	117	1017.1	237	327	11	71	.981	4.99
Roberts,Brian	Bal	154	151	1320.0	289	441	8	110	.989	4.98
Grudzielanek,Mark	KC	85	85	710.2	135	257	4	59	.990	4.96
Uggla,Dan	Fla	144	144	1272.2	297	390	13	82	.981	4.86
Hudson,Orlando	Ari	105	105	904.2	200	284	9	60	.982	4.82
Casilla,Alexi	Min	95	94	833.2	196	247	12	71	.974	4.78
Pedroia,Dustin	Bos	157	155	1376.1	279	448	6	101	.992	4.75
Lopez,Felipe	TOT	101	89	780.0	155	253	11	53	.974	4.71
Iguchi,Tadahito	TOT	78	73	672.1	143	206	1	54	.997	4.67
Durham,Ray	TOT	95	85	738.0	188	190	3	53	.992	4.61
Iwamura,Akinori	TB	152	151	1337.0	284	397	7	109	.990	4.58
Matsui,Kaz	Hou	94	94	806.0	190	219	12	56	.971	4.57
Kent,Jeff	LAD	116	114	885.0	168	279	11	53	.976	4.55
Castillo,Luis	NYM	81	78	689.2	160	186	6	41	.983	4.52
DeRosa,Mark	ChC	95	80	670.0	143	185	8	32	.976	4.41

Second Basemen - The Rest

Player	Tm	G	GS	Inn	PO	A	E	DP	Pct.	Rng
Amezaga,Alfredo	Fla	10	8	73.0	19	18	1	3	.974	4.56
Anderson,Marlon	NYM	1	0	4.0	1	2	0	0	1.000	6.75
Andino,Robert	Fla	15	9	89.2	30	31	2	7	.968	6.12
Antonelli,Matt	SD	18	15	137.1	38	34	2	7	.973	4.72
Arias,Joaquin	Tex	30	26	225.0	48	67	2	19	.983	4.60
Atkins,Garrett	Col	1	0	8.1	3	5	0	2	1.000	8.64
Aurilia,Rich	SF	1	0	3.0	0	0	0	0	-	.00
Ausmus,Brad	Hou	1	0	1.0	0	0	0	0	-	.00
Aviles,Mike	KC	28	9	114.1	26	33	0	5	1.000	4.64
Aybar,Erick	LAA	2	0	2.0	0	1	0	0	1.000	4.50
Aybar,Willy	TB	10	6	70.2	17	19	0	4	1.000	4.58
Baker,Jeff	Col	49	47	369.2	71	131	4	31	.981	4.92
Barden,Brian	StL	1	1	8.0	1	4	1	0	.833	5.63
Barfield,Josh	Cle	9	8	71.0	26	24	0	9	1.000	6.34
Barmes,Clint	Col	61	54	486.0	91	178	6	35	.978	4.98
Bautista,Jose	Tor	2	2	16.0	2	6	0	2	1.000	4.50
Belliard,Ronnie	Was	29	27	229.2	53	60	3	20	.974	4.43
Bernier,Doug	Col	2	1	11.0	5	2	0	0	1.000	5.73
Berroa,Angel	LAD	5	1	12.0	1	4	0	0	1.000	3.75
Betemit,Wilson	NYY	3	3	24.0	4	8	1	2	.923	4.50
Blake,Casey	LAD	1	0	1.0	0	0	0	0	-	.00
Bloomquist,Willie	Sea	4	3	37.0	8	15	0	7	1.000	5.59
Blum,Geoff	Hou	8	5	40.2	9	17	0	2	1.000	5.75
Bonifacio,Emilio	Was	37	37	325.0	78	82	7	25	.958	4.43
Boone,Aaron	Was	1	0	1.1	0	0	0	0	-	.00
Bourgeois,Jason	CWS	1	0	3.0	0	0	0	0	-	.00
Brown,Matt	LAA	1	0	2.0	1	1	0	0	1.000	9.00
Bruntlett,Eric	Phi	5	2	28.0	5	8	1	1	.929	4.18
Burke,Chris	Ari	18	9	92.0	21	34	0	7	1.000	5.38
Burriss,Emmanuel	SF	41	32	282.0	66	80	4	14	.973	4.66
Buscher,Brian	Min	1	0	1.0	0	0	0	0	-	.00
Bynum,Freddie	Bal	1	0	4.0	0	0	0	0	-	.00
Cabrera,Jolbert	Cin	3	2	15.0	4	6	0	3	1.000	6.00
Cairo,Miguel	Sea	5	3	26.0	7	10	0	2	1.000	5.88
Callaspo,Alberto	KC	46	42	365.2	74	119	0	36	1.000	4.75
Carroll,Jamey	Cle	74	66	580.1	105	192	3	46	.990	4.61
Castillo,Jose	SF	9	6	51.0	8	15	1	1	.958	4.06
Castillo,Jose	Hou	3	1	13.0	5	4	0	1	1.000	6.23
Castillo,Wilkin	Cin	2	2	16.0	5	2	0	2	1.000	3.94
Castro,Juan	Cin	2	0	2.0	1	2	0	0	1.000	13.50
Cedeno,Ronny	ChC	43	31	273.0	60	75	2	19	.985	4.45
Cintron,Alex	Bal	7	1	17.0	4	4	0	1	1.000	4.24
Clark,Howie	Min	1	0	3.0	0	2	0	1	1.000	6.00
Conrad,Brooks	Oak	2	2	17.0	4	3	0	1	1.000	3.71
Cora,Alex	Bos	7	3	35.0	6	14	0	3	1.000	5.14
Counsell,Craig	Mil	19	11	112.0	16	42	0	5	1.000	4.66
Crabbe,Callix	SD	5	3	29.2	4	7	3	1	.786	3.34
Cruz,Luis	Pit	2	2	17.0	6	5	0	2	1.000	5.82
Davis,Rajai	Oak	1	0	1.0	0	0	0	0	-	.00
Denker,Travis	SF	13	8	70.0	19	16	1	3	.972	4.50
DeWitt,Blake	LAD	27	24	193.2	41	62	2	9	.981	4.79
Dillon,Joe	Mil	6	5	43.2	9	18	1	5	.964	5.56
Duran,German	Tex	17	9	94.0	24	22	0	3	1.000	4.40
Durham,Ray	SF	70	61	535.1	130	129	3	38	.989	4.35
Durham,Ray	Mil	25	24	202.2	58	61	0	15	1.000	5.28
Easley,Damion	NYM	64	60	539.1	128	160	5	38	.983	4.81
Eckstein,David	Tor	6	5	45.0	7	14	0	4	1.000	4.20
Eckstein,David	Ari	18	18	152.0	30	65	0	14	1.000	5.63
Everett,Adam	Min	1	0	1.0	0	0	0	0	-	.00
Fahey,Brandon	Bal	10	5	48.0	10	11	0	8	1.000	3.94
Figgins,Chone	LAA	9	7	63.0	10	19	0	4	1.000	4.14
Fontenot,Mike	ChC	82	49	498.2	101	143	1	27	.996	4.40
Freel,Ryan	Cin	3	1	12.0	4	5	0	1	1.000	6.75
German,Esteban	KC	35	23	214.0	41	77	3	19	.975	4.96
Getz,Chris	CWS	7	1	23.0	6	9	0	1	1.000	5.87
Gomez,Chris	Pit	18	10	110.2	33	20	2	4	.964	4.31
Gonzalez,Alberto	NYY	4	4	28.0	4	7	0	1	1.000	3.54
Gonzalez,Edgar	SD	72	66	559.2	92	189	4	35	.986	4.52
Gotay,Ruben	Atl	3	3	26.0	3	10	0	2	1.000	4.50
Hairston,Jerry	Cin	5	5	46.0	11	17	0	5	1.000	5.48
Hairston,Scott	SD	1	0	1.2	1	1	0	0	1.000	10.80
Hall,Bill	Mil	6	3	32.0	3	16	2	1	.905	5.34

Player	Tm	G	GS	Inn	PO	A	E	DP	Pct.	Rng
Harman,Brad	Phi	3	2	17.0	2	3	0	0	1.000	2.65
Harris,Brendan	Min	39	37	319.2	56	101	5	24	.969	4.42
Harris,Willie	Was	14	11	86.1	29	30	1	9	.983	6.15
Hernandez,And	Was	16	15	138.0	34	43	0	9	1.000	5.02
Hernandez,Luis	Bal	5	2	21.0	3	9	0	2	1.000	5.14
Herrera,Jonathan	Col	21	12	122.0	34	48	2	13	.976	6.05
Hill,Aaron	Tor	55	53	459.0	87	150	1	27	.996	4.45
Hollimon,Michael	Det	2	1	8.0	3	2	0	0	1.000	5.63
Hu,Chin-lung	LAD	30	7	108.2	15	28	1	4	.977	3.56
Hulett,Tug	Sea	4	1	18.0	4	9	0	2	1.000	6.50
Iguchi,Tadahito	SD	77	72	663.1	142	204	1	54	.997	4.69
Iguchi,Tadahito	Phi	1	1	9.0	1	2	0	1	1.000	3.00
Infante,Omar	Atl	10	9	74.0	14	19	0	6	1.000	4.01
Inglett,Joe	Tor	66	62	541.1	123	176	5	38	.984	4.97
Iribarren,Hernan	Mil	2	1	9.1	1	3	0	1	1.000	3.86
Izturis,Maicer	LAA	23	20	183.2	49	61	2	15	.982	5.39
Johnson,Elliot	TB	1	1	9.0	3	5	0	1	1.000	8.00
Kazmar,Sean	SD	2	0	3.0	2	2	0	1	1.000	12.00
Keppinger,Jeff	Cin	3	3	23.0	5	5	0	2	1.000	3.91
LaRoche,Andy	LAD	3	2	13.0	7	2	0	3	1.000	6.23
Lopez,Felipe	Was	78	69	622.2	128	196	10	39	.970	4.68
Lopez,Felipe	StL	23	20	157.1	27	57	1	14	.988	4.81
Loretta,Mark	Hou	46	41	368.0	85	119	1	28	.995	4.99
Lowrie,Jed	Bos	3	2	16.0	2	4	0	1	1.000	3.38
Macri,Matt	Min	2	1	10.0	1	6	0	1	1.000	6.30
Martinez,Ramon	NYM	5	4	38.0	5	11	0	2	1.000	3.79
Maysonet,Edwin	Hou	3	0	4.0	2	0	0	1	1.000	4.50
Maza,Luis	LAD	35	10	136.1	30	45	2	13	.974	4.95
McDonald,John	Tor	1	0	3.0	0	0	0	0	-	.00
Miles,Aaron	StL	85	49	499.2	91	165	3	47	.988	4.61
Moore,Scott	Bal	1	1	6.0	2	2	0	1	1.000	6.00
Murphy,Donnie	Oak	10	7	61.0	12	20	0	3	1.000	4.72
Newhan,David	Hou	28	19	177.2	33	39	1	11	.986	3.65
Nix,Jayson	Col	20	15	143.1	27	61	0	9	1.000	5.53
Ochoa,Ivan	SF	8	5	48.0	8	14	1	2	.957	4.13
Ojeda,Augie	Ari	44	30	286.0	70	92	0	26	1.000	5.10
Orr,Pete	Was	7	2	31.0	8	10	1	2	.947	5.23
Ozuna,Pablo	CWS	10	6	52.0	10	11	1	0	.955	3.63
Ozuna,Pablo	LAD	27	3	81.2	17	32	0	4	1.000	5.40
Patterson,Eric	ChC	2	1	8.0	3	0	0	0	1.000	3.38
Patterson,Eric	Oak	20	19	169.1	48	49	4	15	.960	5.16
Pennington,Cliff	Oak	16	15	136.0	33	44	0	17	1.000	5.10
Perez,Tomas	Hou	5	1	15.0	2	2	0	2	1.000	2.40
Petit,Gregorio	Oak	4	4	39.0	7	14	0	1	1.000	4.85
Phillips,Andy	Cin	6	1	19.0	5	8	0	3	1.000	6.16
Prado,Martin	Atl	17	15	142.0	33	55	3	7	.967	5.58
Pujols,Albert	StL	1	0	3.1	1	0	0	0	1.000	2.70
Punto,Nick	Min	26	23	215.2	54	79	2	18	.985	5.55
Quintanilla,Omar	Col	40	21	212.2	40	72	1	24	.991	4.74
Raburn,Ryan	Det	16	12	118.0	27	34	5	12	.924	4.65
Ransom,Cody	NYY	2	1	13.0	3	3	1	0	.857	4.15
Reyes,Argenis	NYM	27	20	193.1	48	59	0	17	1.000	4.98
Richar,Danny	Cin	10	6	55.2	12	16	1	4	.966	4.53
Rivas,Luis	Pit	29	19	191.2	51	68	1	22	.992	5.59
Rivera,Juan	LAA	1	0	1.0	0	0	0	0	-	.00
Rodriguez,Luis	SD	7	4	39.0	11	10	0	4	1.000	4.85
Rodriguez,Sean	LAA	51	45	423.2	97	127	2	36	.991	4.76
Rohlinger,Ryan	SF	1	0	3.0	0	0	0	0	-	.00
Rosales,Adam	Cin	2	2	16.0	6	6	0	4	1.000	6.75
Ryan,Brendan	StL	23	18	149.0	23	39	1	5	.984	3.74
Santiago,Ramon	Det	21	13	117.2	30	36	0	13	1.000	5.05
Scutaro,Marco	Tor	50	39	354.1	60	126	1	19	.995	4.72
Smith,Jason	KC	9	3	41.0	5	16	0	2	1.000	4.61
Soriano,Alfonso	ChC	1	0	1.0	0	2	0	0	1.000	18.00
Stansberry,Craig	SD	4	2	24.2	4	3	2	0	.778	2.55
Stewart,Ian	Col	12	12	93.0	16	38	1	5	.982	5.23
Tolbert,Matt	Min	11	8	75.0	15	30	1	7	.978	5.40
Torres,Eider	Bal	1	1	6.0	1	2	0	0	1.000	4.50
Uribe,Juan	CWS	52	39	362.1	104	124	1	34	.996	5.66
Valbuena,Luis	Sea	16	15	125.0	21	41	0	11	1.000	4.46
Vazquez,Ramon	Tex	11	7	59.0	20	15	0	6	1.000	5.34
Velandia,Jorge	Tor	1	1	8.0	1	0	0	0	1.000	1.13
Velandia,Jorge	Cle	1	1	9.0	3	4	0	1	1.000	7.00
Velazquez,Gil	Bos	2	2	19.0	5	9	0	2	1.000	6.63

Player	Tm	G	GS	Inn	PO	A	E	DP	Pct.	Rng
Velez,Eugenio	SF	69	50	449.2	102	104	7	26	.967	4.12
Washington,Rico	StL	1	0	1.0	0	0	0	0	-	.00
Young,Delwyn	LAD	5	1	16.0	3	6	0	0	1.000	5.06
Zobrist,Ben	TB	8	4	41.0	11	11	0	3	1.000	4.83

Third Basemen - Regulars

Player	Tm	G	GS	Inn	PO	A	E	DP	Pct.	Rng
Guillen,Carlos	Det	89	87	749.2	68	195	14	15	.949	3.16
DeWitt,Blake	LAD	95	77	727.2	58	193	8	19	.969	3.10
Bautista,Jose	TOT	99	85	766.1	50	207	11	17	.959	3.02
Zimmerman,Ryan	Was	104	104	910.2	95	199	10	25	.967	2.91
Mora,Melvin	Bal	124	124	1059.2	85	252	14	28	.960	2.86
Lowell,Mike	Bos	110	108	935.2	80	217	10	20	.967	2.86
Crede,Joe	CWS	97	95	834.2	57	207	20	22	.930	2.85
Beltre,Adrian	Sea	139	137	1208.1	100	272	15	27	.961	2.77
Atkins,Garrett	Col	94	92	797.0	47	197	9	21	.964	2.74
Glaus,Troy	StL	146	145	1243.1	99	279	7	27	.982	2.74
Jones,Chipper	Atl	115	115	987.1	64	235	13	21	.958	2.73
Feliz,Pedro	Phi	129	106	978.1	73	223	8	19	.974	2.72
Longoria,Evan	TB	119	118	1045.2	86	230	12	26	.963	2.72
Figgins,Chone	LAA	105	105	914.1	84	185	6	15	.978	2.65
Kouzmanoff,Kevin	SD	154	154	1379.0	128	277	11	34	.974	2.64
Hannahan,Jack	Oak	126	106	983.2	70	218	9	24	.970	2.64
Wigginton,Ty	Hou	82	74	652.0	46	144	6	11	.969	2.62
Hall,Bill	Mil	113	98	899.1	69	193	17	24	.939	2.62
Gordon,Alex	KC	133	133	1180.0	112	230	16	21	.955	2.61
Rolen,Scott	Tor	115	115	1006.2	74	217	11	14	.964	2.60
Rodriguez,Alex	NYY	131	131	1126.1	73	251	10	23	.970	2.59
Blake,Casey	TOT	133	130	1104.2	66	245	14	25	.957	2.53
Wright,David	NYM	159	159	1419.1	114	286	16	21	.962	2.51
Cantu,Jorge	Fla	129	129	1066.2	83	214	20	21	.937	2.51
Castillo,Jose	TOT	110	97	880.0	53	177	15	14	.939	2.35
Reynolds,Mark	Ari	150	149	1288.1	82	240	34	23	.904	2.25
Encarnacion,Edwin	Cin	143	141	1237.0	91	216	23	23	.930	2.23
Ramirez,Aramis	ChC	147	147	1282.2	83	225	18	17	.945	2.16

Third Basemen - The Rest

Player	Tm	G	GS	Inn	PO	A	E	DP	Pct.	Rng
Amezaga,Alfredo	Fla	15	0	25.2	2	5	0	0	1.000	2.45
Andino,Robert	Fla	1	0	1.0	0	0	0	0	-	.00
Aurilia,Rich	SF	63	50	427.2	31	67	5	4	.951	2.06
Ausmus,Brad	Hou	1	0	1.0	0	0	0	0	.000	.00
Aviles,Mike	KC	7	3	29.2	3	3	0	0	1.000	1.82
Aybar,Willy	TB	41	40	358.1	29	84	5	12	.958	2.84
Baisley,Jeff	Oak	10	10	79.0	6	14	0	1	1.000	2.28
Baker,Jeff	Col	9	7	61.0	5	17	0	4	1.000	3.25
Barden,Brian	StL	4	0	7.0	0	2	0	0	1.000	2.57
Barmes,Clint	Col	13	4	48.1	1	10	1	2	.917	2.05
Barton,Daric	Oak	1	0	2.0	1	1	0	1	1.000	9.00
Bautista,Jose	Pit	91	81	726.1	45	196	11	16	.956	2.99
Bautista,Jose	Tor	8	4	40.0	5	11	0	1	1.000	3.60
Belliard,Ronnie	Was	31	25	215.1	16	40	5	3	.918	2.34
Betemit,Wilson	NYY	21	9	100.0	4	21	3	4	.893	2.25
Blake,Casey	Cle	77	74	635.0	39	141	12	15	.938	2.55
Blake,Casey	LAD	56	56	469.2	27	104	2	10	.985	2.51
Blalock,Hank	Tex	31	31	263.0	24	54	4	6	.951	2.67
Bloomquist,Willie	Sea	1	1	7.0	0	0	0	0	-	.00
Blum,Geoff	Hou	75	68	599.2	43	144	4	8	.979	2.81
Boone,Aaron	Was	16	14	113.0	3	23	1	2	.963	2.07
Branyan,Russell	Mil	35	33	276.0	22	63	4	6	.955	2.77
Brown,Matt	LAA	10	3	46.0	3	8	2	2	.846	2.15
Bruntlett,Eric	Phi	27	13	132.0	16	26	2	1	.955	2.86
Burke,Chris	Ari	4	2	20.0	2	5	0	0	1.000	3.15
Burke,Jamie	Sea	1	0	2.0	0	1	0	0	1.000	4.50
Buscher,Brian	Min	64	60	519.1	37	113	10	9	.938	2.60
Cabrera,Jolbert	Cin	3	1	9.1	1	2	0	0	1.000	2.89
Cabrera,Miguel	Det	14	14	116.0	15	30	5	4	.900	3.49
Cairo,Miguel	Sea	19	12	112.0	13	21	1	5	.971	2.73
Callaspo,Alberto	KC	1	1	8.0	1	5	0	1	1.000	6.75
Carroll,Jamey	Cle	43	18	199.2	12	55	6	5	.918	3.02
Cash,Kevin	Bos	4	0	15.0	1	1	0	0	1.000	1.20
Castillo,Jose	SF	103	90	820.0	47	166	15	14	.934	2.34

Player	Tm	G	GS	Inn	PO	A	E	DP	Pct.	Rng
Castillo,Jose	Hou	7	7	60.0	6	11	0	0	1.000	2.55
Casto,Kory	Was	13	11	103.0	12	23	0	1	1.000	3.06
Castro,Juan	Cin	1	0	2.0	0	4	0	0	1.000	18.00
Castro,Juan	Bal	4	0	6.0	1	0	0	0	1.000	1.50
Cedeno,Ronny	ChC	7	0	12.0	1	1	0	0	1.000	1.50
Cervenak,Mike	Phi	2	1	10.0	0	0	0	0	-	.00
Chavez,Eric	Oak	15	15	130.0	12	32	1	4	.978	3.05
Cintron,Alex	Bal	8	0	21.1	1	6	1	0	.875	2.95
Clark,Howie	Min	1	1	8.0	3	2	0	1	1.000	5.63
Conrad,Brooks	Oak	4	4	33.0	1	4	1	1	.833	1.36
Counsell,Craig	Mil	38	30	268.1	23	54	1	6	.987	2.58
Davis,Chris	Tex	32	31	276.0	31	44	3	5	.962	2.45
Denker,Travis	SF	1	0	1.0	0	0	0	0	-	.00
DeRosa,Mark	ChC	22	10	114.1	6	28	2	2	.944	2.68
Dillon,Joe	Mil	1	1	9.0	0	2	0	0	1.000	2.00
Dobbs,Greg	Phi	52	42	327.1	34	67	3	7	.971	2.78
Duran,German	Tex	30	25	223.0	13	45	5	2	.921	2.34
Easley,Damion	NYM	1	1	9.0	3	0	0	0	1.000	3.00
Ensberg,Morgan	NYY	21	13	133.0	8	32	1	2	.976	2.71
Fields,Josh	CWS	12	6	61.2	6	16	2	3	.917	3.21
Freel,Ryan	Cin	4	4	33.0	4	4	1	0	.889	2.18
Gamel,Mat	Mil	1	0	1.0	0	0	0	0	-	.00
Garciaparra,Nomar	LAD	11	9	73.0	2	21	2	0	.920	2.84
German,Esteban	KC	6	5	43.0	2	5	0	2	1.000	1.47
Gillaspie,Conor	SF	2	0	4.0	1	0	0	0	1.000	2.25
Gomez,Chris	Pit	20	6	85.2	5	17	1	1	.957	2.31
Gonzalez,Alberto	NYY	11	6	54.2	6	11	1	2	.944	2.80
Gonzalez,Alberto	Was	3	1	11.0	1	2	0	0	1.000	2.45
Gonzalez,Andy	Cle	2	1	12.0	1	1	1	1	.667	1.50
Gonzalez,Edgar	SD	4	2	23.0	1	3	1	0	.800	1.57
Gotay,Ruben	Atl	10	6	64.0	2	13	2	0	.882	2.11
Hairston,Jerry	Cin	1	0	2.0	0	0	0	0	-	.00
Harman,Brad	Phi	1	0	1.0	0	0	0	0	-	.00
Harris,Brendan	Min	34	28	256.1	18	48	2	4	.971	2.32
Harris,Willie	Was	14	3	44.0	0	6	0	0	1.000	1.23
Headley,Chase	SD	7	6	55.0	3	9	1	0	.923	1.96
Helms,Wes	Fla	60	30	325.0	31	63	1	3	.989	2.60
Hessman,Mike	Det	12	7	70.0	7	20	1	3	.964	3.47
Hinske,Eric	TB	8	4	49.0	1	6	0	0	1.000	1.29
Hollimon,Michael	Det	2	0	2.0	1	0	0	0	1.000	4.50
Huff,Aubrey	Bal	33	31	275.0	23	64	3	4	.967	2.85
Hulett,Tug	Sea	1	0	1.0	0	0	0	0	-	.00
Iannetta,Chris	Col	1	0	8.1	1	1	0	0	1.000	2.16
Infante,Omar	Atl	32	26	228.2	13	55	4	6	.944	2.68
Inge,Brandon	Det	51	33	324.1	38	80	1	14	.992	3.27
Inglett,Joe	Tor	6	5	45.0	5	13	0	1	1.000	3.60
Izturis,Cesar	StL	8	1	15.2	3	3	0	0	1.000	3.45
Izturis,Maicer	LAA	5	5	34.1	1	7	0	0	1.000	2.10
Keppinger,Jeff	Cin	10	7	71.1	3	18	0	2	1.000	2.65
Laird,Gerald	Tex	2	1	10.0	0	3	0	0	1.000	2.70
Lamb,Mike	Min	55	51	458.2	41	88	4	8	.970	2.53
Lamb,Mike	Mil	1	0	2.0	0	2	1	0	.667	9.00
Larish,Jeff	Det	12	12	83.0	10	17	2	1	.931	2.93
LaRoche,Andy	LAD	14	12	105.0	6	25	1	1	.969	2.66
LaRoche,Andy	Pit	45	45	397.1	19	111	9	20	.935	2.94
Lillibridge,Brent	Atl	1	0	2.0	0	1	0	0	1.000	4.50
Lopez,Felipe	StL	13	8	85.1	2	23	2	2	.926	2.64
Loretta,Mark	Hou	17	12	110.2	7	31	1	1	.974	3.09
Lowrie,Jed	Bos	45	22	243.2	16	59	2	8	.974	2.77
Macri,Matt	Min	11	8	64.1	3	14	1	3	.944	2.38
Marte,Andy	Cle	76	68	581.1	43	155	6	19	.971	3.07
Martin,Russell	LAD	11	8	71.0	2	21	3	3	.885	2.92
Mather,Joe	StL	1	0	3.0	0	0	0	0	-	.00
McClain,Scott	SF	4	4	36.0	3	8	0	0	1.000	2.75
McDonald,John	Tor	4	2	23.0	0	5	0	0	1.000	1.96
McGehee,Casey	ChC	6	4	41.2	3	13	0	3	1.000	3.46
McPherson,Dallas	Fla	2	2	17.0	0	1	0	0	1.000	.53
Melhuse,Adam	Tex	2	0	6.0	1	2	0	0	1.000	4.50
Metcalf,Travis	Tex	19	14	130.0	15	18	1	6	.971	2.28
Mientkiewicz,Doug	Pit	33	30	244.2	24	54	7	5	.918	2.87
Miles,Aaron	StL	11	5	61.0	2	16	0	1	1.000	2.66
Moeller,Chad	NYY	3	0	3.2	0	0	0	0	-	.00
Moore,Scott	Bal	1	1	9.0	0	2	0	0	1.000	2.00
Murphy,Donnie	Oak	24	18	143.1	12	27	1	7	.975	2.45
Ojeda,Augie	Ari	28	9	110.1	6	32	0	3	1.000	3.10
Orr,Pete	Was	8	3	37.0	4	16	0	0	1.000	4.86
Ozuna,Pablo	CWS	16	10	100.0	8	29	4	4	.902	3.33
Ozuna,Pablo	LAD	1	0	1.0	0	0	0	0	-	.00
Pennington,Cliff	Oak	9	8	64.0	8	11	1	2	.950	2.67
Peralta,Jhonny	Cle	1	1	9.0	1	2	0	1	1.000	3.00
Perez,Tomas	Hou	1	0	2.0	0	0	0	0	-	.00
Phillips,Andy	Cin	8	5	49.0	1	10	1	2	.917	2.02
Prado,Martin	Atl	24	15	158.2	9	46	1	3	.982	3.12
Punto,Nick	Min	12	6	63.0	3	16	0	1	1.000	2.71
Quinlan,Robb	LAA	39	29	258.2	22	48	4	8	.946	2.44
Raburn,Ryan	Det	18	8	79.0	8	14	3	1	.880	2.51
Ramirez,Alexei	CWS	1	0	1.0	0	1	0	0	1.000	9.00
Ransom,Cody	NYY	4	3	24.0	1	6	0	0	1.000	2.63
Rivas,Luis	Pit	1	0	1.0	0	0	0	0	-	.00
Rodriguez,Luis	SD	1	0	1.1	1	1	0	1	1.000	13.50
Rodriguez,Sean	LAA	1	0	1.0	0	0	0	0	-	.00
Rohlinger,Ryan	SF	14	6	68.1	7	12	3	1	.864	2.50
Rosales,Adam	Cin	4	3	29.0	2	1	0	1	1.000	.93
Ruiz,Carlos	Phi	1	0	1.0	0	0	0	0	-	.00
Ryan,Brendan	StL	5	1	19.1	2	6	1	1	.889	3.72
Salazar,Oscar	Bal	5	5	51.0	3	10	0	3	1.000	2.29
Sandoval,Freddy	LAA	1	1	9.0	0	3	0	0	1.000	3.00
Sandoval,Pablo	SF	12	12	85.0	3	14	0	0	1.000	1.80
Santiago,Ramon	Det	6	1	21.0	2	3	2	0	.714	2.14
Scutaro,Marco	Tor	41	36	332.0	22	84	2	8	.981	2.87
Shelton,Chris	Tex	1	0	1.0	0	0	0	0	-	.00
Smith,Jason	KC	5	1	19.0	5	1	0	0	1.000	2.84
Stewart,Ian	Col	65	59	531.1	40	127	10	15	.944	2.83
Tatis,Fernando	NYM	4	2	22.0	2	2	0	0	1.000	1.64
Teahen,Mark	KC	19	19	166.0	18	24	3	3	.933	2.28
Tolbert,Matt	Min	17	9	89.1	9	24	4	4	.892	3.32
Tracy,Chad	Ari	2	2	16.0	2	2	0	0	1.000	2.25
Tuiasosopo,Matt	Sea	13	12	105.0	11	23	2	4	.944	2.91
Uribe,Juan	CWS	57	52	460.1	41	125	7	10	.960	3.25
Valentin,Javier	Cin	4	1	9.2	0	0	0	0	-	.00
Vazquez,Ramon	Tex	70	60	533.0	30	117	10	16	.936	2.48
Washington,Rico	StL	4	2	19.1	0	9	0	0	1.000	4.19
Wood,Brandon	LAA	32	19	188.0	18	40	2	3	.967	2.78
Youkilis,Kevin	Bos	36	32	252.0	23	70	3	5	.969	3.32
Zobrist,Ben	TB	1	0	4.2	0	2	0	0	1.000	3.86

Shortstops - Regulars

Player	Tm	G	GS	Inn	PO	A	E	DP	Pct.	Rng
Tulowitzki,Troy	Col	101	97	863.1	190	311	8	70	.984	5.22
Wilson,Jack	Pit	80	80	696.1	115	277	5	53	.987	5.02
Izturis,Cesar	StL	130	110	1001.1	170	370	11	77	.980	4.85
Escobar,Yunel	Atl	126	125	1105.2	193	396	16	78	.974	4.79
Aybar,Erick	LAA	96	91	784.2	140	276	18	63	.959	4.77
Cabrera,Orlando	CWS	161	160	1389.2	242	472	16	101	.978	4.62
Young,Michael	Tex	152	151	1289.0	193	465	11	113	.984	4.59
Aviles,Mike	KC	91	89	747.2	141	238	10	66	.974	4.56
Peralta,Jhonny	Cle	146	143	1271.1	217	427	14	104	.979	4.56
Rollins,Jimmy	Phi	132	132	1168.0	193	393	7	71	.988	4.52
Guzman,Cristian	Was	136	132	1174.0	192	394	17	75	.972	4.49
Hardy,J.J.	Mil	145	143	1268.1	202	430	15	86	.977	4.48
Ramirez,Hanley	Fla	150	150	1302.0	236	401	22	89	.967	4.40
Betancourt,Yuniesky	Sea	153	150	1325.1	237	401	21	98	.968	4.33
Renteria,Edgar	Det	138	134	1173.1	197	365	16	91	.972	4.31
Bartlett,Jason	TB	125	122	1097.0	204	309	16	69	.970	4.21
Greene,Khalil	SD	105	103	934.0	146	289	8	66	.982	4.19
Tejada,Miguel	Hou	157	154	1354.1	187	442	11	97	.983	4.18
Crosby,Bobby	Oak	145	144	1263.0	202	384	17	99	.972	4.18
Reyes,Jose	NYM	158	158	1420.1	221	422	17	89	.974	4.07
Jeter,Derek	NYY	148	147	1258.2	220	347	12	69	.979	4.05
Keppinger,Jeff	Cin	108	101	880.2	145	246	8	72	.980	4.00
Drew,Stephen	Ari	151	147	1294.1	190	378	14	85	.976	3.95
Vizquel,Omar	SF	84	76	657.2	100	179	2	43	.993	3.93
Theriot,Ryan	ChC	149	141	1266.0	207	341	14	69	.975	3.90
Lugo,Julio	Bos	81	79	671.1	100	176	16	34	.945	3.70

Shortstops - The Rest

Player	Tm	G	GS	Inn	PO	A	E	DP	Pct.	Rng
Amezaga,Alfredo	Fla	19	11	125.1	22	31	0	3	1.000	3.81
Andino,Robert	Fla	4	0	8.0	0	2	0	0	1.000	2.25
Aybar,Willy	TB	2	2	18.0	2	6	0	1	1.000	4.00
Barmes,Clint	Col	36	32	285.0	57	113	3	28	.983	5.37
Belliard,Ronnie	Was	5	4	33.0	6	11	1	3	.944	4.64
Berroa,Angel	LAD	79	64	591.2	91	219	8	39	.975	4.72
Betemit,Wilson	NYY	14	4	57.0	10	19	0	5	1.000	4.58
Bixler,Brian	Pit	39	32	278.0	53	121	8	28	.956	5.63
Blake,Casey	Cle	1	0	2.0	0	1	0	0	1.000	4.50
Bloomquist,Willie	Sea	12	11	93.0	17	23	0	2	1.000	3.87
Blum,Geoff	Hou	4	3	26.0	2	7	0	0	1.000	3.12
Bocock,Brian	SF	29	26	227.0	39	73	4	23	.966	4.44
Brignac,Reid	TB	4	2	21.1	4	7	2	3	.846	4.64
Bruntlett,Eric	Phi	35	30	279.2	39	92	4	16	.970	4.22
Burke,Chris	Ari	2	2	13.2	2	4	1	2	.857	3.95
Burriss,Emmanuel	SF	47	34	315.0	50	93	5	11	.966	4.09
Bynum,Freddie	Bal	37	32	283.1	56	81	5	28	.965	4.35
Cabrera,Asdrubal	Cle	20	18	154.2	38	59	5	17	.951	5.64
Cabrera,Jolbert	Cin	9	7	60.1	7	14	0	5	1.000	3.13
Cairo,Miguel	Sea	1	0	2.0	0	1	0	0	1.000	4.50
Callaspo,Alberto	KC	18	9	84.0	18	30	2	8	.960	5.14
Cannizaro,Andy	TB	1	0	1.0	1	0	0	0	1.000	9.00
Casilla,Alexi	Min	2	1	10.0	2	3	0	1	1.000	4.50
Castillo,Jose	SF	4	0	4.1	1	1	0	0	1.000	4.15
Castro,Juan	Cin	3	2	18.0	1	4	0	0	1.000	2.50
Castro,Juan	Bal	54	46	390.2	72	136	5	22	.977	4.79
Cedeno,Ronny	ChC	27	20	182.2	41	50	3	10	.968	4.48
Cintron,Alex	Bal	45	28	257.0	50	92	7	21	.953	4.97
Cora,Alex	Bos	69	38	386.0	74	136	6	39	.972	4.90
Counsell,Craig	Mil	24	19	185.1	30	73	2	13	.981	5.00
Crabbe,Callix	SD	3	2	18.0	3	4	0	1	1.000	3.50
Cruz,Luis	Pit	20	18	163.1	32	61	1	14	.989	5.12
DeRosa,Mark	ChC	1	0	1.0	0	1	0	0	1.000	9.00
Duran,German	Tex	2	1	13.0	2	6	0	1	1.000	5.54
Easley,Damion	NYM	8	4	44.0	7	14	0	1	1.000	4.30
Eckstein,David	Tor	57	56	484.1	69	146	9	33	.960	4.00
Escobar,Alcides	Mil	2	0	2.0	0	0	0	0	-	.00
Everett,Adam	Min	44	41	364.0	61	145	7	30	.967	5.09
Fahey,Brandon	Bal	46	27	248.0	43	87	5	19	.963	4.72
Feliz,Pedro	Phi	1	0	2.0	1	0	0	0	1.000	4.50
Fontenot,Mike	ChC	1	0	1.0	0	0	0	0	-	.00
Furcal,Rafael	LAD	36	35	296.0	46	92	4	17	.972	4.20
Garciaparra,Nomar	LAD	31	29	238.0	29	89	4	14	.967	4.46
German,Esteban	KC	3	3	22.0	2	4	1	0	.857	2.45
Gomez,Chris	Pit	13	10	94.1	16	34	3	7	.943	4.77
Gonzalez,Alberto	NYY	14	5	63.0	12	15	0	2	1.000	3.86
Gonzalez,Alberto	Was	12	10	93.0	13	28	0	7	1.000	3.97
Gonzalez,Edgar	SD	3	1	16.1	1	11	0	0	1.000	6.61
Hairston,Jerry	Cin	34	31	271.0	61	68	4	18	.970	4.28
Harris,Brendan	Min	55	51	464.1	84	159	6	42	.976	4.71
Harris,Willie	Was	3	1	13.0	3	2	0	1	1.000	3.46
Hernandez,And	Was	3	3	24.0	3	3	3	0	.667	2.25
Hernandez,Luis	Bal	30	26	223.0	52	75	3	19	.977	5.13
Herrera,Jonathan	Col	2	1	9.0	2	4	0	0	1.000	6.00
Hollimon,Michael	Det	6	5	44.0	1	12	1	2	.929	2.66
Hu,Chin-lung	LAD	35	23	229.0	46	75	0	14	1.000	4.76
Hulett,Tug	Sea	4	1	13.0	2	1	0	0	1.000	2.08
Infante,Omar	Atl	20	15	138.0	27	45	5	12	.935	4.70
Inglett,Joe	Tor	2	0	2.0	0	2	0	0	1.000	9.00
Izturis,Maicer	LAA	52	50	448.0	69	147	2	31	.991	4.34
Janish,Paul	Cin	36	20	204.1	31	78	3	13	.973	4.80
Johnson,Elliot	TB	2	2	18.0	4	6	1	3	.909	5.00
Kazmar,Sean	SD	15	11	98.2	26	24	1	5	.980	4.56
Lillibridge,Brent	Atl	23	20	182.0	39	61	6	13	.943	4.95
Longoria,Evan	TB	1	1	9.0	0	1	0	0	1.000	1.00
Lopez,Felipe	Was	8	7	54.0	3	21	0	4	1.000	4.00
Lopez,Felipe	StL	5	3	25.0	3	7	0	1	1.000	3.60
Loretta,Mark	Hou	5	4	36.0	3	18	2	3	.913	5.25
Lowrie,Jed	Bos	49	45	386.0	46	109	0	21	1.000	3.61
Maysonet,Edwin	Hou	4	0	9.0	0	6	1	0	.857	6.00
Maza,Luis	LAD	16	11	86.0	23	35	2	6	.967	6.07
McDonald,John	Tor	67	52	478.0	80	134	9	33	.960	4.03

Player	Tm	G	GS	Inn	PO	A	E	DP	Pct.	Rng
Metcalf,Travis	Tex	1	0	2.0	0	0	0	0	-	.00
Miles,Aaron	StL	27	24	172.1	32	56	1	14	.989	4.60
Mora,Melvin	Bal	1	0	1.0	0	0	0	0	-	.00
Murphy,Donnie	Oak	13	9	88.0	10	27	2	6	.949	3.78
Ochoa,Ivan	SF	35	26	238.0	45	71	3	20	.975	4.39
Ojeda,Augie	Ari	22	13	126.2	17	39	3	6	.949	3.98
Orr,Pete	Was	8	4	43.0	9	10	2	4	.905	3.98
Ozuna,Pablo	LAD	4	0	6.2	0	4	0	0	1.000	5.40
Pena,Tony F	KC	94	61	592.0	74	180	9	35	.966	3.86
Pennington,Cliff	Oak	10	6	56.0	10	16	4	5	.867	4.18
Petit,Gregorio	Oak	8	2	28.0	7	12	2	5	.905	6.11
Prado,Martin	Atl	2	2	15.0	2	2	1	1	.800	2.40
Punto,Nick	Min	61	60	530.2	103	187	8	46	.973	4.92
Quintanilla,Omar	Col	39	32	288.2	42	100	3	20	.979	4.43
Ramirez,Alexei	CWS	16	2	53.0	8	15	1	4	.958	3.91
Ransom,Cody	NYY	9	6	63.0	12	22	2	4	.944	4.86
Richar,Danny	Cin	1	1	8.0	1	1	0	1	1.000	2.25
Rivas,Luis	Pit	31	22	223.0	37	70	6	24	.947	4.32
Rodriguez,Luis	SD	45	34	391.1	79	121	3	33	.985	4.60
Rodriguez,Sean	LAA	4	2	20.0	5	12	0	2	1.000	7.65
Ryan,Brendan	StL	40	25	255.1	42	91	1	18	.993	4.69
Salazar,Oscar	Bal	1	0	1.0	0	0	0	0	-	.00
Santiago,Ramon	Det	33	23	227.2	45	70	3	15	.975	4.55
Scutaro,Marco	Tor	56	53	472.1	71	165	5	30	.979	4.50
Tolbert,Matt	Min	14	10	90.0	14	26	1	4	.976	4.00
Torres,Eider	Bal	5	2	18.0	2	5	3	1	.700	3.50
Uribe,Juan	CWS	4	1	15.0	2	2	0	0	1.000	2.40
Valbuena,Luis	Sea	1	0	2.0	1	1	0	1	1.000	9.00
Vazquez,Ramon	Tex	26	10	138.0	23	52	3	15	.962	4.89
Velandia,Jorge	Tor	2	1	10.0	1	1	0	0	1.000	1.80
Velandia,Jorge	Cle	2	1	9.0	1	4	0	2	1.000	5.00
Velazquez,Gil	Bos	1	0	3.0	0	1	0	0	1.000	3.00
Wood,Brandon	LAA	28	19	198.2	42	50	2	20	.979	4.17
Zobrist,Ben	TB	35	33	293.1	51	78	7	22	.949	3.96

Left Fielders - Regulars

Player	Tm	G	GS	Inn	PO	A	E	DP	Pct.	Rng
Crawford,Carl	TB	108	103	920.2	231	2	4	0	.983	2.28
Francisco,Ben	Cle	83	71	643.0	150	7	2	2	.987	2.20
Scott,Luke	Bal	106	100	840.1	200	3	2	1	.990	2.17
Damon,Johnny	NYY	87	75	659.1	155	2	1	0	.994	2.14
Ibanez,Raul	Sea	153	153	1340.0	302	9	5	1	.984	2.09
Jackson,Conor	Ari	77	75	656.0	146	5	3	3	.981	2.07
Anderson,Garret	LAA	82	80	689.1	144	9	0	2	1.000	2.00
Headley,Chase	SD	82	82	713.0	156	2	5	0	.969	1.99
Young,Delmon	Min	151	147	1324.0	282	11	8	2	.973	1.99
Dunn,Adam	TOT	119	118	980.2	210	5	7	1	.968	1.97
Braun,Ryan	Mil	149	148	1310.1	275	9	0	0	1.000	1.95
Soriano,Alfonso	ChC	108	107	937.1	186	10	5	5	.975	1.88
Lewis,Fred	SF	112	101	905.2	178	11	6	1	.969	1.88
Lee,Carlos	Hou	110	110	915.1	187	4	1	0	.995	1.88
Quentin,Carlos	CWS	130	130	1147.0	228	5	7	2	.971	1.83
Holliday,Matt	Col	139	139	1229.1	240	9	3	3	.988	1.82
Willingham,Josh	Fla	98	97	855.1	166	7	0	0	1.000	1.82
Ramirez,Manny	TOT	119	119	974.0	190	7	3	2	.985	1.82
Pierre,Juan	LAD	84	71	622.2	125	0	3	0	.977	1.82
Bay,Jason	TOT	154	153	1344.2	254	8	4	0	.985	1.75
Burrell,Pat	Phi	155	154	1198.1	202	12	2	1	.991	1.61

Left Fielders - The Rest

Player	Tm	G	GS	Inn	PO	A	E	DP	Pct.	Rng
Abercrombie,Reggie	Hou	12	2	32.0	7	0	0	0	1.000	1.97
Aguila,Chris	NYM	6	2	26.0	5	1	0	0	1.000	2.08
Alou,Moises	NYM	13	13	92.1	18	0	0	0	1.000	1.75
Anderson,Brian	CWS	3	2	16.0	3	0	0	0	1.000	1.69
Anderson,Josh	Atl	6	3	33.2	9	0	0	0	1.000	2.41
Anderson,Marlon	NYM	25	20	165.2	45	1	2	1	.958	2.50
Ankiel,Rick	StL	17	16	131.0	22	0	3	0	.880	1.51
Bailey,Jeff	Bos	5	2	23.0	3	0	0	0	1.000	1.17
Baldelli,Rocco	TB	1	0	7.0	1	0	0	0	1.000	1.29
Balentien,Wladimir	Sea	5	5	43.0	13	1	0	0	1.000	2.93
Barton,Brian	StL	36	27	209.0	43	2	1	0	.978	1.94

Player	Tm	G	GS	Inn	PO	A	E	DP	Pct.	Rng
Bay,Jason	Pit	105	105	921.1	178	3	3	0	.984	1.77
Bay,Jason	Bos	49	48	423.1	76	5	1	0	.988	1.72
Bernadina,Roger	Was	6	6	56.0	19	2	0	0	1.000	3.38
Blanco,Gregor	Atl	77	55	512.2	86	3	2	0	.978	1.56
Bloomquist,Willie	Sea	8	1	17.2	3	0	0	0	1.000	1.53
Boggs,Brandon	Tex	76	59	579.0	131	7	3	2	.979	2.15
Bohn,T.J.	Phi	12	0	22.0	6	1	1	0	.875	2.86
Bonifacio,Emilio	Ari	1	0	2.0	0	0	0	0	-	.00
Botts,Jason	Tex	4	1	14.0	3	0	0	0	1.000	1.93
Bowker,John	SF	5	3	27.0	5	0	0	0	1.000	1.67
Bradley,Milton	Tex	1	1	8.0	1	0	0	0	1.000	1.13
Brown,Emil	Oak	65	40	413.0	89	6	1	1	.990	2.07
Bruce,Jay	Cin	11	4	41.0	3	0	0	0	1.000	.66
Bruntlett,Eric	Phi	29	0	52.1	11	0	0	0	1.000	1.89
Buck,Travis	Oak	12	3	47.0	11	1	0	0	1.000	2.30
Burke,Chris	Ari	18	13	116.1	43	1	0	0	1.000	3.40
Byrd,Marlon	Tex	31	30	236.0	61	0	0	0	1.000	2.33
Byrnes,Eric	Ari	51	50	419.2	76	1	1	0	.987	1.65
Cabrera,Jolbert	Cin	17	15	124.0	21	2	1	0	.958	1.67
Cabrera,Melky	NYY	8	1	18.0	4	0	0	0	1.000	2.00
Cairo,Miguel	Sea	2	0	4.0	0	0	0	0	-	.00
Callaspo,Alberto	KC	3	1	14.0	0	0	0	0	-	.00
Carroll,Brett	Fla	7	0	10.0	4	0	0	0	1.000	3.60
Carroll,Jamey	Cle	1	0	3.0	0	0	0	0	-	.00
Carter,Chris	Bos	3	1	17.0	3	0	0	0	1.000	1.59
Castillo,Wilkin	Cin	5	5	38.0	6	0	0	0	1.000	1.42
Casto,Kory	Was	8	6	53.2	11	0	0	0	1.000	1.84
Catalanotto,Frank	Tex	26	20	168.1	29	0	1	0	.967	1.55
Cedeno,Ronny	ChC	1	0	2.0	0	0	0	0	-	.00
Chavez,Endy	NYM	54	13	197.1	62	2	0	0	1.000	2.92
Choo,Shin-Soo	Cle	26	25	223.0	40	3	1	0	.977	1.74
Christian,Justin	NYY	9	6	53.0	5	0	1	0	.833	.85
Clark,Brady	NYM	2	2	14.2	2	0	0	0	1.000	1.23
Clevlen,Brent	Det	10	2	39.0	16	1	0	0	1.000	3.92
Coats,Buck	Tor	7	1	23.0	6	0	0	0	1.000	2.35
Crabbe,Callix	SD	1	0	2.0	0	0	0	0	-	.00
Cruz,Jose	Hou	10	1	24.0	5	0	0	0	1.000	1.88
Cunningham,Aaron	Oak	18	18	150.0	41	1	3	0	.933	2.52
Cust,Jack	Oak	78	77	585.2	129	4	4	0	.971	2.04
Davis,Rajai	SF	3	1	7.0	2	0	0	0	1.000	2.57
DeJesus,David	KC	71	54	482.2	136	1	0	0	1.000	2.55
Dellucci,David	Cle	56	46	383.0	75	1	0	0	1.000	1.79
Denorfia,Chris	Oak	13	7	70.1	9	1	0	0	1.000	1.28
DeRosa,Mark	ChC	27	21	185.0	39	0	1	0	.975	1.90
Diaz,Matt	Atl	37	33	288.2	59	2	1	1	.984	1.90
Dickerson,Chris	Cin	28	19	182.2	38	0	0	0	1.000	1.87
Dillon,Joe	Mil	2	1	9.0	1	0	0	0	1.000	1.00
Dobbs,Greg	Phi	3	2	16.0	4	0	0	0	1.000	2.25
Dukes,Elijah	Was	10	7	57.2	16	0	1	0	.941	2.50
Duncan,Chris	StL	43	40	321.1	73	1	2	0	.974	2.07
Dunn,Adam	Cin	110	110	915.2	191	5	7	1	.966	1.93
Dunn,Adam	Ari	9	8	65.0	19	0	0	0	1.000	2.63
Duran,German	Tex	6	2	21.0	7	0	0	0	1.000	3.00
Easley,Damion	NYM	7	2	26.0	2	0	1	0	.667	.69
Ellison,Jason	Tex	2	1	11.0	5	0	0	0	1.000	4.09
Ellsbury,Jacoby	Bos	58	36	346.1	89	1	0	1	1.000	2.34
Erstad,Darin	Hou	56	17	205.0	37	1	0	1	1.000	1.67
Ethier,Andre	LAD	41	29	277.1	48	3	2	0	.962	1.66
Evans,Nick	NYM	28	25	186.1	37	2	0	0	1.000	1.88
Freel,Ryan	Cin	13	2	46.1	6	0	0	0	1.000	1.17
Gardner,Brett	NYY	17	15	145.1	25	1	0	0	1.000	1.61
Gathright,Joey	KC	3	0	9.0	2	0	0	0	1.000	2.00
German,Esteban	KC	39	25	235.0	54	0	2	0	.964	2.07
Gload,Ross	KC	8	8	64.0	18	0	0	0	1.000	2.53
Gomes,Jonny	TB	9	4	40.0	13	0	0	0	1.000	2.93
Gonzalez,Edgar	SD	2	1	7.0	2	0	0	0	1.000	2.57
Gonzalez,Luis	Fla	64	60	503.2	105	0	4	0	.963	1.88
Gross,Gabe	Mil	2	0	4.0	2	0	0	0	1.000	4.50
Guillen,Carlos	Det	2	2	17.0	6	0	0	0	1.000	3.18
Guillen,Jose	KC	45	43	373.0	83	3	1	1	.989	2.08
Gutierrez,Franklin	Cle	11	8	78.0	14	0	0	0	1.000	1.62
Gwynn,Tony	Mil	1	0	4.0	1	0	0	0	1.000	2.25
Hairston,Jerry	Cin	24	4	63.1	10	0	0	0	1.000	1.42
Hairston,Scott	SD	49	30	310.0	70	2	0	0	1.000	2.09

Player	Tm	G	GS	Inn	PO	A	E	DP	Pct.	Rng
Harris,Willie	Was	86	58	562.0	145	4	2	2	.987	2.39
Haynes,Nathan	TB	2	1	12.0	2	0	0	0	1.000	1.50
Helms,Wes	Fla	1	0	1.0	0	0	0	0	-	.00
Hinske,Eric	TB	40	37	265.0	45	2	1	0	.979	1.60
Hoffpauir,Micah	ChC	7	3	38.0	6	0	1	0	.857	1.42
Hopper,Norris	Cin	8	3	31.1	5	0	0	0	1.000	1.44
Horwitz,Brian	SF	9	7	63.1	20	0	0	0	1.000	2.84
Huber,Justin	SD	22	17	139.1	27	0	1	0	.964	1.74
Infante,Omar	Atl	34	26	225.0	44	0	1	0	.978	1.76
Inge,Brandon	Det	2	0	6.0	0	0	0	0	-	.00
Inglett,Joe	Tor	22	5	73.0	15	0	0	0	1.000	1.85
Jimerson,Charlton	Sea	1	0	1.0	0	0	0	0	-	.00
Johnson,Dan	TB	1	1	6.0	3	0	0	0	1.000	4.50
Johnson,Reed	ChC	26	12	124.2	35	1	0	0	1.000	2.60
Jones,Brandon	Atl	29	27	219.2	45	2	0	0	1.000	1.93
Jones,Jacque	Det	23	22	172.0	38	1	1	0	.975	2.04
Jones,Jacque	Fla	4	2	20.1	4	0	0	0	1.000	1.77
Joyce,Matt	Det	60	41	409.1	94	2	3	0	.970	2.11
Kapler,Gabe	Mil	17	12	118.1	22	1	0	0	1.000	1.75
Kennedy,Adam	StL	1	0	1.0	0	0	0	0	-	.00
Kubel,Jason	Min	18	16	130.0	24	1	2	1	.926	1.73
Langerhans,Ryan	Was	24	13	141.2	26	1	0	0	1.000	1.72
Lind,Adam	Tor	71	71	590.2	113	2	0	1	1.000	1.75
Lo Duca,Paul	Was	5	4	23.2	11	0	1	0	.917	4.18
Lopez,Felipe	Was	8	6	49.0	9	1	0	0	1.000	1.84
Lopez,Felipe	StL	8	7	58.0	3	1	0	0	1.000	.62
Ludwick,Ryan	StL	29	17	169.2	42	2	0	0	1.000	2.33
Lugo,Julio	Bos	1	0	1.0	0	0	0	0	-	.00
Macias,Drew	SD	4	2	21.0	7	0	0	0	1.000	3.00
Mackowiak,Rob	Was	12	9	73.1	11	0	0	0	1.000	1.35
Mather,Joe	StL	25	12	124.2	30	1	0	0	1.000	2.24
Matsui,Hideki	NYY	21	20	176.1	40	2	1	1	.977	2.14
Matthews Jr.,Gary	LAA	37	36	313.1	57	1	2	0	.967	1.67
McAnulty,Paul	SD	35	30	266.0	48	1	0	0	1.000	1.66
McLouth,Nate	Pit	4	1	18.0	2	0	0	0	1.000	1.00
Mench,Kevin	Tor	21	14	125.0	28	0	0	0	1.000	2.02
Michaels,Jason	Cle	15	11	97.0	23	2	0	0	1.000	2.32
Michaels,Jason	Pit	19	13	128.2	29	0	0	0	1.000	2.03
Miles,Aaron	StL	4	3	26.0	3	0	0	0	1.000	1.04
Monroe,Craig	Min	1	0	1.0	0	0	0	0	-	.00
Montanez,Lou	Bal	26	20	174.1	30	1	2	0	.939	1.60
Morgan,Nyjer	Pit	23	18	166.2	40	0	1	0	.976	2.16
Moss,Brandon	Bos	11	8	78.0	17	0	0	0	1.000	1.96
Moss,Brandon	Pit	25	25	216.1	43	2	1	1	.978	1.87
Murphy,Daniel	NYM	32	30	249.0	50	1	2	1	.962	1.84
Murphy,David	Tex	54	48	404.2	86	3	1	0	.989	1.98
Murphy,Donnie	Oak	1	0	2.0	0	0	0	0	-	.00
Murton,Matt	ChC	10	6	62.0	13	0	0	0	1.000	1.89
Murton,Matt	Oak	7	7	61.0	27	1	0	1	1.000	4.13
Nady,Xavier	NYY	46	45	389.2	87	2	2	0	.978	2.06
Newhan,David	Hou	2	0	2.0	0	0	0	0	-	.00
Nix,Laynce	Mil	2	1	10.0	4	0	0	0	1.000	3.60
Nixon,Trot	NYM	6	6	44.1	11	1	0	0	1.000	2.44
Norton,Greg	Atl	25	15	137.2	29	0	0	0	1.000	1.90
Orr,Pete	Was	2	1	9.0	2	0	0	0	1.000	2.00
Ortmeier,Dan	SF	13	10	80.1	13	1	0	0	1.000	1.57
Owens,Jerry	CWS	7	1	25.0	3	0	0	0	1.000	1.08
Ozuna,Pablo	LAD	2	0	5.0	0	0	0	0	-	.00
Pagan,Angel	NYM	21	20	169.2	28	0	1	0	.966	1.49
Patterson,Eric	ChC	9	8	68.0	13	1	3	0	.824	1.85
Patterson,Eric	Oak	8	7	63.0	15	0	1	0	.938	2.14
Payton,Jay	Bal	71	41	407.1	132	2	0	1	1.000	2.96
Pearce,Steve	Pit	1	0	4.0	1	0	0	0	1.000	2.25
Pena,Wily Mo	Was	54	51	408.0	99	3	3	0	.971	2.25
Perez,Fernando	TB	8	2	32.2	5	0	0	0	1.000	1.38
Phelps,Josh	StL	3	3	21.0	1	0	0	0	1.000	.43
Phillips,Andy	NYM	2	1	9.0	1	0	0	0	1.000	1.00
Pie,Felix	ChC	1	1	8.2	3	0	0	0	1.000	3.12
Podsednik,Scott	Col	10	2	30.0	7	0	0	0	1.000	2.10
Prado,Martin	Atl	3	3	23.0	7	0	0	0	1.000	2.74
Pridie,Jason	Min	3	0	4.0	0	0	0	0	-	.00
Quinlan,Robb	LAA	3	0	7.1	1	0	0	0	1.000	1.23
Raburn,Ryan	Det	30	9	127.2	29	2	1	0	.969	2.19
Ramirez,Manny	Bos	66	66	537.2	99	6	1	2	.991	1.76

305

Player	Tm	G	GS	Inn	PO	A	E	DP	Pct.	Rng
Ramirez,Manny	LAD	53	53	436.1	91	1	2	0	.979	1.90
Reed,Jeremy	Sea	6	3	29.2	5	1	0	0	1.000	1.82
Repko,Jason	LAD	12	0	18.0	6	0	0	0	1.000	3.00
Resop,Chris	Atl	1	0	0.1	0	0	0	0	-	.00
Riggans,Shawn	TB	1	0	1.0	0	0	0	0	-	.00
Rivera,Juan	LAA	41	35	307.0	59	3	2	1	.969	1.82
Roberts,Dave	SF	32	23	205.2	54	3	0	2	1.000	2.49
Romero,Alex	Ari	13	3	42.1	5	0	0	0	1.000	1.06
Ross,Cody	Fla	17	2	45.0	10	1	0	0	1.000	2.20
Ruggiano,Justin	TB	26	6	94.0	23	0	0	0	1.000	2.20
Ryan,Brendan	StL	1	0	1.0	1	0	0	0	1.000	9.00
Salazar,Jeff	Ari	27	13	133.1	17	2	0	0	1.000	1.28
Schumaker,Skip	StL	56	31	338.1	85	4	1	0	.989	2.37
Scutaro,Marco	Tor	3	3	25.0	4	1	0	0	1.000	1.80
Sheffield,Gary	Det	6	6	47.0	13	0	0	0	1.000	2.49
Smith,Jason	KC	1	0	1.0	0	0	0	0	-	.00
Smith,Seth	Col	8	1	17.2	5	0	0	0	1.000	2.55
Snider,Travis	Tor	13	11	99.0	14	2	0	1	1.000	1.45
Spilborghs,Ryan	Col	22	20	166.2	30	0	0	0	1.000	1.62
Stairs,Matt	Tor	9	8	62.0	10	0	0	0	1.000	1.45
Stavinoha,Nick	StL	13	6	53.0	9	0	0	0	1.000	1.53
Stewart,Shannon	Tor	40	36	310.1	56	3	0	3	1.000	1.71
Sullivan,Cory	Col	2	0	2.1	0	0	0	0	-	.00
Sweeney,Mark	LAD	1	0	1.0	0	0	0	0	-	.00
Sweeney,Ryan	Oak	13	2	43.0	12	0	0	0	1.000	2.51
Swisher,Nick	CWS	18	16	137.0	31	1	0	0	1.000	2.10
Taguchi,So	Phi	38	2	89.2	22	0	2	0	.917	2.21
Tatis,Fernando	NYM	51	28	284.0	47	0	2	0	.959	1.49
Teahen,Mark	KC	31	31	267.0	75	3	0	1	1.000	2.63
Thames,Marcus	Det	73	69	488.0	120	3	5	1	.961	2.27
Thomas,Clete	Det	25	11	139.0	40	4	2	1	.957	2.85
Thurston,Joe	Bos	4	1	19.0	5	0	0	0	1.000	2.37
Tiffee,Terry	LAD	1	0	1.0	0	0	0	0	-	.00
Timpner,Clay	SF	1	0	2.0	0	0	0	0	-	.00
Tyner,Jason	Cle	1	1	10.0	0	0	0	0	-	.00
Van Every,Jonathan	Bos	1	0	1.0	0	0	0	0	-	.00
Velez,Eugenio	SF	8	4	43.1	5	0	1	0	.833	1.04
Ward,Daryle	ChC	6	3	25.0	7	0	0	0	1.000	2.52
Washington,Rico	StL	1	0	0.0	0	0	0	0	-	-
Werth,Jayson	Phi	28	4	71.1	15	0	0	0	1.000	1.89
Wigginton,Ty	Hou	31	31	247.0	46	2	0	0	1.000	1.75
Wilkerson,Brad	Tor	29	13	138.2	24	0	0	0	1.000	1.56
Willits,Reggie	LAA	30	11	134.1	24	0	0	0	1.000	1.61
Winn,Randy	SF	15	13	107.2	30	1	0	0	1.000	2.59
Wise,Dewayne	CWS	24	14	132.2	28	2	2	0	.938	2.04
Young,Delwyn	LAD	15	9	86.0	16	2	0	0	1.000	1.88
Zobrist,Ben	TB	14	8	79.1	21	1	0	0	1.000	2.50

Center Fielders - Regulars

Player	Tm	G	GS	Inn	PO	A	E	DP	Pct.	Rng
Gomez,Carlos	Min	151	143	1271.2	436	9	8	4	.982	3.15
Suzuki,Ichiro	Sea	69	69	601.2	195	4	1	1	.995	2.98
Rowand,Aaron	SF	149	148	1275.1	412	6	4	0	.991	2.95
Upton,B.J.	TB	143	141	1248.2	378	16	7	5	.983	2.84
Gerut,Jody	SD	80	64	605.2	189	2	2	1	.990	2.84
Granderson,Curtis	Det	140	131	1188.0	366	5	4	1	.989	2.81
Jones,Adam	Bal	129	123	1102.0	336	4	3	1	.991	2.78
Patterson,Corey	Cin	124	82	798.0	242	3	3	1	.988	2.76
Beltran,Carlos	NYM	158	158	1407.1	418	8	3	1	.993	2.72
Ross,Cody	Fla	109	101	866.0	254	7	0	2	1.000	2.71
Bourn,Michael	Hou	130	111	1009.0	291	9	5	2	.984	2.68
Hamilton,Josh	Tex	111	107	912.0	268	3	5	3	.982	2.67
Hunter,Torii	LAA	137	137	1193.1	350	4	0	0	1.000	2.67
McLouth,Nate	Pit	149	148	1300.1	380	5	1	1	.997	2.66
Milledge,Lastings	Was	134	134	1185.2	348	1	5	0	.986	2.65
Taveras,Willy	Col	124	110	993.0	282	6	7	2	.976	2.61
Edmonds,Jim	TOT	103	99	840.0	242	1	6	1	.976	2.60
Sizemore,Grady	Cle	151	151	1338.0	382	2	2	1	.995	2.58
Cabrera,Melky	NYY	117	109	973.2	272	7	4	1	.986	2.58
Young,Chris	Ari	159	157	1390.0	393	5	3	2	.993	2.58
Ankiel,Rick	StL	89	84	766.1	213	4	5	1	.977	2.55
Gathright,Joey	KC	100	75	720.0	197	5	1	0	.995	2.53
Cameron,Mike	Mil	119	119	1057.0	293	3	1	0	.997	2.52

Player	Tm	G	GS	Inn	PO	A	E	DP	Pct.	Rng
Crisp,Coco	Bos	114	98	886.0	234	4	2	1	.992	2.42
Victorino,Shane	Phi	139	134	1195.1	314	7	2	2	.994	2.42
Kemp,Matt	LAD	101	92	825.2	209	10	1	3	.995	2.39
Kotsay,Mark	TOT	84	80	696.0	173	3	0	1	1.000	2.28
Wells,Vernon	Tor	100	99	889.0	217	5	3	1	.987	2.25

Center Fielders - The Rest

Player	Tm	G	GS	Inn	PO	A	E	DP	Pct.	Rng
Abercrombie,Reggie	Hou	11	10	77.1	29	2	0	1	1.000	3.61
Ambres,Chip	SD	3	3	22.1	3	0	0	0	1.000	1.21
Amezaga,Alfredo	Fla	79	48	457.1	144	6	1	1	.993	2.95
Anderson,Brian	CWS	94	37	447.1	102	0	0	0	1.000	2.05
Anderson,Josh	Atl	30	27	236.0	55	1	2	0	.966	2.14
Andino,Robert	Fla	1	0	6.0	2	0	0	0	1.000	3.00
Balentien,Wladimir	Sea	29	25	218.2	60	0	0	0	1.000	2.47
Barton,Brian	StL	2	0	2.0	0	0	0	0	-	.00
Bernadina,Roger	Was	14	12	108.0	27	0	1	0	.964	2.25
Blanco,Gregor	Atl	69	54	494.1	128	4	0	0	1.000	2.40
Bloomquist,Willie	Sea	23	16	161.1	48	1	3	0	.942	2.73
Boggs,Brandon	Tex	5	0	9.0	4	0	0	0	1.000	4.00
Brown,Emil	Oak	1	0	1.0	0	0	0	0	-	.00
Bruce,Jay	Cin	35	35	285.0	77	3	2	1	.976	2.53
Byrd,Marlon	Tex	57	46	433.0	149	4	3	0	.981	3.18
Byrnes,Eric	Ari	1	0	3.1	2	0	0	0	1.000	5.40
Cedeno,Ronny	ChC	1	0	1.0	0	0	0	0	-	.00
Chavez,Endy	NYM	10	2	38.1	9	1	0	0	1.000	2.35
Christian,Justin	NYY	3	3	22.1	5	1	0	0	1.000	2.42
Clevlen,Brent	Det	3	3	21.0	6	0	0	0	1.000	2.57
Crawford,Carl	TB	1	1	7.0	2	0	0	0	1.000	2.57
Cruz,Jose	Hou	5	5	35.0	9	0	0	0	1.000	2.31
Cuddyer,Michael	Min	1	1	8.0	3	1	0	1	1.000	4.50
Damon,Johnny	NYY	34	33	285.0	77	1	1	0	.987	2.46
Davis,Rajai	SF	4	2	22.2	6	0	0	0	1.000	2.38
Davis,Rajai	Oak	84	41	465.0	147	4	1	2	.993	2.92
DeJesus,David	KC	68	64	507.0	151	2	1	1	.994	2.72
Denorfia,Chris	Oak	12	8	73.2	26	0	0	0	1.000	3.18
Dickerson,Chris	Cin	7	6	45.0	10	0	0	0	1.000	2.00
Drew,J.D.	Bos	1	0	5.2	0	0	0	0	-	.00
Dukes,Elijah	Was	1	1	9.0	5	0	0	0	1.000	5.00
Edmonds,Jim	SD	26	24	212.1	63	1	1	1	.985	2.71
Edmonds,Jim	ChC	77	75	627.2	179	0	5	0	.973	2.57
Ellison,Jason	Tex	2	0	3.0	0	0	0	0	-	.00
Ellsbury,Jacoby	Bos	66	63	546.2	171	3	0	1	1.000	2.86
Erstad,Darin	Hou	40	35	304.0	97	1	0	0	1.000	2.90
Fiorentino,Jeff	Oak	2	0	4.0	0	0	0	0	-	.00
Fowler,Dexter	Col	9	5	49.2	12	1	0	1	1.000	2.36
Francisco,Ben	Cle	2	0	2.0	0	0	0	0	-	.00
Freel,Ryan	Cin	23	19	151.2	45	1	0	0	1.000	2.73
Fukudome,Kosuke	ChC	12	5	59.0	10	0	0	0	1.000	1.53
Gardner,Brett	NYY	22	17	160.2	53	4	0	0	1.000	3.19
Giles,Brian	SD	2	0	2.0	0	0	0	0	-	.00
Golson,Greg	Phi	2	1	13.0	2	0	1	0	.667	1.38
Gonzalez,Carlos	Oak	69	66	528.2	176	5	2	1	.989	3.08
Griffey Jr.,Ken	CWS	32	32	250.0	62	1	0	1	1.000	2.27
Gross,Gabe	Mil	13	13	98.2	28	1	1	1	.967	2.65
Gross,Gabe	TB	5	4	30.0	6	1	0	0	1.000	2.10
Gutierrez,Franklin	Cle	12	11	97.0	30	1	1	0	.969	2.88
Gwynn,Tony	Mil	7	5	46.0	14	0	0	0	1.000	2.74
Hairston,Jerry	Cin	17	15	116.2	27	1	1	0	.966	2.16
Hairston,Scott	SD	51	45	378.0	114	2	2	0	.983	2.76
Harris,Willie	Was	17	14	131.1	46	0	1	0	.979	3.15
Haynes,Nathan	TB	2	1	13.0	4	0	0	0	1.000	2.77
Hopper,Norris	Cin	7	5	46.0	12	0	0	0	1.000	2.35
Infante,Omar	Atl	3	1	14.1	4	0	0	0	1.000	2.51
Inge,Brandon	Det	13	12	94.0	26	2	0	0	1.000	2.68
Inglett,Joe	Tor	1	1	7.0	1	0	0	0	1.000	1.29
Iribarren,Hernan	Mil	1	0	3.0	1	0	0	0	1.000	3.00
Johnson,Elliot	TB	1	0	3.0	1	0	0	0	1.000	3.00
Johnson,Reed	ChC	78	64	563.2	144	2	1	1	.993	2.33
Jones,Andruw	LAD	66	55	496.1	133	1	1	0	.993	2.43
Jones,Jacque	Fla	5	5	41.0	13	0	0	0	1.000	2.85
Kapler,Gabe	Mil	36	25	251.0	70	0	1	0	.986	2.51
Lewis,Fred	SF	14	5	69.0	16	0	0	0	1.000	2.09

306

Player	Tm	G	GS	Inn	PO	A	E	DP	Pct.	Rng
Ludwick,Ryan	StL	14	10	64.0	20	0	1	0	.952	2.81
Maier,Mitch	KC	33	23	217.2	69	0	1	0	.986	2.85
Mather,Joe	StL	15	9	67.0	19	0	1	0	.950	2.55
Matthews Jr.,Gary	LAA	31	23	221.0	66	3	4	0	.945	2.81
Maybin,Cameron	Fla	8	7	63.0	23	0	0	0	1.000	3.29
Michaels,Jason	Pit	8	6	57.1	22	0	0	0	1.000	3.45
Miles,Aaron	StL	1	0	2.0	0	0	0	0	-	.00
Miller,Jai	Fla	1	0	2.0	0	0	0	0	-	.00
Monroe,Craig	Min	7	6	56.2	13	1	0	1	1.000	2.22
Montanez,Lou	Bal	5	2	19.0	4	0	0	0	1.000	1.89
Morgan,Nyjer	Pit	17	8	97.1	31	0	0	0	1.000	2.87
Murphy,David	Tex	13	9	85.0	30	0	0	0	1.000	3.18
Owens,Jerry	CWS	4	2	18.0	4	0	0	0	1.000	2.00
Pagan,Angel	NYM	2	2	18.2	8	0	0	0	1.000	3.86
Patterson,Eric	ChC	1	0	2.0	0	0	0	0	-	.00
Payton,Jay	Bal	38	36	301.0	99	6	0	0	1.000	3.14
Perez,Fernando	TB	15	11	112.0	47	1	0	1	1.000	3.86
Pie,Felix	ChC	39	17	197.1	58	1	0	0	1.000	2.69
Pierre,Juan	LAD	18	14	116.1	28	1	0	1	1.000	2.24
Podsednik,Scott	Col	36	21	201.1	55	1	2	0	.966	2.50
Punto,Nick	Min	3	0	6.0	1	0	0	0	1.000	1.50
Raburn,Ryan	Det	6	4	30.0	12	0	0	0	1.000	3.60
Ramirez,Alexei	CWS	11	6	63.0	16	1	1	0	.944	2.43
Reed,Jeremy	Sea	58	52	453.2	132	1	1	0	.993	2.64
Repko,Jason	LAD	2	1	9.0	7	0	0	0	1.000	7.00
Rios,Alex	Tor	62	59	522.2	156	10	3	1	.982	2.86
Rivera,Juan	LAA	1	0	3.0	3	0	0	0	1.000	9.00
Romero,Alex	Ari	2	2	13.2	4	0	0	0	1.000	2.63
Ruggiano,Justin	TB	5	1	17.0	5	2	0	1	1.000	3.71
Salazar,Jeff	Ari	4	3	27.2	3	1	0	0	1.000	1.30
Schumaker,Skip	StL	79	59	552.2	136	5	1	2	.993	2.30
Smith,Seth	Col	9	7	46.1	19	0	1	0	.950	3.69
Span,Denard	Min	19	13	116.2	34	1	1	0	.972	2.70
Spilborghs,Ryan	Col	17	16	130.2	34	0	0	0	1.000	2.34
Sullivan,Cory	Col	5	3	25.0	3	0	0	0	1.000	1.08
Sweeney,Ryan	Oak	51	46	362.2	95	0	0	0	1.000	2.36
Swisher,Nick	CWS	70	69	535.1	138	2	4	0	.972	2.35
Taguchi,So	Phi	1	1	8.0	0	0	0	0	-	.00
Teahen,Mark	KC	1	0	1.0	0	0	0	0	-	.00
Thomas,Clete	Det	16	12	112.0	40	0	2	0	.952	3.21
Van Every,Jonathan	Bos	1	1	8.0	1	0	0	0	1.000	1.13
Velez,Eugenio	SF	2	0	4.0	3	0	0	0	1.000	6.75
Venable,Will	SD	27	26	238.0	84	1	0	0	1.000	3.21
Werth,Jayson	Phi	31	26	233.1	73	2	2	1	.974	2.89
Wilkerson,Brad	Tor	5	3	28.0	7	0	0	0	1.000	2.25
Willits,Reggie	LAA	9	2	34.0	10	0	0	0	1.000	2.65
Winn,Randy	SF	10	7	71.0	18	1	0	0	1.000	2.41
Wise,Dewayne	CWS	23	17	144.0	40	0	0	0	1.000	2.50
Zobrist,Ben	TB	5	3	27.0	8	0	0	0	1.000	2.67

Right Fielders - Regulars

Player	Tm	G	GS	Inn	PO	A	E	DP	Pct.	Rng
Gutierrez,Franklin	Cle	97	85	763.2	224	4	2	0	.991	2.69
Span,Denard	Min	85	77	686.2	192	5	3	2	.985	2.58
Winn,Randy	SF	133	127	1108.1	309	5	3	2	.991	2.55
Nady,Xavier	TOT	89	88	763.2	199	10	2	5	.991	2.46
Pence,Hunter	Hou	156	154	1366.1	340	16	1	4	.997	2.34
Kearns,Austin	Was	85	83	734.0	187	3	4	0	.979	2.33
Church,Ryan	NYM	83	81	724.0	180	7	1	1	.995	2.32
Markakis,Nick	Bal	156	155	1367.0	327	17	3	3	.991	2.26
Ludwick,Ryan	StL	124	105	962.1	231	10	2	3	.992	2.25
Gross,Gabe	TOT	121	75	768.1	186	6	1	0	.995	2.25
Teahen,Mark	KC	92	84	756.1	185	4	2	2	.990	2.25
Hermida,Jeremy	Fla	132	124	1092.1	266	4	5	0	.982	2.22
Dukes,Elijah	Was	69	66	602.2	137	9	5	1	.967	2.18
Suzuki,Ichiro	Sea	91	90	788.1	175	7	4	1	.978	2.08
Jenkins,Geoff	Phi	90	72	642.0	140	7	5	1	.967	2.06
Fukudome,Kosuke	ChC	137	121	1103.2	245	6	5	0	.980	2.05
Werth,Jayson	Phi	88	73	661.1	143	7	0	1	1.000	2.04
Hart,Corey	Mil	156	156	1376.2	302	8	5	2	.984	2.03
Guerrero,Vladimir	LAA	99	99	839.0	180	8	4	2	.979	2.02
Francoeur,Jeff	Atl	152	151	1328.2	282	14	4	2	.987	2.01
Giles,Brian	SD	144	142	1263.0	276	3	7	1	.976	1.99

Player	Tm	G	GS	Inn	PO	A	E	DP	Pct.	Rng
Griffey Jr.,Ken	TOT	91	90	763.0	157	7	5	0	.970	1.93
Drew,J.D.	Bos	106	105	886.0	184	6	4	1	.979	1.93
Abreu,Bobby	NYY	150	148	1310.0	270	10	2	3	.993	1.92
Rios,Alex	Tor	93	92	820.0	170	4	1	2	.994	1.91
Upton,Justin	Ari	101	100	860.1	175	6	11	2	.943	1.89
Dye,Jermaine	CWS	151	151	1312.2	266	5	1	0	.996	1.86
Ethier,Andre	LAD	109	102	881.0	171	8	0	0	1.000	1.83
Ordonez,Magglio	Det	135	134	1144.0	220	8	5	0	.979	1.79
Hawpe,Brad	Col	133	132	1172.0	186	9	9	0	.956	1.50

Right Fielders - The Rest

Player	Tm	G	GS	Inn	PO	A	E	DP	Pct.	Rng
Ambres,Chip	SD	7	6	50.0	16	0	1	0	.941	2.88
Anderson,Brian	CWS	2	0	6.0	0	0	0	0	-	.00
Anderson,Josh	Atl	1	0	0.1	0	0	0	0	-	.00
Ankiel,Rick	StL	1	0	2.0	1	0	0	0	1.000	4.50
Bailey,Jeff	Bos	1	0	1.0	0	0	0	0	-	.00
Baker,Jeff	Col	3	3	21.0	2	0	1	0	.667	.86
Baldelli,Rocco	TB	6	3	29.2	5	0	1	0	.833	1.52
Balentien,Wladimir	Sea	35	32	293.0	76	5	2	0	.976	2.49
Barmes,Clint	Col	1	1	6.0	2	0	0	0	1.000	3.00
Barton,Brian	StL	10	6	48.0	15	0	1	0	.938	2.81
Blanco,Gregor	Atl	5	4	34.0	8	0	0	0	1.000	2.12
Bloomquist,Willie	Sea	13	7	74.1	14	0	0	0	1.000	1.70
Boggs,Brandon	Tex	3	1	11.1	3	0	0	0	1.000	2.38
Bonifacio,Emilio	Ari	2	2	16.0	1	0	0	0	1.000	.56
Bowker,John	SF	14	10	91.1	22	0	0	0	1.000	2.17
Bradley,Milton	Tex	19	19	157.1	42	4	3	3	.939	2.63
Brown,Emil	Oak	55	55	433.1	111	4	3	2	.975	2.39
Bruce,Jay	Cin	78	64	590.0	143	5	9	3	.943	2.26
Bruntlett,Eric	Phi	7	1	12.2	3	0	0	0	1.000	2.13
Buck,Travis	Oak	34	34	287.0	73	2	0	0	1.000	2.35
Burke,Chris	Ari	9	7	62.2	9	0	0	0	1.000	1.29
Burriss,Emmanuel	SF	1	0	2.1	0	0	0	0	-	.00
Byrd,Marlon	Tex	39	33	279.0	71	3	3	0	.961	2.39
Cabrera,Jolbert	Cin	3	2	17.0	1	0	0	0	1.000	.53
Cabrera,Melky	NYY	5	2	23.2	8	0	0	0	1.000	3.04
Cairo,Miguel	Sea	1	0	2.0	0	0	0	0	-	.00
Carroll,Brett	Fla	8	3	28.1	9	2	0	0	1.000	3.49
Casto,Kory	Was	1	1	9.0	4	1	0	1	1.000	5.00
Chavez,Endy	NYM	60	41	400.0	109	4	1	2	.991	2.54
Choo,Shin-Soo	Cle	51	45	398.1	88	1	1	0	.989	2.01
Christian,Justin	NYY	5	1	17.0	6	0	0	0	1.000	3.18
Clark,Brady	NYM	2	0	2.0	0	0	0	0	-	.00
Clevlen,Brent	Det	1	1	9.0	1	0	0	0	1.000	1.00
Crabbe,Callix	SD	2	1	10.0	3	0	0	0	1.000	2.70
Cruz,Jose	Hou	3	1	11.0	4	0	0	0	1.000	3.27
Cruz,Nelson	Tex	31	31	274.0	72	1	2	1	.973	2.40
Cuddyer,Michael	Min	58	57	501.2	123	6	1	4	.992	2.31
Cunningham,Aaron	Oak	2	2	18.1	6	0	0	0	1.000	2.95
Cust,Jack	Oak	5	5	39.0	4	0	0	0	1.000	.92
Davis,Rajai	SF	1	0	2.0	1	0	0	0	1.000	4.50
DeJesus,David	KC	23	11	123.0	23	0	0	0	1.000	1.68
Denorfia,Chris	Oak	2	1	10.0	2	0	0	0	1.000	1.80
DeRosa,Mark	ChC	38	32	266.2	72	0	0	0	1.000	2.43
Dobbs,Greg	Phi	4	0	4.2	1	0	0	0	1.000	1.93
Duncan,Chris	StL	2	2	15.0	4	0	0	0	1.000	2.40
Duncan,Shelley	NYY	4	3	23.0	4	0	0	0	1.000	1.57
Dunn,Adam	Ari	23	22	182.2	29	0	1	0	.967	1.43
Duran,German	Tex	2	1	9.0	4	0	0	0	1.000	4.00
Ellison,Jason	Tex	3	1	15.0	6	0	0	0	1.000	3.60
Ellsbury,Jacoby	Bos	36	30	281.0	72	0	0	0	1.000	2.31
Erstad,Darin	Hou	6	6	48.0	12	0	0	0	1.000	2.25
Fowler,Dexter	Col	1	0	1.0	0	0	0	0	-	.00
Francisco,Ben	Cle	32	27	230.0	46	5	2	1	.962	2.00
Freel,Ryan	Cin	5	0	10.1	4	0	0	0	1.000	3.48
Gerut,Jody	SD	9	7	63.0	17	0	0	0	1.000	2.43
Gload,Ross	KC	3	1	13.0	3	0	0	0	1.000	2.08
Golson,Greg	Phi	1	0	0.1	0	0	0	0	-	.00
Gomes,Jonny	TB	21	17	125.0	25	0	1	0	.962	1.80
Gonzalez,Carlos	Oak	36	10	160.2	43	0	0	0	1.000	2.41
Gonzalez,Edgar	SD	3	1	16.2	5	1	0	1	1.000	3.24
Gonzalez,Luis	Fla	22	20	147.1	30	1	0	0	1.000	1.89

Player	Tm	G	GS	Inn	PO	A	E	DP	Pct.	Rng
Griffey Jr.,Ken	Cin	90	89	755.0	156	7	5	0	.970	1.94
Griffey Jr.,Ken	CWS	1	1	8.0	1	0	0	0	1.000	1.13
Gross,Gabe	Mil	1	0	6.2	3	0	0	0	1.000	4.05
Gross,Gabe	TB	120	75	761.2	183	6	1	0	.995	2.23
Guillen,Jose	KC	67	65	539.1	121	7	3	1	.977	2.14
Gwynn,Tony	Mil	2	0	6.1	0	0	0	0	-	.00
Hairston,Jerry	Cin	12	5	47.0	17	0	0	0	1.000	3.26
Hamilton,Josh	Tex	34	33	289.0	77	4	1	2	.988	2.52
Haynes,Nathan	TB	15	8	83.0	19	0	1	0	.950	2.06
Hinske,Eric	TB	49	47	339.1	88	2	1	0	.989	2.39
Hoffpauir,Micah	ChC	5	5	36.0	6	0	0	0	1.000	1.50
Hopper,Norris	Cin	4	2	23.0	6	0	0	0	1.000	2.35
Horwitz,Brian	SF	2	1	9.0	6	0	0	0	1.000	6.00
Inglett,Joe	Tor	12	9	87.1	14	0	0	0	1.000	1.44
Johnson,Elliot	TB	1	1	8.0	3	0	0	0	1.000	3.38
Johnson,Reed	ChC	6	1	23.1	4	0	0	0	1.000	1.54
Jones,Brandon	Atl	7	3	34.2	8	0	0	0	1.000	2.08
Jones,Jacque	Fla	3	1	13.2	3	0	0	0	1.000	1.98
Joyce,Matt	Det	25	16	161.0	42	0	1	0	.977	2.35
Kapler,Gabe	Mil	14	6	66.0	9	0	0	0	1.000	1.23
Kemp,Matt	LAD	63	52	478.2	97	6	2	0	.981	1.94
Kennedy,Adam	StL	9	6	55.0	15	0	0	0	1.000	2.45
Kotsay,Mark	Bos	19	18	151.2	32	0	0	0	1.000	1.90
Kubel,Jason	Min	32	26	238.2	74	1	1	0	.987	2.83
Langerhans,Ryan	Was	12	9	74.1	23	1	0	1	1.000	2.91
Lewis,Fred	SF	2	2	18.0	5	0	0	0	1.000	2.50
Lopez,Felipe	StL	1	0	2.0	1	0	1	0	.500	4.50
Macias,Drew	SD	3	0	7.1	4	0	0	0	1.000	4.91
Mackowiak,Rob	Was	2	2	14.0	2	0	0	0	1.000	1.29
Maier,Mitch	KC	4	1	14.0	2	0	0	0	1.000	1.29
Mather,Joe	StL	15	6	64.2	17	0	0	0	1.000	2.37
Matsui,Hideki	NYY	3	2	18.0	2	0	0	0	1.000	1.00
Matthews Jr.,Gary	LAA	43	36	344.0	77	2	2	0	.975	2.07
McAnulty,Paul	SD	15	5	48.1	18	0	0	0	1.000	3.35
McLouth,Nate	Pit	2	1	12.0	2	0	0	0	1.000	1.50
Mench,Kevin	Tor	15	11	98.0	22	1	0	0	1.000	2.11
Michaels,Jason	Cle	6	5	45.0	15	1	1	0	.941	3.20
Michaels,Jason	Pit	37	25	248.0	73	1	3	0	.961	2.69
Mientkiewicz,Doug	Pit	10	6	60.0	20	1	0	0	1.000	3.15
Miles,Aaron	StL	1	0	3.2	3	0	0	0	1.000	7.36
Monroe,Craig	Min	3	3	25.0	5	0	0	0	1.000	1.80
Montanez,Lou	Bal	5	2	23.0	1	0	0	0	1.000	.39
Morales,Kendry	LAA	12	4	60.0	19	0	0	0	1.000	2.85
Morgan,Nyjer	Pit	6	5	47.0	14	0	0	0	1.000	2.68
Morse,Mike	Sea	5	3	25.0	6	2	0	0	1.000	2.88
Moss,Brandon	Bos	14	8	86.0	19	2	0	0	1.000	2.20
Moss,Brandon	Pit	18	16	148.0	39	4	0	1	1.000	2.61
Murphy,David	Tex	56	43	407.1	107	1	1	1	.991	2.39
Murton,Matt	ChC	2	0	4.0	1	0	0	0	1.000	2.25
Nady,Xavier	Pit	82	82	713.2	189	10	2	5	.990	2.51
Nady,Xavier	NYY	7	6	50.0	10	0	0	0	1.000	1.80
Nixon,Trot	NYM	5	4	37.2	9	0	0	0	1.000	2.15
Norton,Greg	Sea	1	0	3.0	0	0	0	0	-	.00
Norton,Greg	Atl	1	1	2.0	0	0	0	0	-	.00
Ortmeier,Dan	SF	2	0	5.0	1	0	0	0	1.000	1.80
Pagan,Angel	NYM	1	1	8.0	3	0	0	0	1.000	3.38
Payton,Jay	Bal	4	4	32.0	8	0	0	0	1.000	2.25
Pearce,Steve	Pit	29	27	226.1	49	1	2	0	.962	1.99
Perez,Fernando	TB	2	2	17.0	1	0	0	0	1.000	.53
Perry,Jason	Atl	4	3	41.0	13	0	0	0	1.000	2.85
Phelps,Josh	StL	2	2	10.0	4	0	0	0	1.000	3.60
Podsednik,Scott	Col	1	0	3.0	1	0	0	0	1.000	3.00
Pridie,Jason	Min	3	0	7.0	3	0	1	0	.750	3.86
Quinlan,Robb	LAA	3	0	5.1	1	0	0	0	1.000	1.69
Raburn,Ryan	Det	22	6	84.0	22	0	1	0	.957	2.36
Reed,Jeremy	Sea	14	12	101.0	19	0	2	0	.905	1.69
Repko,Jason	LAD	7	0	15.0	2	0	0	0	1.000	1.20
Rivera,Juan	LAA	19	15	115.0	19	1	1	0	.952	1.57
Romero,Alex	Ari	38	23	221.0	39	1	1	0	.976	1.63
Ross,Cody	Fla	35	13	153.2	37	0	1	0	.974	2.17
Ruggiano,Justin	TB	15	8	87.0	21	0	1	0	.955	2.17
Ryan,Brendan	StL	3	3	19.0	4	0	0	0	1.000	1.89
Salazar,Jeff	Ari	18	8	92.0	16	0	0	0	1.000	1.57
Schierholtz,Nate	SF	19	18	161.2	40	1	0	0	1.000	2.28

Player	Tm	G	GS	Inn	PO	A	E	DP	Pct.	Rng
Schumaker,Skip	StL	33	30	249.1	64	1	1	1	.985	2.35
Smith,Seth	Col	14	11	86.0	18	1	0	0	1.000	1.99
Snider,Travis	Tor	7	7	60.0	11	0	0	0	1.000	1.65
Spilborghs,Ryan	Col	22	15	146.0	37	0	2	0	.949	2.28
Stairs,Matt	Tor	6	6	45.0	9	0	0	0	1.000	1.80
Stairs,Matt	Phi	4	3	16.2	5	0	0	0	1.000	2.70
Stavinoha,Nick	StL	5	2	20.0	2	0	0	0	1.000	.90
Sullivan,Cory	Col	5	0	11.0	1	0	0	0	1.000	.82
Sweeney,Ryan	Oak	75	54	486.2	136	6	1	0	.993	2.63
Swisher,Nick	CWS	18	11	118.0	25	0	1	0	.962	1.91
Taguchi,So	Phi	11	9	72.0	11	0	0	0	1.000	1.38
Tatis,Fernando	NYM	39	35	292.2	55	2	0	0	1.000	1.75
Thames,Marcus	Det	7	2	25.0	8	0	0	0	1.000	2.88
Thomas,Clete	Det	3	3	22.0	8	0	0	0	1.000	3.27
Van Every,Jonathan	Bos	8	1	32.0	15	0	0	0	1.000	4.22
Velez,Eugenio	SF	7	4	44.1	8	1	0	0	1.000	1.83
Victorino,Shane	Phi	5	4	40.0	14	0	0	0	1.000	3.15
Ward,Daryle	ChC	3	2	17.0	4	0	0	0	1.000	2.12
Washington,Rico	StL	1	0	3.0	0	0	0	0	-	.00
Wilkerson,Brad	Sea	19	18	148.2	18	1	0	0	1.000	1.15
Wilkerson,Brad	Tor	45	37	336.1	77	3	1	0	.988	2.14
Willits,Reggie	LAA	22	8	88.0	12	0	0	0	1.000	1.23
Wise,Dewayne	CWS	6	0	13.0	4	0	0	0	1.000	2.77
Youkilis,Kevin	Bos	2	0	8.2	3	0	0	0	1.000	3.12
Young,Delwyn	LAD	11	8	72.2	8	2	0	1	1.000	1.24
Zobrist,Ben	TB	2	1	7.0	0	0	0	0	-	.00

Catchers - Regulars

Player	Tm	G	GS	Inn	PO	A	E	DP	PB	Pct.
Iannetta,Chris	Col	100	96	837.0	606	51	0	4	6	1.000
Snyder,Chris	Ari	112	106	922.2	777	69	0	5	7	1.000
Mauer,Joe	Min	139	135	1203.0	831	52	3	1	4	.997
Varitek,Jason	Bos	131	120	1041.1	903	42	4	7	4	.996
Molina,Jose	NYY	81	77	737.0	634	52	3	6	7	.996
Soto,Geovany	ChC	136	131	1150.1	1011	55	5	9	5	.995
Molina,Bengie	SF	136	132	1128.1	987	71	5	6	5	.995
Kendall,Jason	Mil	149	149	1328.1	1025	95	6	13	4	.995
Barajas,Rod	Tor	90	90	785.1	674	47	4	5	2	.994
Navarro,Dioner	TB	117	113	1011.1	837	55	5	10	6	.994
Coste,Chris	Phi	78	69	612.2	488	23	3	6	1	.994
Napoli,Mike	LAA	75	71	625.0	469	21	3	3	7	.994
Suzuki,Kurt	Oak	141	136	1215.0	927	53	6	4	5	.994
Schneider,Brian	NYM	109	99	881.0	741	41	5	3	4	.994
Bako,Paul	Cin	96	88	770.2	679	39	5	7	9	.993
Ruiz,Carlos	Phi	110	92	828.0	623	58	5	2	4	.993
Rodriguez,Ivan	TOT	112	105	930.0	620	58	5	9	6	.993
Pierzynski,A.J.	CWS	131	127	1134.1	913	54	9	8	5	.991
McCann,Brian	Atl	138	132	1143.1	879	70	9	9	7	.991
Martin,Russell	LAD	149	138	1238.0	1042	65	11	8	6	.990
Flores,Jesus	Was	82	78	673.0	474	29	5	6	7	.990
Buck,John	KC	107	106	950.1	751	24	8	6	4	.990
Shoppach,Kelly	Cle	110	94	872.2	586	34	7	2	8	.989
Hernandez,Ramon	Bal	127	119	1039.1	714	45	9	8	10	.988
Johjima,Kenji	Sea	100	95	833.1	632	34	8	8	7	.988
Doumit,Ryan	Pit	106	103	909.0	596	59	8	8	9	.988
Zaun,Gregg	Tor	79	67	612.1	515	28	7	7	4	.987
Molina,Yadier	StL	119	114	1002.0	653	70	10	7	5	.986
Laird,Gerald	Tex	88	86	753.0	523	35	8	7	6	.986
Mathis,Jeff	LAA	94	90	793.1	624	57	13	5	3	.981

Catchers - The Rest

Player	Tm	G	GS	Inn	PO	A	E	DP	PB	Pct.
Alfonzo,Eliezer	SF	2	2	17.0	10	1	1	0	0	.917
Ardoin,Danny	LAD	24	17	145.1	126	11	1	4	2	.993
Ausmus,Brad	Hou	77	62	569.2	428	33	2	4	4	.996
Baker,John	Fla	59	54	496.0	402	22	4	0	3	.991
Bard,Josh	SD	49	47	416.2	329	20	3	1	1	.991
Barrett,Michael	SD	30	29	252.1	205	16	2	0	3	.991
Bellorin,Edwin	Col	2	0	6.0	4	0	0	0	0	1.000
Bennett,Gary	LAD	10	6	54.0	43	3	1	0	1	.979
Blanco,Henry	ChC	45	28	257.2	235	15	2	2	3	.992
Bowen,Rob	Oak	31	25	220.0	147	9	2	1	3	.987

Player	Tm	G	GS	Inn	PO	A	E	DP	PB	Pct.
Budde,Ryan	LAA	7	1	17.0	13	2	0	0	0	1.000
Burke,Jamie	Sea	43	25	246.0	181	10	1	0	2	.995
Cancel,Robinson	NYM	15	9	93.0	81	1	0	0	1	1.000
Carlin,Luke	SD	36	27	259.2	206	14	3	2	3	.987
Casanova,Raul	NYM	13	13	118.0	89	7	0	0	1	1.000
Cash,Kevin	Bos	57	42	372.0	280	26	4	5	14	.987
Castro,Ramon	NYM	47	40	354.1	286	19	4	2	1	.987
Cervelli,Francisco	NYY	3	1	13.2	11	0	0	0	0	1.000
Chavez,Raul	Pit	35	31	278.0	188	23	1	2	3	.995
Clement,Jeff	Sea	38	35	292.0	195	7	1	0	5	.995
Diaz,Robinzon	Pit	1	1	8.0	5	1	0	1	0	1.000
DiFelice,Mike	TB	7	6	54.0	42	3	0	1	0	1.000
Ellis,A.J.	LAD	3	1	10.0	7	1	0	0	0	1.000
Estrada,Johnny	Was	14	12	94.1	78	8	2	0	0	.977
Fasano,Sal	Cle	15	14	117.0	102	9	2	1	3	.982
Hall,Toby	CWS	37	36	315.1	231	15	2	0	1	.992
Hammock,Robby	Ari	15	11	107.1	92	3	0	0	1	1.000
Hanigan,Ryan	Cin	30	25	229.1	186	19	1	4	1	.995
Hernandez,Michel	TB	4	4	33.0	20	1	1	0	0	.955
Hill,Koyie	ChC	9	2	42.2	40	1	1	0	0	.976
Holm,Steve	SF	42	19	210.1	190	5	0	0	1	1.000
Hoover,Paul	Fla	13	12	104.1	84	8	0	0	2	1.000
Hundley,Nick	SD	59	55	486.1	366	32	4	4	4	.990
Inge,Brandon	Det	60	56	493.2	370	33	0	4	11	1.000
Jaso,John	TB	3	1	16.0	11	1	0	0	0	1.000
Johnson,Mark	StL	10	4	40.0	34	0	0	0	0	1.000
Johnson,Rob	Sea	10	7	64.0	44	7	0	0	0	1.000
Jorgensen,Ryan	Min	2	0	3.0	1	0	0	0	0	1.000
Kottaras,George	Bos	2	0	8.0	5	0	0	0	0	1.000
LaRue,Jason	StL	57	44	412.0	289	16	2	1	2	.993
Lo Duca,Paul	Was	20	19	161.0	114	6	0	0	1	1.000
Lo Duca,Paul	Fla	6	6	47.2	49	1	2	0	0	.962
Marson,Lou	Phi	1	1	9.0	9	1	0	0	0	1.000
Martinez,Victor	Cle	55	54	447.1	328	16	3	1	2	.991
Melhuse,Adam	Tex	6	5	42.0	18	2	0	0	0	1.000
Melhuse,Adam	Col	4	2	22.0	17	5	0	0	0	1.000
Miller,Corky	Atl	29	17	164.1	129	18	3	0	4	.980
Moeller,Chad	NYY	33	25	225.0	159	15	3	2	0	.983
Molina,Gustavo	NYM	2	2	18.0	19	0	0	0	0	1.000
Montero,Miguel	Ari	53	45	404.2	352	23	4	2	0	.989
Montz,Luke	Was	8	6	56.0	44	4	1	1	1	.980
Morton,Colt	SD	7	4	43.1	26	5	0	0	0	1.000
Nieves,Wil	Was	61	46	449.2	359	31	3	4	3	.992
Olivo,Miguel	KC	58	56	494.1	378	32	5	6	4	.988
Paulino,Ronny	Pit	32	27	260.0	198	16	2	3	1	.991
Phillips,Paul	CWS	4	0	8.0	7	0	0	0	0	1.000
Posada,Jorge	NYY	30	28	234.1	197	7	1	1	2	.995
Quintero,Humberto	Hou	59	52	447.1	373	26	1	3	1	.998
Quiroz,Guillermo	Bal	54	39	354.1	229	17	1	3	5	.996
Rabelo,Mike	Fla	32	29	262.2	179	11	1	1	3	.995
Ramirez,Max	Tex	12	8	82.0	56	5	1	2	0	.984
Redmond,Mike	Min	30	28	253.0	180	9	0	2	0	1.000
Riggans,Shawn	TB	41	38	343.1	268	5	5	0	4	.982
Rivera,Mike	Mil	17	13	127.1	112	11	3	2	1	.976
Rodriguez,Ivan	Det	81	79	706.1	447	44	4	8	4	.992
Rodriguez,Ivan	NYY	31	26	223.2	173	14	1	1	2	.995
Ross,David	Cin	46	43	374.2	323	29	3	4	6	.992
Ross,David	Bos	8	0	25.0	23	0	0	0	0	1.000
Ryan,Dusty	Det	15	14	122.1	99	5	0	0	1	1.000
Saltalamacchia,J	Tex	54	52	464.1	345	17	9	6	6	.976
Sammons,Clint	Atl	22	13	133.0	106	3	0	0	3	1.000
Sandoval,Pablo	SF	11	9	86.1	76	6	0	1	2	1.000
Santos,Omir	Bal	9	3	28.1	19	0	0	0	0	1.000
Sardinha,Dane	Det	17	13	122.2	109	8	1	1	0	.992
Stewart,Chris	NYY	1	1	8.0	8	0	0	0	0	1.000
Teagarden,Taylor	Tex	12	11	100.2	67	6	3	0	1	.961
Thigpen,Curtis	Tor	9	5	49.0	36	3	0	2	0	1.000
Torrealba,Yorvit	Col	67	64	581.0	433	26	2	4	4	.996
Towles,J.R.	Hou	53	47	408.2	312	13	2	1	3	.994
Treanor,Matt	Fla	65	60	524.2	453	29	8	3	2	.984
Tupman,Matt	KC	1	0	1.0	0	0	0	0	0	
Valentin,Javier	Cin	17	6	67.2	67	5	0	0	1	1.000
Wilson,Bobby	LAA	7	0	16.0	15	1	0	0	0	1.000

Catchers Special - Regulars

Player	Tm	G	GS	Inn	SBA	CS	PCS	CS%	ER	CERA
Molina,Jose	NYY	97	81	737.0	75	33	1	.43	302	3.69
Kendall,Jason	Mil	149	149	1328.1	96	41	5	.40	568	3.85
Navarro,Dioner	TB	117	113	1011.1	73	28	3	.36	438	3.90
Molina,Yadier	StL	119	114	1002.0	52	18	2	.32	470	4.22
Molina,Bengie	SF	136	132	1128.1	104	36	4	.32	539	4.30
Rodriguez,Ivan	TOT	112	105	930.0	77	25	2	.31	473	4.58
Snyder,Chris	Ari	112	106	922.2	71	22	2	.29	393	3.83
Barajas,Rod	Tor	98	90	785.1	64	22	5	.29	290	3.32
Schneider,Brian	NYM	109	98	881.0	63	21	5	.28	402	4.11
Laird,Gerald	Tex	88	86	753.0	74	21	1	.27	436	5.21
Johjima,Kenji	Sea	100	95	833.1	77	25	6	.27	423	4.57
Bako,Paul	Cin	96	88	770.2	77	22	2	.27	373	4.36
Mauer,Joe	Min	139	135	1203.0	80	29	11	.26	564	4.22
Zaun,Gregg	Tor	79	67	612.1	54	14	2	.23	259	3.81
Suzuki,Kurt	Oak	141	136	1215.0	87	32	16	.23	521	3.86
Mathis,Jeff	LAA	94	90	793.1	77	20	4	.22	323	3.66
Shoppach,Kelly	Cle	110	94	872.2	47	10	6	.21	424	4.37
Soto,Geovany	ChC	136	131	1150.1	94	25	7	.21	486	3.80
Martin,Russell	LAD	149	138	1238.0	93	23	6	.20	499	3.63
Flores,Jesus	Was	82	78	673.0	64	17	6	.19	337	4.51
Varitek,Jason	Bos	131	120	1041.1	72	16	3	.19	424	3.66
Ruiz,Carlos	Phi	110	92	828.0	85	20	6	.18	354	3.85
McCann,Brian	Atl	138	132	1143.1	120	27	6	.18	540	4.25
Doumit,Ryan	Pit	106	103	909.0	93	25	10	.18	512	5.07
Hernandez,Ramon	Bal	127	119	1039.1	123	24	3	.18	579	5.01
Iannetta,Chris	Col	100	96	837.0	53	12	4	.16	429	4.61
Coste,Chris	Phi	78	69	612.2	57	13	5	.15	270	3.97
Napoli,Mike	LAA	75	71	625.0	63	11	2	.15	309	4.45
Buck,John	KC	107	106	950.1	71	12	5	.11	480	4.55
Pierzynski,A.J.	CWS	131	127	1134.1	117	21	10	.10	533	4.23

Catchers Special - The Rest

Player	Tm	G	GS	Inn	SBA	CS	PCS	CS%	ER	CERA
Alfonzo,Eliezer	SF	2	2	17.0	3	0	0	.00	10	5.29
Ardoin,Danny	LAD	24	17	145.1	13	3	0	.23	61	3.78
Ausmus,Brad	Hou	77	62	569.2	24	5	1	.17	235	3.71
Baker,John	Fla	59	54	496.0	48	8	2	.13	233	4.23
Bard,Josh	SD	49	47	416.2	63	10	1	.15	197	4.26
Barrett,Michael	SD	30	29	252.1	49	6	1	.10	125	4.46
Bellorin,Edwin	Col	2	0	6.0	0	0	0	-	4	6.00
Bennett,Gary	LAD	10	6	54.0	2	0	0	.00	27	4.50
Blanco,Henry	ChC	45	28	257.2	22	10	1	.43	112	3.91
Bowen,Rob	Oak	31	25	220.0	24	9	4	.25	119	4.87
Budde,Ryan	LAA	7	1	17.0	0	0	0	-	7	3.71
Burke,Jamie	Sea	43	25	246.0	20	8	3	.29	131	4.79
Cancel,Robinson	NYM	15	9	93.0	2	0	0	.00	48	4.65
Carlin,Luke	SD	36	27	259.2	32	7	0	.22	112	3.88
Casanova,Raul	NYM	13	13	118.0	5	2	0	.40	61	4.65
Cash,Kevin	Bos	57	42	372.0	54	16	2	.27	199	4.81
Castro,Ramon	NYM	47	40	354.1	23	5	0	.22	145	3.68
Cervelli,Francisco	NYY	3	1	13.2	1	0	0	.00	12	7.90
Chavez,Raul	Pit	35	31	278.0	25	4	1	.38	147	4.76
Clement,Jeff	Sea	38	35	292.0	20	2	2	.00	164	5.05
Diaz,Robinzon	Pit	1	1	8.0	1	1	0	1.00	8	9.00
DiFelice,Mike	TB	7	6	54.0	6	2	0	.33	22	3.67
Ellis,A.J.	LAD	3	1	10.0	0	0	0	-	5	4.50
Estrada,Johnny	Was	14	12	94.1	19	6	2	.24	54	5.15
Fasano,Sal	Cle	15	14	117.0	12	4	1	.27	74	5.69
Hall,Toby	CWS	37	36	315.1	52	9	6	.07	129	3.68
Hammock,Robby	Ari	15	11	107.1	13	2	1	.08	37	3.10
Hanigan,Ryan	Cin	30	25	229.1	23	8	0	.35	106	4.16
Hernandez,Michel	TB	4	4	33.0	3	0	0	.00	12	3.27
Hill,Koyie	ChC	9	2	42.2	7	1	0	.14	26	5.48
Holm,Steve	SF	42	19	210.1	23	2	1	.09	110	4.71
Hoover,Paul	Fla	13	12	104.1	8	3	0	.38	69	5.95
Hundley,Nick	SD	59	55	486.1	56	14	1	.24	257	4.76
Inge,Brandon	Det	60	56	493.2	37	11	1	.28	308	5.62
Jaso,John	TB	3	1	16.0	0	0	0	-	8	4.50
Johnson,Mark	StL	10	4	40.0	2	0	0	.00	15	3.38
Johnson,Rob	Sea	10	7	64.0	12	2	1	.09	36	5.06
Jorgensen,Ryan	Min	2	0	3.0	0	0	0	-	0	0.00

Player	Tm	G	GS	Inn	SBA	CS	PCS	CS%	ER	CERA
Kottaras,George	Bos	2	0	8.0	0	0	0	-	7	7.88
LaRue,Jason	StL	57	44	412.0	21	8	3	.28	194	4.24
Lo Duca,Paul	Was	20	19	161.0	15	2	1	.07	90	5.03
Lo Duca,Paul	Fla	6	6	47.2	5	0	0	.00	16	3.02
Marson,Lou	Phi	1	1	9.0	1	1	0	1.00	3	3.00
Martinez,Victor	Cle	55	54	447.1	35	13	3	.31	214	4.31
Melhuse,Adam	Tex	6	5	42.0	4	2	0	.50	32	6.86
Melhuse,Adam	Col	4	2	22.0	2	2	0	1.00	2	0.82
Miller,Corky	Atl	29	17	164.1	15	6	0	.40	70	3.83
Moeller,Chad	NYY	33	25	225.0	24	9	2	.32	105	4.20
Molina,Gustavo	NYM	2	2	18.0	1	0	0	.00	7	3.50
Montero,Miguel	Ari	53	45	404.2	34	7	1	.18	206	4.58
Montz,Luke	Was	8	6	56.0	9	3	0	.33	32	5.14
Morton,Colt	SD	7	4	43.1	6	1	0	.17	23	4.78
Nieves,Wil	Was	61	46	449.2	49	10	1	.19	230	4.60
Olivo,Miguel	KC	58	56	494.1	33	14	2	.39	243	4.42
Paulino,Ronny	Pit	32	27	260.0	31	8	0	.26	157	5.43
Phillips,Paul	CWS	4	0	8.0	0	0	0	-	3	3.38
Posada,Jorge	NYY	30	28	234.1	41	7	4	.08	121	4.65
Quintero,Humberto	Hou	59	52	447.0	24	9	2	.32	243	4.89
Quiroz,Guillermo	Bal	54	39	354.1	39	9	2	.19	220	5.59
Rabelo,Mike	Fla	32	29	262.2	22	6	1	.24	121	4.15
Ramirez,Max	Tex	12	8	82.0	15	3	0	.20	72	7.90
Redmond,Mike	Min	30	28	253.0	23	5	2	.14	113	4.02
Riggans,Shawn	TB	41	38	343.1	25	1	0	.04	138	3.62
Rivera,Mike	Mil	17	13	127.1	20	4	2	.11	58	4.10
Rodriguez,Ivan	Det	81	79	706.1	50	18	1	.35	333	4.24
Rodriguez,Ivan	NYY	31	26	223.2	27	7	1	.23	140	5.63
Ross,David	Cin	46	43	374.2	34	10	0	.29	212	5.09
Ross,David	Bos	8	0	25.0	2	0	0	.00	15	5.40
Ryan,Dusty	Det	15	14	122.1	13	6	2	.36	83	6.11
Saltalamacchia,J	Tex	54	52	464.1	49	9	2	.15	265	5.14
Sammons,Clint	Atl	22	13	133.0	13	2	2	.00	105	7.11
Sandoval,Pablo	SF	11	9	86.1	10	3	0	.30	42	4.38
Santos,Omir	Bal	9	3	28.1	1	0	0	.00	15	4.76
Sardinha,Dane	Det	17	13	122.2	5	1	0	.20	64	4.70
Stewart,Chris	NYY	1	1	8.0	1	0	0	.00	6	6.75
Teagarden,Taylor	Tex	12	11	100.2	9	2	0	.22	55	4.92
Thigpen,Curtis	Tor	9	5	49.0	5	1	0	.20	12	2.20
Torrealba,Yorvit	Col	67	64	581.0	61	16	4	.21	331	5.13
Towles,J.R.	Hou	53	47	408.2	20	7	2	.28	217	4.78
Treanor,Matt	Fla	65	60	524.2	59	15	3	.21	269	4.61
Tupman,Matt	KC	1	0	1.0	0	0	0	-	0	0.00
Valentin,Javier	Cin	17	6	67.2	1	0	0	.00	38	5.05
Wilson,Bobby	LAA	7	0	16.0	0	0	0	-	6	3.38

The Baserunners

Bill James

Who would be the best baserunner in the major leagues?   Who would be the worst baserunner in the major leagues?

We are not essentially in the business of rating or ranking ballplayers. We are in the business of keeping track of the facts, and making those available to you.   It would, however, be somewhat absurd to report each player's hits and at bats, and not bother to figure the batting average, or the slugging percentage, or the on base percentage.   A certain amount of primitive analysis is essential to record-keeping.

Hence, the baserunning data that follows.   Let us compare Curtis Granderson, who is a really good baserunner, with Magglio Ordonez, who is a great hitter but, at 34, not quite what he used to be on the bases.

Granderson was on first base when a single was hit to the outfield 34 times, and went to third base 10 times.   Magglio was on first when a single was hit 21 times, and made it to third only 4 times.

Granderson was on second when a single was hit 26 times, and scored 21 times (81%).   Magglio was on second when a single was hit 20 times, and scored 10 times.

Granderson was on first when a double was hit 9 times, and scored 6 times.   Magglio was also on first when a double was hit 9 times, and scored only 3 times.

We compare all of these to the averages, which in all of these cases is a percentage better than Ordonez', but less than Granderson's.   An average baserunner goes from first to third 27% of the time, Granderson 29%, Ordonez 19%.   Granderson is +1, Ordonez –2.   In these three areas Granderson is +1, +6 and +2; Ordonez is –2, –2 and –1.

We also look at how often the baserunner moves up on a Wild Pitch, A Passed Ball, a Balk, a Sacrifice Fly or Defensive Indifference.   These things, taken together, we call "Bases Taken".   Curtis Granderson took 23 bases; Magglio Ordonez took 6.

We look at how many times the player is doubled off on the bases, and how often he runs into an out. We look at how many times he bats in a potential Double Play situation, and how often he grounds into a Double Play.

Finally, we add in base stealing—one point for a stolen base, minus two points for a caught stealing. Adding all that together, Curtis Granderson is +31, making him. . .well, not one of the top 10 base runners in the majors, but pretty close to that. Magglio comes in at –35, making him grateful for Dioner Navarro's late-season leg injuries. These are the best and worst baserunners of 2008:

1.	Willy Taveras	+70	1.	Dioner Navarro	-39
2.	Ichiro	+56	2.	Magglio	-35
3.	Matt Holliday	+52	3.	Edgar Gonzalez	-27
4.	Grady Sizemore	+50	4.	Yorvit Torrealba	-26
5.	Jimmy Rollins	+46	5.	Yunel Escobar	-25
6.	Nate McLouth	+44	6.	Mike Lowell	-23
7.	Ian Kinsler	+41	7.	Ramon Hernandez	-22
	Randy Winn	+41		Prince Fielder	-22
9.	Jacoby Ellsbury	+40		Billy Butler	-22
10.	Carlos Beltran	+35	10.	Long List of Guys	-21

2008 Baserunning

Player	1st to 3rd Moved	1st to 3rd Chances	2nd to Home Moved	2nd to Home Chances	1st to Home Moved	1st to Home Chances	Bases Taken	Out Adv	Doubled Off	BR Outs	GDP	GDP Opps	BR Gain	SB Gain	Net Gain
Abreu,Bobby	7	26	16	26	4	9	21	4	2	7	14	166	+1	0	+1
Amezaga,Alfredo	2	9	6	13	4	6	14	0	0	0	6	64	+13	+4	+17
Anderson,Brian	3	5	5	5	0	0	8	1	0	1	2	27	+9	+3	+12
Anderson,Garret	4	21	11	15	1	8	15	1	0	1	11	118	+9	-1	+8
Anderson,Josh	4	5	2	7	0	1	5	2	0	2	1	23	0	+8	+8
Ankiel,Rick	5	18	6	11	2	2	9	3	3	6	8	93	-8	0	-8
Atkins,Garrett	6	22	13	19	4	10	11	1	2	3	20	157	-2	-1	-3
Aurilia,Rich	4	21	3	6	1	2	3	2	1	3	11	78	-13	-1	-14
Ausmus,Brad	0	8	0	3	1	3	9	0	0	0	4	50	+5	-4	+1
Aviles,Mike	10	19	15	20	4	5	16	1	1	2	12	99	+17	+2	+19
Aybar,Erick	12	20	14	17	1	3	14	5	1	6	2	75	+11	+3	+14
Aybar,Willy	3	6	3	7	2	4	7	6	0	6	7	71	-11	-2	-13
Baker,Jeff	4	20	7	10	3	5	7	0	0	0	5	64	+8	+4	+12
Baker,John	2	9	3	9	1	3	11	1	0	1	6	48	+3	0	+3
Bako,Paul	1	6	3	9	0	0	5	1	1	2	9	64	-7	-4	-11
Balentien,Wladimir	2	8	2	5	1	2	5	0	0	0	12	55	-3	-2	-5
Barajas,Rod	3	22	4	12	1	4	5	3	0	3	9	82	-12	0	-12
Bard,Josh	3	6	3	6	0	0	2	1	0	1	5	42	-1	0	-1
Barmes,Clint	4	10	5	7	2	2	13	0	0	0	9	57	+12	+5	+17
Bartlett,Jason	6	15	6	12	6	10	11	2	0	3	9	92	+3	+8	+11
Barton,Brian	3	9	3	4	2	2	7	1	0	2	5	34	+1	+1	+2
Barton,Daric	2	13	13	18	5	8	12	0	1	1	6	97	+14	0	+14
Bautista,Jose	5	15	9	14	0	2	3	3	3	6	12	97	-17	-1	-18
Bay,Jason	8	27	17	33	5	11	24	2	1	3	7	130	+17	+10	+27
Belliard,Ronnie	3	12	6	9	1	3	5	1	0	1	6	69	+2	-1	+1
Beltran,Carlos	10	33	15	23	7	10	13	0	1	1	11	136	+16	+19	+35
Beltre,Adrian	5	24	11	17	2	3	6	3	0	3	11	115	-4	+4	+0
Berkman,Lance	6	28	16	24	3	7	25	2	0	2	13	120	+16	+10	+26
Berroa,Angel	3	5	8	12	0	2	7	2	2	4	13	54	-12	0	-12
Betancourt,Yuniesky	6	28	12	24	2	3	14	4	1	5	23	124	-16	-4	-20
Betemit,Wilson	1	10	6	9	0	0	6	1	0	1	7	43	-1	-2	-3
Blake,Casey	8	23	10	14	1	3	11	3	0	3	12	100	+1	+3	+4
Blalock,Hank	0	10	3	9	1	2	5	4	0	4	10	64	-16	+1	-15
Blanco,Gregor	8	21	11	17	3	4	13	1	5	6	3	87	+3	+3	+6
Bloomquist,Willie	6	14	9	10	2	4	15	2	1	3	1	34	+13	+8	+21
Blum,Geoff	1	11	5	7	1	4	2	1	0	1	5	64	-2	-3	-5
Boggs,Brandon	3	9	6	8	0	3	6	1	1	2	3	59	+2	-1	+1
Bonifacio,Emilio	2	5	6	6	1	1	5	0	0	0	2	23	+8	-1	+7
Boone,Aaron	0	4	3	5	0	2	4	3	1	4	8	50	-14	-2	-16
Bourn,Michael	2	11	13	26	5	7	11	2	0	2	3	72	+6	+21	+27
Bowker,John	3	8	7	11	0	1	5	3	2	5	7	77	-9	-1	-10
Bradley,Milton	3	21	7	17	0	4	13	1	1	2	10	103	-2	-1	-3
Braun,Ryan	9	26	11	12	3	5	11	0	2	2	13	129	+10	+6	+16
Brown,Emil	3	12	8	17	2	3	11	5	1	6	16	100	-16	0	-16
Bruce,Jay	4	11	4	6	4	7	13	0	0	0	8	90	+15	-8	+7
Bruntlett,Eric	2	8	8	10	3	4	8	1	0	1	7	52	+6	+5	+11
Buck,John	2	11	11	20	1	3	5	2	2	4	12	76	-15	-6	-21
Burke,Chris	2	3	4	7	1	3	6	1	0	1	2	27	+4	+5	+9
Burrell,Pat	1	17	8	13	1	5	11	2	1	3	10	112	-3	0	-3
Burriss,Emmanuel	2	15	11	15	5	7	10	2	1	3	7	52	+0	+3	+3
Buscher,Brian	4	10	5	6	2	4	5	1	0	1	6	60	+4	-4	+0
Butler,Billy	3	11	6	12	2	10	19	6	1	7	23	91	-20	-2	-22
Byrd,Marlon	3	13	13	18	4	7	21	4	0	5	10	99	+7	+3	+10
Byrnes,Eric	2	3	4	8	0	0	3	1	0	1	5	44	-1	-4	-5
Cabrera,Asdrubal	9	17	5	7	1	4	10	6	0	7	8	94	-6	-4	-10
Cabrera,Melky	4	15	5	10	0	5	11	2	0	2	11	90	-1	+5	+4
Cabrera,Miguel	3	26	7	22	1	6	9	1	4	5	16	131	-22	+1	-21
Cabrera,Orlando	10	37	17	24	1	5	22	5	3	8	16	133	-5	+7	+2
Cairo,Miguel	5	13	4	13	2	5	9	2	1	3	6	51	-4	+1	-3
Callaspo,Alberto	1	10	6	9	0	1	13	0	0	0	6	37	+8	0	+8
Cameron,Mike	1	9	10	15	1	2	11	3	2	5	4	78	-2	+7	+5
Cano,Robinson	6	23	13	16	2	6	11	0	3	3	18	124	-2	-6	-8

313

2008 Baserunning

Player	1st to 3rd Moved	Chances	2nd to Home Moved	Chances	1st to Home Moved	Chances	Bases Taken	Out Adv	Doubled Off	BR Outs	GDP	GDP Opps	BR Gain	SB Gain	Net Gain
Cantu,Jorge	1	14	11	21	2	4	23	1	2	3	15	134	+7	+2	+9
Carroll,Jamey	4	20	13	19	3	5	22	1	1	2	2	78	+21	+1	+22
Casey,Sean	2	11	3	6	0	1	5	3	0	3	6	46	-8	+1	-7
Cash,Kevin	0	5	1	4	0	1	2	1	0	1	6	35	-7	0	-7
Casilla,Alexi	9	21	12	16	2	7	15	1	2	3	8	79	+9	+3	+12
Castillo,Jose	4	17	7	13	1	8	6	1	0	1	16	82	-10	-2	-12
Castillo,Luis	3	8	7	11	1	3	13	0	2	2	13	59	0	+13	+13
Casto,Kory	0	2	3	6	0	0	4	0	1	1	5	34	-2	+1	-1
Catalanotto,Frank	2	8	3	3	2	3	5	1	0	1	6	51	+2	-1	+1
Cedeno,Ronny	1	8	7	13	1	4	10	4	0	4	6	58	-6	+2	-4
Chavez,Endy	2	11	4	6	3	5	9	2	1	3	6	55	-1	+4	+3
Choo,Shin-Soo	4	18	16	20	4	5	20	0	0	0	5	71	+26	-2	+24
Church,Ryan	2	15	8	11	2	5	11	0	0	0	9	73	+8	-4	+4
Clark,Tony	0	4	0	1	0	3	5	0	1	1	8	46	-5	0	-5
Clement,Jeff	2	6	1	6	0	0	2	1	0	1	4	39	-4	-2	-6
Cora,Alex	1	10	3	5	1	3	4	0	0	0	3	37	+2	-1	+1
Coste,Chris	2	6	2	7	1	1	6	2	1	3	7	66	-5	-2	-7
Counsell,Craig	2	15	6	10	1	3	10	0	0	0	5	51	+7	+1	+8
Crawford,Carl	4	15	13	16	3	6	16	2	1	4	10	116	+8	+11	+19
Crede,Joe	1	8	3	6	0	2	17	1	1	2	10	79	+6	-6	0
Crisp,Coco	2	8	10	13	1	7	15	1	1	2	6	95	+11	+6	+17
Crosby,Bobby	1	14	18	26	5	7	16	0	2	2	18	134	+6	+1	+7
Cruz,Nelson	2	4	1	1	1	2	2	0	0	0	1	26	+5	+1	+6
Cuddyer,Michael	2	8	2	8	2	3	7	2	1	3	7	57	-6	+3	-3
Cust,Jack	1	22	9	17	2	4	17	1	0	1	7	117	+11	0	+11
Damon,Johnny	11	30	8	25	4	6	18	3	3	6	6	74	-3	+13	+10
Davis,Chris	1	5	9	14	1	3	9	3	2	5	5	61	-6	-3	-9
Davis,Rajai	2	3	8	11	1	2	5	0	0	0	1	41	+10	+17	+27
DeJesus,David	8	30	8	19	4	7	24	4	3	7	10	88	-3	-5	-8
Delgado,Carlos	4	26	11	24	1	5	12	1	3	4	16	140	-11	-1	-12
Dellucci,David	2	13	7	8	0	2	9	0	0	0	12	73	+3	-1	+2
DeRosa,Mark	6	28	12	22	2	6	20	1	3	4	9	133	+7	+6	+13
DeWitt,Blake	3	15	10	14	2	5	13	3	0	3	6	74	+5	+3	+8
Dobbs,Greg	3	7	3	11	1	3	5	1	1	2	4	53	-3	+1	-2
Doumit,Ryan	5	18	13	19	4	6	14	5	0	5	10	96	+1	-2	-1
Drew,J.D.	7	20	15	20	2	6	18	1	4	5	11	101	+5	+2	+7
Drew,Stephen	8	31	10	20	0	5	16	4	3	7	5	95	-7	-3	-10
Dukes,Elijah	3	7	10	12	0	0	7	3	2	5	10	87	-6	+5	-1
Duncan,Chris	1	16	6	8	1	1	9	2	2	4	9	52	-9	0	-9
Dunn,Adam	2	27	8	14	1	7	21	2	1	3	7	107	+6	0	+6
Durham,Ray	8	16	11	18	2	2	16	5	2	7	7	77	-1	0	-1
Dye,Jermaine	4	14	8	17	0	9	17	1	0	1	18	134	+2	-1	+1
Easley,Damion	5	20	5	7	0	2	7	1	0	1	15	73	-5	0	-5
Eckstein,David	3	17	8	15	2	4	11	2	1	3	7	56	-3	0	-3
Edmonds,Jim	7	18	5	6	3	6	8	4	1	5	8	75	-5	-2	-7
Ellis,Mark	3	16	9	20	2	5	13	2	0	2	11	86	-1	+10	+9
Ellsbury,Jacoby	5	15	11	21	5	10	23	2	1	3	10	98	+12	+28	+40
Encarnacion,Edwin	6	20	4	15	3	7	14	1	0	1	13	112	+3	+1	+4
Erstad,Darin	2	18	4	6	2	5	9	1	0	1	3	47	+4	-4	+0
Escobar,Yunel	11	33	16	20	6	9	10	4	3	7	24	118	-17	-8	-25
Ethier,Andre	7	27	14	18	7	11	13	3	1	4	6	107	+9	0	+9
Everett,Adam	2	5	2	3	0	2	5	1	0	1	0	31	+5	0	+5
Feliz,Pedro	0	14	4	9	2	3	9	3	2	5	14	91	-16	0	-16
Fielder,Prince	2	21	4	14	2	7	18	8	1	9	12	112	-21	-1	-22
Figgins,Chone	6	19	9	21	2	2	27	1	7	8	7	63	-1	+8	+7
Flores,Jesus	0	9	5	12	1	1	3	3	0	3	7	67	-11	-2	-13
Floyd,Cliff	2	11	1	4	1	4	5	1	1	2	4	52	-4	+1	-3
Fontenot,Mike	8	20	7	14	0	0	11	1	1	2	1	59	+10	+2	+12
Francisco,Ben	4	11	11	14	6	6	17	2	2	4	10	120	+13	-2	+11
Francoeur,Jeff	7	22	14	20	6	8	13	2	2	4	18	141	+1	-2	-1
Freel,Ryan	2	6	1	1	0	0	2	1	1	2	3	17	-5	-2	-7
Fukudome,Kosuke	7	24	15	20	4	5	18	1	1	2	7	123	+21	+4	+25
Furcal,Rafael	4	14	7	11	0	0	9	1	1	2	3	18	+2	+2	+4
Garciaparra,Nomar	0	4	3	8	2	5	7	1	0	1	12	46	-7	-1	-8

314

2008 Baserunning

Player	1st to 3rd Moved	Chances	2nd to Home Moved	Chances	1st to Home Moved	Chances	Bases Taken	Out Adv	Doubled Off	BR Outs	GDP	GDP Opps	BR Gain	SB Gain	Net Gain
Gardner,Brett	1	2	7	9	0	0	5	2	1	3	0	23	+0	+11	+11
Garko,Ryan	0	21	7	14	2	10	16	2	0	2	10	116	+1	0	+1
Gathright,Joey	6	13	10	13	0	0	11	1	0	1	3	57	+14	+13	+27
German,Esteban	7	13	7	12	1	3	7	1	1	2	5	49	+3	+1	+4
Gerut,Jody	7	16	7	8	1	2	3	1	0	1	1	42	+7	-2	+5
Giambi,Jason	3	15	4	8	1	6	7	3	2	5	6	111	-8	0	-8
Giles,Brian	11	27	13	18	4	7	19	3	3	6	18	121	0	-2	-2
Glaus,Troy	6	30	7	23	3	5	15	1	3	4	14	123	-8	-2	-10
Gload,Ross	4	22	7	18	0	3	15	1	1	2	12	72	-4	-5	-9
Gomes,Jonny	2	7	6	7	0	2	6	3	1	4	1	30	-3	+6	+3
Gomez,Carlos	5	16	22	27	1	3	11	3	3	6	7	101	+1	+11	+12
Gomez,Chris	2	7	7	7	1	3	7	1	0	1	3	38	+7	0	+7
Gonzalez,Adrian	6	29	11	22	3	7	14	5	1	6	24	147	-19	0	-19
Gonzalez,Carlos	3	8	9	13	2	2	6	3	1	4	7	62	-4	+2	-2
Gonzalez,Edgar	2	19	9	12	1	3	5	2	5	7	11	73	-22	-5	-27
Gonzalez,Luis	2	9	2	13	0	2	11	1	1	2	10	68	-6	-3	-9
Gordon,Alex	6	22	18	21	6	7	24	5	0	5	8	120	+20	+5	+25
Granderson,Curtis	10	34	21	26	6	9	23	0	2	2	7	103	+27	+4	+31
Greene,Khalil	2	10	4	9	1	2	4	1	0	1	7	80	-1	+3	+2
Griffey Jr.,Ken	1	22	9	20	0	5	13	2	0	2	13	104	-7	-2	-9
Gross,Gabe	2	10	7	14	2	2	13	0	2	2	6	73	+6	0	+6
Grudzielanek,Mark	6	16	11	15	2	6	10	2	2	4	8	59	-2	0	-2
Guerrero,Vladimir	9	25	13	22	1	6	15	4	2	6	27	122	-19	-1	-20
Guillen,Carlos	7	18	11	15	3	5	21	4	2	6	11	111	+7	+3	+10
Guillen,Jose	9	24	5	14	1	9	14	2	1	3	23	133	-10	0	-10
Gutierrez,Franklin	4	12	5	7	3	5	14	3	1	4	10	80	+1	+3	+4
Guzman,Cristian	9	30	11	22	3	6	14	3	1	4	10	106	0	-4	-4
Hafner,Travis	2	13	3	5	1	1	1	2	1	3	4	41	-9	-1	-10
Hairston,Jerry	6	10	8	14	3	3	13	1	2	3	0	38	+11	+9	+20
Hairston,Scott	3	18	2	7	2	3	4	1	0	1	2	54	+0	+1	+1
Hall,Bill	1	9	9	11	6	6	10	0	2	2	4	77	+11	-7	+4
Hamilton,Josh	13	32	11	18	7	11	13	0	0	0	8	147	+25	+7	+32
Hannahan,Jack	0	15	15	19	0	4	10	2	0	2	5	105	+6	+2	+8
Hardy,J.J.	4	23	5	10	3	5	10	5	1	6	18	132	-17	0	-17
Harris,Brendan	7	25	11	19	1	2	10	2	1	3	13	94	-4	-1	-5
Harris,Willie	4	19	10	13	1	3	10	0	0	0	8	69	+8	+7	+15
Hart,Corey	3	10	9	14	4	6	21	5	0	5	17	124	+2	+9	+11
Hawpe,Brad	4	15	16	23	1	4	16	4	2	6	7	120	+3	-2	+1
Headley,Chase	3	11	4	11	1	3	9	1	0	1	5	77	+5	+2	+7
Helms,Wes	0	11	5	9	1	2	6	0	0	0	6	62	+2	0	+2
Helton,Todd	2	17	5	10	2	5	12	4	0	4	9	65	-7	0	-7
Hermida,Jeremy	6	26	6	16	2	8	24	2	0	2	12	103	+9	+4	+13
Hernandez,Ramon	4	19	10	14	0	3	7	6	2	9	9	89	-22	0	-22
Hill,Aaron	3	8	3	5	2	2	4	1	1	2	4	52	+1	0	+1
Hinske,Eric	2	13	9	13	1	2	10	1	1	2	13	90	-1	+4	+3
Holliday,Matt	15	26	17	24	5	6	23	2	1	3	9	117	+28	+24	+52
Howard,Ryan	3	28	8	18	0	6	15	1	3	4	11	128	-6	-1	-7
Hu,Chin-lung	1	4	7	8	0	1	5	0	0	0	5	18	+3	+2	+5
Hudson,Orlando	7	18	11	14	2	3	10	1	1	2	18	97	0	+2	+2
Huff,Aubrey	8	20	18	25	1	5	14	2	2	4	9	128	+9	+4	+13
Hundley,Nick	2	7	4	7	1	1	6	0	0	0	1	39	+9	0	+9
Hunter,Torii	13	18	12	20	4	8	17	4	2	6	15	118	+3	+9	+12
Iannetta,Chris	3	9	6	13	0	3	8	0	1	1	6	75	+3	0	+3
Ibanez,Raul	0	18	19	25	5	10	8	0	1	1	13	156	+6	-6	0
Iguchi,Tadahito	3	15	3	8	4	5	6	3	0	3	11	72	-9	+6	-3
Infante,Omar	2	15	11	18	1	3	5	1	2	3	4	69	-4	-2	-6
Inge,Brandon	1	13	5	11	1	2	8	0	0	0	4	70	+6	-2	+4
Inglett,Joe	3	11	11	17	4	6	16	1	1	2	5	66	+13	+5	+18
Iwamura,Akinori	11	38	9	19	2	6	22	2	2	4	2	91	+12	-4	+8
Izturis,Cesar	5	18	8	17	2	4	13	4	4	8	6	76	-12	+12	0
Izturis,Maicer	11	16	8	19	1	2	13	1	1	4	9	52	0	+7	+7
Jackson,Conor	9	25	12	18	3	6	28	1	2	3	14	106	+17	+6	+23
Jacobs,Mike	1	7	5	12	0	6	7	2	0	2	7	102	-2	+1	-1
Jenkins,Geoff	2	9	4	8	3	5	4	0	0	0	6	56	+2	-1	+1

315

2008 Baserunning

Player	1st to 3rd		2nd to Home		1st to Home		Bases Taken	Out Adv	Doubled Off	BR Outs	GDP	GDP Opps	BR Gain	SB Gain	Net Gain
	Moved	Chances	Moved	Chances	Moved	Chances									
Jeter,Derek	10	30	11	20	7	9	19	5	3	8	24	134	-14	+1	-13
Johjima,Kenji	2	13	2	8	1	4	10	0	1	1	12	70	-4	+2	-2
Johnson,Kelly	5	18	14	22	5	7	17	1	0	1	3	137	+26	-1	+25
Johnson,Nick	0	2	3	5	0	0	3	0	0	0	2	23	+2	0	+2
Johnson,Reed	8	20	11	16	2	4	11	1	0	1	3	77	+16	-7	+9
Jones,Adam	4	15	9	14	4	6	14	4	0	4	12	94	+0	+4	+4
Jones,Andruw	2	8	5	5	0	2	7	3	0	3	5	45	-2	-2	-4
Jones,Chipper	8	32	9	15	4	7	10	1	1	2	13	119	+1	+4	+5
Joyce,Matt	3	9	6	7	0	1	4	1	0	1	3	56	+5	-4	+1
Kapler,Gabe	3	6	4	9	1	2	10	3	1	4	3	53	0	+1	+1
Kearns,Austin	4	17	7	13	1	1	6	0	0	0	11	67	+0	-2	-2
Kemp,Matt	7	16	17	24	3	3	19	5	3	8	11	134	+3	+13	+16
Kendall,Jason	2	10	9	17	1	3	8	1	3	4	5	92	-4	+2	-2
Kendrick,Howie	4	11	9	12	1	2	11	0	1	1	8	79	+10	+3	+13
Kennedy,Adam	9	14	5	9	4	5	11	2	1	3	13	77	+2	+5	+7
Kent,Jeff	7	24	6	9	1	3	8	0	0	1	13	88	+0	-2	-2
Keppinger,Jeff	3	13	5	9	2	6	6	0	2	2	14	79	-9	+1	-8
Kinsler,Ian	14	24	19	24	5	7	24	2	3	5	12	100	+19	+22	+41
Konerko,Paul	1	13	4	14	1	4	13	2	0	2	17	100	-9	+2	-7
Kotchman,Casey	7	27	6	13	2	10	7	5	0	5	18	104	-21	0	-21
Kotsay,Mark	5	10	7	8	2	4	14	2	1	3	14	94	+4	-6	-2
Kouzmanoff,Kevin	4	28	7	15	3	8	16	1	3	4	14	116	-6	0	-6
Kubel,Jason	5	25	8	16	2	8	18	1	1	2	12	103	+4	-2	+2
Laird,Gerald	10	16	9	16	1	5	9	2	4	6	5	71	-4	-6	-10
Lamb,Mike	3	6	5	10	2	2	6	0	1	1	3	49	+6	-2	+4
Langerhans,Ryan	2	4	5	7	0	0	3	0	0	0	1	30	+6	+2	+8
LaRoche,Adam	3	21	9	16	2	3	13	2	2	4	9	114	0	-1	-1
LaRoche,Andy	2	6	4	6	1	1	1	0	0	0	8	40	-2	+2	0
LaRue,Jason	0	2	1	4	1	4	2	1	0	2	6	42	-9	0	-9
Lee,Carlos	3	15	4	16	0	1	7	5	0	5	8	84	-16	+2	-14
Lee,Derrek	6	32	9	19	4	9	12	2	1	3	27	180	-13	+4	-9
Lewis,Fred	8	23	19	24	2	4	15	4	1	5	5	65	+6	+7	+13
Lind,Adam	4	11	6	13	3	6	11	1	0	1	8	69	+6	+2	+8
Lo Duca,Paul	1	4	3	6	1	2	3	2	0	2	10	40	-10	+1	-9
Loney,James	6	24	12	20	3	4	17	5	2	7	25	132	-17	-1	-18
Longoria,Evan	6	15	11	19	2	2	13	1	0	1	8	93	+13	+7	+20
Lopez,Felipe	2	13	9	17	1	5	16	4	2	6	13	101	-10	-8	-18
Lopez,Jose	5	26	8	19	4	10	13	3	0	3	14	129	-5	0	-5
Loretta,Mark	1	8	6	11	2	3	6	2	0	2	9	72	-4	0	-4
Lowell,Mike	1	14	4	15	1	10	7	4	0	4	14	106	-21	-2	-23
Lowrie,Jed	4	10	10	15	0	0	9	3	1	4	8	64	-3	+1	-2
Ludwick,Ryan	9	29	16	23	0	2	19	3	0	3	9	136	+16	-4	+12
Lugo,Julio	2	14	3	10	1	2	9	2	0	2	13	69	-9	+4	-5
Markakis,Nick	7	35	21	32	3	11	15	4	1	5	10	133	-1	-4	-5
Marte,Andy	2	8	3	3	0	1	4	0	1	1	5	49	+1	-3	-2
Martin,Russell	8	25	15	23	4	7	19	3	0	3	16	124	+8	+6	+14
Martinez,Victor	2	11	1	6	2	2	7	0	0	0	12	59	-2	0	-2
Mathis,Jeff	3	14	4	9	0	1	6	0	1	1	1	50	+4	-2	+2
Matsui,Hideki	3	20	6	7	3	6	7	1	1	2	10	72	-3	0	-3
Matsui,Kaz	9	20	15	18	4	6	10	3	0	3	3	54	+11	+10	+21
Matthews Jr.,Gary	3	17	12	20	3	6	10	5	0	5	12	104	-9	+2	-7
Mauer,Joe	13	34	14	26	9	13	30	0	1	2	21	137	+20	-1	+19
McAnulty,Paul	5	7	1	2	0	0	2	1	1	2	0	27	+1	0	+1
McCann,Brian	3	17	4	19	0	5	8	3	3	6	17	142	-25	+5	-20
McDonald,John	1	13	2	3	0	2	3	3	0	3	3	30	-10	+1	-9
McLouth,Nate	5	18	16	25	3	4	26	2	0	2	5	113	+27	+17	+44
Michaels,Jason	2	12	3	7	2	3	6	1	0	1	9	68	-2	0	-2
Mientkiewicz,Doug	5	18	6	12	2	2	18	6	1	7	6	70	-3	0	-3
Miles,Aaron	8	23	13	20	3	4	9	2	1	3	13	87	-1	-3	-4
Millar,Kevin	2	16	5	17	1	6	14	5	1	6	8	121	-10	-2	-12
Milledge,Lastings	2	15	11	17	3	4	10	4	1	6	19	135	-15	+6	-9
Molina,Bengie	2	19	8	19	0	3	9	2	1	3	23	120	-20	0	-20
Molina,Jose	2	9	5	10	1	1	6	0	1	1	9	56	-2	0	-2
Molina,Yadier	2	19	2	10	1	7	8	0	0	0	21	93	-14	-4	-18

2008 Baserunning

Player	1st to 3rd Moved	Chances	2nd to Home Moved	Chances	1st to Home Moved	Chances	Bases Taken	Out Adv	Doubled Off	BR Outs	GDP	GDP Opps	BR Gain	SB Gain	Net Gain
Montero,Miguel	2	6	3	7	2	4	5	1	0	1	1	32	+3	0	+3
Mora,Melvin	7	19	9	14	2	6	12	1	0	1	14	124	+8	-11	-3
Morgan,Nyjer	4	7	4	5	0	0	12	0	2	2	0	18	+10	-1	+9
Morneau,Justin	1	12	13	24	1	5	28	3	0	3	20	177	+10	-2	+8
Moss,Brandon	1	7	1	4	2	2	8	1	0	1	2	50	+6	-3	+3
Murphy,Daniel	3	11	2	4	2	3	6	0	0	0	4	25	+4	-4	+0
Murphy,David	2	11	12	17	1	4	14	3	2	5	7	93	+0	+3	+3
Nady,Xavier	2	20	8	21	1	8	15	2	2	4	14	108	-12	0	-12
Napoli,Mike	3	12	3	8	0	1	4	0	0	0	3	51	+3	+1	+4
Navarro,Dioner	2	13	6	17	0	4	6	7	0	7	16	88	-31	-8	-39
Nieves,Wil	1	4	6	9	1	1	0	0	0	0	7	46	-2	-2	-4
Norton,Greg	1	10	4	8	0	3	3	0	0	0	7	49	-3	0	-3
Ojeda,Augie	2	9	5	8	0	2	9	1	0	1	6	48	+3	0	+3
Olivo,Miguel	1	9	4	7	1	1	4	3	0	3	6	59	-7	+7	+0
Ordonez,Magglio	4	21	10	20	3	9	6	3	1	4	27	135	-26	-9	-35
Ortiz,David	2	15	5	11	2	10	5	0	3	3	11	111	-11	+1	-10
Overbay,Lyle	5	20	9	21	3	8	18	2	0	2	24	142	-4	-3	-7
Ozuna,Pablo	1	5	2	4	2	3	4	1	0	1	3	22	0	-5	-5
Patterson,Corey	6	10	6	10	0	0	11	2	1	3	3	74	+9	-4	+5
Payton,Jay	3	11	10	13	3	3	11	1	2	3	7	69	+5	+6	+11
Pedroia,Dustin	4	20	19	23	4	9	12	5	0	5	17	117	-7	+18	+11
Pena,Carlos	6	22	7	15	3	8	10	3	1	4	6	107	-1	-1	-2
Pena,Tony F	3	9	7	9	0	2	4	1	2	4	4	46	-6	+1	-5
Pena,Wily Mo	1	8	1	6	0	0	1	1	0	1	5	39	-7	-2	-9
Pence,Hunter	6	18	14	19	2	5	12	2	3	5	14	110	-4	-9	-13
Peralta,Jhonny	8	26	19	28	3	7	15	6	1	7	26	136	-17	+1	-16
Phillips,Brandon	6	12	9	12	0	2	15	4	1	5	13	101	-1	+3	+2
Pierre,Juan	6	16	10	15	2	4	9	2	0	2	3	49	+6	+16	+22
Pierzynski,A.J.	3	16	7	20	0	2	16	8	0	8	14	117	-19	+1	-18
Podsednik,Scott	0	5	6	8	2	2	5	0	1	1	3	22	+2	+4	+6
Polanco,Placido	8	32	16	21	3	8	23	1	1	2	14	133	+17	+5	+22
Posada,Jorge	1	7	3	7	0	1	5	1	0	1	7	41	-4	0	-4
Prado,Martin	3	17	9	14	1	4	11	2	0	2	3	39	+3	+1	+4
Pujols,Albert	6	22	15	21	1	3	18	5	2	7	16	173	-1	+1	0
Punto,Nick	7	16	9	17	2	3	18	3	0	3	10	81	+8	+3	+11
Quentin,Carlos	9	21	9	16	5	8	16	2	0	2	16	111	+8	+1	+9
Quinlan,Robb	4	5	3	4	0	0	5	1	0	1	5	31	+3	0	+3
Quintanilla,Omar	1	4	9	9	0	0	12	1	0	1	3	42	+13	0	+13
Quintero,Humberto	0	5	2	3	1	1	4	0	1	1	5	36	-1	0	-1
Raburn,Ryan	2	4	6	9	2	3	5	0	0	0	2	34	+8	+1	+9
Ramirez,Alexei	9	21	5	12	2	2	18	3	1	4	14	111	+4	-5	-1
Ramirez,Aramis	6	20	9	20	1	9	15	0	0	0	13	143	+9	-2	+7
Ramirez,Hanley	9	26	18	25	6	6	20	5	0	5	5	87	+15	+11	+26
Ramirez,Manny	4	24	16	28	3	8	17	4	4	8	17	151	-15	+3	-12
Reed,Jeremy	7	16	8	11	2	4	8	1	2	3	5	68	+4	-4	+0
Renteria,Edgar	5	20	10	15	1	5	13	2	1	3	19	112	-6	0	-6
Reyes,Jose	9	24	16	29	1	2	36	5	5	10	9	102	+6	+26	+32
Reynolds,Mark	4	13	8	15	3	9	19	4	0	4	10	130	+8	+7	+15
Rios,Alex	7	18	15	22	3	3	16	4	2	6	20	156	-2	+16	+14
Rivas,Luis	4	6	7	9	0	1	5	1	0	1	7	40	+2	-1	+1
Rivera,Juan	0	7	3	4	0	4	4	0	2	2	10	60	-10	-1	-11
Roberts,Brian	10	23	21	31	4	10	14	1	3	4	8	97	+7	+20	+27
Rodriguez,Alex	6	14	17	25	3	5	19	5	2	7	16	117	-3	+12	+9
Rodriguez,Ivan	3	15	6	9	2	6	14	4	0	4	15	70	-8	+8	0
Rodriguez,Luis	3	7	2	4	2	2	7	1	0	1	9	45	+1	-1	0
Rodriguez,Sean	1	6	3	5	0	1	6	0	2	2	3	25	-2	+1	-1
Rolen,Scott	4	14	4	11	1	2	14	6	0	6	12	96	-10	+5	-5
Rollins,Jimmy	7	14	6	12	2	3	20	2	2	4	11	73	+5	+41	+46
Ross,Cody	5	14	5	10	0	0	12	1	0	1	5	85	+11	+4	+15
Ross,David	0	6	2	7	0	4	3	0	0	0	3	43	-2	-2	-4
Rowand,Aaron	10	21	6	15	3	8	9	1	2	3	21	120	-10	-6	-16
Ruiz,Carlos	3	7	10	13	1	1	7	0	2	2	14	65	-4	-3	-7
Ryan,Brendan	2	8	3	5	2	2	11	0	0	0	4	31	+10	+3	+13
Salazar,Jeff	0	3	1	3	0	0	9	0	0	0	2	24	+7	-4	+3

2008 Baserunning

Player	1st to 3rd Moved	Chances	2nd to Home Moved	Chances	1st to Home Moved	Chances	Bases Taken	Out Adv	Doubled Off	BR Outs	GDP	GDP Opps	BR Gain	SB Gain	Net Gain
Saltalamacchia,J.	3	8	6	9	0	2	6	2	0	2	1	38	+3	-4	-1
Sanchez,Freddy	8	29	11	17	5	10	14	2	4	6	13	98	-7	-2	-9
Sandoval,Pablo	1	9	5	8	0	1	3	2	0	2	6	38	-7	0	-7
Santiago,Ramon	2	9	5	7	2	2	8	1	0	1	1	29	+8	+1	+9
Schneider,Brian	2	13	3	7	0	0	1	2	0	2	11	72	-13	0	-13
Schumaker,Skip	11	38	13	19	3	6	13	1	0	1	19	90	+1	+4	+5
Scott,Luke	3	12	12	21	1	3	10	3	4	7	7	100	-10	-2	-12
Scutaro,Marco	5	23	11	23	2	7	15	4	3	7	8	119	-9	+3	-6
Sexson,Richie	2	10	0	6	1	2	4	1	0	1	9	68	-6	+1	-5
Sheffield,Gary	1	13	7	12	1	1	10	5	1	6	19	114	-19	+5	-14
Shoppach,Kelly	2	16	12	18	1	5	13	2	0	2	7	79	+5	0	+5
Sizemore,Grady	6	24	19	26	4	6	16	0	1	1	5	118	+22	+28	+50
Snyder,Chris	1	11	7	13	1	3	7	2	1	3	7	77	-5	0	-5
Soriano,Alfonso	7	17	7	19	1	2	14	1	2	3	9	66	-1	+13	+12
Soto,Geovany	0	10	3	15	3	6	7	2	0	2	11	131	-7	-2	-9
Span,Denard	8	20	7	17	0	2	18	2	3	5	3	56	+3	+4	+7
Spilborghs,Ryan	4	9	5	9	0	1	7	2	1	3	8	52	-5	-1	-6
Stairs,Matt	2	14	6	8	3	7	11	2	0	2	10	77	+1	-1	+0
Stewart,Ian	4	9	4	8	1	3	11	3	1	4	3	63	+2	-1	+1
Stewart,Shannon	2	9	3	4	0	1	3	1	0	1	8	40	-5	+1	-4
Suzuki,Ichiro	11	42	23	30	3	5	30	3	2	5	8	113	+21	+35	+56
Suzuki,Kurt	6	20	9	16	4	5	15	3	0	4	20	119	-5	-4	-9
Sweeney,Mike	1	6	2	2	0	1	4	2	1	3	3	31	-6	0	-6
Sweeney,Ryan	2	11	9	15	5	7	8	0	0	0	9	82	+7	+7	+14
Swisher,Nick	7	18	9	16	3	5	7	1	1	2	14	111	-1	-3	-4
Taguchi,So	4	9	2	2	0	0	1	0	0	0	2	15	+2	+3	+5
Tatis,Fernando	4	11	2	4	0	1	5	2	0	2	7	65	-2	+3	+1
Taveras,Willy	9	16	15	21	1	2	17	3	0	3	4	64	+16	+54	+70
Teahen,Mark	10	24	9	15	3	7	9	2	0	2	6	104	+9	-2	+7
Teixeira,Mark	4	21	11	18	2	12	16	0	1	1	17	158	+5	+2	+7
Tejada,Miguel	9	28	10	21	2	5	23	5	0	5	32	150	-12	-7	-19
Thames,Marcus	2	12	4	11	2	3	6	2	1	3	6	60	-7	-6	-13
Theriot,Ryan	13	30	16	22	8	12	22	1	3	4	19	118	+11	-4	+7
Thomas,Clete	2	6	2	3	0	0	1	1	0	1	1	27	0	+2	+2
Thomas,Frank	2	19	1	10	0	3	8	1	1	2	9	54	-12	0	-12
Thome,Jim	4	19	8	16	2	7	14	4	2	6	18	130	-14	+1	-13
Torrealba,Yorvit	2	6	3	5	1	1	1	3	2	5	10	53	-18	-8	-26
Tracy,Chad	1	4	2	6	0	0	9	0	0	0	5	59	+8	0	+8
Treanor,Matt	3	9	2	5	1	1	4	2	0	2	2	53	+1	+1	+2
Tulowitzki,Troy	7	17	12	17	0	2	9	3	1	4	16	95	-7	-11	-18
Uggla,Dan	7	20	11	18	5	10	17	7	1	8	10	105	-6	-5	-11
Upton,B.J.	8	15	12	18	1	3	22	6	2	9	13	131	-2	+12	+10
Upton,Justin	3	5	11	17	4	8	11	0	1	1	3	55	+12	-7	+5
Uribe,Juan	7	14	4	8	0	3	5	0	1	1	5	55	+3	-5	-2
Utley,Chase	12	22	17	20	4	7	12	4	1	5	9	133	+11	+10	+21
Varitek,Jason	1	17	3	18	0	1	5	2	1	3	13	107	-19	-2	-21
Vazquez,Ramon	1	14	6	13	1	2	9	1	0	1	4	75	+4	-2	+2
Velez,Eugenio	3	8	5	7	1	3	11	3	2	5	11	61	-8	+3	-5
Victorino,Shane	6	17	15	19	8	10	23	0	4	4	8	107	+20	+14	+34
Vidro,Jose	3	8	3	8	1	3	2	1	0	1	5	73	-1	0	-1
Vizquel,Omar	3	8	6	7	0	3	2	1	0	1	4	50	+1	-3	-2
Votto,Joey	5	23	12	16	2	7	6	2	2	4	7	112	-3	-3	-6
Weeks,Rickie	9	19	22	24	2	6	19	3	3	6	5	69	+12	+9	+21
Wells,Vernon	6	15	10	18	2	4	13	4	0	4	16	84	-6	0	-6
Werth,Jayson	4	25	8	12	3	4	13	2	0	2	2	73	+10	+18	+28
Wigginton,Ty	1	10	6	12	1	4	9	1	2	3	9	79	-6	-8	-14
Wilkerson,Brad	2	7	3	10	0	0	9	2	2	4	4	57	-5	-7	-12
Willingham,Josh	5	12	5	9	3	7	5	1	2	3	7	71	-4	-1	-5
Willits,Reggie	4	11	4	5	0	1	4	0	1	1	1	19	+3	0	+3
Wilson,Jack	4	7	4	6	1	3	5	1	1	2	6	49	-1	-2	-3
Winn,Randy	16	36	13	26	5	7	17	0	1	2	6	112	+20	+21	+41
Wright,David	8	22	11	18	4	10	20	6	3	9	15	153	-7	+5	-2
Youkilis,Kevin	11	23	11	18	2	9	19	3	2	5	11	152	+10	-7	+3

2008 Baserunning

Player	1st to 3rd Moved	1st to 3rd Chances	2nd to Home Moved	2nd to Home Chances	1st to Home Moved	1st to Home Chances	Bases Taken	Out Adv	Doubled Off	BR Outs	GDP	GDP Opps	BR Gain	SB Gain	Net Gain
Young,Chris	3	15	13	19	2	6	15	3	4	7	10	123	-5	+4	-1
Young,Delmon	8	26	19	28	2	8	23	6	2	8	19	128	-7	+4	-3
Young,Delwyn	1	4	1	6	1	2	6	0	0	0	2	28	+4	0	+4
Young,Dmitri	0	6	1	4	0	1	2	2	0	2	8	39	-12	0	-12
Young,Michael	5	39	18	23	8	13	24	1	2	3	19	126	+8	+10	+18
Zaun,Gregg	2	11	5	10	2	3	8	2	0	2	6	51	-1	0	-1
Zimmerman,Ryan	1	18	10	12	1	2	12	3	1	4	12	111	-3	-1	-4
Zobrist,Ben	2	5	4	7	1	3	4	1	1	2	4	49	-1	+3	+2

2008 Team Baserunning

Team	1st to 3rd Moved	Chances	2nd to Home Moved	Chances	1st to Home Moved	Chances	Bases Taken	Out Adv	Doubled Off	BR Outs	GDP	GDP Opps	BR Gain	SB Gain	Net Gain
Philadelphia Phillies	55	195	98	163	29	55	142	18	18	36	108	1107	+28	+86	+114
Colorado Rockies	69	202	132	204	25	51	161	28	17	45	118	1168	+36	+67	+103
Texas Rangers	74	239	138	214	32	71	181	28	16	45	117	1255	+58	+31	+89
New York Mets	64	236	105	184	21	54	154	19	15	34	129	1203	+19	+66	+85
Cleveland Indians	56	232	132	193	32	65	177	28	9	39	123	1210	+56	+19	+75
Florida Marlins	47	186	90	179	27	62	173	27	6	33	98	1113	+52	+20	+72
Minnesota Twins	82	245	139	233	28	66	211	29	17	47	144	1254	+50	+18	+68
Chicago Cubs	73	254	107	204	29	62	161	20	12	32	134	1379	+44	+19	+63
Arizona D-Backs	49	173	100	170	18	58	172	23	13	36	105	1119	+49	+12	+61
Oakland Athletics	32	183	128	215	33	64	135	23	10	34	126	1209	+0	+46	+46
Milwaukee Brewers	43	176	107	166	30	54	147	31	16	47	97	1080	+11	+32	+43
Los Angeles Dodgers	64	220	125	193	29	57	155	31	11	43	152	1193	-4	+40	+36
Tampa Bay Rays	60	199	105	185	24	62	161	37	12	52	111	1187	-6	+42	+36
Pittsburgh Pirates	60	220	119	202	25	48	163	30	16	46	111	1146	+16	+19	+35
Los Angeles Angels	85	235	121	202	14	61	169	26	21	49	140	1140	-11	+33	+22
Cincinnati Reds	47	187	81	145	17	52	145	19	14	33	100	1105	+26	-9	+17
Boston Red Sox	47	213	119	219	26	83	163	31	16	47	148	1338	-42	+50	+8
Seattle Mariners	59	242	107	200	29	62	132	23	11	34	136	1177	-21	+26	+5
Houston Astros	46	201	105	182	25	57	138	28	10	38	115	1068	-11	+10	-1
New York Yankees	62	230	110	192	28	64	150	27	20	48	149	1207	-44	+40	-4
Kansas City Royals	78	246	129	213	25	67	181	34	17	52	144	1128	-13	+3	-10
Detroit Tigers	52	239	119	198	28	62	163	29	14	43	144	1238	-13	+1	-12
Atlanta Braves	70	252	115	205	34	71	127	20	18	38	142	1327	-16	+4	-12
Toronto Blue Jays	52	228	107	198	30	61	167	38	10	48	150	1224	-38	+26	-12
St Louis Cardinals	72	272	112	200	26	53	161	28	17	47	151	1273	-26	+9	-17
Chicago White Sox	62	209	91	173	14	51	168	30	9	40	158	1210	-19	-1	-20
Baltimore Orioles	54	202	133	212	23	65	131	31	18	50	111	1144	-31	+7	-24
San Diego Padres	64	242	84	153	26	55	123	23	16	39	129	1181	-27	+2	-25
San Francisco Giants	71	239	113	196	22	55	121	31	17	49	139	1118	-69	+16	-53
Washington Nationals	37	203	113	188	16	35	120	28	9	38	153	1247	-54	-5	-59
MLB Totals	1786	6600	3384	5781	765	1783	4652	818	425	1262	3882	35748			

The 21st Century Bullpen

Bill James

The modern bullpen is still evolving very rapidly. I would put it this way: that if you compare a typical bullpen of 1938 to a bullpen of 1948, compare 1948 to 1958, compare 1958 to 1968, etc. until today, that in every ten-year period there been obvious changes in the way that bullpens have been staffed and used—but that never before have those changes been as large as in the last ten years.

These rapid changes are leaving the stat books in their wake. We evaluate relievers by ERA, but a modern reliever can do a lot of damage with runs charged to somebody else. In the 1950s and 60s we developed the concept of the "Save", and since then have added the derivative concepts of "Blown Saves" and "Holds", but the modern bullpen contains one pitcher who is assigned to save the game and six or seven whose job is something else entirely—something not measured by Saves or anything in their line.

The modern bullpen is staffed by two or three lefties whose job it is to get out lefties, by an eighth-inning guy whose job it is to be a bridge to the closer, by a seventh-inning guy, and by two or three pudknockers whose job is to pitch in where they can. You can have a lot of different guys, doing a lot of different jobs, whose records all look pretty much the same.

We're trying to stretch the record book here to cover more of the modern bullpen. This table has 21 categories, not counting the pitcher's name or his team. These are the 21 categories:

Position: We assign all major league relievers to one of six "positions" in the bullpen:

1—Closer (CL)
2—Set Up Man (SU)
3—Lefty (LT)
4—Long Man (LM)
5—Utility Reliever (UR)
6—Emergency Reliever (ER)

Think about what this means. There have been "field positions" in record books for a hundred years. But, just in the last generation,

a) Positions have evolved within the bullpen, and
b) Nobody has officially categorized them.

That's what we're doing: we're adding "positions" to the bullpen. It's an obvious step, and I don't really know why we didn't do it before now.

We have developed a set of protocols to classify a reliever's position; it's generally obvious, but sometimes it's a close call whether a pitcher is a Set Up Man—the eighth inning guy—or just a long man having a good year. We'll post the protocols on my web site for anybody who cares (BillJamesOnline.com); for the rest of you, it's just a long list of rules that say things like "A pitcher is considered a 'Set Up Man' if he isn't an emergency reliever, isn't a closer, has saves, holds or blown saves in 30% of his appearances, and has a Leverage Index at least 1.00."

Relief Games: No explanation needed

Early Entry: A count of the number of times the reliever entered the game in the sixth inning or earlier. 19% of major league relief appearances are in the sixth inning or earlier, and Lance Cormier of Baltimore led the majors in Early Entries, with 28.

Consecutive Days: A count of how many times the pitcher was used after having pitched on the previous day or (in a few cases) in an earlier game on the same day. This varies with managers. Some managers avoid using relievers on consecutive days; others don't mind.

Pedro Feliciano of the Mets led the majors in appearances on consecutive days, with 34.

Long Outings: Anything more than 25 pitches is considered a Long Outing. Whoever leads a team in early entries will also generally lead the team in Long Outings. 20% of relief appearances are Long Outings.

Josh Rupe of Texas led the majors in Long Outings, with 32.

Leverage Index: Leverage is the amount of swing in the possible change in win probability, compared to the average swing in all situations. The average swing value, by definition, is indexed to 1.00.

If the score of the game is 12-0 or 14-1 the possible changes in win probability will be very close to negligible. Whether the pitcher gives up a home

322

run or gets a double play ball...doesn't really change the outcome of the game. There won't be much swing in either direction for the probability of the win. But in the late innings of a close game, the change in win probability among the various events will have rather wild swings. With a runner on first, two outs, down by one, and in the bottom of the ninth, the game can hinge on one swing of the bat. A home run and an out will both end the game, but with different outcomes for the teams involved. The Leverage Index we use (LI) was developed at the website Tangotiger.net, and compiled at the website Fangraphs.com.

The highest Leverage Index for any pitcher making 40 or more appearances in 2008 was 2.5, by K-Rod. The lowest was 0.5, by several pitchers.

Inherited Runners: A count of the number of runners on base when the reliever entered the fray. Feliciano also led the majors in this area, entering the game with 71 runners on base. Almost all of the highest totals in this area are by lefties.

Inherited Runners Scored: No explanation needed.

Percentage: The major league reliever who did the best job of stranding inherited runners in 2008, among pitchers who came in with 20 or more runners on base, is a surprise. Clay Rapada of the Tigers entered the game with 25 runners on base, of whom only 2 scored—8%. On the other hand, Juan Rincon of the Twindians entered the game with 18 runners on base, of whom 15 eventually scored. For the majors as a whole, 32% of inherited runners score.

Easy Saves: Any Save Opportunity is considered an "Easy" Save if the reliever enters the game with three outs or less remaining, and the first batter he faces does not represent the potential tying or winning run. Relievers are credited with Saves in 87% of their Easy Save opportunities, and 58% of all saves are Easy Saves.

Easy Save Opportunities: The number after the dash is the number of Opportunities the pitcher has been given for an Easy Save. The number before the dash is the number of actual Easy Saves that he was credited with.

Regular Saves: Any save which does not meet the definition either of an Easy Save or a Tough Save is a "Regular" Save. Major league relievers are credited with Saves in 57% of "Regular" Save Opportunities, and "Regular" Saves account for 37% of all major league saves.

Regular Save Opportunities: No explanation needed.

Tough Saves: A "Tough" Save is one in which the reliever enters with the potential tying or winning run on base. Relievers are credited with Saves on only 22% of "Tough Save" Opportunities, and only 5% of Saves are Tough Saves. Mariano Rivera led the majors in Tough Saves, with 5.

Tough Save Opportunities: No explanation needed.

Clean Outing: A Clean Outing is a game in which the reliever is not charged with a run (earned or otherwise) AND does not allow an inherited runner to score. 64% of relief appearances are Clean Outings. Will Ohman of Atlanta had 64 Clean Outings, the most in the majors.

BS Win: A Blown Save/Win is a "win" credited to a reliever who has blown a save opportunity. Suppose that the starter pitches 7 1/3 innings and leaves with a 3-1 lead, runner on base. The reliever gives up a home run, tying the game 3-3, but the reliever's team scores in their next at bat, making the reliever who has given up the home run the "winning" pitcher. That's a BS Win—a Blown Save Win.

Saves: Don't make me explain the Save Rule. I know people.

Holds: A "Hold" is credited to any reliever who inherits a Save Situation, records at least one out, and passes along the Save Situation to the next reliever. Scot Shields of the Angels led the majors in Holds with 31.

Save Opportunities: The sum of Saves and Blown Saves.

Save/Hold Percentage: The sum of Saves and Holds, divided by the sum of Saves, Holds, and Blown Saves.

For several years we figured "Save Percentage", which is simply Saves divided by Save Opportunities, and this stat has some currency in the game. But the Save Percentage severely discriminates against middle relievers, who have no real chance to be credited with the Save, since they will be taken out of the game and replaced by the Closer even if they throw 110 miles an hour and strike out everybody they see. Middle relievers typically have Save Percentages of zero, even if they pitch well. The Save/Hold Percentage is a much more realistic evaluation of a pitcher's success in Save situations.

Opposition OPS: The OPS of the hitters facing the pitcher.

ERA: No explanation necessary.

Relief Pitching

Pitcher	Pos	T	Usage Rel G	Early Entry	Cons Days	Long	Lev Ind	Inherited Runners #	Scrd	Pct	Saves Easy	Reg	Tough	Relief Results Clean	BS Win	Saves	Opps	Holds	Sv/Hld Pct	Opp OPS	Rel ERA
Arizona Diamondbacks																					
Rauch, Jon, Was-Ari	CL	R	74	1	23	4	1.3	14	4	.29	9 - 10	8 - 11	1 - 3	46	2	18	24	6	.80	.742	4.14
Lyon, Brandon, Ari	CL	R	61	0	14	9	1.7	5	4	.80	16 - 18	10 - 12	0 - 1	44	1	26	31	3	.85	.792	4.70
Qualls, Chad, Ari	SU	R	77	3	20	1	1.4	32	11	.34	7 - 7	1 - 7	1 - 3	57	0	9	17	22	.79	.601	2.81
Pena, Tony, Ari	SU	R	72	1	17	5	1.4	14	6	.43	1 - 2	1 - 5	1 - 1	48	1	3	8	23	.84	.748	4.33
Slaten, Doug, Ari	LT	L	45	4	11	2	0.5	10	3	.30	0 - 0	0 - 0	0 - 0	30	0	0	0	4	1.00	.790	4.73
Ledezma, Wil, SD-Ari	LT	L	22	6	2	9	0.5	17	6	.35	0 - 0	0 - 0	0 - 0	15	0	0	0	0		.648	2.41
Cruz, Juan, Ari	UR	R	57	15	16	9	0.9	27	12	.44	0 - 0	0 - 2	0 - 0	41	1	0	2	8	.80	.658	2.61
Rosales, Leo, Ari	UR	R	27	10	6	4	0.7	15	6	.40	0 - 0	0 - 1	0 - 0	16	0	0	1	1	.50	.762	4.20
Medders, Brandon, Ari	UR	R	18	9	3	4	0.7	4	1	.25	0 - 0	0 - 1	0 - 0	11	0	0	1	0	.00	.720	4.58
Petit, Yusmeiro, Ari	UR	R	11	3	0	4	0.4	4	2	.50	0 - 0	0 - 0	0 - 0	5	0	0	0	0		.711	4.20
Gonzalez, Edgar, Ari	UR	R	11	4	3	8	0.4	0	0	.00	0 - 0	0 - 0	0 - 0	4	0	0	0	0		.839	6.00
Buckner, Billy, Ari	UR	R	10	4	1	5	0.3	3	2	.67	0 - 0	0 - 0	0 - 0	6	0	0	0	0		.874	3.21
Scherzer, Max, Ari	UR	R	9	4	0	6	0.3	5	0	.00	0 - 0	0 - 0	0 - 0	6	0	0	0	0		.540	2.37
Peguero, Jailen, Ari	UR	R	7	3	2	3	0.3	4	0	.00	0 - 0	0 - 0	0 - 0	3	0	0	0	0		.753	4.82
Robertson, Connor, Ari	UR	R	6	2	0	2	1.2	4	2	.50	0 - 0	0 - 0	0 - 0	3	0	0	0	0		.855	5.14
Atlanta Braves																					
Gonzalez, Mike, Atl	CL	L	36	0	6	3	1.1	7	2	.29	10 - 10	3 - 4	1 - 2	25	0	14	16	0	.88	.702	4.28
Ohman, Will, Atl	LT	L	83	10	29	3	0.9	35	6	.17	1 - 1	0 - 1	0 - 2	64	0	1	4	23	.89	.640	3.68
Ring, Royce, Atl	LT	L	42	7	15	1	0.8	34	6	.18	0 - 0	0 - 0	0 - 0	25	0	0	0	4	1.00	.921	8.46
Ridgway, Jeff, Atl	LT	L	10	4	2	2	0.6	8	3	.38	0 - 0	0 - 0	0 - 1	5	0	0	1	0	.00	.709	3.72
Bueno, Francisley, Atl	LT	L	1	0	0	1	0.0	0	0		0 - 0	0 - 0	0 - 0	0	0	0	0	0		1.128	7.71
Carlyle, Buddy, Atl	LM	R	45	26	8	16	0.8	36	8	.22	0 - 0	0 - 0	0 - 0	29	0	0	0	0		.661	3.59
Campillo, Jorge, Atl	LM	R	14	7	1	8	0.6	6	4	.67	0 - 0	0 - 0	0 - 0	9	0	0	0	4	1.00	.510	1.25
Boyer, Blaine, Atl	UR	R	76	10	20	11	1.0	26	11	.42	0 - 1	1 - 4	0 - 0	48	0	1	5	14	.79	.774	5.88
Bennett, Jeff, Atl	UR	R	68	19	18	16	1.1	42	14	.33	1 - 1	1 - 1	1 - 2	41	1	3	4	15	.95	.629	3.12
Tavarez, Julian, Bos-Mil-Atl	UR	R	52	10	10	12	0.9	25	9	.36	0 - 0	0 - 0	0 - 0	29	0	0	0	6	1.00	.851	5.10
Acosta, Manny, Atl	UR	R	46	4	10	8	1.2	13	2	.15	1 - 2	2 - 2	0 - 1	34	0	3	5	4	.78	.745	3.57
Julio, Jorge, Cle-Atl	UR	R	27	7	4	9	0.6	13	7	.54	0 - 0	0 - 1	0 - 0	18	1	0	1	0	.00	.756	3.60
Nunez, Vladimir, Atl	UR	R	23	10	5	9	0.6	9	3	.33	0 - 0	0 - 0	0 - 0	14	0	0	0	0		.714	3.86
Resop, Chris, Atl	UR	R	16	3	2	4	0.5	9	4	.44	0 - 0	0 - 0	0 - 0	9	0	0	0	2	1.00	.768	5.89
Soriano, Rafael, Atl	UR	R	14	0	2	0	1.7	0	0		2 - 2	1 - 2	0 - 0	10	0	3	4	0	.75	.575	2.57
Moylan, Peter, Atl	UR	R	7	0	3	0	2.2	2	1	.50	1 - 1	1 - 0	0 - 1	5	0	1	2	4	.83	.628	1.59
Stockman, Phil, Atl	UR	R	6	2	1	2	0.2	2	0	.00	0 - 0	0 - 0	0 - 0	6	0	0	0	0		.424	.00
Dessens, Elmer, Atl	UR	R	4	1	0	2	0.7	0	0		0 - 0	0 - 1	0 - 0	1	0	0	1	0	.00	1.388	22.50
DeSalvo, Matt, Atl	UR	R	2	1	0	2	0.1	0	0		0 - 0	0 - 0	0 - 0	0	0	0	0	0		1.410	31.50
Smoltz, John, Atl	UR	R	1	0	0	0	3.8	0	0		0 - 0	0 - 1	0 - 0	0	0	0	1	0	.00	1.167	18.00
Hudson, Tim, Atl	ER	R	1	0	0	0	0.0	0	0		0 - 0	0 - 0	0 - 0	1	0	0	0	0		.000	.00
Reyes, Jo-Jo, Atl	ER	L	1	1	0	1	1.1	0	0		0 - 0	0 - 0	0 - 0	0	0	0	0	0		1.472	16.88
Morton, Charlie, Atl	ER	R	1	1	0	1	0.9	0	0		0 - 0	0 - 0	0 - 0	1	0	0	0	0		.333	.00
Baltimore Orioles																					
Sherrill, George, Bal	CL	L	57	0	16	5	2.0	22	9	.41	20 - 20	9 - 14	2 - 3	36	1	31	37	0	.84	.708	4.73
Johnson, Jim, Bal	SU	R	54	3	12	12	1.4	20	3	.15	0 - 0	1 - 1	0 - 0	40	0	1	1	19	1.00	.539	2.23
Albers, Matt, Bal	SU	R	25	12	3	11	1.1	18	4	.22	0 - 1	0 - 0	0 - 1	14	0	0	2	6	.75	.643	2.63
Walker, Jamie, Bal	LT	L	59	5	14	3	1.1	51	16	.31	0 - 2	0 - 1	0 - 1	32	0	0	4	9	.69	.981	6.87
Bass, Brian, Min-Bal	LM	R	45	17	6	16	0.5	42	12	.29	0 - 0	1 - 2	0 - 0	20	0	1	2	3	.80	.853	5.01
Cormier, Lance, Bal	LM	R	44	28	3	24	0.7	47	16	.34	0 - 0	1 - 2	0 - 0	20	0	1	3	0	.33	.738	4.19
Bierd, Randor, Bal	LM	R	29	14	4	11	0.5	39	21	.54	0 - 0	0 - 0	0 - 0	12	0	0	0	0		.869	4.91
Castillo, Alberto, Bal	LM	L	28	12	7	7	0.5	33	12	.36	0 - 0	0 - 0	0 - 1	16	0	0	1	0	.00	.758	3.81
Cabrera, Fernando, Bal	LM	R	22	10	2	8	0.5	21	14	.67	0 - 0	0 - 0	0 - 1	13	0	0	0	0		.938	5.40
Sarfate, Dennis, Bal	UR	R	53	17	13	18	0.8	50	19	.38	0 - 1	0 - 0	0 - 1	31	0	0	2	3	.60	.624	3.38
Cherry, Rocky, Bal	UR	R	18	3	2	5	1.6	12	3	.25	0 - 0	1 - 2	0 - 1	8	0	1	3	2	.60	.873	6.35
Mickolio, Kam, Bal	UR	R	9	0	2	2	0.6	6	6	1.00	0 - 0	0 - 0	0 - 1	4	0	0	1	0	.00	.743	5.87
Burres, Brian, Bal	UR	L	9	5	0	4	0.6	8	4	.50	0 - 0	0 - 1	0 - 0	3	0	0	1	0	.00	1.004	13.00
Aquino, Greg, Bal	UR	R	9	1	1	3	0.5	6	3	.50	0 - 0	0 - 0	0 - 0	3	0	0	0	0		1.114	12.54
Miller, Jim, Bal	UR	R	8	1	0	2	1.4	6	4	.67	1 - 1	0 - 0	0 - 1	3	0	1	2	0	.50	.750	1.17
McCrory, Bob, Bal	UR	R	8	1	1	2	0.4	4	0	.00	0 - 0	0 - 0	0 - 0	4	0	0	0	0		.907	15.63
Bukvich, Ryan, Bal	UR	R	4	3	0	1	0.7	3	2	.67	0 - 0	0 - 0	0 - 0	0	0	0	0	0		1.208	6.75
Simon, Alfredo, Bal	UR	R	3	2	1	3	0.4	3	2	.67	0 - 0	0 - 0	0 - 0	0	0	0	0	0		1.262	10.13
Loewen, Adam, Bal	UR	L	3	2	0	0	1.3	3	2	.67	0 - 0	0 - 0	0 - 0	2	0	0	0	1	1.00	.950	9.00
Trachsel, Steve, Bal	UR	R	2	1	0	2	0.2	0	0		0 - 0	0 - 0	0 - 0	0	0	0	0	0		.990	6.00
Boston Red Sox																					
Papelbon, Jonathan, Bos	CL	R	67	0	18	5	1.6	30	4	.13	22 - 22	15 - 20	4 - 4	48	1	41	46	0	.89	.561	2.34
Delcarmen, Manny, Bos	SU	R	73	10	12	11	1.2	45	16	.36	0 - 0	2 - 4	0 - 1	49	0	2	5	18	.87	.605	3.27
Okajima, Hideki, Bos	SU	L	64	1	12	8	1.5	25	13	.52	1 - 2	0 - 3	0 - 4	47	0	1	9	23	.75	.612	2.61

Relief Pitching

Pitcher	Pos	T	Rel G	Early Entry	Cons Days	Long	Lev Ind	#	Scrd	Pct	Easy	Reg	Tough	Clean	BS Win	Saves	Opps	Holds	Sv/Hld Pct	Opp OPS	Rel ERA
Lopez, Javier, Bos	LT	L	70	21	19	6	0.9	46	12	.26	0 - 0	0 - 1	0 - 0	51	0	0	1	10	.91	.699	2.43
Aardsma, David, Bos	LM	R	47	23	7	14	0.7	32	13	.41	0 - 1	0 - 0	0 - 0	27	0	0	1	4	.80	.822	5.55
Timlin, Mike, Bos	UR	R	47	8	9	8	0.7	17	5	.29	0 - 0	1 - 1	0 - 0	27	0	1	1	0	1.00	.891	5.66
Masterson, Justin, Bos	UR	R	27	5	2	7	1.1	17	3	.18	0 - 0	0 - 1	0 - 0	17	0	0	1	3	.75	.645	2.36
Smith, Chris, Bos	UR	R	12	5	1	6	0.2	9	4	.44	0 - 0	0 - 0	0 - 0	5	0	0	0	0		.904	7.85
Pauley, David, Bos	UR	R	4	0	0	2	0.0	0	0		0 - 0	0 - 0	0 - 0	1	0	0	0	0		.948	8.44
Hansack, Devern, Bos	UR	R	4	1	0	2	0.3	2	1	.50	0 - 0	0 - 0	0 - 0	2	0	0	0	0		.603	4.05
Snyder, Kyle, Bos	UR	R	2	2	0	0	0.9	0	0		0 - 0	0 - 1	0 - 0	0	0	0	1	0	.00	1.333	21.60
Buchholz, Clay, Bos	ER	R	1	1	0	0	0.0	0	0		0 - 0	0 - 0	0 - 0	0	0	0	0	0		.900	9.00
Chicago Cubs																					
Wood, Kerry, ChC	CL	R	65	0	19	11	2.0	12	2	.17	21 - 24	13 - 16	0 - 0	50	1	34	40	0	.85	.632	3.26
Marmol, Carlos, ChC	SU	R	82	1	27	17	1.5	47	10	.21	4 - 5	2 - 3	1 - 1	59	1	7	9	30	.95	.508	2.68
Cotts, Neal, ChC	LT	L	50	11	16	3	0.9	33	7	.21	0 - 0	0 - 0	0 - 2	35	0	0	2	9	.82	.786	4.29
Marshall, Sean, ChC	LT	L	27	10	2	4	0.7	15	5	.33	1 - 1	0 - 1	0 - 0	15	0	1	2	3	.80	.740	3.42
Pignatiello, Carmen, ChC	LT	L	2	1	0	0	1.1	2	1	.50	0 - 0	0 - 0	0 - 0	0	0	0	0	0		1.464	13.50
Lieber, Jon, ChC	LM	R	25	11	3	9	0.8	3	2	.67	0 - 0	0 - 0	0 - 1	14	0	0	1	3	.75	.801	3.22
Hart, Kevin, ChC	LM	R	21	9	2	11	0.7	8	4	.50	0 - 0	0 - 0	0 - 0	7	0	0	0	1	1.00	.917	6.51
Howry, Bob, ChC	UR	R	72	6	17	9	1.0	28	5	.18	0 - 0	1 - 3	0 - 2	42	2	1	5	15	.80	.882	5.35
Wuertz, Mike, ChC	UR	R	45	15	12	7	1.0	40	12	.30	0 - 1	0 - 1	0 - 1	25	0	0	3	3	.50	.740	3.63
Gaudin, Chad, Oak-ChC	UR	R	44	13	10	11	0.8	16	5	.31	0 - 0	0 - 1	0 - 0	27	1	0	1	4	.80	.785	4.83
Samardzija, Jeff, ChC	UR	R	26	6	3	8	1.3	10	6	.60	0 - 0	1 - 4	0 - 0	14	0	1	4	3	.57	.599	2.28
Ascanio, Jose, ChC	UR	R	6	0	0	2	0.5	0	0		0 - 0	0 - 0	0 - 0	3	0	0	0	0		1.057	7.94
Guzman, Angel, ChC	UR	R	5	3	0	2	0.3	2	0	.00	0 - 0	0 - 0	0 - 0	3	0	0	0	0		.847	7.04
Wells, Randy, Tor-ChC	UR	R	4	1	1	0	0.4	3	1	.33	0 - 0	0 - 0	0 - 0	3	0	0	0	0		.167	.00
Fox, Chad, ChC	UR	R	3	1	0	1	1.9	5	2	.40	0 - 0	0 - 0	0 - 0	1	0	0	0	0		.885	5.40
Marquis, Jason, ChC	ER	R	1	0	0	0	1.9	0	0		0 - 0	0 - 0	0 - 0	0	0	0	0	1	1.00	1.467	54.00
Cincinnati Reds																					
Cordero, Francisco, Cin	CL	R	72	0	22	11	1.8	15	9	.60	19 - 22	14 - 17	1 - 1	54	1	34	40	0	.85	.682	3.33
Weathers, David, Cin	SU	R	72	2	22	6	1.3	15	2	.13	0 - 0	0 - 3	0 - 1	48	0	0	4	19	.83	.778	3.25
Affeldt, Jeremy, Cin	LT	L	74	24	22	15	0.6	36	12	.33	0 - 1	0 - 0	0 - 0	45	0	0	5	5	.83	.733	3.33
Bray, Bill, Cin	LT	L	63	15	20	2	0.9	48	14	.29	0 - 0	0 - 0	0 - 4	41	0	0	4	9	.69	.779	2.87
Mercker, Kent, Cin	LT	L	15	1	4	1	0.4	1	0	.00	0 - 0	0 - 0	0 - 0	11	0	0	0	0		.756	3.29
Herrera, Daniel Ray, Cin	LT	L	7	2	1	2	0.4	5	0	.00	0 - 0	0 - 0	0 - 0	5	0	0	0	0		.962	7.36
Pettyjohn, Adam, Cin	LT	L	2	1	0	1	0.0	0	0		0 - 0	0 - 0	0 - 0	1	0	0	0	0		.900	4.50
Majewski, Gary, Cin	LM	R	37	17	7	7	0.4	37	14	.38	0 - 0	0 - 0	0 - 1	18	0	0	1	2	.67	.963	6.53
Lincoln, Mike, Cin	UR	R	64	18	9	10	1.0	49	12	.24	0 - 0	0 - 0	0 - 1	42	1	0	1	10	.91	.714	4.48
Burton, Jared, Cin	UR	R	54	7	10	13	1.1	17	9	.53	0 - 1	0 - 1	0 - 0	34	0	0	2	11	.85	.712	3.22
Masset, Nick, CWS-Cin	UR	R	41	13	5	13	0.8	26	13	.50	0 - 0	0 - 1	1 - 2	22	0	1	3	2	.60	.812	3.72
Fogg, Josh, Cin	UR	R	8	5	0	4	0.3	2	0	.00	0 - 0	0 - 0	0 - 0	5	0	0	0	1	1.00	.683	5.06
Roenicke, Josh, Cin	UR	R	5	1	1	0	0.9	5	4	.80	0 - 0	0 - 0	0 - 0	1	0	0	0	0		1.167	9.00
Adkins, Jon, Cin	UR	R	4	1	0	0	0.8	4	0	.00	0 - 0	0 - 0	0 - 0	3	0	0	0	0		1.050	2.45
Ramirez, Ramon A, Cin	UR	R	1	1	0	1	0.6	0	0		0 - 0	0 - 0	0 - 0	1	0	0	0	0		.000	.00
Owings, Micah, Ari-Cin	ER	R	4	0	0	1	1.0	2	0	.00	0 - 0	0 - 0	0 - 0	3	0	0	0	1	1.00	.543	11.25
Volquez, Edinson, Cin	ER	R	1	0	0	1	2.5	0	0		0 - 0	0 - 0	0 - 0	0	0	0	0	0		.821	.00
Harang, Aaron, Cin	ER	R	1	0	0	1	2.4	0	0		0 - 0	0 - 0	0 - 0	1	0	0	0	0		.414	.00
Cleveland Indians																					
Borowski, Joe, Cle	CL	R	18	0	4	1	2.0	0	0		4 - 6	2 - 4	0 - 0	12	1	6	10	0	.60	.978	7.56
Perez, Rafael, Cle	SU	L	73	8	20	13	1.3	44	14	.32	0 - 0	1 - 2	1 - 5	45	1	2	7	25	.84	.649	3.54
Rundles, Rich, Cle	LT	L	8	3	1	0	0.9	4	2	.50	0 - 0	0 - 0	0 - 0	7	0	0	0	1	1.00	.679	1.80
Betancourt, Rafael, Cle	UR	R	69	5	18	12	1.4	33	12	.36	4 - 4	0 - 2	0 - 2	40	1	4	8	12	.80	.789	5.07
Kobayashi, Masa, Cle	UR	R	57	3	14	5	1.0	16	7	.44	3 - 3	2 - 2	1 - 4	33	0	6	9	2	.73	.757	4.53
Lewis, Jensen, Cle	UR	R	51	16	8	18	1.0	34	12	.35	8 - 8	5 - 5	0 - 1	29	0	13	14	4	.94	.771	3.82
Rincon, Juan, Min-Cle	UR	R	47	14	7	16	0.8	18	15	.83	0 - 0	0 - 0	0 - 0	21	0	0	0	3	1.00	.831	5.86
Mujica, Edward, Cle	UR	R	33	7	6	9	0.6	18	6	.33	0 - 1	0 - 0	0 - 1	20	1	0	2	1	.33	.849	6.75
Donnelly, Brendan, Cle	UR	R	15	1	1	0	0.9	0	0		0 - 0	0 - 0	0 - 0	10	0	0	0	4	1.00	.941	8.56
Mastny, Tom, Cle	UR	R	13	7	0	6	0.4	6	3	.50	0 - 0	0 - 1	0 - 0	6	0	0	1	0	.00	.845	9.16
Reyes, Anthony, StL-Cle	UR	R	10	2	0	4	0.8	1	1	1.00	0 - 0	1 - 1	0 - 0	6	0	1	1	2	1.00	.794	4.91
Elarton, Scott, Cle	UR	R	8	4	0	4	0.3	5	2	.40	0 - 0	0 - 0	0 - 0	3	0	0	0	0		.685	3.52
Bauer, Rick, Cle	UR	R	4	1	0	3	0.2	0	0		0 - 0	0 - 0	0 - 0	1	0	0	0	0		1.137	13.50
Slocum, Brian, Cle	UR	R	2	1	0	1	0.0	3	0	.00	0 - 0	0 - 0	0 - 0	0	0	0	0	0		1.754	27.00
Meloan, John, Cle	UR	R	2	0	0	0	0.2	0	0		0 - 0	0 - 0	0 - 0	2	0	0	0	0		.167	.00
Jackson, Zach, Mil-Cle	UR	L	2	0	0	2	0.2	2	0	.00	0 - 0	0 - 0	0 - 0	1	0	0	0	0		.701	4.91
Bullington, Bryan, Cle	UR	R	1	1	0	1	0.8	0	0		0 - 0	0 - 0	0 - 0	1	0	0	0	0		.250	.00
Colorado Rockies																					
Fuentes, Brian, Col	CL	L	67	0	14	7	2.0	5	3	.60	19 - 20	11 - 13	0 - 1	54	0	30	34	6	.90	.569	2.73
Corpas, Manny, Col	SU	R	76	7	14	8	1.4	21	10	.48	0 - 1	4 - 11	0 - 1	47	0	4	13	19	.72	.777	4.52
Buchholz, Taylor, Col	SU	R	63	0	13	5	1.3	10	1	.10	0 - 0	1 - 3	0 - 0	47	0	1	3	21	.92	.550	2.17

Relief Pitching

Pitcher	Pos	T	Rel G	Early Entry	Cons Days	Long	Lev Ind	#	Scrd	Pct	Easy	Reg	Tough	Clean	BS Win	Saves	Opps	Holds	Sv/Hld Pct	Opp OPS	Rel ERA
Bowie, Micah, Col	LT	L	10	2	4	3	0.9	9	1	.11	0 - 0	0 - 0	0 - 0	5	0	0	0	0		.970	9.00
Bowers, Cedrick, Col	LT	L	5	1	0	2	0.3	4	2	.50	0 - 0	0 - 0	0 - 0	2	0	0	0	0		1.323	13.50
Rusch, Glendon, SD-Col	LM	L	26	10	4	13	0.9	21	10	.48	0 - 0	0 - 1	0 - 0	11	0	0	1	1	.50	.711	5.30
Grilli, Jason, Det-Col	UR	R	60	18	6	18	0.8	30	9	.30	0 - 0	1 - 1	0 - 1	41	0	1	2	4	.83	.673	3.00
Herges, Matt, Col	UR	R	58	21	11	13	1.0	20	11	.55	0 - 0	0 - 3	0 - 2	32	1	0	5	4	.44	.830	5.04
Speier, Ryan, Col	UR	R	43	16	7	7	0.7	29	10	.34	0 - 0	0 - 0	0 - 1	26	0	0	1	3	.75	.714	4.06
Vizcaino, Luis, Col	UR	R	43	14	9	10	0.6	21	6	.29	0 - 0	0 - 0	0 - 1	26	0	0	1	1	.50	.837	5.28
Register, Steven, Col	UR	R	10	3	2	3	0.2	5	1	.20	0 - 0	0 - 0	0 - 0	3	0	0	0	0		1.054	9.00
de la Rosa, Jorge, Col	UR	L	5	2	0	3	0.3	2	0	.00	0 - 0	0 - 0	0 - 0	4	0	0	0	0		.664	2.25
Hirsh, Jason, Col	UR	R	3	2	0	2	0.2	1	1	1.00	0 - 0	0 - 0	0 - 0	1	0	0	0	0		1.212	10.38
Morillo, Juan, Col	UR	R	1	0	0	0	0.0	0	0		0 - 0	0 - 0	0 - 0	1	0	0	0	0		.750	.00
Reynolds, Greg, Col	UR	R	1	1	0	0	0.1	0	0		0 - 0	0 - 0	0 - 0	1	0	0	0	0		.000	.00
Capellan, Jose, Col	UR	R	1	0	0	1	0.0	0	0		0 - 0	0 - 0	0 - 0	0	0	0	0	0		.778	4.50
Redman, Mark, Col	UR	L	1	0	0	0	0.1	1	0	.00	0 - 0	0 - 0	0 - 0	1	0	0	0	0		.000	.00
Chicago White Sox																					
Jenks, Bobby, CWS	CL	R	57	0	14	3	1.8	9	2	.22	17 - 18	12 - 15	1 - 1	45	0	30	34	0	.88	.620	2.63
Thornton, Matt, CWS	SU	L	74	8	21	7	1.2	56	21	.38	1 - 1	0 - 1	0 - 4	50	1	1	6	20	.81	.544	2.67
Dotel, Octavio, CWS	SU	R	72	7	16	9	1.4	43	12	.28	0 - 3	1 - 1	0 - 1	49	0	1	5	21	.85	.687	3.76
Linebrink, Scott, CWS	SU	R	50	0	15	3	1.2	10	2	.20	1 - 2	0 - 1	0 - 1	35	0	1	4	19	.87	.677	3.69
Logan, Boone, CWS	LT	L	55	10	13	3	0.8	44	12	.27	0 - 1	0 - 0	0 - 0	35	0	0	1	3	.75	.891	5.95
Ramirez, H., CWS-KC-CWS	LT	L	32	10	4	8	0.9	16	4	.25	0 - 0	0 - 0	0 - 0	18	0	0	0	2	1.00	.718	4.34
Carrasco, D.J., CWS	LM	R	31	14	7	9	0.9	32	12	.38	0 - 0	0 - 0	0 - 1	16	0	0	1	7	.88	.611	3.96
Wassermann, Ehren, CWS	UR	R	24	8	4	5	0.5	26	10	.38	0 - 0	0 - 0	0 - 0	9	0	0	0	2	1.00	.914	7.78
Russell, Adam, CWS	UR	R	22	0	2	8	0.3	12	6	.50	0 - 0	0 - 0	0 - 0	11	0	0	0	0		.741	5.19
MacDougal, Mike, CWS	UR	R	16	2	1	4	0.5	9	2	.22	0 - 0	0 - 0	0 - 0	11	0	0	0	0		.697	2.12
Loaiza, Esteban, LAD-CWS	UR	R	7	3	0	3	0.4	2	0	.00	0 - 0	0 - 0	0 - 0	3	0	0	0	0		.584	2.87
Broadway, Lance, CWS	UR	R	6	2	0	2	0.1	4	2	.50	0 - 0	0 - 0	0 - 0	1	0	0	0	0		1.219	9.35
Richard, Clayton, CWS	UR	L	5	2	0	2	0.1	1	1	1.00	0 - 0	0 - 0	0 - 0	2	0	0	0	0		.649	4.50
Detroit Tigers																					
Jones, Todd, Det	CL	R	45	1	8	2	1.5	8	3	.38	15 - 17	3 - 4	0 - 0	28	0	18	21	0	.86	.827	4.97
Rodney, Fernando, Det	CL	R	38	1	7	9	2.0	15	4	.27	8 - 9	3 - 6	2 - 4	24	0	13	19	5	.75	.733	4.91
Farnsworth, Kyle, NYY-Det	SU	R	61	1	11	7	1.2	14	7	.50	0 - 1	1 - 3	0 - 0	41	0	1	4	14	.83	.907	4.48
Zumaya, Joel, Det	SU	R	21	1	1	5	1.9	11	7	.64	0 - 1	1 - 4	0 - 0	11	0	1	5	5	.60	.854	3.47
Seay, Bobby, Det	LT	L	60	13	12	12	1.1	52	16	.31	0 - 0	0 - 0	0 - 1	35	0	0	1	13	.93	.741	4.47
Fossum, Casey, Det	LT	L	31	9	4	12	0.7	34	10	.29	0 - 1	0 - 0	0 - 0	17	0	0	1	6	.86	.806	5.66
Rapada, Clay, Det	LT	L	25	6	3	2	0.6	24	2	.08	0 - 0	0 - 0	0 - 0	19	0	0	0	2	1.00	.660	4.22
Lopez, Aquilino, Det	LM	R	48	21	7	20	0.5	57	29	.51	0 - 0	0 - 0	0 - 1	18	1	0	1	4	.80	.771	3.55
Miner, Zach, Det	LM	R	32	14	5	16	1.1	26	11	.42	0 - 0	0 - 0	0 - 3	18	0	0	3	6	.67	.714	4.23
Glover, Gary, TB-Det	UR	R	47	9	11	14	0.8	30	7	.23	0 - 1	0 - 0	0 - 0	26	0	0	1	5	.83	.825	5.30
Dolsi, Freddy, Det	UR	R	42	7	7	13	1.2	34	12	.35	0 - 0	2 - 2	0 - 1	24	0	2	3	7	.90	.719	3.97
Cruceta, Francisco, Det	UR	R	13	0	3	1	1.8	8	6	.75	0 - 0	0 - 1	0 - 1	7	0	0	2	1	.33	.880	5.40
Beltran, Francis, Det	UR	R	11	0	3	3	0.4	8	3	.38	0 - 0	0 - 0	0 - 0	6	0	0	0	2	1.00	.839	4.85
Lambert, Chris, Det	UR	R	5	3	0	3	0.6	4	4	1.00	0 - 0	0 - 0	0 - 0	1	0	0	0	0		.890	5.00
Bazardo, Yorman, Det	UR	R	3	0	0	2	0.1	0	0		0 - 0	0 - 0	0 - 0	1	0	0	0	0		1.386	24.00
Willis, Dontrelle, Det	UR	L	1	0	0	1	0.3	0	0		0 - 0	0 - 0	0 - 0	0	0	0	0	0		1.250	9.00
Robertson, Nate, Det	ER	L	4	1	0	3	0.1	0	0		0 - 0	0 - 0	0 - 0	1	0	0	0	0		1.009	11.74
Galarraga, Armando, Det	ER	R	2	2	0	1	1.5	1	1	1.00	0 - 0	0 - 0	0 - 1	0	0	0	1	0	.00	.708	12.00
Florida Marlins																					
Gregg, Kevin, Fla	CL	R	72	0	20	13	2.1	15	1	.07	15 - 17	10 - 16	4 - 5	54	2	29	38	4	.79	.585	3.41
Lindstrom, Matt, Fla	SU	R	66	7	18	2	1.1	18	2	.11	4 - 4	1 - 2	0 - 0	51	0	5	6	14	.95	.688	3.14
Rhodes, Arthur, Sea-Fla	SU	L	61	1	11	1	1.5	45	8	.18	0 - 0	1 - 1	1 - 2	51	0	2	3	24	.96	.566	2.04
Pinto, Renyel, Fla	LT	L	67	6	22	13	1.4	28	9	.32	0 - 0	0 - 1	0 - 1	44	0	0	2	17	.89	.707	4.45
Tankersley, Taylor, Fla	LT	L	25	4	5	2	0.9	20	6	.30	0 - 0	0 - 1	0 - 1	16	0	0	2	4	.67	.995	8.15
Kensing, Logan, Fla	LM	R	48	18	7	15	0.8	31	17	.55	0 - 0	0 - 2	0 - 1	28	0	0	3	5	.63	.727	4.23
Waechter, Doug, Fla	LM	R	48	22	8	18	0.8	15	5	.33	0 - 0	0 - 1	0 - 0	30	0	0	1	9	.90	.718	3.69
Hendrickson, Mark, Fla	LM	L	17	12	2	8	0.6	20	4	.20	0 - 0	0 - 0	0 - 0	9	0	0	0	3	1.00	.608	3.03
Nelson, Joe, Fla	UR	R	59	7	18	5	1.2	39	16	.41	1 - 1	0 - 0	0 - 4	40	0	1	5	11	.75	.616	2.00
Miller, Justin, Fla	UR	R	46	7	9	10	1.1	30	6	.20	0 - 0	0 - 1	0 - 0	28	0	0	1	7	.88	.763	4.24
Miller, Andrew, Fla	UR	L	9	2	2	0	0.9	6	1	.17	0 - 0	0 - 0	0 - 0	5	0	0	0	2	1.00	.695	9.45
Gardner, Lee, Fla	UR	R	7	6	2	2	0.4	5	3	.60	0 - 0	0 - 0	0 - 0	2	0	0	0	0		1.244	10.80
Tucker, Ryan, Fla	UR	R	7	2	1	2	0.2	0	0		0 - 0	0 - 1	0 - 0	4	0	0	1	0	.00	.809	7.88
Badenhop, Burke, Fla	UR	R	5	3	0	2	0.3	8	2	.25	0 - 0	0 - 0	0 - 0	3	0	0	0	0		.741	3.12
de la Cruz, Frankie, Fla	UR	R	5	2	0	3	0.3	1	1	1.00	0 - 0	0 - 0	0 - 0	1	0	0	0	0		1.341	24.00
Delgado, Jesus, Fla	UR	R	2	1	0	0	0.7	0	0		0 - 0	0 - 0	0 - 0	1	0	0	0	0		.611	4.50
Volstad, Chris, Fla	UR	R	1	1	0	1	1.9	0	0		0 - 0	0 - 0	0 - 0	1	0	0	0	0		.873	.00
Nolasco, Ricky, Fla	ER	R	2	2	0	2	0.3	3	1	.33	0 - 0	0 - 0	0 - 0	1	0	0	0	0		.446	.00

Relief Pitching

Pitcher	Pos	T	Usage					Inherited Runners			Saves			Relief Results							
			Rel G	Early Entry	Cons Days	Long	Lev Ind	#	Scrd	Pct	Easy	Reg	Tough	Clean	BS Win	Saves	Opps	Holds	Sv/Hld Pct	Opp OPS	Rel ERA
Houston Astros																					
Valverde, Jose, Hou	CL	R	74	0	22	10	1.6	16	6	.38	33 - 35	10 - 12	1 - 4	56	3	44	51	0	.86	.686	3.38
Brocail, Doug, Hou	SU	R	72	3	17	7	1.2	30	8	.27	0 - 1	2 - 4	0 - 0	51	0	2	5	22	.89	.682	3.93
Wright, Wesley, Hou	LT	L	71	13	17	9	1.0	43	9	.21	1 - 1	0 - 0	0 - 0	47	0	1	1	13	1.00	.733	5.01
Byrdak, Tim, Hou	LT	L	59	21	18	7	0.8	32	6	.19	0 - 0	0 - 0	0 - 0	42	0	0	0	8	1.00	.777	3.90
Sampson, Chris, Hou	LM	R	43	19	5	9	0.9	27	3	.11	0 - 1	0 - 1	0 - 0	29	1	0	2	11	.85	.581	2.92
Borkowski, Dave, Hou	LM	R	26	15	4	13	0.7	11	4	.36	0 - 0	0 - 1	0 - 0	13	0	0	1	0	.00	1.006	7.50
Hawkins, LaTroy, NYY-Hou	UR	R	57	12	13	7	0.7	17	7	.41	1 - 1	0 - 1	0 - 0	42	0	1	2	13	.93	.626	3.92
Geary, Geoff, Hou	UR	R	55	11	9	12	1.1	20	3	.15	0 - 0	0 - 1	0 - 1	43	0	0	2	12	.86	.570	2.53
Villarreal, Oscar, Hou	UR	R	35	11	9	7	0.5	11	1	.09	0 - 0	0 - 1	0 - 0	19	0	0	1	2	.67	.950	5.02
Arias, Alberto, Col-Hou	UR	R	13	6	3	1	0.3	13	3	.23	0 - 0	0 - 0	0 - 0	8	0	0	0	0		.791	5.14
Nieve, Fernando, Hou	UR	R	11	5	0	3	0.6	14	4	.29	0 - 1	0 - 0	0 - 0	4	0	0	1	0	.00	.941	8.44
Paronto, Chad, Hou	UR	R	6	4	0	3	0.3	3	2	.67	0 - 0	0 - 0	0 - 0	2	0	0	0	0		.904	4.35
Cassel, Jack, Hou	UR	R	6	5	0	5	0.5	5	3	.60	0 - 0	0 - 0	0 - 0	2	0	0	0	0		.784	4.50
Moehler, Brian, Hou	UR	R	5	3	0	2	0.6	2	0	.00	0 - 0	0 - 0	0 - 0	1	0	0	0	0		.883	7.04
Kansas City Royals																					
Soria, Joakim, KC	CL	R	63	0	18	10	1.8	6	2	.33	25 - 25	16 - 18	1 - 2	54	1	42	45	0	.93	.503	1.60
Ramirez, Ramon, KC	SU	R	71	6	17	12	1.4	52	12	.23	1 - 2	0 - 1	0 - 2	48	1	1	5	21	.85	.590	2.64
Mahay, Ron, KC	SU	L	57	20	12	13	1.1	47	16	.34	0 - 0	0 - 0	0 - 1	35	0	0	1	21	.95	.695	3.48
Gobble, Jimmy, KC	LT	L	39	6	7	6	0.4	28	15	.54	1 - 1	0 - 1	0 - 0	22	0	1	2	4	.83	.906	8.81
Newman, Josh, Col-KC	LT	L	12	5	1	6	0.2	6	2	.33	0 - 0	0 - 0	0 - 0	5	0	0	0	0		1.102	8.62
Bale, John, KC	LT	L	10	2	1	0	0.9	5	0	.00	0 - 0	0 - 0	0 - 0	10	0	0	0	2	1.00	.337	.00
Musser, Neal, KC	LT	L	1	0	0	0	0.0	0	0		0 - 0	0 - 0	0 - 0	1	0	0	0	0		.333	.00
Peralta, Joel, KC	LM	R	40	17	3	12	0.5	31	7	.23	0 - 0	0 - 1	0 - 0	19	0	0	1	1	.50	.867	5.98
Wells, Kip, Col-KC	LM	R	23	8	0	8	0.8	11	2	.18	0 - 0	0 - 0	0 - 0	12	0	0	0	1	1.00	.766	5.06
Nunez, Leo, KC	UR	R	45	4	6	4	0.9	20	11	.55	0 - 0	0 - 1	0 - 2	33	2	0	3	7	.70	.665	2.98
Yabuta, Yasuhiko, KC	UR	R	31	6	6	12	0.5	12	6	.50	0 - 0	0 - 0	0 - 1	17	0	0	1	0	.00	.817	4.78
Tejeda, Robinson, Tex-KC	UR	R	28	6	5	11	0.6	22	9	.41	0 - 0	0 - 0	0 - 1	14	0	0	1	1	.50	.591	4.24
Fulchino, Jeff, KC	UR	R	12	2	2	3	0.4	4	1	.25	0 - 0	0 - 0	0 - 0	6	0	0	0	0		.981	9.00
Lowery, Devon, KC	UR	R	5	0	0	1	0.1	0	0		0 - 0	0 - 0	0 - 0	2	0	0	0	0		1.013	10.38
Nomo, Hideo, KC	UR	R	3	1	0	2	0.6	4	4	1.00	0 - 0	0 - 0	0 - 0	0	0	0	0	0		1.519	18.69
Rosa, Carlos, KC	UR	R	2	1	0	1	0.5	3	3	1.00	0 - 0	0 - 0	0 - 0	1	0	0	0	0		.667	2.70
Pena, Tony, KC	ER	R	1	0	0	0	0.0	0	0		0 - 0	0 - 0	0 - 0	1	0	0	0	0		.000	.00
Los Angeles Angels																					
Rodriguez, Francisco, LAA	CL	R	76	0	29	5	2.5	18	7	.39	39 - 42	22 - 26	1 - 1	60	1	62	69	0	.90	.630	2.24
Shields, Scot, LAA	SU	R	64	0	20	9	1.8	15	3	.20	3 - 4	1 - 5	0 - 0	45	1	4	9	31	.88	.669	2.70
Arredondo, Jose, LAA	SU	R	52	7	12	10	1.3	31	14	.45	0 - 0	0 - 3	0 - 4	38	3	0	7	16	.70	.533	1.62
Oliver, Darren, LAA	LT	L	54	17	8	15	1.0	34	14	.41	0 - 0	0 - 1	0 - 1	33	0	0	2	12	.86	.682	2.88
O'Day, Darren, LAA	LM	R	30	10	3	11	0.4	17	5	.29	0 - 0	0 - 0	0 - 0	19	0	0	0	1	1.00	.719	4.57
Speier, Justin, LAA	UR	R	62	12	11	14	0.9	32	8	.25	0 - 0	0 - 0	0 - 2	33	0	0	2	10	.83	.839	5.03
Bulger, Jason, LAA	UR	R	14	1	2	4	0.4	1	1	1.00	0 - 0	0 - 0	0 - 0	7	0	0	0	0		.856	7.31
Bootcheck, Chris, LAA	UR	R	10	3	1	6	0.4	5	2	.40	0 - 0	0 - 0	0 - 0	3	0	0	0	1	1.00	.992	10.13
Jepsen, Kevin, LAA	UR	R	9	6	1	2	1.4	9	4	.44	0 - 0	0 - 0	0 - 0	5	0	0	0	3	1.00	.677	4.32
Loux, Shane, LAA	UR	R	7	3	0	5	0.2	2	2	1.00	0 - 0	0 - 0	0 - 0	4	0	0	0	0		.685	2.81
Moseley, Dustin, LAA	UR	R	2	1	0	1	1.1	2	1	.50	0 - 0	0 - 0	0 - 0	1	0	0	0	0		.980	11.25
Thompson, Rich, LAA	UR	R	2	0	0	1	0.1	0	0		0 - 0	0 - 0	0 - 0	1	0	0	0	0		1.100	22.50
Serrano, Alex, LAA	UR	R	1	0	0	0	0.6	0	0		0 - 0	0 - 0	0 - 0	1	0	0	0	0		.750	.00
Los Angeles Dodgers																					
Broxton, Jonathan, LAD	CL	R	70	0	19	3	1.7	31	7	.23	7 - 9	4 - 8	3 - 5	50	0	14	22	13	.77	.595	3.13
Saito, Takashi, LAD	CL	R	45	1	10	8	1.7	3	1	.33	9 - 9	9 - 13	0 - 0	33	0	18	22	0	.82	.594	2.49
Kuo, Hong-Chih, LAD	SU	L	39	14	5	19	1.1	19	3	.16	0 - 0	1 - 2	0 - 1	28	0	1	3	12	.87	.535	1.69
Beimel, Joe, LAD	LT	L	71	11	25	3	1.1	60	20	.33	0 - 0	0 - 0	0 - 0	48	0	0	0	12	1.00	.672	2.02
Elbert, Scott, LAD	LT	L	10	4	0	0	0.6	5	1	.20	0 - 0	0 - 0	0 - 0	6	0	0	0	2	1.00	1.067	12.00
Park, Chan Ho, LAD	LM	R	49	16	5	20	1.0	21	4	.19	0 - 0	2 - 5	0 - 0	29	0	2	5	5	.70	.775	3.84
Wade, Cory, LAD	UR	R	55	10	9	13	0.8	22	5	.23	0 - 0	0 - 1	0 - 0	37	0	0	1	9	.90	.584	2.27
Proctor, Scott, LAD	UR	R	41	13	7	4	0.6	26	12	.46	0 - 1	0 - 0	0 - 0	22	0	0	1	2	.67	.833	6.05
Troncoso, Ramon, LAD	UR	R	32	8	6	10	0.5	19	8	.42	0 - 0	0 - 0	0 - 0	20	0	0	0	2	1.00	.717	4.26
Johnson, Jason, LAD	UR	R	14	5	2	6	0.6	10	5	.50	0 - 0	0 - 0	0 - 0	3	0	0	0	1	1.00	.946	6.63
McDonald, James, LAD	UR	R	4	2	0	2	0.4	0	0		0 - 0	0 - 0	0 - 0	4	0	0	0	0		.534	.00
Sturtze, Tanyon, LAD	UR	R	3	1	0	0	0.0	0	0		0 - 0	0 - 0	0 - 0	3	0	0	0	0		.472	.00
Brazoban, Yhency, LAD	UR	R	2	0	0	1	0.0	0	0		0 - 0	0 - 0	0 - 0	1	0	0	0	0		.976	6.00
Billingsley, Chad, LAD	ER	R	3	1	0	1	1.0	0	0		0 - 0	0 - 0	0 - 0	2	0	0	0	1	1.00	.771	2.08
Penny, Brad, LAD	ER	R	2	0	0	0	0.5	0	0		0 - 0	0 - 0	0 - 0	0	0	0	0	0		1.625	27.00
Kershaw, Clayton, LAD	ER	L	1	1	0	0	2.7	0	0		0 - 0	0 - 0	0 - 0	1	0	0	0	1	1.00	1.350	.00
Milwaukee Brewers																					
Torres, Salomon, Mil	CL	R	71	5	18	12	2.0	26	7	.27	16 - 17	10 - 15	2 - 3	45	3	28	35	5	.83	.680	3.49
Gagne, Eric, Mil	CL	R	50	0	13	8	1.7	7	1	.14	7 - 10	3 - 7	0 - 0	35	1	10	17	7	.71	.841	5.44

Relief Pitching

Pitcher	Pos	T	Usage Rel G	Early Entry	Cons Days	Long	Lev Ind	Inherited Runners #	Scrd	Pct	Saves Easy	Reg	Tough	Relief Results Clean	BS Win	Saves	Opps	Holds	Sv/Hld Pct	Opp OPS	Rel ERA
Riske, David, Mil	SU	R	45	10	8	7	1.2	26	8	.31	0-1	2-4	0-2	28	1	2	7	11	.72	.849	5.31
Villanueva, Carlos, Mil	SU	R	38	19	4	18	1.1	16	1	.06	0-0	1-1	0-0	24	0	1	1	11	1.00	.604	2.12
Shouse, Brian, Mil	LT	L	69	5	18	2	1.1	60	20	.33	0-0	2-3	0-2	46	0	2	5	15	.85	.656	2.81
Stetter, Mitch, Mil	LT	L	30	6	3	5	0.9	12	1	.08	0-0	0-1	0-0	22	0	0	1	4	.80	.613	3.20
McClung, Seth, Mil	LM	R	25	10	2	16	0.5	3	2	.67	0-0	0-0	0-0	14	0	0	0	1	1.00	.682	3.67
Mota, Guillermo, Mil	UR	R	58	4	8	9	1.4	25	5	.20	1-2	0-2	0-0	40	0	1	4	11	.80	.725	4.11
Coffey, Todd, Cin-Mil	UR	R	26	9	8	3	0.5	9	2	.22	0-0	0-0	0-0	17	0	0	0	1	1.00	.822	4.39
DiFelice, Mark, Mil	UR	R	15	8	1	5	0.4	7	2	.29	0-0	0-0	0-0	10	0	0	0	1	1.00	.688	2.84
Dillard, Tim, Mil	UR	R	13	4	2	2	0.4	7	2	.29	0-0	0-0	0-0	7	0	0	0	1	1.00	.802	4.40
Turnbow, Derrick, Mil	UR	R	8	0	1	1	0.9	0	0		0-0	1-1	0-0	4	0	1	1	0	1.00	1.260	15.63
Parra, Manny, Mil	ER	L	3	1	0	1	0.1	0	0		0-0	0-0	0-0	2	0	0	0	0		1.000	6.43
Bush, David, Mil	ER	R	2	2	0	1	0.3	2	1	.50	0-0	0-0	0-0	1	0	0	0	0		.220	.00
Minnesota Twins																					
Nathan, Joe, Min	CL	R	68	0	19	5	1.9	8	4	.50	21-21	17-22	1-2	58	0	39	45	0	.87	.521	1.33
Guerrier, Matt, Min	SU	R	76	10	22	13	1.3	37	8	.22	0-1	1-2	0-2	48	1	1	5	20	.84	.802	5.19
Crain, Jesse, Min	SU	R	66	8	12	4	1.1	42	11	.26	0-0	0-2	0-1	43	0	0	3	17	.85	.744	3.59
Guardado, Eddie, Tex-Min	SU	R	65	0	19	5	1.3	18	5	.28	4-4	0-1	0-0	47	0	4	5	25	.97	.699	4.15
Neshek, Pat, Min	SU	R	15	0	2	1	1.5	8	4	.50	0-0	0-0	0-2	11	0	0	2	6	.75	.751	4.73
Reyes, Dennys, Min	LT	L	75	5	28	0	1.3	68	20	.29	0-0	0-1	0-2	54	0	0	3	17	.85	.658	2.33
Breslow, Craig, Cle-Min	LT	L	49	15	11	11	0.6	47	9	.19	0-0	1-1	0-1	35	0	1	2	5	.86	.516	1.91
Mijares, Jose, Min	LT	L	10	0	3	0	0.8	2	0	.00	0-0	0-0	0-0	9	0	0	0	2	1.00	.206	.87
Bonser, Boof, Min	UR	R	35	15	4	12	0.5	19	3	.16	0-0	0-2	0-0	16	0	0	2	2	.50	.828	5.88
Korecky, Bobby, Min	UR	R	16	2	4	1	0.5	13	0	.00	0-0	0-0	0-0	11	0	0	0	0		.819	4.58
Humber, Philip, Min	UR	R	5	3	1	3	0.3	3	2	.67	0-0	0-0	0-0	1	0	0	0	0		.885	4.63
New York Mets																					
Wagner, Billy, NYM	CL	L	45	0	14	3	1.7	5	3	.60	22-26	5-7	0-1	36	0	27	34	0	.79	.517	2.30
Ayala, Luis, Was-NYM	SU	R	81	1	22	10	1.4	25	9	.36	7-9	2-6	0-0	47	0	9	15	19	.82	.788	5.71
Sanchez, Duaner, NYM	SU	R	66	4	17	4	1.3	20	5	.25	0-0	0-0	0-1	49	0	0	1	21	.95	.681	4.32
Feliciano, Pedro, NYM	LT	L	86	3	34	1	1.2	71	20	.28	0-0	2-3	0-1	60	0	2	4	21	.92	.790	4.05
Schoeneweis, Scott, NYM	LT	L	73	8	22	3	1.0	46	17	.37	0-1	1-3	0-1	52	0	1	5	15	.80	.751	3.34
Rincon, Ricardo, NYM	LT	L	8	2	2	0	0.8	9	2	.22	0-0	0-0	0-0	6	0	0	0	1	1.00	.846	4.50
Sosa, Jorge, NYM	LM	R	20	7	8	7	1.0	15	3	.20	0-0	0-0	0-0	12	0	0	0	1	1.00	.921	7.06
Muniz, Carlos, NYM	LM	R	18	10	2	7	0.6	4	0	.00	0-0	0-1	0-0	11	0	0	1	1	.50	.786	5.40
Smith, Joe, NYM	UR	R	82	14	25	5	1.2	63	11	.17	0-0	0-2	0-1	57	0	0	3	18	.86	.658	3.55
Heilman, Aaron, NYM	UR	R	78	7	25	16	1.4	37	14	.38	1-3	2-3	0-2	49	0	3	8	15	.78	.793	5.21
Stokes, Brian, NYM	UR	R	23	3	7	6	1.0	10	5	.50	0-0	1-2	0-1	15	0	1	3	4	.71	.685	2.93
Figueroa, Nelson, NYM	UR	R	10	4	1	2	0.7	6	5	.83	0-0	0-1	0-0	4	0	0	1	0	.00	.846	3.00
Wise, Matt, NYM	UR	R	8	0	2	1	0.7	1	0	.00	0-0	0-0	0-0	4	0	0	0	1	1.00	.963	6.43
Vargas, Claudio, NYM	UR	R	7	5	1	4	0.6	2	0	.00	0-1	0-0	0-0	3	0	0	1	1	.50	.695	4.85
Parnell, Bobby, NYM	UR	R	6	1	0	1	0.4	1	0	.00	0-0	0-0	0-0	4	0	0	0	0		.440	5.40
Kunz, Eddie, NYM	UR	R	4	1	0	0	0.5	3	1	.33	0-0	0-0	0-0	1	0	0	0	0		1.357	13.50
Armas Jr., Tony, NYM	UR	R	2	1	0	1	0.1	1	0	.00	0-0	0-0	0-0	1	0	0	0	0		1.000	11.57
Knight, Brandon, NYM	UR	R	2	2	0	0	1.1	0	0		0-0	0-0	0-0	1	0	0	0	0		.393	4.50
New York Yankees																					
Rivera, Mariano, NYY	CL	R	64	0	21	5	1.9	20	4	.20	19-19	15-16	5-5	51	0	39	40	0	.98	.423	1.40
Marte, Damaso, Pit-NYY	SU	L	72	8	19	9	1.4	46	9	.20	3-4	2-3	0-0	53	0	5	7	25	.94	.608	4.02
Bruney, Brian, NYY	SU	R	31	7	5	6	1.0	24	10	.42	0-0	1-2	0-0	22	1	1	2	12	.93	.490	1.95
Chamberlain, Joba, NYY	SU	R	30	1	3	6	1.4	10	2	.20	0-0	0-1	0-0	22	0	0	1	19	.95	.570	2.31
Traber, Billy, NYY	LT	L	19	4	5	3	0.3	10	6	.60	0-0	0-0	0-0	10	0	0	0	1	1.00	.893	7.02
Coke, Phil, NYY	LT	L	12	8	0	3	0.8	3	0	.00	0-0	0-0	0-0	11	0	0	0	5	1.00	.392	.61
Giese, Dan, NYY	LM	R	17	10	1	8	0.5	7	2	.29	0-0	0-0	0-0	10	0	0	0	0		.679	3.38
Veras, Jose, NYY	UR	R	60	3	13	6	1.0	13	4	.31	0-1	0-1	0-0	45	0	0	2	10	.83	.738	3.59
Ramirez, Edwar, NYY	UR	R	55	19	10	9	0.8	39	14	.36	1-2	0-0	0-2	43	1	1	4	5	.67	.685	3.90
Robertson, David, NYY	UR	R	25	9	4	8	0.7	14	8	.57	0-0	0-0	0-0	15	0	0	0	0		.690	5.34
Britton, Chris, NYY	UR	R	15	2	1	6	0.1	6	2	.33	0-0	0-0	0-0	7	0	0	0	0		.941	5.09
Albaladejo, Jonathan, NYY	UR	R	7	5	0	4	0.6	5	1	.20	0-0	0-0	0-0	4	0	0	0	1	1.00	.839	3.95
Aceves, Alfredo, NYY	UR	R	2	1	0	1	0.2	3	2	.67	0-0	0-0	0-0	1	0	0	0	0		.596	1.29
Sanchez, Humberto, NYY	UR	R	2	0	0	0	0.0	0	0		0-0	0-0	0-0	1	0	0	0	0		.542	4.50
Igawa, Kei, NYY	UR	L	1	0	0	0	0.0	0	0		0-0	0-0	0-0	1	0	0	0	0		1.000	.00
Kennedy, Ian, NYY	UR	R	1	1	0	1	0.2	0	0		0-0	0-0	0-0	0	0	0	0	0		.580	6.00
Rasner, Darrell, NYY	ER	R	4	1	0	2	1.1	2	0	.00	0-0	0-0	0-0	2	0	0	0	0		.590	5.40
Ponson, Sidney, Tex-NYY	ER	R	1	0	0	0	0.2	0	0		0-0	0-0	0-0	1	0	0	0	0		.000	.00
Oakland Athletics																					
Street, Huston, Oak	CL	R	63	4	14	9	1.9	13	2	.15	10-10	7-13	1-2	44	0	18	25	6	.77	.670	3.73
Ziegler, Brad, Oak	CL	R	47	7	13	10	1.7	22	5	.23	3-3	7-9	1-1	37	1	11	13	9	.91	.638	1.06
Embree, Alan, Oak	SU	L	70	11	14	6	1.3	45	9	.20	0-1	0-4	0-0	44	1	0	5	18	.78	.769	4.96
Devine, Joey, Oak	SU	R	42	12	7	5	1.4	22	7	.32	1-1	0-0	0-1	31	0	1	2	11	.92	.395	.59

Relief Pitching

Pitcher	Pos	T	Rel G	Early Entry	Cons Days	Long	Lev Ind	#	Scrd	Pct	Easy	Reg	Tough	Clean	BS Win	Saves	Opps	Holds	Sv/Hld Pct	Opp OPS	Rel ERA
Foulke, Keith, Oak	SU	R	31	2	8	5	1.0	9	5	.56	1-1	0-0	0-1	19	0	1	2	8	.90	.810	4.06
Blevins, Jerry, Oak	LT	L	36	14	12	4	1.1	24	5	.21	0-0	0-1	0-0	25	0	0	1	5	.83	.639	3.11
DiNardo, Lenny, Oak	LT	L	9	1	1	4	0.5	4	1	.25	0-0	0-0	0-0	3	0	0	0	0		.877	6.89
Meyer, Dan, Oak	LT	L	7	2	2	4	0.3	0	0		0-0	0-0	0-0	4	0	0	0	0		.782	4.97
Casilla, Santiago, Oak	UR	R	51	15	7	6	0.9	31	14	.45	1-1	1-1	0-1	27	1	2	3	7	.90	.810	3.93
Brown, Andrew, Oak	UR	R	31	6	3	9	0.8	11	6	.55	0-1	0-0	0-0	24	0	0	1	2	.67	.609	3.09
Braden, Dallas, Oak	UR	L	9	2	1	5	0.3	3	1	.33	0-0	0-0	0-0	5	0	0	0	0		.804	4.80
Saarloos, Kirk, Oak	UR	R	7	6	0	5	0.3	7	4	.57	0-0	0-0	0-0	3	0	0	0	0		.705	4.30
Calero, Kiko, Oak	UR	R	5	0	0	1	0.1	1	0	.00	0-0	0-0	0-0	4	0	0	0	0		.594	3.86
Gray, Jeff, Oak	UR	R	5	2	1	0	0.0	3	2	.67	0-0	0-0	0-0	2	0	0	0	0		1.053	7.71
Gonzalez, Gio, Oak	UR	L	3	1	0	2	0.1	0	0		0-0	0-0	0-0	3	0	0	0	0		.308	.00
Hernandez, Fernando, Oak	UR	R	3	0	0	2	0.4	2	1	.50	0-0	0-0	0-0	1	0	0	0	0		.911	18.00
Outman, Josh, Oak	UR	L	2	2	0	2	0.2	1	1	1.00	0-0	0-0	0-0	1	0	0	0	0		.965	6.23
Gallagher, Sean, ChC-Oak	ER	R	2	1	0	1	0.1	1	0	.00	0-0	0-0	0-0	1	0	0	0	0		.908	4.50
Philadelphia Phillies																					
Lidge, Brad, Phi	CL	R	72	0	25	10	1.9	1	1	1.00	25-25	16-16	0-0	60	0	41	41	0	1.00	.565	1.95
Romero, J.C., Phi	SU	L	81	2	32	1	1.5	58	16	.28	0-0	0-2	0-3	58	0	1	5	24	.86	.647	2.75
Durbin, Chad, Phi	SU	R	71	20	17	17	1.3	49	16	.33	1-2	0-2	0-3	45	0	1	7	17	.75	.675	2.87
Gordon, Tom, Phi	SU	R	34	0	7	2	1.9	12	4	.33	2-2	0-0	0-1	23	0	2	3	14	.94	.783	5.16
Eyre, Scott, ChC-Phi	LT	L	38	11	9	3	0.8	36	7	.19	0-0	0-0	0-2	30	0	0	2	8	.80	.733	4.21
Walrond, Les, Phi	LT	L	6	3	0	5	0.8	4	1	.25	0-0	0-0	0-0	2	0	0	0	0		.915	6.10
Swindle, R.J., Phi	LT	L	3	2	1	2	0.2	4	4	1.00	0-0	0-0	0-0	0	0	0	0	0		1.140	7.71
Madson, Ryan, Phi	UR	R	76	15	17	13	1.1	37	13	.35	1-1	0-2	0-0	52	0	1	3	17	.90	.675	3.05
Condrey, Clay, Phi	UR	R	56	15	10	9	0.5	21	6	.29	0-0	1-1	0-0	33	0	1	1	1	1.00	.792	3.26
Seanez, Rudy, Phi	UR	R	42	10	8	6	0.7	14	3	.21	0-0	0-1	0-0	29	0	0	1	2	.67	.682	3.53
Happ, J.A., Phi	UR	L	4	2	0	3	0.4	0	0		0-0	0-0	0-0	2	0	0	0	1	1.00	.914	7.88
Carpenter, Andrew, Phi	UR	R	1	0	0	0	0.2	0	0		0-0	0-0	0-0	1	0	0	0	0		.833	.00
Eaton, Adam, Phi	ER	R	2	2	1	1	0.5	0	0		0-0	0-0	0-0	1	0	0	0	0		1.648	9.00
Kendrick, Kyle, Phi	ER	R	1	0	0	0	0.0	0	0		0-0	0-0	0-0	0	0	0	0	0		1.250	9.00
Pittsburgh Pirates																					
Capps, Matt, Pit	CL	R	49	0	14	4	1.7	5	2	.40	12-12	9-14	0-0	37	2	21	26	0	.81	.633	3.02
Grabow, John, Pit	SU	L	74	8	17	13	1.4	33	8	.24	4-4	0-4	0-0	53	1	4	8	16	.83	.651	2.84
Burnett, Sean, Pit	LT	L	58	16	17	10	0.7	44	13	.30	0-0	0-0	0-0	37	0	0	0	8	1.00	.816	4.76
Bautista, Denny, Det-Pit	LM	R	51	15	12	17	0.8	21	6	.29	0-1	0-0	0-0	30	0	1	1	10	.91	.829	5.22
Osoria, Franquelis, Pit	LM	R	43	18	10	16	0.7	19	5	.26	0-0	0-2	0-0	19	0	0	2	3	.60	.927	6.08
Beam, T.J., Pit	LM	R	32	18	5	11	0.9	21	7	.33	1-1	0-0	0-0	15	0	1	1	2	1.00	.784	4.14
Ohlendorf, Ross, NYY-Pit	LM	R	25	14	3	11	0.9	20	10	.50	0-0	0-0	0-0	10	0	0	0	4	1.00	.847	6.53
Yates, Tyler, Pit	UR	R	72	6	18	12	1.1	28	4	.14	1-2	0-2	0-1	50	0	1	5	14	.79	.737	4.66
Hansen, Craig, Bos-Pit	UR	R	48	7	8	7	1.1	17	7	.41	3-4	0-1	0-2	28	1	3	7	7	.71	.707	6.22
Chavez, Jesse, Pit	UR	R	15	5	2	3	0.9	5	3	.60	0-0	0-1	0-1	7	0	0	2	0	.00	.900	6.60
Salas, Marino, Pit	UR	R	13	6	2	7	0.4	9	1	.11	0-0	0-0	0-0	4	0	0	0	0		1.043	8.47
Dumatrait, Phil, Pit	UR	L	10	6	2	8	0.8	7	4	.57	0-0	0-0	0-0	5	0	0	0	0		.833	3.92
Davis, Jason, Pit	UR	R	10	6	2	4	0.9	8	0	.00	0-0	0-0	0-0	5	0	0	0	0		.841	6.91
Sanchez, Romulo, Pit	UR	R	10	1	1	3	0.4	7	1	.14	1-1	0-0	0-0	4	0	1	1	0	1.00	.764	4.05
Meek, Evan, Pit	UR	R	9	1	0	4	0.5	2	2	1.00	0-0	0-0	0-0	4	0	0	0	0		.922	6.92
Van Benschoten, John, Pit	UR	R	4	1	1	1	1.6	0	0		0-0	0-0	0-0	2	0	0	0	0		.703	3.86
San Diego Padres																					
Hoffman, Trevor, SD	CL	R	48	0	8	2	1.9	7	0	.00	19-20	11-14	0-0	35	1	30	34	0	.88	.657	3.77
Bell, Heath, SD	SU	R	74	0	20	10	1.8	11	4	.36	0-0	0-4	0-3	55	1	0	7	23	.77	.639	3.58
Thatcher, Joe, SD	SU	L	25	5	5	6	1.2	16	9	.56	0-0	0-2	0-1	8	0	0	3	5	.63	1.018	8.42
Hampson, Justin, SD	LT	L	35	15	6	8	0.7	27	9	.33	0-0	0-0	0-0	24	0	0	0	0		.679	2.93
Henn, Sean, SD	LT	L	4	2	0	4	0.2	3	1	.33	0-0	0-0	0-0	1	0	0	0	0		.840	7.71
Falkenborg, Brian, LAD-SD	LM	R	25	11	7	4	0.9	20	8	.40	0-0	0-0	0-1	13	0	0	1	1	.50	.823	5.24
Meredith, Cla, SD	UR	R	73	18	27	8	1.1	42	21	.50	0-0	0-4	0-2	43	0	0	6	11	.65	.736	4.09
Adams, Mike, SD	UR	R	54	15	14	13	0.9	19	6	.32	0-0	0-0	0-2	39	0	0	2	10	.83	.609	2.48
Corey, Bryan, Bos-SD	UR	R	46	12	9	7	0.9	19	7	.37	0-0	0-1	0-1	24	0	0	2	4	.67	.820	6.80
Hensley, Clay, SD	UR	R	31	10	8	3	0.8	9	4	.44	0-0	0-1	0-0	18	0	0	1	3	.75	.686	4.50
Tomko, Brett, KC-SD	UR	R	12	5	1	6	0.5	4	2	.50	0-0	0-2	0-0	5	0	0	2	0	.00	.840	6.75
Baek, Cha Seung, Sea-SD	UR	R	11	9	1	7	0.4	7	4	.57	0-0	0-0	0-0	4	0	0	0	0		.817	5.46
Cameron, Kevin, SD	UR	R	10	3	0	4	1.0	3	2	.67	0-0	0-0	0-0	7	0	0	0	0		.724	3.60
Guevara, Carlos, SD	UR	R	10	1	1	4	0.2	6	4	.67	0-0	0-0	0-0	3	0	0	0	0		.801	5.84
Ekstrom, Mike, SD	UR	R	8	6	4	4	1.0	7	2	.29	0-0	0-0	0-0	2	0	0	0	0		.972	7.45
Hayhurst, Dirk, SD	UR	R	7	2	2	1	0.4	8	3	.38	0-0	0-0	0-0	3	0	0	0	0		1.161	11.81
Germano, Justin, SD	UR	R	6	3	1	3	0.1	2	1	.50	0-0	0-0	0-0	3	0	0	0	0		.945	4.66
Gonzalez, Enrique, SD	UR	R	4	0	1	0	0.8	0	0		0-0	0-1	0-0	2	1	0	1	0	.00	1.015	10.80
Patterson, Scott, NYY-SD	UR	R	4	1	1	3	1.4	7	2	.29	0-0	0-0	0-0	1	0	0	0	0		.614	1.93
Haeger, Charlie, SD	UR	R	4	2	1	2	0.1	6	0	.00	0-0	0-0	0-0	1	0	0	0	0		1.202	16.62

Relief Pitching

Pitcher	Pos	T	Rel G	Early Entry	Cons Days	Long	Lev Ind	#	Scrd	Pct	Easy	Reg	Tough	Clean	BS Win	Saves	Opps	Holds	Sv/Hld Pct	Opp OPS	Rel ERA
						Usage			Inherited Runners			Saves					Relief Results					
Banks, Josh, SD	UR	R	3	1	1	2	1.6	0	0		0-0	0-0	0-0	2	0	0	0	0		.819	1.00
Estes, Shawn, SD	UR	L	1	1	0	1	1.2	0	0		0-0	0-0	0-0	0	0	0	0	0		.583	.00
Reineke, Chad, SD	UR	R	1	0	0	1	0.1	0	0		0-0	0-0	0-0	0	0	0	0	0		1.016	9.00
LeBlanc, Wade, SD	UR	L	1	1	0	1	0.8	0	0		0-0	0-0	0-0	0	0	0	0	0		1.306	6.75
Seattle Mariners																					
Putz, J.J., Sea	CL	R	47	0	8	10	2.2	9	5	.56	9-10	6-12	0-1	34	2	15	23	0	.65	.749	3.88
Rowland-Smith, Ryan, Sea	LT	L	35	13	8	11	0.6	30	10	.33	0-0	0-0	2-3	17	0	2	3	1	.75	.669	3.30
Jimenez, Cesar, Sea	LT	L	29	6	9	3	1.2	21	13	.62	0-0	0-2	0-2	15	0	0	4	4	.50	.724	3.90
Woods, Jake, Sea	LT	L	15	5	2	4	0.2	11	5	.45	0-0	0-1	0-0	8	0	0	1	1	.50	.964	6.16
Thomas, Justin, Sea	LT	L	8	2	2	1	1.4	10	5	.50	0-0	0-0	0-1	4	0	0	1	1	.50	1.103	6.75
O'Flaherty, Eric, Sea	LT	L	7	1	3	2	0.9	5	4	.80	0-0	0-0	0-0	1	0	0	0	2	1.00	1.324	20.25
Corcoran, Roy, Sea	LM	R	50	17	8	22	1.1	28	13	.46	2-2	1-3	0-1	28	0	3	6	8	.79	.649	3.22
Dickey, R.A., Sea	LM	R	18	8	1	10	0.4	10	4	.40	0-0	0-0	0-0	10	0	0	0	0		.594	2.00
Green, Sean, Sea	UR	R	72	16	18	18	1.2	49	10	.20	0-0	1-2	0-2	37	1	1	4	17	.86	.690	4.67
Lowe, Mark, Sea	UR	R	57	11	7	21	0.8	32	7	.22	1-1	0-1	0-3	34	0	1	5	1	.33	.838	5.37
Morrow, Brandon, Sea	UR	R	40	0	12	4	1.4	13	4	.31	4-5	4-5	2-2	34	0	10	12	3	.87	.504	1.47
Batista, Miguel, Sea	UR	R	24	1	7	2	1.3	17	9	.53	1-1	0-1	0-2	13	0	1	4	4	.63	.742	4.56
Messenger, Randy, Sea	UR	R	13	5	3	3	1.1	10	3	.30	0-0	0-0	1-1	8	0	1	1	2	1.00	.798	3.55
Wells, Jared, SD-Sea	UR	R	8	3	2	2	0.6	6	3	.50	0-0	0-0	0-0	3	0	0	0	0		.943	8.64
Washburn, Jarrod, Sea	ER	L	2	1	0	0	1.6	0	0		0-0	1-1	0-0	2	0	1	1	0	1.00	.619	.00
Burke, Jamie, Sea	ER	R	1	0	0	0	1.6	0	0		0-0	0-0	0-0	0	0	0	0	0		.917	9.00
San Francisco Giants																					
Wilson, Brian, SF	CL	R	63	0	18	10	2.3	22	3	.14	21-24	16-19	4-4	43	2	41	47	0	.87	.732	4.62
Walker, Tyler, SF	SU	R	65	0	17	3	1.6	32	7	.22	0-1	0-1	0-2	47	0	0	4	19	.83	.706	4.56
Taschner, Jack, SF	LT	L	67	9	19	4	1.1	57	19	.33	0-0	0-1	0-3	42	0	0	4	14	.78	.812	4.88
Hinshaw, Alex, SF	LT	L	48	13	11	5	0.8	36	9	.25	0-0	0-0	0-0	31	0	0	0	4	1.00	.736	3.40
Espineli, Geno, SF	LT	L	15	4	2	5	0.2	8	2	.25	0-0	0-0	0-0	11	0	0	0	0		.920	5.06
Misch, Pat, SF	LT	L	8	3	0	3	0.1	3	1	.33	0-0	0-0	0-0	4	0	0	0	0		.592	2.20
Threets, Erick, SF	LT	L	7	1	1	2	0.6	2	1	.50	0-0	0-0	0-0	2	0	0	0	0		.956	3.60
Sadler, Billy, SF	LM	R	33	9	2	14	0.6	24	8	.33	0-0	0-0	0-0	18	0	0	0	1	1.00	.727	4.06
Matos, Osiris, SF	LM	R	20	10	4	2	0.5	9	3	.33	0-1	0-0	0-0	9	0	0	1	0	.00	.931	4.79
Yabu, Keiichi, SF	UR	R	60	19	10	16	0.8	41	12	.29	0-0	0-0	0-1	35	0	0	1	9	.90	.677	3.57
Romo, Sergio, SF	UR	R	29	4	5	4	1.0	22	3	.14	0-0	0-0	0-0	22	0	0	0	5	1.00	.470	2.12
Chulk, Vinnie, SF	UR	R	27	8	4	8	0.8	25	7	.28	0-0	0-0	0-2	14	0	0	2	2	.50	.800	4.83
Valdez, Merkin, SF	UR	R	16	2	4	1	1.1	12	1	.08	0-0	0-0	0-0	12	0	0	0	2	1.00	.748	1.93
Hennessey, Brad, SF	UR	R	13	4	0	6	0.6	3	3	1.00	0-1	0-0	0-0	3	0	0	1	0	.00	1.209	12.46
Correia, Kevin, SF	UR	R	6	4	0	3	0.2	6	1	.17	0-0	0-0	0-0	2	0	0	0	0		1.394	15.26
Lincecum, Tim, SF	ER	R	1	1	0	1	2.4	0	0		0-0	0-0	0-0	0	0	0	0	0		.873	2.25
St Louis Cardinals																					
Franklin, Ryan, StL	CL	R	74	1	14	15	1.7	22	9	.41	10-11	7-12	0-2	48	2	17	25	13	.79	.805	3.55
Isringhausen, Jason, StL	CL	R	42	6	10	8	1.5	8	2	.25	8-11	4-7	0-1	28	1	12	19	2	.67	.811	5.70
Perez, Chris, StL	CL	R	41	3	6	8	1.3	11	3	.27	4-4	2-4	1-3	26	0	7	11	6	.76	.751	3.46
McClellan, Kyle, StL	SU	R	68	17	12	16	1.6	33	10	.30	0-0	1-5	0-1	40	0	1	6	30	.86	.727	4.04
Flores, Randy, StL	SU	L	43	7	10	3	1.3	27	11	.41	0-0	1-2	0-1	24	1	1	3	14	.88	.883	5.26
Villone, Ron, StL	LT	L	74	11	22	11	0.9	45	10	.22	0-0	0-1	1-1	53	0	1	2	16	.94	.754	4.68
Garcia, Jaime, StL	LT	L	9	1	0	3	0.6	3	2	.67	0-0	0-0	0-0	6	0	0	0	3	1.00	.762	5.73
Mulder, Mark, StL	LT	L	2	0	0	0	1.3	1	1	1.00	0-0	0-0	0-1	1	0	0	1	0	.00	1.127	13.50
Thompson, Brad, StL	LM	R	20	9	3	7	0.8	12	2	.17	0-0	0-0	0-1	8	1	0	1	1	.50	.793	5.35
Springer, Russ, StL	UR	R	70	14	18	4	1.1	51	11	.22	0-0	0-0	0-2	54	0	0	2	15	.88	.595	2.32
Jimenez, Kelvin, StL	UR	R	15	5	2	5	0.6	6	3	.50	0-0	0-0	0-0	9	0	0	0	0		.910	5.63
Motte, Jason, StL	UR	R	12	2	3	0	1.3	10	2	.20	0-0	0-0	1-1	10	0	1	1	4	1.00	.344	.82
Parisi, Mike, StL	UR	R	10	3	0	7	0.9	0	0		0-0	0-0	0-0	4	0	0	0	0		.835	4.41
Kinney, Josh, StL	UR	R	7	1	0	0	0.2	0	0		0-0	0-0	0-0	7	0	0	0	0		.327	.00
Worrell, Mark, StL	UR	R	4	3	1	2	0.5	2	0	.00	0-0	0-0	0-0	2	0	0	0	0		1.052	7.94
Boggs, Mitchell, StL	UR	R	2	0	0	1	0.0	0	0		0-0	0-0	0-0	0	0	0	0	0		1.212	6.00
Carpenter, Chris, StL	UR	R	1	0	0	0	0.3	0	0		0-0	0-0	0-0	1	0	0	0	0		1.000	.00
Pineiro, Joel, StL	ER	R	1	0	0	1	0.0	0	0		0-0	1-1	0-0	0	0	1	1	0	1.00	.900	6.00
Miles, Aaron, StL	ER	R	1	0	0	0	0.0	0	0		0-0	0-0	0-0	1	0	0	0	0		.000	.00
Tampa Bay Rays																					
Percival, Troy, TB	CL	R	50	0	13	5	1.8	2	2	1.00	20-21	8-11	0-0	31	0	28	32	4	.89	.700	4.53
Wheeler, Dan, TB	SU	R	70	2	20	5	1.7	25	4	.16	8-10	3-6	2-2	51	2	13	18	26	.89	.608	3.12
Bradford, Chad, Bal-TB	SU	R	68	7	14	2	1.6	49	18	.37	0-0	0-0	0-0	40	0	0	2	21	.91	.653	2.12
Howell, J.P., TB	SU	L	64	26	13	21	1.3	35	4	.11	0-0	2-4	1-1	45	0	3	5	14	.89	.579	2.22
Balfour, Grant, TB	SU	R	51	13	16	12	1.3	44	9	.20	1-1	0-0	3-4	37	0	4	5	14	.95	.463	1.54
Miller, Trever, TB	LT	L	68	3	21	1	0.8	37	6	.16	0-0	1-2	1-1	51	0	2	3	11	.93	.687	4.15
Birkins, Kurt, TB	LT	L	6	4	1	2	0.3	5	1	.20	0-0	0-0	0-0	5	0	0	0	0		.432	.90
Price, David, TB	LT	L	4	3	0	2	0.5	6	2	.33	0-0	0-0	0-0	3	0	0	0	1	1.00	.502	2.08

Relief Pitching

Pitcher	Pos	T	Rel G	Early Entry	Cons Days	Long	Lev Ind	#	Scrd	Pct	Easy	Reg	Tough	Clean	BS Win	Saves	Opps	Holds	Sv/Hld Pct	Opp OPS	Rel ERA
			Usage					**Inherited Runners**			**Saves**			**Relief Results**							
Hammel, Jason, TB	UR	R	35	6	2	14	0.7	12	8	.67	0 - 0	1 - 1	1 - 1	11	0	2	2	1	1.00	.790	4.44
Reyes, Al, TB-NYM	UR	R	26	0	8	4	0.9	16	6	.38	0 - 0	0 - 1	0 - 0	19	0	0	1	2	.67	.719	4.37
Dohmann, Scott, TB	UR	R	12	3	3	4	0.4	12	3	.25	0 - 0	0 - 0	0 - 0	6	0	0	0	0		.862	6.14
Salas, Juan, TB	UR	R	5	1	1	3	0.1	3	0	.00	0 - 0	0 - 0	0 - 0	3	0	0	0	0		.681	7.11
Niemann, Jeff, TB	UR	R	3	2	0	2	0.8	1	0	.00	0 - 0	0 - 0	0 - 0	1	0	0	0	0		.729	4.05
Talbot, Mitch, TB	UR	R	2	2	0	2	0.5	2	2	1.00	0 - 0	0 - 0	0 - 0	0	0	0	0	0		1.492	15.19
Ryu, Jae Kuk, TB	UR	R	1	0	0	1	0.0	0	0		0 - 0	0 - 0	0 - 0	1	0	0	0	0		.200	.00
Jackson, Edwin, TB	ER	R	1	0	0	1	2.9	0	0		0 - 0	0 - 1	0 - 0	0	1	0	1	0	.00	1.155	9.00
Texas Rangers																					
Wilson, C.J., Tex	CL	L	50	0	13	6	2.3	6	3	.50	11 - 11	13 - 16	0 - 1	33	1	24	28	1	.86	.842	6.02
Wright, Jamey, Tex	SU	R	75	16	21	22	1.2	42	18	.43	0 - 0	0 - 1	0 - 5	42	3	0	6	17	.74	.739	5.12
Francisco, Frank, Tex	SU	R	58	16	13	15	1.5	35	9	.26	2 - 2	2 - 6	1 - 3	38	0	5	11	12	.74	.634	3.13
Benoit, Joaquin, Tex	SU	R	44	3	7	10	1.3	14	3	.21	1 - 2	0 - 2	0 - 0	30	2	1	4	13	.82	.769	5.00
White, Bill, Tex	LT	L	8	2	0	1	0.3	4	2	.50	0 - 0	0 - 0	0 - 0	3	0	0	0	0		1.337	20.25
Rupe, Josh, Tex	LM	R	46	24	2	32	0.6	26	10	.38	0 - 0	0 - 1	0 - 1	18	1	0	2	2	.50	.819	5.14
Nippert, Dustin, Tex	LM	R	14	9	0	12	0.5	11	2	.18	0 - 0	0 - 0	0 - 0	4	0	0	0	0		.924	7.03
Loe, Kameron, Tex	LM	R	14	7	1	10	0.6	13	7	.54	0 - 0	0 - 0	0 - 1	5	0	0	1	2	.67	.768	3.23
Madrigal, Warner, Tex	UR	R	30	8	5	9	0.8	21	9	.43	0 - 0	1 - 2	0 - 1	17	0	1	3	3	.67	.749	4.91
German, Franklyn, Tex	UR	R	17	4	3	6	1.0	18	10	.56	0 - 0	0 - 1	0 - 0	9	0	0	1	0	.00	.655	2.08
Mendoza, Luis, Tex	UR	R	14	6	0	4	0.9	13	7	.54	0 - 0	1 - 2	0 - 0	7	0	1	2	0	.50	.796	6.87
Littleton, Wes, Tex	UR	R	12	5	1	6	0.7	15	9	.60	0 - 0	0 - 0	0 - 1	5	0	0	1	0	.00	.701	6.00
Mathis, Doug, Tex	UR	R	4	0	0	1	0.7	0	0		0 - 0	0 - 0	0 - 0	4	0	0	0	0		.596	.00
Fukumori, Kazuo, Tex	UR	R	4	1	0	2	0.4	0	0		0 - 0	0 - 0	0 - 0	1	0	0	0	0		1.441	20.25
Gordon, Brian, Tex	UR	R	3	0	0	1	0.1	0	0		0 - 0	0 - 0	0 - 0	2	0	0	0	0		.563	2.25
Ramirez, Elizardo, Tex	UR	R	1	1	0	1	1.0	0	0		0 - 0	0 - 0	0 - 0	0	0	0	0	0		1.329	30.38
Diaz, Joselo, Tex	UR	R	1	0	0	1	0.1	0	0		0 - 0	0 - 0	0 - 0	0	0	0	0	0		.833	.00
Feldman, Scott, Tex	ER	R	3	1	0	2	0.4	1	0	.00	0 - 0	0 - 0	0 - 0	0	0	0	0	0		.899	7.71
Toronto Blue Jays																					
Ryan, B.J., Tor	CL	L	60	0	13	7	2.2	2	0	.00	19 - 22	13 - 14	0 - 0	47	0	32	36	1	.89	.650	2.95
Accardo, Jeremy, Tor	CL	R	16	1	2	0	1.8	10	3	.30	4 - 4	0 - 1	0 - 1	11	0	4	6	2	.75	.857	6.57
Carlson, Jesse, Tor	SU	L	69	18	19	7	1.2	49	9	.18	1 - 1	1 - 1	0 - 0	52	0	2	2	19	1.00	.620	2.25
Downs, Scott, Tor	SU	L	66	2	18	10	1.6	28	14	.50	3 - 3	2 - 4	0 - 2	53	0	5	9	24	.88	.590	1.78
Tallet, Brian, Tor	LT	L	51	19	9	10	0.7	24	8	.33	0 - 0	0 - 0	0 - 0	34	0	0	0	4	1.00	.664	2.88
Parrish, John, Tor	LT	L	7	5	0	4	0.9	8	0	.00	0 - 0	0 - 0	0 - 0	5	0	0	0	0		.656	1.46
Frasor, Jason, Tor	UR	R	49	12	8	9	0.7	32	4	.13	0 - 0	0 - 1	0 - 0	34	0	0	1	4	.80	.679	4.18
Camp, Shawn, Tor	UR	R	40	8	5	6	0.9	26	9	.35	0 - 0	0 - 0	0 - 0	24	0	0	0	7	1.00	.694	4.12
League, Brandon, Tor	UR	R	31	4	5	4	1.1	15	5	.33	1 - 1	0 - 0	0 - 0	22	0	1	1	5	1.00	.624	2.18
Wolfe, Brian, Tor	UR	R	20	7	3	2	1.0	13	5	.38	0 - 0	0 - 0	0 - 0	12	0	0	0	3	1.00	.662	2.45
Benitez, Armando, Tor	UR	R	8	0	1	0	1.3	3	1	.33	0 - 0	0 - 1	0 - 0	5	0	0	1	2	.67	.814	5.68
Halladay, Roy, Tor	ER	R	1	1	0	0	1.6	2	0	.00	0 - 0	0 - 0	0 - 0	1	0	0	0	1	1.00	.286	.00
Litsch, Jesse, Tor	ER	R	1	1	0	1	0.1	0	0		0 - 0	0 - 0	0 - 0	0	0	0	0	0		1.231	6.00
Burnett, A.J., Tor	ER	R	1	0	0	0	2.4	0	0		0 - 0	0 - 0	0 - 0	0	0	0	0	0		1.405	18.00
Washington Nationals																					
Rivera, Saul, Was	SU	R	76	14	22	17	1.5	37	15	.41	0 - 0	0 - 6	0 - 0	46	1	0	6	17	.74	.687	3.96
Manning, Charlie, Was	LT	L	57	9	15	7	0.8	35	8	.23	0 - 0	0 - 0	0 - 2	41	0	0	2	7	.78	.782	5.14
Hinckley, Mike, Was	LT	L	14	1	6	1	1.2	7	1	.14	0 - 0	0 - 0	0 - 0	12	0	0	0	4	1.00	.445	.00
King, Ray, Was	LT	L	12	3	4	1	0.4	9	5	.56	0 - 0	0 - 1	0 - 0	6	0	0	1	4	.80	.956	5.68
O'Connor, Mike, Was	LT	L	4	3	1	1	1.0	3	1	.33	0 - 0	0 - 0	0 - 1	2	0	0	1	0	.00	.800	6.35
Colome, Jesus, Was	LM	R	61	18	10	19	0.7	29	11	.38	0 - 0	0 - 0	0 - 2	36	0	0	2	1	.33	.695	4.31
Estrada, Marco, Was	LM	R	11	7	1	5	0.6	12	6	.50	0 - 0	0 - 1	0 - 0	4	0	0	1	3	.75	.952	7.82
Hanrahan, Joel, Was	UR	R	69	9	13	23	1.2	34	16	.47	5 - 6	3 - 3	1 - 4	38	2	9	13	3	.75	.697	3.95
Shell, Steven, Was	UR	R	39	15	10	12	0.8	21	6	.29	1 - 1	1 - 1	0 - 1	29	0	2	3	7	.90	.603	2.16
Mock, Garrett, Was	UR	R	23	10	3	3	0.5	9	6	.67	0 - 0	0 - 0	0 - 0	15	0	0	0	0		.553	2.42
Sanches, Brian, Was	UR	R	12	6	2	5	0.6	13	9	.69	0 - 0	0 - 1	0 - 0	5	0	0	1	0	.00	.918	7.36
Bergmann, Jason, Was	UR	R	8	7	1	5	0.3	3	0	.00	0 - 0	0 - 0	0 - 0	3	0	0	0	0		.854	5.52
Speigner, Levale, Was	UR	R	7	3	1	2	0.5	0	0		0 - 0	0 - 0	0 - 0	3	0	0	0	0		1.088	11.25
Cordero, Chad, Was	UR	R	6	0	0	0	0.9	1	0	.00	0 - 0	0 - 0	0 - 0	5	0	0	0	1	1.00	.778	2.08
Schroder, Chris, Was	UR	R	6	3	0	2	0.3	3	1	.33	0 - 0	0 - 0	0 - 0	2	0	0	0	0		1.062	5.40
Chico, Matt, Was	UR	L	3	1	1	2	0.1	0	0		0 - 0	0 - 0	0 - 0	2	0	0	0	0		.589	1.42
Martis, Shairon, Was	UR	R	1	1	0	1	0.7	1	0	.00	0 - 0	0 - 0	0 - 0	0	0	0	0	0		.667	3.86

Pitchers Hitting, Fielding & Holding Runners, and Hitters Pitching

The 2008 All-Star Game was a real barnburner. The backdrop was perfect: a July night in Yankee Stadium during what would be the final season for The House That Ruth Built. The game lived up to its magical environs as the AL outlasted the NL 4-3 in 15 innings. When it was finally over, at 1:38 AM EST, it was the longest All-Star Game ever played—four hours and fifty minutes.

Late that night, his bullpen exhausted, NL manager Clint Hurdle had asked his third baseman, David Wright, if he had the "stuff" to close out the All-Star Game if needed. Not only that—but did he think the Mets' brass would mind?

"Don't worry," Wright told him. "They're probably sleeping by now. Nobody will know."

Wright didn't have to pitch the 16th inning—and yes, Omar Minaya would have definitely minded—but every year during the regular season a few hitters do take the mound in a pinch. Which hitters took the mound in 2008 and showed they might still have the Wright stuff? Combined, they pitched three innings. They only allowed one hit, one run, and walked none. Pretty impressive.

In this section, you can also see how pitchers fared when it was time to take their turn at the plate. Why did Cubs manager Lou Piniella seriously consider using his marquee pitcher, Carlos Zambrano, as the designated hitter in interleague play? Why might Micah Owings give Big Z a run for his money next season, now that he'll be hitting in Great American Ballpark (Cincinnati)?

We also have 2008 fielding statistics for pitchers and data on how well they held runners in 2008. Greg Maddux has won the NL Gold Glove in 17 of the last 18 seasons; Kenny Rogers has won the AL Gold Glove in five of the last eight. Are they really that much better with the glove than the rest of their pitching cohorts? And if they are, why does Rogers do such a great job holding runners—while Maddux doesn't seem to care at all?

All active position players who have pitched have their career pitching statistics listed, as well as any 2008 pitching statistics that they may have accrued.

Pitchers Hitting, Fielding and Holding Runners

Pitcher	T	2008 Hitting Avg	AB	H	HR	RBI	SH	Career Hitting Avg	AB	H	2B	3B	HR	RBI	BB	SO	SH	2008 Fielding and Holding Runners G	Inn	PO	A	E	DP	Pct	SBA	CS	PCS	PPO	CS%
Aardsma,David, Bos	R	.000	1	0	0	0	0	.000	3	0	0	0	0	0	0	1	1	47	48.2	3	6	0	0	1.000	2	0	0	0	.00
Accardo,Jeremy, Tor	R	-	0	0	0	0	0	.143	7	1	0	0	0	0	0	1	0	16	12.1	1	0	0	1	1.000	1	0	0	0	.00
Aceves,Alfredo, NYY	R	-	0	0	0	0	0	-	0	0	0	0	0	0	0	0	0	6	30.0	3	2	0	2	1.000	4	2	0	0	.50
Acosta,Manny, Atl	R	.000	5	0	0	0	0	.000	5	0	0	0	0	0	0	3	0	46	53.0	7	13	2	3	.909	7	0	0	0	.00
Adams,Mike, SD	R	.000	2	0	0	0	0	.000	2	0	0	0	0	0	0	0	0	54	65.1	9	5	0	1	1.000	6	1	0	0	.17
Adenhart,Nick, LAA	R	-	0	0	0	0	0	-	0	0	0	0	0	0	0	0	0	3	12.0	0	1	0	0	1.000	0	0	0	0	-
Adkins,Jon, Cin	R	-	0	0	0	0	0	.000	1	0	0	0	0	0	0	1	0	4	3.2	0	0	0	0	-	2	1	0	0	.50
Affeldt,Jeremy, Cin	L	.000	1	0	0	0	0	.200	10	2	0	0	0	2	1	2	0	74	78.1	7	22	1	2	.967	8	1	0	0	.13
Albaladejo,J, NYY	R	-	0	0	0	0	0	-	0	0	0	0	0	0	0	0	0	7	13.2	0	0	0	0	-	4	2	0	0	.50
Albers,Matt, Bal	R	-	0	0	0	0	0	.061	33	2	0	0	0	0	0	20	3	28	49.0	5	6	0	0	1.000	4	1	0	0	.25
Aquino,Greg, Bal	R	-	0	0	0	0	0	.000	2	0	0	0	0	0	0	0	0	9	9.1	0	1	0	0	1.000	1	0	0	0	.00
Arias,Alberto, Col-Hou	R	.000	3	0	0	0	0	.000	5	0	0	0	0	0	0	4	0	15	21.2	2	1	1	1	.750	1	0	0	0	.00
Armas Jr.,Tony, NYM	R	.000	3	0	0	0	0	.097	268	26	2	1	0	10	4	99	27	3	8.1	1	2	0	0	1.000	1	0	0	0	.00
Arredondo,Jose, LAA	R	-	0	0	0	0	0	-	0	0	0	0	0	0	0	0	0	52	61.0	2	1	0	0	1.000	5	2	0	0	.40
Arroyo,Bronson, Cin	R	.197	61	12	1	6	9	.131	267	35	10	0	4	16	10	115	28	34	200.0	18	32	0	0	1.000	7	2	1	1	.29
Ascanio,Jose, ChC	R	-	0	0	0	0	0	-	0	0	0	0	0	0	0	0	0	6	5.2	0	2	1	0	.667	0	0	0	0	-
Ayala,Luis, Was-NYM	R	.000	1	0	0	0	0	.286	14	4	1	0	0	0	0	3	2	81	75.2	2	12	0	1	1.000	3	1	0	0	.33
Backe,Brandon, Hou	R	.277	47	13	2	3	5	.258	132	34	5	2	4	16	9	47	13	31	166.2	15	17	1	2	.970	10	6	1	0	.60
Badenhop,Burke, Fla	R	.083	12	1	0	0	2	.083	12	1	0	0	0	0	0	7	2	13	47.1	3	9	0	0	1.000	7	3	0	0	.43
Baek,Cha Seung, Sea-SD	R	.172	29	5	1	2	8	.167	30	5	1	0	1	2	1	8	8	32	141.0	18	13	2	2	.939	14	5	1	1	.36
Bailey,Homer, Cin	R	.100	10	1	0	0	2	.190	21	4	2	0	0	2	0	10	3	8	36.1	2	3	1	0	.833	9	1	0	0	.11
Baker,Scott, Min	R	.500	2	1	0	0	3	.091	11	1	0	0	0	0	0	5	3	28	172.1	10	11	1	2	.955	13	5	0	0	.38
Bale,John, KC	L	-	0	0	0	0	0	.118	17	2	0	0	0	0	0	8	0	13	26.2	0	9	0	1	1.000	4	1	1	0	.25
Balester,Collin, Was	R	.200	15	3	0	1	8	.200	15	3	0	0	0	1	1	8	8	15	80.0	5	5	2	1	.833	6	3	0	1	.50
Balfour,Grant, TB	R	.000	1	0	0	0	0	.000	1	0	0	0	0	0	0	1	0	51	58.1	0	5	0	0	1.000	3	1	0	0	.33
Banks,Josh, SD	R	.130	23	3	0	0	2	.130	23	3	0	0	0	0	2	6	2	17	85.1	9	14	0	0	1.000	20	3	0	0	.15
Bannister,Brian, KC	R	.250	4	1	0	0	1	.316	19	6	3	0	0	2	0	4	2	32	182.2	12	28	2	3	.952	9	3	0	0	.33
Barthmaier,Jimmy, Pit	R	.000	3	0	0	0	0	.000	3	0	0	0	0	0	0	1	0	3	10.1	0	0	0	0	-	2	1	0	0	.50
Bass,Brian, Min-Bal	R	-	0	0	0	0	0	-	0	0	0	0	0	0	0	0	0	49	89.1	11	19	0	0	1.000	3	2	1	0	.67
Batista,Miguel, Sea	R	-	0	0	0	0	1	.093	290	27	5	0	2	9	11	161	24	44	115.0	10	14	1	0	.960	21	2	0	0	.10
Bauer,Rick, Cle	R	-	0	0	0	0	0	-	0	0	0	0	0	0	0	0	0	4	6.0	1	1	0	1	1.000	2	0	0	0	.00
Bautista,Denny, Det-Pit	R	.200	5	1	0	1	0	.143	7	1	0	0	0	1	0	4	0	51	60.1	6	3	0	0	1.000	9	2	0	0	.22
Bazardo,Yorman, Det	R	-	0	0	0	0	0	.000	1	0	0	0	0	0	0	1	0	3	3.0	0	2	0	0	1.000	1	1	0	1	1.00
Beam,T.J., Pit	R	.000	4	0	0	0	1	.000	5	0	0	0	0	0	0	1	0	32	45.2	4	4	1	1	.889	4	1	0	0	.25
Beckett,Josh, Bos	R	.000	6	0	0	0	1	.147	211	31	9	0	2	15	10	77	26	27	174.1	15	18	2	2	.943	12	5	1	0	.42
Bedard,Erik, Sea	L	.500	4	2	0	0	0	.267	15	4	0	0	0	1	1	6	1	15	81.0	4	6	0	2	1.000	6	1	0	0	.17
Beimel,Joe, LAD	L	-	0	0	0	0	0	.233	43	10	1	0	0	1	2	17	6	71	49.0	5	9	0	1	1.000	8	3	3	0	.38
Belisle,Matt, Cin	R	.125	8	1	0	0	3	.070	71	5	1	0	0	1	3	41	14	6	29.2	6	1	1	0	.875	4	1	0	0	.25
Bell,Heath, SD	R	-	0	0	0	0	0	.000	5	0	0	0	0	0	0	2	0	74	78.0	8	7	0	1	1.000	12	2	0	0	.17
Beltran,Francis, Det	R	-	0	0	0	0	0	.250	4	1	0	0	0	0	0	1	0	11	13.0	1	0	0	0	1.000	0	0	0	0	-
Benitez,Armando, Tor	R	-	0	0	0	0	0	.000	8	0	0	0	0	0	2	0	4	8	6.1	0	0	0	0	-	1	0	0	0	.00
Bennett,Jeff, Atl	R	.222	9	2	0	1	1	.133	15	2	1	0	0	1	2	6	1	72	97.1	4	11	2	0	.882	3	0	0	0	.30
Benoit,Joaquin, Tex	R	-	0	0	0	0	0	.000	9	0	0	0	0	0	0	4	0	44	45.0	3	4	0	0	1.000	2	1	0	0	.50
Bergmann,Jason, Was	R	.000	40	0	0	0	2	.068	88	6	0	0	0	3		39	10	30	139.2	5	10	1		.938	10	1	0	0	.10
Betancourt,Rafael, Cle	R	-	0	0	0	0	0	.000	1	0	0	0	0	0	0	1	0	69	71.0	2	6	1	0	.889	11	1	0	0	.09
Bierd,Randor, Bal	R	-	0	0	0	0	0	-	0	0	0	0	0	0	0	0	0	29	36.2	1	3	0	0	1.000	0	0	0	0	-
Billingsley,Chad, LAD	R	.095	63	6	0	3	5	.098	123	12	1	0	0	7	7	70	10	35	200.2	12	19	2	2	.939	12	4	0	0	.33
Birkins,Kurt, TB	L	-	0	0	0	0	0	-	0	0	0	0	0	0	0	0	0	6	10.0	0	2	0	1	1.000	0	0	0	0	-
Blackburn,Nick, Min	R	.333	3	1	0	0	0	.333	3	1	0	0	0	0	0	0	0	33	193.1	14	22	0	4	1.000	4	2	0	0	.50
Blanton,Joe, Oak-Phi	R	.059	17	1	0	1	6	.077	26	2	0	0	0	1	0	15	9	33	197.2	16	25	1	4	.976	5	1	0	0	.20
Blevins,Jerry, Oak	L	-	0	0	0	0	0	-	0	0	0	0	0	0	0	0	0	36	37.2	0	3	3	1	.500	4	2	2	0	.50
Boggs,Mitchell, StL	R	.000	8	0	0	0	0	.000	8	0	0	0	0	0	0	5	0	8	34.0	5	6	1	0	.917	2	0	0	0	.00
Bonderman,Jeremy, Det	R	.000	1	0	0	0	1	.038	26	1	0	0	0	0	0	15	1	12	71.1	6	9	1	2	.938	7	5	0	0	.71
Bonine,Eddie, Det	R	.000	2	0	0	0	0	.000	2	0	0	0	0	0	0	2	0	26	52.2	2	3	1	2	.833	3	1	0	0	.33
Bonser,Boof, Min	R	-	0	0	0	0	0	.000	6	0	0	0	0	0	0	1	3	47	118.1	6	16	3	2	.880	11	0	0	0	.00
Bootcheck,Chris, LAA	R	-	0	0	0	0	0	-	0	0	0	0	0	0	0	0	0	10	16.0	0	0	0	0	-	1	0	0	0	.00
Borkowski,Dave, Hou	R	-	0	0	0	0	0	.000	7	0	0	0	0	0	0	2	0	26	36.0	4	5	0	0	1.000	0	0	0	0	-
Borowski,Joe, Cle	R	-	0	0	0	0	0	.222	9	2	0	0	0	0	0	7	1	18	16.2	0	0	0	0	-	6	0	0	0	.00
Bowden,Michael, Bos	R	-	0	0	0	0	0	-	0	0	0	0	0	0	0	0	0	1	5.0	1	1	0	1	1.000	0	0	0	0	-
Bowers,Cedrick, Col	L	-	0	0	0	0	0	-	0	0	0	0	0	0	1	0	0	5	6.2	0	2	0	0	1.000	0	0	0	0	-
Bowie,Micah, Col	L	-	0	0	0	0	0	.154	26	4	0	0	0	4	1	7	2	10	16.0	1	0	0	0	1.000	0	0	0	0	-
Boyer,Blaine, Atl	R	.000	2	0	0	0	0	.000	2	0	0	0	0	0	0	1	0	76	72.0	1	8	0	0	1.000	10	2	0	0	.20
Braden,Dallas, Oak	L	-	0	0	0	0	0	-	0	0	0	0	0	0	0	0	0	19	71.2	2	14	1	0	.941	3	2	0	7	.67
Bradford,Chad, Bal-TB	R	-	0	0	0	0	0	-	0	0	0	0	0	0	0	0	0	68	59.1	3	13	0	0	1.000	7	4	1	0	.57
Bray,Bill, Cin	L	-	0	0	0	0	0	.000	1	0	0	0	0	0	0	1	0	63	47.0	2	4	0	0	1.000	4	0	0	0	.00
Brazoban,Yhency, LAD	R	-	0	0	0	0	0	.000	3	0	0	0	0	0	0	2	0	2	3.0	0	1	0	0	1.000	0	0	0	0	-
Breslow,Craig, Cle-Min	L	-	0	0	0	0	0	.000	1	0	0	0	0	0	0	0	0	49	47.0	1	11	0	0	1.000	7	5	3	0	.71
Britton,Chris, NYY	R	-	0	0	0	0	0	-	0	0	0	0	0	0	0	0	0	15	23.0	1	0	0	0	1.000	0	0	0	0	-

Pitchers Hitting, Fielding and Holding Runners

Pitcher	T	2008 Hitting						Career Hitting										2008 Fielding and Holding Runners										
		Avg	AB	H	HR	RBI	SH	Avg	AB	H	2B	3B	HR	RBI	BB	SO	SH	G	Inn	PO	A	E	DP	Pct	SBA	CS	PCS	PPO	CS%
Broadway,Lance, CWS	R	-	0	0	0	0	0	-	0	0	0	0	0	0	0	0	0	7	14.0	3	3	0	0	1.000	1	1	1	0	1.00
Brocail,Doug, Hou	R	-	0	0	0	0	1	.148	81	12	0	1	0	1	0	19	16	72	68.2	9	8	1	1	.944	4	1	0	0	.25
Brown,Andrew, Oak	R	-	0	0	0	0	0	-	0	0	0	0	0	0	0	0	0	31	35.0	2	4	0	0	1.000	1	1	0	0	1.00
Broxton,Jonathan, LAD	R	.000	2	0	0	0	0	.000	4	0	0	0	0	0	2	2	1	70	69.0	3	3	1	0	.857	13	3	0	0	.23
Bruney,Brian, NYY	R	-	0	0	0	0	0	.000	1	0	0	0	0	0	0	0	0	32	34.1	1	4	0	0	1.000	3	0	0	0	.00
Buchholz,Clay, Bos	R	-	0	0	0	0	0	-	0	0	0	0	0	0	0	0	0	16	76.0	3	6	0	0	1.000	5	2	0	1	.40
Buchholz,Taylor, Col	R	-	0	0	0	1	0	.075	53	4	0	0	0	2	4	22	5	63	66.1	7	7	1	0	.933	8	2	0	0	.25
Buckner,Billy, Ari	R	.000	1	0	0	0	0	.000	1	0	0	0	0	0	0	0	0	10	14.0	0	0	0	0	-	0	0	0	0	-
Buehrle,Mark, CWS	L	.167	6	1	0	0	2	.083	36	3	0	0	0	1	1	20	6	34	218.2	18	34	0	5	1.000	12	7	5	2	.58
Bueno,Francisley, Atl	L	-	0	0	0	0	0	-	0	0	0	0	0	0	0	0	0	1	2.1	0	0	0	0	-	0	0	0	0	-
Bukvich,Ryan, Bal	R	-	0	0	0	0	0	-	0	0	0	0	0	0	0	0	0	4	5.1	0	0	0	0	-	0	0	0	0	-
Bulger,Jason, LAA	R	-	0	0	0	0	0	-	0	0	0	0	0	0	0	0	0	14	16.0	2	1	0	0	1.000	1	0	0	0	.00
Bullington,Bryan, Cle	R	-	0	0	0	0	0	.333	3	1	0	0	0	0	0	0	1	3	14.2	1	0	0	0	1.000	2	0	0	0	.00
Burnett,A.J., Tor	R	.000	3	0	0	0	1	.130	261	34	6	3	3	9	12	125	34	35	221.1	18	29	7	1	.870	31	9	4	1	.29
Burnett,Sean, Pit	L	.333	3	1	0	0	0	.038	26	1	1	0	0	0	2	8	2	58	56.2	3	14	0	1	1.000	8	3	2	0	.38
Burres,Brian, Bal	L	-	0	0	0	0	0	.500	2	1	0	0	0	1	0	1	1	31	129.2	8	17	1	1	.962	13	2	1	0	.15
Burton,Jared, Cin	R	.000	1	0	0	0	0	.000	1	0	0	0	0	0	0	1	0	54	58.2	6	9	1	0	.938	5	1	0	0	.20
Bush,David, Mil	R	.088	57	5	0	0	5	.131	176	23	6	0	0	11	1	57	20	31	185.0	12	18	1	1	.968	26	9	0	0	.35
Byrd,Paul, Cle-Bos	R	.000	5	0	0	0	0	.154	156	24	0	0	0	10	12	39	27	30	180.0	6	19	2	1	.926	10	5	0	3	.50
Byrdak,Tim, Hou	L	.167	6	1	0	0	0	.167	6	1	0	0	0	0	0	2	0	59	55.1	7	7	0	1	1.000	5	1	1	1	.20
Cabrera,Daniel, Bal	R	.000	5	0	0	0	0	.000	14	0	0	0	0	0	0	14	1	30	180.0	8	11	1	0	.950	31	4	0	0	.13
Cabrera,Fernando, Bal	R	-	0	0	0	0	0	-	0	0	0	0	0	0	0	0	0	22	28.1	3	2	0	1	1.000	6	2	0	0	.33
Cain,Matt, SF	R	.113	62	7	2	3	6	.105	191	20	4	0	4	8	7	100	22	34	217.2	14	24	0	3	1.000	23	10	0	0	.43
Calero,Kiko, Oak	R	-	0	0	0	0	0	.167	6	1	0	0	0	1	0	2	0	5	4.2	0	0	0	0	-	0	0	0	0	-
Cameron,Kevin, SD	R	.000	1	0	0	0	0	.000	5	0	0	0	0	0	0	4	0	10	10.0	3	2	0	0	1.000	1	1	0	0	1.00
Camp,Shawn, Tor	R	-	0	0	0	0	1	-	0	0	0	0	0	0	0	0	0	40	39.1	3	6	0	2	1.000	3	0	0	0	.00
Campillo,Jorge, Atl	R	.178	45	8	0	2	5	.178	45	8	1	0	0	2	1	16	5	39	158.2	11	22	5	2	.868	10	2	0	0	.20
Capellan,Jose, Col	R	.000	1	0	0	0	0	.000	5	0	0	0	0	0	0	4	0	1	2.0	0	0	0	0	-	0	0	0	0	-
Capps,Matt, Pit	R	.000	1	0	0	0	0	.250	4	1	0	0	0	0	1	2	0	49	53.2	2	3	0	0	1.000	5	1	0	0	.20
Carlson,Jesse, Tor	L	-	0	0	0	0	0	-	0	0	0	0	0	0	0	0	0	69	60.0	2	8	0	1	1.000	4	3	2	0	.75
Carlyle,Buddy, Atl	R	.222	9	2	0	0	0	.156	45	7	0	0	0	3	1	13	7	45	62.2	4	8	0	0	1.000	6	1	0	0	.17
Carmona,Fausto, Cle	R	.000	3	0	0	0	0	.000	7	0	0	0	0	0	0	4	1	22	120.2	14	16	2	4	.938	7	1	0	0	.14
Carpenter,Andrew, Phi	R	-	0	0	0	0	0	-	0	0	0	0	0	0	0	0	0	1	1.0	0	0	0	0	-	0	0	0	0	-
Carpenter,Chris, StL	R	.000	5	0	0	0	0	.093	227	21	2	0	0	5	7	79	25	4	15.1	0	5	0	0	1.000	0	0	0	0	-
Carrasco,D.J., CWS	R	-	0	0	0	0	0	.000	9	0	0	0	0	0	0	2	1	31	38.2	1	3	1	0	.800	5	2	0	0	.40
Casilla,Santiago, Oak	R	-	0	0	0	0	0	-	0	0	0	0	0	0	0	0	0	51	50.1	7	3	0	1	1.000	9	0	0	0	.00
Cassel,Jack, Hou	R	.222	9	2	0	1	0	.176	17	3	0	0	0	1	0	7	0	9	30.1	2	5	1	0	.875	1	1	0	0	1.00
Castillo,Alberto, Bal	L	-	0	0	0	0	0	-	0	0	0	0	0	0	0	0	0	28	26.0	2	7	0	0	1.000	2	0	0	0	.00
Chacon,Shawn, Hou	R	.125	24	3	0	0	2	.152	198	30	4	0	1	10	5	78	20	15	85.2	3	9	1	0	.923	5	3	1	1	.60
Chamberlain,Joba, NYY	R	.000	3	0	0	0	1	.000	3	0	0	0	0	0	1	1	1	42	100.1	3	13	0	1	1.000	12	4	1	0	.33
Chavez,Jesse, Pit	R	-	0	0	0	0	0	-	0	0	0	0	0	0	0	0	0	15	15.0	1	3	0	0	1.000	3	0	0	0	.00
Cherry,Rocky, Bal	R	-	0	0	0	0	0	.000	1	0	0	0	0	0	0	0	0	18	17.0	0	2	1	0	.667	2	1	0	0	.50
Chico,Matt, Was	L	.154	13	2	0	0	2	.164	61	10	0	0	0	3	0	15	11	11	48.0	0	9	0	0	1.000	4	2	1	0	.50
Chulk,Vinnie, SF	R	-	0	0	0	0	0	.250	4	1	0	0	0	0	0	0	0	27	31.2	3	4	0	0	1.000	1	0	0	0	.00
Clippard,Tyler, Was	R	1.000	1	1	0	0	0	.667	3	2	1	0	0	0	0	1	1	2	10.1	0	0	0	0	-	0	0	0	0	-
Coffey,Todd, Cin-Mil	R	-	0	0	0	0	0	.000	3	0	0	0	0	0	0	3	0	56	26.2	1	6	0	0	1.000	3	1	0	0	.33
Coke,Phil, NYY	L	-	0	0	0	0	0	-	0	0	0	0	0	0	0	0	0	12	14.2	0	3	0	1	1.000	0	0	0	0	-
Colome,Jesus, Was	R	-	0	0	0	0	0	.000	2	0	0	0	0	0	0	2	1	61	71.0	1	10	0	0	1.000	11	3	0	0	.27
Colon,Bartolo, Bos	R	.000	2	0	0	0	0	.118	85	10	0	0	0	5	0	49	5	7	39.0	2	4	2	0	.750	0	0	0	0	-
Condrey,Clay, Phi	R	.333	3	1	0	0	0	.120	25	3	1	0	0	0	0	15	0	56	69.0	7	9	0	1	1.000	6	3	0	0	.50
Contreras,Jose, CWS	R	.000	1	0	0	0	0	.000	20	0	0	0	0	0	3	13	0	20	121.0	5	14	0	1	1.000	17	1	1	0	.06
Cook,Aaron, Col	R	.233	60	14	0	4	16	.159	264	42	4	1	0	10	14	88	56	32	211.1	15	43	2	4	.967	13	8	0	4	.62
Corcoran,Roy, Sea	R	.000	1	0	0	0	0	.000	3	0	0	0	0	0	1	3	0	50	72.2	4	11	2	3	.882	1	0	0	0	.00
Cordero,Chad, Was	R	-	0	0	0	0	0	.000	5	0	0	0	0	0	0	4	2	6	4.1	0	0	0	0	-	0	0	0	0	-
Cordero,Francisco, Cin	R	.000	1	0	0	0	0	.000	2	0	0	0	0	0	0	1	0	72	70.1	1	6	1	0	.875	10	3	1	0	.30
Corey,Bryan, Bos-SD	R	-	0	0	0	0	0	-	0	0	0	0	0	0	0	0	0	46	45.0	6	4	1	0	.909	3	1	0	0	.33
Cormier,Lance, Bal	R	.000	4	0	0	0	0	.109	46	5	1	0	0	2	2	17	4	45	71.2	5	10	1	0	.938	8	2	0	0	.25
Corpas,Manny, Col	R	.000	1	0	0	0	0	.000	1	0	0	0	0	0	0	0	0	76	79.2	7	8	0	1	1.000	2	0	0	0	.00
Correia,Kevin, SF	R	.111	27	3	0	2	3	.107	84	9	1	0	0	4	6	35	8	25	110.0	13	7	1	0	.952	11	7	1	0	.64
Cotts,Neal, ChC	L	.000	1	0	0	0	0	.500	2	1	1	0	0	0	0	1	0	50	35.2	2	4	2	0	.750	3	0	0	0	.00
Crain,Jesse, Min	R	-	0	0	0	0	0	-	0	0	0	0	0	0	0	0	0	66	62.2	1	10	3	2	.786	7	1	0	0	.14
Cruceta,Francisco, Det	R	-	0	0	0	0	0	-	0	0	0	0	0	0	0	0	0	13	11.2	0	2	0	0	1.000	1	0	0	0	.00
Cruz,Juan, Ari	R	-	0	0	0	0	0	.114	70	8	1	1	0	2	4	28	7	57	51.2	2	4	2	0	.750	10	5	0	0	.50
Cueto,Johnny, Cin	R	.044	45	2	0	1	8	.044	45	2	0	0	0	1	2	15	8	31	174.0	15	16	3	2	.912	13	6	0	1	.46
Danks,John, CWS	R	.167	6	1	0	0	0	.125	8	1	0	0	0	0	1	4	0	33	195.0	12	28	0	1	1.000	31	8	6	0	.26
Davies,Kyle, KC	R	.000	2	0	0	0	1	.136	66	9	1	0	2	9	4	24	14	21	113.0	4	10	1	0	.933	9	1	0	0	.11
Davis,Doug, Ari	L	.095	42	4	0	3	8	.074	326	24	3	1	0	9	4	145	38	26	146.0	4	27	0	1	1.000	11	3	1	1	.27
Davis,Jason, Pit	R	.000	8	0	0	0	0	.059	17	1	0	0	1	1	0	9	2	14	34.0	5	5	1	1	.909	6	1	0	0	.17
de la Cruz,Frankie, Fla	R	.000	2	0	0	0	0	.000	2	0	0	0	0	0	0	2	0	6	9.0	1	4	0	1	1.000	3	0	0	0	.00
de la Rosa,Jorge, Col	L	.150	40	6	0	6	4	.107	56	6	0	0	0	6	0	25	5	28	130.0	1	18	0	0	1.000	18	5	3	0	.28

Pitchers Hitting, Fielding and Holding Runners

Pitcher	T	2008 Hitting						Career Hitting										2008 Fielding and Holding Runners											
		Avg	AB	H	HR	RBI	SH	Avg	AB	H	2B	3B	HR	RBI	BB	SO	SH	G	Inn	PO	A	E	DP	Pct	SBA	CS	PCS	PPO	CS%
de los Santos,Valerio, Col	L	.000	3	0	0	0	1	.000	12	0	0	0	0	0	1	8	3	2	8.0	0	0	0	0	-	0	0	0	0	
Delcarmen,Manny, Bos	R	-	0	0	0	0	0	-	0	0	0	0	0	0	0	0	0	73	74.1	6	5	0	0	1.000	7	0	0	0	.00
Delgado,Jesus, Fla	R	-	0	0	0	0	0	-	0	0	0	0	0	0	0	0	0	2	2.0	0	1	0	0	1.000	0	0	0	0	-
Dempster,Ryan, ChC	R	.164	61	10	0	2	19	.091	375	34	7	1	0	9	8	154	51	33	206.2	18	34	1	2	.981	15	4	0	0	.27
DeSalvo,Matt, Atl	R	-	0	0	0	0	0	-	0	0	0	0	0	0	0	0	0	2	2.0	0	0	0	0	-	0	0	0	0	-
Dessens,Elmer, Atl	R	-	0	0	0	0	0	.163	240	39	4	1	0	16	22	65	38	4	4.0	0	1	0	0	1.000	1	0	0	0	.00
Devine,Joey, Oak	R	-	0	0	0	0	0	.000	1	0	0	0	0	0	0	1	0	42	45.2	2	1	0	0	1.000	4	1	0	0	.25
Diaz,Joselo, Tex	R	-	0	0	0	0	0	-	0	0	0	0	0	0	0	0	0	1	1.0	0	0	0	0	-	1	0	0	0	.00
Dickey,R.A., Sea	R	.250	4	1	0	0	0	.400	5	2	0	0	0	0	0	0	0	32	112.1	6	23	0	1	1.000	13	7	4	1	.54
DiFelice,Mark, Mil	R	-	0	0	0	0	2	-	0	0	0	0	0	0	0	0	2	15	19.0	1	1	0	0	1.000	1	0	0	0	.00
Dillard,Tim, Mil	R	1.000	1	1	0	0	0	1.000	1	1	0	0	0	0	0	0	0	13	14.1	1	0	0	1	1.000	1	1	0	0	1.00
DiNardo,Lenny, Oak	L	-	0	0	0	0	0	.200	5	1	0	0	0	0	0	3	0	11	23.0	3	3	0	1	1.000	2	0	0	0	.00
Dohmann,Scott, TB	R	-	0	0	0	0	0	.000	3	0	0	0	0	0	0	2	1	12	14.2	2	0	0	1	1.000	4	0	0	0	.00
Dolsi,Freddy, Det	R	.000	1	0	0	0	0	.000	1	0	0	0	0	0	0	1	0	42	47.2	1	4	0	0	1.000	12	2	0	0	.17
Donnelly,Brendan, Cle	R	-	0	0	0	0	0	.000	1	0	0	0	0	0	0	0	0	15	13.2	1	0	0	0	1.000	2	1	0	0	.50
Dotel,Octavio, CWS	R	-	0	0	0	0	0	.068	74	5	0	0	0	1	5	42	9	72	67.0	3	5	1	0	.889	17	1	0	0	.06
Downs,Scott, Tor	L	-	0	0	0	0	0	.068	44	3	0	0	0	1	3	17	10	66	70.2	10	14	1	1	.960	2	0	1	0	.00
Duchscherer,Justin, Oak	R	.000	6	0	0	0	0	.000	6	0	0	0	0	0	0	0	6	22	141.2	5	13	0	1	1.000	6	2	0	1	.33
Duckworth,Brandon, KC	R	-	0	0	0	0	0	.221	113	25	4	0	0	8	10	22	10	7	38.0	2	5	0	1	1.000	6	3	1	0	.50
Duke,Zach, Pit	L	.158	57	9	0	1	6	.184	185	34	3	0	0	12	5	74	18	31	185.0	11	39	2	3	.962	12	6	4	0	.50
Dumatrait,Phil, Pit	L	.048	21	1	0	1	5	.037	27	1	0	0	0	1	0	11	5	21	78.2	3	10	0	1	1.000	4	2	0	0	.50
Durbin,Chad, Phi	R	.111	9	1	0	0	0	.067	15	1	0	0	0	1	0	3	1	71	87.2	6	12	0	3	1.000	7	4	0	1	.57
Eaton,Adam, Phi	R	.179	28	5	0	1	3	.194	341	66	16	1	3	25	32	113	26	21	107.0	10	14	0	3	1.000	9	5	0	0	.56
Ekstrom,Mike, SD	R	.000	1	0	0	0	0	.000	1	0	0	0	0	0	0	1	0	8	9.2	2	2	0	0	1.000	1	0	0	0	.00
Elarton,Scott, Cle	R	-	0	0	0	0	0	.139	165	23	3	0	0	3	5	53	28	8	15.1	1	4	0	0	1.000	1	0	0	0	.00
Elbert,Scott, LAD	L	.000	1	0	0	0	0	.000	1	0	0	0	0	0	0	0	0	10	6.0	1	0	0	0	1.000	2	0	0	0	.00
Embree,Alan, Oak	L	-	0	0	0	0	0	.000	3	0	0	0	0	0	1	2	0	70	61.2	2	6	0	0	1.000	7	1	1	0	.14
Espineli,Geno, SF	L	-	0	0	0	0	0	-	0	0	0	0	0	0	0	0	0	15	16.0	2	0	0	0	1.000	2	0	0	0	.00
Estes,Shawn, SD	L	.222	9	2	0	0	5	.159	498	79	15	2	4	28	15	166	78	9	43.2	4	6	0	0	1.000	7	1	0	0	.14
Estrada,Marco, Was	R	-	0	0	0	0	1	-	0	0	0	0	0	0	1	0	1	11	12.2	1	2	0	0	1.000	1	1	0	0	1.00
Eveland,Dana, Oak	L	.250	4	1	0	0	1	.083	12	1	0	0	0	1	6	4	0	29	168.0	5	18	0	2	1.000	17	4	2	0	.24
Eyre,Scott, ChC-Phi	L	-	0	0	0	0	0	.154	13	2	0	0	0	1	6	4	0	38	25.2	1	0	0	0	1.000	4	0	0	0	.00
Falkenborg,B, LAD-SD	R	.000	1	0	0	0	0	.000	5	0	0	0	0	0	1	5	0	25	22.1	1	5	0	1	1.000	2	0	0	0	.00
Farnsworth,Kyle, NYY-Det	R	-	0	0	0	0	0	.074	54	4	1	0	0	3	2	18	8	61	60.1	4	5	0	0	1.000	13	7	0	0	.54
Feierabend,Ryan, Sea	L	-	0	0	0	0	0	-	0	0	0	0	0	0	0	0	0	8	39.2	2	10	0	0	1.000	5	4	3	3	.80
Feldman,Scott, Tex	R	.333	3	1	0	0	0	.333	3	1	0	0	0	0	0	1	0	28	151.1	13	21	2	2	.944	27	5	0	0	.19
Feliciano,Pedro, NYM	L	-	0	0	0	0	0	.000	6	0	0	0	0	0	1	2	1	86	53.1	7	10	1	1	.944	0	0	0	0	-
Figueroa,Nelson, NYM	R	.083	12	1	0	0	1	.162	68	11	1	0	0	5	4	30	7	16	45.1	4	6	1	0	.909	3	0	0	0	.00
Flores,Randy, StL	L	-	0	0	0	0	0	.000	8	0	0	0	0	0	0	5	0	43	25.2	1	2	1	0	.750	4	0	0	0	.00
Floyd,Gavin, CWS	R	.000	3	0	0	0	1	.044	45	2	0	0	0	0	0	25	1	33	206.1	18	23	2	3	.953	42	5	1	0	.12
Fogg,Josh, Cin	R	.136	22	3	0	0	3	.120	326	39	4	0	0	11	12	112	53	22	78.1	6	9	2	2	.882	5	2	0	0	.40
Fossum,Casey, Det	L	-	0	0	0	0	0	.087	46	4	0	0	0	0	1	16	4	31	41.1	1	5	0	0	1.000	1	1	1	0	1.00
Foulke,Keith, Oak	R	-	0	0	0	0	0	.125	16	2	0	0	0	0	0	5	2	31	31.0	3	0	0	0	1.000	1	0	0	0	.25
Fox,Chad, ChC	R	-	0	0	0	0	0	.000	7	0	0	0	0	0	0	3	1	3	3.1	0	1	0	0	1.000	1	0	0	1	.00
Francis,Jeff, Col	L	.128	39	5	0	1	10	.129	232	30	6	0	0	14	17	82	42	24	143.2	8	21	1	0	.967	11	2	1	0	.18
Francisco,Frank, Tex	R	-	0	0	0	0	0	-	0	0	0	0	0	0	0	0	0	58	63.1	2	1	1	0	.750	8	1	0	0	.13
Franklin,Ryan, StL	R	-	0	0	0	0	0	.118	17	2	0	0	0	1	2	8	2	74	78.2	11	12	0	2	1.000	3	1	0	0	.33
Frasor,Jason, Tor	R	-	0	0	0	0	0	-	0	0	0	0	0	0	0	0	0	49	47.1	3	7	0	0	1.000	7	2	0	0	.29
Fuentes,Brian, Col	L	-	0	0	0	0	0	.000	1	0	0	0	0	0	0	0	0	67	62.2	1	9	0	0	1.000	5	1	1	1	.20
Fukumori,Kazuo, Tex	R	-	0	0	0	0	0	-	0	0	0	0	0	0	0	0	0	4	4.0	0	0	0	0	-	0	0	0	0	.00
Fulchino,Jeff, KC	R	-	0	0	0	0	0	-	0	0	0	0	0	0	0	0	0	12	14.0	0	0	0	0	-	1	0	0	0	.00
Gabbard,Kason, Tex	L	.250	4	1	0	0	0	.250	4	1	0	0	0	0	0	1	0	12	56.0	5	8	1	1	.929	2	0	0	0	.00
Gagne,Eric, Mil	R	-	0	0	0	0	0	.140	86	12	2	1	1	3	1	25	12	50	46.1	3	6	0	0	1.000	8	1	0	0	-
Galarraga,Armando, Det	R	.000	2	0	0	0	1	.000	2	0	0	0	0	0	0	3	1	30	178.2	13	11	2	2	.923	8	1	0	0	.13
Gallagher,Sean, ChC-Oak	R	.000	10	0	0	0	3	.000	11	0	0	0	0	0	0	6	3	23	115.1	8	13	1	2	.955	9	4	0	0	.44
Gallardo,Yovani, Mil	R	.111	9	1	0	0	0	.224	49	11	4	0	2	6	1	11	1	4	24.0	1	4	0	1	1.000	1	1	0	0	1.00
Garcia,Freddy, Det	R	-	0	0	0	0	0	.207	58	12	2	0	0	4	2	19	13	3	15.0	0	1	0	0	1.000	2	1	0	0	.50
Garcia,Jaime, StL	L	.000	1	0	0	0	0	.000	1	0	0	0	0	0	2	1	0	16	16.0	1	2	0	0	1.000	0	0	0	0	-
Gardner,Lee, Fla	R	.000	1	0	0	0	0	.000	5	0	0	0	0	0	0	3	0	7	6.2	1	2	0	0	1.000	0	0	0	0	-
Garland,Jon, LAA	R	.000	2	0	0	1	0	.158	19	3	0	0	1	4	2	5	7	32	196.2	25	26	1	3	.981	6	3	0	1	.50
Garza,Matt, TB	R	.000	4	0	0	0	1	.000	6	0	0	0	0	0	1	4	2	30	184.2	14	11	2	0	.926	6	1	0	0	.17
Gaudin,Chad, Oak-ChC	R	-	0	0	0	0	0	.000	4	0	0	0	0	0	1	2	2	50	90.0	7	10	5	0	.773	4	3	1	1	.75
Geary,Geoff, Hou	R	.000	1	0	0	0	0	.118	17	2	1	0	0	1	1	10	0	55	64.0	4	7	0	0	1.000	1	0	0	0	.00
Geer,Josh, SD	R	.111	9	1	0	1	0	.111	9	1	0	0	0	1	1	4	0	5	27.0	2	2	0	0	1.000	2	1	0	0	.50
German,Franklyn, Tex	R	-	0	0	0	0	0	.000	1	0	0	0	0	0	0	1	0	17	21.2	0	2	0	0	1.000	4	2	0	0	.50
Germano,Justin, SD	R	.444	9	4	0	1	3	.180	50	9	2	0	0	3	3	21	11	10	43.2	9	4	0	1	1.000	11	2	0	0	.18
Giese,Dan, NYY	R	-	0	0	0	0	0	-	0	0	0	0	0	0	0	0	0	20	43.1	1	2	2	0	.600	10	1	0	0	.10
Ginter,Matt, Cle	R	-	0	0	0	0	0	.214	14	3	0	0	0	1	2	5	3	4	21.0	1	2	0	0	1.000	1	0	0	0	.00
Glavine,Tom, Atl	L	.105	19	2	0	1	3	.186	1323	246	25	2	1	90	101	329	216	13	63.1	4	16	0	1	1.000	5	4	3	0	.80
Glover,Gary, TB-Det	R	-	0	0	0	0	0	.071	28	2	0	0	0	1	2	14	3	47	54.1	6	4	1	0	.909	1	1	0	0	1.00

Pitchers Hitting, Fielding and Holding Runners

Pitcher	T	2008 Hitting Avg	AB	H	HR	RBI	SH	Career Hitting Avg	AB	H	2B	3B	HR	RBI	BB	SO	SH	2008 Fielding and Holding Runners G	Inn	PO	A	E	DP	Pct	SBA	CS	PCS	PPO	CS%
Gobble,Jimmy, KC	L	-	0	0	0	0	0	.000	2	0	0	0	0	0	0	1	0	39	31.2	0	2	0	0	1.000	2	0	0	0	.00
Gonzalez,Edgar, Ari	R	.100	10	1	0	2	2	.148	61	9	1	0	0	2	0	13	7	17	48.0	1	9	0	0	1.000	3	1	0	0	.33
Gonzalez,Enrique, SD	R	-	0	0	0	0	0	.281	32	9	1	0	0	3	0	8	3	4	3.1	0	0	0	0	-	0	0	0	0	-
Gonzalez,Gio, Oak	L	-	0	0	0	0	0	-	0	0	0	0	0	0	0	0	0	10	34.0	1	5	0	1	1.000	2	2	2	0	1.00
Gonzalez,Mike, Atl	L	.000	1	0	0	0	0	.333	3	1	1	0	0	2	0	0	0	36	33.2	0	1	0	0	1.000	1	0	0	0	.00
Gordon,Brian, Tex	R	-	0	0	0	0	0	-	0	0	0	0	0	0	0	0	0	3	4.0	1	1	0	0	1.000	0	0	0	0	-
Gordon,Tom, Phi	R	-	0	0	0	0	0	.000	2	0	0	0	0	0	0	0	0	34	29.2	1	3	2	0	.667	1	0	0	0	.00
Gorzelanny,Tom, Pit	L	.107	28	3	0	3	6	.063	111	7	0	0	0	7	5	55	14	21	105.1	6	18	1	4	.960	20	4	2	1	.20
Grabow,John, Pit	L	.000	1	0	0	0	0	.000	4	0	0	0	0	0	0	1	0	74	76.0	3	9	1	1	.923	5	2	1	0	.40
Gray,Jeff, Oak	R	-	0	0	0	0	0	-	0	0	0	0	0	0	0	0	0	5	4.2	1	1	0	0	1.000	0	0	0	0	-
Green,Sean, Sea	R	.000	1	0	0	0	0	.000	1	0	0	0	0	0	0	1	0	72	79.0	3	6	2	1	.818	4	1	0	0	.25
Gregg,Kevin, Fla	R	.000	1	0	0	0	0	.000	6	0	0	0	0	0	0	5	0	72	68.2	1	9	2	0	.833	8	2	0	0	.25
Greinke,Zack, KC	R	.286	7	2	0	0	1	.250	12	3	1	0	1	0	0	3	1	32	202.1	11	24	1	1	.972	6	4	1	2	.67
Grilli,Jason, Det-Col	R	.000	3	0	0	0	1	.000	3	0	0	0	0	0	0	0	0	60	75.0	3	7	1	2	.909	6	2	0	0	.33
Guardado,Eddie, Tex-Min	L	-	0	0	0	0	0	.000	1	0	0	0	0	0	0	0	0	65	56.1	0	5	0	0	1.000	3	0	0	0	.00
Guerrier,Matt, Min	R	-	0	0	0	0	0	.000	2	0	0	0	0	0	0	1	0	76	76.1	5	10	1	0	.938	9	1	0	1	.11
Guevara,Carlos, SD	R	-	0	0	0	0	0	-	0	0	0	0	0	0	0	0	0	10	12.1	0	2	0	0	1.000	0	0	0	0	-
Guthrie,Jeremy, Bal	R	.200	5	1	0	0	0	.083	12	1	1	0	0	0	0	7	0	30	190.2	19	21	3	1	.930	17	4	0	0	.24
Guzman,Angel, ChC	R	-	0	0	0	0	0	.105	19	2	1	0	0	2	0	6	4	6	9.2	0	2	0	0	1.000	0	0	0	0	-
Haeger,Charlie, SD	R	1.000	1	1	0	0	0	1.000	1	1	0	0	0	0	0	0	0	4	4.1	0	0	0	0	-	1	0	0	0	.00
Halladay,Roy, Tor	R	.000	4	0	0	0	0	.081	37	3	0	0	0	1	0	16	2	34	246.0	33	26	1	2	.983	20	5	0	0	.25
Hamels,Cole, Phi	L	.224	76	17	0	3	8	.168	184	31	4	0	0	8	8	79	15	33	227.1	11	33	3	3	.936	17	2	1	0	.12
Hammel,Jason, TB	R	-	0	0	0	0	0	1.000	1	1	1	0	0	1	0	0	0	40	78.1	7	5	0	0	1.000	12	1	0	0	.08
Hampson,Justin, SD	L	.000	1	0	0	0	0	.000	8	0	0	0	0	0	1	3	1	35	30.2	1	2	0	0	1.000	4	1	0	0	.25
Hampton,Mike, Atl	L	.208	24	5	0	4	3	.241	688	166	21	5	15	72	45	187	62	13	78.0	3	17	1	2	.952	8	4	1	1	.50
Hanrahan,Joel, Was	R	.000	2	0	0	0	1	.250	16	4	2	1	0	3	0	5	4	69	84.1	4	5	2	0	.818	11	0	0	0	.00
Hansack,Devern, Bos	R	-	0	0	0	0	0	-	0	0	0	0	0	0	0	0	0	4	6.2	0	1	0	0	-	0	0	0	0	-
Hansen,Craig, Bos-Pit	R	-	0	0	0	0	0	-	0	0	0	0	0	0	0	0	0	48	46.1	1	6	0	0	1.000	5	1	0	0	.20
Happ,J.A., Phi	L	.000	7	0	0	0	2	.000	8	0	0	0	0	0	0	5	2	8	31.2	1	4	0	0	1.000	1	0	0	0	.00
Harang,Aaron, Cin	R	.130	54	7	0	2	5	.082	354	29	3	0	0	9	2	170	29	30	184.1	16	11	1	0	.964	21	4	0	0	.19
Harden,Rich, Oak-ChC	R	.111	27	3	0	1	4	.094	32	3	0	0	0	1	0	16	4	25	148.0	9	6	0	0	1.000	14	7	0	0	.50
Haren,Dan, Ari	R	.211	76	16	0	6	5	.155	129	20	10	0	0	9	4	34	8	33	216.0	9	20	0	2	1.000	11	2	0	0	.18
Harrison,Matt, Tex	L	-	0	0	0	0	0	-	0	0	0	0	0	0	0	0	0	15	83.2	1	8	0	0	1.000	6	3	0	0	.50
Hart,Kevin, ChC	R	.000	5	0	0	0	0	.000	5	0	0	0	0	0	0	2	0	21	27.2	6	4	0	1	1.000	4	0	0	0	.00
Hawkins,L., NYY-Hou	R	-	0	0	0	0	0	.000	6	0	0	0	0	0	0	5	1	57	62.0	1	7	0	0	1.000	4	2	0	0	.50
Hayhurst,Dirk, SD	R	.000	3	0	0	0	0	.000	3	0	0	0	0	0	1	3	0	10	16.2	1	0	0	0	1.000	6	1	0	0	.17
Heilman,Aaron, NYM	R	.000	1	0	0	0	0	.023	44	1	0	0	0	1	2	23	5	78	76.0	2	14	0	0	1.000	2	0	0	0	.00
Hendrickson,Mark, Fla	L	.257	35	9	0	1	1	.134	97	13	3	1	1	3	6	53	4	36	133.2	3	22	0	0	1.000	19	3	2	0	.16
Henn,Sean, SD	L	-	0	0	0	0	0	.000	1	0	0	0	0	0	0	1	0	4	9.1	2	1	0	0	1.000	0	0	0	0	-
Hennessey,Brad, SF	R	.250	8	2	0	1	2	.227	88	20	3	0	2	8	1	27	7	17	40.1	8	2	0	0	1.000	7	3	0	0	.43
Hensley,Clay, SD	R	.000	2	0	0	0	1	.114	70	8	2	0	0	4	3	40	8	32	39.0	1	6	0	0	1.000	4	0	0	0	.00
Herges,Matt, Col	R	.000	3	0	0	0	0	.167	36	6	0	0	0	1	1	22	2	58	64.1	4	6	1	2	.909	3	2	0	0	.67
Hernandez,Felix, Sea	R	1.000	1	1	1	4	1	.222	9	2	0	0	1	5	0	6	2	31	200.2	14	31	1	4	.978	23	4	0	1	.17
Hernandez,Fern., Oak	R	-	0	0	0	0	0	-	0	0	0	0	0	0	0	0	0	3	3.0	0	1	0	0	1.000	0	0	0	0	-
Hernandez,Livan, Min-Col	R	.263	19	5	0	2	3	.233	808	188	34	2	9	75	6	108	88	31	180.0	8	31	1	0	.975	8	5	2	0	.63
Hernandez,Run., Hou	R	.250	4	1	0	1	1	.111	9	1	0	0	0	1	1	3	1	4	19.1	1	4	0	0	1.000	1	0	0	0	.00
Herrera,Daniel Ray, Cin	L	-	0	0	0	0	0	-	0	0	0	0	0	0	0	0	0	7	7.1	1	4	0	0	1.000	0	0	0	0	-
Herrera,Yoslan, Pit	R	.143	7	1	0	0	0	.143	7	1	0	0	0	0	0	0	0	5	18.1	2	7	0	1	1.000	1	0	0	0	.00
Hill,Rich, ChC	L	.000	7	0	0	0	0	.123	106	13	3	0	0	5	2	48	6	5	19.2	0	2	0	0	1.000	3	1	1	0	.33
Hill,Shawn, Was	R	.000	7	0	0	0	5	.073	41	3	0	0	0	0	6	18	15	12	63.1	7	17	2	0	.923	11	3	0	0	.27
Hinckley,Mike, Was	L	-	0	0	0	0	0	-	0	0	0	0	0	0	0	0	0	14	13.2	1	1	0	1	1.000	1	0	0	0	.00
Hinshaw,Alex, SF	L	-	0	0	0	0	0	-	0	0	0	0	0	0	0	0	0	48	39.2	2	4	1	0	.857	2	1	0	0	.50
Hirsh,Jason, Col	R	.000	4	0	0	0	0	.060	50	3	0	0	0	2	1	28	4	4	8.2	0	1	0	0	1.000	0	0	0	0	.00
Hochevar,Luke, KC	R	.000	3	0	0	0	1	.000	3	0	0	0	0	0	0	3	1	22	129.0	6	11	1	2	.944	18	4	0	0	.22
Hoffman,Trevor, SD	R	-	0	0	0	0	0	.121	33	4	2	0	0	5	0	10	2	48	45.1	3	6	0	0	1.000	3	0	0	0	.00
Howell,J.P., TB	L	.000	1	0	0	0	0	.200	10	2	0	0	0	1	0	4	0	64	89.1	7	9	1	0	.941	13	3	1	0	.23
Howry,Bob, ChC	R	.000	1	0	0	0	0	.333	3	1	0	0	0	0	0	1	0	72	70.2	2	6	0	0	1.000	5	0	0	0	.00
Hudson,Tim, Atl	R	.146	41	6	0	2	7	.162	271	44	8	1	0	21	11	85	29	23	142.0	7	22	1	2	.967	10	4	0	0	.40
Hughes,Phil, NYY	R	-	0	0	0	0	0	-	0	0	0	0	0	0	0	0	0	8	34.0	2	3	0	0	1.000	8	0	0	0	.00
Humber,Philip, Min	R	-	0	0	0	0	0	.000	1	0	0	0	0	0	0	0	1	5	11.2	1	1	0	0	1.000	0	0	0	0	-
Hunter,Tommy, Tex	R	-	0	0	0	0	0	-	0	0	0	0	0	0	0	0	0	3	11.0	0	1	1	0	.500	2	1	1	0	.50
Hurley,Eric, Tex	R	.500	2	1	0	0	0	.500	2	1	0	0	0	0	0	1	0	5	24.2	0	1	0	0	1.000	2	2	0	0	1.00
Igawa,Kei, NYY	L	-	0	0	0	0	0	-	0	0	0	0	0	0	1	0	1	2	4.0	0	1	0	0	1.000	0	0	0	0	-
Isringhausen,Jason, StL	R	.000	2	0	0	0	0	.202	104	21	4	1	2	16	5	36	8	42	42.2	8	10	1	1	.947	8	2	0	0	.25
Jackson,Edwin, TB	R	.000	4	0	0	0	0	.154	26	4	0	0	0	2	3	7	3	32	183.1	19	11	1	5	.968	18	6	0	1	.33
Jackson,Zach, Mil-Cle	L	-	0	0	0	0	0	.111	9	1	0	0	0	0	0	2	4	11	58.1	5	14	2	2	.905	1	0	0	0	.00
James,Chuck, Atl	L	.000	8	0	0	0	0	.082	97	8	1	0	0	3	3	34	12	7	29.2	1	3	0	0	1.000	4	0	0	0	.00
Jenks,Bobby, CWS	R	-	0	0	0	0	0	-	0	0	0	0	0	0	0	0	0	57	61.2	4	12	0	1	1.000	5	0	0	2	.00
Jennings,Jason, Tex	R	-	0	0	0	0	0	.207	328	68	14	0	2	26	19	80	28	6	27.1	4	3	1	0	.875	1	1	0	0	1.00
Jepsen,Kevin, LAA	R	-	0	0	0	0	0	-	0	0	0	0	0	0	0	0	0	9	8.1	2	2	0	0	1.000	1	0	0	0	.00

337

Pitchers Hitting, Fielding and Holding Runners

Pitcher	T	2008 Hitting						Career Hitting										2008 Fielding and Holding Runners											
		Avg	AB	H	HR	RBI	SH	Avg	AB	H	2B	3B	HR	RBI	BB	SO	SH	G	Inn	PO	A	E	DP	Pct	SBA	CS	PCS	PPO	CS%
Jimenez,Cesar, Sea	L	-	0	0	0	0	0	-	0	0	0	0	0	0	0	0	0	31	34.1	2	8	0	1	1.000	4	3	1	1	.75
Jimenez,Kelvin, StL	R	.000	3	0	0	0	0	.000	5	0	0	0	0	0	1	3	0	15	24.0	3	5	0	0	1.000	2	0	0	0	.00
Jimenez,Ubaldo, Col	R	.045	67	3	0	0	7	.064	94	6	0	0	0	6	35	11	34	198.2	16	32	4	1	.923	22	3	1	2	.14
Johnson,Jason, LAD	R	.000	7	0	0	0	1	.094	32	3	0	0	1	1	2	20	4	16	29.1	1	4	0	0	1.000	1	0	0	0	.00
Johnson,Jim, Bal	R	-	0	0	0	0	0	-	0	0	0	0	0	0	0	0	0	54	68.2	4	10	0	1	1.000	5	2	0	0	.40
Johnson,Josh, Fla	R	.133	30	4	0	2	3	.115	78	9	4	0	0	5	2	44	10	14	87.1	6	10	0	1	1.000	7	2	0	0	.29
Johnson,Randy, Ari	L	.140	50	7	0	5	6	.127	599	76	14	0	1	40	18	280	43	30	184.0	1	13	3	0	.824	24	3	2	0	.13
Jones,Todd, Det	R	-	0	0	0	0	0	.211	19	4	1	0	0	1	6	0	45	41.2	2	5	0	1	1.000	2	0	0	0	.00
Julio,Jorge, Cle-Atl	R	.000	0	0	0	0	0	.000	1	0	0	0	0	0	2	1	0	27	30.0	0	2	0	0	1.000	3	0	0	0	.00
Jurrjens,Jair, Atl	R	.103	58	6	0	0	7	.103	58	6	0	1	0	6	18	7	31	188.1	9	35	1	1	.978	31	3	0	0	.10
Karstens,Jeff, Pit	R	.143	14	2	0	0	2	.143	14	2	0	0	0	2	8	2	9	51.1	3	6	2	1	.818	6	3	1	0	.50
Kazmir,Scott, TB	L	.000	2	0	0	0	2	.125	8	1	0	0	0	1	0	3	0	27	152.1	5	9	2	0	.875	10	3	2	2	.30
Kendrick,Kyle, Phi	R	.100	50	5	0	2	6	.124	89	11	1	0	0	4	6	41	11	31	155.2	9	33	1	0	.977	20	5	1	0	.25
Kennedy,Ian, NYY	R	-	0	0	0	0	0	-	0	0	0	0	0	0	0	0	0	10	39.2	1	6	0	0	1.000	7	2	0	1	.29
Kensing,Logan, Fla	R	.000	2	0	0	0	0	.000	6	0	0	0	0	0	0	2	1	48	55.1	1	2	2	0	.600	11	0	0	0	.00
Kershaw,Clayton, LAD	L	.069	29	2	0	0	9	.069	29	2	0	0	0	0	13	9	22	107.2	1	18	1	2	.950	7	2	2	0	.29
King,Ray, Was	L	-	0	0	0	0	0	.000	6	0	0	0	0	0	0	3	0	12	6.1	0	2	1	0	.667	2	0	0	0	.00
Kinney,Josh, StL	R	-	0	0	0	0	0	-	0	0	0	0	0	0	0	0	0	7	7.0	1	0	0	0	1.000	0	0	0	0	-
Knight,Brandon, NYM	R	.000	3	0	0	0	1	.000	3	0	0	0	0	0	0	2	1	4	12.0	1	2	0	0	1.000	0	0	0	0	-
Kobayashi,Masa, Cle	R	-	0	0	0	0	0	-	0	0	0	0	0	0	0	0	0	57	55.2	8	3	0	0	1.000	2	0	0	0	.00
Korecky,Bobby, Min	R	1.000	1	1	0	0	0	1.000	1	1	0	0	0	0	0	0	0	16	17.2	1	5	0	1	1.000	2	0	0	0	.00
Kunz,Eddie, NYM	R	-	0	0	0	0	0	-	0	0	0	0	0	0	0	0	0	4	2.2	0	2	1	0	.667	0	0	0	0	-
Kuo,Hong-Chih, LAD	L	.250	12	3	0	0	2	.192	26	5	2	0	1	1	0	13	7	42	80.0	2	7	1	0	.900	2	0	0	0	.00
Kuroda,Hiroki, LAD	R	.148	54	8	0	2	6	.148	54	8	1	0	0	2	5	16	6	31	183.1	18	38	2	2	.966	9	2	0	2	.22
Lackey,John, LAA	R	.000	6	0	0	0	0	.000	22	0	0	0	0	0	0	7	0	24	163.1	9	10	5	3	.792	14	3	1	0	.21
Laffey,Aaron, Cle	L	.500	2	1	0	0	0	.500	2	1	0	0	0	0	0	0	0	16	93.2	3	11	1	0	.933	4	2	0	0	.50
Lambert,Chris, Det	R	-	0	0	0	0	0	-	0	0	0	0	0	0	0	0	0	8	20.2	1	3	0	0	1.000	7	0	0	0	.00
Lannan,John, Was	L	.022	45	1	0	0	6	.052	58	3	1	0	0	1	4	29	6	31	182.0	10	31	2	2	.953	25	7	5	0	.28
League,Brandon, Tor	R	-	0	0	0	0	0	-	0	0	0	0	0	0	0	0	0	31	33.0	8	4	0	0	1.000	0	0	0	0	-
LeBlanc,Wade, SD	L	.375	8	3	0	0	1	.375	8	3	0	0	0	0	3	1	0	5	21.1	2	3	0	0	1.000	1	0	0	0	.00
Ledezma,Wil, SD-Ari	L	.000	10	0	0	0	2	.000	12	0	0	0	0	0	1	6	2	28	58.1	3	6	1	0	.900	14	2	0	0	.14
Lee,Cliff, Cle	L	.000	5	0	0	0	0	.074	27	2	0	0	0	0	0	11	0	31	223.1	16	14	1	2	.968	3	0	0	0	.00
Lester,Jon, Bos	L	.000	5	0	0	0	0	.000	9	0	0	0	0	0	0	5	0	33	210.1	19	21	2	3	.952	13	5	3	0	.38
Lewis,Jensen, Cle	R	-	0	0	0	0	0	-	0	0	0	0	0	0	0	0	0	51	66.0	6	9	0	0	1.000	2	1	0	0	.50
Lewis,Scott, Cle	L	-	0	0	0	0	0	-	0	0	0	0	0	0	0	0	0	4	24.0	3	3	0	0	1.000	1	1	0	0	1.00
Lidge,Brad, Phi	R	-	0	0	0	0	0	.286	7	2	1	0	0	2	0	4	0	72	69.1	3	7	0	1	1.000	9	1	0	0	.11
Lieber,Jon, ChC	R	.000	5	0	0	0	1	.139	612	85	17	0	0	25	30	234	55	26	46.2	1	6	0	0	1.000	0	0	0	0	-
Lilly,Ted, ChC	L	.177	62	11	0	5	12	.139	158	22	3	0	0	10	2	71	19	34	204.2	6	21	0	0	1.000	20	8	6	0	.40
Lincecum,Tim, SF	R	.157	70	11	0	5	6	.133	113	15	2	1	0	5	7	53	12	34	227.0	9	17	0	1	1.000	23	3	0	0	.13
Lincoln,Mike, Cin	R	.000	2	0	0	0	0	.083	12	1	0	0	0	0	0	5	1	64	70.1	6	11	1	0	.944	2	1	0	0	.50
Lindstrom,Matt, Fla	R	-	0	0	0	0	0	.000	1	0	0	0	0	0	0	1	0	66	57.1	6	11	1	0	.944	2	1	0	0	.50
Linebrink,Scott, CWS	R	-	0	0	0	0	0	.222	18	4	1	0	0	0	0	10	2	50	46.1	2	6	0	0	1.000	2	0	0	0	.00
Liriano,Francisco, Min	L	-	0	0	0	0	0	.200	5	1	0	0	0	1	1	3	1	14	76.0	2	11	0	0	1.000	9	3	3	0	.33
Litsch,Jesse, Tor	R	.000	3	0	0	0	0	.000	4	0	0	0	0	0	0	0	0	29	176.0	23	36	3	2	.952	9	6	0	1	.67
Littleton,Wes, Tex	R	-	0	0	0	0	0	.000	1	0	0	0	0	0	0	1	0	12	18.0	1	2	1	0	1.000	0	0	0	0	-
Liz,Radhames, Bal	R	.000	6	0	0	0	0	.000	6	0	0	0	0	0	0	3	0	17	84.1	3	7	3	0	.769	14	2	0	1	.14
Loaiza,E., LAD-CWS	R	.333	6	2	0	1	3	.170	271	46	4	1	0	18	3	69	36	10	27.0	2	3	0	0	1.000	0	0	0	0	-
Loe,Kameron, Tex	R	-	0	0	0	0	0	.500	2	1	0	0	0	1	0	0	0	14	30.2	3	1	1	0	.800	0	0	0	1	-
Loewen,Adam, Bal	L	-	0	0	0	0	0	.000	2	0	0	0	0	0	0	0	0	7	21.1	4	0	1	0	1.000	5	2	1	0	.40
Logan,Boone, CWS	L	-	0	0	0	0	0	-	0	0	0	0	0	0	0	0	0	55	42.1	3	6	0	0	1.000	5	1	1	0	.20
Lohse,Kyle, StL	R	.111	63	7	0	5	9	.148	155	23	3	0	0	11	2	50	26	33	200.0	23	26	0	0	1.000	12	3	1	0	.25
Looper,Braden, StL	R	.254	63	16	0	4	13	.222	126	28	6	1	0	10	8	45	19	33	199.0	20	15	0	0	1.000	1	0	0	0	.00
Lopez,Aquilino, Det	R	-	0	0	0	0	0	.000	1	0	0	0	0	0	0	0	0	48	78.2	6	10	0	0	1.000	5	1	0	0	.20
Lopez,Javier, Bos	L	.000	1	0	0	0	0	.125	8	1	0	0	0	1	0	4	1	70	59.1	7	10	4	0	.810	4	3	1	0	.75
Loux,Shane, LAA	R	-	0	0	0	0	0	-	0	0	0	0	0	0	0	0	0	7	16.0	2	2	0	0	1.000	0	0	0	0	-
Lowe,Derek, LAD	R	.138	65	9	0	5	7	.125	273	34	5	0	0	14	16	81	35	34	211.0	15	39	2	3	.964	17	3	0	0	.18
Lowe,Mark, Sea	R	.000	1	0	0	0	0	.000	1	0	0	0	0	0	0	1	0	57	63.2	2	5	1	0	.875	5	0	0	0	.00
Lowery,Devon, KC	R	-	0	0	0	0	0	-	0	0	0	0	0	0	0	0	0	5	4.1	0	0	0	0	-	1	0	0	0	.00
Lyon,Brandon, Ari	R	-	0	0	0	0	0	-	0	0	0	0	0	0	0	1	0	61	59.1	4	4	0	0	1.000	2	1	0	0	.50
MacDougal,Mike, CWS	R	-	0	0	0	0	0	-	0	0	0	0	0	0	0	0	0	16	17.0	0	0	0	0	-	1	0	0	0	.00
Maddux,Greg, SD-LAD	R	.109	55	6	0	3	6	.171	1591	272	35	2	5	84	34	419	180	34	194.0	17	57	3	4	.961	29	5	1	0	.17
Madrigal,Warner, Tex	R	-	0	0	0	0	0	-	0	0	0	0	0	0	0	0	0	31	36.0	4	3	0	1	1.000	6	2	0	0	.33
Madson,Ryan, Phi	R	.000	2	0	0	0	0	.128	47	6	1	0	0	2	2	19	7	76	82.2	4	12	0	0	1.000	8	1	0	0	.13
Mahay,Ron, KC	L	-	0	0	0	0	0	.250	8	2	1	0	0	0	1	8	0	57	64.2	0	8	1	1	.889	4	2	0	0	.50
Maholm,Paul, Pit	L	.123	65	8	0	3	2	.139	194	27	1	0	0	10	11	94	6	31	206.1	7	30	2	2	.949	12	7	3	0	.58
Maine,John, NYM	R	.109	46	5	0	3	5	.093	129	12	1	0	1	6	11	67	22	25	140.0	7	17	1	0	.960	13	6	1	0	.46
Majewski,Gary, Cin	R	.000	1	0	0	0	0	.000	14	0	0	0	0	0	0	8	2	37	40.0	3	2	0	0	1.000	1	0	0	0	.00
Manning,Charlie, Was	L	-	0	0	0	0	0	-	0	0	0	0	0	0	0	0	0	57	42.0	3	3	0	1	1.000	4	0	0	0	.00
Marcum,Shaun, Tor	R	.000	2	0	0	0	0	.000	6	0	0	0	0	0	1	2	0	25	151.1	18	17	0	1	1.000	7	2	0	0	.29
Marmol,Carlos, ChC	R	.000	1	0	0	0	1	.200	30	6	1	0	1	0	11	3	82	87.1	8	6	1	1	.933	4	1	0	0	.25

Pitchers Hitting, Fielding and Holding Runners

Pitcher	T	2008 Hitting						Career Hitting										2008 Fielding and Holding Runners											
		Avg	AB	H	HR	RBI	SH	Avg	AB	H	2B	3B	HR	RBI	BB	SO	SH	G	Inn	PO	A	E	DP	Pct	SBA	CS	PCS	PPO	CS%
Marquis,Jason, ChC	R	.203	59	12	2	10	4	.206	441	91	25	2	5	40	11	109	23	29	167.0	14	31	1	4	.978	12	1	0	0	.08
Marshall,Sean, ChC	L	.333	15	5	0	1	0	.155	84	13	1	0	1	3	1	39	7	34	65.1	3	9	0	0	1.000	7	2	0	0	.29
Marte,Damaso, Pit-NYY	L	-	0	0	0	0	0	.000	8	0	0	0	0	0	0	2	0	72	65.0	3	9	0	1	1.000	4	1	0	0	.25
Martinez,Pedro, NYM	R	.154	39	6	0	4	7	.100	420	42	6	2	0	17	14	184	62	20	109.0	6	17	0	1	1.000	17	2	0	1	.12
Martis,Shairon, Was	R	.000	7	0	0	0	0	.000	7	0	0	0	0	0	1	2	0	5	20.2	0	4	0	0	1.000	3	0	0	0	.00
Masset,Nick, CWS-Cin	R	.000	3	0	0	0	0	.000	4	0	0	0	0	0	0	4	1	42	62.0	3	11	3	3	.824	3	1	0	1	.33
Masterson,Justin, Bos	R	.000	5	0	0	0	0	.000	5	0	0	0	0	0	0	4	0	36	88.1	3	10	1	2	.929	10	1	0	0	.10
Mastny,Tom, Cle	R	-	0	0	0	0	0	-	0	0	0	0	0	0	0	0	0	14	20.0	5	0	0	0	1.000	1	0	0	0	.00
Mathis,Doug, Tex	R	-	0	0	0	0	0	-	0	0	0	0	0	0	0	0	0	8	22.1	2	2	0	0	1.000	2	1	0	0	.50
Matos,Osiris, SF	R	.000	2	0	0	0	0	.000	2	0	0	0	0	0	0	2	0	20	20.2	1	2	1	0	.750	3	1	0	0	.33
Matsuzaka,Daisuke, Bos	R	.000	2	0	0	0	0	.000	6	0	0	0	0	0	0	4	0	29	167.2	16	19	1	2	.972	20	5	0	0	.25
McCarthy,Brandon, Tex	R	-	0	0	0	0	0	.000	5	0	0	0	0	0	0	4	1	5	22.0	0	1	0	0	1.000	7	1	0	0	.14
McClellan,Kyle, StL	R	.000	5	0	0	0	1	.000	5	0	0	0	0	0	0	4	1	68	75.2	7	5	0	0	1.000	3	1	0	0	.33
McClung,Seth, Mil	R	.263	19	5	0	0	2	.250	20	5	1	0	0	0	0	10	3	37	105.1	2	12	1	0	.933	9	4	0	0	.44
McCrory,Bob, Bal	R	-	0	0	0	0	0	-	0	0	0	0	0	0	0	0	0	8	6.1	1	0	0	0	1.000	0	0	0	0	-
McDonald,James, LAD	R	-	0	0	0	0	0	-	0	0	0	0	0	0	0	0	0	4	6.0	1	0	0	0	1.000	0	0	0	0	-
McGowan,Dustin, Tor	R	.000	2	0	0	0	0	.200	10	2	0	0	0	0	0	4	1	19	111.1	11	11	3	4	.880	16	4	0	0	.25
Meche,Gil, KC	R	.250	4	1	0	1	0	.143	21	3	0	0	0	2	0	8	0	34	210.1	6	28	4	1	.895	14	2	0	0	.14
Medders,Brandon, Ari	R	-	0	0	0	0	0	.000	3	0	0	0	0	0	0	1	0	18	19.2	1	3	0	0	1.000	6	1	0	0	.17
Meek,Evan, Pit	R	-	0	0	0	0	0	-	0	0	0	0	0	0	0	0	0	9	13.0	0	5	1	0	.833	2	0	0	0	.00
Meloan,John, Cle	R	-	0	0	0	0	0	-	0	0	0	0	0	0	0	0	0	2	2.0	0	0	0	0	-	0	0	0	0	-
Mendoza,Luis, Tex	R	.000	1	0	0	0	1	.000	1	0	0	0	0	0	0	1	1	25	63.1	7	12	2	2	.905	9	2	1	0	.22
Mercker,Kent, Cin	L	-	0	0	0	0	0	.113	248	28	5	2	1	18	11	115	22	15	13.2	1	0	0	0	1.000	0	0	0	0	-
Meredith,Cla, SD	R	.000	1	0	0	0	0	.000	2	0	0	0	0	0	0	1	1	73	70.1	5	15	2	0	.909	13	1	0	0	.08
Messenger,Randy, Sea	R	-	0	0	0	0	0	.167	6	1	0	0	0	0	1	3	1	13	13.2	0	2	1	0	.667	6	2	0	0	.33
Meyer,Dan, Oak	L	-	0	0	0	0	0	-	0	0	0	0	0	0	0	0	0	11	27.2	0	1	1	0	.500	2	1	0	1	.50
Mickolio,Kam, Bal	R	-	0	0	0	0	0	-	0	0	0	0	0	0	0	0	0	9	7.2	1	1	0	0	1.000	1	0	0	0	.00
Mijares,Jose, Min	L	-	0	0	0	0	0	-	0	0	0	0	0	0	0	0	0	10	10.1	0	2	0	0	1.000	0	0	0	0	-
Miller,Andrew, Fla	L	.067	30	2	0	3	2	.057	35	2	0	0	0	3	0	21	2	29	107.1	5	8	1	0	.929	16	3	1	0	.19
Miller,Jim, Bal	R	-	0	0	0	0	0	-	0	0	0	0	0	0	0	0	0	8	7.2	2	0	2	0	.500	2	0	0	0	.00
Miller,Justin, Fla	R	.000	1	0	0	0	0	.000	5	0	0	0	0	0	0	2	0	46	46.2	2	3	0	0	1.000	5	1	0	0	.20
Miller,Trever, TB	L	-	0	0	0	0	0	.167	6	1	1	0	0	0	1	2	0	68	43.1	2	4	0	2	1.000	2	2	0	0	1.00
Millwood,Kevin, Tex	R	.250	4	1	0	0	1	.122	441	54	15	0	2	24	20	202	52	29	168.2	8	24	2	1	.941	30	4	0	0	.13
Miner,Zach, Det	R	-	0	0	0	0	0	.167	6	1	1	0	0	0	0	3	0	45	118.0	5	17	0	2	1.000	12	4	0	0	.33
Misch,Pat, SF	L	.111	9	1	0	1	4	.111	18	2	0	0	0	1	1	5	5	15	52.1	2	3	0	0	1.000	5	0	0	0	.00
Mock,Garrett, Was	R	.000	4	0	0	0	1	.000	4	0	0	0	0	0	0	3	1	26	41.0	2	2	1	0	.800	2	0	0	0	.00
Moehler,Brian, Hou	R	.023	44	1	0	0	2	.047	150	7	2	0	0	5	8	72	15	31	150.0	14	10	1	0	.960	9	0	0	0	.00
Morales,Franklin, Col	L	.100	10	1	0	0	1	.217	23	5	0	0	0	1	1	7	2	5	25.1	1	4	0	0	1.000	5	0	0	0	.00
Morillo,Juan, Col	R	-	0	0	0	0	0	.000	1	0	0	0	0	0	0	0	0	1	1.0	0	0	0	0	-	0	0	0	0	-
Morris,Matt, Pit	R	.286	7	2	0	1	0	.169	543	92	18	0	2	38	27	216	81	5	22.1	2	2	0	0	1.000	6	3	0	0	.50
Morrow,Brandon, Sea	R	.000	1	0	0	0	0	.000	1	0	0	0	0	0	0	0	0	45	64.2	1	2	0	0	1.000	4	1	0	0	.25
Morton,Charlie, Atl	R	.059	17	1	0	0	3	.059	17	1	1	0	0	0	0	9	3	16	74.2	3	7	0	0	1.000	9	2	1	0	.22
Moseley,Dustin, LAA	R	-	0	0	0	0	0	-	0	0	0	0	0	0	0	0	0	12	50.1	4	7	0	0	1.000	6	2	1	1	.33
Mota,Guillermo, Mil	R	-	0	0	0	0	0	.206	34	7	1	0	2	6	0	17	0	58	57.0	2	13	0	1	1.000	5	1	1	1	.20
Motte,Jason, StL	R	-	0	0	0	0	0	-	0	0	0	0	0	0	0	0	0	12	11.0	1	1	0	0	1.000	0	0	0	0	-
Moyer,Jamie, Phi	L	.078	51	4	0	1	12	.132	319	42	5	0	0	10	25	108	46	33	196.1	18	22	2	1	.952	19	6	4	0	.32
Moylan,Peter, Atl	R	-	0	0	0	0	0	.000	4	0	0	0	0	0	1	3	0	7	5.2	0	1	0	0	1.000	1	0	0	0	.00
Mujica,Edward, Cle	R	-	0	0	0	0	0	-	0	0	0	0	0	0	0	0	0	33	38.2	1	3	0	0	1.000	1	1	0	1	1.00
Mulder,Mark, StL	L	-	0	0	0	0	0	.162	111	18	2	0	1	9	9	45	8	3	1.2	0	0	0	0	-	1	0	0	0	.00
Muniz,Carlos, NYM	R	-	0	0	0	0	0	-	0	0	0	0	0	0	0	0	0	18	23.1	1	1	1	0	.667	0	0	0	1	-
Murray,A.J., Tex	L	-	0	0	0	0	0	-	0	0	0	0	0	0	0	0	0	2	7.2	0	1	0	0	1.000	0	0	0	0	-
Musser,Neal, KC	L	-	0	0	0	0	0	.000	1	0	0	0	0	0	0	0	0	1	1.0	0	0	0	0	-	0	0	0	0	-
Mussina,Mike, NYY	R	.200	5	1	0	0	0	.173	52	9	1	0	0	5	1	9	1	34	200.1	18	23	1	4	.976	19	7	0	0	.37
Myers,Brett, Phi	R	.069	58	4	0	1	9	.116	328	38	8	0	0	10	18	110	44	30	190.0	16	22	0	3	1.000	20	3	1	0	.15
Nathan,Joe, Min	R	-	0	0	0	0	0	.159	63	10	3	0	2	4	3	17	10	68	67.2	3	6	1	0	.900	5	0	0	0	.00
Nelson,Joe, Fla	R	.000	1	0	0	0	0	.000	1	0	0	0	0	0	0	0	0	59	54.0	2	6	0	0	1.000	4	0	0	0	.00
Neshek,Pat, Min	R	-	0	0	0	0	0	-	0	0	0	0	0	0	0	0	0	15	13.1	0	3	0	0	1.000	0	0	0	0	-
Newman,Josh, Col-KC	L	-	0	0	0	0	0	-	0	0	0	0	0	0	0	0	0	12	15.2	1	2	0	0	1.000	1	0	0	0	.00
Niemann,Jeff, TB	R	-	0	0	0	0	0	-	0	0	0	0	0	0	0	0	0	5	16.0	0	1	0	0	1.000	3	1	0	0	.33
Niese,Jonathon, NYM	L	.167	6	1	0	0	0	.167	6	1	0	0	0	0	0	0	0	3	14.0	1	3	0	0	1.000	0	0	0	0	-
Nieve,Fernando, Hou	R	.000	1	0	0	0	0	.118	17	2	0	0	0	1	2	8	5	11	10.2	1	1	0	0	1.000	0	0	0	0	-
Nippert,Dustin, Tex	R	-	0	0	0	0	0	.125	8	1	0	0	0	0	1	6	0	20	71.2	4	5	1	0	.900	7	2	0	0	.29
Nolasco,Ricky, Fla	R	.143	63	9	0	5	10	.145	110	16	2	0	1	10	4	57	17	34	212.1	14	15	0	1	1.000	12	5	0	0	.42
Nomo,Hideo, KC	R	-	0	0	0	0	0	.134	485	65	14	1	4	26	13	222	44	3	4.1	0	0	0	0	-	1	0	0	0	.00
Nunez,Leo, KC	R	-	0	0	0	0	0	-	0	0	0	0	0	0	0	0	0	45	48.1	1	4	1	0	.833	2	1	0	0	.50
Nunez,Vladimir, Atl	R	.000	1	0	0	0	0	.133	60	8	0	0	1	5	1	20	8	23	32.2	2	5	0	0	1.000	4	2	0	0	.50
O'Connor,Mike, Was	L	.000	2	0	0	0	0	.061	33	2	0	0	0	1	1	19	1	5	9.0	1	0	0	0	1.000	1	0	0	0	.00
O'Day,Darren, LAA	R	-	0	0	0	0	0	-	0	0	0	0	0	0	0	0	0	30	43.1	3	9	1	1	.923	3	0	0	0	.33
O'Flaherty,Eric, Sea	L	-	0	0	0	0	0	.000	1	0	0	0	0	0	0	1	0	7	6.2	0	4	0	0	1.000	4	1	1	0	.25
Ohlendorf,Ross, NYY-Pit	R	.000	7	0	0	0	0	.000	7	0	0	0	0	0	0	2	0	30	62.2	0	4	0	1	1.000	3	1	1	0	.33

Pitchers Hitting, Fielding and Holding Runners

Pitcher	T	2008 Hitting						Career Hitting										2008 Fielding and Holding Runners											
		Avg	AB	H	HR	RBI	SH	Avg	AB	H	2B	3B	HR	RBI	BB	SO	SH	G	Inn	PO	A	E	DP	Pct	SBA	CS	PCS	PPO	CS%
Ohman,Will, Atl	L	-	0	0	0	0	0	1.000	1	1	0	0	0	0	1	0	0	83	58.2	2	7	0	1	1.000	3	2	1	0	.67
Okajima,Hideki, Bos	L	-	0	0	0	0	0		0	0	0	0	0	0	0	0	0	64	62.0	3	4	0	0	1.000	1	1	0	0	1.00
Oliver,Darren, LAA	L	-	0	0	0	0	0	.221	217	48	11	0	1	20	8	74	15	54	72.0	3	11	0	2	1.000	7	2	1	0	.29
Olsen,Scott, Fla	L	.129	62	8	0	3	8	.161	174	28	5	0	0	14	4	70	24	33	201.2	6	23	2	0	.935	15	7	3	1	.47
Olson,Garrett, Bal	L	.333	3	1	0	1	1	.333	3	1	0	0	0	1	0	0	1	26	132.2	8	13	4	1	.840	22	2	1	0	.09
Osoria,Franquelis, Pit	R	.333	6	2	0	1	1	.133	15	2	0	0	0	1	0	9	2	43	60.2	6	6	2	1	.857	0	0	0	0	-
Oswalt,Roy, Hou	R	.214	70	15	0	5	5	.162	507	82	7	0	1	31	19	142	73	32	208.2	24	30	0	4	1.000	2	1	0	0	.50
Outman,Josh, Oak	L	-	0	0	0	0	0	-	0	0	0	0	0	0	0	0	0	6	25.2	1	2	1	0	.750	1	0	0	0	.00
Owings,Micah, Ari-Cin	R	.288	52	15	1	3	1	.313	112	35	9	1	5	18	7	37	2	22	104.2	13	12	1	1	.962	5	2	0	0	.40
Padilla,Vicente, Tex	R	.000	1	0	0	0	2	.096	209	20	3	1	0	13	14	110	22	29	171.0	9	21	4	2	.882	13	4	0	2	.31
Palmer,Matt, SF	R	.250	4	1	0	0	0	.250	4	1	0	0	0	0	1	2	0	3	12.2	1	3	0	2	1.000	0	0	0	0	-
Papelbon,Jonathan, Bos	R	-	0	0	0	0	0	-	0	0	0	0	0	0	0	0	0	67	69.1	5	5	3	0	.769	2	0	1	0	.00
Parisi,Mike, StL	R	.250	4	1	0	2	0	.250	4	1	1	0	0	2	0	1	0	12	23.0	3	5	0		1.000	1	1	0	0	1.00
Park,Chan Ho, LAD	R	.111	9	1	0	0	3	.181	415	75	15	1	2	30	17	150	53	54	95.1	11	20	0	5	1.000	6	1	0	0	.17
Parnell,Bobby, NYM	R	-	0	0	0	0	0	-	0	0	0	0	0	0	0	0	0	6	5.0	0	1	0	0	1.000	0	0	0	0	-
Paronto,Chad, Hou	R	.000	2	0	0	0	0	.000	3	0	0	0	0	0	0	3	0	6	10.1	0	1	0	0	1.000	0	0	0	0	-
Parr,James, Atl	R	.250	8	2	0	0	0	.250	8	2	0	0	0	0	0	2	0	5	22.1	0	3	0	0	1.000	1	1	1	0	1.00
Parra,Manny, Mil	L	.226	53	12	0	6	3	.226	62	14	7	1	0	8	2	21	4	32	166.0	3	16	0	2	1.000	13	5	2	0	.38
Parrish,John, Tor	L	-	0	0	0	0	0	.000	1	0	0	0	0	0	0	0	0	13	42.1	3	6	1	0	.900	3	1	0	2	.33
Patterson,Scott, NYY-SD	R	-	0	0	0	0	0	-	0	0	0	0	0	0	0	0	0	4	4.2	0	0	0	0	-	1	0	0	0	.00
Pauley,David, Bos	R	-	0	0	0	0	0	-	0	0	0	0	0	0	0	0	0	6	12.1	0	1	0	0	1.000	2	0	0	0	.00
Pavano,Carl, NYY	R	-	0	0	0	0	0	.139	295	41	8	2	2	14	4	116	34	7	34.1	0	7	0	0	1.000	6	1	0	0	.17
Peavy,Jake, SD	R	.265	49	13	0	2	5	.186	382	71	14	1	2	26	17	112	41	27	173.2	13	25	2	3	.950	27	9	1	0	.33
Peguero,Jailen, Ari	R	-	0	0	0	0	0	-	0	0	0	0	0	0	0	0	0	7	9.1	0	3	0	1	1.000	0	0	0	0	-
Pelfrey,Mike, NYM	R	.085	59	5	0	2	8	.079	89	7	1	0	0	2	5	31	8	32	200.2	14	33	0	3	1.000	11	6	0	4	.55
Pena,Tony, Ari	R	-	0	0	0	0	0	.167	6	1	0	0	0	1	0	2	0	72	75.2	7	10	0	1	1.000	2	0	0	0	.00
Penny,Brad, LAD	R	.192	26	5	0	2	6	.158	480	76	16	2	2	30	3	155	38	19	94.2	6	17	1	2	.958	11	3	0	0	.27
Peralta,Joel, KC	R	-	0	0	0	0	0	1.000	1	1	1	0	0	2	0	0	0	40	52.2	3	2	0	0	1.000	4	1	0	0	.25
Percival,Troy, TB	R	-	0	0	0	0	0	.000	5	0	0	0	0	0	0	5	0	50	45.2	2	0	0	0	1.000	9	2	0	0	.22
Perez,Chris, StL	R	.000	1	0	0	0	0	.000	1	0	0	0	0	0	0	1	0	41	41.2	1	2	0	0	1.000	4	1	0	0	.25
Perez,Odalis, Was	L	.151	53	8	0	2	3	.132	340	45	10	0	1	12	6	85	44	30	159.2	9	26	0	1	1.000	20	7	4	0	.35
Perez,Oliver, NYM	L	.107	56	6	0	3	7	.152	310	47	1	0	0	14	12	105	37	34	194.0	7	15	0	3	1.000	9	1	0	0	.11
Perez,Rafael, Cle	L	-	0	0	0	0	0	-	0	0	0	0	0	0	0	0	0	73	76.1	2	16	1	2	.947	5	3	0	0	.60
Perkins,Glen, Min	L	.000	3	0	0	0	1	.000	3	0	0	0	0	0	0	3	1	26	151.0	2	25	1	0	.964	7	4	3	0	.57
Petit,Yusmeiro, Ari	R	.000	13	0	0	0	2	.059	34	2	0	0	0	1	0	17	4	19	56.1	0	7	0	0	1.000	3	1	0	0	.33
Pettitte,Andy, NYY	L	.000	2	0	0	0	0	.133	181	24	5	0	1	12	6	58	31	33	204.0	6	30	2	2	.947	28	8	6	4	.29
Pettyjohn,Adam, Cin	L	.000	1	0	0	0	0	.000	1	0	0	0	0	0	0	2	0	3	4.0	2	0	0	0	1.000	0	0	0	0	-
Pignatiello,Carmen, ChC	L	-	0	0	0	0	0	-	0	0	0	0	0	0	0	0	0	2	0.2	0	0	0	0	-	0	0	0	0	-
Pineiro,Joel, StL	R	.098	51	5	0	4	3	.086	93	8	4	0	0	6	5	58	11	26	148.2	15	28	1	0	.977	9	4	1	1	.44
Pinto,Renyel, Fla	L	.000	1	0	0	0	2	.000	5	0	0	0	0	0	1	3	2	67	64.2	2	9	2	0	.846	2	1	0	0	.50
Ponson,Sidney, Tex-NYY	R	.000	2	0	0	0	1	.138	65	9	3	0	0	1	3	22	12	25	135.2	7	21	3	1	.903	8	5	1	0	.63
Price,David, TB	L	-	0	0	0	0	0	-	0	0	0	0	0	0	0	0	0	5	14.0	0	1	0	0	1.000	0	0	0	0	-
Proctor,Scott, LAD	R	-	0	0	0	0	0	.000	3	0	0	0	0	0	0	3	0	41	38.2	0	2	1	0	.667	2	1	0	0	.50
Purcey,David, Tor	L	.000	1	0	0	0	0	.000	1	0	0	0	0	0	0	1	0	12	65.0	2	4	0	0	1.000	5	3	1	0	.60
Putz,J.J., Sea	R	-	0	0	0	0	0	-	0	0	0	0	0	0	0	0	0	47	46.1	1	7	1	0	.889	3	2	1	0	.67
Qualls,Chad, Ari	R	.000	2	0	0	0	0	.000	4	0	0	0	0	0	0	3	0	77	73.2	4	7	2	0	.846	3	0	0	0	.00
Ramirez,Edwar, NYY	R	-	0	0	0	0	0	-	0	0	0	0	0	0	0	0	0	55	55.1	4	3	0	0	1.000	6	4	0	0	.67
Ramirez,Elizardo, Tex	R	-	0	0	0	0	0	.154	39	6	1	0	0	3	2	12	2	1	2.2	0	0	0	0	-	0	0	0	0	-
Ramirez,H., CWS-KC	L	-	0	0	0	0	0	.151	179	27	3	1	0	5	2	36	13	32	37.1	3	10	0	0	1.000	5	0	0	0	.00
Ramirez,Ramon, KC	R	-	0	0	0	0	0	.500	4	2	0	0	0	0	0	2	1	71	71.2	2	8	1	1	.909	4	1	1	0	.25
Ramirez,Ramon A, Cin	R	.100	10	1	0	0	0	.100	10	1	0	0	0	0	0	3	0	5	27.0	4	2	0	0	1.000	5	3	0	0	.60
Rapada,Clay, Det	L	-	0	0	0	0	0	-	0	0	0	0	0	0	0	0	0	25	21.1	3	5	2	0	.800	1	1	1	1	1.00
Rasner,Darrell, NYY	R	.000	1	0	0	0	0	.000	1	0	0	0	0	0	2	1	0	24	113.1	5	19	0	0	1.000	6	0	0	0	.50
Rauch,Jon, Was-Ari	R	.000	1	0	0	0	0	.095	21	2	0	0	1	3	0	15	1	74	71.2	2	7	0	0	1.000	4	1	0	0	.25
Redding,Tim, Was	R	.170	47	8	0	3	13	.148	196	29	5	0	0	10	7	85	27	33	182.0	6	19	2	2	.926	20	7	0	0	.35
Redman,Mark, Col	L	.000	12	0	0	0	3	.052	155	8	0	0	0	3	6	70	13	10	45.1	2	7	0	2	1.000	2	0	0	0	.00
Register,Steven, Col	R	-	0	0	0	0	0	-	0	0	0	0	0	0	0	0	0	10	10.0	0	0	0	0	-	0	0	0	0	-
Reineke,Chad, SD	R	.167	6	1	0	1	0	.167	6	1	0	0	0	1	0	4	0	4	18.0	0	0	0	0	-	0	0	0	0	-
Resop,Chris, Atl	R	-	0	0	0	0	0	.000	1	0	0	0	0	0	0	1	0	16	18.1	0	3	0	0	1.000	1	0	0	0	.00
Reyes,Al, TB	R	-	0	0	0	0	0	.250	12	3	0	0	0	0	1	6	2	26	22.2	0	2	0	0	1.000	2	0	0	0	.00
Reyes,Anthony, StL-Cle	R	.000	1	0	0	0	0	.089	56	5	0	0	0	1	1	22	8	16	49.0	2	7	0	0	1.000	4	1	0	0	.25
Reyes,Dennys, Min	L	-	0	0	0	0	0	.074	54	4	1	0	0	0	2	25	2	75	46.1	1	7	0	0	1.000	8	2	2	0	.25
Reyes,Jo-Jo, Atl	L	.133	30	4	0	2	3	.143	49	7	2	0	0	2	1	15	7	23	113.0	3	13	0	0	1.000	13	4	1	0	.31
Reynolds,Greg, Col	R	.200	15	3	0	0	1	.200	15	3	2	0	0	0	1	5	1	14	62.0	4	6	0	1	1.000	3	0	0	0	.00
Rhodes,Arthur, Sea-Fla	L	-	0	0	0	0	0	.250	4	1	0	0	0	0	0	3	0	61	35.1	1	3	0	0	1.000	6	0	0	0	.00
Richard,Clayton, CWS	L	-	0	0	0	0	0	-	0	0	0	0	0	0	0	0	0	13	47.2	3	7	3	0	.769	6	0	0	0	.00
Richmond,Scott, Tor	R	-	0	0	0	0	0	-	0	0	0	0	0	0	0	0	0	5	27.0	2	0	0	0	1.000	2	1	0	0	.50
Ridgway,Jeff, Atl	L	-	0	0	0	0	0	-	0	0	0	0	0	0	0	0	0	10	9.2	2	1	0	0	1.000	0	0	0	0	-
Rincon,Juan, Min-Cle	R	-	0	0	0	0	0	.500	2	1	0	0	0	0	0	1	0	47	55.1	1	5	0	1	1.000	7	1	0	0	.14
Rincon,Ricardo, NYM	L	-	0	0	0	0	0	.000	4	0	0	0	0	0	0	1	1	8	4.0	0	0	0	0	-	1	1	0	0	1.00

Pitchers Hitting, Fielding and Holding Runners

Pitcher	T	2008 Hitting						Career Hitting										2008 Fielding and Holding Runners											
		Avg	AB	H	HR	RBI	SH	Avg	AB	H	2B	3B	HR	RBI	BB	SO	SH	G	Inn	PO	A	E	DP	Pct	SBA	CS	PCS	PPO	CS%
Ring,Royce, Atl	L	-	0	0	0	0	0	-	0	0	0	0	0	0	0	0	0	42	22.1	1	3	0	0	1.000	3	0	0	0	.00
Riske,David, Mil	R	.000	1	0	0	0	0	.000	1	0	0	0	0	0	0	0	0	45	42.1	1	2	0	0	1.000	4	2	1	0	.50
Rivera,Mariano, NYY	R	-	0	0	0	0	0	.000	1	0	0	0	0	0	0	1	0	64	70.2	6	8	0	1	1.000	7	1	0	0	.14
Rivera,Saul, Was	R	.000	1	0	0	0	0	.000	6	0	0	0	0	0	1	2	0	76	84.0	8	21	0	3	1.000	13	0	0	0	.00
Robertson,Connor, Ari	R	-	0	0	0	0	1	-	0	0	0	0	0	0	0	1	6	7.0	1	1	0	0	1.000	0	0	0	0	-
Robertson,David, NYY	R	-	0	0	0	0	0	-	0	0	0	0	0	0	0	0	0	25	30.1	1	3	0	0	1.000	7	3	0	0	.43
Robertson,Nate, Det	L	.000	4	0	0	0	0	.056	18	1	0	0	0	1	0	9	1	32	168.2	8	20	1	1	.966	11	4	1	0	.36
Rodney,Fernando, Det	R	-	0	0	0	0	0	.000	1	0	0	0	0	0	0	0	0	38	40.1	4	2	0	0	1.000	4	0	0	0	.00
Rodriguez,Francisco, LAA	R	-	0	0	0	0	0	-	0	0	0	0	0	0	0	0	0	76	68.1	4	6	2	1	.833	8	0	0	0	.00
Rodriguez,Wandy, Hou	L	.122	41	5	0	1	4	.120	167	20	2	0	0	5	5	52	22	25	137.1	9	14	0	2	1.000	7	3	1	0	.43
Roenicke,Josh, Cin	R	-	0	0	0	0	0	-	0	0	0	0	0	0	0	0	0	5	3.0	0	0	0	0	-	0	0	0	0	-
Rogers,Kenny, Det	L	.000	1	0	0	0	1	.136	66	9	1	1	0	4	4	25	5	30	173.2	26	50	1	11	.987	3	2	0	3	.67
Romero,J.C., Phi	L	-	0	0	0	0	0	.250	4	1	1	0	0	0	0	1	0	81	59.0	9	13	0	0	1.000	12	2	2	1	.17
Romo,Sergio, SF	R	.000	1	0	0	0	0	.000	1	0	0	0	0	0	0	0	0	29	34.0	2	5	0	0	1.000	5	1	0	0	.20
Rosa,Carlos, KC	R	-	0	0	0	0	0	-	0	0	0	0	0	0	0	0	0	2	3.1	0	0	0	0	-	1	1	0	0	1.00
Rosales,Leo, Ari	R	-	0	0	0	0	0	-	0	0	0	0	0	0	0	0	0	27	30.0	1	3	1	0	.800	2	0	0	0	.00
Rowland-Smith,R., Sea	L	-	0	0	0	0	0	-	0	0	0	0	0	0	0	0	0	47	118.1	4	6	1	0	.909	6	2	0	0	.33
Rundles,Rich, Cle	L	-	0	0	0	0	0	-	0	0	0	0	0	0	0	0	0	8	5.0	0	0	0	0	-	1	0	0	0	.00
Rupe,Josh, Tex	R	-	0	0	0	0	0	-	0	0	0	0	0	0	0	0	0	46	89.1	5	10	0	2	1.000	1	1	0	0	1.00
Rusch,Glendon, SD-Col	L	.050	20	1	0	0	3	.148	325	48	4	0	3	19	9	102	41	35	83.2	4	7	0	1	1.000	3	0	0	0	.00
Russell,Adam, CWS	R	-	0	0	0	0	0	-	0	0	0	0	0	0	0	0	0	22	26.0	0	5	0	0	1.000	0	0	0	0	-
Ryan,B.J., Tor	L	-	0	0	0	0	0	.000	2	0	0	0	0	0	0	0	0	60	58.0	1	4	0	1	1.000	4	0	0	0	.00
Ryu,Jae Kuk, TB	R	-	0	0	0	0	0	.000	1	0	0	0	0	0	0	1	0	1	1.1	0	0	0	0	-	0	0	0	0	-
Saarloos,Kirk, Oak	R	-	0	0	0	0	0	.073	41	3	2	0	0	5	1	12	9	8	26.1	1	4	0	1	1.000	1	0	0	0	.00
Sabathia,CC, Cle-Mil	L	.235	51	12	2	7	2	.261	88	23	3	0	3	13	1	22	3	35	253.0	5	28	1	5	.971	15	3	2	0	.20
Sadler,Billy, SF	R	.000	1	0	0	0	0	.000	1	0	0	0	0	0	0	1	0	33	44.1	3	3	0	0	1.000	6	3	0	0	.50
Saito,Takashi, LAD	R	.000	1	0	0	0	0	.000	1	0	0	0	0	0	0	1	0	45	47.0	1	5	0	0	1.000	2	1	1	0	.50
Salas,Juan, TB	R	-	0	0	0	0	0	-	0	0	0	0	0	0	0	0	0	5	6.1	1	0	0	0	1.000	0	0	0	0	-
Salas,Marino, Pit	R	-	0	0	0	0	0	-	0	0	0	0	0	0	0	0	0	13	17.0	0	1	0	0	1.000	0	0	0	0	-
Samardzija,Jeff, ChC	R	.000	1	0	0	0	0	.000	1	0	0	0	0	0	0	1	0	26	27.2	3	4	0	0	1.000	6	1	1	0	.17
Sampson,Chris, Hou	R	.136	22	3	0	0	3	.132	53	7	0	0	0	1	1	21	13	54	117.1	15	7	1	2	.957	4	2	0	0	.50
Sanches,Brian, Was	R	-	0	0	0	0	0	-	0	0	0	0	0	0	0	0	0	12	11.0	0	1	0	0	1.000	1	0	0	0	.00
Sanchez,Anibal, Fla	R	.000	17	0	0	0	1	.079	63	5	0	0	0	2	3	28	5	10	51.2	2	5	4	0	.636	7	0	0	1	.00
Sanchez,Duaner, NYM	R	-	0	0	0	0	1	.111	9	1	1	0	0	2	0	2	2	66	58.1	2	6	1	0	.889	4	0	0	0	.00
Sanchez,Humberto, NYY	R	-	0	0	0	0	0	-	0	0	0	0	0	0	0	0	0	2	2.0	1	0	0	0	1.000	0	0	0	0	-
Sanchez,Jonathan, SF	L	.102	49	5	0	4	5	.097	62	6	2	0	0	5	2	29	6	29	158.0	1	16	0	1	1.000	22	3	1	0	.14
Sanchez,Romulo, Pit	R	-	0	0	0	0	0	.000	1	0	0	0	0	0	0	0	0	10	13.1	0	3	0	0	1.000	0	0	0	0	-
Santana,Ervin, LAA	R	.000	6	0	0	0	0	.133	15	2	1	0	0	2	0	8	0	32	219.0	19	13	0	0	1.000	20	4	0	0	.20
Santana,Johan, NYM	L	.141	78	11	0	1	2	.174	109	19	6	1	0	4	4	28	2	34	234.1	13	27	1	1	.976	11	5	2	0	.45
Sarfate,Dennis, Bal	R	-	0	0	0	0	0	-	0	0	0	0	0	0	0	0	0	57	79.2	4	6	2	1	.833	8	2	0	1	.25
Saunders,Joe, LAA	L	.000	3	0	0	0	0	.000	3	0	0	0	0	0	0	2	0	31	198.0	8	33	0	3	1.000	25	7	3	0	.28
Scherzer,Max, Ari	R	.000	13	0	0	0	1	.000	13	0	0	0	0	0	1	4	1	16	56.0	4	5	1	2	.900	1	1	0	0	1.00
Schoeneweis,Scott, NYM	L	.000	1	0	0	0	0	.250	8	2	1	0	1	2	2	2	0	73	56.2	4	9	0	0	1.000	4	2	2	0	.50
Schroder,Chris, Was	R	-	0	0	0	0	0	.000	4	0	0	0	0	0	2	0	4	4	5.0	0	2	0	0	1.000	0	0	0	0	-
Seanez,Rudy, Phi	R	-	0	0	0	0	0	.000	5	0	0	0	0	0	1	5	0	42	43.1	4	3	2	1	.778	8	1	1	0	.13
Seay,Bobby, Det	L	-	0	0	0	0	0	.000	1	0	0	0	0	0	0	1	0	60	56.1	2	7	0	1	1.000	3	1	0	0	.33
Serrano,Alex, LAA	R	-	0	0	0	0	0	-	0	0	0	0	0	0	0	0	0	1	1.0	0	0	0	0	-	0	0	0	0	-
Sheets,Ben, Mil	R	.075	67	5	0	5	5	.076	433	33	3	0	0	12	18	204	41	31	198.1	10	16	2	0	.929	20	7	0	2	.35
Shell,Steven, Was	R	.000	4	0	0	0	0	.000	4	0	0	0	0	0	0	2	0	39	50.0	3	7	0	1	1.000	3	1	0	0	.33
Sherrill,George, Bal	L	-	0	0	0	0	0	-	0	0	0	0	0	0	0	0	0	57	53.1	1	2	1	0	.750	3	0	0	0	.00
Shields,James, TB	R	.250	4	1	0	1	0	.278	18	5	0	0	0	1	1	3	1	33	215.0	19	19	1	3	.974	13	6	0	1	.46
Shields,Scot, LAA	R	-	0	0	0	0	0	.000	3	0	0	0	0	0	0	2	0	64	63.1	5	4	0	1	1.000	9	1	0	0	.11
Shouse,Brian, Mil	L	-	0	0	0	0	0	-	0	0	0	0	0	0	0	0	0	69	51.1	5	14	1	2	.950	2	1	1	0	.50
Silva,Carlos, Sea	R	.000	4	0	0	0	0	.111	27	3	1	0	0	1	1	10	3	28	153.1	11	12	1	0	.958	10	2	0	0	.20
Simon,Alfredo, Bal	R	-	0	0	0	0	0	-	0	0	0	0	0	0	0	0	0	4	13.0	5	2	0	0	1.000	0	0	0	0	.00
Slaten,Doug, Ari	L	-	0	0	0	0	0	-	0	0	0	0	0	0	0	0	0	45	32.1	0	5	2	1	.714	0	0	0	0	-
Slocum,Brian, Cle	R	-	0	0	0	0	0	-	0	0	0	0	0	0	0	0	0	2	2.0	0	0	0	0	-	0	0	0	0	-
Slowey,Kevin, Min	R	.250	8	2	0	2	0	.250	8	2	1	0	0	2	0	1	0	27	160.1	7	18	1	1	.962	8	4	0	1	.50
Smith,Chris, Bos	R	-	0	0	0	0	0	-	0	0	0	0	0	0	0	0	0	12	18.1	3	2	0	0	1.000	0	0	0	1	-
Smith,Greg, Oak	L	.500	2	1	0	0	1	.500	2	1	0	0	0	0	1	1	1	32	190.1	7	31	0	1	1.000	23	12	11	5	.52
Smith,Joe, NYM	R	.000	1	0	0	0	0	.000	2	0	0	0	0	0	0	2	0	82	63.1	3	18	0	0	1.000	8	2	0	0	.25
Smoltz,John, Atl	R	.000	8	0	0	0	1	.161	933	150	26	2	5	61	78	358	136	6	28.0	2	3	3	0	.625	1	0	0	0	.00
Snell,Ian, Pit	R	.125	48	6	0	1	7	.083	169	14	2	0	0	5	7	74	29	31	164.1	9	19	0	3	1.000	24	4	0	0	.17
Snyder,Kyle, Bos	R	-	0	0	0	0	0	.000	2	0	0	0	0	0	0	0	0	2	1.2	0	0	0	0	-	0	0	0	0	-
Sonnanstine,Andy, TB	R	.400	5	2	0	0	2	.400	10	4	0	0	0	1	2	5	2	32	193.1	19	19	0	1	1.000	4	3	0	0	.75
Soria,Joakim, KC	R	-	0	0	0	0	0	-	0	0	0	0	0	0	0	0	0	63	67.1	6	6	0	0	1.000	3	1	1	1	.33
Soriano,Rafael, Atl	R	-	0	0	0	0	0	.000	4	0	0	0	0	0	0	1	0	14	14.0	1	1	0	0	1.000	2	1	0	0	.50
Sosa,Jorge, NYM	R	.000	1	0	0	0	0	.136	81	11	2	0	3	4	7	36	11	20	21.2	1	2	0	0	1.000	0	0	0	1	.00
Sowers,Jeremy, Cle	L	.000	1	0	0	0	1	.500	2	1	0	0	0	0	2	1	1	22	121.0	7	18	2	2	.926	15	6	1	0	.40
Speier,Justin, LAA	R	-	0	0	0	0	0	.176	17	3	0	0	0	0	1	8	0	62	68.0	8	3	0	0	1.000	8	1	0	0	.13

Pitchers Hitting, Fielding and Holding Runners

Pitcher	T	2008 Hitting						Career Hitting										2008 Fielding and Holding Runners											
		Avg	AB	H	HR	RBI	SH	Avg	AB	H	2B	3B	HR	RBI	BB	SO	SH	G	Inn	PO	A	E	DP	Pct	SBA	CS	PCS	PPO	CS%
Speier,Ryan, Col	R	.000	3	0	0	0	0	.000	5	0	0	0	0	0	0	3	0	43	51.0	2	5	0	0	1.000	8	2	0	0	.25
Speigner,Levale, Was	R	-	0	0	0	0	0	.000	4	0	0	0	0	0	1	2	3	7	8.0	1	2	0	0	1.000	2	2	0	0	1.00
Springer,Russ, StL	R	-	0	0	0	0	0	.074	27	2	0	0	0	0	0	17	4	70	50.1	2	7	2	0	.818	3	2	0	0	.67
Stetter,Mitch, Mil	L	.000	1	0	0	0	0	.000	1	0	0	0	0	0	0	1	0	30	25.1	2	2	0	1	1.000	4	2	1	0	.50
Stockman,Phil, Atl	R	-	0	0	0	0	0	-	0	0	0	0	0	0	0	0	0	6	7.1	1	0	0	0	1.000	1	0	0	0	.00
Stokes,Brian, NYM	R	.667	3	2	0	0	0	.667	3	2	0	0	0	0	0	1	0	24	33.1	2	5	0	0	1.000	3	0	0	0	.00
Street,Huston, Oak	R	-	0	0	0	0	0	-	0	0	0	0	0	0	0	0	0	63	70.0	3	8	0	1	1.000	9	3	1	0	.33
Stults,Eric, LAD	L	.133	15	2	0	2	0	.281	32	9	2	0	0	2	2	12	1	7	38.2	2	4	1	0	.857	3	1	0	0	.33
Sturtze,Tanyon, LAD	R	.000	0	0	0	0	0	.063	16	1	0	0	0	0	0	5	2	3	2.1	0	1	0	0	1.000	0	0	0	0	-
Suppan,Jeff, Mil	R	.140	50	7	0	1	10	.177	361	64	5	0	1	18	18	82	57	31	177.2	10	30	1	2	.976	11	7	1	1	.64
Swindle,R.J., Phi	L	.000	2	0	0	1	0	.000	2	0	0	0	0	1	0	0	0	3	4.2	0	0	0	0	-	0	0	0	0	-
Talbot,Mitch, TB	R	-	0	0	0	0	0	-	0	0	0	0	0	0	0	0	0	3	9.2	1	1	0	0	1.000	2	0	0	0	.00
Tallet,Brian, Tor	L	-	0	0	0	0	0	.000	2	0	0	0	0	0	0	1	0	51	56.1	3	3	1	0	.857	7	1	0	0	.14
Tankersley,Taylor, Fla	L	-	0	0	0	0	0	.000	2	0	0	0	0	0	0	2	0	25	17.2	0	1	1	0	.500	1	0	0	0	.00
Taschner,Jack, SF	L	-	0	0	0	0	0	.000	1	0	0	0	0	0	0	0	1	67	48.0	2	6	0	1	1.000	8	2	1	0	.25
Taubenheim,Ty, Pit	R	.500	2	1	0	1	0	.400	5	2	1	0	0	1	0	2	0	1	6.0	0	0	0	0	-	2	1	0	0	.50
Tavarez,J., Bos-Mil-Atl	R	.000	0	0	0	0	0	.115	139	16	0	0	0	8	7	60	21	52	54.2	5	7	1	1	.923	5	0	0	0	.00
Tejeda,Robinson, Tex-KC	R	-	0	0	0	0	0	.080	25	2	0	1	0	0	0	13	7	29	45.1	2	2	2	0	.667	7	1	1	1	.14
Thatcher,Joe, SD	L	.000	1	0	0	0	0	.000	1	0	0	0	0	0	0	1	0	25	25.2	0	3	0	0	1.000	1	0	0	0	.00
Thomas,Justin, Sea	L	-	0	0	0	0	0	-	0	0	0	0	0	0	0	0	0	8	4.0	0	1	0	0	1.000	0	0	0	0	-
Thompson,Brad, StL	R	.250	12	3	0	2	3	.205	44	9	0	0	0	2	2	20	11	26	64.2	8	11	0	1	1.000	2	1	0	1	.50
Thompson,Daryl, Cin	R	.000	2	0	0	0	0	.000	2	0	0	0	0	0	0	0	0	3	14.1	0	1	0	0	1.000	0	0	0	0	-
Thompson,Rich, LAA	R	-	0	0	0	0	0	-	0	0	0	0	0	0	0	0	0	2	2.0	0	1	0	0	1.000	1	0	0	0	.00
Thornton,Matt, CWS	L	-	0	0	0	0	0	.000	1	0	0	0	0	0	0	1	0	74	67.1	1	8	0	1	1.000	3	0	0	0	.00
Threets,Erick, SF	L	-	0	0	0	0	0	-	0	0	0	0	0	0	0	0	0	7	10.0	0	1	0	0	1.000	1	0	0	0	.00
Timlin,Mike, Bos	R	-	0	0	0	0	0	.000	7	0	0	0	0	0	0	4	0	47	49.1	1	9	0	0	1.000	6	0	0	0	.00
Tomko,Brett, KC-SD	R	.000	4	0	0	0	0	.156	454	71	9	0	4	29	19	179	71	22	70.0	3	12	0	0	1.000	3	0	0	0	.00
Torres,Salomon, Mil	R	.000	1	0	0	0	0	.146	103	15	1	1	0	1	2	46	12	71	80.0	7	15	0	3	1.000	3	2	0	0	.67
Traber,Billy, NYY	L	-	0	0	0	0	0	.048	21	1	0	0	0	0	1	13	2	19	16.2	2	2	0	0	1.000	4	1	0	0	.25
Trachsel,Steve, Bal	R	-	0	0	0	0	0	.163	651	106	17	1	3	40	26	200	87	10	39.2	2	2	0	0	1.000	9	3	0	0	.33
Troncoso,Ramon, LAD	R	-	0	0	0	0	0	-	0	0	0	0	0	0	0	0	0	32	38.0	3	5	0	1	1.000	5	0	0	0	.00
Tucker,Ryan, Fla	R	.000	7	0	0	0	0	.000	7	0	0	0	0	0	0	4	0	13	37.0	2	5	0	0	1.000	3	1	0	0	.33
Turnbow,Derrick, Mil	R	-	0	0	0	0	0	.000	2	0	0	0	0	0	0	1	0	8	6.1	0	1	0	0	1.000	2	0	0	0	.00
Valdez,Merkin, SF	R	-	0	0	0	0	1	-	0	0	0	0	0	0	0	0	1	17	16.0	0	0	0	0	-	2	1	0	0	.50
Valverde,Jose, Hou	R	.000	1	0	0	0	0	.500	2	1	1	0	0	0	0	1	0	74	72.0	6	3	1	0	.900	8	0	0	0	.00
Van Benschoten,J, Pit	R	.000	6	0	0	0	0	.095	21	2	1	0	1	2	3	8	4	9	22.1	0	2	0	0	1.000	5	1	0	0	.20
VandenHurk,Rick, Fla	R	.000	3	0	0	0	2	.038	26	1	0	0	0	0	1	14	5	4	14.0	0	1	1	0	.500	0	0	0	0	-
Vargas,Claudio, NYM	R	.000	8	0	0	0	1	.081	185	15	4	0	0	7	3	57	33	11	37.0	4	6	0	1	1.000	3	1	0	0	.33
Vazquez,Javier, CWS	R	.000	2	0	0	0	0	.211	435	92	10	2	1	24	17	71	74	33	208.1	17	29	0	3	1.000	12	3	1	0	.25
Veras,Jose, NYY	R	-	0	0	0	0	0	-	0	0	0	0	0	0	0	0	0	60	57.2	3	6	0	0	1.000	8	3	0	0	.38
Verlander,Justin, Det	R	.000	5	0	0	0	0	.000	10	0	0	0	0	0	0	0	0	34	201.0	7	24	2	1	.939	17	9	1	1	.53
Villanueva,Carlos, Mil	R	.118	17	2	0	2	3	.089	45	4	0	0	0	3	1	20	9	47	108.1	11	10	1	0	.955	7	2	0	0	.29
Villarreal,Oscar, Hou	R	.000	1	0	0	0	0	.067	15	1	0	0	0	0	0	7	3	35	37.2	3	5	0	0	1.000	3	1	0	0	.33
Villone,Ron, StL	L	.000	1	0	0	0	0	.129	170	22	3	1	1	7	1	51	12	74	50.0	4	8	1	2	.923	0	0	0	0	-
Vizcaino,Luis, Col	R	.000	2	0	0	0	0	.000	6	0	0	0	0	0	0	5	0	43	46.0	2	5	0	0	1.000	2	0	0	0	.00
Volquez,Edinson, Cin	R	.098	61	6	0	1	8	.098	61	6	0	0	0	1	0	31	8	33	196.0	10	24	1	2	.971	33	12	0	0	.36
Volstad,Chris, Fla	R	.115	26	3	0	0	2	.115	26	3	2	0	0	0	0	14	2	15	84.1	6	7	0	0	1.000	14	2	0	0	.14
Wade,Cory, LAD	R	-	0	0	0	0	0	-	0	0	0	0	0	0	1	0	0	55	71.1	7	7	0	0	1.000	2	0	0	0	.00
Waechter,Doug, Fla	R	.167	6	1	0	0	1	.125	8	1	0	0	0	0	1	2	4	48	63.1	2	1	1	0	.750	7	1	0	0	.14
Wagner,Billy, NYM	L	-	0	0	0	0	0	.100	20	2	0	0	0	1	1	12	0	45	47.0	1	2	0	0	1.000	1	1	0	0	1.00
Wainwright,Adam, StL	R	.267	60	16	1	6	2	.289	128	37	6	0	3	13	5	38	11	20	132.0	7	20	1	1	.964	6	4	2	0	.67
Wakefield,Tim, Bos	R	.000	3	0	0	0	0	.119	101	12	2	0	1	4	2	40	13	30	181.0	7	15	1	1	.957	37	10	0	1	.27
Walker,Jamie, Bal	L	-	0	0	0	0	0	-	0	0	0	0	0	0	0	0	0	59	38.0	4	6	0	1	1.000	3	1	1	0	.33
Walker,Tyler, SF	R	-	0	0	0	0	0	.000	10	0	0	0	0	0	1	6	0	65	53.1	2	4	1	0	.857	3	1	0	0	.33
Walrond,Les, Phi	L	.000	1	0	0	0	0	.000	3	0	0	0	0	0	0	1	1	6	10.1	2	5	0	0	1.000	1	1	0	0	1.00
Wang,Chien-Ming, NYY	R	.000	3	0	0	0	0	.000	11	0	0	0	0	0	0	8	0	15	95.0	7	13	0	0	1.000	11	3	0	0	.27
Washburn,Jarrod, Sea	L	.000	6	0	0	0	0	.237	38	9	0	0	0	4	5	11	7	28	153.2	11	20	1	2	.969	9	4	2	0	.44
Wassermann,E., CWS	R	-	0	0	0	0	0	-	0	0	0	0	0	0	0	0	0	24	19.2	0	4	0	0	1.000	6	1	0	0	.17
Waters,Chris, Bal	L	-	0	0	0	0	0	-	0	0	0	0	0	0	0	0	0	11	64.2	11	5	1	1	.941	3	0	0	0	.00
Weathers,David, Cin	R	-	0	0	0	0	0	.101	139	14	0	0	2	4	7	85	16	72	69.1	6	2	2	2	.778	3	0	0	0	.00
Weaver,Jered, LAA	R	.000	4	0	0	0	0	.125	8	1	0	0	0	0	3	0	0	30	176.2	10	11	2	0	.913	25	5	0	2	.20
Webb,Brandon, Ari	R	.149	67	10	0	11	13	.113	389	44	9	0	0	29	10	181	55	34	226.2	18	54	2	4	.973	34	10	1	0	.29
Wellemeyer,Todd, StL	R	.155	58	9	0	5	12	.148	81	12	0	0	0	6	2	41	16	32	191.2	19	15	2	0	.944	13	6	1	1	.46
Wells,Jared, SD-Sea	R	-	0	0	0	0	0	-	0	0	0	0	0	0	0	0	0	9	8.1	1	2	0	0	1.000	2	0	0	0	.00
Wells,Kip, Col-KC	R	.000	5	0	0	0	1	.198	308	61	10	1	4	17	4	134	27	25	37.2	1	7	1	0	.889	3	2	1	0	.67
Wells,Randy, Tor-ChC	R	-	0	0	0	0	0	-	0	0	0	0	0	0	0	0	0	4	5.1	0	0	0	0	-	0	0	0	0	-
Westbrook,Jake, Cle	R	-	0	0	0	0	0	.167	12	2	1	0	0	1	1	8	3	5	34.2	3	8	1	1	.917	2	2	1	0	1.00
Wheeler,Dan, TB	R	-	0	0	0	0	0	.143	7	1	0	0	0	0	0	1	1	70	66.1	4	2	1	0	.857	2	1	0	0	.50
White,Bill, Tex	L	-	0	0	0	0	0	-	0	0	0	0	0	0	0	0	0	8	4.0	1	0	0	0	1.000	0	0	0	0	-
Willis,Dontrelle, Det	L	-	0	0	0	0	0	.234	351	82	10	5	8	35	21	64	29	8	24.0	1	2	0	0	1.000	0	0	0	0	-

Pitchers Hitting, Fielding and Holding Runners

Pitcher	T	2008 Hitting						Career Hitting											2008 Fielding and Holding Runners											
		Avg	AB	H	HR	RBI	SH	Avg	AB	H	2B	3B	HR	RBI	BB	SO	SH	G	Inn	PO	A	E	DP	Pct	SBA	CS	PCS	PPO	CS%
Wilson,Brian, SF	R	-	0	0	0	0	0	.000	2	0	0	0	0	0	0	1	1	63	62.1	3	6	0	1	1.000	3	1	0	0	.33
Wilson,C.J., Tex	L	-	0	0	0	0	0	-	0	0	0	0	0	0	0	0	0	50	46.1	4	8	1	0	.923	2	1	0	0	.50
Wise,Matt, NYM	R	-	0	0	0	0	0	.286	7	2	0	0	0	1	0	2	1	8	7.0	0	1	0	0	1.000	1	0	0	0	.00
Wolf,Randy, SD-Hou	L	.138	58	8	0	2	5	.184	441	81	22	0	4	38	29	148	57	33	190.1	9	24	2	2	.943	13	5	1	1	.38
Wolfe,Brian, Tor	R	-	0	0	0	0	0	-	0	0	0	0	0	0	0	0	0	20	22.0	3	4	0	0	1.000	1	0	0	0	.00
Wood,Kerry, ChC	R	-	0	0	0	0	0	.171	345	59	6	0	7	32	11	113	46	65	66.1	4	3	0	0	1.000	1	0	0	0	.00
Woods,Jake, Sea	L	-	0	0	0	0	0	-	0	0	0	0	0	0	0	0	0	15	19.0	1	1	0	1	1.000	0	0	0	0	-
Worrell,Mark, StL	R	.500	2	1	1	3	0	.500	2	1	0	0	1	3	0	0	0	4	5.2	0	1	0	0	1.000	0	0	0	0	-
Wright,Jamey, Tex	R	-	0	0	0	0	0	.147	436	64	15	1	1	17	12	175	51	75	84.1	12	21	2	1	.943	10	1	0	2	.10
Wright,Wesley, Hou	L	-	0	0	0	0	0	-	0	0	0	0	0	0	0	0	0	71	55.2	2	7	0	1	1.000	5	0	0	0	.00
Wuertz,Mike, ChC	R	.000	1	0	0	0	0	.000	6	0	0	0	0	0	0	5	1	45	44.2	5	6	1	0	.917	7	3	0	0	.43
Yabu,Keiichi, SF	R	.000	1	0	0	0	0	.000	2	0	0	0	0	0	1	0	0	60	68.0	6	6	3	0	.800	3	0	0	0	.00
Yabuta,Yasuhiko, KC	R	-	0	0	0	0	0	-	0	0	0	0	0	0	0	0	0	31	37.2	4	2	1	0	.857	4	0	0	0	.00
Yates,Tyler, Pit	R	-	0	0	0	0	0	.083	12	1	0	0	0	0	0	6	1	72	73.1	4	10	1	0	.933	5	1	0	0	.20
Young,Chris, SD	R	.107	28	3	1	2	6	.120	133	16	4	1	1	8	6	55	20	18	102.1	7	8	1	1	.938	17	2	0	1	.12
Zambrano,Carlos, ChC	R	.337	83	28	4	14	2	.239	494	118	19	3	16	47	5	175	30	30	188.2	21	21	3	1	.933	19	9	0	3	.47
Ziegler,Brad, Oak	R	-	0	0	0	0	0	-	0	0	0	0	0	0	0	0	0	47	59.2	0	14	0	2	1.000	1	0	0	2	.00
Zink,Charlie, Bos	R	-	0	0	0	0	0	-	0	0	0	0	0	0	0	0	0	1	4.1	0	2	0	0	1.000	0	0	0	0	-
Zito,Barry, SF	L	.118	51	6	0	2	4	.099	142	14	0	0	0	5	6	41	11	32	180.0	7	20	1	0	.964	10	4	1	1	.40
Zumaya,Joel, Det	R	-	0	0	0	0	0	-	0	0	0	0	0	0	0	0	0	21	23.1	0	1	0	0	1.000	1	0	0	0	.00

Hitters Pitching

Player	2008 Pitching											Career Pitching										
	G	W	L	Sv	IP	H	R	ER	BB	SO	ERA	G	W	L	Sv	IP	H	R	ER	BB	SO	ERA
Ankiel,Rick, StL	0	0	0	0	0.0	0	0	0	0	0	-	51	13	10	1	242.0	198	119	105	130	269	3.90
Burke,Jamie, Sea	1	0	1	0	1.0	1	1	1	0	0	9.00	1	0	1	0	1.0	1	1	1	0	0	9.00
Loretta,Mark, Hou	0	0	0	0	0.0	0	0	0	0	0	-	1	0	0	0	1.0	1	0	0	1	2	0.00
Miles,Aaron, StL	1	0	0	0	1.0	0	0	0	0	0	0.00	3	0	0	0	3.0	3	2	2	0	0	6.00
Nunez,Abraham, NYM	0	0	0	0	0.0	0	0	0	0	0	-	1	0	0	0	0.1	0	0	0	0	0	0.00
Ojeda,Augie, Ari	0	0	0	0	0.0	0	0	0	0	0	-	1	0	0	0	1.0	0	0	0	0	0	0.00
Pena,Tony F, KC	1	0	0	0	1.0	0	0	0	0	1	0.00	1	0	0	0	1.0	0	0	0	0	1	0.00
Perez,Tomas, Hou	0	0	0	0	0.0	0	0	0	0	0	-	1	0	0	0	0.1	0	0	0	0	0	0.00
Wood,Jason, Fla	0	0	0	0	0.0	0	0	0	0	0	-	1	0	0	0	1.0	0	0	0	0	0	0.00

Manufactured Runs

Bill James

Look at this: The Minnesota Twins in 2008 manufactured 213 runs—the most of any major league team—while allowing only 139 manufactured runs, one of the lowest totals in the majors. The Twins outscored their opponents by only 28 runs on the season, but by 74 manufactured runs.

What is a Manufactured Run, you ask? (Kick him again, Johnny; he didn't ask loud enough.) A Manufactured Run, by our definition, is

a) any run on which two or more of the bases come from something other than playing station-to-station baseball, or

b) a run that scores without a hit, or with only infield hits.

If two or more of the four bases come from infield hits, moving up on a ground ball, moving up on a fly ball, stolen base, bunt, wild pitch, passed ball, anything like that. . .that's a manufactured run.

Actually, in a lame effort to satisfy everybody, we track two types of manufactured runs. MR1 are *deliberately* manufactured runs, manufactured runs that involve a stolen base, a bunt, or a pinch runner. MR2 are manufactured runs that don't involve a manager's gambit. A little more than 60% of manufactured runs are MR2.

These are a few of the things we learn from studying these Manufactured Run charts:

1) The best teams in the majors at manufacturing a run were the Twins, the Mets, the Dodgers, and the Angels.

2) The teams least inclined to manufacture a run were the Padres, Marlins, White Sox, D-Backs and Orioles.

3) The most difficult teams to manufacture a run against were the Blue Jays, Cubs, Astros, Rays and A's.

4) The easiest teams against which to manufacture a run were the Orioles, Rangers, Nationals, Pirates and D-Backs.

5) The standard deviation of manufactured runs is higher from a defensive standpoint than from an offensive standpoint (meaning that manufactured runs occur a little more because of what the defense doesn't do than because of what the offense does.)

6) The major league players who contributed the most to manufactured runs were Ichiro, Jose Reyes, Carlos Beltran, Carlos Gomez, Ian Kinsler, Willy Taveras and Shane Victorino. Reyes led the majors in 2007.

7) An average major league team manufactures about one run per game—156 in 162 games, on average.

8) Manufactured runs do not appear to have a disproportionate impact on wins. The teams that had manufactured run advantages do not appear, overall, to be especially efficient teams in terms of producing wins from runs.

American League

Team	MR	MR1	MR2
Minnesota Twins	213	95	118
Los Angeles Angels	181	65	116
Seattle Mariners	173	68	105
Kansas City Royals	173	51	122
Tampa Bay Rays	168	62	106
New York Yankees	166	52	114
Toronto Blue Jays	157	54	103
Texas Rangers	157	46	111
Detroit Tigers	145	41	104
Boston Red Sox	145	57	88
Cleveland Indians	144	41	103
Oakland Athletics	137	38	99
Baltimore Orioles	136	38	98
Chicago White Sox	129	31	98

American League Opponents

Team	MR	MR1	MR2
Baltimore Orioles	214	74	140
Texas Rangers	202	68	134
Seattle Mariners	174	55	119
Kansas City Royals	172	46	126
Boston Red Sox	164	60	104
Detroit Tigers	162	46	116
Los Angeles Angels	151	51	100
New York Yankees	147	54	93
Chicago White Sox	144	54	90
Cleveland Indians	142	51	91
Minnesota Twins	139	36	103
Oakland Athletics	127	41	86
Tampa Bay Rays	125	43	82
Toronto Blue Jays	116	40	76

National League

Team	MR	MR1	MR2
New York Mets	207	82	125
Los Angeles Dodgers	186	87	99
San Francisco Giants	172	74	98
Houston Astros	162	63	99
Cincinnati Reds	161	74	87
Colorado Rockies	158	72	86
Chicago Cubs	154	53	101
Philadelphia Phillies	153	70	83
Pittsburgh Pirates	152	44	108
Washington Nationals	152	56	96
St Louis Cardinals	152	35	117
Milwaukee Brewers	143	54	89
Atlanta Braves	139	51	88
Arizona Diamondbacks	133	38	95
Florida Marlins	125	40	85
San Diego Padres	104	27	77

National League Opponents

Team	MR	MR1	MR2
Washington Nationals	195	79	116
Pittsburgh Pirates	180	67	113
Arizona Diamondbacks	176	65	111
San Diego Padres	173	76	97
Atlanta Braves	171	69	102
Cincinnati Reds	169	58	111
Los Angeles Dodgers	167	70	97
San Francisco Giants	164	66	98
Florida Marlins	162	73	89
Colorado Rockies	161	62	99
Milwaukee Brewers	149	51	98
New York Mets	132	47	85
Philadelphia Phillies	131	41	90
St Louis Cardinals	128	38	90
Houston Astros	124	35	89
Chicago Cubs	116	43	73

American League Top Ten

Player	Tm	MRC	MRC1	MRC2
Suzuki, Ichiro	Sea	44	26	18
Gomez, Carlos	Min	34	29	5
Kinsler, Ian	Tex	32	10	22
Ellsbury, Jacoby	Bos	30	20	10
Figgins, Chone	LAA	29	18	11
Granderson, Curtis	Det	29	10	19
Span, Denard	Min	28	14	14
Cabrera, Orlando	CWS	27	9	18
Iwamura, Akinori	TB	26	5	21
Rodriguez, Alex	NYY	25	4	21
Upton, B.J.	TB	25	11	14

National League Top Ten

Player	Tm	MRC	MRC1	MRC2
Reyes, Jose	NYM	42	31	11
Beltran, Carlos	NYM	37	10	27
Taveras, Willy	Col	32	25	7
Victorino, Shane	Phi	32	17	15
McLouth, Nate	Pit	31	9	22
Lewis, Fred	SF	29	11	18
Ramirez, Hanley	Fla	29	16	13
Winn, Randy	SF	28	15	13
Kemp, Matt	LAD	26	15	11
Berkman, Lance	Hou	24	6	18

MRC= Manufactured Run Contributions

Top Three From Each Team

Arizona Diamondbacks

Player	MRC	MRC1	MRC2
Jackson, Conor	22	7	15
Drew, Stephen	16	4	12
Reynolds, Mark	15	4	11

Atlanta Braves

Player	MRC	MRC1	MRC2
Blanco, Gregor	20	12	8
Johnson, Kelly	17	6	11
Francoeur, Jeff	15	3	12

Baltimore Orioles

Player	MRC	MRC1	MRC2
Roberts, Brian	20	12	8
Markakis, Nick	19	3	16
Huff, Aubrey	16	3	13

Boston Red Sox

Player	MRC	MRC1	MRC2
Ellsbury, Jacoby	30	20	10
Pedroia, Dustin	20	3	17
Crisp, Coco	15	10	5

Chicago Cubs

Player	MRC	MRC1	MRC2
Theriot, Ryan	22	7	15
Soriano, Alfonso	19	8	11
Ramirez, Aramis	18	2	16

Chicago White Sox

Player	MRC	MRC1	MRC2
Cabrera, Orlando	27	9	18
Ramirez, Alexei	19	6	13
Quentin, Carlos	13	2	11

Cincinnati Reds

Player	MRC	MRC1	MRC2
Phillips, Brandon	23	9	14
Patterson, Corey	17	11	6
Hairston, Jerry	17	9	8

Cleveland Indians

Player	MRC	MRC1	MRC2
Sizemore, Grady	23	11	12
Carroll, Jamey	16	3	13
Peralta, Jhonny	15	4	11

Colorado Rockies

Player	MRC	MRC1	MRC2
Taveras, Willy	32	25	7
Holliday, Matt	20	7	13
Quintanilla, Omar	14	8	6

Detroit Tigers

Player	MRC	MRC1	MRC2
Granderson, Curtis	29	10	19
Polanco, Placido	21	6	15
Guillen, Carlos	13	3	10
Renteria, Edgar	13	6	7

Florida Marlins

Player	MRC	MRC1	MRC2
Ramirez, Hanley	29	16	13
Uggla, Dan	21	5	16
Hermida, Jeremy	11	1	10

Houston Astros

Player	MRC	MRC1	MRC2
Berkman, Lance	24	6	18
Bourn, Michael	21	15	6
Pence, Hunter	17	7	10

Kansas City Royals

Player	MRC	MRC1	MRC2
Gathright, Joey	20	11	9
Aviles, Mike	19	3	16
Gordon, Alex	17	2	15
DeJesus, David	17	5	12

Los Angeles Angels

Player	MRC	MRC1	MRC2
Figgins, Chone	29	18	11
Hunter, Torii	24	7	17
Aybar, Erick	21	5	16

Los Angeles Dodgers

Player	MRC	MRC1	MRC2
Kemp, Matt	26	15	11
Pierre, Juan	22	17	5
Martin, Russell	21	6	15

Milwaukee Brewers

Player	MRC	MRC1	MRC2
Weeks, Rickie	22	11	11
Hart, Corey	18	8	10
Hardy, J.J.	16	4	12

Minnesota Twins

Player	MRC	MRC1	MRC2
Gomez, Carlos	34	29	5
Span, Denard	28	14	14
Young, Delmon	22	9	13

New York Mets

Player	MRC	MRC1	MRC2
Reyes, Jose	42	31	11
Beltran, Carlos	37	10	27
Wright, David	19	5	14

New York Yankees

Player	MRC	MRC1	MRC2
Rodriguez, Alex	25	4	21
Abreu, Bobby	22	8	14
Damon, Johnny	21	6	15

Oakland Athletics

Player	MRC	MRC1	MRC2
Crosby, Bobby	20	3	17
Suzuki, Kurt	14	3	11
Cust, Jack	14	3	11

Philadelphia Phillies

Player	MRC	MRC1	MRC2
Victorino, Shane	32	17	15
Rollins, Jimmy	20	9	11
Werth, Jayson	19	10	9

Pittsburgh Pirates

Player	MRC	MRC1	MRC2
McLouth, Nate	31	9	22
Mientkiewicz, Doug	16	3	13
Bay, Jason	13	6	7
Sanchez, Freddy	13	1	12

San Diego Padres

Player	MRC	MRC1	MRC2
Giles, Brian	11	3	8
Kouzmanoff, Kevin	11	1	10
Gonzalez, Adrian	10	1	9

San Francisco Giants

Player	MRC	MRC1	MRC2
Lewis, Fred	29	11	18
Winn, Randy	28	15	13
Burriss, Emmanuel	14	11	3

Seattle Mariners

Player	MRC	MRC1	MRC2
Suzuki, Ichiro	44	26	18
Ibanez, Raul	18	3	15
Betancourt, Yuniesky	18	5	13
Lopez, Jose	18	3	15

St Louis Cardinals

Player	MRC	MRC1	MRC2
Ludwick, Ryan	19	2	17
Izturis, Cesar	16	10	6
Schumaker, Skip	16	2	14

Tampa Bay Rays

Player	MRC	MRC1	MRC2
Iwamura, Akinori	26	5	21
Upton, B.J.	25	11	14
Crawford, Carl	16	9	7

Texas Rangers

Player	MRC	MRC1	MRC2
Kinsler, Ian	32	10	22
Laird, Gerald	18	7	11
Young, Michael	15	3	12

Toronto Blue Jays

Player	MRC	MRC1	MRC2
Scutaro, Marco	20	6	14
Inglett, Joe	17	8	9
Rios, Alex	17	9	8

Washington Nationals

Player	MRC	MRC1	MRC2
Guzman, Cristian	18	4	14
Harris, Willie	17	7	10
Milledge, Lastings	16	9	7

The Manager's Record

Bill James

Tony LaRussa in 2008 issued only one intentional walk that blew up in his face. Ron Washington and Bobby Cox, on the other hand, issued 20 each.

What does that mean, that an intentional walk "exploded" on the manager who had issued it? It means that multiple runs scored in the inning after the walk. An intentional walk is scored as a "good" walk if

a) the next batter grounds into a double play, or

b) they get out of the inning with no additional runs scoring.

It is scored as "not good" if a run scores after the walk (except in the case of a double play. . .the double play always controls), and it is scored as a "bomb" if multiple runs score.

We are trying to assemble a factual record to distinguish how one manager differs from another. Last year in this article we pointed out that Bruce Bochy had let his starting pitcher throw more than 110 pitchers 36 times, whereas Ron Washington had done so only 4 times. In 2008 Washington was up to 11, but Bochy was up to 42.

Last year in this article we pointed out that Bob Melvin had used 146 different lineups, whereas Charlie Manuel had used only 87. In 2008 Melvin trimmed down to 134 different lineups, but Manuel used only 77.

We may, then, be beginning to identify some actual managerial tendencies: Bochy is willing to let his starter work, Washington errs on the side of caution, Manuel likes a set lineup, Melvin likes to experiment more. That's what we're trying to do: we're trying to pollute the discussion of managers with actual facts.

But the facts only become meaningful when there are standards, and the standards are slow to come into focus. A .270 batting average, .295. . .it looks about the same unless you understand the standard. 65 RBI, 80...what difference does it make? We're trying to establish the standards. It's a slow process, but we think we're gaining a little traction.

Categories of this record are Games Managed (G), Number of Different Lineups Used (LUp), the percentage of players who had the platoon advantage at the start of the game (PL%), Pinch Hitters Used (PH), Pinch Runners Used (PR), Defensive Substitutes Used (DS), Quick Hooks (Quick), Slow Hooks (Slow), Long Outings by Starting Pitchers (LO), Relievers Used on Consecutive Days (RCD), Long Saves (LS), Relievers Used (Rel), Stolen Base Attempts (SBA), Sacrifice Bunts Attempts (SacA), Runners Moving with the Pitch (RM), Pitchouts ordered (PO), Intentional Walks issued (#), Intentional Walks resulting in a Good Outcome (Good), Intentional Walks resulting Not in a Good Outcome (NG), Intentional Walks Blowing up on the Manager (Bomb), Wins (W), Losses (L) and Winning Percentage (Pct.).

Manny Acta

Year	Team	Lg	G	LUp	PL%	PH	PR	DS	Quick	Slow	LO	RCD	LS	Rel	SBA	SacA	RM	PO	#	Good	NG	Bomb	W	L	Pct
				LINEUPS		**SUBSTITUTION**			**PITCHER USAGE**						**TACTICS**				**INTENTIONAL BB**				**RESULTS**		
2007	Nationals	NL	162	101	.65	295	32	**78**	53	28	5	183	1	**588**	92	86	70	28	44	28	16	8	73	89	.451
2008	Nationals	NL	161	133	.62	293	31	39	38	46	6	119	4	517	124	95	63	24	44	27	17	8	59	**102**	.366
	162-Game Average			117	.64	295	32	59	46	37	6	151	3	554	108	91	67	26	44	28	17	8	66	96	.407

Felipe Alou

Year	Team	Lg	G	LUp	PL%	PH	PR	DS	Quick	Slow	LO	RCD	LS	Rel	SBA	SacA	RM	PO	#	Good	NG	Bomb	W	L	Pct
				LINEUPS		**SUBSTITUTION**			**PITCHER USAGE**						**TACTICS**				**INTENTIONAL BB**				**RESULTS**		
1994	Expos	NL	114	72	.48	143	33	7	51	18	0	60	26	259	173	72		20	24	17	7	3	74	40	.649
1995	Expos	NL	144	116	.49	200	36	10	48	28	7	80	18	396	169	74		22	20	7	13	6	66	78	.458
1996	Expos	NL	162	113	.49	240	31	30	**60**	27	13	85	18	433	142	97		25	25	16	9	2	88	74	.543
1997	Expos	NL	162	138	.58	205	22	40	**52**	41	15	78	13	390	121	91		30	33	16	17	9	78	84	.481
1998	Expos	NL	162	133	.50	235	27	37	56	26	2	109	15	443	137	**111**		18	30	21	9	7	65	97	.401
1999	Expos	NL	162	**143**	.49	247	33	**55**	45	36	5	101	10	432	121	84		26	28	16	12	5	68	94	.420
2000	Expos	NL	162	120	.61	211	24	32	51	36	5	113	15	452	106	103		18	29	19	10	5	67	95	.414
2001	Expos	NL	53	40	.58	84	4	5	18	12	1	37	1	171	39	28		7	10	6	4	0	21	32	.396
2003	Giants	NL	161	127	.56	202	32	42	46	27	26	113	5	461	90	93	33	9	34	19	15	7	100	61	.621
2004	Giants	NL	162	**138**	.67	239	47	60	25	50	**45**	154	8	**521**	66	105	109	2	35	21	14	8	91	71	.562
2005	Giants	NL	162	**139**	.62	242	33	49	29	46	37	**145**	6	**511**	106	109	120	12	42	26	16	7	75	87	.463
2006	Giants	NL	161	123	.64	215	57	57	23	50	**44**	98	5	438	83	100	84	14	37	24	13	6	76	85	.472
	162-Game Average			129	.56	226	35	39	46	36	18	108	13	450	124	98	87	19	32	19	13	6	80	82	.494

Dusty Baker

Year	Team	Lg	G	LUp	PL%	PH	PR	DS	Quick	Slow	LO	RCD	LS	Rel	SBA	SacA	RM	PO	#	Good	NG	Bomb	W	L	Pct
				LINEUPS		**SUBSTITUTION**			**PITCHER USAGE**						**TACTICS**				**INTENTIONAL BB**				**RESULTS**		
1994	Giants	NL	115	76	.53	177	16	9	29	25	2	86	12	288	154	88		78	24	8	16	8	55	60	.478
1995	Giants	NL	144	96	.41	230	36	13	32	50	8	90	8	381	184	101		77	33	14	19	14	67	77	.465
1996	Giants	NL	162	129	.51	250	17	15	24	**58**	15	94	8	425	166	103		**96**	45	22	23	15	68	94	.420
1997	Giants	NL	162	114	**.71**	212	17	22	46	25	17	132	4	**481**	170	85		**93**	37	16	21	12	90	72	.556
1998	Giants	NL	163	130	.62	224	20	12	43	38	8	113	5	433	153	**111**		41	**51**	25	26	9	89	74	.546
1999	Giants	NL	162	120	.62	233	16	16	30	**51**	27	111		450	165	**113**		40	28	12	16	10	86	76	.531
2000	Giants	NL	162	82	.56	233	26	22	38	**50**	25	91	3	384	118	86		37	16	7	9	2	**97**	65	.599
2001	Giants	NL	162	122	.48	261	22	19	40	**48**	10	114	4	439	99	95		45	32	16	16	6	90	72	.556
2002	Giants	NL	162	118	.43	223	32	38	29	56	53	106	8	417	95	89	42	41	44	28	16	10	95	66	.590
2003	Cubs	NL	162	114	.49	227	25	43	24	58	65	111	3	420	104	93	31	24	36	23	13	4	88	74	.543
2004	Cubs	NL	162	113	.44	254	16	19	37	41	42	129	8	460	94	108	71	62	33	22	11	7	89	73	.549
2005	Cubs	NL	162	121	.59	240	21	29	40	46	36	103	2	457	104	88	107	70	48	27	21	7	79	83	.488
2006	Cubs	NL	162	133	.56	271	9	26	45	39	22	**165**	2	**542**	170	108	139	46	44	28	16	11	66	**96**	.407
2008	Reds	NL	162	119	.58	285	28	27	26	**63**	39	124	2	507	132	100	101	37	40	28	12	4	74	88	.457
	162-Game Average			117	.54	247	22	23	36	48	27	115	5	447	140	101	82	58	38	20	17	9	83	79	.512

Buddy Bell

Year	Team	Lg	G	LUp	PL%	PH	PR	DS	Quick	Slow	LO	RCD	LS	Rel	SBA	SacA	RM	PO	#	Good	NG	Bomb	W	L	Pct
				LINEUPS		**SUBSTITUTION**			**PITCHER USAGE**						**TACTICS**				**INTENTIONAL BB**				**RESULTS**		
1996	Tigers	AL	162	128	.50	123	29	17	17	27	26	82	8	**426**	137	63		13	40	6	34	19	53	**109**	.327
1997	Tigers	AL	162	116	.61	163	19	22	24	7	12	113	11	417	**233**	44		32	24	8	16	10	79	83	.488
1998	Tigers	AL	137	88	.58	102	25	7	15	15	10	89	4	362	143	24		38	29	8	21	15	52	85	.380
2000	Rockies	NL	162	106	**.64**	285	21	8	12	18	10	106	8	480	192	100		40	**53**	20	33	16	82	80	.506
2001	Rockies	NL	162	116	**.61**	314	27	14	18	30	8	117	6	476	186	108		43	43	12	31	13	73	89	.451
2002	Rockies	NL	22	15	.55	42	1	5	5	11	3	21	0	69	17	10	8	5	11	5	6	4	6	16	.273
2005	Royals	AL	112	93	.61	97	18	8	32	23	3	50	4	310	48	38	80	25	17	9	8	6	43	69	.384
2006	Royals	AL	152	132	.57	87	27	25	40	37	13	86	6	439	95	**63**	84	13	40	20	20	10	58	94	.382
2007	Royals	AL	162	**141**	.55	119	30	28	49	28	16	74	10	448	122	59	125	25	54	33	21	9	69	93	.426
	162-Game Average			123	.58	175	26	18	28	26	13	97	7	450	154	67	107	31	41	16	25	13	68	94	.420

Bud Black

Year	Team	Lg	G	LUp	PL%	PH	PR	DS	Quick	Slow	LO	RCD	LS	Rel	SBA	SacA	RM	PO	#	Good	NG	Bomb	W	L	Pct
				LINEUPS		**SUBSTITUTION**			**PITCHER USAGE**						**TACTICS**				**INTENTIONAL BB**				**RESULTS**		
2007	Padres	NL	163	115	.62	279	18	13	**63**	28	13	122	0	485	79	85	73	56	48	28	20	11	89	74	.546
2008	Padres	NL	162	113	.63	286	25	20	55	36	17	109	0	491	53	75	78	31	61	30	31	17	63	99	.389
	162-Game Average			114	.62	282	21	16	59	32	15	115	0	486	66	80	75	43	54	29	25	14	76	86	.469

Bruce Bochy

Year	Team	Lg	G	LUp	PL%	PH	PR	DS	Quick	Slow	LO	RCD	LS	Rel	SBA	SacA	RM	PO	#	Good	NG	Bomb	W	L	Pct
1995	Padres	NL	144	96	.59	262	30	23	44	41	17	38	3	337	170	68		38	26	8	18	11	70	74	.486
1996	Padres	NL	162	114	.52	289	29	15	51	33	10	67	12	411	164	73		65	42	24	18	12	91	71	.562
1997	Padres	NL	162	111	.60	291	26	9	45	45	3	81	11	426	200	84		58	24	7	17	11	76	86	.469
1998	Padres	NL	162	110	.65	280	62	44	44	45	9	81	12	369	116	84		27	30	16	14	10	98	64	.605
1999	Padres	NL	162	137	.60	298	51	21	44	36	4	68	5	403	241	60		29	39	20	19	13	74	88	.457
2000	Padres	NL	162	134	.52	285	44	14	41	47	14	105	5	443	184	52		27	40	11	29	11	76	86	.469
2001	Padres	NL	162	116	.60	255	54	27	32	47	6	85	10	422	173	43		23	40	17	23	13	79	83	.488
2002	Padres	NL	162	123	.66	259	44	56	39	40	17	106	4	459	115	63	74	14	61	38	23	14	66	96	.407
2003	Padres	NL	162	134	.58	339	20	29	34	43	16	100	3	473	115	63	41	6	52	33	19	12	64	98	.395
2004	Padres	NL	162	96	.54	261	28	47	47	32	15	76	3	437	77	75	96	14	39	24	15	10	87	75	.537
2005	Padres	NL	162	128	.58	285	31	49	46	36	23	87	1	456	143	89	111	16	45	33	12	8	82	80	.506
2006	Padres	NL	162	111	.60	264	64	48	43	42	24	111	2	475	154	77	110	21	63	43	20	10	88	74	.543
2007	Giants	NL	162	128	.72	264	50	45	26	50	36	132	2	496	152	86	119	10	41	29	12	3	71	91	.438
2008	Giants	NL	162	134	.68	276	32	39	24	59	42	97	6	478	154	77	155	5	59	40	19	8	72	90	.444
	162-Game Average			120	.60	281	41	34	40	43	17	89	6	438	155	72	101	25	43	25	19	11	79	83	.488

Cecil Cooper

Year	Team	Lg	G	LUp	PL%	PH	PR	DS	Quick	Slow	LO	RCD	LS	Rel	SBA	SacA	RM	PO	#	Good	NG	Bomb	W	L	Pct
2007	Astros	NL	31	26	.42	63	8	23	10	5	2	11	0	88	19	16	20	4	14	8	6	4	15	16	.484
2008	Astros	NL	161	115	.58	252	16	47	60	35	14	108	2	488	166	81	112	5	53	35	18	11	86	75	.534
	162-Game Average			119	.55	266	20	59	59	34	14	100	2	486	156	82	111	8	57	36	20	13	85	77	.525

Bobby Cox

Year	Team	Lg	G	LUp	PL%	PH	PR	DS	Quick	Slow	LO	RCD	LS	Rel	SBA	SacA	RM	PO	#	Good	NG	Bomb	W	L	Pct
1994	Braves	NL	114	64	.60	163	30	25	22	31	5	60	5	244	79	83		44	39	20	19	9	68	46	.596
1995	Braves	NL	144	59	.56	224	48	40	41	34	13	80	6	339	116	77		41	38	23	15	4	90	54	.625
1996	Braves	NL	162	89	.62	254	32	27	48	43	19	110	9	408	126	90		34	48	22	26	14	96	66	.593
1997	Braves	NL	162	87	.64	276	58	29	40	37	23	90	4	374	166	112		13	46	32	14	10	101	61	.623
1998	Braves	NL	162	80	.64	245	28	25	44	33	14	70	1	354	141	97		40	26	11	15	8	106	56	.654
1999	Braves	NL	162	76	.58	272	51	34	44	39	13	99	6	394	214	89		54	37	17	20	11	103	59	.636
2000	Braves	NL	162	103	.59	252	72	11	52	41	6	81	13	376	204	109		59	34	17	17	5	95	67	.586
2001	Braves	NL	162	113	.57	278	50	23	49	40	4	93	8	412	131	84		90	55	27	28	13	88	74	.543
2002	Braves	NL	161	105	.48	282	33	44	60	30	20	113	9	469	115	89	47	51	63	41	22	12	101	59	.631
2003	Braves	NL	162	69	.52	262	49	45	40	45	23	113	10	489	90	85	23	49	69	51	18	11	101	61	.623
2004	Braves	NL	162	105	.70	243	57	28	50	34	25	128	16	483	118	105	87	25	50	30	20	14	96	66	.593
2005	Braves	NL	162	110	.69	247	54	35	46	20	125	7		484	124	104	93	11	52	34	18	11	90	72	.556
2006	Braves	NL	162	85	.58	299	24	35	44	38	24	144	3	522	87	99	58	24	69	48	21	12	79	83	.488
2007	Braves	NL	162	86	.68	290	33	21	60	24	10	143	1	528	94	77	68	28	89	58	31	16	84	78	.519
2008	Braves	NL	162	117	.67	294	31	17	59	34	6	134	6	545	85	90	77	23	80	45	35	20	72	90	.444
	162-Game Average			92	.61	266	45	30	48	36	15	109	7	440	130	95	65	40	55	33	22	12	94	68	.580

Billy Doran

Year	Team	Lg	G	LUp	PL%	PH	PR	DS	Quick	Slow	LO	RCD	LS	Rel	SBA	SacA	RM	PO	#	Good	NG	Bomb	W	L	Pct
2006	Royals	AL	10	10	.50	5	2	0	4	1	0	4	0	34	4	7	4	0	5	4	1	0	4	6	.400
	162-Game Average			162	.50	81	32	0	65	16	0	65	0	551	65	113	65	0	81	65	16	0	65	97	.401

Terry Francona

Year	Team	Lg	G	LUp	PL%	PH	PR	DS	Quick	Slow	LO	RCD	LS	Rel	SBA	SacA	RM	PO	#	Good	NG	Bomb	W	L	Pct
1997	Phillies	NL	162	98	.66	288	19	28	28	54	22	102	9	409	148	91		30	31	12	19	9	68	94	.420
1998	Phillies	NL	162	84	.53	256	20	19	34	57	20	88	7	385	142	85		16	23	6	17	8	75	87	.463
1999	Phillies	NL	162	85	.51	239	13	31	29	41	16	111	7	441	160	81		27	17	7	10	6	77	85	.475
2000	Phillies	NL	162	108	.53	278	17	14	38	43	25	102	5	414	132	89		16	17	7	10	7	65	97	.401
2004	Red Sox	AL	162	141	.65	116	65	58	41	48	32	105	8	437	98	18	91	28	28	22	6	4	98	64	.605
2005	Red Sox	AL	162	104	.67	110	46	37	25	55	30	99	3	442	57	21	79	11	28	18	10	5	95	67	.586
2006	Red Sox	AL	162	116	.59	93	54	49	36	44	13	94	9	454	74	33	98	16	25	11	14	7	86	76	.531
2007	Red Sox	AL	162	109	.60	84	34	23	41	35	32	89	4	451	120	45	90	14	20	14	6	4	96	66	.593
2008	Red Sox	AL	162	131	.59	62	40	40	50	30	20	90	11	466	155	40	87	8	17	10	7	4	95	67	.586
	162-Game Average			108	.59	170	34	33	36	45	23	98	7	433	121	56	89	18	23	12	11	6	84	78	.519

Ron Gardenhire

Year	Team	Lg	G	LUp	PL%	PH	PR	DS	Quick	Slow	LO	RCD	LS	Rel	SBA	SacA	RM	PO	#	Good	NG	Bomb	W	L	Pct
2002	Twins	AL	161	111	.69	141	36	42	54	25	10	84	1	435	141	48	44	11	24	16	8	4	94	67	.584
2003	Twins	AL	162	126	.63	144	50	26	49	33	13	85	2	399	138	59	37	14	35	16	19	6	90	72	.556
2004	Twins	AL	162	131	.59	129	45	29	56	21	20	106	4	435	162	66	121	18	27	15	12	7	92	70	.568
2005	Twins	AL	162	135	.58	104	45	26	50	21	5	87	1	396	146	59	138	16	38	28	10	3	83	79	.512
2006	Twins	AL	162	97	.62	93	36	21	60	31	3	82	5	421	143	48	130	11	25	14	11	4	96	66	.593
2007	Twins	AL	162	139	.63	104	42	25	45	30	8	99	4	438	142	45	148	11	33	14	19	9	79	83	.488
2008	Twins	AL	163	103	.64	109	26	12	47	29	5	115	3	485	144	73	143	17	38	25	13	8	88	75	.540
162-Game Average				120	.62	118	40	26	52	27	9	94	3	430	145	57	109	14	31	18	13	6	89	73	.549

Phil Garner

Year	Team	Lg	G	LUp	PL%	PH	PR	DS	Quick	Slow	LO	RCD	LS	Rel	SBA	SacA	RM	PO	#	Good	NG	Bomb	W	L	Pct
1994	Brewers	AL	115	94	.53	53	33	24	31	35	0	44	5	252	96	46		23	16	6	10	9	53	62	.461
1995	Brewers	AL	144	120	.58	83	67	52	42	42	10	52	4	321	145	64		52	23	2	21	12	65	79	.451
1996	Brewers	AL	162	114	.58	115	48	46	50	36	13	61	12	385	149	72		82	20	1	19	11	80	82	.494
1997	Brewers	AL	161	128	.59	190	42	36	51	34	6	93	6	367	158	65		55	21	11	10	6	78	83	.484
1998	Brewers	NL	162	125	.59	265	54	46	52	43	6	90	9	416	140	85		59	21	12	9	4	74	88	.457
1999	Brewers	NL	112	69	.57	182	15	5	28	26	4	45	5	294	75	85		57	19	10	9	8	52	60	.464
2000	Tigers	AL	162	128	.53	126	30	25	35	38	8	109	3	429	121	58		26	13	5	8	6	79	83	.488
2001	Tigers	AL	162	116	.64	93	40	14	25	51	9	81	3	391	194	58		36	29	10	19	11	66	96	.407
2002	Tigers	AL	6	3	.63	1	1	0	1	3	3	2	0	15	4	2	3	0	2	0	2	2	0	6	.000
2004	Astros	NL	74	31	.54	142	20	35	27	15	14	71	4	241	78	40	40	7	24	20	4	1	48	26	.649
2005	Astros	NL	163	101	.48	251	40	63	55	34	21	118	3	434	159	99	148	10	29	17	12	7	89	73	.549
2006	Astros	NL	162	111	.47	287	17	47	55	36	18	157	2	497	115	123	114	26	65	31	34	17	82	80	.506
2007	Astros	NL	131	99	.52	230	14	36	31	44	17	120	0	388	79	88	84	23	48	27	21	11	58	73	.443
162-Game Average				117	.55	191	40	41	46	41	12	99	5	418	143	84	118	43	31	14	17	10	78	84	.481

Cito Gaston

Year	Team	Lg	G	LUp	PL%	PH	PR	DS	Quick	Slow	LO	RCD	LS	Rel	SBA	SacA	RM	PO	#	Good	NG	Bomb	W	L	Pct
1994	Blue Jays	AL	115	59	.55	41	16	21	7	14	2	23	5	221	105	44		48	16	8	8	6	55	60	.478
1995	Blue Jays	AL	144	82	.65	85	24	7	15	27	40	29	10	265	91	47		57	26	8	18	10	56	88	.389
1996	Blue Jays	AL	162	87	.70	126	23	11	12	27	23	41	4	303	154	63		34	19	5	14	9	74	88	.457
1997	Blue Jays	AL	157	90	.59	71	19	6	13	22	36	74	6	322	177	50		30	21	12	9	2	72	85	.459
2008	Blue Jays	AL	88	65	.59	36	18	30	18	19	25	40	0	216	37	41	37	11	16	8	8	6	51	37	.580
162-Game Average				93	.62	87	24	18	16	27	31	50	6	323	137	60	68	44	24	10	14	8	75	87	.463

Bob Geren

Year	Team	Lg	G	LUp	PL%	PH	PR	DS	Quick	Slow	LO	RCD	LS	Rel	SBA	SacA	RM	PO	#	Good	NG	Bomb	W	L	Pct
2007	Athletics	AL	162	140	.57	64	31	24	39	43	14	112	9	446	72	31	91	22	60	38	22	10	76	86	.469
2008	Athletics	AL	161	133	.59	91	57	37	49	32	5	87	8	441	109	44	62	18	45	25	20	10	75	86	.466
162-Game Average				137	.58	78	44	31	44	38	10	100	9	445	91	38	77	20	53	32	21	10	76	86	.469

John Gibbons

Year	Team	Lg	G	LUp	PL%	PH	PR	DS	Quick	Slow	LO	RCD	LS	Rel	SBA	SacA	RM	PO	#	Good	NG	Bomb	W	L	Pct
2004	Blue Jays	AL	50	36	.68	42	3	2	16	8	7	22	1	130	34	2	47	21	11	5	6	3	20	30	.400
2005	Blue Jays	AL	162	124	.66	148	11	37	55	18	9	77	12	432	107	28	128	45	29	13	16	9	80	82	.494
2006	Blue Jays	AL	162	120	.53	112	32	40	59	33	17	94	16	482	98	20	127	40	56	32	24	12	87	75	.537
2007	Blue Jays	AL	162	131	.46	139	48	33	45	37	31	75	9	420	79	35	99	37	34	17	17	6	83	79	.512
2008	Blue Jays	AL	74	60	.48	53	15	18	12	20	12	43	0	205	70	23	39	10	26	16	10	6	35	39	.473
162-Game Average				125	.56	131	29	35	50	31	20	83	10	443	103	29	117	41	41	22	19	10	81	81	.500

Joe Girardi

Year	Team	Lg	G	LUp	PL%	PH	PR	DS	Quick	Slow	LO	RCD	LS	Rel	SBA	SacA	RM	PO	#	Good	NG	Bomb	W	L	Pct
2006	Marlins	NL	162	117	.50	250	44	66	46	40	28	76	3	438	168	97	108	42	58	37	21	7	78	84	.481
2008	Yankees	AL	162	114	.63	97	37	42	60	37	12	88	10	475	157	38	173	36	37	22	15	8	89	73	.549
162-Game Average				116	.56	174	41	54	53	39	20	82	7	457	163	68	141	39	48	30	18	8	84	78	.519

Fredi Gonzalez

Year	Team	Lg	G	LINEUPS LUp	PL%	SUB PH	PR	DS	Quick	Slow	LO	RCD	LS	Rel	SBA	SacA	RM	PO	IBB #	Good	NG	Bomb	W	L	Pct
2007	Marlins	NL	162	96	.50	284	29	34	33	56	20	138	5	560	139	91	79	22	60	36	24	**16**	71	91	.438
2008	Marlins	NL	161	106	.51	255	38	49	38	39	8	120	3	511	104	61	75	17	66	42	24	14	84	77	.522
	162-Game Average			101	.51	270	34	42	36	48	14	129	4	537	122	76	77	20	63	39	24	15	78	84	.481

Ozzie Guillen

Year	Team	Lg	G	LINEUPS LUp	PL%	SUB PH	PR	DS	Quick	Slow	LO	RCD	LS	Rel	SBA	SacA	RM	PO	IBB #	Good	NG	Bomb	W	L	Pct
2004	White Sox	AL	162	134	.58	**132**	35	15	28	**65**	48	86	8	399	129	**84**	97	17	36	15	**21**	8	83	79	.512
2005	White Sox	AL	162	112	.51	100	32	21	31	56	35	114	5	412	204	68	148	15	**42**	27	15	6	**99**	63	.611
2006	White Sox	AL	162	87	.60	**135**	42	38	28	68	35	83	7	398	141	61	85	27	**59**	39	20	9	90	72	.556
2007	White Sox	AL	162	124	.56	100	26	23	26	53	33	**131**	2	463	123	54	92	13	50	24	**26**	**15**	72	90	.444
2008	White Sox	AL	163	100	.52	75	49	37	42	48	14	100	3	463	101	44	98	8	42	29	13	6	89	74	.546
	162-Game Average			111	.55	108	37	27	31	58	33	103	5	426	139	62	104	16	46	27	19	9	86	76	.531

Mike Hargrove

Year	Team	Lg	G	LINEUPS LUp	PL%	SUB PH	PR	DS	Quick	Slow	LO	RCD	LS	Rel	SBA	SacA	RM	PO	IBB #	Good	NG	Bomb	W	L	Pct
1994	Indians	AL	113	53	.67	79	18	31	23	31	3	41	4	222	179	43		40	22	8	14	7	66	47	.584
1995	Indians	AL	144	64	.66	101	34	21	36	23	12	61	3	335	185	40		22	12	5	7	3	**100**	44	.694
1996	Indians	AL	161	96	.56	115	20	25	39	31	14	70	5	382	210	58		41	31	11	20	11	**99**	62	.615
1997	Indians	AL	161	109	.58	86	17	14	34	46	14	101	9	429	177	60		37	30	7	23	10	86	75	.534
1998	Indians	AL	162	108	**.62**	88	21	32	29	39	19	104	9	423	203	53		47	**39**	17	22	13	89	73	.549
1999	Indians	AL	162	123	**.66**	99	25	22	41	44	15	99	3	**466**	**197**	82		28	**36**	14	22	13	97	65	.599
2000	Orioles	AL	162	107	.54	77	42	19	25	**55**	24	84	2	396	**191**	36		31	21	10	11	2	74	**88**	.457
2001	Orioles	AL	162	**139**	.53	82	27	20	39	42	3	74	10	392	186	57		**71**	17	7	10	7	63	**98**	.391
2002	Orioles	AL	162	125	.52	127	22	22	36	46	32	74	6	407	158	54	26	42	34	22	12	6	67	95	.414
2003	Orioles	AL	163	120	.52	78	37	22	29	52	48	89	5	425	125	67	45	16	43	20	**23**	11	71	91	.438
2005	Mariners	AL	162	97	.52	125	24	18	30	45	31	73	1	433	149	61	120	36	32	21	11	7	69	93	.426
2006	Mariners	AL	162	84	.51	121	21	20	24	52	24	81	14	429	143	40	124	17	50	26	**24**	**16**	78	84	.481
2007	Mariners	AL	78	48	.47	41	18	21	20	26	9	44	7	209	55	22	58	13	20	12	8	4	45	33	.577
	162-Game Average			106	.57	101	27	24	34	44	21	83	6	411	179	56	83	37	32	15	17	9	83	79	.512

Trey Hillman

Year	Team	Lg	G	LINEUPS LUp	PL%	SUB PH	PR	DS	Quick	Slow	LO	RCD	LS	Rel	SBA	SacA	RM	PO	IBB #	Good	NG	Bomb	W	L	Pct
2008	Royals	AL	162	134	.55	71	44	34	35	48	19	78	2	439	117	50	96	15	15	9	6	3	75	87	.463
	162-Game Average			134	.55	71	44	34	35	48	19	78	2	439	117	50	96	15	15	9	6	3	75	87	.463

Clint Hurdle

Year	Team	Lg	G	LINEUPS LUp	PL%	SUB PH	PR	DS	Quick	Slow	LO	RCD	LS	Rel	SBA	SacA	RM	PO	IBB #	Good	NG	Bomb	W	L	Pct
2002	Rockies	NL	140	100	.52	274	28	41	33	45	17	104	3	437	139	46	50	13	38	22	16	11	67	73	.479
2003	Rockies	NL	162	108	.47	317	17	32	35	40	5	87	4	500	100	82	26	16	51	31	20	13	74	88	.457
2004	Rockies	NL	162	131	.57	289	18	35	36	**63**	20	74	1	473	77	**128**	67	12	**84**	**54**	**30**	12	68	94	.420
2005	Rockies	NL	162	135	.60	273	21	40	32	**60**	17	89	2	459	97	114	119	22	54	28	26	**15**	67	95	.414
2006	Rockies	NL	162	111	.49	259	17	22	34	**52**	17	107	2	499	135	**156**	114	28	81	45	**36**	**23**	76	86	.469
2007	Rockies	NL	163	96	.51	283	32	29	45	37	13	112	1	**529**	131	**112**	109	26	61	30	**31**	14	90	73	.552
2008	Rockies	NL	162	131	.49	253	20	31	40	43	16	85	2	485	**178**	**111**	116	**43**	49	31	18	6	74	87	.457
	162-Game Average			118	.52	284	22	33	39	49	15	96	2	492	125	109	87	23	61	35	26	14	75	87	.463

Tony LaRussa

Year	Team	Lg	G	LINEUPS LUp	PL%	SUB PH	PR	DS	Quick	Slow	LO	RCD	LS	Rel	SBA	SacA	RM	PO	IBB #	Good	NG	Bomb	W	L	Pct
1994	Athletics	AL	114	97	.62	89	28	14	43	21	5	60	4	308	130	31		32	23	13	10	4	51	63	.447
1995	Athletics	AL	144	120	.54	113	38	24	33	38	19	46	7	358	158	42		42	17	9	8	4	67	77	.465
1996	Cardinals	NL	162	120	.52	246	25	13	32	48	**24**	90	8	413	207	**117**		41	38	23	15	7	88	74	.543
1997	Cardinals	NL	162	**146**	.54	**307**	17	18	34	42	16	81	2	399	**224**	77		79	26	18	8	2	73	89	.451
1998	Cardinals	NL	162	**146**	.52	259	7	18	**62**	31	13	82	14	429	174	85		34	32	19	13	8	83	79	.512
1999	Cardinals	NL	161	138	.47	264	32	28	50	41	13	96	14	**454**	182	103		30	31	13	18	11	75	86	.466
2000	Cardinals	NL	162	**137**	.53	240	35	25	40	31	11	63	18	386	138	107		34	21	14	7		95	67	.586
2001	Cardinals	NL	162	117	.47	256	26	13	46	36	7	140	7	**485**	126	102			25	11	15	4	93	69	.574
2002	Cardinals	NL	162	117	.52	**340**	27	41	58	33	23	110	6	472	128	106	75	13	39	25	14	8	97	65	.599
2003	Cardinals	NL	162	126	.50	352	28	51	38	49	36	113	9	460	114	**108**	56	9	36	28	8	2	85	77	.525
2004	Cardinals	NL	162	119	.53	275	25	69	30	48	31	120	**16**	469	158	88	**158**	9	24	17	7	4	**105**	57	.648
2005	Cardinals	NL	162	138	.55	270	25	48	40	38	22	88	4	436	119	92	**153**	9	27	16	11	7	**100**	62	.617

Year	Team	Lg	G	LUp	PL%	PH	PR	DS	Quick	Slow	LO	RCD	LS	Rel	SBA	SacA	RM	PO	#	Good	NG	Bomb	W	L	Pct
2006	Cardinals	NL	161	131	.56	272	11	53	50	34	21	95	6	469	91	86	123	13	35	21	14	3	83	78	.516
2007	Cardinals	NL	162	150	.60	317	19	37	46	44	8	102	5	516	89	85	120	23	25	10	15	11	78	84	.481
2008	Cardinals	NL	162	153	.64	275	26	57	52	40	16	101	11	506	105	87	114	18	21	13	8	1	86	76	.531
	162-Game Average			134	.54	266	25	35	45	39	18	95	9	450	147	90	114	28	29	17	12	6	86	76	.531

Jim Leyland

Year	Team	Lg	G	LUp	PL%	PH	PR	DS	Quick	Slow	LO	RCD	LS	Rel	SBA	SacA	RM	PO	#	Good	NG	Bomb	W	L	Pct
1994	Pirates	NL	114	94	.56	170	16	13	12	9	1	48	4	285	78	48		38	31	8	23	15	53	61	.465
1995	Pirates	NL	144	124	.56	282	8	4	13	12	11	71	4	391	139	69		51	36	16	20	10	58	86	.403
1996	Pirates	NL	162	117	.53	299	18	14	27	8	11	60	11	422	175	101		46	31	4	27	13	73	89	.451
1997	Marlins	NL	162	105	.59	258	36	31	21	12	18	65	2	404	173	91		38	31	15	16	9	92	70	.568
1998	Marlins	NL	162	96	.59	277	13	15	18	24	31	73	8	420	172	91		31	45	20	25	11	54	108	.333
1999	Rockies	NL	162	124	.56	294	11	12	11	29	21	72	5	421	113	88		11	29	7	22	14	72	90	.444
2006	Tigers	AL	162	120	.53	81	34	38	52	32	16	52	3	390	100	57	128	9	35	23	12	9	95	67	.586
2007	Tigers	AL	162	108	.53	77	31	49	46	43	14	70	5	443	133	35	123	20	41	24	17	13	88	74	.543
2008	Tigers	AL	162	131	.51	66	25	50	29	47	20	72	7	440	94	40	114	10	63	37	26	13	74	88	.457
	162-Game Average			119	.55	210	22	26	27	25	17	68	6	421	137	72	122	30	40	18	22	12	77	85	.475

Grady Little

Year	Team	Lg	G	LUp	PL%	PH	PR	DS	Quick	Slow	LO	RCD	LS	Rel	SBA	SacA	RM	PO	#	Good	NG	Bomb	W	L	Pct
2002	Red Sox	AL	162	120	.59	127	51	23	63	28	18	53	11	338	108	35	38	50	29	18	11	3	93	69	.574
2003	Red Sox	AL	162	118	.64	130	80	32	43	36	19	78	8	437	123	32	42	28	41	22	19	13	95	67	.586
2006	Dodgers	NL	162	118	.67	291	34	37	56	27	11	106	9	454	177	82	144	63	40	22	18	7	88	74	.543
2007	Dodgers	NL	162	112	.61	273	35	61	44	31	11	125	4	483	187	77	133	45	34	21	13	7	82	80	.506
	162-Game Average			117	.63	205	50	38	52	31	15	91	8	428	149	57	89	47	36	21	15	8	90	72	.556

Ken Macha

Year	Team	Lg	G	LUp	PL%	PH	PR	DS	Quick	Slow	LO	RCD	LS	Rel	SBA	SacA	RM	PO	#	Good	NG	Bomb	W	L	Pct
2003	Athletics	AL	162	111	.57	140	29	23	44	38	30	72	12	364	62	31	28	9	42	25	17	10	96	66	.593
2004	Athletics	AL	162	119	.60	123	13	14	37	47	39	94	5	414	69	30	63	2	49	31	18	9	91	71	.562
2005	Athletics	AL	162	127	.62	83	17	11	43	36	30	79	13	410	53	29	53	13	42	27	15	6	88	74	.543
2006	Athletics	AL	162	121	.58	62	33	23	39	47	28	104	8	444	81	29	70	22	47	26	21	11	93	69	.574
	162-Game Average			120	.59	102	23	18	41	42	32	87	10	408	66	30	54	12	45	27	18	9	92	70	.568

Pete Mackanin

Year	Team	Lg	G	LUp	PL%	PH	PR	DS	Quick	Slow	LO	RCD	LS	Rel	SBA	SacA	RM	PO	#	Good	NG	Bomb	W	L	Pct
2005	Pirates	NL	26	24	.52	54	1	5	11	4	1	22	0	94	19	19	20	2	5	2	3	1	12	14	.462
2007	Reds	NL	80	57	.59	130	10	26	20	22	9	58	3	266	62	44	36	12	18	10	8	3	41	39	.513
	162-Game Average			124	.57	281	17	47	47	40	15	122	5	550	124	96	86	21	35	18	17	6	81	81	.500

Joe Maddon

Year	Team	Lg	G	LUp	PL%	PH	PR	DS	Quick	Slow	LO	RCD	LS	Rel	SBA	SacA	RM	PO	#	Good	NG	Bomb	W	L	Pct
1996	Angels	AL	22	19	.64	21	5	0	7	6	6	10	3	48	11	20		6	4	3	1	1	8	14	.364
1998	Angels	AL	8	4	.57	4	4	0	1	5	3	5	3	12	2	7		0	1	0	1	0	6	2	.750
1999	Angels	AL	29	19	.58	29	4	1	6	0	4	20	0	85	23	12		7	3	1	2	1	19	10	.655
2006	Devil Rays	AL	162	145	.54	81	26	51	41	39	16	79	10	444	186	51	132	48	39	19	20	13	61	101	.377
2007	Devil Rays	AL	162	122	.53	80	19	16	31	56	19	113	1	483	179	40	118	50	31	18	13	4	66	96	.407
2008	Rays	AL	162	115	.69	133	16	39	48	37	14	112	7	448	192	31	113	26	29	15	14	8	97	65	.599
	162-Game Average			126	.59	103	22	32	40	43	18	101	7	452	176	48	121	41	32	17	15	8	76	86	.469

Charlie Manuel

Year	Team	Lg	G	LUp	PL%	PH	PR	DS	Quick	Slow	LO	RCD	LS	Rel	SBA	SacA	RM	PO	#	Good	NG	Bomb	W	L	Pct
2000	Indians	AL	162	102	.64	73	40	26	21	12	20	104	7	462	147	59		30	38	21	17	9	90	72	.556
2001	Indians	AL	162	114	.61	105	30	49	28	17	10	120	3	484	120	67		43	34	20	14	11	91	71	.562
2002	Indians	AL	86	67	.61	57	10	19	14	17	25	47	0	222	57	21	34	3	21	12	9	4	39	47	.453
2005	Phillies	NL	162	80	.64	265	36	19	42	28	13	119	6	442	143	86	76	11	51	35	16	9	88	74	.543
2006	Phillies	NL	162	81	.65	301	42	49	28	43	22	126	2	500	117	79	74	16	63	35	28	12	85	77	.525

Year	Team	Lg	G	LUp	PL%	PH	PR	DS	Quick	Slow	LO	RCD	LS	Rel	SBA	SacA	RM	PO	#	Good	NG	Bomb	W	L	Pct
2007	Phillies	NL	162	87	.64	264	56	75	40	40	19	128	6	498	157	84	90	30	62	41	21	16	89	73	.549
2008	Phillies	NL	162	77	.65	291	62	60	33	42	24	124	1	468	161	88	92	34	64	46	18	11	92	70	.568
162-Game Average				93	.64	208	42	45	32	30	20	118	4	471	138	74	81	26	51	32	19	11	88	74	.543

Jerry Manuel

Year	Team	Lg	G	LUp	PL%	PH	PR	DS	Quick	Slow	LO	RCD	LS	Rel	SBA	SacA	RM	PO	#	Good	NG	Bomb	W	L	Pct
1998	White Sox	AL	162	110	.56	65	19	31	43	35	6	72	14	405	173	54		26	13	7	6	4	80	82	.494
1999	White Sox	AL	161	109	.58	79	35	39	35	42	9	78	8	409	160	69		22	22	11	11	7	75	86	.466
2000	White Sox	AL	162	84	.53	84	35	20	41	31	8	91	18	466	161	75		32	26	15	11	10	95	67	.586
2001	White Sox	AL	162	115	.53	104	34	50	45	39	5	93	16	406	182	95		41	30	16	14	9	83	79	.512
2002	White Sox	AL	162	104	.55	86	10	39	50	44	17	86	10	423	106	73	38	18	31	17	14	11	81	81	.500
2003	White Sox	AL	162	105	.55	146	40	71	39	36	27	74	10	361	106	66	39	20	30	18	12	7	86	76	.531
2008	Mets	NL	93	58	.76	167	7	31	12	30	23	95	2	324	89	54	81	6	37	18	19	6	55	38	.591
162-Game Average				104	.57	111	27	43	40	39	14	90	12	425	149	74	61	25	29	16	13	8	85	77	.525

Lee Mazzilli

Year	Team	Lg	G	LUp	PL%	PH	PR	DS	Quick	Slow	LO	RCD	LS	Rel	SBA	SacA	RM	PO	#	Good	NG	Bomb	W	L	Pct
2004	Orioles	AL	162	105	.60	89	44	18	47	35	17	95	4	452	142	57	106	34	43	22	21	7	78	84	.481
2005	Orioles	AL	107	81	.57	57	18	30	21	26	16	75	3	294	79	31	63	25	29	15	14	12	51	56	.477
162-Game Average				112	.59	88	37	29	41	37	20	102	4	449	133	53	102	36	43	22	21	11	78	84	.481

Lloyd McClendon

Year	Team	Lg	G	LUp	PL%	PH	PR	DS	Quick	Slow	LO	RCD	LS	Rel	SBA	SacA	RM	PO	#	Good	NG	Bomb	W	L	Pct
2001	Pirates	NL	162	131	.51	255	17	32	45	38	2	85	5	410	166	83		52	49	19	30	19	62	100	.383
2002	Pirates	NL	161	121	.45	261	38	65	62	30	3	98	2	458	135	93	73	67	93	61	32	22	72	89	.447
2003	Pirates	NL	162	114	.57	315	27	59	46	35	27	114	10	457	123	99	55	73	58	34	24	13	75	87	.463
2004	Pirates	NL	161	114	.50	278	13	58	50	40	26	133	1	464	103	100	91	61	64	37	27	16	72	89	.447
2005	Pirates	NL	136	123	.53	218	8	19	37	34	15	86	5	357	84	62	83	37	60	32	28	16	55	81	.404
162-Game Average				125	.51	275	21	48	50	37	15	107	5	445	127	91	79	60	67	38	29	18	70	92	.432

Jack McKeon

Year	Team	Lg	G	LUp	PL%	PH	PR	DS	Quick	Slow	LO	RCD	LS	Rel	SBA	SacA	RM	PO	#	Good	NG	Bomb	W	L	Pct
1997	Reds	NL	63	50	.46	102	18	7	23	11	5	44	3	154	79	42		18	12	2	10	7	33	30	.524
1998	Reds	NL	162	132	.55	288	30	25	49	25	10	107	20	366	137	98		7	31	18	13	8	77	85	.475
1999	Reds	NL	163	95	.50	251	30	38	58	23	9	93	28	381	218	88		14	43	27	16	5	96	67	.589
2000	Reds	NL	163	117	.51	270	31	41	52	27	10	96	24	387	137	82		24	43	26	17	10	85	77	.525
2003	Marlins	NL	124	57	.43	171	26	21	32	35	33	63	6	280	150	92	41	17	28	16	12	10	75	49	.605
2004	Marlins	NL	162	90	.48	224	27	34	42	37	20	95	12	404	139	104	96	19	61	40	21	13	83	79	.512
2005	Marlins	NL	162	82	.43	246	24	36	44	35	36	103	7	449	134	106	106	16	57	37	20	10	83	79	.512
162-Game Average				101	.49	252	30	33	49	31	20	98	16	393	161	99	88	19	45	27	18	10	86	76	.531

John McLaren

Year	Team	Lg	G	LUp	PL%	PH	PR	DS	Quick	Slow	LO	RCD	LS	Rel	SBA	SacA	RM	PO	#	Good	NG	Bomb	W	L	Pct
2007	Mariners	AL	84	52	.48	55	40	18	17	23	19	49	6	247	56	20	76	18	19	10	9	5	43	41	.512
2008	Mariners	AL	72	48	.50	31	16	4	17	24	9	45	1	197	65	17	63	11	12	6	6	5	25	47	.347
162-Game Average				104	.49	89	58	23	35	49	29	98	7	461	126	38	144	30	32	17	16	10	71	91	.438

Bob Melvin

Year	Team	Lg	G	LUp	PL%	PH	PR	DS	Quick	Slow	LO	RCD	LS	Rel	SBA	SacA	RM	PO	#	Good	NG	Bomb	W	L	Pct
2003	Mariners	AL	162	111	.62	81	62	33	27	46	43	56	6	366	145	44	37	5	24	14	10	4	93	69	.574
2004	Mariners	AL	162	151	.59	109	66	26	26	63	43	82	5	414	152	56	123	24	32	18	14	8	63	99	.389
2005	Diamondbacks	NL	162	120	.68	310	26	38	26	56	36	123	11	458	93	93	101	30	43	27	16	9	77	85	.475
2006	Diamondbacks	NL	162	114	.72	278	11	35	37	42	15	86	0	461	106	83	61	30	44	28	16	8	76	86	.469
2007	Diamondbacks	NL	162	146	.57	243	11	61	35	42	31	96	2	469	133	74	70	25	38	30	8	4	90	72	.556
2008	Diamondbacks	NL	162	134	.57	263	27	30	41	39	16	102	0	444	81	87	79	28	41	27	14	9	82	80	.506
162-Game Average				129	.62	214	34	37	32	48	31	91	4	435	118	73	79	24	37	24	13	7	80	82	.494

Dave Miley

Year	Team	Lg	G	LUp	PL%	PH	PR	DS	Quick	Slow	LO	RCD	LS	Rel	SBA	SacA	RM	PO	#	Good	NG	Bomb	W	L	Pct
				LINEUPS		SUBSTITUTION			PITCHER USAGE						TACTICS				INTENTIONAL BB				RESULTS		
2003	Reds	NL	57	52	.61	98	12	18	22	10	2	35	3	168	27	25	13	7	21	17	4	3	22	35	.386
2004	Reds	NL	162	132	.60	265	25	50	42	44	14	122	2	497	102	79	73	11	55	38	17	8	76	86	.469
2005	Reds	NL	70	55	.61	104	10	7	15	20	11	38	1	204	45	19	20	5	22	15	7	4	27	43	.386
	162-Game Average			134	.60	262	26	42	44	41	15	109	3	487	98	69	59	13	55	39	16	8	70	92	.432

Jerry Narron

Year	Team	Lg	G	LUp	PL%	PH	PR	DS	Quick	Slow	LO	RCD	LS	Rel	SBA	SacA	RM	PO	#	Good	NG	Bomb	W	L	Pct
				LINEUPS		SUBSTITUTION			PITCHER USAGE						TACTICS				INTENTIONAL BB				RESULTS		
2001	Rangers	AL	134	94	.66	92	14	19	9	18	6	60	5	340	106	29		5	16	2	14	8	62	72	.463
2002	Rangers	AL	162	128	.52	154	59	30	33	54	26	121	5	487	96	58	58	6	32	19	13	3	72	90	.444
2005	Reds	NL	93	73	.61	156	9	14	13	22	12	71	5	287	50	45	53	7	25	21	4	2	46	46	.500
2006	Reds	NL	162	140	.56	273	23	46	33	47	41	121	2	476	157	86	91	11	55	38	17	9	80	82	.494
2007	Reds	NL	82	63	.58	135	6	26	11	33	21	74	8	256	66	56	45	8	29	16	13	7	31	51	.378
	162-Game Average			128	.58	208	28	35	25	45	27	115	6	473	122	70	80	9	40	25	16	7	75	87	.463

Tony Pena

Year	Team	Lg	G	LUp	PL%	PH	PR	DS	Quick	Slow	LO	RCD	LS	Rel	SBA	SacA	RM	PO	#	Good	NG	Bomb	W	L	Pct
				LINEUPS		SUBSTITUTION			PITCHER USAGE						TACTICS				INTENTIONAL BB				RESULTS		
2002	Royals	AL	126	102	.66	90	28	13	28	35	21	74	1	339	160	57	44	7	43	23	20	9	49	77	.389
2003	Royals	AL	162	125	.60	92	31	16	53	39	10	54	6	407	162	79	35	8	33	16	17	8	83	79	.512
2004	Royals	AL	162	141	.57	53	27	14	37	46	15	49	5	409	115	56	91	7	49	33	16	7	58	104	.358
2005	Royals	AL	33	33	.60	23	4	1	10	12	3	13	0	88	27	15	23	2	13	5	8	3	8	25	.242
	162-Game Average			134	.61	87	30	15	43	44	16	64	4	417	156	69	65	8	46	26	20	9	66	96	.407

Sam Perlozzo

Year	Team	Lg	G	LUp	PL%	PH	PR	DS	Quick	Slow	LO	RCD	LS	Rel	SBA	SacA	RM	PO	#	Good	NG	Bomb	W	L	Pct
				LINEUPS		SUBSTITUTION			PITCHER USAGE						TACTICS				INTENTIONAL BB				RESULTS		
2005	Orioles	AL	55	47	.61	28	23	26	15	11	5	46	2	180	41	24	25	8	3	1	2	1	23	32	.418
2006	Orioles	AL	162	124	.56	72	46	49	29	47	14	102	10	472	153	58	79	30	26	15	11	7	70	92	.432
2007	Orioles	AL	69	48	.60	29	26	25	16	15	13	64	1	211	62	30	29	13	8	3	5	5	29	40	.420
	162-Game Average			124	.58	73	54	57	34	41	18	120	7	489	145	63	75	29	21	11	10	7	69	93	.426

Lou Piniella

Year	Team	Lg	G	LUp	PL%	PH	PR	DS	Quick	Slow	LO	RCD	LS	Rel	SBA	SacA	RM	PO	#	Good	NG	Bomb	W	L	Pct
				LINEUPS		SUBSTITUTION			PITCHER USAGE						TACTICS				INTENTIONAL BB				RESULTS		
1994	Mariners	AL	112	98	.49	113	24	6	30	35	4	54	9	252	69	54		37	28	10	18	9	49	63	.438
1995	Mariners	AL	145	98	.56	137	41	22	37	39	30	58	20	324	151	66		40	32	13	19	12	79	66	.545
1996	Mariners	AL	161	99	.55	190	28	14	56	21	15	91	14	403	129	65		40	40	19	21	13	85	76	.528
1997	Mariners	AL	162	84	.57	147	35	27	38	47	25	79	11	392	129	61		32	30	12	18	10	90	72	.556
1998	Mariners	AL	161	111	.53	99	38	43	38	54	32	81	4	368	154	58		20	18	3	15	7	76	85	.472
1999	Mariners	AL	162	130	.46	122	38	30	31	40	21	51	10	346	175	49		31	27	3	24	8	79	83	.488
2000	Mariners	AL	162	130	.50	109	43	52	51	37	1	64	11	383	178	73		22	32	15	17	8	91	71	.562
2001	Mariners	AL	162	115	.64	121	44	64	55	33	5	62	9	392	216	62		33	23	14	9	3	116	46	.716
2002	Mariners	AL	162	129	.64	95	129	50	49	39	34	52	7	343	195	61	43	25	34	15	19	11	93	69	.574
2003	Devil Rays	AL	162	124	.60	188	43	26	38	41	29	59	5	372	184	53	52	23	37	21	16	10	63	99	.389
2004	Devil Rays	AL	161	137	.63	97	25	36	51	34	23	57	15	401	174	45	104	16	35	16	19	9	70	91	.435
2005	Devil Rays	AL	162	135	.54	127	18	52	38	54	32	67	10	401	200	53	128	16	41	19	22	13	67	95	.414
2007	Cubs	NL	162	125	.51	263	52	51	35	38	33	98	3	478	119	60	89	17	46	28	18	4	85	77	.525
2008	Cubs	NL	161	112	.47	286	22	31	42	37	27	111	3	478	121	93	98	15	45	28	17	9	97	64	.602
	162-Game Average			120	.55	154	43	37	43	40	23	73	10	393	162	63	86	27	35	16	19	9	84	78	.519

Willie Randolph

Year	Team	Lg	G	LUp	PL%	PH	PR	DS	Quick	Slow	LO	RCD	LS	Rel	SBA	SacA	RM	PO	#	Good	NG	Bomb	W	L	Pct
				LINEUPS		SUBSTITUTION			PITCHER USAGE						TACTICS				INTENTIONAL BB				RESULTS		
2005	Mets	NL	162	105	.64	222	10	51	47	34	20	74	5	392	193	89	118	18	43	28	15	9	83	79	.512
2006	Mets	NL	162	101	.68	247	9	24	40	40	15	119	4	474	181	102	106	16	39	25	14	9	97	65	.599
2007	Mets	NL	162	102	.68	269	21	28	26	44	27	122	3	499	246	97	100	10	40	26	14	7	88	74	.543
2008	Mets	NL	69	46	.77	104	3	11	12	20	11	73	1	233	85	44	48	4	16	10	6	2	34	35	.493
	162-Game Average			103	.68	246	13	33	36	40	21	113	4	466	206	97	109	14	40	26	14	8	88	74	.543

Jim Riggleman

Year	Team	Lg	G	LUp	PL%	PH	PR	DS	Quick	Slow	LO	RCD	LS	Rel	SBA	SacA	RM	PO	# Good	NG	Bomb	W	L	Pct
1994	Padres	NL	117	93	.63	184	28	19	11	5	3	53	10	273	116	80		52	41	13	28	11	47	70	.402
1995	Cubs	NL	144	92	.56	196	9	30	15	8	13	119	12	414	142	90		53	51	28	23	12	73	71	.507
1996	Cubs	NL	162	87	.54	326	34	21	17	11	7	114	11	**439**	158	79		65	38	16	22	10	76	86	.469
1997	Cubs	NL	162	127	.50	280	40	**44**	13	5	2	113	9	441	176	103		74	37	24	13	6	68	**94**	.420
1998	Cubs	NL	163	104	.60	273	26	35	16	14	20	133	6	**449**	109	89		26	36	10	26	15	90	73	.552
1999	Cubs	NL	162	122	.61	**312**	25	30	16	19	8	105	4	441	104	94		20	35	8	27	15	67	95	.414
2008	Mariners	AL	90	70	.60	75	30	22	21	25	19	50	4	272	57	27	88	10	25	17	8	3	36	54	.400
	162-Game Average			113	.57	267	31	33	18	14	12	111	9	442	140	91	158	49	43	19	24	12	74	88	.457

Frank Robinson

Year	Team	Lg	G	LUp	PL%	PH	PR	DS	Quick	Slow	LO	RCD	LS	Rel	SBA	SacA	RM	PO	# Good	NG	Bomb	W	L	Pct
2002	Expos	NL	162	121	.60	254	47	40	48	40	34	109	**11**	437	182	**126**	58	24	80	57	23	11	83	79	.512
2003	Expos	NL	162	134	.63	248	55	31	50	44	44	98	4	437	**139**	85	50	8	51	27	24	13	83	79	.512
2004	Expos	NL	162	131	.67	254	17	26	48	39	36	109	4	462	147	121	112	1	78	**54**	24	10	67	95	.414
2005	Nationals	NL	162	121	.63	266	48	35	45	47	**42**	140	3	470	90	**115**	109	4	**77**	**50**	27	9	81	81	.500
2006	Nationals	NL	162	110	.58	**314**	37	26	46	33	19	137	3	517	**185**	95	**150**	14	93	57	36	**23**	71	91	.438
	162-Game Average			123	.62	267	41	32	47	41	35	119	5	465	149	108	96	10	76	49	27	13	77	85	.475

John Russell

Year	Team	Lg	G	LUp	PL%	PH	PR	DS	Quick	Slow	LO	RCD	LS	Rel	SBA	SacA	RM	PO	# Good	NG	Bomb	W	L	Pct
2008	Pirates	NL	162	128	.51	290	17	13	29	47	15	111	0	497	76	92	54	19	31	21	10	4	67	95	.414
	162-Game Average			128	.51	290	17	13	29	47	15	111	0	497	76	92	54	19	31	21	10	4	67	95	.414

Bob Schaefer

Year	Team	Lg	G	LUp	PL%	PH	PR	DS	Quick	Slow	LO	RCD	LS	Rel	SBA	SacA	RM	PO	# Good	NG	Bomb	W	L	Pct
2005	Royals	AL	17	15	.57	13	3	2	4	5	0	4	0	46	11	3	12	4	3	2	1	0	5	12	.294
	162-Game Average			143	.57	124	29	19	38	48	0	38	0	438	105	29	114	38	29	19	10	0	48	114	.296

Mike Scioscia

Year	Team	Lg	G	LUp	PL%	PH	PR	DS	Quick	Slow	LO	RCD	LS	Rel	SBA	SacA	RM	PO	# Good	NG	Bomb	W	L	Pct
2000	Angels	AL	162	75	.62	110	41	4	56	42	6	95	9	441	145	63		40	32	16	16	7	82	80	.506
2001	Angels	AL	162	130	.62	118	30	8	29	41	5	81	9	384	168	66		50	33	8	25	12	75	87	.463
2002	Angels	AL	162	102	.64	**162**	57	26	36	33	34	88	8	400	168	62	52	30	24	15	9	5	99	63	.611
2003	Angels	AL	162	130	.64	134	54	40	50	48	11	60	4	375	190	64	79	25	38	26	12	3	77	85	.475
2004	Angels	AL	162	126	.57	94	32	44	37	40	22	61	11	343	189	70	**229**	33	27	18	9	3	92	70	.568
2005	Angels	AL	162	124	.65	92	37	37	47	37	24	88	9	379	**218**	58	**160**	43	24	15	9	4	95	67	.586
2006	Angels	AL	162	114	.63	103	45	38	38	49	21	99	9	380	**205**	37	**166**	22	27	18	9	6	89	73	.549
2007	Angels	AL	162	127	.66	103	26	19	39	40	14	94	4	396	**194**	41	**166**	44	22	12	10	5	94	68	.580
2008	Angels	AL	162	125	.63	74	30	36	37	48	**21**	87	1	383	177	39	151	31	32	22	10	6	**100**	62	.617
	162-Game Average			117	.63	110	39	28	41	42	18	84	7	387	184	56	143	35	29	17	12	6	89	73	.549

Buck Showalter

Year	Team	Lg	G	LUp	PL%	PH	PR	DS	Quick	Slow	LO	RCD	LS	Rel	SBA	SacA	RM	PO	# Good	NG	Bomb	W	L	Pct
1994	Yankees	AL	113	79	.59	95	31	3	24	30	0	38	7	241	95	34		22	18	7	11	4	70	43	.619
1995	Yankees	AL	145	107	.68	124	30	20	29	42	37	57	6	302	80	27		29	15	8	7	1	79	65	.549
1998	Diamondbacks	NL	162	124	.62	252	17	15	34	40	7	43	6	368	111	68		13	18	2	16	9	65	97	.401
1999	Diamondbacks	NL	162	97	**.63**	220	20	17	37	48	25	74	3	382	176	75		15	34	15	19	8	100	62	.617
2000	Diamondbacks	NL	162	99	.60	250	32	11	46	26	18	74	12	390	141	89		10	36	11	25	16	85	77	.525
2003	Rangers	AL	162	133	.61	88	51	41	35	39	12	93	7	**494**	90	35	**80**	12	45	24	21	**14**	71	91	.438
2004	Rangers	AL	162	120	.64	86	15	24	53	30	12	82	10	468	105	30	88	5	29	19	10	3	89	73	.549
2005	Rangers	AL	162	98	.59	57	22	11	42	39	17	79	8	**454**	82	11	103	5	31	10	21	**16**	79	83	.488
2006	Rangers	AL	162	95	.57	39	34	22	41	27	10	85	4	**489**	77	30	72	8	18	11	7	5	80	82	.494
	162-Game Average			111	.62	141	29	19	40	37	16	73	7	418	111	46	86	14	28	12	16	9	84	78	.519

Dale Sveum

Year	Team	Lg	G	LUp	PL%	PH	PR	DS	Quick	Slow	LO	RCD	LS	Rel	SBA	SacA	RM	PO	#	Good	NG	Bomb	W	L	Pct
				LINEUPS		SUBSTITUTION			PITCHER USAGE						TACTICS				INTENTIONAL BB				RESULTS		
2008	Brewers	NL	12	3	.48	32	2	1	7	2	1	12	0	46	5	13	6	1	2	1	1	0	7	5	.583
	162-Game Average			41	.48	432	27	14	95	27	14	162	0	621	68	176	81	14	27	14	14	0	94	68	.580

Joe Torre

Year	Team	Lg	G	LUp	PL%	PH	PR	DS	Quick	Slow	LO	RCD	LS	Rel	SBA	SacA	RM	PO	#	Good	NG	Bomb	W	L	Pct
				LINEUPS		SUBSTITUTION			PITCHER USAGE						TACTICS				INTENTIONAL BB				RESULTS		
1994	Cardinals	NL	115	79	.68	192	9	0	36	29	6	106	4	330	122	57		33	13	3	10	6	53	61	.465
1995	Cardinals	NL	47	36	.51	99	6	4	17	11	1	41	2	146	42	26		14	11	5	6	2	20	27	.426
1996	Yankees	AL	162	131	.57	92	62	55	59	23	22	97	10	411	142	53		19	27	9	18	14	92	70	.568
1997	Yankees	AL	162	118	.61	75	70	23	35	41	19	84	14	368	157	54		14	29	11	18	10	96	66	.593
1998	Yankees	AL	162	96	.62	94	36	28	43	38	27	71	17	334	216	44		9	18	10	8	4	114	48	.704
1999	Yankees	AL	162	76	.63	103	57	10	29	51	26	80	12	276	129	31		12	15	5	10	8	98	64	.605
2000	Yankees	AL	161	112	.63	86	49	27	43	53	27	92	16	382	147	22		8	16	2	14	7	87	74	.540
2001	Yankees	AL	161	94	.56	76	33	14	37	45	10	77	17	362	214	41		21	22	13	9	6	95	65	.594
2002	Yankees	AL	161	108	.58	89	53	31	39	49	44	86	13	334	138	35	46	18	44	33	11	4	103	58	.640
2003	Yankees	AL	163	104	.65	118	48	18	26	51	52	75	10	367	131	39	69	33	36	21	15	8	101	61	.623
2004	Yankees	AL	162	116	.65	86	35	46	48	35	29	129	10	436	117	50	126	36	32	16	16	9	101	61	.623
2005	Yankees	AL	162	117	.64	94	65	47	44	45	28	92	7	418	111	40	123	50	25	11	14	9	95	67	.586
2006	Yankees	AL	162	120	.66	108	50	59	50	30	9	109	7	489	174	48	118	50	41	22	19	4	97	65	.599
2007	Yankees	AL	162	102	.68	99	34	22	51	29	10	113	13	522	163	51	152	41	33	17	16	7	94	68	.580
2008	Dodgers	NL	162	124	.53	277	43	66	61	30	17	94	8	461	169	75	133	38	58	46	12	5	84	78	.519
	162-Game Average			110	.62	121	47	32	44	40	23	96	11	403	155	48	110	28	30	16	14	7	95	67	.586

Jim Tracy

Year	Team	Lg	G	LUp	PL%	PH	PR	DS	Quick	Slow	LO	RCD	LS	Rel	SBA	SacA	RM	PO	#	Good	NG	Bomb	W	L	Pct
				LINEUPS		SUBSTITUTION			PITCHER USAGE						TACTICS				INTENTIONAL BB				RESULTS		
2001	Dodgers	NL	162	111	.50	264	34	20	46	42	8	84	4	409	131	81		10	25	7	18	9	86	76	.531
2002	Dodgers	NL	162	102	.52	317	39	37	49	36	21	118	9	423	133	81	46	18	45	31	14	5	92	70	.568
2003	Dodgers	NL	162	103	.64	269	22	64	52	29	22	148	11	438	116	97	32	10	35	23	12	8	85	77	.525
2004	Dodgers	NL	162	94	.70	295	25	19	49	34	16	128	16	459	143	81	93	7	47	32	15	8	93	69	.574
2005	Dodgers	NL	162	129	.64	303	31	37	44	40	20	126	2	459	93	76	97	17	34	21	13	6	71	91	.438
2006	Pirates	NL	162	121	.43	264	22	22	37	43	12	156	3	505	91	80	75	12	62	39	23	15	67	95	.414
2007	Pirates	NL	162	124	.49	240	12	26	33	40	13	113	0	495	98	80	90	12	55	30	25	11	68	94	.420
	162-Game Average			112	.56	279	26	32	44	38	16	125	6	455	115	82	72	12	43	26	17	9	80	82	.494

Alan Trammell

Year	Team	Lg	G	LUp	PL%	PH	PR	DS	Quick	Slow	LO	RCD	LS	Rel	SBA	SacA	RM	PO	#	Good	NG	Bomb	W	L	Pct
				LINEUPS		SUBSTITUTION			PITCHER USAGE						TACTICS				INTENTIONAL BB				RESULTS		
2003	Tigers	AL	162	129	.72	138	29	14	48	39	15	73	14	451	161	92	66	18	35	22	13	7	43	119	.265
2004	Tigers	AL	162	131	.65	105	29	19	47	36	26	79	6	432	136	62	99	9	33	16	17	10	72	90	.444
2005	Tigers	AL	162	119	.49	75	26	16	35	39	13	87	2	425	94	56	129	11	33	21	12	7	71	91	.438
	162-Game Average			126	.62	106	28	16	43	38	18	80	7	436	130	70	98	16	34	20	14	8	62	100	.383

Dave Trembley

Year	Team	Lg	G	LUp	PL%	PH	PR	DS	Quick	Slow	LO	RCD	LS	Rel	SBA	SacA	RM	PO	#	Good	NG	Bomb	W	L	Pct
				LINEUPS		SUBSTITUTION			PITCHER USAGE						TACTICS				INTENTIONAL BB				RESULTS		
2007	Orioles	AL	93	71	.60	63	29	16	21	25	16	47	3	279	124	32	83	32	29	15	14	8	40	53	.430
2008	Orioles	AL	161	119	.58	117	36	25	41	44	11	87	4	492	118	38	143	11	44	18	26	12	68	93	.422
	162-Game Average			121	.59	115	41	26	40	44	17	85	4	492	154	45	144	27	47	21	26	13	69	93	.426

Ron Washington

Year	Team	Lg	G	LUp	PL%	PH	PR	DS	Quick	Slow	LO	RCD	LS	Rel	SBA	SacA	RM	PO	#	Good	NG	Bomb	W	L	Pct
				LINEUPS		SUBSTITUTION			PITCHER USAGE						TACTICS				INTENTIONAL BB				RESULTS		
2007	Rangers	AL	162	139	.60	89	30	53	47	46	4	78	9	467	113	76	61	13	38	19	19	11	75	87	.463
2008	Rangers	AL	162	129	.64	118	16	14	31	53	11	85	3	458	106	53	74	20	44	19	25	20	79	83	.488
	162-Game Average			134	.62	104	23	34	39	50	8	82	6	463	110	65	71	17	41	19	22	16	77	85	.475

Eric Wedge

Year	Team	Lg	G	LUp	PL%	PH	PR	DS	Quick	Slow	LO	RCD	LS	Rel	SBA	SacA	RM	PO	#	Good	NG	Bomb	W	L	Pct
				LINEUPS		SUBSTITUTION			PITCHER USAGE						TACTICS				INTENTIONAL BB				RESULTS		
2003	Indians	AL	162	145	.67	117	43	27	47	34	18	89	5	428	147	67	54	12	37	22	15	8	68	94	.420
2004	Indians	AL	162	114	.72	91	34	20	44	38	22	121	0	479	149	57	129	28	47	26	21	18	80	82	.494
2005	Indians	AL	162	111	.66	88	18	16	45	45	15	90	3	409	98	53	79	9	20	11	9	7	93	69	.574

Year	Team	Lg	G	LINEUPS		SUBSTITUTION			PITCHER USAGE						TACTICS				INTENTIONAL BB				RESULTS		
				LUp	PL%	PH	PR	DS	Quick	Slow	LO	RCD	LS	Rel	SBA	SacA	RM	PO	#	Good	NG	Bomb	W	L	Pct
2006	Indians	AL	162	111	.59	98	13	13	31	52	27	48	1	377	78	40	83	15	35	21	14	11	78	84	.481
2007	Indians	AL	162	117	.60	116	41	25	34	38	20	79	2	395	113	40	108	16	42	24	18	9	96	66	.593
2008	Indians	AL	162	136	.54	112	31	18	40	35	17	78	4	399	106	56	98	5	28	6	22	11	81	81	.500
162-Game Average				122	.63	104	30	20	40	40	20	84	3	415	115	52	92	14	35	18	17	11	83	79	.512

Ned Yost

Year	Team	Lg	G	LINEUPS		SUBSTITUTION			PITCHER USAGE						TACTICS				INTENTIONAL BB				RESULTS		
				LUp	PL%	PH	PR	DS	Quick	Slow	LO	RCD	LS	Rel	SBA	SacA	RM	PO	#	Good	NG	Bomb	W	L	Pct
2003	Brewers	NL	162	97	.44	304	22	39	23	59	18	90	6	460	138	85	40	23	43	28	15	9	68	94	.420
2004	Brewers	NL	161	131	.60	283	25	20	39	41	27	63	2	423	178	79	108	8	27	16	11	8	67	94	.416
2005	Brewers	NL	162	99	.46	259	18	35	26	41	42	71	2	395	113	89	97	50	52	23	29	10	81	81	.500
2006	Brewers	NL	162	106	.48	238	12	14	33	44	18	77	4	427	108	80	82	16	34	14	20	12	75	87	.463
2007	Brewers	NL	162	109	.60	259	11	41	37	42	18	117	7	492	128	74	94	19	37	28	9	9	83	79	.512
2008	Brewers	NL	150	93	.48	217	5	16	37	39	23	69	5	399	141	61	105	31	30	17	13	7	83	67	.553
162-Game Average				107	.51	264	16	28	33	45	25	82	4	439	136	79	89	25	38	21	16	9	77	85	.475

Categories of this record are Games Managed (G), Number of Different Lineups Used (LUp), the percentage of players who had the platoon advantage at the start of the game (PL%), Pinch Hitters Used (PH), Pinch Runners Used (PR), Defensive Substitutes Used (DS), Quick Hooks (Quick), Slow Hooks (Slow), Long Outings by Starting Pitchers (LO), Relievers Used on Consecutive Days (RCD), Long Saves (LS), Relievers Used (Rel), Stolen Base Attempts (SBA), Sacrifice Bunts Attempts (SacA), Runners Moving with the Pitch (RM), Pitchouts ordered (PO), Intentional Walks issued (#), Intentional Walks resulting in a Good Outcome (Good), Intentional Walks resulting Not in a Good Outcome (NG), Intentional Walks Blowing up on the Manager (Bomb), Wins (W), Losses (L) and Winning Percentage (Pct.).

2008 American League Managers

Manager	G	LUp	PL%	PH	PR	DS	Quick	Slow	LO	RCD	LS	Rel	SBA	SacA	RM	PO	#	Good	NG	Bomb	W	L	Pct
		LINEUPS		SUBSTITUTION			PITCHER USAGE						TACTICS				INTENTIONAL BB				RESULTS		
Terry Francona, Bos	162	131	.59	62	40	40	50	30	20	90	11	466	155	40	87	8	17	10	7	4	95	67	.586
Ron Gardenhire, Min	163	103	.64	109	26	12	47	29	5	115	3	485	144	73	143	17	38	25	13	8	88	75	.540
Bob Geren, Oak	161	133	.59	91	57	37	49	32	5	87	8	441	109	44	62	18	45	25	20	10	75	86	.466
Joe Girardi, NYY	162	114	.63	97	37	42	60	37	12	88	10	475	157	38	173	36	37	22	15	8	89	73	.549
Ozzie Guillen, CWS	163	100	.52	75	49	37	42	48	14	100	3	463	101	44	98	8	42	29	13	6	89	74	.546
Trey Hillman, KC	162	134	.55	71	44	34	35	48	19	78	2	439	117	50	96	15	15	9	6	3	75	87	.463
Jim Leyland, Det	162	131	.51	66	25	50	29	47	20	72	7	440	94	40	114	10	63	37	26	13	74	88	.457
Joe Maddon, TB	162	115	.69	133	16	39	48	37	14	112	7	448	192	31	113	26	29	15	14	8	97	65	.599
Mike Scioscia, LAA	162	125	.63	74	30	36	37	48	21	87	1	383	177	39	151	31	32	22	10	6	100	62	.617
Dave Trembley, Bal	161	119	.58	117	36	25	41	44	11	87	4	492	118	38	143	11	44	18	26	12	68	93	.422
Ron Washington, Tex	162	129	.64	118	16	14	31	53	11	85	3	458	106	53	74	20	44	19	25	20	79	83	.488
Eric Wedge, Cle	162	136	.54	112	31	18	40	35	17	78	4	399	106	56	98	5	28	6	22	11	81	81	.500
162-Game Average		122	.58	95	35	33	40	42	18	90	5	448	128	47	113	18	37	21	16	9	81	81	.500

Manager	G	LUp	PL%	PH	PR	DS	Quick	Slow	LO	RCD	LS	Rel	SBA	SacA	RM	PO	#	Good	NG	Bomb	W	L	Pct
		LINEUPS		SUBSTITUTION			PITCHER USAGE						TACTICS				INTENTIONAL BB				RESULTS		
Cito Gaston, Tor	88	65	.59	36	18	30	18	19	25	40	0	216	37	41	37	11	16	8	8	6	51	37	.580
John Gibbons, Tor	74	60	.48	53	15	18	12	20	12	43	0	205	70	23	39	10	26	16	10	6	35	39	.473
John McLaren, Sea	72	48	.50	31	16	4	17	24	9	45	1	197	65	17	63	11	12	6	6	5	25	47	.347
Jim Riggleman, Sea	90	70	.60	75	30	22	21	25	19	50	4	272	57	27	88	10	25	17	8	3	36	54	.400

2008 National League Managers

Manager	G	LUp	PL%	PH	PR	DS	Quick	Slow	LO	RCD	LS	Rel	SBA	SacA	RM	PO	#	Good	NG	Bomb	W	L	Pct
		LINEUPS		SUBSTITUTION			PITCHER USAGE						TACTICS				INTENTIONAL BB				RESULTS		
Manny Acta, Was	161	133	.62	293	31	39	38	46	6	119	4	517	124	95	63	24	44	27	17	8	59	102	.366
Dusty Baker, Cin	162	119	.58	285	28	27	26	63	39	124	2	507	132	100	101	37	40	28	12	4	74	88	.457
Bud Black, SD	162	113	.63	286	25	20	55	36	17	109	0	491	53	75	78	31	61	30	31	17	63	99	.389
Bruce Bochy, SF	162	134	.68	276	32	39	24	59	42	97	6	478	154	77	155	5	59	40	19	8	72	90	.444
Cecil Cooper, Hou	161	115	.58	252	16	47	60	35	14	108	2	488	166	81	112	5	53	35	18	11	86	75	.534
Bobby Cox, Atl	162	117	.67	294	31	17	59	34	6	134	6	545	85	90	77	23	80	45	35	20	72	90	.444
Fredi Gonzalez, Fla	161	106	.51	255	38	49	38	39	8	120	3	511	104	61	75	17	66	42	24	14	84	77	.522
Clint Hurdle, Col	162	131	.49	253	20	31	40	43	16	85	2	485	178	111	116	43	49	31	18	6	74	88	.457
Tony LaRussa, StL	162	153	.64	275	26	57	52	40	16	101	11	506	105	87	114	18	21	13	8	1	86	76	.531
Charlie Manuel, Phi	162	77	.65	291	62	60	33	42	24	124	1	468	161	88	92	34	64	46	18	11	92	70	.568
Bob Melvin, Ari	162	134	.57	263	27	30	41	39	16	102	0	444	81	87	79	28	41	27	14	9	82	80	.506
Lou Piniella, ChC	161	112	.47	286	22	31	42	37	27	111	3	478	121	93	98	15	45	28	17	9	97	64	.602
John Russell, Pit	162	128	.51	290	17	13	29	47	15	111	0	497	76	92	54	19	31	21	10	4	67	95	.414
Joe Torre, LAD	162	124	.53	277	43	66	61	30	17	94	8	461	169	75	133	38	58	46	12	5	84	78	.519
Ned Yost, Mil	150	93	.48	217	5	16	37	39	23	69	5	399	141	61	105	31	30	17	13	7	83	67	.553
162-Game Average		114	.59	282	26	35	43	42	20	118	3	503	127	92	100	22	49	30	18	8	81	81	.500

Manager	G	LUp	PL%	PH	PR	DS	Quick	Slow	LO	RCD	LS	Rel	SBA	SacA	RM	PO	#	Good	NG	Bomb	W	L	Pct
		LINEUPS		SUBSTITUTION			PITCHER USAGE						TACTICS				INTENTIONAL BB				RESULTS		
Jerry Manuel, NYM	93	58	.76	167	7	31	12	30	23	95	2	324	89	54	81	6	37	18	19	6	55	38	.591
Willie Randolph, NYM	69	46	.77	104	3	11	12	20	11	73	1	233	85	44	48	4	16	10	6	2	34	35	.493
Dale Sveum, Mil	12	3	.48	32	2	1	7	2	1	12	0	46	5	13	6	1	2	1	1	0	7	5	.583

Categories of this record are Games Managed (G), Number of Different Lineups Used (LUp), the percentage of players who had the platoon advantage at the start of the game (PL%), Pinch Hitters Used (PH), Pinch Runners Used (PR), Defensive Substitutes Used (DS), Quick Hooks (Quick), Slow Hooks (Slow), Long Outings by Starting Pitchers (LO), Relievers Used on Consecutive Days (RCD), Long Saves (LS), Relievers Used (Rel), Stolen Base Attempts (SBA), Sacrifice Bunts Attempts (SacA), Runners Moving with the Pitch (RM), Pitchouts ordered (PO), Intentional Walks issued (#), Intentional Walks resulting in a Good Outcome (Good), Intentional Walks resulting Not in a Good Outcome (NG), Intentional Walks Blowing up on the Manager (Bomb), Wins (W), Losses (L) and Winning Percentage (Pct.).

2008 Park Indices

2008 bid farewell to two New York ballparks: Yankee Stadium and Shea Stadium. The Yankees and Mets will open their 2009 seasons in entirely new digs. Up in the Bronx the stadium will still be known as Yankee Stadium (although some will feel obligated to add the word "New" beforehand in order to differentiate), while out in Queens the Mets will open their season at Citi Field. But what effects will these new parks have on performance? We'll track and measure it all with park indices.

Park indices are calculated in a way that neutralizes the effect of a team's makeup and isolates the effects of the park. The isolation is figured by comparing what both the team and its opponents accomplished at home, and comparing that to what the same team and its opponents accomplished on the road.

To calculate the park index for home runs in a given ballpark, we take the total home runs of both the home team and its opponents at the ballpark and compare it to the total home runs of the home team and its opponents in other games. We then divide each of those totals by the at-bats in the equivalent situations, so that if there are more at-bats in either situation the index is not skewed. The result is then multiplied by 100 to yield the familiar form.

The park indices for doubles, triples, walks, strikeouts and home runs by lefties and righties are determined like home runs above—relative to at-bats. Indices of at-bats runs, hits, errors and infield fielding errors (E-Infield) are calculated relative to games. The three batting average indices are calculated as is, since these are already relative to at-bats.

A park with an index of exactly 100 is neutral and can be said to have had no effect on that particular stat. An index above 100 means the ballpark favors that statistic. For example, if a park has a home run index of 120, it was 20% easier to hit home runs in that park then the rest of the parks in that team's league.

Each year there are twists and turns in the data. 2008 is no different. The historical data for Nationals Park shows only one-year data instead of three—three years of RFK Stadium data are shown for comparison. As for the complexities, the nearly four-month long, rain-delayed game between the White Sox and Orioles begun at U.S. Cellular Field but finished in Camden Yards—with the Sox as the home team—is counted a home game for the Sox and an away game for the Orioles. Two games between the Cubs and Astros, held in Milwaukee's Miller Park due to Hurricane Ike, are counted as away games for both teams because none of the games were played in either team's home park. Likewise for the two-game series between the Athletics and Red Sox that opened the season in the Tokyo Dome in Japan.

Arizona Diamondbacks - Chase Field

	2008 Season							2006-2008						
	Home Games			Away Games				Home Games			Away Games			
	D'Backs	Opp	Total	D'Backs	Opp	Total	Index	D'Backs	Opp	Total	D'Backs	Opp	Total	Index
G	81	81	162	81	81	162		243	243	486	243	243	486	
Avg	.268	.254	.261	.234	.258	.245	106	.271	.264	.267	.242	.259	.250	107
AB	2651	2816	5467	2758	2665	5423	101	8056	8535	16591	8396	8093	16489	101
R	392	366	758	328	340	668	113	1181	1169	2350	1024	1057	2081	113
H	711	716	1427	644	687	1331	107	2180	2257	4437	2031	2095	4126	108
2B	172	157	329	146	119	265	123	505	467	972	430	427	857	113
3B	34	11	45	13	19	32	139	92	60	152	33	53	86	176
HR	77	81	158	82	66	148	106	254	271	525	236	213	449	116
BB	291	216	507	296	235	531	95	818	786	1604	805	747	1552	103
SO	593	633	1226	694	596	1290	94	1528	1743	3271	1835	1689	3524	92
E	54	43	97	59	48	107	91	160	142	302	163	141	304	99
E-Infield	25	13	38	25	19	44	86	78	57	135	64	57	121	112
LHB-Avg	.280	.245	.261	.256	.276	.267	98	.282	.273	.277	.257	.272	.265	105
LHB-HR	23	24	47	30	18	48	93	107	125	232	85	91	176	129
RHB-Avg	.261	.261	.261	.221	.245	.233	112	.262	.258	.260	.231	.248	.239	109
RHB-HR	54	57	111	52	48	100	113	147	146	293	151	122	273	108

Atlanta Braves - Turner Field

	2008 Season							2006-2008						
	Home Games			Away Games				Home Games			Away Games			
	Braves	Opp	Total	Braves	Opp	Total	Index	Braves	Opp	Total	Braves	Opp	Total	Index
G	81	81	162	81	81	162		243	243	486	243	243	486	
Avg	.278	.263	.270	.263	.262	.263	103	.275	.263	.269	.269	.267	.268	100
AB	2792	2854	5646	2812	2626	5438	104	8239	8500	16739	8637	8137	16774	100
R	384	405	789	369	373	742	106	1175	1154	2329	1237	1162	2399	97
H	775	750	1525	739	689	1428	107	2264	2234	4498	2322	2176	4498	100
2B	148	177	325	168	148	316	99	439	453	892	517	448	965	93
3B	19	22	41	14	20	34	116	45	53	98	41	64	105	94
HR	62	82	144	68	74	142	98	244	265	509	284	246	530	96
BB	326	307	633	292	279	571	107	863	855	1718	815	840	1655	104
SO	502	564	1066	521	512	1033	99	1619	1720	3339	1722	1511	3233	103
E	64	57	121	43	43	86	141	162	160	322	151	134	285	113
E-Infield	26	23	49	18	17	35	140	68	69	137	67	62	129	106
LHB-Avg	.286	.255	.272	.278	.267	.273	99	.279	.265	.272	.277	.273	.275	99
LHB-HR	40	31	71	44	30	74	92	114	105	219	150	109	259	85
RHB-Avg	.268	.269	.269	.244	.260	.253	106	.272	.261	.266	.262	.263	.263	101
RHB-HR	22	51	73	24	44	68	104	130	160	290	134	137	271	107

Baltimore Orioles - Oriole Park at Camden Yards

	2008 Season							2006-2008						
	Home Games			Away Games				Home Games			Away Games			
	Orioles	Opp	Total	Orioles	Opp	Total	Index	Orioles	Opp	Total	Orioles	Opp	Total	Index
G	80	80	160	81	81	162		242	242	484	243	243	486	
Avg	.275	.277	.276	.260	.277	.268	103	.282	.277	.279	.263	.276	.269	104
AB	2727	2835	5562	2832	2716	5548	102	8289	8565	16854	8511	8105	16616	102
R	398	443	841	384	426	810	105	1200	1322	2522	1106	1314	2420	105
H	750	785	1535	736	753	1489	104	2335	2370	4705	2236	2238	4474	106
2B	155	142	297	167	137	304	97	427	427	854	489	421	910	93
3B	9	10	19	21	13	34	56	35	29	64	45	39	84	75
HR	96	108	204	76	76	152	134	279	298	577	199	263	462	123
BB	259	331	590	274	356	630	93	733	972	1705	774	1024	1798	93
SO	463	472	935	527	450	977	95	1296	1516	2812	1511	1509	3020	92
E	46	42	88	54	56	110	81	127	143	270	154	153	307	88
E-Infield	18	18	36	21	30	51	71	48	57	105	60	71	131	80
LHB-Avg	.279	.256	.267	.284	.286	.285	94	.285	.274	.279	.273	.283	.277	101
LHB-HR	45	44	89	39	27	66	134	119	116	235	94	112	206	111
RHB-Avg	.272	.293	.283	.240	.271	.256	111	.279	.279	.279	.255	.271	.263	106
RHB-HR	51	64	115	37	49	86	134	160	182	342	105	151	256	133

Boston Red Sox - Fenway Park

	2008 Season							2006-2008						
	Home Games			Away Games				Home Games			Away Games			
	Red Sox	Opp	Total	Red Sox	Opp	Total	Index	Red Sox	Opp	Total	Red Sox	Opp	Total	Index
G	81	81	162	81	81	162		243	243	486	243	243	486	
Avg	.292	.253	.272	.268	.246	.257	106	.291	.263	.277	.261	.254	.258	107
AB	2725	2810	5535	2871	2675	5546	100	8238	8483	16721	8566	8099	16665	100
R	461	337	798	384	357	741	108	1358	1099	2457	1174	1077	2251	109
H	795	712	1507	770	657	1427	106	2399	2229	4628	2237	2060	4297	108
2B	211	183	394	142	106	248	159	588	568	1156	444	364	808	143
3B	16	10	26	17	9	26	100	41	34	75	43	33	76	98
HR	79	68	147	94	79	173	85	241	211	452	290	268	558	81
BB	343	281	624	303	267	570	110	1015	751	1766	992	788	1780	99
SO	490	596	1086	578	589	1167	93	1475	1719	3194	1691	1685	3376	94
E	44	51	95	41	47	88	108	103	151	254	129	133	262	97
E-Infield	19	21	40	19	13	32	125	46	66	112	55	47	102	110
LHB-Avg	.283	.264	.274	.245	.235	.240	114	.285	.268	.276	.250	.248	.249	111
LHB-HR	29	33	62	37	37	74	84	93	99	192	127	122	249	76
RHB-Avg	.300	.244	.271	.289	.255	.272	100	.296	.259	.278	.269	.259	.264	105
RHB-HR	50	35	85	57	42	99	86	148	112	260	163	146	309	84

Chicago Cubs - Wrigley Field

	2008 Season							2006-2008						
	Home Games			Away Games				Home Games			Away Games			
	Cubs	Opp	Total	Cubs	Opp	Total	Index	Cubs	Opp	Total	Cubs	Opp	Total	Index
G	81	81	162	80	80	160		243	243	486	242	242	484	
Avg	.290	.242	.266	.266	.241	.254	105	.282	.246	.264	.262	.249	.256	103
AB	2711	2827	5538	2877	2668	5545	99	8262	8472	16734	8556	7959	16515	101
R	454	339	793	401	332	733	107	1236	1138	2374	1087	1057	2144	110
H	787	685	1472	765	644	1409	103	2333	2082	4415	2245	1983	4228	104
2B	153	151	304	176	132	308	99	477	449	926	463	390	853	107
3B	9	15	24	12	24	36	67	46	50	96	49	50	99	96
HR	106	80	186	78	80	158	118	271	290	561	230	245	475	117
BB	321	256	577	315	292	607	95	782	872	1654	749	936	1685	97
SO	563	676	1239	623	588	1211	102	1553	2010	3563	1615	1715	3330	106
E	50	41	91	49	45	94	96	160	175	335	139	170	309	108
E-Infield	23	18	41	22	18	40	101	76	72	148	52	77	129	114
LHB-Avg	.264	.250	.256	.246	.248	.247	103	.259	.251	.255	.254	.251	.253	101
LHB-HR	27	39	66	24	29	53	126	68	115	183	67	85	152	122
RHB-Avg	.300	.237	.271	.273	.237	.258	105	.295	.243	.269	.267	.248	.258	104
RHB-HR	79	41	120	54	51	105	114	203	175	378	163	160	323	114

Chicago White Sox - U.S. Cellular Field

	2008 Season							2006-2008						
	Home Games			Away Games				Home Games			Away Games			
	White Sox	Opp	Total	White Sox	Opp	Total	Index	White Sox	Opp	Total	White Sox	Opp	Total	Index
G	82	82	164	81	81	162		244	244	488	243	243	486	
Avg	.272	.242	.257	.253	.280	.267	96	.267	.264	.265	.260	.275	.267	99
AB	2773	2892	5665	2780	2749	5529	101	8206	8728	16934	8445	8208	16653	101
R	472	347	819	339	382	721	112	1284	1185	2469	1088	1177	2265	109
H	754	700	1454	704	771	1475	97	2189	2305	4494	2196	2256	4452	101
2B	145	147	292	151	167	318	90	394	449	843	442	458	900	92
3B	3	13	16	10	18	28	56	16	38	54	37	60	97	55
HR	143	83	226	92	73	165	134	389	284	673	272	246	518	128
BB	284	240	524	256	220	476	107	811	714	1525	763	678	1441	104
SO	497	640	1137	519	507	1026	108	1528	1693	3221	1693	1481	3174	100
E	52	54	106	56	36	92	114	152	156	308	154	129	283	108
E-Infield	28	21	49	18	11	29	167	63	64	127	54	55	109	116
LHB-Avg	.262	.253	.257	.244	.275	.262	98	.261	.263	.262	.271	.274	.273	96
LHB-HR	44	37	81	30	36	66	119	128	113	241	91	95	186	125
RHB-Avg	.276	.235	.256	.257	.285	.270	95	.270	.265	.268	.253	.275	.264	101
RHB-HR	99	46	145	62	37	99	144	261	171	432	181	151	332	129

Cincinnati Reds - Great American Ballpark

	2008 Season							2006-2008						
	Home Games			Away Games				Home Games			Away Games			
	Reds	Opp	Total	Reds	Opp	Total	Index	Reds	Opp	Total	Reds	Opp	Total	Index
G	81	81	162	81	81	162		243	243	486	243	243	486	
Avg	.253	.272	.263	.241	.278	.260	101	.263	.273	.268	.252	.285	.268	100
AB	2669	2860	5529	2796	2746	5542	100	8127	8664	16791	8460	8302	16762	100
R	377	400	777	327	400	727	107	1194	1268	2462	1042	1186	2228	111
H	676	778	1454	675	764	1439	101	2138	2361	4499	2128	2362	4490	100
2B	134	164	298	135	158	293	102	416	509	925	437	490	927	100
3B	12	15	27	12	14	26	104	26	33	59	33	45	78	76
HR	103	111	214	84	90	174	123	344	342	686	264	270	534	128
BB	291	271	562	269	286	555	101	901	735	1636	809	768	1577	104
SO	539	635	1174	586	592	1178	100	1676	1756	3432	1754	1592	3346	102
E	44	50	94	70	40	110	85	166	133	299	171	139	310	96
E-Infield	10	21	31	20	18	38	82	61	59	120	54	59	113	106
LHB-Avg	.254	.269	.261	.243	.277	.259	101	.269	.271	.270	.251	.273	.262	103
LHB-HR	59	44	103	59	35	94	111	172	137	309	149	102	251	123
RHB-Avg	.252	.274	.264	.240	.279	.260	102	.259	.274	.267	.252	.292	.272	98
RHB-HR	44	67	111	25	55	80	137	172	205	377	115	168	283	133

Cleveland Indians - Progressive Field

	2008 Season							2006-2008						
	Home Games			Away Games				Home Games			Away Games			
	Indians	Opp	Total	Indians	Opp	Total	Index	Indians	Opp	Total	Indians	Opp	Total	Index
G	81	81	162	81	81	162		239	239	478	247	247	494	
Avg	.272	.268	.270	.254	.278	.266	102	.276	.272	.274	.265	.277	.271	101
AB	2727	2853	5580	2816	2746	5562	100	8023	8432	16455	8743	8448	17191	99
R	426	355	781	379	406	785	99	1274	1077	2351	1212	1170	2382	102
H	741	766	1507	714	764	1478	102	2215	2290	4505	2320	2342	4662	100
2B	167	150	317	172	140	312	101	476	437	913	519	452	971	98
3B	11	6	17	11	15	26	65	31	26	57	45	40	85	70
HR	89	65	154	82	105	187	82	278	207	485	267	275	542	93
BB	312	233	545	248	211	459	118	883	653	1536	823	630	1453	110
SO	572	529	1101	641	457	1098	100	1696	1591	3287	1923	1390	3313	104
E	51	56	107	43	48	91	118	152	150	302	152	133	285	110
E-Infield	30	18	48	20	17	37	130	80	60	140	73	54	127	114
LHB-Avg	.277	.278	.278	.232	.276	.255	109	.285	.284	.284	.263	.283	.273	104
LHB-HR	41	25	66	30	46	76	92	129	78	207	121	102	223	99
RHB-Avg	.268	.263	.266	.266	.280	.272	98	.270	.264	.267	.267	.273	.270	99
RHB-HR	48	40	88	52	59	111	76	149	129	278	146	173	319	90

Colorado Rockies - Coors Field

	2008 Season							2006-2008						
	Home Games			Away Games				Home Games			Away Games			
	Rockies	Opp	Total	Rockies	Opp	Total	Index	Rockies	Opp	Total	Rockies	Opp	Total	Index
G	81	81	162	81	81	162		244	244	488	243	243	486	
Avg	.278	.280	.279	.249	.271	.260	107	.290	.278	.284	.253	.267	.260	109
AB	2742	2912	5654	2815	2702	5517	102	8330	8723	17053	8480	8111	16591	102
R	411	420	831	336	402	738	113	1345	1229	2574	1075	1163	2238	115
H	761	814	1575	701	733	1434	110	2415	2428	4843	2142	2165	4307	112
2B	167	163	330	143	172	315	102	493	508	1001	455	456	911	107
3B	21	22	43	7	24	31	135	76	76	152	42	70	112	132
HR	92	82	174	68	66	134	127	270	257	527	218	210	428	120
BB	289	253	542	281	309	590	90	903	764	1667	850	855	1705	95
SO	552	523	1075	657	518	1175	89	1564	1486	3050	1905	1474	3379	88
E	46	56	102	50	64	114	89	130	181	311	125	168	293	106
E-Infield	13	23	36	26	27	53	68	49	57	106	52	67	119	89
LHB-Avg	.255	.285	.272	.241	.278	.261	104	.278	.276	.277	.257	.279	.269	103
LHB-HR	29	36	65	23	27	50	123	80	114	194	78	97	175	109
RHB-Avg	.288	.276	.282	.253	.267	.259	109	.296	.280	.288	.250	.259	.254	113
RHB-HR	63	46	109	45	39	84	129	190	143	333	140	113	253	127

Detroit Tigers - Comerica Park

	2008 Season							2006-2008						
	Home Games			Away Games				Home Games			Away Games			
	Tigers	Opp	Total	Tigers	Opp	Total	Index	Tigers	Opp	Total	Tigers	Opp	Total	Index
G	81	81	162	81	81	162		243	243	486	243	243	486	
Avg	.287	.276	.281	.256	.273	.264	106	.282	.267	.275	.273	.264	.269	102
AB	2778	2877	5655	2863	2740	5603	101	8344	8633	16977	8696	8143	16839	101
R	437	433	870	384	424	808	108	1275	1199	2474	1255	1130	2385	104
H	797	793	1590	732	748	1480	107	2356	2308	4664	2373	2151	4524	103
2B	148	161	309	145	173	318	96	444	447	891	495	438	933	95
3B	23	16	39	18	17	35	110	77	63	140	54	54	108	129
HR	112	90	202	88	82	170	118	292	259	551	288	247	535	102
BB	267	301	568	305	343	648	87	726	840	1566	750	859	1609	97
SO	480	523	1003	596	468	1064	93	1493	1557	3050	1770	1484	3254	93
E	55	51	106	58	36	94	113	162	154	316	156	133	289	109
E-Infield	25	14	39	24	15	39	100	76	56	132	65	62	127	104
LHB-Avg	.278	.278	.278	.262	.276	.270	103	.279	.262	.269	.280	.265	.272	99
LHB-HR	28	39	67	20	36	56	120	70	95	165	69	95	164	100
RHB-Avg	.290	.274	.283	.253	.271	.261	108	.284	.271	.278	.270	.264	.267	104
RHB-HR	84	51	135	68	46	114	117	222	164	386	219	152	371	103

Florida Marlins - Dolphins Stadium

	2008 Season							2006-2008						
	Home Games			Away Games				Home Games			Away Games			
	Marlins	Opp	Total	Marlins	Opp	Total	Index	Marlins	Opp	Total	Marlins	Opp	Total	Index
G	81	81	162	80	80	160		243	243	486	242	242	484	
Avg	.247	.257	.252	.261	.259	.260	97	.259	.267	.263	.265	.274	.269	98
AB	2658	2811	5469	2841	2693	5534	98	8108	8567	16675	8520	8100	16620	100
R	369	386	755	401	381	782	95	1131	1216	2347	1187	1214	2401	97
H	656	723	1379	741	698	1439	95	2099	2284	4383	2256	2219	4475	98
2B	135	152	287	167	139	306	95	452	463	915	499	398	897	102
3B	20	10	30	8	12	20	152	68	55	123	40	45	85	144
HR	94	76	170	114	85	199	86	288	234	522	303	269	572	91
BB	281	294	575	262	292	554	105	810	985	1795	751	884	1635	109
SO	720	620	1340	651	507	1158	117	1991	1878	3869	1961	1479	3440	112
E	61	55	116	56	37	93	123	190	163	353	190	151	341	103
E-Infield	22	16	38	25	16	41	92	62	49	111	74	55	129	86
LHB-Avg	.236	.266	.252	.253	.252	.252	100	.238	.270	.256	.263	.265	.264	97
LHB-HR	27	34	61	39	37	76	78	70	96	166	80	98	178	90
RHB-Avg	.253	.251	.252	.266	.264	.265	95	.269	.264	.267	.265	.280	.272	98
RHB-HR	67	42	109	75	48	123	92	218	138	356	223	171	394	92

Houston Astros - Minute Maid Park

	2008 Season							2006-2008						
	Home Games			Away Games				Home Games			Away Games			
	Astros	Opp	Total	Astros	Opp	Total	Index	Astros	Opp	Total	Astros	Opp	Total	Index
G	78	78	156	83	83	166		240	240	480	245	245	490	
Avg	.277	.261	.269	.249	.268	.258	104	.266	.259	.262	.253	.270	.261	100
AB	2584	2720	5304	2867	2777	5644	100	8021	8534	16555	8556	8264	16820	100
R	366	358	724	346	385	731	105	1099	1092	2191	1071	1183	2254	99
H	717	710	1427	715	743	1458	104	2131	2213	4344	2165	2231	4396	101
2B	147	160	307	137	149	286	114	429	485	914	423	490	913	102
3B	13	13	26	9	20	29	95	51	43	94	28	55	83	115
HR	92	98	190	75	99	174	116	273	300	573	235	285	520	112
BB	211	250	461	238	242	480	102	781	728	1509	800	754	1554	99
SO	477	571	1048	574	524	1098	102	1485	1826	3311	1685	1538	3223	104
E	33	39	72	34	48	82	93	120	109	229	130	155	285	82
E-Infield	17	18	35	16	23	39	95	69	53	122	56	65	121	103
LHB-Avg	.274	.280	.277	.257	.262	.260	107	.266	.271	.269	.275	.263	.269	100
LHB-HR	26	38	64	26	39	65	105	94	117	211	101	98	199	108
RHB-Avg	.279	.248	.264	.245	.271	.257	103	.265	.251	.259	.243	.274	.258	100
RHB-HR	66	60	126	49	60	109	123	179	183	362	134	187	321	115

Kansas City Royals - Kauffman Stadium

	2008 Season							2006-2008						
	Home Games			Away Games				Home Games			Away Games			
	Royals	Opp	Total	Royals	Opp	Total	Index	Royals	Opp	Total	Royals	Opp	Total	Index
G	81	81	162	81	81	162		243	243	486	243	243	486	
Avg	.275	.260	.267	.263	.269	.266	100	.277	.279	.278	.258	.277	.267	104
AB	2752	2834	5586	2856	2738	5594	100	8199	8597	16796	8532	8203	16735	100
R	338	371	709	353	410	763	93	1117	1269	2386	1037	1261	2298	104
H	756	736	1492	751	737	1488	100	2271	2396	4667	2198	2272	4470	104
2B	159	147	306	144	135	279	110	498	557	1055	440	446	886	119
3B	12	19	31	16	22	38	82	59	48	107	52	50	102	105
HR	50	73	123	70	86	156	79	164	254	418	182	286	468	89
BB	197	252	449	195	263	458	98	660	854	1514	634	818	1452	104
SO	467	514	981	538	571	1109	89	1463	1458	2921	1651	1524	3175	92
E	49	50	99	47	45	92	108	147	156	303	153	160	313	97
E-Infield	22	16	38	19	18	37	103	64	55	119	59	57	116	103
LHB-Avg	.282	.265	.273	.262	.275	.269	102	.280	.272	.276	.260	.272	.265	104
LHB-HR	22	37	59	25	47	72	82	63	107	170	71	121	192	88
RHB-Avg	.268	.255	.262	.263	.263	.263	99	.275	.284	.279	.256	.281	.268	104
RHB-HR	28	36	64	45	39	84	76	101	147	248	111	165	276	90

Los Angeles Angels - Angel Stadium of Anaheim

	2008 Season							2006-2008						
	Home Games			Away Games				Home Games			Away Games			
	Angels	Opp	Total	Angels	Opp	Total	Index	Angels	Opp	Total	Angels	Opp	Total	Index
G	81	81	162	81	81	162		243	243	486	243	243	486	
Avg	.277	.260	.268	.260	.262	.261	103	.287	.259	.273	.264	.262	.263	104
AB	2716	2843	5559	2824	2728	5552	100	8223	8524	16747	8480	8151	16631	101
R	383	354	737	382	343	725	102	1209	1048	2257	1144	1112	2256	100
H	752	739	1491	734	716	1450	103	2361	2206	4567	2242	2139	4381	104
2B	137	135	272	137	137	274	99	461	447	908	446	414	860	105
3B	10	14	24	15	14	29	83	36	35	71	41	50	91	77
HR	72	82	154	87	78	165	93	202	222	424	239	247	486	87
BB	213	206	419	268	251	519	81	735	662	1397	739	743	1482	94
SO	470	540	1010	517	566	1083	93	1334	1717	3051	1450	1709	3159	96
E	41	51	92	50	64	114	81	157	164	321	159	158	317	101
E-Infield	13	18	31	18	27	45	69	62	65	127	70	61	131	97
LHB-Avg	.286	.256	.270	.263	.254	.258	104	.297	.259	.277	.259	.265	.262	106
LHB-HR	23	40	63	29	41	70	88	68	99	167	83	130	213	80
RHB-Avg	.271	.263	.267	.258	.269	.263	101	.280	.258	.270	.268	.260	.264	102
RHB-HR	49	42	91	58	37	95	97	134	123	257	156	117	273	91

Los Angeles Dodgers - Dodger Stadium

	2008 Season							2006-2008						
	Home Games			Away Games				Home Games			Away Games			
	Dodgers	Opp	Total	Dodgers	Opp	Total	Index	Dodgers	Opp	Total	Dodgers	Opp	Total	Index
G	81	81	162	81	81	162		243	243	486	243	243	486	
Avg	.266	.228	.247	.263	.275	.269	92	.279	.252	.265	.265	.270	.267	99
AB	2673	2749	5422	2833	2743	5576	97	8163	8452	16615	8584	8223	16807	99
R	351	265	616	349	383	732	84	1165	1004	2169	1090	1122	2212	98
H	710	627	1337	745	754	1499	89	2275	2131	4406	2276	2217	4493	98
2B	120	126	246	151	133	284	89	402	426	828	452	435	887	94
3B	9	8	17	20	20	40	44	43	25	68	79	55	134	51
HR	71	49	120	66	74	140	88	228	199	427	191	222	413	105
BB	267	215	482	276	265	541	92	873	727	1600	782	763	1545	105
SO	509	666	1175	523	539	1062	114	1381	1893	3274	1474	1564	3038	109
E	42	58	100	59	49	108	93	160	167	327	170	143	313	104
E-Infield	21	23	44	21	20	41	107	65	65	130	69	64	133	98
LHB-Avg	.274	.239	.255	.281	.297	.289	88	.285	.254	.270	.274	.275	.274	98
LHB-HR	21	25	46	24	24	48	102	94	89	183	88	75	163	114
RHB-Avg	.260	.220	.241	.250	.258	.254	95	.273	.251	.261	.258	.265	.262	100
RHB-HR	50	24	74	42	50	92	81	134	110	244	103	147	250	98

Milwaukee Brewers - Miller Park

	2008 Season							2006-2008						
	Home Games			Away Games				Home Games			Away Games			
	Brewers	Opp	Total	Brewers	Opp	Total	Index	Brewers	Opp	Total	Brewers	Opp	Total	Index
G	81	81	162	81	81	162		243	243	486	243	243	486	
Avg	.251	.252	.251	.254	.260	.257	98	.260	.251	.255	.255	.275	.265	96
AB	2677	2813	5490	2858	2717	5575	98	8018	8462	16480	8504	8182	16686	99
R	372	327	699	378	362	740	94	1187	1088	2275	1094	1210	2304	99
H	672	708	1380	726	707	1433	96	2081	2128	4209	2172	2254	4426	95
2B	151	119	270	173	142	315	87	476	442	918	459	495	954	97
3B	18	15	33	17	7	24	140	47	37	84	45	43	88	97
HR	100	76	176	98	99	197	91	317	245	562	292	268	560	102
BB	287	285	572	263	243	506	115	823	809	1632	730	740	1470	112
SO	605	590	1195	598	520	1118	109	1753	1848	3601	1820	1581	3401	107
E	51	56	107	50	62	112	96	174	162	336	153	152	305	110
E-Infield	24	21	45	24	26	50	90	66	67	133	67	65	132	101
LHB-Avg	.270	.261	.264	.232	.254	.246	108	.260	.259	.260	.251	.271	.262	99
LHB-HR	31	42	73	20	39	59	126	109	110	219	98	105	203	110
RHB-Avg	.245	.245	.245	.261	.265	.263	93	.259	.247	.253	.257	.278	.267	95
RHB-HR	69	34	103	78	60	138	76	208	135	343	194	163	357	97

Minnesota Twins - Hubert H. Humphrey Metrodome Surface: FieldTurf

	2008 Season							2006-2008						
	Home Games			Away Games				Home Games			Away Games			
	Twins	Opp	Total	Twins	Opp	Total	Index	Twins	Opp	Total	Twins	Opp	Total	Index
G	81	81	162	82	82	164		243	243	486	244	244	488	
Avg	.289	.255	.272	.269	.294	.281	97	.283	.254	.268	.270	.287	.279	96
AB	2720	2849	5569	2921	2866	5787	97	8171	8545	16716	8594	8344	16938	99
R	431	304	735	398	441	839	89	1179	954	2133	1169	1199	2368	90
H	787	726	1513	785	842	1627	94	2316	2169	4485	2324	2394	4718	95
2B	156	137	293	142	158	300	101	414	425	839	432	447	879	97
3B	28	9	37	21	18	39	99	70	35	105	49	42	91	117
HR	56	82	138	55	101	156	92	173	243	416	199	307	506	83
BB	246	179	425	283	227	510	87	724	544	1268	807	638	1445	89
SO	444	518	962	535	477	1012	99	1267	1728	2995	1423	1525	2948	103
E	45	48	93	63	62	125	75	135	156	291	152	180	332	88
E-Infield	12	18	30	20	25	45	67	46	53	99	57	75	132	75
LHB-Avg	.297	.258	.279	.284	.297	.289	96	.288	.268	.278	.286	.298	.292	96
LHB-HR	35	24	59	35	42	77	81	86	101	187	103	132	235	81
RHB-Avg	.281	.253	.265	.251	.291	.274	97	.279	.244	.260	.256	.279	.268	97
RHB-HR	21	58	79	20	59	79	102	87	142	229	96	175	271	86

New York Mets - Shea Stadium

	2008 Season							2006-2008						
	Home Games			Away Games				Home Games			Away Games			
	Mets	Opp	Total	Mets	Opp	Total	Index	Mets	Opp	Total	Mets	Opp	Total	Index
G	81	81	162	81	81	162		243	243	486	243	243	486	
Avg	.267	.236	.251	.265	.273	.269	93	.265	.242	.253	.272	.266	.269	94
AB	2741	2817	5558	2865	2748	5613	99	8139	8461	16600	8630	8193	16823	99
R	388	348	736	411	367	778	95	1150	1071	2221	1287	1125	2412	92
H	733	664	1397	758	751	1509	93	2153	2051	4204	2350	2181	4531	93
2B	131	129	260	143	135	278	94	427	413	840	464	421	885	96
3B	15	5	20	23	17	40	50	48	30	78	58	43	101	78
HR	95	79	174	77	84	161	109	274	240	514	275	268	543	96
BB	339	291	630	280	299	579	110	881	839	1720	834	848	1682	104
SO	502	624	1126	522	557	1079	105	1477	1810	3287	1599	1666	3265	102
E	34	61	95	49	53	102	93	138	157	295	150	173	323	91
E-Infield	15	29	44	21	27	48	92	58	69	127	50	70	120	106
LHB-Avg	.258	.258	.258	.269	.281	.274	94	.259	.258	.259	.271	.268	.270	96
LHB-HR	48	36	84	46	39	85	102	139	99	238	156	104	260	93
RHB-Avg	.280	.221	.245	.258	.269	.264	93	.270	.232	.249	.274	.265	.269	93
RHB-HR	47	43	90	31	45	76	117	135	141	276	119	164	283	99

New York Yankees - Yankee Stadium

| | 2008 Season | | | | | | | 2006-2008 | | | | | | |
| | Home Games | | | Away Games | | | | Home Games | | | Away Games | | | |
	Yankees	Opp	Total	Yankees	Opp	Total	Index	Yankees	Opp	Total	Yankees	Opp	Total	Index
G	81	81	162	81	81	162		243	243	486	243	243	486	
Avg	.281	.253	.267	.262	.280	.271	98	.288	.256	.272	.276	.275	.275	99
AB	2754	2795	5549	2818	2752	5570	100	8284	8457	16741	8656	8266	16922	99
R	412	361	773	377	366	743	104	1382	1097	2479	1305	1174	2479	100
H	773	707	1480	739	771	1510	98	2388	2166	4554	2388	2273	4661	98
2B	144	144	288	145	144	289	100	449	453	902	493	456	949	96
3B	10	13	23	10	12	22	105	29	30	59	44	44	88	68
HR	92	68	160	88	75	163	99	310	234	544	281	229	510	108
BB	258	254	512	277	235	512	100	906	761	1667	915	802	1717	98
SO	485	603	1088	530	538	1068	102	1428	1660	3088	1631	1509	3140	99
E	38	63	101	45	33	78	129	138	170	308	137	140	277	111
E-Infield	12	27	39	21	16	37	105	57	78	135	61	61	122	111
LHB-Avg	.288	.237	.266	.268	.279	.273	97	.288	.247	.271	.279	.279	.279	97
LHB-HR	56	33	89	48	28	76	115	182	111	293	164	82	246	120
RHB-Avg	.270	.267	.268	.254	.281	.269	100	.289	.263	.274	.272	.272	.272	101
RHB-HR	36	35	71	40	47	87	84	128	123	251	117	147	264	97

Oakland Athletics - McAfee Coliseum

| | 2008 Season | | | | | | | 2006-2008 | | | | | | |
| | Home Games | | | Away Games | | | | Home Games | | | Away Games | | | |
	Athletics	Opp	Total	Athletics	Opp	Total	Index	Athletics	Opp	Total	Athletics	Opp	Total	Index
G	79	79	158	82	82	164		241	241	482	244	244	488	
Avg	.243	.240	.241	.241	.266	.253	95	.247	.253	.250	.258	.273	.265	94
AB	2639	2705	5344	2812	2691	5503	101	7983	8380	16363	8545	8204	16749	99
R	316	310	626	330	380	710	92	1019	1006	2025	1139	1169	2308	89
H	641	649	1290	677	715	1392	96	1974	2119	4093	2203	2238	4441	93
2B	138	126	264	132	158	290	94	393	412	805	438	443	881	94
3B	8	11	19	15	20	35	56	33	47	80	28	63	91	90
HR	59	66	125	66	69	135	95	220	196	416	251	239	490	87
BB	274	280	554	300	296	596	96	911	814	1725	977	821	1798	98
SO	580	531	1111	646	530	1176	97	1508	1529	3037	1813	1571	3384	92
E	45	49	94	53	32	85	115	131	134	265	141	126	267	100
E-Infield	15	24	39	12	8	20	202	43	58	101	42	57	99	103
LHB-Avg	.236	.237	.236	.233	.263	.245	96	.245	.252	.248	.244	.279	.260	96
LHB-HR	32	32	64	38	16	54	111	117	81	198	123	73	196	100
RHB-Avg	.249	.242	.245	.248	.267	.258	95	.249	.254	.252	.269	.269	.269	94
RHB-HR	27	34	61	28	53	81	83	103	115	218	128	166	294	78

Philadelphia Phillies - Citizens Bank Park

| | 2008 Season | | | | | | | 2006-2008 | | | | | | |
| | Home Games | | | Away Games | | | | Home Games | | | Away Games | | | |
	Phillies	Opp	Total	Phillies	Opp	Total	Index	Phillies	Opp	Total	Phillies	Opp	Total	Index
G	81	81	162	81	81	162		243	243	486	243	243	486	
Avg	.262	.258	.260	.249	.261	.255	102	.272	.269	.270	.259	.271	.265	102
AB	2703	2880	5583	2806	2683	5489	102	8207	8597	16804	8677	8285	16962	99
R	412	338	750	387	342	729	103	1306	1179	2485	1250	1134	2384	104
H	707	744	1451	700	700	1400	104	2232	2311	4543	2251	2249	4500	101
2B	139	153	292	152	153	305	94	436	495	931	475	491	966	97
3B	18	8	26	18	17	35	73	54	35	89	64	56	120	75
HR	109	80	189	105	80	185	100	337	326	663	306	243	549	122
BB	305	252	557	281	281	562	97	904	783	1687	949	820	1769	96
SO	539	557	1096	578	524	1102	98	1667	1731	3398	1858	1538	3396	101
E	43	50	93	47	52	99	94	139	173	312	144	155	299	104
E-Infield	19	23	42	24	17	41	102	58	80	138	66	68	134	103
LHB-Avg	.279	.282	.280	.260	.257	.259	108	.280	.282	.281	.268	.271	.269	104
LHB-HR	60	35	95	55	34	89	107	186	127	313	170	92	262	122
RHB-Avg	.246	.242	.244	.239	.263	.252	97	.264	.260	.262	.250	.272	.262	100
RHB-HR	49	45	94	50	46	96	95	151	199	350	136	151	287	122

Pittsburgh Pirates - PNC Park

| | 2008 Season | | | | | | | 2006-2008 | | | | | | |
| | Home Games | | | Away Games | | | | Home Games | | | Away Games | | | |
	Pirates	Opp	Total	Pirates	Opp	Total	Index	Pirates	Opp	Total	Pirates	Opp	Total	Index
G	81	81	162	81	81	162		243	243	486	243	243	486	
Avg	.263	.282	.273	.254	.291	.272	100	.273	.279	.276	.250	.292	.270	102
AB	2775	2951	5726	2853	2742	5595	102	8297	8699	16996	8458	8154	16612	102
R	361	405	766	374	479	853	90	1114	1162	2276	1036	1365	2401	95
H	729	832	1561	725	799	1524	102	2263	2426	4689	2116	2377	4493	104
2B	159	189	348	155	172	327	104	490	527	1017	432	471	903	110
3B	14	12	26	7	21	28	91	36	33	69	33	52	85	79
HR	74	79	153	79	97	176	85	209	219	428	233	287	520	80
BB	226	333	559	248	324	572	95	686	865	1551	710	930	1640	92
SO	481	475	956	558	488	1046	89	1588	1514	3102	1786	1506	3292	92
E	45	57	102	62	43	105	97	118	155	273	176	151	327	83
E-Infield	26	27	53	26	16	42	126	63	64	127	82	55	137	93
LHB-Avg	.271	.285	.278	.265	.299	.281	99	.266	.278	.272	.244	.283	.264	103
LHB-HR	38	24	62	31	28	59	101	81	82	163	70	90	160	99
RHB-Avg	.257	.280	.270	.248	.288	.268	101	.276	.279	.278	.253	.296	.274	102
RHB-HR	36	55	91	48	69	117	77	128	137	265	163	197	360	72

San Diego Padres - PETCO Park

| | 2008 Season | | | | | | | 2006-2008 | | | | | | |
| | Home Games | | | Away Games | | | | Home Games | | | Away Games | | | |
	Padres	Opp	Total	Padres	Opp	Total	Index	Padres	Opp	Total	Padres	Opp	Total	Index
G	81	81	162	81	81	162		243	243	486	244	244	488	
Avg	.239	.246	.242	.260	.281	.270	90	.240	.242	.241	.268	.267	.267	90
AB	2714	2854	5568	2854	2720	5574	100	8071	8520	16591	8685	8244	16929	98
R	289	332	621	348	432	780	80	927	947	1874	1182	1162	2344	80
H	648	702	1350	742	764	1506	90	1935	2058	3993	2328	2199	4527	89
2B	117	113	230	147	148	295	78	361	357	718	523	438	961	76
3B	15	12	27	12	17	29	93	56	44	100	40	58	98	104
HR	66	70	136	88	95	183	74	213	207	420	273	253	526	81
BB	283	263	546	235	298	533	103	833	719	1552	806	784	1590	100
SO	620	589	1209	639	511	1150	105	1805	1784	3589	1787	1549	3336	110
E	48	34	82	37	35	72	114	126	107	233	143	134	277	84
E-Infield	14	14	28	10	16	26	108	44	37	81	53	61	114	71
LHB-Avg	.248	.257	.252	.282	.282	.282	89	.258	.244	.251	.274	.269	.272	92
LHB-HR	27	22	49	50	38	88	55	87	85	172	140	113	253	70
RHB-Avg	.230	.238	.235	.241	.280	.261	90	.225	.240	.233	.263	.265	.264	88
RHB-HR	39	48	87	38	57	95	92	126	122	248	133	140	273	92

San Francisco Giants - AT&T Park

| | 2008 Season | | | | | | | 2006-2008 | | | | | | |
| | Home Games | | | Away Games | | | | Home Games | | | Away Games | | | |
	Giants	Opp	Total	Giants	Opp	Total	Index	Giants	Opp	Total	Giants	Opp	Total	Index
G	81	81	162	81	81	162		243	243	486	242	242	484	
Avg	.264	.259	.261	.260	.257	.258	101	.262	.261	.262	.254	.259	.257	102
AB	2696	2829	5525	2847	2666	5513	100	8107	8521	16628	8446	7957	16403	101
R	314	401	715	326	358	684	105	1032	1150	2182	1037	1119	2156	101
H	712	732	1444	740	684	1424	101	2128	2221	4349	2149	2059	4208	103
2B	162	163	325	149	138	287	113	457	475	932	418	433	851	108
3B	22	23	45	15	9	24	187	72	69	141	54	51	105	132
HR	45	75	120	49	72	121	99	160	207	367	228	226	454	80
BB	229	331	560	223	321	544	103	752	886	1638	726	943	1669	97
SO	492	624	1116	552	616	1168	95	1327	1683	3010	1515	1606	3121	95
E	58	59	117	38	43	81	144	152	160	312	123	131	254	122
E-Infield	34	22	56	18	17	35	160	81	60	141	52	60	112	125
LHB-Avg	.282	.256	.270	.267	.252	.261	104	.270	.257	.264	.260	.260	.260	102
LHB-HR	15	23	38	18	22	40	101	67	64	131	90	77	167	78
RHB-Avg	.249	.260	.255	.253	.259	.257	100	.255	.263	.259	.249	.258	.254	102
RHB-HR	30	52	82	31	50	81	96	93	143	236	138	149	287	81

Seattle Mariners - Safeco Field

	2008 Season							2006-2008						
	Home Games			Away Games				Home Games			Away Games			
	Mariners	Opp	Total	Mariners	Opp	Total	Index	Mariners	Opp	Total	Mariners	Opp	Total	Index
G	81	81	162	81	81	162		244	244	488	242	242	484	
Avg	.271	.268	.269	.260	.285	.272	99	.273	.266	.269	.276	.285	.280	96
AB	2768	2858	5626	2875	2729	5604	100	8240	8584	16824	8757	8220	16977	98
R	337	378	715	334	433	767	93	1076	1156	2232	1145	1260	2405	92
H	750	765	1515	748	779	1527	99	2250	2281	4531	2417	2341	4758	94
2B	150	155	305	135	196	331	92	397	492	889	438	517	955	94
3B	12	10	22	8	10	18	122	42	29	71	42	48	90	80
HR	59	76	135	65	85	150	90	217	237	454	232	254	486	94
BB	201	326	527	216	300	516	102	606	907	1513	604	825	1429	107
SO	435	558	993	455	458	913	108	1365	1689	3054	1360	1414	2774	111
E	39	57	96	60	62	122	79	127	177	304	150	196	346	87
E-Infield	15	22	37	26	31	57	65	49	66	115	66	88	154	74
LHB-Avg	.278	.260	.268	.277	.320	.299	90	.294	.263	.278	.285	.290	.288	96
LHB-HR	23	39	62	23	47	70	93	74	104	178	83	111	194	94
RHB-Avg	.266	.274	.270	.248	.255	.251	107	.261	.267	.264	.270	.281	.275	96
RHB-HR	36	37	73	42	38	80	87	143	133	276	149	143	292	95

St Louis Cardinals - Busch Stadium

	2008 Season							2006-2008						
	Home Games			Away Games				Home Games			Away Games			
	Cardinals	Opp	Total	Cardinals	Opp	Total	Index	Cardinals	Opp	Total	Cardinals	Opp	Total	Index
G	81	81	162	81	81	162		242	242	484	243	243	486	
Avg	.285	.261	.273	.277	.279	.278	98	.280	.261	.270	.269	.279	.274	99
AB	2731	2847	5578	2905	2776	5681	98	8143	8506	16649	8544	8208	16752	100
R	374	356	730	405	369	774	94	1138	1089	2227	1147	1227	2374	94
H	779	742	1521	806	775	1581	96	2281	2220	4501	2301	2286	4587	99
2B	126	169	295	157	183	340	88	398	472	870	456	509	965	91
3B	16	14	30	10	20	30	102	37	45	82	29	61	90	92
HR	79	82	161	95	81	176	93	226	240	466	273	284	557	84
BB	272	256	528	305	240	545	99	796	753	1549	818	756	1574	99
SO	471	477	948	514	480	994	97	1315	1434	2749	1501	1438	2939	94
E	42	38	80	43	42	85	94	165	139	304	139	144	283	108
E-Infield	15	12	27	13	16	29	93	70	56	126	56	63	119	106
LHB-Avg	.286	.252	.269	.280	.273	.276	97	.279	.262	.269	.263	.283	.274	98
LHB-HR	22	39	61	26	34	60	105	75	112	187	90	124	214	86
RHB-Avg	.285	.266	.275	.276	.284	.280	98	.281	.260	.271	.273	.275	.274	99
RHB-HR	57	43	100	69	47	116	87	151	128	279	183	160	343	83

Tampa Bay Rays - Tropicana Field Surface: FieldTurf

	2008 Season							2006-2008						
	Home Games			Away Games				Home Games			Away Games			
	Rays	Opp	Total	Rays	Opp	Total	Index	Rays	Opp	Total	Rays	Opp	Total	Index
G	78	78	156	84	84	168		237	237	474	249	249	498	
Avg	.273	.231	.251	.250	.259	.254	99	.263	.264	.263	.260	.284	.272	97
AB	2539	2633	5172	3002	2861	5863	95	7796	8291	16087	8812	8484	17296	98
R	383	297	680	391	374	765	96	1107	1135	2242	1138	1336	2474	95
H	692	608	1300	751	741	1492	94	2047	2191	4238	2291	2407	4698	95
2B	125	127	252	159	162	321	89	370	458	828	472	499	971	92
3B	20	15	35	17	17	34	117	59	48	107	47	49	96	120
HR	87	67	154	93	99	192	91	280	254	534	277	291	568	101
BB	315	254	569	311	272	583	111	801	828	1629	811	872	1683	104
SO	556	562	1118	668	581	1249	101	1679	1692	3371	1975	1624	3599	101
E	46	49	95	44	58	102	100	152	153	305	171	139	310	103
E-Infield	12	23	35	18	30	48	79	62	65	127	75	60	135	99
LHB-Avg	.282	.231	.259	.242	.262	.250	104	.270	.268	.269	.257	.285	.270	100
LHB-HR	51	26	77	60	39	99	87	126	105	231	133	113	246	101
RHB-Avg	.259	.231	.243	.263	.257	.259	94	.256	.262	.259	.263	.283	.273	95
RHB-HR	36	41	77	33	60	93	95	154	149	303	144	178	322	101

Texas Rangers - Rangers Ballpark in Arlington

	2008 Season							2006-2008						
	Home Games			Away Games				Home Games			Away Games			
	Rangers	Opp	Total	Rangers	Opp	Total	Index	Rangers	Opp	Total	Rangers	Opp	Total	Index
G	81	81	162	81	81	162		243	243	486	243	243	486	
Avg	.297	.289	.293	.268	.287	.277	106	.286	.275	.280	.263	.286	.274	102
AB	2833	2930	5763	2895	2792	5687	101	8363	8695	17058	8579	8188	16767	102
R	485	511	996	416	456	872	114	1334	1324	2658	1218	1271	2489	107
H	842	846	1688	777	801	1578	107	2391	2391	4782	2259	2339	4598	104
2B	189	184	373	187	171	358	103	521	489	1010	510	463	973	102
3B	24	25	49	11	11	22	220	59	49	108	35	37	72	147
HR	107	97	204	87	79	166	121	295	254	549	261	239	500	108
BB	322	297	619	273	328	601	102	826	873	1699	777	916	1693	99
SO	590	507	1097	617	456	1073	101	1730	1522	3252	1762	1389	3151	101
E	74	57	131	58	41	99	132	188	154	342	166	146	312	110
E-Infield	28	24	52	23	17	40	130	87	67	154	61	69	130	118
LHB-Avg	.300	.282	.291	.264	.294	.278	105	.281	.269	.275	.260	.291	.275	100
LHB-HR	59	43	102	48	37	85	121	131	130	261	124	111	235	109
RHB-Avg	.295	.294	.295	.273	.281	.277	106	.289	.280	.284	.266	.281	.273	104
RHB-HR	48	54	102	39	42	81	122	164	124	288	137	128	265	107

Toronto Blue Jays - Rogers Centre Surface: FieldTurf

	2008 Season							2006-2008						
	Home Games			Away Games				Home Games			Away Games			
	Blue Jays	Opp	Total	Blue Jays	Opp	Total	Index	Blue Jays	Opp	Total	Blue Jays	Opp	Total	Index
G	81	81	162	81	81	162		243	243	486	243	243	486	
Avg	.264	.234	.249	.264	.253	.259	96	.273	.241	.257	.265	.264	.265	97
AB	2728	2802	5530	2775	2658	5433	102	8174	8418	16592	8461	8086	16547	100
R	359	289	648	355	321	676	96	1188	972	2160	1088	1091	2179	99
H	721	657	1378	732	673	1405	98	2234	2026	4260	2244	2134	4378	97
2B	153	151	304	150	130	280	107	509	423	932	486	401	887	105
3B	23	18	41	9	13	22	183	52	47	99	31	29	60	165
HR	69	56	125	57	78	135	91	280	233	513	210	243	453	113
BB	264	254	518	257	213	470	108	779	727	1506	789	723	1512	99
SO	477	647	1124	461	537	998	111	1451	1806	3257	1437	1521	2958	110
E	29	52	81	55	48	103	79	116	136	252	169	121	290	87
E-Infield	14	21	35	24	23	47	74	50	54	104	67	56	123	85
LHB-Avg	.276	.250	.261	.259	.274	.267	98	.277	.251	.262	.258	.271	.265	99
LHB-HR	25	32	57	24	34	58	93	91	114	205	70	100	170	119
RHB-Avg	.257	.219	.240	.267	.234	.252	95	.271	.232	.253	.269	.258	.264	96
RHB-HR	44	24	68	33	44	77	89	189	119	308	140	143	283	109

Washington Nationals - Nationals Park

	2008 Season							2005-2007						
	Home Games			Away Games				Home Games			Away Games			
	Nationals	Opp	Total	Nationals	Opp	Total	Index	Nationals	Opp	Total	Nationals	Opp	Total	Index
G	80	80	160	81	81	162		243	243	486	243	243	486	
Avg	.251	.269	.261	.250	.270	.260	100	.252	.256	.254	.261	.281	.271	94
AB	2653	2861	5514	2838	2684	5522	101	7951	8505	16456	8490	8231	16721	98
R	316	426	742	325	399	724	104	986	1087	2073	1072	1241	2313	90
H	667	770	1437	709	726	1435	101	2006	2178	4184	2213	2315	4528	92
2B	126	161	287	143	144	287	100	450	434	884	492	450	942	95
3B	15	10	25	11	12	23	109	51	39	90	34	51	85	108
HR	51	97	148	66	93	159	93	168	234	402	236	286	522	78
BB	280	280	560	254	308	562	100	795	788	1583	814	915	1729	93
SO	517	523	1040	578	540	1118	93	1574	1548	3122	1800	1340	3140	101
E	59	46	105	64	63	127	84	151	152	303	181	118	299	101
E-Infield	26	24	50	24	23	47	108	63	59	122	65	51	116	105
LHB-Avg	.243	.281	.264	.237	.257	.247	107	.258	.260	.259	.262	.276	.269	96
LHB-HR	9	42	51	23	35	58	84	66	104	170	92	120	212	81
RHB-Avg	.256	.260	.258	.257	.280	.268	96	.248	.253	.250	.259	.285	.272	92
RHB-HR	42	55	97	43	58	101	99	102	130	232	144	166	310	76

2008 American League Ballpark Index Rankings - Runs

Home Park	TOTALS											LHB		RHB	
	Avg	AB	R	H	2B	3B	HR	BB	SO	E	E-Inf	Avg	HR	Avg	HR
Rangers (Rangers Ballpark in Arlington)	106	101	114	107	103	220	121	102	101	132	130	105	121	106	122
White Sox (U.S. Cellular Field)	96	101	112	97	90	56	134	107	108	114	167	98	119	95	144
Red Sox (Fenway Park)	106	100	108	106	159	100	85	110	93	108	125	114	84	100	86
Tigers (Comerica Park)	106	101	108	107	96	110	118	87	93	113	100	103	120	108	117
Orioles (Oriole Park at Camden Yards)	103	102	105	104	97	56	134	93	95	81	71	94	134	111	134
Yankees (Yankee Stadium)	98	100	104	98	100	105	99	100	102	129	105	97	115	100	84
Angels (Angel Stadium of Anaheim)	103	100	102	103	99	83	93	81	93	81	69	104	88	101	97
Indians (Progressive Field)	102	100	99	102	101	65	82	118	100	118	130	109	92	98	76
Blue Jays (Rogers Centre)	96	102	96	98	107	183	91	108	111	79	74	98	93	95	89
Rays (Tropicana Field)	99	95	96	94	89	117	91	111	101	100	79	104	87	94	95
Mariners (Safeco Field)	99	100	93	99	92	122	90	102	108	79	65	90	93	107	87
Royals (Kauffman Stadium)	100	100	93	100	110	82	79	98	89	108	103	102	82	99	76
Athletics (McAfee Coliseum)	95	101	92	96	94	56	95	96	97	115	202	96	111	95	83
Twins (Hubert H. Humphrey Metrodome)	97	97	89	94	101	99	92	87	99	75	67	96	81	97	102

2008 National League Ballpark Index Rankings - Runs

Home Park	TOTALS											LHB		RHB	
	Avg	AB	R	H	2B	3B	HR	BB	SO	E	E-Inf	Avg	HR	Avg	HR
Diamondbacks (Chase Field)	106	101	113	107	123	139	106	95	94	91	86	98	93	112	113
Rockies (Coors Field)	107	101	113	110	102	135	127	90	89	89	68	104	123	109	129
Reds (Great American Ballpark)	101	100	107	101	102	104	123	101	100	85	82	101	111	102	137
Cubs (Wrigley Field)	105	99	107	103	99	67	118	95	102	96	101	103	126	105	114
Braves (Turner Field)	103	104	106	107	99	116	98	107	99	141	140	99	92	106	104
Astros (Minute Maid Park)	104	100	105	104	114	95	116	102	102	93	95	107	105	103	123
Giants (AT&T Park)	101	100	105	101	113	187	99	103	95	144	160	104	101	100	96
Nationals (Nationals Park)	100	101	104	101	100	109	93	100	93	84	108	107	84	96	99
Phillies (Citizens Bank Park)	102	102	103	104	94	73	100	97	98	94	102	108	107	97	95
Marlins (Dolphins Stadium)	97	98	95	95	95	152	86	105	117	123	92	100	78	95	92
Mets (Shea Stadium)	93	99	95	93	94	50	109	110	105	93	92	94	102	93	117
Brewers (Miller Park)	98	98	94	96	87	140	91	115	109	96	90	108	126	93	76
Cardinals (Busch Stadium)	98	98	94	96	88	102	93	99	97	94	93	97	105	98	87
Pirates (PNC Park)	100	102	90	102	104	91	85	95	89	97	126	99	101	101	77
Dodgers (Dodger Stadium)	92	97	84	89	89	44	88	92	114	93	107	88	102	95	81
Padres (PETCO Park)	90	100	80	90	78	93	74	103	105	114	108	89	55	90	92

2008 AL Home Runs

Home Park	Index
Orioles	134
White Sox	134
Rangers	121
Tigers	118
Yankees	99
Athletics	95
Angels	93
Twins	92
Blue Jays	91
Rays	91
Mariners	90
Red Sox	85
Indians	82
Royals	79

2008 AL LHB Home Runs

Home Park	Index
Orioles	134
Rangers	121
Tigers	120
White Sox	119
Yankees	115
Athletics	111
Blue Jays	93
Mariners	93
Indians	92
Angels	88
Rays	87
Red Sox	84
Royals	82
Twins	81

2008 AL RHB Home Runs

Home Park	Index
White Sox	144
Orioles	134
Rangers	122
Tigers	117
Twins	102
Angels	97
Rays	95
Blue Jays	89
Mariners	87
Red Sox	86
Yankees	84
Athletics	83
Royals	76
Indians	76

2008 NL Home Runs

Home Park	Index
Rockies	127
Reds	123
Cubs	118
Astros	116
Mets	109
Diamondbacks	106
Phillies	100
Giants	99
Braves	98
Nationals	93
Cardinals	93
Brewers	91
Dodgers	88
Marlins	86
Pirates	85
Padres	74

2008 NL LHB Home Runs

Home Park	Index
Brewers	126
Cubs	126
Rockies	123
Reds	111
Phillies	107
Cardinals	105
Astros	105
Dodgers	102
Mets	102
Giants	101
Pirates	101
Diamondbacks	93
Braves	92
Nationals	84
Marlins	78
Padres	55

2008 NL RHB Home Runs

Home Park	Index
Reds	137
Rockies	129
Astros	123
Mets	117
Cubs	114
Diamondbacks	113
Braves	104
Nationals	99
Giants	96
Phillies	95
Padres	92
Marlins	92
Cardinals	87
Dodgers	81
Pirates	77
Brewers	76

2008 AL Avg	
Home Park	Index
Tigers	106
Red Sox	106
Rangers	106
Orioles	103
Angels	103
Indians	102
Royals	100
Mariners	99
Rays	99
Yankees	98
Twins	97
Blue Jays	96
White Sox	96
Athletics	95

2008 AL LHB Avg	
Home Park	Index
Red Sox	114
Indians	109
Rangers	105
Angels	104
Rays	104
Tigers	103
Royals	102
White Sox	98
Blue Jays	98
Yankees	97
Twins	96
Athletics	96
Orioles	94
Mariners	90

2008 AL RHB Avg	
Home Park	Index
Orioles	111
Tigers	108
Mariners	107
Rangers	106
Angels	101
Yankees	100
Red Sox	100
Royals	99
Indians	98
Twins	97
Blue Jays	95
White Sox	95
Athletics	95
Rays	94

2008 NL Avg	
Home Park	Index
Rockies	107
Diamondbacks	106
Cubs	105
Astros	104
Braves	103
Phillies	102
Reds	101
Giants	101
Nationals	100
Pirates	100
Cardinals	98
Brewers	98
Marlins	97
Mets	93
Dodgers	92
Padres	90

2008 NL LHB Avg	
Home Park	Index
Phillies	108
Brewers	108
Nationals	107
Astros	107
Rockies	104
Giants	104
Cubs	103
Reds	101
Marlins	100
Braves	99
Pirates	99
Diamondbacks	98
Cardinals	97
Mets	94
Padres	89
Dodgers	88

2008 NL RHB Avg	
Home Park	Index
Diamondbacks	112
Rockies	109
Braves	106
Cubs	105
Astros	103
Reds	102
Pirates	101
Giants	100
Cardinals	98
Phillies	97
Nationals	96
Marlins	95
Dodgers	95
Brewers	93
Mets	93
Padres	90

2008 AL Doubles	
Home Park	Index
Red Sox	159
Royals	110
Blue Jays	107
Rangers	103
Twins	101
Indians	101
Yankees	100
Angels	99
Orioles	97
Tigers	96
Athletics	94
Mariners	92
White Sox	90
Rays	89

2008 AL Triples	
Home Park	Index
Rangers	220
Blue Jays	183
Mariners	122
Rays	117
Tigers	110
Yankees	105
Red Sox	100
Twins	99
Angels	83
Royals	82
Indians	65
Athletics	56
White Sox	56
Orioles	56

2008 AL Errors	
Home Park	Index
Rangers	132
Yankees	129
Indians	118
Athletics	115
White Sox	114
Tigers	113
Red Sox	108
Royals	108
Rays	100
Orioles	81
Angels	81
Mariners	79
Blue Jays	79
Twins	75

2008 NL Doubles	
Home Park	Index
Diamondbacks	123
Astros	114
Giants	113
Pirates	104
Rockies	102
Reds	102
Nationals	100
Braves	99
Cubs	99
Marlins	95
Mets	94
Phillies	94
Dodgers	89
Cardinals	88
Brewers	87
Padres	78

2008 NL Triples	
Home Park	Index
Giants	187
Marlins	152
Brewers	140
Diamondbacks	139
Rockies	135
Braves	116
Nationals	109
Reds	104
Cardinals	102
Astros	95
Padres	93
Pirates	91
Phillies	73
Cubs	67
Mets	50
Dodgers	44

2008 NL Errors	
Home Park	Index
Giants	144
Braves	141
Marlins	123
Padres	114
Pirates	97
Cubs	96
Brewers	96
Cardinals	94
Phillies	94
Astros	93
Mets	93
Dodgers	93
Diamondbacks	91
Rockies	89
Reds	85
Nationals	84

2006-2008 American League Ballpark Index Rankings - Runs

Home Park	TOTALS											LHB		RHB	
	Avg	AB	R	H	2B	3B	HR	BB	SO	E	E-Inf	Avg	HR	Avg	HR
Red Sox (Fenway Park)	107	100	109	108	143	98	81	99	94	97	110	111	76	105	84
White Sox (U.S. Cellular Field)	99	101	109	101	92	55	128	104	100	108	116	96	125	101	129
Rangers (Rangers Ballpark in Arlington)	102	102	107	104	102	147	108	99	101	110	118	100	109	104	107
Orioles (Oriole Park at Camden Yards)	104	102	105	106	93	75	123	93	92	88	80	101	111	106	133
Royals (Kauffman Stadium)	104	100	104	104	119	105	89	104	92	97	103	104	88	104	90
Tigers (Comerica Park)	102	101	104	103	95	129	102	97	93	109	104	99	100	104	103
Indians (Progressive Field)	101	99	102	100	98	70	93	110	104	110	114	104	99	99	90
Angels (Angel Stadium of Anaheim)	104	101	100	104	105	77	87	94	96	101	97	106	80	102	91
Yankees (Yankee Stadium)	99	99	100	98	96	68	108	98	99	111	111	97	120	101	97
Blue Jays (Rogers Centre)	97	100	99	97	105	165	113	99	110	87	85	99	119	96	109
Rays (Tropicana Field)	97	98	95	95	92	120	101	104	101	103	99	100	101	95	101
Mariners (Safeco Field)	96	98	92	94	94	80	94	107	111	87	74	96	94	96	95
Twins (Hubert H. Humphrey Metrodome)	96	99	90	95	97	117	83	89	103	88	75	96	81	97	86
Athletics (McAfee Coliseum)	94	99	89	93	94	90	87	98	92	100	103	96	100	94	78

2006-2008 National League Ballpark Index Rankings - Runs

Home Park	TOTALS											LHB		RHB	
	Avg	AB	R	H	2B	3B	HR	BB	SO	E	E-Inf	Avg	HR	Avg	HR
Rockies (Coors Field)	109	102	115	112	107	132	120	95	88	106	89	103	109	113	127
Diamondbacks (Chase Field)	107	101	113	108	113	176	116	103	92	99	112	105	129	109	108
Reds (Great American Ballpark)	100	100	111	100	100	76	128	104	102	96	106	103	123	98	133
Cubs (Wrigley Field)	103	101	110	104	107	96	117	97	106	108	114	101	122	104	114
Phillies (Citizens Bank Park)	102	99	104	101	97	75	122	96	101	104	103	104	122	100	122
Nationals (Nationals Park) *	100	101	104	101	100	109	93	100	93	84	108	107	84	96	99
Giants (AT&T Park)	102	101	101	103	108	132	80	97	95	122	125	102	78	102	81
Astros (Minute Maid Park)	100	100	99	101	102	115	112	99	104	82	103	100	108	100	115
Brewers (Miller Park)	96	99	99	95	97	97	102	112	107	110	101	99	110	95	97
Dodgers (Dodger Stadium)	99	99	98	98	94	51	105	105	109	104	98	98	114	100	98
Marlins (Dolphins Stadium)	98	100	97	98	102	144	91	109	112	103	86	97	90	98	92
Braves (Turner Field)	100	100	97	100	93	94	96	104	103	113	106	99	85	101	107
Pirates (PNC Park)	102	102	95	104	110	79	80	92	92	83	93	103	99	102	72
Cardinals (Busch Stadium)	99	100	94	99	91	92	84	99	94	108	106	98	86	99	83
Mets (Shea Stadium)	94	99	92	93	96	78	96	104	102	91	106	96	93	93	99
Padres (PETCO Park)	90	98	80	89	76	104	81	100	110	84	71	92	70	88	92

2006-2008 AL Home Runs			2006-2008 AL LHB Home Runs			2006-2008 AL RHB Home Runs	
Home Park	Index		Home Park	Index		Home Park	Index
White Sox	128		White Sox	125		Orioles	133
Orioles	123		Yankees	120		White Sox	129
Blue Jays	113		Blue Jays	119		Blue Jays	109
Rangers	108		Orioles	111		Rangers	107
Yankees	108		Rangers	109		Tigers	103
Tigers	102		Rays	101		Rays	101
Rays	101		Tigers	100		Yankees	97
Mariners	94		Athletics	100		Mariners	95
Indians	93		Indians	99		Angels	91
Royals	89		Mariners	94		Royals	90
Athletics	87		Royals	88		Indians	90
Angels	87		Twins	81		Twins	86
Twins	83		Angels	80		Red Sox	84
Red Sox	81		Red Sox	76		Athletics	78

2006-2008 NL Home Runs			2006-2008 NL LHB Home Runs			2006-2008 NL RHB Home Runs	
Home Park	Index		Home Park	Index		Home Park	Index
Reds	128		Diamondbacks	129		Reds	133
Phillies	122		Reds	123		Rockies	127
Rockies	120		Phillies	122		Phillies	122
Cubs	117		Cubs	122		Astros	115
Diamondbacks	116		Dodgers	114		Cubs	114
Astros	112		Brewers	110		Diamondbacks	108
Dodgers	105		Rockies	109		Braves	107
Brewers	102		Astros	108		Nationals *	99
Braves	96		Pirates	99		Mets	99
Mets	96		Mets	93		Dodgers	98
Nationals *	93		Marlins	90		Brewers	97
Marlins	91		Cardinals	86		Padres	92
Cardinals	84		Braves	85		Marlins	92
Padres	81		Nationals *	84		Cardinals	83
Pirates	80		Giants	78		Giants	81
Giants	80		Padres	70		Pirates	72

* Data since 2008

2006-2008 AL Avg	
Home Park	Index
Red Sox	107
Royals	104
Orioles	104
Angels	104
Tigers	102
Rangers	102
Indians	101
White Sox	99
Yankees	99
Blue Jays	97
Rays	97
Twins	96
Mariners	96
Athletics	94

2006-2008 AL LHB Avg	
Home Park	Index
Red Sox	111
Angels	106
Indians	104
Royals	104
Orioles	101
Rangers	100
Rays	100
Tigers	99
Blue Jays	99
Yankees	97
Mariners	96
White Sox	96
Athletics	96
Twins	96

2006-2008 AL RHB Avg	
Home Park	Index
Orioles	106
Red Sox	105
Royals	104
Rangers	104
Tigers	104
Angels	102
White Sox	101
Yankees	101
Indians	99
Twins	97
Blue Jays	96
Mariners	96
Rays	95
Athletics	94

2006-2008 NL Avg	
Home Park	Index
Rockies	109
Diamondbacks	107
Cubs	103
Pirates	102
Giants	102
Phillies	102
Astros	100
Nationals *	100
Braves	100
Reds	100
Dodgers	99
Cardinals	99
Marlins	98
Brewers	96
Mets	94
Padres	90

2006-2008 NL LHB Avg	
Home Park	Index
Nationals *	107
Diamondbacks	105
Phillies	104
Rockies	103
Pirates	103
Reds	103
Giants	102
Cubs	101
Astros	100
Brewers	99
Braves	99
Dodgers	98
Cardinals	98
Marlins	97
Mets	96
Padres	92

2006-2008 NL RHB Avg	
Home Park	Index
Rockies	113
Diamondbacks	109
Cubs	104
Giants	102
Pirates	102
Braves	101
Astros	100
Phillies	100
Dodgers	100
Cardinals	99
Reds	98
Marlins	98
Nationals *	96
Brewers	95
Mets	93
Padres	88

2006-2008 AL Doubles	
Home Park	Index
Red Sox	143
Royals	119
Angels	105
Blue Jays	105
Rangers	102
Indians	98
Twins	97
Yankees	96
Tigers	95
Mariners	94
Athletics	94
Orioles	93
White Sox	92
Rays	92

2006-2008 AL Triples	
Home Park	Index
Blue Jays	165
Rangers	147
Tigers	129
Rays	120
Twins	117
Royals	105
Red Sox	98
Athletics	90
Mariners	80
Angels	77
Orioles	75
Indians	70
Yankees	68
White Sox	55

2006-2008 AL Errors	
Home Park	Index
Yankees	111
Rangers	110
Indians	110
Tigers	109
White Sox	108
Rays	103
Angels	101
Athletics	100
Red Sox	97
Royals	97
Orioles	88
Twins	88
Mariners	87
Blue Jays	87

2006-2008 NL Doubles	
Home Park	Index
Diamondbacks	113
Pirates	110
Giants	108
Cubs	107
Rockies	107
Astros	102
Marlins	102
Nationals *	100
Reds	100
Brewers	97
Phillies	97
Mets	96
Dodgers	94
Braves	93
Cardinals	91
Padres	76

2006-2008 NL Triples	
Home Park	Index
Diamondbacks	176
Marlins	144
Giants	132
Rockies	132
Astros	115
Nationals *	109
Padres	104
Brewers	97
Cubs	96
Braves	94
Cardinals	92
Pirates	79
Mets	78
Reds	76
Phillies	75
Dodgers	51

2006-2008 NL Errors	
Home Park	Index
Giants	122
Braves	113
Brewers	110
Cubs	108
Cardinals	108
Rockies	106
Dodgers	104
Phillies	104
Marlins	103
Diamondbacks	99
Reds	96
Mets	91
Padres	84
Nationals *	84
Pirates	83
Astros	82

* Data since 2008

2008 Lefty/Righty Statistics

Someday maybe major league teams will employ platoon players like Las Vegas employs comedy acts. Two guys who platoon in left field, say, for the Atlanta Braves, will be better known in tandem (like Tim and Tom) than individually. Their cumulative stats will be so impressive they'll both be elected to the All-Star Game—but only absorb one roster spot.

So who are some individuals that missed out on the 2008 All-Star Game, but would easily be voted in for 2009 if only they were part of one of our dream platoons? Here are five recommendations, along with predictions for their 2009 performances:

Torii Edmonds. A combination of Torii Hunter and Jim Edmonds not only flashes Gold Glove skills in center field but owns a .304/.372/.493 line against lefties (Hunter) and a .250/.362/.521 line against righties (Edmonds). He also crashes recklessly into walls—and never gets hurt.

Armando Lackey. A two-headed pitching monster made up of Armando Galarraga and John Lackey stifles lefties to a .221/.279/.379 line (Lackey) and utterly dominates righties to the tune of .174/.252/.291 (Galarraga).

Yadier "Salty" Saltalamacchia. A mash-up of Yadier Molina and Jarrod Saltalamacchia behind the dish results in a .323/.390/.469 line verse lefties (Molina) and a .311/.426/.451 line against righties (Salty). The downside of this combination is that despite Yadier's 2007 and 2008 Fielding Bible Awards, together they make only a league-average defensive catcher.

Dustin Zito. Combining Dustin McGowan with the enigmatic Barry Zito produces a pitcher who, while still not worth $18.5m a year, holds lefties to .213/.316/.287 (Zito) and handcuffs right-handed hitters to a line of .252/.298/.327 (McGowan).

J.J. Drew. A perennial All-Star shortstop, created by combining J.J. Hardy with Stephen Drew, produces .304/.402/.574 against lefties (Hardy) and .300/.348/.520 versus righties (Drew). Unfortunately, he also frequently gets confused with Stephen's older brother, J.D, until he finally just changes his name to Sam.

In the following section are lefty/righty splits for all batters and pitchers who appeared during the 2008 season. The batting side of each hitter is shown below his name; for pitchers, the hand that he throws with is indicated.

Read it and dream.

Batters vs. Left-Handed and Right-Handed Pitchers

Batter	vs	Avg	AB	H	2B	3B	HR	RBI	BB	SO	OBP	Slg
Abercrombie,Reggie	L	.353	34	12	1	0	2	5	0	10	.343	.559
Bats Right	R	.238	21	5	4	0	0	0	1	13	.333	.429
Abreu,Bobby	L	.315	184	58	11	2	6	30	16	32	.370	.495
Bats Left	R	.287	425	122	28	2	14	70	57	77	.372	.461
Aguila,Chris	L	.167	6	1	0	0	0	0	2	2	.375	.167
Bats Right	R	.167	6	1	0	0	0	0	0	2	.167	.167
Alfonzo,Eliezer	L	.000	2	0	0	0	0	0	0	1	.000	.000
Bats Right	R	.111	9	1	0	0	0	1	0	3	.111	.111
Alou,Moises	L	.462	13	6	1	0	0	0	1	0	.533	.538
Bats Right	R	.306	36	11	1	0	0	9	1	4	.333	.333
Ambres,Chip	L	.160	25	4	1	0	0	0	6	12	.323	.200
Bats Right	R	.250	16	4	0	0	0	0	1	3	.294	.250
Amezaga,Alfredo	L	.254	67	17	3	0	1	8	2	11	.275	.343
Bats Both	R	.266	244	65	10	5	2	24	17	36	.322	.373
Anderson,Brian	L	.225	80	18	3	0	8	20	4	15	.262	.563
Bats Right	R	.238	101	24	10	0	0	6	6	30	.280	.337
Anderson,Garret	L	.290	124	36	3	2	1	15	8	23	.333	.371
Bats Left	R	.293	433	127	24	1	14	69	21	54	.323	.450
Anderson,Josh	L	.200	45	9	1	0	0	3	1	16	.234	.222
Bats Left	R	.341	91	31	6	1	3	9	7	17	.388	.527
Anderson,Marlon	L	.000	2	0	0	0	0	0	0	1	.000	.000
Bats Left	R	.213	136	29	6	0	1	10	9	26	.259	.279
Andino,Robert	L	.250	20	5	1	0	0	4	1	6	.286	.300
Bats Right	R	.186	43	8	1	0	2	5	3	17	.239	.349
Ankiel,Rick	L	.224	116	26	5	0	7	15	6	27	.268	.448
Bats Left	R	.279	297	83	16	2	18	56	36	73	.362	.529
Antonelli,Matt	L	.083	12	1	0	0	0	0	1	2	.214	.083
Bats Right	R	.222	45	10	2	0	1	3	4	9	.314	.333
Ardoin,Danny	L	.320	25	8	1	0	1	2	1	4	.346	.480
Bats Right	R	.154	26	4	0	0	0	2	1	6	.214	.154
Arias,Joaquin	L	.417	24	10	2	1	0	3	3	1	.481	.583
Bats Right	R	.256	86	22	5	2	0	6	4	11	.304	.360
Atkins,Garrett	L	.357	140	50	7	0	9	32	14	20	.414	.600
Bats Right	R	.265	471	125	25	3	12	67	26	80	.302	.408
Aubrey,Michael	L	.000	2	0	0	0	0	0	0	0	.000	.000
Bats Left	R	.209	43	9	0	0	2	3	5	5	.292	.349
Aurilia,Rich	L	.321	137	44	13	0	5	15	13	17	.377	.526
Bats Right	R	.263	270	71	8	1	5	37	17	39	.308	.356
Ausmus,Brad	L	.277	65	18	3	0	2	7	8	13	.365	.415
Bats Right	R	.192	151	29	5	0	1	17	17	28	.276	.245
Aviles,Mike	L	.348	141	49	12	4	4	23	11	17	.392	.574
Bats Right	R	.313	278	87	15	0	6	28	7	41	.333	.432
Aybar,Erick	L	.286	105	30	8	0	0	10	5	8	.324	.362
Bats Both	R	.274	241	66	10	5	3	29	9	37	.310	.394
Aybar,Willy	L	.266	124	33	10	0	4	11	16	20	.350	.444
Bats Both	R	.245	200	49	7	2	6	22	16	24	.312	.390
Bailey,Jeff	L	.269	26	7	0	1	2	5	2	8	.321	.577
Bats Right	R	.292	24	7	1	0	0	1	7	9	.452	.333
Baisley,Jeff	L	.188	16	3	0	0	0	0	1	3	.235	.188
Bats Right	R	.296	27	8	1	0	0	5	3	4	.367	.333
Baker,Jeff	L	.290	100	29	9	0	7	23	9	23	.336	.590
Bats Right	R	.256	199	51	13	1	5	25	17	62	.315	.407
Baker,John	L	.213	47	10	2	0	1	8	6	19	.316	.319
Bats Left	R	.327	150	49	12	0	4	24	24	29	.417	.487
Bako,Paul	L	.197	71	14	2	2	3	10	3	28	.240	.408
Bats Left	R	.224	228	51	9	0	3	25	31	62	.315	.303
Baldelli,Rocco	L	.292	48	14	4	0	2	9	5	15	.382	.500
Bats Right	R	.219	32	7	1	0	2	4	2	10	.286	.438
Balentien,Wladimir	L	.218	78	17	4	0	2	9	6	24	.274	.346
Bats Right	R	.194	165	32	9	0	5	15	10	55	.239	.339
Bankston,Wes	L	.300	20	6	3	0	1	3	0	6	.286	.600
Bats Right	R	.154	39	6	0	0	0	1	2	9	.214	.154
Barajas,Rod	L	.204	108	22	7	0	3	15	1	13	.239	.352
Bats Right	R	.270	241	65	16	0	8	34	16	48	.318	.436
Bard,Josh	L	.135	52	7	2	0	1	5	4	11	.196	.231
Bats Both	R	.230	126	29	7	0	0	11	14	14	.312	.286
Barden,Brian	L	.200	5	1	0	0	0	0	0	2	.200	.200
Bats Right	R	.250	4	1	0	0	0	1	0	2	.250	.250
Barfield,Josh	L	.182	11	2	1	0	0	1	0	1	.182	.273
Bats Right	R	.182	22	4	0	0	0	1	0	9	.182	.182
Barmes,Clint	L	.307	114	35	11	3	6	18	5	16	.333	.614
Bats Right	R	.283	279	79	14	3	5	26	12	53	.317	.409
Barrett,Michael	L	.296	27	8	2	0	2	5	5	2	.394	.593
Bats Right	R	.164	67	11	1	0	0	4	4	14	.219	.179
Bartlett,Jason	L	.379	132	50	12	1	1	17	7	19	.411	.508
Bats Right	R	.248	322	80	13	2	0	20	15	50	.296	.301
Barton,Brian	L	.258	89	23	5	1	1	9	16	20	.374	.371
Bats Right	R	.281	64	18	4	1	1	4	3	19	.324	.422
Barton,Daric	L	.273	128	35	5	2	3	15	18	27	.373	.414
Bats Left	R	.208	318	66	12	3	6	32	47	72	.308	.321
Bautista,Jose	L	.250	108	27	5	0	9	18	16	27	.339	.546
Bats Right	R	.233	262	61	12	0	6	36	24	64	.301	.347
Bay,Jason	L	.252	131	33	11	1	5	17	29	37	.387	.466
Bats Right	R	.296	446	132	24	3	26	84	52	100	.369	.538
Belliard,Ronnie	L	.307	88	27	6	0	7	17	15	18	.408	.614
Bats Right	R	.279	208	58	16	0	4	29	22	40	.356	.413
Bellorin,Edwin	L	.000	1	0	0	0	0	0	0	0	.000	.000
Bats Right	R	.500	2	1	0	0	0	0	0	0	.500	.500
Beltran,Carlos	L	.326	178	58	19	0	10	41	27	28	.413	.601
Bats Both	R	.266	428	114	21	5	17	71	65	68	.360	.458
Beltre,Adrian	L	.340	150	51	11	0	8	22	21	18	.421	.573
Bats Right	R	.239	406	97	18	1	17	55	29	72	.290	.414
Bennett,Gary	L	.167	12	2	1	0	0	1	2	0	.286	.250
Bats Right	R	.222	9	2	0	0	1	3	0	0	.222	.556
Berkman,Lance	L	.276	156	43	6	0	7	27	18	29	.354	.449
Bats Both	R	.327	398	130	40	4	22	79	81	79	.444	.613
Bernadina,Roger	L	.300	10	3	0	0	0	0	0	2	.300	.300
Bats Left	R	.197	66	13	1	1	0	2	9	19	.293	.242
Bernier,Doug	L	.000	3	0	0	0	0	0	0	1	.000	.000
Bats Both	R	.000	1	0	0	0	0	0	0	0	.000	.000
Berroa,Angel	L	.219	64	14	6	0	1	6	9	11	.315	.359
Bats Right	R	.235	162	38	7	1	0	10	11	30	.299	.290
Betancourt,Yuniesky	L	.275	160	44	12	1	2	15	3	11	.284	.400
Bats Right	R	.281	399	112	24	2	5	36	14	31	.306	.388
Betemit,Wilson	L	.233	43	10	1	0	2	4	1	15	.250	.395
Bats Both	R	.274	146	40	12	0	4	21	5	41	.301	.438
Bixler,Brian	L	.182	22	4	0	0	0	0	3	8	.280	.182
Bats Right	R	.151	86	13	2	1	0	2	3	28	.215	.198
Blake,Casey	L	.287	129	37	10	0	4	11	15	23	.366	.457
Bats Right	R	.270	407	110	26	1	17	70	34	97	.338	.464
Blalock,Hank	L	.277	83	23	4	1	6	17	6	13	.337	.566
Bats Left	R	.291	175	51	15	0	6	21	13	27	.339	.480
Blanco,Gregor	L	.248	105	26	3	3	0	6	14	31	.360	.333
Bats Left	R	.252	325	82	11	1	1	32	60	68	.369	.302
Blanco,Henry	L	.316	57	18	3	0	1	7	3	10	.350	.421
Bats Right	R	.270	63	17	0	0	2	5	3	12	.303	.365
Bloomquist,Willie	L	.351	74	26	1	0	0	3	12	9	.442	.365
Bats Right	R	.220	91	20	0	0	0	6	13	20	.324	.220
Blum,Geoff	L	.229	48	11	3	0	0	8	6	10	.322	.292
Bats Both	R	.242	277	67	11	1	14	45	15	44	.279	.440
Bocock,Brian	L	.000	11	0	0	0	0	1	5	5	.313	.000
Bats Right	R	.167	66	11	1	0	0	1	7	24	.247	.182
Boggs,Brandon	L	.227	88	20	6	3	4	15	12	34	.327	.500
Bats Both	R	.226	195	44	11	1	4	26	32	59	.336	.354
Bohn,T.J.	L	1.000	1	1	1	0	0	2	0	0	1.000	2.000
Bats Right	R	.250	4	1	0	0	0	0	1	0	.250	.250
Bonifacio,Emilio	L	.163	43	7	1	2	0	3	1	16	.178	.279
Bats Both	R	.270	126	34	5	3	0	11	13	30	.333	.357
Boone,Aaron	L	.275	91	25	5	1	3	8	12	18	.365	.451
Bats Right	R	.220	141	31	8	0	3	20	6	34	.253	.340
Botts,Jason	L	.231	13	3	2	0	0	3	2	4	.333	.385
Bats Both	R	.120	25	3	1	0	0	2	6	14	.290	.400
Bourgeois,Jason	L	-	0	0	0	0	0	0	0	0	-	-
Bats Right	R	.333	3	1	0	0	0	0	0	0	.333	.667
Bourn,Michael	L	.190	116	22	4	0	1	7	10	35	.258	.250
Bats Left	R	.242	351	85	6	4	4	22	27	76	.298	.316
Bowen,Rob	L	.167	30	5	1	0	0	3	1	15	.194	.200
Bats Both	R	.180	61	11	4	1	1	6	3	23	.231	.328
Bowker,John	L	.152	33	5	0	0	1	1	1	12	.171	.152
Bats Left	R	.266	293	78	14	3	10	42	18	62	.314	.437
Bradley,Milton	L	.341	129	44	10	0	10	25	29	33	.476	.651
Bats Both	R	.312	285	89	22	1	12	52	51	79	.417	.523
Branyan,Russell	L	.000	14	0	0	0	0	0	0	8	.000	.000
Bats Left	R	.280	118	33	8	0	12	20	19	34	.377	.653
Braun,Ryan	L	.287	171	49	13	1	9	29	14	26	.341	.532
Bats Right	R	.284	440	125	26	6	28	77	28	103	.333	.561
Brignac,Reid	L	.000	2	0	0	0	0	0	1	1	.333	.000
Bats Left	R	.000	8	0	0	0	0	0	0	4	.000	.000
Broussard,Ben	L	.125	8	1	0	0	0	0	0	4	.222	.125
Bats Left	R	.162	74	12	0	0	3	6	5	16	.225	.284
Brown,Emil	L	.295	156	46	4	0	8	25	8	19	.337	.474
Bats Right	R	.211	246	52	10	2	5	34	19	46	.272	.329

Batters vs. Left-Handed and Right-Handed Pitchers

Batter	vs	Avg	AB	H	2B	3B	HR	RBI	BB	SO	OBP	Slg
Brown,Matt	L	.111	9	1	1	0	0	2	0	6	.111	.222
Bats Right	R	.000	10	0	0	0	0	1	1	4	.091	.000
Bruce,Jay	L	.190	137	26	6	0	3	9	11	46	.263	.299
Bats Left	R	.286	276	79	11	1	18	43	22	64	.340	.529
Bruntlett,Eric	L	.254	71	18	6	0	1	5	12	8	.361	.380
Bats Right	R	.199	141	28	3	1	1	10	9	27	.261	.255
Buck,John	L	.236	110	26	10	0	3	16	19	32	.356	.409
Bats Right	R	.219	260	57	13	1	6	32	19	64	.280	.346
Buck,Travis	L	.196	46	9	1	1	1	4	1	12	.220	.326
Bats Left	R	.239	109	26	8	0	6	21	10	26	.320	.477
Budde,Ryan	L	.000	2	0	0	0	0	0	0	0	.000	.000
Bats Right	R	-	0	0	0	0	0	0	0	0	-	-
Burke,Chris	L	.209	86	18	2	1	2	7	12	13	.317	.326
Bats Right	R	.177	79	14	3	0	0	5	15	20	.302	.215
Burke,Jamie	L	.341	41	14	2	0	1	5	0	2	.341	.463
Bats Right	R	.196	51	10	1	0	0	3	5	5	.276	.216
Burrell,Pat	L	.279	154	43	16	2	7	20	35	36	.406	.545
Bats Right	R	.238	382	91	17	1	26	66	67	100	.351	.492
Burriss,Emmanuel	L	.292	89	26	3	1	0	8	6	7	.340	.348
Bats Both	R	.278	151	42	3	0	1	10	17	17	.366	.318
Buscher,Brian	L	.205	44	9	0	0	0	7	3	12	.250	.205
Bats Left	R	.316	174	55	9	0	4	40	16	30	.362	.437
Butler,Billy	L	.340	144	49	12	0	8	27	13	15	.395	.590
Bats Right	R	.244	299	73	10	0	3	28	20	42	.290	.308
Bynum,Freddie	L	.118	17	2	0	0	0	0	0	7	.118	.118
Bats Left	R	.189	95	18	3	1	0	8	5	24	.238	.242
Byrd,Marlon	L	.277	137	38	8	1	6	24	17	14	.359	.482
Bats Right	R	.308	266	82	20	3	4	29	29	48	.391	.451
Byrnes,Eric	L	.258	62	16	5	0	3	10	7	10	.333	.484
Bats Right	R	.188	144	27	8	1	3	13	9	26	.245	.319
Cabrera,Asdrubal	L	.349	83	29	9	0	2	17	12	11	.427	.530
Bats Both	R	.230	269	62	11	0	4	30	34	66	.322	.316
Cabrera,Jolbert	L	.238	42	10	2	1	2	4	3	12	.283	.476
Bats Right	R	.260	73	19	4	0	1	8	5	17	.325	.356
Cabrera,Melky	L	.213	127	27	5	0	2	11	11	16	.279	.299
Bats Both	R	.265	287	76	7	1	6	26	18	42	.311	.359
Cabrera,Miguel	L	.311	151	47	9	1	9	34	16	33	.376	.563
Bats Right	R	.286	465	133	27	1	28	93	40	93	.340	.529
Cabrera,Orlando	L	.273	165	45	10	1	3	19	23	17	.354	.400
Bats Right	R	.284	496	141	23	0	5	38	33	54	.327	.361
Cairo,Miguel	L	.270	89	24	6	2	0	7	11	6	.356	.382
Bats Right	R	.235	132	31	8	0	0	16	7	26	.287	.295
Callaspo,Alberto	L	.333	72	24	4	0	0	7	5	4	.372	.389
Bats Both	R	.291	141	41	4	3	0	9	14	10	.355	.362
Cameron,Mike	L	.282	110	31	7	1	7	16	19	32	.397	.555
Bats Right	R	.231	334	77	18	1	18	54	35	110	.309	.452
Cancel,Robinson	L	.429	21	9	1	0	1	3	3	1	.500	.619
Bats Right	R	.107	28	3	1	0	0	2	0	5	.107	.143
Cannizaro,Andy	L	-	0	0	0	0	0	0	0	0	-	-
Bats Right	R	.000	1	0	0	0	0	0	0	0	.000	.000
Cano,Robinson	L	.292	171	50	9	1	5	22	11	22	.349	.444
Bats Left	R	.263	426	112	26	2	9	50	15	43	.286	.397
Cantu,Jorge	L	.293	147	43	8	0	8	18	15	26	.359	.510
Bats Right	R	.272	481	131	33	0	21	77	25	85	.317	.472
Carlin,Luke	L	.167	18	3	1	0	0	1	5	.211	.222
Bats Both	R	.145	76	11	2	1	1	6	9	29	.244	.237
Carroll,Brett	L	.000	9	0	0	0	0	0	0	2	.000	.000
Bats Right	R	.125	8	1	0	1	0	1	1	4	.222	.375
Carroll,Jamey	L	.261	111	29	4	0	0	8	12	19	.333	.297
Bats Right	R	.284	236	67	9	4	1	28	22	46	.364	.369
Carter,Chris	L	1.000	2	2	0	0	0	0	0	0	1.000	1.000
Bats Left	R	.250	16	4	0	0	0	3	2	5	.333	.250
Casanova,Raul	L	.333	15	5	1	0	0	1	3	2	.444	.400
Bats Both	R	.250	40	10	1	0	1	5	3	8	.302	.350
Casey,Sean	L	.324	37	12	5	0	0	3	1	4	.359	.459
Bats Left	R	.321	162	52	9	0	0	14	16	21	.385	.377
Cash,Kevin	L	.361	36	13	3	0	0	4	6	13	.442	.444
Bats Right	R	.179	106	19	4	0	3	11	12	37	.261	.302
Casilla,Alexi	L	.264	129	34	3	0	2	14	7	8	.304	.333
Bats Both	R	.289	256	74	12	0	5	36	24	37	.346	.395
Castillo,Jose	L	.238	130	31	9	0	3	11	12	22	.301	.377
Bats Right	R	.250	296	74	20	4	3	26	15	59	.288	.375
Castillo,Luis	L	.211	76	16	1	0	3	9	13	5	.337	.342
Bats Both	R	.257	222	57	6	1	0	19	37	30	.362	.293
Castillo,Wilkin	L	.200	5	1	0	0	0	0	2	.200	.400
Bats Both	R	.296	27	8	0	0	0	1	1	3	.321	.296

Batter	vs	Avg	AB	H	2B	3B	HR	RBI	BB	SO	OBP	Slg
Casto,Kory	L	.048	21	1	0	0	0	0	2	11	.130	.048
Bats Left	R	.239	142	34	10	0	2	16	17	25	.321	.352
Castro,Juan	L	.185	54	10	4	0	0	3	7	6	.279	.259
Bats Right	R	.196	107	21	2	0	2	13	4	20	.228	.271
Castro,Ramon	L	.277	65	18	3	0	3	9	4	15	.319	.462
Bats Right	R	.218	78	17	4	0	4	15	9	19	.307	.423
Catalanotto,Frank	L	.167	12	2	1	0	0	0	2	4	.286	.250
Bats Left	R	.280	236	66	22	1	2	21	18	25	.345	.407
Cedeno,Ronny	L	.257	113	29	5	0	1	12	8	22	.306	.327
Bats Right	R	.282	103	29	7	0	1	16	10	19	.351	.379
Cervelli,Francisco	L	-	0	0	0	0	0	0	0	0	-	-
Bats Both	R	.000	5	0	0	0	0	0	0	3	.000	.000
Cervenak,Mike	L	.200	5	1	0	0	0	0	0	3	.200	.200
Bats Right	R	.125	8	1	0	0	0	1	0	2	.125	.125
Chavez,Endy	L	.194	36	7	2	0	0	1	3	5	.256	.250
Bats Left	R	.278	234	65	8	2	1	11	14	17	.316	.342
Chavez,Eric	L	.333	24	8	3	0	0	4	1	5	.360	.458
Bats Left	R	.215	65	14	4	0	2	10	5	13	.271	.369
Chavez,Raul	L	.240	25	6	1	0	0	2	2	5	.296	.280
Bats Right	R	.264	91	24	3	0	1	8	2	9	.284	.330
Choo,Shin-Soo	L	.286	77	22	4	3	0	14	6	26	.345	.455
Bats Left	R	.317	240	76	24	3	11	52	38	52	.413	.579
Christian,Justin	L	.333	27	9	3	0	0	6	2	2	.379	.444
Bats Right	R	.077	13	1	0	0	0	0	1	2	.143	.077
Church,Ryan	L	.264	106	28	3	0	4	11	7	34	.319	.406
Bats Left	R	.282	213	60	11	1	8	38	26	49	.360	.455
Cintron,Alex	L	.250	40	10	1	1	0	3	3	4	.302	.325
Bats Both	R	.301	93	28	4	0	1	7	4	11	.330	.376
Clark,Brady	L	.167	6	1	0	0	0	1	1	2	.286	.167
Bats Right	R	.500	2	1	0	0	0	0	0	0	.667	.500
Clark,Howie	L	.333	3	1	1	0	0	0	1	0	.333	.667
Bats Left	R	.200	5	1	1	0	0	1	0	1	.200	.400
Clark,Tony	L	.280	50	14	3	0	2	11	6	19	.368	.460
Bats Both	R	.198	101	20	2	0	1	13	25	36	.354	.248
Clement,Jeff	L	.289	45	13	5	0	1	6	1	11	.319	.467
Bats Left	R	.209	158	33	5	1	4	17	14	52	.288	.329
Clevlen,Brent	L	.100	10	1	0	0	0	0	3	4	.308	.100
Bats Right	R	.286	14	4	0	0	1	0	4	.286	.286
Coats,Buck	L	-	0	0	0	0	0	0	0	0	-	-
Bats Left	R	.200	5	1	0	0	0	0	1	2	.333	.200
Conrad,Brooks	L	.000	2	0	0	0	0	0	0	2	.000	.000
Bats Both	R	.176	17	3	1	0	0	2	0	7	.176	.235
Cora,Alex	L	.286	28	8	0	0	0	0	0	5	.333	.286
Bats Left	R	.266	124	33	8	2	0	9	16	18	.378	.363
Coste,Chris	L	.296	81	24	6	0	4	18	7	18	.363	.519
Bats Right	R	.249	193	48	11	0	5	18	9	33	.308	.383
Counsell,Craig	L	.190	21	4	1	0	0	4	4	4	.333	.238
Bats Left	R	.229	227	52	13	1	1	10	42	38	.358	.308
Crabbe,Callix	L	.250	12	3	1	0	0	2	2	3	.400	.333
Bats Both	R	.136	22	3	0	0	0	0	2	3	.208	.136
Crawford,Carl	L	.248	141	35	1	2	3	22	7	26	.293	.348
Bats Left	R	.285	302	86	11	8	5	35	23	34	.330	.424
Crede,Joe	L	.122	82	10	2	0	0	2	8	10	.207	.146
Bats Right	R	.289	253	73	16	1	17	53	22	35	.349	.561
Crisp,Coco	L	.295	95	28	8	0	3	14	4	20	.317	.474
Bats Both	R	.278	266	74	10	3	4	27	31	39	.353	.383
Crosby,Bobby	L	.222	158	35	11	0	3	16	16	21	.293	.348
Bats Right	R	.244	398	97	28	1	4	45	31	75	.297	.349
Cruz,Jose	L	.150	20	3	1	0	0	0	5	3	.320	.200
Bats Both	R	.103	29	3	0	0	0	1	6	6	.257	.103
Cruz,Luis	L	.000	1	0	0	0	0	0	0	1	.000	.000
Bats Right	R	.259	58	15	3	0	0	3	2	2	.306	.310
Cruz,Nelson	L	.419	31	13	6	1	1	7	6	8	.514	.774
Bats Right	R	.298	84	25	3	1	6	19	11	20	.385	.548
Cuddyer,Michael	L	.250	68	17	3	1	0	5	12	14	.370	.324
Bats Right	R	.249	181	45	10	3	3	31	13	26	.313	.387
Cunningham,Aaron	L	.208	24	5	3	0	0	2	0	8	.208	.333
Bats Right	R	.268	56	15	4	1	1	12	6	16	.349	.429
Cust,Jack	L	.235	136	32	5	0	8	20	31	58	.373	.449
Bats Left	R	.229	345	79	14	0	25	57	80	139	.375	.487
Damon,Johnny	L	.258	163	42	5	2	3	12	14	34	.342	.368
Bats Left	R	.321	392	126	22	3	14	56	44	49	.389	.500
D'Antona,Jamie	L	.200	10	2	0	0	0	1	1	1	.273	.200
Bats Right	R	.143	7	1	0	0	0	0	0	2	.250	.143
Davis,Chris	L	.279	86	24	8	2	5	17	5	29	.323	.593
Bats Left	R	.287	209	60	15	0	12	38	15	59	.335	.531

Batters vs. Left-Handed and Right-Handed Pitchers

Batter	vs	Avg	AB	H	2B	3B	HR	RBI	BB	SO	OBP	Slg
Davis,Rajai	L	.232	82	19	3	1	2	8	3	19	.256	.366
Bats Right	R	.250	132	33	2	3	1	11	5	21	.283	.333
DeJesus,David	L	.302	202	61	11	2	1	24	10	22	.336	.391
Bats Left	R	.310	316	98	14	5	11	49	36	49	.384	.491
Delgado,Carlos	L	.267	210	56	9	1	12	41	7	50	.299	.490
Bats Left	R	.273	388	106	23	0	26	74	65	74	.378	.534
Dellucci,David	L	.000	17	0	0	0	0	0	0	5	.056	.000
Bats Left	R	.251	319	80	19	2	11	47	24	71	.319	.426
Denker,Travis	L	.267	15	4	2	0	1	3	1	6	.313	.600
Bats Right	R	.227	22	5	2	1	0	0	4	4	.346	.409
Denorfia,Chris	L	.241	29	7	0	0	0	3	1	6	.267	.241
Bats Right	R	.333	33	11	3	0	1	6	5	10	.436	.515
DeRosa,Mark	L	.310	145	45	10	1	5	23	23	33	.398	.497
Bats Right	R	.275	360	99	20	2	16	64	46	73	.367	.475
DeWitt,Blake	L	.286	84	24	3	1	3	13	17	18	.402	.452
Bats Left	R	.257	284	73	10	1	6	39	28	50	.326	.363
Diaz,Matt	L	.319	72	23	1	0	2	7	1	11	.338	.417
Bats Right	R	.159	63	10	1	0	0	7	2	21	.182	.175
Diaz,Robinson	L	1.000	3	3	0	0	0	1	0	0	1.000	1.000
Bats Right	R	.000	7	0	0	0	0	0	0	2	.000	.000
Dickerson,Chris	L	.286	21	6	3	0	0	2	4	6	.423	.429
Bats Left	R	.309	81	25	6	2	6	13	13	29	.411	.654
DiFelice,Mike	L	.600	5	3	0	0	0	1	0	0	.600	.600
Bats Right	R	.200	15	3	1	0	0	3	1	1	.294	.267
Dillon,Joe	L	.357	28	10	3	0	1	5	8	8	.500	.571
Bats Right	R	.128	47	6	0	0	0	1	5	13	.226	.128
Dobbs,Greg	L	.111	9	1	0	0	0	0	1	3	.200	.111
Bats Left	R	.309	217	67	14	1	9	40	10	37	.339	.507
Doumit,Ryan	L	.330	103	34	5	0	5	16	5	14	.364	.524
Bats Both	R	.314	328	103	29	0	10	53	18	41	.355	.494
Drew,J.D.	L	.284	74	21	5	1	3	17	18	25	.426	.500
Bats Left	R	.279	294	82	18	3	16	47	61	55	.403	.524
Drew,Stephen	L	.267	165	44	9	2	6	23	7	38	.293	.455
Bats Left	R	.300	446	134	35	9	15	44	34	71	.348	.520
Dukes,Elijah	L	.231	78	18	2	1	4	12	13	23	.361	.436
Bats Right	R	.278	198	55	14	1	9	32	37	56	.397	.495
Duncan,Chris	L	.147	34	5	2	0	1	4	2	12	.194	.294
Bats Right	R	.266	188	50	6	0	5	23	32	40	.371	.378
Duncan,Shelley	L	.225	40	9	3	0	1	5	5	9	.304	.375
Bats Right	R	.059	17	1	0	0	0	1	2	4	.158	.059
Dunn,Adam	L	.195	154	30	5	0	10	22	33	60	.351	.422
Bats Left	R	.253	363	92	18	0	30	78	89	104	.400	.551
Duran,German	L	.271	70	19	4	0	1	6	6	12	.342	.371
Bats Right	R	.192	73	14	2	1	2	10	1	20	.203	.329
Durham,Ray	L	.238	80	19	7	0	1	10	5	18	.365	.363
Bats Both	R	.303	290	88	28	0	5	35	38	54	.385	.452
Dye,Jermaine	L	.285	158	45	11	0	11	27	16	23	.354	.563
Bats Right	R	.294	432	127	30	2	23	69	28	81	.340	.532
Easley,Damion	L	.287	108	31	4	0	2	16	5	11	.328	.380
Bats Right	R	.260	208	54	6	2	4	28	14	27	.319	.365
Eckstein,David	L	.313	96	30	10	0	1	7	8	5	.383	.448
Bats Right	R	.246	228	56	11	0	1	20	23	27	.327	.307
Edmonds,Jim	L	.146	48	7	1	0	1	1	4	15	.212	.229
Bats Left	R	.250	292	73	18	2	19	54	51	67	.362	.521
Ellis,A.J.	L	-	0	0	0	0	0	0	0	0	-	
Bats Right	R	.000	3	0	0	0	0	0	0	2	.000	.000
Ellis,Mark	L	.176	125	22	5	0	1	11	20	20	.295	.240
Bats Right	R	.256	317	81	15	3	11	30	33	45	.331	.426
Ellison,Jason	L	.333	3	1	0	0	0	0	1	1	.500	.333
Bats Right	R	.200	10	2	0	0	0	2	0	0	.200	.200
Ellsbury,Jacoby	L	.295	139	41	7	1	1	11	8	21	.347	.381
Bats Left	R	.275	415	114	15	6	8	36	33	59	.332	.398
Encarnacion,Edwin	L	.292	144	42	10	0	7	16	26	30	.401	.507
Bats Right	R	.235	362	85	19	1	19	52	35	72	.315	.450
Ensberg,Morgan	L	.167	30	5	0	0	0	4	4	11	.265	.167
Bats Right	R	.227	44	10	0	0	1	4	2	11	.261	.295
Erstad,Darin	L	.243	70	17	3	0	1	8	1	15	.270	.329
Bats Left	R	.286	252	72	13	0	3	23	13	53	.320	.373
Escobar,Alcides	L	.667	3	2	0	0	0	0	0	0	.667	.667
Bats Right	R	.000	1	0	0	0	0	0	0	0	.000	.000
Escobar,Yunel	L	.262	149	39	4	1	2	8	14	12	.329	.342
Bats Right	R	.299	365	109	20	1	8	52	45	50	.380	.425
Estrada,Johnny	L	.100	10	1	0	0	0	1	0	1	.100	.100
Bats Both	R	.186	43	8	0	0	0	3	1	3	.222	.186
Ethier,Andre	L	.243	136	33	8	0	3	15	15	24	.325	.368
Bats Left	R	.326	389	127	30	5	17	62	44	64	.392	.560
Evans,Nick	L	.319	72	23	8	0	2	5	6	15	.380	.514
Bats Right	R	.135	37	5	2	0	0	4	1	9	.150	.189
Everett,Adam	L	.310	29	9	2	0	0	4	4	1	.394	.379
Bats Right	R	.184	98	18	4	1	2	16	8	14	.243	.306
Fahey,Brandon	L	.200	25	5	1	1	0	2	1	6	.250	.320
Bats Left	R	.235	81	19	8	1	0	10	2	19	.253	.358
Fasano,Sal	L	.235	17	4	3	0	0	2	0	7	.278	.412
Bats Right	R	.276	29	8	1	0	0	4	3	10	.371	.310
Feliz,Pedro	L	.288	139	40	7	2	6	21	13	16	.349	.496
Bats Right	R	.231	286	66	12	0	8	37	20	38	.279	.357
Fielder,Prince	L	.239	205	49	5	1	10	35	17	55	.313	.420
Bats Left	R	.295	383	113	25	1	24	67	67	79	.401	.554
Fields,Josh	L	.273	11	3	1	0	0	2	1	4	.333	.364
Bats Right	R	.095	21	2	0	0	0	0	2	13	.174	.095
Figgins,Chone	L	.272	125	34	4	0	0	8	12	15	.336	.304
Bats Both	R	.277	328	91	10	1	1	14	50	65	.378	.323
Fiorentino,Jeff	L	-	0	0	0	0	0	0	0	0	-	
Bats Left	R	1.000	1	1	0	0	0	1	0	0	1.000	1.000
Flores,Jesus	L	.308	78	24	4	1	3	15	3	21	.329	.500
Bats Right	R	.238	223	53	14	0	5	44	12	57	.285	.368
Floyd,Cliff	L	.100	10	1	1	0	0	0	2	4	.250	.200
Bats Right	R	.275	236	65	12	0	11	39	26	54	.353	.466
Fontenot,Mike	L	.333	21	7	3	0	0	2	2	6	.417	.476
Bats Left	R	.302	222	67	19	1	9	38	32	45	.393	.518
Fowler,Dexter	L	.364	11	4	0	0	0	0	0	2	.364	.364
Bats Both	R	.000	15	0	0	0	0	0	0	3	.063	.000
Francisco,Ben	L	.269	119	32	6	0	5	15	14	21	.348	.445
Bats Right	R	.265	328	87	26	0	10	39	26	65	.326	.436
Francoeur,Jeff	L	.210	176	37	6	1	3	14	15	33	.273	.307
Bats Right	R	.251	423	106	27	2	8	57	24	78	.303	.381
Frandsen,Kevin	L	-	0	0	0	0	0	0	0	0	-	
Bats Right	R	.000	1	0	0	0	0	0	0	0	.000	.000
Freel,Ryan	L	.339	62	21	6	0	0	4	4	7	.388	.435
Bats Right	R	.261	69	18	2	0	0	6	4	11	.297	.290
Fukudome,Kosuke	L	.276	127	35	8	1	6	16	21	26	.371	.354
Bats Left	R	.251	374	94	17	2	10	42	60	78	.355	.388
Furcal,Rafael	L	.365	52	19	3	1	3	8	6	4	.431	.635
Bats Both	R	.352	91	32	9	1	2	8	14	13	.443	.538
Gamel,Mat	L	-	0	0	0	0	0	0	0	0	-	
Bats Left	R	.500	2	1	1	0	0	0	0	1	.500	1.000
Garciaparra,Nomar	L	.339	56	19	5	0	4	15	9	5	.424	.643
Bats Right	R	.224	107	24	4	0	4	13	6	6	.270	.374
Gardner,Brett	L	.125	24	3	0	0	0	0	0	1	.125	.125
Bats Left	R	.252	103	26	5	2	0	15	8	22	.316	.340
Garko,Ryan	L	.315	124	39	8	1	3	27	13	12	.389	.468
Bats Right	R	.259	371	96	13	0	11	63	32	74	.332	.383
Gathright,Joey	L	.250	72	18	1	0	0	8	9	8	.333	.264
Bats Left	R	.256	207	53	2	1	0	14	11	32	.304	.275
German,Esteban	L	.255	110	28	6	1	0	11	16	16	.317	.327
Bats Right	R	.236	106	25	8	2	0	11	7	26	.287	.349
Gerut,Jody	L	.308	65	20	3	3	3	10	3	11	.338	.585
Bats Right	R	.293	263	77	12	1	11	33	25	41	.354	.471
Getz,Chris	L	.500	2	1	0	0	0	1	0	0	.500	.500
Bats Left	R	.200	5	1	0	0	0	0	0	0	.200	.200
Giambi,Jason	L	.231	130	30	7	0	8	27	18	34	.373	.469
Bats Left	R	.253	328	83	12	1	24	69	58	77	.374	.515
Giles,Brian	L	.301	196	59	11	3	1	13	31	24	.397	.403
Bats Left	R	.309	363	112	29	1	11	50	56	28	.399	.485
Gillaspie,Conor	L	-	0	0	0	0	0	0	0	0	-	
Bats Left	R	.200	5	1	0	0	0	0	2	0	.429	.200
Glaus,Troy	L	.221	154	34	8	0	8	18	26	32	.337	.429
Bats Left	R	.290	390	113	25	1	19	81	61	72	.386	.505
Gload,Ross	L	.263	99	26	4	0	0	12	3	10	.286	.303
Bats Left	R	.277	289	80	14	1	3	25	20	29	.327	.363
Golson,Greg	L	.000	3	0	0	0	0	0	0	3	.000	.000
Bats Right	R	.000	3	0	0	0	0	0	0	1	.000	.000
Gomes,Jonny	L	.182	99	18	1	1	7	16	9	29	.281	.424
Bats Right	R	.182	55	10	4	0	1	5	6	17	.286	.309
Gomez,Carlos	L	.270	159	43	8	2	3	16	8	33	.310	.403
Bats Right	R	.254	418	106	16	5	4	43	17	109	.291	.344
Gomez,Chris	L	.226	62	14	2	0	0	7	7	13	.314	.258
Bats Right	R	.298	121	36	6	0	1	13	6	17	.326	.372
Gonzalez,Adrian	L	.213	235	50	5	0	12	38	21	62	.287	.387
Bats Left	R	.320	381	122	27	1	24	81	53	80	.405	.585
Gonzalez,Alberto	L	.219	32	7	1	0	0	2	3	6	.286	.250
Bats Right	R	.275	69	19	7	0	1	8	5	8	.333	.420

Batters vs. Left-Handed and Right-Handed Pitchers

Batter	vs	Avg	AB	H	2B	3B	HR	RBI	BB	SO	OBP	Slg
Gonzalez,Andy	L	.231	13	3	0	0	1	2	6	4	.474	.462
Bats Right	R	.182	11	2	0	0	0	0	0	1	.182	.182
Gonzalez,Carlos	L	.188	85	16	2	0	1	7	2	23	.207	.247
Bats Left	R	.263	217	57	20	1	3	19	11	58	.298	.406
Gonzalez,Edgar	L	.283	127	36	9	0	2	12	15	25	.359	.402
Bats Right	R	.268	198	53	6	0	5	21	10	51	.308	.374
Gonzalez,Luis	L	.239	71	17	4	0	1	9	11	8	.333	.338
Bats Left	R	.267	270	72	22	1	7	38	30	35	.337	.433
Gordon,Alex	L	.234	167	39	11	0	1	10	18	41	.312	.317
Bats Left	R	.273	326	89	24	1	15	49	48	79	.370	.491
Gotay,Ruben	L	.154	26	4	0	0	0	0	5	11	.290	.154
Bats Both	R	.263	76	20	5	0	2	8	8	21	.333	.408
Granderson,Curtis	L	.259	147	38	6	2	5	14	9	29	.310	.429
Bats Left	R	.288	406	117	20	11	17	52	62	82	.383	.517
Greene,Khalil	L	.188	101	19	4	1	1	7	9	24	.252	.277
Bats Right	R	.222	288	64	11	1	9	28	13	76	.263	.361
Griffey Jr.,Ken	L	.202	163	33	12	0	4	23	21	39	.299	.350
Bats Left	R	.272	327	89	18	1	14	48	57	50	.379	.462
Gross,Gabe	L	.191	68	13	2	1	2	5	5	23	.247	.338
Bats Left	R	.249	277	69	14	2	11	35	45	59	.356	.433
Grudzielanek,Mark	L	.395	86	34	11	0	0	7	9	12	.459	.523
Bats Right	R	.265	245	65	13	0	3	17	10	29	.301	.355
Guerrero,Vladimir	L	.286	140	40	5	0	7	18	15	18	.355	.471
Bats Right	R	.309	401	124	26	3	20	73	36	59	.369	.539
Guillen,Carlos	L	.287	87	25	5	0	3	16	12	14	.370	.448
Bats Both	R	.285	333	95	24	2	7	38	48	53	.377	.432
Guillen,Jose	L	.305	174	53	14	0	11	41	14	30	.361	.575
Bats Right	R	.248	424	105	28	1	9	56	9	76	.274	.382
Gutierrez,Franklin	L	.252	131	33	10	0	5	25	10	32	.313	.443
Bats Right	R	.246	268	66	16	2	3	16	17	55	.305	.354
Guzman,Cristian	L	.354	181	64	13	3	4	20	8	10	.380	.525
Bats Both	R	.299	398	119	22	2	5	35	15	47	.329	.402
Gwynn,Tony	L	1.000	2	2	0	0	0	0	1	0	1.000	1.000
Bats Left	R	.150	40	6	1	0	0	1	3	7	.222	.175
Hafner,Travis	L	.220	50	11	3	0	0	7	7	15	.322	.280
Bats Left	R	.189	148	28	7	0	5	17	20	40	.299	.338
Hairston,Jerry	L	.345	84	29	8	0	3	12	11	11	.418	.548
Bats Right	R	.316	177	56	12	2	3	24	12	25	.366	.458
Hairston,Scott	L	.280	143	40	11	1	10	14	8	31	.316	.580
Bats Right	R	.224	183	41	7	2	7	17	20	53	.309	.399
Hall,Bill	L	.306	157	48	13	0	7	25	17	45	.371	.522
Bats Right	R	.174	247	43	9	1	8	30	20	79	.242	.316
Hall,Toby	L	.377	53	20	1	0	2	5	3	1	.411	.509
Bats Right	R	.176	74	13	2	0	0	2	3	18	.228	.203
Hamilton,Josh	L	.288	205	59	7	2	8	37	17	46	.342	.459
Bats Left	R	.313	419	131	28	3	24	93	47	80	.384	.566
Hammock,Robby	L	.158	19	3	1	0	0	2	2	4	.238	.211
Bats Right	R	.217	23	5	0	0	0	0	3	5	.333	.217
Hanigan,Ryan	L	.237	38	9	1	0	1	4	3	4	.293	.342
Bats Right	R	.298	47	14	1	0	1	5	7	5	.421	.383
Hannahan,Jack	L	.204	108	22	6	0	0	8	15	34	.298	.259
Bats Left	R	.223	328	73	21	0	9	39	40	97	.307	.369
Hardy,J.J.	L	.304	148	45	6	2	10	26	25	21	.402	.574
Bats Right	R	.276	421	116	25	2	14	48	27	77	.320	.444
Harman,Brad	L	.167	6	1	1	0	0	1	1	1	.286	.333
Bats Right	R	.000	4	0	0	0	0	0	0	0	.000	.000
Harris,Brendan	L	.265	151	40	14	1	1	14	13	33	.323	.391
Bats Right	R	.265	283	75	15	2	6	35	26	65	.329	.396
Harris,Willie	L	.240	100	24	6	0	5	13	11	29	.327	.450
Bats Left	R	.255	267	68	8	4	8	30	39	37	.351	.404
Hart,Corey	L	.281	167	47	14	0	6	22	10	25	.324	.473
Bats Right	R	.263	445	117	31	6	14	69	17	84	.291	.454
Hatteberg,Scott	L	.100	10	1	0	0	0	2	1	2	.167	.100
Bats Left	R	.190	42	8	3	0	0	5	6	5	.286	.262
Hawpe,Brad	L	.282	124	35	6	0	6	15	13	40	.350	.476
Bats Left	R	.283	364	103	18	3	19	70	63	94	.391	.505
Haynes,Nathan	L	.250	4	1	0	0	0	0	0	1	.250	.250
Bats Left	R	.225	40	9	0	0	0	3	3	11	.279	.225
Headley,Chase	L	.276	116	32	6	1	4	15	6	38	.309	.448
Bats Both	R	.265	215	57	13	1	5	23	24	66	.351	.405
Helms,Wes	L	.258	97	25	6	0	2	13	12	20	.342	.381
Bats Right	R	.234	154	36	5	0	3	18	5	45	.269	.325
Helton,Todd	L	.246	69	17	0	0	1	7	16	17	.388	.290
Bats Left	R	.270	230	62	16	0	6	22	45	33	.391	.417
Hermida,Jeremy	L	.240	121	29	1	2	5	17	11	34	.324	.405
Bats Left	R	.252	381	96	21	1	12	44	37	104	.322	.407

Batter	vs	Avg	AB	H	2B	3B	HR	RBI	BB	SO	OBP	Slg
Hernandez,Anderson	L	.366	41	15	3	0	0	9	4	6	.422	.439
Bats Both	R	.300	40	12	1	0	0	8	6	2	.391	.325
Hernandez,Luis	L	.200	15	3	0	0	0	2	2	2	.263	.200
Bats Both	R	.250	64	16	1	0	0	1	5	9	.304	.266
Hernandez,Michel	L	.200	5	1	0	0	0	0	0	1	.200	.200
Bats Right	R	.200	10	2	0	0	0	0	0	2	.200	.200
Hernandez,Ramon	L	.283	145	41	10	0	1	13	6	18	.316	.372
Bats Right	R	.245	318	78	12	1	14	52	26	44	.305	.421
Herrera,Jonathan	L	.200	20	4	0	0	0	1	3	4	.304	.200
Bats Both	R	.244	41	10	1	1	0	2	1	6	.262	.317
Hessman,Mike	L	.231	13	3	0	0	1	1	2	6	.412	.462
Bats Right	R	.357	14	5	1	0	4	6	0	3	.357	1.286
Hill,Aaron	L	.286	42	12	4	0	0	4	10	8	.426	.381
Bats Right	R	.258	163	42	10	0	2	16	6	23	.292	.356
Hill,Koyie	L	.333	3	1	0	0	0	0	0	1	.333	.333
Bats Both	R	.056	18	1	1	0	0	1	0	11	.056	.111
Hinske,Eric	L	.143	49	7	1	0	1	5	8	10	.263	.224
Bats Left	R	.262	332	87	20	1	19	55	39	78	.344	.500
Hoffpauir,Micah	L	.273	11	3	0	0	1	3	0	4	.273	.545
Bats Left	R	.355	62	22	8	0	1	5	6	20	.420	.532
Holliday,Matt	L	.293	123	36	7	1	5	18	23	26	.408	.488
Bats Right	R	.329	416	137	31	1	20	70	51	78	.410	.553
Hollimon,Michael	L	.000	1	0	0	0	0	0	0	0	.000	.000
Bats Both	R	.273	22	6	2	1	1	2	1	6	.292	.591
Holm,Steve	L	.235	17	4	3	0	1	5	4	4	.381	.588
Bats Right	R	.269	67	18	6	0	0	1	6	12	.351	.358
Hoover,Paul	L	.286	14	4	0	0	0	1	1	5	.333	.286
Bats Right	R	.154	26	4	1	0	0	1	1	12	.185	.192
Hopper,Norris	L	.269	26	7	0	0	0	0	2	3	.321	.269
Bats Right	R	.125	24	3	0	0	0	1	3	3	.250	.125
Horwitz,Brian	L	.235	17	4	0	0	1	2	4	4	.381	.412
Bats Right	R	.211	19	4	0	0	1	2	1	6	.238	.368
House,J.R.	L	.000	1	0	0	0	0	0	0	1	.000	.000
Bats Right	R	.000	2	0	0	0	0	1	0	0	.000	.000
Howard,Ryan	L	.224	237	53	6	3	14	49	23	96	.294	.451
Bats Left	R	.268	373	100	20	1	34	97	58	103	.366	.601
Hu,Chin-lung	L	.158	19	3	0	0	0	0	6	1	.360	.158
Bats Right	R	.186	97	18	2	2	0	9	5	22	.225	.247
Huber,Justin	L	.250	44	11	2	0	2	6	2	13	.313	.432
Bats Right	R	.235	17	4	1	0	0	2	1	6	.278	.294
Hudson,Orlando	L	.269	130	35	7	1	2	12	12	15	.336	.385
Bats Both	R	.321	277	89	22	2	6	29	28	47	.382	.480
Huff,Aubrey	L	.270	196	53	15	0	6	26	12	30	.313	.439
Bats Left	R	.321	402	129	33	2	26	82	41	59	.382	.607
Hulett,Tug	L	.000	3	0	0	0	0	0	0	3	.000	.000
Bats Left	R	.239	46	11	1	0	1	2	5	14	.327	.326
Hundley,Nick	L	.224	58	13	1	1	1	8	4	16	.270	.328
Bats Right	R	.243	140	34	6	0	4	16	7	36	.281	.371
Hunter,Torii	L	.304	148	45	16	0	4	17	16	32	.372	.493
Bats Right	R	.268	403	108	21	2	17	61	34	76	.333	.457
Iannetta,Chris	L	.275	80	22	4	0	6	19	13	22	.398	.550
Bats Right	R	.261	253	66	18	2	12	46	43	70	.388	.490
Ibanez,Raul	L	.305	197	60	13	2	7	37	18	41	.368	.497
Bats Left	R	.288	438	126	30	1	16	73	46	69	.353	.470
Iguchi,Tadahito	L	.190	79	15	3	1	0	6	9	26	.273	.253
Bats Right	R	.247	231	57	12	0	2	18	17	49	.298	.325
Infante,Omar	L	.325	123	40	11	3	0	14	8	18	.361	.463
Bats Right	R	.273	194	53	13	0	3	26	14	26	.324	.387
Inge,Brandon	L	.232	82	19	5	3	2	12	5	19	.281	.439
Bats Right	R	.196	265	52	11	1	9	39	38	75	.310	.347
Inglett,Joe	L	.276	29	8	2	0	0	3	3	6	.364	.345
Bats Left	R	.298	315	94	13	7	3	36	25	37	.355	.413
Iribarren,Hernan	L	.000	1	0	0	0	0	0	0	0	.000	.000
Bats Left	R	.154	13	2	1	0	0	1	1	3	.214	.231
Ishikawa,Travis	L	.000	2	0	0	0	0	0	1	1	.333	.000
Bats Left	R	.280	93	26	6	0	3	15	8	26	.337	.441
Iwamura,Akinori	L	.260	192	50	7	2	1	22	20	47	.335	.333
Bats Left	R	.280	435	122	23	7	5	26	50	84	.356	.400
Izturis,Cesar	L	.304	161	49	3	2	1	13	10	8	.356	.366
Bats Both	R	.237	253	60	7	1	0	11	19	18	.296	.273
Izturis,Maicer	L	.258	62	16	2	1	1	11	2	5	.281	.371
Bats Both	R	.272	228	62	12	1	2	26	24	22	.341	.360
Jackson,Conor	L	.315	130	41	12	1	3	17	30	15	.446	.492
Bats Right	R	.295	410	121	19	5	9	58	29	46	.351	.432
Jacobs,Mike	L	.218	119	26	4	0	7	23	5	36	.248	.429
Bats Left	R	.257	358	92	23	2	25	70	31	83	.315	.542

Batter	vs	Avg	AB	H	2B	3B	HR	RBI	BB	SO	OBP	Slg
Janish,Paul	L	.323	31	10	2	0	0	3	4	5	.400	.387
Bats Right	R	.102	49	5	0	0	1	3	3	13	.185	.163
Jaso,John	L	.500	2	1	0	0	0	0	0	1	.500	.500
Bats Left	R	.125	8	1	0	0	0	0	0	1	.125	.125
Jenkins,Geoff	L	.130	23	3	0	0	1	1	7		.160	.130
Bats Left	R	.256	270	69	16	0	9	28	23	61	.313	.415
Jeter,Derek	L	.302	172	52	9	1	4	18	21	22	.386	.436
Bats Right	R	.300	424	127	16	2	7	51	31	63	.353	.396
Jimerson,Charlton	L	.000	1	0	0	0	0	0	0	0	.000	.000
Bats Right	R	-	0	0	0	0	0	0	0	0	-	-
Johjima,Kenji	L	.205	117	24	7	0	6	19	6	8	.260	.419
Bats Right	R	.237	262	62	12	0	1	20	13	25	.285	.294
Johnson,Dan	L	.111	9	1	0	0	0	0	2	3	.273	.111
Bats Left	R	.235	17	4	0	0	2	4	1	4	.278	.588
Johnson,Elliot	L	.167	12	2	0	0	0	0	0	5	.167	.167
Bats Both	R	.143	7	1	0	0	0	0	0	2	.143	.143
Johnson,Kelly	L	.333	150	50	10	1	1	15	8	28	.366	.433
Bats Left	R	.270	397	107	29	5	11	54	44	85	.342	.451
Johnson,Mark	L	1.000	1	1	0	0	0	1	0	0	1.000	1.000
Bats Left	R	.250	16	4	0	0	1	1	1	2	.294	.250
Johnson,Nick	L	.167	36	6	2	0	1	5	8	10	.354	.306
Bats Left	R	.247	73	18	6	0	4	15	25	15	.444	.493
Johnson,Reed	L	.333	147	49	11	0	2	21	12	30	.399	.449
Bats Right	R	.280	186	52	10	0	4	29	7	38	.323	.398
Johnson,Rob	L	.091	11	1	0	0	1	2	0	3	.091	.364
Bats Right	R	.150	20	3	0	0	0	0	0	3	.150	.150
Jones,Adam	L	.256	121	31	6	2	0	7	11	26	.321	.339
Bats Right	R	.275	356	98	15	5	9	50	12	82	.307	.421
Jones,Andruw	L	.178	73	13	3	1	2	8	13	25	.302	.329
Bats Right	R	.147	136	20	5	0	1	6	14	51	.230	.206
Jones,Brandon	L	.267	15	4	2	0	0	0	2	4	.353	.400
Bats Left	R	.267	101	27	8	1	1	17	5	24	.306	.396
Jones,Chipper	L	.394	155	61	9	1	5	23	26	17	.478	.561
Bats Both	R	.349	284	99	15	0	17	52	64	44	.466	.581
Jones,Jacque	L	.000	15	0	0	0	0	0	1	5	.063	.000
Bats Left	R	.168	101	17	2	1	1	7	13	21	.263	.238
Jorgensen,Ryan	L	-	0	0	0	0	0	0	0	0	-	-
Bats Right	R	.000	1	0	0	0	0	0	0	0	.000	.000
Joyce,Matt	L	.227	22	5	2	0	0	1	6	6	.393	.318
Bats Left	R	.255	220	56	14	3	12	32	25	59	.333	.509
Ka'aihue,Kila	L	.500	2	1	0	0	0	0	0	0	.500	.500
Bats Left	R	.263	19	5	0	0	1	1	3	2	.364	.421
Kapler,Gabe	L	.354	82	29	10	0	4	22	3	12	.379	.622
Bats Right	R	.272	147	40	7	2	4	16	10	27	.318	.429
Kazmir,Sean	L	.095	21	2	0	0	0	1	3	10	.200	.095
Bats Right	R	.333	18	6	1	0	0	1	2	4	.400	.389
Kearns,Austin	L	.153	85	13	3	0	1	4	13	16	.273	.224
Bats Right	R	.241	228	55	7	0	6	28	22	47	.326	.351
Kemp,Matt	L	.369	168	62	14	1	6	31	16	41	.417	.571
Bats Right	R	.260	438	114	24	4	12	45	30	112	.309	.416
Kendall,Jason	L	.250	136	34	10	0	1	16	16	13	.335	.346
Bats Right	R	.245	380	93	20	2	1	33	34	32	.324	.316
Kendrick,Howie	L	.300	100	30	8	0	1	10	4	12	.333	.410
Bats Right	R	.308	240	74	18	2	2	27	8	46	.333	.425
Kennedy,Adam	L	.270	74	20	2	0	0	6	3	13	.299	.297
Bats Left	R	.283	265	75	15	4	2	30	18	30	.326	.392
Kent,Jeff	L	.288	118	34	7	1	3	20	10	19	.341	.441
Bats Right	R	.276	322	89	16	0	9	39	15	33	.322	.410
Keppinger,Jeff	L	.360	139	50	8	2	2	20	13	3	.412	.489
Bats Right	R	.225	320	72	16	0	1	23	17	21	.265	.284
Kinsler,Ian	L	.281	135	38	8	2	5	16	13	15	.347	.481
Bats Right	R	.332	383	127	33	2	13	55	32	52	.385	.530
Konerko,Paul	L	.236	127	30	9	0	7	21	22	16	.353	.472
Bats Right	R	.241	311	75	10	1	15	41	43	64	.341	.424
Koshansky,Joe	L	.250	4	1	1	0	0	0	0	0	.400	.500
Bats Left	R	.206	34	7	2	0	3	8	1	17	.229	.529
Kotchman,Casey	L	.303	142	43	10	0	5	22	7	9	.340	.479
Bats Left	R	.261	383	100	18	1	9	52	29	30	.324	.384
Kotsay,Mark	L	.250	124	31	6	1	1	13	7	12	.290	.339
Bats Left	R	.288	278	80	19	3	5	36	25	33	.345	.432
Kottaras,George	L	.500	2	1	1	0	0	0	0	0	.500	1.000
Bats Left	R	.000	3	0	0	0	0	0	0	2	.000	.000
Kouzmanoff,Kevin	L	.237	186	44	11	1	4	14	10	42	.290	.371
Bats Right	R	.269	438	118	20	3	19	70	13	97	.303	.459
Kubel,Jason	L	.232	99	23	5	0	3	17	15	22	.330	.374
Bats Left	R	.283	364	103	17	5	17	61	32	69	.336	.497

Batter	vs	Avg	AB	H	2B	3B	HR	RBI	BB	SO	OBP	Slg
LaHair,Bryan	L	.091	22	2	0	0	0	0	5	6	.259	.091
Bats Left	R	.281	114	32	4	0	3	10	8	34	.328	.395
Laird,Gerald	L	.245	94	23	9	0	2	10	10	22	.314	.404
Bats Right	R	.288	250	72	15	0	4	31	13	41	.335	.396
Lamb,Mike	L	.067	30	2	1	1	0	0	1	7	.097	.167
Bats Left	R	.258	217	56	11	2	1	32	16	26	.299	.341
Langerhans,Ryan	L	.217	23	5	0	0	2	3	6	7	.379	.478
Bats Left	R	.239	88	21	5	2	1	9	19	24	.380	.375
Larish,Jeff	L	.250	4	1	0	0	0	0	0	2	.250	.250
Bats Left	R	.260	100	26	6	0	2	16	7	32	.308	.380
LaRoche,Adam	L	.241	137	33	11	1	6	24	11	42	.298	.467
Bats Left	R	.282	355	100	21	2	19	61	43	80	.357	.513
LaRoche,Andy	L	.143	63	9	1	0	1	3	8	11	.239	.206
Bats Right	R	.175	160	28	4	0	4	15	16	26	.257	.275
LaRue,Jason	L	.196	46	9	3	0	0	3	3	5	.288	.261
Bats Right	R	.220	118	26	5	1	4	18	12	15	.299	.381
Lee,Carlos	L	.330	106	35	6	0	7	26	7	12	.374	.585
Bats Right	R	.309	330	102	21	0	21	74	30	37	.366	.564
Lee,Derrek	L	.306	144	44	13	1	6	27	27	22	.413	.535
Bats Right	R	.286	479	137	28	2	14	63	44	97	.344	.441
Lewis,Fred	L	.270	100	27	4	2	1	5	12	33	.348	.380
Bats Left	R	.285	368	105	21	9	8	35	39	91	.352	.457
Lillibridge,Brent	L	.171	35	6	1	0	1	1	1	11	.194	.286
Bats Right	R	.222	45	10	5	1	0	7	2	12	.271	.378
Lind,Adam	L	.253	91	23	2	2	2	10	6	25	.303	.385
Bats Left	R	.294	235	69	14	2	7	30	10	34	.321	.460
Lo Duca,Paul	L	.254	59	15	3	0	0	4	4	2	.302	.305
Bats Right	R	.237	114	27	6	0	0	11	11	9	.331	.289
Loney,James	L	.249	169	42	5	1	4	28	13	30	.300	.361
Bats Left	R	.305	426	130	30	5	9	62	32	55	.353	.462
Longoria,Evan	L	.242	120	29	8	0	8	18	15	35	.321	.508
Bats Right	R	.284	328	93	23	2	19	67	31	87	.350	.540
Lopez,Felipe	L	.306	170	52	11	0	1	18	12	29	.348	.388
Bats Both	R	.270	311	84	17	2	5	28	31	53	.341	.386
Lopez,Jose	L	.299	177	53	9	0	5	32	9	16	.328	.435
Bats Right	R	.296	467	138	32	1	12	57	18	51	.319	.445
Loretta,Mark	L	.330	97	32	12	0	1	16	17	6	.419	.485
Bats Right	R	.250	164	41	3	0	3	22	12	24	.306	.323
Lowell,Mike	L	.318	88	28	6	0	5	12	14	10	.404	.557
Bats Right	R	.263	331	87	21	0	12	61	24	51	.319	.435
Lowrie,Jed	L	.338	80	27	10	1	1	22	11	14	.409	.525
Bats Both	R	.222	180	40	15	2	1	24	24	54	.308	.344
Ludwick,Ryan	L	.266	177	47	10	0	15	38	24	44	.353	.576
Bats Right	R	.316	361	114	30	3	22	75	38	102	.386	.598
Lugo,Julio	L	.283	53	15	4	0	0	4	10	11	.391	.358
Bats Right	R	.264	208	55	9	0	1	18	24	40	.346	.322
Luna,Hector	L	-	0	0	0	0	0	0	0	0	-	-
Bats Right	R	1.000	1	1	0	0	0	0	0	0	1.000	1.000
Macias,Drew	L	.333	3	1	0	0	0	0	0	0	.333	.333
Bats Left	R	.176	17	3	0	0	2	5	2	6	.238	.529
Mackowiak,Rob	L	.000	2	0	0	0	0	0	0	2	.000	.000
Bats Left	R	.137	51	7	1	0	1	4	8	15	.262	.216
Macri,Matt	L	.375	24	9	1	0	1	4	0	7	.375	.542
Bats Right	R	.200	10	2	0	0	0	0	2	3	.333	.200
Maier,Mitch	L	.273	33	9	1	0	0	3	0	6	.314	.303
Bats Left	R	.293	58	17	0	1	0	6	2	12	.317	.328
Markakis,Nick	L	.297	195	58	17	0	5	23	25	36	.381	.462
Bats Left	R	.310	400	124	31	1	15	64	74	77	.418	.505
Marson,Lou	L	.500	2	1	0	0	0	0	0	1	.500	.500
Bats Right	R	.500	2	1	0	0	1	2	0	1	.500	2.000
Marte,Andy	L	.293	58	17	4	1	1	9	7	13	.379	.448
Bats Right	R	.198	177	35	7	0	2	8	7	39	.228	.271
Martin,Russell	L	.253	154	39	8	0	5	24	25	16	.365	.403
Bats Right	R	.291	399	116	17	0	8	45	65	67	.392	.393
Martinez,Ramon	L	.000	3	0	0	0	0	0	0	0	.000	.000
Bats Right	R	.308	13	4	3	0	0	3	2	3	.400	.538
Martinez,Victor	L	.339	62	21	7	0	1	9	9	11	.423	.500
Bats Both	R	.260	204	53	10	0	1	26	15	21	.309	.324
Mather,Joe	L	.219	64	14	2	0	3	7	4	16	.292	.391
Bats Right	R	.261	69	18	5	0	5	11	6	18	.320	.551
Mathis,Jeff	L	.224	76	17	3	0	4	9	12	24	.326	.421
Bats Right	R	.184	207	38	5	0	5	33	18	66	.255	.280
Matsui,Hideki	L	.315	108	34	5	0	1	17	8	11	.362	.389
Bats Left	R	.284	229	65	12	0	8	28	30	36	.374	.441
Matsui,Kaz	L	.291	103	30	5	2	1	7	9	16	.345	.408
Bats Both	R	.294	272	80	21	1	5	26	28	37	.358	.434

Batters vs. Left-Handed and Right-Handed Pitchers

Batter	vs	Avg	AB	H	2B	3B	HR	RBI	BB	SO	OBP	Slg
Matthews Jr.,Gary	L	.285	130	37	5	0	4	15	14	25	.359	.415
Bats Both	R	.223	296	66	14	3	4	31	31	70	.301	.331
Mauer,Joe	L	.361	183	66	7	1	7	38	18	16	.415	.525
Bats Left	R	.312	353	110	24	3	2	47	66	34	.412	.414
Maybin,Cameron	L	.375	8	3	1	0	0	0	1	2	.444	.500
Bats Right	R	.542	24	13	1	0	0	2	2	6	.577	.583
Maysonet,Edwin	L	.000	1	0	0	0	0	0	0	0	.000	.000
Bats Right	R	.167	6	1	0	0	0	0	0	2	.167	.167
Maza,Luis	L	.286	21	6	1	0	0	1	2	3	.348	.333
Bats Right	R	.207	58	12	0	0	1	3	3	8	.258	.259
McAnulty,Paul	L	.000	5	0	0	0	0	1	0	1	.167	.000
Bats Left	R	.215	130	28	7	1	3	12	26	40	.348	.354
McCann,Brian	L	.299	164	49	15	0	3	21	17	22	.375	.445
Bats Left	R	.301	345	104	27	1	20	66	40	42	.373	.559
McClain,Scott	L	.167	12	2	0	0	1	3	3	3	.333	.417
Bats Right	R	.333	21	7	1	0	1	4	2	5	.391	.524
McDonald,John	L	.250	72	18	2	0	1	7	5	9	.304	.319
Bats Right	R	.184	114	21	6	0	0	11	5	16	.223	.237
McGehee,Casey	L	.125	8	1	1	0	0	0	0	4	.125	.250
Bats Right	R	.188	16	3	0	0	0	5	0	4	.176	.188
McLouth,Nate	L	.261	165	43	8	2	3	15	12	30	.322	.388
Bats Left	R	.282	432	122	38	2	23	79	53	63	.368	.539
McPherson,Dallas	L	.000	3	0	0	0	0	0	0	1	.000	.000
Bats Left	R	.250	8	2	2	0	0	0	4	4	.500	.500
Melhuse,Adam	L	.250	8	2	0	0	0	1	1	5	.333	.250
Bats Both	R	.136	22	3	1	0	0	1	1	10	.174	.182
Mench,Kevin	L	.237	76	18	9	0	0	6	11	13	.326	.355
Bats Right	R	.256	39	10	2	1	0	4	3	5	.310	.359
Metcalf,Travis	L	.162	37	6	1	0	4	10	0	8	.179	.514
Bats Right	R	.368	19	7	1	0	2	4	3	4	.455	.737
Michaels,Jason	L	.187	91	17	2	0	1	7	10	23	.267	.242
Bats Right	R	.241	195	47	11	1	7	46	17	42	.303	.415
Mientkiewicz,Doug	L	.250	48	12	5	1	0	7	5	6	.321	.396
Bats Left	R	.283	237	67	14	1	2	23	39	22	.384	.376
Miles,Aaron	L	.315	111	35	7	0	0	6	11	15	.377	.378
Bats Both	R	.317	268	85	8	2	4	25	12	22	.345	.407
Millar,Kevin	L	.238	147	35	8	0	5	18	24	24	.341	.395
Bats Right	R	.232	384	89	17	0	15	54	47	69	.316	.393
Milledge,Lastings	L	.258	159	41	3	0	5	16	9	28	.300	.371
Bats Right	R	.272	364	99	21	2	9	45	29	68	.342	.415
Miller,Corky	L	.120	25	3	0	0	0	2	2	8	.185	.120
Bats Right	R	.057	35	2	0	0	1	3	3	7	.128	.143
Miller,Jai	L	-	0	0	0	0	0	0	0	0	-	-
Bats Right	R	.000	1	0	0	0	0	0	0	1	.000	.000
Miranda,Juan	L	1.000	1	1	1	0	0	0	1	0	1.000	2.000
Bats Left	R	.333	9	3	0	0	0	1	1	4	.417	.333
Moeller,Chad	L	.185	27	5	0	0	0	2	4	7	.313	.185
Bats Right	R	.250	64	16	6	0	1	7	3	11	.310	.391
Molina,Bengie	L	.297	138	41	8	0	2	15	8	5	.340	.399
Bats Right	R	.291	392	114	25	0	14	80	11	33	.315	.462
Molina,Gustavo	L	.000	2	0	0	0	0	0	0	1	.000	.000
Bats Right	R	.200	5	1	0	0	0	0	1	0	.333	.200
Molina,Jose	L	.188	85	16	4	0	1	5	5	18	.250	.271
Bats Right	R	.230	183	42	13	0	2	13	7	34	.269	.333
Molina,Yadier	L	.323	130	42	7	0	4	23	14	7	.390	.469
Bats Right	R	.296	314	93	11	0	3	33	18	22	.330	.360
Monroe,Craig	L	.138	87	12	2	0	2	10	9	21	.219	.230
Bats Right	R	.276	76	21	7	0	6	19	7	27	.337	.605
Montanez,Lou	L	.283	53	15	4	0	0	4	1	9	.296	.358
Bats Right	R	.305	59	18	2	1	3	10	3	11	.333	.525
Montero,Miguel	L	.286	28	8	1	0	1	1	4	10	.375	.429
Bats Left	R	.250	156	39	15	1	4	17	15	39	.322	.436
Montz,Luke	L	.000	5	0	0	0	0	0	1	1	.167	.000
Bats Right	R	.188	16	3	0	0	1	3	4	8	.350	.375
Moore,Scott	L	-	0	0	0	0	0	0	0	0	-	-
Bats Left	R	.125	8	1	0	0	1	1	1	3	.222	.500
Mora,Melvin	L	.314	156	49	10	1	12	35	11	18	.365	.622
Bats Right	R	.272	357	97	19	1	11	69	26	52	.332	.423
Morales,Kendry	L	.214	14	3	1	0	1	2	2	3	.313	.500
Bats Both	R	.213	47	10	1	0	2	6	2	4	.260	.362
Morgan,Nyjer	L	.240	25	6	2	0	0	0	3	3	.321	.320
Bats Left	R	.304	138	41	11	0	0	7	7	27	.349	.385
Morneau,Justin	L	.284	236	67	17	1	7	52	14	29	.324	.453
Bats Left	R	.310	387	120	30	3	16	77	62	56	.401	.527
Morse,Mike	L	.250	4	1	0	0	0	0	0	1	.250	.250
Bats Right	R	.200	5	1	1	0	0	0	1	3	.429	.400

Batter	vs	Avg	AB	H	2B	3B	HR	RBI	BB	SO	OBP	Slg
Morton,Colt	L	.200	5	1	0	0	0	0	0	1	.200	.200
Bats Right	R	.000	10	0	0	0	0	1	2	4	.154	.000
Moss,Brandon	L	.267	60	16	5	1	1	11	8	18	.338	.433
Bats Left	R	.239	176	42	10	2	7	23	13	52	.292	.438
Murphy,Daniel	L	.400	10	4	0	0	1	3	2	1	.462	.700
Bats Left	R	.306	121	37	9	3	1	14	16	27	.391	.455
Murphy,David	L	.258	124	32	5	2	2	20	6	20	.290	.379
Bats Left	R	.282	291	82	23	1	13	54	25	50	.333	.502
Murphy,Donnie	L	.196	46	9	2	0	0	5	6	15	.288	.239
Bats Right	R	.175	57	10	1	0	3	8	5	23	.262	.351
Murton,Matt	L	.125	24	3	1	0	0	5	1	4	.160	.167
Bats Right	R	.217	46	10	2	0	0	3	1	8	.250	.261
Myrow,Brian	L	.000	3	0	0	0	0	0	0	0	.000	.000
Bats Left	R	.167	18	3	0	0	1	3	5	5	.238	.333
Nady,Xavier	L	.262	126	33	5	0	6	21	17	25	.361	.444
Bats Right	R	.317	429	136	32	1	19	76	22	78	.357	.529
Napoli,Mike	L	.286	49	14	2	0	4	10	11	16	.406	.571
Bats Right	R	.270	178	48	7	1	16	39	24	54	.364	.590
Navarro,Dioner	L	.257	109	28	8	0	3	13	9	12	.314	.413
Bats Both	R	.308	318	98	19	0	4	41	25	37	.361	.406
Nelson,Brad	L	.000	1	0	0	0	0	0	0	0	.000	.000
Bats Left	R	.333	6	2	2	0	0	0	1	0	.429	.667
Newhan,David	L	.286	7	2	1	0	0	0	0	3	.286	.429
Bats Left	R	.258	97	25	4	2	2	12	6	25	.298	.402
Nieves,Wil	L	.304	56	17	3	0	0	8	6	10	.365	.357
Bats Right	R	.242	120	29	6	1	1	12	7	19	.281	.333
Nix,Jayson	L	.000	17	0	0	0	0	1	3	9	.150	.000
Bats Right	R	.179	39	7	2	0	1	4	4	8	.273	.231
Nix,Laynce	L	.000	1	0	0	0	0	0	0	1	.000	.000
Bats Left	R	.091	11	1	0	0	0	0	1	2	.167	.091
Nixon,Trot	L	.000	1	0	0	0	0	0	0	1	.500	.000
Bats Left	R	.176	34	6	1	0	1	1	5	9	.282	.294
Norton,Greg	L	.192	52	10	3	0	3	12	9	18	.311	.423
Bats Both	R	.289	135	39	8	0	4	23	24	26	.396	.444
Nunez,Abraham	L	-	0	0	0	0	0	0	0	0	-	-
Bats Both	R	.000	2	0	0	0	0	0	0	0	.000	.000
Ochoa,Ivan	L	.244	45	11	2	0	0	2	0	8	.244	.289
Bats Right	R	.173	75	13	6	0	0	1	4	20	.244	.253
Ojeda,Augie	L	.250	60	15	3	0	0	2	9	8	.357	.300
Bats Both	R	.240	171	41	6	2	0	15	17	16	.338	.298
Olivo,Miguel	L	.262	103	27	7	0	7	16	5	24	.296	.534
Bats Right	R	.251	203	51	15	0	5	25	2	58	.268	.399
Ordonez,Magglio	L	.328	137	45	6	0	4	14	17	20	.406	.460
Bats Right	R	.314	424	133	26	2	17	89	36	56	.365	.505
Orr,Pete	L	.286	7	2	0	1	0	2	0	3	.286	.571
Bats Left	R	.250	68	17	2	0	0	5	2	13	.282	.279
Ortiz,David	L	.221	104	23	5	1	5	19	14	19	.308	.433
Bats Left	R	.279	322	87	25	0	18	70	56	55	.389	.532
Ortmeier,Dan	L	.238	42	10	5	0	0	4	4	13	.304	.357
Bats Right	R	.182	22	4	1	0	0	1	3	5	.333	.227
Overbay,Lyle	L	.215	149	32	6	0	3	13	13	41	.285	.255
Bats Left	R	.291	395	115	26	2	15	61	61	75	.384	.481
Owens,Jerry	L	.333	3	1	0	0	0	0	0	2	.333	.333
Bats Left	R	.231	13	3	0	0	0	1	0	2	.231	.231
Ozuna,Pablo	L	.387	31	12	3	0	1	3	1	3	.406	.581
Bats Right	R	.200	65	13	0	1	0	6	2	5	.235	.231
Pagan,Angel	L	.250	40	10	4	0	0	6	1	10	.256	.350
Bats Both	R	.294	51	15	3	1	0	7	10	8	.410	.392
Patterson,Corey	L	.188	64	12	1	1	1	6	1	15	.209	.281
Bats Left	R	.209	302	63	16	1	9	28	15	42	.244	.358
Patterson,Eric	L	.217	23	5	1	0	0	4	0	4	.217	.261
Bats Left	R	.187	107	20	3	0	1	11	17	32	.296	.243
Paulino,Ronny	L	.235	34	8	2	0	1	10	4	5	.308	.382
Bats Right	R	.202	84	17	3	0	1	8	7	19	.264	.274
Payton,Jay	L	.248	109	27	6	0	6	20	6	7	.287	.468
Bats Right	R	.240	229	55	4	2	1	21	16	46	.293	.288
Pearce,Steve	L	.321	28	9	3	0	2	5	1	9	.345	.643
Bats Right	R	.222	81	18	4	0	2	10	4	13	.278	.346
Pedroia,Dustin	L	.313	163	51	13	2	6	16	16	12	.376	.528
Bats Right	R	.331	490	162	41	0	11	67	34	40	.375	.482
Pena,Brayan	L	.333	3	1	0	0	0	0	0	0	.500	.333
Bats Both	R	.273	11	3	1	0	0	0	0	2	.273	.364
Pena,Carlos	L	.190	179	34	5	0	8	27	22	67	.302	.352
Bats Left	R	.280	311	87	19	2	23	75	74	99	.418	.576
Pena,Tony F	L	.243	70	17	2	0	1	6	3	13	.270	.314
Bats Right	R	.135	155	21	2	1	0	8	3	36	.151	.161

Batters vs. Left-Handed and Right-Handed Pitchers

Batter	vs	Avg	AB	H	2B	3B	HR	RBI	BB	SO	OBP	Slg
Pena,Wily Mo	L	.241	83	20	4	0	0	5	2	15	.256	.289
Bats Right	R	.179	112	20	2	0	2	5	8	33	.233	.250
Pence,Hunter	L	.250	152	38	6	0	7	19	9	27	.294	.428
Bats Right	R	.275	443	122	28	4	18	64	31	97	.326	.479
Pennington,Cliff	L	.289	38	11	2	0	0	4	1	6	.325	.342
Bats Both	R	.213	61	13	3	0	0	5	12	12	.347	.262
Peralta,Jhonny	L	.247	146	36	9	0	7	20	14	34	.309	.452
Bats Right	R	.285	459	131	33	4	16	69	34	92	.338	.479
Perez,Fernando	L	.292	24	7	1	0	1	4	5	4	.414	.458
Bats Both	R	.222	36	8	1	0	2	4	3	12	.300	.417
Perez,Tomas	L	.000	1	0	0	0	0	0	0	0	.000	.000
Bats Right	R	.222	9	2	0	0	0	0	0	2	.222	.222
Perry,Jason	L	.000	4	0	0	0	0	0	0	2	.000	.000
Bats Left	R	.154	13	2	0	1	0	1	0	2	.154	.308
Petit,Gregorio	L	.364	11	4	1	0	0		1	5	.417	.455
Bats Right	R	.333	12	4	1	0	0	0	1	4	.385	.417
Phelps,Josh	L	.316	19	6	1	0	0	1	2	6	.381	.368
Bats Right	R	.200	15	3	0	0	0	0	0	5	.200	.200
Phillips,Andy	L	.244	41	10	3	0	1	7	2	7	.295	.390
Bats Right	R	.216	37	8	0	0	2	3	4	7	.293	.378
Phillips,Brandon	L	.296	162	48	8	3	11	34	15	20	.358	.586
Bats Right	R	.247	397	98	16	4	10	44	24	73	.293	.383
Phillips,Paul	L	-	0	0	0	0	0	0	0	0	-	
Bats Right	R	.000	2	0	0	0	0	0	0	1	.000	.000
Pie,Felix	L	.091	11	1	0	0	0	2	3	4	.286	.091
Bats Left	R	.264	72	19	2	1	1	8	4	25	.316	.361
Pierre,Juan	L	.346	107	37	2	1	0	8	7	7	.388	.383
Bats Left	R	.257	268	69	8	1	1	20	15	17	.302	.306
Pierzynski,A.J.	L	.286	133	38	7	1	5	20	2	14	.305	.466
Bats Left	R	.279	401	112	24	0	8	40	17	57	.315	.399
Podsednik,Scott	L	.167	18	3	0	0	0	1	0	5	.167	.167
Bats Left	R	.264	144	38	8	1	1	14	16	23	.340	.354
Polanco,Placido	L	.321	162	52	11	0	4	19	12	13	.373	.463
Bats Right	R	.301	418	126	23	3	4	39	23	30	.342	.400
Posada,Jorge	L	.255	51	13	3	0	1	7	9	13	.361	.373
Bats Both	R	.274	117	32	10	1	2	15	15	25	.366	.427
Prado,Martin	L	.283	99	28	10	3	1	12	11	11	.355	.475
Bats Right	R	.349	129	45	8	1	1	21	10	18	.394	.450
Pridie,Jason	L	-	0	0	0	0	0	0	1	0	1.000	
Bats Left	R	.000	4	0	0	0	0	0	0	1	.000	.000
Pujols,Albert	L	.411	158	65	15	0	11	32	35	11	.518	.715
Bats Right	R	.333	366	122	29	0	26	84	69	43	.437	.626
Punto,Nick	L	.302	126	38	9	0	0	11	5	12	.328	.373
Bats Both	R	.274	212	58	10	4	2	17	27	45	.353	.387
Quentin,Carlos	L	.246	130	32	5	0	12	30	25	22	.375	.562
Bats Right	R	.303	350	106	21	1	24	70	41	58	.401	.574
Quinlan,Robb	L	.282	78	22	1	1	0	6	5	11	.329	.321
Bats Right	R	.244	86	21	0	1	1	5	9	17	.323	.302
Quintanilla,Omar	L	.209	43	9	1	0	0	4	3	10	.261	.233
Bats Left	R	.246	167	41	16	0	2	11	12	36	.294	.377
Quintero,Humberto	L	.273	33	9	2	0	0	1	0	3	.294	.333
Bats Right	R	.215	135	29	4	0	2	11	6	31	.264	.289
Quiroz,Guillermo	L	.200	25	5	0	0	2	3	3	5	.286	.440
Bats Right	R	.183	109	20	5	0	0	11	9	29	.252	.229
Rabelo,Mike	L	.222	18	4	0	0	1	1	3	3	.333	.389
Bats Both	R	.198	91	18	1	0	2	9	5	22	.240	.275
Raburn,Ryan	L	.238	84	20	6	0	3	10	5	20	.281	.417
Bats Right	R	.235	98	23	4	1	1	10	11	29	.312	.327
Ramirez,Alexei	L	.312	138	43	10	1	6	20	7	14	.342	.529
Bats Right	R	.281	342	96	12	1	15	57	11	45	.307	.453
Ramirez,Aramis	L	.239	134	32	11	0	3	27	18	23	.333	.388
Bats Right	R	.305	420	128	33	1	24	84	56	71	.394	.560
Ramirez,Hanley	L	.258	132	34	10	0	3	8	26	40	.389	.402
Bats Right	R	.313	457	143	24	4	30	59	66	82	.403	.580
Ramirez,Manny	L	.308	133	41	7	1	5	21	18	20	.391	.489
Bats Right	R	.339	419	142	29	0	32	100	69	104	.441	.637
Ramirez,Max	L	.071	14	1	0	0	0	2	5	5	.316	.071
Bats Right	R	.281	32	9	1	0	2	7	1	10	.361	.500
Ransom,Cody	L	.214	14	3	2	0	0	0	1	4	.313	.357
Bats Right	R	.345	29	10	1	0	4	8	5	8	.441	.793
Redmond,Mike	L	.277	65	18	3	0	0	7	2	6	.304	.323
Bats Right	R	.297	64	19	3	0	0	5	3	5	.338	.344
Reed,Jeremy	L	.115	26	3	0	0	0	2	0	7	.115	.115
Bats Left	R	.285	260	74	18	1	2	29	18	31	.332	.385
Renteria,Edgar	L	.366	123	45	7	1	5	18	17	12	.443	.561
Bats Right	R	.239	380	91	15	1	5	37	20	52	.274	.324
Repko,Jason	L	.400	5	2	1	0	0	0	0	2	.400	.600
Bats Right	R	.077	13	1	0	0	0	0	2	7	.200	.077
Reyes,Argenis	L	.167	24	4	0	0	0	1	0	6	.167	.167
Bats Both	R	.233	86	20	0	0	1	2	4	14	.283	.267
Reyes,Jose	L	.280	200	56	15	3	5	15	23	26	.356	.460
Bats Both	R	.303	488	148	22	16	11	53	43	56	.358	.482
Reynolds,Mark	L	.279	140	39	12	0	11	36	23	46	.382	.600
Bats Right	R	.226	399	90	16	3	17	61	41	158	.298	.409
Richar,Danny	L	.000	1	0	0	0	0	0	0	1	.000	.000
Bats Left	R	.229	35	8	2	0	0	3	0	8	.229	.286
Riggans,Shawn	L	.233	60	14	5	0	3	10	8	14	.314	.467
Bats Right	R	.213	75	16	2	0	3	14	4	16	.263	.360
Rios,Alex	L	.289	152	44	10	0	3	17	7	26	.321	.414
Bats Right	R	.292	483	141	37	8	12	62	37	86	.342	.476
Rivas,Luis	L	.288	52	15	2	1	2	10	4	11	.339	.481
Bats Right	R	.195	154	30	4	1	1	10	9	16	.242	.253
Rivera,Juan	L	.233	90	21	6	0	5	14	4	11	.263	.467
Bats Right	R	.253	166	42	7	0	7	31	12	22	.292	.422
Rivera,Mike	L	.176	17	3	1	0	0	2	4	3	.333	.235
Bats Right	R	.356	45	16	4	0	1	12	2	7	.396	.511
Roberts,Brian	L	.313	182	57	19	1	2	15	24	30	.389	.462
Bats Both	R	.289	429	124	32	7	7	42	58	74	.373	.445
Roberts,Dave	L	.000	2	0	0	0	0	0	1	1	.333	.000
Bats Left	R	.229	105	24	2	2	0	9	19	17	.341	.286
Roberts,Ryan	L	.000	1	0	0	0	0	0	0	1	.000	.000
Bats Right	R	-	0	0	0	0	0	0	0	0	-	
Rodriguez,Alex	L	.263	137	36	7	0	8	23	26	29	.395	.489
Bats Right	R	.316	373	118	26	0	27	80	39	88	.391	.603
Rodriguez,Ivan	L	.289	97	28	4	1	1	8	4	13	.343	.381
Bats Right	R	.272	301	82	16	2	6	27	15	54	.312	.399
Rodriguez,Luis	L	.238	63	15	3	0	0	5	3	3	.269	.286
Bats Both	R	.309	139	43	8	1	0	7	10	10	.351	.381
Rodriguez,Sean	L	.178	45	8	2	0	0		2	14	.245	.222
Bats Right	R	.213	122	26	6	1	3	10	12	41	.287	.352
Rohlinger,Ryan	L	.250	8	2	1	0	0	1	0	2	.250	.375
Bats Right	R	.042	24	1	0	1	0		1	6	.080	.125
Rolen,Scott	L	.250	100	25	8	0	2	8	15	19	.370	.390
Bats Right	R	.266	308	82	22	3	9	42	31	52	.342	.445
Rollins,Jimmy	L	.288	163	47	13	1	3	18	10	10	.341	.436
Bats Both	R	.272	393	107	25	8	8	41	48	45	.352	.438
Romero,Alex	L	.174	23	4	0	0	0	1	0	4	.174	.174
Bats Left	R	.241	112	27	8	2	1	11	3	16	.265	.375
Rosales,Adam	L	.273	11	3	0	0	0	1	0	1	.273	.273
Bats Right	R	.167	18	3	1	0	0	1	1	3	.211	.222
Ross,Cody	L	.285	144	41	9	1	10	27	11	26	.342	.569
Bats Right	R	.249	317	79	20	4	12	46	22	90	.305	.451
Ross,David	L	.206	63	13	1	0	1	6	16	19	.363	.270
Bats Right	R	.241	79	19	8	0	2	7	16	20	.375	.418
Rottino,Vinny	L	.000	1	0	0	0	0	0	0	0	.000	.000
Bats Right	R	-	0	0	0	0	0	0	0	0	-	
Rowand,Aaron	L	.286	147	42	13	0	8	25	9	38	.340	.537
Bats Right	R	.266	402	107	24	0	5	45	35	88	.339	.363
Ruggiano,Justin	L	.174	46	8	2	0	1	2	2	16	.208	.283
Bats Right	R	.233	30	7	2	0	1	5	2	11	.303	.400
Ruiz,Carlos	L	.212	66	14	5	0	1	7	14	4	.346	.333
Bats Right	R	.220	254	56	9	0	3	24	30	34	.313	.291
Ruiz,Randy	L	.273	33	9	1	0	1	5	4	10	.351	.394
Bats Right	R	.276	29	8	1	0	0	2	2	11	.323	.310
Ryan,Brendan	L	.261	92	24	3	0	0	6	7	14	.327	.293
Bats Right	R	.229	105	24	6	0	0	4	9	17	.289	.390
Ryan,Dusty	L	.429	14	6	2	0	2	4	3	4	.529	1.000
Bats Right	R	.267	30	8	0	0	0	3	2	9	.303	.267
Saccomanno,Mark	L	.000	3	0	0	0	0	0	0	2	.000	.000
Bats Right	R	.286	7	2	1	0	1	2	0	1	.286	.857
Salazar,Jeff	L	.300	10	3	0	0	0	1	0	3	.300	.300
Bats Left	R	.203	118	24	5	3	2	11	21	38	.333	.347
Salazar,Oscar	L	.211	38	8	1	0	1	4	5	7	.302	.316
Bats Right	R	.349	43	15	2	0	4	11	7	6	.431	.674
Salome,Angel	L	.000	2	0	0	0	0	0	0	0	.000	.000
Bats Right	R	.000	1	0	0	0	0	0	0	1	.000	.000
Saltalamacchia,J.	L	.158	76	12	5	0	0	6	6	29	.220	.224
Bats Right	R	.311	122	38	8	0	3	20	25	45	.426	.451
Sammons,Clint	L	.176	17	3	0	0	0	1	0	3	.333	.176
Bats Right	R	.135	37	5	0	0	1	3	1	10	.158	.216
Sanchez,Freddy	L	.289	121	35	8	0	4	14	8	11	.333	.455
Bats Right	R	.266	448	119	18	2	5	38	13	52	.289	.348

Batters vs. Left-Handed and Right-Handed Pitchers

Batter	vs	Avg	AB	H	2B	3B	HR	RBI	BB	SO	OBP	Slg
Sanchez,Gaby	L	.000	1	0	0	0	0	0	0	1	.000	.000
Bats Right	R	.429	7	3	2	0	0	1	0	1	.429	.714
Sandoval,Freddy	L	-	0	0	0	0	0	0	0	0	-	
Bats Both	R	.167	6	1	0	0	0	0	1	0	.286	.167
Sandoval,Pablo	L	.237	38	9	2	0	0	2	2	3	.268	.289
Bats Both	R	.383	107	41	8	1	3	22	2	11	.389	.561
Santiago,Ramon	L	.320	25	8	1	0	2	3	4	2	.414	.600
Bats Both	R	.273	99	27	5	2	2	15	18	15	.410	.424
Santos,Omir	L	-	0	0	0	0	0	0	0	0	-	
Bats Right	R	.100	10	1	0	0	0	0	0	2	.100	.100
Sardinha,Dane	L	.000	7	0	0	0	0	0	3	4	.300	.000
Bats Right	R	.189	37	7	0	1	0	3	1	7	.211	.243
Schierholtz,Nate	L	.333	21	7	1	1	0	1	0	1	.364	.476
Bats Left	R	.315	54	17	7	0	1	4	3	7	.373	.500
Schneider,Brian	L	.187	75	14	1	0	0	7	10	16	.291	.200
Bats Left	R	.277	260	72	9	0	9	31	32	37	.354	.415
Schumaker,Skip	L	.168	119	20	2	0	0	6	11	22	.238	.185
Bats Left	R	.340	421	143	20	5	8	40	36	38	.393	.468
Scott,Luke	L	.215	107	23	3	1	5	11	10	24	.300	.402
Bats Left	R	.269	368	99	26	1	18	54	43	78	.346	.492
Scutaro,Marco	L	.268	142	38	4	1	4	15	15	14	.338	.394
Bats Right	R	.267	375	100	19	0	3	45	42	51	.343	.341
Sexson,Richie	L	.325	83	27	3	0	6	18	14	23	.414	.578
Bats Right	R	.178	197	35	6	0	6	18	29	63	.281	.299
Shealy,Ryan	L	.273	33	9	0	0	3	7	2	9	.333	.545
Bats Right	R	.325	40	13	1	0	4	13	3	10	.372	.650
Sheffield,Gary	L	.239	109	26	4	0	6	19	12	19	.314	.440
Bats Right	R	.220	309	68	12	0	13	38	46	64	.330	.385
Shelton,Chris	L	.184	49	9	3	0	0	3	6	20	.273	.245
Bats Right	R	.250	48	12	2	0	2	8	11	13	.390	.417
Shoppach,Kelly	L	.304	92	28	10	0	5	11	8	35	.373	.576
Bats Right	R	.246	260	64	17	0	16	44	28	98	.339	.496
Sizemore,Grady	L	.224	183	41	7	1	7	21	27	41	.347	.388
Bats Left	R	.286	451	129	32	4	26	69	71	89	.386	.548
Smith,Jason	L	.167	6	1	0	0	0	0	0	2	.167	.167
Bats Left	R	.227	22	5	2	0	0	1	0	10	.227	.318
Smith,Seth	L	.000	11	0	0	0	0	2	1	3	.083	.000
Bats Left	R	.289	97	28	7	0	4	13	14	20	.378	.485
Snelling,Chris	L	-	0	0	0	0	0	0	0	0	-	
Bats Left	R	.500	4	2	1	0	1	1	0	0	.500	1.500
Snider,Travis	L	.286	14	4	1	0	0	0	2	5	.375	.357
Bats Left	R	.305	59	18	5	0	2	13	3	18	.328	.492
Snow,J.T.	L	-	0	0	0	0	0	0	0	0	-	
Bats Left	R	-	0	0	0	0	0	0	0	0	-	
Snyder,Chris	L	.250	100	25	7	1	6	25	18	33	.358	.520
Bats Right	R	.231	234	54	15	0	10	39	38	68	.344	.423
Soriano,Alfonso	L	.351	131	46	11	0	12	27	12	20	.404	.710
Bats Right	R	.252	322	81	16	0	17	48	31	83	.319	.460
Soto,Geovany	L	.312	125	39	12	0	5	25	16	33	.387	.528
Bats Right	R	.276	369	102	23	2	18	61	46	88	.356	.496
Span,Denard	L	.283	106	30	5	3	3	22	18	21	.402	.472
Bats Right	R	.299	241	72	11	4	3	25	32	39	.380	.415
Spilborghs,Ryan	L	.326	86	28	7	0	3	13	11	17	.402	.512
Bats Right	R	.306	147	45	7	2	3	23	27	24	.410	.442
Stairs,Matt	L	.235	34	8	2	0	1	5	1	13	.257	.382
Bats Left	R	.254	303	77	10	1	12	44	41	77	.349	.413
Stansberry,Craig	L	.143	7	1	0	0	0	1	1	1	.250	.143
Bats Right	R	.556	9	5	1	0	0	1	1	2	.600	.667
Stavinoha,Nick	L	.240	25	6	1	0	0	2	2	3	.286	.280
Bats Right	R	.156	32	5	0	0	0	2	0	8	.156	.156
Stewart,Chris	L	.000	3	0	0	0	0	0	0	1	.000	.000
Bats Right	R	-	0	0	0	0	0	0	0	0	-	
Stewart,Ian	L	.370	54	20	6	0	4	17	4	14	.433	.704
Bats Left	R	.231	212	49	12	2	6	24	26	80	.328	.392
Stewart,Shannon	L	.286	49	14	1	1	1	7	5	6	.345	.408
Bats Right	R	.222	126	28	3	1	0	7	17	12	.317	.262
Sullivan,Cory	L	.250	4	1	0	0	0	0		2	.250	.250
Bats Left	R	.211	19	4	0	1	0	4	0	3	.250	.316
Suzuki,Ichiro	L	.288	208	60	7	1	1	13	13	24	.332	.346
Bats Left	R	.320	478	153	13	6	5	29	38	41	.373	.404
Suzuki,Kurt	L	.246	138	34	7	0	3	15	7	14	.303	.319
Bats Right	R	.291	392	114	18	1	6	37	27	55	.351	.388
Sweeney,Mark	L	.071	14	1	1	0	0	0	1	7	.133	.143
Bats Left	R	.141	78	11	2	0	0	5	14	21	.269	.167
Sweeney,Mike	L	.321	53	17	2	0	0	5	4	0	.373	.358
Bats Right	R	.260	73	19	6	0	2	7	3	6	.299	.425

Batter	vs	Avg	AB	H	2B	3B	HR	RBI	BB	SO	OBP	Slg
Sweeney,Ryan	L	.216	88	19	1	0	0	7	9	20	.290	.227
Bats Left	R	.307	296	91	17	2	5	38	29	47	.369	.429
Swisher,Nick	L	.197	132	26	5	1	6	16	32	29	.359	.386
Bats Both	R	.227	365	83	16	0	18	53	50	106	.321	.419
Taguchi,So	L	.184	49	9	2	0	0	6	3	5	.231	.224
Bats Right	R	.262	42	11	3	1	0	3	5	9	.340	.381
Tatis,Fernando	L	.311	106	33	8	0	1	19	14	20	.393	.415
Bats Right	R	.287	167	48	8	1	10	28	15	39	.353	.527
Taveras,Willy	L	.266	128	34	6	0	0	4	10	20	.321	.313
Bats Right	R	.245	351	86	9	2	1	22	26	59	.303	.291
Teagarden,Taylor	L	.091	11	1	0	0	1	1	5	4	.412	.364
Bats Right	R	.386	36	14	5	0	5	16	0	15	.389	.944
Teahen,Mark	L	.262	191	50	13	1	5	27	11	56	.311	.419
Bats Left	R	.252	381	96	18	3	10	32	35	75	.314	.394
Teixeira,Mark	L	.303	195	59	14	0	7	41	39	27	.419	.482
Bats Both	R	.311	379	118	27	0	26	80	58	66	.405	.588
Tejada,Miguel	L	.282	163	46	13	0	3	14	11	14	.326	.417
Bats Right	R	.284	469	133	25	3	10	52	13	58	.310	.414
Thames,Marcus	L	.234	124	29	4	0	13	28	11	38	.296	.581
Bats Right	R	.245	192	47	8	0	12	28	13	57	.290	.474
Theriot,Ryan	L	.305	141	43	7	1	0	12	25	12	.410	.369
Bats Right	R	.308	439	135	12	3	1	26	48	46	.379	.355
Thigpen,Curtis	L	.250	8	2	0	0	1	1	1	3	.400	.625
Bats Right	R	.111	9	1	0	0	0	0	0	5	.111	.111
Thomas,Clete	L	.368	19	7	2	0	0	2	2	3	.429	.474
Bats Left	R	.268	97	26	7	1	1	7	12	23	.355	.392
Thomas,Frank	L	.205	73	15	2	0	1	5	10	21	.301	.274
Bats Right	R	.254	173	44	5	1	7	25	29	36	.369	.416
Thome,Jim	L	.233	146	34	12	0	10	26	22	50	.337	.521
Bats Left	R	.249	357	89	16	0	24	64	69	97	.372	.496
Thurston,Joe	L	.000	1	0	0	0	0	0	0	1	.000	.000
Bats Left	R	.000	7	0	0	0	0	0	0	0	.125	.000
Tiffee,Terry	L	.000	2	0	0	0	0	0	0	0	.000	.000
Bats Both	R	.500	2	1	0	0	0	0	0	0	.667	.500
Timpner,Clay	L	-	0	0	0	0	0	0	0	0	-	
Bats Left	R	.000	2	0	0	0	0	0	0	2	.000	.000
Tolbert,Matt	L	.306	36	11	2	0	0	2	2	7	.342	.361
Bats Both	R	.273	77	21	4	3	0	4	5	12	.313	.403
Torrealba,Yorvit	L	.279	61	17	6	0	1	10	3	7	.313	.426
Bats Right	R	.234	175	41	11	0	5	21	9	37	.286	.383
Torres,Eider	L	.333	3	1	0	0	0	0	0	1	.333	.333
Bats Both	R	.167	6	1	0	0	0	0	0	0	.167	.167
Towles,J.R.	L	.222	27	6	1	0	1	5	4	7	.344	.370
Bats Right	R	.118	119	14	4	0	3	11	12	33	.228	.227
Tracy,Andy	L	-	0	0	0	0	0	0	0	0	-	
Bats Left	R	.000	2	0	0	0	0	0	1	1	.250	.000
Tracy,Chad	L	.243	37	9	2	0	3	9	2	11	.275	.541
Bats Left	R	.271	236	64	14	0	5	30	14	38	.313	.394
Treanor,Matt	L	.197	61	12	3	0	0	3	7	17	.279	.246
Bats Right	R	.255	145	37	4	0	2	20	11	36	.317	.324
Tuiasosopo,Matt	L	.133	15	2	1	0	0	1	0	5	.133	.200
Bats Right	R	.172	29	5	1	1	0	1	2	11	.250	.276
Tulowitzki,Troy	L	.330	88	29	7	1	3	13	12	9	.412	.534
Bats Right	R	.242	289	70	17	1	5	33	26	47	.306	.360
Tupman,Matt	L	-	0	0	0	0	0	0	0	0	-	
Bats Left	R	1.000	1	1	0	0	0	0	0	0	1.000	1.000
Tyner,Jason	L	-	0	0	0	0	0	0	0	0	-	
Bats Left	R	.000	2	0	0	0	0	0	0	0	.333	.000
Uggla,Dan	L	.191	131	25	11	0	2	12	23	41	.310	.321
Bats Right	R	.283	400	113	26	1	30	80	54	130	.377	.578
Upton,B.J.	L	.269	156	42	11	2	2	18	38	39	.415	.404
Bats Right	R	.275	375	103	26	0	7	49	59	95	.369	.400
Upton,Justin	L	.253	99	25	2	2	5	16	21	41	.380	.465
Bats Right	R	.249	257	64	17	4	10	26	33	80	.341	.463
Uribe,Juan	L	.254	71	18	4	1	3	11	8	13	.325	.465
Bats Right	R	.245	253	62	18	0	4	29	14	51	.287	.364
Utley,Chase	L	.277	231	64	11	3	13	33	21	47	.368	.519
Bats Left	R	.301	376	113	30	1	20	71	43	57	.387	.545
Valbuena,Luis	L	.429	7	3	0	0	0	1	1	1	.500	.429
Bats Left	R	.214	42	9	5	0	0	3	2	10	.283	.333
Valentin,Javier	L	.182	22	4	3	0	0	5	2	4	.250	.318
Bats Both	R	.271	107	29	5	0	4	13	12	23	.342	.430
Van Every,Jonathan	L	.333	3	1	0	0	0	2	0	0	.333	.333
Bats Left	R	.214	14	3	0	1	0	3	1	6	.267	.357
Varitek,Jason	L	.284	95	27	4	0	5	14	13	20	.378	.484
Bats Both	R	.201	328	66	16	0	8	29	39	102	.293	.323

Batters vs. Left-Handed and Right-Handed Pitchers

Batter	vs	Avg	AB	H	2B	3B	HR	RBI	BB	SO	OBP	Slg
Vazquez,Ramon	L	.188	48	9	1	0	0	5	5	15	.259	.208
Bats Left	R	.310	252	78	17	3	6	35	33	51	.385	.472
Velandia,Jorge	L	.000	10	0	0	0	0	0	0	3	.000	.000
Bats Right	R	.600	5	3	1	0	0	0	1	1	.667	.800
Velazquez,Gil	L	.000	1	0	0	0	0	0	0	0	.000	.000
Bats Right	R	.143	7	1	0	0	0	1	0	0	.143	.143
Velez,Eugenio	L	.235	51	12	0	1	0	4	5	9	.316	.275
Bats Both	R	.268	224	60	16	6	1	26	9	31	.295	.406
Venable,Will	L	.324	34	11	0	1	0	3	4	3	.395	.382
Bats Left	R	.237	76	18	4	1	2	7	9	18	.314	.395
Victorino,Shane	L	.282	177	50	14	2	9	27	13	21	.345	.537
Bats Both	R	.298	393	117	16	6	5	31	32	48	.355	.407
Vidro,Jose	L	.232	82	19	4	0	1	12	2	11	.247	.317
Bats Both	R	.235	226	53	7	0	6	33	16	25	.284	.345
Vizquel,Omar	L	.121	58	7	1	0	0	1	8	6	.227	.138
Bats Both	R	.250	208	52	9	1	0	22	16	23	.300	.303
Votto,Joey	L	.292	171	50	9	1	8	39	18	47	.365	.497
Bats Left	R	.299	355	106	23	2	16	45	41	55	.370	.510
Ward,Daryle	L	.200	10	2	0	0	0	1	1	7	.273	.200
Bats Left	R	.217	92	20	7	0	4	16	15	17	.324	.424
Washington,Rico	L	-	0	0	0	0	0	0	1	0	1.000	-
Bats Left	R	.158	19	3	2	0	0	3	2	6	.238	.263
Weeks,Rickie	L	.250	140	35	9	1	4	8	28	33	.391	.414
Bats Right	R	.227	335	76	13	6	10	38	38	82	.319	.391
Wells,Vernon	L	.333	99	33	6	0	2	14	9	12	.394	.455
Bats Right	R	.290	328	95	16	1	18	64	20	34	.328	.509
Werth,Jayson	L	.303	155	47	6	0	16	36	16	40	.368	.652
Bats Right	R	.255	263	67	10	3	8	31	41	79	.360	.407
Whitesell,Josh	L	-	0	0	0	0	0	0	0	0	-	-
Bats Left	R	.286	7	2	0	0	1	1	1	2	.444	.714
Wigginton,Ty	L	.340	103	35	9	0	7	15	14	14	.424	.631
Bats Right	R	.265	283	75	13	1	16	43	18	55	.322	.488
Wilkerson,Brad	L	.214	42	9	2	0	0	4	5	13	.292	.262
Bats Left	R	.221	222	49	10	2	4	24	30	55	.311	.338
Willingham,Josh	L	.242	95	23	5	0	5	16	17	23	.371	.453
Bats Right	R	.258	256	66	16	5	10	35	31	59	.361	.477
Willits,Reggie	L	.200	20	4	0	0	0	0	7	4	.407	.200
Bats Both	R	.193	88	17	4	0	0	7	14	22	.298	.239
Wilson,Bobby	L	.500	2	1	0	0	0	0	0	0	.500	.500
Bats Right	R	.000	4	0	0	0	0	1	1	3	.200	.000
Wilson,Jack	L	.228	57	13	2	0	0	8	5	5	.297	.263
Bats Right	R	.282	248	70	16	1	1	14	8	22	.315	.367
Winn,Randy	L	.289	166	48	9	0	7	15	14	17	.343	.470
Bats Both	R	.313	432	135	29	2	3	49	45	71	.371	.410
Wise,Dewayne	L	.143	14	2	0	0	0	1	0	3	.143	.143
Bats Left	R	.261	115	30	4	2	6	17	8	29	.310	.487
Wood,Brandon	L	.094	32	3	1	0	0	0	3	13	.171	.125
Bats Right	R	.229	118	27	3	0	5	13	1	30	.240	.381
Wood,Jason	L	.000	1	0	0	0	0	0	1	1	.500	.000
Bats Right	R	.000	1	0	0	0	0	0	0	0	.000	.000
Wright,David	L	.382	157	60	18	1	9	34	37	26	.497	.682
Bats Right	R	.275	469	129	24	1	24	90	57	92	.351	.484
Youkilis,Kevin	L	.288	104	30	12	0	7	28	22	21	.403	.606
Bats Right	R	.318	434	138	31	4	22	87	40	87	.386	.560
Young,Chris	L	.285	158	45	18	1	6	26	19	30	.361	.525
Bats Right	R	.236	467	110	24	6	16	59	43	135	.298	.415
Young,Delmon	L	.300	170	51	10	1	4	19	14	32	.349	.441
Bats Right	R	.286	405	116	18	3	6	50	21	73	.330	.390
Young,Delwyn	L	.231	39	9	3	0	1	2	7	9	.348	.385
Bats Both	R	.253	87	22	6	0	0	5	7	25	.309	.322
Young,Dmitri	L	.318	44	14	3	0	3	3	7	8	.412	.591
Bats Both	R	.264	106	28	3	0	1	7	21	20	.388	.321
Young,Michael	L	.305	174	53	10	1	6	24	17	24	.365	.477
Bats Right	R	.276	471	130	26	1	6	58	38	85	.329	.374
Zaun,Gregg	L	.163	49	8	1	0	1	4	11	5	.317	.245
Bats Both	R	.255	196	50	11	0	5	26	27	33	.347	.388
Zimmerman,Ryan	L	.333	138	46	7	0	5	15	8	13	.370	.493
Bats Right	R	.259	290	75	17	1	9	36	23	58	.316	.417
Zobrist,Ben	L	.269	78	21	5	0	3	6	11	11	.356	.449
Bats Both	R	.242	120	29	5	2	9	24	14	26	.328	.542
AL	L	.267	-	-	-	-	-	-	-	-	.337	.418
	R	.268	-	-	-	-	-	-	-	-	.335	.421
NL	L	.262	-	-	-	-	-	-	-	-	.335	.417
	R	.260	-	-	-	-	-	-	-	-	.329	.411
MLB	L	.264	-	-	-	-	-	-	-	-	.336	.417
	R	.264	-	-	-	-	-	-	-	-	.332	.416

Pitchers vs. Left-Handed and Right-Handed Batters

Pitcher	vs	Avg	AB	H	2B	3B	HR	RBI	BB	SO	OBP	Slg
Aardsma,David	L	.289	83	24	6	1	0	14	14	16	.400	.386
Throws Right	R	.250	100	25	9	0	4	20	21	33	.392	.460
Accardo,Jeremy	L	.300	20	6	0	1	1	2	2	4	.391	.550
Throws Right	R	.300	30	9	3	1	0	6	2	1	.333	.467
Aceves,Alfredo	L	.238	63	15	3	0	3	6	4	6	.284	.429
Throws Right	R	.213	47	10	2	0	1	4	6	10	.302	.319
Acosta,Manny	L	.280	93	26	3	1	4	10	7	12	.330	.462
Throws Right	R	.218	101	22	5	0	3	14	19	19	.344	.356
Adams,Mike	L	.228	114	26	5	0	1	7	9	31	.282	.298
Throws Right	R	.190	121	23	4	1	6	17	10	43	.248	.388
Adenhart,Nick	L	.300	20	6	4	0	0	3	9	3	.517	.500
Throws Right	R	.400	30	12	2	0	0	7	4	1	.471	.467
Adkins,Jon	L	.250	4	1	0	0	0	0	1	2	.400	.250
Throws Right	R	.375	8	3	0	0	1	1	2	1	.500	.750
Affeldt,Jeremy	L	.269	108	29	6	2	3	19	5	25	.301	.444
Throws Left	R	.255	192	49	8	0	6	18	20	55	.335	.391
Albaladejo,Jonathan	L	.304	23	7	4	1	0	5	1	7	.333	.565
Throws Right	R	.286	28	8	0	0	1	2	5	6	.394	.393
Albers,Matt	L	.163	86	14	0	0	1	5	13	13	.270	.198
Throws Right	R	.312	93	29	4	0	3	13	9	13	.377	.452
Aquino,Greg	L	.333	18	6	2	0	0	3	4	5	.435	.444
Throws Right	R	.478	23	11	2	0	1	9	5	4	.600	.696
Arias,Alberto	L	.361	36	13	4	0	1	8	3	6	.410	.556
Throws Right	R	.213	47	10	2	0	0	3	7	7	.339	.255
Armas Jr.,Tony	L	.412	17	7	3	0	2	6	0	2	.412	.941
Throws Right	R	.235	17	4	1	0	0	1	1	4	.263	.294
Arredondo,Jose	L	.148	115	17	2	1	1	14	9	35	.210	.209
Throws Right	R	.236	106	25	4	0	2	12	13	20	.325	.330
Arroyo,Bronson	L	.314	357	112	27	6	16	47	29	45	.367	.557
Throws Right	R	.254	421	107	16	2	13	55	39	118	.321	.394
Ascanio,Jose	L	.300	10	3	1	0	1	3	2	3	.429	.700
Throws Right	R	.385	13	5	2	0	0	0	2	0	.467	.538
Ayala,Luis	L	.285	137	39	7	0	4	23	14	18	.355	.423
Throws Right	R	.288	163	47	11	1	5	29	10	32	.335	.460
Backe,Brandon	L	.304	313	95	22	3	16	50	38	56	.381	.546
Throws Right	R	.301	356	107	24	1	20	57	39	71	.373	.542
Badenhop,Burke	L	.298	94	28	5	0	5	19	16	11	.402	.511
Throws Right	R	.281	96	27	4	0	2	12	5	24	.327	.385
Baek,Cha Seung	L	.280	264	74	21	3	8	32	26	48	.346	.473
Throws Right	R	.256	281	72	13	1	10	35	17	44	.296	.416
Bailey,Homer	L	.305	59	18	1	0	6	12	4	6	.349	.627
Throws Right	R	.423	97	41	8	0	2	19	13	12	.482	.567
Baker,Scott	L	.263	331	87	16	0	9	30	25	75	.318	.393
Throws Right	R	.230	322	74	10	1	11	27	17	66	.269	.370
Bale,John	L	.275	40	11	2	0	0	3	5	6	.356	.325
Throws Left	R	.305	59	18	3	1	1	8	1	8	.306	.441
Balester,Collin	L	.278	158	44	8	1	8	29	18	25	.350	.494
Throws Right	R	.298	161	48	13	0	4	21	10	25	.358	.453
Balfour,Grant	L	.120	83	10	4	0	0	4	8	36	.196	.169
Throws Right	R	.159	113	18	4	0	3	12	16	46	.260	.274
Banks,Josh	L	.293	147	43	8	1	7	18	16	22	.364	.503
Throws Right	R	.287	178	51	7	1	5	23	16	21	.347	.421
Bannister,Brian	L	.313	364	114	23	2	15	64	33	54	.366	.511
Throws Right	R	.274	368	101	16	3	14	55	25	59	.328	.448
Barthmaier,Jimmy	L	.357	28	10	2	0	1	5	6	5	.471	.536
Throws Right	R	.375	16	6	0	0	2	6	2	1	.444	.750
Bass,Brian	L	.240	150	36	3	3	4	12	16	15	.315	.380
Throws Right	R	.310	200	62	12	2	8	40	15	30	.370	.510
Batista,Miguel	L	.293	242	71	21	2	11	44	55	38	.419	.533
Throws Right	R	.298	215	64	16	0	8	40	24	35	.372	.484
Bauer,Rick	L	.250	12	3	2	0	1	4	1	3	.308	.667
Throws Right	R	.467	15	7	2	1	0	5	2	1	.529	.733
Bautista,Denny	L	.279	68	19	2	0	0	9	21	13	.440	.309
Throws Right	R	.275	153	42	12	2	6	26	21	31	.365	.497
Bazardo,Yorman	L	.500	2	1	0	0	0	2	4	1	.714	.500
Throws Right	R	.500	12	6	2	1	0	6	1	2	.538	.833
Beam,T.J.	L	.310	71	22	8	1	3	17	13	11	.412	.577
Throws Right	R	.210	100	21	6	0	3	9	7	13	.273	.360
Beckett,Josh	L	.260	377	98	19	2	12	44	18	105	.293	.416
Throws Right	R	.252	298	75	20	0	6	24	16	67	.307	.379
Bedard,Erik	L	.253	75	19	3	0	3	11	14	12	.380	.413
Throws Left	R	.224	228	51	12	1	6	22	23	60	.299	.364
Beimel,Joe	L	.278	90	25	3	0	0	9	5	17	.330	.311
Throws Left	R	.263	95	25	5	1	0	17	16	15	.363	.337
Belisle,Matt	L	.296	71	21	3	1	3	11	5	4	.338	.493
Throws Right	R	.419	62	26	8	0	1	13	1	10	.422	.597

Pitcher	vs	Avg	AB	H	2B	3B	HR	RBI	BB	SO	OBP	Slg
Bell,Heath	L	.207	150	31	4	1	0	7	20	38	.298	.247
Throws Right	R	.254	138	35	8	1	5	25	8	33	.307	.435
Beltran,Francis	L	.176	17	3	0	0	1	3	4	3	.333	.353
Throws Right	R	.303	33	10	3	0	2	6	2	6	.343	.576
Benitez,Armando	L	.250	8	2	1	0	1	3	1	3	.333	.750
Throws Right	R	.125	16	2	0	0	2	3	1	6	.176	.500
Bennett,Jeff	L	.269	130	35	4	1	4	24	20	19	.362	.408
Throws Right	R	.228	224	51	11	0	1	26	27	49	.326	.290
Benoit,Joaquin	L	.184	87	16	3	1	2	15	16	25	.311	.310
Throws Right	R	.282	85	24	7	0	4	13	19	18	.413	.506
Bergmann,Jason	L	.309	298	92	22	1	10	49	26	38	.359	.490
Throws Right	R	.243	251	61	11	0	15	33	21	58	.301	.466
Betancourt,Rafael	L	.252	119	30	6	1	4	15	17	23	.343	.420
Throws Right	R	.295	156	46	9	0	7	32	8	41	.321	.487
Bierd,Randor	L	.333	69	23	5	2	0	15	8	12	.392	.464
Throws Right	R	.301	83	25	6	0	3	21	11	13	.398	.482
Billingsley,Chad	L	.274	350	96	22	2	5	32	50	83	.369	.391
Throws Right	R	.225	408	92	11	4	9	38	30	118	.283	.338
Birkins,Kurt	L	.083	12	1	0	0	0	0	2	4	.214	.083
Throws Left	R	.211	19	4	0	0	0	2	3	3	.304	.211
Blackburn,Nick	L	.295	339	100	21	2	7	35	26	40	.349	.431
Throws Right	R	.289	429	124	17	2	16	54	13	56	.315	.450
Blanton,Joe	L	.256	394	101	24	1	12	50	28	52	.304	.414
Throws Right	R	.286	385	110	23	4	10	51	38	59	.355	.444
Blevins,Jerry	L	.193	57	11	2	0	0	7	3	16	.254	.228
Throws Left	R	.256	82	21	6	0	2	7	10	19	.344	.402
Boggs,Mitchell	L	.321	78	25	6	2	5	22	13	6	.419	.641
Throws Right	R	.283	60	17	4	0	0	3	9	7	.386	.350
Bonderman,Jeremy	L	.291	134	39	5	0	2	15	25	19	.401	.373
Throws Right	R	.255	141	36	6	0	7	14	11	25	.316	.447
Bonine,Eddie	L	.340	47	16	4	0	2	13	4	4	.392	.553
Throws Right	R	.328	61	20	5	0	1	6	1	5	.354	.459
Bonser,Boof	L	.315	219	69	14	0	8	33	22	48	.378	.489
Throws Right	R	.260	269	70	13	1	8	40	14	49	.295	.405
Bootcheck,Chris	L	.406	32	13	3	0	0	5	5	4	.486	.500
Throws Right	R	.370	46	17	2	0	2	14	7	10	.453	.543
Borkowski,Dave	L	.339	62	21	3	1	2	8	9	8	.423	.516
Throws Right	R	.355	93	33	7	0	7	25	5	16	.394	.656
Borowski,Joe	L	.333	24	8	1	0	0	3	5	5	.448	.375
Throws Right	R	.333	48	16	5	0	4	11	3	4	.365	.688
Bowden,Michael	L	.222	9	2	1	0	0	1	0	2	.222	.333
Throws Right	R	.417	12	5	2	1	0	1	1	1	.462	.750
Bowers,Cedrick	L	.571	7	4	0	0	0	1	0	1	.625	.571
Throws Left	R	.368	19	7	4	0	2	10	5	4	.480	.895
Bowie,Micah	L	.308	13	4	1	0	1	1	0	2	.308	.615
Throws Left	R	.350	20	7	4	0	0	7	3	3	.440	.550
Boyer,Blaine	L	.271	107	29	5	2	4	19	12	26	.339	.467
Throws Right	R	.256	172	44	10	2	6	32	13	41	.312	.442
Braden,Dallas	L	.319	69	22	2	0	4	11	6	14	.377	.522
Throws Left	R	.272	202	55	10	1	4	24	19	27	.336	.391
Bradford,Chad	L	.313	67	21	1	0	2	14	8	7	.380	.418
Throws Right	R	.255	149	38	3	0	1	16	7	10	.289	.295
Bray,Bill	L	.260	73	19	6	0	1	9	12	21	.360	.384
Throws Left	R	.274	113	31	9	1	3	10	12	33	.349	.451
Brazoban,Yhency	L	.333	6	2	2	0	0	1	1	1	.429	.667
Throws Right	R	.286	7	2	1	0	0	1	2	2	.444	.429
Breslow,Craig	L	.183	82	15	1	0	1	9	5	23	.230	.232
Throws Left	R	.221	86	19	1	0	0	5	14	16	.330	.233
Britton,Chris	L	.391	46	18	4	3	1	8	7	7	.472	.674
Throws Right	R	.213	47	10	3	0	3	7	4	5	.269	.468
Broadway,Lance	L	.308	26	8	2	0	1	3	3	1	.379	.500
Throws Right	R	.343	35	12	4	0	3	9	2	6	.378	.714
Brocail,Doug	L	.305	105	32	6	2	3	14	10	23	.371	.486
Throws Right	R	.200	155	31	1	0	5	17	11	41	.260	.303
Brown,Andrew	L	.183	60	11	1	0	0	8	17	14	.359	.200
Throws Right	R	.190	63	12	4	0	3	10	4	14	.250	.397
Broxton,Jonathan	L	.270	100	27	6	2	1	15	22	28	.400	.400
Throws Right	R	.181	149	27	4	0	1	17	5	60	.217	.228
Bruney,Brian	L	.106	47	5	2	0	0	8	10	15	.271	.149
Throws Right	R	.183	71	13	2	0	2	7	6	18	.244	.296
Buchholz,Clay	L	.293	157	46	5	1	8	28	22	39	.378	.490
Throws Right	R	.305	154	47	9	1	3	24	19	33	.384	.435
Buchholz,Taylor	L	.198	106	21	3	1	3	10	5	29	.246	.330
Throws Right	R	.180	133	24	7	0	2	9	13	27	.252	.278
Buckner,Billy	L	.231	26	6	1	0	1	4	1	4	.259	.385
Throws Right	R	.357	28	10	2	0	2	3	3	7	.438	.643

Pitchers vs. Left-Handed and Right-Handed Batters

Pitcher	vs	Avg	AB	H	2B	3B	HR	RBI	BB	SO	OBP	Slg
Buehrle,Mark	L	.293	239	70	13	4	6	33	11	43	.331	.456
Throws Left	R	.277	614	170	28	3	16	65	41	97	.322	.410
Bueno,Francisley	L	-	0	0	0	0	0	0	1	0	1.000	-
Throws Left	R	.417	12	5	0	0	1	2	0	1	.417	.667
Bukvich,Ryan	L	.600	10	6	2	0	2	4	4	3	.714	1.400
Throws Right	R	.214	14	3	0	0	0	2	2	2	.313	.214
Bulger,Jason	L	.229	35	8	0	1	2	7	2	10	.289	.457
Throws Right	R	.259	27	7	3	1	1	4	7	10	.429	.556
Bullington,Bryan	L	.333	30	10	1	1	2	3	1	5	.355	.633
Throws Right	R	.192	26	5	0	0	2	6	1	7	.241	.423
Burnett,A.J.	L	.262	481	126	36	2	11	47	51	134	.337	.414
Throws Right	R	.231	368	85	19	1	8	50	35	97	.303	.353
Burnett,Sean	L	.171	76	13	2	0	2	7	7	16	.238	.276
Throws Left	R	.328	134	44	13	0	5	32	27	26	.442	.537
Burres,Brian	L	.321	162	52	8	1	4	27	17	20	.390	.457
Throws Left	R	.306	369	113	26	2	13	53	33	43	.363	.493
Burton,Jared	L	.247	93	23	5	1	3	8	11	18	.330	.419
Throws Right	R	.250	132	33	6	0	3	22	14	40	.322	.364
Bush,David	L	.244	336	82	21	4	16	46	29	52	.308	.473
Throws Right	R	.224	362	81	17	0	13	38	19	57	.275	.378
Byrd,Paul	L	.317	363	115	24	1	17	49	25	38	.361	.529
Throws Right	R	.255	349	89	15	1	14	41	9	44	.283	.424
Byrdak,Tim	L	.135	89	12	4	0	2	5	9	30	.222	.247
Throws Left	R	.289	114	33	13	0	8	21	20	17	.397	.614
Cabrera,Daniel	L	.308	380	117	22	2	14	56	58	57	.403	.487
Throws Right	R	.259	316	82	16	0	10	37	32	38	.343	.405
Cabrera,Fernando	L	.304	46	14	3	0	3	10	10	14	.429	.565
Throws Right	R	.269	67	18	2	0	6	16	7	17	.329	.567
Cain,Matt	L	.268	395	106	25	3	10	47	48	85	.346	.423
Throws Right	R	.235	426	100	24	5	9	42	43	101	.312	.378
Calero,Kiko	L	.500	6	3	2	0	0	0	2	0	.625	.833
Throws Right	R	.000	11	0	0	0	0	0	1	7	.083	.000
Cameron,Kevin	L	.286	14	4	1	0	0	3	4	0	.444	.357
Throws Right	R	.250	24	6	3	0	0	6	2	5	.296	.375
Camp,Shawn	L	.356	59	21	8	1	1	11	4	8	.400	.576
Throws Right	R	.204	93	19	1	0	1	11	7	23	.267	.247
Campillo,Jorge	L	.249	277	69	12	3	5	23	25	50	.310	.368
Throws Right	R	.274	325	89	28	0	13	46	13	57	.300	.480
Capellan,Jose	L	.333	6	2	0	0	0	1	0	1	.333	.333
Throws Right	R	.333	3	1	1	0	0	0	0	1	.333	.667
Capps,Matt	L	.222	99	22	2	2	2	9	3	19	.245	.343
Throws Right	R	.245	102	25	7	0	3	13	2	20	.274	.402
Carlson,Jesse	L	.205	112	23	5	1	2	14	9	26	.278	.321
Throws Left	R	.186	97	18	6	0	4	8	12	29	.273	.371
Carlyle,Buddy	L	.247	93	23	5	1	3	13	11	28	.333	.419
Throws Right	R	.215	135	29	6	0	2	14	15	31	.293	.304
Carmona,Fausto	L	.303	261	79	18	2	5	42	34	22	.387	.444
Throws Right	R	.230	204	47	10	0	2	21	36	36	.358	.309
Carpenter,Andrew	L	.500	2	1	0	0	0	0	1	0	.667	.500
Throws Right	R	.000	1	0	0	0	0	0	0	1	.000	.000
Carpenter,Chris	L	.158	19	3	1	0	0	0	3	1	.273	.211
Throws Right	R	.351	37	13	2	0	0	3	1	6	.359	.405
Carrasco,D.J.	L	.186	59	11	1	0	0	3	2	17	.222	.203
Throws Right	R	.244	78	19	4	0	2	18	12	13	.372	.372
Casilla,Santiago	L	.308	91	28	7	0	2	10	3	17	.326	.451
Throws Right	R	.291	110	32	5	1	3	18	17	26	.397	.436
Cassel,Jack	L	.333	48	16	1	1	2	7	3	4	.373	.521
Throws Right	R	.297	74	22	6	1	3	15	5	10	.350	.527
Castillo,Alberto	L	.256	39	10	1	0	2	8	4	8	.356	.436
Throws Left	R	.262	65	17	4	0	1	14	6	15	.368	.369
Chacon,Shawn	L	.270	152	41	10	2	6	24	23	21	.364	.480
Throws Right	R	.270	174	47	10	0	10	27	18	32	.345	.500
Chamberlain,Joba	L	.247	186	46	7	1	2	15	23	59	.332	.328
Throws Right	R	.219	187	41	4	0	3	13	16	59	.284	.289
Chavez,Jesse	L	.217	23	5	0	0	1	1	6	5	.379	.348
Throws Right	R	.395	38	15	4	0	1	13	3	11	.429	.579
Cherry,Rocky	L	.167	24	4	2	1	0	5	12	5	.432	.333
Throws Right	R	.268	41	11	4	0	3	8	4	10	.340	.585
Chico,Matt	L	.351	57	20	4	0	4	8	3	11	.377	.632
Throws Left	R	.312	138	43	12	1	6	25	14	20	.377	.543
Chulk,Vinnie	L	.233	43	10	3	0	2	7	3	3	.298	.442
Throws Right	R	.274	84	23	8	0	4	17	5	13	.319	.512
Clippard,Tyler	L	.333	18	6	4	0	1	3	4	4	.455	.722
Throws Right	R	.261	23	6	1	0	1	2	3	4	.346	.435
Coffey,Todd	L	.290	31	9	3	0	0	2	4	4	.371	.387
Throws Right	R	.301	73	22	3	0	4	10	4	11	.342	.507

Pitcher	vs	Avg	AB	H	2B	3B	HR	RBI	BB	SO	OBP	Slg
Coke,Phil	L	.207	29	6	2	0	0	1	1	9	.233	.276
Throws Left	R	.095	21	2	0	0	0	0	1	5	.136	.095
Colome,Jesus	L	.226	115	26	5	0	4	20	23	23	.364	.374
Throws Right	R	.241	145	35	6	1	2	16	16	32	.321	.338
Colon,Bartolo	L	.309	81	25	5	0	5	15	9	13	.385	.556
Throws Right	R	.253	75	19	3	0	0	6	1	14	.266	.293
Condrey,Clay	L	.320	125	40	10	0	2	12	10	12	.370	.448
Throws Right	R	.288	156	45	9	1	4	15	9	22	.335	.436
Contreras,Jose	L	.286	234	67	12	1	10	27	21	38	.351	.474
Throws Right	R	.258	244	63	12	2	2	30	14	32	.297	.348
Cook,Aaron	L	.297	441	131	28	6	6	50	27	55	.340	.429
Throws Right	R	.276	380	105	18	2	7	41	21	41	.315	.389
Corcoran,Roy	L	.258	132	34	9	0	1	15	19	12	.351	.348
Throws Right	R	.221	140	31	6	2	0	24	17	27	.309	.293
Cordero,Chad	L	.250	12	3	1	0	0	0	1	3	.308	.333
Throws Right	R	.429	7	3	0	0	0	0	2	2	.556	.429
Cordero,Francisco	L	.212	113	24	2	1	0	11	19	33	.321	.248
Throws Right	R	.252	147	37	7	0	6	22	19	45	.347	.422
Corey,Bryan	L	.274	84	23	4	0	2	16	6	13	.315	.393
Throws Right	R	.309	97	30	7	0	6	19	6	9	.350	.567
Cormier,Lance	L	.240	121	29	3	1	1	12	23	27	.361	.306
Throws Right	R	.308	159	49	9	0	3	26	11	19	.351	.421
Corpas,Manny	L	.285	158	45	12	0	1	25	16	20	.354	.380
Throws Right	R	.308	156	48	9	0	6	26	7	30	.339	.481
Correia,Kevin	L	.307	192	59	13	2	3	26	26	24	.386	.443
Throws Right	R	.312	263	82	14	1	12	43	21	42	.368	.510
Cotts,Neal	L	.269	67	18	3	1	4	11	7	22	.338	.522
Throws Left	R	.263	76	20	1	0	3	8	6	21	.325	.395
Crain,Jesse	L	.250	80	20	5	1	1	10	11	19	.344	.375
Throws Right	R	.261	161	42	10	2	5	23	13	31	.314	.441
Cruceta,Francisco	L	.350	20	7	0	0	1	7	5	5	.480	.500
Throws Right	R	.250	24	6	1	0	1	5	5	6	.379	.417
Cruz,Juan	L	.159	82	13	4	1	0	6	17	35	.310	.232
Throws Right	R	.221	95	21	5	0	5	19	14	36	.327	.432
Cueto,Johnny	L	.249	269	67	16	1	11	43	43	69	.359	.439
Throws Right	R	.275	404	111	23	2	18	47	25	89	.330	.475
Danks,John	L	.264	193	51	7	1	3	24	17	42	.324	.358
Throws Left	R	.240	546	131	38	0	12	39	40	117	.295	.375
Davies,Kyle	L	.251	215	54	13	3	5	26	25	39	.331	.409
Throws Right	R	.300	223	67	10	2	5	26	18	32	.352	.430
Davis,Doug	L	.321	137	44	8	1	2	11	12	28	.384	.438
Throws Left	R	.269	431	116	23	3	11	52	52	84	.348	.413
Davis,Jason	L	.342	73	25	1	1	2	13	5	5	.380	.466
Throws Right	R	.241	54	13	5	0	0	8	12	8	.394	.333
de la Cruz,Frankie	L	.400	20	8	2	0	1	7	8	1	.571	.650
Throws Right	R	.350	20	7	2	1	1	7	3	3	.417	.700
de la Rosa,Jorge	L	.289	121	35	4	2	4	22	12	33	.353	.455
Throws Left	R	.253	368	93	26	0	9	44	50	95	.347	.397
de los Santos,Valerio	L	.444	9	4	0	0	1	3	3	1	.583	.778
Throws Left	R	.100	20	2	1	0	0	0	8	9	.357	.150
Delcarmen,Manny	L	.190	126	24	8	1	0	16	15	33	.275	.270
Throws Right	R	.218	142	31	6	0	5	19	13	39	.292	.366
Delgado,Jesus	L	.000	2	0	0	0	0	0	2	0	.500	.000
Throws Right	R	.250	4	1	0	0	0	1	1	0	.400	.250
Dempster,Ryan	L	.243	362	88	17	3	9	35	34	95	.312	.381
Throws Right	R	.213	404	86	18	2	5	36	42	92	.293	.304
DeSalvo,Matt	L	.700	10	7	0	0	0	3	1	2	.727	.700
Throws Right	R	.667	6	4	0	0	0	4	1	0	.714	.667
Dessens,Elmer	L	.500	12	6	1	1	0	2	3	1	.600	.750
Throws Right	R	.500	8	4	1	0	1	6	1	1	.455	1.000
Devine,Joey	L	.197	61	12	2	0	0	11	8	14	.286	.230
Throws Right	R	.120	92	11	1	0	0	1	7	35	.182	.130
Diaz,Joselo	L	.000	1	0	0	0	0	0	0	1	.000	.000
Throws Right	R	.500	2	1	0	0	0	1	1	1	.600	.500
Dickey,R.A.	L	.259	220	57	14	1	10	27	27	39	.336	.468
Throws Right	R	.309	217	67	11	0	5	33	24	19	.378	.429
DiFelice,Mark	L	.333	27	9	0	0	4	5	1	5	.357	.778
Throws Right	R	.170	47	8	0	1	0	2	3	15	.220	.213
Dillard,Tim	L	.269	26	7	2	0	2	6	5	4	.387	.577
Throws Right	R	.313	32	10	1	0	0	6	1	1	.324	.344
DiNardo,Lenny	L	.303	33	10	1	0	0	2	1	1	.343	.333
Throws Left	R	.323	65	21	2	0	3	15	12	11	.436	.492
Dohmann,Scott	L	.250	24	6	1	0	1	7	2	3	.308	.417
Throws Right	R	.353	34	12	3	0	1	6	5	9	.425	.529
Dolsi,Freddy	L	.364	66	24	2	0	2	10	16	9	.494	.485
Throws Right	R	.215	121	26	4	0	1	9	12	20	.296	.273

Pitchers vs. Left-Handed and Right-Handed Batters

Pitcher	vs	Avg	AB	H	2B	3B	HR	RBI	BB	SO	OBP	Slg
Donnelly,Brendan	L	.286	21	6	1	0	0	4	6	4	.444	.333
Throws Right	R	.400	35	14	1	0	2	7	4	4	.439	.600
Dotel,Octavio	L	.240	75	18	2	0	4	14	11	20	.337	.427
Throws Right	R	.194	175	34	6	0	8	22	18	72	.288	.366
Downs,Scott	L	.194	108	21	4	1	1	13	7	25	.263	.278
Throws Left	R	.226	146	33	5	0	2	12	20	32	.323	.301
Duchscherer,Justin	L	.227	286	65	12	1	10	29	23	60	.287	.381
Throws Right	R	.188	224	42	10	0	1	14	11	35	.244	.246
Duckworth,Brandon	L	.299	67	20	4	2	0	6	12	13	.402	.418
Throws Right	R	.237	76	18	2	1	2	9	7	7	.318	.368
Duke,Zach	L	.279	111	31	8	0	2	12	10	18	.344	.405
Throws Left	R	.308	646	199	50	3	17	89	37	69	.349	.474
Dumatrait,Phil	L	.206	63	13	2	0	0	7	12	16	.351	.238
Throws Left	R	.288	240	69	21	0	7	40	30	36	.363	.463
Durbin,Chad	L	.311	132	41	8	0	1	13	18	26	.401	.394
Throws Right	R	.214	187	40	3	1	4	22	17	37	.284	.305
Eaton,Adam	L	.318	223	71	9	2	8	35	28	28	.402	.484
Throws Right	R	.300	200	60	17	0	7	27	16	29	.356	.490
Ekstrom,Mike	L	.357	14	5	0	0	1	5	5	2	.526	.571
Throws Right	R	.346	26	9	1	0	1	4	2	4	.393	.500
Elarton,Scott	L	.280	25	7	2	0	0	2	8	7	.455	.360
Throws Right	R	.250	36	9	2	0	0	6	1	8	.270	.306
Elbert,Scott	L	.417	12	5	1	0	0	1	2	3	.500	.500
Throws Left	R	.286	14	4	0	0	2	4	2	5	.412	.714
Embree,Alan	L	.232	82	19	3	0	4	14	7	20	.304	.415
Throws Left	R	.265	151	40	6	4	4	23	23	37	.358	.437
Espineli,Geno	L	.158	19	3	0	0	1	1	4	2	.304	.316
Throws Left	R	.333	42	14	2	0	4	9	4	6	.391	.667
Estes,Shawn	L	.195	41	8	1	0	1	2	7	8	.313	.293
Throws Left	R	.311	135	42	6	1	5	20	11	11	.372	.481
Estrada,Marco	L	.348	23	8	3	0	2	7	2	4	.400	.739
Throws Right	R	.273	33	9	0	0	2	9	3	6	.368	.455
Eveland,Dana	L	.248	153	38	9	1	1	18	11	35	.306	.340
Throws Left	R	.275	487	134	30	0	9	52	66	83	.371	.392
Eyre,Scott	L	.220	50	11	6	0	1	7	3	17	.264	.400
Throws Left	R	.267	45	12	4	1	1	8	4	15	.340	.467
Falkenborg,Brian	L	.265	34	9	0	0	1	5	6	10	.375	.353
Throws Right	R	.315	54	17	1	0	3	11	6	9	.383	.500
Farnsworth,Kyle	L	.275	102	28	2	1	9	19	17	30	.375	.578
Throws Right	R	.318	132	42	7	1	6	20	5	31	.348	.523
Feierabend,Ryan	L	.386	57	22	6	0	0	12	3	12	.417	.491
Throws Left	R	.339	109	37	10	1	7	19	11	14	.402	.642
Feldman,Scott	L	.291	292	85	18	3	11	49	27	31	.360	.486
Throws Right	R	.269	283	76	14	1	11	41	29	43	.339	.442
Feliciano,Pedro	L	.210	105	22	3	0	2	17	8	34	.280	.295
Throws Left	R	.357	98	35	5	0	5	18	18	16	.453	.561
Figueroa,Nelson	L	.371	70	26	5	0	2	13	11	10	.451	.529
Throws Right	R	.200	110	22	6	0	1	15	15	26	.307	.282
Flores,Randy	L	.314	51	16	6	0	2	14	11	9	.422	.549
Throws Left	R	.316	57	18	2	1	0	8	9	8	.418	.386
Floyd,Gavin	L	.259	371	96	23	2	19	61	44	61	.340	.485
Throws Right	R	.226	416	94	25	3	11	35	26	84	.279	.380
Fogg,Josh	L	.299	147	44	12	0	4	16	14	19	.362	.463
Throws Right	R	.305	174	53	11	1	13	38	13	26	.368	.603
Fossum,Casey	L	.243	74	18	3	0	2	14	6	11	.309	.365
Throws Left	R	.310	84	26	11	0	2	13	12	17	.408	.512
Foulke,Keith	L	.200	55	11	2	0	2	6	6	14	.286	.345
Throws Right	R	.279	61	17	6	0	5	12	7	9	.348	.623
Fox,Chad	L	.333	6	2	0	0	1	2	0	0	.333	.833
Throws Right	R	.000	4	0	0	0	0	2	3	1	.429	.000
Francis,Jeff	L	.248	113	28	6	3	4	15	10	26	.312	.460
Throws Left	R	.295	461	136	30	4	17	58	39	68	.350	.488
Francisco,Frank	L	.193	114	22	5	2	2	10	16	43	.292	.325
Throws Right	R	.207	121	25	5	1	5	17	10	40	.261	.388
Franklin,Ryan	L	.268	123	33	11	0	2	9	17	21	.357	.407
Throws Right	R	.285	186	53	13	1	8	27	13	30	.338	.495
Frasor,Jason	L	.266	64	17	5	1	1	4	16	16	.420	.422
Throws Right	R	.174	109	19	5	0	3	16	16	26	.276	.303
Fuentes,Brian	L	.184	49	9	0	0	1	5	3	20	.226	.245
Throws Left	R	.211	180	38	9	1	2	17	19	62	.290	.306
Fukumori,Kazuo	L	.250	8	2	0	0	0	1	2	0	.400	.250
Throws Right	R	.643	14	9	2	0	2	7	2	1	.688	1.214
Fulchino,Jeff	L	.364	33	12	3	1	1	6	5	7	.447	.606
Throws Right	R	.310	29	9	3	0	1	6	3	5	.382	.517
Gabbard,Kason	L	.233	43	10	1	0	1	7	9	11	.358	.326
Throws Left	R	.307	176	54	10	0	4	23	30	22	.409	.432

Pitcher	vs	Avg	AB	H	2B	3B	HR	RBI	BB	SO	OBP	Slg
Gagne,Eric	L	.241	87	21	3	0	6	13	10	21	.333	.483
Throws Right	R	.275	91	25	6	0	5	12	12	17	.359	.505
Galarraga,Armando	L	.267	374	100	20	3	21	52	35	64	.329	.505
Throws Right	R	.174	299	52	8	3	7	19	26	62	.252	.291
Gallagher,Sean	L	.266	248	66	13	5	6	35	42	58	.374	.431
Throws Right	R	.259	201	52	15	1	7	29	16	45	.320	.448
Gallardo,Yovani	L	.324	37	12	1	0	1	1	6	5	.419	.432
Throws Right	R	.204	49	10	3	0	2	4	2	15	.231	.388
Garcia,Freddy	L	.100	20	2	0	0	1	3	4	7	.280	.250
Throws Right	R	.265	34	9	2	0	2	4	2	5	.306	.500
Garcia,Jaime	L	.250	16	4	1	0	0	0	3	0	.400	.313
Throws Left	R	.227	44	10	1	0	4	11	5	8	.306	.523
Gardner,Lee	L	.412	17	7	3	0	1	4	3	2	.500	.765
Throws Right	R	.438	16	7	2	0	1	6	1	2	.471	.750
Garland,Jon	L	.300	413	124	18	5	16	61	27	46	.345	.484
Throws Right	R	.307	368	113	24	2	7	45	32	44	.367	.440
Garza,Matt	L	.244	332	81	14	4	11	40	32	69	.311	.410
Throws Right	R	.245	363	89	11	1	8	39	27	59	.301	.347
Gaudin,Chad	L	.273	165	45	7	0	3	16	12	18	.320	.370
Throws Right	R	.258	182	47	11	0	8	29	15	53	.323	.451
Geary,Geoff	L	.220	91	20	4	0	0	6	18	16	.349	.264
Throws Right	R	.182	137	25	4	1	3	15	10	29	.247	.292
Geer,Josh	L	.146	48	7	0	1	1	3	4	6	.212	.250
Throws Right	R	.367	60	22	2	1	1	5	5	10	.415	.483
German,Franklyn	L	.300	30	9	3	0	0	8	7	9	.421	.400
Throws Right	R	.205	44	9	2	0	0	5	6	6	.288	.250
Germano,Justin	L	.268	71	19	3	1	3	9	6	7	.321	.465
Throws Right	R	.330	106	35	4	1	5	17	7	10	.377	.528
Giese,Dan	L	.209	91	19	6	0	2	7	11	16	.288	.341
Throws Right	R	.260	77	20	4	0	1	10	3	13	.293	.351
Ginter,Matt	L	.308	52	16	1	2	0	4	3	8	.345	.404
Throws Right	R	.290	31	9	2	0	3	7	0	4	.290	.645
Glavine,Tom	L	.290	69	20	3	0	3	11	7	13	.355	.464
Throws Left	R	.287	164	47	15	0	8	26	30	24	.394	.524
Glover,Gary	L	.304	92	28	5	1	2	9	8	16	.366	.446
Throws Right	R	.279	129	36	7	2	5	28	14	21	.354	.481
Gobble,Jimmy	L	.200	65	13	1	2	1	11	4	18	.257	.323
Throws Left	R	.382	68	26	8	0	4	24	19	9	.517	.676
Gonzalez,Edgar	L	.259	85	22	3	0	4	13	14	15	.366	.435
Throws Right	R	.336	107	36	6	2	4	19	7	17	.388	.542
Gonzalez,Enrique	L	.333	6	2	0	1	0	0	1	0	.429	.667
Throws Right	R	.286	7	2	2	0	0	3	1	1	.375	.571
Gonzalez,Gio	L	.194	36	7	1	1	0	3	6	14	.302	.278
Throws Left	R	.260	96	25	7	1	9	26	19	20	.398	.635
Gonzalez,Mike	L	.259	27	7	1	1	4	8	0	13	.250	.815
Throws Left	R	.196	97	19	2	1	2	10	14	31	.301	.299
Gordon,Brian	L	.100	10	1	0	0	0	0	0	1	.100	.100
Throws Right	R	.500	6	3	1	0	0	1	0	0	.500	.667
Gordon,Tom	L	.246	57	14	6	0	0	6	8	14	.333	.351
Throws Right	R	.266	64	17	3	2	3	10	9	12	.356	.516
Gorzelanny,Tom	L	.261	69	18	4	1	1	9	12	21	.373	.391
Throws Left	R	.299	341	102	22	2	19	60	58	46	.396	.543
Grabow,John	L	.239	71	17	1	0	1	3	8	18	.321	.296
Throws Left	R	.207	208	43	8	0	8	26	29	44	.303	.361
Gray,Jeff	L	.444	9	4	3	0	0	4	0	2	.444	.778
Throws Right	R	.308	13	4	0	0	1	2	1	2	.400	.538
Green,Sean	L	.299	134	40	8	0	3	19	21	16	.401	.425
Throws Right	R	.233	172	40	9	0	0	21	15	46	.298	.285
Gregg,Kevin	L	.181	116	21	5	0	3	13	23	32	.319	.302
Throws Right	R	.222	135	30	3	0	0	14	14	26	.309	.244
Greinke,Zack	L	.287	362	104	23	8	11	43	28	87	.338	.486
Throws Right	R	.232	423	98	13	1	10	39	28	96	.284	.338
Grilli,Jason	L	.237	114	27	5	2	2	16	25	32	.373	.368
Throws Right	R	.242	165	40	9	2	0	16	13	37	.300	.321
Guardado,Eddie	L	.210	81	17	3	0	3	9	7	18	.270	.358
Throws Left	R	.268	123	33	15	0	1	15	12	15	.331	.415
Guerrier,Matt	L	.282	110	31	4	2	3	17	15	16	.365	.436
Throws Right	R	.272	195	53	9	0	9	22	22	43	.346	.456
Guevara,Carlos	L	.190	21	4	0	0	0	2	7	6	.393	.190
Throws Right	R	.321	28	9	2	0	2	10	2	5	.355	.607
Guthrie,Jeremy	L	.241	373	90	16	3	12	36	36	64	.309	.397
Throws Right	R	.243	354	86	14	0	12	38	22	56	.298	.384
Guzman,Angel	L	.263	19	5	2	0	0	1	3	4	.364	.368
Throws Right	R	.250	20	5	1	0	1	5	1	6	.318	.450
Haeger,Charlie	L	.333	9	3	0	0	1	4	0	1	.455	.667
Throws Right	R	.417	12	5	0	0	1	5	5	3	.588	.667

Pitchers vs. Left-Handed and Right-Handed Batters

Pitcher	vs	Avg	AB	H	2B	3B	HR	RBI	BB	SO	OBP	Slg
Halladay,Roy	L	.243	536	130	17	3	11	48	19	115	.275	.347
Throws Right	R	.230	391	90	17	3	7	36	20	91	.278	.343
Hamels,Cole	L	.262	210	55	8	0	12	25	13	51	.308	.471
Throws Left	R	.215	641	138	36	3	16	57	40	145	.261	.356
Hammel,Jason	L	.281	139	39	8	1	5	20	18	21	.367	.460
Throws Right	R	.265	166	44	7	1	6	27	17	23	.333	.428
Hampson,Justin	L	.250	48	12	2	0	0	8	4	8	.291	.292
Throws Left	R	.302	63	19	3	0	1	5	6	11	.357	.397
Hampton,Mike	L	.339	59	20	5	1	2	7	4	11	.369	.559
Throws Left	R	.267	236	63	18	1	8	34	24	27	.337	.453
Hanrahan,Joel	L	.228	136	31	5	0	4	18	24	44	.333	.353
Throws Right	R	.237	177	42	13	0	5	29	18	49	.310	.395
Hansack,Devern	L	.308	13	4	0	0	0	3	1	1	.333	.308
Throws Right	R	.182	11	2	2	0	0	0	0	4	.182	.364
Hansen,Craig	L	.230	74	17	4	0	1	9	18	12	.387	.324
Throws Right	R	.225	102	23	4	0	2	17	25	20	.380	.324
Happ,J.A.	L	.209	43	9	2	0	2	7	3	10	.261	.395
Throws Left	R	.247	77	19	2	0	1	4	11	16	.344	.312
Harang,Aaron	L	.298	299	89	21	1	13	37	28	58	.355	.505
Throws Right	R	.274	424	116	31	2	22	62	22	95	.310	.512
Harden,Rich	L	.198	252	50	6	2	5	21	32	77	.295	.298
Throws Right	R	.168	274	46	12	0	6	16	29	104	.246	.277
Haren,Dan	L	.241	406	98	21	3	6	35	23	107	.282	.352
Throws Right	R	.253	419	106	24	1	13	42	17	99	.290	.408
Harrison,Matt	L	.310	87	27	10	2	3	15	13	16	.396	.575
Throws Left	R	.297	246	73	19	2	9	38	18	26	.344	.500
Hart,Kevin	L	.367	49	18	3	3	2	9	8	7	.483	.673
Throws Right	R	.296	71	21	5	0	0	11	10	16	.383	.366
Hawkins,LaTroy	L	.293	99	29	8	0	3	14	14	19	.374	.465
Throws Right	R	.189	127	24	4	0	0	13	8	29	.235	.220
Hayhurst,Dirk	L	.394	33	13	3	0	0	5	4	7	.459	.485
Throws Right	R	.341	41	14	4	0	2	12	6	7	.426	.585
Heilman,Aaron	L	.308	120	37	5	1	8	30	24	27	.425	.567
Throws Right	R	.222	171	38	10	0	2	21	22	53	.337	.316
Hendrickson,Mark	L	.248	141	35	4	0	5	19	17	25	.335	.383
Throws Left	R	.296	382	113	27	0	12	65	31	56	.350	.461
Henn,Sean	L	.100	10	1	0	0	0	1	3	3	.308	.100
Throws Left	R	.370	27	10	1	0	1	5	6	6	.485	.519
Hennessey,Brad	L	.333	72	24	7	0	3	12	9	7	.402	.556
Throws Right	R	.375	104	39	10	1	5	25	6	14	.414	.635
Hensley,Clay	L	.288	66	19	4	1	0	11	13	11	.400	.379
Throws Right	R	.221	77	17	6	0	2	9	12	15	.326	.377
Herges,Matt	L	.280	125	35	8	2	2	19	11	23	.333	.424
Throws Right	R	.326	135	44	8	3	3	26	13	23	.400	.496
Hernandez,Felix	L	.275	429	118	34	0	13	41	53	106	.353	.445
Throws Right	R	.242	330	80	14	0	4	33	27	69	.311	.321
Hernandez,Fernando	L	.333	9	3	0	0	0	4	1	1	.400	.333
Throws Right	R	.250	4	1	1	0	0	1	4	1	.667	.500
Hernandez,Livan	L	.340	359	122	20	2	11	48	25	27	.377	.499
Throws Right	R	.344	393	135	33	1	14	70	18	40	.373	.539
Hernandez,Runelvys	L	.364	33	12	2	1	4	9	7	6	.475	.848
Throws Right	R	.377	53	20	6	1	0	10	4	9	.421	.528
Herrera,Daniel Ray	L	.000	8	0	0	0	0	0	1	3	.200	.000
Throws Left	R	.455	22	10	3	0	1	2	2	5	.520	.727
Herrera,Yoslan	L	.474	38	18	6	0	0	10	6	3	.545	.632
Throws Right	R	.386	44	17	1	1	1	10	6	7	.453	.523
Hill,Rich	L	.154	13	2	1	0	0	0	7	4	.450	.231
Throws Left	R	.200	55	11	2	0	2	8	11	11	.333	.345
Hill,Shawn	L	.294	143	42	10	2	3	18	11	21	.340	.455
Throws Right	R	.374	123	46	11	2	2	21	12	18	.431	.545
Hinckley,Mike	L	.222	18	4	1	0	0	0	0	4	.263	.278
Throws Left	R	.148	27	4	0	0	0	0	3	5	.233	.148
Hinshaw,Alex	L	.205	73	15	2	0	1	10	12	28	.318	.274
Throws Left	R	.235	68	16	3	1	4	9	17	19	.402	.485
Hirsh,Jason	L	.450	20	9	3	0	1	3	2	2	.500	.750
Throws Right	R	.273	22	6	2	1	2	7	2	4	.333	.727
Hochevar,Luke	L	.314	261	82	14	2	8	42	23	32	.371	.475
Throws Right	R	.244	250	61	14	0	4	31	24	40	.319	.348
Hoffman,Trevor	L	.291	79	23	2	1	5	11	6	28	.341	.532
Throws Right	R	.165	91	15	1	0	3	8	3	18	.191	.275
Howell,J.P.	L	.188	117	22	4	0	1	7	15	30	.286	.248
Throws Left	R	.197	203	40	9	0	5	20	24	62	.290	.315
Howry,Bob	L	.328	116	38	9	2	4	16	7	29	.362	.543
Throws Right	R	.297	175	52	12	2	9	32	6	30	.322	.543
Hudson,Tim	L	.255	271	69	18	3	8	29	25	29	.318	.432
Throws Right	R	.223	251	56	9	0	3	16	15	56	.268	.295
Hughes,Phil	L	.333	60	20	7	0	1	4	10	10	.437	.500
Throws Right	R	.299	77	23	5	0	2	16	5	13	.329	.442
Humber,Philip	L	.150	20	3	1	0	2	3	4	3	.320	.500
Throws Right	R	.333	24	8	0	0	2	5	1	3	.360	.583
Hunter,Tommy	L	.393	28	11	1	0	3	11	3	4	.469	.750
Throws Right	R	.414	29	12	4	0	1	8	0	5	.414	.655
Hurley,Eric	L	.269	52	14	4	0	3	8	6	7	.345	.519
Throws Right	R	.267	45	12	5	0	2	7	3	6	.327	.511
Igawa,Kei	L	.000	1	0	0	0	0	0	0	0	.000	.000
Throws Left	R	.591	22	13	4	0	0	6	0	0	.565	.773
Isringhausen,Jason	L	.186	59	11	4	0	1	8	11	14	.319	.305
Throws Right	R	.327	113	37	4	2	4	18	11	22	.406	.504
Jackson,Edwin	L	.295	342	101	15	1	8	42	48	42	.379	.415
Throws Right	R	.268	365	98	21	4	15	43	29	66	.326	.471
Jackson,Zach	L	.348	69	24	3	1	1	8	4	14	.408	.464
Throws Left	R	.271	166	45	9	0	6	24	12	17	.318	.434
James,Chuck	L	.148	27	4	0	0	2	2	7	8	.324	.370
Throws Left	R	.360	89	32	5	2	8	28	13	14	.444	.730
Jenks,Bobby	L	.219	114	25	5	1	0	8	12	23	.299	.281
Throws Right	R	.241	108	26	7	0	3	12	5	15	.272	.389
Jennings,Jason	L	.333	57	19	4	0	4	12	11	6	.441	.614
Throws Right	R	.281	57	16	4	0	4	13	7	6	.369	.561
Jepsen,Kevin	L	.235	17	4	1	0	0	3	2	4	.316	.294
Throws Right	R	.267	15	4	0	1	0	2	2	3	.353	.400
Jimenez,Cesar	L	.317	60	19	4	0	1	14	5	13	.379	.433
Throws Left	R	.203	64	13	2	0	1	8	8	13	.288	.281
Jimenez,Kelvin	L	.233	43	10	6	0	1	4	8	5	.353	.442
Throws Right	R	.340	53	18	1	0	4	13	7	6	.419	.585
Jimenez,Ubaldo	L	.248	395	98	19	4	8	54	60	85	.349	.377
Throws Right	R	.241	349	84	17	0	3	32	43	87	.335	.315
Johnson,Jason	L	.300	50	15	4	1	2	6	5	7	.375	.540
Throws Right	R	.262	65	17	3	1	3	14	7	13	.342	.477
Johnson,Jim	L	.227	110	25	2	0	0	10	16	15	.328	.245
Throws Right	R	.212	137	29	2	0	0	7	12	23	.285	.226
Johnson,Josh	L	.288	184	53	5	4	2	14	16	38	.343	.391
Throws Right	R	.259	147	38	3	1	5	18	11	39	.314	.395
Johnson,Randy	L	.215	107	23	7	2	0	10	6	26	.265	.318
Throws Left	R	.267	602	161	32	0	24	77	38	147	.313	.440
Jones,Todd	L	.289	76	22	5	0	3	12	11	6	.371	.474
Throws Right	R	.304	92	28	4	1	2	18	7	8	.379	.435
Julio,Jorge	L	.255	55	14	4	0	2	7	12	18	.382	.436
Throws Right	R	.236	55	13	4	0	1	9	7	16	.328	.364
Jurrjens,Jair	L	.261	376	98	25	6	5	36	43	67	.333	.399
Throws Right	R	.260	346	90	15	2	6	44	27	72	.320	.367
Karstens,Jeff	L	.265	102	27	5	1	3	15	9	13	.316	.422
Throws Right	R	.293	99	29	4	2	4	11	4	10	.317	.495
Kazmir,Scott	L	.198	131	26	5	1	1	7	7	34	.239	.275
Throws Left	R	.227	427	97	28	3	22	50	63	132	.329	.461
Kendrick,Kyle	L	.334	329	110	28	2	12	45	38	23	.404	.541
Throws Right	R	.271	310	84	12	1	11	44	19	45	.335	.423
Kennedy,Ian	L	.236	89	21	7	1	1	13	17	16	.355	.371
Throws Right	R	.397	73	29	8	1	4	21	9	11	.458	.699
Kensing,Logan	L	.208	106	22	5	0	4	11	15	30	.303	.368
Throws Right	R	.259	108	28	6	0	3	22	18	25	.382	.398
Kershaw,Clayton	L	.250	80	20	7	1	3	11	11	30	.337	.475
Throws Left	R	.269	331	89	15	1	8	34	41	70	.349	.393
King,Ray	L	.235	17	4	2	0	0	2	0	1	.235	.353
Throws Left	R	.500	10	5	0	0	1	4	4	0	.667	.800
Kinney,Josh	L	.125	8	1	0	0	0	0	1	3	.222	.125
Throws Right	R	.125	16	2	1	0	0	0	0	5	.125	.188
Knight,Brandon	L	.435	23	10	1	0	0	5	4	3	.536	.478
Throws Right	R	.167	24	4	0	0	0	2	3	7	.276	.167
Kobayashi,Masa	L	.280	107	30	5	0	6	18	7	18	.325	.495
Throws Right	R	.292	120	35	3	0	2	12	7	17	.333	.367
Korecky,Bobby	L	.310	29	9	4	0	0	3	5	2	.412	.448
Throws Right	R	.270	37	10	1	0	2	3	3	4	.325	.459
Kunz,Eddie	L	.500	8	4	0	0	1	2	0	1	.500	.875
Throws Right	R	.333	3	1	1	0	0	1	1	0	.600	.667
Kuo,Hong-Chih	L	.202	94	19	2	1	3	12	2	44	.216	.340
Throws Left	R	.205	200	41	13	0	1	8	19	52	.284	.285
Kuroda,Hiroki	L	.260	361	94	23	0	9	45	22	43	.306	.399
Throws Right	R	.246	354	87	12	1	4	31	20	73	.292	.319
Lackey,John	L	.221	317	70	10	2	12	25	19	68	.279	.379
Throws Right	R	.301	302	91	16	0	14	40	21	62	.353	.493
Laffey,Aaron	L	.244	90	22	2	0	3	13	7	15	.327	.367
Throws Left	R	.292	277	81	16	0	7	30	24	28	.359	.426

Pitchers vs. Left-Handed and Right-Handed Batters

Pitcher	vs	Avg	AB	H	2B	3B	HR	RBI	BB	SO	OBP	Slg
Lambert,Chris	L	.372	43	16	2	2	1	10	4	6	.429	.581
Throws Right	R	.306	49	15	3	0	2	8	3	9	.358	.490
Lannan,John	L	.259	174	45	12	1	7	22	13	33	.317	.460
Throws Left	R	.250	508	127	16	1	16	56	59	84	.331	.380
League,Brandon	L	.263	57	15	3	0	2	6	7	11	.364	.421
Throws Right	R	.200	65	13	2	0	0	6	8	12	.297	.231
LeBlanc,Wade	L	.318	22	7	1	0	2	3	4	4	.423	.636
Throws Left	R	.333	66	22	5	1	5	16	11	10	.429	.667
Ledezma,Wil	L	.255	55	14	1	1	1	6	8	14	.359	.364
Throws Left	R	.233	159	37	10	1	3	26	33	39	.364	.365
Lee,Cliff	L	.272	243	66	10	3	2	22	7	43	.299	.362
Throws Left	R	.245	604	148	23	3	10	44	27	127	.279	.343
Lester,Jon	L	.217	235	51	11	0	3	14	13	52	.269	.302
Throws Left	R	.273	554	151	33	1	11	58	53	100	.341	.395
Lewis,Jensen	L	.267	135	36	10	1	4	17	14	29	.338	.444
Throws Right	R	.264	121	32	5	0	4	19	13	23	.353	.405
Lewis,Scott	L	.130	23	3	0	0	1	2	0	6	.130	.261
Throws Left	R	.254	67	17	4	0	3	6	6	9	.315	.448
Lidge,Brad	L	.273	139	38	7	0	1	15	17	54	.354	.345
Throws Right	R	.105	114	12	3	1	1	2	18	38	.227	.175
Lieber,Jon	L	.368	68	25	4	1	6	13	5	11	.411	.721
Throws Right	R	.272	125	34	9	1	4	13	1	16	.287	.456
Lilly,Ted	L	.307	179	55	9	3	9	27	19	30	.386	.542
Throws Left	R	.219	603	132	34	3	23	60	45	154	.275	.400
Lincecum,Tim	L	.221	407	90	20	1	4	22	45	134	.300	.305
Throws Right	R	.221	417	92	19	2	7	36	39	131	.293	.326
Lincoln,Mike	L	.225	111	25	3	1	5	15	6	26	.269	.405
Throws Right	R	.268	153	41	4	0	5	17	18	31	.349	.392
Lindstrom,Matt	L	.324	108	35	8	0	1	9	10	14	.387	.426
Throws Right	R	.214	103	22	3	0	0	6	16	29	.317	.243
Linebrink,Scott	L	.200	80	16	2	0	4	7	6	19	.256	.375
Throws Right	R	.263	95	25	2	1	4	11	3	21	.286	.432
Liriano,Francisco	L	.217	69	15	5	0	1	6	8	17	.304	.333
Throws Left	R	.266	222	59	12	1	6	29	24	50	.335	.410
Litsch,Jesse	L	.270	371	100	19	3	9	34	22	66	.315	.410
Throws Right	R	.250	312	78	18	1	11	33	17	33	.296	.420
Littleton,Wes	L	.241	29	7	1	0	0	8	4	5	.378	.276
Throws Right	R	.282	39	11	1	0	1	9	4	9	.349	.385
Liz,Radhames	L	.318	179	57	10	1	8	32	35	38	.428	.520
Throws Right	R	.269	156	42	6	0	8	24	16	19	.345	.462
Loaiza,Esteban	L	.385	39	15	3	0	1	8	2	5	.395	.538
Throws Right	R	.176	68	12	4	1	3	8	3	5	.219	.397
Loe,Kameron	L	.400	55	22	3	2	2	15	6	5	.459	.636
Throws Right	R	.200	70	14	3	0	1	7	2	15	.219	.286
Loewen,Adam	L	.296	27	8	1	0	1	7	3	6	.355	.444
Throws Left	R	.309	55	17	3	0	4	11	15	8	.451	.582
Logan,Boone	L	.291	103	30	5	1	5	20	5	30	.324	.505
Throws Left	R	.351	77	27	7	1	2	16	9	12	.425	.545
Lohse,Kyle	L	.254	331	84	25	1	6	32	26	52	.311	.390
Throws Right	R	.285	446	127	27	3	12	51	23	67	.319	.439
Looper,Braden	L	.279	326	91	18	2	12	40	28	46	.343	.457
Throws Right	R	.279	448	125	24	1	13	50	17	62	.312	.424
Lopez,Aquilino	L	.298	114	34	14	1	2	12	11	24	.360	.491
Throws Right	R	.265	196	52	11	0	7	42	11	37	.297	.429
Lopez,Javier	L	.182	110	20	3	1	2	11	19	26	.305	.282
Throws Left	R	.311	106	33	5	2	2	12	8	12	.365	.453
Loux,Shane	L	.379	29	11	2	1	1	5	2	1	.438	.621
Throws Right	R	.156	32	5	0	0	0	3	0	3	.182	.156
Lowe,Derek	L	.251	374	94	23	1	3	28	23	56	.293	.342
Throws Right	R	.240	416	100	13	2	11	47	22	91	.278	.361
Lowe,Mark	L	.354	127	45	9	1	6	23	15	23	.427	.583
Throws Right	R	.250	132	33	10	0	0	16	19	32	.350	.326
Lowery,Devon	L	.444	9	4	0	0	1	1	2	1	.545	.778
Throws Right	R	.200	10	2	0	0	1	2	0	5	.200	.500
Lyon,Brandon	L	.278	115	32	4	2	1	11	6	17	.314	.374
Throws Right	R	.321	134	43	8	1	6	24	7	27	.352	.530
MacDougal,Mike	L	.350	20	7	1	0	0	3	4	5	.458	.400
Throws Right	R	.205	44	9	3	0	0	1	8	7	.352	.273
Maddux,Greg	L	.272	345	94	17	0	8	33	19	42	.310	.391
Throws Right	R	.271	406	110	20	4	13	64	11	56	.295	.436
Madrigal,Warner	L	.323	65	21	6	0	0	8	11	9	.421	.415
Throws Right	R	.208	72	15	2	1	4	18	3	13	.234	.431
Madson,Ryan	L	.268	138	37	5	1	3	13	16	25	.344	.384
Throws Right	R	.243	173	42	11	0	3	24	7	42	.273	.358
Mahay,Ron	L	.255	94	24	4	0	3	13	11	22	.327	.394
Throws Left	R	.250	148	37	6	0	3	19	18	27	.327	.351

Pitcher	vs	Avg	AB	H	2B	3B	HR	RBI	BB	SO	OBP	Slg
Maholm,Paul	L	.183	131	24	1	0	4	19	6	41	.232	.282
Throws Left	R	.279	634	177	38	2	17	63	57	98	.341	.426
Maine,John	L	.238	256	61	14	0	10	33	46	52	.356	.410
Throws Right	R	.229	266	61	8	1	6	28	21	70	.288	.335
Majewski,Gary	L	.348	66	23	4	0	1	16	5	12	.394	.455
Throws Right	R	.373	102	38	9	0	5	24	10	15	.429	.608
Manning,Charlie	L	.203	79	16	1	1	4	13	9	23	.284	.392
Throws Left	R	.247	77	19	5	0	4	8	22	14	.414	.468
Marcum,Shaun	L	.244	287	70	15	0	7	21	29	61	.324	.369
Throws Right	R	.200	280	56	12	2	14	34	21	62	.261	.407
Marmol,Carlos	L	.182	132	24	4	0	7	22	18	53	.297	.371
Throws Right	R	.098	164	16	2	0	3	13	23	61	.215	.165
Marquis,Jason	L	.244	291	71	18	1	4	34	45	49	.348	.354
Throws Right	R	.287	352	101	16	3	11	41	25	42	.339	.443
Marshall,Sean	L	.269	67	18	5	1	2	10	7	14	.354	.463
Throws Left	R	.236	178	42	10	0	7	18	16	44	.301	.410
Marte,Damaso	L	.247	85	21	4	1	1	9	9	33	.326	.353
Throws Left	R	.196	158	31	3	0	4	19	17	38	.278	.291
Martinez,Pedro	L	.304	230	70	13	0	11	39	23	42	.371	.504
Throws Right	R	.282	202	57	12	1	8	25	21	45	.357	.470
Martis,Shairon	L	.295	44	13	0	2	3	9	7	12	.385	.591
Throws Right	R	.143	35	5	0	1	2	3	5	11	.250	.371
Masset,Nick	L	.262	84	22	3	1	5	15	15	18	.374	.500
Throws Right	R	.316	155	49	10	0	2	25	11	25	.367	.419
Masterson,Justin	L	.238	147	35	9	0	6	20	25	28	.365	.422
Throws Right	R	.196	168	33	5	0	4	12	15	40	.274	.298
Mastny,Tom	L	.326	46	15	4	0	3	10	8	8	.418	.609
Throws Right	R	.310	42	13	2	0	3	11	3	11	.356	.571
Mathis,Doug	L	.396	53	21	5	0	0	5	10	5	.492	.491
Throws Right	R	.364	44	16	3	1	3	12	4	4	.417	.682
Matos,Osiris	L	.296	27	8	2	0	1	7	5	6	.412	.481
Throws Right	R	.316	57	18	8	1	2	11	4	10	.349	.596
Matsuzaka,Daisuke	L	.225	315	71	19	2	7	24	62	87	.353	.365
Throws Right	R	.195	293	57	10	0	5	30	32	67	.284	.280
McCarthy,Brandon	L	.293	41	12	2	1	2	6	7	6	.400	.537
Throws Right	R	.195	41	8	2	0	1	2	1	4	.209	.317
McClellan,Kyle	L	.238	122	29	9	0	3	11	14	24	.321	.385
Throws Right	R	.291	172	50	2	2	4	22	12	35	.346	.395
McClung,Seth	L	.251	179	45	11	0	7	24	29	41	.358	.430
Throws Right	R	.235	204	48	8	0	3	22	26	46	.331	.319
McCrory,Bob	L	.294	17	5	0	0	0	2	6	3	.458	.294
Throws Right	R	.500	10	5	1	0	0	4	2	2	.583	.600
McDonald,James	L	.118	17	2	0	0	0	0	1	2	.167	.118
Throws Right	R	.600	5	3	1	0	0	0	0	0	.600	.800
McGowan,Dustin	L	.295	207	61	11	2	8	32	26	47	.371	.483
Throws Right	R	.252	214	54	11	1	1	18	12	38	.298	.327
Meche,Gil	L	.238	407	97	23	1	9	43	37	110	.298	.366
Throws Right	R	.273	392	107	21	3	10	50	36	73	.330	.418
Medders,Brandon	L	.286	28	8	1	0	2	9	4	3	.371	.536
Throws Right	R	.205	44	9	3	0	0	1	7	5	.327	.273
Meek,Evan	L	.160	25	4	1	0	1	2	3	4	.250	.320
Throws Right	R	.333	21	7	1	1	2	9	9	3	.531	.762
Meloan,John	L	.000	3	0	0	0	0	0	0	2	.000	.000
Throws Right	R	.000	2	0	0	0	0	0	1	0	.333	.000
Mendoza,Luis	L	.336	146	49	14	0	3	35	12	15	.391	.493
Throws Right	R	.350	137	48	14	1	4	32	13	20	.419	.555
Mercker,Kent	L	.333	18	6	1	0	1	4	2	0	.400	.556
Throws Left	R	.226	31	7	2	0	0	1	6	6	.351	.290
Meredith,Cla	L	.351	94	33	3	0	1	16	11	14	.425	.415
Throws Right	R	.258	178	46	6	0	5	33	13	35	.304	.376
Messenger,Randy	L	.250	24	6	1	0	0	0	3	3	.333	.292
Throws Right	R	.370	27	10	1	0	1	4	2	4	.433	.519
Meyer,Dan	L	.314	35	11	4	0	0	6	4	10	.385	.429
Throws Left	R	.300	80	24	4	3	6	20	10	10	.376	.650
Mickolio,Kam	L	.214	14	3	1	0	0	3	1	4	.250	.286
Throws Right	R	.313	16	5	3	0	0	4	3	4	.421	.500
Mijares,Jose	L	.143	14	2	0	0	0	0	0	1	.143	.143
Throws Left	R	.050	20	1	1	0	0	0	0	4	.050	.100
Miller,Andrew	L	.226	93	21	4	0	3	12	22	33	.378	.366
Throws Left	R	.307	322	99	27	2	4	56	34	56	.372	.441
Miller,Jim	L	.333	15	5	1	0	0	4	4	2	.474	.400
Throws Right	R	.250	16	4	1	0	0	1	1	6	.316	.313
Miller,Justin	L	.310	71	22	6	2	2	9	6	16	.380	.535
Throws Right	R	.224	107	24	7	0	2	16	14	27	.317	.346
Miller,Trever	L	.209	91	19	4	1	1	4	10	30	.305	.308
Throws Left	R	.286	70	20	5	0	1	9	10	14	.383	.400

Pitchers vs. Left-Handed and Right-Handed Batters

Pitcher	vs	Avg	AB	H	2B	3B	HR	RBI	BB	SO	OBP	Slg
Millwood,Kevin	L	.273	363	99	23	4	12	49	34	77	.338	.457
Throws Right	R	.354	342	121	17	2	6	45	15	48	.386	.468
Miner,Zach	L	.269	223	60	14	3	7	21	23	34	.341	.453
Throws Right	R	.256	227	58	11	2	3	33	23	28	.332	.361
Misch,Pat	L	.281	64	18	1	0	3	11	3	14	.309	.438
Throws Left	R	.270	141	38	4	0	8	21	12	24	.333	.468
Mock,Garrett	L	.279	68	19	5	0	0	7	10	17	.372	.353
Throws Right	R	.207	87	18	4	0	4	13	13	29	.307	.391
Moehler,Brian	L	.307	277	85	20	2	11	40	23	27	.359	.513
Throws Right	R	.255	318	81	17	1	9	35	13	55	.285	.399
Morales,Franklin	L	.200	10	2	0	1	0	1	0	1	.182	.400
Throws Left	R	.295	88	26	9	1	2	15	17	8	.411	.489
Morillo,Juan	L	.500	2	1	1	0	0	0	0	0	.500	1.000
Throws Right	R	.000	2	0	0	0	0	0	0	0	.000	.000
Morris,Matt	L	.422	45	19	6	0	2	14	5	5	.481	.689
Throws Right	R	.367	60	22	6	1	4	13	2	4	.391	.700
Morrow,Brandon	L	.198	116	23	3	1	6	16	21	29	.321	.397
Throws Right	R	.149	114	17	1	0	4	11	13	46	.236	.263
Morton,Charlie	L	.306	134	41	9	3	6	23	17	21	.392	.552
Throws Right	R	.245	159	39	11	0	3	28	24	27	.337	.371
Moseley,Dustin	L	.366	101	37	8	1	2	18	10	18	.416	.525
Throws Right	R	.300	110	33	6	0	4	17	10	19	.366	.464
Mota,Guillermo	L	.287	87	25	3	0	4	13	16	17	.390	.460
Throws Right	R	.216	125	27	2	3	3	14	12	33	.283	.352
Motte,Jason	L	.125	16	2	0	0	0	0	2	7	.222	.125
Throws Right	R	.150	20	3	0	0	0	2	1	9	.190	.150
Moyer,Jamie	L	.240	200	48	6	1	8	24	15	36	.321	.400
Throws Left	R	.270	559	151	34	3	12	53	47	87	.328	.406
Moylan,Peter	L	.273	11	3	0	0	0	0	0	3	.333	.273
Throws Right	R	.167	12	2	0	0	1	1	1	2	.231	.417
Mujica,Edward	L	.277	65	18	4	3	2	11	8	8	.360	.523
Throws Right	R	.318	88	28	7	0	3	21	2	19	.323	.500
Mulder,Mark	L	1.000	3	3	0	0	0	1	1	0	1.000	1.000
Throws Left	R	.200	5	1	0	0	0	1	1	2	.286	.200
Muniz,Carlos	L	.294	34	10	2	0	3	8	5	7	.385	.618
Throws Right	R	.250	56	14	3	0	1	4	2	9	.295	.357
Murray,A.J.	L	.600	5	3	0	0	0	0	0	1	.600	.600
Throws Left	R	.300	30	9	2	0	0	4	3	4	.364	.367
Musser,Neal	L	.000	1	0	0	0	0	0	1	0	.500	.000
Throws Left	R	.000	1	0	0	0	0	0	0	0	.000	.000
Mussina,Mike	L	.236	368	87	15	1	2	25	23	84	.284	.299
Throws Right	R	.317	401	127	32	1	15	57	8	66	.336	.514
Myers,Brett	L	.235	336	79	22	4	11	39	40	87	.317	.423
Throws Right	R	.293	403	118	27	0	18	52	25	76	.341	.494
Nathan,Joe	L	.167	120	20	1	0	5	11	12	36	.248	.300
Throws Right	R	.192	120	23	6	1	0	2	6	38	.236	.258
Nelson,Joe	L	.227	97	22	4	1	1	15	9	26	.292	.320
Throws Right	R	.189	106	20	3	0	4	15	13	34	.289	.330
Neshek,Pat	L	.250	20	5	1	1	1	2	1	5	.273	.550
Throws Right	R	.233	30	7	0	1	1	8	3	10	.303	.400
Newman,Josh	L	.273	22	6	2	0	2	7	6	3	.448	.636
Throws Left	R	.404	47	19	5	0	2	11	6	5	.473	.638
Niemann,Jeff	L	.200	25	5	1	0	2	4	5	7	.333	.480
Throws Right	R	.325	40	13	4	0	1	7	3	7	.386	.500
Niese,Jonathon	L	.353	17	6	2	0	1	6	0	2	.353	.647
Throws Left	R	.326	43	14	4	0	1	4	8	9	.431	.488
Nieve,Fernando	L	.636	11	7	1	0	0	3	0	2	.636	.727
Throws Right	R	.278	36	10	2	0	2	8	2	10	.316	.500
Nippert,Dustin	L	.263	152	40	9	1	5	18	19	30	.343	.434
Throws Right	R	.354	147	52	11	1	5	23	18	25	.428	.544
Nolasco,Ricky	L	.238	433	103	18	3	20	47	27	87	.285	.432
Throws Right	R	.239	372	89	26	2	8	36	15	99	.270	.384
Nomo,Hideo	L	.167	12	2	0	0	1	2	2	3	.286	.417
Throws Right	R	.800	10	8	3	0	2	8	2	0	.769	1.700
Nunez,Leo	L	.272	81	22	2	2	2	13	9	11	.355	.420
Throws Right	R	.230	100	23	6	0	0	12	6	15	.284	.290
Nunez,Vladimir	L	.211	57	12	3	0	0	7	11	11	.324	.263
Throws Right	R	.303	66	20	9	0	0	8	8	13	.387	.439
O'Connor,Mike	L	.167	12	2	0	0	0	1	0	0	.167	.167
Throws Left	R	.409	22	9	1	0	3	6	11	4	.588	.864
O'Day,Darren	L	.275	80	22	3	1	2	12	8	13	.352	.413
Throws Right	R	.290	93	27	4	0	0	11	6	16	.347	.333
O'Flaherty,Eric	L	.500	16	8	3	0	1	5	1	1	.579	.875
Throws Left	R	.421	19	8	3	0	1	10	3	3	.478	.737
Ohlendorf,Ross	L	.370	138	51	10	2	7	29	19	21	.443	.623
Throws Right	R	.273	128	35	4	0	3	22	12	28	.340	.375

Pitcher	vs	Avg	AB	H	2B	3B	HR	RBI	BB	SO	OBP	Slg
Ohman,Will	L	.200	105	21	4	1	2	8	8	28	.257	.314
Throws Left	R	.256	117	30	7	1	1	14	14	25	.341	.359
Okajima,Hideki	L	.184	103	19	4	0	3	8	6	31	.236	.311
Throws Left	R	.234	128	30	5	0	3	21	17	29	.318	.344
Oliver,Darren	L	.229	109	25	10	0	2	18	6	25	.277	.376
Throws Left	R	.271	155	42	8	0	3	13	10	23	.321	.381
Olsen,Scott	L	.187	134	25	3	0	3	10	13	29	.262	.276
Throws Left	R	.266	638	170	45	2	27	85	56	84	.326	.470
Olson,Garrett	L	.310	126	39	9	0	1	12	16	18	.392	.405
Throws Left	R	.309	417	129	30	0	16	69	46	65	.384	.496
Osoria,Franquelis	L	.373	102	38	14	1	3	21	3	6	.390	.618
Throws Right	R	.312	157	49	10	0	7	22	9	25	.365	.510
Oswalt,Roy	L	.262	401	105	23	1	10	43	19	84	.293	.399
Throws Right	R	.243	387	94	12	2	13	40	28	81	.307	.385
Outman,Josh	L	.217	23	5	2	0	0	1	2	7	.280	.304
Throws Left	R	.358	81	29	7	2	1	12	6	12	.407	.531
Owings,Micah	L	.268	213	57	12	1	7	28	24	38	.347	.432
Throws Right	R	.242	194	47	9	0	7	34	17	49	.329	.397
Padilla,Vicente	L	.312	327	102	18	3	16	49	45	52	.411	.532
Throws Right	R	.240	346	83	14	0	10	40	20	75	.288	.367
Palmer,Matt	L	.333	21	7	0	0	0	2	10	0	.548	.333
Throws Right	R	.333	30	10	3	0	1	10	3	3	.429	.533
Papelbon,Jonathan	L	.235	136	32	8	0	2	17	6	43	.268	.338
Throws Right	R	.210	124	26	4	0	2	10	2	34	.220	.290
Parisi,Mike	L	.370	46	17	6	0	1	7	8	8	.463	.565
Throws Right	R	.357	56	20	4	1	1	13	7	5	.422	.518
Park,Chan Ho	L	.301	153	46	8	1	5	18	23	33	.399	.464
Throws Right	R	.237	215	51	9	0	7	19	13	46	.287	.377
Parnell,Bobby	L	.000	6	0	0	0	0	1	1	1	.143	.000
Throws Right	R	.273	11	3	0	0	0	0	1	2	.333	.273
Paronto,Chad	L	.200	15	3	1	0	0	0	1	2	.250	.267
Throws Right	R	.348	23	8	2	1	2	7	1	2	.375	.783
Parr,James	L	.304	46	14	5	0	0	5	5	9	.373	.413
Throws Right	R	.326	46	15	7	0	4	8	4	5	.380	.739
Parra,Manny	L	.233	120	28	4	0	4	17	14	36	.313	.367
Throws Left	R	.288	532	153	26	2	14	61	61	111	.362	.423
Parrish,John	L	.305	59	18	4	0	3	10	6	9	.364	.525
Throws Left	R	.279	104	29	6	1	2	8	9	12	.336	.413
Patterson,Scott	L	.111	9	1	0	0	0	0	1	4	.200	.111
Throws Right	R	.143	7	1	0	1	0	3	5	3	.500	.429
Pauley,David	L	.400	30	12	5	0	1	8	5	6	.486	.667
Throws Right	R	.367	30	11	2	0	1	7	0	5	.367	.533
Pavano,Carl	L	.324	74	24	6	0	2	12	8	8	.393	.486
Throws Right	R	.283	60	17	2	0	3	9	2	7	.328	.467
Peavy,Jake	L	.263	323	85	13	2	8	29	28	85	.327	.390
Throws Right	R	.194	314	61	6	0	9	25	31	81	.271	.299
Peguero,Jailen	L	.444	9	4	1	0	0	3	1	0	.545	.556
Throws Right	R	.217	23	5	2	0	0	3	3	5	.308	.304
Pelfrey,Mike	L	.307	371	114	24	2	7	45	42	34	.376	.439
Throws Right	R	.245	387	95	21	2	5	32	22	76	.305	.349
Pena,Tony	L	.296	135	40	9	4	2	20	9	23	.340	.467
Throws Right	R	.267	150	40	9	0	3	20	8	29	.309	.387
Penny,Brad	L	.328	174	57	6	1	5	32	24	26	.416	.460
Throws Right	R	.284	194	55	10	1	8	30	18	25	.343	.469
Peralta,Joel	L	.247	85	21	1	1	9	18	10	17	.330	.600
Throws Right	R	.294	119	35	7	0	6	18	4	21	.317	.504
Percival,Troy	L	.185	81	15	5	2	4	11	13	17	.302	.444
Throws Right	R	.171	82	14	1	0	5	11	14	21	.289	.366
Perez,Chris	L	.220	59	13	4	2	2	6	12	17	.347	.458
Throws Right	R	.231	91	21	5	1	3	12	10	25	.308	.407
Perez,Odalis	L	.218	142	31	3	1	5	16	13	30	.293	.359
Throws Left	R	.306	493	151	44	2	17	66	42	89	.367	.507
Perez,Oliver	L	.158	177	28	3	1	5	17	16	63	.250	.271
Throws Left	R	.258	538	139	25	4	19	68	89	117	.365	.426
Perez,Rafael	L	.222	117	26	3	0	2	13	13	32	.300	.299
Throws Left	R	.243	169	41	5	1	6	23	10	54	.293	.391
Perkins,Glen	L	.352	122	43	8	1	2	11	17	16	.440	.484
Throws Left	R	.288	486	140	30	1	23	65	22	58	.318	.496
Petit,Yusmeiro	L	.231	91	21	2	1	2	8	7	17	.280	.341
Throws Right	R	.205	117	24	6	0	10	21	7	25	.256	.513
Pettitte,Andy	L	.203	231	47	10	0	3	19	8	66	.241	.286
Throws Left	R	.325	573	186	31	4	16	88	47	92	.376	.476
Pettyjohn,Adam	L	.000	2	0	0	0	0	0	0	0	.000	.000
Throws Left	R	.524	21	11	2	0	2	6	2	1	.583	.905
Pignatiello,Carmen	L	-	0	0	0	0	0	1	2	0	1.000	-
Throws Left	R	.500	4	2	1	0	0	1	0	0	.500	.750

Pitchers vs. Left-Handed and Right-Handed Batters

Pitcher	vs	Avg	AB	H	2B	3B	HR	RBI	BB	SO	OBP	Slg
Pineiro,Joel	L	.297	263	78	20	4	10	34	18	41	.343	.517
Throws Right	R	.304	335	102	27	1	12	45	17	40	.338	.499
Pinto,Renyel	L	.264	87	23	2	0	7	16	12	28	.371	.529
Throws Left	R	.203	143	29	3	0	2	13	27	28	.324	.266
Ponson,Sidney	L	.344	302	104	24	1	9	43	38	29	.416	.520
Throws Right	R	.269	245	66	14	1	5	36	10	29	.307	.396
Price,David	L	.158	19	3	0	0	0	2	1	6	.200	.158
Throws Left	R	.188	32	6	1	0	1	3	3	6	.270	.313
Proctor,Scott	L	.263	57	15	3	0	3	9	10	16	.373	.474
Throws Right	R	.260	100	26	6	2	4	23	14	30	.345	.480
Purcey,David	L	.284	67	19	3	0	3	13	8	12	.364	.463
Throws Left	R	.261	184	48	13	0	6	25	21	46	.343	.429
Putz,J.J.	L	.258	97	25	9	0	3	17	15	33	.360	.443
Throws Right	R	.253	83	21	3	0	1	7	13	23	.361	.325
Qualls,Chad	L	.220	132	29	4	1	1	13	9	31	.271	.288
Throws Right	R	.229	140	32	7	1	3	22	9	40	.283	.357
Ramirez,Edwar	L	.229	118	27	7	0	4	21	16	28	.321	.390
Throws Right	R	.195	87	17	6	0	3	11	8	35	.283	.368
Ramirez,Elizardo	L	.333	6	2	1	0	1	4	2	1	.556	1.000
Throws Right	R	.600	10	6	0	0	0	4	0	0	.600	.600
Ramirez,Horacio	L	.350	60	21	1	2	0	10	6	8	.403	.433
Throws Left	R	.258	93	24	5	0	1	4	3	5	.296	.344
Ramirez,Ramon	L	.300	120	36	4	1	1	12	14	32	.370	.375
Throws Right	R	.153	137	21	5	0	1	9	17	38	.244	.212
Ramirez,Ramon A	L	.297	37	11	0	0	3	6	6	7	.395	.541
Throws Right	R	.107	56	6	0	0	0	2	5	14	.194	.107
Rapada,Clay	L	.237	38	9	1	0	0	3	7	9	.370	.263
Throws Left	R	.250	40	10	3	0	0	5	7	6	.362	.325
Rasner,Darrell	L	.279	258	72	10	4	6	28	32	45	.362	.419
Throws Right	R	.312	202	63	12	1	8	31	7	22	.341	.500
Rauch,Jon	L	.268	142	38	5	1	6	18	8	31	.307	.444
Throws Right	R	.242	128	31	8	2	5	19	8	35	.281	.453
Redding,Tim	L	.277	358	99	25	1	13	47	38	54	.348	.461
Throws Right	R	.274	351	96	15	0	14	46	27	66	.332	.436
Redman,Mark	L	.283	46	13	3	1	1	9	4	6	.353	.457
Throws Left	R	.338	142	48	10	1	6	30	12	14	.387	.549
Register,Steven	L	.375	24	9	2	0	3	9	6	2	.484	.833
Throws Right	R	.222	18	4	1	0	1	2	0	6	.222	.444
Reineke,Chad	L	.267	30	8	1	0	0	4	7	9	.395	.300
Throws Right	R	.176	34	6	2	1	1	6	5	4	.282	.382
Resop,Chris	L	.192	26	5	0	0	0	1	5	3	.323	.192
Throws Right	R	.268	41	11	4	1	2	15	5	10	.367	.561
Reyes,Al	L	.300	30	9	2	0	1	4	4	6	.382	.467
Throws Right	R	.226	53	12	3	0	1	11	6	13	.306	.340
Reyes,Anthony	L	.240	100	24	2	0	3	9	3	15	.262	.350
Throws Right	R	.267	86	23	8	1	1	7	12	10	.364	.419
Reyes,Dennys	L	.202	94	19	2	0	2	13	5	23	.250	.287
Throws Left	R	.276	76	21	4	1	2	10	10	16	.368	.434
Reyes,Jo-Jo	L	.255	94	24	2	2	3	12	7	23	.314	.415
Throws Left	R	.313	351	110	25	2	15	57	45	55	.392	.524
Reynolds,Greg	L	.344	131	45	9	1	7	33	18	14	.423	.588
Throws Right	R	.299	127	38	7	2	7	21	8	8	.355	.551
Rhodes,Arthur	L	.157	70	11	3	0	0	6	9	23	.253	.200
Throws Left	R	.309	55	17	1	0	0	5	7	17	.381	.327
Richard,Clayton	L	.274	73	20	5	0	0	9	4	15	.308	.342
Throws Left	R	.320	128	41	11	0	5	20	9	14	.365	.523
Richmond,Scott	L	.426	61	26	9	2	2	5	1	10	.453	.738
Throws Right	R	.128	47	6	0	1	0	6	1	10	.143	.170
Ridgway,Jeff	L	.133	15	2	1	0	0	0	0	4	.133	.200
Throws Left	R	.238	21	5	0	0	3	6	1	4	.304	.667
Rincon,Juan	L	.323	96	31	6	0	4	20	14	19	.414	.510
Throws Right	R	.279	129	36	6	0	4	24	10	20	.340	.419
Rincon,Ricardo	L	.182	11	2	1	0	1	3	1	2	.250	.545
Throws Left	R	.500	4	2	0	0	0	1	0	1	.500	.500
Ring,Royce	L	.264	53	14	4	0	1	11	5	13	.339	.396
Throws Left	R	.419	43	18	6	1	1	10	5	3	.471	.674
Riske,David	L	.359	64	23	2	0	2	13	14	12	.468	.484
Throws Right	R	.240	100	24	7	2	4	14	11	15	.307	.470
Rivera,Mariano	L	.147	129	19	0	0	2	5	4	39	.173	.194
Throws Right	R	.183	120	22	5	0	2	9	2	38	.208	.275
Rivera,Saul	L	.271	170	46	5	0	1	16	15	33	.326	.318
Throws Right	R	.284	155	44	7	0	2	25	20	32	.365	.368
Robertson,Connor	L	.250	8	2	1	0	0	1	2	0	.400	.375
Throws Right	R	.300	20	6	2	0	1	5	0	2	.333	.550
Robertson,David	L	.259	54	14	1	0	0	4	8	15	.349	.278
Throws Right	R	.254	59	15	1	0	3	16	7	21	.324	.424

Pitcher	vs	Avg	AB	H	2B	3B	HR	RBI	BB	SO	OBP	Slg
Robertson,Nate	L	.323	223	72	13	1	8	34	12	34	.360	.498
Throws Left	R	.311	470	146	40	4	18	70	50	74	.378	.528
Rodney,Fernando	L	.256	82	21	3	0	2	15	13	23	.354	.366
Throws Right	R	.186	70	13	7	2	1	8	17	26	.363	.386
Rodriguez,Francisco	L	.227	128	29	8	0	2	15	22	46	.346	.336
Throws Right	R	.205	122	25	5	0	2	10	12	31	.276	.295
Rodriguez,Wandy	L	.282	124	35	6	3	5	15	5	34	.311	.500
Throws Left	R	.248	407	101	19	2	9	46	39	97	.318	.371
Roenicke,Josh	L	.600	5	3	2	0	0	4	0	1	.667	1.000
Throws Right	R	.300	10	3	2	0	0	3	2	5	.417	.500
Rogers,Kenny	L	.293	184	54	12	1	6	24	24	41	.379	.467
Throws Left	R	.315	501	158	43	2	16	76	47	41	.376	.505
Romero,J.C.	L	.102	98	10	2	0	1	9	11	24	.193	.153
Throws Left	R	.282	110	31	7	0	4	21	27	28	.444	.455
Romo,Sergio	L	.083	48	4	2	0	0	3	5	10	.170	.125
Throws Right	R	.176	68	12	3	0	3	12	3	23	.240	.353
Rosa,Carlos	L	.333	6	2	2	0	0	4	0	2	.333	.667
Throws Right	R	.167	6	1	0	0	0	0	0	1	.167	.167
Rosales,Leo	L	.286	42	12	2	0	0	2	11	6	.444	.333
Throws Right	R	.263	76	20	6	1	2	15	4	12	.296	.447
Rowland-Smith,Ryan	L	.311	148	46	7	0	6	20	19	30	.392	.480
Throws Left	R	.224	303	68	20	1	7	25	29	47	.291	.366
Rundles,Rich	L	.167	12	2	0	0	0	1	3	6	.333	.167
Throws Left	R	.429	7	3	1	0	0	1	0	0	.429	.571
Rupe,Josh	L	.308	159	49	13	1	3	30	24	16	.394	.459
Throws Right	R	.262	168	44	7	2	5	21	22	37	.371	.417
Rusch,Glendon	L	.257	109	28	5	1	2	11	1	19	.261	.376
Throws Left	R	.296	223	66	16	2	8	39	24	36	.359	.493
Russell,Adam	L	.292	48	14	4	0	1	6	7	12	.375	.438
Throws Right	R	.291	55	16	2	0	0	10	3	10	.350	.327
Ryan,B.J.	L	.230	61	14	2	1	2	7	11	20	.373	.393
Throws Left	R	.211	152	32	7	1	2	11	17	38	.292	.309
Ryu,Jae Kuk	L	.000	2	0	0	0	0	0	0	0	.000	.000
Throws Right	R	.000	2	0	0	0	0	0	1	1	.333	.000
Saarloos,Kirk	L	.385	52	20	2	0	1	8	3	5	.411	.481
Throws Right	R	.283	60	17	2	0	1	12	1	7	.295	.367
Sabathia,CC	L	.205	234	48	7	1	5	21	15	89	.261	.308
Throws Left	R	.247	708	175	31	0	14	56	44	162	.293	.350
Sadler,Billy	L	.193	57	11	2	0	1	5	10	14	.313	.281
Throws Right	R	.228	101	23	3	1	5	20	17	28	.375	.426
Saito,Takashi	L	.244	86	21	3	0	1	9	7	24	.298	.314
Throws Right	R	.209	91	19	7	0	0	5	9	36	.291	.286
Salas,Juan	L	.300	10	3	1	0	0	1	3	0	.462	.400
Throws Right	R	.154	13	2	2	0	0	1	1	8	.214	.308
Salas,Marino	L	.519	27	14	2	0	2	9	7	2	.600	.815
Throws Right	R	.256	43	11	1	0	2	7	7	7	.385	.419
Samardzija,Jeff	L	.167	48	8	2	0	0	5	8	12	.281	.208
Throws Right	R	.276	58	16	3	0	0	8	7	13	.364	.328
Sampson,Chris	L	.273	172	47	12	0	4	22	17	22	.333	.413
Throws Right	R	.261	272	71	21	0	4	35	6	39	.283	.382
Sanches,Brian	L	.368	19	7	1	0	0	8	3	1	.458	.421
Throws Right	R	.321	28	9	1	0	2	10	2	9	.367	.571
Sanchez,Anibal	L	.340	106	36	6	0	4	19	21	21	.458	.509
Throws Right	R	.188	96	18	4	0	3	14	6	29	.255	.323
Sanchez,Duaner	L	.200	100	20	4	0	3	9	13	19	.292	.330
Throws Right	R	.268	127	34	7	0	3	12	10	25	.333	.394
Sanchez,Humberto	L	.000	3	0	0	0	0	0	2	0	.400	.000
Throws Right	R	.333	3	1	0	0	0	1	0	1	.333	.333
Sanchez,Jonathan	L	.235	132	31	6	2	5	16	7	46	.287	.424
Throws Left	R	.263	467	123	33	1	9	62	68	111	.359	.396
Sanchez,Romulo	L	.294	17	5	1	0	0	4	2	1	.333	.353
Throws Right	R	.290	31	9	2	1	0	1	4	2	.389	.419
Santana,Ervin	L	.240	420	101	20	2	14	48	31	108	.302	.398
Throws Right	R	.234	414	97	12	2	9	37	16	106	.263	.338
Santana,Johan	L	.247	239	59	10	0	8	19	13	60	.289	.389
Throws Left	R	.227	648	147	26	5	15	48	50	146	.285	.352
Sarfate,Dennis	L	.198	131	26	4	1	3	16	36	38	.373	.313
Throws Right	R	.234	154	36	3	1	5	28	26	48	.362	.364
Saunders,Joe	L	.260	169	44	3	0	2	12	12	26	.319	.314
Throws Left	R	.250	571	143	29	1	19	60	41	77	.304	.405
Scherzer,Max	L	.319	91	29	3	0	2	12	13	20	.396	.418
Throws Right	R	.167	114	19	2	0	3	8	8	46	.252	.263
Schoeneweis,Scott	L	.178	101	18	1	0	3	11	6	25	.243	.277
Throws Left	R	.333	111	37	8	1	4	21	17	9	.423	.532
Schroder,Chris	L	.300	10	3	0	0	1	2	4	3	.500	.600
Throws Right	R	.300	10	3	0	0	1	2	2	0	.417	.600

Pitchers vs. Left-Handed and Right-Handed Batters

Pitcher	vs	Avg	AB	H	2B	3B	HR	RBI	BB	SO	OBP	Slg
Seanez,Rudy	L	.247	77	19	3	0	2	10	13	16	.355	.364
Throws Right	R	.232	82	19	5	1	0	9	12	14	.330	.317
Seay,Bobby	L	.303	109	33	8	0	1	18	10	28	.366	.404
Throws Left	R	.252	103	26	3	0	3	12	15	30	.342	.369
Serrano,Alex	L	.500	2	1	1	0	0	0	0	0	.500	1.000
Throws Right	R	.000	2	0	0	0	0	0	0	1	.000	.000
Sheets,Ben	L	.256	379	97	28	4	7	40	25	80	.302	.406
Throws Right	R	.226	372	84	21	2	10	31	22	78	.266	.374
Shell,Steven	L	.253	75	19	4	1	2	6	8	12	.341	.413
Throws Right	R	.150	100	15	1	0	3	12	12	29	.239	.250
Sherrill,George	L	.190	63	12	2	0	1	9	7	30	.264	.270
Throws Left	R	.254	138	35	7	0	5	26	26	28	.373	.413
Shields,James	L	.255	408	104	29	3	12	37	24	85	.306	.429
Throws Right	R	.253	411	104	18	1	12	45	16	75	.291	.389
Shields,Scot	L	.209	115	24	5	0	1	6	15	43	.300	.278
Throws Right	R	.262	122	32	3	0	5	16	14	21	.345	.410
Shouse,Brian	L	.180	100	18	5	0	2	11	2	28	.196	.290
Throws Left	R	.301	93	28	5	0	3	21	12	5	.377	.452
Silva,Carlos	L	.348	348	121	25	1	15	55	20	40	.381	.555
Throws Right	R	.312	295	92	17	4	5	50	12	29	.342	.447
Simon,Alfredo	L	.243	37	9	1	1	2	5	1	7	.275	.486
Throws Right	R	.412	17	7	0	1	2	7	1	1	.474	.882
Slaten,Doug	L	.232	56	13	2	0	2	3	7	14	.317	.375
Throws Left	R	.282	71	20	9	0	2	11	7	6	.373	.493
Slocum,Brian	L	.571	7	4	1	0	0	4	0	1	.500	.714
Throws Right	R	.667	6	4	0	0	2	2	0	0	.714	1.667
Slowey,Kevin	L	.277	285	79	19	3	13	40	21	66	.330	.502
Throws Right	R	.246	334	82	19	0	9	29	3	57	.254	.383
Smith,Chris	L	.200	40	8	3	0	1	7	3	7	.256	.350
Throws Right	R	.345	29	10	1	0	5	11	4	6	.412	.897
Smith,Greg	L	.232	168	39	9	3	4	20	7	32	.270	.393
Throws Left	R	.247	527	130	29	2	17	58	80	79	.342	.406
Smith,Joe	L	.320	50	16	5	1	0	3	11	7	.443	.460
Throws Right	R	.192	182	35	4	2	4	23	20	45	.286	.302
Smoltz,John	L	.226	62	14	4	1	2	7	5	20	.284	.419
Throws Right	R	.234	47	11	3	0	0	0	3	16	.280	.298
Snell,Ian	L	.314	309	97	19	4	10	46	55	46	.415	.498
Throws Right	R	.295	353	104	22	5	8	52	34	89	.356	.453
Snyder,Kyle	L	.333	3	1	0	0	1	2	0	0	.333	1.333
Throws Right	R	.333	3	1	0	0	0	0	2	1	.600	.333
Sonnanstine,Andy	L	.265	359	95	23	1	11	51	20	55	.303	.426
Throws Right	R	.289	405	117	31	5	10	47	17	69	.319	.464
Soria,Joakim	L	.167	120	20	1	0	4	9	14	32	.261	.275
Throws Right	R	.171	111	19	4	0	1	5	5	34	.233	.234
Soriano,Rafael	L	.222	18	4	1	0	1	3	6	6	.417	.444
Throws Right	R	.103	29	3	2	0	0	1	3	10	.212	.172
Sosa,Jorge	L	.375	32	12	4	0	2	13	5	4	.459	.688
Throws Right	R	.295	61	18	3	0	2	11	6	8	.358	.443
Sowers,Jeremy	L	.258	124	32	10	0	7	20	12	18	.333	.508
Throws Left	R	.303	360	109	28	0	11	57	27	46	.350	.472
Speier,Justin	L	.288	118	34	7	1	10	21	16	26	.382	.619
Throws Right	R	.240	146	35	9	0	5	21	11	30	.303	.404
Speier,Ryan	L	.272	81	22	4	0	2	15	12	14	.379	.395
Throws Right	R	.273	110	30	4	1	1	11	6	19	.314	.355
Speigner,Levale	L	.300	20	6	0	1	0	5	4	0	.440	.400
Throws Right	R	.583	12	7	0	0	1	3	2	1	.667	.833
Springer,Russ	L	.277	65	18	5	0	3	9	7	18	.356	.492
Throws Right	R	.176	119	21	1	0	1	9	11	27	.246	.210
Stetter,Mitch	L	.158	38	6	1	0	1	2	7	19	.304	.263
Throws Left	R	.170	47	8	2	0	1	7	12	12	.371	.277
Stockman,Phil	L	.000	7	0	0	0	0	0	1	1	.222	.000
Throws Right	R	.125	16	2	0	1	0	0	3	8	.263	.250
Stokes,Brian	L	.316	57	18	2	0	3	7	7	15	.391	.509
Throws Right	R	.250	68	17	2	0	2	11	1	11	.250	.368
Street,Huston	L	.200	105	21	4	1	5	11	16	30	.309	.400
Throws Right	R	.250	148	37	9	1	1	18	11	39	.298	.345
Stults,Eric	L	.314	35	11	2	0	2	6	0	6	.314	.543
Throws Left	R	.233	116	27	5	0	4	8	13	24	.315	.379
Sturtze,Tanyon	L	.000	3	0	0	0	0	0	1	0	.250	.000
Throws Right	R	.200	5	1	1	0	0	0	0	1	.200	.400
Suppan,Jeff	L	.288	354	102	18	0	15	56	36	49	.354	.466
Throws Right	R	.308	341	105	19	1	15	47	31	41	.368	.501
Swindle,R.J.	L	.333	9	3	0	0	0	3	0	2	.333	.333
Throws Left	R	.462	13	6	0	0	2	5	2	2	.533	.923
Talbot,Mitch	L	.364	11	4	1	0	2	7	7	2	.611	1.000
Throws Right	R	.387	31	12	4	0	1	6	4	3	.472	.613

Pitcher	vs	Avg	AB	H	2B	3B	HR	RBI	BB	SO	OBP	Slg
Tallet,Brian	L	.257	101	26	5	1	0	9	10	19	.327	.327
Throws Left	R	.230	113	26	4	0	4	13	12	28	.302	.372
Tankersley,Taylor	L	.360	25	9	1	1	0	9	4	5	.467	.480
Throws Left	R	.265	49	13	3	0	6	11	4	8	.321	.694
Taschner,Jack	L	.279	104	29	2	2	2	21	10	23	.339	.394
Throws Left	R	.308	91	28	8	0	3	15	14	16	.406	.495
Taubenheim,Ty	L	.286	14	4	1	0	0	1	1	2	.333	.357
Throws Right	R	.333	9	3	1	0	0	1	2	2	.417	.444
Tavarez,Julian	L	.374	107	40	5	2	2	21	15	20	.447	.514
Throws Right	R	.270	122	33	7	0	3	21	13	31	.353	.402
Tejeda,Robinson	L	.225	80	18	4	1	3	16	6	19	.276	.413
Throws Right	R	.115	78	9	1	0	1	9	18	26	.283	.167
Thatcher,Joe	L	.414	29	12	4	0	3	14	2	9	.424	.862
Throws Left	R	.370	81	30	4	1	1	15	11	8	.441	.481
Thomas,Justin	L	.571	14	8	0	1	0	6	1	0	.600	.714
Throws Left	R	.200	5	1	0	0	0	0	1	2	.333	.200
Thompson,Brad	L	.279	104	29	7	2	3	16	9	11	.330	.471
Throws Right	R	.303	142	43	11	1	2	19	10	21	.359	.437
Thompson,Daryl	L	.308	26	8	2	0	1	2	6	5	.438	.500
Throws Right	R	.343	35	12	2	0	2	7	1	1	.378	.571
Thompson,Rich	L	.400	5	2	1	0	0	2	1	0	.500	.600
Throws Right	R	.400	5	2	1	0	0	3	1	1	.500	.600
Thornton,Matt	L	.170	112	19	0	0	2	14	11	46	.256	.223
Throws Left	R	.218	133	29	7	0	3	20	8	31	.261	.338
Threets,Erick	L	.400	5	2	1	0	0	2	3	1	.667	.600
Throws Left	R	.281	32	9	3	0	1	3	6	5	.425	.469
Timlin,Mike	L	.337	95	32	6	3	6	23	9	17	.394	.653
Throws Right	R	.269	104	28	6	0	3	12	11	15	.336	.413
Tomko,Brett	L	.283	145	41	9	0	6	25	12	27	.333	.469
Throws Right	R	.298	141	42	13	1	5	24	6	22	.327	.511
Torres,Salomon	L	.258	132	34	3	0	3	19	22	25	.363	.348
Throws Right	R	.250	164	41	7	0	3	19	11	26	.306	.348
Traber,Billy	L	.410	39	16	3	0	2	10	6	8	.511	.641
Throws Left	R	.219	32	7	0	0	1	5	1	3	.242	.313
Trachsel,Steve	L	.244	82	20	4	1	4	11	15	8	.361	.463
Throws Right	R	.398	83	33	10	0	6	24	12	8	.479	.735
Troncoso,Ramon	L	.254	59	15	3	0	2	11	4	16	.297	.407
Throws Right	R	.278	79	22	5	1	0	13	8	22	.359	.367
Tucker,Ryan	L	.342	79	27	4	1	4	21	11	17	.429	.570
Throws Right	R	.264	72	19	4	0	4	10	12	11	.372	.486
Turnbow,Derrick	L	.500	12	6	2	0	1	6	5	0	.667	.917
Throws Right	R	.353	17	6	2	0	0	5	8	5	.560	.471
Valdez,Merkin	L	.346	26	9	1	0	1	2	3	4	.414	.500
Throws Right	R	.152	33	5	2	0	0	2	4	9	.282	.212
Valverde,Jose	L	.190	121	23	6	1	4	9	16	37	.293	.355
Throws Right	R	.252	155	39	6	2	6	21	7	46	.282	.432
Van Benschoten,John	L	.418	55	23	5	0	6	18	10	14	.522	.836
Throws Right	R	.304	46	14	4	0	1	10	10	7	.439	.457
VandenHurk,Rick	L	.300	30	9	1	0	0	3	8	10	.462	.333
Throws Right	R	.367	30	11	2	0	1	6	2	10	.424	.533
Vargas,Claudio	L	.323	62	20	3	1	1	12	4	6	.364	.452
Throws Right	R	.178	73	13	0	0	3	4	7	14	.265	.301
Vazquez,Javier	L	.259	413	107	30	5	14	56	39	110	.326	.458
Throws Right	R	.266	402	107	24	2	11	45	22	90	.308	.418
Veras,Jose	L	.217	92	20	1	1	5	16	19	36	.354	.413
Throws Right	R	.254	126	32	10	1	2	5	10	27	.319	.397
Verlander,Justin	L	.254	355	90	17	0	8	40	56	72	.353	.369
Throws Right	R	.254	414	105	22	1	10	56	31	91	.324	.384
Villanueva,Carlos	L	.227	198	45	6	2	6	14	15	47	.285	.369
Throws Right	R	.300	223	67	11	0	12	35	15	46	.349	.511
Villarreal,Oscar	L	.258	62	16	0	0	6	11	4	7	.313	.548
Throws Right	R	.306	85	26	2	3	6	12	13	14	.400	.612
Villone,Ron	L	.176	85	15	4	1	2	17	16	27	.311	.318
Throws Left	R	.300	100	30	8	0	2	14	21	23	.421	.440
Vizcaino,Luis	L	.372	86	32	4	2	8	19	8	21	.432	.744
Throws Right	R	.170	94	16	4	0	2	10	11	28	.252	.277
Volquez,Edinson	L	.249	374	93	17	3	6	40	47	94	.342	.358
Throws Right	R	.214	346	74	19	1	8	35	46	112	.316	.344
Volstad,Chris	L	.243	169	41	7	1	1	16	19	25	.325	.314
Throws Right	R	.236	148	35	8	0	2	10	17	27	.327	.331
Wade,Cory	L	.211	109	23	1	2	2	9	3	25	.243	.312
Throws Right	R	.194	144	28	4	1	5	12	12	26	.266	.340
Waechter,Doug	L	.303	109	33	6	1	4	18	9	14	.358	.486
Throws Right	R	.216	139	30	8	0	3	12	12	32	.281	.338
Wagner,Billy	L	.220	41	9	1	0	0	3	4	18	.283	.244
Throws Left	R	.174	132	23	5	0	4	16	6	34	.210	.303

Pitchers vs. Left-Handed and Right-Handed Batters

Pitcher	vs	Avg	AB	H	2B	3B	HR	RBI	BB	SO	OBP	Slg
Wainwright,Adam	L	.264	193	51	14	3	6	20	14	43	.311	.461
Throws Right	R	.234	304	71	15	1	6	27	20	48	.285	.349
Wakefield,Tim	L	.243	280	68	8	2	9	32	23	44	.306	.382
Throws Right	R	.218	395	86	20	0	16	45	37	73	.299	.390
Walker,Jamie	L	.304	92	28	3	1	7	25	4	17	.327	.587
Throws Left	R	.352	71	25	4	1	5	15	7	7	.418	.648
Walker,Tyler	L	.319	72	23	6	1	4	12	6	19	.372	.597
Throws Right	R	.186	129	24	4	0	3	13	15	30	.274	.287
Walrond,Les	L	.154	13	2	1	0	0	4	3	6	.313	.231
Throws Left	R	.440	25	11	3	0	0	3	6	6	.548	.560
Wang,Chien-Ming	L	.261	176	46	6	0	4	24	23	20	.347	.364
Throws Right	R	.238	185	44	13	0	0	15	12	34	.290	.308
Washburn,Jarrod	L	.252	159	40	7	2	3	15	10	30	.298	.377
Throws Left	R	.299	448	134	35	2	16	63	40	57	.361	.493
Wassermann,Ehren	L	.364	22	8	2	1	0	3	4	5	.444	.545
Throws Right	R	.322	59	19	4	2	0	15	10	4	.429	.458
Waters,Chris	L	.303	66	20	6	1	3	12	9	8	.385	.561
Throws Left	R	.263	190	50	10	1	6	20	20	25	.338	.421
Weathers,David	L	.245	106	26	6	0	0	5	14	18	.333	.302
Throws Right	R	.296	169	50	11	3	6	17	16	28	.365	.503
Weaver,Jered	L	.243	342	83	16	2	14	37	33	72	.313	.424
Throws Right	R	.266	338	90	22	4	6	37	21	80	.313	.408
Webb,Brandon	L	.265	434	115	19	2	6	51	46	65	.336	.359
Throws Right	R	.219	416	91	14	1	7	34	19	118	.265	.308
Wellemeyer,Todd	L	.256	309	79	22	0	12	30	28	46	.318	.443
Throws Right	R	.237	417	99	25	1	13	48	34	88	.302	.396
Wells,Jared	L	.333	12	4	1	0	0	2	3	1	.467	.417
Throws Right	R	.304	23	7	0	0	2	7	4	4	.407	.565
Wells,Kip	L	.266	64	17	5	0	1	11	15	12	.405	.391
Throws Right	R	.286	77	22	4	0	3	12	15	19	.415	.455
Wells,Randy	L	.000	7	0	0	0	0	0	0	0	.000	.000
Throws Right	R	.000	8	0	0	0	0	1	3	1	.273	.000
Westbrook,Jake	L	.238	63	15	2	0	1	4	5	7	.290	.317
Throws Right	R	.273	66	18	2	0	4	9	2	12	.300	.485
Wheeler,Dan	L	.215	93	20	7	0	3	13	9	18	.282	.387
Throws Right	R	.163	147	24	3	1	7	13	13	35	.230	.340
White,Bill	L	.200	5	1	1	0	0	0	3	1	.500	.400
Throws Left	R	.429	14	6	3	0	1	8	8	0	.636	.857
Willis,Dontrelle	L	.125	24	3	1	1	0	1	6	9	.300	.250
Throws Left	R	.242	62	15	3	1	4	16	29	9	.489	.516
Wilson,Brian	L	.202	114	23	1	0	2	11	17	31	.301	.263
Throws Right	R	.320	122	39	4	2	5	22	11	36	.381	.508
Wilson,C.J.	L	.265	49	13	3	2	1	8	11	13	.400	.469
Throws Left	R	.269	134	36	7	0	7	28	16	28	.353	.478
Wise,Matt	L	.364	11	4	0	0	1	4	1	1	.417	.636
Throws Right	R	.300	20	6	2	0	1	1	2	5	.364	.550
Wolf,Randy	L	.283	152	43	10	0	5	21	16	35	.368	.447
Throws Left	R	.258	574	148	33	0	16	68	55	127	.329	.399
Wolfe,Brian	L	.273	33	9	2	0	1	4	3	6	.324	.424
Throws Right	R	.205	44	9	3	0	1	5	3	8	.255	.341
Wood,Kerry	L	.209	115	24	8	0	1	8	10	42	.300	.304
Throws Right	R	.227	132	30	10	2	2	18	8	42	.278	.379
Woods,Jake	L	.317	41	13	3	0	2	10	2	4	.364	.537
Throws Left	R	.265	34	9	3	0	3	8	9	5	.419	.618
Worrell,Mark	L	.222	9	2	0	0	1	3	2	2	.364	.556
Throws Right	R	.462	13	6	2	0	0	0	2	2	.533	.615
Wright,Jamey	L	.286	147	42	7	1	1	30	27	25	.403	.367
Throws Right	R	.280	182	51	7	0	4	27	8	35	.323	.385
Wright,Wesley	L	.207	92	19	6	1	1	15	8	29	.295	.326
Throws Left	R	.220	118	26	7	0	7	19	26	28	.361	.458
Wuertz,Mike	L	.230	61	14	2	1	3	10	7	11	.309	.443
Throws Right	R	.288	104	30	6	0	1	16	13	19	.358	.375
Yabu,Keiichi	L	.355	93	33	6	0	1	12	15	13	.450	.452
Throws Right	R	.181	166	30	6	1	2	15	17	35	.284	.265
Yabuta,Yasuhiko	L	.185	65	12	1	0	4	9	8	13	.274	.385
Throws Right	R	.345	84	29	8	1	2	8	9	12	.404	.536
Yates,Tyler	L	.303	109	33	8	1	2	14	14	20	.387	.450
Throws Right	R	.224	174	39	9	0	4	18	27	43	.330	.345
Young,Chris	L	.259	174	45	12	1	7	23	28	39	.365	.460
Throws Right	R	.189	206	39	9	0	6	16	20	54	.260	.320
Zambrano,Carlos	L	.235	361	85	15	2	7	32	48	57	.328	.346
Throws Right	R	.247	352	87	13	3	11	45	24	73	.303	.395
Ziegler,Brad	L	.280	93	26	4	2	2	6	13	11	.370	.430
Throws Right	R	.198	106	21	4	0	0	6	9	19	.256	.236
Zink,Charlie	L	.400	10	4	1	0	0	5	0	0	.400	.500
Throws Right	R	.500	14	7	3	0	0	1	1	1	.533	.714

Pitcher	vs	Avg	AB	H	2B	3B	HR	RBI	BB	SO	OBP	Slg
Zito,Barry	L	.213	150	32	4	2	1	21	22	28	.316	.287
Throws Left	R	.285	540	154	36	3	15	86	80	92	.373	.446
Zumaya,Joel	L	.161	31	5	1	0	1	5	13	9	.400	.290
Throws Right	R	.317	60	19	5	1	2	12	9	13	.406	.533
AL	L	.267	-	-	-	-	-	-	-	-	.341	.421
	R	.264	-	-	-	-	-	-	-	-	.326	.412
NL	L	.266	-	-	-	-	-	-	-	-	.341	.421
	R	.260	-	-	-	-	-	-	-	-	.328	.414
MLB	L	.267	-	-	-	-	-	-	-	-	.341	.421
	R	.262	-	-	-	-	-	-	-	-	.327	.413

2008 Leader Boards

Many of our leader boards are derived from the complex pitch data collected by Baseball Info Solutions. The pitch charting data at BIS is the most complete and thorough in baseball, and the information found in these leader boards cannot be found anywhere else. We have everything from which batters put up the highest OPS on sliders, to which second basemen had the highest pivot percentages in 2008.

Sometimes these leader boards are enough to see what went right—or wrong—with an entire ballclub. For example, many baseball fans are used to seeing intentional walks given out to the big boppers—guys who hit in the heart of the order. But last year, Cleveland Indians leadoff man Grady Sizemore was third in the AL in intentional bases on balls (14). Clearly, pitchers were not afraid of anyone that was hitting behind him.

Likewise, the much-maligned New York Mets bullpen shouldered much of the blame when they missed the postseason again in 2008. But do the leader boards bear this out? We show the leaders for things like Easy Saves, Relief Losses, Relief Games, Relief Opponent Batting Average, and Relief OBP (1st Batter Faced). Did the Mets' bullpen earn the criticism, or was the criticism unfairly placed?

Here are some definitions to help clarify parts of the leader boards that may not be familiar to all readers:

OPS stands for "On-Base Plus Slugging." In the past we measured hitter performance against various pitch types by result pitch only. The problem with that approach was that if a hitter regularly looked silly on non-result-pitch curveballs, but mashed just a few along the way, he could look like a great curveball hitter, even though nothing was further from the truth. Bill James designed a formula to rate hitters not only on the result pitches, but on every pitch the batter faced. The hitters you'll now see in these leader boards are a much better representation of the guys who mastered each pitch type this past year.

OutZ is "Pitches Outside the Strike Zone."

Holds Adjusted Saves Percentage is calculated by dividing holds plus saves by holds plus save opportunities. This percentage is also shown in the new Relief Pitchers section as Save/Hold Percentage.

Many of the great storylines from last season are evident in these leader boards—from the tight batting races in both the American and National Leagues, to how Blue Jays starter Roy Halladay redefined the definition of "workhorse" and should arguably be the AL's Cy Young Award winner. Our leader boards offer the great winners and losers of 2008; there are tons of fascinating stories to be found in the statistics that follow.

2008 American League Batting Leaders

Batting Average
(minimum 502 PA)

Mauer,Joe, Min	.328
Pedroia,Dustin, Bos	.326
Bradley,Milton, Tex	.321
Kinsler,Ian, Tex	.319
Ordonez,Magglio, Det	.317
Youkilis,Kevin, Bos	.312
Suzuki,Ichiro, Sea	.310
DeJesus,David, KC	.307
Polanco,Placido, Det	.307
Markakis,Nick, Bal	.306

On Base Percentage
(minimum 502 PA)

Bradley,Milton, Tex	.436
Mauer,Joe, Min	.413
Markakis,Nick, Bal	.406
Quentin,Carlos, CWS	.394
Rodriguez,Alex, NYY	.392
Youkilis,Kevin, Bos	.390
Upton,B.J., TB	.383
Roberts,Brian, Bal	.378
Pena,Carlos, TB	.377
Ordonez,Magglio, Det	.376

Slugging Average
(minimum 502 PA)

Rodriguez,Alex, NYY	.573
Quentin,Carlos, CWS	.571
Youkilis,Kevin, Bos	.569
Bradley,Milton, Tex	.563
Huff,Aubrey, Bal	.552
Dye,Jermaine, CWS	.541
Cabrera,Miguel, Det	.537
Longoria,Evan, TB	.531
Hamilton,Josh, Tex	.530
Guerrero,Vladimir, LAA	.521

Home Runs

Cabrera,Miguel, Det	37
Quentin,Carlos, CWS	36
Rodriguez,Alex, NYY	35
Dye,Jermaine, CWS	34
Thome,Jim, CWS	34
Cust,Jack, Oak	33
Sizemore,Grady, Cle	33
Giambi,Jason, NYY	32
Hamilton,Josh, Tex	32
Huff,Aubrey, Bal	32

Games

Morneau,Justin, Min	163
Ibanez,Raul, Sea	162
Suzuki,Ichiro, Sea	162
Cabrera,Orlando, CWS	161
Cabrera,Miguel, Det	160
Cano,Robinson, NYY	159
Lopez,Jose, Sea	159
Overbay,Lyle, Tor	158
3 tied with	157

Plate Appearances

Suzuki,Ichiro, Sea	749
Sizemore,Grady, Cle	745
Cabrera,Orlando, CWS	730
Pedroia,Dustin, Bos	726
Morneau,Justin, Min	712
Young,Michael, Tex	708
Ibanez,Raul, Sea	707
Iwamura,Akinori, TB	707
Hamilton,Josh, Tex	704
Roberts,Brian, Bal	704

At Bats

Suzuki,Ichiro, Sea	686
Cabrera,Orlando, CWS	661
Pedroia,Dustin, Bos	653
Young,Michael, Tex	645
Lopez,Jose, Sea	644
Ibanez,Raul, Sea	635
Rios,Alex, Tor	635
Sizemore,Grady, Cle	634
Iwamura,Akinori, TB	627
Hamilton,Josh, Tex	624

Hits

Pedroia,Dustin, Bos	213
Suzuki,Ichiro, Sea	213
Lopez,Jose, Sea	191
Hamilton,Josh, Tex	190
Morneau,Justin, Min	187
Cabrera,Orlando, CWS	186
Ibanez,Raul, Sea	186
Rios,Alex, Tor	185
Young,Michael, Tex	183
2 tied with	182

Singles

Suzuki,Ichiro, Sea	180
Cabrera,Orlando, CWS	144
Jeter,Derek, NYY	140
Pedroia,Dustin, Bos	140
Polanco,Placido, Det	133
Young,Michael, Tex	133
Lopez,Jose, Sea	132
Mauer,Joe, Min	132
Iwamura,Akinori, TB	127
Young,Delmon, Min	125

Doubles

Pedroia,Dustin, Bos	54
Roberts,Brian, Bal	51
Huff,Aubrey, Bal	48
Markakis,Nick, Bal	48
Morneau,Justin, Min	47
Rios,Alex, Tor	47
Ibanez,Raul, Sea	43
Youkilis,Kevin, Bos	43
Guillen,Jose, KC	42
Peralta,Jhonny, Cle	42

Triples

Granderson,Curtis, Det	13
Crawford,Carl, TB	10
Iwamura,Akinori, TB	9
Rios,Alex, Tor	8
Roberts,Brian, Bal	8
7 tied with	7

Total Bases

Cabrera,Miguel, Det	331
Hamilton,Josh, Tex	331
Huff,Aubrey, Bal	330
Pedroia,Dustin, Bos	322
Dye,Jermaine, CWS	319
Sizemore,Grady, Cle	318
Morneau,Justin, Min	311
Youkilis,Kevin, Bos	306
Ibanez,Raul, Sea	304
Rios,Alex, Tor	293

Runs Scored

Pedroia,Dustin, Bos	118
Granderson,Curtis, Det	112
Roberts,Brian, Bal	107
Markakis,Nick, Bal	106
Peralta,Jhonny, Cle	104
Rodriguez,Alex, NYY	104
Suzuki,Ichiro, Sea	103
Kinsler,Ian, Tex	102
Young,Michael, Tex	102
Sizemore,Grady, Cle	101

RBI

Hamilton,Josh, Tex	130
Morneau,Justin, Min	129
Cabrera,Miguel, Det	127
Youkilis,Kevin, Bos	115
Ibanez,Raul, Sea	110
Huff,Aubrey, Bal	108
Mora,Melvin, Bal	104
Ordonez,Magglio, Det	103
Rodriguez,Alex, NYY	103
Pena,Carlos, TB	102

Walks

Cust,Jack, Oak	111
Markakis,Nick, Bal	99
Sizemore,Grady, Cle	98
Upton,B.J., TB	97
Pena,Carlos, TB	96
Thome,Jim, CWS	91
Mauer,Joe, Min	84
Roberts,Brian, Bal	82
Swisher,Nick, CWS	82
Bradley,Milton, Tex	80

Strikeouts

Cust,Jack, Oak	197
Pena,Carlos, TB	166
Thome,Jim, CWS	147
Gomez,Carlos, Min	142
Swisher,Nick, CWS	135
Upton,B.J., TB	134
Shoppach,Kelly, Cle	133
Hannahan,Jack, Oak	131
Iwamura,Akinori, TB	131
Teahen,Mark, KC	131

2008 American League Batting Leaders

Intentional Walks			BA Bases Loaded			Sacrifice Hits			Sacrifice Flies	
			(minimum 10 PA)							
Guerrero,Vladimir, LAA	16		Payton,Jay, Bal	.636		Casilla,Alexi, Min	13		Mauer,Joe, Min	11
Morneau,Justin, Min	16		Blake,Casey, Cle	.600		Cabrera,Asdrubal, Cle	11		Morneau,Justin, Min	10
Sizemore,Grady, Cle	14		DeJesus,David, KC	.556		Carroll,Jamey, Cle	10		Cabrera,Miguel, Det	9
Bradley,Milton, Tex	13		Aybar,Erick, LAA	.500		Gathright,Joey, KC	10		Cabrera,Orlando, CWS	9
Ortiz,David, Bos	12		Drew,J.D., Bos	.500		Aybar,Erick, LAA	9		Giambi,Jason, NYY	9
Suzuki,Ichiro, Sea	12		Iwamura,Akinori, TB	.500		Eckstein,David, Tor	9		Hamilton,Josh, Tex	9
Ibanez,Raul, Sea	11		Kubel,Jason, Min	.500		5 tied with	8		Lopez,Jose, Sea	9
Beltre,Adrian, Sea	10		Pedroia,Dustin, Bos	.500					Pedroia,Dustin, Bos	9
Scott,Luke, Bal	10		Quentin,Carlos, CWS	.500					Pena,Carlos, TB	9
4 tied with	9		Span,Denard, Min	.500					Youkilis,Kevin, Bos	9

BA Close & Late			Batting Average w/ RISP			SLG vs. LHP			SLG vs. RHP	
(minimum 50 PA)			(minimum 100 PA)			(minimum 125 PA)			(minimum 377 PA)	
Lowell,Mike, Bos	.391		DeJesus,David, KC	.419		Bradley,Milton, Tex	.651		Huff,Aubrey, Bal	.607
Bradley,Milton, Tex	.380		Kinsler,Ian, Tex	.413		Mora,Melvin, Bal	.622		Rodriguez,Alex, NYY	.603
Anderson,Garret, LAA	.371		Blake,Casey, Cle	.393		Youkilis,Kevin, Bos	.606		Pena,Carlos, TB	.576
Pedroia,Dustin, Bos	.368		Choo,Shin-Soo, Cle	.386		Butler,Billy, KC	.590		Quentin,Carlos, CWS	.574
Abreu,Bobby, NYY	.361		Ramirez,Alexei, CWS	.380		Thames,Marcus, Det	.581		Hamilton,Josh, Tex	.566
Quentin,Carlos, CWS	.351		Youkilis,Kevin, Bos	.374		Guillen,Jose, KC	.575		Youkilis,Kevin, Bos	.560
Guerrero,Vladimir, LAA	.350		Mauer,Joe, Min	.362		Aviles,Mike, KC	.574		Sizemore,Grady, Cle	.548
Izturis,Maicer, LAA	.348		Mora,Melvin, Bal	.360		Beltre,Adrian, Sea	.573		Guerrero,Vladimir, LAA	.539
Matsui,Hideki, NYY	.348		Morneau,Justin, Min	.348		Dye,Jermaine, CWS	.563		Dye,Jermaine, CWS	.532
Sheffield,Gary, Det	.339		Span,Denard, Min	.346		Cabrera,Miguel, Det	.563		Kinsler,Ian, Tex	.530

Leadoff Hitters OBP			Cleanup Hitters SLG			BA vs. LHP			BA vs. RHP	
(minimum 150 PA)			(minimum 150 PA)			(minimum 125 PA)			(minimum 377 PA)	
Roberts,Brian, Bal	.379		Guerrero,Vladimir, LAA	.612		Bartlett,Jason, TB	.379		Kinsler,Ian, Tex	.332
Span,Denard, Min	.378		Cabrera,Miguel, Det	.600		Renteria,Edgar, Det	.366		Pedroia,Dustin, Bos	.331
Kinsler,Ian, Tex	.377		Bradley,Milton, Tex	.577		Mauer,Joe, Min	.361		Damon,Johnny, NYY	.321
DeJesus,David, KC	.376		Rodriguez,Alex, NYY	.569		Aviles,Mike, KC	.348		Huff,Aubrey, Bal	.321
Damon,Johnny, NYY	.376		Youkilis,Kevin, Bos	.569		Bradley,Milton, Tex	.341		Suzuki,Ichiro, Sea	.320
Sizemore,Grady, Cle	.374		Huff,Aubrey, Bal	.555		Butler,Billy, KC	.340		Youkilis,Kevin, Bos	.318
Figgins,Chone, LAA	.373		Dye,Jermaine, CWS	.551		Beltre,Adrian, Sea	.340		Rodriguez,Alex, NYY	.316
Granderson,Curtis, Det	.363		Ramirez,Manny, Bos	.533		Ordonez,Magglio, Det	.328		Ordonez,Magglio, Det	.314
Suzuki,Ichiro, Sea	.360		Peralta,Jhonny, Cle	.506		Polanco,Placido, Det	.321		Hamilton,Josh, Tex	.313
Eckstein,David, Tor	.354		Cust,Jack, Oak	.500		Abreu,Bobby, NYY	.315		Mauer,Joe, Min	.312

Home BA			Away BA			OBP vs. LHP			OBP vs. RHP	
(minimum 251 PA)			(minimum 251 PA)			(minimum 125 PA)			(minimum 377 PA)	
Mauer,Joe, Min	.362		Markakis,Nick, Bal	.330		Bradley,Milton, Tex	.476		Pena,Carlos, TB	.418
Ordonez,Magglio, Det	.350		Peralta,Jhonny, Cle	.318		Renteria,Edgar, Det	.443		Markakis,Nick, Bal	.418
Hamilton,Josh, Tex	.345		Polanco,Placido, Det	.315		Beltre,Adrian, Sea	.421		Mauer,Joe, Min	.412
Pedroia,Dustin, Bos	.344		Morneau,Justin, Min	.314		Upton,B.J., TB	.415		Quentin,Carlos, CWS	.401
Dye,Jermaine, CWS	.336		Guerrero,Vladimir, LAA	.312		Mauer,Joe, Min	.415		Morneau,Justin, Min	.401
Kinsler,Ian, Tex	.335		DeJesus,David, KC	.311		Bartlett,Jason, TB	.411		Rodriguez,Alex, NYY	.391
Renteria,Edgar, Det	.328		Pedroia,Dustin, Bos	.309		Ordonez,Magglio, Det	.406		Damon,Johnny, NYY	.389
Youkilis,Kevin, Bos	.326		Ibanez,Raul, Sea	.309		Youkilis,Kevin, Bos	.403		Youkilis,Kevin, Bos	.386
Rodriguez,Alex, NYY	.324		Suzuki,Ichiro, Sea	.305		Span,Denard, Min	.402		Sizemore,Grady, Cle	.386
Sizemore,Grady, Cle	.322		Kinsler,Ian, Tex	.303		Rodriguez,Alex, NYY	.395		Kinsler,Ian, Tex	.385

2008 American League Batting Leaders

Stolen Bases

Ellsbury,Jacoby, Bos	50
Upton,B.J., TB	44
Suzuki,Ichiro, Sea	43
Roberts,Brian, Bal	40
Sizemore,Grady, Cle	38
Figgins,Chone, LAA	34
Gomez,Carlos, Min	33
Rios,Alex, Tor	32
Damon,Johnny, NYY	29
Kinsler,Ian, Tex	26

Caught Stealing

Upton,B.J., TB	16
Figgins,Chone, LAA	13
Abreu,Bobby, NYY	11
Ellsbury,Jacoby, Bos	11
Gomez,Carlos, Min	11
Roberts,Brian, Bal	10
Ramirez,Alexei, CWS	9
Damon,Johnny, NYY	8
DeJesus,David, KC	8
Rios,Alex, Tor	8

Highest SB Success Pct
(minimum 20 SBA)

Pedroia,Dustin, Bos	95.2
Kinsler,Ian, Tex	92.9
Suzuki,Ichiro, Sea	91.5
Sizemore,Grady, Cle	88.4
Rodriguez,Alex, NYY	85.7
Gathright,Joey, KC	84.0
Ellsbury,Jacoby, Bos	82.0
Davis,Rajai, Oak	80.6
Rios,Alex, Tor	80.0
Roberts,Brian, Bal	80.0

Lowest SB Success Pct
(minimum 20 SBA)

Ramirez,Alexei, CWS	59.1
Abreu,Bobby, NYY	66.7
Punto,Nick, Min	71.4
Span,Denard, Min	72.0
Figgins,Chone, LAA	72.3
Upton,B.J., TB	73.3
Crisp,Coco, Bos	74.1
Gomez,Carlos, Min	75.0
Cabrera,Orlando, CWS	76.0
Bartlett,Jason, TB	76.9

Steals of Third

Suzuki,Ichiro, Sea	12
Bartlett,Jason, TB	9
Rios,Alex, Tor	9
Roberts,Brian, Bal	9
Cabrera,Orlando, CWS	8
Ellsbury,Jacoby, Bos	8
Kinsler,Ian, Tex	8
4 tied with	6

Grounded Into DP

Guerrero,Vladimir, LAA	27
Ordonez,Magglio, Det	27
Peralta,Jhonny, Cle	26
Jeter,Derek, NYY	24
Overbay,Lyle, Tor	24
Betancourt,Yuniesky, Sea	23
Butler,Billy, KC	23
Guillen,Jose, KC	23
Mauer,Joe, Min	21
3 tied with	20

Grounded Into DP Pct
(minimum 50 GIDP Ops)

Mathis,Jeff, LAA	2.00
Iwamura,Akinori, TB	2.20
Carroll,Jamey, Cle	2.56
Aybar,Erick, LAA	2.67
Sizemore,Grady, Cle	4.24
Hannahan,Jack, Oak	4.76
Boggs,Brandon, Tex	5.08
Gathright,Joey, KC	5.26
Vazquez,Ramon, Tex	5.33
2 tied with	5.36

Hit By Pitch

Giambi,Jason, NYY	22
Quentin,Carlos, CWS	20
Garko,Ryan, Cle	15
Rodriguez,Alex, NYY	14
Pena,Carlos, TB	12
Youkilis,Kevin, Bos	12
5 tied with	11

Pitches Seen

Sizemore,Grady, Cle	3051
Abreu,Bobby, NYY	2937
Iwamura,Akinori, TB	2930
Roberts,Brian, Bal	2844
Ibanez,Raul, Sea	2749
Pedroia,Dustin, Bos	2708
Markakis,Nick, Bal	2687
Granderson,Curtis, Det	2678
Young,Michael, Tex	2678
Suzuki,Ichiro, Sea	2672

At Bats Per Home Run
(minimum 502 PA)

Quentin,Carlos, CWS	13.3
Giambi,Jason, NYY	14.3
Rodriguez,Alex, NYY	14.6
Cust,Jack, Oak	14.6
Thome,Jim, CWS	14.8
Pena,Carlos, TB	15.8
Longoria,Evan, TB	16.6
Cabrera,Miguel, Det	16.6
Dye,Jermaine, CWS	17.4
Youkilis,Kevin, Bos	18.6

Highest GB/FB Ratio
(minimum 502 PA)

Suzuki,Ichiro, Sea	2.54
Jeter,Derek, NYY	2.45
Young,Delmon, Min	1.98
Ellsbury,Jacoby, Bos	1.85
Mauer,Joe, Min	1.74
Upton,B.J., TB	1.65
Teahen,Mark, KC	1.60
DeJesus,David, KC	1.59
Abreu,Bobby, NYY	1.59
Figgins,Chone, LAA	1.56

Lowest GB/FB Ratio
(minimum 502 PA)

Millar,Kevin, Bal	0.59
Pena,Carlos, TB	0.63
Giambi,Jason, NYY	0.66
Gordon,Alex, KC	0.66
Ellis,Mark, Oak	0.73
Kinsler,Ian, Tex	0.75
Sizemore,Grady, Cle	0.76
Barton,Daric, Oak	0.77
Youkilis,Kevin, Bos	0.77
Swisher,Nick, CWS	0.78

Pitches Per Plate App
(minimum 502 PA)

Swisher,Nick, CWS	4.53
Cust,Jack, Oak	4.38
Giambi,Jason, NYY	4.30
Abreu,Bobby, NYY	4.29
Granderson,Curtis, Det	4.26
Garko,Ryan, Cle	4.15
Thome,Jim, CWS	4.15
Iwamura,Akinori, TB	4.14
Damon,Johnny, NYY	4.10
Sizemore,Grady, Cle	4.10

Pct Pitches Taken
(minimum 1500 Pitches)

Mauer,Joe, Min	64.6
Abreu,Bobby, NYY	64.5
Drew,J.D., Bos	63.1
Cust,Jack, Oak	62.1
Swisher,Nick, CWS	62.0
Figgins,Chone, LAA	62.0
Carroll,Jamey, Cle	61.6
Granderson,Curtis, Det	60.6
Thome,Jim, CWS	60.5
Sheffield,Gary, Det	60.4

Best BPS on OutZ
(minimum 502 PA)

Scutaro,Marco, Tor	.687
Pedroia,Dustin, Bos	.659
DeJesus,David, KC	.626
Anderson,Garret, LAA	.599
Roberts,Brian, Bal	.595
Polanco,Placido, Det	.588
Renteria,Edgar, Det	.569
Ordonez,Magglio, Det	.556
Guerrero,Vladimir, LAA	.539
Ibanez,Raul, Sea	.536

Worst BPS on OutZ
(minimum 502 PA)

Cust,Jack, Oak	.184
Thome,Jim, CWS	.186
Bradley,Milton, Tex	.207
Pena,Carlos, TB	.225
Hunter,Torii, LAA	.241
Swisher,Nick, CWS	.259
Garko,Ryan, Cle	.270
Millar,Kevin, Bal	.283
Gordon,Alex, KC	.283
Giambi,Jason, NYY	.298

2008 American League Batting Leaders

Best OPS vs Fastballs		Best OPS vs Curveballs		Best OPS vs Changeups		Best OPS vs Sliders	
(minimum 251 PA)		(minimum 50 PA)		(minimum 50 PA)		(minimum 32 PA)	
Quentin,Carlos, CWS	1.101	Quentin,Carlos, CWS	1.063	Ortiz,David, Bos	1.262	Rodriguez,Alex, NYY	1.168
Youkilis,Kevin, Bos	1.053	Hamilton,Josh, Tex	.926	Mora,Melvin, Bal	1.140	Napoli,Mike, LAA	1.100
Huff,Aubrey, Bal	1.038	Kinsler,Ian, Tex	.922	Cabrera,Miguel, Det	1.112	Bradley,Milton, Tex	1.037
Cust,Jack, Oak	1.027	Upton,B.J., TB	.903	Ordonez,Magglio, Det	1.063	Cano,Robinson, NYY	1.034
Hamilton,Josh, Tex	1.016	Markakis,Nick, Bal	.893	Sizemore,Grady, Cle	1.062	Davis,Chris, Tex	.980
Longoria,Evan, TB	.985	Iwamura,Akinori, TB	.865	Thome,Jim, CWS	1.057	Morneau,Justin, Min	.977
Mauer,Joe, Min	.970	Young,Delmon, Min	.861	Aybar,Willy, TB	1.040	Mora,Melvin, Bal	.958
Rodriguez,Alex, NYY	.967	Rodriguez,Alex, NYY	.857	Upton,B.J., TB	.984	Ramirez,Manny, Bos	.958
Kinsler,Ian, Tex	.949	Roberts,Brian, Bal	.845	Kotchman,Casey, LAA	.983	Cabrera,Asdrubal, Cle	.957
Bradley,Milton, Tex	.942	Pena,Carlos, TB	.829	Pena,Carlos, TB	.980	Huff,Aubrey, Bal	.957

OPS		OPS First Half		OPS Second Half		OPS by Catchers	
(minimum 502 PA)		(minimum 260 PA)		(minimum 201 PA)		(minimum 251 PA)	
Bradley,Milton, Tex	.999	Bradley,Milton, Tex	1.049	Teixeira,Mark, LAA	1.081	Napoli,Mike, LAA	.971
Rodriguez,Alex, NYY	.965	Drew,J.D., Bos	.984	Mora,Melvin, Bal	1.073	Shoppach,Kelly, Cle	.877
Quentin,Carlos, CWS	.965	Rodriguez,Alex, NYY	.972	Choo,Shin-Soo, Cle	1.038	Mauer,Joe, Min	.876
Youkilis,Kevin, Bos	.958	Kinsler,Ian, Tex	.945	Youkilis,Kevin, Bos	.998	Navarro,Dioner, TB	.755
Huff,Aubrey, Bal	.912	Youkilis,Kevin, Bos	.933	Pena,Carlos, TB	.978	Laird,Gerald, Tex	.742
Hamilton,Josh, Tex	.901	Hamilton,Josh, Tex	.919	Guerrero,Vladimir, LAA	.972	Pierzynski,A.J., CWS	.731
Markakis,Nick, Bal	.897	Dye,Jermaine, CWS	.915	Huff,Aubrey, Bal	.964	Hernandez,Ramon, Bal	.729
Kinsler,Ian, Tex	.892	Giambi,Jason, NYY	.915	Shoppach,Kelly, Cle	.957	Rodriguez,Ivan, Det-NYY	.715
Cabrera,Miguel, Det	.887	Sizemore,Grady, Cle	.913	Rodriguez,Alex, NYY	.955	Barajas,Rod, Tor	.707
Guerrero,Vladimir, LAA	.886	Ramirez,Manny, Bos	.908	Cabrera,Miguel, Det	.951	Suzuki,Kurt, Oak	.693

OPS by First Basemen		OPS by Second Basemen		OPS by Third Basemen		OPS by Shortstops	
(minimum 251 PA)		(minimum 251 PA)		(minimum 251 PA)		(minimum 251 PA)	
Youkilis,Kevin, Bos	.949	Kinsler,Ian, Tex	.891	Rodriguez,Alex, NYY	.961	Peralta,Jhonny, Cle	.806
Cabrera,Miguel, Det	.893	Pedroia,Dustin, Bos	.864	Longoria,Evan, TB	.867	Aviles,Mike, KC	.800
Morneau,Justin, Min	.872	Roberts,Brian, Bal	.832	Mora,Melvin, Bal	.827	Jeter,Derek, NYY	.763
Pena,Carlos, TB	.872	Ramirez,Alexei, CWS	.812	Lowell,Mike, Bos	.809	Young,Michael, Tex	.745
Giambi,Jason, NYY	.844	Inglett,Joe, Tor	.779	Blake,Casey, Cle	.805	Cabrera,Orlando, CWS	.706
Konerko,Paul, CWS	.792	Polanco,Placido, Det	.770	Gordon,Alex, KC	.786	Renteria,Edgar, Det	.700
Kotchman,Casey, LAA	.775	Kendrick,Howie, LAA	.754	Beltre,Adrian, Sea	.785	Aybar,Erick, LAA	.695
Overbay,Lyle, Tor	.766	Lopez,Jose, Sea	.750	Rolen,Scott, Tor	.780	Betancourt,Yuniesky, Sea	.690
Garko,Ryan, Cle	.753	Grudzielanek,Mark, KC	.746	Guillen,Carlos, Det	.778	Lugo,Julio, Bos	.687
Millar,Kevin, Bal	.737	Iwamura,Akinori, TB	.729	Crede,Joe, CWS	.773	Bartlett,Jason, TB	.679

OPS by Left Fielders		OPS by Center Fielders		OPS by Right Fielders		OPS by Designated Hitters	
(minimum 251 PA)		(minimum 251 PA)		(minimum 251 PA)		(minimum 125 PA)	
Quentin,Carlos, CWS	.965	Sizemore,Grady, Cle	.873	Drew,J.D., Bos	.923	Bradley,Milton, Tex	.972
Ramirez,Manny, Bos	.916	Granderson,Curtis, Det	.863	Markakis,Nick, Bal	.897	Ramirez,Manny, Bos	.971
Scott,Luke, Bal	.869	Hunter,Torii, LAA	.835	Dye,Jermaine, CWS	.895	Guerrero,Vladimir, LAA	.969
Ibanez,Raul, Sea	.847	Ellsbury,Jacoby, Bos	.834	Ordonez,Magglio, Det	.872	Huff,Aubrey, Bal	.926
Cust,Jack, Oak	.839	Hamilton,Josh, Tex	.830	Rios,Alex, Tor	.860	Ortiz,David, Bos	.879
Damon,Johnny, NYY	.810	Wells,Vernon, Tor	.819	Guerrero,Vladimir, LAA	.850	Thome,Jim, CWS	.868
Lind,Adam, Tor	.781	Swisher,Nick, CWS	.802	Abreu,Bobby, NYY	.838	Kubel,Jason, Min	.843
Anderson,Garret, LAA	.761	Upton,B.J., TB	.790	Span,Denard, Min	.825	Cust,Jack, Oak	.829
Young,Delmon, Min	.737	Crisp,Coco, Bos	.755	Gross,Gabe, TB	.798	Guillen,Jose, KC	.823
Crawford,Carl, TB	.722	Suzuki,Ichiro, Sea	.744	Suzuki,Ichiro, Sea	.731	Floyd,Cliff, TB	.806

2008 American League Batting Leaders

OPS Batting Left vs. LHP (minimum 125 PA)		OPS Batting Left vs. RHP (minimum 377 PA)		OPS Batting Right vs. LHP (minimum 125 PA)		OPS Batting Right vs. RHP (minimum 377 PA)	
Mauer,Joe, Min	.939	Pena,Carlos, TB	.994	Bradley,Milton, Tex	1.129	Rodriguez,Alex, NYY	.994
Span,Denard, Min	.873	Huff,Aubrey, Bal	.989	Youkilis,Kevin, Bos	1.009	Quentin,Carlos, CWS	.975
Ibanez,Raul, Sea	.866	Hamilton,Josh, Tex	.950	Renteria,Edgar, Det	1.004	Youkilis,Kevin, Bos	.946
Abreu,Bobby, NYY	.865	Sizemore,Grady, Cle	.934	Beltre,Adrian, Sea	.994	Kinsler,Ian, Tex	.915
Thome,Jim, CWS	.858	Morneau,Justin, Min	.928	Mora,Melvin, Bal	.987	Guerrero,Vladimir, LAA	.907
Markakis,Nick, Bal	.843	Markakis,Nick, Bal	.923	Butler,Billy, KC	.985	Dye,Jermaine, CWS	.873
Giambi,Jason, NYY	.842	Granderson,Curtis, Det	.900	Aviles,Mike, KC	.967	Ordonez,Magglio, Det	.870
Cust,Jack, Oak	.821	Damon,Johnny, NYY	.889	Cabrera,Miguel, Det	.939	Cabrera,Miguel, Det	.869
Hamilton,Josh, Tex	.801	Giambi,Jason, NYY	.889	Quentin,Carlos, CWS	.937	Pedroia,Dustin, Bos	.857
Cano,Robinson, NYY	.794	Thome,Jim, CWS	.868	Guillen,Jose, KC	.936	Rios,Alex, Tor	.818

OPS vs. LHP (minimum 125 PA)		OPS vs. RHP (minimum 377 PA)		RC Per 27 Outs vs. LHP (minimum 125 PA)		RC Per 27 Outs vs. RHP (minimum 377 PA)	
Bradley,Milton, Tex	1.127	Pena,Carlos, TB	.994	Bradley,Milton, Tex	9.2	Pena,Carlos, TB	8.9
Youkilis,Kevin, Bos	1.009	Rodriguez,Alex, NYY	.994	Span,Denard, Min	9.1	Huff,Aubrey, Bal	8.1
Renteria,Edgar, Det	1.004	Huff,Aubrey, Bal	.989	Aviles,Mike, KC	8.9	Kinsler,Ian, Tex	8.0
Beltre,Adrian, Sea	.994	Quentin,Carlos, CWS	.975	Bartlett,Jason, TB	8.8	Quentin,Carlos, CWS	8.0
Mora,Melvin, Bal	.987	Hamilton,Josh, Tex	.950	Youkilis,Kevin, Bos	8.7	Youkilis,Kevin, Bos	8.0
Butler,Billy, KC	.985	Youkilis,Kevin, Bos	.946	Garko,Ryan, Cle	8.5	Markakis,Nick, Bal	7.9
Aviles,Mike, KC	.967	Sizemore,Grady, Cle	.934	Mauer,Joe, Min	8.0	Damon,Johnny, NYY	7.8
Cabrera,Miguel, Det	.939	Morneau,Justin, Min	.928	Butler,Billy, KC	7.9	Morneau,Justin, Min	7.7
Mauer,Joe, Min	.939	Markakis,Nick, Bal	.923	Renteria,Edgar, Det	7.9	Sizemore,Grady, Cle	7.6
Quentin,Carlos, CWS	.937	Kinsler,Ian, Tex	.915	Beltre,Adrian, Sea	7.5	Granderson,Curtis, Det	7.6

Highest RBI % (minimum 502 PA)		Lowest RBI % (minimum 502 PA)		Highest Strikeout per PA (minimum 502 PA)		Lowest Strikeout per PA (minimum 502 PA)	
Quentin,Carlos, CWS	11.98	Figgins,Chone, LAA	3.17	Cust,Jack, Oak	.329	Polanco,Placido, Det	.068
Hamilton,Josh, Tex	11.62	Suzuki,Ichiro, Sea	3.98	Pena,Carlos, TB	.273	Betancourt,Yuniesky, Sea	.071
Cabrera,Miguel, Det	11.45	Suzuki,Kurt, Oak	4.72	Thome,Jim, CWS	.244	Pedroia,Dustin, Bos	.072
Youkilis,Kevin, Bos	11.39	Iwamura,Akinori, TB	4.90	Longoria,Evan, TB	.240	Mauer,Joe, Min	.079
Mora,Melvin, Bal	11.14	Ellsbury,Jacoby, Bos	5.09	Gomez,Carlos, Min	.231	Suzuki,Ichiro, Sea	.087
Pena,Carlos, TB	10.65	Betancourt,Yuniesky, Sea	5.31	Swisher,Nick, CWS	.230	Cabrera,Orlando, CWS	.097
Morneau,Justin, Min	10.63	Cabrera,Orlando, CWS	5.39	Bradley,Milton, Tex	.220	Lopez,Jose, Sea	.098
Giambi,Jason, NYY	10.52	Ellis,Mark, Oak	5.52	Gordon,Alex, KC	.210	Cano,Robinson, NYY	.103
Rodriguez,Alex, NYY	10.38	Polanco,Placido, Det	5.96	Jones,Adam, Bal	.210	Scutaro,Marco, Tor	.110
Longoria,Evan, TB	10.34	Barton,Daric, Oak	6.04	Teahen,Mark, KC	.210	Kinsler,Ian, Tex	.115

Home Runs At Home		Home Runs Away		Longest Avg Home Run (min 10 over the wall)		Shortest Avg Home Run (min 10 over the wall)	
Quentin,Carlos, CWS	21	Cabrera,Miguel, Det	18	Rodriguez,Alex, NYY	413	Millar,Kevin, Bal	368
Rodriguez,Alex, NYY	21	Pena,Carlos, TB	17	Napoli,Mike, LAA	406	Lowell,Mike, Bos	369
Sizemore,Grady, Cle	21	Dye,Jermaine, CWS	16	Hamilton,Josh, Tex	406	Kotchman,Casey, LAA	370
Cust,Jack, Oak	20	Giambi,Jason, NYY	16	Thome,Jim, CWS	405	Damon,Johnny, NYY	371
Cabrera,Miguel, Det	19	Beltre,Adrian, Sea	15	Hunter,Torii, LAA	405	Lopez,Jose, Sea	374
Hamilton,Josh, Tex	19	Quentin,Carlos, CWS	15	Cano,Robinson, NYY	404	Ellis,Mark, Oak	374
Swisher,Nick, CWS	19	Thames,Marcus, Det	15	Upton,B.J., TB	402	Hernandez,Ramon, Bal	377
Thome,Jim, CWS	19	Thome,Jim, CWS	15	Giambi,Jason, NYY	402	Aybar,Willy, TB	377
3 tied with	18	4 tied with	14	Bay,Jason, Bos	401	Pedroia,Dustin, Bos	377
				Ortiz,David, Bos	401	Crede,Joe, CWS	378

2008 American League Batting Leaders

Under Age 26: AB Per HR
(minimum 502 PA)

Longoria,Evan, TB	16.6
Cabrera,Miguel, Det	16.6
Markakis,Nick, Bal	29.8
Gordon,Alex, KC	30.8
Lopez,Jose, Sea	37.9
Pedroia,Dustin, Bos	38.4
Cano,Robinson, NYY	42.6
Barton,Daric, Oak	49.6
Jones,Adam, Bal	53.0
Young,Delmon, Min	57.5

Under Age 26: OPS
(minimum 502 PA)

Markakis,Nick, Bal	.897
Cabrera,Miguel, Det	.887
Longoria,Evan, TB	.874
Pedroia,Dustin, Bos	.869
Mauer,Joe, Min	.864
Upton,B.J., TB	.784
Gordon,Alex, KC	.783
Lopez,Jose, Sea	.764
Young,Delmon, Min	.741
Ellsbury,Jacoby, Bos	.729

Under Age 26: RC/27 Outs
(minimum 502 PA)

Markakis,Nick, Bal	7.0
Mauer,Joe, Min	7.0
Cabrera,Miguel, Det	6.3
Pedroia,Dustin, Bos	6.0
Longoria,Evan, TB	5.6
Upton,B.J., TB	5.5
Gordon,Alex, KC	5.0
Lopez,Jose, Sea	4.6
Young,Delmon, Min	4.5
Ellsbury,Jacoby, Bos	4.4

Longest Home Run

Rodriguez,Alex, NYY, 6/30	467
Thome,Jim, CWS, 6/4	464
Thome,Jim, CWS, 9/30	461
Rodriguez,Alex, NYY, 4/16	460
Rodriguez,Alex, NYY, 6/7	460
Hamilton,Josh, Tex, 5/16	451
Giambi,Jason, NYY, 7/2	450
Hamilton,Josh, Tex, 5/12	450
Hamilton,Josh, Tex, 8/31	450
Hunter,Torii, LAA, 4/6	450
Laird,Gerald, Tex, 4/6	450
Thames,Marcus, Det, 6/17	450

Swing and Miss %
(minimum 1500 Pitches Seen)

Shoppach,Kelly, Cle	36.0
Cust,Jack, Oak	34.9
Pena,Carlos, TB	30.0
Thome,Jim, CWS	29.6
Hamilton,Josh, Tex	26.0
Bradley,Milton, Tex	25.8
Stairs,Matt, Tor	24.8
Buck,John, KC	24.8
Rodriguez,Alex, NYY	24.4
Inge,Brandon, Det	24.3

Highest First Swing %
(minimum 502 PA)

Guerrero,Vladimir, LAA	47.4
Young,Delmon, Min	47.4
Ramirez,Alexei, CWS	43.2
Hamilton,Josh, Tex	43.0
Ordonez,Magglio, Det	40.9
Gomez,Carlos, Min	40.6
Bradley,Milton, Tex	39.0
Cabrera,Miguel, Det	36.9
Pierzynski,A.J., CWS	36.9
Scott,Luke, Bal	35.5

Lowest First Swing %
(minimum 502 PA)

Abreu,Bobby, NYY	6.2
Mauer,Joe, Min	9.3
Granderson,Curtis, Det	10.1
Damon,Johnny, NYY	10.6
Youkilis,Kevin, Bos	13.5
Pedroia,Dustin, Bos	14.1
Swisher,Nick, CWS	14.1
Suzuki,Kurt, Oak	14.2
Polanco,Placido, Det	15.2
Figgins,Chone, LAA	15.8

Home RC Per 27 Outs
(minimum 251 PA)

Sizemore,Grady, Cle	9.7
Youkilis,Kevin, Bos	8.7
Hamilton,Josh, Tex	8.7
Mauer,Joe, Min	8.2
Rodriguez,Alex, NYY	7.9
Dye,Jermaine, CWS	7.8
Giambi,Jason, NYY	7.7
Damon,Johnny, NYY	7.6
Kinsler,Ian, Tex	7.4
Mora,Melvin, Bal	7.3

Road RC Per 27 Outs
(minimum 251 PA)

Markakis,Nick, Bal	8.2
Quentin,Carlos, CWS	7.9
Kinsler,Ian, Tex	7.5
Youkilis,Kevin, Bos	7.4
Guerrero,Vladimir, LAA	7.4
Morneau,Justin, Min	7.3
Huff,Aubrey, Bal	7.1
Damon,Johnny, NYY	6.9
Thome,Jim, CWS	6.7
Bradley,Milton, Tex	6.6

2008 National League Batting Leaders

Batting Average (minimum 502 PA)		On Base Percentage (minimum 502 PA)		Slugging Average (minimum 502 PA)		Home Runs	
Jones,Chipper, Atl	.364	Jones,Chipper, Atl	.470	Pujols,Albert, StL	.653	Howard,Ryan, Phi	48
Pujols,Albert, StL	.357	Pujols,Albert, StL	.462	Ludwick,Ryan, StL	.591	Dunn,Adam, Cin-Ari	40
Holliday,Matt, Col	.321	Berkman,Lance, Hou	.420	Jones,Chipper, Atl	.574	Delgado,Carlos, NYM	38
Guzman,Cristian, Was	.316	Holliday,Matt, Col	.409	Berkman,Lance, Hou	.567	Braun,Ryan, Mil	37
Berkman,Lance, Hou	.312	Ramirez,Hanley, Fla	.400	Braun,Ryan, Mil	.553	Ludwick,Ryan, StL	37
Theriot,Ryan, ChC	.307	Giles,Brian, SD	.398	Howard,Ryan, Phi	.543	Pujols,Albert, StL	37
Winn,Randy, SF	.306	Wright,David, NYM	.390	Ramirez,Hanley, Fla	.540	Gonzalez,Adrian, SD	36
Giles,Brian, SD	.306	Theriot,Ryan, ChC	.387	Holliday,Matt, Col	.538	Fielder,Prince, Mil	34
Ethier,Andre, LAD	.305	Dunn,Adam, Cin-Ari	.386	Utley,Chase, Phi	.535	4 tied with	33
Wright,David, NYM	.302	Martin,Russell, LAD	.385	Wright,David, NYM	.534		

Games		Plate Appearances		At Bats		Hits	
Gonzalez,Adrian, SD	162	Reyes,Jose, NYM	763	Reyes,Jose, NYM	688	Reyes,Jose, NYM	204
Howard,Ryan, Phi	162	Wright,David, NYM	736	Tejada,Miguel, Hou	632	Wright,David, NYM	189
Beltran,Carlos, NYM	161	Utley,Chase, Phi	707	Cantu,Jorge, Fla	628	Pujols,Albert, StL	187
Loney,James, LAD	161	Beltran,Carlos, NYM	706	Wright,David, NYM	626	Guzman,Cristian, Was	183
Wright,David, NYM	160	Gonzalez,Adrian, SD	700	Young,Chris, Ari	625	Winn,Randy, SF	183
Young,Chris, Ari	160	Howard,Ryan, Phi	700	Kouzmanoff,Kevin, SD	624	Lee,Derrek, ChC	181
5 tied with	159	Young,Chris, Ari	699	Lee,Derrek, ChC	623	Tejada,Miguel, Hou	179
		Lee,Derrek, ChC	698	Gonzalez,Adrian, SD	616	Drew,Stephen, Ari	178
		Fielder,Prince, Mil	694	Hart,Corey, Mil	612	Theriot,Ryan, ChC	178
		Ramirez,Hanley, Fla	693	3 tied with	611	2 tied with	177

Singles		Doubles		Triples		Total Bases	
Theriot,Ryan, ChC	154	Berkman,Lance, Hou	46	Reyes,Jose, NYM	19	Pujols,Albert, StL	342
Guzman,Cristian, Was	134	McLouth,Nate, Pit	46	Drew,Stephen, Ari	11	Braun,Ryan, Mil	338
Winn,Randy, SF	133	Hart,Corey, Mil	45	Lewis,Fred, SF	11	Wright,David, NYM	334
Reyes,Jose, NYM	132	Drew,Stephen, Ari	44	Rollins,Jimmy, Phi	9	Howard,Ryan, Phi	331
Schumaker,Skip, StL	128	Pujols,Albert, StL	44	Victorino,Shane, Phi	8	Reyes,Jose, NYM	327
Tejada,Miguel, Hou	125	Ramirez,Aramis, ChC	44	Braun,Ryan, Mil	7	Utley,Chase, Phi	325
Atkins,Garrett, Col	119	McCann,Brian, Atl	42	Phillips,Brandon, Cin	7	Ludwick,Ryan, StL	318
Loney,James, LAD	118	Wright,David, NYM	42	Velez,Eugenio, SF	7	Ramirez,Hanley, Fla	318
3 tied with	117	Young,Chris, Ari	42	Weeks,Rickie, Mil	7	Berkman,Lance, Hou	314
		3 tied with	41	Young,Chris, Ari	7	Gonzalez,Adrian, SD	314

Runs Scored		RBI		Walks		Strikeouts	
Ramirez,Hanley, Fla	125	Howard,Ryan, Phi	146	Dunn,Adam, Cin-Ari	122	Reynolds,Mark, Ari	204
Beltran,Carlos, NYM	116	Wright,David, NYM	124	Pujols,Albert, StL	104	Howard,Ryan, Phi	199
Wright,David, NYM	115	Gonzalez,Adrian, SD	119	Burrell,Pat, Phi	102	Uggla,Dan, Fla	171
Berkman,Lance, Hou	114	Pujols,Albert, StL	116	Berkman,Lance, Hou	99	Young,Chris, Ari	165
McLouth,Nate, Pit	113	Delgado,Carlos, NYM	115	Wright,David, NYM	94	Dunn,Adam, Cin-Ari	164
Reyes,Jose, NYM	113	Ludwick,Ryan, StL	113	Beltran,Carlos, NYM	92	Kemp,Matt, LAD	153
Utley,Chase, Phi	113	Beltran,Carlos, NYM	112	Ramirez,Hanley, Fla	92	Ludwick,Ryan, StL	146
Holliday,Matt, Col	107	Ramirez,Aramis, ChC	111	Jones,Chipper, Atl	90	Cameron,Mike, Mil	142
Howard,Ryan, Phi	105	Berkman,Lance, Hou	106	Martin,Russell, LAD	90	Gonzalez,Adrian, SD	142
Ludwick,Ryan, StL	104	Braun,Ryan, Mil	106	2 tied with	87	Kouzmanoff,Kevin, SD	139

2008 National League Batting Leaders

Intentional Walks			BA Bases Loaded			Sacrifice Hits			Sacrifice Flies		
			(minimum 10 PA)								
Pujols,Albert, StL		34	Loretta,Mark, Hou		.800	Dempster,Ryan, ChC		19	Molina,Bengie, SF		11
Delgado,Carlos, NYM		19	McLouth,Nate, Pit		.714	Cook,Aaron, Col		16	Wright,David, NYM		11
Fielder,Prince, Mil		19	DeWitt,Blake, LAD		.600	Taveras,Willy, Col		15	Atkins,Garrett, Col		10
Berkman,Lance, Hou		18	Johnson,Reed, ChC		.556	Looper,Braden, StL		13	Fielder,Prince, Mil		10
Gonzalez,Adrian, SD		18	Teixeira,Mark, Atl		.545	Redding,Tim, Was		13	Hart,Corey, Mil		9
Howard,Ryan, Phi		17	Uggla,Dan, Fla		.524	Webb,Brandon, Ari		13	Winn,Randy, SF		9
Jones,Chipper, Atl		16	Belliard,Ronnie, Was		.500	Lilly,Ted, ChC		12	5 tied with		8
Ramirez,Manny, LAD		16	Gonzalez,Luis, Fla		.500	Moyer,Jamie, Phi		12			
Utley,Chase, Phi		14	Hermida,Jeremy, Fla		.462	Wellemeyer,Todd, StL		12			
3 tied with		13	3 tied with		.455	3 tied with		10			

BA Close & Late			Batting Average w/ RISP			SLG vs. LHP			SLG vs. RHP		
(minimum 50 PA)			(minimum 100 PA)			(minimum 125 PA)			(minimum 377 PA)		
Ramirez,Aramis, ChC		.423	Doumit,Ryan, Pit		.407	Pujols,Albert, StL		.715	Pujols,Albert, StL		.626
Schneider,Brian, NYM		.396	Flores,Jesus, Was		.370	Soriano,Alfonso, ChC		.710	Berkman,Lance, Hou		.613
Hardy,J.J., Mil		.386	Johnson,Reed, ChC		.358	Wright,David, NYM		.682	Howard,Ryan, Phi		.601
Dobbs,Greg, Phi		.380	Berkman,Lance, Hou		.345	Werth,Jayson, Phi		.652	Ludwick,Ryan, StL		.598
Teixeira,Mark, Atl		.358	Infante,Omar, Atl		.341	Beltran,Carlos, NYM		.601	Gonzalez,Adrian, SD		.585
Berkman,Lance, Hou		.354	Molina,Yadier, StL		.340	Atkins,Garrett, Col		.600	Ramirez,Hanley, Fla		.580
Jones,Chipper, Atl		.354	Pujols,Albert, StL		.339	Reynolds,Mark, Ari		.600	Uggla,Dan, Fla		.578
Iannetta,Chris, Col		.353	Lee,Carlos, Hou		.338	Phillips,Brandon, Cin		.586	Braun,Ryan, Mil		.561
Miles,Aaron, StL		.350	Hudson,Orlando, Ari		.333	Hairston,Scott, SD		.580	Ethier,Andre, LAD		.560
Fielder,Prince, Mil		.349	Ethier,Andre, LAD		.328	Ludwick,Ryan, StL		.576	Ramirez,Aramis, ChC		.560

Leadoff Hitters OBP			Cleanup Hitters SLG			BA vs. LHP			BA vs. RHP		
(minimum 150 PA)			(minimum 150 PA)			(minimum 125 PA)			(minimum 377 PA)		
Furcal,Rafael, LAD		.434	Berkman,Lance, Hou		.644	Pujols,Albert, StL		.411	Schumaker,Skip, StL		.340
Hairston,Jerry, Cin		.427	Delgado,Carlos, NYM		.623	Jones,Chipper, Atl		.394	Pujols,Albert, StL		.333
Giles,Brian, SD		.402	Lee,Carlos, Hou		.608	Wright,David, NYM		.382	Holliday,Matt, Col		.329
Ramirez,Hanley, Fla		.400	Ludwick,Ryan, StL		.587	Kemp,Matt, LAD		.369	Berkman,Lance, Hou		.327
Winn,Randy, SF		.375	Bay,Jason, Pit		.568	Keppinger,Jeff, Cin		.360	Ethier,Andre, LAD		.326
Blanco,Gregor, Atl		.371	Howard,Ryan, Phi		.550	Atkins,Garrett, Col		.357	Gonzalez,Adrian, SD		.320
Schumaker,Skip, StL		.370	Doumit,Ryan, Pit		.537	Guzman,Cristian, Was		.354	Ludwick,Ryan, StL		.316
Guzman,Cristian, Was		.363	Beltran,Carlos, NYM		.527	Soriano,Alfonso, ChC		.351	Ramirez,Hanley, Fla		.313
McLouth,Nate, Pit		.362	Ramirez,Aramis, ChC		.524	3 tied with		.333	Winn,Randy, SF		.313
Drew,Stephen, Ari		.361	Fielder,Prince, Mil		.521				Giles,Brian, SD		.309

Home BA			Away BA			OBP vs. LHP			OBP vs. RHP		
(minimum 251 PA)			(minimum 251 PA)			(minimum 125 PA)			(minimum 377 PA)		
Jones,Chipper, Atl		.399	Pujols,Albert, StL		.335	Pujols,Albert, StL		.518	Berkman,Lance, Hou		.444
Pujols,Albert, StL		.380	Schumaker,Skip, StL		.321	Wright,David, NYM		.497	Pujols,Albert, StL		.437
Guzman,Cristian, Was		.348	Hardy,J.J., Mil		.316	Jones,Chipper, Atl		.478	Holliday,Matt, Col		.410
Atkins,Garrett, Col		.342	Giles,Brian, SD		.316	Jackson,Conor, Ari		.446	Gonzalez,Adrian, SD		.405
Wright,David, NYM		.336	Lopez,Felipe, Was-StL		.316	Kemp,Matt, LAD		.417	Ramirez,Hanley, Fla		.403
Holliday,Matt, Col		.332	Holliday,Matt, Col		.308	Atkins,Garrett, Col		.414	Fielder,Prince, Mil		.401
Lewis,Fred, SF		.331	Gonzalez,Adrian, SD		.308	Beltran,Carlos, NYM		.413	Dunn,Adam, Cin-Ari		.400
Ramirez,Aramis, ChC		.324	Ethier,Andre, LAD		.307	Lee,Derrek, ChC		.413	Giles,Brian, SD		.399
Drew,Stephen, Ari		.321	Berkman,Lance, Hou		.306	Keppinger,Jeff, Cin		.412	Ramirez,Aramis, ChC		.394
Ludwick,Ryan, StL		.320	Ramirez,Hanley, Fla		.305	Theriot,Ryan, ChC		.410	Schumaker,Skip, StL		.393

2008 National League Batting Leaders

Stolen Bases		Caught Stealing		Highest SB Success Pct (minimum 20 SBA)		Lowest SB Success Pct (minimum 20 SBA)	
Taveras,Willy, Col	68	Reyes,Jose, NYM	15	Werth,Jayson, Phi	95.2	Pence,Hunter, Hou	52.4
Reyes,Jose, NYM	56	Theriot,Ryan, ChC	13	Rollins,Jimmy, Phi	94.0	Patterson,Corey, Cin	60.9
Rollins,Jimmy, Phi	47	Pierre,Juan, LAD	12	Holliday,Matt, Col	93.3	Theriot,Ryan, ChC	62.9
Bourn,Michael, Hou	41	Ramirez,Hanley, Fla	12	Winn,Randy, SF	92.6	Phillips,Brandon, Cin	69.7
Pierre,Juan, LAD	40	Kemp,Matt, LAD	11	Taveras,Willy, Col	90.7	Velez,Eugenio, SF	71.4
Victorino,Shane, Phi	36	Victorino,Shane, Phi	11	Beltran,Carlos, NYM	89.3	Milledge,Lastings, Was	72.7
Kemp,Matt, LAD	35	Bourn,Michael, Hou	10	McLouth,Nate, Pit	88.5	Ramirez,Hanley, Fla	74.5
Ramirez,Hanley, Fla	35	Pence,Hunter, Hou	10	Soriano,Alfonso, ChC	86.4	Lewis,Fred, SF	75.0
Holliday,Matt, Col	28	Phillips,Brandon, Cin	10	Berkman,Lance, Hou	81.8	Martin,Russell, LAD	75.0
2 tied with	25	2 tied with	9	Bourn,Michael, Hou	80.4	Wright,David, NYM	75.0

Steals of Third		Grounded Into DP		Grounded Into DP Pct (minimum 50 GIDP Ops)		Hit By Pitch	
Taveras,Willy, Col	19	Tejada,Miguel, Hou	32	Fontenot,Mike, ChC	1.69	Utley,Chase, Phi	27
Reyes,Jose, NYM	13	Lee,Derrek, ChC	27	Johnson,Kelly, Atl	2.19	Kouzmanoff,Kevin, SD	15
Beltran,Carlos, NYM	12	Loney,James, LAD	25	Werth,Jayson, Phi	2.74	Iannetta,Chris, Col	14
Pierre,Juan, LAD	10	Escobar,Yunel, Atl	24	Blanco,Gregor, Atl	3.45	Milledge,Lastings, Was	14
Hairston,Jerry, Cin	9	Gonzalez,Adrian, SD	24	Bay,Jason, Pit	3.57	Rowand,Aaron, SF	14
Hart,Corey, Mil	9	Molina,Bengie, SF	23	Hairston,Scott, SD	3.70	Weeks,Rickie, Mil	14
Rollins,Jimmy, Phi	9	Molina,Yadier, StL	21	Treanor,Matt, Fla	3.77	Willingham,Josh, Fla	14
Ramirez,Hanley, Fla	7	Rowand,Aaron, SF	21	Johnson,Reed, ChC	3.90	Kendall,Jason, Mil	13
Braun,Ryan, Mil	6	Atkins,Garrett, Col	20	Patterson,Corey, Cin	4.05	3 tied with	12
3 tied with	5	3 tied with	19	Bourn,Michael, Hou	4.17		

Pitches Seen		At Bats Per Home Run (minimum 502 PA)		Highest GB/FB Ratio (minimum 502 PA)		Lowest GB/FB Ratio (minimum 502 PA)	
Wright,David, NYM	2930	Howard,Ryan, Phi	12.7	Schumaker,Skip, StL	2.88	Ludwick,Ryan, StL	0.59
Ramirez,Hanley, Fla	2865	Dunn,Adam, Cin-Ari	12.9	Theriot,Ryan, ChC	2.80	Soriano,Alfonso, ChC	0.60
Dunn,Adam, Cin-Ari	2815	Pujols,Albert, StL	14.2	Escobar,Yunel, Atl	2.35	Ramirez,Aramis, ChC	0.65
Reyes,Jose, NYM	2814	Ludwick,Ryan, StL	14.5	Guzman,Cristian, Was	2.15	Encarnacion,Edwin, Cin	0.69
Howard,Ryan, Phi	2785	Jacobs,Mike, Fla	14.9	Lewis,Fred, SF	1.95	Cameron,Mike, Mil	0.71
Young,Chris, Ari	2778	Soriano,Alfonso, ChC	15.6	Blanco,Gregor, Atl	1.89	McLouth,Nate, Pit	0.74
Utley,Chase, Phi	2769	Delgado,Carlos, NYM	15.7	Bourn,Michael, Hou	1.84	Jacobs,Mike, Fla	0.74
Lee,Derrek, ChC	2760	Burrell,Pat, Phi	16.2	Keppinger,Jeff, Cin	1.82	Uggla,Dan, Fla	0.75
McLouth,Nate, Pit	2736	Braun,Ryan, Mil	16.5	Taveras,Willy, Col	1.81	Molina,Bengie, SF	0.75
Beltran,Carlos, NYM	2731	Uggla,Dan, Fla	16.6	Martin,Russell, LAD	1.73	Cantu,Jorge, Fla	0.76

Pitches Per Plate App (minimum 502 PA)		Pct Pitches Taken (minimum 1500 Pitches)		Best BPS on OutZ (minimum 502 PA)		Worst BPS on OutZ (minimum 502 PA)	
Dunn,Adam, Cin-Ari	4.32	Castillo,Luis, NYM	68.7	Jones,Chipper, Atl	.730	Cameron,Mike, Mil	.167
Fukudome,Kosuke, ChC	4.29	Snyder,Chris, Ari	63.8	Rollins,Jimmy, Phi	.632	Dunn,Adam, Cin-Ari	.187
Cameron,Mike, Mil	4.24	Bay,Jason, Pit	61.9	Schumaker,Skip, StL	.609	Young,Chris, Ari	.225
Reynolds,Mark, Ari	4.24	DeWitt,Blake, LAD	61.8	Hardy,J.J., Mil	.592	Milledge,Lastings, Was	.226
Lewis,Fred, SF	4.23	Dunn,Adam, Cin-Ari	61.6	Loney,James, LAD	.591	Kouzmanoff,Kevin, SD	.259
Uggla,Dan, Fla	4.22	Werth,Jayson, Phi	61.4	Giles,Brian, SD	.570	Reynolds,Mark, Ari	.260
Burrell,Pat, Phi	4.19	Pujols,Albert, StL	61.3	Drew,Stephen, Ari	.557	Encarnacion,Edwin, Cin	.271
Ethier,Andre, LAD	4.16	Jones,Chipper, Atl	61.3	Ethier,Andre, LAD	.545	Phillips,Brandon, Cin	.290
Hawpe,Brad, Col	4.15	Harris,Willie, Was	61.3	Wright,David, NYM	.534	Jacobs,Mike, Fla	.297
Weeks,Rickie, Mil	4.14	Glaus,Troy, StL	60.9	Guzman,Cristian, Was	.533	Hermida,Jeremy, Fla	.304

2008 National League Batting Leaders

Best OPS vs Fastballs
(minimum 251 PA)

Pujols,Albert, StL	1.196
Jones,Chipper, Atl	1.082
Ludwick,Ryan, StL	1.072
Holliday,Matt, Col	1.011
Dunn,Adam, Cin-Ari	.990
DeRosa,Mark, ChC	.962
Howard,Ryan, Phi	.960
Lee,Carlos, Hou	.950
Votto,Joey, Cin	.942
Beltran,Carlos, NYM	.924

Best OPS vs Curveballs
(minimum 50 PA)

Utley,Chase, Phi	1.257
Berkman,Lance, Hou	1.238
Braun,Ryan, Mil	1.179
Ethier,Andre, LAD	1.018
Gonzalez,Adrian, SD	.968
Fielder,Prince, Mil	.936
Jackson,Conor, Ari	.875
Drew,Stephen, Ari	.871
Votto,Joey, Cin	.835
Young,Chris, Ari	.829

Best OPS vs Changeups
(minimum 50 PA)

Ramirez,Hanley, Fla	1.219
McCann,Brian, Atl	1.203
Berkman,Lance, Hou	1.200
Ludwick,Ryan, StL	1.176
Ankiel,Rick, StL	1.129
Encarnacion,Edwin, Cin	1.118
Bowker,John, SF	1.095
Teixeira,Mark, Atl	1.076
Burrell,Pat, Phi	1.048
Delgado,Carlos, NYM	1.021

Best OPS vs Sliders
(minimum 32 PA)

Gerut,Jody, SD	1.124
Hawpe,Brad, Col	1.073
Stewart,Ian, Col	1.063
Rollins,Jimmy, Phi	1.053
Ethier,Andre, LAD	1.026
Spilborghs,Ryan, Col	1.019
Wright,David, NYM	1.008
Votto,Joey, Cin	1.006
Hundley,Nick, SD	.993
Kotsay,Mark, Atl	.986

OPS
(minimum 502 PA)

Pujols,Albert, StL	1.114
Jones,Chipper, Atl	1.044
Berkman,Lance, Hou	.986
Ludwick,Ryan, StL	.966
Holliday,Matt, Col	.947
Ramirez,Hanley, Fla	.940
Wright,David, NYM	.924
Utley,Chase, Phi	.915
Dunn,Adam, Cin-Ari	.898
Ramirez,Aramis, ChC	.898

OPS First Half
(minimum 260 PA)

Berkman,Lance, Hou	1.096
Jones,Chipper, Atl	1.086
Pujols,Albert, StL	1.074
Burrell,Pat, Phi	.979
Uggla,Dan, Fla	.978
Holliday,Matt, Col	.975
Ludwick,Ryan, StL	.962
Ramirez,Hanley, Fla	.957
Utley,Chase, Phi	.955
McCann,Brian, Atl	.940

OPS Second Half
(minimum 201 PA)

Ramirez,Manny, LAD	1.232
Pujols,Albert, StL	1.162
Delgado,Carlos, NYM	.991
Ethier,Andre, LAD	.991
Wright,David, NYM	.988
LaRoche,Adam, Pit	.975
Ludwick,Ryan, StL	.971
Votto,Joey, Cin	.959
Howard,Ryan, Phi	.954
Hawpe,Brad, Col	.931

OPS by Catchers
(minimum 251 PA)

McCann,Brian, Atl	.897
Soto,Geovany, ChC	.876
Doumit,Ryan, Pit	.875
Iannetta,Chris, Col	.864
Snyder,Chris, Ari	.808
Martin,Russell, LAD	.791
Molina,Bengie, SF	.779
Coste,Chris, Phi	.773
Molina,Yadier, StL	.736
Schneider,Brian, NYM	.702

OPS by First Basemen
(minimum 251 PA)

Pujols,Albert, StL	1.098
Berkman,Lance, Hou	.985
Teixeira,Mark, Atl	.900
Howard,Ryan, Phi	.892
Fielder,Prince, Mil	.886
Jackson,Conor, Ari	.879
Gonzalez,Adrian, SD	.872
Votto,Joey, Cin	.872
Delgado,Carlos, NYM	.857
LaRoche,Adam, Pit	.838

OPS by Second Basemen
(minimum 251 PA)

Utley,Chase, Phi	.924
Uggla,Dan, Fla	.875
Durham,Ray, SF-Mil	.842
DeRosa,Mark, ChC	.825
Hudson,Orlando, Ari	.823
Johnson,Kelly, Atl	.787
Matsui,Kaz, Hou	.785
Lopez,Felipe, Was-StL	.747
Phillips,Brandon, Cin	.746
Easley,Damion, NYM	.744

OPS by Third Basemen
(minimum 251 PA)

Jones,Chipper, Atl	1.036
Wright,David, NYM	.927
Ramirez,Aramis, ChC	.904
Glaus,Troy, StL	.849
Atkins,Garrett, Col	.824
Encarnacion,Edwin, Cin	.810
Wigginton,Ty, Hou	.804
Cantu,Jorge, Fla	.801
Reynolds,Mark, Ari	.780
Zimmerman,Ryan, Was	.778

OPS by Shortstops
(minimum 251 PA)

Ramirez,Hanley, Fla	.945
Drew,Stephen, Ari	.835
Reyes,Jose, NYM	.833
Hardy,J.J., Mil	.822
Rollins,Jimmy, Phi	.789
Guzman,Cristian, Was	.788
Escobar,Yunel, Atl	.771
Theriot,Ryan, ChC	.749
Tulowitzki,Troy, Col	.734
Tejada,Miguel, Hou	.731

OPS by Left Fielders
(minimum 251 PA)

Holliday,Matt, Col	.947
Lee,Carlos, Hou	.928
Braun,Ryan, Mil	.893
Dunn,Adam, Cin-Ari	.889
Bay,Jason, Pit	.884
Soriano,Alfonso, ChC	.876
Burrell,Pat, Phi	.865
Willingham,Josh, Fla	.838
Lewis,Fred, SF	.814
Jackson,Conor, Ari	.783

OPS by Center Fielders
(minimum 251 PA)

Ankiel,Rick, StL	.891
Gerut,Jody, SD	.871
Beltran,Carlos, NYM	.866
McLouth,Nate, Pit	.845
Johnson,Reed, ChC	.832
Edmonds,Jim, SD-ChC	.829
Cameron,Mike, Mil	.811
Victorino,Shane, Phi	.805
Ross,Cody, Fla	.776
Kemp,Matt, LAD	.768

OPS by Right Fielders
(minimum 251 PA)

Ethier,Andre, LAD	.950
Ludwick,Ryan, StL	.938
Nady,Xavier, Pit	.915
Hawpe,Brad, Col	.890
Dukes,Elijah, Was	.876
Giles,Brian, SD	.857
Werth,Jayson, Phi	.830
Upton,Justin, Ari	.820
Winn,Randy, SF	.806
Church,Ryan, NYM	.795

OPS by Pitchers
(minimum 66 PA)

Zambrano,Carlos, ChC	.947
Looper,Braden, StL	.651
Haren,Dan, Ari	.530
Arroyo,Bronson, Cin	.518
Hamels,Cole, Phi	.476
Cook,Aaron, Col	.474
Oswalt,Roy, Hou	.429
Lincecum,Tim, SF	.413
Lilly,Ted, ChC	.400
Cain,Matt, SF	.392

2008 National League Batting Leaders

OPS Batting Left vs. LHP
(minimum 125 PA)

Utley,Chase, Phi	.888
Votto,Joey, Cin	.862
Hawpe,Brad, Col	.826
McCann,Brian, Atl	.820
Giles,Brian, SD	.800
Johnson,Kelly, Atl	.800
Delgado,Carlos, NYM	.789
Dunn,Adam, Cin-Ari	.773
LaRoche,Adam, Pit	.765
Drew,Stephen, Ari	.748

OPS Batting Left vs. RHP
(minimum 377 PA)

Berkman,Lance, Hou	1.059
Gonzalez,Adrian, SD	.991
Howard,Ryan, Phi	.966
Fielder,Prince, Mil	.955
Ethier,Andre, LAD	.953
Dunn,Adam, Cin-Ari	.951
McCann,Brian, Atl	.932
Utley,Chase, Phi	.932
Delgado,Carlos, NYM	.912
McLouth,Nate, Pit	.908

OPS Batting Right vs. LHP
(minimum 125 PA)

Pujols,Albert, StL	1.233
Wright,David, NYM	1.179
Soriano,Alfonso, ChC	1.114
Jones,Chipper, Atl	1.040
Werth,Jayson, Phi	1.020
Beltran,Carlos, NYM	1.015
Atkins,Garrett, Col	1.014
Kemp,Matt, LAD	.989
Reynolds,Mark, Ari	.982
Hardy,J.J., Mil	.977

OPS Batting Right vs. RHP
(minimum 377 PA)

Pujols,Albert, StL	1.063
Ludwick,Ryan, StL	.985
Ramirez,Hanley, Fla	.983
Holliday,Matt, Col	.963
Uggla,Dan, Fla	.955
Ramirez,Aramis, ChC	.954
Braun,Ryan, Mil	.894
Glaus,Troy, StL	.891
Soto,Geovany, ChC	.852
Burrell,Pat, Phi	.843

OPS vs. LHP
(minimum 125 PA)

Pujols,Albert, StL	1.233
Wright,David, NYM	1.179
Soriano,Alfonso, ChC	1.114
Jones,Chipper, Atl	1.040
Werth,Jayson, Phi	1.020
Beltran,Carlos, NYM	1.015
Atkins,Garrett, Col	1.014
Kemp,Matt, LAD	.989
Reynolds,Mark, Ari	.982
Hardy,J.J., Mil	.977

OPS vs. RHP
(minimum 377 PA)

Pujols,Albert, StL	1.063
Berkman,Lance, Hou	1.057
Gonzalez,Adrian, SD	.991
Ludwick,Ryan, StL	.985
Ramirez,Hanley, Fla	.983
Howard,Ryan, Phi	.966
Holliday,Matt, Col	.963
Fielder,Prince, Mil	.955
Uggla,Dan, Fla	.955
Ramirez,Aramis, ChC	.954

RC Per 27 Outs vs. LHP
(minimum 125 PA)

Pujols,Albert, StL	12.1
Wright,David, NYM	10.6
Soriano,Alfonso, ChC	9.4
Kemp,Matt, LAD	9.3
Keppinger,Jeff, Cin	8.9
Jones,Chipper, Atl	8.6
Jackson,Conor, Ari	8.6
Atkins,Garrett, Col	8.5
Beltran,Carlos, NYM	8.1
Reynolds,Mark, Ari	7.9

RC Per 27 Outs vs. RHP
(minimum 377 PA)

Berkman,Lance, Hou	9.9
Gonzalez,Adrian, SD	8.7
Pujols,Albert, StL	8.6
Ethier,Andre, LAD	8.2
Dunn,Adam, Cin-Ari	8.1
Ramirez,Hanley, Fla	7.9
Howard,Ryan, Phi	7.8
Holliday,Matt, Col	7.7
Ramirez,Aramis, ChC	7.7
Ludwick,Ryan, StL	7.3

Highest RBI %
(minimum 502 PA)

Howard,Ryan, Phi	13.27
Pujols,Albert, StL	11.93
Ludwick,Ryan, StL	11.48
Ramirez,Aramis, ChC	10.89
Jacobs,Mike, Fla	10.83
Gonzalez,Adrian, SD	10.82
Wright,David, NYM	10.71
Dunn,Adam, Cin-Ari	10.71
Berkman,Lance, Hou	10.57
Delgado,Carlos, NYM	10.52

Lowest RBI %
(minimum 502 PA)

Taveras,Willy, Col	3.46
Theriot,Ryan, ChC	3.98
Bourn,Michael, Hou	4.01
Blanco,Gregor, Atl	5.18
Kendall,Jason, Mil	5.42
Schumaker,Skip, StL	5.52
Lewis,Fred, SF	5.53
Lopez,Felipe, Was-StL	5.64
Keppinger,Jeff, Cin	5.80
Sanchez,Freddy, Pit	5.88

Highest Strikeout per PA
(minimum 502 PA)

Reynolds,Mark, Ari	.333
Howard,Ryan, Phi	.284
Cameron,Mike, Mil	.280
Uggla,Dan, Fla	.276
Dunn,Adam, Cin-Ari	.252
Hermida,Jeremy, Fla	.247
Lewis,Fred, SF	.238
Ludwick,Ryan, StL	.237
Hawpe,Brad, Col	.236
Young,Chris, Ari	.236

Lowest Strikeout per PA
(minimum 502 PA)

Keppinger,Jeff, Cin	.048
Molina,Bengie, SF	.067
Kendall,Jason, Mil	.077
Giles,Brian, SD	.080
Pujols,Albert, StL	.084
Rollins,Jimmy, Phi	.088
Theriot,Ryan, ChC	.088
Guzman,Cristian, Was	.093
Jackson,Conor, Ari	.100
Schumaker,Skip, StL	.101

Home Runs At Home

Howard,Ryan, Phi	26
Braun,Ryan, Mil	23
Delgado,Carlos, NYM	21
Dunn,Adam, Cin-Ari	21
Wright,David, NYM	21
Utley,Chase, Phi	20
Pujols,Albert, StL	19
Cantu,Jorge, Fla	18
Fielder,Prince, Mil	18
Ludwick,Ryan, StL	18

Home Runs Away

Gonzalez,Adrian, SD	22
Howard,Ryan, Phi	22
Burrell,Pat, Phi	21
Dunn,Adam, Cin-Ari	19
Ludwick,Ryan, StL	19
Cameron,Mike, Mil	18
Jacobs,Mike, Fla	18
Pujols,Albert, StL	18
3 tied with	17

Longest Avg Home Run
(min 10 over the wall)

Upton,Justin, Ari	417
Holliday,Matt, Col	412
Branyan,Russell, Mil	409
Ramirez,Hanley, Fla	407
Dunn,Adam, Cin-Ari	406
Hall,Bill, Mil	404
Reynolds,Mark, Ari	404
Ramirez,Manny, LAD	402
Ankiel,Rick, StL	402
Ludwick,Ryan, StL	402

Shortest Avg Home Run
(min 10 over the wall)

Victorino,Shane, Phi	367
Tejada,Miguel, Hou	373
Blum,Geoff, Hou	373
Rollins,Jimmy, Phi	373
Feliz,Pedro, Phi	374
Wigginton,Ty, Hou	374
Hermida,Jeremy, Fla	377
Edmonds,Jim, SD-ChC	377
Hairston,Scott, SD	378
Harris,Willie, Was	378

2008 National League Batting Leaders

Under Age 26: AB Per HR
(minimum 502 PA)

Braun,Ryan, Mil	16.5
Fielder,Prince, Mil	17.3
Ramirez,Hanley, Fla	17.8
Wright,David, NYM	19.0
Reynolds,Mark, Ari	19.3
Encarnacion,Edwin, Cin	19.5
Soto,Geovany, ChC	21.5
Votto,Joey, Cin	21.9
McCann,Brian, Atl	22.1
Pence,Hunter, Hou	23.8

Under Age 26: OPS
(minimum 502 PA)

Ramirez,Hanley, Fla	.940
Wright,David, NYM	.924
McCann,Brian, Atl	.896
Braun,Ryan, Mil	.888
Fielder,Prince, Mil	.879
Votto,Joey, Cin	.874
Soto,Geovany, ChC	.868
Drew,Stephen, Ari	.836
Reyes,Jose, NYM	.833
Encarnacion,Edwin, Cin	.807

Under Age 26: RC/27 Outs
(minimum 502 PA)

Ramirez,Hanley, Fla	7.2
Wright,David, NYM	6.7
Votto,Joey, Cin	6.4
Fielder,Prince, Mil	6.3
Reyes,Jose, NYM	6.1
McCann,Brian, Atl	6.0
Soto,Geovany, ChC	5.9
Braun,Ryan, Mil	5.9
Drew,Stephen, Ari	5.8
Martin,Russell, LAD	5.7

Longest Home Run

Upton,Justin, Ari, 7/6	480
Howard,Ryan, Phi, 4/5	479
Delgado,C., NYM, 6/27	470
Dunn,Adam, Cin, 5/17	468
Branyan,Russell, Mil, 5/31	465
Dunn,Adam, Cin, 5/5	463
Votto,Joey, Cin, 9/19	462
Berkman,Lance, Hou, 6/8	460
Delgado,Carlos, NYM, 9/7	460
Braun,Ryan, Mil, 6/14	455

Swing and Miss %
(minimum 1500 Pitches Seen)

Reynolds,Mark, Ari	37.7
Howard,Ryan, Phi	33.4
Upton,Justin, Ari	31.8
Uggla,Dan, Fla	29.5
Bruce,Jay, Cin	28.6
Dunn,Adam, Cin-Ari	28.3
Hawpe,Brad, Col	27.8
Headley,Chase, SD	27.4
Soriano,Alfonso, ChC	27.3
Iannetta,Chris, Col	26.2

Highest First Swing %
(minimum 502 PA)

Francoeur,Jeff, Atl	42.9
Phillips,Brandon, Cin	40.3
Holliday,Matt, Col	40.0
Hart,Corey, Mil	39.1
Pence,Hunter, Hou	37.9
Kouzmanoff,Kevin, SD	37.3
Hawpe,Brad, Col	36.7
Berkman,Lance, Hou	36.5
Votto,Joey, Cin	36.4
Delgado,Carlos, NYM	36.0

Lowest First Swing %
(minimum 502 PA)

Hardy,J.J., Mil	7.8
McLouth,Nate, Pit	12.0
Hermida,Jeremy, Fla	12.9
Rollins,Jimmy, Phi	13.4
Utley,Chase, Phi	14.9
Atkins,Garrett, Col	16.0
Kendall,Jason, Mil	16.4
Pujols,Albert, StL	16.8
Young,Chris, Ari	17.1
Keppinger,Jeff, Cin	17.3

Home RC Per 27 Outs
(minimum 251 PA)

Pujols,Albert, StL	11.3
Jones,Chipper, Atl	10.6
Ramirez,Aramis, ChC	9.4
Berkman,Lance, Hou	9.3
Wright,David, NYM	8.5
Beltran,Carlos, NYM	8.3
Holliday,Matt, Col	8.0
Ethier,Andre, LAD	7.9
Howard,Ryan, Phi	7.6
DeRosa,Mark, ChC	7.5

Road RC Per 27 Outs
(minimum 251 PA)

Berkman,Lance, Hou	7.9
Pujols,Albert, StL	7.9
Gonzalez,Adrian, SD	7.5
Utley,Chase, Phi	7.5
Dunn,Adam, Cin-Ari	7.5
Lee,Carlos, Hou	7.4
Uggla,Dan, Fla	7.1
Glaus,Troy, StL	7.0
Reyes,Jose, NYM	7.0
Ramirez,Hanley, Fla	6.9

2008 American League Pitching Leaders

Earned Run Average (minimum 162 IP)		Winning Percentage (minimum 15 Decisions)		Opponent Batting Average (minimum 162 IP)		Baserunners Per 9 IP (minimum 162 IP)	
Lee,Cliff, Cle	2.54	Lee,Cliff, Cle	.880	Matsuzaka,Daisuke, Bos	.211	Halladay,Roy, Tor	9.91
Halladay,Roy, Tor	2.78	Matsuzaka,Daisuke, Bos	.857	Galarraga,Armando, Det	.226	Lee,Cliff, Cle	10.20
Matsuzaka,Daisuke, Bos	2.90	Perkins, Glen, Min	.750	Wakefield,Tim, Bos	.228	Santana,Ervin, LAA	10.40
Lester,Jon, Bos	3.21	Baker,Scott, Min	.733	Halladay,Roy, Tor	.237	Baker,Scott, Min	10.76
Danks,John, CWS	3.32	Lester,Jon, Bos	.727	Santana,Ervin, LAA	.237	Shields,James, TB	10.88
Mussina,Mike, NYY	3.37	Saunders,Joe, LAA	.708	Floyd,Gavin, CWS	.241	Galarraga,Armando, Det	11.03
Saunders,Joe, LAA	3.41	Lackey,John, LAA	.706	Guthrie,Jeremy, Bal	.242	Beckett,Josh, Bos	11.15
Baker,Scott, Min	3.45	Santana,Ervin, LAA	.696	Smith,Greg, Oak	.243	Saunders,Joe, LAA	11.18
Hernandez,Felix, Sea	3.45	Mussina,Mike, NYY	.690	Garza,Matt, TB	.245	Danks,John, CWS	11.22
Greinke,Zack, KC	3.47	Floyd,Gavin, CWS	.680	Danks,John, CWS	.246	Wakefield,Tim, Bos	11.29

Games		Games Started		Complete Games		Shutouts	
Guerrier,Matt, Min	76	Buehrle,Mark, CWS	34	Halladay,Roy, Tor	9	Garza,Matt, TB	2
Rodriguez,Francisco, LAA	76	Burnett,A.J., Tor	34	Lee,Cliff, Cle	4	Halladay,Roy, Tor	2
Reyes,Dennys, Min	75	Meche,Gil, KC	34	Garza,Matt, TB	3	Lee,Cliff, Cle	2
Wright,Jamey, Tex	75	Mussina,Mike, NYY	34	Lackey,John, LAA	3	Lester,Jon, Bos	2
Thornton,Matt, CWS	74	9 tied with	33	Millwood,Kevin, Tex	3	Litsch,Jesse, Tor	2
Delcarmen,Manny, Bos	73			Sabathia,CC, Cle	3	Sabathia,CC, Cle	2
Perez,Rafael, Cle	73			Shields,James, TB	3	Shields,James, TB	2
Dotel,Octavio, CWS	72			Slowey,Kevin, Min	3	Slowey,Kevin, Min	2
Green,Sean, Sea	72			7 tied with	2	8 tied with	1
Ramirez,Ramon, KC	71						

Wins		Losses		No Decisions		Wild Pitches	
Lee,Cliff, Cle	22	Verlander,Justin, Det	17	Baker,Scott, Min	13	Cabrera,Daniel, Bal	15
Halladay,Roy, Tor	20	Bannister,Brian, KC	16	Cabrera,Daniel, Bal	12	Padilla,Vicente, Tex	12
Mussina,Mike, NYY	20	Smith,Greg, Oak	16	Danks,John, CWS	12	Wakefield,Tim, Bos	12
Burnett,A.J., Tor	18	Vazquez,Javier, CWS	16	Blackburn,Nick, Min	11	Burnett,A.J., Tor	11
Matsuzaka,Daisuke, Bos	18	Silva,Carlos, Sea	15	Eveland,Dana, Oak	11	Dickey,R.A., Sea	11
Floyd,Gavin, CWS	17	Batista,Miguel, Sea	14	Feldman,Scott, Tex	11	Floyd,Gavin, CWS	9
Saunders,Joe, LAA	17	Pettitte,Andy, NYY	14	Hernandez,Felix, Sea	11	5 tied with	8
Lester,Jon, Bos	16	Washburn,Jarrod, Sea	14	Lester,Jon, Bos	11		
Santana,Ervin, LAA	16	Rogers,Kenny, Det	13	Ponson,Sidney, Tex-NYY	11		
Buehrle,Mark, CWS	15	5 tied with	12	Shields,James, TB	11		

Strikeouts		Walks Allowed		Intentional Walks Allowed		Hit Batters	
Burnett,A.J., Tor	231	Matsuzaka,Daisuke, Bos	94	Guerrier,Matt, Min	9	Cabrera,Daniel, Bal	18
Santana,Ervin, LAA	214	Cabrera,Daniel, Bal	90	Verlander,Justin, Det	8	Padilla,Vicente, Tex	15
Halladay,Roy, Tor	206	Smith,Greg, Oak	87	Carlson,Jesse, Tor	7	Verlander,Justin, Det	14
Vazquez,Javier, CWS	200	Verlander,Justin, Det	87	Downs,Scott, Tor	7	Wakefield,Tim, Bos	13
Greinke,Zack, KC	183	Burnett,A.J., Tor	86	Hernandez,Felix, Sea	7	Eveland,Dana, Oak	12
Meche,Gil, KC	183	Hernandez,Felix, Sea	80	Robertson,Nate, Det	7	Halladay,Roy, Tor	12
Hernandez,Felix, Sea	175	Batista,Miguel, Sea	79	Seay,Bobby, Det	7	Shields,James, TB	12
Beckett,Josh, Bos	172	Eveland,Dana, Oak	77	9 tied with	6	4 tied with	10
Lee,Cliff, Cle	170	Jackson,Edwin, TB	77				
Kazmir,Scott, TB	166	Meche,Gil, KC	73				

2008 American League Pitching Leaders

Runs Allowed

Bannister,Brian, KC	127
Robertson,Nate, Det	124
Verlander,Justin, Det	119
Rogers,Kenny, Det	118
Garland,Jon, LAA	116
Silva,Carlos, Sea	114
Vazquez,Javier, CWS	113
Pettitte,Andy, NYY	112
Burnett,A.J., Tor	109
Cabrera,Daniel, Bal	109

Hits Allowed

Buehrle,Mark, CWS	240
Garland,Jon, LAA	237
Pettitte,Andy, NYY	233
Blackburn,Nick, Min	224
Halladay,Roy, Tor	220
Millwood,Kevin, Tex	220
Robertson,Nate, Det	218
Bannister,Brian, KC	215
3 tied with	214

Doubles Allowed

Burnett,A.J., Tor	55
Rogers,Kenny, Det	55
Sonnanstine,Andy, TB	54
Vazquez,Javier, CWS	54
Robertson,Nate, Det	53
Floyd,Gavin, CWS	48
Hernandez,Felix, Sea	48
Mussina,Mike, NYY	47
Shields,James, TB	47
Danks,John, CWS	45

Home Runs Allowed

Byrd,Paul, Cle-Bos	31
Floyd,Gavin, CWS	30
Bannister,Brian, KC	29
Galarraga,Armando, Det	28
Lackey,John, LAA	26
Padilla,Vicente, Tex	26
Robertson,Nate, Det	26
Perkins,Glen, Min	25
Vazquez,Javier, CWS	25
Wakefield,Tim, Bos	25

Run Support Per Nine IP
(minimum 162 IP)

Padilla,Vicente, Tex	6.58
Floyd,Gavin, CWS	6.54
Garland,Jon, LAA	6.41
Matsuzaka,Daisuke, Bos	6.23
Lee,Cliff, Cle	6.13
Galarraga,Armando, Det	6.04
Lester,Jon, Bos	5.95
Litsch,Jesse, Tor	5.88
Baker,Scott, Min	5.80
Jackson,Edwin, TB	5.69

% Pitches In Strike Zone
(minimum 162 IP)

Byrd,Paul, Cle-Bos	56.5
Sonnanstine,Andy, TB	56.1
Lee,Cliff, Cle	55.9
Mussina,Mike, NYY	55.6
Blackburn,Nick, Min	55.3
Baker,Scott, Min	54.8
Wakefield,Tim, Bos	54.5
Beckett,Josh, Bos	54.2
Lackey,John, LAA	53.2
Millwood,Kevin, Tex	52.6

Pitches Per Start
(minimum 30 GS)

Halladay,Roy, Tor	107.2
Santana,Ervin, LAA	107.1
Verlander,Justin, Det	106.9
Burnett,A.J., Tor	106.6
Lee,Cliff, Cle	106.1
Meche,Gil, KC	104.6
Hernandez,Felix, Sea	103.2
Vazquez,Javier, CWS	102.3
Guthrie,Jeremy, Bal	102.1
Weaver,Jered, LAA	101.4

Pitches Per Batter
(minimum 162 IP)

Byrd,Paul, Cle-Bos	3.33
Blackburn,Nick, Min	3.50
Robertson,Nate, Det	3.51
Millwood,Kevin, Tex	3.53
Sonnanstine,Andy, TB	3.57
Shields,James, TB	3.57
Lackey,John, LAA	3.59
Halladay,Roy, Tor	3.61
Rogers,Kenny, Det	3.64
Eveland,Dana, Oak	3.64

Quality Starts

Buehrle,Mark, CWS	24
Greinke,Zack, KC	23
Halladay,Roy, Tor	23
Lee,Cliff, Cle	23
Santana,Ervin, LAA	22
Saunders,Joe, LAA	22
Shields,James, TB	22
Meche,Gil, KC	21
Mussina,Mike, NYY	21
Lester,Jon, Bos	20

Batters Faced

Halladay,Roy, Tor	987
Burnett,A.J., Tor	957
Buehrle,Mark, CWS	918
Santana,Ervin, LAA	897
Lee,Cliff, Cle	891
Vazquez,Javier, CWS	890
Meche,Gil, KC	886
Pettitte,Andy, NYY	881
Verlander,Justin, Det	880
Floyd,Gavin, CWS	878

Innings Pitched

Halladay,Roy, Tor	246.0
Lee,Cliff, Cle	223.1
Burnett,A.J., Tor	221.1
Santana,Ervin, LAA	219.0
Buehrle,Mark, CWS	218.2
Shields,James, TB	215.0
Lester,Jon, Bos	210.1
Meche,Gil, KC	210.1
Vazquez,Javier, CWS	208.1
Floyd,Gavin, CWS	206.1

Most Pitches in a Game

Halladay,Roy, Tor	130
Lester,Jon, Bos	130
Verlander,Justin, Det	130
Meche,Gil, KC	129
Bannister,Brian, KC	127
McGowan,Dustin, Tor	125
Sabathia,CC, Cle	123
Vazquez,Javier, CWS	122
8 tied with	121

Stolen Bases Allowed

Floyd,Gavin, CWS	37
Cabrera,Daniel, Bal	27
Wakefield,Tim, Bos	27
Millwood,Kevin, Tex	26
Danks,John, CWS	23
Burnett,A.J., Tor	22
Feldman,Scott, Tex	22
Olson,Garrett, Bal	20
Pettitte,Andy, NYY	20
Weaver,Jered, LAA	20

Caught Stealing Off

Smith,Greg, Oak	12
Wakefield,Tim, Bos	10
Burnett,A.J., Tor	9
Verlander,Justin, Det	9
Danks,John, CWS	8
Pettitte,Andy, NYY	8
5 tied with	7

Stolen Base Pct Allowed
(minimum 162 IP)

Sonnanstine,Andy, TB	25.0
Greinke,Zack, KC	33.3
Litsch,Jesse, Tor	33.3
Rogers,Kenny, Det	33.3
Buehrle,Mark, CWS	41.7
Verlander,Justin, Det	47.1
Smith,Greg, Oak	47.8
Blackburn,Nick, Min	50.0
Byrd,Paul, Cle-Bos	50.0
Garland,Jon, LAA	50.0

Pickoffs

Smith,Greg, Oak	16
Pettitte,Andy, NYY	10
Braden,Dallas, Oak	7
Buehrle,Mark, CWS	7
Danks,John, CWS	6
Feierabend,Ryan, Sea	6
Burnett,A.J., Tor	5
Dickey,R.A., Sea	5
Kazmir,Scott, TB	4
8 tied with	3

2008 American League Pitching Leaders

Strikeouts Per 9 IP
(minimum 162 IP)

Burnett,A.J., Tor	9.39
Beckett,Josh, Bos	8.88
Santana,Ervin, LAA	8.79
Vazquez,Javier, CWS	8.64
Matsuzaka,Daisuke, Bos	8.27
Greinke,Zack, KC	8.14
Hernandez,Felix, Sea	7.85
Meche,Gil, KC	7.83
Weaver,Jered, LAA	7.74
Halladay,Roy, Tor	7.54

Opp On-Base Percentage
(minimum 162 IP)

Halladay,Roy, Tor	.276
Santana,Ervin, LAA	.283
Lee,Cliff, Cle	.285
Baker,Scott, Min	.294
Galarraga,Armando, Det	.294
Shields,James, TB	.299
Beckett,Josh, Bos	.300
Wakefield,Tim, Bos	.302
Danks,John, CWS	.303
Guthrie,Jeremy, Bal	.304

Opp Slugging Average
(minimum 162 IP)

Matsuzaka,Daisuke, Bos	.324
Halladay,Roy, Tor	.345
Lee,Cliff, Cle	.348
Lester,Jon, Bos	.368
Santana,Ervin, LAA	.368
Danks,John, CWS	.371
Garza,Matt, TB	.377
Verlander,Justin, Det	.377
Eveland,Dana, Oak	.380
Baker,Scott, Min	.381

Opponent OPS
(minimum 162 IP)

Halladay,Roy, Tor	.621
Lee,Cliff, Cle	.633
Matsuzaka,Daisuke, Bos	.645
Santana,Ervin, LAA	.651
Danks,John, CWS	.674
Baker,Scott, Min	.675
Garza,Matt, TB	.683
Lester,Jon, Bos	.688
Wakefield,Tim, Bos	.689
Saunders,Joe, LAA	.691

Home Runs Per Nine IP
(minimum 162 IP)

Lee,Cliff, Cle	0.48
Eveland,Dana, Oak	0.54
Lester,Jon, Bos	0.60
Matsuzaka,Daisuke, Bos	0.64
Halladay,Roy, Tor	0.66
Danks,John, CWS	0.69
Hernandez,Felix, Sea	0.76
Mussina,Mike, NYY	0.76
Burnett,A.J., Tor	0.77
Verlander,Justin, Det	0.81

Batting Average vs. LHB
(minimum 125 BF)

Rivera,Mariano, NYY	.147
Nathan,Joe, Min	.167
Soria,Joakim, KC	.167
Thornton,Matt, CWS	.170
Lopez,Javier, Bos	.182
Howell,J.P., TB	.188
Delcarmen,Manny, Bos	.190
Francisco,Frank, Tex	.193
Morrow,Brandon, Sea	.198
2 tied with	.198

Batting Average vs. RHB
(minimum 225 BF)

Galarraga,Armando, Det	.174
Duchscherer,Justin, Oak	.188
Matsuzaka,Daisuke, Bos	.195
Howell,J.P., TB	.197
Marcum,Shaun, Tor	.200
Wakefield,Tim, Bos	.218
Bedard,Erik, Sea	.224
Rowland-Smith,Ryan, Sea	.224
Floyd,Gavin, CWS	.226
Kazmir,Scott, TB	.227

Opp BA w/ RISP
(minimum 125 BF)

Matsuzaka,Daisuke, Bos	.164
Kazmir,Scott, TB	.182
Lackey,John, LAA	.200
Rowland-Smith,Ryan, Sea	.204
Beckett,Josh, Bos	.209
Halladay,Roy, Tor	.214
Garza,Matt, TB	.218
Galarraga,Armando, Det	.222
Hernandez,Felix, Sea	.223
Baker,Scott, Min	.225

OBP vs. Leadoff Hitter
(minimum 150 BF)

Beckett,Josh, Bos	.230
Wakefield,Tim, Bos	.246
Galarraga,Armando, Det	.247
Vazquez,Javier, CWS	.251
Litsch,Jesse, Tor	.255
Marcum,Shaun, Tor	.272
Mussina,Mike, NYY	.275
Pettitte,Andy, NYY	.280
Lester,Jon, Bos	.284
Lee,Cliff, Cle	.293

Strikeouts / Walks Ratio
(minimum 162 IP)

Halladay,Roy, Tor	5.28
Beckett,Josh, Bos	5.06
Lee,Cliff, Cle	5.00
Mussina,Mike, NYY	4.84
Santana,Ervin, LAA	4.55
Shields,James, TB	4.00
Baker,Scott, Min	3.36
Sonnanstine,Andy, TB	3.35
Vazquez,Javier, CWS	3.28
Greinke,Zack, KC	3.27

Highest GB/FB Ratio
(minimum 162 IP)

Halladay,Roy, Tor	2.00
Pettitte,Andy, NYY	1.80
Garland,Jon, LAA	1.79
Hernandez,Felix, Sea	1.77
Eveland,Dana, Oak	1.68
Mussina,Mike, NYY	1.64
Buehrle,Mark, CWS	1.57
Litsch,Jesse, Tor	1.52
Burnett,A.J., Tor	1.52
Lester,Jon, Bos	1.49

Lowest GB/FB Ratio
(minimum 162 IP)

Weaver,Jered, LAA	0.71
Baker,Scott, Min	0.72
Wakefield,Tim, Bos	0.73
Smith,Greg, Oak	0.75
Byrd,Paul, Cle-Bos	0.86
Matsuzaka,Daisuke, Bos	0.89
Vazquez,Javier, CWS	0.92
Bannister,Brian, KC	0.92
Santana,Ervin, LAA	0.93
Verlander,Justin, Det	0.94

Sacrifice Flies Allowed

Cabrera,Daniel, Bal	12
Batista,Miguel, Sea	11
Bannister,Brian, KC	10
Lopez,Aquilino, Det	10
Meche,Gil, KC	10
Rogers,Kenny, Det	10
Smith,Greg, Oak	10
4 tied with	9

Sacrifice Hits Allowed

Burnett,A.J., Tor	8
Garland,Jon, LAA	8
Pettitte,Andy, NYY	8
Floyd,Gavin, CWS	7
Perkins,Glen, Min	7
Rogers,Kenny, Det	7
Howell,J.P., TB	6
Lester,Jon, Bos	6
Shields,James, TB	6
Washburn,Jarrod, Sea	6

GIDP Induced

Buehrle,Mark, CWS	34
Blackburn,Nick, Min	31
Hernandez,Felix, Sea	28
Saunders,Joe, LAA	28
Jackson,Edwin, TB	27
Lee,Cliff, Cle	27
Lester,Jon, Bos	27
Carmona,Fausto, Cle	26
Rogers,Kenny, Det	26
Garland,Jon, LAA	25

GIDP Per Nine IP
(minimum 162 IP)

Blackburn,Nick, Min	1.44
Buehrle,Mark, CWS	1.40
Rogers,Kenny, Det	1.35
Jackson,Edwin, TB	1.33
Robertson,Nate, Det	1.28
Saunders,Joe, LAA	1.27
Hernandez,Felix, Sea	1.26
Eveland,Dana, Oak	1.18
Lackey,John, LAA	1.16
Lester,Jon, Bos	1.16

414

2008 American League Pitching Leaders

Saves			Blown Saves			Save Pct			Save Opportunities		
						(minimum 20 Save Ops)					
Rodriguez,Francisco, LAA	62		Okajima,Hideki, Bos	8		Rivera,Mariano, NYY	97.5		Rodriguez,Francisco, LAA	69	
Soria,Joakim, KC	42		Putz,J.J., Sea	8		Soria,Joakim, KC	93.3		Papelbon,Jonathan, Bos	46	
Papelbon,Jonathan, Bos	41		Arredondo,Jose, LAA	7		Rodriguez,Francisco, LAA	89.9		Nathan,Joe, Min	45	
Nathan,Joe, Min	39		Rodriguez,Francisco, LAA	7		Papelbon,Jonathan, Bos	89.1		Soria,Joakim, KC	45	
Rivera,Mariano, NYY	39		Street,Huston, Oak	7		Ryan,B.J., Tor	88.9		Rivera,Mariano, NYY	40	
Ryan,B.J., Tor	32		Francisco,Frank, Tex	6		Jenks,Bobby, CWS	88.2		Sherrill,George, Bal	37	
Sherrill,George, Bal	31		Nathan,Joe, Min	6		Percival,Troy, TB	87.5		Ryan,B.J., Tor	36	
Jenks,Bobby, CWS	30		Rodney,Fernando, Det	6		Nathan,Joe, Min	86.7		Jenks,Bobby, CWS	34	
Percival,Troy, TB	28		Sherrill,George, Bal	6		Jones,Todd, Det	85.7		Percival,Troy, TB	32	
Wilson,C.J., Tex	24		Wright,Jamey, Tex	6		Wilson,C.J., Tex	85.7		Wilson,C.J., Tex	28	

Easy Saves			Regular Saves			Tough Saves			Holds Adjusted Saves %		
									(minimum 20 Save Ops)		
Rodriguez,Francisco, LAA	39		Rodriguez,Francisco, LAA	22		Rivera,Mariano, NYY	5		Rivera,Mariano, NYY	97.5	
Soria,Joakim, KC	25		Nathan,Joe, Min	17		Papelbon,Jonathan, Bos	4		Soria,Joakim, KC	93.3	
Papelbon,Jonathan, Bos	22		Soria,Joakim, KC	16		Balfour,Grant, TB	3		Rodriguez,Francisco, LAA	89.9	
Nathan,Joe, Min	21		Papelbon,Jonathan, Bos	15		Morrow,Brandon, Sea	2		Ryan,B.J., Tor	89.2	
Percival,Troy, TB	20		Rivera,Mariano, NYY	15		Rodney,Fernando, Det	2		Papelbon,Jonathan, Bos	89.1	
Sherrill,George, Bal	20		Ryan,B.J., Tor	13		Rowland-Smith,Ryan, Sea	2		Percival,Troy, TB	88.9	
Rivera,Mariano, NYY	19		Wilson,C.J., Tex	13		Sherrill,George, Bal	2		Jenks,Bobby, CWS	88.2	
Ryan,B.J., Tor	19		Jenks,Bobby, CWS	12		Wheeler,Dan, TB	2		Nathan,Joe, Min	86.7	
Jenks,Bobby, CWS	17		Sherrill,George, Bal	9		14 tied with	1		Wilson,C.J., Tex	86.2	
Jones,Todd, Det	15		Percival,Troy, TB	8					Jones,Todd, Det	85.7	

Relief Wins			Relief Losses			Relief Games			Holds		
Arredondo,Jose, LAA	10		Guerrier,Matt, Min	9		Guerrier,Matt, Min	76		Shields,Scot, LAA	31	
Wright,Jamey, Tex	8		Speier,Justin, LAA	8		Rodriguez,Francisco, LAA	76		Wheeler,Dan, TB	26	
Carlson,Jesse, Tor	7		Wright,Jamey, Tex	7		Reyes,Dennys, Min	75		Guardado,Eddie, Tex-Min	25	
Oliver,Darren, LAA	7		Rodney,Fernando, Det	6		Wright,Jamey, Tex	75		Perez,Rafael, Cle	25	
Street,Huston, Oak	7		Wheeler,Dan, TB	6		Thornton,Matt, CWS	74		Downs,Scott, Tor	24	
8 tied with	6		11 tied with	5		Delcarmen,Manny, Bos	73		Okajima,Hideki, Bos	23	
						Perez,Rafael, Cle	73		Bradford,Chad, Bal-TB	21	
						Dotel,Octavio, CWS	72		Dotel,Octavio, CWS	21	
						Green,Sean, Sea	72		Mahay,Ron, KC	21	
						Ramirez,Ramon, KC	71		Ramirez,Ramon, KC	21	

Relief Innings			Inherited Runners Scrd %			Relief Opp On Base Pct			Relief Opp Slugging Avg		
			(minimum 30 IR)			(minimum 50 IP)			(minimum 50 IP)		
Howell,J.P., TB	89.1		Howell,J.P., TB	11.4		Rivera,Mariano, NYY	.190		Balfour,Grant, TB	.230	
Rupe,Josh, Tex	89.1		Frasor,Jason, Tor	12.5		Balfour,Grant, TB	.233		Rivera,Mariano, NYY	.233	
Wright,Jamey, Tex	84.1		Papelbon,Jonathan, Bos	13.3		Nathan,Joe, Min	.242		Johnson,Jim, Bal	.235	
Green,Sean, Sea	79.0		Miller,Trever, TB	16.2		Papelbon,Jonathan, Bos	.245		Soria,Joakim, KC	.255	
Lopez,Aquilino, Det	78.2		Carlson,Jesse, Tor	18.4		Soria,Joakim, KC	.248		Arredondo,Jose, LAA	.267	
Guerrier,Matt, Min	76.1		Breslow,Craig, Cle-Min	19.1		Wheeler,Dan, TB	.250		Sarfate,Dennis, Bal	.276	
Perez,Rafael, Cle	76.1		Embree,Alan, Oak	20.0		Thornton,Matt, CWS	.258		Nathan,Joe, Min	.279	
Delcarmen,Manny, Bos	74.1		Green,Sean, Sea	20.4		Arredondo,Jose, LAA	.266		Thornton,Matt, CWS	.286	
Corcoran,Roy, Sea	72.2		Balfour,Grant, TB	20.5		Carlson,Jesse, Tor	.275		Ramirez,Ramon, KC	.288	
Oliver,Darren, LAA	72.0		Guerrier,Matt, Min	21.6		Francisco,Frank, Tex	.277		Howell,J.P., TB	.291	

2008 American League Pitching Leaders

Relief Opp BA Vs LHB
(minimum 50 AB)

Balfour,Grant, TB	.120
Rivera,Mariano, NYY	.147
Arredondo,Jose, LAA	.148
Albers,Matt, Bal	.159
Sarfate,Dennis, Bal	.165
Nathan,Joe, Min	.167
Soria,Joakim, KC	.167
Thornton,Matt, CWS	.170
Lopez,Javier, Bos	.182
Breslow,Craig, Cle-Min	.183

Relief Opp BA Vs RHB
(minimum 50 AB)

Morrow,Brandon, Sea	.099
Devine,Joey, Oak	.120
Tejeda,Robinson, Tex-KC	.130
Ramirez,Ramon, KC	.153
Balfour,Grant, TB	.159
Wheeler,Dan, TB	.163
Percival,Troy, TB	.171
Soria,Joakim, KC	.171
Frasor,Jason, Tor	.174
Bruney,Brian, NYY	.179

Relief Opp Batting Average
(minimum 50 IP)

Balfour,Grant, TB	.143
Rivera,Mariano, NYY	.165
Soria,Joakim, KC	.169
Nathan,Joe, Min	.179
Wheeler,Dan, TB	.183
Arredondo,Jose, LAA	.190
Howell,J.P., TB	.194
Sarfate,Dennis, Bal	.195
Thornton,Matt, CWS	.196
Carlson,Jesse, Tor	.196

Relief Earned Run Average
(minimum 50 IP)

Ziegler,Brad, Oak	1.06
Nathan,Joe, Min	1.33
Rivera,Mariano, NYY	1.40
Balfour,Grant, TB	1.54
Soria,Joakim, KC	1.60
Arredondo,Jose, LAA	1.62
Downs,Scott, Tor	1.78
Bradford,Chad, Bal-TB	2.12
Howell,J.P., TB	2.22
Johnson,Jim, Bal	2.23

Rel OBP 1st Batter Faced
(minimum 40 BF)

Devine,Joey, Oak	.167
Francisco,Frank, Tex	.172
Soria,Joakim, KC	.190
Wheeler,Dan, TB	.214
Carlson,Jesse, Tor	.217
Frasor,Jason, Tor	.224
Nathan,Joe, Min	.235
Street,Huston, Oak	.238
Papelbon,Jonathan, Bos	.239
Percival,Troy, TB	.240

Rel Opp BA w/ Runners On
(minimum 50 IP)

Nathan,Joe, Min	.128
Rivera,Mariano, NYY	.143
Balfour,Grant, TB	.169
Ziegler,Brad, Oak	.174
Howell,J.P., TB	.178
Carlson,Jesse, Tor	.183
Dotel,Octavio, CWS	.183
Rodriguez,Francisco, LAA	.183
Shields,Scot, LAA	.184
Johnson,Jim, Bal	.200

Relief Opp BA w/ RISP
(minimum 50 IP)

Balfour,Grant, TB	.109
Ziegler,Brad, Oak	.116
Nathan,Joe, Min	.154
Dotel,Octavio, CWS	.165
Veras,Jose, NYY	.167
Howell,J.P., TB	.169
Ryan,B.J., Tor	.172
Shields,Scot, LAA	.177
Tallet,Brian, Tor	.182
2 tied with	.192

Fastest Avg Fastball-Relief
(minimum 50 IP)

Delcarmen,Manny, Bos	95.5
Thornton,Matt, CWS	95.3
Papelbon,Jonathan, Bos	95.3
Farnsworth,Kyle, NYY-Det	94.9
Veras,Jose, NYY	94.9
Francisco,Frank, Tex	94.7
Balfour,Grant, TB	94.6
Sarfate,Dennis, Bal	94.6
Casilla,Santiago, Oak	94.4
Lowe,Mark, Sea	94.3

Fastest Average Fastball
(minimum 162 IP)

Hernandez,Felix, Sea	94.6
Santana,Ervin, LAA	94.4
Beckett,Josh, Bos	94.3
Burnett,A.J., Tor	94.3
Jackson,Edwin, TB	93.9
Verlander,Justin, Det	93.6
Greinke,Zack, KC	93.3
Guthrie,Jeremy, Bal	93.2
Garza,Matt, TB	93.2
Halladay,Roy, Tor	92.7

Slowest Average Fastball
(minimum 162 IP)

Wakefield,Tim, Bos	72.9
Rogers,Kenny, Det	85.2
Byrd,Paul, Cle-Bos	85.7
Mussina,Mike, NYY	86.4
Buehrle,Mark, CWS	86.5
Sonnanstine,Andy, TB	87.0
Smith,Greg, Oak	87.6
Robertson,Nate, Det	88.4
Pettitte,Andy, NYY	88.5
Bannister,Brian, KC	89.0

Pitches 100+ Velocity

Zumaya,Joel, Det	18
League,Brandon, Tor	4
Chamberlain,Joba, NYY	3
Hernandez,Felix, Sea	3
Morrow,Brandon, Sea	3
Papelbon,Jonathan, Bos	2
Rodney,Fernando, Det	2
Jenks,Bobby, CWS	1
Santana,Ervin, LAA	1

Pitches 95+ Velocity

Hernandez,Felix, Sea	1035
Burnett,A.J.,`Tor	925
Santana,Ervin, LAA	896
Beckett,Josh, Bos	747
Jackson,Edwin, TB	718
Farnsworth,Kyle, NYY-Det	714
Verlander,Justin, Det	673
Delcarmen,Manny, Bos	634
Thornton,Matt, CWS	630
Chamberlain,Joba, NYY	590

Pitches Less Than 80 MPH

Wakefield,Tim, Bos	2594
Byrd,Paul, Cle-Bos	1506
Dickey,R.A., Sea	1254
Sonnanstine,Andy, TB	925
Mussina,Mike, NYY	890
Bradford,Chad, Bal-TB	804
Rogers,Kenny, Det	777
Buehrle,Mark, CWS	724
Hernandez,Livan, Min	701
Halladay,Roy, Tor	676

Lowest % Fastballs
(minimum 162 IP)

Wakefield,Tim, Bos	13.1
Litsch,Jesse, Tor	23.4
Sonnanstine,Andy, TB	32.2
Halladay,Roy, Tor	39.8
Shields,James, TB	44.4
Buehrle,Mark, CWS	46.5
Galarraga,Armando, Det	48.5
Blackburn,Nick, Min	49.2
Mussina,Mike, NYY	49.7
Byrd,Paul, Cle-Bos	49.9

Highest % Fastballs
(minimum 162 IP)

Cabrera,Daniel, Bal	81.3
Padilla,Vicente, Tex	71.9
Garza,Matt, TB	71.2
Millwood,Kevin, Tex	70.3
Lee,Cliff, Cle	69.2
Jackson,Edwin, TB	68.3
Beckett,Josh, Bos	66.3
Burnett,A.J., Tor	64.2
Hernandez,Felix, Sea	64.1
Guthrie,Jeremy, Bal	63.0

Highest % Curveballs
(minimum 162 IP)

Burnett,A.J., Tor	28.9
Lackey,John, LAA	24.2
Mussina,Mike, NYY	24.1
Beckett,Josh, Bos	23.5
Halladay,Roy, Tor	22.3
Verlander,Justin, Det	20.1
Floyd,Gavin, CWS	18.3
Meche,Gil, KC	17.0
Lester,Jon, Bos	16.9
Vazquez,Javier, CWS	12.6

2008 American League Pitching Leaders

Highest % Changeups
(minimum 162 IP)

Shields,James, TB	26.1
Rogers,Kenny, Det	22.9
Saunders,Joe, LAA	21.0
Smith,Greg, Oak	20.2
Danks,John, CWS	19.9
Garland,Jon, LAA	17.0
Weaver,Jered, LAA	16.9
Verlander,Justin, Det	15.5
Buehrle,Mark, CWS	15.3
Robertson,Nate, Det	15.2

Highest % Sliders
(minimum 162 IP)

Galarraga,Armando, Det	38.3
Santana,Ervin, LAA	33.4
Robertson,Nate, Det	24.5
Matsuzaka,Daisuke, Bos	22.9
Eveland,Dana, Oak	22.8
Vazquez,Javier, CWS	22.5
Byrd,Paul, Cle-Bos	22.2
Sonnanstine,Andy, TB	21.5
Jackson,Edwin, TB	21.5
Floyd,Gavin, CWS	20.2

Balks

Padilla,Vicente, Tex	3
Verlander,Justin, Det	3
Burnett,A.J., Tor	2
Cabrera,Daniel, Bal	2
Chamberlain,Joba, NYY	2
Feldman,Scott, Tex	2
Garza,Matt, TB	2
Harrison,Matt, Tex	2
Sabathia,CC, Cle	2
45 tied with	1

Strikeout/Hit Ratio
(minimum 50 IP)

Balfour,Grant, TB	2.93
Morrow,Brandon, Sea	1.88
Rivera,Mariano, NYY	1.88
Dotel,Octavio, CWS	1.77
Francisco,Frank, Tex	1.77
Nathan,Joe, Min	1.72
Soria,Joakim, KC	1.69
Harden,Rich, Oak	1.61
Thornton,Matt, CWS	1.60
Howell,J.P., TB	1.48

Opp OPS vs Fastballs
(minimum 251 BF)

Danks,John, CWS	.605
Garza,Matt, TB	.614
Chamberlain,Joba, NYY	.617
Lee,Cliff, Cle	.637
Halladay,Roy, Tor	.648
Wang,Chien-Ming, NYY	.654
Kazmir,Scott, TB	.658
Beckett,Josh, Bos	.659
Lester,Jon, Bos	.679
Matsuzaka,Daisuke, Bos	.682

Opp OPS vs Curveballs
(minimum 100 BF)

Halladay,Roy, Tor	.480
Lackey,John, LAA	.508
Duchscherer,Justin, Oak	.551
Bedard,Erik, Sea	.573
Burnett,A.J., Tor	.578
Cormier,Lance, Bal	.639
Greinke,Zack, KC	.643
Mussina,Mike, NYY	.648
Verlander,Justin, Det	.651
Lester,Jon, Bos	.658

Opp OPS vs Changeups
(minimum 100 BF)

Marcum,Shaun, Tor	.545
Saunders,Joe, LAA	.564
Smith,Greg, Oak	.618
Hernandez,Felix, Sea	.640
Lee,Cliff, Cle	.655
Danks,John, CWS	.675
Verlander,Justin, Det	.684
Miner,Zach, Det	.712
Rogers,Kenny, Det	.731
Robertson,Nate, Det	.738

Opp OPS vs Sliders
(minimum 64 BF)

Breslow,Craig, Cle-Min	.385
Gaudin,Chad, Oak	.439
Guerrier,Matt, Min	.439
Sabathia,CC, Cle	.449
Matsuzaka,Daisuke, Bos	.488
Perez,Rafael, Cle	.518
Galarraga,Armando, Det	.521
Ponson,Sidney, Tex-NYY	.525
Greinke,Zack, KC	.526
Baker,Scott, Min	.549

Earned Runs

Robertson,Nate, Det	119
Bannister,Brian, KC	117
Rogers,Kenny, Det	110
Silva,Carlos, Sea	110
Vazquez,Javier, CWS	108
Verlander,Justin, Det	108
Garland,Jon, LAA	107
Cabrera,Daniel, Bal	105
Pettitte,Andy, NYY	103
Burnett,A.J., Tor	100

Hits Per Nine Innings
(minimum 162 IP)

Matsuzaka,Daisuke, Bos	6.87
Galarraga,Armando, Det	7.66
Wakefield,Tim, Bos	7.66
Smith,Greg, Oak	7.99
Halladay,Roy, Tor	8.05
Santana,Ervin, LAA	8.14
Floyd,Gavin, CWS	8.29
Garza,Matt, TB	8.29
Guthrie,Jeremy, Bal	8.31
Danks,John, CWS	8.40

2008 National League Pitching Leaders

Earned Run Average
(minimum 162 IP)

Santana,Johan, NYM	2.53
Lincecum,Tim, SF	2.62
Peavy,Jake, SD	2.85
Dempster,Ryan, ChC	2.96
Sheets,Ben, Mil	3.09
Hamels,Cole, Phi	3.09
Billingsley,Chad, LAD	3.14
Volquez,Edinson, Cin	3.21
Lowe,Derek, LAD	3.24
Webb,Brandon, Ari	3.30

Winning Percentage
(minimum 15 Decisions)

Lincecum,Tim, SF	.783
Webb,Brandon, Ari	.759
Dempster,Ryan, ChC	.739
Volquez,Edinson, Cin	.739
Lohse,Kyle, StL	.714
Zambrano,Carlos, ChC	.700
Moyer,Jamie, Phi	.696
Santana,Johan, NYM	.696
Haren,Dan, Ari	.667
Lilly,Ted, ChC	.654

Opponent Batting Average
(minimum 162 IP)

Lincecum,Tim, SF	.221
Hamels,Cole, Phi	.227
Dempster,Ryan, ChC	.227
Peavy,Jake, SD	.229
Volquez,Edinson, Cin	.232
Santana,Johan, NYM	.232
Bush,David, Mil	.234
Perez,Oliver, NYM	.234
Nolasco,Ricky, Fla	.239
Lilly,Ted, ChC	.239

Baserunners Per 9 IP
(minimum 162 IP)

Hamels,Cole, Phi	9.78
Nolasco,Ricky, Fla	10.17
Lowe,Derek, LAD	10.24
Sheets,Ben, Mil	10.39
Haren,Dan, Ari	10.42
Santana,Johan, NYM	10.49
Bush,David, Mil	10.75
Lincecum,Tim, SF	10.78
Peavy,Jake, SD	10.88
Oswalt,Roy, Hou	11.04

Games

Feliciano,Pedro, NYM	86
Ohman,Will, Atl	83
Marmol,Carlos, ChC	82
Smith,Joe, NYM	82
Ayala,Luis, Was-NYM	81
Romero,J.C., Phi	81
Heilman,Aaron, NYM	78
Qualls,Chad, Ari	77
4 tied with	76

Games Started

Arroyo,Bronson, Cin	34
Cain,Matt, SF	34
Jimenez,Ubaldo, Col	34
Lilly,Ted, ChC	34
Lowe,Derek, LAD	34
Perez,Oliver, NYM	34
Santana,Johan, NYM	34
Webb,Brandon, Ari	34
11 tied with	33

Complete Games

Sabathia,CC, Mil	7
Sheets,Ben, Mil	5
Oswalt,Roy, Hou	3
Santana,Johan, NYM	3
Webb,Brandon, Ari	3
7 tied with	2

Shutouts

Sabathia,CC, Mil	3
Sheets,Ben, Mil	3
Hamels,Cole, Phi	2
Kuroda,Hiroki, LAD	2
Oswalt,Roy, Hou	2
Santana,Johan, NYM	2
16 tied with	1

Wins

Webb,Brandon, Ari	22
Lincecum,Tim, SF	18
Dempster,Ryan, ChC	17
Lilly,Ted, ChC	17
Oswalt,Roy, Hou	17
Volquez,Edinson, Cin	17
5 tied with	16

Losses

Harang,Aaron, Cin	17
Zito,Barry, SF	17
Lannan,John, Was	15
Backe,Brandon, Hou	14
Cain,Matt, SF	14
Cueto,Johnny, Cin	14
Duke,Zach, Pit	14
Looper,Braden, StL	14
Maddux,Greg, SD-LAD	13
Myers,Brett, Phi	13

No Decisions

Perez,Oliver, NYM	17
Olsen,Scott, Fla	14
Maholm,Paul, Pit	13
Cain,Matt,SF	12
Davis,Doug,Ari	12
Duke,Zach,Pit	12
Kuroda,Hiroki,LAD	12
Lohse,Kyle,StL	12
Maddux,Greg,SD-LAD	12
Redding,Tim,Was	12
Snell,Ian,Pit	12

Wild Pitches

Lincecum,Tim, SF	17
Parra,Manny, Mil	17
Jimenez,Ubaldo, Col	16
de la Rosa,Jorge, Col	14
Haren,Dan, Ari	11
Billingsley,Chad, LAD	10
Maine,John, NYM	10
Redding,Tim, Was	10
Volquez,Edinson, Cin	10
Perez,Oliver, NYM	9
Santana,Johan, NYM	9

Strikeouts

Lincecum,Tim, SF	265
Haren,Dan, Ari	206
Santana,Johan, NYM	206
Volquez,Edinson, Cin	206
Billingsley,Chad, LAD	201
Hamels,Cole, Phi	196
Dempster,Ryan, ChC	187
Cain,Matt, SF	186
Nolasco,Ricky, Fla	186
Lilly,Ted, ChC	184

Walks Allowed

Perez,Oliver, NYM	105
Jimenez,Ubaldo, Col	103
Zito,Barry, SF	102
Volquez,Edinson, Cin	93
Cain,Matt, SF	91
Snell,Ian, Pit	89
Lincecum,Tim, SF	84
Billingsley,Chad, LAD	80
Backe,Brandon, Hou	77
Dempster,Ryan, ChC	76

Intentional Walks Allowed

Olsen,Scott, Fla	13
Zito,Barry, SF	10
Cain,Matt, SF	9
Jurrjens,Jair, Atl	9
Condrey,Clay, Phi	8
Feliciano,Pedro, NYM	8
Heilman,Aaron, NYM	8
Kuroda,Hiroki, LAD	8
Weathers,David, Cin	8
8 tied with	7

Hit Batters

Cueto,Johnny, Cin	14
Kendrick,Kyle, Phi	14
Volquez,Edinson, Cin	14
Pelfrey,Mike, NYM	13
Owings,Micah, Ari-Cin	12
Webb,Brandon, Ari	12
Wolf,Randy, SD-Hou	12
Looper,Braden, StL	11
Moyer,Jamie, Phi	11
Perez,Oliver, NYM	11

2008 National League Pitching Leaders

Runs Allowed		Hits Allowed		Doubles Allowed		Home Runs Allowed	
Arroyo,Bronson, Cin	116	Cook,Aaron, Col	236	Duke,Zach, Pit	58	Backe,Brandon, Hou	36
Zito,Barry, SF	115	Duke,Zach, Pit	230	Harang,Aaron, Cin	52	Harang,Aaron, Cin	35
Backe,Brandon, Hou	114	Arroyo,Bronson, Cin	219	Lohse,Kyle, StL	52	Lilly,Ted, ChC	32
Duke,Zach, Pit	111	Looper,Braden, StL	216	Cain,Matt, SF	49	Olsen,Scott, Fla	30
Redding,Tim, Was	110	Lohse,Kyle, StL	211	Myers,Brett, Phi	49	Suppan,Jeff, Mil	30
Suppan,Jeff, Mil	110	Pelfrey,Mike, NYM	209	Sheets,Ben, Mil	49	Arroyo,Bronson, Cin	29
Snell,Ian, Pit	107	Suppan,Jeff, Mil	207	Olsen,Scott, Fla	48	Bush,David, Mil	29
Olsen,Scott, Fla	106	Cain,Matt, SF	206	Perez,Odalis, Was	47	Cueto,Johnny, Cin	29
Maddux,Greg, SD-LAD	105	Santana,Johan, NYM	206	Pineiro,Joel, StL	47	Myers,Brett, Phi	29
Harang,Aaron, Cin	104	Webb,Brandon, Ari	206	Wellemeyer,Todd, StL	47	2 tied with	28

Run Support Per Nine IP (minimum 162 IP)		% Pitches In Strike Zone (minimum 162 IP)		Pitches Per Start (minimum 30 GS)		Pitches Per Batter (minimum 162 IP)	
Marquis,Jason, ChC	6.09	Maddux,Greg, SD-LAD	55.3	Lincecum,Tim, SF	109.0	Maddux,Greg, SD-LAD	3.20
Zambrano,Carlos, ChC	6.01	Nolasco,Ricky, Fla	55.1	Cain,Matt, SF	106.1	Cook,Aaron, Col	3.47
Dempster,Ryan, ChC	5.84	Oswalt,Roy, Hou	55.0	Santana,Johan, NYM	105.8	Duke,Zach, Pit	3.53
Arroyo,Bronson, Cin	5.81	Cook,Aaron, Col	54.5	Volquez,Edinson, Cin	104.6	Kuroda,Hiroki, LAD	3.53
Lilly,Ted, ChC	5.80	Lilly,Ted, ChC	54.5	Hamels,Cole, Phi	103.8	Webb,Brandon, Ari	3.56
Pelfrey,Mike, NYM	5.70	Santana,Johan, NYM	54.3	Pelfrey,Mike, NYM	103.8	Maholm,Paul, Pit	3.57
Jurrjens,Jair, Atl	5.59	Olsen,Scott, Fla	54.2	Billingsley,Chad, LAD	101.4	Oswalt,Roy, Hou	3.59
Volquez,Edinson, Cin	5.56	Harang,Aaron, Cin	53.8	Dempster,Ryan, ChC	101.2	Bush,David, Mil	3.59
Redding,Tim, Was	5.54	Sheets,Ben, Mil	53.7	Haren,Dan, Ari	101.2	Marquis,Jason, ChC	3.60
Moyer,Jamie, Phi	5.50	Myers,Brett, Phi	53.7	Arroyo,Bronson, Cin	101.1	Suppan,Jeff, Mil	3.62

Quality Starts		Batters Faced		Innings Pitched		Most Pitches in a Game	
Santana,Johan, NYM	28	Santana,Johan, NYM	964	Santana,Johan, NYM	234.1	Lincecum,Tim, SF	138
Lincecum,Tim, SF	26	Webb,Brandon, Ari	944	Hamels,Cole, Phi	227.1	Lincecum,Tim, SF	132
Webb,Brandon, Ari	24	Cain,Matt, SF	933	Lincecum,Tim, SF	227.0	Nolasco,Ricky, Fla	132
Hamels,Cole, Phi	23	Lincecum,Tim, SF	928	Webb,Brandon, Ari	226.2	Sabathia,CC, Mil	130
Haren,Dan, Ari	23	Hamels,Cole, Phi	914	Cain,Matt, SF	217.2	Zambrano,Carlos, ChC	130
Nolasco,Ricky, Fla	23	Cook,Aaron, Col	886	Haren,Dan, Ari	216.0	Wolf,Randy, SD-Hou	128
Oswalt,Roy, Hou	22	Haren,Dan, Ari	881	Nolasco,Ricky, Fla	212.1	Lincecum,Tim, SF	127
4 tied with	21	Arroyo,Bronson, Cin	871	Cook,Aaron, Col	211.1	Peavy,Jake, SD	127
		Jimenez,Ubaldo, Col	868	Lowe,Derek, LAD	211.0	Wainwright,Adam, StL	127
		Nolasco,Ricky, Fla	868	Oswalt,Roy, Hou	208.2	Cain,Matt, SF	126

Stolen Bases Allowed		Caught Stealing Off		Stolen Base Pct Allowed (minimum 162 IP)		Pickoffs	
Jurrjens,Jair, Atl	28	Volquez,Edinson, Cin	12	Suppan,Jeff, Mil	36.4	Lilly,Ted, ChC	6
Maddux,Greg, SD-LAD	24	Cain,Matt, SF	10	Cook,Aaron, Col	38.5	Lannan,John, Was	5
Webb,Brandon, Ari	24	Webb,Brandon, Ari	10	Backe,Brandon, Hou	40.0	Cook,Aaron, Col	4
Johnson,Randy, Ari	21	Bush,David, Mil	9	Maholm,Paul, Pit	41.7	Duke,Zach, Pit	4
Volquez,Edinson, Cin	21	Peavy,Jake, SD	9	Pelfrey,Mike, NYM	45.5	Moyer,Jamie, Phi	4
Lincecum,Tim, SF	20	Zambrano,Carlos, ChC	9	Duke,Zach, Pit	50.0	Olsen,Scott, Fla	4
Snell,Ian, Pit	20	Cook,Aaron, Col	8	Oswalt,Roy, Hou	50.0	Pelfrey,Mike, NYM	4
Jimenez,Ubaldo, Col	19	Lilly,Ted, ChC	8	Zambrano,Carlos, ChC	52.6	Perez,Odalis, Was	4
Sanchez,Jonathan, SF	19	8 tied with	7	Olsen,Scott, Fla	53.3	8 tied with	3
2 tied with	18			2 tied with	53.8		

2008 National League Pitching Leaders

Strikeouts Per 9 IP
(minimum 162 IP)

Lincecum,Tim, SF	10.51
Volquez,Edinson, Cin	9.46
Billingsley,Chad, LAD	9.01
Peavy,Jake, SD	8.60
Haren,Dan, Ari	8.58
Johnson,Randy, Ari	8.46
Perez,Oliver, NYM	8.35
Cueto,Johnny, Cin	8.17
Dempster,Ryan, ChC	8.14
Lilly,Ted, ChC	8.09

Opp On-Base Percentage
(minimum 162 IP)

Hamels,Cole, Phi	.272
Nolasco,Ricky, Fla	.278
Sheets,Ben, Mil	.284
Lowe,Derek, LAD	.285
Santana,Johan, NYM	.286
Haren,Dan, Ari	.286
Bush,David, Mil	.291
Lincecum,Tim, SF	.297
Kuroda,Hiroki, LAD	.299
Peavy,Jake, SD	.299

Opp Slugging Average
(minimum 162 IP)

Lincecum,Tim, SF	.316
Webb,Brandon, Ari	.334
Dempster,Ryan, ChC	.341
Peavy,Jake, SD	.345
Jimenez,Ubaldo, Col	.348
Volquez,Edinson, Cin	.351
Lowe,Derek, LAD	.352
Kuroda,Hiroki, LAD	.359
Santana,Johan, NYM	.362
Billingsley,Chad, LAD	.363

Opponent OPS
(minimum 162 IP)

Lincecum,Tim, SF	.612
Webb,Brandon, Ari	.636
Lowe,Derek, LAD	.637
Dempster,Ryan, ChC	.642
Peavy,Jake, SD	.645
Santana,Johan, NYM	.648
Hamels,Cole, Phi	.657
Kuroda,Hiroki, LAD	.659
Haren,Dan, Ari	.667
Sheets,Ben, Mil	.674

Home Runs Per Nine IP
(minimum 162 IP)

Lincecum,Tim, SF	0.44
Jimenez,Ubaldo, Col	0.50
Webb,Brandon, Ari	0.52
Jurrjens,Jair, Atl	0.53
Pelfrey,Mike, NYM	0.54
Cook,Aaron, Col	0.55
Lowe,Derek, LAD	0.60
Dempster,Ryan, ChC	0.61
Billingsley,Chad, LAD	0.63
Kuroda,Hiroki, LAD	0.64

Batting Average vs. LHB
(minimum 125 BF)

Perez,Oliver, NYM	.158
Harden,Rich, ChC	.167
Gregg,Kevin, Fla	.181
Marmol,Carlos, ChC	.182
Maholm,Paul, Pit	.183
Olsen,Scott, Fla	.187
Valverde,Jose, Hou	.190
Wilson,Brian, SF	.202
Bell,Heath, SD	.207
Wood,Kerry, ChC	.209

Batting Average vs. RHB
(minimum 225 BF)

Young,Chris, SD	.189
Peavy,Jake, SD	.194
Kuo,Hong-Chih, LAD	.205
Grabow,John, Pit	.207
Dempster,Ryan, ChC	.213
Volquez,Edinson, Cin	.214
Hamels,Cole, Phi	.215
Webb,Brandon, Ari	.219
Lilly,Ted, ChC	.219
Lincecum,Tim, SF	.221

Opp BA w/ RISP
(minimum 125 BF)

Lincecum,Tim, SF	.167
Wellemeyer,Todd, StL	.182
Peavy,Jake, SD	.184
Nolasco,Ricky, Fla	.192
Sheets,Ben, Mil	.198
Hudson,Tim, Atl	.204
Lannan,John, Was	.210
Webb,Brandon, Ari	.211
Billingsley,Chad, LAD	.219
Lilly,Ted, ChC	.222

OBP vs. Leadoff Hitter
(minimum 150 BF)

Dempster,Ryan, ChC	.236
Hamels,Cole, Phi	.252
Haren,Dan, Ari	.256
Santana,Johan, NYM	.258
Sheets,Ben, Mil	.261
Bush,David, Mil	.266
Kuroda,Hiroki, LAD	.268
Campillo,Jorge, Atl	.272
Nolasco,Ricky, Fla	.273
Lilly,Ted, ChC	.274

Strikeouts / Walks Ratio
(minimum 162 IP)

Haren,Dan, Ari	5.15
Nolasco,Ricky, Fla	4.43
Johnson,Randy, Ari	3.93
Hamels,Cole, Phi	3.70
Oswalt,Roy, Hou	3.51
Sheets,Ben, Mil	3.36
Santana,Johan, NYM	3.27
Lowe,Derek, LAD	3.27
Maddux,Greg, SD-LAD	3.27
Lincecum,Tim, SF	3.15

Highest GB/FB Ratio
(minimum 162 IP)

Webb,Brandon, Ari	3.15
Lowe,Derek, LAD	2.63
Cook,Aaron, Col	2.36
Lannan,John, Was	2.03
Jimenez,Ubaldo, Col	1.94
Jurrjens,Jair, Atl	1.94
Parra,Manny, Mil	1.94
Maholm,Paul, Pit	1.93
Kuroda,Hiroki, LAD	1.79
Oswalt,Roy, Hou	1.72

Lowest GB/FB Ratio
(minimum 162 IP)

Perez,Oliver, NYM	0.70
Lilly,Ted, ChC	0.75
Cain,Matt, SF	0.76
Harang,Aaron, Cin	0.77
Olsen,Scott, Fla	0.88
Zito,Barry, SF	0.90
Nolasco,Ricky, Fla	0.92
Backe,Brandon, Hou	0.92
Cueto,Johnny, Cin	0.95
Johnson,Randy, Ari	0.96

Sacrifice Flies Allowed

Zito,Barry, SF	14
Nolasco,Ricky, Fla	9
Oswalt,Roy, Hou	9
Webb,Brandon, Ari	9
Bergmann,Jason, Was	8
Maddux,Greg, SD-LAD	8
Maholm,Paul, Pit	8
Moehler,Brian, Hou	8
8 tied with	7

Sacrifice Hits Allowed

Duke,Zach, Pit	14
Arroyo,Bronson, Cin	13
Johnson,Randy, Ari	13
Lannan,John, Was	13
Jurrjens,Jair, Atl	12
Perez,Odalis, Was	12
Harang,Aaron, Cin	11
Lincecum,Tim, SF	11
Pelfrey,Mike, NYM	11
8 tied with	10

GIDP Induced

Cook,Aaron, Col	29
Pelfrey,Mike, NYM	29
Maholm,Paul, Pit	27
Webb,Brandon, Ari	26
Lincecum,Tim, SF	23
Looper,Braden, StL	23
Suppan,Jeff, Mil	22
Arroyo,Bronson, Cin	20
Marquis,Jason, ChC	20
3 tied with	19

GIDP Per Nine IP
(minimum 162 IP)

Pelfrey,Mike, NYM	1.30
Cook,Aaron, Col	1.24
Maholm,Paul, Pit	1.18
Suppan,Jeff, Mil	1.11
Marquis,Jason, ChC	1.08
Looper,Braden, StL	1.04
Webb,Brandon, Ari	1.03
Parra,Manny, Mil	0.98
Lannan,John, Was	0.94
Snell,Ian, Pit	0.93

2008 National League Pitching Leaders

Saves			Blown Saves			Save Pct			Save Opportunities	
						(minimum 20 Save Ops)				
Valverde,Jose, Hou	44		Corpas,Manny, Col	9		Lidge,Brad, Phi	100.0		Valverde,Jose, Hou	51
Lidge,Brad, Phi	41		Gregg,Kevin, Fla	9		Fuentes,Brian, Col	88.2		Wilson,Brian, SF	47
Wilson,Brian, SF	41		Broxton,Jonathan, LAD	8		Hoffman,Trevor, SD	88.2		Lidge,Brad, Phi	41
Cordero,Francisco, Cin	34		Franklin,Ryan, StL	8		Wilson,Brian, SF	87.2		Cordero,Francisco, Cin	40
Wood,Kerry, ChC	34		Qualls,Chad, Ari	8		Valverde,Jose, Hou	86.3		Wood,Kerry, ChC	40
Fuentes,Brian, Col	30		6 tied with	7		Cordero,Francisco, Cin	85.0		Gregg,Kevin, Fla	38
Hoffman,Trevor, SD	30					Wood,Kerry, ChC	85.0		Torres,Salomon, Mil	35
Gregg,Kevin, Fla	29					Lyon,Brandon, Ari	83.9		Fuentes,Brian, Col	34
Torres,Salomon, Mil	28					Saito,Takashi, LAD	81.8		Hoffman,Trevor, SD	34
Wagner,Billy, NYM	27					Capps,Matt, Pit	80.8		Wagner,Billy, NYM	34

Easy Saves			Regular Saves			Tough Saves			Holds Adjusted Saves %	
									(minimum 20 Save Ops)	
Valverde,Jose, Hou	33		Lidge,Brad, Phi	16		Gregg,Kevin, Fla	4		Lidge,Brad, Phi	100.0
Lidge,Brad, Phi	25		Wilson,Brian, SF	16		Wilson,Brian, SF	4		Fuentes,Brian, Col	90.0
Wagner,Billy, NYM	22		Cordero,Francisco, Cin	14		Broxton,Jonathan, LAD	3		Hoffman,Trevor, SD	88.2
Wilson,Brian, SF	21		Wood,Kerry, ChC	13		Torres,Salomon, Mil	2		Wilson,Brian, SF	87.2
Wood,Kerry, ChC	21		Fuentes,Brian, Col	11		13 tied with	1		Valverde,Jose, Hou	86.3
Cordero,Francisco, Cin	19		Hoffman,Trevor, SD	11					Lyon,Brandon, Ari	85.3
Fuentes,Brian, Col	19		Gregg,Kevin, Fla	10					Cordero,Francisco, Cin	85.0
Hoffman,Trevor, SD	19		Lyon,Brandon, Ari	10					Wood,Kerry, ChC	85.0
Lyon,Brandon, Ari	16		Torres,Salomon, Mil	10					Torres,Salomon, Mil	82.5
Torres,Salomon, Mil	16		Valverde,Jose, Hou	10					Saito,Takashi, LAD	81.8

Relief Wins			Relief Losses			Relief Games			Holds	
Brocail,Doug, Hou	7		Ayala,Luis, Was-NYM	10		Feliciano,Pedro, NYM	86		Marmol,Carlos, ChC	30
Gregg,Kevin, Fla	7		Gregg,Kevin, Fla	8		Ohman,Will, Atl	83		McClellan,Kyle, StL	30
Howry,Bob, ChC	7		Heilman,Aaron, NYM	8		Marmol,Carlos, ChC	82		Romero,J.C., Phi	24
Torres,Salomon, Mil	7		Qualls,Chad, Ari	8		Smith,Joe, NYM	82		Bell,Heath, SD	23
8 tied with	6		Rauch,Jon, Was-Ari	8		Ayala,Luis, Was-NYM	81		Ohman,Will, Atl	23
			Walker,Tyler, SF	8		Romero,J.C., Phi	81		Pena,Tony, Ari	23
			McClellan,Kyle, StL	7		Heilman,Aaron, NYM	78		Brocail,Doug, Hou	22
			10 tied with	6		Qualls,Chad, Ari	77		Qualls,Chad, Ari	22
						4 tied with	76		3 tied with	21

Relief Innings			Inherited Runners Scrd %			Relief Opp On Base Pct			Relief Opp Slugging Avg	
			(minimum 30 IR)			(minimum 50 IP)			(minimum 50 IP)	
Durbin,Chad, Phi	87.2		Marte,Damaso, Pit	16.7		Kuo,Hong-Chih, LAD	.246		Marmol,Carlos, ChC	.257
Marmol,Carlos, ChC	87.1		Ohman,Will, Atl	17.1		Buchholz,Taylor, Col	.249		Lidge,Brad, Phi	.269
Hanrahan,Joel, Was	84.1		Smith,Joe, NYM	17.5		Marmol,Carlos, ChC	.251		Gregg,Kevin, Fla	.271
Rivera,Saul, Was	84.0		Ring,Royce, Atl	17.6		Wade,Cory, LAD	.256		Geary,Geoff, Hou	.281
Madson,Ryan, Phi	82.2		Byrdak,Tim, Hou	18.8		Capps,Matt, Pit	.260		Kuo,Hong-Chih, LAD	.289
Bennett,Jeff, Atl	80.2		Eyre,Scott, ChC-Phi	19.4		Adams,Mike, SD	.265		Fuentes,Brian, Col	.293
Torres,Salomon, Mil	80.0		Miller,Justin, Fla	20.0		Sampson,Chris, Hou	.265		Broxton,Jonathan, LAD	.297
Corpas,Manny, Col	79.2		Wright,Wesley, Hou	20.9		Villanueva,Carlos, Mil	.274		Bennett,Jeff, Atl	.299
Franklin,Ryan, StL	78.2		Cotts,Neal, ChC	21.2		Fuentes,Brian, Col	.277		Buchholz,Taylor, Col	.301
Affeldt,Jeremy, Cin	78.1		Marmol,Carlos, ChC	21.3		Qualls,Chad, Ari	.277		Springer,Russ, StL	.310

2008 National League Pitching Leaders

Relief Opp BA Vs LHB
(minimum 50 AB)

Romero,J.C., Phi	.102
Byrdak,Tim, Hou	.135
Cruz,Juan, Ari	.159
Kuo,Hong-Chih, LAD	.167
Burnett,Sean, Pit	.171
Villone,Ron, StL	.176
Schoeneweis,Scott, NYM	.178
Shouse,Brian, Mil	.180
Gregg,Kevin, Fla	.181
Marmol,Carlos, ChC	.182

Relief Opp BA Vs RHB
(minimum 50 AB)

Marmol,Carlos, ChC	.098
Lidge,Brad, Phi	.105
Shell,Steven, Was	.150
Mock,Garrett, Was	.155
Hoffman,Trevor, SD	.165
Vizcaino,Luis, Col	.170
Wagner,Billy, NYM	.174
Romo,Sergio, SF	.176
Springer,Russ, StL	.176
Buchholz,Taylor, Col	.180

Relief Opp Batting Average
(minimum 50 IP)

Marmol,Carlos, ChC	.135
Buchholz,Taylor, Col	.188
Cruz,Juan, Ari	.192
Kuo,Hong-Chih, LAD	.194
Shell,Steven, Was	.194
Romero,J.C., Phi	.197
Geary,Geoff, Hou	.197
Lidge,Brad, Phi	.198
Wade,Cory, LAD	.202
Gregg,Kevin, Fla	.203

Relief Earned Run Average
(minimum 50 IP)

Kuo,Hong-Chih, LAD	1.69
Lidge,Brad, Phi	1.95
Nelson,Joe, Fla	2.00
Villanueva,Carlos, Mil	2.12
Shell,Steven, Was	2.16
Buchholz,Taylor, Col	2.17
Wade,Cory, LAD	2.27
Springer,Russ, StL	2.32
Adams,Mike, SD	2.48
Geary,Geoff, Hou	2.53

Rel OBP 1st Batter Faced
(minimum 40 BF)

Marmol,Carlos, ChC	.185
Hoffman,Trevor, SD	.188
Buchholz,Taylor, Col	.190
Wagner,Billy, NYM	.200
Sampson,Chris, Hou	.209
Smith,Joe, NYM	.210
Mota,Guillermo, Mil	.224
Lincoln,Mike, Cin	.234
Isringhausen,Jason, StL	.238
Romero,J.C., Phi	.241

Rel Opp BA w/ Runners On
(minimum 50 IP)

Marmol,Carlos, ChC	.148
Grabow,John, Pit	.172
Romero,J.C., Phi	.172
Villanueva,Carlos, Mil	.179
Springer,Russ, StL	.181
Kuo,Hong-Chih, LAD	.181
Geary,Geoff, Hou	.183
Lidge,Brad, Phi	.183
Shell,Steven, Was	.189
Bell,Heath, SD	.203

Relief Opp BA w/ RISP
(minimum 50 IP)

Villanueva,Carlos, Mil	.125
Marmol,Carlos, ChC	.133
Grabow,John, Pit	.146
Valverde,Jose, Hou	.159
Kuo,Hong-Chih, LAD	.160
Geary,Geoff, Hou	.172
Romero,J.C., Phi	.173
Wade,Cory, LAD	.174
Speier,Ryan, Col	.177
Cordero,Francisco, Cin	.187

Fastest Avg Fastball-Relief
(minimum 50 IP)

Lindstrom,Matt, Fla	96.9
Broxton,Jonathan, LAD	96.3
Wilson,Brian, SF	95.8
Valverde,Jose, Hou	95.5
Hanrahan,Joel, Was	95.2
Pena,Tony, Ari	95.1
Colome,Jesus, Was	94.9
Wood,Kerry, ChC	94.8
Cordero,Francisco, Cin	94.6
Affeldt,Jeremy, Cin	94.6

Fastest Average Fastball
(minimum 162 IP)

Jimenez,Ubaldo, Col	94.9
Lincecum,Tim, SF	94.1
Volquez,Edinson, Cin	93.6
Cueto,Johnny, Cin	93.4
Pelfrey,Mike, NYM	92.7
Oswalt,Roy, Hou	92.6
Sheets,Ben, Mil	92.6
Parra,Manny, Mil	92.4
Cain,Matt, SF	92.4
Wellemeyer,Todd, StL	92.3

Slowest Average Fastball
(minimum 162 IP)

Moyer,Jamie, Phi	81.2
Maddux,Greg, SD-LAD	83.7
Zito,Barry, SF	84.9
Suppan,Jeff, Mil	86.9
Lilly,Ted, ChC	87.4
Lannan,John, Was	87.5
Olsen,Scott, Fla	87.8
Webb,Brandon, Ari	88.0
Arroyo,Bronson, Cin	88.3
Bush,David, Mil	88.7

Pitches 100+ Velocity

Broxton,Jonathan, LAD	28
Lindstrom,Matt, Fla	16
Wilson,Brian, SF	6
Jimenez,Ubaldo, Col	4
Morillo,Juan, Col	3
Lincecum,Tim, SF	1
Valdez,Merkin, SF	1

Pitches 95+ Velocity

Jimenez,Ubaldo, Col	1342
Lincecum,Tim, SF	881
Broxton,Jonathan, LAD	655
Valverde,Jose, Hou	651
Hanrahan,Joel, Was	635
Lindstrom,Matt, Fla	590
Wilson,Brian, SF	590
Sabathia,CC, Mil	559
Volquez,Edinson, Cin	514
Kershaw,Clayton, LAD	493

Pitches Less Than 80 MPH

Wolf,Randy, SD-Hou	1750
Moyer,Jamie, Phi	1531
Arroyo,Bronson, Cin	1381
Zito,Barry, SF	1345
Maddux,Greg, SD-LAD	1062
Campillo,Jorge, Atl	947
Webb,Brandon, Ari	836
Hamels,Cole, Phi	805
Nolasco,Ricky, Fla	805
Lilly,Ted, ChC	730

Lowest % Fastballs
(minimum 162 IP)

Moyer,Jamie, Phi	40.4
Arroyo,Bronson, Cin	45.7
Lilly,Ted, ChC	46.4
Backe,Brandon, Hou	47.1
Myers,Brett, Phi	47.3
Haren,Dan, Ari	49.6
Suppan,Jeff, Mil	49.8
Bush,David, Mil	50.4
Johnson,Randy, Ari	50.6
Nolasco,Ricky, Fla	50.9

Highest % Fastballs
(minimum 162 IP)

Cook,Aaron, Col	80.4
Pelfrey,Mike, NYM	80.2
Harang,Aaron, Cin	70.2
Webb,Brandon, Ari	69.7
Jimenez,Ubaldo, Col	68.9
Perez,Oliver, NYM	67.7
Maddux,Greg, SD-LAD	67.0
Lincecum,Tim, SF	64.9
Oswalt,Roy, Hou	64.4
Cain,Matt, SF	64.0

Highest % Curveballs
(minimum 162 IP)

Sheets,Ben, Mil	32.2
Nolasco,Ricky, Fla	26.4
Myers,Brett, Phi	22.9
Arroyo,Bronson, Cin	18.4
Wolf,Randy, SD-Hou	18.2
Oswalt,Roy, Hou	17.6
Billingsley,Chad, LAD	16.8
Parra,Manny, Mil	16.8
Bush,David, Mil	16.5
Zito,Barry, SF	15.8

2008 National League Pitching Leaders

Highest % Changeups
(minimum 162 IP)

Volquez,Edinson, Cin	31.5
Hamels,Cole, Phi	31.1
Santana,Johan, NYM	28.2
Jurrjens,Jair, Atl	25.9
Moyer,Jamie, Phi	23.5
Maddux,Greg, SD-LAD	21.3
Zito,Barry, SF	20.0
Olsen,Scott, Fla	19.4
Lincecum,Tim, SF	18.2
Dempster,Ryan, ChC	16.5

Highest % Sliders
(minimum 162 IP)

Johnson,Randy, Ari	34.6
Snell,Ian, Pit	32.2
Cueto,Johnny, Cin	31.4
Lowe,Derek, LAD	31.1
Dempster,Ryan, ChC	27.1
Perez,Oliver, NYM	26.3
Kuroda,Hiroki, LAD	25.6
Haren,Dan, Ari	24.8
Suppan,Jeff, Mil	23.6
Wellemeyer,Todd, StL	23.4

Balks

Lilly,Ted, ChC	4
Morales,Franklin, Col	3
Nolasco,Ricky, Fla	3
Rodriguez,Wandy, Hou	3
10 tied with	2

Strikeout/Hit Ratio
(minimum 50 IP)

Marmol,Carlos, ChC	2.85
Harden,Rich, ChC	2.28
Cruz,Juan, Ari	2.09
Lidge,Brad, Phi	1.84
Fuentes,Brian, Col	1.74
Broxton,Jonathan, LAD	1.63
Kuo,Hong-Chih, LAD	1.60
Wood,Kerry, ChC	1.56
Adams,Mike, SD	1.51
Lincecum,Tim, SF	1.46

Opp OPS vs Fastballs
(minimum 251 BF)

Sheets,Ben, Mil	.599
Sabathia,CC, Mil	.610
Lincecum,Tim, SF	.628
McClung,Seth, Mil	.630
Bush,David, Mil	.632
Kuroda,Hiroki, LAD	.643
Young,Chris, SD	.643
Hudson,Tim, Atl	.646
Rodriguez,Wandy, Hou	.646
Dempster,Ryan, ChC	.650

Opp OPS vs Curveballs
(minimum 100 BF)

Bergmann,Jason, Was	.483
Nolasco,Ricky, Fla	.556
Myers,Brett, Phi	.584
Hamels,Cole, Phi	.599
Lincecum,Tim, SF	.602
Zito,Barry, SF	.630
Parra,Manny, Mil	.669
Billingsley,Chad, LAD	.681
Lilly,Ted, ChC	.719
Oswalt,Roy, Hou	.737

Opp OPS vs Changeups
(minimum 100 BF)

Glavine,Tom, Atl	.473
Grabow,John, Pit	.492
Webb,Brandon, Ari	.513
Parra,Manny, Mil	.520
Santana,Johan, NYM	.533
Duke,Zach, Pit	.555
Sabathia,CC, Mil	.558
Lohse,Kyle, StL	.564
Olsen,Scott, Fla	.580
Hamels,Cole, Phi	.596

Opp OPS vs Sliders
(minimum 64 BF)

Marmol,Carlos, ChC	.302
Bennett,Jeff, Atl	.384
Sabathia,CC, Mil	.417
Seanez,Rudy, Phi	.420
Grilli,Jason, Col	.459
Lowe,Derek, LAD	.469
Haren,Dan, Ari	.473
Lidge,Brad, Phi	.486
Gonzalez,Mike, Atl	.491
Olsen,Scott, Fla	.504

Earned Runs

Backe,Brandon, Hou	112
Arroyo,Bronson, Cin	106
Zito,Barry, SF	103
Redding,Tim, Was	100
Duke,Zach, Pit	99
Snell,Ian, Pit	99
Harang,Aaron, Cin	98
Suppan,Jeff, Mil	98
Myers,Brett, Phi	96
Kendrick,Kyle, Phi	95

Hits Per Nine Innings
(minimum 162 IP)

Lincecum,Tim, SF	7.22
Peavy,Jake, SD	7.57
Dempster,Ryan, ChC	7.58
Hamels,Cole, Phi	7.64
Volquez,Edinson, Cin	7.67
Perez,Oliver, NYM	7.75
Santana,Johan, NYM	7.91
Bush,David, Mil	7.93
Nolasco,Ricky, Fla	8.14
Webb,Brandon, Ari	8.18

2008 American League Fielding Leaders

2B Pivot %
(minimum 98 G)

Ellis,Mark, Oak	0.707
Iwamura,Akinori, TB	0.706
Lopez,Jose, Sea	0.662
Kinsler,Ian, Tex	0.661
Ramirez,Alexei, CWS	0.658
Pedroia,Dustin, Bos	0.645
Cano,Robinson, NYY	0.634
Roberts,Brian, Bal	0.574
Polanco,Placido, Det	0.542

SS Pivot %
(minimum 98 G)

Crosby,Bobby, Oak	0.662
Peralta,Jhonny, Cle	0.634
Betancourt,Yuniesky, Sea	0.628
Renteria,Edgar, Det	0.627
Cabrera,Orlando, CWS	0.625
Young,Michael, Tex	0.602
Jeter,Derek, NYY	0.552
Bartlett,Jason, TB	0.540

Highest Pct CS by Catchers
(minimum 600 INN or 50 SBA)

Molina,Jose, NYY	43.2
Navarro,Dioner, TB	35.7
Rodriguez,Ivan, Det-NYY	30.7
Barajas,Rod, Tor	28.8
Laird,Gerald, Tex	27.4
Cash,Kevin, Bos	26.9
Mauer,Joe, Min	26.1
Johjima,Kenji, Sea	25.7
Zaun,Gregg, Tor	23.1
Suzuki,Kurt, Oak	22.5

Lowest Pct CS by Catchers
(minimum 600 INN or 50 SBA)

Pierzynski,A.J., CWS	10.3
Buck,John, KC	10.6
Napoli,Mike, LAA	14.8
Hernandez,Ramon, Bal	17.5
Varitek,Jason, Bos	18.8
Shoppach,Kelly, Cle	21.3
Mathis,Jeff, LAA	21.9
Suzuki,Kurt, Oak	22.5
Zaun,Gregg, Tor	23.1
Johjima,Kenji, Sea	25.7

2B Double Play %
(minimum 98 G)

Ellis,Mark, Oak	0.618
Iwamura,Akinori, TB	0.608
Kinsler,Ian, Tex	0.562
Lopez,Jose, Sea	0.523
Pedroia,Dustin, Bos	0.508
Roberts,Brian, Bal	0.498
Polanco,Placido, Det	0.497
Ramirez,Alexei, CWS	0.496
Cano,Robinson, NYY	0.494

3B Double Play %
(minimum 98 G)

Hannahan,Jack, Oak	0.450
Mora,Melvin, Bal	0.424
Longoria,Evan, TB	0.424
Figgins,Chone, LAA	0.368
Beltre,Adrian, Sea	0.364
Rodriguez,Alex, NYY	0.357
Lowell,Mike, Bos	0.356
Gordon,Alex, KC	0.327
Rolen,Scott, Tor	0.317

SS Double Play %
(minimum 98 G)

Crosby,Bobby, Oak	0.682
Cabrera,Orlando, CWS	0.637
Peralta,Jhonny, Cle	0.634
Betancourt,Yuniesky, Sea	0.620
Young,Michael, Tex	0.616
Renteria,Edgar, Det	0.587
Bartlett,Jason, TB	0.549
Jeter,Derek, NYY	0.547

Errors

Betancourt,Yuniesky, Sea	21
Crede,Joe, CWS	20
Aybar,Erick, LAA	18
Kinsler,Ian, Tex	18
Crosby,Bobby, Oak	17
6 tied with	16

Fielding Errors

Betancourt,Yuniesky, Sea	12
Crede,Joe, CWS	12
Kinsler,Ian, Tex	12
Guillen,Carlos, Det	11
Renteria,Edgar, Det	11
Beltre,Adrian, Sea	10
Cabrera,Miguel, Det	10
Cabrera,Orlando, CWS	10
Gordon,Alex, KC	10
Ramirez,Alexei, CWS	10

Throwing Errors

Crosby,Bobby, Oak	13
Mathis,Jeff, LAA	12
Aybar,Erick, LAA	11
Bartlett,Jason, TB	11
Harris,Brendan, Min	10
Betancourt,Yuniesky, Sea	9
Lugo,Julio, Bos	9
Mora,Melvin, Bal	9
Saltalamacchia,J, Tex	9
2 tied with	8

Range Factor for 2B
(minimum 98 games)

Kinsler,Ian, Tex	5.77
Lopez,Jose, Sea	5.32
Polanco,Placido, Det	5.22
Cano,Robinson, NYY	5.15
Ellis,Mark, Oak	5.02
Ramirez,Alexei, CWS	4.99
Roberts,Brian, Bal	4.98
Pedroia,Dustin, Bos	4.75
Iwamura,Akinori, TB	4.58

Range Factor for 3B
(minimum 98 games)

Lowell,Mike, Bos	2.86
Mora,Melvin, Bal	2.86
Beltre,Adrian, Sea	2.77
Longoria,Evan, TB	2.72
Figgins,Chone, LAA	2.65
Hannahan,Jack, Oak	2.64
Gordon,Alex, KC	2.61
Rolen,Scott, Tor	2.60
Rodriguez,Alex, NYY	2.59

Range Factor for SS
(minimum 98 games)

Cabrera,Orlando, CWS	4.62
Young,Michael, Tex	4.59
Peralta,Jhonny, Cle	4.56
Betancourt,Yuniesky, Sea	4.33
Renteria,Edgar, Det	4.31
Bartlett,Jason, TB	4.21
Crosby,Bobby, Oak	4.18
Jeter,Derek, NYY	4.05

2008 National League Fielding Leaders

2B Pivot %
(minimum 98 G)

Hudson,Orlando, Ari	0.722
Uggla,Dan, Fla	0.671
Utley,Chase, Phi	0.658
Phillips,Brandon, Cin	0.644
Johnson,Kelly, Atl	0.628
Sanchez,Freddy, Pit	0.592
Lopez,Felipe, Was-StL	0.583
Weeks,Rickie, Mil	0.557
Kent,Jeff, LAD	0.519

SS Pivot %
(minimum 98 G)

Guzman,Cristian, Was	0.726
Greene,Khalil, SD	0.621
Drew,Stephen, Ari	0.619
Hardy,J.J., Mil	0.605
Tejada,Miguel, Hou	0.605
Theriot,Ryan, ChC	0.597
Tulowitzki,Troy, Col	0.589
Reyes,Jose, NYM	0.588
Izturis,Cesar, StL	0.571
Rollins,Jimmy, Phi	0.552

Highest Pct CS by Catchers
(minimum 600 INN or 50 SBA)

Kendall,Jason, Mil	39.6
Molina,Bengie, SF	32.0
Molina,Yadier, StL	32.0
Snyder,Chris, Ari	29.0
Schneider,Brian, NYM	27.6
Bako,Paul, Cin	26.7
Hundley,Nick, SD	23.6
Treanor,Matt, Fla	21.4
Torrealba,Yorvit, Col	21.1
Soto,Geovany, ChC	20.7

Lowest Pct CS by Catchers
(minimum 600 INN or 50 SBA)

Bard,Josh, SD	14.5
Coste,Chris, Phi	15.4
Iannetta,Chris, Col	16.3
Ruiz,Carlos, Phi	17.7
Doumit,Ryan, Pit	18.1
McCann,Brian, Atl	18.4
Flores,Jesus, Was	19.0
Martin,Russell, LAD	19.5
Soto,Geovany, ChC	20.7
Torrealba,Yorvit, Col	21.1

2B Double Play %
(minimum 98 G)

Sanchez,Freddy, Pit	0.503
Hudson,Orlando, Ari	0.500
Uggla,Dan, Fla	0.481
Utley,Chase, Phi	0.466
Weeks,Rickie, Mil	0.460
Johnson,Kelly, Atl	0.456
Phillips,Brandon, Cin	0.437
Lopez,Felipe, Was-StL	0.437
Kent,Jeff, LAD	0.414

3B Double Play %
(minimum 98 G)

Glaus,Troy, StL	0.500
Jones,Chipper, Atl	0.435
Hall,Bill, Mil	0.396
Feliz,Pedro, Phi	0.395
Encarnacion,Edwin, Cin	0.392
Reynolds,Mark, Ari	0.388
Kouzmanoff,Kevin, SD	0.379
Zimmerman,Ryan, Was	0.370
Ramirez,Aramis, ChC	0.348
Cantu,Jorge, Fla	0.333

SS Double Play %
(minimum 98 G)

Guzman,Cristian, Was	0.645
Greene,Khalil, SD	0.629
Tejada,Miguel, Hou	0.625
Drew,Stephen, Ari	0.609
Keppinger,Jeff, Cin	0.600
Theriot,Ryan, ChC	0.598
Reyes,Jose, NYM	0.577
Izturis,Cesar, StL	0.570
Ramirez,Hanley, Fla	0.564
Tulowitzki,Troy, Col	0.544

Errors

Reynolds,Mark, Ari	35
Encarnacion,Edwin, Cin	23
Cantu,Jorge, Fla	22
Ramirez,Hanley, Fla	22
Hall,Bill, Mil	19
Howard,Ryan, Phi	19
Ramirez,Aramis, ChC	18
Fielder,Prince, Mil	17
Guzman,Cristian, Was	17
Reyes,Jose, NYM	17

Fielding Errors

Reynolds,Mark, Ari	17
Fielder,Prince, Mil	15
Howard,Ryan, Phi	14
Ramirez,Hanley, Fla	14
Johnson,Kelly, Atl	13
Ramirez,Aramis, ChC	13
Cantu,Jorge, Fla	11
Guzman,Cristian, Was	11
Hall,Bill, Mil	11
Reyes,Jose, NYM	11

Throwing Errors

Reynolds,Mark, Ari	18
Encarnacion,Edwin, Cin	16
Martin,Russell, LAD	12
Cantu,Jorge, Fla	11
Escobar,Yunel, Atl	10
Zimmerman,Ryan, Was	10
5 tied with	8

Range Factor for 2B
(minimum 98 games)

Utley,Chase, Phi	5.18
Johnson,Kelly, Atl	5.16
Sanchez,Freddy, Pit	5.12
Phillips,Brandon, Cin	5.08
Weeks,Rickie, Mil	5.02
Uggla,Dan, Fla	4.86
Hudson,Orlando, Ari	4.82
Lopez,Felipe, Was-StL	4.71
Kent,Jeff, LAD	4.55

Range Factor for 3B
(minimum 98 games)

Zimmerman,Ryan, Was	2.91
Glaus,Troy, StL	2.74
Jones,Chipper, Atl	2.73
Feliz,Pedro, Phi	2.72
Kouzmanoff,Kevin, SD	2.64
Hall,Bill, Mil	2.62
Cantu,Jorge, Fla	2.51
Wright,David, NYM	2.51
Castillo,Jose, SF-Hou	2.35
Reynolds,Mark, Ari	2.25

Range Factor for SS
(minimum 98 games)

Tulowitzki,Troy, Col	5.22
Izturis,Cesar, StL	4.85
Escobar,Yunel, Atl	4.79
Rollins,Jimmy, Phi	4.52
Guzman,Cristian, Was	4.49
Hardy,J.J., Mil	4.48
Ramirez,Hanley, Fla	4.40
Greene,Khalil, SD	4.19
Tejada,Miguel, Hou	4.18
Reyes,Jose, NYM	4.07

2008 Active Career Batting Leaders

Batting Average (minimum 1000 PA)		On Base Percentage (minimum 1000 PA)		Slugging Average (minimum 1000 PA)		Home Runs	
Pujols,Albert	.334	Helton,Todd	.428	Pujols,Albert	.624	Griffey Jr.,Ken	611
Suzuki,Ichiro	.331	Pujols,Albert	.425	Ramirez,Manny	.593	Rodriguez,Alex	553
Helton,Todd	.328	Thomas,Frank	.419	Howard,Ryan	.590	Thome,Jim	541
Guerrero,Vladimir	.323	Berkman,Lance	.413	Braun,Ryan	.588	Ramirez,Manny	527
Holliday,Matt	.319	Ramirez,Manny	.411	Rodriguez,Alex	.578	Thomas,Frank	521
Mauer,Joe	.317	Giambi,Jason	.408	Guerrero,Vladimir	.575	Sheffield,Gary	499
Jeter,Derek	.316	Jones,Chipper	.408	Helton,Todd	.574	Delgado,Carlos	469
Ramirez,Manny	.314	Thome,Jim	.406	Thome,Jim	.560	Jones,Chipper	408
Garciaparra,Nomar	.314	Abreu,Bobby	.405	Berkman,Lance	.560	Giambi,Jason	396
Pedroia,Dustin	.313	Giles,Brian	.404	Thomas,Frank	.555	Guerrero,Vladimir	392

Games		At Bats		Hits		Total Bases	
Vizquel,Omar	2680	Vizquel,Omar	9745	Griffey Jr.,Ken	2680	Griffey Jr.,Ken	5092
Gonzalez,Luis	2591	Griffey Jr.,Ken	9316	Vizquel,Omar	2657	Sheffield,Gary	4616
Griffey Jr.,Ken	2521	Gonzalez,Luis	9157	Sheffield,Gary	2615	Thomas,Frank	4550
Sheffield,Gary	2476	Sheffield,Gary	8949	Rodriguez,Ivan	2605	Rodriguez,Alex	4543
Thomas,Frank	2322	Rodriguez,Ivan	8645	Gonzalez,Luis	2591	Ramirez,Manny	4516
Kent,Jeff	2298	Kent,Jeff	8498	Jeter,Derek	2535	Gonzalez,Luis	4385
Rodriguez,Ivan	2267	Thomas,Frank	8199	Thomas,Frank	2468	Kent,Jeff	4246
Thome,Jim	2160	Jeter,Derek	8025	Kent,Jeff	2461	Thome,Jim	4116
Ramirez,Manny	2103	Anderson,Garret	7989	Rodriguez,Alex	2404	Rodriguez,Ivan	4110
Rodriguez,Alex	2042	Rodriguez,Alex	7860	Ramirez,Manny	2392	Jones,Chipper	4020

Doubles		Triples		Runs Scored		RBI	
Gonzalez,Luis	596	Damon,Johnny	92	Griffey Jr.,Ken	1612	Griffey Jr.,Ken	1772
Kent,Jeff	560	Rollins,Jimmy	90	Rodriguez,Alex	1605	Ramirez,Manny	1725
Rodriguez,Ivan	524	Crawford,Carl	84	Sheffield,Gary	1592	Thomas,Frank	1704
Ramirez,Manny	507	Durham,Ray	79	Thomas,Frank	1494	Sheffield,Gary	1633
Griffey Jr.,Ken	503	Guzman,Cristian	78	Jeter,Derek	1467	Rodriguez,Alex	1606
Thomas,Frank	495	Vizquel,Omar	72	Ramirez,Manny	1444	Kent,Jeff	1518
Anderson,Garret	489	Pierre,Juan	71	Thome,Jim	1431	Delgado,Carlos	1489
Delgado,Carlos	476	Reyes,Jose	71	Gonzalez,Luis	1412	Thome,Jim	1488
Helton,Todd	471	Gonzalez,Luis	68	Jones,Chipper	1378	Gonzalez,Luis	1439
2 tied with	454	Suzuki,Ichiro	64	Damon,Johnny	1376	Jones,Chipper	1374

Walks		Intentional Walks		Hit By Pitch		Strikeouts	
Thomas,Frank	1667	Griffey Jr.,Ken	244	Kendall,Jason	231	Thome,Jim	2190
Thome,Jim	1550	Guerrero,Vladimir	239	Delgado,Carlos	168	Delgado,Carlos	1725
Sheffield,Gary	1435	Ramirez,Manny	191	Giambi,Jason	157	Griffey Jr.,Ken	1682
Jones,Chipper	1242	Delgado,Carlos	186	Rodriguez,Alex	141	Edmonds,Jim	1669
Griffey Jr.,Ken	1240	Helton,Todd	170	Jeter,Derek	138	Ramirez,Manny	1667
Ramirez,Manny	1212	Thomas,Frank	168	Sheffield,Gary	133	Cameron,Mike	1642
Giambi,Jason	1205	Thome,Jim	159	Easley,Damion	132	Rodriguez,Alex	1641
Abreu,Bobby	1160	Pujols,Albert	154	Eckstein,David	125	Kent,Jeff	1522
Giles,Brian	1157	Gonzalez,Luis	150	Kent,Jeff	125	Jones,Andruw	1470
Gonzalez,Luis	1155	Jones,Chipper	137	Guillen,Jose	123	Abreu,Bobby	1405

2008 Active Career Batting Leaders

Sacrifice Hits	
Vizquel, Omar	239
Glavine, Tom	216
Maddux, Greg	180
Smoltz, John	136
Schilling, Curt	102
Pierre, Juan	101
Castillo, Luis	93
Schmidt, Jason	89
Hernandez, Livan	88
Trachsel, Steve	87

Sacrifice Flies	
Thomas, Frank	121
Sheffield, Gary	109
Kent, Jeff	103
Gonzalez, Luis	98
Griffey Jr., Ken	98
Delgado, Carlos	91
Ramirez, Manny	86
Vizquel, Omar	86
Alou, Moises	82
Giambi, Jason	80

Stolen Bases	
Pierre, Juan	429
Vizquel, Omar	385
Damon, Johnny	362
Castillo, Luis	342
Abreu, Bobby	318
Suzuki, Ichiro	315
Crawford, Carl	302
Rollins, Jimmy	295
Reyes, Jose	290
Cameron, Mike	289

Seasons Played	
Maddux, Greg	23
Glavine, Tom	22
Moyer, Jamie	22
Johnson, Randy	21
Sheffield, Gary	21
6 tied with	20

At Bats Per Home Run	
(minimum 1000 AB)	
Howard, Ryan	11.7
Thome, Jim	13.6
Dunn, Adam	13.9
Rodriguez, Alex	14.2
Pujols, Albert	14.4
Ramirez, Manny	14.4
Thames, Marcus	14.7
Braun, Ryan	15.0
Branyan, Russell	15.0
Griffey Jr., Ken	15.2

Grounded Into DP	
Rodriguez, Ivan	286
Ramirez, Manny	230
Thomas, Frank	226
Sheffield, Gary	225
Kent, Jeff	224
Guerrero, Vladimir	219
Tejada, Miguel	216
Gonzalez, Luis	213
Konerko, Paul	209
Renteria, Edgar	209

Highest SB Success Pct	
(minimum 100 SBA)	
Beltran, Carlos	88.1
Byrnes, Eric	85.6
Rollins, Jimmy	82.9
Crawford, Carl	82.5
Taveras, Willy	82.4
Suzuki, Ichiro	81.8
Rodriguez, Alex	80.9
Victorino, Shane	80.8
Roberts, Dave	80.7
Wright, David	80.7

Lowest SB Success Pct	
(minimum 100 SBA)	
Edmonds, Jim	56.5
Gonzalez, Luis	59.5
Kent, Jeff	61.0
Kotsay, Mark	62.3
Anderson, Garret	62.4
Guillen, Carlos	63.4
Mora, Melvin	63.8
Jones, Jacque	64.6
Ordonez, Magglio	64.7
Ausmus, Brad	65.6

Strikeouts / Walks Ratio	
(minimum 1000 AB)	
Giles, Brian	.695
Pujols, Albert	.727
Helton, Todd	.778
Sheffield, Gary	.784
Mauer, Joe	.798
Thomas, Frank	.838
Hatteberg, Scott	.895
Kendall, Jason	.914
Theriot, Ryan	.914
Jones, Chipper	.919

At Bats Per GIDP	
(minimum 1000 AB)	
Iwamura, Akinori	279.5
Matsui, Kaz	175.5
Drew, Stephen	136.3
Taveras, Willy	131.5
Suzuki, Ichiro	130.0
Roberts, Dave	117.7
Branyan, Russell	117.6
Granderson, Curtis	114.6
Patterson, Corey	108.3
Reyes, Jose	106.9

OPS	
(minimum 1000 PA)	
Pujols, Albert	1.049
Ramirez, Manny	1.004
Helton, Todd	1.002
Thomas, Frank	.974
Berkman, Lance	.973
Howard, Ryan	.970
Rodriguez, Alex	.967
Thome, Jim	.966
Guerrero, Vladimir	.963
Jones, Chipper	.955

Secondary Average	
(minimum 1000 PA)	
Thome, Jim	.495
Dunn, Adam	.493
Howard, Ryan	.472
Cust, Jack	.470
Thomas, Frank	.461
Berkman, Lance	.457
Pujols, Albert	.451
Ramirez, Manny	.443
Giambi, Jason	.441
Rodriguez, Alex	.433

Highest Strikeout per PA	
(minimum 1000 PA)	
Branyan, Russell	.344
Cust, Jack	.330
Reynolds, Mark	.324
Smoltz, John	.311
Pena, Wily Mo	.301
Howard, Ryan	.283
Gomes, Jonny	.281
Dunn, Adam	.264
Fasano, Sal	.263
Werth, Jayson	.263

Lowest Strikeout per PA	
(minimum 1000 PA)	
Pierre, Juan	.055
Polanco, Placido	.065
Lo Duca, Paul	.069
Pedroia, Dustin	.072
Eckstein, David	.073
Kendall, Jason	.076
Johjima, Kenji	.082
Molina, Yadier	.085
4 tied with	.086

Plate Appearances	
Vizquel, Omar	11082
Griffey Jr., Ken	10742
Sheffield, Gary	10635
Gonzalez, Luis	10531
Thomas, Frank	10074
Kent, Jeff	9537
Rodriguez, Ivan	9264
Jeter, Derek	9093
Rodriguez, Alex	9076
Thome, Jim	9029

At Bats Per RBI	
(minimum 1000 AB)	
Howard, Ryan	4.2
Ramirez, Manny	4.4
Pujols, Albert	4.7
Ortiz, David	4.8
Thomas, Frank	4.8
Delgado, Carlos	4.8
Rodriguez, Alex	4.9
Thome, Jim	4.9
Giambi, Jason	5.0
Hafner, Travis	5.0

2008 Active Career Pitching Leaders

Earned Run Average
(minimum 750 IP)

Rivera,Mariano	2.29
Wagner,Billy	2.40
Hoffman,Trevor	2.78
Martinez,Pedro	2.91
Santana,Johan	3.11
Oswalt,Roy	3.13
Benitez,Armando	3.13
Maddux,Greg	3.16
Webb,Brandon	3.24
Peavy,Jake	3.25

Winning Percentage
(minimum 100 Decisions)

Martinez,Pedro	.684
Santana,Johan	.681
Oswalt,Roy	.668
Halladay,Roy	.665
Lee,Cliff	.661
Hudson,Tim	.655
Johnson,Randy	.648
Mussina,Mike	.638
Mulder,Mark	.632
Pettitte,Andy	.629

Opponent Batting Average
(minimum 750 IP)

Wagner,Billy	.189
Benitez,Armando	.195
Hoffman,Trevor	.210
Rivera,Mariano	.212
Martinez,Pedro	.213
Wood,Kerry	.215
Johnson,Randy	.220
Santana,Johan	.223
Foulke,Keith	.223
Zambrano,Carlos	.228

Baserunners Per 9 IP
(minimum 750 IP)

Wagner,Billy	9.40
Rivera,Mariano	9.50
Hoffman,Trevor	9.51
Martinez,Pedro	9.90
Santana,Johan	10.10
Foulke,Keith	10.18
Schilling,Curt	10.38
Maddux,Greg	10.53
Smoltz,John	10.67
Mussina,Mike	10.88

Games

Timlin,Mike	1058
Jones,Todd	982
Hoffman,Trevor	930
Weathers,David	896
Gordon,Tom	887
Guardado,Eddie	860
Rivera,Mariano	851
Embree,Alan	846
Tavarez,Julian	786
Wagner,Billy	765

Games Started

Maddux,Greg	740
Glavine,Tom	682
Johnson,Randy	586
Moyer,Jamie	584
Mussina,Mike	536
Rogers,Kenny	474
Smoltz,John	466
Schilling,Curt	436
Pettitte,Andy	426
Trachsel,Steve	417

Complete Games

Maddux,Greg	109
Johnson,Randy	100
Schilling,Curt	83
Mussina,Mike	57
Glavine,Tom	56
Smoltz,John	53
Martinez,Pedro	46
Hernandez,Livan	45
Halladay,Roy	40
Rogers,Kenny	36

Shutouts

Johnson,Randy	37
Maddux,Greg	35
Glavine,Tom	25
Mussina,Mike	23
Schilling,Curt	20
Martinez,Pedro	17
Smoltz,John	16
Carpenter,Chris	12
Halladay,Roy	11
Hudson,Tim	11

Wins

Maddux,Greg	355
Glavine,Tom	305
Johnson,Randy	295
Mussina,Mike	270
Moyer,Jamie	246
Rogers,Kenny	219
Schilling,Curt	216
Pettitte,Andy	215
Martinez,Pedro	214
Smoltz,John	210

Losses

Maddux,Greg	227
Glavine,Tom	203
Moyer,Jamie	185
Johnson,Randy	160
Trachsel,Steve	159
Wakefield,Tim	157
Rogers,Kenny	156
Mussina,Mike	153
Smoltz,John	147
Schilling,Curt	146

Innings Pitched

Maddux,Greg	5008.1
Glavine,Tom	4413.1
Johnson,Randy	4039.1
Moyer,Jamie	3746.2
Mussina,Mike	3562.2
Smoltz,John	3395.0
Rogers,Kenny	3302.2
Schilling,Curt	3261.0
Wakefield,Tim	2802.0
Martinez,Pedro	2782.2

Batters Faced

Maddux,Greg	20421
Glavine,Tom	18604
Johnson,Randy	16655
Moyer,Jamie	15943
Mussina,Mike	14593
Rogers,Kenny	14280
Smoltz,John	13927
Schilling,Curt	13284
Wakefield,Tim	12080
Pettitte,Andy	11617

Strikeouts

Johnson,Randy	4789
Maddux,Greg	3371
Martinez,Pedro	3117
Schilling,Curt	3116
Smoltz,John	3011
Mussina,Mike	2813
Glavine,Tom	2607
Moyer,Jamie	2248
Vazquez,Javier	2015
Pettitte,Andy	2002

Walks Allowed

Glavine,Tom	1500
Johnson,Randy	1466
Rogers,Kenny	1175
Moyer,Jamie	1074
Wakefield,Tim	1072
Maddux,Greg	999
Smoltz,John	992
Gordon,Tom	974
Trachsel,Steve	943
Nomo,Hideo	908

Hit Batters

Johnson,Randy	188
Wakefield,Tim	163
Maddux,Greg	137
Martinez,Pedro	137
Park,Chan Ho	130
Moyer,Jamie	128
Rogers,Kenny	127
Wright,Jamey	127
Tavarez,Julian	94
Padilla,Vicente	91

Wild Pitches

Smoltz,John	145
Gordon,Tom	110
Nomo,Hideo	109
Johnson,Randy	104
Wakefield,Tim	104
Schmidt,Jason	93
Batista,Miguel	90
Estes,Shawn	79
Rogers,Kenny	79
Lackey,John	77

2008 Active Career Pitching Leaders

Saves	
Hoffman, Trevor	554
Rivera, Mariano	482
Wagner, Billy	385
Percival, Troy	352
Jones, Todd	319
Isringhausen, Jason	293
Benitez, Armando	289
Cordero, Francisco	211
Rodriguez, Francisco	208
Nathan, Joe	200

Save Pct	
(minimum 50 Save Ops)	
Gagne, Eric	91.7
Smoltz, John	91.1
Soria, Joakim	89.4
Nathan, Joe	89.3
Hoffman, Trevor	89.2
Saito, Takashi	89.0
Rivera, Mariano	88.9
Papelbon, Jonathan	88.3
Jenks, Bobby	88.0
Rodriguez, Francisco	86.3

Home Runs Allowed	
Moyer, Jamie	464
Johnson, Randy	392
Mussina, Mike	376
Wakefield, Tim	362
Glavine, Tom	356
Maddux, Greg	353
Trachsel, Steve	348
Schilling, Curt	347
Rogers, Kenny	339
Vazquez, Javier	300

Strikeouts Per 9 IP	
(minimum 750 IP)	
Wagner, Billy	11.73
Benitez, Armando	10.93
Johnson, Randy	10.67
Wood, Kerry	10.39
Martinez, Pedro	10.08
Hoffman, Trevor	9.61
Santana, Johan	9.26
Perez, Oliver	9.25
Peavy, Jake	8.96
Rhodes, Arthur	8.89

Opp On-Base Percentage	
(minimum 750 IP)	
Wagner, Billy	.263
Hoffman, Trevor	.265
Rivera, Mariano	.266
Martinez, Pedro	.275
Santana, Johan	.279
Foulke, Keith	.280
Schilling, Curt	.286
Maddux, Greg	.291
Smoltz, John	.292
Johnson, Randy	.297

Opp Slugging Average	
(minimum 750 IP)	
Rivera, Mariano	.290
Wagner, Billy	.300
Martinez, Pedro	.335
Benitez, Armando	.338
Hoffman, Trevor	.340
Johnson, Randy	.350
Isringhausen, Jason	.350
Webb, Brandon	.351
Zambrano, Carlos	.352
Smoltz, John	.357

Hits Per Nine Innings	
(minimum 750 IP)	
Wagner, Billy	6.11
Benitez, Armando	6.30
Hoffman, Trevor	6.94
Wood, Kerry	6.99
Martinez, Pedro	7.03
Rivera, Mariano	7.03
Johnson, Randy	7.24
Santana, Johan	7.43
Foulke, Keith	7.46
Zambrano, Carlos	7.54

Home Runs Per Nine IP	
(minimum 750 IP)	
Rivera, Mariano	0.47
Webb, Brandon	0.62
Maddux, Greg	0.63
Cook, Aaron	0.70
Hudson, Tim	0.71
Isringhausen, Jason	0.71
Lowe, Derek	0.72
Glavine, Tom	0.73
Smoltz, John	0.73
Tavarez, Julian	0.74

Strikeouts / Walks Ratio	
(minimum 750 IP)	
Schilling, Curt	4.38
Martinez, Pedro	4.14
Wagner, Billy	3.95
Sheets, Ben	3.85
Hoffman, Trevor	3.85
Rivera, Mariano	3.83
Santana, Johan	3.72
Foulke, Keith	3.70
Lieber, Jon	3.68
Oswalt, Roy	3.61

Stolen Base Pct Allowed	
(minimum 750 IP)	
Carpenter, Chris	38.3
Buehrle, Mark	41.4
Rogers, Kenny	41.6
Zambrano, Carlos	47.9
Santana, Johan	50.0
Garland, Jon	50.5
Colon, Bartolo	51.5
Redman, Mark	51.6
Oswalt, Roy	52.4
Meche, Gil	52.6

GIDP Induced	
Maddux, Greg	422
Glavine, Tom	421
Rogers, Kenny	349
Moyer, Jamie	309
Pettitte, Andy	306
Mussina, Mike	293
Hampton, Mike	274
Johnson, Randy	244
Estes, Shawn	240
Smoltz, John	240

GIDP Per Nine IP	
(minimum 750 IP)	
Cook, Aaron	1.32
Estes, Shawn	1.29
Westbrook, Jake	1.28
Tavarez, Julian	1.26
Wright, Jamey	1.23
Silva, Carlos	1.20
Hampton, Mike	1.15
Mulder, Mark	1.14
Schoeneweis, Scott	1.11
Robertson, Nate	1.11

Complete Game %	
(minimum 100 GS)	
Schilling, Curt	0.19
Johnson, Randy	0.17
Halladay, Roy	0.16
Maddux, Greg	0.15
Mulder, Mark	0.12
Hernandez, Livan	0.12
Martinez, Pedro	0.12
Smoltz, John	0.11
Ponson, Sidney	0.11
Carpenter, Chris	0.11

Quality Start Pct	
(minimum 100 GS)	
Oswalt, Roy	69.7
Johnson, Randy	67.7
Martinez, Pedro	67.5
Peavy, Jake	67.3
Webb, Brandon	67.0
Santana, Johan	67.0
Schilling, Curt	66.1
Maddux, Greg	64.9
Halladay, Roy	64.3
Hudson, Tim	64.0

Walks Per 9 IP	
(minimum 750 IP)	
Silva, Carlos	1.66
Lieber, Jon	1.73
Maddux, Greg	1.80
Schilling, Curt	1.96
Sheets, Ben	1.97
Mussina, Mike	1.98
Bush, David	2.03
Oswalt, Roy	2.05
Buehrle, Mark	2.07
Halladay, Roy	2.09

Games Finished	
Hoffman, Trevor	774
Rivera, Mariano	718
Wagner, Billy	637
Jones, Todd	619
Percival, Troy	536
Benitez, Armando	527
Timlin, Mike	467
Isringhausen, Jason	463
Foulke, Keith	406
Guardado, Eddie	390

2008 American League Bill James Leaders

Top Game Scores

Pitcher	Date	Opp	IP	H	R	ER	BB	SO	GS
Lester,Jon, Bos	5/19	KC	9.0	0	0	0	2	9	94
Shields,James, TB	5/9	LAA	9.0	1	0	0	0	8	93
Garza,Matt, TB	8/15	Tex	9.0	2	0	0	2	9	90
Garza,Matt, TB	6/26	Fla	9.0	1	1	1	1	10	90
Halladay,Roy, Tor	7/11	NYY	9.0	2	0	0	1	8	90
Lee,Cliff, Cle	4/24	KC	9.0	3	0	0	0	9	90
Shields,James, TB	4/27	Bos	9.0	2	0	0	1	7	89
Slowey,Kevin, Min	6/29	Mil	9.0	3	0	0	0	8	89
Harden,Rich, Oak	6/26	Phi	8.0	2	0	0	1	11	88
Santana,Ervin, LAA	5/5	KC	9.0	4	0	0	0	9	88

Worst Game Scores

Pitcher	Date	Opp	IP	H	R	ER	BB	SO	GS
Bannister,Brian, KC	8/17	NYY	1.0	10	10	10	3	0	-10
Lackey,John, LAA	9/26	Tex	2.2	12	10	10	2	1	-7
Washburn,Jarrod, Sea	5/21	Det	2.1	12	9	9	0	2	-1
Feldman,Scott, Tex	8/12	Bos	2.2	10	12	6	3	2	1
Mendoza,Luis, Tex	7/7	LAA	1.1	9	8	8	2	0	2
Sabathia,CC, Cle	4/11	Oak	3.1	12	9	9	2	4	2
Contreras,Jose, CWS	6/21	ChC	3.1	10	9	9	2	1	3
Buehrle,Mark, CWS	8/2	KC	4.1	14	8	8	0	1	4
Eveland,Dana, Oak	8/2	Bos	2.0	8	9	9	2	2	4
Gallagher,Sean, Oak	8/19	Min	5.0	11	10	10	3	2	4
Trachsel,Steve, Bal	5/24	TB	1.2	7	9	9	2	1	4

Runs Created

Morneau,Justin, Min	122
Sizemore,Grady, Cle	121
Youkilis,Kevin, Bos	120
Hamilton,Josh, Tex	119
Markakis,Nick, Bal	113
Huff,Aubrey, Bal	111
Cabrera,Miguel, Det	109
Damon,Johnny, NYY	109
Abreu,Bobby, NYY	108
2 tied with	107

Runs Created Per 27 Outs

Youkilis,Kevin, Bos	8.1
Bradley,Milton, Tex	8.0
Quentin,Carlos, CWS	7.6
Kinsler,Ian, Tex	7.4
Damon,Johnny, NYY	7.2
Hamilton,Josh, Tex	7.0
Markakis,Nick, Bal	7.0
Mauer,Joe, Min	7.0
Morneau,Justin, Min	7.0
Huff,Aubrey, Bal	6.9

Offensive Winning %

Youkilis,Kevin, Bos	.730
Bradley,Milton, Tex	.721
Quentin,Carlos, CWS	.705
Mauer,Joe, Min	.705
Morneau,Justin, Min	.705
Kinsler,Ian, Tex	.690
Damon,Johnny, NYY	.689
Markakis,Nick, Bal	.677
Sizemore,Grady, Cle	.673
DeJesus,David, KC	.673

Secondary Average
(minimum 502 PA)

Cust,Jack, Oak	.476
Sizemore,Grady, Cle	.448
Bradley,Milton, Tex	.447
Pena,Carlos, TB	.445
Thome,Jim, CWS	.441
Quentin,Carlos, CWS	.435
Rodriguez,Alex, NYY	.433
Giambi,Jason, NYY	.426
Upton,B.J., TB	.394
Youkilis,Kevin, Bos	.377

Isolated Power
(minimum 502 PA)

Quentin,Carlos, CWS	.283
Rodriguez,Alex, NYY	.271
Longoria,Evan, TB	.259
Thome,Jim, CWS	.258
Youkilis,Kevin, Bos	.257
Giambi,Jason, NYY	.255
Dye,Jermaine, CWS	.249
Huff,Aubrey, Bal	.247
Pena,Carlos, TB	.247
Cust,Jack, Oak	.245

Power / Speed Number

Sizemore,Grady, Cle	35.3
Rodriguez,Alex, NYY	23.8
Damon,Johnny, NYY	21.4
Kinsler,Ian, Tex	21.3
Abreu,Bobby, NYY	21.0
Rios,Alex, Tor	20.4
Hunter,Torii, LAA	20.0
Pedroia,Dustin, Bos	18.4
Ramirez,Alexei, CWS	16.1
Granderson,Curtis, Det	15.5

Speed Scores (2007-2008)

Granderson,Curtis, Det	8.90
Crawford,Carl, TB	8.02
Suzuki,Ichiro, Sea	7.65
Sizemore,Grady, Cle	7.46
Damon,Johnny, NYY	7.45
Crisp,Coco, Bos	7.36
Roberts,Brian, Bal	7.28
Kinsler,Ian, Tex	7.03
Iwamura,Akinori, TB	6.99
Figgins,Chone, LAA	6.75

Cheap Wins

Garland,Jon, LAA	6
Olson,Garrett, Bal	6
Rogers,Kenny, Det	6
Burnett,A.J., Tor	5
Jackson,Edwin, TB	5
Robertson,Nate, Det	5
Sonnanstine,Andy, TB	5
6 tied with	4

Tough Losses

Guthrie,Jeremy, Bal	6
Vazquez,Javier, CWS	6
Beckett,Josh, Bos	5
Duchscherer,Justin, Oak	5
Halladay,Roy, Tor	5
7 tied with	4

2008 National League Bill James Leaders

Top Game Scores

Pitcher	Date	Opp	IP	H	R	ER	BB	SO	GS
Zambrano,Carlos, ChC	9/14	Hou	9.0	0	0	0	1	10	96
Nolasco,Ricky, Fla	8/19	SF	9.0	2	0	0	1	11	93
Sabathia,CC, Mil	8/31	Pit	9.0	1	0	0	3	11	93
Hudson,Tim, Atl	5/2	Cin	9.0	3	0	0	0	10	91
Kuroda,Hiroki, LAD	7/7	Atl	9.0	1	0	0	0	6	91
Kuroda,Hiroki, LAD	6/6	ChC	9.0	4	0	0	0	11	90
Haren,Dan, Ari	9/16	SF	9.0	4	0	0	2	12	89
Johnson,Randy, Ari	9/28	Col	9.0	2	1	0	1	9	89
Oswalt,Roy, Hou	9/6	Col	9.0	1	0	0	2	6	89
Lincecum,Tim, SF	9/13	SD	9.0	4	0	0	3	12	88
Oswalt,Roy, Hou	8/17	Ari	8.0	1	0	0	2	10	88
Santana,Johan, NYM	8/17	Pit	9.0	3	0	0	0	7	88

Worst Game Scores

Pitcher	Date	Opp	IP	H	R	ER	BB	SO	GS
Arroyo,Bronson, Cin	6/24	Tor	1.0	11	10	10	1	1	-9
Backe,Brandon, Hou	8/6	ChC	3.1	9	11	11	6	0	-8
Hernandez,Run, Hou	7/7	Pit	4.0	13	10	10	4	3	-5
Germano,Justin, SD	4/21	Hou	3.1	10	10	10	3	1	-2
Suppan,Jeff, Mil	4/30	ChC	3.2	11	11	8	1	1	1
Penny,Brad, LAD	5/7	NYM	4.2	10	10	10	3	2	3
Lowe,Derek, LAD	8/6	StL	3.1	13	8	8	0	2	4
Hendrickson,Mark, Fla	5/30	Phi	3.2	7	10	10	3	1	5
Hernandez,Livan, Col	8/10	SD	2.2	7	9	9	4	1	5
Myers,Brett, Phi	9/19	Fla	4.0	9	10	10	2	3	5

Runs Created

Pujols,Albert, StL	130
Berkman,Lance, Hou	129
Howard,Ryan, Phi	117
Reyes,Jose, NYM	117
Beltran,Carlos, NYM	116
Ramirez,Hanley, Fla	116
Wright,David, NYM	116
Utley,Chase, Phi	113
Ramirez,Aramis, ChC	108
Gonzalez,Adrian, SD	107

Runs Created Per 27 Outs

Pujols,Albert, StL	9.6
Jones,Chipper, Atl	8.9
Berkman,Lance, Hou	8.6
Holliday,Matt, Col	7.4
Ramirez,Hanley, Fla	7.2
Ramirez,Aramis, ChC	7.0
Ethier,Andre, LAD	7.0
Beltran,Carlos, NYM	6.8
Utley,Chase, Phi	6.7
Ludwick,Ryan, StL	6.7

Offensive Winning %

Pujols,Albert, StL	.817
Jones,Chipper, Atl	.787
Berkman,Lance, Hou	.770
Ramirez,Hanley, Fla	.719
Ethier,Andre, LAD	.716
Holliday,Matt, Col	.700
Beltran,Carlos, NYM	.693
Ludwick,Ryan, StL	.687
Gonzalez,Adrian, SD	.686
Ramirez,Aramis, ChC	.686

Secondary Average

(minimum 502 PA)

Dunn,Adam, Cin-Ari	.516
Pujols,Albert, StL	.508
Berkman,Lance, Hou	.466
Ramirez,Hanley, Fla	.455
Burrell,Pat, Phi	.448
Howard,Ryan, Phi	.426
Jones,Chipper, Atl	.424
Ludwick,Ryan, StL	.414
Beltran,Carlos, NYM	.409
Uggla,Dan, Fla	.409

Isolated Power

(minimum 502 PA)

Pujols,Albert, StL	.296
Ludwick,Ryan, StL	.292
Howard,Ryan, Phi	.292
Dunn,Adam, Cin-Ari	.277
Braun,Ryan, Mil	.268
Jacobs,Mike, Fla	.266
Burrell,Pat, Phi	.257
Berkman,Lance, Hou	.255
Uggla,Dan, Fla	.254
Soriano,Alfonso, ChC	.252

Power / Speed Number

Ramirez,Hanley, Fla	34.0
Holliday,Matt, Col	26.4
Beltran,Carlos, NYM	26.0
Reyes,Jose, NYM	24.9
McLouth,Nate, Pit	24.4
Kemp,Matt, LAD	23.8
Soriano,Alfonso, ChC	23.0
Berkman,Lance, Hou	22.2
Phillips,Brandon, Cin	22.0
Hart,Corey, Mil	21.4

Speed Scores (2007-2008)

Taveras,Willy, Col	8.70
Reyes,Jose, NYM	8.52
Rollins,Jimmy, Phi	8.28
McLouth,Nate, Pit	7.94
Weeks,Rickie, Mil	7.94
Pierre,Juan, LAD	7.71
Victorino,Shane, Phi	7.54
Ramirez,Hanley, Fla	7.23
Beltran,Carlos, NYM	7.18
Byrnes,Eric, Ari	7.17

Cheap Wins

Cook,Aaron, Col	5
Marquis,Jason, ChC	5
Kendrick,Kyle, Phi	4
Looper,Braden, StL	4
8 tied with	3

Tough Losses

Lannan,John, Was	7
Harang,Aaron, Cin	6
Bergmann,Jason, Was	5
Hamels,Cole, Phi	5
Looper,Braden, StL	5
Lowe,Derek, LAD	5
Perez,Odalis, Was	5
9 tied with	4

Additional Bill James Leaders

AL Batters Win Shares (2008)		NL Batters Win Shares (2008)		AL Pitchers Win Shares (2008)		NL Pitchers Win Shares (2008)	
Mauer,Joe, Min	30	Berkman,Lance, Hou	36	Lee,Cliff, Cle	24	Lincecum,Tim, SF	25
Morneau,Justin, Min	28	Pujols,Albert, StL	34	Halladay,Roy, Tor	23	Santana,Johan, NYM	21
Youkilis,Kevin, Bos	27	Ramirez,Hanley, Fla	32	Rivera,Mariano, NYY	20	Webb,Brandon, Ari	21
Hamilton,Josh, Tex	26	Utley,Chase, Phi	30	Santana,Ervin, LAA	19	Haren,Dan, Ari	19
Pedroia,Dustin, Bos	26	Beltran,Carlos, NYM	29	Lester,Jon, Bos	18	Dempster,Ryan, ChC	18
Sizemore,Grady, Cle	26	Reyes,Jose, NYM	28	Saunders,Joe, LAA	18	Hamels,Cole, Phi	18
Kinsler,Ian, Tex	24	Wright,David, NYM	27	Mussina,Mike, NYY	17	5 tied with	16
4 tied with	23	Ramirez,Aramis, ChC	25	Soria,Joakim, KC	17		
		6 tied with	24	4 tied with	16		

Batters Win Shares (Career)		Pitchers Win Shares (Career)		2008 AL Component ERA (minimum 162 IP)		2008 NL Component ERA (minimum 162 IP)	
Sheffield,Gary	422	Maddux,Greg	398	Halladay,Roy, Tor	2.62	Lincecum,Tim, SF	2.69
Thomas,Frank	405	Johnson,Randy	322	Lee,Cliff, Cle	2.75	Lowe,Derek, LAD	2.72
Rodriguez,Alex	399	Glavine,Tom	314	Santana,Ervin, LAA	3.00	Hamels,Cole, Phi	2.76
Griffey Jr.,Ken	396	Smoltz,John	288	Danks,John, CWS	3.26	Sheets,Ben, Mil	2.89
Ramirez,Manny	379	Mussina,Mike	270	Baker,Scott, Min	3.31	Santana,Johan, NYM	2.93
Jones,Chipper	349	Martinez,Pedro	252	Matsuzaka,Daisuke, Bos	3.36	Haren,Dan, Ari	2.96
Thome,Jim	341	Schilling,Curt	252	Shields,James, TB	3.41	Dempster,Ryan, ChC	3.03
Kent,Jeff	339	Moyer,Jamie	215	Beckett,Josh, Bos	3.45	Nolasco,Ricky, Fla	3.03
Rodriguez,Ivan	321	Rivera,Mariano	212	Garza,Matt, TB	3.47	Webb,Brandon, Ari	3.04
Jeter,Derek	320	Rogers,Kenny	206	Saunders,Joe, LAA	3.49	Peavy,Jake, SD	3.12

Highest Avg Game Score (AL - minimum 30 GS)		Lowest Avg Game Score (AL - minimum 30 GS)		Lowest Offensive Win % (AL)	
Halladay,Roy, Tor	60.48	Rogers,Kenny, Det	41.87	Crosby,Bobby, Oak	.318
Lee,Cliff, Cle	59.87	Bannister,Brian, KC	43.66	Betancourt,Yuniesky, Sea	.326
Santana,Ervin, LAA	57.88	Cabrera,Daniel, Bal	44.43	Cano,Robinson, NYY	.368
Shields,James, TB	54.88	Garland,Jon, LAA	44.97	Jones,Adam, Bal	.411
Lester,Jon, Bos	54.76	Byrd,Paul, Cle-Bos	47.20	Renteria,Edgar, Det	.415
Greinke,Zack, KC	54.63	Blackburn,Nick, Min	47.91	Pierzynski,A.J., CWS	.420
Danks,John, CWS	54.52	Jackson,Edwin, TB	48.16	Guillen,Jose, KC	.428
Burnett,A.J., Tor	53.97	Pettitte,Andy, NYY	48.58	Gomez,Carlos, Min	.428
Hernandez,Felix, Sea	53.97	Verlander,Justin, Det	48.88	Millar,Kevin, Bal	.435
Saunders,Joe, LAA	53.23	Sonnanstine,Andy, TB	49.03	Ellis,Mark, Oak	.438

Highest Avg Game Score (NL - minimum 30 GS)		Lowest Avg Game Score (NL - minimum 30 GS)		Lowest Offensive Win % (NL)	
Lincecum,Tim, SF	62.06	Kendrick,Kyle, Phi	42.63	Francoeur,Jeff, Atl	.261
Santana,Johan, NYM	60.12	Backe,Brandon, Hou	42.97	Bourn,Michael, Hou	.293
Hamels,Cole, Phi	58.82	Snell,Ian, Pit	43.77	Tejada,Miguel, Hou	.330
Dempster,Ryan, ChC	57.42	Duke,Zach, Pit	44.68	Taveras,Willy, Col	.331
Haren,Dan, Ari	57.21	Suppan,Jeff, Mil	44.84	Keppinger,Jeff, Cin	.395
Sheets,Ben, Mil	56.71	Zito,Barry, SF	45.44	Milledge,Lastings, Was	.398
Webb,Brandon, Ari	56.18	Redding,Tim, Was	46.64	Sanchez,Freddy, Pit	.413
Volquez,Edinson, Cin	55.97	Perez,Odalis, Was	47.70	Kendall,Jason, Mil	.431
Nolasco,Ricky, Fla	55.94	Arroyo,Bronson, Cin	48.38	Lopez,Felipe, Was-StL	.433
Billingsley,Chad, LAD	55.84	Maddux,Greg, SD-LAD	48.91	Rowand,Aaron, SF	.443

Win Shares

Bill James initially devised Win Shares as a way to relate a player's individual statistics to the number of wins he contributed to his team. As a single number, Win Shares allows us to easily compare the accomplishments of each player and to compare players across positions.

We credit a team with three Win Shares for each win. If a team wins 100 games, the players on the team will be credited with 300 Win Shares—or 300 thirds-of-a-win. If a team wins 70 games, the players on the team will be credited with 210 Win Shares, and so on.

The following pages contain the sum of a player's Win Shares prior to 1999, followed by his individual season totals from 1999 through 2008. Career totals are also included for each player.

The quality of the team does not affect an individual player's Win Shares. A great player on a bad team will rate just as well as a great player on a good team. In 2008 for example, Pat Burrell's 20 Win Shares for NL East champion Philadelphia Phillies were the absolute equivalent of Miguel Cabrera's 20 Win Shares for the last place Detroit Tigers.

Win Shares are also a great tool for evaluating award voting and Hall of Fame credentials. Do this year's Most Valuable Player or Cy Young Award winner match up with the leaders in Win Shares? Generally, 30 Win Shares indicates an MVP-caliber season; 20 Win Shares indicates a season worthy of the Cy Young Award.

Based on Win Shares, the 2008 National League MVP should be the Astros' Lance Berkman (36) while in the American League, Twins backstop Joe Mauer (30) should garnish the award. Cliff Lee posted the most Win Shares of any pitcher in the American League (24) and should win the AL Cy Young, while in the National League, Giant Tim Lincecum led all pitchers with 25 Win Shares, but might lose out on the actual NL Cy Young to either the Diamondbacks' Brandon Webb or the Mets' Johan Santana (21). As for NL Rookie of the Year, Cubs catcher Geovany Soto (21) will get a little competition from the Reds' Joey Votto (19), while in the AL, Evan Longoria (19) should nudge out The Cuban Missile, Alexei Ramirez (18).

Win Shares can also be used to assess the value of trades. Does your favorite team have a net gain or loss from their transactions? Win Shares also adjusts for offensive environment, so it is a great tool to use for looking at the greatest individual seasons in baseball history, as well as the greatest players of all time. For a complete description of how Win Shares are calculated as well as countless essays using Win Shares to analyze various facets of the game, check out Bill James' book, *Win Shares*.

Left Table

Player	<99	99	00	01	02	03	04	05	06	07	08	Career
Aardsma,David							0		4	1	1	6
Abercrombie,Reggie								3	1	3		7
Abreu,Bobby	32	26	23	26	29	28	33	25	27	18	22	289
Abreu,Tony										4		4
Accardo,Jeremy							2	14	0			20
Aceves,Alfredo										3		3
Acosta,Manny									2	4		6
Adams,Mike						5	1	0		6		12
Adenhart,Nick										0		0
Adkins,Jon					0	3	0	3	0	1		7
Affeldt,Jeremy				5	12	4	1	3	5	6		36
Aguila,Chris					0	0	0					0
Albaladejo,J									2	1		3
Albers,Matt							0	0	4			4
Alfonzo,Eliezer							9	1	0			10
Alou,Moises	141		17	21	9	20	23	18	14	12	2	277
Ambres,Chip							1		0	0		1
Amezaga,Alfredo				2	1	1	0	5	5	9		23
Anderson,Brian							0	5	0	3		8
Anderson,Garret	51	16	15	17	23	25	14	16	14	13	19	223
Anderson,Josh									3	4		7
Anderson,Marlon	2	8	2	16	10	12	3	4	8	4	1	70
Andino,Robert							0	0	0	1		1
Ankiel,Rick		3	14	0		0			8	13		38
Antonelli,Matt										1		1
Aquino,Greg					6	0	3	0	0			9
Ardoin,Danny			0			0	3	2		1		6
Arias,Alberto									0	1		1
Arias,Joaquin									1		3	4
Armas Jr.,Tony	0	5	12	7	4	2	2	4	1	0		37
Arredondo,Jose										11		11
Arroyo,Bronson			0	3	2	2	11	11	20	11	10	70
Ascanio,Jose									0	0		0
Atkins,Garrett					0	2	13	23	18	13		69
Aubrey,Michael										0		0
Aurilia,Rich	25	18	20	33	15	13	7	16	15	5	9	176
Ausmus,Brad	56	17	16	10	10	12	7	15	7	7	8	165
Aviles,Mike										17		17
Ayala,Luis					11	10	8		4	2		35
Aybar,Erick									1	2	15	18
Aybar,Willy							6	6		6		18
Backe,Brandon				0	1	5	7	3	3	2		21
Badenhop,Burke										0		0
Baek,Cha Seung					0			3	3	4		10
Baez,Danys			6	11	9	10	10	6	1			53
Bailey,Homer									2	0		2
Bailey,Jeff									0	1		1
Baisley,Jeff										1		1
Baker,Jeff							1	3	1	7		12
Baker,John										9		9
Baker,Scott							4	0	8	13		25
Bako,Paul	5	5	5	3	3	6	2	1	2	2	7	41
Baldelli,Rocco					14	14		12	2	2		44
Bale,John		0	0	2		2			3	1		8
Balentien,Wladimir									0	1		1
Balester,Collin										1		1
Balfour,Grant				0		2	3		0	11		16
Banks,Josh									0	2		2
Bankston,Wes									0			0
Bannister,Brian								3	11	2		16
Barajas,Rod		1	0	1	3	5	9	11	7	3	10	50
Bard,Josh				1	7	2	2	10	16	2		40
Barden,Brian									0			0
Barfield,Josh								18	8	1		27
Barmes,Clint						1	3	9	6	0	12	31
Barrett,Michael	1	11	1	2	12	7	14	18	13	3	1	83
Barthmaier,Jimmy									0			0
Bartlett,Jason							0	6	13	16	14	49
Barton,Brian										3		3
Barton,Daric									3	9		12
Bass,Brian									3			3
Batista,Miguel	6	6	0	11	9	14	11	8	10	12	0	87
Bauer,Rick			0	5	2	3	0	6		0		16

Right Table

Player	<99	99	00	01	02	03	04	05	06	07	08	Career
Bautista,Denny							0	1	1	0	3	5
Bautista,Jose							0	0	9	12	8	29
Bay,Jason				5	15	30	21	12	24			107
Bazardo,Yorman					0		3	0				3
Beam,T.J.						0		2				2
Beckett,Josh		3	5	11	9	12	11	18	11			80
Bedard,Erik			0		6	8	13	17	6			50
Beimel,Joe		4	3	2	0	1	7	6	7			30
Belisle,Matt			0			4	3	5	0			12
Bell,Heath					2	0	1	13	6			22
Belliard,Ronnie	0	15	17	13	1	12	18	18	11	15	11	131
Bellorin,Edwin							0	0	0			0
Beltran,Carlos	2	18	5	27	20	28	29	21	34	25	29	238
Beltran,Francis					0		2			1		3
Beltre,Adrian	4	15	22	12	16	13	33	13	17	16	13	174
Benitez,Armando	26	19	17	14	12	10	18	4	6	2	0	128
Bennett,Gary	1	2	3	1	4	6	2	5	2	2	0	28
Bennett,Jeff						2			1	7		10
Benoit,Joaquin			0	3	5	4	6	4	10	2		34
Benson,Kris		12	14		5	2	10	10	8			61
Bergmann,Jason							2	0	5	2		9
Berkman,Lance		1	10	32	29	25	30	20	31	24	36	238
Bernadina,Roger										1		1
Bernier,Doug									0	0		0
Berroa,Angel			1	1	15	12	12	4	0	3		48
Betancourt,Rafael			4	5	7	5	16	3				40
Betancourt,Yuniesky					3	13	19	8				43
Betemit,Wilson			0		1	7	9	8	2			27
Bierd,Randor										1		1
Billingsley,Chad							6	12	16			34
Birkins,Kurt							2	0	1			3
Bixler,Brian										1		1
Blackburn,Nick								0	10			10
Blake,Casey		1	0	1	0	11	17	9	11	11	18	79
Blalock,Hank				1	17	24	14	13	8	6		83
Blanco,Gregor										11		11
Blanco,Henry	0	6	9	6	4	2	5	5	6	0	3	46
Blanton,Joe							0	13	10	13	7	43
Blevins,Jerry									0	3		3
Bloomquist,Willie				3	3	2	4	5	2	5		24
Blum,Geoff		3	10	8	15	5	3	7	6	9	9	75
Bocock,Brian										1		1
Boggs,Brandon										5		5
Boggs,Mitchell										0		0
Bohn,T.J.								0		1		1
Bonderman,Jeremy					2	8	9	13	7	4		43
Bonifacio,Emilio									1	2		3
Bonine,Eddie										1		1
Bonser,Boof							6	4	0			10
Boone,Aaron	6	15	10	13	19	23		9	7	7	2	111
Bootcheck,Chris					0		1	0	4	0		5
Borkowski,Dave		1	0	0		2		4	3	0		10
Borowski,Joe	4		0	8	14	0	3	9	8	0		46
Botts,Jason							0	1	2	1		4
Bourgeois,Jason									0	0		0
Bourn,Michael							0	4	7			11
Bowden,Michael										1		1
Bowen,Rob					0	1		2	5	1		9
Bowers,Cedrick									0	0		0
Bowie,Micah		0			2	0			3	3	0	8
Bowker,John										7		7
Boyer,Blaine							4	0	0	1		5
Braden,Dallas									0	4		4
Bradford,Chad	3	0	2	3	9	9	5	2	7	6	8	54
Bradley,Milton		3	3	6	18	16	10	13	11	19		99
Branyan,Russell	0	1	5	10	8	5	5	9	6	5	5	59
Braun,Ryan									22	23		45
Bray,Bill									3	1	4	8
Brazoban,Yhency						4	4	0	0	0		8
Breslow,Craig							1	1		6		8
Brignac,Reid										0		0
Britton,Chris								4	1	1		6
Broadway,Lance									2	0		2

WIN SHARES BY YEAR												
Player	<99	99	00	01	02	03	04	05	06	07	08	Career
Brocail,Doug	23	12	5				4	3	1	6	7	61
Broussard,Ben				0	8	16	10	11	5	0		50
Brown,Andrew									1	2	3	6
Brown,Emil	1	0	1	2				18	13	8	7	50
Brown,Matt										0	0	0
Broxton,Jonathan								0	9	10	10	29
Bruce,Jay											7	7
Bruney,Brian							2	0	3	2	6	13
Bruntlett,Eric					1	2	3	4	4	3		17
Buchholz,Clay										3	0	3
Buchholz,Taylor								1	5	9		15
Buck,John							4	10	8	7	8	37
Buck,Travis										10	5	15
Buckner,Billy										1	1	2
Budde,Ryan										0	0	0
Buehrle,Mark			4	18	17	13	17	22	9	17	16	133
Bueno,Francisley											0	0
Bukvich,Ryan				1	0	1	0			2	0	4
Bulger,Jason								1	0	1	0	2
Bullington,Bryan							0		0	0	0	0
Burgos,Ambiorix							4	3	2			9
Burke,Chris							0	6	10	5	2	23
Burke,Jamie			0		1	5	0			6	2	14
Burnett,A.J.		3	5	9	14	0	7	11	9	11	14	83
Burnett,Sean							2				2	4
Burrell,Pat			12	17	25	8	14	24	15	20	20	155
Burres,Brian									1	3	2	6
Burriss,Emmanuel											4	4
Burton,Jared										5	6	11
Buscher,Brian										1	8	9
Bush,David							7	6	12	6	8	39
Butler,Billy										7	8	15
Bynum,Freddie							0	3	2	1		6
Byrd,Marlon				0	16	5	6	2	13	12		54
Byrd,Paul	13	10	0	6	19		7	13	6	12	9	95
Byrdak,Tim	0	0	0					1	0	4	4	9
Byrnes,Eric			0	1	2	16	17	9	13	24	2	84
Cabrera,Asdrubal										7	12	19
Cabrera,Daniel							8	7	7	6	6	34
Cabrera,Fernando							0	4	2	1	1	8
Cabrera,Jolbert	0	0	2	6	1	8	8				2	27
Cabrera,Melky								0	13	12	5	30
Cabrera,Miguel						12	19	27	33	29	20	140
Cabrera,Orlando	6	8	9	26	14	19	11	15	18	25	19	170
Cain,Matt								5	11	12	14	42
Cairo,Miguel	10	10	10	4	3	14	5	5	4	4		72
Calero,Kiko						3	6	5	7	1	0	22
Callaspo,Alberto								1	1	6		8
Cameron,Kevin									4	0		4
Cameron,Mike	23	19	19	29	18	21	15	11	25	20	17	217
Camp,Shawn							4	0	5	0	3	12
Campillo,Jorge							0	0	0	9		9
Cancel,Robinson	0										0	0
Cannizaro,Andy								0		0	0	0
Cano,Robinson								12	17	21	12	62
Cantu,Jorge							4	18	5	1	19	47
Capellan,Jose							0	1	5	0	0	6
Capps,Matt								0	7	14	7	28
Capuano,Chris						2	4	13	14	5		38
Carlin,Luke											1	1
Carlson,Jesse											9	9
Carlyle,Buddy		0	0					0		3	4	7
Carmona,Fausto									1	22	3	26
Carpenter,Andrew											0	0
Carpenter,Chris	13	9	5	13	3		12	20	19	0	1	95
Carrasco,D.J.						6	1	4			3	14
Carroll,Brett										0	0	0
Carroll,Jamey					3	3	6	9	13	5	10	49
Carter,Chris										0		0
Casanova,Raul	2		8	6	1		0			1	2	20
Casey,Sean	10	23	17	18	6	17	28	13	10	9	5	156
Cash,Kevin				0	1	3	0			0	1	5
Casilla,Alexi								0	1	9		10

WIN SHARES BY YEAR												
Player	<99	99	00	01	02	03	04	05	06	07	08	Career
Casilla,Santiago							0	0	0	4	3	7
Cassel,Jack										1	1	2
Castillo,Alberto										2		2
Castillo,Jose							9	9	7	2	6	33
Castillo,Luis	9	14	18	14	20	23	22	18	18	16	8	180
Castillo,Wilkin										0		0
Casto,Kory										0	1	1
Castro,Juan	6	0	3	1	2	7	5	7	6	1	2	40
Castro,Ramon		1	3	0	4	2	1	7	2	6	6	32
Catalanotto,Frank	5	5	8	17	7	15	5	16	14	9	4	105
Cedeno,Ronny								2	5	1	5	13
Cervelli,Francisco										0		0
Cervenak,Mike										0		0
Chacon,Shawn				7	4	8	2	11	1	6	2	41
Chamberlain,Joba										5	11	16
Chavez,Endy			0	3	9	10	1	13	4	3		43
Chavez,Eric	2	9	16	26	24	23	18	20	16	6	3	163
Chavez,Jesse										0		0
Chavez,Raul	0		0		0	1	3	2	0		3	9
Cherry,Rocky										1	0	1
Chico,Matt										5	0	5
Choo,Shin-Soo								0	4	1	16	21
Christian,Justin										1		1
Chulk,Vinnie					0	4	5	2	5	1		17
Church,Ryan							1	8	9	16	10	44
Cintron,Alex			0	1	14	8	7	6	4	2		42
Clark,Brady			0	4	1	6	12	22	8	2	0	55
Clark,Howie					0	3	1		0	0	0	4
Clark,Tony	49	19	6	16	1	4	7	18	0	4	3	127
Claussen,Brandon					1	0	7	1				9
Clement,Jeff										2	3	5
Clement,Matt	1	6	5	4	11	11	12	11	1			62
Clevlen,Brent									2	0	0	2
Clippard,Tyler										1	1	2
Coats,Buck										0	0	0
Coffey,Todd								3	9	1	1	14
Coke,Phil											3	3
Colome,Jesus					4	0	4	5	2	0	5	23
Colon,Bartolo	18	16	15	14	22	17	10	18	1	1	2	134
Condrey,Clay					2	0			2	3	5	12
Conrad,Brooks										0		0
Contreras,Jose						7	6	17	13	5	7	55
Cook,Aaron					2	3	6	6	12	9	15	53
Cora,Alex	1	0	6	6	13	12	17	5	6	4	5	75
Corcoran,Roy					1	0		0			7	8
Cordero,Chad					2	12	15	12	10	0		51
Cordero,Francisco		2	3	0	8	12	17	11	12	12	11	88
Corey,Bryan	0			0				3	1	0		4
Cormier,Lance							0	4	2	0	4	10
Corpas,Manny										3	15	6	24
Correia,Kevin						3	0	2	6	8	0	19
Coste,Chris										8	4	9	21
Cotts,Neal						0	2	9	2	1	2	16
Counsell,Craig	21	2	5	14	15	5	10	22	9	6	6	115
Crabbe,Callix										0		0
Crain,Jesse							4	10	7	0	5	26
Crawford,Carl				6	13	20	22	21	20	11		113
Crede,Joe			0	1	6	13	8	15	19	4	10	76
Crisp,Coco				3	8	14	20	9	16	11		81
Crosby,Bobby					0	14	12	8	4	10		48
Cruceta,Francisco							0	0	0	0		0
Cruz,Jose	23	11	15	16	13	17	14	11	4	5	0	129
Cruz,Juan				4	3	0	7	0	6	6	6	32
Cruz,Luis										1		1
Cruz,Nelson							0	3	4	7		14
Cuddyer,Michael			0	3	1	10	7	22	16	7		66
Cueto,Johnny										6		6
Cunningham,Aaron										3		3
Cust,Jack				0	0	4	0		0	19	17	40
Damon,Johnny	43	18	26	17	22	19	26	25	21	15	23	255
Danks,John										4	17	21
D'Antona,Jamie										0		0
Davies,Kyle							4	0	1	7		12

435

Player	<99	99	00	01	02	03	04	05	06	07	08	Career
WIN SHARES BY YEAR												
Davis,Chris											8	8
Davis,Doug		0	5	8	3	7	16	12	8	11	7	77
Davis,Jason					2	5	2	2	4	1	0	16
Davis,Rajai									0	5	5	10
De Aza,Alejandro											1	1
de la Cruz,Frankie										0	0	0
de la Rosa,Jorge							0	2	2	3	5	12
de los Santos,Valerio	2	0	3	0	4	4	0	0				13
DeJesus,David						0	9	16	14	15	22	76
Delcarmen,Manny							1	3	6	7		17
Delgado,Carlos	57	21	36	23	26	32	16	29	22	13	23	298
Delgado,Jesus										0	0	0
Dellucci,David	11	5	1	7	4	4	10	15	8	2	5	72
Dempster,Ryan	0	6	17	7	4	0	2	14	6	8	18	82
Denker,Travis											1	1
Denorfia,Chris							0	2			2	4
DeRosa,Mark	0	0	1	6	7	5	2	4	14	16	23	78
DeSalvo,Matt										0	0	0
Dessens,Elmer	3		10	10	15	7	5	4	5	0		59
Devine,Joey								0	0	1	9	10
DeWitt,Blake											12	12
Diaz,Joselo								0	0			0
Diaz,Matt					0	0	2	7	11		1	21
Diaz,Robinzon											1	1
Dickerson,Chris											5	5
Dickey,R.A.				0		7	4	0	0		3	14
DiFelice,Mark											2	2
DiFelice,Mike	11	8	2	1	4	6	0	0	0	1	1	34
Dillard,Tim											0	0
Dillon,Joe							0		3	2		5
DiNardo,Lenny							1	1	0	6	0	8
Dobbs,Greg							1	2	1	7	8	19
Dohmann,Scott							3	1	1	3	0	8
Dolsi,Freddy											3	3
Donnelly,Brendan					6	11	5	6	5	2	0	35
Dotel,Octavio		3	7	12	17	12	14	2	0	3	6	76
Doumit,Ryan								6	2	6	20	34
Downs,Scott			3			0	0	5	6	8	11	33
Drew,J.D.	3	10	18	22	15	13	31	12	19	12	16	171
Drew,Stephen								6	16	21		43
Duchscherer,Justin			0		1	9	11	10	1	13		45
Duckworth,Brandon			5	2	2	0	0	0	2	2		13
Duke,Zach						10	10	2	3			25
Dukes,Elijah									2	9		11
Dumatrait,Phil									0	1		1
Duncan,Chris							0	10	17	5		32
Duncan,Shelley									3	0		3
Dunn,Adam				10	20	13	29	25	18	18	21	154
Duran,German											1	1
Durbin,Chad		0	0	8	0	0	1		1	6	8	24
Durham,Ray	63	20	19	21	20	16	19	14	20	6	13	231
Dye,Jermaine	9	16	21	18	13	2	12	17	25	11	17	161
Easley,Damion	62	13	14	15	5	0	8	9	5	8	7	146
Eaton,Adam			9	5	0	7	6	5	4	2	1	39
Eckstein,David			12	21	10	10	27	13	12	8		113
Edmonds,Jim	90	5	29	30	29	21	33	25	11	9	11	293
Ekstrom,Mike										0	0	0
Elarton,Scott	5	10	11	0		0	5	7	4	0	1	43
Elbert,Scott											0	0
Ellis,A.J.											0	0
Ellis,Mark				14	18		21	14	20	13		100
Ellison,Jason						0	1	6	0	0		7
Ellsbury,Jacoby										6	16	22
Embree,Alan	10	6	3	2	7	5	4	0	5	8	2	52
Encarnacion,Edwin							4	14	16	14		48
Ensberg,Morgan			0		2	15	11	27	16	6	1	78
Erstad,Darin	43	9	30	14	17	4	15	15	1	5	8	161
Escobar,Alcides											0	0
Escobar,Alex				1		1	3		4			9
Escobar,Kelvim	13	7	8	11	9	12	14	5	12	18		109
Escobar,Yunel										12	13	25
Espineli,Geno											1	1
Estes,Shawn	23	6	10	7	4	0	9	5	0		1	65

Player	<99	99	00	01	02	03	04	05	06	07	08	Career
WIN SHARES BY YEAR												
Estrada,Johnny		5	0	0	18	9	13	7	0			52
Estrada,Marco										0		0
Ethier,Andre								11	13	23		47
Evans,Nick											1	1
Eveland,Dana								0	0	0	8	8
Everett,Adam			0	1	11	12	14	13	4	4		59
Eyre,Scott	4	0	0	2	4	5	4	9	5	3	3	39
Fahey,Brandon									4	1	1	6
Falkenborg,B		0					0	0	0		0	0
Farnsworth,Kyle		5	0	9	0	7	3	14	5	3	3	49
Fasano,Sal	12	3	2	2	0		3	3	0	1		26
Feierabend,Ryan								1	0	0		1
Feldman,Scott							1	3	1	4		9
Feliciano,Pedro				0	3	1		8	6	3		21
Feliz,Pedro		0	0	2	7	9	9	13	12	8		60
Fielder,Prince							2	16	27	23		68
Fields,Josh								0	12	0		12
Figgins,Chone				0	9	20	22	17	21	12		101
Figueroa,Nelson		0	6	1	3	0				2		12
Fiorentino,Jeff								0	1		0	1
Flores,Jesus										6	9	15
Flores,Randy				1		2	3	1	3	0		10
Floyd,Cliff	40	9	19	26	22	15	13	24	9	8	6	191
Floyd,Gavin						2	0	0	2	15		19
Fogg,Josh			2	10	4	7	3	6	6	0		38
Fontenot,Mike							0		5	12		17
Fossum,Casey			2	6	3	0	5	4	0	2		22
Foulke,Keith	9	16	16	17	9	21	18	3	4		2	115
Fowler,Dexter											0	0
Fox,Chad	6	0		9	0	4	0	0			0	19
Francis,Jeff							2	6	13	14	5	40
Francisco,Ben										1	9	10
Francisco,Frank					6		0	3	6			15
Francoeur,Jeff						12	15	20	5			52
Frandsen,Kevin							0	4	0		4	4
Franklin,Ryan		1		5	6	13	6	6	4	8	8	57
Frasor,Jason						9	6	4	3	2		24
Freel,Ryan			0		3	19	11	11	4	4		52
Fuentes,Brian			1	2	10	2	14	12	10	12		63
Fukudome,Kosuke										15		15
Fukumori,Kazuo										0	0	0
Fulchino,Jeff							0	0			0	0
Furcal,Rafael		17	9	20	26	20	26	27	15	8		168
Gabbard,Kason								2	5	2		9
Gagne,Eric		3	2	4	20	25	19	3	1	7	2	86
Galarraga,Armando									0	13		13
Gallagher,Sean									0	2		2
Gallardo,Yovani									9	2		11
Gamel,Mat										0		0
Garcia,Freddy		16	8	18	11	8	15	17	14	1	1	109
Garcia,Jaime										1	1	1
Garciaparra,Nomar	55	32	29	3	26	25	11	5	17	11	4	218
Gardner,Brett										3		3
Gardner,Lee			0			0		7	0			7
Garko,Ryan							0	6	12	15		33
Garland,Jon			1	8	8	10	11	20	15	13	9	95
Garza,Matt								1	4	12		17
Gathright,Joey					0	4	7	6	6			23
Gaudin,Chad				3	1	0	7	9	5			25
Geary,Geoff				0	1	3	10	3	7			24
Geer,Josh										2		2
German,Esteban				0	0	2	1	11	8	5		27
German,Franklyn				2	1	0	4	1		2		10
Germano,Justin					0			0	4	0		4
Gerut,Jody				14	10	3				13		40
Getz,Chris										0	0	0
Giambi,Jason	61	30	38	38	34	27	8	24	22	6	14	302
Giese,Dan									0	2		2
Giles,Brian	34	27	27	29	31	25	23	32	21	17	20	286
Gillaspie,Conor										0		0
Ginter,Matt			0	2	2	0	2	0			1	7
Glaus,Troy	3	16	25	21	22	10	8	23	16	14	20	178
Glavine,Tom	185	14	21	16	19	7	14	14	13	10	1	314

Player	<99	99	00	01	02	03	04	05	06	07	08	Career

Left table:

Player	<99	99	00	01	02	03	04	05	06	07	08	Career
Gload,Ross			0		0		7	0	4	7	5	23
Glover,Gary			0		4	5	3	1	1		4	1	19
Gobble,Jimmy						3	5	1	4	5	0	18
Golson,Greg											0	0
Gomes,Jonny					0	0	14	6	8	2		30
Gomez,Carlos										2	13	15
Gomez,Chris	49	6	1	8	11	2	8	4	5	4	4	102
Gonzalez,Adrian							1	1	16	25	24	67
Gonzalez,Alberto										0	3	3
Gonzalez,Alex	1	11	3	10	3	20	15	14	10	10		97
Gonzalez,Andy										1	0	1
Gonzalez,Carlos											6	6
Gonzalez,Edgar G.					1	0	0	3	5	0		9
Gonzalez,Edgar										7		7
Gonzalez,Enrique								3	0	0		3
Gonzalez,Gio											0	0
Gonzalez,Luis	115	26	27	37	27	24	10	19	12	12	9	318
Gonzalez,Mike						0	8	6	11	3	3	31
Gordon,Alex										12	15	27
Gordon,Brian											0	0
Gordon,Tom	114	2		8	3	11	15	10	10	4	2	179
Gorzelanny,Tom								0	3	11	0	14
Gotay,Ruben						3	5			6	1	15
Grabow,John				0	1	2	5	3	6		17
Granderson,Curtis						0	6	20	25	20		71
Gray,Jeff										0		0
Green,Sean								2	5	4		11
Greene,Khalil				1	20	16	13	19	4		73
Gregg,Kevin				2	6	2	4	10	11		35
Greinke,Zack					9	3	1	9	15	37
Griffey Jr.,Ken	244	31	24	14	5	6	15	19	9	14	15	396
Grilli,Jason			0	1		0	1	4	4	7	17
Gross,Gabe						2	2	10	4	10	28
Grudzielanek,Mark	47	13	15	17	12	18	8	18	13	12	10	183
Guardado,Eddie	19	4	8	12	14	14	8	10	3	0	6	98
Guerrero,Vladimir	39	28	29	23	28	18	27	27	24	29	22	294
Guerrier,Matt						0	5	5	9	2	21
Guevara,Carlos											0	0
Guillen,Carlos	2	0	8	14	12	12	22	8	25	19	13	135
Guillen,Jose	18	3	6	2	2	20	20	15	3	18	10	117
Guthrie,Jeremy						1	0	0	12	13	26
Gutierrez,Franklin						0	1	6	5	12
Guzman,Angel							0	2	0		2
Guzman,Cristian			5	12	18	14	14	16	6		7	20	112
Gwynn,Tony									1	3	0	4
Haeger,Charlie									2	0		2
Hafner,Travis				1	7	21	26	24	16	2		97
Hairston,Jerry	0	5	4	10	12	7	8	9	1	2	12	70
Hairston,Scott						3	0	0	7	9	19
Hall,Bill					1	3	7	17	20	10	8	66
Hall,Toby			0	6	7	10	8	11	3	0	2	47
Halladay,Roy	2	10	0	9	21	23	9	15	20	16	23	148
Hamels,Cole								8	15	18	41
Hamilton,Josh									11	26	37
Hammel,Jason							0	2	3	5
Hammock,Robby						7	3		0	1	1	12
Hampson,Justin							0	4	2	6
Hampton,Mike	48	26	19	11	5	11	10	6			3	139
Hanigan,Ryan									1	4	5
Hannahan,Jack							0	5	5	10
Hanrahan,Joel									2	7	9
Hansack,Devern							1	0	0	1
Hansen,Craig					0	0		1	1
Happ,J.A.									0	2	2
Harang,Aaron				4	3	5	11	18	17	6	64
Harden,Rich				4	14	12	4	2	16	52
Hardy,J.J.					11	3	19	20	53
Haren,Dan				1	2	13	14	17	19	66
Harman,Brad									0	0
Harris,Brendan					0	1	0	13	11	25
Harris,Willie			0	2	2	10	4	1	9	10	38
Harrison,Matt										3	3
Hart,Corey					0	0	5	21	16	42

Right table:

Player	<99	99	00	01	02	03	04	05	06	07	08	Career
Hart,Kevin										2	0	2
Hatteberg,Scott	17	4	5	5	16	15	17	8	15	10	0	112
Hawkins,LaTroy	8	3	12	3	11	13	16	5	4	5	6	86
Hawpe,Brad					1	8	15	20	16	60
Hayhurst,Dirk										0	0
Haynes,Nathan									1	0	1
Headley,Chase									0	8	8
Heilman,Aaron					0	0	10	8	8	2	28
Helms,Wes	1		0	5	1	14	4	5	10	2	5	47
Helton,Todd	19	19	29	26	27	35	30	25	21	22	8	261
Hendrickson,Mark				4	5	7	4	8	3	3	34
Henn,Sean						0	0	0	0	0
Hennessey,Brad						1	6	6	10	0	23
Hensley,Clay							5	11	0	0	16
Herges,Matt		1	10	9	4	7	3	1	3	5	2	45
Hermida,Jeremy							3	6	13	13	35
Hernandez,And							0	1	0	4	5
Hernandez,Felix							8	8	14	13	43
Hernandez,Fern									0	0	0
Hernandez,Livan	15	9	14	5	7	22	19	13	10	10	3	127
Hernandez,Luis									1	1	2
Hernandez,Michel				0		0		0	0	0
Hernandez,Orlando	13	14	12	4	11		8	5	7	9		83
Hernandez,Ramon		6	10	13	12	18	13	10	21	11	11	125
Hernandez,Run				5	7		4	1		0	17
Herrera,Daniel Ray										0	0
Herrera,Jonathan										1	1
Herrera,Yoslan										0	0
Hessman,Mike					1	0			1	2	4
Hill,Aaron								9	14	20	5	48
Hill,Koyie						0	1	1		1	0	3
Hill,Rich							0	5	13	1	19
Hill,Shawn						0		1	6	0	7
Hinckley,Mike									2	2
Hinshaw,Alex									4	4
Hinske,Eric				22	12	6	11	7	3	10	71
Hirsh,Jason							0	5	0	5
Hochevar,Luke								1	3	4
Hoey,Jim							0	0		0
Hoffman,Trevor	78	14	13	9	8	1	11	10	14	11	7	176
Hoffpauir,Micah										3	3
Holliday,Matt						9	17	19	27	21	93
Hollimon,Michael										0	0
Holm,Steve										2	2
Hoover,Paul			0	0			0	0	0	0
Hopper,Norris								2	7	0	9
Horwitz,Brian									1	1
House,J.R.					0	0		0	0	0	0
Howard,Ryan							1	10	29	26	24	90
Howell,J.P.							1	2	0	11	14
Howry,Bob	7	10	9	5	3	0	4	11	9	11	3	72
Hu,Chin-lung									1	1	2
Huber,Justin						0	0	0	2	2
Hudson,Luke				0		4	1	5	0	10
Hudson,Orlando					7	17	16	15	20	21	17	113
Hudson,Tim	12	15	17	23	23	16	14	7	17	10	154
Huff,Aubrey		3	5	12	21	20	14	9	12	21	117
Hughes,Phil								4	0	4
Hulett,Tug									0	0
Humber,Philip							0	0	0	0
Hundley,Nick									3	3
Hunter,Tommy									0	0
Hunter,Torii	0	5	8	19	20	16	13	11	17	22	21	152
Hurley,Eric									1	1
Iannetta,Chris								1	5	17	23
Ibanez,Raul	1	4	1	9	12	15	12	17	25	23	21	140
Igawa,Kei								1	0	1
Iguchi,Tadahito						18	19	15	4	56
Infante,Omar				3	3	12	7	5	4	9	43
Inge,Brandon			3	4	4	13	17	17	12	10	80
Inglett,Joe								6	1	12	19
Iribarren,Hernan									0	0
Ishikawa,Travis								1	4	5

437

WIN SHARES BY YEAR												
Player	<99	99	00	01	02	03	04	05	06	07	08	Career
Isringhausen,Jason	14	4	10	14	13	7	15	12	8	12	1	110
Iwamura,Akinori										13	21	34
Izturis,Cesar				4	4	10	25	6	3	5	9	66
Izturis,Maicer						1	6	13	16	11		47
Jackson,Conor								0	12	13	17	42
Jackson,Edwin						2	0	0	1	2	10	15
Jackson,Zach										1	1	2
Jacobs,Mike								5	12	7	14	38
James,Chuck								1	8	8	0	17
Janish,Paul											1	1
Janssen,Casey									4	10		14
Jaso,John											0	0
Jenkins,Geoff	1	18	20	11	4	19	12	20	15	11	4	135
Jenks,Bobby								6	12	16	13	47
Jennings,Jason				3	14	8	9	5	14	0	0	53
Jepsen,Kevin											0	0
Jeter,Derek	65	35	23	28	24	19	26	26	32	24	18	320
Jimenez,Cesar										0	2	2
Jimenez,Kelvin										0	0	0
Jimenez,Ubaldo									0	4	11	15
Jimerson,Charlton								0	0	1	0	1
Johjima,Kenji									20	17	8	45
Johnson,Dan								9	5	10	1	25
Johnson,Elliot											0	0
Johnson,Jason	2	4	0	9	5	10	6	8	2		0	46
Johnson,Jim									0	0	8	8
Johnson,Josh								1	12	0	6	19
Johnson,Kelly									9	19	19	47
Johnson,Mark	0	5	5	5	4	0	0				1	20
Johnson,Nick				0	11	14	6	20	25		4	80
Johnson,Randy	148	26	26	26	29	7	21	15	8	4	12	322
Johnson,Reed						11	9	10	16	3	13	62
Johnson,Rob										0	0	0
Johnson,Tyler							0	1	2			3
Jones,Adam									1	0	9	10
Jones,Andruw	42	28	30	22	27	23	17	21	22	15	2	249
Jones,Brandon										0	3	3
Jones,Chipper	98	32	27	29	31	26	18	18	22	25	23	349
Jones,Jacque	9	11	10	25	14	13	13	15	14	0		124
Jones,Todd	46	10	10	5	6	1	6	15	9	8	3	119
Jorgensen,Ryan							0		1	0		1
Joyce,Matt											6	6
Julio,Jorge				1	13	6	8	1	7	4	2	42
Jurrjens,Jair										2	11	13
Ka'aihue,Kila											1	1
Kapler,Gabe	0	8	10	13	7	4	5	1	2		8	58
Karstens,Jeff									3	0	1	4
Kazmar,Sean											1	1
Kazmir,Scott							1	10	13	13	12	49
Kearns,Austin					16	12	5	10	17	20	3	83
Kemp,Matt									3	10	19	32
Kendall,Jason	60	13	24	9	14	21	25	14	23	7	19	229
Kendrick,Howie									6	9	15	30
Kendrick,Kyle										9	3	12
Kennedy,Adam			2	11	8	17	13	13	17	15	2	8	106
Kennedy,Ian										2	0	2
Kensing,Logan							0	0	2	2	3	7
Kent,Jeff	110	23	37	27	28	20	22	28	18	17	9	339
Keppinger,Jeff								2		1	9	10	22
Kershaw,Clayton											5	5
King,Ray		0	4	5	5	4	8	3	2	2	0	33
Kinney,Josh									2	1		3
Kinsler,Ian									12	17	24	53
Knight,Brandon		0	0									0
Kobayashi,Masa											4	4
Konerko,Paul	2	14	15	17	17	4	20	24	21	16	10	160
Korecky,Bobby											1	1
Koshansky,Joe										0	1	1
Kotchman,Casey							2	4	0	15	14	35
Kotsay,Mark	14	6	12	16	22	13	21	19	11	3	9	146
Kottaras,George											0	0
Kouzmanoff,Kevin									1	15	14	30
Kroon,Marc	0				0							0

WIN SHARES BY YEAR												
Player	<99	99	00	01	02	03	04	05	06	07	08	Career
Kubel,Jason						3		1	12	12		28
Kunz,Eddie											0	0
Kuo,Hong-Chih								0	3	0	10	13
Kuroda,Hiroki											10	10
Lackey,John				7	7	10	16	16	21	13		90
Laffey,Aaron										3	4	7
LaHair,Bryan											2	2
Laird,Gerald					1	3	1	5	10	9		29
Lamb,Mike		6	8	7	0	12	6	9	10	5		63
Lambert,Chris											0	0
Langerhans,Ryan				0	0		12	8	5	4		29
Lannan,John										2	9	11
Larish,Jeff											2	2
LaRoche,Adam							7	11	16	16	16	66
LaRoche,Andy										2	2	4
LaRue,Jason		2	3	9	11	10	15	17	5	2	4	78
League,Brandon								1	0	5	0	4	10
LeBlanc,Wade											0	0
Ledezma,Wil					2	3	0	4	2	2		13
Lee,Carlos		10	14	15	17	20	22	21	22	21	22	184
Lee,Cliff				1	3	6	13	10	1	24	58
Lee,Derek	12	1	16	16	22	25	19	34	4	21	17	187
Lerew,Anthony								0	0	0		0
Lester,Jon								5	4	18		27
Lewis,Colby				0	1	1		0	0			2
Lewis,Fred								1	5	13		19
Lewis,Jensen									4	6		10
Lewis,Scott										3		3
Lidge,Brad				1	8	22	15	7	10	15	78
Lieber,Jon	32	13	12	16	7		10	12	6	3	2	113
Lillibridge,Brent										1		1
Lilly,Ted		0	0	3	6	10	15	4	11	15	12	76
Lincecum,Tim										8	25	33
Lincoln,Mike		1	0	4	6	2	1				4	18
Lind,Adam									3	7	7	17
Lindstrom,Matt										5	6	11
Linebrink,Scott		1	1	0	6	10	11	8	5	5		47
Liriano,Francisco								0	16		4	20
Litsch,Jesse										7	12	19
Littleton,Wes									6	3	0	9
Liz,Radhames										0	0	0
Lo Duca,Paul	0	2	2	28	19	18	20	11	16	9	2	127
Loaiza,Esteban	24	8	12	8	4	23	7	12	7	2	0	107
Loe,Kameron								0	8	2	3	2	15
Loewen,Adam									4	2	0	6
Logan,Boone									0	3	1	4
Lohse,Kyle				3	11	11	6	10	4	9	12	66
Loney,James									3	16	14	33
Longoria,Evan											19	19
Looper,Braden	0	5	5	7	11	11	13	6	8	6	11	83
Lopez,Aquilino						10	1	1		1	6	19
Lopez,Felipe					5	6	3	9	21	16	11	10	81
Lopez,Javier						6	0	0	2	4	6	18
Lopez,Jose							3	5	16	10	18	52
Lopez,Rodrigo			0		15	2	14	8	4	4		47
Loretta,Mark	31	14	12	9	10	25	32	15	17	12	9	186
Loux,Shane					0	0				1		1
Lowe,Derek	8	19	19	11	22	12	6	11	15	11	16	150
Lowe,Mark									3	0	1	4
Lowell,Mike	0	8	20	20	19	22	22	8	16	23	12	170
Lowery,Devon											0	0
Lowrie,Jed											7	7
Lowry,Noah						1	6	15	7	10		39
Ludwick,Ryan					0	6	0	0		10	24	40
Lugo,Julio		9	9	9	15	20	24	13	11	2		112
Luna,Hector						4	5	9	0	0		18
Lyon,Brandon				4	0	5		0	6	11	6	32
MacDougal,Mike		1	0	9	0	8	5	0	2	25
Macias,Drew									0	0		0
Mackowiak,Rob				4	12	6	14	12	6	7	0	61
Macri,Matt										1		1
Maddux,Greg	256	17	24	20	19	11	13	11	12	9	6	398
Madrigal,Warner											1	1

438

	WIN SHARES BY YEAR											
Player	<99	99	00	01	02	03	04	05	06	07	08	Career
Madson,Ryan						0	9	6	4	5	8	32
Mahay,Ron	5	3	1	2	0	5	8	0	4	7	6	41
Maholm,Paul								4	7	5	9	25
Maier,Mitch										0	1	1
Maine,John							0	0	6	11	7	24
Majewski,Gary						1	8	4	0	0		13
Manning,Charlie											1	1
Marcum,Shaun								1	3	10	12	26
Markakis,Nick									12	20	23	55
Marmol,Carlos									1	11	12	24
Marquis,Jason			1	8	3	1	14	12	2	8	8	57
Marshall,Sean									2	6	4	12
Marson,Lou											1	1
Marte,Andy								0	4	0	2	6
Marte,Damaso		0		1	9	15	9	4	4	5	6	53
Martin,Russell									14	22	20	56
Martinez,Pedro	99	27	29	12	21	20	16	19	6	2	1	252
Martinez,Ramon	0	5	7	9	9	8	6	2	5	2	0	53
Martinez,Victor					1	3	20	22	18	29	7	100
Martis,Shairon											0	0
Masset,Nick									1	0	4	5
Masterson,Justin											7	7
Mastny,Tom									1	4	0	5
Mather,Joe											4	4
Mathieson,Scott									0			0
Mathis,Doug											0	0
Mathis,Jeff								0	0	2	7	9
Matos,Osiris											0	0
Matsui,Hideki						19	28	23	6	16	10	102
Matsui,Kaz							13	5	7	14	12	51
Matsuzaka,Daisuke										12	16	28
Matthews Jr.,Gary		1	1	10	10	9	11	11	21	14	8	96
Mauer,Joe							6	22	30	21	30	109
Maybin,Cameron										0	3	3
Maysonet,Edwin											0	0
Maza,Luis											1	1
McAnulty,Paul								0	1	0	4	5
McBride,Macay								0	4	1		5
McCann,Brian								6	22	15	18	61
McCarthy,Brandon								5	5	3	1	14
McClain,Scott	0								0	0	1	1
McClellan,Kyle											4	4
McClung,Seth				2				1	2	0	7	12
McCrory,Bob											0	0
McDonald,James											1	1
McDonald,John		0	0	0	5	3	1	4	3	8	1	25
McGehee,Casey											0	0
McGowan,Dustin								0	0	11	5	16
McLouth,Nate								1	2	10	24	37
McPherson,Dallas							1	6	3	0		10
Meche,Gil		6	6			9	5	5	8	13	14	66
Medders,Brandon								5	6	2	1	14
Meek,Evan											0	0
Melhuse,Adam			0	0		4	5	2	1	2	0	14
Meloan,John										0	0	0
Mench,Kevin					10	4	13	12	9	8	2	58
Mendoza,Luis										2	0	2
Mercker,Kent	57	6	1			1	6	7	5	2	1	86
Meredith,Cla								0	9	5	3	17
Messenger,Randy								1	1	3	1	6
Metcalf,Travis										3	1	4
Meyer,Dan						0			0	0	0	0
Michaels,Jason				0	3	4	10	12	9	7	7	52
Mickolio,Kam											0	0
Mientkiewicz,Doug	0	3	0	18	17	20	6	4	8	4	10	90
Mijares,Jose											1	1
Miles,Aaron						1	12	8	10	10	9	50
Millar,Kevin	0	12	10	20	14	16	17	11	13	12	10	135
Milledge,Lastings									4	6	11	21
Miller,Andrew									0	2	0	2
Miller,Corky				2	5	1	0	0	0	1	1	10
Miller,Jai											0	0
Miller,Jim											1	1

	WIN SHARES BY YEAR											
Player	<99	99	00	01	02	03	04	05	06	07	08	Career
Miller,Justin				3		2	0			5	3	13
Miller,Trever	4	2	0			4	4	2	6	2	3	27
Millwood,Kevin	13	22	10	5	19	12	5	14	13	5	6	124
Milton,Eric	6	12	11	15	9	2	9	0	7	1		72
Miner,Zach									4	5	8	17
Miranda,Juan										1		1
Misch,Pat									0	2	1	3
Mitre,Sergio						0	0	2	0	4		6
Mock,Garrett										2		2
Moehler,Brian	26	10	10	1	2	0		5	0	3	7	64
Moeller,Chad			2	0	6	6	5	3	1	0	3	26
Molina,Bengie	0	3	13	7	10	16	11	15	11	13	19	118
Molina,Gustavo										0	0	0
Molina,Jose		0		1	2	2	6	7	5	4	9	36
Molina,Yadier							5	14	9	12	15	55
Monroe,Craig				1	0	9	11	13	13	3	3	53
Montanez,Lou											3	3
Montero,Miguel									0	3	4	7
Montz,Luke											1	1
Moore,Scott									1	1	0	2
Mora,Melvin		0	12	11	16	15	24	20	18	10	17	143
Morales,Franklin										4	0	4
Morales,Kendry									2	2	0	4
Morgan,Nyjer										4	3	7
Morillo,Juan									0	0	0	0
Morneau,Justin						1	9	7	26	18	28	89
Morris,Matt	26		6	17	14	10	7	9	8	7	0	104
Morrow,Brandon										5	7	12
Morse,Mike								5	2	2	0	9
Morton,Charlie											0	0
Morton,Colt										0	0	0
Moseley,Dustin									0	6	0	6
Moss,Brandon										1	5	6
Mota,Guillermo		5	1	2	2	14	12	3	3	1	4	47
Motte,Jason											2	2
Moyer,Jamie	95	18	5	15	16	18	5	12	10	8	13	215
Moylan,Peter									1	9	1	11
Mujica,Edward									1	0	0	1
Mulder,Mark			5	18	19	17	15	13	1	0	0	88
Muniz,Carlos										0	1	1
Murphy,Daniel											6	6
Murphy,David									0	5	11	16
Murphy,Donnie							0	0		3	1	4
Murray,A.J.										1	1	2
Murton,Matt								4	13	5	1	23
Musser,Neal										1	0	1
Mussina,Mike	126	17	18	20	15	18	9	10	14	6	17	270
Myers,Brett					3	9	4	14	12	9	7	58
Myrow,Brian									1	0	0	1
Nady,Xavier		0				7	1	8	12	10	20	58
Napoli,Mike									10	8	12	30
Nathan,Joe	5	2			1	11	19	17	20	16	16	107
Navarro,Dioner							0	4	5	6	17	32
Nelson,Brad										0	0	0
Nelson,Joe			0			0			5		6	11
Neshek,Pat									6	8	1	15
Newhan,David	1	0	0				13	2	0	1	1	18
Newman,Josh										0	0	0
Niemann,Jeff											0	0
Niese,Jonathon											0	0
Nieve,Fernando									6	0		6
Nieves,Wil					1			0	0	1	4	6
Nippert,Dustin								1	0	1	1	3
Nix,Jayson										1		1
Nix,Laynce						4	7	4	0	0	0	15
Nixon,Trot	0	10	14	20	16	19	4	15	10	4	0	112
Nolasco,Ricky									5	0	14	19
Nomo,Hideo	45	10	10	11	14	18	0	0			0	108
Norton,Greg	5	11	3	3	3	4	0		9	5	6	49
Nunez,Abraham	2	4	1	6	5	4	2	12	4	3	0	43
Nunez,Leo								0	1	3	5	9
Nunez,Vladimir	0	5	0	8	14	0	1				2	30
Ochoa,Ivan											2	2

Player	<99	99	00	01	02	03	04	05	06	07	08	Career
WIN SHARES BY YEAR												
O'Connor,Mike									3	0		3
O'Day,Darren											2	2
O'Flaherty,Eric									0	4	0	4
Ohlendorf,Ross										1	0	1
Ohman,Will			0	0				4	5	2	5	16
Ojeda,Augie		2	2	1	0	3				4	6	18
Okajima,Hideki										11	8	19
Oliver,Darren	37	13	0	3	3	10	1		6	5	9	87
Olivo,Miguel					1	8	7	7	13	7	7	50
Olsen,Scott								1	10	1	8	20
Olson,Garrett										0	1	1
Ordonez,Magglio	16	20	22	25	25	23	8	10	19	34	16	218
Orr,Pete								3	2	0	1	6
Ortiz,David	11	0	8	7	11	14	24	30	27	27	15	174
Ortiz,Russ	3	12	7	15	13	16	12	0		1	1	80
Ortmeier,Dan									0	3	0	3
Osoria,Franquelis								1	0	1	1	3
Oswalt,Roy				15	20	10	18	21	20	17	16	137
Outman,Josh											1	1
Overbay,Lyle				0	0	6	17	17	17	6	14	77
Owens,Henry									0	3		3
Owens,Jerry									0	6	0	6
Owings,Micah										13	2	15
Ozuna,Pablo			1		1	1		4	6	0	2	15
Padilla,Vicente		0	6	3	14	13	5	6	12	2	8	69
Pagan,Angel									3	5	3	11
Palmer,Matt											0	0
Papelbon,Jonathan								4	19	15	15	53
Parisi,Mike											0	0
Park,Chan Ho	33	6	18	16	5	0	4	5	4	0	6	97
Parnell,Bobby											0	0
Paronto,Chad				0	2	0			4	3	0	9
Parr,James											1	1
Parra,Manny										2	8	10
Parrish,John			0	0	2	6	2			2	2	14
Patterson,Corey			0	3	8	13	17	4	13	8	2	68
Patterson,Eric										0	2	2
Patterson,Scott										0		0
Patton,Troy										1		1
Pauley,David									0	0	0	0
Paulino,Felipe											0	0
Paulino,Ronny								0	14	10	3	27
Pavano,Carl	6	3	8	0	3	9	19	3		1	1	53
Payton,Jay	0	0	14	3	15	15	15	12	15	7	6	102
Pearce,Steve										2	2	4
Peavy,Jake					3	7	15	16	12	21	13	87
Pedroia,Dustin									2	18	26	46
Peguero,Jailen										0	0	0
Pelfrey,Mike									0	1	12	13
Pena,Brayan							0	1	0	0		1
Pena,Carlos				3	11	9	11	7	0	28	22	91
Pena,Tony									1	11	6	18
Pena,Tony F									0	11	3	14
Pena,Wily Mo					0	1	14	6	8	5	1	35
Pence,Hunter										18	19	37
Penn,Hayden								0	0			0
Pennington,Cliff											3	3
Penny,Brad			5	12	4	10	10	9	11	20	0	81
Peralta,Jhonny						5	0	25	15	21	19	85
Peralta,Joel								2	5	6	0	13
Percival,Troy	50	11	8	14	13	8	9	2		4	6	125
Perez,Chris											4	4
Perez,Fernando											3	3
Perez,Odalis	1	1		3	17	7	13	4	2	3	6	57
Perez,Oliver					4	1	16	2	0	10	8	41
Perez,Rafael									1	9	8	18
Perez,Tomas	6		1	5	4	5	4	1	3	0		29
Perkins,Glen									1	2	7	10
Perry,Jason											0	0
Petit,Gregorio											1	1
Petit,Yusmeiro									0	3	3	6
Pettitte,Andy	62	10	14	13	11	14	5	21	12	13	10	185
Pettyjohn,Adam				0							0	0

Player	<99	99	00	01	02	03	04	05	06	07	08	Career
WIN SHARES BY YEAR												
Phelps,Josh		0	0	10	10	5	4			5	0	34
Phillips,Andy						0	0	1	3	0		4
Phillips,Brandon				1		4	0	0	14	17	19	55
Phillips,Paul						0	2	2	0	0		4
Pie,Felix										5	2	7
Pierre,Juan			3	17	15	20	22	14	15	12	9	127
Pierzynski,A.J.	1	0	3	15	18	22	12	11	14	8	8	112
Pignatiello,Carmen										0	0	0
Pineiro,Joel			0	7	14	13	5	3	0	5	3	50
Pinto,Renyel									2	4	3	9
Podsednik,Scott		0		1	22	13	12	9	1		2	60
Polanco,Placido	2	3	11	14	16	18	17	22	14	24	15	156
Ponson,Sidney	5	10	11	4	10	16	8	0	3	0	5	72
Posada,Jorge	21	10	29	23	22	28	21	19	24	24	5	226
Prado,Martin									2	1	9	12
Price,David											1	1
Pridie,Jason										0		0
Prior,Mark					8	22	7	12	0			49
Proctor,Scott							1	0	9	6	0	16
Pujols,Albert				29	32	41	37	34	37	32	34	276
Punto,Nick				0	0	1	4	6	12	5	10	38
Purcey,David										1		1
Putz,J.J.						0	3	5	17	20	5	50
Qualls,Chad							4	7	9	9	11	40
Quentin,Carlos								5	5	23		33
Quinlan,Robb						1	8	2	8	1	3	23
Quintanilla,Omar								1	0	1	3	5
Quintero,Humberto						0	1	1	0	1	3	6
Quiroz,Guillermo							0	0	0	1	1	2
Rabelo,Mike									0	2	1	3
Raburn,Ryan								0		4	3	7
Ramirez,Alexei											18	18
Ramirez,Aramis	2	0	3	27	6	20	19	18	21	21	25	162
Ramirez,Edwar										0	5	5
Ramirez,Elizardo							1	0	3	0	0	4
Ramirez,Hanley								0	25	27	32	84
Ramirez,Horacio						9	5	8	3	0	2	27
Ramirez,Manny	105	35	27	25	29	28	25	33	27	14	31	379
Ramirez,Max											2	2
Ramirez,Ramon									7	0	9	16
Ramirez,Ramon A											3	3
Ransom,Cody			0	0	0	2				2	3	7
Rapada,Clay										0	2	2
Rasner,Darrell								0	1	1	3	5
Rauch,Jon					0		4	2	8	10	9	33
Ray,Chris								4	12	6		22
Redding,Tim				2	1	10	1	0		5	6	25
Redman,Mark		0	10	3	10	12	10	4	6	2	0	57
Redmond,Mike	4	12	5	6	13	1	6	7	6	11	3	74
Reed,Jeremy						3	9	1	0	4		17
Register,Steven											0	0
Reineke,Chad											1	1
Renteria,Edgar	41	13	15	13	26	25	16	15	19	19	11	213
Repko,Jason								5	4		0	9
Resop,Chris								0	1	0	0	1
Reyes,Al	9	5	1	2	2	1	2	9		6	1	38
Reyes,Anthony								1	3	0	5	9
Reyes,Argenis											1	1
Reyes,Dennys	4	5	2	1	4	0	4	1	9	2	6	38
Reyes,Jo-Jo										0	0	0
Reyes,Jose						12	4	16	28	24	28	112
Reynolds,Greg											0	0
Reynolds,Mark										14	17	31
Rhodes,Arthur	33	2	6	12	11	4	2	6	3		6	85
Richar,Danny										3	0	3
Richard,Clayton											0	0
Richmond,Scott											1	1
Ridgway,Jeff										0	1	1
Riggans,Shawn									1	0	4	5
Rincon,Juan				0	0	7	12	10	8	2	1	40
Rincon,Ricardo	16	3	3	6	6	6	4	2	0			46
Ring,Royce								0	1	2	0	3
Rios,Alex							7	9	18	22	20	76

WIN SHARES BY YEAR

Player	<99	99	00	01	02	03	04	05	06	07	08	Career
Riske,David		0		3	2	10	7	5	4	8	1	40
Rivas,Luis			1	8	6	7	9	4		0	1	36
Rivera,Juan				0	1	4	12	9	18	1	4	49
Rivera,Mariano	49	17	16	19	9	17	18	19	16	12	20	212
Rivera,Mike				0	1	0			4	0	4	9
Rivera,Saul									5	7	6	18
Roberts,Brian				3	2	14	16	28	13	22	20	118
Roberts,Dave		2	0	0	19	9	12	14	19	10	2	87
Roberts,Ryan									0	0	0	0
Robertson,Connor										0	0	0
Robertson,David											2	2
Robertson,Nate				0	1	8	7	14	8	1		39
Rodney,Fernando					0	1		6	8	3	4	22
Rodriguez,Alex	88	23	37	37	35	31	29	34	25	37	23	399
Rodriguez,Francisco					1	9	17	14	17	15	16	89
Rodriguez,Ivan	141	28	19	18	11	25	22	10	24	12	11	321
Rodriguez,Luis								6	1	1	4	12
Rodriguez,Sean											3	3
Rodriguez,Wandy								2	2	7	9	20
Roenicke,Josh											0	0
Rogers,Kenny	101	12	15	2	15	11	14	15	14	3	4	206
Rohlinger,Ryan											0	0
Rolen,Scott	61	15	18	29	26	24	35	5	21	11	11	256
Rollins,Jimmy			1	20	17	18	24	21	25	28	24	178
Romero,Alex											1	1
Romero,J.C.		1	0	1	14	3	8	5	0	8	7	47
Romo,Sergio											4	4
Rosa,Carlos											0	0
Rosales,Adam											0	0
Rosales,Leo											2	2
Rosario,Francisco									0	0		0
Ross,Cody							1	0	6	10	16	33
Ross,David				1	4	2	3	13	7	5		35
Rottino,Vinny									0	0	0	0
Rowand,Aaron			5	7	6	20	18	7	21	14		98
Rowland-Smith,Ryan										2	9	11
Ruggiano,Justin										0	1	1
Ruiz,Carlos									2	13	6	21
Ruiz,Randy											2	2
Rundles,Rich											1	1
Rupe,Josh								1	2		3	6
Rusch,Glendon	10	0	11	6	7	0	10	6	0		3	53
Ryan,B.J.		2	2	3	3	6	11	14	19	0	10	70
Ryan,Brendan										5	2	7
Ryan,Dusty											3	3
Ryu,Jae Kuk									0	0	0	0
Saarloos,Kirk					1	2	2	9	6	0	1	21
Sabathia,CC				12	13	13	11	12	15	24	23	123
Saccomanno,Mark											0	0
Sadler,Billy										0	2	2
Saito,Takashi									18	17	9	44
Salas,Juan									0	2	0	2
Salas,Marino											0	0
Salazar,Jeff									2	4	3	9
Salazar,Oscar				1							3	4
Salome,Angel											0	0
Saltalamacchia,J										5	6	11
Samardzija,Jeff											3	3
Sammons,Clint										0	0	0
Sampson,Chris									4	5	7	16
Sanches,Brian									0	0	0	0
Sanchez,Anibal									10	1	0	11
Sanchez,Duaner					0	0	6	7	6		4	23
Sanchez,Freddy					0	1	0	12	23	21	11	68
Sanchez,Gaby											1	1
Sanchez,Humberto											0	0
Sanchez,Jonathan									2	0	6	8
Sanchez,Romulo										1	1	2
Sandoval,Freddy											0	0
Sandoval,Pablo											6	6
Santana,Ervin								6	12	3	19	40
Santana,Johan			2	2	10	16	26	23	24	17	21	141

WIN SHARES BY YEAR

Player	<99	99	00	01	02	03	04	05	06	07	08	Career
Santiago,Ramon					4	5	0	0	1	2	6	18
Santos,Omir											0	0
Sardinha,Dane						0		0			1	1
Sarfate,Dennis									0	2	4	6
Saunders,Joe								0	4	7	18	29
Scherzer,Max											4	4
Schierholtz,Nate										2	3	5
Schilling,Curt	108	15	16	24	24	15	21	4	15	10		252
Schmidt,Jason	21	13	1	9	10	23	19	9	15	0		120
Schneider,Brian			1	2	7	13	17	16	9	11	10	86
Schoeneweis,Scott		1	6	9	5	3	4	6	6	2	4	46
Schroder,Chris									0	3	0	3
Schumaker,Skip								0	0	7	16	23
Scott,Luke								0	11	11	11	33
Scutaro,Marco					0	2	11	11	11	8	15	58
Seanez,Rudy	8	7	2	3	1	0	4	7	2	6	3	43
Seay,Bobby			0			1	2	0	0	6	3	12
Serrano,Alex										0		0
Sexson,Richie	5	10	16	19	21	26	3	24	19	7	4	154
Shealy,Ryan								2	6	1	3	12
Sheets,Ben			6	8	10	21	11	7	10	15		88
Sheffield,Gary	191	24	31	30	26	34	30	31	4	16	5	422
Shell,Steven											6	6
Shelton,Chris						0	13	8		1		22
Sherrill,George						1	2	3	8	7		21
Shields,James									6	12	15	33
Shields,Scot			2	6	12	11	13	11	8	8		71
Shoppach,Kelly								0	3	7	14	24
Shouse,Brian	0				0	6	6	2	3	5	6	28
Silva,Carlos					7	5	14	14	2	11	0	53
Simon,Alfredo										0		0
Sisco,Andy								5	0	0		5
Sizemore,Grady							5	24	24	29	26	108
Slaten,Doug									1	4	1	6
Slocum,Brian									0	0	0	0
Slowey,Kevin										3	10	13
Smith,Chris										0	0	0
Smith,Greg											9	9
Smith,Jason				0	0	0	2	1	3	2	0	8
Smith,Joe										3	6	9
Smith,Seth										1	3	4
Smoltz,John	163	18		8	17	16	16	19	15	14	2	288
Snell,Ian							0	1	8	11	2	22
Snelling,Chris					0			1	2	2	0	5
Snider,Travis											3	3
Snow,J.T.	75	18	16	6	11	14	19	10	1		0	170
Snyder,Chris							2	4	7	16	15	44
Snyder,Kyle						4		0	1	3	0	8
Sonnanstine,Andy										3	10	13
Soria,Joakim										13	17	30
Soriano,Alfonso		0	0	16	28	27	16	16	26	20	16	165
Soriano,Rafael					1	7	0	1	7	9	2	27
Sosa,Jorge					2	5	3	14	2	6	0	32
Soto,Geovany								0	0	3	21	24
Sowers,Jeremy									7	0	2	9
Span,Denard											16	16
Speier,Justin	0	1	7	5	7	8	7	7	6	7	2	57
Speier,Ryan							2			2	3	7
Speigner,Levale									0	0		0
Spilborghs,Ryan								0	3	9	8	20
Springer,Russ	15	5	3	0		0	1	3	5	8	6	46
Stairs,Matt	41	20	10	11	7	12	11	14	7	13	6	152
Stansberry,Craig										0	1	1
Stauffer,Tim								0	1	0		1
Stavinoha,Nick											0	0
Stetter,Mitch										1	3	4
Stewart,Chris									0	1	0	1
Stewart,Ian										1	9	10
Stewart,Shannon	25	17	17	18	17	18	13	11	5	13	2	156
Stockman,Phil									0	1		1
Stokes,Brian									1	0	3	4
Street,Huston								16	14	10	10	50
Stults,Eric									1	1	2	4

Player	<99	99	00	01	02	03	04	05	06	07	08	Career
Sturtze,Tanyon	0	1	6	11	6	2	3	4	0		0	33
Sullivan,Cory								10	6	4	0	20
Suppan,Jeff	7	12	12	12	9	13	9	13	12	9	5	113
Suzuki,Ichiro				36	26	23	27	22	24	33	19	210
Suzuki,Kurt										7	17	24
Sweeney,Mark	16	2	1	1	0	2	6	9	5	2	0	44
Sweeney,Mike	17	16	26	18	18	14	14	16	5	5	3	152
Sweeney,Ryan									0	0	12	12
Swindle,R.J.											0	0
Swisher,Nick							1	12	20	18	12	63
Taguchi,So					1	3	6	12	6	9	1	38
Talbot,Mitch											0	0
Tallet,Brian					2	0		0	4	4	5	15
Tankersley,Taylor								5	4	0		9
Taschner,Jack								3	0	2	2	7
Tatis,Fernando	12	23	11	2	6	1			2		13	70
Taubenheim,Ty									1	0	1	2
Tavarez,Julian	25	1	10	6	2	10	9	6	5	4	1	79
Taveras,Willy							0	13	13	11	6	43
Teagarden,Taylor											4	4
Teahen,Mark								9	18	15	11	53
Teixeira,Mark						12	24	33	21	25	28	143
Tejada,Miguel	8	20	23	25	32	26	28	26	23	14	14	239
Tejeda,Robinson								5	4	0	3	12
Thames,Marcus				0	0	6		1	11	6	7	31
Thatcher,Joe									2	0		2
Theriot,Ryan							0	6	11	16		33
Thigpen,Curtis									2	1		3
Thomas,Clete										3		3
Thomas,Frank	257	16	34	1	16	23	12	3	21	17	5	405
Thomas,Justin										0		0
Thome,Jim	115	26	20	31	33	29	20	4	25	21	17	341
Thompson,Brad								5	5	4	3	17
Thompson,Daryl											0	0
Thompson,Rich							0	0				0
Thornton,Matt						2	1	7	4	10		24
Threets,Erick								0	1			1
Thurston,Joe				1	0	0			0	0		1
Tiffee,Terry							1	0	1			2
Timlin,Mike	55	9	6	5	8	8	7	14	6	5	1	124
Timpner,Clay											0	0
Tolbert,Matt											3	3
Tomko,Brett	19	6	5	1	6	6	10	8	5	1	1	68
Torrealba,Yorvit				1	4	7	4	4	6	6	4	36
Torres,Eider										0		0
Torres,Salomon	6			3	6	11	10	9	3	12		60
Towles,J.R.										3	2	5
Traber,Billy					3			0	1	0		4
Trachsel,Steve	52	6	11	8	10	13	10	1	6	8	0	125
Tracy,Andy		5	0		0							5
Tracy,Chad						11	19	14	6	4		54
Treanor,Matt						1	2	5	6	5		19
Troncoso,Ramon											2	2
Tucker,Ryan											0	0
Tuiasosopo,Matt											0	0
Tulowitzki,Troy									1	24	9	34
Tupman,Matt										0		0
Turnbow,Derrick			2			2	1	17	2	6	0	30
Tyner,Jason			1	6	1	2		2	7	4	0	23
Uggla,Dan								23	16	24		63
Upton,B.J.					4			2	22	23		51
Upton,Justin										1	8	9
Uribe,Juan				7	10	9	18	17	11	13	11	96
Utley,Chase						5	8	25	27	28	30	123
Valbuena,Luis										1		1
Valdez,Merkin					0				2		2	2
Valentin,Javier	2	5			0	2	4	11	3	6	3	36
Valverde,Jose					11	3	13	4	14	14		59
Van Benschoten,J					0			0	0	0		0
Van Every,Jonathan										1	1	1
VandenHurk,Rick									0	0		0
Vargas,Claudio						7	3	6	7	5	2	30
Varitek,Jason	5	12	7	8	12	16	18	18	7	14	8	125

Player	<99	99	00	01	02	03	04	05	06	07	08	Career
Vazquez,Javier	0	8	14	21	13	21	9	12	11	18	11	138
Vazquez,Ramon			0	14	10	1	1	1	6	10		43
Velandia,Jorge	0	1	0	0		2				3	0	6
Velazquez,Gil										0		0
Velez,Eugenio										1	4	5
Venable,Will											3	3
Veras,Jose									1	1	5	7
Verlander,Justin							0	15	16	8		39
Victorino,Shane					0		1	11	11	20		43
Vidro,Jose	5	11	25	18	29	18	11	10	12	16	2	157
Villanueva,Carlos									4	8	6	18
Villarreal,Oscar				11	0	1	7	3	1			23
Villone,Ron	12	8	5	3	2	5	6	5	3	2	2	53
Vizcaino,Luis		0	0	2	8	1	6	6	7	6	2	38
Vizquel,Omar	116	22	16	12	21	5	18	20	20	12	5	267
Volquez,Edinson							0	0	2	16		18
Volstad,Chris										7		7
Votto,Joey									3	19		22
Wade,Cory									7		7	7
Waechter,Doug					3	1	3	0		4		11
Wagner,Billy	30	20	1	13	16	19	10	18	14	12	10	163
Wagner,Ryan				3	2	1	1	0				7
Wainwright,Adam							0	9	13	11		33
Wakefield,Tim	62	8	5	11	15	12	8	15	7	10	10	163
Walker,Jamie	2			4	6	6	4	5	8	0		35
Walker,Tyler			0		4	7	3	3	4			21
Walrond,Les			0			0	0		0			0
Wang,Chien-Ming							7	16	15	7		45
Ward,Daryle	0	3	3	5	10	0	7	7	6	4	1	46
Washburn,Jarrod	4	3	7	15	18	9	8	14	7	10	5	100
Washington,Rico										0		0
Wassermann,Ehren									3	0		3
Waters,Chris									2		2	2
Weathers,David	12	6	7	10	7	8	5	8	10	13	6	92
Weaver,Jered								14	12	11		37
Webb,Brandon					17	11	17	20	22	21		108
Weeks,Rickie					0		9	10	14	16		49
Wellemeyer,Todd					0	1	0	4	4	12		21
Wells,Jared										0		0
Wells,Kip			3	2	6	13	15	6	3	0	2	1	51
Wells,Randy										1	1	1
Wells,Vernon			1	0	3	18	26	13	20	24	15	15	135
Werth,Jayson				1	1	11	9		13	17		52
Westbrook,Jake			0	2	1	6	15	8	13	9	3	57
Wheeler,Dan			1	1	0		3	3	10	12	4	12	46
White,Bill									1	0		1
Whitesell,Josh										0		0
Wigginton,Ty					3	14	10	4	13	11	14	69
Wilkerson,Brad				1	17	18	19	19	5	11	3	93
Willingham,Josh						0	0	14	19	13		46
Willis,Dontrelle						14	9	22	13	7	0	65
Willits,Reggie									1	14	1	16
Wilson,Bobby										0		0
Wilson,Brian									1	5	9	15
Wilson,C.J.								0	3	9	2	14
Wilson,Jack				5	12	12	22	14	12	19	7	103
Wilson,Vance			0	0	1	5	7	5	3	5		26
Winn,Randy	5	4	2	10	23	21	17	22	13	16	19	152
Wise,Dewayne			0		1		3		0	0	2	6
Wise,Matt			2	2	1		3	7	4	4	0	23
Wolf,Randy	4	13	11	15	12	6	4	2	5	7		79
Wolfe,Brian									4	2		6
Wood,Brandon									0	2		2
Wood,Jason	0	0						1	3	0		4
Wood,Kerry	14		7	13	12	18	9	4	2	2	12	93
Woods,Jake							1	6	0	0		7
Worrell,Mark										0		0
Wright,David							9	26	30	34	27	126
Wright,Jamey	16	7	9	7	2	2	5	4	4	5	3	64
Wright,Wesley											3	3
Wuertz,Mike						2	6	4	6	3		21
Yabu,Keiichi				3						5		8
Yabuta,Yasuhiko										1		1

Player	<99	99	00	01	02	03	04	05	06	07	08	Career
Yates,Tyler							0		3	2	3	8
Youkilis,Kevin							8	3	22	20	27	80
Young,Chris							2	10	12	12	5	41
Young,Chris									2	14	17	33
Young,Delmon									2	17	13	32
Young,Delwyn									0	2	1	3
Young,Dmitri	21	10	14	13	5	19	8	9	2	16	2	119
Young,Michael			0	7	11	22	25	29	26	23	20	163
Zambrano,Carlos			0	5	18	20	18	17	16	16		110
Zaun,Gregg	18	3	9	4	2	2	11	14	8	9	8	88
Ziegler,Brad											12	12
Zimmerman,Ryan							2	24	20	9		55
Zink,Charlie											0	0
Zito,Barry			9	15	25	18	12	13	17	8	5	122
Zobrist,Ben									2	1	8	11
Zumaya,Joel									12	3	1	16

Young Talent Inventory

Bill James

A year ago in these pages we introduced a new concept, which is the Young Talent Inventory.

There are three levels of questions here. The entry level query is an assessment of each young player. How good is this young player? Who are the best young players in baseball? Who is the best young player on the Rockies? Who are the best young pitchers in baseball, the best young infielders, the best young outfielders?

The second level is trying to look at the Big Picture of Young Talent. We're trying to cast our eyes all around baseball and ask, "Where is the young talent? Who has the young talent now? Is there more young talent than normal?"

The third level is the general questions that can only be addressed when you have solid answers at the second level. How significant is the possession of young talent? Do the teams that have the most young talent tend to do well over the next five years 80% of the time, or 55% of the time? Is developing young talent more important than being able to afford free agents, or less? Is it more important than having talent in the farm system, or less? What causes the amount of young talent in baseball to go up or go down? Is it just cyclical, or are there definable causes? Which is better: to be the team with the young pitchers, or to be the team with the young hitting?

The entry level question is a complex question, because it requires that we combine two unlike things—youth and talent—in a single measurement. Since "youth" and "talent" are inherently unlike, there is no perfect way to do this. Is a 22-year-old pitcher who is 12-10 ahead of or behind a 24-year-old who is 15-9, as a combination of youth and talent? It's an arbitrary question.

We are evaluating here only proven major league talents, not prospects or young players who are not yet proven as major league players. A year ago, when we presented our first list of the games most talented young players, I got a lot of feedback about players who had been left off the list—Atlanta fans upset that Jeff Francoeur didn't make the top 25, Philadelphia fans irritated that I didn't include Howard and Utley, etc. I think I heard from the fans of 14 teams who felt that I had slighted their guy.

It's my own fault; I didn't quite explain what we're trying to do. One list of great young players is not objectively better than another. I'm not saying that we couldn't improve our process; I'm sure we could. But. . .anybody can look around and tick off the names, and we're not arguing that our list is better than your list or your local columnist's list. That's really not the point of doing this.

Anybody can look around and pick out the best young players, but how do you stand on that list to reach the second level of questions? What we are really trying to do here is to take a list of the best young players (which is as good as anybody else's list, but not better) and use that to study the second and third level of questions, which are issues that are difficult to access by seat-of-the-pants analysis. By formalizing the process, we make the level-one answers solid enough to be used to construct answers to the second- and third-level questions. The second-level questions now; eventually, in theory, we could get to the third-level questions.

So anyway, without further apologies, this is our list of the top 25 young major league players of 2008, with their 2008 ages:

1. Prince Fielder, Milwaukee (24)
2. Hanley Ramirez, Florida (24)
3. Tim Lincecum, San Francisco (24)
4. David Wright, Mets (25)
5. Ryan Braun, Milwaukee (24)
6. Dustin Pedroia, Boston (24)
7. Matt Kemp, Dodgers (23)
8. Francisco Rodriguez, Angels (26)
9. Jose Reyes, Mets (25)
10. Nick Markakis, Baltimore (24)
11. Joakim Soria, Kansas City (24)
12. Ryan Zimmerman, Nationals (23)
13. Cole Hamels, Philadelphia (24)
14. Troy Tulowitzki, Rockies (23)
15. Felix Hernandez, Seattle (22)
16. Jon Lester, Boston (24)
17. Evan Longoria, Rays (22)
18. John Danks, White Sox (23)
19. Adrian Gonzalez, Padres (26)
20. James Loney, Dodgers (24)
21. Stephen Drew, Arizona (25)
22. Brian McCann, Atlanta (24)
23. Miguel Cabrera, Detroit (25)
24. Grady Sizemore, Cleveland (25)
25. Joey Votto, Cincinnati (24)

Prince Fielder and Hanley Ramirez, who ranked 1 and 2 a year ago, still do, while David Wright, who ranked fourth a year ago behind a pitcher, still does.

446

Which brings up a point: 2008 really was not a great year for young talent, except pitchers. Fielder and Ramirez had good years, not great years, but they had lesser seasons in 2008 than they had in 2007—plus they are a year older, which is a huge thing in this system, which is youth-centered. They remained at the top of the list because nobody did enough to push them aside. Some young stars took a step forward (Pedroia, Matt Kemp, James Loney, Stephen Drew, Joey Votto, Josh Hamilton, Jose Lopez, Geovany Soto, Nate McLouth); others took a step backward (Tulowitzki, Ryan Zimmerman, Alex Gordon, Jeff Francoeur.) But the only really huge talent to emerge in 2008 was Longoria. Longoria probably would rank as the number one guy on our list, were it not for an injury, but the system relies on major league production; when part of his season is missing, his position drops.

In pitching, on the other hand, it was a good year: Lincecum, Jon Lester, John Danks and others emerged as major young talents—others including Jair Jurrjens, Ricky Nolasco, Mike Pelfrey and Edinson Volquez. It was a good year for young pitchers; it was not really a good year for young position players. This is a level-two conclusion—a conclusion that would be difficult to reach with confidence by intuitive analysis.

Of the 25 players who were on our list of the best young players in baseball last year, 13 are still on the list this year. Virtually everyone who is on this list now will drop off within two years. In baseball, you get over being "young" really quickly.

Why does John Danks rank ahead of, let's say, Edinson Volquez? Danks was 12-9, 3.32 ERA, Volquez was 17-6, 3.21. Danks struck out 159, Volquez 206. Shouldn't Volquez rank ahead?

Again, we're not necessarily saying our system is right, and we're not necessarily saying that Edinson won't have a better career than Danks; you rank Volquez ahead of Danks if you want to. Danks and Volquez are almost even in terms of games and innings pitched (33 and 195 for Danks, 33 and 196 for Volquez.) Our system ignores won-lost records, and it is based on RUNS allowed, rather than earned runs allowed. Danks allowed 72 earned runs and 74 total runs; Volquez allowed 70 earned but 82 total. Danks is almost two years younger. They're both really good, but. . .our math puts Danks ahead. Take it for what it is worth.

We made some changes in the way we calculate "youth value"; I'm not going to explain them all here, but one change was calculating ages based on month of birth, rather than year of birth. By baseball tradition, and by the method we used last year, a player born in June, 1983 or in July, 1982, would be considered 25 years old in 2008. We changed that so that a player born in June, 1983, would be considered 25.0 years of age, whereas a player born in July, 1982 would be 25.92 years old in 2008. Another change, which could be called the

Tulowitzki rule, is that if a player has an injury season, we substitute a value based on his previous season (discounted, obviously), rather than basing the ranking 100% on 2008 stats.

Anyway, we have a list of the top 25 players, which nobody will be happy with because Nate McLouth isn't in the top 25, or Josh Hamilton, or Edinson Volquez, or Curtis Granderson or Andre Ethier or Clayton Kershaw or Zack Greinke or Justin Upton or his brother or Hunter Pence or Jay Bruce or Matt Garza or Jacoby Ellsbury. My point is that there are 75 players who could be on the list, but there are only 25 spots. The second-level question, which is really what we're trying to get to, is "Who has the young talent now? Which teams have the most young talent?"

1. Minnesota Twins The Twins have not a single player in the top 25, but they have 6 players in the top 100, 8 in the top 120, and 10 in the top 150. The average team has five players in the top 150; the Twins have ten—Joe Mauer (33), Delmon Young (40), Justin Morneau (50), Kevin Slowey (82), Scott Baker (85), Carlos Gomez (93), Nick Blackburn (109), Jason Kubel (120), Denard Span (136) and Glen Perkins (141). And then they have Michael Cuddyer, and Francisco Liriano, and Boof Bonser, and Craig Breslow, and then they have a bunch of other guys. The Twins rank seventh in the majors in young pitching talent, and first in non-pitching talent. The Twins ranked 11th on this list last year, and moved forward basically because of the development of the young pitchers. They're loaded.

2. Arizona Diamondbacks. The Diamondbacks are basically even with the Twins in young position players, a little behind them in young pitching. The Snakes have five outstanding young position players—Drew (21st), Chris Young (36), Justin Upton (48), Mark Reynolds (54) and Conor Jackson (56). Their top pitchers, Haren and Webb, are still on the young players list, but are closing in on 30, and are not really young anymore. In our system a player drops off the list at age 30. My gut instinct is that the D'Backs will win the World Series in 2009, but you know. . .with that and $1.50 you can get a cup of coffee, but not at Starbucks.

3. Tampa Bay. The Rays ranked second last year (behind Colorado), and obviously justified our faith in their young talent with their remarkable season. In fact, this is perhaps the most interesting thing that happened in regard to this list in 2008: the Rays, who our system had identified as the team with the most young talent in the American League, vaulted over the league. And added Longoria, which keeps them near the top of the list.

448

4. Florida Marlins. Jorge Cantu, who has been up and down several times already in his career, is still only 26 years old, 27 in January. The Marlins have six good young players (Hanley, Cantu, Hermida, Ugly Dan Uggla, Mike Jacobs and Cody Ross) plus at least four good young pitchers (Nolasco, Olsen, Volstad, and Kevin Gregg. OK, Gregg is not really "young".) If Andrew Miller figures it out, the Marlins could make some noise again.

5. Kansas City Royals. The Royals have arguably baseball's best closer, in Soria (11th on our list), and they have a young starting pitcher, Greinke, who may be as good as anybody in baseball.

  I've always loved watching Greinke pitch; occasionally I do those lists of the most-fun pitchers to watch, and Greinke has always been on my list. When he was a kid he had a big, slow curve ball that was almost like El Duque's. He lost confidence, re-emerged last year, still only 24 years old. He has junked the curve ball, but the fast ball comes out of his hand 95-96 MPH with just *no* apparent effort. It looks like he's playing catch with his father, but the ball just zooms. And, because it is so effortless for him to throw hard, he can move the ball up and down and in and out and hit the corners pretty reliably. I saw him pitch twice late in the season, and honestly, he was as good as anybody I saw in 2008. Greinke and Jon Lester were the best I saw.

  Behind those two they have Alex Gordon (58th on our list), Billy Butler (69) and Mark Teahen (131), plus Aviles, who was sensational at shortstop although he is late emerging, Kyle Davies, David DeJesus, Brian Bannister, Luke Hochevar. They have little veteran talent, but if a couple of guys step forward, they could win 85-90 games in 2009.

6. Milwaukee Brewers. A complication of figuring out who "has" the most young talent is, do the Brewers have CC Sabathia or do they not? They have him at the moment, which is all we're measuring at the moment. They have Fielder (1), Braun (5), Sabathia (29), J.J. Hardy (41), Corey Hart (81), Rickie Weeks (134), Ben Sheets (135), Manny Parra (164) and David Bush (178). They'll have an outstanding lineup in 2009. Whether they'll be able to hold onto enough pitching to stay in the playoffs is a question to be determined over the winter, and revealed in the summer.

7. Cleveland Indians. One of the announcers during the post-season said that the Indians had missed their moment, and their opportunity was getting away from them. Our analysis suggests that this is untrue, that the Indians, despite the injuries and the loss of Sabathia, are still well stocked. Sizemore (24th on our list), Peralta (61), Cliff Lee (76), Shin-Soo Choo (133), Aswhuppin Cabrera (162), Jensen Lewis (175), Victor Martinez (177. . .not much youth left), Ben Francisco

(180), Ryan Garko (190), Franklin Gutierrez, Aaron Laffey, Kelly Shoppach, Fausto Carmona. I think the Indians are still very capable of challenging the Twins and the Royals for the future of this division.

8. Colorado Rockies. The Rockies had a tough season, dropping from 1st place in our survey to 8th, but there is still a solid foundation in place here with Tulowitzki, Matt Holliday, Iannetta, Garret Atkins, Brad Hawpe, plus pitchers Ubaldo Jimenez and Aaron Cook.

9. Atlanta Braves. The Braves ranked 16th in our survey last year, but shot up the list due to a solid year by McCann and the emergence of Jurrjens (34th on our list), Yunel Escobar (103rd) and others (Gregor Blanco, Jorge Campillo, Martin Prado, Jo-Jo Reyes, Josh Anderson.) Francoeur and Kelly Johnson are still young players. They just need for some of these guys to pump up the volume.

10. Boston Red Sox. Everybody knows the Red Sox. Four young players in the top 100—Pedroia, Lester, Papelbon and Ellsbury.

11. Los Angeles Angels. The Angels, like the Brewers, have a huge issue about possession. They have three players in the top 50, but two of them are free agents already (Teixeira and K-Rod.) But the Angels will be really good even if they lose those two players, because they have young pitching and Arredondo to step into K-Rod's shoes and Howie Kendrick, who is still capable of MVP performance if he can stay healthy. The Angels rank first in the majors in young pitching.

12. Oakland A's. Nobody here is all that good, at least not yet, but they lead the world in guys who should get better.

13. Los Angeles Dodgers. The Dodgers are the exact opposite of the A's; they have very impressive young talent in Kemp, Ethier, Billingsley, Loney and Kershaw, Broxton and Martin, but the issue is depth.

14. St. Louis Cardinals. The Cardinals best young player, by far, is Pujols, who as we all know is not really "young" anymore. He is just SO good that he almost makes the top 25 young players anyway (27th). The Cardinals don't really have any young studs, but they have a bunch of guys in their late 20s who are pretty decent.

15. Cincinnati Reds. And the Reds are the exact opposite of the Cardinals. They have four young lions that everybody would love to have (Votto, Volquez,

Jay Bruce and Johnny Cueto), but only two late-twenties guys who can really play (Encarnacion and Phillips.) Dickerson will make a splash in '09, if he's the player we think he is.

16. New York Mets. Similar to the Reds. Two top-ten guys (Reyes and Wright), four good young pitchers (Pelfrey, Santana, Maine and Perez) and one guy who could make a splash in '09 (Daniel Murphy).

17. Pittsburgh Pirates. Maholm and McLouth are top 100, although McLouth isn't exactly a baby, other guys have ability but haven't produced yet. Gorzelanny's big step backward is a disappointment. McLouth replaces Bay in the way that Bay replaced Giles, but the Pirates don't appear to be close to getting out of this rut.

18. Seattle Mariners. The Mariners lead the world in "buts". Jose Lopez had a big year in 2008, but nobody noticed. Lopez has ability as a hitter, and so does Betancourt and Balentien and Jeff Clement, but none of them has any control of the strike zone. Felix Hernandez and Brandon Morrow look like world-beaters half the time, but lose the other half.

19. Texas Rangers. Hamilton and Kinsler are MVP candidates, but not all that young. Young isn't young at all. Chris Davis is young and could hit 40 homers, but hasn't done it yet. They have traded away a couple of the best young pitchers in baseball, and don't really seem to have anybody else you would put in the same cattle call.

20. Philadelphia Phillies. Cole Hamels is among the best young pitchers in the game (duh.); otherwise their best "young" players are Howard and Utley, who are pushing 30.

21. San Diego Padres. Three good young players—Adrian Gonzalez, Jake Peavy and Kevin Kouzmanoff. Chase Headley could help. Talent depth is a real issue.

22. San Francisco Giants. Lincecum and Cain and pray for rain.

23. Washington Nationals. Three guys in the top 100—Zimmerman (12), Lastings Milledge (64) and John Lannan (70). Elijah Dukes will be an All-Star if he can stay out of trouble and in the lineup. After that it's not pretty.

24. Baltimore Orioles. Markakis is the real deal, one of the best young players in baseball. Adam Jones (113) has a lot to prove. Jeremy Guthrie (120) is a little bit young and pretty good, but, you know. …he's the same age as Johan Santana, and not making hundreds of millions yet. Otherwise, just a bunch of older guys and second-line pitching prospects.

25. Chicago White Sox. Danks (18), Carlos Quentin (42—would be top 15 if he hadn't gotten hurt), Gavin Floyd (73), Bobby Jenks (117), Swisher (118), Mark Buehrle (126), Alexei Ramirez (153). The aging of Thome, Konerko, Dye and Pierzynski may drag the White Sox out of contention in 2009.

26. Chicago Cubs. The Cubs key players are not really old, but they're not really young, either. . .Derrek Lee, Aramis, DeRosa, Soriano, Fukudome. They're all past 30; they could hang together to keep the Cubs at the top for a year or two, but they don't have time to be wasting their bullets. Young guys are Soto (51st on our list...don't really know why he isn't higher), Rich Harden (80th), Zambrano (101) and Carlos Marmol (173). Ryan Theriot is 29 years old.

27. Detroit Tigers. Miguel Cabrera (23rd on our list) and Curtis Granderson (30) are hosses. The young pitching has fallen apart and the rest of the team is fighting the calendar.

28. Toronto Blue Jays. The young pitching is good, Litsch and Marcum. Alex Rios is a good young player but not exactly Evan Longoria or David Wright. Adam Lind could help out. Travis Snider should be on our list next year; he's a "prospect" now, as opposed to a young player of proven value.

29. New York Yankees.   This is the really interesting problem that we face: Will the Yankees other resources ultimately prove more important than their lack of young talent? The Yankees have a fling of young pitchers, of course, but they're having all kinds of trouble getting those guys tires running on the major league highway, which is the normal thing; most young pitchers struggle for several years before they get going, and very often the guys who look like they're going to be great and the guys who are great aren't the same guys. A year ago, who was talking about Edinson Volquez and Jair Jurrjens and Ricky Nolasco?

Anyway, the Yankees basically have no young talent of proven ability; they've got Melky (83) and Cano (104) and Joba (121). But there are four elements of this equation: Young major league talent, prospects, veterans, and other resources that can be converted into talent. The Yankees' farm system isn't the best in the majors, but it's certainly not 29th out of 30. Their veteran core is still very impressive.

452

And, of course, their other resources are formidable: they've got a fan base, and a new stadium, and a tradition, and a city, and a TV contract, and committed ownership. If they sign CC Sabathia and Mark Teixeira this winter, does that offset the lack of young talent, or not? We'll see.

30. Houston Astros. Among the 30 teams the Astros rank dead last in young pitching talent, and dead last in young non-pitching talent. They're in a sorry state, but they were in the same position last year, and they managed to stay in contention until the closing weeks of the season.

I've suggested here a way to take an inventory of young talent. We could also do a "prospect inventory", and a "veteran talent inventory", and an inventory of a team's other resources. In theory, we could learn to put these together, so that we could project the course of a franchise over a period of the next several years, not with 100% reliability, obviously.

Another One Bites the Dust

Bill James

OK, here's a story problem for you. If we projected 33 players to drive in 100 runs in 2008, and 29 players did in fact drive in 100 runs in 2008, and 19 of those were the same players, then why in the sacred name of Allan Roth did we project Andruw Jones to drive in 103 runs?

We had projected that Ryan Howard would lead the majors in RBI in 2008, with 144, and he did, with 146, although the funny thing is that we actually had a lousy projection on him; we were 50 points off on his batting average, 100 points off on his slugging percentage—among our worst projections of 2008—we just happened to be about right on his RBI.

The 19 players that we projected to drive in 100 runs who actually did push home 100 runs were Carlos Beltran (106 projected, 112 actual), Lance Berkman (113 and 106), Ryan Braun (122 and 106), Miguel Cabrera (128 and 127), Carlos Delgado (101 and 115), Adam Dunn (103 and 100), Prince Fielder (111 and 102), Ryan Howard (144 and 146), Raul Ibanez (100 and 110), Carlos Lee (108 and 100), Justin Morneau (112 and 129), Magglio Ordonez (111 and 103), Albert Pujols (126 and 116), Aramis Ramirez (108 and 111), Manny Ramirez (113 and 121), Alex Rodriguez (133 and 103), Mark Teixeira (120 and 121), Chase Utley (109 and 104), and David Wright (115 and 124). I'll give you the projected/actual on a couple of those, just to establish the principle that we're not ALWAYS completely wrong:

David Wright

	G	AB	R	H	D	T	HR	RBI	BB	SO	SB	Avg	Slg
Actual	160	626	115	189	42	2	33	124	94	118	15	302	534
Projected	160	603	111	192	45	2	31	115	84	113	27	318	554

Adam Dunn

	G	AB	R	H	D	T	HR	RBI	BB	SO	SB	Avg	Slg
Actual	158	517	79	122	23	0	40	100	122	164	2	236	513
Projected	158	566	107	142	31	1	43	103	118	183	8	251	537

That leaves ten players who drove in 100 runs that we didn't *project* to drive in 100 runs. Those were:

Player	Projected	Actual
Bobby Abreu	99	100
Carlos Pena	87	102
Jason Bay	91	101
Adrian Gonzalez	87	119
Melvin Mora	67	104
Josh Hamilton	71	130
Kevin Youkilis	78	115
Aubrey Huff	67	108
Carlos Quentin	59	100
Ryan Ludwick	40	113

Bobby Abreu, we actually had a very good projection for, we just missed that last RBI and didn't anticipate that he would stop taking walks:

Bobby Abreu

	G	AB	R	H	D	T	HR	RBI	BB	SO	SB	Avg	Slg
Actual	156	609	100	180	39	4	20	100	73	109	22	296	471
Projected	160	596	107	170	42	2	20	99	110	130	25	285	463

And Carlos Pena, we actually did very, very well on, considering the up and down nature of his career, we just shorted him by 15 RBI:

Carlos Pena

	G	AB	R	H	D	T	HR	RBI	BB	SO	SB	Avg	Slg
Actual	139	490	76	121	24	2	31	102	96	166	1	247	494
Projected	140	469	78	123	25	2	31	87	78	134	2	262	522

On the other hand, we were inexplicably dense about Josh Hamilton and Carlos Quentin:

Josh Hamilton

	G	AB	R	H	D	T	HR	RBI	BB	SO	SB	Avg	Slg
Actual	156	624	98	190	35	5	32	130	64	126	9	304	530
Projected	115	410	77	125	23	2	31	71	47	82	7	305	598

Carlos Quentin

	G	AB	R	H	D	T	HR	RBI	BB	SO	SB	Avg	Slg
Actual	130	480	96	138	26	1	36	100	66	80	7	288	571
Projected	110	380	60	100	30	2	13	59	37	65	4	263	455

We had about the same projection last year for Carlos Quentin that we did for Dan Ortmeier, which brings up an interesting question: Who, exactly, is Dan Ortmeier? Hamilton, we achieved the remarkable double dumb combination of over-projecting his slugging percentage by 68 points while under-projecting his RBI by 59. That's hard to do. I suppose we could alibi that both of these players were traded after we printed the projections, but. . ..philosophically, I don't know why in the world we project young studs to play 110 or 115 games, anyway. It's off the subject, but another one of those is Geovany Soto. We would have had a killer projection for Soto, except that we projected him to play in only 110 games.

Ryan Ludwick, I don't suppose anyone saw that one coming:

Ryan Ludwick

	G	AB	R	H	D	T	HR	RBI	BB	SO	SB	Avg	Slg
Actual	152	538	104	161	40	3	37	113	62	146	4	299	591
Projected	89	235	35	62	15	0	11	40	20	58	2	264	468

Or anyway, if anyone did see it coming, he doesn't work for us. We just missed the boat on the two old Orioles, Melvin Mora and Aubrey Huff, projecting them for 67 RBI apiece:

Melvin Mora

	G	AB	R	H	D	T	HR	RBI	BB	SO	SB	Avg	Slg
Actual	135	513	77	146	29	2	23	104	37	70	3	285	483
Projected	130	505	74	139	26	1	16	67	50	94	8	275	426

Aubrey Huff

	G	AB	R	H	D	T	HR	RBI	BB	SO	SB	Avg	Slg
Actual	154	598	96	182	48	2	32	108	53	89	4	304	552
Projected	138	472	59	130	27	2	18	67	43	72	2	275	456

Back to the story problem; that leaves fourteen players that we projected to drive in 100 runs who didn't quite do it. Those were:

Player	Projected	Actual
Garrett Atkins	113	99
Pat Burrell	104	86
Vladimir Guerrero	118	91
Travis Hafner	115	24
Brad Hawpe	105	85
Matt Holliday	121	88
Andruw Jones	103	14
Paul Konerko	105	62
Nick Markakis	106	87
Victor Martinez	102	35
David Ortiz	130	89
Hunter Pence	100	83
Miguel Tejada	105	66
Ryan Zimmerman	102	51

Which certainly explains a lot about what happened to the Rockies and the Indians. Many of these guys played about the way we thought they would, but were out a few weeks with an injury and pulled up short of 100 RBI. Pat Burrell we had a nearly perfect projection for, but he just didn't drive in runs:

Pat Burrell

	G	AB	R	H	D	T	HR	RBI	BB	SO	SB	Avg	Slg
Actual	157	536	74	134	33	3	33	86	102	136	0	250	507
Projected	156	540	82	138	29	1	31	104	107	149	0	256	485

Miguel Tejada may need a few days off:

Miguel Tejada

	G	AB	R	H	D	T	HR	RBI	BB	SO	SB	Avg	Slg
Actual	158	632	92	179	38	3	13	66	24	72	7	283	415
Projected	153	608	90	183	34	1	24	105	46	72	4	301	479

And Andruw Jones. . .man, that has to be the worst projection we have ever published:

Andruw Jones

	G	AB	R	H	D	T	HR	RBI	BB	SO	SB	Avg	Slg
Actual	75	209	21	33	8	1	3	14	27	76	0	158	249
Projected	154	558	90	141	29	1	34	103	68	129	5	253	491

From now on, we will refer to the inexplicable loss of all ability in mid-career as "pulling an Andruw on us." He was one of my favorite players, too.

One of the interesting things about doing projections is that we're actually more accurate in projecting young players than we are in projecting older players. One might think, intuitively, that it would be the opposite: that after players had been around a few years, we would have enough information to project them more accurately. But actually, while there is a problem with young players because it's hard to guess how much playing time they're going to get, there is a bigger problem with older players because they get hurt more and their production becomes unreliable. I don't know that we missed too badly on any of the rookies and first-year regulars of 2008:

Rick Ankiel

	G	AB	R	H	D	T	HR	RBI	BB	SO	SB	Avg	Slg
Actual	120	413	65	109	21	2	25	71	42	100	2	264	506
Projected	131	456	67	117	19	2	29	94	29	97	4	257	498

Erick Aybar

	G	AB	R	H	D	T	HR	RBI	BB	SO	SB	Avg	Slg
Actual	98	346	53	96	18	5	3	39	14	45	7	277	384
Projected	60	175	23	45	8	1	2	16	8	22	10	257	349

Jeff Baker

	G	AB	R	H	D	T	HR	RBI	BB	SO	SB	Avg	Slg
Actual	104	299	55	80	22	1	12	48	26	85	4	268	468
Projected	96	227	29	62	13	2	9	35	17	51	2	273	467

Brian Buscher

	G	AB	R	H	D	T	HR	RBI	BB	SO	SB	Avg	Slg
Actual	70	218	29	64	9	0	4	47	19	42	0	294	390
Projected	102	336	39	90	18	1	9	43	34	45	3	268	408

Asdrubal Cabrera

	G	AB	R	H	D	T	HR	RBI	BB	SO	SB	Avg	Slg
Actual	114	352	48	91	20	0	6	47	46	77	4	259	366
Projected	110	347	61	96	21	2	6	42	35	55	15	277	401

Alberto Callaspo

	G	AB	R	H	D	T	HR	RBI	BB	SO	SB	Avg	Slg
Actual	74	213	21	65	8	3	0	16	19	14	2	305	371
Projected	74	201	27	57	11	2	3	21	16	14	2	284	403

Alexi Casilla

	G	AB	R	H	D	T	HR	RBI	BB	SO	SB	Avg	Slg
Actual	98	385	58	108	15	0	7	50	31	45	7	281	374
Projected	98	312	44	80	12	1	2	20	28	46	24	256	321

Jeff Clement

	G	AB	R	H	D	T	HR	RBI	BB	SO	SB	Avg	Slg
Actual	66	203	17	46	10	1	5	23	15	63	0	227	360
Projected	50	114	15	29	8	0	4	16	12	23	0	254	430

Elijah Dukes

	G	AB	R	H	D	T	HR	RBI	BB	SO	SB	Avg	Slg
Actual	81	276	48	73	16	2	13	44	50	79	13	264	478
Projected	72	233	40	59	9	3	11	36	34	46	6	253	459

Jacoby Ellsbury

	G	AB	R	H	D	T	HR	RBI	BB	SO	SB	Avg	Slg
Actual	145	554	98	155	22	7	9	47	41	80	50	280	394
Projected	125	463	78	148	29	5	5	46	39	55	42	320	436

Yunel Escobar

	G	AB	R	H	D	T	HR	RBI	BB	SO	SB	Avg	Slg
Actual	136	514	71	148	24	2	10	60	59	62	2	288	401
Projected	120	410	59	126	27	2	5	46	42	60	9	307	420

Jesus Flores

	G	AB	R	H	D	T	HR	RBI	BB	SO	SB	Avg	Slg
Actual	90	301	23	77	18	1	8	59	15	78	0	256	402
Projected	79	231	29	59	12	0	6	35	19	56	0	255	385

Chris Iannetta

	G	AB	R	H	D	T	HR	RBI	BB	SO	SB	Avg	Slg
Actual	104	333	50	88	22	2	18	65	56	92	0	264	505
Projected	67	237	33	65	13	2	7	32	33	50	0	274	435

Adam Jones

	G	AB	R	H	D	T	HR	RBI	BB	SO	SB	Avg	Slg
Actual	132	477	61	129	21	7	9	57	23	108	10	270	400
Projected	98	270	43	73	14	2	11	38	20	69	7	270	459

Fred Lewis

	G	AB	R	H	D	T	HR	RBI	BB	SO	SB	Avg	Slg
Actual	133	468	81	132	25	11	9	40	51	124	21	282	440
Projected	109	326	53	88	16	4	7	37	38	70	15	270	408

Evan Longoria

	G	AB	R	H	D	T	HR	RBI	BB	SO	SB	Avg	Slg
Actual	122	448	67	122	31	2	27	85	46	122	7	272	531
Projected	147	500	92	142	29	0	27	93	64	111	5	284	504

Lastings Milledge

	G	AB	R	H	D	T	HR	RBI	BB	SO	SB	Avg	Slg
Actual	138	523	65	140	24	2	14	61	38	96	24	268	402
Projected	139	538	85	154	33	4	18	78	48	117	21	286	463

Nyger Morgan

	G	AB	R	H	D	T	HR	RBI	BB	SO	SB	Avg	Slg
Actual	58	160	26	47	13	0	0	7	10	32	9	294	375
Projected	62	193	31	58	5	3	1	10	16	29	22	301	373

David Murphy

	G	AB	R	H	D	T	HR	RBI	BB	SO	SB	Avg	Slg
Actual	108	415	64	114	28	3	15	74	31	70	7	275	465
Projected	75	208	27	57	15	2	5	27	20	35	3	274	438

Skip Schumaker

	G	AB	R	H	D	T	HR	RBI	BB	SO	SB	Avg	Slg
Actual	153	540	87	163	22	5	8	46	47	60	8	302	406
Projected	70	130	16	37	7	1	2	11	9	16	2	285	400

Geovany Soto

	G	AB	R	H	D	T	HR	RBI	BB	SO	SB	Avg	Slg
Actual	141	494	66	141	35	2	23	86	62	121	0	285	504
Projected	110	423	55	123	30	1	17	71	47	103	0	291	487

Ian Stewart

	G	AB	R	H	D	T	HR	RBI	BB	SO	SB	Avg	Slg
Actual	81	266	33	69	18	2	10	41	30	94	1	259	455
Projected	132	494	66	134	34	3	13	65	43	106	10	271	431

Kurt Suzuki

	G	AB	R	H	D	T	HR	RBI	BB	SO	SB	Avg	Slg
Actual	148	530	54	148	25	1	7	42	44	69	2	279	370
Projected	123	432	60	112	26	0	10	63	49	70	1	259	389

Justin Upton

	G	AB	R	H	D	T	HR	RBI	BB	SO	SB	Avg	Slg
Actual	108	356	52	89	19	6	15	42	54	121	1	250	463
Projected	130	490	76	136	32	9	19	74	56	100	16	278	496

Joey Votto

	G	AB	R	H	D	T	HR	RBI	BB	SO	SB	Avg	Slg
Actual	151	526	69	156	32	3	24	84	59	102	7	297	506
Projected	135	460	71	141	30	1	23	81	61	96	16	307	526

Jay Bruce, after a red-hot start, did not hit what we had projected that he would hit:

Jay Bruce

	G	AB	R	H	D	T	HR	RBI	BB	SO	SB	Avg	Slg
Actual	108	413	63	105	17	1	21	52	33	110	4	254	453
Projected	143	535	77	165	41	4	36	82	46	141	9	308	602

And Chase Headley did not:

Chase Headley

	G	AB	R	H	D	T	HR	RBI	BB	SO	SB	Avg	Slg
Actual	91	331	34	89	19	2	9	38	30	104	4	269	420
Projected	126	467	85	145	37	4	18	81	77	130	1	310	522

And Daric Barton did not:

Daric Barton

	G	AB	R	H	D	T	HR	RBI	BB	SO	SB	Avg	Slg
Actual	140	446	59	101	17	5	9	47	65	99	2	226	348
Projected	127	496	75	136	38	3	10	61	69	66	4	274	423

But players just have subpar seasons sometimes; that's just baseball. Kenji Johjima hit 74 points less than we had projected, Austin Kearns 55 points less, Andruw Jones 95 points less. We have to expect that a few of the rookies would do the same. Carlos Gomez was traded after the book had been out for a couple of months, and got playing time we hadn't anticipated:

Carlos Gomez

	G	AB	R	H	D	T	HR	RBI	BB	SO	SB	Avg	Slg
Actual	153	577	79	149	24	7	7	59	25	142	33	258	360
Projected	72	181	24	49	9	2	3	19	13	35	20	271	392

And, of course, some rookies and young players didn't get the playing time that we had projected for them.   I look at it this way: when we projected that Brandon Wood would have these numbers in 2008:

Brandon Wood

	G	AB	R	H	D	T	HR	RBI	BB	SO	SB	Avg	Slg
Projected	122	392	53	98	26	1	17	58	33	115	11	250	452

We weren't really trying to say that Brandon Wood would play 122 games and bat almost 400 times, because we don't have any control of that, and we don't really have any way of knowing how much he will play.   What we are really trying to say is that *if* he gets a chance to play, that's what we expect him to hit.   If he doesn't get a chance to play, well. . .that's not my department.

We are not seers, psychics, prophets or geniuses; we just predict that players will mostly continue to do what they have done in the past.   And we're pretty much right most of the time.

2009 Hitter Projections

Hitter	Team	Age	G	AB	H	2B	3B	HR	R	RBI	RC	RC27	BB	SO	SB	CS	SB%	Avg	OBP	Slg	OPS
Abreu,Bobby	NYY	35	159	604	173	41	2	19	104	100	107	6.32	98	125	22	9	.71	.286	.389	.455	.844
Amezaga,Alfredo	Fla	31	127	342	89	14	3	3	42	28	36	3.61	25	51	10	6	.62	.260	.316	.345	.661
Anderson,Brian	CWS	27	95	222	55	13	1	9	31	28	29	4.46	18	51	4	2	.67	.248	.307	.437	.744
Anderson,Garret	LAA	37	140	525	148	30	1	16	62	83	72	4.94	28	79	4	2	.67	.282	.318	.434	.753
Anderson,Josh	Atl	26	132	502	143	21	4	4	66	38	62	4.37	28	69	39	10	.80	.285	.324	.367	.690
Anderson,Marlon	NYM	35	74	115	29	6	0	2	14	13	13	3.89	9	21	2	1	.67	.252	.312	.357	.669
Andrus,Elvis	Tex	20	94	324	88	13	1	2	46	36	37	3.88	21	62	40	12	.77	.272	.316	.336	.652
Ankiel,Rick	StL	29	139	502	132	24	2	31	77	96	81	5.66	43	110	3	2	.60	.263	.324	.504	.828
Arias,Joaquin	Tex	24	138	415	116	17	7	5	49	39	50	4.23	16	48	21	8	.72	.280	.308	.390	.698
Atkins,Garrett	Col	29	158	617	183	41	1	22	90	105	104	6.22	57	95	1	1	.50	.297	.359	.473	.832
Aurilia,Rich	SF	37	114	335	90	18	1	9	39	41	44	4.67	25	49	1	0	1.00	.269	.323	.409	.732
Ausmus,Brad	Hou	40	63	186	42	7	0	2	17	17	16	2.87	19	35	1	1	.50	.226	.311	.296	.607
Aviles,Mike	KC	28	148	580	167	38	5	16	78	72	82	5.10	28	65	10	5	.67	.288	.322	.443	.765
Aybar,Erick	LAA	25	143	436	117	21	4	4	63	45	47	3.73	19	53	17	9	.65	.268	.303	.362	.666
Aybar,Willy	TB	26	95	314	84	19	1	9	35	40	44	4.93	33	40	2	2	.50	.268	.343	.420	.763
Bailey,Jeff	Bos	30	72	185	50	12	1	8	29	28	31	5.93	24	42	2	1	.67	.270	.354	.476	.830
Baker,Jeff	Col	28	106	285	78	19	2	11	42	47	44	5.50	23	69	3	1	.75	.274	.330	.470	.800
Baker,John	Fla	28	70	225	59	14	1	5	29	29	30	4.67	23	50	1	1	.50	.262	.333	.400	.733
Bako,Paul	Cin	36	100	310	63	11	1	4	27	27	25	2.63	33	96	0	0	.00	.203	.282	.284	.566
Baldelli,Rocco	TB	27	103	312	87	18	2	12	47	44	47	5.38	20	64	5	2	.71	.279	.330	.465	.795
Balentien,Wladimir	Sea	24	105	426	102	25	1	20	62	69	59	4.68	45	112	7	4	.64	.239	.312	.444	.756
Barajas,Rod	Tor	33	108	384	92	24	0	13	46	51	44	3.92	24	69	0	0	.00	.240	.291	.404	.695
Bard,Josh	SD	31	84	306	82	20	0	6	30	39	40	4.64	32	42	0	0	.00	.268	.337	.392	.729
Barmes,Clint	Col	30	107	351	96	21	2	8	45	36	44	4.42	15	49	7	4	.64	.274	.309	.413	.722
Barrett,Michael	SD	32	109	370	96	23	1	11	40	47	48	4.54	29	56	1	1	.50	.259	.317	.416	.733
Bartlett,Jason	TB	29	141	517	148	29	4	3	71	45	66	4.55	38	69	19	8	.70	.286	.343	.375	.719
Barton,Brian	StL	27	60	115	33	5	1	2	17	14	16	4.95	12	28	4	2	.67	.287	.359	.400	.759
Barton,Daric	Oak	23	149	475	120	27	4	10	69	56	64	4.66	69	80	2	2	.50	.253	.350	.389	.739
Bautista,Jose	Tor	28	110	374	94	22	1	14	51	52	53	4.89	44	80	3	2	.60	.251	.336	.428	.764
Bay,Jason	Bos	30	156	582	163	35	3	30	100	102	109	6.72	83	148	9	3	.75	.280	.376	.505	.881
Belliard,Ronnie	Was	34	129	433	116	29	1	11	53	53	59	4.81	38	75	3	2	.60	.268	.330	.416	.746
Beltran,Carlos	NYM	32	156	593	164	37	3	30	110	107	111	6.65	84	105	23	5	.82	.277	.369	.501	.870
Beltre,Adrian	Sea	30	153	605	165	36	2	27	82	92	93	5.45	47	104	8	4	.67	.273	.329	.473	.802
Berkman,Lance	Hou	33	158	579	171	39	2	33	104	113	127	7.98	109	119	11	6	.65	.295	.413	.541	.954
Berroa,Angel	LAD	31	59	115	30	6	0	2	14	12	12	3.63	6	20	1	1	.50	.261	.331	.365	.696
Betancourt,Yuniesky	Sea	27	157	576	162	36	4	8	70	59	69	4.29	19	47	6	4	.60	.281	.307	.399	.706
Betemit,Wilson	NYY	27	113	274	72	17	1	10	36	40	40	5.15	26	72	0	0	.00	.263	.329	.442	.771
Bixler,Brian	Pit	26	69	193	50	8	2	2	27	17	22	3.92	16	56	11	3	.79	.259	.322	.352	.675
Blake,Casey	LAD	35	110	386	87	20	1	12	45	44	46	4.76	31	77	2	2	.50	.259	.336	.432	.768
Blalock,Hank	Tex	28	145	529	149	33	2	22	77	83	87	5.94	50	95	3	1	.75	.282	.346	.476	.822
Blanco,Gregor	Atl	25	129	398	109	16	4	2	61	31	53	4.62	67	82	16	9	.64	.274	.382	.349	.732
Blanco,Henry	ChC	37	68	172	39	8	0	4	16	19	16	3.13	11	33	0	0	.00	.227	.273	.343	.616
Bloomquist,Willie	Sea	31	92	207	54	7	1	1	31	16	22	3.62	20	38	12	5	.71	.261	.329	.319	.648
Blum,Geoff	Hou	36	112	289	68	15	1	8	31	35	31	3.63	22	50	1	1	.50	.235	.294	.377	.671
Boggs,Brandon	Tex	26	73	186	47	12	2	7	26	26	29	5.35	29	55	3	2	.60	.253	.359	.452	.811
Bonifacio,Emilio	Was	24	132	453	123	19	6	1	60	30	51	3.89	31	85	27	11	.71	.272	.318	.347	.665
Boone,Aaron	Was	36	86	204	49	10	0	6	25	26	23	3.83	16	43	2	1	.67	.240	.317	.377	.695
Bourn,Michael	Hou	26	136	435	110	11	5	5	69	31	50	3.87	42	92	40	11	.78	.253	.320	.336	.656
Bowen,Rob	Oak	28	53	101	22	6	0	2	12	11	10	3.29	12	33	0	0	.00	.218	.307	.337	.644
Bowker,John	SF	25	101	317	88	17	3	11	40	47	46	5.18	21	65	2	2	.50	.278	.326	.454	.781
Bradley,Milton	Tex	31	123	442	127	27	1	20	72	68	83	6.76	70	108	7	4	.64	.287	.391	.489	.879
Branyan,Russell	Mil	33	46	122	29	7	0	8	17	20	20	5.53	18	47	1	1	.50	.238	.340	.492	.832
Braun,Ryan	Mil	25	151	603	187	43	6	44	112	120	134	8.26	46	117	16	6	.73	.310	.364	.620	.984
Brignac,Reid	TB	23	83	262	63	16	2	7	36	33	31	4.01	21	62	5	2	.71	.240	.297	.397	.694
Brown,Dusty	Bos	27	41	106	27	7	0	3	13	16	14	4.61	11	27	0	0	.00	.255	.325	.406	.730
Brown,Emil	Oak	34	102	293	76	15	1	8	36	43	37	4.39	23	55	4	2	.67	.259	.320	.399	.719
Bruce,Jay	Cin	22	159	587	174	30	4	35	94	90	109	6.75	46	145	12	7	.63	.296	.351	.540	.891
Bruntlett,Eric	Phi	31	110	234	57	10	1	2	33	20	24	3.45	25	38	10	4	.71	.244	.319	.321	.640
Buck,John	KC	28	120	396	92	23	1	13	46	54	46	3.93	35	100	0	0	.00	.232	.303	.394	.697
Buck,Travis	Oak	25	135	512	140	36	5	14	69	63	79	5.46	58	106	9	4	.69	.273	.351	.445	.796
Burke,Chris	Ari	29	69	134	34	7	1	3	19	11	17	4.33	13	21	4	2	.67	.254	.342	.388	.730
Burke,Jamie	Sea	37	43	116	31	6	0	2	14	13	13	3.98	7	12	0	0	.00	.267	.315	.371	.685
Burrell,Pat	Phi	32	157	537	136	29	1	32	78	98	98	6.35	104	145	0	0	.00	.253	.377	.490	.867
Burriss,Emmanuel	SF	24	153	562	155	14	4	2	80	43	62	3.83	48	51	29	14	.67	.276	.338	.326	.664
Buscher,Brian	Min	28	128	370	103	19	1	9	44	55	51	4.93	35	52	3	2	.50	.278	.341	.408	.749
Butler,Billy	KC	23	147	563	166	35	2	18	73	87	92	6.03	53	69	0	0	.00	.295	.357	.460	.817
Bynum,Freddie	Bal	29	81	183	44	7	2	1	24	16	17	3.11	14	47	7	3	.70	.240	.298	.317	.615
Byrd,Marlon	Tex	31	129	438	124	26	3	10	65	54	64	5.25	40	83	6	3	.67	.283	.351	.425	.776
Byrnes,Eric	Ari	33	141	540	139	32	3	18	79	66	73	4.65	44	92	20	7	.74	.257	.319	.428	.747
Cabrera,Asdrubal	Cle	23	143	505	140	30	2	10	84	62	71	4.98	54	91	11	6	.65	.277	.349	.404	.753
Cabrera,Melky	NYY	24	134	445	123	19	3	9	53	53	59	4.71	38	55	10	4	.71	.276	.337	.393	.731
Cabrera,Miguel	Det	26	160	608	192	43	2	37	103	130	135	8.42	71	124	2	1	.67	.316	.392	.576	.967
Cabrera,Orlando	CWS	34	159	643	176	38	1	9	86	69	80	4.41	49	69	16	5	.76	.274	.327	.378	.705
Cairo,Miguel	Sea	35	64	101	25	5	1	0	13	10	10	3.38	7	15	3	1	.75	.248	.321	.317	.638
Callaspo,Alberto	KC	26	100	328	92	16	3	3	41	30	41	4.48	27	22	3	2	.60	.280	.335	.375	.710
Cameron,Mike	Mil	36	145	558	132	32	3	24	82	80	77	4.62	67	173	18	7	.72	.237	.325	.434	.759
Cano,Robinson	NYY	26	157	607	179	42	4	17	81	86	92	5.56	31	72	2	2	.50	.295	.333	.461	.795
Cantu,Jorge	Fla	27	152	585	157	42	1	24	76	92	84	5.08	35	107	3	2	.60	.268	.315	.467	.782
Carlin,Luke	SD	28	37	102	21	4	0	1	10	9	8	2.57	14	29	0	0	.00	.206	.302	.275	.576
Carroll,Jamey	Cle	35	123	362	94	15	2	2	57	30	39	3.73	39	63	6	4	.60	.260	.340	.329	.669

2009 Hitter Projections

Hitter	Team	Age	G	AB	H	2B	3B	HR	R	RBI	RC	RC27	BB	SO	SB	CS	SB%	Avg	OBP	Slg	OPS
Casey,Sean	Bos	34	92	195	57	12	0	3	22	24	27	5.09	17	21	1	0	1.00	.292	.361	.400	.761
Cash,Kevin	Bos	31	54	103	21	6	0	2	10	11	9	2.85	10	31	0	0	.00	.204	.281	.320	.601
Casilla,Alexi	Min	24	148	580	153	23	1	7	85	53	66	3.94	55	76	22	9	.71	.264	.329	.343	.672
Castillo,Jose	Hou	28	101	276	70	16	1	5	30	31	31	3.89	17	53	2	1	.67	.254	.302	.373	.675
Castillo,Luis	NYM	33	123	448	126	13	3	3	68	34	57	4.50	56	49	17	7	.71	.281	.362	.344	.706
Casto,Kory	Was	27	62	131	32	7	1	3	17	18	16	4.16	17	29	1	1	.50	.244	.331	.382	.713
Castro,Juan	Bal	37	63	117	26	6	0	2	10	10	10	2.86	6	20	0	0	.00	.222	.260	.325	.585
Castro,Ramon	NYM	33	56	167	43	9	0	8	22	27	25	5.24	17	39	0	0	.00	.257	.330	.455	.785
Catalanotto,Frank	Tex	35	111	338	94	25	2	6	45	38	47	4.99	30	40	2	1	.67	.278	.349	.417	.766
Cedeno,Ronny	ChC	26	109	321	89	15	2	6	41	36	40	4.43	21	57	6	3	.67	.277	.324	.393	.716
Chavez,Endy	NYM	31	105	234	64	11	2	2	29	18	27	4.06	15	23	6	3	.67	.274	.317	.363	.681
Chavez,Eric	Oak	31	144	555	143	34	1	25	80	87	86	5.40	67	117	4	2	.67	.258	.339	.458	.796
Chavez,Raul	Pit	36	52	122	28	6	0	1	11	13	10	2.77	5	15	0	0	.00	.230	.266	.303	.569
Choo,Shin-Soo	Cle	26	132	454	128	27	4	14	78	68	74	5.80	57	103	12	6	.67	.282	.365	.452	.816
Church,Ryan	NYM	30	128	444	122	29	2	16	62	69	69	5.54	46	100	3	2	.60	.275	.348	.457	.805
Cintron,Alex	Bal	30	100	295	81	15	2	4	34	30	34	4.11	14	38	2	1	.67	.275	.310	.380	.689
Clark,Tony	Ari	37	92	152	35	7	0	7	17	26	20	4.44	19	49	0	0	.00	.230	.320	.414	.734
Clement,Jeff	Sea	25	142	520	133	35	2	20	67	78	76	5.11	57	117	0	0	.00	.256	.333	.446	.779
Cora,Alex	Bos	33	102	252	62	10	2	2	28	20	25	3.40	19	29	2	1	.67	.246	.321	.325	.647
Coste,Chris	Phi	36	61	164	44	9	0	5	17	22	21	4.55	9	26	0	0	.00	.268	.326	.415	.740
Counsell,Craig	Mil	38	97	227	53	10	1	2	29	16	23	3.40	31	37	4	2	.67	.233	.338	.313	.651
Crawford,Carl	TB	27	130	485	143	21	9	10	74	59	73	5.42	29	74	33	8	.80	.295	.338	.437	.776
Crede,Joe	CWS	31	96	302	77	16	0	14	38	47	41	4.74	21	42	0	0	.00	.255	.312	.447	.759
Crisp,Coco	Bos	29	138	494	138	28	3	9	74	53	67	4.76	43	78	22	10	.69	.279	.338	.403	.741
Crosby,Bobby	Oak	29	149	567	138	35	1	12	72	64	65	3.91	53	106	8	3	.73	.243	.309	.372	.681
Cruz,Nelson	Tex	28	124	443	123	25	2	28	74	84	82	6.50	50	106	18	8	.69	.278	.352	.533	.885
Cuddyer,Michael	Min	30	119	416	113	26	3	12	62	60	62	5.27	46	83	5	3	.62	.272	.351	.435	.786
Cust,Jack	Oak	30	134	466	116	22	0	29	77	78	87	6.46	106	166	0	0	.00	.249	.389	.483	.872
Damon,Johnny	NYY	35	147	556	156	29	3	14	96	65	83	5.29	62	82	22	8	.73	.281	.355	.419	.774
Davis,Chris	Tex	23	158	566	171	42	3	40	107	118	118	7.69	43	147	8	4	.67	.302	.352	.599	.951
Davis,Rajai	Oak	28	94	206	56	9	2	2	29	15	26	4.31	15	31	25	7	.78	.272	.324	.364	.688
DeJesus,David	KC	29	141	525	151	30	5	10	81	60	77	5.27	51	74	9	6	.60	.288	.362	.421	.783
Delgado,Carlos	NYM	37	151	558	147	32	1	33	85	107	98	6.18	74	128	1	1	.50	.263	.361	.502	.863
Dellucci,David	Cle	35	93	220	53	11	1	8	32	30	28	4.33	23	54	2	1	.67	.241	.329	.409	.738
DeRosa,Mark	ChC	34	153	556	152	32	2	17	87	78	83	5.32	63	114	4	2	.67	.273	.354	.430	.783
DeWitt,Blake	LAD	23	131	373	97	15	2	10	42	48	44	4.54	38	60	3	1	.75	.261	.333	.394	.727
Diaz,Matt	Atl	31	133	351	109	22	2	10	43	47	56	5.92	16	63	7	4	.64	.311	.346	.470	.816
Dickerson,Chris	Cin	27	150	564	151	28	7	21	93	74	94	5.74	80	176	37	13	.74	.268	.360	.454	.814
Dobbs,Greg	Phi	30	125	296	84	16	2	8	37	44	42	5.10	19	49	4	2	.67	.284	.329	.432	.762
Doumit,Ryan	Pit	28	134	534	163	42	1	20	82	87	93	6.48	37	81	3	2	.60	.305	.358	.500	.858
Drew,J.D.	Bos	33	140	495	135	29	3	22	93	79	93	6.68	96	111	5	2	.71	.273	.395	.477	.872
Drew,Stephen	Ari	26	146	560	156	36	7	19	78	66	88	5.64	47	93	4	2	.67	.279	.336	.470	.805
Dukes,Elijah	Was	25	81	284	72	14	3	13	49	44	47	5.61	46	69	12	6	.67	.254	.363	.461	.825
Duncan,Chris	StL	28	103	290	77	15	0	13	41	46	47	5.71	41	71	2	1	.67	.266	.358	.452	.810
Dunn,Adam	Ari	29	159	562	138	30	1	42	100	103	112	6.84	122	183	4	2	.67	.246	.386	.527	.913
Duran,German	Tex	24	52	104	28	6	1	3	16	14	14	4.73	6	18	1	1	.50	.269	.315	.433	.748
Durham,Ray	Mil	37	136	440	114	28	2	11	64	53	60	4.73	52	77	7	4	.64	.259	.341	.407	.748
Dye,Jermaine	CWS	35	153	581	157	33	1	31	86	96	93	5.68	50	118	4	2	.67	.270	.334	.491	.825
Easley,Damion	NYM	39	112	278	69	12	1	8	30	35	33	4.11	22	41	1	0	1.00	.248	.317	.385	.702
Eckstein,David	Ari	34	128	483	134	22	1	3	64	36	55	4.05	38	41	7	4	.64	.277	.346	.346	.692
Edmonds,Jim	ChC	39	105	316	81	19	1	18	49	54	56	6.17	51	84	2	1	.67	.256	.363	.494	.857
Ellis,Mark	Oak	32	138	506	131	26	2	14	72	56	67	4.60	52	79	10	4	.71	.259	.335	.401	.736
Ellsbury,Jacoby	Bos	25	145	559	169	29	6	9	100	53	88	5.68	45	71	52	13	.80	.302	.359	.424	.783
Encarnacion,Edwin	Cin	26	148	539	150	37	1	25	83	85	91	6.05	56	95	4	2	.67	.278	.356	.490	.846
Erstad,Darin	Hou	35	78	157	39	8	0	2	20	15	16	3.50	10	30	2	1	.67	.248	.302	.338	.639
Escobar,Alcides	Mil	22	139	520	153	21	4	6	74	62	68	4.70	26	81	33	9	.79	.294	.328	.385	.712
Escobar,Yunel	Atl	26	141	533	160	30	2	9	78	63	82	5.66	60	66	5	4	.56	.300	.375	.415	.790
Ethier,Andre	LAD	27	143	532	161	36	4	19	81	79	96	6.66	57	82	5	4	.56	.303	.374	.492	.867
Evans,Nick	NYM	23	50	162	46	11	2	6	27	23	27	6.05	13	34	1	0	1.00	.284	.341	.488	.829
Everett,Adam	Min	32	88	263	64	13	1	4	32	26	27	3.49	18	40	4	2	.67	.243	.299	.346	.645
Fahey,Brandon	Bal	28	75	164	40	6	1	1	18	14	15	3.10	13	28	2	2	.50	.244	.303	.311	.614
Feliz,Pedro	Phi	34	136	459	114	28	2	17	52	66	56	4.22	28	71	1	0	1.00	.248	.293	.420	.714
Fielder,Prince	Mil	25	160	595	167	35	1	40	97	110	120	7.26	84	128	4	2	.67	.281	.379	.545	.923
Figgins,Chone	LAA	31	153	627	180	26	6	5	101	56	86	4.82	71	110	43	17	.72	.287	.361	.372	.732
Flores,Jesus	Was	24	135	436	109	26	1	12	43	81	52	4.13	30	108	0	0	.00	.250	.304	.397	.701
Floyd,Cliff	TB	36	81	256	67	14	0	11	36	38	38	5.20	29	55	2	1	.67	.262	.353	.445	.798
Fontenot,Mike	ChC	29	118	358	103	24	3	9	54	43	58	5.87	41	65	4	2	.67	.288	.363	.447	.809
Fowler,Dexter	Col	23	150	564	171	38	8	10	95	63	96	6.16	63	112	28	12	.70	.303	.374	.452	.826
Francisco,Ben	Cle	27	110	388	105	26	1	11	54	47	55	4.98	35	71	9	4	.69	.271	.334	.428	.762
Francoeur,Jeff	Atl	25	139	496	135	29	2	16	65	76	68	4.88	30	93	2	1	.67	.272	.323	.435	.758
Frandsen,Kevin	SF	27	144	503	141	33	2	8	63	54	64	4.51	29	46	11	7	.61	.280	.322	.402	.724
Freel,Ryan	Cin	33	100	327	87	17	2	3	48	21	40	4.19	33	56	19	8	.70	.266	.342	.358	.700
Fukudome,Kosuke	ChC	32	134	467	128	32	3	13	75	64	74	5.61	62	104	9	4	.69	.274	.363	.439	.802
Furcal,Rafael	LAD	31	119	486	139	25	4	9	82	44	71	5.19	50	64	23	9	.72	.286	.354	.409	.763
Gamel,Mat	Mil	23	150	539	163	35	4	18	87	89	94	6.40	52	127	8	6	.57	.302	.364	.482	.846
Garciaparra,Nomar	LAD	35	76	179	51	10	1	6	25	28	27	5.44	13	16	1	1	.50	.285	.344	.453	.796
Gardner,Brett	NYY	25	42	144	39	5	2	1	28	12	20	4.77	21	30	16	4	.80	.271	.367	.354	.722
Garko,Ryan	Cle	28	128	425	120	24	1	15	55	72	65	5.54	39	72	0	0	.00	.282	.358	.449	.807
Gathright,Joey	KC	28	91	224	63	7	1	0	33	17	26	4.05	22	31	16	6	.73	.281	.356	.321	.677
German,Esteban	KC	31	95	225	62	11	2	1	32	22	28	4.36	24	36	9	4	.69	.276	.351	.356	.706
Gerut,Jody	SD	31	96	314	87	19	2	11	45	40	48	5.40	30	41	7	4	.64	.277	.344	.455	.799

2009 Hitter Projections

Hitter	Team	Age	G	AB	H	2B	3B	HR	R	RBI	RC	RC27	BB	SO	SB	CS	SB%	Avg	OBP	Slg	OPS
Giambi,Jason	NYY	38	136	446	109	20	0	29	70	86	80	6.15	89	113	1	1	.50	.244	.388	.484	.873
Giles,Brian	SD	38	149	579	162	36	3	16	85	75	96	5.94	97	65	4	3	.57	.280	.387	.435	.822
Glaus,Troy	StL	32	148	539	140	29	1	31	83	97	96	6.24	87	123	1	1	.50	.260	.367	.490	.856
Gload,Ross	KC	33	123	369	109	22	1	8	45	47	52	5.16	21	38	2	2	.50	.295	.337	.425	.762
Gomes,Jonny	TB	28	77	179	44	10	1	9	28	28	27	5.12	22	54	5	2	.71	.246	.351	.464	.815
Gomez,Carlos	Min	23	155	588	157	28	7	8	81	63	70	4.11	32	127	41	12	.77	.267	.310	.379	.690
Gomez,Chris	Pit	38	75	140	38	7	0	1	15	14	15	3.82	9	19	0	0	.00	.271	.320	.343	.663
Gonzalez,Adrian	SD	27	161	622	172	38	2	31	95	106	106	6.12	65	134	0	0	.00	.277	.349	.494	.842
Gonzalez,Alberto	Was	26	45	132	34	8	1	2	17	14	15	3.94	10	17	2	1	.67	.258	.315	.379	.693
Gonzalez,Carlos	Oak	23	124	487	128	36	2	11	58	60	61	4.38	30	107	7	3	.70	.263	.306	.413	.718
Gonzalez,Edgar	SD	31	98	347	99	20	1	8	40	40	50	5.18	33	65	4	3	.57	.285	.349	.418	.767
Gonzalez,Luis	Fla	41	125	313	81	20	1	9	40	42	45	5.02	42	41	1	1	.50	.259	.354	.415	.769
Gordon,Alex	KC	25	148	535	146	40	2	20	81	73	88	5.82	64	120	12	4	.75	.273	.358	.467	.825
Granderson,Curtis	Det	28	155	599	172	32	13	23	110	76	108	6.50	69	135	14	5	.74	.287	.364	.499	.863
Greene,Khalil	SD	29	150	581	140	36	2	19	68	75	68	3.98	39	135	6	3	.67	.241	.294	.408	.702
Griffey Jr.,Ken	CWS	39	127	412	105	21	0	20	57	64	65	5.50	58	81	1	0	1.00	.255	.351	.451	.802
Gross,Gabe	TB	29	133	332	87	21	2	11	48	43	51	5.37	47	71	4	2	.67	.262	.355	.437	.792
Grudzielanek,Mark	KC	39	78	224	64	13	1	3	29	20	28	4.52	12	31	1	1	.50	.286	.336	.393	.729
Guerrero,Vladimir	LAA	34	153	593	186	37	1	31	94	111	121	7.65	64	77	8	4	.67	.314	.386	.536	.922
Guillen,Carlos	Det	33	144	540	156	34	4	15	86	76	88	5.87	65	91	10	6	.62	.289	.368	.450	.818
Guillen,Jose	KC	33	145	557	151	32	1	21	70	88	76	4.86	30	106	2	1	.67	.271	.322	.445	.767
Gutierrez,Franklin	Cle	26	103	369	100	26	1	10	60	42	51	4.84	29	79	10	5	.67	.271	.329	.428	.757
Guzman,Cristian	Was	31	137	496	145	26	5	7	68	45	65	4.76	24	55	6	4	.60	.292	.329	.407	.736
Hafner,Travis	Cle	32	122	448	121	30	1	23	72	83	83	6.58	76	110	1	1	.50	.270	.384	.496	.880
Hairston,Jerry	Cin	33	93	220	58	14	1	4	31	22	27	4.23	18	32	8	4	.67	.264	.333	.391	.724
Hairston,Scott	SD	29	121	385	102	22	3	19	56	48	61	5.56	35	84	3	2	.60	.265	.328	.486	.814
Hall,Bill	Mil	29	131	418	103	28	2	15	57	54	54	4.39	37	122	6	5	.55	.246	.311	.431	.741
Hall,Toby	CWS	33	65	178	45	9	0	3	14	19	18	3.52	8	20	0	0	.00	.253	.293	.354	.646
Hamilton,Josh	Tex	28	158	619	192	36	4	36	103	126	131	7.92	68	116	9	3	.75	.310	.384	.556	.940
Hanigan,Ryan	Cin	28	33	102	28	5	0	2	12	10	14	4.92	12	14	0	0	.00	.275	.357	.382	.739
Hannahan,Jack	Oak	29	97	277	70	17	0	6	34	35	36	4.50	40	72	2	1	.67	.253	.349	.379	.728
Hardy,J.J.	Mil	26	142	556	152	32	2	23	79	77	86	5.52	51	79	2	1	.67	.273	.336	.462	.798
Harris,Brendan	Min	28	134	482	131	32	2	10	64	59	65	4.80	42	93	3	1	.75	.272	.334	.409	.743
Harris,Willie	Was	31	119	306	78	14	2	7	51	28	40	4.44	38	60	13	6	.68	.255	.341	.382	.723
Hart,Corey	Mil	27	146	518	148	37	6	20	77	83	85	5.85	34	92	21	8	.72	.286	.336	.496	.832
Hawpe,Brad	Col	30	152	540	152	31	3	27	76	99	100	6.67	78	146	2	2	.50	.281	.374	.500	.874
Headley,Chase	SD	25	124	451	130	33	3	16	67	64	79	6.38	52	126	3	1	.75	.288	.367	.481	.848
Helms,Wes	Fla	33	113	229	58	13	1	6	23	30	28	4.26	17	57	0	0	.00	.253	.319	.397	.716
Helton,Todd	Col	35	131	476	145	36	1	17	79	74	98	7.67	93	73	1	1	.50	.305	.421	.492	.913
Hermida,Jeremy	Fla	25	145	516	142	31	2	20	78	72	85	5.86	66	123	8	3	.73	.275	.363	.459	.822
Hernandez,Anderson	Was	26	81	149	37	6	1	1	18	11	14	3.19	9	26	4	2	.67	.248	.291	.322	.613
Hernandez,Ramon	Bal	33	134	482	126	25	1	16	55	74	64	4.67	39	71	0	0	.00	.261	.324	.417	.741
Hill,Aaron	Tor	27	126	463	132	32	2	9	62	57	66	5.14	38	62	5	3	.62	.285	.343	.421	.764
Hinske,Eric	TB	31	123	339	83	21	1	14	51	47	48	4.82	41	84	7	3	.70	.245	.332	.437	.768
Holliday,Matt	Col	29	154	605	192	43	4	29	111	108	128	7.94	66	116	19	6	.76	.317	.392	.545	.937
Holm,Steve	SF	29	41	111	29	8	0	2	13	11	15	4.76	15	18	0	0	.00	.261	.359	.387	.747
Howard,Ryan	Phi	29	158	596	164	31	2	50	101	144	130	7.84	92	202	1	0	1.00	.276	.376	.587	.963
Hu,Chin-lung	LAD	25	140	457	119	22	3	6	63	39	51	3.88	32	60	10	4	.71	.260	.309	.361	.670
Hudson,Orlando	Ari	31	140	533	151	32	4	11	71	59	78	5.27	55	85	6	3	.67	.283	.353	.420	.773
Huff,Aubrey	Bal	32	149	533	151	33	2	23	72	83	88	5.96	48	81	3	2	.60	.283	.347	.482	.829
Hundley,Nick	SD	25	81	216	48	10	1	9	27	34	24	3.71	16	47	0	0	.00	.222	.279	.403	.682
Hunter,Torii	LAA	33	155	593	159	37	1	25	87	93	87	5.12	48	117	16	8	.67	.268	.329	.460	.790
Iannetta,Chris	Col	26	133	463	126	29	4	21	71	79	84	6.48	74	108	0	0	.00	.272	.382	.488	.870
Ibanez,Raul	Sea	37	159	623	173	36	2	22	84	100	95	5.46	60	111	2	2	.50	.278	.343	.448	.791
Iguchi,Tadahito	Phi	34	87	255	65	13	1	5	34	29	31	4.20	23	57	7	2	.78	.255	.326	.373	.699
Infante,Omar	Atl	27	102	296	80	18	3	4	38	32	37	4.43	20	46	3	2	.60	.271	.320	.393	.713
Inge,Brandon	Det	32	134	447	104	22	3	14	54	58	52	3.91	44	119	5	3	.62	.233	.311	.389	.701
Inglett,Joe	Tor	31	95	294	85	15	3	3	39	30	39	4.76	25	39	7	4	.64	.289	.349	.391	.740
Ishikawa,Travis	SF	25	50	170	46	12	1	7	23	30	27	5.57	18	38	3	2	.60	.271	.340	.476	.816
Iwamura,Akinori	TB	30	147	601	172	29	7	7	93	45	85	5.08	70	117	8	6	.57	.286	.364	.393	.756
Izturis,Cesar	StL	29	122	368	97	15	2	1	41	26	37	3.47	24	27	13	6	.68	.264	.314	.323	.637
Izturis,Maicer	LAA	28	119	432	121	24	3	5	64	49	58	4.76	44	41	14	6	.70	.280	.348	.384	.732
Jackson,Conor	Ari	27	148	534	158	36	3	15	81	81	91	6.24	65	59	7	3	.70	.296	.379	.459	.837
Jacobs,Mike	Fla	28	134	452	122	31	1	26	61	80	75	5.89	36	100	1	1	.50	.270	.325	.515	.841
Jenkins,Geoff	Phi	34	126	374	96	22	1	15	45	52	52	4.85	34	99	1	1	.50	.257	.330	.441	.771
Jeter,Derek	NYY	35	156	628	193	32	2	14	102	73	100	5.91	59	101	14	5	.74	.307	.377	.432	.808
Johjima,Kenji	Sea	33	121	400	106	21	0	12	43	52	49	4.32	20	37	2	1	.67	.265	.319	.408	.727
Johnson,Kelly	Atl	27	139	518	147	34	6	15	84	67	86	5.95	63	101	10	5	.67	.284	.364	.459	.823
Johnson,Nick	Was	30	69	198	53	15	0	8	33	31	36	6.41	42	42	2	1	.67	.268	.413	.465	.878
Johnson,Reed	ChC	32	116	369	102	21	1	7	54	42	46	4.43	22	74	4	3	.57	.276	.339	.396	.735
Jones,Adam	Bal	23	150	480	134	24	5	15	71	65	68	5.04	30	108	12	5	.71	.279	.326	.444	.769
Jones,Andruw	LAD	32	101	301	70	14	1	16	45	50	42	4.69	37	80	2	2	.50	.233	.328	.445	.774
Jones,Brandon	Atl	25	82	273	74	18	2	7	36	40	40	5.12	20	60	7	4	.64	.271	.343	.429	.772
Jones,Chipper	Atl	37	121	457	144	28	1	23	82	82	102	8.42	82	72	4	2	.67	.315	.420	.532	.952
Jones,Jacque	Fla	34	51	132	34	7	0	4	17	17	16	4.20	10	27	2	1	.67	.258	.324	.402	.726
Joyce,Matt	Det	25	92	296	76	20	3	15	46	47	48	5.62	34	79	2	2	.50	.257	.335	.497	.832
Ka'aihue,Kila	KC	25	86	304	79	14	0	18	53	57	56	6.44	60	50	2	1	.67	.260	.382	.484	.865
Kapler,Gabe	Mil	33	79	177	49	11	1	4	27	23	24	4.84	13	30	2	1	.67	.277	.333	.418	.751
Kearns,Austin	Was	29	117	384	100	23	1	14	57	57	58	5.27	51	81	2	2	.50	.260	.359	.435	.794
Kemp,Matt	LAD	24	155	562	175	37	5	19	96	80	101	6.60	42	124	32	11	.74	.311	.360	.496	.857
Kendall,Jason	Mil	35	133	445	118	21	1	2	49	39	48	3.77	39	40	6	4	.60	.265	.343	.330	.674

2009 Hitter Projections

PLAYER			BATTING											BASERUNNING			AVERAGES			
Hitter	Team	Age	G	AB	H	2B	3B	HR	R	RBI	RC	RC27	BB	SO	SB	CS	SB%	Avg	OBP	Slg	OPS
Kendrick,Howie	LAA	25	152	612	194	49	4	11	87	82	96	5.86	20	96	18	8	.69	.317	.343	.464	.807
Kennedy,Adam	StL	33	116	348	95	17	2	4	41	34	41	4.15	26	50	8	4	.67	.273	.332	.368	.700
Kent,Jeff	LAD	41	140	519	143	31	1	17	64	78	76	5.24	48	74	1	1	.50	.276	.344	.437	.781
Keppinger,Jeff	Cin	29	117	439	134	24	2	5	53	43	63	5.34	35	23	3	2	.60	.305	.359	.403	.762
Kinsler,Ian	Tex	27	149	581	169	39	3	22	108	82	102	6.34	58	77	25	6	.81	.291	.360	.482	.842
Konerko,Paul	CWS	33	144	524	140	26	0	30	75	90	90	6.08	70	96	1	1	.50	.267	.360	.489	.849
Kotchman,Casey	Atl	26	141	521	147	34	1	14	69	78	77	5.34	46	41	2	1	.67	.282	.346	.432	.778
Kotsay,Mark	Bos	33	94	295	79	17	1	5	34	32	37	4.41	27	35	2	2	.50	.268	.331	.383	.714
Kottaras,George	Bos	26	80	223	54	15	0	9	31	32	32	4.92	31	58	0	0	.00	.242	.335	.430	.765
Kouzmanoff,Kevin	SD	27	152	601	170	37	3	25	76	94	92	5.55	33	114	1	0	1.00	.283	.332	.479	.811
Kubel,Jason	Min	27	145	517	146	33	4	22	78	89	88	6.15	52	90	2	1	.67	.282	.348	.489	.837
LaHair,Bryan	Sea	26	52	156	39	10	0	4	18	20	19	4.22	15	42	0	0	.00	.250	.316	.391	.707
Laird,Gerald	Tex	29	112	369	97	21	2	8	54	45	46	4.36	27	71	4	2	.67	.263	.318	.396	.714
Lamb,Mike	Mil	33	97	237	64	12	1	6	32	32	32	4.81	22	36	0	0	.00	.270	.335	.405	.740
Langerhans,Ryan	Was	29	93	176	45	11	1	4	27	20	25	4.89	28	46	4	2	.67	.256	.364	.398	.762
LaPorta,Matt	Cle	24	144	540	136	31	1	24	76	86	78	5.01	58	110	3	1	.75	.252	.324	.446	.771
Larish,Jeff	Det	26	59	150	37	8	1	8	19	26	23	5.25	19	40	1	1	.50	.247	.331	.473	.805
LaRoche,Adam	Pit	29	151	551	149	40	1	26	76	91	92	5.94	60	135	1	1	.50	.270	.344	.488	.832
LaRoche,Andy	Pit	25	147	516	130	23	0	18	77	71	71	4.73	74	83	7	4	.64	.252	.347	.401	.748
LaRue,Jason	StL	35	68	154	34	8	0	5	17	19	16	3.47	14	39	0	0	.00	.221	.322	.370	.692
Lee,Carlos	Hou	33	148	573	168	36	0	32	85	109	106	6.75	52	68	8	3	.73	.293	.355	.524	.879
Lee,Derrek	ChC	33	146	567	165	38	2	24	87	85	104	6.66	73	119	8	4	.67	.291	.376	.492	.868
Lewis,Fred	SF	28	140	498	138	25	7	10	84	49	74	5.23	57	115	21	8	.72	.277	.353	.416	.768
Lind,Adam	Tor	25	154	597	179	39	4	23	81	105	102	6.31	44	116	3	2	.60	.300	.349	.494	.843
Lo Duca,Paul	Fla	37	73	197	54	11	0	3	22	22	23	4.15	13	17	1	1	.50	.274	.338	.376	.714
Loney,James	LAD	25	161	546	161	34	4	13	66	81	84	5.61	45	75	6	4	.60	.295	.351	.443	.794
Longoria,Evan	TB	23	154	599	168	39	1	37	102	116	114	6.83	69	142	9	3	.75	.280	.358	.534	.892
Lopez,Felipe	StL	29	112	344	92	18	2	7	48	36	45	4.57	35	66	9	4	.69	.267	.340	.392	.733
Lopez,Jose	Sea	25	150	551	155	34	2	14	70	75	73	4.76	24	62	4	3	.57	.281	.316	.426	.743
Loretta,Mark	Hou	37	90	245	69	13	0	3	28	25	31	4.55	23	26	1	1	.50	.282	.355	.371	.727
Lowell,Mike	Bos	35	128	462	128	31	0	16	59	75	70	5.43	42	64	2	1	.67	.277	.343	.448	.791
Lowrie,Jed	Bos	25	148	544	150	37	5	10	79	83	83	5.45	76	114	3	2	.60	.276	.366	.417	.783
Ludwick,Ryan	StL	30	152	540	152	38	1	31	91	100	98	6.52	54	135	3	3	.50	.281	.351	.528	.879
Lugo,Julio	Bos	33	128	463	119	25	2	6	60	46	55	4.07	46	83	18	7	.72	.257	.328	.359	.687
Maier,Mitch	KC	27	50	165	45	10	1	3	22	18	21	4.48	10	24	4	2	.67	.273	.318	.400	.718
Markakis,Nick	Bal	25	159	598	185	46	2	22	104	99	118	7.32	83	99	10	6	.62	.309	.396	.503	.900
Marson,Lou	Phi	23	103	343	100	18	0	6	50	42	53	5.60	56	77	3	3	.50	.292	.391	.397	.787
Marte,Andy	Cle	25	58	125	31	8	0	4	15	17	16	4.43	11	25	0	0	.00	.248	.314	.408	.722
Martin,Russell	LAD	26	147	535	156	30	2	15	91	79	91	6.11	81	75	17	8	.68	.292	.390	.439	.829
Martinez,Fernando	NYM	20	128	436	115	22	3	9	54	45	53	4.24	32	90	8	4	.67	.264	.314	.390	.704
Martinez,Victor	Cle	30	147	547	164	38	0	17	73	92	94	6.38	61	74	0	0	.00	.300	.374	.463	.837
Mather,Joe	StL	26	63	162	41	9	0	10	26	24	26	5.54	17	28	3	1	.75	.253	.328	.494	.822
Mathis,Jeff	LAA	26	73	174	38	9	1	5	23	21	18	3.42	15	43	1	1	.50	.218	.288	.368	.656
Matsui,Hideki	NYY	35	125	466	134	26	1	17	72	77	78	6.09	58	70	1	1	.50	.288	.370	.457	.827
Matsui,Kaz	Hou	33	120	459	126	27	3	8	69	44	61	4.66	37	78	19	7	.73	.275	.330	.399	.729
Matthews Jr.,Gary	LAA	34	125	426	109	23	2	11	60	49	55	4.45	45	91	8	4	.67	.256	.330	.397	.727
Mauer,Joe	Min	26	138	520	168	34	3	11	88	80	99	7.27	78	53	4	2	.67	.323	.412	.463	.876
Maybin,Cameron	Fla	22	141	490	135	21	7	16	86	58	81	5.79	65	151	32	9	.78	.276	.362	.445	.806
McAnulty,Paul	SD	28	68	145	37	9	1	4	17	20	20	4.81	19	33	0	0	.00	.255	.345	.414	.759
McCann,Brian	Atl	25	142	518	156	42	1	24	68	98	99	7.07	53	62	4	2	.67	.301	.370	.525	.896
McCutchen,Andrew	Pit	22	149	557	150	29	2	10	76	53	72	4.42	59	93	35	17	.67	.269	.339	.382	.722
McDonald,John	Tor	34	94	212	48	9	1	1	23	17	16	2.51	10	32	4	2	.67	.226	.268	.292	.560
McLouth,Nate	Pit	27	143	560	154	40	3	21	103	72	92	5.82	57	87	22	5	.81	.275	.350	.470	.820
Mench,Kevin	Tor	31	87	235	62	16	1	7	29	32	32	4.78	18	32	1	1	.50	.264	.322	.430	.751
Michaels,Jason	Pit	33	85	195	50	10	0	5	27	27	24	4.27	20	43	2	1	.67	.256	.332	.385	.716
Mientkiewicz,Doug	Pit	35	113	307	83	20	1	5	38	36	43	4.99	40	39	0	0	.00	.270	.360	.391	.751
Miles,Aaron	StL	32	130	360	105	16	2	3	45	31	44	4.45	22	36	3	2	.60	.292	.334	.372	.706
Millar,Kevin	Bal	37	129	407	103	23	0	14	53	56	57	4.88	52	77	0	0	.00	.253	.348	.413	.760
Milledge,Lastings	Was	24	138	494	139	27	3	15	71	67	73	5.20	41	91	22	10	.69	.281	.347	.439	.787
Molina,Bengie	SF	34	140	527	146	25	0	17	45	83	68	4.64	21	48	0	0	.00	.277	.311	.421	.732
Molina,Jose	NYY	34	84	207	48	12	0	3	20	19	18	2.94	9	45	1	0	1.00	.232	.274	.333	.607
Molina,Yadier	StL	26	126	473	129	22	0	8	40	60	57	4.31	37	40	0	0	.00	.273	.329	.370	.699
Monroe,Craig	Min	32	65	154	37	9	0	6	21	24	19	4.22	11	39	1	0	1.00	.240	.295	.416	.711
Montanez,Lou	Bal	27	70	222	66	13	1	9	35	34	37	6.13	17	32	2	1	.67	.297	.347	.486	.834
Montero,Miguel	Ari	25	95	302	77	18	1	11	35	44	42	4.85	32	57	0	0	.00	.255	.330	.430	.761
Mora,Melvin	Bal	37	146	483	133	25	1	17	71	72	71	5.23	44	80	5	3	.62	.275	.348	.437	.785
Morales,Kendry	LAA	26	158	537	156	30	1	19	67	79	80	5.45	28	72	1	1	.50	.291	.327	.456	.783
Morgan,Nyjer	Pit	28	71	240	70	11	2	1	37	16	31	4.53	15	36	26	8	.76	.292	.339	.367	.705
Morneau,Justin	Min	28	161	615	177	40	3	29	92	120	111	6.59	68	94	0	0	.00	.288	.362	.504	.866
Moss,Brandon	Pit	25	142	463	127	36	3	15	63	69	72	5.52	47	122	4	3	.57	.274	.341	.462	.803
Murphy,Daniel	NYM	24	139	456	135	33	4	14	73	74	80	6.34	53	67	14	7	.67	.296	.371	.478	.849
Murphy,David	Tex	27	151	527	146	38	4	15	73	78	80	5.40	47	84	9	4	.69	.277	.336	.450	.786
Murphy,Donnie	Oak	26	62	144	34	10	0	5	20	19	17	3.98	10	39	2	1	.67	.236	.290	.410	.700
Nady,Xavier	NYY	30	147	546	155	32	1	23	71	86	85	5.64	36	108	2	1	.67	.284	.337	.473	.810
Napoli,Mike	LAA	27	136	449	113	22	1	31	82	85	81	6.16	73	129	11	6	.65	.252	.361	.512	.873
Navarro,Dioner	TB	25	134	472	137	26	1	9	52	55	67	5.18	44	59	1	1	.50	.290	.353	.407	.760
Newhan,David	Hou	35	74	152	42	8	1	4	22	19	21	4.88	11	28	4	2	.67	.276	.329	.421	.750
Nieves,Wil	Was	31	58	125	31	6	0	1	11	11	11	3.04	6	17	0	0	.00	.248	.282	.320	.602
Norton,Greg	Atl	36	115	162	40	8	0	5	20	22	22	4.69	23	41	1	0	1.00	.247	.341	.389	.729
Ochoa,Ivan	SF	26	60	142	36	6	1	1	17	10	14	3.31	11	28	7	4	.64	.254	.312	.331	.643
Ojeda,Augie	Ari	34	93	225	53	9	1	1	27	17	21	3.17	24	23	1	0	1.00	.236	.317	.298	.615

2009 Hitter Projections

Hitter	Team	Age	G	AB	H	2B	3B	HR	R	RBI	RC	RC27	BB	SO	SB	CS	SB%	Avg	OBP	Slg	OPS
Olivo,Miguel	KC	30	117	413	101	23	2	15	45	54	46	3.78	15	110	8	4	.67	.245	.276	.419	.695
Ordonez,Magglio	Det	35	156	599	187	39	1	24	88	110	112	7.03	59	84	2	2	.50	.312	.377	.501	.878
Ortiz,David	Bos	33	142	539	155	39	1	37	98	119	121	8.17	95	107	1	1	.50	.288	.396	.570	.966
Overbay,Lyle	Tor	32	152	520	141	37	1	15	68	69	79	5.41	66	106	1	1	.50	.271	.355	.433	.788
Ozuna,Pablo	LAD	34	65	135	37	6	1	1	16	12	14	3.64	5	12	3	2	.60	.274	.310	.356	.665
Patterson,Corey	Cin	29	118	339	87	17	2	10	47	35	40	4.02	17	62	18	7	.72	.257	.298	.407	.705
Patterson,Eric	Oak	26	43	137	36	8	1	3	20	16	18	4.50	12	29	9	3	.75	.263	.322	.401	.724
Paulino,Ronny	Pit	28	70	184	50	11	0	4	20	24	24	4.66	15	34	1	0	1.00	.272	.330	.397	.727
Payton,Jay	Bal	36	102	277	71	12	1	6	34	32	31	3.88	17	37	4	2	.67	.256	.306	.372	.678
Pearce,Steve	Pit	26	51	114	31	9	0	4	15	18	17	5.26	8	19	3	1	.75	.272	.331	.456	.787
Pedroia,Dustin	Bos	25	158	642	202	52	2	15	107	78	114	6.66	58	46	16	5	.76	.315	.376	.472	.848
Pena,Carlos	TB	31	138	488	124	25	2	31	77	90	90	6.41	85	153	2	1	.67	.254	.372	.504	.877
Pena,Tony F	KC	28	93	215	52	9	1	2	24	16	18	2.84	6	39	4	2	.67	.242	.266	.321	.587
Pena,Wily Mo	Was	27	98	310	79	14	1	13	37	42	41	4.59	22	93	1	1	.50	.255	.310	.432	.743
Pence,Hunter	Hou	26	157	622	183	39	7	29	91	100	110	6.40	47	118	13	8	.62	.294	.346	.519	.865
Pennington,Cliff	Oak	25	55	104	25	4	1	0	16	7	11	3.53	16	16	6	2	.75	.240	.347	.298	.645
Peralta,Jhonny	Cle	27	156	605	166	38	3	23	97	84	94	5.54	58	138	3	2	.60	.274	.341	.461	.802
Perez,Fernando	TB	26	42	109	31	4	2	2	19	8	17	5.46	14	31	10	3	.77	.284	.371	.413	.784
Phillips,Brandon	Cin	28	154	601	158	30	4	21	84	76	80	4.60	39	101	22	9	.71	.263	.313	.431	.744
Pie,Felix	ChC	24	143	498	137	28	6	13	72	60	69	4.84	34	101	19	10	.66	.275	.323	.434	.756
Pierre,Juan	LAD	31	117	394	115	14	4	1	54	26	48	4.27	23	24	34	13	.72	.292	.340	.355	.696
Pierzynski,A.J.	CWS	32	139	525	144	30	1	14	62	65	66	4.49	23	71	1	1	.50	.274	.316	.415	.731
Podsednik,Scott	Col	33	69	155	41	8	1	1	22	12	18	3.93	15	27	11	5	.69	.265	.337	.348	.686
Polanco,Placido	Det	33	146	599	183	32	2	9	91	62	85	5.27	36	42	6	3	.67	.306	.353	.411	.764
Posada,Jorge	NYY	37	139	462	128	29	1	17	65	78	78	6.05	70	104	1	1	.50	.277	.378	.455	.833
Prado,Martin	Atl	25	78	249	75	15	2	2	34	28	35	5.17	21	29	3	2	.60	.301	.356	.402	.757
Pujols,Albert	StL	29	155	575	194	45	1	41	118	125	159	10.77	102	59	6	3	.67	.337	.443	.633	1.076
Punto,Nick	Min	31	127	406	102	18	3	2	53	29	43	3.59	43	73	15	7	.68	.251	.323	.325	.648
Quentin,Carlos	CWS	26	156	553	153	40	2	31	102	103	103	6.65	66	87	7	3	.70	.277	.366	.524	.890
Quinlan,Robb	LAA	32	81	185	52	9	1	4	22	22	24	4.62	12	27	3	2	.60	.281	.328	.405	.734
Quintanilla,Omar	Col	27	86	246	65	17	1	2	31	20	29	4.14	19	43	2	1	.67	.264	.317	.366	.683
Quintero,Humberto	Hou	29	65	161	41	9	0	3	15	17	17	3.68	6	24	0	0	.00	.255	.290	.366	.656
Quiroz,Guillermo	Bal	27	92	244	57	15	0	6	23	32	26	3.61	19	54	0	0	.00	.234	.292	.369	.661
Rabelo,Mike	Fla	29	56	141	35	7	0	3	15	15	15	3.68	9	30	0	0	.00	.248	.303	.362	.664
Raburn,Ryan	Det	28	86	212	57	13	2	8	33	33	33	5.46	23	51	5	2	.71	.269	.340	.462	.803
Ramirez,Alexei	CWS	27	158	574	166	28	4	24	88	97	88	5.49	32	64	14	9	.61	.289	.329	.477	.806
Ramirez,Aramis	ChC	31	152	580	169	40	1	31	88	111	108	6.82	58	87	1	1	.50	.291	.364	.524	.888
Ramirez,Hanley	Fla	25	157	627	194	42	6	30	130	75	131	7.62	75	108	39	14	.74	.309	.388	.539	.927
Ramirez,Manny	LAD	37	150	552	166	34	1	34	95	113	121	8.13	88	125	2	1	.67	.301	.404	.551	.955
Ramirez,Max	Tex	24	86	221	68	12	1	13	37	39	46	7.77	27	57	1	1	.50	.308	.390	.548	.938
Rasmus,Colby	StL	22	135	472	116	27	1	18	75	54	67	4.81	60	99	22	6	.79	.246	.331	.422	.752
Redmond,Mike	Min	38	63	187	54	10	0	1	17	21	22	4.30	10	18	0	0	.00	.289	.338	.358	.697
Reed,Jeremy	Sea	28	92	268	73	16	2	4	35	28	34	4.46	22	33	5	3	.62	.272	.330	.392	.722
Renteria,Edgar	Det	33	146	569	163	33	1	11	84	69	80	5.07	50	81	9	4	.69	.286	.345	.406	.751
Reyes,Jose	NYM	26	160	669	194	34	15	14	117	67	108	5.71	60	79	59	17	.78	.290	.349	.448	.798
Reynolds,Mark	Ari	25	152	553	149	32	4	32	101	105	99	6.31	66	182	10	4	.71	.269	.350	.515	.866
Riggans,Shawn	TB	28	49	150	40	9	0	5	17	22	20	4.73	11	32	0	0	.00	.267	.317	.427	.743
Rios,Alex	Tor	28	156	611	178	42	7	16	91	80	97	5.71	46	108	24	9	.73	.291	.344	.462	.805
Rivas,Luis	Pit	29	67	163	39	7	1	3	20	16	16	3.30	11	25	4	2	.67	.239	.291	.350	.641
Rivera,Juan	LAA	31	99	317	89	20	0	13	40	52	48	5.45	21	41	1	1	.50	.281	.327	.467	.794
Roberts,Brian	Bal	31	156	623	176	44	4	10	100	58	96	5.44	79	99	36	12	.75	.283	.364	.414	.778
Roberts,Dave	SF	37	92	275	70	10	3	2	40	20	32	3.94	33	44	16	6	.73	.255	.337	.335	.671
Rodriguez,Alex	NYY	33	153	577	169	29	1	42	115	120	125	7.85	84	134	17	6	.74	.293	.396	.565	.961
Rodriguez,Ivan	NYY	37	132	445	125	25	2	11	53	52	59	4.75	22	81	6	3	.67	.281	.318	.420	.738
Rodriguez,Luis	SD	29	60	169	46	10	1	1	19	14	20	4.23	15	12	0	0	.00	.272	.332	.361	.692
Rodriguez,Sean	LAA	24	59	210	54	13	1	9	36	28	31	5.10	20	50	5	2	.71	.257	.328	.457	.785
Rolen,Scott	Tor	34	134	488	131	35	2	17	75	80	76	5.49	58	83	5	3	.62	.268	.356	.453	.808
Rollins,Jimmy	Phi	30	154	648	183	41	8	17	107	70	102	5.58	56	74	41	10	.80	.282	.344	.449	.793
Romero,Alex	Ari	26	76	129	35	7	1	2	15	13	15	4.06	7	14	4	2	.67	.271	.309	.388	.696
Ross,Cody	Fla	28	132	428	113	26	3	21	62	67	67	5.50	36	96	5	2	.71	.264	.327	.486	.813
Ross,David	Bos	31	102	294	66	14	1	13	34	38	38	4.33	38	80	0	0	.00	.224	.317	.412	.729
Rowand,Aaron	SF	31	154	580	160	38	1	18	79	74	82	5.04	41	124	5	3	.62	.276	.339	.438	.777
Ruiz,Carlos	Phi	30	108	317	83	18	1	7	40	40	42	4.65	35	37	2	1	.67	.262	.341	.391	.732
Ryan,Brendan	StL	27	88	237	60	11	1	3	36	15	25	3.61	17	34	8	3	.73	.253	.306	.346	.652
Ryan,Dusty	Det	24	112	379	97	21	2	15	51	55	54	4.96	38	118	2	1	.67	.256	.324	.441	.764
Salazar,Jeff	Ari	28	78	161	42	9	2	3	24	17	22	4.73	20	30	4	2	.67	.261	.346	.398	.744
Salome,Angel	Mil	23	90	310	92	24	1	10	49	61	51	6.03	25	50	3	2	.60	.297	.349	.477	.827
Saltalamacchia,Jarrod	Tex	24	95	344	90	21	1	11	46	46	51	5.22	46	94	0	0	.00	.262	.349	.424	.773
Sanchez,Freddy	Pit	31	148	557	163	36	2	8	73	62	74	4.87	29	64	1	1	.50	.293	.332	.408	.740
Sandoval,Pablo	SF	22	150	540	173	42	2	17	90	103	93	6.59	20	53	0	0	.00	.320	.346	.500	.846
Santiago,Ramon	Det	29	87	236	57	10	2	3	32	21	24	3.45	19	36	4	2	.67	.242	.309	.339	.648
Sardinha,Dane	Det	30	56	134	26	5	0	3	11	12	9	2.17	7	36	0	0	.00	.194	.234	.299	.533
Schierholtz,Nate	SF	140	536	160	36	8	17	73	74	86	5.85	24	75	12	6	.67	.299	.331	.491	.822	
Schneider,Brian	NYM	32	125	405	100	20	1	9	35	50	48	4.09	47	64	0	0	.00	.247	.328	.368	.696
Schumaker,Skip	StL	29	128	405	119	20	2	6	55	33	56	5.04	34	45	6	3	.67	.294	.350	.398	.748
Scott,Luke	Bal	31	142	476	130	31	3	25	69	79	85	6.35	57	98	3	2	.60	.273	.354	.508	.863
Scutaro,Marco	Tor	33	125	437	113	23	2	7	58	46	53	4.23	46	61	4	2	.67	.259	.332	.368	.700
Sexson,Richie	NYY	34	96	278	65	14	0	15	36	46	40	4.88	37	79	1	0	1.00	.234	.330	.446	.776
Shealy,Ryan	KC	29	117	402	112	24	1	19	54	69	67	6.01	39	90	0	0	.00	.279	.344	.485	.829
Sheffield,Gary	Det	40	109	352	88	15	0	16	53	55	53	5.16	52	60	7	3	.70	.250	.356	.429	.785
Shelton,Chris	Tex	29	36	112	32	7	1	4	16	16	19	6.18	14	28	0	0	.00	.286	.370	.473	.843

2009 Hitter Projections

Hitter	Team	Age	G	AB	H	2B	3B	HR	R	RBI	RC	RC27	BB	SO	SB	CS	SB%	Avg	OBP	Slg	OPS
Shoppach,Kelly	Cle	29	108	363	93	26	0	19	57	59	57	5.49	35	121	0	0	.00	.256	.328	.485	.813
Sizemore,Grady	Cle	26	160	638	177	41	7	29	117	88	118	6.53	88	137	30	9	.77	.277	.374	.500	.874
Smith,Seth	Col	26	79	211	60	15	1	7	28	29	34	5.78	21	34	5	2	.71	.284	.349	.464	.814
Snider,Travis	Tor	21	127	448	121	29	0	19	69	83	71	5.63	49	143	2	1	.67	.270	.342	.462	.804
Snyder,Chris	Ari	28	121	399	97	26	0	16	49	63	58	4.99	57	95	0	0	.00	.243	.342	.429	.771
Soriano,Alfonso	ChC	33	140	576	160	36	2	33	93	84	98	6.02	41	133	21	7	.75	.278	.332	.519	.851
Soto,Geovany	ChC	26	141	515	151	35	1	23	71	89	95	6.79	62	118	0	0	.00	.293	.370	.499	.869
Span,Denard	Min	25	150	570	162	24	7	6	96	62	78	4.77	63	101	33	17	.66	.284	.357	.382	.740
Spilborghs,Ryan	Col	29	118	370	115	24	2	10	59	53	66	6.60	44	60	9	5	.64	.311	.386	.468	.853
Stairs,Matt	Phi	41	119	327	79	17	0	12	38	46	43	4.49	41	80	1	1	.50	.242	.333	.404	.737
Stewart,Ian	Col	24	81	272	72	18	2	11	40	41	42	5.41	26	70	5	2	.71	.265	.338	.467	.805
Stewart,Shannon	Tor	35	77	226	63	11	1	4	29	21	30	4.73	20	26	3	2	.60	.279	.345	.389	.735
Suzuki,Ichiro	Sea	35	161	679	217	22	5	8	103	54	103	5.69	48	71	34	9	.79	.320	.368	.402	.770
Suzuki,Kurt	Oak	25	148	539	148	30	1	9	66	60	70	4.63	53	71	2	2	.50	.275	.347	.384	.731
Sweeney,Ryan	Oak	24	148	538	151	27	2	11	71	66	74	4.91	51	84	11	5	.69	.281	.344	.400	.744
Swisher,Nick	CWS	28	142	463	111	27	1	23	78	71	74	5.45	80	122	2	1	.67	.240	.359	.451	.810
Taguchi,So	Phi	39	72	130	34	6	0	1	17	14	13	3.48	9	19	3	1	.75	.262	.319	.331	.650
Tatis,Fernando	NYM	34	88	261	66	14	1	10	34	36	36	4.78	28	58	2	1	.67	.253	.330	.429	.759
Taveras,Willy	Col	27	134	514	145	16	3	2	77	29	62	4.23	35	85	56	12	.82	.282	.335	.337	.672
Teagarden,Taylor	Tex	25	139	448	107	18	2	25	64	61	64	4.87	50	153	2	1	.67	.239	.317	.455	.772
Teahen,Mark	KC	27	139	494	135	31	5	12	67	61	72	5.17	50	113	6	3	.67	.273	.342	.429	.772
Teixeira,Mark	LAA	29	154	589	176	41	2	36	102	121	129	8.10	89	110	2	1	.67	.299	.397	.559	.956
Tejada,Miguel	Hou	35	155	613	179	35	1	19	85	92	90	5.35	37	74	5	3	.62	.292	.340	.445	.786
Thames,Marcus	Det	32	117	367	92	19	1	25	59	64	58	5.46	33	92	1	1	.50	.251	.314	.512	.826
Theriot,Ryan	ChC	29	144	533	156	25	3	2	78	42	71	4.78	60	50	20	9	.69	.293	.366	.362	.728
Thigpen,Curtis	Tor	26	75	154	37	10	0	2	16	17	16	3.53	13	26	1	1	.50	.240	.299	.344	.644
Thomas,Clete	Det	25	53	100	26	6	1	2	14	11	13	4.39	11	24	7	3	.70	.260	.339	.400	.739
Thomas,Frank	Oak	41	111	349	85	14	0	17	41	56	53	5.22	58	75	0	0	.00	.244	.358	.430	.787
Thome,Jim	CWS	38	150	530	134	25	0	38	93	102	103	6.76	107	166	1	0	1.00	.253	.382	.515	.897
Tolbert,Matt	Min	27	56	141	39	8	2	1	20	16	18	4.46	11	20	6	3	.67	.277	.329	.383	.712
Torrealba,Yorvit	Col	30	56	134	33	9	0	3	14	17	15	3.86	10	26	0	0	.00	.246	.318	.381	.698
Towles,J.R.	Hou	25	117	439	112	20	2	17	63	70	58	4.53	39	85	8	6	.57	.255	.322	.426	.748
Tracy,Chad	Ari	29	103	325	92	22	1	10	41	44	49	5.47	26	55	1	0	1.00	.283	.340	.449	.789
Treanor,Matt	Fla	33	82	228	54	9	0	3	20	24	22	3.27	24	47	1	1	.50	.237	.318	.316	.633
Tulowitzki,Troy	Col	24	129	500	144	32	3	17	80	71	82	5.92	51	79	4	4	.50	.288	.359	.466	.825
Uggla,Dan	Fla	29	156	606	158	39	3	31	106	93	99	5.69	70	154	5	4	.56	.261	.344	.488	.833
Upton,B.J.	TB	24	140	501	145	30	2	14	86	65	87	6.11	78	122	38	14	.73	.289	.387	.441	.828
Upton,Justin	Ari	21	137	506	133	30	9	22	79	68	86	5.93	70	146	6	4	.60	.263	.356	.488	.844
Uribe,Juan	CWS	30	113	331	81	18	2	11	39	44	39	4.02	20	66	1	2	.33	.245	.294	.411	.705
Utley,Chase	Phi	30	155	615	184	44	3	30	112	109	118	7.05	63	111	12	4	.75	.299	.381	.527	.908
Valentin,Javier	Cin	33	89	167	42	10	0	5	17	23	21	4.37	15	30	0	0	.00	.251	.313	.401	.714
Varitek,Jason	Bos	37	122	395	94	20	1	13	45	52	50	4.30	51	113	1	1	.50	.238	.334	.392	.726
Vazquez,Ramon	Tex	32	105	289	71	15	2	5	40	28	34	4.04	35	67	1	1	.50	.246	.329	.363	.693
Velez,Eugenio	SF	27	86	241	68	13	5	2	32	21	32	4.60	16	38	19	8	.70	.282	.329	.402	.732
Venable,Will	SD	26	46	101	26	4	1	2	13	11	12	4.11	8	22	2	1	.67	.257	.312	.376	.688
Victorino,Shane	Phi	28	150	528	151	24	6	13	88	54	77	5.17	41	63	27	10	.73	.286	.345	.428	.774
Vidro,Jose	Sea	34	94	282	79	15	0	6	35	34	38	4.84	26	32	1	1	.50	.280	.345	.397	.742
Vizquel,Omar	SF	42	90	218	54	9	1	1	24	19	21	3.27	20	23	5	3	.62	.248	.317	.312	.629
Votto,Joey	Cin	25	157	586	180	40	2	30	87	102	120	7.55	74	141	13	7	.65	.307	.386	.536	.922
Ward,Daryle	ChC	34	99	176	44	11	0	6	18	28	24	4.73	19	36	0	0	.00	.250	.327	.415	.741
Weeks,Rickie	Mil	26	137	510	131	28	6	17	100	55	79	5.34	73	118	21	6	.78	.257	.364	.435	.799
Wells,Vernon	Tor	30	139	533	150	33	2	23	78	85	85	5.73	41	70	7	3	.70	.281	.336	.480	.817
Werth,Jayson	Phi	30	147	516	144	25	3	25	88	89	93	6.40	71	137	21	6	.78	.279	.369	.484	.854
Wieters,Matt	Bal	23	133	470	146	25	2	24	68	85	100	8.00	76	63	2	1	.67	.311	.407	.526	.932
Wigginton,Ty	Hou	30	140	520	140	31	1	23	67	75	78	5.28	45	103	5	4	.56	.269	.335	.465	.800
Wilkerson,Brad	Tor	32	101	261	62	16	1	9	38	32	35	4.50	39	77	3	3	.50	.238	.343	.410	.753
Willingham,Josh	Fla	30	138	507	137	31	3	23	76	82	87	6.08	70	109	4	2	.67	.270	.371	.479	.850
Willits,Reggie	LAA	28	81	103	29	5	0	0	18	8	13	4.45	16	18	6	2	.75	.282	.383	.330	.713
Wilson,Jack	Pit	31	132	493	135	25	2	7	57	43	58	4.18	29	52	4	3	.57	.274	.321	.375	.696
Winn,Randy	SF	35	155	586	168	37	3	11	77	63	84	5.15	50	89	17	6	.74	.287	.347	.416	.763
Wise,Dewayne	CWS	31	72	176	45	9	2	6	26	20	23	4.43	12	35	10	4	.71	.256	.303	.432	.735
Wood,Brandon	LAA	24	123	447	113	26	1	23	63	67	64	4.92	34	123	10	4	.71	.253	.307	.470	.777
Wright,David	NYM	26	160	618	192	46	2	33	113	120	136	8.19	89	116	17	6	.74	.311	.402	.552	.953
Youkilis,Kevin	Bos	30	155	608	176	47	2	23	102	101	112	6.69	87	123	4	3	.57	.289	.386	.487	.873
Young,Chris	Ari	25	145	554	141	39	4	26	86	79	86	5.34	56	128	17	6	.74	.255	.325	.480	.805
Young,Delmon	Min	23	135	485	146	27	3	11	66	72	72	5.44	25	84	14	5	.74	.301	.342	.437	.779
Young,Delwyn	LAD	27	65	114	31	9	0	3	15	15	16	5.01	8	25	0	0	.00	.272	.320	.430	.749
Young,Dmitri	Was	35	108	366	104	21	1	12	44	48	57	5.66	37	71	1	0	1.00	.284	.355	.445	.800
Young,Michael	Tex	32	159	654	194	37	3	14	94	85	97	5.45	51	109	8	3	.73	.297	.349	.427	.776
Zaun,Gregg	Tor	38	72	229	55	12	0	6	27	29	28	4.16	33	39	1	1	.50	.240	.341	.371	.712
Zimmerman,Ryan	Was	24	145	576	167	42	2	22	84	87	97	6.14	51	94	3	2	.60	.290	.351	.484	.835
Zobrist,Ben	TB	28	95	345	92	18	3	12	53	41	54	5.46	48	59	9	4	.69	.267	.358	.441	.798

Introduction to the Pitcher Projections

Bill James

Our worst projections each year, as we score ourselves, are those in which we project pitching time for pitchers who get hurt and don't pitch.   These were our five worst pitching projections for 2008:

Chuck James

	G	GS	IP	H	HR	BB	SO	W	L	Pct.	Sv	ERA
Actual	7	7	30	36	10	20	22	2	5	286	0	9.10
Projected	28	28	175	161	27	60	143	12	8	600	0	3.86

Mark Mulder

	G	GS	IP	H	HR	BB	SO	W	L	Pct.	Sv	ERA
Actual	3	1	2	4	0	2	2	0	0	0	0	10.80
Projected	23	23	143	152	17	47	88	7	9	438	0	4.34

Jason Hirsh

	G	GS	IP	H	HR	BB	SO	W	L	Pct.	Sv	ERA
Actual	4	1	9	15	3	4	6	0	0	0	0	8.31
Projected	28	28	169	155	20	64	133	11	8	579	0	3.83

Matt Morris

	G	GS	IP	H	HR	BB	SO	W	L	Pct.	Sv	ERA
Actual	5	5	22	41	6	7	9	0	4	0	0	9.67
Projected	31	31	192	207	21	53	120	10	11	476	0	4.17

Dontrelle Willis

	G	GS	IP	H	HR	BB	SO	W	L	Pct.	Sv	ERA
Actual	8	7	24	18	4	35	18	0	2	0	0	9.37
Projected	34	34	209	219	20	73	153	12	11	522	0	4.22

There were about 15 of those type projections in the majors; these were the worst.   It is, of course, somewhat embarrassing to miss the target by a margin of essentially 100%, but at the same time, most people understand that some pitchers get hurt and you don't know in advance who they will be. Setting those type of projections aside, our worst projections occur when we project a pitcher as a starter, and he winds up in the bullpen, or vice versa. Like Ryan Dempster Diving:

Ryan Dempster

	G	GS	IP	H	HR	BB	SO	W	L	Pct.	Sv	ERA
Actual	33	33	207	174	14	76	187	17	6	739	0	2.96
Projected	65	0	70	69	7	34	58	4	4	500	32	4.37

Or Brett Myers:

Brett Myers

	G	GS	IP	H	HR	BB	SO	W	L	Pct.	Sv	ERA
Actual	30	30	190	197	29	65	163	10	13	435	0	4.55
Projected	65	5	95	94	14	33	83	6	5	545	29	4.17

There were only about ten of those, since not a lot of pitchers run back and forth between the bullpen and a starting role. Oddly enough, I did a search to see if there was any pitcher in the majors whose ERA we had projected perfectly. There wasn't, but there were two guys on whom we had missed by only one point. But both of those, oddly enough, were players that we had projected into entirely the wrong roles:

Jon Lieber

	G	GS	IP	H	HR	BB	SO	W	L	Pct.	Sv	ERA
Actual	26	1	47	59	10	6	27	2	3	400	0	4.05
Projected	27	27	167	185	22	29	107	10	8	556	0	4.04

Chad Gaudin

	G	GS	IP	H	HR	BB	SO	W	L	Pct.	Sv	ERA
Actual	50	6	90	92	11	27	71	9	5	643	0	4.40
Projected	32	32	202	206	20	90	149	10	12	455	0	4.41

Thus creating low-scoring projections despite being right on the ERAs. Then, of course, there are the pitchers that we project to have minor roles, who step up and into larger roles:

Chad Durbin

	G	GS	IP	H	HR	BB	SO	W	L	Pct.	Sv	ERA
Actual	71	0	88	81	5	35	63	5	4	556	1	2.87
Projected	35	10	90	97	14	34	60	4	6	400	0	5.00

J.P. Howell

	G	GS	IP	H	HR	BB	SO	W	L	Pct.	Sv	ERA
Actual	64	0	89	62	6	39	92	6	1	857	3	2.22
Projected	8	8	42	47	5	16	40	2	3	400	0	4.93

There aren't very many of those in a year, since we tend to project pitchers on the assumption that they'll be healthy. In terms of just simply missing, it's hard to beat what we did last year on Cliff Lee:

Cliff Lee

	G	GS	IP	H	HR	BB	SO	W	L	Pct.	Sv	ERA
Actual	31	31	223	214	12	34	170	22	3	880	0	2.54
Projected	30	12	90	93	12	33	68	5	5	500	0	4.40

Although, in all fairness, we were almost equally bad on Gavin Floyd, Joe Saunders and Mike Mussina:

Gavin Floyd

	G	GS	IP	H	HR	BB	SO	W	L	Pct.	Sv	ERA
Actual	33	33	206	190	30	70	145	17	8	680	0	3.84
Projected	25	16	118	138	19	51	87	4	9	308	0	5.87

Joe Saunders

	G	GS	IP	H	HR	BB	SO	W	L	Pct.	Sv	ERA
Actual	31	31	198	187	21	53	103	17	7	708	0	3.41
Projected	25	25	151	160	15	48	108	8	9	471	0	4.05

Mike Mussina

	G	GS	IP	H	HR	BB	SO	W	L	Pct.	Sv	ERA
Actual	34	34	200	214	17	31	150	20	9	690	0	3.37
Projected	28	26	154	159	17	33	124	11	7	611	0	3.74

There are a lot of ways to miss; that's my point. You can project playing time for a pitcher who doesn't pitch, fail to project innings for a pitcher who does pitch, you can project a pitcher into the wrong role, and you can project him to be bad when he turns out to be really good. Or vice versa:

Barry Zito

	G	GS	IP	H	HR	BB	SO	W	L	Pct.	Sv	ERA
Actual	32	32	180	186	16	102	120	10	17	370	0	5.15
Projected	35	33	212	190	24	85	153	12	12	500	0	3.74

But at least we didn't pay him $100 million.

And believe it or not, we're not always *entirely* wrong. Sometimes we're pretty close. Scott Olsen, we had projected he would go 8-11, and he did:

Scott Olsen

	G	GS	IP	H	HR	BB	SO	W	L	Pct.	Sv	ERA
Actual	33	33	202	195	30	69	113	8	11	421	0	4.20
Projected	30	30	165	177	23	74	149	8	11	421	0	4.96

Although that's not a great projection, as we were off some on his innings and his ERA.   We had better overall projections for Ben Sheets and Derek Lowe:

Ben Sheets

	G	GS	IP	H	HR	BB	SO	W	L	Pct.	Sv	ERA
Actual	31	31	198	181	17	47	158	13	9	591	0	3.09
Projected	27	27	185	181	21	40	161	13	8	619	0	3.55

Derek Lowe

	G	GS	IP	H	HR	BB	SO	W	L	Pct.	Sv	ERA
Actual	34	34	211	194	14	45	147	14	11	560	0	3.24
Projected	32	32	212	216	19	61	134	13	11	542	0	3.78

Roy Oswalt, we missed his innings pitched by one and his ERA, strikeouts and walks by tiny margins, although we were off on his won-lost record:

Roy Oswalt

	G	GS	IP	H	HR	BB	SO	W	L	Pct.	Sv	ERA
Actual	32	32	209	199	23	47	165	17	10	630	0	3.54
Projected	31	31	210	209	16	49	167	14	9	609	0	3.51

Although honestly, I don't know why we would miss that, since he's had decisions in 80% of his starts throughout his career. We had good projections for David Bush, Sean Green and Paul Byrd:

David Bush

	G	GS	IP	H	HR	BB	SO	W	L	Pct.	Sv	ERA
Actual	31	29	185	163	29	48	109	9	10	474	0	4.18
Projected	32	31	184	198	25	40	129	11	10	524	0	4.26

Sean Green

	G	GS	IP	H	HR	BB	SO	W	L	Pct.	Sv	ERA
Actual	72	0	79	80	3	36	62	4	5	444	1	4.67
Projected	73	0	75	76	2	38	53	4	4	500	0	4.08

Paul Byrd

	G	GS	IP	H	HR	BB	SO	W	L	Pct.	Sv	ERA
Actual	30	30	180	204	31	34	82	11	12	478	0	4.60
Projected	28	28	180	209	25	33	92	9	11	450	0	4.45

We had good projections for veterans Tim Wakefield and Jose Valverde:

Jose Valverde

	G	GS	IP	H	HR	BB	SO	W	L	Pct.	Sv	ERA
Actual	74	0	72	62	10	23	83	6	3	667	44	3.38
Projected	63	0	67	52	7	29	83	5	3	625	40	3.36

Tim Wakefield

	G	GS	IP	H	HR	BB	SO	W	L	Pct.	Sv	ERA
Actual	30	30	181	154	25	60	117	10	11	476	0	4.13
Projected	29	29	181	174	24	63	123	11	9	550	0	4.03

We had very good projections for Mike Hampton, Yusmeiro Petit, Tyler Yates, Renyel Pinto, Saul Rivera, Jack Taschner, LaTroy Hawkins, and others too humorous to mention.   A blind pig will find an acorn if he hangs out under the oak tree.   Our strategy is to hang out under the oak tree and see what falls on our heads.

2009 Pitcher Projections

PLAYER			HOW MUCH			WHAT HE WILL GIVE UP					THE RESULTS					
Pitcher	Team	Age	G	GS	IP	H	HR	BB	SO	HB	W	L	Pct	Sv	BR/9	ERA
Aardsma,David	Bos	27	36	0	38	37	5	22	36	2	2	2	.500	0	14.4	4.81
Accardo,Jeremy	Tor	27	30	0	30	28	2	9	24	1	2	1	.667	0	11.4	3.37
Acosta,Manny	Atl	28	50	0	54	49	5	36	45	2	3	3	.500	1	14.5	4.43
Adams,Mike	SD	30	64	0	75	69	7	27	73	0	5	4	.556	0	11.5	3.56
Affeldt,Jeremy	Cin	30	65	0	77	79	8	34	59	3	4	5	.444	0	13.6	4.39
Arredondo,Jose	LAA	25	61	0	76	72	6	31	66	1	5	4	.556	32	12.3	3.72
Arroyo,Bronson	Cin	32	32	32	212	222	27	64	152	10	11	12	.478	0	12.6	4.25
Ayala,Luis	NYM	31	78	0	76	79	8	18	49	4	5	4	.556	2	12.0	3.94
Backe,Brandon	Hou	31	24	24	130	144	22	60	91	4	5	9	.357	0	14.4	5.49
Baek,Cha Seung	SD	29	30	25	150	161	20	46	100	5	7	9	.438	0	12.7	4.37
Baker,Scott	Min	27	29	29	181	191	22	41	142	6	10	10	.500	0	11.8	3.93
Balfour,Grant	TB	31	65	0	74	53	5	37	99	1	6	2	.750	0	11.1	3.01
Bannister,Brian	KC	28	30	30	173	183	22	52	107	6	8	11	.421	0	12.5	4.26
Bass,Brian	Bal	27	38	8	85	99	10	28	51	4	4	6	.400	0	13.9	4.97
Batista,Miguel	Sea	38	46	13	94	102	10	42	58	3	4	7	.364	0	14.1	4.81
Bautista,Denny	Pit	28	57	0	64	73	4	37	48	4	2	5	.286	0	16.0	5.47
Beam,T.J.	Pit	28	43	0	54	54	7	20	42	1	3	3	.500	0	12.5	4.14
Beckett,Josh	Bos	29	29	29	189	176	21	55	176	7	13	8	.619	0	11.3	3.57
Bedard,Erik	Sea	30	16	16	89	82	8	35	86	3	5	5	.500	0	12.1	3.72
Beimel,Joe	LAD	32	71	0	52	53	3	22	30	1	3	3	.500	0	13.2	3.98
Bell,Heath	SD	31	68	0	72	63	5	22	74	2	5	3	.625	0	10.9	3.16
Bennett,Jeff	Atl	29	77	2	97	96	8	44	66	7	5	5	.500	1	13.6	4.31
Benoit,Joaquin	Tex	31	36	0	37	34	4	18	34	1	2	2	.500	0	12.9	4.13
Bergmann,Jason	Was	27	33	21	139	138	20	51	113	4	7	9	.438	0	12.5	4.25
Betancourt,Rafael	Cle	34	67	0	72	64	7	18	70	0	5	3	.625	0	10.2	3.19
Billingsley,Chad	LAD	24	33	30	193	174	17	84	189	6	12	9	.571	0	12.3	3.69
Blackburn,Nick	Min	27	33	33	196	222	20	41	104	7	10	12	.455	0	12.4	4.18
Blanton,Joe	Phi	28	32	32	193	207	18	55	110	4	11	10	.524	0	12.4	3.99
Blevins,Jerry	Oak	25	52	0	56	48	3	17	59	3	4	2	.667	0	10.9	3.07
Bonderman,Jeremy	Det	26	24	24	150	157	17	51	123	4	8	8	.500	0	12.7	4.23
Bonser,Boof	Min	27	53	6	103	110	15	36	90	2	5	7	.417	0	12.9	4.61
Boyer,Blaine	Atl	27	63	0	58	64	4	30	51	3	3	4	.429	0	15.1	5.00
Braden,Dallas	Oak	25	21	16	103	107	10	35	79	2	5	6	.455	0	12.6	4.09
Bradford,Chad	TB	34	66	0	61	62	3	16	34	4	4	3	.571	0	12.1	3.55
Bray,Bill	Cin	26	61	0	42	43	4	17	46	1	2	2	.500	0	13.1	4.26
Breslow,Craig	Min	28	60	0	56	52	3	23	53	2	3	3	.500	0	12.4	3.66
Britton,Chris	NYY	26	22	0	30	30	3	11	25	0	2	1	.667	0	12.3	3.76
Brocail,Doug	Hou	42	64	0	63	62	5	22	48	3	4	3	.571	0	12.4	3.78
Broxton,Jonathan	LAD	25	70	0	70	56	4	27	87	2	4	3	.571	30	10.9	3.03
Bruney,Brian	NYY	27	49	0	52	45	5	36	52	3	3	3	.500	0	14.5	4.50
Buchholz,Taylor	Col	27	57	0	59	59	7	17	42	2	4	3	.571	4	11.9	3.92
Buehrle,Mark	CWS	30	34	34	221	239	26	50	128	5	12	12	.500	0	12.0	4.00
Burnett,A.J.	Tor	32	33	32	224	199	21	88	218	11	14	11	.560	0	12.0	3.62
Burnett,Sean	Pit	26	67	0	60	76	7	32	29	2	2	5	.286	0	16.5	6.27
Burres,Brian	Bal	28	35	8	74	86	10	35	50	4	3	5	.375	0	15.2	5.63
Burton,Jared	Cin	28	42	0	45	44	4	20	40	2	2	3	.400	0	13.2	4.11
Bush,David	Mil	29	31	29	192	195	27	44	128	13	11	10	.524	0	11.8	3.99
Byrd,Paul	Bos	38	29	29	188	218	28	33	93	6	10	11	.476	0	12.3	4.51
Byrdak,Tim	Hou	35	59	0	57	52	7	31	56	2	3	3	.500	0	13.4	4.36
Cabrera,Daniel	Bal	28	25	25	141	141	15	78	108	9	7	9	.438	0	14.6	4.85
Cabrera,Fernando	Bal	27	27	0	34	31	6	17	39	0	2	2	.500	0	12.7	4.42
Cain,Matt	SF	24	32	32	213	185	19	92	192	6	13	11	.542	0	12.0	3.57
Camp,Shawn	Tor	33	32	0	32	38	4	9	23	2	1	2	.333	0	13.8	4.97
Campillo,Jorge	Atl	30	35	28	166	173	16	45	111	3	10	8	.556	0	12.0	3.86
Capps,Matt	Pit	25	41	0	47	45	5	6	36	2	3	2	.600	29	10.1	3.20
Carlson,Jesse	Tor	28	67	0	62	60	7	19	58	4	3	3	.500	5	12.0	3.86
Carlyle,Buddy	Atl	31	52	0	75	71	10	25	66	2	5	4	.556	0	11.8	3.90
Carmona,Fausto	Cle	25	25	25	141	146	12	53	88	9	8	8	.500	0	13.3	4.17
Carpenter,Chris	StL	34	8	8	45	42	4	11	36	2	3	2	.600	0	11.0	3.34
Carrasco,D.J.	CWS	32	50	0	57	66	6	25	36	4	2	4	.333	0	15.0	5.40
Casilla,Santiago	Oak	28	49	0	55	49	5	25	57	2	3	3	.500	2	12.4	3.78
Cherry,Rocky	Bal	29	33	0	32	32	4	17	30	2	2	2	.500	0	14.3	4.65
Colome,Jesus	Was	31	58	0	68	66	7	35	51	2	3	4	.429	0	13.6	4.41
Condrey,Clay	Phi	33	56	0	67	79	6	20	36	3	3	4	.429	0	13.7	4.74
Contreras,Jose	CWS	37	11	11	63	65	7	22	44	3	3	4	.429	0	12.9	4.29
Cook,Aaron	Col	30	29	29	182	209	14	51	74	6	11	10	.524	0	13.2	4.34
Corcoran,Roy	Sea	29	57	0	88	83	3	49	71	4	5	5	.500	0	13.9	3.93
Cordero,Francisco	Cin	34	67	0	68	60	5	29	77	2	4	3	.571	34	12.0	3.53
Cormier,Lance	Bal	28	49	2	81	98	11	38	51	2	3	6	.333	0	15.3	5.78
Corpas,Manny	Col	26	77	0	82	82	6	21	60	3	5	4	.556	32	11.6	3.54
Correia,Kevin	SF	28	29	12	110	119	13	47	78	4	5	8	.385	0	13.9	4.79
Cotts,Neal	ChC	29	55	0	42	40	6	21	39	2	2	2	.500	0	13.5	4.50
Crain,Jesse	Min	27	65	0	61	61	6	21	39	2	3	3	.500	0	12.4	3.86
Cruz,Juan	Ari	30	57	0	57	47	5	29	63	5	3	3	.500	0	12.8	3.74
Cueto,Johnny	Cin	23	28	28	154	155	24	52	151	14	8	10	.444	0	12.9	4.56
Danks,John	CWS	24	33	33	201	191	24	72	173	5	12	11	.522	0	12.0	4.00
Davies,Kyle	KC	25	25	25	139	149	18	66	100	3	7	9	.438	0	14.1	4.79
Davis,Doug	Ari	33	29	29	159	165	16	70	121	4	8	10	.444	0	13.5	4.41
Davis,Jason	Pit	29	24	8	66	76	6	26	41	3	3	5	.375	0	14.3	4.86
de la Rosa,Jorge	Col	28	29	24	153	168	19	78	124	5	7	10	.412	0	14.8	5.27

2009 Pitcher Projections

Pitcher	Team	Age	G	GS	IP	H	HR	BB	SO	HB	W	L	Pct	Sv	BR/9	ERA
Delcarmen,Manny	Bos	27	71	0	81	71	5	35	80	3	6	3	.667	1	12.1	3.44
Dempster,Ryan	ChC	32	30	30	195	182	16	90	166	7	12	10	.545	0	12.9	3.89
Devine,Joey	Oak	25	55	0	58	43	2	28	72	3	4	2	.667	21	11.5	3.01
Dickey,R.A.	Sea	34	34	13	102	119	16	42	61	5	3	8	.273	0	14.6	5.58
Dotel,Octavio	CWS	35	65	0	63	51	9	25	81	4	4	3	.571	0	11.4	3.59
Downs,Scott	Tor	33	61	0	67	63	6	24	54	2	4	3	.571	0	12.0	3.70
Duchscherer,Justin	Oak	31	24	24	140	120	13	35	105	6	10	6	.625	0	10.4	3.12
Duckworth,Brandon	KC	33	14	14	76	86	9	32	53	4	3	5	.375	0	14.4	5.07
Duke,Zach	Pit	26	28	28	180	221	17	48	92	6	8	12	.400	0	13.8	4.84
Durbin,Chad	Phi	31	73	0	86	89	12	32	59	5	4	5	.444	0	13.2	4.59
Eaton,Adam	Phi	31	10	9	54	60	8	20	37	3	2	4	.333	0	13.8	5.03
Embree,Alan	Oak	39	50	0	48	46	5	16	42	1	3	3	.500	0	11.8	3.74
Estes,Shawn	SD	36	10	10	51	56	7	25	30	2	2	4	.333	0	14.6	5.21
Eveland,Dana	Oak	25	26	26	152	149	9	70	124	11	8	9	.471	0	13.6	4.03
Eyre,Scott	Phi	37	46	0	34	33	3	16	32	1	2	2	.500	0	13.2	4.09
Farnsworth,Kyle	Det	33	53	0	54	50	8	23	58	1	3	3	.500	0	12.3	4.15
Feierabend,Ryan	Sea	23	15	15	79	97	11	32	58	4	3	6	.333	0	15.2	5.76
Feldman,Scott	Tex	26	28	25	153	161	17	63	88	10	8	9	.471	0	13.8	4.64
Feliciano,Pedro	NYM	32	86	0	50	46	4	22	45	3	3	3	.500	0	12.8	3.90
Figueroa,Nelson	NYM	35	18	3	33	35	5	14	20	2	2	2	.500	0	13.9	4.90
Floyd,Gavin	CWS	26	33	33	217	215	34	87	157	16	12	12	.500	0	13.2	4.00
Fogg,Josh	Cin	32	21	15	83	97	12	28	44	5	3	6	.333	0	14.1	5.28
Fossum,Casey	Det	31	38	0	54	62	8	22	40	5	2	4	.333	0	14.8	5.53
Francis,Jeff	Col	28	29	29	176	191	22	59	120	7	10	10	.500	0	13.1	4.56
Francisco,Frank	Tex	29	57	0	61	51	5	30	69	1	4	3	.571	26	12.1	3.55
Franklin,Ryan	StL	36	71	0	79	83	11	24	42	3	4	5	.444	2	12.5	4.36
Frasor,Jason	Tor	31	43	0	44	39	4	22	42	1	2	2	.500	0	12.7	3.81
Fuentes,Brian	Col	33	63	0	62	50	6	25	70	5	5	2	.714	4	11.6	3.43
Gabbard,Kason	Tex	27	26	26	137	140	15	73	101	6	7	8	.467	0	14.4	4.80
Gagne,Eric	Mil	33	55	0	52	41	6	16	61	2	4	2	.667	5	10.2	3.11
Galarraga,Armando	Det	27	30	28	188	189	28	70	146	12	10	11	.476	0	13.0	4.47
Gallagher,Sean	Oak	23	21	20	109	107	10	60	99	5	5	7	.417	0	14.2	4.52
Gallardo,Yovani	Mil	23	31	31	196	179	13	76	201	3	13	9	.591	0	11.8	3.61
Garcia,Freddy	Det	33	26	26	168	170	23	48	120	6	10	9	.526	0	12.0	4.05
Garland,Jon	LAA	29	30	30	186	203	22	57	93	5	10	11	.476	0	12.8	4.38
Garza,Matt	TB	25	29	29	183	181	16	63	153	8	11	9	.550	0	12.4	3.85
Gaudin,Chad	ChC	26	44	3	68	68	7	28	51	3	4	4	.500	0	13.1	4.19
Geary,Geoff	Hou	32	51	0	57	58	4	18	38	3	3	3	.500	0	12.5	3.87
Glavine,Tom	Atl	43	25	25	139	146	15	50	73	3	8	8	.500	0	12.9	4.23
Glover,Gary	Det	32	49	0	58	64	8	21	39	2	3	4	.429	0	13.5	4.80
Gonzalez,Mike	Atl	31	48	0	45	35	3	21	52	1	3	2	.600	26	11.4	3.19
Gordon,Tom	Phi	41	40	0	35	30	4	13	35	1	2	1	.667	4	11.3	3.42
Gorzelanny,Tom	Pit	26	25	25	157	159	15	70	114	6	8	10	.444	0	13.5	4.34
Grabow,John	Pit	30	73	0	72	71	8	32	63	2	4	4	.500	0	13.1	4.24
Green,Sean	Sea	30	62	0	72	73	2	35	52	4	4	4	.500	0	14.0	4.07
Gregg,Kevin	Fla	31	64	0	61	56	5	25	55	3	4	3	.571	3	12.4	3.71
Greinke,Zack	KC	25	30	30	194	196	23	52	156	7	12	10	.545	0	11.8	3.98
Grilli,Jason	Col	32	59	0	78	81	7	34	55	4	4	4	.500	0	13.7	4.44
Guardado,Eddie	Min	38	57	0	52	49	8	16	43	1	3	3	.500	0	11.4	3.78
Guerrier,Matt	Min	30	73	0	68	68	8	24	48	2	4	4	.500	0	12.4	4.10
Guthrie,Jeremy	Bal	30	30	30	195	194	22	68	131	9	11	11	.500	0	12.5	4.03
Halladay,Roy	Tor	32	32	32	241	228	18	44	172	7	17	10	.630	0	10.4	3.18
Hamels,Cole	Phi	25	32	32	223	192	29	58	214	3	16	8	.667	0	10.2	3.24
Hammel,Jason	TB	26	45	2	72	78	8	30	58	3	3	5	.375	2	13.9	4.73
Hampson,Justin	SD	29	47	0	43	47	4	17	28	2	2	3	.400	0	13.8	4.67
Hampton,Mike	Atl	36	22	22	132	145	14	53	66	2	7	8	.467	0	13.6	4.61
Hanrahan,Joel	Was	27	65	0	77	78	10	30	70	2	3	5	.375	25	12.9	4.00
Hansen,Craig	Pit	25	46	0	47	50	3	32	37	3	2	3	.400	3	16.3	5.26
Harang,Aaron	Cin	31	29	29	184	192	25	50	155	5	10	10	.500	0	12.1	4.11
Harden,Rich	ChC	27	24	24	144	109	11	61	151	2	11	5	.688	0	10.8	3.02
Haren,Dan	Ari	28	32	32	210	206	23	47	174	6	14	10	.583	0	11.1	3.59
Hawkins,LaTroy	Hou	36	62	0	62	60	5	19	44	0	4	3	.571	0	11.5	3.51
Heilman,Aaron	NYM	30	70	0	64	58	6	27	56	4	4	3	.571	0	12.5	3.82
Hendrickson,Mark	Fla	35	38	9	99	113	12	30	57	2	5	6	.455	0	13.2	4.67
Hennessey,Brad	SF	29	17	8	57	62	7	22	31	3	2	4	.333	0	13.7	4.83
Hensley,Clay	SD	29	52	0	60	61	5	27	40	1	3	4	.429	0	13.4	4.27
Herges,Matt	Col	39	47	0	52	57	5	19	35	2	3	3	.500	0	13.5	4.50
Hernandez,Felix	Sea	23	31	31	205	202	19	74	188	6	11	12	.478	0	12.4	3.86
Hernandez,Livan	Col	34	27	27	150	174	19	48	84	4	8	9	.471	0	13.6	4.90
Hill,Shawn	Was	28	15	15	75	83	5	22	45	4	4	5	.444	0	13.1	4.12
Hochevar,Luke	KC	25	26	26	146	163	20	52	100	8	6	10	.375	0	13.7	4.95
Hoffman,Trevor	SD	41	42	0	42	35	4	10	38	0	2	2	.500	41	9.6	2.94
Howell,J.P.	TB	26	64	0	87	87	10	35	84	5	5	5	.500	1	13.1	4.37
Howry,Bob	ChC	35	64	0	63	62	8	16	52	2	4	3	.571	0	11.4	3.72
Hughes,Phil	NYY	23	22	22	125	110	9	46	122	3	9	5	.643	0	11.4	3.35
Isringhausen,Jason	StL	36	28	0	30	24	3	13	27	1	2	1	.667	0	11.4	3.39
Jackson,Edwin	TB	25	31	29	180	197	23	79	125	5	10	11	.476	0	14.0	4.59
Jenks,Bobby	CWS	28	57	0	67	58	3	22	62	2	4	3	.571	30	11.0	3.10
Jimenez,Cesar	Sea	24	41	4	46	48	4	22	34	1	2	3	.400	0	13.9	4.61
Jimenez,Ubaldo	Col	25	32	32	195	190	18	106	165	11	11	11	.500	0	14.2	4.49
Johnson,Jason	LAD	35	27	2	39	45	5	13	22	2	2	3	.400	0	13.8	4.89

478

2009 Pitcher Projections

Pitcher	Team	Age	G	GS	IP	H	HR	BB	SO	HB	W	L	Pct	Sv	BR/9	ERA
Johnson,Jim	Bal	26	58	0	70	82	8	30	47	5	3	5	.375	0	15.0	5.36
Johnson,Josh	Fla	25	21	21	139	139	10	58	119	3	8	7	.533	0	12.9	3.92
Johnson,Randy	Ari	45	28	28	170	153	21	41	178	8	12	7	.632	0	10.7	3.40
Julio,Jorge	Atl	30	30	0	34	32	5	17	33	1	2	2	.500	0	13.2	4.50
Jurrjens,Jair	Atl	23	29	29	178	185	15	64	132	4	10	9	.526	0	12.8	4.02
Karstens,Jeff	Pit	26	24	24	151	167	19	46	105	3	7	10	.412	0	12.9	4.49
Kazmir,Scott	TB	25	29	29	162	144	17	74	177	5	10	8	.556	0	12.4	3.80
Kendrick,Kyle	Phi	24	20	18	110	126	13	33	51	7	5	7	.417	0	13.6	4.82
Kensing,Logan	Fla	26	43	0	46	41	6	25	45	3	2	3	.400	0	13.5	4.33
Kobayashi,Masa	Cle	35	52	0	51	56	7	14	37	0	3	3	.500	2	12.4	4.31
Kuo,Hong-Chih	LAD	27	42	1	69	59	5	27	84	2	5	3	.625	0	11.5	3.34
Kuroda,Hiroki	LAD	34	31	31	192	193	25	54	125	1	12	10	.545	0	11.6	3.87
Lackey,John	LAA	30	26	26	175	175	17	51	141	9	11	9	.550	0	12.1	3.81
Laffey,Aaron	Cle	24	22	22	121	134	10	37	72	9	6	7	.462	0	13.4	4.36
Lannan,John	Was	24	29	29	177	174	18	71	103	7	9	11	.450	0	12.8	4.08
League,Brandon	Tor	26	45	0	48	51	4	19	32	4	2	3	.400	0	13.9	4.45
Ledezma,Wil	Ari	28	29	3	46	48	5	23	34	1	2	3	.400	0	14.1	4.84
Lee,Cliff	Cle	30	29	29	194	197	21	42	146	7	14	9	.609	0	11.4	3.90
Lester,Jon	Bos	25	32	32	212	209	19	88	168	8	12	11	.522	0	12.9	4.02
Lewis,Jensen	Cle	25	58	0	70	65	7	27	70	4	4	4	.500	2	12.3	3.84
Lidge,Brad	Phi	32	71	0	70	54	6	31	96	4	5	3	.625	39	11.4	3.26
Lilly,Ted	ChC	33	32	32	208	194	31	75	176	6	12	11	.522	0	11.9	3.95
Lincecum,Tim	SF	25	34	33	240	192	14	94	272	5	17	9	.654	0	10.9	3.02
Lincoln,Mike	Cin	34	64	0	63	63	8	22	48	2	3	4	.429	0	12.4	4.13
Lindstrom,Matt	Fla	29	68	0	61	64	4	30	54	3	3	4	.429	27	14.3	4.51
Linebrink,Scott	CWS	32	55	0	51	46	6	16	43	1	3	2	.600	0	11.1	3.60
Liriano,Francisco	Min	25	28	28	166	151	14	61	171	2	11	8	.579	0	11.6	3.62
Litsch,Jesse	Tor	24	27	27	180	190	21	45	108	10	9	11	.450	0	12.2	4.06
Liz,Radhames	Bal	26	18	18	98	98	16	62	91	6	4	7	.364	0	15.2	5.59
Loe,Kameron	Tex	27	20	0	46	55	5	18	26	1	2	3	.400	0	14.5	5.24
Lohse,Kyle	StL	30	30	30	191	210	22	56	117	7	10	11	.476	0	12.9	4.41
Looper,Braden	StL	34	30	30	187	197	20	52	104	7	11	10	.524	0	12.3	4.03
Lopez,Aquilino	Det	34	46	0	87	87	13	28	78	3	5	5	.500	0	12.2	4.20
Lopez,Javier	Bos	31	66	0	57	58	3	26	38	4	3	3	.500	0	13.9	4.14
Lowe,Derek	LAD	36	32	32	206	205	17	56	132	4	14	9	.609	0	11.6	3.60
Lowe,Mark	Sea	26	49	0	57	61	5	30	51	3	2	4	.333	0	14.8	4.94
Lyon,Brandon	Ari	29	54	0	55	61	5	15	35	1	3	3	.500	3	12.6	4.16
Maddux,Greg	LAD	43	30	30	186	196	19	29	107	5	11	10	.524	0	11.1	4.01
Madson,Ryan	Phi	28	77	0	84	88	9	26	66	4	5	5	.500	0	12.6	4.15
Mahay,Ron	KC	38	55	0	60	57	6	29	51	1	3	4	.429	0	13.0	4.07
Maholm,Paul	Pit	27	29	29	203	216	21	69	134	9	10	13	.435	0	13.0	4.33
Maine,John	NYM	28	25	25	145	135	18	62	122	4	9	8	.529	0	12.5	3.98
Majewski,Gary	Cin	29	44	0	45	55	4	17	28	3	2	3	.400	0	15.0	5.28
Manning,Charlie	Was	30	64	0	48	43	5	26	45	2	2	3	.400	0	13.3	4.06
Marmol,Carlos	ChC	26	80	0	87	65	9	46	97	7	6	4	.600	8	12.2	3.55
Marquis,Jason	ChC	30	29	27	167	174	22	65	94	9	9	10	.474	0	13.4	4.60
Marshall,Sean	ChC	26	37	9	82	80	11	32	59	3	5	4	.556	0	12.6	4.14
Marte,Damaso	NYY	34	67	0	56	46	4	25	60	3	4	2	.667	0	11.9	3.40
Martinez,Pedro	NYM	37	20	20	120	106	13	32	122	7	9	5	.643	0	10.9	3.36
Masset,Nick	Cin	27	35	0	57	71	6	25	40	3	2	4	.333	0	15.6	5.82
Matsuzaka,Daisuke	Bos	28	30	30	184	160	17	77	174	7	12	8	.600	0	11.9	3.58
McCarthy,Brandon	Tex	25	23	23	121	121	18	44	93	2	7	7	.500	0	12.4	4.26
McClellan,Kyle	StL	25	55	0	63	62	5	20	51	2	4	3	.571	0	12.0	3.77
McClung,Seth	Mil	28	37	7	85	81	10	49	73	5	4	5	.444	0	14.3	4.69
McGowan,Dustin	Tor	27	22	22	128	124	12	52	110	5	7	7	.500	0	12.7	3.95
Meche,Gil	KC	30	32	32	210	212	24	77	160	4	11	13	.458	0	12.6	4.10
Meredith,Cla	SD	26	63	0	64	66	5	17	48	2	4	3	.571	0	12.0	3.74
Miller,Andrew	Fla	24	27	20	114	118	9	61	97	9	5	7	.417	0	14.8	4.78
Miller,Trever	TB	36	66	0	47	43	5	21	45	4	3	3	.500	6	13.0	3.96
Millwood,Kevin	Tex	34	27	27	175	194	18	54	131	5	10	10	.500	0	13.0	4.40
Miner,Zach	Det	27	40	15	130	139	12	59	81	3	7	8	.467	0	13.9	4.57
Misch,Pat	SF	27	13	3	34	38	4	10	26	2	1	2	.333	0	13.2	4.59
Moehler,Brian	Hou	37	31	29	160	191	22	42	86	4	7	11	.389	0	13.3	4.93
Morrow,Brandon	Sea	24	27	27	139	111	15	88	155	1	8	8	.500	0	12.9	3.84
Moseley,Dustin	LAA	27	12	11	50	59	6	18	32	2	2	3	.400	0	14.2	5.19
Mota,Guillermo	Mil	35	57	0	56	52	7	22	47	1	3	3	.500	0	12.1	3.86
Moyer,Jamie	Phi	46	32	32	193	203	26	54	114	7	11	11	.500	0	12.3	4.23
Mujica,Edward	Cle	25	39	0	45	49	4	11	39	1	3	2	.600	0	12.2	3.93
Mussina,Mike	NYY	40	34	34	211	221	22	42	166	6	14	10	.583	0	11.5	3.74
Myers,Brett	Phi	28	30	30	210	211	31	73	182	7	12	12	.500	0	12.5	4.26
Nathan,Joe	Min	34	66	0	68	47	4	20	80	1	5	3	.625	39	9.0	1.99
Nelson,Joe	Fla	34	68	0	64	51	8	30	72	3	4	3	.571	2	11.8	3.58
Nippert,Dustin	Tex	28	21	12	96	106	10	46	82	2	5	6	.455	0	14.4	4.97
Nolasco,Ricky	Fla	26	32	31	205	207	28	52	176	10	12	11	.522	0	11.8	3.98
Nunez,Leo	KC	25	49	0	58	58	7	19	41	2	3	3	.500	0	12.3	4.01
Nunez,Vladimir	Atl	34	40	0	58	61	9	26	43	3	3	4	.429	0	14.0	5.02
Ohlendorf,Ross	Pit	26	13	13	70	89	9	24	52	3	2	5	.286	0	14.9	5.72
Ohman,Will	Atl	31	79	0	50	44	4	23	50	2	3	2	.600	0	12.4	3.69
Okajima,Hideki	Bos	33	61	0	61	51	6	20	57	1	5	2	.714	0	10.6	3.19
Oliver,Darren	LAA	38	48	0	71	75	9	23	45	3	4	4	.500	0	12.8	4.30
Olsen,Scott	Fla	25	32	32	199	205	29	80	153	4	10	12	.455	0	13.1	4.58

479

2009 Pitcher Projections

PLAYER			HOW MUCH			WHAT HE WILL GIVE UP					THE RESULTS					
Pitcher	Team	Age	G	GS	IP	H	HR	BB	SO	HB	W	L	Pct	Sv	BR/9	ERA
Olson,Garrett	Bal	25	26	26	130	142	17	61	102	7	6	9	.400	0	14.5	5.18
Osoria,Franquelis	Pit	27	21	0	30	38	3	9	17	3	1	2	.333	0	15.0	5.63
Oswalt,Roy	Hou	31	33	33	215	212	18	49	170	8	16	11	.593	0	11.3	3.50
Owings,Micah	Cin	26	25	21	118	124	13	43	91	11	6	7	.462	0	13.6	4.52
Padilla,Vicente	Tex	31	26	26	151	161	19	55	105	12	8	9	.471	0	13.6	4.72
Papelbon,Jonathan	Bos	28	64	0	71	53	6	16	78	3	5	3	.625	41	9.1	2.04
Park,Chan Ho	LAD	36	62	2	85	94	14	35	66	6	4	6	.400	0	14.3	5.36
Parra,Manny	Mil	26	30	26	154	156	11	61	142	5	9	8	.529	0	13.0	3.95
Parrish,John	Tor	31	19	6	53	55	4	32	42	2	2	4	.333	0	15.1	4.87
Pavano,Carl	NYY	33	14	14	69	76	7	17	43	4	4	4	.500	0	12.7	4.22
Peavy,Jake	SD	28	32	32	202	173	19	65	202	7	14	8	.636	0	10.9	3.26
Pelfrey,Mike	NYM	25	31	31	211	225	14	82	140	17	11	12	.478	0	13.8	4.35
Pena,Tony	Ari	27	67	0	70	67	6	19	51	3	5	3	.625	2	11.4	3.55
Penny,Brad	LAD	31	22	21	130	134	12	42	90	4	8	7	.533	0	12.5	3.92
Peralta,Joel	KC	33	40	0	53	54	8	14	41	2	3	3	.500	0	11.9	4.09
Percival,Troy	TB	39	47	0	42	30	6	18	38	1	3	2	.600	23	10.5	3.25
Perez,Chris	StL	23	46	0	48	35	5	33	56	5	3	2	.600	8	13.7	3.90
Perez,Odalis	Was	32	30	30	171	192	21	48	113	5	8	11	.421	0	12.9	4.51
Perez,Oliver	NYM	27	34	34	204	186	31	109	205	10	11	12	.478	0	13.5	4.53
Perez,Rafael	Cle	27	71	0	77	70	6	23	71	2	5	3	.625	2	11.1	3.32
Perkins,Glen	Min	26	27	27	158	175	23	56	117	7	7	11	.389	0	13.6	4.91
Petit,Yusmeiro	Ari	24	21	13	76	75	13	21	59	1	4	4	.500	0	11.5	4.05
Pettitte,Andy	NYY	37	30	30	192	205	18	51	147	3	12	10	.545	0	12.1	3.90
Pineiro,Joel	StL	30	24	22	142	159	19	43	87	4	7	9	.438	0	13.1	4.63
Pinto,Renyel	Fla	26	45	0	40	35	4	25	39	3	2	2	.500	0	14.2	4.34
Ponson,Sidney	NYY	32	20	18	106	128	12	36	58	4	5	7	.417	0	14.3	5.22
Proctor,Scott	LAD	32	31	0	30	29	5	13	27	1	2	2	.500	0	12.9	4.44
Putz,J.J.	Sea	32	53	0	55	46	5	19	59	2	4	2	.667	28	11.0	3.23
Qualls,Chad	Ari	30	76	0	77	72	7	22	63	4	5	3	.625	30	11.5	3.52
Ramirez,Edwar	NYY	28	56	0	53	39	6	24	74	4	4	2	.667	0	11.4	3.38
Ramirez,Horacio	CWS	29	43	0	41	47	5	15	18	1	2	3	.400	0	13.8	4.96
Ramirez,Ramon	KC	27	66	0	67	62	6	28	62	1	4	4	.500	1	12.2	3.74
Rasner,Darrell	NYY	28	26	18	109	121	11	30	67	6	6	6	.500	0	13.0	4.33
Rauch,Jon	Ari	30	68	0	66	60	8	19	57	1	4	3	.571	3	10.9	3.48
Ray,Chris	Bal	27	45	0	45	36	6	18	42	2	3	2	.600	17	11.2	3.44
Redding,Tim	Was	31	30	30	168	188	24	63	115	6	7	12	.368	0	13.8	5.01
Reyes,Anthony	Cle	27	29	29	168	159	23	53	135	9	10	9	.526	0	11.8	3.88
Reyes,Dennys	Min	32	77	0	51	50	4	25	43	2	3	3	.500	0	13.6	4.16
Reyes,Jo-Jo	Atl	24	21	21	102	107	14	51	80	3	5	7	.417	0	14.2	4.95
Rhodes,Arthur	Fla	39	66	0	38	34	2	14	39	1	3	2	.600	2	11.6	3.29
Rincon,Juan	Cle	30	46	0	56	55	5	23	50	2	3	3	.500	0	12.9	4.01
Riske,David	Mil	32	38	0	33	30	4	15	27	1	2	2	.500	0	12.5	3.95
Rivera,Mariano	NYY	39	61	0	70	56	3	12	66	4	5	2	.714	43	9.3	2.07
Rivera,Saul	Was	31	74	0	80	80	3	33	60	3	4	5	.444	0	13.0	3.80
Robertson,Nate	Det	31	40	16	116	128	16	41	77	3	6	7	.462	0	13.3	4.77
Rodney,Fernando	Det	32	49	0	54	47	5	29	55	4	3	3	.500	4	13.3	3.96
Rodriguez,Francisco	LAA	27	73	0	66	47	5	30	85	1	4	3	.571	43	10.6	2.90
Rodriguez,Wandy	Hou	30	25	25	136	141	17	51	110	6	7	8	.467	0	13.1	4.45
Rogers,Kenny	Det	44	26	26	149	163	17	49	76	6	8	9	.471	0	13.2	4.52
Romero,J.C.	Phi	33	80	0	53	46	4	31	43	3	3	3	.500	0	13.6	3.96
Rowland-Smith,Ryan	Sea	26	37	20	154	155	14	70	135	5	7	10	.412	0	13.4	4.26
Rupe,Josh	Tex	26	48	0	90	102	10	41	54	8	4	6	.400	0	15.1	5.44
Rusch,Glendon	Col	34	42	10	96	111	13	31	70	2	5	6	.455	0	13.5	4.93
Ryan,B.J.	Tor	33	61	0	61	46	4	27	72	2	4	3	.571	38	11.1	3.02
Saarloos,Kirk	Oak	30	13	2	41	48	5	14	20	2	2	3	.400	0	14.0	5.13
Sabathia,CC	Mil	28	34	34	240	226	21	70	205	8	16	10	.615	0	11.4	3.48
Sadler,Billy	SF	27	36	0	53	42	5	32	59	5	3	3	.500	0	13.4	3.91
Saito,Takashi	LAD	39	50	0	52	44	5	14	55	3	4	2	.667	20	10.6	3.09
Sampson,Chris	Hou	31	57	5	102	107	11	19	51	3	6	5	.545	0	11.4	3.78
Sanchez,Anibal	Fla	25	25	25	131	131	14	58	110	7	7	8	.467	0	13.5	4.36
Sanchez,Duaner	NYM	29	59	0	47	44	4	19	35	3	3	2	.600	0	12.6	3.91
Sanchez,Jonathan	SF	26	24	24	132	121	10	64	140	8	7	8	.467	0	13.2	3.90
Santana,Ervin	LAA	26	31	31	210	206	25	63	177	11	12	11	.522	0	12.0	3.90
Santana,Johan	NYM	30	34	34	230	189	25	58	234	4	18	7	.720	0	9.8	3.01
Sarfate,Dennis	Bal	28	52	2	68	67	7	48	68	5	3	5	.375	0	15.9	5.25
Saunders,Joe	LAA	28	29	29	186	191	19	56	121	4	11	10	.524	0	12.1	3.90
Schmidt,Jason	LAD	36	6	6	34	29	3	13	33	1	2	1	.667	0	11.4	3.37
Schoeneweis,Scott	NYM	35	71	0	51	52	6	21	32	3	3	3	.500	0	13.4	4.43
Seanez,Rudy	Phi	40	36	0	38	36	4	18	38	1	2	2	.500	0	13.0	4.09
Seay,Bobby	Det	31	62	0	60	60	5	24	51	3	4	3	.571	0	13.0	4.01
Sheets,Ben	Mil	30	29	29	186	178	19	41	159	3	13	8	.619	0	10.7	3.39
Shell,Steven	Was	26	57	0	66	74	9	22	50	5	3	5	.375	6	13.8	4.98
Sherrill,George	Bal	32	60	0	53	43	4	27	60	1	4	2	.667	3	12.1	3.42
Shields,James	TB	27	32	32	212	210	24	44	178	10	14	10	.583	0	11.2	3.65
Shields,Scot	LAA	33	64	0	64	55	5	24	60	2	5	3	.625	3	11.4	3.31
Shouse,Brian	Mil	40	62	0	48	47	4	16	31	2	3	2	.600	0	12.2	3.77
Silva,Carlos	Sea	30	28	28	150	187	20	28	63	4	6	11	.353	0	13.1	4.91
Slowey,Kevin	Min	25	29	29	176	180	21	29	137	4	11	9	.550	0	10.9	3.60
Smith,Greg	Oak	25	31	31	190	194	21	79	121	4	9	12	.429	0	13.1	4.32
Smith,Joe	NYM	25	85	0	62	58	4	32	54	6	4	3	.571	0	13.9	4.09
Snell,Ian	Pit	27	29	29	163	173	20	67	139	3	7	11	.389	0	13.4	4.63

2009 Pitcher Projections

PLAYER			HOW MUCH			WHAT HE WILL GIVE UP					THE RESULTS					
Pitcher	Team	Age	G	GS	IP	H	HR	BB	SO	HB	W	L	Pct	Sv	BR/9	ERA
Sonnanstine,Andy	TB	26	31	31	195	206	25	40	145	6	11	10	.524	0	11.6	3.92
Soria,Joakim	KC	25	55	0	61	45	4	17	63	3	4	3	.571	37	9.6	2.16
Sowers,Jeremy	Cle	26	21	15	83	92	8	24	45	3	4	5	.444	0	12.9	4.28
Speier,Justin	LAA	35	59	0	69	62	10	22	59	5	4	3	.571	0	11.6	3.83
Speier,Ryan	Col	29	40	0	47	52	2	19	32	4	3	3	.500	0	14.4	4.52
Springer,Russ	StL	40	69	0	50	41	6	16	43	2	4	2	.667	0	10.6	3.22
Stokes,Brian	NYM	29	46	2	67	76	8	25	47	3	3	4	.429	0	14.0	4.90
Street,Huston	Oak	25	61	0	70	56	5	21	71	1	5	3	.625	28	10.0	2.90
Suppan,Jeff	Mil	34	31	31	184	205	23	62	100	7	9	11	.450	0	13.4	4.70
Tallet,Brian	Tor	31	45	0	55	52	6	22	41	3	3	3	.500	0	12.6	3.96
Taschner,Jack	SF	31	58	0	41	41	4	20	41	1	2	3	.400	0	13.6	4.36
Tavarez,Julian	Atl	36	66	0	69	77	6	28	43	5	3	4	.429	0	14.3	4.80
Tejeda,Robinson	KC	27	36	2	60	59	7	35	49	3	3	4	.429	0	14.6	4.86
Thompson,Brad	StL	27	29	7	67	73	8	20	34	5	3	4	.429	0	13.2	4.58
Thornton,Matt	CWS	32	73	0	71	63	7	33	71	2	4	4	.500	0	12.4	3.73
Tomko,Brett	SD	36	16	5	44	49	6	13	28	1	2	3	.400	0	12.9	4.61
Torres,Salomon	Mil	37	65	0	75	74	7	27	51	5	4	4	.500	23	12.7	3.94
Valverde,Jose	Hou	29	72	0	72	58	8	29	87	2	4	4	.500	43	11.1	3.42
Vazquez,Javier	CWS	32	33	33	214	211	28	54	195	8	13	11	.542	0	11.5	3.80
Veras,Jose	NYY	28	65	0	62	57	6	30	62	3	4	3	.571	0	13.1	3.96
Verlander,Justin	Det	26	30	30	182	173	18	68	147	12	11	9	.550	0	12.5	3.87
Villanueva,Carlos	Mil	25	47	4	92	85	13	32	79	3	6	5	.545	0	11.7	3.85
Villone,Ron	StL	39	76	0	42	39	4	22	36	3	2	2	.500	0	13.7	4.22
Vizcaino,Luis	Col	34	51	0	58	54	8	25	52	2	4	3	.571	0	12.6	4.06
Volquez,Edinson	Cin	25	30	30	192	176	20	95	191	10	11	11	.500	0	13.2	4.08
Waechter,Doug	Fla	28	39	0	44	54	7	15	26	1	2	3	.400	0	14.3	5.65
Wainwright,Adam	StL	27	25	25	150	152	13	45	110	5	9	7	.562	0	12.1	3.80
Wakefield,Tim	Bos	42	28	28	160	151	21	55	107	9	10	8	.556	0	12.1	3.91
Walker,Jamie	Bal	37	59	0	42	44	7	10	30	1	2	2	.500	0	11.8	4.18
Walker,Tyler	SF	33	60	0	46	46	6	19	38	1	2	3	.400	0	12.9	4.28
Wang,Chien-Ming	NYY	29	30	30	200	208	11	58	92	6	13	9	.591	0	12.2	3.70
Washburn,Jarrod	Sea	34	24	21	130	137	16	39	74	5	6	8	.429	0	12.5	4.25
Weathers,David	Cin	39	70	0	71	68	7	30	50	3	4	4	.500	0	12.8	4.00
Weaver,Jered	LAA	26	28	28	166	159	18	47	143	4	11	8	.579	0	11.4	3.63
Webb,Brandon	Ari	30	32	32	222	204	14	71	176	8	15	9	.625	0	11.5	3.37
Wellemeyer,Todd	StL	30	31	31	200	189	24	91	152	7	11	11	.500	0	12.9	4.15
Wells,Kip	KC	32	28	1	37	40	4	17	27	2	2	3	.400	0	14.4	4.92
Westbrook,Jake	Cle	31	11	11	64	69	5	20	35	2	4	4	.500	0	12.8	4.14
Wheeler,Dan	TB	31	69	0	63	55	8	20	57	2	4	3	.571	9	11.0	3.42
Willis,Dontrelle	Det	27	8	8	31	32	3	21	23	2	2	2	.500	0	16.0	5.78
Wilson,Brian	SF	27	61	0	63	55	4	32	62	4	4	3	.571	46	13.0	3.74
Wilson,C.J.	Tex	28	52	0	48	47	5	23	43	3	3	3	.500	9	13.7	4.49
Wolf,Randy	Hou	32	32	32	195	198	25	70	161	10	10	12	.455	0	12.8	4.29
Wolfe,Brian	Tor	28	28	0	30	31	3	10	20	1	2	2	.500	0	12.6	3.92
Wood,Kerry	ChC	32	62	0	66	53	7	28	74	5	5	3	.625	33	11.7	3.51
Woods,Jake	Sea	27	29	0	38	45	6	18	26	2	1	3	.250	0	15.4	6.03
Wright,Jamey	Tex	34	70	0	80	87	8	38	46	6	4	5	.444	0	14.7	5.01
Wright,Wesley	Hou	24	63	0	54	47	7	36	60	2	3	3	.500	0	14.2	4.66
Wuertz,Mike	ChC	30	50	0	49	42	5	22	52	0	3	2	.600	0	11.8	3.58
Yabu,Keiichi	SF	40	58	0	66	65	5	24	45	5	3	4	.429	0	12.8	3.92
Yabuta,Yasuhiko	KC	36	30	0	36	36	5	14	29	0	2	2	.500	0	12.5	4.17
Yates,Tyler	Pit	31	67	0	67	66	6	36	61	2	3	4	.429	0	14.0	4.50
Young,Chris	SD	30	29	29	153	124	17	59	137	5	10	7	.588	0	11.1	3.37
Zambrano,Carlos	ChC	28	28	28	196	166	18	87	163	10	13	9	.591	0	12.1	3.56
Ziegler,Brad	Oak	29	56	0	74	77	6	22	46	3	4	4	.500	7	12.4	3.91
Zito,Barry	SF	31	31	31	197	184	22	84	139	7	10	12	.455	0	12.6	3.94

Career Targets

This section is designed to give probabilities on players achieving important career milestones. The method (formerly under the name of "The Favorite Toy") was developed by Bill James and takes into account a player's age and performance level in predicting the probability that he will accumulate certain career stats. A detailed explanation of how the system works can be found in the glossary.

Viewed in full, the 2008 season was mostly about many star-caliber players taking important steps toward eventually achieving truly noteworthy records, although a few players did end up reaching historic plateaus: Ken Griffey, Jr. moved into fifth place on the all-time home run list (611); Manny Ramirez blasted his 500th home run; and John Smoltz stayed healthy long enough to record his 3,000th strikeout.

Given that 2008 was more of a bridge season (at least as far as the record books are concerned), what should we be keeping our eye on in 2009? With one more homer, Gary Sheffield will reach 500 home runs, and with an MVP-caliber season, Alex Rodriguez might eclipse 600. Luis Gonzalez is only four doubles away from 600, which would be good enough for 14th all-time.

3,000 Hits	
% chance to reach milestone	
Jeter, Derek	93%
Rodriguez, Alex	89%
Guerrero, Vladimir	53%
Pujols, Albert	38%
Damon, Johnny	38%
Renteria, Edgar	32%
Reyes, Jose	31%
Ramirez, Manny	31%
Griffey Jr., Ken	30%
Cabrera, Miguel	30%
Rollins, Jimmy	26%
Suzuki, Ichiro	25%
Wright, David	24%
Beltre, Adrian	22%
Young, Michael	21%
Ramirez, Hanley	20%
Anderson, Garret	20%
Rodriguez, Ivan	19%
Jones, Chipper	16%
Abreu, Bobby	16%
Sizemore, Grady	16%
Ordonez, Magglio	15%
Tejada, Miguel	15%
Markakis, Nick	15%
Crawford, Carl	15%
Beltran, Carlos	13%
Pierre, Juan	13%
Lopez, Jose	13%
Cano, Robinson	13%
Holliday, Matt	12%
Cabrera, Orlando	11%
Ramirez, Aramis	11%
Francoeur, Jeff	10%
Rios, Alex	10%
Lee, Carlos	10%
Morneau, Justin	10%
Polanco, Placido	9%
Teixeira, Mark	9%
Young, Delmon	8%
Fielder, Prince	8%
Gonzalez, Adrian	8%
Pedroia, Dustin	7%
Zimmerman, Ryan	6%
Roberts, Brian	6%
Atkins, Garrett	6%
Peralta, Jhonny	5%
Lee, Derrek	4%
Utley, Chase	4%
Berkman, Lance	4%
Wells, Vernon	2%

Career Targets

762 Home Runs
% chance to break record

Rodriguez,Alex	49%
Howard,Ryan	9%
Pujols,Albert	9%
Dunn,Adam	8%
Fielder,Prince	3%

2,298 RBI
% chance to break record

Rodriguez,Alex	39%
Cabrera,Miguel	13%
Pujols,Albert	11%
Ramirez,Manny	6%
Howard,Ryan	6%
Wright,David	5%
Morneau,Justin	2%
Guerrero,Vladimir	2%

2,296 Runs Scored
% chance to break record

Rodriguez,Alex	36%
Ramirez,Hanley	8%
Reyes,Jose	6%
Pujols,Albert	3%
Sizemore,Grady	2%
Wright,David	2%

4,257 Hits
% chance to break record

Reyes,Jose	< 1%

900 Home Runs
% chance to reach milestone

Rodriguez,Alex	10%

2,000 RBI
% chance to reach milestone

Rodriguez,Alex	91%
Ramirez,Manny	67%
Pujols,Albert	29%
Cabrera,Miguel	27%
Guerrero,Vladimir	23%
Griffey Jr.,Ken	19%
Howard,Ryan	17%
Wright,David	16%
Morneau,Justin	13%
Delgado,Carlos	12%

6,857 Total Bases
% chance to break record

Rodriguez,Alex	19%
Pujols,Albert	9%
Cabrera,Miguel	5%
Wright,David	1%
Ramirez,Hanley	< 1%

4,000 Hits
% chance to reach milestone

Reyes,Jose	5%
Jeter,Derek	3%
Cabrera,Miguel	3%
Pujols,Albert	2%
Rodriguez,Alex	2%
Wright,David	< 1%

800 Home Runs
% chance to reach milestone

Rodriguez,Alex	34%
Howard,Ryan	5%
Pujols,Albert	4%
Dunn,Adam	4%
Fielder,Prince	< 1%

600 Home Runs
% chance to reach milestone

Griffey Jr.,Ken	done
Rodriguez,Alex	97%
Thome,Jim	95%
Ramirez,Manny	77%
Pujols,Albert	43%
Dunn,Adam	37%
Howard,Ryan	32%
Delgado,Carlos	26%
Fielder,Prince	21%
Cabrera,Miguel	18%

793 Doubles
% chance to break record

Pujols,Albert	12%
Wright,David	8%
Cabrera,Miguel	8%
Markakis,Nick	6%
Ramirez,Hanley	5%
Sizemore,Grady	4%
Pedroia,Dustin	3%
Rollins,Jimmy	2%
Rios,Alex	2%
Roberts,Brian	1%

Most Likely No-Hitter
% chance to reach milestone

Lincecum,Tim	28%
Harden,Rich	24%
Volquez,Edinson	18%
Kazmir,Scott	16%
Sabathia,CC	15%
Billingsley,Chad	14%
Burnett,A.J.	13%
Sanchez,Jonathan	12%
Perez,Oliver	12%
Santana,Ervin	12%

700 Home Runs
% chance to reach milestone

Rodriguez,Alex	90%
Pujols,Albert	19%
Dunn,Adam	16%
Howard,Ryan	16%
Fielder,Prince	9%
Thome,Jim	6%
Cabrera,Miguel	5%
Ramirez,Manny	4%
Griffey Jr.,Ken	3%

500 Home Runs
% chance to reach milestone

Griffey Jr.,Ken	done
Rodriguez,Alex	done
Thome,Jim	done
Ramirez,Manny	done
Thomas,Frank	done
Sheffield,Gary	99%
Delgado,Carlos	97%
Pujols,Albert	86%
Guerrero,Vladimir	80%
Dunn,Adam	76%

1,000 Stolen Bases
% chance to reach milestone

Reyes,Jose	27%
Pierre,Juan	4%

Pitchers on Course
For 300 Wins
Bill James

If you are a major league pitcher who is fighting to win 300 games in his career, 2008 was probably a very good year for you. Most of the top candidates had outstanding seasons.

Ancient Randy Johnson had a 5.00 ERA in 2006 and pitched in only ten games in 2007, creating the impression that he might be one of those pitchers, like Ferguson Jenkins and Robin Roberts, who just runs out of time to get to 300 wins. But after a solid season in 2008, he is now poised to reach 300 in 2009.

Mike Mussina, who had a 5.15 ERA in 152 innings in 2007, stunned the baseball world with his first 20-win season—at age 39—increasing his chance of winning 300 from about 10% to about 47%. A year ago he was nearly five years away from 300 wins. Now he's less than two.

Name	2008 Age	R/L	W	L	EWL	Momentum	Chance
Johnson, Randy	44	L	295	160	10.5	.723	.86
Mussina, Mike	39	R	270	153	14.8	.688	.47
Moyer, Jamie	45	L	246	185	12.7	.725	.25
Santana, Johan	29	L	109	51	15.0	.893	.24
Webb, Brandon	29	R	87	62	17.4	.887	.23
Pettitte, Andy	36	L	215	127	12.9	.768	.18
Sabathia, CC	27	L	117	73	16.5	.855	.18
Halladay, Roy	31	R	131	66	16.6	.835	.16
Oswalt, Roy	30	R	129	64	14.5	.820	.10
Lowe, Derek	35	R	126	107	12.2	.810	.05
Buehrle, Mark	29	L	122	87	12.2	.804	.04
Vazquez, Javier	31	R	127	129	12.5	.790	.04
Burnett, A.J.	31	R	87	76	15.1	.746	.02
Wakefield, Tim	41	R	178	157	10.2	.696	.01
Rogers, Kenny	43	L	219	156	7.5	.624	.01
Zito, Barry	30	L	123	93	9.8	.755	.01
Garland, Jon	28	R	106	89	11.1	.742	.01
Hernandez, Livan	33	R	147	139	10.0	.711	.01
Martinez, Pedro	36	R	214	99	5.5	.664	.00
Millwood, Kevin	33	R	142	111	9.1	.670	.00
Suppan, Jeff	33	R	128	123	9.2	.678	.00

Note: EWL = Established Win Level

Jamie Moyer, who is too old to be taken seriously as a 300-win candidate but doesn't seem to know it, had his best season since 2003.

The younger 300-win candidates, further from the goal—Sabathia, Roy Halladay, Johan Santana, Roy Oswalt, Brandon Webb—those guys are not yet in a position where one season makes a big difference to their 300-win chances. It's a marathon, winning 300, and those guys are at about the ten-mile mark. But they're a strong group, and it's unlikely that they will ALL fall out.

Baseball Glossary

% Inherited Scored
The percentage of inherited baserunners a relief pitcher allows to score.

% Pitches Taken
The percentage of pitches that a batter does not swing at out of the total number of pitches thrown to him.

1st Batter Average
The Batting Average that a relief pitcher allows to the first batter he faces when he enters a game.

1st Batter OBP
The On-Base Percentage that a relief pitcher allows to the first batter he faces when he enters a game.

1st to 3rd (Baserunning)
Moved is the number of times a runner goes from 1st base to 3rd base on a SINGLE. Chances are the number of times a runner is on 1st base and a batter is credited with a SINGLE.

1st to Home (Baserunning)
Moved is the number of times a runner goes from 1st base to home on a DOUBLE. Chances are the number of times a runner is on 1st base and a batter is credited with a DOUBLE.

2nd to Home (Baserunning)
Moved is the number of times a runner goes from 2nd base to home on a SINGLE. Chances are the number of times a runner is on 2nd base and a batter is credited with a SINGLE.

Active Career Batting Leaders
A list of batting leaders among active (appearing in the most recent season) players. An active player is eligible when he meets the minimum requirements for the following categories:

> 1,000 At Bats—Batting Average, On-Base Percentage, Slugging Average, At Bats Per HR, At Bats Per GDP, At Bats Per RBI, Strikeout to Walk Ratio
> 100 Stolen Base Attempts—Stolen Base Success Percentage

Active Career Pitching Leaders
A list of pitching leaders among active (appearing in the most recent season) players. An active player is eligible when he meets the minimum requirements for the following categories:

750 Innings Pitched—Earned Run Average, Opponent Batting Average, all "Per 9 Innings" categories, Strikeout to Walk Ratio
250 Games Started—Complete Game Frequency
100 Decisions—Win-Loss Percentage

AVG Allowed ScPos
The Batting Average allowed by a pitcher while pitching with runners in scoring position.

AVG Bases Loaded
The Batting Average of a hitter while batting with the bases loaded.

Base Taken
A player is credited with a Base Taken whenever he moves up a base on a Wild Pitch, Passed Ball, Balk, Sacrifice Fly (other than the runner who scores), or Defensive Indifference.

Batting Average
Hits divided by at bats.

Blown Save
When a relief pitcher enters a game in a Save Situation (see definition for Save Situation) and allows the other team to score the tying or go-ahead run.

Bomb (Intentional Walk)
An Intentional Walk blows up (Bombs) when the next batter after the intentional walk does not ground into a double play and subsequently more than one run scores in the inning.

BR Gain (Baserunning)
BR Gain (or Loss if a negative number) is the total of all the types of extra baserunning advances minus the (triple) penalty for all the BR Outs compared with what would be expected based on the MLB averages.

BR Outs (Baserunning)
BR Outs include the sum of Outs Advancing, Doubled Offs, and when a runner is tagged out on the bases when another runner moves up on a Wild Pitch, Passed Ball, or scores on a Sacrifice Fly.

BS Win
A Blown Save Win is a "win" credited to a reliever who has blown a save opportunity.

Career Targets
This method, once called the Favorite Toy, is a way to estimate the probability that a player will achieve a specific career goal. In this example, 3,000 hits will be used. The four components of the formula are Needed Hits, Years Remaining, Established Hit Level and Projected Remaining Hits.

Needed Hits. This is the number of Hits (or any statistic) that a player needs to reach a desired goal.

Years Remaining. This is the estimated number of years remaining in the player's career. It is determined using the player's age (on June 30th of the previous year; use 2003 when making the calculation after the 2003 season is complete). The formula is (42 - age) divided by two. This means a player who is 20 years old will have 11 remaining seasons, a player who is 25 years old will have 8.5 remaining seasons and a player who is 35 years old will have 3.5 remaining seasons. If the player is a catcher, then multiply his remaining seasons by .7. If a player is older than 39 (the Years Remaining calculation yields less than 1.5), consult the player's statistics for the most recent year. If the player either had 100 Hits or an Offensive Winning Percentage of .500 or greater, then the player will have 1.0 remaining seasons. If the player has both, he has 1.5 remaining seasons. If he has neither, he has .5 remaining seasons.

Established Hit Level. The Established Hit Level is a weighted average of the player's hits over the past three seasons. To calculate the Established Hit Level after the 2003 season is complete, add 2001 Hits, (2002 Hits multiplied by two) and (2003 Hits multiplied by three), then divide by six. If the Established Hit Level is less than 75% of the most recent performance (2003 Hits in this case), then the Established Hit Level is equal to .75 times the most recent performance.

Projected Remaining Hits. This is calculated by multiplying Years Remaining by the Established Hit Level.

The probability of achieving the specified goal is found by dividing Projected Remaining Hits by Need Hits, then subtracting .5. The maximum that any player has of achieving a goal is .97 raised to the power of (Need Hits / Established Hit Level). This prevents the possibility of a player reaching a goal from being higher than 100 percent, which is impossible.

Catcher's ERA
The ERA for a catcher is equal to the ERA of pitchers pitching while the catcher is playing behind the plate. It is calculated exactly like ERA for pitchers. Take the number of earned runs allowed while the catcher is playing, multiply it by 9 and then divide it by the total number of defensive innings that the catcher was behind the plate.

Cheap Win
A starting pitcher who wins the game with a game score under 50 gets credit for a cheap win. See Game Score.

Clean Outing
A Clean Outing is a game in which the reliever is not charged with a run (earned or otherwise) AND does not allow an inherited runner to score.

Cleanup Slugging Average
The Slugging Average of a batter when he bats in the cleanup spot, or fourth, in the batting order.

Close and Late

A situation in a game that is very similar to a Save Situation. The following requirements are necessary for a Close and Late game:

1. The game is in the seventh inning or later AND
2. The batting team is either leading by one run or tied OR
3. The tying run is on base, at bat, or on deck.

Component ERA (ERC)

A statistic that estimates what a pitcher's ERA should have been, based on his pitching performance. The ERC formula is calculated as follows:

1. Subtract the pitcher's Home Runs Allowed from his Hits Allowed.
2. Multiply Step 1 by 1.255.
3. Multiply his Home Runs Allowed by four.
4. Add Steps 2 and 3 together.
5. Multiply Step 4 by .89.
6. Add his Walks and Hit Batsmen.
7. Multiply Step 6 by .475.
8. Add Steps 5 and 7 together.

This yields the pitcher's total base estimate (PTB), which is:

$$PTB = 0.89 \times (1.255 \times (H - HR) + 4 \times HR) + 0.475 \times (BB + HB)$$

For those pitchers for whom there is intentional walk data, use this formula instead:

$$PTB = 0.89 \times (1.255 \times (H - HR) + 4 \times HR) + 0.56 \times (BB + HB - IBB)$$

9. Add Hits and Walks and Hit Batsmen.
10. Multiply Step 9 by PTB.
11. Divide Step 10 by Batters Facing Pitcher. If BFP data is unavailable, approximate it by multiplying Innings Pitched by 2.9, then adding Step 9.
12. Multiply Step 11 by 9.
13. Divide Step 12 by Innings Pitched.
14. Subtract .56 from Step 13.

This is the pitcher's ERC, which is:

$$\frac{(H + BB + HB) \times PTB}{BFP \times IP} \times 9 - 0.56$$

If the result after Step 13 is less than 2.24, adjust the formula as follows:

$$\frac{(H + BB + HB) \times PTB}{BFP \times IP} \times 9 \times 0.75$$

490

Consecutive Days
A count of how many times the pitcher was used after having pitched on the previous day or (in a few cases) in an earlier game on the same day.

Double Play %
Successful Double Plays divided by the number of Double Play opportunities. This statistic includes both the fielder who started the play and the pivot man.

Double Play Opportunity
A fielder is considered to have a double play opportunity when a ground ball is hit with a runner on first base and less than 2 outs and that fielder is involved in the play. This is used to calculate Double Play % and Pivot %.

Doubled Off
A runner is Doubled Off when he is out for failing to get back to his base before he, or the base, is tagged after a ball hit in the air is caught.

Early Entry
A count of the number of times the reliever entered the game in the sixth inning or earlier.

Earned Run Average
The number of earned runs that a pitcher surrenders per nine innings that he pitches. It is calculated by multiplying the total earned runs allowed by nine and dividing by the total number of innings pitched.

Easy Save
This label is used to separate Saves by difficulty level (Easy or Tough). A Save is considered Easy if the relief pitcher enters the game, pitches one inning or less, and the first batter he faces does not at least represent the tying run.

Fielding Percentage
The percentage of plays a player makes in the field without making an error out of the total number of opportunities. It is calculated by adding (Putouts plus Assists) and dividing by (Putouts plus Assists plus Errors).

Games Finished
The relief pitcher who is in the game for each team when the game ends is credited with a Game Finished.

Game Score
To determine the starting pitcher's Game Score:
Start with 50.
Add 1 point for each out recorded by the starting pitcher.
Add 2 points for each inning the pitcher completes after the fourth inning.
Add 1 point for each strikeout.
Subtract 2 points for each hit allowed.
Subtract 4 points for each earned run allowed.
Subtract 2 points for an unearned run.

Subtract 1 point for each walk.

GDP
Grounded into Double Play

GDP Opportunity
This is a situation where the batter has a chance to ground into a double play. It occurs with at least a runner on first base and less than two outs.

Ground / Fly Ratio (Grd/Fly, GB/FB)
Calculated for both batters and pitchers. For batters, it is the number of groundballs hit divided by the number of flyballs hit. For pitchers, it is exactly the same but uses the number of groundballs and flyballs allowed. Every fair batted ball is included except for bunts and line drives.

Hold
A relief pitcher is given a Hold anytime he enters the game in a Save Situation (see definition for Save Situation), records one out or more, and exits the game without giving up the lead. If the pitcher finishes the game, then he will only earn credit for a Save. He cannot receive credit for both a Hold and a Save.

Holds Adjusted Saves Percentage (same as Save/Hold Percentage)
Holds plus Saves divided by Holds plus Saves Opportunities.

Inherited Runner
When a relief pitcher enters the game, any runner who was on base at the time is considered an Inherited Runner.

Isolated Power
Slugging Average minus Batting Average.

K/BB Ratio
Strikeouts divided by Walks.

Leadoff On-Base Percentage
The On-Base Percentage of a batter when he bats leadoff, or first, in the batting order.

Leverage Index
Leverage is the amount of swing in the possible change in win probability, compared to the average swing in all situations. The average swing value, by definition, is indexed to 1.00.

In the score of the game is 12-0 or 14-1 the possible changes in win probability will be very close to negligible. Whether the pitcher gives up a home run or gets a double play ball, doesn't really change the outcome of the game. There won't be much swing in either direction for the probability of the win. But in the late innings of a close game, the change in win probability among the various events will have rather wild swings. With a runner on first, two outs, down by one, and in the bottom of the ninth, the game can hinge on one swing of that bat. A home run and an out will both end the game, but with different outcomes for the teams involved. The Leverage Index we use (LI) was developed at the website Tangotiger.net, and compiled at the website Fangraphs.com.

Long Outing
A Long Outing is one in which the starting pitcher throws more than 110 pitches. Prior to 2002, we used 120 pitches as the cutoff in the Manager's Record section.

Long Save
A Long Save is when the pitcher credited with a save pitches more than one inning.

Manufactured Runs
Manufactured Runs are of two types: Type 1 - Strict Manufactured Runs (MR-1) which involve at least one base resulting from one of four deliberate acts intended to manufacture a run; i.e. a sacrifice bunt, a stolen base, a hit and run play, or a bunt hit. Type 2 - Other Manufactured Runs (MR-2) are ones in which two of the four bases advanced do NOT result from the runner being forced along by a walk, a hit batsman, or a safe hit to the outfield; e.g. double, ground out, ground out, runner scores would be a MR-2. For a complete description with more examples, see the section on Manufactured Runs.

Not Good Outcome (Intentional Walk)
A Not Good Outcome (NG) for an Intentional Walk occurs when one run scored in the inning after the intentional walk (and the next batter after the intentional walk did not ground into a double play).

Offensive Winning Percentage (OWP)
A player's Offensive Winning Percentage is the winning percentage of a hypothetical team which has an offense consisting of nine of that player, and pitching and defense which is average for the player's league. It is calculated by taking the square of RC/27 (see the definition for Runs Created per 27 Outs), dividing it by the sum of RC/27 and the square of the average runs scored per game in the league.

On-Base Percentage
(Hits plus Walks plus Hit by Pitcher) divided by (At Bats plus Walks plus Hit by Pitcher plus Sacrifice Flies).

$$\frac{H + BB + HBP}{AB + BB + HBP + SF}$$

Opponent Batting Average
Hits Allowed divided by (Batters Faced minus Walks minus Hit Batsmen minus Sacrifice Hits minus Sacrifice Flies minus Catcher's Interference).

$$\frac{H}{BFP - BB - HBP - SH - SF - CI}$$

Opposition OPS
The OPS of the hitters facing the pitcher.

Out Advancing

A runner is out advancing when he is tagged out attempting to score from 2nd base on a single or from 1st base on a double, or attempting to go from 1st base to 3rd base on a single.

PA*

Used in the denominator for the calculation of On-Base Percentage. It is calculated by subtracting (Sacrifice Hits plus Times Reached Base on Defensive Interference) from Plate Appearances (see definition for Plate Appearances).

Park Index

The Park Index of a given ballpark is the amount that the ballpark influences a given statistic. The following is a calculation of a park index using runs as the statistic:

1. Add Runs and Opponent Runs in home games.
2. Add At Bats and Opponent At Bats in home games. (If At Bats are unavailable, use home games.)
3. Divide Step 1 by Step 2.
4. Add Runs and Opponent Runs in road games.
5. Add At Bats and Opponent At Bats in road games. (If At Bats are unavailable, use road games.)
6. Divide Step 4 by Step 5.
7. Divide Step 3 by Step 6.
8. Multiply Step 7 by 100.

An index of 100 means the park is completely neutral and does not influence the particular statistic at all. A park index of 112 for runs indicates that teams score 12 percent more runs in this ballpark than a neutral park. A park index of 92 for runs means that teams tend to score 8 percent fewer runs in this ballpark than a neutral park.

PCS (Pitchers' Caught Stealing)

The number of runners officially scored as Caught Stealing where the pitcher initiated the play. The normal Caught Stealing is when a runner is out attempting to steal a base but the play was initiated by the catcher. PCS plays are often referred to as pickoffs, but differ when the runner breaks towards the next base as opposed to returning to the base he was currently on. Pickoffs occur when the pitcher throws to a base that a runner is leading from, and the runner is out attempting to return to that base. Pickoffs are not an official statistic.

Pitches per PA

The total number of pitches a hitter sees divided by his total Plate Appearances.

Pivot %

Successful Double Plays turned by pivot man divided by the number of Double Play opportunities with that pivot man involved.

Plate Appearances

At Bats plus Total Walks plus Hit By Pitcher plus Sacrifice Hits plus Sacrifice Flies plus Times Reached on Defensive Interference.

Platoon Advantage %

Platoon Advantage % is the percentage of players in the starting lineup who have the platoon advantage (i.e. bats right against a left-handed pitcher or bats left against a right-hander) against the starting pitcher; e.g. if the opposing starting pitcher is right handed and the batting team has six left-handed batters in its lineup, the platoon advantage for that game would be 67%.

Plus/Minus System

The Plus/Minus System is a method for evaluating defensive play on batted balls. It is made possible by a game scoring system in which each batted ball is rated for type (line drive, grounder, etc.), velocity within its type (hard, medium or soft), and location on the field. A player gets credit (a "plus" number) if he makes a play that at least one other player at his position missed during the season and he loses credit (a "minus" number") if he misses a play that at least one player made. The size of the credits are proportional to the percentage of times all players make the play, All plays for each player at his position are summed to get his total plus/minus for the season. A total of zero would be average and any other number would approximate how many plays more or less the player made than the average player at the position for the number of chances the player had to field batted balls.

Power/Speed Number

A single number that reflects a combination of power and speed. To achieve a high Power/Speed Number, a player must score high in both power and speed. To calculate the Power/Speed Number, multiply Home Runs by Stolen Bases by two, and divide by the sum of Home Runs and Stolen Bases.

$$\frac{2 \times HR \times SB}{HR + SB}$$

PPO (Pitcher Pickoff)

The number of baserunners thrown out when a pitcher throws to a base with a leading baserunner, and the runner is tagged out attempting to return to the base. PPO is not an official statistic and does not count toward Caught Stealing totals.

Quality Start

A game where the starting pitcher pitches for at least six innings and allows no more than three earned runs.

Quality Start Percentage

Quality Starts divided by Games Started (see the definition for Quality Start).

Quick Hooks

Used in the Manager's Record. For Quick Hooks and Slow Hooks a score is calculated for each game that is the sum of the number of Pitches plus 10 times the number of Runs Allowed. The bottom 25% of scores in the league are considered to be Quick Hooks.

Range Factor

The number of Successful Chances (Putouts plus Assists) times nine divided by the number of Defensive Innings Played. The average for a Regular Player at each position in 2008:

Second Base: 4.91
Third Base: 2.66
Shortstop: 4.41
Left Field: 1.97
Center Field: 2.66
Right Field: 2.14

Regular Saves

Any save which does not meet the definition either of an Easy Save or a Tough Save is a "Regular" Save.

Run Support Per 9 IP

The total number of runs scored by a pitcher's team while he is in the game multiplied by nine and divided by total Innings Pitched.

Runs Created

"Runs Created" is an estimate of the number of a team's runs which are created by each individual hitter. The Cincinnati Reds scored 820 runs last year, let us say. How many of those were created by Adam Dunn? How many by Ken Griffey Jr.? How many by Jason LaRue?

There are many different formulas for estimating runs created. . .did you want the one that involves swinging a dead cat in the cemetery under a full moon? Yeah, I don't blame you. . .worm-eaten persimmons are so hard to find in the modern world.

This is the one we use now; it is complicated enough. First, there is an "A" Factor in the formula, a "B" Factor, and a "C" factor. The "A" Factor, which represents the number of times the hitter is on base, is Hits, Plus Walks, Plus Hit Batsmen, Minus Caught Stealing, Minus Grounded Into Double Play. The "B" Factor, which represents the hitter's ability to advance other runners, is 1.125 times the player's Singles, plus 1.69 times his Doubles, plus 3.02 times his Triples, plus 3.73 times his Home Runs, plus .29 times his Walks and Hit Batsmen, not counting intentional walks, plus .492 times Sacrifice Hits, Sacrifice Flies and Stolen Bases, minus .04 times Strikeouts. The "C" Factor, which represents opportunities, is At Bats, Plus Walks, Plus Hit By Pitch, Plus Sacrifice Hits, Plus Sacrifice Flies.

Having made these initial calculations of the A, B and C factors, we then change the "A" factor to "A plus 2.4 times C".

We change the "B" factor to "B plus 3 times C".

We change the "C" factor to "9 times C".

Multiply A times B, divide by then new C ("9 times C"), and subtract .90 times by the original C.

This is our first, temporary estimate of the player's runs created. We what we have done here is to ask these questions:
1. How many runs would a team probably score that consisted of eight "ordinary" type of hitters, plus this particular hitter?
2. How many of those runs would be created by the eight ordinary type of hitters?
3. What is the difference-and thus, how many runs did our player create?

To estimate this, we have placed our player in the context of eight hitters with a .300 on base percentage (2.4 divided by 8) and a .375 advancement percentage (3 divided by 8). For each trip through the batting order, the eight ordinary-type hitters would produce 9/10 of a run (2.4 times 3, divided by 8). The "9" in the denominator is eight ordinary hitters plus our man. The "-.9" being subtracted at the end is the runs created by the "ordinary" hitters. In essence, we have placed the hitter in a neutral solution, measured the neutral solution without our hitter, measured it with our hitter, and then estimated the contribution of this hitter as being the difference between the two.

We're not quite done. After that, we adjust the player's runs created estimate for his performance in two "run-sensitive" situations. Suppose that a player whose overall batting average is .250 has batted 100 times with runners in scoring position, and has gone 30-for-100. That's five hits better than expected, 30 hits where we would have expected 25. His team will score an extra five runs because he has done that, and so we increase the player's runs created estimate by five runs. If the player has hit poorly with runners in scoring position, we decrease it by the shortfall in the same way.

Suppose that a player has batted 250 times with runners on base, 250 times with the bases empty, and that he has hit 20 home runs overall. We would expect him to have hit 10 with men on base, 10 with the bases empty, right?

Suppose that he didn't. Suppose that he hit 12 with the bases empty, 8 with men on base. His team would score two runs less than expected because he did this, and we would thus penalize him two runs for the shortfall.

This is our second runs created estimate-the player's runs created, adjusted for his batting performance in run-sensitive situations.

Suppose, however, that we figure the runs created for all of the individuals on a team, and we add them up, and it doesn't match the runs actually scored by the team? What if the formulas say that the team should have scored 800 runs, but they actually scored 820?

Then obviously, the formulas missed. We're trying to measure the runs ACTUALLY created by each hitter as best we can, in the real world, not the theoretical impact of some combination of singles, doubles, triples and walks. If the actual number is different than the estimates, we have to adjust the estimates to fit the facts. In this case-820 runs scored with only 800 runs created-we would multiply each runs created estimate by 820/800, or 1.025. Then we round it off to an integer, and that's the player's estimated runs created.

Let go of that cat, Arthur. Heck, the moon isn't full for three weeks, anyway.

Runs Created per 27 Outs (RC/27)

This statistic estimates the number of runs per game that a team made up of nine of the same player would score. To calculate RC/27, multiply Runs Created by league outs per team game, divide the result by outs made by the player (the sum of at bats plus sacrifice hits plus sacrifice flies plus caught stealing plus grounded into double plays, minus hits). The formula written out is:

$$\frac{\frac{RC \times 3 \times LgIP}{2 \times LgG}}{AB - H + SH + SF + CS + GDP}$$

Save Opportunities

The sum of Saves and Blown Saves (see Save Situation).

Save/Hold Percentage (same as Holds Adjusted/Saves Percentage)

The sum of Saves and Holds, divided by the sum of Saves, Holds, and Blown Saves.

For several years we figured "Save Percentage", which is simply Saves divided by Save Opportunities, and this stat has some currency in the game. But the Save Percentage severely discriminates against middle relievers, who have no real chance to be credited with the Save, since they will be taken out of the game and replaced by the Closer even if they throw 110 miles an hour and strike out everybody they see. Middle relievers typically have Save Percentages of zero, even if they pitch well. The Save/Hold Percentage is a much more realistic evaluation of a pitcher's success in Save situations.

Save Percentage

A pitcher's Saves divided by the total number of Save Situations he faces (see definition for Save Situation).

Save Situation

A relief pitcher is in a Save Situation when he enters the game with his team in the lead, has the opportunity to finish the game, is not the winning pitcher of record at the time, and meets any one of the three following conditions:

1. The pitcher's team is leading by no more than three runs and the pitcher has the chance to pitch for at least one inning,

OR

2. The pitcher enters the game with the potential tying run on base, at bat, or on deck,

OR

3. The pitcher pitches three or more effective innings regardless of the lead. The determination of a save in this situation is made by the official scorer.

It is not possible to have more than one save credited to a single team in a game.

SB Gain (Baserunning)

Stolen Base attempts must be successful greater than about two thirds of the time to have a positive result on the number of runs scored. SB gain is therefore the number of bases stolen minus two times the number of caught stealing (SB Gain = SB - 2CS.) For example, a runner steals 30 bases and is caught stealing 7 times. His SB Gain would be 30 - 2*7 = +16. Another runner steals 10 bases and is caught stealing 6 times. His SB Gain (actually a loss) would be 10 - 2*6 = -2.

SB Success Percentage

Stolen Bases divided by the number of Stolen Base attempts (Stolen Bases plus Caught Stealing).

$$\frac{SB}{SB + CS}$$

Secondary Average

A number meant to reflect everything else except for batting average. A player will have a high Secondary Average if he hits for power, takes walks and steals bases. It is calculated with the following formula:

$$\frac{TB - H + BB + SB}{AB}$$

Similarity Score

A number which reflects the similarity between two different statistical lines, either for a player or for a team. A score of 1,000 means that the statistical lines are identical.

Slow Hooks

Used in the Manager's Record. For Quick Hooks and Slow Hooks a score is calculated for each game that is the sum of the number of Pitches plus 10 times the number of Runs Allowed. The top 25% of scores in the league are considered to be Slow Hooks.

Slugging Average

Total Bases divided by At Bats.

$$\frac{TB}{AB}$$

Speed Score

Speed Score is a number which evaluates how fast a player is. To calculate the Speed Score, start with the player's statistics over the last two seasons combined. A value will be found for each of the following six categories and will be combined for a final score at the end:

1.Stolen Base Percentage. The value of this category is:

$$\left(\frac{SB + 3}{SB + CS + 7} - 0.4\right) \times 20$$

2.Frequency of Stolen Base Attempts. The value of this category is:

$$\frac{\sqrt{\dfrac{SB + CS}{Singles + BB + HBP}}}{0.07}$$

3.Percentage of Triples. This is calculated by taking the percentage of triples out of the number of balls put in play. To get the percentage, use this formula:

$$\frac{3B}{AB - HR - SO}$$

From this assign an integer from 0 to 10, based on the following chart:
Less than .0010
.001- .00231
.0023- .00392
.0039- .00583
.0058- .00804
.0080- .01055
.0105- .0136
.013- .01587
.0158- .01898
.0189- .02239
.0223 or more10

4. Runs Scored Percentage. This is calculated by taking the percentage of times the player scores a run out of the number of times the player is on base. To get the percentage, use this formula:

$$\frac{\left(\dfrac{R - HR}{H + HBP + BB - HR} - 0.1\right)}{0.04}$$

5. Grounded Into Double Play Frequency. To get the frequency, use this formula:

$$\frac{0.055 - \left(\dfrac{GIDP}{AB - HR - SO}\right)}{0.005}$$

6. Range Factor. The value of this category depends on the players position:

Catcher—1
First Baseman—2

Designated Hitter—1.5
Second Baseman—1.25 x Range Factor
Third Baseman—1.51 x Range Factor
Shortstop—1.52 x Range Factor
Outfield—3 x Range Factor

For an explanation on Range Factor, consult the definition in this glossary. Remember to figure range factors over a two-year period.

If any category value is greater than 10, then reduce it to 10. If any value is less than zero, then increase the value to zero. All category values must fall within the zero to 10 range. The Speed Score is then calculated by discarding the lowest of the six values, and taking the average of the remaining five.

Total Bases
Hits plus Doubles plus (2 times Triples) plus (3 times Home Runs).

$$H + 2B + (2 \times 3B) + (3 \times HR)$$

Tough Loss
A starting pitcher who loses the game with a game score over 50 gets credit for a tough loss. See Game Score.

Tough Save
This label is used to separate Saves by difficulty level (Easy or Tough). A Save is considered Tough if the relief pitcher enters the game with the tying run on base.

Win Probability
The probability of a team winning the game determined at any time during the game based on the score, inning, outs and base situation.

Winning Percentage
Wins divided by (Wins plus Losses).

Baseball Info Solutions

What will box scores look like in a hundred years? What did they look like a century ago? Whatever the difference, it can almost be entirely attributed to advances in baseball statistical analysis.

But analysis alone is not responsible for the prevalence of advanced statistics now in broadcasts and bar-room arguments across the world; you need to have high quality, innovative data or you may draw the wrong conclusions. Baseball Info Solutions has been supplying top notch, timely, and in-depth baseball data to its customers since 2002.

BIS collects a statistical snapshot of every important moment of ever Major League Baseball game with the most advanced technology, resulting in a database that includes traditional basic data, advanced pitch-by-pitch data, and state-of-the-art defensive positioning data. The company also has the highest quality pitch charting data available anywhere, including pitch type, location, and velocity.

BIS provides comprehensive services to over half of the 30 Major League Baseball teams, as well as many sports agents, media, fantasy services, game companies and private individuals.

John Dewan, the principal owner of BIS, has been on the cutting edge of baseball analysis for over 20 years. His experience goes all the way back to his days as Executive Director of Project Scoresheet, the Bill James-led effort that pioneered the new wave of baseball statistics that are now common terminology. He wonders if he might be the only practicing sports actuary in the country.

President Steve Moyer brings almost twenty years of baseball industry experience to BIS. His hands-on, can-do business demeanor helps set BIS apart from its competition.

The rest of the BIS team includes former professional and collegiate baseball players as well as programming and database management experts. Over the last four seasons, BIS has more than tripled its full-time staff.

BIS continues to grow within the industry while emphasizing personal attention to its customers. This focus on personal attention is evidenced by the fact that if you contact the office with an inquiry you are very likely to be able to speak to the company president directly.

To contact BIS:

Baseball Info Solutions
41 S. 2nd Street
Coplay, PA 18037
610-261-2370
www.baseballinfosolutions.com

Notes

Notes

Notes

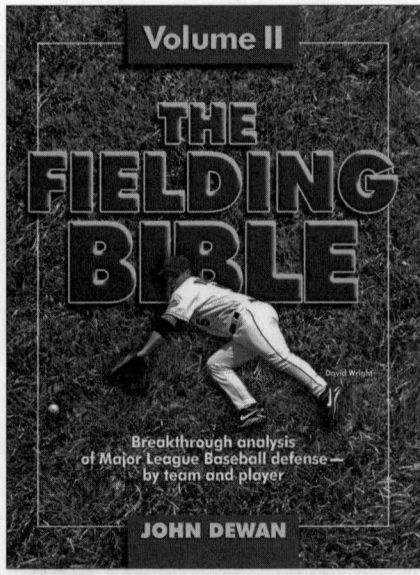